S0-BIP-258

BIBLIOGRAPHY OF COSTUME

EXPLANATIONS

The Bibliography is in the form of a dictionary catalog, with author, title, subject, editor, illustrator, engraver and other entries all in one alphabet.

The main entry is under the name of the author, or, for an anonymous book, under the first word of the title. Here the fullest information about the book is given, in the following order: Author, title, place, publisher, date, number of pages, illustrations, plates, size, series, and descriptive annotations. Here also are given the references to the bibliographies of Colas, and Lipperheide, and numbers by which Library of Congress cards can be ordered.

Under the subject of which the book treats the information is limited to author, title, and date of publication. The subject is followed by the author's name. Turn to entry under author's name for full information.

Titles entries, likewise, are only guides to the main entry. The title is followed by the author's name.

Entries under names of engravers, illustrators, and editors, are also brief, giving only the name of the author (i.e. the main entry) and title of the work.

For example the book *Antike mode,* by Max von Boehn, will be found under 1, the author's name: Boehn, Max von; 2, the title: Antike mode; 3, the subject: Ancient times.

The main entry should always be consulted, since only in the main entry will be found all the titles under which a book and its translations were published, and therefore can be found listed in library catalogs.

The articles *a, an,* and *the* and their equivalents in other languages, have been ignored in filing. i.e. *L'image de la femme* is found under the letter *i,* not under *L.*

ä, ö, ü, å, and ø in the Teutonic languages are filed as if spelled ae, oe, ue, etcetera.

For further explanations see the Introduction, pages vii-ix.

BIBLIOGRAPHY OF COSTUME

A Dictionary Catalog of About Eight Thousand Books and Periodicals

Compiled by
HILAIRE and MEYER HILER

Edited by
HELEN GRANT CUSHING

Assisted by
ADAH V. MORRIS

Benjamin Blom
New York

First Published 1939
Reissued 1967, by Benjamin Blom, Inc., New York 10452
Library of Congress Catalog Card No. 66-12285

Printed in U.S.A. by
NOBLE OFFSET PRINTERS, INC.
NEW YORK 3, N. Y.

PREFACE

The Bibliography, international in scope, is a list of approximately eighty-four hundred works on costume and adornment, including books in all languages.

The books are listed in a dictionary catalog with author, subject, and title entries, and references, in one alphabet. Full bibliographic information is given for each book: the author's name in full, title, illustrator, engraver, place, publisher, date, paging, size, illustrations and plates (with color indicated). The entries include references to the H. W. Wilson Company's *Costume index,* to Colas's *Bibliographie du Costume,* and to Lipperheide's *Katalog der Kostümbibliothek.* Library of Congress card numbers are also given.

The Dictionary catalog form was decided upon after consultation, by the questionnaire method, with a number of librarians and others chiefly interested. The decision in favor of this form was practically unanimous. The main entry for each book is under the name of the author, which has been verified and given in complete form wherever possible. In many cases an effort had to be made to find the complete and best-known form of the name. Research in this connection resulted in many corrections and changes and the discovery of numerous pseudonyms (noms de plumes) in which case entry has been made under the real name with reference from the pseudonym. It was also possible to supply authors' names for many books published anonymously and listed under titles only in other bibliographies. Such names are indicated in the Bibliography by being enclosed in brackets. The same indication is used in the case of the title of the book. A note then tells where the title is to be found, e.g. "cover title," "title on portfolio," "title appears on each plate," "title appears on some plates," "plates are signed." The name of the artist or engraver is given whenever possible. Brief descriptive annotations are given for books whose title does not indicate their costume values, and information is given about other editions, changes in title and translations.

Each phase of costume treated is brought out under subject as fully as possible; e.g. the country and type, military costume, arms and armor, orders of knighthood and chivalry, religious orders, etc. Ecclesiastical costume is arranged by country and period, or by church.

In research of all sorts, a definite knowledge of the necessary bibliographic sources is of incalculable value in saving time and labor. The compilers have found from personal experience that the subject indexes of even the most modern libraries are practically useless in dealing with specialized problems such as those involved in the study of costume. While all the larger libraries are rich in valuable material, it is often obtainable only by much painstaking search.

The compilers believe that this is by far the most extensive and complete bibliography of costume ever offered, covering every period and country from prehistoric times to the present day, as well as every specialized phase of the subject.

In connection with the present work the word costume is used in its broadest sense. Not only is costume treated from the standpoint of clothing and decoration of the human body, but works are included on such allied subjects as masks, tattooing, body-painting, arms and armor, tailoring and cutting, military, naval and civil uniforms, ecclesiastical and academic costume, coiffure, hygiene, esthetics of costume, dress reform, jewelry, and accessories (the umbrella, muff, gloves, corsets, fans, etc.) Books on each subject and country are arranged in groups by period. There are many references for native tribes of Africa, Australia, India, etc., and for American Indians.

Fashion periodicals are listed under title, under country of publication and by date. Under the latter entry it is possible to ascertain exactly what fashion periodicals were published during any particular period. The list also includes some periodicals in the fields of ethnology and history, containing notable costume material.

Painters of historical subjects, illustrators, stage designers, cinema costumers, shoe designers, dress designers, milliners, costume students, historians, bibliographers, sociologists, ethnologists, collectors, museums, libraries, advertising agencies, manufacturers, book dealers, students of dramatics, directors of pageants, and many others, we hope will find this work of value.

The Bibliography is accompanied by an essay, "Costumes and ideologies," discussing the psychological and social factors underlying all costume development.

The compilers wish to express their thanks to the persons who have given much-appreciated advice and assistance in various stages of the work: Charles H. Hastings, chief, Card division, Library of Congress, and John W. Cronin, assistant chief; Harry M. Lydenberg, director, New York Public library; Pauline V. Fullerton, chief, Art division, New York Public library; Victor H. Paltsits, chief, American history division, New York Public library; Jean M. Murphy, Queens Borough Public library; and Paul Otlet, of the Palais Mondiale, Brussels.

MEYER HILER

Contents

INTRODUCTION

The original list was made up prior to the year 1930, from books examined and titles collected from the libraries of New York City and of Paris, Berlin, London, Brussels, Madrid, and other European cities. During the years 1937 and 1938 it was checked with titles in the catalog of the Lipperheide Costume Library, Colas's *Bibliographie du Costume,* and The H. W. Wilson Company's *Costume Index* by Isabel Monro and Dorothy E. Cook. All titles found that were within the scope of the present work have been included. Also all the titles were considered that are listed in the catalog of the Library of Congress under the subject Costume and the subjects there referred to, and also the titles so listed in the New York Public Library, up to June 1937. The list of fashion periodicals in the *Periodicals directory,* edited by Carolyn F. Ulrich (2d ed. 1935) was checked and used to bring the list of fashion periodicals up to date. Various other smaller lists of books on costume have been checked, for example the bibliographies issued by the Boston Public Library and by Detroit Public Library, the catalog of the King collection of the Western Reserve Historical Society, and the unpublished photostat list compiled by the Grosvenor Library, Buffalo, New York. While the smaller lists did not add many titles they sometimes uncovered English editions which might otherwise have been missed.

Altho they have some costume interest this Bibliography does not include books of the classes listed below: (1) Sumptuary laws. Lipperheide devotes a section to them, nos. 3321-3423, and Colas lists a few. (2) Books on textiles that do not show actual dress. Lipperheide lists a number, nos. 3727-3756. (3) General museum guides, unless they are outstanding and contain actual material, text or illustrations on costume. Lipperheide lists them, nos. 4999-5055. (4) Books on coats of arms. Many are listed in Lipperheide in the section on heraldry, nos. 4386-4439. (5) Laundering. Some books on this subject are listed in Lipperheide, nos. 3775-3854. (6) Titles in the Lipperheide sections on metalwork, leather, and woodwork, etc., nos. 4302-4355. Books purely on manufacturing have been omitted, but those on tailoring and cutting are included.

Authors, titles and other items of information were verified from Library of Congress cards whenever possible; otherwise from the bibliographies by Lipperheide and Colas, from cards received from the Union Catalog at the Library of Congress, from the catalogs of libraries in New York City, or from the various national and trade bibliographies and printed library catalogs. If the subject seemed clear from the title, or other information at hand, subjects were assigned without examination of the books. If the subject seemed in doubt an effort was made to find and examine the book in one of the three New York libraries: The New York Public Library, the library of Columbia University, or the Library of the Metropolitan Museum of Fine Arts.

Scope. The items listed include books, periodicals, and portfolios of plates dealing with dress, jewelry, and decoration of the body, in general and for special occasions, of all countries, times, and peoples; also items on such subjects as reform of dress, psychology of dress, art of dress; also needlework and its branches. In addition to books on costume many books of travel, history, and antiquities are listed since they include text or illustrations of costume value.

Editions. An effort has been made to list all editions in the English language, even though English was not the language in which the book was originally published. For example, a book originally in German, but also published in an English translation, will have both editions listed fully. However, if the English edition is the original it alone receives full listing, and information about the German, Spanish and other editions and translations is given in a note. The exact title of the noted books is given and references are made from changed titles to the author and title under which the information will be found.

Main entry. Fullest information is in the main entry, which is under the author's name if that is known, otherwise under the title of the book. Full cataloging information is given. If the name seemed to be complete and correct in Colas and Lipperheide, that form was accepted and used. Reference is made to the *Costume Index* and to the bibliographies of Colas and Lipperheide, for all titles included in these lists; and Library of Congress card numbers are given. Prices and out of print information are given only incidentally, if they were found in the process of verifying some other part of the entry. The price is the publication price.

The main entry should always be consulted. The subject entry gives only the author, title, and date of publication of the edition entered. Descriptive notes and information about other editions and about translations will be found only in the author entry. Anyone who consults the bibliography from the subject side alone will not find all the titles under which a certain book has been published and can be found in libraries.

Subjects. Books on costume in the restricted sense of clothing, will be found under the name of country, e.g. *France, Germany,* etc., further subdivided by period, or by region, e.g. *France—1774-1789,* or *France—Burgundy.* Books on costume not restricted to any one country or period are listed under the heading: *General,* with reference to related subjects. For books on costume of many countries but of one period see the name of the period, e.g. *Seventeenth century;* for books restricted to one section of the world see name of section or country, e.g. *Europe—Middle ages,* or *France—Middle ages. Ecclesiastical costume, Military costume, Naval costume,* and *Academic costume,* are listed under their appropriate headings. They are subdivided by church, country, period, or name of university, as applicable to the subject. *Ceremonial and festival costume* is treated in the same way. Parts of costume, and accessories, are listed under the specific name, e.g. *Footwear, Gloves, Jewelry, Needlework, Lace, Buttons.* Under *Embroidery* will be found the subhead *Monograms and numerals* and both show books of patterns and designs; *Embroidery* is divided by names of countries, e.g. *Embroidery—Russia; Embroidery—India,* making it possible to get a list of books on each particular type. The headings *Reform of dress, Nudity, Philosophy of dress, Fashion, Psychology of dress, Hygiene of dress* will guide to material of a more theoretical nature.

References to all these subjects are made from the subject *General,* under which the user can get a fairly clear idea of the scope and arrangement of the subjects, and how to find quickly the specific information sought.

Fashion periodicals. Several hundred fashion periodicals are listed under the heading Periodicals. They are arranged by the dates they cover in such a way that it is possible to find a list of the fashion periodicals of each quarter (e.g. 1800-1825, 1826-1850, etc.) of the nineteenth and twentieth centuries, and also of the few fashion periodicals begun in the eighteenth century. The entry for each periodical states the exact years during which it was issued and whether or not it contains colored plates. Since these periodicals show authentic fashions for each year, even each season or each month, they form a highly accurate, detailed, and useful source for information about fashionable European dress (wherever worn) from the year 1770, when the *Lady's magazine and museum of the belles-lettres* began publication. Fashion almanacs (annuals) were also issued, beginning somewhat later, but are now so scarce that for the most part they have not been included.

Union list. Altho this Bibliography does not tell in what libraries each book may be found, references to *Colas, Lipperheide,* the *Costume Index,* and the Library of Congress Card numbers provide to some extent a union list. Most of the books for which L. C. card numbers are given can be found in the Library of Congress. If a letter other than A or AC is prefixed to the L.C. card number it means that the book is in one of the other libraries in Washington, D. C. If the prefix is A or AC, it indicates that the book is in an American library outside of Washington. The name of the library in which the book is located is always noted on the card. The Lipperheide library is now a part of the Staatliche Kunstbibliothek in the Museum in der Prinz Albrechtsstrasse (formerly the Kunstgewerbemuseum) in Berlin. Colas frequently tells where he examined the copy he describes, and the *Costume Index* gives for each of its 600 titles a list of American libraries which own it. The *Union List of Serials,* edited by Winifred Gregory, which is widely available in libraries, tells where many of the fashion periodicals can be found.

COSTUMES AND IDEOLOGIES

> "The compilation of a complete bibliography, even the most concise, of the works devoted to the subject of costume, and to the incessant changes of fashion at every period, and in every country in the world, would be a considerable undertaking—a work worthy of such learning as dwelt in the monasteries of the Sixteenth Century. Such a book would, in an abbreviated form, be a sort of 'Dictionary of Origins,' useful for the 'General History of Mankind.'"
>
> OCTAVE UZANNE. *Fashion in Paris* (1898)

Many people might consider that a Bibliography of costume as large in scope as the present work is "much ado about little". The compilers are convinced that such a viewpoint is superficial. The present state of civilization underlines and points the repeated and justified warnings of men of the highest scientific standing that the Social Sciences must be stressed and their study greatly intensified at this time.

The expression of the human ego in all its manifold subtleties and attitudes is perhaps nowhere more evident than in the choice which men and women make of the articles which they use to cover or ornament their persons. The exaggerated use of elaborate or alarming uniforms and fantastic headgear on the part of totalitarian dictators may point, as some claim, to a state of mind bordering on the pathological, or simply clever showmanship. It has in any case a considerable interest. If it were properly understood and analyzed, far reaching and important deductions might be reached.

Women's styles offer another complex but interesting gauge which may tell us much of the psychology of a given epoch. Their relation to the dress of men, and which sex sets the mode, certainly are questions as yet unsolved. Differentiation of the sexes, considered a mark of the degree of civilization, is expressed in dress.

In connection with the newer techniques of Psychology a profound and significant analysis of social implications, as expressed in the rather unconscious exteriorizations of costume, is now theoretically possible. It should prove important for the very reason that many hidden characteristics of the individual are written for those capable of reading them, in the subtle and unapprehended language of the attempt at conformity or adaptation shown on his back.

Two ideologies seem to be struggling for world power at the time of this writing. One, theoretically at least, with a materialistic basis and theory; the other, purportedly, with a more romantic and emotional appeal. Between the extreme polar attitudes represented by these two concepts a vast majority of the world's population continues in an evolutionary rather than a revolutionary way, with more ordinary and therefore more "normal" psychological mechanisms.

Georges Sorel, in his *La Ruine du Monde Antique* and other books, analyzes the part played by the national totem and *mythos* in national expansion and the rise and fall of powers. The outward and plainest aspect of the nation as a godhead is perhaps most clearly demonstrated as may be seen elsewhere, in symbolic appurtenances in the form of raiment and adornment on personages living and dead and their sculptural effigies. The point in question is that these ideologies permeate the lives of individuals living under their rule and influence them in practically every external detail.

When Vienna was embraced in the Anschluss, the ladies of that formerly gay capital, whose international reputation for beauty and charm is unquestioned, were forbidden their millenary use of facial cosmetics on the rather suddenly discovered grounds that these aids to nature are a form of "Jewish eroticism." The accompanying doctrine of "kinder, kirche u. küche" (now replaced by "Kultur") would also have an obvious and thoro effect on the mode, implying certain limitations which could hardly be popular with all the fair sex all of the time. Keyserling might be spared, under such circumstances, the necessity of attempting to follow the peregrinations of post-war morals and the alterations of sex philosophies which replace each other with almost cinematographic rapidity; each one externalized more or less in dress.

Totalitarianism demands identification, as well as obedience in the comparatively negative form of abstinence. Many primitive peoples identify themselves with the totem by symbols attached to or painted on the body. Royce Brier, in the *San Francisco Chronicle* of November 10th, 1937, writes

> "About a year ago the British concluded that a uniform gives a Fascist an unfair advantage in drumming up converts, because it is a matter of common knowledge that fancy garb has been stealing the reason of both wearer and beholder since the Stone Age days when a leopard skin was superior to a wolf skin. So the British banned the black shirts and patent leather boots, and British Fascists had to shout in tweeds, a most extrawd'nary getup for a firebrand seeking overthrow of the House of Commons.
>
> "Sir Oswald Mosley promptly lost the two-thirds of his disciples, to whom a uniform was a uniform but the corporate state was just so much higher algebra, and Sir Oswald groped about in obscurity looking for a stunt."

Facts like these point to a difference of sexual psychology under different social structures. We believe that there is, and must be, a compensatory mechanism at work in every situation. An illusion of some sort is the necessary accompaniment of some state of mind which may, relatively at least, pass for sanity. A well-known psychiatrist, recently returned from a European tour, attempted to classify the forms taken by mental tendencies in the different countries which he studied. For him: Italy was paranoid, Germany megalomaniac, France in the grip of a fear psychosis, etc. Such tendencies, if they had any basis, might be expressed in dress. Can the older escape mechanisms or aids to the illusion for living, in which costume plays such a major part, be changed or replaced by others of equal or superior efficacy? If there is a shift in stress of elaborateness from the feminine back to the masculine are not basic situations involved? Is uniformity a gauge of a primitive stage of social organization; diversity of a higher degree of civilization? With no conclusions drawn, or perhaps to be drawn, as yet, it seems interesting to study all contemporary sources with such thoughts in mind. Little daggers, riding-boots, feathers in hats, etc., hardly seem of much practical use in the twentieth century. What state of mind do they express?

Costume versus Clothing

"Dressing up" implies dressing in a style distinct from that worn habitually. One is costumed rather than merely clothed. Between the terms clothing and costume there is a great distinction. Clothing is bodily covering; costume, raiment.

To elucidate. Let's assume that we have a nice clean blank white page. Drawing a line down the center, it is divided into two equal parts. The half on the left will have printed at the top the word *Material*; on the right, the word *Mental* will appear.

Under the word Material, we will write the terms: Apparel, Clothing and Dress; under the word Mental, the terms: Costume, Adornment and Body Ornament. Thus if we were making a study of the subject we might continue to write in the rest of the left-hand side such phrases as "Environment makes clothing necessary," "Climate furnishing in flora and fauna sufficient to provide materials for the fabrication of garments to protect man from its own temperatures," "Economic side of clothing," "Physiology of clothing," "Technique of manufacture from felting to tanning," "Bodily comfort; physical health."

Then we might cross the line and arrive on the Mental side where we would see such terms as Sex, Religion, Magic, Totem, Trophyism, Taboo, Ego, Aesthetics, Prestige, Imitation, et cetera, all tied up with the subject of clothes.

Clothes are economically, of course, of primary importance. Food, Clothing and Shelter are the three economic "goods" needed, in the order named. Lately I read a newspaper account of a woman who had for some time been in dire financial need, and unbeknown to her friends took poison; upon which her friends at last got together and purchased a silk dress to have her buried in. Man is born naked but dies and is put away with clothes on. Clothes have a practical material hygienic side of great scientific importance. Nothing warmer than fur, ounce for ounce, has ever been discovered. Wool is warmer than silk, silk than cotton, and cotton than linen. Dr. Dearborn, of the U.S. Army Medical Corps, says that the comfort, or lack of it, in clothing means immeasurable loss or gain in the efficiency of people in all sorts of jobs. Measured in terms of money, collectively estimated, it makes the head swim.

Thomas Carlyle had his studious character Diogenes Teufelsdrockh take a look into this business a long while ago. In his book, *Sartor Resartus,* Herr Teufelsdrockh rather longwindedly came to the conclusion that barbarous man spiritually craved decoration while he showed considerable indifference about the warmth and protective qualities of his clothes. He was strong on the esthetic side, and craved that touch of *je ne sais quoi* of necessary decoration (*putz*). It was hinted that man, as Diogenes T. states, changed from a "naked animal" to a clothed animal for some obscure artistic reason.

I think that man took to costume before he took to clothing; he "dressed up" before he clothed himself. Carlyle's Herr T. was right when he said or hinted that ornament, not covering, was the preoccupation of the "hairy savage." There is much evidence that the savage, indifferent concerning the vagaries of temperature, neglected his clothing. The ancient Chinese and the old Greek commentators thought that clothing was adopted for warmth, but this is not a modern scientific view of the matter.

An early traveler describes a Mangai islander as "being clothed with a hunting knife which was stuck through the lobe of his ear." Darwin speaks of giving a good-sized piece of red cloth to a Fuegian who, although "he certainly stood in need of protective clothing" tore it up and distributed it among his companions who used it decoratively.

African safari porters wear all the odds and ends of clothing they can get hold of in the heat of the day, and throw them off in the cool of the evening when camp is reached. The evidence all over the primitive world, with few exceptions, seems to show that clothing plays a secondary role to costume.

Decoration first, protection afterward. Man's origin in the tropics would not point to the use of clothing for economic reasons. The primitives do not "wear clothes." They "dress up."

The assumption of the dressing up proclivity puts by the board theories such as that held by Ratzel and the older school of ethnologists, that clothing was forced upon women by their lords and masters as a means of diminishing the force of their charms. It also does not agree with the Mosaic assumption explained naively by St. Augustine in connection with the serpent and the apple, that modesty is at the bottom of dress. Robert Burton in his somewhat dour *Anatomy of Melancholy,* Dumaurier, Stendhal, Remy de Gourmont, Westermarck, Havelock Ellis and many others, deny this possibility emphatically.

Modesty came after clothing. Ornament preceded clothing and was worn to attract, not to hide. Salomon Reinach denies this possibility, favoring the explanation of a blood taboo as reason for the origin of dress; but it is simpler and just as probable to accept, at least in part, the more intriguing theory that men and women started "dressing up" to make themselves mutually attractive. The behavior of many "savages" supports such an assumption, for more than one people among whom nudity is the habitual state, don body ornaments and garments when about to engage in licentious ceremonies or sexual dances. They do, in fact, "dress up" for every sort of ceremony.

Ceremonial and dressing up scent of the theatre in embryo. Frazer, who gives such an excellent idea of these activities in the *Golden Bough,* hints that magic may have something to do with it. Tree sprites, being present in the tree and in its bark, are present in bark clothing. Clothing is again picturesquely connected with the worship of the serpent, which was the only animal which could change its dress—and therefore its personality. Elliot Smith, whose theories have somewhat more lately romantically revolutionized ethnology, claims that costume originated through the wearing of amulets of sexual power, near the appropriate spot. Crawley, differing with him, yet agrees in his *Mystic Rose.*

Perhaps a hunter carrying his trophy proudly thought of hanging it about his neck, or more conveniently, wearing its skin. Shining ornaments may have been worn because of a purely esthetic attraction which such objects seem to have exerted upon creatures as diversified as jackaws, monkeys, Australian bower birds and Park Avenue dowagers.

Anyway—our material, physical side of the affair, seems, at first at least, to have had very little to do with "dressing up." It is on the mental side of our paper that we find all our terms, now somewhat explained, which have to do with Costume as opposed to Clothing; Raiment as opposed to mere Apparel; Adornment, as opposed to Dress. "Dressing up" then, is the whole artistic side of clothing, the psychological side in its purest connotation—Sexually attractive, Magico-religious, Prestige imitational, Ego Lotzean stimulating, Esthetic, Architectural, War, Theatrical, Ceremonial, Caste-marking, Armorial, Totem-influencing, Trophyistical dressing up.

Costume Developing

If people are assumed as having begun to dress with ornament: The girdle grew into kilt, skirt and trousers; the necklace into cape, robe, cloak and coat. Around the diadem or head-band, feathers sprang up, flaps hung down. Bracelets, rings, anklets, earrings, labrets, garters and armlets pretty well complete the list of ornaments from which clothing stemmed, because they exhaust the places where ornaments could be conveniently worn. The architecture of the human body, as Semper remarks, forms the architecture of costume: Two pendicular ornamental earrings, one on each side; A nodding plume or floating feather leaning backward to accentuate its wearer's movement forward, corresponding with the axis of the human body. Costume, following the path of the other arts, becomes architectural. It reacts mutually with the human body. Ripley draws attention to the Basques who shaved appropriately to the way in which their beards grew. "The ancient Egyptians," says Elliot Smith, "were endowed with a respectable growth of beard only upon the chin." But the Assyrians and the Babylonians were contrastingly hirsute. Thick limbs, thick clothing. Would our friend Gerald Heard then admit that the Minoans in their highly developed anatomic costume, were naturally somewhat slim waisted?

Clothes and Caste

Clothes artistically satisfying, were insufficient. Norman Douglas, in his *Siren Land,* recalls Lotze's observations on the manner in which man enlarged his personality, extending it by a huge headdress and a walking stick. Happy coincidence that economically the headdress and walking stick could so unfit their wearer to perform anything in the nature of productive labor.

Veblen shows that the "canon of wasted effort," when it lent value to the chief's cloak, which was made of the feathers of a rare Pacific bird, lent value to the chief. A leisured man was he, with the leisure of others at his disposal. The rich one then hung his riches 'round his neck. A mighty man's riches were too heavy for one neck? Well, then, other necks were provided—wives, concubines and servants each did their share in aiding the display. God, the mightiest chief, came to have the most leisured servants, the tallest houses and the most preciously dressed butlers—the bishops.

If one was "dressed up"—that is to say, dressed up from every point of view—then one was esthetically satisfying, the naturally esthetic assets being properly stressed; therefore, sexually attractive, with a maximum expansion of the ego in all directions; magically protected by the proper amulets, with metamorphosed trophies visible somewhere about one's person (having taken on the desirable qualities of brightness and shininess); economically conspicuous because of the ability to wear rare and therefore valuable materials; fearless, because protected from demons, possible accusation of poverty, insignificance, or nonconformity; *en règle,* provided with the proper papers for one's class and epoch, pointing always toward the appropriate ideal.

"Plus ça change, plus c'est la même chose." All those things which so elusively through the ages went to make up that indefinable thing called taste. Reflected here, there and everywhere. The tightly corseted figures of the anatomically dressed Aegeans. The beautiful gravitational folds of the Greek robes. Architectural forms repeated on . . . or from humanity, as pointed out by Viollet le Duc, Webb and Heard.

But it seems to us lately that the men at least, and they have until yesterday with one exception set the styles, are becoming more and more clothed and less "dressed up." Does this point to a return to the uniformity of savagery, as Havelock Ellis sometimes seems to fear? Man's choice of clothing appears to be getting instinctively *selbstverständlich.*

There is seemingly little hope offered by a future in a civilization dominated by machinery.

Trotter's rationalization of the belief in the herd idea is here appropriate. It serves to justify the assumption of herd suggestion, which is so rapidly taking on a universal force and scope. "This mechanism," he says, "enables the English lady who, to escape the stigma of having normal feet, subjects them to a formidable degree of lateral compression, to be aware of no logical inconsequence when she subscribes to missions to teach the Chinese lady how absurd it is to compress her feet longitudinally; it enables the European lady who wears rings in her ears, to smile at the barbarism of the colored lady who wears rings in her nose; it enables the Englishman, who is amused by the African chieftain's regard for the top hat as an essential piece of the furniture of state, to ignore the identity of his own behavior when he goes to church beneath the same tremendous ensign."

But the tendency is toward a devolution from costume toward clothing. The "tremendous ensign" itself is becoming old-fashioned. Ever there is less of the real costume psychology in clothes. "Dressing," as a conventional art, is dead or dying.

Costume is too close to dancing, music, poetry and ceremonial, to occupy a place in a world given over more and more exclusively to mass production. It must give way to clothing, and that quickly. The headgear (the last article of costume to be given up is the hat *) is made to disappear when not sacrificed, as it usually is, without a struggle. Turkey and Persia suppressed the national headgear by stern sumptuary edict. Echoes of the "Whisker Rebellion" in Afghanistan are still heard. Verlaine's dire prophecy of the time "when madmen walk the streets all clothed in black" is being everywhere fulfilled.

The effect of unesthetic clothing upon morale is too well known to need stressing. It is mentioned by Robert Louis Stevenson (who says "a change of habit is bloodier than bombardment"), Louis LeFevre, Francis Abell in his account of the preoccupation of prisoners with the decoration of their clothes, Stanley Hall in his report about school children, and hinted at by Sigmund Freud when he remarks "of equal significance to the physician, and worthy of his observation, is everything that one does with his clothing, often without noticing it. Every change in the customary attire, every little negligence, such as an unfastened button, every trace of exposure, means to express something that the wearer of the apparel does not wish to say directly. Usually he is entirely unconscious of it."

Does the disappearance of dressing up indicate the passing of Western Civilization? If so, Spengler is welcome to the suggestion. It is certainly in youth and the virile period that the individual is preoccupied with dress. Which of us might not sneakingly enjoy a real costume, if he dared? Real costume, which is now confined to the theatre and cinema, to be enjoyed by most of us in a somewhat vicarious fashion—May the theatre keep the spark of suggestion alive until some more leisured age when the play spirit reawakens, and we may all again "dress up."

Philosophy and Psychology

There are a number of books purporting to deal with the psychology of clothing. Philosophers of one sort or another have, in their universality of specialization interested themselves in the subject since the time when Pan Kou

* Exception: Japan.

of China said that at the end of the "seventh conjunction . . . men covered themselves with vestments of leaves . . . and with the skins of beasts to preserve themselves from the cold and the winds." Lucretius set forth his theories poetically in *De Rerum Natura* and Saint Augustine rather morally in *Clivitate Dei* (Bk. XIV, Chapter XVII). The psychology of clothing is a complex and highly technical subject that, in our opinion, has baffled all the writers who have so far attempted to deal with it. A more recent and comparatively profound book is that by Flügel of the University of London. Carlyle's classic *Sartor Resartus* is too well known to need more than a passing mention. H. Lotze in his "Microcosmus" interestingly discussed the connection between costumes and the ego, particularly as related to the wearing of the top hat (4th American edition 1897. Bk. V, Chapter II, p592-595).

In the newer psychology and in psychoanalysis a continued interest is shown in costume. Freud discusses it briefly under "Fetichism" in his *Autobiography* (2nd edition 1927-1935, p149) He has made many other observations on clothing and says that he studies the appearance of his patients from this standpoint as carefully as he does from any other one. His views, as might be expected, have a consistently sexual basis, and it must be said with some regret that a lack of acquaintance with Freudian technique prevented my giving to the well-known castration theory, the space which is probably due it in my discussion of the origin of clothing in *From Nudity to Raiment.*

Perhaps some day a synthesis of the different schools of psychoanalysis, including Adlers' "purpose-force" concept, Jung's "energic ego," Steckel's "dynamic mechanism," and the original libido theories may give us a clearer concept of some more profound implications in dress. These theories might very well allow of elaborations on older ideas in the same connections.

In his book *Understanding Human Nature,* (American edition, p248) Adler says, "Untidiness if carried to an extreme may sometimes be an indication of greater vanity than careful dressing." (In this he seems to follow Spinoza's dictum "The humble man goes nearest to the proud.") In some cases the untidiness may be a subconsciously assumed habit—one of the many forms which the alibi of the vain individual may take as the reason for his lack of success in handling the problems of everyday life."

If this sort of thing interests the reader, he would be able to follow it up by consulting specialized bibliographies relating to the literature of the different psychoanalytical schools.* These bibliographies are particularly rich in periodical literature.

We believe that there may be such a thing as an anal-sadistic type of clothing which would be characterized by its tight fit, general stiffness and lack of comfort and something military in its character. For a number of years, women masochists, particularly, subjected themselves to the tortures of the now happily extinct corset as they still do to extremely high heeled shoes. Magnus Hirschfield and O. P. Gilbert, the latter in a book called *Men in Women's Guise,* have studied the relations between homosexuality and clothing. The wearing of womens' clothes by male homosexuals is a carefully studied, and to them doubtless delightful preoccupation which is known in certain circles as "drag."

Clothing fetichism may at times have incestuous implications as one theory purporting to explain shoe fetichism, which is one of the commonest sorts, bases its ideology on the contacts with the mother's shoes which the child established

* See for instance: Flügel, J. C. Clothes, Symbolism and Clothes, Ambivalence, *International Journal of Psycho-Analysis* 10:203, 1929; A Dress Reform Dream. *The same* 11:4-479, 1936; The Psychology of Clothes. *The same* 12:1-98; etc.

while creeping on the floor. Havelock Ellis has many interesting things to say in his *Psychology of Sex,* some, rather surprisingly, touching on masturbation.

Sexual Psychology

The importance of clothing as a sex stimulant is universally admitted. South Sea Island maidens of years gone by put flowers in their tresses to fascinate the shipwrecked sailors, at least so the cinema tells us. The girls of our cities are doing the same thing this summer.

Du Maurier makes the following observation in *Trilby,* "It is well known to all painters and sculptors who have used a nude model (except for a few shady pretenders, whose purity, not being of the right sort, has gone rank from too much watching) that nothing is so chaste as nudity. Venus herself as she drops her garments and steps upon the model throne, leaves behind her on the floor every weapon in her armory by which she can pierce to the grosser passions of men." Stendhal agrees with him when he says in *De l'Amour,* "It is clear that three parts of modesty are taught—modesty that gives to love the aid of the imagination, and in so doing imparts life to it." And the melancholy Robert Burton said years before either of them: "The greatest provocations of lust are from our apparel."

All individuals are not equally affected by the visual refinements of costume as the modes change from year to year and seem to alter to stress by display different portions of the fair anatomy. Perhaps the type most susceptible to such lures would, in extreme cases, trend toward that sort of psychopath which the French describe as a *voyeur.* Krafft-Ebing in his monumental *Psychopathia Sexualis* describes cases which were repeatedly attracted to such diverse articles of apparel as shoes, boots, silken scarves and blacksmiths' aprons.

Metapsychology

Precursors of psychology, sorcerers, magicians, demonologists, etc., have also a considerable connection with dress. Demons were (and still are in some parts of the world) kept at bay by being frightened away by masks. Charms and amulets were used to secure love or fertility or protect the wearer from the evil eye as some forms of tattooing are warranted to do.

If the theories of the late Elliot Smith, Rivers and Perry are to be accepted, search for amuletic substances and their surrogates must have played an incalculable role in the diffusion of culture and perhaps type-forms of clothing.

The buttons on the Costermonger's "pearly" suit may have come through Venice to England from the Indian Ocean. The amuletic cowry shell, thought from its resemblance to the female genetalia to be a guarantor of fertility, evolved into shell buttons worn by the fisherfolk in many places. It is said to be the basis for the Egyptian written symbol for gold. The costermongers were fishmongers before they were Coster—*apple,* Mongers—*sellers,* so their buttons were traced back to Venice where a similar garb was worn in the same vocation, and far beyond.

Further interesting theories might be followed up in connection with the conventionalized dress of Mephistopheles, the survival of the Halloween witch's hat from the medieval hennin, which appears to have been worn by adepts of both sexes. Could there be, as Heard suggests, some connection between this

Gothic hennin and the Gothic spire? If so, the symbolry may be self-explanatory.

Theories

Such considerations take us back to the very origins of clothing which are so closely connected with the generally fundamental psychology of the subject that they may appropriately be treated with it. For a more detailed discussion of these origins the reader is again referred to *From Nudity to Raiment,* Chapter v, and the references therein. Here it may suffice to outline some of the more generally accepted theories referring, for purposes of further study, to the authors who respectively support them.

The Theory of Sex Attraction, based to some extent on Montaigne's statement that "There are certain things which are hidden in order to be shown" is best explained in brief by Westermarck, in his *History of Human Marriage,* where he declares that "we have every reason to believe that mere decorations have also developed into clothes" and that clothing originated mainly "in the desire of men and women to make themselves mutually attractive." This theory is supported by Havelock Ellis (with reservations), Grosse and others.

That it is in direct opposition to the Mosaic Theory as expounded in the Bible, and the Theory of Possession held by Ratzel and other early ethnologists, both the author and the authorities quoted above, are well aware.

The Taboo Theory, self-explanatory in its title, was put forward by Durkheim and supported by Reinach. The latter says that "Durkheim determined it happily in recognizing the *blood taboo* as a particular case." It would seem reasonable to suppose that Freud would be interested in this theory and with the possible exception to be mentioned later, lend it his support.

The Totemistic Theory, as advanced by Crawley in his *Mystic Rose* argues for an amuletic origin, claiming that ornamentation, tattooing, etc., may have originated "for the purpose of magically insulating certain organs." We are unacquainted with any important defense or elaboration of this theory on the part of others.

The Amuletic Theory, is closely related to Crawley's, as may be also the idea that clothing originated in the carrying of trophies or trophyistic surrogates.

I advanced an Esthetic Theory based upon substantiated observations of the behavior of birds and animals with arboreally developed vision, such as bower birds, jackdaws, monkeys and apes. Attraction for shiny objects may have suggested that they might most easily be kept near the possessor by being attached to the person. Köhler, in *The Mentality of Apes*; Edmond Haraucourt, in *Daah, le Premier Homme*; and Johannes V. Jensen in *The Long Journey* directly or indirectly seem to support this theory.

It now seems that an interesting if somewhat complex theory might also be built up on the Castration Fear so important in Freudian Psycho-analysis. Quite apart from any directly protective function of the garment, this fear may well be the basis for the amuletic theory. If men, as their more elaborate dress in primitive stages of society may indicate, wore ornament or clothing before women did, a Castration Theory becomes more plausible.

We can think of a few other factors which come into the psychology of clothing with an advancingly complex social structure. They touch upon economic factors increasingly as these in their turn interact with others. Certain objects and substances which may have owed their first importance to esthetic and amuletic considerations take on an economic value and tend to function as primitive media of exchange. Wampum, shells, teeth, skins, etc., finally leather and metals.

Caste and its heraldry as manifested by dress seem to have an economic basis discernible at some very early stage. Hunting was certainly an economic activity and the prowess of the hunter must have automatically been made evident. Prestige and prestige-imitation, still a powerful conditioner of dress, appear, flourish and evolve in diversified and ever elaborating forms.

Many factors in Paleopsychology are closely paralleled by more nearly contemporary hunting tribes. These parallels are interestingly and humanly discussed by Sollas in his remarkable book, *Ancient Hunters and their Modern Representatives.*

Child Psychology

Children have a very considerable propensity for dressing up. The effect of clothing on their personality is the same as in the case of adults arrayed for a masquerade ball except for its intensity which because of their fresher and more powerful imaginations and lower degree of socialization is considerable. With some children this amounts almost to a mania. Stanley Hall, in a report based on returns from almost a thousand persons, mostly teachers, states that among the three main functions of clothes: protection, ornament and "Lotzean self-feeling"—the second is by far the most conspicuous in childhood. Among sensitive children this is doubtless part of a gradual technique of personality adjustment to reality. In clothing we might hint that the psychology of the child may be studied through the psychology of the primitive. There is a similar pressure toward uniformity within the given group, and parents who insist for the satisfaction of their own ego in distinguishing the child from his fellows, put him to much unnecessary misery, which might increase a trauma already undergone, or in some cases even bring about traumatic results. The child's world does not function by the same or even similar standards of conformity as that of adults. In closing we should like to remark for a possible random benefit to some mothers that ideas of sexual differentiation in dress appear much earlier than may be generally supposed. This fact is generally recognized by people in all culture stages from the most primitive to European peasantry.

Personality and Characterology

Much has been written on personality, physiognomy, and characterology since the days of Nordau and Lombroso. The study of the individual from these standpoints has not been entirely disinterested as there is supposed to be a definitely practical side to such studies in connection with commercial activities, particularly in the hiring of employees and in salesmanship. We remember an outline paper in a course in "Business Psychology" which purported to analyze a man from the standpoint of his clothing by beginning at the hat and working gradually down to the shoes. Such an analysis, while not beyond the bounds of possibility would involve extremely complex factors. The tendency of the vain man toward careless dressing as observed above by Adler, and the fact that people on the fringes of society often compensate for their precarious social position by what they call a "front," should be illuminating. Investigators know that successful criminals often have very large wardrobes in a quiet taste.

Physiognomy undoubtedly affects the dress of the individual, as people instinctively know, at least to some extent, what is fitting, viz: becoming, or, on the other hand, what may help to hide or stress some impossible or favorable feature. Our own opinion of the so-called systems of physiognomy need not be given here and we feel that it would have little connection with clothing except that noted.

Practice in observation and analysis provides at least an interesting and possibly useful pastime. In a city with a climate like that of Paris a lady on the *Metro* wearing light colored shoes in the winter is probably there through inadvertance or temporary misfortune, as her footgear hints that she has been in the habit of taking taxis. The young man next to her with his cap over one eye is certainly not working for a bourgeois establishment as such headgear would be frowned upon if that were the case. A short distance down the aisle a still younger man who wears a *beret* consciously or unconsciously does not care to stress his masculinity, as this type of head covering is also worn quite commonly by women and children. Such observations are endless, as are the techniques of the individual to adjust himself to the group and through it to society in general. It might be safely claimed that the attitude, position and occupation of the great majority of men may be approximated from their dress except in cases where it is profitable for them to take advantage of this very fact by conscious deceit.

Religion and Beliefs

The connection between religious beliefs and dress are manifold and obvious. From the explanations given in the Bible to the latest pronunciamento of his Holiness, religion has concerned itself with modesty and the wickedness of sex attraction as abetted by clothing. It may be interesting to note here that the serpent is connected with these ideas in the Jewish and Christian as well as other religions. Frazier interestingly notes in his observations on serpent worship that this reptile had the unique faculty of changing its skin (clothing). It might seem to some readers that we are drawing rather a long bow if we connect these facts with the Freudian "Castration Theory."

The clothing of the priestly class throughout history has been relatively sexless, and that in a conservative way. Priests and women are the last to give up the concealment of the robe-skirt type of clothing in the process of its gradual disappearance before the spread of so-called civilization.

Readers who are familiar with the monumental *Golden Bough* may find a connection between the priestly robes worn by the God-King, and the concealment and isolation of the ruler and his cult of servitors. This fact was noted by Thorstein Veblen whose theories will be discussed later in connection with their main interest, economics.

The liturgical and general symbolism in religious dress is so complex and interesting that it would provide a good basis for an extended separate work. A book has been written on the Quaker and his particular attitude toward clothing (A. M. Gummere's *The Quaker, a study in costume*), and special laws were passed after the French Revolution granting privileges to this sect, so seriously did they take their rules regulating clothing.

The *Jewish Encyclopedia,* The *Catholic Encyclopedia,* and T. P. Hughes' *Dictionary of Islam* are interesting sources for information on costume in their particular fields.

The striking similarity in type-form in the dress of religious orders the world over is indicative of a common origin in the folkways. Similarities as clear as those which exist in the case of the Catholic and Buddhist orders of monks can hardly be considered fortuitous.

We may now have the opportunity of witnessing the origin and development of new religions and their effect on clothing. The correspondent of the *London Times* gives the following directions for the dress of a wedding party under National Socialism, "who have severed their ties with Christianity and who, as true Germans, wish to marry without a priest's blessing. . . The wedding party are expected to wear Nazi uniforms or peasant costumes or white blouses and dark skirts, or white shirts and dark trousers—thus doing away with the frivolous finery of bygone days." The costume recommended above for the National Socialist wedding would certainly be inconspicuous at a church social presided over by Elmer Gantry.

This attitude toward dress fits in quite well with the theory advanced by Dr. Ernest Jones of London, wherein a distinction is made in the religious symbolism of the national mythos. The typical matriarchal countries are represented by a feminine totem in terminology and caricature, e.g. "Marianne," "La Belle France," or "La Mère Patrie," "Mother Ireland," "Kathleen O'Houlihan," and so forth. These concepts are opposed to the patriarchal ones of the "Vaterland," "John Bull," and "Uncle Sam."

Social Sciences

The social sciences have a basis in economics. The whole aspect of clothing involved therein must be considered as a part of shelter. Schweinfurth and Dr. K. H. Stratz have divided clothing into two main types; the northern and the southern: or arctic and tropic. These are exemplified respectively by the Eskimo and the Arab. The northern type is assumed to be typical of the desire for protection. The upper garment is close fitting and a tight pair of trousers or skirt, may have been derived from the practise of tying skins about the body. It is usually termed the *anatomic* type to distinguish it from the southern or *gravitational,* composed of loose elements hanging in folds and considered as having developed from the ornamental girdle and necklace. Generally speaking, trousers are universal in the far north, confined to the male in the more temperate zones, and practically absent from the southern latitudes where gravitational clothing is worn by both sexes.

Thorstein Veblen, in his book *The Theory of the Leisure Class,* discusses clothing in its economic aspects, and its relation to sociology, caste and class distinction. These factors are very interestingly demonstrated at many points by the formerly distinctive dress of the guilds and crafts which disappeared in most parts of the world with the advent of the industrial revolution. Louis Bourdeau in *Histoire de l'Habillement et de la Parure* discussed many phases of clothing from an economic standpoint and some remarks of Dickens may be relevant, if we remember that the industrial revolution began in England and advanced far more rapidly there than in France.

The following is from *The Uncommercial Traveler* (Chapter 25)

"The mass of London people are shabby. The absence of distinctive dress has, no doubt, something to do with it. The porters of the Vintners' Co., the draymen and the butchers are about the only people who wear distinctive dress and even these do not wear them on holidays. We have nothing which, for cheapness, cleanliness, convenience, can compare with the belted blouse. As to our women, next Easter or Whitsuntide, look at the bonnets at the British Museum or the National Gallery and think of the pretty white French cap, Spanish mantilla, or the Genevese mezzero."

And, again, from the same source:

"Probably there are not more secondhand clothes sold in London than in Paris and yet the mass of the London population have a secondhand look which is not to be detected on the mass of the French population. I think this is mainly because a Parisian workingman does not in the least trouble himself about what is worn by the Parisian idler, but dresses himself in the way of his own class and for his own comfort."

Such considerations have by no means disappeared from the world. The doormen of the great New York hostelries and the ushers of the moving picture palaces, in that same metropolis, are costumed to outdo South American or Balkan *generalissimos* in their fullest dress. The employees of the Mediterranean casinos, where chance may be tempted, wear chains about their necks like medieval mayors. The wealth and social position of the most sophisticated sections of the privileged classes is still displayed indirectly upon the persons of servants and retainers; this situation reaching its apogee in the coronation ceremony of regal Albion. We are here far away indeed from the naïve pretensions of gypsies and peasants who, their material needs in clothing satisfied, can find no more suitable demonstration of their wealth and position than in hanging strings of gold coins around the necks of their women.

Communism

Some years ago, Madam Alexandra Exter, the Russian stage designer, accorded us the privilege of examining a number of lithographic plates issued by the Soviet government as graphic recommendations of what they considered ideal dress in a potentially classless society. It is perhaps fortunate esthetically that these suggestions were never adopted in their entirety by the comrades, as a tendency toward drab uniformity appeared to be the most outstanding characteristic. Certainly Russian official types now show a simplicity more than lacking under the Tsarist regime. Stalin, with his pipe, hunting blouse, cap and leggings, is a walking epitome of an economic social theory.

State Socialism

These conditions do not apply under State Socialism. The trappings of the dictators have already been mentioned. The predominant section of the population brings Kipling's poem *Boots* involuntarily to mind. Dr. Boje Benzon in the *Berlinske Tidende,* a Danish paper of conservative tendencies, gives a description of Herr Goering's idea of dress which is too interesting to skip.

"We saw Marshal Goering leaning against a table. He was dressed in a unique kind of sporting outfit. It consisted of high green suede boots, the front part of which reached above his knees; a dark green, sleeveless leather jacket with silver-edged elk's teeth instead of buttons (contributed by an elk which the Head Huntsman himself had shot); riding breeches of beige-colored suede, and a white shirt with an unusually wide collar and large sleeves which narrowed suddenly at the wrists. A Scot's tartan tie was held in place by an enormous gold pin. In a gold embroidered belt, he carried a golden hunting knife in a golden sheath. On his left breast Goering wore the medal of the German Hunting Society; a stag with a Swastika between the antlers. The stag was of gold; the Swastika consisted of diamonds which sparkled when the Reich Hunting Master moved about . . . Behind each chair stood a waiter in eighteenth century hunting outfit—white boots, green velvet dress suit, lace jabots and cuffs. I was surprised to see that they did not wear wigs. In reply to my question about this, my neighbor at table, who was well informed, told me that during hunts the servants never wore wigs, which might become entangled, like Absalom's, in the branches."

Law

The dress of devotees of justice in all ages, the survival of the jabot in the French courts, the barrister's wig in England and the black robe everywhere, need not be discussed here. Sumptuary laws have been covered to some extent in the Hiler bibliography and more specialized legal sources may be suggested to those who have a particular interest in this phase of the subject.

Uniforms

Three principal factors may be noted in connection with uniforms:

a. The desire to terrify (Grosse's *Schreckschmuck*).

b. The function of protection (in the form of survival of parts of armor and camouflage color).

c. The identification with the group and totem-concept.

Of these, the first mentioned is the least important. To be seen surviving as evolved from the primitive war paint in medieval armour and the metal masks of the samurai, it also appears as exemplified in the busby of the palace guard in England and Denmark and the trappings of Hussar regiments which come from the original death's head and skeleton markings. That it has up until lately played a role, there is little doubt. The American Indians in full array were sufficiently effective to require careful distribution of veterans whose advice and example neutralized to some extent the fear inspired. The history of the Kaffir wars, says Ratzel (*History of Mankind,* v7 p346) teaches that even European troops were not always sufficiently steeled against such a display of warlike savagery. Long range weapons have made any contemporary survival accidental or purely residual.

Regarding the function of protection, it has survived amply in the readopted steel helmet, and through the cuirassier's breastplate; also in the bullet-proof vest used by the German Army in the World War, when relative man power was running low. The horsehair plume and epaulettes are other examples. Carried to its logical conclusion, it would result ultimately in the one-man tank which has so far only appeared in purely experimental form. France, weak in numbers, may resort to some elaboration of this factor.

Gustavus Adolphus is supposed to have been responsible for the use of uniforms in the modern sense of the term. Their psychological value in relation to identification with the group must be very considerable. A number of studies on the effect of uniforms on morale have been made and some twenty years ago I wrote a treatise *The Psychology of Costume in Warfare* which is in manuscript form in the Library of the University of Pennsylvania.

Red has been the outstanding color of Empire. The Roman legions were predominantly dressed in it, as were the forces of expanding Britain. Victorious Roman generals painted their bodies in this color for triumphal processions and it survived on cuffs and emblems in modern mechanized armies. Georges Sorel, in his *La Ruine du Monde Antique* gives a penetrating analysis of the power of a common Totem as a national mythos. It would prove illuminating reading in connection with some of the above observations.

Some survivals in uniform, symbolic and otherwise, help to explain its evolution: the placing of the buttons on the sleeves to keep them from being used as handkerchiefs; the wearing of a certain type of mustache which was formerly considered terrifying; Grenadier buttons to keep the grenadiers from being hoisted with their own petards; the Nelson hook and eye; etc.

This Bibliography has paid particular attention to the uniforms of the American forces which have been neglected in former works.

Non-Military Uniforms

Uniforms of a non-military nature are imposed by society for some reason or other; sometimes from inside a group and sometimes upon a group by a larger and more powerful group. An example of the latter case is furnished by prison uniforms which generate interesting reactions on the part of the wearer. By the imposition of such stigmata society hopes to protect itself. The title of a book, rather difficult to classify bibliographically, translated from the original French, reads: "The Badges of Infamy in the Middle Ages: Jews, Saracens, Heretics, Lepers, Bigots, and Prostitutes." The color of such marks was usually yellow and its use persisted. Francis Abell in his book *Prisoners of War in Britain, 1756 to 1815* (Oxford univ. press 1914 p255) mentions the fact that the prisoners were given clothes of a sulphurous yellow "to prevent them from being sold" (!). He continues "In dress, it was the aim of everyone to disguise the hideous prison garb as much as possible, the results often being ludicrous in the extreme."

This same preoccupation with clothing is evident in the case of Robert Joyce Trasker, a writer, invited by the authorities to pass some time in meditation in the San Quentin Prison near San Francisco. In an article in the *American Mercury,* Volume 10, p39, March 1927, in which he describes his sensations upon entering the institution, he stresses the physical discomforts of the prison garb, but I believe that the possible discomfort involved in the wearing of such garments is accentuated to such a point as a subconscious protest against their hideous appearance, for, save in the case of the underclothing, it is hard to see how their use could result in any serious inconvenience in such a universally uncomfortable environment. His description, with its careful attention to color, texture and cut seems to bear out this assumption.

"At last, I stepped out of the tub and dried myself with a coarse towel. Unseen hands had removed my discarded clothes and placed my new ones on a stool. The underwear was of two pieces; the lower garment reaching to my ankles, and the upper, extending from my throat to my wrist. It was heavy stuff, and, even as I drew it on, I knew that it would bring me hours of torture when the heat of the day set in, for the fabric against my skin was clinging, woolly, irritating. There were trousers of heavy blue material . . . rough, hairy cloth that would fade quickly and lose all semblance of shape in the first rain. They were tailored with no thought to the contours of the body. A shirt of similar but lighter stuff proved to be much too large for me in every part except the sleeves and these were uncomfortably tight about the armpits, were ludicrously full at the elbows and at least two inches short.

"Already, I began to feel as though laced into Arctic clothes. The socks I was given were of heavy white cotton. My feet, if they may be credited with senses of their own, sent up an indignant protest. Then came brogans, high-topped, built on the lines of Boy Scout shoes, but poorly shaped. Followed a cap of the trousers material, the cardboard bill fitting wretchedly against my forehead. Lastly, a coat was slipped on—a sort of jacket—bunchy and out of all proportion as it hung upon me."

A better understanding of how uniforms are voluntarily adopted by groups in societies (particularly in the United States, in fraternal organizations, schools, etc.) may be gained by reading Trotter's *The Instincts of the Herd in Peace and War.* Implications therein are worthy of a profound study. They are, incidentally, very timely.

In uniforms, clothing outwardly shows at least a pretence of adherence and identification with some class, caste or group. "They're hangin' men and women for the wearin' o' the green." In this manner, the illusion of the individual is strengthened and affirmed. His sense, true or false, of his concept of "reality" is surrounded and supported by the thoughts and actions of other individuals with whom he wears a common sign and mark. White hood or edged academic one; red shirt, black, brown or green. Fez, suppressed in Turkey, or caftan in Persia, by their presence or absence, as the case may be, show a mental attitude which in the ultimate analysis goes deeply into the individual psyche.

Customs and Costume

In a less obvious manner, custom influences costume. The less evolved the society, the more stringently are the totem and taboo enforced. Some rule broken in "civilized" society may cause embarrassment, where in primitive circles it would result in serious punishment or death.

Customs and costume are regulated in all the ceremonies and rituals of life. Clothing for betrothals has been shown to be still carefully regulated in some parts of the world. White is worn by the bride at the marriage and a ring after the marriage. Black is a mourning color in the west; white, in China. Clothing is provided carefully for the world beyond and efforts are made to preserve it with the body. Folk dress persists in some few localities, while in others, official efforts are made for its revival or preservation.

Hendrik W. Van Loon, in his *Story of Mankind* (p362) says:

> You may think it absurd that I mention such a detail. But, if you please, the Congress of Vienna was one long succession of such absurdities and for many months the question of "short trousers vs. long trousers" interested the delegates more than the future settlement of the Saxon or Spanish problems. His Majesty, the King of Prussia, went so far as to order a pair of short ones, that he might give public evidence of his contempt of everything revolutionary.

Is it to be supposed that such considerations no longer preoccupy people in the rapid stresses of the Twentieth Century? They did in 1936, as an issue of *The Scotsman* of that year gives the following news item:

> "The controversy over which is the correct tie to wear with Highland evening dress was again raised at a special general meeting of the Kilt Society of Inverness yesterday, when there was a representative attendance of members to consider a motion tabled by The Mackintosh of Mackintosh, Chief of the Society.
>
> "The Mackintosh at a recent meeting took strong exception to the Society's booklet—an official guide on how Highland dress should be properly worn—containing the advice that either a black or a white tie is correct for evening wear.
>
> "He maintained that a black tie was the correct wear, and gave notice of the following motion: 'That the meeting is of the view that the black tie is the correct wear for evening dress, and that the booklet of the Kilt Society be altered accordingly'.
>
> "The Mackintosh, however, was unfortunately unable to be present at yesterday's meeting, but his motion was moved by Dr. Ferguson Watson, Edinburgh, who came to Inverness specially to support it.
>
> "At the outset, Colonel George Mackintosh, C. B., Balvraid, the President, explained that the Society's booklet had been issued after two years' intensive research and was purely a guide.

"An original booklet, which had run out of circulation, contained the advice as regards evening dress, that 'a black tie or jabot' was suitable. The reason why 'black or white' was included in the up-to-date booklet was that a great many Highland gentlemen wore the white tie at a ball, and they felt it was a matter on which the Society could not be too dogmatic.

"Since The Mackintosh had raised the question, members of the Society had been asked to state their opinion, and twenty-four had replied—fourteen in favor of the black tie, and ten in favor of the white. Of the latter, some held that while the black tie was correct with a dinner jacket, the white tie could be worn with a tail-coat.

"In moving The Mackintosh's motion, Dr. Ferguson Watson said he had a feeling that in introducing the white bow there was great danger of the jabot disappearing altogether. It was not so much white against black, as probably the white against the jabot. He considered the black bow preferable to the white for evening wear. He knew the Duke of Atholl favored the white bow, but he had been at several ceremonies where the Duke wore a black tie. It was quite true that they were not issuing regulations in the booklet, but simply guiding facts to people who were not quite sure how to wear Highland dress.

"Mr. E. E. Malcolm, W.S., Fort-William, supported The Mackintosh's motion. Not only from the point of view of correctness, but from that of appearance, the black tie went very much better with a dress kilt, he said. He did not consider the jabot a feminine adornment, but it did not go with a 'boiled' shirt. The latter was altogether foreign, but they had to adapt their dress to modern requirements.

"Mr. Murdoch Mackintosh, Sheriff-Clerk of Invernessshire, who said the white tie was essentially modern dress, supported the amendment.

"On the suggestion of Brigadier-General Macfarlane, it was unanimously agreed that the whole question be remitted to a further meeting of the Society, in view of The Mackintosh's absence."

Philology

The study of the etymology of words connected with dress is an interesting and illuminating one. An etymological glossary on the subject is much to be desired, but, as far as we know, no such work exists. We are somewhat better off in this respect for arms and armor as armorial terms have been explained at some length as will be seen by consulting this portion of the bibliography.

Another interesting study would be that of slang used in different languages as applying to clothing. "Fedora" and "Kelly" and so forth, for hat; "Benny" for overcoat; "Dogs" for shoes, and many other such terms are interesting psychologically. There are also the languages of clothing or accessories, such as the well-known language of the fan, which was formerly used to convey a variety of messages in the form of signals, some of which were not unlike the wig-wag codes as used in the army and navy.

The little beauty spots, which the French appropriately called *"mouches"* also had a language in the eighteenth century. These little spots spoke a language in the manner in which they were placed, as some of the names will indicate. The "Passionate" was placed at the corner of the eye, the "Majestic" in the middle of the forehead, the "Playful" on the little wrinkles formed on the cheek by laughter, the "Gallant" in the middle of the cheek, the "Kissing" in the corner of the mouth, the "Offended" on the nose, the "Coquettish" near the lips. There was a special term used for the spot which the French called "Receleuse" which served to hide pimples. Long, slender beauty spots were called "Assassins."

The angle at which the headgear is worn also speaks a language and to close this brief treatment of the subject, it may be germane to quote Spengler in a self-explanatory statement which follows.

". . . and the language of costume, which is contained in clothing, tattooing and personal adornment; all of which have a uniform significance. The investigators of the Nineteenth Century vainly attempted to trace the origin of clothing to the feeling of shame or to utilitarian motives. It is in fact intelligible only as the means of an expression-speech, and as such it is developed to a grandiose level in all the high civilizations, including our own of today. We need only think of the dominant part played by the "mode" in our whole public life and doings, the regulation attire for important occasions, the nuances of wear for this and that social function, the wedding dress, mourning; of the military uniform, the 'priests' robes, orders and decorations, mitre and tonsure, periwig and queue, powder, rings, styles of hairdressing; of all the significant displays and concealments of person, the costume of the mandarin and the senator, the odalisque and the nun; of the Court-State of Nero, Saladin and Montezuma—not to mention the details of peasant costumes, the language of flowers, colors and precious stones. As for the language of religion, it is superfluous to mention it, for all this is religion."

Biology and Dress

The relation of biology to dress is considerable. The mannish post-war fashions need not be explained here nor need we go into the cut of bodices or v-shaped ornamentations on skirts. Some of the other aspects of biology in dress will not soon be forgotten. We hailed the discovery that modes in beards and hair dressing were biologically controlled, as our own, until the day we ran across Ripley's *Basque Fashions in Shaving.*

As an example of how far exaggerations of natural attributes may be carried, the false chin beards of the Pharaohs may be cited. Elliot Smith correctly states "that the Egyptians were endowed with a reasonable growth of beard on the chin only." Gerald Heard calls our attention to the fact that the slim Egyptians wore little clothing while the more heavily built dwellers of the Tigris and Euphrates valleys clothed themselves in much heavier garments although the climatic situation was similar.

Archaeology and prehistory have provided us with almost unlimited sources for the study of dress, and bibliographies on these subjects should be consulted in connection with the present one. The same may be said for the sciences of anthropology and ethnology which fields must also be intensively studied by anyone wishing to be really expert on clothes. Primitive Costume may be studied to a very large extent in books as there is little of it outside the museums today. Captain MacGillivray Milne, Governor of Samoa, wrote to Secretary Swanson in 1937 that the young people in his care were desirous of substituting American dress for the native lava-lava. He believes that they may have been influenced by a moving picture colony which moved in on them to take a south sea film. All this in spite of the fact that the Samoan people are peculiarly given to maintaining their own culture and customs.

The well meaning missionaries have had a great deal to do with the adoption of clothing. That unesthetic garment the pinafore (Samoan *pina-foa*) sold modesty and Manchester cotton. Overalls are suggested to natives as soon as there is a glut in the bead market. A thriving business is done in England in hopelessly outmoded second hand clothing which is sent overseas to native purchasers.

Robert Louis Stevenson remarks on this situation in an interesting chapter of *In the South Seas,* saying:

"Upon the whole, the problem seems to me to stand thus: when there have been fewest changes, important or unimportant, salutary or hurtful, there the race survives. Where there have been most, important or unimportant, salutary or hurtful, there it perishes. Each change, however small, augments the sum of new conditions to which the race has to become inured. There may seem, *a priori,* no comparison between the change from 'sour toddy' to bad gin and that from the island kilt to a pair of European trousers. Yet I am far from persuaded that one is any more hurtful than the other. . . . Experience begins to show us (at least in the Polynesian Islands) that change of habit is bloodier than a bombardment."

Louis Le Fevre, in an article in *The American Mercury* (Volume 9, no. 23, Sept. 1926, p147, et seq.) discusses the effect of the inferiority feeling upon the primitive's capacity for resistance to disease. If his conclusions have any basis of fact, there can be no more fitting symbolical demonstration of the manner in which the new forces act, than that furnished by clothing.

The savage who attempts to change his personality and allegiance, thru the external processes of dress, sacrifices all the significant and often complicated heraldry which bound him pridefully to the old group, yet finds too late that their efficacy as a passport to the new and assumedly superior one existed only in his imagination. "He-who-sits-by-the-red-stream," member of the "Turtle" clan, of the "Flying-gull" tribe, becomes simply the house-boy of Mrs. Smith, the missionary's wife. He has hauled down his colors and attempted unsuccessfully to desert to the enemy. If his white corpuscles are in any manner affected by comparative mental depression, he is a more ready subject for the ravages of one of the white man's polysyllabled maladies than his proud and less accessible brother who keeps his ensign flying and his group pride and subconscious mentality unaffected.

The most important scientific aspect of clothing is that connected with human ecology: Man's attempt at adaptation to climatic environment. It has been proven for instance that a well-wound turban is several degrees cooler than the best pith helmet. Red underwear was tried out for the American army in the Philippines. Tourists on the French Riviera are sometimes taken very ill when they refuse to take the advice of the natives regarding the proper clothing to be worn in that sun.

Hygiene as a study would of course be carried on under this heading. Pressure, occupational protection, permeability, allergies in certain cases, are said to make or lose millions of dollars to the nation every year. Such considerations have little to do with fashion.

Fashion

Marcel Proust advised us never to be in fashion or we would surely go out of fashion. Charles Morgan voiced a similar note in his article entitled "Epitaph on George Moore." He says "To be fashionable is what Moore did not desire, for to be fashionable today is to be unfashionable tomorrow."

The well-known New York lawyer, Stansfield, asked each member of a jury but one if he had ever thought for himself. The juror excused from the question was wearing a beard.

Being in fashion indicates conformity or a desire for conformity; social adaptation and a certain feeling of superiority or self-assurance. Baggy trousers and long sleeves are for clowns; failure to comply, or the lack of ability to comply, make them ridiculous. We laugh thru a feeling of superior adaptation. The opposite extreme, the over-compensation of the fop, is comic for similar reasons.

Sexual differentiation is part of every *zeitgeist,* differing with each epoch,

The effort of the naïve, to conform with a milieu not habitually their own, is pathetic. Two French terms *endimanché* (in Sunday go-to-meetin' clothes) and *mathurin* (yokelish) hold a world of meaning. Well-meaning efforts at conformity have failed.

At certain stages of sophistication, envy must be aroused in others and praiseworthy expenditure demonstrated. "Fine linen," formerly so expensive to buy and wear, resulted in the gradual increase of the size of the jabot, until it reached the level of the present dress shirt.

Beau Brummel had his valet wear each of his suits once or twice so that they might not have an undesirable look of newness.

Self-consciousness has much to do with fashion, group identification, and snobs. Snobbishness is a form of social cowardice. Dr. Henri Denjean, in the French medical review *Guerir* for November 1933, discussed the "pathology" of snobbishness which he looks upon as a form of neurosis, a viewpoint which is quite obviously not difficult to defend. Elizabeth Hawes says *Fashion is Spinach* showing conformity to her own group in this somewhat remarkable title. She emphasizes the distinction between "style" and "fashion." Style changes only "every seven years or so" and women of wisdom and courage, dress to suit themselves.

There is little doubt that commercial considerations on the part of cloth manufacturers, hairdressers, etc., have a very considerable influence on the unwitting public. The cinema is a great *arbiter dictum.* Individual and group prestige play, of course, a very large part. Spain, France and England, each in their heyday, set the style as did a Spanish princess in interesting condition, and a rather peculiarly built Viennese *danseuse.* Sometimes the utilization of prestige takes an odd or pathetic twist, as the following advertisement illustrates:

Saks Fifth Avenue
Presents
"VAN GOGH COLORS"

"Inspired by the recent brilliant showing of Van Goghs at the Museum of Modern Art, we introduce this series of new colors. We take the liberty of calling them 'Van Gogh' because in his paintings of the Arles period, the clear pure colors are like a fresh breeze blowing. In this freshness and vitality, and in the quality that gives the very texture of things, we found a relationship to these colors we present in clothes for the new season.

"The Van Gogh colors are shown with reproductions of the paintings which inspired them in the full sweep of our twelve Fifth Avenue windows and will be on display until Saturday. They are shown in evening clothes, sport clothes, hats, shoes and costume accessories. All the things displayed can be found in their own departments, but we suggest that the Ensemble Center will be helpful to you in assembling and matching those in which you are most interested.

Ensemble Center . . . Street Floor."

Privilege for leisure is shown in fashion. The walking stick of the overseer, in Egyptian paintings, evolves to immobilize the hands for useful labor, as do the long finger nails formerly affected by Mandarins. The fashion of the master in one generation becomes that of the servant of the next, probably originating from "hand-me-downs" when clothing was expensive and long wearing. The poet, Kenneth Rexroth, says that now the sports clothing of one generation will be the street costume of the next and if this is true, it may at least have the virtue of comfort to recommend it. Equestrian or other expensive sports have made fashionable the "bowler" hat invented by the Earl of Derby to protect the head in case of falls while chasing the fox, and the "polo coat." Inventions such as the automobile and aeroplane have far-reaching effect on clothes.

At the time of this writing, the general reactionary and escapist trend in politics is making itself significantly felt.

Costume and Architecture

Man is Symmetry. His mind has arbitrary geometrical tendencies as definitely crystallized as the snowflake; inherent as the decimal extremities. Within this mathematical complex are biologicoethnic variations. Reflections of nature imposed by the group ego stressing naturally imposed and inescapable characteristics and exaggerating them. How unsatisfactory is a thin and sparse beard when compared to a luxuriantly thick one which has been tended, curled and shampooed with sweet smelling herbs and essences. These factors form the basis for cultivated esthetic fitting each case, an esthetic which grows and develops according to geographic surroundings and their dual effect physically and psychologically thru climate and earth acting and interacting on mind, glands, and bodies, and vice versa. Sunshine or lack of it, water or desert, diet, dank dampness, high wind, and numberless other factors each play an important part.

Otto Rank, in his book *Art and Artist* has a most illuminating chapter on architectural origins. The role played by the human body of both sexes is clearly demonstrated. If this human body was the first of all surfaces to have been decorated, how can some authorities speak of "the influence of Architecture on Costume!" The reverse is more probably true. Costume is a portable architecture, a moving shelter. A cloak propped up on a pole becomes a tent. The step from a large tent to a small house is slight. For our purposes such considerations have only a relative importance; that of point of view.

Development of type forms, and sometimes their origins, has been stimulatingly indicated by Viollet le Duc. The Mongol tentpole with the typical curve it engendered was at the origin of the upturning corners of the pagoda roof as well as of typical headgear. The Cambodian temple spire, obviously organic in origin is repeated on dancers who dance architecturally in flesh and blood, and stone. The turban, or the wound helmet stands out in similar outline against the sky as the dome of the mosque; ancient Babylonian headgear is repeated in pyramidal architecture.

The dual evolution continues. The flat Tudor arch, as pointed out by Heard, is repeated in the contemporary hat and shoes. An old print comes to mind. A train with a black chimney belching black smoke is passing through a forest of factories. On the flat cars provided with benches sit rows of bearded men in "stove-pipe" hats. An old photograph shows the melon-like dome of the *Grand Palais*. In the foreground is a group of little men attired in *chapeaux melons*. Only when the traces of culture pass into a formless thing called by courtesy "civilization" are these profoundly fitting relationships lost.

If you wish to understand the esthetics of Dress, go to the Architect. Gottfried Semper has some appropriate observations which repose in manuscript form in the South Kensington Museum, if memory serves us rightly. He realized the architecture of dress. It is interesting to speculate how some of his conclusions might apply to present a-symetric trends in design. To paraphrase and condense, he speaks in part as follows:

> Man should be esthetically considered, neither in outline nor in mass as a visual image, but as a solid body activated by three forms corresponding to the three dimensions; first, the force of gravity, or weight, which acts from top to bottom, and retains him

to the earth; second, the vegetative force, or force of growth which is independent of his will, and which operates, also vertically, from bottom to top; third, the force of voluntary activity, which gives the body a movement towards a given point, imposed by the will. The first two forces, weight and growth, are diametrically opposed and it is this conflict which determines character, form and grace. But because of the law of inertia, weight also offers a resistance to the third force, that of voluntary activity, as it does to the second force, that of growth. Fourth, we have a superior unity, the cardinal point of the being, the idea which, harmonizing these diverse forces, can make them capable of expression and the manifestation of beauty.

The primary condition of an active and durable existence is that the three interacting forces should be in equilibrium. If man had only developed the vegetative force, like a tree, he would develop in height, and the masses would coil themselves around the trunk obeying the laws of equilibrium. If the axis of growth coincided with the axis of movement, as is the case with a fish, an exact balance of the masses around this axis of direction would be necessary in order to avoid an involuntary deviation of movement. But man participates simultaneously in these two systems. He develops vertically, as the tree, and moves horizontally, as the fish. The result is that he is independent of the rigorous law of equilibrium, in the vertical and forward and backward directions. It is only from right to left, or from left to right, that symmetry, as a static condition, must inevitably obey the laws of equilibrium. This axis of symmetry, (which is horizontal from left to right) cuts the axis of direction (also horizontal, from front to back) at right angles, and the axis of growth (which is vertical).

Thus we have three forces, or axes, which correspond in the human figure to the three dimensions of space, these three forces correspond to three sorts of ornaments which Semper calls respectively, pendicle, annular, and (for want of a better term) ornaments of direction. In order that beauty should manifest itself in man it is necessary that these different centers of action reflect themselves externally in a manner perceptible to the eye.

The pendicles are related to the first force, weight, and establish the stability of the body. They should be essentially symmetrical; the conception of a single earring or two hanging ornaments of an unequal length or weight is, architecturally, difficult. The aesthetic effect of these ornaments is augmented by the moral reaction exerted upon the person of the wearer: he is obliged to exercise a certain moderation in his movements, thus leading towards a dignity of attitude. The rigid hanging forms represented by the hair and beard of the Pharaohs belong to this category.

The annular, or peripheric form of ornament, serves to accentuate the proportions of the individual; it marks the center around which it is worn, and its principal object, the head, is the symbol of the man in his entirety. Crowns, diadems and bandeaux, sometimes accented by a symmetric repetition of motif, fall into this class of ornament. The collar, marking the transition of the head to the shoulders, so important among body ornaments, and the tight belt, marking the junction of the torso and the nether limbs, as well as the bracelets, anklets, and rings, which bring out the fine proportions of the extremities, complete this list.

Liberty and spontaneity of movement attach themselves to an ornament which has the accentuation of them as its raison d'être. It is distinguished from the two aforementioned groups in that it is neither rhythmic nor symmetric. It is based upon the contrast of the front to the rear, and should be designed primarily to be seen in profile. This form or ornament may be divided into two types, fixed and floating. The former is well exemplified by the royal *uraeus,* which decorates the foreheads of the Egyptian God-kings, while the floating type is to be seen in the materials of the headdress of warriors. The lightness of the materials of this latter type renders them mobile, and allows them to express the general direction of the motion of the individual.

Semper's esthetic metaphysics are most conspicuous when costume is relatively free from economic influences and at the height of a conventionally artistic style wave. At times the esthetically engendered features of costume may be remarked side by side with a survival of features to which other influences seem to have given birth. Thus in the esthetically architectural coiffure of the kings of Egypt, the primitive desire to inspire fear, the *Schreckschmuck* of Grosse, may persist as in the ram's horns, which appear again on the medals of Alexander where he is shown as the son of Jupiter-Ammon.

In relation to these theories, the activities of primitive peoples regarding self-decoration show, as might be expected, the richness and variety of form inherent in the experimental early stages of an art. The various ornaments take on the most fantastic and variable forms, which are in most cases exceedingly difficult, if not impossible, to explain. Yet in many cases their beauty and propriety are unquestionable.

Compare this point of view with that of another and more modern architect, Amédée Ozenfant, who writes (in his book *Art* p230) concerning the top hat; first, as to its incorporation into African sculpture which he claims is due to the fact that "their vertical lines and mass are most dignified" and further:

> "The cap will never be appropriate in solemn ceremonies. The Soviets made of it a symbol of proletarian affirmation. Their processions lack solemnity for there is none of this quality inherent in the form of the cap. Its symbolic quality is insufficient to react upon our senses and Moscow has again adopted, among its various types of head covering the 'Russian' cap which shows similarity to the high hat by the elevation of its vertical. . . . The negroes have been able to distinguish the fact that the high hat owes its expression of nobility, not to the function which it is understood to fulfill in Europe, but to the specific expression of a cylinder with vertical dominants . . and, its particularly grave color, black."

Such plastic and esthetic considerations bring us close to the fine arts.

Fine Arts

Painting and Sculpture provide inexhaustible sources for the study of dress. They are indeed the original sources, unique and par excellence. Their use as documentation requires a special training, historical and artistic as well as thoroly archaeological. Happily, there is an enormous literature including very extensive dictionaries of artists which are outside the scope of this bibliography. The student may, and must therefore investigate these rich sources for himself, a task which most of us consider delightful.

In each case, the necessary investigation must be carried on with considerable circumspection and deductive reasoning. In spite of much debunking and successful research in the past two or three decades, popular miseducation remains beyond belief. Maurice Leloir's designs for the dress in a Trojan classic, being based upon the clothing as then actually worn according to the latest discoveries in research, brought a storm of protest because of his incorrectness (!) and departure from the "classic tradition."

Francis Kelly warns us in his review of Enlart's Bibliography (cited p xxxvi) that "In the attribution of pictures to specific artists or schools, the evidence of costume might be invaluable, more especially on the negative side." Planché's notes on a number of pictures in the National Portrait Exhibition of 1866 are quoted to clarify his meaning. There was "Darnley" and "Sir Philip Sidney" in the approved mode of 1635, "Warwick the King Maker" appareled after the style of about 1600, etc. On the other hand, a farthingale served to identify Queen Elizabeth, and a doubly arched lace cap adorned appropriately the forehead of Mary Stuart. In another far more recent exhibition, Kelly adds: "two full-length portraits in private collections, in which every item of costume unmistakably proclaimed a mid-Jacobean date, were accepted as genuine likenesses of Sir Hugh Willoughby (d. 1553) and Henri I, 'le Balafre' Duke of Guise (murdered 1588).

The Theater and Cinema

The theater and cinema might take warning from such examples, but do not, in spite of the ever increasing sums they expend for research. In former days when the Three Musketeers fenced with rapiers which had not yet been invented; or every regiment in the civil war was dressed exactly alike, we excused the "infant industry" on varied grounds. This year when a "Million dollar production" portrays French police in a dress half a century ahead of the time (for a refreshing change) or Victor McLaglen incorrectly dressed in *Wee Willie Winkie,* we can find less excuse. In the latter case, an old soldier wrote to the London Daily Express that "among other things that didn't please them were that the boots were not of army pattern. . . Kilt is too long and denotes a different regiment from his sporran . . . he is wearing white buff walking out belt, yet carrying rifle with fixed bayonet," etc. A proof that both research and criticism are getting down to details, which can hardly be other than a good sign.

There is a rich specialized literature on Costume in the Theatre, ranging from illustrated souvenir programs and periodicals like *Theatre Arts* or *The Mask,* to the famous *Denkmaler* or *Monumenta Scenica* and the great Doucet Collection of the Bibliothèque de l'Arsenal. Works like that of Karl Mantzius in six volumes are well worth consulting for bibliographical sources touching on costume. Other more specialized types such as *La Comédie Italienne* of Pierre Duchartre, or that on the Chinese theater by IAkovlev contain admirable and highly accurate visual documentation of much esthetic merit.

The Lagye Collection, acquired in 1926, was the property of the former *costumiers* of the Théatre Royale de la Monnaie, of Brussels. It consists of hundreds of prints, drawings, watercolors, sketches, clippings, etc., and would warrant examination on the part of anyone in a position to visit the Hiler Costume section of the Queens Borough Public Library, Jamaica, New York.

Colored lithographic plates were formerly published somewhat extensively in France and Germany, in much the same way that similarly printed paper soldiers were circulated. Of very unequal value, they covered such diverse productions as the Barber of Seville and Robinson Crusoe. Very reasonable in price, a collection of such plates would increase in value with the passage of the years. Of a somewhat similar character are the *Masken Albums* and *Travestissements* published respectively in Vienna and Paris from year to year. In a simple way these little booklets illustrate and typify the classic dresses of every "Theatrical Costumer." Pierrots, dominoes, harlequins, etc., which can be traced back through the Commedia del Arte to Medieval Moralities and sometimes beyond these to Rome and ancient Greece.

A special study should be made of the mask, in carnival, primitive religion, the theatre, love and crime. Here there is a psychological connection with the marionette, the *über marionette,* and the classic tradition of the ballet and the dance in general. A great list of names comes to mind which would be easily enlarged and studied in a Theatrical rather than a Costume bibliography. Burnacini, Bertelli, Inigo Jones, Bakst, Craig and Reinhardt, to name, perhaps unfairly, but a few.

Costume in Literature

The vastness of material concerning costume in literature makes this subject impossible of treatment within the present limitations. From Chaucer and

Shakespeare thru the great writers and novelists of every country and historic period, there are a myriad of references to dress, of varying factual value. The diaries of Pepys and Evelyn are examples of important contemporary original sources. Flaubert, Balzac, Scott, Dickens, Thackeray are a few names which come immediately to mind as writers who were particularly interested in dress and its details. There is a whole literature of Dandyism and the History of the Fop; another very extensive one of Travel and Voyages. The classics of Marco Polo and Doughty, Rubruquis and Cook and other somewhat less famous books such as the fine series published by the Hakluyt Society are rich in quaint references to intimate details of clothing and the toilet in general. There are extensive collections of travel volumes such as the *Encyclopédie des Voyages* and the *Tour du Monde* (the latter published regularly for a number of years) which globally considered cover all periods, countries and peoples. The contact with this enormous field carries us out of our own more specialized one.

Compilation of the Bibliography

The cumulative process, involved in the assembling of this bibliography, continued for many years. Time spent in Europe allowed a considerable expansion of the collection which grew into a sizable library. Interest in the subject increased, keeping pace with it. Finally an ambition was born to write a great general history of costume and brought to a head by a visit from C. K. Ogden, then representing a well-known firm of English publishers * as editor of a series on the *History of Civilization.*

Work was begun on an introduction to the study of costume which appeared some ten years ago under the title *From Nudity to Raiment.* The experience and research necessary to the completion of this volume taught me many things. First: that my plan for the general work was somewhat impractical in a world where time was precious, money difficult and interest in the subject slight. Second: among other things that, if any success were to be achieved, a foundation must be first laid out in the form of a general survey of what had already been accomplished in the field.

About this time, for a number of reasons, it was decided that a catalog of the Hiler Costume Library should be printed. My father, Meyer Hiler, co-compiler of the present opus, had become rather thoroly involved in arrangements. The catalog was printed in 1927 and my own attitude towards the general bibliographical situation expressed, perhaps not very accurately, by the following brief introduction:

> This little catalogue makes no pretension towards being a Bibliography of Costume, yet so great is the current ignorance of the subject that it might do so with no great risk of being found ridiculous. In reply to a request for a bibliography to be furnished by the Office Central de Librarie et de Bibliographie, an organization which specializes in finding books on any subject, I was told that "it does not appear that more than 600 works dealing exclusively with costume exist at the present time", and as I already possessed more than this number, the Office hardly seemed in a position to make itself useful. The *opus* entitled "Art in Home Economics"; a bibliography compiled by the combined efforts of "Marion E. Clark and Others", and printed by the academic presses of the University of Chicago, gives a list of 65 books on Costume including the Encyclopedia Britannica . . . Max von Boehn, who is the author of a number of tomes dealing with dress, is given somewhat pathetically as "Von Brehm, Max", in connection with two of his least important efforts. Nor are other esteemed contemporaries in much better case. George Van Ness Dearborn of the Medical Corps of the United States Army, in one of a series

* Kegan Paul, Trench, Truebner & company

of monographs entitled *The Psychology of Clothing,* published by the Psychological Review Publications of Princeton, N.J., admits that the study of clothing is "almost pioneer scientific work", and later states, apparently not without pride, that "Harvard University has more than a hundred volumes on clothes and costume, mostly historical and classed as works on the fine arts". The Bibliothèque Nationale (exclusive of the Cabinet des Estampes) lists somewhat over two hundred works under the heading of costume.

Such seemed the attitude and information on the part of the general public and even persons more particularly interested at that time.

There was no very considerable bibliography of costume. The nearest approach to such a work was the catalogue of the Lipperheide Costume Library, *Katalog der Freiherrlich von Lipperheide'schen Kostümbibliothek,* published in Berlin, 1896-1905. The books are listed in a classified order which, tho in the main reasonable and satisfactory, is nevertheless complex. Consultation is difficult, and a knowledge of German is requisite, in order to make full use of the book. Since it is the catalog of a great bibliophile, its tendency is to stress the material rather than the intellectual aspects of the works included. Of course, it contains inherent and unavoidable weaknesses from the fact that it is, after all, a list of the books in one particular library, and so conceived and executed.

Next to the Lipperheide catalog in value may be placed Colas's *Bibliographie du Costume* published in Paris, 1933. The Hiler bibliography is far more extensive than either of the aforementioned publications.

There has never been any pretense of recognizing the fundamentally important relationships present in allied fields, and indispensable to a serious study, or the valuable sources for enrichment of knowledge offered by the domains of Anthropology, Ethnology, Geography, History, Painting and Sculpture, Folklore, Psychology, etc.

In the *Burlington Magazine,* Volume 33, Pages 89 to 95, F. M. Kelly writes an article in the form of a review of Camille Enlarts' *Critical Bibliography of Costume* which appeared in the *Manuel d'Archéologie Française depuis les Temps Mérovingiens jusqu'à La Renaissance, Tome 3, Le Costume* (Paris, August Picard, 1916. 8vo.) In this review Kelly neglects to mention the great general bibliographical sources. It is interesting to note that he complains: "How little advance has been made for the last forty or fifty years in the study of civilian apparel". A long list of *loci classici,* some of which are almost incunabula, is included. Perhaps the chief interest in the discussion of this somewhat excessively meager bibliographical material, which as far as we know automatically closes treatment of this phase of the subject, comes through the fact that it is a proof of the inaccessibility of general bibliographical material extant at the time. The capacities of Frances Kelly may not fairly be questioned for he is the author of an excellent book on costume, in collaboration with Schwabe, which method and treatment make outstanding.

Small editions, expensive publications, difficulty of cross indexing, etc., render consultation of existing sources extremely difficult. The catalogs of the Rothschild Costume Library; of the compilers' small library now in the Queens Borough Public Library at Jamaica, N.Y.; of the Cabinet des Estampes at the Bibliothèque Nationale; of the British Museum; and so forth, are by no means everywhere available.

In this connection, we wish to mention an excellent and beautifully executed documentation, particularly important in relation to a study of costume and accessories in our own country. This can be furnished by the Index of American Design, collection of pictures of American art objects gathered by a division of the Federal Art Project of the United States Works Progress Administration.

So much for some of the more general bibliographical sources. It is hoped that the above discussion may justify the existence of the bibliography which this article accompanies.

General Works

When one thinks of general works on Costume, the names Racinet, Hottenroth, Kretschmer and Rohrbach, Rosenberg and Tilke, at once come to mind. Their books are typical of encyclopedic attempts to present the subject pictorially in popular form. One or more of these works are to be found in almost any Public Library. Their use, however, with any hope of authenticity, is difficult. Any data found in them must be carefully verified elsewhere.

Sources less known in connection with the subject may well yield richer returns. There is much data, for instance, in the volumes of Herbert Spencer's *Descriptive Sociology,* which, in spite of the dates of their publication, are fully as authentic as the works mentioned above. Very interesting bibliographical data is also to be found there.

Periodicals

Periodicals concerned with costume, and fashion periodicals have been listed fully. The access to materials on costume in general periodicals is considerably facilitated by the Periodical Indexes. Some of the most useful have been named under the subject Periodicals. They are widely available in libraries.

Encyclopedias

The encyclopedias are convenient sources for general and condensed information regarding costume. Articles are often accompanied by illustrations and a more or less extended bibliography. Data should be checked with some caution. As an instance of what is meant here, we cite the doubtful theory that kilts are worn by the Scotch Highlanders because of the dew on the heather. This appeared in a recent edition of a world famous encyclopedia, and would hardly explain the bare knees of the Tyrolese; or the Albanian, Greek or Afghan "kilt".

In the index volume of the *Britannica,* of the eleventh and succeeding editions, a number of related words refer to articles of varied interest. Under the word "robes" for instance, there is a full page double color plate. *Larousse Universel,* volume 5, pages 246 to 261, gives a considerable bibliography, which includes many incunabula. Other continental encyclopedias are of interest. The most extensive special article which has come to our notice appears in the *Enciclopedia Universal Ilustrada Europeo-Americana* (Barcelona, Espasa 1905-33). Under the word "traje" (Volume 63 p582-801) there are over two hundred pages in fine type, with more than that number of black and white and colored illustrations. This lengthy treatise concludes with an extensive bibliography.

Newspapers

There is a great amount of material concerning dress, adornment, fashion and mode in the daily papers, past and present. It would be interesting and valuable if some person or organization had the money and interest to subscribe to one or more good clipping bureaus for the subject.

In the Crocker Art Museum at Sacramento, California, there is a section showing old dresses worn at functions of some eighty-odd years ago. In several cases the newspaper comments on these gowns are framed and displayed next to them. The language like the dresses was somewhat extravagant. Challamel, from 18th century French newspapers, describes some popular colors: "Rash tears, Paris mud, Burnt Opera house, Stifled sigh," nor was England far behind. British publications for the year of 1783 describe as fashionable: "Elliots red-hot bullets", "Smoke of the Camp of St. Roche", and so forth. If these seem quaint, they are almost matched by terms in our present press: "Folly, Lucky stone, Elephants' breath, Tango" and so on, almost inexhaustibly. For a number of years a friend of the late Rudyard Kipling sent him American newspapers. Kipling asked him to be sure to send all the advertising sections, which had been removed to lighten postage. Advertising is interesting in connection with prices and the standard of living. Newspapers of a hundred years ago stressed the wearing quality of materials. One newspaper article which we saw, dated just prior to the Civil War, gave as a gauge of the Franco-American amity at that time, the fact that American gentlemen followed Paris modes. Allegiance has since rather obviously shifted to Bond Street.

Fashion columns such as that of Bettina Bedwell take on interest as the years go by. Syndicated articles, appearing in more or less sensationalized form, usually on Sunday, are less interesting. Most material of this type may be traced quite easily to books. The sources are seldom mentioned and are ordinarily so distorted as to be of little, if any, value.

There is a detailed index to the *New York Times* 1913- date; the *New York Daily Tribune index* covers that paper for the years 1875-1906. There is also an index to the *Times, London* since the year 1906. All of the above indexes will guide the searcher to costume material.

Museums and Societies

There are a few museums which, quite apart from ethnographical displays or arms and armour, show actual or reconstructed historical costumes. In some important cases, their catalogs or guide books are mentioned in the body of the Bibliography. The Victoria and Albert Museum in London, the Musée du Costume in Paris, the collection of uniforms in the Invalides, the extensive theatrical material in the Bibliothèque Doucet and the Musée Carnavalet, also in Paris, are examples, as is the Museum für Völkerskunde in Berlin.

These collections have a unique value. The cut and manner of sewing of old garments are strikingly illustrated when actual examples in a good state of preservation may be examined. Beside the collections mentioned there are numerous smaller collections, such as that of the Museum of the Paris Opera, and the one mentioned in Sacramento, which might really be made the subject of a special work.

There are a few societies which have interested themselves in Historic costume. The now unfortunately defunct Société de l'Histoire du Costume was perhaps the best known. Their publications were excellent of their kind and it is regrettable that because of small editions they have become very difficult to find. The Sabretache was another French society which being of a military nature was chiefly interested in uniforms. The National Geographic Society as before mentioned is too well-known to need comment. The Salmagundi

Club of New York has a collection of costume books for the use of their members who are illustrators. Private collectors connected with the theatre, pageants, the cinema or book illustrators, etc., have interesting collections, which, however, in most cases are difficult of access. It has been our privilege to see a very remarkable and authentic collection of lead soldiers accurately costumed to the smallest detail and covering a period of several hundred years. Another collection consisted of tiny hand-painted terra cotta figurines showing Spanish folk dress; still another of costume dolls which reminded us of the time when these were shipped around Europe as precursors of the more modern fashion magazines.

Special Libraries

Special libraries on the subject are as rare as museum collections. The Lipperheide Library in Berlin is the largest and perhaps the best known. Very considerable sources exist in the great libraries of the world although usually cataloged in such a manner that extended consultation is difficult without bibliographical data. The Cabinet des Estampes of the Bibliothèque Nationale (Paris) is both interesting and what is rarer, satisfactorily cataloged. The Traphagen School of Fashion Design in New York has a costume library. The Hiler collection, as has been mentioned is now in a special division of the Queens Borough Public Library, Jamaica, Long Island, N.Y.

Incunabula, Erotica, etc.

Books on costume following economic and political changes appeared relatively late from a standpoint of the history of early printing. For about a half century, roughly from 1560 to 1600, some dozen or so costume books appeared. Of these, somewhat less than half went into several editions. In the 17th century only one book which might be considered as chiefly devoted to costume was published. Such books are antedated by manuscript accounts of early travelers, some of which are mentioned elsewhere, and drawings and writings of wandering students and errant scholars.

Many illustrated manuscripts are authentic sources for information about dress worn at the period and place where the manuscript was copied. They can be seen in the rare book collections of large public libraries, for example the Spencer Collection at New York Public Library. Libraries which are sufficiently important to be able to possess any considerable number of incunabula or of manuscripts are also usually in a position to offer photostat service so that students who are unable to visit them may, with the help of a documentation such as this bibliography, obtain facsimiles necessary for the study in hand.

Before leaving this portion of the subject another category of rather rare books should be mentioned. These are kept in that portion of the library known to students as the "hell" and may only be consulted by special permission. In some parts of the world such books as the works of Eduard Fuchs fall into this category. Erotica are often interesting in connection with the psychology of clothing and intimate details of sleeping garments and under-garments which are not usually shown in better known publications. For rather obvious reasons the reader must be somewhat reluctantly allowed to shift for himself in this domain.

The study of costume is quite without limits and we regard the present bibliography as only a very imperfect beginning in research which we must, with some regrets consider as here terminated as far as our own efforts are concerned.

HILAIRE HILER

EXPLANATIONS

The Bibliography is in the form of a dictionary catalog, with author, title, subject, editor, illustrator, engraver and other entries all in one alphabet.

The main entry is under the name of the author, or, for an anonymous book, under the first word of the title. Here the fullest information about the book is given, in the following order: Author, title, place, publisher, date, number of pages, illustrations, plates, size, series, and descriptive annotations. Here also are given the references to the bibliographies of Colas, and Lipperheide, and numbers by which Library of Congress cards can be ordered.

Under the subject of which the book treats the information is limited to author, title, and date of publication. The subject is followed by the author's name. Turn to entry under author's name for full information.

Titles entries, likewise, are only guides to the main entry. The title is followed by the author's name.

Entries under names of engravers, illustrators, and editors, are also brief, giving only the name of the author (i.e. the main entry) and title of the work.

For example the book *Antike mode,* by Max von Boehn, will be found under 1, the author's name: Boehn, Max von; 2, the title: Antike mode; 3, the subject: Ancient times.

The main entry should always be consulted, since only in the main entry will be found all the titles under which a book and its translations were published, and therefore can be found listed in library catalogs.

The articles *a, an,* and *the* and their equivalents in other languages, have been ignored in filing. i.e. *L'image de la femme* is found under the letter *i,* not under *L.*

ä, ö, ü, å, and ø in the Teutonic languages are filed as if spelled ae, oe, ue, etcetera.

For further explanations see the Introduction, pages vii-ix.

ABBREVIATIONS

abr.	abridged
aufl.	auflage
Aug.	August
ausg.	ausgabe
c.	copyright
ca.	circa
col.	colored
Colas	René Colas's Bibliographie générale du costume
comp.	compiled, compiler
corr.	corrected
D.	duodecimo (17½-20cm. high)
Dec.	December
diagr.	diagram, diagrams
ea	each
ed.	edition, editor, edited
engr.	engraver
enl.	enlarged
F.	folio (30 or more cm. high)
Feb.	February
front.	frontispiece
hrsg.	herausgegeben, herausgegeber
illus.	illustrations, illustrator, illustrirte, etc.
incl.	including
Jan.	January
jahr.	jahrgang
jt.	joint
L.C.	Library of Congress
Lipp., Lipperheide	Lipperheide's Katalog der. . .kostümbibliothek
l.	leaf, leaves
lithgr.	lithographer
n.d.	no date
n.f.	neue folge
no.	number
Nov.	November
n.s.	new series
O.	octavo (20-25 cm. high)
ob.	oblong
o.p.	out of print
Oct.	October
p.	page, pages
p.l.	preliminary leaves
pl.	plate, plates
port.	portrait, portraits
pseud.	pseudonym
pt., pts.	part, parts
pub.	publisher, published
Q.	quarto (25-30 cm. high)
rev.	revised
S.	16mo (15-17½cm. high)
Sept.	September
ser.	series
sq.	square
t.	tome
T.	24mo. (12-15 cm. high)
t.-p.	title page
unp.	unpaged
tr.	translated, translator, translation
v.	volume, volumes
verb.	verbessert
verm.	vermehrt
+	to date (ie. to June 1937)
[ ]	brackets in the main entry enclose material not found in book
( )	parentheses around L.C. numbers indicate that the card shows an open entry

Bibliography of Costume

A., H. A. von. See Manuale, oder Handgriffe der infanterie

A., M. P.
(ed.) La Roumanie en images, v. 1 1919

A B C book of people. Cole, Walter

A B C des kölnischen maskenfestes; 2. verbesserte aufl. Cöln, Renard & Dübyen ca1830
1 col.pl. D.
Lipperheide 2867

The **A B C** of dress. Collins, Harry

A la caserne. Malliot, T. J. R.

A la danseuse. Jou, Louis

A la gloire des soldats suisses. Arnoux, Guy

A los toros. Perea, Daniel

A magyar nép müvészete. Malonyay, Dezsö

A mi hadseregünk. Danzer, Alfonz

A travers la Bosnie et l'Herzégovine. Capus, Guillaume

A travers le monde. See note under Tour du monde

A travers l'Europe. Vallet, L.

Aa, Pieter van der
Habillemens de plusieurs nations, representez au naturel. Leyde, Vander Aa ca1710
136 pl. Q.
Colas 1367. Lipperheide 34

(ed.) Carracci, Annibale. Divers ouvrages de belles figures

(pub.) Allard, A. Habillemens der paisans et paisannes de Hollande, de Frise, de Braband et autres provinces

(pub.) Effigies virorum ac foeminarum illustrium

Aastraamat, v3. See Manninen, Ilmari. Eesti rahvariiete ajalugu

L'**Abbaye** des Vignerons. Vernes-Prescott, J. F.

Abbesses
Kettner, F. E. Kirchen- und Reformationshistorie des kayserl. freyen weltlichen stiffts Quedlinburg. 1710

Abbildung der churfürstlich-saechsischen armée uniformen. Dresden, J. S. Gerlach 1799
34 col.pl. D. 180fr.
Colas 1. Lipperheide 2198s

Abbildung der churhannöverischen arméeuniformen. Ronnenberg, J. G. F.

Abbildung der chursächsischen truppen in ihren uniformen unter der regierung Fried.-Aug. III. Hess, C. A. H.

Abbildung der Communal-Garde zu Leipzig. Geissler, C. G. H.

Abbildung der gemein-nützlichen hauptstände. Weigel, Christoph

Abbildung der k. k. oesterreichsichen armee durch alle waffengattungen. Stephanie, J.

Abbildung der königlich hannoverschen armee. Leopold, Franz, and Mentzel, C.

Abbildung der königl. preussischen armee uniformen. Müller, C. F.

Abbildung der kurfürstlich sächsischen armee. No place, ca1800
111 col.pl. D.
Colas 3. Lipperheide 2201

Abbildung der neuen adjustirung der k. k. armee. Kininger, V. G., and Mansfeld, J. G.

Abbildung der neuen k. k. oesterreichischen armee uniformen. Mollo, Tranquillo

Abbildung der neuen königl. preuss. armee uniformen. Wolf, L.

Abbildung der veränderten monturen 1799. No place, n.d.
33 col.pl. Q.
Lipperheide 2153

Abbildung der verschiedenen corps des oesterreichischen allgemeinen aufgebothes. Représentation des différens corps de l'Insurrection générale d'Autriche. Wien, T. Mollo 1797
14 col.pl. O.
Colas 4

Abbildung derer VIII. ersten hertzogen zu Sachsen, Jülich, Cleve und Berg, Engern und Westphalen, des H. Römischen Reichs ertz-marschallen und chur-fürsten landgrafen in Thüringen. . . sammt: kurtzer beschreibung ihres . . . lebens und regiments. . . auch der beygefügten zehen-alter des menschen männlichen u. weiblichen-geschlechts mit ihren studiis, verrichtungen und zuneigungen ordentlich beschrieben. No place, 1702
30 illus. Q.
Lipperheide 682

Abbildung des churpfalzbaïerischen militairs nach voriger und gegenwaertiger uniform. No place, 1787
37 pl. (41 illus.) Q.
Colas 5

Abbildung des Normannsthals, in dem königlichen lustgarten zu Friedensburg. See Grund, J. G. Afbildning af Nordmands-Dalen

Abbildung merkwürdiger menschen. Hempel, C. F.

Abbildung und beschreibung der südwest- und östlichen Wenden, Illyrer und Slaven. Hacquet, Balthasar

Abbildung und beschreibung aller hohen ritter-orden in Europa. Eichler, Gottfried

Abbildung und beschreibung der völkerstämme und völker unter des russischen kaisers Alexander I. regierung. Hempel, Friedrich, and Geissler, C. G. H.

Abbildung und bescheibung derer sämtlichen berg-wercks-beamten und bedienten. See Weigel, Christoph. Icones omnium ad rem metallicam spectantium officialium et operariorum

Abbildung und beschreibung derer sämtlichen schmeltz-hütten-beamten und bedienten. See Wiegel, Christoph. Icones omnium ad officinas aerarias pertinentium officialium et operariorum

Abbildung und repraesentation der fürstlichen inventionen, auffzüge, ritter-spiel, auch ballet, so in des herren Johann Georgen, fürsten zu Anhalt ... bey des herrn Georg Rudolph, hertzogen in Schlesien mit fraw Sophia Elizabeth, hertzogin in Schlesien ... Hochzeitlichem frewenfest, und ... beylager ... 1614. Leipzig, S. Grosen 1615
118p. 11 pl. Q.
Lipperheide 2607

Abbildungen aller angeblich: und wirklichen regenten Ungarns mit beygefügten kurzen historischen anmerkungen. Wien, F. Molis 1815
14 col.pl. F.
Lipperheide 866m

Abbildungen Böhmischer und Mährischer gelehrten und künstler. Pelzel, F. M., and Voigt, Adauctus

Abbildungen der k. k. cavallerie-regimenter von 1765. Schmutzer, Jakob

Abbildungen der k. k. oesterreichischen infanterie. Schmutzer, Jakob

Abbildungen der kostüme und uniformen des württembergischen militärs von der zeit des 30jährigen kriegs bis 1854; ein beitrag zur kostümkunde. Stuttgart, H. W. Beck 1860
36 col.pl.(incl. 244 illus.) O.
These plates appeared first as a supplement to L. J. von Stadlinger's *Geschichte der württembergischen kriegswesens* (Stuttgart, 1856)
Colas 6. Lipperheide 2207

Abbildungen der neu organisirten königlich-sächsischen armee. Leipzig, Industrie-comptoir [1810]
20 col.pl. Q.
Plates show 74 military types
Colas 7

Abbildungen der neuen uniformen der königlich sächsischen armee. Heine, Ferdinand

Abbildungen der uniformen aller in Hamburg seit den jahren 1806 bis 1815 einquartiert gewesener truppen. Suhr, Christoffer

Abbildungen der vorzüglichsten geistlichen-orden. Schwan, C. F.

Abbildungen derjenigen ritter-orden. Schwan, C. F.

Abbildungen des königlich-hannoverschen militairs. Osterwald, G.

Abbildungen des württembergischen militärs von der früheren bis zur gegenwärtigen zeit. Stuttgart, Ebner 1857
8 col.pl. Q.
Title on plates: *Württembergisches militär. . .von 1800 bis 1857.* Each plate is signed: Fr. Malté art. anstalt
Colas 10

Abbildungen sämmtlicher geistlichen orden. Wietz, J. K.

Abbildungen sämmtlicher geistlichen und weltlichen ritter- und damenorden. See Wietz, J. K. Abbildungen sämmtlicher geistlichen orden

Abbildungen und beschreib. herumziehender krämer von Constantinopel. Hunglinger von Yngue, A. M.

Abbildungen und beschreibung aller hoher geistlichen, weltlichen, und frauenzimmer ritter-orden in Europa. See note under Eichler, Gottfried. Abbildung und beschreibung aller hohen ritter-orden in Europa

Abbildungen verschiedener völker der erde in ihren eigenthümlichen trachten. Breslau, J. D. Grüson 1826
80 col.pl. D.
Colas 11. Lipperheide 54

Abbildungen von allen uniformen der königl. preuss. armee unter der regierung sr. maj. Friedrich Wilhelm III. See Ramm, A. L. Tabellarische nachweisung

Abbott, John Colby
The days of the Directoire. See entry under Allinson, A. R.

Abbott, Mary
Jewels of romance and renown, by Mary Abbott. London, T. W. Laurie, [1933]
217 p. front. pl. ports. O.
Bibliography: p203-204
LC 34-31994

Abcontersaittung, allerlei ordenspersonen in iren klaidungen. Heldt, Sigmund

Abcontrafactur und bildnis aller gross hertzogen chur und fürsten welche vom jahre nach Christi geburt 842 biss auff das jetztige 1599 jahr das land Sachsen löblich und Christlich regiert haben. Sampt kurtzer erklerung ihres lebens aus glaubwirdigen historien zusamen getragen u. in deutsche reime bracht. Wittenberg, L. Seuberlich 1599
29 l. 60 col.illus. F.
The source of the book is Gabriel Schnellholz's *Sammlung*
Lipperheide 703

Abdeker. Le Camus, Antoine

Abdrücke eines vollständigen kartenspieles auf silberplatten. Bleich, G. H.

À Beckett, Gilbert Abbott
The comic history of England. With ... coloured etchings and ... woodcuts, by John Leech. London, The Punch office, 1847, '48
2v. illus. 20 col.pl. O.
Later edition (London, Bradbury, Agnew & co. [1864?] 2 v in 1 LC 15-14139)
LC 16-17272

L'**Abeille** impériale, littérature, poésie, beaux-arts, théâtres; messager des modes et de l'industrie. 1856-1862. Paris
Col.pl. Q.
Almost 100 colored plates, many by Gavarni
Colas 15

Abendländische künstler zu Konstantinopel im xv. und xvi. jahrhundert. Karabacek, Josef, ritter von

Aberdeen ecclesiological society
Four Scottish coronations. See entry under Cooper, James

Aberli, Johann Ludwig
Costumes de Berne et paysans des environs. ca1782
6 col.pl. on 3 l. D.
Three of the plates are engraved by Dunker
Colas 16

Abhandlung über die beste form der schuhe. Camper, Petrus

Abhandlung über die comödie aus dem stegreif und die italienischen masken. See Valentini, Francesco. Trattato su la commedia dell' arte

Abhandung von der schädlichen wirkung der schnürbrüste. Bonnand

Abiet, Édouard
Réflexions sur la crinoline. [Paris, Ragot 1865]
7 p. D.
Colas 17

Abiti e fogge civili e militari dal i al xviii secolo. Stibbert, Federigo

Abito dei rappresentanti del popolo francese. See note under Grasset de Saint Sauveur, Jacques. Costumes des représentans du peuple

Aborigines of South America. Church, G. E.

The **aborigines** of western Australia. Calvert, A. F.

About Persia and its people. Knanishu, Joseph

Abraham a Santa Clara
Neu eröffnete welt-galleria. . .allerley aufzug und kleidungen unterschiedlicher stande und nationen: Forderist aber ist darinnen in kupffer entworffen die kaiserl. Hoffstatt in Wien, wie dann auch anderer hohen haupter und potentaten biss endlich gar auf den mindesten gemeinen mann. Nürnberg [1703]
100 pl. F.
Colas 2189. Lipperheide 32

See also Centi-folium stultorum (attributed)

Abraham Bosse et la société française au dix-septième siècle. Blum, André

Abrahams, Ethel Beatrice
Greek dress; a study of the costumes worn in ancient Greece, from pre-Hellenic times to the Hellenistic age. London, J. Murray 1908
xvi,134p. illus. 40 pl. diagrs. O. 12s.
Costume index. LC 9-12608

Abrahams, Israel
Jewish life in the middle ages. London, Macmillan 1896
452 p. O. (The Jewish library, v 1)
Costume index. LC 99-1069

Abrégé de la vie des plus fameux peintres. Dezallier d'Argenville, A. J.

Abrégé historique des principaux traits de la vie de Confucius. Helman, I. S.

Abruzzi e Molise. See Italy—Abruzzi e Molise

Abyssinia. See Ethiopia

Abyssinia of to-day. Skinner, R. P.

Abzeichen der koeniglich preussischen armee im jahre 1863. Brügner, C.

R. **Academia de la historia, Madrid.** See Clonard, S. M. de S. y A., conde de. Discurso histórico sobre el trajo de los Españoles

Academic caps, hoods and gowns. Rogers, J. E.

Academic colours. Baty, Thomas

Academic costume
Baty, Thomas. Academic colours. 1934
Delitzsch, F. J. Die akademische amtstracht und ihre farben. 1859
Haycraft, F. W. Degrees and hoods of the world's universities & colleges. 1927
Leonard, G. C. The cap and gown in America. 1896
Monroe, Paul, ed. A cyclopedia of education. 1911-13

See also Students

England

Beaumont, E. T. Academical habit. 1928
Clark, E. C. English academical costume (mediaeval). 1894
Wood, T. W. The degrees, gowns, and hoods of the British, colonial, Indian, and American universities and colleges. 1883

See also Special universities below

Germany

Bauer, Max. Sittengeschichte des deutschen Studententums. 1927
Dyas orationum de ritu depositionis. 1666
Heideloff, K. A. von. Gedenkblätter der Universitäten Heidelberg, Prag und Wien, darstellend die ursprünglichen trachten der landmannschaften mit den rektoren, siegeln und schutzpatronen nebst theilweiser stadtansicht im hintergrund. 1848
Meiners, Christoph. Göttingische akademische annalen. 1804
Schundenius, K. H. Erinnerungen an die festlichen tage der dritten stiftungsfeyer der Akademie zu Wittenberg. 1803
Winterschmidt, A. W. Das studentenleben in 30. kupfern vorgestellet. ca1760

See also Special universities below

Netherlands

Afbeeldingen van den gecostumeerden optogt der studenten van de Utrechtsche Hoogeschool, vorstellende: het bezoek van Maximilian van Oostenrijk en Maria van Bourgondië en feesten bij die gelgenheid gevierd to Brugge, en het jaar 1477, te houden op Dingsdag 25 Junif 1867. 1867

Academic costume—*Continued*

United States

Erwin, John. History of academic costume in America. 193-?

Rogers, J. E. Academic caps, hoods and gowns. 1911

SPECIAL UNIVERSITIES

Altdorf university

Apin, S. J. Vitae et effigies procancellariorum Academiae Altorfinae non solem de hac se etiam de universa Norimbergensium publica cuius consiliarii pro in ordine fuerunt maxime meritorum in publicum datae. 1721

Contains pictures of the chancellors of Altdorf University, 1575-1711

Cambridge university

Almond, A. G. Gowns and gossip. 1925

Combe, William. History of the University of Cambridge. 1815

Costumes of the members of the University of Cambridge. London, H. Hyde 1840?

Harraden, R. B. Costume of the various orders in the University of Cambridge. 1805

Whittock, Nathaniel. Costumes of the members of the University of Cambridge. 1840?

See also Boating costume—Cambridge university

Dublin university

Taylor, W. B. S. History of the University of Dublin. 1845

Frankfurt university

See Academic costume. Viadrina university

Heidelberg university

Chronik der Hirschgasse. 1910

Jena university

Borkowsky, Ernst. Das alte Jena und seine universität. 1908

Kiel university

Torquatus à Frangipani, A. J. Meditatae a gloriosiss. Memoriae in Cimbrica chersoneso academiae divo Friderico Cimbrorum duce ... & providentia ... Christiani Alberti ... Kiloniae fundatae. Ejusdem inaugurationis panegyrica descriptio. 1666

Leiden university

Illustrium Hollandiae & Westfrisiae ordinum alma Academia Leidensis. 1614

Leipzig university

Gruner, Erich. Der historische festzug, anlässlich der jubelfeier des 500 jährigen bestehens der universität zu Leipzig. 1909

Kreussler, H. G. Beschreibung der feierlichkeiten am jubelfeste der Universität Leipzig, den 4. december 1809. 1810

Oxford university

Buxton, L. H. D. and Gibson, Strickland. Oxford university ceremonies. 1935

Combe, William. History of the University of Oxford. 1814

Habitus academicorum Oxoniensium a doctore ad servientem. ca1680

Shrimpton, A. T., pub. Shrimpton's series of the costumes of the members of the University of Oxford. 1885?

Uwins, Thomas. Costume of the University of Oxford. 1815

Whittock, Nathaniel. The costumes of the members of the University of Oxford. 1840?

Whittock, Nathaniel. A topographical and historical description of the university and city of Oxford. 1828

Tübingen university

Cell, Erhard. Imagines professorum Tubigensium. 1596

Neyffer, J. C. Illustrissimi Wirtembergici ducalis novi collegii quod Tubingae quâ situm quâ studia quâ exercitia, accurata delineatio. ca1580

Viadrina university

Becmann, J. C. Notitia universitatis Francofurtanae, una com iconibus personarum aliquot illustrium, aliorumq. virorum egregiorum, qui eam praesentia sua ac meritis. 1707

Würzburg, Bavaria. University

Würzburg, Bavaria. Julius-Maximilian-Universitet. Alma Iulia; illustrirte chronik ihrer dritten säcularfeier. 1882

Academical habit. Beaumont, E. T.

Academie des inscriptions et belles lettres

La miniature carolingienne; son origines, son developpement. See entry under Boinet, Amedée

Academy for grown horsemen. Bunbury, H. W.

Les **accessoires** du costume et du mobilier. Allemagne, H. R. d'

Accessories

Allemagne, H. R. d'. Les accessoires du costume et du mobilier depuis le treizième jusqu'au milieu du dixneuvième siècle. 1928

Boehn, Max von. Das beiwerk der mode. 1928

Boehn, Max von. Modes & manners: ornaments; lace, fans, gloves, walking-sticks, parasols, jewelry and trinkets. 1929

See also Aprons; Buttons; Eyeglasses and lorgnettes; Fans; Footwear; Garters; Gloves; Handkerchiefs; Headdress; Muffs; Neckwear; Negligees; Shawls; Umbrellas and parasols; Underwear; Veils; Waists

Account of a voyage of discovery to the north-east of Siberia. Sarychev, G. A.

An **account** of medieval figure-sculpture in England. Prior, E. S., and Gardiner, Arthur

An **account** of the interior of Ceylon and of its inhabitants. Davy, John

An **account** of the kingdom of Caubul. Elphinstone, Mountstuart

Account of the manners and customs of the modern Egyptians. Lane, E. W.

An **account** of travels into the interior of southern Africa in the years 1797 and 1798. See Barrows, Sir John. Travels into the interior of southern Africa

Accuratae effigies pontificum maximorum, numero XXVIII. Panvinio, Onofrio

Accurate vorstellung der saemtlichen churfürstl. hanoverischen armee, zur eigentlichen kentniss der uniform von jedem regimente. Nebst beygefügter geschichte, worinne von der stiftung, denen chefs, der staercke, und den wichtigsten thaten jedes regiments nachricht gegeben wird. Nürnberg, Raspe, 1763
44p. 50 col.pl. O. 260 fr.
Colas 18. Lipperheide 2218

Accurate vorstellung der sämtlichen chur fürstl. sächss. regimenter und corps, worinnen zur eigentl: kenntnis der uniform von jedem regimente ein officier und ein gemeiner in völliger montirung und ganzer statur nach dem leben abgebildet sind. Nürnberg, Raspe 1769
32p. 33 col.pl. O. 1000 fr.
"Nebst beygefügter nachricht 1, von ihrer stifftung. 2, denen chefs, commendanten, und staabs officiers. 3, der stärcke, und 4, derer in friedens, zeiten habenden quartiere und garnisons, eines jeden regiments und einer kurz gefassten geschichte desselben bis ans ende des jahrs 1769." Subtitle
Colas 18. Lipperheide 2218

Accurate vorstellung der saemtlichen kayserlich koeniglichen armeen, zur eigentlichen kentniss der uniform von jedem regimente. Schmalen, J. C. H. von

Accurate vorstellung der sämtlichen koeniglich preussischen armee. Schmalen, I. C. H. von

Achard, Louis Amédée Eugène. See Grandville, J. I. I. G. Cent proverbes

Achaval, Guillermo de
España, tipos y trajes. See entry under Ortiz Echagüe, José

Ache, Caran d'. See Caran d'Ache, E. P.

The **Achehnese.** Hurgronje, C. S.

38 Steirmark's national-trachten und festanzüge jetztiger und vergangener zeit. Kaiser, Eduard

48 erinnerungs-blätter and die krönuung S.K.H. des erzherzogs kronprinzen Ferdinand zum könig von Ungarn in Presburg, den 28. september 1830. Gurk, Eduard

1826-1896. Der jubiläums festzug der haupt- und residenz-stadt Karlsruhe. Götz, Hermann

L'**acier** de Carme: notes sur le commerce de l'acier à l'époque de la renaissance, suivies des tables du second volume. 1904. See Giraud, J. B. Documents pour servir à l'histoire de l'armement au moyen âge et à la renaissance

Ackermann, Rudolph
Changeable [ladies]; being an assemblage of moveable human features. London, R. Ackermann 1819
24 pl. in box
Title pasted on inside of box reads: *Changeable gentlemen*

[Costumes of the British army] London, The author 1840-58
2v. 76 col.pl. F.
The plates are after drawings by H. Martens, W. Heath, H. de Daubrawa and others, lithographed by J. Harris
Colas 25-26. Lipperheide 2269

[Costumes of the Indian army] London, The author 1844-49
43 col.pl. F.
Some editions have 33 colored plates. Some have the plates in black and white only. Plates are by J. Harris after drawings by H. Martens
Colas 27. Lipperheide 2270

The history of the colleges of Winchester, Eton, and Westminster; with the Charterhouse, the schools of St. Paul's, Merchant Taylors, Harrow, and Rugby and the Freeschool of Christ's hospital. London, R. Ackermann 1816
9 pts. in 1 v. 48 col.pl. F.
Various pagings. Issued in 12 monthly parts, 1816-17. Text by W. Combe, with the exception of Winchester, Eton and Harrow, which are by W. H. Pyne. Plates by W. Westall, F. Mackenzie, A. Pugin, and T. Uwins
LC 7-8737

The microcosm of London. London, R. Ackermann [1808]
3v. 104 col.pl. Q.
Colas 2054. Lipperheide 1022

(pub.) The Repository of arts, literature, commerce, manufactures, fashions and politics

Across Africa. Cameron, V. L.

Across Thibet. Bonvalot, Gabriel

Across unknown South America. Landor, A. H. S.

Across widest Africa. Landor, A. H. S.

I. **Acta** Mechmeti I saracenorum principis. Aussführlicher bericht von ankunfft zunehmen gesatzen regirung und jämerlichem absterben Mechmeti I. Genealogia seiner successorn biss auff den jetztregirenden Mechmetem III. Auss vielen glaubwürdigen autoribus fleissig zusammen getragen. II. Propheceyung. Keysers Seueri uñ Leonis, sampt etlichen andern weissagung vom undergang dess türckischen regiments bey jetzregirenden Mechmete III. Alles mit schönen kunstreichen kupfferstucken gezieret und von neuwem an tag geben durch Hans Dietherich und Hans Israel von Bry gebrüder. [Frankfurt] 1597
101p. 26 illus. sq.D.
Lipperheide 1402. LC 5-2488

Acteurs du théâtre italien. Paris, Hérisset ca1730
6 pl. ob.Q.
Colas 28

Les **actrices.** Damourette, and Talin, H. M.

Actrices des principaux théâtres de Paris. Devéria, Achille

Adam, Eugene. See Adam, Franz, jt. lithgr.

Adam, Frank

The clans, septs and regiments of the Scottish Highlands; 3d ed. Edinburgh and London, W. & A. K. Johnston 1934
xxiv,523p. front. illus.(coast of arms) pl.(part.col.) ports. fold.map. O.
Plates in color show 114 tartans
First edition: 1908. Second edition: 1904
LC 35-6321

What is my tartan? or, The clans of Scotland, with their septs and dependents. Edinburgh and London, W. & A. K. Johnston 1896
112 p. front. (port.) illus.(coats of arms) D.
Second edition 1924
LC 2-30488

Adam, Franz, and Adam, Eugen

(lithgrs.) Hacklaender, F. W., ritter von. Erinnerungen an die feldzüge der k. k. oester. armee in Italien in den jahren 1848-49

Adam, Georg

[Russisches militair] im jahr 1814 in Nürnberg nach dem leben gezeichnet und radiert von Georg Adam. Augsburg, Herzberg 1814?
6 col.pl. F.
Colas 29. Lipperheide 2374

Adam, Jacques

Bildungen des gemeinen volks zu Wien. Les portraits du commun peuple à Vienne. No place, ca1790
100 pl. engraved by Jacques Adam. Q.
Colas 30

Adam, Leonhard

Nordwest-amerikanische Indianerkunst. Berlin, E. Wasmuth a. g. [1923]
44 p. illus. 24 pl. no 12 1. Q. (Orbis pictus; weltkunst-bücherei, bd 17)
Plates printed on both sides
"Literaturverzeichnis": p33-34
LC 24-4232

Adam, Victor

Album de Ste. Pélagie (dette); douze scènes intérieures dessinées et lithographiées d'après nature. Paris, V. Morlot ca1835
12 pl. Q.
Scenes from the debtors' prison Ste. Pélagie in Paris
Lipperheide 3562

Album militar. See note under Villegas, José. Album militar

Un an de la vie de jeune homme, histoire véritable en 17 chapitres écrits par lui-même. Paris, Sazerac & Duval 1824
17 col.pl. Q. 50 fr.
Lipperheide 3561

[Armée russe, cavalerie] Saint-Pétersbourg & Moscou, G. Daziaro ca1860
72 col.pl. Q.
Legends in Russian and French
Colas 36

Les arts et métiers; avec vignettes par Victor Adam. Paris, L. Janet ca1830
100 p. 24 pl. S.
Lipperheide 1977m

[Cavalerie de la Garde impériale du 1er empire] Paris, G. Lemercier ca1840
4 col.pl. F.
Also known with plates in black and white
Colas 32

[Cavalerie sous le règne de Louis-Philippe. Paris, Turgis] ca1840
4 col.pl. F.
Also known with plates in black and white
Colas 33

Collection des costumes militaires, armée française, 1832. Paris, D. Becker ca1840
42 col.pl. ob.Q.
Colas 34

Costumes de la république, de l'empire, de l'armée française et de l'armée d'Afrique de 1830 à 1840. Paris, A. Bès et F. Dubreuilh ca1840
14 col.pl. F.
Especially interesting for French military uniforms of 1830 to 1840
Colas 35

Costumes de l'armée française 1860-1861-1862. Paris, Desgodets ca1863
33 col.pl. Q.
Colas 37

Costumes de marins, dessinés dans les ports de Dunquerque au Havre; par V. Adam. Paris, Rittner et Arrowsmith 1828
12 col.pl. Q.
Colas 31. Lipperheide 1193

(engr.) Föhn. Suisse—costumes anciens

(lithgr.) Föhn. Suisse—costumes modernes

(lithgr.) Graf, Henry. Vues des cérémonies les plus intéressantes du couronnement de Leurs Majestés Impériales l'empereur Nicholas 1er et l'impératrice Alexandre, à Moscou

(lithgr.) Vernet, Carle. Scènes et costumes divers

(lithgr.) Villegas, José. Album militar

Adam; revue de l'homme. v 1, 1925+ Paris
Illus. F. 60 fr.
Periodical of men's fashions. Published monthly. Current 1938

Adami, Casimiro

Arte e storia nel mondo antico monumenti della civiltà classica orientale, greca e romana, scelti, disposti ed illustrati in collaborazione col Ermanno Luckenbach. Bergamo, Istituto italiano [1925?]
xiv,208 p. front. illus. col.pl. F. (Collezione di testi-atlanti per l'insegnamento della storia e dell' arte)

Adamic, Louis

Native's return. New York, Harper 1934
370p. pl. ports. O. $2.75
Costume index. LC 34-2193

Adamo, Max

(illus.) Dowden, Edward. Shakespeare scenes and characters

(illus.) Pecht, Friedrich. Shakespeare-galerie

Adams, Dale

(illus.) Story, Mrs M. McE.-F. Individuality and clothes

Adams, Capt. John

Sketches taken during ten voyages to Africa between the years 1786 and 1800, including observations on the country between Cape Palmas and the River Congo, and cursory remarks on the

Adams, Capt. John—*Continued*
physical and moral character of the inhabitants, with an appendix containing an account of the European trade with the west coast of Africa. London [etc.] Hurst, Robinson and co. [1822?]
119 p. 2 maps, tables. O.
LC A16-1326

Adams, Rudolph
Die farben-harmonie in ihrer anwendung auf die damentoilette. Leipzig, J. J. Weber 1862
xii,322 p. front. 3 pl. (2 col. and fold.) O.
Lipperheide 3266. LC 10-1026

Adams, William
The modern voyager & traveller, through Europe, Asia, Africa, & America. London, H. Fisher, son, and P. Jackson 1835-38
4 v. col.fronts. pl(part col.) maps. S
"Authorities consulted" at beginning of each volume.
Contents v1 Africa. 1837. v2 Asia. 1835. v3 America. 1836. v4 Europe. 1838
LC 1-23939

Adams-Ray, Edward
(tr.) Stockholm. Hallwylska palatset. Catalogue of the collection of arms and armour at Hallwyl house, Stockholm

Addison, Lancelot
The present state of the Jews: wherein is contained an exact account of their customs, secular and religious. To which is annexed a summary discourse of the Misna, Talmud, & Gemara. London, Printed by J. C. for W. Crooke, 1676
6p.l. 247p. D.
Third edition, 1682
Page 10 is on the apparel of Jews in Barbary. Page 97-102 on dress to wear in the synagogue, burial and mourning clothes

Ademollo, Alessandro
I teatri di Roma nel secolo decimosettimo; memorie . . . di fatti ed artisti teatrali, librettisti, commediografi e musicisti, cronologicamente ordinate per servire alla storia del teatro italiano. Roma, L. Pasqualucci 1888
xxviii,283p. O.
Bibliografia: p ix-xv
LC 10-1339

Adelmann, Leofrid
Bayerische trachten, Mittelfranken. Würzburg, Verlag des polytechnischen vereins 1858
18 col.pl. Q.
Colas 39. Lipperheide 759

Bayerischen trachten, Unterfranken. Würzburg, Verlag des polytechnischen vereins 1856
18 col.pl. Q.
Colas 38. Lipperheide 758

Adelphus, Joannes Argentinen Phisicus
Warhafftige sag; oder red von dem rock Jesu Christi; neulich in der heylign̄ Stat Trier erfunden mit anderñ vil köstbarñ heyltumb; in gegewertigkeit des Keysers Maximiliani und ander fürsten uñ herren, da selbs im reychstag versamelt anno dñi. 1512. Nürnberg, Hannsen Weyssenburger Priester 1512
8 l. illus. Q.
Lipperheide 1791

Die **adjustierung** der armee Osterreich-Ungarns mit berücksichtigung der bis zum monate märz 1877. See Franceschini, Friedrich. Militairisches pracht-bilderbuch

Adjustierungs- und ausrüstungsvorschrift für die K. und K. Trabantenleibgarde. Genehmigt mit allerhöchster entschliessung vom 12 märz 1904. Wien, K. K. Hof- und staatsdruckerei 1904
66p. illus. Q.
Colas 40

Adjustierungsblätter des k. u. k. oesterr.-ungar. heeres. Righetti, Camillo

Adjustirungs- und ausrüstungs-vorschrift für das k. k. heer. Wien, Kaiserlich-königlichen hof- und staatsdruckerei 1878
v.p. 380 illus. 11 pl. Q.
Includes supplements 1883 to 1887
Colas 43. Lipperheide 2241

Adjustirungs-vorschrift für die generale, stabs- und ober-officiere . . . der kaiserlich-königlichen armée (sanctionirt . . . vom 17 februar, 1854). Vienne, K. K. Hof- und staatsdruckerei 1855
59p. 32pl. ob.Q.
Colas 42

Adjustirungs-vorschrift für die generale, stabs- und ober-officiere . . . der k. k. armée, vom jahre 1837. Wien, aus der K. K. Druckerei [1837]
76p. Q. and atlas (22pl.) F.
Colas 41, 12?

Adler, Fritz
Pommern. See Deutsche volkskunst. v 11

Adlerblum, Mrs Nima (Hirschensohn)
A perspective of Jewish life through its festivals. New York, The Jewish forum pub. co. 1930
78p. front. illus. pl. O.
Bibliography included in preface
LC 31-6902

Admiranda narratio fida tamen, de commodis et incolarum ritibus Virginiae . . . anno M.D.LXXXV. Harriot, Thomas

Adnet-Molé, Mad.
Steno-tricographie; das ist neueste französische methode stenographischer musterzeichnungen für kunst- und spitzenstrickerei. Grimma & Leipzig, Verlags-comptoirs 1850
20p. 8 illus. O.
Lipperheide 4092

Adonis, Attis, Osiris. Frazer, Sir J. G.

Adriani, Nicolaus, and Kruijt, Alb. C.
Geklopte boomschors als kleedingstof op Midden-Celebes, en hare geographische verspreiding in Indonesië . . . Met aanteekeningen, register, aanvullingen en verbeteringen, van J. D. E. Schmeltz. Leiden, E. J. Brill, 1905
78p. front. illus. col.pl. F. (Rijks ethnographisch museum. Publicatien, ser. 2, no 4)
Reprint from *Internationales archiv für ethnographie* v 14-15
Bibliographical footnotes

Adriatic, Islands of the
Das was verschwindet; trachten aus den bergen und inseln der Adria. 188-?

Adventures among the Dyaks of Borneo. Boyle, Frederick

Advice to young ladies from the London journal of 1855 and 1862. The London journal

Advis sur l'usage des passements d'or et d'argent. Paris, J. Millot [1610]
72p. Q.
Signed S. R.
A criticism of the sumptuary laws. Discusses the economic importance of gold and silver for braid and embroidery
Lipperheide 3429

Der **advokat** in der karikatur. Veth, Cornelis

Aegidius à Sancto Joanne Baptista, Augustinian prior
D. Wenceslao Bohemorum duci ac martyri inclyto sertum ortus, vitae, necis è duabus suprà triginta iconibus, totidemque Tetrastichis, velut è rosis quibusdam contextum . . . cui attexitur floriger fasciculus selectiorum epigrãmatum operâ F.AE. â S.I.B. Prag, Bilina 1644
122 l. illus. O.
Lipperheide 871

Aegypten und aegyptisches leben im altertum. Erman, Adolf

Die **ägyptische** tracht bis zum ende des neuen reiches. Bonnet, Hans

Aelbrecht-hertog in Beieren-graaf van Holland-enz-binnen-Enkhuizen in 1396. Bosch, Etienne

Aelianus, Tacitus. See Vegetius Renatus, Flavius. De re militari

Die **aeltesten** deutschen spielkarten des königlichen kupferstichkabinets zu Dresden. Lehrs, Max

Die **ältesten** glasgemälde des chorherrenstiftes Klosterneuburg und die bildnisse der Babenberger in der Cistercienser-abtei Heiligenkreuz. Camesina, Albert

Die **ältesten** glasgemälde im Dome zu Augsburg. Herberger, Theodor

Die **änfange** der kunst. Grosse, Ernst

Ärtzliche zimmergymnastik. Schreber, D. G. M.

Aesthetics of dress. See Art of dress

Aesthetik und cynismus. Löwenheim-Röhn, E.

Åt solsidan. Larsson, Carl

Ättartal för Swea och Götha konunga hus. Peringskiöld, Johan

Afbeelding van de kaamer en 't parade-bed waar op het lyk van . . . Anna, kroon princesse van Groot-Brittanje . . . 1759. Swart, P. de

Afbeelding van de zaal en 't praalbed waar op het lyk van . . . Willem Karel Hendrik Friso, prinse van Orange en Nassau. Swart, P. de

Afbeeldingen der monteeringen van de gewapende schutterije en burgercorpsen in Nederland. Uniforms de la garde civique et de corps militaires nationaux aux Pays Bas en 1789. Amsterdam, 1789
35 col.pl.

Afbeeldingen van de kleedingen, zeden en gewoonten in Holland, met den aanvang der negentiende eeuw. Maaskamp, Evert

Afbeeldingen van den gecostumeerden optogt der studenten van de Utrechtsche Hoogeschool, vorstellende: het bezoek van Maximilian van Oostenrijk en Maria van Bourgondië en feesten bij die gelegenheid gevierd te Brugge, en het jaar 1477, te houden op Dingsdag 25 Junij 1867. Utrecht, Van Boeckhoven 1867
8pl. O.
Pictures of a procession organized by the students of Utrecht to celebrate the 230th anniversary of the University.
Colas 44. Lipperheide 2837

Afbildning af Nordmands-Dalen, i den kongelige lyst-hauge ved Fredensburg. Grund, J. G.

Afbildningar af nordiska drägter; utgifna af H. Thulstrup, met en kort svensk och fransk text af J. H. Kramer. Stockholm, P. B. Eklund [1888-89]
18 l. 16 col.pl. ob.F.
Swedish costume. Title page in Swedish and French. French title: *Costumes nationaux scandinaves.* Ten of the plates are identical with those in the *Afbildningar af svenska national dräkter*
Colas 2875. Costume index. Lipperheide 1058

Afbildninger af norske nationaldragter. See Keyser, J. R. Om nordmae klaededragt i aeldre tider

Afbildningar af svenska national dräkter. Stockholm, P. B. Eklund [1907]
25 l. 12 col.pl. F.
Title page and text in Swedish, English, French and German. Ten of the plates are identical with those in the *Afbildningar af nordiska drägter*
Costume index

Les **affiches** de recrutements du XVIIe siècle a nos jours. Depréaux, Albert

Afghanistan
Atkinson, James. Sketches in Afghaunistan. 1842
Elphinstone, Mountstuart. An account of the kingdom of Caubul. 1815
Hamilton, Angus. Afghanistan. 1906
Hart, L. W. Character and costumes of Affghanistan. 1843
Rattray, James. The costumes of the various tribes, portraits of ladies of rank, celebrated princes and chiefs, views of the principal fortresses and cities, and interior of the cities and temples of Afghaunistaun. 1848

Aflalo, Frederick George
(ed.) The sports of the world, with illustrations from drawings and photographs. London, Paris, New York & Melbourne, Cassell. 1903
viii,416p. front. illus. pl. Q.
Eighty-seven articles by various authors
LC 3-18932

Africa
Adams, Capt. John. Sketches taken during ten voyages to Africa between the years 1786 and 1800. 1822?
Barbosa, Duarte. A description of the coasts of East Africa and Malabar in the beginning of the sixteenth century. 1866

Africa—*Continued*

Barnim, A. J. B. von, freiherr, and Hartmann, Robert. Reise in Nord-Ost Afrika. 1863

Barth, Heinrich. Travels and discoveries in North and Central Africa. 1857-58

Carpenter, F. G. Uganda to the Cape. 1924

Frobenius, Leo. Das sterbende Afrika. 1923

Henricy, Casimir, and Lacroix, Frédéric. Les moeurs et costumes de tous les peuples. 1847

Junger, Alexander. Kleidung und umwelt in Afrika; eine anthropogeographische studie, zugleich ein beitrag zur frage nach den grundprinzipien der tracht. 1926

See also Africa, North; Africa, South; African tribes; Algeria; Arabs; Ashanti; Dahomey; Egypt; Jewelry, Medieval and modern—Africa; Nubia; Senegal; Tattooing—Africa; Touaregs; Tunisia; Zanzibar

Africa; containing a description... Shoberl, Frederic, ed.

Africa, North

Barnim, A. J. B. von, freiherr, and Hartmann, Robert. Reise in Nord-Ost Afrika. 1863

Carpenter, F. G. From Tangier to Tripoli. 1923

Kühnel, Ernst. Nordafrika; Tripolis, Tunis, Algier, Marokko. 1924

Kühnel, Ernst. North Africa; Tripoli, Tunis, Algeria, Morocco. 1924

Tilke, Max. Oriental costumes. 1923

Tilke, Max. Orientalische kostüme in schnitt und farbe. 1923

See also Sahara; Tripolitania

Africa, South

Alexander, Sir J. E. An expedition of discovery into the interior of Africa. 1838

Arbousset, Thomas. Relation d'un voyage d'exploration au nord-est de la colonie du Cap de Bonne-Espérance. 1842

Barrow, Sir John. Travels into the interior of southern Africa. 1806

Bowler, T. W. The Kafir wars and the British settlers in South Africa. 1865

Carpenter, F. G. Uganda to the Cape. 1924

Christol, Frédéric. L'art dans l'Afrique australe. 1911

African tribes

Alberti, Lodewyk. De Kaffers aan de zuidkust van Afrika. 1810

Andersson, K. J. Lake Ngami. 1856

Angas, G. F. The Kaffirs illustrated in a series of drawings taken among the Amazulu, Amaponda, and Amakosa tribes; also portraits of . . other races inhabiting southern Africa. 1849

Bernatzik, H. A. The dark continent; Africa, the landscape and the people. 1931

Burchell, W. J. Travels in the interior of southern Africa. 1822

Burrows, Guy. The land of the pigmies. 1898

Cameron, V. L. Across Africa. 1877

Carpenter, F. G. Cairo to Kisumu. 1923

Casalis, Eugène. The Basutos; or Twenty-three years in South Africa. 1861

Chapman, James. Travels in the interior of South Africa. 1868

Damberger, C. F., pseud. Christian Friedrich Damberger's Landreise in das innere von Afrika. 1801

Domville-Fife, C. W. Savage life in the black Sudan. 1927

Douville, J. B. Voyage au Congo et dans l'intérieur de l'Afrique equinoxiale, fait dans les années 1828, 1829 et 1830. 1832

Du Chaillu, P. B. Explorations and adventures in equatorial Africa. 1871

Du Chaillu, P. B. A journey to Ashango-Land and further penetration into equatorial Africa. 1867

Eyriès, J. B. B. Voyage pittoresque en Asie et en Afrique; résumé générale des voyages anciens et modernes d'après Erman, Lesseps, J.-F. Gmelin. 1839

Fritsch, G. T. Die eingeborenen Süd-Afrika's, ethnographisch und anatomisch beschrieben. 1872

Geoffroy de Villeneuve, R. C. L'Afrique, ou histoire, moeurs, usages et coutumes des Africains: Le Senegal. 1814

Hartmann, Robert. Les peuples de l'Afrique. 1884

Hartmann, Robert. Die völker Afrikas. 1879

Jacottet, Henri, and Leclerc, Max. Colonies françaises. 1888

Johnston, Sir H. H. George Grenfell and the Congo. 1908

Johnston, Sir H. H. Liberia. 1906

Kidd, Dudley. The essential Kafir. 1904

Kidd, Dudley. Savage childhood. 1906

Landor, A. H. S. Across widest Africa, an account of the country and people of Eastern, Central and Western Africa as seen during a twelve months' journey from Djibuti to Cape Verdi. 1907

Le Vaillant, François. Second voyage dans l'intérieur de l'Afrique. 1794

Lopes, Duarte. Beschrijvinge van 't konninckrijck Congo met 't aenpalende landt Angola. 1650

Lyon, G. F. A narrative of travels in northern Africa, in the years 1818, 19, and 20. 1821

Mansfeld, Alfred. Urwald-dokumente: vier jahre unter den crossflussnegern Kameruns. 1908

Mansfeld, Alfred. Westafrika; aus urwald und steppe zwischen Crossfluss und Benue. 1928

Muraz, Gaston. Sous le grand soleil, chez les primitifs; images d'Afrique équatoriale. 1923

Omboni, Tito. Viaggi nell' Africa occidentale. 1845

African tribes—*Continued*

Pease, Sir A. E., bart. Travel and sport in Africa. 1857

Routledge, W. S., and Routledge, Mrs K. P. With a prehistoric people, the Akikúyu of British East Africa. 1910

Schweinfurth, G. A. The heart of Africa, three years travels and adventures in the unexplored regions of Central Africa, from 1868 to 1871. 1874

Schweinfurth, G. A. Im herzen von Afrika; reisen und entdeckungen im zentralen äquatorial-Afrika während der jahre 1868-1871. 1918

Shoberl, Frederic. Africa, containing a description of the manners and customs, with some historical particulars of the Moors of the Zahara, and of the negro nations between the rivers Senegal and Gambia. 1821

Stuart, Martinus. De mensch, zoo als hij voorkomt op den bekenden aardbol. 1802-07

Tessmann, Günter. Die Pangwe; völkerkundliche monographie eines westafrikanischen negerstammes; ergebnisse der Lübecker Pangwe-expedition 1907-1909 und früherer forschungen 1904-1907. 1913

Tilke, Max. Oriental costumes. 1923

Tilke, Max. Orientalische kostüme in schnitt und farbe. 1923

Torday, Emil. On the trail of the Bushongo; an account of a remarkable & hitherto unknown African people, their origin, art, high social & political organization & culture. 1925

Weiss, Hermann. Geschichte des kostüms. . . 1. abt. Geschichte des kostüms der vornehmsten völker des alterthums. . . .1. theil: Afrika. 1853

See also Hottentots; Ibo tribe; Masks, Africa; Pygmies—Africa

L'**Afrique.** Geoffroy de Villeneuve, R. C.

L'**Afrique.** See note under McLeod, John. A voyage to Africa

L'**Afrique** française, l'empire de Maroc, et les deserts de Sahara. Christian, Pierre

L'**Afrique,** ou Histoire, moeurs, usages et coutumes des Africains. See Lyon, G. F. A narrative of travels in northern Africa, in the years 1818, 19, and 20

Agdá

Tratado sobre o ensino do córte das vestes de ambos os sexos. Rio de Janeiro, A. Lavignasse 1897
79p. 160pl. O.
The second edition (2. aufl. 1898) contains 95 pages and 160 plates
Colas 45. Lipperheide 3852-53

L'**age** du bronze. See Evans, Sir John. The ancient bronze implements, weapons, and ornaments, of Great Britain and Ireland

Age du bronze. Chantre, Ernest. See his Études paléoethnologiques dans le bassin du Rhone

L'**âge** du renne. Paniagua, André de

Les **âges** de la pierre. See Evans, Sir John. The ancient stone implements, weapons and ornaments of Great Britain

Aggiunte e rettificazioni all' opera Il costume antico e moderno. Ferrario, Giulio

Aghion, Janine

The essence of the mode of the day, Paris 1920; a series of fifteen drawings. Paris, The books of La Belle édition [1920?]
15 col.pl. Q.

Aghion, Max

Le théâtre à Paris au XVIIIe siècle. Paris, Librairie de France [1926?]
442p. incl.ports. col.front. illus. pl.(1 col.) Q.
Bibliographical footnotes

Agincourt, Jean Baptiste Louis Georges Seroux d'. See Seroux d'Agincourt, J. B. L. G.

Agnelli, Jacopo

Descrizione delle ... solennità celebrate ... 12. Febbrajo 1736 ... in Ferrara per le . . . nozze di S.A.R. Francesco Steffano Duca di Lorena e della Serenissima Arciduchessa Maria Teresa d'Austria. Ferrara, D. B. Giglio 1736
7 l. 3pl. F.
Lipperheide 2759

Agricola, Georg

Berckwerck buch, darinn nicht allain alle empte instrument gezeug und alles so zu diesem handel gehörig mit figuren vorgebildet und klärlich beschriben, sondern auch wie ein rechtverstendiger berckmann seyn sol und die gäng ausszurichten seyen ... erstlich ... in latein beschriben und in zwölff bücher abgetheilt: nachmals aber ... Philippum Bechium ... verteutscht. Franckfort am Mayn [Getruckt durch P. Schmidt in verlegung Sigmundt Feyrabendts] 1580
ccccxci p. illus. fold.pl. diags. Q
LC GS13-437

Bergwerck buch, darinnen nicht allein alle empter instrument ... gezeug und alles so zu disem handel gehörig mit figuren vorgebildet und klärich beschrieben; sondern auch wie ein rechtverständiger bergmann seyn soll und die gäng ausszurichten seyen ... Basel, L. König 1621
491p. 283 illus. 2pl. F.
Lipperheide 1989

De re metallica libri XII. Basileae [apvd] H. Frobenivm et N. Episcopivm] 1556
538 (i.e. 502) 74p. illus. diags. F.
"Quibus officia, instrumenta, machinae, ac omnia denique ad metallicam specantia, non modo luculentissimè describuntur, sed & per effigies, suis locis insertas, adiunctis latinis, germanicisque appellatonibus ita ob oculos ponuntur, ut clarius tradi non possint." Subtitle
First edition
First German translation *Vom bergwerck.* There are other German and Latin editions, an English translation entitled *De re metallica,* see below, and one in Italian, ***Opera di Georgio Agricola de l'arte de metalli*** (Basilea, Frobenio & Episcopio 1563)
LC 14-21386

De re metallica; tr. from the 1st Latin ed. of 1556, with ... introduction ... appendices upon the development of

Agricola, Georg—*Continued*
mining methods ... from the earliest times to the 16th century, by H. C. Hoover ... and L. H. Hoover. London, Mining magazine 1912
xxxi,640p. illus. pl. F.
LC 13-10108

Vom bergkwerck xij bücher darin alle empter, instrument, bezeuge, unnd alles zu disem handel gehörig ... beschriben seindt . . . jezundt aber verteüscht, durch Philippum Bechium. Basel, Froben & Bischoff 1557
8,ccccxci,10p. illus. pl. F.
First German translation of *De re metallica.* For later editions see his: *Berckwerck buch*
Lipperheide 1989 (Noted)

Agricola, Johann
Warhafftige abcontrafactur und bildnüs aller gros herzogen, chur und fürsten, welche vom jahr ... 842 bis auff das jetzige ... jahr das landt Sachssen löblich und christlich regieret haben. Dressden, G. Bergen 1586
44 l. Q.

Agricultural laborers
Coler, Johann. Oeconomia ruralis et domestica. 1665

Crescenzi, Pietro de. Commoda ruralium. ca1493

Crescenzi, Pietro de. Neu feldt und ackerbau. 1602

Germany

Bartels, Adolf. Der bauer in der deutschen vergangenheit. 1900

Hohberg, W. H., freiherr von. Georgica curiosa aucta, das ist: Umståndlicher bericht und klarer unterricht von dem adelichen land-und feld-leben. Auf alle in Teutschland ûbliche land- und hauswirthschafften gerichtet. 1701-1715

Italy

Cyriax, Tony. Among Italian peasants. 1919

Gallo, Agostino. Le venti giornate dell' agricoltura. 1584

Netherlands

Divers paissans d'Hollande. ca1700

Norway

Grund, J. G. Afbildning af Nordmands-Dalen, i den kongelige lyst-hauge ved Fredensborg... Abbildung des Normannsthals, in dem königlichen lustgarten zu Friedensburg. 1773

Switzerland

Barnard, George. Switzerland; scenes and incidents of travel in the Bernese Oberland. 184-?

Agrippa, Camillo
Trattato di scientia d'arme, con un dialogo di filosofia. Roma, A. Blado [1553]
70 l. 55 illus. Q.
Lipperheide 2948

Ah! que c'est drôle! ou le cabinet de modes; description des costumes nouveaux, entre-mêlée de vaudevilles et de facéties. Paris, chez Ouvrier An VI 1797-1798
Ti.
Colas 46

Ahmad Shāh
Four years in Tibet. Benares, E. J. Lazarus 1906
78p. Q.
LC A35-788

Ahrem, Maximilian
Das weib in der antiken kunst. Jena, E. Diederichs 1924
320p. col.front. illus. Q.

Ahrenberg, Johan Jacob
Fennia illustrata; 1. Finsk ornamentik. Suomalainen ornamentiiki. Ornementation finlandaise. Helsingfors, G. W. Edlund 1878-82
32 col.pl. Q.
Lipperheide 3961

Ahrens, Wilhelm. See Kohfeldt, Gustav, jt. ed.

Aigentliche warhaffte delineatio unnd abbildung aller fürstlichen auffzüg und rütterspilen bey dess ... Johann Friderichen hertzogen zu Württemberg ... jungen printzen und sohns hertzog Ulrichen ... kindtauff ... Hulsen, Esaias von

Aiken, Charlotte Rankin
Millinery. New York, Ronald 1922
xix,188p. front. illus. pl. O. (Merchandise manual series)
Books for reference: p 181
LC 22-14269

Aincourt, Marguerite d'
Études sur le costume féminin; illus. de Cortazzo et Scott. Paris, Rouveyre et Blond 1884
72p. illus. 16pl. O.
Colas 47. Lipperheide 3290

Ainos
Batchelor, John. The Ainu and their folklore. 1901

Ainslie, Douglas
(tr.) Barbey d'Aurevilly, J. A. Of dandyism and of George Brummell. 1897

Ainslie, Sir Robert. See Mayer, Ludwig. Views in Egypt; Views in the Ottoman dominions; and Views in the Ottoman empire ... from the original drawings in the possession of Sir R. Ainslie

Ainsworth, William Harrison
The miser's daughter. with illustrations by G. Cruikshank. London, G. Routledge [1872]
xi,302p. front. pl. O.
First edition 1842 (London, Cunningham & Mortimer) Illustrations show Jacobite costume
LC 1-1782

Aintree. Brown, Paul

The **Ainu** and their folk-lore. Batchelor, John

Ainus. See Ainos

Airy nothings. Egerton, M.

Aitsinger, Michael. See Eitzing, Michael, freiherr von

Ajduklewicz, T.
L'armée roumaine. Bucarest, Socec 1903
2 l. 26 col.pl. 1 col.port. F.
Cataloged from Colas
Colas 48

K. **Akademie der künste.** See Berlin. K. Akademie der künste

Akademiía nauk, Leningrad. See Barons, Krišjānis, ed. Latwju dainas

Akademija umiejętności, Cracow
Ubiory ludu polskiego. Zeszyt I-II. Krakowie, Nakladem Akademii umiejętności 1904-09
2v. in 1. illus. XIV pl. (part col.) F.
Preface signed: Komitet wydawniczy komisyi antropologicznej Akademii umiejętności: Roman Zawiliński, Włodzimierz Tetmajer, Seweryn Udziela
Colas 2925

Die **akademische** amtstracht und ihre farben. Delitzsch, F. J.

Akerlio, [pseud] See Deguerle, Jean Marie Nicolas

Alamodische hobelbanck ... von den jetzigen ... sitten, närrischen gebräuch und missbräuchen als da ist in klaidern, gebärden gehen. Augsburg, A. Aperger [1630]
85p. D.
An enlarged edition was published in 1710 under title: *Renovirte und mercklich vermehrte alamodische hobel-bank* (184p. 1 illus.) Reprinted in 1713 with title: *Neue alamodische sitten-schul* (360p.)
Lipperheide 3432-34

Alaska. See Arctic regions

Alaska, our northern wonderland. Carpenter, F. G.

Alaux, M. M. J., and Duponchel, L.
Théâtre français: recueil de costumes ... lithographiés par Baptiste. Seul recueil publié d'après les dessins manuscrits de la bibliothèque de la Comédie française. Paris, Engelmann n.d.
34 col.pl. Q.
Plates show actors and actresses dressed for various roles. For list see Colas's *Bibliographie*
Colas 49

Alba, André
La révolution française. [Paris] Hachette °1924
64p. 89 illus. (incl. ports. map. facsims.) O. (Encyclopédie par l'image)
"Bibliographie": p63
LC A33-1885

Albania
Barletius, Martinus. Des aller streytparsten vñ theüresten fürsten und herrn Georgen Castrioten genant Scanderbeg ... ritterliche thaten. 1533
Gopčević, Spiridion. Das fürstentum Albanien. 1914

19th-20th centuries

Cartwright, J. Selections of the costume of Albania and Greece. 1822
Degrand, J. A. T. Souvenirs de la Haute-Albanie. 1901
Durham, M. E. The burden of the Balkans. 1905
Durham, M. E. High Albania. 1909
Howe, Fisher. Oriental and sacred scenes. 1856
Lane, Mrs R. W. Peaks of Shala. 1923
Nopcsa, Ferencz, báró. Albanien; bauten, trachten und geräte Nordalbaniens. 1925

Albéca, Alexandre L. d'
La France au Dahomey. Paris, Hachette 1895
236p. front. illus. (incl. maps, port.) F.

Albemarle, George Thomas Keppel, 6th earl of. See Pictures of the uniforms, arms, and equipments of the cavalry of Great Britain

Albert, A.
Le tour du monde: album des costumes de toute la terre. Paris, A. Albert [1892]
1 l. 16pl. ob.Q.
Colas 50

Alberti, Lodewyk
De Kaffers aan de zuidkust van Afrika; natuur en geschiedkundig beschreven. Amsterdam, E. Maaskamp 1810
260p. 2 col.pl. fold.plan
French translation *Description physique et historiques des Cafres* (Amsterdam, E. Maaskamp 1811. xii,255p. front. col.pl. O. and atlas of 4 col.pl. ob.F.)
German edition: *Die Kaffern* (Gotha, Becker 1815)

Albo pittorico di alcune feste modenesi nella fausta occasione delle nozze auguste tra l'A.R. dell'arciduca Francesco Ferdinando, principe ereditario di Modena e S.A.R. la principessa Adelgonda di Baviera. Modena, per gli eredi Soliani 1842
5 l. 13pl. ob.O.
Dedication signed by the engravers: Bruni Geminiano, Cappelli Agostino, Berselli Giovanni
Lipperheide 2778

Alboise de Poujol, Jules Édouard, and Élie, Charles
Fastes des gardes nationales de France. Paris, Goubaud & Olivier 1849
2 l. 554p. 20pl. (2 col.) O.
Published in 15 parts, the first in December 1848. The colored plates show uniforms, the others scenes of battles engaged in from 1789-1848
A second edition was issued (1849. 2v. 22pl. incl. 3 col.) with new colored plates, the others the same as in the first edition
Colas 51-52. Lipperheide 2320

Al'bom" rīsunkov" dlía kanvovykh" rabot". S.-Peterburg", Hermana Hoppe 1882-83
2v. 21 col.pl. Q.
Album of needlepoint designs
Lipperheide 3969

Al'bom rīsunkov" russkīkh ī slavíanskīkh" naríadov" Vypusk" I. naríady Velīkorusskiĭ (Ríazanskoĭ) gub ī chernogorskiĭ. S.-Peterburg", Hermana Hoppe 1884
6 col.pl. F.
Album of drawings of Russian and Slavic costumes, issued as a free supplement to *Modnyĭ sviet ī modnyĭ magazin* 1883, the Russia edition of *Modenwelt*
Lipperheide 1376

Al'bom" russkīkh ī malorossiĭskīkh" rīsunkov". Īvchenko, A.

Al'bom" russkīkh" monogramm" dlía míetkī bíel'ía. S.-Peterburg", Hermana Hoppe 1882
20pl. Q.
Album of Russian monograms for marking linen
Lipperheide 4186

Albrecht, prince of Prussia, 1837-1906
Im Kaukasus 1862. [Berlin, A. W. Hayn 1865]
2v.(603p.) illus. 39 col.pl. O.-F.
Ten of the plates, after T. Horschelt and H. Kretzschmer form a separate atlas in folio size. The greater part of the plates are costume pictures
Colas 53. Lipperheide 1386

Albrecht, Ignatz
(ed.) Spalart, Robert von. Versuch über das kostum der vorzüglichsten völker

L'Album; journal des arts, des modes et des théâtres. v. 1-11; 19 juillet 1821-15 août 1829. Paris, A. Boucher
11 v. col.pl. O.
Volumes 1-8 nos. 1-136, v9-11 nos. 1-52. No numbers published between March 25, 1823 and no.136, November 1828, when title became *L'Ancien Album* v9-11 (nos 1-52) 25 Nov. 1828 to 15 Aug. 1829
Founded and edited by François Grille d'Angers; later (no. 96 on) by J. D. Magallon
Colas 54

Album altdeutscher leinenstickerei. Manteuffel, Erna von

Album amicorum Habitibus mulierum omniu nationu Europae tum tabulis ac scutis vacuis in aes incisis adornatum, ut quisque et sÿmbola et insignia sua gentilitia in ijs depingi commode curare possit. Lovanii, Apud Joannem Baptis, tam Zangrium 1601
70pl. Q.
Colas 56

Album auvergnat. Bouillet, Jean Baptiste

Album colorié des uniformes des grandes armées de l'Europe. Valley, A.

Album comique de pathologie pittoresque, recueil de vingt caricatures médicales dessinées par Aubry, Chazal, Colin, Bellangé et Pigal. Paris, A. Tardieu 1823
[44]p. front. 20 col.pl. ob.Q.

Album de broderies anciennes. Lessing, Julius

Album de broderies au point de croix. Dillmont, Thérèse de

Album de coiffures historiques. Bysterveld, Henri de

Album de coiffures historiques avec descriptions. Nissy, E.

Album de coiffures travesties. Mallemont, A.

Album de costumes des Pays-Bas; dedié a Sa Majesté la Reine des Pays-Bas. Amsterdam, F. Buffa 1849
20 col.pl. F.
Title on cover: *Costumes des Pays Bas*

Album de costumes portuguezes; cincoenta chromos copias de aguarellas originaes de Alfredo Roque Gameiro, Columbano Bordallo Pinheiro, Condeixa, Malhôa, Manuel de Macedo, Raphael Bordallo Pinheiro e outros. Com artigos descriptivos de Fialho d'Almeida, Julio Cesar Machado, Manuel Pinheiro Chagas, Ramalho Ortigão e Xavier da Cunha. Lisboa, D. Corazzi [1888]
52 l. 50 col.pl. F.
Colas 65. LC 16-24884

Album de danses illustrées, anciennes & modernes. Histoire de la danse, théorie, dessin, musique. Paris, Choudens [189-?]
108p. illus. F.
Includes music and directions for each dance. Contents: Pavane; Chacone; Gigue; Passepied; Bourée; Menuet; Gavotte; Cracovienne; Versoviana; Redowa; Schottische; Valse à deux temps; Valse à trois temps; Polka; Polka-mazurka; Quadrille; Les lanciers; Ostendaise; Pas de quatre; Le cotillon

Album de divers travaux exécutés sur la fourche à franges, Deuxième. Paris, Maison Sajou [1885]
32p. 33 illus. S.
Lipperheide 4144

Album de la artilleria española. Madrid, Lit. Marquerie 1862
16 col.pl. F.
LC 34-41459

Album de la caballeria española. Clonard, S. M. de S. y A., conde de

Album de la cavalerie de l'armée espagnole. Madrid, J. Donon ca1850
1 l. 12 col.pl. F.
Colas 57

Album de la cavalerie française, 1635-1861. Armand-Dumaresq, C. É.

Album de la infanteria y caballeria española del ejercito de Filipinas, siendo capitan general de ellas el esĉmo. sor. teniente general D. Manuel Crespo. Madrid, [1856]
1 l 35 col.pl. Q.
Colas 58

Album de la mode. Chronique du monde fashionable, ou choix de morceaux de littérature contemporaine; par Jules Jannin, Henry Martin, Gustave Drouineau, le vicomte de Marquessac, Alexandre Dumas, Gustave Albitte, Émile Deschamps, Jules Lacroix, le vicomte d'Arlincourt, P. L. Jacob, Petrus Borel et Eugène Sue. Paris, L. Janet 1833
376p. 12 col.pl. O. 16 fr
The plates exist also in black and white
Colas 59. Lipperheide 1163

Album de l'armée française. Epinal, Pellerin ca1875
16 col.pl. F.
Colas 61. Lipperheide 2332

Album de l'armée française. Lançon, A.

Album de l'armée française (de 1700 à 1870) Fallou, Louis

Album de l'armée française et la Garde impériale. Paris, Becquet frères ca1860
1 l. 25 col.pl. S.
Colas 60

Album de l'Exposition militaire de la Société des amis des arts de Strasbourg. Seyboth, Adolf, and Binder, C.

Album de l'histoire des modes françaises. See Autour de la table

Album de modèles de tricot; avec explications. Paris, Cabin 1881
72p. 25pl. Q.
Lipperheide 4131

Album de portraits d'après les collections du Département des manuscrits. Paris. Bibliothèque nationale. Département des manuscrits

Album de Ste. Pélagie (dette). Adam, Victor

Album de uniformes exercito e armada; con decoracôes militares. Lisboa, 1890
53 col. pl. map. Q.
Plates show military uniforms of Portugal
Colas 67

Album delle uniformi militari del regno: esercito e marino. Cenni, Quinto

Album départemental ou Bordeaux et ses environs. Galard, Gustave de

Album der bühnen-costüme. Bloch, Eduard

Album der monogramme für kreuzstich. Wien & Leipzig, Verlag der Wiener mode 1894
38pl. Q. (Handarbeits-bibliothek der "Wiener mode." no 1)
Lipperheide 4191

Album des costumes nationaux de la Suisse. No place, J. Jundt [1837]
24 col.pl. Q.
Cover title. Cataloged from Colas's *Bibliographie*
Colas 64

Album des théâtres. Guyot, and Debacq, A.

Album des types et costumes de tous les peuples du monde. Paris, Lib. generale 1869
398p. pl. Q.
As in many old books on costume the pictures are not all true to life

Album des uniformes de l'armée et de la marine françaises. See Lalaisse, Hippolyte. Collection complète des uniformes de l'armée et de la marine françaises

Album des voyages anciens et modernes. Jouhanneaud, Paul

Album descriptif des fêtes et cérémonies religieuses à l'occasion du jubilé de 700 ans du Saint-Sang, à Bruges. Carton, C. L.

Album descriptivo del ejército y la armada de España, publicado por tres oficiales de ejército. Madrid, Fontanet 1884
128p. 32 col.pl. F.
Plates are after designs by E. Soria
Colas 2769

Album deutscher volkstrachten. See note under Kretschmer, Albert. Deutsche volkstrachten

Album di lavori a punto croce. Milano, Fratelli Treves 1890
7p. 27 illus. 60pl. F.
Lipperheide 4013

Album 1861; spécialités de La compagnie Lyonnaise. Lyon [etc] Maisons à cachemire 1861
2 l. 11 col.pl. Q.
Feminine costume of the period
Colas 55

Album du bal costumé au Palais d'hiver, février 1903. Saint Pétersbourg 1904
194pl. F.
Title in Russian and French. Shows fancy dress derived from Russian costume of the 17th century
Colas 68

Album du bon-bock. Bellot, R. P.

Album du cortège des comtes de Flandre. Busscher, Edmond de

Album du cortége historique. Le Gendre, Léonce

Album du Guide à l'usage des artistes et des costumiers, publié en 1904. See Malibran, H. Guide à l'usage des artistes et des costumiers .

Album du jubilé de 875 ans. Vervloet, Victor

Album du progrès; costumes historiques, artistiques et travestis. Paris, A. Picart ca1872
25 col.pl. Q.
Plates each show twelve to sixteen types of costumes historical or fanciful
Colas 69

Album d'un soldat. Clerjon de Champagny

Album estnischer volkstrachten. See Tartu. Eesti rahva muuseum. Eesti rahvariiete album

Album Forain. Forain, J. L.

Album für altdeutsche leinen-stickerei und stickerei auf Java-canevas. Leipzig, Kramer [1878]
8 col.pl. O.
Lipperheide 3990

Album für frauen-arbeit. Hirth, Georg

Album für stickerei. Fischbach, Friedrich

Album für weisse und bunte häkel-und filetarbeiten. Herder, Natalie von

Album hambürgische costüme. Buek, F. G.

Album Henri Monnier. Monnier, Henri

Album hervorragender gegenstände aus der waffensammlung der allerhöchsten kaiserhauses. Boeheim, Wendelin

Album historique. Parmentier, A. É. E.

Album historique de l'armée et de la marine. Paris, J. Leroy 1905-1906
98p. illus.(part col.) 47pl.(part col.) F. 240 fr.
In portfolio. Contains the history of the Musée historique de l'armée
Colas 70. LC 24-1785

Album keepsake des costumes de la cour française depuis Charles VII jusqu'à Louis XVI. Compte-Calix, F. C.

Album lithographié. See Devéria, Achille. Album lithographié

Album lithographié. Grenier, François

Album lithographique. Charlet, N. T.

Album militaire. Paris, Boussod, Valadon & cie [18—]
15 parts in portfolio. col.illus. ob.O.
Portfolio has title: *Illustrated album of the French army and navy.* Each part contains 6 colored pictures of groups of men from the French army and navy, including some of the French foreign troops, such as Zouaves and Spahis. Descriptions are given

Album militaire de l'armée française en action. Moraine, L. P. R. de

Album militaire suisse. See Kindler, Alfred. Die schweizerische armee in bildern

Album militar; album del ejercito español. See Villegas, José. Album militar; coleccion de uniformes del ejercito español

Album militar; coleccion de uniformes del epercito español. Villegas, José

Album mittelalterlicher ornament-stickerei zur zierde für kirche und haus, in autographien ... mit erklärenden. Bock, Franz

Album moderner, nach kunstlerentwürfen ausgeführter damen-kleider; mit einleitung von Frau Maria van de Velde. Düsseldorf, F. Wolfrum [1900]
32pl.(part col.) Q.
Colas 2090. Lipperheide 3311m

Album moderner stick-muster. Kühn, Heinrich

Album of drawing, in pencil and water-colors, made during the Sioux troubles of 1851-52, and the Sioux rising of 1863 under Little Crow. One of the drawings is signed "White, fecit." No place, 1863?
48 l. pl. ob.F.

Album of the life sized figures. Tokyo. Imperial museum

Album of the weapons, tools, ornaments, articles of dress, etc. of the natives of the Pacific islands. Edge-Partington, James

Album ou collection complète et historique des costumes de la cour de Rome. Perugini, G.

Album pittoresque du nord. Forsell, C. D.

Album pour ouvrages de fleurs au crochet. Paris, Maison Sajou ca1858
24p. 6 illus. O.
Lipperheide 4093

Album pour ouvrages de travaux à la fourche; nouv. éd. Paris, Maison Sajou [1883]
21p. 28 illus. S.
Lipperheide 4145

Album russe ou fantaisies dessinées lithographiquement. Orlowski, A. O.

Album valaque. Bouquet, Michel

Album vendéen. Drake, T.

Album wojska polskiego z 1831. See note under Kozłowski, Karol. Wojsko polskie w roku 1831

Album "Ziemi." Warszawa, Polskie Tow. Krajoznawcz 191-?
2v. pl. ob.O.
Volume 2 shows Polish costume. No more published?

Album-annuaire de l'armée française. Beauvoir, H. R. de

Albums pour ouvrages au tricot. Paris, Maison Sajou [1886]
26p. 8pl. S.
Lipperheide 4149

Albums pour ouvrages en frivolité. Paris, Maison Sajou [1886]
11p. illus. 8pl. S.
Lipperheide 4148

Albumul armatei romane. Bucuresci, Stab. lith. M. B. Baer 1873
[19]p. 28 col.pl. sq.Q.
Colas 71

Alby hebet sich an dy grosse lege. See Legenda der heiligen Hedwig

Alcega, Juan de
Libro de geometria practica y traça; el que trata de lo tocante. Madrid, G. Drouy 1580
104 l. illus.
Reprinted 1589

Alciati, Andrea
Les emblèmes ... mis en rime francoyse, et puis nagueres reimprime avec curieuse correction. Paris, C. Wechel 1540
245p. illus. O.
This version first published in Paris in 1534. Text in Latin and French

Aldegrever, Heinrich
Ornamente; facsimiles in gleicher grösse der im Kgl. kupferstich-cabinet-München vorhandenen originalstiche. Zusammengestellt auf 25 tafeln nach den nummern von Bartsch. Hrsg. in unveränderlichem photographischen druck von J. B. Obernetter in München. München, H. Manz [1876]
61pl. mounted on 25 l. F.
In portfolio. Portrait of author on portfolio
Lipperheide 4356. LC 20-11623

Aldenkirchen, Joseph
Früh-mittelalterliche leinenstickereien. Bonn, Universitäts buchdruckerei von C. Georgi 1885
19p. 3pl. O.
Reprint from the *Jahrbuch* of the Vereins von alterthumsfreunden im Rheinland v79
Lipperheide 3867

Aldin, Cecil Charles Windsor
(ed.) The omnibus book of sports for young and old. New York, Coward-McCann [1937]
178,125,147p. illus. pl. ports. fold.map. O.
Originally published as three separate works in the Aldin series: each part has also special title page
Contents: Elements of lawn tennis, by J H. Doeg and Allison Danzig; Riding, by Lady Hunloke and Cecil Aldin; Golf, by T. H. Cotton
LC 37-4150

Alensis, A. d'
L'enseignement professionnel de la mode; méthode moderne et pratique permettant d'exécuter ses chapeaux soi-même et les réparer. Paris, A. Jeandé 1911
48p. illus. D. 1 fr.
Colas 73

Alessandro, Giuseppe d'
Opera. Napoli, A. Muzio 1723
811p. illus. F.
On cavalry, swordsmen, etc. Illustrations are full-page copper engravings of prominent men of the time (p319-45), cavalry officers (p291-317), horses, accoutrements and fencers

Alexander, Christine. See New York. Metropolitan museum of art. Jewelry

Alexander, Sir James Edward
An expedition of discovery into the interior of Africa, through the hitherto undescribed countries of the Great Namaquas, Boschmans, and Hill Damaras. Performed under the auspices of Her Majesty's government, and the Royal geographical society. London, H. Colburn 1838
2v. fronts. illus. pl. fold.map. O.
Describes dress of the explorers and their servants, and of some native tribes
LC 5-15398

Alexander, Vera Constance
Cross-stitch. London, Pitman 1932
88p. col.front. illus. O. (Pitman's craft for all series)
LC 32-25119

Alexander, Virginia M.
Appropriate clothes for the high school girl. [Denton, Tex. 1920]
26p. illus. O. (College of industrial arts. Denton, Texas. Bulletin no 74)
LC 24-14861

Alexander, William

The costume of China, illus. in forty-eight coloured engravings. London, W. Miller 1805

48p. 48 col.pl. F.
Colas 74

The costume of Turkey, illustrated by a series of engravings; with descriptions in English and French. London, W. Miller [etc] 1802

[134]p 60 col.pl. F.
Supposed author
Added t.-p. in French: *Costume de la Turquie.* The drawings, from which these plates have been engraved, were made by Octavian Dalvimart. Some of them are reproduced in Castellan's *Moeurs*
Colas 782. Lipperheide 1422. LC 16-25725

Costume et vues de la Chine, gravés par Simon, d'après les dessins de W. Alexandre. Paris, Nepveu 1815

2v. 54 col.pl. D.
French edition of his *Picturesque representations of the Chinese.* The title page of v2 reads *Vues de la Chine et de la Tartarie*
Colas 77. Lipperheide 1528

Histoire des femmes . . . chez tous les peuples barbares et civilisés, anciens et modernes. Tr. de l'anglois, par M. de Cantwell. Paris, Chez Briand 1791-94

4v. fronts. D.
Translation of his *History of women*
LC 9-1571

The history of women, from the earliest antiquity, to the present time; giving some account of almost every interesting particular concerning that sex, among all nations, ancient and modern. London, Printed for W. Strahan and T. Cadell 1779

2v. sq.Q.
Third edition (London, C. Dilly 1782) Also an edition (Philadelphia, J. H. Dobelbower 1796. LC 7-5692)
LC 9-3473

Picturesque representations of the dress and manners of the Austrians; illus. in 50 coloured engravings, with descriptions. London, T. McLean 1813

15p. 50 col.pl. O.
Plates are marked: Published June 1, 1813, by J. Murray and are copies in reduced size of those in Bertrande de Moleville's *Costume of the hereditary states of the house of Austria*
Colas 78. Costume index. Lipperheide 832

Picturesque representations of the dress and manners of the Chinese; illus. in 50 coloured engravings with descriptions. London, J. Murray 1814

50 l. 50 col.pl. Q.
Editions also published by J. Goodwin and by T. McLean. A new edition of the author's *The costume of China* which contains 48 of the same plates. Some of the plates are reproduced in Malpière's *La Chine*
Colas 75. Lipperheide 1527-28

Picturesque representations of the dress and manners of the English. Illustrated in sixty-four coloured engravings, with descriptions. London, Murray 1814

[51] l. 50 col.pl. F.
Supposed author William Alexander
Colas 2357. Costume index

Picturesque representations of the dress and manners of the Russians. London, J. Murray 1814

64 l. 64 col.pl. O. o.p.
Plates almost identical with those in *Costume of the Russian empire* (London, William Miller 1803) and the same title (London, E. Harding 1803) The source of all is Georgi's *Beschreibung aller nationen des russischen reichs*
Reprinted (London, T. M'Lean 1815. 64 l. 64 col.pl. O.)
Colas 2358-59 Costume index. Lipperheide 1351

Picturesque representations of the dress and manners of the Turks. London, Printed for J. Goodwin by W. Lewis [1814?]

vi p. 60 l. 60 col.pl. Q.
A reproduction of his *Costume of Turkey* with illustrations reduced in size. The French translation has been omitted
Reprinted (Istanbul, Zaman, bookseller 1932-33. 60 l. 60 col.pl.)
Colas 783. Lipperheide 1423

Vues, costumes, moeurs et usages de la Chine. No place, ca1815

48p. 24pl. O.
Contains 24 of the plates that are in his *Costumes et vues de la Chine*
Lipperheide 1528a

Alexandre, Arsène

L'art du rire et de la caricature ... 300 similés en noir et 12 planches en couleurs d'après les originaux. Paris, Quantin [1892]

350p. illus. 12 col.pl. Q.
Lipperheide 3515. LC 13-12189

Histoire de la peinture militaire en France. Paris, H. Laurens [1889]

332p illus. pl. O. [Biblithèque d'histoire et d'art]

Honoré Daumier, l'homme et l'œuvre; ouvrage orné d'un portrait à l'eau-forte, de deux héliogravures et de 47 illustrations. Paris, H. Laurens 1888

383p. front.(port.) illus. pl.(part double) Q.
Lipperheide 3512 LC 9-24578

Alexandre, Paul

La beauté de la chevelure; orné de 75 bois et dessins originaux par Henry Gazan. Paris, Javailier 1924

188p. illus. D. (On cover: Les manuels de science et de beauté)
LC 24-10318

Alfabetos adornados. Peñafiel, Antonio

Alfieri, Francesco Fernando

La picca, e la bandiera; nella quale si mostra per via di figure una facile nuova pratica, et il maneggio, e l'uso di essa, con la diffessa della spada. Padova, S. Sardi 1641

2v. 40 illus. Q.
Also published separately as *La bandiera* (1638) and *La picca* (1641)
Lipperheide 2962

La scherma ... dove con nove ragione e con figure si mostra la perfezione di quest' arte, e in che modo secondo l'arme e l'sito possa il cavaliere restar al suo nemico superiore. Padova, S. Sardi 1640

168p. 35 illus. 1 pl. Q.
Lipperheide 2961

Alford, Marianne Margaret (Compton) Cust, viscountess
Needlework as art. London, S. Low, Marston, Searle, and Rivington 1886
xxiii,422p. illus. 86pl. O.
Lipperheide 3868
(ed.) Higgin, L. Handbook of embroidery

Alford, Violet
Peeps at English folk-dances. London, A. & C. Black 1923
87p. col.front. illus. pl.(part col.) O. [The peeps series]
LC 24-8886

Alford, Violet, and Gallop, Rodney
The traditional dance. London, Methuen [1935]
xv,204p. front. pl. D.
LC 39-916

Algardi, Alessandro
(engr.) Carracci, Annibale. Le arti di Bologna

Algemeen handelsblad
In kleuren en kleeren. Nederlandsche volksdrachten. . . Met beschrijving van C. K. Elout. [Amsterdam, 1930]
75p. illus. 16pl.(15 col.) F.

Alger; tableau de royaume. Renaudot

Algeria. Commissariat général du centenaire
L'armée d'Afrique, 1830-1930; son évolution—ses uniformes ... avec préface du maréchal Franchet-d'Esperey. [Alger, M. Léon] 1930?
[24]p. col.illus. Q.

Algeria
Aperçu historique, statistique et topographique sur l'état d'Alger, à l'usage de l'armée expéditionnaire d'Afrique, avec . . . costumes. 1830
Archinard, L. Q. L'autre France (Tunisie, Algérie, Maroc) 1914
Barclay, Edgar. Mountain life in Algeria. 1882
Berbrugger, L. A. Algérie historique, pittoresque et monumentale. Recueil de vues, monuments, cérémonies, costumes, armes et portraits . . . avec texte descriptif. 1843-45
Christian, Pierre. L'Afrique française, l'empire de Maroc, et les deserts de Sahara. 1846
Galibert, Leon. L'Algérie, ancienne et moderne depuis les premiers éstablissements des Carthaginois jusqu'à la prise de la Smalah d'Abd-el-Kader. 1844
Guillaumet, G. A. Tableaux algériens. 1888
Hilton-Simpson, M. W. Among the hill-folk of Algeria. 1921
Jungmann, Robert. Costumes, moeurs et usages des Algériens. . . Trachten, sitten, und gebräuche der Algierer. 1837
Lessore, A. E., and Wyld, W. Voyage pittoresque dans la régence d'Alger pendant l'année 1833. 1835
Marçais, Georges. Le costume musulman d'Alger. 1930
Piesse, Louis. Costumes algériens. ca1835
Renaudot. Alger; tableau du royaume, de la ville d'Alger et de ses environs. 1830
Ricard, Prosper. Les merveilles de l'autre France; Algérie, Tunisie, Maroc; le pays—les monuments—les habitants. c1924
Vaillant. Costumes algériens. 1847-49
Wolffgang, A. M. Costumes algériens. ca1796

L'**Algérie,** ancienne et moderne. Galibert, Léon

Algérie historique, pittoresque et monumentale. Berbrugger, L. A.

Algonquian Indians. See Indians of North America—Algonquian Indians

Algué, José
(ed.) El archipiélago filipino

Aliev, Umar D.
Karachaĭ; istorico-ekonomichesk. i kul'turno-ekonomicheskiĭ ocherk. Rostov na Donu, Kraĭnatsizdat "Severo-Kavkaszk 1927g
8,30p. illus. col.map. 10r. 50k.
Shows dress worn in Karachai, a district of the Russian Caucasus

Alix, Pierre Michel
(engr.) Le Vacher de Charnois, J. C. Recherches sur les costumes et sur les théatres de toutes les nations, tant anciennes que modernes

Alkemade, Kornelis van
Inleidinge tot het ceremonieel, en de plegtigheden der begraavenissen, en der wapen-kunde; uit deszelfs oorspronkelykheid . . . door Cornelis van Alkemade. Delft, A. Voorstad 1713
266p. 3pl. O.
Burial customs in Friesland and Holland
Lipperheide 2470

Alken, Henry Thomas
The national sports of Great Britain. London, T. McLean 1821
51 l. 50 col.pl. F.
Added title page: *British sports* (1920). French title *Chasse et amusemens nationaux de la Grande Bretagne.* Plates are signed H. Alken, Alken, or I. Clark
LC 19-509
Symptoms, of being amused. v 1. London, T. McLean 1822
1 p.l. 41 col.pl. F.
No more published
Lipperheide 3556. LC 11-29543

All the Russias. Norman, Sir Henry, bart.

Allan, Charles Stuart Hay. See Stuart, C. E.

Allan, John Hay. See Stuart, J. S. S.

Allard, A.
Habillemens des païsans et païsannes de Hollande, de Frise, de Braband et autres provinces; Dragten der Boeren en Boerinner, in Holland, Vriesland, Braband, en elders. Leyden, P. Vander Aa [1713]
1 l. 16pl.
Legends on the plates are in Dutch and in French. The plates are copied from Van den Berge's *Costumes hollandois*
Colas 79

Allard, Carel
Orbis habitabilis oppida et vestitus, centenario numero complexa, summo studio collecta. Des bewoonden waerelds steden en dragten. Amsterdam, C. Allard 170-?
9pl. 100 double pl. F.
Binder's title: *Hondert steden en dragten*
The full views are engraved by T. Doesburgh and the costume views are by A. Meijer. Issued after 1700, and, it may be, as late as 1710. Descriptive table of plates, in Latin and Dutch, signed: Ludolph Smids. Views of American towns and costumes, pl. 77-100

Allardt, Hugo. See Eeckhout, Guillielmus vanden. Le nouvelle figure à la mode de ce tempts de fine

Allegorical and imaginary figures
Amman, Jost, Wapen und stammbuch darinnen du keys. maiest. chur und fürsten, graffen, freyherrn, deren vom adel, etc. mit kunstreichen figuren. 1589
Art workers guild, London. Beauty's awakening, a masque of winter and of spring. ₍1899₎
Bartsch, Gustav. Deutsche mährchengestalten. ₍1857₎
Boissard, J. J. Iani Iacobi Boissardi Vesuntini emblematum liber. 1593
Oeri, J. J. Der onyx von Schaffhausen; jubiläums-schrift des historisch-antiquarischen vereins Schaffhausen. 1882
Passe, Crispijn van de. Le vrais pourtraits de quelques unes des plus grandes dames de la chrestiente, desguisees en bergeres. 1640
Pistrucci, Filippo. Iconologia ovvero immagini di tutte le cose principali a cui l'umano talento ha finto un corpo. 1819-21

See also Angels; Mythological characters

Allegri, Girolamo Maria
Esercizio di preparazione alla visita. In Casotti, G. B. Memorie istoriche della miracolosa. v2, pt 2

Allemagne, Henry René d'
Les accessoires du costume et du mobilier depuis le treizième jusqu'au milieu du dixneuvième siècle; ouvrage contenant 393 phototypies, reproduisant plus de 3.000 documents. Paris, Schemit 1928
3v. front. pl. F.
Paged continuously
Contents: v 1 Bijouterie, bagues, bracelets, boucles d'oreilles, bijoux en acier & en fonte de Berlin, boutons, châtelaines, cachets, pommes de cannes, éventails, miroirs, escarelles & sacs, boîtes & tabatières, coffrets, luminaire, objets en tôle vernie; v2 Outils & instruments de précision, bésicles & lunettes, lorgnettes, écritoires, horloges, montres, ciseaux, navettes, accessoires de fumeurs, ustensiles de table & de cuisine: couteaux, cuillers & fourchettes, bassinoires, mortiers, moulins à café, paniers, clavandiers; v3 Description détaillée des sujets figurés dans les planches. Table analytique. Table méthodique
Bibliographie: v3, p₍565₎-67
Colas 81. Costume index. LC 29-7460

Les cartes à jouer du XIVe au XXe siècle . . . Ouvrage contenant 3200 reproductions de cartes dont 956 en couleur, 12 planches hors texte coloriées à l'aquarelle, 25 phototypies, 116 enveloppes illustrées pour jeux de cartes et 340 vignettes et vues diverses. Paris, Hachette 1906
2v. col.front. illus. pl(part col.) ports. plans, facsims. ob.O.
"Bibliographie des ouvrages sur les cartes à jouer": v2 p₍551₎-54; "Table analytique": v2 p₍555₎-624
LC 6-20330

Du Khorassan au pays des Backhtiaris, trois mois de voyage en Perse; ouvrage contenant 960 clichés dans le texte et 255 planches hors texte, dont 47 en couleur. Paris, Hachette 1911
4v. mounted col.front. illus. 255pl.(part mounted, 47 col.) maps, plans. F.
"Bibliographie de la Perse": v2 p₍185₎-204
LC 17-13837

Récréations et passe-temps; ouvrage contenant 249 illustrations dans le texte et 132 gravures hors texte dont 30 planches coloriées à l'aquarelle. Paris, Hachette ₍1905₎
380p. illus. (incl.facsims.) 41pl.(part col. 1 double) ob.Q.
LC 20-14732

Allemand, Fritz. See L'Allemand, Fritz

Allen, Edward Heron-. See Heron-Allen, Edward

Allen, Frederick Lewis. See Rogers, Agnes, comp. The American procession

Allerhand kurtzweilige stücklein. See Heyden, Jacob van der. Pugillus facetiarum iconographicarū

Allerhand mödel zum stricken und nähen. No place, 1748
4pl. Q.
Each sheet signed with monogram A. R. P. The important designs are copied from Quentel (1527), Steyner (1534) und Sibmacher
Lipperheide 4059

Allerhöchst-feyerlichste festivitäten welche bey dem . . . beylager . . . Leopoldi I. Römischen Kaysers . . . und Margaritae . . . Infantin von Hispanien . . . eins theils bey . . . empfahung und . . . einzug infantin . . . in . . . Wien . . . andern theils in eim . . . feuerwercke . . . und denn in einem . . . thurnier und ballet zu ross . . . gehalten worden. No place, 1667
36,99p. 35pl. Q.
Part 1 The arrival and reception of the bride in Vienna; part 2 The fireworks, tournament and equestrian ballet
The festivities are described separately in *Von himmeln entzindete* and *Sieg-streit dess lufft*, listed below. The plates are mediocre copies of those in the other two works
Lipperheide 2622

Der **allerneueste** staat von Sibirien, einer grossen und zuvor wenig bekannten Moscowitischen provinz in Asien, entdeckend . . . die sitten und gebräuche der Samojeden, Wagullen, Calmucken, Ostiaken, Tungusen, Buratten, Mongalen und anderer tartarischen völcker. Nürnberg, W. M. Endter 1725
246p. O.
Lipperheide 1387

Allers, Christian Wilhelm
La bella Napoli. Stuttgart, Union deutsche verlagsgesellschaft ₍1893₎
213p. illus. ports. pl. facsims. F.

Allerton, Thomas, pseud. See Allom, Thomas

Allgemeine culturwissenschaft. See note under Klemm, G. F. Werkzeuge und waffen

Das **allgemeine** deutsche schützenfest. Weismann, Heinrich

Allgemeine geschichtforschende gesellschaft der Schweiz. See Zeitschrift für schweizerische geschichte

Allgemeine modenzeitung; eine zeitschrift für die gebildete welt. 1799-1903. Leipzig, Industrie-comptoir
105v. col.illus. Q.
Title varies: 1801, *Magazin des neuesten geschmackes in kunst und mode*; 1802-06 *Charis*
Edited by J A. Bergk; 1837-64 by Dr. A. Diezmann; last volumes by O. F. Durr. Later volumes published by Baumgärtner and later still by Dürr

Allgemeine muster-zeitung; album für weibliche arbeiten und moden. 1.-22. jahrg.; 1844-1865. Stuttgart, Engelhorn & Hochdanz
Illus. O.-Q.
Volumes 17-21 published by E. Hochdanz; v22 by J. B. Metzler
Contains fashion engravings
Colas 82. Lipperheide 4651

Allgemeine schilderung des Othomanischen Reichs. See Mouradgea d'Ohsson, Ignatius. Tableau général de l'Empire Othoman

Allgemeine theaterzeitung und originalblatt für kunst, literatur, musik, mode und geselliges leben. v 1-50; 1806-56. Wien & Trieste
Publication suspended, 1809-10. Volumes for 1812+ published as year 6+
Changes in title: 1807-08 *Zeitung für theater, musik und poesie*; 1811-15 *Theater zeitung*; 1816-22 *Wiener theater zeitung*; 1823-28 *Allgemeine theaterzeitung und unterhaltungsblatt für freunde der kunst. . .*

Allgemeine theaterzeitung und unterhaltungsblatt für freunde der kunst... See Allgemeine theaterzeitung und originalblatt

Allgemeine trachtenkunde. Köhler, Bruno

Allgemeine weltchronik unserer zeit; hrsg. von T. Strahlheim. 1.-3. jahrg.; 1832-1834. Frankfurt am Main, Verlagsmagazin für litteratur und kunst
Col.pl. O.
Contains colored fashion engravings
Colas 85. Lipperheide 4621

Allgemeiner militär-almanach, erster jahrgang mit acht colorirten militärgruppen, nach zeichnungen von Monten, und vier portraits berühmter generals ... von Ernst Rauch und Fleischmann. Darmstadt, C. W. Leske 1828
xii,xxii,88,276p. 12pl.(8 col.) D.
Colas 83. Lipperheide 2119

Allgemeines europäisches journal. 1794-1798. Brunn, J. Trassler
3v. col.illus. O.
Contains fashion plates
Colas 84. Lipperheide 4579

Les **alliés** à Paris en 1815, scènes de moeurs. Finart, N.

Allinson, Alfred Richard
The days of the Directoire; with a photogravure frontispiece & 48 other illustrations of which the costume plates have been selected by J. C. Abbott. London, New York, J. Lane 1910
387p. 25pl. 22 port.(incl.front.) O.
Costume index. LC 10-35139

Allmodischer kleyder teuffel. Ellinger, Johann

Allmogens byggnadssätt. Hammarstedt, Edvard

Allom, Thomas
Character and costume in Turkey and Italy. Designed and drawn from nature by Thomas Allom . . . with descriptive letterpress by Emma Reeve. London, Fisher 1845
47p. 20pl. F. 31s 6d, o.p.
Colas 86 (1839 ed.) Costume index. Lipp. 1282

Allom, Thomas
China, in a series of views, displaying the scenery, architecture and social habits, of that ancient empire. . . With descriptive notices by . . . G. N. Wright. London, Fisher 1843
4v. pl. Q.
Contains the same plates as his *The Chinese empire.* A German partial translation is entitled *China, historisch, romantisch, malerisch* (Karlsruhe ca1843. xlviii, 351p. 35pl.)
Colas 88. LC 4-24783

The Chinese empire, historical and descriptive, illustrating the manners and customs of the Chinese, in a series of steel engravings from original sketches. London and New York, London print. and pub. co. 184-?
2v. pl. Q.
Cover and half-title. *China, its scenery,* etc. German translation *China, historisch, romantisch, malerisch* (1843. 36pl.)

Constantinople and the scenery of the seven churches of Asia Minor; illustrated . . . from nature by Thomas Allom. With an historical account of Constantinople, and descriptions of the plates, by Robert Walsh. London & Paris, Fisher [1838]
2v. in 1 fronts. 92pl. 2 maps (1 fold.) Q.
Engr. t.-p.: *Fisher's illustrations of Constantinople and its environs*
LC 5-7225

L'empire chinois . . . description . . . par Clement Pellé. Londres & Paris, Fisher ca1845
4v. 120pl. Q.
English and German editions are listed above

Die **allzeit** fertige stickerin, ein geschenk für das schöne geschlecht, oder, anweisung, wie eine stickerin sich selbst, ohne zeichnen zu können, jedes muster ab- und auf-zeichnen und fortführen kann; 2.aufl. Meissen, F. W. Goedsche ca1825
15pl. D.
Lipperheide 3947

Alma Julia; illustrirte chronik ihrer dritten säcularfeier. Würzburg, Bavaria. Julius-Maximilian-Universitet

Almack, Edward
The history of the Second dragoons, Royal Scots greys. With forty-four illustrations. London 1908
xix,312p. front. pl.(part col.) ports. facsims. Q.
Illustrations include color plates of early uniforms
LC 24-1791

Regimental badges worn in the British army one hundred years ago. . . The regiments identified, and notes bearing on their history added. London, Blades, East & Blades 1900
92p. front. pl. port. facsim. Q.
LC 2-21913

An **Almain** armourer's album. Selections from an original ms. in Victoria and Albert museum, South Kensington. With introduction and notes by Viscount Dillon. Reproduced and printed by W. Griggs. London 1905
33pl.(32 col.) 2fold.facsim.(1 col.) F.
Thirty-two of the plates preceded by leaves with descriptions and a few illustrations
"The title An Almain armourer's album has been chosen . . . as it is very probable that the ms. from which the following plates have been taken, represents the output of a famous German armourer working in England in Elizabeth's reign . . . Jacob Topf [is] the presumed author of this ms." Introduction
LC 19-573

Almanacco illustrato delle maschere italiane dalla loro origine sino ai nostri tempi. Milano, E. Sonzogno 1863
116p. 21 illus. O.
Lipperheide 3224

Almanacco pittorico anno III. See Manuale dei pittori . . . per l'anno 1792 [and 1794]

Almanach de la mode de Paris; tablettes du monde fashionable. 1. année, 1834. Paris, au bureau de La mode de Paris
246p. 2pl. T.
Text edited by M. de Saint-Maurice
Colas 89

Almanach de la toilette et de la coëffure des dames françoises, suivie d'une dissertation sur celle des dames romaines. Paris, Desnos 1777
20p. 24pl. T.
Illustrations show French hair styles of the 16th, 17th and 18th centuries
A second part was published: *Le bijou des dames*, which see. Both parts are included in *Recueil des coeffures depuis 1589 jusqu'en 1778*
Colas 90. Lipperheide 1676

Almanach der mode und das geschmacks für damen auf das jahr 1802. Berlin, Oehmigke 1802
col.pl. O.
"Zur kunde eleganter gegenstände, und zur beurtheilung des schönen in der tanzkunst, schauspielkunst, musik, zeichenkunst, malerei, stickerei u.s.w." Subtitle
Colas 94. Lipperheide 4507

Almanach der ritter-orden. Gottschalck, Friedrich

Almanach des augsburgischen bürgermilitärs. Augsburg, Brinhausserischen 1796-[98]
3v. 34 col.pl. D.
Colas 95. Lipperheide 2216

Almanach des luxus und der moden auf 1801 mit zehn illuminirten kupfern nach Hogarth; ein beytrag zu Lichtenbergs nachlass. Mainz & Hamburg, G. Wollmer 1801?
80p. 10 col.pl. Ti.
Colas 96

Almanach des modes. 1.-9. années; 1814-1822. Paris, Rosa
col.pl. D.
Volume 6 has title: *Almanach des modes et des moeurs parisiennes*
Each volume contains six colored fashion plates, some by H. Vernet, engraved by Gatine. According to Colas, Barbier attributes the work to Pierre de Lamésangère
Colas 97. Lipperheide 4526

Almanach des modes de la saison. Alq, Louise d', pseud.

Almanach des modes et de la parure. Paris, Marcilly 1805
illus. T.
Colas 99. Lipperheide 4516

Almanach des modes nouvelles de Paris pour 1911. 150 modèles inédits par Bianca et Bill. Paris, Nilsson 1911?
60p. illus. O.
Colas 100

Almanach galant des costumes français des plus à la mode; dessinés d'après nature. Paris, Boulanger [1782]
18pl. Ti.
Colas 101

Almanach welt-sitten-staat-marter-calender. Callenbach, Franz

Les **almanachs** de modes de 1814 à 1830. Savigny de Moncorps, de

Les **almanachs** français: bibliographie—iconographie des almanachs. Grand-Carteret, John

Almeida, Fialho d'. See Album de costumes portuguezes

Almeida, Pierre Joseph Camena d'. See Camena d'Almeida, P. J.

Alméras, Henri d'
La vie parisienne pendant le siège et sous la commune. Paris, A. Michel [1927]
541p. incl. pl. illus.(incl. ports.) O.

La vie parisienne sous la republique de 1848. Paris, A. Michel 1921?
521p. ports. illus. D.

La vie parisienne sous la restauration. Paris, A. Michel [1910]
418p. illus.(incl. music) pl. port. O.

La vie parisienne sous la révolution et le directoire. Paris, A. Michel 1909
432p. illus. pl. ports. O.
On cover: 4. éd.
LC 11-27799

La vie parisienne sous le consulat et l'empire. Paris, A. Michel [1909]
496p. illus.(incl.facsim.) pl. ports. O.
On cover: 7 éd.
LC 11-27800

La vie parisienne sous le règne de Louis-Philippe. Paris, A. Michel [1923]
506p. illus. pl. port. D.

La vie parisienne sous le second empire. Paris, A. Michel [1933]
518p. illus.(incl.ports. facsims.) O.
LC 35-35911

Alméras, Henri d', and Quentin, Henri
Les théâtres libertins au XVIIIe siècle; l'amour sur la scène et dans les coulisses, spectacles des petits appartements, théâtres de société de Collé à Laujon et de la Du Barry à la Guimard, répertoires galants, parades et pièces badines. . . Paris, H. Daragon 1905
360p. pl. ports. O. (Bibliothèque du vieux Paris)
Joint author's pseudonym, Paul d'Estrée, at head of title
Bibliographical footnotes

Almond, A. G.
Gowns & gossip. Cambridge, [Eng] Bowes & Bowes 1925
31p. front. illus. col.pl. diagrs. D.
Sequel to his: *Robes* 1906

Along the Paraná and the Amazon, Paraguay, Uruguay, Brazil. Carpenter, F. G.

Alophe, pseud. See Menut, Adolphe

Alpenländer, Trachten der. Hammerstein, Hans von

Les **Alpes** pittoresques. Forestier, Alc. de, ed.

Alphabet des cris de Paris. Paris, Fourquemin [1840]
25pl. D.
For list of plates see Colas's *Bibliographie* Colas 104

Alphabet des dames. Grévedon, P. L. H.

Alphabet varié. Devéria, Achille

Alphabets. See Embroidery—Monograms and numerals

Alphabets et monogrammes. Dillmont, Thérèse de

Alpinus, Marcus Tatius
(tr.) Vergilius, Polydorus. Von den erfyndern der dyngen

The **Alps,** the Danube and the Near East. Carpenter, F. G.

Alq, Louise d', pseud.
Almanach des modes de la saison, ou Le véritable almanach de la mode et de la femme, 1871. Dessins sur bois par les artistes du journal Les Modes de la saison. Paris, E. Plon 1871
Illus. O.
Colas 98

Les ouvrages de main en famille. Le tricot—le filet—le filet-guipure—le crochet—la frivolité—le travail au métier. 2. éd. Paris, F. Ebhart 1877
380p. 309 illus. O.
Lipperheide 4117

Les secrets du cabinet de toilette, conseils et recettes, par une femme du monde sous la direction de Madame Louise d'Alq. Paris, Bureau des causeries familières 1881
240p. illus. O.
Nouv. éd. rev. & augm. de dessins nouveaux

Alsace
Edwards, G. W. Alsace-Lorraine. 1918
Evidens designatio receptissimarum consuetudinem ornamenta quaedam et insignia continens magistratui et academiae Argentinensi à maioribus relicta. 1605
Grad, Charles. L'Alsace; le pays et ses habitants. 1919
Hanauer, C. A. Les paysans de l'Alsace au moyen-âge. 1865
Kassel, August. Über elsässische trachten. 1907
Kauffmann, P. A. L'Alsace traditionaliste. 1931
Kauffmann, P. A. Les costumes de l'Alsace. 1918
Laugel, Anselme. Trachten und sitten im Elsass. 1902
Représentation des modes et particularitez de l'habillement en Alsace. 1705
Spindler, Charles. Ceux d'Alsace; types et coutumes. 1928
Terence. Works. 1496

See also subhead Alsace under Arms and armor; Ceremonial and festival costume

Strasbourg

L'Alsace françoise; ou Nouveau recueil de ce qu'il y a de plus curieux dans la ville de Strasbourg. 1706
Arnold, J. G. D. Der pfingstmontag, lustspiel in Strasburger mundart. 1867
Berger-Levrault, Oscar. Les costumes strasbourgeois. 1889
Dieterlin, Petrus. Strasburgisch trachtenbuchlein. La mode de Strasbourg. ca.1680
Eigentliche vorstellung der heutiger strassburgische mode und kleÿdertrachten. Représentation des modes et habillemens qui sont en usage à Strasbourg. 1731
Hollar, Wenceslaus. Strassburger ansichten und trachtenbilder aus der zeit des dreissigjahrigen krieges. 1931
Piton, Frédéric. Strasbourg illustré. 1855
Seyboth, Adolf. Costumes des femmes de Strasbourg (XVIIe et XVIIIe siècles). 1880
Seyboth, Adolf. Costumes strasbourgeois (hommes) XVIe, XVIIe et XVIIIe siècles. 1881
Strasburger trachtenbüechlein darinnen von man und weibs personen aussgangen ihm jhar 1660. 1660
Stridbeck, J. F. Representation des modes et habillements de Strasbourg. 1756
Weis, J. M. Costumes d'hommes et de femmes de Strasbourg. 1740
Weis, J. M. Nouveau calendrier du diocèse de Strasbourg pour l'an 1760 avec une représentation des modes et habillements de Strasbourg. 1745
Welper, Eberhard. Neu gestellter schreibkalender auf das jahr . . . 1748. 1749?

Alsace françoise. See Berger-Levrault, Oscar. Les costumes strasbourgeois

L'**Alsace** françoise; ou Nouveau recueil, de ce qu'il y a de plus curieux dans la ville de Strasbourg. Strasbourg, G. Bouches 1706
6 l. 15 pl. F.
Has also German title. *Das frantzösische Elsass; oder newe beschreibung der Stadt-Strassburg*
Some of the plates are reproduced from Dieterlin's *Strasburgisch tractenbuchlein*
Colas 105. Lipperheide 791, 791a

L'**Alsace** traditionaliste. Kauffmann, P. A.

Alsace-Lorraine. Edwards, G. W.

Les **Alsaciens** dans la Garde impériale et dans les corps d'élite. Ganier, Henry

Alt, Georg
(tr.) Schedel, Hartmann. Das buch der chroniken

Alt-Berlin, anno 1740. Consentius, Ernst

Alt-Berliner humor um 1830. Pniower, O. S.

Alt Kreta. Bossert, H. T.

Alt-Stambuler hof- und volksleben. Taeschner, Franz

Alt- und neues- Preussen. Hartknoch, Christoph

Die **altägyptische** schurztracht. See Bonnet, Hans. Die ägyptische tracht bis zum ende des neuen reiches

Ein **altdeutscher** totentanz. Bossert, H. T.

Altdorf university. See Academic costume—Altdorf university

Das **alte** Jena und seine universität. Borkowsky, Ernst

Alte kunstvolle spitzen. Claesen, Joseph

Alte spitzen . . . photographien nach originalen. Berlin, C. Claesen [1886]
36pl. F.
Lipperheide 4050

Alte Testament, in funfzig holzschnitten. Holbein, Hans, the younger

Alte und neue fächer. Rosenberg, Marc

Alte waffen. Haenel, Erich

Alte waffen aus d. Schweiz. See note under Boissonnas, Jean. Armes anciennes

Die **alten** jüdischen heiligthümer gottesdienste und gewohnheiten. Lund, Johann

Die **alten** trachten der männlichen und weiblichen orden sowie der geistlichen mitglieder der ritterlichen orden. Doyé, F. von S.

Die **alten** zunft- und verkehrs-ordnungen der stadt Krakau. Benn, Balcer

Alteneck, Jakob Heinrich von Hefner. See Hefner-Alteneck, J. H. von

Die **altenglischen** kleidernamen. Stroebe, L. L.

Der **altenn** weisenn exempel sprüch und underweisungen. Bīdpāÿ

Alterskrud og messeklaer i Norge. Bugge, A. R., and Kielland, T. B.

Alterthümer der bronzezeit in Ungarn. Hampel, József

Die **alterthümer** unserer heidnischen vorzeit. Lindenschmit, Ludwig

Die **alterthümer** von Kertsch in der Kaiserlichen Eremitage. Petrograd. Ėrmitazh

Altfrankfurter trachten. Hottenroth, Friedrich

Die **altfranzösischen** bildteppiche. Fels, Florent

Altgriechische plastik; eine einführung in die griechische kunst der archaischen und gebundenen stils. Lermann, Wilhelm

Althann, Michael Franciscus Ferdinandus ab, count
Imago principum Bohemiae LXI; elogiis ducum, regum, interregum, adumbrata, in novam patriae splendorem, & publicum regni decus, spectatum proposita ab . . . Michaele Francisco Ferdinando S.R.I. comite ab Althann. Praga, Typis universitatis Carolo-Ferdinandeae 1673
65 l. 61pl. Q.
The plates are head and shoulder portraits of nobles and kings of Bohemia to the time of Leopold I
Lipperheide 856

Die **altlettischen** färbmethoden. Bielenstein, Martha

Altman, Georg. See Alt-Nürnberg, schwänke, lieder und tänze d. Hans Sachs

Altnorwegische bildteppiche. See Oslo. Kunstindustrimuseet. Gamle norska billedtæpper

Alt-Nürnberg, schwänke, lieder und tänze d. Hans Sachs u. seiner zeitgenossen in e. bühneneinrichtg. v. Georg. Altman. Berlin, Drei masken verlag [1918]
88p. 8 pl. sq.F.
Illustration by A. Dürer, H. S. Beham, S. Heldt and E. M. Engert

Altoviti, Giovanni
Essequie della sacra cattolica, e real maesta di Margherita d'Austria, regina di Spagna; celebrate dal serenissimo don Cosimo II, Gran Duca di Toscana IIII. Firenze, Bartolemo Sermartelli 1612
51p. 29 illus. F.
Lipperheide 2744

Altsteirische trachten. Sann, Hans von der

Die **altthüringischen** funde von Weimar. Götze, Alfred

Altwestnordische kleiderkunde. Falk, H. S.

Alves de Noronha, José Eduardo. See Noronha, Eduardo de

Am japanischen hofe. Mohl, Ottmar von

Amades, Joan
Gegants, nans i altres entremesos. Barcelona, Direcció: P. Pujol i Casademont, Impremta La Neotípia [1934]
227p. illus.(part col.) 87 (*i.e.* 88) pl.(part col. 1 double) F.
At head of title: Costumari popular català
Bibliografia: p209-12
LC 35-20478

Amades, Joan; Colominas, Josep, and Vila, Pau
Els soldats, i altres papers de rengles. Barcelona, Editorial Orbis 1933-36
2v. illus.(part col.) C double pl.(part col.) F.
At head of title: *Imatgeria popular catalana*
Shows many uniforms of Spanish soldiers in the 18th and 19th centuries, and some soldiers of other nations
Contents: v 1 Text; v2 Facsimils
LC 36-33093

Amaral, Bras do
(ed.) Vilhena, L. dos S. Recopilção de noticias soteropolitanas e brasilicas

Amaranthes, pseud. See Corvinus, G. S.

Amateur's costume book. Guptill, Mrs E. F. E. and Wormwood, E. M.

Amato, Cintio d', and Riccio, Tomaso Antonio
Nuova, et utilissima prattica di tutto quello ch' al diligēte barbiero s'appartiene. Napoli, Geronimo 1671
168 p. 13 pl. Q.
The first edition was published in Naples in 1630, the second in Venice in 1669
Lipperheide 2005

L'ambassade de la Compagnie orientale des Provinces Unies vers l'empereur de la Chine. Nieuhof, Johan

Ambert, Joachim Marie Jean Jacques Alexander Jules, baron
Esquisses historiques des différents corps qui composent l'armée française; illus. by Charles Aubry. Saumur, Degouy 1835
128p. illus. 16pl. F.
A second edition was published (Saumur, A Degouy 1837. 16 col.pl. O.) the plates reduced in size
Colas 106-07. Lipperheide 2315

Ambrosiana, XI. See Magistretti, Marco. Delle vesti ecclesiastiche in Milano

Ambrosoli, Solone
Numismatica. Milano, U. Hoepli 1891
214p. 100 illus. 4pl. O.
Lipperheide 4436

Amelung, Walther
Die gewandung der alten Griechen und Römer. Leipzig, Koehler 1903
61p. illus. 5 col.pl. Q.
Plates marked: Tabulae quibus antiquitates . . . illustrantur. Taf. 16-20

America, Central. See Central America

America dancing. Martin, J. J.

Americae pars quarta[-sexta.] Benzoni, Girolamo

Americae tertia pars memorabilē provinciae Brasiliae historiam continēs. Staden, Hans, and Lery, Jean de

The **American** costume book. Haire, F. H.

American Asiatic association, New York
Journal. See Asia; journal of the American Asiatic association

American costumes. Sellmer, Eudora

The **American** Egypt. Channing, Arnold, and Frost, F. J. T.

American fashion review. See Sartorial art journal and American tailor and cutter

American fashion review and Tailor's art journal. See Sartorial art journal and American tailor and cutter

American fur designer. v 1, 1920+ New York, Herzberg pub. co.
Illus. F. $30
Published monthly. Current 1938

The **American** garment cutter. Regal, Samuel

The **American** garment cutter for women's garments. Engelmann, Gustav

American gentleman and sartorial art journal. v 1-29, no.4, 1901-May 1929; v 55 no.1, Sept. 1929+ New York, American gentleman pub. corp.
Illus. pl. F. $15 a year
A tailoring periodical on men's fashions. Published monthly, Feb. to June and Sept. to Dec. Current 1938
Title varies: v 1-29 no4, *American gentleman.* Sept. 1929 absorbed the *Sartorial art journal,* took the title *American gentleman and Sartorial art journal* and changed its volume numbering to continue as v55+, the volume numbering of the *Sartorial art journal.* Numbers 29 no5, to 54 omitted in the volume numbering
Styles for men is a supplement

American Indian costumes in the United States National museum. Krieger, H. W.

American Indian dance steps. Evans, Bessie, and Evans, M. G.

American Indian designs. Westlake, Mrs I. B.

The **American** Indian, North, South, and Central America. Verrill, A. H.

American Indians. Harvey, Fred

American Indians, tribes of the prairies and the East. Dengler, Hermann

American jockey club. See American racing colors

American lace & lace-makers. Vanderpoel, Mrs E. N.

The **American** ladies' magazine; edited by Sarah J. Hale. v. 1-9; Jan. 1828-Dec. 1836. Boston, Putnam & Hunt [etc.]
9v. pl.(part col.) ports. O.
Published monthly
Title varies: 1828-31, *The Ladies' magazine* (caption title, 1830-31, *Ladies' magazine and literary gazette*) 1832-33, *The Ladies' magazine, and literary gazette.* 1834-36, *The American ladies' magazine* (caption title, Jan. 1834, *The Ladies' magazine*) Merged into *Godey's Lady's book*
LC 16-16947

American ladies' tailor and Les Parisiennes. 1903+ New York, American-Mitchell style corp.
Illus. F. $30 a year
Published monthly, Feb.-June and Sept.-Dec. Current 1938. H. W. Rosley, editor
Absorbed *Les Parisiennes* Sept. 1929 and added subtitle

The **American** metropolis. Moss, Frank

American monthly magazine of literature, art, and fashion. See Graham's American monthly magazine

American museum of natural history, New York
Anthropological papers. v 1, 1907+ New York
Illus. pl. O.
Published irregularly. Current 1938. Contains material on Indians of North and South America and Mexico
LC (9-7462)

Costumes of the Plains Indians. See entry under Wissler, Clark

Distribution of moccasin decorations among the Plains tribes. See entry under Wissler, Clark

Indian costumes in the United States. See entry under Wissler, Clark

North American Indians of the Plains. See entry under Wissler, Clark

Structural basis to the decoration of costumes among the Plains Indians. See entry under Wissler, Clark

American national Red cross. See Red cross. United States. American national Red cross

American Paragon scientific system
The improved American "Paragon" scientific system of dress cutting and dress fitting. Melbourne, Inglis [1884]
11p. O.

The **American** procession. Rogers, Agnes, comp.

American racing colors. Colors of the owners of racing horses as worn by their jockeys at the meetings of the American jockey club. New York, T. K. Miller 1884
1 p.l. 10 col.pl. S.
Shows jockeys in costume
LC 13-2314

American Scandinavian review. v 1, 1913+ New York, American-Scandinavian foundation
Illus.(part col.) pl.(part col.) O.
Published quarterly. Bimonthly 1913-19; monthly 1920-Sept. 1933
LC (16-23752)

American scientific system of dress cutting. London, 1883-84
9 pieces(5 mounted) F.

American ski annual. Brattleboro, Vt., Stephen Daye press 1936
v[2] illus. pl. ports. diagrs. O. 75c
"Edited by the United States eastern amateur ski association, Nathaniel L. Goodrich, editor-in-chief for the National ski association."
Volume for 1935 entitled: *United States eastern ski annual* (Bellows Falls, Vt. U.S. eastern amateur ski assn. 1935)
LC (37-105)

Das **amerikanische** theater und kino. Gregor, Joseph, and Fülöp-Miller, René

Amerika's Nordwest-küste. Bastian, Adolf

Ames sword company, Chicago
Regalia, paraphernalia, and supplies for encampments I. O. O. F. Chicago, Ames sword company 1893
99p. illus. Q.
LC CA22-152

L'**ami** des femmes. Marie de Saint-Ursin, P. J.

Amiconi, Jacob
Londoner ausrufer. [London] 1739
4pl. F.
Plates show lamplighter, chimney sweeper, shoe black, golden pippins
Lipperheide 1020

Amictus senatus tam politi. Ringle, J. J.

Amigues. See Japhet

Amil, Genaro Pedez de Villa-. See Villa-Amil, G. P. de

Amiot, Joseph Marie
(tr.) Art militaire des Chinois, ou Recueil d'anciens traités sur la guerre, composés avant l'ere chrétienne, par différents généraux chinois; tr. en françois, par le P. Amiot ... rev. & pub. par M. Deguignes. Paris, Didot l'ainé 1772
xii,397p. 33 col.pl. Nar.Q.
"Ouvrages sur lesquèls les aspirants aux grades militaires sont obligés de subir des examens. On y a joint dix préceptes adressés aux troupes par l'empereur Yong-tcheng, pere de l'empereur régnant. Et des planches gravées pour l'intelligence des exercices, des evolutions, des habillements, des armes & des instruments militaires des Chinois." Subtitle
Also published as v7 of *Mémoires concernant l'histoire, les sciences, les arts, les moeurs, les usages, &c., des Chinois: par les missionnaires de Pekin* (Paris, Nyon 1782) A brief supplement is included in v8 of the same collection
Contents: Discours préliminaire du traducteur; Les dix préceptes de l'empereur Yong-tcheng aux gens de guerre; Les XIII articles sur l'art militaire, par Sun-tse; Les VI articles sur l'art militaire, par Ou-tse; Les V articles sur l'art militaire, par Se-ma; Extrait du livre intitulé Lou-tao, sur l'art militaire; Instruction sur l'exercice militaire
LC 18-8078

Amman, Jost
Bildnuss oder contrafactur der zwölff ersten alten teutschen königen und fürsten. Franckfort am Mayn, J. Fischer 1622
6 l. 12 illus. F.
Portraits of twelve German rules from Tuisco to Charlemagne
Lipperheide 701

Cleri totius romanæ ecclesiæ subiecti. Francoforti, sumtib. S. Feyrabendij 1585
113 l. 103 illus. O.
The Latin edition of Amman's *Ständ und orden*
Colas 120-122. Lipperheide 1853. LC 28-22508

De omnibus illiberalibus sive mechanicis artibus, humani ingenii sagacitate atque industria iam inde ab exordio nascentio mundi usque ad nostram aetatem adinuentis, luculentus atque succinctus. Liber: auctore Hartmanno Schoppero. Francofurti ad Moenum, S. C. Feyerabent 1574
147 l. 132 illus. O.
The first Latin edition had title: *Panoplia omnium illiberalium mechanicarum aut sedentarium artium genera* (Francofurti ad Moenum, S. Feyerabent 1568. 148 l. 130 illus. O.)
Colas 112, 111. Lipperheide 1948

Ehebrecherbrücke des Königs Artus; facsimile-reproduction des aus 8 blättern bestehenden original-holtzschnittes. München & Leipzig, G. Hirth 1883
8 pl. F.
Sixteenth century woodcuts reproduced from the only known complete example, in the collection of the Ritter von Hauslab, Vienna
Lipperheide 666

Eygentliche beschreibung aller stände auff erden hoher und nidriger, geistlicher und weltlicher, aller künsten, handwercken unnd händeln, &c. vom grössten biss zum kleinesten ... Hans Sachsen ... beschrieben ... mit kunstreichen figuren deren gleichen zuvor niemals gesehen allen ständen so in diesem buch begriffen zu ehren und wolgefallen allen kunstlern aber als malern, goldschmiden zu sonderlichem dienst in druck verfertigt. Franckfurt am Mayn, S. Feyerabend 1568
119, 114 l. 114 illus. O.
The second edition (1574) had the same plates with a few changes
For Latin editions see his *De omnibus*
Colas 108-109. Lipperheide 1947 (2. aufl.)

Genuinae icones ducum Bavariae . . . ex principi familia Bavarica illustrissima et vetustissima oriundorum, ab anno virginei partus 493 usq. ad annum 1583. Noriberg, [1583]
79pl. F.
Full-length figures of the Bavarian rulers, mostly in armor, including some duchesses
Lipperheide 700

Amman, Jost—*Continued*

Gynaeceum, sive Theatrum mulierum . . . Additis ad singulas figuras singulis octostichis Francisci Modii Brug. Francoforti, S. Feyramendij 1586
118 l. 122 illus. O.
Latin edition of *Im frauwenzimmer*
Colas 125. Lipperheide 19. LC 14-17725

Icones Livianae: praecipuas romanorum historias magno artificio ad vivum expressas oculis repraesentantes, succinctis versibus; illus. per Phillipum Lonicerum. Francofurti ad Moenum, G. Corvinus 1573
103 l. 75 illus. Q.
Reprinting of Amman's woodcut illustrations for the history of Rome by Titus Livius. Published also with German title: *Livische figuren* and *Nieuwe Livische figuren*
Some of the illustrations appear also in Lonicer's *Chronicorum turcicorum*
Lipperheide 636

Im frauwenzimmer wirt vermeldt von allerley schönen kleidungen unnd trachten der weiber hohes und niders stands wie man fast an allen orten geschmückt unnd gezieret ist. Franckfort am Mayn, S. Feyrabends 1586
118 l. 122 illus. Q.
"Als teutsche, welsche, frantsösische, engelländische, niderländische böhemische, ungerische, und alle anstossende länder." Subtitle
Published at the same time with Latin text and title *Gynaeceum!* An English reprint is entitled *The theatre of women*
Woodcuts by Jost Amman show women of all classes in Western Europe: Patricians, burghers, peasants and nuns in the costume of the sixteenth century
Colas 126. Lipperheide 19

Insignia sacrae Caesareae maiestatis, principum electorum, ac aliquot illustrissimarum, illustrium, nobilium et aliarum familiarum, formis artificiosissimis. Francofurti ad Moenum, S. Feyerabendij 1579
112 l. 225 illus. Q.
Original of his *Stam und wappenbuch.* The author of the Latin verses is Philippus Lonicer. Besides Amman the illustrators were Christoph Stimmer, Lucas Mayer, Ludwig Frig, and an unknown wood engraver with initials M B
Lipperheide 638

Kartenspielbuch. Charta lusoria. Nürnberg, L. Huessler 1588. Neudruck. München, G. Hirth 1880
64 l. 55 illus. O. (Liebhaber-Bibliothek facsimile reproduction)
Facsimile reproduction of *Charta lusoria tetrastichis illustrata per Janum Heinricum Scroterum de Gustrou . . . & P. L. Caesarum kunstliche uñ wolgerissene figuren in ein new kartenspiel* (Nürnberg, L. Heussler 1588. 64 l. 55 illus. O.)
Text in Latin and German
Colas 129-30

Künstliche wolgerissene new figuren, von allerlei jag und weidtwerck . . . auch durchauss mit lateinischen und teutschen reymen . . . Franckfort am Mayn, S. Feyerabend 1582
39 l. illus. Q.
Lipperheide 3021

Kunstbüchlin darinnenn neben fürbildung vieler geistlicher unnd weltlicher hohes und niderstands personen, so dann auch der türckischen, käyser unnd derselben obersten, allerhandt kunstreiche stück unnd figuren; auch die sieben planeten, zehen alter, rittermeister unnd befelchshaber, reuterey und contrafactur der pferde, allerley thurnier fechten, und dann etliche helm und helmdecken begriffen. Franckfurt am Mayn, Feyrabend 1599
147p. 293 illus. Q.
Fourth and most inclusive edition. The first collection of his works was entitled: *Kunst und lehrbüchlein* (Franckfurt am Mayn, S. Feyrabend 1578. 101 l. 102 illus.) Published later with title *Enchiridion artis pingendi fingendi et sculpendi* (1878)
Another collection was entitled *Kunst und lehrbüchlein* (Franckfurt am Mayn, S. Feyerabend 1580. 2v. 156 illus.) the second volume with title *Der ander theil dess neuwen kunstbuchs*
Colas 115-119. Lipperheide 498

Ständ und orden der H. Römischen Catholischen kirchen . . . fleissig beschrieben durch I. A. Lonicerum. Franckfort am Mayn, S. Feyrabend 1585
115 l. 102 illus. Q.
"Darinn aller geistlichen personen, h. ritter und dero verwandten herkommen constitution regeln habit und kleidung beneben schönen und künstlichen figurn." Subtitle
Also known with the illustrations in color
An edition in Latin was published simultaneously with title: *Cleri totius romanae ecclesiae*
Colas 121-22. Lipperheide 1851-1852

Stände und handwerker mit versen von Hans Sachs. München, G. Hirth 1884
114 illus. 119pl. Q.
A facsimile reprint of his *Eygentliche beschreibung aller stände* (1568)
Colas 110. Lipperheide 1946

Das ständebuch. Leipzig, Insel-verlag ₍1934₎
13p. 114 illus. D. M.80 (Insel-bücherei)
Woodcuts, illustrating in accurate detail many trades and professions, are by Jost Amman with verses by Hans Sachs
An inexpensive modern edition of *Eygentliche beschreibung aller stände auff erden*

Stam und wapenbuch hochs und nieders standts, darinnen der römischen keys. mt. dess heiligen röm. reychs, churfürsten, grafen, freyen und herrn . . . wapen mit iren schilt und helmen . . . mit angehengten vilen ledigen schildten und helmen; zusammen getragen durch Sigmund Feyrabend. Franckfurt a. M., S. Feyrabend 1579
123 l. illus. Q.
First German edition of his *Insignia*

Stamm- und wappenbuch; neu herausgegeben und geordnet von Friedrich Warnecke . . . Goerlitz, C. A. Starke 1877
13p. 49pl. Q.
Facsimile edition of the first German edition of 1579 together with additions from the second German edition of 1589, listed below as *Wapen und stammbuch*
Lipperheide 640

Theatre of women; designed by Jobst Amman; ed. by Alfred Aspland. Manchester, For the Holbein society 1872
₍131₎p. illus. O. (The Holbein society's facsimile reprints. v7)
Added title page: Gynæceum; or, The theatre of women: wherein may be seen the female costumes of all the principal nations, tribes, and peoples of Europe ₍etc.₎ This book is a facsimile reprint of *Gynaeceum,* the Latin edition of *Im frauenzimmer*
List of Amman's works: p₍xiii₎-xxvi
Colas 127. LC 3-24581

Amman, Jost—*Continued*

Wapen und stammbuch darinnen der keys. maiest. chur und fürsten, graffen, freyherrn, deren vom adel, etc. mit kunstreichen figuren. Franckfort am Mayn, S. Feyrabend 1589

59 l. 120 illus. O.

Second German ed. of his *Stam und wapenbuch.* Latin original entitled *Insignia sacrae caesareae maiestatis* listed above

Besides nobles and their coats of arms, the illustrations show men of various occupations, e.g. jurists, soldiers, a doctor, a merchant, etc. and 32 allegorical figures. Altogether 27 costume pictures

Lipperheide 639

Wappen- & stammbuch. Franckfort a. M., S. Feyrabend 1589. München, Hirth 1881

178p. illus. O. (Liebhaber-bibliothek alter illustratoren in facsimile-reproduction, 3)

Facsimile of 1589 edition. Reprinted 1923

(illus.) Creccelius, Johannes. Collectanea ex historijs, de origine et fundatione omnium ferè monasticorum ordinum

(illus.) Fronsperger, Leonhard. Kriegszbuch

(illus.) Garzoni, Tommaso. Piazza universale: Das ist: Allgemeiner schauplatz, marckt und zusammenkunfft aller professionen, künsten, geschafften, händeln und handwercken

(illus.) Giovio, Paolo, bp. of Nocera. Die moscouitische chronica

(illus.) Inventarium . . . was in . . . herrn Marx Fuggers . . . rüst: und sattel cammer

(illus.) Kellner, Heinrich. Chronica, das ist: Wahrhaffte eigentliche und kurtze beschreibung aller hertzogen zu Venedig leben

(illus.) Livius, Titus. Titi Livii Patavini, Romanae historiae principis

(illus.) Megiser, Hieronymus. Ein tractat von dem dreyfachen ritterstand und allen ritter orden der Christenheit

(illus.) Mergenthaler linotype company. A true description of all trades

(illus.) Modius, Francois. Francisci Modii Liber singularis

(illus.) Neuw jag unnd weydwerck buch

(illus.) Paracelsus. Opus chyrurgicum

(illus.) Pomay, Fr. Ein sehr artig büchlein von dem weydwerck und der falcknerey

(illus.) Rüxner, Georg. Thurnier buch

(illus.) Weigel, Hans. Habitus praecipuorum populorum

See also Solis, Virgil, jt. auth.

Ammirabile promozione all' arcivescovato di Milano. Perabò, Gabrio

Amon von Treuenfest, Gustav, ritter

Armee-album zur erinnerung an das 40jähr. regierungs-jubiläum . . . Franz Joseph I. Wien, Administration des "Armee-album" 1889

16p. 12pl. F.

Geschichte des k.k. dragoner-regimentes Feldmarschall Alfred fürst zu Windisch-Graetz nr. 14. Wien, Verlag d. regiments 1886

734,lx p. 2 port. pl.(part col.) Q.

Uniforms and equipment are described on p4-5

Geschichte des k. und k. dragoner-regimentes, General der cavallerie freiherr Piret de Bihain nr. 9, von seiner errichtung 1682 bis 1892. Wien, Verlag des regimentes 1892

Front. O.

Geschichte des k. und k. Husaren-regimentes Kaiser nr.1 (1756-1898) [Wien] Verlag d. regimentes 1898

545p. ports. O.

Geschichte des k. u. k. Huszaren-regimentes nr. 3, feldmarschall Andreas graf Hadik von Futak. Wien, St. Norbertus buch- und kunstdruckerei 1893

Port.

Geschichte des k. u. k. Husaren-regiments nr.4, Arthur herzog von Connaught und Strathearn, (1733-1901) Wien, Verlag d. regiments 1903

663p.

Geschichte des k.k. Huszaren-regimentes Freiherr von Edelsheim-Gyulai nr. 4, von seiner errichtung 1734-1882. Wien, Verlag d. regiments 1882

561p. port. O.

Geschichte des k.k. Feldmarschall graf Radetzky huszaren-regimentes nr. 5. Wien, Verlag d. regiments 1885

460p. col.pl. 1 port. Q.

Uniform regulations, p3-6

Geschichte des k.k. Huszaren-regimentes Alexander freiherr v. Koller nr. 8. Von seiner errichtung 1696-1880; nach den feldakten und sonstigen originalquellen der k.k. archive. Wien, L. Mayer 1880

603p. 6 col.pl. O.

Lipperheide 2243

Geschichte der k. und k. Husaren-regimentes nr. 10, Friedrich Wilhelm III, könig von Preussen; zum 150 jährigen regiments-jubiläum... Wien, Verlag d. regiments 1878

736p. port.

Geschichte des k. k. 11. Huszaren-regimentes Herzog Alexander v. Württemberg 1762 bis 1850. Székler Grenzhuszaren. Wien, Verlag des regiments 1878

432p. col.pl. O.

Detailed uniform regulations issued in 1768, p 10-11

Geschichte des k. k. 12. Huszaren-regiments. Wien, Verlag des regiments 1876

Port.

Geschichte des k. u. k. Huszaren-regimentes nr. 15 Feldmarschall-lieutenant Moriz Graf Pálffy ab Erdöd. Wien, Verlag d. regimentes 1894

324p. port. O.

Geschichte des k.k. Infanterie-regimentes hoch- und deutschmeister nr.4, ergänzungs-bezirks-station, Wien. Wien, Verlag d. regiments 1879

726p. 2 ports. col.pl. Q.

Amon von Treuenfest, Gustav, ritter—*Continued*
Geschichte des kaiserl. und königl. Kärnthnerischen infanterie-regimentes Feldmarschall graf von Khevenhüller nr.7. Wien, Verlag d. regiments 1891
1005,cvp. port.
Geschichte des k.u.k. Infanterie-regimentes nr.18, Constantin grossfürst von Russland, von 1682 bis 1882, ergänzungsbezirks-station Königgrätz. Wien, Verlag d. regiments 1882
724p. ports. col.pl. maps. Q.
Description of uniforms and arms, p5-6
Geschichte des k.k. Infanterie-regiments nr.20 Friedrich Wilhelm, Kronprinz ... ergänzungsbezirk Neu-Sandec in Galizien. Wien, Verlag d. regiments 1878
736p.
Gechichte des k.u.k. Infanterie-regimentes nr.46 feldzeugmeister Géza frh. Fejerváry de Komós-Keresztes, 1762 bis 1850, erstes Siebenbürger romanen-grenz-infanterie-regiment nr.16. Wien, Verlag d. regiments 1890
524,lxix p.
Geschichte des k.u.k. Infanterie-regimentes nr.47. Wien, Verlag. d. regimentes 1882
787p. port. O.
Geschichte des k.k. Infanterie-regimentes nr.50, Friedrich Wilhelm Ludwig, grossherzog von B[aden] 1762 bis 1850 zweites Siebenbürger Romanen-Grenz-infanterie-regimentes nr.17. Wien, Verlag des regimentes 1882
Col.pl. O.
Geschichte des k. und k. Uhlanen-regimentes Kaiser nr.4 (1813-1900) Wien, Verlag d. regiments 1901
345p. ports.

Among Italian peasants. Cyriax, Tony

Among pagoda and fair ladies. Gascoigne, G. T.

Among the Danes. Butlin, F. M.

Among the Eskimos of Labrador. Hutton, S. K.

Among the hill-folk of Algeria. Hilton-Simpson, M. W.

Among the Ibos of Nigeria. Basden, G. T.

Among the Indians of Guiana. Im Thurn, Sir E. F.

Among unknown Eskimo. Bilby, J. W.

Amongst the Shans. Colquhoun, A. R.

Amor vehementer quidem flagrans. Schübler, J. J.

Amore prigioniero in Delo. Lodi, Giacinto

Am Ort, Caspar
(illus.) Churfürstlich bayrisches frewdenfest

Amory de Langerack
Histoire anecdotique des fêtes et jeux populaires au moyen-age. Lille, J. Lefort 1870
334p. 1 pl. O.
Lipperheide 2493

L'**amour** badin ou les ruses de Cupidon; dédiés à la jeunesse. Paris, Boulanger [1788]
Illus. Tt.
Lipperheide 4467

Amplissimi ornatissimique triumphi. Panvinio, Onofrio

Amplissimo hoc apparatu et pulchro ordine pompa funebris Bruxellis a palatio ad Divae Gudulae templum processit cum rex hispaniarum Philippus Carolo. v. rom. imp. Cock, Hieronymus

Amtskleidungen der stellvertreter des französischen volks und der übrigen staatsbeamten der republik Frankreich. See note under Grasset de Saint Sauveur, Jacques. Costumes des représentans du peuple

Amulets and talismans
Holmboe, C. A. Tillæg til en afhandling om amuletter og stormænds begravelse blandt Skandinaver i hedenold og blandt Mellemasiens Buddhister. 1863
Petrie, Sir W. M. F. Amulets, illustrated by the Egyptian collection in University college, London. 1914
Reisner, G. A. Amulets. 1907

The **amusements** of old London ... 19th century. Boulton, W. B.

Un **an** à Rome et dans ses environs. Thomas, J. B.

Un **an** de la vie de jeune homme. Adam, Victor

Anacephalaeoses. Vasconcellos, Antonio de

Analecta de re vestiaria. Ferrari, Ottavio

The **anatomy** of dandyism. Barbey d'Aurevilly, J. A.

The **anatomy** of melancholy. Burton, Robert

Ancel, Henri
(tr.) L'art populaire hongrois

Ancessi, Victor
L'Egypte et Moïse. Première partie: Les vêtements du grand prêtre et des Levites, le sacrifice des colombes, d'après les peintures et les monuments, etc. Paris, Leroux 1875
151p. 9pl. O. 10 fr.

Anchorites. See Hermits

L'**Ancien** Album. See L'Album, journal des arts, des modes et des théâtres

Ancien armorial équestre de la Toison d'or et de l'Europe au 15. siècle. Larchey, Lorédan

L'**ancien** royaume du Dahomey. Le Herissé, A.

L'**ancienne** Auvergne et le Velay. Michel, Adolphe

L'**ancienne** France. L'armée, depuis le moyen age jusqu'à la revolution. Étude illustrée d'après l'ouvrage de m. Paul Lacroix, sur le moyen age, la renaissance, le XVII et le XVIII siècle. Paris, Firmin Didot 1886
288p. illus. col.pl. O.
The history of the French army from the Middle Ages to the 18th century, with 165 gravure illustrations and a colored frontispiece

L'ancienne France: La justice et les tribunaux; Impôts, monnaies et finances. Ouvrage illustré de 178 gravures et d'une chromolithographie. Paris, Firmin-Didot 1888
338p. front. illus. Q. (Bibliothèque historique illustrée)
Shows dress of judges, police and criminals, and instruments of punishment used in France from the middle ages to the eighteenth century
LC 27-10379

L'ancienne France: La marine et les colonies; Commerce. Ouvrage illustré de 149 gravures et d'une chromolithographie. Paris, Firmin-Didot 1888
294p. col.front. illus. (ports. map, plans, facsim.) Q. [Biblithèque historique illustrée]
"Collection . . . publiée sous la direction de M. Louisy"
LC 4-266

L'ancienne France. Le théâtre: mystères, tragédie, comédie, et la musique: instruments, ballet, opéra, jusqu'en 1789. Ouvrage illustré de 228 gravures et d'une chromolithographie. Paris, Firmin-Didot 1887
304p. col.front. illus.(incl. ports. plan, facsims. music) Q.
Pictures show scenes and costumes in the theater from Roman times thru the 18th century. They are taken from prints and book illustrations
LC 31-30009

Les **anciennes** armées françaises. Thoumas, C. A.

Les **anciennes** tapisseries historiées. Jubinal, Achille

Les **anciennes** villes du Nouveau monde. Charnay, Désiré

Les **anciens** costumes de l'Empire ottoman. Arif Pasha

Les **anciens** costumes des Alpes du Dauphiné. Delaye, Edmond

Les **anciens** uniformes du Ministère des affaires étrangères. Extrait de la Revue d'histoire diplomatique. Paris, Plon-Nourrit 1901
24p. 2pl. O.
Colas 131

Anciens vêtements sacerdotaux et anciens tissus conservés en France. Linas, Charles de

Ancient and modern beards. Price, George

Ancient armour and weapons in Europe. Hewitt, John

The **ancient** bronze implements, weapons, and ornaments of Great Britain and Ireland. Evans, Sir John

Ancient cities and modern tribes. Gann, T. W. F.

The **ancient** cities of the New World. Charnay, Désiré

Ancient costume of Great Britain and Ireland, from the seventh to the sixteenth century. See Smith, C. H. Selections of the ancient costume of Great Britain and Ireland

Ancient customs, sports, and pastimes of the English. See Aspin, Jehoshaphat. A picture of the manners ... of the inhabitants of England

Ancient Egypt or Mizraïm. Binion, S. A.

Ancient Egyptian, Assyrian, and Persian costumes and decorations. Houston, M. G., and Hornblower, F. S.

Ancient Egyptian dances. Lexová, Irena

Ancient Egyptian works of art. Weigall, A. E. P. B.

Ancient Greek female costume. Smith, J. M., comp.

Ancient Greek, Roman and Byzantine costume and decoration (including Cretan costume). Houston, M. G.

Ancient heraldic and antiquarian tracts. Balfour, Sir James, bart.

Ancient memorial brasses. Beaumont, E. T.

Ancient Mexican feather work. Nuttall, Mrs Zelia

Ancient needlepoint and pillow lace. Cole, A. S.

Ancient Scottish weapons. Drummond, James

The **ancient** stone implements, weapons and ornaments of Great Britain. Evans, Sir John

Ancient times

General works

Baïf, Lazare de. De re vestiaria libellus ex Bayfio excerptus. 1535

Boehn, Max von. Antike mode. 1926

Cavaro, Richard. Les costumes des peuples anciens. 1887

Dandré-Bardon, M. F. Costume des anciens peuples, à l'usage des artistes. 1784-86

Debay, Auguste. Hygiène vestimentaire; les modes et les parures chez les Français depuis l'établissement de la monarchie jusqu'à nos jours, précédé d'un curieux parallèle des modes chez les anciennes dames grecques et romaines. 1857

Diego y González, J. N. de, and Léon Salmerón, Africa. Compendio de indumentaria española, con un preliminar de la historia del traje y el mobiliario en los principales pueblos de la antigüedad. 1915

Ferrari, Ottavio. De re vestiaria libri septem, 1654

Ferrari, Ottavio. Octavii Ferrarii Analecta de re vestiaria. 1670

Forster, J. R. Liber singularis de bysso antiquorum, quo, ex Aegyptia lingua, res vestiaria antiquorum, imprimis in s. codice Hebraeorum occurrens, explicatur: additae ad calcem Mantissae Aegypticae. 1776

Fosbroke, T. D. Synopsis of ancient costume, Egyptian, Greek, Roman, British, Anglo-Saxon, Norman, and English. 1825

Genoni, Rosa. La storia della mode. 1925

Granier de Cassagnac, B. A. Danaë; roman historique. Suivi du costume des anciens, analyse raisonné de l'architecture, des meubles, de la vie intérieure, toilette, cuisine, poterie cu-

Ancient times—General works—*Continued*
linaire, du costume militaire, des armes offensives et défensives, et de la manière de combattre des Grecs homériques. 1840
Heuzey, L. A. Du principe de la draperie antique. 1893
Hope, Thomas. Costume of the ancients. 1841
Jacquemin, Raphael. Histoire générale du costume civil, religieux et militaire du IV. au XII. siècle: Occident (315-1100). 1879
Kerr, R. N. Miniature costume folios. c1937. v 1
Klemm, Heinrich. Versuch einer urgeschichte des kostüms mit beziehung auf das allgemeine culturleben der ältesten völker der erde. 1860
Lapaume, Jean. De la parure au temps jadis. 1866
Lens, A. C. Le costume des peuples de l'antiquité prouvé par les monuments. 1785
Lens, A. C. Das kostum der meisten völker des alterthums. 1784
Malliot, Joseph, and Martin, P. Recherches sur les costumes, les usages religieux, civils et militaires des anciens peuples d'après les auteurs célèbres, et les monuments antiques. 1804
Mannlich, J. C. von. Versuch über gebräuche, kleidung und waffen der ältesten völker bis auf Constantin den Grossen; nebst einigen anmerkungen über die schaubühne. 1802
Manoni, Alessandro. Il costume e l'arte delle acconciature nell'antichità. 1895
Peters, Emil. Entwicklungs-geschichte der tracht. I. teil: Das altertum. 1907
Pinelli, Bartolommeo. Raccolta di cento costumi antichi ricavati dai monumenti, e dagli autori antichi. 1809
Pronti, Domenico. Nuova raccolta rappresentante i costumi religiosi, civili, e militari degli antichi Egiziani, Etruschi, Greci, e Romani, tratti dagli antichi monumenti. ca1805
Roccheggiani, Lorenzo. Nuova raccolta di cento tavole rappresentante i costumi religiosi civili e militari degli antichi Egiziani, Etruschi, Greci e Romani. 1805-09
Roccheggiani, Lorenzo. Raccolta di cento tavole rappresentanti i costumi religiosi civili, e militari degli antichi Egiziani, Etruschi, Greci, e Romani, tratti dagli antichi monumenti. 1804
Rosa, Michele. Delle porpore e delle materie vestiarie presso gli antichi. 1786
Rubens, Albert. Albert Rubeni. De re vestiaria veterum. 1665
Spalart, Robert von. Versuch über das kostum der vorzüglichsten völker. 1796-1837
Speleers, Louis. Le costume oriental ancien. 1923
Willemin, N. X. Choix de costumes civils et militaires des peuples de l'antiquité. 1798-1802

Supplementary works

Adami, Casimiro. Arte e storia nel mondo antico monumenti della civiltà classica, orientale, greca e romana. 1925?
Ancona, Amilcare. Catalogo della collezione di antichità. 1892
Baïf, Lazare de. Lazari Bayfi annotationes in l. II. De captivis, et postliminio reversis. 1536
Bartoli, P. S., and Bellori, G. P. Columna Cochlis. 1704
Beissel, Stephan. Vaticanische miniaturen. 1893
Blümner, Hugo. Das kunstgewerbe im altertum. 1885
Cambridge ancient history. 1927-34
Cichorius, Conrad. Die reliefs der Traianssäule. 1896-1900
Forrer, Robert. Reallexikon der prähistorischen, klassischen und frühchristlichen altertümer. 1907
Friederichs, Karl. Kleinere kunst und industrie im alterthum. 1871
Friedlaender, Julius, and Sallet, A. F. C. von. Das Königliche münzkabinet. 1877
Fröhner, Wilhelm. Collection H. Hoffmann. Catalogue des objets d'art antiques. 1886-1888
Ginzrot, J. C. Die wagen und fahrwerke der Griechen und Römer und anderer alten völker. 1817
Göll, Hermann. Kulturbilder aus Hellas und Rom. 1880
Hastings, James. Dictionary of the Bible. 1898-1902
Herodianus. Der fürtrefflich griechisch geschicht-schreiber Herodianus . . . Wellicher Herodianus von Marco Elio Antonino philosopho an untz auff Gordianum de jüngern römischen keysern unnd irer regierung die sich wunderbarlich zůtragen geschriben hatt. 1532
Krause, J. H. Angeiologie; die gefässe der alten völker insbesondere der Griechen und Römer aus den schrift- und bildwerken des alterthums. 1854
Kulturhistorischer bilderatlas. 1883-88
Lilienfeld, C. J. Die antike kunst. 1875
Lindenschmit, Ludwig. Die alterthümer unserer heidnischen vorzeit. 1868-1900
Lübker, F. H. C. Friedrich Lübker's Reallexikon des classischen alterthums, für gymnasien. 1891
Ménard, R. J. La vie privée des anciens. 1880-83
Menestrier, C. F. Description de la belle et grande colonne historiée, dressée à l'honneur de l'empereur Theodose. 1702
Mongez, Antoine, ed. Recueil d'antiquités. 1804
Montfaucon, Bernard de. L'antiquité expliquée et representée en figures. 1722
Montfaucon, Bernard de. Antiquity explained, and represented in sculptures. 1721-22
Müller, K. O. Denkmäler der alten kunst. 1854-56

Ancient times—Supp. works—*Continued*
Mužik, Hugo, and Perschinka, Franz. Kunst und leben im altertum. 1909
Naples. Museo nazionale. Collection of the most remarkable monuments of the National museum. 1870
Naples. Museo nazionale. Recueil des monumens les plus intéressans du Musée national. 1863?
New York. Metropolitan museum of art. The daily life of the Greeks and Romans, as illustrated in the classical collections, by Helen McClees. 1933
Overbeck, Johannes. Gallerie heroischer bildwerke der alten kunst. Erster band: Die bildwerke zum thebischen und troischen heldenkreis. 1853
Panofka, Theodor, ed. Terracotten des Königlichen museums zu Berlin. 1842
Paris. Bibliothèque nationale. Catalogue des bronzes antiques de la Bibliothèque nationale. 1895
Perrot, Georges, and Chipiez, Charles. Histoire de l'art dans l'antiquité. 1882-1914
Les plaisirs et les fêtes. 1929-30
Rawlinson, George. The five great monarchies of the ancient eastern world; or, The history, geography, and antiquities of Chaldaea, Assyria, Babylon, Media, and Persia. 1871
Rossi, Domenico de. Gemme antiche figurate. 1707-09
Sittl, Karl. Archäologie der kunst. 1895-97

See also Assyria; Babylonia; Byzantine empire; Ear-rings; Egypt; Etruria; Irak; Jews; Nubia; Phenicia; Troy; also subdivision Ancient times under Dance costume; Greece; Helmets; Military costume; Rings; Styria; Syria; Sport costume

The **ancient** use of liturgical colours. Rolfe, C. C.

Ancona, Amilcare
Catalogo della collezione di antichità . . . Oggetti preistorici, etruschi, greci, romani in bronzo, terra cotta, vetro. Milan, C. Bebeschini 1892
x,82p. port. 12pl. O.

Ancona, Paolo d'
Les primitifs italiens du XIe au XIIIe siècle. Paris, Les Éditions d'art et d'histoire 1935
159p. 88pl. Q.
Bibliographical foot-notes
LC AC35-3149

Andalusia. See Spain—Andalusia

Andalusian annual for MDCCCXXXVII; edited by M. B. Honan. London, J. Macrone 1836
161p. 12 col.pl. Q.
Plates show dress worn in Andalusia. They are lithographs by Jose I. Becquer
Colas 1476. Lipperheide 1223

Andaman Islands
Kloss, C. B. In the Andamans and Nicobars. 1903

Der **ander** theil dess neuwen kunstbuchs. See Amman, Jost. Kunstbüchlin

Andersen, Carl Christian Thorwald
The chronological collection of the kings of Denmark. Copenhagen, Forlagsbureauet 1878
126p. illus. O.
Contains full length portraits of some of the Danish kings from Christian IV to Frederik VII. Also illustrations of swords, the insignia of the Order of the Elephant, the Order of the Armed hand, and a falcon hood
Translation of *Die chronologische sammlung der dänischen könige* (Kjøbenhavn, Thiele 1872)
Lipperheide 5023 (ed. in German)

Andersen, Ingeborg
(tr.) Poulsen, Frederik. Etruscan tomb paintings

Anderson, Edward Lowell
Die mittlere reitschule, ein reit-und dresser-system für gebrauchszwecke. Aus dem englischen ubersetzt von Berghaus. Dresden, Friese & von Puttkamer 1889
74p. pl. O.

Anderson, Mrs Isabel Weld (Perkins)
The spell of Belgium. Boston, Page 1915
xii,442p. col.front. pl.(part col.) ports. fold.map. O. [The spell series]
Illustrated lining-papers
Bibliography: p429-30
LC 32-32188

Anderson, J. A.
(tr.) Bouillane de Lacoste, E. A. H. de. Around Afghanistan

Anderson, John William
Notes of travel in Fiji and New Caledonia, with some remarks on South Sea Islanders and their languages. illus. from sketches by the author. London, Ellissen. 1880
xii,288p. front.(map) illus. col.pl. O.

Anderson, Joseph. See Drummond, James. Ancient Scottish weapons

Anderson, William
The pictorial arts of Japan. With a brief historical sketch of the associated arts, and some remarks upon the pictorial art of the Chinese and Koreans. Boston and New York, Houghton. 1886
276p. illus. 80pl.(part col.) F.
Issued in 4 parts. Some of the plates show costume
LC 13-11464

Andersson, Karl Johan
Lake Ngami; or, Explorations and discoveries during four years' wanderings in the wilds of southwestern Africa. By Charles John Andersson. New York, Harper; London, Hurst & Blackett 1856
xviii,[19]-521p. front. illus. D.
Several editions. Pictures of members of the Damaras, Ovambos and other tribes
LC 5-15397

Andras barn. Larsson, C. O.

Andreä, Nanette
Leicht fassliche anweisungen zu verschiedenen weiblichen kunstarbeiten. Erfurt, Hennings & Hopf 1843
3v. illus. D.
Lipperheide 4079

Andreä, Nanette—*Continued*
Sammlung von leicht ausführbaren vorschriften zu den schönsten und elegantesten strumpf-rändern und andern seinen strickereien. Erfurt, Hennings & Hopf 1843
36p. D.
Lipperheide 4078

Andree, Richard
Die masken in der völkerkunde.
p[477]-506 1 pl.
From *Archiv für anthropologie,* v 16, 1886
The author classifies masks as religious, war, death masks, masks of justice and punishment, and theatrical and dance masks. The plate shows a dance mask from Borneo, a Peruvian death mask, a Japanese war mask and an Aleutian mask

Andree-Eysen, Marie
Die perchten im Salzburgischen. Braunschweig, F. Vieweg 1905
p122-141. 9 illus. 2pl. Q.
From *Archiv für anthropologie* neue folge 3.bd. 2.heft
Mainly the masks and costumes used in the Salzburg mountains in parades on the sixth of January in honor of "Frau Percht," with some treatment of similar customs in other parts of Austria and Germany. Costumes and their colors, are described in detail

Andrews, Alexander
The eighteenth century; or, Illustrations of the manners and customs of our grandfathers. London, Chapman and Hall 1856
x,334p. O.
Chapter III, p20-40, deals with costume
LC 2-24354

Andrews, Benjamin Richard
(ed.) Costume design. See entry under Gallemore, Margaret; Harris, V. A., and Morris, Maria
(ed.) Latzke, Alpha, and Quinlan, Elizabeth. Clothing
(ed.) Trilling, M. B., and Nicholas, Mrs F. W. Art in home and clothing

Andrews, Eliza Frances
The war-time journal of a Georgia girl, 1864-1865; illustrated from contemporary photographs. New York, Appleton 1908
387p. front. pl. ports. O. $2.50 o.p.
Costume index. LC 8-27163

Andrews, Roy Chapman, and Andrews, Mrs Yvette Borup
Camps and trails in China; a narrative of exploration, adventure, and sport in little-known China. New York, London, D. Appleton 1918
xxv,334p. front. 1 illus. pl. ports. 2 fold. maps. O. $3
A popular narrative of the Asiatic zoölogical expedition of the American museum of natural history to China in 1916-17. Parts of the book have been published as separate articles in the American museum *Journal, Harper's magazine,* and *Asia*
LC 18-14668

Andrews, William
Bygone punishments. London, W. Andrews 1899
311p. front. illus. pl. O.
An account of the ducking stool, brank, pillory, stocks, drunkard's cloak, whipping post, riding the stang, etc.
Lipperheide 2012w. LC 5-3965

Old time punishments. Hull, W. Andrews 1890
x,251p. front. illus. Q.
The second edition of *Bygone punishments*
LC 15-25764

Punishments in the olden time. London. W. Stewart 1881?
76p. front. illus. D.
The first edition of *Bygone punishments*
LC 30-8744

Andrews, Mrs Yvette Borup. See Andrews, R. C., jt. auth.

Andriessen, Andreas
Plegtige inhuldiging van zyne doorlugtigste hoogheidt, Willem Karel Henrik Friso, prinse van Oranje en Nassau ... als markgraaf van Vere; op den 1. juny des jaars 1751.
[10],52p. 11pl.(1 fold.) F.
Lipperheide 2671

Anecdotes of the manners and customs of London...to the year 1700. Malcolm, J. P.

Anecdotes of the manners and customs of London, during the eighteenth century. Malcolm, J. P.

Anekdoten und charakterzüge, luxus und moden...unsrer teutschen vorältern im mittelalter. Jena, Voigt 1812
xii,226p. O.

Anfangsgründe der fechtkunst. Kahn, A. F.

Die **anfertigung** der damen garderobe. Lechner, Hedwig, and Beeg, Gunda

Die **anfertigung** der damen-kleider. Lenniger, F. F.

Die **anfertigung** der kinder-garderobe. Lechner, Hedwig, and Beeg, Gunda

Angas, George French
The Kaffirs illustrated in a series of drawings taken among the Amazulu, Amaponda, and Amakosa tribes; also portraits of...other races inhabiting southern Africa. London, J. Hogarth 1849
10,50p. front.(port.) illus. 30 col.pl. F.
Colas 134?

The New Zealanders illustrated. London, T. M'Lean 1847
66 l. front. 60 col.pl. F.
More than half the plates are paintings of the aboriginal inhabitants
Colas 132

Polynesia; a popular description of the physical features, inhabitants, natural history, and productions of the islands of the Pacific; with an account of their discovery, and of the progress of civilization and Christianity amongst them. London, Society for promoting Christian knowledge [1866]
xii,436p. front.(fold.map) illus. pl. S.
LC A21-118

South Australia illustrated. London, McLean 1847
66 l. front. 60 col.pl. F.
Nineteen of the plates show aboriginal inhabitants. Two of these show figures with the bodies painted for native dances
Colas 133

Angeiologie. Krause, J. H.

Angelino, P. de Kat. See Kat Angelino, P. de

Angelo, Domenico
L'ecole des armes, avec l'explication générale des principales attitudes et positions concernant l'escrime. Londres, R. & J. Dodsley 1763
[110]p. 47pl. ob.F.
Lipperheide 2974. LC 19-17248

Angels in art. Waters, Mrs C. E. C.

Angelucci, Angelo
Documenti inediti per la storia delle armi da fuoco italiane. Torino, G. Cassone 1869
476p. 13 illus. 10pl. O.
From the 13th to the 17th century
Lipperheide 2421

(ed.) Italy. Ministero della casa reale. Catalogo della armeria reale

Angeordtneter grosser umbang, und procession auf das hohe fest des Zarten Fronleichnambs Jesu Christi. In ... Landshut, mit denen handwerchszunfften, fähnen, stangen, und kertzen sambt figuren und persohnen auch mit bruderschafften und clerisey. No place, R. Schmidt 1733
38p. 3pl. Q.
Lipperheide 2799

Anger, Gilbert
Illustrirte geschichte der K. K. Armee. Wien, G. Anger 1886-87
3v. illus. 87pl.(64 col.) O.
Shows uniforms of the Austrian army from its origin until 1867
Second edition (Wien, Halm und Goldmann 1888. 3v. 86pl.)
Colas 135-136

Angermayer, Fred Antoine
(tr.) Fels, Florent. Die altfranzösischen bildteppiche

Angers, François Grille d'
(ed.) L'Album, journal des arts, des modes et des théâtres

Les **Anglais** peints par eux-mêmes. See Meadows, Kenny. Heads of the people

L' **Angleterre.** Eyriès, J. B. B.

Angleterre ancienne. See Strutt, Joseph. Horda Angelcynnan

Anglican church. See Ecclesiastical costume—Anglican and Episcopal churches

An **Anglican** study in Christian symbolism. Neff, E. C.

Anglo-Saxon costume. See England—To 1066

Die **angriffswaffen** in den altfranzösischen Artus- und abenteuer-romanen. Bach, Volkmar

Anhalt. See Ceremonial and festival costume—Germany—Anhalt

Aniota-kifwebe; les masques des populations du Congo Belge et le materiel des rites de circoncision. Maes, Joseph

Anker, Erna
Muster-album für haekel-arbeiten. Leipzig, H. Barsdorf 1887
18pl. F.
Lipperheide 4154

Anleitung, den menschlichen körper, besonders aber den weiblichen. Bernhardt, J. S.

Anleitung zu wettkämpfen, spielen und turnerischen vorführungen bei volks- und jugendfesten. Schmidt, F. A.

Anmuth und schönheit aus den misterien der natur und kunst für ledige und verheirathete frauenzimmer. Berlin, Oehmigke der jüngere 1797
xvi,301p. 2 col.pl. O.
Lipperheide 3243

Annales. Roo, Gerardus de

Annales bambergensis episcopatus. Hoffmann, Martin

Les **annales** de la danse et du théâtre. Guérard, Eugène

Annales ducum seu principum Brabantiae totivsq. Belgii. Haraeus, Franciscus

Annales Ferdinandei. Khevenhiller. F. C.

Annals and occurrences of New York city and state. See note under Watson, J. F. Historic tales of olden time

Annals of horsemanship. See Bunbury, H. W. Academy for grown horsemen

Annals of Philadelphia, and Pennsylvania, in the olden time. Watson, J. F.

Annals of Philadelphia, being a collection of memoirs. See Watson, J. F. Annals of Philadelphia, and Pennsylvania, in the olden time

Annals of the Swedes on the Delaware. Clay, J. C.

Une **année** en Suède. Grafström, A. A.

Anneis. Teixeira de Aragão, A. C.

Annereau
(engr.) Dubois. Principes d'allemandes

Annotations. Baïf, Lazare de

Annuaire des modes de Paris; orné de douze gravures. 1. année. 1814. Paris, Au bureau du Journal des dames, & chez Delaunay
288p. 12 col.pl. D.
Colas 137

Annual customs and festivals in Peking. Tun, Li-ch'ên

Ansbach. See Germany—By region or province—Bavaria—Ansbach

Anselmus, bishop of Marsico. See Joachim, abbot of Fiore. Profetie dell' abbate Gioachino et di Anselmo

Anteckningar, förda under tiden från år 1785 til år 1816 jemte relation om Savolaksbrigadens operationer under 1808 och 1809 års krig. Burman, J. J.

Anteckningar rörande svenska regementernas historia. Mankell, Julius

Anthologie de coiffes. Bianchi de Médicis de Manville, prince

Anthonia Margaretha, pseud.
Onze kleeding. Utrecht, G. J. A. Ruys 1910
187p. O. f.1.75

Anthropological papers. American museum of natural history, New York

Anthropologische studien über die urbewohner Brasiliens. Ehrenreich, P. M. A.

L'**antica** Roma ovvero Descrizione storica e pittorica di tutto cio che riguarda il popolo romano. See Grasset de Saint-Sauveur, Jacques. L'antique Rome

Antiche trine italiane. Ricci, Signora Elisa

Antike gesichtshelme und sepulcralmasken. Benndorf, Otto

Antike handarbeiten. Schinnerer, Luise

Die **antike** kunst. Lilienfeld, C. J.

Antike mode. Boehn, Max von

Antike und frühmittelalterliche fussbekleidungen aus Achmim-Panopolis. Frauberger, Heinrich

Antilles islands

Jacottet, Henri, and Leclerc, Max. Colonies françaises. 1888

Anti-maquignonage, pour éviter les surprises dans l'emplette des chevaux. See Eisenberg, von, baron. La perfezione e i difetti del cavallo

Ein **antiphonarium** mit bilderschmuck. Lind, Karl

Antiqua; unterhaltungsblatt für freunde der alterthumskunde. Herausgegeben von H. Messikommer und R. Forrer. 1884-1891. Zürich, F. Lohbaur

2v. illus. pl. O.
The numbers for 1886-1891 were later published under title *Urgeschichtliche nachrichten und forschungen* (Dresden, Zähn und Jänsch)
Volume 1, 1882-1883 was later republished in a separate edition entitled *Praehistorische varia*
Lipperheide 299

Antiquarian, architectural, and landscape illustrations of the history of Java. Raffles, Sir T. S.

Antique gems and rings. King, C. W.

Antique jewellery and trinkets. Burgess, F. W.

Antique jewelry and its revival. Castellani, Alessandro

Antique laces of American collectors. Morris, Frances, and Hague, Marian

Antique point and Honiton lace. Treadwin, Mrs

Antique portraits from the Hellenistic times. Graf, Theodor

L'**antique** Rome. Grasset de Saint-Sauveur, Jacques

Antiquitates gandersheimenses. Leuckfeld, J. G.

Antiquitates graecae et romanae. See Montfaucon, Bernard de. L'antiquité expliquée et representée en figures

Antiquitates sacræ & civiles Romanorum explicatæ. Sive commentarii historici, mythologici, philologici, in varia monumenta prisca, & maxime in plures statuas, aras, tumulos, inscriptiones &c . . . Autore M. A. V. N. Hagæ-Comitum, apud R. C. Alberts 1726

xlix,307p. 87pl. (incl.ports.)
Also title page in French: *Antiquitez sacrées & profanes des Romaines expliquées.* Text in Latin and French, in parallel columns. Author alleged to be van Nartow or van Nideck
Lipperheide 226

L'**antiquité** expliquée. Montfaucon, Bernard de

Antiquités de la Nubie. Gau, F. C.

Antiquités de l'Empire de Russie. See note under Russia. Komitet dlîa îzdaniîa drevnosteĭ Rossiĭkago gosudarstva. Drevnostī Rossiĭskago gosudarstva

Antiquités des Pays-Bas. See Kellen, David van der. Nederlands-oudheden

Antiquités et Guerre des Juifs de Josèphe. Paris. Bibliothèque nationale. Département des manuscrits

Antiquités nationales. Millin, A. L.

Antiquités norvégiennes. See Rygh, Oluf. Norse oldsager

Antiquités suédoises. Montelius, Oskar

Antiquitez sacrées & profanes des Romains expliquées. See Antiquitates sacrae & civiles Romanorum explicatae

Antiquities and views in Greece and Egypt. Dalton, Richard

Antiquities of Mexico. Kingsborough, E. K., viscount

Antiquities of the Jews. Brown, William

Antiquities of the New England Indians. Willoughby, C. C.

Antiquity explained, and represented in sculptures. Montfaucon, Bernard de

Anti-Titus. Rothe de Nugent, D.

Antonioli, Giovanni

Raccolta di costumi di Roma e vicinanze: incisi all' acqua-forte da Gio. Antonioli. No place, ca1820

12pl. O.
Most of the plates are copies from Pinnelli
Colas 139. Lipperheide 1308

Antrobus, Mrs Mary (Symonds) and Preece, Louisa

Needlework in religion; an introductory study of its inner meaning, history, and development; also a practical guide to the construction and decoration of altar clothing and of the vestments required in church services. London, New York [etc.] Pitman [1924]

xxiii,229p. illus.(part col.) 35pl. (incl. col.front.) O. 21s o.p.
Costume index LC 24-23722

Needlework through the ages, a short survey of its development in decorative art, with particular regard to its inspirational relationship with other methods of craftsmanship. London, Hodder & Stoughton 1928

xxxiii,413p. col.front. 103pl.(part col.) 32x25cm. 210s
Bibliography: p391-398
Costume index. LC 29-16752

Anweisung, wie eine stickerin sich selbst, ohne zeichnen zu können, jedes muster . . . aufzeichnen, und fortführen oder verlängern kann; mit 50 neuen geschmackvollen stickmustern. Meissen, F. W. Goedsche ca1820

26p. 12pl. D.
Lipperheide 3946

Anweisung zum hiebfechten mit graden und krummen klingen. Roux, F. A. W. L.

Anweisung zur kunst-strickerei. Hennings, Emma

Anweisung zum sticken und illuminiren, mit ausgemalten und schwarzen zeichnungen von bouquets, körbchen, arabesquen, desseins zu granirungen und kleinen kanten. Halle, Dreyssig [1795]

24p. 16pl.(8 col.) O.
Lipperheide 3930

Anzeiger des germanischen nationalmuseums. Nuremberg. Germanisches national-museum

Aperçu historique, statistique et topographique sur l'état d'Alger, à l'usage de l'armée expéditionnaire d'Afrique, avec ... costumes. Paris, C. Picquet 1830
216p. D. and Atlas (11pl.) F.
Colas 140

Aperçu historique sur les moeurs et coutumes des nations. Depping, G. B.

Aperçu pittoresque de la Régence de Tunis. Chassiron, Charles, baron de

Aperçu sur les variations du costume militaire. Steyert, André

Apin, Siegmund Jakob
Dissertatio de loricis linteis veterum et novo loricarum invento. Altorfii, J. G. Kohlesius 1719
32p. illus. Q.

Vitae et effigies procancellariorum Academiae Altorfinae non solem de hac sed etiam de universa Norimbergensium publica cuius consiliarii pro in ordine fuerunt maxime meritorum in publicum datae. Norimbergae et Altorfii, apud Haeredes Tauberi 1721
87p. 8 col.pl. Q.
Pictures of the chancellors of Altdorf university, 1575-1711
Lipperheide 2021

Apokalypsis. Niessen, Johannes

Apologia de barbis. Burchardus, abbot of Bellevaux

Apologie des dames, les jolies françaises, leurs coëffures et habillemens. Paris, Desnos 1781
1 l. 12 col.illus. Ti.
Illustrations are from *Recueil général de coëffures de différents goûts*
Colas 141

Apothecaries
Peters, Hermann. Aus pharmazeutischer vorzeit in bild und wort. 1889-91

Les **appartements** du roi Louis XIV. Trouvain, Antoine

Appelgren-Kivalo, Hjalmar
Suomalaisia pukuja ... Finnische trachten aus der jüngeren Eisenzeit. Helsingissä, Tilgmann 1907
60p. 6 illus. 15pl.(part col.) F.

Appell, J. W. See Colonna, Francesco. The dream of Poliphilus fac-similes of one hundred and sixty-eight woodcuts in the "Hypernerotomachia Poliphili," Venice 1499

Apperçu sur les modes françaises. Ponce, Nicolas

Applegate, Frank Guy
Indian stories from the Pueblos; illus. from original Pueblo Indian paintings. Philadelphia, J. B. Lippincott. 1929
178p. col.front. col.pl.(1 double) O. $2.50
Costume index. LC 29-25487

Applied design in the precious metals. Davidson, P. W.

Appropriate clothes for the high school girl. Alexander, V. M.

Aprons and house dresses. Kneeland, Natalie

L'**Aquarelle-mode;** compositions, nouveautés. 1.-11. année. 1866?-1876. [Paris] L. Sault
11v. col.pl. F.
Contains fashion plates
Colas 142. Lipperheide 4717

Aquarelles de Job. Onfroy de Bréville, J. M. G.

Aquila austriaca; das ist historische beschreibung und abbildung alles römischen kaiser und könige welche von Rudolpho I. biss auff Leopoldum I. auss dem Hause des Graven von Habspurg sind erwöhlet worden. Nürnberg, Paulus Fürsten kunsthändlern ca.1660
4 l. 15pl. F.
Plates are the work of Jakob von der Heyden
Lipperheide 852

Arabia
Barbosa, Duarte. A description of the coasts of East Africa and Malabar in the beginning of the sixteenth century. 1866
Blunt, Lady Anne. Bedouin tribes of the Euphrates. 1879
Breton de la Martinière, J. B. J. L'Égypte et la Syrie, ou moeurs, usages, costumes et monumens des Égyptiens, des Arabes et des Syriens. 1814
Burckhardt, J. L. Notes on the Bedouins and Wahábys. 1831
Bury, G. W. The land of Uz. 1911
Dozy, R. P. A. Dictionnaire détaillé des noms des vêtements chez les Arabes. 1845
Gröber, Karl. Picturesque Palestine, Arabia and Syria. c1925
Nicolay, Nicolas de, sieur d'Arfeuille. The navigations, peregrinations and voyages, made into Turkie. 1585
Nicolay, Nicolas de, sieur d'Arfeuille. Les navigations, peregrinations et voyages, faicts en la Turquie. 1576
Nicolay, Nicolas de, sieur d'Arfeuille. Les quatre premiers livres des Navigations et peregrinations orientales. 1568
Ruete, Frau Emilie. Memoirs of an Arabian princess. 1907

See also Arabs; Arabs in Syria; Lace—Macramé; also subdivision Arabia under Arms and armor; Decoration and ornament

Arabs
Used for Arabs living outside Arabia
Baker, Sir S. W. The Nile tributaries of Abyssinia, and the sword hunters of the Hamran Arabs. 1868
Field, Henry. Arabs of central Iraq, their history, ethnology, and physical characters. 1935
Leeder, S. H. The Desert gateway, Biskra and thereabouts. 1910

See also Hair-dressing—Arabs

Arabs in Syria
Goodrich-Freer, A. M. Arabs in tent & town. 1924

Aragão, A. C. T. de. See Teixeria de Aragão, A. C.

Arago, Jacques. See Pigal, E. J., jt. auth.

Aragon, Henry
Le costume dans les temps anciens et au moyen âge (v[e]-xiiie siècle) Partie 1-4. [Perpignan] Barrière 1921
4v. D.
Cover-title. Each part has separate title-page
Contents: v1 L'habillement en Grèce et à Rome. Les vêtements de dessus; v2 L'habillement en Grèce et à Rome. Les vêtements de dessous.—Les ceinture; v3 L'habillement en Grèce et à Rome. Parures.—Ornements divers de la personne. v4 Des Gaulois à la renaissance

Aragon. See Spain—Aragon

Araucanian Indians. See Indians of South America — Araucanian Indians

Arbeau, Thoinot, pseud. See Tabourot, Jehan

Die **arbeitstunden** im stricken, nähen und sticken. Leipzig, G. Voss 1810
60p. 29pl. (11 col.) Q.
Lipperheide 4066

Arbousset, Thomas
Relation d'un voyage d'exploration au nord-est de la colonie du Cap de Bonne-Espérance ... 1836. Paris, A. Bertrand 1842
x,620p. 11 pl. map. O.
Eight plates show full length figures, two in Europeanized, the rest in native costume, described in detail

Arc, Édouard Gauttier du Lys. See Gauttier du Lys d'Arc, Louis Édouard

Archäologie der kunst. Sittl, Karl

Archäologisches institut des Deutschen Reichs
Griechische thonfiguren aus Tanagra. See entry under Kekule von Stradonitz, Reinhard

Archaeology. Maudslay, A. P.

Archaiologikē hetaireia en Athēnais. See Société archéologique d'Athènes

Archbishops

Catholic church

Das ruhmwürdige triumvirat der Johannischen verehrung. 1829

Archdall, Mervyn
Monasticon hibernicum: or, A history of the abbeys, priories, and other religious houses in Ireland . . . to the time of their final suppression . . . Ed. by Patrick F. Moran . . . Three volumes, v 1-2. Dublin, W. B. Kelly 1873-76
2v. front. pl(part col.) port. 2 fold. maps, 2 fold. plans. Q.
No more published

Archer, James Henry Lawrence-. See Lawrence-Archer, J. H.

Archers
Hansard, G. A. The book of archery. 1840
Stein, Henri. Archers d'autrefois; archers d'aujourd'hui. 1925

Archers (Military)
Delaunay, L. A. Étude sur les anciennes compagnies d'archers, d'arbaletriers et d'aruebusiers. 1879

Archers (Sport)
Ford, H. A. Archery: its theory and practice. 1880
Longman, C. J., and Walrond, Henry. Archery. 1894

Archers d'autrefois; archers d'aujourd'hui. Stein, Henri

Archery. Ford, H. A.

Archery. Longman, C. J., and Walrond, Henry

Archibald, James Francis Jewell
Blue shirt and khaki; a comparison. New York, Silver, Burdett 1901
269p. incl.front. illus. ports. D.
LC 1-31814

Archinard, Louis Quérouil
(ed) L'autre France (Tunisie, Algérie, Maroc). Publiée ... de Henri Lorin . . . Marcel Nési . . . Jean Garoby . . . Préfaces de MM. Charles Chaumet, Victor Margueritte — Général Lyautey. Bordeaux, Feret et fils 1914
408p. illus.(incl. maps) 2 col.pl. F.

El **archipiélago** filipino ... por algunos padres de la Misión de la Compañía de Jesús en estas islas. Washington, Impr. del gobierno 1900
2v. col.front. pl. (part fold.) maps (part fold.) diagrs. (part fold.) Q.
Edited by José Algué. Volume one has costume value
LC 1-8390

Architecture. See Fancy dress — Architecture

Archiv für deutsche schützengesellschaften. Hendel, J. C.

Archiv weiblicher hauptkenntnisse für diejenigen jedes standes. 1.-4. jahrg.; 1787-1790. Leipzig
4v. col.pl. O.
"Welche angenehme freundinnen, liebenswürdige gattinnen, gute mütter u. wahre hauswirtinnen seyn und werden wollen." Subtitle
Edited by A. F. Geisler
Plates show fashions of the period
Colas 145. Lipperheide 4571

Arco, Ricardo del
Costumbres y trajes en los Pirineos. Zaragoza, Artes gráficas E. Berdejo Casañal 1930
108p. illus. O. (Publicaciones de la Academia de ciencias, de Zaragoza)
Reprint from the Academy's *Curso de conferencias para un congreso y exposición internacional de los Pirineos que tiene en proyecto la Academia . . . 1930.*
Bibliografia: p105-08
LC 32-24345

El traje popular Altoaragonés; aportación al estudio del traje regional español. Madrid, Huesca 1924
71p. pl. O.
Colas 146

Arctic regions
Carpenter, F. G. Alaska, our northern wonderland. 1923
Hatt, Gudmund. Arktiske skinddragter i Eurasien og Amerika. 1914
Hatt, Gudmund. Moscasins and their relation to the Arctic footwear. 1916
United States. Quartermaster corps. Illustrations of Alaskan clothing. 1914

Arcy, Gabriel d', pseud. See Letainturier-Fradin, Gabriel

Ardenne de Tizac, Jean Henri d'
The stuffs of China, weavings and embroideries; fifty-two collotype plates reproducing 84 fine examples in French collections. London, E. Benn 1924
14p. 52pl. F.
LC 24-32076

Ardenne de Tisac, Jean H. d'—*Continued*

See also Étoffes de la Chine

Arène, Paul Auguste, and Tournier, Albert
Des Alpes aux Pyrénées, étapes félibréennes. Paris, E. Flammarion 1891?
286p. illus. D.
On the fetes of Gascony and the departments of the Pyrenees, 1890
LC 22-11153

Aretz, Frau Gertrude (Kuntze-Dolton)
The elegant woman, from the rococo period to modern times; tr. with a preface by James Laver. London, G. G. Harrap [1932]
314p. col.front. pl. (part col.) ports. O. $5. o.p.
Bibliography: p303-05
Costume index. LC 32-33977

Argenter, José Ignacio Miró y. See Miró y Argenter, José Ignacio

Argentine republic. Laws, statutes, etc.
Reglamento de uniformes para el ejercito. Buenos Aires, 1904
29p. 71 col.pl. Q.

Argentine republic. Ministerio de guerra y marina
Reglamento propuesto por la comandancia jeneral de armas prescribiendo el uniforme que debe usar el ejército de la República. Buenos Aires, Imprenta americana 1872
93p. fold.pl. diagrs. O.
LC CA10-2011

Argentine republic. Ministerio de marina
Uniformes navales de la marina de guerra Argentina. Buenos Aires, 1901
36p. 46 col.pl. Q.

Uniformes para el personal subalterno de la marina de guerra de la Republica Argentina. Buenos Aires, 1896
42 col.pl. Q.
"Declarado reglamentario por decreto del superior gobierno de Fecha, 13 de Mayo de 1896." Subtitle
Colas 2940

Argentine Republic
Koebel, W. H. The romance of the river Plate. 1914

MacCann, William. Two thousand miles' ride through the Argentine provinces. 1853

Trages y costumbres de la provincia de Buenos Aires. 1833-34

Uriarte, J. R. de, ed. Los baskos en la Nacion Argentina. 1919

Vidal, E. E. Picturesque illustrations of Buenos Ayres and Monte Video. 1820

See also subdivision Argentine republic under Military costume; Naval costume

Argentoratensis Lapponia. Scheffer, Johannes

Argenville, Antoine Joseph Dezallier d'. See Dezallier d'Argenville, Antoine Joseph

Argoli, Giovanni
(ed) Panvinio, Onofrio. De ludis circensibus

Aria, Mrs Eliza (Davis)
Costume: fanciful, historical, and theatrical; illus. by Percy Anderson. London and New York, Macmillan 1906
xiii,259p. illus. 16 col.pl. O. $2.50 o.p.
Colas 147. Costume index. LC 7-8553

Arif Pasha
Les anciens costumes de l'Empire ottoman, depuis l'origine de la monarchie jusqu'à la réforme du sultan Mahmoud ... Imprimé en couleurs par Lemercier. Paris, Impr. Lainé et Havard [1864]
47p. 16 col.pl. F. 80 fr.
Also published in Turkish (17 p. 1 port. 16 col.pl.)
The plates represent 80 types of costume. Published also with plates in black and white, at 40 fr.
Colas 148. Lipperheide 1440m

Aristotile, Nicolo d'. See Zoppino, Nicolo d'Aristotile, called

Arktiske skinddragter i Eurasien og Amerika. Hatt, Gudmund

L'**Arlequin;** journal de pièces et de morceaux. 15 thermidor An VII-10 vendémiaire An VIII. [2 aout 1799- 2 octobre 1799] Paris, Deferrière 1799
Illus. O.
Illustrated periodical of fashions and customs
Continuation of *Correspondance des dames.* Merged with *Gazette des salons, journal des dames et des modes,* 3 brumaire An VIII (25 Oct. 1799)
Colas 149

Arlington, Lewis Charles
The Chinese drama from the earliest times until today; a panoramic study of the art in China, tracing its origin and describing its actors (in both male and female rôles): their costumes and make-up, superstitions and stage slang. Shanghai, Kelly and Walsh 1930
xxxi, 177, xxxv-xli p. incl. illus. pl. col.front. 115 col.pl. Q.
Bibliography p xli
LC 30-30921

Armand-Dumaresq, Charles Édouard
Album de la cavalerie française, 1635-1881. Paris, J. Baudoin 1881
66 l. 66 col.pl. F.
Each plate shows six uniforms of one regiment from the time of its establishment
Colas 406. Lipperheide 2333

Uniformes de la Garde impériale en 1857, dessinés par Armand Dumaresq. Paris, Imprimerie impériale 1858
1 l. 55 col.pl. 78x57 cm.
Also exists with plates in black and white, published by Lemercier. The sets with colored plates were not put on sale but used by the emperor as presentation copies
Colas 150

Uniformes de l'armée française en 1861 ... Troupes de ligne. Paris, Lemercier 1861
1 p.l. 56 col.pl. 78x57 cm.
Colas 151. Lipperheide 2327

Uniformes de l'armée française en 1884; texte par M. de Bouillé. [Paris, 1885]
2v. (15, 14 p.) 16 col.illus. O.
Lipperheide 2337

Uniformes de l'armée française en 1887; texte par M. de Bouillé. Paris, Baschet 1887
2v. in 1 col.pl. O. [Cahiers d'enseignement illustrés. No. 1-2]

Armand-Dumaresq, Charles É.—*Continued*
Uniformes des écoles du gouvernement. [Paris, Baschet 1887]
111p. 240 illus.(20 col.) O. [Cahiers d'enseignement illustrés. No. 25-29]
Five parts. Part 5, text by H. Barthélemy
Deals mainly with military schools
Lipperheide 2347

Armata sarda. Galateri, Pietro

L'**arme** blanche de guerre française au XVIIIe siècle. Bottet, Maurice

Armee-album zur erinnerung an des 40jähr. regierungs-jubiläum ... Franz Joseph I. Amon von Treuenfest, Gustav, ritter

L'**armée** allemande sous l'empereur Guillaume II. Lange, Gustav

L'**armée** américaine, 1918. Jonas, Lucien

L'**armée** anglaise vers 1830. Mansion, L. M., and Saint-Eschauzier

[**Armée** bavaroise vers 1840. Leipzig, G. Bach] 1840?
9 col.pl. F.
Colas 153

L'**armée** belge. Rouen, Charles

Armée belge. See Madou, J. B. Collection des costumes de l'armée belge en 1832 et 1833

L'**armée** d'Afrique, 1830-1930. Algeria. Commissariat général du centenaire

L'**armée** danoise. Dally, Aristide

Armée de ligne. See Hecquet, F. Tracé descriptif des divers objets d'habillement ... de l'armée française en 1828

Die **armee** der Vereinigten Staaten von Amerika. Falls, De W. C.

Die **armee** der Vereinigten Staaten von Nord-Amerika. Bresler, A. L.

L'**armée** du Duché da Varsovie. Chelminski, J. V.

L'**armée** et la Garde impériale. See Lalaisse, Hippolyte. Empire français

L'**armée** et la Garde impériale, 1860-1870. Lalaisse, Hippolyte

L'**armée** et la Garde nationale. Poisson, S. J. C., baron

L'**armée** et la marine danoises. See Brock, Gustav. Den Danske haer og flaade

L'**armée** française. Gaildrau, Jules

Armée française. See Lalaisse, Hippolyte. Collection complète des uniformes de l'armée et de la marine françaises

Armée française. See Lançon, A. Album de l'armée française

Armée française. Mouillard, Lucien

Armée française. Pajol, C. P. V., comte

L'**armée** française à travers les âges; ses traditions—ses gloires—ses uniformes
See entries under individual authors: v 1 Vidal, J. J. G. P. L'artillerie; v2 Riols de Fonclare, J. E. de. L'infanterie; v3 Payard, Pol. Les chasseurs à pied; v4 Brécard, C. T. La cavalerie

L'**armée** française, Album-annuaire de. See Beauvoir, H. R. de. Album-annuaire de l'armée française

L'**armée** française en 1848. Bastin, Ferdinand

L'**armée** française en 1854. Bastin, Ferdinand

L'**armée** française et ses cantinières. Lalaisse, Hippolyte

See also Lalaisse, Hippolyte. Types de l'armée française et de ses cantinières

[**Armée** française (1844-1846). Paris, Sinnet 184?-]
16 col.pl. O.
Colas 156

Armée française, 1831. Swebach, E.

L' **armée** française représentée en 18 feuilles. Berka, J.

Die **armee** Friedrich's des Grossen in ihrer uniformirung. Menzel, A. F. E. von

L'**armée** hollandaise. Dally, Aristide

L'**armée** norvégienne. Dally, Aristide

Armée polonaise. Straszewicz, Joseph

L'**armée** roumaine. Ajduklewicz, T.

Armée royale de Prusse. Randel

L'**armée** russe. Camena d'Almeida, P. J., and Jongh, Francis de

L'**armée** russe. Dally, Aristide

Armée russe, cavalerie. Adam, Victor

Armée russe de 1855 à 1867. Piratzky, A., and Goubarev

Armée russe 1854-1862. Gebens

Armée russe, 1856. Pajol, C. P. V., comte

Armée russe vers 1815. Sauerweid, Alexandre

L'**armée** saxonne depuis ses origines jusqu'en 1832. Schmid, H., and Patzschke, Carl

L'**armée** saxonne représentée en 30 feuilles. Sauerweid, Alexandre

Armée suédoise. Bagge, Göran

L'**armee** suisse. Estoppey, D.

Armée suisse. Perron, Ch.

Armée suisse. See Wolf, E. Schweizerische armee

Armée Toscane. Gaglier

Die **armeen** der Balkan-staaten. Leipzig, M. Ruhl [1914]
3v. 16 col.pl.(part fold.) D.
Contents: v 1 Serbien u. Montenegro; v2 Türkei u. Griechenland; v3 Rumänien u. Bulgarien
Colas 2595

Die **armeen** der Türkei und Griechenlands. Sussmann, Anton

Die **armeen** Rumäniens und Bulgariens. Sussmann, Anton

Die **armeen** Serbiens und Montenegros. Rottmann, Hans

Les **armées** britanniques. Jonas, Lucien

Armeés des souverains alliés, années 1814 et 1815. Godefroy, A. P. F.

Les **armées** d'Europe representées en groupes charactéristiques. See Eckert, H. A., Monten, Dietrich, and Schelver, F. Saemmtliche truppen von Europa

Armées étrangères. Finart, N. and others

Les **armées** étrangères en campagne. Dally, Aristide

Les **armées** françaises d'outre-mer. Depréaux, Albert

[**Armées** françaises et étrangères (de 1800 à 1804) Prag, F. K. Wolf] ca1804
25 col. pl. D.
These plates are copied in part in *Charakteristiche darstellung der vorzüglichsten europäischen militairs*
Colas 155

Armelhault, J., pseud. See Mahérault, M. J. F.

Armenia

Curtis, W. E. Around the Black Sea. 1911

Dupré, Louis. Voyage à Athènes et à Constantinople. 1825

Filian, G. H. Armenia and her people. 1896

Hacouni. Patmouthiun hin haj tarazan patkerazard. 1923

Porter, Sir R. K. Travels in Georgia, Persia, Armenia, ancient Babylonia, &c. &c. during the years 1817, 1818, 1819, and 1820. 1821-22

See also Embroidery—Armenia

Armenia and her people. Filian, G. H.

Armenian church. See Ecclesiastical costume—Armenian church

La **Armeria** real. Jubinal, Achille

Armeria reale di Torino. Turin. Armeria reale

Armerie des ducs de Lorraine, en 1629; nouv. éd. 1900. See Giraud, J. B. Documents pour servir à l'histoire de l'armement au moyen âge et à la renaissance

Les **armes.** Maindron, M. G. R.

Armes anciennes de la Suisse. Boissonnas, Jean

Armes & armures anciennes. Paris. Musée de l'armée

Armes et armures. Nesselrode, C. R., comte de

Armes et armures du moyen age et de la renaissance. Asselineau, L. A.

Les **armes** et le duel. Grisier, A. E. F.

Les **armes** et les armures. Lacombe, Paul

Armies. See Military costume

Armies of Europe. Köppen, Fedor von

Armies of India. MacMunn, Sir G. F.

The **Armies** of to-day; a description of the armies of the leading nations at the present time. New York, Harper 1893
438p. front. illus. pl. O. $3.50, o.p.
Contents: The army of the United States, by W. Merritt; The standing army of Great Britain, by Viscount Wolseley; The German army, by Lieutenant-Colonel Exner; The French army, by General Lewal; The Russian army, by a Russian general; The Austro-Hungarian army, by Baron von Kuhn; The Italian army, by G. Goiran; The Mexican army, by T. A. Janvier; Appendix: Military situation in Europe, by Lieutenant-Colonel Exner
Costume index. LC 19-9218

Armont, Paul

Soldats d'hier et d'aujourd'hui; planches en couleurs d'après la collection de soldats de plomb de M. Paul Armont. Paris, M. Lesage [1929-31]
44pl. (part col.) ob.F.
Title from publisher's announcement, 2 leaves inserted at front. Each col'd plate accompanied by a replica in phototype. Plates colored by J. Saudé

Armor. See Arms and armor

Armor and arms club, New York

Catalogue of a loan exhibition of Japanese sword fittings, held at the Metropolitan museum of art, New York city, August 1 to December 31, 1922. [New York, R. A. Haag, printer, c1924]
xix p. 59 l. 43 pl. ob.O.
"In the present volume are illustrated and described over six hundred examples of Japanese metal-work"
Introduction by Howard Mansfield; text, glossary and chronological index by Robert Hamilton Rucker; illustrations from photographs by George Cameron Stone
LC 24-4035

Catalogue of a loan exhibition of Japanese sword guards, held at the Metropolitan museum of art, New York city, July 15 to October 15, 1921. [New York, R. A. Haag, printer c1922]
xxi p. 73 l. ob. O.
Robert Hamilton Rucker, compiler
LC 22-12977

A miscellany of arms and armor, presented by fellow members of the Armor and arms club to Bashford Dean in honor of his sixtieth birthday, October twenty-eight, MCMXXVII. [New York city, Printing house of W. E. Rudge c1927]
109, incl.front.(port.) illus. pl. Q.
Contents: The barbute, by G. A. Douglass; Malay krisses, by S. V. Grancsay; Weapons of the buccaneers and pirates, by D. Franklin; Notes on Japanese chronology, by R. H. Rucker; The double set trigger, by T. T. Hoopes; The American military pike of '76, by R. W. Bingham; The story of a Kaneiyé sword guard, by H. Mansfield; Notes on the development of the Baltic flintlock, by T. T. Hoopes; The Indian gauntlet sword-pata, by G. C. Stone; A Nuremberg casque, by C. O. v. Kienbusch; Nathan Starr, American swordsmith, by R. W. Bingham; A decimal classification of the discharge mechanism of hand firearms, by W. G. Renwick; Arms and armor of the Hebrews, by F. G. Blakeslee
LC 28-1701

Armorial des cardinaux, archevêques et évêques français. Cosson, André

Armour & weapons. Ffoulkes, C. J.

Armour and weapons in the middle ages. Ashdown, C. H.

Armour in England from the earliest times to the reign of James the First. Gardner, J. S.

The **armourer** and his craft from the XIth to the XVIth century. Ffoulkes, C. J.

The **armoury** of Windsor castle; European section. Laking, Sir G. F., bart.

Arms and armor

An Almain armourer's album. Selections from an original ms. in Victoria and Albert museum. 1905

Armor and arms club, New York. A miscellany of arms and armor, presented ... to Bashford Dean. [c1927]

Angelucci, Angelo. Documenti inediti per la storia delle armi da fuoco italiane. 1869

Ashdown, C. H. Arms & armour ... Illustrated ... from actual examples, missals, illuminated mss., brasses, effigies, etc. 1909

Arms and armor—*Continued*

Asselineau, L. A. Armes et armures du moyen age et de la renaissance; choix et reproduction des plus remarquables spécimens conservés dans les principaux musées et cabinets de l'Europe. 1864

Asselineau, L. A. Meubles et objets divers du moyen âge et de la Renaissance. 1854?

Boeheim, Wendelin. Handbuch der waffenkunde ... vom beginn des mittelalters biz zum ende des 18. jahrhunderts. 1890

Boeheim, Wendelin. Meister der waffenschmiedekunst vom XIV. bis ins XVIII. jahrhundert. 1897

Bouly de Lesdain, Louis. Les variantes dans les armoiries. 1897

Brett, E. J. A pictorial and descriptive record of the origin and development of arms and armour. 1894

Carré, J. B. L. Panoplie, ou réunion de tout ce qui a trait à la guerre, depuis l'origine de la nation française jusqu'à nos jours. 1795

Claesen, Charles. Recueil d'ornements et de sujets pour être appliqués à l'ornementation des armes. 1857

Clephan, R. C. The defensive armour and the weapons and engines of war of mediaeval times and of the "renaissance." 1900

Cripps-Day, F. H. A record of armour sales. 1925

Demmin, A. F. Encyclopédie d'armurerie avec monogrammes, guide des amateurs d'armes et armures anciennes. 1869

Demmin, A. F. Weapons of war. 1870

Egerton, W. E., earl. Description of Indian and Oriental armour. 1896

Extraits de L'art pour tous, encyclopédie de l'art industriel & décoratif. Armes et armures. ca1880

Ffoulkes, C. J. Armour & weapons. 1909

Ffoulkes, C. J. The armourer and his craft from the XIth to the XVIth century. 1912

Gardner, J. S. Foreign armour in England. 1898

Gessler, E. A. Die trutzwaffen der Karolingerzeit vom VIII bis zum XI. jahrhundert. 1908

Gimbel, Karl. Tafeln zur entwicklungsgeschichte der schutz- und trutzwaffen in Europa mit ausschluss der feuerwaffen vom VIII. bis XVII. jahrhundert. 1894

Giraud, J. B. Documents pour servir à l'histoire de l'armement au moyen âge et à la renaissance. 1895-99

Gohlke, Wilhelm. Die blanken waffen und die schutzwaffen, ihre entwicklung von der zeit der landsknechte bis zur gegenwart, mit besonderer berücksichtigung der waffen in Deutschland, Österreich-Ungarn und Frankreich. 1912

Haenel, Erich. Alte waffen. 1920

Hefner-Altereck, J. H. von. Waffen; ein beitrag zur historischen waffenkunde vom beginn des mittelalters bis gegen ende des siebzehnten jahrhunderts. 1903

Hewitt, John. Ancient armour and weapons in Europe: from the iron period of the northern nations to the end of the seventeenth century. 1855-60

Jackson, H. J. European hand firearms of the sixteenth, seventeenth & eighteenth centuries. 1923

Kelly, F. M. and Schwabe, Randolph. A short history of costume & armour, chiefly in England, 1066-1800. 1931

Lacombe,. Paul. Les armes et les armures. 1877

Lacombe, Paul. Arms and armour in antiquity and the middle ages: also a descriptive notice of modern weapons. 1870

Laking, Sir G. F., bart. A record of European armour and arms through seven centuries. 1920-22. 5v.

Laufer, Berthold. Chinese clay figures, part I: Prolegomena on the history of defensive armour. 1914

Leber, F. O., edler von. Wien's Kaiserliches zeughaus, zum ersten male aus historisch-kritischem gesichtspunkte betrachtet, für alterthumsfreunde und waffenkenner. 1846

Maindron, M. G. R. Les armes. 1890

Meyrick, Sir S. R. A critical inquiry into antient armour, as it existed in Europe, but particularly in England, from the Norman conquest to the reign of King Charles II, with a glossary of military terms of the middle ages. 1824

Meyrick, Sir S. R. Engraved illustrations of antient arms and armour. 1830

Miquel y Badia, Francisco. Industrias artísticas; alfarería, terra cotta, mayólica, loza, porcelana, vidrio, bronce, orfebrería, joyería, armas. 1892

Paris. Musée de l'armée. Armes & armures anciennes et souvenirs historiques les plus précieux. 1917-27

Pistofilo, Bonaventura. Oplomachia di Bonaventura Pistofilo ... Nella quale con dottrina morale, politica, e militare, e col mezzo delle figure si tratta per via di teorica, e di pratica del maneggio, e dell' uso delle armi. 1621

Schön, Julius. Geschichte der handfeuerwaffen; eine darstellung des entwickelungsganges der handfeuerwaffen von ihrem entstehen bis auf die neuzeit. 1858

Schrenck von Nozing, Jacob. Augustissimorum, serenissimorum regum, atque archiducum, illustrissimorum principum ... gestarum succinctae descriptiones. 1601

Specht, F. A. K. von. Geschichte der waffen. 1869-77

Arms and armor—*Continued*

Stone, G. C. A glossary of the construction, decoration and use of arms and armor in all countries and in all times. 1934

See also Creese; Cuirass; Heraldic costume; Sword; Tournament costume

Bibliography

Cripps-Day, F. H. A record of armour sales. 1925

Edinburgh. Royal Scottish museum. Library. List of books, &c. relating to armour and weapons in the library of the Museum. 1891

Schott, C. M. Catalogue of the choice and valuable collection of rare antique guns and pistols, edge weapons, accessories, etc. 1918

Collections

Berthold, F. R. von. Katalog der kunst- und waffen-sammlung. 1898

Brett, E. J. Catalog of collection of armour and arms sold March 18th, 1895. n.d.

Brussels. Musées royaux des arts décoratifs et industriels. Catalogue des armes et armures du Musée de la Porte de Hal, par Hermann van Duyse. 1897

Cleveland museum of art. A catalogue of the collection of arms and armor presented to the Cleveland museum of art by Mr and Mrs John Long Severance. 1924

Cosson, C. A., baron de. Le cabinet d'armes de Maurice Tallyrand-Périgord. 1901

Dresden. Historisches museum und gewehrgalerie. Führer durch das Königliche historische museum. 1897

Dresden. Historisches museum und gewehrgalerie. Kostbare waffen aus der Dresdner rüstkammer. 1923

Ffoulkes, C. J. European arms and armour in the University of Oxford. 1912

Ffoulkes, C. J. Inventory and survey of the armouries of the Tower of London. 1916

Ffoulkes, C. J. Tower of London; guide to the armouries. 1930

Gille, Floriant. Musée de Tzarskoe-Selo, ou Collection d'armes de sa majesté l'empereur de toutes les Russies. 1835-53

Hans majestät konung Carl xv[s] vapensamling. 1861

Hardy, E. A. Le musée de l'armée. Section des armes et armures ... collections renfermées dans les salles d'armures et dans la galerie des costumes de guerre. 1911

Hiltl, Georg. Die waffensammlung Sr. königlichen Hoheit des prinzen Carl von Preussen. 1879

Hiltl, Georg. Waffen-sammlung Sr. königlichen hoheit des prinzen Carl von Preussen; mittelalterliche abtheiling. 1877

Jubinal, Achille. La Armeria real; ou Collection des principales pièces de la galerie d'armes anciennes de Madrid. 1837-42

Laking, Sir G. F., bart. The armoury of Windsor castle; European section. 1904

Leber, F. O., edler von. Wien's Kaiserliches zeughaus, zum ersten male aus historisch-kritischem gesichtspunkte betrachtet, für alterthumsfreunde und waffenkenner. 1846

Leiden, H. K. Waffensammlung konsul a. d. Hans C. Leiden. 1934

Leitner, Quirin, ritter von. Die waffensammlung des osterreichischen kaiserhauses im k.k. Artillerie-arsenal-museum in Wien. 1866-70

Lenz, E. von. Die waffensammlung des grafen S. D. Scheremetew in St Petersburg. 1897

Madrid. Armería real. Catálogo de la Real armería. 1849

New York. Metropolitan museum of art. The Bashford Dean collection of arms and armor in the Metropolitan museum of art. 1933

New York. Metropolitan museum of art. Catalogue of a loan exhibition of arms and armor. 1911

New York. Metropolitan museum of art. Handbook of arms and armor, European and oriental, by Bashford Dean; 4th ed. 1930

New York. Metropolitan museum of art. Historical arms and armor. 1935

Paris. Musée d'artillerie. Catalogue des collections composant le Musée d'artillerie en 1889. 1889-93

Pichler, Fritz, and Meran, F. graf von. Das landes-zeughaus in Graz. 1880

Richards, Raoul. Catalogue de la riche collection d'armes antiques, du moyen âge, de la renaissance et des temps modernes. 1890

Sacken, Eduard, freiherr von. Die vorzüglichsten rüstungen und waffen der K.K. Ambraser-sammlung in originalphotographien. 1859-62

Schott, C. M. Catalogue of the choice and valuable collection of rare antique guns and pistols, edge weapons, accessories, etc. 1918

Schwerzenbach, Carl von. Die schwerter und schwertknäufe der Sammlung Carl von Schwerzenbach — Bregenz. 1905

Stockholm. Hallwyliska palatset. Catalogue of the collection of arms and armour at Hallwyl house, Stockholm. 1928

Stockholm. Livrustkammaren. Kongl. lifrustkammaren och därmed förenade samlingar. 1897-1901

Stuyvesant, Rutherfurd. The collection of arms and armor of Rutherfurd Stuyvesant, 1843-1909, by Bashford Dean. 1914

Periodical

Zeitschrift für historische waffen- und kostumkunde. 1896+

Arms and armor—*Continued*

Prehistoric

British museum. Department of British and mediaeval antiquities. Guide to the antiquities of the bronze age. 1920

British museum. Department of British and mediaeval antiquities. Guide to antiquities of the early iron age. 1925

Middle ages

Ashdown, C. H. Armour and weapons in the middle ages. 1925

Gautier, Léon. La chevalerie. 1895

Kottenkamp, F. J. History of chivalry and ancient armour. 1857

Kottenkamp, F. J. Der rittersaal; eine geschichte des ritterthums. 1842

Kugler, Bernhard. Geschichte der kreuzzüge. 1880

Musée des armes rares, ancieñs et orientales de Sa Majesté l'Empereur de toutes les Russies. 1835?

Peigné-Delacourt, Achille. Recherches sur le lieu de la Bataille d'Attila en 451. 1860

Reibisch, F. M. von. Deutscher rittersaal. 1836

15th-17th centuries

Baillie-Grohman, W. A. The land in the mountains; being an account of the past & present of Tyrol. 1907

Benham, William. Tower of London. 1906

Burgkmair, Hans. Hans Burgkmair des jüngeren turnierbuch von 1529. 1910

Harmand, Adrien. Jeanne d'Arc, ses costumes, son armure. 1929

Hefner-Alteneck, J. H. von. Originalzeichnungen deutscher meister des sechzehnten jahrhunderts. 1889

Iselberg, Peter. Künstliche waffenhandlung der musqueten uñ piquen oder langen spiessen ... Maniement des mousquets & piques. 1620

Larchey, Lorédan. Ancien armorial équestre de la Toison d'or et de l'Europe au 15. siècle. 1890
Reprint of a 15th century mss

Lostelneau, de. Le mareschal de bataille, contenant le maniment des armes, les evolutions, plusieurs bataillons, tant contre l'infanterie que contre la cavalerie. 1647

Maximilian I, emperor of Germany. Freydal. Des kaisers Maximilian I. turniere und mummereien. 1880-82

Mieth, Michael. Neue curieuse beschreibung der gantzen artillerie, worinnen ... gehandelt wird ... wie ... man aus stücken ... glüend- und andere kugeln ... werffen soll. 1736

19th-20th centuries

Bley, Wulf. Moderne heere, moderne waffen. c1935

Paulin-Désormeaux, A. O. Nouveau manuel complet de l'armurier, du fourbisseur et de l'arquebusier. 1852

Dean, Bashford. Helmets and body armor in modern warfare. 1920

OF SPECIAL COUNTRIES

Alsace

Seyboth, Adolf, and Binder, C. Album de l'Exposition militaire de la Société des amis des arts de Strasbourg (fondée en 1832). 1904

Arabia

Egerton, W. E., earl. Description of Indian and Oriental armour. 1896

Asia

Egerton, W. E., earl. Description of Indian and Oriental armour. 1896

Moser, Henri. Collection Henri Moser, Charlottenfels ... oriental arms and armour. 1912

China

Werner, E. T. C. Chinese weapons. 1932

Czechoslovakia

Kunstgewerbliches aus der vom Mähr. gewerbe-museum im jahre 1885 veranstalteten ausstellung von waffen, kriegs- und jagdgeräthen. 1886

Egypt

Petrie, Sir W. M. F. Tools and weapons illustrated by the Egyptian collection in University college, London, and 2,000 outlines from other sources. 1917

Wolf, Walther. Die bewaffnung des altägyptischen heeres. 1926

England

Ashdown, C. H. Arms & armour ... Illustrated ... from actual examples, missals, illuminated mss., brasses, effigies, etc. 1909

Deters, Friedrich. Die englischen angriffswaffen zur zeit der einführung der feuerwaffen (1300-1350). 1913

Druitt, Herbert. A manual of costume as illustrated by monumental brasses. 1906

Gardner, J. S. Armour in England from the earliest times to the reign of James the First

Grose, Francis. Military antiquities respecting a history of the English army, from the conquest to the present time. 1801

Grose, Francis. A treatise on ancient armour and weapons, illustrated by plates taken from the original armour in the Tower of London, and other arsenals, museums, and cabinets. 1786

Kelly, F. M., and Schwabe, Randolph. A short history of costume & armour, chiefly in England, 1066-1800. 1931

Lacombe, Paul. Arms and armour in antiquity and the middle ages: also a descriptive notice of modern weapons. 1870

Lehmann, Hans. Brünne und helm im angelsächsischen beowulfliede. 1885

Meyrick, Sir S. R. A critical inquiry into antient armour, as it existed in Europe, but particularly in England, from the Norman conquest to the reign of King Charles II, with a glossary of military terms of the middle ages. 1824

Arms and armor—England—*Continued*

Meyrick, Sir S. R. Observations on the body-armour anciently worn in England. 1818

Meyrick, Sir S. R. Observations on the military garments formerly worn in England. 1821

Scott, Sir J. S. D., bart. The British army: its origin, progress, and equipment. 1868

Suffling, E. R. English church brasses from the 13th to the 17th century. 1910

See also subdivisions Ireland, and Scotland under Arms and armor

Europe

New York. Metropolitan museum of art. Catalogue of European arms and armor, by Bashford Dean. 1905

France

Bach, Volkmar. Die angriffswaffen in den altfranzösischen Artus- und abenteuer-romanen. 1887

Beaunier, F. and Rathier, L. Recueil des costumes français. 1810-13

Margerand, J. Les cuirasses des carabiniers (1810-1870). 1911

Monstrelet, Enguerrand de. The chronicles of Enguerrand de Monstrelet. 1810

Roger, P. A. La noblesse de France aux croisades. 1845

Viel-Castel, Horace, comte de. Collection des costumes, armes et meubles pour servir à l'histoire de France depuis le commencement du veme siècle jusqu'à nos jours. 1827-1845

Viollet-Le-Duc, E. E. Dictionnaire raisonné du mobilier français de l'époque carlovingienne à la renaissance. 1858-75

Germany

Bagensky, C. H. L. von, and Klaatsch, K. H. Das preussische infanterie-gewehr. 1820

Boeheim, Wendelin. Album hervorragender gegenstände aus der waffensammlung der allerhöchsten kaiserhauses. 1894-1898

Boeheim, Wendelin. Augsburger waffenschmiede, ihre werke und ihre beziehungen zum kaiserlichen und zu anderen höfen. 1891

Boeheim, Wendelin. Nürnberger waffenschmiede. 1895

Braun, Kaspar. Das landwehr-zeughaus in München. 1866

Breen, A. v. Le maniement d'armes de Nassau, avecq rondelles, piques, espees, & targes. 1618

Diener-Schönberg, Alfons. Die waffen der Wartburg. 1912

Geisberg, Max. Die prachtharnische des goldschmiedes Heinrich Cnoep aus Münster i. W. 1907

Gimbel, Karl. Die reconstructionen der gimbel'schen waffensammlung. 1902

Gimbel, Karl. Waffen und kunst-sammlung. 1904

Gurlitt, Cornelius. Deutsche turniere, rüstungen und plattner des XVI. jahrhunderts. 1889

Hocker, J. L. Hailsbronnischer antiquitäten-schatz. 1731

Jahn, Martin. Die bewaffnung der Germanen in der älteren eisenzeit, etwa von 700 v. Chr. bis 200 n. Chr. 1916

Klingsohr, C. F. Kurze geschichte des ehemaligen klosters Heilsbronn, und biographien derer sämtlich in der münsterkirche daselbst beigesetzten fürsten und kurfürsten aus dem burggraflichen fürsten hause, Nürnberg Hohenzollern. 1806

Kuppelmayr, Hans. Waffen-sammlung Kuppelmayr. 1895

Mair, P. H. Bericht und anzeigen aller Herren Geschlecht der loblichen statt Augspurg. 1538?

Potier, Othmar, baron. Fürhrer durch die rüstkammer der stadt Emden. 1903

Reibisch, F. M. von. Eine auswahl merkwürdiger gegenstände aus der königl. sächsischen rüstkammer. 1825-27

Schulz, Albert. Zur waffenkunde des älteren deutschen mittelalters. 1867

Greece—Ancient times

Hagemann, Arnold. Griechische panzerung. 1919

Reichel, Wolfgang. Homerische waffen. 1901

India

India. Army department. Photographs of types of the native Indian arms. 1895?

Sandringham House, Norfolk, England. Arms and armour at Sandringham. 1910

Indians of North America

Hough, Walter. Primitive American armor. 1895

Ireland

Walker, J. C. An historical essay on the dress of the ancient and modern Irish; to which is subjoined a memoir on the armour and weapons of the Irish. 1818

Italy

Italy. Ministero della casa reale. Catalogo della armeria reale. 1890

Turin. Armeria reale. Armeria reale di Torino. 1865

Japan

Armor and arms club, New York. Catalogue of a loan exhibition of Japanese sword fittings. c1924

Armor and arms club, New York. Catalogue of a loan exhibition of Japanese sword guards. c1922

Japan society, London. Catalogue of an exhibition of the arms and armour of old Japan, held ... London, in June 1905. 1905

New York. Metropolitan museum of art. Catalogue of the loan collection of Japanese armor. 1903

Arms and armor—*Continued*

Mexico

Peñafiel, Antonio. Indumentaria antigua; vestidos guerreros y civiles de los Mexicanos. 1903

Persia

Nesselrode, C. R., comte de. Armes et armures de la collection du comte de Nesselrode au château de Tzarevtchina Saratov (Russie). 1909

Philippine islands

Krieger, H. W. The collection of primitive weapons and armor of the Philippine islands in the United States National museum. 1926

Poland

Dziewanowski, Władysław. Zarys dziejów uzbrojenia w Polsce. 1935

Rome

Forestier, Amédée. The Roman soldier; some illustrations representative of Roman military life with special reference to Britain. 1928

Scotland

Drummond, James. Ancient Scottish weapons. 1881

Spain

Calvert, A. F. Spanish arms and armour. 1907

Danvila y Collado, Francisco. Trajes y armas de los españoles desde los tiempos prehistóricos hasta los primeros años del siglo XIX. 1877

Jubinal, Achille. La Armeria real; ou Collection des principales pièces de la gallerie d'armes anciennes de Madrid. 1837-42

Jubinal, Achille. La Armeria real, ou Collection des principales pièces du Musée d'artillerie de Madrid. 1861

Madrid. Armería real. Catálogo de la Real armería. 1849

Madrid. Armería real. Catalogo históricodescriptivo de la Real armería de Madrid. 1898

Switzerland

Boissonnas, Jean. Armes anciennes de la Suisse. 1900

Arms and armor, Primitive

Breton, W. H. Excursions in New South Wales, Western Australia, and Van Diemen's Land, during the years 1830, 1831, 1832, and 1833. 1834

British museum. Department of British and mediaeval antiquities. Handbook to the ethnographical collections. 1910

Bonnet, Hans. Die waffen der völker des alten Orients. 1926

Lindblom, Gerhard. Fighting-bracelets and kindred weapons in Africa. 1927

Meyer, A. B., and Uhle, Max. Seltene waffen aus Afrika, Asien und Amerika. Herausgegeben mit unterstützung der Generaldirection der königlichen sammlungen für kunst und wissenschaft zu Dresden. 1885

See also Arms and armor—Philippine Islands; Bracelets

Arms and armour at Sandringham House, Norfolk, England

Arms and armour in antiquity and the middle ages: also a descriptive notice of modern weapons. Lacombe, Paul

Armstrong, Sir Walter

Gainsborough and his place in English art. London, W. Heinemann; New York, C. Scribner's sons [etc.] 1898
297p. front. 47 pl. (incl.ports.) O.
Popular edition (Scribner 1906)
LC 12-35682

Sir Joshua Reynolds, first president of the Royal academy. London, Heinemann; New York, Scribner; [etc.] 1900
x,235p. front. 51pl. (incl.ports.) fold. facsim. O.
Popular edition 1905
LC 12-15572

(ed. and tr.) Perrot, Georges and Chipiez, Charles. A history of art in ancient Egypt

(ed. and tr.) Perrot, Georges, and Chipiez, Charles. A history of art in Chaldaea & Assyria

(ed. and tr.) Perrot, Georges, and Chipiez, Charles. History of art in Phoenicia

Une **armure** de joute en 1514. See Giraud, J. B. Documents pour servir à l'histoire de l'armement au moyen âge et à la renaissance

L'**armurie** royale et les collections y incorporées. See Stockholm. Livrustkammaren. Kongl. lifrustkammaren

Les **armuriers** français et étrangers en Touraine. 1897. See Giraud, J. B. Documents pour servir à l'histoire de l'armement au moyen âge et à la renaissance

Army and navy gazette, London

British military types. See Simkin, Richard. British military types

Coloured military types which were issued as supplements to the "Army and navy gazette" between March 1888 and September 1902. London, The army and navy gazette [1910?]
172 pl. Q.

Army and navy information. Falls, De W. C.

Army and navy of the United States. Walton, William

Army and navy uniforms and insignia. Williams, Dion

Army of Russia containing the uniforms in portrait of the Russian soldiery. London, Longman [1807]
20 col.pl. Q.
Colas 158

The **army** of the United States. United States. Quartermaster corps

Army transport service. See Military costume—United States—Army transport service

Army uniforms of the world. Blakeslee, F. G.

Armytage, Mrs Fenella Fitz Hardinge (Berkeley)
Old court customs and modern court rule. London, R. Bentley 1883
xv,272p. front. 3pl. O.
Lipperheide 2497. LC 4-18726

Arnaud, Ch. See Gellé, P., jt. auth.

Arnault, Antoine Vincent
Les souvenirs et les regrets du Vieil amateur dramatique [pseud], ou Lettres d'un oncle à son neveu sur l'ancien théâtre français, depuis Bellecour, Lekain, ... Préville ... jusqu'à Molé, Larive, Monvel ... Vestris ... Ouvrage orné ... d'après les miniatures ... de Foëch de Basle et de Whirsker, ces différens acteurs dans les rôles où ils ont excellé. Paris, C. Froment 1829
214p. 36 col.pl. O. 250 fr.
First edition. Some of the plates appeared in an earlier collection entitled *Les metamorphoses de Melipomène et de Thalie, by Whirsker.* Some editions have the plates in black and white only
A second edition (Paris, A. Leclere 1861. 219p. 49 col.pl. O) is described by Colas as less brilliant in coloring. Some copies have the plates in black and white only
Colas 159-60

Vie politique et militaire de Napoléon ... Ouvrage orné de planches lithographiées, d'après les dessins originaux de premiers peintres de l'école française, imprimées par C. Motte. Paris, Émile Babeuf 1822-26
2 v. ca120 plates. F.
Lipperheide 1156

[**Arnay, Jean Rodolphe d'**]
De la vie privée des romains. Lausanne, Chez M. M. Bousquet & compagnie 1757
207p. D.
Published later under title: *Habitudes et mœurs ...* (Paris 1795)
LC 7-11325

Habitudes et moeurs privées des Romains ... nouv. éd. rev. et corrigée. Paris, Maillard 1795
278p. O.
Earlier edition, 1757, entitled *De la vie privée des Romains*
LC 7-11324

The private life of the Romans, tr. from the French. Edinburgh, The translator & A. Donaldson 1761
378p. D.
Translation of *De la vie privée des Romains*
Third edition (Dublin, D. Chamberlaine 1771. 264p. D.) also another edition (illus. with notes, etc. Edinburgh, P. Cairns 1808. 257p. D.)
An Italian translation was published, *della vita privata de' Romani* tr. di Domenico Amato (Napoli, 1763) also (Napoli, 1783)

Arndt, E. M.
Deutsche trachten; erstes heft. Berlin, L. W. Wittich 1815
2 l. 4 col.pl. Q.
Costumes of the sixteenth and seventeenth centuries. No further numbers of this work appeared
Colas 162. Lipperheide 655

Ueber sitte, mode und kleidertracht; ein wort aus der zeit. Frankfurt am Main, B. Körner 1814
88p. O.
Colas 161. Lipperheide 3485

Arneberg, Halfdan
(illus.) Garborg, Fru H. B. Norsk klaedebunad

Arnold, Carl Franklin
Die vertreibung der Salzburger protestanten und ihre aufnahme bei den glaubensgenossen. Ein kulturgeschichtliches zeitbild aus dem achtzehnten jahrhundert. Leipzig, E. Diederichs 1900
246p. 41 illus. 1 pl. O.
Lipperheide 697e

Arnold, Channing, and Frost, Frederick J. Tabor
The American Egypt; record of travel in Yucatan. New York, Doubleday 1909
391p. 16pl. map Q. $3.80, o.p.

Arnold, Sir Edwin
Japonica; illus. by Robert Blum. New York, Scribner 1891
xv,128p. incl.front. illus. pl. Q.
Essays on Japan reprinted from Scribner's magazine
LC 4-19319

Seas and lands. New York, Longmans, Green 1891.
x,530p. front.illus. pl. O.
Reprinted from letters published in the Daily telegraph under the title *By sea and land*
The greater part of the work relates to Japan
LC 5-38888

Arnold, Johann Georg Daniel
Der pfingstmontag, lustspiel in Strasburger mundart, in fünf aufzügen und in versen; dritte ... verb. ausg. mit einem wörtebuche eigenthümlicher Strassburger ausdrücke. Strassburg, E. Simon 1867
88p. 42 pl. F.
A reprint of the second edition of 1816 was issued in 1914 (Strassburg, K. J. Trübner) in the series Jahresgaben der gesellsschaft für elsäsassische literatur
Lipperheide 792

Arnold, Karl
Kriegsflugblätter der Liller kriegszeitung. [Lille] Liller kriegszeitung [1915]
3p.l. 100pl. ob.F.
LC 23-2716

Arnold, Mme Paula. See Kellner, Leon, jt. auth.

Arnold, Sir Thomas Walker, and Grohmann, Adolf
The Islamic book; a contribution to its art and history from the VII-XVIII century. [Paris] Pegasus press [New York, Harcourt, Brace and company] 1929
xxi,130p. illus. (part mounted) 104 pl. (part col.) F.
Each plate accompanied by guard sheet with descriptive letterpress, not included in collation. In 2 parts: 1 The early Islamic period from the VII-XII century, by A. Grohmann (written in German, translated by J. Allan) 2 XIII-XVIII century by Sir T. W. Arnold
Part 2 is a rich collection of Persian paintings and pictures from manuscripts, many of which show costume
Bibliographies p 116
LC 30-5360

Arnold, Wilhelm
Deutsche geschichte. Gotha, Perthes 1881-83
2v. in 3 (462, 329, 314p.) D.
Describes costume from the early period to the death of Charlemagne
Part 2 of volume 2 was edited after the death of the author by Andreas Heusler
Contents: v 1. Deutsche urzeit: 1. buch Der urzeit bis zur gründung der fränkischen monarchie; 2. buch Innere zustände während dieser zeit. v2 Fränkische zeit 1. hälfte Fränkischen reichs bis zum tode Karls des Grossen 481-814; 2. Fortschritte der inneren entwickelung

Arnold, Xaver and Knoll, Eduard
Sammlung von initialen aus dem 12.-17. jahrh. endnommen der königl. Hof-u. staats-bibliothek zu München, der Biblioteca nacional u. der Biblioteca de la Universidad central zu Madrid; bd. 1. Leipzig, L. Denicke 1869
39pl. Q.
The second edition (Leipzig, Brehse 1889-90. 30pl.) is entitled *Sammlung . . . aus dem 11.-17. jahrhundert*

Arnould, Charles Albert d'. See Bertall, C. A. d'A.

Arnould, Georg
Das deutsche heer und die marine. Militair-typen ... mit erläuterndem text von Félix von Olberg. Hamburg, [1891-94]
60 col.pl. F.
Colas 163

Arnoux, Guy
A la gloire des soldats suisses (hommage français). Paris, Société litteraire de France 1917
10 col.pl. Q.
Swiss soldiers of various periods

Les soldats français dans les guerres. [Paris] Société litteraire de France 1916
17 col.pl. Q.
Of various periods from Vercingetorix to the World war

Tambours et trompettes; images de Guy Arnoux. Paris, Devambez 1919
10 col.pl. F.
French uniforms of various periods

Arnz & compagnie, Düsseldorf
Bilder aus dem schwedischen volksleben: 12 blatt nach originalgemälden schwedischer künstler in farbendruck ausgeführt; mit beschreibendem text in deutscher, englischer und schwedischer sprache. Gothenburg, D. F. Bonnier 1855
12 col. pl. ob.F.
Contents: Das innere einer lapländischen hütte; Die leser-sekte; Sennhütte in Dalekarlien; Dalekarlier auf wanderschaft; Der taufakt; Die schmuggler; Der heringsfang; Der brautzüg in Wärend; Holländische bauerstube; Der pferdemarkt; Die abendsmahlsfeier; Das erntefest

Aromunes. See Greece—20th century

Arosa, Gustave. See Froehner, Wilhelm. La Colonne Trajane d'après le surmoulage executé à Rome en 1861-62

Around Afghanistan. Bouillane de Lacoste, É. A. H. de

Around the Black Sea. Curtis, W. E.

The **art** & craft of old lace. Henneberg, Alfred, freiherr von

The **art** and craft of ribbonwork. New York, The Illustrated milliner co. [1921]
71p. illus. (part col.) F.
LC 22-21339

The **art** & ethics of dress. Farnsworth, E. O.

Art and fundamentals of hairdressing. Korf, Frederick

Art as applied to dress. Higgin, L.

L'**art** capillaire dans l'Inde, à la Chine et au Japon. Blondel, Spire

L'**art** chrétien en Egypte. Dillmont, Thérèse de

L'**art** dans la parure et dans sle vêtement. Blanc, Charles

L'**art** dans l'Afrique australe. Christol, Frédéric

L'**art** de composer les livrées au milieu du XIX. siècle. Saint-Épain, de

L'**art** de décorer les tissus. Cox, Raymond

L'**art** de faire les armes. Saint-Martin, J. de

Art de la chaussure. See Nouvelle encyclopédie des arts et métiers

L'**art** de la coëffure des dames dans le nouveau goût d'à-présent. See Legros, coiffeur. L'art de la coëffure des dames françoises

L'**art** de la coëffure des dames françoises. Legros, coiffeur

L'**art** de la coiffure féminine. Stéphane

L'**art** de la lingère. Garsault, F. A. P. de

Art de la mode. See Art et la mode; revue de l'élégance

L'**art** de la toilette. Mariette, Pauline

L'**art** de la toilette chez la femme, breviaire de la vie élégante. Laincel-Vento, Alix, comtesse de

L'**art** de mettre sa cravate de toutes les manières connues et usitées. Saint-Hilaire, É. M. H.

L'**art** de monter a cheval. Delcampe, and Fouquet, Samuel

L'**art** de monter à cheval. See Eisenberg, von, baron. Description du manège moderne

L'**art** de reconnaître les bijoux anciens, pierres précieuses, métal précieux. Bayard, Émile

L'**art** de reconnaître les dentelles, guipures, etc. Bayard, Émile

L'**art** de se coiffer soi-même enseigné aux dames. Villaret, P.

L'**art** de se raser. Malet, Georges

L'**art** de tricoter. Netto, J. F., and Lehmann, F. L.

L'**art** décoratif de Léon Bakst. Bakst, Léon

L'**art** des armes. Danet, Guillaume

L'**art** des armes simplifié. See Olivier, J. Fencing familiarized

L'**art** du brodeur. Saint-Aubin, Augustin de

L'**art** du coëffeur. An XI-XV?; 1803-07. [Paris]
Col.illus. col.pl. ob.O.
Shows fashions and styles of hair-dressing of the period
Colas 165. Lipperheide 4592

Art du cordonnier. Garsault, F. A. P. de

L'**art** du maquillage. Bitterlin, A.

Art du perruquier. Garsault, F. A. P. de

L'**art** du militaire, ou traité complet de l'exercice de l'infanterie, cavalerie, du canon, de la bombe, et des piques. Paris, F. Dufart; Bordeaux, Bergeret 1793
173p. 7pl. D.
Lipperheide 2301m

L'**art** du peuple roumain ... suivie d'un Aperçu historique du Prof. Alexandre Tzigara-Samurcas. Genève, A. Kündig 1925
122p. illus. 4pl. Q. 3fr. 50

L'**art** du rire et de la caricature. Alexandre, Arsène

Art du tailleur. Garsault, F. A. P. de

L'**art** égyptien. Capart, Jean

Art et la mode; revue de l'élégance. 1. annee, v 1, août, 1880+ Paris, 1881+
Illus. pl. (part col.) ports. F.
Published monthly. Current 1938
Title changes: v 1-3 *Art de la mode.*
Suspended publication Aug. 1914-June, 1915
Editors: 1880-81, Étincelle (pseud. of Baroness H. M. A. Double); 1881-82, Ernest Hoschedé
Colas 164. Lipperheide 4766. LC 13-11927

L'**art** et la parure féminine dans l'ancienne Egypte. Capart, Jean

L'**art** étrusque. Martha, Jules

L'**art** gaulois. Hucher, E. F. F.

Art, goût, beauté; feuillets de l'élégance féminine. Année 4-13; avr., 1924-avr. 1933. Paris, A. Godde, Bedin
Illus. pl. (part col.) F.
Published monthly, numbering continuous. Can be had with text in English, French or Spanish

See also Voici la mode

Art in costume design. Shover, E. M.

Art in dress. Bolmar, Lydia, and McNutt, Kathleen

Art in dress. Brown, P. C.

Art in Egypt. Maspero, Sir G. C. C.

Art in every day life. Goldstein, H. I., and Goldstein, Vetta

Art in home and clothing. Trilling, M. B., and Nicholas, Mrs F. W.

Art in home economics. Clark, M. E., and others, comps.

Art in needlework. Day, L. F., and Buckle, Mary

Art in ornament and dress. Blanc, Charles

The **Art** index, 1929+ See note at head of subject: Periodicals, yearbooks, etc.

Art industriel. Dupont-Auberville, A.

Art militaire des Chinois. Amiot, J. M.

L'**art** militaire françois, pour l'infanterie. Contenant l'exercice & le maniement des armes, tant des officiers. Paris, P. Giffart 1696
178p. 85pl. O.
Lipperheide 2289

The **art** of bobbin lace. Tebbs, L. A.

The **art** of colour. Jacobs, Michel

The **art** of defence on foot with the broad sword and sabre. Roworth, C.

Art of dress

See also Beauty, Personal; Color in dress; Designing

18th century

Anmuth und schönheit aus den misterien der natur und kunst für ledige und verheirathete frauenzimmer. 1797

19th century

Ballin, A. S. Health and beauty in dress; from infancy to old age. 1893

Ballin, A. S. The science of dress in theory and practice. 1885

Banze, Angela. Der zauber des fleisses; die kunst mit wenig mitteln eine geschmackvolle toilette herzustellen; nebst anleitung zum schnittzeichnen. 1871

Barras, Easton de. Home dressmaking and the art of good dressing. 1898

Barrett, W. H. Hint's about men's dress, right principles economically applied. 1888

Bayle-Mouillard, Mme. É. F. Manuel des dames. 1827

Bernhardt, J. S. Anleitung, den menschlichen körper, besonders aber den weiblichen. 1820

Blanc, Charles. L'art dans la parure et dans le vêtement. 1875

Blanc, Charles. Art in ornament and dress. 1877

Clasen-Schmid, Mathilde. Das frauencostüm in praktischer, conventioneller und ästhetischer beziehung. 1888

Cook, M. W. How to dress on £ 15 a year. 1874

Dewing, M. R. O. Beauty in dress. 1881

Douglas, Mrs Fanny. The gentlewoman's book of dress. 1894

Ecob, H. G. The well-dressed woman. 1893

Falke, Jacob von. Zur cultur und kunst. 1878

Gale, E. C. Hints on dress. 1872

Grünwald-Zerkovitz, Frau Sidonie. Die mode in der frauenkleidung. 1889

Hauff, Ludwig. Die menschliche schönheit. 1866

Haweis, Mrs M. E. J. The art of dress. 1879

Higgin, L. Art as applied to dress, and to harmonious colour. 1885

Hohenheim, A., and Richards, E. Chic! Ein ratgeber für damen in allen toilettenfragen mit besonderer berücksuchtigung der farben. 1890

Klemm, Heinrich. Unterricht im arrangement der damen-toiletten von standpunkte der kleider-aesthetik und der farben-harmonie. 1876

Laincel-Vento, Alix, comtesse de. L'art de la toilette chez la femme; breviaire de la vie élégante. 1885

Art of dress—19th cent—*Continued*
The mirror of the graces. 1811
Quigley, Dorothy. What dress makes of us. 1897
Raisson, H. N. Code de la toilette. 1828
Saint-Hilaire, É. M. H. Manuel complet de la toilette, ou L'art de s'habiller avec élégance et méthode, contenant L'art de mettre sa cravate. 1828
Sydow, Johanna von. Im toilettenzimmer; plaudereien und enthüllungen aus dem gebiete der eleganz und aus dem salon ... 1882
Sylvia's book of the toilet: a ladies' guide to dress and beauty, with a fund of information of importance to gentlemen. ca1880
Walker, Mrs A. Female beauty as preserved and improved by regimen, cleanliness and dress; and especially by the adaptation, colour and arrangement of dress. c1840
The whole art of dress. 1830

20th century

Baldt, L. I. Clothing for women; selection and construction. c1935
Bolmar, Lydia, and McNutt, Kathleen. Art in dress. 1916
Bruns, M. S. Der stil unserer kleidung. 1902
Burbank, Emily. The smartly dressed woman; how she does it. 1925
Burbank, Emily. Woman as decoration. 1917
Buttrick, H. G. Principles of clothing selection. 1930
Collins, Harry. The A B C of dress. 1923
De Garmo, Charles, and Winslow, L. L. Essentials of design. 1924
Farnsworth, E. O. The art & ethics of dress. c1915
Goldstein, H. I., and Goldstein, Vetta. Art in every day life. 1925
Gould, G. M. The magic of dress. 1911
Gratz, Josefine. Der gute geschmack in der frauenkleidung. 1922
Hallmark, Harrydele. The well-dressed woman. 1924
Hopkins, Mrs M. S. Dress design and selection. 1935
Jéglot, Cécile. La jeune fille et la mode. 1928
Jordan, Mrs L. E. B. Clothing: fundamental problems; a practical discussion in regard to the selection, construction and use of clothing. 1927
Joy, Lilian. The well dressed woman. 1907
Klickmann, Flora, ed. How to dress; a handbook for women of modest means. 1900
Knoll, Carl, and Reuther, Fritz. Die kunst des schmückens; eine klärung des schmuck-problems durch wort und bild für schaffende und geniessende. 1910
Krapf, Anton. Durchdachte frauenkleidung; eine schönheitsfibel. 1934
L'Heureux, Mme M. A. Pour bien s'habiller. 1911
McFarland, Mrs F. W. Good taste in dress. 1936
Matthews, M. L. Clothing; selection and care. 1936
Miller, F. S., and Laitem, Mrs H. H. Personal problems of the high school girl. c1935
Picken, Mrs M. B. The secrets of distinctive dress. 1918
Shover, E. M. Art in costume design; practical suggestions for those interested in art, sewing, history and literature. 1920
Story, Mrs M. McE.-F. Individuality and clothes, the blue book of personal attire. 1930
Stote, Dorothy. Making the most of your looks. 1935
Trilling, M. B., and Nicholas, Mrs F. W. Art in home and clothing. c1936
Velde, Henry van de. Die künstlerische hebung der frauentracht. 1900
Wells, J. W. Dress and look slender. c1924
Wells, Margery. Clothes economy for well dressed women. 1927
Winterburn, Mrs F. H. Principles of correct dress. 1914

The **art** of dress. Haweis, Mrs M. E. J.

The **art** of dress. Parsons, F. A.

The **art** of dress; or, Guide to the toilette: with directions for adapting the various parts of the female costume to the complexion and figure ... [With] engravings from designs by Frank Howard. London, C. Tilt 1839
68p. 6 col.pl. O.
Plates show coiffures, hats and neckwear
Colas 166. Lipperheide 3263

Art of dressmaking. Byron, E.

The **art** of Greece. Gardner, E. A.

The **art** of heraldry. Fox-Davies, A. C.

The **art** of hunting. Dryden, Alice, ed.

The **art** of Japan. Brinkley, Frank

The **art** of needle-work. Wilton, M. M. E., countess of

The **art** of old Peru. Lehmann, Walter, and Doering, Heinrich

The **art** of portrait painting. Collier, John

The **art** of producing pageants. Bates, E. W.

The **art** of theatrical make-up. Morton, Cavendish

The **art** of tying the cravat. Le Blanc, H.

The **art** of wig-making. See Creer, Edwin. Board work, or the art of wig-making

Art populaire. International congress of popular arts, Prague, 1928

L'**art** populaire en Europe. See Bossert, H. T. Volkskunst in Europa

L'art populaire hongrois; édité par la Section ethnographique du Musée national hongrois et l'Imprimerie de l'Université. [Budapest, Impr. de l'Université royale hongroise 1928]
xxx p. 240pl.(part mounted col.) on 120 l. F.
"L'introduction de cet ouvrage est due à Charles Viski, les notes explicatives des figures à Sigismond Bátky et Étienne Györffy. Les matériaux on été recueillis en commun par les trois auteurs. Traduction de Henri Ancel." The illustrations show Hungarian dress and embroidery
"Historique des recherches; notice bibliographique": p vi-viii
LC 29-7463

L'art populaire russe à la seconde exposition koustare. Russia. Glavnve upravlenīe

L'Art pour tous. See Extraits de L'Art pour tous, encyclopédie de l'art industriel & decoratif; Armes et armures

L'art religieux de la fin du moyen âge en France. Mâle, Émile

L'art religieux du XIIIe siècle en France. Mâle, Émile

L'art rustique en France. Las Cases, Philippe, vicomte de, ed.

Art workers guild, London
Beauty's awakening, a masque of winter and of spring. [London, New York, The Studio 1899]
44p. illus. pl. (4 col. 1 double) Q.
The Studio summer number, 1899. Walter Crane, chairman of the Committee of designers
Lipperheide 2846. LC 16-21645

Arta ţărănească la Români. Oprescu, George

Artaria & compagnie, Vienna
Schema aller uniform der kaiserl. königl. kriegsvölkern. Wienn, Artaria compaÿ 1781
1 l. 133 col.pl. O.
This collection was republished in 1783, 1785, 1786, 1791 with some variations in the number of plates. According to Colas these plates bear some resemblance to those in the *Schema* published by H. Löschenkohl
Colas 2655-59. Lipperheide 2227 (1785 ed)
(pub.) Stubenrauch, Philipp von; Schindler, J. J., and Höchle, J. N. Darstellung der k. k. österr. armee

Arte de andar a cavallo. Bernard, Francisco

L'arte del cappello et della berretta a Monza e a Milano nei secolo XVI-XVIII. Riva, Giuseppe

L'arte del taglio e la confezione d'abiti per signora. Bonetti, Emelia

Arte dell' armi. Marozzo, Achille

L'arte di mettere la propria cravatta in tutte le foggie conosciute. See Saint-Hilaire, É. M. H. L'art de mettre sa cravate de toutes les manières connues et usitées

Arte e storia nel mondo antico monumenti della civiltà classica orientale, greca e romana. Adami, Casimiro

Arte militare terestre, e maritima. Savorgnano, Mario, conte di Belgrado

L'arte negli arredi sacri della Lombardia. Beltrami, Luca

El **arte** popular en Europa. See Bossert, H. T. Volkskunst en Europa

Arthurian costume. See England—To 1066; Kings and rulers—England

Arthus, Gotthard
Electio et coronatio ... Matthiae I. electi Rom. imperat ... eiusq ... coniugis Annae Austriacae ... Wahl undt krönung des ... herrn Matthiae ... Matthiae I ... hanc ... delineationem, carminicè à Gatardo Arthusio ... descriptam ... dedicant J. T. de Bry, J. de Zettra, J. Gelle. Frankfurt, 1612
13 pl. Q.
With inscriptions in Latin and German verse
Lipperheide 2507

Le **arti** che vanno per via nella citta di Venezia. Zompini, Gaetano

L'arti communi che vanno per Londra. See Lauron, Marcellus. The cryes of the city of London

Le **arti** di Bologna. Carracci, Annibale

L'arti per via. Carracci, Annibale

Artículos de Fausto Vigil sobre los trajes y costumbres asturianas. Vigil, Fausto

L'artillerie. Vidal, J. J. G. P.

L'artillerie française, costumes, uniformes, matériel depuis le moyen-âge jusqu'à nos jours. See Moltzheim, A. de. Esquisse historique de l'artillerie française

L'artillerie française en 1829. Foussereau

Artillerie, Garde royale. Mareschal

Artisanne, grisette, jeune fille et dame. Grévedon, P. L. H.

Artist and lady's world. See Peterson magazine

Artistic embroidery. Church, Mrs E. R. M.

Artistic Japan: a monthly illustrated journal. See Bing, Samuel. Artistic Japan

Artists
Adam, Victor. Les arts et métiers; avec vignettes par Victor Adam. ca1830
Balzer, Johann. 87 abbildungen böhmischer und mährischer gelehrten und künstler. 1773

The **arts** & crafts of ancient Egypt. Petrie, Sir W. M. F.

The **arts** and crafts of older Spain. Williams, Leonard

The **arts** and crafts of our Teutonic forefathers. Brown, G. B.

Les **arts** au moyen âge. Du Sommerard, Alexandre

Les **arts** au moyen âge. Lacroix, Paul

Les **arts** et métiers. Adam, Victor

The **arts** in the middle ages. Lacroix, Paul

Arts, métiers et cris de Paris. See Joly, Adrien. Les petits acteurs du Grand théâtre ou recueil des divers Cris de Paris

Arts, métiers et cultures de la Chine; representés dans une suite de gravures ... d'après les dessins originaux envoyés de Pékin; accompagnés des explications données par les missionaires français et étrangers. Paris, Nepveu 1814-15
2v. 24 col.pl. D.
v 1 Art du vernis par le P. d'Incarville (84 p. 11 col.pl.) 1814; v2 Papier de bambou (71p. 13 col.pl.) 1815
Lipperheide 1526

Les **arts** somptuaires. Louandre, C. L.

Artus, Thomas, sieur d' Embry. See Chalcondylas, Laonicus. Histoire generale des Turcs

Artzenei spiegel gemeyner inhalt. Dryander, Johann

Arundel society, London
Cole, A. S. Les dentelles anciennes. 1878

Arvidsson, Adolf Ivar
Svenska konungar och deras tidehvarf, en samling af portraitter öfver namkunniga personer med bifogade korta lefnadsteckningar. Stockholm, [P. A. Norstedt & söner 1830-43]
2v. 156 pl. (ports.) F.
Illustrations are head and shoulder portraits of rulers and other outstanding men and women of the 16th to the 19th centuries
Lipperheide 1047

Der **arzt** in der karikatur. Veth, Cornelis

Der **arzt** und die heilkunst in der deutschen vergangenheit. Peters, Hermann

Asbóth, János de
An official tour through Bosnia and Herzegovina, with an account of the history, antiquities, agrarian conditions, religion, ethnology, folk lore, and social life of the people. Authorized English ed. London, S. Sonnenschein 1890
xx,496p. illus. fold. map. O.
Translated from the Hungarian
Bibliography: p[xiii]-xx
LC 3-29165

Ascani, D.
Costumi della corte pontificia (attributed author)

Aschenborn, Heinrich Anton Louis Karl Richard
Die flotte (*In* Boguslawski, Albrecht von. Deutschland)

Ashanti
Dupuis, Joseph. Journal of a residence in Ashantee. 1824

Ashbee, Charles Robert, and Harwood, Edith
The masque of the Edwards of England, [being a coronation pageant to celebrate the crowning of the king] [London] E. Arnold; New York, S. Buckley 1902
45p. incl.pl. 29x40cm.
"The drawings of the pageants of the kings are by Edith Harwood and have been in part printed from stones by Sprague & co., and in part are touched by hand, while the vellum copies are all painted by Edith Harwood."
LC A13-984

Ashby, Thomas
Some Italian scenes and festivals. London, Methuen [1929]
xv,179p. 18pl.(incl.front.) D.
LC 29-28815

Ashdown, Mrs Charles A. See Ashdown, E. J.

Ashdown, Charles Henry
Armour & weapons in the middle ages. London [etc.] G. G. Harrap [1925]
219p. front. illus. D. (The home antiquary series)
Bibliography: p201-02
LC 25-14310

Arms & armour ... Illustrated ... from actual examples, missals, illuminated mss., brasses, effigies, etc., and from original research in the British museum, the Tower of London, Wallace collection, rotunda at Woolwich, many private collections, etc. New York, Dodge pub. co. [1909]
xv,384p. front. illus. pl. O.
English edition: *British and foreign arms & armour* (London & Edinburgh, T. C. & E. C. Jack 1909
LC A10-1, 9-30462(English ed.)

Ashdown, Emily Jessie
British costume during XIX centuries (civil and ecclesiastical) By Mrs. Charles A. Ashdown; illustrated ... from original costumes and from illuminated mss., missals, brasses, effigies, etc., from original research in the Manuscript department of the British museum and in various national collections. London and Edinburgh, T. C. & E. C. Jack 1910
xiii,376p. 459 illus. 119pl.(9 col., incl. front.) ports. O. 12s 6d
Colas 168. Costume index. LC 10-25109

Ashley, Sir William James
An introduction to English economic history and theory. London, New York [etc.] Longmans, Green 1923-25
2v. map. O.
First edition 1888-1893. Lettered on cover: Economic history, v 1, part I-II. "Authorities" at beginning of each chapter
Contents: v 1 The middle ages; v2 The end of the middle ages
Liveries of the craft gilds and of retainers during the Middles Ages, v2 p 124-34
LC 26-923

Ashmole, Elias
The institution, laws & ceremonies of the most noble Order of the Garter. Collected and digested into one body by Elias Ashmole. London, Printed by J. Macock, for Nathanael Brooke 1672
720(i.e. 716),[102]p. front. (port.) illus. pl. (part fold. and double) coats of arms. F.
Pages 131-134 omitted in numbering. Some of the plates are printed on both sides
Numerous engravings by W. Hollar
Lipperheide 1892. LC 22-11820

Ashton, John
The dawn of the XIXth century in England, a social sketch of the times ... with 114 illustrations drawn by the author from contemporary engravings; 5th ed. London, T. F. Unwin 1916
xx,476p. incl.front. illus. D. 2s 6d o.p.
Costume index. LC 17-4479

Ashton, John—*Continued*

Men, maidens and manners a hundred years ago; with thirty-four contemporary illustrations. London, Field & Tuer [etc.]; New York, Scribner & Welford 1888
124p. illus. sq. T.
Divided into 12 chapters, one for each month of 1787
LC 2-24355

Old times; a picture of social life at the end of the eighteenth century, collected and illustrated from the satirical and other sketches of the day; with eighty-eight illustrations. London, J. C. Nimmo 1885
xii,354p. front. pl. O. 21s o.p.
Costume index. LC 2-24356

Social England under the regency; with 90 illustrations. London, Ward and Downey 1890
2v. illus. pl. O.
Costume index. LC 2-27327
Covers the period 1810-1820

Social life in the reign of Queen Anne; taken from original sources. New York, C. Scribner's sons; London, Chatto & Windus 1919
xix,474p. front. (facsim.) illus.(incl. music.) D. $2.50
On the period 1702-1714
Costume index. LC 2-26103

Asia

Asia; journal of the American Asiatic association. 1898+
Bastian, Adolf. Die voelker des oestlichen Asien. 1866-71
Blakeslee, F. G. Eastern costume. 1935
Bourges, Jacques de. Wahrhaffte und eigendliche erzehlung von der reise des bischofs von Beryte auss Franckreich ... nach China. 1671
Bruyn, Cornelis de. Cornelis de Bruins Reisen over Moskovie, door Persie en Indie. 1711
Bruyn, Cornelis de. Travels into Muscovy, Persia, and part of the East-Indies. 1737
Bruyn, Cornelis de. Voyage au Levant; c'est-à-dire dans les principaux endroits de l'Asia Mineure, dans les isles de Chio, Rhodes, Chypre, etc., de même que dans les plus considérables villes d'Egypte, Syrie, & Terre Sainte. 1725
Churchill, Awnsham, and Churchill, John. A collection of voyages and travels. 1732
Cooper, Mrs E. G. The harim and the purdah. 1915
Dapper, Olfert. Naukeurige beschryving van Asie. 1680
Eyriès, J. B. B. Voyage pittoresque en Asie et en Afrique; résumé générale des voyages anciens et modernes d'après Erman, Lesseps, J.-F. Gmelin. 1839
Hürlimann, Martin. Burma, Ceylon, Indo-China, Siam, Cambodia, Annam, Tongking, Yunnan; landscape, architecture, inhabitants. 1930
Kerr, R. N. Miniature costume folios. c1937. v2
Laurent, and Perrot, Georges. Les femmes de l'Asie. [18-?]
Linschoten, J. H. van. Itinerario, voyage ofte schipvaert ... naer Oost ofte Portugaels Indien. 1595-96
Milne, Mrs L. J. When we were strolling players in the east. 1894
Norman, Sir Henry. The peoples and politics of the Far East; travels and studies in the British, French, Spanish and Portuguese colonies, Siberia, China, Japan, Korea, Siam and Malaya. 1900
Orlich, Leopold von. Reise in Ostindien in briefen an Alexander von Humboldt und Carl Ritter. 1845
Pécheux, and Manzoni. Costumes orientaux. 1813
Penfield, F. C. East of Suez: Ceylon, India, China and Japan. 1907
Petit album des peuples de l'Asie avec une description de leurs moeurs et usages. n.d.
Schweiger-Lerchenfeld, Amand, freiherr von. Die frauen des Orients in der geschichte, in der dichtung und im leben. 1904
Tilke, Max. Oriental costumes. 1923
Tilke, Max. Orientalische kostüme in schnitt und farbe. 1923
Tilke, Max. Studien zu der entwicklungsgeschichte des orientalischen kostüms. 1923
Varthema, Ludovico de. Die ritterlich vñ lobwirdig rayss des gestrengen vñ uber all ander weyt erfarnen ritters und lantfarers herzen Ludovico vartomans vo Bolonia Sagent vo den landen Egypto, Syria vo bayden Arabia Parsia India uñ Ethiopia vo den gestalte syte. 1515

See also Dutch East Indies; East (Near East); China; Japan; Korea; Malay archipelago; Malay peninsula; Manchuria; Mongolia; Persia; Phenicia; Riu Kiu islands; Tibet; also subdivision Asia under Arms and armor; Decoration and ornament; Jewelry, Ancient; Jewelry, Medieval and modern; Theatrical costume

Asia; journal of the American Asiatic association. v 1, July 1898+ New York
Illus. pl. (part col.) ports. maps. sq.F.
Issued irregularly July 1898-Feb. 1902; monthly, Apr. 1902+
Title varies: July 1898-Jan. 1917, *Journal of the American Asiatic association.* Present title since March 1917
Photographs show dress in various parts of Asia
LC 18-13913

Asia, Central

Atkinson, T. W. Travels in the regions of the upper and lower Amoor, and the Russian acquisitions on the confines of India and China. 1860
Hellwald, F. A. H. von. Centralasien. Landschaften und völker in Kaschgar, Turkestan, Kaschmir und Tibet. 1880
Le Coq, Albert von. Bilderatlas zur kunst und kulturgeschichte Mittel-Asiens. 1925

See also Turkestan

Asia Minor. See East (Near East)

Asiatic costumes. Smith, Captain

The **Asiatic** Islands and New Holland. Shoberl, Frederic, ed.

Das **asiatische** Russland. Roskoschny, Hermann

Asociación artistico-arqueologica barcelonesa. See Barcelona. Asociación artistico-arqueologica barcelonesa

Art. See Costume and art; Costume in art

The **art** and craft of hairdressing. Foan, G. A., ed.

L'**Aspic,** moniteur générale des modes, littérature, beaux-arts, théâtres; rédacteur en chef: Jules Leroy. 1.-2. année; 1837-38. Paris
O.
Colas 169

Aspin, Jehoshaphat

Cosmorama: a view of the costumes and peculiarities of all nations. London, J. Harris 1826
404p. 15 col.pl.(60 illus.) D.

A picture of the manners, customs, sports, and pastimes, of the inhabitants of England, from the arrival of the Saxons down to the eighteenth century. London, J. Harris 1825
296p. front. pl. D.
Based on Joseph Strutt's *Sports and pastimes*
Another edition is entitled *Ancient customs, sports, and pastimes of the English* (London, Harris 1832. viii,256p. illus. pl. sq.T.)
LC 2-8626

Aspland, Alfred

(ed.) Burgkmair, Hans. The triumphs of the Emperor Maximilian I

Aspruck, Franz

(engr.) Custos, Dominicus. Tirolensium. Principum comitum. Ab. an. ... 1229 usq. ad ann. 1599

Assam. See India—Assam

Asselineau, Léon Auguste

Armes et armures du moyen age et de la renaissance; choix et reproduction des plus remarquables spécimens conservés dans les principaux musées et cabinets de l'Europe. Paris, A. Lévy 1864
54pl. F.
Lipperheide 2416

Meubles et objets divers du moyen âge et de la Renaissance. Paris, 1854?
2v. 186pl. F.
Some of the plates show arms and armor

(lithgr.) Gille, Floriant. Musée de Tzarskoe-Selo, ou Collection d'armes de sa majesté l'empereur de toutes les Russies

Assemblage nouveau des manouvriers habilles. Engelbrecht, Martin

Assner, Leopold

Neueste abbildung aller kayserl. königl. regimenter; 2. verb. aufl. Pressburg, A. Löwen 1778
126 col.pl. O.
Colas 170

Associació d'amics dels museus de Catalunya, Barcelona

Catàleg de la col·lecció d'indumentària de Manuel Rocamora. See entry under Rocamora, Manuel

Assum, Johann Augustin

Warhaffte relation und ... discours uber dess ... herren Johann Friderichen, hertzogen zu Würtemberg ... jungen sohns Printz Friderichen ... kind tauff: sampt darbey begangnem ... fürstlichem ritterlichem frewden fest zu Stuttgardten: Den 8.9.10.11.12.13.14. etc. Martij, anno 1616, verfertigt durch Philopatrida Charitinum [pseud] [Stuttgart] J. W. Rösslin & J. A. Cellio [1616]
40,65p. F.
Lipperheide 2585

Assyria

Bonomi, Joseph. Nineveh and its palaces; the discoveries of Botta and Layard. 1852

Botta, P. E. Monument de Ninive. 5v. 1850

British museum. Department of Egyptian and Assyrian antiquities. A guide to the Babylonian and Assyrian antiquities. 1908

Gosse, P. H. Assyria. 1852

Hommel, Fritz. Geschichte Babyloniens und Assyriens. 1885-88

Houston, M. G., and Hornblower, F. S. Ancient Egyptian, Assyrian, and Persian costumes and decorations. 1920

Layard, Sir A. H. Nineveh and its remains. 1849

Layard, Sir A. H. A second series of the Monuments of Nineveh. 1853

Lutz, H. F. Textiles and costumes among the peoples of the ancient Near east. 1923

Maspero, Sir G. C. C. Life in ancient Egypt and Assyria. 1892

Perrot, Georges, and Chipiez, Charles. A history of art in Chaldaea & Assyria. 1884

Place, Victor. Ninive et l'Assyrie. 1867-70

Reimpell, Walter. Geschichte der babylonischen und assyrischen kleidung. 1921

Vaux, W. S. W. Nineveh and Persepolis: an historical sketch of ancient Assyria and Persia. 1850

See also Syria

Astley, Thomas

(pub.) A new general collection of voyages and travels

Aston, Ed.

(tr.) Boemus, Johann. The manners, lawes, and customes of all nations

Asturias. See Spain—Asturias

Atchley, Edward Godfrey Cuthbert Frederic. See Hope, Sir W. H. St. J., jt. auth.

Athletic costume. See Gymnasium dress

Atkinson, George Francklin

The campaign in India, 1857-58, from drawings made during the period of the great mutiny, illustrating the military operations ... with descriptive letter press. London, Day & son 1859

26pl. F.

"Curry & rice," on forty plates; or, The ingredients of social life at "our station" in India. London, Day & son [1859]

[90]p. 39 col.pl.(incl. front.) Q.
Other editions. Fourth edition (London [etc] Thacker 1911)
Plates show both native and English costume, including some English uniformed figures
LC 5-10080

Indian spices for English tables. London, Day & son [1860]

4p.l. xxvii col.pl. ob.Q.
"A rare relish of fun from the Far East. Being, the adventures of 'our special correspondent' in India, illustrated in a series of one hundred and twenty humorous sketches, and exhibiting, in all its phases, the peculiarity of life in that country." Subtitle
LC 11-29145

Atkinson, James

Sketches in Afghaunistan. London, H. Graves 1842

3p.l. 25pl. F.
Lettered on cover: Atkinson's sketches in Afghanistan. One plate contains costume pictures of Kabul
Colas 173. Lipperheide 1493. LC 22-24333

Atkinson, John Augustus, and Walker, James

A picturesque representation of the manners, customs, and amusements of the Russians. London, W. Bulmer [etc.] 1803-04

3v. in 1 front.(port.) 100 col.pl. F.
Explanation of each plate is in English and French. Some of the plates have been copied for A. C. Houbigant's *Moeurs et costumes des Russes*
Colas 171. Lipperheide 1343. LC 11-19833

A picturesque representation of the military and miscellaneous costumes of Great Britain. v 1. London, W. Miller 1807

34 l. 33 col.pl. F.
Planned as a three-volume work but only volume 1 appeared. Explanations of the plates are in English and French
Colas 172

Atkinson, Thomas Witlam

Travels in the regions of the upper and lower Amoor, and the Russian acquisitions on the confines of India and China. London, Hurst and Blackett 1860

xiii,570p. illus. fold.map. O.
Has costume pictures of members of various tribes and also describes their dress
LC 5-14116

Atkinson's Casket. See Graham's American monthly magazine

Atlante militare organizzazione. Cenni, Quinto

Atlas ou collection de 43 costumes persanes, militaires et civil; dessinés par A. Orlowski. Drouville, Gaspard

Atlas zur weltlichen altertumskunde des deutschen mittelalters. Philippi, Friedrich

Atrebatensis, Carolus Clusius. See L'Écluse, Charles de

The **Attic** theatre. Haigh, A. E.

Les **attraits.** Grévedon, P. L. H.

Die **attribute** des neuen deutschen reiches. Stillfried und Rattonitz, R. M. B., graf von

Au bal masqué. Beaumont, C. E. de

Au quartier Latin. Vernier, Charles

Aubé, Mme Antonine

Traité complet du filet et du filet-guipure. Bruxelles, A. N. Lebégue [1876]

64p. 126 illus. 1 pl. O.
Lipperheide 4116

Traité de couture. Paris, J. Baudry 1875

2v. illus. 3pl. O.
Lipperheide 3804

Aubel, Hermann, and Aubel, Marianne

Der künstlerische Tanz unserer Zeit. Königstein im Taunus; Karl Robert Langewiesche 1930

110p. front. illus. port. Q. (Die blauen bücher)

Aubel, Marianne. See Aubel, Hermann, jt. auth.

Aubert

(engr.) Dezallier d'Argenville, A. J. Abregé de la vie des plus fameux peintres

Aubert, David

Les cronicques et conquestes de Charlemaine. See entry under Le Tavernier, Jean

Histoire de Charles Martel. See entry under Liédet, Loyset

Aubert, Édouard

Trésor de l'abbaye de Saint-Maurice d'Agaune. Paris, Vve. A. Morel 1872

263p. illus.(incl. plans) 45 (i.e. 33) pl. (part col., incl. facsim.) ob.F.
Lipperheide 1839. LC 12-15111

Aubert, Octave Louis

Les costumes bretons; leur histoire, leur évolution. Saint-Brieuc, Prud'homme & Guyon 1936

167p. illus. Q.

Aubert, P. A.

Équitation des dames. Paris, Gaultier-Laguionie 1842

xii,135p. 20pl. O.
Lipperheide 2936

Aubert & cie

Musée de costumes. Paris, Aubert & cie ca1850-60

444 col.pl. Q.
A series of atlases of colored plates, illustrating costumes of the leading nations: Algérie (61pl.), Allemagne (29pl.), Amérique (27pl.), Belgique & Hollande (14pl.), Espagne et Portugal (37pl.), France (100pl.), Italie (42pl.), Russie (38pl.), Suède, Norwège et Danemark (10pl.), Suisse & Tyrol (26pl.), Turquie, Egypte, Grèce (60pl.)
Illustrated by Compte-Calix, Pingret, Girardet, Belin, Sharles and others. Some of the earlier plates were issued under title *Musée cosmopolite*
Colas 2161. Lipperheide 68

(pub.) Galerie royale de costumes

Auberteuil, Michel René Hilliard d'. See Hilliard d'Auberteuil, Michel René

Auberville, A. Dupont-. See Dupont-Auberville, A.

Aubry, A.

Uniformes et costumes officiels de la 3e République: Service militaire du chemins de fer. Paris, Clavreuil 1909

The first part was planned to be published in ten parts at 5fr. each

Aubry, Charles

Chasses anciennes d'après les manuscrits des XIVe & XVe siècles 1837. Paris. Chles Motte [1837]

[1]l. 12pl. F.
Lipperheide 3031

Collection des uniformes de l'armée française présentée au Roi par S. E. M. le maréchal duc de Bellune, ministre de la guerre. Paris, Picquet 1823

57pl.(27 col.) F.
Another edition (1823) has 84 colored plates; the 1828 edition (97 col.pl.) has the same plates with thirteen new ones
Colas 177-79

[Cris de Paris] Paris, Genty 1818

13 col.pl. Q.
Plates engraved by C. Naudet, after C. Aubry. For list of plates see Colas's *Bibliographie*
Colas 176

Histoire pittoresque de l'équitation, ancienne et moderne. Paris, C. Motte 1833-34

24pl. F.
Lipperheide 2935

(illus.) Ambert, J. M. J. J. A. J., baron. Esquisses historiques des différents corps qui composent l'armée française. 1835

Aubry, Charles and others

(illus.) Album comique de pathologie pittoresque, recueil de vingt caricatures médicales dessinées par Aubry, Chazal, Colin, Bellangé et Pigal

Aubry, Charles, [and Loeillot, Karl]

[Maison du roi et garde royale (Louis XVIII) Paris, lithogr. de Delpech 1816-17]

20 col.pl. Q.
Uniforms from the beginning of the second restoration, 1816-17
Colas 175

Aubry, Félix

Rapport sur les dentelles, les blondes, les tulles et les broderies, fait à la commission française du jury international de l'exposition universelle de Londres. Paris, Imprimerie Impériale [1854]

158p. O.
Lipperheide 4024

Aubry, Petrus

Effigies omnium legatorum, deputatorum, consiliariorum, qui pacem universalem monasterij anno salutis 1648 nomine suorum principalium, pontificis, imperatoris, regum, principum, rerum publicarum, partim mediati sunt, partim concluserunt et subscripserunt. Argentorati, P. Aubry ca1655

93pl. Q.
Plates are after portraits by Anselm van Hulle and only ten show variations from those in Hulle's *Pacis* and *Les hommes illustres*
Lipperheide 535

Aucupatorium Herodiorum. Hicfelt, Eberhard

Audebrand, Philibert and others. See Autrefois; ou, Le bon vieux temps, types français du dix-huitième siècle

Audebrand, Philibert; Beauvoir, Roger de, and La Bédollière, Émile Gigaut de

Les Français sous Louis XIV et Louis XV. Paris, Challamel 185-?

316p. illus. col.pl. Q.

Audeoud, Alfred

Notre armée; [illus.] par Eric de Coulon. Genève, Atar [1915]

41p. 20 illus.(ports.) 40 col.pl. F.

Audot, Louis Eustache

L'Italie, la Sicile, les Iles Éoliennes, l'Ile d'Elbe, la Sardaigne, Malte, l'Ile de Calypso, etc ... Sites, monumens, scènes et costumes. Recueillis et publiés par Audot père. Paris, Audot 1834-37

6v. pl. O.
Contains many good engravings which show costume of various regions
Contents: v 1 Toscane, by Saint-Germain Leduc; v2 Royaume de Naples, by C. D. de La Chavanne; v3 Rome, by D. D. Farjasse; v4 Venise, Milan, Royaume-Lombardo-Venitien et états voisins, by Hyp. Hostein rev. by Alexandre Duchesne; v5 Piémont, Sardaigne, Simplon, by Hyp. Hostein

Audsley, George Ashdown

Colour harmony in dress. New York, McBride 1922

132p. diagrs. D.
The American edition of *Colour in dress*
LC 23-3156

Colour in dress; a manual for ladies on all matters connected with the proper selection and harmonious combination of colours suitable for the various complexions. Based on the indisputable phenomena of colour. London, S. Low, Marston and co. 1912

132p. 2 diagr. D.
Colas 180. LC 13-13134

Auerswald, Fabian von

Ringer kunst: fünff und achtzig stücke. Wittemberg, H. Lufft 1539

85 illus. Q.
Full-page woodcuts by Lucas Cranach show wrestlers in sixteenth century costume
Two facsimile editions have been published: (Berlin, 1887 edited by Ernst Wasmuth) also, with introduction by K. Wassmansdorf (Leipzig, M. G. Priber 1869 47pl.)

Auf deutschlands hohen schulen. Fick, Richard, ed.

Aufgedeckete rosztäuscherkunst. See Eisenberg, Baron d'. La perfezione e i difetti del cavallo

Das **aufkommen** der pulverwaffe. Rathgen, Bernhard

Augrand, Parfait

Métiers féminins. Paris, Tessari ca1810

20 col.pl. F.
Plates are engraved by Augrand after his designs and those of G. Busset, Coeuré, Dubrusle, and Duthé
Colas 181

Augsburg. See subdivision Augsburg under Germany—By region or province—Bavaria; Military costume—Germany—Bavaria

Augsburger waffenschmiede. Boeheim, Wendelin

Augsburgische kleider tracht. See Engelbrecht, Martin. La mode d'Augsbourg

Augspurgische kleider tracht. Augsburg, P. D. Danner ca1720
20 col.pl. O.
Colas 182. Lipperheide 766m

Ausspriiche der heiligen schrift und der kirchenväter über kleiderpracht und moden zur warnung und belehrung gesammelt. Lohmann, Hermann

Augusta quinque Carolorum historia ... Carolo VI. Pichler, Le P. Joseph

Augusta Vindelicorum. Grimm, Simon

Le **auguste** alleanze fra le case sovrane di Savoia e di Baviera nei secolo XV, XVII, XVIII. Promis, Vincenzo

Les **augustes** representations de tous les rois de France depuis Pharamond, jusqu'à Louys XIIII. Larmessin, Nicolas

Augusti corona augustissima Augustae coronata. Leucht, C. L.

Augustin, Felix Paul
(tr.) Velde, T. H. van de. Die frauenkleidung

Augustinian canons. See Canons (Members of chapters)

Augustissimorum imperatorum. Schrenck von Nozing, Jacob

Aujourd'hui; journal des modes ridicules et d'annonces illustrées, dessinées par Gérard-Fontallard. 1838-1841. Paris, Hautecoeur-Martinet
78 col.pl. ob.Q.
Edited by H. Gérard-Fontallard
Colas 1228

Aula veneris. Hollar, Wenceslaus

Aureli, Aurelio
La gloria d'amore; spettacolo festivo fatto rappresentare dal ... Duca di Parma sopra l'acque della gran peschiera novamente fatta nel suo giardino. Parma, Stampa ducale 1690
30p. 15pl. Q.
Lipperheide 2753

Aurelius, Cornelius. See Die cronycke van Hollant, Zeelant, ende Vrieslant (supposed author)

Aurevilly, Jules Amédée, Barbey d'. See Barbey d'Aurevilly, J. A.

Arouze, J.
Le costume en Provence, à propos de l'ouvrage récent de Jules Charles Roux. Avignon, F. Seguin 1908
15p. D.
Colas 183

Aus allen weltteilen. See note under Globus

Aus altrömischer zeit. Simons, Theodor

Aus dem alten Rom. Lambert, André

Aus dem inneren leben der zigeuner. Wlislocki, Heinrich von

Aus könig Friedrich's zeit, kriegs- und friedens-helden. Menzel, A. F. E. von

Aus pharmazeutischer vorzeit in bild und wort. Peters, Hermann

Aus Rom und Byzanz. Danz, A. H. E.

Auserlesene griechische vasenbilder. Gerhard, Eduard

Auserlesenes blumen-zeichen-buch für frauenzimmer. Knorr, G. W.

Ausführliche beschreibung der feierlichkeiten bei gelegenheit der ... dem könige Friedrich Wilhelm III ... zu Königsberg in Preussen 1798 geleisteten erbhuldigung; nach den akten ... herausgegeben von der königl. deutschen gesellschaft. Königsberg, Hartungschen büchdrukkerei n.d.
214p. O.
Lipperheide 2532m

Ausführliche beschreibung des- zu Bayreuth im september 1748 vorgegangenen ... beylagers. Schönhaar, W. F.

Ausführliche geschichte aller geistlichen und weltlichen kloster und ritterorden. See Hélyot, Pierre. Histoire des ordres monastiques, religieux et militaires

Das **Ausland.** See note under Globus

Aus'm Weerth, Ernst. See Weerth, Ernst aus'm

Der **ausruf** in Hamburg. Suhr, Christoffer

Ausruffende personen in Nürnberg. See Gabler, Ambrosius. Nürnberger ausrufer

Aussführlich beschreibung der königlich-böheimischen Crönungen ... Caroli VI Römischen Kaysers ... und ... Elizabethae Christinae ... so geschehen den 5. und 8. Sept. 1723 in Prag. Augspurg, J. C. Kolb [1723]
8 l. 1 pl. Q.
Lipperheide 2627

Aussführlicher bericht von ankunfft zunehmen gesatzen regirung und jam̃erlichen absterben Mechmeti I. See Acta Mechmeti I

Aussfürliche und warhaffte beschreibung des durchlauchtigsten ... herrn Christians, des vierden dieses namens, zu Dennemark, norwegen ... königes ... zu Koppenhagen den 29. augusti anno 1596 glücklich ... krönung. Erich, Augustus

Australia. Department of defence. Clothing factory
Report. [Melbourne]
Published annually. First published 1912-13
LC (15-6836)

Australia
Carpenter, F. G. Australia, New Zealand and some islands of the South Seas. 1924
Shoberl, Frédéric, ed. The Asiatic Islands and New Holland. 1824

See also subdivision Australia under Military costume; Naval costume

Native races

Angas, G. F. South Australia illustrated. 1847

Bonwick, James. Daily life and origin of the Tasmanians. 1870

Bonwick, James. The last of the Tasmanians. 1870

Calvert, A. F. The aborigines of western Australia. 1894

Australia—Native races—*Continued*
Dawson, James. Australian aborigines, the languages and customs of several tribes of aborigines in the western district of Victoria, Australia. 1881
Melville, H. S. Sketches in Australia and the adjacent islands. ca1850

Australia, New Zealand and some islands of the South Seas. Carpenter, F. G.

Australian aborigines. Dawson, James

Austrasiae reges et duces epigrammatis. Clément, Nicolas, de Treille

Austria. Kriegsministerium
Uniformen distinctions- und sonstige abzeicher der gesammten k.k. osterr.-ungar. wehrmacht sowie orden' und ehrenzeichen Oesterreich-Ungarns. 2. aufl. Troppau, Aug. Strasilla 1887
61p. 24 col.pl. D.

Austria. Laws, statutes, etc.
Constitutio criminals Theresiana, oder Der Römisch-kaiserl. zu Hungarn und Böheim ... Königl. Apost. Majestät Mariä Theresiä, erzherzogin zu Oesterreich ... Peinliche gerichtsordnung. Wien, Gedruckt bey J. T. edlen von Trattnern 1769
282,lvi p. incl. 16 plates (part fold.) F.
Latin summary of paragraphs in margin. The plates (mostly printed on both sides) are illustrations of instruments of torture and their application
Lipperheide 2012. LC 30-23452

Austria
For material on the period 1867 to 1919 this subject includes Austria-Hungary

Hammerstein, Hans von. Trachten der Alpenländer. 1937
Kellner, Leon; Arnold, Mme Paula, and Delisle, A. L. Austria of the Austrians and Hungary of the Hungarians. 1914
Masner, Carl. Die costüm-ausstellung im K.K. Oesterreichischen museum 1891. 1892-93
Scheurer, J. E. Wiener-costume vom mittel-alter bis zur gegenwart. 1890

See also Illyria; Tyrol; also subdivision Austria under Ceremonial and festival costume; Coronations and coronation robes; Embroidery; Lace; Military costume; Nobles; Shooting costume; Theatrical costume; Uniforms, Civil; Weddings and wedding dress

Caricature and satire

Grand-Carteret, John. Les moeurs et la caricature en Allemagne—en Autriche —en Suisse. 1885

13th century

Camesina, Albert. Die ältesten glasgemälde des chorherren-stiftes Klosterneuburg und die bildnisse der Babenberger in der Cistercienser-abtei Heiligenkreuz. 1857

16th century

Käysserliche freyhaitten d schneyder und ab cunderfectur irer matteri auf allerley stuck zue endwerffen und zue sagen &c. 1590

18th century

Arnold, C. F. Die vertreibung der Salzburger protestanten und ihre aufnahme bei den glaubensgenossen. 1900
Höchle, illus. Hauptmomente aus dem leben Sr. majestät Franz I. kaisers von Oesterreich, apostol. königs. 1835-1836
Schwarz, Ignaz, ed. Wiener strassenbilder im zeitalter des rokoko; die Wiener ansichten von Schultz, Ziegler, Janscha, 1779-1798. 1914
Will, J. M., engr. Samlung europaeischer national trachten. ca1780

19th century

Adam, Jacques. Bildungen des gemeinen volks zu Wien: Les portraits du commun peuple à Vienne. ca1790
Alexander, William. Picturesque representations of the dress and manners of the Austrians. 1813
Bertrand de Moleville, A. F., marquis de. The costume of the hereditary states of the house of Austria. 1804
Dopler, J. and Müller, C. Vollständige bildliche darstellung der gesammten löblichen uniformirten bürgerschaft der K. auch K. K. haupt- und residenzstadt Wien nach dem neuesten costume 1806. [1806]
Eyriès, J. B. B. L'Autriche, ou Costumes, moeurs et usages des Autrichiens. ca1821
Gaul, Franz. Österreichisch-ungarische national-trachten. 1881-88
Gross-Hoffinger, A. J. Wien wie es ist. 1847
Heksch, A. F. Die Donau von ihrem ursprung bis an die mündung. Eine schilderung von land und leuten des Donaugebietes. 1881
Kininger, V. G. Costumes des différentes nations composant les états héréditaires de S.M. et R. ca1821
Kininger, V. G. Kleidertrachten der kaiserl. könig,staaten. Habillemens des états de S. M. l'Empereur roi. ca1830
Die Österreichisch-ungarische monarchie in wort und bild. 1886-1902
Pelcoq, Jules. Souvenir de l'Exposition universelle de Vienne. 1873
Selb, August, and Tischbein, A. Memoire di un viaggio pittorico nel littorale Austriaco. 1842
Serres, Marcel de. L'Autriche, ou Moeurs, usages et costumes des habitans de cet empire. 1821
Shoberl, Frédéric. Austria (World in miniature) 1823
XVII vorstellungen von deutschen nationaltrachten. 1800
Trollope, Mrs F. M. Vienna and the Austrians. 1838
Wienerstadt, lebensbilder aus der gegenwart. 1895

Caricature and satire

Moser, J. B. Das Wiener volksleben, in komischen scenen mit eingelebten liedern. 1842-44

Austria—19th century—*Continued*

Periodicals

Allgemeine theaterzeitung und originalblatt für kunst, literatur, musik, mode und geselliges leben. 1806-56

Die Elegante. 1842-71

Iris; illustrirte blätter für mode, haushaltung und praktisches leben. 1849-65

Die Wiener elegante. 1842-67

Wiener hausfrauen-zeitung. 1875-1907

Wiener mode. 1887+

Wiener zeitschrift für kunst, litteratur, theater und mode. 1816-48

20th century

Haberlandt, Michael. Textile volkskunst aus Österreich. 1912

Mitton, G. E. Austria-Hungary. 1914

Periodical

Wiener hausfrauen-zeitung. 1875-1907

BY REGION OR PROVINCE

Das Kaiser-Album. Viribus unitis. 1858

Schedler, J. G. Nationaltrachten von Tirol und Vorarlberg. ca1824

Trachten-album, nach der natur gezeichnet und lithogr. von Ranftl. Kollarz, Gerasch, Kaliwoda, etc. ca1860

Valerio, Théodore. Souvenirs du Tyrol, du Vorarlberg et de la Haute Bavière ... Erinnerungen von Tyrol Vorarlberg und Ober Baiern. 1842

Salzburg

See Masks—Salzburg

Styria

Kaiser, Eduard. 38 Steirmark's nationaltrachten und fest-anzüge jetztiger und vergangener zeit. ca1820

Vienna

See Street venders—Austria—Vienna

Austria of the Austrians and Hungary of the Hungarians. Kellner, Leon; Arnold, Mme Paula, and Delisle, A. L.

Austria-Hungary. See Austria; Hungary; also subdivision Austria under Military costume; Naval costume

Austria, Lower. Kammer für handel, gewerbe und industrie, Vienna

Lehr- und lesebuch für männer- und frauenkleidermacher. Wien, Handels und gewerbekammer 1880
798p. illus. 38pl. O.
Colas 1822. Lipperheide 3821

Austria s. r. imperii conjux. Leucht, C. L.

Auswahl böhmischer nationalstickerei. See Koula, Jan. Výběr národního českého vyšívání

Eine **auswahl** merkwürdiger gegenstände aus der königl. sächsischen rüstkammer. Reibisch, F. M. von

An **authentic** history of the coronation of His Majesty, King George the Fourth. Huish, Robert

Authenticated tartans of the clans and families of Scotland. Painted by machinery. With map of the Highlands, showing the territories of the clans. Mauchline, W. and A. Smith [1850]
161p. 69 col.pl. map. Q.
LC 2-2196

Authentische und vollständige beschreibung aller feyerlichkeiten, welche in dem hannoverschen lande bey der anwesenheit ... Georgs des vierten während dem monate october 1821 veranstaltet worden sind. Dittmer, Heinrich

Automobile costume. See Motoring costume

Autour de la table; album de l'histoire des modes françaises: Johannot, Valentin, Janet-Lange, Forest, Cham, Fragonard, etc. 110 dessins. Paris, Garnier [1851]
54p. 50pl. Q.
Plates show groups of people
Colas 184

L'**autre** France (Tunisie, Algérie, Maroc). Archinard, L. Q.

Un **autre** monde. Grandville, J. I. I. G., called

Autrefois; ou, Le bon vieux temps, types français du dixhuitième siècle; texte par Ph. Audebrand [et autres] Vignettes par MM. Tony Johannot, Th. Fragonard, Gavarni, Ch. Jacques, Ch. Marville et Émile Wattier. Paris, Challamel [1842]
316p. illus. col.pl. Q.
Originally issued in 40 parts
Colas 185. Lipperheide 1135. LC 2-13305

L'**Autriche.** Eyriès, J. B. B.

L'**Autriche.** Serres, Marcel de

Auvergne. See France—By region or province—Auvergne

Auvergne, Puy-de-Dôme. Talbot, ed.

Aux héros polonais. Heideloff, K. A. von

Avancinus, Nicolas

Imperium Romano-Germanicum, sive Quinquaginta imperatorum ac Germaniæ regum elogia, imperatori Leopoldo ab Universitate Viennensi oblata. Viennæ Austriæ, M. Cosmerovij 1663
487p. 50pl. illus.(ports.) Q.
Lipperheide 713

Leopoldi Guilielmi, Archiducis Austriae ... virtutes. Antverpiae, B. Moreti 1665
309p. illus. 3pl. Q.
Leopold lived from 1614 to 1662
Lipperheide 854

Avanda, Jim

[Costumes espagnols. Paris, Londres, La Haye, Berlin, Goupil; New York, M. Knoedler] 1876
5pl. F.
Plates signed by the artist, Valencia, 1876
Colas 186

Avary, Mrs Myrta (Lockett)

Dixie after the war; an exposition of social conditions existing in the South, during the twelve years succeeding the fall of Richmond ... Illus. from old paintings, daguerreotypes and rare photographs. New York, Doubleday, Page 1906
435p. front. pl. ports. O.
LC 6-29042

Aveelen, Jan van den
(engr.) Dahlberg, E. J. Suecia antiqua et hodierna

Avenarius, Toni
Historischer festzug veranstaltet bei der feier der vollendung des Kölner domes am 16. October 1880. ⌊Köln, Warnitz 1881⌋
8 l. 29 col.pl. F.
Lipperheide 2814

See also Weerth, Ernst aus'm, ed. Der mosaikboden in St Gereon zu Cöln

Avenel, Georges d'
Le mécanisme de la vie moderne; 4. série: L'habillement féminin. Paris, A. Colin 1902
416p. O.
Lipperheide 582e

L'**Avenir**, revue politique, littéraire et des modes. Nos. 1-10, 20 decembre 1841-31 mars 1842. Paris, E. Brière
Editor in chief: H. Bonnellier
Colas 187

Avery, Elroy McKendree
A history of the United States and its people, from their earliest records to the present time. Cleveland, The Burrows brothers company 1904-10
7v. col.fronts. illus.(part col.) pl.(part fold.) ports.(part col.) maps(part fold.) plans(part fold.) facsims.(part fold.) Q.
Bibliographical appendix at end of each volume
On title page of v 1 "in twelve volumes"; on title page of v2-4, "in fifteen volumes"; on title page of v5-7, "in sixteen volumes". No more published
A *Complete index* is available (Tarrytown, N.Y. W. Abbatt 1915. 106 l. Q.)
Costume index. LC 4-32329

Avis important au sexe. Reisser

Avis très-important au public. Dôffémont

Avril, Paul
(illus.) Uzanne, L. O. L'éventail
(illus.) Uzanne, L. O. The fan
(illus.) Uzanne, L. O. L'ombrelle, le gant, le manchon

Axon, William Edward Armitage. See Procter, R. W. The barber's shop

Azerbaijan. See Russia—Azerbaijan

Aznar y García, Francisco
Indumentaria española, documentos para su estudio desde la época visigoda hasta nuestros dias; obra subvencionada por el Ministerio de fomento y premiada en la Exposicion de bellas artes de 1881. Doscientas ochenta y ocho estampas, la mayor parte al cromo, reproduccion de los códices, cuadros, estátuas, estampas raras, muebles, armas, etc., que se conservan en España. 2. ed. Madrid, Administracion ⌊1881⌋
3p.l. 96pl.(part col.) F.
Volume I only, issued in 48 "entregas"; projected second and third volumes (48 "entregas" each) were never published
LC 33-22393

Aztecs
Arnold, Channing, and Frost, F. J. T. The American Egypt; record of travel in Yucatan. 1909
Biart, Lucien. The Aztecs. 1887
Biart, Lucien. Les Aztèques. 1885
Brasseur de Bourbourg, C. É. Histoire des nations civilisées du Mexique et de l'Amérique-Centrale, durant les siècles antérieurs à Christophe Colomb. 1857-59
Cortés, Hernando. Historia de Nueva-España. 1770
Durán, Diego. Historia de las Indias de Nueva-España y islas de Tierra Firme. 1867-80
Hoffmann, Anton. Die eroberung von Mexiko durch Ferdinand Cortez 1519-1521. 1922
Humboldt, Alexander, freiherr von. Vues des Cordillères, et monumens des peuples indigènes de l'Amérique. 1810
Kingsborough, E. K., viscount. Antiquities of Mexico. 1830-48
Peñafiel, Antonio. Monumentos del arte mexicano antiguo. 1890

See also subdivision Aztecs under Gods; Masks—Indians of America

The **Aztecs.** Biart, Lucien

Les **Aztèques.** Biart, Lucien

B

B., E.
(comp.) Collection d'éventails anciens des XVIIe et XVIIIe siècles, d'après éventails authentiques Louis XIV, Louis XV, Louis XVI. Paris, 1890
80pl. ob.F.

B., J. L. See Saultereau, Anthoine, comp. Chronologie et sommaire des souverains pontifes, anciens pères, empereurs, roys, princes

B., T. L. See Busby, Thomas Lord

Baader, Joseph
Die fehde des Hanns Thomas von Absberg wider den schwäbischen bund; ein beitrag zur culturgeschichte des sechszehnten jahrhunderts. München, Max Kellerer 1880
128p. 23 col.pl. Q.
Lipperheide 2101

Bab, Julius
Das theater der gegenwart; geschichte der dramatischen bühne seit 1870. Leipzig, J. J. Weber 1928
247p. 78 illus.(incl.ports.) O. (Illustrierte theatergeschichtliche monographien. bd 1)
"Quellennachweis": p⌊231⌋-33
LC 34-18900

Babelon, Ernest Charles François
Catalogue des bronzes antiques de la Bibliothèque nationale. See entry under Paris. Bibliothèque nationale

Baber, Edward Colborne
Travels and researches in the interior of China. London, Royal geographical society 1886
201p. illus. pl. maps, plans, tables. O. (Supplementary papers v 1)

Babies. See Children

Baby; eine zeitschrift für mütter. Hrsg. Frau Kath. John. 1.-2. jahrg. 1899-1900. Berlin & Leipzig, C. Messer 1899-1900
2v. illus. O.
Published fortnightly
Merged with *Kinder-modenwelt* 1900

Baby, an illustrated magazine for mothers. See Lloyd's magazine

Babylonia
Botta, P. E. Monument de Ninive. 5v. 1850

British museum. Department of Egyptian and Assyrian antiquities. A guide to the Babylonian and Assyrian antiquities. 1908

Hommel, Fritz. Geschichte Babyloniens und Assyriens. 1885-88

Lutz, H. F. Textiles and costumes among the peoples of the ancient Near east. 1923

Perrot, Georges, and Chipiez, Charles. A history of art in Chaldaea & Assyria. 1884

Porter, Sir R. K. Travels in Georgia, Persia, Armenia, ancient Babylonia, &c. &c. during the years 1817, 1818, 1819, and 1820. 1821-22

Reimpell, Walter. Geschichte der babylonischen und assyrischen kleidung. 1921

See also Irak

Baca, Francisco Martínez. See Martínez Baca, Francisco

Bach, Emilie
Muster stilvoller handarbeiten für schule und haus. Wien, R. V. Waldheim 1879-81
2v. 285 illus. Q.
Volume 1 was issued also in a third edition (1883. 125p. 146 illus.)
Lipperheide 4124-25

Neue muster in altem stil. Dornach, T. de Dillmont [1894]
3v. 202 illus. Q.
Lipperheide 4173

Bach, Volkmar
Die angriffswaffen in den altfranzösischen Artus- und abenteuer-romanen. Marburg, N. G. Elwert 1887
58p. O. (Ausgaben und abhandlungen aus dem gebiete der romanischen philologie . . . 70)
Published also as the author's inaugural dissertation, Marburg, 1887
"Verzeichnis der vorliegender abhandlung zu grunde gelegten texte": p[3]-4
LC 22-18513

Bacha, Eugène
(ed.) Brussels. Bibliothèque royale de Belgique. Section des manuscrits. Les très belles miniatures de la Bibliothèque royale de Belgique

The **bachelor's** own book. Cruikshank, George

Bacher, Moritz
Trachtenpavillon der Berliner gewerbe-ausstellung 1896; ein jahrhundert der mode 1796-1896. Berlin, M. Bacher 1896
2 l. 20pl. Q.
Colas 2904. Lipperheide 582

Bachiller y Morales, Antonio
Coleccion de artículos; tipos y costumbres de la isla de Cuba. Primera serie. Habana, M. de Villa 1881
255p. pl.(part.col.) F.
Illustrated by Victor Patricio de Landaluze

Bachou, Jean
(tr.) Boodt, A. B. de. Le parfait ioaillier

Bachoué, E. Lostalot-. See Lostalot-Bachoué, E.

The **back** blocks of China. Jack, R. L.

Backhouse, Edmund. See Bland, J. O. P., jt. auth.

Backman, Gustaf
(tr.) Costumes nationaux des provinces de la Suède

Backmanson, H.
L'empereur Nicolas Alexandrovitch en tenue de 10 régiments dont sa majesté est chef. Saint-Pétersbourg, P. Paetz n.d.
10 col.pl. F.
Descriptive notes in Russian and French
Colas 188

[**Backus, Mary**]
(ed.) Siam and Laos, as seen by our American missionaries. Philadelphia, Presbyterian board of publication [1884]
552p. incl.front.(port.)illus. fold.map. D.
LC 5-6169

Bacle, César Hippolyte
(pub.) Trages y costumbres de la provincia de Buenos Aires

Bacqueville de la Potherie, Claude Charles Le Roy
History of the savage peoples who are allies of New France (In Blair, E. H., ed. Indian tribes of the upper Mississippi valley and region of the Great lakes)

Badelló, Francisco. See Costums de Catalunya

Baden. See Germany—By region or province—Baden; also subdivision Baden under Ceremonial and festival costume

Badenia, oder, Das badische land und volk; eine zeitschrift für vaterländische geschichte und landeskunde mit karten, lithographien und colorierten abbildungen und landestrachten. Jahrg. 1-3; 1839-1844. Karlsruhe & Freiburg, Herder 1839-44
3v. 54pl.(9 col.) O.
The colored plates show folk dress of Baden
Colas 189. Lipperheide 745

Badenia, oder Das badische land und volk; [neue folge] bd. 1-2 Heidelberg, A. Emmerling 1859-62
2v. illus. pl. O.
Some of the plates were published later in Bader's *Badische volkssitten*
Colas 189. Lipperheide 746

Badenia; zeitschrift des vereins für badische ortsbeschreibung; erster band. Heidelberg, A. Emmerling 1864
393p. 1 pl. O.
Lipperheide 747

Bader, Joseph
Badische volkssitten und trachten. Karlsruhe, Kunstverlag 1843-44
24 l. 28pl. (12 col.) O.
Some of the plates have appeared previously in the periodical *Badenia*
Colas 190. Lipperheide 748

Badges of honor. See Decorations of honor

Badía, Francisco Miquel y. See Miquel y Badía, Francisco

Badische landestrachten im auftrage des grossherzog. badischen handelsministeriums. Gleichauf, R.

Badische uniformen 1807 und 1809. Rosenberg, Marc

Badische volkssitten und trachten. Bader, Joseph

Badische volks-trachten. Freiburg ca1870
16 col.pl. S.
Lipperheide 752

Der **badische** wehrstand. Schreiber, Guido

Baerland, Adriaan van
Hollandiae comitum historia et icones: cum selectis scholiis ad lectoris lucem. Eiusdem Barlandi Caroli Burgundiae ducis vita. Item Ultraiectensium episcoporum catalogus et res gestae. Eiusdem argumenti libellus Gerardo Noviomago auctore. Lugduni Batavorum, C. Plantini 1584
127,31p. illus.(ports.) tab. F.
Running title *Hollandiae et Zelandiae comitum*
"Had. Barlandi Traiectensium episcoporum catalogus et eorum res gestae" has special title-page, and separate pagination
Reproduces the portraits in Vosmer's *Princepes* up to Herzog Johann von Bayern and King Philip II
Lipperheide 924

Baerle, Kaspar van
Marie de Medicis, entrant dans Amsterdam; ou, Histoire de la reception faicte à la reyne mère du roy tres-Chrestien, par les bourgmaistres & bourgeoisie de la ville d'Amsterdam; tr. du Latin de Gaspar Barleus. Amsterdam, J. & C. Blaev 1638
97p. 1 illus. 17pl. F.
An edition in Latin, with title *Medicea hospes*, and also one in French, were published at the same time
Lipperheide 2665

Bäseler, Gerda
Die kaiserkrönungen in Rom und die Römer von Karl dem Grossen bis Friedrich II. (800-1220). Freiburg im Breisgau [etc.] Herder 1919
xiv,135p. O.
"Literatur": p ix-xiii
"Tabelle der kaiserkrönungen": p128-30
LC 33-39504

Bäuerle, Adolf
(ed.) Gallerie drolliger und interessanter scènen der Wiener-bühnen. Wien, Büreau der theaterzeitung 1827-28
2v. 50 col.pl. Q.
Colas 247. Lipperheide 3214

Bagensky, Carl Heinrich Leopold von, and Klaatsch, K. H.
Das Preussische infanterie-gewehr; 2. verm. aufl. Berlin, E. W. Starck 1820
139p. illus. 3pl. O.
Lipperheide 2405

Bagge, Göran
Armée suédoise. Paris, L. Baschet [1887]
3v. 24 col.illus. O. (Cahiers d'enseignement illustrés, no35-37)
Illustrations by Gustave Bagge
Lipperheide 2286

Bagge, Gustave
(illus.) Bagge, Göran. Armée suédoise
(illus.) Dally, Aristide. L'armée danoise
(illus.) Dally, Aristide. L'armée norvégienne

La **bague** en France à travers l'histoire. Deloche, Maximin

Baïf, Lazare de
De re vestiaria libellus ex Bayfio excerptus: addita vulgaris linguae interpretatione, in adolescêtulorû gratiam atq. utilitatem. Parisiis, officina Rob. Stephani 1535
66p. O.
Part 2 of Lazari Baysii *Annotationes* listed below
Also published (Parisiis, A. Girault 1535)
Other editions published Paris, London and elsewhere, 1536-1542, are listed by Colas
Colas 191-92

Lazari Bayfii annotationes in l. II. De captivis, et postliminio reversis. In quibus tractatur de re navali. Eiusdem annotationes in tractatum De auro & argẽto leg. quibus, vestimentorũ, & vasculorum genera explicantur. Antonii Thylesii De coloribus libellus, à coloribus vestium non alienus. Parisiis, officina Rob. Stephani 1536
168,203,13p. illus. O.
Edited by Charles Estienne
First edition, 1526. Another edition (Basil, H. Frobenius & N. Episcopium 1541)
Three parts issued with this title: pt [1] *De re navali* (168p.) pt[2] *De re vestiaria* (p[1]-105) pt3 *De vasculis* (p107-203) Index [13]p. at end
Lipperheide 99. LC 13-3362

Baierische volkstrachten. Rheinwald, J. L. C.

Les **baigneurs.** Daumier, H. V.

Baikie, James
The sea-kings of Crete. With 32 full-page illustrations from photographs. London, A. and C. Black 1910
xiv,273p. 32pl.(incl.front.) map, fold. plan. O.
Bibliography: p262-63
LC A10-1400

Baillie-Grohman, William Adolph
The land in the mountains; being an account of the past & present of Tyrol, its people and its castles. Illustrated with eighty-two plates and maps of modern Tyrol and ancient Raetia. London, Simpkin, Marshall, Hamilton, Kent; Philadelphia, J. B. Lippincott 1907
xxxi,288p. (incl.facsim.) col.front. 80(i.e. 59)numb.pl.(incl.ports., plans) 2 double maps. O.
Plates accompanied by guard sheets with descriptive letterpress. "Introduction, by Charles Landis, giving an account of the author's personality and life"
LC 7-31993

(ed.) Maximilian I, emperor of Germany. Das jagd-buch kaiser Maximilians I

Bailliot, Marcel
Du détatouage; différent procédés de destruction des tatouages. Paris, Steinheil 1894
41p. O.

Baily, J. T. Herbert

Napoleon, illustrated with prints from contemporary and other portraits. London, Pub. by the Connoisseur magazine 1908

126p. front.illus. ports.(part col.) Q.
LC 12-21860

Baĭsutov, Nikolaĭ Ivanovich

Tam gde rastet khlopok; kak zhivut i chem promyshliaiut uzbeki. Moskva, Izd-vo "Rabotnik Prosveshcheniia" 1927

64p. illus. 40k.
On the dress of Turkoman women of Stavropol

V peschanykh stepiakh. Kak zhivut i chem promyshliaiut turkmeny. Moskva, Izd-vo "Rabotnik Prosveshcheniia 1927g

49p. illus. 35k.
Showing Turkomans of middle Asia

V strane samykh bol'shikh morozov; kak zhivut i chem promyshliaiut iakuty; oblozhka V. Berga. Moskva, Izd-vo "Rabotnik Prosveshcheniia" 1928

64p. illus. 25k.
On the Iakuty tribe of Eastern Siberia

Baker, Mrs Blanch (Merritt)

Dramatic bibliography; an annotated list of books on the history and criticism of the drama and stage and on the allied arts of the theatre. New York, The H. W. Wilson company 1933

xvi,320p. O.
List of books on costume p98-121, including a list of customers and rental companies. Make-up p122-23. Dance and dancers p132-36
Contents: pt 1 Drama and theatre; pt II Production and stagecraft; pt III Pageantry, religious drama, entertainment; pt IV Anthologies, bibliographies, directories
LC 33-3167

Baker, Sir Richard

A chronicle of the kings of England from the time of the Romans government unto the death of King James ... with a continuation to ... King George the First. London, S. Ballard 1730

11 l. 918p. 1 pl. F.
Earlier editions: to the reign of Charles I (London, D. Frere 1643. 4v). Thru the first thirteen years of Charles II (London 1674. 23 l. 772p. reprinted 1679) Title pages show a Roman, a Saxon, and a Norman. The last two editions have a portrait of Charles II
Two editions in Dutch were published in 1649. *Cronyke van het leven en hedryff van alle de coningen van Engeland.* (Amsterdam, C. Dankertz 3v. illus. F.) and *Kronyk der koningen van Engeland* (2v.)

Baker, Sir Samuel White

The Nile tributaries of Abyssinia, and the sword hunters of the Hamran Arabs. 4th ed. Philadelphia, J. B. Lippincott 1868

xix,413p. 2 maps (incl.front. 1 fold.) pl. D.
The author travelled from Cairo to Lake Albert Nyanza and gives material on dress, hair-dressing, and the use of perfume, etc. of Arabs and other native peoples
LC 17-9531

Baker, William Henry

A dictionary of men's wear. Cleveland, W. H. Baker 1908

326p. O.
Authorities consulted: p[ix]-x. A general diagram of correct attire, p301. Periods of mourning, p305. Livery chart . . . for city and country, arranged by vehicles p306-307. British peers' robes and coronets p315. Uniforms of famous independent military organizations p316-22
LC 8-34827

Bakst, Léon

L'art décoratif de Léon Bakst; essai critique par Arsène Alexandre; notes sur les ballets par Jean Cocteau. Paris, Brunoff 1913

49p. 95 col.pl. F.
Among the designs represented are Cléopâtre, Schéherazade, Narcisse, Le martyre de S. Sébastien, Hélène de Sparte, Daphnis et Chloë
Colas 193

The designs of Léon Bakst for The sleeping princess. London, Benn 1923

18p. 54 col.pl. F.
Published first in French with title: *L'oeuvre de Léon Bakst pour La belle au bois dormant*
Colas 195, 194

Inedited works of Bakst: Essays on Bakst by Louis Réau, Denis Roche, V. Svietlov and A. Tessier. New York, Brentano 1927

127p. 17 illus.(7 col.) 30pl.(part col.) F.
Published in Paris by G. Lang
Most of the illustrations and plates contain designs for the scenery and costuming of the Russian ballet
Colas 2490

Leon Bakst. Einl. v. Carl Einstein. Berlin, E. Wasmuth [1927]
42p. 42 col.pl. Q.

Synthèse de l'oeuvre du maitre. Paris, 1928

25pl.(20 col.) Q.

About

Inedited works ... essays on Bakst; by L. Réau, and others. 1927

See also Ivchenko, V. I., jt. auth.

Bakst, the story of the artist's life. Levinson, A. I.

[Balachev]

Dessins d'uniformes de l'histoire du regiment de cuirassiers de la garde de S.M. l'Empereur, 1702-1871. St-Pétersbourg, Balachev 1872

25 col.pl. F.
Title and legends also in Russian. Cataloged from Colas
Colas 196

Balaschoff, Pierre de

(tr.) Lange, Gustave. L'armée allemande sous l'empereur Guillaume II

Balbin, Bohuslav

Historia de ducibus ac regibus Bohemiae ... anno MDCLXXXVII, in miscellaneorum historicorum regni Bohemiae, decade 1, libro 7. Vetero-Praga, typis Universitatis Carolo-Ferdinandeae 1735

282p. 56pl. ports. F.
Lipperheide 863

Balch, Edwin Swift
Savage and civilized dress. Philadelphia, 1904
322p. O.
Reprinted from the *Journal* of the Franklin Institute, May 1904

Baldt, Laura Irene
Clothing for women; selection and construction; 8 color plates, 367 illustrations, in text, by M. R. Pritchard and Emily H. Schreiber. Chicago, Philadelphia, J. B. Lippincott company c1935
552p. incl.col.front. illus.(part col.) diagrs. 7 col.pl. O.
First edition 1916. Revised and enlarged 1924, 1929 and 1935
Bibliography: p513-29
LC 35-2178

Balduino, Giacomo
Imagini degl' abiti con cui va vestita la nobilta' della serenis'ma Republica di Venezia. Venezia, L. Ragheno 1702
12pl. F.
These plates are reprinted in Freschot's *La nobilita*
Colas 198. Lipperheide 1328

Balduinus, B. See Baudouin, Benoît

Baldwin, of Luxemburg, abp. and elector of Treves
Die romfahrt Kaiser Heinrich's VII im bildercyclus des Codex Balduini Trevirensis ... erläuternder text ... von dr. Georg Irmer. Berlin, Weidmann 1881
xii,120p. 39pl.(37 col.) Q.
Shows costume of the 14th century
Lipperheide 400

Baldwin, Muriel
Costume 1400-1600: an exhibition in the Spencer room. New York, Public library 1937
p8-14. illus. O.
In New York. Public library, *Bulletin* v41, Jan. 1937

Balearic Islands
Grasset de Saint-Sauveur, André. Voyage dans les îles Baléares et Pithiuses; fait dans les années 1801, 1802, 1803, 1804 et 1805. 1807

Balfour, Sir James, bart.
Ancient heraldic and antiquarian tracts. Edinburgh, T. G. Stevenson 1837
liv,145p. O.
LC 22-5668

Bali
Kat Angelino, P. de. Mudras auf Bali; handhaltungen der priester. 1923
Krause, Gregor, and With, Karl. Bali: volk, land, tänze, feste, tempel. 1926

Balkan home life. Garnett, L. M. J.

Balkan peninsula
Die armeen der Balkan-staaten. 1914
Fox, Frank. The Balkan Peninsula. 1915
Garnett, L. M. J. Balkan home life. 1917
Grasset de Saint-Sauveur, André. Voyage historique, littéraire et pittoresque dans les isles et possessions ci-devant vénitiennes du Levant. 1800
Masner, Carl. Die costüm-ausstellung im k.k. Oesterreichischen museum 1891. 1892-93
Mayer, Ludwig. Views in Turkey, in Europe and Asia comprising Romelia, Bulgaria, Walachia, Syria and Palestine. 1801
Moore, Frederick. The Balkan trail. 1906
Tilke, Max. The costumes of eastern Europe. 1926
Tilke, Max. Osteuropäische volkstrachten in schnitt und farbe. 1925

See also Albania; Bulgaria; Greece; Rumania; Yugoslavia

The **Balkan** trail. Moore, Frederick

Ball, James Dyer
The Chinese at home, or the man of Tong and his land. New York [etc.] Fleming H. Revell 1912
xii,370p. 23pl.(incl.front.) O.
LC A12-304

Things Chinese; being notes on various subjects connected with China. London [etc.] S. Low, Marston, and co. [etc.] 1892
419,xiii p. O.
Dress is described p137-43
LC 1-11150

The **ballad** of Beau Brocade. Dobson, Austin

Il **ballarino.** Caroso, M. F.

Ballassa, Constantin
Die militärische fechtkunst vor dem feinde; eine darstellung der im kriege vorkommenden fechtarten des bajonets gegen bajonet, des säbels gegen den säbel, und der lanze gegen die lanze. Pest, Engel & Mandello 1860
67p. 27pl. Q.
Lipperheide 2991

Le **ballet contemporain.** Ivchenko, V. I., and Bakst, Léon

Ballet profile. Deakin, Irving

Ballet, Russian. See Theatrical costume—Special plays, ballets, etc.—Russian ballet

Ballett und pantomime. Schnackenberg, Walther

Ballhorn, Albert
Das polizei-präsidium zu Berlin. Berlin, Decker 1852
204p. 8 col.pl. O.
Plates show uniforms of the Berlin police from 1787 to 1851
Colas 201

Balli di Sfessania. Callot, Jacques

Ballin, Ada S.
Children's dress. London, W. Clowes 1884
27p. O.
Health and beauty in dress; from infancy to old age. London, J. Flack 1893
xii,244p. illus. O.
A revised edition of *The science of dress*
The science of dress in theory and practice. London, S. Low, Marston, Searle & Rivington 1885
xvi,273p. 28 illus. 8pl.(incl.front) O.
Colas 202. Lipperheide 3292. LC 12-1900

Bals bourgeois. Monta

Bals de l'opéra; costumes du quadrille historique. Paris, Rittner and Goupil [1834]
17 col.pl. F.
Costumes of men and women of the sixteenth to the nineteenth centuries
Colas 203. Lipperheide 3175

Bals masqués de Paris. Paris, Maison Martinet 1835-55
255 col.pl. Q.
Plates show fancy dress and are lithographed by Bertrand, Ed. Morin, A. Lacauchie, Eustache Lorsay, E. Mille and each is marked with the name of one of the following printers: Destouches, Fernique, Godard. Lithographed by Lemercier
Colas notes also a collection of 70 plates on this subject by Lacauchie
Colas 204

Bals masqués de Paris. Paris, Maison Martinet 1859?
15 col.pl. F.
Six plates signed A. Lacauchie, four signed Eustache Lorsay. Probably part of the collection with same title listed above
Colas 204 (part)

Balsan, Auguste
Catalogue de costumes militaires français et étrangers. Paris, H. Leclerc 1909
94p. 1 l. O.
Subtitle: "Recueils, suites, estampes detachees, livres, états et annuaires, aquarelles composant la collection de feu M. A. B. [Auguste Balsan]" Subtitle
Describes 559 works
Colas 550

Baltic states
Carpenter, F. G., and Harmon, Dudley. The British isles and the Baltic states. 1926

Hansen, Gotthard von. Die sammlungen inländischer alterthümer und anderer auf die baltischen provinzen bezüglichen gegenstände des Estländischen provinzial-museums, beschrieben. 1875

Heikel, A. O. Die volkstrachten in den Ostseeprovincen und in Setukesien. 1909

See also Estonia; Latvia; Lithuania

Baluchistan. See India—Baluchistan

Balzac, Honoré de
Paris marié; philosophie de la vie conjugale. Paris, J. Hetzel 1846
84p. front. illus. 20pl. O.
Illustrated by Gavarni
Also published in the series: *Romans du jours illustrés* (Paris, S. Raçon 1851)

Petites misères de la vie conjugale; illus. par Bertall. Paris, Chlendowski [1846]
392p. front. illus. pl. O.
LC 12-11389

Traité de la vie élégante, suivi de la Théorie de la démarche; introduction et notes de Claude Varèze [pseud.] Paris, Éditions Bossard, 1922
193p. front.(port.) D. (Collection des chefs-d'œuvre méconnus no28)
LC 31-19599

See also La grande ville

Balzer, Anton and Walenta, J.
Sammlung der merkwürdigsten städte und festungen, welche in den jahren 1788, 1789 und 1790 von den k.k. österreichischen, und kais. russischen armée der pforte abgenommen worden, nach ihrer wahren lage. Prag, Widtmann 1790
2v. 35 col.pl. F.
Colas 205. Lipperheide 2113

Balzer, Johann
87 abbildungen bömischer und mährischer gelehrten und künstler. Prag, mit von Schönfeldischen schriften [1773]
19p. 87pl. Q.
Lipperheide 872

Neueste Pariser moden, bestehend aus 103 verschiedenen frisuren und frauenzimmer aufsätzen, wie auch 72 figuren, von verschiedenen kleidertrachten für kavaliers und damen. No place, ca1780
1 l. 92pl. Q.
Colas 206

Schema der kaisl. königl. armee. No place, 1784
127 col.pl. D.
Cataloged from Ridder's *Catalogue* where a list of the plates is also given
Colas 207

(engr.) Lens, A. C. Le costume des peuples de l'antiquité prouvé par les monuments

Bambergensis constitutio criminalis
Bambergische halszgerichts und rechtlich ordnung in̄ peinlichen sachen. Meyntz, J. Schöffer 1531
xliii l. 22 illus. F.
In 1508 three editions were published by Johann Schöffer in Mainz. The criminal code of Bamberg, Bavaria was compiled by Johann von Schwarzenberg and first published in Bamberg in 1507
The illustrations show instruments of punishment, executioners, judges and officials of the law courts. The 1510 edition (Wentz [i.e. Mentz] J. Schöffer) contains 6 woodcuts from Schöffer's edition of Livy (1505) The 1531 edition substitutes for the Livy pictures five new engravings showing judges and court scenes. Three of the new pictures are from the Livy of 1530
Lipperheide 608-9

Bambergensium episcoporum. See Hoffmann, Martin. Annales bambergensis episcopatus

Bambergische halszgerichts und rechtlich ordnung in̄ peinlichen sachen. Bambergensis contitutio criminalis

Bance & Aumont, firm, Paris
(pub.) Coiffures de femmes

Bancroft, Hubert Howe
The native races of the Pacific states of North America. New York, D. Appleton and company 1874-76
5v. illus. fold.maps, fold. tab. O.
Authorities quoted: v 1 p[xvii]-xlix
Contents; v 1 Wild tribes. 1874; v2 Civilized nations. 1875; v3 Myths and languages. 1875; v4 Antiquities. 1875; v5 Primitive history. 1876
LC 7-23985

Band uniforms. See Military costume—England—1914-date—Musicians; Musicians

La **bandiera.** See note under Alfieri, F. F. La picca, e la bandiera

Bandits

Italy

Pinelli, Bartolommeo. Costumi e fatti dei briganti che infestano le compagne degl' Appenini fra Roma e Napoli. 1822

Pinelli, Bartolommeo. Nuova raccolta di cinquanta costumi de' contorni di Roma compresi diversi fatti di briganti. 1823

Bandits—Italy—*Continued*

Pinelli, Bartolommeo. Raccolta de' fatti li più interessanti eseguiti dal Capo Brigante Massaroni per la strada che da Roma, conduce a Napoli, dall' anno 1818, fino al 1822. 1823

Bands of the British army. Gordon, W. J.

Bankel, Johannes Bankel

(engr.) Dowden, Edward. Shakespeare scenes and characters

The **Bankside** costume book for children. Stone, Melicent

Banze, Angela

Der zauber des fleisses; die kunst mit wenig mitteln eine geschmackvolle toilette herzustellen; nebst anleitung zum schnittzeichnen. Wien, Pest, Leipzig, A. Hartleben 1871

239p. 16 illus. 29pl. O. (Deutsche frauenwelt. v8)
Lipperheide 3799

Bapst, Germain

Deux éventails du Musée du Louvre. Paris, Morgand et Fatout 1882

p89-96 2pl. O.
From Société des amis des livres. *Annuaire,* 1881
Lipperheide 1724

Essai sur l'histoire du théatre; La mise en scène, le décor, le costume, l'architecture, l'éclairage, l'hygiène. Paris, Hachette 1893

693p. 53 illus. 32pl. Q. 30fr.
Extraits des rapports du jury international de l'Exposition universelle de 1889
Colas 208. Lipperheide 3232

Das **Bapstum** mit seinen gliedern gemalet und beschrieben. Witteberg, 1563

40 l. 67 illus. O.
See Lipperheide for discussion of authorship. Contains pictures of officials of the church and members of religious brotherhoods. The verses which serve as descriptions sometimes give the color of the costumes pictured
A book with the same title and 74 woodcuts by Hans Sebald Beham, superior to those in the work listed here, was published by Hans Wandereisen in 1526
Lipperheide 1794

Bar, Jacques Charles

Coleccion de los trages de todas las ordenes religiosas y militares de todo el mundo; tr. a de la que publica en frances. [Madrid] ca1790

60 l. 81 col.pl. F.

Mascarades monastiques et religieuses de toutes les nations du globe; représentées par des figures coloriées dans la plus exacte verité, avec l'abrégé historique chronologique et critique de chacque ordre, enrichi de notes sur l'origine de toutes ces pieuses folies; par Giacomo Carlo Rabelli [pseud] Paris, 1793

254p. 26 col.pl. O.
Begun as a revision of the author's *Recueil* listed below. Only this one volume was published
Colas 210. Lipperheide 1873

Receuil de tous les costumes des ordres religieux et militaires, avec un abrégé historique et chronologique enrichi de notes et de planches coloriées. Paris, L'auteur 1778-89

6v. 600 col.pl. F.
Contents: v 1 Costumes religieux et militaires des Mameluks, Arabes, Turcs, Orientaux, etc. v2 Costumes religieux et militaires des peuples de l'Orient, des templiers, des chanoins et chevaliers de la Syrie, de la Palestine d'Egypte, d'Ethiopie, d'Afrique et de l'Inde; v3 Les ordres de chevalerie d'Europe; v4-5 Les ordres monastiques masculins; v6 Les ordres monastiques féminins
Colas 209. Lipperheide 1848

Barado y Font, Francisco

Museo militar: historia del ejercito español armas, uniformes, sistemas de combate, instituciones, organizacion del mismo desdo los tempos más remotos hasta nuestros diâs. Barcelona, Vuida é hijos de E. Ullastres 1889

3v. col.front. 78pl.(part col.) F.
Colas 212

La vida militar en España; cuadros y dibujos de José Cusachs ... texto de Francisco Barado. Barcelona, Tip. de los sucesores de N. Ramirez y C. Pasaje 1888

xi,343p. illus. 24pl. F.
Colas 211

Barbara Uttmann, die begründoun der spitzen-industrie im Erzgebirge. Finck, Emil

Barbault, Jean

12 costumes d'Italie d'aprės les peintures faîtes par Barbault à Rome en 1750, gravées par Léon Gaucherl. Paris, Cadart & Chevalier 1862

12pl. T.
The pictures show members of the papal household and peasant and society women
Colas 213. Lipperheide 1314

Barbeau, Charles Marius

Indian days in the Canadian Rockies. illus. by W. Langdon Kihn. Toronto, Macmillan 1923

207p. col.front. col.ports. O. $3, o.p.
Sources and references: p205-[08]
Costume index. LC 24-3550

Barber, Mrs Mary

Some drawings of ancient embroidery; thirty specimens. London [etc] H. Sotheran 1880

33 l. col.front. 29pl.(26 col.) F.
English ecclesiastical needlework
Lipperheide 3863. LC 12-15126

Barber-surgeons.. See Physicians

Barberi

Costumes de la ville de Nice Maritime. Nice, Société typographiques et L'auteur 1831

10 col.pl. F.
Colas 214. Lipperheide 1197

Barbers

Procter, R. W. The barber's shop. 1883

Barbes du dix-huitième siècle. See Lescure, Alfred. Collection. A. Lescure

Barbey d'Aurevilly, Jules Amédée

The anatomy of dandyism ... translated from the French ... by D. B. Wyndham Lewis. London, P. Davies 1928

xv,84p. illus. pl. O.
Translation of *Du dandysme.* Illustrated by Hermine David

Du dandysme et de G. Brummell. Caen, B. Mancel 1845

118p. S.
Many editions. Also contained in the author's *Oeuvres* v9 (Paris, F. Bernouard 1926)

Barbey d'Aurevilly, Jules A.—*Continued*
Of dandyism and of George Brummell; tr. by Douglas Ainslie. London, J. M. Dent; Boston, Copeland & Day 1897
xxiii,140p. S.
Translation of *Du dandysme*
LC 9-1781

Barbiani, Francesco
Relazione del funerale celebrato nella Chiesa Metropolitana di Milano il giorno 8. febraro 1741; per comando della reale maestà di Maria Teresa, regina d'Ongheria, alla sacra reale cesarea, cata. maestà dell' imperadore Carlo VI, suo padre. Milano, Malatesta 1741?
16 l. 21pl. F.
Lipperheide 2763

Barbié de Bocage, Jean Denis. See Choiseul-Gouffier, M. G. A. F., comte de

Barbier, George
Designs on the dances of Vaslav Nijinsky. Foreword by Francis de Miomandre, tr. from the French by C. W. Beaumont. London, C. W. Beaumont 1913
Illus. pl. Q.

Panorama dramatique: Casanova. Décors et costumes. Paris, Vogel [1921]
6,iv p. 24 col.pl. O.
In portfolio. Settings and costumes for Maurice Rostand's play Casanova
Reprinted (Paris, Jules Meynial. 140fr)
Colas 215

Vingt-cinq costumes pour le théâtre; préface par Edmond Jaloux. Paris, C. Block & J. Meynial 1927
24p. 25 col.pl. Q. 300fr.
Colas 218

(illus.) Falbalas et fanfreluches
(illus.) Flament, Albert. Personnages de comédie
(illus.) Gazette du bon genre. Le bon genre
(illus.) Guirlande des mois

Barbier de Montault, Xavier
Le costume épiscopal et prélatice selon l'étiquette romaine. Marseille, Imprimerie Saint-Joseph 1876
22p. O.
Colas 220

Le costume et les insignes du pape ... Extrait du Dimanche, semaine religieuse du diocèse d'Amiens. Amiens, Librairie Langlois 1874
16p. O.
Colas 219

Le costume et les usages ecclésiastiques selon la tradition romaine. Paris, Letouzey et Ané [1897-1901]
2v. (491,527p.) illus. O. ea 7fr 50
Contents: V 1, Règles générales, Le costume usuel, Le costume de choeur; v2 Les ornements, Les pontificaux
Colas 223

Les gants pontificaux. Tours, P. Bouserez 1877
183p. 4pl. O.

Particularités du costume des évêques de Poitiers au XIIe siècle. Tours, P. Bouserez 1877
32p. O.
From *Bulletin monumental* no7, 1877
Colas 221

Traité pratique de la construction, de l'ameublement et de la décoration des églises, selon les règles canoniques et les traditions romaines, avec un appendice sur le costume ecclésiastique. Paris, L. Vivès 1885
2v. O.
On cover: 2. édition
Colas 222. LC 11-33397

Barbosa, Duarte, supposed author
A description of the coasts of East Africa and Malabar in the beginning of the sixteenth century. Tr. from an early Spanish manuscript in the Barcelona library; by the Hon. Henry E. J. Stanley. London, Printed for the Hakluyt society 1866
xi,336(i.e. 236)p. 2 facsim. O. (Works issued by the Hakluyt society no xxxv)
"Translated into Spanish from the original Portuguese in 1524, at Vittoria, by Martin Centurion": p[i] The preface is translated from the Portuguese edition, Lisbon, 1812. Attributed also to Fernão de Magalhães
LC 5-40434

Barbot, E. See Bida, Alexandre, jt. auth.

Barbuò Soncino, Scipione
Sommario delle vite de' duchi di Milano, cosi Visconti, comte Sforzeschi, raccolto da diversi auttori ... col natural ritratto di ciascun d'essi, intagliato in rame. Venetia, Presso G. Porro 1574
15 numb. l. illus. Q.
Full-length portraits in architectural settings
Lipperheide 1239. LC 27-4447

Barcelona. Asociación artistico-arqueologica barcelonesa
Estudios de indumentaria española concreta y comparada. Puiggari, José

Barclay, Alexander
(tr.) Brant, Sebastian. The Ship of fools

Barclay, Edgar
Mountain life in Algeria; with illustrations by the author. London, K. Paul, Trench 1882
xviii,119p. 15pl.(incl. front.) Q.
LC 3-29167

Barde, F. A.
Traité encyclopédique de l'art du tailleur. Paris, Chez l'auteur 1834
268p. 57pl. O.
Plates lithographed by Engelmann
Colas 224

Bardeleben, Karl von. See Pflugk-Harttung, J. A. G. von, ed. Napoleon I: Das erwachen der völker

Bardon, Michel François Dandré-. See Dandré-Bardon, M. F.

Baret, L.
Le costume et la toilette au Japon. Paris, [Imprimerie central de chemin de fer; imprimerie Chaix] 1892
18p. O.
Colas 225

Barfield, T. C.
Longmans' historical illustrations. England in the middle ages. Drawn and

Barfield, T. C.—*Continued*
described by T. C. Barfield. London, New York [etc.] Longmans, Green & co. 1909-10
6 l. 72pl. F. ea $1.50
Published in six portfolios
Contents: 1 The XI century; 2 The XII century; 3 The XIII century; 4 The XIV century; 5 The XIV and XV centuries; 6 The XV century
Costume index. LC A11-2150

Bark as clothing
Adriani, Nicolaus, and Kruijt, A. C. Geklopte boomschors als kleedingstof op Midden-Celebes, en hare geographische verspreiding in Indonesië. 1905

Barker, Albert Winslow
A classification of the chitons worn by Greek women as shown in works of art. Philadelphia, 1923
48p. O.
Thesis, University of Pennsylvania, 1921
Reprint from Proceedings of the Delaware County institute of science, v9 no3, Media, Pa
Partial list of works consulted: p47-48
Colas 226. LC 23-13845

Barker, Bligh, jt. auth. See Crocker, Sydney

Barker, Thomas
Forty lithographic impressions from drawings selected from his studies of rustic figures after nature. Bath, Wood & co. 1813
3 l. 40pl. F.

Barlaeus, Caspar. See Baerle, Kaspar

Barlandus, Hadrianus. See Baerland, Adriaan van

[**Barletius, Martinus**]
Des aller streytparsten vñ theüresten fürsten und herr Georgen Castrioten genañt Scanderbeg, hertzogen zü Epiro und Albanien etc. ritterliche thaten. Augsberg, H. Steiner 1533
241 l. 105 illus. F.
Another edition (Franckfurt am Mayn, H. and G. Reben 1561)
Illustrations are by Jörg Breu
A Latin edition with woodcuts by Jost Amman is entitled: *Vita, indoles, et adversus Turcas res gestae Georgii Castrioti* was published as volume 3 of Lonicer's *Chronicorum Turcicorum*
Lipperheide 1397

Barleus, Gaspar. See Baerle, Kaspar van

Barlow, Francis
Several wayes of hunting, hawking, and fishing, according to the English manner; etched by W. Hollar. London, J. Overton 1671
12pl. Q.
Lipperheide 3023

Barlow, Jane
Irish ways, by Jane Barlow. With illustrations in colour and black and white by Warwick Goble. London, G. Allen 1909
262p. col.front. col.pl. O.
Plates protected by guard sheets with descriptive letterpress. Illustrations show costume
LC A10-2423

Barnard, Francis Pierrepont
(ed.) Mediaeval England, a new ed. of Barnard's "Companion to English history", ed. by H. W. C. Davis. Oxford, The Clarendon press 1924
xxi,632p. front. illus. (incl. maps, plans, facsims.) O. $7
Costume is shown in many of the illustrations and is treated in the following chapters: IV Costume, civil: Anglo-Saxon period, Norman and Plantagenet periods, Period of York and Lancaster, Tudor period; V Costume, military; X: 1 The monks, friars and secular clergy, 2 The mendicant orders
"Books for reference" at end of each article
Costume index. LC 24:26449

Barnard, George
[Switzerland; scenes and incidents of travel in the Bernese Oberland, etc ... London, T. McLean 184-?]
1 l. 4p. col.front. 25 col.pl. O.
Without title page. Plates signed by the artist. Frontispiece gives costume of some of the principal Swiss cantons. Other plates are especially good for Swiss peasant costume

Barnett, Edith A.
Common-sense clothing. London, New York, Ward, Lock 1882?
150p. front. illus. D.

Barnim, Adalbert Johann Baptiste von, freiherr, and Hartmann, Robert
Reise in Nord-Ost Afrika; skizzen nach der natur gemalt 1859-1860. Berlin, G. Reimer [1863]
24pl. (12 col.) F.
Ten of the plates show costume
Colas 227. Lipperheide 1605

Barocci, Luigi, and Fabi-Montani, Francesco, count
Collezione di quaranta sacre ceremonie usate principalmente in Roma; incise dal ... Barocci ... e descritte da ... Fabi Montani. Rome, P. Brognòli [1841-50]
41 l. 40pl. F.
Plates after drawings by J. Riepenhausen, N. Panini, J. Meli, L. Lolli, C. Masini, V. Pasqualoni and others
Lipperheide 1822

Baron, Auguste Alexis Floréal
Lettres à Sophie sur la danse, suivies d'entretiens sur les danses ancienne, moderne, religieuse, civile et théâtrale. Paris, Dondey-Dupré 1825
344p. front. (fold.facsim.) O.
Published in 1824 under title *Lettres et entretiens sur la danse ancienne, moderne, religieuse, civile et théâtrale*
Lipperheide 3094. LC 15-8911

See also La Belgique monumentale, historique et pittoresque

Baron, Henri Charles Antoine
(illus.) Challamel, Augustin, and Ténint, Wilhelm. Les Français sous la révolution

Barons, Krišjānis, and Wissendorffs, Henri
(eds.) Latwju dainas. Kr.. Barona un H. Wissendorffa isdotas. Jelgawâ, H. J. Drawin-Drawneeka general-komisijâ 1894-1915
6v. in 8 front. (ports., v5) 2 fold.maps (v5) O.
Added t.-p.: Chansons nationales lataviennes. Mitau, H. I. Drawiņ-Drawneeks, imprimeur-commissionnaire

Barons, K., and Wissendorffs, H.—*Continued*
Vol. 1, pt5-10 have imprint: Rigâ, Speeduschi Kalninsch & Deutschmans. Vols. 2-5 have imprint: Peterburgâ (v6, Petrogradâ) Keisariskâs sinibu akademijas speestawâ. Vols. 2-6: Imprimé par ordre de l'Académie impériale des sciences. Vol. 5 includes table of contents of first five volumes in Russian and of the whole work in German
LC 21-5234

Barr, Estelle De Young
A psychological analysis of fashion motivation. New York, 1934
100p. diagrs. 25cm. (Archives of psychology. no171)
Issued also as thesis. Columbia university
Bibliography: p99-100
LC 35-2472

Barras, Easton de
Home dressmaking and the art of good dressing. London, Iliffe [1898]
99p. diagrs. T. (Nutshell series)

Barraud, Pierre Constant
Des gants portés par les évêques, par d'autres members du clergé et même par les laïques dans les cérémonies religieuses. Caen, F. Le Blanc-Hardel 1867
57p. 5 illus. O.
Taken from the *Bulletin monumental*
Colas 228. Lipperheide 1836

Barrès, Maurice
La vieille garde imperiale; illus. par Job [pseud] Tours, Mame [1901]
38 illus.(part col.) 19pl.(part col.) Q.
The Imperial guard of Napoleon is described by Barrès, Houssaye and others

[**Barrett, W. H.**]
Hint's about men's dress, right principles economically applied, by a New York clubman. New York, D. Appleton 1888
83p. illus. T.
LC 10-1028

Barrière-Flavy, C.
Le costume et l'armement du Wisigoth aux cinquième et seizième siècles. Toulouse, E. Privat 1902
21p. illus. O.
Colas 229

Barrois, J.
Le livre du très chevalereux comte d'Artois et de sa femme, fille au comte de Boulogne ... publié d'après les manuscrits. Paris, Techener 1837
xxviii,207p. 28pl. Q.
The miniatures which are made after the originals by Onghena, are of costume interest
Lipperheide 448

Barron, Louis
Paris pittoresque, 1800-1900. La vie—les moeurs—les plaisirs. Ouvrage orné de 500 reproductions d'estampes et de 20 gravures hors texte tirées en couleur. Paris, L. H. May [1899]
412p. illus. pl.(part col.) plans, facsims. F.

Barrow, Sir John, bart.
Travels into the interior of southern Africa. In which are described the character and condition of the Dutch colonists of the cape of Good Hope, and of the several tribes of natives beyond its limits .. 2d ed., with additions and alterations, illus. with several engravings and charts. London, T. Cadell and W. Davies 1806
2v in 1 col.pl. fold.maps. Q.
First edition published, 1801-04, under title: *An account of travels into the interior of southern Africa, in the years 1797 and 1798*
LC 31-4122

Barteau, L. R.
Die K. K. Oesterreichisch-ungarische armee; bildlich dargestellt nach den neuesten adjustierungs vorschriften. Nach original. skizzen von ... Barteau. Wien, L. W. Seidel [1893]
XXIV col.pl. ob.Q.
Colas 230

Bartels, Adolf
... Der bauer in der deutschen vergangenheit. Mit einhundert acht und sechzig abbildungen und beilagen nach den originalen aus dem 15.—18. jahr. Leipzig, E. Diederichs 1900
142p. illus. pl. Q. (Monographien zur deutschen kulturgeschichte ... 6. bd)
Lipperheide 1988. LC G-1209

Barth, Heinrich
Travels and discoveries in North and Central Africa: being a journal of an expedition undertaken ... in the years 1849-1855. London, Longman, Brown, Green, Longmans, & Roberts 1857-58
5v. col.fronts. illus. col.pl. fold.maps plans(1 fold.) O.
Published also in German: *Reisen und entdeckungen in Nord- und Central-Afrika* 5v. Gotha, Perthes 1857-58) Also other editions
LC 5-3610

Barth, Hermann
Das geschmeide; schmuck- und edelsteinkunde. Berlin, A. Schall [1903-04]
2v. col.fronts. (1 double) 24pl. D.
Contents: Die geschichte des schmucks; v2 Das material des schmucks
LC 5-11630

Barth, J. A.
Hoyer, J. G. von. Pragmatische geschichte der saechsischen truppen (attributed)

Barthélemy, Hyacinth Eugène
Uniformes des écoles du gouvernement. See entry under Armand-Dumaresq, C. E.

Barthema, Ludovico de. See Varthema, Ludovico de

Barthold, Friedrich Wilhelm
George von Frundsberg oder das deutsche kriegshandwerk zur zeit der reformation. Hamburg, F. Perthes 1833
x,516p. 1 pl.(port.) O.
Lipperheide 2094

Geschichte der kriegsverfassung und des kriegswesens der Deutschen; neue ausg. Leipzig, T. O. Weigel 1864
2v.(254,302p.) O.
First edition 1854-55
Lipperheide 2037

Bartholdy, Jakob Ludwig Salomo
Bruchstücke zur nähern kenntniss des heutigen Griechenlands gesammelt auf einer reise ... im Jahre 1803-1804. Erster theil. Berlin, Realschulbuchhandlung 1805
xii,518p. illus. 9pl.(part col., part fold.) D.
No more published

Bartholin, Bertelli
De paenula; accessit ... Henrici Ernstii ejusdem argumenti epistola. Editio altera priori auctior. Hafniae, D. Paulli 1670
11 l. 120p. 3pl. O.
First edition 1655
Lipperheide 219m

Bartholin, Caspar
De inauribus veterum syntagma. Accedit Mantissa ex Thomæ Bartholini Miscellaneis medicis de annulis narium. Amstelodami, H. Wetstenii 1676
148,17p. illus. T.
LC 6-8690

(ed.) Bartholin, Thomas. De armillis veterum

Bartholin, Thomas
De armillis veterum schedion. Accessit Olai Wormii De aureo cornu danico ad Licetum responsio. Editio novissima, figuris æneis illustrata. Amstelodami, H. Wetstenii 1676
114,14,40p. illus. fold.pl. T.
Edited by Caspar Bartholin
Including bracelets as ornaments and also as weapons; and pictures of hand bandages, studded with metal and attached to wrist bands, used like brass knuckles
LC 6-8692

Miscellaneis medicis de annulis varium (In Bartholin, Caspar. De inauribus veterum syntagma. 1676. Part 2)

Bartoli, Pietro Santi, and Bellori, Giovanni Pietro
Columna Cochlis, M. Aurelio Antonino Augusto dicata, eius rebus gestis in Germanicâ, atque Sarmaticâ expeditione insignis, ex S. C. Romae ad viam Flaminiam erecta, ac utriusque belli imaginibus anaglyphice insculpta Romae, D. de Rubeis 1704
80pl. F.
Lipperheide 224

Bartolozzi, Francesco
(engr.) Chamberlaine, John. Imitations of original drawings by Hans Holbein, in the collection of His Majesty, for the portraits of illustrious persons of the court of Henry VIII

Barton, Lucy
Historic costume for the stage. illus. by David Sarvis. Boston, Walter H. Baker 1935
605p. col.front. illus. Q.
Bibliography: p[587]-95; bibliography at end of each chapter
Costume index. LC 35-34454

Barton, R.
(tr.) Blasis, Carlo. Manuel complet de la danse

(tr.) Blasis, Carlo. The code of Terpsichore

Bartsch, Adam
Die verschiedenen uniformen der sächsischen armee 1806 und 1823. No place, ca1823
88 col.pl. Q.
Colas 231

Bartsch, Adam von, and Kininger, Vincent George
[Heldenthaten von soldaten der k.k. armee in den Feldzügen gegen die franzosen in den jahren 1792 bis 1799] T. Mollo ca1800
12 col.pl. F.
Each plate has descriptive text in both French and German
Lipperheide 2230

Bartsch, Gustav
Deutsche mährchengestalten; erfunden und gezeichnet von Gustav Bartsch. Berlin, F. Lobeck [1857]
1 l. 4 col.pl. F.
The fairy tale characters: Cinderella, Red Riding Hood, Snow White and The Sleeping Beauty. Text is by Rudolf Dehnike
Lipperheide 3182

Bartsch, L.
Sächsische kleiderordnungen aus der zeit von 1450-1750. Annaberg, C. O. Schreiber 1882-[83]
27,40p. Q.
From *Neununddreissigster (und Vierzigster) bericht über die Königliche realschule zu Annaberg*
Lipperheide 3338

Baruël, Euchaire
(tr.) Boye, V. C. Fund af Egekister fra bronzealdern i Danemark

[Baschet, Armand, and Feuillet de Conches, Félix Sébastien]
Les femmes blondes selon les peintres de l'école de Venise, par deux Vénitiens. Paris, A. Aubry 1865
326p. O.
"Recettes", p[269]-301, in Italian and French. Bibliographical foot-notes
LC 21-10992

Basden, George Thomas
Among the Ibos of Nigeria, an account of the curious & interesting habits, customs, & beliefs of a little known African people. Philadelphia, J. B. Lippincott; London, Seeley, Service & co. 1921
315p. incl.front. pl. fold.map. O.
Published 1920; printed in Great Britain
LC 20-20653

Baseball costume
Chadwick, Henry. Base-ball. 1888

Church, S. R. Base ball; the history, statistics and romance of the American national game from its inception to the present time. 1902

Claudy, C. H. The battle of base-ball. 1912

Harper. C. D., and Mussey, W. P. The pictorial base ball album. 1888

Base-ball. Chadwick, Henry

Base ball; the history, statistics and romance. Church, S. R.

Basedow, Johann Bernhard
Elementarwerk mit den kupfertafeln Chodowieckis u. a. kritische bearbeitung ... (enthaltend u. a. die listen der beförderer des werkes aus den jahren 1768ff. und die beurteilungen aus alter und neuer zeit), mit ungedruckten

Basedow, Johann B.—*Continued*
briefen, porträts, faksimiles und verschiedenen registern hrsg. von Theodor Fritzsch. Leipzig, E. Wiegandt 1909
3v. fronts.(ports., v 1-2) pl. maps, plans, facsims.(1 fold.) O.
Volume 3, containing the engravings, has an introduction by Hermann Gilow
For the illustrations alone see Chodowiecki, D. N. Daniel Chodowiecki; 62 bisher unveroffentlichte handzeichnungen zu dem Elementarwerk
LC E11-1157

Basel. See Switzerland—By region or province—Basel

Die **Baseler** todtentänze in getreuen abbildungen. Dance of death

Basilica Carolina ... Aedificata; a Carolo Philippo e ducali domo neoburgico ... anno MDCCXXXIII ... dedicata ... anno MDCCLX. Mannhemii, ex typ. electorali aulico 1760
80p. 19pl. F.
Contains six portraits of counts Palatine
Lipperheide 723

Los **baskos** en la Nacion Argentina. Uriarte, J. R. de, ed.

Basler kleidung aller hoh und nidriger standts, persone nach deren grad auff jetzige art fleissig corrigiert. Basell, H. H. Glaser 1634
14 l. 56pl. Q.
Colas 232

Basler portraits aller jahrhunderte. Staehelin, W. R.

Baslerische ausruff-bilder. Herrliberger, David

Basque provinces
Bernoville, Gaëtan. Le pays des Basques, types et coutumes; dessins originaux de Inigo Bernoville. 1930

Boissel, W. Le Pays Basque: sites, arts et coutumes. 1930

Crocker, Sydney, and Barker, Bligh. Sketches from the Basque Provinces of Spain. 1839

Basques in the Argentine Republic
Uriarte, J. R. de, ed. Los baskos en la Nacion Argentina

Bassaget, Pierre Numa
Caricatures anti-cholériques. Paris, Aubert [1832]
12 col.pl. Q.
Lipperheide 3670

Costumes civils et militaires depuis le ve siècle, origine de la monarchie française, jusqu'à nos jours; lithographiés par Numa ... Civil and military costumes from the vth century, beginning of the French monarchy, till our days. Paris, Gihaut frères; London, C. Tilt [1833-35]
101 col.pl. F.
Colas 2228

Costumes cosmopolites, lithographiés par Régnier et Bettannier. Paris, Bulla ainé et Tony 184-?
24 col.pl. F.
Plates are portraits of women in Swiss, Italian, Spanish, Algerian and other costume
Colas 2230

Fantaisies gracieuses; suite des travestissements composés par Numa. Paris, Gache ca1850
16pl. F.
Colas 2229

Basse-Pyrenees. See France—Basses-Pyrenees

Bassermann-Jordan, Ernst
Der schmuck. Leipzig, Klinkhardt & Biermann 1909
134p. col.front. illus. Q. (Half-title: Monographien des kunstgewerbes. 12)
"Literatur": p[129]-31
LC 10-24471

Basset, Paris, publisher
Modes d'hommes et de femmes de l'époque Louis XVI. Paris, Basset n.d.
55? pl. F.
Colas lists the plates in this series and describes them as interesting for fashions at the end of the reign of Louis XVI
This publisher has also issued a series of plates with title *Costumes français.* Colas gives a list of the plates
Colas 233

Troupes françaises; 1er empire. Paris, Basset [1805-14]
col.pl. O.
Colas 235

[Troupes françaises; Restauration] Paris Basset n.d.
54 col.pl. O.
Some of the plates are variants of those in the First empire series
Colas 236

[Uniformes français; Restauration] Paris, Basset [1830]
128 col.pl. O.
To July 1830
Colas 237

Uniformes français sous le règne de Louis-Phillippe. Paris, Basset n.d.
54 col.pl. Q.
Colas 238

Les **Bassoutos.** Casalis, Eugène. The Basutos

Bastard d'Estang, Auguste, comte de
Costumes de la cour de Bourgogne sous le règne de Philippe III dit le Bon (1455-1460) Paris, Imprimerie nationale 1881
3 l. 1 illus. 25pl. F.
Issued in five parts. The plates are reproductions of leaves from the illuminated manuscript: *Histoire de Girart, comte de Nevers, et de la belle Euriant, sa mie*
La publication, interrompue en 1848, avait pour titre: *Costumes, mœurs et usages de la Cour de Bourgogne, sous la règne de Philippe III, dit le Bon*
Colas 239. LC 19-18880

Peintures et ornements des manuscrits classés dans un ordre chronologique pour servir à l'histoire des arts du dessin depuis le quatrième siècle de l'ère chrétienne jusqu'à la fin du seizième; manuscrits français. [Paris, Priv. print. 1837-46]
3 cover-titles, half-title, 48pl.(part col.) in 1 v. F.
Plates signed: Le comte Auguste de Bastard direxit; part of plates dated, 1837-46
Selection of plates exhibited in London at the Great exhibition of 1851 by the Bastard family. The "édition française" of the whole work comprised 160 plates issued in 20 fascicles, to which later some sixty more plates were added. Further additions of "inedited" plates were made to the copy presented by the count to the Bibliothèque nationale, and to the still more complete

Bastard d' Estang, Auguste—*Continued*
copy made for his son, eventually presented, after the latter's death, to the Bibliothèque nationale by the countess. James Ludovic Lindsay, 26th earl of Crawford, describes a copy assembled by him as containing "362 plates of subjects, or counting the various 'states' of the plates . . . 546", of which a full description was printed
LC 32-9812

Bastholm, Christian
Historische nachrichten zur kenntniss des menschen in seinem wilden und rohen zustande; aus dem Dänischen übersetzt von H. E. Wolf. Altona, J. F. Hammerich 1818-21.
4v. O.
Original edition in Danish about 1805. On clothing, customs and practices of the Polynesians and American Indians
Lipperheide 53

Bastian, Adolf
Amerika's Nordwest-küste. Neueste ergebnisse ethnologischer reisen; aus der sammlungen der Königlichen museen zu Berlin. Berlin, Asher 1883-84
2v. 24pl.(part col.) map. F.
The titles under the pictures are by E. Krause and Grunwedel

Die culturländer des alten America. Berlin, Weidmannsche buchhandlung 1878-89
3v in 4 6 col.pl. 7 port. on 1 pl. 3 fold. maps. O.
Contents: v 1 Ein jahr auf reisen. Kreuzfahrten zum sammelbehuf auf transatlantischen feldern der ethnologie. 1878; v2 Beiträge zu geschichtlichen vorarbeiten auf westlicher hemisphäre. 1878; v3 I.-II. abth. Nachträge und ergänzungen aus den sammlungen des Ethnologischen museums. 1886-89
Plates (contained in last volume only) show ancient Peruvian pottery decorated with or fashioned in the shape of human figures. One plate shows part of an embroidered coat
LC 5-3804

Die voelker des oestlichen Asien. Studien und reisen von dr. Adolf Bastian. Leipzig, O. Wigand [etc.] 1866-71
6v. fold.map. O.
Volumes 3-6: Jena, H. Costenoble
Contents: 1. bd. Die geschichte der indochinesen; 2. bd. Reisen in Birma in den jahren 1861-1862; 3. bd. Reisen in Siam im jahre 1863. Nebst einer karte Hinterindiens von . . . dr. Kiepert; 4. bd. Reise durch Kambodja nach Cochinchina; 5. bd. Reisen im indischen archipel. Singapore, Batavia, Manilla und Japan; 6. bd. Reisen in China von Peking zur mongolischen grenze und rueckkehr nach Europa
LC G-1131

(ed.) Die bronzeschwerter des Königlichen museums zu Berlin. See Berlin. Staatliche museen

Bastin, Ferdinand
L'armée française en 1848. Paris, Lordereau 1848?
6pl. Q.
Colas 240

L'armée française en 1854. Paris, 1854?
60 col.pl. Q.
Colas 241

Costumes militaires des armées françaises de 1790 à 1856. Paris, J. Rigo ca1857
57 col.pl. F.
Listed by Glasser under title *Collection d'uniformes militaires français de 1789 à 1857*
Colas 242

Uniformes français sous Napoléon Ier, la restauration et Napoléon III. Paris, Hautecoeur frères 1860?
12 col.pl. F.
Colas 243

Basutos. See African tribes

The **Basutos;** or Twenty-three years in South Africa. Casalis, Eugène

Batailles gagnées par le serenissime prince Fr. Eugene de Savoye. Dumont, Jean, baron de Carlscroon

Les **bataillans** scolaires. Geoffroy, J. J. H.

Batchelor, John
The Ainu and their folk-lore. London, The Religious tract society 1901
xxvi,603p. front. illus. pl. O.
LC 2-9187

Bates, Esther Willard
The art of producing pageants. Boston, W. H. Baker 1925
269p. front. illus. pl. D.
Bibliography: p253-69
LC 26-1207

Bates, Henry Walter
(ed.) Humbert, Aimé. Japan and the Japanese, illustrated

Bateson, Gregory
Naven; a survey of the problems suggested by a composite picture of the culture of a New Guinea tribe. Cambridge, [Eng.] University press 1936
xvii,286p. front. 27pl. diagrs. O.

Bath, Order of the
Johnston, M. M. Coronation of a king; or The ceremonies, pageants and chronicles of coronations of all ages. 1902

Pine, John. The procession and ceremonies observed at the time of the installation of the Knights Companions of the . . . Military order of the Bath: Upon Thursday, June 17th 1725. 1730

Batik. See Decoration and ornament—Dutch East Indies

De **batik-kunst** in Nederlandsch-Indië en haar geschiedenis. Rouffaer, G. P., and Juynboll, H. H.

Die **batik-kunst** in Niederländisch-Indien und ihre geschichte. See Rouffaer, G. P., and Juynboll, H. H. De batik-kunst in Nederlandsch-Indië en haar geschiedenis

The **batiks** of Java. Réal, Daniel

Batissier, Louis
Les douze dames de rhétorique, publiées . . . d'après les manuscrits de La bibliothèque royale; avec une introduction par Louis Batissier et ornées de gravures par Schall. Moulins, P. A. Desrosiers fils 1838
28p. illus. pl. Q.
Illustrations show feminine costume of the 15th century
Lipperheide 449

Bátky, Zsigmond. See Magyarság tárgyi néprajza

Batsch, Carl Ferdinand
Russland: Das heer, die flotte. See entry under Drygalski, Albert von, and Zepelin, Constantin von

Batsch, Carl Ferdinand, and Meuss, Johann Friedrich
Frankreich: Die flotte. Berlin, A. Schall [1900]
x,269p. front. illus.(incl. ports.) pl.(part col.) 2 fold.plans. O. (Die heere und flotten der gegenwart ... hrsg. von C. von Zepelin. VI)
"Quellennachweis": p[259]
LC 19-5745

Batt, and others
Teutsche denkmäler; herausgegeben und erklärt von Batt., v. Babo, Eitenbenz, Mone und Weber. Lief. 1: Die bilder zum sächsischen land-und lehnrecht. Heidelberg, Mohr und Winter 1820
108p. 34pl. (1 col.) F.
Plates 1-32 reproduce miniatures from the Pfälzer (Heidelberger) *Handschrift des Sachsenspiegels*, 33-34 from the Dresden *Handschrift*. Pictures of the early thirteenth century
Lipperheide 375

Battaglia navale rappresentata in Arno ... 1608. See Le manifique carousel fait sur le fleuve de l'Arno

The **battle** of base-ball. Claudy, C. H.

The **battle** of Waterloo. Booth, John, comp.

Baty, Thomas
Academic colours. Tokio, Kenkyusha press 1934
172p. Q.
Short bibliography: p ii
LC 35-19371

Baud-Bovy, Daniel
Peasant art in Switzerland; by Arthur Palliser. London, The Studio ltd. 1924
xxiv,76p. col.front. illus. pl(part col. mounted) Q. 10s 6d o.p.
Bibliography of works consulted: p xvii-xix
Costume index. LC 24-14035

Baudier, Michel. See Chalcondylas, Laonicus. Histoire general des Turcs

Baudouin, Benoît, and Negrone, Giulio
B. Balduinus De calceo antiquo, et Jul. Nigronus De caliga veterum. Accesserunt ex Q. Sept. Fl. Tertulliani, Cl. Salmasi, & Alb. Rubeni scripts plurima ejusdem argumenti. In his scriptores veteres quamplurimi explicantur, & emendantur, nec non res ipsæ adjects æneis figuris illustrantur. Amstelodami, A. Frisi 1667
2v. (330,210p.) illus. fold.pl. T.
Vol. 2 has title: *Genuensis De caliga veterum dissertatio subseciva. Qua declaratur, quid ea sit latinis scriptoribus, in Sacra Scriptura, iure civili, ac lapidibus vetustis. Editio novissima aucta, emendata, & figuris æneis exornata*
Other editions were published (Leyden, 1711) and (Lipsiae, J. G. Loewium 1733. 2v. 28pl.)
Colas 200-200bis. LC 19-11860

Baudouin, Marcel Édouard, and Lacouloumère, Georges
Le coeur vendéen; bijou populaire ancien. Paris, Institut international de bibliographie 1903
72p. illus. S.

Baudouin, Pierre Antoine
(illus.) Bocher, Emmanuel. Les gravures françaises de XVIIIe siècle; v2.

Baudouin, Simon René, comte de
Exercice de l'infanterie françoise ordonnée par le roy le VI may MDCCLV. Dessiné d'après nature dans toutes ses positions et gravé par S. R. Baudouin. Paris, 1757
63pl. F.
Colas 245. Lipperheide 2294

Exercice de l'infanterie françoise ... copié d'après l'original. Paris, S. Fessard 1759
8 l. 61pl. O.
Copy of preceding, reduced in size
Colas 246. Lipperheide 2294

Bauer. See Lommel, Georg, jt. auth.

Bauer, Max
Deutscher frauenspiegel; bilder aus dem frauenleben in der deutschen vergangenheit. München [etc.] G. Müller 1917
2v. illus. pl. O.

Sittengeschichte des deutschen studententums. Dresden, P. Aretz 1927?
219p. front. 39pl. Q.

(ed.) Scherr, Johannes. Kulturgeschichte der deutschen frau

Der **bauer** in der deutschen vergangenheit. Bartels, Adolf

Bauern-trachten aus dem bayerischen hochland. Zell, Franz

Bauernpelze in der tschechoslowakischev republik. See Úprka, Joža. Peasants' furs in Czechoslovakia

Baukunst u. landschaft in China. See Boerschmann, Ernst. Picturesque China

Baulich und volkskundlich beachtenswertes aus dem kulturgebiete des silberbergbaues zu Freiberg, Schneeberg und Johanngeorgenstadt im sächs. erzgebirge. Bleyl, Fritz

Baumann, Erich
Die reform der männerkleidung. Der weg z. befreiung d. männerwelt v. d. fesseln d. kragens u. d. ungesunden bekleidungsweise. Gettenbach, Lebensweiser verlag 1929
30p. O.

Baumeister, August
Denkmäler des klassischen altertums zur erläuterung des lebens der Griechen und Römer in religion, kunst und sitte. München und Leipzig, R. Oldenbourg 1885-88
3v. illus. pl. maps, plans, tables. Q.
Lipperheide 174. LC 4-35149

Baumeister, Johann Sebald
Familienbilder des Hauses Hohenzollern von den in dem Hochfürstlichen Schlosse zu Hechingen befindlich originalien copirt. Wirtemberg, 1817
28 l. 25 col.pl. (ports.) Q.
Portraits of the Counts von Zollern from the 9th to the 17th century
Lipperheide 727

Baumgärtner, F. G. See Müller, Ernst, jt. auth.

Baur, Johann Wilhelm
[Costumes of various peoples] Wien, 1640
20pl. D.
Eleven of these plates are on the same subjects as his: *Livre nouveau*
Lipperheide 521

Baur, Johann W.—*Continued*
Livre nouveau de diverses nations. No place, ca1630
8pl. Q.
Costumes of the seventeenth century
Colas 248. Lipperheide 520

Bautz, Rudolf
Formenstudien; musterzeichnungen für schule, haus und gewerbe. Frankfurt a. M., A. Frey 1891
30p. 110 patterns Q.
Lipperheide 4381

Bavaria. See Germany—Bavaria; also Ceremonial and festival costume—Germany—Bavaria

Bavaria sancta Maximiliani sereniss. principis imperii. Sadeler, Raphael

Bavaria. K. Hof- und staatsbibliothek, Munich. See Munich. Bayerische staatsbibliothek

Bavaria. Staatsbibliothek, Munich. See Munich. Bayerische staatsbibliothek

Baxter, Thomas
Darstellung des aegyptischen, griechischen und römischen costums; aus dem englischen, herausgegeben von Christian Friedrich Michaelis. Leipzig, Im Industrie-comptoir 1815
15p. front. 40pl. Q.
German translation of his *An illustration*
Colas 251. Lipperheide 116. LC 33-8620

An illustration of the Egyptian, Grecian, and Roman costume. London, W. Miller 1810
16p. front. 40pl. O.
Also published (London, H. Setchell 1814)
Colas 249-50. LC 33-8613

Bayard, Émile
L'art de reconnaître les bijoux anciens, pierres précieuses, métal précieux; ouvrage illustré de 115 planches et gravures d'après la collection Georges Chapsal. Paris, E. Gründ 1924
313p. illus. D. (Guides pratiques de l'amateur et du collectionneur d'art)
LC 32-30057

L'art de reconnaître les dentelles, guipures, etc. Paris, R. Roger and F. Chernoviz 1914
345p. illus. D. (Guides pratiques de l'amateur)

Bayard, Émile Antoine
(illus.) Regnard, J. F. Oeuvres complètes

Baye, Joseph, baron de
Études archéologiques. Époque des invasions barbares. Industrie anglo-saxonne. Paris, Nilsson 1889
133p. pl. Q.

The industrial arts of the Anglo-Saxons ... Tr. by T. B. Harbottle. London, S. Sonnenschein; New York, Macmillan 1893
17 l. xii,135p. illus. XVII pl. F.
A translation of his *Études archéologiques ... industrie anglo-saxonne*
LC 2-229

Die **bayerische** armee, nach der ordonnanz von jahre 1825. Monten, Dietrich

Das **bayerische** bürger-militär. Hohfelde Carl

Bayerische chevaux legers. Gillig, Victor

Bayerische trachten Mittelfranken. Adelmann, Leofrid

Bayerischen trachten Unterfranken. Adelmann, Leofrid

Die **bayerischer** armee unter König Maximilien II. Behringer, Ludwig

Bayeux, George Louis. L'antiquité pittoresque [extract from] (*In* Meiners, Christoph. Recherches historiques sur le luxe chez les Athéniens)

The **Bayeux** tapestry. Fowke, F. R.

The **Bayeux** tapestry elucidated. Bruce, J. C.

Bayeux tapisserie de la Reine Mathilde. Queen Matilda's tapestry. Conquête de l'Angleterre par Guillaume le Conquérant, 1066. Edition reservée au gardien de la tapisserie R. Falue. Texte français-anglais. Paris, Levy de Reurdein n.d.
1 fold. pl. Q.
Reproduction in colors

Bayf, Lazare. See Baïf, Lazare de

Bayle-Mouillard, Mme Élisabeth Félicie (Canard)
Manuel des dames, ou l'art de la toilette, suivi de l'art du modiste, et du mercier-passementier ... par Mme. Celnart. Paris, Roret 1827
366p. 1 col.pl. (showing patterns and hats) D.
Discusses beauty culture, cosmetics, millinery, care of furs, etc. The patterns and illustrations show hats
Colas 568. Lipperheide 3257

Nouveau manuel complet de la broderie, indiquant la manière de dessiner et d'exécuter tout ce qui est relatif à cet art ... Par Mme Celnart [pseud] Paris, Roret 1840
309p. 40pl. D.

Nouveau manuel complet des demoiselles, ou arts et métiers qui leur conviennent, et dont elles peuvant s'occuper avec agrément, tels que la couture, la broderie, le tricot, la dentelle ... par Mme. Celnart; nouvelle ed. Paris, Roret 1837
308p. 3 col.pl. (part col.) D.
Lipperheide 4072

Bayley, Frank William
Five colonial artists of New England: Joseph Badger, Joseph Blackburn, John Singleton Copley, Robert Feke, John Smibert. Boston, Priv. print. 1929
448p. ports. F.
Shows colonial costume of the United States
LC 29-14568

Bayo, Joaquín Ezquerra del. See Ezquerra del Bayo, Joaquín

Bayot, A.
(lithgr.) Vidal, J., pub. Collection des costumes du Roussillon dédiée à la ville de Perpignan

Der **Bazar;** erste damen- und modenzeitung. 1.+ jahrg.; jan. 1854+ Berlin, Bazar-Actien-gesellschaft 1855+
Col.illus. F.
A fashion periodical. Published fortnightly. Current 1937. Subtitle varies. For supplement 1881 and 1882 see *Illustrirte coiffeur*
Colas 252. Lipperheide 4674

De **Bazar**; geillustreerd tijdschrift voor modes en handwerken. 1.-44. jaargang; 1857-1900. s'Gravenhage, Gebr. Belinfante
42v. col.illus. F.
Colas 253. Lipperheide 4706

Bazin, H.
(illus.) Brunet. Théorie pratique du danseur de société

Bazin de Malpière, D. See Malpière, D. Bazin de

Beach, Belle
Riding and driving for women. New York, C. Scribner's sons 1912
xiv,295p. front.(port.) illus. O.
LC 12-25232

Beads

See entry below; *also* Beadwork

Greece—Minoan and Mycenaean ages

Evans, Sir A. J. 'The ring of Nestor'. 1925

Beads and beadwork of the American Indians. Orchard, W. C.

Beadwork
Biggart, Helen. Leathercraft and beading, adapted for Camp fire girls. 1930
Griswold, L. E. Handbook of craftwork in leather, horsehair, bead, porcupine quill and feather, Indian (Navajo) silver and turquoise. 1928
Orchard, W. C. Beads and beadwork of the American Indians. 1929

Beamish, North Ludlow
History of the King's German legion. London, T. & W. Boone 1832-37
2v. col.pl. O.
A group of Hanoverian troops which served the English king during the Napoleonic wars
German translation by G. Nagel *Geschichte des königlich deutschen legion* (Hannover, Hahn'schen hofbuchhandlung)
Colas 254 (German ed.)

Beard
Das buch der haare und bärte. 1844
Burchardus, abbot of Bellevaux. Apologia de barbis. 1935
Canel, Alfred. Histoire de la barbe et des cheveux en Normandie. 1859
Fangé, Augustin. Mémoires pour servir à l'histoire de la barbe de l'homme. 1774
Geschichte des männlichen barts unter allen völkern der erde bis auf die neueste zeit. 1797
Histoire philosophique, anecdotique et critique de la cravate, et du col, précédé d'une notice sur la barbe. 1854
Hotman, Antoine. Jucundus & verè lectu dignus de barba et coma. 1628
Kirchmaier, G. C. De majestate juribusque barbae. 1698
Lacroix, Paul, and others. Le livre d'or des métiers. 1850-58. v5
Motteley, J. C. Histoire des révolutions de la barbe des Français, depuis l'origine de la monarchie. 1826
Pagenstecher, J. F. W. De barba, liber singularis. 1746
Paris. Musée des monumens français. Musée royal des monumens français, ou Mémorial de l'histoire de France et de ses monumens. 1815
Permoser, Balthasar. Der ohne ursach verworffene und dahero von rechts wegen auff den thron der ehren wiederum erhabene barth ... sambt anhang eines schönen lustig und ausführlichen real-discurs von den bärthen. 1714
Phillippe, Adrien. Histoire philosophique, politique et religieuse de la barbe, chez les principaux peuples de la terre, depuis les temps les plus reculés jusqu'à nos jours. 1845
Price, George. Ancient and modern beards. 1893
Saggio di storia sulle vicendo della barba, con un' appendice sopra i mostacchj. 1801
Ulmus, M. A. Physiologia barbae humanae. 1602

See also Shaving

Béarn. See France—By region or province—Basse-Pyrénées

[**Beatus, M. Georgius, and Bischius, Johannes Ludovicus**]
[Book of designs. Frankfort on Main, 1601]
3 l. 80pl. O.
Plates are copied from Quentel (1527), Sibmacher (1597), Vecellio and others
Lipperheide 3908

Beau Brummell and his times. Boutet de Monvel, Roger

Le **beau** monde. See Moses, Henry. Designs of modern costume

Le **Beau** monde; or, Literary and fashionable magazine. v. 1-5? Nov. 1806-Apr. 1810. London, J. B. Bell [etc.]
5v. pl.(part col.) ports. O.
Published monthly
Final date from Colas' *Bibliographie.* Library of Congress card has v 1-5, no. 1-31, Nov. 1806-Feb. 1809 only
Contains fashion plates in color
Colas 255. LC 28-6273

Beauchamp, Frederick Lygon, 6th earl
(ed.) Liber regalis. See Catholic church. Liturgy and ritual

Beauchamp, Richard de. Pageants. See Pageants of Richard Beauchamp, earl of Warwick

Beauclerk, Lord Charles
Lithographic views of military operations in Canada under his excellency Sir John Colborne during the late insurrection. London, A. Flint 1840
24p. front.(map) 6 col.pl. F.
LC 1-13533

Beaulieu, Michèle
Contribution à l'étude de la mode à Paris; les transformations du costume élégant sous le règne de Louis XIII (1610-1643) Paris, R. Munier 1936
196p. incl. xv pl. O.
Descriptive letterpress on versos facing plates (except XIII and XV)
"Bibliographie": p[151]-160
LC 38-11499

Beaumont, coëffeur, pseud. See Marchand, J. H.

Beaumont, Adalbert de. See Collinot, E., jt. auth.

Beaumont, Charles Édouard de
Au bal masqué. Paris, Bureau de Charivari ca1850
30 col.pl. Q.
According to Colas there is another set of Beaumont's plates with this title and containing about 150 plates
Colas 258. Lipperheide 3564

Les jolies femmes de Paris. Paris, Aubert [1846]
40 col.pl. Q.
Colas 257

[L'opéra au XIXme siècle] Paris, Aubert ca1845
57 col.pl. Q.
Colas 256. Lipperheide 3563

Nos jolies parisiennes. Paris, Bureau de Charivari ca1860
30 col.pl. Q.
Colas 259. Lipperheide 3565

Beaumont, Cyril William
The history of Harlequin ... with ... illustrations from contemporary sources. London, C. W. Beaumont 1926
155p. col.front. pl.(part col.) ports. facsims. Q.
A chacoon for a harlequin by F: Le Roussau dancing-master (London) reproduced in facsimile: p121-32
List of principal works consulted: p115-17
LC 28-10128

(ed.) Lambranzi, Gregorio. New and curious school of theatrical dancing

(tr.) Tabourot, Jehan. Orchesography

Beaumont, Edouard de
(illus.) Grisier, A. E. F. Les armes et le duel

Beaumont, Edward Thomas
Academical habit; illustrated by ancient armorial brasses. [Oxford] 1928
91p. front.(port.) 21 facsims. Q.
Typewritten on both sides of leaves

Ancient memorial brasses. London, New York [etc.] H. Milford, Oxford university press 1913
xvi,197p. incl. front. illus. D. 3s 6d, o.p.
English costume from the thirteenth to the seventeenth century as shown in brass memorials. Each piece is pictured, described and dated. Illustrations are from rubbings
Costume index. LC A15-698

Beaunier, André
Visages de femmes. Paris, Plon-Nourrit 1913
377p. D. 3fr. 50
Pages 338-73: La mode sous le deuxième empire
Colas 261. LC 13-15227

Beaunier, F., and Rathier, L.
Recueil des costumes français, ou collection des plus belles statues et figures françaises ... devant servir à l'histoire de l'art du dessin en France, depuis Clovis jusqu'à Napoléon Premier inclusivement. Paris, Rathier 1810-13
2v. 216 col.pl. F.
"Des armes, des armures, des instruments, des meubles, etc., dessinés d'après des monuments, manuscrits, peintures et vitraux, avec un texte explicatif suivi d'un notice historique et cronologique." Subtitle
Published also with the plates in black and white. The work was not finished, but goes to the end of the reign of Louis XII, 1515
Colas 260. Lipperheide 1072

Beaurain, Georges
Le portail de l'église de Mimizan étudié dans ses rapports avec l'histoire du costume et du mobilier au moyen age. Dax and Paris, H. Labèque n.d.
58p. illus. 3pl. O.
Colas 262

Beaurepaire, Sieur de. See Fouquet, Samuel

La **Beauté** de la chevelure. Alexandre, Paul

Beautés de l'histoire d'Angleterre. Nougaret, P. J. B.

Les **beautés** de l'opéra. Gautier, Théophile

Beautés historiques, chronologiques, politiques et critiques de la ville de Paris. Propiac, C. J. F. G. de

Beautiful children immortalised by the masters. Macfall, Haldane

Beautiful Holland. See Vries, R. W. P. de. Dutch national costumes

Beautiful women in history & art. Erskine, Mrs Beatrice

Beauty, Personal
Adams, Rudolph. Die farben-harmonie in ihrer anwendung auf die damentoilette. 1862
Alq, Louise d' Les secrets du cabinet de toilette, conseils et recettes. 1881
Caraccioli, L. A. de. Le livre de quatre couleurs. 1760
Cooley, A. J. The toilet and cosmetic arts in ancient and modern times. 1866
Cunliffe-Owen, M. de G. Eve's glossary. 1897
Flittner, C. G. Die kunst der toilette. 1833
Franklin, A. L. A. La vie privée d'autrefois; arts et métiers, modes, moeurs, usages des Parisiens du XII. au XVIII. siècle. [v 1]
Larisch, Rudolf von. Der "schönheitsfehler" des weibes. 1896
Le Camus, Antoine. Abdeker; ou, L'art de conserver la beauté. 1774
Orchamps, baronin d', pseud.? Die geheimnisse der frau. 1908
Raisson, H. N. Code de la toilette. 1828
Schultze-Naumburg, Paul. Die kultur des weiblichen körpers als grundlage der frauenkleidung. 1922
Stote, Dorothy. Making the most of your looks. 1935

See also Art of dress; Color in dress; Cosmetics; Make-up

Periodical

Women; the hairstyle and beauty review. 1933+

Beauty begins at home. Wellman, Katharine

Beauty in dress. Dewing, M. R. O.

The **beauty** of skating. Curry, Manfred

Beauty's awakening. Art workers guild, London

Beauty's costume: a series of female figures in the dresses of all times and nations. Ritchie, Leitch

Beauvoir, Henri Roger de
Album-annuaire de l'armée française. 1889-1909? Paris, Plon,Nourrit 1889-1909?
Illus. ports. Q. 1 fr. 50
No more published?

Beauvoir, Ludovic, marquis de
Pékin, Yeddo, San Francisco; voyage autour du monde ... 15 gravures-photographies par Deschamps. 6. éd. Paris, Plon-Nourrit 1902
359p. front. pl. ports. maps, plan. D.
Originally published as v3 of the author's *Voyage autour du monde* (6. ed 1872)
LC 5-38342

Beauvoir, Roger de. See Audebrand, Philibert, jt. auth.

Beaven, Arthur Henry
Crowning the king. London, C. A. Pearson 1902
209p. front. pl. ports. D.
LC 2-21040

Becanus, Guilielmo
Serenissimi principis Ferdinandi Hispaniarum infantis S.R.E. cardinalis triumphalis introitus in Flandreae metropolim Gandavum. Antverpia, J. Meursi [1636]
68p. 42pl. F.
Lipperheide 2663

Becatelli, Lorenzo
(ed.) I riti nuziali degli antichi Romani [by Diomede Egeriaco, Pastor Arcade i.e. Flaminio Scarselli and others. Ed. by L. Becatelli] Per le nozze di Don Giovanni Lambertini con ... Donna Lucrezia Savorgnan. Bologna, Lelio dalla Volpe 1762
xvi,100p. 21 illus. Q.
Lipperheide 230

Bechius, Philippus
(tr.) Agricola, Georg. Berckwerck buch
(tr.) Agricola, Georg. Vom bergkwerck XII bucher

Bechlin, Louise Thormann-. See Thormann-Bechlin, Louise

Bechmannus; enucleatus, suppletus et continuatus. Lentz, Samuel

Bechstein, L.
Phantasie-costüme. München, Braun & Schneider [1880]
16 col.pl. Q.
Colas 263. Lipperheide 3190

[**Béchu, Marcel Ernest**]
Nos vieux houzards. Paris, Berger-Levrault 1933
184p. col.front. pl.(part col.) ports.(1 col.) O.
Author's pseudonym, Marcel Dupont, at head of title
LC 35-808

Beck, August
Die königlich sächsische armee in ihrer neuesten uniformirung; 24 colorirte abbildungen nach originalzeichnungen von August Beck. Dresden, C. C. Meinhold [1867]
24 col.pl. Q.
Colas 265. Lipperheide 2204m

Lose blätter zur geschichte der königlich sächsischen armee [from 1806-1868] Dresden, C. C. Meinhold 1873
41pl. Q.
Lipperheide 2205

Schweizer militair album. Düsseldorf, Kunst-anstalt ca1860
12 col.pl. Q.
Descriptive matter is in German and in French
Colas 264. Lipperheide 2253

Beck, Leonard. See Burgkmair, Hans. Images de saints et saintes issus de la famille de l'Empereur Maximilian I (attributed)

Beck, S. William
Gloves, their annals and associations: a chapter of trade and social history. London, Hamilton, Adams 1883
xvii,263p. incl.illus. pl. O. 7s 6d, o.p.
Costume index. Lipperheide 1727. LC 2-26626

Becker, Albert
Pfälzer volkskunde. Bonn & Leipzig, K. Schroeder 1925
xv,413p. 153 illus. 5 maps. O.

Becker, C., and Hefner-Alteneck, Jacob Heinrich von
Kunstwerke und geräthschaften des Mittelalters und der Renaissance. Frankfurt am Main, Schmerber'schen 1852[-63]
3v. 216 col.pl. Q.
The same plates have been reproduced in Hefner-Alteneck's *Trachten*
Colas 270. Lipperheide 322

Becker, Hermann
Das Dortmunder wandschneider-buch. Dortmund, W. Crüwell 1871
31p. O.
Lipperheide 1980

Becker, Marie Luise
Der tanz. Leipzig, H. Seemann nachfolger [1901]
210p. front. illus. Q.
A history of the dance from ancient times thru the 19th century, profusely illustrated
LC 3-8853

Becker, Rudolph Zacharias
Bildnisse der urheber und beförderer auch einiger gegner der religions- und kirchenverbesserung im sechzehnten jahrhundert. Gotha, Becker 1817
2 l. 23pl. F.
"Nebst andern darauf bezug habenden bildern in gleichzeitigen holzschnitten, zum andenken des dritten jubelfestes der evangelisch lutherischen kirche am 31sten October 1817." Subtitle
Lipperheide 507

Das deutsche feyerkleid zur erinnerung des einzugs der Deutschen in Paris am 31sten märz 1814 eingeführt von deutschen frauen. Gotha, Becker'schen buchhandlung 1814
20p. 1 col.pl. O.
Suggestion for a national woman's garment for ceremonial occasions
Lipperheide 690

Becker, Walter M. F.
Der herr von heute; ein neues herrenbrevier. Berlin, Selle-Eysler 1927
88p. 90 illus. O.

Becker, Wilhelm Adolf
Charicles; or, Illustrations of the private life of the ancient Greeks. With notes and excursuses; tr. by Frederick Met-

Becker, Wilhelm A.—*Continued*
calfe. 3d ed. New York, D. Appleton 1866
xxi,512p. illus. pl. plans. O.
Often reprinted. Taken over by Longmans and now o.p. First published by J. W. Parker at 12s
LC 15-23679

Charikles, bilder altgriechischer sitte. Zur genaueren kenntniss des griechischen privatlebens. Leipzig, F. Fleischer 1854
3v. 2 fold.pl. plans. O.
First edition 1840. See English translation above
Chapter in volume 3 is entitled Die kleidung, die beschuhung, haar und bart
Lipperheide 189. LC 4-35178

Gallus, oder Römische scenen aus der zeit Augusts. Zur genaueren kenntniss des römischen privatlebens. 3. ausg. von Wilh. Rein. Leipzig, F. Fleischer 1863
3v. illus. pl. plans. O.
First edition 1838
Volume 3, chapter 8: Die kleidung
Colas 269. Lipperheide 240. LC 18-15575

Gallus; or, Roman scenes in the time of Augustus; tr. by Frederick Metcalfe. [2d ed.] London, J. W. Parker 1849
xxiii,535p. illus. 12s
Dress of men p408-30; of women p431-50
Costume index. Lipperheide 240

[**Becker, Wilhelm Gottlieb**]
Vom costume an denkmälern. Leipzig, J. C. Müller 1776
80p. O.
Colas 266. Lipperheide 3238

Beckmann, Johann Christoph. See Becmann, J. C.

Beckwith, Martha Warren
Christmas mummings in Jamaica. Poughkeepsie, N. Y. Vassar college 1923
46p. front. illus. O. (Publications of the Folk-lore foundation. no2)
LC 24-2162

The Hussay festival in Jamaica. Poughkeepsie, N. Y. Vassar college 1924
17p. front. illus. O. (Publications of the Folklore foundations. no4)
At head of cover-title: Vassar college field-work in folk-lore
LC 24-29648

Becmann, Johann Christoph
Beschreibung des ritterlichen Johanniter-Orden und dessen absonderlicher beschaffenheit im Herrn-Meistertum in der Marck Sachsen, Pommern und Wendland ... mit nöthigen anmerckungen. 3. aufl. verm. von J. C. Dithmar. Franckfurt an der Oder, J. G. Conradi 1726
10 l. 312,98p. front.(port.) O.
The first edition was published in 1693
Lipperheide 1896

Notitia universitatis Francofurtanae, una cum iconibus personarum aliquot illustrium, aliorumq. virorum egregiorum, qui eam praesentia sua ac meritis. Francofurti ad Viadrum, Schrey & Hartmann 1707
284,39p. 38pl. F.
The plates are half-length portraits
Lipperheide 2020

Becquer, Jose I.
(lithgr.) Andalusian annual for MDCCCXXXVII

Becquier, José
Spanish costumes. Paris, Bulla 1830
12 col.pl. F.
Each plate marked D. José Becquer, pinto, Bayot dibujo
Colas 271

Bedford, Jessie
English children in the olden time, by Elizabeth Godfrey [pseud.] 2d ed. London, Methuen 1907
xvii,336p. 32pl. O.
LC W8-3

Home life under the Stuarts, 1603-1649, by Elizabeth Godfrey [pseud] London, G. Richards; New York, E. P. Dutton 1903
xx,312p. front. 18pl.(incl. ports. facsim.) O. $3.50 o.p.
Costume index. LC 3-15115

Social life under the Stuarts, by Elizabeth Godfrey [pseud.] London, G. Richards; New York, E. P. Dutton 1904
xxiv,273p. 18pl(incl. front. ports.) O.
Authorities: p xvii-xviii
LC 5-4480

Bedinger, Margery
Navajo Indian silver-work. Denver, Col. J. VanMale c1936
43p. front. pl. O. (Old West series of pamphlets, no8)
Bibliography: p42-43
LC 37-1851

La Bédollière, Émile Gigaut de. See Audebrand, Philibert, jt. auth.

Bedouin tribes of the Euphrates. Blunt, Lady Anne

Bedouins. See Arabia

Bedoya, Fernando Gomez de. See Gomez de Bedoya, Fernando

Beeg, Gunda. See Lechner, Hedwig, jt. auth.

Beeg-Aufsess, and others, eds. See Muster altdeutscher und moderner stickereien

Beely, F., and Kirchhoff, E.
Der menschliche fuss, seine bekleidung und pflege. Tübingen, H. Laupp [1891]
112p. 35 illus. O.
Lipperheide 1744o

Beer, C.
(illus.) Buek, F. G. Album hambürgische costüme

Beer, Johann Christoph
Der ... erz-hertzogen zu Oesterreich leben, regierung und gross-thaten: von dem ... urheber ... Rudolpho, grafen von Habsburg ... erstem römischen kayser an biss in die ... regierung ... Leopoldi und Josephi. Nürnberg, M. Endter 1695
1146p. 51pl. Q.
Lipperheide 860

Beer, Thomas Leonhard
(tr.) Siemienowicz, Kazimierz. Vollkommene geschütz-feuerwerck-und büchsenmeistereykunst

Beeton, Samuel Orchart
Book of needlework; new and rev. ed. London, Ward, Lock 1886
622p. 665 illus. 8pl. O.
Contains designs and illustrations. The frontispiece is a sixteenth century engraving showing a group of women spinning and doing various kinds of needlework
An earlier edition was published 1870
Lipperheide 4150

Beger, Lorenz

Cranae insula Laconica, Eadem & Helena dicta, & Minyarum posteris habitata; ex numismatibus Goltzianis, contra communem opionem, quae ad Helenam Atticae respexit. Coloniae Brandenburgicae, U. Liebpertus 1696
26p. illus. (incl. 16 pictures of coins) Q.
Lipperheide 183

Meleagrides et Aetolia, ex numismate Kyrieon apud Goltzium; interspersis marmoribus quibusdam, de Meleagri interitu, & apri Calydonii venatione. Coloniae Brandenburgicae, U. Liebpertus 1696
26p. 16 illus. Q.
Lipperheide 184

Beggars

England

Smith, J. T. Etchings of remarkable beggars, itinerant traders, and other persons of notoriety in London and its environs. 1815-16

France

Duplessi-Bertaux, Jean. Recueil de cent sujets de divers genres. 1814. Part 7

Callot, Jacques. Italian beggars, men and women. 1622

Bégin, Émile Auguste Nicolas Jules

Voyage pittoresque en Espagne et en Portugal ... Illus. de MM. Rouargue frères. Paris, Belin-Leprieur et Morizot [1852]
xii,556p. front. pl.(part col.) Q.
Colas 272. Lipperheide 1233. LC 19-3382

Voyage pittoresque en Suisse, en Savoie et sur les Alpes. Illus. de MM. Rouargue frères. Paris, Belin-Leprieur et Morizot [1852]
560p. front. 24pl.(8 col.) Q.
The colored plates show costumes
Colas 273. LC 19-3384

The **beginnings** of art. Grosse, Ernst

Begraeffenisse van ... Frederick Henrick ... prince van Orange. Post, Pieter

Begründeter aufweis des plazes bei der stadt Constanz. Eiselein, Josua

Behaim, Paulus

Briefe eines Leipziger studenten aus den jahren 1572 bis 1574; herausgegeben von W. Loose ... Beigabe zum Jahresbericht der realschule zu Meissen. Meissen, C. E. Klinkicht 1880
23p. Q.
On materials, style and cost of a student's wardrobe of this period
Lipperheide 634m

Beham, Hans Sebald

Biblicae historiae artificiosissimè depictae. Biblische historien figürlich fürgebildet. Franckfurt, C. Egenolph 1537
40 l. 81 illus. Q.
Lipperheide 624

Biblicae historiae, artificiocissimus picturis effigiatae ... Biblische historien kunstlich furgemalet. Franckfurt, C. Egenolph [1536]
40 l. 81 illus. Q.
Many editions published 1533-1557. One other with variation in title is listed here
Lipperheide 623

... Holzschnitte zum Alten Testament. Zwickau, F. Ullmann 1910
3p.l. facsim.: [79]p. illus. D. (Zwickauer facsimiledrucke no 1)
Facsimile reprint of his: *Biblicae historiae.* Preface signed Otto Clemen
LC 12-8193

(illus.) Das Bapstum. See note under Das Bapstum

Behind the smile in real Japan. Venables, E. K.

Behringer, Ludwig

Die bayerischer armee unter König Maximilian II. München, Mey & Widmayer 1854
19 col.pl.(incl. 157 illus.) F.
Colas 274. Lipperheide 2194

Uniformen des bayerischen heeres nach der neuen bekleidungsvorschrift. München, Mey & Widmayer ca1864
24 col.pl. Q.
Colas 276. Lipperheide 2196

See also Münich, Friedrich, jt. auth.

Beier, W.

(lithgr.) Mannheimer maskenzug im jahr 1841

Beijer, Agne. See Stockholm. Nationalmuseum. Recueil de plusieurs fragments des premières comédies italiennes

Beisbarth, Karl Friedrich. See Heideloff, K. A. von, ed. Die kunst des mittelalters in Schwaben

Beissel, Stephan

Die bilder der handschrift des Kaisers Otto im Münster zu Aachen ... herausgegeben und mit den bildern der evangelienbücher von Trier, Gotha, Bremen und Hildesheim. Aachen, R. Barth 1886
109p. 33pl. Q.
Lipperheide 366

Vaticanische miniaturen ... Quellen zur geschichte der miniaturmalerei. Mit XXX tafeln in lichtdruck. Miniatures choisies de la Bibliothèque du Vatican. Freiburg im Breisgau, St. Louis, Mo. [etc.] Herder 1893
59p. 30pl. F.
German and French in parallel columns
Bibliographical foot-notes
Lipperheide 362. LC 14-17461

Beiträge zur geschichte der altgriechischen tracht. Studniczka, Franz

Beitrage zur teutschen kunst- und geschichts-kunde durch kunstdenkmale mit vorzüglicher berücksichtigung des mittelalters. Müller, F. H.

Das **beiwerk** der mode. Boehn, Max von

Die **bekleidung.** Kratschmer, Florian

Die **bekleidung,** ausrüstung und bewaffnung der königlich bayerischen armee von 1806 bis zur neuzeit. Müller, Karl, and Braun, Louis

Bekleidung und ausrüstung der preussischen feuerwehren. Scholl, Edouard

Bekleidungs vorschrift für die kaiserlichen schutztruppen in Afrika. Berlin, S. Mittler 1896
48p. O.
Lipperheide 2142

Bekleidungs-vorschrift für offiziere. Donat, F. M. von

Bekleidungskunst und mode. Boehn, Max von

Bekleidungsvorschrift für die staatliche schutzpolizei Preussens. Berlin, Kameradschaft 1923
37p. O.

Die **belagerung** der stadt Augsburg. Rugendas, G. P.

Der **belehrende** bergmann. Ein fassliches lese- und bildungsbuch für kinder und erwachsene, lehrer und laien, besonders aber für jünglinge. Mit 9 schwarzen und colorirten, von C. Biechling gestochenen kupfern. Pirna, A. R. Friese 1830
232p. col.front. pl.(part col.) sq.T.

Belevitch-Stankevitch, H.
Le goût chinois en France au temps de Louis XIV. Paris, J. Chemit 1910
xliv,272p. 14pl. Q.
The plates show Siamese and Chinese of various classes

Belgian life in town and country. Boulger, D. C. de K.

La **Belgique** monumentale, historique et pittoresque, par mm. H. G. Moke, Victor Joly, Eugène Gens, [and others.] Ouvrage suivi d'un Coup d'oeil sur l'état actuel des arts, des sciences et de la littérature en Belgique, par A. Baron. Bruxelles, A. Jamar et C. Hen 1844
2v. 196 illus. 67pl.(7 col.) port. Q. (Panthéon national [v5-6])
The colored plates show costume
Lipperheide 966. LC 2-22246

Die **belgische** armee in ihrer gegenwärtigen uniformierung ... gezeichnet von J. Hohmann. Leipzig, M. Ruhl 1908
20p. fold.col.pl. D.

Belgium
Anderson, Mrs I. W. P. The spell of Belgium. 1915
Busscher, Edmond de. Album du cortège des comtes de Flandre, personnages et costumes. 1852-53
Madou, J. B., and Hemelryck, J. L. van. Costumes belgiques, anciens et modernes, militaires civils et religieux. 1830
Vlaanderen door de eeuwen heen. 1912-1913

See also Netherlands; also subdivision Belgium under Ceremonial and festival costume; Funerals; Lace; Military costume; Monastic and religious orders; Nobles; Tattooing; Theatrical costume; Weddings and wedding dress

Middle ages

Vigne, Félix de. Vade-mecum du peintre, ou Recueil de costumes du moyen-âge, pour servir à l'histoire de la Belgique et pays circonvoisins. 1844

16th century

Winkler, Friedrich. Die flämische buchmalerei des XV. und XVI. jahrhunderts. 1925

17th century

Hannema, Dirk, and Schendel, A. van. Noorden Zuid- Neterlandsche schilderkunst der XVII. eeuw. 1936
Illustrium quos Belgium habuit pictorum effigies, ad vivum accurate delineatae. ca1600
Winkler, Friedrich. Die flämische buchmalerei des XV. und XVI. jahrhunderts. 1925

18th century

Ehrmann, T. F. Print-Geschenkjen voor myn kinderen, bestaande in afbeeldingen van Hollandsche, Friesche, Brabandsche en Fransche dragten en costumes. 1804
Recueil des devotions et divertissements de ... Marie Elisabeth archiduchesse d'Aûtriche ... dans sa residence à Bruxelles. 1736

Periodicals

L'Indicateur; contenant toutes les productions de l'esprit, les pièces de poésie fugitives, les bon-mots ... et surtout les modes. 1778-80

19th century

La Belgique monumentale, historique et pittoresque. 1844
Madou, J. B., and Eeckhout, J. J. Collection des provinces de la Belgique. 1835

20th century

Boulger, D. C. de K. Belgian life in town and country. 1904
Edwards, G. W. Some old Flemish towns. 1911
Omond, G. W. T. Belgium; painted by Amédée Forestier. 1908

Belgium. Bibliothèque royale de Belgique, Brussels. See Brussels. Bibliothèque royale de Belgique

Belgium. Ministère de la guerre
Tenues des officiers et assimilés. Bruxelles, Guyot frères 1914
66p. O.
LC 15-12687

Belgrado, Mario Savorgnano, conte di. See Savorgnano, Mario, conte di Belgrado

Belin, A., and others
Costumes de Suède, Norvège, Danemark, Hollande et Allemagne; dessinés par Belin, Karl Girardet, H. Sharles, Elchanon Verveer, et gravés par Geoffroy, Girardet, Lallemand, Metzmacher, Nargeot et Varin. Paris, Aux bureaux des journaux, Les Modes parisiennes, La Toilette de Paris & Le Petit journal pour rire 186-?
20 col.pl. F.
At head of title: Prime du journal Les Modes parisiennes
Colas 712

Belisario, L. M.
Sketches of character in illustration of the habits, occupation and the costume of the Negro population in the Island Jamaica. Kingston, Jamaica 1837
8 col.pl. Q.
Colas 279

Bell, Archie
A trip to Lotus land. New York, John Lane company [etc.] 1917
287p. front. 32pl. O.
Bibliography: p284
LC 17-30747

Bell, Mrs Arthur. See Bell, Mrs N. R. E. M.

Bell, Aubrey Fitz Gerald
Portugal of the Portuguese. New York, C. Scribner's sons 1915
x,268p. front. pl. fold.map. D. (Countries and peoples series) $1.50 o.p.
Costume index. LC A16-423

Bell, Sir Charles Alfred
The people of Tibet. Oxford, The Clarendon press 1928
xix,319p. front. pl.(1 col.) maps(part fold.) O. $7
Bibliography: p[305]-06
Costume index. LC 29-26164

Bell, Gertrude Lowthian
The desert and the sown. New York, E. P. Dutton 1907
xvi,347p. col.fronts. illus. pl. O.
Shows costume of Syria
LC 7-35188

Bell, Mrs Nancy R. E. (Meugens)
Lives and legends of the English bishops and kings, mediæval monks, and other later saints. London, G. Bell 1904
xiii,377p. front. 52pl. O. (The saints in Christian art, [v. III])
Contains pictures of the saints
LC 4-19635

(ed.) Perl, Frau Henriette. Venezia

(tr.) Nadaillac, J. F. A. du P., marquis de. Manners and monuments of prehistoric peoples

Bella, Stefano della. See Della Bella, Stefano

La **bella** Napoli. Allers, C. W.

Bellangé, Joseph Louis Hippolyte
Collection des types de tous les corps et des uniformes militaires de la république et de l'empire. Paris, J. J. Dubochet 1844
112p. 50 col.pl. port. Q.
Forty-four of the plates appeared first in P. M. Laurent d'Ardèche's *Histoire de l'Empereur Napoléon*
German translation entitled: *Die soldaten der französischen republik und des kaisserreichs* (Leipzig, J. J. Weber 1843)
Colas 287. Lipperheide 2316 (German ed.)

Costumes de l'armée française depuis 1830 jusqu'à nos jours. Paris, Gihaut frères [1831]
61pl. Q.
Plates are modified from his *Uniformes ... depuis 1815*
Colas 285

[Croquis divers; lith. de Villain] Paris, Gihaut 1828-30
4v. 54pl. Q.
Sketches of popular and military life
Lipperheide 1158

Les jolis soldats français, chant guerrier par Ch. Plantade. Paris, Gihaut 1824
5pl. Q.
Colas 283

Uniformes de l'armée française depuis 1815 jusqu'à ce jour. Paris, Gihaut frères 1831
1 p.l. 115 col.pl. F.
Binder's title: *Costumes militaires.* Published also with plates in black and white
Colas 284. LC 11-20042

La **Belle** assemblée, or Bell's court and fashionable magazine, addressed particularly to the ladies. v 1-7, 1806-10; new ser. v 1-30, 1810-24; ser.3 v 1-15, 1825-32. London, J. Bell, 1806-32
[52]v. col.pl. O.
Continued as *Court magazine and monthly critic*
Colas 289. Lipperheide 4596

A **belle** of the fifties. Clay-Clopton, Mrs Virginia

Bellermann, Christian Friedrich
Über die ältesten christlichen begräbnissstätten und besonders die katakomben zu Neapel mit ihren wandgemälden; ein beitrag zur christlichen alterthumskunde. Hamburg, F. Perthes 1839
120p. 15pl. (12 col.) Q.
Lipperheide 235

Les **belles** marchandes; almanach historiques, proverbiale et chantant. Paris, Jubert 1783-84
2v. 24 illus. Ti.
Illustrations show costume
Colas 290

Belleval, René, marquis de
Du costume militaire des Français en 1446. Paris, A. Aubry 1866
91p. 7pl. Q.
Colas 291. Lipperheide 2098

Bellezze de recami, et dessegni, opera nova, nellaquale si ritrovano, varie, & diverse sorti de mostre, di punti tagliati, & punti in aiere, à fogliami, punti in stuora, & altre sorte. Venetia 1558
20,19 l. illus. Q.
Embroidery designs
Lipperheide 3889

Bellini, Gentile
(illus.) Menestrier, C. F. Description de la belle et grande colonne historiée, dressée à l'honneur de l'empereur Theodose

Bellinzoni, Luigi
Usi e costumi antichi e moderne, di tutti i popoli del mondo. Roma, Perino 1884
4v. Q.

Il **bellissimo** torneo à piedi, overo la barriera fatta dalla nobilta di Vicenza nel theatro Delli Signori Academici Olimpice il carnevale dell' anno MDCXII. Vicenza, F. Grossi [1612]
43p. Q.
Lipperheide 2816

Belloc, Hilaire
The book of the Bayeux tapestry, presenting the complete work in a series of colour facsimiles: the introduction & narrative by Hilaire Belloc. New York, G. P. Putnam's sons 1914
xix,[76]p. front.(map) col.illus. Q.
Illustrations colored by hand
LC 14-20288

Bellori, Giovanni Pietro. See Bartoli, P. S., jt. auth.

[**Bellot, R. P.**]
Album du bon-bock. Paris, L. Baschet 1878
49pl. Q.
Lipperheide 3566

Belmonte y García, Juan
Juan Belmonte, killer of bulls; the autobiography of a matador ... as told to Manuel Chaves Nogales. Tr. from the Spanish and with a note on bull-fighting by Leslie Charteris. Garden City, N. Y., Doubleday, Doran 1937
x,340p. illus. pl. ports. O.
LC 37-27179

Belnos, Mrs S. C.
The Sundhya, or the daily prayers of the Brahmins; illus. in a series of original drawings from nature, demonstrating their attitudes and different signs and figures performed by them during the ceremonies of their morning devotions; and likewise their poojas. [London,] 1851
20 l. 24 col.pl. F.
Lipperheide 1499

Twenty four plates illustrative of Hindoo and European manners in Bengal; drawn on the stone by A. Colin from sketches by Mrs Belnos. London, Smith and Elder; Paris, A. Colin ca1832
24 l. 24 col.pl. F.
Plates have legends in French and English. Also known with plates in black and white
Colas 292

Beltrami, Luca
D'arte negli arredi sacri della Lombardia; con note storiche e descrittive. Milano, W. Hoepli 1897
55p. 80pl. F.
Seventeen of the plates show church vestments

Belts and belt buckles
Peteva, Yelena. Ceintures populaires bulgares. 1931
Roth, H. L. Oriental silverwork, Malay and Chinese. 1910

See also Cestus; Netsukes

Bem, Balcer
Die alten zunft- und verkehrs-ordnungen der stadt Krakau. Nach Balthasar Behem's Codex picturatus in der K. K. Jagellonischen bibliothek hrsg. von Bruno Bucher. Wien, C. Gerold's sohn 1889
xxxvi,112p. front. xxvi pl. F.
Festschrift zum jubiläum des K. K. Oesterreich. museums für kunst und industrie
Plates are miniature paintings of the various gilds of Krakow
LC 11-7629

Bemerkungen auf einer reise in die südlichen statthalterschaften des Russischen reichs in den jahren 1793 und 1794. Pallas, P. S.

Bemerkungen über die monumente der ritter zu Vellberg. Gräter, F. D.

Benavides, Antonio. See Carramolino, J. M. Discursos leidos ante la Real academia de ciencias morales y politicas en la recepcion publica

Bender, Ferdinand
Fünf lebende bilder vor ... dem Könige und der Königin am 9ten September 1840 zur vorfeyer der huldigung von Preussens ständen dargestellt im dazu errichten festsaale. Königsberg, H. L. Voigt [1840]
18p. 5pl. F.
Title of the text: *Preussens vorzeit in lebenden bildern dargestellt*
Lipperheide 2543

Bender, Hermann
Rom und römisches leben im alterthum ... mit zahlreichen abbildungen nach zeichnungen von A. Gnauth ... professor Riess und A. Schill ... und anderen. Tübingen, H. Laupp [1880]
599p. double front. illus. (incl. plans) pl. Q.
Lipperheide 251. LC 35-22816

Bender, Paul
(illus.) Netto, Curt. Papier-schmetterlinge aus Japan

Die **benennung** der wichtigeren bestandteile der modernen französischen tracht. Esau, Hubert

Bengal. See India—Bengal

Benham, William
The tower of London. London, Seeley and co.; New York, E. P. Dutton 1906
104p. 28pl. (4 col.) plan. Q. (Portfolio artistic monographs no47)
Three of the plates are of costume interest: Assault on a fortress, from a manuscript of Boccaccio's *De casibus*; Artillery of the fifteenth century; and A tournament, from a manuscript of the romance of Sire Jehan de Saintré
LC 6-46330

Benhazera, Maurice
Six mois chez les Touareg du Ahaggar. Illustrations photographiques d'après les clichés de Laperrine, Voinot et Cannac. Alger, A. Jourdan 1908
xxiii,233p. 1 map, 1 pl. Q.

Benigni, P.
(illus.) Margerand, J. Les cuirasses des carabiniers (1810-1870)

Benito
(illus.) Zamacoïs, Miguel. Dernière lettre persane mise en français par M. Zamacoïs

Benjamin, Mrs Caroline (Gilbert). See National society of the colonial dames of America. Report of the Committee on relics

Benndorf, Otto
Antike gesichtshelme und sepulcralmasken. Wien, K. Gerold's sohn 1878
77p. 12 illus. 17pl. Q.
From Vienna. Kaiserliche Akademie der wissenschaften. *Denkschriften der philosophisch-historischen classe* v28, p301-75
On masks found in various parts of Europe
Lipperheide 172

Bennet, H. Graham
(ed.) Great Britain. Lord chamberlain. Dress worn by gentlemen at His Majesty's court

Bennett, Frank Marion
The steam navy of the United States. A history of the growth of the steam vessel of war in the U.S. navy, and of the naval engineer corps. Pittsburgh, Pa. Press of W. T. Nicholson 1896
xi,953p. illus. pl. (part col. part fold.) ports. facsim. O.
Illustrations show insignia, and officers and cadets in the uniform of different periods
LC 8-32073

Benoist, Antoine

(illus.) Fête publique donnée par la ville de Paris à l'occasion du mariage de monseigneur le Dauphin le 13. fevrier M.DCC.XLVII

(illus.) Highmore, Joseph. Plates illustrating the "Pamela" of Samuel Richardson

Benoist, Félix

La Bretagne contemporaine ... Dessins d'après nature; texte par Aurélien de Courson, Pol de Courcy [et autres] Paris, Charpentier 1865

3v in 1 pl. F.
"Sites pittoresques, monuments, costumes, scènes de moeurs, histoire, légendes, traditions et usages des cinq départements." Subtitle
Contents: v[1] Loire-Inférieure. v[2] Ille-et-Vilaine. v[3] Côtes-du-Nord
Colas 295

Nantes et la Loire Inférieure. Nantes, Charpentier 1850

2v. (33,45 l.) 76pl.(part col.) F. 70fr.
"Dessinés d'après nature ... Les costumes dessinés et lithographiés par Hte Lalaisse ... accompagnés de notices ... par Pitre Chevalier, Emile Souvestre et une société d'hommes de lettres du pays." Subtitle
Work published in 35 parts
Colas 293

(illus.) La Normandie illustrée

See also Lalaisse, Hippolyte, jt. auth.

Bensusan, Samuel Levy

Morocco, painted by A. S. Forrest. London, A. and C. Black 1904

xv,230p. 72 col.pl.(incl. front.) O. 42s o.p.
Costume index. LC 5-21055

[Bentley, John]

Essays relative to the habits, character, and moral improvement of the Hindoos. London, Printed for Kingsbury, Parbury & Allen 1823

351p. O.
Essays originally published in the *Friend of India,* a periodical work, conducted by the Serampore missionaries
Colas 983. LC 5-12912

Benvenuti, Leo

La situla Benvenuti nel Museo di Este. Este, A. Stratico 1886

11p. 2pl.(1 col.) F.
The plaque reproduced shows priests, a potter's shop, wrestlers, soldiers with prisoners and hunting scenes of prehistoric times
Lipperheide 258

Benziger brothers, New York

Catalogue of church ornaments, New York, Benziger brothers [1889]

200,[12]p. incl.front. illus. F.
LC CA10-5425

Catalogue of vestments, banners and regalia. New York, Benziger brothers [1893]

88,[8]p. incl.front. illus. F.
LC 10-19919

Benzinger, Immanuel

Hebräische archäologie; ... 2. vollständig neu bearb. aufl., mit 253 abbildungen im text und einem plan von Jerusalem. Tübingen, Mohr 1907

xx,450p. illus. plan. Q. (Grundriss der theologischen wissenschaften. 2. reihe. 1. bd)
LC 7-35615

Hebraeische archäologie; 3d ed. rev. Leipzig, E. Pfeiffer 1927

xxiv,437pl. illus. Q. (Angelos lehrbücher, bd 1, Jews)

Benzoni, Girolamo

Americae pars quarta [-sexta] Francofurti ad Moenum, typis I. Feyrabend, impensis T. de Bry [1594-96]

3v. maps, 74pl. F. (In Bry, Theodor de. [Grands voyages] pts4-6)
Translated by U. Chauveton
Plates show Christopher Columbus and the early Spanish conquerors
Second Latin edition published 1594-1617. German edition: *Das vierdte-[sechste] theil der neuwen welt* (1594-97)
Lipperheide 1612-13 (pts4, 6)

History of the New world ... shewing his travels in America, from A. D. 1541 to 1556: with some particulars of the island of Canary. Now first tr. and ed. by Rear-Admiral W. H. Smyth. London, Printed for the Hakluyt society, 1857

280p. illus. O. (Works issued by the Hakluyt society [no XXI])
LC 5-40265

Der **Beobachter** der herrenmoden. Jahrg. 1, 1855+ Berlin, Expedition d. europäische modenzeitung

Col.illus. col.pl. O.-F.
A periodical of men's fashions. Published monthly. Current 1937. Some numbers contain patterns
Title varies: v 1-9, 1856-64: *Der Beobachter französischer, deutscher u. englischer herrenmoden*; v10-48, 1865-1903: *Der Beobachter deutscher, französischer u. englischer herrenmoden*
Absorbed *Moden-telegraph* 1923
Colas 296. Lipperheide 4677

Der **Beobachter** deutscher, französischer u. englischer herrenmoden. See Der Beobachter der herrenmoden

Der **Beobachter** französischer, deutscher u. englischer herrenmoden. See Der Beobachter der herrenmoden

Bérain, Jean Louis

Costumes de ballet, gravés par Jacques Le Pautre. Paris, ca1690

11pl. Q.
Colas 297

Maskenanzüge. [engr. by J. Le Pautre] Paris, ca1670-80

20pl.

Berbrugger, Louis Adrien

Algérie historique, pittoresque et monumentale. Recueil de vues, monuments, cérémonies, costumes, armes et portraits ... avec texte descriptif. Paris, J. Delahaye 1843-[45]

5v. front. illus. 125pl.(part col.) 6 port. maps, plan. F.
Contents: v 1 Province d'Alger; v2 Province d'Oran; v3 Province de Bone; v4 Province de Constantine; v5 Races algériennes, monnaies, flore d'Algérie
Colas 298. Lipperheide 1594. LC 5-8633

Berckwerck buch. Agricola, Georg

Berendsohn, B. S.

(pub.) Buek, F. G. Album hambürgische costüme

(pub.) Erinnerung an Hamburg

Berensberg, Franz von Pelser-. See Pelser-Berensberg, Franz von

Berg, Johan August
Bilder ur svenska folklifvet. Götheborg, D. F. Bonnier 1855
12 l. 12 col.pl. F.
"Teckningar efter originaler af B. Nordenberg, K. Zoll, J. W. Wallander, J. Höckert och B. Wennerberg" Subtitle
Text in Swedish, German and English
Colas 299. Lipperheide 1051

Berge, P. A. van den
[Costumes hollandois] No place, 16—?
26pl. Q.
Cataloged from Colas's *Bibliographie* where a list of plates is given. The plates were copied for A. Allard's *Habillemens*
Colas 2966

Berger, Anatoliĭ Ksaver'yevich
V gorakh Vostochnogo Zakavkaz'îa Azerbaĭdzhan. Moskva, Izdatel'stvo "Rabotnik Prosveshcheniîa" 1927g
60p. illus. 35k.
On the inhabitants of the mountains of Azerbaijan, Russia

Berger, Christoph Heinrich, edler herr von
Commentatio de personis vulgo larvis seu mascheris von der carnavals-lust, critico, historico, morali atque iuridico modo. Francofurti et Lipsiae, apud G. M. Knochium [1723]
340p. front. illus. pl.(part fold.) O.
An enlarged edition of the author's *Dissertatio de iure personarum* (Vitembergae, literis viduae Gerdesiae 1720) Includes (between p128 and 129) reproduction of the miniatures in the illustrated codex Terence manuscript (Vaticanus 3868) 153 plates on 85 leaves
Lipperheide 3169. LC 17-11521

Berger-Levrault, Oscar
(ed.) Les costumes strasbourgeois ... Reproduits en fac-similés d'après les recueils originaux. Paris and Nancy, Berger-Levrault 1889
20p. 1 illus.102pl. 60fr.
"Éd. au dix-septième siècle par Frederic Guillaume Schmuck et au dix-huitième siècle par ses fils Frédéric Schmuck et Guillaume Schmuck." Subtitle
Contains reproductions from five books on costume published in Strasbourg in the 17th and 18th centuries, namely, the three editions of *Strassburgisch trachtenbüchlein, Alsace françoise,* and *Strassburger Sackkalender*
Colas 300. Lipperheide 795

Berggruen, Oscar
Huldigungs-festzug der stadt Wien zur feier der silberne hochzeit ihrer majestäten des kaisers Franz Joseph I. und der kaiserin Elizabeth, 27 April 1879 ... mit illustr. text v. Osc. Berggruen. Wien, Im selbstverlag des gemeinderathes der stadt Wien 1881
43p. illus. 15pl. and atlas 37pl. F.
French edition has title *27 avril 1879; cortège historique* (Paris, Quantin [1879] 26 l. 45pl. O.) Plates are after Makart
Lipperheide 2647

Bergh, Th.
Den danske armee og marine i tegninger af Th. Bergh. Kjobenhavn, Stinck 1859
1 l. 24 col.pl. Q.
Colas 301

Die uniformen d. königl. dänischen armee. Kjobenhavn, ca1860
23 col.pl. O.

Berghaus, Heinrich Karl Wilhelm
Die völker des erdballs nach ihrer abstammung und verwandtschaft, und ihren eigenthumlichkeiten in regierungsform, religion, sitte und tracht. Brüssel und Leipzig, C. Muquardt 1845-47
2v 150 col.pl. Q.
Later edition by the same publisher (1861. 3v.)
Colas 302

(tr.) Catlin, George. Die Indianer. See note under his North American Indians

Die **bergknappen** in ihren berufs- und familienleben. Heuchler, Eduard

Bergwerck buch. Agricola, Georg

Bericht und anzeigen aller Herren Geschlecht der loblichen Statt Augspurg. Mair, P. H.

Bericht vom bergwerck. Löhneyss, G. E.

[**Berka, J.**]
L'armée française représentée en 18 feuilles. Prague, F. Zimmer ca1810
Front. 18 col.pl. O.
According to Colas a facsimile reprint also exists
Colas 303

Berkhey, Johannes le Francq van. See Chalon, Christina. Zinspelende gedigtjes

Berlepsch, Hermann Alexander von
Chronik vom ehrbaren schuhmachergewerk, nebst einer kurzen geschichte der vorzüglichsten fussbekleidungen früherer zeiten. St Gallen, Scheitlin und Zollikofer [1850]
176p. 24 illus. O.
Volume 4 of his *Chronik der gewerke*
Lipperheide 1738

Chronik vom ehrbaren und uralten schneidergewerk; nebst einer kurzen geschichte der trachten und moden. St Gallen, Scheitlin und Zollikofer [1850]
244p. 12 illus. Q.
Volume 2 of his: *Chronik der gewerke*
Contains excerpts from sumptuary laws, material on wedding dress, biographies of famous tailors, etc. and illustrations of costumes from the Middle Ages to the eighteenth century
Lipperheide 65

Berlien, Johann Heinrich Friedrich
Der Elephanten-orden und seine ritter ... Kopenhagen, Gedruckt in der Berlingschen officin 1846
188p. front.(port.) 9pl. O.
Lipperheide 1929. LC 9-32595

Berlin. See subdivision Berlin under Police—Germany; Street venders—Germany

Berlin. K. Akademie der künste. See Chodowiecki, D. N. Von Berlin nach Danzig

Berlin. Königliche museen. See Berlin. Staatliche museen

Berlin. Museum für deutsche volkstrachten und erzeugnisse des hausgewerbes
Mittheilungen. [Band 1] Berlin, R. Mosse 1897-[1901]
339p. 152 illus. on 1 l. O.
Lipperheide 742c

Berlin. Museum für völkerkunde. See Berlin. Staatliche museen. Museum für völkerkunde

Berlin. Staatliche kunstbibliothek. See Lipperheide, F. J., freiherr von. Katalog der Freiherrlich von Lipperheide'schen kostümbibliothek

Berlin. Staatliche museen

Amerika's Nordwest-küste. See entry under Bastian, Adolf

Die bronzeschwerter des Königlichen museums zu Berlin; hrsg. im auftrage der generalverwaltung durch A. Bastian und A. Voss. Berlin, Weidmann 1878
xvi,79p. 16pl. F.
Lipperheide 292. LC 19-1612

Sport und spiel bei Griechen und Römern; bildwerke aus den Staatlichen museen zu Berlin. Berlin, Verlag für kunstwissenschaft [1934]
15p. 58pl.(incl. facsim.) Q.
Collection in the Kaiser Friedrich museum, Berlin. "Literaturangaben": p15
LC 35-14284

Terracotten des Königlichen museums zu Berlin. See entry under Panofka, Theodor, ed.

Berlin. Staatliche museen. Museum für völkerkunde

Führer durch das Museum für völkerkunde. Berlin, W. de Gruyter 1929
203p. 48 illus. pl. maps. plans. O.

Berlin. Staatliche museen. Museum für völkerkunde. Ethnologisches forschungs-u. lehr- institute

The art of old Peru. See entry under Lehmann, Walter, and Doering, Heinrich

Kunstgeschichte des alten Peru. See entry under Lehman, Walter, and Doering, Heinrich

Berlin. Zeughaus

Die waffensammlung Sr. königlichen Hoheit des prinzen Carl von Preussen. See entry under Hiltl, Georg

Waffensammlung Sr. koniglichen Hoheit des prinzen Carl von Preussen; mittelalterliche abtheilung. See entry under Hiltl, Georg

Berlin; eine zeitschrift für freunde der schönen künste, des geschmacks und der moden. 1.-2. jahrg.; 1799-1800. Berlin, H. Fröhlich
2v. col.pl. O.
Contains fashion plates
Colas 304. Lipperheide 4587

Berlin und die Berliner. Eichler, Ludwig

Berlin und die Berliner. Löffler, Ludwig

Berlin und die Berlinerin. Ostwald, H. O. A.

Berlin und die Hohenzollern. Rapsilber, Maximilian

Berlin vor hundert jahren. 1800. Secularheft von "Berliner leben"; illustrierte zeitschrift fur schönheit und kunst. Berlin, Freier verlag [1900]
16 l. 3p. 102 illus. F.
Lipperheide 820c

Berlin wie es ist und trinkt. Glasbrenner, Adolf

Berliner ausrufer. Dörbeck, B.

Berliner modenblatt. 1.-3. jahrg., 1879-1881. Berlin, Verlag des Berliner modenblatt
3v. illus. col.pl. F.
Published fortnightly. Contains colored fashion plates. Editor: Frz. Ebhardt
Colas 305. Lipperheide 4765

Stick-album des Berliner modenblatt; sammlung farbiger musterblätter für handarbeiten. Berlin, F. Ebhardt [1880]
3pts. 16 illus. 18 col.pl. F.
Lipperheide 4002

Berliner modenspiegel in- und ausländischer originale; eine zeitschrift für die elegante welt. 1.-18. jahrgang; 1832-1849. Berlin
18v. col.pl. Q.
Contains colored fashion plates
Colas 306. Lipperheide 4618

Berliner muster zur weissen stickerei; auswahl des modernstern und geschmackvollsten für alle gegenstände dieser kunst. Berlin, L. W. Wittich [1817-33]
20pts. 170pl. Q.
Lipperheide 3942

Berliner redensarten. Dörbeck, B.

Berliner witze und anecdoten. Dörbeck, B.

Berlinische relation, was beym sieg- und freudenreichen einzug sr. churfl. durchl. zu Brandenburg ... als ... se: churfl. durchl. nach glücklich-vollendeter pommerischer expedition ... in dero residentzstädte Berlin Cölln ... am 31 decembr. ... 1677, passiret. Berlin(?) [1678]
11 l. 1 pl. Q.
Lipperheide 2524

Berlinischer damen-kalender auf das jahr 1798-1810. Berlin, J. F. Unger
13v. illus. D.
Colas 308. Lipperheide 4495

Berlinisches archiv der zeit und ihres geschmacks; hrsg. von F. L. W. Meyer, F. E. Rambach und I. A. Fessler. 1.-6. jahrg. v 1-12, 1795-1800. Berlin, F. Maurer
12v. col.illus. O.
Contains fashion plates
Colas 309. Lipperheide 4580

Berlins antike bildwerke. See Friederichs, Karl. Kleinere kunst und industrie im alterthum

Bern. See Switzerland—Bern

Bernard, Charles

Généalogie de la maison royale de Bourbon, avec les éloges et les portraits des princes qui en sont sortis. [Éd. by Charles Sorel.] Paris, N. de Sercy 1644
58p. port. F.

Bernard, Francisco

Arte de andar a cavallo. Madrid, Vda de Josepha de Orga 1757
198p. 5pl. Q.

Bernard, Frédéric

Les fêtes célèbres de l'antiquité du moyen âge et des temps modernes; ouvrage illustré de 25 vignettes par Goutzwiller. Paris, Hachette 1878
306p. incl. illus. pl. D. (Bibliothèque des merveilles)
LC 27-6028

Bernatzik, Hugo Adolf

The dark continent; Africa, the landscape and the people. London, The Studio limited [1931]
xv p 256pl. on 128 l. F. (Orbis terrarum) $7.50
Contains pictures of members of many African tribes
German edition (Berlin, Atlantis-verlag, 1930) published under title: *Der dunkle erdteil; Afrika, landschaft, volksleben*
Costume index. LC 31-12232

Bernhardi, Karl. See note under Kulturhistorischer bilderatlas

Bernhardt, Johan Samuel

Anleitung, den menschlichen körper, besonders aber den weiblichen, seinem verschiedenen abweichungen gemäss, zu kleiden und zu verschönern; ein handbuch; 2. unveranderte ausg. Dresden, Arnoldischen buchhandlung 1820
112,120p. 15pl. tables O.
First edition, 1811
Lipperheide 3786m

Bernoulli, Johann Jacob B.

Museum in Basel; catalog für die antiquärische abtheilung (mit ausschluss der pfahlbauten und ethnographischen alterthümer) Basle, F. Wassermann 1880
O.
Lipperheide 5005

Bernoville, Gaëten

... Le pays des Basques, types et coutumes; dessins originaux de Iñigo Bernoville. Paris, Horizons de France 1930
149p. col.front. col.illus. ob.Q. (Provinces de France, types et coutumes. 7)
Costume index. LC 32-21359

Berrin, Emilie, and Savin, Jacques Christophe

Neueste englische und französische muster zu aller art der stickerei. Leipzig, Industrie-comptoir [1803]
40pl. (20 col.) F.
Lipperheide 3936

Berry, Jean de France, duc de

Durrieu, Paul, comte. Les très belles Heures de Notre-Dame du duc Jean de Berry

Durrieu, Paul, comte. Les très riches heures de Jean de France, duc de Berry

Berry, Mary

Extracts of the journals and correspondence of Miss Berry, from the year 1783 to 1852; ed. by Lady Theresa Lewis. London, Longmans 1865
3v. fronts.(ports.) 2pl. O.
LC 5-663

Berryman, J.

(engr.) Douce, Francis. Illustrations of Shakespeare, and of ancient manners

Bertall, Charles Albert d'Arnould

La comédie de notre temps ... études au crayon et à la plume; [1st]-2d series. Paris, E. Plon 1874-75
2v. fronts. illus. pl. Q.
Contents: La civilité, les habitudes, les mœurs, les coutumes, les manières et les manies de notre époque; v2 Les enfants, les jeunes, les mûrs, les vieux
Lipperheide 3568-69. LC 17-29318

The communists of Paris 1871; types, physiognomies, characters ... with explanatory text descriptive of each design written expressly for this edition by an Englishman, eye-witness of the scenes and events of that year. Paris, London, Buckingham [1873]
43 l. 40 col.pl. Q.
Several editions with French text were published, same collation, entitled *Les communeux en 1871* (Paris, Lemonnyer 1871) and *Les communeux, 1871* (Plon, 1880)
Colas 311-313. Lipperheide 3567

La vie hors de chez soi (comédie de notre temps). L'hiver, le printemps, l'été, l'automne; études au crayon et à la plume. Paris, E. Plon 1876
667p. 581 illus. Q.
Lipperheide 3570

La vigne; voyage autour des vins de France; étude physiologique, anecdotique, historique, humoristique et même scientifique. Paris, E. Plon 1878
659p. front.illus.95pl. O.
Rich in pictures of French costume of all classes during this period

(illus.) Balzac, Honoré de. Petites misères de la vie conjugale

(illus.) Briffault, E. V. Paris dans l'eau

Bertarelli, Achille

L'imagerie populaire italienne. Paris, Duchartre & Van Buggenhoudt [1929]
105p. pl.(part col.) illus. Q.
Illustrations show Italian costume of the 17th, 18th, and 19th centuries

Bertaux, Jean Duplessi-. See Duplessi-Bertaux, Jean

Bertelli, Ferdinando

Ferdinando Bertelli's trachtenbuch. Venedig 1563. Zwickau, F. Ullmann 1913
2p.l. facsim.(60p. illus.) Q. (Zwickauer facsimiledrucke no17)
Facsimile reproduction of *Omnium fere gentium*, 1563 edition
LC 16-8683

Omnium fere gentium nostrae aetatis habitus, nunquam ante hac aediti. Venetijs, F. Bertelli 1563
60pl. Q.
The second edition published 1569 has 64 plates
Colas 314-15. Lipperheide 2z, 3

Bertelli, Francesco

Il carnevale Italiano mascherato, oue si veggono in figura varie inueutione di capritii. [Venice] 1642
23pl. O.
The plates are copied from Pietro Bertelli's *Diversaru nationum habitus*
Colas 317. Lipperheide 3168

Bertelli, Pietro

Diversarũ nationum habitus. Patauij, A. Alcia & P. Bertelli 1589-96
3v. 106,79,76pl. O.
The first volume begun in 1589 was finished in 1592; the second was begun in 1592 and finished in 1594; vol. 3 appeared in 1596. Three large folded plates show processions, of the Turks, the Doges of Venice, and the popes. Five plates are arranged with flaps in such a manner that in the picture of a gondola or palanquin the flap can be raised showing the occupants; in another plate which shows a woman with large skirt, the flap can be raised showing underclothing and shoes
Some of the plates are in Francesco Bertelli's *Carnevalo italiano mascherato*. See also entry under Fabri, Alexandro de. *Diversarum*
Colas 316. Lipperheide 20

Bertelli, Pietro—*Continued*
Vite de gl'imperatori di Turchi; con le loro effiggie intalgiate. Vicenza, G. Greco 1599
56p. illus. F.
Head and shoulder pictures of emperors of Turkey of the 14th to the 16th centuries
Lipperheide 1403

Berthold, Friedrich Rudolph von
Katalog der kunst- und waffen-sammlung. Köln, M. D. Schanberg 1898
72p. 25p.l. Q.
Auction catalog
Lipperheide 2456

Bertini, A.
Costumi di Roma e dei contorni ... V. Mochetti, inc. Roma, 1846
30 col.pl. S.
Colas 318. Lipperheide 1312

Bertius, Petrus
Commentariorum rerum germanicarum libri tres. Primus est Germaniæ veteris. Secundus, Germaniæ posterioris, a Karolo Magno ad nostra usque tempora, cum principum genealogijs. Tertius est præcipuarum Germaniæ urbium cum earum iconismis et descriptionibus. Amstelodami, apud Ioannem Ianssonium 1616
732p. illus.(incl. maps, coat of arms) 18x24cm
Includes 26 maps and 99? views of cities. Many of the views show people in the costume of the time
Lipperheide 677. LC 32-18757

Bertoli, Antonio Daniele
Desseins (*In* Denkmäler des theaters. v3)

Bertolini, Francesco
Storia di Roma dalle origini italiche sino alla caduta dell' impero d'occidente; illustrata da Lodovico Pogliaghi. Milano, Fratelli Treves 1886
1058p. 229 illus. Q.
Lipperheide 259

Bertolotti, Antonino
Divertimenti pubblici nelle feste religiose del secolo XVIII dentro e fuori delle porte di Roma. Roma, Tipografia delle scienze mathematiche e fisiche 1887
32p. Q.
From the periodical: *Il Buonarroti*, ser 3, v2 pts9-11
Lipperheide 2499

Bertrand, Alexander Louis Joseph
Les Celtes dans les vallées du Pô et du Danube. Paris, E. Leroux 1894
241p. F. (Bibl. archéologique)

Bertrand de Moleville, Antoine François, marquis de
The costume of the hereditary states of the house of Austria, displayed in fifty coloured engravings; with descriptions, and an introduction. Tr. by R. C. Dallas. London, Printed for W. Miller by W. Bulmer and co. 1804
xxviii,[100]p. 50 col.pl. F.
Added t.-p. in French: *Costumes des états héréditaires de la maison de l'Autriche.* Text in English and French
Plates engraved by William Ellis and William Poole. William Alexander's *Picturesque representations of the dress and manners of the Austrians* contains reproductions of the same plates reduced in size Some of the plates appeared originally in Kininger's *Kleidertrachten*
Colas 2112. Costume index. Lipperheide 831. LC 28-31165

[Bertuch, Friedrich Justin]
Beschreibung der feierlichkeiten welche ... in Weimar und Jena am 6sten und 7ten October 1808 von dem Herzoge Carl August von Sachsen-Weimar veranstaltet wurden. Weimar, im verlage des H. S. priv. Landes-industrie-comptoirs 1809
24p. 5pl.(4 col.) F.
Added t.-p. in French. German and French in parallel columns

Besant, Sir Walter
Early London, prehistoric, Roman, Saxon and Norman. London, A. & C. Black 1908
x,370p. front. illus. pl. facsim. 29x22cm. 30s o.p. (The survey of London)
Costume index. LC 8-28407

London in the eighteenth century. London, A. & C. Black. 1902
xvii,667p. front. illus. pl. port. fold.map. 29x24cm 30s o.p. (The survey of London)
Contents: Historical notes; The city and the streets; Church and chapel; Government and trade of the city; Manners and customs; Society and amusements; Crime, police, justice, debtors' prisons; Appendices; Chronicle of the eighteenth century; Index
Costume index. LC 3-2034

London in the nineteenth century. London, A. & C. Black 1909
421p. front. illus. pl. 29x22cm. 30s o.p. (The survey of London)
Contents: History and government; Education and entertainment; Open spaces; Societies and clubs; Charitable work; General improvements; Miscellaneous
Costume index. LC 10-8968

London in the time of the Stuarts. London, A. & C. Black 1903
xiii,384p. front. illus.(incl.facsims.) 19pl. ports. plans. 29x24cm. 30s o.p. (The survey of London)
Costume index. LC 4-3050

London in the time of the Tudors. London, A. & C. Black 1904
x,430p. front. illus. pl.(part fold.) ports. plans(part fold.) 29x24cm. 30s o.p. (The survey of London)
Costume index. LC 5-6023

Mediæval London. London, A. & C. Black 1906
2v. front. illus. pl. ports. facsims. 29x23cm. ea 30s o.p. (The survey of London)
Contents: v 1 pt 1 Mediæval sovereigns. pt 2 Social and general. Appendices. Index; v 2 pt 1 The government of London. pt 2 Ecclesiastical London. pt 3 Religious houses. Appendices. Index
Costume index. LC 6-22389

Die **beschäftigung** des weiblichen geschlechts in der hand-arbeit. Daul, A.

Beschreibender katalog einer sammlung von spitzen und kanten. Bock, Franz

Beschreibung aller nationen des russischen reichs. Georgi, J. G.

Beschreibung aller sowohl noch heutiges tages florirenden als bereits verloschenen. Rammelsberg, J. W.

Beschreibung der aegyptischen sammlung. Leyden. Rijksmuseum van oudheden

Beschreibung der feierlichkeiten am jubelfeste der Universität Leipzig, den 4 december 1809. Kreussler, H. G.

Beschreibung der feierlichkeiten, welche bei der vermählung des Kronprinzen von Preussen K.H. mit der Prinzessin Elisabeth von Baiern K.H. so wie bei der ankunft der Prinzessin K.H. in Berlin und an andern Orten statt gefunden haben. Berlin, T. C. F. Enslin 1824
164p. 3pl.(1 col.) O.
Lipperheide 2539

Beschreibung der feierlichkeiten welche ... in Weimar und Jena am 6ten und 7ten October 1808 von dem Herzoge Carl August von Sachsen-Weimar veranstaltet wurden. Bertuch, F. J.

Beschreibung der festlichkeiten, welche bei der zu Dessau vollzogenen vermählung ... des Erbprinzen Ernst von Sachsen-Altenburg Herzogs zu Sachsen ... und der Prinzessin Agnes von Anhalt-Dessau ... sowie höchstderen einzuge in Altenburg stattgefunden haben. Altenburg, 1853
124p. O.
Lipperheide 2582e

Beschreibung der feyrlichkeiten, welche bey gelegenheit der durchreise ... der ... Frau Dauphine, Marien Antonien Erzherzoginn zu Oesterreich ... von den Vorderöstreich-Breissgauischen landständen veranstaltet worden. Freiburg, J. A. Satron 1770
8 l. 3pl. F.
Lipperheide 2631

Beschreibung der gemeineidgenossischen truppensendung nach Basel. Meister, Léonard

Beschreibung der illumination zu Dreszden bey der königlichen Sicilianischen in vollmacht vollzogenen vermählung, nebst andern dahin gehörigen vorstellungen. Dresden, Hekel & Walter 1738
140p. 11pl. Q.
Lipperheide 2580

Beschreibung der reise und des einzuges sr. majestät des Königs Friedrich Wilhelm II. von Preussen etc. in der ehemaligen fürstlichen residenzstadt Ansbach; der daselbst ... errichteten ... ehrenpforte; nebst einer ... abbildung dieses ... gebäues, von einem Brandenburger. Nürnberg, 1792
83p. 1 pl. O.
Lipperheide 2531w

Beschreibung der reisz: Empfahuñg desz ritterlichen ordens; volbringung des heyraths ... Gehaltener ritterspiel und frewdenfests, des ... Herrn Friederichen desz fünften, Pfaltzgraven bey Rhein. mit Elisabetheñ ... Jacobi desz Ersten, königs in Gross Britannien einigen tochter. [Heidelberg] G. Vögelin 1613
205,99p. 25 col.pl. Q.
Lipperheide 2556

Beschreibung der sämtlichen reichskleinodien und heiligthümer welche in Nürnberg aufbewahret werden. Murr, C. G. von

Beschreibung der XXII. Schweizer-kantone. Sommerlatt, C. V. von

Beschreibung des festes Der zauber der weissen rose gegeben in Potsdam am 13 July 1829 zum geburtstage Ihrer majestät der Kaiserin von Russland; die ansichten nach der natur gezeichnet ... von Gaertner. Berlin, Gropius 1829?
7 l. 24pl.(13 col.) F.
Lipperheide 2540c

Beschreibung des Kaiserl. gnaden- und freyschiessen, welche von Ihro ... Majestät Carolo Sexto der wienerischen burgerschaft durch vierzehen täg gegeben worden. Wien, J. P. v. Ghelen [1739]
69p. 10pl. F.
Lipperheide 3002

Beschreibung des Ritterlichen Johanniter-Orden. Becmann, J. C.

Beschreibung und abbildung aller königl. und churfürstl. ein-züge wahl und crönungs acta, so geschehen zu Franckfurt am Mayn im jahr 1658. Merian, Caspar

Beschreibung und abbildung der nonnen- und münch- orden; ein beytrag zur kirchengeschichte. See Handbuch fürs schöne geschlecht, zum nutzen und vergnügen

Beschreibung und abrisz der fürstlichen leich procession ... desz ... herrn Christiani marggraffens zu Brandenburg. Schnitzer, Lucas

Beschreibung und vorstellung des solennen stuck-schiessens, welches auf ... befehl eines ... raths des Heil. Röm. Reichs Freyer Stadt Nürnberg ... 1733 den 8 Junii ... gehalten ... worden. Nürnberg, L. Bieling 1734
12p. 14pl. F.
Lipperheide 2219

Beschreibung was auf ableiben weyland ihrer keyserl. majestät Josephi, bisz nach vorgegangener erb-huldigung. Mairn, J. B. von

Beschrijvend programma van den feestelijken optocht. Wüppermann, W. E. A.

Beschrijving der kleeding, equipment en wapening van de Nederlandsche land-, zeemagt en schutterijen, zoo binnen het koningrijk, als in deszelfs overseesche bezittingen. Amsterdam, L. S. Leman 1845
78 l. 63 col.pl. Q.
Colas 319. Lipperheide 2259

Beschrijving hoedanig de koninklijke Nederlandsche troepen en alle in militaire betrekking staande personen gekleed, geëquipeerd en gewapend zijn. Teupken, J. F.

Beschrijvinge van 't koninckrijck Congo. Lopes, Duarte

Beschryving der nieuwlijks uitgewonden en geoctrojeerde slang-brand-spuiten. Heyden, Jan van der

Beschryving der voornaamste vreugde-bedryven in 's Gravenhage, ter gelegenheid van de krooning van ... Franciscus I. See Description des principales rejoussances, faites à la Haye à l'occasion du couronnement de sa majesté ... François I

Beschryving van het plechtige volksfeest, gehouden te Amsterdam, op den 19 Juny, 1795; by gelegenheid van het installeeren, der door de volksstem verkozene representanten dier stad, en de alliantie gesloten tusschen de Fransche en Bataafsche Republieken. Amsterdam, D. M. Langeveld 1795
68p. 12 col.pl. O.
Lipperheide 2824

Beschryving van 's Graven-hage. Riemer, Jacob de

Beskrivelse over Finmarkens Lapper, deres Tungemaal. Leems, Knud

Besselièvre, de

Collection Besselièvre spitzen & stickereien. Plauen i. Vogtland, C. F. Schulz 192-?
52pl. Q.
No text. Collection is now in the Museum of the Brooklyn institute of arts and sciences

Étoffes & broderies du XVe au XVIIIe siècles. Préface et notice de M. Paul Cornu ... Cent-seize planches reproduisant les pièces les plus remarquables de cette collection. Plauen i. V., C. Stoll 1914?
[8],7p. 116pl. F. (La collection Besselièvre)

Besser, Johann von

Preussische krönungs-geschichte, oder Verlauf der ceremonien, mit welchen ... Friderich der Dritte, marggraf und churfürst zu Brandenburg, die königliche würde des von ihm gestiffteten königreichs Preussen angenommen ... Aufs sorgfältigste beschrieben, und im jahr 1702 das erstemahl gedrucket, itzo aber in diesem andern druck an vielen orten gebessert. Cölln an der Spree, U. Liebpert 1712
76,13p. 27pl. F.
Illustrated by J. F. Wentzel and engraved by J. G. Wolffgang
First edition (Cölln an der Spree, U. Liebpert 1702. 95,87p. 1 illus.) Reprint of first edition (Berlin, Verlag des Vereins für die geschichte Berlins 1901. 100p. 4pl.) Lipperheide also lists the plates of the 1712 edition separately, under the name of the engraver, with title: *Der königlich-preuszischen crönung hochfeyerliche solemnitäten*
Lipperheide 2526-29. LC 4-36408

Best-dressed man: a gossip on manners and modes. London, Doré 1892
144p. illus. pl. S.

Besterman, Theodore

(ed.) Crawley, A. E. Dress, drinks, and drums

Beta, Heinrich, pseud. See Bettziech, Heinrich

Béthencourt, Jean de, baron de Saint-Martin-le-Gaillard

The Canarian. See entry under Bontier, Pierre, and Le Verrier, Jean

Bettanier

(lithgr.) Henry, Elisa. Le charme

Bettziech, Heinrich

Physiologie Berlins; mit federzeichnungen von W. Scholz. Berlin, Weinholz 1846-47
46,48,52,48p. 8 col.illus. O.

Beuther von Carlstatt, Michael

Kurtz begriffene anzeigung, vom leben und wesen der könige zu Dänemarck, Sueden, Nordwagen etc. Basel, C. Waldkirch 1587
80p. 9 illus. F.
Darneben vom stannde und leben der ... Johann Ranzawen Ritters treier könige zu Danemarck etc. gewesenen feldobersten; Hainrich Ranzawen seines sohns ... Dessgleichen Daniel Ranzawen
Lipperheide 1035

Beveren, Jacques Joseph van. See Van Beveren, Jacques Joseph

Bévy, Charles Joseph

Histoire des inaugurations des rois, empereurs, et autres souverains de l'univers, depuis leur origine jusqu'à présent; suivie d'un précis de l'état des arts & des sciences ... des principaux faits, moeurs, coutumes & usages les plus remarquables des François, depuis Pépin jusqu'à Louis XVI. Paris, Moutard 1776
xvi,559p. 14pl. O.
The plates picture about 80 French costumes from the 13th to the 18th century
Colas 320. Lipperheide 2479

Die **bewaffnung** der Germanen in der älteren eisenzeit etwa von 700 v. Chr. bis 200 n. Chr. Jahn, Martin

Die **bewaffnung** des altägyptischen heeres. Wolf, Walther

Beyer, Leopold

Kriegsscenen aus den jahren 1813 bis 1815, zur erinnerung für ehemalige krieger und zum nachzeichnen und illuminiren für kleine leute in 12 herrlichen skizzen. Dresden, R. Friese ca1815
12pl. Q.
Lipperheide 2117

Beyschlag, Robert

Female costume pictures; figures of female grace and beauty in costumes of various centuries. London, Sampson Low, Marston, Searle and Rivington New York, Scribner & Welford 1880
1 p.l. 12 mounted pl. F.
Issued in portfolio
Colas 321

Beytrag zur unterhaltung beim nachttische für frauenzimmer vom stande. Prag J. Balzer 1782
67p. 110pl. O.
Most of the plates are reproduced from French fashion magazines, particularly from *Gallerie des modes et costumes françai[s]* and show fashions in dress and hair-dressing
Colas 322. Lipperheide 567

Bèze, Théodore de

Icones, id est verae imagines virorum doctrina simul et pietate illustrium [Geneva] I. Laonium 1580
318p. 135 illus.(incl. ports.) O.
For French translation see his *Les vrai[s] portraits*
"Quorum praecipuè ministerio partim bonarum literarum studia sunt restituta, partim vera religio in variis orbis christiani regionibus, nostra patrúmque memoria fuit instaurata: additis eorumdem vitae & operae descriptionibus, quibus adiectae sunt nonnulae picturae quas emblemata vocant." Subtitle
Lipperheide 490. LC 14-17774

Bèze, Théodore de—*Continued*

Les vrais portraits des hommes illustres en piete et doctrine, du travail desquels Dieu s'est ferui en ces derniers temps, pour remettre fus la vraye religion en divers pays de la Chréstienté ... Tr. du Latin ... [par Simon Goulart] [Genève] Jean de Laon 1581
284p. illus. Q.
Forty nine portraits and forty-four Christian emblems
For Latin edition see his: *Icones*

Bianchi de Médicis de Manville, prince

Anthologie de coiffes et types actuels du peuple Breton, appliquée à ses origines ethniques ... dessins documentaires de Noëlie Couillaud. Saint-Brieuc, Editions de la Bretagne touristique [1925]
91p. col.front. illus. 80pl.
Colas 323

Bianchi, Lorenzo. See Cuciniello, Michele, jt. auth.

Bianchini, Charles

(illus.) Le costume au théâtre et à la ville

Bianchini, Giuseppe [Maria]

Dei gran duchi di Toscana della reale casa de' Medici, protettori delle lettere, e delle belle arti, ragionamenti istorici. Venezia, G. B. Recurti 1741
xxiv,192,[13]p. ports. F.
Plates are head and shoulder portraits of members of the Medici family
Lipperheide 1252. LC 4-32851

Biart, Lucien

The Aztecs; their history, manners, and customs; authorized translation by J. L. Garner. Chicago, A. C. McClurg 1887
343p. illus. fold.map fold.facsim. O.
Translation of *Les Aztèques*
LC 2-7336

Les Aztèques; histoire, mœurs, coutumes. Paris, A. Hennuyer 1885
xi,304p. illus. col.pl. maps, plan. Q. (Bibliothèque ethnologique)
LC 8-21108

Biasioli. See Raccolta di 30 costumi con altretante vedute le piú interessanti della cittá di Milano

Bibesco, Marthe Lucie (Lahovary) Princesse Bibesco

Noblesse de robe. Paris, B. Grasset 1928
220p. D.
LC 29-5853

Bible, Daniel P. See Bible, G. W., jt. auth.

Bible, George W., and Bible, Daniel P.

Looking backward at woman's fashionable dress. New York, Dry goods chronicle publishing co. 1892
116p. illus. F.
LC 7-32066

Bible. German

Biblia; das ist: Die gantze Heilige Schrifft: deudsch. d. Mart. Luth. Wittemberg, H. Lufft 1556
2v. 175 col.illus. F.
Illustrated by Hans Brosamer and Gottfried Leigel. The same woodcuts were used in the Bible published by H. Lufft in 1550
Lipperheide 631

Biblia, das ist: Die gantze Heilige Schrift, Altes und Neues Testaments. Verteutscht von doctor Martin Luther. Nürnberg, J. A. Endters seel. sohn und erben 1708
23p.l. 11 numb.l. 1652p. illus. port. pl. (part double) plans, maps. nar.F.
Eleventh edition of the so-called Ernestine, Kurfürsten, or Weimar Bible, edited under the auspices of Duke Ernst of Saxe-Weimar, and first published in 1641. New plates were added in some of the editions and other plates changed
Lipperheide lists the 1649-1653 edition which differs slightly in illustrations
Lipperheide 712 (1652 ed.) LC 20-17705

Die gantze Bibel der ursprüngliche ebraischen und griechischen waarheyt nach auffs aller treüwlichest verteütschet. Zürich, G. Froschouer 1531
2v. 199 illus. F.
This edition is rich in illustrations. C. Froschouer used for the Old Testament wood vignettes from his edition of 1525, which in part are copies in reverse from Holbein's *Icones veteris testamenti*, with 45 additional illustrations of the same size. For the New Testament Froschouer included vignettes from his edition of 1524. He also borrowed from Thomas Wolff in Basel 21 woodcuts by Holbein to illustrate the apocalypse
Lipperheide 617

Die neunte deutsche Bibel. Nürnberg, A. Koberger 1483
583p. 109 col.illus. F.
Translated by Nicolas Syber
Lipperheide 413

Bible, Wendic

Tv ie, vse svetv pismv, stariga inu Noviga Testamenta, Slovenski, tolmazhena, skusi ivria Dalmatina. Bibel, das ist die gantze Heilige Schrifft, windisch. Wittemberg, H. Kraffts erben 1584
3v. 220 illus. F.
Lipperheide 644

Bible characters. See Biblical characters

La bible des poètes metamorphosée. Ovid

Biblia, das ist die gantze Heilige Schrift. Bible. German

Biblia pauperum

Biblia pauperum; nach dem original in der Lyceumsbibliothek zu Constanz hrsg. und mit einer einleitung begleitet von Laib und Schwarz. Zürich, L Wörl 1867
26,17p. 4 illus. 17 col.facsim. on 9 l. F.
Reproduction of a block-book in the Bibliothek des Lyceums at Constance, of about the year 1300
Lipperheide 392. LC 8-20988

Biblia Pauperum; reproduced in facsimile from one of the copies in the British Museum with an historical and bibliographical introduction by J. Ph. Berjeau. London, J. R. Smith 1859
38p. 40 facsim. F.
Facsimile of a blockbook by Laurenz Coster, printed in the Netherlands about 1465, the drawings by Jan van Eyck
Lipperheide 404. LC 23-15685

Biblicae historiae artificiosissimè depictae. Beham, H. S.

Biblicae historiae, artificiocissimus picturis effigiatae. Beham, H. S.

Biblical characters

Barton, Lucy. Historic costume for the stage. 1935. p19-46

Beham, H. S. Biblicae historiae artificiosissimè depictae. 1537

Beham, H. S. Biblicae historiae, artificiocissimus picturis effigiatae. 1536

Biblical characters—*Continued*

Beham, H. S. Holzschnitte zum Alten Testament. 1910

Bellermann, C. F. Über die ältesten christlichen begrabnissstatten und besonders die katakomben zu Neapel mit ihren wandgemälden. 1839

Bible. German. Biblia; das ist: Die gantze Heilige Schrifft: deudsch. d. Mart. Luth. 1556

Bible. German. Die gantze Bibel der ursprüngliche ebraischen und griechischen waarheyt nach auffs aller treüwlichest verteutschet. 1531

Bible. German. Die neunte deutsche Bibel. 1483

Biblia pauperum. Biblia pauperum; nach dem original in der Lyceumsbibliothek zu Constanz. 1867

Catholic church. Liturgy and ritual. Hours. Heures. ca1502

Catholic church. Liturgy and ritual. Hours. Le livre d'heures de la reine Anne de Bretagne. 1841

Copping, Harold. The gospel in the Old Testament. 1908

Doré, Gustave. The Doré Bible gallery. 1883

Engelbrecht, Martin. Biblische und religiöse darstellungen. 172-?

Friederich, Adolf. Der teppich aus dem kloster Drübeck. 1877

Geldart, Ernest. Ecclesiastical decoration. 1889

Griffith, William, ed. Great painters and their famous Bible pictures. 1925

Historia S. Joannis Evangelistae ejusque visiones apocalypticae. ca1465

Holbein, Hans, illus. Historiarum veteris instrumenti icones ... Ymagines de las historias del viejo testamento. 1540

Holbein, Hans, the younger. Hans Holbeins Alte Testament in funfzig holzschnitten getreu nach den originalen copirt. 1850

Jameson, Mrs A. B. M., and Eastlake, E. R., lady. The history of Our Lord as exemplified in works of art: with that of His types; St. John the Baptist; and other persons of the Old and New Testament. 1864

Liber regum ... zum ersten male. 1892

Methodius, Saint, bp of Olympus. Revelationes. 1498

Paris. Bibliothèque nationale. Mss. (Lat. 8846). Psautier illustré (XIIIe siècle). 1906

Paris. Bibliothèque nationale. Mss. (Lat. 10525) Psautier de Saint Louis. 190-

Das Passional. Passional. 1488

Perret, Louis. Catacombes de Rome. 1851-55

Pinder, Ulrich. Speculum passionis domine nostri Ihesu christi. 1507

Rahn, J. R. Geschichte der bildenden künste in der Schweiz von den ältesten zeiten bis zum schlusse des mittelalters. 1876

Richter, J. P., and Taylor, A. C. The golden age of classic Christian art. 1904

Ritter, Georges, and Lafond, Jean. Manuscrits à peintures de l'école de Rouen; livres d'heures normands; recueil de facsimiles et texte. 1913

Westwood, J. O. Fac-similes of the miniatures and ornaments of Anglo-Saxon & Irish manuscripts. 1868

Wright, M. L. Biblical costume, with adaptations for use in plays. 1936

See also Jesus Christ; Jews; Mary, Virgin—Dress

Biblical costume. Wright, M. L.

Bibliografia generale della scherma. Gelli, Jacopo

La **bibliographie** de l'escrime ancienne et moderne. Vigeant, Arsène

Bibliographie générale du costume et de la mode. Colas, René

Bibliographie méthodique. Vinet, Ernest

Bibliographies of costume

Bibliographies of special phases of costume will be found listed under the phase, with subhead: Bibliography. E.g. Military costume—Bibliography

Baker, Mrs B. M. Dramatic bibliography. 1933

Baldwin, Muriel. Costume 1400-1600. (In New York. Public library. Bulletin. 41:8-14, January 1937)

Boston. Public library. Costume; a selected list of books in the Public library of the city of Boston. 1928

Boyd, A. M., and Miller, M. V., comps. A reading list. 1920

Brooklyn. Public library. A reading and reference list on costume. 1909

Clark, M. E., and others, comps. Art in home economics. 1925

Colas, René. Bibliographie générale du costume et de la mode. 1933

Detroit. Public library. Costume, a list of books. 1928

Doege, Heinrich. Die trachtenbücher des 16. jahrhunderts. 1903

Edinburgh. Royal Scottish museum. Library. List of books, &c. in the library of the Museum; part 3 Costume. 1892

Jonghe, J. de, vicomte. Catalogue d'une très belle collection de recueils de costumes, XVIIIe et début du XIXe siècles. 1930

Küp, Karl. Some early costume books (In New York. Public library. Bulletin 40:926-32 November 1936

Lacroix, Paul. Recueil curieux de pièces originales rares ou inédites, en prose et en vers, sur le costume et les révolutions de la mode en France. 1852

Lipperheide, F. J., freiherr von. Katalog der Freiherrlich von Lipperheide'scher kostümbibliothek. 1896-1905

Monro, I. S., and Cook, D. E., eds. Costume index; a subject index to plates and to illustrated text. 1937

Bibliographies of costume—*Continued*
Racinet, A. C. A. Le costume historique. v 1 p 141-65
Salmagundi club, New York. Library. Catalogue of the costume books in the library of the Salmagundi club, New York. 1906
Traphagen, Ethel. Costume design and illustration. 1932. p 165-223
Victoria and Albert museum, South Kensington. Costume. 1936
Vinet, Ernest. Bibliographie méthodique et raisonnée des beaux-arts. 1874-77
Western reserve historical society, Cleveland, Ohio. King collection. The Charles G. King collection of books on costume. 1914

Criticism

Kelly, F. M. The bibliography of costume. 1918

Bibliography of colonial costume. Meyers, C. L., comp.

Biblioteca delle tradizioni popolari siciliane. Pitrè, Giuseppe, ed.

Bibliotheca accipitraria. Harting, J. E.

Bibliothèque régionaliste: Le costume en Provence. Roux, J. C.

Bibliothèque universelle des voyages effectués par mer ou par terre. See Montémont, A. É. de. Histoire universelle des voyages effectués par mer et par terre

Biblische historien figürlich fürgebildet. See Beham, H. S. Biblicae historiae artificiocissimus picturis effigiatae

Biblische historien kunstlich furgemälet. See Beham, H. S. Biblicae historiae, artificiocissimus picturis effigiatae

Biblische und religiöse darstellungen. Engelbrecht, Martin

Bibra, Ernst, freiherr von
Ueber alte eisen- und silber-funde; archäologisch-chemische skizze. Nürnberg & Leipzig, Verlag von Richter & Kappler 1873
75p. O.
Lipperheide 125

Bicci, Antonio
I contadini della Toscana, espressi al naturale secondo le diverse loro vestiture. Firenze, N. Pagni e G. Bardi 1796
60 col.pl. F.
Engravings from designs by Antonio and Gaetano Bicci, Antonio Fedi and Piattoli
Colas 325. Lipperheide 1320

Bicci, Gaetano
(illus.) Bicci, Antonio. I contadini della Toscana, espressi al naturale secondo le diverse loro vestiture

Les **biches.** Dyagilev, S. P.

Bickham, George
The musical entertainer. London, C. Corbett ca1740
2v. 200pl. F.
Lipperheide 560

Bicycle costume
Schönberger, Käthe. Reiterinnen und radlerinnen. 1901

Bida, Alexandre, and Barbot, E.
Souvenirs d'Égypte. Paris, Lemercier ca1850
24pl. F.
Twelve of the plates are costume pictures, the others views with figures
Colas 326. Lipperheide 1600

Biddle, C. Harry. See Lindsey, Ben, jt. auth.

[**Bidloo, Govard**]
Komste van Zyne Majesteit Willem III koning van Groot Britanje, enz. in Holland. Gravenhaage, A. Leers [1691]
127p. 15pl. F.
"Of Te omstandelyke beschryving van alles, het welke op des zelfs komste en geduurende zyn verblyf, in's Graavenhaage en elders, ten teeken van vreugde en eere, is opgerecht en voorgevallen." Subtitle
Lipperheide 2667. LC 3-29466

Bīdpāy
Der altenn weisenn exempel sprüch und underweisungen. No place, 1548
148 l. 108 illus. Q.
"Wie sich einem jeden frommen ehrliebenden vor der untrewen hinderlistigen geschwinden bösen welt unnd weltkindern zuhüten vorzusehẽ; auch weiszheyt und vorsichtigkeyt darausz zu lernen durch schöne alte beispil unnd weltweise lehren unuergrifflich uff historien der gethier gewendt und fürgestelt." Subtitle
Lipperheide 445

Bidrag til den danske krigsmagts histoire. Blom, Carl

Bie, Oskar
Der gesellschaftstanz in der Renaissance. Berlin, S. Fischer
p920-46 O.
From *Neue deutsche rundschau* v14, no9. 1903
Lipperheide 3138

Die oper. Berlin, S. Fischer 1913
571p. illus. (incl. ports. facsims.) pl. (part col.) Q. M. 25
LC 14-5089

Der tanz; 2. aufl.; mit hundert kunstbeilagen; buchausstattung von Karl Walser. Berlin, J. Bard [c1919]
394p. col.front. illus. pl. (part col.; incl. music) ports. O.
LC 21-11566

Das theater: bühnenbilder und kostüme von Karl Walser; mit text von Oskar Bie. Berlin, Cassirer [1912]
35p. col.illus. 33 col.pl. Q.
Relates to various operas
Colas 3049

Bieber, Margarete
Die denkmäler zum theaterwesen im altertum ... mit 142 abbildungen im text und 109 tafeln. Berlin und Leipzig, Vereinigung wissenschaftlicher verleger 1920
212p. illus. (incl. plans) 109pl. (part fold.) Q.
"Literatur": p[179]-98
LC 21-19434

Das Dresdner schauspielerrelief; ein beitrag zur geschichte des tragischen kostüms und der griechischen kunst. Bonn, F. Cohen 1907
91p. illus. pl. O.
Inaugural dissertation, Bonn
LC 9-14613

Bieber, Margarete—*Continued*
Entwicklungsgeschichte der griechischen tracht von der vorgriechischen zeit bis zur römischen kaiserzeit. Berlin, Gebr. Mann 1934
63p. illus. 54pl. F.
Contains bibliographies
LC AC34-2389

Griechische kleidung. Berlin und Leipzig, Walter de Gruyter 1928
100p. illus. 64pl. diagrs. F.
"Literatur": p95
Costume index. LC A30-173

Biedenfeld, Ferdinand Leopold Carl, freiherr von
Geschichte und verfassung aller geistlichen und weltlichen, erloschenen und blühenden ritterorden. Nebst einer übersicht sämmtlicher militär- und civilehrenzeichen, medaillen &. &. und einem atlas mit beinahe 500 illuminirten abbildungen der ordensinsignien, bänder u. ketten. Zugleich als fortsetzung von dessen geschichte der mönchs- und klosterfrauenorden im Orient und Occident. Weimar, B. F. Voigt 1841
2v. 53 col.pl. fold.tab. O.
The material on the British orders is published separately as John Hunter's *Concise description of the insignia of the orders of British knighthood*
Colas 328. Lipperheide 1924. LC 8-37148

Ursprung, aufleben, grösse, herrschaft, verfall und jetzige zustände sämmtlicher mönchs- und klosterfrauen-orden im Orient und Occident. Nebst den illuminirten abbildungen von 77 verschiedenen geistlichen orden. Weimar, B. F. Voigt 1837-39
2v. 21 col.pl. O.
Companion volume to his *Geschichte und verfassung aller geistlichen und weltlichen . . . ritterorden*
Colas 327. Lipperheide 1879

Biedermann, E. Schellenberg-. See Schellenberg-Biedermann, E.

Biedermeier. Boehn, Max von

Bielenstein, Martha
Die altlettischen färbmethoden. Rīgā, a.-g. E. Plates 1935
176p. col.front. 1 col.pl. O. (Herder-institut, Riga. Volkskundliche forschungsstelle. Veröffentlichungen, v2)
Frontispiece and plate show Lettish costume

Biggart, Helen
Leathercraft and beading, adapted for Camp fire girls ... from the Hand book of craft work in leather, by Lester Griswold. [New York, The Camp fire outfitting co. c1930]
58p. front. illus. O. (Camp fire girls library of the seven crafts)
Contents: Leather craft; Suggested projects: Beading; Moccasin making; Thong plaiting
LC 30-19402

Bignon, Jean Paul. See Danchet, Antoine, ed. sacre de Louis xv

Bigot, Maurice
Les coiffes bretonnes, 100 modèles différents. Saint-Brieuc, O. L. Aubert [1928]
17p. 101pl. D.
Colas 330

Bijdrage tot de geschiedenis der kerkelijke en wereldlijke kleeding. Schotel, G. D. J.

Bijdrage tot de kennis van de Noord-Nederlandsche costuum-geschiedenis. Jonghe, C. H. de

Bijou; original Pariser musterblätter weiblicher kunstarbeiten ... Mignon-begleiter der damen-zeitschrift Iris. 1.-2. bd., 1851-1852. Gratz & Leipzig
2v. col.pl. O.
No more published?
Colas 331. Lipperheide 4660

Le **bijou** des dames. Nouveau costume français et de la connaissance des diamans, des perles et des parfums les plus précieux. Paris, Desnos [1779]
33,48p. 24 l. 24 col.pl. (numbered 25 to 48) T.
Part 2 of *Almanach de la toilette et la coëffure*. Both parts are included in *Recueil des coeffures depuis 1589 jusqu'en 1778*
Plates show coiffures and headdress of the sixteenth to the eighteenth centuries
Colas 91

Bijou populaire ancien. See Baudouin, M. E., and Lacouloumère, Georges. Le coeur vendéen

La **bijouterie** et la joaillerie egyptiennes. Vernier, E. S.

La **bijouterie** française au XIXe siècle (1800-1900). Vever, Henri

Les **bijoux** anciens. Blanchot, I. L.

Les **bijoux** anciens et modernes. Fontenay, E.

Bikessy, J. Heimbucher von. See Heimbucher von Bikessy, J.

Bilbergh, Joanne
Orchestra sive de saltationibus veterum dissertatio. [Upsala] Excudit H. Curio, bibliopola [1685]
4 l. 62p. O.
Lipperheide 3063

Bilby, Julian W.
Among unknown Eskimo; an account of twelve years intimate relations with the primitive Eskimo of ice-bound Baffin Land, with a description of their ways of living, hunting customs & beliefs. With thirty-three illustrations & a map. London, S. Service & co. 1923
280p. front. illus. pl. fold. map. O.
Appendix. Eskimo deities: p265-70
LC 23-8916

Nanook of the North. London, Arrowsmith [1925]
318p. front. 28pl. O.
LC 25-25972

Bildende künste für frauenzimmer, im sticken, waschen, stricken usw. Römhild, 1785
3v. col.pl. O.

Bilder antiken lebens. Panofka, Theodor

Bilder aus dem deutschen studentenleben. Geiling, F. W.

Bilder aus dem ritterleben und aus der ritterdichtung. Hagen, F. H. von der

Bilder aus dem schwedischen volksleben. Arnz & compagnie, Düsseldorf

Bilder aus der Lutherzeit. Hirth, Georg, ed.

Die **bilder** der handschrift des Kaisers Otto im Münster zu Aachen. Beissel, Stephan

Die **bilder** der Hedwigslegende. Wolfskron, Adolf, ritter von

Bilder-sal heutiges tages lebender, und durch gelahrtheit berühmter schrifftsteller. Brucker, J. J., and Haid, J. J.

Bilder-sammlung, Martin Friedrich Seidels. Küster, G. G.

Bilder und schriften der vorzeit. Kopp, U. F.

Bilder ur svenska folklifvet. Berg, J. A.

Bilderatlas zur geschichte der deutschen nationalliteratur. Könnecke, Gustav

Bilderatlas zur kunst und kulturgeschichte Mittel-Asiens. Le Coq, Albert von

Bildersaal altdeutscher dichter. Hagen, F. H. von der

Bildliche darstellung aller bekannten völker. Leonhardi, F. G.

Bildliche darstellung der K. K. Oesterreichischen armee. Papin

Bildliche darstellung der K. K. Oesterreichischen armee aller waffengattungen. See Stephanie, J. Abbildung der K. K. Oesterreichischen armee durch alle waffengattungen

Bildliche darstellung der königlich preussischen civil-uniformen ... nebst ausführlicher erklärung. Berlin, J. W. Schmidt 1804
16p. 8pl. (7 col.) O.
Shows uniforms of the law courts, justices and attendants, the departments of war, taxation, forestry, the post, mines and police
Colas 332. Lipperheide 1773

Bildnerei der gefangenen. Prinzhorn, Hans

Bildnisse aller berg-beambten und bedienten. See Weigel, Christoph. Icones omnium ad rem metallicam spectanium officialium et operariorum

Bildnisse aller hütten-beambten und bedienten. See Weigel, Christoph. Icones omnium ad officinas aerarias pertinentium officialium et operariorum

Bildnisse ausgezeichneter Griechen und Philhellenen. Krazeisen, Karl

Bildnisse der deutschen könige und kaiser von Karl dem Grossen bis Maximilian I. Kohlrausch, Friedrich

Bildnisse der regierenden fürsten und berühmter männer. Heraeus, C. G.

Bildnisse der urheber und beförderer auch einiger gegner der religions- und kirchenserbesserung im sechzehnten jahrhundert. Becker, R. Z.

Bildnisse verdienter Lübecker, nebst deren biographien. Petersen, H.

Bildnuss oder contrafactur der zwölff ersten alten teutschen königen und fürsten. Amman, Jost

Bildungen des gemeinen volks zu Wien. Adam, Jacques

Die **bildwerke** zum thebischen und troischen heldenkreis. See Overbeck, Johannes. Gallerie heroischer bildwerke der alten kunst

Biller, B. See Mansfeld, Heinrich, jt. auth.

[**Billow, Anders**]
Pictorial Sweden; nature and culture of the past and present. Stockholm, Nordisk rotogravyr [1932]
284p. illus. Q.
The pictures are collected, collocated and supplied with text by Anders Billow. Translation by William Savage

Billstein, Emma L.
Fashion in footwear; a brief account of the various ways in which the feet have been clothed at different times by different peoples, from the pyramidal ages of ancient Egypt down to the present period. Philadelphia, Billstein 1886
48p. illus. T.
LC 8-34480

Binder, C. See Seyboth, Adolf, jt. auth.

The **binding** of kerchiefs in Moravia and Slovakia. See Úprka, Joža. Vazani šátků

Bing, Samuel
(ed.) Artistic Japan: illustrations and essays. London, S. Low, Marston, Searle & Rivington [etc., 1888]-91
6v. in 3. illus. pl. (part col.) narF.
Published also New York, Brentano's
Paged continuously. Originally issued as a periodical appearing simultaneously in French and German under the titles *Le Japon artistique* and *Japanischer formenschatz,* (Leipzig, E. A. Seeman 1888-1891)
Separate issues have title *Artistic Japan: a monthly illustrated journal*
Lipperheide 1566e (German ed.) LC 2-26532

Bing, Valentyn, and Ueberfeldt, Braet von
Nederlandsche kleederdragten; naar de natuur geteekend ... Costumes des Pays-Bas ... 1. ser. Amsterdam, F. Buffa en Zonen 1857
15 l. 56 col.pl. F.
Text in Dutch and French
Colas 333. Lipperheide 969m

Binion, Samuel Augustus
Ancient Egypt or Mizraïm. New York, H. G. Allen 1887
2v. illus. pl. (part col.) sq.F.
A few plates show ancient Egyptian costume
LC 7-1065

Biographie der regenten von Württemberg von herzog Eberhard im Bart bis zum könig Friederich. Pfaff, Karl

Biographie einer perüque mit 16 abbildungen der unsterblichen perüque des weltberühmten magisters Sebaldus Nothanker. Bayreuth, A. Lübecks 1806
71p. 5pl. (17 illus.) O.
Lipperheide 1689

Birch, Samuel
(ed.) Wilkinson, Sir J. G. The manners and customs of the ancient Egyptians

Birds-eye views of modern society. Doyle, Richard

Birken, Sigmund von
Chur- und Fürstlicher sächischer heldensaal. 3. ed. Nürnberg, J. Hoffmann 1687
694p. 65pl. D.
"Oder ... beschreibung der ankunfft aufnahme fortpflanzung und vornehmster geschichten dieses hoch-löblichen hauses samt dessen genealogie wappen und kupffer-bild-

Birken, Sigmund von—*Continued*
nissen; als eine sächsische chronik zusammen getragen und vorgestellt durch ein mitglied der ... fruchtbringenden gesellschaft." Subtitle
First published 1677. Contains 56 portraits, the last signed H.I.S., perhaps Hans Jacob Schollenberger. Forty-two coats of arms are shown

(ed.) Fugger, J. J. Spiegel der ehren des ... erzhauses Österreich

Birmingham, George A., pseud. See Hannay, J. O.

Birt, Francis Bradley Bradley-. See Bradley-Birt, F. B.

The **birth** of ballets-russes. Liven, P. A., kniâź

Bischius, Johannes Ludovicus. See Beatus, M. G., jt. auth.

Ein **bischofsgrab** des zwölften jahrhunderts im Wormser dom. Schneider, Friedrich

Bishop, Mrs Isabella Lucy (Bird)

Korea and her neighbors; a narrative of travel. New York [etc.] F. H. Revell 1898
480p. front. illus. pl. O.
LC 4-16694

Unbeaten tracks in Japan; an account of travels on horseback in the interior, including visits to the aborigines of Yezo and the shrines of Nikkô and Isé. New York, G. P. Putnam 1880?
2v. in 1 fronts. illus.(incl.tables) fold. map. D.
LC 4-16697

Bishops

Catholic church

Barbier de Montault, Xavier. Particularités du costume des évêques de Poitiers au XIIe siècle. 1877

Hoeffler, A. R. F. Philosophia Herbipolensis, aeternae episcoporum ... memoriae devota. 1712

Hoffmann, Martin. Annales Bambergensis episcopatus, aborigine ad an MDC. Fide tabularii publica scripti et ex quatuor codicibus manuscriptis emendati continuatique ad MDCC ... Bambergensium episcoporum novissimi seculi continuatio, ab anno 1600 ad annum 1718 cum adnotationibus. 1718

See also Archbishops

Bisi, Avvto Franco

Uniformi militari Italiani a 1° Ottobre 1863. Torino, G. B. Maggi 1863
1 l. 33 col.pl. Q.
Plates by Luigi Crosio
Colas 335. Lipperheide 2368

Bissing, Friedrich Wilhelm, freiherr von

Denkmäler ägyptischer sculptur. München, F. Bruckmann a.-g. 1914
xiii,[344],iii-xxivp. illus. 125(i.e. 149)pl. (1 double) F.
Issued in 13 parts, 1906-14, in portfolios
Bibliographical foot-notes
LC 14-21843

Bitterlin, A.

L'art du maquillage. Paris, Boucoiran 1925
123p. illus. 16 col.pl. ports. O.

Bizet, René

La mode. Paris, F. Rieder 1925
98p. 32pl. O. (L'art français depuis vingt ans)
On fashion and French dress, 1900-1925. Plates show women's dresses by well-known French designers
Colas 336. Costume index. LC 26-2429

Blaauw, A. H.

De tropische natuur in schetsen en kleuren; 2. aufl. Amsterdam, Koloniaal Instituut 1917
xi,191p. illus. maps, col. plates (incl. front.) O.

Black, Charles Christopher

(tr.) Demmin, A. F. Weapons of war

Black, John

(tr.) Buch, Leopold, freiherr von. Travels through Norway and Lapland

Black, John Sutherland. See Cheyne, T. K., jt. ed.

Black eagle, Order of the

Statuten des königlichen preuszischen ordens vom Schwartzen adler. 1701

Black Forest. See Germany—Baden

Blackburn, Henry

Breton folk; an artistic tour in Brittany. With one hundred and seventy illustrations by R. Caldecott. London, S. Low, Marston, Searle, & Rivington 1880
xii,200p. front. illus. pl. map. Q.
LC 4-25967

Blackfeet Indians. Linderman, F. B.

Blackfoot. See Indians of North America—Siksika Indians

Blätter aus meinem portefeuille. Faber du Faur, C. W. von

Blätter für kostümkunde; neue folge; untermitwirkung von Otto Brausewetter [u. and.] hrsg. von A. von Heyden. Berlin, F. Lipperheide 1876-91
4v. in 8 illus. 252 col.pl. Q.
First edition (Berlin, F. Lipperheide 1874-75. 3v. 30pl. incl.27 col. F.) Second edition (1876-78. 2v. 24 col.pl. F.) each plate with ten to twelve costume figures
Colas 342-44 Lipperheide 80-82

Blagdon, Francis William

(tr.) Pallas, P. S. Travels through the southern provinces of the Russian empire, in the years 1793 and 1794

Blair, Emma Helen

(ed.) The Indian tribes of the upper Mississippi valley and region of the Great lakes ... as described by Nicolas Perrot, Bacqueville de la Potherie, Morrell Marston, and Thomas Forsyth, United States agent at Fort Armstrong, tr., ed., annotated, and with bibliography and index by Emma Helen Blair. Cleveland, O., The Arthur H. Clark company 1911
2v. fronts. (v2: map) pl. facsims. O.
Additions to bibliography: v II, p357
Contents: v 1 Memoir on the manners, customs, and religion of the savages of North America, by Nicolas Perrot. Ed. and pub. (in French) for the first time (Leipzig and Paris, 1864) by the Reverend Jules Tailhan: History of the savage peoples who are allies of New France, by Claude Charles Le Roy, Bacqueville de la Potherie, from his *Histoire de l'Amérique septentrionale* (Paris, 1753) tome II and IV. v2 History of the savage peoples who are allies of New France, by Claude Charles Le Roy,

Blair, Emma Helen—*Continued*
Bacqueville de la Potherie, from his *Histoire de l'Amérique septentrionale* (Paris, 1753), tome II and IV, continued and completed from vol.. I; Memoirs relating to the Sauk and Foxes, letter to Reverend Dr. Jedidiah Morse, by Major Morrell Marston, U.S.A., commanding at Fort Armstrong, Ill., November, 1820. From original manuscript in the library of the Wisconsin historical society; *Account of the manners and customs of the Sauk and Fox nations of Indian traditions*. A report on this subject, sent to General William Clarks, superintendent of Indian affairs, by Thomas Forsyth, Indian agent for the U.S. government, St. Louis, January 15, 1827. From the original and hitherto unpublished manuscript in the library of the Wisconsin historical society; Appendices: A. Biographical sketch of Nicolas Perrot, condensed from the notes of Father Tailhan. B. Notes on Indian social organization, mental and moral traits, and religious beliefs; and accounts of three remarkable religious movements among Indians in modern times. Mainly from writings of prominent ethnologists, the remainder by Thomas Forsyth and Thomas R. Roddy. C. Various letters, etc., describing the character and present condition of the Sioux, Potawatomi, and Winnebago tribes, written for this work by missionaries and others who know these peoples well
LC 11-28844

Blair, Matthew
The Paisley shawl and the men who produced it; a record of an interesting epoch in the history of the town. Paisley, A. Gardner 1904
84p. 15pl.(part col.) Q.
Each plate accompanied by leaf with descriptive letterpress
LC 17-19573

Blake, Sir Henry Arthur
China. See entry under Menpes, Mortimer

Blake, William
Chaucers Canterbury pilgrims. Painted in fresco by William Blake & by him engraved & published October 8, 1810. [Photographic copy. London, 189-?]
1 pl. nar.F.

Blakeslee, Fred Gilbert
Army uniforms of the world. [Hartford?] Printed for the author, 1919
183p. O.
Bibliography: p181-83
LC 20-573

Eastern costume. Hollywood, Calif., Printed for the author by Warner publishing company 1935
77p. D.
LC 36-9040

Police uniforms of the world ... illustrations by Bert Offord. Norwood, Mass., Printed for the author, Plimpton press c1934
301p. incl. front. illus. O.
Intended to supplement his *Uniforms of the world*
LC 34-1760

Uniforms of the world. New York, E. P. Dutton c1929
449p. incl.front. pl. ports. O. $6
Bibliography: p441-49
Costume index. LC 29-10410

Blakeslee, Theron J.
Illustrated catalogue of the extensive collection of highly valuable paintings by the great masters of the early English, French, Flemish, Dutch, Italian and Spanish schools, from the ... Blakeslee galleries [for a public sale] [April 21, 22 and 23, 1915] New York [The American art association; Lent & Graff co. printers] 1915
[268]p. illus. pl. Q.
LC 15-21284

[Blanc]
Garde nationale en 1830. Paris, Gobert 1830
11 col.pl. O.
Colas 337

Blanc, Charles
L'art dans la parure et dans le vêtement. Paris, Renouard, H. Loones, successeur, 1875
375,83p. illus. 2 col.pl. diagrs. O.
Part 1 of the author's *Grammaire des arts décoratifs*, which forms a continuation of his *Grammaire des arts du dessin*
Later editions by the same publisher 1882, 1887 (95 illus.) and 1890 (233 illus.)
Colas 338-41. Lipperheide 3276-78. LC 22-4130

Art in ornament and dress; tr. from the French. New York, Scribner 1877
274p. illus.(2 col.) diagrs. O.
Translation of his *L'art dans la parure*
LC 29-24827

Blanchard, Laman
(ed.) Cruikshank, George. George Cruikshank's Omnibus

Blanchet, Adrien
Catalogue des bronzes antiques de la Bibliothèque nationale. See entry under Paris. Bibliothèque nationale

Blanchot, Ivan Léon
Les bijoux anciens. Paris, Les Éditions pittoresques 1929
255p. col.front. illus. 48pl.(incl.ports.) on 24 l. O. (La collection des collectionneurs)
"Bibliographie sommaire": p[11]-14
LC 30-18878

Bland, John Otway Percy, and Backhouse, Edmund
China under the empress dowager, being the history of the life and times of Tzŭ Hsi, compiled from state papers and the private diary of the comptroller of her household. Philadelphia, J. B. Lippincott company; London, William Heinemann 1910
xv,525p. incl.map. front. pl. 13 port. O. 16s o.p.
Under Tzŭ-Hsi, 1834-1908
Costume index. LC A10-1730

Die **blanken** waffen und die schutzwaffen. Gohlke, Wilhelm

Blasis, Carlo
The code of Terpsichore; the art of dancing; comprising its theory and practice, and a history of its rise and progress, from the earliest times; tr. by R. Barton. London, E. Bull 1830
548p. 17pl. O.
Primarily on theatrical dancing and the ballet, with a selection of programs
"The original French edition, from which this is a translation, was apparently the work entitled: *Code complet de la danse* (Paris, 1829)" Library of Congress
Lipperheide 3096

Manuel complet de la danse, comprenant la théorie, la pratique et l'histoire de cet art depuis les temps les plus reculés

Blasis, Carlo—*Continued*
jusqu'à nos jours; trad. de l'anglais de M. Barton, sur l'édit. de 1830, par M. Paul Vergnaud, et revu par M. Gardel. Paris, Roret 1830
412p.; 24p.(music) front. 4 fold.pl. T. (Encyclopédie Roret)
Translation of the author's *Code of Terpsichore*, with illustrations in smaller format
Lipperheide 3097. LC 26-194

Traité élémentaire théorique et pratique de l'art de la danse. Milan, Chez Beati et A. Tenenti 1820
124p. 15pl. O.
Lipperheide 3093. LC 5-39483

Le **blason** des basquines et vertu-galles, avec la belle remonstrance qu'ont faict quelques dames quand on leur a remonstré qu'il n'en failloit plus porter. Lyon, B. Rigaud 1563 [Paris, A. Pinard 1833]
[16]p. O.
Edited by Jérome Pichon

Blau, Friedrich
Die deutschen Landsknechte; ein culturbild. Görlitz, C. U. Starke 1882
144p. 52 illus. 6pl. O.
Costume on page 112-21
Lipperheide 2102

Blaze, Castil. See Blaze, François Henri Joseph

Blaze, François Henri Joseph
La danse et les ballets depuis Bacchus jusqu'à mademoiselle Taglioni; par Castil-Blaze. Paris, Paulin 1832
373p. front. nar.D.
Lipperheide 3099. LC 9-31112

Bleich, Georg Heinrich
Abdrücke eines vollständigen kartenspieles auf silberplatten. hrsg. von Carl Förster ... München, G. Schuh 1881
iii p. 36pl. Q.
In portfolio. Reproductions of playing card designs engraved on silver plates, about 1580
Lipperheide 665. LC 3-31707

Bles, Arthur de
How to distinguish the saints in art by their costumes, symbols, and attributes. New York, Art culture publications 1925
168p. illus. F. $5
"A discussion of symbolism in general and for different groups, monastic orders, etc., with illustrations, and explanations of pictures showing symbols." B. M. Baker's Dramatic bibliography
Appendixes: Alphabetical tables of martyrdoms; Saints classified by habitual costume and by categories; Tables of symbols and attributes with names of those who bear them; Chronological tables of bishops and popes of Rome. Index
"Works consulted in the preparation of this book": p163
LC 25-21075

Bleuettes. Colin, Mme Anaïs

Bleuler, L.
Collection des costumes de la Suisse et de ses pays limitrophes; d'après F. Junghans. Schaffhouse, ca1810
1 l. 28 col.pl.(incl. 58 costume figures) S.
Costumes of different cantons
Colas 345

Bley, Wulf
... Moderne heere, moderne waffen; mit 48 abbildungen. Berlin, R. Hobbing gmbh. [c1935]
126p. pl. O.

Bleyl, Fritz
Baulich und volkskundlich beachtenswertes aus dem kulturgebiete des silberbergbaues zu Freiberg, Schneeberg und Johanngeorgenstadt im sächs. erzgebirge. Dresden, Landesverein sächs. heimatschutz 1917
180p. 6pl. Q.

Bloch, Eduard
Eduard Bloch's album der bühnencostüme; mit erläuterndem texte, von F. Tietz. Berlin, L. Lassar 1859-60
2v. 48 col.pl. Q.
Colas 346 Lipperheide 3222

Blom, Carl
Bidrag til den danske krigsmagts historie. København, Officerskolens forlag [1868]-70
3v. (76,143,186p.) illus. 9pl. O.
Arms, weapons, ships and uniforms to the middle of the 16th century
Lipperheide 2098m

Blondel, François
(illus.) Fête publique donnée par le ville de Paris à l'occasion du mariage de Monseigneur le Dauphin le 13. fevrier M.DCC.XLVII

(illus.) Fêtes publiques données par la ville de Paris à l'occasion du mariage de Monseigneur le Dauphin, les 23. et 26. fevrier M.DCC.XLV

Blondel, J. F.
(engr.) Description des festes données par la ville de Paris, à l'occasion du mariage de Madame Louise-Elisabeth de France, & de Dom Philippe, infant ... d'Espagne

Blondel, Spire
L'art capillaire dans l'Inde, à la Chine et au Japon. Paris, E. Leroux 1889
p[423]-48 O.
From *Revue d'ethnographie*, v7
LC CA22-167

Histoire des éventails chez tous les peuples et à toutes les époques; ouvrage ... suivi de notices sur l'écaille, la nacre et l'ivoire. Paris, Renouard 1875
336p. illus. O.
Costume index. Lipperheide 1722. LC 12-8565

Le tabac; le livre des fumeurs et des priseurs. Paris, Laurens 1891
xvi,293p. illus. col.pl. Q.
Bibliography: p291-93

Bloomer costume
Grand-Carteret, John. La femme en culotte. 1899

Bloxam, Matthew Holbeche
Companion to the Principles of Gothic ecclesiastical architecture, being a brief account of the vestments in use in the church, prior to, and the changes therein in and from, the reign of Edward VI ... illus. by T. O. S. Jewitt. London, G. Bell 1882
403p. illus. pl. D.
LC 11-30705

Blue shirt and khaki. Archibald, J. F. J.

Blümmer, Hugo
The home life of the ancient Greeks; trans. from the German by Alice Zimmern ... London, Cassell; New York, Funk and Wagnalls 1893
xv,548p. front. illus. pl. D. $2.50
Costume index. LC 5-1679

Das kunstgewerbe im altertum. Leipzig, G. Freytag; Prag, F. Tempsky 1885
2v. 276 illus. O. (Das wissen der gegenwart, v30 und v32)
Part 1-2 of *Geschichte des kunstgewerbes* by Hugo Blumner and Otto von Schorn, 1885
Lipperheide 129

Leben und sitten der Griechen. Leipzig, G. Freytag; Prag, F. Tempsky 1887
3v. 206 illus. pl. D. (Das wissen der gegenwart; Deutsche universal-bibliothek für gebildete, bd. LX, LXII, LXIII)
Contents: v 1 Die tracht. Geburt und erste kindheit. Erziehung und unterricht. Eheschliessung und frauenleben; v2 Tägliches leben in und ausser dem hause. Mahlzeiten, trinkgelage und gesellige unterhaltungen. Krankheiten und ärzte, tod und bestattung. Gymnastik. Musik und orchestik. Kultus; v3 Feste und festliche spiele. Das theaterwesen. Kriegs- und seewesen. Landwirtschaft, gewerbe und handel. Die sklaven
Most of the costume is in volume 1, p11-90
Lipperheide 201. LC 3-6503

Die römischen privataltertümer. München, C. H. Beck, O. Beck 1911
677p. illus. Q. (Handbuch der klassischen altertums-wissenschaft)
LC 11-27951

Blüthenzauber. Kramer, Ludwig von

Blum, André
Abraham Bosse et la société françait au dixseptième siècle; préface de Gabriel Hanotaux. [Paris] A. Morancé c1924
xxiii,226p. illus. 23pl.(1 double) O. (Archives de l'amateur)
Bibliography: p[217]-23
LC 25-1585

Histoire du costume en France. Paris, Hachette c1924
64p. incl.front. illus. ports. O. (Encyclopédie par l'image. Arts)
Bibliography: p63
Colas 347. LC 26-6155

Histoire du costume, les modes au XVII. et au XVIII. siècle; illustré de 210 reproductions en couleurs et en noir. [Paris] Hachette [1928]
215p. incl. pl.(part col.) col.front. Q. 35frs.
Bibliography: p209-[10]
Colas 348. Costume index. LC 29-9733

L'oeuvre gravé d'Abraham Bosse. [Paris] A. Morancé [1924]
93p. 44pl. O. (Documents d'art. L'oeuvre graphique du XVIIe siècle)

Histoire du costume; les modes au XIX. siècle; ouvrage illustré de 253 reproductions en couleurs et en noir. [Paris] Hachette c1931
221(i.e. 219)p. incl. col.front. pl.(part col.) Q.
Bibliography: p217
LC 32-6080

Blum, Clara M.
Old world lace; or, A guide for the lace lover. New York, E. P. Dutton c1920
85p. front. 74 illus. O. $3
LC 21-1529

Blumen und kanten zum sticken als beitrag zum unterricht in zeichnen- und stickeschulen. Giem, A. C. S.

Blumenkinder. Nauen, Paul

Blumer, Friedrich Imhoof-. See Imhoof-Blumer, Friedrich

Blunt, Lady Anne
Bedouin tribes of the Euphrates; ed... by W. S. B[lunt] Map and sketches by the author. New York, Harper 1879
445p. front. pl. fold.map, fold.tab. O.
LC 15-23689

Board work. Creer, Edwin

Boardman, Dorothy Cochran
(illus.) Stote, Dorothy. Making the most of your looks

Boas, Franz
Facial paintings of the Indians of northern British Columbia. [New York] 1898
24p. 6pl. map. F. (Memoirs of the American museum of natural history. vol. II. Anthropology. v 1 pt 1)
LC 11-14252

The social organization and the secret societies of the Kwakiutl Indians ... Based on personal observations and on notes made by Mr. George Hunt. Washington, Govt. print. office 1897
p311-738. illus.(incl. plan) 51pl. O.
From the *Annual report* of the United States National museum, 1895
LC 14-19805

Boating costume

Cambridge university

Cambridge university boating costumes. 1907?

Boccaccio, Giovanni
De claris mulieribus. Bernae Helvet. M. Apiarius 1539
81 l. 15 illus. Q.
Lipperheide 628. LC 21-18150

Fornemste historien und exempel von widerwertigem glück mercklichem ... unfahl erbärmklichen verderben unnd sterben groszmächtiger kayser, künig, fürsten unnd anderer namhafftiger herrn. Augsburg, H. Stainer 1545
250 l. 117 illus. F.
Includes many woodcuts from earlier works from the same publisher
Lipperheide 630

Il Decamerone. See Merkel, Carlo. Come vestivano gli uomini del "Decameron"; saggio di storia del costume

Le **Boccace** de Munich. Durrieu, Paul, comte

Boch, Ioannes
Historica narratio profectionis et inaugurationis ... Belgii Principum Alberti et Isabellae, Austriae Archiducum. Antverpia, J. Moretum 1602
500p. 31 illus. F.
"Et eorum ... in Belgium adventus, rerumque gestarum et memorabilium gratulationum, apparatuum, et spectaculorum in ipsorum susceptione et inauguratione hac tenus editorum accurata descriptio." Subtitle
Lipperheide 2657

Bocher, Emmanuel
Les gravures françaises du XVIIIe siècle; ou, Catalogue raisonné des estampes, eaux-fortes, pièces en couleur, au bistre

Bocher, Emmanuel—*Continued*
et au lavis, de 1700 à 1800. Paris, Librairie des bibliophiles [etc.] 1875-82
6v. fronts. (v 1-4, 6; ports. v 1, 3, 4, 6) F.
"Renseignements bibliographiques" at beginning of each volume
Contents: v 1 Nicolas Lavreince; v2 Pierre Antoine Baudouin; v3 Jean Baptiste Siméon Chardin; v4 Nicolas Lancret; v5 Augustin de Saint-Aubin; v6 Jean Michel Moreau le jeune
Lipperheide 4974. LC 10-29188

(ed.) Livres à dentelles

See also Mahérault, M. J. F., jt. auth.

Bock, A.
(engr.) Giem, A. C. S. Blumen und kanten zum sticken als beitrag zum unterricht in zeichnen- und sticke-schulen

Bock, Emil
Die brille und ihre geschichte. Wien, J. Šafář, 1903
62p. front. illus. nar.Q.
LC 5-1688

Bock, Franz
Album mittelalterlicher ornament-stickerei zur zierde für kirche und haus, in autographien ... mit erklärenden. Aachen, A. Jacobi 1866-[69]
41p. 15pl. F.
Lipperheide 3858

Beschreibender katalog einer sammlung von spitzen und kanten, darstellend den geschichtlichen entwickelungsgang der gesammten spitzen-industrie vom XVI. bis zum XIX. jahrhundert, nebst kurzem abriss der geschichte der fabrikation der "passements, dentelles et guipures." Wien, K. K. Oesterreichischen museum 1874
27,66p. O.
Lipperheide 4032

Geschichte der liturgischen gewänder des mittelalters oder entstehung und entwicklung der kirchlichen ornate und paramente in rücksicht auf stoff, gewebe, farbe, zeichnung schnitt und rituelle bedeutung nachgewiesen. Bonn, Henry & Cohen 1859-71
3v. (453,391,237p.) 126pl. (51 col.) O.
Colas 349. Lipperheide 1830

Der kaisermantel Otto's IV., kürzlich wieder aufgefunden in Braunschweig. Köln, DuMont-Schauberg [1860]
4p. pl. Q.
Lipperheide 1764

Die kleinodien des Heil. Römischen Reiches deutscher nation nebst den kroninsignien Böhmens, Ungarns und der Lombardei; mit kunsthistorischen erläuterungen. Wien, K. K. Hof- und staatsdruckerei 1864
217p. 173 illus. and atlas of 47 col.pl. F.
Lipperheide 1765

Bocquin, J.
(lithgr.) Müller, Élisabeth. Le monde en estampes

Bodde, Derk
(tr.) Tun, Li-ch'ên. Annual customs and festivals in Peking

Bode, Wilhelm. See Geschichte der deutschen kunst

Bodemann, Friedrich Wilhelm
Denkwürdigkeiten der elbinsel finkenwerder, sowie der benachbarten eilande und ortschaften. Harburg, R. Dankwerts 1860
215p. 24 l. 1 col.pl. map. O.
Colas 351. Lipperheide 798

Bodenschatz, Johann Christoph Georg
Kirchliche verfassung der heutigen Juden, sonderlich derer in Deutschland ... aus ihren eigenen und andern schriften. Frankfurt & Leipzig, 1748-49
2v. 30pl. Q.
Many reprints exist
Colas 352

Bodin, B.
Echo des casernes. Paris, Genty 1822
8 col.pl. Q.
Lipperheide 3571

Bodmer, Karl
(illus.) Wied-Neuwied, M. A. P., prinz von. Reise in das innere Nord-America

(illus.) Wied-Neuwied, M. A. P., prinz von. Travels in the interior of North America

Body-armour anciently worn in England. See Meyrick, Sir S. R. Observations on the body-armour anciently worn in England

Body mutilation. See Mutilation

Body painting
Boaz, Franz. Facial paintings of the Indians of northern British Columbia. 1898

Cocheris, Mme P. A. W. Les parures primitives avec une introduction sur les temps préhistoriques. 1894

Joest, Wilhelm. Tätowiren, narbenzeichnen und körperbemalen. 1887

See also Tattooing

Boece de Boodt, Anselm. See Boodt, Anselm Boece de

Boeck, Kurt
Durch Indien ins verschlossene land Nepal; ethnographische und photographische studienblätter. Leipzig, F. Hirt 1903
xv,319p. front. illus. (incl.facsim.) pl. map. O.
LC 3-17500

Boeheim, Wendelin
Album hervorragender gegenstände aus der waffensammlung der allerhöchsten kaiserhauses. Wien, J. Löwy 1894-[98]
2v. 65 illus. 100pl. Q.
Lipperheide 2448

Augsburger waffenschmiede, ihre werke und ihre beziehungen zum kaiserlichen und zu anderen höfen. Wien, F. Tempsky 1891
p165-227 36 illus. 2pl. Q.
From the *Jahrbuch der kunsthistorischen sammlungen* v12
Lipperheide 2445

Handbuch der waffenkunde; das waffenwesen in seiner historischen entwickelung vom beginn des mittelalters bis zum ende des 18. jahrhunderts. Leipzig, E. E. Seemann 1890
694p. about 800 illus. O. (Seemanns kunsthandbücher VII)
Lipperheide 2441

Boeheim, Wendelin—*Continued*

Meister der waffenschmiedekunst vom XIV. bis ins XVIII. jahrhundert; ein beitrag zur geschichte der kunst und des kunsthandwerks. Berlin, W. Moeser 1897
246p. 159 illus. 20pl. Q.
Lipperheide 2454. LC 4-8967

Nürnberger waffenschmiede und ihre werke in den kaiserlichen und in anderen sammlungen. ₍Wien, 1895₎
37p. 28 illus. 3pl. Q.
Reprint from: *Jahrbuch der kunsthistorischen sammlungen* v16
Lipperheide 2449

Philippine Welser; eine schilderung ihres lebens und ihres charakters. Innsbruck, verlag des Museum Ferdinandeum ₍1894₎
67p. 17 illus. 7pl. Q.
Portraits of the Guelphs, 1527-1595
Lipperheide 674

See also Kunstgewerbliches aus der vom Mähr. gewerbe-museum im jahre 1885

Boehlau, Johannes

Quaestiones de re vestiaria Graecorum. Wimeriae, H. Boehlau 1884
85p. 45 illus. O.
Bibliographical foot-notes
Colas 353. Lipperheide 197

Böhme, Franz Magnus

Geschichte des tanzes in Deutschland. Beitrag zur deutschen sitten-, litteratur- und musikgeschichte. Leipzig, Breitkopf & Härtel 1886
2v. Q.
"Quellen und litteratur": v 1 p₍325₎-30
Lipperheide 3128. LC 3-22464

Böhme, Fritz

Der tanz der zukunst. München, Delphin-verlag 1926
55p. 4pl. O.

Böhmische volkstrachten. Grüner, V. R.

Boehn, Max von

Antike mode. München, E. Heimeran 1926
57p. O.

Das beiwerk der mode: spitzen, fächer, handschuhe, stöcke, schirme, schmuck. München, F. Bruckmann ₍1928₎
277p. 293 illus. 16pl. O.
For translation see the author's *Modes and manners: ornaments*

Bekleidungskunst und mode. München, Delphin-Verlag 1918
128p. diags. illus. 48pl.(incl. front.) O.
Contents: Die entstehung der kleidung; Die entwickelung der tracht; Ästhetische und psychologische probleme; Die mode; Reformen und revolutionem
Colas 361

Biedermeier; Deutschland von 1815-1847. Berlin, B. Cassirer ₍1911₎
xi,615p. col.front. illus.(incl. facsims.) col.pl. ports.(2 col. mounted) Q.
Has a section entitled: Die mode. Contains many portraits of men and women of the time
LC 35-11252

Das bühnenkostüm in altertum, mittelalter und neuzeit. Berlin, B. Cassirer 1921
495p. front. illus.(part col.) pl. Q.
Bibliography: p57-58, 205-06, 442-45

Deutschland im 18. jahrhundert. Berlin, Askanischer verlag 1922
2v. illus. col.pl. ports.(part col.) O.
Contains many portraits of men and women of the time

Dolls and puppets; tr. by Josephine Nicoll; with a note on puppets by George Bernard Shaw. London ₍etc.₎ G. G. Harrap ₍1932₎
521p. col.front. illus. col.pl. O. $7.50
Translation of *Puppen und puppenspiele*
Bibliography p481-506
Costume index. LC 32-28084

England im 18. jahrhundert; 2. aufl. Berlin, Askanischer verlag 1922
678p. col.front. illus. col.ports. Q.
Contains many portraits of men and women of the time

Miniaturen und silhouetten; ein kapitel als kulturgeschichte und kunst; 3. ed. München, F. Bruckman ₍1919₎
207p. ports. O.

Miniatures and silhouettes. tr. by E. K. Walker. London and Toronto, J. M. Dent; New York, E. P. Dutton 1928
214p. col.front. illus. col.ports. O.
Translation of his *Miniaturen.* Silhouettes from the beginning of the 16th century to the middle of the nineteenth. Jewelry page 133-70
LC 28-13004

La moda; historia del traje en Europa desde los orígenes del cristianismo hasta nuestros días; con un estudio preliminar por el marqués de Lozoya. 1. ed. española, adaptada del alemán y notablemente aumentada. Barcelona, Salvat 1928-29
8v. col.fronts. (v 1-4, 6-8) illus. col.pl. col.ports. O.
Contents: t 1 Edad media; t2 Siglo XVI; t3 Siglo XVII; t4 Siglo XVIII; t5 Siglo XIX, 1790-1817; t6 Siglo XIX, 1818-1842; t7 Siglo XIX, 1843-1878; t8 Siglo XIX y XX, 1879-1914
Spanish translation of *Die mode* for the corresponding periods
LC 32-13849

Die mode; menschen und moden im achtzehnten jahrhundert, nach bildern und stichen der zeit, ausgewählt von Oskar Fischel, text von Max von Boehn, München, F. Bruckmann 1909
251p. illus. pl.(part col. incl.front.) ports. (part col.) O.
Costumes of the Directory and the Empire periods
Colas 356. LC 10-11923

Die mode; menschen und moden im mittelalter vom untergang der alten welt bis zur renaissance, nach bildern und kunstwerken der zeit ausgewählt und geschildert von Max von Boehn. München, F. Bruckmann ₍1925₎
284p. illus. 24 col.pl. (incl. front., ports.) O.
Colas 354. LC 27-6015

Die mode; menschen und moden im neunzehnten jahrhundert nach bildern und kupfern der zeit, ausgewählt von dr. Oskar Fischel, text von Max von Boehn. München, F. Bruckmann 1907-19
4v. illus. col.pl. col.ports. O.
Contents: v 1 1790-1817; v2 1818-1842; v3 1843-1878; v4 1878-1914
Colas 357-60. LC 7-40055

Boehn, Max von—*Continued*

Die mode; menschen und moden im sechzehnten jahrhundert, nach bildern und stichen der zeit ausgewählt und geschildert von Max von Boehn. München, F. Bruckmann [1923]
253p. illus. 16 col.pl. (incl.front. ports.) O.
LC 27-6016

Die mode; menschen und moden im siebzehnten jahrhundert nach bildern und stichen der zeit, ausgewählt und geschildert von Max von Boehn. München, F. Bruckmann 1913
189p. incl.front. illus. col.pl. ports. O. M. 6.50
Colas 355 LC 13-26711

Modes and manners; tr. by Joan Joshua. Illustrated with reproductions of contemporary paintings &c. Philadelphia, J. B. Lippincott; London, G. H. Harrap 1932-[36]
4v. col. front. illus. col.pl. O. ea $4
Contents: I from the decline of the ancient world to the renaissance; II The sixteenth century; III The seventeenth century; IV The eighteenth cenury
Translation of the volumes of *Die mode* which cover corresponding periods
Costume index. LC 33-270

Modes & manners of the nineteenth century as represented in the pictures and engravings of the time, tr. from the German. London, J. M. Dent; New York, E. P. Dutton 1927
4v. col.fronts. illus.(incl. ports.) pl.(part col.) O. ea $5
Volumes 1-3 first published 1909, revised and enl. 1927. Some colored and black and white illustrations have been added, and a short note on American fashions. Volume 4 includes only the chapters on fashions from the German edition. Two chapters by Grace Thompson, on English social history and on sport and sport clothes, have been substituted for the parts omitted
Contents: v 1 1790-1817; v2 1818-1842; v3 1843-1878; v4 1879-1914
Translation of *Die mode; menschen und moden im neunzehnten jahrhundert* (München, 1907-19)
Costume index. LC 28-3478

Modes & manners: ornaments; lace, fans, gloves, walking-sticks, parasols, jewelry and trinkets ... translated from the German. London & Toronto, J. M. Dent; New York, E. P. Dutton [1929]
xix,273p. illus. 16 col.pl.(incl.front.) O. $6; 15s
Half-title: Modes & manners, supplementary volume, ornaments
Translation of *Das beiwerk der mode*
Costume index. LC 30-26605

Modespiegel. Berlin [etc.] G. Westermann c1919
176p. col.front. illus.(part col.) ports. D.
Contents: Die mode; Die entstehung der weltmode; Die mode im neunzehnten jahrhundert; Freiheitskrieg und mode; Vom brautkleide; Kinderkleid und kindermode; Schönheitsabende in alter zeit; Zur geschichte des modejournals

Polizei und mode. Berlin, Gersbach [1926]
119p. illus. col.pl. Q. (Die polizei in einzeldartstellungen. Bd 10)

Puppen und puppenspiele. München, F. Bruckmann ag. [1929]
2v. illus. col.pl. O.
Contents: v 1 Puppen; v2 Puppenspiele. Bibliography at end of each volume
LC 30-10040

Rokoko; Frankreich im XVIII. jahrhundert. [4. aufl.] Berlin, Askanischer verlag 1923
611p. col.front. illus. col.pl. col.ports. O.

Spanien: geschichte, kultur, kunst. Berlin, C. A. Kindle 1924
453p. col.front. illus. pl.(part col.) ports. (part col.) Q.
LC 29-18589

Der tanz. Berlin, Volksverband d. bücherfreunde 1925
268p. 32pl. O.
The latter half of the book consists of selections from works on the dance by other authors, under the title *Dokumente*
"Literatur": p[263]

Vom kaiserreich zur republik; ein kulturgeschichte Frankreichs im 19. jahrhundert. München, Hyperionverlag 1921
490p. front. illus. pl.(part col.) O.
The same title was published (Berlin, 1917. 244 illus. 24pl: 10 col.)

(ed.) Moreau, J. M., dit le jeune, and Freudenberger, Sigmund. Trois suites d'estampes pour servir à l'histoire des modes et du costume des Français dans le 18. siècle

Boemus, Johann

The manners, lawes, and customes of all nations. Collected out of the best writers by Ioannes Boemus Aubanus, a Dutchman ... Written in Latin, tr. by Ed. Aston. London, Printed by G. Eld 1611
589p. O.
"With many other things of the same argument, gathered out of the historie of Nicholas Damascen. The like also out of the history of America, or Brasill, written by Iohn Lerius. The faith, religion and manners of the Aethiopians, and the deploration of the people of Lappia, compiled by Damianus à Goes. With a short discourse of the Aethiopians, taken out of Ioseph Scaliger his seventh booke de Emendatione temporum." Subtitle
Translation of his *Mores*
LC 2-23653

Mores, leges, et ritus omnium gentium ... Lugduni? apud J. Tornaesium 1582
495p. nar.T.
Appendix: Fides, religio, morésque Aethiopum sub imperio preciosi Joannis ... degentium, unà cum enarratione confoederationis ac amicitiae inter ipsos Aethiopum imperatores, & reges Lusitaniae initae ... deploratio Lappianae gentis, ipso etiam Damiano à Goës autore.
Liber I, de Aphrica; II, de Asia; III, de Europa. The part by Boemus appeared first in 1520, the appendix in 1540. For English translation see his *The manners*. Italian version has title *Gli costumi, de legge et le usani* (Venetia 1542 etc.)
Lipperheide 16. LC 10-4411 (1591 ed.)

Bööcke, Robert L.

Shakespearian costumes; illustrations ... compiled from authentic sources ... drawn by Robert L. Bööcke. London, S. Miller 1889[-9-?]
8v. pl. Q.
Contents: v 1 As you like it; v2 Twelfth night; v3 Taming of the shrew; v4 The merry wives of Windsor; v5 The merchant of Venice; v6 Cymbeline; v7 Hamlet; v8 Richard the third

Boerschmann, Ernst
Picturesque China, architecture and landscape; a journey through twelve provinces. New York, Brentano's [1923]
xxvi,288p. pl. mop. F. $4.50
288 pages of illustrations, with titles in English, French, German, Spanish, and Italian
Translated by Louis Hamilton
English title: *China, architecture and landscape* (London, The studio c1925)
French edition: *La Chine pittoresque* (Paris, Calavas. 100fr.) German edition *Baukunst u. landschaft in China* (Berlin, E. Wasmuth)
Costume index (French ed.) LC 24-11591, 32-31223 (English ed.) 32-31222 (German ed.)

Boesch, Hans
Katalog der im Germanischen museum befindlichen originalskulpturen. See entry under Nuremberg. Germanisches national-museum

Katalog der im germanischen museum vorhandenen zum abdrucke bestimmten geschnittenen holzstöcke vom XV.-XVIII. jahrhunderte. Nürnberg, Germanischen museum 1892-96
3v. 1180 illus. pl. Q.
Volume 3 is an atlas of 12 plates
Lipperheide 603

Kinderleben in der deutschen vergangenheit. Mit einhundertneunundvierzig abbildungen und beilagen nach den originalen aus dem 15.-18. jahrhundert. Leipzig, E. Diederichs 1900
131p. 143 illus. pl.(part fold.) Q. (Monographien zur deutschen kulturgeschichte v. bd.)
Lipperheide 605c. LC G-1208

Böttger, Adolf
Die pilgerfahrt der blumengeister; 3. umgearb. und verb. aufl. Leipzig, F. Fleischer 1857
296p. 36 col.pl. O.
Plates are from Grandville's *Les fleurs animées*
First edition: 1850
Lipperheide 3181

Böttiger, Karl August
Sabina, oder morgenscenen im putzzimmer einer reichen Römerin; ein beytrag zur rightigen beurtheilung des privatlebens der Römer und zum bessern verständniss der römischen schriftsteller. Leipzig, G. J. Göschen 1803
505p. 13pl. O.
The toilet and dress of a Roman matron at the time of Nero. The German edition of 1811 entitled *Morgenscenen im putzzimmer der Römerin Sabina* contains only one plate with nine of the illustrations
French translation by Clapier is entitled *Sabine, ou Matinée d'une dame romaine à sa toilette, à la fin du premier siècle de l'ère chrétienne.* (Paris, Maradan 1813. 406p. 13pl. D.)
Lipperheide 233

See also note under Retzsch, F. A. M. Gallerie zu Shakspeare's dramatischen werken

Bogeng, Gustav Adolf Erich
Geschichte des sports aller völker und zeiten. Leipzig, E. A. Seemann 1926
2v. illus. xviii pl.(part col.), ports. Q.

Boguslawski, Albrecht von
Deutschland. Das heer, von Boguslawski ... Die flotte, von R. Aschenborn ... Anhang: Das internationale Rote kreuz, von V. von Strantz ... 2. ausg. ergänzt durch einen nachtrag ... Berlin, A. Schall [1900]
xix,596,128p. front. illus. pl.(part col.) ports. fold. plans. O. (Die heere und flotten der gegenwart ... hrsg. von C. von Zepelin. [I])
LC 19-5739

Bohemia. See Czechoslovakia—Bohemia. Also subdivision Czechoslovakia—Bohemia under Ceremonial and festival costume; Coronations and coronation robes; Crown jewels; Ecclesiastical costume; Military costume. Also Nobles—Bohemia

Bohmann, Peter
(pub.) Wietz, J. K. Abbildungen sämmtlicher geistlichen orden

Boilat, P. D., abbé
Esquisses sénégalaises. Paris, P. Bertrand 1853
2v. (xvi,496p. map; 31p. 24 col.pl.) Q.
Colas 364

Boileau, Étienne
Réglemens sur les arts et métiers de Paris; rédigés au XIIIe siècle, et connus sous le nom du Livre des métiers d'Étienne Boileau. Paris, Crapelet 1837
474p. (Collection de documents inédits sur l'histoire de France ... 1. sér. Historie politique)
Laws governing the various crafts of Paris, including those dealing with clothing

Boileau, Jacques
De l'abus des nuditez de gorge. Bruxelles, F. Foppens 1675
110p. D.
Second edition rev. corr. & augm. (Paris, J. de Laize-de-Bresche 1677. 116p.) and a facsimile reproduction of the second edition entitled *De l'abus des nudités de gorge* (Paris, Delahays 1858. 130p.)
Lipperheide 3440 (1858 ed.) LC 15-22971 (2. ed.)

Boilly, Jules
(illus.) Eyriès, J. B. B. Voyage pittoresque en Asie et en Afrique

Boilly, Julien Léopold
Collection de costumes italiens, dessinés d'après natur en 1827 et lith. par Jul. Boilly. Paris, Daudet 1827?
48 col.pl. Q.
Published in eight parts
Colas 365. Lipperheide 1278

Boilly, Louis Léopold
[Les grimaces] Paris, ca1826
68 col.pl. F.
Lipperheide 3572

Recueil de dessins lithographiques. Paris, Delpech 1822
8 col.pl. F.
Popular French types

[Recueil de sujets moraux] [Paris] Delpech 1827
6pl. Q.
Lipperheide 1157m

About

Harrisse, Henry. L.-L. Boilly ... 1761-1845. 1898

Boinet, Amédée

La miniature carolingienne, son origine, son développement. Paris, Picard 1920

160pl. Q. 200fr.

From French, Italian, Flemish and German Bibles, psalters, etc. published from 751 to 987

"Publié avec le concours de l'Académie des inscriptions et belles-lettres." The projected volume of text has never appeared

Boissard, Jean Jacques

Habitus variarum orbis gentium. Habitz de nations estrãges. Trachten mancherley völcker des erdskreyss. Mecheln, C. Rutz 1581

2 l. 67pl. 3 ports. F.

Each plate shows three figures. Titles and descriptions are in Latin, French and German

Colas 366. Lipperheide 14-15

Iani Iacobi Boissardi Vesuntini emblematum liber; ipsa emblemata ab auctore delineata: a Theodoro de Bry sculpta, & nunc recens in lucem edita. Francofurti ad Moenum, 1593

103p. 53 illus. Q.

Brunet describes an edition of 1588 and also one of 1593 with 55 illustrations

Lipperheide 496

Icones & effigies virorum doctorum. Quotquot celebres fuerunt per Europam artificiosissimè in aes incisae à J. T. de Brij. Francofurti, I. Ammon 1645-50

2v. 289pl. Q.

Volume 2, published 1650 is part 6, entitled Pars bibliothecae chalcographicae, id est continuatio prima, *Iconum virorum virtute atq. eruditione illustrium*

This work was originally published in Frankfurt from 1597 to 1599, in 4 parts with 198 head and shoulder portraits, under the title *Icones virorum illustr. doctrina et eruditione praestantium.* A new edition published from 1650 to 1654, contains 150 more portraits which form parts 7, 8, and 9

Lipperheide 504

Leben und contrafeiten der türckischen un persischen sultanen von Osmane an biss auff den jetztregierenden sultan Mahumet II; auch vieler anderer fürtrefflicher helden und heldinen historische beschreibung und eigentlicher abriss. ... In Latein beschrieben ... jetzo in teutsch gebracht ... von newem an tag geben durch Diterich von Bry Leodien. Franckfurt, 1596

394p. 47 illus. Q.

Half length portraits of the Turkish and Persian princes, generals and their consorts, from Ottoman to Mohammed II

A Latin edition with title *Vitae et icones Sultanorum Turcicorum* appeared also in 1596. Greblinger's *Wahre abbildungen* is an abridgement

Lipperheide 1401

Mascarades; recuilles & mises en taille douce par Robert Boissart. No place, 1597

11p. 24pl. Q.

Each plate shows a man and woman in masquerade costume, for the most part of the type used at the end of the 16th century

Colas 368. Lipperheide 3167

Recueil de costumes etrangers; faisant le 3ᵉ volume de la collection recueillie par J. J. Boissard après 1581? No place, ca1585?

57pl. F.

Described by Colas as a series in the collection of the Cabinet des estampes. Plates are engraved in the manner of his *Habitus*. The title is in manuscript. Colas gives a list of the plates

Colas 367

(illus.) Lonicer, J. A. Pannoniae historia chronologica

Boissart, Robert

(engr.) Boissard, J. J. Mascarades

Boissel, W.

Le Pays basque: sites, arts et coutumes. Paris, A. Calavas [1930]

46p. cviii pl. Q. (Les provinces françaises)

LC 32-8322

Boissevin, Louis

Portraits des rois de France ... depuis Pharamond jusqu'au rois Louis XIV. Paris, L. Boissevin ca1660

Q.

Boissonnas, Charles

Alte waffen aus d. Schweiz. See entry under Boissonnas, Jean

Boissonnas, Jean

Armes anciennes de la Suisse. Paris, Schemit [etc. 1900]

31p. 33pl. (Collection Charles Boissonnas)

Weapons used in Switzerland before the 16th century

Also published in a German edition *Alte waffen aus d. Schweiz* (Berlin, R. C. Schmidt 1914. 32p. 33pl.)

[**Bojardi, F. de**]

L'évolution de l'art dans l'éventail aux 16. 17. et 18. siècles; catalogue illustré de 93 pièces de la collection de F. de B. Rome, Imprimerie Roma [1907]

52 l. illus. O.

At head of cover-title: Esposizione dell' ornamento feminile 1500-1800, Palazzo Rospigliosi, décembre 1907

LC 14-6358

Bokhara

Curtis, W. E. Turkestan: "the heart of Asia". 1911

Grasset de Saint-Sauveur, Jacques. Moeurs, loix et costumes des Tatars-Usbeks. 1795

Bol, Hans

[The twelve months] Joan. Bol inve. Adria. Collaert exc. [Antwerp] ca1590

12pl. O.

Lipperheide 924m

Bolivia

Meyendorff, K. E., and Meyendorff, N. G. L'empire du soleil, Pérou et Bolivie. 1909

United States. Bureau of foreign and domestic commerce. Wearing apparel in Bolivia. 1918

Wright, Mrs M. R. Bolivia. c1907

Bolmar, Lydia, and McNutt, Kathleen

Art in dress, with notes on home decoration. Peoria, Ill. The Manual arts press 1916

46p. illus. fold.pl. O.

LC 16-14652

Bologna. See Italy—Emilia; Street venders—Italy—Bologna

Bolt, Fr.
(engr.) Walter, W. Das preuszische heer in bildern

Bolte, Johannes
Das Danziger theater im 16. und 17. jahrhundert. Hamburg und Leipzig, L. Voss 1895
xxiii,296p. O. (Theatergeschichtliche forschungen, hrsg. von Berthold Litzmann. XII)
LC 3-12720

Bolton, Adelaide. See Louden, Mrs A. B.

Bolton, Charles Knowles
The private soldier under Washington. New York, C. Scribner's sons 1902
xiii,258p. pl. facsim. O.
LC 2-23616

Boltze, Eberh.
Die infanterie Friedrichs d. G. 1785. Dresden, 1927
2v. (64p. 18 col.pl.)
Text is in typewriting

Bombast von Hohenheim. See Paracelsus

Bombelli, Rocco
Storia della corona ferrea dei re d'Italia. Firenze, Tip. Cavour 1870
231p. front. O.
LC 20-13233

Le **bon** genre; a selection of 100 plates of the famous Gazette du bon genre. See entry under Gazette du bon genre

Le **bon** genre, réimpression des 115 gravures, publiée sous ce titre de 1801 à 1822. See Gazette du bon genre. Le bon genre, réimpression du recueil de 1827 comprenant les "Observations."

Le **bon** genre; réimpression du recueil de 1827 comprenant les "Observations". See entry under Gazette du bon genre

Le **Bon** ton and le Moniteur de la mode united. v 1-73, no. 7; 1851-Sept. 1925. v75, no. 3, Mr 1926. New York, S. T. Taylor [etc.]
Illus. pl.(part col.) Q.-F.
No more published?
A fashion periodical. Text in English. Published monthly
Title varies: 1851-1917, *Le Bon ton; journal de modes; monthly report of Paris fashions*
Volume 73 no8- v75 no2 omitted in numbering
Colas 385. LC CA8-3497

Le **Bon** ton, journal des modes. 1.-40. année; 10. novembre 1834-1874. Paris,
Pl.(part col.) O.
Colas 384. Lipperheide 4627

The **Bon** ton magazine; or, Microscope of fashion and folly. v. 1-5 (no. 1-61); Mar. 1791-Mar. 1796. London, Printed for the proprietors, and sold by D. Brewman
5v. pl. O.
Published monthly. Nos. 1-33 have imprint: London, Printed for W. Locke
No more published?
LC 24-15230

Bonanni, Filippo. See Buonanni, Filippo

Bondí di Mazo. See Mazo, Bondí di

Boner, Charles
Transylvania; its products and its people. London, Longmans, Green, Reader, and Dyer 1865
xiv,642p. col.front illus. pl. 5 fold.maps. O.
LC 3-8241

Bonetti, Emilia
L'arte del taglio e la confezione d'abiti per signora: manuale teorico-pratico. Milano, Hoepli 1908
xix,296p. illus. pl. S.

See also G. Peterlongo's *Abiti*

Disegno, taglio e confezione di biancheria: manuale teorico-pratico. Milano, U. Hoepli 1894
216p. 40pl. O.
Lipperheide 3847

Bonin, Louis
Die neueste art zur galanten und theatralischen tantz-kunst: worinnen gründliche nachricht anzutreffen wie dieses ... exercitium. Franckfurt, J. C. Lochner 1712
24 l. 270p. O.
Lipperheide 3068

Bonnaffé, A .A.
Recuerdos de Lima; album: Tipos, trajes y costumbres. Lima, 1857
1 p. 12 col.pl. F.

Bonnand
Abhandlung von der schädlichen wirkung der schnürbrüste. Leipsic, Jacobaer 1773
O.

Bonnard, Camille
Costumes des XIIIe, XIVe et XVe siècles, extraits des monumens les plus authentiques de peinture et de sculpture; 1. éd. française. Paris, Treuttel & Wurtz [etc] [1829-39]
2v.(208,213p.) 200 col.pl. Q. 200-600fr.
First French edition of his *Costumi ecclesiastici civili e militari.* Described by Colas as the most handsome edition
The same work appeared with the following title *Costumes historiques des XIIIe, XIVe et XVe siècles, extraits des monuments les plus authentiques de peinture et de sculpture dessinés et gravés par Paul Mercurj. Avec un texte historique et descriptif par Camille Bonnard. Première édition française.* (Paris, Goupil et Vibert 1845. 2v.) Many of the plates are reproduced in *Costumes historiques* by Le Chevallier Chevignard
Colas 375-376. Lipperheide 334z

Costumes historiques des XIIe, XIIIe, XIVe et XVe siècles tirés des monuments ... de peinture et de sculpture; dessinés et gravés par Paul Mercuri; nouv. éd. rev. Paris, A. Lévy 1860-61
3v. 200pl. Q.
Revision of the first French edition. *Costumes historiques des XVIe, XVIIe et XVIIIe siècles* by G. V. A. G. Duplessis is a supplementary work
Colas 377. Costume index. Lipperheide 335

Costumi ecclesiastici, civili e militari d' secolo XIII, XIV e XV ... Costumes ecclesiastiques, civils et militaires des XIIIe, XIVe, XVe siècles. Roma, Poggioli 1827-28
2v. (xx,99p. 100 l.) 198 col.pl. Q.
"Raccolti par Camille Bonnard, ed accompagnati da un testo istorico e descrittivo." Subtitle
First Italian edition, with text in French and Italian. Plates engraved by Paul Mercuri. Some editions have plates in black and white only. Most of the costumes are French or Italian
The second Italian edition was entitled *Costumi de' secolo XIII, XIV, e XV estratti*

Bonnard, Camille—*Continued*
da' monumenti i più autentici di pittura e scultura; 2. ed. (Roma, Salviucci 1828. 2v. 200 col.pl. Q.)
Colas 374. Lipperheide 334y

Bonnart, Henri
Recueil d'estampes de costume du XVIIe siècle. Paris, N. Bonnart ca1690
58pl. D.
Colas 379?

[**Bonnart, Jean Baptiste**]
[Cris de Paris] Paris, Bonnart ca1700
34pl. F.
Number of plates varies in different copies. Colas lists 34
Colas 380. Lipperheide 1178

[**Bonnart, Jean-Baptiste, and Bonnart, Robert**]
Kostüme aus der zeit Ludwigs XIV. Paris, [Les auteurs] ca1700
167pl.(6 col.) F.
Lipperheide 1116

Bonnart, Robert. See Bonnart, Jean Baptiste, jt. auth.

Bonnaud. Abhandlung von der schädlichen wirkung der schnürbrüste. See Bonnand

La **Bonne** compagnie, sporting and fashionable review. 1852-1855 Paris
Col.illus. O.
Contains colored fashion plates
Colas 381. Lipperheide 4665

Bonnellier, Hippolyte
(ed.) L'Avenir, revue politique, litteraire et des modes

Bonnemère, Lionel. See Bosc, Ernest, jt. auth.

Bonnet, Hans
Die ägyptische tracht bis zum ende des neuen reiches, von Hans Bonnet. Leipzig, J. C. Hinrichs 1917
73p. 9pl.(incl. diagrs.) Q. (Untersuchungen zur geschichte und altertumskunde Aegyptens. 7. bd. hft. 2)
Published also, in part, as the author's inaugural dissertation, Leipzig, 1916, with title: *Die altägyptische schurztracht* (44p.) Also paged continuously with heft 1:83-155p.
Bibliographical foot-notes
Colas 382. LC 21-7622

Die waffen der völker des alten Orients. Mit 107 abbildungen. Leipzig, J. C. Hinrichs 1926
223p. illus.(1 mounted) O.
Bibliographical foot-notes

Bonnet, Jacques
Histoire generale de la danse, sacrée et prophane; ses progrès & ses révolutions, depuis son origine jusqu'à présent. Paris, Houry fils 1724
xl,269p. D.
Lipperheide 3069. LC 5-35050

Bonneville, François, and Quénard, P.
Portraits des personnages célèbres de la révolution avec tableau historique et notices de P. Quénard. Paris, Cercle social 1796-1802
4v. 230pl.(29 col. 200 ports.) Q.
Colas 383

Bonney, Thérèse
(ed.) Remember when—a pictorial chronicle of the turn of the century and of the days known as Edwardian. New York, Coward McCann 1933
[127]p. incl. illus. ports. Q. $2
Costume index. LC 33-36697

Bonomi, Joseph
Nineveh and its palaces. The discoveries of Botta and Layard, applied to the elucidation of Holy Writ. London, Office of the Illustrated London library [pref. 1852]
xx,402p. front. illus. maps. O. (Illustrated London library. v 1)
LC 5-13003

Bontier, Pierre, and Le Verrier, Jean
The Canarian; or, Book of the conquest and conversion of the Canarians in the year 1402, by Messire Jean de Bethencourt; tr. and ed. by R. H. Major. London, Printed for the Hakluyt society 1872
lv,229p. front.(port.) 2pl. map. O. (Works issued by the Hakluyt society. no. XLVI)
Includes title used by Galien de Bethencourt in his manuscript of 1625: *Le Canarien; ou, Livre de la conqueste ... en l'an 1402.*
LC 4-22705

Bonvalot, Gabriel
Across Thibet ... With illustrations from photographs ... tr. by C. B. Pitman. New York, Cassell publishing company c1891
134p. incl.illus. 7pl. O.
A translation of his *De Paris au Tonking*
LC 5-12658

Bonwick, James
Daily life and origin of the Tasmanians. London, S. Low, son, & Marston 1870
304p. incl. col.front. illus. pl. ports. fold.map. O.
LC 3-3739

The last of the Tasmanians; or, The black war of Van Diemen's Land. London, S. Low, son, & Marston 1870
400p. col.front. 6pl. ports. fold.map. O.
LC 8-33923

Bonwit, Teller & co., New York
The philosophy of dress. New York, Bonwit, Teller [c1925]
[16]p. illus. O.
"Written ... for Bonwit, Teller & co. by Mr. M. D. C. Crawford." Introd.
LC 25-21805

Boodt, Anselm Boèce de
Le parfaict ioaillier, ou Histoire des pierreries ... de nouveau enrichi de belles annotations, indices & figures, par André Toll. Lyon, I. A. Huguetan 1644
16p.l. 746,[35]p. illus. 2 fold.tab. D.
Translated from the Latin by Jean Bachou
LC 8-36371

A **book** about doctors. Jeaffreson, J. C.

A **book** about fans. Flory, M. A.

A **book** about lawyers. Jeaffreson, J. C.

A **book** for Shakespeare plays and pageants. Hatcher, O. L.

The **book** of archery. Hansard, G. A.

The **book** of Ceylon. Cave, H. W.

The **book** of costume. Wilton, M. M. S. E., countess of

The **book** of delightful and strange designs. Tuer, A. W.

A **book** of dramatic costume. Dabney, Edith, and Wise, C. M.

The **book** of fancy needlework. Containing clear instructions in embroidery, Berlin wool-work, crewel-work, appliqué-work, netting, guipure d'art, darning on net, lace-work, etc. London, Ward, Lock, & co. [1879]
78p. 106 illus. O.
Lipperheide 4120

The **book** of historical costumes, drawn from specimens and the most authentic documents of each period. Pauquet, H. L. E., and Pauquet, P. J. C.

Book of needlework. Beeton, S. O.

A **book** of old embroidery. Holme, Geoffrey, ed.

Book of opening the mouth
The Book of opening the mouth, the Egyptian texts with English translations, by E. A. W. Budge. London, K. Paul, Trench, Trübner & co. 1909
2v. 100 illus. 1 pl. D. (Books on Egypt and Chaldaea. v26-27)
LC 10-13899

The **book** of orders of knighthood and decorations of honour of all nations. Burke, Sir J. B.

The **book** of perfumes. Rimmel, Eugene

The **book** of sport. Patten, William

The **book** of the American Indian. Garland, Hamlin

Book of the American spirit. Pyle, Howard, illus.

The **book** of the Bayeux tapestry. Belloc, Hilaire

Book of the bench, with 39 reproductions in colour from paintings by "Spy" and other cartoonists. London, J. Mackenzie 1909
unp. 39pl. F.
The plates are portraits of judges and officials of the English courts

The **book** of the Club of true Highlanders. North, C. N. M.

Book of the dead
Facsimile of the Papyrus of Ani, in the British Museum. 2d ed London, British museum, Longmans [etc] 1894
37 col.pl.(double) F.
Fine color plates each with a short descriptive note

The **book** of the feet. Hall, J. S.

The **book** of the Hosroes, history of the kings of Iran. Gálâl ad-Dîn Mîrzâ

The **book** of the ranks and dignities of British society, lately attributed in the press and elsewhere to Charles Lamb; including an introductory note by Clement Shorter. London, J. Cape 1924
135p. 24pl.(8 col.) D. 5s, o.p.
Published in the United States by C. Scribner
Reprint of a book published in 1805 (London, printed for Tabart & co. 24 col.pl.)
Describes dress of the king, the lord chancellor, various ranks of nobility, a bishop, officers of the law, army, navy and officials' court dresses, etc. Plates show many of these in ceremonial dress
Costume index. LC 25-5103

The **book** of weddings. Kingsland, Florence

A **book** of winter sports. Dier, J. C.

The **booke** of falconrie or hawking. Turberville, George

The **books** of Indian crafts & Indian lore. Salomon, J. H.

The **boot** and shoe-maker's assistant; containing a treatise on clicking, and the form and fitting-up of lasts scientically considered; illus. with engravings and pattern plates. Preceded by a history of feet costume. By one who has worked on the seat and at the cutting-board. London, Groombridge 1853
74,30p. illus., 60pl.(part fold.) diagrs. F.
LC 8-36581

Booth, Eric Charles Talbot-. See Talbot-Booth, E. C.

[**Booth, John**]
(comp.) The battle of Waterloo, with those of Ligny and Quatre Bras, described by eye-witnesses and by the series of official accounts published by authority ... Illustrated by maps, plans ... and thirty-four etchings from drawings by George Jones. 11th ed. enl. and corr. London, L. Booth 1852
xii,cxxxiii,[17],475p. front. (ports.) pl. (1 fold.) fold.maps, fold.plans, double facsim. O.
LC 4-11635

The **boots** and shoes of our ancestors. Dutton, W. H.

Boppe, Paul Louis Hippolyte
La Croatie militaire (1809-1813): Les régiments croates à la grande armée. Paris, Berger-Levrault 1900
267p. 6 col.pl. col.map. O.
Colas 388

La Légion portugaise, 1807-1813. Paris, Nancy, Berger-Levrault 1897
xii,518p. front. (port.) col.pl. O.
Each plate accompanied by guard sheet with descriptive letterpress
Colas 387. LC 29-2069

Borchardt, Georg Hermann
Die deutsche karikatur im 19. jahrhundert; von Georg Hermann [pseud] Bielefeld, Velhagen & Klasing 1901
132p. 177 illus. 6pl.(2 col.) (Sammlung illustrierter monographien. 2)
Lipperheide 3517

Borchardt, Ludwig, and Ricke, Herbert
Egypt; architecture, landscape, life of the people. New York, Westermann; London, The Studio limited [1930]
xxviii p 272pl. on 136 l. map. F. (Orbis terrarum) $5
Costume index. LC 30-21825

Borchers, Fr.
Neue zuschneidekunst für damenbekleidung. Hannover, Gőhmann 1889
54p. 35pl. O.
Colas 389. Lipperheide 3843

Bordeaux. See France—By region or province—Bordeaux

Bordeaux, Raymond. See La Normandie illustrée

Bordoli, Ernest
Footwear down the ages. Northampton [Eng] Printed by the Mercury co. [1933]
68p. illus. O.
LC 34-39601

Borel, Lusan-. See Lussan-Borel

Borget, Auguste
La Chine et les Chinois, dessins exécutées d'après nature; lithographiés à deux teintes par Eugène Cicéri. Paris, Goupil & Vibert [1842]
26p. front. 32 views on 25pl. F.
Plates show views, many with costume figures
Colas 390

Sketches of China and the Chinese; from drawings by Auguste Borget. London, Tilt & Bogue [1842]
11p. 32 views on 25pl. F.
Translation of his *La Chine*
LC 4-24776

(illus.) Forgues, P. E. D. La Chine ouverte

Borghi, Camillo Ranier
L'oplomachia pisana, ovvero La battaglia del ponte di Pisa. Lucca, P. Frediani 1713
184p. 4pl. O.

Boris Aronson et l'art du théatre. George, Waldemar

Borkowsky, Ernst
Das alte Jena und seine universität; eine jubiläumsgabe zur universitätsfeier ... mit 107 abbildungen. Jena, E. Diederichs 1908
286p. front. illus.(incl.ports.) double pl. double plan. O.
LC E9-23

[**Born, Ignaz, edler von**]
John Physiophilus's Specimen of the natural history of the various orders of monks, after the manner of the Linnæan system. Tr. from the Latin, printed at Augsburgh. London; J. Johnson 1783
xxxii,48p. pl. O.
Edition in Latin has title *Joannis Physiophili Specimen monachologiae*
A satire against monks. The plates are engraved by J. Schaff and show characteristic parts of monks' dress
Lipperheide 1876 (Latin ed.)

Bornecque, Jules Charles Constant
La coiffure militaire. Paris, J. Dumaine 1880
18p. 3 illus. O.
Colas 391

Borneo
Boyle, Frederick. Adventures among the Dyaks of Borneo. 1865
Gomes, E. H. Seventeen years among the Sea Dyaks of Borneo. 1911
Haddon, A. C., and Start, L. E. Iban or sea Dayak fabrics and their patterns. 1936
Hose, Charles, and McDougall, William. The pagan tribes of Borneo. 1912
Juynboll, H. H. Borneo. 1909
Nieuwenhuis, A. W. Quer durch Borneo; ergebnisse seiner reisen in den jahren 1894, 1896-97 und 1898-1900. 1904-07

See also subdivision Borneo under Decoration and ornament

Borsa, Mario
La caccia nel milanese dalle origini ai giorni nostri. Milano, U. Hoepli [1924]
xv,356p. col.front. illus. pl.(part col.) ports.(1 col.) F.
Illustrations show weapons and hunting scenes from the medieval times to the 20th century

Bosa, Eugenio
Crieurs et autres costumes populaires de Venise. Milan and Venise, P. & J. Vallardi 1835
24pl. Q.
Colas 392. Lipperheide 1332

Gridatori ed altri costumi popolari di Trieste. Milano, E. P. e G. Vallardi 1835
24 col.pl. O.
Colas 393

Sogetti pittoreschi e costumi di Venezia incisi all' acqua forte. Venezia, ca1840
24pl. O.
Same plates reissued with title *Sketch-book by an American in Venice* (1860)
Colas 394. LC 11-2548

Bosaeus, Ernst
Tafvelgalleri från stugor i Dalom; gemaldegallerie aus den bauernstuben Dalekarliens. Stockholm, Wahlström & Widstrand [1905]
4 l. 20 col.pl. Q.
Lipperheide 1059g

Bosc, Ernest, and Bonnemère, Lionel
Histoire nationale des Gaulois sous Vercingétorix. Paris, Firmin-Didot 1882
xvi,466p. illus. O.
Bibliography: p457-60

Bosch, Ant.
(illus.) Deserpz, François. Omnium fere gentium

Bosch, Bernardus
De weelde in Nederland; met ophelderende aanteekeningen en bijvoegzels. Dordrecht, A. Blussé en zoon 1784
72p. O.
Lipperheide 3478

Bosch, Etienne
Aelbrecht-hertog in Beieren-graaf van Holland-enz-binnen Enkhuizen in 1396. Leiden, H. Kleyn [1900]
1 l. 8pl. F.
Lipperheide 2848

Bosch, Johannes van den
De heeren stadhouderen van Vriesland; mitsgaders naukeurige korte beschryvinge van de vorstelyke grafkelder en sepulture binnen Leeuwarden. Leeuwarden, Gedrukt by A. Ferwerda en G. Tresling 1770
87p. 43pl. F.
Twenty-one of the plates are pictures of stadtholders of Friesland. The rest show the funeral procession of Maria Louise, born Princess of Hesse-Cassel, the wife of Stadtholder J. W. Friso
Lipperheide 945m

Bosio, Jean François
Cinq tableaux de costumes parisiens réunissant cent quarante-trois figures. Paris, Journal des dames 1804
1 l. 5 col.pl. O. 33fr.
Colas 395

Bosnia and Herzegovina. See Yugoslavia —Bosnia and Herzegovina

Bosnia and Herzegovina. Holbach, M. M.

Bosse, Abraham
Les cris de Paris. Paris, ca1640
12pl. Q.
Various other collections of his works are of costume interest
Colas 396

Bosse, Abraham—*Continued*

Figures au naturel tant des vestements que des postures des gardes françoises du roy très chretien. Paris, François l'Anglois dit Ciartres 1660?

9pl. O.
Colas 397

(engr.) Blum, André. Abraham Bosse et la société française au dix-septième siècle

(engr.) Blum, André. L'oeuvre gravé d'Abraham Bosse

(engr.) Saint-Igny, Jean de. Le jardin de la noblesse françoise

(engr.) Saint-Igny, Jean de. La noblesse françoise à l'eglise

Bosselt, Rudolf

Krieg und deutsche mode. [Magdeburg, Heinrichshofensche buchh. 1915]

38p. O.
At head of title: Nationaler frauendienst, Magdeburg
LC 22-1260

Bossert, Helmuth Theodor

Alt Kreta. Kunst und kunstgewerbe im ägäischen kulturkreise. Berlin, E. Wasmuth 1921

66p. illus. pl. plans. O.

Ein altdeutscher totentanz. Berlin, E. Wasmuth [1919]

4p. 13pl. Q. (Wasmuths kunsthefte, heft 2)
Facsimiles of woodcuts from the German Dance of death, first published about 1490. Shows Death with persons of various occupations, e.g. Death and the doctor, death and the writer, etc. who are in costume of the 15th century

Peasant art in Europe ... reproducing 2100 examples of peasant ornament and handicraft taken directly from unpublished originals: selected and arranged by H. Th. Bossert. London, E. Benn 1927

xii,44p. 132pl.(part col. part mounted) F.
English edition of his: *Volkskunst in Europa*
Bibliography: p40-43
LC 28-11634

Volkskunst in Europa; nahezu 2100 beispiele unter besonderer berücksichtigung der ornamentik. Berlin, E. Wasmuth [1926]

xii,46p. 132pl.(part col.) F.
Published in French with title: *L'art populaire en Europe* (Paris, A. Calavas 1927) and in Spanish: *El arte popular en Europa* (Barcelona, G. Gili 1928) French edition at 1300fr.
Bibliography: p41-46

(tr.) Kheiri, Sattar. Indische miniaturen der islamischen zeit

Bossi, Benigno

(engr.) Petitot, E. A. Mascarade à la grecque

Bossi, Gerolamo

De toga Romana commentarius. Amstelodami, A. Frisius 1671

84p. 1 illus. 1 pl. D.
"Accedit ex Philippo Rubenio iconismus statuae togatae et praeter indicem geminum, quem adjecimus, de modo gestandi togam ex Ferrario dissertatio." Subtitle
Also included in A. H. de Sallengre's *Novus Thesaurus antiquitatum Romanorum* v2 column 1305-1448
Colas 399. Lipperheide 220

Bossoli, Carlo

The war in Italy. London, Day & son 1859

72p. 40 col.pl. 2 maps. Q.
Lipperheide 2367. LC 4-29988

Boston. Museum of fine arts

Japanese sword guards. See entry under Okabe-Kakuya

Boston. Public library

Costume; a selected list of books in the Public library of the city of Boston. Boston, The Trustees 1928

48p. D. (Brief reading lists. no30. June, 1928)
Compiled by Walter Rowlands
LC 29-5926

Botanisches stick- und zeichen-buch für damen. Leipzig, G. Fleischer [1805-08]

3v. 71pl (35 col.) Q.
Lipperheide 3937

Botho, Conrad

Cronecken der Sassen. Mainz, P. Schöffer 1492

284 l. 811 illus. F.
Woodcuts show cities, a battle scene, royal persons, bishops, banners, etc.
Lipperheide 423

Botsford, Amelia Howard

Child life in all nations; or, The Earlingtons' trip around the world ... showing children in their characteristic national costume. Philadelphia, American book and Bible house [c1901]

278p. incl.illus. pl. (part col.) O.
LC 2-1435

Bott, Alan John

This was England; manners and customs of the ancient Victorians: a survey in pictures and text of their history, morals, wars, inventions, sports, heroes and social and sexual distinctions between 1870 and 1900. Garden City, N. Y., Doubleday, Doran 1931

248p. front. illus. O. $3.50, o.p.
Published in England under title: *Our fathers* (London, Heinemann 1931). For sequel see I. Clephane's *Ourselves,* 1900-1930
Costume index. LC 31-34317

(ed.) Our mothers, edited by Alan Bott, text by Irene Clephane; a cavalcade in pictures, quotation and description of late Victorian women, 1870-1900. London, V. Gollancz 1932

219p. incl. front. illus. ports. O.
Companion volume to *Our fathers*
LC 33-14677

Botta, Paul Émile

Monument de Ninive, découvert et décrit par M. É. Botta; mesuré et dessiné par E. Flandin. Ouvrage pub. ... sous les auspices de M. le ministre de l'intérieur et sous la direction d'une commission de l'Institut ... Paris, Imprimerie nationale 1849-50

5v. pl.(part col. part fold.) plans(part fold.) F.
Issued in installments from 1846 to 1850
Contents: v 1-2 Architecture et sculpture; v3-4 Inscriptions; v5 Texte
LC F-1939

Bottet, Maurice

L'arme blanche de guerre française au XVIIIe siècle. Paris, Leroy 1910
86p. incl. 22pl. F.
Complements the author's *Monographie de l'arme blanche des armées françaises de 1789 à 1870*
Sources principales: p[76]
LC 24-6826

Le bouton de l'armée française. Paris, J. Leroy 1908
126p. 53 col.pl. Q.
Each plate shows 24 buttons. They are arranged by the following periods: Monarchie, 1762-1792; Révolution, 1792-1802; Consulat et Empire, 1802-1815; Les deux Restaurations, 1814-1830; Monarchie de Juillet 1830-1850; Second Empire; Défense nationale; Divers
Colas 400

Bouchard, Alfred. See Bysterveld, Henri de. Album de coiffures historiques. v4

Bouchardon, Edme

Les cris de Paris en 8 suites; gravées d'après les desseins de Mr Bouchardon. Paris, Crêpy 1768
60 col.pl. O.
Published in 10 parts, the 8th published by Juillet
Colas 402. Lipperheide 1180

Études prises dans le bas peuple, ou Les cris de Paris. Paris, Joullain 1737-46
5v in 1 illus. 60pl. F.
Consists of 60 plates designed by Bouchardon and etched by Caylus
Colas 401

Boucher, François

Les cris de Paris. Paris, Huquier ca1735
12pl. F.
Colas 403. Lipperheide 1179

Les oeuvres de Molière; inventées & dessinées par F. Boucher & sculptées par Laurens Cars. [Amsterdam] 1741?
33pl. port. F.
Title page in manuscript

Recueil de diverses figures étrangères; gravées par F. Ravenet. Paris, Huquier ca1740
12pl. Q.
Plates show feminine costume
Colas 404

(illus.) Guer, J. A. Moeurs et usages des Turcs

Boucherit, Renée

(ed.) Modes & travaux féminins

Bouchot, Frédéric

Ce que parler veut dire. Paris, Aubert ca1840
28 col.pl. Q.
Lipperheide 3574

Le chapitre des illusions. Paris, Dupin ca1840
12 col.pl. Q.
Lipperheide 3575

Les contraires. Paris, Gobert et Tirot ca1835
4 col.pl. Q.
Lipperheide 3573

L'école des voyageurs. Paris, Dupin ca1840
12 col.pl. Q.
Lipperheide 3576

Les malheurs d'un amant heureux. Paris, Dupin ca1840
12 col.pl. Q.
Lipperheide 3577

Bouchot, Henri François Xavier Marie

Le cabinet d'estampes de la Bibliothèque nationale; guide ... catalogue general et raisonné. Paris, E. Dentu [1895]
xxiv,392p. O.
Peinture p17-41; Gravure p41-111; Costumes et moeurs, p231-56. References are to books as well as to individual prints
Lipperheide 4989

Catalogue de dessins relatifs à l'histoire du théâtre conservés au département des estampes de la Bibliothèque nationale avec la description d'estampes rares sur le même sujet, récemment acquises de M. Destailleur. Paris, É. Bouillon 1896
82p. O.
From *Revue des bibliothèques*, Oct. 1895-March 1896
Lipperheide 3233. LC 4-7083

L'épopée du costume militaire français; aquarelles et dessins originaux de Job [pseud. of J. M. G. Onfroy de Bréville]. Paris, Société française d'éditions d'art, L.-H. May [1898]
299p. illus. 10 col.pl. Q.
From the early Middle Ages to the nineteenth century
Colas 405

Le luxe français: L'empire; illustration documentaire. Paris, A la librairie illustrée [1892]
214p. illus. pl.(part col.) F.
Contains some pictures of French costume 1804-15

Le luxe français. La restauration; illustration documentaire d'après les originaux de l'époque. Paris, Librairie illustrée [1893]
324p. front. illus. pl. (part col. 1 double) ports. Q.
LC 1-F-2157

La toilette à la cour de Napoléon; chiffons et politique de grandes dames (1810-1815) d'après des documents inédits. Paris, Librairie illustrée [1895]
267p. O.

Le **bouddhisme** au Tibet. See Schlagintweit, Emil. Buddhism in Tibet

Boudier. See Boussenot, jt. auth.

Le **Boudoir;** modes, théâtres, littérature, beaux-arts. 1. fév.-16. nov. 1843. Paris
Q.
Succeeded *Colifichet*
Colas 648

Bouët, Alexandre

Breiz-Izel; ou, Vie des Bretons de l'Armorique, dessins par Olivier Perrin, gravés sur acier par Réveil, texte par M. Alexandre Bouët; 2. éd. Paris, B. Dusillion 1844
3v. 120pl. O.
First edition published under title: *Galerie bretonne, ou Vie (moeurs, usages et costumes) des Bretons de l'Armorique* (Paris, I. Pesron 1835-38). The first 12 notices in the above edition were by Mareschal, the remaining 36 by Bouët
Colas lists editions of 1856 and 1884, same collation
Colas 2315-17. LC 25-6356

Boughton, George Henry

Sketching rambles in Holland; with illustrations by the author and Edwin A. Abbey. New York, Harper 1885
xvi,342p. front. illus. pl. O.
LC 4-5315

Bouillane de Lacoste, Émile Antoine Henri de
Around Afghanistan; with a preface by M. Georges Leygues; tr. from the French by J. G. Anderson. London, I. Pitman 1909
xxxi,217p. front. pl. ports. maps. O.
The author circled Afghanistan through Persia, Baluchistan and Tibet
LC 9-15079

Bouillé, Louis Pierre Amour Marie Henri, comte de
Uniformes de l'armée française en 1884. See entry under Armand-Dumaresq, C. É.
Uniformes de l'armée française en 1887. See entry under Armand-Dumaresq, C. É.

Bouillet, Jean Baptiste
(comp.) Album auvergnat; bourrées, montagnardes, chansons, noels et poèmes en patois d'Auvergne; illus. de gravures représentant des danses et scènes villageoises, où se trouvent reproduits les costumes les plus remarquables du département du Puy-de-Dôme. Moulins, P.-A. Desrosiers 1853
195p. illus. 13pl. Q.
LC 22-21542

Der **Bouillotenleuchter**; eine goldgrube der Pariser damen vom ton; skizze über heutigen sitten der Pariser, ihre spielsucht, ihre hohe wetten, ihre spielfeste und privilegirte lottohäuser, nebst schilderung einer solchen spielscene in einem tripot. Berlin, K. A. Nicolai sohn 1800
32p. 1 pl. O.
Reprint from *London and Paris* v4, no5 p62
Lipperheide 1132

Boulenger. See Deveria, Achille, jt. auth.

Boulenger, Jacques Romain
Monsieur. Paris, G. Carette 1911
39p. illus. O.
On masculine fashions
Sous Louis-Philippe; les dandys. Paris, Calmann-Lévy 1932
216p. front.(port.) pl. D. (Nouvelle collection historique)
Bibliographical footnotes

Boulger, Demetrius Charles de Kavanagh
Belgian life in town and country. New York and London, G. P. Putnam 1904
321p. front. 15pl. D. (Our European neighbours)
LC 4-14601

Boullay, Benoît
Le tailleur sincère, contenant ce qu'il faut observer pour bien tracer, couper & assembler toutes les principales pièces qui se font dans la profession de tailleur. Paris, Antoine de Raffle 1671
92p. illus. O.
A textbook on tailoring with patterns for ceremonial and official clothes for the king, nobility, orders of knighthood, the pope, ecclesiastical costume, etc.
Colas 409. Lipperheide 3778
Le tailleur sincere, contenant les moyens pour bien pratiquer toutes sortes de pieces d'ouvrage pour les habits d'hommes, & la quantité des estoffes qu'il y doit entrer en chaque espece ... Enrichis de plusieurs planches gravées, dans lesquelles sont empreintes les aulnages & mesurages de chaques estoffes. Paris, A. de Rafflé [etc.] 1671
12p.l. 51pl. port. sq.F.
Colas 408. LC 10-23031

Boulton, William B.
The amusements of old London; being a survey of the sports and pastimes, tea gardens and parks, playhouses and other diversions of the people of London from the 17th to the beginning of the 19th century; with 12 illustrations from contemporary sources, all coloured by hand. London, J. C. Nimmo 1901
2v. col.front. col.pl. O.
Color plates show costume of 1776, 1784 and scenes at the sports: bull-baiting, cock-fighting, duck-hunting and bear-baiting
LC 1-3734

Bouly de Lesdain, Louis
Les variantes dans les armoiries. Saint-Amand (Cher) Impr. Destenay 1897
50p. O.
Extrait de *L'Annuaire du Conseil héraldique de France,* 1897
LC 5-16336

Bouquet, Michel
Album valaque; vues et costumes pittoresques de la Valachie. Paris, Goupil & Vibert 1843
11pl. F.
Colas 410. Lipperheide 1451

Bourbourg, Charles Étienne Brasseur de. See Brasseur de Bourbourg, C. É.

Bourcard, Francesco de
(ed.) Usi e costumi di Napoli e contorni descritti e dipinti. Napoli, G. Nobile 1853-58
2v. 100 col.pl. Q.
Colas 411. Costume index. Lipperheide 1304. LC 4-12565

Bourdeau, Louis
Histoire de l'habillement et de la parure. Paris, F. Alcan 1904
302p. O. (Bibliothèque scientifique internationale. 100)
Colas 412. Lipperheide 98i. LC 33-8597

Bourdeille, Pierre de, Seigneur de Brantôme. See Brantôme, Pierre de Bourdeille, seigneur de

Bourdon, Marie Ujfalvy. See Ujfalvy, Marie

Bourgeois, Émile
France under Louis XIV (le grand siècle) its arts—its ideas; [tr. by] Mrs. Cashel Hoey. New York, C. Scribner 1897
xvi,xxvii,470p. front. illus. pl. O.
English title: *The century of Louis* XVI (London, Sampson, Low, Marston [pref. date 1895])
Translation of his *Le grand siècle*
LC A12-1316
Le grand siècle; Louis XIV, les arts, les idées, d'après Voltaire, Saint-Simon, Spanheim, Dangeau, Madame de Sévigné, Choisy, La Bruyère, Laporte, le Mercure de France, la Princesse Palatine, etc. Paris, Hachette 1896
483p. front illus. pl. ports. F.
"Liste alphabétique des principaux peintres, sculpteurs, graveurs, architectes, graveurs en médailles, dessinateurs et ciseleurs d'art dont les œuvres sont reproduites dans ce volume": p[475]-83
Shows French costume of the period
LC 14-22016

Bourgeois, Émile—*Continued*
Ludwig XIV, der Sonnenkönig, oder Das grosse jahrhundert Frankreichs: Die künste, die geistige richtung ...übertragen von Oscar, Marschall von Bieberstein. Leipzig, Schmidt & Gunther 1897
xii,454p. illus. 29pl. Q.
Translation of his *Le grand siècle*

Bourgeois, François. See Mémoires concernant l'histoire, les sciences, les arts, les moeurs, les usages, &c. des Chinois

Bourgeois, Jacques
Advis aux curieux. See note under Heymann, Mme Alfred. Lunettes et lorgnettes de jadis

La **bourgeoisie** de Vienne formée en regimens. See Mansfeld, Heinrich, and Biller, B. Wien's bewaffnete bürger im jahre 1806

Bourges, Jacques de
Wahrhaffte und eigendliche erzehlung von der reise des bischofs von Beryte auss Franckreich zu wasser und lande nach China, nemlich auss Marsilien übers Mittel-meer nach Algier und so ferner durch Syrien, Arabien, Persien, und unterschiedne indianische landschafften mit genauer beschreibung der städte und plätze gottesdienste und sitten der völcker sam̃t derer zu dieser reise nützlichen kosten item von der müntze so in selbigen landen gangbar. Verteuscht durch T. R. C. S. C. S. Leipzig, Ritzschischen buchladen 1671
182p. 8 illus. D.
Translation of his *Relation du voyage de Monseigneur l'évêque de Beryte* [*Pierre de La Mothe Lambert*] (Paris, 1666)
Lipperheide 1513. LC 1-20735

Bourguignon, Hubert François. See Gravelot, H. F. B.

Bourke, John Gregory
The snake-dance of the Moquis of Arizona; being a narrative of a journey from Santa Fé, New Mexico, to the villages of the Moqui Indians ... with an account of the tablet dance of the pueblo of Santo Domingo, New Mexico, etc. New York, C. Scribner's sons 1884
xvi,371p. illus. pl.(part col. 1 fold. O. $5 o.p.
Costume index. LC 2-16830

Bournand, François
Le régiment de sapeurs-pompiers de Paris; dessins de Charles Morel. Paris, J. Moutonnet 1887
34p. illus. (part col.) pl. sq.F. (Galerie militaire illustrée)
Colas 413. LC 21-7293

Bourrilly, Joseph
Le costume en Provence au moyen age. Marseille, Institut historique de Provence 1928
149p. illus. 9pl. O. (Marseille. Bibliothèque. 1928 t 4 p 1-151)
Seven full pages of illustrations show articles of costume, cloaks, caps, etc. each with a descriptive note
Colas 414

Bousfield, Paul
Sex and civilization. London, K. Paul, Trench, Trubner; New York, E. P. Dutton 1925
294p. O.
Criticism of modern women's dress from the point of view of hygiene and suitability
Bibliography: p265-67
LC 25-3958

Boussenot, and Boudier
Les péchés actuels. Paris, Dupin ca1840
12 col.pl. Q.
Lipperheide 3578

Boutell, Charles
Boutell's manual of heraldry, rev. and illus. by V. Wheeler-Holohan. London and New York, F. Warne [c1931]
xx,332p. illus. xxxii col.pl. (incl. front.) O.
Most of the plates are accompanied by guard sheets with descriptive letterpress. Contains material on English crowns
Bibliography: p320
LC 32-7527

The monumental brasses of England; a series of engravings upon wood ... with brief descriptive notices ... Engravings ... by R. B. Utting. London, G. Bell 1849
xii,53,[10]p. front. pl. O.
The brasses, of the fourteenth through the sixteenth century, show knights, in many cases with their wives, and ecclesiastics. Mostly full length figures
Costume index. Lipperheide 1006. LC 11-19797

Boutell, Charles
(ed.) Arms and armour in antiquity and the middle ages: also a descriptive notice of modern weapons. Lacombe, Paul

Boutell's manual of heraldry. Boutell, Charles

Boutet, Henri
Les modes féminines du XIXe siècle. Paris, Edition de la maison d'art 1902
14p. 100 col.pl. O. 100fr.
Also published by E. Flammarion. Sixty copies were published in 2 volumes
Colas 415-16. Costume index. LC 24-2038 (1903 edition)

Boutet de Monvel, Louis Maurice
Jeanne d'Arc. Paris, E. Plon, Nourrit [1896]
47p. col. illus. ob.O.
LC 3-7897

Joan of Arc. New York, Century 1907
47p. col.illus. ob.O.
Translation of his *Jeanne d'Arc.* Also published (Philadelphia, D. McKay 1918. col.illus. col.pl. ob.D.)
LC w8-2, A18-2165 (1918 ed.)

Boutet de Monvel, Roger
Beau Brummell and his times; with a chapter on dress and the dandies, by Mary Craven. London, E. Nash 1908
199p. 15pl. O.
LC 8-34712

La **boutique** de Jean de Vouvray, armurier à Tours, en 1512. See Giraud, J. -B. Documents pour servir à l'histoire de l'armement au moyen âge et à la renaissance

La **boutique** et la mobilier d'un fourbisseur lyonnais en 1555. See Giraud, J. B. Documents pour servir à l'histoire de l'armement au moyen âge et à renaissance

Le **bouton** de l'armée française. Bottet, Maurice

Le **bouton** uniforme français (de l'ancien-régime à fin juillet 1914). Fallou, Louis

Bouvet, Joachim
L'estat présent de la Chine en figures. Paris, Filleul 1697
43 col.pl. F.
Plates engraved by Pierre Giffard
Colas 417

See also Le Comte, L. D., jt. auth.

Bouvier
(illus.) Friedel, Adam. The principal leaders in the Greek revolution

Bove, Giacomo
Patagonia, Terra del Fuoco, mari australi. Pt. 1. Genova, 1883
150p. pl. maps. O.
No more published

Bowdich, Thomas Edward
Excursion in Madeira and Porto Santo, during the autumn of 1823 while on his third voyage to Africa. London, Whittaker 1825
xii,278p. col.front. 21pl. Q. 42s
Two plates show the costume worn in Madeira
French edition: *Excursions dans les isles de Madère et de Porto Santo faîtes dans l'automne de 1823* (Paris, F. G. Levrault 1826)
Colas 418

Bowen, Cyril
Practical hints on stage costume, including instructions and patterns for making hats, boot tops, sword belts, lace ornaments, ballet shirts and all other necessary articles of costume generally supplied by the actor himself. London & New York, S. French 18-?
36p. illus. D.

Bowen, Frank C.
The sea: its history and romance. London, Halton & co. 1927
4v. col. front. illus. pl(part col.) ports. maps. 28x23cm. 60s
Costume index. LC 25-18103

Bowen, Marjorie, pseud.
William Hogarth, the cockney's mirror, by Marjorie Bowen. New York, London, D. Appleton-Century 1936
xii,340p. xxxiii pl. (incl.front. ports. facsim.) on 17 l. O. $5
Bibliography: p323-29
LC 37-6102

Bowler, Thomas William
The Kafir wars and the British settlers in South Africa: a series of picturesque views from original sketches; with descriptive letterpress by W. R. Thomson. London, Day 1865
24 l. 20pl. F.
LC 20-3110

Bowne, Mrs Eliza (Southgate)
A girl's life eighty years ago; selections from letters of Eliza Southgate Bowne ... illus. ... with portraits and views. New York, C. Scribner 1887
xii,239p. 4pl. 13 port. on 11pl.(incl. front.) O.
First published in *Scribner's magazine,* v2 1887
LC 7-11160

Boxhorn, Marcus Zuerius van
Spiegeltjen, vertoonende 't lanck ende cort hayr, by de Hollanders ende Zeelanders ghedragen. Leyden, P. Bonk 1742
60p. illus. O.
First published Middelburgh, 1644, by J. Fierens
Lipperheide 1648

Boyars. See Nobles—Russia

Boyd, Alexander Stuart
Glasgow men and women; their children and some strangers within their gates. A selection from the sketches of Twym. London, Hodder and Stoughton 1905
243p. incl.pl. front. Q.
"Most of these sketches originally appeared in the *Bailie* and *Quiz.*" Introduction
LC A13-1488

Boyd, Anne Morris, and Miller, Mabel Verdilla
(comps.) A reading list: historic and fancy costume for domestic art, amateur theatricals, historical pageants, and festivals. No place, 1920
8 l. sq.Q.
Caption-title. Type-written
LC CA24-919

Boydell, John
(pub.) A collection of the dresses of different nations, antient and modern

Boydell, John, and Boydell, Josiah
The American edition of Boydell's Illustrations of the Dramatic works of Shakspeare, by the most eminent artists of Great Britain. New York: Restored and pub. with original descriptions of the plates, by Shearjashub Spooner 1852
2v. fronts.(port.) 96pl. sq.F.
Printed from the original copper plates, restored. Each design is accompanied by a leaf of descriptive letterpress with quotations from the text it illustrates. The original edition of John and Josiah Boydell, appeared under title: *A collection of prints, from pictures painted for the purpose of illustrating the Dramatic works of Shakspeare,* by the artists of Great Britain (London, 1803. 2v.) The order differs somewhat from that of the original (Lear being transferred to the first volume)
Of the artists, Smirke, Fuseli, and Northcote contributed the largest number of plates; the others including Reynolds, Opie, and Stothard, are represented by from one to five plates each, engraved by R. Thew, T. Ryder, P. Simon and others
LC 20-1253

Boydell's Graphic illustrations of the dramatic works of Shakspeare: consisting of a series of prints ... engraved from pictures. London, Boydell [1798]
102pl. F.

Boydell, Josiah. See Boydell, John, jt. auth.

Boye, Vilhelm Christian
Fund af Egekister fra bronzealderen i Danmark: et monografisk bidrag til Belysning af bronzealderens kultur. Kjøbenhavn, Høst 1896
xxxvi,186p. illus. pl. Q.
Prefixed is a French title-page and translation, by Euchaire Baruël, of the introduction and descriptions of the individual finds

Boyle, Frederick
Adventures among the Dyaks of Borneo. London, Hurst and Blackett 1865
xii,324p. front. O.
LC 5-10733

Boyle, Mary Elizabeth
The cave of Altamira ... English text by M. E. Boyle. See entry under Breuil, Henri, and Obermaier, Hugo

In search of our ancestors; an attempt to retrace man's origin and development from later ages back to their beginnings. With reproductions in colour of cave-paintings and numerous other illustrations. London [etc.] G. G. Harrap [1927]
286p. col.front. illus.(incl. map) col.pl. (1 double) O.
Bibliography: p271-72
LC 28-15137

Boys, Thomas Shotter
Original views of London as it is ... With historical and descriptive notices of the views, by Charles Ollier. London, T. Boys 1842
25 l. 25pl. F.
Each plate accompanied by one leaf of descriptive text in English and French. Added title page, engraved: *London as it is*. Most of the views show costume
LC 3-11555

Braam-Houckgeest, Andreas Everard
Voyage de l'embassade. See note under Grohmann, J. G. Gebräuche und kleidungen der Chinesen

Braatz, Egbert
Ueber die falsche, gewőhnliche schuhform und über die richtige form der fussbekleidung. Königsberg, Thomas und Oppermann 1897
28p. 4 illus. 3pl. O.
Colas 420. Lipperheide 1745m

Brabançons, Volontaires. See Volontaires brabançons

Brabant. See Nobles—Brabant

Brabant and East Flanders. See Omond, G. O. T. Belgium

Bracelets
Bartholin, Thomas. De armillis veterum. 1676

Lindblom, Gerhard. Fighting-bracelets and kindred weapons in Africa. 1927

Bracque, Georges
(illus.) Dyagilev, S. P. Les fâcheux

Bracquet
(engr.) Compte-Calix, F. C. Costumes de l'époque de Louis XVI

(engr.) Compte-Calix, F. C. Costumes historiques français

Bracteates (Ornaments)
Salin, Bernhard. De nordiska guldbrakteaterna. 1895

Worsaae, J. J. A. Forestillingerne paa guldbracteaterne. 1870

Bradford, William
Sketches of the country, character, and costume, in Portugal and Spain, made ... in 1808 and 1809. Engraved and coloured from the drawings by William Bradford ... Esquisse du pays, du caractère et du costume, en Portugal et en Espagne. London, Printed for J. Booth, by Howlett and Brimmer [1812-13]
[74]p. 55 col.pl. F. o.p.
There is a second edition with same title and collation (London, T. M'Lean 1823)
Includes the author's *Sketches of military costume in Spain and Portugal* ([8]p. 13 col.pl. F.)
Colas 421-22. Costume index. Lipperheide 1213, 2358. LC 15-14147

Bradley, Herbert Dennis
The eternal masquerade. London, T. W. Laurie; New York, Boni & Liveright 1922
xx,268p. incl.front.(port.) D.
LC 23-128

Bradley-Birt, Francis Bradley
Chota Nagpore, a little-known province of the empire. London, Smith, Elder 1903
xiv,310p. 40pl.(incl.front.) fold.map. O.
LC 4-1874

Brahaut, Germain Nicolas. See Pascal, Adrien, and others. Galerie des victoires et conquêtes de l'armée française

Brahmans
Belnos, Mrs S. C. The Sundhya, or the daily prayers of the Brahmins. 1851

Brainerd, Mrs Eleanor (Hoyt)
In Vanity Fair; a tale of frocks and femininity. New York, Moffat, Yard & company 1906
xi,15-232p. incl.front. 15pl. D.
LC 6-14476

Brambilla, Ambrosius
Ritratto de quelle che vano vendendo et lavorando per Roma con la nova agionta de tutti quelli che nelle altre mancavano sin al presente. Roma, I. Orladij formis 1582
1 pl. (incl. 200 illus.) sq.F.
Lipperheide 1305

Branchardière, Éléonore Riego de la. See Riego de la Branchardière, Éléonore

Brand, C.
Zeichnungen nach dem gemeinen volke besonders der kaufruf in Wien; études prises dans le bas peuple et principalement les cris de Vienne; nach dem leben gezeichnet. [Wien] 1775
40 col.pl. F.
A reproduction was published in smaller format, and with illustrations in black and white only (Wien, 1924)
Colas 423. Lipperheide 898

Brand, Norton F.
The Mexican southland, by Kamar al-Shimas [pseud.] An account of the author's wanderings upon, and of the plants, animals, people, commerce and

Brand, Norton F.—*Continued*
industries of the Isthmus of Tehuantepec. Fowler, Ind., Benton review shop 1922
xviii,327p. col.front. pl. ports. maps. O.
The last twelve chapters give the semi-legendary history of the Zapotecs as it is found in the works of Burgoa, Gay, Del Valle, and Gracida, and now for the first time translated from the original Spanish
LC 22-24030

Brandenburg. See Germany—Brandenburg

Brandenburg, Hans
Der moderne tanz, mit 129 reproduktionen nach 54 zeichnungen von Hugo Böttinger, Dora Brandenburg-Polster, J. Grandjouan, Erwin Lang, Alexander Sacharoff und nach 75 photographien. München, G. Müller [1913]
161p. 24pl. ports. O.
LC 14-14793

Die **brandenburg-preussische** armee in historischer darstellung. Rabe, Edmund, and Burger, Ludwig

Brandt, Max August Scipio von
Der Chinese in der öffentlichkeit und der familie wie er sich selbst sieht und schildert, in 82 zeichnungen nach chinesischen originalen erläutert. Berlin, D. Reimer [1911]
165p. illus. sq.Q.
LC 22-4498

Brandt, Paul
Schaffende arbeit und bildende kunst. Leipzig, Kröner 1927-28
2v. (324,348p.) 902 illus. 10pl.(part col.) O.
Contents: v 1 Im altertum und mittelalter; v2 Vom mittelalter bis zur gegenwart
Illustrations from works of art show people in various occupations from the earliest time to the present. There is an index to artists and subjects

Brant, Sebastian
Sebastian Brands Narrenschiff; ein hausschatz zur ergetzung und erbauung erneuert von Karl Simrock; mit den holzschnitten der ersten ausgaben und dem bildniss Brands aus Reusners Icones. Berlin, F. Lipperheide 1872
30,340p. 116 illus. port. Q.
First edition (Basle, J. B. von Olpe 1494) It has been claimed that *Das Narrenschiff* was the first printed book to give an account of contemporary events and living persons. It was soon translated into French with title: *La nef dez folz du monde* (Paris, J. P. Manstener & G. de Marnef 1497) For the English edition see his *Ship of fools.* The book appeared in many editions. Those with the original illustrations are of costume interest, showing among other things the dress worn at trades and occupations of the period
Lipperheide 460

The Ship of fools; tr. by A. Barclay. Edinburgh, W. Patterson 1874
2v. illus. Q.
A reprint of the Pynson edition of 1509; with introduction, notes, and notice of Barclay and his writings. Edited by T. H. Jamieson. This is a translation of the author's *Das narrenschiff.*

Branting, Agnes
Das goldene gewand der Königin Margareta in der Domkirche, zu Uppsala. Stockholm, P. A. Norstedt [1911]
27p. 7 illus. vi pl (1 col.) F.

Brantôme, Pierre de Bourdeille, seigneur de
Memoires ... contenans les vies des hommes illustres & grands capitaines estrangers de son temps. Leyde, J. Sambix 1665
600p. D.
Lipperheide 1110

Memoires ... contenans les vies des hommes illustres & grands capitaines françois de son temps. Leyde, J. Sambix 1666
4v. (ea ca400p.) D.
Lipperheide 1111

Memoires ... contenant les vies de dames galantes de son temps. Leyde, J. Sambix 1693
2v. D.
Lipperheide 1112

Oeuvres de Brantôme; nouv. éd. rev. d'àpres les meilleurs textes avec une préface historique et critique par H. Vigneau. Paris, A. Delahays 1857
xiv,382p. O.
There are other editions. Brantôme's works contain some interesting references to the dress of his day
Lipperheide 1113

The **brasses** of England. Macklin, H. W.

Brasseur de Bourbourg, Charles Étienne
Histoire des nations civilisées du Mexique et de l'Amérique-Centrale, durant les siècles antérieurs à Christophe Colomb. Paris, A. Bertrand 1857-59
4v. map O.
Costume of Chiapas, Yucatan and Central America as shown in bas-reliefs, v2, p67-68; vestments of the Wiyato priests. v3 p30; costume at the time of the Spanish conquest, p647-51
LC 2-4879

Monuments anciens du Mexique; Palenqué et autres ruines de l'ancienne civilisation du Mexique. Collection de vues, basreliefs, morceaux d'architecture, coupes, vases, terres cuites, cartes et plans, dessinés d'après nature et relevés par M. de Waldeck. Ouvrage publié sous les auspices de ... le ministre de l'instruction publique. Paris, A. Bertrand 1866
23,83p. illus. pl.(part col.) map. F. (Recherches sur les ruines de Palenqué et sur les origines de la civilisation du Mexique)
LC 5-6461

Brauel, Hans Müller-. Müller-Brauel, Hans

Braun, Adolphe Armand
The child in art & nature. London, B. T. Batsford [1921]
175p. illus. sq.Q.
LC 22-14128

Figures, faces and folds, a practical reference book on woman's form and dress, and its application in past and present art for artists, students and designers ... with sections on drapery and anatomy by D. Hartley. London, B. T. Batsford [1928]
152p. incl.front. illus. pl. Q.
LC 30-3212

Braun, Georg
Civitates orbis terrarum. [Coloniae Agrippinae. 1572-1618]
6v. illus. pl.(part col.) F.
Scenes from cities in all parts of the world
Lipperheide 5

Braun, Georg—*Continued*

Urbium totius Germaniae superioris illustriorum clariorumque tabulae antiquae & novae accuratissimè elaboratae. Amstelodami, apud J. Janssonium 1657

2v. pl. F.

Contains reprints of the plates on Germany originally published in his *Civitates orbis terrarum,* plus fifty new plates

Lipperheide 6

Braun, Johannes

... Vestitus sacerdotum hebraeorum; sive commentarius amplissimus in Exodi cap. 28 ac 39 & Levit. cap. 16 aliaque loca S. Scripturae quam plurima. Amstelodami, Abrahamum a Someren 1697-98

2v. illus. 20pl. Q.

Another edition: Editio ultima priori auct. & emend. (Amstelodami, J. Wolters 1701. 2v. in 4, same collation). The first edition (Amstelodami, apud J. Waesbergios 1680. 2v. illus. 5pl.) Volume 2 (Lugduni Batavorum, apud Arnoldum Dondium)

Colas 424-26. Lipperheide 1803

Braun, Joseph

Die liturgische gewandung im Occident und Orient nach ursprung und entwicklung, verwendung und symbolik. Mit 316 abbildungen. Freiburg im Breisgau, St. Louis, Mo. [etc.] Herder 1907

xxiv,797p. front. 315 illus. Q.

"Verzeichnis der häufiger benutzten mittelalterlichen werke": p[xvii] "Verzeichnis bemerkenswerter für die arbeit benutzter inventare": p[xviii]-xxii

Costume index. LC 13-25792

Die pontificalen gewänder des Abendlandes nach ihrer geschichtlichen entwicklung. Freiburg im Breisgau, St. Louis, Mo. [etc.] Herder 1898

191p. illus. pl. O. (Ergänzungshefte zu den "Stimmen aus Maria-Laach." 73)

Colas 428. Lipperheide 1844. LC A14-447

Die priesterlichen gewänder des Abendlandes nach ihrer geschichtlichen entwicklung. Freiburg im Breisgau, St. Louis, Mo. [etc.] Herder 1897

180p. illus. O. (Ergänzungshefte zu den "Stimmen aus Maria-Laach." 71)

Colas 427. Lipperheide 1843. LC A14-446

Braun, Kaspar

Das landwehr-zeughaus in München. München, Braun u. Schneider 1866

115p. 16 illus. O.

Lipperheide 2418

Braun, Louis. See Müller, Karl, jt. auth.

Braun, Reinhold

Königliche württembergische armee. Stuttgart, G. Ebner [1840]

24 col.pl. Q.

Colas 429

Braunschvig, Marcel

La femme et la beauté. Paris, A. Colin 1929

249p. VIII pl. D.

Contents: Le rôle de la beauté dans la nature; La coquetterie; La mode; La galanterie masculine; L'évolution de la beauté feminine

Colas 430. LC 29-29694

Brausewetter, Otto

(ed.) Blätter für kostümkunde

Brazil

Carpenter, F. G. Along the Paraná and the Amazon, Paraguay, Uruguay, Brazil. 1925

Chamberlain. Views and costumes of the city and neighbourhood of Rio de Janeiro, Brazil. 1822

Churchill, Awnsham, and Churchill, John. A collection of voyages and travels. 1732

Koster, Henry. Travels in Brazil. 1816

Nieuhof, Johan. Joan Nieuhofs Gedenkwaerdige zee en lantreize door de voornaemste landschappen van West en Oostindien. 1682

Ribeyrolles, Charles. Brazil pittoresco. 1859-61

Rugendas, J. M. Voyage pittoresque dans le Brésil. 1835

Taunay, Hippolyte, and Denis, Ferdinand. Le Brésil. 1822

See also subdivision Brazil under Indians of South America; Military costume; Naval costume

Brazil pittoresco. Ribeyrolles, Charles

Brebiette, Pierre

Les cris de Paris. [Paris] I. Honervogt ca1640

42pl. Q.

Colas 431

Brécard, Charles Théodore

La cavalerie, par le général Brécard; préface de monsieur le maréchal Pétain; aquarelles de Pierre-Albert Leroux. Paris, Société des éditions militaires 1931

170p. 20 col.pl. F. (L'armée française à travers les âges; ses traditions—ses gloires—ses uniformes. [4])

Colas 157d. LC 36-5858

Breen, Adam van

Le maniement d'armes de Nassau, avecq rondelles, piques, espees & targes; representez par figures, selon le nouveau ordre du tresillustre Prince Maurice de Nassau; avecq instructions par escript pour tous cappitaines & commandeurs, nouvellement mis en lumiere. La Haye, 1618

47pl. F.

Lipperheide 2072

Brehm, Reinhold Bernhard

Das Inka-reich. Beiträge zur staats- und sitten-geschichte des kaiserthums Tahuantinsuyu. Nach den ältesten spanischen quellen. Jena, F. Mauke's verlag (A. Schenk) 1885

842p. illus. pl. fold.map. O.

LC 2-1516

Breiz-Izel. Bouët, Alexandre

Bremen. See Germany—By region or province—Bremen

Bremer, Walther

Die haartracht des mannes in archaischgriechischer zeit. Giessen, R. Lange 1911

72p. O.

Colas 432

Brennecke, F. See Hoyer, K., jt. auth.

Brenner, Eli

Thesaurus nummorum Sueo-Gothicorum. Holmiae, J. L. Horrn. 1731

270p. 226 illus. 63pl. Q.

Lipperheide 1039

Brennglas, Adolf. See Glasbrenner, Adolf

Brennig, Marie Coudert
(ed.) Wedding embassy year book. New York, Wedding embassy, inc. [c1935]
96p. ports. Q.
LC 35-4498

Brentano, Frantz Funck-. See Funck-Brentano, Frantz

Brentel, Fr.
(engr.) La Ruelle, Claude de. Decem insignes tabulae ... Caroli III

Bresciani, Antonio
Dei costumi dell' isola di Sardegna comparati cogli antichissimi popoli orientali. Napoli, All' uffizio della civitá cattolica 1850
2v. 2pl. O.
Lipperheide 1317e

Bresciani, Marin
Li trastulli guerrieri. Brescia, [1668]
90 l. 69 illus. Q.
On how to handle the pike
Lipperheide 2085

Le **Brésil.** Taunay, Hippolyte, and Denis, Ferdinand

Breslau. Museum schlesischer altertümer
Wegweiser durch die urgeschichte Schlesiens und der nachbargebiete. See entry under Mertins, Oskar

Bresler, Arthur L.
Die armee der Vereinigten Staaten von Nord-Amerika. Leipzig, M. Ruhl [1891]
38p. 19 col.pl. D.
Colas 2608. Lipperheide 2395. LC 5-19036

La **Bretagne.** Lalaisse, Hippolyte

La **Bretagne**; sites, arts et coutumes. Gauthier, Joseph

La **Bretagne** ancienne et moderne. Pitre-Chevalier, P. M. F. C., called

La **Bretagne** contemporaine. Benoist, Félix

Bretagne et Vendée. Pitre-Chevalier, P. M. F. C., called

La **Bretagne** pittoresque. Souvestre, Émile

Breton folk. Blackburn, Henry

Breton, William Henry
Excursions in New South Wales, Western Australia, and Van Diemen's Land, during the years 1830, 1831, 1832, and 1833; 2d ed. rev. with additions. London, R. Bentley 1834
xii,420p. front.(incl. 12 illus.) O.
Frontispiece shows boomerangs and other weapons of the native races
LC 4-24180

Breton de la Martinière, Jean Baptiste Joseph
China: its costume, arts, manufactures, &c. ed. principally from the originals in the cabinet of the late M. Bertin: with observations explanatory, historical, and literary, by M. Breton; tr. from the French. London, J. J. Stockdale 1812
4v. 80 col.pl. O. o.p.
Reprinted 1813 and 1824. Translation of and plates reprinted from the first four volumes of the author's *La Chine en miniature.* Tinting of the plates is somewhat different from that of the originals
Colas 435. Costume index. Lipperheide 1525 (1824 ed.). LC 5-9337

La Chine en miniature; ou, Choix de costumes, arts et metiers de cet empire ... gravures ... d'après les originaux inédits du Cabinet de feu M. Bertin. Paris, Nepveu 1811[-12]
6v. 108 col.pl. D.
Originally issued in 4 volumes
Colas 433. Costume index. Lipperheide 1524

Coup d'oeil sur la Chine, ou Nouveau choix de costumes, arts et métiers de cet empire. Paris, Nepveu 1812
2v. 28 col.pl. S.
Contains the same text and plates as volumes 5 and 6 of his: *La Chine en miniature*
Colas 434

L'Égypte et la Syrie, ou moeurs, usages, costumes et monumens des Égyptiens, des Arabes et des Syriens ... Notes [etc] par M. Marcel. Paris, A. Nepveu 1814
6v. 84 col.pl. D.
Illustrated with plates from original designs and also some after designs by Louis Mayer
Colas 438. Lipperheide 1578

L'Espagne et le Portugal, ou moeurs, usages et costumes des habitans de ces royaumes. Précédé d'un précis historique; ouvrage orné de cinquante-quatre planches représentant douze vues et plus de soixante costumes différens, la plupart d'après des dessins exécutés en 1809 et 1810. Paris, A. Nepveu 1815
6v. fold.col.front. col.pl. T.
Colas 439. Lipperheide 1214. LC 3-7746

Le Japon, ou mœurs, usages et costumes des habitans de cet empire, d'après les relations récentes de Krusenstern, Langsdorf, Titzing, etc. ... suivi de la relation du voyage et de la captivité du capitaine russe Golownin. Paris, A. Nepveu 1818
4v. col.fronts.(part fold.) col.pl. S.
Some of the plates also appear in *Japan, eine schilderung von dem anfange,* which is sometimes attributed to Breton
Colas 440. Costume index. Lipperheide 1558. LC 4-28644

La Russie, ou moeurs, usages et costumes des habitans de toutes les provinces de cet empire; orné de planches gravés sur les dessins ... de Damame-Démartrait et Robert Ker-Porter. Paris, A. Nepveu 1813
6v. pl.(part col.) D.
Colas 436. Lipperheide 1350

Russland oder sitten, gebräuche und trachten. Pesth, K. U. Hartleben 1816
6v. 111pl.(part col.) D.
Translation of his *La Russie,* which see
Colas 437. Lipperheide 1350a

(tr.) Broughton, T. D. Les Marattes

(tr.) Tableau du royaume de Caboul. See note under Elphinstone, Mountstuart. An account of the kingdom of Caubul

Les **Bretons.** Martin, Eugène

The **Bretons** at home. Gostling, Mrs F. M P.

Bretschneider, Andreas
Neues modelbuch 1619; neu herausg. mit vorwort von Dr. P. Jessen. Berlin, E. Wasmuth 1892
2 l. 48pl. F.
Facsimile edition of *New Modelbüch darinnen allerley künstliche viesirüng und müster artiger züege und schöner blümmen zü zierlichen uberschlegen* (Leipzigt, H. Grossen 1619)
Lipperheide 3916

Brett, Edwin John
Catalog of collection of armour and arms sold March 18th, 1895. No place, [1895]
42pl. O.

A pictorial and descriptive record of the origin and development of arms and armour. London, Sampson, Low, Marston & co. 1894
xii,120p. 133pl. (1000 illus.) Q.
Plates from the author's collection

Brett, William Henry
The Indian tribes of Guiana; their condition and habits. London, Bell and Daldy 1868
xiii,500p. illus. 19pl.(8 col. incl.front.) fold.map. O.
First edition, New York, 1852
LC 8-11842

Breuil, Henri, and Obermaier, Hugo
The cave of Altamira at Santillana del Mar, Spain. English text by Mary E. Boyle. New edition published by the Junta de las Cuevas de Altamira, the Hispanic society of America and the Academia de la historia. Madrid, Tip. de Archivos 1935
223p. illus. 53pl.(part col.) plan, tables (part double) F.
New and revised text embodying results of late discoveries; with superior reproductions of the drawings and new plates replacing those of the first edition *La caverne d'Altamira à Santillane près Santander* par Émile Cartailhac et Henri Breuil (Monaco, 1906)
LC 37-1506

Breüning, Hanss Jacob
Orientalische Reyss ... in der Türckey ... so wol in Europa als Asia unnd Africa ... benantlich in Griechen Land, Egypten, Arabien, Palestina, das heylige gelobte Land, und Syrien ... verrichtet. Straszburg, Johann Carolo 1612
298p. 60 illus. F.
The illustrations show costumes worn in the countries thru which he travelled, and include also pictures of the fauna
Colas 442. Lipperheide 1404

Breunner-Enkevoërth, August Johann, graf von
Römisch kaiserlicher majestät kriegsvölker im zeitalter der landsknechte ... mit erläuterndem text von Jacob von Falke. Wien, C. I. Wawra 1883
21p. 151pl. F.
Includes portraits of the Emperor Maximilian (1508) and of the Count-Palatine Friedrich (1534) Also pictures of mercenary troops (landsknechte) of the period 1520-30
Colas 443. Lipperheide 2103

Le **Bréviaire** de Philippe le Bon. Brussels. Bibliothèque royale de Belgique. Mss. (9511)

Breviaire Grimani
Fac-simile delle miniature contenute nel Breviario Grimani. See entry under Catholic church. Liturgy and ritual. Breviary

Breviaire Grimani de la Bibliothèque de S. Marco à Venise: reproduction photographique complète. Catholic Church. Liturgy and ritual. Breviary

Brevier der tanzkunst. Czerwinski, Albert

Bréville, Jacques Marie Gaston Onfroy de. See Onfroy de Bréville, J. M. G., called Job

Brevis narratio eorum quae in Florida Americae provĩcia Gallis acciderunt, secunda in illam navigatione, duce Renato de Laudõniere classis praefecto: anno MDLXIIII. Le Moyne de Morgues, Jacques

Brichet, R.
(engr.) Göz, J. F. von. Die heutige sichtbare körperwelt

Brides and bridals. Jeaffreson, J. C.

The **Bride's** magazine; So you're going to be married. v 1, 1934+ New York, Brides house, inc.
Illus. pl. F. $1.50
Published quarterly. Current 1938
Title varies: autumn 1934-winter 1935, *So you're going to be married*
Editor: autumn 1934+ A. F. Wright

The **bride's** own book. New York, McCall's magazine c1922
8p. illus. O. [McCall's service booklets]
LC CA23-235

Bridge, Sir Frederick
The old cryes of London. London, Novello 1921
78p. col.front. illus. double pl. O.
LC 22-12313

Bridgens, Richard
Sketches illustrative of the manners and costumes of France, Switzerland, and Italy. London, Baldwin, Craddock & Joy 1821
45 l. 50pl. Q.
Costumes from Boulogne, Dieppe, Paris, Rome and Turin
Another edition was published under title *Illustrations of the manners and costumes of France, Switzerland, and Italy.* (London, J. Donding 1835. Colas 445)
Colas 444. Lipperheide 572 (1835 ed.)

Brief et utile discours sur l'immodestie et superfluité des habits. Châtillon, Jérôme de

Brief guide to the Chinese embroideries. Victoria and Albert museum, South Kensington

Brief guide to the Chinese woven fabrics. Victoria and Albert museum, South Kensington

Brief guide to the oriental painted, dyed and printed textiles. Victoria and Albert museum, South Kensington

Brief guide to the Persian woven fabrics. Victoria and Albert museum, South Kensington

Brief guide to the Peruvian textiles. Victoria and Albert museum, South Kensington

Brief guide to the Turkish woven fabrics. Victoria and Albert museum, South Kensington

Brief guide to the western painted, dyed and printed textiles. Victoria and Albert museum, South Kensington

Brief list of references on the history of hats and head-dresses. United States. Library of Congress. Division of bibliography

Briefe and true report of the newfoundland of Virginia, of the commodities and of the nature and manners of the natural inhabitants. See Harriot, Thomas. Admiranda narratio

Briefe eines Leipziger studenten aus den jahren 1572 bis 1574. Behaim, Paulus

Briefve histoire de l'institution des ordres religieux. See Fialetti, Odoardo. De gli habiti della religioni

Briffault, Eugène Victor

Paris dans l'eau, par Eugène Briffault; illus. par Bertall. Paris, J. Hetzel 1844
138p. illus. O.
Contains humorous drawings of Parisians fishing and at the baths
LC 4-20930

Brigands. See Bandits

Brigham, William Tufts

Hawaiian feather work. Honolulu, Bishop museum press 1899
81p. illus. 15pl.(part col.) F. (Memoirs of the Bernice Pauahi Bishop museum v 1 no 1)
Additional notes (19p. 4pl.) was issued in 1903 as volume 1, no5 and *Additional notes ... second supplement* (69p. illus. 4 col.pl.) in 1918 as volume 7 no 1 of the same series
LC 1-2995

Die **brille** und ihre geschichte. Bock, Emil

Brinckmann, Justus

Kunst und handwerk in Japan. 1. bd. Berlin, R. Wagner 1889
x,300p. illus. Q.
Clothing p117-34; Arms and armor p135-51
Lipperheide 1566m. LC 25-13008

Brindesi, Jean

Elbicei Atika; musée des anciens costumes turcs de Constantinople. Paris, Lemercier [1855]
22 col.pl. F.
Costumes of Sultans, military and palace officials of the period 1808-38
Colas 446. Lipperheide 1438

Souvenirs de Constantinople. Paris, Lemercier [1855-60]
21 col.pl. ob.F.
Colas 447

Brinkley, Frank

The art of Japan. Boston, J. B. Millet company c1901
2v. illus.(part col.) F.
Printed on double leaves in Japanese style
Contents: v 1 Pictorial art; v2 Applied art
LC 1-31828

Japan, its history, arts and literature. Illustrated. [Library ed.] Boston and Tokyo, J. B. Millet company [1901-02]
8v. fronts.(v3, 5, 6, 8) pl.(part col.) 2 fold.maps. O. (Oriental series. v 1-8)
LC 1-28069

(ed.) Japan; described and illustrated by the Japanese; written by eminent Japanese authorities and scholars; with an essay on Japanese art by Kakuzo Okakura. Boston, J. B. Millet company c1897-98
10v. col.illus. col.pl. F. ea $6, o.p.
Paged continuously. Printed on one side of leaf only. The greater part of the plates preceded by guard sheet with descriptive text. Introduction by Arthur J. Mundy
Costume index. LC 3-31040

Brinton, Selwyn John Curwen

The eighteenth century in English caricature. London, A. Siegle 1904
96p. col.front. illus. 13pl.(part col.) D. (The Langham series; an illustrated collection of art monographs v8)
LC 5-10583

Briot, Isaac

(engr.) Saint-Igny, Jean de. Diversitez d'habillemens à la mode

(engr.) Saint-Igny, Jean de. Le théâtre de France

Briscoe, John Potter

(ed.) Heaton, H. A. The brooches of many nations

Brissac, René Marie Timoléon de Cossé-. See Cossé-Brissac, R. M. T. de

British and foreign arms and armour. See Ashdown, C. H. Arms & armour

The **British** army. Scott, Sir J. S. D., bart.

The **British** army. Talbot-Booth, E. C.

The **British** army, by a lieutenant-colonel in the British army, with an introduction by ... F. Maurice. London, S. Low, Marston & co. 1899
256p. front.(port.) illus. pl.(part col.) Q. 12s 6d o.p.
Costume index. LC 1-14548

The **British** army button in the American revolution. Calver, W. L.

British costume during XIX centuries (civil and ecclesiastical). Ashdown, E. J.

British costume from the first to the nineteenth century. See , Schild, Marie. Old English costumes

British fashions, for the years 1803 and 1804. [London] Ackermann 1803-04
27 col.pl. Q.
Colas 448

The **British** isles and the Baltic states. Carpenter, F. G. and Harmon, Dudley

British military costume. Heath, William

The **British** military library: comprehending a complete body of military knowledge. See The British military library; or, Journal

The **British** military library; or, Journal: comprehending a complete body of military knowledge; and consisting of original communications; with selections from the most approved and respectable foreign military publications ... London, Printed for R. Phillips by J. Rider; pub. by J. Carpenter and co. [etc.] 1799-1801
2v. pl.(part col.) maps. plans. Q.
Second edition is entitled *The British military library; comprehending a complete body of military knowledge.* New edition improved and corrected, published London, 1804
Color plates show uniforms of various regiments
Colas 449-50. LC 6-7114 (v 1 only)

British military prints. Nevill, R. H.

British military types. Simkin, Richard

British monachism. Fosbroke, T. D.

British museum

Coronation exhibition; manuscripts, printed books, prints, drawings and medals exhibited in the King's library of the British museum. [London] Printed by order of the trustees [by Wm. Clowes & sons] 1902

47p. O.
LC 4-10808

British museum. Department of British and mediæval antiquities

Catalogue of the engraved gems of the post-classical periods in the Department ... in the British museum; by O. M. Dalton. London, The trustees 1915

lxxvii,180p. front.(port.) illus. xxxvii pl. Q.
Includes the engraved gems, cameo and intaglio. List of publications useful for the study of post-classical engraved gems: p[x]-xii
LC 16-2614

Franks bequest. Catalogue of the finger rings, early Christian, Byzantine, Teutonic, mediaeval and later, bequeathed by Sir Augustus Wollaston Franks ... in which are included the other rings of the same periods in the museum; by O. M. Dalton. London, The trustees, 1912.

57+366p. illus. 30pl. Q.
List of works useful for the study of rings: p[xi]-xii
LC 13-4889

A guide to antiquities of the early iron age in the Department of British and mediaeval antiquities. 2d ed. [London] The trustees 1925

xii,175p. 200 illus. 13pl.(part col.) O.
The first edition (1905) was published by the Dept. of British and mediæval antiquities and ethnography. The author of the present edition is Reginald A. Smith
LC 27-13082

A guide to the antiquities of the bronze age in the Department of British and mediæval antiquities. [London] The trustees, 1920

xii,159p. 195 illus. x pl.(incl.front.) O.
Preface signed: Charles H. Read
LC A10-1451

Handbook to the ethnographical collections. With 15 plates, 275 illustrations and 3 maps. [London] The trustees 1910

xv,304p 275 illus.(incl.maps) 15pl.(incl.col. front.) O.
By T. A. Joyce in collaboration with O. M. Dalton. Other editions
LC 10-24928

British museum. Department of ceramics and ethnography

Guide to the Maudslay collection of Maya sculptures (casts and originals) from Central America. [London] The trustees 1923

93p. illus. 8pl.(incl.front.) map. O.
Prepared by T. A. Joyce
Bibliography: p[85]
LC 26-13102

British museum. Department of coins and medals

A guide to the principal gold and silver coins of the ancients, from circ. B. C. 700 to A. D. 1. By Barclay V. Head; 4th ed. London, The trustees [etc] 1895

128p. 7pl. O.
Plates are same as in third ed. 1899, but parts of the text have been revised
Coins which picture rulers are of costume interest, since they show styles of hair dressing and head-gear. The text identifies each series
Lipperheide 178. LC 8-5030

British museum. Department of Egyptian and Assyrian antiquities

A guide to the Babylonian and Assyrian antiquities; 2d ed. rev. and enl. [London] The trustees 1908

xiv,275p. illus. 45pl. O.
Prepared and revised by E. A. Wallis Budge and L. W. King
In the 1900 edition plate III shows Sennacherib, king of Assyria receiving tribute; Plate XIII Ashur-bani-pal; Plate XXII Cylinder seals with figures. The catalog is also a guide to other costume material in this department of the British museum, altho it is not shown in illustrations
LC 9-26092

A guide to the Egyptian collections in the British museum. With 53 plates and 180 illustrations in the text. [London] The trustees 1909

xiv,325p. illus.(incl.maps, plans, facsims.) 53pl. O.
Preface signed: E. A. Wallis Budge
LC 9-27285

A guide to the first, second and third Egyptian rooms; 3d ed. rev. and enl. London, The trustees 1924

xvi,180p. xxxv pl.(part col.) O.
Prepared by E. A. Wallis Budge
Plates show Egyptian mummies and coffins, decorated with figures relating to the times

(pub.) Book of the dead. Facsimile of the Papyrus of Ani, in the British museum

British museum. Department of Greek and Roman antiquities

Catalogue of the finger rings, Greek, Etruscan, and Roman, in the departments of antiquities; by F. H. Marshall. London, The trustees 1907.

53+258p. illus. 35pl. Q.
List of the principal works dealing with Greek and Roman finger rings, pref. p51-53
LC 9-10973

Catalogue of the jewellery, Greek, Etruscan, and Roman, in the departments of antiquities, British museum. By F. H. Marshall. London, The trustees 1911

lxii,400p. illus. 73pl. Q. 35s
Costume index. LC 12-26201

A guide to the exhibition illustrating Greek and Roman life. 2d ed. With a frontispiece and two hundred and sixty-four illustrations. London, The trustees 1920

232p. front. illus. O.
LC 24-11336

British museum. Department of manuscripts
Catalogue of the manuscripts in the Cottonian library deposited in the British museum, by J. Planta. London, 1802
[16],618p. 28 l. F.

Chronicler of European chivalry. See entry under Coulton, G. G.

Liber pontificalis. See entry under Catholic church. Liturgy and ritual. Pontifical

Queen Mary's psalter; miniatures and drawings by an English artist of the 14th century; reproduced from royal ms. 2B. VII in the British museum, with introduction by Sir George Warner. London, The trustees 1912
92p. 158pl. F.
Shows English costume of the 14th century

British museum. Department of prints and drawings
Catalogue of the collection of fans and fan-leaves presented ... by the Lady Charlotte Schreiber; comp. by Lionel Cust. London, Longmans 1893
138p. O.
A profusely illustrated book on this collection was written by Lady Schreiber and published in 1888-90. See entry under Schreiber
LC 12-14020

The **British** navy. Stenzel, Alfred

British North America. Hill-Tout, Charles

British soldiers 1550 to 1906. Clark, Christopher

British sporting artists from Barlow to Herring. Sparrow, W. S.

British sports. See Alken, H. T. The national sports of Great Britain

The **British** tar in fact and fiction. Robinson, C. N.

British theatrical gallery. Terry, Daniel

British volunteers, or, a general history of the formation and establishment of the Volunteer and associated corps. London, 1799
Ports. pl. Q.

Brittany. See France—Brittany; also Hairdressing—France—Brittany

Brittany and the Bretons. Edwards, G. W.

Broadsword and quarter-staff without a master. Riboni, Giuseppe

Brocard, Madeleine Rage-. See Rage-Brocard, Madeleine

[Brock, Gustav]
Den Danswe haer og flaade. L'armée et la marine danoises. No place, A. F. Host; C. Ferslew, lith. 1885
9 col.pl. F.
Legends in Danish and French
Colas 451

Brock, Peter Michael Johan
The chronological museum of the Danish kings, in Rosenborg Castle. [Copenhagen] G. E. C. Gad 1899
108p. illus. O.
Supplement (8p.) published in Copenhagen, 1901
French edition published in Copenhagen 1879 under title: *Musée chronologique des rois de Danemark au château de Rosenborg*
Lipperheide 5024 (French ed.)

Brockedon, William
Egypt & Nubia, from drawings made on the spot by David Roberts ... with historical descriptions by William Brockedon ... lithographed by Louis Haghe. London, F. G. Moon 1846-[49]
3v. illus. (part col.) 61pl. (part col.) F.
Also included in George Croly's *The Holy Land*
Lipperheide 1591

See also Croly, George. The Holy Land, Syria, Idumea, Arabia, Egypt & Nubia

Brockhaus, Albert
Netsuke; versuch einer geschichte der japanischen schnitzkunst. Leipzig, F. A. Brockhaus 1905
xiv,482p. illus. 53 col.pl. Q.
Each plate accompanied by guard sheet with descriptive letterpress
LC 6-1084

Netsukes; tr. by M. F. Watty, by E. G. Stillman. New York, Duffield 1924
xvii,175p. front. XVI pl. O.
Partial bibliography: p173-75
Translation of his *Netsuke*
LC 24-28349

Brockhoff, L. E. D.
Die kloster-orden der heiligen katholischen kirche; 2. ausg. Frankfurt a. M., G. Bender [1875]
777p. 10 col.pl. O.
First edition 1870
Lipperheide 1886

La **broderie** du XIe siècle jusqu'à nos jours. Farcy, Louis de

Broderie et dentelles. Lefébure, Ernest

La **broderie** somptuaire. Seligman, G. S., and Hughes, Talbot

Broderies des paysannes de Smolensk. Ténicheva, M. K. P. knyaginya

Broderies et décoration populaires tchécoslovaques. Paris, H. Ernst 192-?
[5]p. illus. 34 col.mounted pl. F.
Introduction signed: L'après mme. Renata Tyrsova et m. Ch. Chotek. Issued in portfolio
LC 31-6419

Broderies hindoues. Estrade, C.

Broderies populaires espagnoles. Villalba, J.

Broderies populaires russes. See Paris. Exposition internationale des arts décoratifs et industriels modernes, 1925. Broderies russes, tartares, armeniennes

Broderies russes, tatares, armeniennes. Paris. Exposition internationale des arts décoratifs et industriels modernes, 1925

Broderies, tissus, soieries, dessins de tissus. Paris. Musée des arts décoratifs

Broke, Sir Arthur de Capell, 2d bart.
A winter in Lapland and Sweden, with various observations relating to Finmark and its inhabitants; made during a residence at Hammerfest, near the North Cape. London, J. Murray 1826
xvi,612p. front. illus. 22pl. (part col.) fold. map, plans. sq.Q.
Colas 452. LC 5-10703

Broke, Sir Arthur de Capell—*Continued*
Winter sketches in Lapland, or illustrations of a journey from Alten ... through Norwegian, Russian, and Swedish Lapland ... a complete view of the mode of travelling with rein-deer ... illus. by D. Dighton and J. D. Harding. London, J. Rodwell 1827
24pl. F.

Die **bronzeschwerter** des Königlichen museums zu Berlin. Berlin. Staatliche museen

Die **bronzezeit** in Oberbayern. Naue, Julius

Brooches
Heaton, H. A. The brooches of many nations. 1904

Rydh, H. A. Dosformiga spännen från vikingetiden. 1919

Ancient

Fairholt, F. W. Rambles of an archaeologist among old books and in old places. 1871. p 159-83

Leeds, E. T. Two types of brooches from the island of Gotland, Sweden. 1910

Brooke, Arthur de Capell. See Broke, Sir A. de C., 2d bart.

Brooke, Iris
English children's costume since 1775, drawn and described by Iris Brooke. London, A. & C. Black 1930
86p. col.front. illus.(part col.) O.
Costume index. LC 31-3299

English costume from the fourteenth through the nineteenth century; drawn by Iris Brooke; described by Iris Brooke and James Laver. New York, Macmillan 1937
426p. illus. O. (Imperial eds) $3.95
Contains five books originally published separately: *English costume of the later Middle ages, English costume in the age of Elizabeth, English costume of the seventeenth century, English costume of the eighteenth century,* and *English costume of the nineteenth century.* The original illustrations in color and black and white. No index
LC 38-27015

English costume in the age of Elizabeth: the sixteenth century. London, A. & C. Black; New York, Macmillan 1933
86p. col.front. illus.(part col.) pl. O. $2; 6s
Costume index. LC 34-625

English costume of the early middle ages; the tenth to the thirteenth centuries; drawn and described by Iris Brooke. London, A. & C. Black; New York, Macmillan 1936
86p. col.front. illus.(part col.) O. 6s; $2.25
Costume index. LC 37-6425

English costume of the eighteenth century; drawn by Iris Brooke, described by James Laver. New York, Macmillan; London, A. & C. Black 1931
86p. col.front. illus.(part col.) O. $2; 6s
Costume index. LC 32-3407 (under Laver)

English costume of the later middle ages: the fourteenth and fifteenth centuries. London, A. & C. Black; New York, Macmillan 1935
86p. col.front. illus.(part col.) pl. O. $1.75
Costume index. LC 36-27161

English costume of the nineteenth century; drawn by Iris Brooke, described by James Laver. New York, Macmillan; London, A. & C. Black. 1929
88p. col.front. illus.(part col.) O. $2; 6s
Costume index. LC 30-12375 (under Laver)

English costume of the seventeenth century. London, A. & C. Black; New York, Macmillan 1934
86p. col.front. illus.(part col.) O. $2
Costume index. LC 35-1665

Brooklyn. Public library
A reading and reference list on costume. Brooklyn, N.Y., Brooklyn public library 1909
64p. O.
A revised edition, 1932, has been included in E. Traphagen's *Costume design and illustration* p165-223
LC 10-4602

Brooks, Vincent
(illus.) Macleay, Kenneth. Highlanders of Scotland

Brosamer, Hans
(illus.) Bible. German. Biblia

Brosin, Fr.
Ein ideal der frauenwelt; beiträge zur bekleidungsfrage. Dresden, D. B. Böhmert 1898
35p. 4pl. O.
Colas 453

Brossard, Charles
Colonies françaises, par un groupe d'écrivains, d'explorateurs et de fonctionnaires, sous la direction de Ch. Brossard. Paris, E. Flammarion 1906
632p. front. illus.(part col.) Q.
At head of title: Géographie pittoresque et monumentale de la France et de ses colonies
LC Agr21-1047

Brosses, Charles de
Lettres familières écrites d'Italie en 1739 & 1740; préface et bibliographie d'Edmond Pilon. nouv. éd. Paris, Les oeuvres représentatives 1929
2v. illus. O.
Earlier edition 1858
Volume 2 contained 6 full page illustrations showing papal guards

Broughton, Thomas Duer
The costume, character, manners, domestic habits, and religious ceremonies of the Mahrattas. With ten coloured engravings from drawings by a native artist. London, J. Murray 1813
358p. 10 col.pl.(incl. front.) Q.
Half-title: Letters written in a Mahrattas camp during the year 1809
Colas 454. Lipperheide 1480. LC 5-6179

Les Marattes, ou moeurs, usages et costumes de ce peuple; tr. de l'anglais par M. Breton. Paris, A. Nepveu 1817
2v. 10 col.pl. D.
Translation of his *Costume ... of the Mahrattas.* The plates are copies of those in the English edition
Colas 455. Lipperheide 1481

Broughton, Urban Huttleston Rogers
The dress of the First regiment of life guards, in three centuries. London, Halton & Truscott Smith 1925
36p. 80pl.(incl. ports., part col. mounted) ob.Q.
Catalog of pictures, original drawings, & engravings of the First regiment of life guards—1670 to 1923 p17-36
Colas 456. LC 26-13066

Brown, Gerard Baldwin
The arts & crafts of our Teutonic forefathers, being the substance of the Rhind lectures for 1909. London & Edinburgh, T. N. Foulis 1910
xviii,250p. front. illus.(incl.maps) 32pl. D. (The arts and crafts of the nations)
Bibliography: p232-[38]
LC w11-39

Brown, Henry
(illus.) De Nederlanden

Brown, Henry Collins. See note under Valentine's manual of old New York

Brown, Horatio Robert Forbes
(tr.) Molmenti, P. G. Venice

Brown, John Macmillan
Maori and Polynesian, their origin, history and culture. London, Hutchinson 1907
vii-xxxi,300p. D.
LC w9-224

Brown, Paul
Aintree; Grand nationals—past and present. New York, Derrydale press 1930
xxi,191p. incl.illus. pl. diagr. front. pl. map, facsims. Q.
Short bibliography included in preface. The illustrations show jockeys in costume
LC 31-456

Brown, Percy Clement
Art in dress. [1st ed] [New York, P. C. Brown c1922]
185p. illus. diagrs. F.
LC 22-18903

Brown, William
Antiquities of the Jews. London, Rodwell and Martin 1820
2v. 2pl. O.
Lipperheide 136

Browne, George Waldo
Japan, the place and the people; with an introduction by the Hon. Kogoro Takahira. Boston, D. Estes [1904]
438p. col.front. illus. pl.(part col.) map. Q.
Published in 1901 in his *The Far East and the new America* v2 (in part) and v3
LC 4-9142

The new America and the Far East; a picturesque and historic description of these lands and peoples ... Illustrated by about 1,200 photogravures, colored plates, engravings & maps. Boston, Marshall Jones company c1907
6v. fronts. illus. pl.(part col.) fold. maps. Q.
Paged continuously. Earlier edition entitled *The Far East and the new America*
Contents: v 1 Hawaii; The Philippines; v2 The Philippines, continued; Japan; v3 Japan, continued; v4-5 China; v6 Cuba; Porto Rico
LC 7-7537

Browne, James
A history of the Highlands and of the Highland clans; with an extensive selection from the hitherto inedited Stuart papers; new ed. London, Edinburgh, and Dublin, A. Fullarton 1849-50
4v. fronts. illus. 55pl.(part col.) 8 port. fold.map. O.
LC 3-29896

Browne, Miss M. Prince
Dress-cutting, drafting, and French pattern modelling ... preface by the Hon. Mrs. Colborne. Westminster, A. Constable 1902.
122p. illus. diagrs. O.

The new and simplified system of dress-cutting and tailoring. London, Black 1896
64p. illus. O.-F. 1s
Illustrations are separate, in folio size

The practical work of dressmaking & tailoring, with illustrations. 3d and rev. ed. London, H. Cox 1908
xix,194p. diagrs. D.
LC w9-108

"Up-to-date" dress cutting and drafting; with diagrams. Part I-IV. London, H. Cox 1907-08
4v. illus. diagrs. D.
Contents: pt 1 Bodices and sleeves. 1907; 72p. pt2 Skirts and adaptations. 1908, 52p. pt3 Tailoring and French pattern modelling. 1908. 54p. pt4 Adaptation of patterns to the cutting out of under garments. 1908. x,84p.

Brownell, Charles De Wolf
The Indian races of North and South America, comprising an account of the principal aboriginal races; a description of their national customs, mythology, and religious ceremonies; the history of their most powerful tribes, and of their most celebrated chiefs and warriors. Cincinnati, Morse & Gordon; Hartford, L. Stebbins 1853
720(i.e. 640)p. 24 col.pl. 15 port.(part col.) O. $2.75, o.p.
Many later editions published with the same plates
Costume index. LC 2-12679

Brownlow, William Robert Bernard, bp.
(ed.) Rossi, G. B. de. Roma sotterranea

Bruant, Aristide
Dans la rue; chansons et monologues ... dessins de Steinlen. Paris, A. Bruant [1889-95]
2v. illus. D.
LC 6-27322

Bruce, John Collingwood
The Bayeux tapestry elucidated. London, J. R. Smith 1856
166p. XVII col.pl.(incl.front.) Q.
LC 10-4984

Bruce, Philip Alexander
Economic history of Virginia in the seventeenth century; an inquiry into the material condition of the people, based upon original and contemporaneous records. New York, P. Smith 1935
2v. O.
Contains material on Indian style of dress and other clothing of colonial times
Bibliography: v 1 p xv-xix
LC 35-27241

Bruchstücke aus einigen reisen nach dem südlichen Ruszland, in den jahren 1822 bis 1828. Schlatter, Daniel

Bruchstücke zur nähern kentniss des heutigen Griechenlands gesammelt auf einer reise. Bartholdy, J. L. S.

Bruck-Auffenberg, Frau Natalie

Dalmatien und seine volkskunst; muster und kunsttechniken aus altem volks- u. kirchengebrauch; spitzen, stickarbeit, teppichweberei, schmuck, trachten u. gebrauchsgegenstände der Dalmatiner. Wien, A. Schroll [1911]
72p. illus. and atlas of 68pl.(part col.) 36x29cm.
Descriptive letterpress in Croatian, German and Italian
LC 28-58

Brucker, Johann Jakob and Haid, Johann Jacob

Bilder-sal heutiges tages lebender und durch gelahrheit berühmter schriftsteller; in welchem derselbigen nach wahren original-malereyen entworfene bildnisse in schwarzer kunst in natürlicher aehnlichkeit vorgestellet und ihre lebens-umstände verdienste um die wissenschafften und schrifften aus glaubwürdigen nachrichten erzählet werden. Augspurg, J. J. Haid 1741-66
11pts. 110pl. F.
An edition in Latin published at the same time, entitled: *Pinacotheca scriptorum nostra aetate litteris illustrium,* lacks volume 11 which is a supplement
Lipperheide 561. LC 33-38509

Ehren-tempel der deutschen gelehrsamkeit, in welchem die bildnisse gelehrter, und um die schönen und philologischen wissenschafften verdienter männer unter den Deutschen aus dem XV., XVI. und XVII. jahrhunderte aufgestellet, und ihre geschichte, verdienste und merckwürdigkeiten entworfen sind von Jacob Brucker ... in kupfer gebracht von J. J. Haid ... Augspurg, J. J. Haid 1747
210p. 50 port. O.
Head and shoulder portraits of German scholars
Lipperheide 585. LC 33-38511

Brueck, O von

Erinnerungen an Schleswig; skizzen aus dem album eines sächsischen offiziers. Dresden, Adler und Dietze 1850
12pl. F.
Lipperheide 2129

Brückmann, H. W.

Lehrkursus für damen-garderobe; 2. aufl. Köln, H. W. Brückmann 1878
72p. 16pl. O.
Colas 459. Lipperheide 3812

Brückner, Éduard. See Dalmatien und das österreichische küstenland

Brügner, C.

Abzeichen der koeniglich preussichen armee im jahre 1863. Berlin, J. H. Neumann [1863]
3pl. F.
First part only published
The plates contain patterns of the uniforms of the corps of guards and of the first and second army
Colas 460. Lipperheide 2184

Bruehl, Anton

Photographs of Mexico. New York, Delphic studios [c1933]
4 l. 25pl. F.
LC 34-1135

Brühl, Karl Friedrich Moritz Paul, graf von

Darstellung d. festspiels Lalla Rukh, welches am 27. januar 1822 im königl. schlosse zu Berlin gegeben wurde. Berlin, L. W. Wittich 1822
Illus. Q.

Lalla Rûkh; ein festspiel mit gesang und tanz aufgeführt auf dem königl. schlosse in Berlin am 27sten januar 1821. Berlin, L. W. Wittich 1822
27p. 21 col.pl. Q.
French translation with title: *Lalla Roûkh,* and same plates was published by Wittich simultaneously (23p. 23pl.[22 col.])
Lipperheide 2536-37

Neue kostüme auf den beiden königlichen theatern in Berlin unter der General-Intendantur dess Herrn Grafen von Brühl. Berlin, L. W. Wittich 1819-31
2v. 193pl.(192 col.) Q.
Plates are engraved by Brühl and Jügel after C. F. Thiele and Sturmer
Colas 461. Lipperheide 3210

See also Hirt, A. L., jt. auth.

Bruel, François Louis

Un siècle d'histoire de France par l'estampes, 1799-1871. See entry under Paris. Bibliothèque nationale. Département des estampes

Brüll, Adolph

Trachten der Juden im nachbiblischen alterthume; ein beitrag zur allgemeinen kostümkunde. 1. theil. Frankfurt a/M, I. St. Goar 1873
90p. O.
No more published. This volume contains only undergarments, outer clothing and trousers. A second volume on hats, shoes, hair, etc. was planned but never published
Colas 462. Lipperheide 141

Brünn. Mähr. gewerbemuseum

Proben weiblicher handarbeiten mährischländlicher haus-industrie. Brünn, W. Burkart 1885
7p. 26pl. F.
Lipperheide 3970

Brünne und helm im angelsächsischen Beowulfliede. Lehmann, Hans

Bruges and West Flanders. See Omond, G. W. T. Belgium

Brugsch, Émile

La tente funéraire de la princesse Isimkheb provenant de la trouvaille de Déir el-Baharî. Le Caire, L'auteur 1889
8p. illus. 7pl.(5 col.) Q.
Lipperheide 145m

Bruhn, Wolfgang

Das frauenkleid in mode und malerei seit zwei jahrhunderten. Berlin, Kunstgewerbe museum 1926
16p. col.illus. Q.

Die mode in fünf jahrhunderten. Leipzig, Bibliographisches institut c1936
57p. 25 illus.(16 col.) D. (Meyers buntebändchen) 90pf.
Sold by Westermann, N.Y. 25c
From the fifteenth century thru the nineteenth
LC 37-449

Bruin, Cornelis de. See Bruyn, Cornelis de

Bruin, Georg. See Braun, Georg

Brummell, George Bryan
Male and female costume; Grecian and Roman costume, British costume from the Roman invasion until 1822 and the principles of costume applied to the improved dress of the present day, by Beau Brummell; illustrated from the manuscript, ed. by Eleanor Parker. Garden City, N.Y., Doubleday, Doran 1932
xviii,316p. incl. pl. Q. $25
Costume index. LC 32-4722

Brun, Charles
Costumes des provinces françaises. 1: Audessous de la Loire. Paris, R. Ducher 1932
64p. illus. O. (Les arts décoratifs)

Uniformes militaires anciens et actuels ... Nos soldats. Paris, Delandre [1916]
4 l. 15 col.pl. ob.F.
Plates accompanied by descriptive letter press
Colas 463

Brun, Corneille Le. See Bruyn, Cornelis de

Brunel, Georges. See Le costume, la mode: Encyclopédie populaire illustrée du vingtième siècle

Brunel, Noré. See Roux, Claudius, jt. auth.

Brunelleschi, Umberto
(ed.) La Guirlande

See also Regnier, Mme. M. L. A. de H. de, jt. auth.

Brunet
Théorie pratique du danseur de société, ou l'art d'apprendre sans maître les figures de la contre-danse française, et la valse. Paris, Chaumerot 1839
113p. 34 illus. 17pl. Q.
Drawings by H. Bazin
Lipperheide 3103

Brunet, Charles
(ed.) Restif de La Bretonne, N. E. Monument du costume physique & moral de la fin du XVIIIe siècle

Brunet, Gustave
Étude sur Francisco Goya sa vie et ses travaux. Paris, Aubry 1865
65p. front. pl. F.
Binder's title: *Études sur Goya*

Brunet, Romuald, and Chaperon, Eugène
Les grandes manoeuvres de cavalerie. Paris, L. Baschet [1887]
2v. illus. O. (Cahiers d'enseignement illustrés no30-31)
Lipperheide 2344

La science des armes dans la cavalerie. Paris, L. Baschet 1887
6v. illus. O. (Cahiers d'enseignement illustrés no49, 51-55)
Lipperheide 2343

Brunings, Pieter Frederik
Onze krijgsmacht met bijschriften. s'Gravenhage, C. Ewings 1887
108p. 26 col.pl. Q.
Colas 464. Lipperheide 2260

Brunn, Heinrich von
Greek vases: their system of form and decoration. Twelve plates, in colors, selected from the forty-four illustrations taken from the originals in the royal collection of vases at Munich, ed. by T. Lau ... With translations of the accompanying text, by E. H. Greenleaf. Boston, S. W. Tilton & company 1879
69p. 12 col.pl. Q.
"Greek vases. Historical survey of system," signed H. Brunn: p11-40
Contains a selection from the plates in *Die griechischen vasen* by Brunn and Krell
LC 12-8572

Griechische kunstgeschichte. München, Verlagsanstalt f. kunst und wissenschaft 1893-97
2v. 142 illus. O.
No more published. Contents: v 1 Die anfänge und die älteste decorative kunst; v2 Die archaische kunst
Lipperheide 204

Brunn, Heinrich von, and Krell, Paul Friedrich
Die griechischen vasen ihr formen- und decorationssystem ... aufgenommen nach originalen der K. vasensammlung in München ... mit einer historischen einleitung und erläuterndem texte von dr. Heinrich Brunn ... und dr. P. F. Krell. Leipzig, E. A. Seemann 1877
38p. 44 col.pl. F.
Lipperheide 192

Brunner, Andrea
Excubiae tutelares LX heroum, qui ab anno Ch. DVIII. Theodonem in principatu Boariae secuti cum elogiis suis et rerum gestarum compendio ad felicissimas cunas serenissimi principis Ferdinandi Marli Francisci Ignatii Wolfgangi utr. Boiariae ducis. Monachii, Typis C. Lesserii [1637]
613p. 60pl. O.
Portraits of the dukes of Bavaria from the eighth to the seventeenth century
Lipperheide 711

Brunner, Karl
Ostdeutsche volkskunde. Mit 69 abbildungen auf 32 tafeln. Leipzig, Quelle & Meyer 1925
xi,279p. pl. O. (Half-title: Deutsche stämme, deutsche lande)

Brunoff, Jacques De. See Brunoff, Maurice de, jt. ed.

Brunoff, Maurice de, and Brunoff, Jacques de
(eds.) Collection des plus beaux numéros de Comœdia illustré et des programmes consacrés aux ballets & galas russes, depuis le début à Paris, 1909-1921. Paris, M. de Brunoff 1922?
[380]p. illus. pl. ports. (part col.) F.
LC 23-15133

Bruns, Margarete Sieckmann
Der stil unserer kleidung; eine ästhetische studie. Minden in Westf. J. C. C. Bruns [1902]
117p. illus. pl. front. (port.) O.
Colas 466. Lipperheide 3315

Brunton, Guy
Lahun. [v. 1-2] London, British school of archaeology in Egypt, University college 1920-23
2v. col.front. pl.(part col.) plans(1 fold.) sq.F. (British school of archaeology in Egypt and Egyptian research account. Publication no27, 33)
Volume 1 contains colored plates and descriptions of ancient Egyptian jewelry
LC 22-14840

Brunton, Mrs Winifred
(illus.) Kings and queens of ancient Egypt

Brusasorci, pseud. See Riccio, Domenico, known as Il Brusasorci

Brusasorzi, Domenico Riccio, known as. See Riccio, Domenico, known as Il Brusasorci

Brussels. Bibliothèque royale de Belgique. Mss. (9511)
Le Bréviaire de Philippe le Bon, bréviaire parisien du xve siècle. Bruxelles, 1929
2v. col.illus.(coat of arms) pl. ports. map, plans (1 double) facsims.(part col.) F. (Œuvre national pour la reproduction de manuscrits à miniatures de Belgique. Publication no7)
The Breviary of the Bibliothèque royale is preserved in 2 volumes (mss. 9511, 9026) The paintings and miniatures are generally ascribed to Guillaume Vrelant and his atelier. The introduction includes chapters on Jean Tavernier (p144-50), Guillaume Vrelant (p150-53), L'atelier de Guillaume Vrelant (p153-54) and on Manuscrits avec images d'imitateurs de Vrelant (p175-77)
Contents: [1] Étude du texte et des miniatures, par l'abbé V. Leroquais; [2] Planches
LC 30-6855

—Mss. (6-9)
Histoire de Charles Martel, reproduction des 102 miniatures de Loyset Liédet. See entry under Liédet, Loyset

—Mss. (9392)
Christine de Pisan. Épître d'Othéa

—Mss. (9967)
L'ystoire de Helayne: reproduction des 26 miniatures du manuscrit; par J. Van den Gheyn. Bruxelles, Vromant 1913
14p. pl. sq.O.

Brussels. Bibliothèque Royale de Belgique. Mss. Bibliothèque de Bourgogne no. 9066-9068
Cronicques et conquestes de Charlemaine. See entry under Le Tavernier, Jean

Brussels. Bibliothèque royale de Belgique. Section des manuscrits
Deux livres d'heures (n°s. 10767 et 11051 de la Bibliothèque royale de Belgique) attribués à l'enlumineur Jacques Coene; par J. van den Gheyn. Bruxelles, Vromant 1911?
16p. 51pl. O.
In portfolio
Shows fifteenth century costume
LC 11-18820

Les très belles miniatures de la Bibliothèque royale de Belgique, par Eugène Bacha ... choix de cinquante-sept miniatures, reproduites en héliotypie. Bruxelles et Paris, G. van Oest 1913
viii,5p. LVI pl. F.
In portfolio
The miniatures show fifteenth century costume
LC 21-17777

Brussels. Exposition de l'art ancien, 1884
La dentelle. See Claesen, Joseph. Alte kunstvolle spitzen

Brussels. Musées royaux des arts décoratifs et industriels
Catalogue des armes et armures du Musée de la Porte de Hal, par Hermann van Duyse ... Ouvrage illustré de 20 reproductions photographiques et de 45 dessins de l'auteur. [Bruxelles, Imprimerie Van Assche] 1897
402p. illus. O.
LC 21-10822

Dentelles anciennes des Musées royaux des arts décoratifs et industriels à Bruxelles. See entry under Overloop, Eugène van

Donation d'antiquités égyptiennes aux Musées royaux de Bruxelles. See entry under Capart, Jean

Bruun, Chr.
Danske uniformer. Kjöbenhavn, 1837-42
3v. 207 col.pl. O.
v 1 contains illustrations of army uniforms, v2 of dress of orders, courtiers and officials, and v3 of the militia
Colas 467. Lipperheide 2277

Bruun, Daniel
(ed.) Danmark; Land og folk. Historisk-topografisk-statistisk Haandbog, udgivet ved Daniel Bruun, under medvirking af en Række Fagmænd. Bind 1-2. Kjøbenhavn, Gyldendal 1919-23
6v. facsims. illus. pl.(part col.) fold. maps. fold.plan. Q.

Den islandske Kvinde og hendes dragt. [København, 1903]
Signed: Daniel Bruun
Excerpt: Tidsskrift for Industri 1903.

Bruyère, Henri Étienne Paul, comte
1635-1885. Historique du 2. régiment de dragons; [illus] par E. Penon & L. Gaudibert ... Chant et marche, par A. Kopff. Chartres, Garnier 1885
222p. illus.(incl. music) 18 col.pl.(incl. front.) Q.
LC 21-11904

Bruyn, Abraham de
Costumes civils et militaires de XVIe siècle; reproduction fac-simile de l'édition de 1581 coloriée d'après des documents contemporains; texte traduit et annoté par Auguste Schoy. Bruxelles, G. A. van Trigt 1875
20p. 33 col.pl. F.
Plates are facsimile reproductions of those in his *Omnium pene* (1581)
Colas 478. Costume index. Lipperheide 11

Diversarum gentium armatura equestris; ubi fere Europae Asiae atque Africae equitandi ratio propria expressa est. Coloniae, [1577]
8 l. 52pl. Q.
Text on the plates is by Adrien Damman. Lipperheide lists a copy of the same date with title beginning *Divesarum.* An undated edition with title: *Divesarum gentium*

Bruyn, Abraham de—*Continued*
armatura equestris (52,23pl.) is a collection of plates from earlier editions and from the author's *Equitum. Diversarum gentium armatura equestris* (Amstelodami, N. J. Visscheri 1617) has 76 plates, the same as the preceding edition with some changes in order
Colas 469-70. Lipperheide 2897-98

Equitum descripcio; quomodo equestres copie, nostra hac aetate, in sua armatura, per cunttas, videlicet Europae, Asiae et Affrice. [1576]
5 l. 52pl. Q.
Horsemen of different European countries. The author's *Diversarum gentium* 1577 contains the same collection of plates
Colas 468. Lipperheide 2899

Imperii ac sacerdotii ornatus; diversarum item gētium peculiaris vestitus; excudebat Abr. Bruin; his adiunxit cōmentariolos Caesar. Pontif. ac sacerdotū Hadr. Damman. Gand, [1578]
281p. 50pl.(incl. 200 costume figures) F.
Published first as a supplement to the *Omnium pene* (1577) and united with it in the second edition of *Omnium pene* (1581)
Colas 476. Lipperheide 10

Omnium pene Europae, Asiae, Africae et Americae gentium habitus ... quibus accedunt Romani pontificis, cardinalum, episcoporum, una cum omnium ordinum monachorum et religiosorum habitu; [2. ausg] [Antwerpiae] 1581
79pl. F.
The first 61 plates appeared in the 1577 edition. The added 18 plates show 108 figures in religious costume
Also published under the title: *Omnium pene Europae, Asiae, Aphricae atque Americae gentium habitus* (Antwerpiae, M. Colÿn, ex. 1581)
Colas 473-74

Omnium pene Europae, Asiae, Aphricae atque Americae gentium habitus; [4.ausg.] Michiel Colyn excudit. [Antwerpen] ca1610
75pl.(incl. 458 costume figures) Q.
Has title also in French: *Habits de diverses nations* and in German: *Trachtenbuch der furnembsten nationen und volcker kleyrungen.* Explanations of the figures are in three languages
Fourth edition of *Omnium pene.* The plates are those of the earlier editions with additional costume figures
Colas 475. Lipperheide 12

Omnium poene gentium imagines, ubi oris totiusque corporis & vestium habitus, in ordinis cuiuscunque, ac loci hominibus diligentissime experimuntur. [Coloniae, 1577]
22 l. 50pl.(incl. 206 costume figures) F.
Each plate shows four or five different costumes
Colas 472. Lipperheide 9

Sacri Romani imperi ornatus, item Germanorum diversarumq. gentium peculiares vestitus; quibus accedunt ecclesiasticorum habitus varii. [Antwerpiae] exc. C. Rutz 1588
69pl. ob.F.
Contains the plates of the author's *Omnium pene* and *Imperii ac sacerdotii ornatus.* Two other editions are known dated 1592 and 1595
Colas 477

Bruyn, Cornelis de
Cornelis de Bruins Reizen over Moskovie, door Persie en Indie. Amsterdam, W. and D. Goeree 1711
472p. (incl. 37 illus.) 110pl.(incl. 260 illus.) port. 3 maps. F.
French edition published in Amsterdam in 1718 under title: *Voyages de Corneille Le Brun par la Moscovie, en Perse et aux Indes Orientales.* For English edition see his *Travels into Muscovy*
Lipperheide 547

Reizen van Cornelis de Bruyn, door de vermaardste deelen van Klein Asia, de eylanden Scio, Rhodus, Cyprus, Metelino, Stanchio, etc. mitsgaders de voornaamste steden van Aegypten, Syrien en Palestina. Delft, H. van Krooneveld. 1698
398p. 102pl.(incl. 210 illus.) F.
French edition published at Delft in 1700 and at Paris in 1714 under title: *Voyage au Levant*
Lipperheide 546

Travels into Muscovy, Persia, and part of the East-Indies ... to which is added an account of the journey of Mr. Isbrants, ambassador from Muscovy, through Russia and Tartary, to China; together with remarks on the travels of Sir John Chardin, and Mr. Kempfer, and a letter written to the author on that subject. Tr. from the original French. London, A. Bettesworth [etc.] 1737
2v. front. pl.(part fold.) ports. maps(part fold.) F.
Translation of his *Reizen over Moskovie*
LC 5-3706

Voyage au Levant; c'est-à-dire, dans les principaux endroits de l'Asie Mineure, dans les isles de Chio, Rhodes, Chypre, etc., de même que dans les plus considérables villes d'Egypte, Syrie, & Terre Sainte ... par Corneille le Bruyn; nouv. ed. Rouen, C. Ferrand [1725]
5v. illus. pl. Q.
This edition combines in French the two titles originally issued as: *Reizen ... door de vermaardste deelen van Klein Asia* and *Reizen over Moskovie.* Volumes 3-5 of the present French edition have title: *Voyages par la Moscovie, en Perse et aux Indes Orientales*
Lipperheide 548. LC 5-3708

Bry, Johann Israel de. See Bry, J. T., jt. auth.; also Acta Mechmeti I saracenorum principiis

Bry, Johann Theodor de
Emblemata nobilitatis; Stamm und wappenbuch ... mit einem vorwort über die geschichtliche entwickelung der stammbücher bis zum ende des XVI. jahrhunderts. Berlin, J. A. Stargardt 1894
31p. 60pl. Q.
Facsimile of the edition published in Frankfurt in 1593
Lipperheide 502

Emblemata secularia, mira et jucunda varietate seculi hujus mores ita emprimentia, ut sodalitatum symbolis in-

Bry, Johann Theodor de—*Continued*
signiisque conscribendis & depingendis peraccommoda sint. Oppenheim, H. Galleri 1611
56p. 2 illus. 144pl. O.
Title also in German: *Weltliche lustige newe kunststück der jetzigen welt lauff fürbildende mit artlichen lateinischen teutischen frantzösischen und niderländischen carminibus und reimen geziert fast dienstlich zu einem zierlichen stamm und wapenbüchlein.* The edition published 1596 in Frankfort had 101 plates. There is also a facsimile edition *Emblemata saecularia, life and manners of the XVIth century in emblems designed by J. T. de Bry* (Berlin, J. A. Stargardi 1895. 101pl.)
Lipperheide 501

Repraesentatio & explicatio duorum arcuum triumphalium ... abriss und beschreibung zwoer triumph: oder ehren pforten welche ... herrn Friderichen den fünfften pfaltzgraffen bey Rhein ... und frauen Elisabethen ... als beyde ... zu Oppenheim eingezogen ... auffrichten lassen. Oppenheim, H. Galleri [1613]
12p. 8pl. F.
Lipperheide 2555

(engr.) Boissard, J. J. Icones & effigies virorum doctorum

(engr.) Creccelius, Johannes. Colectanea ex historijs, de origine et fundatione

See also Acta Mechmeti I saracenorum principis

Bry, Johann Theodor de, and Bry, Johann Israel de
Wahrhafftige unnd eygentliche beschreibung der allerschrecklichsten verrätherey ... wieder die Königliche Majestät ... zu Londen. Franckfurt am Mayn, M. Beckern 1606
32p. illus. 3pl. O.
On the Gunpowder plot of 1605
Lipperheide 973. LC 2-23828

Bry, Theodor de
[Grands voyages. pars I-VI] Francoforti ad Moenum, typis I. Wecheli, sumtibus vero T. de Bry [1590-96]
6v. F.
The *Grands voyages* comprise thirteen volumes of the author's *Collectiones peregrinationum in Indian orientalem et Indiam occidentalem* and relate entirely to North and South America, although often referred to as *India occidentalis,* sometimes also *Historia Americae, sive novi orbis.* The entire series is published in a German edition of fourteen volumes. Parts 1-6 relate to costume and each has been entered separately in this catalog. For full information about any volume see entry under name of author as given below: v 1 Harriot, Thomas. Admiranda narratio fida tamen, de commodis et incolarum ritibus Virginiae; v2 Le Moyne de Morgues, Jacques. Brevis narratio eorum quae in Florida Americae provĩcia Gallis acciderunt; v3 Staden, Hans. Americae tertia pars memorabilẽ provinciae Brasiliae historiam continẽs; v4-6 Benzoni, Girolamo. Americae pars quarta [-sexta]

See also Album amicorum habitibus mulierum omniu nationu Europae (attributed)

(engr.) Boissard, J. J. Leben und contrafeiten der türckischen un persischen sultanen

(engr.) Lonicer, J. A. Pannoniae historia chronologica

Bryan, Michael
Bryan's dictionary of painters and engravers. New ed., rev. and enl. under the supervision of George C. Williamson. London, G. Bell 1903-05
5v. fronts. pl. ports. Q.
The reproductions of paintings, many of which are portraits of the artist's period, make this cyclopedia a source of costume material
LC 5-11698

Bryson, Mrs Mary Isabella
Child life in China. [London] Religious tract society 1900
160p. incl.front. illus. D.
LC 2-24407

Der **bubikopf** von Agamemnon bis Stresemann. Handke, Hermann

Buch, Leopold, freiherr von
Reise durch Norwegen und Lappland. Berlin, G. C. Nauck 1810
2v. maps
Describes dress of southern Norway, and discusses the decreasing use of national costume, v 1 p63-8
For English translation see his *Travels* below. There is a French translation: *Voyage en Norvège et en Laponie 1806, 1807 et 1808* (Paris, Gide 1816)

Travels through Norway and Lapland, during the years 1806, 1807 and 1808 ... Tr ... by John Black. With notes and illustrations, chiefly mineralogical, and some account of the author, by Robert Jameson. London, Printed for H. Colburn 1813
xviii,460(i.e. 440)p. maps. Q.
Translation of his *Reise*
LC 4-25545

Das **buch** der chroniken. Schedel, Hartmann

Das **buch** der haare und bärte; humoristische abhandlungen. Leipzig, I. Jackowitz 1844
85p. O.
Lipperheide 1702

Buch der livreen. Klemm, Heinrich

Das **buch** der marionetten. Rehm, H. S.

Das **buch** der ritterorden und ehrenzeichen. Brüssel und Leipzig, C. Muquardt 1848
388p. 98 col.pl.(incl. front.) Q.
"Geschichte, beschreibung und abbildungen der insignien aller ritterorden, militair- und civil- ehrenzeichen, medaillen &c., nebst einer auswahl der vorzüglichsten costüme." Subtitle

Das **buch** reizender und merkwürdiger zeichnungen. See Tuer, A. W. The book of delightful and strange designs

Das **buch** vom deutschen heere. Vogt, Hermann

Das **buch** vom preussischen soldaten. Gerstmann, Maximilian

Das **buch** vom Schwanenorden. Stillfried und Rattonitz, R. M. B., graf von, and Haenle, S.

Das **buch** vom tabak. Cudell, Robert

Buchanan, Francis Hamilton
A journey from Madras through the countries of Mysore, Canara, and Malabar; pub. under the authority ... of the East India company. London, T. Cadell and W. Davies [etc] 1807
3v. front. pl.(part col.) fold.map. tables (part fold.) F.
LC 4-32964

Bucher, Bruno
(ed.) Bem, Balcer. Die alten zunft- und verkehrs-ordnungen der stadt Krakau

Les **bûcherons** et les schlitteurs des Vosges. Michiels, Alfred

Buchholtz, Hermann
Die tanzkunst des Euripides. Leipzig, B. G. Teubner 1871
191p. O.
Lipperheide 3119

Buck, Henry A. See Heathcote, J. M., and others. Skating

Buck, Peter Henry
The evolution of Maori clothing, by Te Rangi Hiroa (P. H. Buck) ... printed under the authority of the Board of Maori ethnological research. New Plymouth, N. Z., T. Avery 1926
xxiii,248p. illus. pl. O. (Polynesian society. Memoirs 7)
Bibliography: p231-32

Buckland, A. W.
On tattooing. London, Harrison 1888
318-327p. 1 map. O.
Reprint from the Anthropological Institute. *Journal* May 1888
Title from cover

Buckle, Charles Randolph
(ed.) Rousselet, Louis. India and its native princes

Buckle, Mary. See Day, L. F., jt. auth.

Bucquoy, Eugène Louis
Les gardes d'honneur du premier empire. Nancy, A. Crépin-Leblond 1908
24,487p. 8 col.pl. Q.
Index bibliographique: p[ix]-xxiii
LC 9-14810

Les uniformes de l'armée française; terre, mer, air; illustrations de Maurice Toussaint. Paris, Les Éditions militaires illustrées 1935
269p. illus. 120 col.pl. facsim. 33x25cm.
Imprint date changed in manuscript to 1936. On cover: Ouvrage publié sous le haut patronage du Ministère de la guerre
LC 36-17459

Budapest. Exposition hongroise, 1881
Kiváló diszitmények az 1881. évi Országos magyar nöiparkiállitából. See entry under Hungary. Földmívelesügyi ministerium

Budapest. Magyar nemzeti múzeum
Néprajzi ostályának értesítöje. v 1, 1900+ Budapest, A Magyar nemzeti múzeum kiadása
Illus.(incl.music) pl.(part col.) ports. maps, plans. O. Q.
Issued in 10 numbers annually, 1900-04; in 4 numbers annually, 1905+ (in some cases two or more numbers are combined) Volumes 6+ are also numbered "új folyam" 1+
Editors: 1900-June 1902, János Jankó. Sept. 1902-? Villibáld Semayer
In Hungarian and German. German title: *Ethnographische sammlungen.* Volumes 1-5 were issued in same covers with *Ethnographia; a Magyar néprajzi társaság értesítöje*

See also L'art populaire hongrois

Budapest, the city of the Magyars. Smith, F. B.

Budapesti bazar. See note under Die Modenwelt

Buddeus, Carl
Volksgemälde und charakterköpfe des russischen volks ... Tableau des moeurs et des usages ... des russes. Leipzig, J. F. Gleditsch 1820
12p. 16 col.pl. F.
Colas 481. Lipperheide 1351s

Buddhism in Tibet. Schlagintweit, Emil

The **Buddhism** of Tibet. Waddell, L. A.

Buddhist monks
Schlagintweit, Emil. Buddhism in Tibet illustrated by literary documents and objects of religious worship. 1863

See also Lamas

Budé, Guillaume
(ed.) Vegetius Renatus, Flavius. De re militari

Budge, Sir Ernest Alfred Thompson Wallis
The mummy, a handbook of Egyptian funerary archaeology; 2d ed. rev. & greatly enl. Cambridge, The University press 1925
xxiv,513p. fold.front. illus. XXXIII pl. O.
First edition: 1893; 2d edition: 1894
LC 26-22236

(ed.) Book of opening the mouth
(ed.) Book of the dead. Facsimile of the Papyrus of Ani, in the British museum
(ed.) Liturgy of funeral offerings. The liturgy of funerary offerings

See also British museum. Department of Egyptian and Assyrian antiquities. A guide to the Egyptian collections in the British museum; and their Guide to the first, second and third Egyptian rooms

Büchner, B. J. Römer-. See Römer-Büchner, B. J.

Büchner, Elise
Gründlicher selbstunterricht die damenbekleidungskunst in 1-2 stunden zu erlernen. 2. aufl. Eisenach, Druck der hofbuchdruckerei ca1865
28p. 11pl. O.
Colas 479. Lipperheide 3793

Büchsenmeisterey. Dambach, Christoff

Das **bühnenkostüm** in altertum. Boehn, Max von

Buek, F. Georg
Album hambürgische costüme; in sechs und neunzig von mehreren künstlern nach der natur gezeichneten ... blättern ... Text vom F. G. Buek. Hamburg, B. S. Berendsohn [1843-47]
94 l. 97 col.pl. O.
Most of the plates are by H. Jessen, a few by C. Beer. They show uniforms, military and civil, and regional costume
Colas 482. Lipperheide 808

Buel, Mrs Elizabeth Cynthia (Barney)
(ed.) Vanderpoel, Mrs E. N. American lace & lace-makers

Bürger-militär almanach. Lipowsky, F. J.

Bürkner, Hugo. See Holbein, Hans, the younger. Hans Holbeins Alte Testament

Bürmann, Fritz. See note under Die Modenwelt. Zum fünfundzwanzigjährigen bestehen der Modenwelt, 1865-1890

Li **buffoni.** Costa, Margherita

Bugge, Anders Ragnar, and Kielland, Thor Bendz

Alterskrud og messeklær i Norge. Kristiania, Norsk folkemuseum 1919
43p. D. (Norsk folkemuseums særudstilling nr 10)
On cover: Norsk folkemuseum. Særudstilling X. Paramenter
LC 22-7808

Building of Britain and the empire. See Traill, H. D., and Mann, J. S., eds. Social England

Buisson, Ferdinand and others. See Le costume, la mode: Encyclopédie populaire illustrée du vingtième siècle

Bujack, Georg

Zur bewaffnung und kriegführung der ritter des Deutschen Ordens in Preussen. Königsberg, Hartungsche buchdruckerei 1888
22p. 1 col.pl. Q.
From Königsberg. Altstädtisches gymnasium. *Bericht* 1887-88
The plate is a reproduction of a medieval wall painting in the cathedral of Königberg showing a knight of the order in armor
Lipperheide 2104

Bulgaria

Filov, Bogdan. Geschichte der bulgarischen kunst unter der türkischen herrschaft und in der neueren zeit. 1933

Fox, Frank. Bulgaria. 1915

Macdonald, John. Czar Ferdinand and his people. 1913

Monroe, W. S. Bulgaria and her people, with an account of the Balkan wars, Macedonia, and the Macedonian Bulgars. 1914

See also Military costume—Bulgaria

Bull-fighters

Spain

Belmonte y Garcia, Juan. Juan Belmonte, killer of bulls. 1937

Brunet, Gustav. Étude sur Francisco Goya. 1865

Carnicero, Antonio. Colleccion de las principales suertes de una corrida de toros. 1790

Estadística taurina anual ... año [1]+ 1931+

Gail, Wilhelm. Erinnerungen aus Spanien. Nach der natur und auf stein gezeichnete skizzen aus dem leben in den provinzen Catalonien, Valencia, Andalusien, Granada und Castilien. 1837

Gomez de Bedoya, Fernando. Historia del toreo, y de las principales ganaderias de España. 1850

Goya y Lucientes, F. J. de. Tauromachia. c1923

Oduaga-Zolarde, G. Les courses de taureaux expliquées, manuel tauromachique à l'usage des amateurs de courses. 1854

Perea, Daniel. Á los toros. 1894

Price, Lake, and Ford, Richard. Tauromachia, or The bull-fights of Spain, illustrated by ... plates, representing the most remarkable incidents and scenes in the arenas of Madrid, Seville, and Cadiz. 1852

Vindel, Pedro. Estampas de toros; reproducción y descripción de las más importantes publicadas en los siglos XVIII y XIX relativas a las fiesta nacional. 1931

Bulletin de la Société. Société de l'histoire du costume, Paris

Bullot, Maximilien. See Hélyot, Pierre. Histoire des ordres monastiques, religieux et militaires

[**Bulwer, John**]

A view of the people of the whole world. London, 1658
590p. 2 fronts.(1 port.) illus.
"A short survey of their policies, dispositions, naturall deportments, complexions, ancient and moderne customes, manners, habits, and fashions. A worke everywhere adorned with philosophicall, morall and historicall observations on the occasions of their mutations & changes throughout all ages." Subtitle
Running title: Man transform'd: or, The artificial changling

Bunbury, Henry William

Academy for grown horsemen; by Geoffry Gambado, [pseud] London, R. Ackermann [1825]
2v. in 1. 26 col.pl. S.
Plates are reproductions of original plates, designed by H. Bunbury, engraved by T. Rowlandson
Part 2 has title: *Annals of horsemanship.*
Earlier editions 1787, and 1808. German edition issued under title: *Reiter-karikaturen*
LC 12-22452 (1808 ed.)

Das **bunden** von kopftüchern in Mähren und der Slowakei. See Úprka, Joža. Vazani, šátků

Bunkley, Joel William

Military and naval recognition book, a handbook on the organization, insignia of rank, and customs of the service of the world's important armies and navies. 60 full-page plates, 20 in colors. 2d ed., rev. and enl. New York, D. Van Nostrand 1918
xi,268p. col.front. illus.(part col.) D. $1, o.p.
First edition 1917 (51pl., 18 col.)
Costume index. LC 19-848

Bunte stickmuster in weiss. Hennings, Emma

Buonaiuti, B. Serafino

Italian scenery. See entry under Godby, James

Buonanni, Filippo

Descrizione degl' istromenti armonici d'ogni generi. 2. ed. riveduta, corr. ed accreciuta dall' Abbate Giacinta Ceruti,

Buonanni, Filippo—*Continued*
ornata con ... rami incisi d'Arnoldo Wanwesterout. Rome, V. Monaldini 1776
214p. 142pl. Q.
Text in French and Italian. French title: *Description des instrumens harmoniques en tout genre.* First edition 1722, had Italian text only and title: *Gabinetto armonico pieno d'istrumenti*
Lipperheide 2000

La gerarchia ecclesiastica considerata nelle vesti sagre e civili: con le imagini di ciascun grado. Roma, 1720
2v. 160pl. Q.

Histoire du clergé séculier et régulier, des congrégations de chanoines et de clercs et des ordres religieux de l'un et de l'autre sexe qui ont été établis jusques à présent ... nouvelle éd. Amsterdam, P. Brunel 1716
4v. pl. O.

Ordinum equestrium et militarium catalogus in imaginibus expositus & cum brevi narratione. Romæ, typis G. Plachi 1711
18p.l. 144 l, 164pl. O.
Added t.-p. in Italian: *Catalogo degli ordini equestri e militari.* Latin and Italian in parallel numbered columns, printed on one side of leaf only and each leaf preceded by numbered plate (1-141) Plates 142-64: Primi elementi delle croci dalle quali procedono tutte le altre degli ordini equestri, con la nota delli colori
The plates were engraved by Giovanni Battista Sintes after Andrea Orazi
Several times reprinted. For edition with German text see his *Verzeichnis der geist und weltlichen ritter-orden*
Colas 372. Lipperheide 1900. LC 12-31644

Ordinum religiosorum in ecclesia militanti catalogus, eorumque indumenta in iconibus expressa. Romæ, typis A. de Rubeis 1706-10
3v. 324pl. O.
Latin and Italian in parallel columns. Added t.-p.: *Catalogo degli ordini religiosi della chiesa militante.* Vol. 2 has imprint: Romae, typis Georgii Plachi
Plates are engraved by Arnold van Westerhout after designs by A. Orazi and show the costumes of both masculine and feminine orders
For German translation see his *Verzeichnüss*
Contents: pars 1 Complectens virorum ordines; 2 Continens virgines Deo dicatas; 3 Ordines in prima editiones omissi
Colas 370-71. Lipperheide 1863 (1738-42 ed.) LC 21-3007

Verzeichniss der geist und weltlichen ritter-orden in netten abbildungen und einer kurtzen erzehlung in lateinisch und italienischer sprache. Nürnberg, C. Weigel 1720
154p. 164pl. Q.
German translation of his *Ordinum equestrum,* plates reduced in size
Lipperheide 1901

Verzeichnüss der geistlichen ordens-personen in der streitenden kirchen in nette abbildungen und einer kurtzen erzehlung verfasset ... Andere und verbesserte aufl. Nürnberg, C. Weigel 1720-24
3v. 325pl. Q.
German translation of his *Ordinum religiosorum.* According to Colas there was a German edition dated 1711
Colas 371. Lipperheide 1864

Buoninsegni, Francesco
Satyra Menippea, oder straff-schrifft weiblicher pracht; auss dem italiänischen ins deutsche versetzt ... von J. D. Majorn. Hamburg, G. Wulffen [1683]
130p. illus. D.
First Italian edition published 1637
Lipperheide 3435

Burato. Paganino Alessandro

Burbank, Emily
The smartly dressed woman; how she does it. New York, Dodd, Mead 1925
264p. incl. 24 pl. O.
LC 25-17562

Woman as decoration. New York, Dodd, Mead 1917
29,326p. incl. 33pl. O.
LC 17-29164

Burchard, A.
Musterblätter für kreuzstichstickereien. Berlin, Winckelmann 1892
24pl. O.
Lipperheide 4018

Burchardus, abbot of Bellevaux, d. 1163?
Apologia de barbis; nunc primum ex ms. add. 41997 Musaei britannici editit E. Ph. Goldschmidt. Cantabrigiae, typis Academiae 1935
x,96p. front.(facsim.) O.
LC 36-22528

Burchell, William John
Travels in the interior of southern Africa. London, Printed for Longman, Hurst, Rees, Orme, and Brown 1822
2v. front. illus. col.pl. map. Q.
Color plates of members of several native tribes
LC 4-19484

Burckhardt, Jakob Christoph
The civilization of the renaissance in Italy, by Jacob Burckhardt; tr. by S. G. C. Middlemore. London [etc.] G. G. Harrap; New York, Harper
526p. col.front. illus.(incl. facsims.) pl. (part col.) port. fold.plan. Q. $12, o.p.
Translation of his *Die cultur* with additions by Ludwig Geiger and Walther Götz
Costume index. LC 30-26611

Die cultur der renaissance in Italien. 4. aufl. besorgt von Ludwig Geiger. Leipzig, E. A. Seemann 1885
2v. O.
The second volume contains a section on Clothes and fashions. For English translation see his *The civilization*
Bibliographical foot-notes
Lipperheide 1287. LC 29-18583

Burckhardt, John Lewis
Notes on the Bedouins and Wahábys; collected during his travels in the East. London, H. Colburn and R. Bentley 1831
2v. front.(fold.map) O.
LC 5-10093

Burckhardt, Rudolf Friedrich
Gewirkte bildteppiche des XV. und XVI. jahrhunderts im Historischen museum zu Basel; 25 tafeln in farbigem lichtdruck. Leipzig, K. W. Hiersemann 1923
65p. illus. 25 col.mounted pl. F.
Most of the plates are costume pictures
LC 25-13026

The **burden** of the Balkans. Durham, M. E.

Buren, Hendrik van
Drilkonst, of hedendaaghsche wapen-oeffening. 2. dr. verb. Amsterdam, M. Doornick 1672
98p. 17pl. O.
Lipperheide 2087

Burford, Robert
Description of a view of the city of Moscow, with the gorgeous entry of His Imperial Majesty the Emperor Alexander II. into the Kremlin. Painted by the proprietor, Robert Burford, and Henry C. Selous and assistants, from drawings taken by a Russian artist. London, Printed by W. J. Godbourn 1857
20p. fold.front. O.
LC 10-33971

Burger, Ludwig
Das emancipirte amazonen-heer. Berlin, A. von Schröter ca1850
8pl. Q.
Colas 485. Lipperheide 3545m

Die königl. preussische armee in ihrer neuesten uniformirung. Berlin, Mitscher & Röstell 1860
48 col.pl. D.
Colas 487

See also Kaiser, Friedrich, jt. auth.; also Rabe, Edmund, jt. auth.

[**Burger, Ludwig, and Müller, H.**]
[Garde royale prussienne, 1861. Berlin, 1861]
52 col.pl. Q.
Plates show uniforms of the following regiments, thirteen for each regiment: 3e régiment de la garde à pied; Régiment des fusiliers de la garde; 2e régiment des dragons de la garde; 2e régiment des Uhlans de la garde
Colas 488

Burgess, Frederick William
Antique jewellery and trinkets. London, G. Routledge; New York, G. P. Putnam's sons 1919
x,399p. front. pl. O. (Home connoisseur ser. 3) 7s 6d
Costume index. LC 20-11517

Burggraaff, van den
(pub.) Madou, J. B., and Eeckhout, J. J. Collection de costumes du peuple des provinces de la Belgique

Burgkmair, Hans
Hans Burgkmair des jüngeren turnierbuch von 1529. Sechszehn blätter in handkolorit mit erläuterndem text hrsg. von Heinrich Pallmann. Leipzig, K. W. Hiersemann 1910
22 columns. 16 col.pl. F.
Plates except the first are from Burgkmair's *Kaiser Maximilians I triumph,* and have been hand-colored by Burkmair's son. The plates show competitors in full armor with their heraldic devices

Images de saints et saintes issus de la famille de l'Empereur Maximilian I. en une suite de ... planches gravées en bois par differens graveurs d'après les dessins de Hans Burgkmaier. Vienne, F. X. Stöckl 1799
11p. 119pl. F.
Text by Jacob Mennel. Illustrations are from plates by Hans Frank, Cornelius and Wilhelm Lieferinck, etc. cut from 1516 to 1518. The work has also been attributed to Leonhard Beck
Lipperheide 1793

Kaiser Maximilians I. triumph. Le triomphe de l'empereur Maximilien I ... gravées en bois d'après les desseins de Hans Burgmair, accompagnées de l'ancienne description dictée par l'empereur à son secrétaire Marc Treitzsaurwein. Vienne, M. A. Schmidt; Londres, J. Edwards 1796
30p. 135pl. F.
Plates reproduce the woodcuts only. The verses are printed on separate pages. Some of the plates, hand colored, are in the *Turnierbuch* listed below
Lipperheide 2503

The triumphs of the Emperor Maximilian I., by Hans Burgmair. Ed. by Alfred Aspland. ... Manchester, Published for the Holbein society by A. Brothers [etc.] 1873
2v. 137pl. 36x45cm. (The Holbein society's facsimile reprints. vol. IX-X)
Collation; pt I: 2p.l. pl. 1-68; pt II: 2p.l. pl. 69-135a. Nos. 124 and 135 followed, in numbering of plates, by 124a and 135a
LC 3-25490

Triumph of the Emperor Maximilian I., with woodcuts designed by Hans Burgmair. Ed. by Alfred Aspland. [Manchester] Reproduced by the Holbein society 1875
177p. 2 illus. O. (The Holbein society's facsimile reprints. vol. XI)
Explanatory volume to the 2 vols. of plates. Contains an introduction, reproduction of the t.-p., and translation of preface of Vienna edition of 1796, and of "the ancient description dictated by the emperor to his secretary Marc Treitzsaurwein"
LC 3-24590-1

(illus.) Cicero, M. T. Officia M. T. C. Ein buch so Marcus Tullius Cicero der Römer zů seynem sune Marco

(illus.) Dürer, Albrecht. Triumph des kaisers Maximilian I

(illus.) Treitz-Saurwein, Marx, von Ehrentreitz. Der weisz kunig

Der **burgundische** paramentenschatz des Ordens von goldenen vliesse. Schlosser, Julius, ritter von

Die **Burgundischen** gewänder der k.k. schatzkammer. Vienna. K.K. Österreichisches museum fur künst und industrie

Buried Norsemen at Herjolfsnes. Nørlund, Poul

Burke, Ashworth Peter. See Burke, Sir J. B., jt. auth.

Burke, Henry Farnham
Historical record of Coronation of their Majesties Edward VII. and Queen Alexandra ... 9 August 1902. London, Harrison 1904
32pl.(11 col.) F. 336s

The historical record of the coronation of Their Majesties King George the Fifth and Queen Mary, 1911. London, McCorquodale [1911]
264p. front.(port.) 20 col.port. F.
Shows members of the royal family and other participants in the ceremony, in coronation regalia and describes the costumes
LC A13-2584

Burke, Sir John Bernard
The book of orders of knighthood and decorations of honour of all nations, comprising an historical account of each order, military, naval, and civil, from the earliest to the present time, with lists of the knights and companions of each British order. London, Hurst and Blackett 1858
411p. 100 col.pl. O.
Plates show insignia only
LC 9-26290

Burke, Sir John Bernard, and Burke, Ashworth Peter
A genealogical and heraldic history of the peerage and baronetage, the Privy council, and knightage. Ed. by E. M. Swinhoe. London, Burke's peerage 1935
illus. (incl. coats of arms) ports. Q.
Coats of arms and badges of the various orders
LC 35-9756

Burlin, Mrs. Natalie (Curtis)
(ed.) The Indians' book; ... recorded and ed. by Natalie Curtis; illus. from photographs and from original drawings by Indians. New York and London, Harper and brothers c1923
xxxvi,582p. illus. facsims. pl. (part col.) ports. facsims. (part col.) Q. $7.50
LC 23-5612

Burlington fine arts club, London
Exhibition of English embroidery executed prior to the middle of the XVI century. London, Printed for the Burlington fine arts club, 1905
87p. XXX pl. (10 col.) Q.
Plates show church embroidery
LC 10-8854

Burma. See India—Burma; also Tattooing—Burma

Burma, Ceylon, Indo-China, Siam, Cambodia, Annam, Tongking, Yunnan. Hürlimann, Martin

Burman, Johan Jakob
Anteckningar, förda under tiden från år 1785 till år 1816 jemte relation om Savolaks-brigadens operationer under 1808 och 1809 års krig. Stockholm, Typografiska föreningens boktryckeri 1865
323p. 8 col.pl. O.
Lipperheide 2281

The **Burman.** Scott, Sir J. G.

A **Burmese** arcady. Enríquez, C. M. D.

Burnacini, Ludovico Ottavio
Maschere (In Denkmäler des theaters. v 1)

Burnouf, Eugène
L'Inde française, ou Collection de dessins lithographiés, représentant les divinités, temples, costumes, physionomies, meubles, armes, et ustensiles des peuples hindous qui habitent les possessions françaises de l'Inde, et en général la côte de Coromandel et le Malabar. Paris, Chabrelie 1827-35
2v. col.pl. col.ports. F.
Text of vol. 2 by E. Burnouf and E. Jacquet
Colas 490. LC 20-22145

Burrows, Guy
The land of pigmies. London, C. A. Pearson 1898
xxx,3-299p. illus. pl. ports. front. O.
LC 5-15410

Burton, Harry. See Carter, Howard, and Mace, A. C. The tomb of Tut.ankh. Amen

Burton, John Wear
The Fiji of to-day. London, C. H. Kelly [1910]
364p. pl. ports. O.
LC A11-580

Burton, Robert
The anatomy of melancholy, what it is, with all the kinds, causes, symptoms, prognostics, and several cures of it. By Democritus junior [pseud.] A new ed. Corrected. Boston, W. Veazie; New York, Hurd and Houghton 1864-65
3v. O.
First edition 1621. Many other editions
LC 32-8884

Bury, Lady Charlotte (Campbell)
The diary of a lady-in-waiting, by Lady Charlotte Bury; being the Diary illustrative of the times of George the Fourth, interspersed with original letters; ed. with an introduction by A. Francis Steuart. London, J. Lane; New York, J. Lane company 1908
2v. 18 port. (incl. fronts.) O.
First published, anonymously, in 1838 under the title *Diary illustrative of the times of George the Fourth*
Portraits of Queen Caroline and women of the English nobility from 1820-30
LC 8-29183

Bury, George Wyman
The land of Uz. London, Macmillan 1911
xxviii,354p. front. (ports.) pl. fold.map. O.
On Arabia
LC A12-698

Bury John Bagnell
(ed.) Cambridge ancient history

Busby, Thomas Lord
Civil and military costume of the city of London; painted and engr. by T. L. B. London, 1824-25
nos 1-4. illus. F.
Colas 494

Costume of the lower orders in Paris [by] T. L. B. [London] ca1820
28 col.pl. D.
Plates show street venders and have titles in French and English. Plates are after Rowlandson
Colas 493

Costume of the lower orders of London; painted and engraved from nature. London, Baldwin, Cradock and Joy [1820]
11 l. 24 col.pl. Q.
Colas 491. Lipperheide 1025

Costume of the lower orders of the metropolis. London, ca1820
24 col.pl. D.
Different from his *Costume of the lower orders of London.* Some of the plates are the same, revised; thirteen are new
Colas 492. Lipperheide 1026

Busby, Thomas Lord—*Continued*
The fishing costume and local scenery of Hartlepool in the county of Durham. London, printed for J. Nichols and Son 1819
3,5,2,p. 6 col.pl. Q.

Buschan, Georg Hermann Theodor
(ed.) Die sitten der völker; liebe, ehe, heirat, geburt, religion, aberglaube, lebensgewohnheiten, kultureigentümlichkeiten, tod und bestattung bei allen völkern der erde, bearb. aug grund der beiträge hervorragender fachgelehrter wie T. J. Albridge, Baudesson, E. Eylmann. Stuttgart [etc.] Union deutsche verlagsgesellschaft [1914-16]
3v. fronts.(2 col. 1 double) illus. pl.(part col. part double) Q.
Costume pictures of all parts of the world
Contents: v 1 Australien und Ozeanien. Asien; v2 Asien (fortsetzung) Afrika; v3 Afrika (schluss) Amerika. Europa
The author's *Illustrierte völkerkunde* (Stuttgart, Strecker und Schröder 1922-26) is on the ethnology of the same peoples and contains some pictures of costume interest. Some of the illustrations are reproductions, in reduced size, of those used in *Die sitten der völker*
LC 20-14746

Buschmann, Hedwig
Neue frauentracht. Berlin; Leipzig, Fritzsche & Schmidt 1910
25p. 16pl. O.

Buschor, Ernst. See Furtwängler, Adolf, and Reichhold, Karl. Griechische vasenmalerei

Bushongo. See African tribes

Buss, Georg
Der fächer. Bielefeld und Leipzig, Velhagen & Klasing 1904
139p. 120 illus.(part col.) 2pl. Q. (Sammlung illustrierter monographien 14)
LC 33-23460

Das kostüm in vergangenheit und gegenwart. Bielefeld, Velhagen & Klasing 1906
171p. illus. Q. (Sammlung illustrierter monographien, 17)
A history of costume traced by selections from the art of the various countries and periods

Buss, Kate
Studies in the Chinese drama. Boston, The Four seas company 1922
77p. front. illus. pl. ports. facsim. O.
LC 22-16215

Busscher, Edmond de
Album du cortège des comtes de Flandre, personnages et costumes; dessinés par Felix de Vigne ... et texte historique et descriptif par Edmond de Busscher. Gand, Busscher 1852-53
2v. 88 col.pl. Q.
Handsome colored plates show rulers, members of guilds, judges, nobles and others of Flanders from the ninth to the fifteenth century, in robes of their rank. Also published with plates in black and white
A text is published separately: *Description du cortège historique des comtes de Flandre* (Gand, Busscher 1849. 83p. 1 pl. O.)
Colas 3011. Lipperheide 2832-33

Busse, B. E .
Baden. See Deutsche volkskunst. v 13

[Bussemecher, Johann]
[Folge von reitern verschiedener volker] No place, ca1590
22pl. O.
Lipperheide 2903

Bussenius, Arno
(tr.) Harva, Uno. Die religion der Tscheremissen

Busuttil, Salvatore
Nuova raccolta di costumi di Napoli disegnati dal vero. Roma, P. Datri [1828-30]
28pl. Q.
Colas 496

Raccolta di costumi dello Stato Pontificio; incisi in accquaforte. Lanno, D. Minelli 1826
35 col.pl. ob.O.
Some of the plates are dated 1827
Colas 495

Raccolta di costumi dello Stato Romano. Roma, G. Antonelli [1836-38]
25pl. F.
Colas 497. Lipperheide 1311m

Raccolta di costumi religiosi e civile della corte pontificia ... incise 1833. Roma, Mineli 1833?
112 col.pl.(part fold.) O.

Raccolta di sessanta piu belle vestiture che si costumono nelle provincie del regno di Napoli divisa in due parti. Napoli, V. Talani & N. Gervasi 1793
1 l. 60 col.pl. F.
Women's costume from all the cities and regions which made up the kingdom of Naples. Published also with plates in black and white
In two parts of 30 plates each numbered 1-30. In addition to the picture the first plate of each part has title: *Raccolta di varie vestiture ... del regno di Napoli.* Colas gives a list of the plates. They are engraved from designs by Alesando and Olivia d'Anna, Lumicisi and others
Colas 2468

(illus.) Pistolesi, Erasmo. La Colonna Trajana

Bute, John Patrick Crichton Stuart, 3d marquis of
Scottish coronations. Paisley, London, A. Gardner 1902
310p. O.
The first three of the following papers appeared originally in the tenth and eleventh volumes of the Scottish review (1887-88)
Contents: The earliest Scottish coronations; The coronation of Charles I. at Holyrood; The coronation of Charles II. at Scone; Three illustrative coronation rituals; Appendix [Report by Sir James Balfour, lyon king of arms, to the privy council of Scotland, July, 1628, on "The forme of the coronation of the kings of Scotland"]
LC 2-17269

Butler, John
Travels and adventures in the province of Assam, during a residence of fourteen years. London, Smith, Elder, and co. [etc.] 1855
268p. front. pl. fold.map. O.
A continuation of the author's *A sketch of Assam*
LC 5-14307

Butlin, F. M.
Among the Danes; with twelve illustrations in colour by Ellen Wilkinson, and fifteen other illustrations. New York, J. Pott [etc.] 1909
xi,278p. 27pl.(12 col.) O.
LC 9-35857

Butron, Francisco Antonio Lorenzano y. See Lorenzano y Butron, F. A.

Butsch, Albert Fidelis
(ed.) Inventarium ... was in ... herrn Marx Fuggers ... rüst: und sattel cammer

Butterfield, William
(ed.) Barber, Mrs Mary. Some drawings of ancient embroidery

Butterick fashion magazine. v 1, 1908+ New York, Butterick co.
Col.illus. F. $1.25 a year
Published five times a year. Current 1938
Title varies: Spring-Summer 1916, *Butterick fashions*; Autumn 1916-Spring 1932, *Butterick quarterly*; Summer 1932-Early Spring 1933, *Butterick Paris fashions:* Spring/Early summer 1933-Winter 1934 *Butterick fashion book*

Butterick fashions. See Butterick fashion magazine

Butterick Paris fashions. See Butterick fashion magazine

Butterick publishing company, limited
The dressmaker ... new ed. rev. and enl. New York [etc.] The Butterick publishing company c1916
138p. illus. Q. $1.00
"A complete book on all matters connected with sewing and dressmaking from the simplest stitches to the cutting, making, altering, mending and caring for the clothes." Subtitle
LC 16-2238

(pub.) Wandle, Mrs J. T. Masquerade and carnival

Butterick quarterly. See Butterick fashion magazine

Butterick's moden revue. See Butterick's modenblatt

Butterick's modenblatt. Jahrg. 38-50? 1896-1900. London & New York, Butterick pub. co.
Illus. F.
Absorbed by *Butterick's moden revue*
Lipperheide 4816

Buttons
Essex institute, Salem, Massachusetts. The Emilio collection of military buttons, American, British, French and Spanish, with some of other countries, and non-military, in the museum of the Essex institute, Salem, Mass. 1911
Manchester, Herbert. The evolution of dress fastening devices from the bone pin to the koh-i-noor. c1922
Wrschowitz, Austria. Knopf-museum Heinrich Waldes. Berichte. 1916-1919

Buttons, Military
Bottet, Maurice. Le bouton de l'armée française. 1908
Calver, W. L. The British army button in the American revolution. 1923
Fallou, Louis. Le bouton uniforme français (de l'ancien-régime à fin juillet 1914). 1915

Buttrick, Helen Goodrich
Principles of clothing selection; rev. ed. Drawings by Gertrude Spaller Kinder. New York, Macmillan 1930
xiii,219p. illus. diagrs. D.
Bibliography at end of most of the chapters
LC 30-33964

Buxton, Leonard Halford Dudley, and Gibson, Strickland
Oxford university ceremonies. Oxford, Clarendon press; New York, Oxford univ. press 1935
xii,168p. IV pl.(incl. facsim.) D. $2.25
Costume index. LC 35-14863

Buyers yardgoods review. See note under McCall fashion book

Buytewech, Willem
Sieben edelleute verschiedener nationen. Berlin, Reichsdruckerei 1926
8p. 7pl. Q.
Facsimile of an edition published in Haarlem, about 1614

[Trachten der Holländerinnen. G. v. Scheindel, fecit H. Hondius, exc. 1645]
8 illus. Q.
Nagler in his *Künstler-Lexicon* XV 204 mentions a series of twelve leaves signed Clement de Jonghe with which the corresponding leaves of the Lipperheide copy are identical
Colas 498. Lipperheide 935

By sea and land. See Arnold, Sir Edwin. Seas and lands

Bygone punishments. Andrews, William

Bynaeus, Anthony
De calceis Hebraeorum libri duo, curis secundis recogniti, et aucti. Accedit ejusdem Somnium, tertio recusum. Dordraci, ex officina T. Goris 1715
267,[37],24p. illus. 3pl. Q.
First edition was published in 1682
Lipperheide 129y. LC 8-36579

Byne, Mrs Mildred (Stapley)
Popular weaving and embroidery in Spain, by Mildred Stapley. New-York, W. Helburn c1924
xii,60p. illus. 124pl.(3 col.) Q.
Printed in Spain
LC 25-19394

Tejidos y bordados populares españoles, por Mildred Stapley. Madrid, Editorial Voluntad [c1924]
xii,56p. illus. 121pl.(3 col.) Q.
LC 32-34456

Byrne, John J.
Perfection; an illustrated manual for artist tailors. London, Trübner 1899
129p. ob.F.

Practical tailoring; rev. by Z. W. Shaw. Pt. 1-5. London, The J. Williamson co. [1895]
5v. O.

Byron, E.
Art of dressmaking. Dublin, Wood 1897
15p. O.

Bysterveld, Henri de
Album de coiffures historiques ... Dessiné par Rigolet. Paris, P. Dupont 1863-67
5v. 120 col.pl. D.
Volume 3 has the explanations on the plates in French and English and the notice "agent at Paris, Léon Pelleray, agent in London, Hovenden & sons." The historical notes in volume 4 are by Alfred Bouchard
Colas 499

Byvanck, Alexander Willem, and Hoogewerff, Godfried Joannes
Noord-Nederlandsche miniaturen in handschriften der 14e, 15e en 16e eeuwen. 's-Gravenhage, M. Nijhoff 1922-25
3v. 240pl. (part col.) F.
LC 22-21747

Byzantine empire
Danz, A. H. E. Aus Rom und Byzanz. 1867

Gayet, A. J. Exposition universelle de 1900. Palais du costume. Le costume en Égypte de IIIe au XIIIe siècle. 1900

Houston, M. G. Ancient Greek, Roman and Byzantine costume and decoration (including Cretan costume). 1931

Kondakov, N. P. Histoire de l'art byzantin considéré principalement dans les miniatures. 1886-91

See also Kings and rulers—Byzantine empire

C

C., E. M. See The lady's crochet-book; also The lady's knitting-book

Le **cabinet** d'armes de Maurice Tallyrand-Périgord. Cosson, C. A., baron de

Le **cabinet** de toutes les modes d'habits. See Pfeffel, J. A. Schweitzerisches trachtencabinet

Cabinet des modes. See Magazin des modes nouvelles, françaises et anglaise

Le **cabinet** d'estampes de la bibliothèque nationale. Bouchot, H. F. X. M.

Cabrera y su ejército. Lopez, J. A.

Cabris
Le costume de la Parisienne au XIX. siècle. Paris, Société anonyme des publications scientifiques & industrielles 1901
293p. illus. O.
Cover dated 1902. Running title: *Le vêtement de la Parisienne au* XIX. *siècle*
Colas 501. LC 4-12422

La **caccia** nel Milanese. Borsa, Mario

Caddo Indians. See Indians of North America—Caddo Indians

Cadets, Military. See Military cadets

[**Cadoux, Gaston**]
Relation officielle des fêtes organisées par la ville de Paris pour la visite des officiers et marins de l'escadre russe de la Méditerranée les 17, 19, 20 et 24 Octobre 1893. Paris, Imprimerie nationale [1896]
244p. 17pl. (1 col.) Q.
Lipperheide 2728

Caesar, Caius Julius
The Gallic war, with an English translation, by H. J. Edwards. London, W. Heinemann; New York, G. P. Putnam's sons 1917
xxii,619p. front. O. (The Loeb classical library)
LC 17-28110

... Historien vom Gallier uñ der Römer burgeriche krieg: so er selbst beschriben. Meyntz, J. Schöffer 1530
31,clxiii l. 115 illus. F.
At head of title: Caii Julii Cesaris des grossmechtigen ersten römischen keysers
Translation by Ringmannus Philesius. Some of the illustrations are from the *Romische historien* of Livius published 1505. They show German dress of the sixteenth century
Lipperheide 616

Die **Cäsar-teppiche** im Historischen museum zu Bern. Weese, Arthur

Cahier, Charles, and Martin, Arthur
Mélanges d'archéologie, d'histoire et de littérature ... Collection de mémoires sur l'orfévrerie et les émaux des trésors d'Aix-la-Chapelle, de Cologne, etc.; sur les miniatures et les anciens ivoires sculptés de Bamberg, Ratisbonne, Munich, Paris, Londres, etc.; sur des étoffes byzantines, siciliennes, etc.; sur des peintures et bas-reliefs mystérieux de l'époque carlovingienne, romane, etc. Paris, Mme Ve Poussielgue-Rusand 1847-56
4v. illus. 154pl. (part col. part fold.) F.
Illustrations show decoration and ornament of the middle ages
Lipperheide 4216. LC 16-13417

Cahier de costumes suisses. Paris, Delarue [1833]
10pl. Q.
Plates show masculine and feminine dress of the cantons of Berne, Basel, Zurich, Lucerne, Soleure, Fribourg and Schaffhausen
Colas 503

Cahusac, Louis de
La danse ancienne et moderne, ou Traité historique de la danse. A La Haye [i. e. Paris] chez J. Neaulme 1754
3v. T.
Lipperheide 3073. LC 8-12053

Caiger, G.
Dolls on display; Japan in miniature, being an illustrated commentary on the girls' festival and the boys' festival. Tokyo, Hokuseido press [1933]
141p. col.front. illus. 3 col.pl. (2 fold.) Q.
LC 34-11221

(comp.) Japan, a pictorial interpretation. Tokyo & Osaka, Japan, Asahi shimbun pub. co. 1932
272p. incl.pl. Q.
Preface signed: G. Caiger, Tokio, 1932
LC 33-14728

Cailliaud, Frédéric
Recherches sur les arts et métiers, les usages de la vie civile et domestique des anciens peuples de l'Égypte, de la Nubie et de l'Éthiopie, suivies de détails sur les moeurs et coutumes de peuples modernes des mêmes contrées. Paris, Debures frères 1831
89pl. map. F.
Listed in the catalog of the Paris Bibliothèque nationale with 11 pages, 66 plates

Caillot, Antoine
Mémoires pour servir à l'histoire des moeurs et usages des Français, depuis les plus hautes conditions, jusqu'aux classes inférieures de la société, pendant

Caillot, Antoine—*Continued*
le règne de Louis XVI, sous le Directoire exécutif, sous Napoléon Bonaparte, et jusqu'à nos jours. Paris, Dauvin 1827
2v. O.
LC 3-23592

Cain, Georges
Musée rétrospectif des classes 85 et 86; le costume et ses accessoires. See entry under Paris. Exposition universelle, 1900

Le **Caire**, moeurs et costumes. Preziosi, A.

Cairo. Lane-Poole, Stanley

Cairo to Kisumu. Carpenter, F. G.

Calamandrei, E. Polidori. See Polidori Calamandrei, E.

Calchaqui; con ilustraciones de F. Gonzales. Quiroga, Adán

Calchaqui Indians. See Indians of South America—Calchaqui Indians

Caldecott, Randolph
(illus.) Blackburn, Henry. Breton folk; an artistic tour in Brittany

Calderini, Emma
Il costume popolare in Italia. Milano, Sperling & Kupfer [1934]
166p. 4 l.(incl.illus.) XIV pl. 200 col.pl. Q.
'Pubblicato sotto gli auspici del Comitato nazionale per le arti popolari (O. N. D. e C. N. I. C. I.)"
Fourteen plates show jewelry and patterns. The colored plates show costume of all sections of Italy
Costume index. LC 35-12046

Calderini, Guglielmo. See Petersen, E. A. H., jt. ed.

Calendario del esercito, 1936. Italy. Ministero della guerra

California. See United States—California

California stylist. v1, July 1937+ Los Angeles
Illus. F.
Published monthly. Current 1938

Caliga veterum. See Baudouin, Benoît and Negrone, Giulio. Balduinus de calceo antico

Calina, Josephine
(tr.) Boehn, Max von. Dolls and puppets.

Calix, François Claudius Compte- See Compte-Calix, F. C.

Callenbach, Franz
Almanach welt-sitten-staat-marter-calender; gerichtet auf alle schalt-jahr. Allen ... zur nachricht, warnung und glimpflicher bestraffung. [Nürnberg, Lochner 1714]
187p. D.
Lipperheide 3451

Callot, Jacques
Balli di Sfessania di Jacomo Callot. [Nancy, 1621]
24pl. T.
The engravings are of figures from Italian plays
Lipperheide lists an edition, published about 1635, 6 plates, each with 6 figures
Colas 505. Lipperheide 3195

Capricci di varie figure. Fiorentia, ca1617
48pl. S.
Colas notes a series *Les caprices* with 100 plates (Colas 507)
Lipperheide 514

Exercices militaires. Paris, Israel 1635
13pl. S.
The plates show officers, halberdiers, drummers, musketeers, pikemen, and three artillerymen
Colas 507 (noted) Lipperheide 2078

Les fantasies de Noble I. Callot. No place, Israel 1635
12pl. S.
Figures of both men and women, three on each plate
Colas 507. Lipperheide 515

[Italian beggars, men and women. Nancy, 1622]
26pl. O.
Lipperheide 1951

Livre d'esquisses de Jacques Callot dans la Collection albertine à Vienne, avec cinquante heliogravures en facsimile et huit vignettes, publié par Moriz Thausing. Wien, H. O. Miethke [etc.] 1880
20p. illus.(incl. mounted port.) 50pl. on 25 l. F.
Miscellaneous sketches made about 1624-25. Five plates (Callot 1-5) from the Collection Mariette, Paris, Impr. de Ch. Gillot, inserted at end
Lipperheide 517. LC 25-6755

Les miseres et les mal-hevrs de la gverre, representez par Iacqves Callot ... et mis en lumiere par Israel, son amy. Paris, 1633
18 mounted pl. ob.Q.
Pictures of soldiers during the Thirty years' war, 1618-48
Lipperheide 2077. LC 29-25383

La noblesse de Lorraine. [Nancy, 1624]
12pl. O.
Colas 506

Varie figure. No place, 1630?
16pl. S.
Lipperheide 516

Il **Callotto** resuscitato, oder Neü eingerichtes zwerchen cabinet. No place, ca1720
49pl. F.
Plates are copies from the original which appeared in Amsterdam in 1716 under title: *Le monde plein de fols, ou Le théâtre des nains*
Lipperheide 3548

Calthrop, Dion Clayton
English costume. London, A. and C. Black; New York, Macmillan 1907
xvi,453p. col. fronts. illus. pl.(part col.) O. $4
First published 1906 in 4 volumes. Reissued with the same plates but different paging in a one volume edition 1907, 1913, 1917 and 1923
Colas 508-09. LC 24-12397

English dress from Victoria to George V. London, Chapman & Hall [1934]
xv,172p. illus. col.pl. O. 15s.
Bibliography: p39
Costume index. LC 34-36803

Calvenfeier, Zürich. Organisations-comité
Rätische trachtenbilder. Zürich, Polygraphisches institut 189-?
12 col.pl. O.
Cover title

Calver, William L.
The British army button in the American revolution. [New York] 1923
29p. O.
Reprinted from the New York historical society *Quarterly bulletin* 1923
LC 24-13543

Calvert, Albert Frederick
The aborigines of western Australia. London, Simpkin, Marshall, Hamilton, Kent & co. 1894
55p. music. D.
LC 2-9211

Spanish arms and armour, being a historical and descriptive account of the Royal armoury of Madrid. London, New York, J. Lane 1907
xxx,142p. 248(i.e. 291)pl. on 146 l. O. (The Spanish series)
Based on the *Catalogo* by Valencia de San Juan
LC 7-41545

Valladolid, Oviedo, Segovia, Zamora, Avila, & Zaragoza; an historical & descriptive account. London & New York, J. Lane 1908
xxiii,162p. 413pl. on 207 l. D.
Plates 155-65 are photographs of peasants of Segovia
LC 8-26390

Calvert, W. E.
(tr.) Nørlund, Poul. Viking settlers in Greenland and their descendants during five hundred years

Calvo, y Sánchez, Ignacio
Retratos de personajes del siglo XVI, relacionados con la historia militar de España. Madrid, J. Cosano 1919
xx,291p. illus. pl. ports. O.
Shows costume of Spain in the 16th century

Calvocoressi, Michel D.
(tr.) Ivchenko, V. I., and Bakst, Léon. Le ballet contemporain

Cambodge et Cambodgiens. Collard, Paul

Cambodia
Collard, Paul. Cambodge et Cambodgiens. 1925?

Groslier, George. Danseuses cambodgiennes anciennes et modernes. 1913

Groslier, George. Recherches sur les Cambodgiens d'après les textes et les monuments depuis les premiers siècles de notre ère. 1921

Leclère, Adhémard. Cambodge: la crémation et les rites funéraires. 1906

Marchal, Sappho. Costumes et parures khmèrs. 1927

Mouhot, Henri. Travels in the central parts of Indo-China (Siam), Cambodia, and Laos, during the years 1858, 1859, and 1860. 1864

See also Dance costume—Cambodia

The **Cambrian** popular antiquities. Roberts, Peter

Cambridge. University. See Academic costume—Cambridge university; Boating costume—Cambridge university

Cambridge. University. Corpus Christi college. Lewis collection.
The Lewis collection of gems and rings in the possession of Corpus Christi college, Cambridge; with an introductory essay on ancient gems by J. Henry Middleton. London, C. J. Clay 1892
93p. illus. O.
Works on antique gems: p43-5
LC 1-2008

Cambridge. University. Museum of archaeology and ethnology
Iban or sea Dayak fabrics. See entry under Haddon, A. C., and Start, L. E.

Cambridge ancient history; plates prepared by C. T. Seltman. v 1-4. New York, Macmillan 1927-34
v 1-4. pl. O.
Separate volumes of plates. Many of the plates are interesting for costume of primitive peoples and of the Egyptians, Babylonians, Greeks, and other peoples of ancient times. References are given to the volumes of the text of the *Cambridge ancient history* where explanation of the plates will be found
Costume index. LC 23-11667

Cambridge university boating costumes. Cambridge, W. Metcalf 1907?
1 fold.pl. F.

Camden, William
The funeral procession of Queen Elizabeth, from a drawing of the time, supposed to be by the hand of William Camden. London, Soc. antiquar. 1791
7pl. F.
From *Vetusta monumenta* issued by the London antiquarian society (London 1796. v3)
Lipperheide 2685

Camena d'Almeida, Pierre Joseph, and Jongh, Francis de
L'armée russe d'après photographies instantanées exécutés par Mm. de Jongh frères. Texte et notices historiques par P. Camena d'Almeida et F. de Jongh. Paris, Imprimeries Lemercier [1896]
151p. illus. 8 col.pl. F.
Colas 510

Cameos and inspiration jewellery. Good, Edward

Camerino, J. G.
Collection J. G. Camerino, Paris: Les points de Venise. Point de Venise relief, point de Venise plat à l'aiguille et aux fuseaux, point à la rose. Venise gothique, broderie de Venise sur toile, point de Burano. Paris, Librairie des arts décoratifs [1907]
1 l. 40pl. F.

Cameron, Verney Lovett
Across Africa. New York, Harper 1877
xvi,508p. front. illus. pl. fold.map, 4 facsim.(3 fold.) O.
LC 17-11500

Camesina, Albert
Die ältesten glasgemälde des chorherrenstiftes Klosterneuburg und die bildnisse der Babenberger in der Cistercienserabtei Heiligenkreuz. Wien, Kaiserl. königl. Hof- und staatsdruckerei 1857
34p. 22 illus. 27pl. F.
Reprinted from the *Jahrbuch* der k. k. Central-Commission zur erforschung und erhaltung der baudenkmale
Costume figures from thirteenth century windows
Lipperheide 388. LC 11-7113

(illus.) Lind, Karl. Ein antiphonarium

Camino, Charles, and Régamey, Frederic
Costumes suédois; dessinés par Mm. Camino et Regamey d'après les dessins originaux communiqués par M. de

Camino, Charles, and Régamey, F.—*Continued*
D....l, et gravées par Charles Geoffroy. Paris, Aux bureau des journeaux Les modes parisiennes 187-?
20 col.pl. F.
Colas 511. Costume index. Lipperheide 1052

Campagnes des français sous le consulat & l'empire. Vernet, Carle, and others

The **campaign** in India, 1857-58. Atkinson, G. F.

Campaigns of ... Arthur, Duke of Wellington ... from Seringapatam to ... Waterloo. Duplessi-Bertaux, Jean

Campaigns of the British army in Portugal. L'Évêque, Henry

Campana, Cesare
(ed.) Savorgnano, Mario, conte di Belgrado. Arte militare terrestre, e maritima

Campania. See Italy—Campania

Campbell, *Lord* **Archibald**
The children of the mist; or, The Scottish clansmen in peace and war. Edinburgh, W. & A. K. Johnston 1890
55p. 1 pl. O.

Highland dress, arms and ornament. Westminster, A. Constable 1899
xv,176p. pl. O.

(ed.) [Craignish tales and others] ... Edited with notes on the war dress of the Celts. London, D. Nutt 1889
xv,98p. front. 1 illus. pl. O. (Waifs and strays of Celtic tradition. Argyllshire series. I)
Illustrated with a picture of Irish soldiers' from a drawing by Dürer, and effigies of knights from tombs in Oransay, Iona and Queen's county, Ireland. Page 84-96 on the war dress of the Celt
LC 1-5312

Campbell, Donald Maclaine
Java: past & present; a description of ... its ancient history, people, antiquities, and products. London, W. Heinemann [1915]
2v. front. pl. ports. fold.map, plan. Q.
Paged continuously. Edited by G. C. Wheeler
Costume index. LC 16-10490

Campbell, James
Excursions, adventures, and field-sports in Ceylon; its commercial and military importance, and numerous advantages to the British emigrant. By Lieut.-Colonel James Campbell. London, T. and W. Boone 1843
2v. fronts.(fold.maps) pl.(part col.) O.
LC 5-13879

Campbell, Jean
(illus.) Shakespeare, William. The Swan Shakespeare

Campbell, Sir John
A personal narrative of thirteen years' service amongst the wild tribes of Khondistan. London, Hurst and Blackett 1864
320p. front. pl. O.
Plates show dress and weapons of the Khonds, a tribe of Orissa, India

Camper, Petrus
Abhandlung über die beste form der schuhe; aus der Französischen [tr. von Trost] Berlin, F. Nicolai 1783
103p. 1 pl. O.
German translation of his: *Dissertation.* First published at Vienna in 1782
Colas 513. Lipperheide 1736

Dissertation sur la meilleure forme des souliers. No place, [1781]
80p. 1 pl. D.
Colas 512

Campfire and battle-field. Johnson, Rossiter

Campillo, J.
(illus.) México y sus alrededores

Campion, Samuel S.
Delightful history of Ye gentle craft: an illustrated history of feet costume ... frontispiece by George Cruikshank; 2d. ed. rev. and enl. Northampton, Taylor 1876
84p. fold.pl. O.

Campo, Antonio
Cremona fedelissima citta, et nobilissima colonia di Romani. Cremona, In casa dell' istesso auttore 1585
lxxviii,120p. 34 illus. 1 pl. F.
Pictures of the members of the city government of Cremona
Lipperheide 1241

Camps and trails in China. Andrews, R. C., and Andrews, Mrs Y. B.

Canada. Geological survey
Memoir 91. See Hawkes, E. W. The Labrador Eskimo

Canada
Carpenter, F. G. Canada and Newfoundland. 1924

Carrel, Frank, and Feiczewicz, Louis. The Quebec tercentenary commemorative history. 1908

Illustrations of the historical ball given by ... the Earl and Countess of Aberdeen in the Senate Chamber, Ottawa, 17th Feb. 1896. 1896

See also Indians of Canada; also subdivision Canada under Military costume

Quebec

Chambers, William. Things as they are in America. 1854

Canada. Hamilton, Louis

Canada and Newfoundland. Carpenter, F. G.

The **Canarian.** Bontier, Pierre and Le Verrier, Jean

Canary islands
Benzoni, Girolamo. History of the New world ... shewing his travels in America, from A. D. 1541 to 1556: with some particulars of the island of Canary. 1857

Bontier, Pierre and Le Verrier, Jean. The Canarian; or, Book of the conquest and conversion of the Canarians in the year 1402 by Messire Jean de Benthencourt. 1872.

Verneau, René. Cinq années de séjour aux îles Canaries. 1891

Les **cancans.** Compte-Calix, F. C.

Candeur et bonté. Legrand, Augustin

Candler, Edmund

The unveiling of Lhasa, by Edmund Candler. 3d impression. London, E. Arnold 1905

xvi,304p. col.front. pl. fold.map. O.
LC 5-8759

Canel, Alfred

Histoire de la barbe et des cheveux en Normandie. Rouen, A. Lebrument 1859

86p. D.
Lipperheide 1707

Canes, walking-sticks, etc.

Cazal, R. M. Essai historique, anecdotique sur la parapluie, l'ombrelle et la canne et sur leur fabrication. 1844

Fernand-Michel, F. F. The story of the stick in all ages and lands. 1875

Franklin, A. L. A. La vie privée d'autrefois; arts et métiers, modes, moeurs, usages des Parisiens du XII. au XVIII. siècle. [v 18]

Hints to the bearers of walking sticks and umbrellas. 1908

Jeaffreson, J. C. A book about doctors. 1861

Cannon, Richard

Historical records of the British army; comprising the history of every regiment in Her Majesty's service. London, Printed by authority 1837-53

70v. col.pl. O.

Each volume is concerned with one regiment and plates show flags and uniforms. The series was compiled by order of the Adjutant general's office. Volume numbers below are as given in the press marks: 8829. C. 1-70

[v 1] Life guards. 1660 to 1835; [v2] The Cape mounted riflemen; [v3] Royal regiment of horse guards, or Oxford Blues, from the first establishment to 1847, by Edmund Packe; [v4] The first, or Kings regiment of dragoon guards, 1685-1836; 2d ed to 1838; [v5] The second or Queen's regiment of dragoon guards (Queen's Bays) 1685-1837. [v6] Third or Prince of Wales' regiment of dragoon guards. 1685-1838. [v7] Fourth, or Royal Irish regiment of dragoon guards. 1685-1838. [v8] Fifth, or Princess Charlotte of Wales regiment of dragoon guards. 1685-1838. [v9] Sixth regiment of dragoon guards, or Carabineers. 1685-1839; [v10] Seventh, or Princess Royal's regiment of dragoon guards. 1688-1839; [v 11] First, or Royal regiment of dragoons. From its formation to 1839; [v 12] Second, or Royal North British dragoons, 1840; [v 13] The Third, or King's Own regiment of light dragoons. 1685-1846 [1st ed to 1842]; [v 14] Fourth, or Queen's Own regiment of light dragoons, 1685-1846; [v 15] The Sixth, or Inniskilling regiment of dragoons. 1689-1843 [v 16] Same 1689-1846; [v 17] Seventh, or Queen's Own regiment of Hussars. 1690-1842; [v 18] Eighth, or the King's Royal Irish regiment of Hussars. 1693-1843; [v 19] Ninth, or Queen's Royal regiment of light dragoons; lancers. 1715-1841.

[v20] The Tenth, the Prince of Wales's Own Royal regiment of Hussars. 1715-1842. 1843. [21] Eleventh, or Prince Albert's Own regiment of Hussars. 1715-1842. [v22] Twelfth, or Prince of Wales' Royal regiment of lancers. 1715-1842; [v23] Thirteenth regiment of light dragoons.' 1715-1842; [v24] Fourteenth, or King's regiment of light dragoons. (LC 22-25660); [v25] Fifteenth, or King's regiment of light dragoons, Hussars. 1759-1841. [v26] Sixteenth, or Queen's regiment of light dragoons, lancers. 1759-1841; [v27] Seventeenth regiment of light dragoons, lancers. 1759-1841; [v28] First, or Royal regiment of foot ... to 1838; [v29] First, or Royal regiment of foot ... to 1846.

[v30] Second, or Queen's Royal regiment of foot. 1661-1837; [v31] Third regiment of foot, or the Buffs; [v32] Fourth, or King's Own regiment of foot. 1839; [v33] Fifth regiment of foot, or Northumberland fusiliers 1838; [v34] Sixth, or Royal First Warwickshire regiment or foot. 1674-1838; [v35] Seventh regiment, or Royal fusiliers. 1847. [v36] Eighth, or King's regiment of foot, 1685-1841 (LC 26-19802 2d ed.); [v37] Ninth, or East Norfolk regiment of foot. 1848; [v38] Tenth, or North Lincolnshire regiment of foot. 1847; [v39] Eleventh, or North Devon regiment of foot. 1685-1845.

[v40] Twelth, or East Suffolk regiment of foot. 1685-1848; [v41] Thirteenth, First Somerset, or Prince Albert's regiment of light infantry; 1685-1848; [v42] Fourteenth or Buckinghamshire regiment. 1685-1845; [v43] Fifteenth, or Yorkshire East Riding regiment of foot. 1685-1848; [v44] Sixteenth, or Bedfordshire regiment of foot. 1688-1848; [v45] Seventeenth, or Leicestershire regiment of foot. 1688-1848; [v46] Eighteenth, or Royal North British fusiliers. 1678-1849. [v47] Nineteenth, or first Yorkshire, North Riding regiment of foot. 1688-1848; [v48] Twentieth, or East Devonshire regiment of foot. 1688-1848; [v49] Twenty-first regiment or Royal North British fusiliers. 1678-1849; [v50] Twenty-second, or Cheshire regiment of foot. 1689-1849; [v51] Twenty-third or Royal Welsh fusiliers. 1689-1850; [v52] Thirty-first, or Huntingdonshire regiment of foot, 1702-1850. Marine corps. 1664-1748; [v53] Thirty-fourth, or Cumberland regiment of foot. 1702-1844; [v54] Thirty-sixth, or Herefordshire regiment of foot. 1701-1852. 1852-1881 (LC A14-123) [v55] Thirty-ninth, or Dorsetshire regiment of foot. 1702-1853; [v56] Forty-second, or The Royal highland regiment of foot, The Black watch. 1729-1844; [v57] Forty-sixth, or South Devonshire regiment of foot. 1741-1851; [v58] Fifty-third, or Shropshire regiment of foot. 1755-1848; [v59] Fifth-sixth, or West Essex regiment of foot. 1755-1844.

[v60] Sixty-first, or South Gloucestershire regiment of foot. 1758-1844; [v61] Sixty-seventh, or South Hampshire regiment 1758-1849; [v62] Seventieth, or Surrey regiment of foot. 1758-1848; [v63] Seventy-first regiment, Highland light infantry. 1777-1852 (LC A14-124 [v64] Seventy-second regiment, or Duke of Albany's Own Highlanders. 1778-1848; [v65] Seventy-third regiment ... the second battalion of the Forty-second Royal Highlanders. 1780-1851; [v66] Seventy-fourth regiment, Highlanders. 1787-1850 (LC A14-125); [v67] Eighty-sixth, or Royal County Down regiment of foot. 1793-1842; [v68] Eighty-seventh regiment, or Royal Irish fusiliers. 1793-1853; [v69] Eighty-eighth regiment of foot, or Connaught rangers 1793-1837; [v70] Ninety-second regiment, originally termed "The Gordon Highlanders" and numbered the hundredth regiment. 1794-1851

Colas 514. Lipperheide 2268. LC (see contents note)

Canonia Rohrensis documents, monumentis et observationibus historico-criticis. Dalhammer, Patritius

Canons (Members of chapters)

Du Moulinet, Claude. Figures de différents habits de chanoines réguliers en ce siècle. Avec un discours sur les habits anciens et modernes des chanoines tant séculiers que réguliers. 1666

Canstein, E. R. von. See Warnecke, Friedrich, ed. Sammlung historischer bildnisse

Canteen women

French army

Lalaisse, Hippolyte. L'armée française et ses cantinières. ca1857

Lalaisse, Hyppolyte. Types de l'armée française et de ses cantinières. 1860

Maurice, C. Les cantinières de France. 184-?

Cantemir, Dumitru

The history of the growth and decay of the Othman empire ... Written originally in Latin, by Demetrius Cantemir, late prince of Moldavia. Tr. into English, from the author's own manuscript, by N. Tindal ... Adorn'd with the heads of the Turkish emperors, ingraven from copies taken from originals in the grand seignor's palace, by the late sultan's painter. London, James, John, and P. Knapton 1734-35

2v. in 1. 22 port. (incl.front.) fold.plan. F.

Portraits show the emperors seated in the Turkish fashion, which shows the costume about three-quarter length

Contents: pt 1 Containing the growth of the Othman empire, from the reign of Othman the founder, to the reign of Mahomet IV. that is, from the year 1300, to the siege of Vienna, in 1683; pt2 The history of the decay of the Othman empire, from the reign of Mahomet IV. to the reign of Ahmed III (to 1711)

The German translation *Geschichte des osmanischen reichs ... nach seinem anwachse und abnehmen* (Hamburg, C. Herold 1745) contains the same portraits

Lipperheide 1417 (German ed.). LC 5-2485

Les **cantinières** de France. Maurice, C.

Cantwell, Andre Samuel Michel

(tr.) Alexander, William. Histoire des femmes

[**Canu**]

[Collection des uniformes français. Paris, Canu 1816-25]

89pl. Q.

Above title is found on the plates: La Garde royale, infanterie, tambour. Another edition, keeping the date 1816, has been published by the Vve. Turgis. The plates have been altered in accordance with the change in costume for the period

Colas 515

Canziani, Estella

Costumes, moeurs et légendes de Savoie. Adapté de l'anglais par A. Van Gennep. Chambéry, 1920

96p. 54 col.pl. Q.

English translation of *Costumes, traditions and songs of Savoy*

Colas 517

Costumes, traditions and songs of Savoy. London, Chatto & Windus 1911

179p. col.mounted front. illus. col.pl. (46 mounted) map, facsim. Q. 21s

Colas 516. Costume index. LC 12-15

Through the Apennines and the lands of the Abruzzi; landscape and peasant life, described and drawn by Estella Canziani. Cambridge [Eng.] W. Heffer & sons 1928

xiv,339p. illus. 24 mounted pl. (part col. incl.front.) O.

Each plate accompanied by guard sheet with descriptive letterpress

Costume index. LC 29-9908

Canziani, Estella, and Rohde, Eleanour

Piedmont. London, Chatto & Windus 1913

203p. 48 col.pl. Q. 21s

Costume index

Caonersin, Wilhelm. See Caorsin, Wilhelm

Caorsin, Wilhelm

Historia von Rhodis wie ritterlich sie sich gehaltẽ mit dem tyrannischen keiser Machomet uss Türckyẽ ... Wilhelm Caonersin cãtzler zü Rhodis hatt dise hystory gedichtet ... Johãnes Adelphus Argẽtiñ ... hat sie in teutsche zungẽ transfferiert uñ interpretiert. Strassburg, M. Flach 1513

67 l. 34 illus. F.

The woodcuts are partly copies from the Latin original (Ulm, Beger 1496) They show a knight of the Order of St John of Jerusalem and scenes from campaigns of this Order against the Turks

Lipperheide 1888

Caoursin, Wilhelm. See Caorsin, Wilhelm

The **cap** and gown in America. Leonard, G. C.

Capart, Jean

L'art égyptien; choix de documents, accompagnés d'indications bibliographiques. Bruxelles, Vromant [etc] 1909

31p. 100pl. O.

LC 9-10304

L'art et la parure féminine dans l'ancienne Egypte. Bruxelles, Vromant 1907

20p. 7pl. Q.

Reprint from the *Annales de la Société d'archéologie de Bruxelles* v21, 1907

Donation d'antiquités égyptiennes aux Musées royaux de Bruxelles. Bruxelles, Vromant [1911]

51p. 1 illus. 22pl. (1 fold.) D.

Reprinted from the *Bulletin* of the Musées royaux des arts décoratifs et industriels 1908-1909

LC 28-20698

Egyptian art; introductory studies. Tr. from the French by Warren R. Dawson. London, G. Allen & Unwin [1923]

179p. front. LXIV pl. on 32 l. O.

Contains bibliographies

A translation of the introductory chapters of his *Leçons sur l'art égyptien*

LC 23-7188

Capellan, Antonio

Chronologia summor. romrum. pontificum, in quâ habentur verae eor. effigies ex antiqis numismatib. et picturis delineatae, ac nomna cognomna patriae, anni, menses, ac dies, creatnis pontificat. obit ac sedes vactes, ab Anastasio, Lvitprando, Panvinio, Baronio, et Ciaconio, excerpta. No place, ca1800

17pl. (port.) F.

The portraits show the popes up to Pius VI

Lipperheide 1816

Capes and cloaks

Caylus, A. C. P., comte de. Les manteaux; recueil. 1746

Hispanic society of America. Men's capes and cloaks: La Alberca, Salamanca. 1931

Wirsching, Joseph. Die manteltracht im mittelalter. 1915

Capiaumont, A.
Manuel d'escrime à la baïonette, simplifiée. Liège, F. Oudart 1848
44p. 18pl. O.
Lipperheide 2990

Capitaine, Joseph
(ed.) Women

Capitan, Louis
La préhistoire; ed. rev. et augm. par Michel Faguet. Paris, Payot 1931
223p. illus.(incl.maps) 16pl. on 8 l. O. (Bibliothèque scientifique)
Bibliography p[214]-17
An edition was published in 1922 as no28 of the Collection Payot. (157p. illus. incl. map, D.)
LC 23-8008 (1922 ed.)

Capitani illustri. See Totti, Pompilio. Ritratti et elogii di Capitani illustri; also Capriolo, A. Ritratti

Caplin, Jessie F.
The lace book. New York, Macmillan 1932
xi,166p. front. illus. port. O.
Bibliography: p163-64
LC 32-25123

Capoferro, R.
Gran simulacro dell' arte e dell' uso della scherma di Ridolfo Capo Ferro. Siena, S. Marchetti 1610
67 l. 45 illus. Q.
Lipperheide 2955

Capparoni, Giuseppe
Raccolta degli ordini religiosi che esistono nella città di Roma. Disegnati ed incisi all'acquaforte da Giuseppe Capparoni. Roma, Presso G. Antonelli 1826
54 l. 54 col.pl. O.
Italian and French in opposite columns. Eighteen of the plates are copied after Ferrari's *Costumi ecclesiastici*
Colas 518. Lipperheide 1877. LC 13-14597

Raccolta degli ordini religiosi delle vergini a Dio dedicate. Roma, Presso G. Antonelli 1828
60 l. 60 col.pl. O.
Italian and French in opposite columns. Six of the plates are copied after Ferrari's *Costumi ecclesiastici*
Colas 519. Lipperheide 1878. LC 13-14596

Raccolta della gerarchia ecclesiastica considerata nelle vesti sagre, e civili usate da quelli li quali la compongono. Disegnata ed incisa da Giuseppe Capparoni. Roma, G. Antonelli 1827
2v. 100 col.pl. O.
Some of the plates are copied from Ferrari's *Costumi ecclesiastici*
Colas 520. Lipperheide 1819. LC 13-14598

Capricci di varie figure. Callot, Jacques

Capricci di varie figure. Gerardini, Melchion

Le **Caprice;** journal de la lingerie, revue des modes, des théâtres et des arts. Nov. 1836-1854. Paris
Col.pl. O.
Publication suspended Dec. 1837-1840
First series 1836-37 had subtitle: journal des modes contenant les articles sur le costume. . . 2.sér. 1841-mars 1844; 3.sér. avr. 1844-54
Colas 521

Les **caprices.** See Callot, Jacques. Capricci di varie figure

Caprichos inventados y grabados al agua forte. Goya y Lucientes, F. J. de

Caprin, Giuseppe
I nostri nonni; pagina della vita triestina dal 1800 al 1830. Trieste, Stab. art. tip., G. Caprin 1888
234p. 15 illus. 4pl. O.
Bibliography p231-36
Lipperheide 884

Tempi andanti; pagine della vita triestina, 1830-1848. Trieste, Stab. art. tip., G. Caprin 1891
527p. 113 illus. O.
Illustrations are by E. Croci, N. Girotto, etc. After E. Bosa, L. F. Cassas, and others. Many show costume
Lipperheide 885

Capriolo, Aliprando
Ritratti di cento capitani illustri con li lor fatti in guerra brevemente scritti. Roma, Thomassino & Turpino per D. Gigliotti 1600
111 l. 100 ports. Q.
From Kaiser Frederick I to Stephen Bathory, king of Poland. Pictures of Italians predominate. The colophon dated 1596
Lipperheide 1244

Capus, Guillaume
À travers la Bosnie et l'Herzégovine; études et impressions de voyage. Paris, Hachette 1896
350p. illus. fold.map. F.

Caracci, Anibale. See Carracci, Annibale

[**Caraccioli, Louis Antoine de**]
Le livre à la mode. [Paris, Duchesne 1759]
xxii,86p. O.
Printed in green. A satire on the fickleness of fashion
New edition published eight days later, printed in red (LC 18-21586) German edition, printed in green, published in 1760 under title: *Das mode-buch,* translated by E. G. Küster
Lipperheide 3467-69

Le livre de quatre couleurs. [Paris, Duchesne 1760]
xxxiv,114p. O.
Printed in orange, green, brown and red
Lipperheide 3470

Caractères dramatiques ou portraits divers du théâtre anglois. Londres, R. Sayer 1770
38 col.pl. D.
For list of plates see Colas's *Bibliographie*
Colas 523

Caragueuz en Turquie. See Fleury, Jules. Le musée secret de la caricature

Caran d'Ache, Emmanuel Poiré, known as
Caran d'Ache, the supreme; with an introduction by H. M. Bateman. London, Methuen [1933]
vii p. incl. front. 79pl. on 40 l. sq.Q.
Many examples of his work show French costume of the nineteenth century
LC 35-24231

Nos soldats du siècle. Paris, E. Plon, Nourrit [1889]
24 col.pl. Q.
French army uniforms 1789-1889. Plates printed on both sides
Lipperheide 2353

Caravanne du sultan à la Mecque. Vien, J. M.

Cardalucius, Johannes Hiskias
(ed.) Ercker, Lazarus. Aula subterranea domina dominantium subdita subditorum

Carderera y Solano, Valentín
Iconografía española. Coleccion de retratos, estatuas, mausoleos y demas monumentos inéditos de reyes, reinas, grandes capitanes, escritores, etc. desde el siglo XI hasta el XVII, copiados de los originales. Madrid, Impr. de R. Campuzano 1855-64
2v. 92pl. (part col.) F.
Pictures of statues, monuments, etc. showing kings, queens, military officers, writers, and others, from the eleventh to the seventeenth century
Costume index. LC 10-4454

Cardinals
Conlin, J. R. Roma sancta sive Benedicti XIII. 1726-30
Lonigo, Michel. Delle vesti purpuree d'altri colori con quali adorna la dignità cardinalitia. 1623

Cards, Costume on. See Playing cards

Carey, William Paulet
Critical description of the procession of Chaucer's pilgrims to Canterbury, painted by Thomas Stothard. London, Cadell & Davies 1808
77p. O.
Stothard's painting "The procession of the Canterbury pilgrims" is in the National gallery, London

Caricature and satire
Damourette. Penseurs & propos; grand album de caricatures. ca.1855
Flögel, K. F. Floegels Geschichte des grotesk komischen. 1888

See also names of countries and periods with subhead Caricature and satire, e.g. Eighteenth century—Caricature and satire; England—18th century—Caricature and satire

La **caricature** [morale, religieuse, littéraire et scénique]; journal fondé et dirigé par C. Philipon. 1-10 (1830/31-1835) Paris, 1830-35
10v. pl. F.
Published weekly. Volume 1-10 also called année 1-5
Suppressed with tome 10, 1835

Caricatures. Isabey, J. B.

Caricatures anti-cholériques. Bassaget, P. N.

The **caricaturist's** scrap book. Heath, Henry

Carleton, George Washington
Our artist in Cuba, fifty drawings on wood; leaves from the sketch-book of a traveler, during the winter of 1864-5. New York, Carleton [etc.] 1665 [i. e. 1865]
viii p. 50pl. D.
Letterpress on plates
LC 3-11693

Our artist in Peru; leaves from the sketch-book of a traveller, during the winter of 1865-6. New York, Carleton [etc.] 1866
50p. 50 illus. D.
LC 11-25507

Carleton, William
Traits and stories of the Irish peasantry; new ed. With an autobiographical introduction, explanatory notes, and numerous illustrations on wood and steel, by Harvey, Phiz, Franklin, Macmanus, Gilbert, and other artists of eminence ... London, G. Routledge 1852
2v. fronts. illus. pl. O.
LC 6-20152

Carlier, Alfred
Histoire du costume civil (de 80 avant J.-C. à 1930 après J.-C.) en France; trois cent vingt costumes. Paris, A. Lesot [1931]
2p.l. 32 col.pl. F.
Colas 527. LC 32-13848

Carlisle, E. M. F.
A practical method of dress cutting, especially designed for technical classes, schools, and self teaching. Part 1, Dressmaking for adults. Westminster, Roxburghe press [1893]
100p. D.

Carlyle, Thomas
Sartor Resartus: The life and opinions of Herr Teufelsdröckh. New York, Scribner's 1897
xxii,250p. front. (port.) O. (Centenary ed. v 1)
A philosophical treatise on clothes. Many editions

Carmen de motibus siculis. See Petrus, de Ebulo. De rebus siculis carmen

Carmichael, Montgomery
In Tuscany; Tuscan towns, Tuscan types and the Tuscan tongue. New York, E. P. Dutton; London, J. Murray 1901
355p. front. illus. pl. ports. maps, facsim. O.
LC 2-8829

Carmontelle, Louis Carrogis, dit
Jardin de Monceau. Paris, M. Delafosse 1779
12p. 18pl. F.
Lipperheide 1130

Il **carnavale** di Roma. Pinelli, Bartolommeo

Carnegie institution of Washington. See Textile arts of the Guatemalan natives

Carnegie institution of Washington. News service bulletin. See note under Shattuck, G. C. The peninsula of Yucatan

Carnet de La Sabre-tache; revue militaire rétrospective publiée par la société La Sabretache. v 1-9, 1893-1901; ser. 2 v 1, 1902+ Paris, Berger-Levrault 1893+
Illus. pl. (part col.) O.
Published bi-monthly. Current 1937. Publication suspended July 1914-July 1919
Contains sketches and plates which show uniforms
Colas 529

Il **carnevale** di Roma, 1820. Mörner, Hjalmar

Il **carnevale** Italiano mascherato. Bertelli, Francesco

Die **carnevals-freuden,** oder Kleines ideenmagazin zu geistreichen und leicht ausführbaren masken. Nürnberg, F. Campe 1839
66p. 24 col.pl. O.
Colas 531. Lipperheide 3176

Carnicero, Antonio
Colleccion de las principales suertes de una corrida de toros. Madrid, Libreria di Quiroga 1790
12 col.pl. F.
Lipperheide 2860

Carniola. See Yugoslavia—Carniola

Caroline Islands
Christian, F. W. The Caroline Islands. 1899

Carolus Clusius Atrebatensis. See L'Écluse, Charles de

Caroso, Marco Fabrizio
Il ballarino. Venetia, F. Ziletti 1581
2v. illus. Q.
First edition. Plates engraved by Giacomo Franco
Colas 532. Lipperheide 3055

Nobiltà di dame; libro, altra volta, chiamato Il ballarino: nuouamente dal proprio auttore corretto, ampliato. Venetia, Presso il Muschio 1600
10p.l. 370p. 37 illus. Q.
The illustrations consist of 10 full-page engravings by Giacomo Franco; 8 of them, figures of dancers, occur from 2 to 7 times each
The second edition of *Il ballarino.* Also published in 1605. An edition (evidently a reissue of the 2d) is entitled: *Raccolta di varij balli fatti in occorenze di nozze, e festini* (Roma, G. Facciotti 1630)
Colas 533-535. Lipperheide 3056. LC 30-3284

Das **caroussel** welches am 27. Oktober 1846 ... in Stuttgart abgehalten wurde. Hacklaender, F. W.

Caroussel zur anwesenheit J. J. K. K. majestäten in Prag den 5. juni 1854. Franceschini, Girolamo

Carpenter, Frank George
Alaska, our northern wonderland. Garden City, N.Y., Doubleday, Page 1923
xv,319p. front. pl. ports. fold.maps. O. (Carpenter's world travels) $4
Costume index. LC 23-26131

Along the Paraná and the Amazon, Paraguay, Uruguay, Brazil. Garden City, N.Y., Doubleday, Page 1925
xiv,314p. front. pl. O. (Carpenter's world travels)
LC 25-10888

The Alps, the Danube and the Near East; Switzerland, Czechoslovakia, Austria, Hungary, Yugoslavia, Bulgaria, Rumania, Italy, Greece, Turkey. Garden City, N.Y., Doubleday, Page 1924
xiv,310p. front. pl. ports. O. (Carpenter's world travels) $4
Costume index. LC 24-20629

Australia, New Zealand and some islands of the South seas; Australia, New Zealand, Thursday island, the Samoas, New Guinea, the Fijis, and the Tongas. Garden City, N.Y., Doubleday, Page 1924
xiii,294p. front. pl. O. (Carpenter's world travels) $4
Costume index. LC 24-10230

Cairo to Kisumu; Cairo—the Sudan—Kenya colony. Garden City, N.Y., Doubleday, Page 1923
xiv,313p. front. pl. fold.maps. 23½cm. (Carpenter's world travels) $4
Bibliography: p305-07
Costume index. LC 23-26432

Canada and Newfoundland. Garden City, N.Y., Doubleday, Page 1924
xiv,311p. incl. front. pl. O. (Carpenter's world travels)
LC 24-26448

China. Garden City, N.Y., Doubleday, Page 1925
xiv,310p. front. pl. O. (Carpenter's world travels) $4
Costume index. LC 25-19730

France to Scandinavia; France, Belgium, Holland, Denmark, Norway and Sweden. Garden City, N.Y., Doubleday, Page 1923
xiii,273p. front. pl. ports. 2 fold.maps. O. (Carpenter's world travels) $4
Costume index. LC 23-17546

From Bangkok to Bombay; Siam, French Indo-China, Burma, Hindustan. Garden City, N.Y., Doubleday, Page 1924
xiv,311p. front. pl. O. (Carpenter's world travels) $4
Costume index. LC 25-22

From Tangier to Tripoli; Morocco, Algeria, Tunisia, Tripoli, and the Sahara. Garden City, N.Y., Doubleday, Page 1923
xiv,277p. front. pl. fold.map. O. (Carpenter's world travels) $4
Bibliography: p270-72
Costume index. LC 23-2190

The Holy Land and Syria. Garden City, N.Y., Doubleday, Page 1922
xiv,297p. front. pl. fold.maps. O. (Carpenter's world travels) $4
Bibliography: p289-90
Costume index. LC 22-24097

How the world is clothed. New York, Cincinnati [etc.] American book company c1908
340p. illus. D. (His: Readers on commerce and industry)
LC 8-30026

Japan and Korea. Garden City, N.Y., Doubleday, Page 1925
xiv,310p. front. pl. O. (Carpenter's world travels) $4
Costume index. LC 25-26895

Java and the East Indies; Java, Sumatra, Celebes, the Moluccas, New Guinea, Borneo, and the Malay peninsula. Garden City, N.Y., Doubleday, Page 1923
xv,280p. front. pl. 2 fold.maps. O. (Carpenter's world travels) $4
Bibliography: p270-73
Costume index. LC 23-13278

Lands of the Caribbean. Garden City, N.Y., Doubleday, Page 1925
xiv,309p. front. pl. O. (Carpenter's world travels)
"The Canal zone, Panama, Costa Rica, Nicaragua, Salvador, Honduras, Guatemala, Cuba, Jamaica, Haiti, Santo Domingo, Porto Rico, and the Virgin islands." Subtitle
LC 26-2175

Mexico. Garden City, N.Y., Doubleday, Page 1924
xiii,287p. front.(port.) pl. O. (Carpenter's world travels)
LC 24-6666

South America, social, industrial, and political; a twenty-five-thousand-mile journey in search of information. Akron, O., New York [etc.] The Saalfield pub. co. 1900
625p. illus. pl. front. Q.
LC 0-6886

Through the Philippines and Hawaii. Garden City, N.Y., Doubleday, Page 1925
xiv,314p. front. pl. ports. O. (Carpenter's world travels)
LC 25-9410

Carpenter, Frank George—*Continued*

Uganda to the Cape; Uganda, Zanzibar, Tanganyika territory, Mozambique, Rhodesia, Union of South Africa. Garden City, N.Y., Doubleday, Page 1924
xiv,263p. front. pl. O. (Carpenter's world travels)
LC 24-26946

Carpenter, Frank George, and Harmon, Dudley

The British isles and the Baltic states; England, Wales, Scotland, Northern Ireland, the Irish free state, Germany, Poland, Latvia, Russia, Esthonia, and Finland. Garden City, N.Y., Doubleday, Page 1926
xiv,320p. front. pl. maps. O. (Carpenter's world travels)
The chapters relating to England, Wales, Scotland, Northern Ireland and the Irish free state were prepared by Dudley Harmon, who visited these countries after the death of Frank G. Carpenter
LC 26-10537

Carpenter, Margaret Boyd

The child in art. London, Methuen [1906]
200p. front. L pl. O.
Includes many pictures of the Madonna
LC 7-28524

Carr, Lucien

Dress and ornaments of certain American Indians. Worcester, Mass., C. Hamilton 1897
76p. O.
From the Proceedings of the American antiquarian society April, 1897
LC 17-22223

Carracci, Annibale

Le arti di Bologna; originale de Anibale Caracci per utile di tutti li virtuosi e le intendenti della professione della pittura e disegno. [Romae, 1646]
3 l. 80pl. F.
Second printing of the plates in *Diverse figure*
Colas 537

Le arti di Bologna disegnate da Annibale Caracci ed intagliate da Simone Guilini coll'assistenza di Alessandro Algardi, aggiuntavi la vita del sudetto Annibale Caracci. Roma, G. Roisecco. 1740
8p. 80pl. port. F.
Issued in portfolio. Third printing of the plates in *Diverse figure* and described by Colas as inferior to the others
Colas 538. Lipperheide 1290. LC 33-3363

L'arti per via; disegnate ... dal sig. G. M. Mitelli, Franco Curti, intagliò. Bologna, G. Longhi ca1740
40pl. F.
Plates copied from *Di Bologna*
Lipperheide 1292

Di Bologna, l'arti per via d'Anibal Caraci; disegnate, intagliate ... da Gioseppe Ma. Mitelli. Roma, G. J. Rossi 1660
1 l. 40pl. F.
Each plate shows a street vender of Bologna, is signed with the monogram of Mitelli, and is accompanied by a four line verse. Not a replica of the series of engravings in *Le arti di Bologna.*—Colas (adapted)
Colas 539. Lipperheide 1291

Divers ouvrages de belles figures, peints, dessinées ou gravées par divers maîtres tres-renomées, savoir: A. Carats ... Leide, 1690?
F.
Edited by P. van der Aa

Diverse figure al numero di ottanta. Roma, L. Grigniani 1646
81pl. F.
Colas 536. Lipperheide 1289. LC 14-16263

Carracci, Augustin

(illus.) Campo, Antonio. Cremona fedelissima citta

Carrache

(engr.) Compte-Calix, F. C. Les modes parisiennes sous le Directoire

Carramolino, Juan Martin

Discursos leidos ante la Real academia de ciencias morales y politicas en la recepcion publica. Madrid, Impr. del Colegio de sordo-mudos y de ciegos 1868
51p. O.
"Contestacion del Excmo. Sr. D. Antonio Benavides": p[31]-51
LC 10-21382

Carranza, Alonso

Rogacion en detestacion de los grandes abusos en los traxes y adornos nuevamente introducidos en España. Madrid, Impr. de M. de Quiñones 1636
Half-title: Discurso contra malos trages y adornos lascivos
56 l. 19½x14½cm.
LC 34-41547

Carrara, Francesco

La Dalmazia descritta; con 48 tavole miniate rappresentanti i principali costumi nazionali. Zara, Fratelli Battara 1846
192p. 24 col.pl. Q.
The work was not completed. Lithographs are by Jocosi. Text on the plates is in Croatian, Italian and German. For a separate printing of 20 of the plates see Jocosi's *Costumi*
Colas 540. Lipperheide 882

Carré, Jean Baptiste Louis

Panoplie, ou réunion de tout ce qui a trait à la guerre, depuis l'origine de la nation française jusqu'à nos jours. Chaalons-sur-Marne, Pinteville-Bouchard; Paris, Fuchs 1795
558p. 41pl. Q.
Title page is marked: Tome premier, but the work is complete
Colas 541. Lipperheide 2403

Carré, Léon

(illus.) Uzanne, L. O. Les parfums et les fards à travers les âges

Carré de Montgeron, Louis Basile. See Montgeron, L. B. C. de

Carrel, Frank, and Feiczewicz, Louis

The Quebec tercentenary commemorative history; comp. and ed. by Frank Carrel and Louis Feiczewicz; rev. by E. T. D. Chambers, with introduction by Dr. A. G. Doughty. Quebec, The Daily telegraph printing house 1908
176p. illus.(incl.ports.) col.pl. F.
LC 9-2247

Carrington-Peirce, P.
A handbook of court and hunting swords, 1660-1820. London, B. Quaritch 1937
100p. front. illus. O.
LC 37-39528

Carrogis, Louis. See Carmontelle, L. C. dit

[**Carrousel,** geritten in Potsdam am 13. Juli 1829] Lithogr. von Emil Pracht. Leipzig, C. C. Böhme n.d.
11 col.pl. F.
Celebration in honor of the birthday of the Empress Charlotte
Lipperheide 2540

Das **carroussel** zu Wien 1894; festblatt herausgegeben von Comité des carroussels. Wien, Steyrermühl [1894]
24p. 27 illus. 1 pl. Q.
Lipperheide 2843

Carruthers, Alexander Douglas Mitchell
Unknown Mongolia; a record of travel and exploration in north-west Mongolia and Dzungaria ... with three chapters on sport by J. H. Miller. 2d ed. London, Hutchinson 1914
2v. fronts. illus. pl. (part fold.) maps. O.
Paged continuously
Bibliography: v2 p635-39
LC 20-7104

Cars, Laurens
(engr.) Boucher, François, illus. Les oeuvres de Molière

Carson, William English
Mexico; the wonderland of the south. Rev. ed. New York, Macmillan 1914
xiii,449p. front. illus. pl. ports. map. O. $2.50, o.p.
First edition 1909
Costume index. LC 14-4204

Carta, Maria Stella
Tessuti fogge e decorazioni nell' abito muliebre in Grecia e a Roma. Palermo, A. Trìmarchi [1934]
62p. pl. Q. (Saggi e studi critici. n2)
Bibliographical footnotes

Carta Raspi, Raimondo
Costumi sardi. Cagliari, Fondazione Il Nuraghe 1932?
48p. front. illus. 3 col.pl. O.
Bibliography: p47

Cartailhac, Émile, and Breuil, Henri
La caverne d'Altamira. See note under Breuil, Henri, and Obermaier, Hugo. The cave of Altamira

Cartarius, Marius
Icones operum misericordiae; cum Julii Roscii Hortini sententiis et explicationibus. Roma, B. Grassi 1586
2v. 16 illus. F.
Lipperheide 1242

Carter, Howard, and Mace, Arthur Cruttenden
The tomb of Tut.ankh.Amen, discovered by the late Earl of Carnarvon and Howard Carter. London, New York Cassell 1923-33
3v. front. illus.(incl. plan, facsim.) pl. ports. O.
Illustrations, from photographs by Harry Burton, show costume and jewelry of ancient Egypt
LC 24-3985

Carter, John
Specimens of English ecclesiastical costume, from the earliest period down to the sixteenth century; selected from sculptures, paintings and brasses remaining in this kingdom. London, J. Nichols 1817
p386-96. 7pl. Q.
Separate from Fosbroke's *British monachism*
Colas 543

Specimens of the ancient sculpture and painting now remaining in England, from the earliest period to the reign of Henry VIII, consisting of statues, bas-reliefs, busts, sculptures; brasses ... etc. Plates drawn and etched by John Carter ... With critical and historical illustrations by Francis Douce [and others] New and improved ed., arranged in topographical order. London, H. G. Bohn 1838
2v. in 1. fronts. illus. cxv pl.(part col. part fold. incl.ports.) F.
"Designed to shew the rise and progress of sculpture and painting in England; to explain obscure and doubtful parts of history, and to preserve the portraits of great and eminent personages" Subtitle
The original edition was published in parts, 1780-94
Lipperheide 980 (1780 ed.) LC 30-18227

Carter, Matthew
Honor redivivus; or, The analysis of honor and armory; reprinted with many useful and necessary additions; and supply'd with the names and titles of honour of the present nobility of England, the bishops, baronets, members of Parliament, &c. 3d ed., adorned with several sculptures. London, A. Herringman 1673
351p. front. illus. pl. D.
Added t.-p., engr., has name of author. The plates are engraved by Gaywood and are reduced copies of the whole length figures in Milles, *Catalogue of honor*. They show creation robes of a Knight of the Garter, a baron, a viscount, an earl, a marquis and the Prince of Wales. Induction ceremonies are described
LC 15-18502

Carteret, John Grand-. See Grand-Carteret, John

Les **cartes** à jouer du XIV. au XX. siècle. Allemagne, Henry René d'

Carthage and Tunis. Sladen, D. B. W.

Cartland, Bernice M.
The dress of the ancient Egyptian. New York, Gilliss press 1916
6 l. illus. Q.
Reprint from the *Bulletin* of the Metropolitan museum of art, New York, Aug. and Sept. 1916

Carton, Charles Louis
Album descriptif des fêtes et cérémonies religieuses à l'occasion du jubilé de 700 ans du Saint-Sang, à Bruges, précédé de l'abrégé d'un essai sur l'histoire du Saint-Sang. Bruges, Daveluy 1850
29p. 28 col.pl. O.
Lipperheide 2809

Cartwright, J.
Selections of the costume of Albania and Greece with explanatory quotations from the poems of Lord Byron and Gally Knight. London, R. Havell [1822]
1 l. 12 col.pl. F.
Illustrations by Cartwright engraved by Robert Havell, and son
Colas 544

Cary, Elisabeth Luther
Honoré Daumier; a collection of his social and political caricatures, together with an introductory essay on his art. New York and London, G. P. Putnam 1907
185p. (incl. 75pl.) front.(port.) Q.
LC 7-36960

Casa, Giovanni della, abp.
Trattato de costumi, fatto nouvamente italiano & franceze a commune utilita di quelli che si dilettano dell' una & l'altra lingua, & delle buone creanze; Le Galathée, faict nouvellement en italien & français. Lione, A. de Marsilii 1573
83p. T.
Italian and French in parallel columns

Casalis, Eugène
The Basutos; or Twenty-three years in South Africa. London, J. Nisbet 1861
xix,355p. front. illus. map. pl. O.
Translation of his *Les Bassoutos* (Paris, Meyrueis 1859. LC 5-16932)

Casberg, Paul
(illus.) Osten-Sacken und von Rhein, Ottomar, freiherr von der. Deutschlands armee in feldgrauer kriegs- und friedens-uniform

Cases, Philippe, vicomte de Las. See Las Cases, Philippe, vicomte de

Casket. See Graham's American monthly magazine

Casorti, Louis
Der instructive tanzmeister für herren und damen. Ilmenau, B. F. Voigt 1826
x,110p. S.
Lipperheide 3095

Casotti, Giovanni Battista
Memorie istoriche della miracolosa immagine di Maria Vergine dell' Impruneta. Firenze, G. Manni 1714
2v. fronts. fold.pl. fold.plans. Q.
Appended to v2, with special t.-p. and separate paging: Allegri, G. M. *Esercizio di preparazione alla visita* (Firenze, 1714. 30p.) It is included in the "Tavola delle cose" and in the "Registro" at end
Plates show Italian festivals and processions
Lipperheide 2797. LC CA29-848

Cassagnac, Bernard Adolphe Granier de. See Granier de Cassagnac, B. A.

Cassal, Charles
Litterateurs français. See note under Langley, E. F. Romantic figures in pen and color

Casse de Saint Prosper, André Augustin. See Saint Prosper, A. A. C. de

Cassock and gown. Clayton, H. J.

Castel, Horace, comte de Viel. See Viel-Castel, Horace, comte de

Castell, graf
Die soldaten d. Königl. deutschen legion. Berlin, H. Barsdorf 1906
2p. 18 col.pl. O.

Castellan, Antoine Laurent
Moeurs, usages, costumes des Othomanes et abrégé de leur histoire. Paris, Nepveu 1812
6v. 72pl.(70 col.) D.
Plates are by Dalvimart, most of them reduced from those in William Alexander's *Costume of Turkey*
There is an English translation by Frederic Shoberl, entitled *Turkey* (Philadelphia, H. Cowperthwait 1829. 24 col.pl. LC 15-3529) For an English translation and adaptation with a full set of 72 plates see Frederic Shoberl's *Turkey*, in the World in miniature series
Colas 545. Lipperheide 1427

Sitten, gebräuche und trachten der Osmanen; nebst einem abrisse der osmanischen geschichte; mit erläuterungen aus morgenländischen schriften von Langlès. Leipzig, G. Fleischer 1815
3v. 72 col.pl. O.
German translation of his *Moeurs* with corresponding plates
Colas 546. Lipperheide 1428

Castellani, Alessandro
Antique jewelry and its revival. Philadelphia, For the Penna. museum and school of industrial art, by J. H. Coates 1862?
19p. O.
LC 4-334

Castil-Blaze. See Blaze, François Henri Joseph

Castillon, A. See Vanauld, Alfred, jt. auth.

Castillon de Saint-Victor, Marie Émilien de
Historique du 5ᵉ régiment de hussards ... 9 gravures en couleur par M. H. de Bouillé ... Reproductions photographiques de 23 portraits de colonels et de la Prise de la flotte du Texel. Paris, Lobert et Person 1889
210p. pl.(part col.) ports. sq.F.
Each plate and portrait accompanied by guard sheet with descriptive letterpress
LC 22-9268

Castle, Egerton
Schools and masters of fence, from the middle ages to the eighteenth century ... Illus. with reproductions of old engravings and carbonplates of ancient swords. London, G. Bell 1885
lii,254p. front. illus. 6pl. O.
Bibliography, sixteenth, seventeenth, and eighteenth centuries: p[xv]-lii
Lipperheide 2994. LC A13-2314

Castro, C.
(illus.) México y sus alrededores

Castro, Fernández de
Cuadernos militares; illus. por Eduardo Serrano. Madrid, 1886
205p. col.pl. F.

Castro, José Villaamil y. See Villaamil y Castro, José

Catacombes de Rome. Perret, Louis

Catacombes de Rome. Roller, Théophile

Catàleg de la collecció d'indumentària. Rocamora, Manuel

Catalog of brilliant old robes from the late court of the Manchus. Moore, Frederick

Catalog of collection of armour and arms sold March 18th, 1895. Brett, E. J.

Catálogo de la Real armería. Madrid. Armeria real

Catalogo degli ordini religiosi della chiesa militante. See Buonanni, Filippo. Ordinum religiosorum in ecclesia militanti catalogus

Catalogo della armeria reale. Italy. Ministero della casa reale

Catalogo della collezione di antichità. Ancona, Amilcare

Catálogo histórico-descriptivo de la Real armería de Madrid. Madrid. Armería real

Catalogue de costumes militaires français et étrangers. Balsan, Auguste

Catalogue de dessins relatifs à l'histoire du théâtre conservés au département des estampes de la Bibliothèque nationale. Bouchot, H. F. X. M.

Catalogue de la riche collection d'armes antiques, du moyen âge, de la renaissance et des temps modernes. Richards, Raoul

Catalogue des armes et armures du Musée de la Porte de Hal. Brussels. Musées royaux des arts décoratifs et industriels

Catalogue des bronzes antiques. Paris. Bibliothèque nationale

Catalogue des bronzes de la Société archéologique d'Athènes. Ridder, A. H. P. de

Catalogue des collections composant le Musée d'artillerie en 1889. Paris, Musée d'artillerie

Catalogue des collections des costumes de theatres, fantaisies, historiques et nationaux. Martinet, pub.

Catalogue des livres rares et précieux. Ruggieri, E. F. D.

Catalogue des ouvrages composant la bibliothèque. Chambre syndicale de la bijouterie, de la joaillerie et de l'orfèvrerie de Paris

Catalogue descriptif et illustré de la collection de bagues. Tarnóczy, Mme Gustave de

Catalogue du musée archéologique. Société archéologique du Finistère

Catalogue d'une collection de miniatures gothiques et persanes. Rosenberg, Léonce

Catalogue d'une collection importante de costumes militaires français et étrangers. Glasser

Catalogue d'une très belle collection de recueils de costumes, xviiie et début du xixe siècles. Jonghe, J. de, vicomte

Catalogue et description bibliographique d'une collection de livres et gravures sur les costumes militaires: Autriche Hongrie. Ridder, G. de

Catalogue of a collection of ancient and mediaeval rings and personal ornaments. Londesborough, U. L. G. B. D., baroness

Catalogue of a loan exhibition of arms and armor. New York. Metropolitan museum of art

Catalogue of a loan exhibition of Japanese sword fittings. Armor and arms club, New York

Catalogue of a loan exhibition of Japanese sword guards. Armor and arms club, New York

Catalogue of American historical costumes. See Hoes, Mrs R. G. Dresses of the mistresses of the White House

Catalogue of an exhibition of the arms and armour of old Japan. Japan society, London

Catalogue of church ornaments. Benziger brothers, New York

Catalogue of competitive exhibitions of fans. London. Fanmakers

Catalogue of early German and Flemish woodcuts. Dodgson, Campbell

Catalogue of English ecclesiastical embroideries of the xiii. to xvi. centuries. Victoria and Albert museum, South Kensington

Catalogue of European arms and armor. New York. Metropolitan museum of art

A **catalogue** of German paintings of the middle ages and renaissance in American collections. Kuhn, C. L.

The **catalogue** of honor. Milles, Thomas

Catalogue of loan collection of art fans. Edinburgh. Royal Scottish museum

Catalogue of rings. Victoria and Albert museum, South Kensington

Catalogue of the choice and valuable collection of rare antique guns and pistols. Schott, C. M.

A **catalogue** of the collection of arms and armor presented to the Cleveland museum of art by Mr and Mrs John Long Severance. Cleveland museum of art

Catalogue of the collection of arms and armour at Hallwyl house. Stockholm. Hallwylska palatset

Catalogue of the collection of fans and fanleaves presented by the Lady Charlotte Schreiber. British museum. Department of prints and drawings

Catalogue of the collection of jewels and precious works of art. Morgan, J. P.

Catalogue of the costume books in the library of the Salmagundi club, New York. Salmagundi club, New York. Library

Catalogue of the engraved gems of the post-classical periods. British museum. Department of British and mediaeval antiquities

Catalogue of the finger rings, Greek, Etruscan, and Roman. British museum. Department of Greek and Roman antiquities

Catalogue of the jewellery, Greek, Etruscan, and Roman. British museum. Department of Greek and Roman antiquities

Catalogue of the loan collection of Japanese armor. New York. Metropolitan museum of art

Catalogue of the manuscripts in the Cottonian library. British museum. Department of manuscripts

A catalogue of 250 coloured etchings. Solvyns, F. B.

Catalogue of vestments, banners and regalia. Benziger brothers, New York

Catalogue sommaire des bijoux antiques. Paris. Musée national du Louvre

Catalogus Sanctorum. Natalibus, Petrus de, bp. of Equilio

Catalonia. See Spain—Catalonia

Catenacci, H.
(illus.) Lacombe, Paul. Les armes et les armures

Catholic church. Liturgy and ritual
Liber regalis; seu, Ordo consecrandi regem solum; ordo consecrandi reginam cum rege; ordo consecrandi reginam solam; rubrica de regis exequiis; e codice westmonasteriensi editus. Printed for the Roxburghe club. London, J. B. Nichols 1870
xvi,67p. front.(illum. facsim.) Q.
Edited by Frederick, earl Beauchamp
LC 3-1800

Catholic church. Liturgy and ritual. Breviary
Breviaire Grimani de la Bibliothèque de S. Marco à Venise: reproduction photographique complète; ed. par Scato de Vries ... Pref. du Sal. Morpurgo. Leyde, Sijthoff; Paris, C. Delagrave 1904-08
1 v. of text and 12v. of pl. (1581 pl., part col.) F.
Text by Giulio Coggiola
The text of the *Breviaire Grimani* was written about 1484. The miniatures belong to a somewhat later period and are of the school of Hans Memling. They are pictures of Bible characters and of social life among all classes of the fifteenth century

Fac-simile delle miniature contenute nel Breviario Grimani conservati nella biblioteca di S. Marco esequito in fotografia da A. Perini. Venise, A. Perini 1862-78
1 v. of text, 2v. of pl.(110pl.) F.
Published also with French title *Fac-simile des miniatures contenues dans le Bréviaire Grimani* (Venise, F. Ongania 1880. 2v. xlvi,300p. and facsimile 4 col.pl. 112pl. Q.) Lipperheide 462
Reproduces without color 110 pages from the Grimani breviary

Catholic church. Liturgy and ritual. Hours
Heures. Paris, S. Vostre ca1502
98 l. illus. Q.
First leaf begins: Ces presentes heures a lusaige de Rome
Pictures in the borders of the text show Bible scenes and characters. Another series shows a Dance of death
Lipperheide 436

Le livre d'heures de la reine Anne de Bretagne, traduit du Latin ... par M. l'abbé Delauney. Paris, L. Curmer 1841
2v. col.illus. 32 col.pl. F.
Plates are miniatures by unknown French artists, showing Biblical costume and costume of the saints
Lipperheide 458

Catholic church. Liturgy and ritual. Pontifical
Liber pontificalis. [Glasgow, 1924]
facsim: 197 l. 24x37½cm.
Photostat facsimile of British museum Cottonian manuscript Tiberius BVIII. 13th century; Fol. 35-80 (33-78) Livre du sacre des roys de France, with autograph subscription, fol. 74 (72) verso, of Charles V, king of France
For contents see Planta's *Catalogue of the manuscripts in the Cottonian library in the British museum,* 1802, p36-7
LC 28-23375

Catholic church. See Ecclesiastical costume—Catholic church

Catlin, George
Catlin's North American Indian portfolio; hunting scenes and amusements of the Rocky mountains and prairies of America. London, G. Catlin 1844
2 l. 31 col.pl. F.
"From drawings and notes of the author, made during eight years' travel amongst forty-eight of the wildest and most remote tribes of savages in North America." Subtitle
Contains six unnumbered plates in addition to the 25 of the earlier editions
Colas 562. Lipperheide 1617
Also published New York, J. Ackermann 1845 (LC 11-10441)

Illustrations of the manners, customs, and condition of the North American Indians: in a series of letters and notes written during eight years of travel. With three hundred and sixty engravings from the author's original paintings. 5th ed. London, H. G. Bohn 1845
2v. fronts. pl. ports. maps(1 fold.) Q.
Same plates as his *Letters and notes* but colored by hand. Some copies are in black and white
Sixth edition 1848; 7th ed. 1848; 8th ed. 1851; 9th ed. 1857; 10th ed. 1866. Also published London, Chatto & Windus 1876
Colas 561. Lipperheide 1618. LC 2-14233, 7-23805 (8th ed.) 2-14234(1876 ed.)

Letters and notes on the manners, customs, and condition of the North American Indians. New-York, Wiley and Putnam 1841
2v.(264,266p.) 312pl. maps. O.
First edition. English edition (London, The author, printed by Tosswill and Myers 1841) 2d ed. 1842; 3d ed. 1842; 4th ed. 1843; 5th ed. 1845; 6th ed. 1846. A reproduction was published Edinburgh, W. and A. K. Johnston for J. Grant 1892
The plates were sold to H. G. Bohn who issued the *Illustrations* listed above
Colas 560. LC 11-9430

North American Indians; being letters and notes on their manners, customs, and conditions, written during eight years' travel amongst the wildest tribes of Indians in North America, 1832-39. Edinburgh, John Grant 1926
2v. col.pl. ports. O.
Also a 1903 edition (Edinburgh, Grant) without color. And one published 1913 (Philadelphia, Leary, Stuart & co. LC 14-30805) with colored plates
A German translation: *Die Indianer,* made by Heinrich Berghaus, from the fifth English edition, was published (Brüssel, C. Muquardt 1848. x,382p. 24pl.) without color. There are later printings including one (Berlin c1924)
Costume index

Catlin, George—*Continued*

Souvenir of the N. American Indians as they were in the middle of the nineteenth century. A numerous and noble race of human beings, fast passing to extinction, leaving no monuments or records of their own in existence. London, The author 1850

3v. pl. F.

A collection of pencil drawings showing costume of North American Indians according to tribe

(illus.) Donaldson, Thomas. The George Catlin Indian gallery in the U. S. National museum

Catologo degli ordini equestri e militari. See Buonanni, Filippo. Ordinum equestrium et militarium catalogus in imaginibus expositus & cum brevi narratione

Cats, Jacob

Alle de wercken ... De laatste druck; waar in het Twee-en-tachtig jaarig leeven des dichters, beneffens desselfs Slaapeloose nachten, met printverbeeldingen sijn verrijkt. Amsterdam, J. Ratelband [etc.] 1726

2v. 428 illus. 3 fold.pl. 2 port. F.

Most of the illustrations, including added title-pages and 11 special half-titles, are engraved from the original designs of Adriaan van de Venne, twelve are by J. Goeree

Lipperheide 942. LC 18-631

Cats, Jacob, and Farley, Robert

Moral emblems, with aphorisms, adages, and proverbs, of all ages and nations, from Jacob Cats and Robert Farlie. Translated ... by Richard Pigot. London, Longman, Green, Longman and Roberts 1860

ix-xvi,239p. front. illus. Q.

"The original designs of Adrian van de Venne, in a few instances only, have been deviated from." Introduction p xii

Second edition 1862

LC 29-114

Le **Caucase** pittoresque. Gagarīn, G. G., kn͡iaz, and Stackelberg, Ernest, count

Caucasus. See Russia—Caucasus

Caulfeild, S. F. A. and Saward, Blanche C.

The dictionary of needlework, an encyclopedia of artistic, plain, and fancy needlework. London, L. U. Gill 1882

528p. 822 illus. Q.

Plain sewing etc. by Caulfeild. Church embroidery, lace, by Saward

Lipperheide 4138

Caumont, Aroisse, comte de

Cours d'antiquités monumentales professé à Caen. Paris, Lance 1830-41

6v. illus. D.

Illustrations show effigies from tombs of the 11th to the 16th centuries, v6 chapter 4

Causerie sur les dentelles de Normandie au debut du xxe siècle. Drouet, P. L. M.

Cauwelaert, Frans van. See Vlaanderen door de eeuwen heen

Cavalcade religieuse. Vervloet, J.

La **cavalerie.** Brécard, C. T.

Cavalerie de la Garde impériale du 1er empire. Adam, Victor

Cavalerie française en 1846. Paris, Bouvenne, imp. J. Rigo 1846?

6 col.pl. O.

Colas 564

Cavalerie sous le règne de Louis-Philippe. Adam, Victor

La **cavalerie** suisse de 1694 à 1880. See Escher, A. von. Die schweizerische cavallerie

Die **cavallerie** Deutschland's. Schindler, C. F.

Cavalleriis, Johan Baptista de

Pontificum romanorum effigies. [Roma] D. Basa 1585

11,235 l. 233 illus. O.

First edition was published in Rome, F. Zanetti 1580

Contains portraits of 231 popes from Peter to Gregory XIII, and a brief text on the back of each plate

Lipperheide 1796

Romanorum imperatorium effigies; elogijs, ex diversis scriptoribus, per Thomam Treteru ... collectis, illustratae opera et studio Io. Baptae de Cavallerijs aeneis tabulis incisae. Roma, [V. Accoltus] 1538

5 l. 152pl. O.

Portraits of the emperors of Rome and of the Holy Roman empire from Julius Caesar to Rudolph II. The latter reigned from 1576 to 1606

Lipperheide 214

Il **cavallo** da maneggio. Galiberto, G. B. di

Cavaro, Richard

Les costumes des peuples anciens. Paris, Librairie de l'art 1887

2v. illus. D. (Bibliothèque populaire des écoles de dessin. 3. ser. Histoire des arts décoratifs)

Contents: 1 Egypte, Asie; 2 Grèce, Etrurie, Rome

Colas 565

Cave, Henry William

The book of Ceylon ... illus. from photographs by the author. London, Paris, New York, Toronto and Melbourne, Cassell 1908

xii,664p. col.front. pl. plans. fold.map, fold.plan. 22cm.

LC 8-29426

The **cave** of Altamira. Breuil, Henri, and Obermaier, Hugo

La **caverne** d'Altamira. See note under Breuil, Henri, and Obermaier, Hugo. The cave of Altamira at Santillana del Mar, Spain

Caxton, William

(tr.) Cessolis, Jacobus de. The game of the chesse

Caylus, Anne Claude Philippe, comte de

Les manteaux; recueil. La Haye, 1746

2v. front. D.

Colas 566

(engr.) Bouchardon, Edme. Études prises dans le bas peuple, ou Les cris de Paris

Cazal, René Marie

Essai historique, anecdotique sur la parapluie, l'ombrelle et la canne et sur leur fabrication. Paris, Lacrampe 1844

106p. 9pl. D.

Lipperheide 1720

Ce que parler veut dire. Bouchot, Frédéric

Ce qu'on dit et ce qu'on pense. Scheffer, J. G.

Cecchetti, Bartolomeo

Il doge di Venezia. Venezia, P. Naratovich 1864
xix,341p. O.
Lipperheide 1766

La vita dei Veneziani nel 1300; le vesti. Venezia, Tipografia Emiliana 1886
133p. 3pl.(1 double) O.
In continuation of his articles, "Vita dei Veneziani", in the *Archivio veneto,* t. 2, t. 27-30 and t. 35:428-38
LC 22-1793

Cederblom, Gerda

(ed.) Svenska allmogedräkter; med illus. efter original av Emelie von Walterstorff. Stockholm, Gen. lit. anst. förlag 1921
79p. 48 col.pl. D. kr. 18 (Nordiska museet, Stockholm)

(ed.) Svenska folklivsbilder. Stockholm, 1923
40p. 100pl.(part col.) Q. (Nordiska museet, Stockholm)

Ceintures populaires bulgares. Peteva, Yelena

Celebes. See Dutch East Indies

Célébrités contemporaines. Paris, Delpech [1842]
94pl. O.
Portraits of illustrious Frenchmen by contemporary artists. Plates are copies, reduced in size, from a folio edition of *Iconographie des contemporaines*
Lipperheide 1170

Cell, Erhard

Imagines professorum Tubigensium, senatorii praecipue ordinis: qui, hoc altero academiae seculo, anno 1577. inchoato, in ea & hodie, anno (1596.) vivunt, ac florent: & interea mortui sunt. Tubingae, E. Cell 1596
67 l. 37 illus.(ports.) Q.
The half-length portraits are by Jakob Lederlein from designs by Helias Alt von Herenberg and Jakob Züberlein
Lipperheide 2015

Cellarius, Henri

La danse des salons. Paris, J. Hetzel 1847
174p. 10pl. O.
Lipperheide 3106

Celler, Ludovic, pseud. See Leclercq, Louis

Celnart, Élisabeth Félicie. See Bayle-Mouillard, Mme É. F.

Les **Celtes** dans les vallées du Pô et du Danube. Bertrand, A. L. J.

Celts

Campbell, Lord Archibald. Craignish tales and others. 1889

See also Gauls

Cendrillon, ou La fée du foyer; journal des petites demoiselles. v 1-12; Nov. 1850-1872. Paris, Goubaud
12v. pl.(part col.) D.
Plates show designs for needlework, and fashions of the day. Subtitle varies: v 1, revue encyclopédique de tous les travaux de dames: tricot, crochet, frivolité, lacet, filet, tapisseries, broderies, modes, recettes, hygiène, etc. No more published?
Colas 569

Cenni, Italo

L'esercito Italiano. Milano [etc.] Vallardi 1914
16 col.pl. ob.F.
Title from the library of the United States war department

Cenni, Quinto

Album delle uniformi militari del regno: esercito e marino. Milano, 1879
8 col.pl. ob.Q.
Colas 570

L'Arma del genio nel 4°. esercito italiano; storia dell' ingegneria, etc. ... illus. di Quinto Cenni, 1903. Milano, Mauri e Ghirlanda 1903
28p. illus.(part col.) ports. Q.

Atlante militare organizzazione, uniforme e distintivi degli eserciti et delle armate d'Europa. Milano, U. Hoepli [1890]
68pl. 18 col.pl. Q.
Each plate shows several types. Illustrations are after designs by Cenni and R. Knötel
Colas 574

Eserciti d'oltremare; skizzi militari. Milano, Vallardi [1880]
1 l. 12pl. ob.Q.
Military costume of China, Japan, Algeria, Egypt, Persia, Siam, etc.
Colas 573

Eserciti europei; skizzi militari. Milano, A. Vallardi [1880]
1 l. 18 col.pl. ob.F.
Each plate shows several types
Colas 572

L'esercito Italiano; schizzi militari. Milano, A. Vallardi [1880]
1 l. 18 col.pl. F.
Colas 571. Lipperheide 2369

Gl' ordini equestri religioso-militari; studi storico sui loro costumi ed armi; per commissione ed a spese del H. J. Vinkhuizen. Maccagno Superiore? [1909]
12p. 21pl.(part col.) F.
Shows costume of the Knights of Malta

Cenni sulla Sardegna ovvero usi e costumi amministrazione, industria e prodotti dell' isola. Luciano, Baldassarre

Cent ans de modes françaises (1800-1900) ... Documents du XIX. siècle commentés et interprétés au goût du jour. Cornil, Mme

Cent cinq costumes des départemens de la Seine, Inférieure, du Calvados, de la Manche et de l'Orne. See Lanté, L. M. Costumes des femmes du pays de Caux

Cent proverbes. Grandville, J. I. I. G., called

Les **cent** Robert Macaire. Daumier, H. V.

Les **cent**-un coiffeurs de tous les pays. Croisat, ed.

Les **centennales** parisiennes. See Cleemputte, P. A. van. Paris de 1800 à 1900

The **centennial** of the United States Military academy at West Point, New York, 1802-1902. United States. Military academy, West Point

Centi-folium stultorum in quarto; oder, hundert ausbündige narren in folio. Neu aufgewärmet ... Auch mit einer delicaten brühe vieler artigen historien

Centi-folium, etc.—*Continued*
lustiger fablen kurtzweiliger discursen und erbaulichen sitten-lehren angerichtet ... Wien, J. C. Megerle; [etc.] [1709]
404p. 101pl. O.
Plates engraved by C. Weigel. Work is ascribed to Abraham a Santa Clara (Johann Ulrich Megerle)
Lipperheide 3519

Central America
Carpenter, F. G. Lands of the Caribbean. 1925
Davis, R. H. Three gringos in Venezuela and Central America. 1896
Domville-Fife, C. W. Guatemala and the states of Central America. 1913

See also Indians of Central America

The **Central** criminal court of London. Hooper, W. E., comp.

Central provinces, India. See India—Central provinces

Centralasien. Hellwald, F. A. H. von

A **century** of fashion. Worth, J. P.

A **century** of French fashion and costume. See La mode féminine de 1490 à 1920

A **century** of hats and the hats of the century. Woolley, E. M.

Century of Louis XIV. See Bourgeois, Émile. France under Louis XIV

Cerchiari, G. Luigi
Chiromanzia e tatuaggio, note de varietà, ricerche storiche e scientifiche, coll' appendice di un'inchiesta con riposte de Ferrero, Lombroso, Mantegazza, Morselli, ed altri. Milano, Hoepli 1903
xx,323p. 82 illus. 29pl. S.

Ceremonial and festival costume
Bernard, Frédéric. Les fêtes célèbres de l'antiquité du moyen âge et des temps modernes. 1878
Modius, François. Pandectae triumphales, sive, Pomparum, et festorum ac solennium apparatuum, conviviorum, spectaculorum, simulacrorum bellicorum equestrium, et pedestrium. 1586
Picart, Bernard. Ceremonies and religious customs of the various nations of the known world, together with historical annotations. 1733-39
Picart, Bernard. Cérémonies et coutumes religieuses de tous les peuples du monde. 1723-1743
Promis, Vincenzo. Le auguste alleanze fra le case sovrane di Savoia e di Baviera nei secolo XV, XVII, XVIII; documenti e memorie. 1883

See also Coronations and coronation robes; Court dress; Funerals; Masks; Weddings and wedding dress

Bibliography

Ruggieri, E. F. D. Catalogue des livres rares et précieux composant la bibliothèque de m. E. F. D. Ruggieri. Sacres des rois et des empereurs, entrées triomphales, mariages, tournois, joutes, carrousels, fêtes populaires et feux d'artifice. 1873

Alsace

Arnold, J. G. D. Der pfingstmontag lustspiel in Strasburger mundart. 186[illegible]
Fargès-Méricourt, P. J. Relation d[u] voyage de sa majesté Charles X e[n] Alsace. 1829
Glück, E. Fètes de Gutenberg. Cortèg[e] industriel de Strasbourg 25. juin 1840 1840?
Relation des fêtes données par la ville de Strasbourg à leurs majestés impériales et royales, les 22 et 23 janvie[r] 1806. 1806
Weis, J. M. Représentation des fêtes données par la ville de Strasbourg pour l[a] convalescence du roy; à l'arrivée e[t] pendant le séjour de sa majesté en cette ville. 1750?

Austria

Allerhöchst-feyerlichste festivitäten .. bey dem . . . beylager . . . Leopoldi [I] Römischen Kaysers ... und ... Margaritae ... Infantin von Hispanien 1667
Andree-Eysen, Marie. Die perchten im Salzburgischen. 1905
Berggruen, Oscar. Huldigungs-festzug der stadt Wien zur feier der silbern[en] hochzeit ihrer majestäten des kaiser[s] Franz Joseph I. und der kaiserin Elizabeth, 27 April 1879. 1881
Beschreibung der feyrlichkeiten, welche bey gelegenheit der durchreise ... de[r] ... Frau Dauphine, Marien Antonie[n] Erzherzoginn zu Oesterreich ... von den Vorderösttreich-Breissgauischen landständen veranstaltet worden. 177[illegible]
Das carroussel zu Wien 1894. 1894
Deyersperg, G. J. von. Erb-huldigung welche dem ... römischen kayse[r] Carolo dem sechsten ... als herzogen in Steyer, von denen gesamten steyrischen landständen den sechsten juli[i] 1728 ... abgeleget und ... zusammen getragen worden. 1740
Franceschini, Girolamo. Caroussel zu[r] anwesenheit J. J. K. K. majestäten in Prag den 5. juni 1854
Gülich, Ludwig von. Erb-huldigung s[o] ... Josepho dem ersten von den[en] gesambten nider-oesterreichischen ständen ... an dem auff den 22. des[s] monats septembris anno 1705 angesetzten tag abgelegt und ... zusammen getragen worden. 1705?
Kriegl, G. C. Erb-huldigung, welche .. Mariae Theresiae, zu Hungarn, und Böheim königin, als ertz-hertzogin zu Oesterreich, von denen gesammten nider-oesterreichischen ständen ... abgeleget den 22. novembris anno 1740 1742
Mairn, J. B. von. Beschreibung was au[f] ableiben weyland ihrer keyserl. majestät Josephi, bisz nach vorgegangener erb-huldigung welche dem ... römischen keyser Carolo dem sechsten ..

Ceremonial and festival . . .—Austria—*Cont.* als erz-herzogen zo Oesterreich die gesamte nider-oesterreichische stände den 8. novembris A:1712. 1712?

Makart, Hans. Festzug zur feier der silbernen hochzeit des kaiserpaares Franz Joseph und Elisabeth. 1879

Makart, Hans. Festzug zur fünfundzwanzigjährigen vermählungs-feier des allerhöchsten kaiserpaares veranstaltet von der haupt- und residenzstadt Wien, April 1879. 1879

Neues Wiener tagblatt. Festzug der stadt Wien zur silbernen hochzeit des kaiserpaares. 1879

Reise a. h. ihrer k.k. apostolischen majestäten Franz Joseph und Elizabeth durch Kärnthen im september 1856. 1859

Sieg-streit dess lufft und wassers freudenfest zu pferd. 1667

Von himmeln entzindete und durch allgemainen zuruff der erde sich himmelwerts erschwingende frolokhungs flammen zur begengnus des hochzeitlichen beylägers ... Leopoldi des Ersten, Römischen Kaisers ... und Margarita, geborner Infantin aus Hispanien 1666. [1666]

Wirrich, Heinrich. Ordenliche beschreibung des ... beylags oder hochzeit so da gehalten ist worden durch ... Herrn Carolen ertzhertzog zu Osterreich ... mit ... Maria geborne hertzogin zu Bayrn den XXVI. Augusti in ... Wienn. 1571

Belgium

Becanus, Guilielmo. Serenissimi principis Ferdinandi Hispaniarum infantis S.R.E. cardinalis triumphalis introitus in Flandreae metropolim Gandavum [1636]

Carton, C. L. Album descriptif des fêtes et ceremonies religieuses à l'occasion du jubilé de 700 ans du Saint-Sang, à Bruges. 1850

Dupuys, Remy. La tryumphante et solemnelle entree faicte sur le nouvel et joyeux advenement de ... Charles prince des Hespaignes ... en sa ville de Bruges lan 1515 le XVIIIe jour dapvril après Pasques. 1850

Geets, Willem. Ommegang de Saint-Rombaut (1875). Cavalcade historique organisée par la ville de Malines, à l'occasion du jubilé de Saint-Rombaut, patron de la commune. 1875

Gevaerts, J. G. Pompa introitus honori ... Ferdinandi Austriaci Hispaniarum infantis S.R.E. card ... a S.P.Q. Antverp. decreta et adornata; cum ... Antverpiam ... adventu suo bearet xv. kal. maii, ann. 1635. 1642

Hymans, Louis. XXVe anniversaire de l'inauguration du roi. Les fêtes de juillet ... celebrées à Bruxelles les 21, 22 et 23 juillet 1856. 1856

La joyeuse & magnifique entrée de Monseigneur Françoys, fils de France, et frere unique du roy ... duc de Brabant, d'Anjou, Alençon, Berri &c. en ... Anvers. 1582

Le Gendre, Léonce. Album du cortège historique, qui aura lieu à Bruges le 31 aout 1853, à l'occasion du mariage de ... monseigneur le duc de Brabant avec ... Marie-Henriette-Anne, archiduchesse d'Autriche. 1853

Prael-treyn ... aen het duyzend-jaerig jubilé van ... den Heyligen Rumoldus. 1775

Prael-treyn, plegtigheden, vreugde-feesten en vercieringen van het vyftigjaerig jubilé der martelie van den Heyligen Rumoldus, apostel en patroon der stad Mechelen MDCCCXXV. 1825

Relation de l'inauguration solemnelle de ... Charles VI. empereur des Romains ... et troisiéme du nom roy des Espagnes, comme comte de Flandres, celebrée à Gand ... le XVIII. Octobre 1717. 1719

Schryver, Cornelis. La tresadmirable, tresmagnificque, & triumphante entree, du ... Prince Philipes, Prince d'Espaignes, filz de Lempereur Charles V[e]. ... en ... ville d'Anvers, anno 1549. 1550

Vervloet, J. Cavalcade religieuse à l'occasion du jubilé de 850 ans célébré ... en l'honneur de Notre Dame d'Hanswyck à Malines pendant la dernière quinzaine du mois d'août 1838. 1838

Vervloet, Victor. Album du jubilé de 875 ans, en l'honneur de Notre Dame d'Hanswyk, ou description historique de la grande cavalcade et des fêtes publiques qui seront célébrées ... à Malines pendant la dernière quinzaine du mois d'août 1863. 1863

China

Hodous, Lewis. Folkways in China. 1929

Czechoslovakia—Bohemia

Glaser, Rudolph. Denkbuch über die anwesenheit ihrer K. K. majestäten Franz des ersten und Carolin Auguste in Böhmen im jahre 1833. 1836

Ramhoffsky, J. H. Drey beschreibungen, erstens: des königlichen einzugs, welchen ... Maria Theresia, zu Hungarn und Böheim königin ... in dero königliche drey Prager-städte gehalten; andertens: der erbhuldigung, welche ... die gesammte. ... stände des königreichs Böheim ... abgegeleget; drittens ... ihro ... majestät königlich-böhmischen crönung. 1743

France

17th century

Discours de l'entrée faicte par ... Henry IIII, roi de France et de Navarre, et ... Marie de Médicis, la royne son epouse, en leur ville de Caen, au mois de septembre 1603. 1842

Félibien, André, sieur des Avaux et de Javercy. Relation de la feste de Versailles. 1679

Ceremonial and festival . . .—France—17th century—*Continued*

La Ruelle, Claude de. Decem insignes tabulae, complexae icones justorum ac honorum supremorum, corpori ... Caroli III ... Dix grandes tables, contenantes les pourtraictz des ceremonies, honneurs, et pompe funebres, faitz au corps de Charles 3 ... duc le Lorraine. 1611?

Menestrier, C. F. Les rejouissances de la paix, faites dans la ville de Lyon le 20.mars 1660. 1660

18th century

Description des festes données par la ville de Paris, à l'occasion du mariage de Madame Louise-Elisabeth de France, & de Dom Philippe, infant ... d'Espagne, les vingtneuvième & trentième août mil sept cent trente-neuf. 1740

Fête publique donnée par la ville de Paris à l'occasion du mariage de Monseigneur le Dauphin le 13. fevrier MDCC.XLVII. [1747?]

Fêtes publiques données par la ville de Paris à l'occasion du mariage de Monseigneur le Dauphin, les 23. et 26. fevrier M.DCC.XLV

Grégoire, Gaspard. Explication des cérémonies de la Fête-Dieu d'Aix en Provence. 1777

19th century

Arène, P. A. and Tournier, Albert. Des Alpes aux Pyrénées, étapes félibréennes. 1891?

Cadoux, Gaston. Relation officielle des fêtes organisées par la ville de Paris pour la visite des officiers et marins de l'escadre russe de la Méditerranée les 17, 19, 20 et 24 Octobre 1893. 1896

Dinaux, A. M. Description des fêtes populaires données à Valenciennes les 11, 12, 13 mai 1851. 1854

Drumont, E. A. Les fêtes nationales à Paris. 1879

Goulet, Nicolas. Fêtes à l'occasion du mariage de S. M. Napoléon, empereur des Français ... avec Marie Louise, archiduchesse d'Autriche. 1810

Hitorff, J. I., and Lecointe, J. F. J. Description des cérémonies et des fêtes qui ont eu lieu pour le baptême de . . . Henri-Charles-Ferdinand-Marie-Dieudonné d'Artois, duc de Bordeaux. 1827

Lafitte, Louis. Entrée triomphale ... le duc d'Angoulême, généralissime de l'armée des Pyrenées. 1825

Germany

Andree-Eysen, Marie. Die perchten im Salzburgischen. 1905

Becker, R. Z. Des deutsche feyerkleid zur erinnerung des einzugs der Deutschen in Paris am 31sten März 1814 eingeführt von deutschen frauen. 1814

Fehrle, Eugen. Deutsche feste und volksbrauche. 1927

Hüsing, Georg. Die deutschen hochgezeiten. 1927

Reinsberg-Dueringsfeld, Otto, freiherr von. Das festliche jahr; in sitten gebraüchen, aberglauben und festen der germanischen völker. 1898.

16th century

Dilich, Wilhelm. Historische beschreibung der fürstlichen kindtauff fräulein Elisabethen zu Hessen ... welche im augusto des 1596 jahrs zu Cassel gehalten worden. 1598

17th century

Abbildung und repraesentation der fürstlichen inventionen, auffzüge, ritterspiel auch ballet, so in des Herren Johann Georgen, fürsten zu Anhalt, bey des Herrn Georg Rudolph, Hertzogen in Schlesien mit Fraw Sophia Elizabeth Hertzogin in Schlesien ... hochzeitlichem frewdenfest ... beylager. 1615

Assum, J. A. Warhaffte relation und .. discours uber dess ... herzen Johann Friderichen, Hertzogen zu Würtemberg ... jungen sohns Printz Friderichen ... kind tauff: sampt darbey begangnem ... fürstlichem ritterlichem Frewden fest zu Stuttgardten: Den 8 9. 10. 11. 12. 13. 14. etc. Martij, anno 1616. [1616]

Berlinische relation, was beym sieg- und freudenreichen einzug sr. churfl. durchl zu Brandenburg ... als ... se: churfl durchl. nach glücklich-vollendeter pommerischer expedition ... in dero residentz-städte Berlin, Cölln ... am 3 decembr 1677 ... eingezogen passiret [1678]

Bry, J. T. de. Repraesentatio & explicatio duorum arcuum triumphalium. 161[illegible]

Churfürstlich bayrisches frewden-fest 1662. n.d.

Ehren-seule ... Hn. Wilhelmen des Sechsten, landgraffen zu Hessen .. alss sr. fürstlichen durchleutchtigkei[t] seeligst verblichener cörper den 27ten octobris des 1663ten jahrs ... zu Cassel ... beygesetzt worden. 1669

Hulsen, Esaias von. Aigentliche warhaffte delineatio unnd abbildung aller fürstlichen auffzüg und rütterspilen bey dess ... Johann Friderichen hertzogen zu Württemberg ... jungen printzen und sohns hertzog Ulrichen ... kind tauff: und bey ... dess ... Ludwige[n] Friderichen hertzogën zu Württemberg &c. Mit ... Magdalena Elizabeth landtgräffin auss Hessen &c. hoch zeytlichem frewdenfest celebrirt i[n] Stuetgartt Julii, 1617. 1618

Hulsen, Esaias von. Repræsentatio der furstlichen aufzug und ritterspil. So .. Johan Friderich hertzog zu Württemberg ... beij ihr ... neüwgebornen soh[n] Friderich ... kindtauffen, 1616. Inn .. Stuetgarten .. gehalten. 1616

Klai, Johann. Irene, das ist Vollständig[e] aussbildung dess zu Nürnberg geschlossenen friedens 1650. 1650

Ceremonial and festival . . .—Germany—17th century—*Continued*

Kuchler, Balthasar. Repraesentatio der fürstlichen auffzug und ritterspil ... des ... Johann Friedrichen, hertzogen zu Wurttenberg ... und ... Barbara Sophien geborne Marggravin zu Brandēburg r̃ hochzeitlich ehrnfest den 6 Novemb. 1609. 1611

Kurtze und eygentliche beschreibung dess jenigen so bey der verlöbnus, heimführ- und vermählung ... Caroli, pfaltzgrafens bey Rhein ... mit ... Wilhelmina Ernestina ... erb-princessin zu Dennemarck ... vorgangen. 1672

Mayr, J. B. Zwey-einiger Hymenaeus, oder oesterreich-lüneburgischer ... vermählungs-gott denen ... Josepho I ... und Wilhelminae Amaliae ... durch ruhm- oder ehren-pforten ... hierbefor eröffnet. 1699

18th century

Angeordtneter grosser umbgang, und procession auf das hohe fest des Zarten Fronleichnambs Jesu Christi. In ... Landshut, mit denen handwerchszunfften, fähnen, stangen, und kertzen sambt figuren und persohnen auch mit bruderschafften und clerisey. 1733

Ausführliche beschreibung der feierlichkeiten bei gelegenheit der ... dem Könige Friedrich Wilhelm III ... zu Königsberg in Preussen 1798 geleisteten erbhuldigung. n.d.

Beschreibung der reise und des einzuges sr. majestät des Königs Friedrich Wilhelm II von Preussen. 1792

Louisens und Friederikens, kronprinzessin, und gemahlin des prinzen Ludwig von Preussen, geborner prinzessinnen von Mecklenburg-Strelitz, ankunft und vermählung in Berlin im december 1793. 1794

Saeculum octavum, oder Acht-tägisches hoch-feyrliches jubel-fest ... mit ungemeinen kirchen-gepräng ... processionen triumphierlicher einholung der heiligen zweyen römischen martyrer Marii und Caelestini. 1702

Schönhaar, W. F. Ausführliche beschreibung des- zu Bayreuth im september 1748 vorgegangenen ... beylagers, und derer- ... heimführungs festivitaeten, des ... herrn Carls, regierenden herzogs zu Württemberg ... und der ... frauen Elisabethae Fridericae Sophiae. 1749

Vollständiges diarium, alles dessen was vor, in und nach denen ... wahl- und crönungssolennitaeten ... Caroli des VI. erwehlten römischen kaysers. 1712

19th century

ABC des kölnischen maskenfestes. ca1830

Avenarius, Toni. Historischer festzug veranstaltet bei der feier der vollendung des Kölner domes am 17. October 1880. 1881

Bender, Ferdinand. Fünf lebende bilder vor ... dem Könige und der Königin am 9ten September 1840 zur vorfeyer der huldigung von Preussens ständen dargestellt im dazu errichten festsaale. 1840

Bertuch, F. J. Beschreibung der feierlichkeiten welche ... in Weimar und Jena am 6ten und 7ten October 1808 von dem Herzoge Carl August von Sachsen-Weimar veranstaltet wurden. 1809

Beschreibung des festes Der zauber der weissen rose gegeben in Potsdam am 13 July 1829 zum geburtstage Ihrer majestät der Kaiserin von Russland. [1829?]

Carrousel, geritten in Potsdam am 13. Juli 1829. n.d.

Des königs Friedrich August des gerechten heimkehr und empfang am 7ten juni 1815. 1815?

Des Rheinkreises jubelwoche, oder Geschichtliche darstellung der reise ihrer majestäten des königs Ludwig und der königin Therese von Bayern durch die gaue des Rheinkreises vom 7ten bis zum 14ten junius 1829. 1829

Dittmer, Heinrich. Authentische und vollständige beschreibung aller feyerlichkeiten, welche in dem hannoverschen lande bey der anwesenheit. ... Georgs des vierten während dem monate october 1821 veranstaltet worden sind. 1822

Das dritte brandenburgische reformations-jubiläum oder ausführliche beschreibung aller bei gelegenheit der 300 jährigen jubelfeier am 1., 2. und 3. november 1839 in Spandow, Berlin und mehreren andern städten der mark stattgefundenen festlichkeiten. 1839

Der einzug des ... herzogs Friedrich von Sachsen-Altenburg nebst seiner ... familie in sein neues land und seine neue residenz im november 1826. 1827

Ernst August album. 1862

Feier des fünf und zwanzig jährigen regierungs jubiläums seiner majestät Maximilian Joseph I königes von Baiern. 1824

Festzug zur feier der fünfundzwanzigjährigen regierung des königs Wilhelm von Württemberg am 28. september 1841, in Stuttgart. 1841

Förster, Friedrich. Die perle auf Lindahaide. Fest-spiel in romanzen und lebenden bildern zur feier der ... vermählung ... des kronprinzen Friedrich von Dänemark mit ... herzogin Karoline von Mecklenburg. 1841

Förster, Friedrich. Vollständige beschreibung aller feste und huldigungen ... zur vermählungsfeier des kronprinzen Friedrich Wilhelm von Preussen. 1824

Frederich, E. Gedenkblätter des festcarrousels welches zur vorfeier des allerhöchsten geburtsfestes ihrer majestät der königinn Maria am 13ten april 1853 im königlichen reithause zu Hannover statt fund. 1854

Ceremonial and festival . . .—Germany—19th century—*Continued*

Gedenkbuch zu Friedrich v. Schiller's 100 jähriger geburtsfeier, begangen in Frankfurt a. M. den 10 november 1859. 1860

Götz, Hermann. 1826-1896. Der jubiläums festzug der haupt- und residenzstadt Karlsruhe, zum siebenzigsten geburtstage seiner königlichen hoheit des grossherzogs Friedrich von Baden. 1896

Hacklaender, F. W. Das caroussel welches am 27. Oktober 1846 aus veranlassung der hohen vermaelung ... des Kronzprinzen Karl von Würtemberg mit ... der Grossfürstin Olga Nikolajéwna in Stuttgart abgehalten wurde. 1846?

Heyberger, G., and Füsslen, J. Festzug zur vollendung des [Ulmer] Münsters 1377-1890. 1890

Huldigungen ihren majestaeten Anton und Theresia könig und königin von Sachsen am 16n. October 1827. 1827?

Illustrirte zeitung. Die Kölner dom-feier. 1880

Kopisch, August. Die kunstheroen der vorzeit, ein geisterzug, bei der 25. stiftungsfeier des Berliner Kunstlervereins am 18. october 1839. 1840

Kraus, Gustav. Festzug zur feyer der jubelehe I.I.M.M. des königs Ludwig und der königin Therese beym octoberfeste zu München am 4. october 1835. 1836

Mannheimer maskenzug im jahr 1841. 1841?

Quadrilles du carnaval à Berlin 1836 1836

Vorläufer zum ersten theresienvolksfeste in Bamberg, oder Die öffentliche maskerade in Bamberg am fastnachtsmontage 1833. 1833?

20th century

Crass, Eduard. Deutsches brauchtum im jahreslauf, eine bilderfolge. 1935

Sutter, Conrad. Gutenberg-feier Mainz 1900. 1900

Italy

15th century

Pippi, Giulio. L'entrée de l'empereur Sigismond a Mantouë. 1675

16th century

Fontana, Publio. Il sontuoso apparato, fatto dalla magnifica citta di Brescia nel filice ritorno dell' ... il cardinale Morosini. 1591

Gualterotti, Raffaello. Descrizione del regale apparato per le nozze della serenissima Madama Cristiana di Loreno, moglie del serenissimo Don Ferdinando Medici III. granduca di Toscana. 1589

Gualterotti, Raffaello. Feste nelle nozze del serenissimo Don Francesco Medici gran duca di Toscana; et della sereniss. sua consorte. . . Bianca Capello. 1579

Pagani, Mattio. La processione del Doge nella domenica delle palme. 1880

Riccio, Domenico. La gran cavalcata di Clemente VII. e Carlo V. della Sala Ridolfi. ca1825?

17th century

Aureli, Aurelio. La gloria d'amore; spettacolo festivo fatto rappresentare dal ... duca di Parma sopra l'acque della gran peschiera novamente fatta nel suo giardino. 1690

Il bellissimo torneo à piedi, ouero la barriera fatta dalla nobilta di Vicenza nel theatro Delli Signori Academici Olimpice il Carnevale dell' anno MDCXII. 1612

Certani, Giacomo. Maria Vergine coronata. 1675

Coppola, G. C. Le nozze degli dei favola ... nelle ... nozzi de ... Ferdinando II. 1637

Della Bella, Stefano. Entrata in Roma dell' eccelmo ambasciatore di Pollonia l anno MDCXXXIII. 163-?

Forcella, Vincenzo. Spectacula ossia caroselli, tornei, cavalcate e ingressi trionfali. 1896

Isachi, Alfonso. Relatione di Alfonso Isachi intorno l'origine, solennita, traslatione, et miracoli della Madonna di Reggio. 1619

Le manifique carousel fait sur le fleuve de l'Arno, à Florence, pour le mariage du Grand Duc. ca1690

Mascardi, Vitale. Festa, fatta in Roma, alli 25. febraio MDCXXXIV. 1635

Patino, Carlo. Le pompose feste di Vicenza, fatte nel mese di giugno, del 1680. 1680

Sartorio, B. C. I numi a diporto su l'Adriatico; descrizione della regatta solenne disposta in Venezia a godimento dell' altezza serenissima di Ferdinando terzo prencipe di Toscanna. 1688

18th century

Bertolotti, Antonino. Divertimenti pubblici nelle feste religiose del secolo XVIII dentro e fuori delle porte di Roma. 1887

Borghi, C. R. L'oplomachia pisana, ovvero La battaglia del ponte di Pisa 1713

Casotti, G. B. Memorie istoriche della miracolosa immagine di Maria Vergine dell' Impruneta. 1714

Descrizione delle feste fatte in Bologna il giorno XVII agosto dell' anno MDCCXXXVIII ... in occasione delle ... nozze de' monarchi delle due Sicilie. 1738

In espettazione delle loro altezze reali Ferdinando III ... gran duca di Toscana e Luisa Maria di Borbone ... sua consorte; feste pubbliche ... Siena 1791. 1791

Mitelli, G. M. Entrata solenne dell' ... Confaloniero di Giustizia, che si fà ogni bimestre nel palazzo publico di Bologna. 1700?

Narrazione delle solenni reali feste fatte celebrare in Napoli da Sua Maestà il re Due Sicile, Carlo infante di Spagna. 1749

Ceremonial and festival costume—Italy—18th century—*Continued*

Paciaudi, P. M. Descrizione delle feste celebrate in Parma l'anno MDCCLXIX per le auguste nozze di ... l'infante Don Ferdinando colla ... arciduchessa Maria Amalia. 1769

Perabò, Gabrio. Ammirabile promozione all' arcivescovato di Milano, ed alla sagra porpora dell' ... Cardinale Don Gioseppe Pozzobonelli, e suo solenne ingresso adì 21. giugno 1744. 1744

Scamozzi, O. B. Descrizione dell' arco trionfale e della illuminazione fatta nella pubblica piazza di Vicenza la notte 12 novembre 1758. 1758

Ubilla y Medina, Antonio, marqués de Rivas. Succession de el rey D. Phelipe v. nuestro Señor en la corona de España. 1704

19th century

Chiappa, G. P. Disegni d'alcune opere eseguite in occasione della fausta venuta in Lombardia di S. M. l'imperatore e re Ferdinando primo. 1838

Cibrario, G. A. L., conte. La feste torinesi dell' aprile 1842. 1842

Costumi e descrizione delle processioni conosciute in Genova sotto il nome di Casacce. 1828

Descrizione dell' apparato fatto in Firenze ... nell' occasione del ... ritorno in Toscana di ... il granduca Ferdinando III. 1814

Graf, Rainer. Die feste der republik Venedig. 1865

Hercolani, Antonio. Storia e costumi delle contrade di Siena. 1845

Morelli, Jacopo. Descrizione delle feste celebrate in Venezia per la venuta di S.M.I.R. Napoleone, il massimo imperatore de' Francesi. 1808

Mörner, Hjalmar. Il carnevale di Roma, 1820. 1820

Pinelli, Bartolommeo. Il carnavale di Roma 1820

Pinelli, Bartolommeo. Pinelli's five last days of the Carnival of Rome, in a series of five plates, drawn on the spot. 1830

Raccolta di scene carnevalesche di Roma. 18—

Ventimiglia, Domenico. Il torneo di Caserta nel carnevale dell' anno 1846 descritto ed illustrato. 1850

20th century

Ashby, Thomas. Some Italian scenes and festivals. 1929

Costumi, musica, danze e feste popolari italiane. 1935

Jamaica

Beckwith, M. W. The Hussay festival in Jamaica. 1924

Japan

Caiger, G. Dolls on display. 1933

Clement, E. W. The Japanese floral calendar. 1911

Jews

Adlerblum, Mrs N. H. A perspective of Jewish life through its festivals. 1930

Levinger, Mrs E. C. E. With the Jewish child in home and synagogue. 1930

Middle ages

Amory de Langerack. Histoire anecdotique des fêtes et jeux populaires au moyen-age. 1870

Netherlands

Beschryving van het plechtige volksfeest, gehouden te Amsterdam, op den 19 Juny, 1795; by gelegenheid van het installeeren, der door de volksstem verkozene representanten dier stad, en de alliantie gesloten tusschen de Fransche en Bataafsche Republieken. 1795

Cérémonies et fêtes qui ont eu lieu à Bruxelles, du 21 au 23 juillet 1856 à l'occasion du XXVe anniversaire de l'inauguration de ... Leopold 1er. 1856

14th century

Bosch, Etienne. Aelbrecht-hertog in Beieren-graaf van Holland-enz-binnen Enkhuizen in 1396. [1900]

16th century

Dankerts, C. Delineatio pompae triumphalis qua Robertus Dudlaeus comes Leicestrensis Hagae comitis fuit exceptus. 1586

17th century

Baerle, Kaspar van. Marie de Medicis, entrant dans Amsterdam. 1638

Bidloo, Govard. Komste van Zyne Majesteit Willem III. koning van Groot Britanje, enz. in Holland. [1691]

Const-thoonende ivweel, by de lofijcke stadt Haerlem ten versoecke van Trou moet blijcken, in't licht gebracht. 1607

Haerlems ivweel, tot nut vande arme uyt liefde ten thoon ghestelt nae de voorghegevene caerte van 't speelcorentken. 1608

La Serre, J. P. de. Histoire curieuse de tout ce qui c'est passé à l'entrée de la reyne mere du roy treschrestien dans les villes des Pays Bas. 1632

18th century

Andriessen, Andreas. Plegtige inhuldiging van zyne doorlugtigste hoogheidt, Willem Karel Henrik Friso, prinse van Oranje en Nassau. 1751

Huet, D. T. Inhuldiging van ... Willem Karel Hendrik Friso, prins van Oranje en Nassau ... als erf-heer van Vlissingen, op den V. junij MDCCLI. 1753

Kok, W. Illumination in Amsterdam am 8. märz 1788. 1788?

La Fargue, P. C. Lyk-staetsie van ... Anna kroon princesse van Groot Brittanien princesse douariere van Orange en Nassau. 1761

Ceremonial and festival costume—Netherlands—18th century—*Continued*

Swart, P. de. Afbeelding van de kaamer en 't parade-bed waar op het lyk van ... Anna, kroon princesse van Groot-Brittanje, princesse douariere van Orange en Nassau ... 1759. 1759

19th century

Wüppermann, W. E. A. Beschrijvend programma van den feestelijken optocht, gehouden te Haarlem, op Maandag 1 April 1872. 1872

Rome

Fowler, W. W. The Roman festivals of the period of the Republic. 1899

Russia

Chalif, L. H. Russian festivals and costumes for pageant and dance. 1921

Sicily

Le feste di S. Rosalia in Palermo l'anno 1841. 1841

Spain

Amades, Joan. Gegants, nans i altres entremesos. [1934]

Mascara real, executada por los colegios y gremios de Barcelona para festejar el feliz desseado arribo de ... dn. Carlos tercero y da. Maria Amalia de Saxonia, con el real principe e infantes [October, 1759] 1764

Ragguaglio delle nozze delle maestà di Filippo quinto, e di Elisabetta Farnese. ... celebrate in Parma l'anno 1714. 1717

Relacion de la entrada de los reyes nuestros señores en la ciudad de Barcelona, la mañana del 4 de diciembre de 1827, y de los demas festejos públicos, que tributó á ss. mm. la junta de reales obsequios, en nombre y representacion de dicha ciudad. 1828

Sweden

Floding, P. G. Solemniteter ... i ... Stockholm, aren 1771 och 1772 ... Solemnités, qui se sont passées à Stockholm ... dans les années 1771 et 1772. 1772

Klöcker von Ehrenstrahl, David. Das grosse carrosel und prächtige ringrännen ... was ... zu sehen war alss ... Carl der Eylffte ... anno M.DC.LXXII. den XVIII. decembris ... zu Stockholm antratt. 1672?

Switzerland

Description de la fête des vignerons, célébrée à Vevey, le 5 aoust 1819. 1819

Description de la fête des vignerons célébrée à Vevey les 8 et 9 août 1833. 1833

Jauslin, Carl, and Roux, G. 400 jährige jubelfeier der schlacht bei Murten am 22 Juni 1876. 1877

Jenny, Heinrich. Historischer festzug in Winterthur den 22. Juni 1864, erinnerungsfeier des 22. Juni 1264. 1864

Vernes-Prescott, J. F. L'Abbaye des Vignerons, son histoire et ses fêtes jusqu'à et y compris la fête de 1865, les toillettes de bal de 1783 à 1865. 1865?

Cérémonial de l'empire française; par L.-I. P. Paris, À la librairie economique 1805
502p. 3 col.pl. O.
Plates show the pope, and the French emperor and empress in coronation robes
Lipperheide 2482

Ceremonial of the coronation of His most Sacred Majesty King George the Fourth in the abbey of St. Peter, West-Minster. West-Minster, J. Whittaker 1823
27 col.pl. F.
Printed in gold

Ceremonial pictured in photographs; a companion volume to the 'Directory of ceremonial' (Tract XIII) London, A. R. Mowbray; Milwaukee, Morehouse [1924]
[44]p. incl.front. 17 illus. O. (Alcuin club tracts. XIV)
LC 25-5223

Ceremoniel und privilegia derer trompeter und paucker. Friese, Friedrich

Das **ceremoniell** der kaiserkrönungen von Otto I. bis Friedrich II. Diemand, Anton

Ceremonies and religious customs of the various nations of the known world. Picart, Bernard

Cérémonies et coutumes religieuses de tous les peuples du monde. Picart, Bernard

Cérémonies et fêtes du mariage de ... Duc de Brabant, et de ... Marie Henriette Anne Archiduchesse d'Autriche, célébré à Bruxelles le 22 aout, 1853 Bruxelles, J. Géruzet 1853
30p. 20pl.(18 col.) F.
Lipperheide 2680

Cérémonies et fêtes qui ont eu lieu à Bruxelles, du 21 au 23 juillet 1856, à l'occasion du XXVe anniversaire de l'inauguration de ... Leopold 1er. Bruxelles, J. Géruzet 1856
41p. 24pl.(2 col.) F.
Lipperheide 2682

Cérémonies et prières du sacre des rois de France. Paris, Firmin-Didot 1825
108p. D.
Lipperheide 2486

The **ceremonies** of a Japanese marriage. [Kobe, Japan, Tamamura, photographer] 19—?
1 l. 19 col.pl. 18x26cm.
Descriptive text at foot of each plate. Japanese t.-p. at end
LC CA11-1402

Cerémonies usitées au Japon. Titsingh, Isaac

Céresole, Victor

Origines de la dentelle de Venise et l'École du point de Burano en 1878. Venise, imp. Antonelli 1878
14p. O.
Lipperheide 4040

Cernitius, Johannes
Decem, è familiâ burggraviorum Nurnbergensium, electorum Brandenburgicorum eicones ad vivum expressæ, eorumque res gestæ, una cum genealogiis, fide optimâ collectæ publicatæque. Berlini, typ. Rungianis 1626
8,110p. illus. F.
Lipperheide 709

Cernuschi, and others
Le costume au théâtre par Cernuschi, Mesplés, Mucha, etc. Paris, A. Lévy [1865]
50 col.pl. Q. 25fr.
Colas 579

[**Cerrone, F.**]
[Scenes from Italian life; lithographed by A. Ledoux after designs by F. Cerrone] No place, ca1830
10 col.pl. Q.
Plates show a fisherman, porter, brigand, etc., and women of Procida, Ischia and Capri
Colas 580. Lipperheide 1280

Certain Caddo sites in Arkansas. Harrington, M. R.

Certani, Giacomo
Maria Vergine coronata ... Descrizione, e dichiarazione della divota solemnità fatta in Reggio li 13. Maggio 1674. Reggio, P. Vedrotti 1675
137p. 16pl. F.
Lipperheide 2791

Cervio, Vincenzo
Il trinciante; ampliato et ridotto a perfettione dal cavallier Reale Fusoritto da Narni. Venetia, F. Tramezzini 1581
44 l. 2 illus. 1 fold.pl. D.
Several later editions. Also published as part of Bartholomeo Scappi's *Dell' arte cucinare* (1643) and of his *Opera* (1622) listed below
Lipperheide 3151w

Ces messieurs. Morel-Retz, L. P. G. B.

Česká vesnice. Žalud, August

Český lid. Sbornik věnovaný studiu lidu českého v Čechách, na Moravě, ve Slezsku a na Slovensku. v 1, 1892+ Praze, F. Šimáček 1891+
Illus. pl. ports. O.
Current 1937. Suspended publication 1915-22
Editor: 1892- Čeněk Zíbrt (with Lubor Niederle 1892-95)

Cesnola, Luigi Palma di
Cyprus: its ancient cities, tombs, and temples. A narrative of researches and excavations during ten years' residence in that island. New York, Harper 1878
xix,465p. front.(port.) illus. pl. maps, facsims. O.
Contains material on the jewelry of ancient Cyprus
LC 5-7102

[**Cessolis, Jacobus de**]
The game of the chesse, by William Caxton. Reproduced in facsimile from a copy in the British museum. With a few remarks on Caxton's typographical productions. By Vincent Figgins. London, J. R. Smith 1860
2p.l. facsim.(165p. illus.) 13p. 1 l. Q.
Translated by William Caxton from Jean de Vignay's French version of Jacobus de Cessolis' *De ludo scacchorum.* Italian edition: *Libro de scacchi* (Florence, A. Miscomini 1493)
Facsimile of Caxton's 2d edition [Westminster] 1481 (1st edition Bruges, 1476)
"A list of the works ascribed to Caxton: p[9]-11. List of places where, and persons by whom the art of printing was practised at the time Caxton commenced it in England: p12-13
Woodcuts show players in fifteenth century dress
LC 5-24316

Volgarizzamento del libro de' costumi e degli offizii de' nobili sopra il giuoco degli scacchi di frate Jacopo da Cessole, tratto nuovamente da un codice Magliabechiano. Milano, Tip. del dottore G. Ferrario 1829
xx,162p. illus. O.
The illustrations, reproduced from the Florence edition of 1493, show men in costume of the fifteenth century. They are not the same as those in the English translation *The game of chess,* listed above. A Catalan translation is entitled: *De les costumes dels homes ...* (Barcelona, La marca de l'Avenc [1900] xii,159p. illus.)
LC 32-13868

C'est ici les différens jeux des petits polissons de Paris. Saint-Aubin, Augustin de

Cestus (girdle)
Mohler, S. L. The cestus. 1926

Ceux d'Alsace. Spindler, Charles

Ceux d'Auvergne. Pourrat, Henri

Ceux de Yorktown. Malo, Servan

Ceylan. Gauttier du Lys d'Arc, L. E.

Ceylon
Campbell, James. Excursions, adventures, and field-sports in Ceylon. 1843
Cave, H. W. The book of Ceylon. 1908
Churchill, Awnsham, and Churchill, John. A collection of voyages and travels. 1732
Corner, Mrs Caroline. Ceylon, the paradise of Adam. 1908
Daniell, Samuel. A picturesque illustration of the scenery, animals and native inhabitants of the island of Ceylon. 1808
Davy, John. An account of the interior of Ceylon. 1821
Gauttier du Lys d'Arc, L. E. Ceylan, ou, Recherches sur l'histoire, la littérature, les moeurs et les usages des Chingulais. 1823

Chabrelie, J. J.
(ed.) Burnouf, Eugène. L'Inde française

Chacobo Indians. See Indians of South America—Chacobo Indians

A **chacoon** for a harlequin. See Beaumont, C. W. The history of Harlequin. p 121-32

[**Chadwick, Henry**]
Base-ball. Philadelphia, J. B. Lippincott company 1888
8p. illus. D.
Reprinted from *Chambers's encyclopædia*
LC 5-23916

Chadwick, Luie M.
Fashion drawing & design, a practical manual for art students and others. London, B. T. Batsford [1926]
xi,262p. incl.col.front. illus. pl.(part double, part col.) O. 15s
LC 27-14475

Chalcondylas, Laonicus
Histoire generale des Turcs. Paris, D. Bechet 1662
2v. (907,208p.) 106 illus. 2pl. F.
Lipperheide 1407

Chaleyé, Joannès
Dentelles du Puy. Paris, A. Calavas 1910?
2p.l. 30pl. F.
Issued in portfolio
LC 31-22073

Chalif, Louis Harvy
Russian festivals and costumes for pageant and dance. New York, Chalif Russian school of dancing c1921
176p. incl.front. pl. ports. O. $3
Colas 581. Costume index. LC 21-18330

Challamel, Augustin
La France et les Français à travers les siècles. Paris, Roy 1881
4v. 256 illus. 96 col.pl. O.

Histoire de la mode en France; la toilette des femmes depuis l'époque gallo-romaine jusqu'à nos jours; nouv. éd. Paris, A. Hennuyer 1881
327p. 21 col.pl. Q. 16fr.
Earlier edition by the same publisher (1875. 240p. 17 col.pl. O.)
Colas 583-84. Lipperheide 1094 (1875 ed.) LC 32-20466

Histoire-musée de la République française, depuis l'Assemblée des notables jusqu'à l'empire. Avec les estampes, costumes, médailles, caricatures, portraits historiés et autographes les plus remarquables du temps. 3. éd., entièrement refondue et considerablement augmentée. Paris, G. Havard 1857-58
2v. illus. pl. ports. facsims. Q.
LC 4-21521

The history of fashion in France; or, The dress of women from the Gallo-Roman period to the present time. Tr. by Cashel Hoey and John Lillie. London, S. Low, Marston, Searle, & Rivington 1882
xii,293p. col.pl. Q. 28s, o.p.
Translation of his *Histoire de la mode en France*
Costume index. LC 35-14165

Challamel, Augustin, and Ténint, Wilhelm
Les Français sous la révolution; avec quarante scènes et types dessinés par M. H. Baron, gravés sur acier par M. L. Massard. Paris, Challamel 1843?
316p. front. 40pl. Q.
Colas 582. Lipperheide 1136. LC 16-3907

Challaye, Félicien
Le Japon illustré. Paris, Larousse 1915
303p. 677 illus. 8pl. (4 col.) maps, plans. 33x26cm.
Costume index. LC 33-5163

Challiot
[Modèles pour les uniformes et l'équipement des officiers et fonctionnaires de l'armée française] Paris? ca1800
14pl. F.
Plates are signed Challiot and engraved by Gautier and P. Boutrois. They give details of buttons, insignia, etc.
Colas 585. Lipperheide 2304m

Chalmers, Helena
Clothes, on and off the stage; a history of dress from the earliest times to the present day. New York, London, D. Appleton 1928
292p. front. illus. O. $3.50
Costume index. LC 28-4399

Chalon, Christina
Tweeëndertig stuks studien of Ordonnantien naar de origineele Tekeningen; in het koper gebragt door Pieter de Mare. Leyden, K. en P. Delfos 1779
20pl.(incl. 32 illus.) Q.
Dutch figures and scenes showing children. In the style of Adrian van Ostade
Lipperheide 946

Zinspelende gedigtjes, ob de geestige printjes ge-etst door Pieter de Mare, na de teekeningen van Mejufvrouw Christina Chalon ... berijmt door J. le Francq van Berkhey. Amsteldam, W. van Vliet 1806
28p. 28 col.pl.(incl. 32 illus.) O.
A later edition of his *Tweeëndertig stuks*, with verses added
Colas 587. Lipperheide 947

Chalon, John James
Twenty four subjects exhibiting the costume of Paris, the incidents taken from nature, designed and drawn on stone by J. J. Chalon. London, Rodwell and Martin 1822
24 col.pl. F.
Published in four parts. The plates show people of various occupations, shoeblacks, venders, politicians, general scenes, etc.
Colas 588. Lipperheide 1185 (pt 1 only)

Cham, pseud. See Noé, Amédée, comte de

Chamberlain
Views and costumes of the city and neighbourhood of Rio de Janeiro, Brazil, from drawings taken ... during the years 1819 and 1820. London, T. M'Lean 1822
38 l. 36 col.pl.(part fold.) F.
Plates engraved by J. Clarke, Halken, G. Hunt and T. Hunt
Colas 591

Chamberlain, Basil Hall
Things Japanese, being notes on various subjects connected with Japan for the use of travellers and others; 5th ed. rev. London, J. Murray; [etc.] 1905
552p. illus. fold.map. O.
"Books on Japan" p64-73. "Books recommended" with special subjects

Chamberlain, James Franklin
How we are clothed; a geographical reader. New York and London, Macmillan 1923
x,189p. illus. D. (Home and world series)
LC 23-12261

Chamberlaine, John

Imitations of original drawings by Hans Holbein, in the collection of His Majesty, for the portraits of illustrious persons of the court of Henry VIII. With biographical tracts [by E. Lodge] London, W. Bulmer 1792

[142]p. 84 col.port. on 83 l. F.
Originally published in parts
"The plates are stipple engravings, printed in colors, and with the exception of four are by F. Bartolozzi; three were engraved by C. Metz, and one by C. Knight. Most of the prints are mounted." Library of Congress
Lipperheide 984. LC 10-1936

Portraits of illustrious personages of the court of Henry VIII. Engraved in imitation of the original drawings of Hans Holbein, in the collection of His Majesty. With biographical and historical memoirs by Edmund Lodge. London, W. Bulmer 1828

[144]p. 84 col.port. F.
"This is evidently an imitation of a similar edition by Chamberlaine published first in 1792 and in inferior form in 1812. The plates are stipple engravings, printed in colors, and are by various engravers, only two being by F. Bartolozzi." Leland Stanford Jr. University
LC A12-196

Chamberlen, Paul

(tr.) Dumont, Jean, baron de Carlscroon, and Rousset de Missy, Jean. The military history of Prince Eugene of Savoy.

Chambers, Sir Edmund Kerchever

The mediaeval stage, by E. K. Chambers. New York, Oxford univ press; Oxford, Clarendon press 1903

2v. fronts. O. 36s; $12
List of authorities: p[xiii]-xlii
Contents: v 1 Minstrelsey, Folk drama; v2 Religious drama, The interlude, Appendices
LC 4-1915

Chambers, Edward Thomas Davies

(ed.) Carrel, Frank, and Feiczewicz, Louis. The Quebec tercentenary commemorative history

Chambers, Sir William, 1726-1796

Designs of Chinese buildings, furniture, dresses, machines, and utensils, engraved by the best hands from the originals in China; to which is annexed a description of their temples, houses, gardens, &c. London, Pub. for the author [etc.] 1757

19,19p. 21pl. F.
English and French. French title: *Desseins des edifices, meubles, habits ... des chinois.* Four of the plates show costume
Colas 592. LC 1-19408

Traité des edifices, meubles, habits, machines et ustensiles des Chinois; compris une description de leurs temples, maison, jardins, etc. Paris, Le Rouge 1776

30p. 20pl. Q.
A new edition of his *Designs* with some plates redrawn and in a different arrangement
Colas 593. Lipperheide 1518

Chambers, William, 1800-1883

Things as they are in America. London and Edinburgh, W. and R. Chambers; Philadelphia, Lippincott, Grambo 1854

364p. D.
The first part of the book (p 1-141) relates principally to Quebec, Canada. A second edition was published 1857 (376p.)
LC 2-2201

Chambre syndicale de la bijouterie, de la joaillerie et de l'orfèvrerie de Paris. Bibliothèque

Catalogue des ouvrages composant la bibliothèque de la Chambre syndicale de la bijouterie, de la joaillerie et de l'orfèvrerie de Paris. [Paris, Impr. M. Villain & M. Bar] 1914

157p. O.
LC 15-22496

Chambre syndicale de la confection et de la couture pour dames et enfants

Les toilettes de la Collectivité de la couture. See entry under Paris. Exposition universelle, 1900

Chamfort, Sébastien Roch. See Collection complète des tableaux historiques de la révolution française

Champagny, Clerjon de. See Clerjon de Champagny

Champeaux, Alfred de

Dessins et modèles; les arts du tissu: Étoffes—tapisseries — broderies—dentelles—reliures. Paris, J. Rouam [1892]

144p. 149 illus. Q.
Lipperheide 3871

Champfleury, pseud. See Fleury, Jules

Champier, Victor

Le Caire, moeurs et costumes. See entry under Preziosi, A.

(ed.) Preziosi, A. Stamboul

Champlin, John Denison

(ed.) Cyclopedia of painters and paintings ... Critical editor, Charles C. Perkins. New York, C. Scribner 1887

4v. fronts. illus. (incl.ports. facsims.) Q.
More than 2000 reproductions of paintings, many of which are portraits of the artist's period, make this cyclopedia a rich source of costume material
Bibliography: v 1 p xix-xxxvi
LC 4-18452

Champollion, Jean François

Monuments de l'Égypte et de la Nubie, d'après les dessins exécutés sur les lieux; pub. sous les auspices de m. Guizot et de m. Thiers ... par une commission spéciale. Planches. Paris, Firmin Didot 1835-45

4v. CCCCXLVI(i.e. 511) pl. (part col.) F.
Plates, with brief descriptions. Editor's preface signed: J. J. Champollion-Figeac. A. C. T. E. Prisse d'Avennes's *Monuments egyptiens* is a continuation of this work
LC 10-98

Champollion-Figeac, Jacques Joseph

(ed.) Champollion, J. F. Monuments de l'Egypte et de la Nubie

Champvans, Frédéric Guigue de. See Guigue de Champvans, Frédéric

Chancellor, Edwin Beresford
Life in Regency and early Victorian times; an account of the days of Brummel and D'Orsay, 1800-1850. London, B. T. Batsford [1926]
130p. illus. ports. pl.(1 col.) O. 12s 6d
Costume index

Change of the uniform regulations of the Czechoslovak armed forces. Czechoslovakia. Minister of national defense

Changeable ladies. Ackermann, Rudolph

Changing horizons. Foran, W. R.

Chansons nationales lataviennes. See Barons, Krišjānis, and Wissendorffs, Henri, eds. Latwju dainas

Chantilly. Notices des peintures; les quarante Fouquet. Gruyer, F. A.

Chantre, Ernest
Études paléoethnologiques dans le bassin du Rhône. Âge du bronze; recherches sur l'origine de la métallurgie en France. Paris, J. Baudry 1875-76
3v. illus. maps, tables. sq.F. and album of lxxiii (i.e. 79) pl.
Each plate has a guard-sheet with explanatory letterpress
The album contains illustrations of prehistoric weapons and jewelry
Contents: v 1 Industries de l'âge du bronze; v2 Gisements de l'âge du bronze; v3 Statistique
LC 3-23121

Premier âge du fer; nécropoles et tumulus: Album. Paris, J. Baudry 1880
col.front. L pl. F.
Plates accompanied by guard sheets with descriptive letterpress
Illustrations show jewelry, buttons and toilet articles found in different parts of France

Recherches anthropologiques dans le Caucase. Paris, C. Reinwald; Lyon, H. Georg 1885-87
4v. in 5. illus. 143pl.(part double) col.pl. 2 port. 2 maps. sq.F.
The plates of v2 form a separate atlas
Contents: v 1 Période préhistorique; v2 Période protohistorique, 2v; v3 Période historique; v4 Populations actuelles
LC 3-27695

Chapeaux du Très parisien. Année 1-16; 1921-1936. Paris
Col.illus. col.pl. Q. 52fr. a year
Published quarterly. Supplement to *Très parisien.* Ceased publication with année 16, no3 (automne 1936)

Chapeaux élégants. 1927+ Paris, Éditions Bell
Q. 58fr. a year
Published quarterly. Current 1938

Chapeaux modernes. no 1, 1904?+ New York, Classique modes; Paris, G. Lyons
Illus. pl.(part col., mounted) F.
Published semi-annually. Current 1938

Chaperon, Eugène. See Brunet, Romuald, jt. auth.

Le **chapitre** des illusions. Bouchot, Frédéric

Chapman, Arthur Percy Frank. See The game of cricket

Chapman, James
Travels in the interior of South Africa, comprising fifteen years' hunting and trading; with journeys across the continent from Natal to Walvisch Bay, and visits to Lake Ngami and the Victoria Falls. London, Bell & Daldy [etc.] 1868
2v. fronts. illus. pl. 2 fold.maps. O.
A few of the illustrations show costume of native tribes
LC 5-15264

Chapman, Kenneth Milton. See note under Traphagen, Ethel. Costume design and illustration

Chappon, Louis
Theoretisch-practische anleitung zur fecht-kunst. Pesth, Der verfasser 183?
54p. 80pl. port. Q.
Lipperheide 2987

Chapsal, Georges. See Bayard, Émile L'art de reconnaître les bijoux anciens pierres précieuses, métal précieux

Chapters on Greek dress. Evans, M. M L., lady

Chapuis, F.
Uniformes de l'armée française. Paris & Nancy, Berger-Levrault 1892?
ix fold.col.pl. F.

Character and costume in Turkey and Italy Allom, Thomas

Character and costumes of Affghanistan Hart, L. W.

Character sketches from the works of Charles Dickens. Darley, F. O. C.

The **characteristic** costume of France Peake, R. B.

Characteristic portraits of the various tribes of Cossacks attached to the allied armies in the campaign of 1815, taken from life at Paris, and accompanied by ... descriptions of their manners costumes, etc. London, R. Ackermann 1820
24 col.pl. Q.
Colas 598

Characteristic sketches of the lower orders Rowlandson, Thomas

Characters at the west end of the town Dighton, Richard

Characters from Dickens. Fraser, C. L.

Characters in literature. See subdivision Characters under Dickens, Charles

The **characters** of Charles Dickens. Clark J. C.

Charakteristiche darstellung der vorzüglichsten europaeischen militairs. Augsburg, Academischen kunsthandlung [1800-10]
1 l. 97 col.pl. Q.
Published in 19 series, each with title page and 5 plates, except one which has seven. Illustrations by Seele, Ebner, Mettenleither, J. Volz and Rugendas
Contents: Armée autrichienne; Armée prussienne; Armée française (République) Armée française (Empire); Armée russe Armée anglaise; Armée turque; Armée de l'Electorat de Bavière; Armée du Royaume de Bavière; Milice du Royaume de Bavière Armée de l'Electorat de Saxe; Armée du royaume de Saxe; Armée suédoise; Armée Wurtembergeoise; Armée danoise; Armée Badoise; Armée espagnole; Armée hollandaise; Troupes alliées de la France
Colas 597

Chardin, Jean Baptiste Simeon
(illus.) Boucher, Emmanuel. Les gravures françaises du XVIIIe siècle, v3

Charicles; or, illustrations of the private life of the ancient Greeks. Becker, W. A.

Charikles, bilder altgriechischer sitte. Becker, W. A.

Charioteers

Rome

Panvinio, Onofrio. De ludis circensibus. 169-?

Charis. See Allgemeine modenzeitung

Charitable remonstrance addressed to the wives and maidens of France touching their dissolute adornments. Mineur, A. E.

Charitinum, Philopatrida, pseud. See Assum, J. A.

Charlemagne, A., and Ladurner, A.

Garde impériale Russe. Saint-Pétersbourg, Moscou et Paris, Daziaro [1848-52]
12 col.pl. F.
Plates lithographed by Bastin, Chevalier, Huot and Victor
Colas 599

Charles G. King collection of books on costume. Western reserve historical society, Cleveland, O. King collection

Charles V, king of France

The coronation book of Charles V of France. (Cottonian ms. Tiberius B.VIII) With collotypes of all miniatures and reproductions of seven in colours and gold by W. Griggs. London, Harrison 1899
xx p. 102 columns. pl.(part. col.) facsims. Q. (Henry Bradshaw society, 16)
The ordinance and oaths are in French; the ordo itself is in Latin
Edited by E. S. Dewick
Bibliography p vii-viii

Charles-Roux. See Roux, Jules Charles

Charlet, Nicolas Toussaint

Album lithographique. Paris, Gihaut frères 185-?
62pl. ob.Q.

[Costumes de corps militaires faisant partie de l'armée française avant et pendant la révolution et de la garde impériale. Paris, A. Bry] ca1842
43 col.pl. Q.
Also known with plates in black and white and in editions with fewer plates
Colas 606 (part)

[Costumes de l'ex-garde impériale. Paris, F. Delpech 1819-20]
30 col.pl. Q.
There is another edition published by Delpech in which the figures are smaller but with the same titles. The plates, unsigned, exist in black and white and in color
Colas 604

Costumes militaires. Paris, C. de Lasteytie [1817-18]
17 col.pl. F.
Colas 602

Costumes militaires 1789-1815, dessinés et lithographiés par Charlet. 50 planches en couleurs. Notice par A. Guillaumot fils. Paris, J. Cahen 1886
5p.l. 50 col.pl. F.
Colas 609. LC 10:2710

Costumes militaires français. [Paris, Delpech 1818]
28 col.pl. Q.
Colas notes also an edition in smaller format with plates in black and white, (Octavo) published 1821, each plate signed D. L. D.
Colas 603

[Croquis à la manière noire dédiés à Béranger. Paris, Gihaut 1840]
9pl. F.
Lithographs by Villain
Lipperheide 1168m

Croquis inédits de Charlet. Reproduits d'après l'album de Mr. le ... Vte. de Rigny, par Isidore Meyer. Paris, I. Meyer 1846
16pl. Q.
Lipperheide 1170i

[Croquis lithographiques] Paris, Gihaut 1824
16pl. F.
Lipperheide 3612

L'empereur et la garde impériale. Paris, A. Bry ca1845
36? pl.(numbered irreg. 1-84) F.
Cataloged from Colas
Colas 607

L'empereur et la garde impériale ... avec un précis historique ... par M. Adrien Pascal. Paris, Perrotin 1853
16p. 46pl.(part col.) F.
Plates are signed: Charlet, and printed by A. de Bry and are the enlarged plates of the ex-garde to which have been added the plates relating to the army of Napoleon I
Colas 608

Vie civile, politique et militaire du caporal Valentin. Paris, Gihaut [1842]
1 l. 51pl. 1 facsim. ob.Q.
Shows French costume of the period

La vieille armée française. Paris, C. Motte 1820
13pl. F.
The French army of 1809
There are other collections of Charlet's work which show French costume of the first half of the 19th century
Colas 605

Charlet, Nicolas Toussaint, and Jaime, Ernest

Scènes des mémorables journées des 27, 28, 29 juillet 1830. Paris, Gihaut ca1831
1 l. 18 illus.(on 1 l.) 4pl. F.
French and English text. The streets, houses, etc. are by Jaime, the figures by Charlet
Lipperheide 1161

Charlotte de Belgique. Reinach-Foussemagne, H. de, comtesse

The **charm** of Kashmir. O'Connor, V. C. S.

Le **charme.** Henry, Elisa

Charnay, Désiré

Les anciennes villes du Nouveau monde; voyages d'explorations au Mexique et dans l'Amérique Centrale ... 1857-1882. Paris, Hachette 1885
469p. illus. pl. maps. front.(port.) map. O.

The ancient cities of the New World; tr. from the French by J. Gonino and Helen S. Conant. London, Chapman and Hall 1887
xxxii,514p. illus. port. map. Q.
LC 2-13483

Charnay, Désiré—*Continued*

Cités et ruines américaines: Mitla, Palenqué, Izamal, Chichen-Itza, Uxmal; recueillies et photographiées par Désiré Charnay; avec un texte par M. Viollet-le-Duc ... suivi du voyage et des documents de l'auteur. Paris, Gide [etc.] 1863
543p. illus. O. and atlas of 49 pl. F.
"Antiquités américaines, par Viollet-le-Duc": p 1-104
LC 2-4883

Le Mexique; souvenirs et impressions de voyage. Paris, E. Dentu [etc.] 1863
439p. D.
On Mexico 1858-61
LC 2-408

Charnois, Jean Charles Le Vacher de. See Le Vacher de Charnois, J. C.

Charpentier, Amédée
(lithgr.) Colin, Mme Anaïs. Les dames cosmopolites

Charpentier, Eugène
Costumes militaires sous la deuxième république. Paris, Lebrasseur & Hautecoeur; Londres, Gambart ca1850
20 col.pl. Q.
Colas 611

(lithgr.) Foussereau. Milices révolutionnaires sous le gouvernement provisoire [du 24 Fevrier au 4 Mai 1848]

Charpentier, Henri Désiré
Recueil des costumes de la Bretagne & les autres contrées de la France; où la mise des habitans offre quelque singularité remarquable. Nantes, Charpentier [1829-31]
2v. 120 col.pl. Q.
Colas 612. Lipperheide 1195

Charpentier, L. See Molé, G. F. R. Essais historiques sur les modes et sur le costume en France

Charta lusoria tetrastichis. See Amman, Jost. Kartenspielbuch

Charteris, Leslie
(tr.) Belmonte y Garcia, Juan. Juan Belmonte, killer of bulls

Chase, Mrs Lewis
A vagabond voyage through Brittany. Philadelphia, J. B. Lippincott company; London, Hutchinson 1915
316p. front. pl. O.
LC A16-61

Chasles, Philarète. See Gautier, Théophile. Les beautés de l'opéra

Chassé, Charles. See Blum, André, jt. auth.

La **châsse** de Sainte Ursule gravée ... d'après Jean Memling. Delepierre, Octave and Voisin, Auguste

Chasse et amusemens nationaux de la Grande Bretagne. See Alken, H. T. The national sports of Great Britain

Chasses anciennes d'après les manuscrits des XIV. & XV. siècles. Aubry, Charles

Les **chasseurs** à pied. Payard, Pol

Chassiron, Charles, baron de
Aperçu pittoresque de la Régence de Tunis. Paris, Bénard 1849
27p. 42 col.pl. F.

Chassiron, Gustave Charles Alexandre Martin, baron de. See Chassiron, Charles, baron de

Chataignier
[Costumes militaires et civil] Paris, Chataignier An 8-an 13 (1800-15?)
131 numbered pl. (and others unnumb.) F.
A series of prints showing French official and military costume from the Consulate to the Restoration
Colas 613

[Costumes officiels des fonctionnaires du Directoire] Paris, Chataignier 1796
20 col.pl. Q.
Costume of members of the Directoire, ministers, the executive secretary, etc.
Lipperheide 1786

Chatelain
(engr.) Dalton, Richard. Antiquities and views in Greece and Egypt

[**Châtillon, Jérôme de**]
Brief et utile discours sur l'immodestie et superfluité des habits. Lyon, A. Gryphius 1577
71p. Q.

Châtiments usetés chez les Chinois. See Hempel, Friedrich. Die strafen der Chinesen

Châtiments usités en Russie. Richter, J. G., and Geissler, C. G. H.

Chats on costume. Rhead, G. W.

Chats on old jewellery and trinkets. Percival, MacIver

Chats on old lace and needlework. Lowes, Mrs E. L.

Chaucer, Geoffrey, characters. See England —14th century

Chaucers Canterbury pilgrims. Blake, William

Chauvet, Stéphen
La Normandie ancestrale; ethnologie, vie, coutumes, meubles, ustensiles, costumes, patois. Paris, Boivin c1921
170p. illus. O. 12fr.
LC 22-5235

Chauveton, U.
(tr.) Benzoni, Girolamo. Americae pars quarta-sexta

Chaveau, François
(engr.) Félibien, André, sieur des Avaux et de Javercy. Les divertissemens de Versailles

Chavez Nogales, Manuel. See Belmonte y Garcia, Juan. Juan Belmonte, killer of bulls

Chefs-d'Oeuvre dramatiques du XVIIIe siècle ou choix des pièces les plus remarquables de Régnard, Lesage, Destouches, Beaumarchais, Marivaux ... Édition ornée de portraits. Dessinés par M. Geffroy; introd. par Jules Janin Paris, Laplace, Sanchez et cie 1872
674p. 20 col.pl. O.
Pictures of actors in costume of their roles
Lipperheide 3225

Chełminski, Jan V.
L'armée du duché de Varsovie; texte par le commandant A. Malibran. Paris, J. Leroy 1913
314p. front. illus. 52pl.(50 col.) ports. F
"Notices biographiques sur les généraux et officiers polonais dont les portraits sont reproduits dans cet ouvrage": p[285]-95
"Ouvrages consultés": p[297]-98
Colas 614. LC 16-15733

Cheney, Sheldon
The theatre; three thousand years of drama, acting and stagecraft. New York, Tudor publishing co. 1929
558p. front. illus. pl. ports. O.
Reprinted October 1930; January 1935
Bibliography: p547-49
LC A36-282

Chenu, Jean Charles, and Oeillet des Murs, Marc Athanase Parfait
La fauconnerie ancienne et moderne, par J. C. Chenu et O. des Murs. Supplément au tome deuxième des Leçons élémentaires sur l'histoire naturelle des oiseaux. Paris, L. Hachette 1862
176p. illus. diagrs. D.
"Observations sur le vol des oiseaux": p[121]-49
LC 30-32268

Chéreau, F.
(pub.) Eisen, C. D. J. Nouveau recueil des troupes qui forment la garde et maison du roy
(pub.) La Rue, P. D. Nouveau recueil des troupes légères de France

Chéreau, J.
(pub.) Costumes français

Chéreau, Mme Vve.
(pub.) Garde royale. Paris, Mme Vve. Chéreau 1825?
12 col.pl.
Described by Glasser, p103, as inferior to the suites by Martinet, Genty, Basset and Canu
Colas 615

Cheremisses
Harva, Uno. Die religion der Tscheremissen. 1926

Chertablon, de
La maniere de se bien preparer a la mort par des considerations sur la cene, la passion, & la mort de Jesus-Christ; avec de trés-belles estampes emblematiques. Anvers, G. Gallet 1700
63p. 42pl.(incl.front.) Q.
Engravings are by Romein de Hooghe
Lipperheide 940. LC CA18-1687

Chéruel, Pierre Adolph
(tr.) See note under Rich, Anthony. The illustrated companion to the Latin dictionary and Greek lexicon

Chery, Philippe
(illus.) Le Vacher de Charnois, J. C. Recherches sur les costumes et sur les théatres de toutes les nations, tant anciennes que modernes

Chesneau, Ernest Alfred. See Guichard, Édouard. Dessins de décoration des principaux maîtres

Chesson, Wilfrid Hugh. See Pennell, Joseph. The work of Charles Keene

Chester, S. Beach
Secrets of the tango; its history and how to dance it. London, T. W. Laurie 1914
62p. 8pl. O. 6d

La **chevalerie.** Gautier, Léon

Chevalier de *, pseud.** See Villiers, Henri de

Chevalier, Pierre Michel. See Pitre-Chevalier, P. M. F. C., called

Chevallier, Guillaume Sulpice. See Gavarni, G. S. C.

Chevigny, de
La science des personnes de la cour, de l'épée et de la robe; 6. éd ... [éd] par M. de Limiers. Amsterdam, Honoré et Chatelain 1723
4v. pl. maps. O.

Chevreul, Michel Eugène
De la loi du contraste simultané des couleurs, et de l'assortiment des objets colorés. Paris, Pitois-Levrault 1839
xv,735p. 2 fold.tab. O. and atlas of 40pl.(part col. and fold.) sq.Q.
"Cet ouvrage ... a été l'objet de huit leçons publiques, faites aux Gobelins ... 1836 et ... 1838" page xv
German translation: *Die farbenharmonie* (Stuttgart, Neff 1847) For a later edition see Jaennicke's *Die farbenharmonie*
LC 10-19705

The principles of harmony and contrast of colours, and their applications to the arts; tr. by Charles Martel [pseud.]. 3d ed. London, G. Bell 1899
xlvi,465p. 2pl. diagr. D. (Bohn's scientific library)
Translation of his *De la loi du contraste.* Section III pages 657-730, on clothing
LC 4-11699

Cheyne, Thomas Kelly, and Black, John Sutherland
(eds.) Encyclopaedia biblica; a critical dictionary of the literary, political and religious history, the archaeology, geography, and natural history of the Bible. New York, The Macmillan company [etc.] 1899-1903
4v. illus. maps(part double) plan. Q.
Contains a large amount of material on religious costume, special garments, festival dress, and ornaments
LC 2-705

Chiappa, Giovanni Battista
Disegni d'alcune opere eseguite in occasione della fausta venuta in Lombardia di S. M. l'imperatore e re Ferdinando primo. Milano, Pirotta 1838
[8]p. 4pl. F.

Chiavacci, Vincenz. See Wienerstadt, lebensbilder aus der gegenwart

Chic! Hohenheim, A., and Richards, E.

Le **chic** à cheval. Vallet, L.

Chic et pratique; combined with Jardin des modes. v 1-3; mars, 1933-oct. 1935. Paris, Condé Nast
Illus. Q. 40fr. a year
Published monthly. Each issue includes a pattern supplement
Formed by the union of the subsections: Les ouvrages, and Les patrons of *Les Albums ... du Jardin des modes*
Title varies: Mar. 1933-Feb. 1934, *Soyons pratiques*; Mar.-Aug. 1924, *Soyons chic et pratiques*; Sept. 1934-Oct. 1935, *Chic et pratique.* Absorbed by *Le Jardin des modes* Nov. 1935

Chicago. World's Columbian exposition, 1893. See Oriental and occidental northern and southern portrait types of the Midway plaisance

Chicago apparel gazette. See Men's wear; the retailer's newspaper

Les **chiffres** au XIXme siècle. Leborgne, Paul

Chiffres Louis XV. Fougeadoire, Paris

Chiffres modernes. Fougeadoire, Paris

Chiffres renaissance. Fougeadoire, Paris

Child, Théodore

Les peintures de la jeunesse ... gravures sur bois par Méaulle. Paris, Ducrocq 1889

289p. 60pl. Q.
Shows children of Italy, Spain, Flanders, Holland, England, Germany, France

Wimples and crisping pins: being studies in the coiffure and ornaments of women, by Theodore Child. New York, Harper and brothers 1895

xi,209p. illus. pl. ports. O. $1.50, o.p.
Costume index. LC 8-34023

The **child** in art. Carpenter, M. B.

The **child** in art & nature. Braun, A. A.

Child life in all nations. Botsford, A. H.

Child-life in art. Hurll, E. M.

Child life in China. Bryson, Mrs M. I.

The **childhood** of man. Frobenius, Leo

Child-life in colonial days. Earle, Mrs A. M.

Child life in pictures: heliotypes with descriptive letterpress. Boston, Osgood 1877

illus. D. $3
From paintings of the 15th to 18th centuries

Children

Ballin, A. S. Children's dress. 1884

Botsford, A. H. Child life in all nations. c1901

Braun, A. A. The child in art & nature. 1921

Carpenter, M. B. The child in art. 1906

Child, Théodore. Les peintures de la jeunesse. 1889

Child life in pictures. 1877

Entwistle, Mary. Children of other lands. 1923

Hurll, E. M. Child-life in art. 1898

Jackson, Margaret. What they wore. 1936

Macfall, Haldane. Beautiful children immortalised by the masters. 1909

Macquoid, Percy. Four hundred years of children's costume from the great masters, 1400-1800. 1923

Menpes, Mortimer. World's children. 1903

Moore, Mrs H. H. Children of other days. 1905

Müllerheim, Robert. Die wochenstube in der kunst. 1904

Ploss, H. H. Das kleine kind von tragbett bis zum ersten schritt. 1881

Sauerlandt, Max. Kinderbildnisse aus fünf jahrhunderten der europäischen malerei von etwa 1450 bis etwa 1850. 1921

Schwartz, J. A. Famous pictures of children. c1907

Fancy dress

Schild, Marie. Children's fancy costumes. 1886

China

Bryson, Mrs M. I. Child life in China. 1900

Headland, I. T. The Chinese boy and girl. 1901

England

Bedford, Jessie. English children in the olden time. 1907

Brooke, Iris. English children's costumes since 1775. 1930

Fleming, J. A. Garment making. The cutting-out and making-up of common-sense comfortable clothing for children 1912

Lloyd's magazine. 1887+

May, Phil. Phil Mays' gutter-snipes. 1896

The Queen, the Lady's newspaper 1847+

Stone, Melicent. The Bankside costume book for children. 1913

France

Charlet, N. T. Album lithographique. 185-?

Franklin, A. L. A. La vie privée d'autrefois; arts et métiers, modes, moeurs, usages des Parisiens du XII. au XVIII. siècle. [v 19-20]

Grévedon, P. L. H. XII portraits d'enfants. 183-?

Legrand, Augustin. Candeur et bonté, ou Les quatre âges d'une femme. ca1820

Modes de Paris. Costumes d'enfans. ca1810

Periodical

Les Enfants du Jardin des modes. 1928+?

Germany

Boesch, Hans. Kinderleben in der deutschen vergangenheit. Mit einhundertneunundvierzig abbildungen und beilagen nach den originalen aus dem 15.-18. jahrhundert. 1900

Donner, Mizi, ed. Stil im kinderkleid. 1924

Familien-spiele aus dem im besitz ... des kronprinzen und der kronprinzessin des deutschen reiches und von Preussen befindlichen spielschrein. 1886

Klemm, Heinrich. Die gesammte kindergarderobe. 1876

Musäus, J. K. A. Moralische kinderklapper für kinder und nichtkinder. 1823

Periodicals

Baby; eine zeitschrift für mütter. 1899-1900

Kindergarderobe. 1894-1919

India

Marston, A. W. The children of India. 1883

Japan

Caiger, G. Dolls on display. 1933

Chōkōrō, Hōshun. ... Jimbuts' gafu. n.d.

Collection of Children's sports. 1888

Children—*Continued*

Netherlands

Chalon, Christina. Tweeëndertig stuks studien ordonnantien. 1779

Sweden

Larsson, C. O. Andras barn. 1913

United States

Colonial period, 1607-1775

Earle, Mrs A. M. Child-life in colonial days. 1899

Hart, A. B., and Hazard, B. E. Colonial children. 1901

New York life insurance company. Colonial children's costumes. 1900

United States. George Washington bicentennial commission. George Washington play and pageant costume book, c1931

20th century

Alexander, V. M. Appropriate clothes for the high school girl. 1920

Carpenter, F. G., and Carpenter, Frances. The clothes we wear. 1926

Kneeland, Natalie. Infants' and children's wear. 1925

Synge, M. B. Simple garments for infants. 1914

Periodicals

Children's vogue. 1919-25

Designer and manufacturer; a magazine devoted to the designing and manufacture of men's, boys' and children's clothing. 1933+

Infants' and children's review. 1926+

The **children** of India. Marston, A. W.

Children of other days. Moore, Mrs H. H.

Children of other lands. Entwistle, Mary

The **children** of the cold. Schwatka, Frederick

The **children** of the mist. Campbell, Lord Archibald

The **children's** book of Edinburgh. Grierson, E. W.

Children's costume royal. See Children's vogue

Children's dress. Ballin, A. S.

Children's fancy costumes. Schild, Marie

Children's royal. See Children's vogue

Children's vogue. v 1-7, Sept. 1917-Aug./Sept. 1925. Greenwich, Conn., Condé Nast pub. inc.
7v.
Title varies: v 1-3, no 1 *Children's costume royal*; v3 no2-v5 no3 *Children's royal.* Absorbed by *Vogue pattern book*

Chile

Schmidtmeyer, Peter. Travels into Chile, over the Andes, in the years 1820 and 1821. 1824

Chimani, Leopold

Das portefeuille des wissbegierigen: ein werk für die jugend; Enthaltend: sitten und trachten verschiedener völker, das ritterthum, die Stephanskirche zu Wien und den Dom zu Mailand. Wien, H. F. Müller [1841]
84p. 24 col.pl.(incl.front.) O.
LC 20-14729

China. President

Specifications for the uniforms of the Chinese navy; promulgated by Presidential mandate on Jan. 18, 1913. No place, 1913?
68p. col.illus.

China

Arlington, L. C. The Chinese drama from the earliest times until to-day. 1930

Doré, Henri. Recherches sur les superstitions en Chine. 1911-36

Doré, Henri. Researches into Chinese superstitions. 1914-33

Gray, J. H. China: a history of the laws, manners, and customs of the people. 1878

Kircher, Athanasius. China monumentis. 1667

McNabb, R. L. The women of the Middle kingdom. 1903

Mémoires concernant l'histoire, les sciences, les arts, les moeurs, les usages, &c. des Chinois. 1776-91

Moore, Frederick. Catalog of brilliant old robes from the late court of the Manchus. 1917

New York. Metropolitan museum of art. Chinese textiles. 1934

Tun, Li-ch'ên. Annual customs and festivals in Peking as recorded in the Yen-ching Suishih-chi by Tun Li-ch'en. 1936

See also Chinese in the United States; Manchuria; Prisoners; Sungaria; Tatars; also subdivision China under Arms and armor; Ceremonial and festival costume; Children; Decoration and ornament; Embroidery; Hair-dressing; Legal costume; Military costume; Naval costume; Occupations; Workmen

Early period, to 1643

Barbosa, Duarte. A description of the coasts of East Africa and Malabar in the beginning of the sixteenth century. 1866

Helman, I. S. Abrégé historique des principaux traits de la vie de Confucius. ca 1790

17th century

Belevitch-Stankevitch, H. Le goût chinois en France au temps de Louis XIV. 1910

Bouvet, Joachim. L'estat présent de la Chine en figures. 1697

Dapper, Olfert. Gedenkwaerdig bedryf der Nederlandsche Oost-Indische maetschappye, op de kuste en in het keizerrijk van Taising of Sina. 1670

China—17th century—*Continued*

Le Comte, L. D. Nouveau memoires sur l'etat present de la Chine. 1696

Le Comte, L. D., Le Gobien, Charles, and Bouvet, Joachim. Das heutige Sina. 1699-1700

Nieuhof, Johan. L'ambassade de la Compagnie orientale des Provinces Unies vers l'empereur de la Chine, ou grand cam de Tartarie. 1665

Wagner, J. C. Das mächtige kayser-reich Sina und die asiatische Tartarey vor augen gestellet. 1688

18th century

Chambers, Sir William. Designs of Chinese buildings, furniture, dresses, machines, and utensils. 1757

Chambers, Sir William. Traité des edifices meubles, habits, machines et ustensiles des Chinois. 1776

Du Halde, J. B. Description géographique, historique, chronologique, politique, et physique de l'empire de la Chine et de la Tartarie chinoise. 1735

Helman, I. S. Faits mémorables des empereurs de la Chine, tirés des annales chinoises. 1788

Schenk, Peter. Nieuwe geinventeerde Sineesen, met groote moeyte geteekent en in 't ligt gegeven. ca1740

Watteau, J. A. Diverses figures chinoises et tartares. ca1740

19th century

Alexander, William. The costume of China. 1805

Alexander, William. Costumes et vues de la Chine. 1815

Alexander, William. Picturesque representations of the dress and manners of the Chinese. 1814

Alexander, William. Vues, costumes, moeurs et usages de la Chine. ca.1815

Allom, Thomas. China, in a series of views, displaying the scenery, architecture and social habits, of that ancient empire. 1843

Allom, Thomas. The Chinese empire, historical and descriptive. 184-?

Baber, E. C. Travels and researches in the interior of China. 1886

Beauvoir, Ludovic, marquis de. Pékin, Yeddo, San Francisco. 1902

Bland, J. O. P., and Backhouse, Edmund. China under the empress dowager. 1910

Borget, Auguste. La Chine et les chinois. 1842

Borget, Auguste. Sketches of China and the Chinese

Breton de la Martinière, J. B. J. China: its costume, arts, manufactures, etc. 1812

Breton de la Martinière, J. B. J. La Chine en miniature. 1811[-1812]

Breton de la Martinière, J. B. J. Coup d'oeil sur la Chine, ou Nouveau choix de costumes, arts et métiers de cet empire. 1812

China in miniature. 1833

Colin, Mme Anais. Les filles du celeste empire. ca 1850

Corti, E. C. Chinesisches bilderbuch. c1935

Dagneau, L. De la Chine au point de vue commercial, social et moral. 1844

Daniell, Thomas, and Daniell, William. A picturesque voyage to India, by the way of China. 1810

Davis, Sir J. F., bart. The Chinese: a general description of the empire of China and its inhabitants. 1848

Doolittle, Justus. Social life of the Chinese. 1868

Escayrac de Lauture, Stanislas, comte d'. Mémoires sur la Chine. 1865

Eyriès, J. B. B. La Chine, ou costumes, moeurs et usages des Chinois. ca1822

Forgues, P. E. D. La Chine ouverte. 1845

Holmes, Samuel. Voyage en Chine et en Tartarie à la suite de l'ambassade de lord Macartney. 1805

Malpière, D. B. de. La Chine: moeurs, usages, costumes. 1825-27

Mason, G. H. The costume of China. 1800

Northrop, H. D. The flowery kingdom and the land of the mikado. 1894

Pauthier, J. P. G. Chine; ou, Description historique, géographique et littéraire de ce vaste empire, d'après des documents chinois. 1837

Perry, M. C. Narrative of the expedition of an American squadron to the China seas and Japan, performed in the years 1852, 1853 and 1854. 1856

Shoberl, Frédéric, ed. China. 1823

Thomson, John. Illustrations of China and its people. 1873-74

20th century

Andrews, R. C., and Andrews, Mrs Y. B. Camps and trails in China. 1918

Ball, J. D. The Chinese at home. 1912

Ball, J. D. Things Chinese. 1892

Bland, J. O. P., and Backhouse, Edmund. China under the empress dowager. 1910

Boerschmann, Ernst. Picturesque China, architecture and landscape; a journey through twelve provinces. 1923

Brandt, M. A. S. von. Der Chinese in der öffentlichkeit und der familie wie er sich selbst sieht und schildert. [1911]

Browne, G. W. The new America and the Far East. 1907 v7-8

Carpenter, F. G. China. 1925

Chitty, J. R. Things seen in China. 1909

Fisher, Mrs W. H. Twins travelogues. v4. 1924

Franck, H. A. Roving through southern China. 1925

Franck, H. A. Wandering in northern China. 1923

Grohmann, J. G. Gebräuche und kleidungen der Chinesen. 1800-10

Hardy, E. J. John Chinaman at home. 1905

Hodous, Lewis. Folkways in China. 1929

China—20th century—*Continued*
Hosie, D. S., lady. Two gentlemen of China. 1924
Hubrecht, Alph. Grandeur et suprématie de Peking. 1928
Jack, R. L. The back blocks of China. 1904
Kemp, E. G. The face of China. 1909
Little, A. H. N. B. Round about my Peking garden. 1905
Menpes, Mortimer. China. 1909
Payer von Thurn, Rudolf, ritter. Chinesische miniaturen. 1924
Tafel, Albert. Meine Tibetreise. 1914

China. Carpenter, F. G.

China: a general description of that empire and its inhabitants. See Davis, Sir J. F., bart. The Chinese: a general description of the empire of China and its inhabitants

China, architecture and landscape. See Boerschmann, Ernst. Picturesque China

China, historisch, romantisch, malerisch. See Allom, Thomas. China in a series of views; also Allom, Thomas. The Chinese empire

China in a series of views. Allom, Thomas

China in miniature; containing illustrations of the manners, customs, character, and costumes of the people of that empire. With sixteen colored engravings. Boston, Carter, Hendee and co. 1833
127p. incl.front. col.pl. T.
LC 5-9324

China: its costume, arts, manufactures, etc. Breton de la Martinière, J. B. J.

China, its scenery. See Allom, Thomas. The Chinese empire

China monumentis. Kircher, Athanasius

China under the empress dowager. Bland, J. O. P., and Backhouse, Edmund

La **Chine.** Eyriès, J. B. B.

La **Chine.** Malpière, D. B. de

Chine. Pauthier, J. P. G.

La **Chine** en miniature. Breton de la Martinière, J. B. J.

La **Chine** et les Chinois. Borget, Auguste

La **Chine** et les Chinois. Malpière, D. B. de. See note under Malpière, D. B. de. La Chine: moeurs, usages, costumes

La **Chine,** ou description générale. See Davis, Sir J. F., bart. The Chinese: a general description of the empire of China and its inhabitants

La **Chine** ouverte. Forgues, P. E. D.

La **Chine** pittoresque. See Boerschmann, Ernst. Picturesque China

The **Chinese** at home. Ball, J. D.

The **Chinese** boy and girl. Headland, I. T.

Chinese clay figures. Laufer, Berthold

The **Chinese** drama. Johnston, R. F.

The **Chinese** drama from the earliest times until to-day. Arlington, L. C.

The **Chinese** empire. Allom, Thomas

Der **Chinese** in der öffentlichkeit und der familie wie er sich selbst sieht und schildert. Brandt, M. A. S. von

Chinese in the United States
Irwin, W. H. Old Chinatown. 1913

Chinese textiles. New York. Metropolitan museum of art

The **Chinese** theatre. Chu Chia-Chien

Chinese weapons. Werner, E. T. C.

Die **chinesische** armee in ihrer neu-organisation und neu-uniformierung. Hill, J. C.

Chinesische miniaturen. Payer von Thurn, Rudolf, ritter

Chinesisches bilderbuch. Corti, E. C.

Chiodi, Pasquale. See Dura, Gaetano. Tarantella ballo napolitano

Chipiez, Charles. See Perrot, Georges, jt. auth.

Chiromanzia e tatuaggio. Cerchiari, G. L.

Chisman, Isabel, and Raven-Hart, Hester Emilie
Manners and movements in costume plays. London, H. F. W. Deane, the Year book press; Boston, Mass., Baker international play bureau [1934]
122p. illus. diagrs. D.
LC 35-1072

Chitty, J. R.
Things seen in China. New York, E. P. Dutton 1909 [1908]
251p. illus. pl. front. D.
LC 9-5229

Chivalry. See Gautier, Léon. La chevalerie

Chivalry, Age of. See Knights; Europe—Middle ages; Orders of knighthood and chivalry

Chmury, B. See Khmuryĭ, V.

Chodowiecki, Daniel Nikolaus
Daniel Chodowiecki; 25 bisher unveröffentlichte handzeichnungen zu dem Moralischen elementarbuche von Christian Gotthelf Salzmann ... vorworte von Max von Boehn. Frankfurt am Main, Voigtländer-Tetzner 1922
15p. 25 mounted pl. O. (Veröffentlichung der Prestel-gesellschaft, XI)
LC 22-14083

Daniel Chodowiecki; 62 bisher unveröffentlichte handzeichnungen zu dem Elementarwerk von Johann Bernhard Basedow. Frankfurt am Main, Voigtländer-Tetzner 1922
4p.l. 62pl. mounted on 39 l. Q. (Veröffentlichung der Prestelgesellschaft, x)
LC 22-14084

Von Berlin nach Danzig; eine künstlerfahrt im jahre 1773. 108 lichtdrucke nach den originalen in der Königl. akademie der künste in Berlin, mit erläuterndem text und einer einführung von ... W. von Oettingen. [2. ausg.] Berlin, Amsler & Ruthardt [1895]
[94]p. 44pl. 16½x26cm.
Plates printed on both sides
Lipperheide 822c. LC 13-11474

(illus.) Basedow, J. B. Elementarwerk mit den kupfertafeln Chodowieckis u. a. kritische bearbeitung. 1909

Chodzko, Leonard Jakób Borejko
(ed.) La Pologne historique, littéraire, monumentale et pittoresque ... rédigée par une société de littérateurs sous la direction de Leonard Chodzko. Paris, I. S. Grabowski 1835-42
3v. ports. pl. nar.Q.
Volume 1, p 1-425 of this title has the same text and illustrations as the author's *La Pologne; scènes historiques, monumens,* etc. published 1835
One supplementary volume issued under the title: *La Pologne historique, littéraire, monumentale et illustrée;* 3. ed., 1843

[**Choiseul-Gouffier, Marie Gabriel Auguste Florent, comte de**]
Voyage pittoresque de la Grèce. Paris, 1782-[1824]
2v. (518p.) front. port. 82pl. maps(part fold.) plans, fold.geneal.tab. F.
Volume 2, issued in 4 "livraisons" is in 2 parts, paged continuously. Imprint [pt 1]: Paris, 1809; pt2: Paris, J. J. Blaise 1822
After Choiseul's death, MM. Barbié du Bocage and Letronne completed and edited the work. Notices on Choiseul's life and works: v2, ix p.
LC 4-34788

Choix de costumes civils et militaires des peuples de l'antiquité. Willemin, N. X.

Choix de costumes de l'époque de Charles V. Schaepkens, A.

Choix de costumes italiens. Scheffer, J. G.

Chōkōrō Hōshun
Jimbuts' gafu. Tōkyō, Ohashidō n.d.
21p. 53 col.illus. O.
Title in Japanese characters
Picture-book of figures from daily life. Dancing, festivities, performances by acrobats, dancers and other entertainers, and children playing
Lipperheide 1569

[**Chopin**]
[Costumes persans] Paris, lith. de Engelmann ca1830
25 col.pl. Q.
Colas 618

[Costumes russes modernes]. Paris, lith. de G. Engelmann. ca1828
16 col.pl. Q.
Colas 617. Lipperheide 1357

Chopin, Jean Marie. See Eyriès, J. B. B. Danemark

Choppin, Henri
Les hussards, les vieux régiments, 1692-1792. Illus. de M. de Fonrémis. [Paris] Berger-Levrault [1899]
x,428p. illus.(part col.) pl. (part col.) ports.(part col.) fold.facsim. sq.Q.
LC 22-9269

Chorégraphie. Feuillet, R. A.

Choricero costume. Hispanic society of America

Les **choses** de Paul Poiret. Lepape, Georges

Chota Nagpore, a little-known province of the empire. Bradley-Birt, F. B.

Chotek, Ch. See Broderies et décoration populaires tchéco-slovaques

Chotscho. Le Coqq, Albert von

Choudens, fils
(pub.) Album de danses illustrées

Chrapovitsky, L.
Russisches musterbuch gesammelt aus den gouvernements Tschernigow, Poltawa and Kiew. Riga, 1887
15 col.pl. Q.
Lipperheide 3974

Chrieger, Christoph. See note under Vecellio, Cesare. De gli habiti antichi

Christ. See Jesus Christ

Christ in art. French, J. L.

Christensen, Sigrid Flamand
Die männliche kleidung in der süddeutschen renaissance. Berlin, Deutscher kunstverlag 1934
80p. illus. pl. O. (Kunstwissenschaftliche studien. bd XV)
LC AC34-3658

Christian, Frederick William
The Caroline Islands; travel in the sea of the little lands. London, Methuen
xiii,412p. front. pl. ports. fold.map, plans (part fold.) O.
LC 1-5285

Eastern Pacific lands: Tahiti and the Marquesas Islands. London, R. Scott 1910
269p. front. pl. ports. maps(part fold.) O.
LC A11-266

Christian, Pierre
L'Afrique française, l'empire de Maroc, et les deserts de Sahara; conquêtes, victoires et découvertes des Français, depuis la prise d'Alger jusqu'à nos jours. Paris, A. Barbier [1846]
500p. illus. 29pl.(incl. 12 costume pl., 11 col.) fold.map. Q.
Colas 619. Lipperheide 1603. LC 5-9809

Christian art and archaeology. See Lowrie, Walter. Monuments of the early church

Christiansen, Rasmus
Danske uniformer for haer og flaade; tegnede af Rs. Christiansen udgivet med tilladelse af krigsministeriet og marineministeriet. Kobenhavn, C. F. Romers forlag 1911
12p. col.pl. T.
Plates are in a separate part

Christie, Mrs Grace
Samplers and stitches: a handbook of the embroiderer's art. London, B. T. Batsford [1920]
xiv,142p. col.front. illus. pl. Q.

Christine de Pisan. Épître d'Othéa, déese de la prudence, à Hector, chef des Troyens; reproduction des 100 miniatures du manuscrit 9392 de Jean Miélot, par J. van den Gheyn. Bruxelles, Vromant 1913
16p. 100pl. O.
In portfolio
Reproduction of a manuscript with 15th century costumes
LC 13-13945

Christ-königliches trauer- und ehren-gedächtnüs der Weyland ... Sophien Charlotten, königin in Preussen. Cölln, U. Liebpert 1705
114p. 89pl. F.
Lipperheide 2530

Der **christliche** welt-weise beweinent die thorheit der neuentdeckten narrn-welt. Conlin, A. J.

Christlicher abschiede; erster [bis der vierthe] theil. Hamburg, P. Cretzeri 1593
4v. (240,256p.) 37 illus. D.
Most of the illustrations show famous persons of the sixteenth century
Lipperheide 497

Christmas mummings in Jamaica. Beckwith, M. W.

Christol, Frédéric
L'art dans l'Afrique australe; impressions et souvenirs de mission. Paris [etc] Berger-Levrault 1911
xxi,144p. front.(port.) illus. 11 col.pl.(1 double) Q.
Contents: Les Bushmen; A la recherche de peintures de Bushmen; Intailles et graffites; Des nègres du sud de l'Afrique; Art nègre; Figurines; A propos d'un parasol; Un peu de folklore; Noms, prénoms, surnoms; Mon voyage au Zambèze; L'art au Zambèze; Adieux à mon wagon; Adieux à Hermon
LC 13-2353

Christy, H[oward] C[handler]
Men of the army and navy; characteristic types of our fighting men. New York, C. Scribner 1899
6 col.pl. F.
Contents: An artillery officer; A rough rider; A cavalry officer; A naval officer; An infantry officer; A jack tar
LC 99-23

Chromotypographisches album ... enthaltend 80 miniaturen des mittelalters. See Reiss, Heinrich, ed. Sammlung der schönsten miniaturen

Chronica, das ist: Wahrhaffte eigentliche und kurtze beschreibung aller hertzogen zu Venedig leben. Kellner, Heinrich

A **chronicle** of England. Doyle, J. W. E.

A **chronicle** of the kings of England. Baker, Sir Richard

The **chronicler** of European chivalry. Coulton, G. G.

Chronicles of England, France, Spain, and adjoining countries. Froissart, Jean

The **chronicles** of Enguerrand de Monstrelet. Monstrelet, Enguerrand de

Chronicles of fashion. Stone, Mrs Elizabeth

Chronicon militaris ordinis Equitum Templariorum. Kolinovics, Gabriel

Chronicorum mundi epitome in singulos annos curiose degesta. See note under Franck, Sebastian. Teutscher nation chronic

Chronicorum turcicorum. Lonicer, Phillip, comp.

Chroniicke van de hertoghen van Brabant. Haecht Goidtsenhoven, Laurens van

Chronik der gewerke. See Berlepsch, H. A. von. Chronik vom ehrbaren schuhmachergewerk; also Berlepsch, H. A. von. Chronik vom 'ehrbaren und uralten schneidergewerk

Chronik der Hirschgasse. Heidelberg, O. Petters 1910
90p. illus.(incl.port.) 2pl.(1 double) O.
LC 18-220

Chronik sämmtlicher bekannten ritterorden und ehrenzeichen. Schulze, H.

Chronik vom ehrbaren schuhmachergewerk. Berlepsch, H. A. von

Chronik vom ehrbaren und uralten schneidergewerk. Berlepsch, H. A. von

Chronique de tous les ordres de chevalerie et marques d'honneur. See Schulze, H. Chronik sämmtlicher bekannten ritterorden und ehrenzeichen

Les **chroniques** de J. Froissart. Froissart, Jean

[**Chroniques** dites Martiniennes. Written on vellum in A.D. 1458]
237 l. col.illus. F.
A French manuscript translation and reworking of the Latin chronicle of emperors and popes, to 1394, by Martin of Troppau, or Martinus Polonius. Contains 24 miniatures. Costume and arms are of the middle of the 15th century reflecting the civilization of the south of France

Les **chroniqueurs** de l'histoire de France. Witt, H. G., dame de

Chronisten der mode. Fischel, Oskar

Chronologia summor. romrum pontificum. Capellan, Antonio

The **chronological** collection of the kings of Denmark. Andersen, C. C. T.

Chronological museum of the Danish kings, in Rosenborg castle. Brock, P. M. J.

Chronologie et sommaire des souverrains pontifes, anciens pères, empereurs, roys, princes. Saultereau, Anthoine, comp.

Die **chronologische** sammlung der dänischen könige. See note under Andersen, C. C. T. The chronological collection

Chronologische übersicht der geschichte des preussischen heers. Ciriacy, L. F. von

Chu Chia-Chien
The Chinese theatre. Translated from the French by James A. Graham. With illustrations from paintings, sketches and crayon drawings by Alexandre Jacovleff. London, J. F. Lane 1922
35p. pl.(part col.) F.
LC 23-6453

Le théâtre chinois, peintures, sanguines et croquis d'Alexandre Jacovleff. Paris, M. de Brunoff 1922
30p. pl.(part col.) Q.

Chubb, Perclval
Festivals and plays in schools and elsewhere; by [a] former director of festivals in the Ethical culture school, New York, and ... associates of the school staff. New York, Harper 1912
xxi,402p. front. illus. pl. O.
Part IV p237-57 is on Costuming in the festival. General bibliography p355-58; Costume bibliography: p391-92
LC 12-18545

Chur- und fürstlicher sächsischer heldensaal. Birken, S. von

Church, Mrs Ella Rodman (MacIlvaine)
Artistic embroidery: containing practical instructions in the ornamental branches of needlework, with nearly two hundred illustrations and explanatory diagrams. New York, Adams & Bishop [1880]
129p. 142 illus. O.
Lipperheide 3999. LC 8-23952

Church, George Earl
Aborigines of South America; ed. by Clements R. Markham. London, Chapman and Hall 1912
xxiv,314p. front.(port.) fold.map. O.
Contents: Introduction; Caraios or Caraïbes; Brazilian coastal tribes; Tapuyas; South-western Amazonia; Lowland Amazonia; Eastern slopes of the Andes; The Chiriguanos; Tribes of the Gran Chacu; The Abipones and the southern tribes
LC 14-5827

Church, Seymour Roberts
Base ball; the history, statistics and romance of the American national game from its inception to the present time. v. 1. San Francisco, S. R. Church 1902
v 1, illus. ports.(part col.) sq.F.
Contents: v 1 1845-1871. No more published
LC 2-24095

Church embroidery. See Embroidery, Church; Needlework, Church

Church embroidery, ancient and modern. Dolby, Mrs A. M.

Church needlework. See Needlework, Church

Church needlework with practical remarks on its arrangement and preparation. Lambert, Miss A.

Church of England. See Ecclesiastical costume—Anglican and Episcopal churches

Church ornaments and their civil antecedents. Legge, J. W.

Church vestments. See Vestments, Church

Church vestments. Darby, W. A.

Church vestments. Dolby, Mrs A. M.

Churchill, Awnsham, and Churchill, John
(comps.) A collection of voyages and travels, some now first printed from original manuscripts, others now first published in English. London, J. Walthoe 1732
6v. in 12 fronts. illus. pl. maps. F.
First edition: London 1704
The plates of volume 2, part 1 show costume of the natives of Brazil and the East Indies; volume 3, part 2 shows costume of Ceylon

Churchill, John. See Churchill, Awnsham, jt. comp.

Churfürstlich bayrisches frewden-fest ... welches alles in dem hierzu erbauten churfürstl. comedi- unnd thurnierhauss den 24 und 26. herbstmonat dann das Fewrwerck den ersten weinmonat under freyem himmel gehalten und fürgestellt worden. Bey den vorgangnen tauff-ceremonien dess ... erstgebohrnen chur-printzens dess ... Herrn Ferdinand Maria in Ober- und Nidern Bayern hertzogens in München 1662. No place, n.d.
35pl. F.
Illustrations by Caspar Am Ort, engraved by Melchior and Matthaeus Küsel
Lipperheide 2558

Chuse, Anne R.
Costume design. Pelham, N.Y., Bridgman publishers c1930
64p. illus. Q.
Costume index. LC 30-28277

Ciappori-Puche, Claudius
(illus.) Louandre, C. L. Les arts somptuaires

Cibrario, Giovanni Antonio Luigi, conte
Descrizione storica degli ordini cavallereschi. Torino, stab. tip. Fontana 1846
2v.(337,425p.) 97 col.pl. Q.
Eighty-four of the plates are from Loumyer's *Ordres de chevalerie*
The author's *Breve storia degli ordini di San Maurizio e di San Lazzaro avanti et dopo l'unione dei medesimi* (8 col.pl.) is in volume 1, page 17-68. Published separately in French translation by Humbert Ferrand with title *Précis historique des ordres religieux et militaires de S. Lazare et S. Maurice* (Lyon, L. Perrin 1860. 144p. 4 col. pl. O.)
Colas 622-23. Lipperheide 1930

Descrizione storica degli ordini religiosi comp. sulle opere di Bonanni, l'Helyot, dell' ab. Tiron ed altre sì edite che inedite per cura del cav. Luigi Cibrario. Torino, Stabilimento tipografico Fontana 1845
2v.(345,446p.) 95 col.pl. Q.
The text is a revision and translation of Tiron's *Histoire*. According to Lipperheide the pictures are the same with somewhat less color
Colas 621. Costume index. Lipperheide 1882

Le feste torinesi dell'aprile 1842. Torino, A. Fontana 1842
123p. 12pl. O.
Celebrating the marriage of Victor Emmanuel II and Maria Adelaide, archduchess of Austria

Cicéri, Eugène
(lithgr.) Borget, Auguste. La Chine et les chinois
(lithgr.) Borget, Auguste. Sketches of China and the Chinese

Cicero, Marcus Tullius
Officia M. T. C. Ein buch so Marcus Tullius Cicero der Römer zů seynem sune Marco. Augspurg, H. Steyner [1531]
91 l. 103 illus. F.
Translated by Johannes Neuber. Plates are usually ascribed to Hans Burgkmair
A later edition *Officia Ciceronis, Teutsch. Des fürtreflichen hochberhümpten römischen redners Marci Tullii Ciceronis drey bücher an seinen son Marcum...* (Franckfurt, C. Egenolffs erben 1565) omits five of the woodcuts, adds five by Steiner from Petrarch's *Trostspiegel*. The prints are from old plates and less clear than those of the earlier edition
Lipperheide 618-19

Cichorius, Conrad
Die reliefs der Traianssäule. Berlin, G. Reimer, 1896-1900
3v. illus. maps. O. and 2 atlases (113pl.) F.
LC (12-4035)

Cieza de Leon, Pedro de
The travels of Pedro de Cieza de Leon, A. D. 1532-50, contained in the first part of his Chronicle of Peru. Tr. and ed ... by Clements R. Markham. London, Printed for the Hakluyt society 1864
xvi,lvii,438p. front.(fold.map) O. (Works issued by the Hakluyt society. no33)
A source book for material on the Indians of South America at the time of the Spanish conquest. Costume is mentioned frequently and described on page 146
LC 5-40432

Cigogna, Giovan Mattheo
Il primo libro del trattato militare; nel quale si contengono varie regole, & diversi modi, per fare con l'ordinanza Battaglie nuove di fanteria. Venetia, C. Castelli 1583
65 l. 21 illus. Q.
First edition: 1567
Lipperheide 2049m

Cinq années de séjour aux îles Canaries. Verneau, René

Cinq tableaux de costumes parisiens. Bosio, J. F.

LII figure nelle arnese di guerre dell' hussari. See Cinquante-deux figures en habit de guere des hussarts

Cinquanta maschere italiane illustrate nei loro costumi. Frizzi, Arturo

50 leçons de coiffure: coupe, mise en plis, ondulation. Ledoux, Hector

LII figures en habit de guere des hussarts, Écossois montagnards, Pandours, Tolpats, Morlacs, Croats, Warasdins Licaniens et d'autres qui habitent de long de la rivière Sari—LII figure nelle arnese di guerra dell' hussari, Scozzési di montagna [etc] No place, ca1850
1 l. 52pl. Q.
Legends on the plates are in French, Italian and German. The suite seems to be reproduced from an earlier one
Colas 1066

Ciotti, Giovanni Battista
Prima parte de' fiori, e disegni di varie sorti di ricami moderni. Venetia, F. di Franceschi 1591
15pl. ob.D.
Later edition, published in Berlin, E. Wasmuth, 1891 under title: *Vorlagen für nadelarbeiten*
Lipperheide 3898 (German ed.)

Cipriani, Giovanni Battista
Costumi di Roma, incisi da Gio. Batt. Cipriani co' disegni del Sig. Filippo Ferrari. Roma, 1822
1 p.l. 16pl. ob.O.
Engr. t.-p. No text
With this is bound his: *Piccoli costumi di vario disegno*
LC 11-11955

Piccoli costumi di vario disegno, incisi da Gio. Batt. Cipriani. Roma, 1821
1 p.l. 12pl. ob.O. Bound with his *Costumi di Roma* (Roma, 1822)
LC 11-11956

Circassians
Curtis, W. E. Around the Black Sea. 1911

A **circumstantial** account of the preparations for the coronation of His Majesty King Charles the Second. Walker, Sir Edward

Circus parade. Clarke, J. S.

Circus performers
Clarke, J. S. Circus parade. 1937
Escudier, Gaston. Les saltimbanques. Leur vie—leurs moeurs. 1875
Lang, Heinrich. Kunstreiter und gaukler. 1881

See also Clowns

Ciriacy, Ludwig Friedrich von
Chronologische übersicht der geschichte des preussischen heers ... seit den letzen kurfursten von Brandenburg bis auf die jetzigen zeiten mit vielen erläuternden zusätzen von F. v. Ciriacy. Berlin & Posen, E. S. Mittler 1820
xii,478p. 2pl. O.
The illustrations show the development of the Prussian uniform
Lipperheide 2160

Cirino, Antonio. See Rose, A. F., jt. auth.

Cisalpine republic. See Military costume—Cisalpine republic; Naval costume—Cisalpine republic

Cités et ruines américaines: Mitla, Palenqué, Izamal, Chichen-Itza, Uxmal. Charnay, Désiré

[**Ciuli, E.**]
[Folk-costume of Rome and the provinces of Italy] Roma, 1830
12pl. F.
Colas 624. Lipperheide 1311e

Civil and military costume of the city of London. Busby, T. L.

Civil and military costumes from the vth century beginning of the French monarchy till our days. See Bassaget, P. N. Costumes civils et militaires depuis le ve siècle

Civil costume of England, from the conquest to the present time. Martin, Charles, and Martin, Leopold

Civil uniforms. See Uniforms, Civil

La **civilisation** égéenne. Glotz, Gustave

La **civilisation** primitive en Italie. Montelius, Oskar

Les **civilisations** de l'Inde. Le Bon, Gustave

La **civilité** l'étiquette, la mode, le bon ton, du XIIIe au XIXe siècle. Franklin, A. L. A.

The **civilization** of the renaissance in Italy. Burckhardt, J. C.

Civitates orbis terrarum. Braun, Georg

Claesen, Charles
Recueil d'ornements et de sujets pour être appliqués à l'ornementation des armes. Liège, Etab. lith. de C. Claesen [1857]
xxv pl. (part col.) F.
In portfolio

Claesen, Joseph
Alte kunstvolle spitzen auf der ausstellung zu Brüssel 1884. Berlin & Paris, C. Claesen 1884
7p. 30pl. F.
Also French title-page: *La dentelle.* At head of title: *Album de l'Exposition de l'art ancien*
Contains seven pages of text signed Chanoine Reusens
Lipperheide 4043

The **clans** of the Highlands of Scotland. Smibert, Thomas

The **clans** of the Scottish Highlands. Logan, James

See also Logan, James. McIan's costumes of the clans of Scotland

The **clans,** septs and regiments of the Scottish Highlands. Adam, Frank

Clapham, Richard
Foxhunting on the Lakeland fells ... with an introduction by the Right Hon. J. W. Lowther. London, New York [etc] Longmans, Green 1920
xvi,113p. front. pl. ports. O. $4.25
LC 20-17000

Clar
(engr.) Dahling, illus. Der grosse maskenball in Berlin ... 1804

Clara, Donna. See Donna Clara, pseud.

Clarac, Charles Othon Frédéric Jean Baptiste, comte de
Musée de sculpture antique et moderne. Paris, Imprimerie royale 1826-53
6v. in 7. pl. Q. and atlas (6v.) of 1136(i.e. 859)pl. ob.O.
"Description historique et graphique du Louvre et de toutes ses parties, des statues, bustes, bas-reliefs et inscriptions du Musée royal des antiques et des Tuileries et de plus de 2500 statues antiques ... tirées des principaux musées et des diverses collections de l'Europe, accompagnée d'une iconographie égyptienne, grecque et romaine et terminée par l'iconographie française du Louvre et des Tuileries." Subtitle
Volumes 3-7 of the text and v6 of the plates are edited by Alfred Maury from the author's manuscripts, and published by V. Texier
Many of the cuts of ancient bas-reliefs and statues have been reproduced in S. Reinach's *Répertoire de la statuaire grecque et romaine,* volume one of which is entitled: *Clarac de poche*
Lipperheide 119. LC 10-19696

Clarac de poche. See Reinach, Salomon. Répertoire de la statuaire grecque et romaine. v 1

Clarendon, Edward Hyde, 1st earl of
The history of the rebellion and civil wars in England, begun in the year 1641. Oxford, Printed at the Theater 1732
3v. in 1. illus.(83 port.) F.
First edition 1702-04. Most of the plates are engraved by Michael van der Gucht
Lipperheide 979. LC 2-23359

Claretie, Léo
Nos petites grand'mères: La jeune fille au XVIIIe siècle. Tours, A. Mame [1901]
318p. incl.illus. pl. ports. col.front. Q.
"200 reproductions de peintures et dessins de l'époque." Subtitle
LC 25-18932

Clark, Christopher
British soldiers 1550 to 1906. London, F. C. Southwood [1907]
12pl. F.
Colas 625

Clark, Edwin Charles
English academical costume (mediaeval). Exeter, W. Pollard 1894
73p. O.
Cover title

Clark, John Heaviside
(engr.) Williamson, Thomas. The costume and customs of modern India

Clark, Marion Elizabeth, and others
(comps.) Art in home economics; a bibliography of costume design, history of costume, interior decoration, history of furniture, architecture, art principles, and art appreciation. Chicago, Ill., The University of Chicago press c1925
x,66p. O. (The University of Chicago Home economics series)
Prepared by the Bibliography committee of the Related arts section of the American home economics association
Bibliography of costume design p 1-7; History of costume (by peoples and periods) p8-16
LC 25-21195

Clarke, Henri Jacques Guillaume, duc de Feltre. See Feltre, H. J. G., duc de

[**Clarke, J. Clayton**]
The characters of Charles Dickens pourtrayed in a series of original water colour sketches by "Kyd" [pseud.] London, New York [etc] R. Tuck & sons 1898?
20 l. 20 col.pl. Q.
LC 6-24732

Clarke, John Smith
Circus parade ... illustrated from old prints and pictures, and modern photographs. New York, C. Scribner's sons; London, B. T. Batsford [1937]
120p. col.front. illus. pl. ports. O.
LC 37-11642

Clarke, Mary Cowden-. See Cowden-Clarke, Mary

Clasen, Karl Heinz
Ost-preussen. See Deutsche volkunst. v 10

Clasen-Schmid, Mathilde
Das frauencostüm in praktischer, conventioneller und ästhetischer beziehung. Leipzig, Hoffmann & Ohnstein 1888
151p. 24 illus. O.
Colas 626. Lipperheide 3297

Musterbuch für frauenarbeiten. Leipzig, Hoffmann & Ahnstein 1881
2v. illus. Q.
Second edition, 1887
Lipperheide 4133

Neues system des zuschneidens der damenkleider auf grundlage des dreiecks. Methode Vaillant. In's deutsche übertragen von M. Clasen-Schmid. Leipzig, Hoffmann & Ohnstein [1880]
28p. 41 illus. Q.
Lipperheide 3819

(tr.) Handbuch der frauenarbeiten. See entry under Journal des demoiselles. Manuel du Journal des demoiselles

A **classical** and topographical tour through Greece. Dodwell, Edward

A **classification** of the chitons worn by Greek women. Barker, A. W.

Claudius, Georg Karl
Philosophie der toilette. Leipzig, J. G. Graffe 1800
262p. O.
Colas 627. Lipperheide 3484

Claudy, Carl Harry
The battle of base-ball. New York. Century co. 1912
xvi,377p. incl.pl. ports. front. D.
LC 12-12145

Clausel de Coussergues, Jean Claude
Du sacre des rois de France. Paris, A. Egron 1825
xi,493,cxv p. O.
Lipperheide 2483

Clauss, Josef M. B.
Rabat und chorrock: ein beitrag zur geschichte des geistlichen kostüms. Strassburg, F. X. Le Roux 1904
29p. 2pl. O.
From the *Strassburger diözesanblatt*
Colas 628. Lipperheide 1844e

Claveau, Eugene. See Galard, Gustave de, jt. auth.

Clay, Jehu Curtis
Annals of the Swedes on the Delaware, from their first settlement in 1636, to the present time; 2d ed. cor. and enl. Philadelphia, F. Foster 1858
179p. front. pl. ports. D.
LC 1-5964

Clay-Clopton, Mrs Virginia
A belle of the fifties; memoirs of Mrs. Clay, of Alabama, covering social and political life in Washington and the South, 1853-66, put into narrative form by Ada Sterling. Illus. from contemporary portraits. New York, Doubleday, Page 1905
xxi,386p. 24 port.(part col. incl.front.) O.
LC 13-24517

[Clayton, B.]
The Grenadier guards. [London, Ackermann & co. 1854]
cover-title, 12 col.pl. 42x58cm.
Costumes of the First regiment of Grenadier guards from 1660
Colas 630. LC 19-40

Clayton, Henry James
Cassock and gown. London, J. R. Mowbray 1929
16p. 6pl.(incl.front. ports.) Q. 2s 6d (Alcuin club tracts. no XVIII)
Costume index. LC 29-12725

The ornaments of the ministers as shown on English monumental brasses. London, A. R. Mowbray; Milwaukee, Morehouse 1919
190p. illus. Q. (Alcuin club collections. 22)
LC 19-12353

Cleaveland, Nehemiah
(tr.) Grandville, J. I. I. G., called. The flowers personified

[Cleemputte, Paul Adolphe van]
Paris de 1800 à 1900. Les centennales parisiennes; panorama de la vie de Paris à travers le XIXe siècle, publié sous la direction de Charles Simond [pseud.] ... illustré d'après les documents. Paris, Plon-Nourrit 1903
192p. illus. Q.
A companion volume to the author's *La vie parisienne*
LC 3-22064

La vie parisienne à travers le XIXe siècle. Paris de 1800 à 1900 d'après les estampes et les mémoires du temps publié sous la direction de Charles Simond [pseud.] ... illustré ... d'après les documents. Paris, E. Plon, Nourrit 1900-01
3v. illus.(incl. ports. maps, plans, facsims.) pl. Q.
Published 1900-1902. Some of the plates are accompanied by leaf with descriptive letterpress
Each volume has 3 indexes: Tables des gravures and Table des matières arranged chronologically, and Table des portraits de célébrités arranged alphabetically. The 3 volumes include 1211 portraits. A supplementary volume was published by the author under title: *Paris de 1800 à 1900*
Contents: v 1 1800-1830: Le consulat, Le premier empire, La restauration; v2 1830-1870: La monarchie de juillet, La seconde république, Le second empire; v3 1870-1900: Troisième république
Lipperheide 1177 l. LC 3-22252

La **clef** de tous les ouvrages de dames. Verboom, Agnès

Clemen, Otto Constantin. See Beham, H. S. Holzschnitte zum alten Testament. 1910

Clement, Clara Erskine. See Waters, Mrs Clara (Erskine) Clement

Clement, Ernest Wilson
The Japanese floral calendar. 2d and rev. ed. Chicago, The Open court publishing company 1911
66p. front. illus. O.
LC 11-8367

Clément, Nicolas, de Treille
Austrasiae reges et duces epigrammatis. Coloniae, 1591
130p. illus.(incl. 63 port.) Q.
Medallion portraits of the kings and dukes of Lorraine engraved by Pierre Woeiriot
Edited by François Guibaudet, who also translated the book into French under the title *Les rois et ducs d'Austrasie* (Coulogne, 1591. v.p. 63 illus. Q.)
Lipperheide 1064(French ed.)

Clephan, Robert Coltman
The defensive armour and the weapons and engines of war of mediæval times, and of the "renaissance." With 51 illustrations from specimens in his own and in other English collections, and also from others in some of the great collections of Europe. London, W. Scott 1900
237p. front. pl. O.
LC 2-7555

The tournament; its periods and phases; with a preface by Charles J. Ffoulkes. London, Methuen [1919]
xxiii,195p. col.front. illus. XII pl. F.
Bibliography: p xix-xxiii
LC 19-17734

Clephane, Irene
Our mothers. See entry under Bott, A. J., ed.

Ourselves, 1900-1930, by Irene Clephane. London, John Lane [1933]
xiii,240p. front. illus.(incl.ports.) O.
"A sequel to *Our fathers* and *Our mothers* ... undertaken by arrangement with Alan Bott, author of the former and part-author of the latter"
LC 34-40305

Clerck, Nicolaes de
Princelyck cabinet; verthoonende t'leven afcomste ende afbeeldingen, der voornaemste vorstē, princen, graven en heeren van Europa jegenwoordig regierende. Delf, Erffghenamen van N. de Clerck 1625
140p. 54 port. Q.
Portraits of European rulers and nobles with their wives, about 1620
Lipperheide 518

Cleri totius romanae ecclesiae. Amman, Jost

[Clerjon de Champagny]
Album d'un soldat pendant la campagne d'Espagne en 1823. Paris, Imprimerie de Cosson 1829
118p. 40 col.pl. O.
Shows costume in various parts of Spain

Cleveland, William Frederick
The prophylactic clothing of the body chiefly in relation to cold. London, H. K. Lewis 1896
15p. O.

Cleveland museum of art
A catalogue of the collection of arms & armor presented to the Cleveland museum of art by Mr. and Mrs. John Long Severance; 1916-1923; written by Helen Ives Gilchrist. Cleveland, The Cleveland museum of art 1924
294p. front. illus. 51pl. F.
LC 25-576

Clifford, Chandler Robbins
The lace dictionary; pocket ed., including historic and commercial terms, technical terms, native and foreign. New York, Clifford & Lawton [c1913]
156p. front. illus. S. $2
LC 14-7

Clinch, George
English costume from prehistoric times to the end of the eighteenth century. London, Methuen; Chicago, McClurg [1909]
xxii,295p. incl.illus. pl. front. pl. ports. O. (The antiquary's books) $2.50 o.p.
Costume index. LC 9-30145

Cloaks. See Capes and cloaks

Clodt von Jürgensburg, Michael Petrowitsch, baron
Costumes petit-russiens; dess. par M. Klodt; publié par Velten. St Pétersbourg; Paris, Lemercier ca1865
6 col.pl. F.
Title from the legend on plates
Lipperheide 1368m

Costumes russes, lithogr. par C. Schulz. St Petersbourg, Velten 1865?
16 col.pl. F.
Cataloged from Colas
Colas 1629

Clonard, Serafín María de Soto y Abbach, conde de
Album de la caballeria española desde sus primitivos tiempos hasta el dia. [Madrid, Imprenta y litografia militar 1861]
40 l. 69 col.pl. F.
Lithographs by J. Villegas
Colas 632. Lipperheide 2363

Album de la infantiera española desde sus primitivos tiempos hasta el dia. Publicado por la Dirección general del Arma. [Madrid, Imprenta y litografia militar 1861]
31p. 92 col.pl. ob.Q.
Lithographs by J. Villegas
Colas 633. Lipperheide 2364

Discurso histórico sobre el trajo de los Españoles, desde los tiempos más remotos hasta el rienado de los reyes catolicos. Publicado por la Real academia de la historia. Madrid, impr. de M. Tello 1879
217p. Q.

Historia organica de las armas de infanteria y caballeria españolas desde la creacion del ejercito permanente hasta el dia, por el teniente general conde de Clonard [Madrid, D. B. Gonzalez] 1851-59?
16v. pl.(part col.) ports. plans, col. coats of arms. Q.
Colas 631. Lipperheide 2362. LC 16-24179

Memorias para la historia de las tropas de la casa real de Espana. Madrid, Imprenta real 1828
xx,239p. 25 col.pl. Q.
"Subdivida en seis épocas, y adornada con una coleccion de laminas grabadas sacadas de varios monumentos, que representan los trages militares de los distintos cuerpos que han servido de custodia a los soberanos desde la restauracion de la monarquia goda por el rey Don Pelayo. Escritas por un oficial de la antigua Guardia Real." Subtitle
Colas 2771. Lipperheide 2359

Clothes and the man: hints on the wearing and caring of clothes: By the 'Major' of 'Today' London, Richards 1900
200p. D. 2s 6d

Clothes economy for well dressed women. Wells, Margery

Clothes, on and off the stage. Chalmers, Helena

Clothes that count. Field, Bradda

Clothing. Latzke, Alpha, and Quinlan, Elizabeth

Clothing and style. Dooley, W. H.

Clothing designer and manufacturer. See Clothing trade journal

Clothing for women. Baldt, L. I.

Clothing: fundamental problems. Jordan, Mrs L. E. B.

Clothing; selection and care. Matthews, M. L.

Clothing trade journal; a technical monthly magazine and review of the cutting-up and allied industries. v 1, 1912+ New York,
Illus. diagrs. Q.
A periodical of men's fashions. Published monthly. Current 1938
Title varies: 1912-July 1918, *Clothing designer and manufacturer.* Dec. 1928 absorbed *The manufacturing clothier*

Clouet, François
Three hundred French portraits, representing personages of the courts of Francis I., Henry II., and Francis II., by Clouet. Auto-lithographed from the originals at Castle Howard, Yorkshire, by Lord Ronald Gower. London, S. Low, Marston, Low & Searle; Paris, Hachette 1875
2v. 303 port.(incl.fronts.) F.
LC 3-15869

(illus.) Moreau-Nélaton, Étienne. Les Clouet et leurs émules

Clouet, Jean
(illus.) Moreau-Nélaton, Étienne. Les Clouet et leurs émules

Les **Clouet** et leurs émules. Moreau-Nélaton, Étienne

Clouzot, Henri. See Libron, Fernand, jt. auth.

Clowns
Disher, M. W. Clowns & pantomimes. 1925
Otto, H. W. Pauvres saltimbanques. 1891

See also Harlequin

Clowns & pantomimes. Disher, M. W.

[**Clucas, Charles**]
The etiquette of men's dress. New York, The Men's outfitter 1888
92p. incl.illus. pl. O. pa 25c
LC 10-1029

Clugny de Nuis, baron de
(illus.) Jorio, Andrea de. La mimica degli antichi investigata nel gestire napoletano

See also Costumes français depuis Clovis jusqu'à nos jours

Clyde and Black, firm, New York
Umbrellas and their history; with illustrations by Bennett. [Cambridge, Mass.] Riverside press, Printed by H. O. Houghton, 1864
74p. incl.front. 26 illus. D.
Lipperheide 1721. LC 10-25012

Coast guard, United States
United States. Coast guard. Regulations governing the uniforms for commissioned and warrant officers and enlisted men of the United States Coast guard, 1930. 1930
United States. Coast guard. Regulations governing the uniforms for enlisted persons of the United States Coast guard, 1922. 1922
United States. Coast guard. Regulations governing the uniforms for warrant officers and enlisted persons of the United States Coast guard, 1916. 1916

Coats. See Capes and cloaks

Coats of arms. See Heraldic costume

Cocheris, Hippolyte François Jules Marie
Patrons de broderie et de lingerie du XVIe siècle, reproduits ... pub. d'après les éditions conservées à la Bibliothèque Mazarine, par Hippolyte Cocheris. Paris, Librairie de l'Écho de la Sorbonne 1872
19,[135]p. illus. D. (Recueil de documents graphiques pour servir à l'histoire des arts industriels)
Cover-title: *Patrons de broderies, dentelles & guipures du XVIe siècle;* fac-simile des éditions originales avec une introduction par Hippolyte Cocheris. The illustrations consist of facsimile reproductions of the title-pages and plates of four books of patterns, published in Lyons during the first half of the 16th century
Lipperheide 3882. LC 13-12181 (2d ed.)

Cocheris, Mme Pauline Augustine (Wagrez)
L'empire d'Allemagne, précis historique et géographique. Paris, Librairie de l'Écho de la Sorbonne [1875]
352p. illus.(ports.) 3 fold.maps. D. (Bibliothèque de l'Écho de la Sorbonne)

Les parures primitives avec une introduction sur les temps préhistoriques. Paris, Jouvet et cie 1894
226p. 209? illus. Q. 12fr.
Illustrations by P. Sellier
Contents: I Bijoux préhistoriques. Tatouages. Peintures corporelles; II Déformations et mutilations au point de vue de l'esthétique; III Rôle des écorces d'arbres, des feuillages et des fleurs dans le costume et la parure; IV Peaux des bêtes employees comme vêtements
Colas 634. Lipperheide 98

Cochin, Charles Nicolas, 1715-1790
Galerie françoise, ou Portraits des hommes et des femmes célèbres. See entry under Restout, Jean
(ed.) Dandré-Bardon, M. F. Costume des anciens peuples

Cochin, Nicolas
(engr.) La Chapelle, George de. Recueil de divers portraits de principales dames de la Porte du grand Turc

Cochius, Christianus
Davids des königs in Israel heilige fürbereitung zum tode ... betrachtet bey dem todes-fall des ... herrn Friderich Wilhelmen, marggraffen zu Brandenburg ... In einer leich-predigt. Cölln, U. Liebpert ca1688
230p. 59 l. 92pl. F.
In addition to the funeral oration this contains a detailed description of the funeral procession and in an appendix eleven elegies by various authors
Lipperheide 2525

Cock, Hieronymus
Amplissimo hoc apparatu et pulchro ordine pompa funebris Bruxellis á palatio ad Divae Gudulae templum processit cum rex hispaniarum Philippus Carolo v. rom. imp. The Hague, H. Hondius 1619
37pl. F.
Later edition published under French title: *La magnifique et sumpteuse pompe funèbre faite aux obsèques et funérailles du tresgrand et tresvictorieux empereur Charles V^e célébrées en la ville de Bruxelles, la XXIXe jour du mois de décembre M.D.LVIII, par Philippes, roy catholique d' Espaigne, son fils*
Lipperheide 2654

Code de la cravate; traité complet des formes, de la mise, des couleurs de la cravate. Paris, Audin 1828
127p. 2pl.(incl. 50 illus.) D.
Colas 636. Lipperheide 1698

Le **code** de la mode. Despaigne, H.

Code de la toilette. Raisson, H. N.

The **code** of Terpsichore. Blasis, Carlo

Codex chiromantiae. Heron-Allen, Edward

Codrington, Robert Henry
The Melanesians: studies in their anthropology and folk-lore. Oxford, Clarendon press 1891
xv,419p. front. illus. fold.map. O.
LC 5-38953

Coeffures de dames. Depain

Coene, Jacques, 15th cent.
(illus.) Brussels. Bibliothèque royale de Belgique. Section des manuscrits. Deux livres d'heures (nos. 10767 et 11051 de la Bibliothèque royale de Belgique) attribués à l'enlumineur Jacques Coene

Le **coeur** vendéen; bijou populaire ancien. Baudouin, M. E., and Lacouloumère, Georges

Coffignon, A.
Paris-vivant: Les coulisses de la mode. Paris, à la librairie illustrée 1888
290p. 9pl.(incl.front.) D. 3fr. 50
Colas 637

Coggiola, Giulio
Breviaire Grimani de la Bibliothèque de S. Marco à Venise: reproduction photographique complète. See Catholic Church. Liturgy and ritual. Breviary

Cogniat, Raymond
Décors de théâtre. Paris, Éditions des Chroniques du jour c1930
37,[12]p. illus.(part col.) pl.(part col.) Q.
"Édité sous la direction de m. G. di San Lazzaro"
LC 31-17626

Cogniet, Léon, and Raffet, Denis Auguste Marie
Illustration de l'armée française depuis 1789 jusqu'en 1832 d'après Léon Cogniet et Raffet, et lith. par Llanta et Ad. Midy. Paris, V. Delarue ca1837
18 col.pl. F.
Plates are marked: "Peint par Raffet, Lith. par Llanta." Colas gives a list of them
Colas 638

Cohen, Gustave
Le théâtre en France au moyen âge. Paris, Rieder c1928-31
2v. 119pl.(incl.facsims.) on 60 l. O. (Half-title: Bibliothèque générale illustrée. 6, 18)
Contents: I Le théâtre religieux; II Le théâtre profane. Bibliography 1:77, 2:107
The author's *Le costume dans le théâtre religieux du moyen âge* (Bruxelles, P. Weissenbruch 1903. 27p.) is a preliminary edition of part of volume 1, and exists as an extract from *Revue de Belgique,* 1903. (Colas 639)
LC 28-20032

Les **coiffes** bretonnes. Bigot, Maurice

Les **coiffes** poitevines, les bijoux poitevins. Gelin, Henri

Le **coiffeur** de la cour et de la ville. Villaret, P.

Coiffure. See Hair-dressing

Die **Coiffure**; zeitschrift für kopfputz und frisur. 1.-34 jahrg. 1868-1901. Berlin, S. Cronach
34v. illus. col.pl. Q.-F.
Succeeded by *Der Damenputz.* Volumes 15-32 have subtitle: *specialzeitschrift für die gesammtinteressen des damenputzfaches.* Absorbed *Illustrirte coiffure* 1892
Editors: v 1-14 Friederike Lesser; 15-34 Therese Mauser
Colas 641. Lipperheide 4724

Le **Coiffure** de Paris. 1910+ Paris, Pronnier & Chimot
Published monthly

La **coiffure** militaire. Bornecque, J. C. C.

[**Coiffures** de femmes] Paris, Bance & Aumont ca1825
51pl. Q.
Plates are by Choubard, Negelin, Leroy, A. Z. Hubert, and Schenker
Colas 642

Coiffures de femmes. Mark, Quirin

Les **coiffures** de l'armée française. Margerand, J.

Coiffures de style. Uzanne, L. O.

Coindre, A.
(lithgr.) Les Français; costumes des principales provinces de la France

Colas, René
Bibliographie générale du costume et de la mode; description des suites, recueils, séries, revues et livres français et étrangers relatifs au costume civil, militaire et religieux, aux modes, aux coiffures et aux divers accessoires de l'habillement, avec une table méthodique et un index alphabetique. Paris, R. Colas 1933
2v. illus. O.
"Les . . . principales bibliographies": v 1, p vii-viii
LC 33-11496

Cole, Alan Summerly
Ancient needlepoint and pillow lace. With notes on the history of lacemaking and descriptions of thirty examples. London, Arundel society 1875
12p. 30pl. F.

Les dentelles anciennes, avec introduction, texte descriptif et trente-deux spécimens de dentelles ... Tr. par Ch. Haussoullier avec la collaboration de l'auteur. Paris, V. A. Morel 1878
50p. 20pl. F.
Published by the Arundel society under the auspices of the Science and art department of the Committee of Council on Education

(comp.) Dentelles d'Irlande, recueillies et annotées par Alan S. Cole. Paris, Librarie des arts décoratifs 1915?
30pl. F.
Also published in a German translation: *Irische spitzen* (Stuttgart, C. Stoll 1902)

A descriptive catalogue of the collections of tapestry and embroidery in the South Kensington museum. London, Eyre and Spottiswoode 1888
432p. 8 illus. O.
Lipperheide 3870

Embroidery and lace. See entry under Lefébure, Ernest

Hand-made laces from the South Kensington museum. London, R. Sutton [1890]
2 l. 30pl. F. (Studies from the museums)
Lipperheide 4054

Ornament in European silks. London, Debenham and Freebody 1899
xv,220p. incl.front. illus. pl. Q.
LC 9-1341

Cole, Fay Cooper
The Tinguian; social, religious, and economic life of a Philippine tribe. With a chapter on music by Albert Gale, 83 plates and 26 text-figures. Chicago, 1922
p231-493. front.(map) illus.(incl. music) 83pl. O. (Field museum of natural history. Publication 209. Anthropological series, v. xiv no2)
LC 23-2203

The wild tribes of Davao district, Mindanao. Chicago, 1913
49-203p. front.(map) illus. 75pl. O. (Field museum of natural history. Publication 170. Anthropological ser. v. xii no2)
Some of the plates accompanied by guard sheets with descriptive letterpress
LC 13-24658

Cole, Robert
Particulars relative to that portion of the regalia of England which was made for the coronation of King Charles the Second. [London, J. B. Nichols 1842]
p262-66. F.
From Society of antiquaries of London. *Archaeologia* v29
LC 2-20491

Cole, Walter
A B C book of people, by Walter Cole. New York, Minton, Balch c1932
[59]p. col.illus. F. $2.50
Costume index. LC 32-24037

Coleçaõ de estampas intitulada Ruas de Lisboa; contem figuras iluminadas que representaõ os diversos trajest, e maneiras mais constantes das gentes que servem, e habitaõ a Cidade 1819. Lisbon, L. de Carvalho 1826
1 l. 30 col.pl. O.
Colas 644. Lipperheide 1215

Coleccion de artículos. Bachiller y Morales, Antonio

Coleccion de los trages de todas las ordenes religiosas y militares de todo el mundo. Bar, J. C.

Coleccion de trages. Vecellio, Cesare

Coleccion de trages de España. [Madrid] [1832-36]
112 col.pl. O.
Colas 646. Lipperheide 1224

Coleccion de uniformes del egercito español. Zambrano, marques de

Coler, Johann
Oeconomia ruralis et domestica. Darin das gantz ampt aller treuer hauszvätter, hausz-mütter, beständiges und allgemeines hausz-buch vom haushalten wein-ackergärten-blumen und feld-bau begriffen ... auch eines calendarii perpetui ... jetzo aber auff ... corrigirt, vermehret und verbessert. Mäyntz, N. Heyll 1665
2v. 102 illus. 24pl. F.
First edition: 1609. The engravings, especially in the calendar, show peasant workmen in house and field
Lipperheide 1986

Le **Colifichet,** indicateur des modes et nouveautés manufacturières. 1.-6. annee; 1. juil. 1838-16 jan. 1843. Paris
In 1840 the subtitle was changed to: *modes, litterature, théâtre.* Absorbed the following: Jan. 15 1840, *Le Monde élégant;* June 1 1840, *Le Messager des salons;* June 16 1840, *Le Bon goût.* Succeeded by *Le Boudoir*
Colas 647

Colin, Mme Anaïs
Bleuettes. Paris, H. Cache; London, G. Junin [1844-45]
12 col.pl. F.
Plates show feminine dress of the period. They are from paintings by Colin, lithographed by Mlle Dreys and Jules Champagne. Title from the plates
Colas 655

Costumes de diverses provinces d'Italie. Paris, Giraldon-Bovinet; London, McLean 1830
12 col.pl. Q.
Also known with plates in black and white
Colas 650. Lipperheide 1279m

Costumes des reines de France. Paris, Lemercier [1845]
5 col.pl. F.
Plates are lithographed by Régnier and Bettanier, after Colin
Colas 656

Les dames cosmopolites; album de costumes aristocratiques et artistiques; lithographiés par Amédée Charpentier. Paris, R. Lebrasseur; London, J. Bouvier [1843-45]
1 l. 60 col.pl. Q.
Plates show feminine costume of different periods and countries
Colas 653

Les filles du celeste empire; lithographiées par Gsell. Paris, H. Cache ca1850
6 col.pl. F.
Colas 657. Lipperheide 1534

Groupes de costumes de différens pays. Paris and London, Gihaut frères [1834]
12 col.pl. F. 36fr.
Also published in black and white at 18fr.
Costume of Turkey, China, India, Japan, Naples, etc.
Colas 651

Groupes de costumes de la cour de France. Paris and London, Gihaut frères [1835]
12 col.pl. F. 36fr.
Also published in black and white at 18fr.
Colas 652

Le maître à danser. Paris, Goupil & Vibert; London, Anaglyphic co. [etc.] [1844]
12 col.pl. F.
Ball gowns of the period
Colas 654

Colin, Mme Anaïs, and Marin, L.
Portraits d'acteurs et d'actrices dans différents rôles. Paris, F. Nöel ca1825
70 col.pl. F.
Colas 649. Lipperheide 3212

Coline, Line. See Keim, Aline. Les costumes du pays de France

Collado, Francisco Danvila y. See Danvila y Collado, Francisco

Collard, Paul
Cambodge et Cambodgiens. Paris, Société d'éditions géographiques, maritimes et coloniales [1921]
xiv,312p. incl.front. (map) illus. ports. O.

Collars. See Neckwear

Collas, baron. See Knötel, Herbert; Pietsch, Paul, and Jantke, Egon. Uniformkunde

Çollecao dos trajos, uzos, costumes mais motaveis, e caracteristicos dos habitans de Lisbo e Provincias de Portugal. See Costumes portuguezes

Colleccâo de dezenhos das figuras de detalhes que designâo os differentes uniformes para todos os corpos do exercito. Lecor, L. P.

Colleccion de trajes de España. Cruz Cano y Olmedilla, Juan de la

Colleccion general de los trages. Rodriguez, A.

Colleccion general de los trages que en la actualidad se usan en España; principiada en el año 1801. Rodriguez, A.

Collectanea ex historijs. Creccelius, Johannes

Collection A. Lescure. See titles listed under Lescure, Alfred

Collection Besselièvre, spitzen & stickereien. Besselièvre, de

Collection complète des costumes de la cour de Rome. See Perugini, G. Album ou collection complète et historique des costumes de la cour de Rome

Collection complète des différens genres de voitures dont les Russes se servent dans leur empire et particulièrement à Saint-Pétersbourg. See Damame-Démartrais, M. F. Collection complète des divers jardins

Collection complète des divers jardins et points de vue des maisons de plaisance impériales de Russie. Damame-Démartrais, M. F.

Collection complète des tableaux historiques de la révolution française, composée de cent treize numéros, en trois volumes. Paris, Auber 1804
3v. fronts. 153pl. 66 port. F.
V. 1-2 paged continuously. 1st edition pub. about 1791-96
Text by Claude Fauchet, Sebastien R. N. Chamfort, Pierre L. Ginguené, and F. X. Pagès
Lipperheide 1133. LC 4-21524

Collection complète des uniformes de la marine et de l'armée danoise. Hyllested, H. C.

Collection complète des uniformes de l'armée et de la marine françaises. Lalaisse, Hippolyte

Collection complette de costumes et occupations suisses. See König, F. N. Nouvelle collection de costumes suisses des XXII cantons

Collection de chevaux de tous pays montés. Vernet, Carle

Collection de 54 costumes originaux de la Suisse. Schabelitz, J. C.

Collection de costumes. Vernet, Carle

Collection de costumes, armes et meubles pour servir à l'histoire de la revolution française et de l'empire. See Viel-Castel, Horace, comte de. Collection

Collection de costumes civils et militaires, scenes populaires, portraits, et vues de l'Asie-Mineure. Fulgenzi, Eugène

Collection de costumes de tous les ordres monastiques. Maillart, P. J.

Collection de costumes des cantons de la Suisse. Volmar, G.

Collection de costumes des diverses provinces de l'Espagne. Pigal, E. J.

Collection de costumes du peuple des provinces de la Belgique. Madou, J. B., and Eeckhout, J. J.

Collection de costumes du royaume de Naples. Damame-Démartrais, M. F.

Collection de costumes italiens. Boilly, J. L.

Collection de costumes militaires. Raffet, D. A. M.

Collection de costumes nationaux. Diehl, C. P.

Collection de costumes polonais. See Norblin de la Gourdaine, J. P. Zbior wzorowy rozmaitych polskick

Collection de costumes suisses. König, F. N.

Collection de costumes suisses. Lucerne, ca1820
30 col.pl. O.
Colas 658

Collection de costumes suisses dans leurs genres actuels. Wisard

Collection de costumes suisses d'après les dessins de Reinhardt. See Reinhardt, J. C. A collection of Swiss costumes in miniature

Collection de costumes suisses des XXII cantons. Reinhardt, J. C.

Collection de cris et costumes de paysans et paysannes de St. Pétersbourg. St. Pétersbourg, A. Pluchart 1823
16 col.pl. F.
Some of the plates signed: C. Kollmann
Colas 659. Lipperheide 1378

Collection de dentelles anciennes. Geneva. Musée d'art et d'histoire. Section des arts décoratifs

Collection de dentelles antiques. München, S. Helbing 1874]
12pl. Q.
Lipperheide 4033

La **collection** de dentelles au Musée des tissus de Lyon. Lyons. Musée historique des tissus

Collection de dessins lithographiés représentant les principales positions du canonnier. See Mareschal. Artillerie, Garde royale

Collection de divers habits, usités dans la ville d'Augsbourg. See Rohbausch, H. R. Sam̃lung Augspurgischer kleider trachten

Collection de figures theatrales. Martin, J. B.

Collection de las principales suretes de una corrida de toros. Carnicero, Antonio

Collection de manières de se vetir de la nation russienne. See Will, J. M., engr. Samlung der ruszischen national-trachten

Collection de manières de se vêtir des nations de l'Europe. See Will, J. M., engr. Samlung europaeischer national trachten

Collection de types coloriés représentant les uniformes français. See Pascal, Adrien and others. Galerie des victoires et conquêtes de l'armée française

Collection des costumes, armes et meubles pour servir à l'histoire de France depuis le commencement du V. siècle jusqu'à nos jours. Viel-Castel, Horace, comte de

Collection des costumes de la Suisse et de ses pays limitrophes. Bleuler, L.

Collection des costumes de la Suisse et de ses pays limitrophes. Zurich, Keller & Fussli 1820?
24 col.pl. S.
Cataloged from Colas. The same series has been published in quarto
Colas 660

Collection des costumes de l'armée belge en 1832 et 1833. Madou, J. B.

Collection des costumes des Pays-Bas. See Last, H. W. Verzameling van nederlandsche kleederdragten

Collection des costumes des provinces septentrionales du royaume des Pays-Bas. Greeven, H.

Collection des costumes du Roussillon. Vidal, J., pub.

Collection des costumes espagnols anciens et moderns. Cruz Cano y Olmedilla, Juan de la

Collection des costumes militaires, armée française, 1832. Adam, Victor

Collection des costumes militaires de l'armée, de la marine et de la garde nationale françaises depuis août 1830. Raffet, D. A. M.

Collection des costumes suisses. See Hegi, Franz. Sammlung von schweitzertrachten

Collection des costumes suisses. Zürich, Trachslerschen buch- u. kunsthandlung n.d.
24 col.pl. S.
Title in French and German
Colas 662

Collection des différents portraits d'hommes illustres. Polanzani, Felix

Collection des divers costumes composant les quadrilles du bal masqué donné à Munic le 15 fév. 1827. Nachtmann, X

Collection des nouveaux costumes des autorités constituées civils et militaires. Garneray, J. F.

Collection des plus beaux numéros de Comoedia illustré. Brunoff, Maurice de, and Brunoff, Jacques de, eds.

[**Collection** des prospects. Augsburg] ca1780
100pl. (2 col.) F.
Most of the plates engraved by Balth. Freder. Leizelt
Plates represent various countries as follows: Germany 27, Austria 4, Switzerland 11, Netherlands 8, Batavia 4, England 8, Sweden 4, France 12, Spain 9, Italy 12, Russia 1
Lipperheide 565m

Collection des types de tous les corps et des uniformes militaires de la république et de l'empire. Bellangé, J. L. H.

Collection des uniformes actuels de l'artillerie européenne. Moltzheim, A. de

Collection des uniformes de l'armée française. Aubry, Charles

Collection des uniformes de l'armée française. Mallet, and Lameau

Collection des uniformes des armées françaises, de 1791 à 1814. Vernet, Horace, and Lami, L. E.

Collection des uniformes français. Canu

Collection des uniformes militaires danois; avec 6 feuilles supplémentaires. See Husher, Th. v. Samling af danske militaire uniformer

Collection d'éventails anciens des XVIIe et XVIIIe siècles. B., E.

Collection d'habillements modernes et galants avec les habillements des princes et seigneurs. Paris, Basset ca1775-81
42pl. F.
Plates engraved by Deny, Desrais, Fauche, Joly, A. Léveillé and Meusnier
Colas 663

Collection d'uniformes militaires français de 1789 à 1857. See Bastin, Ferdinand. Costumes militaires des armées françaises de 1790 à 1856

Collection générale de costumes suisses. Snoeck

Collection H. Hoffmann; catalogue des objets d'art antiques. Fröhner, Wilhelm

Collection Henri Moser, Charlottenfels. Moser, Henri

Collection historique des ordres de chevalerie civils et militaires. Perrot, A. M.

Collection of arms and armor of Rutherfurd Stuyvesant. Stuyvesant, Rutherfurd

Collection of Children's sports. Tokyo, The Hakubunsha [1888]
2 l. 12 col.pl. Q.
Lipperheide 1566

A **collection** of eastern & other foreign dresses. Tinney, John

A **collection** of engravings containing views ... by A. Perelle ... portraits, costumes ... by A. Dieu. Perelle, Adam

A **collection** of interesting subjects of military occurences, costumes etc. Heath, William

[**Collection** of New Year's plates of the Company of constabulary and firemen in Zurich, 1689-1779. Zurich] 1780?
89pl. sq.F.
Cataloged by Lipperheide under the supplied title: *Sammlung der Neujahrs-kupfer der gesellschaft der constabler und feuerwerker in Zürich, 1689-1779*
Plates are by Johann Meyer, Joh. Melchior Füssly, D. Herliberger, J. B. Bullinger, and others. They show weapons, battle scenes, etc., with soldiers in the foreground, and are rich in pictures of uniforms of the Zurich artillery corps during this period
Lipperheide 2250

The **collection** of primitive weapons and armor of the Philippine islands in the United States National museum. Krieger, H. W.

A **collection** of prints, from pictures painted for the purpose of illustrating the Dramatic works of Shakspeare. See Boydell, John, and Boydell, Josiah. The American edition of Boydell's Illustrations of the Dramatic works of Shakspeare

A **collection** of Swiss costumes in miniature. Reinhardt, J. C.

Collection of swords of ... M. Dreger. See Dreger, Max. Schwerter-sammlung

A **collection** of the dresses of different nations, antient and modern, particularly old English dresses. London, T. Jefferys 1757-1772
4v. 240 col.pl. Q.
"After the designs of Holbein, Vandyke, Hollar, and others; with an account of the authorities, from which the figures are taken; and some short historical remarks on the subject. To which are added The habits of the principal characters on the English stage." Subtitle
Text in English and French. Title also in French: *Recueil des habillements de différentes nations, anciens et modernes*
Republished (London, J. Boydell 1773)
Colas lists (no2469) a collection with title: *Raccolta di stampe che rappresentano figure ed abiti di varie nazioni secondo gli*

A collection of the dresses—*Continued*
originali e le descrizioni di piu recenti viaggiatori e degli scopritori di paesi nuovi (Venezia, 1783-90) which he says may be an Italian edition of Jefferys's collection
Colas 2507. Lipperheide 37

Collection of the most remarkable monuments of the National museum. Naples. Museo nazionale

A collection of two hundred and fifty coloured etchings descriptive of the manners, customs, and dresses of the Hindoos. Solvyns, F. B.

A collection of voyages and travels Churchill, Awnsham, and Churchill, John

Collection raisonnée des uniformes français de 1814 à 1824. Vernet, Horace; Vernet, Carle, and Lami, L. E.

Collectiones peregrinationum in Indiam orientalem et Indiam occidentalem. See Bry, Theodor de. Grands voyages

Collections of costumes
Lipperheide 4977 to 5055 lists catalogs and guides to museums that contain costume material. These books are listed by the city in which each museum is situated. Since they do not contain actual costume material they have been omitted from the present bibliography

Gilder, Rosamond, and Freedley, George. Theatre collections in libraries and museums. 1936
Contains references to costume collections

Rocamora, Manuel. Catàleg de la col·lecció d'indumentària de Manuel Rocamora, exposada per l'Associació d'amics dels museus de Catalunya. 1933

Collectivité de la couture. See Paris. Exposition universelle de 1900. Les toilettes de la Collectivité de la couture

Colleges. See Academic costume

Collezione degli uniformi del reale esercito, della real marina napoletana. Napoli, 1844
26 col.pl. Q.
Cataloged from Colas's *Bibliographie*
Colas 664

Collezione dei costumi militari pontifici. Ferrara, Pomatelli [1834]
24 col.pl. Q.
Colas 665

Collezione di quaranta sacre ceremonie usate principalmente in Roma. Barocci, Luigi, and Fabi-Montani, Francesco, count

Collier, John
The art of portrait painting. London, New York, Cassell 1905
108p. col.front. 40pl.(13 col.) Q.
Colored plates accompanied by leaves with descriptive letterpress
Contains portraits by famous English, Dutch, Italian, and Spanish masters
LC 6-5468

Collinot, E., and Beaumont, Adalbert de
Ornements arabes; recueil de dessins pour l'art et l'industrie. Paris, Canson 1883
40pl.(port col.) F. (Encyclopédie des arts décoratifs de l'Orient. sér2)
Lipperheide 4372. LC F-2181

Ornements de la Chine. Paris, Canson 1883
40 col.pl. F. (Encyclopédie des arts décoratifs de l'Orient. sér5)
Lipperheide 4373. LC F-2415

Ornements de la Perse. Paris, Canson 1883
60pl.(part col.) F. (Encyclopédie des arts décoratifs de l'Orient sér 1)
Lipperheide 4375. LC 9-34358

Ornements du Japon. Paris, Canson 1883
40 col.pl. F. (Encyclopédie des arts décoratifs de l'Orient. sér4)
Lipperheide 4374. LC F-2183

Ornements turcs. Paris, Canson 1883
30pl.(part col.) F. (Encyclopédie des arts décoratifs de l'Orient. sér3)
Lipperheide 4376. LC F-2182

Ornements vénitiens, hindous, russes, etc. Paris, Canson 1883
40pl.(part col.) F. (Encyclopédie des arts décoratifs de l'Orient. sér6)
Lipperheide 4377: LC F-2414

Collins, Harry
The A B C of dress. New York, Modern modes corporation 1923
xvi,129p. front. illus. Q.
LC 23-13554

Collombar, A.
(illus.) Emmanuel, Maurice. La danse grecque antique d'après les monuments figures

Collombon, Jacques
Traité de l'exercice militaire, ou est l'instruction des jeux de toutes sortes d'armes, celuy du drapeau. Lyon, P. Anard 1650
116p. 1 port. 13pl. O.
The plates show uniforms of officers and soldiers of the French army
Lipperheide 2081

Collum, Vera Christina Chute
(tr.) Morgan, J. J. M. de. Prehistoric man

Collyer, James N., and Pocock, John Innes
An historical record of the Light Horse volunteers of London and Westminster ... 1779 to 1829. London, Wright 1843
55 l. 279p. 11pl.(8 col.) O.

Cologne, Germany. Städtisches museum Wallraff-Richartz
Katalog des museums. Köln, 1869
2v. in 1
Contents: [v 1] Verzeichniss der gemälde, sammlung von J. Niessen; [v2] Verzeichniss der römischen alterthümer von H. Düntzer

Cologne. Schnütgen-museum
Die liturgischen gewänder und kirchlichen stickereien; von Fritz Witte. Berlin, Verlag für kuntwissenschaft [1926]
22p. 81pl. F.
"Öfter zitierte werke": p[6]
LC 30-15463

Colombia
Torres Méndez, Ramón. Costumbres santafereñas. 1910?

Colominas, Josep. See Amades, Joan, jt. auth.

Colonial children. Hart, A. B., and Hazard, B. E.

Colonial children's costumes. New York life insurance company

Colonial colors for the bicentennial year. Textile color card association of the United States

Colonial days & dames. Wharton, A. H.

Colonial Virginia. Stanard, Mrs M. M. P. N.

Colonies françaises. Brossard, Charles

Colonies françaises. Jacottet, Henri, and Leclerc, Max

[**Colonna, Francesco**]

The dream of Poliphilus; fac-similes of one hundred and sixty-eight woodcuts in the "Hypnerotomachia Poliphili," Venice, 1499 with an introductory notice and descriptions by J. W. Appell ... reproduced for the Department of science and art in photolithography by W. Griggs. London, 1889

12p. 80pl.(incl. 168 illus.) F.
Lipperheide 471

Poliphili Hypnerotomachia, ubi humana omnia non nisi somnium esse ostendit, atque obiter plurima scitu sanequam digna commemorat. London, Methuen 1904

236 l. 172 illus. F.
Contains facsimile reproductions of the original edition: *Hypnerotomachia Poliphili* (Venice, Aldus 1499)
French edition: *Hypnerotomachie* (Paris, I. Keruer 1546); for an English edition see the author's *Dream of Poliphilus*

La **colonna** Trajana. Pistolesi, Erasmo

La **colonne** trajane. Froehner, Wilhelm

Color and design. Gillum, Mrs L. W.

Color and line in dress. Hempstead, Laurene

Color in dress

Adams, Rudolph. Die farben-harmonie in ihrer anwendung auf die damentoilette. 1862
Audsley, G. A. Colour harmony in dress. 1922
Audsley, G. A. Colour in dress. 1912
Chevreul, M. E. De la loi du contraste simultané des couleurs, et de l'assortiment des objets colorés. 1839
Chevreul, M. E. The principles of harmony and contrast of colours, and their applications to the arts. 1899
Gillum, Mrs L. W. Color and design, a practical art book. 1931
Gillum, Mrs L. W. Color secrets. 1929
Hempstead, Laurene. Color and line in dress. 1931
Higgin, L. Art as applied to dress, and to harmonious colour. 1885
Hohenheim, A., and Richards, E. Chic! Ein ratgeber für damen in allen toilettenfragen mit besonderer berücksichtigung der farben. 1890
Jacobs, Michel. The art of colour. 1923
Jaennicke, Friedrich. Die farbenharmonie mit besonderer rücksicht auf den gleichzeitigen contrast in ihrer anwendung in der malerei ... sowie in kostüm & toilette. 1878
Kellam, S. B. Color in personality and dress characterizes charming and distinctive women. 1933
Klemm, Heinrich. Unterricht im arrangement der damen-toiletten von standpunkte der kleider-aesthetik und der farben-harmonie. 1876
Moncrieffe, Mona, pseud. The magic of colour harmony in dress. 1927
Piergiovanni, Bruno. Enciclopedia dell'abbigliamento femminile. v2 p[5]-187. 1924
Schröder, Severin. Die farbenharmonie in der damen-toilette. 1897
Snow, B. E., and Froehlich, H. B. The theory and practice of color. c1918
Textile color card assocation of the United States. Colonial colors for the bicentennial year. 1932?
Weinberg, Louis. Color in everyday life. 1918

See also Art of dress

Color in everyday life. Weinberg, Louis

Color in personality and dress characterizes charming and distinctive women. Kellam, S. B.

Color secrets. Gillum, Mrs L. W.

[**Colored** wood engravings showing scenes of social life in China, and of Chinese trades-people working at their trades] No place, 1880?

50 col.pl. Q.
Title page lacking. Inclosure to dispatch no180, dated Feb. 2, 1888, from Consul General at Shanghai

Colour harmony in dress. Audsley, G. A.

Colour in dress. Audsley, G. A.

Coloured military types. Army and navy gazette, London

Colours, Academic. See Baty, Thomas. Academic colours

Colquhoun, Archibald Ross

Amongst the Shans. With ... an historical sketch of the Shans, by H. S. Hallett ... Preceded by an introduction on The cradle of the Shan race, by Terrien de Lacouperie. London, Field & Tuer [etc]; New York, Scribner & Welford 1885

lv,392p. incl.front. pl. fold.map. O.
LC 5-7349

Colquhoun, Archibald Ross, and Colquhoun, Mrs Ethel Maud (Cookson)

The whirlpool of Europe, Austria-Hungary and the Habsburgs. New York, Dodd, Mead 1907

xvi,349p. front. pl. fold.maps. diagrs. O. $3.50, o.p.
Plates show Hungarian and Bohemian costume, chiefly the peasant and gypsy types
List of principal authorities consulted: p341
Costume index. LC 7-10613

Colquhoun, Mrs Ethel Maud (Cookson). See Colquhoun, A. R., jt. auth.

Cols en broderies et en dentelles, milieu du dix-neuvième siècle. See Lescure, Alfred. Collection A. Lescure

Columna Cochlis. Bartoli, P. S., and Bellori, G. P.

Comandini, Alfredo

L'Italia nei cento anni del secolo XIX (1801-1900) giorno per giorno illustrata. Milano, A. Vallardi 1900-29

v 1-4. illus. pl. maps. facsims. D.
Contents: v 1 1801-1825; v2 1826-1849; v3 1850-1860; v4 1861-1870
LC (10-9787)

[**Combe, William**]

A history of Madeira. With a series of twenty-seven coloured engravings, illustrative of the costumes, manners, and occupations. London, R. Ackermann 1821

118p. col.front. 26 col.pl. Q.

Colas 1455. Lipperheide 1581. LC 4-34208

The history of the colleges of Winchester, Eton, and Westminster. See entry under Ackermann, Rudolph

A history of the University of Cambridge, its colleges, halls, and public buildings. London, R. Ackermann 1815

2v. col.front. 76 col.pl. 17 port.(16 col.) sq.F. £12, 12s o.p.

Authorship ascribed to Combe in *Notes and queries*, 1869 (article by W. Papworth) and in the *Dictionary of national biography* v11, p432, 434. The latter (v52, p147) also gives the work in the list of Frederick Shoberl's writings

Plates by W. Westall, F. Mackenzie, A. Pugin and T. Uwins

Costume index. Lipperheide 2030. LC 7-9202

A history of the University of Oxford, its colleges, halls, and public buildings. London, R. Ackermann 1814

2v. col.fronts. 78 col.pl. 34 port.(33 col.) sq.F. £12, 12s o.p.

This work is included in Combe's list of his own writings, published in *Gentleman's magazine* for May, 1852. The *Dict. nat. biog* (v11, p432, 434) ascribes the authorship to Combe, but also includes the work in list of Frederic Shoberl's writings (v52, p147) British museum *Catalogue of printed books* enters it under both Combe and Shoberl

Plates by A. Pugin, F. Nash, F. Mackenzie, W. Westall and T. Uwins

An extract has been published: Thomas Uwin's *Costume of the University of Oxford*

Costume index. Lipperheide 2029. LC 7-9203

Combs

Winter, Ferdinand. Die kämme aller zeiten von der steinzeit bis zur gegenwart. 1907

The **combs** of all times. See Winter, Ferdinand. Die kämme aller zeiten

Come vestivano gli uomini del "Decameron"; saggio di storia del costume. Merkel, Carlo

La **comédie** de notre temps. Bertall, C. A. d'A.

La **comedie** italienne. Duchartre, P. L.

La **comédie** parisienne. Forain, J. L.

Comédies de Térence. Paris. Bibliothèque nationale. Mss. (Lat. 7899)

The **comic** history of England. À Beckett, G. A.

Comic-prints of characters, caricatures, macaronies, etc. Darly, Mary

Comines, Philippe de, sieur d'Argenton

Mémoires; ... nouvelle ed. rev. sur un manuscrit ayant appartenu à Diane de Poitieres et à la famille de Montmorency-Luxembourg par R. Chantelauze. Paris, Firmin-Didot 1881

xii,789p. 82 illus. 4 col.pl. Q.

An English edition entitled *Memoirs ... containing the histories of Louis XI and Charles VIII, kings of France, and of Charles the Bold, duke of Burgundy ...* (London, H. G. Bohn 1855-56. 2v. 2 ports. D.) contains half-length portraits of Louis XI and Charles the Bold

Lipperheide 464

Comitium gloriae centum qua sanguine qua virtute illustrium heroum iconibus instructum. Wideman, Elias

The **commedia** dell' arte. Smith, Winifred

[**Commelin, Izaäk**]

Histoire de la vie & actes memorables de Frédéric Henry de Nassau, Prince d'Orange; enrichie de figures en taille douce & fidelement translatée du flamand en françois. Amsterdam, Vefve & heretiers de I. Ianssonius 1656

360,197p. 1 illus. 34pl. F.

The plates show battle scenes on land and at sea and the funeral of the prince

Lipperheide 2083

Comment discerner les styles du VIIIe au XIXe siècle. Roger-Milès, Léon

Comment on noue les fichus de tête. See Úprka, Joža. Vazani šátků

Commentario degli ordini equestri esistenti negli stati di santa chiesa. Giacchieri, Pietro

Commentariorum rerum germanicarum. Bertius, Petrus

Commentatio de honoratissimo ordine militari de Balneo. See Dithmar, J. C. Justus Christoph Dithmars Nachrichten von dem englischen kriegs- und ritterorden des Budes

Commentatio de personis vulgo laruis seu mascheris von der carnavals-lust. Berger, C. H., edler herr von

Commoda ruralium. Crescenzi, Pietro de

Common sense clothing. Barnett, E. A.

Les **communeux,** 1871. See Bertall, C. A. d'A. The communists of Paris, 1871

The **communists** of Paris, 1871. Bertall, C. A. d'A.

Comoediae. Plautus

La Compagnie Lyonnaise, Lyons, France. See Album 1861

Compaing, Charles, and Devère, Louis

The complete manual of cutting. London, Simpkin, Marshall & co. 1883-84

5v. in 4. illus. diagrs. F.

On the cutting of men's garments. Part 5: Waistcoat cutting. Several other titles by this author deal with cutting

The French edition is entitled *Méthode complete de coup d'habillements* (Paris, n.d.)

Companion to English history. See Barnard, F. P. ed. Mediaeval England

Companion to Greek studies. Whibley, Leonard, ed.

A **companion** to Latin studies. Sandys, Sir J. E., ed.

Companion to the Principles of Gothic ecclesiastical architecture, being a brief account of the vestments. Bloxam, M. H.

A **comparative** study of the Mayas and the Lacandones. Tozzer, A. M.

Compendio de indumentaria española. Diego y Gozález, J. N. de, and León Salmerón, Africa

A **complete** account of the ceremonies observed in the coronations of the kings and queens of England. London, J. Roberts 1727
67p. fold.front. illus. fold.pl. O.
LC 12-4995

A **complete** bibliography of fencing and duelling, as practised by all European nations. Thimm, C. A.

The **complete** coiffeur. Lafoy, J. B. M. D.

The **complete** manual of cutting. Compaing, Charles, and Devère, Louis

Complete view of the dress and habits of the people of England. Strutt, Joseph

The **complete** woodcuts of Albrecht Dürer. Dürer, Albrecht

Complexion. See Beauty, Personal

Compositions from Shakespeare's Tempest. Paton, Sir J. N., illus.

Compte-Calix, François Claudius

Album keepsake des costumes de la cour française depuis Charles VII jusqu'à Louis XVI. Paris, Journal Les modes parisiennes 1854
20 col.pl. Q.
Plates engraved by A. Portier
Colas 672

Les cancans. Paris, R. Lebrasseur ca1840
1 l. 6 col.pl. F.
Groups of women of all classes in the costume of the period
Colas 670

Costumes de l'époque de Louis XVI. Paris, aux bureau des Modes parisiennes, de la Toilette de Paris [1869]
15 col.pl. Q.
Prime du journal *Les modes parisiennes,* 1869
Plates engraved by Bracquet, Carrache, Lacourrière, Paquin
Colas 677. Lipperheide 1139

Costumes historiques français. Paris, [H. Plon 1864]
15 col.pl. Q. 10fr.
Plates engraved by Bracquet, Carrache, C. Geoffroy, and Lacourrière. Another edition was published with title: *Recueil de planches de costumes historiques de Charles VII à Louis XVI.* "Prime du journal *Les modes parisiennes,* 1865"
Feminine costume from the time of Louis XI to Louis XVI
Colas 675. Lipperheide 1091

Les douze mois. Paris, Goupil et Vibert [1840]
12 col.pl. F.
Plates show peasant dress
Colas 669

Les modes parisiennes sous le Directoire; dessins ... d'après Moreau, les tableaux et les estampes de l'époque. Paris, aux bureaux des Modes parisiennes, de la Toilette de Paris [1872]
1 l. 15 col.pl. Q.
Prime du journal *Les modes parisiennes,* 1871 and 1872
Plates engraved by Carrache, Bracquet, Lacourrière
Colas 678. Lipperheide 1140

Le musée des dames. Paris, Aubert [1851]
40p. 12 col.pl. F.
Colas 671

Portes et fenêtres ... lithographiées par Regnier et Bettannier. Paris, R. Labrasseur; London, E. Gambart [1840]
6 col.pl. F.
Shows groups in city and country dress
Colas 668

Proverbes en action. Paris, R. Lebrasseur; [etc.] 1840
6 col.pl. F.
Colas 667

Six tableaux. Paris, Journal Les modes parisiennes ca1865
6 col.pl. F.
Colas 676. Lipperheide 1173

Les travestissements élégants. Paris, Journaux Les modes parisiennes, La toilette de Paris et Le petit journal pour rire 1864
15 col.pl. Q.
Prime du journal *Les modes parisiennes,* 1864
Plates engraved by Geoffroy, Ferdinand, Monnin, Carrache, Millin
Colas 674. Lipperheide 3183

Vie élégante de la société parisienne. Paris, Journal les modes parisiennes ca1860
12 col.pl. ob.F.
Fashions and costumes of the second Empire
Colas 673

[**Compte-Calix, François Claudius; Mille, E., and Morlon, A.**]

Les délices de l'hiver. Paris, Martinet n.d.
24 col.pl. Q.
Plates 1-17 each present two feminine subjects; plates 18-24 present a masculine and feminine subject: for list of plates see Colas' *Bibliographie*
Colas 679

Comptes de l'écurie de François d'Angoulême. 2. éd. 1899. See Giraud, J. B. Documents

Comptes d'un budget parisien: Toilette et mobilier d'une élégante de 1869. Paris, F. Henry 1870
64p. O. 1 fr.

Comunn an Fheilidh

Comunn an Fheilidh (The Kilt society). Inverness, R. Carruthers 1932
23p. port. O.
A treatise on Highland dress

Conant, Helen Peters Stevens

(tr.) Charnay, Désiré. The ancient cities of the New World

Concilium so zû Constantz gehalten. Richental, Ulrich.

A **concise** description of the insignia of the orders of British knighthood. Hunter, John, robe-maker

Confederate army. See Military costume—United States—1860-1865—Confederate army

Confederate States of America. War department

Regulations for the army of the Confederate States, and for the Quartermaster's and Pay departments. The uniform and dress of the army. As pub. by authority of the secretary of war. Rev. ed. New-Orleans, Bloomfield & Steel 1861
262,107p. incl.forms. D.
"The only correct edition published. This edition has been carefully revised and cor-

Confederate States of America—*Continued*
rected from the 'Regulations for the army of the Confederate States, and for the Quartermaster's department and Pay department,' as issued by authority of the secretary of war. It also contains, all the laws appertaining to the army—both regular and volunteer"
LC 18-2671

Uniform and dress of the army of the Confederate States. Richmond, C. H. Wynne 1861
15pl.(9 col.) sq.F.
LC 5-25942

Confezione d'abiti par signora e l'arte del taglio. Cova, Emilia

Conhertius, Theodorus. See Coornhert, Dierick

La Confianza, Madrid
[Plates illustrating uniforms and insignia in the Spanish army.] Madrid, Sociedad de maestros sastres ca1919
9pl.(1 fold.) F.

Conlin, Albert Joseph
Der christliche welt-weise beweinent die thorheit der neuentdeckten narrn-welt ... Vorgestellt von Alberto Josepho Loncin von Gominne. Augsburg, J. Stretter 1706
390p. 20pl. Q.
Lipperheide 3518

Conlin, Johann Rudolph
Roma sancta, sive Benedicti XIII, pontificis maximi & ... cardinalium viva virtutum imago aeri & literis in perennaturam virtutum memoriam incisa. Continentur vitae ... qui ultimo conclavi anno 1724 interfuêre ... Omnia desumpta ex fidis manuscriptis, relationibus, publicis monumentis. Historicam relationem adumbrante Joan. Rudolph. Conlin ... icones caelante Joanne Christophoro Kolb. Augustae Vindelicorum, 1726-30
266p. front. 93 port. F.
Continuatio I-II Romae sanctae auctore F. Augustino Fabri ... 1729-30 p203-66
Lipperheide 1810

Connolly, Thomas William J.
The history of the corps of royal Sappers and Miners. London, Longman, Brown, Green, and Longmans 1855
2v. 17 col.pl. O.
Second edition published 1857 under title: *History of the Royal Sappers and Miners, from ... March 1772 to ... October 1856*
Colas 680. Lipperheide 2272

The **conquest** of Virginia. Sams, C. W.

Conrad de Meyendorff. See Meyendorff, K. E.

Conrady, Alexander
Geschichte der Revolutionen, vom niederländischen Aufstand bis zum vorabend der französischen revolution. Berlin, Buchhandlung Vorwärts [1911]
2v. illus. Q.
Paging continuous
On cover: *Kulturbilder* 4
An illustrated history with pictures of the participants in revolutions from the end of the 15th thru the eighteenth centuries

Conring, Friedrich Franz
Das deutsche militär in der karikatur. Stuttgart, Schmidt [1907]
470p. illus. 72pl.(part. col.) F.

Le **Conseiller** des dames et des demoiselles; journal d'économie domestique et de travaux l'aiguille. v 1-16; Nov. 1847-Oct. 1863? Paris
Col.illus. O.
Contains fashion plates by Anaïs Toudouze
Colas 681

Le **Conseiller** des familles: littérature, travaux à l'aiguille, modes, etc. Avr. 1874-dec. 1879. Paris, Périsse
Col.pl. Q.
Contains fashion plates
Colas 682

Consentius, Ernst
Alt-Berlin, anno 1740. 2. verm. aufl. Berlin, Gebrüder Paetel 1911
287p. front. pl.(fold.) fold.plan. O. M.6
LC 12-10656

Le **conservatoire** de la danse moderne. Sarcus, C. M. de

Const-thoonende ivweel, by de loflijcke stadt Haerlem ten versoecke van Trou moet blijcken, in't licht gebracht. Waer inne duydelick verclaert ende verthoont wordt alles wat den mensche mach wecken om den armen te troosten ende zijnen naesten by te staen. Zwol, Z. Heyns, drucker 1607
265p. illus. 13pl. Q.
Lipperheide 2853. LC 15-16942

Constantinople. See Street venders—Turkey—Constantinople

Constantinople and the scenery of the seven churches of Asia Minor. Allom, Thomas

Constantinople et la Mer Noire. Méry, J. P. A.

Constantinople, painted by Warwick Goble. Van Millingen, Alexander

Consten, Hermann
Weideplätze der Mongolen im reiche der Chalcha. Berlin, D. Reimer 1919-20
2v. fronts.(v2: facsim.) 126pl.(incl.ports.) 2 fold.maps. O.
LC 21-20238

Constitutio criminalis Theresiana. Austria. Laws, statutes, etc.

Constitutiones insignis ordinis equitum S. Stephanis regis apostolici. Viennae, J. Kurzböck 1764
35p. 5pl. F.
The plates show insignia and dress of the order and are by J. Mansfeld
Lipperheide 1913

I **contadini** della Toscana, espressi al naturale secondo le diverse loro vestiture. Bicci, Antonio

Contemporary modes; the magazine of millinery and accessories. v 1, 1934+ New York, Style magazines
Illus. F. $4 a year
Published monthly. Current 1938

Les **contes** du jour de l'an pour 1852. Lespès, Leo

Les **contesses** de van Dyck. Dyck, Sir Anthonie van

The **Continental** army uniform. Fitzpatrick, J. C.

Contrafactur des löblichen freund und nachbarliche stahelschiessens so anno 1586 den 31. julii zu Regenspurg gehalten. Opel, Peter

Contrafeth und abbildungen eines gesambten ministerij und praedig-ampts evangelischer gemein. See Hopffer, Bartholom. Icones sive effigies

Les **contraires.** Bouchot, Frédéric

[Les **Contretems.** Paris] ca1830
24 col.pl. O.
Lithographs by Villain
Lipperheide 3698

Contribution à l'étude de la mode à Paris. Beaulieu, Michèle

Contributions to the ethnography of the Kutchin. Osgood, Cornelius

Contributo allo studio del tatuaggio negli antichi Peruviani. Danielli, Iacopo

Convoi funèbre de son altesse royale, Anne. See La Fargue, P. C. Lyk-staetsie van ... Anna kroon princesse van Groot-Britanien

Conway, Katherine Eleanor
(ed.) Waters, Mrs C. E. C. A handbook of Christian symbols and stories of the saints

Conway, Moncure Daniel
My pilgrimage to the wise men of the East. Boston, Houghton, Mifflin and company 1906
416p. front. pl. ports. facsims. O.
LC 6-38349

Conze, Alexander Christoph Léopold
Heroën- und götter-gestalten der griechischen kunst. Wien, R. v. Waldheim 1875
49p. 106pl. F.

Cook, Dorothy Elizabeth. See Monro, I. S., jt. ed.

Cook, James
A voyage towards the South pole, and round the world. Performed in His Majesty's ships the Resolution and Adventure, in the years, 1772, 1773, 1774, and 1775. Written by James Cook, commander of the Resolution. In which is included, Captain Furneaux's narrative of his proceedings in the Adventure during the separation of the ships ... Illustrated with ... and a variety of portraits ... drawn during the voyage by Mr. Hodges. London, W. Strahan & T. Cadell 1777
2v. pl.(part fold.) ports. maps(part fold.) sq.Q.
Many of the plates of this edition show costume of the natives of New Zealand and islands of the Pacific
LC 5-34850

[**Cook, Millicent Whiteside**]
How to dress on £ 15 a year ... By a lady. London, G. Routledge 1874
123p. S. (Routledge's railway library, v3)

Cook, Theodore Andrea
A history of the English turf. London, H. Virtue [1901-04]
3v. (741p.) fronts. illus. pl. ports. F.
LC 4-31588

Cooks
Cervio, Vincenzo. Il trinciante. 1581
Pandini, Cesare. Il mastro di casa. 1610
Scappi, Bartolomeo. Dell' arte del cucinare, con Il mastro di casa di C. Pandini; ragionamento del cavalier R. Fusorito ... con C. Pandini; e Trinciante by V. Cervio. 1643

Cookson, Mrs Nesfield-. See Nesfield-Cookson, Mrs M. J.-P.

Cooley, Anna Maria. See Kinne, Helen, jt. auth.

Cooley, Arnold James
The toilet and cosmetic arts in ancient and modern times: with a review of the different theories of beauty, and copious allied information, social, hygienic, and medical, including instructions and cautions respecting the selection and use of perfumes, cosmetics, and other toilet articles, and a comprehensive collection of formulæ and directions for their preparation. London, R. Hardwicke 1866
804p. D.
The author's *The toilet in ancient and modern times.* (Philadelphia, J. B. Lippincott 1873. 388p. D.) seems to be an American edition
LC 8-28912

Coomaraswamy, Ananda Kentish
Indian drawings. [London, Essex house press 1910]
32p. illus. XXIX pl. Q.
LC 24-7177

Indian drawings: 2d series, chiefly Rājput. [London, Old Bourne press 1912]
34p. illus. XXVI pl. Q.
LC 24-7176

Cooper, Charles William
The precious stones of the Bible; with an account of the breastplate of the High Priest, the ephod and urim and thummim. London, H. R. Allenson 192-?
127p. front. D.
A description of the precious stones in the breastplate of the Jewish High Priest
Bibliography: p126-27

Cooper, Mrs Elizabeth (Goodnow)
The harim and the purdah; studies of oriental women. New York, Century; London, T. F. Unwin, [1915]
309p. front. pl. O. $3 o.p.; 10s 6d o.p.
Costume index. LC 16-26321

The women of Egypt. London, Hurst & Blackett 1914
380p. front. pl. D.
LC 14-16468

Cooper, James
Four Scottish coronations. Aberdeen, Printed for the two societies 1902
49p. front. Q. (Transactions of the Aberdeen ecclesiological society and of the Glasgow ecclesiological society. Special issue, 1902)
Contents: I Scottish coronations before the reformation; II The coronation of James VI; III The coronation of Anne, queen of James VI; IV The coronation of Charles I; V The coronation of Charles II; Appendix [I] The coronation of Charles II at Scone; Appendix II Translation of the bull of Pope John XXII
LC 17-25181

Cooper, Merian C.
Grass. With sixty-four illustrations from photographs by Ernest Beaumont Schoedsack. New York, G. P. Putnam's sons 1925
xx,362p. incl.pl. ports. map, facsim. front. O. $3
Presents the migration of the Baktyari tribe across mountains and rivers of Persia
Costume index. LC 25-8071

Cooper, R.
(engr.) Terry, Daniel. British theatrical gallery

Coornhert, Dierick
Emblemata moralia, et oeconomica, de rerum usu et abusu, olim inventa et Belgicis rithmis explicata à Theodoro Cornhertio ... illustrata à Richardo Lubbaeo. Arnhemi, apud I. Iansonium bibliopolam 1609
25 l. 25 illus. Q.
The illustrations appeared first in the work: *De rerum usu et abusu* by B. G. Furmerius (Antverpiae, C. Plantinus 1575)
Lipperheide 500

Copia eines unbedachtsamen schreibens über die heutige fontangen-tracht und entblössung des halses. An der Petri Pauli mess eingeloffen sambt darauff erfolgten antwort. No place, 1704
7 l. Q.
Colas 684. Lipperheide 3450

A **copper** mask from Chimbote, Peru. Dorsey, G. A.

Copping, Harold
The gospel in the Old Testament. New York, F. H. Revell c1908
1 p.l. 24pl. O.
LC 8-36412

Coppola, Giovanni Carlo
Le nozze degli deï. Favola rappresentata in musica in Firenze nelle reali nozze de serenismi. Gran Duchi di Toschana, Ferdinando II e Vittoria, principessa d'Urbino. Firenze, A. Massi e L. Landi 1637
104p. 7pl. Q.
Drawings by Alfonso Parigi. Engraved by Stefano Della Bella
Very often there is bound with this a description of the marriage festivities of Ferdinand II
Lipperheide 2746

Coptic cloths. Start, L. E.

Copts
Leeder, S. H. Modern sons of the Pharaohs; a study of the manners and customs of the Copts of Egypt. 1918

See also Decoration and ornament—Egypt; Embroidery—Copts

Le **Coquet**; journal de modes, spécial pour couturières. 1867-1875? Paris
Illus. O.-Q.
Colas 685. Lipperheide 4722

La **Corbeille**; journal des modes. 1840-1855. Paris
Q.
Published also in an English edition: *The Corbeille, journal of fashion* (1852-1855)
Colas 686-87

The **Corbeille,** journal of fashion. See note under La Corbeille, journal des modes

[**Corbesier, Antoine J.**]
Theory of fencing; with the small-sword exercise. Washington, Govt. print. off. 1873
35p. 23pl. O.
By A. J. Corbesier, sword-master of the U.S. Naval academy, Annapolis
LC 9-5086

Coriolano, Gio. B.
(engr.) Lodi, Giacinto. Amore prigioniero in Delo

Coriolanus, Christophorus
(ed.) Mercuriale, Girolamo. De arte gymnastica

Corneille, Pierre
Théâtre ... avec des commentaires et autres morceaux intéressans; nouv. éd. augm. Génève? 1776
10v. front. pl. D.
Edited by Voltaire
One plate for each play shows one character or a group

Cornelis de Bruins Reisen over Moskovie. Bruyn, Cornelis de

Corner, Mrs Caroline
Ceylon, the paradise of Adam. London, J. Lane; New York, J. Lane 1908
xiv,323p. 16pl.(incl.front. ports.) O.
LC 8-16439

Cornhertius, Theodorus. See Coornhert, Dierick

Cornil, Mme
Cent ans de modes françaises (1800-1900) ... Documents du XIXe siècle commentés et interprétés au goût du jour. Paris, R. Ducher c1932
v 1-3. col.front. pl.
Colas 688. LC 36-33704

Cornu, Paul
Gallerie des modes et costumes français dessinés d'après nature, 1778-1787. See note under Gallerie des modes et costumes français dessinés d'après nature, gravés par les plus célèbres artistes
(ed.) Besselievre, de. Étoffes & broderies XVe au XVIIIe siècles

See also note under Schéfer, Gaston. Documents pour l'histoire du costume de Louis XV à Louis XVIII

Corona delle nobili et virtuose donne. Vecellio, Cesare

Corona duodecim Caesarem ex Augustissimâ domo Austriacâ ... celebrata elogiis latinis, graecis, hebraicis, solutis, ligatis. Vienna, M. Cosmerovium 1654
73 l. 11p. 14pl.(port.) Q.
The illustrations, engraved by Wolfgang and Philipp Kilian, are half-length portraits of Rudolph I and the later emperors up to Ferdinand IV
Lipperheide 851

The **coronation** book. Perkins, J. H. T.

The **coronation** book of Charles V of France. Charles V, king of France

The **coronation** book of Edward VII. king of the Britains and emperor of India. Loftie, W. J.

Coronation exhibition. British museum

Coronation guide. See Debrett's Coronation guide

Coronation of a king. Johnston, M. F.

The **coronation** of Elizabeth Wydeville. The coronation of the Queen

The **coronation** of His Most Sacred Majesty King George IV. Nayler, Sir George

The **coronation** of King George and Queen Mary. The Illustrated London news

The coronation of the Queen

The coronation of Elizabeth Wydeville, queen consort of Edward IV, on May 26th, 1465; a contemporary account now first set forth from a XV century manuscript, by George Smith. London, Ellis 1935

88p. front. (facsim.) O.
Caption title of original manuscript: *The coronacon of the Queene*
Books and manuscripts quoted: p85-88
LC 35-29630

The **coronation** order of King James I. Legg, J. W., ed.

Coronation record number. The Illustrated London news

Coronations and coronation robes

Johnston, M. F. Coronation of a king; or The ceremonies, pageants and chronicles of coronations of all ages. 1902

Menin, Nicolas. The form, order and ceremonies of coronations, used at the investiture of all the sovereign princes of Europe, with the whole ceremony of the grand anointing and coronation of the present king of France. 1727

Menin, Nicholas. Traite historique et chronologique du sacre et couronnement des rois et des reines de France: depuis Clovis I. jusqu'à present, et de tous les princes souverains de l'Europe, augmenté de la relation exacte de la cérémonie du sacre de Louis XV. 1723

See also Crowns; Durbars; Regalia

Austria

Boch, Ioannes. Historica narratio profectionis et inaugurationis ... Belgii Principum Alberti et Isabellae, Austriae Archiducum. 1602

Falk, Max, and Dux, Adolf. Krönungsalbum. 8. juni 1867. 1867

Gurk, Eduard. 48 erinnerungs-blätter an die krönuurg S. K. H. des erzherzogs kronprinzen Ferdinand zum könig von Ungarn in Presburg, den 28. september 1830. 1830

Czechoslovakia—Bohemia

Debrois, Johann. Urkunde über die ... krönung ... des königs von Böhmen Leopold des zweiten und ... der gemahlinn des königs Maria Louise. 1806

Merkwürdigkeiten der feierlichen krönung eines königs von Böhmen; nebst dem krönungszeremoniel einer königinn von Böhmen. 1791

Rink, E. G. Das königliche böhmische crönungs-ceremoniel. 1923

Denmark

Erich, Augustus. Aussfürliche und warhaffte beschreibung des durchlauchtigsten ... herrn Christians, des vierden dieses namens, zu Dennemark, norwegen ... königes ... zu Koppenhagen den 29. augusti anno 1596 glücklich ... krönung. 1597

England

Ashbee, C. R. and Harwood, Edith. The masque of the Edwards of England. 1902

Beavan, A. H. Crowning the king. 1902

The book of the ranks and dignities of British society. 1924

British museum. Coronation exhibition. 1902

Burke, H. F. Historical record of coronation of their Majesties Edward VII. and Queen Alexandra ... 9 August 1902. 1904

Burke, H. F. Historical record of the coronation of Their Majesties King George the Fifth and Queen Mary, 1911. 1911

Catholic church. Liturgy and ritual. Liber regalis. 1870

Ceremonial of the coronation of His most Sacred Majesty King George the Fourth in the abbey of St. Peter, West-Minster. 1823

Cole, Robert. Particulars relative to that portion of the regalia of England which was made for the coronation of King Charles the Second. 1842

A complete account of the ceremonies observed in the coronations of the kings and queens of England. 1727

The coronation of the Queen. The coronation of Elizabeth Wydeville. 1935

Debrett's Coronation guide. 1911

Le grand cortége du couronnement de la reine Victoria. 1838

Heawood, William. The manner and solemnite of the coronation of His Most Gracious Majestie King Charles the Second at Manchester. 1861

Huish, Robert. An authentic history of the coronation of His Majesty, King George the Fourth. 1821

The Illustrated London news. The coronation of King George and Queen Mary: the abbey ceremonies; the processions; and the naval review. 1911

The Illustrated London news. The Illustrated London news coronation record number. King George V. and Queen Mary. 1911

The Illustrated London news. The Illustrated London news record of the coronation service and ceremony, King Edward VII. and Queen Alexandra (June 26, 1902). 1902

Johnston, M. F. Coronation of a king; or The ceremonies, pageants and chronicles of coronations of all ages. 1902

Jones, William. Crowns & coronations; a history of regalia. 1883

Legg, J. W., ed. The coronation order of King James I. 1902

Legg, L. G. W. English coronation records. 1901

Loftie, W. J. The coronation book of Edward VII. king of the Britains and emperor of India. 1902

Coronations and coronation robes—England —*Continued*

The maner of the tryumphe of Caleys and Bulleyn, and The noble tryumphaunt coronacyon of Quene Anne, wyfe unto the most noble kynge Henry VIII. 1884

Nayler, Sir George. The coronation of ... King George the Fourth. 1837

Noppen, J. G. Royal Westminster and the coronation. 1937

Ogilby, John. The entertainment of His most excellent Majestie Charles II, in his passage through the city of London to his coronation. 1662

Perkins, J. H. T. The coronation book; or, The hallowing of the sovereigns of England. 1902

Perkins, J. H. T. The crowning of the sovereign of Great Britain and the dominions overseas. 1937

Planché, J. R. Regal records: or, A chronicle of the coronations of the queens regnant of England. 1838

Robins, Joseph. Robins's panoramic representation of the queen's coronation procession in Westminster abbey, on the 28th June, 1838. 1838?

Sandford, Francis. The history of the coronation of ... James II ... and of his royal consort Queen Mary ... on Thursday the 23 of April ... 1685. 1687

Thomson, Richard, ed. A faithful account of the processions and ceremonies observed in the coronation of the kings and queens of England, exemplified in that of Their late most sacred Majesties King George the Third, and Queen Charlotte. 1820

Twining, E. F. The English coronation ceremony. 1937

Twining, E. F. The English regalia and crown jewels in the Tower of London. 1935

Vollståndige beschreibung der ceremonien ... bey dem crönungsfest ... Georgii des II. 1728

Walker, Sir Edward. A circumstantial account of the preparations for the coronation of His Majesty King Charles the Second. 1820

Ethiopia

Jacoby, Mrs C. M. On special mission to Abyssinia. c1933

France

Bévy, C. J. Histoire des inaugurations des rois, empereurs, et autres souverains. 1776

Catholic church. Liturgy and ritual. Pontifical. Liber pontificalis. 1924

Cérémonial de l'empire français. 1805

Cérémonies et prières du sacre des rois de France. 1825

Charles V, king of France. The coronation book of Charles V of France. 1899

Clausel de Coussergues, J. C. Du sacre des rois de France. 1825

Danchet, Antoine, ed. Le sacre de Louis XV, roy de France & de Navarre, dans l'église de Reims, le dimanche XXV octobre MDCCXII. 1722?

Leber, J. M. C. Des ceremonies du sacre, ou Recherches historiques et critiques sur les moeurs, les coutumes, les institutions et le droit public des Français dans l'ancienne monarchie. 1825

Lenoble, Alexandre. Histoire du sacre et du couronnement des rois et reines de France. 1825

Masson, Frederic. Livre du sacre de l'empereur Napoléon. 1908

Percier, Charles, and Fontaine, P. F. Description des cérémonies et des fêtes qui ont eu lieu pour le couronnement de ... Napoléon ... et Joséphine. 1807

Pichon, T. J., ed. Sacre et couronnement de Louis XVI. roi de France et de Navarre, à Rheims, le 11. juin 1775. 1775

Sacre de sa majesté Charles X. dans la métropole de Reims, le 29 mai 1825. 1825

Le sacre de s. m. l'empereur Napoléon, dans l'Église métropolitaine de Paris le XI frimaire an XIII, dimanche 2 décembre 1804. 1804

Germany

Arthus, Gotthard. Electio et coronatio ... Matthiae I. electi Rom. imperat ... eiusq ... coniugio Annae Austriacae. 1612

Aussführlich beschreibung der königlich-böheimischen Crönungen ... Caroli VI Römischen Kaysers ... und ... Elizabethae Christinae ... so geschehen den 5. und 8. Sept. 1723 in Prag. 1723

Bäseler, Gerda. Die Kaiserkrönungen in Rom und die Römer von Karl dem Grossen bis Friedrich II. (800-1220). 1919

Besser, Johann von. Preussische krönungsgeschichte. 1712

Diemand, Anton. Das ceremoniell der kaiserkrönungen von Otto I. bis Friedrich II. 1894

Eigentliche beschreibung deren zu Franckfurth am Mayn anno 1711 vollzogenen wahl- und crönungs-actuum, ihrer römisch. kayserl. mayest. Caroli VI. 1712

Das hochbeehrte Augspurg wie solches nicht allein mit beeder kayserl. als auch der ungaris. königl. majest. ingleichem der ... churfürsten und churfürstl. gesandten ... ankunfft sondern auch darauf gefolgter der ... römischen kayserin und römischen königs Eleonorae und Josephi, krönungs-festivität beglücket worden. 1690

Krönungs-album ihrer majestäten des königs Wilhelm, der königin Augusta. 1861

Lallemand, Charles. Lettres sur les fêtes du couronnement à Koenigsberg et Berlin, October 1861. 1861

Coronations and coronation robes—Germany—*Continued*

Leucht, C. L. Augusti corona augustissima Augustae coronata; das ist: Die crone ... des Leopoldi ... käyserliche gemahlin ... Frau Eleonora Magdalena Theresia ... als römische käyserin ... in Augspurg den 9. (19.) jenner des 1690sten jahrs gesalbet ... worden. 1690

Leucht, C. L. Austria s. r. imperii conjux; das ist: des Heil. Röm. Reichs mit dem ... herzoglichen ertz-hause Oesterreich beständige ehe welche ... als ... Herr Josephus ... den 14.(24.) Januarii zum römischen könig ... erwöhlet ... wurde. 1690

Leucht, C. L. Cronen zur zierd und schutz des Heiligen Römischen Reichs auf denen häuptern ... Eleonorä und Josephi &c. so auf das richtigste beschrieben nach allen umstanden der wahl- und cronungs-solennitäten die vor- mit- und nachgegangen ... nebenst der wahl-capitulation. 1690

Merian, Caspar. Beschreibung und abbildung aller königl. und churfürstl. ein-züge wahl und crönungs acta, so geschehen zu Franckfurt am Mayn im jahr 1658. Sampt andern darzu gehörigen und beygefügten sachen. 1658

Olenschlager, J. D. von. Vollständiges diarium von der ... erwehlung des ... herrn Franciscus ... zum römischen könig und kayser. 1746

Römer-Büchner, B. J. Die wahl und krönung der deutschen kaiser zu Frankfurt am Main. 1858

Schulin, J. P. Vollständiges diarium der römisch-königlichen wahl und kayserlichen krönung ... Leopold des zweiten. 1791

Stillfried und Rattonitz, R. M. B., graf von. Die kroenung ihrer majestaeten des koenigs Wilhelm und der koenigin Augusta von Preussen zu Koenigsberg am 18. october 1861. 1868

Vollständiges diarium, alles dessen was vor, in und nach denen ... wahl- und crönungs-solennitaeten ... Caroli des VI. erwehlten römischen kaysers. 1712

Vollständiges diarium von den merckwürdigsten begebenheiten, die sich vor, in und nach der ... wahl und crönung ... Carls des VII. erwehlten römischen kaysers. 1742-43

Holy Roman empire

See Coronations and coronation robes—Germany

Hungary

Festschmuck für die königskrönung in Budapest 1916. 1917

Italy

Bombelli, Rocco. Storia della corona ferrea dei re d'Italia. 1870

Lewald, August. Die krönung in Mailand im jahre 1838. 1838

Sanquirico, Alessandro. Incoronazione di ... Ferdinando I. a re del Regno Lombardo-Veneto ... celebrata nell' insigne metropna. di Milano il VI settre. MDCCCXXXVIII. 1838

See also Coronations, etc.—Naples (Kingdom)

Japan

The Japan advertiser. Enthronement of the one hundred twenty-fourth emperor of Japan. 1928

Naples (Kingdom)

La Placa, Pietro. La reggia in trionfo per l'acclamazione e coronazione ... di Carlo infante di Spagna, re di Sicilia. 1736

Netherlands

Description des principales rejouissances, faites à La Haye, à l'occasion du couronnement de sa majesté ... François I. 1747

Russia

Burford, Robert. Description of a view of the city of Moscow, with the gorgeous entry of His Imperial Majesty the Emperor Alexander II. into the Kremlin. 1857

Description du sacre et du couronnement de ... l'empereur Alexandre II et l' imperatrice Marie Alesandrovna, MDCCCLVI. 185-?

Graf, Henry. Vues des cérémonies les plus intéressantes du couronnement de Leurs Majestés Imperiales l'empereur Nicolas 1er et l'impératrice Alexandra, à Moscou. 1828

Russia. Ministerstvo Imperatorskago dvora. Les solennités du saint couronnement. 1899

Umständliche beschreibung der ... salbung und crönung der ... frauen, Anna Joannowna kayserin und selbstherrscherin von gantz Ruszland ... 28. april 1730, in Moscau. 1731

V" pami͡at' svi͡ashchennago koronovanii͡a Īkh" Īmperatorskīkh" Velīchestv" v" Moskvi͡e 1896g. 1896?

Vi͡enchanie russkīkh" gosudareĭ na TSarstvo, nachīnai͡a s" tsari͡a Mīkhaīla Fedorovīcha do Īmperatora Aleksandra III ... Couronnement des Souverains Russes à partir du Tsar Michel Fédorovitch jusqu'à l'empereur Alexandre III. 1883

Balfour, Sir James, bart. Ancient heraldic and antiquarian tracts. 1837

Bute, J. P. C. S., 3d marquis of. Scottish coronations. 1902

Cooper, James. Four Scottish coronations. 1902

Spain

Madrid. Descripcion de los ornatos públicos con que la corte de Madrid ha solemnizado la feliz exâltacion al trono de los reyes nuestros Señores Don Carlos IIII. y Doña Luisa de Borbon. 1789

Coronations and coronation robes—Spain—*Continued*
Routier, Gaston. Le couronnement d'Alphonse XIII, roi d'Espagne. 1902

Coronelli, Marco Vincenzo
Ordinum equestrium, ac militarium brevis narratio ... Degli ordini equestri, e militari. Venezia, Orlandi 1715
71 l. 80pl.(incl.715 illus.) Q.
Text in Latin and Italian
Contains the following appendices omitted from earlier editions: *Ecclesiasticorum antiquae legis, nempe sacerdotum Hebraeorum institutio et habitus* (4 l. incl. 23 illus.); *Graecorum ecclesiasticorum institutio et habitus* (6 l. incl. 12 illus.); *Curia romana* (27 l. incl. 51 illus.)
Lipperheide 1902
Ordinum religiosorum in ecclesia militanti catalogus. Roma, 1708
2v. in 1. 257pl. Q.
Explanation of plates is in Latin and Italian

Correct social usage; a course of instruction in good form, style and deportment, by eighteen distinguished authors. New York, The New York society of selfculture 1906
2v. fronts. illus. pl. D.
Contains references and figures showing the correct dress of servants
LC 6-12584

La **Correspondance** des dames, ou Journal des modes et spectacles de Paris; rédigée par J. J. Lucet. 1799-1800. Paris, Gide An VII
2v. 27pl.(18 col.) O.
The colored plates show fashions
Continuation of *Tableau général du goût;* was continued with title: *L'Arlequin*
Colas 690

Corset
Bonnand. Abhandlung von der schädlichen wirkung der schnürbrüste. 1773
Dôffémont. Avis très important au public. Sur différentes espèces de corps & de ceintures, d'une nouvelle invention. 1775
Fowler, O. S. Intemperance and tight lacing, considered in relation to the laws of life. 1849
Gâches-Sarraute, Mme Inèz. Le corset. Étude physiologique et pratique. 1900
Leóty, Ernest. Le corset à travers les âges. 1893
Libron, Fernand, and Clouzet, Henri. Le corset dans l'art et les moeurs du XIIIe au XXe siècle. 1933
Lord, W. B. The corset and the crinoline. 1868
Lorentz, Mme E., and Lacroix, A. Cours complet d'enseignement professionel de le coupe du corset. 1911?
O'Followell, Ludovic. Le corset, médecine, hygiène. 1905
Reisser. Avis important au sexe, ou Essai sur les corps baleinés pour former & conserver la taille aux jeunes personnes. 1770

Le **corset** à travers les âges. Leóty, Ernest

The **corset** and the crinoline. Lord, W. B.

Le **corset** dans l'art et les moeurs. Libron Fernand, and Clouzot, Henri

Le **corset;** histoire, médecine, hygiène. O'Followell, Ludovic

Corsica
Este, Margaret d' Through Corsica with a camera. 1905
Feydel, Gabriel. Moeurs et coutumes des Corses. 1799

Corsini, Andrea
Il costume del medico nelle pitture fiorentine del rinascimento. Firenze, Istituto micrografico italiano 1912
39p. 14pl. O.
Colas 693. LC 13-21365

Cortambert, Richard
Essai sur la chevelure des différents peuples. Paris, Challamel ainé 1861
64p. O.
Extrait de la *Revue orientale et américaine*
LC 4-12568

Cortazzo
(illus.) Darfeu. Hygiène de la parisienne

La **corte** di Alphonso I di Aragona. Montalto, Lina

Corte pontificia. Milano, F. Tensi ca1860
12 col.pl. S.
The plates show the pope in his state coach, and officials and soldiers of the papal state
Lipperheide 1833

Cortège funébre de feu Sa Majesté l'Émpereur Alexandre Ier ... Saint-Petersbourg, 13 Mars 1826. No place, Pluchart n.d.
10 col.pl. F.
Lipperheide 2785

Cortège historique de la ville de Vienne, à l'occasion des noces d'argent de leurs majestés Francois-Joseph Ier, et Elisabeth. See Berggruen, Oscar. 27 avril 1879

Cortés, Hernando
Historia de Nueva-España, escrita por su esclarecido conquistador; augmentada con otros documentos y notas por ... Francisco Antonio Lorenzana. Mexico City, J. A. de Hogal 1770
10 l. xvi,400,18p. pl. maps, facsim. on 31pl. Q.
Contains facsimiles of Aztec hieroglyphics, many of which show costume and ornaments
Lipperheide 1621

Corti, Egon Caesar, conte
Chinesisches bilderbuch. Leipzig, Bibliographisches institut ag c1935
55p. 19 col. illus. D. (Meyers bunte bändchen)
Illustrations are reduced in size from G. H. Mason's *The costume of China*
LC 35-19583

Corvinus, Gottlieb Siegmund
Nutzbares, galantes und curiöses frauenzimmer-lexicon; worinnen ... nahmen und thaten gelehrter frauenzimmer, künstlerinnen dererselben trachten und moden, und was zum putz und kleidung des frauenzimmers, und auszierung der gemächer gehöret ... wie auch ein koch-buch. Verm. und verb. aufl. Frankfurt und Leipzig, bey J. F. Gleditschens seel. sohn 1739
1768p. 16 l. 16 illus. O.
First edition published in 1715 under the pseudonym Amaranthes
Lipperheide 682e

Corvinus, J. A.
(engr.) Decker, Paul. Repraesentatio belli, ob successionem in Regno Hispanico

Cosmetics
Bayle-Mouillard, Mme É. F. Manuel des dames. 1827
Cooley, A. J. The toilet and cosmetic arts in ancient and modern times. 1866
Cunliffe-Owen, M. de G. Eve's glossary. 1897
Dachauer, Gustav. Kosmetische receptirkunst. 1872
Franklin, A. L. A. La vie privée d'autrefois; arts et métiers, modes, moeurs, usages des Parisiens du XII. au XVIII. siècle. [v 17]
James, Constantin. Toilette d'une Romaine au temps d'Auguste, et cosmétiques d'une Parisienne au XIXe siècle. 1865
Marie de Saint-Ursin, P. J. L'ami des femmes, ou Lettres d'un médecin, concernant l'influence de l'habillement des femmes sur leurs moeurs et leur santé. 1805
Orchamps, baronin d', pseud.? Die geheimnisse der frau. 1908
Schreger, C. H. T. Kosmetisches taschenbuch für damen. 1810
Uzanne, L. O. Les parfums et les fards à travers les âges. c1927
Wellman, Katharine. Beauty begins at home; how to make and use cosmetics. c1936

See also Beauty, Personal; Perfumery

Cosmography, oder beschreibung aller länder. See Münster, Sebastian. Cosmographia, das ist: beschreibung der gantzen welt

Cosmographia. Münster, Sebastian

Cosmorama. Aspin, Jehoshaphat

Cossacks
Die Kosaken, oder Historische darstellung ihrer sitten, gebräuche, kleidung, waffen und art krieg zu führen. c1812

Cossé-Brissac, J. de
(illus.) Cossé-Brissac, R. M. T. de. Historique du 7e régiment de dragons

Cossé-Brissac, René Marie Timoléon de
Historique du 7e régiment de dragons [1673-1909] Illustrations de Louis Vallet, J. de Cossé-Brissac. Paris, Leroy 1909
184p. illus.(incl.ports.) pl.(part col.) maps. Q.
LC 22-17671

Cosson, André
Armorial des cardinaux, archevêques et évêques français actuels résidentiels et titulaires au 1er janvier 1917. Paris, H. Daragon 1917
288p. illus. 182 port. O.
Plates show modern ecclesiastical costume worn in the various French provinces
LC 18-113

Cosson, Charles Alexander, baron de
Le cabinet d'armes de Maurice Tallyrand-Périgord ... reproduction de 200 pièces par P. Dujardin. Paris, E. Rouveyre 1901
118p. 23pl. F.
The collection is now in the Metropolitan Museum, New York

Costa, Margherita
Li buffoni. Fiorenza, A. Massi e L. Landi 1641
177p. front. Q.
This title is included because frontispiece shows a stage scene engraved in the manner of Callot. The same plate is reproduced in Lipperheide's *Katalog* p483
Lipperheide 3196

Costa Rica. See Military costume—Costa Rica

Costa Rica. Laws, statutes, etc.
Reglamento de uniformes. San José, Tipografía nacional, 1903
29p. pl.(1 fold.) O.
LC CA10-858

Costa Rica. Ministerio de guerra y marina
Reglamento de uniformes. See entry under Costa Rica. Laws, statutes, etc.

Costa Rica. Secretaría de la guerra
Reglamento de uniformes para el ejército. San José, Tipografia nacional 1907
175p. col.pl. D.

Coste, Z.
Keepsake-Breton; scènes familières. Nantes, Charpentier ca1850
6 col.pl. F.
Plates show peasants from six sections of Brittany
Colas 694

Costenoble, Carl Ludwig
Dramatische spiele von C. Costenoble. Ein taschenbuch für 1811. Hamburg, [1811]
col.illus. S.
Lipperheide 4523

Costere, Pieter de
(illus.) Martin, Cornelis. Les genealogies et anciennes descentes des forestiers et comtes de Flandre

Die **costüm-ausstellung** im k.k. Oesterreichischen museum 1891. Masner, Carl

Costüm-buch für künstler. Sammlung der interessanten gegenstände des costüms aller zeiten und völker der christlichen zeitrechnung; herausgegeben von einem verein von künstlern. Düsseldorf, J. Buddeus [1839]
64pl. Q.
Colas 695. Lipperheide 57

Costüme des Königlichen hof-theaters zu Berlin. Lange, Eduard

Costüme zur Lessing-feier. [Carlsruhe, 1878]
4pl.(169 illus.) Q.
Lipperheide 3189

Costümgeschichte der culturvölker. Falke, Jacob von

Der **costum-ball** am schlusse des carnevals 1826. Weidmann, F. C.

Costum des deutschen ritterthums. Heideloff, K. A. von

Costumari popular català. See Amades, Joan. Gegants, nans i altres entremesos

Costumbres santafereñas. Torres Méndez, Ramón

Costumbres y trajes en los Pirineos. Arco, Ricardo del

Costume. London. Museum

Le **costume.** Ruppert, Jacques

Le **costume.** Zamacoïs, Miguel

Le **costume** à la cour et à la ville. Kerckhoff, Émile

Le **costume** à l'armée de Condé. La Chanonie, L. C. de

Costume, a list of books. Detroit. Public library

Costume; a selected list of books in the Public library of the city of Boston. Boston. Public library

Costume; an index to the more important material in the library. Victoria and Albert museum, South Kensington

Le **costume** ancien et moderne. See Ferrario, Giulio. Il costume antico e moderno

Costume and art

Declaration of the artists of the nineteenth century on the influence of costume and fashion upon high art. 1862

Costume and conduct in the laws of Basel, Bern, and Zurich, 1370-1800. Vincent, J. M.

The **costume** and customs of modern India. Williamson, Thomas

Costume & fashion. Norris, Herbert

Il **costume** antico e moderno. Ferrario, Giulio

Le **costume** au moyen âge d'après les sceaux. Demay, Germain

Le **costume** au moyen âge et à la renaissance. Jean, René

Le **costume** du théâtre. Cernuschi, and others

Le **costume** au theatre. Lamé, Émile

Le **costume** au théâtre et à la ville. no 1-45; 15 dec. 1886-1888. Paris, Aubert

3v. col.pl. F. 60fr. a year
Published semi-monthly
Plates after Bianchini, Thomas Lacoste, etc.
Colas 324. Lipperheide 3230

The **costume** book. Nesfield-Cookson, Mrs M. J.-P.

Costume caracteristique de France. See Peake, R. B. The characteristic costume of France

The **costume,** character, manners, domestic habits, and religious ceremonies of the Mahrattas. Broughton, T. D.

Le **costume** chez les peuples anciens et modernes. Hottenroth, Friedrich

Costume civil, costume ecclesiastique, costume monastique. Crépon, Théophile

Le **costume** civil en France, du XIIIe au XIXe siècle. Piton, Camille

Le **costume** dans le théâtre religieux du moyen âge. See Cohen, Gustave. Le théâtre en France au moyen âge

Le **costume** dans les armées royalistes. La Chanonie, L. C. de

Le **costume** dans les temps anciens et au moyen âge. Aragon, Henry

[**Costume** d'Auvergne.] Paris, Martinet, Lith. de A. Cheyère n.d.

5pl. Q.
Contents: Laitière des environs de Clermont; Nourrice de Cressini près Clermont; Vigneron de Clermont; Cultivateur de St-Alyre; Electeur de l'arrondissement d'Issoire
Colas 699

Le **costume** de guerre en Basse Champagne au XIIIe et au XIVe siècle. Leclert, Louis

Le **costume** de guerre et d'apparat d'après les sceaux du moyen âge. See Demay, Germain. Le costume au moyen âge d'après les sceaux

Le **costume** de la garde suisse pontificale et la Renaissance italienne. Repond, Jules

Le **costume** de la Parisienne au XIX. siècle. Cabris

Le **costume** de la revolution à nos jours. Sée, Raymonde

El **costume** de le donne, incomenzando da la pueritia per fin al maritar ... con un capitolo de le trentatre cose che convien alla donna a esser bella. Firenze, Libreria Dante 1889

36p. (Collezione de operette edite eel inedite opera nuova, 2)
Edited by S. Morpurgo

Costume de l'Empire russe. See Costume of the Russian empire illustrated by upwards of seventy richly coloured engravings. London, E. Harding 1803

Costume de l'Empire de Russie. See The costume of the Russian empire, illustrated by a series of seventy-three engravings. London, W. Miller 1803

Le **costume** de l'Europe orientale. See Tilke, Max. Osteuropäische volkstrachten

Il **costume** del medico nelle pitture fiorentine del rinascimento. Corsini, Andrea

Costüme der ältesten völker. See Dandré-Barden, M. F. Costume des anciens peuples

Costume des anciens peuples. Dandré-Bardon, M. F.

Le **costume** des femmes en Bretagne. Petitville, Mme de

Das **costume** des mittelalters. Hegi, Franz

Le **costume** des peuples de l'antiquité prouvé par les monuments. Lens, A. C.

Costume design. Chuse, A. R.

Costume design. Gallemore, Margaret, Harris, V. A., and Morris, Maria

Costume design and home planning. Izor, E. P.

Costume design as an occupation. Federated council on art education

Il **costume** di tutte le nazioni e di tutti i tempi. Menin, Lodovico

Costume du moyen âge d'après les manuscrits les peintures et les monuments contemporains. Van Beveren, J. J., and Du Pressoir, Charles

Il **costume** e l'arte delle acconciature nell'antichità. Manoni, Alessandro

Le **costume** en Égypte du IIIe au XIIIe siècle. Gayet, A. J.

Le **costume** en France. Renan, Ary

Le **costume** en orient. See Tilke, Max. Orientalische kostüme

Le **costume** en Provence. Aurouze, J.

Le **costumen** en provence. See Roux, J. C. Bibliothèque régionaliste: Le costume en Provence

Le **costume** en Provence. See Roux, J. C. Souvenirs du passé: Le costume en Provence

Le **costume** en Provence au moyen age. Bourilly, Joseph

Le **costume** épiscopal et prélatice selon l'étiquette romaine. Barbier de Montault, Xavier

Le **costume** et la toilette au Japon. Baret, L.

Le **costume** et l'armement du Wisigoth aux cinquième et seizième siècles. Barrière-Flavy, C.

Le **costume** et les insignes du pape. Barbier de Montault, Xavier

Le **costume** et les usages ecclésiastiques selon la tradition romain. Barbier de Montault, Xavier

Costume: fanciful, historical and theatrical. Aria, Mrs E. D.

Le **costume** féminin. Montaillé

Costume 1400-1600. Baldwin, Muriel

Le **costume** historique. Racinet, A. C. A.

Costume in England; a history of dress to the end of the eighteenth century. Fairholt, F. W.

Costume in literature

Album de la mode. Chronique du monde fashionable, ou choix de morceaux de littérature contemporaine. 1833

Fairholt, F. W. Satirical songs and poems on costume: from the 13th to the 19th century. 1849

Costume in Roman comedy. Saunders, Catharine

Costume in the drama of Shakespeare and his contemporaries. Linthicum, M. C.

Costume index. Monro, I. S., and Cook, D. E., eds.

Le **costume,** la mode; encyclopédie populaire illustrée du vingtième siècle publiée sous la direction de Mm. Buisson, Denis, Larroumet, Stanislas Meunier; Georges Brunel, secrétaire. Paris, Soc. française d'éditions d'art 1899
160p. D.
According to Colas the author is Mlle. H. Daux
Colas 483, 724

Le **costume,** les armes, les bijoux, la céramique, les ustensiles, outils, objets mobiliers, etc. chez les peuples anciens et modernes. See Hottenroth, Friedrich. Le costume, les armes, ustensiles, outils des peuples anciens et modernes

Le **costume,** les armes, ustensiles, outils des peuples anciens et modernes. Hottenroth, Friedrich

Le **costume** liturgique arménien. Muyldermans, Joseph

Le **costume** militaire en France. Herlaut, A. P.

Le **costume** militaire en France et les premiers uniformes. Quarré de Verneuil, A. H. R.

Le **costume** musulman d'Alger. Marçais, Georges

Costume of Candelario, Salamanca. Hispanic society of America

Costume of China. Alexander, William

The **costume** of China. Mason, G. H.

Costume of colonial times. Earle, Mrs A. M.

The **costume** of Great Britain. Pyne, W. H.

Costume of Illyria and Dalmatia; Les costumes de l'Illyrie et de la Dalmatie. London, 1824
2v. 36 col.pl. Q.
Colas 731

The **costume** of Indostan. Solvyns, F. B.

The **costume** of Nō play in Japan. Kongow, Iwao

Costume of Paris. See Chalon, J. J. Twenty four subjects exhibiting the costume of Paris

The **costume** of Persia. Orlowski, A. O.

Costume of Portugal. L'Évêque, Henry

Costume of prelates of the Catholic church. Nainfa, J. A. F. P.

Costume of Shakespeare's ... King John [etc] Planché, J. R.

Costume of Sweden. Svedman, K. V.

Costume of the ancients. Hope, Thomas

Costume of the army of the British Empire, according to the last regulations, 1812. London, 1813
75 col.pl. F.
Colas 732

Costume of the army of the British Empire according to the regulations, 1814. Smith, C. H.

Costume of the British army. Hayes, M. A.

Costume of the British Army in 1828. Hull, Edward

Costume of the British navy in 1828. Hull, Edward

The **costume** of the clans. Stuart, J. S. S., and Stuart, C. E.

Costume of the hereditary states of the house of Austria. Bertrand de Moleville, A. F., marquis de.

The **costume** of the inhabitants of Russia. Porter, Sir R. K.

Costume of the ladies of England, 1810-1829. London, R. Ackermann 1829?
3v. 153 col.pl. O.
Water color drawings by Thomas Uwins and others
Colas 734

Costume of the lower orders in Paris. Busby, T. L.

Costume of the lower orders of London. Busby, T. L.

Costume of the lower orders of the metropolis. Busby, T. L.

Costume of the Madras army. Hunsley, W.

The **costume** of the Netherlands. Semple, Miss

Costume of the original inhabitants of the British islands. Meyrick, Sir S. R., and Smith, C. H.

Costume of the Royal navy and marines. Mansion, L. M., and Saint-Eschauzier

The **costume** of the Russian army, from a collection of drawings made on the spot, and now in the possession of the Right Honourable The Earl of Kinnaird. London, E. Orme 1807
3 l. front. 8 col.pl. F.
Colas 735

The **costume** of the Russian empire, illustrated by a series of seventy-three engravings. London, W. Miller 1803
[164]p. 73 col.pl. F.
Plates hand colored. Text in English and French. Added t.-p. in French: *Costume de l'Empire de Russie*
Plates "copied from a series of engravings begun at Petersburg in 1776 and finished in 1779 under the care and at the expense of C. W. Müller [for J. G. Georgi's work: *Beschreibung*]" "The descriptions to the plates have been derived from the most authentic sources": Müller, D'Auteroche, Kracheninnikow, Plescheëf, Pallas and Saür
Plates are almost identical with those in *Costume of the Russian empire* (London, E. Harding 1803) and in William Alexander's *Picturesque representations of the dress and manners of the Russians* (London, John Murray 1814)
Colas 702. Costume index. Lipperheide 1341. LC 16-25727

Costume of the Russian empire illustrated by upwards of seventy richly coloured engravings. London, E. Harding 1803
[154]p. 70(i.e. 72) col.pl. F. 168s
Plates hand colored. Text in English and French. French title: *Costume de l'Empire russe*
"The subjects are partly selected from [Georgi's Beschreibung] and partly from the . . . Travels of Pallas . . . in collecting the materials for the historical descriptions, recourse has been had to the labours of Müller, Pallas, Coxe, Fischer, Krackeninikof"
Plates almost identical with those in *Costume of the Russian empire* (Miller 1802) and in *Picturesque representations of the dress and manners of the Russians* (Murray 1814)
Also published (London, printed by T. Bensley for John Stockdale 1810, some copies dated 1811)
Colas 703-04; Costume index. Lipperheide 1342. LC 16-25726

The **costume** of the theatre. Kommīssarzhevskiĭ, F. F.

Costume of the University of Oxford. Uwins, Thomas

Costume of the various orders in the University of Cambridge. Harraden, R. B.

The **costume** of Turkey, illustrated by a series of engravings. Alexander, William

The **costume** of Yorkshire. Walker, George

Costume on brasses. See Druitt, Herbert. A manual of costume as illustrated by monumental brasses

Le **costume** oriental ancien. Speleers, Louis

Il **costume** popolare in Italia. Calderini, Emma

Costume royal. See Royal

Le **costume** rustique vosgien. Save, Gaston

Costume silhouettés. Evans, Mary

Costume throughout the ages. Evans, Mary

Costumes algériens. Piesse, Louis

Costumes algériens. Vaillant

Costumes algériens. Wolffgang, A. M.

Costumes anciens et modernes. Vecellio, Cesare

Costumes and scenery for amateurs. Mackay, C. D'A.

Costumes and scenery of Afghaunistaun. See Rattray, James. The costumes of the various tribes

Costumes anglais du temps de la révolution et du premier empire 1795-1806. Guillaumot, A. E.

Costumes, arts, métiers et usages de l'Angleterre. Paris, Nepveu 1817
16p. 8pl. O.
"Lithographiés d'après le procédé de G. Engelman et soigneusement coloriés." Subtitle
Only this one part was published
Colas 696

Costumes auvergnats. Delorieux, F. N.

Costumes belgiques. Madou, J. B., and Hemelryck, J. L. van

Costumes bordelais. La Torre, F. de

Les **costumes** bretons. Aubert, O. L.

Costumes bretons. Darjou, H. A.

Costumes bretons. Deshays, Célestin

Costumes bretons. Saint-Germain, Prosper

Costumes civils actuels de tous les peuples connus. Grasset de Saint-Sauveur, Jacques

Costumes civils de tous les peuples. See Maréchal, P. S. Costumes civils actuels de tous les peuples connus

Costumes civils des peuples connus. See Maréchal, P. S. Costumes civils actuels de tous les peuples connus

Costumes civils et militaires de XVIe siècle. Bruyn, Abraham de

Costumes civils et militaires de la monarchie française depuis 1200 jusqu'à 1820. Lecomte, Hippolyte

Costumes civils et militaires depuis le Ve siècle. Bassaget, P. N.

Costumes civils français et hollandais de diverses époques. No place, 1790?
1 l. 10pl. O.
Colas 697

Costumes civils, militaires et religieux du Mexique. Linati, C.

Costumes coloriés des différents peuples d'Italie. Lemercier, Charles

Costumes coloriés des Parisiens à toutes les époques; complément de Paris à travers les âges. Paris, F. Roy 1879-81
112 col.pl. Q.
Appeared in 28 parts with 4 plates in each
Colas 698. Lipperheide 1098

Costumes cosmopolites. Bassaget, P. N.

Costumes d'atelier. Puyo, C.

Costumes de ballet. Bérain, J. L.

Costumes de Berne et paysans des environs. Aberli, J. L.

Costumes de carnaval. Vanier, Léon

Costumes de corps militaires faisant partie de l'armée française. Charlet, N. T.

Costumes de divers nations du monde. Ram, Johannis de

Costumes de divers pays. See note under Lanté, L. M. Costumes des femmes de Hambourg, du Tyrol, etc.

Costumes de divers pays d'Europe. Noort, Adam van, and Snellinck, Joan

Costumes de diverses provinces d'Italie. Colin, Mme Anaïs

Costumes de fantaisie pour un bal travesti. Grévin, Alfred

Costumes de femmes. Lacauchie, A.

Costumes de femmes à Bordeaux. Sewrin, Edmond

Costumes de femmes suisse. Rohr, G.

Costumes de guerre de l'âge du bronze et de l'ère gauloise. Grasset, Eugène

Costumes de Hambourg. See Suhr, Christoffer. Hamburgische trachten

Costumes de la Basse-Normandie. [Paris, G. Lalonde 18-?]
26 col.pl. (folded)
Title taken from cover

Costumes de la Bretagne. Darjou, H. A.

Costumes de la cavalerie française suivant les ordonnances de 1775 et 1779. Hoffmann, Nicolas

Costumes de la Comédie française XVIIe-XVIIIe siècles. Guillaumot, A. E.

Costumes de la cour de Bourgogne sous le règne de Philippe III. Bastard d'Estang, Auguste, comte de

Costumes de la cour impériale de France. Neueste hof- und staats- trachten in Frankreich; vorgeschrieben vom Kaiser Napoleon I. Leipzig, Industrie-Comptoir ca1810
18pl. O.
Three parts each in a separate cover bearing the title. The legend on each plate is in French and German
Colas 701. Lipperheide 1787

Costumes de la Hongrie et des provinces danubiennes, Dalmatie, Monténégro, Croatie, Slavonie, frontières militaires. Valério, Théodore

Costumes de la Palestine. Pierotti, Ermete

Costumes de la Perse. See Orlowski, A. O. The costume of Persia

Costumes de la région pyrénéenne française et espagnole. Gorse, P.

Costumes de la république, de l'empire, de l'armée française et de l'armée d'Afrique de 1830 à 1840. Adam, Victor

Costumes de la Suisse. No place, n.d.
20 col.pl. Ti.
Costume from various cantons. Each plate pictures two persons in an oval and has a legend in French
Lipperheide 913

Costumes de la vallée d'Ossau. Devéria, Eugène

Costumes de la ville de Nice Maritime. Barberi

Les **costumes** de l'Alsace. Kauffmann, P. A.

Costumes de l'armée bavaroise 1813-1825. Voltz, J-M

Costumes de l'armée belge. Hemelryck, J. L. van

Costumes de l'armée belge. Payen, Camille

Costumes de l'armée française depuis 1830 jusqu'à nos jours. Bellangé, J. L. H.

Costumes de l'armée française depuis Louis XIV jusqu'à ce jour. Vernier, Charles

Costumes de l'armée française 1860-1861-1862. Adam, Victor

Costumes de l'Empire Turc. Lachaise

Costumes de l'époque de Louis XVI. Compte-Calix, F. C.

Costumes de l'ex-garde impériale. Charlet, N. T.

Costumes de l'Indostan. See Solvyns, F. B. The costume of Indostan

Les **costumes** de l'opéra. Fischer, Carlos

Costumes de l'opéra, XVIIe-XVIIIe siècles. Guillaumot, A. E.

Costumes de marins de la basse Normandie. Mozin, Ch.

Costumes de marins, dessinés dans les ports de Dunquerque au Havre. Adam, Victor

Costumes de Nice. Lattre, A. de

Costumes de principaux personnages des Scandinaves. Gérard

Costumes de Suède, Norvège, Danemark, Hollande et Allemagne. Belin, A., and others

Costumes de théâtre. Grévin, Alfred

Costumes de théâtre. Paris, Masson ca1815
73 col.pl. O.
Title engraved on each plate. Two plates are signed J. Merle del., one Renausy del., one D. B. and one Maleuvre sc.
Colas 713

Costumes de théâtre, ballets & divertissements. Lepape, Georges

Costumes de théâtre de 1600 à 1820. Lecomte, Hippolyte

Costumes de tous les corps de l'armée et de la marine françaises. Lalaisse, Hippolyte

Costumes de tous les peuples connu. Leonhardi, F. G.

Costumes d'enfans. Modes de Paris

Costumes des anciens. See note under Hope, Thomas. Costume of the ancients

Costumes des armées française, bavaroise et autrichienne en 1809. Engelbrecht, Martin

Costumes des ballets du roy. Guillaumot, A. E.

Costumes des cantons. Lamy, J. P.

Costumes des cantons de la Suisse. Paris, Tessari ca1830
12 col.pl. Q.
Colas 705

Costumes des communautés religieuses de femmes en Canada. Montréal, J. Lovell 1854
8p. D.
"Accompagnés d'un précis historique sur leur formation, but, etc. et d'un tableau de leur état en 1853." Subtitle
Colas 706

Les **costumes** des dames parisiennes, ou l'Ami de la mode. Paris, Janet 1803?
12 illus. S.
Colas 707

Costumes des différens départemens de l'Empire français. Paris, Martinet ca1815
147p. O.
The plates show costume of Switzerland, Italy and other countries, as well as France. For contents see Colas' *Bibliographie.* Many of the plates are engraved by Maleuvre, some by Dubucourt and some are not signed
The Swiss costumes are available in *Recueil de costumes suisses*
Colas 708

Costumes des différens états de l'Italie; lithographiés d'après les dessins originaux de Sgroppo, Pieraccini, Pittaluga, & a. Paris, P. Marino [1826]
6v. 285 col.pl. F.
Contents: États du pape. 30 colored plates, lithographed by Levilly. Plates are copies of those in Ferrari's *Costumi no.XXX di Roma*. . . v2 Grand Duché de Toscane. 50 colored plates after Pieraccini and J. Galli, lithographed by Levilly, E. Langlois and Jacquet. v3 Royaume des deux Siciles. 100 colored plates after Sgroppo, lithographed by Levilly, Pohl, Deruelle, and V. Leprince. v4 Royaume de Sardaigne. 25 colored plates after A. Pittaluga, lithographed by Levilly and Vitasse; v5 Duché de Gênes; v6 Tyrol. The last two, 40 plates each, lithographed by Pieraccini
Colas 2719. Lipperheide 1277

Costumes des différentes nations composant les états héréditaires de S.M. et R. Kininger, V. G.

Costumes des différents peuples de l'Italie. Rémond, C.

Costumes des états heréditaires de la maison d'Autriche. See Bertrand de Moleville, A. F., marquis de. The costume of the hereditary states of the house of Austria

Costumes des femmes de Hambourg, du Tyrol, de la Hollande, de la Suisse, de la Franconie, de l'Espagne, du royaume de Naples. Lanté, L. M.

Costumes des femmes de Strasbourg (XVIIe et XVIIIe siècles). Seyboth, Adolf

Costumes des femmes du pays de Caux. Lanté, L. M.

Costumes des femmes françaises du XIIe au XVIIIe siècle. Lanté, L. M.

Costumes des gentilshommes et des dames nobles venitiennes. See Franco, Giacomo. Habiti d'huomeni et donne venetiane

Costumes des habitans de l'île de Java et des possessions hollandaises dans l'Inde. Grévedon, P. L. H.

Costumes des Pays-Bas. Jager, A.

Costumes des Pays-Bas. See Album de costumes des Pays-Bas

Costumes des Pays-Bas. See Bing, Valentyn, and Ueberfeldt, Braet von. Nederlandsche kleederdragten

Costumes des pays du Nord: Hollande et Danemark. Esménard, Jeanne d'

Costumes des paysans de divers cantons en Suède. Hilleström, Pehr

Les **costumes** des peuples anciens. Cavaro, Richard

Costumes des principaux ballets dessines par Alophe. See Menut, Adolphe. Les danseuses de l'Opéra

Costumes des provinces françaises. Brun, Charles

Costumes des provinces françaises au 18ème siècle. Grasset de Saint-Sauveur, Jacques

Costumes des Pyrénées. Dartiguenave, Alfred

Costumes des Pyrennées. Pingret, Edouard

Costumes des Pyrénées. See Gavarni, G. S. C. Montagnards des Pyrénées, françaises et espagnoles

Costumes des quatres parties du monde gravés dans la manière de Luycken See Ram, Johannis de. Costumes de divers nations du monde

Costumes des régiments et des milices. Ganier, Henry

Costumes des reines de France. Colin, Mme Anaïs

Costumes des représentants du peuple Paris, Basset n.d.
5 col.pl. F.
Cataloged from Colas' *Bibliographie*
Contents: Costume des ministres; Huissier du Directoire exécutif; Huissier des deux Conseils; Secrétaire des deux Conseils; Messager d'État
Colas 709

Costumes des représentans du peuple. Grasset de Saint Sauveur, Jacques

Costumes des représentans du peuple français et fonctionnaires public. Paris, Augrand fils n.d.
1 pl.(16 illus.) sq.F.
Colas notes another plate of the same title published by Canu
Colas 710

Costumes des XIIIe, XIVe et XVe siècles. Bonnard, Camille

Costumes des troupes russes répresentées en (quatorze) gravures et notice sur les différens peuples qui composent l'armée russe. Paris, A. Nepveu 1812
40p. 33 col.pl. O.
Contents of the military plates is given in Glasser's *Costumes militaires;* Colas gives contents of the eight other plates
Colas 711

Costumes des uniformes de l'armée impériale et royale. See Geschichte der kaiserl. königl. regimenter

Costumes d'hommes et de femmes. Quast, P. J.

Costumes d'hommes et de femmes de Strasbourg. Weis, J. M.

Costumes d'hommes et de femmes du temps de Louis XIII. Valegio, Francisco

Costumes du Caucase. Gagarin, G. G., kniaz

Costumes du comté d'York. See Walker, George. The costume of Yorkshire

Costumes du directoire, tirés des Merveilleuses. Guillaumot, A. E.

Costumes du XVIIIe siècle. Renard, Jules

Costumes du XVIIIe siècle, d'après les dessins de Watteau fils, etc. Guillaumot, A. E.

Costumes du XVIIIe siècle tirés des près Saint-Gervais. Guillaumot, A. E.

Costumes du Finistère. Théodore, L.

Costumes du Grand Duché de Bade. Pingret, Edouard

Costumes du grand-duché de Bade et des bords du Rhin. Valerio, Théodore

Costumes du moyen-âge chrétien d'après les monumens contemporains. See Hefner-Alteneck, J. H. von. Trachten des christlichen mittelalters

Les **costumes** du pays de France. Kleim, Aline

Costumes du peuple de toutes les provinces du royaume des Pays-Bas. Madou, J. B., and Eeckhout, J. J.

Costumes du peuple en Allemagne. See Kretschmer, Albert. Deutsche volkstrachten

Les **costumes** du peuple polonais. Zienkowicz, Léon

Costumes du quadrille historique. See Bals de l'opera

[**Costumes** du Royaume de Naples.] No place, ca1825
67 col.pl. Q.
Said by Colas to be copied from a suite published toward the end of the 18th century, which also served as a model for Damame-Démartrais. The first plate is entitled Donna della villa Masciuni
Colas 714

Costumes du temps de la révolution. Guillaumot, A. E.

Costumes du Tyrol. Vienne, Artaria ca1805
24? col.pl. Q.
Each plate has title *Tyrol* and a legend in German, and French
Colas 715

Costumes du Wurtemberg. Eliat, F.

Costumes ecclesiastiques, civils et militaires des XIIIe, XIVe, XVe siècles. See Bonnard, Camille. Costumi ecclesiastici, civili e militari d' secolo XIII, XIV e XV

Costumes espagnols. Avanda, Jim

Costumes et annales des grands théâtres de Paris, accompagnés de notices intéressantes et curieuses. Paris, au bureau du journal des costumes des théâtres 1786-89
4v. 178pl.(part col.) O.
Volumes 2-4 have title: *Costumes et annales des grands théâtres de Paris; en figures au lavis et coloriées* ... Par M. de Charnois; v3-4 were published by Janinet
Colas notes that a quarto edition is known
The plates of the last 3 volumes are not signed. Those of volume 1, are engraved by Janinet, Phelippaux, Chapuis, Carrée, Guyot, etc. after Le Barbier, Duplessis-Bertaux, Dutertre, Desrais, and others
Recherches sur les costumes by J. C. Le Vacher de Charnois is a continuation
Colas 716

Costumes et coiffes de Bretagne. Lalaisse, Hippolyte

Costumes et coiffures de Paris des haute et moyenne classes. Lanté, L. M.

Costumes et manteaux. 1919+ Paris, Editions Bell
Illus. F.
Published semiannually. Current 1938. Numbering continuous

Costumes et moeurs de Mexique. See Linati, C. Costumes civils, militaires et religieux du Mexique

Costumes et moeurs des Italiens d'après Pinelli en cinquante feuilles. See Pinelli, Bartolommeo. Raccolta di cinquanta costumi pittoreschi

Costumes et parures khmèrs. Marchal, Sappho

Costumes & uniformes; revue historique documentaire paraissant mensuellement. Publiée sous le patronage de la Société de l'histoire du costume. nos. 1-10, avr. 1912-Jan. 1914. Paris, J. Leroy 1912-14
88p. illus.(part col.) pl.(part col.) Q.
No more published. Continues the *Bulletin* of the Société
Colas 718bis. LC (24-6705)

Costumes & usages des peuples de la Grèce moderne. See Stackelberg, O. M., freiherr von. Trachten und gebräuche der Neugriechen

Costumes et vues de la Chine. Alexander, William

Costumes européens. Lecomte, Hippolyte

Costumes européens du XVIIe au XIXe siècle ... Aquarelles de Job [pseud] et de Hérouard. Paris, Librairie centrale d'art et d'architecture 1909
26p. 60 col.pl. Q. 80fr.
Colas 1550. Costume index(1915 ed.)

Costumes féminins ... du pays de Caux, dessinés ... en 1811 et 1812. See Lanté, L. M. Costumes des femmes du pays de Caux

Costumes for bazaars and masquerades. [Philadelphia, Curtis publishing co.] c1917
30p. illus. O.
LC 18-785

Costumes for the dance. Joiner, Betty

Costumes français. Mariette, P. J.

Costumes français. See Basset, Paris, pub. Modes d'hommes et de femmes de l'époque Louis XVI

Costumes français civils, militaires et religieux. Herbé, C. A.

Costumes français, de 1200 à 1715. Le Comte, Hippolyte

Costumes français depuis Clovis jusqu'à nos jours, extraits des monumens les plus authentiques de sculpture et de peinture, avec un texte historique et descriptif. Paris, Mifliez frères 1836-39
4v. 640 col.pl. O.
Volumes 2 and 3: "Par M. de Clugny." Plates are engraved by L. and A. Massard and by Lafosse. The complete work has been reproduced as part of Lacroix's *Costumes historiques*
Colas 722. LC 30-33199

Costumes français; en nonante sept gravures, representant les modes des hommes et femmes au commencement du 19. siècle. Paris, Chéreau [1799]-1800?
126pl. F.
Colas 721

Costumes français pour les coeffures depuis 1776. See entry under Gallerie des modes et costumes français dessinés d'après nature, gravés par les plus célèbres artistes

Les **costumes** français répresentans les différens etats du royaume, avec les habillemens propres à chaque etat. Paris, chez le Pere et Avaulez 1776
1 l. 10pl. F.
Contents: Seigneur et dame de cour; L'Evêque et l'abbesse; Le magistrat et le militaire; Les religieux et les religieuses; Le financier et l'abbé; Le bourgeois et la bourgeoise. Le médecin; Artisans: le maçon et la blanchisseuse; Le jardinier et la paysanne; Le pauvre de l'un et de l'autre sexe
The last plate is signed by Dupin
Colas 719. Lipperheide 1128

[**Costumes** françois et la parure des dames] Paris, Mondhare 1776-?
12pl. F.
Colas describes as an incomplete rare set. Each plate shows four pictures of hair and headdress. The first (unnumbered) is entitled: La parure des dames, ou 1re collection des plus belles cöeffures inventées depuis l'année 1776 et ainsi de suite
Colas 720

Costumes historiques. Emy, Henry, engr.

Costumes historiques. Lacauchie, A.

Costumes historiques de femmes du XIVe au XVIIIe siècle. Le Chevallier-Chevignard, Edmond

Costumes historiques de la France. Lacroix, Paul

Costumes historiques de ville ou de théâtre et travestissemens. Devéria, Achille

Costumes historiques des XIIe, XIIIe XIVe et XVe siècles. Bonnard, Camille

Costumes historiques des XIIIe, XIVe et XVe siècles. See Bonnard, Camille. Costumes des XIIIe, XIVe et XVe siècles

Costumes historiques des XVIe, XVII et XVIIIe siècles. Duplessis, G. V. A. G.

Costumes historiques français. Compte-Calix, F. C.

Costumes historiques pour travestissements. See Gavarni, G. S. C. Travestissemens

Costumes hollandois. Berge, P. A. van den

Costumes hongrois. See Pekáry, István. Magyar népviseletek

Costumes in Sachsen. Graenicher, Samuel, and Thiele, C. F.

Costumes in Shakespeare's historical play of King Henry the Eighth; published by ... permission of C. Kean. London, A. & S. Joseph 18-?
18 col.pl. ob.O.

Costumes in Shakespeare's play of the Winter's Tale, as represented at the Princess's Theatre. [London, Joseph, Myers & co] 1861?
24 col.pl. ob.O.
Printed at Vienna by M. Trentsensky. Colored by hand

Costumes inédits de Aine-Montaillé. Mich

Costumes, insignes, cartes, médailles des députés 1789-1898. Launay, Edmond

Costumes italiens. Paris, Martinet ca1810
33 col.pl. O.
Title is at top of each plate
Colas 723

Costumes italiens dessinés à Rome en 1807. Debret

Costumes lyonnais du XIVe au XXe siècle. Vial, Eugène

Costumes militaires. Charlet, N. T.

Costumes militaires. Genty, firm, Paris, pub.

Costumes militaires. Saint-Fal

Costumes militaires. See Bellangé, J. L. H. Uniformes de l'armée française depuis 1815 jusqu'à ce jour

Costumes militaires belges du XIe au XVIIIe siècle. Vinkeroy, E. van

Costumes militaires de France. Hoffmann, Nicolas

Costumes militaires des armées françaises de 1790 à 1856. Bastin, Ferdinand

Costumes militaires des différentes nations. Vernier, Charles

Costumes militaires; catalogue des principales suites de costumes militaires français. Glasser

Costumes militaires des cantons de la Suisse. Feyerabend, Franz

Costumes militaires 1789-1815. Charlet, N. T.

Costumes militaires et civil. Chataignier

Costumes militaires français. Charlet, N. T.

Costumes militaires français, depuis l'organisation des premières troupes régulières en 1439 jusqu'en 1789. Dunoyer de Noirmont, J. A. É. É., baron, and Marbot, A. C. A., baron de

Costumes militaires français depuis 1789 jusqu'à 1814. Marbot, A. C. A., baron de

Costumes militaires français & étrangers, portraits et sujets divers. Raffet, D. A. M.

Costumes militaires: Infanterie anglaise (1815). Genty, firm, Paris, pub.

Costumes militaires russes. Schadow, J. G.

Costumes militaires sous la deuxième république. Charpentier, Eugène

Costumes militaires suivant l'ordonnance de 1786. Hoffmann, Nicolas

Costumes, moeurs et coutumes des Russes. See Gruber, J. G. Sitten, gebräuche und kleidung der Russen, in St Petersburg

Costumes, moeurs et légendes de Savoie. Canziani, Estella

Costumes, moeurs et usages de la cour de Bourgogne. See Bastard d'Estang, Auguste, comte de. Costumes de la cour de Bourgogne

Costumes, moeurs, et usages de tous les peuples ... France—Paris. Eyriès, J. B. B.

Costumes, moeurs et usages de tous les peuples ... Espagne. Eyriès, J. B. B.

Costumes, moeurs et usages des Algériens. Jungmann, Robert

Costumes nationaux. Morel-Retz, L. P. G. B.

Costumes nationaux de Leipzig. Richter, J. G.

Costumes nationaux des provinces de la Suède, avec un aperçu des mœurs et coutumes de leurs habitans; Tr. de Gustave Backman. Stockholm [A. Bonnier, 1850]
34p. 11 col.pl. O.
Added t.-p.: *Pittoreska folkdrägter, från Sveriges provinser*
French and Swedish, in parallel columns. Plates by Hård and A. Weidel
Colas 729. LC 28-31164

Costumes nationaux scandinaves. See Afbildningar af nordiska drägter

Costumes, oeuvres d'art et utensiles. See Hefner-Alteneck, J. H. von. Trachten, kunstwerke und geräthschaften vom frühen mittelalter bis ende des achtzehnten jahrhunderts

The **costumes** of all nations, from the earliest times to the nineteenth century. Rohrbach, Carl

Costumes of all nations: one hundred and twenty-three plates, containing over fifteen hundred coloured costume pictures designed by the first Munich artists. 3d ed. rev. and enl. London, H. Grevel 1910
xii p. 123 double col. and mounted pl. F. o.p.
Plates with descriptive letterpress in German
The plates were originally issued under the title of *Zur geschichte der kostüme*, in the celebrated collection known as the *Münchener bilderbogen*. Illustrations by W. Diez and others
Costume index. LC w10-294

The **costumes** of America; with descriptive notices of the people. Cincinnati, U. P. James [1852]
128p. front. pl. T.

Costumes of Bordeaux. Bordeaux, Maggi ca1828
6pl. Q.
Lithographs signed X. M. Contents: Couturières; Marchandes de volailles; Marchandes de lait; Marchandes de royans; Marchandes de poissons; Grisettes
Colas 700

Costumes of British ladies from the time of William the 1st to the reign of Queen Victoria. [London] Dickinson & son ca1840
50 l. 48 col.pl. F.
Colas 730. Lipperheide 1000. LC 10-373

The **costumes** of eastern Europe. Tilke, Max

The **costumes** of France. Keim, Aline

Costumes of Hamburg. See Suhr, Christoffer. Hamburgische trachten

[**Costumes** of religious orders; sixty-one original colored drawings, with ms. descriptions.] [Rome] 184-?
61 col.pl. Q.

Costumes of Schwitzerland. See Costumes suisses

Costumes of the British army. Ackermann, Rudolph

Costumes of the clans of Scotland. Logan, James

The **costumes** of the French Pyrenees. Johnson, John

Costumes of the Indian army. Ackermann, Rudolph

Costumes of the members of the University of Cambridge. London, H. Hyde ca1840
1 col.pl. in 11 folds. F.

Costumes of the members of the University of Cambridge. Whittock, Nathaniel

The **costumes** of the members of the University of Oxford. Whittock, Nathaniel

The **costumes** of the mistresses of the White House. See Hoes, Mrs R. G. Dresses of the mistresses of the White House

Costumes of the modern stage. Mobisson, Ferdinand, ed.

Costumes of the Plains Indians. Wissler, Clark

Costumes of the time of George II designed for Her Majesty's state ball. Onwhyn, J., and Onwhyn, T.

Costumes of the time of the French revolution 1790-1793. Guillaumot, A. É.

The **costumes** of the various tribes ... of Afghaunistaun. Rattray, James

Costumes of various peoples. Baur, J. W.

Costumes officiels des fonctionnaires du Directoire. Chataignier

Costumes orientaux. Pécheux, and Manzoni

Les **costumes** originaux des provinces de France. Verdun, Paul

Costumes parisiens. Lanté, L. M.

Costumes parisiens pendant les glorieuses journées des 27, 28 et 29 juillet 1830. Paris, chez tous les Mds d'estampes [1830]
15 col.pl. Q.
Colas 736

Costumes patriotiques, ou Souvenirs des 27, 28, 29 Juillet 1830. Gérard-Fontallard, Henri

Costumes paysans. Gauthier, Joseph

Costumes persans. Chopin

Costumes persans modernes. Wattier, Émile

Costumes petit-russiens. Clodt von Jürgensburg, Michael Petrowitsch, baron

Costumes pittoresques. Maurice, C.

Costumes poitevins. Gelin, Henri, and Escudier, Charles

Costumes polonais. Gerson, Aldabert

Costumes populaires de la Turquie en 1873. Hamdī, O., bey, and Launay, Marie de

Costumes populaires et villageois de la Hollande. Amsterdam, C. G. Sulpke n.d.
1 l. 20 col.pl. O.
Plates copied in reduced size from those of Kuyper
Colas 737. Lipperheide 956

Costumes-portraits des actrices des principaux théâtres de Paris. Journal des dames et des modes

Costumes portuguezes, ou Colleçao dos trajos, uzos, costumes mais motaveis, e caracteristicos dos habitantes de Lisbo e Provincias de Portugal. Lissabon, 1832
1 l. 13pl. Q.
Colas 738

Les **costumes** régionaux de la France. Gardilanne, Gratiane de, and Moffat, E. W.

Costumes romains. Vleughels, Nicolas

Costumes russes. Clodt von Jürgensburg, M. P., baron

Costumes russes. Timm, W.

Costumes russes modernes. Chopin

Costumes russes representés en groupes charactéristiques. Knorre, Fr.

Costumes russes, vue de Saint-Pétersbourg. Kollmann, Ch.

Les **costumes** strasbourgeois. Berger-Levrault, Oscar

Costumes strasbourgeois (hommes). Seyboth, Adolf

Costumes suédois. Camino, Charles, and Régamey, Frederic

Costumes suisses. Zurich, J. H. Locher ca1870
22pl. S.
Colas 741. Lipperheide 913m

Costumes suisses ... Costumes of Schwitzerland. London, Telt and Bogne ca1830
22 col.illus. on 1 folded sheet. F.
Cataloged from Lonchamp

[**Costumes** suisses;] T. Richard, phot., Maenedorf. Zurich, Attenhofer & co. n.d.
22 col.pl. Q.
Colas 742. Lipperheide 914

Costumes suisses. See this title under Fuchslin; Graenicher, Samuel; Lory, Gabriel, and Moritz, F. W., eds; Mechel, Christian von; Rullmann; and Suter, Jakob

Costumes suisses d'après les desseins de J. Reinhard. See Reinhardt, J. C. Collection de costumes suisses des XXII cantons

Costumes suisses des différens cantons. Mechel, Christian von

Costumes suisses des 22 cantons. Genève, S. Morel ca1850
22 col.pl. S.
In *Colas (1782)* this title is attributed to Louis Lassalle
In *Colas* (1782) this title is attributed to

Costumes suisses des 22 cantons. Yves

Costumes suisses en mignature. Leuthold, H. F.

Les **costumes** suisses les plus origineaux. Füssli, R. H.

Costumes suisses peints par Reinhard. See Reinhardt, J. C. Collection de costumes suisses des XXII cantons

Costumes, traditions and songs of Savoy. Canziani, Estella

Costumes, uniformes, matérial de l'artillerie française depuis le moyen âge jusqu'à nos jours. See Moltzheim, A. de. Esquisse historique de l'artillerie française

Costumes vénitiens. Dusi, C.

Costumes vrais. Larchey, Lorédan

Costumi de' secolo XIII, XIV, e XV estratti da' monumenti i piu autentici di pittura e scultura. See Bonnard, Camille. Costumi ecclesiastici, civili e militari d' secolo XIII, XIV e XV

Costumi degli ordini religiosi. Roma, 1848
37 col.pl. Ti.
In portfolio
Colas 743

Costumi dei popoli antichi e moderni. Sergent-Marceau, A. F.

Costumi della corte pontificia. Roma, 1846
31 col.pl. Ti.
In portfolio
Plates are engraved by Ascani and Mochetti
Colas 167

Costumi della corte pontificia. Pistolesi, Erasmo

Costumi della festa data da S. Maesta' il di 20 feb. 1854 nella reggia di Napoli. Marta, Luigi

Costumi delle ven: archiconfraternite. Roma, E. Verzaschi 1870
31 col.pl. T.
Colas 744. Lipperheide 1885

Costumi di Roma. Cipriani, G. B.

Costumi di Roma e dei contorni. Bertini, A.

Costumi di Roma e suoi contorni. Marroni, Salvatore

Costumi diversi. Pinelli, Bartolommeo

Costumi diversi di alcune popolazioni de' reale domini di qua del Faro. Milano, G. M.

Costumi e descrizione delle processioni conosciute in Genova sotto il nome di Casacce. Ricavati da quella di San Giacomo il Magiore delle Focine. Genova, 1828
5p. 11 col.pl. ob.F.
Plates show the various companies which form the procession known as La Casaccia

Costumi e fatti dei briganti che infestano le compagne degl' Appenini fra Roma e Napoli. Pinelli, Bartolommeo

Costumi, e vestiture napolitani. Lindström, K. J.

Costumi ecclesiastici, civili e militari d' secolo XII, XIV e XV. Bonnard, Camille

Costumi ecclesiatici civili e militari della corte di Roma disegnati all' acquaforte. Ferrari, Filippo

Gli **costumi,** le leggi et l'usanze di tutte le genti. See Boemus, Johann. Mores, leges, et ritus omnium gentium

Costumi, musica, danze e feste popolari italiane; 2.éd. Roma, Stabilimento tipografico centrale 1935
308p. illus.
First edition: 1931

Costumi nazionali Dalmati. Jocosi

Costumi no. XXX di Roma e di altre paesi dello Stato Pontificio. Ferrari, Filippo

Costumi ornati. Parducci, Amos

Costumi popolari dello Statto Romano e Regno di Napoli tratti dal vero. Roma, A. Depoletti ca1815
20 col.pl. Q.
One man and 18 women in costume. Also a wagon and driver
Colas 745. Lipperheide 1273

Costumi popolari Italiani. Ferrari, Filippo

Costumi religiosi della corte pontificia. Roma, L. M. Garroni ca1850
48 col.pl. D.
Costume of religious orders
Lipperheide 1883

Costumi religiosi e militari della corte pontificia. Roma, T. Cuccioni ca1840
29 col.pl.(162 figures) on 1 strip. Ti.

Costumi sardi. Carta Raspi, Raimondo

Costumi ungheresi. See Pekáry, István. Magyar népviseletek

Costumi vestiti alla festa da ballo data in Milano dal ... Conte Giuseppe Batthyany ... La sera del 30. Genn°. 1828. Milan? 1828?
1 l. 60 col.pl. F.
Fancy dress and folk dress are shown. Descriptive text is in German and Italian
Colas 746. Lipperheide 2826

Costuming a play. Grimball, E. B., and Wells, Rhea

Costuming the amateur show. Saunders, D. L.

Costums de Catalunya; vint dibuixos originals de Josep Ribot, reproduits a tot color, acompanyats de comentaris per Francesc Baldelló ... precedits d'un pròleg de Prudenci Bertrana. Barcelona, Institut gràfic Oliva de Vilanova [1935]
[88]p. illus.(music) xx col.pl. ob.F.
LC 36-13203

Cotman, John Sell
Engravings of sepulchral brasses in Norfolk and Suffolk, tending to illustrate the ecclesiastical, military, and civil costume as well as to preserve memorials of ancient families in that county; with an introductory essay by Dawson Turner. 2d ed. London, H. G. Bohn 1839
2v. col.fronts. col.pl.(part fold.) F. 126s o.p.
124 plates from Norfolk, and 47 from Suffolk, of which 2 are in color. First edition (Yarmouth 1816) The Suffolk volume was not completed
Shows English costume from the 14th to the 17th century, including arms and armor
Colas 747. Costume index. Lipperheide 999. LC 11-32369

Cotrell & Leonard
History of academic costume in America. See entry under Erwin, John

Cottagers' comforts and other recipes in knitting & crochet; by "Grandmother". London, Hatchards [1882]
63p. O.
Lipperheide 4139

Cottafavi, Gaetano
Raccolta di n. costumi di Roma e dei contorni. Roma, P. Datri 1828
30 col.pl. O.
Colas 748. Lipperheide 1310
(engr.) Pinelli, Bartolommeo. Raccolta di cinquanta costumi di Roma e sue vicinanze

Cotton, Thomas Henry
Golf. (In Aldin, C. C. W. The omnibus book of sports for young and old. Part 3)

Cottreau, Gabriel
Les affiches de recrutement. See entry under Depréaux, Albert
Tenues des troupes de France. See Onfroy de Bréville, J. M. G. Aquarelles de Job. v4

Couderc, Camille
(ed.) Paris. Bibliothèque nationale. Mss. (Fr. 616). Livre de la chasse

Les **coulisses** de la mode. See Coffignon, A. Paris-vivant

Coulon, Jean
(illus.) Vial, Eugène. Costumes lyonnais du XIVe au XXe siècle

Coulton, George Gordon
The chronicler of European chivalry. London, The Studio 1930
x,133p. illus. col.pl. Q. $4.50
The illustrations are reproduced from manuscripts Harley 4379 and 4380 in the British museum. Plates accompanied by guard sheets with descriptive letterpress. Special winter number of the *Studio*
"While Dr. Coulton's study of Froissart and his time ranges over the whole period of his life, the miniatures which accompany it are taken from a manuscript of the Fifteenth century, which contains only the Fourth Book of the Chronicles. . . It covers only the last ten years of the reign of Richard II . . . 1389-1399." Introduction
Costume index. LC 31-826
(ed.) Life in the middle ages, selected, translated & annotated by G. G. Coulton. New York, Macmillan; Cambridge (Eng.) University press 1930
4v. in 1. front. illus. pl. D. (The Cambridge anthologies) $4.50
Volumes 2-4 have half-titles only. "Second edition in four volumes, 1928 . . . reprinted in one volume, 1930
New edition, "arranged roughly according to subject", of *A medieval garner* (London, Constable 1910)
Contents: v 1 Religion, folk-lore and superstition; v2 Chronicles, science and art; v3 Men and manners; v4 Monks, friars and nuns
Costume index. LC 31-9494

Counterfet kupffer-stich. Khevenhiller, F. C.

Coup d'oeil sur la Chine. Breton de la Martinière, J. B. J.

Coup d'oeil sur Rome, en 1828. Pigal, E. J.

Courboin, François
(illus.) Uzanne, L. O. Fashion in Paris
(illus.) Uzanne, L. O. Les modes de Paris

Courcy, Margaret De. See De Courcy, Margaret

Le **couronnement** d'Alphonse XIII. Routier, Gaston

Couronnement des Souverains Russes à partir du tsar Michel Fédorovitch jusqu'à l'empereur Alexandre III. See Vi͡enchanie russkīkh" gosudareĭ na Tsarstvo, nachīnai͡a s" tsari͡a Mīkhaīla Fedorovīcha do Īmperatora Aleksandra III

Courrier de la mode, ou Journal du goût. Paris? 1768
O.
An early fashion journal listed by Hatin

Cours complet d'enseignement professionel de la coupe du corset. Lorentz, Mme E., and Lacroix, A.

Cours d'antiquités monumentales. Caumont, Aroisse, comte de

Cours de coupe pour dames. Jacquenod, M. L.

Cours d'histoire naturelle. Daumier, H. V.

Cours élémentaire d'archéologie religieuse. Mallet, Joseph

Les **courses** de taureaux expliquées. Oduaga-Zolarde, G.

Courses de testes et de bague faittes par le roy. Perrault, Charles

Courson de la Villeneuve, Aurélien Marie C. de, and others
La Bretagne contemporaine. See entry under Benoist, Félix

The **Court** album: twelve portraits of the female aristocracy; engraved from drawings by the best artists. London, D. Bogue 1853
56p. 12pl. Q.
Shows women's dress of the period
Lipperheide 1008

The **court** circles of the republic. Ellet, Mrs E. F. L.

Court dress

Chevigny, de. La science des personnes de la cour, de l'épée et de la robe. 1723

Middle ages

Koehler, J. D. Dissertatio historico-critica de imperiali sacra lancea non inter reliquias imperii sed clinodia referenda cum problemate de novo S.R.I. Officio archi-lanciferatu. 1731

Parducci, Amos. Costumi ornati; studi sugli insegnamenti di cortigiania medievali. 1927

Schultz, Alwin. Das höfische leben zur zeit der minnesinger. 1889

18th century

Engelbrecht, Martin. Vornehmste reiche und staaten der welt in zierlichem und theils nach ihrer landes-art gewöhnlichem habit mit ihren wappen und ordens-zeichen vorgestellet. 1717

20th century

Ebart, P. J. von. Der hofmarschall auf der bühne, schauspielern und regisseuren. 1903

BY COUNTRY

England

Armytage, Mrs F. F. H. B. Old court customs and modern court rule. 1883

Barbey d'Aurevilly, J. A. The anatomy of dandyism. 1928

Barbey d'Aurevilly, J. A. Du dandysme et de G. Brummell. 1845

Barbey d'Aurevilly, J. A. Of dandyism and of George Brummell. 1897

Holding, T. H. Uniforms of British army, navy and court. 1894

Nichols, John. The progresses, processions, and magnificent festivities, of King James the First, his royal consort, family, and court. 1828

Onwhyn, J. and Onwhyn, T. Costumes of the time of George II designed for Her Majesty's state ball. 1845

20th century

Great Britain. Lord chamberlain. Dress and insignia worn at His Majesty's court. 1921

Great Britain. Lord chamberlain. Dress and insignia worn at His Majesty's court. 1929

Great Britain. Lord chamberlain. Dress worn at His Majesty's court. 1912

Great Britain. Lord chamberlain. Dress worn by gentlemen at His Majesty's Court and on occasions of ceremony. 1903

Their Majesties' courts holden at Buckingham palace and at the palace of Holyroodhouse, 1934-35. 1934-35

France

Compte-Calix, F. C. Album keepsake des costumes de la cour française depuis Charles VII jusqu'à Louis XVI. 1854

17th century

Trouvain, Antoine. Les appartements du roi Louis XIV. 1694-96

19th century

Colin, Mme Anaïs. Groupes de costumes de la cour de France. 1835

Costumes de la cour impérial de France. Neueste hof- und staats- trachten in Frankreich. ca1810

Defontaine, Henri. Du costume civil officiel et de l'uniforme militaire des officiers à la cour ou auprès des chefs d'état français depuis 1804 jusqu'à nos jours. 1908

Kerckhoff, Émile. La costume à la cour et à la ville; étiquette, tenue officielle et de fantaisie. 1865

Germany

16th century

Schlichtegroll, Franz von. Gallerie altteutscher trachten. 1802

Japan

Kawase Hasui. The Japanese dolls, Goshoningyo. 1935

The **Court** magazine and monthly critic and lady's magazine, and museum of the belles lettres. v. 1-31, 1832-1847. London

31v. col.illus. O.

A general periodical largely concerned with fashions

Continues *La Belle assemblée.* 1-9 as *Court magazine and La Belle assemblée;* 10-11 as *Court magazine and monthly critic;* 12-31 also called *united ser.* 1-20

Absorbed *Lady's magazine and museum of the belles-lettres* 1838?

Colas 749. Lipperheide 4617

Courte description des ordres des femmes et filles religieuses. See Schoonebeek, Adriaan. Kurtze und gründliche histori ... der Gott-geweyhten orden aller closter-jungfrauen

Courte et solide histoire de la fondation des ordres religieux. See note under Schoonebeek, Adriaan. Nette afbeeldingen

Courtin, L.

(lithgr.) Graf, Henry. Vues des cérémonies les plus intéressantes du couronnement de l'empereur Nicolas 1er et l'impératrice Alexandre

Courtois, A. See Madou, J. B., jt. auth.

Cousin, Jean. See Sera, Domenico da. Le livre de lingerie

Cousin, Jules. See Pilinski, Adam, ed. Cris de Paris au XVIe siècle

Coutance, Amadée Guillaume Auguste. See Jannettaz, Édouard, jt. auth.

Couts, Joseph

A practical guide for the tailor's cutting-room. Glasgow, Edinburgh, and London, Blackie and son [1848]

166p. illus. 27pl.(13 col.) diagrs. (1 fold.) Q.

"Being a treatise on measuring and cutting clothing in all styles, and for every period of life from childhood to old age." Subtitle

LC 9-1374

Coutumes des nations plus célèbres du monde. No place, 1750?
5v. 312 costumes on 39 double col.pl. Q.
Contents: [v 1] Hongrois, Suisses, Allemands, Anglois, &c. (10pl.) [v2] Russes, Tartares, Lapons, &c. (6pl.) [v3] Espagnols (6pl.) [v4] Coutumes des États de Vénise, de Toscane, de Rome, de Naples, &c. (8pl.) [v5] Othomans, Morlaques, Grecs, Egyptiens, &c. (9pl.)
LC 8-29090

Cova, Emilia
Confezione d'abiti par signora e l'arte del taglio. Milano, U. Hoepli 1895
91p. 40pl. O.
Colas 750. Lipperheide 3848

Cowden-Clarke, Mary
World-noted women. New York, D. Appleton 1858
407p. illus. Q.
For list of plates see entry for *Les étoiles du monde,* which contains the same plates

Cox, Raymond
L'art de décorer les tissus d'après les collections du Musée historique de la Chambre de commerce de Lyon; ouvrage publié sous le patronage de la Chambre de commerce de Lyon. Paris, P. Mouillot 1900
xxi,39p. 127pl.(part col.) F.
LC 10-2702

Coy, Owen Cochran
Pictorial history of California. Berkeley, University of California extension division [c1925]
4 l. 261pl.(incl.ports. maps, plans, facsims.)
Some of the plates show dress in California in the early days and in the 19th century
LC 25-28064

Cracow. Akademija umiejetności. See Akademija umiejętności, Cracow

Crafty, pseud. See Géruzez, Victor

Craig, Edward Gordon
On the art of the theatre. London, W. Heinemann 1912
xix,295p. front. 15pl. O.
Plates accompanied by guard sheets with descriptive letterpress. Six plates show costumes which are simple but effective in the theater
First printed December 1911
LC 12-22064

Craignish tales and others. Campbell, Lord Archibald

Craik, George Lillie, and MacFarlane, Charles
The pictorial history of England. London, C. Knight 1849
8v. front. illus. port. Q.
Standard edition. Planned and carried out under the auspices of Charles Knight. New edition revised and enlarged (Edinburgh, W. & R. Chambers 1855-58. 7v.)
Each volume has an ornamental t.-p. added (dated 1846 in v 1) In v5-8 (numbered v 1-4 respectively) this title reads: *The pictorial history of England during the reign of George the Third.* v4 has at end a chronological index, B.C. 55-A.D. 1760
Volumes 1-3, 5, 7-8 show costume of the period under the section: Manners and customs
Costume index (new ed.) LC 2-7805

Cranach, Hans Lucas von. See Diener-Schönberg, Alfons. Die waffen der Wartburg

Cranach, Lucas, i. e. Lucas Sunder
Passional Christi und Antichristi. [Wittenberg, J. Grünenberg 1521]
14 l. 26 illus. Q.
The book is a satire against the papacy. The illustrations are woodcuts by Cranach and each picture of an incident in the life of Christ is accompanied by a picture of one of the popes
Also available reproduced in facsimile with introduction by G. Kawerau (Berlin, G. Grote 1885) as volume 3 of the *Deutsche drucke älterer zeit in nachbildungen . . . von Wilhelm Scherer*
Lipperheide 614. LC 12-16039 (facsim. ed.)

(illus.) Auerswald, Fabian von. Ringer kunst

Cranach, Lucas, 1515-1586
(illus.) Reusner, Nicolaus. Icones sive imagines impp. regum, principum, electorum et ducum Saxoniae (attributed)

Cranae insula Laconia. Beger, Lorenz

Crane, Walter
Eight illustrations to Shakespeare's Tempest; designed by Walter Crane. Engraved & printed by Duncan C. Dallas. London, Dent 1894
8pl. F.

Eight illustrations to Shakespeare's Two gentlemen of Verona. Engraved and printed by Duncan C. Dallas. London, Dent 1894
8pl. F.

Flora's feast; a masque of flowers, penned & pictured by Walter Crane. London, Paris & Melbourne, Cassell 1892
40 col.pl. Q.
Plates show fancy dress representing various flowers
Lipperheide 3194

Shakespeare's comedy of the Merry wives of Windsor, presented in eight pen designs by Walter Crane; engraved and printed by Duncan C. Dallas. London, G. Allen 1894
2 l. 8pl. F.

See also Art workers guild, London. Beauty's awakening

Crass, Eduard
Deutsches brauchtum im jahreslauf, eine bilderfolge. Leipzig, Bibliographisches institut [1935]
40p. 48pl. on 24 l. D. (Bilder zur deutschen volkskunde)
"Ein teil des textes und der bilder ist dem . . . werke 'Die deutsche volkskunde' . . . Leipzig 1934/35, entnommen." page 37, foot-note
LC 36-10690

Crasso, Lorenzo
Elogii di capitani illustri. Venezia, Combi e Là Noù 1683
472p. 98 illus. Q.
Lipperheide 544

Crauzat, P. de
(illus.) Escudier, Gaston. Les saltimbanques

Cravatiana, ou traité général des cravates considérées dans leur origine, leur influence politique, physique et morale, leur formes, leurs couleurs et leurs espèces. Paris, Ponthieu 1823
84p. 15 illus. 1 pl. D.
Lipperheide notes that this is freely translated from an English edition which first appeared in 1818. A German translation of the French edition is found with title: *Cravatiana d. i. neueste halstuch-toilette für herren* (Ilmenau, B. F. Voigt 1823)
Colas 752. Lipperheide 1694-95

Cravats. See Neckwear

Craven, Mary. See Boutet de Monvel, Roger. Beau Brummell and his times

Crawford, Morris De Camp
The philosophy of dress. See entry under Bonwit, Teller & co., New York

Crawfurd, John. See Raffles, Sir T. S. Antiquarian, architectural, and landscape illustrations of the history of Java

Crawley, Alfred Ernest
Dress, drinks, and drums; further studies of savages and sex; edited by Theodore Besterman. London, Methuen [1931]
274p. O.
Bibliographical foot-notes
LC 31-29171

Les **créateurs** de la mode. Roger-Milès, Léon

Creations de manteaux. 1931?+ Paris, Société graphique
Col.pl. F.
Published quarterly. Current 1938. Brief descriptive text in French, English and German

Créations parisiennes. 1921+ Paris, Éditions Bell
Illus. F. 135fr. a year
Published monthly Sept. to July. Current 1938

Creccelius, Johannes
Collectanea ex historijs, De origine et fundatione omnium ferè monasticorum ordinum in specie: Simúlq. De fundatione et donatione cathedralium ac collegiatarum ecclesiarum cum suis canonicatibus ... incisae per Ioh. Th. de Bry. Francofurti 1614
203p. 11pl.(99 illus.) Q.
"Quibus accesserunt variorum ac diversorum ordinum ecclesiae papisticae variae ac diversae imagines, habitum et mores tam virorum quam feminarū caenobitarum referentes." Subtitle
Illustrations are copied from those in Jost Amman's *Ständ und orden*
Colas 124. Lipperheide 1854

Creeny, William Frederick
Illustrations of incised slabs on the continent of Europe, from rubbings and tracings. Norwich, Printed by A. H. Goose, for the author 1891
viii p. 69 l. 71-76p. 69pl. F.
The 71 facsimiles have been photo-lithographed by W. Griggs and sons
Plates show costume from 1150 to 1500
LC 1-5081

Creer, Edwin
Board work; or the art of wig-making. London, R. Hovenden 1887
234p. O.

Lessons in hair dressing. London, 1887
129p. illus. O.

Creese
Groneman, Isaäc. Der kris der Javaner. 1910

Crémaillère chez Antenor Joly. Paris, 1837
16 l. illus. Q.
Lipperheide 3699

Cremona fedelissima citta. Campo, Antonio

Crépon, Théophile
Costume civil, costume ecclésiastique, costume monastique. Paris, impr. De Soye et fils 1900
24p. O.
Extract from *Correspondent*
Colas 753

Crescentiis, Petrus de. See Crescenzi, Pietro de

Crescenzi, Pietro de
Commoda ruralium. Strassburg? ca1493
152 l. 312 illus. F.
Written about 1300 but was not printed in Latin until 1471. Later it was translated into German under title: *Neu feldt und ackerbau.* Illustrations show people at rural occupations
Lipperheide 426

Neu feldt und ackerbau dariñen deutlich begriffen wie man ausz rechtem grund der natur auch langwiriger erfahrung so beydes alhier in xv. bücher beschrieben ist jedes landgut bevorab den acker ... vorsorgen: demnach allerley lust und früchtgärten ... anrichten auch in bau und wessen erhalten soll. Erstlich durch ... Petrum de Crescentiis beschrieben. Strazburg, L. Zetzner 1602
646,[24]p. 200 illus. F.
Written about 1300 under the title *Commoda ruralium,* this book was not printed until 1471 and later was translated into German. Most of the drawings of the German edition are by Tobias Stimmer and show persons at rural occupations
Lipperheide 1985. LC Agr31-776

Crespo, Manuel. See Album de la infanteria y caballeria española del ejercito de Filipinas

A **Cretan** statuette in the Fitzwilliam museum, a study in Minoan costume. Wace, A. J. B.

Crete

Ancient

Baikie, James. The sea-kings of Crete. 1910

Bossert, H. T. Alt Kreta. 1921

Glotz, Gustave. La civilisation égéenne. 1923

Houston, M. G. Ancient Greek, Roman and Byzantine costume and decoration (including Cretan costume). 1931

Wace, A. J. B. A Cretan statuette in the Fitzwilliam museum, a study in Minoan costume. 1927

See also Greece—Mycenaean age

Creutz, Max
Die Rheinlande. See Deutsche volkskunst. v3

Creutzing, Caspar
(respondent) Müller, Peter, praeses. Dissertatio de jocalibus

[**Crevaux, Jules Nicolas**]
Voyages dans l'Amérique du Sud; avec 253 gravures sur bois, d'après des photographies ou des croquis pris par les voyageurs, 4 cartes. Paris, Hachette 1883
635p. incl.illus. pl. ports. port. 4 maps, 6 facsim. F.
Previously published in *Le tour du monde* 1879-1882 v37, 40, 41, 43, 44
Excursion du docteur Crevaux chez les Guaraounos; notes communiquées par M. E. Le Janne: p[593]-617
LC 6-42748

Creve, Carl Caspar
Medizinischer versuch einer modernen kleidung die brüste betreffend ... nebst einigen bemerkungen über das schminken. Wien, Heubner 1794
69p. O.
Lipperheide 3242

Cricketers
The game of cricket. 1930

The **cries** of London. Cooperstown, H. and E. Phinney 1839
31p. illus. Fe.
Cover title: *The London cries.* 1836

The **cries** of London. Lauron, Marcellus

The **cries** of London. Roberts, William

The **cries** of London. Smith, J. T.

Cries of London; [published] in aid of the "Daily News" wireless for hospitals fund ... music arranged by H. S. Ryan. Wheatley, Francis

Cries of Venice. See Zompini, Gaetano. Le arti che vanno per via nella città di Venezia

Crieurs et autres costumes populaires de Venise. Bosa, Eugenio

Crinoline
Genthe, F. W. Schutz- und trutzrede für die crinoline oder den steif- und reifrock. 1858
Lord, W. B. The corset and the crinoline. 1868
The origin of the whale bone-petticoat; a satyr. 1925

See also Hoop skirts

Crinoline from 1730 to 1864. London, E. Philpott 1864
12 l. 11pl. ob.O.
Text on one side of leaf only. Cover-title: *Crinoline in our parks and promenades, from 1710 to 1864 with antique illustrations*
Plates show fashions of various years
Colas 754. Lipperheide 1732

Crinoline in our parks and promenades, from 1710 to 1864. See Crinoline from 1730 to 1864

Crinolines et volants. Lamorillière, R. L. de

Crinolinens-einholung in Deutschland, wie alles, was nachher sich zugetragen. Ein humoristisch-satyrischer gesang. 6. aufl. Bad Oeynhausen, Essmann [1858]
22p. D.
Lipperheide 3491

Cripps-Day, Francis Henry
A record of armour sales, 1881-1924. London, G. Bell 1925
lxviii,327p. front. illus. F.
LC 26-489

(ed.) Laking, Sir G. F., bart. A record of European armour and arms through seven centuries

Les **cris** de la ville de Londres. See Lauron, Marcellus. The cryes of the city of London

Les **cris** de Berlin. Rosenberg, J. C. W.

Les **cris** de Londres au XVIIIe siècle ... Avec épigrammes en vers traduites par Mlle X ... Préface, notes, et bibliographie des principaux ouvrages sur les cris de Paris par A. Certeux. Paris, Chamuel 1893
183p. illus. D.
Text in English and French. There are reproductions of the title-pages of the 1799 London edition

[**Cris** de Paris. Paris, Martinet, litho. de C. Motte] ca1825
8 col.pl. F.
Cataloged from Colas where a list of the plates is given. Plates are signed F.
Colas 755

Cris de Paris. See this title under Aubry, Charles; Bonnart, J. B.; Bosse, Abraham; Boucher, François; Brebiette, Pierre; Fournel, F. V.; Poisson, J. B. M.; Vernet, Carle; Wattier, Édouard. *See also* Joly, Adrien. Les petits acteurs du grand théâtre

Cris de Paris au XVIe siècle. Pilinski, Adam, ed.

Les **Cris** de Paris en 8 suites. Bouchardon, Edme

Les **cris** de Vienne. See Brand, C. Zeichnungen nach dem gemeinen volke besonders der kaufruf in Wien

Cris et costumes de Paris. Watteau, L. J.

Cris et divers marchands de Petersbourg et de Moscou, Première suite de. See Le Prince, J. B. Oeuvres

Crisp, Frederick Arthur
Memorial rings, Charles the Second to William the Fourth, in the possession of Frederick Arthur Crisp. [London] Priv. print. ["Grove Park press"] 1908
10p.l. 373p. illus. 33½x26½cm.
Introduction signed: Bower Marsh
LC 13-19912

Critical description of the procession of Chaucer's pilgrims to Canterbury. Carey, W. P.

A **critical** inquiry into antient armour. Meyrick, Sir S. R.

Criticism
Bradley, H. D. The eternal masquerade. 1922

Ancient times

Cyprianus, Saint, bp. of Carthage. Thasci Caecili Cypriani De habitu virginum. 1932

16th century

Le blason des basquines et vertu-galles. 1563

Estienne, Antoine. Remonstrance charitable aux dames et damoyselles de France sur leurs ornemens dissolus. 1867

Criticism—*Continued*

17th century

Alamodische hobelbanck ... von den jetzigen ... sitten, närrischen gebräuch und missbräuchen als da ist in klaidern, gebärden gehen. 1630

Boileau, Jacques. De l'abus des nuditez de gorge. 1675

Carranza, Alonso. Rogacion en detestacion de los grandes abusos en los traxes y adornos nuevamente introducidos en España. 1636

Ellinger, Johann. Allmodischer kleyder teuffel. 1629

Englands vanity: or the voice of God against the monstrous sin of pride in dress and apparel. 1683

Evelyn, John. Mundus muliebris: or, The ladies dressing-room unlock'd, and her toilette spread. In burlesque. 1690

Haenfler, Johann. Ists auch mode? Wenn wil mode modus werden? 1693

Ouw, Wolfgang. Nothwendige erinnerung vom miszbrauch der kleyder da viele Christen in defectu, viele in excessu sündigen. 1663

18th century

Bosch, Bernardus. De weelde in Nederland; met ophelderende aanteekeningen in bijvoegzels. 1784

Feyjoo, B.-J. Théâtre critique, ou discours differens sur toutes sortes de matières pour détruire les erreurs communes. Tr. de l'espagnol ... Les modes. 1744

Gauthier, F. L. Traité contre l'amour des parures, et le luxe des habits. 1780

Gespräch eines doctors in der theologie mit zweyen vornehmen frauen über die neue kleydertragten. 1738

Harris, John, bp. of Llandaff. Treatise upon the modes; or A farewell to French kicks. 1715

Hiltebrandt, J. A. Der unwürdige communicant. 1705

Das lob der mode, eine rede, gehalten und gedruckt nach der mode. 1772

Luxus und modesucht der jezigen zeit. 1799

Oelssner, Gottlieb. Philosophisch-moralisch- und medicinische betrachtung, ueber mancherley zur hoffart und schönheit hervorgesuchte, schädliche **zwang-mittel**. 1754

19th century

Crinolinens-einholung in Deutschland, wie alles, was nachher sich zugetragen. Ein humoristisch-satyrischer gesang. 1858

Löwenheim-Röhn, E. Aesthetik und cynismus; eine entgegnung auf die Vischer'sche schrift "Mode und cynismus". 1879

Lohmann, Hermann. Ausspüche der heiligen schrift und der kirchenväter über kleiderpracht und moden zur warnung und belehrung gesammelt. 1844

Meinert, E. Modethorheiten. 1893

20th century

Bousfield, Paul. Sex and civilization. 1925

Croatia and Slavonia. See Military costume—Yugoslavia—Croatia and Slavonia

La **Croatie** militaire (1809-1813). Boppe, Paul

Crochet, L.

La toilette chez les Romaines au temps des empereurs. Lyon, Sézanne frères 1888

71p. XII pl. F.

"Étude des principaux objets de toilette en os trouvés dans les fouilles de la nécropole de Trion & du coteau de Fourvière." Subtitle

Bibliographical foot-notes

Colas 757. LC A32-1764

Crochet edgings. Myra and son

Crochet lessons. Myra and son

Crocheting

Album pour ouvrages de fleurs au crochet. ca.1858

Anker, Erna. Muster-album für haekelarbeiten. 1887

Cottagers' comforts and other recipes in knitting & crochet. 1882

Fischbach, Friedrich. Stilistische muster für stickerei und hakelei. ca1875

Georgens, J. D. Das häkeln. 1888

Häkel- und stickmuster der modenwelt. 1897

Häkelmuster-album der "Wiener mode". 1896

Hennings, Emma. Häkelschule für damen. 1850

Hennings, Emma. Kleine häkel-schule, oder die kunst sämmtliche häkelarbeiten zu erlernen. 1849

Hennings, Emma. Weisshäkel-muster. 1850

Herder, Natalie von. Album für weisse und bunte häkel- und filetarbeiten. 1870

Hertel, Louise. Neueste vollständige und gründliche anweisung zum häkeln der spitzen, manschetten, hauben, börsen, tücher, handschuhe. 1867

Hochfelden, Frau B. L. Das filet und das filettopfen. 1889

Hochfelden, Frau B. L. Die gabelhäkelei; anleitung zur anfertigung zahlreicher hübscher und leichter muster. 1885

Hochfelden, Frau B. L. Das häkeln; ausführliche anleitung zur erlernung der häkelarbeit und handbuch der gesammten häkelkunst. 1892

Korn, Minna. Minna Korn's Häkel-buch. 1867

The lady's crochet-book. 1884-86

Lambert, Miss A. My crochet sampler. 1847-48

Crocheting—*Continued*

Leach, Mrs. Mrs Leach's complete guide to crochet work. 1890

Manteuffel, Erna von. Filet-guipure-album. 1881

Myra and son. Myra's Crochet lessons, no.1, containing the rudiments of crochet ... with ... original designs. 1889

Myra and son. Myra's Harlequin crochet, containing full descriptions ... of ... designs for the new fancy needlework. 1888

Neue häkelmappe; eine anzahl schöner häkel-muster nebst genauer beschreibung. 1879

Rausche-Rauss, Frieda. Häckel-vorlagen für schule und haus. 1892

Reinle, Sophie. Neue häkel-vorlagen. 1892

Sammlung gehäkelter spitzen und einsätze. 1896

Sylvia's book of new designs in knitting, netting, and crochet, containing a selection of useful articles in crochet, knitting, tatting, and netting, with minute details. 1881

Sylvia's crochet book. ca1879

Crocker, Sydney, and Barker, Bligh

Sketches from the Basque Provinces of Spain. ₍London, T. McLean 1839₎
3 l. 22pl. F.
Plates show scenes with people in Basque costume
Colas 758. Lipperheide 1227

Croisat

Méthode de coiffure. Paris, ₍The author₎ 1831
120p. 6pl. O.
The 2. *édition augmentée* was published 1832 (171p. 22pl. O.)
Colas 759-60

Théorie de l'art du coiffeur, ou méthode à suivre, pour approprier la coiffure aux traits, l'âge et la stature. Paris, ₍The author₎ 1847
32,171p. 25pl. O.
Colas 761. Lipperheide 1699m

(ed.) Les cent-un coiffeurs de tous les pays. v 1-5 Paris, ₍The editor₎ 1836-41
5v. pl.(part col.) O.
Annual publication 1837-₍1841₎
Croisat was a Parisian "professeur de coiffure"
Colas 762

Croly, George

The Holy Land, Syria, Idumea, Arabia, Egypt & Nubia. After lithographs by Louis Haghe from drawings made on the spot by David Roberts, R. A. London, Day 1855-56
6v. in 3. fronts.(v 1, 3, 5-6) pl.(part col.) maps. Q.
Vols. 4-6: Historical descriptions by William Brockedon
Originally published 1842, in 2 vols., with introduction by Rev. G. Croly. In 1847 combined with *Views in ancient Egypt and Nubia* (1846, introduction by W. Brockedon) and issued under general title *Views in the Holy Land, Syria, Idumea*
Lipperheide 1590. LC 4-12302

Crompton, Mrs Rebecca

Modern design in embroidery; edited by Davide C. Minter. New York, C. Scribner; London, B. T. Batsford ₍1937₎
72p. col.front. illus. LI pl.(part col.) on 27 l. diagrs. O. $3.50, 8s 6d
LC 37-27182

Die **crone** ... des Leopoldi ... käyserliche gemahlin. See Leucht, C. L. Augusta corona augustissima Augustae coronata

Cronecken der Sassen. Botho, Conrad

Cronen zur zierd und schutz des Heiligen Römischen Reichs auf denen häuptern ... Eleonorä und Josephi. Leucht, C. L.

Cronica breve de i fatti illustri de' re di Francia. Venetia, B. Giunti 1588
62 l. 63 ports. F.
"Con le loro effigie dal naturale, cominciando da Faramondo, primo re di Francia .... CCCCXX sino a Henrico III ... 1588." Subtitle
According to *Brunet*, Fr. Franco is the engraver
Lipperheide 1063

Cronica van Coellen

Die Cronica van der hilliger stat Coellen. Köln, J. Koelhoff 1499
13,ccliv l. col.illus. F.
Illustrations show 15th century costume, including that of rulers, popes and bishops
Lipperheide 432

Cronicques et conquestes de Charlemaine. Le Tavernier, Jean

Die **cronycke** van Hollant, Zeelant ende Vrieslant. Beghinnende van Adams tijden tot die gheboorte ons Heeren Jesum voortgaende tot den jare M.CCCCC. ende XVJJ ... Hier is by ghevoecht het tweede deel oft vervolch vande Hollandtsche cronijcke Van den jare 1516. totten jare 91 ... Dordrecht, P. Verhaghen 1590-91
3v. in 1. illus. ports. Q.
Volume 1, known as *Divisie chronijk*, was first published in 1517, by Jan Severs; authorship has been attributed to him and to Cornelius Aurelius. v2: Het tweede deel vande Hollandtsche ende Zeelandtsche cronycke ... Vanden jaere XVᶜ. zestien totten jaere een ende tnegentich. Met grooter vlijt by een vergadert, door E. D. V. Ellert de Veer ... In S'Gravenhaghe, By Aelbrecht Hendricksz 1591. v₍3₎ (attributed to E. de Veer): *Historie ofte wiider verclaringhe* vande Nederlantsche gheschiedenissen ... van alles wat sich verloopen heest vanden jare 1566, totten wtganghe vanden jare 90. Dordrecht, P. Verhaghen 1590
Issued also with same dates by A. Heyndricxsz., Delft (v 1) and Corn. Claesz., Amsterdam (v2-3)
Lipperheide 925-26

Cronyke van het leven en bedryff van alle de coningen van Engeland. See note under Baker, Sir Richard. A chronicle of the kings of England

Crooke, William

Natives of northern India. London, A. Constable 1907
xiv,270p. front. pl. ports. map. O. (The native races of the British empire)
Bibliography: p263-65
LC 7-29138

Crooke, William—*Continued*
Things Indian; being discursive notes on various subjects connected with India. New York, C. Scribner 1906
xi,546p. O.
Alphabetically arranged. Bibliographical references at end of most of the articles. Costume p155-67; shawls p416-17; tattooing p460-64
LC 6-22386

Croquis à la manière noire dédiés à Béranger. Charlet, N T

Croquis d'après nature faits ... en Grèce et dans le Levant. Le Blanc, T. P.

Croquis de cavalerie. See Vallet, L. A travers l'Europe

Croquis divers. Bellangé, J. L. H.

Croquis inédits de Charlet. Charlet, N. T.

Croquis lithographiques. Charlet, N. T.

Croquis russes. Mitreuter, H. D., and others

The **crossbow,** mediaeval and modern, military and sporting. Payne-Gallwey, Sir R. W. F., bart.

Cross-stitch. Alexander, V. C.

Cross-stitch embroidery. See Embroidery, Cross-stitch

Crousaz, A. von
Geschichte des königlich preussischen Kadetten-Corps, nach seiner entstehung, seinem entwickelungsgange und seinen resultaten. Berlin, H. Schindler 1857
xx,433,49p. 6 illus.(ports.) 6 col.pl. F.
Lipperheide 2181

Crouzil, Lucien
Le port du costume religieux. Paris, A. Fontemoing 1902
11p. O.
Cover title
Extrait de la *Revue générale du droit*
Colas 763

Crown jewels
Abbott, Mary. Jewels of romance and renown. 1933

See also Regalia

Czechoslovakia

Bohemia

Bock, Franz. Die kleinodien des Heil. Römischen Reiches deutscher nation nebst den kroninsignien Böhmens, Ungarns und der Lombardei; mit kunsthistorischen erläuterungen. 1864

England

Davenport, C. J. H. English regalia. 1897

Garrard's, 1721-1911, crown jewellers and goldsmiths during six reigns and in three centuries. 1912

Younghusband, Sir G. J. The jewel house. 1920?

Younghusband, Sir G. J., and Davenport, C. J. H. The crown jewels of England. 1919

Germany

Bock, Franz. Die kleinodien des Heil. Römischen Reiches deutscher nation nebst den kroninsignien Böhmens, Ungarns und der Lombardei; mit kunsthistorischen erläuterungen. 1864

Delsenbach, J. A. Wahre abbildung der sämtlichen reichskleinodien welche in ... Nürnberg aufbewahret werden. 1790

Murr, C. G. von. Beschreibung der sämtlichen reichskleinodien und heiligthümer welche in Nürnberg aufbewahret werden. 1790

Seidel, Paul. Die insignien und juwelen der preussischen krone. 1913

Hungary

Bock, Franz. Die kleinodien des Heil. Römischen Reiches deutscher nation nebst. den kroninsignien Böhmens, Ungarns und der Lombardei; mit kunsthistorischen erläuterungen. 1864

Italy

Lombardy

Bock, Franz. Die kleinodien des Heil. Römischen Reiches deutscher nation nebst den kroninsignien Böhmens, Ungarns und der Lombardei; mit kunsthistorischen erläuterungen. 1864

Russia

Hammer, Armand. The quest of the Romanoff treasure. 1932

Spain

Miró y Argenter, José Ignacio. Estudio de las peidras preciosas, su historia y caractéres en bruto y labradas con la descripcion de las joyas mas notables de la corona de España y del monasterio del Escorial. 1870

The **crown** jewels of England. Younghusband, Sir G. J., and Davenport, C. J. H.

The **crown** skirts; nouveautés für 1864. Annaberg, Thomas & co. [1864]
11 l. illus. 11pl. O.
Colas 764. Lipperheide 1733

The **crowning** of the sovereign of Great Britain and the dominions overseas. Perkins, J. H. T.

Crowning the king. Beavan, A. H.

Crowninshield, Frank
(ed.) Vanity fair

Crowns
Bombelli, Rocco. Storia della corona ferrea dei re d'Italia. 1870
Boutell, Charles. Boutell's manual of heraldry. c1931
Geldart, Ernest. Ecclesiastical decoration. 1889
The Illustrated London news. Silver jubilee record number, King George v. and Queen Mary, 1910-1935. 1935
Jones, William. Crowns & coronations; a history of regalia. 1883
Noppen, J. G. Royal Westminster and the coronation. 1937
Twining, E. F. The English coronation ceremony. 1937
Zanetti, G. F. Della berretta ducale volgarmente chiamata corno che portasi da' serenissimi dogi di Venezia. 1779

See also Miters

Crowns, Papal. See Papal tiara

Crowns & coronations: a history of regalia. Jones, William

Cruikshank, George

The bachelor's own book, being the progress of Mr. Lambkin, (gent.) in the pursuit of pleasure and amusement, and also in search of health and happiness. London, D. Bogue 1844
1 p.l. 12pl. nar.O.
LC 11-24212

Cruikshank's water colours; with introduction by Joseph Grego. London, Black 1903
xxvi,325p. col.pl. O.
Contents: Introduction. Oliver Twist [selections] by C. Dickens. The miser's daughter [selections] by W. H. Ainsworth. History of the Irish Rebellion in 1798, and Emmet's Insurrection in 1803 [selections] by W. H. Maxwell

Drawings ... prepared by him to illustrate an intended autobiography. London, pub. for B. W. Richardson by Chatto & Windus 1895
49 illus. sq.Q.
The pictures illustrate "Adventures in his own life; Napoleon; Revolution; the course of some social advancements, such as chimney sweeping and ventilation; fashions and customs of his day; and one or two whimsicalities." H. R. Huntington library

George Cruikshank's Omnibus; illus. with one hundred engravings on steel and wood. Ed. by L. Blanchard; new ed. London, Bell and Daldy 1869
300p. 19pl. 3 port. illus. Q.

(illus.) Ainsworth, W. H. The miser's daughter

(illus.) Egan, Pierce. Life in London

(illus.) Jerrold, Blanchard. The life of George Cruikshank

Cruikshank, George, and Cruikshank, Isaac Robert

London characters; twenty-four col'd plates. Comicalities; twenty-four col'd plates by Robert Cruikshank. London, J. Robins 1827-30
48pl. S.
Binder's title

Cruikshank, Isaac Robert

(illus.) Egan, Pierce. Life in London

See also Cruikshank, George, jt. auth.

Cruikshank's water colours. Cruikshank, George

A **cruise**; or, Three months on the continent by a naval officer. London, Law and Whittaker 1818
129p. 4 col.pl. O. 8s
Three of the plates show Dutch costume
Colas 765

Crusaders

Michaud, J. F. History of the crusades. 189-

Øverland, O. A. Korstogehes historie. 1900-01

Cruso, Thalassa. See London. Museum. Costume

Cruz Cano y Olmedilla, Juan dé la

Colleccion de trajes de España, tanto antiguos como modernos, que comprehende todos los de sus dominios ... tomo I. Madrid, M. Copin Carrera 1777-88
82 col.pl. Q.
The collection appeared in seven numbers, of which the last was dated 1788. Plates are engraved and colored by Juan de la Cruz after Manuel de La Cruz, Joseef Muñoz y Frias, etc. Copies of some of the plates were published with the same title about 1785 (64 col.pl.)
Colas 1706, 645. Lipperheide 1209-10

Collection des costumes espagnols anciens et moderns. Paris, Guaguery 1786
48 col.pl. F.
The above title is given on a prospectus for the work. The title *Recueil des plusrs. habillements espagnols* appears on the first plate of each of the seven parts in which the work was published. Plates are engraved by Devère after those in the La Cruz *Colleccion*
Colas 854. Lipperheide 1211

The **cryes** of the city of London. Lauron, Marcellus

Családi Kör. 1865-1866. Pest, Gyorssaitonyomat Khor és Weintól
Col.pl. F.
A Hungarian periodical with fashion plates
Colas 766. Lipperheide 4698

Čtení o Lužici, cesty z roků 1886-1923. Kuba, Ludvík

Cuadernos militares. Castro, Fernández de

Cuba

19th century

Bachiller y Morales, Antonio. Coleccion de artículos. 1881

Carleton, G. W. Our artist in Cuba. 1865

Olivares, José de. Our islands and their people. 1899-1900

20th century

Browne, G. W. The New America and the Far East. 1907 v9-10

Periodical

Gaceta gentleman. 1933+

Cubas, Antonio Garcia. See Garcia Cubas, Antonio

Cuciniello, Michele, and Bianchi, Lorenzo

Voyage pittoresque dans le royaume des deux Siciles. Naples, 1830-33
180pl. F. 300fr.

Cuciniello & Bianchi, firm, Naples

(pub.) Raccolta delle diverse vestiture delle provincie del regno di Napoli

Cudell, Robert

Das buch vom tabak. Coeln a. Rh., Haus Neuerburg 1927
245p. illus. O.
Vom tabakblatt zur zigarette; ein anhang zum "Buch vom tabak" von Rob. Cudell. Coeln a Rh., Haus Neuerburg 1927 (28p. illus. O.) laid in
LC 27-21592

Cudet, François

Histoire des corps de troupe qui ont été spécialement chargés du service de la ville de Paris depuis son origine jusqu'à nos jours; illus ... en couleurs par Eugène Chaperon, Georges Clairin, Eugène Courboin, Édouard Detaille, Ferdinandus, Fournier, Paul Jazet, Jeanniot, Alfred de Marbot, Philippoteaux, Maurice Pillet, Eugène Titeux. Paris, L. Pillet 1887

313p. illus.(incl.music) pl.(part col.) maps. Q.

Contents: Histoire du guet de Paris; Police de Paris depuis la création des lieutenants généraux de police (1667-1789) Garde nationale de Paris; Histoire de la Garde républicaine

Colas 768. LC 22-1187

Cuendias, Manuel Galo de, and Suberwick, Mme de

L'Espagne pittoresque, artistique et monumentale. Mœurs, usages et costumes, par Manuel de Cuendias et V. de Féréal [pseud]; illustrations par Célestin Nanteuil. Paris, Librairie ethnographique 1848

392p. front.(port.) illus. 49pl.(part col.) Q.

The color plates show costume of men and women of different regions of Spain. Most of them were reproduced in *Recuerdos de un viage por España*

Also available in German translation with title: *Spanien und die Spanier, ihre sitten, trachten, volkssagen und legenden* (Brüssel, 1849) with same illustrations

Colas 769-770. Costume index. Lipperheide 1231 (German ed.) LC 4-28860

Cuirass

Apin, S. J. Dissertatio de loricis linteis veterum et novo loricarum invento. 1719

Les **cuirasses** des carabiniers (1810-1870) Margerand, J.

Les **cuirassiers** (1672-1886). Hardoin, Georges

Die **cultur** der renaissance in Italien. Burckhardt, J. C.

Culturistorisch etnografischer atlas des Königreiches Serbien. See Laj Felīks. Kulturno īstorījsko etnografskī atlas kraīevīne Srbīje

Die **culturländer** des alten America. Bastian, Adolf

Cuming, Edward William Dirom

With the jungle folk; A sketch of Brumese[!] village life. Illustrated by a Burmese artist. London, Osgood, McIlvaine 1897

400p. front. pl. O.

[**Cunliffe-Owen, Marguerite (de Godart, comtesse du Planty et de Sourdis)**]

Eve's glossary. [The guide-book of a "mondaine"] By the Marquise de Fontenoy [pseud.] Chicago & New York, H. S. Stone 1897

285p. O.

Der **cur** und fürsten von Sachsen. See Kilian, Wolfgang. Serenissimorum Saxoniae electorum, et quorundam ducum Agnatorum genuinae effigies

Curia romana. See Coronelli, M. V. Ordinum equestrium, ac militarium brevis narratio

Curiöser spiegel; neue aufl. Nürnberg Johann Andreä Endter handlung 1804

xli p. 41 col.illus. F.

"Worinnen der ganze lebenslauf des menschen von der kindheit bis zum alter zu sehen, in figuren mit beygefügten ganz neuen kürzen erklärungen vorgestellt." Subtitle

First edition 1700. Other editions appeared, the latest in 1853. The plates show persons of different occupations, including street criers, at their work. They are by Susanna Maria Sandrart, most of them engraved by Elias Porzel

Lipperheide 1955

Curious fashions. Lewis, Dio

Currier, Charles Warren

History of religious orders. New York Murphy & McCarthy 1895

x,484p. pl.(part col.) ports. O. o.p.

Published also (Boston, MacConnell 1896) with plates in black and white only

Costume index

Curry, Manfred

The beauty of skating; foreword and notes on skaters by T. D. Richardson London, J. Miles [1935]

18p. 96pl. on 48 l. sq.Q. $5

LC 36-12086

"**Curry** & rice," on forty plates; or, The ingredients of social life at "our station" in India. Atkinson, G. F.

Curtis, Edward S.

The North American Indian; being a series of volumes picturing and describing the Indians of the United States and Alaska, written, illustrated, and published by Edward S. Curtis; edited by Frederick Webb Hodge, foreword by Theodore Roosevelt; field research conducted under the patronage of J Pierpont Morgan. [Seattle, Wash. E. S. Curtis; [Cambridge, U. S. A., The University press] 1907-30

20v. fronts.(1 col.) pl. ports. F.

Twenty portfolios containing 722 plates part col.) accompany the bound volumes as a supplement

Contents: I The Apache. The Jicarillas The Navaho; II The Pima. The Papago The Qahatika. The Mohave. The Yuma The Maricopa. The Walapai. The Havasupai. The Apache-Mohave, or Yavapai III The Teton Sioux. The Yanktonai. The Assiniboin; IV The Apsaroke, or Crows The Hidatsa; V The Mandan. The Arikara The Atsina; VI The Piegan. The Cheyenne The Arapaho; VII The Yakima. The Klickitat. Salishan tribes of the interior. The Kutenai; VIII The Nez Percés. Wallawalla Umatilla. Cayuse. The Chinookan tribes IX Salishan tribes of the coast. The Chimakum and the Quilliute. The Willapa X The Kwakiutl; XI The Nootka. The Haida; XII The Hopi; XIII The Hupa. The Yurok. The Karok. The Wiyot. Tolowa and Tututni. The Shasta. The Achomawi The Klamath; XIV The Kato. The Wailaki The Yuki. The Pomo. The Wintun. The Maidu. The Miwok. The Yokuts; XV Southern California Shoshoneans. The Diegueños. Plateau Shoshoneans. The Washo XVI The Tiwa. The Keres; XVII The Tewa The Zuñi; XVIII The Chipewyan. The Western woods Cree. The Sarsi; XIX The Indians of Oklahoma. The Wichita. The southern Cheyenne. The Oto. The Comanche. The Peyote cult; XX The Alaskan Eskimo. The Nunivak Eskimo of Hooper bay. Eskimo of King island. Eskimo of Little Diomede island. Eskimo of Cape Prince of Wales. The Kotzebue Eskimo The Noatak. The Kobuk. The Selawik

LC 8-2173

Curtis, Natalie. See Burlin, Mrs N. C.

Curtis, Oswald. See Norris, Herbert. Costume & fashion, v6

Curtis, William Eleroy

Around the Black Sea; Asia Minor, Armenia, Caucasus, Circassia, Daghestan, the Crimea, Roumania. New York, Hodder & Stoughton, George H. Doran company c1911
456p. pl. port. group, fold.map. O. 12s o.p.
Costume index. LC 11-18104

Egypt, Burma and British Malaysia. Chicago, New York [etc] F. H. Revell company 1905
399p. incl.front.(map) pl. ports. facsim. O.
LC 5-27427

Turkestan: "the heart of Asia" ... pictures by John T. McCutcheon. New York, Hodder & Stoughton, George H. Doran company c1911
344p. front. pl. ports. fold.map. O. $2.00
Costume index. LC 11-15040

Cusachs, Jose

(illus.) Barado y Font, Francisco. La vida militar en España

Cust, Lionel Henry

(comp.) Catalogue of the collection of fans and fan-leaves presented by the Lady Charlotte Schreiber. See entry under British museum. Department of prints and drawings

Customs and traditions of Palestine. Pierotti, Ermete

The **customs** of mankind. Eichler, Lillian

The **customs** of New England. Felt, J. B.

Customs of the world. Hutchinson, Walter, ed.

Custos, Dominicus

Fuggerorum et Fuggerarum quae in familia natae, quaeve in familiam transierunt, quot extant aere expressae imagines. Augustae Vindelicorum, A. Aperger 1618
2 l. 127pl. F.
On verso of title page: Opus, quod . . . D. Custos . . . e suo diagrammate in aere incisum edidit, nuncque Lucas et Wolfgangus Kilian . . . genealogia Fuggaricae prosapiae per alium . . . collecta, et de novo adjecta, ampliarunt
First edition: 1593
Lipperheide 763

Pinacotheca Fuggerorum S.R.I. comitum ac baronum in Khierchperg et Weissenhorn; editio nova multis imaginibus aucta. Ulmae, I. F. Gaum 1754
26 l. 1 pl. 139 ports. F.
Portraits, engraved by Lucas and Wolfgang Kilian, show 16th century costume
Lipperheide 764

Tirolensium principum comitum. Ab. an. ... 1229 usq. ad ann. 1599. Augustae Vindelicorum, ex typographeio I. Praetorij [1599]
36 l. 30 illus. F.
Contains 28 full-length portraits of the counts of Tirol to the time of the emperor Rudolf II. Some of the plates are signed F. A. or Franz Aspruck
A German edition was published with five additional portraits. *Tirolensium principum comitum, Der gefürsten grafen zu Tyrol von anno 1229 biss anno 1623 eigentliche contrafacturen* (Augspurg, W. Kilian 1623)
Lipperheide 846-47

(engr.) Schrenck von Nozing, Jacob. Augustissimorum imperatorum ... thaten

Cutch. Young, Marianne

Cutting. See Tailoring and cutting

Cutts, Edward Lewes

Scenes and characters of the middle ages. London, Simpkin, Marshall 1872
xiii,546p. 81 illus. pl. Q.
"The essays which are collected in this volume were originally published . . . in the . . . *Art-journal,* extending over a period of nearly five-and-twenty years." Preface
Contents: Monks; Hermits and recluses; Pilgrims; Secular clergy; Minstrels; Knights; Merchants
Costume index. Lipperheide 1011. LC 3-13468

Cuyck, Pieter van, the younger

Lyk-staetsie van ... Willem Carel Hendrik Friso, prince van Orange en Nassau ... Gehouden den IV. Februari MDCCLII. Naeuwkeuriglyk nagetekent door P. van Cuyk, junior, en in het kooper gebragt door J. Punt. 's Gravenhage, P. Gosse junior 1755
40p. 27pl. F.
Illustrated title-page. Text in Dutch and French
The plates are steel engravings which show members of various professions and trades, and officials as they marched in the funeral procession
Lipperheide 2674

A **cyclopaedia** of costume or dictionary of dress. Planché, J. R.

Cyclopaedia of the British costumes, from the Metropolitan repository of fashions. v 1-5; 1823-1847. London, G. Walker
5v. ca146 col.pl. ob.Q.
Colas 771

A **cyclopedia** of education. Monroe, Paul, ed.

Cyclopedia of painters and paintings. Champlin, J. D., ed.

Cynismus, Mode und. Vischer, F. T. von

Cyprianus, Saint, bp. of Carthage

Thasci Caecili Cypriani De habitu virginum: a commentary; with an introduction and translation ... by Sister Angela Elizabeth Keenan. Washington, D.C. The Catholic university of America, 1932
xiii,188p. O. (The Catholic university of America. Patristic studies. v34)
Thesis, Catholic university of America, 1932. Latin and English
Written originally about 250 A.D. Advice to women in monastic and religious orders on plainness and simplicity in dress. Includes Latin text, English translation and commentary
Bibliography: p ix-xiii
LC 32-22111

Cyprus

Ancient

Perrot, Georges, and Chipiez, Charles. History of art in Phoenicia and its dependencies. 1885

Modern

Ohnefalsch-Richter, M. H. Griechische sitten und gebräuche auf Cypern. 1913

Cyprus. Cesnola, L. P. di

Cyriax, Tony

Among Italian peasants, written and illustrated by Tony Cyriax. London [etc] W. Collins [1919]
xii,263p. col.front. pl.(part col.) O.
LC 20-6679

Czakó, Elemér

(ed.) Magyarság tárgyi néprajza

Czaplicka, Mary Antoinette

My Siberian years ... illustrations from photographs. London, Mills & Boon [1916]
xii,315p. front. pl. ports. fold.map. O.
LC 17-26074

Czar Ferdinand and his people. Macdonald, John

Czechoslovakia

Heimbucher von Bikessy, J. Pannoniens bewohner in ihren volksthümlichen trachten. 1820

Holme, Charles, ed. Peasant art in Austria and Hungary. 1911

Jaschke, Franz. National-kleidertrachten und ansichten von Ungarn, Croatien, Slavonien, dem Banat, Siebenbürgen und der Bukowina. 1821

Kožmínová, Amalie. Podkarpatská Rus. 1922

Mothersole, Jessie. Czechoslovakia, the land of an unconquerable ideal. 1926

Die Österreichisch-ungarische monarchie in wort und bild. 1886-1902 v 17

Paris Exposition de l'art populaire tchécoslovaque, 1920. Exposition de l'art populaire tchéco-slovaque. 1920

Prague. Národopisné museum československé. Moravské slovensko. 1918-22

Tyršová, R. F. and Hantich, Henri. Le paysan tchèque: Bohême, Moravie, Silésie, costumes et broderies. 1911

Úprka, Joža. Na pouit u Sv. Antoníčka. 1924?

Úprka, Joža. Peasants' furs in Czechoslovakia. 1920

Young women's Christian associations. Bureau of pageantry and the drama. National costumes of the Slavic peoples. 1920

Zíbrt, Čeněk, and Winter, Zikmund. Dějiny kroje v zemích českých. 1892-93

See also subdivision Czechoslovakia under Arms and armor; Embroidery; Military costume

Periodical

Český lid. Sbornik věnovaný studiu lidu českého v Čechácк, na Moravě, ve Slezsku a na Slovensku. 1892+

Bohemia

Aegidius. D. Wenceslao Bohemorum duci ac martyri inclyto sertvm ortus, vitae, necis è duabus suprà triginta iconibus, totidemque Tetrastichis, velut è rosis quibusdam contextum ... cui attexitur floriger fasciculus selectiorum epigrãmatum opera F.Æ. â S.I.B. 1644

Balzer, Johann. 87 abbildungen böhmischer und mährischer gelehrten und künstler. 1773

Colquhoun, A. R., and Colquhoun, Mrs E. M. C. The whirlpool of Europe, Austria-Hungary and the Habsburgs. 1907

Dobrovsky, Josef. Dobrowsky's Slavin. Bothschaft aus Böhmen an alle slawischen volker. 1834

Fišer, Frant. Old Bohemian customs throughout the year. 192-?

Grüner, V. R. Böhmische volkstrachten. ca1830

Die Österreichisch-ungarische monarchie in wort und bild. 1886-1902 v 14-15

Pelzel, F. M., and Voigt, Adauctus. Abbildungen böhmischer und mährischer gelehrten und künstler. 1773-82

Žalud, August. Česká vesnice. 1919

See also Kings and rulers—Bohemia also subdivision Czechoslovakia—Bohemia under Ceremonial and festival costume; Coronations and coronation robes; Crown jewels; Ecclesiastical costume; Headdress

Eger

Grüner, J. S. Über die ältesten sitten und gebräuche der Egerländer. 1901

Pröckl, Vincenz. Eger und das Egerland. 1845

Moravia

Balzer, Johann. 87 abbildungen böhmischer und mährischer gelehrten und künstler. 1773

Pelzel, F. M., and Voigt, Adauctus. Abbildungen böhmischer und mährischer gelehrten und künstler. 1773-82

See also Embroidery—Czechoslovakia—Moravia

Ruthenia

Golovatskĭ, I͡A. F. Narodnyi͡a pi͡esni Galitskoĭ ĭ Ugorskoĭ Rusĭ. 1878

Golovatskĭ, I͡A. F. O narodnoĭ odezhdi͡e ubranstvi͡e Rusĭnov" ĭlĭ Russkĭkh" v' Galĭchĭni͡e ĭ si͡evero-vostochnoĭ Vengriĭ. 1877

Czechoslovakia. Minister of national defense

Change of the uniform regulations of the Czechoslovak armed forces; supplement to service publication no 1. Praha, Nákladem M. N. O. 1920?
23p. illus. tab. F.
"Published ... according to a decision of the minister of national defense C.J., 437 515 of the 27th day of November, 1920." Subtitle
At head of title: *Service regulations of the Czechoslovak army.* Bohemian and English
Catalogued by the library of the United States Department of War

Czerwinski, Albert

Brevier der tanzkunst. Leipzig, O. Spamer [1881]
260p. 50 illus. D.
"Die tänze bei den kulturvölkern, von den ältesten zeiten bis zur gegenwart. Nebst einem anhange: Tanzrepertoir für kleinere und grössere gesellschaftskreise." Subtitle
Lipperheide 3120

Czerwinski, Albert—*Continued*
Geschichte der tanzkunst bei den cultivirten völkern von den ersten anfängen bis auf die gegenwärtige zeit. Leipzig, J. J. Weber 1862
264p. 34 illus. D.
Lipperheide 3112. LC 10-17954

(tr.) Tabourot, Jehan. Die tanze des XVI. jahrhunderts und die alte franzözische tanzschule vor einführung der menuett

Czobor, Béla
Les insignes royaux de Hongrie ... Rédigés par E. de Radisics. Budapest, La société des amis de l'art 1896
p15-26. 5pl. F.
Has also Hungarian title page
Lipperheide 1770

Czynski, Jean
Russie pittoresque. Histoire et tableau de la Russie. Paris, Pilout 1837
2v. pl. Q.

D

D., R. See The London journal. Advice to young ladies

D., J.
(tr.) Schultze, Walter. Ost-indische reyse

D. Wenceslao Bohemorum duci ac martyri inclyto sertum ortus, vitae, necis ... Aegidius

Dabney, Edith, and Wise, Claude Merton
A book of dramatic costume. New York, F. S. Crofts 1930
x,163p. incl.illus. pl. diagrs. O. $3
"Sources" at beginning of most of the chapters; Bibliography: p161-63
Costume index. LC 30-5825

Dachauer, Gustav
Kosmetische receptirkunst. 2.aufl. München, G. Beck 1872
99p. O.
First edition: 1864
Lipperheide 3267

Dachery
(illus.) Uniformes de tous les régiments de Hussards. Paris, L. Pillet 1889
50 col.pl. Q.
Plates cover the period of the Republic, the First Empire, the Restoration, the reigns of Louis Philippe and Napoleon III
Colas 772

Dacier, Émile
Le musée de la Comédie-française, 1680-1905; préface par Jules Claretie. Paris, [E. Martin] 1905.
xii,202p. illus. pl. F.

Dädalus und seine statuen. Hirt, A. L.

[Dähling]
(illus.) Der grosse maskenball in Berlin zur feier des geburtstages ... der regierenden königin von Preussen am 12ten März 1804 im königlichen nationaltheater veranstaltet. Berlin, L. W. Wittich 1805
28p. 10 col.pl. Q.
Plates engraved by Clar and Jügel
Colas 774. Lipperheide 2534

Dänemark, Schweden, Norwegen. Hielscher, Kurt

Dänische national kleidertrachten. See Rieter, Jac. Danske nationale klaededragter

Dafforne, James
(tr.) Lacroix, Paul. The arts in the middle ages

Dagligt liv i Norden i det 16de aarhundrede. Troels-Lund, T. F.

Dagneau, L.
De la Chine au point de vue commercial, social et moral. Etendue, population, production, alimentation, vêtements, ameublements, moeurs, usages, institutions, lois, etc. Paris, Prevot et Drouard 1844
80p. O.
Colas 773

Die **daguerreotype** in Berlin, 1839-1860. Dost, Wilhelm, and Stenger, Erich

Die **daguerreotypie** in Hamburg, 1839-1860. Weimar, Wilhelm

Dahl, Hans
Et varsko til det norske folk og den nordiske rase. Balestrand, Norway, Eget forlag c1932
44p. incl.front.(port.) D.
One chapter deals with clothing and dress
LC 32-23906

Dahlbergh, Erik Jønson
Exequiae ... Caroli Gustavi Suecorum Gothorum et Wandalorum regis d. 3. Nouemb. 1660 Holmiae celebratae. No place, n.d.
13pl. F.
These plates are included in the first edition of *De rebus a Carolo Gustavo gestis,* by S. Pufendorf
Lipperheide 2697

Suecia antiqua et hodierna. [Holmiae, 1691-1715]
3v. 353pl. D.
A collection of drawings by Dahlberg, and possibly some others, which show towns, places, antiquities, weapons, etc., of Sweden, engraved by Jan van den Aveelen, William Swidde, E. Reitz, Jean Marot, and others. "Index figurarum," (13p.) is inserted at end of book
"Descriptive letter-press to the first edition was prepared in Swedish and Latin by Peter Lagerlöf and others, and a few signatures printed. This was never published and never completed. Another description of the same plates was published in Nettelbla's periodical work *Greinir or theim gaumlu Saugum* and in 1856 an edition was published by Riis, Stockholm, with text by C. F. Lindström." Boston public library
Lipperheide 1037

Dahlsteen, August. See Dahlstein, Augustin

Dahlstein, Augustin
Russische trachten und ausrufer in St. Petersburg. Habillemens moscovites et crieurs à St. Petersbourg. Cassel, W. C. Mäÿr [1750]
49pl. F.
Colas 776. Lipperheide 1377

Dahlström, Carl Andreas
Svenska folkets seder, bruk och klädedrägter. Stockholm, Typografiska föreningens boktryckeri 1863
42p. 20 col.pl. Q.
Colas 775. Lipperheide 1053. LC A33-711 (1868 ed.)

Dahomey
Albeca, A. L. d' La France au Dahomey. 1895
Forbes, F. E. Dahomey and the Dahomans. 1851
Le Herissé, A. L'ancien royaume du Dahomey. 1911
McLeod, John. A voyage to Africa. 1820

Dahtsteen, Auguste. See Dahlstein, Augustin

[**Daigremont, Joseph Hon.**]
Description de l'uniforme des sous-lieutenants de l'école d'application de l'artillerie et du génie. Metz, Nouvain 1848
23p. O.
Colas 777

Daily life and origin of the Tasmanians. Bonwick, James

The **daily** life of the Greeks and Romans. New York. Metropolitan museum of art

Daï-Nippon. Hitomi, L.

Dakota Indians. See Indians of North America—Dakota Indians

Dalecaria. See Sweden—Kopparberg

Dalhammer, Patritius
Canonia Rohrensis documentis, monumentis et observationibus historico-criticis. Ratisbonae, [Krüll 1784]
134p. 13pl. F.
Plates show ecclesiastical dress in Bavaria
Lipperheide 1814

Dallas, Alexander Kennedy
(tr.) Köhler, Karl. A history of costume

Dallas, Duncan C.
(engr.) Crane, Walter. Eight illustrations to Shakespeare's Tempest
(engr.) Crane, Walter. Eight illustrations to Shakespeare's Two gentlemen of Verona
(engr.) Crane, Walter. Shakespeare's comedy of the Merry wives of Windsor

Dallas, Robert Charles
(tr.) Bertrand de Moleville, Antoine François, marquis de. The costume of the hereditary states of the house of Austria

Dallaway, James
Inquiries into the origin and progress of the science of heraldry in England. With explanatory observations on armorial ensigns. Gloucester, R. Raikes 1793
xiii,424,cxii p. illus. pl.(part col.) port. facsims. coats of arms(part col.) F.
Lipperheide 4405. LC 28-14089

Dally, Aristide
L'armée danoise. Paris. L. Baschet [1887]
3v. 24 illus. O. (Cahiers d'enseignement, no60-62)
Illustrated by K. Hansen Reistrup and G. Bagge
Lipperheide 2284

L'armée hollandaise. Paris, L. Baschet [1887]
4v. 32 col.illus. O. (Cahiers d'enseignement, no84-87)
Illustrated by E. Mas
Lipperheide 2261

L'armée norvégienne. Paris, L. Baschet [1887]
2v. 16 col.illus. O. (Cahiers d'enseignement, no63-64)
Illustrated by K. Hansen Reistrup and G. Bagge
Lipperheide 2285

L'armée russe. Paris, L. Baschet 1887
6v. illus.(part col.) O. (Cahiers d'enseignement, no72-77)
Lipperheide 2378

Les armées étrangères en campagne; leur formation, leur organisation, leurs effectifs et leurs uniformes. Paris, Société de typographie 1885
166p. illus. pl. D.
Plates show German, English, Austria-Hungarian, Belgian, Spanish, Italian, Russian, and Swiss military costume of the 19th century

La France militaire illustrée. Diverses organisations de l'armée; armures et costumes; armes; drapeaux; décorations et orders militaires. Paris, Vve P. Larousse 1886
378p. 360 illus. D.
Describes organization of the French army from the time of the Gauls to 1885
Lipperheide 2336

Les sapeurs-pompiers. Paris, L. Baschet [1887]
4v. 32 illus.(part col.) O. (Cahiers d'enseignement, no56-59)
Illustrated by Marius Roy
Lipperheide 2345

Uniformes de l'armée allemande. Paris, L. Baschet [1886]
4v. 32 illus.(part col.) O. (Cahiers d'enseignement illustrés, no13-16)
Illustrated by Marius Roy
Lipperheide 2137

Uniformes de l'armée anglaise. Paris, L. Baschet [1886]
4v. 32 col.illus. O. (Cahiers d'enseignement illustrés, no19-22)
Illustrated by Marius Roy
Lipperheide 2274

Uniformes de l'armée autrichienne. Dessins de Myrbach. [Paris, L. Baschet 1887]
4v. in 1. pl.(part col.) O. (Cahiers d'enseignement illustrés, no41-44)
Lipperheide 2245

Uniformes de l'armée espagnole. Paris, L. Baschet [1887]
4v. 32 illus.(part col.) O. (Cahiers d'enseignement illustrés no38-40 bis)
Illustrated by P. Eriz
Lipperheide 2365

Uniformes de l'armée italienne. Paris, L. Baschet 1887
4v. 32 illus.(part col.) O. (Cahiers d'enseignement illustrés, no45-48)
Illustrated by Marius Roy
Lipperheide 2370

Dally, Frédéric Jules Michel Aristide. See Dally, Aristide

Dalmatia. See Yugoslavia—Dalmatia; also subdivision Yugoslavia—Dalmatia under Decoration and ornament

Dalmatien und das österreichische küstenland; vorträge ... von M. Dvořák, M. Haberlandt [and others] hrsg. von E. Brückner. Wien, F. Deuticke 1911
250p. 60 illus. map. O.

Dalmatien und seine volkskunst. Bruch, Auffenberg, Frau Natalie

Dalmatov", K.
Russkiía vyshīvkī ... v" russkī teret" dat skago korolevskago parka Fredensborg" v" 1889 g. Uzory vzíaty īz" ... sobraniía starīnnykh" obraztsov" narodnago shit'ía Velīkorussov" Moskovskoĭ, Novgorodskoĭ, Tverskoĭ i ÍAroslavskoĭ guberniĭ. S. Peterburg", Khromo-līt. Gakshtettera 1889
16 col.pl. sq.F.
Russian embroidery after the folk embroideries of ancient Russia
Lipperheide 3977

La Dalmazia. Carrara, Francesco

Dalsani]
[Galleria di costumi Sardi] Cagliari, Tipografia nazionale 1878
42 col.pl. F.
From *Il buonumore, giornale umoristico con caricature ed illustrazioni di Dalsani.* Anno IV
Colas 778. Lipperheide 1317i

Dalton, Edward Tuite
Descriptive ethnology of Bengal; illus. by lithograph portraits copied from photographs. Calcutta, Supt. of govt. print. 1872
327,12p. front. illus. 39pl. F.
Colas 781. Lipperheide 1506. LC 3-8158

Dalton, Ormonde Maddock
Catalogue of the engraved gems of the post-classical periods. See entry under British museum. Department of British and mediaeval antiquities
Franks bequest. See entry under British museum. Department of British and mediaeval antiquities

See also Joyce, T. A., jt. auth.

Dalton, Richard
Antiquities and views in Greece and Egypt; with the manners and customs of the inhabitants: from drawings made on the spot, A.D. 1749. [London] T. King and H. Chapman 1791
12p. 76pl.(part col.) F.
Engraved by Chatelain, Vivares, Rooker, Basire, Mason, and others
Colas 779

Dalvimart, Octavian
(illus.) Alexander, William. Picturesque representations of the dress and manners of the Turks
(illus.) Alexander, William. Picturesque representations of the dress and manners of the Turks with Turkish translation
(illus.) Alexander. William. The costume of Turkey
(illus.) Castellan, A. L. Moeurs, usages, costumes des Othomanes
(illus.) Castellan, A. L. Sitten, gebräuche und trachten der Osmanen
(illus.) Shoberl, Frédéric, ed. Turkey

Damame-Démartrais, Michel François
Collection complète des divers jardins et points de vue des maisons de plaisance impériales de Russie, et de celles des plus grands seigneurs de cet empire. Paris, Gillé fils 1811
3 l. 36 col.pl. F.
Included in this collection are eight plates published in 1806 under the title: *Collection complète des différens genres de voitures dont les Russes se servent dans leur empire et particulièrement à Saint-Pétersbourg*
Some of plates engraved by P. Debucourt
Colas 784-85

Collection de costumes du royaume de Naples. Paris, Firmin-Didot 1818
3 l. 12pl. F.
This series of plates is probably copied from a series published in Italy at the end of the 18th century. For list of plates see Colas' *Bibliographie*
Colas 787

Vues de Russie et usages divers des habitants de ce genre. Paris, Bassand ca1817
36 col.pl. F.
For a list of plates see Colas' *Bibliographie.* The last eight plates were engraved by P. Debucourt
Colas 786

Damaze de Raymond
Tableau historique, géographique, militaire et moral de l'Empire de Russie. Paris, Le Normant 1812
2v. 14 col.pl. maps. O.
Illustrations by N. Finard, engraved by Blanchard fils after Couché fils, show Russian soldiers, especially Cossacks, Tartars, Kalmucks, and Kirghiz
Colas 788. Lipperheide 2373

Dambach, Christoff
Büchsenmeisterey das ist ... erklärung deren dingen so einem büchsenmeister fürnemlich zu wissen von nöthen: als ihre freyheiten und artickel zu feldt und in besatzungen, auch der rechte gebrauch desz grossen geschütz ... mit fleisz erkündiget. Franckfort, W. Hoffmann 1609
55,165p. 99 illus. 2pl. Q.
Plates show gunners and groups of artillerymen
Lipperheide 2063

Damberger, Christian Friedrich, pseud.
Christian Friedrich Damberger's Landreise in das innere von Afrika ... in den jahren 1781 bis 1797. Leipzig, G. Martini 1801
2v. 3 col.pl. map. O.
The plates, engraved by C. Geissler, show costume of African tribes
Lipperheide 1575

Die **Dame.** v 1, 1873+ Berlin, Ullstein
Illus. F. Rm.1 per no.
Published semi-monthly. Current 1938

Dame Fashion, Paris—London (1786-1912). Price, J. M.

Die **Damen-toilette;** herausgegeben ... unter leitung von Gustav Lyon. 1865-1886? Berlin, Bureau des museum für mode, kunst und industrie
Col.pl. F.
Colas 789. Lipperheide 4700

Damenkleider magazin vereinigt mit Musterzeitung und frauenzeitung. v.1-? 1848-1869. Stuttgart, J. B. Metzler
Col.illus. col.pl. O.-Q.
Published semi-monthly. v 1-18, 1848-65, published monthly
Title varies: 1848-65: *Pariser damenkleider-magazin.* Subtitle, v12-18, 1859-65: journal fur weiblicher arbeiten
Colas 2274. Lipperheide 4657

Les **dames** cosmopolites. Colin, Mme Anaïs

Damhouder, Joost
Praxis rerum civilium. Antwerpiae, ex officina I. Belleri 1569
25,16 l. 472p. 15 illus. Q.
First Latin edition: 1567. French edition: 1572. German edition: 1581
Some of the plates are from the author's *Pupillorum patrocinium*
Lipperheide 2011

Praxis rerum criminalium ... Antwerpiae, apud I. Bellerum 1562
11,26 l. 467p. 69 illus. Q.
First Latin edition: 1554, a French edition in the same year. German edition: 1565
Plates show scenes of the rack, courts of justice, and executions
Lipperheide 2010. LC 25-14426(German ed.)

Pupillorum patrocinium legum et praxeos studiosis non minus utile quam necessarium ... Item. De magnificentia politiae amplissimae civitatis Brugarum, cum eiusdem topographia. Antverpiae, apud I. Bellerum 1564
11,180,18 l. 11 illus. 1 pl. Q.
First edition: Bruges, 1544
Illustrations represent court scenes, judges, jurymen, etc.
Lipperheide 2009

Damman, Adrien
Diversarum gentium armatura equestris. See entry under Bruyn, Abraham de

Damourette
Penseurs & propos; grand album de caricatures. Paris, Martinet, Hautecoeur frère! ca1855
12 col.pl. Q.
Lipperheide 3613

Damourette, and Talin, Henri Meilhac
Les actrices; 1re partie. Paris, Maresq et Philipon fils ca1855
56pl. O.
Lipperheide 3614

Danaë ... Suivi du costume des anciens. Granier de Cassagnac, B. A.

Dance costume
Bals de l'opéra; costumes du quadrille historique. 1834
Becker, M. L. Der tanz. 1901
Blasis, Carlo. The code of Terpsichore; the art of dancing; comprising its theory and practice, and a history of its rise and progress, from the earliest times. 1830
Blasis, Carlo. Manuel complet de la danse. 1830
Blaze, F. H. J. La danse et les ballets depuis Bacchus jusqu'à mademoiselle Taglioni. 1832
Böhme, F. M. Geschichte des tanzes in Deutschland. 1886
Bonnet, Jacques. Histoire generale de la danse, sacrée et prophane; ses progrès & ses révolutions, depuis son origine jusqu'à présent. 1724
Cahusac, Louis de. La danse ancienne et moderne, ou Traité historique de la danse. 1754
Czerwinski, Albert. Geschichte der tanzkunst bei den cultivirten völkern von den ersten anfängen bis auf die gegenwärtige zeit. 1862
Desrat, G. Dictionnaire de la danse historique, theorique, pratique et bibliographique depuis l'origine de la danse jusqu'à nos jours. 1895
Dugazon, Gustave. Danses nationales de chaque pays. n.d.
Lambranzi, Gregorio. New and curious school of theatrical dancing. 1928
Lambranzi, Gregorio. Nuova e curiosa scuola de' balli theatrali ... Neue und curieuse theatralische tanz-schul. 1716
Levinson, A. I. Meister des ballets. 1923
Martinet, J. J. Essai, ou principes élémentaires de l'art de la danse. 1797
Menestrier, C. F. Des ballets anciens et modernes selon les regles du theatre. 1682
Moreck, Curt, ed. Der tanz in der kunst; die bedeutendsten tanzbilder von der antike bis zur gegenwart. 1924
Les quatre nieces et des autres. n.d.
Urlin, E. L. H. Dancing, ancient and modern. 1911
Vuillier, Gaston. La danse. 1898
Vuillier, Gaston. A history of dancing from the earliest ages to our own times. 1898

Ancient times

Buchholtz, Hermann. Die tanzkunst des Euripides. 1871
Gironi, Robustiano. Le danze dei Greci. 1820
Séchan, Louis. La danse grecque antique. 1930

16th century

Caroso, M. F. Il ballarino. 1581
Caroso, M. F. Nobiltà di dame; libro, altra volta, chiamato Il ballarino. 1600

18th century

Dubois. Principes d'allemandes. ca1760
Guillaumot, A. E. Costumes des ballets du roy. 1885
Taubert, Gottfried. Rechtschaffener tantzmeister, oder Gründliche erklärung der frantzösischen tantz-kunst. 1717

19th century

Album de danses illustrées, anciennes & modernes. 189-?
Baron, A. A. F. Lettres à Sophie sur la danse. 1825
Blasis, Carlo. Traité élémentaire théorique et pratique de l'art de la danse 1820
Brunet. Théorie pratique du danseur de société. 1839
Casorti, Louis. Der instructive tanzmeister für herren und damen. 1826
Cellarius, Henri. La danse des salons 1847
Colin, Mme Anaïs. Le maître à danser 1844
Compte-Calix, F. C. Les cancans ca.1840
Czerwinski, Albert. Brevier der tanzkunst. 1881
Haguental, and Fagonde. Les gloires de l'Opéra. n.d.

Dance costume—19th century—*Continued*

Lami, E. L. Quadrille de Marie Stuart. 1829

Renouard, Paul. La danse; vingt dessins. 1892

Rietmann, A. Reigentänze: 21 charakter- und waffentänze. 1892

20th century

Alford, Violet. Peeps at English folk-dances. 1923

Alford, Violet, and Gallop, Rodney. The traditional dance. 1935

Aubel, Hermann, and Aubel, Marianne. Der künstlerische tanz unserer zeit. 1930

Barbier, George. Designs on the dances of Vaslav Nijinsky. 1913

Bie, Oskar. Der tanz. c1919

Böhme, Fritz. Der tanz der zukunst. 1926

Boehn, Max von. Der tanz. 1925

Brandenburg, Hans. Der moderne tanz. 1913

Delius, Rudolf von. Mary Wigman. 1925

Divoire, Fernand. Pour la danse. 1935

Duncan, Isadora. Der tanz der zukunft (The dance of the future) eine vorlesung. 1903

Dyagilev, S. P. Les biches. 1924

Dyagilev, S. P. Les fâcheux. 1924

Ebart, P. J. von. Der hofmarschall auf der bühne, schauspielern und regisseuren. 1903

Fischer, Carlos. Les costumes de l'Opéra. 1931

Giese, Fritz. Girlkultur. 1925

Giese, Fritz. Körperseele; gedanken über persönliche gestaltung. c1927

Hincks, M. A. The Japanese dance. 1910

Joiner, Betty. Costumes for the dance. 1937

Jou, Louis. À la danseuse. 1925

Kellermann, Bernhard. Sassa yo yassa; japanische tänze. 1920

Kimmins, Mrs G. T. H. The Guild of play book of festival and dance. 1907-12

Laban, Rudolf von. Die welt des tänzers. 1920

Levīnson, A. I. La danse d'aujourd'hui. 1929

Levīnson, A. I. Serge Lifar; destin d'un danseur. 1934

Levīnson, A. I. Les visages de la danse. 1933

Lussan-Borel. Traité de danse avec musique contenant toutes les danses de salon avec une théorie nouvelle de valse et boston, du cotillon et du cake-walk. 1903

Martin, J. J. America dancing. 1936

Nikolaus, Paul. Tänzerinnen. 1919

Vala Moro, pseud. Tanz. 1924

BY COUNTRY

Cambodia

Groslier, George. Danseuses cambodgiennes anciennes et modernes. 1913

Egypt

Lexová, Irena. Ancient Egyptian dances. 1935

Indians of North America

Evans, Bessie, and Evans, M. G. American Indian dance steps. 1931

Java

Lelyveld, T. B. van. La danse dans le théâtre javanais. 1931

Lelyveld, T. B. van. De javaansche danskunst. 1931

Dance of death

Die Baseler todtentänze in getreuen abbildungen ... sammt einem anhange: Todtentanz in holzschnitten des fünfzehnten jahrhunderts, von H. F. Massmann. Stuttgart, Verlag des herausgebers 1847

127,[12]p. xiv l. S. and atlas of 49pl. sq.Q. (Der schatzgräber in den literarischen und bildlichen seltenheiten hrsg. von J. Scheible. 5. th.)
LC F-1167

Freund Heins erscheinungen in Holbeins manier von J. R. Schellenberg. Winterthur, H. Steiner 1785

165p. 24pl. O.
Text by J. K. A. Musäus
Lipperheide 1966

La grande danse Macabre des hommes et des femmes, historiée & renouvellée de vieux Gaulois, en langage le plus poli de notre temps. Troyes, J. A. Garnier [1728]

76p. illus. O.
"Avec Le débat du corps & de l'ame; La camplainte de l'ame damnée; l'exhortation de bien vivre & de bien mourir; La vie du mauvais antechrist; Les quinze signes du jugement." Subtitle
Reprinted from original woodcuts of the *Danse macabre de Troyes,* 1486
LC 25-24401

Holbein's todtentanz in den wandbildern zu Chur; einleitender text von S. Plattner, zeichnungen von J. Weber. Chur, 1885

7p. 17pl. O.
Holbein's drawings of the Dance of death, copied in the corridor of the episcopal castle of Chur by an unknown artist in 1543, have been reproduced here
Lipperheide 1960

Les simulachres & historiees faces de la mort: commonly called "The dance of death"; tr. and ed. by Henry Green. With a sketch of Holbein's life and works, and some explanatory notes. Manchester, Pub. for the Holbein-society by A. Brothers 1869

xxx,292p. illus. sq.O. (The Holbein-society's facsimile reprints, v 1)
First edition (Lyon, Melchior and Gaspar Trechsel, 1538) had forty-one woodcuts attributed to Hans Lützelburger after designs by Hans Holbein. An edition with fifty-three woodcuts appeared in 1545 the printing of which was credited to Jean and François Frellon of Basel. A German edition with title: *Der todtentanz* (München, 1832) had fifty three plates; another German edition (Berlin, E. Wasmuth 1879) had forty plates
Contents: Introduction; *Les simulachres & historiees faces de la mort.* Lyon, 1538; *The images and storied aspects of death.* tr. from ... the Lyons ed. of 1538, by Henry Green. To which are added the

Dance of death—*Continued*

German rhymes from Rentz's *Remembrances of death and eternity.* Manchester, 1869; Appendix. Photo-lith. facsimiles: of the title, index, and extra woodcut of *Imagines mortis,* by George Æmylius, Lyons, 1545; of the title and of pl I., XXXVI., LIJ., and LIII., of [the same] Cologne, 1566; of the title, of pl. VII., XVI., XL.-LI., and of colophon of *Simolachri ... de la morte,* Lyons, 1549; Epigrammata, I.- LIII., of *Imagines mortis,* tr. ... into Latin by George Æmylius, in the Lyons ed. of 1545 and the Cologne ed. of 1566; Quotations from the Holy Scriptures of the 12 additional plates, XL.-LI.—Various editions of Holbein's *Images of death;* Stanzas, I.-LIII., from *Simolachri ... de la morte.* Lyons, 1549

Lipperheide 1958-59 (German ed.) LC 3-24592

Todten-tantz wie derselbe in der löblichen und weitberühmten statt Basel als ein spiegel menschlicher beschaffenheit gantz künstlich gemahlet zu sehen ist ... hrsg. durch Matthaeum Merian. Franckfurt, 1649

206p. 43 illus. 1 pl. Q.

The original drawings by an unknown artist upon the walls of a church-yard of a Dominican monastery at Basel were copied by Johann Jacob Merian for an edition which apeapred in Basel in 1621. For the edition of 1649 the plates were newly engraved by Matthaeus Merian. The same illustrations were reproduced in color with title: *Todtentanz der stadt Basel* (Basel, F. Schneider 1875)

Lipperheide 1961-62

The **dance** of the future. See Duncan, Isadora. Der Tanz der zukunft

[Danchet, Antoine]

(ed.) Le sacre de Louis XV, roy de France & de Navarre, dans l'église de Reims, le dimanche XXV octobre MDCCXII. [Paris] 1722?

36 l. illus. 39pl. (9 double) F.

Edited by A. Danchet, under the supervision of J. P. Bignon and C. Gros de Boze. The engravings are mainly after drawings by P. Dulin, were made by Cochin, Larmessin and a number of other engravers. They show each ceremony of the coronation, allegorical pictures, and robes of the king and officials

Lipperheide 2713. LC 12-17872

Dancing, ancient and modern. Urlin, E. L. H.

Danckerts, Cornelis

Delineatio pompae triumphalis qua Robertus Dudlaeus comes Leicestrensis Hagae comitis fuit exceptus. Hague, C. Dankerts [1586]

12pl. F.

Plates show townspeople of The Hague and Delft as they unite in a procession and festival honoring Robert Dudley, the earl of Leicester, sent by Queen Elizabeth to aid the Netherlands in their struggle for independence from Spanish rule

Lipperheide 2656

Danckwerth, Caspar

Helgoland einst und jetzt. Bericht von Caspar Danckwerth vor ungefähr 250 jahren über die insel geschrieben, neu hrsg ... mit einer bibliographie ... von Max Harrwitz. Berlin, M. Harrwitz 1891

22p. 2 maps. O.

The map of 1649 shows Helgoland costume, masculine and feminine

Lipperheide 799

Dandies and Don Juans. Gleichen-Russwurm, Alexander, freiherr von

Dandré-Bardon, Michel François

Costume des anciens peuples, à l'usage des artistes ... Nouv. éd., rédigée par M. Cochin. Paris, A. Jombert 1784-86

4v. 352pl. Q.

First edition: 1772 (3 vols.) An incomplete German edition, translated by W. G. Becker, exists under the title: *Costüme der ältesten völker* (Leipzig, 1776-1777)

Contents: v 1 Usages religieux, civils et domestiques des Grecs et des Romains; v2 Usages militaires des Grecs et des Romains; v3 Usages des Israélites, Hébreux et Egyptiens; v4 Usages des Perses [etc]

Colas 791-3. Lipperheide 107. LC 16-14977

Dandyism

Barbey d'Aurevilly, J. A. The anatomy of dandyism. 1928

Barbey d'Aurevilly, J. A. Du dandysme et de G. Brummell. 1845

Barbey d'Aurevilly, J. A. Of dandyism and of George Brummell. 1897

Boulenger, J. R. Sous Louis-Philippe; les dandys. 1932

Boutet de Monvel, Roger. Beau Brummell and his times. 1908

Gleichen-Russwurm, Alexander, freiherr von. Dandies and Don Juans. 1928

Gleichen-Russwurm, Alexander, freiherr von. Könige des lebens. 1927

Danemark. Eyries, J. B. B.

Danet, Guillaume

L'art des armes, ou la manière la plus certaine de se servir utilement de l'épée soit pour attaquer, soit pour se défendre ... suivant les meilleurs principes de théorie & de pratique adoptés actuellement en France. Paris, Herissant fils 1766-67

2v. 46pl. illus. O.

Plates engraved after Vaxcillere by L. G Taraval

Lipperheide 2975

Danet, Louis

(engr.) Nicolay, Nicolas de, sieur d'Arfeuille. Les quatre premiers livres des Navigations et peregrinations orientales

Daniaud

(lithgr.) Drake, T. Album vendéen

Daniel, Gabriel

Histoire de la milice françoise, et des changemens qui s'y sont faits depuis l'établissement de la monarchie françoise dans les Gaules, jusqu'à la fin du règne de Louis le Grand. Amsterdam, Compagnie de Jésus 1724

2v. 70pl. Q.

First edition: (Paris, Coignard 1721), is described by Colas as better. Also published (Paris, Saugrain & Prault 1728)

Colas 794-6. Lipperheide 2292

Daniell, Samuel

A picturesque illustration of the scenery animals and native inhabitants of the island of Ceylon. London, 1808

12 col.pl. ob.F.

Daniell, Thomas and Daniell, William

A picturesque voyage to India, by the way of China. London, Longman Hurst, Rees, and Orme 1810

50 l. 50 col.pl. Q.

Twenty four plates show Chinese and Javanese costume

Colas 797. Lipperheide 1523. LC 5-1007

Daniell, William. See Daniell, Thomas, jt. auth.

Danielli, Iacopo
Contributo allo studio del tatuaggio negli antichi Peruviani. [Firenze, Fototipia Ciardelli, 1894]
13p. 4pl. O.
From *Archivio per l'antropologia e l'etnologia* v24, 1894
LC 25-14351

Danilowicz, Casimir de
La Lituanie artistique. Lausanne. Bureau d'information de Lituanie 1919
71p. illus. 20pl. F.
Some plates show peasant costume of the fourteenth to eighteenth centuries

Dankerts, C. See Danckerts, C.

Danliard, Lacroix. See Lacroix-Danliard, pseud.

Danmark, land og folk. Bruun, Daniel, ed.

Dans la rue. Bruant, Aristide

La **danse.** Renouard, Paul

La **danse.** Vuillier, Gaston

La **danse** ancienne et moderne. Cahusac, Louis de

La **danse** dans le théâtre javanais. Lelyveld, T. B. van

La **danse** d'aujourd'hui. Levinson, A. I.

La **danse** des noces. Schaeufelein, H. L.

La **danse** des salons. Cellarius, Henri

La **danse** et les ballets depuis Baccus jusqu'à mademoiselle Taglioni. Blaze, F. H. J.

La **danse** grecque antique. Séchan, Louis

La **danse** grecque antique d'après les monuments figures. Emmanuel, Maurice

Danse macabre de Troyes. See Dance of death. La grande danse Macabre

Danses nationales de chaque pays. Dugazon, Gustave

Danseuses cambodgiennes anciennes et modernes. Groslier, George

Les **danseuses** de l'Opéra. Menut, Adolphe

Den **danske** armee. Steen, Chr.

Den **danske** armee og marine. Bergh, Th.

Den **danske** armés uniformer. Møller, Vald.

Danske folkedragter. Ottesen, Louise

Den **danske** haer og flaade. Brock, Gustav

Den **danske** haers histoire til nutiden og den norske haers historie, indtil 1814. Vaupell, O. F.

Danske nationaldragter. Lund, F. C.

Danske nationale klaededragter; Dänische national kleidertrachten. Rieter, Jakob

Danske uniformer. Kjöbenhaven, F. Wöldike 1864
15 col.pl. Q.
Colas 798

Danske uniformer. Bruun, Chr.

Danske uniformer: I Militaire; udgivet af L. P. Kjöbenhavn, C. W. Stirck n.d.
12 col.pl. Q.
Cover title
Colas 799

Danske uniformer for haer og flaade. Christiansen, Rasmus

Dantier, Alphonse
Les femmes dans la société chrétienne. Paris, Firmin-Didot 1879
2v. fronts. illus. pl. ports. Q.
Lipperheide 340. LC 10-8523

Der **Dantzger** frawen und jungfrawen gebreuchliche zierheit und tracht jetziger zeit zu sehen. See Möller, Anton. Omnium statuum foeminei sexus ornatus et usitati habitus Gedanenses

Danvers, Verney L.
Training in commercial art, the principles and technique of the subject, with chapters on fancy-costume designing. London, New York. Sir I. Pitman 1926
177p. col.front. illus. O.
LC 27-5867

Danvila y Collado, Francisco
Trajes y armas de los españoles desde los tiempos prehistóricos hasta los primeros años del siglo XIX; ilustrada por C. Ginér. Tomo I. Madrid, T. Fortanet 1877
160p. 8pl. Q.
No more published?
Colas 800. LC 34-36286

Danz, August Heinrich Emil
Aus Rom und Byzanz. Weimar, H. Böhlau 1867
x,164p. O.
Lipperheide 242

Le **danze** dei Greci. Gironi, Robustiano

Danzel, Theodor Wilhelm
Mexiko. Hagen i. W. und Darmstadt, Folkwang verlag 1923, '22
3v. pl. Q. (Schriften-reihe: Kulturen der erde, material zur kultur- und kunstgeschichte aller völker, bd xi-xiii)
Plates printed on both sides
"Literaturverzeichnis": v 1 p8-10
Contents: v 1 Grundzüge der altmexikanischen geisteskultur. 3.aufl. v2 Kultur und leben im alten Mexiko. 2.aufl. v3 Über die religiösen kulte. Tonatiu. Mexikanische gebete. 2.aufl. Verfasser, Ernst Fuhrmann

Danzer, Alfonz
A mi hadseregünk. Az Osztrák-magyar monarchia népei fegyverben és zászlók alatt. Szécsi Mór, Bankalari Gusztáv, Rieger Ferencz közremüködése mellett szerkesztette Danczer Alfons.
588p. front.(port.) illus. 11 col.pl. O.
The Hungarian army
German edition published under title: *Unter den fahnen; die völker Osterreich-Ungarns in waffen* (Wien, F. Tempsky 1889)
Colas 801(German ed.) Lipperheide 2246 (German ed.) LC CA10-924

Danzig, Allison. See Doeg, J. H., jt. auth.

Danzig. See Street venders—Danzig

Danzig. Stadtmuseum
Kirchliche gewänder und stickereien aus dem schatz der Marienkirche; katalog, austellung okt. 1929. [Danzig, 1929]
63p. 8pl. O.

Danzig

17th century

Möller, Anton. Omnium statuum foeminei sexus ornatus et usitati habitus Gedadenses ... Der Dantzger frawen und jungfrawen gebreuchliche zierheit und tracht jetziger zeit zu sehen. 1601

Danziger ausrufbilder. Deisch, Matthaeus

Danziger frauentrachtenbuch. See Möller, Anton. Omnium statuum foeminei sexus ornatus et usitati habitus Gedanenses

Der **Danziger** paramentenschatz. Mannowsky, Walter

Das **Danziger** theater im 16. und 17. jahrhundert. Bolte, Johannes

Dapper, Olfert

Gedenkwaerdig bedryf der Nederlandsche Oost-Indische maetschappye, op de kuste en in het keizerrijk van Taising of Sina ... Beneffens een beschryving van geheel Sina. Amsterdam, J. van Meurs 1670

3pt. in 1 v. illus. pl.(part fold.) F.
Rich in illustrations of the costume of China
Lipperheide 1512. LC 5-36891

Naukeurige beschryving van Asie ... Mesopotamie, Babylonie, Assyrie, Anatolie ... beneffens eene volkome beschryving van gansch ... Arabie. Amsterdam, J. Van Meurs 1680

2v. in 1. front. pl. F.

Naukeurige beschryving van gansch Syrie en Palestyn. Amsterdam, J. Van Meurs 1677

588p. front. pl. F.

Daragon, Henri

(pub.) Les modes du Directoire et du Consulat; dessins et aquarelles de G. Garcia. Paris, [1911]

80 col.pl. O.

Darby, William Arthur

Church vestments, an examination, scriptural, historical, and ecclesiastical. London, R. Hardwicke 1866

72p. front. O.

Darcel, Alfred. See Guichard, Édouard. Les tapisseries décoratives du Garde-meuble (Mobilier national)

Dardel, Fredrik L. von

Den svenske og den norske armees samt marines uniformer. [Stockholm, Hörbergske bogtrykkeriet 1863]

1 l. 36 col.pl. F.
Some copies, with text in French and Swedish, have title: *Svenska och norska arméerna* (Stockholm, Bonnier; Paris, Lemercier 1863)
Plates drawn by Dardel, lithographed by Bayot, Bureau, Guerard, Bocquin, Vernier and Sorrieu
Colas 802, 2845. Lipperheide 2280

Daremberg, Charles Victor, and Saglio, Edmond

(eds.) Dictionnaire des antiquités grecques et romaines, d'après les textes et les monuments ... ouvrage rédigé par une société d'écrivains spéciaux, d'archéologues et de professeurs ... Paris, Hachette 1877-1919

5v. in 10. illus. maps. plans. facsims. Q.
The editors were assisted by Edmond Pottier in the preparation of volumes 2-4 and by Edmond Pottier and Georges Lafaye in the preparation of volume 5. Originally issued in 53 fascicles 1873-1919
Lipperheide 173. LC 31-10623

Daret, Pierre

Tableaux historiques ou sont gravez les illustres Francois et estrangers de l'un et de l'autre sexe remarquables par leur naissance et leur fortune, doctrine, pieté, charges et emplois; avec les eloges sommaires contenans leurs noms ... et leurs armes blasonées. Paris, Daret 1654

4 l. 1 pl. 97 ports. Q.
Contains portraits of noted persons of the seventeenth century and of the early kings of France. Lipperheide mentions other editions with a greater number of portraits
Lipperheide 537

Darfeu

Hygiène de la parisienne. Paris, E. Rouveyre et G. Blond [1884]

56p. 16 illus. O.
Illustrations by Cortazzo and Scott
Lipperheide 3291

Darjou, Henri Alfred

Costumes bretons. Paris, Journal amusant ca1860

16 col.pl. Q.
Colas 803

Costumes de la Bretagne. Paris, Journal les Modes parisiennes et Journal amusant 1865

20 col.pl. F.
Plates differ entirely from those in his *Costumes bretons.* Some of the plates signed by A. Leroux
Colas 804. Lipperheide 1202

Les plaisirs de Baden. Paris, Hautecoeur frères ca1860

30 col.pl. F.
Lipperheide 3616

The **dark** continent. Bernatzik, H. A.

Darley, Felix Octavius Carr

Character sketches from the works of Charles Dickens. Philadelphia, Porter & Coates 1888

2v. 13pl. sq.F.
Each plate accompanied by guard sheet with descriptive letterpress
Contents: 1st ser. Clemency Newcome and Ben Britain; Little Nell and her grandfather; Tony Weller; Barnaby Rudge; Oliver Twist; Joe Gargery. 2d ser. Caleb Plummer and his blind daughter; Dolly Varden and Hugh of the Maypole inn; Oliver Twist claimed by Bill Sykes and Nancy; John Willet and Rudge the murderer; Mrs. Gargery on the rampage; Dick Swiveller and Quilp; Sam Weller
LC 11-28962

The Darley gallery of Shakespearean illustrations ... with text selected by Horace Howard Furness. New York and Philadelphia, J. M. Stoddart 1884

31 l. 30pl. sq.F.
LC 27-10589

Darling, Charles John Darling, 1st baron

A pensioner's garden. London, Hodder and Stoughton 1926

224p. O. 10s 6d
Contains an essay on judicial robes

Darly, Mary

Darly's comic-prints of characters, caricatures, macaronies, etc. London, M Darly 1776

1 l. 128pl. port. F.

Darstellung aller waffengattungen der kais königl. osterreichischen armee im jahr 1839. Emphinger, Franz

Darstellung der k.k. osterreichischen armee mit allen chargen. Hauslab, Franz von

Darstellung der k. k. österr. armee nach der neuesten adjustirung. Stubenrauch, Ph. von; Schindler, J., and Höchle

Darstellung der königlich preussischen cavallerie. Lieder, Friedrich, and Krüger, F.

Darstellung der königl. preussischen infanterie. Lieder, Friedrich

Darstellung der königl. preussischen infanterie und cavallerie. Lieder, Friedrich

Darstellung des aegyptischen, griechischen und römischen costums. Baxter, Thomas

Darstellung d. festspiels Lalla Rukh. Brühl, K. F. M. P., graf von

Darstellungen aus dem Nibelungen-liede. Preuschen, Erwin

Dartiguenave, Alfred

Costumes des Pyrénées. Pau, A. Bassy ca1860
1 l. 10 col.pl. F.
Lithographs by V. Adam, Champagne, Lemoine, jr. and others
This seems to be the set described in Colas 2449 with title *Pyrénées (Hautes et Basses)*. Colas gives contents
Colas 805. Lipperheide 1236

Pyrénées (Hautes et Basses). See his Costumes des Pyrénées

Dartmann, G. H.

Manuel du tailleur. Paris, Hautecoeur 1837
xx,274p. 80pl.(part col.) O.
Colas 806

Darwin, Bernard Richard Meirion

A golfer's gallery by old masters, introduction by Bernard Darwin. London, Country life, ltd. 1927?
19p. col.front. illus. 17 col.pl. F.
Most of the plates show Dutch golfers of the 16th to 18th century although some Scotch and English figures are included

Das, Sarat Chandra. See Sarachchandra Dāsa

Das was verschwindet; trachten aus den bergen und inseln der Adria. Leipzig, F. A. Brockhaus 188-?
ix p. 87pl.(86 col.) F.
Plates accompanied by guard sheets with descriptive letter press. Illustrated by Franz Bohumil Doubek, Paul Joanowits, Emil Lauffer, Peter Maixner, Guido Manes

Dashkov, Vorontsov

Ocherk" dīeiātel'nostī Mīnīsterstva Īmperatorskago dvora po prīgotovlenīiām ī ustroīstvu torzhestv" svīashchennago koronovanīia Īkh" Imperatorskīkh" Velīchestv" v" 1896. See entry under Russia. Mīnīsterstvo Īmperatorskago dvora

Dass die blosse brüste seyn ein gross gerüste viel böser lüste wird dem züchtigen frauen-zimmern zu ehren und den unverschämten weibs-stücken zur schande erwiesen. No place, 1687
19 l. Q.
A manuscript note on the title page attributes this work to Michael Freud and notes a Swedish translation of 1690
Lipperheide 3444

Daubert, Pierre

Du port illégal de costume et de décoration. Paris, A. Rousseau 1904
141p. Q.

Daubrawa, Henry de

(illus.) Ackermann, Rudolph. Costumes of the British Army

Daudet, Alphonse. See Goncourt, E. L. A. H. de, jt. auth.

Daul, A.

Die beschäftigung des weiblichen geschlechts in der hand-arbeit. Altona, J. F. Hammerich 1867
968p. D. (Die frauen-arbeit, oder der kreis ihrer erwerbsfähigkeit. 1. bd.)
Lipperheide 4096

[**Daumier, Honoré Victorin**]

Les baigneurs. Paris, Aubert ca1840
24 col.pl. Q.
Title taken from plates
Lipperheide 3619

Les cent Robert Macaire. Paris, au Bureau du Journal pour rire [1836-38]
1 l. 100pl. O.
A reprint appeared after the drawings of Daumier signed by Philipon. Later editions note that the series of Robert Macaire was conceived by Philipon and executed by Daumier. An edition of 1839 differs only in a title page signed: Celestin Nanteuil
Lipperheide 3617-18

Cours d'histoire naturelle. Paris, Dupin ca1840
12 col.pl. Q.
Title taken from plates
Lipperheide 3620

Locataires et propriétaires. Paris, Aubert ca1840
29 col.pl. Q.
Title taken from plates
Lipperheide 3621

Honoré Daumier; a collection of his social and political caricatures, together with an introductory essay on his art. See entry under Cary, E. L.

(illus.) Texier, E. A. Physiologie du poëte

Dauphiné. See France—By region or province—Dauphiné

Daux, Henriette. See Le costume, la mode: Encyclopédie populaire illustrée du vingtième siècle

Davenport, Cyril James Humphries

English regalia. London, Kegan Paul, Trench, Trubner 1897
65p. 12 col.pl. Q. 21s o.p.
Costume index

Jewellery, by Cyril Davenport. 2d ed. London, Methuen [1913]
166p. col.front. illus. pl. S. (Little books on art)
Bibliography: p[159]-60
First edition, 1905
Costume index. LC 31-12393

On the history of personal jewellery from prehistoric times. Delivered before the Society of arts on February 10, 17, and 24, 1902. London, W. Trounce 1902
38p. illus. O. (Royal society of arts, London. Cantor lectures)
LC GS34-832

See also Younghusband, Sir G. J., jt. auth.

Davey, Richard Patrick Boyle

Furs and fur garments. London, The International fur store [1895]
108p. front. pl. ports. O.
LC 4-20465

Davey, Richard P. B.—*Continued*
A history of mourning. [London] Jay's [1890]
111p. illus. pl. ports. sq.Q.
LC 2-8745

The pageant of London; illus. by John Fulleylove. London, Methuen 1906
2v. 40 col.pl. O.
Dress during Saxon, Norman and other times up to the Victorian is described but not pictured. See references under Dress in the index
LC w6-228

[David]
[Costumes de la révolution française.] No place, n.d.
7 col.pl. Q.
Engraved by Vivant-Denon. For a list of plates see Colas' *Bibliographie*
Colas 807

(engr.) Villamena. Cris de Rome

David, Fernand. See entry under Paris. Exposition internationale des arts décoratifs et industriels modernes, 1925. Rapport général

David, Hermine
(illus.) Barbey d'Aurevilly, J. A. The anatomy of dandyism

David, Jules
Vice et vertu; album moral. Paris, Jeannin ca1830
12 col.pl. F.
Lipperheide 1159i

Davids des königs in Israel heilige fürbereitung zum tode ... herrn Friderich Wilhelmen, marggraffen zu Brandenburg. Cochius, Christianus

Davidson, Daniel Sutherland
Snowshoes. Philadelphia, American philosophical society 1937
x,207p. illus.(incl. maps) diagrs. O. (Memoirs of the American philosophical society. v6 1937)
Bibliography: p193-98
LC 37-10910

Davidson, James Wheeler
The island of Formosa past and present. London, Macmillan 1903
646,xxviii,46p. col.front. pl. 2 maps. Q.

Davidson, Peter Wylie
Applied design in the precious metals, an educational work in which tool-form and material are utilised in the development of design. Longmans 1929
143p. incl.front. illus. O. (Longmans' technical handicraft series)
LC 29-8506

Davies, Arthur Charles Fox-. See Fox-Davies, A. C.

Davies, J. F.
Pioneer systems of cutting ladies' fashionable garments, of the latest London, Paris, and New York styles. London, J. Williamson [1881]
40p. illus. Q.

Davies, John Langdon-. See Langdon-Davies, John

Davies, Norman de Garis
The Tomb of two sculptors at Thebes ... with plates in color by Norman de Garis Davies, Nina de G. Davies, H. R. Hopgood and Charles K. Wilkinson, of the Egyptian expedition. New York, 1925
xii,76p. XXXI pl.(part col. part fold) F. (Half-title: Publications of the Metropolitan museum of art, Egyptian expedition. Robb de Peyster Tytus memorial series, vol. IV)
LC 25-18176

Davies, R.
English society in the eighteenth century in contemporary art. London, Seeley 1907
88p. 37 illus.(4 col.) O. 7s

Davillier, Charles. See Davillier, Jean Charles, baron

Davillier, Jean Charles, baron
L'Espagne; illus. par Gustave Doré. Paris, Hachette 1874
799p. 310 illus. Q.
English edition: 1876
Lipperheide 1237m

Spain; illus. by Gustave Doré; tr. by J. Thomson. London, S. Low, Marston, Low, and Searle 1876
xiii,512p. illus. pl. F.
French edition: 1874
LC 4-25771

Davis, Sir John Francis, bart.
The Chinese: a general description of the empire of China and its inhabitants. By John Francis Davis. New York, Harper 1848
2v. front.(fold.map) illus. D. (The family library no80, 81)
Binder's title: History of China
Later published under title: *China: a general description of that empire and its inhabitants* (new ed. London, J. Murray 1857) French translation by A. Picard *La Chine, ou description générale* (Paris, Paulin 1837)
Colas 808, 809(French ed) LC 15-25148

Davis, Richard Harding
The rulers of the Mediterranean. New York, Harper 1894
x,228p. front. illus. pl. D.
LC 4-16719

Three gringos in Venezuela and Central America. New York, Harper & brothers 1896
xi,282p. front. illus. pl.(1 double) ports. map. D.
LC 2-8086

Davis, William Stearns
A day in old Rome. Boston, New York, Allyn and Bacon 1925
xxiv,482p. front. illus. D. $1.80
Costume index. LC 25-19296

Life on a mediaeval barony, a picture of a typical feudal community in the thirteenth century. New York, Harper 1923
xi,414p. front. illus. pl. port. O. $3.50
Costume index. LC 34-8806(1933 ed.)

Davison, Thomas Raffles
Gleanings from the past and memorials from the present; being a series of sketches at the Health exhibition, 1884. London, British architect offices [1884]
37p. 30pl. Q.
Some of the plates show old English costume

Davy, John
An account of the interior of Ceylon and of its inhabitants. London, Longman, Hurst, Rees, Orme, and Brown 1821
530p. front.(fold.map) Q.
LC 5-13882

Davydoff, Sophie. See Davydova, S. A.

Davydova, Sofía Aleksandrovna
La dentelle russe; histoire, technique, statistique par Mme Sophie Davydoff ... Tr. du russe sous la direction de l'auteur ... Leipzig, K. W. Hiersemann 1895
28p. 80pl. F.
Lipperheide 4058. LC 3-18435

The **dawn** of the XIXth century in England. Ashton, John

Dawson, James
Australian aborigines, the languages and customs of several tribes of aborigines in the western district of Victoria, Australia. Melbourne G. Robertson 1881
111,ciii p. front. ports. fold.facsim. Q.
Two plates show a tribal chief and his wife
LC 3-5343

Dawson, Thomas
Memoirs of St George, the English patron, and of the most noble Order of the Garter.. London, H. Clements 1714
336p. front. D.
LC 9-32606

Dawson, Warren Royal
(tr.) Capart, Jean. Egyptian art.

Day, Francis Henry Cripps-. See Cripps-Day, F. H.

Day, Lewis Foreman, and Buckle, Mary
Art in needlework; a book about embroidery; with additional chapters by Mary Hogarth. 5th ed. rev. London, B. T. Batsford [1926]
xxii,280p. illus. D.

Day, Thomas Anthony, and Dines, John Henry
Illustrations of medieval costume in England; collected from mss. in the British museum, Bibliothèque nationale de Paris, etc. London, T. Bosworth [1851]
24p. col.front. 19pl.(18 col.) Q. 9s, o.p.
Shows English costume from the Anglo-Saxon period to the time of Henry VIII
Colas 810. Costume index. Lipperheide 1007

A **day** in old Rome. Davis, W. S.

Dayot, Armand Pierre Marie
Histoire contemporaine par l'image, d'après les documents du temps, 1789-1872. Paris, E. Flammarion 1905
368p. illus.ports. facsims. ob.Q.
LC 13-12643

L'image de la femme. [Paris] Hachette 1899
397p. illus. pl. ports. Q.

L'invasion, le siège, la commune, 1870-1871, d'après des peintures, gravures ... objets du temps. Paris, E. Flammarion n.d.
364p. ports. illus. facsims. ob.F.

Journées révolutionnaires: 1830, 1848, d'après des peintures, sculptures, dessins, lithographies, médailles, autographes, objets ... du temps. Paris, E. Flammarion 1897
112,140p. illus.ports. facsims. ob.Q.
LC 32-6872

Louis XIV; illustrations d'après des peintures, sculptures, gravures, objets, etc., du temps. Paris, E. Flammarion 1909
315p. illus. ob.Q. 15fr.
LC 10-751

Les maitres de la caricature française au XIXe siècle. Paris, Quantin 1888
xvii p. 18 illus. 55pl.(5 col.) Q.
Lipperheide 3513. LC 20-12999

La révolution française; constituante, législative, convention, directoire, d'après des peintures, sculptures, gravures, médailles, objets du temps. Paris, E. Flammarion [1896]
495p. illus.ports. facsims. ob.Q.

Le second empire (2 décembre 1851—4 septembre 1870). D'après des peintures, gravures, photographies, sculptures, dessins, medailles, autographes, objets du temps. Paris, E. Flammarion ca1900
348p. 1009 illus. O.
Lipperheide 1177m

The **days** of Dickens. Hayward, A. L.

The **days** of the Directoire. Allinson, A. R.

The **days** when we had tails on us. Hort, Sir J. J., 3d bart.

De anulis antiquis. Liceti, Fortunio

De annulis narium. (In Bartholin, Caspar. De inauribus veterum syntagma. 1676. Part 2, 17p.)

De armillis veterum. Bartholin, Thomas

De arte gymnastica libri sex. Mercuriale, Girolamo

De barba, liber singularis. Pagenstecher, J. F. W.

De calceis Hebraeorum. Bynaeus, Anthony

De calceo antiquo. Baudouin, Benoit, and Negrone, Giulio

De caliga veterum. See Baudouin, Benoît and Negrone, Giulio. Balduinus de calceo antico

De capillamentis seu vulgo parucquen. Rango, K. T.

De capillis veterum collectanea historico-philologica. See Henning, Johann. Trichologia

De claris mulieribus. Boccaccio, Giovanni

De coronis et tonsuris. Stellartius, Prosper

De fuga in persecutione. Tertullianus, Q. S. F.

De gentium aliquot migrationibus. Lazius, Wolfgang

De gli habiti antichi. Vecellio, Cesare

De gli habiti della religioni. Fialetti, Odoardo

De habitu virginum. Cyprianus, Saint, bp. of Carthage

De inauribus veterum syntagma. Bartholin, Caspar

De la Chine au point de vue commercial, social et moral. Dagneau, L.

De la loi du contraste simultané des couleurs. Chevreul, M. E.

De la modestie des femmes et des filles chrétiennes dans leurs habits. Philalethe, Thimothée, pseud.

De la necessité de la coiffure pour les hommes distingués. Duchesne, coiffeur

De la parure au temps jadis. Lapaume, Jean

De la vie privee des romains. See Arnay, J. R. d'. Habitudes et moeurs

De l'abus des nuditez de gorge. Boileau, Jacques

De lamiis et phitonicis mulieribus. Molitor, Ulrich

De Lapponibus Finmarchiae ... commentatio. See Leems, Knud. Beskrivelse over Finmarkens Lapper, deres Tungemaal

De legatione Basilii magni principis Moscoviae. See Giovio, Paolo, bp. of Nocera. Die Moscouitische chronica

De les costumes dels homens. See Cessolis, Jacobus de. Volgarizzamento del libro de' costumi

De l'évolution moderne du chupen et du jilet dans le costume masculin. Picquenard, C. A.

De loricis. Apin, S. J.

De ludis circensibus. Panvinio, Onofrio

De luxu et abusu vestium nostri temporis. Matenesius, J. F.

De luxu Romanorum. Meurs, Johannes van

De magnificentia politiae amplissisimae civitatis Brugarum. See Damhouder, Joost. Pupillorum patrocinium

De majestate juribusque barbae. Kirchmaier, G. C.

De militia equestri antiqua et nova. Hugo, Hermann

De mutatione formarum in vestibus. Loeber, C. G., praeses

De nederlandsche nationale kleederdrachten. Molkenboer, Theodoor

De omnibus illiberalibus sive mechanicis artibus. Amman, Jost

De paenula. Bartholin, Bertelli

De pallio. See Tertullianus, Q. S. F. De fuga in persecutione, De pallio

De Paris à Samarkand. Ujfalvy, Marie

De Paris au Tonking. See Bonvalot, Gabriel. Across Thibet

De pileo. See Raynaud, Théophile. Anselmus Solerius Cemeliensis

De re equaria tractatio nova complectens. Winter, G. S.

De re metallica. Agricola, Georg

De re militari. Vegetius Renatus, Flavius.

De re navali. See Baïf, Lazare de. Lazari Bayfii annotationes

De re vestiaria. See Baïf, Lazare de. Lazari Bayfii annotationes in l. II. De captivis, et postliminio reversis. pt[2]

De re vestiaria. Ferrari, Ottavio

De re vestiaria libellus ex Bayfio excerptus. Baïf, Lazare de

De re vestiaria veterum. Rubens, Albert

De rebus a Carolo Gustavo Sveciae rege gestis ... Pufendorf, Samuel, freiherr von

De rebus siculis carmen. Petrus, de Ebulo

De remediis utriusque fortunae. See Petrarca, Francesco. Trostspiegel in glück und unglück

De Sacri rom. imperii libera Civitate noribergensi commentatio. Wagenseil, J. C.

De stola in archidiaconorum visitationibus. Thiers, J. B.

De toga Romana commentarius. Bossi, Gerolamo

De translatis Habsburgo-Austriacorum principum. Gerbert, Martin, freiherr von Hornau

De vasculis. See Baïf, Lazare de. Lazari Bayfii annotationes

Dea; revista mensile della moda. Anno 1+ Nov. 1932+ Milano, G. P. Cei
Illus. pl.(part col.) F. 65 l. a year
Published monthly. Current 1938

Deakin, Irving

Ballet profile. New York, Dodge publishing. c1936
xiv,368p. pl. ports. O.
LC 37-3478

Dean, Bashford

Helmets and body armor in modern warfare. New Haven, Yale university press 1920
325p. double front. illus.(incl.ports) 2 double tab. Q.
Half-title: The Metropolitan museum of art. Publication of the Committee on education
LC 20-17513

The Bashford Dean collection of arms and armor. See entry under New York. Metropolitan museum of art

Catalogue of a loan exhibition of arms and armor. See entry under New York. Metropolitan museum of art

Catalogue of European arms and armor. See entry under New York. Metropolitan museum of art

Catalogue of the loan collection of Japanese armor. See entry under New York. Metropolitan museum of art

The collection of arms and armor of Rutherfurd Stuyvesant. See entry under Stuyvesant, Rutherford

Handbook of arms and armor. See entry under New York. Metropolitan museum of art

A miscellany of arms and armor. See entry under Armor and arms club, New York

Deane, John Bathurst

Remarks on certain ornaments of gold found near Quentin in Britany in 1832; presumed to have been the *maniakai* of the ancient Gauls; in a letter ... to Sir Henry Ellis. London, J. B. Nicholas 1838
14p. 2pl. Q.
From *Archaeologia, or, Miscellaneous tracts relating to antiquity,* published by the Society of antiquaries of London v27
Lipperheide 278

Dearborn, George Van Ness

The psychology of clothing. Princeton, N.J. Psychological review company
72p. diagrs. O. (Psychological review publications. The psychological monographs. v26, no 1; whole no112)
References: p[71]-72
LC 19-3234

Dearmer, Percy
Ornaments of the ministers; 2d ed. London, A. R. Mowbray 1920
xii,136p. front. pl. D.
Traces the development in ecclesiastical costume beginning with the second century
Costume index

Debacq, Alexandre. See Guyot, jt. auth.

Debay, Auguste
Hygiène vestimentaire. Les modes et les parures chez les Français depuis l'établissement de la monarchie jusqu'à nos jours, précédé d'un curieux parallèle des modes chez les anciennes dames grecques et romaines. Paris, E. Dentu 1857
360p. D.
Colas 811. Lipperheide 3265. LC 32-35433

Deblay, A.
Histoire anecdotique du costume en France de la conquête romaine à nos jours: costume féminin et masculin, coiffure, lingerie, chaussure, la mode et l'art, la mode et l'hygiène, la mode et la politique. Paris, Colin 1924
148p. 32 illus. D. 4fr.
Colas 812

Debray, V.
(pub.) México y sus alrededores

[**Debret**]
[Costumes italiens dessinés à Rome en 1807 par Debret, gravés par L. M. Petit en 1809.] No place, n.d.
30 col.pl. Q.
Plates without legend or name of artist
Colas 813

Debrett's Coronation guide. London, Dean & son, 1911
xxix,253p. illus. O.
LC 11-20489

Debrois, Johann
Urkunde uber die ... krönung ... des königs von Böhmen Leopold des zweiten und ... der gemahlinn des königs Maria Louise. Prag, G. Haase 1806
168,75p. illus. 12pl. F.
Plates engraved by Franz Heger. The 1818 edition has the same plates, with addition of author's name to title page
Lipperheide 2632-33

De Bruin, Cornelis. See Bruyn, Cornelis de

[**Debucourt, Philibert Louis**]
Modes et manières du jour à Paris à la fin du 18ᵉ siècle et au commencement du 19ᵉ. Paris, Journal des dames [1798-1808]
1 l. 52 col.pl. O. 18fr.
Colas describes this as a rare collection and gives a complete list of the plates
Colas 814

Recueil de têtes et coiffures modernes à l'usage des jeunes personnes qui dessinent. No place, [1801-04]
6pl. O.
Title on first plate. Plates exist in black or in red
Colas 815

(engr.) Damame-Démartrais, M. F. Collection complète des divers jardins et points de vue des maisons de plaisance impériales de Russie

(engr.) Damame-Démartrais, M. F. Vues de Russie et usages divers des habitants de ce genre

(engr.) Norblin de la Gourdaine, J. P. Zbior wzorowy rozmaitych polskich

(engr.) Vernet, Carle. Collection de costumes

Il Decamerone. Boccaccio, G. See entry under Merkel, Carlo. Come vestivano gli uomini del "Decameron"; saggio di storia del costume

Decem, è familiâ burggraviorum Nurnbergensium. Cernitius, Johannes

Decem insignes tabulae. La Ruelle, Claude de

Dechelette, Joseph
Manuel d'archéologie préhistorique celtique et gallo-romaine. Paris, A. Picard 1908-34
6v. in 8. illus. pl. maps. plans. O.
Some of the illustrations show costume, weapons and jewelry of the bronze age

Dechend, Hans. See Pflugk-Harttung, J. A. G. von, ed. Napoleon I.: Das erwachen der völker

Decker, Paul
Repraesentatio belli, ob successionem in Regno Hispanico ... gesti ... Der spanische successions-krieg unter drey ... keyszern Leopoldo I, Josepho I und Carolo VI. Augsburg, Jeremias Wolffens erben [after 1714]
56pl. F.
Plates are by Decker and others. They show scenes of battle, sieges, etc. and incidentally uniforms worn in the war of the Spanish succession (1701-1714)
Lipperheide 2107

Declaration of the artists of the nineteenth century on the influence of costume and fashion upon high art. London, 1862
O.
Cataloged from Colas
Colas 816

Decoration and ornament
Bastard d'Estang, August, comte de. Peintures et ornements des manuscrits. 1837-46

Cahier, Charles, and Martin, Arthur. Mélanges d'archéologie, d'histoire et de littérature. 1847-56

Cole, A. S. Ornament in European silks. 1899

Collinot, E., and Beaumont, Adalbert de. Ornements vénitiens, hindous, russes, etc. 1883

Diefenbach, Leonhard. Geometrische ornamentik. 1889

Dupont-Auberville, A. Art industriel: L'ornément des tissus; recueil historique et pratique. 1877

Fischbach, Friedrich. Ornament-album. 1892

Fischbach, Friedrich. Ornamente der gewebe. 1874-80

Flemming, E. R. Textile künste, weberei, stickerei, spitze, geschichte, technik, stilentwickelung. 1923

Guichard, Édouard. Dessins de décoration des principaux maîtres. 1881

Guilmard, Désiré. Les maîtres ornemanistes. 1880-81

Heiden, Max. Motive. Sammlung von einzelformen aller techniken des kunstgewerbes als vorbilder und studienmaterial. 1892

Decoration and ornament—*Continued*

Hoffmann, Wilhelm, and Kellerhoven, Franz. Recueil de dessins relatifs à l'art de la décoration chez tous les peuples et aux plus belles époques de leur civilisation. 1858

Jones, Owen. The grammar of ornament. 1865

Racinet, A. C. A., ed. L'ornement polychrome. 1869-73

See also Embroidery—Finland; Jewelry; Needlework

Plant forms

Botanisches stick- und zeichen-buch für damen. [1805-1808]

Giem, A. C. S. Blumen und kanten zum sticken als beitrag zum unterricht in zeichnen- und sticke-schulen. ca1810

Herdtle, Eduard. Stilisirte blumen aus allen kunstepochen. 1881

Knorr, G. W. Auserlesenes blumenzeichenbuch für frauenzimmer. ca1750

Koch, Rud. Hamburger pflanzen-bilder. 1882

Rococo

Jessen, Peter. Das ornament des rococo und seine vorstufen. 1894

Arabia

Collinot, E., and Beaumont, Adalbert de. Ornements arabes. 1883

Asia

Victoria and Albert museum, South Kensington. Brief guide to the oriental painted, dyed and printed textiles. 1924

Borneo

Haddon, A. C., and Start, L. E. Iban or sea Dayak fabrics and their patterns. 1936

China

Collinot, E., and Beaumont, Adalbert de. Ornements de la Chine. 1883

Les étoffes de la Chine; tissus & broderies. 1914?

Jones, Owen. Examples of Chinese ornament selected from objects in the South Kensington museum and other collections. 1867

Victoria and Albert museum, South Kensington. Brief guide to the Chinese woven fabrics. 1925

Dutch East Indies

Jasper, J. E., and Pirngadie, Mas. De inlandsche kunstnijverheid in Nederlandsch Indië. 1912-16

Réal, Daniel. The batiks of Java. 1924

Rouffaer, G. P., and Juynboll, H. H. De batik-kunst in Nederlandsch-Indië en haar geschiedenis. 1914

Egypt

Forrer, Robert. Die frühchristlichen alterthümer aus dem gräberfelde von Achmin-Panopolis. 1893

Forrer, Robert. Römische und byzantinische seiden-textilien aus dem gräberfelde von Achmin-Panopolis. 1891

Forrer, Robert. Die zeugdrucke der byzantinischen, romanischen, gothischen und spätern kunstepochen. 1894

Gerspach, Édouard. Les tapisseries coptes. 1890

Rosellini, Ippolito. I monumenti dell' Egitto e della Nubia. 1832-44

Stuart, Villiers. The funeral tent of an Egyptian queen. 1882

Europe

Bossert, H. T. Peasant art in Europe. 1927

Bossert, H. T. Volkskunst in Europa. 1926

Victoria and Albert museum, South Kensington. Brief guide to the western painted, dyed and printed textiles. 1924

Finnish

Ahrenberg, J. J. Fennia illustrata. 1878-1882

Tikkanen, J. J. Finnische textilornamentik. 1901

Germany

Aldegrever, Heinrich. Ornamente. 1876

Brown, G. B. The arts and crafts of our Teutonic forefathers. 1910

Fink, Karl. Die geometrische construction und farbengebung des flach-ornamentes. 1875-76

Frickinger, J. M. Nützliches, in lauter auserlesenen, wohl-approbirt- und meistentheils neu-inventirten mustern bestehendes, weber-bild-buch. 1740

Händel, Ernest. Schablonen in natürlicher grösse für decken, wände, säulenschäfte etc. aus dem ende des xv. und anfang des xvi. jahrhunderts. 1888

Lichtwark, Alfred. Der ornamentstich der deutschen frührenaissance nach seinem sachlichen inhalt. 1888

Hungary

Huszka, József. Magyarische ornamentik. 1900

Pulszky, Karoly. Ornamente der hausindustrie Ungarns. 1878

Indians of North America

Westlake, Mrs I. B. American Indian designs. c1925-30

Bibliography

Traphagen, Ethel. Costume design and illustration. 1932. p225-29

Indians of South America

Victoria and Albert museum, South Kensington. Brief guide to the Peruvian textiles. 1926

See also Decoration and ornament—Peru

Italy

Holme, Charles, ed. Peasant art in Italy. 1913

Decoration and ornament--*Continued*

Japan

Bing, Samuel. Artistic Japan. 1888-91

Collinot, E., and Beaumont, Adalbert de. Ornements du Japon. 1883

Dolmetsch, Heinrich, ed. Japanische vorbilder; ein sammelwerk zur veranschaulichung japanischer kunstprodukte ... nach japanischen originalmustern. 1886

Tuer, A. W. The book of delightful and strange designs. 1893

Victoria and Albert museum, South Kensington. Guide to the Japanese textiles. 1919-20

Java

See also Decoration and ornament—Dutch East Indies

Mexico

Peñafiel, Antonio. Alfabetos adornados; aplicaciones decorativas del arte mexicano antiguo. 1898

Morocco

Vogel, Lucien. Soieries marocaines, les ceintures de Fès. 1921

Persia

Arnold, Sir T. W., and Grohmann, Adolf. The Islamic book. 1929

Collinot, E., and Beaumont, Adalbert de. Ornements de la Perse. 1880

Perleberg, H. C., comp. Persian textiles. 1919-31

Victoria and Albert museum, South Kensington. Brief guide to the Persian woven fabrics. 1922

Peru

Lehmann, Walter, and Doering, Heinrich. The art of old Peru. 1924

Lehmann, Walter, and Doering, Heinrich. Kunstgeschichte des alten Peru. 1924

Victoria and Albert museum, South Kensington. Brief guide to the Peruvian textiles. 1926

Primitive

La décoration primitive. 1922-24

Russia

Chrapovitsky, L. Russisches musterbuch. 1887

Holme, Charles, ed. Peasant art in Russia. 1912

Ivchenko, A. Al'bom" russkīkh ī malorossiĭskīkh" rīsunkov". 1875

Lītvīnov", P. ÎA. IUzhno-russkiĭ narodynĭ ornament. Ornement national de la Russie meridional. 1878

Sīmakov", N. Russkiĭ ornament" v" starīnnykh" obraztsakh" khudozhestvenno-promyshlennago proīzvodstva ... L'ornement russe dans les anciens produits de l'art industriel national. 1882

Stasov, V. V. L'ornement slave et oriental d'après les manuscrits anciens et modernes. 1887

Ukraine

Kosacheva, O. P. Ukrainskiĭ narodnyĭ ornament, obraztsy, vyshivok", tkaneĭ i pīsanok, izdanie vtoroe. 1879

Turkey

Collinot, E., and Beaumont, Adalbert de. Ornements turcs. 1883

Victoria and Albert museum, South Kensington. Brief guide to the Turkish woven fabrics. 1923

Yugoslavia

Dalmatia

Bruck-Auffenberg, Frau Natalie. Dalmatien und seine volkskunst. 1911

La **décoration** primitive. Paris, A. Calavas 1922-24

4v. pl.(part col.) sq.Q.

Shows primitive decoration and ornament, also masks of Indians of Alaska, British Columbia, and Mexico

Contents: [1] Lepage, P. C. Afrique; [2] Réal, Daniel. Océanie; [3] Réal, Daniel. Amérique pré-colombienne; [4] Réal, Daniel. Amérique post-colombienne

LC 24-1679

Décorations, médailles, monnaies et cachets du Musée de l'armée. Sculfort, V. C. L. É.

Decorations of honor

Das buch der ritterorden und ehrenzeichen. 1848

Burke, Sir J. B. The book of orders of knighthood and decorations of honour of all nations. 1858

Burke, Sir J. B., and Burke, A. P. A genealogical and heraldic history of the peerage and baronetage, the Privy council, and knightage. 1935

Loumyer, J. F. N. Ordres de chevalerie et marques d'honneur. 1844

France

Sculfort, V. C. L. É. Décorations, médailles, monnaies et cachets du Musée. de l'armée. 1912

Papal

Guigue de Champvans, Frédéric. Histoire et législation des ordres de chevalerie. 1932-33

Decorative art of Indians of the Southwest. Chapman, K. M., comp. See note under Traphagen, Ethel. Costume design and illustration

Die **decorative** kunst-stickerei. Lipperheide, Frieda

Décors de théâtre. Cogniat, Raymond

Les **décors,** les costumes, et la mise en scène au XVIIe siècle. Leclercq, Louis

Decorum. Ruth, J. A., and Snyder, C. S., comps.

De Courcy, Margaret

(ed.) Ladies cabinet of fashion, music and romance

Decret relatif à l'uniforme des officiers et fonctionnaires des différents corps de la marine, corps de troupe exceptés. 3 juin 1891. France. Ministère de la marine

The **defensive** armour and the weapons and engines of war of mediaeval times and of the "renaissance." Clephan, R. C.

Defensorium immaculatae virginitatis. Franciscus, de Retza

Defensorium inviolatae perpetuaeque virginitatis. See Franciscus, de Retza. Defensorium immaculatae virginitatis

Defontaine, Henri
Du costume civil officiel et de l'uniforme militaire des officiers à la cour ou auprès des chefs d'état français depuis 1804 jusqu'à nos jours. Paris, A. Geoffroy frères 1908
xx,309p. front. illus. 34pl.(part col.) O.
Colas 817. Costume index

Deformities
Flower, Sir W. H. Fashion in deformity. 1882
Holländer, Eugen. Wunder, wundergeburt und wundergestalt in ein blattdrucken des fünfzehnten bis achtzehnten jahrhunderts. 1921

De Garmo, Charles, and Winslow, Leon Loyal
Essentials of design [by] Charles De Garmo ... and Leon Loyal Winslow ... with numerous illustrations from the Metropolitan museum of art. New York, Macmillan 1924
255p. illus.(part col.) diagrs. D. $1.60
Art in dress p208-47
LC 24-4977

De Gheyn, Jacob. See Gheyn, Jacob de

Degli abiti sacri del sommo pontefice paonazzi e neri in alc. sol. funzioni della chiesa. Giorgi, Domenico

Degrand, A. See Degrand, J. A. T.

Degrand, Jules Alexandre Théodore
Souvenirs de la Haute-Albanie. Paris, H. Welter 1901
333p. illus. Q.
LC 19-7441

Degrees and hoods of the world's universities & colleges. Haycraft, F. W.

The **degrees,** gowns, and hoods of the British, colonial, Indian, and American universities and colleges. Wood, T. W.

[**Deguerle, Jean Marie Nicolas**]
Éloge des perruques, enrichi de notes plus amples que le texte; par le docteur Akerlio [pseud.] Paris, Maradan [1799]
x,215p. S.
German edition: *Lobrede auf die perrüquen*
Colas 818-819. Lipperheide 1685; 1685a (German ed.) LC 17-5489

Deguignes, Joseph. See Guignes, Joseph de

Dehnike, Rudolf
Deutsche mährchengestalten. See entry under Bartsch, Gustav

De Haenen, F.
(illus.) Dobson, George. St Petersburg
(illus.) Dobson, George; Grove, H. M., and Stewart, Hugh. Russia; painted by F. De Haenen
(illus.) Stewart, Hugh. Provincial Russia

Dei costumi dell' isola di Sardegna comparati cogli antichissimi popoli orientali. Bresciani, Antonio

Dei gran duchi di Toscana della reale casa de' Medici. Bianchini, G. M.

Dei in Göttingen herüm schriende lühe. Heumann, G. D.

Dei veri ritratti degl' habiti di tutte le parti del mondo. Grassi, Bartolomeo

Deis, C.
(engr.) Dürer, Albrecht. Albrecht Dürer's Kleine passion

[**Deisch, Matthaeus**]
[Danziger ausrufbilder] no place, ca1780
40pl. F.
Colas gives the title in French: *Figures des cris de Danzig*
Colas 820. Lipperheide 821

Deiss, F. W.
Das deutsche soldatenbuch, Deutschlands wehr und waffen im wandel der zeiten—von den Germanen bis zur neuzeit. Leipzig, A. Fröhlich 1926
2v. diagrs. fronts.(1 col.) illus. pl.(part col.) F.
Contents: Bd 1 Von den Germanen bis zum Bundesheer; bd 2 Vom deutschen Bundesheer bis zum Reichsheer

Dějiny kroje v zemích českých. Zíbrt, Čeněk, and Winter, Zikmund

Del costume antico e moderno. Ferrario, Giulio

Del costume veneziano. Mutinelli, Fabio

Del paramento de prete. See Manuzzi, Giuseppe, ed. Tratto della messa e della maniera di assistervi

Delacourt, Achille Peigné-. See Peigné-Delacourt, Achille

De La Haye, Guillaume. See La Haye, Guillaume de

De la Jonchère, Ermance Dufaux. See Dufaux de la Jonchère, Ermance

Delarue, Fortuné
Tableaux de Paris ou costumes, habitudes et usages des habitants de cette capitale. Paris, C. Motte [1827]
1 l. 24 col.pl. ob.Q.
A collection which is rarely complete but usually found with 18 or 21 plates
Colas 821

Delarue, Philibert Benoit de. See La Rue, P. B. de

De Las Cases, Philippe, vicomte. See Las Cases, Philippe, vicomte de

Delaunay, Henri
(tr.) Catholic church. Liturgy and ritual. Hours. Le livre d'heures de la reine Anne de Bretagne

Delaunay, L. A.
Étude sur les anciennes compagnies d'archers, d'arbalétriers et d'arquebusiers. Paris, Champion 1879
412p. 54pl. F.

Delaunay, Sonia
Sonia Delaunay; ses peintures, ses objets, ses tissus simultané, ses modes. Paris, Librairie des arts décoratifs 1924?
4 l. 20 col.pl. F.
Introduction by Andre Lhote. English translation by H. C. Perleberg

Delaware Indians. See Indians of North America—Delaware Indians

Delaye, Edmond
Les anciens costumes des Alpes du Dauphiné. Lyon, Grange et Giraud 1922
x,125p. illus. 38pl.(part col.) Q.
Thirteen colored plates are reproductions of pastels of G. C. Michelet showing peasant costume of the 4th to 19th century
Colas 822. LC 22-20159

Delbecchi, Amedée
Nice; vues et costumes. Paris, Lemercier ca1865
1 l. 17pl. Q.
Lithographs by Guiaud and J. Félon. Six plates show folk costume of Nice
Colas 1354. Lipperheide 1203

Delcampe, and Fouquet, Samuel
L'art de monter a cheval, par Sr Delcampe; 2. ed. Augmenté d'une seconde partie, des remedes les plus efficaces pour les maladies des chevaux, par Samuel Fouquet ... Sieur de Beaurepaire. Paris, J. Le Gras [1663-64]
2v. 5pl. O.
The second part has the title: Traité des remèdes les plus utils et nécessaires pour la guérison des chevaux, published 1663
Date of first edition is unknown. A German translation appeared in 1698
Lipperheide 2909

Delegal
(engr.) Stewart, James. Plocacosmos: or, The whole art of hair dressing

Delepierre, Octave, and Voisin, Auguste
La châsse de Sainte Ursule gravée au trait par Charles Onghéna d'après Jean Memling. Bruxelles, Société des beaux-arts 1841
54p. 12pl. Q.
Contains Memling's pictures from the shrine containing the relics of St Ursula in the St. Johann hospital in Bruges, and fourteen of his pictures of saints
Lipperheide 450

Delhi and the durbar. Finnemore, John

Delhi durbars. See Durbars, Delhi

Les **délices** de la mode et du bon goût. Paris, Janet [1805]
12 illus. Ti.
Twelve pictures of fashions
Cataloged from Colas's *Bibliographie*
Colas 824

Les **délices** de l'hiver. Compte-Calix, F. C., Mille, E., and Morlon, A.

Delightful history of Yé gentle craft. Campion, S. S.

Delineatio pompae triumphalis qua Robertus Dudlaeus comes Leicestrensis Hagae comitis fuit exceptus. Dankerts, C.

Delineatio provinciarum Pannoniae et imperii Turcici in oriente. Wagner, J. C.

Delineations of the most remarkable costumes of the different provinces of Spain. Giscard

The **Delineator**; a monthly magazine illustrating European and American fashions. v 1-130; 1873-1937. New York
130v. illus.(part col.) F.
Absorbed *The Designer,* Nov 1926. Merged with *Pictorial review,* May 1937

Delisle, Arthur L. See Kellner, Leon, jt. auth.

Delitzsch, Franz Julius
Die akademische amtstracht und ihre farben. Erlangen, C. H. Kunstmann 1859
11p. Q.
Colas 825. Lipperheide 2032m

Delius, Rudolf von
Mary Wigman. Dresden, C. Reissner 1925
56p. front. pl. ports. Q.

Dell' arte del cucinare. Scappi, Bartolomeo

Della berretta ducale. Zanetti, G. F.

Della porpore e delle materie vestiarie presso gli antichi. Rosa, Michele

Della Bella, Stefano
Diverse figure & paese; fatti per Bella; [plates engraved by Israel Silvestre] Paris, Israel 1649
8pl. O.
Colas 280. Lipperheide 532

Diverses exercices de cavalerie. [Paris, 1642]
13pl. S.
Lipperheide 2079

Entrata in Roma dell' eccelmo ambasciatore di Pollonia l anno MDCXXXIII. Roma, G. J. de Rossi 163-?
6pl. F.
Lipperheide 2745

(engr.) Coppola, G. C. Le nozze degli dei

Della Casa, Giovanni. See Casa, Giovanni della, abp.

Della ornatrici ... nella chioma. Guasco, F. E.

Della vita privata de' Romani. Arnay, J. R. d'

Delle caccie. Raimondi, Eugenio

Delle livree, del modo di comporle e descrizione di quelle di famiglie nobili italiane. Padiglione, Carlo

Delle vesti ecclesiastiche in Milano. Magistretti, Marco

Delle vesti purpuree e d'altri colori con quali adorna la dignità cardinalitia. Lonigo, Michel

Dellenbaugh, Frederick Samuel
The North-Americans of yesterday: a comparative study of North-American Indian life. New York & London, G. P. Putnam's sons 1901
xxvi,487p. front. illus. O. $4, o.p.
"A comparative study of North-American Indian life, customs, and products, on the theory of the ethnic unity of the race." Subtitle
Costume index. LC 1-29467

Del Mar, Walter
The romantic East: Burma, Assam, & Kashmir. London, A. and C. Black 1906
xv,211p. front. pl. ports. O.
LC 8-425

Deloche, Maximin, 1817-1900
Étude historique et archéologique sur les anneaux sigillaires et autres des premiers siècles du moyen âge; description de 315 anneaux, avec dessins dans le texte. Paris, E. Leroux 1900
lxv,397p. illus. Q.
LC 2-27157

Deloche, Maximin, 1859-
La bague en France à travers l'histoire. Paris, Firmin-Didot 1929
104p. 16pl. on 8 l. Q.
LC 30-21420

De Lonlay, Dick, pseud. See Hardoin, Georges

Delord, Taxile
Un autre monde. See entry under Grandville, J. I. I. G.
Cent proverbes. See entry under Grandville, J. I. I. G.
Les fleurs animées. See entry under Grandville, J. I. I. G.

Delorieux, F. N.
Costumes auvergnats. Paris, Gihaut frères ca1835
18 col.pl. F.
Cover title
Colas 826

Delsenbach, Johann Adam
Wahre abbildung der sämtlichen reichskleinodien welche in ... Nürnberg aufbewahret werden. In ihrer wirklichen grösse ... nach den originalen abgezeichnet ... Nebst den Reichsheiligthümern, nach Friedrich Iuvenells abzeichnungen. Nürnberg, A. G. Schneider 1790
11 col.pl. F.
The plates of the crown jewels engraved by Delsenbach in 1740, did not come into the book trade at that time. In 1784 C. G. von Murr, in the same size as the original plates, had engraved for his *Commentatio de sacris Lipsanis* two other plates by J. Georg and J. H. Klinger after drawings made by Friedrich Juvenell in 1645. The entire collection of plates was published in 1790. For description of the jewels pictured see C. G. Murr's *Beschreibung*
Lipperheide 1760

Die **dem** lieben frauenzimmer sehr angenehmen auch commoden contusche und reiffenröcke. Leucorande, E. C.

Demange
Les mésaventures, lithographiées par Demange. [Paris] Gihaut frères 1828
1 l. 6 col.pl. F.
Lipperheide 3622

Démartrais, Michel François Damame-. See Damame-Démartrais, M. F.

Demay, Germain
Le costume au moyen âge d'après les sceaux. Paris, D. Dumoulin 1880
496p. illus. 2 col.pl. facsims. Q.
The chapter entitled *Habillement chevaleresque*, first published in volume 35 of the *Mémoires* de la Société nationale des antiquaires de France, was issued separately in 1875 under the title: *Le costume de guerre et d'apparat d'après les sceaux du moyen âge* (Colas 827, Lipperheide 2099)
Colas 828. Costume index. Lipperheide 358

Demeuse, Nicolas
Nouveau traité de l'art des armes. Liège, F. J. Desoer 1778
181p. 14pl. O.
Lipperheide 2977

Demmin, August Frédéric
Encyclopédie d'armurerie avec monogrammes, guide des amateurs d'armes et armures anciennes, par ordre chronologique, depuis les temps les plus reculés jusqu'à nos jours. Paris, Vve J. Renouard 1869
628p. illus. S.
Translated into English under title: *Weapons of war*, see below. German translation has the title: *Die kriegswaffen* (2d ed. Leipzig, E. A. Seeman 1885; 3d ed. Gera-Untermhaus, F. E. Köhler 1891)
Lipperheide 2422-23(German ed.)

Weapons of war; being a history of arms and armour from the earliest period to the present time, with nearly 2000 illustrations; tr. by C. C. Black. London, Bell & Daldy 1870
595p. illus. O. 12s
Translation of the author's: *Encyclopédie d'armurerie avec monogrammes.* The English edition was later issued with title: *An illustrated history of arms and armour from the earliest period to the present time* (London, G. Bell 1911)
LC 18-23684; 15-20637(1911 ed.)

Denckwürdige gesandtschafften der Ost-Indischen gesellschaft. See note under Montanus, Arnoldus. Gedenwaerdige gesantschappen

Dendrono
Natürlich abschilderung des academischen lebens. Nürnberg, J. J. Wolrab ca1725
1 l. 14pl. F.
Lipperheide 2022

Dengler, Hermann
American Indians, tribes of the prairies and the East ... with 96 illustrations taken from old prints (1590-1850) New York, A. and C. Boni 1923
80p. col.front. illus. ports. map. Q. o.p.
Also published in German with title: *Indianer, die indianerstämme des Ostens und der prärien Nordamerikas* (Stuttgart, Franckh 1924)
Costume index. LC 28-14255

Denike, Borisa Petrovicha
(ed.) Iskusstvo Sredneĭ Azii. Sbornik stateĭ. B. P. Denike, M. M. Denisovoĭ, B. N. Zasypkina, B. V. Krusman, B. M. Nikiforova, N. I. Sokolovoĭ. A. S. Strelkova, V. N. Chepeleva, E. N. Chernîavskogo. Moskva, Ranion 1930g
113p. illus. 3r. (Trudy sektsii istorii iskusstv. Institut arkheologii i iskusstvoznaniîa)
On the art of Central Asia

Deniker, Joseph
Les races et les peuples de la terre. 2. éd. rev. et considérablement augm., avec 340 figures et 2 cartes. Paris Masson 1926
750p. illus.(col.front. maps) Q.
LC 26-13887

Denis, Ferdinand
La Guyane, ou histoire, moeurs et costumes des habitants di cette partie de l'Amérique. Paris, Nepveu 1823
2v. 16pl. S.
Also published with colored plates
Colas 829

Portugal. Paris, Firmin Didot 1846
439p. 32pl.(incl.ports.) O. (L'univers; histoire et description de tous les peuples. 66)
LC 3-10077

See also Taunay, Hippolyte, jt. auth.

Denis, Jean Ferdinand. See Denis, Ferdinand

Denkbuch über die anwesenheit ihrer k. k. majestäten Franz des ersten und Caroline Auguste. Glaser, Rudolph

Denkmäler ägyptischer sculptur. Bissing, F. W., freiherr von

Denkmaeler aus Aegypten und Aethiopien. Lepsius, Richard

Denkmäler der alten kunst. Müller, K. O.

Denkmäler der kunst. See Denkmäler der malerei; also Denkmäler der sculptur

Denkmäler der malerei auf 63 tafeln mit erklärendem text als integrirender theil des werkes: Denkmäler der kunst zur uebersicht ihres entwickelungsganges von den ersten künstlerischen versuchen bis zu den standpunkten der gegenwart. Hrsg. von ... v. Voit, E. Guhl, J. Caspar, W. Lubke und C. v. Lützow. Stuttgart, Ebner & Seubert 1860
55p. 63pl. F.
Lipperheide 73

Denkmäler der sculptur auf 36 tafeln mit erklärendem text. Als integrirender theil des werkes: Denkmäler der kunst zur uebersicht ihres entwickelungsganges von den ersten künstlerischen versuchen bis zu den standpunkten der gegenwart. Hrsg. von ... v. Voit, E. Guhl, J. Caspar, W. Lübke und C. v. Lützow. Stuttgart, Ebner & Seubert 1860
39p. 36pl. F.
Lipperheide 74

Denkmäler des hauses Habsburg in der Schweiz. Huber-Liebenau, Theodor von

Denkmäler des klassischen altertums. Baumeister, August

Denkmäler des theaters; inszenierung, dekoration, kostüm des theaters und der grossen feste aller zeiten, nach originalen der theatersammlung der Nationalbibliothek, der Albertina und verwandter sammlungen, Wien, herausgegeben von der direktion der Nationalbibliothek mit unterstützung der Gesellschaft zur herausgabe der denkmäler des theaters. München, R. Piper [1926-30]
12v. [362]pl. (part col.) F.
Issued in 12 portfolios, each with a fascicle of text by Joseph Gregor. Volumes 1, 3-9, 11-12 are of costume value. An issue with English text added has title *Monumenta scenica; monuments of the theatre, scenery, decorations and costumes* (Vienna, National library [1926-30])
Contents: 1. mappe L. O. Burnacini: Maschere; 2. mappe Szenische architekturen und architekturphantasien; 3. mappe A. D. Bertoli: Desseins; 4. mappe Pompe funèbre de S. A. R. Charles III, duc de Lorraine; 5. mappe Altvlämisches und altniederländisches theater; 6. mappe Courses de testes et de bague faites par le roy en l'année 1662. XXI pl. 7. mappe Theater und garten; 8. mappe Groteskkommödie und stegriefstück; 9. mappe Theater des mittelalters, seine wirkungen in der graphik, miniatur und im tafelbilde; 10. mappe Magna allegoria; Mortis imagines; 11. mappe Feste des sonnenkönigs; 12. mappe Wiens letzte grosse theaterzeit
LC 36-15526

Die **denkmäler** zum theaterwesen im altertum. Bieber, Margarete

Denkmahl der vaterlandsliebe und fürstentreue. Lauber, Joseph

Denkmale der geschichte und kunst der freien Hensestadt Bremen. See Kohl, J. G. Episoden

Denkmale des geschmaks der sitten und gebräuche der alten Schweizer. Maurer, H. R.

Denkmale deutscher bildnerei und malerei von einführung des christenthums bis auf die neueste zeit. Förster, Ernst

Denkmale italienischer malerei vom verfall der antike bis zum sechzehnten jahrhundert. Förster, Ernst

Denkwürdigkeiten der elbinsel finkenwerder. Bodemann, F. W.

Denmark

Bruun, Daniel, ed. Danmark; land og folk. 1919-23

Eckersberg, C. V. Ti Tegninger af Christoffer Wilhelm Eckersberg. 1919

Eyriès, J. B. B. Danemark. 1846

Hambro, C. J., baron. Edda; or, The tales of a grandmother. History of Denmark, from the earliest ages to the accession of the Oldenburg dynasty, A. D. 1448. 1875

Hielscher, Kurt. Dänemark, Schweden, Norwegen; landschaft, baukunst, volksleben. 1932

Ottesen, Louise. Danske folkedragter. 1923

Troels-Lund, T. F. Dagligt liv i Norden i det 16de aarhundrede. 1880-1901

See also Zealand; also subdivision Denmark under Coronations and coronation robes; Kings and rulers; Military costume; Naval costume; Orders of knighthood and chivalry

Prehistoric

Boye, V. C. Fund af Egekister fra bronzealderen i Danmark. 1896

Müller, S. O. Ordning af Danmarks oldsager; système préhistorique du Danemark, résumé en français. 1888-95

19th century

Belin, A., and others. Costumes de Suède, Norvège, Danemark, Hollande et Allemagne. 186-?

Esménard, Jeanne d'. Costumes des pays du Nord: Hollande et Danemark. ca1830

Klaederdragter i Kiöbenhavn. ca1808

Lahde, G. L. Kjøbenhavns kloededragter eller det daglige liv i hovedstaden i characteristiske figurer. ca1800

Lund, F. C. Danske nationaldragter. 1916

National-trachten verschied. völkerschaften in Dänemark. 1815

Rieter, Jakob. Danske nationale klaededragter; Dänische national kleidertrachten. 1805

Denmark—*Continued*

20th century

Butlin, F. M. Among the Danes. 1909

Sprengel, David. Från det moderna Danmark. 1904

Dennison, Walter

A gold treasure of the late Roman period. New York, Macmillan 1918
p89-175. front. illus. pl.(part double) port. Q. (University of Michigan studies. Humanistic ser. v12. Studies in East Christian and Roman art. pt2)
LC 18-5765

Dennison manufacturing company

How to make crepe paper costumes; 2d ed. Framingham, Mass., Dennison manufacturing co. 1925
36p. illus.(part col.) O. 10c
First edition: *How to make paper costumes* (1922)
LC 25-21992

Denon, Dominique Vivant, baron

(engr.) David. Costumes de la revolution française

La **dentelle** à Valenciennes. Malotet, A.

La **dentelle** russe. Davydova, S. A.

Dentelles anciennes. Cole, A. S.

Dentelles anciennes. Overloop, Eugène van

Dentelles anciennes. Paris. Musée des arts décoratifs

Dentelles anciennes des Musées royaux des arts décoratifs et industriels à Bruxelles. Overloop, Eugène van

Les **dentelles** de Normandie en 1913. See Drouet, P. L. M. Causerie sur les dentelles de Normandie au debut du XXe siècle

Dentelles d'Irlande. Cole, A. S.

Dentelles du Puy. Chaleyé, Joannes

Dentelles et broderies d'art, stores & brise-bise. Prévot, Gabriel, and Devresse, G.

Dentelles, guipures, broderies ajourées. Paris. Musée Galliera

Depain

[Coëffures de dames. Paris, Depain] 17-?
1 l. front. 12pl. Q.
Each plate shows a single coiffure. They are without legends and are signed: D.P. inv.
Colas 830

Depping, George Bernhard

Aperçu historique sur les moeurs et coutumes des nations. Paris, Mairet et Fournier 1842
xii,256p. S.
Colas notes an edition of 1826, as part of the *Encyclopédie portative*
"I. Thl. kap. 3: 'De l'habillement, de la parure et des modes' " Lipperheide
Colas 831. Lipperheide 59

Depréaux, Albert

Les affiches de recrutement du XVIIe siècle à nos jours, préface de M. Gabriel Cottreau. Paris, J. Leroy 1911
95p. illus. 48pl.(part col.)facsim. F.
The 48 plates, including 46 facsimiles, are in pasteboard folder
Principales sources consultées: p85-87
LC 24-1786

Les armées françaises d'outre-mer. Les uniformes des troupes de la marine et des troupes coloniales et nord-africaines. Paris, Ateliers d'impressions d'art 1931
[130]p. illus.(part col.) pl.(part col. 1 double) ports.(part col.) Q.
At head of title: Exposition coloniale internationale de Paris, 1931. "Cet ouvrage a été publié sous le patronage du Ministère des colonies et du Service historique de l'armée. Il a été établi et rédigé par M. Albert Depréaux."
"Index chronologique des ouvrages cités": p129-[130]
Colas 833. LC 32-5576

Les gardes d'honneur d'Alsace et de Lorraine à l'époque du premier empire. Paris, J. Leroy 1913
174p. illus. 10pl.(6 col.) O.
"Bibliographie des principales sources consultées": p151-52
Colas 832. LC 24-1787

Les uniformes des troupes coloniales de 1666 à 1875. Paris, Exposition coloniale international 1931
16p. 16pl.(2 col.) O. 12fr.
Colas 834

De Quincey, Thomas

Toilette of a Hebrew lady, exhibited in six scenes. Hartford, Conn., E. V. Mitchell 1926
64p. O.
In *Blackwood's magazine* for March 1828; reprinted by De Quincey in 1859 in volume 12 of his *Collected writings*

Der aller durchleuchtigisten und grossmächtigen kayser ... thaten. See Schrenck von Nozing, Jacob. Augustissimorum imperatorum

Der Madame Beaumont, berühmten putzmacherin zu Paris lehrreiches kopfzeugermagazin zum nutzen des schönen geschlechts in Deutschland eingerichtet. See Marchand, J. H. L'enciclopédie carcassière

Dergny, Dieudonné

Usages, coutumes et croyances ou livre des choses curieuses ... Costumes locaux de France illustrés et gravés par E. Winckler. Abbeville, E. Winckler-Hiver 1885-88
2v. illus. O.
The illustrations show peasant headdress
Colas 835

Dernières créations parisiennes. Louvel

Derrick, Freda

Tales told in church stones; symbolism and legend in medieval architecture and handicrafts; with 54 illustrations by the author. London, Lutterworth press [1935]
127p. col.front. illus. O.
Bibliographical references included in the author's acknowledgements (p11-12)
LC 36-1063

Des aller streytparsten vñ theüresten fürsten und herrn Georgen Castrioten genañt Scanderbeg ... ritterliche thaten. Barletius, Martinus

Des allerdurchleuchtigsten groszmechtigsten unüberwindlichsten Keyser Karls des Fünfften und des Heyligen Römischen Reichs peinlichs gerichts-

Des allerdurchleuchtigsten ... —*Continued*
ordnung auff den reichsstägen zu Augspurg und Regenspurg in jaren dreissig und zwey und dreissig gehalten auffgericht und beschlossen. Franckfurt am Main, J. Raschen [1559]
38 l. 6 illus. F.
Illustrations show scenes at courts of law, and prisoners being tortured
Lipperheide 2008

Des Alpes aux Pyrénées, étapes félibréennes. Arène, P. A., and Tournier, Albert

Des alten Nürnbergs sitten und gebräuche in freud und leid. Mayer, M. M.

Des ballets anciens et modernes selon les regles du theatre. Menestrier, C. F.

Des bewoonden waerelds steden en dragten See Allard, Carel. Orbis habitabilis oppida et vestitus

Des ceremonies du sacre. Leber, J. M. C.

Des gants portés par les évêques, par d'autres membres du clergé et même par les laïques dans les cérémonies religieuses. Barraud, P. C.

Des gold- und silber-gläntzenden himmels erlustigung und beschaffenheit. Menschenhold, C. G.

Des habits, moeurs, ceremonies, façons de faire anciennes & modernes du monde. Glen, J. B. de

Des herrn Beaumont ... lehrreiches Peruquenmagazin. See Marchand, J. H. L'enciclopédie perruquiere

Des hochberümptesten geschicht schreybers Justini warhafftige hystorien. Justinus, M. J.

Des königs Friedrich August des gerechten heimkehr und empfang am 7ten juni 1815. Dresden, Königlichen hofbuchdruckerei 1815?
158p. 6pl. O.
Lipperheide 2580s

[**Des** Maltheser-ritter-ordens teutschen grosspriorats wappen calender, 1770.] No place, 1770
12 l. 60pl. D.
Cataloged from Lipperheide's *Katalog*. Title taken from Bernd's *Allgemeine schriftenkunde der gesammten wappenwissenschaft*
Lipperheide 4402

Des Rheinkreises jubelwoche, oder Geschichtliche darstellung der reise ihrer majestäten des königs Ludwig und der königin Therese von Bayern durch die gaue des Rheinkreises vom 7ten bis zum 14ten junius 1829. Speyer, J. C. Kolb [1829]
203p. 13pl. 1 map. Q.
Lipperheide 2567m

Des vice-lavmands Eggert Olafsens und des landphysici Biarne Povelsens reise durch Island. Ólafsson, Eggert

De Sallieth, Matheus. See Sallieth, Matheus de

Los **desastres** de la guerra. Goya y Lucientes, F. J. de

Descaves, Paul
Historique du 13me régiment de chasseurs et des chasseurs à cheval de la garde. Béziers, A. Bouineau 1891
399p. col.pl. ports. maps. F.
Drawings of the uniforms are by M. de Fonremis

Descripcion de la solemnidad fúnebre con que se honraron las cenizas del héroe de Iguala, don Agustin de Iturbide, en octubre de 1838. Pacheco, J. R.

Descripcion de los ornatos públicos con que la corte de Madrid ha solemnizado la ... exâltacion al trono de ... Don Carlos IIII. y Doña Luisa de Borbon. Madrid

Description de la belle et grande colonne historiée, dressée à l'honneur de l'empereur Theodose. Menestrier, C. F.

Description de la chambre et lit de parade sur lequel le corps d'Anne, Princesse Royale de Grande-Bretagne ... a été exposé. See Swart, P. de. Afbeelding van de kaamer

Description de la fête des vignerons, célébrée à Vevey, le 5 aoust 1819. Vevey, Loertscher 1819
47p. 8pl. O.
Lipperheide 2863

Description de la fête des vignerons célébrée à Vevey les 8 et 9 août 1833. Vevey, Steinlen, A. Monnerat, G. Blanchoud 1833
52p. 30pl. O.
Lipperheide 2870

Description de l'Égypte; ou, Recueil des observations et des recherches qui ont été faites en Égypte pendant l'expédition de l'armée française, pub. par les ordres de Sa Majesté l'empereur Napoleon le grand [rédigé par F. Jomard] Paris, Imprimerie impériale 1809-22
8v. 542pl.(part col.) ports. maps. F.
Many of the plates show costume of ancient Egypt

Description de l'uniforme des sous-lieutenants de l'école d'application de l'artillerie et du génie. Daigremont, J. H.

Description de quelques corps composant les armées françoises. Leipzig, F. A. Leo 1794
10p. 3 col.pl. Q.
Colas 837. Lipperheide 2302

Description de tous les peuples qui se trouvent sous la domination bienfaisante d'Alexandre I. See Hempel, Friedrich, and Geissler, C. G. H. Abbildung und beschreibung der völkerstämme

Description de toutes les nations de l'empire de Russie. Georgi, J. G.

Description des cérémonies et des fêtes qui ont eu lieu pour le baptême de ... Henri-Charles-Ferdinand-Marie-Dieudonné d'Artois, Duc de Bordeaux. Hitorff, J. J., and Lecointe, J. F. J.

Description des cérémonies et des fêtes qui ont lieu pour le couronnement de ... Napoléon ... et Joséphine. Percier, Charles, and Fontaine, Pierre François

Description des cérémonies et des fêtes qui ont eu lieu pour le mariage de ... Napoléon avec ... Marie-Louise d'Autriche. Percier, Charles, and Fontaine, P. F. L.

Description des effets d'habillement, de coiffure, de grand et de petit équipement, de petite monture, de pansage et objets divers à l'usage des corps de troupe. France. Ministère de la guerre

Description des festes données par la ville de Paris, à l'occasion du mariage de Madame Louise-Elisabeth de France, & de Dom Philippe, infant ... d'Espagne, les vingtneuvième & trentième août mil sept cent trente-neuf. Paris, P. G. Le Mercier 1740
22p. illus. 13pl. F.
Engraved by J. F. Blondel after designs by Salley, Servandony and Gabriel
Lipperheide 2714

Description des fêtes populaires données à Valenciennes les 11, 12, 13 mai 1851. Dinaux, A. M.

Description des instrumens harmoniques en tout genre. See Buonanni, Filippo. Descrizione degl' istromenti armonici d'ogni generi

Description des ornemens impériaux et des reliques de Saint empire romain. Murr, C. G. von. See note under Beschreibung der sämtlichen reichskleinodien und heiligthümer welche in Nürnberg aufbewahret werden

Description des planches relatives aux crieurs publics de St Pétersbourg. Shönberg, and Geïssler, C. G. H.

Description des principales rejouissances, faites à La Haye, à l'occasion du couronnement de sa majesté ... François I. La Haye, A. de Groot [1747]
18p. 7pl. F.
Title also in Dutch: *Beschryving der voornaamste vreugde-bedryven in 's Gravenhage, ter gelegenheid van de krooning van ... Franciscus I.* Drawings by M. Schluymer, engraved by J. C. Philips
Lipperheide 2670

Description des XXII cantons de la Suisse. See Sommerlatt, C. V. von. Beschreibung der XXII Schweizer-kantone

Description du bal paré en costume. See Weidmann, F. C. Der costum-ball am schlusse des carnevals 1826

Description du cortège historique des comtes de Flandre. See Busscher, Edmond de. Album du cortège des comtes de Flandre

Description du manége moderne dans sa perfection. Eisenberg, von, baron

Description du sacre et du couronnement de ... l'empereur Alexandre II et l'impératrice Marie Alexandrovna, MDCCCLVI. [St. Petersburg, Imprimerie de l'Académie impériale des sciences] 185-?
125p. 32 illus.(2 col.) 18 col.pl. F.
Illustrated by Zichy and others
Lipperheide 2787

La **description** et ordre du camp & festiemt & ioustes des ... roys de France et Dangleterre la mil. CCCCC. et vingt au moys de iuing. Paris, A. Aubry [1864]
23p. D.
Lipperheide 2703

Description ethnographique des peuples de la Russie. Pauli, F. K.,

Description géographique, historique, chronologique, politique, et physique de l'empire de la Chine et da la Tartarie chinoise. Du Halde, J. B.

Description historique de l'habillement et de l'armement des troupes russes de 862-1855. See Viskovatov, A. V. Istoritcheskoïe oppissanïe odéjedy i vooroujéniia rossiskich voïsk

Description historique des uniformes et des armes des troupes russes. See Viskovatov, A. V. Istoritcheskoïe oppissanïe odéjedy i vooroujéniia rossiskich voïsk

A **description** of a singular aboriginal race. Harkness, Henry

Description of a view of the city of Moscow. Burford, Robert

A **description** of Indian and Oriental armour. Egerton, W. E., earl

A **description** of the coasts of East Africa and Malabar in the beginning of the sixteenth century. Barbosa, Duarte

Description of the collection of gold ornaments from the "huacas". Wright, B. M.

Description of the plates, representing the itinerant traders of London in their ordinary costume. London, [R. Phillips 1804]
63 l. 31 col.pl. Q.

Description of the regalia of Scotland. Scott, Sir Walter, bart.

A **descriptive** catalogue of the collections of tapestry and embroidery in the South Kensington museum. Cole, A. S.

A **descriptive** catalogue of the lace in the South Kensington museum. Palliser, Mrs F. M.

Descriptive ethnology of Bengal. Dalton, E. T.

Descriptive sociology. Spencer, Herbert

Descrizione degl' istromenti armonici d'ogni generi. Buonanni, Filippo

Descrizione del regale apparato per le nozze della serenissima Madame Cristiana di Loreno, moglie del serenissimo Don Ferdinando Medici III. granduca di Toscana. Gualterotti, Raffaello

Descrizione dell' apparato fatto in Firenze ... nell' occasione del ... ritorno in Toscana di ... il granduca Ferdinando III. Firenzi, N. Carli 1814
7p. 3pl. F.
Plates engraved by N. Palmerini, R. Morghen and A. E. Lapi
Lipperheide 2772

Descrizione dell' arco trionfale. Scamozzi, O. B.

Descrizione della Palestina. Ferrario, Giulio

Descrizione delle feste celebrate in Parma l'anno MDCCLXIX. Paciaudi, P. M.

Descrizione delle feste celebrate in Venezia per la venuta di S.M.I.R. Napoleone, il massimo imperatore de' Francesi. Morelli, Jacopo

Descrizione delle feste fatte in Bologna il giorno XVII agosto dell' anno MDCCXXXVIII ... in occasione delle ... nozze de' monarchi delle due Sicilie. Bologna, L. dalla Volpe [1738]
52p. 2pl. F.
Engraved by A. A. Scarselli after drawings by St Orlandi
Lipperheide 2762

Descrizione delle ... solennita celebrate ... 12. febbrajo 1736 ... in Ferrara per le ... nozze di S.A.R. Francesco Steffano Duca di Lorena e della Serenissima Arciduchessa Maria Teresa d'Austria. Agnelli, Jacopo

Descrizione, storia, ed illustrazione degli ornamenti di una donna romana. Riccio, Gennaro

Descrizione storica degli ordini cavallereschi. Cibrario, G. A. L., conte

Descrizione storica degli ordini religiosi. Cibrario, G. A. L., conte

[**Deserpz, François**]

Ominium fere gentium, nostræq. ætatis nationum, habitus & effigies. In eosdem Ioannis Sluperij Herzelensis epigrammata. Adiecta ad singulas icones gallica tetrasticha. Antverpiæ, apud I. Bellerum 1572

16p. 120 l.(incl.120 illus.) S.

An edition, with Latin verses and a dedication to Ioannes Wynter by Iacobus Sluper, of the *Recueil de la diuersité des habits, qui sont de present en usage, tant es pays d'Europe, Asie, Affrique & isles sauvages* (first published Paris, 1562, also 1564, 1567) with French quatrains ascribed to François Descerps. The 120 woodcuts were copied for this edition by Ant. Bosch called Silvius

Colas 2498. Lipperheide 2. LC 33-5049

Recueil de la diversité des habits qui sont de present en usaige tant es pays d'Europe; Asie, Affrique et Illes sauvages, le tout fait aprés le naturel. Paris, R. Breton 1562

64 l.(incl.121 illus.) O.

Dedication to Henry of Navarre by F. Deserpz

Lipperheide describes it as the earliest known work on costume printed in book form. The costumes range from the provinces of rural France to typical costumes of the European and Asiatic countries. Most of the plates appear in pairs, showing masculine and feminine costume of each nationality

Also published in Paris 1564 (2d ed.) and 1567 (3d ed.) A reproduction of the third edition was published (Lyon, Audin 1927)

Colas 2595-97, 2499. Lipperheide 1

The **desert** and the sown. Bell, G. L.

Desert gateway. Leeder, S. H.

Desessarts, Alfred

L'univers illustré. Paris, Janet ca1840

16 col.pl. O.

Lithographs by Louis Lassalle

Colas 842

Deshays, Célestin

Costumes bretons. Paris, Clément ca1840

1 l. 6 col.pl. F.

Colas 844

Souvenirs de Bretagne. Paris, Aubert ca1840

1 l. 12 col.pl. F.

Shows peasant costume of Brittany

Colas 843

The **design** and development of costume from prehistoric times up to the twentieth century. Rosenberg, Adolf

Design, Decorative. See Decoration and ornament

Design in the theater. Sheringham, George, and others

The **Designer.** See The Delineator

Designer and manufacturer; a magazine devoted to the designing and manufacture of men's, boys' and children's clothing. v 1+ May 1933+ New York, H. K. Burnam

Illus. F. $5 a year

Published monthly. Current 1938

Organ of the International association of clothing designers; International clothing factory managers and foremen's association

Designing

Braun, A. A. Figures, faces and folds, a practical reference book on woman's form and dress. 1928

Brown, P. C. Art in dress. 1922

Chadwick, L. M. Fashion drawing & design. 1926

Chuse, A. R. Costume design. c1930

Downs, Marie, and O'Leary, Florence. Elements of costume design for high school students. c1923

Ellsworth, E. P. Textiles and costume design. 1917

Evans, Mary. Draping and dress design. 1935

Federated council on art education. Costume design as an occupation. 1936

Gallemore, Margaret; Harris, V. A., and Morris, Maria. Costume design. 1934

Hall, M. L. Fashion drawing and dress design. 1928

Hammond, E. C. Industrial drawings for girls; design principles applied to dress. 1912

Hartman, E. A. Instructive costume design. 1922

Hopkins, Mrs M. S. Dress design and selection. 1935

Hughes, Talbot. Dress design. 1920

Izor, E. P. Costume design and home planning. c1916

Traphagen, Ethel. Costume design and illustration. 1932

Designs by Inigo Jones, for masques & plays at court. Jones, Inigo

Designs for fancy dresses. Peel, Mrs D. C. B.

Designs for lace making. Hailstone, S. H. L.

Designs of Chinese buildings, furniture, dresses, machines, and utensils. Chambers, Sir William

The **designs** of Leon Bakst for The sleeping princess. Bakst, Léon

Designs of modern costume. Moses, Henry

Designs of the home-industry embroideries in Bukovina. See Kolbenheyer, Erich. Motive der hausindustriellen stickerei in der Bukowina

Designs on the dances of Vaslav Nijinsky. Barbier, George

Desmaisons, E.

(lithgr.) Gerson, Aldabert. Costumes polonais

Désormeaux, A. O. Paulin-. See Paulin-Désormeaux, A. O.

Despaigne, H.

Le code de la mode. Paris, L'auteur 1866

93p. D.

Colas 846

Despierres, Mme Gérasime (Bonnaire)
Histoire du point d'Alençon, depuis son origine jusqu'à nos jours. Paris, Renouard, H. Laurens, succ. 1886
276p. 9 illus. VIII pl. O.
Lipperheide 4046. LC 19-18886

Desrais, Claude Louis
Suites des nouvelles modes françoises depuis 1778 jusqu'à ce jour. Paris, Vve Avaulez [1785]
2 l. 24pl. O.
Colas 847

(illus.) Mode au jour

Desrat, G.
Dictionnaire de la danse historique, théorique, pratique et bibliographique depuis l'origine de la danse jusqu'à nos jours. Paris, Librairies-imprimeries réunies 1895
484p. 7 illus. D.
Lipperheide 3134. LC 3-27303

Dess aller durchleutigsten Haus Ostereich herzogen. Kilian, Wolfgang

Dessault, Marcel
Études variés sur la coupe. Paris, 1903
71p. illus. Q.
The 1st part: Costume pour dames genre tailleur, appeared in *Le progrès*

Traité pratique de la coupe et de la confection des vêtements pour dames et enfants. Paris, Garnier frères 1896
xii,597p. illus. D. (Bibliothèque d'utilité pratique)
Illustrations by Marcel and Paul Dessault

Dessault, Paul
(illus.) Dessault, Marcel. Traité pratique de la coupe et de la confection des vêtements pour dames et enfants

Desseins des edifices, meubles, habits ... des Chinois. See Chambers, Sir William. Designs of Chinese buildings, furniture, dresses, machines, and utensils

Dessins d'anciennes broderies en Russie. See Shakhovskaia, Princess S. N. Uzory starinnago shit'ia v" Rossii

Dessins de broderies, fin du XVIIIe siècle & 1er empire. Paris. Musée des arts décoratifs

Dessins de décoration des principaux maîtres. Guichard, Édouard

Dessins et modèles. Champeaux, Alfred de

Dessins pour ouvrages de dames. Paris, A. Simart ca1870
4v. 17 illus. 33pl. O.
Contents: pt 1 Dessins spéciaux pour tulle; pt2 Crochet tunisien; pt3 Dessins pour crochet; pt4 Guipure sur filet
Lipperheide 4104

Le **dessus** du panier. Jean-Meyan, Maurice, and Socquet, Jean

D'Este, Margaret. See Este, Margaret d'

Desvergers, Marie Joseph Adolphe Noël. See Desvergers, Noël

Desvergers, Noël
L'Étrurie et les Étrusques; ou, Dix ans de fouilles dans les Maremmes toscanes. Paris, Firmin Didot 1862-64
3v. XL pl.(part col.) map. O.
Plates in volume 3 show Etruscan dress

Detaille, Édouard
(illus.) Hoff, Major, pseud. Les grandes manoeuvres

Detaille, Édouard and Maillot, Thomas Jules Richard
Types et uniformes. L'armée française, par Édouard Detaille; texte par Jules Richard [pseud] Paris, Boussod, Valadon et cie 1885-89
2v. illus. 64 col.pl. F.
Issued in 16 parts in portfolios. Paged continuously
French army uniforms from 1789-1889. Contents: t 1 États-majors. Écoles. Infanterie. Cavalerie. t2 Armes spéciales. Corps indigènes. Corps auxiliaires. Marine
A popular edition is described by Colas (849) with the plates and illustrations reproduced in color by zinc-engravings. Published in 16 parts at 160 francs
Colas 848. Lipperheide 2340. LC 6-37634

Detaille, F.
(illus.) Flandreysy, J. M. de. La femme provençale

Deters, Friedrich
Die englischen angriffswaffen zur zeit der einführung der feuerwaffen (1300-1350). Heidelberg, C. Winter 1913
150p. O. (Anglistische forschungen. hft. 38)
"Literatur": pref. p9-16
LC 14-1407

Detmold, Johann Hermann and Schrödter, Adolph
Thaten und meinungen der herrn Piepmeyer. Abgeordneten zur constituirenden nationalversammlung zu Frankfurt am Main. [Frankfurt a. M. C. Jügel 1849]
50pl. Q.
Lipperheide 3538

Detroit. Public library
Costume, a list of books. [Detroit] Detroit public library, Fine arts department 1928
cover-title, 56p. O.
Arranged by subject
LC 28-19604

Le **deuil.** Mercier, Louis

Deutliche und gründliche erklärung der ... fecht-kunst. L'Ange, J. D.

Deutliche vorstellung der nürnbergischen trachten. Luyken, Caspar

Der **Deutsch Orden.** See Teutonic Knights

Die **deutsche** armee; abbildungen von offizieren und soldaten aller truppengattungen, militär-beamtem etc. Uebersichtliche farbendarstellungen der uniformen der deutschen armee. Farbendruck nebst erläuterungen und einer vollständigen armee- und quartier-liste. Leipzig, M. Ruhl 1915?
3v. in 1. 46 col.pl. O.
First edition: Stuttgart, G. Weise 1890
At head of title of Part 1: Militär-Album aller Länder. Heft 1
Contents: [Part 1] Die deutsche Armee. 6. ed. [Part 2-3] Die Uniformen der deutschen Armee. Abt. 1. 35. ed.
Lipperheide 2139 (1892 ed. of pt 1) LC CA 11-3234 (pt 1)

Deutsche bauerntrachten. Retzlaff, Hans

Deutsche bauerntrachten, farbige meisterbilder mit einer einführung von prof. dr. Hans W. Singer; 2. aufl. Bielefeld und Leipzig, Velhagen & Klasing 1924?
3 l. 32 col.pl. Q.

Das **deutsche** bundesheer. See entry under Eckert, H. A.; Monten, Dietrich, and Schelver, F. Saemmtlich truppen von Europa

Die **deutsche** Elite, das blatt der gesellschaft. 1.-7. jahrg. 1924-1930. Berlin, O. Dreyer
7v. col.illus. col.pl. Q.
Title varies: v 1, 1924: *Die elite;* v2,.1927-30: *Die deutsche elite, gesellschaft, mode, kunst, sport*
Editor: Gus. W. Nedowitz

Deutsche feste und volksbrauche. Fehrle, Eugen

Das **deutsche** feyerkleid zur erinnerung des einzugs der Deutschen in Paris am 31sten märz 1814 eingeführt von deutschen frauen. Becker, R. Z.

Die **deutsche** frauenkleidung. Kiesewatter, Doris, and Steffahny, Hermine

Deutsche geschichte. Arnold, Wilhelm

Deutsche geschichte. Stacke, L. C.

Deutsche hausfrauen-zeitung. See Frauen reich

Das **deutsche** heer und die marine. Arnould, Georg

Deutsche heeres-uniformen auf der weltausstellung in Paris 1900. Prussia. Kriegsministerium

Das **deutsche** Helgoland. Lindemann, Emil

Deutsche illustrierte theatergeschichte. See Devrient, Eduard. Geschichte der deutschen schauspielkunst

Die **deutsche** karikatur im 19. jahrhundert. Borchardt, G. H.

Deutsche mährchengestalten. Bartsch, Gustav

Die **deutsche** marine in ihrer gegenwärtigen uniformierung. Schlawe, Karl

Die **deutsche** marine und die deutsche schutztruppe für Ost-Afrika in ihrer neuesten uniformirung. 6. aufl. Leipzig, M. Ruhl [1893]
67,10p. 20 col.pl. O.
First edition issued in 1878 under title: *Die uniformen der deutschen marine*
Colas 2598. Lipperheide 2134

Das **deutsche** militar in der karikatur. Conring, F. F.

Die **deutsche** militair-musik auf der internationalen ausstellung für musik- und theaterwesen Wien 1892. Berlin, Verlag der Expedition der deutschen militair-musiker-zeitung [1892]
16p. 16pl. O.
Lipperheide 2140

Deutsche modenzeitung. v 1, okt. 1891+ Leipzig, O. Beyer
Col.illus. F.
Published bi-weekly. Current 1937
Title varies: jan.-sept. 1891, *Leipziger modenzeitung*
Colas 1823. Lipperheide 4802

Das **deutsche** reichsheer, graphisch dargestellt ... nebst erläuternden und historischen bemerkungen. Karlsruhe, W. Hasper 1879
24 l. 11 col.pl. F.
Colas 851

Das **deutsche** reichsheer in seiner neuesten bekleidung und ausrüstung. Krickel, G., and Lange, G.

Die **deutsche** reichswehr in ihrer uniformierung. Pietsch, Paul

Die **deutsche** reichswehr; organisation, einteilung, truppenteile, bekleidung und ausrüstung d. deutschen reichsheeres. 2. erw. und verb. aufl. Leipzig, M. Ruhl [1924]
23p. 150 illus.(part col.) 16 col.pl. O.

Deutsche Ritter. See Teutonic Knights

Das **deutsche** schützenfest in Frankfurt am Main. Hornfeck, Fr.

Das **deutsche** soldatenbuch. Deiss, F. W.

Die **deutsche** theaterausstellung, Berlin 1910. Stümcke, Heinrich

Deutsche theatergeschichte. See Devrient, Eduard. Geschichte der deutschen schauspielkunst

Deutsche trachten. Arndt, E. M.

Deutsche trachten aus dem sechzehnten jahrhundert. Thaeter, Julius

Die **deutsche** trachten und modenwelt. Falke, Jacob von

Deutsche turniere, rüstungen und plattner des XVI. jahrhunderts. Gurlitt, Cornelius

Deutsche urzeit. See Arnold, Wilhelm. Deutsche geschichte

Das **deutsche** volk in seinen mundarten, sitten, gebräuchen, festen und trachten. Duller, Eduard

Deutsche volkskunst. hrsg. von ... Edwin Redslob. v 1-13 München, Delphin verlag [1923-33]
13v. pl. O.
Each volume contains a few plates from photographs which show festive and ordinary dress of the people of the region
Contents: v 1 Pessler, Wilhelm. Niedersachsen; v2 Lindner, Werner. Mark Brandenburg; v3 Creutz, Max. Die Rheinlande; v4 Karlinger, Hans. Bayern; v5 Gröber, Karl. Schwaben; v6 Ritz, Joseph. Franken; v7 Redslob, Edwin. Thüringen; v8 Grundmann, Günther, and Hahm, Konrad. Schlesien; v9 Uebe, Rudolf. Westfalen; v10 Clasen, K. H. Ost-preussen; v11 Adler, Fritz. Pommern; v12 Zink, Theodor. Die Pfalz; v13 Busse, B. E. Baden

Deutsche volkstracht. Friedrich, T. H.

Deutsche volks-trachten. Leipzig, Verlag von Bernhard Schlicke [ca1847]
50pl.(1 in color) Q.
Colas 852. Lipperheide 738

Deutsche volks-trachten. Duller, Eduard. See note under his Das deutsche volk in seinen mundarten

Deutsche volkstrachten. Erich, O. A.

Deutsche volkstrachten. Kretschmer, Albert

Deutsche volkstrachten, aus der sammlung des Germanischen museums in Nürnberg. Helm, Rudolf

Deutsche volkstrachten, städtische und ländliche. See note under Hottenroth, Friedrich. Deutsche volkstrachten vom XVI bis zum XIX jahrhundert

Deutsche volkstrachten vom XVI bis zum XIX jahrhundert. Hottenroth, Friedrich

Die **deutschen** corps. Fabricius, Wilhelm

Die **deutschen** hochgezeiten. Hüsing, Georg

Die **deutschen** landsknechte. Blau, Friedrich

Die **deutschen** reichs- und königl. preuss. staats- und hofbeamten-uniformen. Dresden, 1897
118p. 1 l.(incl.221 illus.) 12pl. O.
Lipperheide 1779

Die **deutschen** reichsinsignien in ihrer symbolischen bedeutung. Liebusch, Georg

Die **deutschen** schutztruppen in Afrika (Sudwestafrika, Ostafrika, Kamerun und Togo) in ihrer gegenwärtigen uniformirung. Leipzig, M. Ruhl [1897]
32p. col.pl. D.

Die **deutschen** volkstrachten. Spiess, Karl

Die **deutschen** volkstrachten zu beginn des 20 jahrhunderts. Julien, Rose

Deutscher frauenspiegel. Bauer, Max

Deutscher ritter-saal. Reibisch, F. M. von

Deutscher verein für kunstwissenschaft. Der Mainzer goldschmuck der kaiserin Gisela. See entry under Falke, Otto von

Deutsches brauchtum im jahreslauf. Crass, Eduard

Deutsches bundesschiessen. 7.-10. München, Knorr & Hirth 1881-90
illus. pl. Q.
The eighth issue is entitled *Festzeitung für das achte deutsche bundesschiessen* (Leipzig, E. A. Seemann 1884); the ninth *Deutsches bundes- & jubiläums-schiessen* (Frankfurt am Main, A. Osterreich 1887); the tenth *Festzug 10tes deutsches bundesschiessen* (Berlin, Amsler & Ruthardt 1890)
Lipperheide 3010-14

Deutsches ernte-dankfest, 1933. Rosenfeld, Helmut

Deutsches leben. See note under Falke, Jacob von. Die deutsche trachten

Deutsches leben der vergangenheit in bildern. Diederichs, Eugen

Deutsches leben im XIV. und XV. jahrhundert. Schultz, Alwin

Deutsches volksleben in 13 bildern nach Melchior Meyr's erzählungen aus dem Ries. Enhuber, Carl von

Deutschland. Boguslawski, Albrecht von

Deutschland im 18. jahrhundert. Boehn, Max von

Deutschland: landschaft und baukunst. Hürlimann, Martin

Deutschland vor dreihundert jahren in leben und kunst. Eye, August von

Deutschlands armee in feldgrauer kriegs- und friedens-uniform. Osten-Sacken und von Rhein, Ottomar, freiherr von der

Deutschlands heer und flotte. Sigel, G. A.

Deux années à Constantinople et en Morée (1825-1826). Deval, Charles

Deux éventails du Musée du Louvre. Bapst, Germain

Deux livres d'heures. Brussels. Bibliothèque royale de Belgique. Section des manuscrits

Deux témoignages inédits sur le costume des élégants au XIVe siècle. Langfors, Arthur

Deuxième album de divers travaux exécutés sur la fourche à franges. See Album de divers travaux exécutés sur la fourche à franges, Deuxième

[**Deval, Charles**]
Deux années à Constantinople et en Morée (1825-1826) ou esquisses historique sur Mahmoud, les Janissaires, les nouvelles troupes, Ibrahim-Pascha, Solyman-Bey. London, R. G. Jones 1828
219p. 16pl. O.
Each plate included twice, in black and white and in colors
Colas 853. Lipperheide 1435

Devère
(engr.) Cruz Cano y Olmedilla, Juan de la. Collection des costumes espagnols anciens et moderns

Devère, Louis. See Compaing, Charles, jt. auth.

Deveria, Achille
[Actrices des principaux théâtres de Paris] Paris, Aumont [1832]
14pl.
Portraits of Mmes Jawureck, Léontine Fay, Prévost, Noblet, Damoreau-Cinti, Falcon, Grévédon, Malibran, Paradol, Mars, Despréaux, Dupont, Fanny Kemble and Al. Noblet
For a list of Devéria's costume portraits see Henri Beraldi's *Les graveurs du XIXe siècle*. Deveria's *Album lithographié* (1833) and other Albums are listed in the same book

Alphabet varié. Paris, A. Fonrouge [1830]
25pl. Q.
Cover title
A suite showing varies costumes
Colas 854bis

Costumes historique de ville ou de théâtre et travestissemens. Paris, Goupil et Vibert [1831]
125 col.pl. F.
Colas 859

Dix-huit heures de la journée d'une Parisienne. Paris, Fonrouge ca1830
1 l. 18pl. F.
Shows feminine costume only. Colas describes this suite as very rare and almost always incomplete
Colas 855. Lipperheide 1159o

Les femmes, galerie fashionable; Women, fashionable gallery. Paris, F. and L. Janet ca1830
12 col.pl. Q.
For a list of plates see Colas' *Bibliographie*. These exist also in black and white, with legends in English and French
Colas 856. Lipperheide 1159m

Flore des salons ou les fleurs et les femmes de tous les pays. [Paris] F. and L. Janet 1831
1 l. 48 col.pl. Q.
English title given in a separate column: *Flora of saloons or flowers and women of every country* (London, C. Tilt) Legends in English and in French
Colas 858

Deveria, Achille—*Continued*
Le goût nouveau. Paris, Tessari 18-?
24 col.pl. Q.
Title taken from plates, which are also found in black and white. They show feminine costume only
Colas 860

(illus.) Legouvé, G. J. B. E. W., and others. Les hommes célèbres de l'Italie

See also Gavarni, G. S. C., jt. auth.

Devéria, Achille, and Boulenger
Souvenirs du théâtre anglais; dessinés par ... Devéria et Boulenger avec un texte par Moreau. Paris, H. Gaugain ca1830
1 l. ports. 12 col.pl. Q.
Appeared in parts and it seems probable that the text never was published
Colas 857

Devéria, Eugène
Costumes de la vallée d'Ossau. Pau, F. Gudin [1843-44]
6 col.pl. F.
Cover title
Colas 861

Devéria, Gabriel
(tr.) Un mariage impérial chinois

Devresse, G. See Prévot, Gabriel, jt. auth.

Devrient, Eduard
Geschichte der deutschen schauspielkunst ... neu bearbeitet und bis in die gegenwart fortgeführt als "Illustrierte deutsche theatergeschichte," von Intendant Willy Stuhlfeld. Berlin, Eigenbrödlerverlag [1929]
597p. facsims. plans. pl. ports. O.
Half-title: Devrient-Stuhlfeld Deutsche illustrierte theatergeschichte; Binder's title: Deutsche theatergeschichte
Bibliography: last page

De Vries, R. W. P. See Vries, R. W. P. de

Dewick, Edward Samuel
(ed.) Charles v, king of France. The coronation book of Charles v of France

Dewing, Mrs Maria Richards (Oakey)
Beauty in dress. New York, Harper 1881
196p. pl. S.
LC 10-1025

Dewing, Mrs T. W. See Dewing, Mrs M. R. O.

Deyersperg, Georg Jacob von
Erb-huldigung, welche dem ... römischen kayser Carolo dem sechsten ... als hertzogen in Steyer, von denen gesamten steyrischen land-ständen den sechsten julii 1728 ... abgeleget und ... zusammen getragen worden. Grätz, bey denen Widmanstätterischen erben [1740]
91p. 13pl. F.
Plates, after drawings by J. J. Fluerer, engraved by J. H. Störcklin
Lipperheide 2628

Deyeux, Théophile
Physiologie du chasseur; vignettes d'Eugène Forest. Paris, Aubert [1841]
122p. 58 illus. T.
Lipperheide 3709. LC 14-8565

Dezallier d'Argenville, Antoine Joseph
Abrégé de la vie des plus fameux peintures, avec leurs portraits gravés en tailledouce, les indications de leurs principaux ouvrages. Paris, De Bure l'Aîne 1745-52
3v. 224 port. Q.
Portraits engraved by Aubert and Fessard. Lipperheide states that a 2d enlarged edition was published in Paris (4v 1762), with inferior reprints of the plates
Lipperheide 478. LC 11-9778 (2. ed.)

Dhurandhar, M. V.
(illus.) Rothfield, Otto. Women of India

Di Bologna, l'arti per via. Carracci, Annibale

Le **diable** à Paris. Paris et les Parisiens. Mœurs et coutumes, caractères et portraits des habitants de Paris ... etc. Texte par MM. George Sand, P.-J. Stahl ... [et autres] ... précédé d'une histoire de Paris par Théophile Lavallée. Paris. J. Hetzel 1845-46
2v. front. illus. pl. Q.
Illustrated by Gavarni
Volume 2 has been published separately under title: *Le tiroir du diable*
Lipperheide 1170e. LC 4-32083

Diaghilev, Serge de. See Dyagilev, S. P.

Diamant et pierres précieuses. Jannettaz, Édouard, and others

Diary illustrative of the times of George IV. See Bury, Lady C. C. The diary of a lady-in-waiting

The **diary** of a lady-in-waiting. Bury, Lady C. C.

The **diary** of Jörg von Ehingen. Ehingen, Georg von

The **diary** of Samuel Pepys. Pepys, Samuel

Dickens, Charles—Characters
Clark, J. C. The characters of Charles Dickens. 1898
Darley, F. O. C. Character sketches from the works of Charles Dickens. 1888
Fraser, C. L. Characters from Dickens. 1924
Gibson, C. D. People of Dickens. 1897
Smith, J. W., illus. Dickens's children. 1912

Dickens's children. Smith, J. W., illus.

Dictionaries of costume
Eckardt, Theodor. Wörterbuch der bekleidung. Erklärung der auf die kostüme, volkstrachten und moden aller zeiten und völker bezüglichen namen, sowie aller die herstellung der web- und wirkwaren, der putzgegenständte, der weiblichen handarbeiten ... betreffenden bezeichnungen. 1886
Lexikon des kleidermachers enthalend in einzelnen aufsätzen eine ausführliche darstellung des gesammten fachwissens des kleidermachers in wort und bild. 1895-1904
Müller, H. A., and Mothes, Oscar. Illustrirtes archäologisches wörterbuch der kunst des germanischen alterthums, des mittelalters und der renaissance, sowie ... kostümkunde, waffenkunde. 1877-78
Stroebe, L. L. Die altenglischen kleidernamen. 1904

Dictionaries of costume—*Continued*
Williams, John, ab Ithel. Glossary of terms used for articles of British dress and armour. 1851

A **dictionary** of men's wear. Baker, W. H.

The **dictionary** of needlework. Caulfeild, S. F. A., and Saward, B. C.

Dictionary of painters and engravers. Bryan, Michael

Dictionary of Roman and Greek antiquities. See Rich, Anthony. The illustrated companion to the Latin dictionary and Greek lexicon

Dictionary of the Bible. Hastings, James

Dictionnaire critique et raisonné des étiquettes de la cour, des usages du monde. Genlis, S. F. D. de S. A., comtesse de, afterwards marquise de Sillery

Dictionnaire de la danse historique, théorique, pratique et bibliographique depuis l'origine de la danse jusqu'à nos jours. Desrat, G.

Dictionnaire des antiquités chrétiennes. Martigny, J. A., l'abbé

Dictionnaire des antiquités grecques et romaines. Daremberg, C. V., and Saglio, Edmond, eds.

Dictionnaire des antiquités romaines et grecques. See Rich, Anthony. The illustrated companion to the Latin dictionary and Greek lexicon

Dictionnaire des bijoux de l'Afrique du Nord. Eudel, Paul

Dictionnaire détaillé des noms des vêtements chez les Arabes. Dozy, R. P. A.

Dictionnaire historique et biographique de la Suisse. Neuchâtel 1921-34
7v. and suppl.(2v.) illus. pl.(part col.) maps. Q.
Cover-title
Issued in parts
Plates show Swiss military and folk costume
LC 21-5108

Dictionnaire historique et pittoresque du théâtre et des arts qui s'y rattachent. Pougin, Arthur

Dictionnaire raisonné. Viollet-Le-Duc, E. E.

Didot, Ambroise Firmin. See note under Vecellio, Cesare. Costumes anciens et modernes

Diederichs, Eugen
(ed.) Deutsches leben der vergangenheit in bildern; ein atlas mit 1760 nachbildungen alter kupfer- und holzschnitte aus dem 15ten-18ten jahrhundert. Jena, E. Diederichs 1908
2v. illus. F.
Costume index. LC 11-14233

Diefenbach, Leonard
Geometrische ornamentik ... Ein motivenwerk, der griechischen, arabischen, maurischen, gothischen und modernen ornamentik entnommen; 2. aufl. Berlin, C. Claesen [1889]
14p. 87pl.(part col.) F.
First edition: 1875
Lipperheide 4364

Diego y González, Juana Natividad de, and Léon Salmerón, Africa
Compendio de indumentaria española, con un preliminar de la historia del traje y el mobiliario en los principales pueblos de la antigüedad. Madrid, S. de Sales 1915
204p. illus. O.
Contents: Preliminar; Indumentaria española: 1 Epoca ibero-romana, Epoca visigoda, Alhajas; 2 Periodo árabe; Al siglo XII, Siglo XIII, XIV, XV; 3 Renacimiento: Siglo XVI, XVII; 4 Los Borbones, Siglo XVIII, XIX, Trajes populares españoles
LC 36-22542

Diehl, Charles P.
Collection de costumes nationaux. Bucharest 1853
12 col.pl. F.
Plates, lithographed by Wüllner, show Wallachian costume
Colas 862. Lipperheide 1452

Dielmann
Les modes depuis 1515 jusqu'à 1834. Stuttgart, E. Fischhaber ca1834
16pl. O.
Each plate shows a man and woman in the French costume of some special period
Colas 863. Lipperheide 1081

Diemand, Anton
Das ceremoniell der kaiserkrönungen von Otto I. bis Friedrich II. München, H. Lüneburg 1894
149p. O. (Historische abhandlungen. IV. hft.)
A part of this work was published as an inaugural dissertation (München, J. B. Lindl 1893. 39p.)
LC 3-7244

Diener, Walter
Hunsrücker volkskunde. Bonn, F. Klopp 1925
xiv,284p. illus. pl. O. (Volkskunde rheinischer landschaften)

Diener-Schönberg, Alfons
Die waffen der Wartburg. Beschreib. verzeichnis d. waffen-sammlung d. groszherzogs Wilhelm Ernst v. Sachsen-Weimar-Eisenach. Berlin, Histor. verlag Baumgärtel 1912
195p. 78pl. Q.
Plates are after photographs by H. L. von Cranach

Dier, J. C.
(ed.) A book of winter sports. New York, Macmillan 1912
x,351p. col.front. illus. pl.(part col.) D. $1.50
Illustrations show winter sports costumes in various countries
LC 12-24770

Diesel, Matthias
Erlustierender augen-weyde zweyte fortsetzung, vorstellend, die weltberühmte churfürstliche residenz in München, als auch vornemlich die herrliche pallatia und gärten, so ihro churfürstl. durchl. in Bayrn Maximilian Emanuel zu Dero unsterblichem ruhm erbauen lassen. Aug. Vindelicorum, J. Wolff ca1720
[4]p. 42pl. F.
The views show figures in costume of the time
Lipperheide 552

Dieseldorff, Erwin Paul
Kunst und religion der Mayavölker im alten und heutigen Mittelamerika. Berlin, J. Springer 1926
45p. illus. 53pl. Q.
LC 26-13329

Dietell, Christ.
(engr.) Historia ducum Styriae

Dieterich, Albrecht
Pulcinella; pompejanische wandbilder und römische satyrspiele. Leipzig, Teubner 1897
x,306p. 3pl. D.
Contains many references to masks used in the Greek and Roman theater

Dieterlin, Petrus
Strasburgisch trachtenbuchlein; Martinus Hailler sculpsit. La mode de Strasbourg. Strasbourg, F. W. Schmuck [ca.1680]
15pl. O.
Titles in German and French
Colas lists also an edition with German title only, and the titles of the plates in German, which seems to indicate that it was the first edition, published about 1676
The plates were reproduced in 1858 by M. H. Hazard and in 1882 by Paul Buttner. Berger-Levrault's *Costumes strasbourgeois* contains reproductions of some of the plates in this work
Colas 864-65. Lipperheide 790

Dietrich, F.
[Ubiory Wojska Polskiego z csasow kosiestwa Warszawskiego. Varsovie, A. Dal-Trozzo 1831]
30 col.pl. Q.
Plates are unsigned with legends in Polish and French. They show costume of the Polish revolutionary army
Lipperheide enters an edition with supplied title: *Uniformen des polnischen revolutions-heeres* and states that some of the plates are signed by the engraver
Colas 866. Lipperheide 2384 (German title)

Dietrichson, Lorentz Henrik Segelke
Moderna och drägtreformen. Stockholm, H. Geber 1887
112p. illus. O.

Dietz, Conrad
(tr.) Roo, Gerardus de. Annales

Dietzler, Joh. Jos.
(illus.) Ramhoffsky, J. H. Drey beschreibungen

Dieu, A. See Perelle, Adam. A collection of engravings containing views

Diez, Wilhelm von
Königl. bayerische armée. München, M. Ravizza ca1864
30 col.pl. O.
Colas 867

Diez, Wilhelm von, and others
(illus.) Costumes of all nations
(illus.) Zur geschichte der kostüme

Les **différens** goûts et nouvelles modes de coeffures. Augsburg, J. M. Will ca1775
4 l. 96pl. O.
According to Colas this title is composed of 4 series with 24 plates each, engraved by J. M. Will. They show feminine coiffures and also are found in color
Colas 868. Lipperheide 1680 (4th ser.)

Différens soldats. Liagno, T. P.

Differents habillements de Turcs. Silvestre, C. F.

Les **différents** publics de Paris. Doré, Gustave

Dighton, Basil Lewis. See Lawrence, H. W., jt. auth.

Dighton, D.
(illus.) Broke, Sir A. de C., 2d bart. Winter sketches in Lapland
(lithgr.) Svedman. Costume of Sweden

Dighton, Richard
Characters at the west end of the town. London, M'Lean 1825
37 col.pl. F.

Sketches in colors showing costumes of the period. London, T. McLean 1819-22
31 col.pl. F.
Colas 869

[English heads and coiffures. London, printed for R. Sayer, J. Bennet and J. Smith 1778]
12pl. F.
Colas 870

Dilich, Wilhelm [Schäffer] **called**
Historische beschreibung der fürstlichen kindtauff fräulein Elisabethen zu Hessen ... welche im augusto des 1596 jahrs zu Cassel gehalten worden. Cassel, W. Wessel 1598
81p. illus. 29pl. F.
Lipperheide 2598

Krieges-schule worinnen nach ... der alten Römer und Griechen zu wasser und land geführten ... streit-methode ... gewiesen wird. Franckfurt am Mayn, J. D. Zunner 1689
494,410p. 339 illus. 109pl. F.
First written in 1608 but left unpublished until the present revision of 1689. The illustrations show the arming of the infantry and cavalry and the formation of opposing armies on the field
Lipperheide 2090

Dillmont, Thérèse de
Album de broderies au point de croix. [Dornach, T. de Dillmont 1885-90]
3v. 95 illus. 112pl. Q.
An edition with German text
Lipperheide 4009

Alphabets et monogrammes. [Dornach, 1889]
7p. 60pl. Q.
Lipperheide 4188

L'art chrétien en Egypte; motifs de broderie copte. Dornach (Alsace), T. de Dillmont ca1892
2v. illus. 60pl.(2 col.) Q.
German edition: *Muster altchristlicher kunst in Egypten. Koptische stickereien* (Dornach, T. de Dillmont 1894)
Lipperheide 3874 (German ed.)

The embroiderer's alphabet: letters, figures, monograms and ornaments for embroideries on counted threads, followed by a series of patterns with tracings for white embroidery. Mulhouse, T. de Dillmont [1920]
42p. illus. 92pl.(part col.) ob.Fe.
A translation of her: *Alphabets et monogrammes*

Encyclopédie des ouvrages de dames. [Dornach, 1887]
622p. 893 illus. O.
German edition: *Encyklopaedie der weiblichen handarbeiten* (Dornach, 1888)
Lipperheide 4155-56

Encyclopedia of needlework; new ed., rev. and enl. Mulhouse (France) T. de Dillmont [19—]
809p. illus. XIII col.pl. S.
Published in English, French, Italian and German. Translation of her *Encyclopédie des ouvrages de dames*
LC 24-10486

Dillmont, Thérèse de—*Continued*

Die knüpfarbeit. Dornach, T. de Dillmont 1891
15p. 52 illus. 32pl. Q.
Lipperheide 4167

Recueil d'ouvrages divers à exécuter avec les fils et les cotons D. M. C. Dornach, T. de Dillmont [1888]
24p. 24 illus. Q.
Lipperheide 4157

Die stickerei auf netz-canavas. Dornach, T. de Dillmont [1892]
10p. 14 illus. 20pl. Q.
Lipperheide 4019

Die strickarbeit; 1. serie. Mülhausen (Elsass), Th. de Dillmont 1893?
39p. illus. 10pl. F.
In portfolio
LC 14-14838

Vorlagen für die plattstich-arbeit. Dornach, T. de Dillmont [1894]
7p. 6 illus. 40pl. Q.
Lipperheide 4021

Dillon, Harold Arthur Lee-Dillon, 17th viscount

An Almain armourer's album. See entry under An Almain armourer's album

(ed.) Fairholt, F. W. Costume in England; a history of dress to the end of the eighteenth century

(ed.) Pageants of Richard Beauchamp, earl of Warwick. Pageant of the birth, life and death of Richard Beauchamp

Le **dimanche** d'un bon bourgeois, ou Les tribulations de la petite propriété. Grandville, J. I. I. G., called

Dimier, Louis

Histoire de la peinture de portrait en France au XVIe siècle. Paris et Bruxelles, G. van Oest 1924-26
3v. 64pl. Q.
Bibliography: v3 p[281]-89
Volume 1 is useful for French costume of the 16th century
LC 25-6764

Dinaux, Arthur Martin

Description des fêtes populaires données à Valenciennes les 11, 12, 13 mai 1851; par la Société des Incas. Lille, E. Vanackere 1854
218p. front.(port.) 22pl. Q.
Engraved by W. Marks
Lipperheide 2875. LC 6-4088

Dines, John Henry. See Day, T. A., jt. auth.

Dinkel, M., and Locher, N.

Recueil de portraits et costumes suisses les plus élégants, usités dans les 22 cantons, accompagné d'un supplément. Berne et Bâle, J. P. Lamy ca1820
30 l. 30pl.(part col.) Q.
Plates, engraved by Meichelt, show full length figures. Another edition, issued in 1817, shows half length figures
Colas 872, 871 (1817 ed.) Lipperheide 906m, 911 (1817 ed.)

Diplomatic costume

France

Les anciens uniformes du Ministère des affaires étrangères. 1901

Russia

Rovinskiĭ, D. A. Portraits authentiques des tzars Jean III., Basile son fils et Jean IV. le Terrible, et cinq ambassades de leur époque. 1882

Le **directoire.** Rouveyre, Édouard

Directoire and first Empire dress. London, 1889
55p. O.

Directoire, consulat et empire. Lacroix, Paul

Directoire costume. See France—1789-1799; also similar periods under names of other countries

The **directorium** Anglicanum. Purchas, John

A **directory** of ceremonial. 3d ed. London, Oxford university press, H. Milford, 1931
v,1 front. D. (Alcuin club tracts, XIII[b])
Preface signed by the compilers: A. S. Duncan-Jones, Stephen Gaselee, E. G. P. Wyatt
Companion volume to *Ceremonial pictured in photographs*
LC 31-25282

Der **dirigent** im 20. jahrhundert. Weissmann, Adolf

Disceptatio de stola. See Thiers, J. B. Johannis Baptistae Thiers ... De stola

Discorso ... sopra la castrametatione, & bagni antichi. Du Choul, Guillaume

Discours de la religion des anciens Romains. Du Choul, Guillaume

Discours de l'entrée faicte par ... Henry IIII, roi de France et de Navarre, et ... Marie de Médicis, la royne son epouse, en leur ville de Caen, au mois de septembre 1603. Caen, Mancel 1842
48p. O.
Edited by G. S. Trébutien
Lipperheide 2705

Discours et histoire véritable des navigations ... en la Turquie. See Nicolay, Nicolas de, sieur d'Arfeuille. Les navigations, pérégrinations et voyages, faicts en la Turquie

Les **discours** militaires. Du Praissac

Discours nouveau sur la mode. Paris, P. Ramier 1613
32p. O.
From the *Bulletin* of the Societé archéologique et historique de la Charente, v4, 1850
Colas 873. Lipperheide 3430

Discours sur la castrametation et discipline militaire des anciens Romains. See Du Choul, Guillaume. Discours de la religion des anciens Romains

Discoveries in the ruins of Nineveh and Babylon. See Layard, Sir A. H. A second series of the Monuments of Nineveh

Discurso contra malos trages y adornos lascivos. See Carranza, Alonso. Rogacion en detestacion de los grandes abusos en los traxes

Discurso histórico sobre el trajo de los Españoles. Clonard, S. M. de S. y A., conde de

Discurso sobre el luxô de las señoras, y proyecto du un trage nacional. De orden superior. Madrid, Imprenta real 1788
64p. 3 col.pl. S.
Plates colored by hand. A proposed national costume. Bound with it is *Respuesta à las objectiones que se han hecho contra el proyecta de un trage nacional para las damas* (Madrid, Imprenta real 1788)

Discursos leidos ante la Real academia de ciencias morales y politicas en la recepcion publica. Carramolino, J. M.

Disegni d'alcune opere eseguite in occasione della fausta venuta in Lombardia di S. M. l'imperatore e re Ferdinando primo. Chiappa, G. B.

Disegno, taglio e confezione di biancheria. Bonetti, Emilia

Disel, Matthias. See Diesel, Matthias

Disher, Maurice Willson
Clowns & pantomimes. London, Constable 1925
xix,343p. col.front. illus. pl. ports. facsim. Q.
LC 26-3747

Disquisitio de chirothecarum usu & abusu. Nicolai, Johann

Dissertatio de jocalibus. Müller, Peter, praeses

Dissertatio de jure personarum. See Berger, C. H., edler herr von. Commentatio de personis vulgo

Dissertatio de larvis scenicis et figuris comicis antiquorum Romanorum. See Ficoroni, Francesco. Le maschere sceniche e le figure comiche

Dissertatio historica de Saxo-Vinariensi vigilantiae ordine. Haagen, C. E. C.

Dissertatio historico-critica de imperiali sacra lancea. Koehler, J. D.

Dissertatio philologica de toga & sago. Eiler, J. G., praeses

Dissertation sur la meilleure forme des souliers. Camper, Petrus

Distribution of moccasin decorations among the Plains tribes. Wissler, Clark

Dit is die afcoemste ende genalogie der Hertoghen ende Hertoginnen van Brabant. Thantwerpen, J. Mollijns 1565
37 l. 71 illus. F.
"Vande welcke de eerste was Saluius Brabon met zyn huysvrouwe Swana lj. iaer voor Christus geboorte tot op onsen alderdoorluchtichsten Key. Caro. de v. van dien name ende met zynen sone Philippus Coninck van Spaengien." Subtitle
Illustrations are full-length portraits of counts and countesses of Brabant
Lipperheide 922

Ditchett, Samuel Herbert
Historic costumes; their influence on modern fashions. New York, Textile pub. co. c1920
20p. illus. Q. 50c, o.p.
Reprinted from the *Dry goods economist* of April 3, 1920
Costume index. LC A22-408

Dithmar, Justus Christoph
Justus Christoph Dithmars Nachrichten von dem ... englischen kriegs- und ritter orden des Budes, worinn desselben ursprung ... erkläret, und der ... ritter namen, titel und wapenschilder ... dargestellet werden. Frankfurt an der Oder, J. G. Conradi 1744
16,28p. illus. 20pl. F.
The Latin original was entitled *Commentatio de honoratissimo ordine militari de Balneo* (Francofurti, 1729)
Lipperheide 1905

(ed.) Becmann, J. C. Beschreibung des ritterlichen Johanniter-Orden

Dittmer, Heinrich
Authentische und vollständige beschreibung aller feyerlichkeiten, welche in dem hannoverschen lande bey der anwesenheit ... Georgs des vierten während dem monate october 1821 veranstaltet worden sind. Hannover, H. Dittmer 1822
xvi,349p. 22pl.(part col.) Q.
Lipperheide 2611

Ditzinger, Ludwig
(engr.) Neyffer, J. C. Illustrissimi Wirtembergici

Divat-Tükör. Képes közlöny a divat-es kézimunka köreböl ... felelös szerkestö és kiadó-tulajdonos: Király János. 1889-1890. Budapest, J. Király
Illus.(part col.) F.
A Hungarian illustrated periodical of fashion and needlework, edited by Király
No more published?
Lipperheide 4796

Divers adjustements et usages de Russie. Le Prince, J. B.

See also Le Prince, J. B. Oeuvres

Divers costumes français du règne de Louis XIV. Le Clerc, Sébastien

Divers cris de marchands de Russie. See Le Prince, J. B. Oeuvres

Divers habillemens des anciens Grecs et Romains. Le Clerc, Sébastien

Divers habillemens des femmes de Moscovie. See Le Prince, J. B. Oeuvres

Divers habillements des peuples du nord. See Le Prince, J. B. Oeuvres

Divers habillements des prêtres de Russie. Le Prince, J. B.

Divers habillements des prêtres de Russie les mêmes qui étoient généralement en usage avant la desunion des deux eglises. See Le Prince, J. B. Oeuvres

Divers habillements suivant le costume d'Italie. Greuze, J. B.

Divers ouvrages de belles figures. Carracci, Annibale

Divers paissans d'Hollande. Augspourg, J. Wolff ca1700
4pl. Q.
The first plate bears the title. The others are without signature or legend
Colas 874

Diversaru nationum habitus. Bertelli, Pietro

Diversarum gentium armatura equestris. Bruyn, Abraham de

Diversarum nationum ornatus. Fabri, Alexandro de

Le **diverse** et artificiose machine. Ramelli, Agostino

Diverse figure. Carracci, Annibale

Diverse figure & paesi. Della Bella, Stefano

Diverses figures chinoises et tartares. Watteau, J. A.

Diverses modes. Picart, Bernard

Diverses exercices de cavalerie. Della Bella, Stefano

Diverses petitte figure des cris de Paris. Guerard, N.

Diversi pensieri. Rugendas, G. P.

Diversitez d'habillemens à la mode. Saint-Igny, Jean de

Divertimenti pubblici nelle feste religiose del secolo XVIII dentro e fuori delle porte di Roma. Bertolotti, Antonino

Les **divertissemens** de Versailles. Félibien, André, sieur des Avaux et de Javercy

Divesarum gentium armatura equestris. Bruyn, Abraham de

Divisie chronycke. See Die cronycke van Hollant, Zeelant ende Vrieslant

Divoire, Fernand

Pour la danse. Paris, Éditions de la danse 1935

392p. illus. O.

Illustrations show dance costume of all countries, including Asiatic and American

Dix grandes tables ... de Charles 3. See La Ruelle, Claude de. Decem insignes tabulae

Dix-huit heures de la journée d'une parisienne. Devéria, Achille

XVIIIme siècle; institutions, usages et costumes. Lacroix, Paul

XVIIIme siècle; lettres, sciences et arts. Lacroix, Paul

Le **XIX**e siècle. Robida, Albert

XIXe siècle (en France). Grand-Carteret, John

Dixie after the war. Avary, Mrs M. L.

Dixon, Joseph Kossuth

The vanishing race, the last great Indian council; a record in picture and story of the last great Indian council, participated in by eminent Indian chiefs from nearly every Indian reservation in the United States. Garden City, N.Y., Doubleday, Page & company 1913

xviii,231p. front. pl. ports. map. Q. $3.50 o.p.

Costume index. LC 13-24815

XVIIme siècle; institutions, usages et costumes. Lacroix, Paul

XVIIme siècle; lettres, sciences et arts. Lacroix, Paul

Dmitri Donskoy. See Theatrical costume—Special play, ballets, etc.—Dmitri Donskoy

Dobrovský, Josef

Dobrowsky's Slavin. Bothschaft aus Böhmen an alle slawischen völker, oder beiträge zu ihrer charakteristik, zur kenntniss ihrer mythologie, ihrer geschichte und alterthümer, ihrer literatur und ihrer sprachkunde nach allen mundarten. Prag, Mayregg'sche buchhandlung 1834

496p. col.front. pl.(1 col.) ports. fold. facsims. D.

Lipperheide 875. LC 2-2679

Dobson, Austin

The ballad of Beau Brocade, and other poems of the XVIIIth century ... with fifty illustrations by Hugh Thomson. London, K. Paul, Trench, Trübner & co. 1892

xiii,89p. front. illus. 25pl. Q.

LC 12-31857

Dobson, George

St Petersburg, painted by F. De Haenen. London, A. & C. Black 1910

xii,167p. 32pl.(16 col.) fold.map. O.

Colored plates accompanied by guard sheets with descriptive letterpress

LC 10-36067

Dobson, George; Grove, Henry M., and Stewart, Hugh

Russia; painted by F. De Haenen, text by G. Dobson, H. M. Grove, and H. Stewart. London, A. and C. Black 1913

x,479p. col.front. pl.(part col.) col.ports. fold.map. O. 20s, o.p. (Color books of travel and description)

Each colored plate accompanied by guard sheet with descriptive letterpress

Costume index. LC A14-1683

Dobson, W. L.

£20 prize essay on cutting by block patterns. With additions and practical remarks on practical tailoring by T. D. Humphreys; 2d edition. London, Simpkin, Marshall [1884]

15p. diagrs. Q.

Dockery, Mrs S. Roope

(illus.) Koebel, W. H. Portugal

Documenti inediti per la storia delle armi da fuoco italiane. Angelucci, Angelo

Documents pour l'histoire du costume de Louis XV à Louis XVIII. Schéfer, Gaston

Documents pour servir à l'histoire de l'armement. Giraud, J. B.

Documents sur l'importation des armes italiennes à Lyon à l'époque de la renaissance 1897. See Giraud, J. B. Documents pour servir à l'histoire de l'armement au moyen âge et à la renaissance

Dodd, Ira Seymour

The pictorial life of Christ; eighty sculptural reliefs by Dominico Mastroianni; text by Ira S. Dodd. New York city, Christian herald 1912

202p. incl.front. illus. Q. $2

LC 12-29410

Dodge, Louise. See Preston, H. W., jt. auth.

Dodge, Richard Irving

Our wild Indians. Hartford, A. D. Worthington 1882

xxxix,650p. front. pl.(part col.) ports. O. $3.50 o.p.

Reprinted 1883, 1884, 1890 with same plates

Costume index. LC 2-14104

Dodgson, Campbell
Catalogue of early German and Flemish woodcuts, preserved in the Department of prints and drawings in the British museum. London, Longmans 1903-11
2v. 36pl. Q.
Plates show 15th and 16th century costume

Dodwell, Edward
A classical and topographical tour through Greece, during the years 1801, 1805, and 1806. London, Rodwell & Martin 1819
2v. illus. 30pl.(2 col.) map. Q.
Most of the plates show costume
Colas 875. LC 4-35187

Views in Greece, from drawings by Edward Dodwell. London, Rodwell and Martin 1821
[66]p. 30 col.pl. F.
English and French
The same plates are in his: *A classical and topographical tour* but not all in color
Colas 876. Lipperheide 1444. LC 12-19075

Döbel, Heinrich Wilhelm
Heinrich Wilhelm Döbels Neueröffnete jäger-practica; 2. verm. aufl. Leipzig, J. S. Heinsii sel. erben 1754
14,32 l. 148,264,184,108p. illus. 21pl. F.
First edition 1746
Lipperheide 3027

Doeg, John Hope, and Danzig, Allison
Elements of lawn tennis (In Aldin, C. C. W. The omnibus book of sports for young and old. Part 1)

Doege, Heinrich
Die trachtenbücher des 16. jahrhunderts. Leipzig, O. Harrassowitz 1903
p429-44. O.
From *Beitrage zur bücherkunde und philologie,* 1903

Döhner, Kurt Meyer-. See Meyer-Döhner, Kurt

Dörbeck, Franz Burchard
Berliner ausrufer, costüme und locale gebräuche. Berlin, Gropius ca1830
16 col.pl. Q.
Colas 877. Lipperheide 819

Berliner redensarten. Berlin, Gropius ca1830
30 col.pl. Q.
Lipperheide 3530

Berliner witze und anecdoten. Berlin, Gropius ca1830
8 l. 32 col.pl. F.
Engraved by B. Doerbeck, Hosemann and others
Lipperheide 3531

Masken-anzüge zu polter-abenden und bällen. Berlin, Gropius 1831
24 col.pl. Q.
Colas 878. Lipperheide 3173

Dörig, James
La mode et la couture. Paris, chez l'auteur [1925]
318p. S.
Colas 884

Doering, Heinrich. See Lehmann, Walter, jt. auth.

Döring, Julius
(illus.) Duller, Eduard. Das deutsche volk

Dôffémont
Avis très-important au public. Sur différentes espèces de corps & de ceintures, d'un nouvelle invention. Paris, D. C. Couturier père 1775
32p. S.
Colas 879

Dogaressas
Staley, J. E. The dogaressas of Venice (the wives of the doges) 1910

Il **doge** di Venezia. Cecchetti, Bartolomeo

Doges
Misson, F. M. Herrn Maximilian Missons Reisen aus Holland durch Deutschland in Italien. 1701

Venice

Cecchetti, Bartolomeo. Il doge di Venezia. 1864
Kellner, Heinrich. Chronica, das ist: Wahrhaffte eigentliche und kurtze beschreibung aller hertzogen zu Venedig leben ... von den ersten biss auff den jetzt regierenden. 1574
Matina, Leone. Ducalis regiae lararium, sive Ser'me Reipv. Venetae principũ omniũ icones usque ad ... Ioannem Pisaurum qui nunc rerũ feliciter potitur, elogia. 1659

Dohme, Robert. See Geschichte der deutschen kunst

Dolby, Mrs Anastasia Marice
Church embroidery, ancient and modern, practically illustrated by Anastasia Dolby. London, Chapman and Hall 1867
176p. fold.col.front. illus. 20pl. O.
LC 12-12359

Church vestments: their origin, use, and ornament, practically illustrated. London. Chapman & Hall 1868
203p. fold.col.front. illus. 37pl. O. 21s, o.p.
Colas 880. Costume index. LC 12-8567

Dóll, J.
(engr.) Kok, W. Illumination in Amsterdam am 8. märz 1788

The **doll** book. Starr, L. B.

Dollet, Victor
(illus.) Galerie dramatique, costumes de théâtre

Dolls
Boehn, Max von. Dolls and puppets. 1932
Boehn, Max von. Puppen und puppenspiele. 1909
Caiger, G. Dolls on display. 1933
Frankfort-on-Main. International puppenausstellung, 1911. Offizieller führer. 1911
Gröber, Karl. Kinderspielzeug aus alter zeit, eine geschichte des spielzeugs. 1928
Hooper, Elizabeth. Dolls the world over. 1936
Howard, O. O. My life and experiences among our hostile Indians. 1907
Lesser, Friederike. Die kleine puppenschneiderin. 1861
Low, F. H. Queen Victoria's dolls. 1894

Dolls—*Continued*
Muller, Samuel, and Vogelsang, Willem. Holländische patrizierhäuser. 1909
Rumpf, Fritz, and Erich, O. A., illus. Spielzug der völker. 1922
Russia. Glavnve upravlenīe zemleustroīstra ī zemledīê liîâ. L'art populaire russe à la seconde exposition koustare. 1914
Sézan, Claude. Les poupées anciennes. 1930
Singleton, Esther. Dolls. c1927
Starr, L. B. The doll book. 1908
White, Gwen. A picture book of ancient & modern dolls. 1928

See also Puppets

Dolls and puppets. Boehn, Max von
Dolls on display. Caiger, G.
Dolls the world over. Hooper, Elizabeth
Dolly Madison. Goodwin, Mrs M. W.

Dolmetsch, Heinrich
(ed.) Japanische vorbilder. Ein sammelwerk zur veranschaulichung japanischer kunstprodukte ... nach japanischen originalmustern. Stuttgart, J. Hoffmann [1886]
2p.l. 50pl.(part. col.) F.
Lipperheide 4378. LC 2-26055

Der **Dom** zu Halberstadt. Hermes, E.

Domanig, Karl
Porträtmedaillen des erzhauses Oesterreich von Kaiser Friedrich III. bis Kaiser Franz II. Wien, Gilhofer & Ranschburg 1896
40p. 50pl. F. (Kunsthistorische sammlungen des allerhöchsten kaiserhauses)
Lipperheide 870

Domashniĭ byt' russkīkh" tsarīts" v" XVI ī XVII st. Zabīelin, Ī. E.

Domaszewski, Alfred von. See Petersen, E. A. H., jt. ed.

Dombrowski, Ernst, ritter von. See Hicfelt, Eberhard. Aucupatorium Herodiorum

Domeny de Rienzi, Grégoire Louis
Océanie, ou cinquième partie du monde. Revue géographique et ethnographique de la Malaisie, de la Micronésie, de la Polynésie et de la Mélanésie. Paris, Firmin Didot frères 1836-38
3v. illus.(music) pl. ports. fold.maps. O. (L'univers. v19-21)
LC 3-10095

Domestic needlework. Seligman, G. S., and Hughes, Talbot

Domville-Fife, Charles William
Guatemala and the states of Central America. London, F. Griffiths 1913
310p. front.(fold.map) pl. O.
LC War13-259

Savage life in the black Sudan; an account of an adventurous journey of exploration amongst wild & little-known tribes ... with a description of their manner of living, secret societies & mysterious & barbaric rites. London, Seeley, Service 1927
284p. front. illus. pl. 2 fold.maps. O.
LC 27-19492

Donaldson, Anna M. See Manning, Sibylla, jt. auth.

Donaldson, Thomas Corwin
The George Catlin Indian gallery in the U.S. National museum (Smithsonian institution), with memoir and statistics. Washington, Govt. print. off. 1886
939p. 9 facsims. 149pl. 3 ports. O. 80c
Reprint from the report of the Smithsonian institution, U.S. National museum 1885. Contains reprints of the plates from Catlin's *Letters and notes*, etc.
Costume index. LC 2-14082

Moqui Pueblo Indians of Arizona and Pueblo Indians of New Mexico. See entry under United States. Census office. 11th census, 1890

Donat, F. M. von
Bekleidungs-vorschrift für offiziere, sanitätsoffiziere und obere militärbeamte der reserve und landwehr und mit uniform verabschiedete offiziere des XIII (königl. württ.) armeekorps. Stuttgart, J. B. Metzler 1897
42p. O.
Lipperheide 2208

Donation d'antiquités égyptiennes aux Musées royaux de Bruxelles. Capart, Jean

Die **Donau.** Heksch, A. F.

Donauer, Johann Christoph
(ed.) Florin, F. P. Oeconomus prudens et legalis

Doncourt, A. S. de, pseud. See Drohojowska, A. J. F. A. S. de L., comtesse

Doniol, Henri
Voyage pittoresque dans la Basse-Auvergne. See note under Michel, Adolphe. L'ancien Auvergne et le Velay

Donna Clara, pseud.
L'eleganza femminile. Torino, Lattes 1907
251p. O.

La **Donna,** la casa, il bambino; revista mensile di ricamo, moda, biancheria 1930+ Milano
Illus. F. 14.40 l.
Published monthly. Current 1938

Donne, Thomas Edward
Maori, past and present. Philadelphia J. B. Lippincott 1927
287p. front. illus. pl. ports. O. $6 o.p
Contains two chapters on tattooing (p141-57) English edition published by Seeley service, 1927
Costume index. LC 28-8421 (English ed.)

Donne e gioielli in Sicilia. Lanza D Scalea, Pietro

Donner, Mizi
(ed.) Stil im kinderkleid. Leipzig, O Beyer 1924
11 l. col.illus. ob.D.

Donovan, Dulcie Godlove
The mode in dress and home. Boston New York, Allyn and Bacon c193
445p. col.front. illus.(part col.) col.pl diagrs. D.
Bibliographies at end of each chapter
LC 35-10152

Dooley, William Henry
Clothing and style, for dressmakers, milliners, buyers, designers, students of clothing, and stylers. Boston, New York [etc] D.C. Heath c1930
xii,441p. illus. O.
LC 30-13456

Doolittle, Justus
Social life of the Chinese ... Ed. and rev. by the Rev. Paxton Hood. London, S. Low, son, and Marston 1868
xxxii,633p. front. illus. 11pl. D.
Illustrations show costume
LC 5-9319

Dopler, J. and Müller, C.
Vollständige bildliche darstellung der gesammten löblichen uniformirten bürgerschaft der K. auch K. K. haupt- und residenz-stadt Wien nach dem neuesten costume 1806. Wien, im verlage der K.K. priv. chemischen druckerey. [1806]
2 l. 38 col.pl. Q.
Plates are signed by the engravers
Colas 882

Doran, John
Habits and men, with remnants of record touching the makers of both. London, R. Bentley 1854
417p. D.
Colas 883. LC 12-31855

Doré, Gustave
Les différents publics de Paris. Paris, Journal amusant [1854]
20pl. Q.
Lipperheide 3623

The Doré Bible gallery, containing one hundred superb illustrations, and a page of explanatory letter-press facing each. Philadelphia, W. T. Amies 1883
107 l. front.(port.) 100pl. Q.
LC 10-2263

Folies gauloises depuis les Romains jusqu'à nos jours; album de moeurs et de costumes. Paris, Journal amusant 1859
20pl. ob.Q.
Cover-title
The same plates are found in his *Historical cartoons*
Colas 883bis

Histoire pittoresque, dramatique et caricaturale de la Sainte Russie, d'après les chroniqueurs et historiens Nestor, Nikan, Sylvestre, Karamsin, Ségur. Paris, J. Bry 1854
207p. 500 illus. Q.
LC 5-13907

Historical cartoons; or, Rough pencillings of the world's history from the first to the nineteenth century with descriptive text by Thomas Wright. London, J. C. Hotten [1865]
20 l. 20pl. ob.Q.
Plates are the same as those in his *Folies gauloises,* with the legends in English
Colas 883ter

Two hundred sketches, humorous and grotesque. London, F. Warne 1867
86p. front. illus. sq.F.
LC 11-29121

(illus.) Davillier, J. C., baron. L'Espagne

(illus.) Davillier, J. C., baron. Spain

(illus.) E., G. R. Story of Arthur and Guinevere

(illus.) Jerrold, Blanchard. London; a pilgrimage

(illus.) Michaud, J. F. History of the crusades

(illus.) Øverland, O. A. Korstogenes historie

Doré, Henri
Recherches sur les superstitions en Chine. Chang-Hai, La mission catholique 1911-36
17v. illus. col.pl. ports. O. (Variétés sinologiques, no32, 34, 36, 39, 41-42, 44-46, 48-49, 51, 57, 61, 62)
Contents: v 1-4 Les pratiques superstitieuses; v5 La lecture des talismans chinois; v6-12 Le Panthéon chinois; v13 Popularisation du Confucéisme, du Bouddhisme et du Taoïsme en Chine; v14 La doctrine du Confucéisme; v15 Vie illustrée du Bouddha Cakyamouni; v16 Inde-Chine jusqu'aux T'ang; v17 Chine depuis les T'ang jusqu'à nos jours

Researches into Chinese superstitions, by Henry Doré ... translated from the French with notes, historical and explanatory, by M. Kennelly. Shanghai, T'usewei printing press, 1914-33
10v. illus. pl.(part col.) facsims.(part col.) O.
Translation of his *Recherches sur les superstitions en Chine*
LC 26-18204

Doré, Louis Auguste Gustave. See Doré, Gustave

The **Doré** Bible gallery. Doré, Gustave

Dorinda, pseud.
Needlework for ladies for pleasure and profit; 3d ed. rev. and enl. London, S. Sonnenschein, Lowrey & co. 1886
172p. O.
First edition 1882
Lipperheide 4140

Dorn, Anna. See Lipperheide, Frieda, jt. auth.

Dorregaray, José Gil
(ed.) Historia de las órdenes de caballería y de las condecoraciones españolas; redactada por ... Benavides, Cervino [and others] ... Publícala el editor Don José Gil Dorregaray. Madrid, T. Rey 1865
2v. 64 col.pl. F.
"Apéndice" at end (184p. 4pl.)
Thirty-nine plates show dress of the orders and the rest show insignia. Includes orders and decorations of honor of Spain, other European countries, and of some countries outside Europe
Lipperheide 1934

Dorsey, George Amos
A copper mask from Chimbote, Peru. Washington, D.C. Judd & Detweiler, printers 1897
cover-title, [413]-14p. pl. O.
From the American anthropologist for December 1897
LC 8-29783

Dorsey, George Amos, and Voth, Henry R.
The Mishongnovi ceremonies of the snake and antelope fraternities. Chicago, 1902
p[161]-261. LXXV-CXLVII pl.(part col.) O. (Field Columbian museum. Publication 66. Anthropological series. v III no3)
Each plate accompanied by guard sheet with descriptive letterpress
Colored plates show costume of the antelope fraternity of the Hopi Indians
LC 4-12213

The Oraibi Soyal ceremony. Chicago, 1901
59p. XXVII pl. O. (Field Columbian museum. Publication 55. Anthropological series. v III no 1)
Each plate accompanied by guard sheet with descriptive letterpress
Plates show masks of the Hopi Indians
LC 4-12216

Das **Dortmunder** wandschneider-buch. Becker, Hermann

Dosformiga spännen från vikingetiden. Rydh, H. A.

Dost, Wilhelm, and Stenger, Erich
Die daguerreotype in Berlin, 1839-1860. Berlin, R. Bredow 1922
123p. front. illus. O.

Doubek, Franz Bohumil
(illus.) Das was verschwindet

Douce, Francis
Illustrations of Shakspeare, and of ancient manners. London, Longman, Hurst, Rees, and Orme 1807
2v. illus. IX pl. O.
Engraved by J. Berryman
LC 18-4855

See also Smith, J. T. The cries of London

Doucet, Jérôme
Les petits métiers de Paris. Paris, Ollendorff 1901
93p. 140 illus. O. 3fr.
Lipperheide 1190i

Douglas, Mrs Fanny
The gentlewoman's book of dress. London, Henry [1894]
191p. pl. O.
Colas 885. Lipperheide 3304

The imperial macramé lace-book; first, second & third series. London, T. Scott ca1875
41p. 17pl. O.
Lipperheide 4110

Douglas, Loudon MacQueen
The kilt; a manual of Scottish national dress. Edinburgh, A. Elliot 1914
49p. 5pl. 2 port. D.
Bibliography: p38-49

Douville, Jean Baptiste
Voyage au Congo et dans l'intérieur de l'Afrique equinoxiale, fait dans les années 1828, 1829 et 1830. Paris, J. Renouard 1832
3v. front. O. and atlas of 20pl (13 col.) Q.
Seventeen plates show native costume and weapons
Colas 886. Lipperheide 1587

12 costumes d'Italie. Barbault, Jean

Les **douze** dames de rhétorique. Batissier, Louis

Les **douze** mois. Compte-Calix, F. C.

Les **douze** mois de l'année. Romme

XII portraits d'enfants. Grévedon, P. L. H.

XII sujets variés composés et dessinés sur pierre. Grenier, François

Dowd, Francis Joseph
(ed.) Pyle, Howard, illus. Howard Pyle's book of the American spirit

Dowden, Edward
Shakespeare scenes and characters. A series of illustrations designed by Adamo, Hofman, Makart, Pecht, Schwoerer, and Spiess; engraved on steel by Bankel, Bauer, Goldberg, Raab, and Schmidt, with explanatory text selected and arranged by Prof. E. Dowden. London, Macmillan 1876
276p. 36 illus. Q.
The illustrations are the same as in *Shakespeare-galerie* by A. F. Pecht
LC A30-324

Downs, Harold
(ed) Theatre and stage; a modern guide to the performance of all classes of amateur dramatic, operatic, and theatrical work. London, Sir I. Pitman 1934
2v. front. illus. col.pl. ports. fold.plan. O.
Bibliography: v 1 p587-90
Contains a chapter on the creation of modern masks
LC 35-5363

Downs, Marie, and O'Leary, Florence
Elements of costume design for high school students; illus. by Louise Sarrazin. Milwaukee, Wis., Bruce c1923
64p. incl.front. illus. O.
LC 23-12774

Doyé, Franz von Sales
Die alten trachten der männlichen und weiblichen orden sowie der geistlichen mitglieder der ritterlichen orden, mit erläuterungen zu Peter Bohmanns abbildungen von F. [!] K. Wietz zusammengestellt von Franz von Sales Doyè. Leipzig, Vier quellen verlag [1930]
96p. 160 col.pl. on 80 l. O.
Issued also as a supplement in the second volume of the author's *Heilige und selige der römischkatholischen kirche* (Leipzig, 1930)
"Literatur": verso of 2d prelim. leaf
LC 31-5518

Doyle, Alexander
Neu alamodische ritterliche fecht- und schirm-kunst. Nürnberg, P. Lochner 1715
63 l. 1 pl. 59 illus. Q.

Doyle, James William Edmund
A chronicle of England, B. C. 55—A. D. 1485, written and illustrated by James E. Doyle. London, Longman, Green, Longman, Roberts, & Green 1864
462p. col.illus. Q.
Illustrations, engraved by Edmund Evans, show costume
LC 2-13062

Doyle, Richard
Birds-eye views of modern society. London, 1864?
1 l. xvi pl. ob.O.
Reprinted from the *Cornhill magazine*
LC 3-14026

Manners and customs of ye Englyshe. [London] Bradbury & Evans [1849]
[86]p. 40pl. ob.O.
Illustrations are a satire on the life of the English people in 1849

D'Oyley, Sir Charles
(illus.) Williamson, Thomas. The costume and customs of modern India

Dozy, Reinhart Pieter Anne
Dictionnaire détaillé des noms des vêtements chez les Arabes. Amsterdam, J. Müller 1845
444p. 23x23cm.
Colas 889. LC 8-95

Dragten der Boeren en Boerinner, in Holland, Vriesland, Braband, en elders. See Allard, A. Habillemens des païsans et païsannes de Holland, de Frise, de Braband et autres provinces

Drahan, Em.
K.K. Oesterr. museum. Stickmuster. Wien, A. Hartinger 1873
2 l. 29pl. O.
Lipperheide 3986

Drake, Maurice, and Drake, Wilfred
Saints and their emblems ... illus. by XII. plates from photographs and drawings by Wilfred Drake, with a foreword by Aymer Vallance. London, T. W. Laurie 1916
xiii,235p. col.front. XI pl.(3 col.) F.
LC 16-25117

Drake, T.
Album vendéen, illustration des histoires de la Vendée militaire. Dessins par T. Drake, texte par Albert Lemarchand. Angers, Lainé frères 1856-60
2v. 125 col.pl. F.
Plates are marked Drake del., Daniaud, lith.
Colas 890

Drake, Wilfred. See Drake, Maurice, jt. auth.

Dramatic bibliography. Baker, Mrs B. M.

Dramatische spiele. Costenoble, C. L.

Draner, pseud. See Renard, Jules

Draping and dress design. Evans, Mary

A **drawing** book of figures. Watteau, J. A.

Drawings faithfully copied from nature at Naples. Rehberg, Friedrich

Drawings ... prepared ... to illustrate an intended autobiography. Cruikshank, George

The **dream** of Poliphilus; fac-similes of one hundred and sixty-eight woodcuts in the "hypnerotomachia Poliphili," Venice, 1499. Colonna, Francesco

Dreger. See Russia. Komītet dlī͡a īzdanīi͡a drevnosteĭ Rossīĭkago gosudarstva. Drevnostī Rossīĭskago gosudarstva

Dreger, Max
Schwerter-sammlung des herrn ... M. Dreger, Berlin ... Collection of swords of ... M. Dreger. [Zurich, O. Füssli 1927]
23,23p. 24pl. F.
On cover: ... Versteigerung am 2. August 1927 in Luzern durch die Häuser Th. Fischer, Luzern, E. Kahlert & sohn, Berlin
German and English on opposite pages; paged in duplicate

Dreger, Moriz
Die Wiener spitzenausstellung 1906. See entry under Vienna. Österreichisches museum für kunst und industrie

Drei jahrhunderte der fechtkunst in Steiermark. Feeder, J.

Dreier, Johan Friedrich Leonhard
(illus.) Lexow, E. J. Joh. F. L. Dreiers norskefolkedragter

Drescher, Karl
(ed.) Das nürnbergische schönbartbuch nach der Hamburger handschrift

Dresden types. Moré, G.

Dresden. Historisches museum und gewehrgalerie
Führer durch das Königliche historische museum ... von M. v. Ehrenthal. 2. aufl., hrsg. von der generaldirektion der Königlichen sammlungen. Dresden, Druck von W. Baensch 1897
225p. illus. plan. D.
LC 21-12662

Kostbare waffen aus der Dresdner rüstkammer. Leipzig, K. W. Hiersemann 1923
164p. col.front. 80(i.e. 81)pl.(1 col.) F.
At head of title: Erich Haenel
LC 24-24011

Dresden. K. Kunstgewerbemuseum
Posamente des XVI.-XIX. jahrhunderts, hrsg. von ... E. Kumsch. Dresden, Stengel & Markert 1892
25pl. F.
At head of title: K. Kunstgewerbemuseum zu Dresden und Kunstgewerbemuseum zu Leipzig
Lipperheide 4170

Spitzen und weiss-stickereien des XVI.-XVIII. jahrhunderts, hrsg. von Emil Kumsch. Dresden, Stengel & Markert 1889
1 l. 50pl. F.
Lipperheide 4053. LC 10-11197

Dresdner rüstkammer. See Dresden. Historisches museum und gewehrgalerie. Kostbare waffen aus der Dresdner rüstkammer

Das **Dresdner** schauspielerrelief. Bieber, Margarete

Dresdner spielzeug aus den Dresdner werkstätten für handwerkskunst. Dresden, [1904]
16 l.(with 57 illus.) O.
Lipperheide 3151c

Dress. Oliphant, Mrs M. O. W.

Dress and address. By the author of The Greeks, Pigeons, Fashion, Modern belles, Modern beaux, Life, high and low, Tonight, Ton, &c. Dedicated to the merveilleux of either sex; 3d ed. London, J. J. Stockdale 1829
201p. 6 col.pl. D.
Plates engraved by C. Williams

Dress and adornment in the Mountain province of Luzon, Philippine islands. Vanoverbergh, Morice

Dress and care of the feet. Peck, J. L.

Dress and health. Jessop, C. M.

Dress and insignia worn at His Majesty's court. Great Britain. Lord chamberlain

Dress and look slender. Wells, J. W.

Dress and ornaments in ancient Peru. Montell, Gösta

Dress and ornaments of certain American Indians. Carr, Lucien

Dress and Vanity fair. See Vanity fair, 1913-36

Dress as a fine art. Merrifield, Mrs M. P.

Dress: as it has been, is, and will be. Walker, Isaac

Dress cutting. Guerre, Alice

Dress cutting and making on tailors principles. Hicks, Mrs R.

Dress design. Hughes, Talbot

Dress design and selection. Hopkins, Mrs M. S.

Dress, drinks, and drums. Crawley, A. E.

Dress fastening devices from the bone pin to the koh-i-noor, The evolution of. Manchester, Herbert

The **dress** of the ancient Egyptian. Cartland, B. M.

The **dress** of the First regiment of life guards, in three centuries. Broughton, U. H. R.

Dress reform. See Reform of dress

Dress reform. Harman, E. B.

Dress-reform. Woolson, Mrs A. L. G.

Dress reform practically and physiologically considered. Merritt, Mrs M. A.

Dress regulations for the army ... 1911. Great Britain. War office

Dress regulations for the army ... 1934. Great Britain. War office

Dress regulations for the army. (Provisional) 1928. Great Britain. War office

Dress regulations for the officers of the army ... 1900. Great Britain. War office

Dress regulations for the officers of the army ... 1904. Great Britain. War office

Dress worn at court. See Great Britain. Lord chamberlain. Dress worn by gentlemen at His Majesty's court

Dress worn at His Majesty's court. Great Britain. Lord chamberlain

Dress worn by gentlemen at His Majesty's court. Great Britain. Lord chamberlain

The **dress** you wear and how to make it. Rhoe, Mrs M. J.

Dress-cutting, drafting, and French pattern modelling. Browne, M. P.

Dresses and decorations of the middle ages. Shaw, Henry

The **dresses** of the mistresses of the White House. Hoes, Mrs R. G.

Dresses of the representatives of the people. Grasset de Saint Sauveur, Jacques

The **dressmaker.** Butterick publishing company, limited

Dressmaking. Fales, Jane

Dressmaking made easy. Leverton, Mrs Waldemar

Dreux du Radier, Jean François

L'Europe illustre. Paris, Odieuvre [et] Le Breton 1755-65

6v. fronts. ports. Q.

"Contenant l'histoire abrégée des souverains, des princes, des prélats, des ministres, des grands capitaines, des magistrats, des savans, des artistes & des dames célèbres en Europe; dans le xve siècle compris jusqu'à présent." Subtitle

Later edition (Paris, Nyon 1777)

The 600 plates are half-length portraits which show costume from the 15th to the 18th century

Lipperheide 316 (1777 ed.)

Drevnostī Rossīĭskago gosudarstva. Russia. Komītet dlīa īzdanīia drevnosteĭ Rossiĭkago gosudarstva

Drews, Paul

Der evangelische geistliche in der deutschen vergangenheit. Jena, E. Diederichs 1905

145p. illus. facsims. Q. (Monographien zur deutschen kulturgeschichte. XII bd)

LC 5-43021

Drey beschreibungen. Ramhoffsky, J. H.

Drey schöne und lustige bücher von der Hohen Zollerischen hochzeyt, Frischlin, Jacob

Driejaarige reize naar China. Ides, E. Y.

Driesch, Gerhard Cornelius von den

Historische nachricht von der röm. kays. gross-botschaft nach Constantinopel welche Damian Hugo von Virmondt verrichtet. Nürnberg, P. C. Monath 1723

19 l. 494p. 12pl.(ports.) Q.

Portraits of the Emperor Charles VI and and his family and of the Turkish embassy in Vienna, the Turkish sultan and grand-vizier, engraved by G. D. Heumann and A. Nunzer

Lipperheide 1416

Driesen, Otto

Der ursprung des harlekin. Berlin, A. Duncker 1904

xii,286p. illus. O. (Forschungen zur neueren literaturgeschichte. XXV)

Illustrations show Harlequin masks and costumes

LC 4-12138

Drilkonst, of hedendaaghsche wapenoeffening. Buren, Hendrik van

Die **drillkunst.** Gheyn, Jacob de

Das **dritte** Brandenburgische reformationsjubiläum. Frege, Ludwig

Dritte buch America. See Staden, Hans, and Lery, Jean de. Americae tertia pars

Drohojowska, Antoinette Josephine Françoise Anna (Symon de Latreiche) comtesse

La Perse, géographie, histoire, moeurs, gouvernement [by A. S. de Doncourt, pseud] Lille; Paris, J. Lefort [1885]

328p. illus. Q.

Ninety-nine of the illustrations show costume

Colas 881

La vérité aux femmes sur l'excentricité des modes et de la toilette, par le chevalier A. de Doncourt [pseud] Paris, Périsse frères 1858

71p. S. 0.75fr.

Drouet, Paul L. M.

Causerie sur les dentelles de Normandie au debut du xxe siècle. Enquête artistique et industrielle dédiée à la ve session des Assises de Caumont. Caen, L. Jouan [1913]

61p. illus. pl. O.

Cover title: *Les dentelles de Normandie en 1913*

Drouineau, Gustave
L'hygiène et la mode. La Rochelle, A. Siret 1886
16p. O.
Colas 898

Drouville, Gaspard
Atlas ou collection de 43 costumes persanes, militaires et civil; dessinés par A. Orlowski pour orner le voyage en Perse fait ... par Gaspard Drouville ... 3. tirage. St Petersbourg, A. Pluchart 1823
1 l. 36? pl. F.
Probably one of the printings of the atlas which was part of the first edition of Drouville's *Voyage en Perse*
Colas 900

Voyage en Perse, fait en 1812 et 1813; 2. éd. Paris, Librairie nationale et étrangère 1825
2v. 60 col.pl. O.
First edition (St Petersburg, 1819-21) with plates in a separate atlas. Third edition (Paris, Masson & Yonet 1828)
Colas 901. Lipperheide 1465. LC 3-13430 (3. ed.)

Drovetti, Bernardin
Le voyage à l'oasis du Dakel (In Cailliaud, Frederic. Recherches sur les arts et métiers)

Druggists. See Apothecaries

Druitt, Herbert
A manual of costume as illustrated by monumental brasses. London, A. Moring 1906
xxii,384p. front. 96pl. O. 10s 6d, o.p.
Publisher's lettering: Costume on brasses
English armor and dress of the 14th and 15th centuries
Colas 903. Costume index. LC 6-32704

Drummond, James
Ancient Scottish weapons: a series of drawings ... With introduction & descriptive notes by Joseph Anderson. Edinburgh & London, G. Waterston 1881
56 l. 26p. 54 col.pl. ob.F.
Each plate accompanied by leaf of descriptive letterpress
Lipperheide 1034. LC 11-20050

Drummond de Melfort, Louis Hector, comte de
Traité sur la cavalerie. Paris, G. Desprez 1776
11pl. and atlas of 32pl.(part col.) F.
A reprint (Dresden, 1786) is described as inferior in the quality of the plates

Drumont, Édouard Adolphe
Les fêtes nationales à Paris. Paris, L. Baschet 1879
[189]p. 51 illus. 38pl. F.
Lipperheide 2495. LC 11-3025

Drury, Robert
Madagascar; or, Robert Drury's journal, during fifteen years' captivity on that island. London, T. F. Unwin 1890
398p. front. pl. port. fold.map. facsim. O. (The adventure series)
Edited by S. P. Oliver. First edition (London, 1729)
Illustrations show costume of the natives of Madagascar
LC 5-15921

Dryander, Johann
Artzenei spiegel gemeyner inhalt derselbigen wes bede einem leib unnd wundtartzt in der theoric, practic unnd chirurgei zusteht. Frankfurt am Meyn, C. Egenolph [1557]
153 l.(with 200 illus.) F.
First edition 1542
Lipperheide 2003

Dryden, Alice
(ed.) The art of hunting; or, Three hunting mss. A rev. ed. of The art of hunting, by William Twici, huntsman to King Edward the Second, by H. Dryden, 1844. Ed. by Alice Dryden. Northampton, W. Mark 1908
163p. front. facsims. illus. pl. O.
Contains a chapter on costume
"Bibliography of printed books in English and French upon hunting, written prior to ... 1800": p 141-57
LC A11-1669

(ed.) Palliser, Mrs F. M. History of lace

Dryden, Sir Henry Edward Leigh
(tr.) Dryden, Alice, ed. The art of hunting

Drygalski, Albert von, and Zepelin, Constantin von
Russland. Das heer ... Die flotte, von C. F. Batsch. Berlin, A. Schall [1898]
xviii,662p. front. illus. pl.(part col.) ports. fold.map, fold.plan, fold.tab. O. (Die heere und flotten der gegenwart, 3.bd.)
LC 19-5742

Du costume civil officiel et de l'uniforme militaire des officiers à la cour. 1804 jusqu'à nos jours. Defontaine, Henri

Du costume de l'avocat à travers les âges. Marchand, Louis

Du costume et de la toilette dans l'antiquité et de nos jours. Graterolle, Maurice

Du costume militaire des Français en 1446. Belleval, René, marquis de

Du costume monastique antérieurement au XIII. siècle. Piolin, Paul

Du dandysme et de G. Brummell. Barbey d'Aurevilly, J. A.

Du detatouage. Bailliot, Marcel

Du Khorassan au pays des Backhtiaris. Allemagne, H. R. d'

Du luxe des vêtements au XVIe siècle. Villepelet, Ferdinand

Du port illégal de costume et de décoration. Daubert, Pierre

Du sacre des rois de France. Clausel de Coussergues, J. C.

Du tatouage chez les prostituées. Le Blond, A. W. L., and Lucas, Arthur

Du tatouage en Afrique. Verrier, Eugène

Dubech, Lucien
Histoire générale illustrée du théâtre, par Lucien Dubech, avec la collaboration de Jacques de Montbrial et de Madeleine Horn-Monval. Paris, Librairie de France 1931-34
5v. illus.(incl. plans, music) pls.(part col.) ports. facsims. Q.
With volume 3 Claire Elaine Engel became a joint collaborator
Contents: v 1 Le théâtre Grec. Le théâtre Latin; v2 Le théâtre des miracles et

Dubech, Lucien—*Continued*
des mistères, Le théâtre profane au moyen âge; v3 Le théâtre anglais. Le théâtre français; v4 Le théâtre français. Le théâtre européen du dix-huitième siècle; v5 Le théâtre française. Le théâtre européen
LC 32-18695

Dublin university. See Academic costume—Dublin university

Dubois
Principes d'allemandes. Gravés par Mme Annereau. Paris, Chez l'auteur ca1760
13 l. 12pl. O.
Lipperheide 3074. LC 23-1991

Dubois, Edmond
(pub.) État général des troupes de France sur pied en mai 1748 (uniformes, drapeaux, étendards) par le sieur J. B. V. Réimpression textuelle sauf en ce qui concerne la solde par Edmond Dubois, directeur de la curiosité historique et militaire. Paris, E. Dubois 1901
192p. S.
Colas 992

Dubois de Jancigny, Adolphe Philibert
Japon, Indo-Chine, Empire Birman (ou Ava), Siam, Annam (ou Cochinchine), Péninsule Malaise, etc., Ceylan. Paris, Firmin Didot 1850
666p. 20pl. 3 maps(1 fold.) O. (L'univers. Histoire et description de tous les peuples)
LC 3-10441

Dubouchet
(engr.) Freudenberger, Sigmund. Estampes de Freudeberg pour le Monument du costume
(engr.) Restif de La Bretonne, N. E. Estampes de Moreau-le-jeune pour le Monument du costume

Dubourg, C.
(engr.) Williamson, Thomas. The costume and customs of modern India

Dubourg, Matthew
Views of the remains of ancient buildings in Rome and its vicinity. London, J. Taylor 1820
[32]p. XXVI col.pl. sq.F.
LC 4-32835

Ducalis regiae lararium. Matina, Leone

Ducamp, Jules
Histoire de l'armée d'Orient et de tous les régiments qui ont pris part aux campagnes de la Mer Noire et de la Mer Baltique; illus. par Lalaisse. Paris, A. Barbier 1858
495p. col.front. col.pl. map. Q.

See also Pascal, Adrien, and others. Galerie des victoires et conquêtes de l'armée française

Duces supremi qui elapso saeculo decimo septimo, Caesareis augustissimae domus Austriacae exercitibus summa potestate praefuere. Vienna, L. J. Kaliwoda 1735
186p. 20 ports. O.
Lipperheide 2092

Du Chaillu, Paul Belloni
Explorations and adventures in equatorial Africa; with accounts of the manners and customs of the people ... by Paul B. Du Chaillu; rev. and enl. ed. New York, Harper & brothers 1871
535p. incl. double front. illus. pl. fold. map. O.
LC 16-3209

A journey to Ashango-Land and further penetration into equatorial Africa. London, J. Murray 1867
xxiv,501p. 12 illus. 18pl. map. O.
Illustrations show native costume
American edition: New York, Harper 1874
Lipperheide 1604. LC 16-4358 (Amer. ed.)

The viking age: the early history, manners, and customs of the ancestors of the English-speaking nations. New York, Scribner 1889
2v. fronts. 128 illus.(incl. map, facsims.) O. $7.50, o.p.
Costume index. LC 4-14845

Duchartre, Pierre Louis
La comédie italienne; l'improvisation, les canevas, vies, caractères, portraits, masques des illustres personnages de la commedia dell'arte. Paris, Librairie de France c1924
328p. illus. pl.(part col.) ports. sq.Q.
Bibliography: p324-27
Plates show theatrical costume of the sixteenth to eighteenth century
LC 24-16536

See also Stockholm. Nationalmuseum. Recueil de plusieurs fragments des premières comédies italiennes ... suivi de compositions de m. don Arlequin présentées par P. L. Duchartre

Duchartre, Pierre Louis, and Saulnier, René
L'imagerie populaire; les images de toutes les provinces françaises du xve siècle au second empire. Paris, Librairie de France [1925]
447p. illus. pl.(part col.) Q.
Sources bibliographiques: p443-45
Plates show regional costume of France
LC 26-22761

Duchesne, ainé. See Jeux de cartes tarots et de cartes numérales du quatorzième au dix-huitième siècle

Duchesne, coiffeur
De la necessité de la coiffure pour les hommes distingués: ses rapports avec la civilisation suivi de la manière de mettre son chapeau. Paris, L'auteur 1826
12p. O.
Colas 906. Lipperheide 1696

Duchesne, Alphonse. See Lacroix, Paul, jt. auth.

Du Choul, Guillaume
Discorso ... sopra la castrametatione, & bagni antichi de i Greci, & Romani. Con l'aggiunta della figura del Campo Romano. Et una informatione della militia turchesca, & de gli habiti de soldati Turchi, scritta da M. Francesco Sansovino. Vinegia, presso Altobello Salicato 1582
2v.(80, 28 l.) 5pl.(incl. 57 illus.) O.
An Italian edition of the *Discours.* The second volume contains woodcuts showing Turkish soldiers of the sixteenth century
Lipperheide 148

Discours de la religion des anciens Romains, de la castrametation & discipline militaire d'iceux, des bains & antiques exercitations grecques & romaines; il-

Du Choul, Guillaume—*Continued*
lus. de medailles & figures retirées des marbres antiques qui se treuvent à Rome, & par nostre Gaule. Lyon, G. Roville 1567
2v. in 1. illus. O.
First edition Lyon 1555
Title page volume 2: *Discours sur la castrametation et discipline militaire des anciens Romains*. . . This part contains many woodcuts which show military costume. Part one, which reproduces coins, shows modes of dressing the hair
For an Italian edition see his: *Discorso* listed above

Duckett, Sir George Floyd
Monastic and ecclesiastical costume. Lewes, Farncombe 1892?
23p. O.
Reprinted from volume XXXVIII of the Sussex archeological society's collections
A discussion of costume from the 5th to the 16th century
Colas 907

Dudley, Robert
(illus.) Russell, Sir W. H. A memorial of the marriage of H. R. H. Albert Edward, prince of Wales

Düben, Gustaf Vilhelm Johan von
Om Lappland och Lapparne, företrädesvis de svenske. [Stockholm] P. A. Norstedt [1873]
528p. illus. 8pl.(2 col.) fold.map. O.
Bibliography p500-12
LC 5-15793

Le **duel** à travers les âges. Letainturier-Fradin, Gabriel

Dueminchen, Johannes
Die flotte einer aegyptischen koenigin aus dem XVII. jahrhundert vor unserer zeitrechnung; und altaegyptisches militair im festlichen aufzuge auf einem monumente aus derselben zeit abgebildet. Leipzig, J. C. Hinrichs 1868
22p. 33pl.(1 col.) F.
"Beides zum ersten male veroeffentlicht nach einer vom herausgeber im terrasentempel von Dêr-el-Baheri genommenen copie, mit teilweiser reconstruction. Nebst einem anhange . . . als ein beitrag zur geschichte der schifffahrt und des handels im alterthume." Subtitle
Lipperheide 140

Düntzer, H.
Katalog des museums. See entry under Cologne, Germany. Städtisches museum Wallraff-Richartz

Dürer, Albrecht
Albrecht Dürer's Holzschnitt-werk in königlichen museum zu Berlin. Zum 400-jährigen Dürer-jubiläum hrsg. in der originalgrösse photolithographirt von Gebrüder Burchard in Berlin. Nürnberg, S. Soldan [1871]
3v. 72pl. F.
Lipperheide 662

Albrecht Dürer's Holzschnitt-werk in auswahl mit text hrsg. von Carl von Lützow. Nach den originalen aus der kunstsammlung des fürsten von Hohenzollern in Sigmaringen durch lichtdruck als facsimile ausgeführt von Arnold & Zettler in München. Nürnberg, S. Soldan [1883]
xii p. 60pl. F.
Lipperheide 664

Albrecht Dürer's Kleine passion; getreu in holz nachgeschnitten von C. Deis. Stuttgart, E. Schweizerbart'sche verlags-handlung [1859]
2 l. 37pl. Q.
Also published with title in French, English, and Italian. (Eichstätt & Stuttgart, Krüll 1868) A phototype edition has plates the size of the originals with text by Bruno Meyer (Leipzig, L. Zehl 1887)
Lipperheide 661

Albrecht Dürer's Randzeichnungen aus dem Gebetbuche des kaisers Maximilian I mit eingedrucktem original-texte; nebst einer einleitung von Franz Xaver Stöger. München, G. Franz 1850
8p. 45 col.pl. port. F.
A prayer book with many illustrations of saints forming the border of the text
Lipperheide 658

The complete woodcuts of Albrecht Dürer, edited by Dr. Willi Kurth. [New York, Arden book co. 1936]
41p. 345pl. Q. $2.25
Translated by Silvia M. Welsh
Plates show costume of the 16th century
LC 36-27365

Dürer album ... hrsg. von W. v. Kaulbach und A. Kreling. Nürnberg, J. Zeiser [1856-61]
3v. 42pl. F.
Contents: v 1 Die grosse passion; v2 Das leben der Maria; v3 Aus der offenbarung Johannis, aus dem leben der Heiligen, etc.
Lipperheide 659

Dürer vier holzschnittfolgen phototypisch nachgebildet in der grösse der originale, mit einführendem text. Charlottenburg-Berlin, Helios photographische kunst- und verlags-anstalt 1887
8p. 58pl. F.
Contents: Apokalypse (16pl.); Die grosse passion (12pl.); Das Marienleben (20pl.); Die kleine passion (10pl.)
Lipperheide 669

Ehrenpforte des Kaisers Maximilian I. Wien, A. Holzhausen 1885-86
1 l. 36(i.e. 37)pl. 56x73cm.
Supplement to *Jahrbuch der kunsthistorischen sammlungen* v3-4. Explanatory text is in v4 of the *Jahrbuch*
Illustrated with woodcuts by Albrecht and Hans Dürer and Hans Springinklee
Lipperheide 2502. LC 12-13290

Trachten-bilder ... aus der Albertina. Wien, W. Braumüller 1871
1 l. 5 col.pl. F.
Text by M. Thausing
Colas 923. Lipperheide 663

Triumph des Kaisers Maximilian I. Wien, A. Holzhausen 1883-84
1 l. 137pl. 46x59cm.
Supplement to *Jahrbuch der Kunsthistorischen sammlungen* v 1-2. Explanatory text is in v 1 of the *Jahrbuch*
Illustrated with woodcuts by Albrecht Dürer and Hans Burgkmair. The first plans for the work were made 1512 to 1516 and by 1519 there were 137 plates cut. The edition listed here is a reprint from the original plates, except that nos90 and 132 are from new zinc etchings since the original plates were lost
Lipperheide 2504. LC 12-13290

(illus.) Alt-Nürnberg, schwänke, lieder und tänze d. Hans Sachs

(illus.) Hrotsvit, of Gandersheim. Opera

Dürer, Albrecht, and Wolgemut, Michael
Die gemälde von Dürer und Wolgemut in reproductionen nach den originalen, hrsg. von Sigmund Soldan; text von dr. Berthold Riehl. Nürnberg, S. Soldan [1888]
22p. 98pl. F.
Contains reproductions of 77 paintings by Dürer and 25 by Wolgemut
A supplement, with the same title, containing reproductions of 19 of Dürer's illustrations was published (Nürnberg, J. A. Stein 1895) This has text by H. Thode and is edited by T. Schiener
Lipperheide 671-72

Dürer album. Dürer, Albrecht

Dürer vier holzschnittfolgen phototypisch nachgebildet in der grösse der originale. Dürer, Albrecht

Düringsfeld, Otto, freiherr von Reinsberg. See Reinsberg-Düringsfeld, Otto, freiherr von

Düringsfeld, Ida, freifrau von Reinsberg. See Reinsberg-Düringsfeld, Otto, freifrau von

Düsseldorf. Künstler verein Malkasten. See Shakspeare-album

Dufaux de la Jonchère, Ermance
Le travail manuel; traité pratique de la broderie et de la tapisserie. Paris, Garnier [1894]
567p. 415 illus. 14pl.(1 col.) O.
Lipperheide 4174

Dufèy
(illus.) Mazuy, A. Types et caractères anciens

Duff-Gordon, Caroline Lucie
Home life in Italy; letters from the Apennines. London, Methuen [1908]
xiv,390p. front. pl. O.
Illustrations show folk dress
LC 8-35752

Duflos, C.
(engr.) Guer, J. A. Moeurs et usages des Turcs

Duflos, Pierre, le jeune
(pub.) Nouveau recueil des costumes militaires français et autres nations tant anciennes et modernes
(pub.) Recueil d'estampes, représentant les grades, les rangs et les dignités, suivant le costume de toutes les nations existantes

Dufourny, Léon
(ed.) Seroux d'Agincourt, J. B. L. G. Histoire de l'art par les monumens

Du Fresne, Raphael Trichet. See Trichet du Fresne, Raphael

Du Fresnel, Henri Victor Dollin
Un régiment à travers l'histoire: Le 76e, ex-1er léger.. Préface de François Copée. Paris, E. Flammarion 1893
752p. 9pl.(part col.) F.
Illustrated by G. Gostiaux engraved by L. Rose
Plates show uniforms of the 76th regiment of French infantry, 1671-1893

Dugazon, Gustave
Danses nationales de chaque pays. Paris, Gide fils n.d.
6 col.pl. 36p. of music. ob.O.
Includes music and costumes for the national dance of Russia, Spain, England, Scotland, France, Germany, Engraved by Richomme

Du Halde, Jean Baptiste
Description géographique, historique, chronologique, politique, et physique de l'empire de la Chine et de la Tartarie chinoise; enrichie des cartes générales et particulières de ces pays. Paris, P. G. Lemercier 1735
4v. illus. pl.maps. F.
Also published (nouv. éd. La Haye, H. Scheurleer 1736)
Volume 2, page 82-83 is a double plate with 8 pictures of feminine and 8 of masculine dress: Emperor, mandarins, soldiers, Buddhist priests, and peasants. Page 120 shows women at various occupations. There is a section on fashions volume 2, page 80-81
LC 4-1237 (nouv. éd.)

Dujardin
(ed.) Goncourt, E. L. A. H. de, and Goncourt, J. A. H. de. La femme au dix-huitième siècle

Dulaure, Jacques Antoine
Pogonologie, ou Histoire philosophique de la barbe Par m. J. A. D. Paris, Le Jay 1786
xv,210p. front. S.
Lipperheide 1683. LC 7-21783

Duleep Singh, Frederick, prince
Portraits in Norfolk houses, by the late Prince Frederick Duleep Singh; ed. by Rev. Edmund Farrer. Norwich, Jarrold [1928]
2v. fronts. ports. D.
Portraits, from the 15th century to the present, are arranged by the location of the original and each one is dated either on the plate or in the text. An index to portraits is given
LC A30-1068

Dulin, Pierre
(illus.) Danchet, Antoine, ed. Le sacre de Louis xv

Duller, Eduard
Das deutsche volk in seinen mundarten, sitten, gebräuchen, festen und trachten. Leipzig, G. Wigand 1847
332p. col.front. 49 col.pl. O.
Illustrations by J. Doring, M. Mühlig, and C. W. Schurig. The plates alone are issued separately under the title: *Deutsche volks-trachten*
Colas 910. Lipperheide 737

Dumaresq, Charles Édouard Armand. See Armand-Dumaresq, Charles Édouard

Du Maurier, George Louis Palmella Busson
English society at home; From the collection of "Mr. Punch." London, Bradbury, Agnew & co. 1880
42pl. F.
Descriptive letterpress

Pictures of English society ... from "Punch". New York, D. Appleton 1884
front. 40 illus. T.

Dumont, Jean, baron de Carlscroon
Batailles gagnées par le serenissime prince Fr. Eugene de Savoye sur les ennemis de la foi, et sur ceux de l'empereur & de l'empire, en Hongrie, en Italie, en Allemagne & aux Pais-Bas. La Haye, P. Gosse 1725
132p. 16pl. F.
Illustrations by Jan van Huchtenburgh show military costume 1697 to 1717
Published later in 3 volumes, including a supplement by J. Rousset, with title: *Histoire militaire du prince Eugène de Savoye.* For English edition see his *Military history of prince Eugene of Savoy*
Lipperheide 2108. LC 12-14936

Dumont, Jean, baron de Carlscroon, and Rousset de Missy, Jean
Le military history of Prince Eugene of Savoy ... as also of ... the late Duke of Marlborough ... and of ... the Prince of Nassau-Friezland. London, W. Rayner [1736]
754p. 14pl. F.
This is a translation, by Paul Chamberlen, of the first two volumes of the authors' *Histoire militaire du prince Eugène de Savoye*
Lipperheide 2109

Dumont d'Urville, Jules Sebastien César
(ed.) Voyage pittoresque autour du monde; resumé générale des voyages de découvertes de Magelan, Tasman, Dampier. Paris, L. Tenré 1834-35
2v. illus. 142 double pl. Q.
Plates show costume of natives in the countries visited by explorers and navigators from the time of Magellan
Spanish edition: *Viaje pintoresco al rededor del mundo á las dos Amérigas, Asia y África* (Barcelona, J. Oliveres 1842, 1841. 3v.)
Lipperheide 1458

Du Moulinet, Claude, abbé des Thuileries
Figures de différents habits de chanoines réguliers en ce siècle. Avec un discours sur les habits anciens et modernes des chanoines tant séculiers que réguliers. Paris, S. Piget 1666
144p. 31pl. Q.
Colas 911. Lipperheide 1856

Dumoutier, Gustave
(ed.) Grasset, Eugène. Costumes de guerre de l'âge du bronze et de l'ère gauloise

Duncan, Isadora
Der tanz der zukunft (The dance of the future) eine vorlesung; übers. und eingeleitet von Karl Federn. Leipzig, E. Diederichs 1903
46p. front.(port.) pl. O.
English and German; introduction in German
Lipperheide 3139. LC 5-9931

Duncan-Jones, Arthur Stuart. See A directory of ceremonial

Duncker, Alexander Friedrich Wilhelm
Aus könig Friedrich's zeit, kriegs- und friedens-helden. See entry under Menzel, A. F. E. von

Dunhill, Alfred
The pipe book. London, A. & C. Black 1924
x,262p. col.front. illus. XXVIII pl.(part col.) O.

Dunker, Balthasar Anton
Tableau de Paris, ou Explication de différentes figures, gravées a l'eau-forte, pour servir aux différentes editions du Tableau de Paris, par M. Mercier. Yverdon, 1787
63p. front. 95pl. O.
Lipperheide lists an edition with title: *Skizzen für künstler und kunst-liebhaber über Paris ... Esquisses sur Paris* (1786. 96pl.)
Lipperheide 1131m. LC 15-14651

(engr.) Aberli, J. L. Costumes de Berne et paysans des environs.

(illus.) Keller, J. J. Taschenbuch über die Schweiz

Der **dunkle** erdteil. See Bernatzik, H. A. Dark continent

Dunlap, R. & co., New York
A short treatise on head wear, ancient and modern. See entry under Goater, Mrs A. C.

Dunlop, John
Mooltan, during and after the siege, being twenty-one drawings from sketches taken on the spot ... lithographed by Andrew Maclure. London, W. S. Orr 1849
17 l. 21pl. F.
Six of the plates show costumes of India, the others English uniforms, battle scenes and views
Colas 912. Lipperheide 1498

Dunn, Mrs Louise M. See Mills, Mrs W. H., jt. auth.

Dunoyer de Noirmont, Joseph Anne Émile Édouard, baron, and Marbot, Alfred Charles Adolfe, baron de
Costumes militaires français, depuis l'organisation des premières troupes régulières en 1439 jusqu'en 1789; dessins et texte par ... D. de Noirmont & Alfred de Marbot. Paris, Clément; London, E. Gambart [1845]
2v. 300 col.pl. F.
Published in 15 parts at 15fr. each
According to Colas the most important book on French military costume. For the period, 1789-1914, see the same title under Marbot
Colas 1970. Lipperheide 2311. LC 11-20049

XII. primorum caesarum et LXIII. ipsorum uxorum et parentum ex antiquis numismatibus, in aere incisae, effigies. Hulsius, Levinus

Du Paty, Jules
(illus.) Maillot, T. J. R. La jeune armée

Dupin, N.
(engr.) See Les costumes français répresentans les différens etats du royaume, avec les habillemens propres à chaque etat

Duplessi-Bertaux, Jean
Campaigns of ... Arthur, Duke of Wellington ... from Seringapatam to ... Waterloo ... with ... engravings ... by J. Duplessi-Bertaux. Paris, Galignani 1817?
v.p. 24pl. 1 port. F.
Text in English and French

Recueil de cent sujets de divers genres. dessinés et gravés à l'eau forte ... A sett of one hundred original etchings. Paris, chez les éditeurs, rue Boucher no. 1. 1814
9 l. 98pl. port. ob.Q.
"Représentant toutes sortes d'ouvriers occupés de leurs travaux, scènes de comedies, scènes populaires, Mendians, Militaires, Cavaliers, Chevaux à l'abreuvoir, Foires, Danses de village, etc. . ." Subtitle
Plates are signed by J. D. B. They were first published in eight parts, each in a paper cover with title: *Eaux-fortes de J. Duplessis-Bertaux*. Introduction in French and English. Colas lists the parts as follows: 1 Suite d'ouvriers de différentes classes; 2 Suite de militaires de différentes armes; 3 [Divers artisans] 4 Suite des cris des marchands ambulants de Paris, par

Duplessi-Bertaux, Jean—*Continued*

J. B. Bertaux; 5 [Scènes diverses] 6 [Scènes de comédie] 7 Suite de mendiants; 8 [Jeux et bateliers et scènes militaires] Colas lists also titles of many of the plates

The same collection was republished later (Paris, C. Thierry 1846)

Colas 914. Lipperheide 1134. LC 20-11601

Recueil des principaux costumes militaires des armées alliées. Paris, 1816

36 col.pl. Q.

Uniforms of the Russian, English and Prussian armies

Colas 915

Suite de militaires de différentes armes. Paris, chez l'éditeur, rue Saint Lazare no.42 1807

12 col.pl. O.

Cover title: Eaux-fortes de Duplessi-Bertaux

Published later as part 2 of his: *Recueil de cent sujets*

Colas 913

Duplessis, Georges

Costumes historiques des XVIe, XVIIe et XVIIIe siècles, dessinés par E. Lechevallier-Chevignard, gravés par A. Didier, L. Flameng, F. Laguillermie, etc. avec un texte historique et descriptif par Georges Duplessis. Paris, A. Lévy 1867

2v.(xix,151,154p.) 150 col.pl. F. 250-400fr.

On the same plan and supplementary to Camille Bonnard's *Costumes historiques.* Published in 75 parts. Many of the plates are reproduced in *Costumes historiques* by Le Chevallier-Chevignard

Colas 378. Costume index. Lipperheide 336

Histoire de la gravure en Italie, en Espagne, en Allemagne, dans les Pays-Bas, en Angleterre et en France. Paris, Hachette 1880

528p. illus. 37pl. Q.

Shows costume of the 15th to 18th century in various countries

Lipperheide 341. LC 1-18321

Duponchel, L. See Alaux, M. M. J., jt. auth.

Dupont, Marcel, pseud. See Béchu, M. E.

Dupont-Auberville, A.

Art industriel: L'ornément des tissus; recueil historique et pratique. Paris, Ducher 1877

37p. 100 l. 115 illus. 100 col.pl. F.

Lipperheide 3743

Du Praissac

Les discours militaires. Paris, S. Thiboust [1612]

214p. 64 illus. O.

Lipperheide 2067

Dupré, Louis

Voyage à Athènes et à Constantinople, ou Collection de portraits, de vues et de costumes grecs et ottomans, peints sur les lieux. Paris, Dondey-Dupré [1825]

52p. 12 illus. 41 col.pl. F.

Illustrations show Greek, Armenian and Turkish costume. Colas gives list of plates

Colas 916. Lipperheide 1434

Du Pressoir, Charles. See Van Beveren, J. J., jt. auth.

Dupuis, Joseph

Journal of a residence in Ashantee ... Comprising notes and researches relative to the Gold Coast, and the interior of Western Africa; chiefly collected from Arabic mss. and information communicated by the Moslems of Guinea: to which is prefixed an account of the origin and causes of the present war. London, H. Colburn 1824

xxxviii,264,cxxxv p. fold.front. pl.(part fold.) fold.map. Q.

Costumes of Ashanti, Banna, and Gaman, Moslems of Dagomba, Salagab and Kong

LC 5-14607

Dupuy, Jean Raoul

Historique du 12e régiment de chasseurs de 1788 à 1891. Illustrations de M. le lieutenant ... de Frasnois. Paris, E. Person 1891

456p. 12pl.(11 col.) 5 port. O.

Dupuys, Remy

La tryumphante et solemnelle entree faicte sur le nouvel et joyeux advenement de ... Charles prince des Hespaignes ... en sa ville de Bruges l'an 1515 le xviiie jour dapvril après Pasques. [Bruges, Imprimerie de Vandecasteele-Werbrouck 1850]

58p. 32pl. Q.

Original edition: Paris, Gilles de Gourmont 1515

Lipperheide 2651

Dura, Gaetano

Gruppi di costumi napolitani. [Napoli] Gatti e Dura ca1835

1 l. 33 col.pl. Q.

Colas 919. Lipperheide 1299

Naples—Characters. [Napoli, Gatti e Dura] 183-?

11 col.pl. ob.O.

Cover title

Napoli e contorni; album. Napoli? Gatti e Dura ca1835

35 col.pl. F.

Feminine and masculine costume of Naples and its environs, and street types

Colas 918. Lipperheide 1298

Nuova raccolta di costumi e vestiture di Napoli e suoi d'intorni. Napoli, Gatti e Dura 1833-53

1 l. 57 col.pl. Q.

Colas 917. Lipperheide 1297

Raccolta di costumi di provincie diverse. Napoli, 18—?

96 col.pl. Q.

Colas 922

Scènes populaires, 1840. Naples, Gatti e Dura 1840?

64 col.pl. Q.

Colas 1840, 920. Lipperheide 1300

Tarantella ballo napolitano, disegnato da Gaetano Dura, diretto da Pasquale Chiodi. [Napoli] F. Gatti 1854

2 l. 20 col.pl. ob.O.

Colas 921

Du Radier, Jean François Dreux. See Dreux du Radier, J. F.

Durán, Diego

Historia de las Indias de Nueva-España y islas de Tierra Firme. México, J. M. Andrade y F. Escalante 1867-80

2v. and atlas of facsims. on 66pl.(63 col.) F.

Edited by Gumesindo Mendoza. Atlas of facsimiles shows costume of the Aztecs

Lipperheide 1626. LC 3-18023

Durand-Gréville, Émile
Hubert et Jean van Eyck. Bruxelles, G. van Oest 1910
191p. pl. ports. O.
Bibliography: p176-81
LC A11-2525

The **Durbar.** Menpes, Mortimer

Durbars—Delhi
Finnemore, John. Delhi and the Durbar. 1912
The historical record of the imperial visit to India, 1911. 1914
Menpes, Mortimer. The Durbar. 1903
Wheeler, Stephen. History of the Delhi coronation Durbar ... 1903. 1904

Durch Indien ins verschlossene land Nepal. Boeck, Kurt

Durchdachte frauenkleidung. Krapf, Anton

Duret, D., abbé
Mobilier, vases, objets et vêtements liturgiques. Paris, Letouzey et Ané 1932
403p. illus. S.
Traces ecclesiastical vestments by period from early times to the 20th century

Durham, Mary Edith
The burden of the Balkans. London, E. Arnold 1905
xii,331p. front. illus. pl. ports. fold.map. O.
Valuable for illustrations of Albanian costume
LC 5-21049
High Albania. London, E. Arnold 1909
xii,352p. front. illus. 6pl. fold.map. O.
LC 10-8301
Through the lands of the Serb. London, E. Arnold 1904
xi,345p. front. illus. pl. fold.map. O.
LC 4-32188

Durrieu, Paul, comte
Le Boccace de Munich; reproduction des 91 miniatures du célèbre manuscrit de la Bibliothèque royale de Munich. Étude historique et critique et explication détaillée des planches par le comte Paul Durrieu. Munich, J. Rosenthal 1909
130p. XXVIII(i.e. 30)pl. F.
Added title page in German: *Der Münchener Boccaccio*
Reproductions of the miniatures in the Munich manuscript of Laurent de Premierfait's *Des cas des nobles hommes et femmes,* a translation with additions of Boccaccio's *De casibus virorum illustrium.* The miniatures are attributed by the author to Jean Foucquet
Bibliographical foot-notes
LC 9-25645
Les très belles Heures de Notre-Dame du duc Jean de Berry. Paris, Société française de reproductions de manuscrits à peintures 1922
127p. XXX pl. O.
Issued in portfolio. At head of title: Comte Durrieu
Bibliographical foot-notes
LC AC33-3056
Les très riches heures de Jean de France, duc de Berry, par Paul Durrieu. Paris, Plon-Nourrit 1904
260p. col.front. LXIV pl. F.
At head of title: Chantilly. The manuscript is in the Musée Condé, Chantilly
"Héliogravures par Paul Dujardin; héliogravure en couleurs gravée par A. Coret et tirée par Ch. Wittmann."
LC 5-12457

Dusi, C.
Costumes vénitiens. Venise, J. Kier 1840
1 l. 12pl. ob.Q.
Colas 924

Du Sommerard, Alexandre
Les arts au moyen âge. Paris, Hôtel de Cluny 1838-46
5v. O. and atlas of 107pl.(part col.) F. and album of 402pl.(part col.) 2v. F.
Issued in 10 series; arranged in the album in 9 classes: Monumens religieux; monumens civils; mobiliers civils et religieux; sculptures; peintures; miniatures, manuscrits, dessins; tapisseries; émaux, autels d'or; armes, armures, fers. The album is useful for general costume of the 14th and 15th centuries, with some plates showing arms and armor
LC F-2897

Dutch costume. See Netherlands; also United States—Colonial period (to 1775)—Dutch

Dutch East Indies
Adriani, Nicolaus, and Kruijt, A. C. Geklopte boomschors als kleedingstof op Midden-Celebes, en hare geographische verspreiding in Indonesië. 1905
Blaauw, A. H. De tropische natuur in schetsen en kleuren. 1917
Carpenter, F. G. Java and the East Indies. 1923
Grubauer, Albert. Unter kopfjägern in Central-Celebes. 1913
Leyden. Rijks ethnographisch museum. Tentoonstelling van kleederdrachten in Nederlandsch Indië. 1894
Müller, Salomon. Verhandelingen over de natuurlijke geschiedenis der nederlandsche overzeesche besittingen. 1839-44
Nieuhof, Johan. Joan Nieuhofs Gedenkwaerdige zee en lantreize door de voornaemste landschappen van West en Oostindien. 1682
Pers, A. van. Nederlandsch oost-indische typen. Types indiens neerlandais. 1856
Rouffaer, G. P., and Juynboll, H. H. De batik-kunst in Nederlandsch-Indië en haar geschiedenis. 1914
Sarasin, Paul, and Sarasin, Fritz. Reisen in Celebes, ausgeführt in den jahren 1893-1896 und 1902-1903. 1905
Schultze, Walter. Ost-indische reyse ... beschreibung der fürnehmsten ost-indischen landschaften ... ihre gesetze, sitten, religion, kleidung. 1676
Shoberl, Frédéric, ed. The Asiatic Islands and New Holland. 1824

See also Java; Sumatra; also subdivision Dutch East Indies under Decoration and ornament

Dutch national costumes. Vries, R. W. P. de

Dutton, William Henry
The boots and shoes of our ancestors as exhibited by the worshipful company of

Dutton, William Henry—*Continued*
cordwainers; with a brief history of the company. London, Chapman & Hall 1898
8,13p. 38 l. 39pl. Q. 21s, o.p.
Colas 925. Costume index. Lipperheide 1746

Duverger, E.
(engr.) Tiron, abbé. Histoire et costume des ordres religieux, civils et militaires

Dux, Adolf. See Falk, Max, jt. auth.

Duyse, Hermann van
Catalogue des armes et armures du Musée de la Porte de Hal. See entry under Brussels. Musées royaux des arts décoratifs et industriels

Dvor″ russkīkh″ īmperatorov″ v″ ego proshlom″ ī nastoīāshchem″. Volkov″, N. E.

Dvořák, Max. See Dalmatien und das österreichische küstenland

Dwarfs. See Pygmies

Dyagilev, Sergeĭ Pavlovich
Les biches. Paris, Éditions des quatre chemins 1924
2v. 16 col.pl. 20 ports. Q.
Colored illustrations are by Marie Laurencin

Les fâcheux. Paris, Éditions des quatre chemins 1924
2v. 46pl.(23 col.) Q.
Colored plates by Georges Bracque. Black and white plates are photographs of ballet dancers

Dyaks. See Borneo

Dyas orationum de ritu depositionis. Argentorati, P. Aubry [1666]
56p. 20pl. O.
Lipperheide 2018

Dyck, Sir Anthonie van
[Les contesses de van Dyck] Antonius van Dyck, eques, pinxit, P. Lombart sculpsit. Londini, ca1660
12pl. F.
Ten pictures of English noblewomen, two of English noblemen
Lipperheide 977m

Icones principum, virorum doctorum, pictorum, chalcographorum, statuariorum nec non amatorum pictoriæ artis numero centum ab Antonio van Dyck, pictore, ad vivum expressæ eiusq: sumptibus æri incisæ. Antverpiæ, G. Hendricx [1646]
1 p.l. 109 port. F.
Portraits of Dutch artists. Lipperheide lists an edition dated 1645 with 192 plates
Lipperheide 529. LC 14-15841

(illus.) Polanzani, Felix. Collection des différents portraits d'hommes illustres

Dzērvītis, Arvēds, and Ģinters, Valdis
(eds.) Latviešu tautas tērpi; [sējums] 1-4. Rīgā, J. Grīnbergs 1936
pts. 1-4. col.front. illus. col.pl. Q.
Describes and pictures Lettish national costume

Działynski, Adam Tytus, hrabia
(ed.) Liber geneseos illustris familie Schidlovicie. [Parisiis, Crapelet 1849]
15 l. illus. 17pl. F.
From a 16th century manuscript. Plates are engraved by J. F. Piwarski and Q. Feart
Lipperheide 1395

Dziennik domowy wydawany przez N. Kamieńskiego. v 1-9; 1840-1848. Poznań
9v. col.illus. Q.
Contains costume illustrations
Lipperheide 4635

Dziennik podróży do Turcyi. Raczyński, Edward, hrabia

Dziewanowski, Władysław
Zarys dziejów uzbrojenia w Polsce. Warszawa, Główna ksiegarnia wojskowa 1935
xi,224p. illus. O.

Dzungaria. See Sungaria

E

E., G. R.
Story of Arthur and Guinevere, and the fate of Sir Lancelot of the Lake, as told in antique legends and ballads and in modern poetry; with nine illus. by Gustave Doré. London, E. Moxon [1879]
Q.

Ear-rings
Bartholin, Caspar. De inauribus veterum syntagma. 1676

Hadaczek, Karol. Der ohrschmuck der Greichen und Etrusker. 1903

Earle, Mrs Alice (Morse)
Child-life in colonial days. New York Macmillan 1899
xxi,418p. front. illus. pl. ports. facsims O.
Costume index

Costume of colonial times. New York C. Scribner's sons 1894
xiv,264p. D.
LC 12-31991

Home life in colonial days. New York London, Macmillan 1913
xvi,470p. front. illus. pl. O.
Costume index. LC A13-2290

Stage-coach and tavern days. New York, Macmillan 1905
xvi,449p. 27pl. illus. D.

Two centuries of costume in America, MDCXX-MDCCCXX. New York, London, Macmillan 1903
2v. fronts. illus. pl. ports. O.
Colas 926. Costume index. Lipperheide 1619e. LC 3-31011

Early American costume. Warwick, Edward, and Pitz, H. C.

Early American painters. Morgan, J. H.

Early California costumes. Mackey, M G., and Sooy, L. P.

Early Christian church. See Ecclesiastical costume—To 9th century (Early Christian church)

Early London. Besant, Sir Walter

Early Victorian England, 1830-1865. Young, G. M., ed.

East (Far East). See Asia

East (Near East)
Bruyn, Cornelis de. Reizen van Cornelis de Bruyn, door de vermaardste deelen van Klein Asia, de eylanden Scio Rhodus, Cyprus, Metelino, Stanchio etc. mitsgaders de voornaamste steden van Aegypten, Syrien en Palestina 1698

East (Near East)—*Continued*
Bruyn, Cornelis de. Voyage au Levant; c'est-à-dire dans les principaux endroit de l'Asia Mineure, dans les isles de Chio, Rhodes, Chypre, etc. de même que dans les plus considérables villes d'Egypte, Syrie, & Terre Sainte. 1725
Carpenter, F. G. The Alps, the Danube and the Near East; Switzerland, Czechoslovakia, Austria, Hungary, Yugoslavia, Bulgaria, Rumania, Italy, Greece, Turkey. 1924
Croly, George. The Holy Land, Syria, Idumea Arabia, Egypt & Nubia. 1855-56
Forbin, L. N. P. A., comte de. Voyage dans le Levant en 1817 et 1818. 1819
Franck, H. A. The fringe of the Moslem world. 1928
Fulgenzi, Eugène. Collection de costumes civils et militaires, scènes populaires, portraits, et vues de l'Asie-Mineure. 1838
Goupil Fesquet, F. A. A. Voyage d'Horace Vernet en Orient. 1843
Kühnel, Ernst. Miniaturmalerei im islamischen Orient. 1922
Le Blanc, T. P. Croquis d'après nature faits ... en Grèce et dans le Levant. 1833
Mayer, Ludwig. Views in Turkey, in Europe and Asia comprising Romelia, Bulgaria, Walachia, Syria and Palestine. 1801
Mayr, Heinr. von. Malerische ansichten aus dem Orient, gesammelt aus der reise ... des herrn herzogs Maximilian in Bayern, im jahre 1837, nach Nubien, Aegypten, Palästina, Syrien, und Malta im j. 1838. Vues pittoresques de l'Orient. 1839-40
Montfort. Souvenir de l'orient. 1827-29
Moor, J. B. van. Recueil de cent estampes representant differentes nations du Levant tirées sur les tableaux peints d'après nature en 1707. et 1708. 1714
Moor, J. B. van. Wahreste und neueste abbildung des turckischen hofes. 1719-21
Perrot, Georges, and Chipiez, Charles. History of art in Phrygia, Lydia, Caria, and Lycia. 1892
Tilke, Max. Oriental costumes. 1923
Tilke, Max. Orientalische kostüme in schnitt und farbe. 1923

See also Mohammedans; Palestine; Syria; also Street-venders—East (Near East)

East Indies. See Asia; Dutch East Indies
East of Suez. Penfield, F. C.
Eastern costume. Blakeslee, F. G.
Eastern Pacific lands. Christian, F. W.
Eastern women's wear magazine. See Women's wear magazine
Eastlake, Elizabeth (Rigby), lady. See Jameson, Mrs A. B. M., jt. auth.

Eaux-fortes de Duplessi-Bertaux. See Duplessi-Bertaux, Jean. Suite de militaires de différentes armes; also his Recueil de cent sujets de divers genres

Ebart, Paul J. von
Der hofmarschall auf der bühne, schauspielern und regisseuren. Berlin, M. Staegemann 1903
19p. D.
Intended to give actors an understanding of modern court and social dress
LC 25-24108

Ebeling, Friedrich Wilhelm. See Flögel, K. F. Floegels Geschichte des grotesk komischen

[**Eben, Frederic, baron d'**]
The Swedish army; modèles de l'uniforme militaire adopté dans l'armée royale de Suède. London, Rudolph Ackermann 1808
29p. 25pl.(24 col.) F.
Plates engraved by N. Heideloff after designs by Frédéric, baron d'Eben. Text in English and French
Colas 927

Ebers, Georg Moritz
Egypt: descriptive, historical and picturesque; tr. from the original German by Clara Bell. London, Paris [etc] Cassell 1887
2v. fronts. illus. pl. F.
LC 1-17871

Ebhardt, Franz
(ed.) Berliner modenblatt

Ebhardt's handarbeiten. Hochfelden, Frau B. L.

Ebhardts' Moden-album. v 1-30, 1879-1894. Berlin, F. Ebhardt
30v. col.illus. Q.
Editor: Brigitta Hochfelden
Colas 928. Lipperheide 4764

Ebulo, Petrus d'. See Petrus, de Ebulo

Ecclesiastical costume
Antrobus, Mrs M. S. and Preece, Louisa. Needlework in religion. 1924
Benziger brothers, New York. Catalogue of church ornaments. 1889
Benziger brothers, New York. Catalogue of vestments, banners and regalia. 1893
Bock, Franz. Geschichte der liturgischen gewänder des mittelalters oder entstehung und entwicklung der kirchlichen ornate und paramente in rücksicht auf stoff, gewebe, farbe, zeichnung schnitt und rituelle bedeutung nachgewiesen. 1859-1871
Bonnard, Camille. Costumi ecclesiastici, civili e militari d' secolo XIII, XIV e XV. 1827-1828
Braun, Joseph. Die liturgische gewandung im Occident und Orient. 1907
Buonanni, Filippo. La gerarchia ecclesiastica considerata nelle vesti sagre e civili: con le imagini di ciascun grado. 1720
Buonanni, Filippo. Histoire du clergé séculier et régulier, des congrégations de chanoines et de clercs et des ordres religieux de l'un et de l'autre sexe qui ont été établis jusques à présent. 1716
Cartarius, Marius. Icones operum misericordiae; cum Julii Roscii Hortini sententiis et explicationibus. 1586

Ecclesiastical costume—*Continued*

Cheyne, T. K., and Black, J. S. Encyclopaedia biblica. 1899-1903

Clauss, J. M. B. Rabat und chorrock: ein beitrag zur geschichte des geistlichen kostüms. 1904

Crépon, Théophile. Costume civil, costume ecclesiastique, costume monastique. 1900

Crouzil, Lucien. Le port de costume religieux. 1902

Cutts, E. L. Scenes and characters of the middle ages. 1872

Darby, W. A. Church vestments, an examination, scriptural, historical, and ecclesiastical. 1866

Dearmer, Percy. Ornaments of the ministers. 1920

Dolby, Mrs A. M. Church embroidery, ancient and modern. 1867

Dolby, Mrs A. M. Church vestments: their origin, use, and ornament. 1868

Duckett, Sir G. F. Monastic and ecclesiastical costume. 1892?

Duret, D., abbé. Mobilier, vases, objets et vêtements liturgiques. 1932

Gardner, James. The faiths of the world. 1858-60

Guilhermy, R. F. F. M. N., baron de, and Lasteyrie du Saillant, R. C. Inscriptions de la France du v. siècle au xviii. 1873-83

Jacquemin, Raphael. Histoire générale du costume civil, religieux et militaire du iv. au xix. siècle (315-1815). [1876]

Jacquemin, Raphael. Histoire générale du costume civil, religieux et militaire du iv. au xii. siècle: Occident (315-1100) 1879

Jacquemin, Raphael. Iconographie générale et méthodique du costume au iv. au xix. siècle (315-1815) collection gravée à l'eau forte d'après des documents authentiques & inédits. 1863-68

Klemm, H. Die geistlichen gewänder katholischer und evangelischer konfession in mathematisch genauen schnittzeichnungen. 1890

Legg, J. W. Church ornaments and their civil antecedents. 1917

Linas, Charles de. Anciens vêtements sacerdotaux et anciens tissus conservés en France. 1860-63

Macalister, R. A. S. Ecclesiastical vestments; their development and history. 1896

Mallet, Joseph. Cours élémentaire d'archéologie religieuse; mobilier. 1883

Marriott, W. B. Vestiarium Christianum; the origin and gradual development of the dress of holy ministry in the church. 1868

Neff, E. C. An Anglican study in Christian symbolism. 1898

Picart, Bernard. Ceremonies and religious customs of the various nations of the known world, together with historical annotations. 1733-39

Picart, Bernard. Cérémonies et coutumes religieuses de tous les peuples du monde. 1723-1743

Pugin, A. W. N. Glossary of ecclesiastical ornament and costume. 1868

Rogers, Peet & co. New York. Things clerical; being some account of ecclesiastical vestments, their origin and early form. 1902

Rolfe, C. C. The ancient use of liturgical colours. 1879

Schotel, G. D. J. Bijdrage tot de geschiedenis der kerkelijke en wereldlijke kleeding. 1856

Stummel, Helene. Paramentik. 1923

Weingartner, Josef. Das kirchliche kunstgewerbe der neuzeit. 1927

Weston, Mrs L. B. N. F. Vestments and how to make them. 1914

See also Abbesses; Canons (Members of chapters); Embroidery, Church; Hermits; Needlework, Church; Religious costume; Saints

Collections

Bugge, A. R. and Kielland, T. B. Alterskrud og messeklaer i Norge. 1919

Cologne. Schnütgen-museum. Die liturgischen gewänder und kirchlichen stickereien. 1926

Cox, Raymond. L'art de décorer les tissus d'après les collections du Musée historique de la Chambre de commerce de Lyon. 1900

To 9th century
(Early Christian church)

Lowrie, Walter. Monuments of the early church. 1923

Rohault de Fleury, Charles. La messe; études archéologiques sur ses monuments. 1883-89

Roller, Théophile. Les catacombes de Rome; histoire de l'art ... pendant les premiers siècles du christianisme. 1881

Anglican and Episcopal churches

Ceremonial pictured in photographs. 1924

Clayton, H. J. Cassock and gown. 1929

Directory of ceremonial. 1931

Essays on ceremonial, by various authors. 1904

Hall, M. R. English church needlework. 1901

Pictures of the English liturgy. 1916-22

Pinnock, W. H. The laws and usages of the church and the clergy. 1855-63

Pugin, A. W. N. Glossary of ecclesiastical ornament and costume. 1868

Purchas, John. The directorium Anglicanum; being a manual of directions for the right celebration of the Holy Communion, for the saying of matins and evensong, and for the performance of other rites and ceremonies of the Church; according to ancient uses of the Church of England. 1879

Skilbeck, C. O., illus. Illustrations of the liturgy, being thirteen drawings of the celebration of the Holy Communion in a parish church. 1912

Ecclesiastical costume—Anglican and Episcopal churches—*Continued*

Tyack, G. S. Historic dress of the clergy. 1897

See also Ecclesiastical costume—England

Armenian church

Muyldermans, Joseph. Le costume liturgique arménien, étude historique. 1926

Catholic church

Amman, Jost. Cleri totius romanae ecclesiae. 1585

Amman, Jost. Ständ und orden der H: Römischen Catholischen Kirchen. 1585

Aubert, Édouard. Trésor de l'abbaye de Saint-Maurice d'Agaune. 1872

Barbier de Montault, Xavier. Le costume épiscopal et prélatice selon l'étiquette romaine. 1876

Barbier de Montault, Xavier. Le costume et les usages ecclésiastiques selon la tradition romain. 1897-1901

Barbier de Montault, Xavier. Traité pratique de la construction, de l'ameublement et de la décoration des églises. 1885

Barocci, Luigi, and Fabi-Montani, Francesco, count. Collezione di quaranta sacre ceremonie usate principalmente in Roma. 1841-50

Beltrami, Luca. L'arte negli arredi sacri della Lombardia. 1897

Braun, Joseph. Die pontificalen gewänder des abendlandes. 1898

Braun, Joseph. Die priesterlichen gewänder des abendlandes. 1897

Busuttil, Salvatore. Raccolta di costumi religiosi e civile della corte pontificia. 1833?

Creccelius, Johannes. Collectanea ex historijs, de origine et fundatione omnium ferè monasticorum ordinum in specie: Simulq. De fundatione et donatione cathedralium ac collegiatarum ecclesiarum cum suis canonicatibus. 1614

Ferrari, Filippo. Costumi ecclesiastici civili e militari della corte di Roma disegnati all' acquaforte. 1823

Kirchenschmuck, ein archiv für weibliche handarbeit. 1857-1870

Kirchenschmuck, neue folge. Sammlung von vorlagen für kirchliche stickereien ... 1873-1895

Magistretti, Marco. Delle vesti ecclesiastiche in Milano. 1897

Marroni, Salvatore. Raccolta dei principali costumi religio e militari, della corte pontificia. ca1840

Roulin, E. A. Linges, insignes et vêtements liturgiques. 1930

Roulin, E. A. Vestments and vesture, a manual of liturgical art. 1931

Schlichten, I. P. van der. Tableaux de la sainte messe. 1738

Villanueva, A. P. Los ornamentos sagrados en España, su evolución histórica y artística. 1935

Walsh, John. The mass and vestments of the Catholic church; liturgical, doctrinal, historical and archaeological. 1909

Witte, Fritz. Die liturgischen gewänder und kirchlichen stickereien des Schnütgenmuseums Köln. 1926

See also Archbishops—Catholic church; Bishops—Catholic church; Cardinals; Monastic and religious orders Catholic church; Popes

Middle ages

Beissel, Stephan. Die bilder der handschrift des Kaisers Otto im Münster zu Aachen. 1886

Heider, Gustav. Liturgische gewänder aus dem Stifte St. Blasien im Schwarzwalde, dermalen aufbewahrt im Stifte St. Paul in Kärnten. 1860

Hinz, A. Die schatzkammer der Marienkirche zu Danzig. 1870

Kingsford, H. S. Illustrations of the occasional offices of the church in the middle ages from contemporary sources. 1921

Rohault de Fleury, Charles. La messe; études archéologiques sur ses monuments. 1883-89

Schneider, Friedrich. Ein bischofsgrab des zwölften jahrhunderts in Wormser dom. 1888

Villaamil y Castro, José. Pasatiempos eruditos. 1907

14th-16th centuries

Boutell, Charles. The monumental brasses of England. 1849

Bruyn, Abraham de. Imperii ac sacerdotii ornatus; diversarum item gētium peculiaris vestitus. 1578

Bruyn, Abraham de. Omnium pene Europae, Asiae, Aphricae atque Americae gentium habitus. ca1610

Bruyn, Abraham de. Omnium pene Europae, Asiae, Africae et Americae gentium habitus ... quibus accedunt Romani pontificis, cardinalum, episcoporum, una cum omnium ordinum monachorum et religiosorum habitu. 1581

Bruyn, Abraham de. Sacri Romani imperi ornatus, item Germanorum diversarumq. gentium peculiares vestitus; quibus accedunt ecclesiasticorum habitus varii. 1588

Villaamil y Castro, José. Inventarios de mobiliario litúrgico (Catedral de Mondoñedo, años 1579 y 1572. Colegiata de Ribadeo, año 1564. Catedral de Santiago, año 1509. Catedral de Sevilla, siglos XIV á XVII. Catedral de Oviedo, año 1385. Catedral de Toledo, último tercio del siglo XIII. Catedral de Salamanca, año 1275) 1906

17th century to date

Capparoni, Giuseppe. Raccolta della gerarchia ecclesiastica considerata nelle vesti sagre, e civili usate da quelli li quali la compongono. 1827

Ecclesiastical costume—Catholic Church—17th century to date—*Continued*

Costumi religiosi e militari della corte pontificia. ca1840

Giorgi, Domenico. Degli abiti sacri del sommo pontefice paonazzi e neri in alc. sol. funzioni della chiesa. 1724

Gründliche nachricht von denen ceremonien, welche jederzeit nach dem absterben eines pabstes ausser und in dem conclave bis zur wahl und crönung eines neuen pabstes vorgehen. Ingleichen von dem ursprung, hoheit und würde der cardinäle. 1769

Lemonnier, T. P. H. Ordonnance et règlement de Mgr. l'évêque de Bayeux et Lisieux [Lemonnier] sur le costume ecclésiastique, et notamment sur l'habit de choeur (6 mai 1909). 1909

Manuzzi, Giuseppe, ed. Trattato della messa e della maniera di assistervi, e Del paramento del prete. 1850

Nainfa, J. A. F. P. Costume of prelates of the Catholic church, according to Roman etiquette. 1926

A simple explanation of low mass, by a secular priest. 1934

Thiers, J. B. Johannis Baptistae Thiers ... De stola. 1674

Church of England

See Ecclesiastical costume—Anglican and Episcopal churches

Eastern church

See Ecclesiastical costume—Greek church

Greek church

Elssner, Jacob. Neueste beschreibung derer griechischen christen in der Türckey. 1737

King, J. G. The rites and ceremonies of the Greek church in Russia. 1772

Le Prince, J. B. Divers habillements des prêtres de Russie, les mêmes qui étoient general't en usage avant la désunion des deux eglises. 1764

Moscow. Sinodal'naía (byvshaía patrïarshaía) riznitsa. Sacristie patriarcale dite synodale, de Moscou. 1865

Riefstahl, R. M. Greek orthodox vestments and ecclesiastical fabrics. 1932

Robinson, N. F. Monasticism in the orthodox churches. 1916

Valekoff, C. Ornaments and vestments of the church of Russia and Constantinople. 189-?

See also Ecclesiastical costume—Armenian church

Jews

Ancessi, Victor. L'Egypte et Moïse. 1875

Bodenschatz, J. C. G. Kirchliche verfassung der heutigen Juden, sonderlich derer in Deutschland. 1748-49

Braun, Johannes. Vestitus sacerdotum hebraeorum. 1697-1698

Schemel, Siegfried. Die kleidung der Juden im zeitalter der Mischnah, nebst einem anhange: Die priester-kleidung. 1912

See also Ephod; Jewish priests

Orthodox Greek church

See Ecclesiastical costume—Greek church

BY SPECIAL COUNTRY

Czechoslovakia

Bohemia

Aegidius. D. Wenceslao Bohemorum duci ac martyri inclyto sertvm ortus, vitae, necis è Duabus suprà triginta iconibus, totidemque Tetrastichis, velut è rosis quibusdam contextum ... cue attexitur floriger fasciculus selectiorum epigramatum opera F.AE. â S.I.B. 1644

England

Ashdown, Mrs Emily. British costume during XIX centuries (civil and ecclesiastical). 1910

Beaumont, E. T. Ancient memorial brasses. 1913. p78-113

Bloxam, M. H. Companion to the Principles of Gothic ecclesiastical architecture, being a brief account of the vestments in use in the church, prior to, and the changes therein in and from, the reign of Edward VI. 1882

Carter, John. Specimens of English ecclesiastical costume, from the earliest period down to the sixteenth century. 1817

Clayton, H. J. The ornaments of the ministers as shown on English monumental brasses

Hope, Sir W. H. St J. On the tomb of an archbishop recently opened in the Cathedral church of Canterbury. 1893

Hope, Sir W. H. St J., and Atchley, E. G. C. F. English liturgical colours. 1918

Hope, Sir W. H. St J., and Atchley, E. G. C. F. An introduction to English liturgical colours. 1920

Strutt, Joseph. Regal and ecclesiastical antiquities of England. 1842

France

Cosson, André. Armorial des cardinaux, archevêques et évêques français actuels résidentiels et titulaires au 1er janvier 1917. 1917

Herbé, C. A. Costumes français civils, militaires et religieux ... depuis les Gaulois jusqu'en 1834. 1835-37

Germany

Das bapstum mit seinen gliedern gemalet und beschrieben. 1563

Dalhammer, Patritius. Canonia Rohrensis documentis, monumentis et observationibis historico-criticis. 1784

Danzig. Stadtmuseum. Kirchliche gewänder und stickereien aus dem schatz der Marienkirche. 1929

Ecclesistical costume—Germany—*Continued*
Drews, Paul. Der evangelische geistliche in der deutschen vergangenheit. 1905
Gallenstein, Anton von. Zur geschichte der deutschen kleider-trachten bis zum schlusse des 16ten jahrhunderts ... Die priesterliche kleidung. 1863
Hermes, E. Der Dom zu Halberstadt; seine geschichte und seine schätze. 1896
Hopffer, Bartholom. Icones sive effigies omnium & singulorum ecclesiae Augustanae A. Cillibatâ verbi praedicatione, & purâ verorum sacramentorum administratione inservientium ministrorum ... Das ist: Contrafeth und abbildungen eines gesambten ministerij und praedig-ampts evangelischer gemein Augsb. conf. in Augspurg. 1656
Mannowsky, Walter. Der Danziger paramentenschatz; kirchliche gewänder und stickereien aus der Marienkirche. 1931-33
Müller, Jacob. Ornatus ecclesiasticus ... Kirchen geschmuck. 1591

Norway

Bugge, A. R. and Kielland, T. B. Alterskrud og messeklaer i Norge. 1919

Poland

Przezdziecki, Aleksander, and Rastawiecki, Edward, baron. Wzory sztuki średniowiecznej i z epoki odrodzenia po koniec wieku XVII. w dawnej Polsce. 1853-62

Ecclesiastical decoration. Geldart, Ernest

Ecclesiastical gloves. See Gloves, Ecclesiastical

Ecclesiastical vestments. Macalister, R. A. S.

Ecclesiasticorum antiquae legis, nempe sacerdotum Hebraeorum institutio et habitus. See Coronelli, M. V. Ordinum equestrium, ac militarium brevis narratio

Ecclesiological society, Cambridge
Illustrations of monumental brasses, comp. by J. M. Neale. Cambridge, Walters 1846
192p. 33pl. F.
The brasses show costume of bishops, knights, priests, and nobles of England in the 13th to 16th centuries

Eccleston, James
An introduction to English antiquities; intended as a companion to the history of England. London, Printed for Longman, Brown, Green, and Longmans 1847
xii,485p. illus. O.
Costume and armor in England from the Roman conquest to the seventeenth century
"Authors and books of reference": p445-55
LC 2-12611

Echagüe, José Ortiz. See Ortiz Echagüe, José

Echo des casernes. Bodin, B.

Eck, Ch.
Histoire chronologique du vêtement (Homme), ou Jadis et aujourd'hui; suivi de l'art de se vêtir au XIX. siècle. (Paris, C. Vanier; La Haye, Bélinfante 1867.
72p. S.
Published as an advertisement for the house of Coutard. Reprinted (Paris, Maison de Phares de la Bastille 1869) and again 1873. The same text was published (Paris, C. Vanier; La Haye, Bélinfante 1867. 166p. 21pl. D.) but with plates added
Colas 931-33

Eckardt, Theodor
Wörterbuch der bekleidung. Erklärung der auf die kostüme, volkstrachten und moden aller zeiten und völker bezüglichen namen, sowie aller die herstellung der web- und wirkwaren, der putzgegenstände, der weiblichen handarbeiten ... betreffenden bezeichnungen. Wien [etc.] A. Hartleben [1886]
255p. O. (Hauswirtschaftliche bibliothek. Special-wörter- u. handbücher. 2. band)
Colas 934. Lipperheide 92

Eckersberg, Christoffer Vilhelm
Ti Tegninger af Christoffer Wilhelm Eckersberg. Gengivelser i lystryk, med tekst af Karl Madsen. København, A. Marcus 1919
5 l. 10pl. F.
Three plates show Danish costume

Eckersberg, J. F.
(illus.) Tønsberg, N. C., ed. Norske nationaldragter

Eckert, Heinrich Ambros; Monten, Dietrich, and Schelver, F.
Saemmtliche truppen von Europa in characteristischen gruppen dargestellt. München, H. A. Eckert; Würzburg, C. Weiss [1836-43]
2v. col.pl. F.
Contents: v 1 Das deutsche bundesheer (1838) 385 plates; v2 Schweden, 40 plates; Frankreich, 21 plates; Russland, 128 plates; Schweiz, 11 plates
Appeared in parts. French title: *Les armées d'Europe representées en groupes charactéristiques*
Colas 935. Lipperheide 2120. LC 34-19789 (*Das deutsche bundesheer* only)

L'Écluse, Charles de
(tr.) Harriot, Thomas. Admiranda narratio fida tamen, de commodis et incolarum ritibus Virginiae, nuper admodum ad Anglis, qui à dn. Richardo Greinvile ... eò in coloniam anno. M.D.LXXXV
(tr.) Le Moyne de Morgues, Jacques. Brevis narratio eorum quae in Florida Americae provĩcia Gallis acciderunt, secunda in illam navigatione, duce Renato de Laudõniere classis praefecto: anno MDLXIIII. Quae est secunda pars Americae

Ecob, Helen Gilbert
The well-dressed woman: a study in the practical application to dress of the laws of health, art, and morals; 2d ed., rev. and enl. New York, Fowler & Wells 1893
262p. front. illus. pl. D.
LC 11-22826

École de cavalerie. La Guérinière, F. R.

L'ecole des armes. Angelo, Domenico

L'école des voyageurs. Bouchot, Frédéric

École du soldat et de peloton; nouv. éd. par Chrétien de Mechel. Basle, L'editeur 1799
2v. (147,32p.) 13pl. O.
First edition 1791
Lipperheide 2300z

Economic history, An introduction to English. Ashley, Sir W. J.

Economic history of Virginia in the seventeenth century. Bruce, P. A.

Economics of fashion. Nystrom, P. H.

Edda. Hambro, C. J., baron

[Edel, Edmund]
Die krawatte: ein brevier des geschmacks, aus der Galerie der moden ausstellung im Hohenzollern kunstgewerbehaus, 1912. [Berlin, Ce-el-co] c1912
61p. illus. S. M.1.75
On verso of t.-p.: Hrsg. von Edmund Edel . . . mit beiträgen von W. Fred, Hans Heinz Ewers, Roda Roda; sämtliche zeichnungen von Robert L. Leonard
Issued as an advertisement of "Rotsiegelcravatten"
LC 12-25982

Edel, Vittorio
Ricordo delle nozze d'argento delle loro maestà Umberto I e Margherita di Savoia, 22 Aprile 1893. Collezione dei costumi dei cavalieri e degli uomini d'arme del grande torneo storico. Roma, Voghera Enrico 1893
[4]p. 44pl. F.
The plates are mounted photographs

Edelmann, August
Schützenwesen und schützenfeste der deutschen städte vom 13. bis zum 18. jahrhundert. München, E. Pohl 1890
163p. 15 illus. 5pl. O.
Many of the illustrations show hunting scenes after Jost Amman. The plates are copied from Opel's *Warhafte und aigentliche contrafactur*
Lipperheide 3013

(ed.) Flexel, Lienhard. Lienhard Flexel's Lobspruch des fürstlichen freischiessens zu Innsbruck im oktober 1569

Edelsteine und schmucksteine. Eppler, Alfred

Eden, Emily
Portraits of the princes & people of India; drawn on the stone by L. Dickinson. London, J. Dickinson 1844
24 l. 24pl. F.
Colas 936. Lipperheide 1494. LC 11-5277

Edge-Partington, James
Album of the weapons, tools, ornaments, articles of dress, etc. of the natives of the Pacific islands; drawn and described from examples in public and private collections in England. Manchester, J. Edge-Partington & C. Heape 1890-95
3v. illus. ob.O.

Edinburgh. See Scotland—Edinburgh; Street venders—Scotland—Edinburgh

Edinburgh. Royal Scottish museum
Catalogue of loan collection of art fans. Edinburgh, Printed by Neill, for H. M. Stationery office 1878
74p. T.
Preface signed: T. C. A.
"The introduction to this catalogue was written [by Mr. G. A. Audsley] for the Liverpool fine art club last year, and appeared in the catalogue of fans exhibited in their rooms by that club." Preface
LC 11-11367

Edinburgh. Royal Scottish museum. Library
List of books, &c. in the library of the Museum. Edinburgh, Printed by Neill & company, for H. M. Stationery off. 1892
61p. O.
At head of title: Science and art department. Edinburgh museum of science and art
Contents: Pt 1, Textile fabrics; pt2, Lace & needlework; pt3, Costume
LC 11-16825

List of books, &c. relating to armour and weapons in the library of the Museum. Edinburgh, Printed by Neill & company, for H. M. Stationery off. 1891
32p. O.
At head of title: Science and art department. Edinburgh museum of science and art
LC 11-16820

Edlweckh, Johannes
Triumphus virtutum im funere Caroli VII . . . anno . . . MDCCXLV. Monachii, J. J. Vötter 1745
102,20p. 27pl. F.
Plates after drawings by N. Stuber engraved by F. X. Jungwirth
Lipperheide 2564

Edwardes, Marian
(tr.) Boehn, Max von. Modes & manners of the nineteenth century

Edwards, Charles
The history and poetry of finger-rings. New York, Redfield 1855
239p. col.front. illus. D.
LC 9-7468

Edwards, George Wharton
Alsace-Lorraine. Philadelphia, Penn c1918
344p. col.front 1 illus. pl. (part col.) Q.
Bibliography: p336
LC 18-22744

Brittany and the Bretons. [New York] Moffat, Yard 1910
xii,274p. col.front. pl. (part col.) Q. $6, o.p.
Costume index. LC 10-23539

Holland of to-day. New York, Moffat, Yard 1909
xi,217p. 56pl. (part col.) Q.
Costume index

Some old Flemish towns. New York, Moffat, Yard 1911
x,326p. col.front. pl. (part col.) O. $4
Published also in London (Gay and Hancock [1913])
Contents: Characteristics; Oudenaarde; Alost, Dendermonde, Commines and Bergues; Courtrai; Ypres; Dixmude; Furnes and Nieuport; Tournai; Douai and Lille; Bruges and Damme; Ghent; Mechelen; Louvain; The legend of Margaret the Courageous; Conclusion
LC 11-31166

Edwards, Osman
Japanese plays and playfellows. London, W. Heinemann 1901
306p. 12 col.pl. (incl.front.) O.
LC 3-12804

Eeckhout, Guilielmus vanden
Le nouvelle figure à la mode de ce tempts de fine; desine G. vanden Eeckhout, et gravé par I. Troyen, mis en lumière par Hugo Allardt. No place, ca1650
12pl. Q.
The title is from the first plate. Dutch costume of the middle of the seventeenth century
Colas 2967. Lipperheide 936

Eeckhout, J. J. See Madou, J. B., jt. auth.

Eelking, Hermann, freiherr von
Die uniformen der Braunhemden (S. A., S. S., Politische leiter, Hitler-jugend, Jungvolk und B. D. M.). München, Zentralverlag der N. S. d. A. P. 1934
104p. illus.(part col.) O.

Eesti rahva muuseum. See Tartu. Eesti rahva muuseum

Eesti rahvariiete ajalugu. Manninen, Ilmari

Eesti rahvariiete album. Tartu. Eesti rahva muuseum

Eestimaa. See Estonia

"Effects" and adventures of Raby Rattler, gent. Hall, Thomas

Effigies des forestiers et comtes de Flandres. Meÿssens, Jean

Effigies ducum et regum Hungariae. Schad, J. A. X.

Effigies omnium legatorum, deputatorum, consiliariorum, qui pacem universalem monasterij anno salutis 1648. Aubry, Petrus

Effigies regum Francorum omnium, a Pharamundo, ad Henricum usque tertium. Solis, Virgil, and Amman, Jost

Effigies regum Francorum omnium, a Pharamundo, ad Ludovicum XIII. Francofurti, I. de Zetter 1622
139p. 64 ports. Q.
Portraits, which are half length, differ from those in a similar title by Solis
Lipperheide 1062

Effigies Romanorum imperatorum ex antiquis numismatibus. Vianen, Ioannes van

Effigies virorum ac foeminarum illustrium, quibus in Græcis aut Latinis monumentis aliqua ... pars datur ... ex antiquis marmoribus ... numismatibus, gemmisque expressæ. Lugduni Batavorum, P. van der Aa 1724?
9v. in 1. 301pl. F.
A collection of 300 plates first published with the *Thesaurus* of J. Gronovius now republished by P. van der Aa

Egan, Pierce
Life in London; or, The day and night scenes of Jerry Hawthorn, esq. and Corinthian Tom ... in their rambles and sprees through the metropolis; new ed. London, G. Virtue 1821
xvi,376p. 35 col.pl. O.
Plates show English costume of 1820-1821 and are designed and etched by I. R. and G. Cruikshank

Egenolff, Christian
Modelbůch aller art nehewercks und stickens. Dresden, G. Gilbers 1880
2 l. 71pl. Q.
Facsimile edition
Lipperheide 3879

Modelbůch Welscher, Ober uñ Niderländischer arbait. Franckfurt, C. Egenolff ca1530
28 l. illus. Q.
The first edition of Egenolff's *Modelbuch*
Lipperheide 3878

Eger. See Czechoslovakia—Bohemia—Eger

Eger und das Egerland. Pröckl, Vincenz

Egerton, D. T.
The necessary qualifications of a man of fashion. London, T. McLean 1823
24 col.pl. ob.Q. 25s
Colas 937

[**Egerton, M.**]
Airy nothings; or, Scraps and naughts, and odd-cum-shorts; in a circumbendibus hop, step, and jump, by Olio Rigmaroll [pseud.] Drawn and written by M. E., esq. Engraved by Geo. Hunt. 2d ed. London, T. M'Lean 1825
73p. col.front. 22 col.pl. Q.
Humorous illustrations which show masculine and feminine costume
Colas 938. LC 30-19440

Matrimonial ladder or, Such things are a gift for all seasons; twenty-three plates drawn by M. E., esq. engraved by G. Hunt. London, T. M'Lean 1825
3 l. 20 col.pl. O.
Colas 939

Egerton, Mary Margaret (Stanley). See Wilton, M. M. S. E., countess of

Egerton, Wilbraham Egerton, earl
A description of Indian and Oriental armour ... New ed. with considerable additions to illustrations and text. London, W. H. Allen 1896
178p. col.front. illus. pl.(part fold. 1 col.) fold.map. Q.
"Illustrated from the collection formerly in the India office, now exhibited at South Kensington, and the author's private collection. With a map, twenty-three full-page plates and numerous woodcuts. With an introductory sketch of the military history of India."
Weapons of India, Persia, Japan and Arabia
LC 1-558

Eggleston, Edward
The household history of the United States and its people, for young Americans. New York, D. Appleton 1901
xvi,404p. col.front. illus.(incl.ports.) pl. (part col.) maps. O. $2.50, o.p.
Costume index. LC 1-15049

Egypt
Cailliaud, Frédéric. Recherches sur les arts et métiers, les usages de la vie civile et domestique des anciens peuples de l'Égypte, de la Nubie et de l'Éthiopie, suivies de détails sur les moeurs et coutumes des peuples modernes des mêmes contrées. 1831
Dalton, Richard. Antiquities and views in Greece and Egypt. 1791
Davis, R. H. Rulers of the Mediterranean. 1894
Ebers, G. M. Egypt: descriptive, historical and picturesque. 1887

See also Copts; also subhead Egypt under Arms and armor; Dance costume; Decoration and ornament; Jewelry, Ancient; Military costume; Rings

Egypt—*Continued*

Ancient times

Ahrem, Maximilian. Das weib in der antiken kunst. 1924

Baxter, Thomas. Darstellung des aegyptischen, griechischen und römischen costums. 1815

Baxter, Thomas. An illustration of the Egyptian, Grecian, and Roman costume. 1810

Binion, S. A. Ancient Egypt or Mizraïm. 1887

Bissing, F. W., freiherr von. Denkmäler ägyptischer sculptur. 1914

Bonnet, Hans. Die ägyptische tracht bis zum ende des neuen reiches. 1917

Book of the dead. Facsimile of the Papyrus of Ani, in the British Museum. 1894

British museum. Department of Egyptian and Assyrian antiquities. A guide to the Egyptian collections in the British museum. 1909

British museum. Department of Egyptian and Assyrian antiquities. A guide to the first, second and third Egyptian rooms. 1924

Budge, Sir E. A. T. W. The mummy. 1925

Capart, Jean. L'art égyptien; choix de documents, accompagnés d'indications bibliographiques. 1909

Capart, Jean. L'art et la parure féminine dans l'ancienne Egypte. 1907

Capart, Jean. Donation d'antiquités égyptiennes aux Musées royaux de Bruxelles. 1911

Capart, Jean. Egyptian art. 1923

Carter, Howard, and Mace, A. C. The tomb of Tut.ankh.Amen, discovered by the late Earl of Carnarvon and Howard Carter. 1923-33

Cartland, B. M. The dress of the ancient Egyptians. 1916

Champollion, J. F. Monuments de l'Egypte et de la Nubie. 1835-45

Davies, N. de G. The tomb of two sculptors at Thebes. 1925

Description de l'Égypt; ou, Recueil des observations et des recherches qui ont été faites en Égypte pendant l'expédition de l'armée française. 1809-22

Dueminchen, Johannes. Die flotte einer aegyptischen koenigin aus dem XVII. jahrhundert vor unserer zeitrechnung; und altaegyptisches militair im festlichen aufzuge auf einem monumente aus derselben zeit abgebildet. 1868

Erman, Adolf. Aegypten und aegyptisches leben im altertum. 1885-87

Erman, Adolf. Life in ancient Egypt. 1894

Hammerton, Sir J. A., ed. Wonders of the past. 1923-24

Heuzey, L. A., and Heuzey, Jacques. Histoire du costume dans l'antiquité classique. 1935

Houston, M. G., and Hornblower, F. S. Ancient Egyptian, Assyrian, and Persian costumes and decorations. 1920

Leemans, Conradus. Monumens égyptiens du Musée d'antiquités des Pays-Bas à Leyde. 1839-67

Lepsius, Richard. Denkmaeler aus Aegypten und Aethiopien. 1849-56

Leyden. Rijksmuseum van oudheden. Beschreibung der aegyptischen sammlung des Niederländischen reichsmuseums der altertümer in Leiden. 1905-32

Lutz, H. F. Textiles and costumes among the peoples of the ancient Near East. 1923

Maspero, Sir G. C. C. Art in Egypt. 1912

Maspero, Sir G. C. C. Histoire ancienne de peuples de l'Orient classique. 1895-1908

Maspero, Sir G. C. C. Life in ancient Egypt and Assyria. 1892

Perrot, Georges and Chipiez, Charles. A history of art in ancient Egypt. 1883

Prisse d'Avennes, A. C. T. É. Histoire de l'art égyptien d'après les monuments, depuis les temps les plus reculés jusqu'à la domination romaine. 1878-79

Prisse d'Avennes, A. C. T. E. Monuments égyptiens. 1847

Rosellini, Ippolito. I monumenti dell' Egitto e della Nubia. 1832-44

Rue, Lena. Greek and Egyptian costumes. 1931

Smith, Sir G. E. Tutankhamen and the discovery of his tomb by the late Earl of Carnarvon and Mr Howard Carter. 1923

Start, L. E. Coptic cloths. 1914

Stuart, Villiers. The funeral tent of an Egyptian queen. 1882

Weigall, A. E. P. B. Ancient Egyptian works of art. 1924

Wilkinson, Sir J. G. The Egyptians in the time of the Pharaohs. 1857

Wilkinson, Sir J. G. The manners and customs of the ancient Egyptians. 1879

Wilkinson, Sir J. G. A popular account of the ancient Egyptians. 1854

See also Funerals—Egypt; Naval costume—Egypt—Ancient times; Queens and empresses

19th century

Bida, Alexandre, and Barbot, E. Souvenirs d'Égypte. ca.1850

Breton de la Martinière, J. B. J. L'Égypte et la Syrie, ou moeurs, usages, costumes et monumens des Égyptiens, des Arabes et des Syriens. 1814

Brockedon, William. Egypt & Nubia. 1846-49

Fischer, Sébastien. Tableaux de genre recueillis pendant le voyage de ... Monseigneur le duc Maximilien de Bavière. 1846-49

Gouin, Édouard. L'Égypte au XIXe siècle. 1847

Egypt—19th century—*Continued*
Lane, E. W. Account of the manners and customs of the modern Egyptians, written in Egypt during the years 1833, 34, and 35; 5th ed. 1871
Lane-Poole, Stanley. Cairo, sketches of its history, monuments, and social life. 1892
Lane-Poole, Stanley. Social life in Egypt. 1884
Latour, Antoine de. Voyage de S.A.R. Monseigneur le Duc de Montpensier à Tunis en Égypte, en Turquie et en Grèce. 1847
Mayer, Ludwig. Views in Egypt, from the original drawings in the possession of Sir Robert Ainslie, taken during his embassy to Constantinople, by Luigi Mayer. 1804
Minutoli, W. von der S. von W., freiherrn von. Mes souvenirs d'Égypte. 1826
Noé, Amédée, comte de. Mémoires relatifs à l'expédition anglaise partie du Bengale en 1800 pour aller combattre en Égypte l'armée d'Orient. 1826
Preziosi, A. Le Caire, moeurs et costumes. 1883
St. John, J. A. Oriental album; characters, costumes, and modes of life, in the valley of the Nile. 1848
Wilkie, Sir David. Sir David Wilkie's sketches in Turkey, Syria and Egypt, 1840 & 1841. 1843

20th century

Borchardt, Ludwig, and Ricke, Herbert. Egypt; architecture, landscape, life of the people. 1930
Carpenter, F. G. Cairo to Kisumu. 1923
Cooper, Mrs E. G. The women of Egypt. 1914
Curtis, W. E. Egypt, Burma and British Malaysia. 1905
Kelly, R. T. Egypt. 1902
Thackeray, Lance. People of Egypt. 1910

Egypt & Nubia. Brockedon, William

Egypt, Burma and British Malaysia. Curtis, W. E.

L'**Égypte** au XIXe siècle. Gouin, Édouard

L'**Égypte** et la Syrie. Breton de la Martinière, J. B. J.

L'**Egypte** et Moïse. Ancessi, Victor

Egyptian art. Capart, Jean

The **Egyptians** in the time of the Pharaohs. Wilkinson, Sir J. G.

Ehebrecherbrücke des Konigs Artus. Amman, Jost

Ehingen, Georg von

The diary of Jörg von Ehingen, tr. and ed. by Malcolm Letts. London, Oxford 1929

71p. front. pl. ports. Q.
Translation of his *Itinerarium*
"The manuscript ... is preserved in the Landesbibliothek at Stuttgart ... and the nine portraits which give the diary its peculiar value are drawn in colour on parchment sheets at the end ... The diary was printed from the Stuttgart manuscript without the portraits, in vol. 1 of the publications of the Litterarischer verein in Stuttgart in 1842, and it is from this reprint, after comparison with the original manuscript, that my translation has been made." Preface
Contents: Burkard von Ehingen with the tress; The diary of Jörg von Ehingen; The portraits: Ladislaus V, Charles VII of France, Henry IV, 'the Impotent', of Castile, Henry VI of England, Alfonso V, 'the African', of Portugal, Janus III (miscalled Philip) of Cyprus, René of Anjou, John II of Navarre and Aragon, James II of Scotland
LC 29-25178

Itinerarium, das ist Historische beschreibung, weylund herrn Georgen von Ehingen raisens nach der ritterschafft, vor 150. jaren, in x underschidliche königreich verbracht, auch eines kampfs von jme bey der statt Sept in Aphrica gehalten. Neben beygefügten contrafacturn, deren potentaten und könige ... Augspurg, J. Schultes, im verl. D. Custodis 1600

19 l. 10 ports. F.
Portraits are from the author's drawings made during his travels of 1453 to 1457, and show European rulers whom he visited
Lipperheide 446

Die **ehre** desz hertzogthums Crain. Valvasor, J. W.

Das **ehrenkleid** des soldaten. Lezius, Martin

Ehrenpforte des Kaisers Maximilian I. Dürer, Albrecht

Ehrenreich, Paul Max Alexander

Anthropologische studien über die urbewohner Brasiliens vornehmlich der staaten Matto Grosso, Goyaz und Amazonas (Purus-gebiet). Nach eigenen aufnahmen und beobachtungen in den jahren 1887 bis 1889. Braunschweig, F. Vieweg 1897

165p. illus. XXX pl. 9 diagr. F.
Bibliography: 1 p. at end
LC G-82

Ehren-seule ... Hn. Wilhelmen den Sechsten, landgraffen zu Hessen ... alss sr. fürstlichen durchleuchtigkeit seeligst verblichener cörper den 27ten octobris des 1663ten jahrs ... zu Cassel ... beygesetzt worden. Cassel? G. C. Wächtern [1669]

607p. illus. 25pl. F.
Illustrated by J. E. Schäfler and engraved by E. and H. van Lennep and P. Kilian
Lipperheide 2602

Ehrenstrahl, David Klöcker von. See Klöcker von Ehrenstrahl, David

Ehren-tempel der deutschen gelehrsamkeit. Brucker, J. J., and Haid, J. J.

Ehrenthal, Max von

Führer durch das Königliche historische museum. See entry under Dresden. Historisches museum und gewehrgalerie

[**Ehrmann, Theophil Friedrich**]

Die Holländer; eine karakteristische skizze aus der völkerkunde. Leipzig and Jena, A. G. Schneider 1791

58p. 18 col.pl. O.
"Most of the plates are copied from those by Bernard Picart." Colas
Colas 941. Lipperheide 949

Ehrmann, Theophil F.—*Continued*
Print-Geschenkjen voor myn kinderen, bestaande in afbeeldingen van Hollandsche, Friesche, Brabandsche en Fransche dragten en costumes. Amsterdam, G. Roos 1804
2 l. 18pl. O.
Plates are engraved after Picart and eleven are the same as those in Ehrmann's *Die Holländer*
Colas 942. Lipperheide 952

Das **Eibenstocker** stickereigewerbe unter der einwirkung der mode. Rasch, Albert

Eichler, Gottfried
Abbildung und beschreibung aller hohen ritter-orden in Europa. Augspurg, J. A. Fridrich 1756
5 l. 156p. 44pl. D.
An enlarged edition was published with title: *Abbildungen und beschreibung aller hoher geistlichen, weltlichen, und frauenzimmer ritter-orden in Europa* (Augsburg, C. F. Bürglen 1792; 2d ed. 1793)
Lipperheide 1911-12

(engr.) Freudenberger, Sigmund. Premier cahier des différens habillements distinctifs de la ville de Berne

Eichler, Lillian
The customs of mankind, with notes on modern etiquette and the newest trend in entertainment. Garden City, N.Y., Nelson Doubleday 1924
xvii,753p. col.front. illus. pl.(part col.) O.
Pages 500-58 have title: Dress through the centuries, and are accompanied by appropriate illustrations. Other plates also show costume
Authorities consulted: p727-31
Costume index. LC 24-20056

Eichler, Ludwig
Berlin und die Berliner; neue folge. Berlin, C. J. Klemann 1841-42
5v. 5pl. O.
Plates lithographed by Th. Hosemann
Lipperheide 3534

Eickstedt, C. von
Reglements und instructionen für die churfürstlich-brandenburgischen truppen zur zeit der regierung Friedrichs des dritten (ersten) als churfürst und als könig. Berlin, C. Heymann 1837
97.90p. col.front. 26pl. Q.
"Mit beilagen aus der zeit seines vorfahren und seines nachfolgers. Aus archivar. quellen zusammengetragen." Subtitle
Colas 943. Lipperheide 2169

Das **eigenkleid** der frau. Muthesius, Anna

Eigentliche abbildungen beeder römm. kayserl. wie auch der röm. königl. majestäten und dann sämtlicher ... churfürsten dess H. Röm. Reichs wie selbige auf dem röm. königl. wahl-tag in ... Augspurg im jahr 1689 und 1690. Augspurg, L. Kroniger und G. Göbels erben 1690
10pl. F.
Portraits are half length and are engraved by Leonhard Heckenauer
Lipperheide 716

Eigentliche beschreibung deren zu Franckfurth am Mayn anno 1711 vollzogenen wahl- und crönungs-actuum, ihrer römisch. kayserl. mayest. Caroli VI. Mayntz, J. Mayer 1712
40,34,56p. 5pl. F.
Lipperheide 2515

Eigentliche vorstellung aller, sich dermahlen (von anno 1741, da sich das kriegs theatrum eröffnet hat) auf teutschem boden, befindlichen fremden nationen. No place, ca1745
4 l. 24 col.illus. O.
The figures show Austria-Hungarian border troops and volunteer corps including Croats, Morlaks and others, as well as infantrymen of the Scottish Highlands and French lancers
Lipperheide 2110

Eigentliche vorstellung der heutiger strassburgische mode und kleÿdertrachten. Représentation des modes et habillemens qui sont en usage à Strasbourg. Strasbourg, J. D. Dulsecker 1731
1 l. 20pl. O.
Plates show six costumes of men and 24 of women, and are signed by J. M. Weiss. G. F. L. Debrie et Folkema, Fonbonne, and the initials F. B. Colas (945) lists another edition with title *Representation de l'ancien habillement de Strasbourg. Vorstellung der alten Strassburger kleidertracht.* (Strassburg, F. A. Haüssler ca1735) same collation but with the name of Weiss removed from the plates
Colas 944-45. Lipperheide 791e

Eigentlicher, und gründlicher bericht dessen was zu einer volkommenen erkantnusz und wissenschaft desz ... ritterlichen ordens S. Johannis von Jerusalem zu Malta vonnöthen. Osterhausen, Christian von

Eight illustrations to Shakespeare's Tempest. Crane, Walter

Eight illustrations to Shakespeare's Two gentlemen of Verona. Crane, Walter

Eighteen historical and local views illustrative of the operations and positions of the forces in the Birman territories. Moore, Joseph

Eighteenth century
Aa, Pieter van der. Habillemens de plusieurs nations. ca.1710
Abraham a Santa Clara. Neu eröffnete weltgalleria ... allerley aufzug und Kleidungen unterschiedlicher stande und nationen: Forderist aber ist darinnen in kupffer entworffen die Kaiserl. Hoffstatt in Wien, wie dann auch anderer hohen haupter und potentaten biss endlich gar auf den mindesten gemeinen mann. [1703]
Allard, Carel. Orbis habitabilis oppida et vestitus. 1750?
Boucher, François. Recueil de diverses figures étrangères. ca.1740
Coutumes des nations plus célèbres du monde. 1750?
Diesel, Matthias. Erlustierender augenweyde zweyte fortsetzung, vorstellend, die weltberühmte churfürstliche residenz in München. ca1720
Florin, F. P. Oeconomus prudens et legalis. 1750-51
Hausleutner, P. W. G. Gallerie der nationen. 1792-1800
Hausleutner, P. W. G. Gemählde aller nationen. 1796-1800

Eighteenth century—*Continued*

Hirth, Georg, ed. Kulturgeschichtliches bilderbuch aus drei jahrhunderten. 1881-90

La Mottraye, Aubry de. Voyages ... en Europe, Asie & Afrique. 1727

Loutherbourg, P. J. de. 1er recueil de modes et habits galans de différents pays. 1771

Loutherbourg, P. J. de. Seconde suite des figures. ca1770

Représentation, ou l'on voit un grand nombre des isles, côtes, rivières et ports de mer, comme aussi les habillemens & moeurs des peuples, les cérémonies, les pompes et les magnificences. ca1730

Viero, Teodoro. Raccolta di 126 stampe, che rappresentano figure, ed abiti di varie nazioni, secondo gli originali, e le descrizioni dei piu celebri recenti viaggiatori, e degli scopritori di paesi nuovi. 1783-1791

See also Europe—18th century

Eighteenth-century costume in Europe. New York. Metropolitan museum of art

The **eighteenth** century in English caricature. Brinton, S. J. C.

The **XVIII**th century; its institutions, customs and costumes. Lacroix, Paul

Eighteenth century, or, Illustrations of the manners and customs of our grandfathers. Andrews, Alexander

"Eighty" club, London

Hungary, its people, places, and politics, the visit of the Eighty club in 1906. London, T. F. Unwin 1907
421p. incl.front. pl. ports. O.
Slip inserted before t.-p. reads: Edition for America, imported by A. Wessels company, Brooklyn and New York
LC 7-40873

Eiler, Johann Georg, praeses

Dissertatio philologica de toga & sago. Wittebergae, Literis M. Henckelii 1671
8 l. sq.D.
Dissertation, Wittenberg, 1671

Eilpost für moden; nebst beiblatt Der Salon. 1.-5. jahrg. 1837-1841; neue folge 1.-2. jahrg. 1842-1843. Leipzig, Verlag der expedition der Eilpost 1837-43
7v. col.illus. Q.
Published weekly
Title change: 1837-40, v 1-4: *Eilpost, neue zeitschrift für kunst, literatur, theatre und moden*
Editors: 1837-40: N. Bücher and Fd. Stoller; 1841-43: Fd. Stoller
Colas 946. Lipperheide 4632

Die **eingeborenen** Süd-Afrika's. Fritsch, G. T.

Einstein, Carl

Der frühere japanische holzschnitt. Berlin, E. Wasmuth [1922]
24p. 48pl. on 24 l. Q. (Orbis pictus. bd. 16)
Woodcuts are from work of the seventeenth and eighteenth centuries
Literatur: p22
LC 24-1693

See also Bakst, Leon. Leon Bakst

Der **einzug** des ... herzogs Friedrich von Sachsen-Altenburg nebst seiner ... familie in sein neues land und seine neue residenz im november 1826. Altenburg, Literatur-comptoir 1827
48,256p. 8 col.pl. O.
Lipperheide 2581

Eiselein, Josua

Begründeter aufweis des plazes bei der stadt Constanz, auf welchem Johannes Hus und Hieronymus von Prag in den jahren 1415 und 1416 verbrannt worden. Constanz, P. Forster 1847
47p. 3pl.(1 col.) O.
Lipperheide 454

Eisen, Charles Dominique Joseph

Nouveau recueil des troupes qui forment la garde et maison du roy, avec la date de leur creation, le nombre d'hommes dont chaque corps est composé, leur uniforme et leurs armes. Paris, chez la vve. de F. Chéreau 1756
2 l. 13pl. F.
Two plates are by P. B. Delarue
Colas 947. Lipperheide 2293

Eisenberg, baron d'

Description du manége moderne, dans sa perfection, expliqué par des leçons necessaires, et representé par des figures exactes, depuis l'assiette de l'homme à cheval jusqu'à l'arrest accompagné aussi de divers mords pour bien brider les chevaux ... gravé par B. Picart. London? 1727
56 l. LV, 4pl. ob.Q.
Lipperheide notes that other editions were published in 1733, 1737 and 1749. Afterwards republished under title: *L'art de monter à cheval.* A German translation with title: *Des herrn baron von Eisenbergs Wohleingerichtete reitschule, oder beschreibung der allerneuesten reitkunst* (Amsterdam, Arckstee und Merkus 1746) has the same plates. Another German translation (Basel, D. Eckenstein 1748) has copies of the engravings by David Herrliberger
Lipperheide 2919-21. LC 6-31301

La perfezione e i difetti del cavallo. Firenze, G. Allegrini 1753
cxliii p. pl. F.
Text in Italian and French, with half title: *Anti-maquignonage, pour eviter les surprises dans l'emplette des chevaux.* A German translation has title: *Des herrn barons von Eisenberg ... Aufgedeckete rosztäuscherkunst* (Leipzig & Amsterdam, Arckstee & Merkus 1766)
Lipperheide 2927 (Ger. ed.)

Der **eislauf.** Zindel, C. S., ed.

Eitzing, Michael, freiherr von

1588. Novus ... de leone belgico, eiusque topographia atque historica descriptione liber quinque partibus Gubernatorum Philippi Regis Hispaniarum ordine, distinctus Jn super & elegantissimi illius artificis Francisci Hogenbergii ... perpetuà narratione continuatus Michaele Aitsingero. Antwerp? [1596]
499 l. 245 illus. map. F.
History of wars in the Netherlands from 1559 to 1596. The first edition appeared in 1583
Lipperheide 2051

Eklund, P. B.

Svenska arméns och flottans nuvarande uniformer ... Die schwedische armee

Eklund, P. B.—*Continued*
und marine in ihrer gegenwärtigen uniformirung. Stockholm, P. B. Eklund [1890]
1 l. 6 col.pl. F.
Colas 948. Lipperheide 2287

Ekman, Robert Wilhelm
Svenska national drägter. (Lapland-Wingäker-Dalarne); Häft 1-11. Stockholm 1847-49
11pts. col.pl. Q.
No more published

Elbicei Atika. Brindesi, Jean

Elchlepp, Johannes
(ed.) Issel, Heinrich. Volkstrachten aus dem Schwarzwald

[**Elder, Abram P. T.**]
The light of the world; or, Our Saviour in art ... Illustrated with over one hundred superb engravings made direct from the world's greatest paintings of Our Lord. Chicago, Elder 1896
[9]p. 142pl. Q.
Each plate preceded by guard sheet with descriptive letterpress
LC 10-107

Electio et coronatio ... Matthiae I. electi Rom. imperat. Arthus, Gotthard

L'**Élégance** féminine; la lingerie moderne. no30, 1933+ New York, Classique modes
Col.illus. F. $3 a year
Published semi-annually. Current 1938

L'**élégance** masculine. Léger, Abel

L'**Elégance** parisienne. Paris, Bance ca1805
7 col.pl. F.
Title and imprint appear on each plate
The plates are caricatures interesting for fashions of the times
Colas 949

Élégance parisienne; a journal of fashion and instruction for the benefit of ladies' tailors. v 1-24, June 1900-1924. New York, G. Pinsuti [etc]
24v. illus. pl. 41½cm.
Published monthly except July and August. Text in French and English. Organ of the United ladies' tailoring association of America, New York
LC 9-30740

Les **élégances** de la toilette. Grand-Carteret, John

Les **Élégances** parisiennes; publication officielle des Industries françaises de la mode. v 1-4; avr. 1916-1924. Paris, Hachette
4v. illus. pl.(part col.) F.
Published monthly. A continuation of *Style parisien*
Colas 950. LC 17-22104

Elegant modes in the nineteenth century. Holden, Angus

The **elegant** woman, from the rococo period to modern times. Aretz, Frau G. K. D.

Die **Elegante**; herausgegeben unter verantwortlichkeit des F. Kratochwill. 1.-30. jahrg.; 1842-1871. Wien
30v. col.pl. Q.
Colas 952. Lipperheide 4640

Die **Elegante** mode; illustrierte zeitung für mode und handarbeiten. jahrg. 1+ 1890+ Berlin, Bazar-aktien-gesellschaft
Col.pl. F. ea. no. 45pf.
Colas 953. Lipperheide 4799

Die **elegante** stickerin oder pracht muster im neuesten modegeschmack zum sticken und weissnähen. Leipzig, Vetter & Rostosky [1830]
4p. 18pl. O.
Lipperheide 3948

Elegantia; of tydschrift van mode, luxe, en smaak voor dames. 1.-4. jaarg. 1807-1810. Amsterdam, E. Maaskamp
4v. col.pl. Q.
Colas 954. Lipperheide 4597

L'**eleganza** femminile. Donna Clara, pseud.

Elementarwerk mit den kupertafeln Chodowieckis u. a. kritische bearbeitung. Basedow, J. B.

Elements of costume design. Downs, Marie, and O'Leary, Florence

The **elements** of dress pattern-making. Reeve, A. J.

Elements of lawn tennis. Doeg, J. H., and Danzig, Allison

Elephant, Order of the
Berlien, J. H. F. Der Elephanten-orden und seine ritter. 1846

Elgger, Karl von
Kriegswesen und kriegskunst der schweizerischen eidgenossen im XIV.-XVI. jahrhundert. Luzern, Militärisches verlagsbureau 1873
xx,438p. 10pl. O.

[**Eliat, F.**]
[Costumes du Wurtemberg] Stuttgart, G. Ebner ca1830
9 col.pl. Q.
Two of the plates are signed by Eliat
Cataloged from Colas
Colas 955

Élie, Charles. See Alboise de Poujol, J. É., jt. auth.

Eliseev, Sergiei Grigorevich. See Iakovlev, Aleksandr, jt. auth.

Élite. 1908+ Paris
Illus.(part col.) F. 18fr. per no.
Published semi-annually. Current 1938
Printed in Vienna. Editeurs-proprietaires: *Le grand chic* [etc.] Text in French; separate leaflet with English text inserted in each issue

Die **elite.** See Die deutsche elite

Élite; an illustrated society journal addressed to people of culture and fashion v 1, 1881-1907. Chicago
Illus. Q.
Published weekly
No more published?

Elite des almanachs, les modes et conversation que tiennent les dames et les messieurs sur leurs nouveaux habillemens. Paris, Desnos 1786?
24 illus. T.
Cataloged from Colas
Colas 957

Elite des almanachs ou les agrémens de la parure: conversation que tiennent les dames et les messieurs sur leurs nouveaux habillements; avec chansons Paris, Desnos 1787?
12 illus. T.
Cataloged from Colas
Colas 958

Elite des almanachs ou les agrémens de la parure, les nations en gaité; ou les peuples chantant. Conversation des dames et des messieurs sur les nouveaux habillemens. Paris, Desnos [1785]
24pl. T.
Plates engraved by Desrais. Cataloged from Colas
Colas 956

Elizabethan costume. See England—Tudor period, 1485-1603

Elizabethan pageantry. Morse, Mrs H. K., ed.

Eljasz, Walery Radzikowski
Ubiory w Polsce i u sasiadow. Krakowie, W. L. Anczyca 1879-1905
44 col.pl. Q.
A collection of costumes of Poland and the neighboring countries. According to Colas only four parts appeared
Colas 959

Elkington, Ernest Way
The savage South Seas, painted by Norman H. Hardy, described by E. Way Elkington. London, A. & C. Black 1907
xii,211p. col.front. 68 col.pl. fold.map. O.
Each plate is accompanied by guard sheet, with descriptive letterpress
Many of the plates show costume
Contents: pt 1 British New Guinea; pt2 The Solomon Islands; pt3 The New Hebrides
LC 7-37966

Ellet, Mrs. Elizabeth Fries (Lummis)
The court circles of the republic; or, The beauties and celebrities of the nation; illustrating life and society under eighteen presidents; describing the social features of the successive administrations from Washington to Grant ... with sketches by Mrs. R. E. Mack. Hartford, Conn., Hartford publishing co. 1869
586p. front. ports. D.
Portraits show feminine coiffures
LC 6-28022

The queens of American society. New York, C. Scribner 1867
464p. front. ports. O.
LC 12-31969

The women of the American revolution; introduction by Anne Hollingsworth Wharton. Philadelphia, G. W. Jacobs [1900]
2v. fronts. ports. O.
LC 0-6774

Ellinger, Johann
Allmodischer kleyder teuffel. Franckfurt am Mayn, J. C. Onckels 1629
56p. Q.
Lipperheide 3431

Elliot, Margaret M. V. See Hartley, Dorothy, jt. auth.

Ellis, William
Three visits to Madagascar during the years 1853-1854-1856. Including a journey to the capital ... Illustrated by woodcuts from photographs, etc. London, J. Murray 1858
xvii,470p. fold.front. illus. pl. ports. map. O.
LC 5-15927

Ellsworth, Evelyn Peters
Textiles and costume design. San Francisco, P. Elder 1917
xii,85p. 10pl.(part mounted) O.
Bibliography: p[77]-85
LC 17-23963

Éloffe, Mme
Modes et usages au temps de Marie-Antoinette, par le comte de Reiset ... Livre-journal de Madame Éloffe, marchande de modes, couturière lingère ordinaire de la reine et des dames de sa cour. Paris, Firmin-Didot 1885
2v. fronts. illus. pl.(part col.) ports. plan, facsims. Q. 60fr.
Contents: v 1, 1787-1790; v2, 1790-1793
Colas 2533. Costume index. Lipperheide 1150. LC F-3362

Éloge des perruques. Deguerle, J. M. N.

Elogia virorum bellica virtute illustrium. Giovio, Paolo, bp. of Nocera

Elogia virorum literis illustrium. Giovio, Paolo, bp. of Nocera

Elogii di capitani illustri. Crasso, Lorenzo

Elout, C. K. See Algemeen handelsblad. In kleuren en kleeren

Elphinstone, Mountstuart
An account of the kingdom of Caubul, and its dependencies in Persia, Tartary, and India; comprising a view of the Afghaun nation, and a history of the Dooraunee monarchy. By the Hon. Mountstuart Elphinstone ... London, Longman, Hurst, Rees, Orme, and Brown [etc] 1815
xxi,675p. 14 col.pl. 2 maps. Q.
Many editions. Second ed. (1819. 2v. O.) New and rev. ed. (London, R. Bentley 1842. 2v. O.)
French translation: *Tableau du royaume de Caboul* tr. et abr. par M. Breton (Paris, Nepveu 1817. 3v. 14 col.pl. D.)
Colas 960-61. Lipperheide 1483. LC 14-15132

Elrich, Daniel. See Siemienowicz, Kazimierz. Vollkommene geschütz-feuerwerck-und büchsenmeisterey-kunst

Elsholz, L.
(illus.) Walter, W. Das preuszische heer in bildern

Elssner, Jacob
Neueste beschreibung derer griechischen christen in der Türckey. Berlin, C. L. Kunst 1737
380p. 9pl. O.
"Aus glaubwürdiger erzehlung herrn Athanasius Dorostamus, archimandriten des patriarchen zu Constantinopel, nebst von ihm selbst gezeichneten kupfern." Subtitle
Plates, engraved by G. F. Schmidt, show costume of the Greek Catholic clergy in Turkey
Lipperheide 1811

Elster, O.
Die historische schwarze tracht der ... Braunschweigischen truppen. Leipzig, Zuckschwerdt & Co. 1896
48p. 3pl. O.
Colas 962

Elwin, Edward Fenton
India and the Indians. London, J. Murray 1913
xi,352p. front. pl. ports. O. 12s, o.p.
Costume index. LC A13-1618

Elzholz, L.; Rechlin, Karl, and Schulz, J.
Das preussische heer, herausgegeben und Sr Majestät dem Könige Friedrich Wilhelm III allerunterthänigst gewidmet. Berlin, S. Sachse 1836
1 l. 72 col.pl. Q.
Differs only slightly from the 1830 edition
Colas 964

Das preussische heer; herausgegeben ... von der kunsthandlung von L. Sachse & co. Gezeichnet und lithographirt von L. Elzholz [etc] Berlin, Gedruckt im lith. inst. der herausgeber 1830
72 col.pl. Q.
Colas 963. Lipperheide 2165

Elzingre, Édouard
(illus.) Pourrat, Henri. Ceux d'Auvergne
(illus.) Spindler, Charles. Ceux d'Alsace

Ema, Tsutomu
Kimono, one hundred masterpieces of Japanese costumes. Tokyo [etc] Meiji-shobo 193-?
2v. 100 col.pl. F.
In case. Each plate accompanied by guard sheet with descriptive letterpress in English and Japanese
LC 36-20219

Das **emancipirte** amazonen-heer. Burger, Ludwig

Emblemata. Reusner, Nicolaus

Emblemata moralia, et oeconomica, de rerum usu et abusu. Coornhert, Dierick

Emblemata nobilitatis. Bry, J. Theodor de

Emblemata secularia, mira et iucunda varietate seculi huius mores. Bry, J. T. de

Les **emblèmes.** Alciati, Andrea

The **embroiderer's** alphabet. Dillmont, Thérèse de

Embroidery
Aldenkirchen, Joseph. Früh-mittelalterliche leinenstickereien. 1885
Antrobus, Mrs M. S. and Preece, Louisa. Needlework through the ages. 1928
Anweisung, wie eine stickerin sich selbst, ohne zeichnen zu können, jedes muster ... aufzeichnen, und fortführen oder verlängern kann; mit 50 neuen geschmackvollen stickmustern. ca1820
Anweisung zum sticken und illuminiren, mit ausgemalten und schwarzen zeichnungen von bouquets, körbchen, arabesquen, desseins zu granirungen und kleinen kanten. 1795
Aubry, Félix. Rapport sur les dentelles, les blondes, les tulles et les broderies, fait à la commission française du jury international de l'exposition universelle de Londres. 1854
Bayle-Mouillard, Mme E. F. C. Nouveau manuel complet de la broderie, indiquant la manière de dessiner et d'executer tout ce qui est relatif à cet art ... Par Mme Celnart [pseud.] 1840
Berliner muster zur weissen stickerei; auswahl des modernstern und geschmackvollsten fur alle gegenstände dieser kunst. [1817-1833]
Besselièvre, de. Collection Besselièvre, spitzen & stickereien. 192-?
Besselièvre, de. Étoffes & broderies du XVe au XVIIIe siècles. 1914?
Bolmar, Lydia, and McNutt, Kathleen Art in dress. 1916. p29-37
Bretschneider, Andreas. Neues modelbuch 1619. 1892
Champeaux, Alfred de. Dessins et modeles; les arts du tissu: Étoffes—tapisseries—broderies—dentelles, reliures. 1892
Christie, Mrs Grace. Samplers and stitches. 1920
Cole, A. S. A descriptive catalogue of the collections of tapestry and embroidery in the South Kensington museum. 1888
Cocheris, H. F. J. M. Patrons de broderie et de lingerie du XVIe siècle, reproduits. 1872
Dillmont, Thérèse de. Alphabets et monogrammes. 1889
Dillmont, Thérèse de. The embroiderer's alphabet. 1920
Drahan, Em. K.k. oesterr. museum: Stickmuster. 1873
Dresden. K. Kunstgewerbemuseum. Spitzen und weiss-stickereien des XVI.-XVIII. jahrhunderts. 1889
Egenolff, Christian. Modelbůch aller art nehewercks und stickens. 1880
Egenolff, Christian. Modelbůch Welscher Ober un Niderländischer arbait. ca1530
Farcy, Louis de. La broderie du XIe siècle jusqu'à nos jours. 1890
Fischbach, Friedrich. Stilistische muster für stickerei und hakelei. ca1875
Flemming, E. R. Textile künste, weberei, stickerei, spitze, geschichte, technik, stilentwickelung. 1923
Head, Mrs R. E. The lace & embroidery collector. 1922
Holme, Geoffrey, ed. A book of old embroidery. 1921
Kramer's Bazar für stickerei auf leder- und silber-canevas in vorlagen von angefangenen arbeiten. ca1874
Lefébure, Ernest. Broderie et dentelles. 1904?
Lefébure, Ernest. Embroidery and lace. 1888
Lessing, Julius. Album de broderies anciennes. 1879
Lilly's Stickmuster-album ... entworfen und gezeichnet in der Gewerbeschule für mädchen in Hamburg. 1879
Lilly's Stickmusterbüchlein; eine sammlung in farben ausgeführter stylvoller stickmuster bearbeitet von den lehrerinnen der Hamburger gewerbeschule. 1879
Lipperheide, Frieda. Musterblätter für künstlerische handarbeiten. 1889-95
Il monte: opera nova di recami. ca1557
Müntz, Eugène. Tapisseries, broderies et dentelles; recueil de modèles anciens et modernes. 1890
Muster zur weiszen stickerei im neuesten geschmack. 1829
Netto, J. F. Zeichen- mahler- und stickerbuch zur selbstbelehrung für damen. 1795

Embroidery—*Continued*

Neue zeichnungen zur weissen stickerey. 1820

Neues stick und zeichnungs-buch verschiedene neue desseins enthaltend. 1818

Oppenheim, Guido. Neues stick-musterbuch. 1878

Paris. Musée des arts décoratifs. Broderies, tissus, soieries, dessins de tissus. n.d.

Paris. Musée des arts décoratifs. Dessins de broderies, fin du XVIIIe siècle & 1er empire. 1922

Philipson, A. Muster von couleurt gestickten bordüren, zu kleidungsstücken. 1799

Pracht-muster für die weisse stickerei. 1833

Saint-George, Amalie von. Die kunst der goldstickerei. 1896

Sajou, firm, publishers. Ouvrages de dames, dessins de broderies. ca1880

Sammlung neuer muster zum sticken in plattstich und tambourin. 1812-30

Schön neues modelbuch von allerley lustigen mödeln naazunehen zuwürcken uñ zusticke. 1606

Schulze, Heinrich, and Maiss, Karl. Muster-sammlung alter leinen-stickerei. 1887-88

Seligman, G. S., and Hughes, Talbot. La broderie somptuaire; à travers les moeurs et les costumes. 1927

Sibmacher, Johann. Newes modelbuch in kupffer gemacht darinen aller hand arth newes mödel von dün mittel und dick auszgeschnidener arbeit. 1604

Silling, Karl. Grand magazin des plus nouveaux dessins françois de broderie ... Groszes magazin für stickerei. ca1800

Stuhlmann, A. Stickmuster für schule und haus. 1890-93

Sylvia's illustrated embroidery book, containing ... ornamental designs in broderie anglaise, appliqué, cross stitch and the new Holbein work. 1879

Vienna. K. K. Österreichisches museum für kunst und industrie. Original-stickmuster der Renaissance in getreuen copien. 1874

Zeissig, M. C. Neue stickmuster zu allen gegenständen welche in weisz gestickt werden ... Nouveaux modèles. ca1815

Zoppino, N. d'A. Gli universali de i belli recami antichi e moderni. 1876

See also Beadwork; Featherwork; Needlework

Monograms and numerals

Al'bom" russkīkh" monogramm" dlīâ mīētkī bīēl'īâ. 1882

Album der monogramme für kreuzstich. 1894

Arnold, Xaver, and Knoll, Eduard. Sammlung von initialen. 1869

Fougeadoire, Paris. Chiffres Louis XV. 18—?

Fougeadoire, Paris. Chiffres modernes. 18—?

Fougeadoire, Paris. Chiffres renaissance. 18—?

Guichard, Édouard. Les petits alphabets du brodeur. 187-?

Laborgne, Paul. Les chiffres au XIXme siècle. 1884-91

Leipold, Victor. Leutzsch' universal-monogramm-werk für gold-, bunt-, und weiss-stickerei, holz-, und glasmalerei. 1893

Manteuffel, Erna von. Monogramm-album sechshundert stilvoll verschlungene buchstaben für plattstich-stickerei. 1881

Plant forms

See Decoration and ornament—Plant forms

BY PERIOD

Middle ages

Bock, Franz. Album mittelalterlicher ornament-stickerei zur zierde für kirche und haus, in autographien ... mit erklärenden. 1866-1869

Modèles de broderies genre moyen-âge. 1889-92

16th-18th centuries

Advis sur l'usage des passements d'or et d'argent. 1610

Bellezze de recami, et dessegni, opera nova, nellaquale si ritrovano, varie, & diverse sorte de mostre, di punti tagliati, & punti in aiere, à fogliami, punti in stuora, & altre sorte. 1558

Latomus, Sigismund. Schön newes modelbuch von 500. schönen ausserwehlten künstlichen so wol italiänischen frantzösischen niderländischen engeländischen als teutschen mödeln allen nätherin seydenstickern &c. 1606

Saint-Aubin, Augustin de. L'art du brodeur. 1770

Winter- und sommer-gärtlein aller wolkönnenden jungfrauen; aus welchen unterschiedliche frücht und blumen abzubrocken auch zu einem däntzerl gegenwärtiges als musicalische noten allen embsigen frau- und jungfrauen. 1691

Zoppino, Nicolo d'Aristotile, called. Esemplario di lavori dove le tenere fanciulle & altre donne nobile potranno facilmente imparare il modo & ordine di lavorare. 1878

19th century

Die allzeit fertige stickerin, ein geschenk für das schöne geschlicht, oder, Anweisung, wie eine stickerin sich selbst, ohne zeichnen zu können, jedes muster ab- und aufzeichnen und fortführen kann. ca1825

Berrin, Emilie, and Savin, J. C. Neueste englische und französische muster zu aller art der stickerei. [1803]

Church, Mrs E. R. M. Artistic embroidery. 1880

Embroidery—19th century—*Continued*

Day, L. F., and Buckle, Mary. Art in needlework, a book about embroidery. 1926

Dillmont, Thérèse de. Die stickerei auf netz-canavas. 1892

Dillmont, Thérèse de. Vorlagen für die plattstich-arbeit. 1894

Dufaux de la Jonchère, Ermance. Le travail manuel. Traité pratique de la broderie et de la tapisserie. 1894

Die elegante stickerin oder pracht muster im neuesten modegeschmack zum sticken und weissnähen. 1830

Fischbach, Friedrich. Album für stickerei. 1872

Fischbach, Friedrich. Stickerei-album des Bazar. 1879

Häkel- und stickmuster der modenwelt. 1897

Harrison, Mrs C. C. Woman's handiwork in modern homes. 1881

Hennings, Emma. Bunte stickmuster in weiss. 1846-47

Hennings, Emma. Die neuesten und elegantesten stickmuster in weiss. 1845-46

Hennings, Emma. Vorlegeblätter zu modeltüchern. 1846

Higgin, L. Handbook of embroidery. 1880

Kick, Wilhelm. Preisgekrönte stickereiarbeiten der wurttembergerischen frauenarbeitschulen aus der ... landesschulausstellung. 1891

Kûhn, Heinrich. Album moderner stickmuster ... für ornamentale stickereien. 1880

Lescure, Alfred. Collection A. Lescure: Fonds de bonnets du XIXe siècle. 1919?

Lescure, Alfred. Collection A. Lescure: Gestickte kragen; mitte des XIXe jahrhunderts. 1910

Lescure, Alfred. Collection A. Lescure: Mouchoirs brodés, milieu du dixneuvième siècle. 190?

Lessing, C. F., and Lessing, Ida. Musterblätter als vorlagen für stickereien in wolle und perlen. ca1850

Lipperheide, Frieda. Die decorative kunst stickerei. 1890-96

Modèles nouveaux de crochet et filet, broderies en soie, broderies anglaises, plumetis, soutache, laine, etc. ca1850?

Muster altdeutscher und moderner stickereien. 1884

Redtenbacher, M. Farbige stickereivorlagen. 1891-95

Reitz, A., and Reitz, E. Farbige flachtisch-muster. 1891

Townsend, W. G. P., and Pesel, L. F. Embroidery; or, The craft of the needle. 1908

20th century

Crompton, Rebecca. Modern design in embroidery. 1936

Day, L. F., and Buckle, Mary. Art in needlework; a book about embroidery. 1926

Huish, M. B. Samplers and tapestry embroideries. 1913

Prévot, Gabriel. Stores dentelles & broderies dans le style moderne. 1901

Prévot, Gabriel, and Devresse, G. Dentelles et broderies d'art, stores & brisebise. 1905

BY SPECIAL COUNTRY

Armenia

Paris. Exposition internationale des arts décoratifs et industriels modernes, 1925. Broderies russes, tartares, armeniennes. 1925

Austria

Haberlandt, Michael. Textile volkskunst aus Österreich. 1912

China

Ardenne de Tizac, J. H. d'. The stuffs of China, weavings and embroideries. 1924

Les étoffes de la Chine; tissus & broderies. 1914?

New York. Metropolitan museum of art. Chinese textiles. 1934

Victoria and Albert museum, South Kensington. Brief guide to the Chinese embroideries. 1921

Copts

Dillmont, Thérèse de. L'art chrétien en Egypte. Motifs de broderie copte. ca1892

Czechoslovakia

Broderies et décoration populaires tchéco-slovaques. 192-?

Koula, Jan. Výběr národního českého vyšívání z českého průmyslového musea Náprstkových ... Auswahl bömischer nationalstickerei. 1893

Kožmínová, Amalie. Podkarpatská Rus. 1922

Socháň, P. B., pub. Slovenské národnie ornamenty ... Ornaments nationales slovaques. Slowakische national-ornamente. 1896

Socháň, P. B., pub. Vzory staroslovenských vipiviek. Muster altslowakischer leinenstickerei. 1894

Sojková, Berta. Vzory vyšwání lidu slovanského na Moravě ... [Stickereimuster des slavischen volkes in Mähren, nach originalen im patriotischen museum in Olmütz] 1887-95

Wierzbicki, Ludowik. Wzory przemysłu domowego ... włościani na rusi wydane przez muzeum Przemysłowe miejskie ... Ornamente der hausindustrie ... ruthenischern bauern. 1880-89

Moravia

Brünn. Mähr. gewerbemuseum. Proben weiblicher handarbeiten mährisch-ländlicher haus-industrie. 1885

Egypt

See Embroidery—Copts

Embroidery—England—*Continued*

England

Hartshorne, C. H. English medieval embroidery. 1848

Kendrick, A. F. English embroidery. 1905

Marshall, Frances, and Marshall, Hugh. Old English embroidery: its technique and symbolism. 1894

Pesel, L. F. English embroidery. 1931

Victoria and Albert museum, South Kensington. A picture book of English embroideries, Elizabethan and Stuart. 1926

Europe

Cole, A. S. Ornament in European silks. 1899

See also names of European countries under heading Embroidery

Finland

Schvindt, Theodor. Suomalaisia koristeita. Finnische ornamente. 1895-1903

Germany

Album fur altdeutsche leinen-stickerei und stickerei auf Java-canevas. Leipzig, Kramer 1878

Berliner modenblatt. Stick-album des Berliner modenblatt. 1880

Hillardt, Gabriele. Stickmuster in altdeutschem stile für leinenstickerei (Holbeintechnik) und löchleinstickerei in verbindung mit fullstichen und plattstich. 1883

Lessing, Julius. Muster altdeutscher leinenstickerei. 1878-93

Manteuffel, Erna von. Album altdeutscher leinenstickerei. 1883

Rasch, Albert. Das Eibenstocker stickereigewerbe unter der einwirkung der mode. 1910

Schinnerer, Luise. Die kunst der weissstickerei. 1896

Schinnerer, Luise. Lehrgänge für weiszstickerei und knüpfarbeit. 1893

Hungary

L'art populaire hongrois. 1928

Hungary. Földmívelésügyi ministerium. Kiváló diszitmények az 1881. évi Országos magyar nöiparkiállitából ... Ornements remarquables de l'Exposition hongroise industrielle des ouvrages de femmes en 1881. 1882

Malonyay, Dezsö. A magyar nép müvészete. 1913-22

Pentsy, Josef, and Szentgyörgyi, Ludwig. Kalotaszegi varrottas-album. 1888

Undi, Mariska. Magyar himvarró müvészet; a nemes magyar fonalasmunkák története, a honfoglalás korától napjainkig. 1934

India

Estrade, C. Broderies hindoues. 1926

Italy

Lipperheide, Frieda. Muster altitalienischer leinenstickerei. 1881-83

Paganino, Alessandro. Burato ... 1527. 1878-80

Latvia

Latvijas saule. 1923-31

Rumania

L'art du peuple roumain. 1925

Kolbenheyer, Erich. Motive der hausindustriellen stickerei in der Bukowina ... Motifs de la broderie paysanne en Bukovine ... Designs of the home-industry embroideries in Bukovina. 1912

Oprescu, George. Arta ţărănească la Români; lucrare însoţită de cincizeci şi opt tabele de ilustraţii. 1922

Oprescu, George. Peasant art in Roumania. 1929

Russia

Al'bom" risunkov" dli͡a kanvovykh" rabot". 1882-83

Al'bom" russkīkh" monogramm" dli͡a mi͡etkī bi͡el'i͡a. 1882

Dalmatov", K. Russkii͡a vyshīvkī ... v" russkī teret " datskago korolevskago parka Fredensborg" v" 1889 g. Uzory vzi͡aty īz" ... sobranii͡a starīnnykh" obraztsov" narodnago shit'i͡a Velīkorussov" Moskovskoĭ, Novgorodskoi, Tverskoĭ ī I͡Aroslavskoĭ guberneiĭ. 1889

Kalitkin, N. Ornament shit'i͡a kostromskogo polushubka. S predisl. Vas. Smirnova. 1926g

Paris. Exposition internationale des arts décoratifs et industriels modernes, 1925. Broderies russes, tartares, arméniennes. 1925

Shakhovskai͡a, Princess S. N. Uzory starīnnago shīt'i͡a v" Rossiī ... s"predisloviem F. Buslaeva. Dessins d'anciennes broderies en Russie. 1885

Stasov", V. V. Russkiĭ narodnyĭ ornament"; vypusk" nervyĭ, shīt'e tkanī, kruzheva ... S" ob" i͡asnītel'nym" tekstom". L'ornement national russe; Première livraison: Broderies, tissus, dentelles. 1872

Ténicheva, M. K. P. knyaginya. Broderies des paysannes de Smolensk. 1907

Verkhovskoĭ, O. Uzory russkie, malorossiĭskie, ī i͡uzhno-slavi͡anskie. Ornements russes, petit-russiens et slaves méridionaux. Russische, kleinrussische, und südslavonische stickmuster. 1882

Scandinavia

Karlin, G. J. Skånsk textil konstslöjd. 1886

Kulle, Jakob. Jakob Kulles svenska mönster för konst-väfnader och broderier. 1892

Kulle, Jakob. Nordische muster-sammlung. 1895

Spain

Byne, Mrs M. S. Popular weaving and embroidery in Spain. 1924

Embroidery—Spain—*Continued*
Byne, Mrs M. S. Tejidos y bordados populares espanoles. c1924
Villalba, J. Broderies populaires espagnoles. 1929?

Tatary

Paris. Exposition internationale des arts décoratifs et industriels modernes, 1925. Broderies russes, tartares, armeniennes. 1925

United States

Vanderpoel, Mrs E. N. American lace & lace-makers. 1924

Yugoslavia

Lay, Felix. Kulturno īstorījsko etnografskī atlas kraļevīne Srbīje ... Culturhistorisch etnografischer atlas des Königreiches Serbien. 1886
Lay, Felix. Ornamenti jugoslovenske domaće i umjetne obŕtnosti ... Ornamente südslavischer nationaler haus und kunst-industrie. 1875-84
Lay, Felix. Sudslävische ornamente gesammelt ... und nebst einer abhandlung über die verbreitung und cultur der Südslaven; der ornamentale theil von F. Fischbach. 1872

Embroidery, Church
Barber, Mrs Mary. Some drawings of ancient embroidery. 1880
Burlington fine arts club, London. Exhibition of English embroidery executed prior to the middle of the XVI century. 1905
Neff, E. C. An Anglican study in Christian symbolism. 1898
Stiff, A. Stickmuster für kirchl. linnenzeug im styl des XII.-XIII. jahrhunderts. 1884
Versteyl, H. A. Die heiligen monogramme. 1879
Versteyl, H. A. Die kirchliche leinwandstickerei. 1879-83
Victoria and Albert museum, South Kensington. Catalogue of English ecclesiastical embroideries of the XIII. to XVI. centuries. 1930
Vienna. K. K. Österreichisches museum fur künst und industrie. Die Burgundischen gewander der k.k. schatzkammer; messornat fur den Orden vom Goldenen vliess. 1864

Embroidery, Cross-stitch
Album der monogramme für kreuzstich. 1894
Album di lavori a punto croce. 1890
Alexander, V. C. Cross-stitch. 1932
Burchard, A. Musterblätter für kreuzstichstickereien. 1892
Dillmont, Thérèse de. Album de broderies au point de croix. 1885-1890
Freimann, Jenny. Muster-album von kreuzstichmonogrammen. 1890
Lessing, Julius. Mönster för korsstyngsbroderier. 1880

Scheffers, A. Neue muster-vorlagen für farbige kreuzstich-arbeiten. 1887
Teschendorff, Toni. Kreuzstich-muster für leinenstickerei. 1879-84

Embroidery and lace. Lefébure, Ernest

Embroidery; or, The craft of the needle. Townsend, W. G. P. and Pesel, L. F.

Éméric-David, Toussaint Bernard
(ed.) Seroux d'Agincourt, J. B. L. G. Histoire de l'art par les monumens

Emerson, Edwin
German swordplay. Philadelphia, Pa. Graf & Breuninger c1936
80p. front. illus. O.
Pictures German and Scandinavian swords of ancient and medieval times, and fencers of various periods
LC 36-16915

A history of the nineteenth century, year by year ... with an introduction by George Gottfried Gervinus. New York, Dodd, Mead 1902
3v. col.fronts. pl.(part col.) ports. 2 fold. maps. O.
Paged continuously
With the exception of slight changes in the t.-p., identical with the edition published in the same year by P. F. Collier and son
Volume 1 shows military costume of the Napoleonic era; v2-3 show general costume of the 19th century
LC 2-19294

Emilia. See Italy—Emilia

The **Emilio** collection of military buttons. Essex institute, Salem, Massachusetts

Emmanuel, Maurice
La danse grecque antique d'après les monuments figures. Paris, Hachette 1896
xvi,348p. 600 illus. 6 col.pl. O.
Drawings by the author and by A. Collombar
Lipperheide 207

Emonts, Ch.
(illus.) Gayet, A. J. Exposition universelle de 1900. Palais du costume. Le costume en Égypte du IIIe au XIIIe siècle

L'**empereur** et la garde impériale. Charlet, N. T.

L'**empereur** Nicolas Alexandrovitch en tenue de 10 régiments dont sa majesté est chef. Backmanson, H.

Emperors. See Kings and rulers

Emphinger, Franz
(lithgr. Darstellung aller waffengattungen der kais. königl. osterreichischen armee im jahr 1839. Wien, J. Léon ca1840
6 col.pl. Q.
Colas 965

L'**empire.** See Bouchot, H. F. X. M. Le luxe francais: L'Empire

L'**empire** chinois. Allom, Thomas

L'**empire** d'Allemagne. Cocheris, Mme P. A. W.

L'**Empire** de la mode. Paris, Janet [1817]
48p. 6pl. Ti.
Plates engraved by Janet after H. Vernet
Colas 966. Lipperheide 2531

L'**empire** du soleil. Meyendorff, K. E., and Meyendorff, N. G.

Empire français. Lalaisse Hippolyte

Empresses. See Queens and empresses

Emy, Henry
(engr.) Costumes historiques. Paris, Aubert ca1850
6 col.pl. ob.F.
Title is from the inscriptions on the plates
Colas 967. Lipperheide 1086m

En campagne. Maillot, T. J. R.

En la sala de armas. Sanchez-M. Navarro, Francisco

En marge de l'histoire. Puis, Auguste

Enchiridion artis pingendi fingendi et sculpendi. See note under Amman, Jost. Kunstbüchlin

Enciclopedia dell'abbigliamento femminile. Piergiovanni, Bruno

Enciclopedia delle donne; Plocamopoli. See Manuel des toilettes; dedié aux dames

L'enciclopédie carcassière. Marchand, J. H.

L'enciclopédie perruquiere. Marchand, J. H.

Encyclopaedia biblica. Cheyne, T. K., and Black, J. S.

An **encyclopaedia** of freemasonry and its kindred sciences. Mackey, A. G.

Encyclopädie der sämmtlichen frauenkünste. Leonhardt-Lysèr, Caroline, and Seifer, Cäcile

Encyclopedia of needlework. Dillmont, Thérèse de

Encyclopédie d'armurerie avec monogrammes, guide des amateurs d'armes et armures anciennes. Demmin, A. F.

Encyclopédie des ouvrages de dames. Dillmont, Thérèse de

Encyclopédie des voyages. Grasset de Saint-Sauveur, Jacques

Encyclopédie méthodique. Lacombe, Fr.

Encyclopédie populaire illustrée du vingtième siècle. See Le costume, la mode

Encyclopédie portative. See Depping, G. B. Aperçu historique sur les moeurs et coutumes des nations

Encyklopaedie der weiblichen handarbeiten. See Dillmont, Thérèse de. Encyclopédie des ouvrages de dames

Endrulat, Bernhard
Das Schillerfest in Hamburg am 11., 12. u. 13. Novbr. 1859; mit 12 illus. von Otto Speckter. Hamburg, O. Meissner 1860
xv,367p. illus. O.

Les **Enfants** du Jardin des modes. 1928-? Paris, C. Nast
Illus. Q. 15fr. per no.
Supplement to Jardin des modes. Published quarterly. Current 1938

Engel, Claire Elaine. See Dubech, Lucien, jt. auth.

Engel, Johann Jakob
Ideen zu einer mimik. Berlin, Auf kosten des verfassers 1785-86
2v. front. pl. D.
Lipperheide 3201. LC 11-17703

Engelbrecht, Christian
(engr.) Gülich, Ludwig von. Erb-huldigung so ... Josepho dem ersten ... an dem auff den 22. dess monats septembris anno 1705 angesetzten tag abgelegt ... worden

Engelbrecht, Martin
Assemblage nouveau des manouvriers habilles. Neueröffnete samlung der mit ihren eigenen arbeiten und werckzeugen eingekleideten künstlern, handwerckern und professionen A[ugustae] V[indelicorum] ca1730
1 l. 192 col.pl. 34½x23cm.
Copperplate engravings with explanatory subscriptions in French and German; arranged alphabetically by name of occupation: Apoticaire to Vitrier
Colas 969. Lipperheide 1976. LC 25-18232

[Biblische und religiöse darstellungen] Augsburg? 172-?
160 col.pl. ob.O.

[Costumes des armées française, bavaroise et autrichienne en 1809] No place 1809?
15 col.pl. Q.
Colas 972

La mode d'Augsbourg; Augsburgische kleider tracht. Augusta Vindelicorum, M. Engelbrecht 1739
14 col.pl. Q.
Most of the plates show three figures, with explanatory text in French and German
Colas 970. Lipperheide 770

[Pictures of Swiss uniforms] Augusta vindelicorum, M. Engelbrecht ca1792
57 col.pl. Q.
Colas 971. Lipperheide 2252

Vornehmste reiche und staaten der welt in zierlichem und theils nach ihrer landes-art gewöhnlichem habit mit ihren wappen und ordens-zeichen vorgestellet. Augspurg, J. A. Pfeffel 1717
18pl. F.
Plates show women in court costume
Colas 968. Lipperheide 33

(engr.) Meister, Léonard. Beschreibung der gemeineidgenossischen truppensendung nach Basel

(illus.) Manuale, oder Handgriffe der infanterie

Engelhardt, Christian Moritz
Herrad von Landsperg, aebtissin zu Hohenburg, oder St Odilien, im Elsass, im zwölften jahrhundert; und ihr werk: Hortus deliciarum. Ein beytrag zur geschichte der wissenschaften, literatur, kunst, kleidung, waffen und sitten des mittelalters. Stuttgart und Tübingen, J. G. Cotta 1818
xv,200p. O. and atlas of 12 col.pl. F.
Plates are a selection of the most noteworthy from the *Hortus deliciarum*, a source book for costume of the 12th century. They are engraved by Willemin
Lipperheide 373

Engelhart, Gustaf
Svenska arméns och flottans officers—och civilmilitära uniformer jemte gradbeteckingar samt arméns och flottans indelning. Stockholm, Kongl. boktryckeriet, P. A. Norstedt 1886
30p. 7 col.pl. O.
Another edition (Stockholm, R. Blaedel 1888) has the same collation
Colas 973

(lithgr.) Roehn, Adolphe. Nouveaux cris de Paris

Engelmann, Godefroi
(pub.) Chopin. Costumes persans
(pub.) Chopin. Costumes russes modernes

[**Engelmann, Gustav**]
The American garment cutter for women's garments; 2d ed. New York [etc] American fashion company c1913
295p. illus. diagrs. Q. $15
Preface signed: The author, Gustav Engelmann
LC 13-2097

England, Paul
(tr.) Gregor, Joseph, and Fülöp-Miller, René. The Russian theatre

England
Ashdown, E. J. British costume during XIX centuries (civil and ecclesiastical). 1910
Aspin, Jehoshaphat. A picture of the manners, customs, sports and pastimes, of the inhabitants of England. 1825
Beaumont, E. T. Ancient memorial brasses. 1914
Boulton, W. B. The amusements of Old London ... from the 17th to the beginning of the 19th century. 1901
Brooke, Iris. English costume from the fourteenth through the nienteenth century. 1937
Brummell, G. B. Male and female costume. 1932
Calthrop, D. C. English costume. 1907
Carpenter, F. G., and Harmon, Dudley. The British isles and the Baltic states. 1926
Carter, John. Specimens of the ancient sculpture and painting. 1838
Clinch, George. English costume from prehistoric times to the end of the eighteenth century. 1909
Costumes, arts, métiers et usages de l'Angleterre. 1817
Costumes of British ladies from the time of William the I[st] to the reign of Queen Victoria. ca1840
Cotman, J. S. Engravings of sepulchral brasses in Norfolk and Suffolk, tending to illustrate the ecclesiastical, military, and civil costume as well as to preserve memorials of ancient families in that county. 1839
Craik, G. L., and MacFarlane, Charles. The pictorial history of England. 1849
Davey, R. P. B. The pageant of London. 1906
Davison, T. R. Gleanings fom the past and memorials from the present; being a series of sketches at the Health exhibition, 1884. 1884
Day, T. A., and Dines, J. H. Illustrations of medieval costume in England. 1851
Doyle, J. W. E. A chronicle of England, B. C. 55-A. D. 1485. 1864
Duleep Singh, Frederick, prince. Portraits in Norfolk houses. 1928
Eccleston, James. An introduction to English antiquities. 1847
Fairholt, F. W. Costume in England; a history of dress to the end of the eighteenth century. 1896
Garnett, Richard, and Gosse, Sir E. W. English literature; an illustrated record. 1903-04
Giles, E. B. The history of the art of cutting in England; preceded by a sketch of the history of English costumes. 1887
Green, J. M. C. Period costumes and settings for the small stage. 1936
Green, J. R. A short history of the English people. 1893-95
Haines, Herbert. A manual of monumental brasses. 1861
Harding, G. P., and Moule, Thomas. Gallery of English historical personages
Hartley, Dorothy, and Elliot, M. M. V. Life and work of the people of England; a pictorial record from contemporary sources. 1926-31
Hill, Georgiana. A history of English dress from the Saxon period to the present day. 1893
Holland, Henry. Herwologia anglica: hoc est, clarissimorum et doctissimorum, aliqout Anglorum qui floruerunt ab anno Cristi M.D. usq' ad presentem annum. 1620
Hughes, Talbot. Dress design. 1920
Innes, A. D. A history of England from the earliest times to the present day. 1913
Kelly, F. M., and Schwabe, Randolph. A short history of costume & armour, chiefly in England, 1066-1800. 1931
Kelly, Mary. On English costume. 1934
Knight, Charles, ed. London. 1851
Knight, Charles, ed. Old England. 1845
Lennox, Lord W. P. Fashion then and now. 1878
Lodge, Edmund. Portraits of illustrious personages of Great Britain, engraved from authentic pictures in the galleries of the nobility and the public collections of the country. 1835
London. Museum. Costume. 1934
Macklin, H. W. The brasses of England. 1907
Macklin, H. W. Monumental brasses together with a selected bibliography and county lists of brasses remaining in the churches of the United Kingdom. 1913
Malcolm, J. P. Anecdotes of the manners and customs of London from the Roman invasion to the year 1700. 1811
Martin, Charles, and Martin, Leopold. Civil costume of England, from the conquest to the present time. 1842
Meyrick, Sir S. R. A critical inquiry into antient armour, as it existed in Europe, but particularly in England, from the Norman conquest to the reign of King Charles II, with a glossary of military terms of the middle ages. 1824
Mineur, A. E. A charitable remonstrance addressed to the wives and maidens of France, touching their dissolute adornments. 1887

England—*Continued*

Nougaret, P. J. B. Beautés de l'histoire d'Angleterre, ou époques intéressantes et remarquables, origines, usages et moeurs, batailles célèbres, depuis les commencements de la monarchie, jusqu'à la fin du règne de Georges II. 1811

Parrott, Sir J. E. The pageant of British history. 1911

Parrott, Sir J. E. The pageant of English literature. 1914

Phillips, Margaret, and Tomkinson, W. S. English women in life and letters. 1926

Planché, J. R. History of British costume, from the earliest period to the close of the eighteenth century. 1847

Price, Sir H. P. When men wore muffs; the story of men's clothes. 1936

Quennell, Mrs M. C., and Quennell, C. H. B. A history of everyday things in England, 1066-1935. 1922-35

Schild, Marie. Old English costumes; ladies & peasants. 1912

Skeat, W. W. The past at our doors; or, The old in the new around us. 1911

Smith, C. H. Selections of the ancient costume of Great Britain and Ireland from the seventh to the sixteenth century. 1814

Stone, Mrs Elizabeth. Chronicles of fashion, from the time of Elizabeth to the early part of the nineteenth century, in manners, amusements, banquets, costume, &c. 1845

Strutt, Joseph. Complete view of the dress and habits of the people of England. 1842

Strutt, Joseph. Horda Angelcynnan: or A compleat view of the manners, customs, arms, habits &c. of the inhabitants of England from the arrival of the Saxons to the present time. 1775-76

Strutt, Joseph. Regal and ecclesiastical antiquities of England. 1842

Suffling, E. R. English church brasses from the 13th to the 17th century. 1910

Thornely, J. L. The monumental brasses of Lancashire and Cheshire, with some account of the persons represented. 1893

Traill, H. D., and Mann, J. S., eds. Social England. 1901-04

Truman, Nevil. Historic costuming. 1936

Victoria and Albert museum, South Kensington. Guide to the collection of costumes. 1924

Waller, J. G., and Waller, L. A. B. A series of monumental brasses, from the thirteenth to the sixteenth century. 1864

Wingfield, L. S. Notes on civil costume in England from the conquest to the regency. 1884

Wright, Thomas. The homes of other days; a history of domestic manners and sentiments in England from the earliest known period to modern times. 1871

See also Scotland; Wales; also subdivision England under Academic costume; Arms and armor; Beggars; Children; Coronations and Coronation robes; Court dress; Crown jewels; Ecclesiastical costume; Embroidery; Funerals; Heraldic costume; Hunting costume; Kings and rulers; Legal costume; Military costume; Monastic and religious orders; Naval costume; Nobles; Officials; Orders of knighthood and chivalry; Regalia; Rings; Servants; Students; Universities and colleges; Theatrical costume; Weddings and wedding dress; Workmen

Caricature and satire

À Beckett, G. A. The comic history of England. 1847-48

Everitt, Graham. English caricaturists and graphic humourists of the nineteenth century. 1886

To 1066

Baker, Sir Richard. A chronicle of the kings of England. 1730

Baye, Joseph, baron de. Études archéologiques. Époque des invasions barbares. Industrie anglo-saxonne. 1889

Baye, Joseph, baron de. The industrial arts of the Anglo-Saxons. 1893

Bayeux tapisserie de la Reine Mathilde. n.d.

Belloc, Hilaire. The book of the Bayeux tapestry. 1914

Besant, Sir Walter. Early London, prehistoric, Roman, Saxon and Norman. 1908

Brooke, Iris. English costume of the early middle ages: 10th to 13th centuries. 1936

Bruce, J. C. The Bayeux tapestry elucidated. 1856

E., G. R. Story of Arthur and Guinevere, and the fate of Sir Lancelot of the Lake, as told in antique legends and ballads and in modern poetry. 1879

Faussett, Bryan. Inventorium sepulchrale [antiquities found in Anglo-Saxon cemeteries] 1856

Fowke, F. R. The Bayeux tapestry; a history and description. 1898

Meyrick, Sir S. R., and Smith, C. H. Costume of the original inhabitants of the British islands, from the earliest periods to the 6th century; to which is added that of the Gothic nations of the western coasts of the Baltic, the ancestors of the Anglo-Saxons and Anglo-Danes. 1821

Notice historique sur la tapisserie brodée par la reine Mathilde, épouse de Guillaume le Conquérant. 1804

England—To 1066—*Continued*

Quennell, Mrs M. C., and Quennell, C. H. B. Everyday life in Anglo-Saxon, viking, and Norman times. 1927

Quennell, Mrs M. C., and Quennell, C. H. B. Everyday life in Roman Britain. 1925

Medieval period, 1066-1485

Barfield, T. C. England in the middle ages. 1909-10

Barnard, F. P. ed. Mediaeval England. 1924

Besant, Sir Walter. Mediaeval London. 1906

Blake, William. Chaucers Canterbury pilgrims. 189-?

Brooke, Iris. English costume of the early middle ages: 10th to 13th centuries 1936

Brooke, Iris. English costume of the later middle ages: The fourteenth and fifteenth centuries. 1935

Druitt, Herbert. A manual of costume as illustrated by monumental brasses. 1906

Ecclesiological society, Cambridge. Illustrations of monumental brasses. 1846

Hartley, Dorothy. Mediaeval costume and life. 1931

Hodgetts, J. F. The English in the middle ages; from the Norman usurpation to the days of the Stuarts. 1885

Perkins, Mrs L. F., comp. Robin Hood; his deeds and adventures as recounted in the old English ballads. 1906

Prior, E. S., and Gardiner, Arthur. An account of medieval figure-sculpture in England. 1912

Salzman, L. F. English life in the middle ages. 1929

Shaw, Henry. Dresses and decorations of the middle ages. 1843

Stothard, C. A. The monumental effigies of Great Britain; selected from our cathedrals and churches ... from the Norman conquest to the reign of Henry the Eighth. 1817

14th century

British Museum. Department of manuscripts. Queen Mary's psalter; miniatures and drawings by an English artist of the 14th century. 1912

Carey, W. P. Critical description of the procession of Chaucer's pilgrims to Canterbury, painted by Thomas Stothard. 1808

15th century

Derrick, Freda. Tales told in church stones. 1935. p81-105

Pageants of Richard Beauchamp, earl of Warwick. Pageant of the birth, life and death of Richard Beauchamp, earl of Warwick, K. G., 1389-1439. 1914

Tudor period, 1485-1603

Besant, Sir Walter. London in the time of the Tudors. 1904

Brooke, Iris. English costume in th age of Elizabeth: the sixteenth century 1933

Chamberlaine, John. Imitations of origi nal drawings by Hans Holbein, in th collection of His Majesty, for the por traits of illustrious persons of the cour of Henry VIII. 1792

Chamberlaine, John. Portraits of illus trious personages of the court o Henry VIII. 1828

Ecclesiological society, Cambridge. Illus trations of monumental brasses. 184

Gosson, Stephen. Pleasant quippes fo upstart newfangled gentlewomen. 1596 1847

Hatcher, O. L. A book for Shakespear plays and pageants. 1916

Linthicum, M. C. Costume in the dram of Shakespeare and his contemporaries 1936

Morse, Mrs H. K., ed. Elizabetha pageantry. 1934

Salzman, L. F. England in Tudor times an account of its social life and in dustries. 1926

Shakespeare's England; an account o the life & manners of his age. 191

17th century

Bedford, Jessie. Home life under th Stuarts, 1603-1649. 1903

Bedford, Jessie. Social life under th Stuarts. 1904

Besant, Sir Walter. London in the tim of the Stuarts. 1903

Brooke, Iris. English costume of th seventeenth century. 1934

Bry, J. T. de, and Bry, J. I. de. Wahr hafftige unnd eygentliche beschreibun der allerschrecklichsten verrätherey .. wieder die Königliche Majestät ... z London. 1606

Clarendon, E. H., 1st earl of. Th history of the rebellion and civil war in England, begun in the year 164 1732

Gibb, William. The royal house o Stuart. 1890

Hollar, Wenceslaus. Aula veneris, siv Varietas foeminini sexus diversarun Europae nationum differentiag habi tuum. 1644

Hollar, Wenceslaus. Ornatus muliebri Anglicanus, or The Severall Habit of English Women, from the Nobilit to the contry woman, as they are i these times. 1640

Hollar, Wenceslaus. Theatru mulierum sive Varietas atque differentia habituun foeminei sexus diversorum Europa nationum hodierno tempore vulgo. 164

Linthicum, M. C. Costume in the dram of Shakespeare and his contemporaries 1936

Macaulay, T. B. M., 1st baron. Th history of England, from the accessio of James the Second. 1913-15

Morse, Mrs H. K., ed. Elizabetha pageantry. 1934

England—17th century—*Continued*

Parkes, Joan. Travel in England in the seventeenth century. 1925

Pepys, Samuel. The diary of Samuel Pepys. 1885

18th century

Ainsworth, W. H. The miser's daughter. 1872

Andrews, Alexander. The eighteenth century; or, Illustrations of the manners and customs of our grandfathers. 1856

Armstrong, Sir Walter. Gainsborough and his place in English art. 1898

Armstrong, Sir Walter. Sir Joshua Reynolds, first president of the Royal academy. 1900

Ashton, John. Men, maidens and manners a hundred years ago. 1888

Ashton, John. Old times: a picture of social life at the end of the eighteenth century. 1885

Ashton, John. Social life in the reign of Queen Anne. 1919

Berry, Mary. Extracts of the journals and correspondence of Miss Berry, from the year 1783 to 1852. 1865

Besant, Sir Walter. London in the eighteenth century. 1902

Bickham, George. The musical entertainer. ca.1740

Boehn, Max von. England im 18. jahrhundert. 1922

Bowen, Marjorie, pseud. William Hogarth, the cockney's mirror. 1936

Brooke, Iris. English costume of the eighteenth century. 1931

Davies, R. English society in the eighteenth century in contemporary art. 1907

Dobson, Austin. The ballad of Beau Brocade, and other poems of the XVIIIth century. 1892

Gaunt, William. English rural life in the eighteenth century. 1925

Gravelot, H. F. B. Four costume suites. ca1744

Guillaumot, A. E. Costumes anglais du temps de la révolution et du premier empire 1795-1806. 1879

Guillaumot, A. É. Costumes of the time of the French revolution 1790-1793, together with English costumes during the years 1795-1806. 1889

Highmore, Joseph. Plates illustrating the "Pamela" of Samuel Richardson. 1745?

Hogarth, William. The works of William Hogarth, from the original plates restored by James Heath ... with the addition of many subjects not before collected: to which are prefixed, a biographical essay on the genius and productions of Hogarth, and explanations of the subjects of the plates, by John Nichols. 1822

Hogarth, William. The works of William Hogarth ... with descriptions by the Rev. John Trusler. 18—

Hughes, Talbot. Old English costumes, selected from the collection formed by Talbot Hughes: a sequence of fashions through the 18th & 19th centuries. 1914

Jesse, William. The life of Beau Brummell. 1927

Loftie, W. J. Kensington, picturesque and historical. 1888

Malcolm, J. P. Anecdotes of the manners and customs of London. 1808

Mitton, G. E. Jane Austen and her times. 1905

Richardson, A. E. Georgian England; a survey of social life, trades, industries & art from 1700 to 1820. 1931

Turberville, A. S. English men and manners in the eighteenth century; an illustrated narrative. 1929

Turberville, A. S., ed. Johnson's England; an account of the life & manners of his age. 1933

Periodicals

The Bon ton magazine; or, Microscope of fashion and folly. 1791-96

Fashions of London & Paris; v 1, 1798/1800-v3 1804/06. 1800-06

Gallery of fashion. 1794-1803

Lady's magazine and museum of the belles-lettres. 1770-1837

Ladies' museum. 1798-1832

London und Paris. 1798-1810

Caricature and satire

Brinton, S. J. C. The eighteenth century in English caricature. 1904

Darly, Mary. Darly's comic-prints of characters, caricatures, macaronies, etc. 1776

Grego, Joseph. Rowlandson the caricaturist. 1880

19th century

Berry, Mary. Extracts of the journals and correspondence of Miss Berry, from the year 1783 to 1852. 1865

Besant, Sir Walter. London in the nineteenth century. 1909

Brooke, Iris. English costume of the nineteenth century. 1929

Chancellor, E. B. Life in Regency and early Victorian times. 1926

Hayward, A. L. The days of Dickens. 1926

Hughes, Talbot. Old English costumes, selected from the collection formed by Talbot Hughes: a sequence of fashions through the 18th & 19th centuries. 1914

Peel, Mrs D. C. B. A hundred wonderful years: social and domestic life of a century, 1820-1920. 1926

Quennell, Peter. Victorian panorama; a survey of life & fashion from contemporary photographs. 1937

Young, G. M., ed. Early Victorian England, 1830-1865. 1934

See also Dandyism

Periodicals

The Court magazine and monthly critic and lady's magazine, and museum of the belles lettres. 1832-47

England—19th century—Periodicals—*Cont.*

Gentleman's magazine of fashions, fancy costumes, and the regimentals of the army. 1828-94

Ladies pocket magazine. 1824-40

Monde élégant, or The world of fashion. 1824-91

New monthly Belle assemblée. 1834-70

Townsend's monthly selection of Parisian costumes. 1825-88

See also subdivision Periodicals under parts of the nineteenth century, e.g. Nineteenth century—1800-1837—Periodicals

1800-1837

Ackermann, Rudolph. Changeable ladies; being an assemblage of moveable human features. 1819

Ackermann, Rudolph. The microcosm of London. 1808

Alexander, William. Picturesque representations of the dress and manners of the English. 1814

Ashton, John. The dawn of the XIXth century in England. 1916

Ashton, John. Social England under the regency. 1890

Atkinson, J. A. A picturesque representation of the naval military and miscellaneous costumes of Great Britain. 1807

Barbey d'Aurevilly, J. A. The anatomy of dandyism. 1928

Barbey d'Aurevilly, J. A. Du dandysme et de G. Brummell. 1845

Barbey d'Aurevilly, J. A. Of dandyism and of George Brummell. 1897

Barker, Thomas. Forty lithographic impressions from drawings selected from his studies of rustic figures after nature. 1813

Boutet de Monvel, Roger. Beau Brummell and his times. 1908

British fashions, for the years 1803 and 1804. 1803-1804

Bury, Lady Charlotte (Campbell) The diary of a lady-in-waiting. 1908

Costume of the ladies of England, 1810-1829. 1829?

Cruikshank, George, and Cruikshank, I. R. London characters; twenty-four col'd plates. 1827-30

Cyclopaedia of the British costumes, from the Metropolitan repository of fashions. 1823-47

Dighton, Richard. Sketches in colors showing costumes of the period. 1819-22

Egan, Pierce. Life in London. 1821

Egerton, M. Airy nothings. 1825

Egerton, M. Matrimonial ladder or, Such things are a gift for all seasons. 1825

Egerton, D. T. The necessary qualifications of a man of fashion. 1823

Eyriès, J. B. B. L'Angleterre, ou costumes, moeurs, et usages des Anglais. ca1821

Guillaumot, A. E. Costumes anglais du temps de la révolution et du premier empire 1795-1806. 1879

Hunt, Mrs M. R. Our grandmothers' gowns. 1884

Jesse, William. The life of Beau Brummell. 1927

Lami, E. L., and Monnier, Henry. Voyage en Angleterre. 1829

Mitford, John. My cousin in the army: or Johnny Newcome on the peace establishment; a poem. 1822

Moses, Henry. Designs of modern costume. 1823?

Pyne, W. H. The costume of Great Britain. 1808

Pyne, W. H. Etchings of rustic figures for the embellishment of landscape 1815

Richardson, A. E. Georgian England; a survey of social life, trades, industries & art from 1700 to 1820. 1931

Shoberl, Frédéric, ed. England, Scotland and Ireland 1827

Strutt, Joseph. The sports and pastimes of the people of England. 1876

Tuer, A. W. The follies and fashions of our grandfathers (1807); embellished with ... plates including ladies' and gentlemen's dress. 1886-87

Walker, George. The costume of Yorkshire. 1885

Wilkins, W. H. Mrs Fitzherbert and George IV. 1905

Periodicals

Le Beau monde; or Literary and fashionable magazine. 1806-09

La Belle assemblée, or Bell's court and fashionable magazine. 1806-32

Fashions of London & Paris; v 1 1798/1800-v3 1804/06. 1800-06

Gallery of fashion. 1794-1803

Lady's magazine and museum of the belles-lettres. 1770-1837

Ladies' museum. 1798-1832

London und Paris, 1798-1810

The New bon ton magazine. 1818-21

Record of fashion and court elegance for 1807, 1808-1809. 1807-09

The Repository of arts, literature, commerce, manufactures, fashions and politics. 1809-29

Townsend's quarterly selection of French costumes. 1822-24

Caricature and satire

Alken, H. T. Symptoms, of being amused. 1822

Dighton, Richard. Characters at the west end of the town. 1825

Figures of fun; or comical pictures and droll verses, for little girls and boys 1833

Heath, William. Parish characters in ten plates. 1829

1837-1900

Bott, A. J., ed. Our mothers. 1932

Bott, A. J. This was England 1931

Boys, T. S. Original views of London as it is. 1842

England—1837-1900—*Continued*
Calthrop, D. C. English dress from Victoria to George v. 1934
The Court album: twelve portraits of the female aristocracy. 1853
Cruikshank, George. Cruikshank's water colours. 1903
Cruikshank, George. Drawings ... prepared by him to illustrate an intended autobiography. 1895
Cruikshank, George. George Cruikshank's Omnibus. 1869
Gavarni, G. S. C. Gavarni in London. 1849
Gray, William. Social contrasts. 1865
Gronow, R. H. The reminiscences and recollections of Captain Gronow. 1892
Jerrold, Blanchard. London; a pilgrimage. 1872
Loftie, W. J. Kensington, picturesque and historical. 1888
London interiors, with their costumes & ceremonies. 1841
The London journal. Advice to young ladies from the London journal of 1855 and 1862, with illustrations from the same and other sources, selected by R. D. 1933
McCarthy, Justin. Portraits of the sixties. 1903
Nevill, R. H. The world of fashion, 1837-1922
Nicholson, William. London types. 1898
Pingret, Édouard. Voyage de S. M. Louis-Philippe Ier, roi des Français, au Chateau de Windsor. 1846
The private life of King Edward VII (Prince of Wales, 1841-1901) by a member of the royal household. 1901
Victorian costumes; a record of ladies' attire 1837 to 1897. 1897

Periodicals

The Englishwoman's domestic magazine. 1852-79
The Illustrated household journal and Englishwoman's domestic magazine. 1880-81
Lady's pictorial, a newspaper for the home. 1881-1907
The Lion; a journal of gentlemen's newest fashions. 1845-48
The Little messenger of fashions and the Confident united. 1852-54
London tailor and record of fashion. 1876-1914
Madame. 1895-97
Master tailor and cutters' gazette. 1893-1908
The Milliner and dressmaker, and warehouseman's gazette, and illustrated journal of the new modes. 1870-81
The Milliner, dressmaker and draper. 1881-82
Minister's Gazette of fashion. 1846+
Le Moniteur de la mode: a fashionable journal appearing monthly. 1882-89
The Queen, the Lady's newspaper. 1847+
The St. James's budget. 1880-1911
Sylvia's home journal. 1878-94
Vogue, incorporating Vanity fair. 1892+
Woman's world. 1888-90
Women's wear, incorporating the Ladies tailor. 1898? +
The Young Englishwoman. 1865-77
The Young ladies' journal. 1864-1920

Caricature and satire

Cruikshank, George. The bachelor's own book. 1844
Doyle, Richard. Birds-eye views of modern society. 1864?
Doyle, Richard. Manners and customs of ye Englyshe. 1849
Du Maurier, G. L. P. B. English society at home. 1880
Du Maurier, G. L. P. B. Pictures of English society ... from "Punch." 1884
Grego, Joseph. Rowlandson the caricaturist. 1880
Heath, Henry. The caricaturist's scrap book. 1840
Jerrold, Blanchard. The life of George Cruikshank, in two epochs. 1882
Leech, John. Pictures of life & character. 1854-69
Meadows, Kenny. Heads of the people, or Portraits of the English. 1841
Pennell, Joseph. The work of Charles Keene ... to which is added a bibliography of the books Keene illustrated, and a catalogue of his etchings. 1897

20th century

Calthrop, D. C. English dress from Victoria to George v. 1934
Chester, S. B. Secrets of the tango. 1914
Clephane, Irene. Ourselves, 1900-1930. 1933

Periodicals

Fashion age. 1934+
Lady's pictorial, a newspaper for the home. 1881-1907
London art fashions for ladies. 1937+
London tailor and record of fashion. 1876-1914
Man and his clothes. 1926+
Master tailor and cutters' gazette. 1893-1908
Minister's gazette of fashion. 1846+
The Queen, the Lady's newspaper. 1847+
The St. James's budget. 1880-1911
Sartorial gazette. 1909+
Vogue, incorporating Vanity fair. 1892+
The Young ladies' journal. 1864-1920
Women's wear, incorporating the Ladies tailor. 1898?+

London

See subdivision England—London under Street venders; Uniforms, Civil

England, Church of. See Ecclesiastical costume—Anglican and Episcopal churches

England im 18. jahrhundert. Boehn, Max von

England in Tudor times. Salzman, L. F.

England, Scotland and Ireland. Shoberl, Frédéric, ed.

Englands vanity: or the voice of God against the monstrous sin of pride in dress and apparel. London, Printed for J. Dunton 1683
144p. front. O.
"Wherein naked breasts and shoulders, antick and fantastick garbs, patches, and painting, long perriwigs, towers, bulls, shades, curlings, and crispings, with an hundred more fooleries of both sexes, are condemned as notoriously unlawful. With pertinent addresses to the court, nobility, gentry, city, and country. Directed especially to the professors in London." Subtitle

Die **englische** armee in ihrer gegenwärtigen uniformirung ... Nebst erläuterungen zu denselben und mittheilungen über eintheilung, organisation etc. der englischen armee sowie mit einer liste der sämmtlichen regulären regimenter. Leipzig, M. Ruhl [1894]
42p. 17pl.(16 col.) on fold.sheet. D.
Colas 2599. Lipperheide 2276. LC 13-5873

Die **englischen** angriffswaffen zur zeit der einführung der feuerwaffen (1300-1350). Deters, Friedrich

Die **englischen** armee- und marine-uniformen im kriege, sowie die abzeichen an denselben. Leipzig, M. Ruhl [1912]
28p. 2 col.fold.pl. D.

English academical costume (mediaeval). Clark, E. C.

English caricaturists and graphic humorists of the nineteenth century. Everitt, Graham

English children in the olden time. Bedford, Jessie

English costume from the fourteenth through the nineteenth century. Brooke, Iris

English jewellery from the fifth century A. D. to 1800. Evans, Joan

English children's costume since 1775. Brooke, Iris

English church brasses. Suffling, E. R.

English church needlework. Hall, M. R.

The **English** coronation ceremony. Twining, E. F.

English coronation records. Legg, L. G. W.

English costume. Calthrop, D. C.

English costume from prehistoric times to the end of the eighteenth century. Clinch, George

English costume in the age of Elizabeth: the sixteenth century. Brooke, Iris

English costume of the early middle ages: 10th to 13th centuries. Brooke, Iris

English costume of the eighteenth century. Brooke, Iris

English costume of the later middle ages. Brooke, Iris

English costume of the nineteenth century. Brooke, Iris

English costume of the seventeenth century. Brooke, Iris

English dress from Victoria to George v. Calthrop, D. C.

English economic history and theory, An introduction to. Ashley, Sir W. J.

English embroidery. Kendrick, A. F.

English embroidery. Pesel, L. F.

The **English** governess at the Siamese court. Leonowens, Mrs A. H. C.

English heads and coiffures. Dighton, Robert

English in India
Atkinson, G. F. "Curry & rice," on forty plates; or, The ingredients of social life at "our station" in India. 1859
Atkinson, G. F. Indian spices for English tables. 1860
Tayler, W. Sketches illustrating the manners and customs of the Indians and Anglo-Indians. 1842

The **English** in the middle ages. Hodgetts, J. F.

English life in the middle ages. Salzman, L. F.

English literature; an illustrated record. Garnett, Richard, and Gosse, Sir E. W.

English liturgical colours. Hope, Sir W. H. St. J., and Atchley, E. G. C. F.

English medieval embroidery. Hartshorne, C. H.

English men and manners in the eighteenth century. Turberville, A. S.

English monastic life. Gasquet, F. A., cardinal

English regalia. Davenport, C. J. H.

The **English** regalia and crown jewels in the Tower of London. Twining, E. F.

English rural life in the eighteenth century. Gaunt, William

English society at home. Du Maurier, G. L. P. B.

English society in the eighteenth century in contemporary art. Davies, R.

English trade in the middle ages. Salzman, L. F.

English wayfaring life in the middle ages (xiv[th] century). Jusserand, J. A. A. J.

English women in life and letters. Phillips, Margaret, and Tomkinson, W. S.

The **Englishwoman's** domestic magazine. v 1-8, 1852-59; new ser. v 1-9, 1860-64; new ser. (ser.3) v 1-27, 1865-79. London, 1852-79
44v. O.-F.
Succeeded by *Illustrated household journal and Englishwoman's domestic magazine*

Engraved illustrations of antient arms and armour. Meyrick, Sir S. R.

Engravings of sepulchral brasses in Norfolk and Suffolk. Cotman, J. S.

Enhuber, Carl von
Deutsches volksleben in 13 bildern nach Melchior Meyr's erzählungen aus dem Ries. Berlin, G. Grote [1869]
4p. 13pl. ob.F.
Lipperheide 760

Enkevoërth, August Johann Breunner, graf von. See Breunner-Enkevoërth, A. J., graf von

Enlart, Camille
Manuel d'archéologie française depuis les temps mérovingiens jusqu'à la renaissance. Tome 3: Le costume. Paris, A. Picard 1916
Illus. pl. plans. O.
"Bibliographie critique": v3, pref. p21-29
Colas 974. Costume index. LC 6-46313

Der **Enndkrist** der Stadt-bibliothek zu Frankfurt am Main. Facsimile-wiedergabe; hrsg. und bibliographisch beschrieben von dr. Ernst Kelchner. Frankfurt a. M., H. Keller 1891
8p. 20 l. (incl. 62 illus.) Q.
A facsimile reproduction of the first printed edition of the *Enndkrist* (Strassburg, 1475)
Lipperheide 412

21. bataillons historie 1788-1918. Michelsen, P. U.

Enríquez, Colin Metcalfe Dallas
A Burmese arcady, an account of a long & intimate sojourn amongst the mountain dwellers of the Burmese hinterland & of their engaging characteristics and customs. London, Seeley, Service 1923
282p. col.front. pl. fold.map. O.
"This book is devoted chiefly to the Kachins." Preface
Costume index. LC 23-9510

L'**enseignement** professionnel de la mode. Alensis, A. d'

The **entertainment** of His most excellent Majestie Charles II. Ogilby, John

Enthronement of the one hundred twenty-fourth emperor of Japan. The Japan advertiser

Entrata in Roma dell' eccelmo ambasciatore di Pollonia l anno MDCXXXIII. Della Bella, Stefano

Entrata solenne dell' ... Confaloniero di Giustizia, che si fà ogni bimestre nel palazzo publico di Bologna. Mitelli, G. M.

Entrée de la Reine Bérengère au Mans en 1204. Le Mans, Monnoyer frères 1865
21p. 82 illus. F.
Lipperheide 2836

L'**entrée** de l'empereur Sigismond a Mantouë. Pippi, Giulio

Entrée triomphale ... le duc d'Angoulême. Lafitte, Louis

Die **entwickelung** der tracht in Deutschland während des mittelalters und der neuzeit. Köhler, Karl

Entwicklungsgeschichte der alten trutzwaffen. Jähns, Max

Entwicklungsgeschichte der griechischen tracht. Bieber, Margarete

Entwicklungs-geschichte der tracht. Peters, Emil

Entwistle, Mary
Children of other lands. London, H. Milford [1923]
118p. illus. D. (Friends of all the world. I)
LC 24-19335

Entwurf einer vorstellung der russisch-kayserlichen armee. No place, ca1760
1 l. 16 col.pl. O.
Colas 975. Lipperheide 2372

Les **épées** de Bordeaux, archéologie comparée des industries du fer dans la Biscaye française, le pays de Guyenne et le duché de Savoie. See Giraud, J. B. Documents pour servir à l'histoire de l'armement au moyen âge et à la renaissance

Les **épées** de Rives, étude archéologique sur les industries du fer en Dauphiné. See Giraud, J. B. Documents pour servir à l'histoire de l'armement au moyen âge et à la renaissance

Ephod
Foote, T. C. The ephod: its form and use. 1902

Episcopal church. See Ecclesiastical costume—Anglican and Episcopal churches

Episoden aus der cultur- und kunstgeschichte Bremens. Kohl, J. G.

Epitome chronicorum mundi. See note under Franck, Sebastian. Teutscher nation chronic

Epitome de las historias portuguezas. See Faria e Sousa, Manuel de. Historia del reyno de Portugal

Epitome regii ac vetustissimi artus sacrae caesareae ac Catholice maiestatis ... principis ... Ferdinandi ... Bohemiae regis, omniumque archiducum Austriae, ac Habsburgensium comitum. Gebwiler, Hieronymus

Épître d'Othéa. See Christine de Pisan

L'**épopée** du costume militaire français. Bouchot, H. F. X. M.

Époques remarquables de la vie de la femme. Suite de têtes. Grévedon, P. L. H.

Eppler, Alfred
Edelsteine und schmucksteine; 2., vollständig neu bearb. aufl., mit ausführlichen angaben über die natürlichen und gezüchteten perlen, über die edelsteinindustrie und den edelstein-handel von W. Fr. Eppler. Leipzig, W. Diebener 1934
554p. illus. 4 col.pl. diagrs. O.
The first edition was published under title: *Die schmuck-und edelsteine* as volume 2 of *Gewerblichen materialkunde*
LC 34-41249

Eppler, Wilhelm Friedrich
(ed.) Eppler, Alfred. Edelsteine und schmucksteine

L'**équipment** de l'armée Austro-Hongroise. See Franceschini, Friedrich. Militairisches pracht-bilderbuch

Équitation des dames. Aubert, P. A.

Equitum descripcio. Bruyn, Abraham de

Erb-huldigung. Kriegl, G. C.

Erb-huldigung so ... Josepho dem ersten ... an dem auff den 22. dess monats septembris anno 1705 angesetzten tag abgelegt ... worden. Gülich, Ludwig von

Erb-huldigung, welche dem ... römischen kayser Carolo dem sechsten ... als herzogen in Steyer, von denen gesamten steyrischen land-ständen den sechsten julii 1728 ... abgeleget und ... zusammen getragen worden. Deyersperg, G. J. von

Ercker, Lazarus
Aula subterranea domina dominantium subdita subditorum. Das ist: untererdische hofhaltung ... oder gründliche beschreibung derjenigen sachen so in der tieffe der erden wachsen als aller ertzen der königlichen und gemeinen

Ercker, Lazarus—*Continued*
metallen, auch fürnehmster mineralien ... auffs neue mercklich vermehret, zusambt angehängter auszlegung der terminorum und redarten der bergleute. Franckfurt, J. D. Zunners, gedruckt bei P. Hummen 1672
332p. 41 illus. F.
The first edition (Prag 1574) also contains the illustrations. Later editions 1684, 1703, 1736
Edited and enlarged by Johannes Hiskias Cardalucius
Some of the woodcuts show metal workers in seventeenth century smelteries
Lipperheide 1990

Erckert, Roderich von
Der Kaukasus und seine völker. Leipzig, P. Frohberg 1887
385p. illus. pl. fold.map, fold.tab. O.
LC 14-19121

Erclerung der preüssischen grössern landtaffel oder wappen. Henneberg, Caspar

Erdélyi magyarság. See Viski, Károly. Transylvanian Hungarians, peasant art

Der **erdkreis.** Hürlimann, Martin

Erich, Augustus
Aussfürliche und warhaffte beschreibung des durchlauchtigsten ... herrn Christians, des vierden dieses namens, zu Dennemark, Norwegen ... königes ... zu Koppenhagen den 29. augusti anno 1596 glücklich ... krönung. Koppenhagen, M. Weingardt 1597
168p. 11pl. Q.

Erich, Oswald Adolf
Deutsche volkstrachten. Leipzig, Bibliographisches institut c1934
55p. col.illus. D. [Meyers bunte bändchen]
LC 34-31250

See also Rumpf, Fritz, jt. illus.

Erinnerung an Hamburg. 20 hamburg. volkstrachten. Hamburg, B. S. Berendsohn ca1840
20pl. S.
Plates are signed H. I.
Colas 976

Erinnerung an süd Tirol. Botzen, J. Thuille 186-?
27pl. O.
Nine plates show costume

Erinnerungen an den feldzug in der Rheinpfalz und Baden ... 1849. Kaiser, Friedrich

Erinnerungen an die feldzüge der k. k. oester armee in Italien in den jahren 1848-49. Hacklaender, F. W., ritter von

Erinnerungen an die festlichen tage der dritten stiftungsfeyer der Akademie zu Wittenberg. Schundenius, K. H.

Erinnerungen an Schleswig. Brueck, O. von

Erinnerungen aus Spanien. Gail, Wilhelm

Erinnerungen eines waffensammlers. Wilczek, J. N., graf von

Erinnerungen von Tyrol, Vorarlberg und Ober Baiern. See Valério, Théodore. Souvenirs du Tyrol, du Vorarlberg et de la Haute Bavière

Eriz, P.
(illus.) Dally, Aristide. Uniformes de l'armée espagnole

Erlustierender augen-weyde zweyte fortsetzung, vorstellend, die weltberühmbte churfürstliche residenz in München. Diesel, Matthias

Erman, Adolf
Aegypten und aegyptisches leben im altertum. Tübingen, Laupp [1885-87]
2v. 400 illus. 12pl. O.
Bibliography: p[741]-42
Lipperheide 144

Life in ancient Egypt; translated by H. M. Tirard. London and New York, Macmillan 1894
xii,570p. illus. 11pl. O. $6, o.p.
Translation of his *Aegypten.* Pages 200-233 are on costume, with illustrations
Costume index. LC 1-600

Ernst, Henricus. See Bartholin, Bertelli. De paenula

Ernst August album. Hannover, Klindworth [1862]
xi,157p. col.front. 25pl.(part col.) Q.
The book describes the unveiling of the statue of King Ernst August of Hannover on Sept. 21, 1861 and the ensuing festivities
Lipperheide 2613

Die **eroberung** von Mexiko durch Ferdinand Cortez 1519-1521. Hoffmann, Anton

Der **eröffnete** teutsche audientz-saal. See Leucht, C. L. Cronen zur zierd und schutz des Heiligen Römischen Reichs auf denen häuptern ... Eleonorä und Josephi

Erskine, Mrs. Beatrice
Beautiful women in history & art, by Mrs. Steuart Erskine. London, G. Bell 1905
xii,282p. front. illus. 28pl.(part col.) Q.
Plates show costume of famous women in France and England from the time of Henry VIII until the 20th century
LC 6-35612

Erskine, Mrs Steuart. See Erskine, Mrs Beatrice

Erskine, John Elphinstone
Journal of a cruise among the islands of the western Pacific, including the Feejees and others inhabited by the Polynesian negro races, in Her Majesty's ship Havannah. London, J. Murray 1853
488p. col.front. illus. 6pl.(part col.) fold. map. O.
LC 4-32227

Das **erste** niedersächsische volkstrachtenfest zu Scheessel. Müller-Brauel, Hans

Erwin, John
History of academic costume in America. Albany, N.Y. Cotrell & Leonard 193-?
16p. illus.
Cover title
First published in 1902
Costume index

Der ... **erz-hertzogen** zu Oesterreich leben, regierung und gross-thaten: von dem ... urheber ... Rudolpho, grafen von Habsburg ... erstem römischen kayser an biss in die ... regierung ... Leopoldi und Josephi. Beer, J. C.

Esau, Hubert
Die benennung der wichtigeren bestandteile der modernen französischen tracht: ein sprach- und kulturgeschichtlicher versuch. Kiel, P. Peters 1902
69p. O.
"Litteratur": p[7]-10
LC 5-22861

Escayrac de Lauture, Stanislas, comte d'
Mémoires sur la Chine. Paris, Magazin pittoresque 1865
[545]p. illus. pl. maps(2 fold.) F.
Various pagings
LC 4-28632

Eschauzier, Saint-. See Saint-Eschauzier

Escher, A. von
Die Helvetische legion, 1798-1804. [Zürich, 1903]
16 col.pl. F.
Cataloged from Colas
Colas 978

Die Schweizer milizen im 18 und 19 jahrhundert. Les milices suisses aux XVIIIe et XIXe siècles. [Zürich, 1903]
100 col.pl. F.
Published in four series of 25 plates each. Each plate shows five types of uniforms
Cataloged from Colas
Colas 979

Die Schweizer regimenter in fremden diensten 1515-1860. Les régiments suisses au service étranger. Leipzig, K. Hiersemann [1903]
75 col.pl. F.
Colas 981

Die schweizerische cavallerie im XVII, XVIII und XIX jahrhundert. La cavalerie suisse de 1694 à 1880. [Zürich] ca1903
50 col.pl. F.
Published in two series of 25 plates each
Colas 980

Uniformierung und ausrüstung der schweizerischen armee von II januar 1898. [Zürich] ca1900
50 col.pl. F.
Cataloged from Colas
Colas 977

Escosura, Patricio de la
España artística y monumental. Vistas y descripcion de los sitios y monumentos mas notables de España. Paris, A. Hauser 1842-50
3v. 144pl. F.
Text in Spanish and French. Edited by G. P. de Villa-Amil
Lipperheide 1229

Escudier, Charles. See Gelin, Henri, jt. auth.

Escudier, Gaston
Les saltimbanques; leur vie—leurs moeurs ... Dessins ... par P. de Crauzat. Paris, Lévy 1875
480p. illus. pl. O.

Esequie della serenissima Elisabetta Carlotta d'Orleans duchessa vedova di Lorena fatte celebrare in Firenze dall' ... Francesco III. duca di Lorena ... granduca di Toscana. Firenze, nella stamperia granducale per i tartini, e franchi 1745
15,12p. 2pl. Q.
Lipperheide 2764

Eserciti d'oltremare. Cenni, Quinto

Eserciti europei. Cenni, Quinto

L'**esercito** abissino. Sambon, L.

L'**esercito** italiano. Cenni, Italo

L'**esercito** italiano. Cenni, Quinto

Esercizio di preparazione alla visita. Allegri, Girolamo Maria

Eskimo life. Nansen, Fridtjof

Eskimoleben. Nansen, Fridtjof

Eskimos
Bilby, J. W. Among unknown Eskimo. 1923
Bilby, J. W. Nanook of the North. 1925
Carpenter, F. G. Alaska, our northern wonderland. 1923
Curtis, Edward S. The North American Indians. 1907-30
Gordon, G. B. In the Alaskan wilderness. 1917
Hamilton, Louis. Canada. 1926
Hawkes, E. W. The Labrador Eskimo. 1916
Hutton, S. K. Among the Eskimos of Labrador. 1912
Kaladlit assilialiait; or, Woodcuts, drawn and engraved by Greenlanders. 1860
Nansen, Fridtjof. Eskimo life. 1893
Nansen, Fridtjof. Eskimoleben. 1910?
Paris. Exposition internationale des arts décoratifs et industriels modernes, 1925. Ornements et perles des peuples finnois et siberiens. 1927?
Parry, Sir W. E. Journal of a second voyage for the discovery of a north-west passage from the Atlantic to the Pacific; performed in the years 1821-22-23, in His Majesty's ships Fury and Hecla. 1824
Rasmussen, K. J. V. The people of the Polar north. 1908
Schwatka, Frederick. The children of the cold. 1899
Stefánsson, Vilhjálmur. My life with the Eskimo. 1913
United States. Bureau of American ethnology. Annual report and accompanying papers. 1881+

[**Esménard, Jeanne d'**]
[Costumes des pays du Nord: Hollande et Danemark.] Paris, lithogr. de Villain ca1830
24 col.pl. Q.
Colas 982

L'**Espagne.** Davillier, J. C., baron

L'**Espagne** et le Portugal. Breton de la Martinière, J. B. J.

L'**Espagne,** pittoresque, artistique et monumentale. Cuendias, M. G. de, and Suberwick, Mme de

España artística y monumental. Escosura, Patricio de la

La **España** incognita. See Hielscher, Kurt. Picturesque Spain

España, tipos y trajes. Ortiz Echagüe, José

Esquise historique de l'artillerie française. Moltzheim, A. de

Esquisse du pays, du caractère et du costume, en Portugal et en Espagne. See Bradford, William. Sketches of the country, character, and costume, in Portugal and Spain

Esquisses historiques des différents corps qui composent l'armée française. Ambert, J. M. J. J. A. J., baron.

Esquisses sénégalaises. Boilat, P. D., abbé

Esquisses sur Paris. See Dunker, B. A. Tableau de Paris

Essai historique, anecdotique sur la parapluie, l'ombrelle et la canne et sur leur fabrication. Cazal, R. M.

Essai, ou principes élémentaires de l'art de la danse. Martinet, J. J.

Essai sur la chevelure des différents peuples. Cortambert, Richard

Essai sur l'art de parer la beauté naturelle et de créer la beauté factice. See note under Lafoy, J. B. M. D. The complete coiffeur

Essai sur l'histoire du théatre. Bapst, Germain

Essai typographique et bibliographique sur l'histoire de la gravure sur bois. See note under Vecellio, Cesare. Costumes anciens et modernes

Essais historiques sur les modes et la toilette française. Villiers, Henri de

Essais historiques sur les modes et sur le costume en France. Molé, G. F. R.

An **essay**, philosophical and medical, concerning modern clothing. Vaughan, Walter

Essays on ceremonial, by various authors. London, The De La More press 1904
311p. illus. pl. O. (Library of liturgiology & ecclesiology for English readers v4)
Contents: English ceremonial, by E. G. C. F. Atchley; On some ancient liturgical customs now falling into disuse, by J. W. Legg; On English liturgical colours, by E. G. C. F. Atchley; Church vestments, by Percy Dearmer; The altar and its furniture, by Percy Dearmer; Some remarks on the Edwardian prayer-book, by E. G. C. F. Atchley; The genius of the Roman rite, by E. Bishop
LC 4-19175

Essays relative to the habits, character and moral improvement of the Hindoos. Bentley, John

The **essence** of the mode of the day. Aghion, Janine

The **essential** Kafir. Kidd, Dudley

Essentials of design. De Garmo, Charles, and Winslow, L. L.

[**Essenwein, August Ottomar**]

Quellen zur geschichte der feuerwaffen ... hrsg. vom Germanischen museum. Leipzig, F. A. Brockhaus 1877
178p. 9 illus. 157pl. O.
"Facsimilierte nachbildungen alter originalzeichnungen, miniaturen, holzschnitte und kupferstiche, nebst aufnahmen alter originalwaffen und modelle." Subtitle
Lipperheide 2425

Die holzschnitte des 14. und 15. jahrhunderts im Germanischen museum. See entry under Nuremberg. Germanisches nationalmuseum

Katalog der im Germanischen museum befindlichen glasgemälde aus älterer zeit. See entry under Nuremberg. Germanisches nationalmuseum

Katalog der im Germanischen museum befindlichen kartenspiele und spielkarten. See entry under Nuremberg. Germanisches nationalmuseum

See also note under Kulturhistorischer bilderatlas

Essequie delle sacra cattolica, e real maesta di Margherita d'Austria, regina di Spagna. Altoviti, Giovanni

Essex institute, Salem, Massachusetts

The Emilio collection of military buttons, American, British, French and Spanish, with some of other countries, and non-military, in the museum of the Essex institute, Salem, Mass. Salem, Mass. Essex institute 1911
xx,264p. 10pl. O. $3
"A descriptive catalog with historical notes and ten plates illustrating two hundred and forty important specimens, by Luis Fenollosa Emilio." Subtitle
LC 12-540

Estaçâo; jornal illustrado para a familia. See note under Die Modenwelt

La **Estaciôn**; periôdico para senoras. See note under Die Modenwelt

Estadística taurina anual ... año [1] 1931+ Madrid, E. Giménez 1932+
illus.(incl.ports.) O.
1931 has title: *Estadística taurina*
LC 34-9144

L'**Estafette** des modes. v 1-17; oct. 1836-1853. Paris
17v. O.
Editor: E. Champeaux. Subtitle varies
Colas 986

Estampas de toros. Vindel, Pedro

Estampes de Freudeberg pour le Monument du costume. Freudenberger, Sigmund

Estampes de Moreau-Le-jeune. Restif de La Bretonne, N. E.

L'**estat** présent de la Chine. Bouvet, Joachim

Este, Margaret d'

Through Corsica with a camera. London, Putnam 1905
156p. illus. O. 7s 6d

Esteves Saguí, Miguel

(ed.) Saguí, Francisco. Los últimos cuatro años de la dominacion española

Esthetics of dress. See Art of dress

Esthonia. See Estonia

[**Estienne, Antoine**] **Minim.**

Remonstrance charitable aux dames et damoyselles de France sur leurs ornemens dissolus, par le frère Antoine Estienne, mineur. Réimpression textuelle de l'édition de Paris, 1585. Genève, J. Gay 1867
77p. S.
1st edition, 1570 or 1571
With reproduction of original t.-p.: Remonstrance charitable aux dames et damoyselles de France sur leurs ornemens dissolus, pour les induire a laisser l'habit du paganisme et prendre celuy de la femme pudique et chrestienne, avec une élégie de la Femme se complaignant de la dissolution desdites damoyselles, par F. A. E. M. Pour la quatrième edition. Paris, S. Nivelle 1585
LC 16-23723

Estienne, Charles
(ed.) Baïf, Lazare de. De re vestiaria libellus ex Bayfio excerptus
(ed.) Baïf, Lazare de. Lazari Bayfii annotationes

Estonia
Manninen, Ilmari. Eesti rahvariiete ajalugu. 1927?
Rutter, Owen. The new Baltic states and their future. 1926
Schlichting, H. E. Trachten der Schweden an den küsten Ehstlands und auf Runö. 1854
Tartu. Eesti rahva muuseum. Eesti rahvariiete album. Album estnischer volkstrachten. 1927
Die trachten der XII kirchspiele des Oeselschen kreises. ca1840

See also Military costume—Estonia

Estonia. Kaitsevägede staap
Pionerieeskiri. Tallinnas [Eesti kirj.-ühisuse trükikoda] 1932
v. 1. illus. tables. D.
"Kaitsevägede staabi VI osakonna väljaanne"
LC 34-34226

Estoppey, D.
L'armée suisse; illustrations de D. Estoppey; lettre-préface de M. le colonel Frey. Texte de Mm. les colonels Feiss ... Wille ... Schumacher ... Lochmann ... Keller ... Ziégler ... De Grenus ... et Potterat. Genève, C. Eggimann 1894
73p. 34 col.pl. F.
Plates have titles in French and in German
Also published with German title page and title: *Die schweizerische armee* (Genf, C. Eggimann 1894)
Colas 987, 988 (German ed.) Lipperheide 2254 (German ed.)

[**Estrade, C.**]
Broderies hindoues. Paris, E. Henri [1926]
3 l. 38pl. F.

Estrée, Paul, pseud. See Quentin, Henri

Estremadura. See Spain—Estremadura

Estudio de las piedras preciosas. Miró y Argenter, José Ignacio

Estudios de indumentario española concreta y comparada. Puiggari, José

Et varsko til det norske folk og den nordiske rase. Dahl, Hans

État actuel de l'armée de Sa Majesté le roi de Pologne ainsi qu'il a été stipulé à la Diète tenue en 1775. Nuremberg, G. N. Raspe 1781
76 col.pl. S.
"Où l'on trouve la force et l'uniforme de tous les régiments, brigades, pulks, corps, drapeaux et compagnies, tant nationaux qu'allemands, qui sont en garnison en Pologne et dans le grand-duché de Lithuanie." Subtitle
Text in German and French
Colas 989

État général des troupes de France sur pied en mai 1748. Dubois, Edmond, pub.

État général des troupes sur pied en 1760 et 1761. Augsbourg, 1761?
24 col.pl. F.
Plates engraved by J. A. Frédéric
Colas 990

État général des uniformes de toutes les troupes de France. Isnard, P. Fr. d'

Etat général des uniformes des troupes de S. M. le roi de Sardaigne. Stagnon, A. M.

État militaire de l'Europe en 1762. Augsbourg, 1762?
18 col.pl. F.
Colas 991

État militaire des troupes de France en 1789. No place 1789?
6 col.pl. F.
Cataloged from Colas
Colas 993

Etchings illustrative of Scottish character and scenery. Geikie, Walter

Etchings of remarkable beggars, itinerant traders, [etc] Smith, J. T.

Etchings of rustic figures. Pyne, W. H.

Etchings to the illustrated Shakspere. Meadows, Kenny

L'**été** à Bade. Guinot, Eugène

The **eternal** masquerade. Bradley, H. D.

Ethiopia
Cailliaud, Frédéric. Recherches sur les arts et métiers, les usages de la vie civile et domestique des anciens peuples de l'Égypte, de la Nubie et de l'Éthiopie, suivies de détails sur les moeurs et coutumes des peuples modernes des mêmes contrées. 1831

See also subdivision Ethiopia under Coronations and coronation robes

Ancient

Lepsius, Richard. Denkmaeler aus Aegypten und Aethiopien. 1849-56

Modern

Baker, Sir S. W. The Nile tributaries of Abyssinia, and the sword hunters of the Hamran Arabs. 1868
Kulmer, Friedrich von. Im reiche Kaiser Menelik's tagebuch einer abessinischen reise. 1910
Parkyns, Mansfield. Life in Abyssinia. 1853
Skinner, R. P. Abyssinia of to-day; an account of the first mission sent by the American government to the court of the King of Kings (1903-1904). 1906
Stern, H. A. Wanderings among the Falashas in Abyssinia. 1862

See Military costume—Ethiopia, Modern

Ethnographia; a Magyar néprajzi társaság értesítöje. Supplement. See note under Budapest. Magyar nemzeti múzeum. Néprajzi

Ethnographic notes in southern India. Thurston, Edgar

Ethnological researches, respecting the red man of America. See Schoolcraft, H. R. Information respecting

Etiquet of dress
Baker, W. H. A dictionary of men's wear. 1908
Best-dressed man: a gossip on manners and modes. 1892

Etiquet of dress—*Continued*
Hall, Mrs F. M. H. Good form for all occasions. 1914
Moltke, E. M.-H. von, comtesse. Richtig angezogen in Deutschland und im Ausland? 1912
Praga, Mrs Alfred. What to wear and when to wear it. 1908
Ruth, J. A., and Snyder, C. S., comps. Decorum, a practical treatise on etiquette and dress of the best American society. 1877

The **etiquette** of men's dress. Clucas, Charles

Etnografía española. Hoyos Sáinz, Luis de

Les **étoffes** de la Chine; tissus & broderies. Préface et notice de M. H. d'Ardenne de Tizac. Paris, Librairie des arts decoratifs 1914?
4p.l. 4p. 54pl. F.

Étoffes & broderies du XVe au XVIIIe siecles. Besselievre, de

Les **étoiles.** Grandville, J. I. I. G.

Les **étoiles** du monde; galerie historique des femmes les plus célèbres de tous les temps et de tous les pays. Texte par Messieurs d'Araquy, Dufayl, Alexandre Dumas, de Geurupt, Arsène Houssaye, Miss Clarke. Dessins de G. Staal. Paris, Garnier 1858
xvi,340p. front. 17 ports. Q.
Contains three quarter length portraits of Laure de Noves, Mlle. de la Vallière, Isabelle de Castille; Cléopatre; Catherine II; Jeanne d'Arc; Sainte Cécile; Marguerite d'Anjou; Aspasie; Héloïse; Lucrèce; Marie-Thérèse d'Autriche; Jeanne Gray; Valentine de Milan; Sappho; Pocahontas; Miss Nightingale. The same plates are in M. Cowden-Clarke's *World-noted women*

Eton, William
W. Eton's Schilderung des Türkischen reiches in politischer, moralischer, historischer, religiöser, wissenschaftl. statistischer, merkantiler, u.s.w. hinsicht. Leipzig, Rein 1805
xvi,448p. 6 col.pl. O.
The text is translated from the author's *Survey of the Turkish empire* (London, T. Cadell 1799) but we have not found any English edition with the plates which give it costume value
Lipperheide 1424

Etrennes aux héros futurs ou présent d'un militaire à son fils. Paris, Le Coeur ca1810
[38] l. 16 col.pl. O.
Colas 994

Etrennes chantantes, avec des couplets analogues aux modes parisiennes ... faisant suite à l'Almanach de toilette, et au Bijou. Paris, Desnos [1780]
front. 24pl. S.
Colas 995. Lipperheide 4451

Etrennes des jolies femmes, ou almanach de la beauté. Paris, chez ceux qui vendent des almanachs 1783
1 l. 24pl. S.
Cataloged from Colas
Colas 996

Etrennes géographiques, ou costumes des principaux peuples de l'Europe; nouv. éd. Paris, Saintin 1815
32 col.pl. S.
Cataloged from Colas
Colas 997

Etrennes pour les personnes de tout l'âge et de toute condition. Pour l'an de grâce 1792-1793. Lausanne, J. B. Heubach [1792-93]
2v. col. fronts. 24 col.pl. S.
Colas 998-99

Etruria
Desvergers, Noël. L'Étrurie et les Étrusques. 1862-64
Inghirami, Francesco. Pitture di vasi etruschi esibite dal cavaliere Francesco Inghirami, per servire di studio alla mitologia ed alla storia degli antichi popoli. 1852-56
Martha, Jules. L'art étrusque, illustré. 1889
Maximis, F. X. de. Musei Etrusci quod Gregorius XVI. pont. max. in aedibus Vaticanis constituit monimenta. 1842
Poulsen, Frederik. Etruscan tomb paintings, their subjects and significance. 1922
Zannoni, Antonio. Gli scavi della Certosa di Bologna. 1876-84

L'Étrurie et les Étrusques. Desvergers, Noël

Etruscan tomb paintings. Poulsen, Frederik

Ett år i Sverge. Grafström, A. A.

Ett hem. Larsson, Carl

Étude historique et archéologique sur les anneaux sigillaires et autres des premiers siècles du moyen âge. Deloche, Maximin

Étude sur Francisco Goya. Brunet, Gustav

Étude sur l'armée belge, 1896. Viatour, Gustave

Étude sur les anciennes compagnies d'archers, d'arbaletriers et d'arquebusiers. Delaunay, L. A.

Études archéologiques ... Industrie anglo-saxonne. Baye, Joseph, baron de

Études contemporaines. Yves

Études de types militaires. Paris, Legras n.d.
109 col.pl. F.
Cataloged from Colas
Colas 1000

Études et motifs d'après nature. Grenier, François

Études militaires faîtes au Caucase (1858). Horschelt, Theodor

Études paléoethnologiques dans le bassin du Rhone: Age du bronze. Chantre, Ernest

Études prises dans le bas peuple et principalement les cris de Vienne. See Brand, C. Zeichnungen nach dem gemeinen volke

Études prises dans le bas peuple, ou Les cris de Paris. Bouchardon, Edme

Études sur Goya. See Brunet, Gustav. Étude sur Francisco Goya

Études sur le costume féminin. Aincourt, Marguerite d'

Études sur le rituel funéraire des anciens Égyptiens. Rougé, Emmanuel, vicomte de

Études variés sur la coupe. Dessault, Marcel

Etwas über kleidertracht. Rougemont, J. C.

Eudel, Paul

Dictionnaire des bijoux de l'Afrique du Nord, Maroc, Algérie, Tunisie, Tripolitaine. Paris, E. Leroux 1906
242p. illus. O.
LC 8-29322

L'orfévrerie algérienne et tunisienne. Alger, A. Jourdan 1902
xx,544p. illus. plan, facsim, geneal.tables. pl.(part col. 1 fold.) Q.
Bibliography: pref. p15-20
LC 31-6431

Europa; chronik der gebildeten welt; hrsg. von August Lewald. v 1-38, 1835-44; [new ser.] v 1-?, 1845-85. Leipzig [etc] J. Scheible 1835-85
Col.pl. O.-Q.
New series volume 1-v2 no.13 published as *Neue Europa*
Colas 1002-03. Lipperheide 4628

Europa in waffen; die sämmtl. europ. heere in ihrer jetz. uniformirg. ... Für junge und alte soldatenfreunde [illus] nach original-aquarellen v. L. Burger, W. Emelé, O. Fickentscher, H. Lüders u. a. Stuttgart, Nietzschke 1874
12p. 14 col.pl. Q.
Colas 1004

Europäische modenzeitung für herrengarderobe. jahrg. 1, 1850+ Dresden, Klemm & Weisz
Col.pl. F.
Colas 1005. Lipperheide 4663

Die **europäischen** heere der gegenwart. Vogt, Hermann

Europäischen modenzeitung, Expedition der. See Lexicon des kleidermachers

Europe

Aretz, Frau G. K. D. The elegant woman, from the rococo period to modern times. 1932

Barton, Lucy. Historic costume for the stage. 1935

Berlepsch, H. A. von. Chronik vom ehrbaren und uralten schneidergewerk. 1850

Boehn, Max von. Bekleidungskunst und mode. 1918

Boehn, Max von. Modes and manners. 1932-36

Boehn, Max von. Modespiegel. 1919

Bonnard, Camille. Costumes des XIIIe, XIVe et XVe siècles, extraits des monuments les plus authentiques de peinture et de sculpture. 1829-1830

Bonnard, Camille. Costumes historiques des XIIe, XIIIe, XIVe et XVe siècles. 1860-61

Bonnard, Camille. Costumi ecclesiastici, civili e militari d' secolo XIII, XIV e XV. 1827-1828

Bossert, H. T. Peasant art in Europe. 1927

Bossert, H. T. Volkskunst in Europa. 1926

Braun, A. A. Figures, faces and folds, a practical reference book on woman's form and dress. 1928

Bruhn, Wolfgang. Das frauenkleid in mode und malerei seit zwei jahrhunderten. 1926

Bruhn, Wolfgang. Die mode in fünf jahrhunderten. c1936

A collection of the dresses of different nations, antient and modern. 1757-1772

Collier, John. The art of portrait painting 1905

Conrady, Alexander. Geschichte der revolutionen. 1911

Costumes européens du XVIIe au XIXe siècle. 1909

Dezallier d'Argenville, A. J. Abregé de la vie des plus fameux peintres. 1745-1752

Duplessis, Georges. Costumes historiques des XVIe, XVIIe et XVIIIe siècles. 1867

Duplessis, Georges. Histoire de la gravure en Italie, en Espagne, en Allemagne, dans les Pays-Bas, en Angleterre et en France. 1880

Erskine, Mrs Beatrice. Beautiful women in history & art. 1905

Glen, J. B. de. Des habits, moeurs, ceremonies, façons de faire anciennes & modernes du monde ... Partie première. Des principales nations, provinces, regions, & villes de l'Europe. 1601

Haire, F. H. The folk costume book. 1934

Havard, Henry. Les quatre derniers siècles: étude artistique. 1873

Hempel, C. F. Abbildung merkwürdiger menschen, mit rücksicht auff die trachten verschiedener zeitaltern nach den gemählden und zeichnungen eines Van Dyk, Holbein, Rubens, Hollart und andrer meister. 1810?

Heyden, August von. Die tracht der kulturvölker Europas vom zeit-alter Homers bis zum beginne des XIX jahrhunderts. 1889

Hirth, Georg, and Muther, Richard, eds. Meister-holzschnitte aus vier jahrhunderten. 1893

Kelly, F. M. and Schwabe, Randolph. Historic costume, a chronicle of fashion in western Europe, 1490-1790. 1929

Le Chevallier-Chevignard, Edmond. Costumes historiques de femmes du XIVe au XVIIIe siècle. 1889

Lecomte, Hippolyte. Costumes européens. 1817-19

Madou, J. B. Physionomie de la société en Europe, depuis 1400 jusqu'à nos jours. 1837

Mann, Kathleen. Peasant costume in Europe. 1931-36

Massmann, H. F. Geschichte des mittelalterlichen, vorzugsweise des deutschen schachspieles. 1839

Mazuy, A. Types et caractères anciens d'après des documents peints ou écrits. 1841

Parmentier, A. É. E. Album historique. 1897-1907

Philippson, Martin. Geschichte der neueren zeit. 1886-89

Planché, J. R. A cyclopaedia of costume or dictionary of dress. 1876-79

Price, J. M. Dame Fashion, Paris—London (1786-1912). 1913

Europe—*Continued*

Recueil des habillements anciens et modernes des differents nations d'après les dessins de Holbein [and others]. Sammlung von trachten bey verschiedenen ältern und neuern völkern. 1805

Rhead, G. W. Chats on costume. 1906

Roscio, Giulio, and others. Ritratti et elogii di capitani illustri, che ne' secoli moderni hanno gloriosamente guerreggiato. 1646

Schultz, Alwin. Das häusliche leben der europäischen kulturvölker vom mittelalter bis zur zweiten hälfte der XVIII. jahrhunderts. 1903

Tetzner, F. O. Die Slawen in Deutschland. 1902

Totti, Pompilio. Ritratti et elogii di Capitani illustri. 1635

Wright, Thomas. Womankind in western Europe from the earliest times to the seventeenth century. 1869

See also Names of European countries; Periodicals; also subhead Europe under Arms and armor; Decoration and ornament; Embroidery; Jewelry, Ancient; Jewelry, Medieval and modern; Military costume; Theatrical costume

Caricature and satire

Wendel, Friedrich. Die mode in der karikatur. 1928

To 476

Antiqua; unterhaltungsblatt für freunde der alterthumskunde. 1884-91

Lazius, Wolfgang. De gentium aliquot migrationibus. 1557

Meyrick, Sir S. R., and Smith, C. H. Costume of the original inhabitants of the British islands, from the earliest periods to the 6th century; to which is added that of the Gothic nations on the western coasts of the Baltic, the ancestors of the Anglo-Saxons and Anglo-Danes. 1821

Middle ages

General works

Aragon, Henry. Le costume dans les temps anciens et au moyen âge. 1921

Becker, C., and Hefner-Alteneck, J. H. von. Kunstwerke und geräthschaften des Mittelalters und der Renaissance. 1852[-1863]

Bock, Franz. Geschichte der liturgischen gewänder des mittelalters oder entsbehung und entwicklung der kirchlichen ornate und paramente in rücksicht auf stoff, gewebe, farbe, zeichnung schnitt und rituelle bedeutung nachgewiesen. 1859-1871

Boehn, Max von. La moda. 1928-29. v 1

Boehn, Max von. Die mode; menschen und moden im mittelalter. 1925

Coulton, G. G. Life in the middle ages. 1930

Cutts, E. L. Scenes and characters of the middle ages. 1872

Demay, Germain. Le costume au moyen âge d'après les sceaux. 1880

Hartley, Dorothy. Mediaeval costume and life. 1931

Hefner-Alteneck, J. H. von. Trachten des christlichen mittelalters. 1840-54

Hinton, H. L. Select historical costumes. 1868

Jacquemin, Raphael. Histoire générale du costume civil, religieux et militaire du IV. au XII. siècle: Occident (315-1100). 1879

Jean, René. Le costume au moyen âge et à la renaissance. 1905

Kerr, R. N. Miniature costume folios. c1937. v3

Kingsford, H. S. Illustrations of the occasional offices of the church in the middle ages from contemporary sources. 1921

Kleinpaul, R. A. R. Das mittelalter. 1895

Lacroix, Paul. Les arts au moyen âge et à l'époque de la renaissance. 1877

Lacroix, Paul. The arts in the middle ages and at the period of the renaissance. 1870

Lacroix, Paul. Manners, customs, and dress during the middle ages and during the renaissance period. 1874

Lacroix, Paul. Military and religious life in the middle ages and at the period of the renaissance. 1874

Lacroix, Paul. Moeurs, usages et costumes au moyen âge et à l'époque de la renaissance. 1878

Lacroix, Paul. Sciences & lettres au moyen âge et à l'époque de la renaissance. 1877

Lacroix, Paul. Vie militaire et religieuse au moyen âge et à l'époque de la renaissance. 1873

Lacroix, Paul, and Séré, Ferdinand. Le moyen âge et la renaissance. 1848-51

Lonsdale, H. W., and Tarver, E. M. Illustrations of medieval costume. 1874

Post, Paul. Die französich-niederländische männertracht, einschliesslich der ritterrustung im zeitalter der spätgotik 1350 bis 1475. 1910

Prelle de la Nieppe, Edgar de. Notes sur les costumes chevaleresques et les armes offensives des XIIe, XIIIe et XIVe siècles. 1901

Spalart, Robert von. Versuch über das kostum der vorzüglichsten völker. 1796-1837

Van Beveren, J. J., and Du Pressoir, Charles. Costume du moyen âge d'après les manuscrits les peintures et les monuments contemporains. 1847

Wagner, Heinrich. Trachtenbuch des mittel-alters, eine sammlung von trachten, waffen, geraethen. 1830-33

Supplementary material

Baldwin, of Luxemburg, abp. and elector of Treves. Die romfahrt Kaiser Heinrich's VII im bildercyclus des Codex Balduini Trevirensis. 1881

Europe—Middle ages—Supp. works—*Cont.*
Beissel, Stephan. Die bilder der handschrift des Kaisers Otto im Münster zu Aachen. 1886
Beissel, Stephan. Vaticanische miniaturen. 1893
Bīdpāy. Der altenn weisenn exempel sprüch und underweisungen. 1548
Boinet, Amédée. La miniature carolingienne, son origine, son développement. 1920
Caumont, Aroisse, comte de. Cours d'antiquités monumentales. 1830-1841
Creeny, W. F. Illustrations of incised slabs on the continent of Europe, from rubbings and tracings. 1891
Dance of death. Die Baseler todtentänze in getreuen abbildungen. 1847
Dance of death. Freund Heins erscheinungen in Holbeins manier von J. R. Scheltenberg. 1785
Dance of death. La grande danse macabre. 1728
Dance of death. Holbein's todtentanz in den wandbildern zu Chur. 1885
Dance of death. Les simulachres & historiees faces de la mort: commonly called "The dance of death". 1869
Dance of death. Todten-tanz wie derselbe in der löblichen und weitberühmten statt Basel als ein spiegel menschlicher beschaffenheit gantz künstlich gemahlet zu sehen ist. 1649
Durand-Gréville, Émile. Hubert et Jean van Eyck. 1910
Durrieu, Paul, comte. Les très belles Heures de Notre-Dame du duc Jean de Berry. 1922
Durrieu, Paul, comte. Les très riches heures de Jean de France, duc de Berry. 1904
Du Sommerard, Alexandre. Les arts au moyen âge. 1838-46
Fasti Limburgenses. Fasti Limpurgenses. Das ist: Eine wohlbeschriebene chronick von der stadt und den herren zu Limpurg. 1720
Franciscus, de Retza. Defensorium immaculatae virginitatis. 1925
Friedlaender, Julius, and Sallet, A. F. C. von. Das Königliche münzkabinet. 1877
Froissart, Jean. Les chroniques de J. Froissart. 1881
Froissart, Jean. Sir John Froissart's chronicles of England, France, Spain, and adjoining countries, from the latter part of the reign of Edward II. to the coronation of Henry IV. 1805-06
Gay, Victor. Glossaire archéologique du moyen âge et de la renaissance. 1887-1928
Gerbert, Martin, freiherr von Hornau. De translatis Habsburgo-Austriacorum principum, eorumque conjugum cadaveribus ex ecclesia cathedrali Basileensi et monasterio Koenigsveldensi in Helvetia ad conditorium novum monasterii S. Blasii in Silva Nigra. 1772
Gropp, Ignaz. Monumenta sepulchralia ecclesiae Ebracensis. 1730
Herberger, Theodor. Die ältesten glasgemälde im Dome zu Augsburg mit der geschichte des Dombaus in der romanischen kunstperiode. 1860
Humphreys, H. N. The illuminated books of the middle ages. 1859
Jeux de cartes tarots et de cartes numérales du quatorzième au dixhuitième siècle. 1844
Jubinal, Achille. Les anciennes tapisseries historiées. 1838
Jusserand, J. A. A. J. English wayfaring life in the middle ages (XIVth century). 1931
Kraus, F. X. Die miniaturen der Manesseschen liederhandschrift. 1887
Kraus, F. X. Die miniaturen des Codex Egberti in der Stadtbibliothek zu Trier. 1884
Kulturhistorischer bilderatlas. 1883-88
Labarte, Jules. Histoire des arts industriels au moyen âge et à l'époque de la renaissance. 1864-66
Lazius, Wolfgang. De gentium aliquot migrationibus. 1557
Lind, Karl. Ein antiphonarium mit bilderschmuck aus der zeit des XI. und XII. jahrhunderts im stifte St Peter zu Salzburg befindlich. 1870
Lind, Karl. Die grabdenkmale während des mittelalters. 1870
Medio-evo pittoresco; supplemento alla Galleria universale di tutti i popoli del mondo. 1844
Meller, W. C. A knight's life in the days of chivalry. 1924
Müller, F. H. Beitrage zur teutschen kunst- und geschichtskunde durch kunstdenkmale mit vorzüglicher berücksichtigung des mittelalters. 1837
Münchausen, A. F. von. Teppiche des jungfrauenstifts Marienberg bei Helmstedt. 1874
Munich. Bayerische staatsbibliothek. Meisterwerke der buchmalerei; aus handschriften der bayerischen staatsbibliothek München. 1920
Niessen, Johannes. Apokalypsis; zehn lithographisch vervielfältigte federzeichnungen ... aus der Felix'schen sammlung, in die des Germanischen museums zu Nürnberg übergegangenen originalen. 1886
Nuremberg. Germanisches nationalmuseum. Die holzschnitte des 14. und 15. jahrhunderts im Germanischen museum. 1874
Nuremberg. Germanisches nationalmuseum. Katalog der im germanischen museum befindlichen gewebe und stickereien, nadelarbeiten und spitzen aus älterer zeit. 1869
Nuremberg. Germanisches nationalmuseum. Katalog der im germanischen museum befindlichen glasgemälde aus älterer zeit. 1884

Europe—Middle ages—Supp. works—*Cont.*

Olschki, Leonardo. Die romanischen literaturen des mittelalters. c1928

Prüfer, Theodor. Der todtentanz in der Marien-kirche zu Berlin. 1883

Rahn, J. R. Geschichte der bildenden künste in der Schweiz von den ältesten zeiten bis zum schlusse des mittelalters. 1876

Rahn, J. R. Katalog der ... kunst-sammlung der herren C. und P. N. Vincent in Konstanz am Bodensee. 1891

Rahn, J. R. Das Psalterium aureum von Sanct Gallen; ein beitrag zur geschichte der karolingischen miniaturmalerei. 1878

Renier, Rodolfo. Il tipo estetico della donna nel medioevo. 1885

Richental, Ulrich. Das concilium so zů Constantz gehalten, MCCCCXIII. 1536

Ritter, Georges, and Lafond, Jean. Manuscrits à peintures de l'école de Rouen; livres d'heures normands; recueil de facsimiles et texte. 1913

Robert, U. L. L. Les signes d'infamie au moyen âge: Juifs, Sarrasins, hérétiques, lépreux, Cagots et filles publiques. 1891

Rosenberg, Léonce. Catalogue d'une collection de miniatures gothiques et persanes. 1913

Salzman, L. F. English trade in the middle ages. 1931

Schwind, Moritz von. Die wandgemaelde des landgrafensaales auf der Wartburg. 1863

Seroux d'Agincourt, J. B. L. G. Histoire de l'art par les monumens, depuis sa décadence au IVe siècle jusqu'à son renouvellement au XIVe. 1823

Seroux d'Agincourt, J. B. L. G. History of art by its monuments, from its decline in the fourth century to its restoration in the sixteenth. 1847

Viel-Castel, Horace, comte de. Statuts de l'ordre du Saint Esprit au droit desir ou du noeud institué à Naples en 1352 par Louis d'Anjou ... Manuscrit du XIVme siècle conservé au Louvre. 1853

Weerth, Ernst aus'm, ed. Der mosaikboden in St Gereon zu Cöln, restaurirt und gezeichnet von Toni Avenarius, nebst den damit verwandten mosaikböden Italiens. 1873

See also Crusaders; Gaule; Infamy, Signs of; Knights; Troubadours; Visigoths. Also subdivision Middle Ages under Embroidery; Helmets; Theatrical costume

12th century

Engelhardt, C. M. Herrad von Landsperg, aebtissin zu Hohenburg, oder St Odilien, im Elsass, im zwölften jahrhundert; und ihr werk: Hortus deliciarum. 1818

Grimm, Wilhelm. Ruolandes liet, mit einem facsimile und den bildern der pfälzischen handschrift. 1838

Herrad von Landsberg, abbess of Hohenburg. Hortus deliciarum. 1879-99

Petrus, de Ebulo. De rebus siculis carmen. 1904

Petrus, de Ebulo. Liber ad honorem Augusti. 1905-06

13th century

Gerbert, Martin, freiherr von Hornau. De translatis Habsburgo-Austriacorum principum, eorumque coniugum cadaveribus ex ecclesia cathedrali Basileensi et monasterio Koenigsveldensi in Helvetia ad conditorium novum monasterii S. Blasii in Silva Nigra. 1772

Paris. Bibliothèque nationale. Mss. fr. nouv. acq. 1098. Vie et histoire de Saint Denys. 1905

15th century

Batissier, Louis. Les douze dames de rhétorique. 1838

Benham, William. Tower of London. 1906

Botho, Conrad. Cronecken der Sassen. 1492

Brant, Sebastian. Sebastian Brands Narrenschiff; ein hausschatz zur ergetzung und erbauung erneuert von Karl Simrock; mit den holzschnitten der ersten ausgaben und dem bildniss Brands aus Reusners Icones. 1872

Brant, Sebastian. The Ship of fools. 1874

Brussels. Bibliothèque royale de Belgique. Le Bréviaire de Philippe le Bon. 1929

Brussels. Bibliothèque royale de Belgique. Mss(9967). L'ystoire de Helayne; reproduction des 26 miniatures du manuscrit. 1913

Brussels. Bibliothèque royale de Belgique. Section des manuscrits. Deux livres d'heures (nos. 10767 et 11051 de la Bibliothèque royale de Belgique) attribués à l'enlumineur Jacques Coene. 1911?

Brussels. Bibliothèque royale de Belgique. Section des manuscrits. Les très belles miniatures de la Bibliothèque royale de Belgique. 1913

Burckhardt, R. F. Gewirkte bildteppiche des XV. und XVI. jahrhunderts im Historischen museum zu Basel. 1923

Catholic church. Liturgy and ritual. Breviary. Breviaire Grimani de la Bibliothèque de S. Marco à Venise: reproduction photographique complète. 1904-1908

Catholic church. Liturgy and ritual. Breviary. Fac-simile delle miniature contenute nel Breviario Grimani conservati nella biblioteca di S. Marco esequito in fotografia da A. Perini. 1862-1878

Cessolis, Jacobus de. The game of the chesse. 1860. Original ed. 1490

Cessolis, Jacobus de. Volgarizzamento del libro de' costumi. 1829

Europe—15th century—*Continued*
Christine de Pisan. Épître d'Othéa, déese de la prudence, à Hector, chef des Troyens; reproduction des 100 miniatures du manuscrit 9392 de Jean Miélot, par J. van den Gheyn. 1913
Colonna, Francesco. The dream of Poliphilus; fac-similes of one hundred and sixty-eight woodcuts in the "Hypnerotomachia Poliphili," Venice, 1499. 1889
Colonna, Francesco. Poliphili Hypnerotomachia. 1904
Coulton, G. G. Chronicler of European chivalry. 1930
Cronica van Coellen. Die Cronica van der hilliger stat Coellen. 1499
Delepierre, Octave, and Voisin, Auguste. La chasse de Sainte Ursule gravée au trait par Charles Onghéna d'après Jean Memling. 1841
Dodgson, Campbell. Catalogue of early German and Flemish woodcuts. 1903-11
Dreux du Radier, J. F. L'Europa illustre. 1755-65
Eiselein, Josua. Begründeter aufweis des plazes bei der stadt Constanz, auf welchem Johannes Hus und Hieronymus von Prag in den jahren 1415 und 1416 verbrannt worden. 1847
Der Enndkrist der Stadt-bibliothek zu Frankfurt am Main. Facsimile-wiedergabe; hrsg. und bibliographisch beschrieben von dr. Ernst Kelchner. 1891
Exercitium super Pater noster (Blockbook). Exercitium super Pater noster, suite de gravures avec légendes. 188-?
Forrer, Robert. Spätgothische wohnräume und wandmalereien aus Schloss Issogne. 1896
Gruyer, F. A. Chantilly. Notices des peintures; les quarante Fouquet. 1900
Harff, Arnold, ritter von. Die pilgerfahrt des ritters Arnold von Harff von Cöln durch Italien, Syrien, Aegypten, Arabien, Aethiopien, Nubien, Palastina, die Turkei, Frankreich und Spanien, wie er sie in den jahren 1496 bis 1499 vollendet, beschrieben und durch zeichnungen erläutert hat. 1860
Hind, A. M. An introduction to a history of woodcut. 1935
Historie von Pontus und Sidonia. 1539
Horologium devotionis circa vitam Christi. ca1480-90?
Huon Capet. Der Huge Scheppel der gräfin Elisabeth von Nassau-Saarbrücken, nach der handschrift der Hamburger Stadtbibliothek. 1905
Jäklin, Dietrich. Geschichte der Kirche St. Georg bei Räzüns und ihre wandgemälde. 1880
Legenda der heiligen Hedwig. 1504
Lehrs, Max. Die aeltesten deutschen spielkarten des Königlichen kupferstichkabinets zu Dresden. 1886
Le Tavernier, Jean. Cronicques et conquestes de Charlemaine: reproduction de 105 miniatures de Jean Le Tavernier. 1909
Liber regum ... zum ersten male. 1892
Liédet, Loyset. Histoire de Charles Martel, reproduction des 102 miniatures by Loyset Liédet (1470). 1910
Lippmann, Friedrich. The seven planets. 1895
Lippmann, Friedrich. Die sieben planeten. 1895
Locher, Jakob. Panegyricus ad Maximilianum. 1497
Eyn loszbuch ausz der karten gemacht und alleyn durch kurtzweyl erdacht, wer aber zu glauben sich daran wolt keren das selbig liesz sich unrecht leren. 1890
Luchs, Hermann. Ueber die bilder der Hedwigslegende. 1861
Ludolphus de Saxonia. Das leben Christi. 1488
Melusine. ca1483
Mittelalterliches hausbuch; bilderhandschrift des 15. jahrhunderts mit vollständigem text und facsimilierten abbildungen. 1887
Molitor, Ulrich. De lamiis et phitonicis mulieribus. ca1489
Natalibus, Petrus de, bp. of Equilio. Catalogus Sanctorum. 1514
Nuremberg. Germanisches nationalmuseum. Die holzschnitte des 14. und 15. jahrhunderts im Germanischen museum. 1874
Nuremberg. Germanisches nationalmuseum. Katalog der im Germanischen museum befindlichen originalskulpturen. 1890
Ovid. La bible des poètes metamorphosée. 1493
Paris, Louis. Toiles peintes et tapisseries de la ville de Reims; ou, La mise en scène du théâtre des Confrères de passion. 1843
Paris. Musée national du Louvre. Les tapisseries des chasses de Maximilien. 1920
Plautus. Comoediae. 1511
Ricci, Signora Elisa. Antiche trine italiane ... Trine a fuselli. 1911
Ricci, Signora Elisa. Antiche trine italiane ... Trine ad ago. 1908
Ricci, Signora Elisa. Old Italian lace. 1913
Der Schatzbehalter. 1491
Schmidt, W. Die frühesten und seltensten denkmale des holz- und metallschnittes aus dem vierzehnten und fünfzehnten jahrhundert. 1886
Schreiber, W. L. Manuel de l'amateur de la gravure sur bois et sur métal au xve siècle. 1891-1911
Speculum humanæ salvationis. Speculum humanae salvationis cum speculo S. Mariae virginis, latine et germanice. 1472?
Spiegel der menschlichen behaltniss. 1492

Europe—15th century—*Continued*

Vergilius Maro, Publius. Opera. 1502
Vindler, Hans. Flores virtutum, oder das buch der Tugent. 1486
Wolfskron, Adolf, ritter von. Die bilder der Hedwigslegende, nach einer handschrift von jahre MCCCLIII in der bibliothek der p. p. Piaristen zu Schlackenwerth. 1846
Zingerle, I. V., edler von Summersberg. Fresken-cyklus des schlosses Runkelstein bei Bozen. 1857

Renaissance period, 1453-1517

Becker, C., and Hefner-Alteneck, J. H. von Kunstwerke und geräthschaften des Mittelalters und der Renaissance. 1852[-1863]
Gay, Victor. Glossaire archéologique du moyen âge et de la renaissance. 1887-1928
Jean, René. Le costume au moyen âge et à la renaissance. 1905
Lacroix, Paul. Les arts au moyen âge et à l'époque de la renaissance. 1877
Lacroix, Paul. The arts in the middle ages and at the period of the renaissance. 1870
Lacroix, Paul. Manners, customs, and dress during the middle ages and during the renaissance period. 1874
Lacroix, Paul. Moeurs, usages et costumes au moyen âge et à l'époque de la renaissance. 1878
Lacroix, Paul. Sciences & lettres au moyen âge et à l'époque de la renaissance. 1877
Lacroix, Paul, and Séré, Ferdinand. Le moyen âge et la renaissance. 1848-51

16th century

Album amicorum habitibus mulierum omniu nationu Europae, tum tabulis ac scutis vacuis in aes incisis adornatum, ut quisque et sÿmbola et insignia sua gentilitia in ijs depingi commode curare possit. 1601
Amman, Jost. Gynaeceum, sive Theatrum mulierum. 1586
Amman, Jost. Im frauwenzimmer wirt vermeldt von allerley schönen kleidungen annd trachten der weiber hohes und niders stands. 1586
Amman, Jost. Kunstbüchlin darinnenn neben fürbildung vieler geistlicher unnd weltlicher hohes und niderstands personen, so dann auch der türckischen käyser unnd derselben obersten, allerhandt kunstreiche stück und figuren. 1599
Amman, Jost. The theatre of women. 1872
Auerswald, Fabian von. Ringer kunst. 1539
Bie, Oskar. Der gesellschaftstanz in der Renaissance
Boehn, Max von. La moda. 1928-29. v3
Boehn, Max von. Die mode; menschen und moden im sechzehnten jahrhundert. 1923
Burckhardt, R. F. Gewirkte bildteppiche des XV. und XVI. jahrhunderts im Historischen museum zu Basel. 1923
Capriolo, Aliprando. Ritratti di cento capitani illustri. 1600
Catholic church. Liturgy and ritual. Hours. Heures. ca1502
Christlicher abschiede. 1593
Coornhert, Dierick. Emblemata moralia, et oeconomica, de rerum usu et abusu. 1609
Costüme zur Lessing-feier. 1878
Dodgson, Campbell. Catalogue of early German and Flemish woodcuts. 1903-11
Dreux du Radier, J. F. L'Europe illustre. 1755-65
Dürer, Albrecht. Albrecht Dürer's Handzeichnungen im königlichen museum zu Berlin. 1871
Dürer, Albrecht. Albrecht Dürer's Holzschnitt-werk in auswahl. 1883
Dürer, Albrecht. The complete woodcuts of Albrecht Dürer. 1936
Dürer, Albrecht. Trachten-bilder ... aus der Albertina. 1871
Dürer, Albrecht, and Wolgemut, Michael. Die gemälde von Dürer und Wolgemut in reproductionen nach den originalen. 1888
Gualla, Giacopo. Papie sanctuarium. 1505
Guichard, Édouard. Les tapisseries décoratives du Garde-meuble (Mobilier national). 1881
Henricpetri, Adam. General historien der aller namhafftigsten ... geschichten, thaten und handlungen, so sich bey ubergebung und ende des ... keyser Carols des Fünfften und anfange Ferdinanden seines bruders regierung. 1577
Hogenberg, Hans. The procession of Pope Clement VII. and the Emperor Charles V. after the coronation at Bologna on the 24th February 1530. 1875
Holbein, Hans, the younger. Hans Holbeins Alte Testament in funfzig holzschnitten getreu nach den originalen copirt. 1850
Holbein, Hans, the elder. Hans Holbein's des aelteren feder- und silberstiftzeichnungen in den kunstsammlung zu Basel, Bamberg, Dessau, Donaueschingen, Erlangen, Frankfurt, Kopenhagen, Leipzig, Sigmaringen, Weimar, Wien. 1885
Isenberg, Walther. Wie die mechtige erbkünigreich unnd fürstentumb Hispania, Hunngern unnd Gelldern zu den loblichen heüsern Osterreich uñ Burgundi kommen sein. 1520
Kerr, R. N. Miniature costume folios. c1937. v5
Labarte, Jules. Histoire des arts industriels au moyen âge et à l'époque de la renaissance. 1864-66
Lacroix, Paul. Military and religious life in the Middle ages and at the period of the renaissance. 1874

Europe—16th century—*Continued*

Lacroix, Paul. Vie militaire et religieuse au moyen âge et à l'époque de la renaissance. 1873

Lippmann, Friedrich. The seven planets 1895

Lippmann, Friedrich. Die sieben planeten. 1895

Eyn loszbuch ausz der karten gemacht und alleyn durch kurtzweyl erdacht, wer aber zu glauben sich daran wolt keren das selbig liesz sich unrecht leren. 1890

Monnoyeur, J. B. Recueil de costumes. 1590?

Nuremberg. Germanisches nationalmuseum. Katalog der im Germanischen museum befindlichen glasgemälde aus älterer zeit. 1884

Nuremberg. Germanisches nationalmuseum. Katalog der im Germanischen museum befindlichen originalskulpturen. 1890

Petrarca, Francesco. Trostspiegel in glück und unglück. 1584

Reusner, Nicolaus. Icones sive imagines vivae, literis cl. virorum, Italiae, Graeciae, Germaniae, Galliae, Angliae, Ungariae. 1589

Ricci, Signora Elisa. Antiche trine italiane ... Trine a fuselli. 1911

Ricci, Signora Elisa. Antiche trine italiane ... Trine ad ago. 1908

Ricci, Signora Elisa. Old Italian lace. 1913

Schwanthaler, Ludwig. Künstler-gestalten aus der blüthezeit der kunst. 1879

Tabourot, Jehan. Orchésographie. 1888

Tabourot, Jehan. Orchesography, a treatise in the form of a dialogue whereby all manner of persons may easily acquire and practice the honourable exercise of dancing. 1925

Tabourot, Jehan. Die tanze des XVI. jahrhunderts und die alte französiche tanzschule vor einführung der menuett. 1878

Theuerdank. Die geuerlicheiten und eins teils der geschichten des loblichẽ streitbaren und hochberümbten helds und ritters Tewrdannckhs. 1519

Treitz-Saurwein, Marx, von Ehrentreitz. Der weisz kunig. 1775

Villepelet, Ferdinand. Du luxe des vêtements au XVIe siècle. 1869

17th century

Bie, Oskar. Der gesellschaftstanz in der Renaissance

Bilbergh, Joanne. Orchestra sive de saltationibus veterum dissertatio. 1685

Blum, André. Histoire du costume, les modes au XVIIe et au XVIIIe siècle. 1928

Boehn, Max von. La moda. v3. 1928-29

Boehn, Max von. Die mode; menschen und mode im siebzehnten jahrhundert. 1913

Boissard, J. J. Icones & effigies virorum doctorum. Quotquot celebres fuerunt per Europam artificiosissimè in aes incisae à J. T. de Brij. 1645-1650

Brantôme, Pierre de Bourdeille, seigneur de. Memoires ... contenans les vies des hommes illustres & grands capitaines. 1665

Brantôme, Pierre de Bourdeille, seigneur de. Memoirs ... contenant les vies de dames galantes de son temps. 1693

Brantôme, Pierre de Bourdeille, seigneur de. Oeuvres de Brantôme. 1857

Callot, Jacques. Les fantasies de Noble I. Callot. 1635

Callot, Jacques. Livre d'esquisses. 1880

Callot, Jacques. Varie figure. 1630

Della Bella, Stefano. Diverse figure & paesi. 1649

Dreux du Radier, J. F. L'Europe illustre. 1755-65

Gerardini, Melchion. Capricci di varie figure. ca1650

Gualdo Priorato, Galeazzo, conte. Historia di Ferdinando Terzo imperatore. 1672

Gualdo Priorato, Galeazzo, conte. Historia di Leopoldo Cesare, continente le cose piu memorabili successe in Europa, dal 1656 fino al 1670. 1670

Gualdo Priorato, Galeazzo, conte. Vite, et azzioni di personaggi militari, e politici. 1673

Guichard, Édouard. Les tapisseries décoratives du Garde-meuble (Mobilier national). 1881

Happel, E. W. Historia moderna Europae, oder eine historische beschreibung dess heutigen Europae. 1691

Hefner-Alteneck, J. H. von. Trachten, kunstwerke und geräthschaften des siebzehnten und achtzehnten jahrhunderts. 1889

Helwig, Nicolaus. Theatrum hystoriae universalis Catholico Protestantiv. Das ist wahrhafftige hÿstorische beschreibung aller gedenckwürdigen geschichten, welche sich von dem 1517 jahr und von anfang des religionstreits zwischen der Römischen Catholischen kirchen und D. Martino Luthero ... zugetragẽ v. 1641

Heyden, Jacob van der. Pugillus facetiarum iconographicarũ ... 1618. Allerhand kurtzweilige stücklein, allen studenten furnemblich zu lieb aufs ihren eigenen stambüchern zusamen gelesen. 1618

Historisch interessante bildnisse und trachten nach alten meistern der letzten drei jahrhunderte. 1893

Hollar, Wenceslaus. Aula veneris, sive Varietas foeminini sexus diversarum Europae nationum differentiag habituum. 1644

Hollar, Wenceslaus. Theatru Mulierum, sive Varietas atque differentia habituum foeminei sexus diversorum Europae nationum hodierno tempore vulgo. 1643

Europe—17th century—*Continued*

Kolb, Ambrosius. Kriegs unnd friedens unserer zeiten kurtz begriffene history dessen was im Heil. Röm. Reich und durch gantz Europam denckwürdiges sich zugetragen bisz in das jahr 1653. 1653

Leloir, Maurice. Histoire du costume de l'antiquité à 1914. 1934-35. v8-10

Noort, Adam van, and Snellinck, Joan. Costumes de divers pays d'Europe. ca1630

Passe, Crispijn van de. Die zwölf monate. ca1640

Philalethe, Thimothée, pseud. De la modestie des femmes et des filles chrétiennes, dans leurs habits & dans tout leur exterieur. 1686

Les plaisirs et les fêtes. 1929-30

Theatrum europaeum. 1646-1738

Wideman, Elias. Comitium gloriae centum qua sanguine qua virtute illustrium heroum iconibus instructum. 1649

Criticism

Matenesius, J. F. De luxu et abusu vestium nostri temporis. 1612

18th century

Blum, Andre. Histoire du costume, les modes au XVIIe et au XVIIIe siècle. 1928

Boehn, Max von. La moda. 1928-29. v4.

Boehn, Max von. Die mode; menschen und moden im achtzehnten jahrhundert, nach bildern und stichen der zeit, ausgewählt von Oskar Fischel. 1909

Boehn, Max von. Die mode; menschen und moden im neunzehnten jahrhundert nach bildern und kupfern der zeit. 1907-19. v 1

Boehn, Max von. Modes & manners of the nineteenth century. 1927. v 1

Collection des prospects. ca.1780

Corvinus, G. S. Nutzbares, galantes und curiöses frauenzimmer-lexicon. 1739

Crinoline from 1730 to 1864. 1864

Dreux du Radier, J. F. L'Europe illustre. 1755-65

Etrennes pour les personnes de tout l'âge et de toute condition; pour l'an de grâce 1792-1793. 1792-93

Hefner-Alteneck, J. H. von. Trachten, kunstwerke und geräthschaften des siebzehnten und achtzehnten jahrhunderts. 1889

Historisch interessante bildnisse und trachten nach alten meistern der letzten drei jahrhunderte. 1893

Keyssler, J. G. Neueste reisen durch Deutschland, Böhmen, Ungarn, die Schweiz, Italien und Lothringen, worinnen der zustand und das merkwürdigste dieser länder beschrieben ... wird. 1741

Le Prince, J. B. Oeuvres de Jean-Baptiste Le Prince. 1782

Martini, Angela. Moda, 1790-1900. 1933

New York. Metropolitan museum of art. Eighteenth-century costume in Europe. 1937

Puis, Auguste. En marge de l'histoire, 1re série: essai sur les moeurs, les goûts et les modes au XVIIIe siècle. 1914

Un siècle de modes féminines, 1794-1894. 1894

Theatrum europaeum. 1646-1738

Caricature and satire

Il Callotto resuscitato, oder Neü eingerichtes zwerchen cabinet. ca1720

Het groote tafereel der dwaasheid, vertoonende de opkomst, voortgang en ondergang der actie, bubbel en windnegotie, in Vrankryk, Engeland, en de Nederlanden, gepleegt in jaare MDCCXX. 1720

19th century

Bassaget, P. N. Costumes cosmopolites. 184-?

Blum, André. Histoire du costume; les modes au XIX. siècle. [c1931]

Boehn, Max von. La moda. 1928-29. v5-8.

Boehn, Max von. Die mode; menschen und moden im neunzehnten jahrhundert nach bildern und kupfern der zeit. 1907-19

Boehn, Max von. Modes & manners of the nineteenth century. 1927

Crinoline from 1730 to 1864. 1864

Devéria, Achille. Les femmes; galerie fashionable. ca1830

Dubourg, Matthew. Views of the remains of ancient buildings in Rome and its vicinity. 1820

Emerson, Edwin. A history of the nineteenth century, year by year. 1902

Etrennes géographiques, ou costumes des principaux peuples de l'Europe. 1815

Gavarni, G. S. C., and Devéria, Achille. Nouveaux travestissements pour le théâtre et pour le bal. 1830

Geszler, J. Die moden des XIX jahrhunderts. 1895-96

Holden, Angus. Elegant modes in the nineteenth century, from high waist to bustle. 1935

Jacottet, L. J. Souvenirs des eaux de Baden-Baden et des environs. 1860

Keezer, Ro. Feminine toilettes and knickknacks of the romantic age. 1930

Kohl, J. G. Die völker Europas. 1872

Lanté, L. M. Costumes des femmes de Hambourg, du Tyrol, de la Hollande, de la Suisse, de la Franconie, de l'Espagne, du royaume de Naples, etc. 1827

Malo, Charles. Les femmes et les fleurs. 1831

Menzel, A. F. E. von. Aus könig Friedrich's zeit, kriegs- und friedens-helden 1856

Die Modenwelt. Zum fünfundzwanzigjährigen bestehen der Modenwelt, 1865-1890. 1890

Evans, Sir Arthur John

'The ring of Nestor'; a glimpse into the Minoan after-world, and a sepulchral treasure of gold signet-rings and bead-seals from Thisbê, Boeotia. London, Macmillan 1925

75p. illus. 5pl.(1 col.fold.) Q.

Reprinted from the *Journal of Hellenistic studies,* April 1925

LC 26-13303

Evans, Bessie, and Evans, May Garrettson

American Indian dance steps. introduction by Frederick Webb Hodge; illustrated in color by Poyege, San Ildefonso Indian. New York, A. S. Barnes 1931

xviii,104p. col.front. illus.(incl.music) col. pl. Q.

"Concerned chiefly with elements of the art observed in certain Pueblo tribes of New Mexico—especially those of San Ildefonso, Tesuque, Santa Clara, Cochiti, and Santo Domingo." Foreword

Costume index. LC 32-960

Evans, Edmund

(engr.) Doyle, J. W. E. A chronicle of England

Evans, Joan

English jewellery from the fifth century A. D. to 1800. London, Methuen [1921]

xxxi,168p. 34pl.(2 col. incl.front.) F. 52s 6d

Bibliographical foot-notes

Costume index. LC 22-2231

Life in mediaeval France. London, Oxford univ. press 1925

234p. XLVIII pl.(incl.front.) fold.map. plan. O. 15s

Costume index. LC 25-22127

Magical jewels of the middle ages and the renaissance, particularly in England. Oxford, The Clarendon press 1922

264p. III pl.(incl.front.) O.

LC 23-6879

Evans, Sir John

The ancient bronze implements, weapons, and ornaments, of Great Britain and Ireland. London, Longmans, Green 1881

xix,509p. illus. O.

Also published in New York (D. Appleton 1881) French edition has title: L'âge du bronze (Paris, G. Baillière 1882)

LC 1-5390

The ancient stone implements, weapons and ornaments of Great Britain; 2d ed. rev. London, Longmans, Green 1897

747p. illus. O. 28s

First edition, 1872. Translated into French under title: *Les âges de la pierre* (Paris, G. Baillière 1878)

Colas 290 (French ed.)

Evans, Sir John—*Continued*
Posy-rings; a Friday evening discourse at the Royal Institution of Great Britain March 25, 1892. London, Longmans, Green 1892
30p. D.
On rings engraved with verses, poesy-rings

Evans, Maria Millington (Lathbury) lady
Chapters on Greek dress. London and New York, Macmillan 1893
xvii,84p. fold.front. illus. 18pl. O. $2, o.p.
Descriptions of Greek dress from the period of Homer through the fifth century, including accessories, as girdles, coverings for the head and feet, etc. Illustrations and line drawings show the construction of the garments
Bibliography: pref. p16-17
Costume index. LC 4-4629

Evans, Mary
Costume silhouettes; with 19 illustrations of historic and modern silhouettes of costume. Philadelphia [etc.] J. B. Lippincott c1923
51p. illus. Q. (Lippincott's unit texts)
Bibliography: p43-49
LC 24-4948

Costume throughout the ages. 2d ed rev. Philadelphia [etc.] J. B. Lippincott c1938
xv,360p. incl.col.front. illus. pl. O. $3.50; 15s
First edition 1930. References at end of each chapter; Bibliography of history of costume: p320-31
Costume index. LC 38-3997

Draping and dress design; sketches by Eva M. Darden. Ann Arbor, Mich. Edwards brothers 1935
89p. illus. Q.
Bibliography: p89; bibliography at end of chapter one
LC 35-24290

Evans, May Garrettson. See Evans, Bessie, jt. auth.

[**Evelyn, John**]
Mundus muliebris: or, The ladies dressing-room unlock'd, and her toilette spread. In burlesque. Together with the Fop-dictionary, compiled for the use of the fair sex. London, R. Bentley 1690
3 l. 22p. Q.
Lipperheide attributes this book to Mary Evelyn
Lipperheide 3447

Tyrannus, or The mode, in a discourse of sumptuary laws. London, for G. Bedel, T. Collins and J. Crook 1661
30p. O.

Evelyn, Mary. See Evelyn, John. Mundus muliebris

Évènements de Bruxelles. Anvers, 1830
44pl. Q.
Binder's title. Plates show scenes from the Belgian war for independence of 1830
Lipperheide 2258

L'**éventail.** Uzanne, L. O.

Un **éventail** historique du XVIIIe siècle. Marcel, G. A.

L'**éventail**, l'ombrelle, le gant, le manchon. See Uzanne, L. O. Les ornements de la femme

Everard, Harry Stirling Crawfurd
A history of the Royal & ancient golf club, St. Andrews, from 1754-1900. Edinburgh and London, W. Blackwood 1907
xi,306p. incl.pl. ports.(part col.) facsims. front. Q.
"This book consists for the most part of articles originally contributed to 'Golf illustrated' "; it includes "Mr. Cunningham's article on Dutch golf." Preface
LC 15-11964

Everitt, Graham
English caricaturists and graphic humourists of the nineteenth century. How they illustrated and interpreted their times. London, S. Sonnenschein, Le Bas & Lowrey 1886
xx,427p. front. pl. facsim. Q.
Appendices (p401-16): 1 Some illustrative work of Isaac Robert Cruikshank; 2 Some miscellaneous work of Robert Seymour executed between 1822 and 1836; 3 Some of the illustrated work of John Leech; 4 Some miscellaneous work of Alfred Henry Forrester (Alfred Crowquill) 5 Some works illustrated by Hablot Knight Browne
LC 9-34365

Everyday life in Anglo-Saxon, viking and Norman times. Quennell, Mrs M. C., and Quennell, C. H. B.

Everyday life in Homeric Greece. Quennell, Mrs M. C., and Quennell, C. H. B.

Everyday life in prehistoric times. See Quennell, Mrs M. C., and Quennell, C. H. B.

Everyday life in Roman Britain. Quennell, Mrs M. C., and Quennell, C. H. B.

Everyday life in the new stone, bronze & early iron ages. Quennell, Mrs M. C., and Quennell, C. H. B.

Everyday things in archaic Greece. Quennell, Mrs M. C., and Quennell, C. H. B.

Everyday things in England. See Quennell, Mrs M. C., and Quennell, C. H. B. A history of everyday things in England

Everyday things in Homeric Greece. See Quennell, Mrs M. C., and Quennell, C. H. B. Everyday life in Homeric Greece

Eve's glossary. Cunliffe-Owen, M. de G.

Evidens designatio receptissimarum consuetudinem ornamenta quaedam et insignia continens magistratui et academiae Argentinensi à maioribus relicta. Argentorati, J. Carolus 1605
1 l. 60pl. O.
Costume of Alsace
Preface signed: J. F. An edition dated 1606 with 61 plates is described by Lipperheide
Colas 1006. Lipperheide 789m

The **evils** of fashionable dress. Kellogg, J. H.

L'**évolution** de l'art dans l'éventail aux 16. 17. et 18. siècles. Bojardi, F. de

The **evolution** of dress fastening devices from the bone pin to the koh-i-noor. Manchester, Herbert

The **evolution** of fashion. Gardiner, F. M

The **evolution** of Maori clothing. Buck, P. H.

Ewald, Paulus
Reise des evangelischen missionar Christian Ferdinand Ewald, von Tunis über Soliman, Nabal, Hammamet, Susa, Sfar, Gabis, Gerba nach Tripolis, und von da wieder zurück nach Tunis, im jahre 1835. Nürnberg, F. von Ebner 1837
240p. 14pl.(5 col.) O.
The color plates show costume and are engraved after Obermüller
Colas 1007. Lipperheide 1588

Ewers, Hanns Heinz
Musik im bild; hrsg. von H. H. Ewers. Begleitender text von J. E. Poritzky; 3. aufl. München, G. Müller ca1920
128p. 73 illus. 50pl. F.

Ex emendationibus, adque comentariis Bernardi Saraceni. See Plautus. Comoediae

Examples of Chinese ornament. Jones, Owen

Excella fashion quarterly. no. 1-44; 1922-Spring 1936. New York, Excella pattern co.
Illus. F. $1 a year
Published quarterly. Ceased with no44, Spring 1936

Excubiae tutelares LX heroum. Brunner, Andrea

Excursion in Madeira and Porto Santo. Bowdich, T. E.

Excursions, adventures, and field-sports in Ceylon. Campbell, James

Excursions dans les isles de Madère et de Porto Santo faîtes dans l'automne de 1823. See Bowdich, T. E. Excursion in Madeira and Porto Santo

Excursions in New South Wales ... Breton, W. H.

Exemplario di lavori. Zoppino, Nicolo d'Aristotile, called

Exequiae ... Caroli Gustavi Suecorum Gothorum et Wandalorum regis d. 3. Nouemb. 1660 Holmiae celebratae. Dahlbergh, E. J.

Exequias feitas em Roma a magestade fidelissima do senhor rey Dom Joaõ V. por ordem do fidelissimo senhor rey Dom Jozé I. seu filho, e successor. Roma, J. M. Salvioni 1751
xxiv p. 13 illus. 19pl. F.
Lipperheide 2767

Exercice de l'infanterie françoise ... copié d'après l'original. Baudouin, S. R., comte de

Exercice de l'infanterie françoise ordonnée par le roy le VI may MDCCLV. Baudouin, S. R., comte de

L'**exercice** des armes ou le maniement du fleuret. Le Perche

Exercice et révolutions de l'infanterie françoise. Lattré, pub.

Exércices d'imagination de différens caractères et formes humaines. See Göz, J. F. von. Die heutige sichtbare körperwelt

Exercices militaires. Callot, Jacques

The **exercise** of armes for calivres, muskettes, and pikes. Gheyn, Jacob de

Exercises for ladies. Walker, Donald

Exercitium super Pater noster (Blockbook)
Exercitium super Pater noster, suite de gravures avec légendes; reproduction photographique d'une publication xylographique du XVe siècle. Notice par Benjamin Pifteau. Paris, Delarue 188-?
x p. 10 facsim. sq.Q.
"L'original existe à la Bibliothèque nationale." p x
Lipperheide 406. LC 33-36752

Exercitium zu pferd und zu fuss. See Khevenhüller, L. A., graf von. Observationspuncten

Exerzier-reglement für die Eidgenössische linien u. leichte infanterie. Abt I. Soldaten-schule. Basel, 1799-1804
78,21p. 8 col.pl. O.
Plates show military uniforms. They are by Wellstein, engraved by Ch. de Mechel
Colas 1008

Exhibition of English embroidery executed prior to the middle of the XVI century. Burlington fine arts club, London

The **exhibition** of the Rational dress association, Prince's Hall, Piccadilly, W. Catalogue of exhibits and list of exhibitors. London, Wyman [1883]
36p. 1 illus. 16pl. Q.
Lipperheide 3289

Exler, Max
(ed.) Lübker, F. H. C. Friedrich Lübker's Reallexikon des classischen alterthums, für gymnasien

Exner, Moritz. See Hepke, F. V. von. Frankreich. Das heer am ende des neunzehnten jahrhunderts

Expedition der europäischen modenzeitung. See Lexikon des kleidermachers

An **expedition** of discovery into the interior of Africa. Alexander, Sir J. E.

Explication des cent estampes qui representent differentes nations du Levant. Moor, J. B. van

Explication des cérémonies de la Fête-Dieu d'Aix en Provence. Grégoire, Gaspard

Exploration of the valley of the Amazon. Herndon, W. L., and Gibbon, Lardner

Explorations and adventures in equatorial Africa. Du Chaillu, P. B.

Explorations in the interior of the Labrador peninsula. Hind, H. Y.

Exposicion de "el abanico en España". Sociedad española de amigos del arte, Madrid

Exposition de l'art ancien, 1884. See Brussels. Exposition de l'art ancien, 1884

Exposition de l'art populaire tchéco-slovaque. Paris. Exposition de l'art populaire tchéco-slovaque, 1920

Exposition rétrospective du mobilier et du costume poitevins, 20 sept. 1902. See Farault, Alphonse. Ville de St-Maixent

Exposition universelle de 1900, Paris. See Paris. Exposition universelle, 1900

Extracts of the journals and correspondence of Miss Berry. Berry, Mary

Extraits de L'Art pour tous, encyclopédie de l'art industriel & décoratif. Armes et armures. Paris, Librairie des imprimeries réunies ca1880
1 l. 60pl. F.
Plates, showing arms and armor from the 2d to the 16th century have been selected from the periodical *L'Art pour tous.* Legends are in French, German and English
Lipperheide 2430

Extremadura costume. Hispanic society of America

Eyck, Jan van
(illus.) Biblia pauperum. Biblia Pauperum; reproduced in facsimile from one of the copies in the British Museum

Eye, August von
Deutschland vor dreihundert jahren in leben und kunst. [Leipzig, 1857]
14p. 20pl. F.
Shows German costume from 1557 to 1857

Eye, August von, and Falke, Jacob von
Kunst und leben der vorzeit vom beginn des mittelalters bis zu anfang des 19. jahrhunderts in skizzen nach original denkmälern; 2. ausg. Nürnberg, Bauer & Raspe 1859-62
3v. 288pl.(10 col.) Q.
Illustrated by Willibald Maurer
First edition: 1855-59
Lipperheide 334

Eyeglasses and lorgnettes
Allemagne, H. R. d'. Les accessoires du costume et du mobilier depuis le treizième jusqu'au milieu du dixneuvième siècle. v2 1928

Bock, Emil. Die brille und ihre geschichte. 1903

Heymann, Mme Alfred. Lunettes et lorgnettes de jadis. 1911

Phillips, R. J. Spectacles and eyeglasses. 1923

Rasmussen, O. D. History of Chinese spectacles. 1915

Rasmussen, O. D. Old Chinese spectacles. c1915

Eygentliche beschreibung aller stände auff erden. Amman, Jost

Eyre-Todd, George
The Highland clans of Scotland: their history and traditions ... with ... illustrations including reproductions of M'Ian's celebrated paintings of the costumes of the clans. London, Heath, Cranton 1923
2v. col.fronts. pl.(part col.) ports. O.
LC 24-8529

Eyriès, Jean Baptiste Benoît
L'Angleterre, ou costumes, moeurs, et usages des Anglais. Paris, Gide fils ca1821
24 l. 24 col.pl. O.
Colas 1013

L'Autriche ou costumes, moeurs et usages des Autrichiens. Paris, Gide fils ca1821
24 l. 24 col.pl. O.
Plates are from Marcel Serres's *L'Autriche*
Colas 1014

La Chine, ou costumes, moeurs et usages des Chinois. Paris, Gide fils ca1822
24 l. 24 col.pl. O.
Also known in smaller format (72p. 24 col.pl. T.)
The plates are taken from William Alexander's *Picturesque representations of the dress and manners of the Chinese*
Colas 1015

Costumes, moeurs et usages de tous les peuples: suite de gravures coloriées avec un texte explicatif. Espagne. Paris, Gide fils ca1815
2v. 36 col.pl. O.
Each plate is signed: Chasselat del. Mme Couët, sc.
Colas 1012

Costumes, moeurs, et usages de tous les peuples: suite de gravures coloriées avec un texte explicatif. France—Paris. Paris, Gide fils ca1815
18 l. 18 col.pl. O.
Each plate signed: Chasselat, del, Mme Couët, sc.
Also published with title: *La France, ou costumes, moeurs et usages des Français*
Colas 1011

Danemark ... continué par M. Chopin. Paris, Firmin Didot 1846
415p. 24pl. O. (L'univers, histoire et description de tous les peuples)
Six plates show Danish costume in 1588
LC 3-10086

La Russie, ou costumes, moeurs et usages des Russes. Paris, Gide fils ca1823
24 l. 24 col.pl. O.
Plates numbered 1-18, and 15, 16, 17, and 18 bis
Plates are from *The costume of the Russian empire* published London, W. Miller 1803
Colas 1016

La Suisse, ou costumes, moeurs et usages des Suisses. Paris, Gide fils [1825]
54 l. 63 col.pl. O.
Also known in smaller format (72p. 24pl. T.) Plates are reproduced from those in *Costumes suisses dédié à son altesse royale ...* edited by Gabriel Lory and F. W. Moritz
Colas 1017

La Turquie ou costumes, moeurs et usages des Turcs. Paris, Gide fils ca1827
24 l. 24 col.pl. O.
Plates are from William Alexander's *Picturesque representations of the dress and manners of the Turks*
Colas 1018

Voyage pittoresque en Asie et en Afrique; résumé générale des voyages anciens et modernes d'après Erman, Lesseps, J.-F. Gmelin [illus] ... d'après les dessins de J. Boilly. Paris, Furne [1839]
423,160p. 68pl. maps. Q.
Plates are double and most of them contain four costume figures
Colas 1019. Lipperheide 1459

Eze, Mme Marie Gabrié, dit Gabriel d', and Marcel, A.
Histoire de la coiffure des femmes en France ... illustré de 242 gravures par J. Rocault. Paris, P. Ollendorf 1886
368p. 205 illus. D.
Colas 1020. Lipperheide 1714

Ezquerra del Bayo, Joaquín
Exposicion de "el abanico en España". See entry under Sociedad española de amigos del arte, Madrid

F

F.
(illus.) Cris de Paris

Faber du Faur, Christian Wilhelm von
Blätter aus meinem portefeuille, im laufe des feldzugs 1812 in Russland ... Feuilles extraites de mon portefeuille, esquissées sur les lieux dans le courant de la campagne de 1812 en Russie. Stuttgart, C. F. Autenrieth 1831-34
100pl. ob.F.
Shows French army uniforms of 1812

Fabi-Montani, Francesco, count. See Barocci, Luigi, jt. auth.

Fabri, Alexandro de
Diversarum nationum ornatus. [Padoue, Fabri 1593]
3v. 80,104,82pl. O.
Copied from the series by Pierre Bertellius entitled *Diversaru nationum habitus*
Colas 1021

Fabri, Augustin. See Conlin, J. R. Roma sancta sive Benedicti XIII

Fabricius, Wilhelm
Die deutschen corps. Berlin, H. L. Thilo 1898
431p. 183 illus. 1 pl. O.
A history of German student organisations (corps) showing distinctive costumes
Lipperheide 2034

Fabris, Pietro
Raccolta di varii vestimenti ed arti del regno di Napoli. Naples, 1773
35pl. F.
Cataloged from Colas
Colas 1022

Fabronius, Hermann
Newe summarische welt historia ... Was für land and leute in der gantzen welt, was ihre gestalt, kleidung, sprachen unnd handthierung ... seyen. Schmalkalden, W. Ketzeln 1612
2v. 33 illus. 2pl. Q.
Illustrations show dress of various peoples with explanatory text
Lipperheide 28

Face. See Make-up

The **face** of China. Kemp, E. G.

Les **fâcheux.** Dyagilev, S. P.

Facial paintings of the Indians of northern British Columbia. Boaz, Franz

Fac-simile delle miniature contenute nel Breviario Grimani. Catholic church. Liturgy and ritual. Breviary

Fac-simile des miniatures contenues dans le Bréviaire Grimani. See Catholic Church. Liturgy and ritual. Breviary. Fac-simile delle miniature contenute nel Breviario Grimani

Facsimile of the Papyrus of Ani. Book of the dead

Fac-similes of the miniatures and ornaments of Anglo-Saxon & Irish manuscripts. Westwood, J. O.

Der **fächer.** Buss, Georg.

Fagonde. See Haguental, jt. auth.

Faguet, Michel
(ed.) Capitan, Louis. La préhistoire

Die **fahrenden** leute in der deutschen vergangenheit. Hampe, Theodor

Fahrnbauer, J. G.
(illus.) Leitner, Quirin, ritter von. Die waffensammlung des osterreichischen kaiserhauses im K.K. Artillerie-arsenal-museum in Wien

The **fair** land Tyrol. See McCracken, W. D. The spell of Tyrol

Fairchild's magazine. See Man's book, a magazine

Fairholt, Frederick William
Costume in England; a history of dress to the end of the eighteenth century. 4th ed. enl. and rev. by H. A. Dillon. Illustrated with above seven hundred engravings. London, G. Bell 1896
2v. illus. D. (Bohn's artists' library) 10s, o.p.
First edition 1846. Second edition 1860. Third edition enl. and rev. by H. A. Dillon, 2v 1885
Contents: v 1, History; v2, Glossary. Books treating of costume: v 1, pref. p11-14
Colas 1023-25. Lipperheide 1008z, 1009. Costume index. LC 4-18450

Rambles of an archæologist among old books and in old places. London, Virtue 1871
259p. incl.front. 259 illus. O.
The papers originally appeared in the Art journal
Contents: Rambles of an archæologist among old books and in old places; Grotesque design, as exhibited in ornamental and industrial art; Facts about finger-rings; Ancient brooches and dress fastenings; Albert Dürer: his works, his compatriots, and his times
LC 1-5392

(ed.) Satirical songs and poems on costume: from the 13th to the 19th century. London, Printed for the Percy society by Richards 1849
267p. illus. D. (Percy society. Early English poetry ... v27, pt2)
LC A10-923

See also Merrifield, Mrs M. P. Dress as a fine art

A **faithful** account of the processions and ceremonies observed in the coronation of the kings and queens of England. Thomson, Richard, ed.

The **faiths** of the world. Gardner, James

Faits mémorables des empereurs de la Chine. Helman, I. S.

Fal, Saint. See Saint-Fal

Falbalas et fanfreluches; almanach des modes, présentes, passés, futures pour 1922-[1925 ou 1926]. Paris, Meynial 1922-26
5v. col.pl. O.
Published annually. Each volume contains ten or twelve pages of text and twelve colored plates engraved after pictures by George Barbier which are humorous treatments of the costume of the time
The text of volume 1, is by comtesse Mathieu de Noailles, v2 by Colette, v3 by Cécile Sorel, v4 by Gérard d'Houville and v6 by the baronne de Brimont
Colas 1026

Falconer, John
A series of tables and diagrams illustrating economy in cutting; ed. by J. Williamson. 3d ed. enl. London, J. Williamson [1889]
Diagrs. Q.

Falconers

Chenu, J. C., and Oeillet des Murs, M. A. P. La fauconnerie. 1862

Harting, J. E. Bibliotheca accipitraria; a catalogue of books ancient and modern relating to falconry. 1891

Hicfelt, Eberhard. Aucupatorium Herodiorum; eine deutsche abhandlung über die beizjagd aus der ersten hälfte des 15. jahrhundertes. 1886

Latham, Simon. The whole work of Mr. Latham's books of faulconry. 1662

Menino, Pero. Livro de falcoaria. 1924 (From a 14th century manuscript)

Pomay, Fr. Ein sehr artig büchlein von dem weydwerck und der falcknerey; traitté fort curieux de la vénerie et de la fauconnerie. 1886

Turberville, George. The booke of falconrie or hawking. 1611

Falda, Giovanni Battista

Der römischen fontanen wahre abbildung, wie solche so wohl auf offentlichen plätzen und palatien als auch zu Frescada Tiuoli und denen lust-gärten mit ihren prospecten der zeit allda zu ersehen sind. Gezeichnet von ... J. B. Falti. Nürnberg, In Sandrartischem verlag. Gedruckt bey C. S. Froberg 1685
11p. xxxxii pl. (part fold.) F.
Edited, with descriptions, by J. von Sandrart
Lipperheide 1306. LC 10-4461

Fales, Jane

Dressmaking, a manual for schools and colleges. New York, [etc] C. Scribner's c1917
xiii,508p. illus. D.
Bibliography: p486-88
LC 17-1600

Falk, Hjalmar Sejersted

Altwestnordische kleiderkunde, mit besonderer berücksichtigung der terminologie. Kristiania, J. Dybwad 1919
234p. Q. (Videnskapsselskapets skrifter. II. Hist.-filos. klasse. 1918. no3)
Shows old Norse costume

Falk, Max, and Dux, Adolf

Krönungs-album, 8. juni 1867, mit ... illustrationen von Kolarz, Kriehuber, Katzler und Jankó. Pest, Gebrüder Deutsch [1867]
60p. front. illus. 20pl. F.
Lipperheide 2639

Falke, Jacob von

Costümgeschichte der culturvölker. Stuttgart, W. Spemann [1881]
480p. 377 illus. 1 col.pl. Q. (Histoire du costumes des peuples civilisés)
Colas 1029. Lipperheide 88

Die deutsche trachten und modenwelt. Leipzig, G. Meyer 1858
2v. O.
These two volumes from part 1 of his *Deutsches leben*
Contents: v 1 Die alte zeit und das mittelalter; v2 Die neuzeit
Colas 1027. Lipperheide 589

Greece and Rome their life and art; tr. by William Hand Browne. New York, H. Holt 1882
xii,351p. illus. pl. F.
Personal appearance and dress, Greece p55-72; Dress and personal ornament, Rome p240-50

Die ritterliche gesellschaft im zeitalter des frauencultus; neue ausg. Berlin, F. Henschel [1872]
172p. O.
First edition: 1862
Lipperheide 390m

Römisch kaiserlicher majestät kriegsvölker im zeitalter der landsknechte. See entry under Breunner-Enkevoërth, A. J., graf von

Zur costumgeschichte des mittelalters. Wien, Prendel & Meyer 1861
46p. 156 illus. Q.
Contents: Die männliche kopftracht; Die weibliche kopftracht
Colas 1028. Lipperheide 1708

Zur cultur und kunst. Wien, C. Gerold's sohn 1878
353p. 34 illus. O.
Pages 70-180 give a critical discussion of costume from viewpoint of aesthetics
Lipperheide 3279

See also Geschichte der deutschen kunst; also Eye, August von, jt. auth.

Falke, Otto von

Der mainzer goldschmuck der kaiserin Gisela. Berlin, In kommission des Verlags für kunstwissenschaft 1913
30p. illus. 8pl. (incl.mounted col.front.) F.
Edition of the Deutscher verein für kunstwissenschaft. The treasure of the Empress Gisela, d. 1043 consort of Konrad II, emperor of Germany, was found in Mainz in 1880
LC 15-21303

See also Le Coq, Albert von. Volkskundliches aus Ost-Turkistan

Fallou, Louis

Album de l'armée française (de 1700 à 1870) Texte par L. Fallou. Paris, La Gibirne 1902
40 col.pl. O.
"Quarante planches en couleurs de Aubry, Bellangé, Chaperon, Geens, Grammont, Morel, Orange, Rouffet, Vallet, et quarante planches en noir pour colorier." Subtitle
Colas 1032

Le bouton uniforme français (de l'ancien-régime à fin juillet 1914) Ouvrage illustré de 10 planches d'uniformes en couleurs, hors texte, d'après les aquarelles de Maurice Orange et de 3700 dessins par Jacques Hilpert. Colombes (Seine) La Giberne, 1915
327p. illus. 10 col.pl. (incl.front.) F.
Colas 1033. LC 19-597

La Garde impériale (1804-1815) ouvrage illustré de 450 dessins dans le texte par: E. Grammont, M. Orange, L. Vallet et de 60 compositions, hors-texte, en couleurs, d'après les aquarelles de: J. Chelminski, E. Grammont, H. Dupray, M. Orange, Rouffet et L. Vallet. Paris, La Giberne 1901
xii,378p. illus. 60 col.pl. F.
Colas 1030. LC 3-7495

Fallou, Louis—*Continued*
Nos hussards (1692-1902) Formations, uniformes, équipements, armements, harnachements. Paris, La Giberne 1902
300p. 20 col.pl. tables. F.
Colas 1031. LC 3-23264

Falls, De Witt Clinton
Die armee der Vereinigten Staaten von Amerika. Leipzig, M. Ruhl [1914]
23p. 16 col.pl. on 1 fold.sheet. D.
LC 15-7057

Army and navy information; uniforms, organizations, arms and equipment of the warring powers. New York, E. P. Dutton & company c1917
xxii,192p. 30 illus. 6 col.pl. D. $1.50 o.p.
This author's personal collection of books and notes on uniforms is now in the New York public library
Costume index. LC 17-29353

Falti, Johann Baptista. See Falda, G. B.

Famiglie celebri d'Italia. Litta, Pompeo

Familienbilder des Hauses Hohenzollern. Baumeister, J. S.

Familien-spiele aus dem im besitz ... des kronprinzen und der kronprinzessin des deutschen reiches und von Preussen befindlichen spielschrein. Berlin, Vereins für deutsches kunstgewerbe 1886
10p. 36pl. F.
Lipperheide 3147m

Famous bands of the British Empire. Zealley, A. E., and Hume, J. O.

Famous pictures of children. Schwartz, J. A.

The **fan.** Uzanne, L. O.

The **fan** book. Percival, MacIver

The **fan** in all ages; a brief history of its evolution. Grolier club, New York

Fancy ball dress. Mansion, L. M.

Fancy dress
Aria, Mrs E. D. Costume: fanciful, historical and theatrical. 1906
Bals masqués de Paris. 1835-1855
Bals masqués de Paris. 1859?
Costumes for bazaars and masquerades. c1917
Dennison manufacturing company. How to make crepe paper costumes. 1925
Grévin, Alfred. Les nouveaux travestissements parisiens. 1873
Hirt, A. L. Dädalus und seine statuen. 1802
Hirt, A. L., and Brühl, K. F. M. P., graf von. Die weihe des Eros Uranios; ein festlicher aufzug mit tänzen gegeben den 8ten januar 1818 im weissen saale des königlichen schlosses, zur vermählungsfeuer ... des prinzen Friederich von Preussen ... und der prinzessin Wilhelmine Luise von Anhalt-Bernburg. 1818

15th century

De intogt van hertog Jan van Beijeren binnen Leyden, op den 18^den^ augustus 1420, in maskerade voorgesteld door H. H. studenten der Leydsche hoogeschool, op den 8sten februarij 1840. 1840?
Das nürnbergische schönbartbuch nach der Hamburger handschrift. 1908
Nürnbergisches schönbart-buch und gesellenstechen. 1765

16th century

Boissard, J. J. Mascarades; recuillies & mises en taille douce. 1597
Das nürnbergische schönbartbuch nach der Hamburger handschrift. 1908
Nürnbergisches schönbart-buch und gesellenstechen. 1765

17th century

Bérain, J. L. Maskenanzüge. ca1670-80
Bertelli, Francesco. Il carnevale Italiano mascherato. 1642

18th century

Goethe, Johann Wolfgang. Das römische carneval. 1789

19th century

Bassaget, P. N. Fantaisies gracieuses. ca1850
Bechstein, L. Phantasie-costüme. [1880]
Die carnevals-freuden, oder Kleines ideenmagazin zu geistreichen und leicht ausführbaren masken. 1839
Compte-Calix, F. C. Les travestissements élégants. 1864
Costumi vestiti alla festa da ballo data in Milano Dal ... Conte Giuseppe Batthyany ... 1828
Dahling, illus. Der grosse maskenball in Berlin zur feier des geburtstages ... der regierenden königin von Preussen am 12ten Marz 1804 im königlichen nationaltheater veranstaltet. 1805
Dörbeck, F. B. Masken-anzüge zu polter-abenden und bällen. 1831
Fries, and Nachtmann. Quadrilles parées et costumées exécutées à la cour de sa majesté le roi de Bavière le 3 février 1835 représentant les divers pays des quatre parties du mond. 1835?
Frizzi, Arturo. Cinquanta maschere italiane illustrate nei loro costumi. 1888
Gavarni, G. S. C. Travestissemens. ca1838
Goebels, W. Der grosse cölnische maskenzug im jahr 1824. 1824
Grandville, J. I. I. G. Les étoiles. 1849
Grevin, Alfred. Costumes de fantaisie pour un bal travesti. 1870
Holt, Ardern. Fancy dresses described, or What to wear at fancy balls. 1896
Holt, Ardern. Gentlemen's fancy dress. 1898
Körber, Philipp. Volksbelustigungen und mummenschanz der alten ehemaligen reichsstadt Nürnberg. 1859
Lange, Eduard. Das hoffest zu Ferrara in den saelen des koeniglichen schlosses zu Berlin dargestellt am 28. februar 1843. 1846
Léo. Travestissements enfantins. 1880?
Male character costumes. 1884
Mansion, L. M. Fancy ball dress. 1831?

Fancy dress—19th century—*Continued*
Marta, Luigi. Costumi della festa data da S. Maesta' il di 20 feb. 1854 nella reggia di Napoli. 1854
Masken-costüme; 70 costüm-entwürfe für damen- u. kinder-masken ... nebst erläuterungen und beschreibungen. 1883
Méry, J. P. A. Les parures: Fantaisie par Gavarni, texte par Méry, histoire de la mode par le Cte Foelix [pseud] ca1850
Morel-Retz, L. P. G. B. Ces messieurs; travestissements fantaisistes. ca1870
Morghen, Luigi. Programma e figure delle mascherata dé quattro principali poeti d'Italia, mostratasi alla festa data in Napoli ... la sera del 19 febbraio 1827. ca1830
Nachtmann, F. X. Collection des divers costumes composant les quadrilles du bal masqué donné à Munic le 15 fév. 1827. 1827?
Neueste und geschmackvollste masken-anzüge. 1839-53
Planché, J. R., and Smyth, Coke. Souvenir of the bal costumé given by ... Queen Victoria at Buckingham palace, May 12, 1842. 1843
Renard, Jules. Travestissements comiques. 1870?
Robida, Albert. La grande mascarade parisienne. 1881-82
Robin. Travestissements. ca1868
Valentini, Francesco. Trattato su la commedia dell' arte, ossia improvvisa maschere italiane. 1826
Vanier, Léon. Costumes de carnaval. 1885
Wandle, Mrs J. T. Masquerade and carnival: their customs and costumes. 1892
Weidmann, F. C. Der costum-ball am schlusse des carnevals 1826. 1826

20th century

Beaumont, C. E. de. Au bal masqué. ca1850
Danvers, V. L. Training in commercial art. 1926
McCormick, Olive. Water pageants, games and stunts. 1933
Nice-carnaval. 192-?
Peel, Mrs D. C. B. Designs for fancy dresses. 1905
Romme. Les douze mois de l'année. 1928?
Schnackenberg, Walther. Kostueme, plakate und dekorationen. 1920
Zamacoïs, Miguel. Dernière lettre persane mise en français par M. Zamacoïs et accompagnée de douze dessins exécutés dans le goût persan par Benito. ca1925

SPECIAL REPRESENTATIONS

Architecture

Petitot, E. A. Mascarade à la grecque. 1771

Flowers

Böttger, Adolf. Die pilgerfahrt der blumengeister. 1857
Crane, Walter. Flora's feast. 1892
Grandville, J. I. I. G., called. Les fleurs animées. 1847
Grandville, J. I. I. G., called. The flowers personified. 1847-49
Kramer, Ludwig von. Blüthenzauber. 1885-87
Nauen, Paul. Blumenkinder. 1884-87

Shepherdesses

Passe, Crispijn van de. Les vrais pourtraits de quelques unes des plus grandes dames de la chrestiente, desguisees en bergeres. 1640

Fancy dress for children. See Children—Fancy dress

Fancy dresses described. Holt, Ardern

Fancy work. See Needlework

Fangé, Augustin
Mémoires pour servir à l'histoire de la barbe de l'homme. Liège, J. F. Broncart 1774
320p. O.

Fanmakers, London. See London. Fanmakers

Fans
Allemagne, H. R. d'. Les accessoires du costume et du mobilier depuis le treizième jusqu'au milieu du dixneuvième siècle. 1928
B., E. Collection d'éventails anciens des xviie et xviiie siècles, d'après éventails authentiques Louis xiv, Louis xv, Louis xvi. 1890
Bapst, Germain. Deux éventails du Musée du Louvre. 1882
Blondel, Spire. Histoire des éventails ... Ouvrage suivi de notices sur l'ecaille, la nacre et l'ivoire. 1875
Bojardi, F. L'évolution de l'art dans l'éventail aux 16. 17. et 18. siècles. 1907
British museum. Department of prints and drawings Catalogue of the collection of fans and fan-leaves presented by the Lady Charlotte Schreiber. 1893
Buss, Georg. Der fächer. 1904
Edinburgh. Royal Scottish museum. Catalogue of loan collection of art fans. 1878
Flory, M. A. A book about fans. 1895
Frauberger, Heinrich. Die geschichte des fächers. 1878
Grolier club, New York. The fan in all ages; a brief history of its evolution. To accompany an exhibition of fans, mostly French, of the xviiith century, illustrating the decorative art of that period as applied to fans. 1891
Holme, Charles, ed. Modern design in jewellery and fans. 1902
London. Fanmakers. Catalogue of competitive exhibitions of fans. 1897
Marcel, G. A. Un éventail historique du xviiie siècle. 1901

Fans—*Continued*
Mineur, A. E. A charitable remonstrance addressed to the wives and maidens of France, touching their dissolute adornments. 1887
Percival, MacIver. The fan book. 1921
Rhead, G. W. History of the fan. 1910
Rosenberg, Marc. Alte und neue fächer. 1891
Salwey, Mrs C. M. B. Fans of Japan. 1894
Schreiber, Lady Charlotte Elizabeth (Bertie) Guest. Fans and fan leaves. 1888-90
Sociedad española de amigos del arte, Madrid. Exposicion de "el abanico en España", catalogo general ilustrado. 1920
Uzanne, L. O. L'éventail. 1882
Uzanne, L. O. The fan. 1884
Uzanne, L. O. Les ornements de la femme ... L'éventail, l'ombrelle, le gant, le manchon. 1892
Waern, Cecilia. A short historical sketch of fans. 1895
Walker, Robert. Old fans from Mr. R. Walker's cabinet. 1882?
Wells, Rosalie. Fans. 1928

Fans and fan leaves. Schreiber, Lady C. E. B. G.

Fans of Japan. Salwey, Mrs C. M. B.

Les **fantaisies** aimables ou les caprices des belles répresentés par les costumes les plus nouveaux. Paris, Jubert 1786
1 l. 12pl. T.
"Plates are copied from those in *Les belles marchandes.*" Colas
Colas 1034

Fantaisies gracieuses. Bassaget, P. N.

Fantaisies, localités bordelaises. Galard, Gustave de, and Claveau, Eugene

Les **fantasies** de Noble I. Callot. Callot, Jacques

Fantassins et cavaliers sous Louis xv. Grandmaison, Henri de

Farault, Alphonse
Ville de St-Maixent (Deux-Sèvres). Exposition rétrospective du mobilier et du costume poitevins, 20 septembre 1902: Catalogue des objets exposés. Saint Maixent, E. Payet 1902
80p. O.
Colas 1035

Die **farbenharmonie.** Jaennicke, Friedrich

Die **farbenharmonie.** See note under Chevreul, M. E. De la loi du contraste simultané des couleurs

Die **farbenharmonie** in der damen-toilette. Schröder, Severin

Die **farben-harmonie** in ihrer anwendung auf die damentoilette. Adams, Rudolph

Farbige flachtisch-muster. Reitz, A., and Reitz, E.

Farbige schweizer trachten-bilder. Schmid, D. A.

Farbige stickerei-vorlagen. Redtenbacher, M.

Farcy, Louis de
La broderie du XIe siècle jusqu'à nos jours. Paris, E. Leroux 1890
144p. 181pl. F.
Lipperheide 3872

Fargès-Méricourt, P. J.
Relation du voyage de sa majesté Charles x en Alsace. Strasbourg, F. G. Levrault 1829
184p. 12pl. 1 map. Q.
Lipperheide 2727

Faria e Sousa, Manuel de.
Historia del reyno de Portugal; nueva ed. Brusselas, F. Foppens 1730
xxiv,456,xlix,15p. 2 illus. 25pl. F.
"Dividida en cinco partes, que contienen en compendio, sus poblaciones, las entradas de las naciones setentrionales en el reyno ... las vidas y las hazañas de sus reyes con sus retratos." Subtitle
Full length portraits of the kings of Portugal to Don Juan v. The last four portraits are engraved by Franz Harrewijn
First edition appeared in Madrid in 1628 under title: *Epitome de las historias portuguezas,* another edition in Brussels in 1678, and the last edition in the year 1779
Lipperheide 1208

Farjasse, D. D.
Rome. See Audot, L. E. L'Italie. v3

Farley, Robert. See Cats, Jacob, jt. auth.

Farmers. See Agricultural laborers

Farnsworth, Eva Olney
The art & ethics of dress, as related to efficiency and economy; illus. by Audley B. Wells. San Francisco, Cal., P. Elder c1915
xvi,53p. incl.pl. front. pl. D. $1
LC 15-13388

Farrer, Edmund
(ed.) Duleep Singh, Frederick, prince. Portraits in Norfolk houses

Fashion
Aincourt, Marguerite d'. Études sur le costume féminin. 1884
Aretz, Frau G. K. D. The elegant woman, from the rococo period to modern times. 1932
Barr, E. De Y. A psychological analysis of fashion motivation. 1934
Beaulieu, Michèle. Contribution à l'étude de la mode à Paris; les transformations du costume élégant sous la règne de Louis XIII (1610-1643). 1936
Bibesco, M. L. L. princesse. Noblesse de robe. 1928
Boehn, Max von. Das beiwerk der mode. 1928
Boehn, Max von. Bekleidungskunst und mode. 1918
Boehn, Max von. Modes and manners. 1932-36
Boehn, Max von. Modes & manners: ornaments; lace, fans, gloves, walking-sticks, parasols, jewelry and trinkets. 1929
Boehn, Max von. Modespiegel. 1919
Bosselt, Rudolf. Krieg und deutsche mode. 1915
Bradley, H. D. The eternal masquerade. 1922
Braunschvig, Marcel. La femme et la beauté. 1929
Caraccioli, L. A. de. Le livre à la mode. 1759

Fashion—*Continued*

El costume de le donne, incomenzando da la pueritia per fin al maritar. 1889

De Garmo, Charles, and Winslow, L. L. Essentials of design. 1924

Despaigne, H. Le code de la mode. 1866

Discours nouveau sur la mode. 1613

Ditchett, S. H. Historic costumes; their influence on modern fashions. 1920

Dörig, James. La mode et la couture. 1925

Drohojowska, A. J. F. A. S. de L., comtesse. La vérité aux femmes sur l'excentricité des modes et de la toilette. 1858

Fox, G. P. Fashion: the power that influences the world. 1872

Hurlock, E. B. Motivation in fashion. 1929

Hurlock, E. B. The psychology of dress; an analysis of fashion and its motive. c1929

Keezer, Ro. Feminine toilettes and knick-knacks of the romantic age. 1930

Kleinwächter, Friedrich. Zur philosophie der mode. 1880

Lacroix, Paul. History of prostitution among all the peoples of the world, from the most remote antiquity to the present day. 1926

Langlade, Émile. La marchande de modes de Marie-Antoinette, Rose Bertin. 1911

Langlade, Émile. Rose Bertin, the creator of fashion at the court of Marie-Antoinette. 1913

Loeber, C. G., praeses. Dissertationem academicam de mutatione formarum in vestibus; i.e., Von veränderung der kleidermoden. 1722

Miomandre, Francis de. La mode. 1927

Mustoxidi, T. M. Qu'est-ce que la mode? 1920

Neuburger, Otto. Die mode; wesen, entstehen und wirken. 1913

Nystrom, P. H. Economics of fashion. 1928

Porada, Käthe von. Mode in Paris. 1932

Stern, Norbert. Mode und kultur. c1915

Vischer, F. T. von. Mode und cynismus. 1879

See also Designing; Dolls

History

Bizet, Rene. La mode. 1925

Robida, Albert. Mesdames nos aïeules; dix siècles d'élégances. 1891

Robida, Albert. Yester-year; ten centuries of toilette. 1891

Uzanne, L. O. Fashion in Paris; the various phases of feminine taste and aesthetics from 1797 to 1897. 1898

Uzanne, L. O. La Française du siècle, la femme et la mode. 1892

Uzanne, L. O. The Frenchwoman of the century [1792-1892] 1886

Uzanne, L. O. Les modes de Paris, variations du goût et de l'esthétique de la femme, 1797-1897. 1898

Young, A. B. Recurring cycles of fashion 1760-1937. 1937

Periodicals

See Periodicals

Fashion age, incorporating Fashions & fabrics. v 1, Aug. 1934+ London, Textile journals, ltd
Illus. Q. 1s 6d per no.
Published monthly. Current 1938
Volume 1 no.2-12 lack numbering
Supersedes *Fashions and fabrics*

Fashion drawing. Hodgkin, Eliot

Fashion drawing & design. Chadwick, L. M.

Fashion drawing and dress design. Hall, M. L.

La **Fashion**, guide journal des gens du monde; édition des dames. See L'Oriflamme des modes

La **Fashion**, guide-journal des gens du monde; édition du commerce, réd. générale E. Champeaux. 1.-24. année (no.1-160) août 1839-1852. Paris
O.
Subtitle varies
An *édition des elegants* was published (no 1-11, août 1839-juin 1840)
Colas 1037

Fashion in deformity. Flower, Sir W. H.

Fashion in footwear. Billstein, E. L.

Fashion in France, The history of. Challamel, Augustin

Fashion in Paris. Uzanne, L. O.

Fashion motivation. See Barr, E. De Y. A psychological analysis of fashion motivation

Fashion service. See Fashion service magazine

Fashion service magazine. v 1, 1920+ Scranton, Pa. Woman's institute of domestic arts and sciences.
Illus. Q. 75c a year
Published bi-monthly. Current 1938. Published semiannually 1920-24; quarterly 1925-30; monthly 1931-June 1932
Title varies: fall, 1920, *Woman's institute fashion service*; spring & summer, 1921-May 1931, *Fashion service*; June 1931+ *Fashion service magazine*
Editors: fall, 1920-summer, 1925, Mary B. Picken; autumn 1925+, Laura MacFarlane

Fashion then and now. Lennox, Lord, W. P.

Fashions and fabrics. See Fashion age

Fashions art. v 1-2, no 2; fall, 1934-winter 1935/36. New York, Weil, McGinniss and Sloman 1934-36
Illus.(part col.) F. $5 a year
Published quarterly. Ceased publication with v2, no2, winter 1935/36
Editor: Fall, 1934-winter 1935/36, Dessie M. Barr

Fashions of London & Paris; v 1-3, 1798/1800-1804/06. London, R. Phillips [1800-06]
3v. 324 col.pl. O.
Published monthly
Colas 1041

See also Record of fashion and court elegance for 1807, 1808-1809

Fashions of the hour. 1929+ Chicago, Marshall Field
Illus.(part col.) F. free
Published irregularly, four to six times a year. Current 1938

Fastes des gardes nationales de France. Alboise de Poujol, J. E., and Élie, Charles

Les **fastes** du peuple français. Grasset de Saint-Sauveur, Jacques

Fasti Limburgenses
Fasti Limpurgenses. Das ist: Eine wohlbeschriebene chronick von der stadt und den herren zu Limpurg auff der lahn, darin ... geschichten, veränderungen der sitten, kleidung, musik, krieg ... beschrieben werden. Im jahr 1617; anjetzo ... von neuem auffgelegt. Wetzlar, G. E. Winckler 1720
7 l. 141,25p. O.
Costume is treated in parts 36-38, 46-47, 85, 110, 115, 155, 159, 175
Lipperheide 346

Fatio, Antoine Léon Morel-. See Morel-Fatio, A. L.

Fau, Fernand
(illus.) Grand-Carteret, John. La femme en culotte

Fauchet, Claude. See note under Collection complète des tableaux historiques de la révolution française

La **fauconnerie** ancienne et moderne. Chenu, J. C., and Oeillet des Murs, M. A. P.

Faulhaber, Johann
Neue geometrische und perspectinische inventiones etlicher sonderbahrer instrument die zum perspectinischen grundreissen der pasteyen unnd vestungen ... deszgleichen zur büchsenmeisterey ... gebrauchsam seynd. Franckfurt am Mayn, W. Richter 1610
38p. 4 illus. 3pl. Q.
Plates show army engineers with instruments
Lipperheide 2065

Fauqueux, (Lavergne de Labarrière). See Pour bien travailler chez soi

Faur, Christian Wilhelm von Faber du. See Faber du Faur, C. W. von

Faussett, Bryan
Inventorium sepulchrale: an account of some antiquities dug up at Gilton, Kingston, Sibertswold, Barfriston, Beakesbourne, Chartham, and Crundale, in the county of Kent, from A. D. 1757 to A. D. 1773 ... Edited, from the original manuscript in the possession of Joseph Mayer ... by C. R. Smith. London, Printed for the subscribers only [T. Richards] 1856
lvi,230p. front.(port.) illus. 20pl.(7 col.) map. Q.
List of books relating especially to the antiquities found in the Anglo-Saxon cemeteries, and in the similar interments on the continent: p lv-lvi
LC 2-30224

Le **faux-luxe** et l'abandon des costumes locaux dans les campagnes. Fontenouille, G. de

Le **Favori** des dames; messager des salons, modes, industrie, littérature, théâtres, beaux-arts. 1845-1853. Paris
Col.pl. Q.
Colas 1043

Fawcett, Frank Burlington
(ed.) Their Majesties' courts holden at Buckingham palace and at the palace of Holyroodhouse, 1934-35

Fayolle, L. T. See note under Perrot, A. M. Collection historique des ordres de chevalerie civils et militaires

Feather work

Hawaiian islands

Brigham, W. T. Hawaiian feather work. 1899-1918

South America

Mead, C. W. Technique of some South American feather-work. 1907

Feathers used in costume
Lacroix-Danliard, pseud. La plume des oiseaux. 1891

Die **fechtkunst** im XV. und XVI. jahrhunderte. Hergsell, Gustav

Feder- und silberstift-zeichnungen. Holbein, Hans, the elder

Federated council on art education
Costume design as an occupation. New York, N.Y., Federated council on art education; New London, Conn., Institute of women's professional relations, Connecticut college. 1936
59p. O.
Professional schools, vocational schools, trade schools offering instruction in costume design: p42-46; Colleges and universities offering instruction in costume design. p47-55
Some books and articles to read and some costume designs to look at: p57-58
LC 36-14728

Fedi, Antonio
(illus.) Bicci, Antonio. I contadini della Toscana, espressi al naturale secondo le diverse loro vestiture

La **fée** du foyer. See Cendrillon

Feeder, J.
Drei jahrhunderte der fechtkunst in Steiermark. Graz, Leuschner & Lubensky 1905
49p. 8pl. O.
Lipperheide 2996e

Die **Fehde** des Hanns Thomas von Absberg wider den schwabischen bund. Baader, Joseph

Die **fehler** der menschen nebst deren verbesserung in saubern kupfern und moralischen versen vorgestellet. Nürnberg, G. P. Monath 1751
1 l. 37pl. F.
Name of the engraver. D. C. C. Fleischman, junior, is found on plate 16
Lipperheide 1956

Fehr, Hans Adolf
Das recht im bilde. Erlenbach-Zürich, E. Rentsch [1913]
194p. pl. Q.

Fehrle, Eugen
Deutsche feste und volksbräuche; 3. durchgesehene und erg. aufl. Leipzig und Berlin, B. G. Teubner 1927
108p. illus. D. (Aus natur und geisteswelt; sammlung wissenschaftlichgemeinverständlicher darstellungen. 518. bd)
Literatur: p102-05
First edition 1916

Feiczewicz, Louis. See Carrel, Frank, jt. auth.

Feier des fünf und zwanzig jährigen regierungs jubiläums seiner majestät Maximilian Joseph I, königes von Baiern. München, 1824
58p. 45pl.(13 col.) F.
Lipperheide 2566

Feier zur eröffnung der Schweizerischen landesmuseums. Jauslin, Carl

Feijoo, Benoît-Jerôme. See Feyjoo, B.-J.

Feillet
(lithgr.) Gerard. Costumes de principaux personnages des Scandinaves

Feinhals, Joseph
(ed.) Schranka, E. M., comp. Tabakanekdoten

Feiss, Joachim
L'armée suisse. See entry under Estoppey, D.

Feldgrau in krieg und frieden. Weisz, Otto

Die **feldgraue** friedens- und kriegs- bekleidung d. k. bayer. armee. Helm, Seb., and Ströbel, Christian

Félibien, André, sieur des Avaux et de Javercy
Les divertissemens de Versailles donnez par le roy a toute sa cour au retour de la conqueste de la Franche-Comté en l'année M.DC.LXXIV. Paris, Imprimerie royale 1676
34p. 4 double pl. F.
Signed: Felibien
Lipperheide 2711. LC 15-1207

Relation de la feste de Versailles, du 18. juillet, 1668. Paris, L'imprimerie royale 1679
43p. 5pl. F.
The text without the plates appeared in 1668. Plates are by Le Pautre
Lipperheide 2710

Félix, E.
(ed.) What she wore; a pictorial history of woman's dress. An object lesson in colors, showing the principal eras of fashion from the twelfth century to the present day, illustrated by Amigues (Japhet) of Paris. New York city, Paris [etc] The Baldwin syndicate c1899
2p.l. 24 illus. on 12 l. [3]p. incl.front. (port.) O.

Fellner, Friedrich
(ed.) Weingartner liederhandschrift

Félon, J.
(lithogr.) Delbecchi, Amedee. Nice; vues et costumes

Fels, Florent
Die altfranzösischen bildteppiche, mit einer einleitung von Florent Fels. Berlin, E. Wasmuth 1923?
16p. 48pl. on 24 l. O. (Orbis pictus. bd.18)
On verso of t.-p.: Aus dem französischen übertragen von Fred Antoine Angermayer
Reproductions of French tapestries of the 14th, 15th and 16th centuries. Many of the designs show costume
Bibliography: p14-15
LC 24-13899

Felt, Joseph Barlow
The customs of New England. Boston, Press of T. R. Marvin 1853
208p. O.
Part 2 Fashions of dress, p79-208
LC 1-7575

Feltre, Henri Jacques Guillaume, duc de
Notice sur l'uniforme des officiers d'état-major général, et des aides-de-camp, du 22 mai 1816. Paris, Magimel, Anselin et Pochard 1816
8p. O.
Colas 1045

Female beauty as preserved and improved by regimen, cleanliness and dress. Walker, Mrs A.

Female costume pictures. Beyschlag, Robert

Female costumes, historical, national and dramatic. Lacy, T. H., ed.

Femina. v 1,1901+ Paris
Illus. F.
Journal of women's fashions. Published monthly. Current 1938

Feminine toilettes and knick-knacks of the romantic age. Keezer, Ro

La **femme** au dix-huitième siècle. Goncourt, E. L. A. H. de, and Goncourt, J. A. H. de

Femme chic. no.1, 1911+ Paris, A. Louchel
Illus. F. 95fr. a year
Published monthly. Current 1937

La **femme** dans l'antiquité grecque. Notor, G.

La **femme** dans l'art. Vachon, Marius

Femme élégante à Paris; album spécial de haute mode pour tailleurs et couturières, costumes, manteaux, robes. 1907+ Paris, Union des journaux de modes
Illus. F. 45fr. a year
Published quarterly. Current 1938. Beginning date taken from *Argus de la presse*

La **femme** en Allemagne. Grand-Carteret, John

La **femme** en culotte. Grand-Carteret, John

La **femme** et la beauté. Braunschvig, Marcel

La **femme** et le costume masculin. Flobert, Mme L. P.

La **femme** italienne à l'époque de la renaissance. See Rodocanachi, E. P. La femme italienne avant, pendant et après la renaissance.

La **femme** italienne avant, pendant et après la renaissance. Rodocanachi E. P.

La **femme** provençale. Flandreysy, J. M. de

Les **femmes** blondes selon les peintres de l'école de Venise. Baschet, Armand, and Feuillet de Conches, F. S

Les **femmes** célèbres de l'ancienne France Le Roux de Lincy, A. J. V.

Les **femmes** cosmopolites. Grévedon, P. L. H.

Les **femmes** dans la société chrétienne. Dantier, Alphonse

Les **femmes** de l'Asie. Laurent, and Perrot, Georges

Les **femmes** de ménage. Gédéon

Les **femmes** du second empire. Loliée, F. A.

Les **femmes** et les fleurs. Malo, Charles

Les **femmes**; galerie fashionable. Devéria, Achille

Fencers, fighters with bayonets, etc.

Castle, Egerton. Schools and masters of fence. 1885

Chronik der Hirschgasse. 1910

Emerson, Edwin. German swordplay. c1936

Feeder, J. Drei jahrhunderte der fechtkunst in Steiermark. 1905

Hergsell, Gustav. Die fechtkunst im xv. und xvi. jahrhunderte. 1896

Heussler, Sebastian. Künstliches abprobirtes und nutzliches fecht-buch von einfachen und doppelten degenfechten. 1665

Hutton, Alfred. Old sword-play; the systems of fence in vogue during the xvi[th], xvii[th], and xviii[th] centuries. 1892

Kahn, A. F. Anfangsgründe der fechtkunst nebst einer vorrede, in welcher eine kurze geschichte der fechtkunst vorgeträgen ... wird. 1761

Letainturier-Fradin, Gabriel. Le duel à travers les âges: Histoire et législation, duels célèbres, code du duel. 1892

Letainturier-Fradin, Gabriel. Les joueurs d'épée à travers les siècles; maîtres d'armes, escrimisseurs, capitans, rodomonts, bravaches et ferailleurs. 1905

Mérignac, Émile. Histoire de l'escrime dans tous les temps et dans tous les pays. 1883-86

See also Gladiators

Bibliography

Gelli, Jacopo. Bibliografia generale della scherma. 1890

Thimm, C. A. A complete bibliography of fencing and duelling, as practised by all European nations from the middle ages to the present day. 1896

Vigeant, Arsène. La bibliographie de l'escrime ancienne et moderne. 1882

Middle ages

Schlichtegroll, Nathanael. Talhofer; ein beytrag zur literatur der gerichtlichen zweykaempfe im mittelalter. 1817

16th century

Agrippa, Camillo. Trattato di scientia d'arme. 1553

Grassi, Giacomo di. Ragione di adoprar sicuramente l'arme si da offesa, come da difesa. 1570

Marozzo, Achille. Arte dell' armi. 1568

Meyer, Joachim. Gründtliche beschreibung der freyen ritterlichen unnd adelichen kunst des fechtens. 1570

17th century

Alfieri, F. F. La picca, e la bandiera. 1641

Alfieri, F. F. La scherma ... dove con nove ragione e con figure si mostra la perfezione di quest' arte, e in chè modo secondo l'arme e l'sito possa il cavaliere restar al suo nemico superiore. 1640

Bresciani, Marin. Li trastulli guerrieri. 1668

Capoferro, R. Gran simulacro dell' arte e dell' uso della scherma. 1610

Heussler, Sebastian. New künstlich fechtbuch ... Als dess: Sign. Salvator. Fabri de Padua und Sign. Rudol. Capo di Ferr, wie auch anderer italienischen und frantzösischen fechter beste kunststücklein im dolchen und rappier. 1630

Köppe, Joachim. Neuer discurs von der rittermessigen und weitberümbten kunst des fechtens sowol im rapier alleine als in dolchen und rapier pede firmo und per caminada ... beschrieben. 1619

L'Ange, J. D. Deutliche und gründliche erklärung der ... fecht-kunst. 1664

Marcelli, F. A. Regole della scherma insegnate da Lelio, e titta Marcelli, scritte da Francesco Antonio Marcelli. 1686

Mazo, Bondí di. La spada maestra. 1696

Pallavicini, G. M. La scherma illustrata. 1670

Pascha, J. G. Kurtze jedoch deutliche beschreibung handlend vom fechten auf den stosz und hieb ... auffgesetzet. 1664

Sutor, Jakob. Neu künstliches fechtbuch. 1849

18th century

Alessandro, Giuseppe d'. Opera. 1723 p758-76

Angelo, Domenico. L'ecole des armes, avec l'explication generale des principales attitudes et positions concernant l'escrime. 1763

Danet, Guillaume. L'art des armes, ou la manière la plus certaine de se servir utilement de l'épée, soit pour attaquer, soit pour se défendre. 1766-1767

Demeuse, Nicolas. Nouveau traité de l'art des armes. 1778

Doyle, Alexander. Neu alamodische ritterliche fecht- und schirm-kunst. 1715

Girard, P. J. F. Traité des armes. 1740

Le Perche. L'exercice des armes ou le maniement du fleuret. 1750

Olivier, J. Fencing familiarized: or, A new treatise on the art of small sword. 1780

Roworth, C. The art of defence on foot with the broad sword and sabre. 1798

Fencers . . . etc.—18th century—*Continued*
Schmidt, J. A., fencing master. Leib-beschirmende und feinden trotz-bietende fecht-kunst. 1713

Schmidt J. A., fencing master. Mit . . . bewilligung der hochfürstl. Würtemb. ober-vormundschafft und administration, solte die fecht-kunst . . . nebst einem . . . unterricht vom voltigiren und ringen . . . an das licht stellen. 1737

19th century

Ballassa, Constantin. Die militarische fechtkunst vor dem feinde; eine darstellung der im kriege vorkommenden fechtarten des bayonets gegen bajonet, des säbels gegen den säbel, und der lanze gegen die lanze. 1860

Capiaumont, A. Manuel d'escrime à la baïonette, simplifiée. 1848

Chappon, Louis. Theoretisch-practische anleitung zur fecht-kunst. 1839

Corbesier, A. J. Theory of fencing. 1873

Florio, Blasco. La scienza della scherma. 1844

Gordon, Anthony. A treatise on the science of defence, for the sword, bayonet, and pike, in close action. 1805

Grisier, A. E. F. Les armes et le duel. 1847

Katkoff, Paul. Manuel de l'enseignement de l'escrime au sabre à l'usage de la cavalerie Russe. 1895

Muller, Alexandre. Théorie sur l'escrime à cheval. 1816

O'Rourke, M. J. Sword exercise illustrated. 1865

Riboni, Giuseppe. Broadsword and quarterstaff without a master. 1862

Rolando, Guzman. The modern art of fencing. 1822

Roux, F. A. W. L. Anweisung zum hiebfechten mit graden und krummen klingen. 1849

Saint-Martin, J. de. L'art de faire les armes. 1804

Vaux, Ludovic, baron de. Les hommes d'épée. 1882

20th century

Sanchez-M. Navarro, Francisco. En la sala de armas y en el terreno. 1907

Fencing familiarized. Olivier, J.

Fennia illustrata. Ahrenberg, J. J.

Fer, Nicolas de
Histoire des rois de France depuis Pharamond jusqu'à . . . Louis quinze. Paris, Danet 1722
63 l. 66pl. Q.
Lipperheide 1069

Féréal, V. de, pseud. See Suberwick, Mme de

Ferenczy, Ferenc
Magyaros ifjúsági ruhák. Budapest, A "Magyar izlés" kiadása 1935
71p. illus. O. (A "Magyar izlés" könyvei, [szám]1)

Fernand-Michel, François Fortune
The story of the stick in all ages and lands; tr. and adapted from the French of Antony Réal (Fernand-Michel) New York, J. W. Bouton, 1875
x,254p. D.
"A philosophical history and lively chronicle of the stick as the friend and the foe of man. Its uses and abuses. As sceptre and as crook. As the warrior's weapon and the wizard's wand. As stay, as stimulus, and as scourge." Subtitle
LC 15-22478

Ferogio, P.
(engr.) Lagarrigue. Nouvelle suite de costumes des Pyrénées

Féron, Louis. See Rey, Alfred

Ferrari, Filippo, 1819-1897
Costumi ecclesiastici civili e militari della corte di Roma disegnati all' acquaforte. Roma, presso L. Nicoletti [1823]
68 col.pl. Q.
Some of the plates have been copied for Capparoni's three *Raccolta's*
Lipperheide notes an edition dated 1842 with 79 colored plates (Roma, N. Monaldini)
Colas 1047. Lipperheide 1817

Costumi no. xxx di Roma e di altre paesi dello Stato Pontificio. Roma presso L. Nicoletti 1825
1 l. 30 col.pl. Q.
Also known with plates in black and white. The plates have been reproduced in color for [part 1] of *Costumes des différens états de l'Italie*
Colas 1046. Lipperheide 1276

Costumi popolari Italiani. Roma, presso G. Antonelli 1825
12pl. ob.F.
Colas 1048. Lipperheide 1275

Nuova raccolta di costumi di Roma e suoi contorni, disegnati e incisi all acqua forte. Roma, 1838
42pl. ob.S.
Bound with Parboni, A. *Nuova raccolta delle principali veduti antichi, e moderne dell' alma città di Roma e sue vicinage* which has plates of views only, no costume

(illus.) Cipriani, G. B. Costumi di Roma

Ferrari, Ottavio
Octavii Ferrarii Analecta de re vestiaria siue exercitationes ad Alberti Rubeni commentarium de re vestiaria. Patavii P. M. Frambotti 1670
155p. illus. 19pl. Q.
Colas says this work is a reply to Rubens *De re vestiaria veterum* and that many of the plates are taken from the author's *De re vestiaria*
Colas 1056. Lipperheide 151

Octavii Ferrarii De re vestiaria libri septem. Patavii, P. Frambotti 1654
2v. 29 illus. 5pl. O.
First edition: 1654, 217p.
Engraved by J. Georg and J. Ruffonus
Colas 1055, 1055 bis. Lipperheide 149

Ferrario, Giulio
Aggiunte e rettificazioni all' opera Il costume antico e moderno di tutti i popoli cogli analoghi disengi del dottore Giulio Ferrario, Milano, tip. dell' autore 1831-34
3v. 212 col.pl. O.
Published also with plates in black and white. Published in 25 livraisons at 253fr

Ferrario, Giulio—*Continued*
with black and white and 336fr. with colored plates
Volume 1, Asia; v2 Africa; v3 America and Europe
Colas 1053. Costume index

Il costume antico e moderno. Milano, tip. dell' editore 1827
14v in 17. col.pl. Q.
"O storia del governo, della milizia, della religione, delle arti, scienze ed uzanze di tutti i popoli antichi e moderni provata coi monumenti dell' antichita e rappresentata cogli analoghi disegni." Subtitle
First edition 1816-27. Published also with plates in black and white
Contents: Asia (4v. 351 col.pl.) Africa (2v. 160 col.pl.) América (2v. 167 col.pl.) Europa (6v. in 9. 759 col.pl.)
Published simultaneously in French with title: *Le costume ancien et moderne* (14v in 17. Milano, imp. de l'auteur 1816-17) also (1827)
Republished in smaller format, the plates reduced in size, *ed. 2, riveduta et accresciuta* (Firenze, Batelli 1823-38. 30v. 1571 col.pl. O.) Published also with plates in black and white. There are other Italian editions
Colas 1049-52. Costume index. Lipperheide 51

Del costume antico e moderno del dottore Giulio Ferrario: Indice generale per alfabeto e per materie; preceduto da un saggio di supplimento alla detta opera e dall' indicazione delle più importante scoperte e relazioni fatte dai recenti viaggiatori dal 1820 al 1829. Milano, tip. del G. Ferrario 1829
67,452p. 5pl. Q.
Index to *Il costume*, with a supplement on Sardinian costume
Colas 1052

Descrizione della Palestina, o storia del vangelo; illustrata coi monumenti. Milano, Società tip. de' classici italiani 1831
171p. 33pl.(31 col.) O.
Eighteen of the plates are copied from L. Mayer's *Views in Palestine*
Lipperheide 1462

Storia ed analisi degli antichi romanzi di cavalleria e dei poemi romanzeschi d'Italia, con dissertazioni sull' origine, sugl' istituti, sulle cerimonie de' cavalieri, sulle corti d'amore, sui tornei, sulle giostre ed armature de' paladini, sull' invenzione e sull' uso degli stemmi ecc. con figure tratte dai monumenti d'arte del dottore Giulio Ferrario. Milano, tip. dell' autore 1828
3v. 40 col.pl.(part double) 3 fold.tab. O.
Illustrations show knights, ladies and blazons of the days of chivalry
Lipperheide 347m. LC 15-9526

Ferrarius, Sigismundus, pseud. See Leucht, C. L.

Ferriman, Z. Duckett
Home life in Hellas, Greece and the Greeks. London, Mills & Boon [1910]
338p. front. pl. ports. O.
LC A11-1622

Ferriol, Charles, marquis d'Argental, comte de
Recueil de cent estampes representant differentes nations du Levant. See entry under Moor, J. B. van

Wahreste und neueste abbildung des turckischen hofes. See entry under Moor, J. B. van

Ferro, R. Capo. See Capoferro, R.

Ferry, Ramon
La madre de familia o tratado de corte para confeccion de trajes de señora y niños basado en la geometria. Madrid, Astort hermanos 1882
128p. 119 illus. O.
Lipperheide 3826

Fesquet, Frédéric Auguste Antoine Goupil. See Goupil Fesquet, F. A. A.

Fessard
(engr.) Dezallier d'Argenville, A. J. Abregé de la vie des plus fameux peintres

Festa, fatta in Roma, alli 25. fabraio MDCXXXIV. Mascardi, Vitale

Die **feste** der republik Venedig. Graf, Rainer

Le **feste** di S. Rosalia in Palermo ... 1841. Palermo, F. Lao 1841
20p. 2pl. O.
Lipperheide 2808

Feste nelle nozze del serenissimo Don Francesco Medici gran duca di Toscana; et della sereniss. sua consorte ... Bianca Cappello. Gualterotti, Raffaello

La **feste** torinesi dell' aprile 1842. Cibrario, G. A. L., conte

Festiva ad capita annulumque decursio, a rege Ludovico XIV ... 1662. See Perrault, Charles. Courses de testes et de bague faittes par le roy

Festival costume. See Ceremonial and festival costume

Festivals and plays in schools and elsewhere. Chubb, Percival

Das **festliche** jahr; in sitten gebraüchen, aberglauben und festen der germanischen völker. Reinsberg-Dueringsfeld, Otto, freiherr von

Festschmuck für die königskrönung in Budapest 1916. Darmstadt, 1917
4p. 6pl. F.
Reprint from *Innendekoration*

Festzeitung für das achte deutsche bundesschiessen. See Deutsches bundesschiessen

Festzeitung für das 10. Deutsche turnfest zu Nürnberg, 1903. nr. 1-14; 15. mai-28. nov. 1903. Nürnberg, W. Tümmel 1903
292p. illus. F.
Reports on other turnfests have been issued at irregular intervals. Caption title. Title-page reads: *10. Deutsches turnfest.* Nürnberg, 1903. Festzeitung
No more published
LC 10-366

Festzug der stadt Wien zur silbernen hochzeit des kaiserpaares. Neues Wiener tagblatt

[**Festzug** zur feier der fünfundzwanzigjährigen regierung des königs Wilhelm von Württemberg am 28. september 1841, in Stuttgart. Stuttgart 1841]
48 col.pl. sq.F.
Lipperheide 2596

Festzug zur feier der silbernen hochzeit des kaiserpaares Franz Joseph und Elisabeth. Makart, Hans

Festzug zur feyer der jubel-ehe I.I.M.M. des königs Ludwig und der königin Therese beym october-feste zu München am 4. october 1835. Kraus, Gustav

Festzug zur fünfundzwanzigjährigen vermählungsfeier des allerhöchsten kaiserpaares veranstaltet von der haupt- und residenzstadt Wien. Makart, Hans

Festzug; jubiläum. Kley, Heinrich

Festzug 10tes deutsches bundesschiessen. See Deutsches bundesschiessen

Festzug zur vollendung des [Ulmer] Münsters 1377-1890. Heyberger, G., and Füsslen, J.

Fête publique donnée par la ville de Paris à l'occasion du mariage de Monseigneur le Dauphin le 13. fevrier M.DCC.XLVII. Paris, 1747?
12p. 7pl. F.
Plates after drawings by François Blondel and A. Benoist, engraved by Marvye, N. Le Mire and P. F. Tardieu
Lipperheide 2717

Fêtes à l'occasion du mariage de S. M. Napoléon, empereur des Français ... avec Marie Louise, archiduchesse d'Autriche. Goulet, Nicolas

Les **fêtes** célèbres de l'antiquité du moyen âge et des temps modernes. Bernard, Frédéric

Fêtes de Gutenberg. Glück, E.

Fêtes et cérémonies siamoises. Plion, Raymond

Les **fêtes** nationales à Paris. Drumont, É. A.

Fêtes publiques données par la ville de Paris à l'occasion du mariage de Monseigneur le Dauphin, les 23. et 26. fevrier. M.DCC.XLV. Paris, 1745?
18p. 19pl. F.
Plates after drawings by François Blondel
Lipperheide 2716

Fett, Harry Per
Nationaldragter; udstillingen ordnet og katalogen udarbeidet af Harry Fett. Kristiania, S. M. Brydes bogtrykkeri 1903
43p. 9pl. D. (Norsk folkemuseum. Særudstilling nr. 1)
LC 13-33979

Feuilles extraites de mon portefeuille, esquissées sur les lieux dans le courant de la campagne de 1812 en Russie. See Faber du Faur, C. W. von. Blätter aus meinem portefeuille

Feuillet, Laurent François
(ed.) Seroux d'Agincourt, J. B. L. G. Histoire de l'art par les monumens

Feuillet, Raoul Augur
Chorégraphie. (In Taubert, Gottfried. Rechtschaffener tantzmeister, p745-915)

Feuillet de Conches, Félix Sébastien. See Baschet, Armand, jt. auth.

Feydel, Gabriel
Moeurs et coutumes des Corses. Paris, Garnery [1799]
112p. 1 pl. O.
"Mémoire tiré en partie d'un grand ouvrage sur la politique, la législation et la morale des diverses nations de l'Europe." Subtitle
Lipperheide 1316

[**Feyel, Paul**]
Jeanne d'Arc. [Paris] Hachette c1925
64p. incl.front. 93 illus. O. (Encyclopédie par l'image. Histoire)
Signed: Paul Feyel
Bibliography: p63
LC 26-6185

[**Feyerabend, Franz**]
[Costumes militaires des cantons de la Suisse. Die eidgenössischen truppen. Basel] 1792
26 col.pl. F.
Portraits of officers and men of different units, in uniform. A list of plates is given in Colas's *Bibliographie.* Volmar's *Officiers et soldats* is designed and colored after this collection
Colas 1058

Feyerabend, Sigmund
Stam und wapenbuch. See entry under Amman, Jost

Feyjoo, Benoît Jérôme
Théâtre critique, ou discours differens sur toutes sortes de matières pour détruire les erreurs communes. Tr. de l'espagnol ... Les modes. Paris, Prault 1744
42,4p. T.
Extract translated from *Teatro critico universal* (Madrid, 1726-60)
Colas 1059

Feyzi, Muharrem
(tr.) Alexander, William. Picturesque representations of the dress and manners of the Turks

Ffoulkes, Charles John
Armour & weapons; with a preface by Viscount Dillon. Oxford, Clarendon press 1909
112p. front. illus. 11pl. O.
List of authorities: p[10]

The armourer and his craft from the XIth to the XVIth century. London, Methuen [1912]
xxii,199p. front. illus. 31pl. 33x27cm.
Enlarged from a thesis offered for the degree of bachelor of letters in the University of Oxford in the Michaelmas term, 1911
Short biographies of notable armourers: p131-46
LC 21-10152

European arms and armour in the University of Oxford (principally in the Ashmolean and Pitt-Rivers museums) catalogued, with introductory notes, by Charles Ffoulkes ... Oxford, Clarendon press 1912
64p. illus. 19pl. (incl.fold. front. 2 port.) F.
LC 13-1463

Inventory and survey of the armouries of the Tower of London. London, His Majesty's stationery office [1916]
2v. 2 col.fronts. illus. 37pl. Q.

Tower of London. Guide to the armouries. [London, H M Stationery off., Harrison and sons, printers 1930]
25p. illus. plan. D.
LC 33-17613

Fialetti, Odoardo
De gli habiti della religioni; con le armi, a breve descrittion. Venetia, M. Sadeler 1626
3v.(3,74 l.) 75 illus. Q.
Monastic orders only
Two editions in French were published with titles: *Briefve histoire de l'institution des ordres religieux* (Paris, A. Menier 1658. 45p. front. 72pl. Q.) and *Histoire de l'institution des ordres religieux dispersés par tout le monde* (Paris, 1680. 72pl.)
Colas 1060-62. Lipperheide 1855

La **fiamme accese** dal cielo. See Von himmeln entzindete

Fiaschi, Cesare
Trattato dell' imbrigliare, maneggiare et ferrare cavalli. Bologna, A. Giaccarelli 1556
171p. 84 illus. Q.
Lipperheide 2894

Fibulae. See Brooches

Fick, Richard
(ed.) Auf Deutschlands hohen schulen. Eine illustrierte kulturgeschichtliche darstellung deutschen hochschul- und studentenwesens. Berlin, H. L. Thilo [1900]
xiii,488p. illus. Q.
Illustrations show student costume of various groups and locations in Germany between the 16th and 20th centuries
Bibliography: p473-80
LC E11-939

Fickelscherer, Martin
Das kriegswesen der alten. Leipzig, A. Seemann 1888
234p. illus. 6 fold.pl. D. (Kulturbilder aus dem klassischen altertume. IV)
Lipperheide 176. LC 4-20049

Ficoroni, Francesco
Le maschere sceniche e le figure comiche d'antichi romani descritte brevemente. Roma, A. de' Rossi 1736
228p. 85pl. Q.
Zweite ausgabe 1748
A Latin translation is available *Dissertatio de larvis scenicis et figuris comicis antiquorum Romanorum* (ed. 2. auct. et emend. Romae, A. Rotilii 1754) with same plates. First edition 1750
Lipperheide 228. LC 4-20713 (Latin ed.)

Fictitious and legendary characters. See Allegorical and imaginary figures

Fidelis certa verissimaqz narratio de Monasterio beate Marie ad littus martirum. Johann von St Wendel

Fieffé, Eugène
Histoire des troupes étrangères au service de France depuis leur origine jusqu'à nos jours, et de tous les régiments levés dans les pays conquis sous la première république et l'empire. Paris, Dumaine 1854
2v. 30 col.pl. tab. O.
Plates are engraved by Sorrieu
Translated into German with title: *Geschichte der fremd-truppen im dienste Frankreichs, von ihrer entstehung bis auf unsere tage;* deutsch von F. Symon de Carneville (München, J. Deschler'chen buchdruckerei 1860) and same plates
Colas 1064. Lipperheide 2321 (Ger. ed.)
LC 3-4257

Napoléon Ier et la Garde impériale ... Dessins par Raffet. Paris, Furne fils 1859
16,170p. 20 col.pl. Q.
Colas 1063. Lipperheide 2323

Field, Bradda
Clothes that count and how to make them. Illustrations by Mary Stewart. London, J. Murray 1923
152p. illus. O.
LC 24-901

Field, Henry
Arabs of central Iraq, their history, ethnology, and physical characters ... with introduction by Sir Arthur Keith ... Field museum-Oxford university joint expedition to Kish, Iraq ... Chicago, 1935
474p. front. (map) illus. CLVI pl. on 78 l. diagrs. ob.O. (Field museum of natural history ... Anthropology, Memoirs, v. IV)
Bibliography: p464-66
LC 36-23511

Field, Marshall, and co., Chicago. See Fashions of the hour

Field museum of natural history, Chicago
Japanese sword-mounts in the collections of Field museum, by Helen C. Gunsaulus. Chicago, 1923
195p. LXI pl. O. (Field museum of natural history. Publication 216. Anthropological series. v. XVI)
LC 24-4950

Fierabras
Eyn schöne kurtzweilige historí von eym mächtigẽ riesen auss Hispaniẽ, Fierrabras genant, der eyn heyd gewest und bei zeiten des durchleuchtigsten grossen keyser Karls gelebt sich in kämpffen unnd in streitten dapfferlich grossmütig, mañlich unnd eerlich gehalten hat. Getruckt zu Siem̃ern, I. Rodler 1533
52 l. 20 illus. F.
This is the first German edition, with woodcuts by an unknown artist. A French edition appeared at Geneva in 1478, a German edition at Frankfort, undated, and another German edition dated 1594
Lipperheide 622

Figaro-modes, à la ville, au théâtre, arts décoratifs. no. 1-38, jan. 1903-fev. 1906. Paris
4v. illus. col.pl. F.
Published monthly. No more published. Successor to *Modes* (v 1-2, 1901-02. Paris)
LC 11-10708

Figgins, Vincent
(ed.) Cessolis, Jacobus de. The game of the chesse

Fighting-bracelets and kindred weapons in Africa. Lindblom, Gerhard

Figuier, Louis
L'homme primitif; ouvrage illustré de 30 scènes de la vie de l'homme primitif, composé par Émile Bayard, et de 232 figures représentant les objets usuels des premiers âges de l'humanité, dessinées par Delahaye. Paris, L. Hachette 1870
446p. front. illus. pl. O.
LC 33-5064

The human race. London, Chapman & Hall 1872
xvi,548p. 243 illus. 8 col.pl. (incl.front.) O.
Translation of *Les races humaines*
LC 5-29759

Les races humaines. Paris, Hachette 1880
612p. 269 illus. 8 col.pl. O.
Illustrations show native costume in all parts of the world

Figure disegnate. See Lorich, Melchior. Des kunstreichen und weitberühmten Melchior Lorichs ... türckische figuren

Figure originali. Labruzzi, Carlo

Figures à la mode. Hooghe, Romein de

Les **figures** à la mode. Le Clerc, Sébastien

Figures au naturel ... des gardes françoises. Bosse, Abraham

Figures de différents habits de chanoines réguliers en ce siècle. Du Moulinet, Claude

Figures de modes. Watteau, J. A.

Figures des cris de Danzig. See Deisch, Matthaeus. Danziger ausrufbilder

Figures dessinées d'après nature du bas peuple à Rome. Pierre, J. B. M.

Figures, faces and folds. Braun, A. A.

Figures françoises et comiques. Watteau, J. A.

Figures françoises nouvellement inventées. Octavien, François

Figures of fun; or comical pictures and droll verses for little girls and boys; part I. London, C. Tilt 1833
  8 l. 8 col.pl. O.
  Colas 1067. Lipperheide 3174

Figurini di moda. Volpini, Angelo

Figurinos do exercito de conformidade com o decreto N. 3620, 28 fevereiro de 1866. Rio de Janeiro, 1866
  2 l. 24 col.pl. F.
  "Mandado executar pelo governo imperial desenhados na lithographia do archivo militar pelo systema cromo-lithographico sob as determinações do general Conselheiro A. N. de Aguiar." Subtitle
  Plates show Brazil army uniforms. They are lithographed by "Alvaro e Laréé"
  Colas 1068

Fiji Islands
  Anderson, J. W. Notes of travel in Fiji and New Caledonia. 1880
  Burton, J. W. The Fiji of to-day. 1910

The **Fiji** of to-day. Burton, J. W.

Filet-guipure-album. Manteuffel, Erna von

Das **filet** und das filettopfen. Hochfelden, Frau B. L.

Filet- und haeckel-spitzen-muster für kirchliche zwecke. Regensburg, A. Coppenrath [1867]
  30pl. F.
  Lipperheide 4097

Filet-schule. Hennings, Emma

Filian, George H.
  Armenia and her people; or, The story of Armenia by an Armenian. Hartford, Conn. American publishing company 1896
  376p. front. illus. pl. ports. map. O.
  LC 5-6175

Filimonov", Georg
  Opīsanie pamîâtnīkov' drevnostī tserkovnago ī grazhdanskago byta russkago muzeîâ P. Koroanova. Moskva, V" Universitetskoĭ tīp. 1849
  32p. 60pl.(22 col.) F.
  Description of the monuments of religious and civil life in the Russian museum of P. Karabanov
  Lipperheide 1363

Les **filles** d'Ève. Grévin, Alfred

Les **filles** du celeste empire. Colin, Mme Anais

Filov, Bogdan
  Geschichte der bulgarischen kunst unter der türkischen herrschaft und in der neueren zeit. Berlin und Leipzig, W. de Gruyter 1933
  94p. illus.(plan) 64pl. on 32 l. O. (Grundriss der slavischen philologie und kulturgeschichte, hrsg. von R. Trautmann und M. Vasmer. bd. XI)
  Includes bibliographies
  LC 34-32464

Finard, N.
  (illus.) Damaze de Raymond. Tableau historique, géographique, militaire et moral de l'Empire de Russie

[**Finart, Noël Dieudonné**]
  [Les alliés à Paris en 1815, scènes de moeurs. Paris, Basset] 1815?
  14 col.pl. F.
  Colas gives a list of the plates which show soldiers and Parisians. They are engraved by Blanchart fils, Thiebaut and Rulhières
  Colas 1070

  [Garde royale et maison du Roi. Paris, Basset] ca1816
  4 col.pl. F.
  Colas 1071

  [Troupes étrangères.] Paris, Basset ca1835
  10 col.pl. Q.
  Colas 1073

  [Uniformes des armées alliées.] No place, ca1815
  12 l. 36 col.pl. Q.
  Troupes russes, Troupes anglaises and *Troupes prussiennes,* six plates each
  Cataloged from Colas
  Colas 1069

  (illus.) Costumes des troupes russes

[**Finart, Noël Dieudonné, and others**]
  [Armées étrangères. Paris, Dero-Becker] ca1840
  30 col.pl. ob.Q.
  Plates are lithographed by Finart, Lehnert, Le Pan, Madou and Roland
  Colas 1072

Finck, Emil
  Barbara Uttmann, die begründoun der spitzenindustrie im erzgebirge. Annaberg, Rudolph & Dieterici 1886
  39p. 2pl. O.
  Lipperheide 4047

Finden, Edward Francis. See Finden, William, jt. auth.

Finden, William, and Finden, Edward Francis
  Findens' tableaux of national character, beauty, and costume ... With original tales in prose and poetry, written expressly for the work, by the Countess of Blessington, Miss Mitford, L. E. L. ... and others. London, Pub. for the proprietor by T. G. March 1843
  2v. 60pl. F.
  "The work is designed to illustrate by a series of pictorial groups, accompanied by original tales, the character and costumes of all nations." Preface
  Much enlarged since first edition: *Findens' tableaux; a series of picturesque scenes* (London, C. Tilt 1838. 56p. 12pl.)
  LC 10-15120

Finger nails
  Foan, G. A., ed. The art and craft of hairdressing. 1931

Finger-ring lore. Jones, William

Fink, Karl
Die geometrische construction und farbengebung des flach-ornaments. Carlsruhe, 1875-76
1 l. 48pl.(part col.) F.
Lipperheide 4365

Finland
Appelgren-Kivalo, Hjalmar. Suomalaisia pukuja ... Finnische trachten aus der jüngeren Eisenzeit. 1907

Norman, Sir Henry, bart. All the Russias; travels and studies in contemporary European Russia, Finland, Siberia, the Caucasus, and Central Asia. 1902

Paris. Exposition internationale des arts décoratifs et industriels modernes, 1925. Ornements et perles des peuples finnois et siberiens. 1927?

Russia. Glavnve upravlenīe zemleustroīstra i zemledīe lia. L'art populaire russe à la seconde exposition koustare. 1914

Schvindt, Theodor. Finnische volkstrachten. 1905

See also Cheremisses; Decoration and ornament—Finnish; Embroidery—Finland

Finley, Mrs Ruth (Ebright)
The lady of Godey's, Sarah Josepha Hale, by Ruth E. Finley. Philadelphia & London, J. P. Lippincott 1931
318p. col.front. pl.(part col.) ports. facsims. O. $3.50
Plates from *Godey's Lady's book* show feminine fashions from 1835-1877
Costume index. LC 31-28307

Finnemore, John
Delhi and the durbar, by John Finnemore; with twelve full-page illustrations in colour by Mortimer Menpes. London, A. and C. Black 1912
87p. col.front. col.pl. O. (Peeps at great cities)
LC 12-29129

Finnische ornamente. See Schvindt, Theodor. Suomalaisia koristeita

Finnische textilornamentik. Tikkanen, J. J.

Finnische trachten aus der jüngeren eisenzeit. See Applegren-Kivalo, Hjalmar. Suomalaisia pukuja

Finnische volkstrachten. Schvindt, Theodor

Finsch, Otto
Südseearbeiten. Gewerbe- und kunstfleiss, tauschmittel und "geld" der eingeborenen, auf grundlage der rohstoffe und der geographischen verbreitung. [Illus.] vom verfasser u. A. Strohmeyer. Hamburg, L. Friederichsen 1914
xii,605,[60]p. xxx pl.(2 col.) Q. (Abhandlungen des Hamburgischen kolonialinstituts. bd XIV. Reihe B. Völkerkunde, kulturgeschichte und sprachen. bd. 9)
Some of the plates show jewelry and ornamental design from the South Sea islands
"Schriftennachweis": p[567]-73
LC 14-17651

Ueber bekleidung, schmuck, und tätowirung der Papuas der südostküste von Neu-Guinea. Wien, A. Hölder 1885
23p. illus. Q.
From *Mittheilungen der anthropologischen gesellschaft* im Wien, v15 (New ser. v5) Wien 1885

Finx, E. See Francisci, Erasmus

Il fiore di Venezia. Paoletti, Ermolao

Fiori di ricami nuovamente posti in luce. Florimi, Matteo

Firemen

France

Album militaire. 18—. pt. 10

Bournand, François. Le régiment de sapeurs-pompiers de Paris. 1887

Dally, Aristide. Les sapeurs-pompiers. 1887

See also Military costume—France
The firemen (sapeurs-pompiers) are part of the army

Germany

Scholl, Edouard. Bekleidung und ausrüstung der preuszischen feuerwehren. 1926

Netherlands

Heyden, Jan van der, 1637-1712, and Heyden, Jan van der, 1662-1726. Beschryving der nieuwlijks uitgewonder en geoctrojeerde slang-brand-spuiten, en haare wijze van brand-blussen ... nevens beschrijving der brand-ordres der stad Amsterdam. 1690

Fischbach, Friedrich
Album für stickerei; 3. aufl. Leipzig, R. Weigel 1872
1 l. 20 col.pl. Q.
Lipperheide 3985

Ornament-album. Wiesbaden, Selbstverlag [1892]
1 l. 27 col.pl. Q.
Lipperheide 4382

Ornamente der gewebe. Hanau, G. M. Alberti [1874-80]
x p. 160(i.e. 161)col.pl. sq.F.
Lettered: Ornament of textile fabrics. Prefixed are 4 pages containing description of plates in English, signed: Bernard Quaritch
Lipperheide 3741. LC 4-3659

Stickerei-album des Bazar. 1. sammlung. Berlin, Verlag der Bazar-a.-g. 1879
1 l. 9 col.pl. O.
Lipperheide 3992

Stilistische muster für stickerei und häkelei. No place, ca1875
48 col.pl. S.
Lipperheide 3988

(illus.) Lay, Felix. Sudslävische ornamente

(illus.) Pulszky, Karoly. Ornamente der hausindustrie Ungarns

Fischel, Oskar
Chronisten der mode; mensch und kleid in bildern aus drei jahrtausenden. Potsdam, Müller 1923
101p. front. illus. 113pl.(6 col.) Q.

Fischel, Oskar—*Continued*
Die mode; menschen und moden im achtzehnten jahrhundert. See entry under Boehn, Max von

Modes & manners of the nineteenth century. See entry under Boehn, Max von

Fischer, Carl August
Geschichte der Stuttgarter stadgarde zu pferd. Stuttgart, Kröner 1887
4 col.pl. Q.
Uniforms of the municipal guard of Stuttgart
Colas 1074

Fischer, Carlos
Les costumes de l'Opéra. Paris, Librairie de France [1931]
324p. illus. col.pl.(1 fold.) 28½x23cm. 130fr.
Bibliography included in "Notes" p[281]-319
Colas 1075. LC 32-17281

Fischer, Frederik Henrik. See Jong, Jo de. 50 eeuwen costuum

Fischer, Johann Bernhard
Statistische und topographische beschreibung des burggraftums Nürnberg, unterhalb des gebürgs; oder des fürstentums Brandenburg-Anspach. Anspach, der Verfasser 1787
2v. 4pl. O.
Two plates show folk costume of Ansbach
Lipperheide 762

Fischer, Joseph, and Ly'chdorff, Vincenz
Der ornat der ritter des erhabenen kaiserl. österreichischen Leopolds ordens. Innsbruck, 1892
3 l. 9pl.(6 col.) F.
Three plates are by J. Fischer, attributed to the year 1808, and six plates in color are by V. Lýchdorff. All show commanders and knights of the Austrian Order of Leopold
Lipperheide 1942

Fischer, Sébastien
Tableaux de genre recueillis pendant le voyage de ... Monseigneur le duc Maximilien de Bavière. [Stuttgart, Ebner & Seubert 1846-49]
70p. 48pl.(33 col.) F.
The colored plates are pictures of life in Egypt, and views. Those in black and white show dress, jewelry, arms and equipment for horses and camels
Published simultaneously in German with title: *Genrebilder aus dem Orient,* same publisher and collation
Lipperheide 1598

Fischer, Th.
Schwerter-sammlung. See entry under Dreger, Max

Das **fischereibuch** kaiser Maximilians I. Maximilian I, emperor of Germany

Fischerin, Dorothea
Strick buch; worinnen nicht nur viele neue zwickel, sondern nebst dem alphabet und zahlen auch viele zierrathen befindlich. Nürnberg, 1803
1 l. 37pl. Q.
This is a manuscript pattern book. According to Lipperheide most of the designs are original, although some are direct copies from Weigel's *Neues neh- und strickbuch*
Lipperheide 4063

Fischof, Mme A. A. de
La réforme du costume féminin. Paris, Maloine 1900
O.
Colas 1076

Fišer, Frant
Old Bohemian customs throughout the year, illus. by Frant. Fisher; ed. by R. D. Szalatnay. [New York, R. D. Szalatnay] 192-?
[14]p. col.illus. 18½x24cm.
LC 28-26726

Fishberg, Maurice
The Jews: a study of race and environment. London, New York, The Walter Scott publishing co. 1911
xix,578p. illus. D. (The contemporary science series. Ed. by Havelock Ellis)
Many of the illustrations show costume
Bibliography: p557-66
LC 11-8850

Fisher, Frant. See Fišer, Frant

Fisher, Sydney George
Men, women & manners in colonial times. Illus ... by Edward Stratton Holloway. Philadelphia & London, J. B. Lippincott 1898
2v. front. illus. pl. D.
LC 2-5480

Fisher, Mrs Welthy (Honsinger)
Twins travelogues. New York, Abingdon press 1924
4v. illus. ea 50c
Contents: v 1 The travels of Kim and Chin Chu, Korean twins; v2 The travels of Tan and Tara, Japanese twins; v3 The travels of Mona and Mani, Indian twins; v4 The travels of Wen Chi and Wen Bao, Chinese twins
An idea for costuming children's plays illustrated with paper dolls. Included in the portfolio are stories of the twins who introduce the dolls

Fishermen
Busby, T. L. The fishing costume and local scenery of Hartlepool in the county of Durham. 1819
Maximilian I, emperor of Germany. Das fischereibuch kaiser Maximilians I. 1901

Fisher's illustrations of Constantinople and its environs. See Allom, Thomas. Constantinople and the scenery of the seven churches of Asia Minor

The **fishing** costume and local scenery of Hartlepool in the county of Durham. Busby, T. L.

Fishmongers
Fishwives and fishgirls' costumes: a souvenir of Fisheries Exhibition, 1883. 1883

Fishwives and fishgirls' costumes; a souvenir of Fisheries Exhibition, 1883. London, S. Miller [1883]
99p. illus. Q. 2s 6d

Fiske, Mrs
(ed.) Record of fashion and court elegance

Fitz-Gerald, John Driscoll
Rambles in Spain. New York, T. Y. Crowell [1910]
xviii,310p. front. pl. ports. map. O. o.p.
Costume index. LC 10-22786

Fitz-Gerald, Shafto Justin Adair
How to "make up." A practical guide for amateurs and beginners. London, New York, S. French c1901
106p. front. illus. D.
LC 8-14810

Fitzpatrick, John Clement
The Continental army uniform
p629-39. illus.
From *Daughters of the American revolution magazine,* v54 1920

Five colonial artists of New England. Bayley, F. W.

The **five** great monarchies of the ancient eastern world. Rawlinson, George

Fladt, Wilhelm Jakob
Volksleben im Schwarzwald. See entry under Retzlaff, Hans

Die **flämische** buchmalerei des XV. und XVI. jahrhunderts. Winkler, Friedrich

Flament, Albert
Personnages de comédie; illustrations de Georges Barbier. Paris, Meynial 1922
58p. 12pl. Q. 500fr.
Colas 216

Flanders. See Belgium; also Netherlands (thru 16th century)

Flandin, Eugène Napoléon
Monument de Ninive. See entry under Botta, P. E.

Flandreysy, Jeanne (Mellier) de
La femme provençale; illustrations de F. Detaille. Marseille, F. Detaille 1922
150p. 180 illus. 8 col.pl. F. 60fr.

Fleischer, Ernst Gerhard
(pub.) Retzsch, F. A. M. Gallerie zu Shakspeare's dramatischen werken

Fleischmann,
(engr.) Allgemeiner militär-almanach; erster jahrgang mit acht colorirten militärgruppen, nach zeichnungen von Monten, und vier portraits berühmter generale. 1828
(engr.) Heideloff, K. A. von. Aux héros polonais
(engr.) Heideloff, K. A. von. Costum des deutschen ritterthums
(engr.) Heideloff, K. A. von, ed. Polnisches militair

Fleischman, D. C. C.
(engr.) Die fehler der menschen nebst deren verbesserung in saubern kupfern und moralischen versen vorgestellet

Fleming, Hanns Friedrich von
Der vollkommene teutsche jäger ... Dann auch die ... hunde, und der völlige jagd-zeug; letzlich die hohe und niedere jagd-wissenschaft nebst einem immerwährenden jäger-calender. Leipzig, J. C. Martini 1719
10 1,400,111p. 16 l. 2 illus. 61pl. F.
Some of the plates show hunting costume
Lipperheide 3026

Der vollkommene teutsche soldat, welcher die gantze kriegs-wissenschaft, insonderheit was bey der infanterie vorkommt ... die einem soldaten nöthige vorbereitungs-wissenschafften, künste und exercitia, die chargen und verrichtungen aller kriegs-bedienten, von dem mousquetier an bis auf den general. Leipzig, J. C. Martini 1726
20,808p. 20 l. 63pl. F.
Plates show soldiers on military duty and at recreation
Lipperheide 2127

Fleming, Jane A.
Garment making; the cutting-out and making-up of common-sense comfortable clothing for children. Leeds and Glasgow, E. J. Arnold [1912]
vii,151p. 126 illus. sq.O.

Flemming, Ernst Richard
Textile künste, weberei, stickerei, spitze, geschichte, technik, stilentwickelung. Berlin, Verlag für kunst-wissenschaft [1923]
384p. incl.illus. pl. col.front. col.pl. diagrs. O.
A survey of textile designs from ancient times to the present, arranged by countries
"Literatur": p[379]-80
LC 32-9801

Fletcher, Robert
Tattooing among civilized people. Read before the Anthropological society of Washington, December 19, 1882. Washington, Judd & Detweiler 1883
27p. O.
LC 5-31181

Fletcher, S. P.
(illus.) Hall, Thomas. "Effects" and adventures of Raby Rattler, gent.

Fletcher, Ursula
Stage costumes. Leicester, England, Dryad handicrafts n.d.
11p. 6d (Dryad handicrafts leaflet no37)
"A pamphlet on making costumes for amateur productions, with explanation of the method of stenciling, and making wigs, head-dresses and ornaments inexpensively."
B. M. Baker's Dramatic bibliography

Fleurer, J. J.
(illus.) Deyerlsperg, G. J. von. Erbhuldigung

Les **fleurs** animées. Grandville, J. I. I. G., called

Fleury, Charles Rohault de. See Rohault de Fleury, Charles

[**Fleury, Jules**]
Le musée secret de la caricature, par Champfleury [pseud.] Paris, E. Dentu, 1888
x,249p. illus. pl. col.front. D.
The first part: *Caragueuz en Turquie,* p2-116, contains pictures of marionettes
LC F-684

Fleury, Maurice, comte, and Sonolet, Louis
La société du second empire, 1851-1870 d'après les mémoires contemporains et des documents nouveaux. v 1-4. Paris, A. Michel 1917-24?
4v. illus. pl. ports. O.
Contains many portraits and scenes of the period
Contents: v 1 1851-1858; v2 1858-1863; v3 1863-1867; v4 1867-1870

Flexel, Lienhard
Lienhard Flexel's Lobspruch des fürstlichen freischiessens zu Innsbruck im oktober 1569; hrsg. und eingeleitet von August Edelmann. Innsbruck, Wagner 1885
63p. 3 illus.(2 col.) Q.
Lipperheide 2997

Die **fliegenden** blätter des XVI. und XVII. jahrhunderts. Scheible, Johann, ed.

Flinn, David Edgar
Our dress and our food in relation to health. Dublin, M. H. Gill 1886
59p. S.

Flitner, Johann
(tr.) Murner, Thomas. Nebulo nebulonum

Flittner, Christian Gottfried
Die kunst der toilette; ein taschenbuch für junge damen die durch anzug und putz ihre schönheit erhöhen wollen; 2. ausz. Berlin, C. F. Kecht 1833
x,181p. 2pl. O.
Lipperheide 3258

Flobert, Mme Laure Paul
La femme et le costume masculin. Lille, Lefebvre-Ducrocq 1911
31p. 1 pl. O.
"Causerie faîte à la Société archéologique, historique et artistique 'Le vieux papier' 28 mars 1911." Subtitle
From the *Bulletin* of the Société archéologique
Colas 1077

Floding, Per Gustaf
Solemniteter ... i ... Stockholm, åren 1771 och 1772 ... Solemnités, qui se sont passées à Stockholm ... dans les années 1771 et 1772. Stockholm 1772
1 l. 18pl. F.
Lipperheide 2699

Flögel, Karl Friedrich
Floegels Geschichte des grotesk komischen, bearbeitet, erweitert und bis auf die neueste zeit fortgeführt von Friedrich W. Ebeling. 5. aufl. Leipzig, H. Barsdorf 1888
xiv,478p. front.(port.) 41pl.(21 col.) O.
Printed in blue
First edition: 1788. A new edition edited by Max Bauer was published: München, G. Muller 1914
Lipperheide 3502 (4th ed.) LC 2-11029

Floerke, Hanns
Die moden der italienischen renaissance. München, G. Müller 1917
112p. 132pl. O. M.20
Reprinted 1924
Colas 1078. Costume index

Flora of saloons or flowers and women of every country. See Devéria, Achille. Flore des salons

Flora's feast. Crane, Walter

Flore des salons ou les fleurs et des femmes de tous les pays. Devéria, Achille

Florence. See Italy—Tuscany—Florence

Flores virtutum. Vindler, Hans

Floriger fasciculus selectiorum epigramatum opera F. Ae. à S. I. B[aptista]. See Aegidius, à Sancto Joanne Baptista, Augustinian prior. D. Wenceslao bohemorum duci ac martyri

Florimi, Matteo
Fiori di ricami nuovamente posti in luce. Siena, M. Florimi 1603
17pl. Q.
"Ne i quali sono varii, et diversi disegni di lavori. Come merli, bavari, manichetti, & altre sorte di opera, che al presente sono in uso, utilissimi ad ogni stato di donne." Subtitle
Lipperheide 3911

Florin, Franz Philipp
Oeconomus prudens et legalis, oder Allgemeiner kluger und rechts-verständiger hausz-vatter ... mit rechtlichen anmerckungen ... versehen, durch herrn Johann Christoph Donauern. Nürnberg, Franckfurt, und Leipzig, C. Riegel 1750-51
4v. front. 179 illus. 56pl. F.
Plates are noteworthy for costume of the 18th century
It appears to be well established that the actual editor of this composite work was the field marshal count Philipp of Sulzbach. cf. *Allgemeine deutsche biographie* 7:131-132, 48:601-602
Lipperheide 563

Florinus, Franciscus Philippus. See Florin, F. P.

Florio, Blasco
La scienza della scherma. Catania, Tipographia de R. ospizio di beneficenza 1844
230p. 4pl. O.
Lipperheide 2989

Flory, M. A.
A book about fans; the history of fans and fan-painting ... with a chapter on fan-collecting by Mary Cadwalader Jones. New York and London, Macmillan 1895
xiii,141p. illus. pl. O. $2.50 o.p.
Costume index. Lipperheide 1730. LC 12-8566

Flotow, Gustav von
Das schuhmacher-handwerk im seiner entwickelung. München, C. Fritsch 1890
122p. 44 illus. 4pl. Q.
"Ein beitrag zur kultur-geschichte Münchens. Als festschift zum 600 jährigen jubiläum der Schuhmachermeister-innung. München." Subtitle
Lipperheide 1744m

Die **flotte.** Jedina, R., ritter von. See Kählig, Eduard von. Österreich-Ungarn: Das heer, von E. von Kählig ... Die flotte, von R. ritter von Jedina

Die **flotte** einer aegyptischen koenigin aus dem XVII. jahrhundert. Dueminchen, Johannes

Flower, Sir William Henry
... Fashion in deformity, as illustrated in the customs of barbarous and civilized races. To which is added: Manners and fashion. By Herbert Spencer. [New York, J. Fitzgerald & co. 1882]
49p. illus. O. (Humboldt library of popular science literature. no28. v2)
Caption title
LC 6-24706

Flowers. See Fancy dress—Flowers

The **flowers** personified. Grandville, J. I. I. G., called

The **flowery** kingdom and the land of the mikado. Northrop, H. D.

Flügel, John Carl
The psychology of clothes. London, L. & V. Woolf at the Hogarth press, and the Institute of psychoanalysis 1930
257p. front. 21pl. O. (The international psycho-analytical library, no18)
Bibliography: p239-42
LC 31-20782

[Flutre, Fernand]
... Molière. [Paris] Hachette [c1925]
64p. incl.front. illus. ports. facsims. O (Encyclopédie par l'image. [Littérature])
Signed: F. Flutre
Bibliography: p63
LC 26-6287

Foan, Gilbert Arthur
(ed.) The art and craft of hairdressing; a standard and complete guide to the technique of modern hairdressing, manicure, massage and beauty culture, edited by Gilbert A. Foan ... assisted by leading specialists. London, New York [etc.] Sir I. Pitman & sons, ltd., 1931.
xix,529p. incl.front. illus. IX pl.(incl. ports.) on 7 l. sq.Q. 60s
Costume index. LC 32-1441

Focosi, Robert
(illus.) Zanoli, Allessandro, baron. Sulla milizia cisalpino italiana

Föhn, Michael
[Suisse—Costumes anciens. Paris, lith. de Engelmann 18-?]
12 col.pl. Q.
Plates are lithographed and colored by Victor Adam after Föhn. They show costume of the twelfth century to the seventeenth
Colas 1079

[Suisse—Costumes modernes. Paris, lith. de Engelmann 1826]
21 col.pl. Q.
Plates are lithographed and colored by Victor Adam after Föhn and show costumes of the different cantons
Cataloged from Colas
Colas 1080

[Suisse—jeux et usages. Paris, lith. de Engelmann 1827]
13 col.pl. Q.
Plates are lithographed in color by Weber and Zwinger after Föhn
Cataloged from Colas
Colas 1081

Föhr. See Frisian islands

Foelix, comte, pseud. See Raban, L. F.

Förster, Carl
(ed.) Bleich, G. H. Abdrücke eines vollständigen kartenspieles

Förster, Ernst
Denkmale deutscher bildnerei und malerei von einführung des christenthums bis auf die neueste zeit. Leipzig, T. O. Weigel 1858-1870
6v. 2 illus. 294pl.(3 col.) F.
Each volume is divided into 2 parts: I Sculptors, II Painters
Lipperheide 588

Denkmale italienischer malerei vom verfall der antike bis zum sechzehnten jahrhundert. Leipzig, T. O. Weigel 1870-1874
3v. 150pl. F.
Lipperheide 354

Förster, Friedrich
Die perle auf Lindahaide; fest-spiel in romanzen und lebenden bildern zur feier der ... vermählung ... des kronprinzen Friedrich von Dänemark mit ... herzogin Karoline von Mecklenburg auf dem grossherzoglichen schlosse zu Neu-Strelitz dargestellt, im juni 1841. Berlin, F. Dümmler [1841]
16p. 7pl. Q.
Illustrated by C. Stürmer
Lipperheide 2606

Vollständige beschreibung aller feste und huldigungen, welche in ... Preussen und Baiern zur ... vermählungsfeier des ... kronprinzen Friedrich Wilhelm von Preussen ... und der ... prinzessin Elisa Ludovika von Baiern ... statt gefunden haben. Berlin, Im verlage der Maurerschen buchhandlung 1824
219p. 5 col.pl. Q.
Lipperheide 2538

Förster, L.
(lithgr.) Zimmermann, C. F. Russische militair gruppen

Foillet, Jacques
Das musterbuch. Berlin, E. Wasmuth 1891
5 l. 83pl. sq.O.
A facsimile reprint of his *Nouveaux pourtraicts de point coupé* (Montbeliard 1598)

Foix, Gaston III, Phoebus, comte de. See Gaston III, Phoebus, comte de Foix

Fokke, Simon
(engr.) La Fargue, P. C. Lyk-staetsie van ... Anna kroon princesse van Groot-Britanien
(engr.) Swart, P. de. Afbeelding van de kaamer en 't parade-bed waar op het lyk van ... Anna, kroon princesse van Groot-Brittanje

Folge von reitern verschiedener volker. Bussemecher, Johann

Folies gauloises depuis les Romains jusqu'à nos jours. Doré, Gustave

Folk costume. See the subdivision: By region or province, under names of European countries; e.g. France—By region or province—Brittany. Folk costume will also often be found in books listed under names of countries with subdivisions 18th century and 19th century

The **folk** costume book. Haire, F. H.

Folk-costume of Rome and the provinces of Italy. Ciuli, E.

Folk-costumes of Asiatic Russia. Martuinov, A. E.

Folkedragter i Nordvestsjælland. Møller, J. S.

Folklore y costumbres de España. Barcelona, A. Martín 1931-33
3v. col.front. illus. pl.(part col.) Q.

Folkways in China. Hodous, Lewis

Der **Follet,** courrier des salons; damenmodenjournal. See note under Le Follet, courrier des salons; journal des modes

Le **Follet,** courrier des salons; journal des modes. 1.-50. année; 1. ser. nov. 1829-juin 1831; 2. ser. juillet 1831-1875. Paris, 1829-75
Col.pl. O.
Title varies: 1872-75 *Follet et le courrier de la mode*
Plates by Anaïs Toudouze and Laure Colin
English edition: *Le Follet, courrier des salons; the newest Paris fashions for ladies, published weekly* (Paris, A. Appert 1843-53)
German edition: *Der Follet, courrier des salons; damen-modenjournal* (Aachen, M. Urlichs sohn 1848-71)
Italian edition: *Il Folletto, corriere de' saloni, giornale delle mode* (Parigi, 1851-52)
Colas 1083-86. Lipperheide 4611-12

Le **Follet,** courrier des salons; the newest Paris fashions for ladies published weekly. See note under Le Follet, courrier des salons; journal des modes

Il **Folletto,** corriere de' saloni, giornale delle mode. See note under Le Follet, courrier des salons; journal des modes

The **follies** and fashions of our grandfathers (1807). Tuer, A. W.

Folliot de Crenneville-Poutet, Franz Maria Johann, graf
Freydal. Des kaisers Maximilian. I. turniere und mummereien. See entry under Maximilian I, emperor of Germany

Foltz, Philipp
IV blaetter aus dem Münchner volksleben. München, L. Lacroix 1829
4pl. Q.
Lipperheide 3529

Fonclare, Jacques Élie de Riols de. See Riols de Fonclare, J. É. de

Fonds de bonnets du XIXe siècle. See Lescure, Alfred. Collection A. Lescure

Fonremis,
(illus.) Choppin, Henri. Les hussards, les vieux régiments, 1692-1792. 1899

Fonta, Laure. See Tabourot, Jehan. Orchésographie

Fontaine, Pierre François Léonard
(illus.) Description des cérémonies et des fêtes qui ont eu lieu pour le couronnement de ... Napoléon ... et Joséphine

See also Percier, Charles, jt. auth.

Fontallard, Henri Gérard. See Gérard-Fontallard, Henri

Fontana, Giovanni Battista
(illus.) Schrenck von Nozing, Jacob. Augustissimorum imperatorum ... thaten

Fontana, J. B. See Fontana, Giovanni Battista

Fontana, Publio
Il sontuoso apparato, fatto dalla magnifica citta di Brescia nel felice ritorno dell' ... il cardinale Morosini. Brescia, V. Sabbio [1591]
76p. 12pl. F.
Lipperheide 2789

Fontenay, Eugène
Les bijoux anciens et modernes. Preface par V. Champier ... illus. par M. Saint-Elme Gautier. Paris, Maison Quantin 1887
xxiv,520p. illus. Q.

See also Jannettaz, Édouard, jt. auth.

Fontenouille, G. de
Le faux-luxe et l'abandon des costumes locaux dans les campagnes. Besançon, Impr. catholique de l'Est 1913
13p. O.
Colas 1087

Fontenoy, Marquise de, pseud. See Cunliffe-Owen, M. de G.

Football costume
Marshall, Francis. Football; the Rugby union game. 1895
Schnell, H. Handbuch der ballspiele. 1899-1901

Foote, Theodore Clinton
The ephod: its form and use; an investigation in Biblical archaeology. Baltimore, 1902
47,v-viii p. O.
Reprinted from the *Journal of Biblical literature* v31, 1902
Bibliography: p v-viii
LC 2-20263

Footwear
Beely, F., and Kirchhoff, E. Der menschliche fuss, seine bekleidung und pflege. [1891]
Camper, Petrus. Abhandlung über die beste form der schuhe. 1783
Camper, Petrus. Dissertation sur la meilleure forme des souliers. 1781
Dutton, W. H. The boots and shoes of our ancestors as exhibited by the worshipful company of cordwainers. 1898
Flotow, Gustav von. Das schuhmacherhandwerk in seiner entwickelung. 1890
Goater, W. H. A short treatise on boots and shoes, ancient and modern. 1884
Manchester, Herbert. Historic beauties and their footwear. 1927
Meyer, G. H. von. Die richtige gestalt der schuhe; eine abhandlung aus der angewandten anatomie für aerzte und laien. 1858
Redfern, W. B. Royal and historic gloves and shoes. 1904
Rosenthal, Doris, comp. Pertaining to costume. 1929

See also Footwear, Military; Footwear, Moccasins; Snowshoes

History

Baudouin, Benoît, and Negrone, Giulio. B. Balduinus De calceo antiquo, et Jul. Nigronus De caliga veterum. 1667

Berlepsch, H. A. von. Chronik vom ehrbaren schuhmachergewerk. 1850

Billstein, E. L. Fashion in footwear. 1886

The boot and shoe-maker's assistant. 1853

Bordoli, Ernest. Footwear down the ages. 1933

Bynaeus, Anthony. De calceis Hebraeorum libri duo, curis secundis recogniti, et aucti. 1715

Campion, S. S. Delightful history of Ye gentle craft: an illustrated history of feet costume. 1876

Franklin, A. L. A. La vie privée d'autrefois; arts et métiers, modes, moeurs, usages des Parisiens du XII. au XVIII. siècle. [v 18]

Frauberger, Heinrich. Antike und frühmittelalterliche fussbekleidungen aus Achmim-Panopolis. 1896

Greig, T. W. Ladies old-fashioned shoes. 1885
—Supplement. 1889

Hall, J. S. The book of the feet; a history of boots and shoes. 1846

Jackson, Margaret. What they wore. 1936

Footwear—History—*Continued*

Lacroix, Paul, and Duchesne, Alphonse. Histoire de la chaussure depuis l'antiquité la plus reculée jusqu'à nos jours. 1862

Morgan, W. C. Shoes and shoemaking illustrated. 1897

Towle, H. C. The shoe in romance and history. c1915

Vincent, Charles. Histoire de la chaussure, de la cordonnerie et des cordonniers célèbres depuis l'antiquité jusqu'à nos jours. Antiquité. 1880

Wright, Thomas. The romance of the shoe, being the history of shoemaking in all ages, and especially in England and Scotland. 1922

18th century

Garsault, F. A. P. de. Art du cordonnier. 1767

19th century

Braatz, Egbert. Ueber die falsche, gewöhnliche schuhform und über die richtige form der fussbekleidung. 1897

Greig, T. W. Ladies' dress shoes, of the nineteenth century. 1900

Günther, G. B. Ueber den bau des menschlichen fusses und dessen zweckmässigste bekleidung. 1863

Nouvelle encyclopédie des arts et métiers; Art de la chaussure considéré dans toutes ses parties. 1824

Peck, J. L. Dress and care of the feet: showing their natural perfect shape and construction. 1871

Pestel, Bernhard. Deh menschliche fuss und seine naturgemässe bekleidung. 1885

Voetsch, August. Fussleiden und rationelle fussbekleidung. 1883

20th century

Lapidoth, Frits. Een schoeisel verzameling. 1902

Footwear down the ages. Bordoli, Ernest

Footwear, Military

Munson, E. L. The soldier's foot and the military shoe. 1912

Salquin, S. A. Die militarische fussbekleidung. 1883

Salquin, S. A. The militaary shoe. 1883

Starcke, Paul. Der naturgemässe stiefel ... mit specieller berücksichtigung der bekleidung und pflege des fusses bei der armee. 1881

Webb-Johnson, Cecil. The soldiers' feet and footgear. 1915

Footwear, Moccasins

Biggart, Helen. Leathercraft and beading, adapted for Camp fire girls. 1930

Griswold, L. E. Handbook of craftwork in leather, horsehair, bead, porcupine quill and feather, Indian (Navajo) silver and turquoise. 1928

Hatt, Gudmund. Moccasins and their relation to the Arctic footwear. 1916

Verrill, A. H. The American Indian, North, South, and Central America. 1927

Wissler, Clark. Distribution of moccasin decorations among the Plains tribes. 1927

Forain, Jean Louis

Album Forain; avant-propos de Maurice Talmeyr. Paris, Plon [1896]
3 l. illus. 54pl. Q.
Lipperheide 3628

La comédie parisienne. Paris, G. Charpentier et E. Fasquelle 1892
248p. 250 illus. D.
Lipperheide 3627. LC 22-8823

Foran, William Robert

Changing horizons ... covering over thirty years' wanderings up and down the seven seas. London, Hutchinson [1937]
288p. front. pl. O.
LC 37-3535

Forbes, Frederick Edwyn

Dahomey and the Dahomans; being the journals of two missions to the king of Dahomey, and residence at his capital, in the year 1849 and 1850. London, Longman, Brown, Green, and Longmans 1851
2v. col.fronts. pl.(part col.) col.ports. D.
LC 5-14405

Forbes, Henry Ogg

A naturalist's wanderings in the Eastern archipelago; a narrative of travel and exploration fom 1878 to 1883. With numerous illustrations ... by John B. Gibbs. New York, Harper 1885
xix,536p. col.front. illus. 1 pl. maps(part fold.) O.
Brief descriptions of costume in various parts of the Malay peninsula and pictures of hair dress among various tribes
LC 5-9729

Forbes-Leith, William

The Scots men-at-arms and life-guards in France. From their formation until their final dissolution A. D. MCCCCXVIII-MDCCCXXX. With etched plates by Major H. de Grandmaison. Edinburgh, W. Paterson 1882
2v. fronts. illus. pl.(part double) facsim. Q.
Colas 1088. LC 3-8858

Forbin, [Louis Nicolas Philippe Auguste] comte de

Voyage dans le Levant en 1817 et 1818. 2. éd. Paris, Delaunay 1819
460p. fold.plan and atlas(fold.l. of 80pl. 11 col.)
Thirteen of the plates show costume. The first edition (Paris, L'imprimerie royale 1819) contains the same plates
Colas 1089-1090. Lipperheide 1596. LC 4-12194

Forcella, Vincenzo

Spectacula ossia caroselli, tornei, cavalcate e ingressi trionfali. Milano, M. Kantorowicz [1896]
xi,169p. 40 illus. Q.
Contains a description of three processions known as Amore e Gloria, Corsa del Saracino, and La Contesa dell'aria e dell' acqua, held in Milan, Rome, and Vienna in 1669, 1634, and 1667
Lipperheide 2500

Ford, Horace A.
Archery: its theory and practice. Ed. by Dean V. R. Manley; American ed. Toledo [O.] F. E. Roff 1880
x,175p. front.(port.) illus. pl.
First edition: London, J. Buchanan, 1856; second edition, 1859
Lipperheide 3006 (2d ed.) LC 5-23442

Ford, Richard. See Price, Lake, jt. auth.

Foreign armour in England. Gardner, J. S.

Foreign military costume. Heath, William

Foresters. See Lumbermen

Forestier, Alc. de
(ed.) Les Alpes pittoresques; description de la Suisse, par Lullin de Châteauvieux, Zschokke, Meyer de Knonau, publiée par A. de Forestier. Paris, 1837-38
2v. 96pl. maps. Q.

Forestier, Amédée
The Roman soldier; some illustrations representative of Roman military life with special reference to Britain. London, A. & C. Black; New York, Macmillan 1928
144p. col.front. illus. mounted col.plates. O. $2
Some authorities consulted in connection with the illustrations: p6
Costume index. LC 29-14515

(illus.) Omond, G. W. T. Belgium

Forestillingerne paa guldbracteaterne. Worsaae, J. J. A.

Forgues, Paul Émile Daurand
Cent proverbes. See entry under Grandville, J. I. I. G.

La Chine ouverte; aventures d'un fankouei dans le pays de Tsin, par Old Nick [pseud.] Ouvrage illustré par Auguste Borget. Paris, H. Fournier 1845
396p. illus. 24pl. O.
Lipperheide 1532. LC 33-18112

The **form,** order and ceremonies of coronations. Menin, Nicolas

Forman, Harrison
Through forbidden Tibet; an adventure into the unknown, by Harrison Forman. New York, Toronto, Longmans, Green 1935
xii,275p. front. pl. ports. facsims. O. $3.50
Costume index. LC 35-25394

Die **formations-** und uniformirungs-geschichte des preussischen heeres. Pietsch, Paul

Formenstudien; musterzeichnungen für schule, haus und gewerbe. Bautz, Rudolf

Formosa
Davidson, J. W. The island of Formosa past and present. 1903
Franck, H. A. Glimpses of Japan and Formosa. 1924
Psalmanazar, George. An historical and geographical description of Formosa. 1705
Trautz, F. M. Japan, Korea and Formosa. 1931?

Fornemste historien und exempel ... grossmächtiger kayser, künig, fürsten. Boccaccio, Giovanni

Forno, F.
Storia e costumi delle diciassette contrade di Siena; opera pubblicata a cura del F. Forno. Firenze, Stab. Benelli e Gambi 1887
34 l. 36 col.pl. ob.F.
Colas 1091. Lipperheide 2879

Forrer, Robert
Die frühchristlichen alterthümer aus dem gräberfelde von Achmin-Panopolis. Strassburg 1893
29p. illus. 18pl.(part col.) F.
Lipperheide 266

Reallexikon der prähistorischen, klassischen und frühchristlichen altertümer. Mit 3000 abbildungen. Berlin & Stuttgart, W. Spemann [1907]
viii,943p. front. illus. pl. Q.
LC 8-18621

Römische und byzantinische seidentextilien aus dem gräberfelde von Achmim-Panopolis. Strassburg E. Birkhäuser 1891
28p. 120 illus. XVII pl.(part col.) F.
Illustrations show textile designs
Lipperheide 3752. LC 33-14786

Spätgothische wohnräume und wandmalereien aus Schloss Issogne. Strassburg, F. Schlesier 1896
11p. 12pl. facsim. Q.
Plates 8-12 have costume value. They are reproductions of murals in the Castle of Issogne which dates from about 1490
Lipperheide 475

Die zeugdrucke der byzantinischen, romanischen, gothischen und spätern kunstepochen. Strassburg, Druck der aktiengesellschaft Konkordia in Bühl 1894
39p. 12 illus. 57 col.pl. Q.
Lipperheide 3754

(ed.) Schwerzenbach, Carl von. Die schwerter und schwentknäufe der Sammlung Carl von Schwerzenbach

See also Zschille, Richard, jt. auth.

Forrest, A. S.
(illus.) Bensusan, S. L. Morocco

Forschungen und urkunden zur geschichte der uniformirung der preussischen armee 1713-1807. Lehmann, Gustav

Forschungen zur deutschen theater-geschichte des mittelalters und der renaissance. Herrmann, Max

Forssell, Christian Didrik
Album pittoresque du nord; tableaux des costumes, moeurs et usages des paysans de la Suède. Londres & Berlin, A. Asher 1843
24p. 15 col.pl. F.
Illustrated by I. G. Sandberg. Thirteen of the plates show costume
Colas 1092. Lipperheide 1048

(engr.) Grafström, A. A. Ett år i Sverge

(engr.) Grafström, A. A. Une année en Suède

Forster, Johann Reinhold
Liber singularis de bysso antiquorum, quo, ex Aegyptia lingua, res vestiaria antiquorum, imprimis in s. codice Hebraeorum occurrens, explicatur: additae ad calcem Mantissae Aegyptiacae. Londini, G. Bowyer and J. Nichols 1776
133p. O.
Colas 1093. Lipperheide 133

Forsyth, J. S.
(ed.) Rolando, Guzman. The modern art of fencing

Forsyth, James
The highlands of central India; notes on their forests and wild tribes, natural history and sports. New ed. London, Chapman and Hall 1919
xi,387p. front. illus. pl. fold.map. O.
Two plates, facing p108 and p124, show costume of the Gonds
LC 20-7667

Forsyth, Thomas. See Blair, E. H. ed. The Indian tribes of the upper Mississippi valley and region of the Great lakes

Fort, E.
Recueil d'uniformes. Gardes d'honneur du voyage impérial de 1808. [Paris] no pub. n.d.
20 col.pl. Q.
Cataloged from Colas
Colas 1094

Forti, Alberto
Abbate Alberto Fortis Reise in Dalmatien ... aus dem italiänischen. Bern, bey der typographischen gesellschaft 1776
2v. 15pl. O.
Four plates engraved by T. Wocher show costume
Lipperheide 877

Fortitudo leonina in utraque fortuna Maximiliani Emmanuelis, V. B. ac Sup. Palat. ducis, comitis Palatini Rheni. Monachii apud M. S. Jaeklinin 1715
14 l., 232,124p. 65 illus. 16pl. F.
Four plates are full length, and forty plates are half length portraits of dukes of Bavaria. Plates are engraved by A. M. Wolffgang and F. I. Spätt
Lipperheide 719

Forty lithographic impressions. Barker, Thomas

Fosbroke, Thomas Dudley
British monachism, or, Manners and customs of the monks and nuns of England; new ed. London, J. Nichols 1817
560p. illus. 12pl. Q.
"To which are added, I. Peregrinatorium religiosum; or, Manners and customs of ancient pilgrims. II. The consuetudinal of anchorets and hermits. III. Some account of the continentes, or persons who had made vows of chastity. IV. Four select poems." Subtitle
Drawings by T. D. Fosbrooke, J. Carter and W. Alexander, engraved by Audinet and J. Basire
Chapter 60 contains a discussion by J. Carter: *Specimens of English ecclesiastical costume,* also issued separately
Lipperheide 1875. LC 16-8274 (3d ed.)

Synopsis of ancient costume, Egyptian, Greek, Roman, British, Anglo-Saxon, Norman, and English. Extracted from the Encyclopedia of Antiquities, with additional remarks. London, J. Nichols 1825
48p. 4pl.(incl. 68 illus.) Q.
From the *Encyclopedia of antiquities and elements of archaeology, classical and medieval* (London, 1823-25 2v.)
Colas 1095. Lipperheide 118

Fosbrooke, Thomas Dudley. See Fosbroke, T. D.

Fossil man in Spain. Obermaier, Hugo

Foucquet, Jehan
(illus.) Durrieu, Paul, comte. Le Boccace de Munich

Fougeadoire, Paris
Chiffres Louis XV; Fougeadoire. Paris. [Paris, 18—?]
30p. illus. sq.O.
LC 12-6406

Chiffres modernes; Fougeadoire. Paris. [Paris, 18—?]
43p. illus. sq.O.
LC 12-6405

Chiffres renaissance; Fougeadoire. Paris. Paris, Imp. Prissette [18—?]
30p. illus. sq.O.
Lipperheide 4180. LC 12-12361

Fougerat, L.
La pelleterie et le vêtement de fourrures dans l'antiquité; La préhistoire, les barbares, la Grèce, Rome ... illus. d'après les documents authentiques, par P. Savigny. Lyon, Ch. Beranger 1914
xi,353p. illus. O. 25fr.

Foulquier, J. F.
(engr.) Loutherbourg, P. J. de. 1er recueil de modes et habits galans de différents pays

Fouquet, Samuel. See Delcampe, jt. auth.

Fouquier, Marcel
Paris au XVIIIe siècle, ses divertissements, ses moeurs, directoire et consulat. Paris, Émile-Paul [1912?]
146p. illus. pl.(part col.) F.

Fouquières, André de. See Léger, Abel. L'élégance masculine

Four costume suites. Gravelot, H. F. B.

400 outstanding women of the world and costumology of their time. Schmidt, Mrs M. M.

Four hundred years of children's costume from the great masters. Macquoid, Percy

Four Scottish coronations. Cooper, James

Four years in Tibet. Ahmad Shāh

Fourdrignier, Edouard
Notes archéologiques. Double sépulture gauloise de la Gorge-Meillet, territoire de Somme-Tourbe (Marne). Étude sur les chars gaulois et les casques dans la Marne. Paris, Menu 1878
36p. 3 illus. 10 double col.pl. Q.
Lipperheide 291

Fournel, François Victor
Les cris de Paris, types et physionomies d'autrefois. Paris, Firmin-Didot 1887
221p. illus. pl. O.
Lipperheide 1190e. LC 34-19212

Fournier, August. See Pflugk-Harttung, J. A. G. von, ed. Napoleon I.: Das erwachen der völker

Fournier, Édouard
(ed.) Regnard, J. F. Oeuvres complètes

Fourrures et pelleteries. Hanau, Ch.

Foussemagne, H. de, comtesse Reinach. See Reinach-Foussemagne, H. de, comtesse

Foussereau, Joseph Marie
[L'artillerie française en 1829; Garde royale et ligne. Paris, lith. de Engelmann] n.d.
13 col.pl.(incl.front.) F.
Colas 1097

Fousserau, Joseph Marie—*Continued*
Milices révolutionnaires sous le gouvernement provisoire [du 24 Février au 4 Mai 1848] Paris, Goupil, Vibert [1848]
12 col.pl. F.
Plates are lithographed by E. Charpentier
Colas 1099

Uniformes de la garde nationale de l'armée et de la marine françaises de 1830-1832. Paris, Desmaisons [1832?]
100 col.pl. O.
Plates 1-56 are signed Foussereau, the rest E. D. A list of the plates is given in Glasser's *Catalogue*
Colas 1098

Fowke, Frank Rede
The Bayeux tapestry; a history and description. London & New York, G. Bell 1898
ix,139p. LXXIX pl. D. (Ex-libris series)
Scenes from the Middle ages
LC 12-3922

Fowler, Orson Squire
Intemperance and tight lacing, considered in relation to the laws of life. London, J. Watson 1849
37p. O.

Fowler, William Warde
The Roman festivals of the period of the Republic; an introduction to the study of the religion of the Romans. London and New York, Macmillan 1899
ix,373p. illus. O. (Handbooks of archaeology and antiquities)
LC 3-5803

Fox, Frank
The Balkan Peninsula. London, A. & C. Black 1915
xi,213p. front. pl. ports. O.
LC 16-1064

Bulgaria. London, A. and C. Black 1915
viii,208p. 32 col.pl. fold.map. O.
LC A16-701

Fox, George Patrick
Fashion: the power that influences the world. The philosophy of ancient and modern dress and fashion; rev. and enl. 3d ed. New York, American news; London, Trübner 1872
277p. D.

Fox-Davies, Arthur Charles
The art of heraldry; an encyclopædia of armory. London, T. C. & E. C. Jack; New York, Brentano's 1904
viii,503p. illus. CLIII pl.(part col.) F.
Plates 1 and 2 (in color) show heralds in official dress. The other plates show armorial bearings
LC 4-12432

Fox Indians. See Indians of North America—Fox Indians

Foxhunting on the Lakeland fells. Clapham, Richard

Fradin, Gabriel Jules Adrien Paul Letainturier-. See Letainturier-Fradin, G. J. A. P.

Från det moderna Danmark. Sprengel, David

Fragmente aus der geschichte der klöster und stiftungen Schlesiens von ihrer entstehung bis zur zeit ihrer aufhebung im november 1810. Breslau, Grasz und Barth [1811]
656p. 41 col.pl. O.
Lipperheide 1876

Fragonard, Théophile
(illus.) Mazuy, A. Types et caractères anciens

Les **Français;** costumes des principales provinces de la France, d'après nature par Gavarni, H. Emy, Pauquet, Ferogio, R. Pelez, Loubon, P. Saint-Germain, etc. Lith. par A. Coindre. Paris, L. Curmer 1842
16 l. 32pl. Q.
Copies of the plates, reduced in size, are in *Les Français peints par eux-mêmes*
Colas 1100. Lipperheide 1200

Les **Français** peints par eux-mêmes; encyclopédie morale du dix-neuvième siècle. Paris, L. Curmer 1841-50
9v. illus. plates, port. col.map. Q.
Originally issued in parts (fascicules) 1839-42. Vol. 3 has t.-p. without the subtitle, as originally printed for the first 3 vols
Text by Achard, Balzac, Janin, Karr, Nodier, Soulié, and many others. Illustrations (408 plates, 1,000 illustrations, in the text) by Gavarni, Grandville, Johannot, Meissonnier, and others. The first 5 vols. deal with general types. The next 3 [6-8] contain provincial and colonial types and have title: *Les Français peints par eux-mêmes; encyclopédie morale du dix-neuvième siècle. Province.*
The ninth volume, issued free to subscribers, and frequently wanting in sets, has title: *Le Prisme; encyclopédie morale du dix-neuvième siècle.* It is included in the index at the end of the eighth volume.
For detailed bibliographical description see Vicaire, *Manuel de l'amateur de livres du* XIX *siècle* t. 3, 1897, col. 793-804
Lipperheide 1168-1169, 1199. Colas 1101. LC 15-22215

See also Pictures of the French

Les **Français** sous la révolution. Challamel, Augustin, and Ténint, Wilhelm

Les **Français** sous Louis XIV et Louis XV. Audebrand, Philibert; Beauvoir, Roger de, and La Bédollière, E. G. de

La **Française** du siècle; la femme et la mode. Uzanne, L. O.

La **Française** du siècle, modes, moeurs, usages. See note under Uzanne, L. O. La Française du siècle

France. Armée. Infanterie. Légion étrangère
Livre d'or de la Légion étrangère, 1831-1931. Paris, [Frazier-Soye] 1931
367p. 60pl.(22 col.) Q.
At head of title: Centenaire de la Légion étrangère. Bibliography p357-63
Colas 575

France. Laws, statutes, etc.
Ordonnance du Roi, pour régler l'exercice de ses troupes d'infanterie; du 1. juin 1776. Paris, Imprimerie royale 1776
223p. 17pl. Q.
Lipperheide 2299

France. Ministère de la guerre
Collection des uniformes de l'armée française. See entry under Mallet, and Lameau

Description des effets d'habillement, de coiffure, de grand et de petit équipement, de petite monture, de pansage et

France. Ministère de la guerre—*Continued*
objets divers à l'usage des corps de troupe. 15 mars 1879. Paris, Impr. J. Dumaine 1879
599p. incl. tables. 125(i.e. 136)pl.(part col.) on 55 l. F.
Colas 838. LC 20-16309

Historiques des corps de troupe de l'armée française (1569-1900) Paris, Berger-Levrault 1900
xxxvii,782p. front. illus. 34pl. Q.
Colas 1454. Lipperheide 2356. LC 32-35665

Règlement concernant les uniformes des généraux et officiers des etats-majors des armées de la République française. Paris, Imprimerie de Ballard [1798]
16p. 12pl. Q.
Plates are engraved by Godefroy from designs by Challiot. They show decorations, badges used on uniforms and the equipment of the period
Colas 2516-18. Lipperheide 2304e

Règlement sur l'uniforme des généraux, des officiers des états-majors des armées et des places, des officiers du corps du génie [etc.] Paris, 1803
2v. 13pl. Q.
Colas 2517

Tracé descriptif des divers objets d'habillement. See entry under Hecquet, F.

Les uniformes de l'armée française; terre, mer, air. See entry under Bucquoy, E. L.

France. Ministère de la maison de l'empéreur et des beaux-arts
Ninive et l'Assyrie. See entry under Place, Victor

France. Ministère de la marine
Décret relatif à l'uniforme des officiers et fonctionnaires des différents corps de la marine, corps de troupe exceptés. 3 juin 1891, suivi d'un arrêté ministériel 6 juin 1891. Paris, Impr. et librarie militaires de L. Baudoin 1891
Cover-title, 72,[2]p. 66pl. O.
LC 8-16976

France
Album du progrès; costumes historiques, artistiques et travestis. ca1872

Autour de la table; album de l'histoire des modes françaises: Johannot, Valentin, Janet-Lange, Forest, Cham, Fragonard, etc. 100 dessins. 1851

Bassaget, P. N. Costumes civils et militaires depuis le ve siècle, origine de la monarchie française, jusqu'à nos jours .... Civil and military costume from the vth century, beginning of the French monarchy, till our days. 1833-35

Blum, André. Histoire du costume en France 1924

Carlier, Alfred. Histoire du costume civil (de 80 avant J.-C. à 1930 après J.-C.) en France. 1931

Callamel, Augustin. Histoire de la mode en France. 1881

Challamel, Augustin. History of fashion in France. 1882

Challamel, J. B. M. A. La France et les Français à travers les siècles. 1881

Compte-Calix, F. C. Costumes historiques français. 1864

Costumes civils français et hollandais de diverses époques. 1790?

Costumes coloriés des Parisiens à toutes les époques. 1879-1881

Costumes français depuis Clovis jusqu'à nos jours. 1836-39

Debay, Auguste. Hygiène vestimentaire; les modes et les parures chez les Français depuis l'établissement de la monarchie jusqu'à nos jours, précédé d'un curieux parallèle des modes chez les anciennes dames grecques et romaines. 1857

Deblay, A. Histoire anecdotique du costume en France de la conquête romaine à nos jours. 1924

Desrais, C. L. Suites des nouvelles modes françoises depuis 1778 jusqu'à ce jour. 1785

Dielmann. Les modes depuis 1515 jusqu'à 1834. ca1834

Doré, Gustave. Folies gauloises depuis les Romains jusqu'à nos jours. 1859

Doré, Gustave. Historical cartoons. 1865

Fels, Florent. Die altfranzösischen bildteppiche. 1923?

Franklin, A. L. A. La civilité, l'étiquette, la mode, le bon ton, du XIIIe au XIXe siècle. 1908

Franklin, A. L. A. La vie privée d'autrefois; arts et métiers, modes, moeurs, ages des Parisiens du XII. au XVIII. siècles d'après des documents originaux ou inédits. 1887-1902. [v15]

Fréchon, Henri. Traité théorique et pratique de travaux à l'aiguille. 1913

Giafferri, P. L. V. de, marquis. L'histoire du costume féminin français de l'an 1037 à l'an 1870. 1922-23

Giafferri, P. L. V. de, marquis. Histoire du costume masculin français de l'an 420 à l'an 1870. 1927

Giafferri, P. L. V. de, marquis. The history of French masculine costume. 1927

Gourdon de Genouillac, Henri. Paris à travers les siècles. 1879-82

Herbé, C. A. Costumes français civils, militaires et religieux ... depuis les Gaulois jusqu'en 1834. 1835-37

Iconographie françoise, ou Portraits des personnages les plus illustres qui ont paru en France depuis François premier, (et quelques années avant) jusqu'à la fin du régne de Louis XVI. 1828-40

Koenig, Marie. Poupées et légendes de France. 1900?

La Bédollière, É. G. de. Histoire de la mode en France. 1858

Laborde, Alexandre de, comte, Versailles ancien et moderne. 1839

Lacauchie, A. Costumes historiques. 1846?

Lacroix, Paul. Costumes historiques de la France. 1852

France—*Continued*

Lacroix Paul. Histoire de la vie privée des Français depuis les temps les plus reculés jusqu'à nos jours, comprenant l'histoire des moeurs, usages et costumes de la nation française. 1852

Lacroix, Paul. Recueil curieux de pièces originales rares ou inédites, en prose et en vers, sur le costume et les révolutions de la mode en France. 1852

Lanté, L. M. Costumes des femmes françaises du xiie au xviiie siècle. 1900

Lanté, L. M. Galerie française de femmes célèbres par leurs talens, leur rang ou leur beauté. 1827

Lavisse, Ernest, ed. Histoire de France contemporaine depuis la révolution jusqu'à la paix de 1919

Lavisse, Ernest, ed. Histoire de France depuis les origines jusqu'à la révolution. 1900-11

Lecomte, Hippolyte. Costumes civile et militaires de la monarchie française depuis 1200 jusqu'à 1820. 1820

Le Comte, Hippolyte. Costumes français, de 1200 à 1715. ca1830

Lenoir, Alexandre. Monumens des arts libéraux, mécaniques et industriels de la France, depuis les Gaulois jusqu'au règne de François i^{er}. 1840

Le Roux de Lincy, A. J. V., and Leynadier, Camille. Les femmes célèbres de l'ancienne France. 1858

Lyons. Bibliothèque municipale. Les gravures de mode à la Bibliothèque de la ville de Lyon. 1928

Maigron, Louis. Le romantisme et la mode. 1911

Malliot, Joseph, and Martin, P. Recherches sur les costumes, les usages religieux, civils et militaires des anciens peuples d'après les auteurs célèbres, et les monuments antiques. 1804

Malet, Albert. Nouvelle histoire de France. 1922

Mennechet, Édouard, ed. Le Plutarque français; vies des hommes et femmes illustres de la France. 1835?-41?

Millin, A. L. Antiquités nationales, ou Recueil de monumens pour servir à l'histoire générale et particulière de l'empire françois, tels que tombeaux, inscriptions, statues, vitraux, fresques, etc. 1790-99

La mode féminine de 1490 à 1920. 1926

Die moden der alten und neuern zeit seit dem verfall der Griechen und Römer. 1869-70

Modes françaises: leur origine et leurs variations jusqu'à nos jours. 1822

Molé, G. F. R. Essais historiques sur les modes et sur le costume en France. 1776

Molé, G. F. R. Histoire des modes françaises, ou révolutions du costume en France, depuis l'établissement de la monarchie jusqu'à nos jours. 1773

Montaillé. Le costume féminin, depuis l'époque gauloise jusqu'à nos jours; tome 1. Allant jusqu'à la fin du règne de Louis xvi. 1894

Paris. Bibliothèque nationale. Département des manuscrits. Album de portraits d'après les collections du Département des manuscrits. 1910

Paris. Exposition universelle, 1900. Musée rétrospectif des classes 85 et 86; le costume et ses accessoires. 1900?

Paris. Musée des monumens français. Musée royal des monumens français, ou Mémorial de l'histoire de France et des ses monumens. 1815

Pauquet, H. L. E., and Pauquet, P. J. C. The book of historical costumes, drawn from specimens and the most authentic documents of each period. 1868

Pauquet, H. L. É., and Pauquet, P. J. C. Modes et costumes historiques. 1864?

Pictures of the French: a series of literary and graphic delineations of French character. 1840

Piton, Camille. Le costume civil en France, du xiiie au xixe siècle. 1895

Prod'homme, J. G. La toilette féminine à travers les ages. 1932-33

Propiac, C. J. F. G. de. Beautés historiques, chronologiques, politiques et critiques de la ville de Paris, depuis le commencement de la monarchie jusqu'au 1er novembre. 1822

Propiac, C. J. F. G. de. Petit tableau de Paris et des français aux principales époques de la monarchie ... avec une notice explicative des vêtemens, coiffures et armures des français depuis Pharamond jusqu'à ce jour. 1820

Quicherat, J. É. J. Histoire du costume en France depuis les temps les plus reculés jusqu'à la fin du xviiie siècle. 1875

Renan, Ary. Le costume en France. 1890

Robida, Albert. Mesdames nos aïeules; dix siècles d'élégances. 1894

Robida, Albert. Yester-year; ten centuries of toilette. 1891

Rodier, Paul. The romance of French weaving. 1931

Schéfer, Gaston. Documents pour l'histoire du costume de Louis xv à xviii. 1911

Sée, Raymonde. Le costume de la revolution à nos jours. 1929

Storia delle mode: Italia dagli Etruschi circa 800 anni avanti l'era Cristiana fino al secolo xviii; Francia dal secolo xv al 1854. 1854

Tableau historique des monumens, costumes et usages des Français, depuis les Gaulois jusqu'à nos jours. 1822

Teissier, Octave. Meubles et costumes (xvie, xviie, et xviiie siècles). 1904

Uzanne, L. O. Son altesse la femme. 1885

France—*Continued*

Viel-Castel, Horace, comte de. Collection des costumes, armes et meubles pour servir à l'histoire de France depuis le commencement du v. siècle jusqu'à nos jours. 1827-1845

Villiers, Henri de. Essais historiques sur les modes et la toilette française. 1824

Viollet-Le-Duc, E. E. Dictionnaire raisonné du mobilier français de l'époque carlovingienne à la renaissance. 1858-75

Willemin, N. X. Monuments français inédits pour servir à l'histoire des arts depuis le VIe siècle jusqu'au commencement du XVIIe. Choix de costumes civils et militaires, d'armes, armures. 1839

Witt, H. G., dame de. Les chroniqueurs de l'histoire de France depuis les origines jusqu'au XVIe siècle. 1883-95

See also subdivision France under: Arms and armor; Beggars; Ceremonial and festival costume; Children; Coronations and coronation robes; Court dress; Decorations of honor; Diplomatic costume; Ecclesiastical costume; Firemen; Headdress; Headdress, Military; Hunting costume; Kings and rulers; Lace; Legal costume; Military costume; Naval costume; Nobles; Officials; Orders of knighthood and chivalry; Rings; Theatrical costume; Uniforms, Civil; Watchmen; Workmen

Caricature and satire

Alexandre, Arsène. L'art du rire et de la caricature. 1892

Grand-Carteret, John. Les moeurs et la caricature en France. 1888

Jaime, E. Musée de la caricature ou recueil des caricatures les plus remarquables publiées en France depuis le quatorzième siècle jusqu'à nos jours. 1838

Early period to 987

Beaunier, F. and Rathier, L. Recueil des costumes français. 1810-13

Medieval period, to 1515

Bayeux tapisserie de la Reine Mathilde. n.d.

Beaunier, F. and Rathier, L. Recueil des costumes français. 1810-13

Beaurain, Georges. Le portail de l'église de Mimizan étudié dans ses rapports avec l'histoire du costume et du mobilier au moyen age. n.d.

Belloc, Hilaire. The book of the Bayeux tapestry. 1914

Bourrilly, Joseph. Le costume en Provence au moyen age. 1928

Bruce, J. C. The Bayeux tapestry elucidated. 1856

Davis, W. S. Life on a mediaeval barony. 1923

Enlart, Camille. Manuel d'archéologie française depuis les temps mérovingiens jusqu'à la renaissance. 1916

Entrée de la Reine Bérengère au Mans en 1204. 1865

Evans, Joan. Life in mediæval France. 1925

Ferrario, Giulio. Storia ed analisi degli antichi romanzi di cavalleria e dei poemi romanzeschi d'Italia. 1828

Fowke, F. R. The Bayeux tapestry; a history and description. 1898

Goddard, E. R. Women's costume in French texts of the eleventh and twelfth centuries. 1927

Mâle, Émile. L'art religieux de la fin du moyen âge en France; étude sur l'iconographie du moyen âge et sur ses sources d'inspiration. 1908

Miélot, Jean. Vie de Ste Catherine d'Alexandrie. 1881

Notice historique sur la tapisserie brodée par le reine Mathilde, épouse de Guillaume le Conquérant. 1804

Shaw, Henry. Dresses and decorations of the middle ages. 1843

Winter, Max. Kleidung und putz der frau nach den altfranzösischen chansons de geste. 1886

13th century

Lecoy de la Marche, Albert. Le treizième siècle artistique. 1892

Mâle, Émile. L'art religieux du XIIIe siècle en France. 1931

Mâle, Émile. Religious art in France, XIII century; a study in mediaeval iconography and its sources of inspiration. 1913

14th century

Barrois, J. Le livre du très chevalereux comte d'Artois et de sa femme, fille au comte de Boulogne. 1837

Langfors, Arthur. Deux témoignages inédits sur le costume des élégants au XIVe siècle. 1913

15th century

Bastard d'Estang, Auguste, comte de. Costumes de la cour de Bourgogne sous le règne de Philippe III dit le Bon, 1455-1460. 1881

Boutet de Monvel, L. M. Jeanne d'Arc. 1896

Boutet de Monvel, L. M. Joan of Arc. 1907

Croniques dites Martiniennes; written on vellum in A.D. 1458

Durrieu, Paul, comte. Le Boccace de Munich. 1909

Feyel, Paul. Jeanne d'Arc. 1925

Funck-Brentano, Frantz. Jeanne d'Arc. 1912

Harmand, Adrien. Jeanne d'Arc, ses costumes, son armure. 1929

Montorgueil. Georges. Louis XI. 1905

Morant, Georges de, comte. Le sang glorieux de Jeanne d'Arc. 1912

Müntz, Eugène. La renaissance en Italie et en France a l'époque de Charles VIII. 1885

René I, d'Anjou, king of Naples and Jerusalem. Oeuvres complètes du roi René. 1843-46

Wallon, H. A. Jeanne d'Arc. 1876

France—*Continued*

16th century

Alciati, Andrea. Les emblèmes. 1540

Clouet, Francois. Three hundred French portraits. 1875

Dimier, Louis. Histoire de la peinture de portrait en France au XVIe siècle. 1924-26

Estienne, Antoine. Remonstrance charitable aux dames et damoyselles de France sur leurs ornemens dissolus. 1867

Le grand calendrier, et compost des bergiers. 1579

Moreau-Nélaton, Étienne. Les Clouet et leurs émules. 1924

Müller, W. J. Sketches of the age of Francis I. 1841

Niel, P. G. J. Portraits des personnages français les plus illustres du XVIe siècle. 1848-56

Pilinski, Adam, ed. Cris de Paris au XVIe siècle. 1885

17th century

Blum, André. Abraham Bosse et la société française au dix-septième siècle c1924

Blum, André. Histoire du costume, les modes au XVIIe et au XVIIIe siècle. 1928

Blum, André. L'oeuvre gravé d'Abraham Bosse. 1924

Bonnart, Henri. Recueil d'estampes de costume du XVIIe siècle. ca1690

Bonnart, J. B. and Bonnart, R. Kostüme aus der zeit Ludwigs XIV. ca. 1700

Boullay, Benoît. Le tailleur sincère, contenant ce qu'il faut observer. 1671

Boullay, Benoît. Le tailleur sincere, contenant les moyens pour bien pratiquer toutes sortes de pieces d'ouvrage pour les habits d'hommes, & la quantité des estoffes qu'il y doit entrer en chaque espece. 1671

Brantôme, Pierre de Bourdeille, seigneur de. Memoires ... contenans les vies des hommes illustres & grands capitaines françois de son temps. 1666

Daret, Pierre. Tableaux historiques ou sont gravez les illustres Francois et estrangers ... remarquables par leur naissance et leur fortune, doctrine, pieté, charges et emplois. 1654

Dayot, A. P. M. Louis XIV. 1909

Genlis, S. F. D. de S. A., comtesse de. Dictionnaire critique et raisonné des étiquettes de la cour, des usages du monde. 1818

Lacroix, Paul. XVIIme siècle; institutions, usages et costumes, France 1590-1700. 1880

Lacroix, Paul. XVII siècle, lettres, sciences et arts, France 1590-1700. 1882

Leloir, Maurice. Histoire du costume de l'antiquité à 1914. 1934 35

Perrault, Charles. Les hommes illustres qui ont paru en France pendant ce siecle: avec leurs portraits au naturel. 1696-1700

Rabel, Daniel. Voici comment l'on s'accomode ... ca1630

Restout, Jean. Galerie françoise, ou Portraits des hommes et des femmes célèbres. 1771-72

Saint-Igny, Jean de. Diversitez d'habillemens à la mode; naifuement portraits, sur la differente condition de la noblesse, des magistrats, et du tiers estat. ca1630

Saint-Igny, Jean de. Le théâtre de France contenant la diversitez des habits selon les qualitez & conditions des personnes. 1629

Louis XIII, 1610-1643

Beaulieu, Michèle. Contribution à l'étude de la mode à Paris; les transformations du costume élégant sous la règne de Louis XIII (1610-1643). 1936

Valegio, Francisco. Costumes d'hommes et de femmes du temps de Louis XIII. ca1635

Louis XIV, 1643-1715

Audebrand, Philibert; Beauvoir, Roger de, and La Bédollière, E. G. de. Les Français sous Louis XIV et Louis XV. 185-?

Bourgeois, Émile. France under Louis XIV. 1897

Bourgeois, Émile. Le grand siècle; Louis XIV, les arts, les idées. 1896

Bourgeois, Émile. Ludwig XIV, des Sonnenkönig, oder, Das grosse jahrhundert Frankreichs. 1897

Le Clerc, Sébastien. Divers costumes français du règne de Louis XIV. ca1695

Le Clerc, Sébastien. Les figures à la mode. 1685

Perelle, Adam. A collection of engravings containing views ... by A. Perelle ... portraits, costumes ... by A. Dieu ... and others. 1685?

18th century

General works

Blum, André. Histoire du costume, les modes au XVIIe et au XVIIIe siècle. 1928

Boehn, Max von. Rokoko. 1923

Les costumes français répresentans les différens etats du royaume, avec les habillemens propres à chaque etat. 1776

Courrier de la mode, ou Journal du goût. 1768

Éloffe, Mme. Modes et usages au temps de Marie-Antoinette. 1885

Les fantaisies aimables ou les caprices des belles répresentés par les costumes les plus nouveaux. 1786

Freudenberger, Sigmund. Estampes de Freudeberg pour le Monument du costume. 1882

Freudenberger, Sigmund. Histoire des moeurs & du costume des Français dans le dix-huitième siècle. 1888

France—18th century—*Continued*

Freudenberger, Sigmund. Première suite d'estampes, pour servir à l'histoire des modes et du costhume en France, dans le xviii siecle. 1775

Freudenberger, Sigmund. Suites d'estampes pour servir à l'histoire des moeurs et du costume des Français dans le dix-huitième siècle. 1774

Gallerie des modes et costumes français dessinés d'après nature, gravés par les plus célèbres artistes en ce genre, et colorés avec le plus grand soin par Madame Le Beau. 1778-1788

Goncourt, E. L. A. H. de, and Goncourt, J. A. H. de. La femme au dix-huitième siècle. 1887

Grand-Carteret, John. Les élégances de la toilette: robes—chapeaux—coiffures de style, Louis xvi—directoire—empire—restauration (1780-1825). 1911

Guillaumot, A. F. Costumes du xviiie siècle, d'après les dessins de Watteau fils, etc. 187-?

Guillaumot, A. E. Costumes du xviiie siècle tirés des près Saint-Gervais. 1874

Hennezel, Henri d'. La mode féminine au xviiie siècle. 1924

Lacroix, Paul. xviiime siècle; institutions, usages et costumes, France 1700-1789. 1875

Lacroix, Paul. The xviiith century; its institutions, customs, and costumes, France, 1700-1789. 1876

Langlade, Émile. La marchande de modes de Marie-Antoinette, Rose Bertin. 1911

Langlade, Émile. Rose Bertin, the creator of fashion at the court of Marie-Antoinette. 1913

Lawrence, H. W., and Dighton, B. L. French line engravings of the late xviii century. 1910

Lesage, L. E. Paris au xixe siècle et la fin du xviiie; costumes, scènes et élégances parisiennes. 1907

Mariette, P. J. Costumes français. ca1730

Moreau, J. M. Monument du costume physique & moral de la fin du xviiie siecle. 1888

Moreau, J. M. Seconde suite d'estampes pour servir a l'histoire des modes et du costume en France, dans le dix-huitième siècle. Année 1776. 1777

Moreau, J. M., dit le jeune. Troisième suite d'estampes pour servir a l'histoire des moeurs et du costumes des François, dans le dix-huitième siècle. Année 1784. 1784

Moreau, J. M., dit le jeune, and Freudenberger, Sigmund. Trois suites d'estampes pour servir à l'histoire des modes et du costume des Français dans le 18. siècle. 1920

Naudet, T. C. Costumes du directoire et du consulat. ca1799

Picart, Bernard. Diverses modes dessinées d'après nature. ca1710

Recueil des différentes modes du temps. 1729

Renard, Jules. Costumes du xviiie siècle, d'après les dessins de m. Draner [pseud.] 1874

Restif de La Bretonne, N. E. Estampes de Moreau-le-jeune pour le Monument du costume. 1881

Restif de La Bretonne, N. E. Histoire des moeurs et du costume des Français dans le dix-huitième siècle. 1878

Restif de La Bretonne, N. E. Monument du costume physique & moral de la fin du xviiie siècle. 1876

Restif de La Bretonne, N. E. Monument du costume physique et moral de la fin du dix-huitième siècle. 1789

Restout, Jean. Galerie françoise, ou Portraits des hommes et des femmes célèbres. 1771-72

Saint-Aubin, Augustin de. Habillemens à la mode de Paris en l'année 1761. 1761?

Schéfer, Gaston. Moreau le jeune, 1741-1814. 1915

Sorrieu, Frédéric. Galerie des modes et costumes français. 1867

Uzanne, L. O. La Française du siècle; la femme et la mode. 1892

Uzanne, L. O. The Frenchwoman of the century [1792-1892] 1886

Watteau, J. A. Figures de modes. ca1720

Supplementary material

Alméras, Henri d'. La vie parisienne sous la révolution et le directoire. 1909

Alméras, Henri d'. La vie parisienne sous le consulat et l'empire. 1909

Audebrand, Philibert; Beauvoir, Roger de, and La Bédollière, E. G. de. Les Français sous Louis xiv et Louis xv. 185-?

Autrefois; ou, Le bon vieux temps, types français du dix-huitième siècle. 1842

Les belles marchandes; almanach historiques, proverbiale et chantant. 1783-84

Beytrag zur unterhaltung beim nachttische für frauenzimmer vom stande. 1782

Bocher, Emmanuel. Les grávures françaises du xviiie siècle. 1875-82

Der bouillotenleuchter; eine goldgrube der Pariser damen vom ton. 1800

Caillot, Antoine. Memoires pour servir a l'histoire des moeurs et usages des Français. 1827

Carmontelle, L. C. dit. Jardin de Monceau. 1779

Célébrités contemporaines. 1842

Claretie, Leo. Nos petites grand'mères: La jeune fille au xviii. siècle. 1901

Dunker, B. A. Tableau de Paris. 1787

Genlis, S. F. D. de S. A., comtesse de. Dictionnaire critique et raisonné des étiquettes de la cour, des usages du monde. 1818

Grand-Carteret, John. Les almanachs français: bibliographie—inconographie des almanachs. 1896

France—18th century—Supplementary works—*Continued*

Gurlitt, Cornelius. Das französische sittenbild des achtzehnten jahrhunderts im kupferstich. 1913

Harrisse, Henry. L.-L. Boilly ... 1761-1845. 1898

Iconographie des contemporains. 1832

Lacroix, Paul. XVIIIme siècle: lettres, sciences et arts, France 1700-1789. 1878

La Cuisse, de, 18th cent. Le répertoire des bals, ou Theorie-pratique des contredanses. 1762-65

Model, Julius, and Springer, Jaro. Der französische farbenstich des XVIII. jahrhunderts. 1912

Montgeron, L. B. C. de. La verité des miracles operés par l'intercession de m. de Paris, demontrée contre m. l'archevêque de Sens. 1739

Nouvion, Pierre de, and Liez, Émile. Un ministre des modes sous Louis XVI: Mademoiselle Bertin, marchande de modes de la reine (1747-1813). 1911

Octavien, François. Figures françoises nouvellement inventées. 1725

Paris. Bibliothèque nationale. Département des estampes. Un siècle d'histoire de France par l'estampes, 1700-1871. 1909-29

Restif de La Bretonne, N. E. Tableaux de la bonne compagnie. 1787-88

Restif de La Bretonne, N. E. Tableaux de la vie, ou Les moeurs du dix-huitième siècle. 1791

Rigaud, Jean. Recueil de cent vingt-une des plus belles vues de palais, chateaux et maisons royales de Paris et de ses environs. 1780

Saint-Aubin, Augustin de. C'est ici les différens jeux des petits polissons de Paris. 1766-70

Saint-Aubin, Augustin de. Types du dix-huitième siècle. ca1760

Tinney, John. A collection of eastern & other foreign dresses. ca1750

Watteau, J. A. A drawing book of figures. 1728

Watteau, J. A. Figures françoises et comiques. ca1720

Watteau, J. A. Gemälde und zeichnungen. 1886-89

Watteau, J. A. Pièces choisies. 1850

Caricature and satire

Modes-caricatures. 1794

Nouvelles étrennes curieuses des incroyables, merveilleuses, inconcevables, et des raisonnables de Paris. 1796

Criticism

Lettres critiques et morales sur les modes du tems. 1760

Louis XVI, 1774-1789

Almanach galant des costumes françois des plus à la mode. 1782

L'amour badin ou les ruses de Cupidon; dédiés a la jeunesse. 1788

Balzer, Johann. Neueste Pariser moden, bestehend aus 103 verschiedenen frisuren und frauenzimmer aufsätzen, wie auch 72 figuren, von verschiedenen kleidertrachten für kavaliers und damen. ca1780

Basset, Paris, pub. Modes d'hommes et de femmes de l'époque Louis XVI. n.d.

Collection d'habillements modernes et galants avec les habillements des princes et seigneurs. ca1775-81

Compte-Calix, F. C. Costumes de l'époque de Louis XVI. 1869

Elite des almanachs, les modes et conversation que tiennent les dames et les messieurs sur leurs nouveaux habillements. 1786?

Elite des almanachs ou les agrémens de la parure. 1785

Elite des almanachs ou les agrémens de la parure: conversation que tiennent les dames et les messieurs sur leurs nouveaux habillemens; avec chansons. 1787?

Etrennes chantantes, avec des couplets analogues aux modes parisiennes ... faisant suite à l'Almanach de toilette, et au Bijou. 1780

Nouveaux costumes, étrennes les plus utiles aux dames. 1781

Le prototype des ames sensibles, ou Les épargnes de la pudeur; almanach nouveau. 1789

La pythonisse de Lutèce, ou Les secrets découverts. 1789

Le quart d'heure des jolies Françaises. 1782

Suite de nouvelles modes françoises; avec les différentes grandeurs de boucles, chapeaux retapez à la Suisse, à la Corse; bourses longues, crapeaux, etc. 1776

Suite d'estampes, pour servir à l'histoire des modes, et du costume en France, dans le XVIIIe siècle. 1778

Union centrale des arts décoratifs, Paris. Le costume 190-

Periodical

Magasin des modes nouvelles, françaises et anglaise. 1785-89

1789-1799

Ah! que c'est drôle! ou le cabinet de modes; description des costumes nouveaux, entre-mêlée de vaudevilles et de facéties. An VI 1797-1798

Alba, André. La révolution française. 1924

Allinson, A. R. The days of the Directoire. 1910

Alméras, Henri d'. La vie parisienne pendant le siège et sous la commune. 1927

Bonneville, François, and Quénard, P. Portraits des personnages célèbres de la révolution. 1796-1802

Challamel, Augustin. Histoire-musée de la République française, depuis l'Assemblée des notables jusqu'à l'empire. 1857-58

Challamel, Augustin, and Ténint, Wilhelm. Les Français sous la révolution. 1843?

France—1789-1799—*Continued*

Collection complète des tableaux historiques de la révolution française. 1804

Compte-Calix, F. C. Les modes parisiennes sous le Directoire. 1872

Daragon, Henri. Les modes du Directoire et du Consulat. 1911

David. Costumes de la révolution française. n.d.

Dayot, A. P. M. La révolution française; constituante, législative, convention, directoire, d'après des peintures, sculptures, gravures, médailles, objets du temps. 1896

Directoire and first Empire dress. 1889

Fouquier, Marcel. Paris au XVIIIe siècle, ses divertissements, ses moeurs, directoire et consulat. 1925

Garcia, G. Les modes du Directoire et du Consulat. 1911

Goncourt, E. L. A. H. de, and Goncourt, J. A. H. de. Histoire de la société francaise pendant la révolution. 1889

Guillaumot, A. É. Costumes du Directoire, tirés des Merveilleuses, avec ... 30 eaux-fortes. 1875

Guillaumot, A. É. Costumes du temps de la révolution, 1790-1791-1792-1793. 1876

Guillaumot, A. É. Costumes of the time of the French revolution 1790-1793, together with English costumes during the years 1795-1806. 1889

Lacroix, Paul. Directoire, consulat et empire. 1884

Pflugk-Harttung. J. A. G. von, ed. Napoleon I.: Revolution und kaiserreich. 1900

Ponce, Nicolas. Apperçu sur les modes françaises. ca1795

Rouveyre, Édouard. Le directoire. 1880

Uzanne, L. O. Les modes de Paris, variations du goût et de l'esthétique de la femme, 1797-1897. 1898

Uzanne, L. O. Fashion in Paris; the various phases of feminine taste and aesthetics from 1797 to 1897. 1898

See also France—19th century—Consulate and empire, 1799-1815

Periodicals

L'Arlequin; journal de pièces et de morceaux. 1799

La Correspondance des dames, ou Journal des modes et spectacles de Paris. 1799-1800

Fashions of London & Paris; v 1 1798/1800-v3 1804/06. 1798-1806

Gazette des salons; journal des dames et des modes. 1797-1839

Journal de la mode et du goût. 1790-93

Tableau général du goût, des modes, et costumes de Paris. 1797-99

19th century

Barron, Louis. Paris pittoresque, 1800-1900. 1899

Blum, André. Histoire du costume; les modes au XIX. siècle. [c1931]

Boehn, Max von. Vom kaiserreich zur republik. 1917

Boehn, Max von. Vom kaiserreich zur republik. 1921

Boutet, Henri. Les modes féminines du XIXe siècle. 1902

Cabris. Le costume de la Parisienne au XIX. siècle. 1901

Cleemputte, P. A. van. Paris de 1800 à 1900: Les centennales parisiennes; panorama de la vie de Paris à travers le XIXe siècle. 1903

Cleemputte, P. A. van. La vie parisienne à travers le XIXe siècle. Paris de 1800 à 1900 d'après les estampes et les mémoires du temps. 1900-01

Cornil, Mme. Cent ans de modes françaises (1800-1900) ... Documents du XIX. siècle commentés et interprétés au goût du jour. c1932

Debucourt, P. L. Modes et manières du jour a Paris à la fin du 18e siècle et au commencement du 19e. 1798-1808

Les Français peints par eux-mêmes; encyclopédie morale du dix-neuvième siècle. 1841-50

Gazette du bon genre. Trente neuf aquarelles. 1930

Grand-Carteret, John. XIXe siecle (en France); classes—moeurs—usages—costumes—inventions. 1893

Grand-Carteret, John. Les élégances de la toilette: robes—chapeaux—coiffures de style, Louis XVI—directoire—empire—restauration (1780-1825). 1911

Gronow, R. H. The reminiscences and recollections of Captain Gronow. 1892

Harrisse, Henry. L.-L. Boilly ... 1761-1845. 1898

Hugo, Abel. France militaire. Histoire des armées françaises de terre et de mer de 1792 à 1837. 1838

Lacauchie, A. Costumes de femmes. 1853-54

Laincel-Vento, Alix, comtesse de. Les grandes dames d'aujourd'hui. 1886

Lesage, L. E. Paris au XIXe siècle et la fin du XVIIIe; costumes, scènes et élégances parisiennes. 1907

Lewis, George. A series of groups illustrating the physiognomy, manners, and character of the people of France and Germany. 1823

Maurin, Antoine. Iconographie française et étrangée. 1835-37

Paris. Bibliothèque nationale. Département des estampes. Un siècle d'histoire de France par l'estampes, 1700-1871. 1909-29

Peake, R. B. The characteristic costume of France. 1819-22

Robida, Albert. Le XIXe siècle. 1888

Schéfer, Gaston. Moreau le jeune, 1741-1814. 1915

Toilettes de nos grand'mères d'après les meilleurs journaux du temps: Le journal des dames et Le petit courrier des dames. 1860

France—19th century—*Continued*

Uzanne, L. O. Fashion in Paris; the various phases of feminine taste and aesthetics from 1797 to 1897. 1898
Uzanne, L. O. La française du siècle; la femme et la mode. 1892
Uzanne, L. O. The Frenchwoman of the century [1792-1892] 1886
Uzanne, L. O. Les modes de Paris variations du goût et de l'esthétique de la femme, 1797-1897. 1898
Worth, J. P. A century of fashion. 1928

Periodicals

Almanach des modes et de la parure. 1805
L'Aquarelle-mode; compositions, nouveautés. 1866?-76
Le Bon ton, journal des modes. 1834-74
Le Caprice; journal de la lingerie, revue des modes, des théâtres et des arts. 1836-54
Cendrillon. 1850-72
Le Conseiller des dames et des demoiselles; journal d'économie domestique et de travaux l'aiguille. 1847-63?
La Corbeille; journal des modes. 1840-55
L'Estafette des modes. 1836-53
La Fashion, guide-journal des gens du monde. 1839-52
Le Favori des dames. 1845-53
Le Follet, courrier des salons; journal des modes. 1829-75
Gazette des salons; journal des dames et des modes. 1797-1839
L'Illustrateur des dames et des demoiselles. 1861-74
Journal des dames. 1849-57
Journal des demoiselles. 1833-92
Journal des jeunes personnes. 1832-63?
Le Lion; journal des nouveautés et des modes d'hommes. 1842-53
Magazin des demoiselles. 1844-93
Le Magasin pittoresque. 1833+
La Mode artistique. 1869-99?
La Mode de Paris. 1859-82?
La Mode illustrée. 1860+
La Mode nouvelle. 1829-62
Les Modes parisiennes illustrées. 1843-68
Le Monde élégante; estafette des modes. 1856-82
Le Moniteur de la coiffure. 1858-91
Le Moniteur de la mode. 1843-1910
Le Moniteur des dames et des demoiselles. 1845-78
Musée des familles. 1833-91
L'Observateur des modes et Le Narcisse réunis. 1830-56
Le Paris élégant, journal de modes 1836-54
Petit courrier des dames. 1821-68
Psyché, journal des modes, littérature, théâtres et musique. 1834-54
Le Souvenir. 1849-66?
La Toilette de Paris. 1859-73?
La Vie parisienne. 1863+

See also Periodicals, under subdivisions of the 19th century, e.g. 1799-1815; 1815-1848

Periodicals—Bibliography

Grand-Carteret, John. Les almanachs français: bibliographie—inconographie des almanachs. 1896
Savigny de Moncorps, de. Les almanachs de modes de 1814 à 1830. 1897

Caricature and satire

Alexandre, Arsène. Honoré Daumier, l'homme et l'oeuvre. 1888
Balzac, Honoré de. Paris marié. 1846
Bassaget, P. N. Caricatures anti-cholériques. 1832
Bellot, R. P. Album du bon-bock. 1878
Bertall, C. A. d'A. La comédie de notre temps. 1874-75
Bertall, C. A. d'A. La vie hors de chez soi (comédie de notre temps). 1876
Bertall, C. A. d'A. La vigne, voyage autour des vins de France; étude physiologique, anecdotique, historique, humoristique et même scientifique. 1878
Bodin, B. Echo des casernes. 1822
Boilly, L. L. Les grimaces. ca1826
Bouchot, Frédéric. Ce que parler veut dire. 1840
Bouchot, Frédéric. Le chapitre des illusions. 1840
Bouchot, Frédéric. L'école des voyageurs. 1840
Bouchot, Frédéric. Les contraires. 1835
Boussenot, and Boudier. Les péchés actuels. ca1840
Caran d'Ache, E. P., known as. Caran d'Ache, the supreme. 1933
La caricature [morale, religieuse, littéraire et scénique]. 1830-35
Cary, E. L. Honoré Daumier. 1907
Charlet, N. T. Croquis lithographiques. 1824
Les Contretems. ca1830
Crémaillère chez Antenor Joly. 1837
Daumier, H V. Les baigneurs. 1840
Daumier, H. V. Les cent Robert Macaire. 1836-1838
Daumier, H. V. Cours d'histoire naturelle. 1840
Daumier, T. V. Locataires et proprietaires. ca1840
Dayot, A. P. M. Les maîtres de la caricature française au XIXe siècle. 1888
Demange. Les mésaventures. 1828
Doré, Gustave. Les différents publics de Paris. 1854
Doré, Gustave. Two hundred sketches, humorous and grotesque. 1867
Forain, J. L. Album Forain. 1896
Forain, J. L. La comédie parisienne. 1892
Gavarni, G. S. C. Oeuvres choisies de Gavarni. 1848
Gédéon. Les femmes de ménage. ca1860
Grandville, J. I. I. G., called. Un autre monde ... et autres choses. 1844

France—19th century—Caricature and satire —*Continued*

Grandville, J. I. I. G., called. Cent proverbes. 1845
Grandville, J. I. I. G., called. Le dimanche d'un bon bourgeois ou Les tribulations de la petite propriété. ca 1827
Grandville, J. I. I. G., called. Les métamorphoses du jour. 1830
Grandville, J. I. I. G., called. Petites misères de la vie humaine. 1843
Grandville, J. I. I. G., called. Scènes de la vie privée et publique des animaux; études des moeurs contemporaines. 1842
Grévin, Alfred. Les filles d'Ève. 1867
Grévin, Alfred. Le monde amusant. ca 1873
Grévin, Alfred, and Huart, Adrien. Les Parisiennes. 1879
Huart, Louis. Muséum parisien; histoire physiologique, pittoresque, philosophique et grotesque de toutes les bêtes curieuses de Paris et de la banlieue. 1841
Huart, Louis. Physiologie du tailleur. 1841
Isabey, J. B. Caricatures. 1818
Jossot. Mince de trognes!!! 1896
Lami, E. L. Tribulations des gens à équipages. 1827
La lanterne magique. ca1840
Marie, Aristide. Henry Monnier, 1799-1877. 1931
Moeurs du temps. ca1830
Monnier, Henri. Album Henri Monnier. 1843
Monnier, Henri. Les grisettes, leurs moeurs, leurs habitudes. 1827
Monnier, Henri. Moeurs administratives, dessinées d'après nature. 1828
Monnier, Henri. Rencontres parisiennes; Macédoine pittoresque. 1839-40
Monta. Bals bourgeois. 1854
Parades, 1791-1826. ca1826
Pigal, E. J.; Pajou, A. D., and Arago, Jacques. Proverbes et bons mots mis en action d'après les moeurs populaires. 1822-24
Randon, Gilbert. Messieurs nos fils & mesdemoiselles nos filles. ca1860
Randon, Gilbert. Les petites misères. 1860
Sarcus, C. M. de. Le conservatoire de la danse moderne; charges parisiennes. 1844-45
Scheffer, J. G. Ce qu'on dit et ce qu'on pense, petites scènes du monde. 1829
Vernier, Charles. Au quartier Latin. ca1860

Consulate and empire 1799-1815

Arnault, A. V. Vie politique et militaire de Napoléon. 1822-1826
Bosio, J. F. Cinq tableaux de costumes parisiens réunissant cent quarante-trois figures. 1804
Bouchot, H. F. X. M. Le luxe français: L'empire. 1892
Bouchot, H. F. X. M. La toilette à la cour de Napoléon, 1810-1815. 1895
Les costumes des dames parisiennes, ou l'Ami de la mode. 1803?
Costumes français; en nonante sept gravures, representant les modes des hommes et femmes au commencement du 19. siècle. 1799-1800?
Daragon, Henri. Les modes du Directoire et du Consulat. 1911
Les délices de la mode et du bon goût. 1805
Directoire and first Empire dress. 1889
Duplessi-Bertaux, Jean. Recueil de cent sujets de divers genres. 1814
L'elégance parisienne. ca1805
Eyriès, J. B. B. Costumes, moeurs et usages de tous les peuples: suite de gravures coloriées avec un texte explicatif. ca1815
Fouquier, Marcel. Paris au XVIIIe siècle, ses divertissements, ses moeurs, directoire et consulat. 1925
Garcia, G. Les modes du Directoire et du Consulat. 1911
Garde à vous; caricatures parisiennes. 1802-1815
Gazette du bon genre. Le bon genre. 1929
Gazette du bon genre. Observations sur les modes et les usages de Paris. 1817
Le goût du jour. ca1808
Kircheisen, F. M. Napoleon I.; ein lebensbild. 1927-29
Lacroix, Paul. Directoire, consulat et empire. 1884
Laurent de l'Ardèche, P. M. Histoire de l'Empereur Napoléon. 1840
Manners & customs of the French. 1893
Masson, Frederic. Livre du sacre de l'empereur Napoléon. 1908
Mode du jour. ca1815
Paris et ses modes. 1803
Percier, Charles, and Fontaine, P. F. L. Description des cérémonies et des fêtes qui ont eu lieu pour le mariage de S. M. l'empereur Napoléon avec S. A. I. Madame l'archiduchesse Marie-Louise d'Autriche. 1810
Pflugk-Harttung, J. A. G. von, ed. Napoleon I.: Das erwachen der völker. 1901
Pflugk-Harttung, J. A. G. von ed. Napoleon I.: Revolution und kaiserreich. 1900
Reichardt, J. F. Vertraute briefe aus Paris geschrieben in den jahren 1802 und 1803. 1804

Periodicals

Annuaire des modes de Paris. 1814
L'art du coëffeur. 1803-07
Fashions of London & Paris; v 1, 1798/1800-v3 1804/06. 1800-06

Restoration, 1815-1848

Adam, Victor. Un an de la vie de jeune homme. 1824

France—Restoration, 1815-1848—*Continued*

Album de la mode. Chronique du monde fashionable, ou choix de morceaux de littérature contemporaine. 1833

Almeras, Henri d'. La vie parisienne sous la republique de 1848. 1921?

Almeras, Henri d'. La vie parisienne sous le règne de Louis-Philippe. 1923

Balzac, Honoré de. Petites misères de la vie conjugale; illus. par Bertall. [1846]

Beaumont, C. E. de. Les jolies femmes de Paris. 1846

Bellangé, J. L. H. Croquis divers. 1828-1830

Boilly, L. L. Recueil de dessins lithographiques. 1822

Boilly, L. L. Recueil de sujets moraux. 1827

Bouchot, Frédéric. Les malheurs d'un amant heureux. ca1840

Bouchot, H. F. X. M. Le luxe français. [1893]

Bridgens, Richard. Sketches illustrative of the manners and costumes of France, Switzerland, and Italy. 1821

Briffault, E. V. Paris dans l'eau. 1844

Caillot, Antoine. Mémoires pour servir à l'histoire des moeurs et usages des Français. 1827

Célébrités contemporaines. 1842

Chalon, J. J. Twenty four subjects exhibiting the costume of Paris. 1822

Charlet, N. T. Album lithographique. 185-?

Charlet, N. T. Croquis à la manière noire dédiés à Béranger. 1840

Charlet, N. T. Croquis inédits de Charlet. 1846

Charlet, N. T. Vie civile, politique et militaire du caporal Valentin. 1842

Charlet, N. T., and Jaime. Scènes des mémorables journées des 27, 28, 29 juillet 1830. ca1831

Colin, Mme Anaïs. Bleuettes. 1844-45

Compte-Calix, F. C. Les douze mois. 1840

Compte-Calix, F. C. Portes et fenêtres. 1840

Compte-Calix, F. C. Proverbes en action. 1840

Costumes parisiens pendant les glorieuses journées des 27, 28 et 29 juillet 1830. 1830

David, Jules. Vice et virtu. Album moral. 1830

Dayot, A. P. M. Journées révolutionnaires: 1830, 1848, d'après des peintures, sculptures, dessins, lithographies, médailles, autographes, objets ... du temps. 1897

Delarue, Fortuné. Tableaux de Paris. 1827

Devéria, Achille. Alphabet varié. 1830

Devéria, Achille. Dix-huit heures de la journée d'une parisienne. ca1830

Devéria, Achille. Le goût nouveau. 18-?

Le diable à Paris. 1845-46

Finart, N. Les alliés à Paris en 1815, scènes de moeurs. 1815?

Le furet des salons. ca1840

Gatine, G. J., engr. Travestissemens. ca1825

Gavarni, G. S. C. Physionomie de la population de Paris. 1832

Gazette du bon genre. Le bon genre. 1929

Gazette du bon genre. Observations sur les modes et les usages de Paris. 1817

Gérard-Fontallard, Henri. Costumes patriotiques, ou Souvenirs des 27, 28, 29 Juillet 1830. 1830

La grande ville; nouveau tableau de Paris, comique, critique et philosophique. 1842-43

Grenier, François. Album lithographié. 1828

Grenier, François. XII sujets variés composés et dessinés sur pierre. 1826

Grenier, François. Le genre, études variées. 1884

Grévedon, P. L. H. Alphabet des dames ou, Recueil de vingt cinq portraits de fantaisie. 1833

Grévedon, P. L. H. Les attraits. 1839

Grévedon, P. L. H. Le miroir des dames. 1834

Grévedon, P. L. H. Les quatre éléments, portraits de femmes. 1833

Grévedon, P. L. H. Le vocabulaire des dames. 1833

Henry, Elisa. Le charme. ca1840

Iconographie des contemporains. 1832

Janin, J. G. Un hiver à Paris. 1846

Jazet, A. Mon village. ca1840

Langley, E. F. Romantic figures in pen and color. 1935

Lanté, L. M. Costumes parisiens; les ouvrières de Paris. ca1824

Legrand, Augustin. Candeur et bonté, ou Les quatre âges d'une femme. ca1820

Le Lys, chronique de la cour; modes, theâtres, littérature. 1830

Madou, J. B. Sujets composés et dessinés sur pierre. 1835

Mazeret, Constantin, and Perrot, A. M. Miroir des graces, dédié aux dames; ou Dictionnaire de parure et de toilette. ca1821

Les modes; almanach des dames pour 1832, première année. 1832

Les modes et les belles; almanach nouveau, rédigé par le Caprice. 1822

Modes françaises, ou Histoire pittoresque du costume en France depuis 1818. 1818-23

Mörner, Hjalmar. Scenes from Naples, Rome, and Paris. 1829

Paris et ses modes. 1821

Le petit magasin de modes. ca1826

Philipon, Charles. Le lavater des dames. Ladies lavater. ca1830

Philipon, Charles. Mascarade improvisée. ca1835

Philipon, Charles. Miroir des dames. ca1834

France—Restoration, 1815-1848—*Continued*
Pigal, E. J. Scènes de société. 1822
Pigal, E. J. Scènes populaires. 1822
Pigal, E. J. Moeurs parisiennes. ca1823
Pigal, E. J. Vie d'un gamin. 1825
A tour through Paris. 1822-24

Periodicals

L'Album, journal des arts, des modes et des théâtres. 1821-28
Almanach de la mode de Paris; tablettes du monde fashionable. 1834
Almanach des modes. 1814-22
L'Aspic, moniteur générale des modes, littérature, beaux-arts, théâtres. 1837-38
Aujourd'hui; journal des modes ridicules et d'annonces illustrées. 1838-41
L'Avenir, revue politique, littéraire et des modes. 1841-42
Le Boudoir; modes, théâtres, littérature, beaux-arts. 1843
Le Colifichet, indicateur des modes et nouveautés manufacturières. 1838-43
L'Empire de la mode. 1817
Gazette des salons, journal des modes et de la musique. 1835-37
L'Iris, album de l'élégance. 1832-34
Mercure des salons, revue française et étrangère; album des modes. 1830-31
Le Messager des salons, journal des modes et des nouveautés parisiennes. 1832-38
Miroir des modes parisiennes. ca1824
La Mode des demoiselles. 1845-48
Le Monde élégant; journal des modes. 1838-39
L'Observateur des modes. 1818-23
L'Oriflamme des modes. 1840-44
Le Papillon, journal des modes. 1842-48
Le Petit messager des modes et le Confident réunis. 1842-54
La Renaissance, journal du monde élégante. 1840-42
La Sylphide; littérature, beaux-arts, modes. 1839-54

Second republic and second empire (1848-1870)

Album 1861. Spécialités de La compagnie Lyonnaise. 1861
Alméras, Henri d'. La vie parisienne sous la restauration. 1910
Alméras, Henri d'. La vie parisienne sous le second empire. 1933
Beaumont, C. E. de. Nos jolies parisiennes. ca1860
Beaunier, André. Visages de femmes. 1913
Compte-Calix, F. C. Le musée des dames. 1851
Compte-Calix, F. C. Six tableaux. ca1865
Compte-Calix, F. C. Vie élégante de la société parisienne. ca1860
Comptes d'un budget parisien: Toilette et mobilier d'une élégante de 1869. 1870
Dayot, A. P. M. Le second empire (2 décembre 1851—4 septembre 1870) ca1900
Fleury, Maurice, comte, and Sonolet, Louis. La société du second empire, 1851-1870 d'après les mémoires contemporains et des documents nouveaux. 1917-1924?
Janet, G. Vie d'une Parisienne. ca1854
Loliée, F. A. Les femmes du second empire. 1906
Talin, H. M., and Damourette. Les lorettes. ca1855
Vernier, Charles. Travestissements parisiens. ca1850
Yves. Études contemporaines; types parisiens. 1850

Periodicals

L'Abeille impériale, littérature, poésie, beaux-arts, théâtres; messager des modes et de l'industrie. 1856-62
La Bonne compagnie, sporting and fashionable review. 1852-55
Le Coquet; journal de modes, spécial pour couturières. 1867-75?
Neue Pariser moden- und modell-zeitung für damen- und kinder-garderobe. 1860-70

Third republic, 1870-1899

Alq, Louise d', pseud. Almanach des modes de la saison, ou le véritable almanach de la mode et de la femme, 1871. 1871
Bertall, C. A. d'A. La comédie de notre temps. 1874-75
Bertall, C. A. d'A. The communists of Paris 1871. [1873]
Bertall, C. A. d'A. La vie hors de chez soi (comédie de notre temps). 1876
Bertall, C. A. d'A. La vigne, voyage autour des vins de France; étude physiologique, anecdotique, historique, humoristique et même scientifique. 1878
Bruant, Aristide. Dans la rue. 1889-95
Coffignon, A. Paris-vivant: Les coulisses de la mode. 1888
Dayot, A. P. M. L'invasion, le siège, la commune, 1870-1871, d'après des peintures, gravures ... objets du temps. n.d.
La France pittoresque, ou description par Départment de la France et de ses colonies. 1884-85
Goncourt, E. L. A. H. de; Daudet, Alphonse, and Zola, Émile. Les types de Paris. 1889
Goudeau, Émile. Tableaux de Paris. 1893
Grenier, François. Études et motifs d'après nature. ca1850
Grenier, François. Nouvelle collection variée de sujets de genre. ca1850
Léo. Travestissements parisiens. 1880?
Leroy, Louis. Les pensionnaires du Louvre. 1880
Louvel. Dernières créations parisiennes. 1884
Mariette, Pauline. L'art de la toilette; méthode nouvelle pour tailler, éxécuter ou diriger avec économie et élégance tous les vêtements de dames et d'enfants. 1866
Renard, Jules. Paris assiégé; scènes de la vie parisienne pendant le siège. ca1871

France—Third republic, 1870-1899—*Cont.*
Rosary, Eugène, pseud. Nos vêtements. 1881

Periodicals

Art et la mode; revue de l'élégance. 1881+
Conseiller des familles: littérature, travaux à l'aiguille, modes, etc. 1874-79
Le Costume au théâtre et à la ville. 1886-88
La Mode française. 1875-86?
La Mode nationale. 1885-1930
La Mode pratique; journal de la femme et de la maison. 1891+
La Mode universelle, journal illustré des dames. 1874-85
Les Modes de la saison. 1871-85?
Paris charmant artistique. 1877-84
Paris-illustré. 1883-90
Le Petit écho de la mode. 1879+
Revue de la mode: gazette de la famille. 1872-98
Le Salon de la mode. 1876-1900?
Vogue, incorporating Vanity fair. 1892+

20th century

Aghion, Janine. The essence of the mode of the day, Paris 1920. 1920?
Almanach des modes nouvelles de Paris pour 1911. 1911?
Bizet, René. La mode. 1925
Brainerd, Mrs E. H. In Vanity Fair. 1906
Esau, Hubert. Die benennung der wichtigeren bestandteile der modernen französischen tracht. 1902
Gazette du bon genre. Le bon genre; a selection of 100 plates of the famous Gazette du bon genre. 1922
Green, E. M. La mode et la coquetterie. 1912
Iribe, Paul. Les robes de Paul Poiret. 1908
Jean-Meyan, Maurice, and Socquet, Jean. Le dessus du panier. 1914
Jégoudez, Mme. La mode. 1926
Marsan, Eugène. Pour habiller Eliante ou Le nouveau secret des dames. 1927
Mich. Costumes inédits de Aine-Montaillé ... Dessins fantaisistes de Mich, hiver 1906. 1906?
Modes et manières d'aujourd'hui. 1912-23
Paris. Exposition internationale des arts décoratifs et industriels modernes, 1925. Rapport général. 1927
Paris. Exposition universelle, 1900. Les toilettes de la Collectivité de la couture. 1900
Porada, Käthe von. Mode in Paris. 1932
Puyo, C. Costumes d'atelier. 191-?
Riotor, Léon. Le mannequin. 1900
Roger-Milès, Léon. Les créatures de la mode. c1910

Periodicals

Adam; revue de l'homme. 1925+
Art et la mode; revue de l'élégance. 1881+
Art, goût, beauté; feuillets de l'élégance féminine. 1924-33
Chic et pratique. 1933-35
Costumes et manteaux. 1919+
Creations de manteaux. 1931?
Créations parisiennes. 1921+
Les élégances parisiennes; publication officielle des industries françaises de la mode. 1916-24
Élite. 1908+
Femina. 1901+
Femme chic. 1911+
Femme élégante à Paris; album spécial de haute mode pour tailleurs et couturières, costumes, manteaux, robes. 1907+
Figaro-modes, à la ville, au thèâtre, arts décoratifs. 1903-06
Gazette du bon genre. 1912-25
La Guirlande; album mensuel d'art et de littérature sous la direction littéraire de monsieur Jean Hermanovits, sous la direction artistique de monsieur Brunelleschi. 1919-20
Guirlande des mois. 1917-1921
Les Idées nouvelles de la mode. 1922-32
Iris; journal périodique. 1932+
Jardin des modes. 1920-35
Journal des dames et des modes. 1912-14
La mode chic. 1928+
La Mode nationale. 1885-1930
La Mode pratique; journal de la femme et de la maison. 1891+
Les Modes; revue mensuelle illustrée des arts decoratifs appliqués à la femme. 1901+
Modes & travaux féminins. 1919+
Le Moniteur de la mode. 1843-1910
Pages de mode. 1924-36
Perfection; album pratique de la mode. 1920+?
Le Petit écho de la mode. 1879+
Plaisirs de France; art, ameublement, jardins, mode, tourisme, mondanités. 1934+
Primerose. 1935+
Robes elegantes. 1933+
Style, combined with Paris fashion magazine. 1916+
Le Style parisien. 1915-16
Très parisien; la mode, le chic, l'élégance. 1920-36
La Vie parisienne. 1863+
Vogue, incorporating Vanity fair. 1892+
Voici la mode. 1933-36

BY REGION OR PROVINCE

Brun, Charles. Costumes des provinces françaises. 1932
Charpentier, H. D. Recueil des costumes de la Bretagne et des autres contrées de la France. 1829-1831
Dergny, Dieudonné. Usages, coutumes et croyances ou livre des choses curieuses. 1885-88
Duchartre, P. L., and Saulnier, René L'imagerie populaire. 1925
Les Français; costumes des principales provinces de la France. 1842
Gallois, Émile. Provinces françaises costumes décoratifs. 1937

France—By region or province—*Continued*
Gardilanne, Gratiane de, and Moffat, E. W. Les costumes régionaux de la France. 1929
Gauthier, Joseph. Costumes paysans. 1930
Grasset de Saint-Sauveur, Jacques. Costumes des provinces françaises au 18ème siècle. 1932
Keim, Aline. Les costumes du pays de France. 1929
Keim, Aline. The costumes of France. 1930
Las Cases, Philippe, vicomte de, ed. L'art rustique en France
Lespès, Leo. Les contes du jour de l'an pour 1852. 1852
Verdun, Paul. Les costumes originaux des provinces de France. 1897

See also Headdress—France—By region or province

Alsace-Lorraine

See Alsace; Lorraine

Auvergne

Bouillet, Jean Baptiste. Album auvergnat. 1853
Costume d'Auvergne. n.d.
Delorieux, F. N. Costumes auvergnats. ca1835
Michel, Adolphe. L'ancienne Auvergne et le Velay. 1843-51
Pourrat, Henri. Ceux d'Auvergne. 1928
Talbot, ed. Auvergne, Puy-de-Dôme. ca1865

Basses-Pyrenees

Devéria, Eugène. Costumes de la vallée d'Ossau. 1843-44

Béarn

See France—By region or province—Basse-Pyrénées

Bordeaux

Costumes of Bordeaux. ca1828
Galard, Gustave de. Album départemental ou Bordeaux et ses environs. 1829
Galard, Gustave de, and Claveau, Eugene. Fantaisies, localités bordelaises. 1827-1830
Galard, Gustave de, and Géraud, S. E. Recueil des divers costumes des habitans de Bordeaux et des environs. 1818-1819
La Torre, F. de. Costumes bordelais. 1828
Sewrin, Edmond. Costumes de femmes à Bordeaux. 1837

Brittany

Aubert, O. L. Les costumes bretons; leur histoire, leur evolution. 1936
Benoist, Félix. La Bretagne contemporaine. 1865
Benoist, Félix. Nantes et la Loire Inférieure. 1850
Bianchi de Médicis de Manville, prince. Anthologie de coiffes et types actuels du peuple breton appliquée à ses origines ethniques. 1925
Blackburn, Henry. Breton folk; an artistic tour in Brittany. 1880
Bouët, Alexandre. Breiz-Izel; ou, Vie des Bretons de l'Armorique. 1844
Chase, Mrs Lewis. Vagabond voyage through Brittany. 1915
Coste, Z. Keepsake-Breton; scènes familières. ca1850
Darjou, H. A. Costumes bretons. ca1860
Darjou, H. A. Costumes de la Bretagne. 1865
Deshays, Célestin. Costumes bretons. ca1840
Deshays, Célestin. Souvenirs de Bretagne. ca1840
Edwards, G. W. Brittany and the Bretons. 1910
Gauthier, Joseph. La Bretagne; sites, arts et coutumes; clichés originaux de Marius Gravot. 1928
Gostling, Mrs F. M. P. The Bretons at home. 1925
Lalaisse, Hippolyte. La Bretagne, scènes de moeurs, sujets pittoresques et traits caractéristiques de cette contrée. ca1840
Lalaisse, Hippolyte. Costumes et coiffes de Bretagne. 1932?
Lalaisse, Hippolyte, and Benoist, Felix. Gallerie armoricaine: costumes et vues pittoresques de la Bretagne. 1820?
Lalaisse, Hippolyte, and Ropartz, Sigismond. Scènes de la vie rurale en Bretagne. 1840
Mansfield, M. F. Rambles in Brittany. 1906
Martin, Eugène. Les Bretons, moeurs et coutumes. 1868
Menpes, Mortimer. Brittany. 1905
Perrin, O. S., and Mareschal, L. A. Galerie des moeurs, usages et costumes des Bretons de l'Armorique. 1808
Petitville, Mme de. Le costume des femmes en Bretagne. 1909
Picquenard, C. A. De l'évolution moderne du chupen et du jilet dans le costume masculin. 1904
Pitre-Chevalier, P. M. F. C., called. La Bretagne ancienne et moderne. 1844
Pitre-Chevalier, P. M. F. C., called. Bretagne et Vendée; histoire de la revolution française dans l'ouest. 184-?
Saint-Germain, Prosper. Costumes bretons. 1841
Société archéologique du Finistère. Catalogue du musée archéologique et du musée des anciens costumes bretons de la ville de Quimper. 1885
Souvenir de Bretagne: costumes de Cornouaille. n.d.
Souvestre, Émile. La Bretagne pittoresque, ou Choix de monuments, de costumes et de scènes de moeurs de la Bretagne. 1841
Théodore, L. Costumes du Finistère. 1848?

France—Brittany—*Continued*

Valerio, Théodore. Souvenirs de l'ouest de la France: costumes bretons. 1843-44

Valerio, Théodore. Le touriste ou souvenir de l'ouest de la France. 1843-44

Colonies

See French colonies

Dauphiné

Delaye, Edmond. Les anciens costumes des Alpes du Dauphiné. 1922

Gascony

See France—By region or province—Basses-Pyrénées

Languedoc

Michel, Adolphe. L'ancienne Auvergne et le Velay. 1843-51

Lorraine

Save, Gaston. Le costume rustique vosgien. 1888

Lyonnais

Roux, Claudius, and Brunel, Noré. La vie galante à Lyon au bon vieux temps, histoire anecdotique et illustrée des moeurs intimes lyonnaises à toutes les époques. 1928

Vial, Eugène. Costumes lyonnais du XIVe au XXe siècle. 1935

Nice

Barberi. Costumes de la ville de Nice, maritime. 1831

Delbecchi, Amedée. Nice; vues et costumes. 1865

Lattre, A. de. Costumes de Nice. 1849-68

Normandy

Benoist, Félix. La Normandie illustrée; monuments, sites et costumes de la Seine-Inférieure, de l'Eure, de Calvados, de l'Orne et de la Manche; dessinés par F. Benoist. 1852-55

Chauvet, Stéphen. La Normandie ancestrale; ethnologie, vie, coutumes, meubles, ustensiles, costumes, patois. 1921

Costumes de la Basse-Normandie. 18—?

Langlois, E. H. Recueil de quelques vues de sites et monuments de France, spécialement de Normandie, et des divers costumes des habitans de cette province. 1817

Lanté, L. M. Costumes des femmes du pays de Caux, et de plusieurs autres parties de l'ancienne province de Normandie. 1827

Loritz. Dieppe. ca1830

Maurice, C. Costumes pittoresques. 1859

Mitton, G. E. Normandy. 1905

Mozin, Ch. Scènes de Normandie. 1828

Philippe, P. La Normandie en 1834; moeurs, usages, antiquités, costumes et statistique des cinq départemens composant cette ancienne province. 1834

See also Hairdressing—France—Normandy

Poitou

Drake, T. Album vendéen, illustration des histoires de la Vendée militaire. 1856-60

Farault, Alphonse. Ville de St-Maixent (Deux-Sèvres). Exposition rétrospective du mobilier et du costume poitevins, 20 septembre 1902: Catalogue des objets exposés. 1902

Gelin, Henri, and Escudier, Charles. Costumes poitevins. 1898

Gellé, P., and Arnaud, Ch. Vues et costumes pittoresques du départ des Deux-Sèvres. 1844

Pitre-Chevalier, P. M. F. C., called. Bretagne et Vendée; histoire de la revolution française dans l'ouest. 184-?

See also Hair-dressing—France—Poitou

Provence

Aurouze, J. Le costume en Provence, à propos de l'ouvrage ... de J. C. Roux. 1908

Flandreysy, J. M. de. La femme provençale. 1922

Roux, J. C. Bibliothèque régionaliste: Le costume en Provence. 1909

Roux, J. C. Souvenirs du passé: Le costume en Provence. 1907

Pyrenees

See Pyrenees

Roussillon

Vidal, J., pub. Collection des costumes du Roussillon dédiée à la ville de Perpignan. 1833-34

Savoy

Bégin, E. A. N. J. Voyage pittoresque en Suisse, en Savoie et sur les Alpes. 1852

Canziani, Estella. Costumes, moeurs et légendes de Savoie. 1920

Canziani, Estella. Costumes, traditions and songs of Savoy. 1911

Raverat, Achille, baron. Savoie; promenades historiques, pittoresques et artistiques en Maurienne, Tarentaise, Savoie-Propre, et Chautagne. 1872

Strasbourg

See Alsace—Strasbourg

Touraine

Macdonell, Anne. Touraine and its story. 1906

Vendée

See France—Poitou

Vosges

See Lumbermen

Paris

See Street venders—France—Paris

La **France** au Dahomey. Albeca, A. L. d'

La **France** en campagne. Rozat de Mandres, C. N. L.

La **France** et les Français à travers les siècles. Challamel, J. B. M. A.

France militaire. Hugo, Abel

La **France** militaire illustrée. Dally, Aristide

La **France,** ou costumes, moeurs et usages des Français. See Eyriès, J. B. B. Costumes, moeurs

La **France** pittoresque, ou description par département de la France et de ses colonies. Paris, La librairie illustrée 1884-85
2v. 95 col.illus. 101 maps. Q.
The illustrations are all costume figures
Lipperheide 1206

France to Scandinavia. Carpenter, F. G.

France under Louis XIV. Bourgeois, Émile

Franceschi, Domenico de
Serena opera nova di recami, nella quale si ritrova varie & diverse sorte di punti in stuora, & punti a filo, & medesimamenta di punto scritto & a fogliami, & punto in stuora a scacchetti, & alcuni groppi incordonati, & rosete. Venezia, F. Ongania 1879
1 l. 27pl. Q.
Facsimile of the edition published in Venice in 1564
Lipperheide 3892

Franceschini, Friedrich
Militairisches pracht-bilderbuch. Wien, M. Perles [1875-76]
1 l. 22 col.pl. ob.F.
Each plate shows seven to twelve uniforms. The last two are by F. V. Kuhn and show decorations and badges of rank
Published later with title *Die adjustierung der armee österreich-Ungarns mit berücksichtigung der bis zum monate märz 1877* (Wien, S. Czeiger [1877] 2 l. 22 col.pl. ob.F.) and also with a French title *L'équipement de l'armée Austro-Hongroise.* (Vienna, Haupt & Czeiger [1877])
Colas 1102-1104, 2057? Lipperheide 2244?

Franceschini, Girolamo
Caroussel zur anwesenheit J. J. K. K. majestäten in Prag den 5. juni 1854. Wien [1854]
3 l. col.front. 25 col.pl. F.
Lithographs by V. Katzler after drawings by G. Franceschini
This festival is in imitation of the tournament held in Grätz in 1572 in honor of the marriage of Duke Carl of Steiermark with Marie of Bavaria
Lipperheide 2637

Franceschini, Girolamo, and Hagemann, A.
Neueste adjustirung des Wiener bürger militärs ... lithographirt von Franceschini. Wien, auf der Wieden im Freihause 1842
24 col.pl. Q.
Colas 1105

Francisci, Erasmus
Leben und tapffere thaten der aller-berühmtesten see-helden admiralen und land-erfinder unserer zeiten angefangen mit Cristoforo Colombo ... und geendigt mit ... M. A. de Ruyter ... in niderteutscher sprache aufgesetzet durch V. D. B. Nürnberg, C. Endters seel. handlungs erben 1681
1090p. 32pl. Q.
Contains nine pictures of famous seamen
Lipperheide 543

Neu-polirter geschichte- kunst- und sitten spiegel ausländischer völcker, fürnemlich der Sineser, Japaner, Indostaner, Javaner ... und theils anderer nationen mehr. Nürnberg, J. A. Endters und W. Endters 1670
15 l. 1550p. 15 l. 51pl. F.
Most of the plates are engraved by C. N. Schurtz. They show Japanese costume
Lipperheide 476

[**Franciscus, de Retza**]
Defensorium immaculatae virginitatis. Leipzig, Insel-verlag 1925
10 l. about 50 col.illus. Q.
Facsimile reproduction of *Defensorium inviolatae perpetuaeque virginitatis Mariae* published 1470
Lipperheide 409 (1470 ed.)

Franck, Harry Alverson
The fringe of the Moslem world. New York & London, Century [1928]
xiv,426p. front. pl. port. O. $4
"Being the tale of a random journey by land from Cairo to Constantinople, with enough of present conditions to suggest the growing antagonistic attitude of the followers of Mohammed toward those who profess Christianity." Subtitle
Costume index. LC 28-21929

Glimpses of Japan and Formosa. New York & London, Century [c1924]
xi,235p. front. pl. O.
Costume index. LC 24-22806

Roving through southern China. New York & London, Century [c1925]
xxi,649p. incl.front. pl. fold.map. O. $5
Costume index. LC 25-19913

Wandering in northern China. New York & London, Century [c1923]
xx,502p. front. pl. fold.map. O. $5
Costume index. LC 23-16480

Franck, Sebastian
Teutscher nation chronic alt und neu vorbilde. Des gantzen teutschenn landes und völcker anfenglich herkomen, grentze und gelegenheit der reiche, fürstenthumb, bisthumb, stett und herschafften. Franckfurt, C. Egenolff 1539
15,402 l. 73 illus. F.
The 70 medallion portraits of Roman and German emperors included in this book were printed by Egenolff in 1533 under title *Epitome chronicorum mundi* and in 1534 under title *Chronicorum mundi epitome in singulos annos curiose degesta.* They are in part copies in reverse after Huttichius' *Imperatorum romanorum libellus.* In 1538 the first edition of the present work was published by Egenolff with title: *Germaniae chronicon; von des gantzen Teutschlands aller teutschen völcker herkomen* (332 l.)
Lipperheide 698

Franckfurther burger-lust im stück-schiessen, oder Ausführliche beschreibung was bey dem ... ertz-hertzog von Oesterreich ... Leopoldo zu ... ehren den 10. aug. 1716. gehaltenen stückschiessen. Franckfurth, F. W. Förstern [1716?]
68p. 3pl. Q.
Lipperheide 2217

Franco, Fr.
(engr.?) Cronica breve de i fatti illustri de' re di Francia

Franco, Giacomo
Habiti delle donne venetiane intagliate in rame nuovamente. Venedig 1610
20 l. 20pl. F.
Text in Latin and Italian
Colas 1106. Lipperheide 1322

Franco, Giacomo—*Continued*

Habiti delle donne venetiane intagliate in rame nuovamente. [Venetia, 1610. Venezia, F. Ongania, 1877]

1 p.l., 20 numb. l. front. (port.) 19pl. F.

Facsimile reproduction of the 1610 edition. The frontispiece is a portrait of Franco. A leaf has been added to accompany each plate with descriptive text in French, German and English

Colas 1107. Costume index. Lipperheide 1323. LC 10-4410

Habiti d'huomeni et donne venetiane con la processione della ser'ma signoria et altri particolari cioae trionfi feste et cerimonie publiche della noblissima città di Venetia. Frezzaria, G. Franco 1610

1 l. 25pl. F.

Plates show 34 figures of men and women in rich Venetian dress

This edition dedicated to Vincent de Gonzague de Mantoue. Another printing (Venetia, A. Turini [1610]) has on the dedication page "di Venetia, adi I. Zener 1610" and is described by Colas (no.1109)

A much later edition also is described by Lipperheide with 28pl., all from the earlier editions

A reprint is available (Venezia, F. Ongania 1878) It includes second part entitled *La città di Venetia con l'origine e governo di quella* which contains only views, no costume. It contains a half-title with title in French, German and English. French title given by Colas: *Costumes des gentilshommes et des dames nobles venitiennes*

Colas 1108. Lipperheide 1324-27

Nuova inventione; de diverse mostre cosi di punto in aere come de retticelli hoggi di usate per tutte le parte del mondo. Con merletti, mostrette da colari, e da manegheti et merli per cantoni de fazoletti. Venetia, G. Franco 1596

24pl. Q.

Facsimile reprint: *Raccolta di opere antiche sui disegni di merletti di Venezia* I. bis Venezia, F. Ongania 1876

Lipperheide 3904

(engr.) Caroso, M. F. Il ballarino

(engr.) Caroso, M. F. Nobiltà di dame; libro, altra volta, chiamato Il ballarino

Francq van Berkhey, Johannes de. See Chalon, Christina. Zinspelende gedigtjes

Francquart, Jacques

Pompa funebris ... Albertii Pii, archiducis Austriae. Bruxellae, apud J. Mommartium 1623

12 l. 64pl. F.

Plates engraved by C. Galle

Lipperheide 2660

Frangipani, Alexander Julius Torquatus A. See Torquatus à Frangipani, A. J.

Frank Leslie's ladies' gazette of fashion and fancy needle work. v. 1-7; Jan. 1854-1857. New-York, F. Leslie

7v. illus. col.pl. F.

Published monthly

LC 5-23325

Frank Leslie's modenwelt; illustrirte zeitung für toilette und handarbeiten. bd. 1; 16. nov. 1870-28, okt. 1871. New York, F. Leslie

336p. illus. pl. F.

Published weekly, Nov. 16, 1870-Feb. 1, 1871; biweekly, Feb. 1-Oct. 28, 1871

No more published

LC 11-24774

Frankfort on Main. See Germany—Prussia—Frankfort on Main

Frankfort-on-Main. Internationale puppenausstellung, 1911

Offizieller führer. Frankfurt am Main, Englert & Schlosser 1911

55p. illus.

"Veranst. v. Frankfurter frauenclub E. V. mit beitr. v. Rich. Dehmel, Hanns Heinz Ewers, Fritz Hoeber, Elisabeth Mentzel, Julia Virginia." Subtitle

Frankfurt university. See Academic costume—Viadrina university

Franklin, Alfred Louis Auguste

... La civilité, l'étiquette, la mode, le bon ton, du XIIIe au XIXe siècle. Paris, Émile-Paul 1908

2v. 325,71p.) O.

At head of title: Alfred Franklin

Bibliographical foot-notes

LC 26-2957

La vie privée d'autrefois; arts et métiers, modes, mœurs, usages des Parisiens du XIIe au XVIIIe siècle d'après des documents originaux ou inédits. [sér. 1-2] Paris, E. Plon, Nourrit et c^{ie}, 1887-1902

27v. illus. plates, ports. plans, facsims. D.

Contents: Series I, [v 1] Les soins de toilette. La savoir-vivre. 1887; [v2] L'annonce et la réclame. Les cris de Paris. 1887; [v3] La cuisine. 1888; [v4] La mesure du temps. 1888; [v5] Comment on devenait patron. 1889; [v6] Les repas. 1889; [v7] L'hygiène. 1890; [v8] Variétés gastronomiques. 1891; [v9] Les médicaments 1891; [v 10] Écoles et collèges. 1892; [v 11] Les médecins. 1892; [v 12] Les chirurgiens. 1893; [v 13] Le café, le thé & le chocolat. 1893; [v 14] Variétés chirurgicales. 1894; [v 15-18] Les magasins de nouveautés: [15] Introduction. Le vêtement. 1894; [16] La ganterie et la parfumerie. La mercerie. La draperie. 1895; [17] Teinturerie et deuil. Chapellerie et modes. La bonneterie. 1896; [18] La lingerie. La cordonnerie. Les fourrures. Cannes et parapluies. 1898; [v 19-20] L'enfant. 1895-96: [19] La naissance. Le baptême; [20] La layette. La nourrice. La vie de famille. Les jouets et les jeux; [v21-22] Les animaux. 1897-99; [v23] Variétés parisiennes. 1901. Series II, [v 1] Nemeitz, J. C. La vie de Paris sous la régence. 1897 (Lipperheide 1152. LC 3-17833); [v2] La vie de Paris sous Louis XIV. 1898 (LC 5-21994); [v3] La vie de Paris sous Louis XV. 1899 (LC 5-21995); La vie de Paris sous Louis XVI. 1902

Colas 1111. Lipperheide 1101 (1101 v 15-17). LC 26-8914 (ser. 1)

Frankreich; das heere am ende neunzehnten jahrhunderts. Hepke, F. V. von

Frankreich; die flotte. Batsch, C. F., and Meuss, J. F.

Franks, Sir Augustus Wollaston

Franks bequest. See entry under British museum. Department of British and mediaeval antiquities

Frank's bequest; catalogue of the finger rings. British museum. Department of British and mediaeval antiquities

Frantzösische Elsass; oder newe beschreibung der Stadt-Strassburg. See entry under L'Alsace françoise.

Die **französich-niederländische** männertracht. Post, Paul

Das **französisch** kaiserl. militair, 1805. No place [1805]

49 col.pl. Q.

Binder's title

Legends of plates are in German with French translations. Most of them are signed: C. V. and C. M. or C. Müller

Lipperheide 2305

Die **französische** armee in ihrer gegenwärtigen uniformierung. Mit 18 tafeln in lithographischen farbendruck. 3. neubearb. aufl. Leipzig, M. Ruhl [1903]
56p. 18pl. (17 col.) on fold.sheet. D.
LC CA17-2457

Die **französische** armee in ihrer gegenwärtigen uniformirung dargestellt in 183 chromolithographischen abbildungen von offizieren und soldaten aller truppengattungen; 2. aufl. Leipzig, M. Ruhl 1891
26p. 17pl. O.
The first edition appeared in 1888
Colas 2600. Lipperheide 2351

Der **französische** farbenstich des XVIII. jahrhunderts. Model, Julius, and Springer, Jaro

Das **französische** sittenbild des achtzehnten jahrhunderts im kupferstich. Gurlitt, Cornelius

Fraser, Claud Lovat

Characters from Dickens. Drawn by Claud Lovat Fraser. London, T. C. & E. C. Jack [1924]
10,83p. illus. col.pl. Q. 25s
Foreword by Haldane MacFall

Frasnois, de

(illus.) Dupuy, J. R. Historique du 12e régiment de chasseurs de 1788 à 1891

Fraternal orders. See Freemasons; Maccabees, Knights of; Odd-fellows, Independent order of; Pythias, Knights of

Frauberger, Heinrich

Antike und frühmittelalterliche fussbekleidungen aus Achmim-Panopolis. Düsseldorf [1896]
48p. 97 illus. 25 col.pl. Q.
Colas 1112. Lipperheide 267

Die geschichte des fächers. Leipzig, K. Scholtze 1878
122p. 72 illus. O.
Lipperheide 1723

Die **frauen** des Orients. Schweiger-Lerchenfeld, Amand, freiherr von

Frauen reich; deutsche hausfrauen-zeitung; begrundet von Lina Morgenstern. 1.-37. jahrg. 1874-1910. Berlin
37v. illus. Q.
Published weekly
Title change: 1874-1898, v 1-25, *Deutsche hausfrauen-zeitung*. Subtitle varies
Editors: 1874-76 Frau Lina Morgenstern and Frau Maria Gubitz; 1877-1904 Lina Morgenstern; 1905-190? Paul Lorenz; 190?-1910 Cäcilie Meyer
Lipperheide 4742

Frauen-zeitung für hauswesen, weibliche arbeiten und moden. 1.-14 jahrg. 1852-1865. Stuttgart, Verlag der frauenzeitung
14v. illus. col.pl. patterns. O.-Q.
Published monthly. 1852-1860, published semi-monthly; 1861-1862, 48 numbers a year
Colas 1113. Lipperheide 4666

Das **frauencostüm.** Clasen-Schmid, Mathilde

Das **frauenkleid** in mode und malerei. Bruhn, Wolfgang

Die **frauenkleidung.** Reichel, Emil

Die **frauenkleidung.** Stratz, C. H.

Die **frauenkleidung.** Velde, T. H. van de

Die **frauenkleidung** vom standpunkte der hygiene. Kuhnow, Anna

Das **frauenleben** der erde. Schweiger-Lerchenfeld, Amand, freiherr von

Die **frauenreform-kleidung.** Pudor, Heinrich

Frauenschule; das A B C der schneiderskunst. Link, J. C. E.

Frazer, Sir James George

Adonis, Attis, Osiris; studies in the history of oriental religion. London, Macmillan; New York, Macmillan 1906
xvi,339p. O.
"These studies are an expansion of the corresponding sections in my book 'The golden bough', and they will form part of the third edition of that work." p v
Contains material on the psychology of dress
LC 7-15462

The golden bough; a study in magic and religion. 3d ed. ... [New York, The Macmillan company, 1935]
12v. front. O.
Half-title
LC 35-35398

Freaks. See Deformities

The **freaks** of fashion. See The corset and the crinoline

Fréchon, Henri

Traité théorique et pratique de travaux à l'aiguille; dans l'enseignement primaire supérieur et dans l'enseignement secondaire. Paris, Masson 1913
103p. illus. Q.
"Couture, lingerie, tricot, crochet, tapisserie, coupe, modes, précis d'histoire du costume, répondant aux derniers programmes du travail manuel." Subtitle

Fred, W., pseud. See Wechsler, Alfred

Frédéric, J. A.

(engr.) État général des troupes sur pied en 1760 et 1761

Frederich, Eduard

Gedenkblätter des festcarrousels welches zur vorfeier des allerhöchsten geburtsfestes ihrer majestät der königinn Maria am 13ten april 1853 im königlichen reithause zu Hannover statt fund. Gemalt v. E. Frederich. Farbendruck v. J. Giere. [Hannover 1854]
1 l. 5 col.pl. F.
Lipperheide 2612

Freedley, George. See Gilder, Rosamond, jt. auth.

Freemasons

Geheime unternehmungen der Freymaurer darinne ihr ursprung und fortgang, ihr aufdingen, loszsprechen, die dabey vorkommenden ceremonien enthalten sind, und alle bey ihnen gebräuchliche allegorien erklärt werden. 1787

Hammond, William. Masonic emblems & jewels. 1917

Lilley, M. C. & co., Columbus, O. Supplies for Royal arch chapters and councils of R. and S. masters. 1899

Mackey, A. G. An encyclopaedia of freemasonry and its kindred sciences. 1912

Freer, Adela M. Goodrich. See Goodrich-Freer, A. M.

Frege, Ludwig

Das dritte Brandenburgische reformationsjubiläum oder ausführliche beschreibung aller bei gelegenheit der

Frege, Ludwig—*Continued*
300 jährigen jubelfeier am 1., 2. und 3. november 1839 in Spandow, Berlin und mehreren andern städten der mark stattgefundenen festlichkeiten. Berlin, G. Gropius 1839
xii,176p. 3pl.(1 col.) O.
The colored plate shows four marshalls of the festival and two Protestant bishops
Lipperheide 2807

Die **freiheitskriege** in bildern. Mundt, Albert

Freimann, Jenny
Muster-album von kreuzstichmonogrammen. ⌊Berlin 1890⌋
1 l. 36 col.pl. Q.
Lipperheide 4189

Die **Freiwilligen-corps** Österreich's im jahre 1859. Wien, K. K. hof- und staatsdruckerei 1860
xxx,48p. 18 col.pl. Q.
Colas 1115. Lipperheide 2240

Freja; illustrerad Skandinavisk modetidning. See note under Die Modenwelt

Frémaux, Léon J.
New Orleans characters. ⌊New Orleans?⌋ Peychaud & Garcia 1876
1 l. 16 col.pl. F.

Fremde völker. Oberländer, Richard

Frémy, Arnould. See Grandville, J. I. I. G., called. Cent proverbes

French, Joseph Lewis
Christ in art. Boston, L. C. Page 1900
267p. front. 32pl. D. ⌊Art lovers' series⌋
Bibliography: p259-60
LC 99-5400

French characteristic costumes. See Peake, R. B. The characteristic costume of France

French colonies
Brossard, Charles. Colonies françaises. 1906

See also French Guiana; Indo-China; Madagascar; Senegal

French Guiana
Denis, Ferdinand. La Guyane, ou histoire, moeurs et costumes des habitants di cette partie de l'Amérique. 1823
Jacottet, Henri, and Leclerc, Max. Colonies françaises. 1888

French India. See India, French

French line engravings of the late XVIII century. Lawrence, H. W., and Dighton, B. L.

French pattern modelling for professionals. Reeve, A. J.

The **Frenchwoman** of the century. Uzanne, L. O.

Frenzel, Wilhelm
(illus.) Lange, Eduard. Das hoffest zu Ferrara

Freschot, Casimir
La nobilta' veneta, o' sia Tutte le famiglie patrizie con le figure de suoi scudi & arme; historia di D. Casimiro Freschot. 2. ed. rinovata, & accresciuta della nobiltà, ò sia famiglie nuovamente aggregate sino all'anno 1706. Con un discorso del blasone. Venetia, G. G Hertz 1707⌊-1722?⌋
12p.l. 448,31,18p. plates, coats of arms D.
"Published in 1682 under title : *Li preg della nobilta' veneta.* Appended: Famiglie venete nuovamente aggregate alla nobilta sino all' anno 1707 (31p.) Famiglie venete aggregate alla nobilta' dal 1707 sino all anno 1719 (18p.)"—Library of Congress
Twelve of the plates are copied from Balduino's *Imagini*
Colas 199. Lipperheide 1329. LC 24-19251

Fresken-cyklus des schlosses Runkelstein bei Bozen. Zingerle, I. V., edler von Summersberg

Fresnel, Henri Victor Dollin du. See Du Fresnel, H. V. D.

Freud, Michael,
Dass die blosse brüste. See Dass die blosse brüste

Freudeberg, Sigmund. See Freudenberger Sigmund

Freudenberger, Sigmund
Estampes de Freudeberg pour le Monument du costume; gravées par Dubouchet. Paris, L. Conquet 1883
xxix,24p. 12pl. O.
Contains a study of Freudenberger by Grand-Carteret
There is also an edition with the plates and portrait of Freudenberger in triple proof (Paris, L. Conquet 1885. 48pl. F.)
Colas 1128

Histoire des mœurs & du costume des Français dans le dix-huitième siècle Stuttgart, J. Scheible ⌊1888⌋
2p.l. iv p. 12pl. F.
Reproduction of plates from his *Suites d'estampes*
LC 3-6634

Premier cahier des différens habillements distinctifs de la ville de Berne; dessinés d'après nature par S. Freudenberg et gravés par G. Eichler. Berne 1785
6 col.pl. Q.
Colas 1117

Première suite d'estampes, pour servir à l'histoire des modes et du costhume en France, dans le XVIII siècle. Année 1775. Chez Mr., A. P. D. R. avec privilege du roi
12pl. D.
Reduced in size, and printed in reverse from the *Suite d'estampes*
Lipperheide 1125

Suites d'estampes pour servir à l'histoire des moeurs et du costume des Français dans le dix-huitième siècle. Année 1774. Paris, J. Barbou 1774
3p. 12 l. 12pl. F.
The same title and plates published also (Paris, Prault 1775) and in other editions
The series was completed by Jean Michel Moreau, see entries under his name, and the complete series was published with text by N. E. Restif de La Bretonne, with title *Monument du costume.* It is also reproduced in *French line engravings of the late XVIII century* by H. W. Lawrence and B. L. Dighton
Colas 1118. Lipperheide 1122

(illus.) Restif de La Bretonne, N. E Histoire des moeurs et du costume des Français dans le dix-huitième siècle

Freudenberger, Sigmund—*Continued*
(illus.) Restif de La Bretonne, N. E. Tableaux de la bonne compagnie

See also Moreau, J. M., dit le jeune, jt. auth.

Freund Heins erscheinungen in Holbein's manier. Dance of death

Frewer, Ellen Elizabeth
(tr.) Schweinfurth, G. A. The heart of Africa

Freya; illustrirte blätter für die gebildete welt. 1.-7. jahrg. 1861-1867. Stuttgart, Expedition
7v. illus. Q.
Published monthly
Subtitle varies: 1861, illustrirte blätter fur deutschlands frauen und jungfrauen; 1862-64, illustrirte familien blätter
Lipperheide 4691

Freycinet, Louis Claude Desaulses de
(ed.) Péron, François. Voyage de découvertes aux terres Australes

Freydal. Maximilian I, emperor of Germany

Freydorf, Rudolf von
Die geschichtlichen uniformen des jetzigen Bad. Leib-Grenadier. Régiments; illus. von Gustav Crecelius. Karlsruhe 1903
220p. 12 col.pl. Q.
Colas 1130. Lipperheide 2210e

Frich, Joachim
(illus.) Tønsberg, N. C., ed. Norske nationaldragter

Frickinger, Johann Michael
Nützliches, in lauter auserlesenen, wohlapprobirt- und meistentheils neu-inventirten mustern bestehendes, weber-bildbuch. Schwabach und Leipzig, J. J. Enderes 1740
4 l. 2 illus. 100pl. F.
Lipperheide 3730

Friderich, Jacob Andreas
[Costumes of Nuremberg] Augsbourg, J. Wolff ca1720
12pl. F.
Plates are signed by the artist and have legends in German, French and Italian
Colas 1131. Lipperheide 782

Friedel, Adam
The principal leaders in the Greek revolution ... drawn on stone by Bouvier. London, R. Martin 1827
25pl.(24 col.) F.
Plates are half length portraits of men and women with legends in English and French
Lipperheide 1446

Friedenthal, Albert
Das weib im leben der völker. 3. verm. und verb. aufl. Berlin-Grunewald, Verlagsanstalt für litteratur und kunst [1911]
2v. illus. col.pl. fold.tab. Q.
Feminine costume from all parts of the world, primitive and civilized
LC 12-4198

Friederich, Adolf
Der teppich aus dem kloster Drübeck. Wernigerode, B. Angerstein 1877
6p. illus. 23pl. ob.F.
A tapestry of 1529 showing Bible characters

Friederichs, Karl
Kleinere kunst und industrie im alterthum. Düsseldorf, J. Buddeus 1871
xii,521p. O.
Also published under title: *Berlins antike bildwerke*
The following sections are of costume interest: Toiletten- und schmuck-geräth (p18-134), Waffen (p218-49), Broncen (p377-510)
Lipperheide 167

Friedlaender, Julius, and Sallet, Alfred Friedrich Constantin von
Das Königliche münzkabinet. Geschichte und übersicht der sammlung nebst erklärender beschreibung der auf schautischen ausgelegten auswahl; 2. verm. aufl. Berlin, Weidmann 1877
336p. illus. xi pl. O.
First edition: Berlin, G. Schade 1873
A description of ancient coins with a selection of coins and medallions of the middle ages
Lipperheide 168 (1st ed.) LC 10-10764

Friedrich, Theodor Heinrich
Deutsche volkstracht, oder Geschichte der kleiderreformation in der residenzstadt flottleben; ein satyrisches gemälde. Berlin, Maurerschen buchhandlung 1815
60p. 2pl. D.
Colas 1132. Lipperheide 3486

Friedrichs II königs von Preussen. Armee montirungen sauber gemahlt wie selbige unter dessen regierung waren. Potsdam, C. C. Horvath 1789
1,4 l. 103 col.pl. O.
Colas 1485. Lipperheide 2152

Friends, Society of
Gummere, Mrs A. M. The Quaker; a study in costume. 1901

Fries, Ernest, and Nachtmann, Franz Xaver
Quadrilles parées et costumées exécutées à la cour de sa majesté le roi de Bavière le 3 février 1835 représentant les divers pays des quatre parties du monde, et les principaux personnages de Quentin Durward. Munich, I. M. Hermann 1835?
4 l. 36,14pl. F.
Water color drawings by J. Kurzinger
Colas 1133. Lipperheide 2568

Friese, Friedrich
Ceremoniel und privilegia derer trompeter und paucker. No place, ca1720
43p. 1 pl. O.
Lipperheide 1999

Historische nachricht von den merkwürdigen ceremonien der altenburgischen bauern, 1703; neudruck, mit einleitung und anmerkungen versehen. Schmölln, R. Bauer 1887
39p. 2pl. O.
First edition was published in Leipzig, Groschuffs buchladen, 1703 (60p. 1 pl.)
Lipperheide 2855-56

Der vornehmsten künstler und handwercker ceremonial-politica, in welcher nicht allein dasjenige was bey dem auffdingen, losssprechen und meister werden ... observiret worden, sondern auch diejenigen ... actus wie auch examina bey dem gesellen-machen ...

Friese, Friedrich—*Continued*
vorstellen und mit ... anmerckungen ... ausführen wollen; 1. theil. Leipzig, Groschuffs buchladen 1708
940p. 29pl. O.
A second part was not published. Plates show various hand workers of the early 16th century at their trades and in their societies
Lipperheide 1975

Friesische heimatkunst. Jessen, K. L.

The **fringe** of the Moslem world. Franck, H. A.

Frischlin, Jacob
Drey schöne und lustige bücher von der Hohen Zollerischen hochzeyt welcher gestalt ... herr Eytel Friderich, graffe zu Hohen Zollern ... seiner gnaden geliebten son, herrn Johann Georgen ... hochzeyt gehalten hab mit ... Fräwlin Francisca ... herrn Friderichs ... graffens zu Dhaum und Kürburg ... tochtern: Wie die gantze hochzeyt zu Hechingen den 11. octobris Anno 1598 gehalten worden. Augspurg, V. Schönigk 1599
251p. 26 illus. Q.
A Latin translation appeared at Lauingen in 1601
Lipperheide 2521

Frisia. Hamckem, Martin

Frisian islands
Haeberlin, Carl. Inselfriesische volkstrachten vom XVI. bis XVIII. jahrhundert. 1926
Haeberlin, Carl. Trauertrachten und trauergebräuche auf der insel Föhr. 1909
Haeberlin, Carl. Volkstrachten d. nordfriesischen inseln. 1909?
Jensen, Christian. Die nordfriesischen insel Sylt, Föhr, Amrum und die Halligen, vormals und jetzt. 1891
Jessen, K. L. Friesische heimatkunst. 1913

Fritsch, Gustav Theodor
Die eingeborenen Süd-Afrika's, ethnographisch und anatomisch beschrieben. Breslau, F. Hirt 1872
xxiv,528p. 77 illus.(incl. 8pl.) 20pl. map. tables. O. and atlas of 30pl. 60 ports. Q.
The second section of the text deals with clothing and weapons
Colas 1134. Lipperheide 1606. LC 8-14641

Fritsch, Theodor
(ed.) Basedow, J. B. Elementarwerk mit den kupfertafeln Chodowieckis u. a. kritische bearbeitung. 1909

Fritze, C. E.
(pub.) Svenska arméens och flottans nuvarande uniformer. Stockholm, C. E. Fritze ca1880
30 col.pl. Q.
Colas 2843

Frizzi, Arturo
Cinquanta maschere italiane illustrate nei loro costumi. Codogno, Cairo 1888
64p. illus. T.

Frobenius, Leo
The childhood of man; a popular account of the lives, customs and thoughts of the primitive races. Tr. by A. H. Keane. London, Seeley 1909
xviii p. 21-504p. front. illus. pl.(part double) O.
Chapter I Personal adornment; II Tattooing and III Tests of manhood, are interesting for costume
LC 9-2054
Die masken und geheimbünde Afrikas Halle, E. Karras 1898
278p. illus. col.pl. Q.
Das sterbende Afrika, v 1. München, O C. Recht 1923
Col.front. illus. 86pl.(22 col.) Q.
Illustrations show costume and tattooing of West African natives

Froehlich, Hugo B. See Snow, B. E., jt auth.

Fröhner, Wilhelm
Collection H. Hoffmann. Catalogue des objets d'art antiques. Paris 1886-1888
2v. 60 illus. 44pl.(2 col.) Q.
Lipperheide 175
La Colonne Trajane, d'après le surmoulage exécuté à Rome en 1861-1862, reproduite en phototypographie par Gustave Arosa. Paris, J. Rothschild 1872-74
5v. illus. 220pl. F.
In portfolio. Published in 120 parts. Plates in 4 volumes each with separate title-page
"Inscriptions relatives aux guerres daciques": p[27]-29. Bibliographical footnotes
Reproduction of the sculptures of Trajan's column in Rome, built to celebrate the wars against the Dacians 101-102 A.D.
LC 10-30230

Frölich, Franz
Die mode im alten Rom; vortrag, gehalten am 28. november 1883 zu Aarau Basel, B. Schwabe 1884
35p. O.
Colas 1135. Lipperheide 256

Frönsperger, Lienhart. See Fronsperger, Leonhard

Froissart, Jean
Les chroniques de J. Froissart. Édition abrégée avec texte rapproché du français moderne par Mme De Witt; née Guizot. Paris, Hachette 1881
840p. col.front. illus. 2 maps. 11 col.pl. Q.
Illustrations of this edition are reproductions of miniatures, coins, seals showing costume of the 14th century. Miniatures from the Froissart manuscripts are especially noteworthy
Lipperheide 399
Sir John Froissart's chronicles of England, France, Spain, and adjoining countries, from the latter part of the reign of Edward II. to the coronation of Henry IV ... translated by Thomas Johnes ... 2d ed. London, Longman 1805-06
12v. and atlas of plates. O.-Q.
Plates show costume of men and women civilian and military, of the fourteenth century. Other illustrated editions of Froissart also show dress of the period
LC 3-17190

From Bangkok to Bombay. Carpenter, F. G.

From Carpathian to Pindus. Stratilescu, Tereza

From everglade to cañon with the second dragoons. Rodenbough, T. F., comp.

From nudity to raiment. Hiler, Hilaire

From Tangier to Tripoli. Carpenter, F. G.

Fromm, F. L. v.
Würtembergischer militär-almanach; erster jahrgang. Ulm, Stettin 1825
xiv,341p. 8 col.pl. O.
Colas 1136. Lipperheide 2206

Frond, Victor
Brazil pittoresco. See entry under Ribeyrolles, Charles

Frontinus, Sextus Julius. See Vegetius Renatus, Flavius. Fl. Vegetii Renati viri illustris De re militari

Fronsperger, Leonhard
Fünff bücher. Voñ kriegss regiment und ordnung wie sich ein jeder kriegzman inn seinem ampt und beuelch halten soll und was zů anfang eines kriegs zůerwegen unnd zůbetrachten sey. Franckfurt am Mayn, D. Schöffel 1555
131 l. 20 illus. F.
A later edition was issued (Franckfurt, Zephelius 1558) An edition with 21 illustrations by Jost Amman was published (Feyerabend 1564)
Lipperheide 2048

Kriegszbuch. Franckfurt am Mayn, S. Feyerabend und S. Hüter 1565-73
3v. 601 illus. 21pl. F.
Illustrations are by Jost Amman. They give a realistic picture of military life and of the mercenary troops of the 16th century
Lipperheide 2049

Frost, Arthur Burdett
Sports and games in the open; pictured by A. B. Frost. New York and London, Harper & brothers 1899
6 numbered leaves. 53pl. port. F.
LC 99-4398

Frost, Frederick J. Tabor. See Arnold, Channing, jt. auth.

Frucht, Lotte, and Schneehagen, Christian
Unsere kleidung; anregungen zur neuen männer- und frauentracht. 2. aufl. Hamburg, A. Saal 1914
45p. 1 pl. O.

Früh-mittelalterliche leinenstickereien. Aldenkirchen, Joseph

Die **frühchristlichen** alterthümer aus dem gräberfelde von Achmin-Panopolis. Forrer, Robert

Der **frühere** japanische holzschnitt. Einstein, Carl

Die **frühesten** und seltensten denkmale. Schmidt, W.

Fuchs, Eduard
Illustrierte sittengeschichte vom mittelalter bis zur gegenwart. München, A. Langen [1909-12]
3v. in 6. illus.pl.(part col. part fold.) Q.
Useful in the study of undergarments
Contents: v 1 and Ergänzungsband: Renaissance. [1909] 2v. v2 and Ergänzungsband: Die galante zeit. [1910-11] 2v. v3 and Ergänzungsband: Das bürgliche zeitalter. [1912] 2v.
LC 12-33880

Die Juden in der karikatur. München, A. Langen [1921]
309p. 307 illus. 31pl.(part col., part double) facsims. Q.
LC 25-6738

Die karikatur der europäischen völker vom jahre 1848 bis zur gegenwart. Berlin, A. Hofmann [1903]
x,487p. 515 illus. 65pl.(part col.) Q.
Issued in 20 parts. Each part has cover-title: *Die karikatur der europäischen völker vom altertum bis zur neuzeit.* Neue folge, 1848-1900
Bibliography: p[485]
LC 4-6356

[Fuchslin]
[Costumes suisses] Paris, Dusacq ca1860
22 col.pl. Q.
Colas reports some of these plates exist with imprint: Paris, Wild. The plates are half-length portraits of women in the dress of the various cantons. They are lithographed by Schultz and Grenier, after Fuchslin, and printed by Lemercier
Colas 1136 bis

Führer durch das Königliche historische museum. Dresden. Historisches museum und gewehrgalerie

Führer durch das Museum für völkerkunde. Berlin. Staatliche museen. Museum für völkerkunde

Führer durch die rüstkammer der stadt Emden. Potier, Othmar, baron

Fülöp-Miller, René. See Gregor, Joseph, jt. auth.

Fünf bücher deutscher hausaltertümer. Heyne, Moritz

Fünf lebende bilder vor ... dem Könige und der Königin am 9ten September 1840 zur vorfeyer der huldigung von Preussens ständen dargestellt im dazu errichten festsaale. Bender, Ferdinand

Fünff bücher: Von kriegss regiment und ordnung. Fronsperger, Leonhard

XV bücher von dem feldbaw. Sebizius, Melchior

Fuentes, Manuel Atanasio
Lima; or, Sketches of the capital of Peru, historical, statistical, administrative, commercial and moral. London, Trübner 1866
ix,224p. illus. 43 col.pl. ports. Q.
Also published (Paris, Firmin-Didot)
A French edition also was published *Lima: esquisses historiques* (Paris, Firmin-Didot 1866)
Colas 1137-1139. Lipperheide 1636. LC 4-11987

Für frauen und töchter. Rötter, Henriette

Fürst, Paulus
Neues modelbuch von unterschiedlicher art der blumen und anderer genehten mödel nach itziger manier allen liebhaberinnen dieser kunst zumbesten vorgestellt. Nürnberg, P. Fürst 1666-89
4v. 188pl. Q.
A later edition was published at Nürnberg in 1728 by J. C. Weigel
Lipperheide 3920

Das **fürstentum** Albanien. Gopčević, Spiridion

Fürstliches Hessen-Holsteinisches ehrengedächtnuss. Darmbstadt 1665
89,131p. 5pl. F.
A memorial for the death of Maria Elisabeth of Hessen on June 17, 1665. Plates engraved by Christoph Metzger
Lipperheide 2603

Der **fürtreffich** griechisch geschicht-schreiber Herodianus. Herodianus

Füsslen, J. See Heyberger, G., jt. auth.

Füssli, Rudolf Heinrich
Les costumes suisses les plus origineaux et les plus intéressants dessinés d'après nature. Zurich, Keller & Fussli [1830]
10p. 30 col.pl. Q.
Colas 1142

Fugger, Johann Jacob
Spiegel der ehren des ... erzhauses Osterreich oder ausführliche geschicht schrift von desselben ... mit Käys. Rudolphi I geburts jahr 1212 anfahend und mit Käys. Maximiliani I todes jahr 1519 sich endend. Aus dem original ... durch Sigmund von Birken. Nürnberg, M. and J. F. Endter 1668
15 l. 1416p. 17 l. 200 illus. 10pl. F.
Illustrations include portraits, coats of arms, genealogical tables and scenes from the lives and wars of the Austrian emperors. Plates are engraved by P. Kilian and C. N. Schurtz
Lipperheide 855

Fugger, Marx
Von der gestüterey, das ist ein grundtliche beschreibung wie unnd wa man ein gestüt von guten edlen kriegsrossen auffrichten, underhalten, und wie man die jungen von einem jar zu dem andern erziehen soll ... gestellet und an tag geben. Franckfurt am Mayn, S. Feyrabend 1584
129 l. 39 illus. F.
First edition: 1578
Illustrations are after those in Jost Amman's *Kunstbüchlin*
Lipperheide 2900

Fuggerorum et Fuggerarum quae in familia natae, quaeve in familiam transierunt. Custos, Dominicus

Fuhrmann, Ernst
Mexiko. See entry under Danzel, T. W.

Fuku sen shiryo kenkyi kai, Tokio
Specimens of Japanese classical dresses, no. 1-2. [Tokio, Fuku sen shiryo kenkyi kai 1935]
Col.pl. F.
In portfolio. Accompanied by descriptive text in Japanese (6p.) Title from letterpress on guard sheet for each plate

Fulgenzi, Eugène
Collection de costumes civils et militaires, scènes populaires, portraits, et vues de l'Asie-Mineure. Smyrne, 1838
30 col.pl. Q.
Colas 1140

Fulleylove, John
(illus.) Davey, R. P. B. The pageant of London
(illus.) Kelman, John. The Holy Land

Fulop, Jean
Système théorique et pratique de la coupe des vêtements pour dames. Paris, A. Müller 1896
59p. illus. 41pl. sq.Q. 15fr.

Funck-Brentano, Frantz
Jeanne d'Arc. Paris, C. Boivin [1912]
83p. col.illus. sq.F. 50fr.
LC 13-1685

Fund af Egekister fra bronzealdern i Danmark. Boye, V. C.

Fundamentals of dress construction. Manning, Sibylla, and Donaldson, A. M.

Funebris memoria Mariae Amaliae ... rom. imperatricis, utriusque Bavariae ... ducis ... viduae, die 11. decembris 1756. Monachii, J. J. Vötter [1757]
78,29p. 23pl. F.
Plates engraved by F. X. Jungwirth after drawings by I. Schilling
Lipperheide 2565

Funérailles de S. A. R. Louise-Marie-Thérèse-Caroline-Isabelle, princesse d'Orléans, reine des Belges. Bruxelles J. Géruzet 1850
19p. 11pl.(1 col.) F.
Lipperheide 2679

[**Funeral** ceremonies for George II, Landgrave of Hesse, June 1661] Darmbstadii Typis C. Abelii [1662]
56,480,238p. 34pl. F.
Most of the plates show the funeral procession. They are engraved by Johann Schweizer and Adrian Haelwegh and are signed
Lipperheide 2600

Funeral customs. Puckle, B. S.

The **funeral** procession of King Edward VII The Illustrated London news

The **funeral** procession of Queen Elizabeth Camden, William

The **funeral** tent of an Egyptian queen Stuart, Villiers

Funerali antichi di diversi popoli, et nationi Porcacchi, Tommaso

Funerals
Perucci, Francesco. Pompe funebri di tutte le nationi del mondo. 1639
Porcacchi, Tommaso. Funerali antichi di diversi popoli, et nationi; forma, ordine et pompa di sepolture, di essequie, di consecrationi antiche et d'altro, descritti in dialogo. 1574
Puckle, B. S. Funeral customs; their origin and development. 1926

See also Mourning costume

Belgium

Funérailles de S. A. R. Louise-Marie-Thérèse-Caroline-Isabelle, princesse d'Orléans, reine des Belges. 1850

Egypt

Liturgy of funeral offerings. The liturgy of funerary offerings. 1909
Rougé, Emmanuel, vicomte de. Études sur le rituel funeraire des anciens Égyptiens. 1860

England

Camden, William. The funeral procession of Queen Elizabeth, from a drawing of the time. 1791
The Illustrated London news. The funeral procession of King Edward VII. 1910
The order and ceremonies used for the solemn interment of ... George late Duke of Albemarle ... in the year ... 1670. 1670

Germany

16th century

Graminaeus, Dietrich. Spiegel und abbildung der vergengligkeit. Darinnen was der toden recht und gebürnuss begriffen ... und wie ... Johan Wilhelm hertzog zu Gülich ... da ... hertzog Wilhelm am fünfften tag jannuarij, im jahr 1592 ... entschlaffen am zehenden tag martij in der collegiat kirchen zu Düsseldorff begraben und zur erden bestellen lassen. 1592

Funerals—Germany—16th century—*Cont.*

17th century

Cochius, Christianus. Davids des königs in Israel heilige fürbereitung zum tode ... betrachtet bey dem todes-fall des ... herrn Friderich Wilhelmen, marggraffen zu Brandenburg. ca1688

Fürstliches Hessen-Holsteinisches ehrengedächtnuss. 1665

Funeral ceremonies for George II. Landgrave of Hesse, June 1661. 1662

Gärtner, Georg. Ordnung Weyland desz ... herrn Joachim Ernsten marggrafen zu Brandenburg ... furstlicher leichbegängnusz ... anno 1625. 1625

Justa funebria serenissimo principi Ioanni Friderico Brunsvicensium et Luneburge-duci a revermo. et sermo. fratre Ernesto Augusto ... duci Brunsv: et Luneb: persoluta. 1685

Olearius, Adam. Die hoch fürstl: leichbegengnis des durchleuchtigsten furstẽ ... herrn Friederich erben zu Norwegen, hertzogẽ zu Sleszwig Holstein ... so gestorben den 10 aug 1659 beigesetzt den 30. janua 1661. 1661

Schnitzer, Lucas. Beschreibung und abrisz der fürstlichen leich procession ... desz ... herrn Christiani marggraffens zu Brandenburg ... den 11 septembris anno 1655, zu Bayreuth vorgangen. 1655?

18th century

Christ-königliches trauer- und ehren-gedächtnüs der Weyland ... Sophien Charlotten, königin in Preussen. 1705

Edelweckh, Johannes. Triumphus virtutum in funere Caroli VII ... anno ... MDCCXLV. 1745

Funebris memoria Mariae Amaliae ... rom. imperatricis, utriusque Bavariae ... ducis ... viduae, die 11. decembris 1756. 1757

Italy

17th century

Altoviti, Giovanni. Essequie della sacra cattolica, e real maesta di Margherita d'Austria, regina di Spagna; celebrate dal serenissimo don Cosimo II, Gran Duca di Toscana IIII. 1612

18th century

Barbiani, Francesco. Relazione del funerale celebrato nella Chiesa Metropolitana di Milano il giorno 8. febraro 1741 ... alla sacra reale cesarea, cata. maestà dell' imperadore Carlo VI. 1741?

Esequie della serenissima Elisabetta Carlotta d'Orleans duchessa vedova di Lorena fatte celebrare in Firenze. 1745

Exequias feitas em Roma a magestade fidelissima do senhor rey Dom Joaõ V. por ordem do fidelissimo senhor rey Dom Jozé I. seu filho, e successor. 1751

Ragguaglio delle solenni esequie fatte celebrare in Roma nella Basiñca di S. Clemente alla sacra real maestà di Federigo Augusto re di Polonia. 1733

Relazione delle solenni esequie celebrate nel duomo di Milano a sua maestà la reina di Sardigna, Polissena Giovanna Cristina. 1735

19th century

Memorie ed omaggi funebri per la morte dell' Arciduchessa Maria Beatrice Vittoria di Savoja ... duchessa di Modena. 1841

Macedonia

Müller, K. F. Der leichenwagen Alexanders des Grossen. 1905

Mexico

Pacheco, J. R. Description de la solemnidad fúnebre con que se honraron las cenizas del héroe de Iguala, don Agustin de Iturbide, en octubre de 1838. 1849

Netherlands

Alkemade, Cornelis van. Inleidinge tot het ceremonieel, en de plegtigheden der begraavenissen, en der wapenkunde. 1713

Cock, Hieronymus. Amplissimo hoc apparatu et pulchro ordine pompa funebris Bruxellis a palatio ad Divae Gudulae templum processit cum rex hispaniarum Philippus Carolo V. rom. imp. 1619

Francquart, Jacques. Pompa funebris ... Albertii Pii, archiducis Austriae. 1623

Russia

Cortège funèbre de feu Sa Majesté l'Empereur Alexandre Ier. n.d.

Scotland

Balfour, Sir James, bart. Ancient heraldic and antiquarian tracts. 1837

Spain

Relazione del funerale celebrato in Parma nelle chiesa conventuale della Beata Vergine della Steccata ... il giorno 28 di febbrajo dell' anno MDCCL. dalla ... real maestà di Elisabetta Farnese regina vedova di Spagna. 1750

Sweden

Dahlbergh, E. J. Exequiae ... Caroli Gustavi Suecorum Gothorum et Wandalorum regis d. 3. Nouemb. 1660 Holmiae celebratae. n.d.

Funke, Karl

(engr.) Walter, W. Das preuszische heer in bildern

Fur in costume

Cocheris, Mme P. A. W. Les parures primitives avec une introduction sur les temps préhistoriques. 1894

Davey, R. P. B. Furs and fur garments. 1895

Fougerat, L. La pelleterie et le vêtement de fourrures dans l'antiquité. 1914

Hanau, Ch. Fourrures et pelleteries. 1913

Fur in costume—*Continued*

Larisch, Paul. Die kürschner und ihre zeichen; beiträge zur geschichte der kürschnerei. 1928

Larisch, Paul, and Schmidt, Joseph. Das kürschner-handwerk. 1902-04

Piergiovanni, Bruno. Enciclopedia dell'abbigliamento femminile. 1924. v2 p305-80.

Uprka, Joža. Peasants' furs in Czechoslovakia. 1920

Periodical

American fur designer. 1920+

Le **furet** des salons. Paris, Marcilly ca1840
8 col.pl. Ti.
Color plates show fashions
Colas 1141

Furmerius, Bernard Gebrands. See note under Coornhert, Dierick. Emblemata moralia

Furness, Horace Howard. See Darley, F. O. C. The Darley gallery of Shakespearean illustrations

Furs and fur garments. Davey, R. P. B.

Furtwängler, Adolf

Masterpieces of Greek sculpture ... ed. by Eugénie Sellers. London, W. Heinemann 1895
xxiii,487p. front. illus. XVIII pl. F.
Plates accompanied by guard sheets with descriptive letterpress
A translation of his *Meisterwerke der griechischen plastik*
LC 1-4107

Meisterwerke der griechischen plastik. Leipzig, Giesecke 1893
2v. 40pl. F.

Die sammlung Sabouroff. See entry under Saburov, P. A.

Furtwängler, Adolf, and Reichhold, Karl

Griechische vasenmalerei; auswahl hervorragender vasenbilder, mit unterstützung aus dem Thereianos-fonds der Kgl. bayerischen akademie der wissenschaften. Serie 1-3 München, F. Bruckmann 1904-1932
2v. of text. illus. 11pl.(part fold.) F. and 12 portfolios of 150pl.(part col. part fold.) F.
Series 2, 1909 continued after Furtwängler's death by Friedrich Hauser; Series 3, 1932 continued after the death of Reichhold and Hauser, by Ernst Buschor. Each volume issued in 6 parts, consisting of plates in portfolios accompanied by the corresponding pages of text in loose signatures in a pocket of the back cover. The third series contains plates 121-180
Illustrations are from Greek vases, many of them showing costume of Ancient Greece. Most of the plates have descriptive notes which tell what person or event is depicted. The text is also descriptive
LC 9-26103

Fuseli, Henry

(illus.) Boydell, John, and Boydell, Josiah. The American edition of Boydell's Illustrations of the Dramatic works of Shakspeare

See also Cervio, Vincenzo. Il trinciante

Fusoritto, reale da Narni

(illus.) Pandini, Cesare. Il mastro di casa

(illus.) Scappi, Bartolomeo. Dell' arte del cucinare

Fussleiden und rationelle fussbekleidung. Voetsch, August

G

G., A. P. D. See Sketches of Portuguese life, manners, costume, and character

Die **gabelhäkelei.** Hochfelden, Frau B. L.

Gaber, August

(engr.) Schwind, Moritz von. Die wandgemaelde des landgrafensaales auf der Wartburg

Gabinetto armonico pieno d'istrumenti. See Buonanni, Filippo. Descrizione degl'istromenti armonici d'ogni generi

Gabler, Ambrosius

160 Nürnberger schimpfwörter. Nürnberg, J. L. Lotzbeck ca1795
16pl. Q.
Lipperheide 3523

[Nürnberger ausrufer mit darstellung der vornehmsten stadttheile Nürnbergs] Nürnberg 1789
9 col.pl. F.
Colas lists an edition with title: *Ausruffende personen in Nürnberg* (Nürnberg, C. Weigel 1790. 6 col.pl.) and the same title (Nürnberg, Homanns erben 1805. 8 col.pl)
Colas 1143-1144. Lipperheide 785

Gabriel, Ralph Henry

(ed.) Pageant of America; a pictorial history of the United States

Gaceta gentleman. Año 1, Feb. 1933+ La Habana, C. M. Ayala
Illus. F. $4.50
A Cuban journal of masculine fashions. Published monthly except Feb. and Aug. Current 1938

Gâches-Sarraute, Mme Inèz

Le corset. Étude physiologique et pratique. Paris, Masson 1900
131p. illus. Q.

Gaedechens, C. F.

Das hamburgische militär bis zum jahre 1811 und die hanseatische legion. Hamburg, L. Gräfe 1889
220p. 1 illus. 8 col.pl. O.
From *Zeitschrift des Vereins für hamburgische geschichte,* vol. 8
Colas 1146. Lipperheide 2215

Hamburgs bürgerbewaffnung. Ein geschichtlicher rückblick ... hrsg. vom Verein für hamburgische geschichte. Hamburg, W. Mauke 1872
60p. 4pl.(3 col.) Q.
Colas 1145. Lipperheide 2214

Gaelic gatherings. Logan, James

Gärtner, Georg

Ordnung Weyland desz ... herrn Joachim Ernsten marggrafen zu Brandenburg ... furstlicher leichbegängnusz ... anno 1625. Nürmberg, L. Lochnern [1625]
46pl. F.
Contains more than half of the 44 pictures of the funeral procession of Georg Friedrich von Brandenburg, first published in Nuremberg in 1603
Lipperheide 2522

Gagarīn, Grīgoriĭ Grīgor̃evīch, knîaz'
Costumes du Caucase. Paris, A. Hauser ca1840
66 col.pl. F.
Planned as part of *Scènes, paysages, moeurs et costumes du Caucase* of which only these 66 plates were published. Plates are lithographs by Janet-Lange, Bachmann, Springer and Gagarin
Colas 1147. Lipperheide 1384

Gagarīn, Grīgoriĭ Grīgor̃evīch, knîaz, and Stackelberg, Ernest, count
Le Caucase pittoresque; dessiné d'après nature par le prince Grégoire Gagarine, avec une introduction et un texte explicatif par le comte Ernest Stackelberg. Paris, Plon 1847
22,33p. 80pl.(part col.) F.
Published in 20 parts, one or two leaves and four plates in each part
Colas 1148. Lipperheide 1385

Gageur, Karl
Das trachtenfest zu Haslach im Kinzigthal am 4. juni 1899. Freiburg im Breisgau, H. M. Poppen [1899]
48p. 17 illus. O.
Colas 1149. Lipperheide 752e

Gaglier
[Armée Toscane.] No place, lith. Targioni [1827]
16 col.pl. F.
Cataloged from Colas
Colas 1150

Gagnier, G.
Survivance du culte solaire dans les coiffures féminines en Bretagne, Auvergne, Savoie, Bourbonnais, etc. St-Brieuc, E. Hamonic; Paris, Champion [1910]
[8]p. 1 l. 4pl. O.
Colas 1151. LC 19-20001

Gaignières, Roger de
(illus.) Tableau historique des monumens

Gail, Wilhelm
Erinnerungen aus Spanien. Nach der natur und auf stein gezeichnete skizzen aus dem leben in den provinzen Catalonien, Valencia, Andalusien, Granada und Castilien. München [1837]
viii,8p. 5 illus. 30pl. F.
The last 10 plates are views of Spanish bull fights
Lipperheide 1225

Gaildrau, Jules
L'armée française: recueil contenant toutes les tenues des différentes armes, les écoles militaires et les écoles de marine, les equipages et les trains de l'armée, l'administration militaire etc. dessiné et lith ... par Jules Guildrau. Paris, L'auteur [1855-56]
27 col.pl. F.
Nine parts only were published at 4 francs each. Glasser gives a list of the plates
Colas 1152

Gainsborough and his place in English art. Armstrong, sir Walter

[**Gálâl ad-Dîn Mîrzâ**]
[The book of the Hosroes, history of the kings of Iran from the beginning of the Abbadides until the end of the Sassanid dynasty] Wien 1880
408p. 56 illus. O.
Title is in Persian. Illustrations show portraits of the Persian kings
Lipperheide 1470

Galanterieen der Türken. Kindleben, C. W.

Galanis, D.
(illus.) Ivchenko, V. I. Anna Pavlova

Galard, Gustave de
Album départemental, ou Bordeaux et ses environs. Bordeaux, lith. de Légé [1829]
60 col.pl. F.
Also known with plates in black and white and with part only in color
Colas 1155

[**Galard, Gustave de, and Claveau, Eugene**]
[Fantaisies, localités bordelaises] Bordeaux, Magi impr. lith. de Légé 1827-1830
12 col.pl. F.
Colas gives a list of the plates. All are known also in black and white
Colas 1154

Galard, Gustave de, and Géraud, S. E.
Recueil des divers costumes des habitans de Bordeaux et des environs; dessinés ... par M. G. de Galard; précédés de notices ... par M. S. E. Geraud. Bordeaux, Lavigne jeune, imp. [1818-1819]
36 col.pl. F.
Published in nine parts, each of two leaves and four plates
Colas gives a list of 32 plates in a variant edition of the same dates
Colas 1153. Lipperheide 1191

Galateri, Pietro
Armata sarda; uniformi antichi et moderni. Album ... comandato presso il Ministerio di guerra e marina. Torino & Roma, Maggi 1844
[2] l. 33 col.pl. ob.F.
Colas 1156

Le **Galathee.** See Casa, Giovanni della, abp. Trattato de costumi

Gale, Albert. See Cole, F. C. The Tinguian

Gale, Ethel C.
Hints on dress; or, What to wear, when to wear it, and how to buy it. New York, G. P. Putnam 1872
107p. D.
LC 10-1024

Gale & Polden, ltd
Regimental ribbons & buttons of the British army. London, Gale & Polden [1915]
1 col.fold.pl. Q.
(pub.) Stripes and types of the Royal navy

Galerie bretonne. See Bouët, Alexandre. Breiz-Izel

Galerie de costumes. Lacauchie, A.

Galerie des artistes dramatiques de Paris. Lacauchie, A.

Galerie des enfants de Mars. Martinet, pub.

Galerie des militaires français qui, à differentes époques, se sont distingués par leur courage. Paris, G. Engelmann ca1820
43pl. F.
This suite is lithographed by H. Bellangé, Bosis, Gaillot and others
Lipperheide 2306

Galerie des modes et costumes français. Sorrieu, Frédéric

Galerie des modes et costumes français dessinés d'après nature, 1778-1787. See entry under Gallerie des modes et costumes français dessinés d'après nature, gravés par les plus célèbres artistes

Galerie des moeurs, usages et costumes des Bretons de l'Armorique. Perrin, O. S., and Mareschal, L. A.

Galerie des uniformes des gardes nationales de France. Tardieu, Ambroise

Galerie des victoires et conquêtes de l'armée française et de tous les régiments depuis les premiers temps de la monarchie jusqu'à nos jours. Pascal, Adrien, and others

Galerie dramatique; costumes des théâtres de Paris. Paris, Martinet [1844-70]
10v. 993pl. O.
Illustrated by Dollet, Lacauchie and Lassalle
This collection is preceded by *Petite galerie dramatique* (1796-1843) and continued by *Nouvelle galerie dramatique* (1872-80)
Colas 1159. Lipperheide 3205

Galerie dramatique, ou Acteurs et actrices. Grasset de Saint-Sauveur, Jacques

Galerie fashionnable de costumes, de fleurs et de femmes, de tous les pays. See Leloir, Mme Héloise. Le Sélam

Galerie française de femmes célèbres par leurs talens, leur rang ou leur beauté. Lanté, L. M.

Galerie françoise. Restout, Jean

Galerie illustrée des célébrités contemporaines. Lorsay, Eustache

Galerie militaire. Martinet, pub.

Galerie militaire. Vernet, Pierre

Galerie militaire; armées européennes. Paris, Déro Becker [1845]
14 col.pl. F.
Each plate shows four uniforms. They are signed Bour, Luna, A. Regnier and Ch. Vogt and printed in the margin: A. Collin, editeur. A list of the plates is given in Glasser
Colas 1160

Galerie militaire; collection des costumes militaires de toutes les nations. Paris, Déro-Becker [1840-1855]
2v. 395 col.pl. Q.
Volume 1 contains plates 1 to 302, 52 bis, and 57 bis. Volume 2 published by Martinet-Hautecoeur contains plates numbered 301 to 391
According to Colas the plates for the German, Austrian and Russian uniforms are copies of those in Eckert, Monten and Schelver's *Saemmtliche truppen*, the English from E. Hull's *Costume of the British army in 1828*. Other plates were made especially for this collection by V. Adam and others
Colas 1161-1162

Galerie militaire: troupes françaises. Martinet, pub.

Galerie royale de costumes peints d'après nature par divers artistes et lithographiés par Alophe, Janet-Lange et Dollet. Paris, Aubert ca[1842-43]
245 col.pl. F.
Cover title
A fine collection of colored plates showing costume of many different countries. Colas gives a list of the plates he has seen and of the illustrators. In addition plates exist with titles: *Amerique du sud*, and *Palestine, Egypte* et *Asie-Mineure*. There are probably others
Colas 1163. Lipperheide 60

Galerie théâtrale, ou Collection des portraits en pied des principaux acteurs des premiers théâtres de la capitale; gravées par les plus célèbres artistes. Paris, Bance [1812-1834]
3v. 144 col.pl. Q.
These plates were published later with some new explanatory notes. (Galerie théâtrale, collection de 144 portraits en pied des principaux acteurs et actrices qui ont illustré la scène française depuis 1552 jusqu'à nos jours. Paris, A. Barraud 1873. 2v. 144 col.pl. F.)
Also published with plates in black and white
Colas 1164-1165

Galerij van beroemde Nederlanders. Lennep, Jakob van

Galibert, Léon
L'Algérie, ancienne et moderne depuis les premiers éstablissements des Carthaginois jusqu'à la prise de la Smalah d'Abd-el-Kader. Vignettes par Raffet et Rouargue frères. Paris, Furne 1844
637p. front. 63 illus. 36pl.(13 col.) fold. map. O.
Twenty-four plates, after Raffet, Biard and Rouargue, deal with camp scenes in Algeria. The others show uniforms of French troops and of the troops of Abd-el-Kader
First edition: *Histoire de l'Algérie ancienne et moderne depuis les premiers établissements des Carthaginois jusques et y compris les dernières campagnes du général Bugeaud* (Paris, Furne 1843. 637p. 63 illus. 36pl. map. O.)
Colas 1166 (1st ed.) Lipperheide 1592. LC 5-9812

Galiberto, Giovan Battista di
Il cavallo da maneggio. Vienna, G. G. Kyrneri 1659
106p. 30 illus. F.
Lipperheide 2908

Galicia. See Poland—Galicia

Galland, V. A.
Der vollkommene damen-friseur; eine ... anweisung ... den kopfputz der damen, ohne beihülfe eines friseurs, aufs vollkommenste herzustellen; 2. verm. aufl. Hanau, C. J. Edler 1830
62p. 4 col.pl. O.
First edition was published in 1828
Lipperheide 1698m

Gallardo, Carlos R.
Tierra del Fuego; Los Onas. Buenos Aires, Cabaut 1910
395p. illus.(part. col.) O.
LC 18-20623

Galle, Corneille
(engr.) Francquart, Jacques. Pompa funebris ... Albertii Pii, archiducis Austriae

Galle, Philippe
Les vies et alliances des comtes de Holande et Zélande, seigneurs de Frise. Anvers, C. Plantin 1586
75p. 36 ports. Q.
Shows Dutch costume

Gallemore, Margaret; Harris, Vida Agnes, and Morris, Maria
Costume design; a student's handbook. Chicago, Philadelphia, J. B. Lippincott [c1934]
xi,126p. illus. F.
Reference books recommended for the library: p viii; Additional references: p126; Selected references at end of each lesson except lessons 19 and 22
LC 34-29305

Gallenstein, Anton von
Zur geschichte der deutschen kleidertrachten bis zum schlusse des 16ten jahrhunderts ... Die priesterliche kleidung. Klagenfurt, F. von Kleinmayr [1863]
13p. Q.
From the review *Carinthia*
Colas 1167. Lipperheide 1834

Galleria di costumi Sardi. Dalsani

Gallerie altteutscher trachten. Schlichtegroll, Franz von

Gallerie armoricaine: costumes et vues pittoresques de la Bretagne. Lalaisse, Hippolyte, and Benoist, Félix

Gallerie der costüme. Schneider, Louis

Gallerie der menschen; ein bilderbuch zur erweiterung der kenntnisse über länder und völker; neue verb. und verm. aufl. Pest, K. A. Hartleben 1813
2v. 80 col.pl. O.
The first edition appeared in Leipzig in 1806 in 3 volumes with 123 plates
Colas 1168. Lipperheide 50

Gallerie der nationen. Hausleutner, P. W. G.

Gallerie der sitten, geräthschaften, religiösen, bürgerlichen und kriegerischen gebräuche. See note under Malliot, Joseph, and Martin, P. Recherches sur les costumes, les moeurs, les usages religieux, civil et militaires des anciens peuples

Gallerie der stånde. Kerndörffer, H. A.

Gallerie des kurhessischen militärs. Tackmann, E.

Gallerie des modes et costumes français dessinés d'après nature, gravés par les plus célèbres artistes en ce genre, et colorés avec le plus grand soin par Madame Le Beau; ouvrage commencé de l'année 1778. Paris, Esnauts & Rapilly [1778-1788]
4v. 436 col.pl. F.
Described by Colas as the most handsome collection of plates on 18th century costume. Colas gives a list of the 73 parts (cahiers) in which it was published, and the title of each plate
Some of the early plates have title: *Costumes français pour les coeffures depuis 1776*
Complete sets of the original are very rare. A reprint exists: *Galerie des modes et costumes français dessinés d'après nature, 1778-1787* (Paris, E. Levy [1912] 2 l. xv,16p. 325 l. 325 col.pl. Q.) The plates concerned exclusively with hair dressing, and hats, and some plates of street or theatrical costume were omitted in the reprint
Colas 1169, 1158. Costume index. Lipperheide 1129. LC 15-8907 (reprint)

Gallerie dramatischer künstler der königlichen hofbühne zu Berlin. I. heft, Charlotte von Hagn. Berlin, A. Duncker 1838
4pl. Q.
Lipperheide 3219

Gallerie drolliger und interessanter scenen der Wiener-bühnen. Bäuerle, Adolf, ed.

La **Gallerie** du Palais du Luxembourg. Rubens, Sir P. P.

Gallerie heroischer bildwerke der alten kunst. Overbeck, Johannes

Gallerie zu Shakspeare's dramatischen werken. Retzsch, F. A. M.

Gallery of English historical personages. Harding, G. P., and Moule, Thomas

Gallery of fashion. v 1-9; Apr. 1794-Mar. 1803. London, N. Heideloff
9v. 217 col.pl. Q.
Published monthly. Explanations for the plates are in English, German and French. Shows Engish fashions in a collection of plates which compare favorably with those of the French *Gallerie des modes*
Colas 1170. Lipperheide 4578

Gallery to Shakespeare's dramatic works in outlines. See Retzsch, F. A. M. Gallerie zu Shakspeare's dramatischen werken

The **Gallic** war. Caesar, C. J.

Gallo, Agostino
Le venti giornate dell' agricoltura. Venetia, C. Borgomienero 1584
10 l. 447p. 10 illus. O.
Several editions. Another (Brescia, G. Bossini 1775. xx,570p. front. 6pl. Q.)
The illustrations are full-page woodcuts and picture agricultural instruments and a few agricultural laborers of the 16th century
LC A17-1972 (1775 ed.)

Gallo, Emanuele
Il valore sociale dell' abbigliamento. Torino, Fratelli Bocca 1914
331,41p. 2 l. D.
Colas 1171

Gallois, Émlie
Provinces françaises costumes décoratifs; preface de Maurice Genevoix. New York, French and European publications [1937]
6p. 40 col.pl. F. $12

Gallop, Rodney
Portugal; a book of folk-ways. Illustrated with photographs by the author and drawings by Marjorie Gallop. Cambridge [Eng.] The University press 1936
xv,291p. front. ilus. XVI pl. on 8 l. O
Bibliography: p[281]-84
LC 37-6108

See also Alford, Violet, jt. auth.

Gallus, oder Römische scenen aus der Zeit Augusts. Becker, W. A.

Gallus, or Roman scenes in the time of Augustus. Becker, W. A.

Gallwey, Sir Ralph William Frankland Payne-. See Payne-Gallwey, Sir R. W. F., bart.

Gamba, Jacques François
Voyage dans la Russie méridionale et particulièrement dans les provinces situées au-delà du Caucase, fait depuis 1820 jusqu'en 1824. Paris, C. J. Trouvé 1826
2v. maps. O. and atlas of 60pl.(34 col.) F.
The colored plates show costume
Colas 1172

Gambado, Geoffrey, pseud. See Bunbury, Henry William

Gambier-Parry, Thomas Robert. See Legg, J. W. Church ornaments and their civil antecedents

The **game** of cricket, by A. P. F. Chapman ... [and others] with fifty-five illustrations. London, Seeley, Service 1930
255p. illus 41pl. (incl.front.) O. (The Lonsdale library)
Contents: Batsmanship, by D. R. Jardine; Bowling, by E. G. Martin; The placing of the field, by some famous bowlers; A note on swerve and spin, by R. C. Robertson-Glasgow; Wicket-keeping, by W. B. Franklin; Fielding, by A. P. F. Chapman; Captaincy in cricket, by P. G. H. Fender; Umpiring, by H. D. G. Leveson-Gower; Scoring, by H. Strudwick; Cricket-coaching, by D. J. Knight; Test match cricket, by D. R. Jardine; Club cricket, by E. A. C. Thomson; The care and maintenance of cricket grounds, by H. E. White; The laws of cricket
LC 31-11703

The **game** of the chesse. Cessolis, Jacobus de

Gamla bröllopsseder hos svenska allmogen. Norlind, Tobias

Gamla Stockholm anteckningar ur tryckta och otryckta källor framletade. Lundin, Claës, and Strindberg, August

Gamle norske billedtæpper. Oslo. Kunstindustrimuseet

Gamle smykker i Norge. Oslo. Kunstindustrimuseet

Ganier, Henry
Les Alsaciens dans la Garde impériale et dans les corps d'élite. Strasbourg, Imprimerie alsacienne 1914
54 l. 50 col.pl. F.
Plates are by Tanconville and Maurice Taussaint
Colas 1175

Costumes des régiments et des milices recrutés dans les anciennes provinces d'Alsace et de la Sarre, les républiques de Strasbourg et de Mulhouse, la principauté de Montbéliard et de duché de Lorraine pendant les XVIIe et XVIIIe siècles. Epinal, C. Froereisen 1882
xi,121p. 20 col.pl. Q.
Colas 1174. Lipperheide 2334

Gann, Thomas William Francis
Ancient cities and modern tribes: exploration and adventure in Maya lands. New York, C. Scribner's sons 1926
256p. front. illus. (map) pl. ports. O.
Contains photographs of statues, monuments, etc. showing costume of the Mayas
LC 27-26446

Les **gants** pontificaux. Barbier de Montault, Xavier

Gantz new modelbuch künstlicher und lustiger visirung und muster von allerhand schöner artiger zügen und blumwerck. See Hoffmann, Wilhelm. Spitzen-musterbuch

Die **gantze** Bibel der ursprüngliche ebraischen und griechischen warrheyt nach auffs aller treüwlichest verteutschet. Bible. German

Garborg, Fru Hulda (Bergersen)
Norsk klædebunad; med 100 bilæte og 8 fargelagde mynsterteikningar av Halfdan Arneberg. Kristiania, H. Aschehoug 1917
2p.l. 91p. illus. 8 col.pl. Q.
Norwegian folk dress. Includes patterns
LC 21-2018

Garcia, G.
Les modes du Directoire et du Consulat; dessins et aquarelles de G. Garcia, d'après les estampes de l'époque. Preface de Maurice Vitrac. Paris, H. Daragon 1911
xi p. col.front. 88 col.pl. O. 6fr.
Colas 1177

(illus.) Daragon, Henri. Les modes du Directoire et du Consulat

García Cubas, Antonio
The republic of Mexico in 1876. A political and ethnographical division of the population, character, habits, costumes and vocations of its inhabitants; tr. ... by G. F. Henderson. Mexico, "La Enseñanza" print. office 1876
130,[8]p. 8 col.pl. double map. Q.
Contains specimens of popular music
Colas 767. Costume index. Lipperheide 1625. LC 2-4837

Garcin, J.
Le vrai patineur ou principes sur l'art de patiner avec grâce. Paris, Delespinasse 1813
xxiv,93p. 8 col.pl. D.
Lipperheide 3042w

Garde à vous; caricatures parisienne. Paris, Martinet [1802-1815]
38 col.pl. ob.F.
Title from the plates which show Parisian costume of the period. Colas gives a list of the plates
Colas 1178

Garde des Consuls. Paris, Potrelle [1799-1804]
14 col.pl. O.
Gives exact details of the uniform of the Consular guard
Colas 1179

La **Garde** impériale (1804-1815). Fallou, Louis

Garde impériale Russe. Charlemagne, A., and Ladurner, A.

Garde municipale et garde nationale. Noguès, S.

Garde nationale en 1830. Blanc

Garde royale. Chéreau, Mme Vve.

Garde royale dessiné par Ch. L. Paris, Plancher n.d.
7 col.pl. Q.
Colas 1180

Garde royale, 1828. Raffet, D. A. M.

Garde royale et maison du Roi. Finart, N.

Garde royale prussienne. Winckelmann

Garde royale prussienne, 1861. Bürger, L., and Müller, H.

Les **gardes** d'honneur d'Alsace et de Lorraine à l'époque du premier empire. Depréaux, Albert

Les **gardes** d'honneur du premier empire. Bucquoy, Eugène Louis

Les **gardes** impériales et royales de l'armée française en 1810. Henschel, W., and Henschel, F. A.

Gardilanne, Gratiane de, and Moffat, Elisabeth Whitney

Les costumes régionaux de la France, deux cents aquarelles par G. de Gardilanne et E. W. Moffat; avec un texte historique par Henry Royère. New York, Harcourt, Brace 1929

4v. 200 col.pl. F. $330 o.p.

Also published in Paris by the Pegasus press

Masculine and feminine costume of all the French provinces

Colas 2590. Costume index. LC 29-16681

The national costumes of Holland; fifty studies reproduced by lithography in full colours from the originals of Gratiane de Gardilanne and Elizabeth Whitney Moffatt; with an introduction and explanatory letterpress by Alma Oakes. London [etc.] G. G. Harrap [1932]

2p.l. 3-115,[1]p. incl.map. 50 col.pl. F. 325s

Costume index. LC 32-31951

Gardiner, Arthur. See Prior, E. S., jt. auth.

Gardiner, Asa Bird

The uniforms of the American army. New York and Chicago, A. S. Barnes 1877

p461-92. O.

From *Magazine of American history,* August 1877, v 1, no8, with addenda, 2 pages

A discussion of American uniforms from 1775-1832, including regulations governing styles of hair dressing of the soldiers

LC 3-18436

Gardiner, F. Mary

The evolution of fashion; ed. de luxe. London, Cotton press 1897

98p. illus. 2pl. Q. 10s 6d

Gardner, Ernest Arthur

The art of Greece. London, The Studio 1925

viii,54p. LVI pl. diagrs. O.

Chapter VI is on dress, chapter VII on gems, coins and jewelry

Bibliography: p53-54

LC 26-5493

Gardner, James

The faiths of the world; an account of all religions and religious sects, their ... rites, ceremonies, and customs. Edinburgh, Glasgow, London, A. Fullarton [1858-60]

2v. pl. Q.

Shows some ecclesiastical costumes

Dutch edition: *De geloofsbelijdenissen der wereld* (Rotterdam, D. Bolle ca1865)

Lipperheide 1829 (Dutch ed.)

Gardner, John Starkie

Armour in England from the earliest times to the reign of James the First. London, Seeley; New York, Macmillan 1898

100p. col.front. pl.(7 col.) Q. (Portfolio artistic monographs no33)

Lipperheide 2457

Foreign armour in England. London, Seeley; New York, Macmillan 1898

96p. col.front. illus. pl.(7 col.) Q. (Portfolio artistic monographs no38)

Lipperheide 2457

Gardner, Percy

Sculptured tombs of Hellas. London; New York, Macmillan 1896

xix,259p. illus. xxx pl.(incl. front.) Q.

LC 11-13924

Gargiulo, Raffaele

(ed.) Naples. Museo nazionale. Collection of the most remarkable monuments of the National museum

(ed.) Naples. Museo nazionale. Recueil des monumens les plus intéressans du Musée national

Garland, Hamlin

The book of the American Indian; pictured by Frederic Remington. [1st ed.] New York and London, Harper 1923

274p. col.front. pl.(part col.) F.

LC 23-12977

Garment making. Fleming, J. A.

Garmo, Charles de. See De Garmo, Charles

Garner, John Leslie

(tr.) Biart, Lucien. The Aztecs. 1887

Garneray, Auguste

(illus.) Vizentini, Augustin. Recueil des costumes de tous les ouvrages dramatiques représentés avec succès sur les grands théâtres de Paris

Garneray, Jean François

Collection des nouveaux costumes des autorités constituées civils et militaires. Paris, L'imprimerie de Boiste [ca1796]

26 col.pl. Q.

A second edition with thirty plates by Alix after Garneray was published about 1798. List of plates is given by Colas

Colas 1181

Garnett, Lucy Mary Jane

Balkan home life. London, Methuen [1917]

309p. front. pl. O.

LC 18-1521

Garnett, Richard, and Gosse, Sir Edmund William

English literature; an illustrated record. New York, Macmillan; London, Macmillan 1903-04

4v. fronts.(1 col.) illus. pl.(part col.) ports. facsims. (part col.) Q.

A history of English literature which contains many portraits of writers in costume of their time. A chronological record

Contents: v 1 From the beginnings to the age of Henry VIII; v2 From the age of Henry VIII to the age of Milton; v3 From Milton to Johnson; v4 From the age of Johnson to the age of Tennyson

LC 4-1596

Les **garnisons** d'Alsace au 19. siècle. Kieffer, Fritz, ed.

Garoby, Jean. See Archinard, L. Q. L'autre France (Tunisie, Algérie, Maroc). 1914

Garrard's, 1721-1911, crown jewellers and goldsmiths during six reigns and in three centuries. London, S. Paul [1912]

182,[2]p. illus. plates, plans, facsims. O.

LC 12-10156

Garrett, Edmund H.
(illus.) Smith, J. H., ed. The historie booke, done to keep in lasting remembrance the joyous meeting of the Honourable artillery company of London ... 1903

Garsault, François Alexandre Pierre de
L'art de la lingère. Paris, L. F. Delatour 1771
58p. 4pl. F. (Acad. royale des sciences. Description des arts et métiers)
Lipperheide 3784

Art du cordonnier. [Paris] 1767
51p. 5pl. F. (Acad. royale des sciences. Description des arts et métiers v12)
Some of the plates show sandals and footwear

Art du perruquier contenant la façon de la barbe; la coupe des cheveux; la construction des perruques d'hommes et de femmes; le perruquier en vieux; & le baigneur-etuviste. [Paris] 1767
44p. 5pl. F. (Acad. royale des sciences. Description des arts et métiers v12)
One plate shows feminine coiffures; another plate shows several styles of wigs
Lipperheide 1671

Art du tailleur, contenant le tailleur d'habits d'hommes; les culottes de peau; le tailleur des corps de femmes & enfants; la couturière; & la marchande des modes. [Paris, L. F. Delatour 1769]
60p. 16pl. F. (Acad. royale des sciences. Description des arts et métiers v17)
Lipperheide 3783

Die **Gartenlaube;** illustriertes familienblatt. 1. jahrg, 1853+ Leipzig, E. Keil [etc.]
Illus. pl. (part col.) ports. F.
Published weekly. Current 1937
Die Welt der frau has been issued as a supplement since 1905. In September 1905, *Vom fels zum meer* was united with *Die Gartenlaube,* the two being continued under their former titles, with contents identical
Lipperheide 4668. LC 11-22964

Garter, Order of the
Ashmole, Elias. The institution, laws & ceremonies of the most noble Order of the garter. 1672

Dawson, Thomas. Memoirs of St George, the English patron, and of the most noble Order of the Garter. 1714

Garzoni, Tommaso
Piazza universale; Das ist: Allgemeiner schauplatz, marckt und zusammenkunfft aller professionen, künsten, geschäfften, händeln und handt-wercken. Franckfurt am Mayn, M. Merian 1641
1084p. 148 illus. Q.
Woodcuts by Jost Amman had appeared before in his *De omnibus illiberalibus sive mechanicis artibus*
This is a translation from the Italian original published without illustrations under title: *La piazza universale di tutte le professioni del mondo* (Venetia 1585). Another German edition with 147 woodcuts was published in 1659
Lipperheide 1949-50

Gascoigne, Gwendolen T.
Among pagoda and fair ladies; tour through Burma. London, Innes 1896
318p. illus. O. 12s
Costume p33-36 and in many of the illustrations

Gascony. See France—Basse-Pyrénées

Gaselee, Stephen. See A directory of ceremonial

Gasquet, Francis Aidan, cardinal
English monastic life. London, Methuen 1904
xix,326p. front. illus. XVIII pl. (incl. ports. facsims.) 5 maps, 3 fold. plans. O. (The Antiquary's books)
List of manuscripts and printed books: p xv-xix
List of English religious houses: p251-317
LC 4-19648

Henry VIII and the English monasteries; 5th ed. London, J. Hodges 1893
2v. 33pl. 1 port. 6 maps. O.
Many of the plates show dress of the English monastic and religious orders
LC 12-32384

Gaston III, Phoebus, comte de Foix
Livre de la chasse. See entry under Paris. Bibliothèque nationale. Mss. (Fr. 616)

Gatine, Georges Jacques
Travestissemens. [Paris] ca1825
22 col.pl. Q.
Sometimes attributed to Lanté
Colas 1184

(engr.) Lanté, L. M. Costumes des femmes de Hambourg, du Tyrol, etc.

(engr.) Lanté, L. M. Costumes des femmes du pays de Caux

(engr.) Lanté, L. M. Costumes des femmes françaises du XIIe au XVIIIe siècle

(engr.) Lanté, L. M. Costumes et coiffures de Paris des haute et moyenne classes

(engr.) Lanté, L. M. Costumes parisiens

(engr.) Lanté, L. M. Galerie française de femmes célèbres

(engr.) Le Roux de Lincy, A. J. V., and Leynadier, Camille. Les femmes célèbres de l'ancienne France

(engr.) Pécheux, and Manzoni. Costumes orientaux

(engr.) Vernet, Horace. Incroyables et merveilleuses de 1814

Gatti
[Uniformes de l'armée des Deux-Siciles. No place] Lith. Gatti & Dura ca1840
30 col.pl. F.
Two of the plates are signed, one by A. Terranova, and one by Dom La Greca
Colas 1185

Gau, François Chrétien
Antiquités de la Nubie, ou, Monumens inédits des bords du Nil, situés entre la première et la seconde cataracte, dessinés et mesurés, en 1819 ... Ouvrage faisant suite au grand ouvrage de la Commission d'Égypte. Stuttgart, J. G. Cotta; [etc.] 1822-[27]
[84]p. illus. 78pl. (part col.) F.
Plates 21, 45, 60 and 61, in color, are pictures of kings, servants, charioteers and soldiers of ancient Nubia, and show dress
LC 5-8297

Gaucherel, Léon
(engr.) Barbault, Jean. 12 costumes d'Italie d'après les peintures faîtes par Barbault à Rome en 1750

Gauci, M.
(lithgr.) Hull, Edward. Costume of the British Army in 1828
(lithgr.) Hull, Edward. Costume of the British navy in 1828

Gaudy, Franz Bernhard Heinrich Wilhelm, freiherr von
Karikaturenbuch; hrsg. von Fedor von Zobeltitz. Berlin, E. Frensdorff 1906
4 p.l. 62pl. ob.O.

Gaujean, Eugene
(engr.) Uzanne, L. O. La Française du siècle

Gaul, Franz
Österreichisch-ungarische national-trachten. Wien, R. Lechner 1881-88
24 col.pl. Q.
Colas 1187. Lipperheide 841

Gaullieur, Eusèbe Henri Alban. See La Suisse historique et pittoresque

Gaulon, Cyprien Charles Marie Nicolas
(lithgr.) La Torre, F. de. Costumes bordelais

Gauls
Bosc, Ernest, and Bonnemère, Lionel. Histoire nationale des Gaulois sous Vercingetorix. 1882
Caesar, C. J. The Gallic war. 1917
Dechelette, Joseph. Manuel d'archéologie préhistorique celtique et gallo-romaine. 1908-34
Hucher, E. F. F. L'art gaulois, ou, Les Gaulois d'après leurs médailles. 1868

See also Helmets—Gauls

Gaunt, William
English rural life in the eighteenth century ... London, The Connoisseur 1925
viii,34p. col. mounted front. 18 illus. 15pl. (part col., mounted) sq.O. (The Connoisseur series of books for collectors)
LC 26-3246

Gauthier, François Louis
Traité contre l'amour des parures, et le luxe des habits; 2. éd. Paris, A. M. Lottin 1780
xii,250p. S.
First edition: 1779
Lipperheide 3476 (1st ed.). LC 20-6272

Gauthier, Joseph
La Bretagne; sites, arts et coutumes; clichés originaux de Marius Gravot. Paris, Librairie des arts décoratifs [1928]
41p. 109pl. Q.
Five plates show costume of Brittany
Bibliography: p[43-45]

Costumes paysans. Paris, C. Massin [1930]
28p. illus. 40pl. (7 col.) F. 150fr. (L'art populaire français)
Colas 1188. Costume index

Gautier, Léon
La chevalerie; nouv. éd. accompagnée d'une table par ordre alphabétique des matières. Paris, Sanard & Derangeon [1895]
xv,850p. front. illus. pl. Q.
"Index bibliographique": p[785]-86
The English edition has the same illustrations reduced in size: *Chivalry* tr. by Henry Frith (London, New York, G. Routledge 1891. xii,499p. front. illus. pl. O.)
LC F-1774, A12-1084 (English ed.)

Gautier, Rodolphe
[Troupes françaises. Paris, Gautier 1814-1816]
4pl. F.
Plates are signed P. L. C.
Colas 1189

(illus.) Uniformes de la garde de sa majesté le roi de Westphalie (attributed)

Gautier, Saint Elme
(illus.) Laincel-Vento, Alix, comtesse de. Les grandes dames d'aujourd'hui
(illus.) Paris. Bibliothèque nationale. Catalogue des bronzes antiques

Gautier, Théophile
Les beautés de l'opéra, ou Chefs-d'oeuvre lyriques, illustrés par les premiers artistes de Paris et de Londres sous la direction de Giraldon, avec un texte explicatif rédigé par Théophile Gautier, Jules Janin et Philarète Chasles. Paris, Soulié 1845
263p. illus. ports. Q.
Various paging
Costumes used in nine operas: Les Huguenots; Giselle; Le barbier de Séville; Le diable boiteux; Norma; La sylphide; Don Juan; Ondine; La Juive
LC 8-11671

Gauttier, Édouard. See Gauttier du Lys d'Arc, Louis Édouard

Gauttier du Lys d'Arc, Louis Édouard
Ceylan, ou, Recherches sur l'histoire, la littérature, les mœurs et les usages des Chingulais. Paris, Nepveu 1823
291p. col.front. 14 col.pl. T.
Colas 1190. LC 5-13887

See also Perrin, Narcisse, jt. auth.

Gavarni, Guillaume Sulpice Chevallier, known as
Gavarni in London: sketches of life and character, with illustrative essays by popular writers. Ed. by Albert Smith. London, D. Bogue 1849
115p. front. 22pl. port. Q.
The illustrations, designed by Gavarni and engraved by Henry Vizetelly, are the same as those in La Bédollière's *Londres et les Anglais*. In some copies the plates are colored by hand
LC 3-12165

Montagnards des Pyrénées, françaises et espagnoles; Montañeses de la Frontera de Francia. Paris & London, Rittner 1829
24 col.pl. Q.
Plate no4 marked: Lith. de Lemercier
Plates show costume of the regions Béarn, Bigorre and Aragon. Legends are in Spanish and French. For a list and description of the plates see Maherault and Boche's *L'oeuvre de Gavarni* p531 where the set is described, under title: *Costumes des Pyrénées*
Colas 1191

Œuvres choisies de Gavarni, rev. cor. et nouvellement classées par l'auteur. Études de mœurs contemporaines; La vie de jeune homme; Les débardeurs. Avec des notices en tête de chaque série, par M. P.-J. Stahl [pseud.] Paris, J. Hetzel [etc.] 1848
[14]p. 80pl. Q.
In two parts, each with special title page. The plates are caricatures which show French costume of the nineteenth century
LC 11-8040

Gavarni, Guillaume S. C.—*Continued*

Physionomie de la population de Paris. Paris, Rittner et Goupil; London, C. Tilt 1832

12 col.pl. Q.

Contents: Laitière; Élégante; Charretier; Porteuse d'eau; Cuisinière; Garde nationale; Ouvrier peintre; Bourgeoise; Avocat; Femme de chambre; Boulanger; Garde nationale

Colas 1194. Lipperheide 1162i

Travestissemens. Paris, de Kaeppelin; London, Ch. Tilt ca1838

12 col.pl. Q.

The second state of these plates was published (Paris, Rittner)

Feminine costume. Contents: Paysanne d'Altenbourg; Siennoise en 1300; Femme du Duché de Wenden; Fiancée de Berne; Italienne en 1300; Modes de Paris en 1787; Soubrette; Cracovienne; Paysanne de Rochersberg; Franconienne; Bavaroise; Duchesse en 1400; Paysanne du Canton de Soleure

The same plates slightly modified are included in a portfolio with title *Costumes historiques pour travestissements* (Paris, Beauger, lith. Coulon ca1840). The name of the artist appears on the first plate only and the lithographs have been enclosed in an oval

For a list of Gavarni's sets and plates which show costume and fashions see Mahérault and Bocher's *L'oeuvre de Gavarni*

Colas 1195-1196

(illus.) Balzac, Honoré de. Paris marié

(illus.) Le diable à Paris

(illus.) Huart, Louis. Muséum parisien

(illus.) Huart, Louis. Physiologie du tailleur. 1841

(illus.) Méry, J. P. A. Les parures

Catalogs

Mahérault, M. J. F., and Bocher, Emmanuel. L'oeuvre de Gavarni; ... catalogue raisonné. 1873

Gavarni, Guillaume Sulpice Chevallier, known as, and Devéria, Achille

Nouveaux travestissements pour le théâtre et pour le bal. Paris, Rittner & Goupil 1831; London, Ch. Tilt 1830

68pl. Q.

Each plate bears the title: Nouveau travestissemens. The plates exist in various states, for description see Mahérault and Boche's *L'oeuvre de Gavarni* p559. They show costume of many countries of Europe, various occupations and folk dress of various regions. Twelve of the plates are by Devéria

Colas 1193

Gavarni, Guillaume Sulpice Chevallier, known as, and others

(illus.) Les Français; costumes des principales provinces de la France

Gavarni in London. Gavarni, G. S. C.

Gay, Victor

Glossaire archéologique du moyen âge et de la renaissance. Paris, Société bibliographique 1887-1928

2v. illus. Q.

Volume 1 originally issued in five fascicules, 1882-87; v2 published 1928. v2, texte revu et complété par Henri Stein ... illustration dirigée par Marcel Aubert. Paris, A. Picard 1928

An illustrated dictionary of archeology which describes and gives the history of many articles of dress

LC F-1844

Gayet, Albert Jean

Exposition universelle de 1900, Palais du costume. Le costume en Égypte du IIIe au XIIIe siècle ... dessins de Ch. Emonts. Paris, E. Leroux 1900

251p. 110 illus. O.

This treats of Byzantine costume

Colas 1199. Lipperheide 1608e

Gayet, Georges Lacour-. See Lacour-Gayet, Georges

Gayette-Georgens, Frau Jeanne Marie von. See Georgens, J. D., jt. auth.

Gaywood, Richard

(illus.) Carter, Matthew. Honor redivivus; or, The analysis of honor and armory

Gazette anecdotique du regne de Louis XVI. Rouveyre, Édouard

Gazette des salons; journal des dames et des modes. v 1-34; 30 Ventôse An V [20 mars 1797]-5 janvier 1839. Paris, 1797-1839

3624 col.pl. O.

Founded by Sellèque and Madame Clément (née Hemery) with La Mésangère as collaborator on the engravings

Published 1797-Oct. 15, 1837 with title: *Journal des dames et des modes;* absorbed *L'Arlequin,* 2 Oct. 1799; and *Gazette des salons,* 15 Oct. 1837, when the title changed to *Gazette des salons, Journal des dames et des modes, fondé par M. La Mésangère*

Various extracts and collections of plates from the *Journal des dames* have been published separately (Colas 1562-64)

Colas 1561. Lipperheide 4583

Gazette des salons, journal des modes et de la musique, artistique, littéraire et théâtrale. Janvier 1835-1. octobre 1837 Paris

Pl. O.

Merged with *Gazette des salons, Journal des dames et des modes,* October 15, 1837

Colas 1201. Lipperheide 4583

Gazette du bon genre; arts modes & frivolités. 1.-7. année; nov. 1912-été 1915, jan. 1920-dec. 1925. Paris, Librairie centrale des beaux-arts 1912-25

12v. (70 fasc.) col.illus. col.pl. O.

Published monthly except January and August. Suspended 1915-19

Volume 1, 1912 to v2 no7, July 1914 as *Gazette du bon ton*

Colas 1202. LC (CA22-274)

Le bon genre; a selection of 100 plates of the famous Gazette du bon genre, by G. Barbier, Benito, R. Bonfils, P. Brissaud, J. G. Domergue, Drian, Iacovleff, G. Lepape, Ch. Martin, A. E. Marty, Siméon, Thayaht, etc. ... from the years 1920, 1921, 1922. [Paris, 1922]

100 col.pl. Q.

Contains both masculine and feminine costume but predominantly the latter

Le bon genre; réimpression du recueil de 1827 comprenant les "Observations" ... Préface de Léon Moussinac. Paris, Ed. A. Lévy [1929]

4v. col.pl. F.

"Paraît en 5 fascicules [with cover title: *Le bon genre, réimpression des 115 gravures, publiée sous ce titre de 1801 à 1822*] le dernier comprenant *Observations sur les modes et usages de Paris pour servir d'explication aux 115 caricatures.* Préface de Jean Robiquet." Subtitle

A reproduction of the *Observations.* Plates are engraved by E. Doisteau and

Gazette du bon genre—*Continued*
colored by J. Saudé. A correction slip at end explains that Robiquet did not write the preface
Colas 2241

Observations sur les modes et les usages de Paris, pour servir d'explication aux caricatures publiée sous le titre de Bon genre, depuis le commencement du dix-neuvième siècle. Paris, L. G. Michaud 1817
29p. 104 col.pl. F.
Each plate marked *Le bon genre.* For contents see Colas
The second edition (Paris, Crapelet 1822) contains the same plates and in addition seven new ones. Another edition (Paris, Vassal & Essling, or Settier 1827) contains the same plates, or in some examples new impressions, with a few of the titles changed.
Colas 2238-40

Trente neuf aquarelle originales de Harriet, Pasquier, Garbrizza, Vernet, Dutailly, Garneray, et Lanté, pour Le bon genre. Paris, Denis 1930
6 l. 39 col.pl. F.
Preface by Charles Martyne and Jacques Megret
Colas 2242

Gazette du bon ton. See Gazette du bon genre

Gazette of fashion and cutting room companion. See Minister's Gazette of fashion

The **gazetteer** of the Central Provinces of India. Grant, Sir Charles

Gebbie, George. See Paul, Howard, jt. ed.

[**Gebens**]
[Armée russe 1854-1862] St. Petersbourg, bureau de la Chronique militaire [1862?]
58 col.pl. F.
Fifty-five of the plates show the Imperial Guard and three show infantry
Colas 1204, 1511

Gebräuche und kleidungen der Chinesen. Grohmann, J. G.

Gebser, Clara
Leitfaden zum selbstunterricht im spitzenklöppeln nebst praktischen winken für erfahrenere klöppelerinnen. Hannover, Helwingsche verlagsbuchhandlung [1892]
27p. 10 illus. 8pl. Q.
Lipperheide 4055

Gebweiler, Hieronymus. See Gebwiler, Hieronymus

Gebwiler, Hieronymus
... Epitome regii ac vetustissimi artus sacrae caesareae ac Catholice maiestatis ... principis ... Ferdinandi ... Bohemiae regis, omniumque archiducum Austriae, ac Habsburgensium comitum. Haganoae, ex officina I. Secerii 1530
103 l. 24 illus. Q.
Illustrations include 32 portraits of the Hapsburgs
A Latin and a German edition were published in Strassburg in 1527
Lipperheide 844

Gedenk boek der inhuldiging en feesttogten van Zijne Majesteit Wilhelm II, 1840-1842. St. Hertogenbosch, J. F. Demelinne [1842?]
2 l. 9 col.pl. O.
Plates show uniforms of the civic guard
Colas 1205

Gedenkblätter der Universitäten Heidelberg, Prag und Wien. Heideloff, K. A. von

Gedenkblätter des festcarrousels. Frederich, E.

Gedenkbuch zu Friedrich v. Schiller's 100 jähriger geburtsfeier, begangen in Frankfurt a. M. den 10 november 1859. Frankfurt a.M. Keller 1860
xxiv,76p. 16pl. Q.
Plates are engraved by F. C. Klimsch

Gedenkwaerdig bedryf der Nederlandsche Oost-Indische maetschappye. Dapper, Olfert

Gedenkwaerdige gesantschappen der Oost-Indische maatschappy in 't Vereenigde Nederland, aan de kaisaren van Japan. Montanus, Arnoldus

Gedenkwaerdige zee en lantreize door de voornaemste landschappen van West en Oostindien. Nieuhof, Johan

Gedenkweerdige Brasiliaense zee- en lantreize. See Nieuhof, Johan. Joan Nieuhofs Gedenkwaerdige zee en lantreize door de voornaemste landschappen van West en Oostindien

Gédéon
Les femmes de ménage. Paris, A. de Vresse ca1860
19pl. Q.
Lipperheide 3640

Gee, James, hatter
(pub.) Sala, G. A. H. The hats of humanity

Geelen, G. V.
Relation succincte et veritable de tout ce qui s'est passé pendant le siège de Vienne ... assiegée par les Turcs depuis le 14. juillet jusqu'au 12. de septembre 1683 ... traduit en françois par N. J. D. N. Bruxelles, J. Leonard 1684
89p. 11pl. 1 plan. Q.
Plates 1-10 are engraved by R. de Hooghe
Lipperheide 2089

Geens, Louis
(illus.) Viatour, Gustave. Étude sur l'armée belge, 1896

Geets, Willem
Ommegang de Saint-Rombaut (1875). Calvalcade historique organisée par la ville de Malines, à l'occasion du jubilé de Saint-Rombaut, patron de la communne. Plans et dessins de M. Willem Geets; texte français par M. Emmanuel Neeffs. Bruxelles, Simonau-Toovey [1875]
7 l. 7pl.(3 col.) F.
Lipperheide 2812

Geffroy
(illus.) Chefs-d'oeuvre dramatiques du XVIIIe siècle

Der **gefursten** grafen zu Tyrol. See note under Custos, Dominicus. Tirolensium principum comitum

Gegants, nans i altres entremesos. Amades, Joan

Geheime unternehmungen der Freymaurer darinne ihr ursprung und fortgang, ihr aufdingen, loszsprechen, die dabey vorkommenden ceremonien enthalten sind,

Geheime unternehmungen ... —*Continued*
und alle bey ihnen gebräuchliche allegorien erklärt werden. London and Berlin 1787
230p. 7pl. O.
Lipperheide 1945

Die **geheimnisse** der frau. Orchamps, baronin d', pseud.

Gehrig, Oscar
Hiler theater- und ballettentwürfe; zusammengestellt und eingeleitet von Dr. Oscar Gehrig. Berlin [Carl Michaal'schen hof- und ratsdruckerei] 1922
15p. XII mounted pl. O.
Costumes for an acrobatic ballet and a play, *Der kleine Klaus und der grosse Klaus,* based on Hans Christian Andersen's story

Gehrts, Johs
(illus.) Jostes, Franz. Westfälisches trachtenbuch

Geiger, Ludwig
(ed.) Burckhardt, J. C. Die cultur der renaissance in Italien. 1885

Geiger, Peter Johann Nepomuk
(illus.) Das Kaiser-Album

Geikie, Walter
Etchings illustrative of Scottish character and scenery; Sir Thomas Dick Lauder's edition, with additional plates and letterpress. Edinburgh, W. Paterson 1885
xiii,136p. 3 l. front. 89pl. sq.Q.

Geiling, F. W.
Bilder aus dem deutschen studentenleben ... von F. W. G. Jena & Berlin 1865
16pl. ob.F.

Geisberg, Max
... Die prachtharnische des goldschmiedes Heinrich Cnoep aus Münster i. W. Strassburg, J. H. E. Heitz 1907
59p. 1 illus. XIV pl. O. (Studien zur deutschen kunstgeschichte, 85. hft.)
LC 12-11877

Geisler, Adam Friedrich
(ed.) Archiv weiblicher hauptkenntnisse für diejenigen jedes standes

Geissler, Christian Gottfried Heinrich
Abbildung der Communal-Garde zu Leipzig in ihren verschiedenen uniformen. Leipzig, P. Lenz [1831]
1 l. 35 col.pl. Q.
Plates are marked: C. G. H. Geissler, del. They show the civic guard of Leipzig
Colas 1210. Lipperheide 2203

Leipziger meszscenen. Leipzig, E. F. Steinacker 1804-1805
3v. 16 col.pl. Q.
Lipperheide 828

Mahlerische darstellungen der sitten, gebräuche und lustbarkeiten bey den russischen, tartarischen, mongolischen und andern völkern im russischen reich ... Deutsch und französisch. Leipzig, Baumgärtner [1804]
4v. 40 col.pl. Q.
Explanatory text of volumes 1-2 by F. Hempel, of volumes 3-4 by J. Richter
French title: *Tableaux pittoresque des moeurs, des usages, et des divertissements des Russes, Tartares, Mongols et autres nations de l'empire russe*
Colas 1208. Lipperheide 1344

Représentation des uniformes de l'armée impériale de la Russie en 88 estampes enluminées. [No place] 1793
2 l. 88 col.pl. O.
Colas 1206

(engr.) Damberger, C. F., pseud. Christian Friedrich Damberger's Landreise in das innere von Afrika

(illus.) Gruber, J. G. Sitten, gebräuche und kleidung der Russen, in St Petersburg

(illus.) Hacquet, Balthaser. Abbildung und beschreibung der südwest- und östlichen Wenden, Illyrer und Slaven

(illus.) Hacquet, Balthasar. L'Illyrie et la Dalmatie, ou Moeurs usages et costumes des habitants et des ceux des contrées voisines

(illus.) Richter, J. G. Sitten, gebräuche und kleidung der Russen aus den niedern ständen

(illus.) Richter, J. G. Spiele und belustigungen der Russen

See also Richter, J. G., jt. auth.; Hempel, Friedrich, jt. auth.; Shönberg, jt. auth.

Geissler, Christian Gottfried Heinrich, and Menzel, A.
Leipziger volksscenen. Berlin, Gebrüder Gropius im Diorama ca1830
12 col.pl. Q.
Plates show scenes at the Leipzig fair. Each plate bears the title, the statement: "Lith. Anst. v. Winckelmann & Söhne" and a legend in German
Colas 1209

Geissler, J. G. H. See Geissler, Christian Gottfried Heinrich

Die **geistlichen** gewänder katholischer und evangelischer konfession in mathematisch genauen schnitt-zeichnungen. Klemm, H.

Geklopte boomschors als kleedingstof op Midden-Celebes. Adriani, Nicolaus, and Kruijt, A. C.

Gelbke, Carl Heinrich von
Ritterorden und ehrenzeichen erlaütert durch die vorhandenen urkunden. Als anhang des werkes: Abbildungen und beschreibung der ritterorden und ehrenzeichen sämmtlicher souveraine und regierungen ... I. Preussen. Berlin, G. Reimer 1834
66p. 1 col.pl. Q.
Lipperheide 1923

Geldart, Ernest
Ecclesiastical decoration. London, Mowbray 1889
206p. front. 52pl. O. o.p.
Plate 32 shows costume of the twelve apostles; plate 51, crowns used in various periods; plate 52, the mitre

Geldenhauer, Gerardus. Noviomagus. (In Baerland, Adriaan van. Hollandiae comitum historia et icones)

Der **gelehrte** in der deutschen vergangenheit. Reicke, Emil

Gelin, Henri
Les coiffes poitevines, les bijoux poitevins. Collection de la société du costume poitevin. Ligugé, Aux bureaux du pays poitevin 1898
22p. illus. O.
Colas 1212

Gelin, Henri, and Escudier, Charles
Costumes poitevins, études dessinées et gravées par Ch. Escudier; texte explicatif, par H. Gelin. Niort, L'auteur 1896
40p. 30pl. Q.
Colas 1211

Gellé, P., and Arnaud, Ch.
Vues et costumes pittoresque du départ des Deux-Sèvres; par Gellé. Texte par Ch. Arnaud. Niort, Morrisset [1844]
8p. 13? pl. Q.
Colas gives a list of the plates
Colas 1213

Gelli, E. See Gelli, Jacopo. Bibliografia generale della scherma

Gelli, Jacopo
Bibliografia generale della scherma, con note critiche, biografiche e storiche. Testo italiano e francese. Illustrazioni originali di E. Gelli Firenze, L. Niccolai 1890
xliii,582p. 31 illus. O.
Lipperheide 2995. LC 5-12780

De **geloofsbelijdenissen** der wereld. See Gardner, James. The faiths of the world

Gemähde aller nationen. Hausleutner, P. W. G.

Gemälde und zeichnungen. Watteau, J. A.

Die **gemälde** von Dürer and Wolgemut. Dürer, Alb recht, and Wolgemut, Michael

Gemäldegallerie aus den bauernstuben Dalekarliens. See Bosaeus, Ernst. Tafvelgalleri från stugor i Dalom

Gembarzewski, Bronislaw
Wojsko Polskie. Krôlestwo Polskie 1815-1830. Opracowal i rysowal Bronislaw Gembarzewski z przedmowa Aleksandra Rembowskiego. Warsawa, K. Trepte 1903
xv,192,xxxvi p. 8 col.pl. Q.
Colas 1214

Wojsko Polskie. Ksiestvoo Warszawskie 1807-1814. Warszawa, Gebethner i Wolff 1905
Pl.(part col.) Q.
Cataloged from Colas's *Bibliographie*
Colas 1215

Gemme antiche figurate. Rossi, Domenico de

Genaue darstellung saemmtliche branchen der kaiserl. koenigl. armee. See Geschichte der kaiserl. königl. regimenter

La **gendarmerie** de France. Isnard, P. Fr. d'

Genealogia comitum Flandriae. Vred, Oliverius

Genealogia illustrissimorum comitum Nassoviae. Orlers, Jan

Genealogia serenissimor. Boiarlae ducum. Kilian, Wolfgang

A **genealogical** and heraldic history of the peerage. Burke, Sir J. B., and Burke, A. P.

Généalogie de la maison royal de Bourbon. Bernard, Charles

Les **genealogies** et anciennes descentes des forestiers et comtes de Flandre. Martin, Cornelis

Genée, Rudolf
Hans Sachs und seine zeit; ein lebens- und kulturbild aus der zeit der reformation. Leipzig, J. J. Weber 1894
xvi,524p. 166 illus. 21 facsims. O.
Lipperheide 675

General
Under this subject are entered works that are not confined to any one country, continent, or period

General works

Albert, A. Le tour du monde; album des costumes de toute la terre. 1892
Album des types et costumes de tous les peuples du monde. 1869
Alexander, William. Histoire des femmes. 1791-94
Alexander, William. History of women. 1779. v2 p 111-204
Aria, Mrs E. D. Costume: fanciful, historical and theatrical. 1906
Aspin, Jehoshaphat. Cosmorama; a view of the costumes and peculiarities of all nations. 1826
Aubert & cie. Musée de costumes. ca1850-60
Balch, E. S. Savage and civilized dress. 1904
Barton, Lucy. Historic costume for the stage. 1935
Becker, W. G. Vom costume an denkmälern. 1776
Bellinzoni, Luigi. Usi e costumi antichi e moderni di tutti i popoli del mondo. 1884
Beyschlag, Robert. Female costume pictures; figures of female grace and beauty in costumes of various centuries. 1886
Bible, G. W., and Bible, D. P. Looking backward at woman's fashionable dress. 1892
Blätter für kostümkunde; historische und volks-trachten. 1876-91
Bonwit, Teller & co., New York. The philosophy of dress. c1925
Bourdeau, Louis. Histoire de l'habillement et de la parure. 1904
Brossard, Charles. Colonies françaises. 1906
Brummell, G. B. Male and female costume. 1932
Bulwer, John. A view of the people of the whole world. 1658
Buss, Georg. Das kostum in vergangenheit und gegenwart. 1906
Chalmers, Helena. Clothes, on and off the stage. 1928
Chisman, Isabel and Raven-Hart, H. E. Manners and movements in costume plays. 1934
Chuse, A. R. Costume design. c1930
Cole, Walter. A B C book of people. 1932
Colin, Mme Anais. Les dames cosmopolites. 1843-45

General—*Continued*

Costüm-buch für künstler; sammlung der interessanten gegenstände des costüms aller zeiten und völker der christlichen zeitrechnung. 1839

Costumes of all nations: one hundred and twenty-three plates, containing over fifteen hundred coloured costume pictures designed by the first Munich artists. 1910

Coutumes des nations plus célèbres du monde. 1750?

Crépon, Théophile. Costume civil, costume ecclesiastique, costume monastique. 1900

Dooley, W. H. Clothing and style. c1930

Eck, Ch. Histoire chronologique du vêtement (Homme). 1866

Eichler, Lillian. The customs of mankind. 1924

Emy, Henry, engr. Costumes historiques. ca1850

Erskine, Mrs Beatrice. Beautiful women in history & art. 1905

Evans, Mary. Costume silhouettes. c1923

Evans, Mary. Costume throughout the ages. 1930

Eye, August von, and Falke, Jacob von. Kunst und leben der vorzeit vom beginn des mittelalters bis zu anfang des 19. jahrhunderts. 1859-62

Fabronius, Hermann. Newe summarische welt historia ... Was für land and leute in der gantzen welt, was ihre gestalt, kleidung, sprachen annd handthierung ... seyen. 1612

Fales, Jane. Dressmaking, a manual for schools and colleges. 1917

Falke, Jacob von. Costümgeschichte der culturvölker. 1881

Félix, E., ed. What she wore. 1899

Ferrario, Giulio. Aggiunte e rettificazioni all' opera Il costume antico e moderno di tutti i popoli cogli analoghi disegni del dottore Giulio Ferrario. 1831-34

Ferrario, Giulio. Il costume antico e moderno. 1827

Felt, J. B. The customs of New England. 1853. p79-208

Finden, William, and Finden, E. F. Findens' tableaux of national character, beauty, and costume. 1843

Fischel, Oskar. Chronisten der mode: mensch und kleid in bildern aus drei jahrtausenden. 1923

Gardiner, F. M. The evolution of fashion. 1897

Giafferri, P. L. V. de, marquis. L'histoire du costume feminin mondial de l'an 5318 avant J.-C. à nos jours. 1925

Giafferri, P. L. V. de, marquis. The history of the feminine costume of the world, from the year 5318 B. C. to our century. 1926-27

Grasset de Saint-Sauveur, Jacques. Costumes civils actuels de tous les peuples connus, dessinés d'après nature, gravés et coloriés, accompagnés d'un abrégé historique de leurs coutumes, moeurs, religions, sciences, arts, commerce, monnoïes. 1784

Grasset de Saint-Sauveur, Jacques. Costumes civils actuels de tous les peuples connus, dessinés d'après nature, gravés et coloriés, accompagnés d'une notice historique sur leurs coutumes, moeurs, religions. 1788

Grasset de Saint-Sauveur, Jacques. Tableaux des principaux peuples de l'Europe, de l'Asie, de l'Afrique, de l'Amerique; et les découvertes des capitaines Cook, La Pérouse, etc. 1798

Graterolle, Maurice. Du costume et de la toïlette dans l'antiquité et de nos jours. 1897

Grévedon, P. L. H. Mosaïque de costumes, ou Alphabet étranger. ca1830

Happel, E. W., ed. Thesaurus exoticum. 1688

Hauff, H. Moden und trachten; fragmente zur geschichte des costüms. 1840

Hefner-Alteneck, J. H. von. Trachten, kunstwerke und geräthschaften vom frühen mittelalter bis ende des achtzehnten jahrhunderts. 1879-89

History of feminine costume; tracing its evolution from earliest times to the present. 1896

Hottenroth, Friedrich. Le costume, les armes, ustensiles, outils des peuples anciens et modernes. 1886-91?

Hottenroth, Friedrich. Trachten, haus-, feld- und kriegsgeräthschaften der völker alter und neuer zeit. 1884?-91

Jacquemin, Raphael. Histoire générale du costume civil, religieux et militaire du IV au XIX. siècle (315-1815). [1876]

Jacquemin, Raphael. Iconographie générale et mèthodique du costume du IV. au XIX. siècle (315-1815) collection gravée à l'eau forte d'après des documents authentiques & inédits. 1863-68

Jong, Jo de. 50 eeuwen costuum. 1927

Jossic, Y. F. A revival of the past ages; costumes, accessories, architecture, social life and various activities. 1932-35

Köhler, Bruno. Allgemeine trachtenkunde. 1900-1902

Köhler, Karl. A history of costume. 1928

Köhler, Karl. Praktische kostümkunde in 600 bildern und schnitten. 1926

Kraus, G. M. Nationaltrachten verschied. völker. 1805

Lacauchie, A. Galerie de costumes. 1851

Lacauchie, A. Les nations. 1853

Lacy, T. H., ed. Female costumes, historical, national and dramatic. 1865

Lacy, T. H., ed. Male costumes, historical, national, and dramatic. 1868

Lampert, Kurt. Die völker der erde. 1902

Leonhardi, F. G. Bildliche darstellung aller bekannten völker nach ihren kleidertrachten, sitten, gewohnheiten. 1798

Leonhardi, F. G. Costumes de tous les peuples connu. 1815

Lester, K. M. Historic costume; a résumé of the characteristic types of costume from the most remote times to the present day. c1933

General—*Continued*
Le Vacher de Charnois, J. C. Recherches sur les costumes et sur les théatres de toutes les nations, tant anciennes que modernes. 1790
Lippmann, Friedrich. Kupferstiche und holzschnitte aller meister in nachbildungen. 1889-95
Llanta, J. F. G. Les jeunes fiancées; suite de portraits et costumes variés de tous les pays. 1834
Lorenzini, Paolo. Storia del costume dei popoli attraverso i secoli. 1934
Louandre, C. L. Les arts somptuaires; histoire du costume et de l'ameublement et des arts et industries qui s'y rattachent. 1857-58
Louden, Mrs A. B., and Louden, N. P. Historic costumes through the ages. 1936
Loumyer, J. F. N. Moeurs, usages et costumes de tous les peuples du monde ... par Auguste Wahlen [pseud.] 1843-44
Marais, Paul. Trois causeries sur l'histoire du costume. 1914
Menin, Lodocico. Il costume di tutte le nazioni e di tutti i tempi. 1834-37
Les modes anciennes et modernes; coup d'oeil sur l'origine et les progrès du vêtement, depuis l'antiquité jusqu'à nos jours, par D. M. J. H. ca1860
La mode par l'image du XIIe au XVIIe siècle. 1903
Moeurs et costumes de différens peuples de la terre. ca1840
Moeurs et coutumes des peuples, ou Collection de tableaux représentant les usages remarquables, les mariages, funérailles, supplices et fêtes des diverses nations du monde. 1811-14
Mohrbutter, Alfred. Das kleid der frau. 1904
Morel-Retz, L. P. G. B. Costumes nationaux. ca1875
Müller, Élisabeth. Le monde en estampes; types et costumes des principaux peuples de l'univers. 1858
Mützel, H. H. H. E. Kostümkunde für sammler. 1921
Mützel, H. H. H. E. Vom lendenschurz zur modetracht, aus der geschichte des kostüms. 1925
Neu-eingerichtete und vermehrte bildergeographie von Europa, Asia, Africa und America worinnen alle nationen nach ihrem habit in saubern figuren ... vorgestellt werden. 1738
Noronha, Eduardo de. O vestuario, historia do traje desde os tempos mais remotes até á idade-média. 1911
Norris, Herbert. Costume & fashion. 1924-33
Northrup, Belle, comp. The story of costume told in pictures. c1935
Northrup, Belle, and Green, A. L. A short description of historic fashion. 1925
Pachinger, A. M. Die mutterschaft in der malerei und graphik. 1906
Parsons, F. A. The art of dress. 1928
Pauquet, H. L. É., and Pauquet, P. J. C. Illustrations of English and foreign costumes from the fifteenth century to the present day. 1875
Pauquet, H. L. É., and Pauquet, P. J. C. Modes et costumes historiques étrangers. 1875?
Le petit cosmopolite, ou Recueil des costumes de différents peuples. ca1830
Price, Sir H. P. When men wore muffs; the story of men's clothes. 1936
Puiggarí, José. Monografía histórica é iconográfica del traje. 1886
Quincke, Wolfgang. Handbuch der kostümkunde. 1908
Racinet, A. C. A. Le costume historique. 1888
Recueil d'estampes, représentant les grades, les rangs et les dignités, suivant le costume de toutes les nations existantes. 1779-84
Ritchie, Leitch. Beauty's costume: a series of female figures in the dresses of all times and nations. 1838
Rodriguez, A. Colleccion general de los trages; que usan actualmente todas las naciones del mundo descubierto. 1799
Roger-Milès, Léon. Comment discerner les styles du VIIIe au XIXe siècle: histoire—philosophie—document. ca1906
Rohrbach, Carl. The costumes of all nations from the earliest times to the nineteenth century. 1882
Rohrbach, Carl. Die trachten der völker vom beginn der geschichte bis zum 19. jahrhundert. 1882
Rosenberg, Adolf. The design and development of costume from prehistoric times up to the twentieth century. 1925
Rosenberg, Adolf. Geschichte des kostüms. 1905-23
Rosenthal, Doris, comp. Pertaining to costume. 1929
Rouit, H. La mode féminine à travers les âges. 1925
Roujoux, P. G., baron de. Le monde en estampes ou Géographie des cinq parties du monde. 1830
Rumpf, Fritz. Der mensch und seine tracht ihrem wesen nach geschildert. 1905
Ruppert, Jacques. Le costume. c1930-31
Ruppert, Jacques. Histoire du costume de l'antiquité au XIX. siècle. 1930
Sage, Elizabeth. A study of costume, from the days of the Egyptians to modern times. c1926
Saultereau, Anthoine, comp. Chronologie et sommaire des souverrains pontifes, anciens pères, empereurs, roys, princes, et hommes illustres, dés le commencement du monde, jusques à l'an de grace mil six cens vingtdeux. 1631
Schmidt, Mrs M. M. 400 outstanding women of the world and costumology of their time. 1933
Sellner, Eudora. History of costume design. c1928

General—*Continued*

Sergent-Marceau, A. F. Costumi dei popoli antichi e moderni... con discorsi analoghi sulla forma degli abiti e la maniera di vestirli. 1813-17

Stibbert, Federigo. Abiti e fogge civili e militari dal I al XVIII secolo. 1914

Thirifocq. Histoire universelle du costume ... d'après les grands peintres de chaque époque. 1863-64

Trachten oder Stambuch: dariñen alle fürnemste nationen, völckern, manns unnd weibs personen in ihren kleydern artlich abgemahlt nach jedes landes sitten und gebrauch. 1600

Traphagen, Ethel. Costume design and illustration. 1932

Truman, Nevil. Historic costuming. 1936

Usi e costumi di tutti i popoli dell' universo. 1856-62

Vachon, Marius. La femme dans l'art. 1893

Vecellio, Cesare. Coleccion de trages que usaron todas las naciones conocidas hasta el siglo XV. 1794

Vecellio, Cesare. Costumes anciens et modernes; Habiti antichi et moderni di tutto il mondo. 1860

Vecellio, Cesare. De gli habiti antichi, et moderni di diverse parti del mondo. 1590

Villard, Georges. Le théâtre d'amateurs; manuel d'art théâtral. c1919

Walkup, Mrs F. P. Outline history of costume, based on authentic and historic sources, illustrated by plates with patterns. 1933

Webb, W. M. The heritage of dress; being notes on the history and evolution of clothes. 1912

Weiss, Hermann. Kostümkunde. 1860-72

Wilson, M. M. S. E., countess of. The book of costume: or, Annals of fashion, from the earliest period to the present time. 1847

Zamacoïs, Miguel. Le costume. c1936

Zur geschichte der costüme, nach zeichnungen von W. Diez, C. Fröhlich, C. Häberlin M. Heil, A. Müller, F. Rothbart, J. Watter. [1895?]

Supplementary material

Berlin. Staatliche museen. Museum für völkerkunde. Führer durch das Museum für völkerkunde

Boehn, Max von. Miniaturen und silhouetten. 1919

Boehn, Max von. Miniatures and silhouettes. 1928

Bouchot, H. F. X. M. Le cabinet d'estampes de la bibliothèque nationale. 1895

Bryan, Michael. Bryan's dictionary of painters and engravers. 1903-05

Buschan, G. H. T. Die sitten der völker. 1914-16

Cartarius, Marius. Icones operum misericordiae; cum Julii Roscii Hortini sententiis et explicationibus. 1586

Champlin, J. D., ed. Cyclopedia of painters and paintings. 1887

Chimani, Leopold. Das portefeuille des wissbegierigen. 1841

Clarac, C. O. F. J. B., comte de. Musée de sculpture antique et moderne. 1826-53

Compte-Calix, F. C.; Mille, E., and Morlon, A. Les délices de l'hiver. n.d.

Conrady, Alexander. Geschichte der revolutionen vom niederländischen aufstand bis zum vorabend der französischen revolution. 1911

Cowden-Clarke, Mary. World-noted women. 1858

Dantier, Alphonse. Les femmes dans la société chrétienne. 1879

Dass die blosse brüste seyn ein gross gerüste viel böser lüste wird dem züchtigen frauen-zimmern zu ehren und den unverschämtem weibs-stücken zur schande erwiesen. 1687

Dayot, A. P. M. L'image de la femme. 1899

Denkmäler der malerei auf 63 tafeln mit erklärendem text. 1860

Denkmäler der sculptur auf 36 tafeln mit erklärendem text. 1860

Depping, G. B. Aperçu historique sur les moeurs et coutumes des nations. 1842

Desessarts, Alfred. L'univers illustré ca1840

Devéria, Achille. Flore des salons ou les fleurs et les femmes de tous les pays 1831

Doran, John. Habits and men. 1854

Dumont d'Urville, J. S. C., ed. Voyage pittoresque autour du monde; resumé générale des voyages de découvertes de Magelan, Tasman, Dampier. 1834-35

Les étoiles du monde; galerie historique des femmes les plus célèbres de tous les temps et de tous les pays. 1858

Figuier, Louis. The human race. 1872

Figuier, Louis. Les races humaines. 1880

Friedenthal, Albert. Das weib im leben der völker. 1911

Grévedon, P. L. H. Les femmes cosmopolites. ca1831

Hale, P. L. Great portraits, women. 1909

Hammerton, Sir J. A., ed. Manners & customs of mankind. 1931-32

Hatin, L. E. Histoire pittoresque des voyages autour du monde. 1847

Hürlimann, Martin. Der erdkreis. 1935

Hutchinson, H. N.; Gregory, J. W., and Lydekker, Richard, eds. The living races of mankind. 1901

International congress of popular arts Prague, 1928. Art populaire. 1931

Jouhanneaud, Paul. Album des voyage anciens et modernes. 1854

Lands and peoples; the world in color 1932

Larned, J. N. The new Larned History for ready reference, reading and re search. 1922-24

Malerische studien; eine reise um die welt in . . . photographien nach naturaufnah men. 1899

General—Supplementary works—*Continued*
Mongez, Antoine. Tableaux, statues, bas reliefs et camées de la Galerie de Florence et du Palais Pitti. 1789-1807
Montémont, A. É. de. Histoire universelle des voyages effectués par mer et par terre dans les cinq parties du monde. 1833-37
Münster, Sebastian. Cosmographia, das ist: beschreibung der gantzen welt. 1628
The mythology of all races. 1916-32
A new general collection of voyages and travels. 1745-47
Nuremberg. Germanisches nationalmuseum. Katalog der im Germanischen museum befindlichen kartenspiele und spielkarten. 1886
Peoples of all nations; their life to-day and the story of their past. 1922-24
Ratzel, Friedrich. The history of mankind. 1896-98
Ratzel, Friedrich. Völkerkunde. 1894
Ridpath, J. C. Great races of mankind. 1893
Rimmel, Eugene. The book of perfumes. 1867
Saint Prosper, A. A. C. de, and others. Histoire de tous les peuples et des revolutions du monde depuis les temps les plus reculés jusqu'à nos jours. 1841?
Schedel, Hartmann. Das buch der chroniken. 1493
Schweiger-Lerchenfeld, Amand, freiherr von. Das frauenleben der erde. 1881
Simpson, William. Picturesque people: being groups from all quarters of the globe. 1876
Spencer, Herbert. Descriptive sociology. 1873-1934
The world displayed; or, A curious collection of voyages and travels. 1795-96

See also Ecclesiastical costume; Military costume; also names of countries; and of periods as Middle ages, Seventeenth century; also parts of dress as Footwear, Capes and Cloaks; also Art of dress, Collections of costume, Costume in art, Criticism, Designing, Dictionaries of costume, Etiquet of dress, Fancy dress, Fashion, Hospital garments, Hygiene of dress, Nudity, Philosophy of dress, Playing cards, Prehistoric, Primitive dress, Psychology of dress, Reform of dress

Periodicals

Globus; illustrierte zeitschrift für länder- und völkerkunde. 1867-1910
Le magasin pittoresque. 1833+
The National geographic magazine. 1888+
Peterson magazine. 1840-98
Société de l'histoire du costume, Paris. Bulletin. 1907-11
Tour du monde. 1860-1914
Tygodnik illustrowany. 1859+
Zeitschrift für bildende kunst. 1866-1931/32
Vsemirnaía illíustratsiía. 1869-97

General historien der aller namhafftigsten ... geschichten ... keyser Carols des Fünfften und anfange Ferdinanden seines bruders regierung. Henricpetri, Adam

General history of the North American Indians. See Schoolcraft, H. R. Information respecting ... the Indian tribes of the United States, v6

General regulations for the government of the army of the Republic of Texas. Texas (Republic) War department

Geneva. Musée d'art et d'histoire. Section des arts décoratifs
Collection de dentelles anciennes. Paris, Librairie générale de l'architecture et des arts decoratifs 190-?
2 l. 36pl. F.

Genin, John Nicholas
An illustrated history of the hat. From the earliest ages to the present time. New York [E. N. Grossman, printer] 1848
54p. incl.illus. pl. S.
LC 36-24754

Genlis, Stéphanie Félicité Ducrest de Saint Aubin, comtesse de, afterwards Marquise de Sillery
Dictionnaire critique et raisonné des étiquettes de la cour, des usages du monde. Paris, P. Mongie aîné 1818
2v. O.
"Des amusemens, des modes, des moeurs, etc., des François, depuis la mort de Louis XIII jusqu'à nos jours, contenant le tableau de la cour, de la société, et de la littérature du dix-huitième siècle." Subtitle
Colas 1216. Lipperheide 1073. LC 9-27225

Genoni, Rosa
La storia della moda attraverso i secoli (dalla preistoria ai tempi odierni) volume 1. Bergamo, Istituto italiano d'arti grafiche [c1925]
1 v. illus. pl.(part col.) fold.diagrs. Q.
Contents of volume 1: Preistoria; La veste egizia; La veste Assiro-Babilonese; Età minoico-micenica; Grecia
"Bibliografia": v 1, 1 leaf at end
LC 25-7994

Genouillac, Henri Gourdon de. See Gourdon de Genouillac, Henri

Le **genre**, études variées. Grenier, François

Genre parisien (métiers). Philipon, Charles

Genrebilder aus dem Orient. See Fischer, Sébastien. Tableaux de genre

Genthe, Arnold
(illus.) Irwin, W. H. Old Chinatown

Genthe, Friedrich Wilhelm
Schutz- und trutzrede für die crinoline oder den steif- und reifrock. Eisleben, G. Reichardt. 1858
24p. O.
Colas 1217. Lipperheide 3492

Gentleman's journal. See Man's book; a magazine

Gentleman's magazine of fashions, fancy costumes, and the regimentals of the army. v 1- , May 1828-Dec. 1894. London Bell
Pl.(part col.) O.
Merged into *London tailor and record of fashion*
Colas 1218

Gentlemen's fancy dress. Holt, Ardern

The **gentlewoman's** book of dress. Douglas, Mrs Fanny

Genty, firm, Paris

(pub.) Costumes militaires. Paris, Genty 1814-1815
3v. col.pl. Q.
Contents: 1. suite, Infanterie russe. ([1815] 22 col.pl.) 2. suite, Infanterie prussienne 1815. (34 col.pl.) 3. suite, Infanterie allemande (1815. 57 col.pl.)
Colas 725-27

(pub.) Costumes militaires. Infanterie anglaise (1815). Paris, Genty [1815?]
9 col.pl. Q.
According to Colas a tenth plate exists, not described by Glasser. The title is: *Troupes anglaises. Garde du corps du roi 1815*
Colas 728

(pub.) [Troupes françaises] Paris, Genty 1814-16
3v. 101 col.pl. Q.
Published in three series: 1814 (12pl.) 1815 (22pl.) 1816 (67pl.)
In 1832 fourteen colored plates were issued, with the same title, by Richard and Berrieux, the successors of Genty. For the most part these were the Genty plates brought up to date
Colas 2914-2917

Genuinae icones ducum Bavariae. Amman, Jost

Geoffroy, Charles

(engr.) Camino, Charles, and Régamey, Frederic. Costumes suédois

(engr.) Compte-Calix, F. C. Les travestissements élégants

Geoffroy, Jean Jules Henri

Les bataillons scolaires ... Texte par Désiré Lacroix. [Paris, L. Baschet 1887]
15p. 8 col.illus. O. (Cahiers d'enseignement illustrés, no34)
Lipperheide 2348

Geoffroy de Villeneuve, René Claude

L'Afrique, ou histoire, moeurs, usages et coutumes des Africains: Le Senegal. Paris, Nepveu 1814
4v. 44pl.(40 col.) D.
For an English translation with the same plates see Frederic Shoberl's *Africa*
Colas 1219. Lipperheide 1579

A **geographical** present: being descriptions of the principal countries of the world; with representations of the various inhabitants in their respective costumes. London, Darton, Harvey & Darton 1817
120p. 60 col.pl. D.
Colas 1220. Lipperheide 480

La **géographie** en estampes, ou, Mœurs et costumes des différens peuples de la terre. Paris, Lecerf [etc., 1816?]
196p. front. 28pl. maps. ob.O.
Colas 1221. LC 8-29092

Géographie pittoresque et monumentale de la France et de ses colonies. See Brossard, Charles. Colonies françaises

Die **geometrische** construction und farbengebung des flach-ornamentes. Fink, Karl

Geometrische ornamentik. Diefenbach, Leonhard

Georg, J.

(engr.) Delsenbach, J. A. Wahre abbildung der sämtlichen reichskleinodien welche in ... Nürnberg aufbewahret werden

(engr.) Ferrari, Ottavio. Ottavii Ferrarii De re vestiaria libri septem

George, Waldemar

Boris Aronson et l'art du théatre. Paris, Éditions des Chroniques du jour 1928
xv p. illus. pl.(part col.) sq.Q. (Maîtres de l'art étranger)

The **George** Catlin Indian gallery in the U.S. National museum. Donaldson, Thomas

George Grenfell and the Congo. Johnston, Sir H. H.

George von Frundsberg oder das deutsch kriegshandwerk zur zeit der reformation. Barthold, F. W.

George Washington play and pageant costume book. United States. George Washington bicentennial commission

Georgens, Jan Daniel

Das häkeln; mit einer ornamentik aus drei jahrhunderten ... unter mitwirkung von Marie Sturm und Florentine Sturm; 3. aufl. Leipzig, O. Schneider [1888]
113p. 168 illus. 4 col.pl. Q.
Lipperheide 4142

Das stricken; mit einer ornamentik aus drei jahrhunderten ... unter mitwirkung von Marie Sturm ... und Florentine Sturm; 4. aufl. Leipzig, O. Schneider 1882 [-1885]
4v. 187 illus.(part col.) Q.
Lipperheide 4141

Georgens, Jan Daniel, and Gayette-Georgens, Frau Jeanne Marie von

Die schulen der weiblichen handarbeit. 2. verm. aufl. Leipzig, Richter 1878
58p. 82 illus. 146pl. Q.
First edition: Berlin, O. Loewenstein 1869. (64pl.)
Lipperheide 4100-4101

Georgens, Frau Jeanne Marie Von Gayette. See Gayette-Georgens, Frau J. M. von

Georgi, Johann Gottlieb

Beschreibung aller nationen des russischen reichs, ihrer lebensart, religion, gebräuche, wohnungen, kleidungen und übrigen merkwürdigkeiten. St. Petersburg, C. W. Müller, 1776-[80]
530,[10]p. 1 illus. (music) and atlas of 95pl. Q.
Issued in 4 volumes, each with separate t.-p. and "Nachricht" and paged continuously. Atlas has title: *Kupfer zur Beschreibung aller nationen des russischen reichs.* The edition described by Lipperheide has the plates in color
Contents: 1. ausg. Nationen vom finnischen stamm; 2. ausg. Tatarische nationen; 3. ausg. Samojedische, mandshurische und ostlichste sibirische nationen; 4. ausg. Mongoliische völker, Russen und die noch übrigen nationen
Also issued in Russian with title *Opisanie vsiekh" obitaiushchikh" v" Rossiiskom' gosudarstvie narodov"* (Sanktpeterburgie I. Akademii nauk" 1799) LC CA15-193
The plates have been copied for several other books including *Costume of the Russian empire* (London, E. Harding 1803) the

Georgi, Johann G.—*Continued*
same title (London, W. Miller 1803) and William Alexander's *Picturesque representations of the dress and manners of the Russians*
Colas 1223. Lipperheide 1337. LC 18-18725

Description de toutes les nations de l'empire de Russie, ou l'on expose leurs moeurs, religions, usages, maisons, habillemens et autres curiosités; tr. de l'allemand. St. Petersbourg, C. W. Müller 1776-80
An edition of *Beschreibung* with French text
Colas 1224

La Russie ouverte ou collection complette des habillemens de toutes les nations que se trouvent dans l'empire de Russie. Saint Petersburg, C. W. Muller 1774-75
18 l. 45pl. F.
Title also in German: *Das eroffnete Russland oder sammlung von kleidertrachten aller im Russischen Reiche wohnenden volker,* and in Russian. Said by Colas to be the first edition of *Beschreibung*
Colas 1222

Russland: Beschreibung aller nationen des russischen Reiches. Leipzig, Dukischen buchhandlung 1783
2v. 530p. 2pl. (incl. 39 illus.) Q.
The text of *Beschreibung* with two new plates which reproduce 39 illustrations in reduced size
Colas 1225

Georgia. See Russia—Georgia

Georgian England. Richardson, A. E.

Georgica curiosa aucta. Hohberg, W. H., freiherr von

La **gerarchia** ecclesiastica considerata nelle vesti sagre e civili. Buonanni, Filippo

Gérard
Costumes de principaux personnages des Scandinaves, tragédie en 5 actes de M. Victor; lith. par Feillet d'après les dessins de Mr Gérard. Paris [1824]
1 l. 8 col.pl. Q.
Cataloged from Colas
Colas 1226

Gerard, Emily
The land beyond the forest: facts, figures and fancies from Transylvania. Edinburgh and London, W. Blackwood 1888
2v. fronts. illus. 9pl. O.
LC 3-8239

Gérard, Jean Ignace Isidore. See Grandville, J. I. I. Gérard, called

Gérard-Fontallard, Henri
Costumes patriotiques, ou Souvenirs des 27, 28, 29 juillet 1830. Paris, Dauty [1830]
6 col.pl. Q.
Colas 1227

(ed.) Aujourd'hui; journal des modes ridicules et d'annonces illustrées

Gerardini, Melchion
Capricci di varie figure. No place, ca1650
1 l. 48pl. O.
Plates engraved in the manner of Callot show allegorical figures, types of various professions, hunting and festival scenes
Lipperheide 534m

Gerasch, August. See Richter, Wilhelm, jt. auth.

Gerasch, Franz
Die kaiserl. koenigl. oesterreichische armee seit dem jahre 1849. Wien, J. Bermann 1851
12 col.pl. ob.F.
Colas 1229

Das oesterreichische heer von Ferdinand II. römisch deutschen kaiser, bis Franz Josef I. kaiser von Oesterreich. Wien, L. T. Neumann ca1854
1 l. 152 col.pl. F.
The same plates with a few variations are found in the author's *Das oesterreichische heer von Ferdinand II. römisch deutschen kaiser, bis Ferdinand I., kaiser von Oesterreich* (Wien, L. T. Neumann ca1854. 153pl.)
Colas 1230-1231. Lipperheide 2239

Géraud, S. E. See Galard, Gustave de, jt. auth.

Gerbert, Martin, freiherr von Hornau
De translatis Habsburgo-Austriacorum principum, eorumque coniugum cadaveribus ex ecclesia cathedrali Basileensi et monasterio Koenigsveldensi in Helvetia ad conditorium novum monasterii S. Blasii in Silva Nigra. Typis San-Blasianis 1772
150p. 2 illus. 9pl. Q.
Plates are engraved by I. B. Haas and are reproductions of monuments and seals of the 13th and 14th centuries
Lipperheide 370

Gerbing, Frau Luise
Die Thüringer trachten. Erfurt, Thüringer vereinigung für wohlfahrts- und heimatpflege 1925
135p. 83 illus. 17 col.pl. O.

Gerhäuser, Emil
Stuttgarter bühnenkunst; inszenierungen der Königlich württembergischen hofoper von werken Mozarts und von Schillings' Mona Lisa; hrsg. und verlegt von Wilhelm Meyer-Ilschen. Stuttgart, 1917
418p. front. illus. (incl. music) pl.(part col.) 3 col.port. diagrs. F.
LC 21-7955

Gerhard, Eduard
Auserlesene griechische vasenbilder, hauptsächlich etruskischen fundorts. Berlin, G. Reimer 1840-58
4v. CCCXXX(i.e. 285)pl.(partly fold.) F.
The folded plates have, with few exceptions, been given two numbers each
Contents: 1 th Götterbilder; 2 th Heroenbilder; 3 th Heroenbilder, meistens Homerisch; 4 th Griechisches alltagsleben
LC 11-7912

Germain, Prosper Saint-. See Saint-Germain, Prosper

German swordplay. Emerson, Edwin

Germaniae chronicon; von des gantzen Teutschlands, aller teutschen völcker herkomen. See Franck, Sebastian. Teutscher nation chronic

Germanic tribes. See Europe—To 476; also Europe—Middle ages

Germanischer schmuck des frühen mittelalters. Jenny, W. A., ritter von, and Volbach, W. F.

Die **Germanisierung** der frauenkleidung. Gratz, Josefine

Germany

Bauer, Max. Deutscher frauenspiegel. 1917

Berlin. Museum für deutsche volkstrachten und erzeugnisse des hausgewerbes. Mittheilungen. 1897-1901

Bösch, Hans. Katalog der im germanischen museum vorhandenen zum abdrucke bestimmten geschnittenen holzstöcke vom XV-XVIII jahrhunderte. 1892-1896

Brucker, J. J. Ehren-tempel der deutschen gelehrsamkeit, in welchem die bildnisse gelehrter, und um die schönen und philologischen wissenschafften verdienter männer unter den Deutschen aus dem XV, XVI, und XVII jahrhunderte aufgestellet, und ihre geschichte, verdienste und merckwürdigkeiten entworfen sind von Jacob Brucker ... in kupfer gebracht von J. J. Haid. 1747

Deutsche volks-trachten. ca1847

Diederichs, Eugen. Deutsches leben der vergangenheit in bildern; ein atlas mit 1760 nachbildungen alter kupfer- und holzschnitte aus dem 15ten-18ten jahrhundert. 1908

Eye, August von. Deutschland vor dreihundert jahren in leben und kunst. 1857

Falke, Jacob von. Die deutsche trachten und modenwelt. 1858

Förster, Ernst. Denkmale deutscher bildnerei und malerei von einführung des christenthums bis auf die neueste zeit. 1858-1870

Geschichte der deutschen kunst. 1887-91

Hagen, F. H. von der. Bildersaal altdeutscher dichter; bildnisse, wappen und darstellungen aus dem legen und den liedern der deutschen dichter des XII. bis XIV. jahrhunderts. 1856-1861

Hampe, Theodor. Die fahrenden leute in der deutschen vergangenheit. 1902

Helm, Rudolf. Deutsche volkstrachten aus der sammlung des Germanischen museum in Nürnberg. 1932

Henne am Rhyn, Otto. Kulturgeschichte des deutschen volkes. 1886

Heyne, Moritz. Fünf bücher deutscher hausaltertümer von den ältesten geschichtlichen zeiten bis zum 16. jahrhundert. 1901-03

Hottenroth, Friedrich. Le costume chez les peuples anciens et modernes. 189-?

Hottenroth, Friedrich. Deutsche volkstrachten vom XVI bis zum XIX jahrhundert. 1923

Hottenroth, Friedrich. Handbuch der deutschen tracht. 1893-1896?

Köhler, Karl. Die entwickelung der tracht in Deutschland während des mittelalters und der neuzeit. 1877

Könnecke, Gustav. Bilderatlas zur geschichte der deutschen nationalliteratur. 1895

Kuhn, C. L. A catalogue of German paintings of the middle ages and renaissance in American collections. 1936

Nuremberg. Germanisches nationalmuseum. Anzeiger. 1884/86+

Nuremberg. Germanisches national museum. Mitteilungen aus dem Germanischen nationalmuseum. 1886-1921

Pantaleon, Heinrich. Teutscher nation heldenbuch. 1567-71

Reicke, Emil. Der gelehrte in der deutschen vergangenheit. 1900

Scheible, Johann. Die gute alte zeit geschildert in historischen beiträgen zur nähern kenntnisz der sitten, gebräuche und denkart ... in den letzten fünf jahrhunderten. Erster band: Zur geschichte hauptsächlich des stadtlebens, der kleidertrachten ... der kinderspiele, tanzfreuden. 1847

Scheible, Johann, ed. Das schaltjahr; welches ist der teutsch kalendar mit den figuren, und hat 366 tag. 1846-47

Scherr, Johannes. Kulturgeschichte der deutschen frau. 1928

Stacke, L. C. Deutsche geschichte. 1880-81

Steinhausen, Georg. Geschichte der deutschen kultur. 1904

See also Austria; also subdivision Germany under Academic costume; Agricultural laborers; Arms and armor; Ceremonial and festival costume; Children; Coronations and coronation robes; Court dress; Crown jewels; Decoration and ornament; Ecclesiastical costume; Embroidery; Firemen; Funerals; Heraldic costume; Hunting costume; Kings and rulers; Lace; Legal costume; Masks; Military costume; Officials; Orders of knighthood and chivalry; Police; Regalia; Shooting costume; Students; Theatrical costume; Uniforms, Civil; Weddings and wedding dress; Workmen

Caricature and satire

Conring, F. F. Das deutsche militär in der karikatur. 1907

Grand-Carteret, John. Les moeurs et la caricature en Allemagne—en Autriche—en Suisse. 1885

Early period to 843

Arnold, Wilhelm. Deutsche geschichte. 1881-83

Girke, Georg. Die tracht der Germanen in der vor- und frühgeschichtlichen zeit. 1922

Götzinger, Ernst. Reallexicon der deutschen altertümer. 1885

Klemm, G. F. Handbuch der germanischen alterthumskunde. 1836

Lindenschmit, Ludwig. Handbuch der deutschen alterthumskunde. 1880-89

Lindenschmit, Ludwig. Das Römisch-germanische central-museum in bildlichen darstellungen aus seinen sammlungen. 1889

Mestorf, Johanna. Die vaterländischen alterthümer Schleswig-Holsteins. 1877

Mestorf, Johanna, ed. Vorgeschichtliche alterthümer aus Schleswig-Holstein. 1885

Germany—Early period to 843—*Continued*

Reynitzsch, Wilhelm. Uiber truhten und truhtensteine, barden, und bardenlieder, feste, schmäuse und gerichte des Teutschen. 1802

843-1300

Anekdoten und charakterzuge, luxus und moden ... unsrer teutschen vorältern im mittelalter. 1812

Kopp, U. F. Bilder und schriften der vorzeit. 1819-21

Philippi, Friedrich. Atlas zur weltlichen altertumskunde des deutschen mittelalters. 1923-24

Preuschen, Erwin. Darstellungen aus dem Nibelungen-liede. 1847

Weerth, Ernst aus'm, ed. Kunstdenkmäler des christlichen mittelalters in den Rheinlanden. 1857-80

See also Minnesingers

14th century

Grupen, C. U. Teutsche alterthümer, zur erleuterung der sächsischen auch schwäbischen land- und lehn-rechts, wobey der gebrauch der dresdenschen, wolfenbüttelschen, und oldenburgschen ... durch einige abbildungen ... unter augen gestellet worden. 1746

Reiss, Heinrich, ed. Sammlung der schönsten miniaturen des mittelalters aus dem 14. u. 15. jahrhundert. 1867

Schultz, Alwin. Deutsches leben im XIV. und XV. jahrhundert. 1892

15th century

Bossert, H. T. Ein altdeutscher totentanz. 1919. From 15th century drawings

Lehrs, Max. Katalog der im germanischen museum befindlichen deutschen kupferstiche des XV. jahrhunderts. 1887

Maximilian I, emperor of Germany. Freydal. Des kaisers Maximilian I. turnier und mummereien. 1880-82

Reiss, Heinrich, ed. Sammlung der schönsten miniaturen des mittelalters aus dem 14. u. 15. jahrhundert. 1867

Schultz, Alwin. Deutsches leben im XIV. und XV. jahrhundert. 1892

16th century

Amman, Jost. Kartenspielbuch. 1588

Arndt, E. M. Deutsche trachten; erstes heft. 1815

Becker, R. Z. Bildnisse der urheber und beförderer auch einiger gegner der religions- und kirchenserbesserung im sechzehnten jahrhundert. 1817

Behaim, Paulus. Briefe eines Leipziger studenten aus den jahren 1572 bis 1574. 1880

Beham, H. S. Biblicae historiae, artificiosissimis picturis effigiatae. [1536]

Beham, H. S. Biblicae historiae artificiosissimè depictae. 1537

Beham, H. S. Holzschnitte zum Alten Testament. 1910

Bleich, G. H. Abdrücke eines vollständigen kartenspieles auf silberplatten. 1881

Boccaccio, Giovanni. De claris mulieribus. 1539

Caesar, C. J. Historien vom Gallier un der Römer burgerische krieg. 1530

Christensen, S. F. Die männliche kleidung in der süddeutschen renaissance. 1934

Cranach, Lucas. Passional Christi und Antichristi. 1521

Custos, Dominicus. Fuggerorum et Fuggerarum quae in familia natae, quaeve in familiam transierunt, quot extant aere expressae imagines. 1618

Custos, Dominicus. Pinacotheca Fuggerorum S.R.I. comitum ac baronum in Khierchperg et Weissenhorn. 1754

Fierabras. Eyn schöne kurtzweilige histori von eym mächtigẽ riesen auss Hispaniẽ, Fierrabras genant, der eyn heyd gewest und bei zeiten des durchleuchtigsten grossen keyser Karls gelebt sich in kämpffen unnd in streitten dapfferlich grossmütig, mañlich unnd eerlich gehalten hat. 1533

Genée, Rudolf. Hans Sachs und seine zeit. 1894

Gräter, F. D. Bemerkungen über die monumente der ritter zu Vellberg. 1797

Grellmann, H. M. G. Historische kleinigkeiten zum vergnügen und unterricht aus der zerstruung gesammelt. 1794

Herberstein, Sigmund, freiherr von. Picturae variae. 1560

Hirth, Georg, ed. Bilder aus der Lutherzeit; eine sammlung von porträts aus der zeit der Reformation in getreuen facsimilenachbildung. 1883

Hocker, J. L. Hailsbronnischer antiquitäten-schatz. 1731

Hrotsvit, of Gandersheim. Opera . 1501

Livius, Titus. Römische historien. 1505

Livius, Titus. Titi Livii Patavini, Romanae historiae principis, libri omnes quotquot ad nostram aetatem pervenerunt. 1568

Musculus, Andreas. Hosedjaevelen paa Dansk ved Peder Palladius, 1556. 1920

Reichard, E. C. Matthäus und Veit Konrad Schwarz nach ihren merkwürdigsten lebensumständen und vielfältig abwechselnden kleidertrachten aus zwey im Herzoglich-Braunschweigischen kunst- und naturalienkabinette befindlichen originalien. 1786

Reusner, Nicolaus. Emblemata ... cum symbolis & inscriptionibus illustrium & clarorum virorum. 1581

Scheible, Johann, ed. Die fliegenden blätter des XVI. und XVII. jahrhunderts. 1850

Tengler, Ulrich. Der neü Layenspiegel. 1511

17th century

Arndt, E. M. Deutsche trachten; erstes heft. 1815

Bertius, Petrus. Commentariorum rerum germanicarum libri tres. 1616

Germany—17th century—*Continued*

Braun, Georg. Urbium totius Germaniae superioris illustriorum clariorumque tabulae antiquae & novae accuratissimè elaboratae. 1657

Geyer, Andrea. Gründlicher abriss der jenigen zimmer in welchen bey noch fürwährendem reichs-tag der an. 1663. angefangen und biss date continuiret die sessiones und deliberationes gehalten werden. ca1722

Khevenhiller, F. C. Annales Ferdinandei, oder Wahrhaffte beschreibung, käysers Ferdinandi des Andern ... geburth, auferziehung und bisshero in krieg und friedenszeiten vollbrachten thaten. 1721-26

Khevenhiller, F. C. Counterfet kupfferstich ... deren jenigen regierenden grossen herren, so von käysers Ferdinand dess Andern geburt, biss zu desselben seeligsten tödtlichen abschied successivè regiert, davon ertz hertzog Carl, vatter käysers Ferdinand dess Andern zum ersten gestellet worden. 1721

Kleiner, Salomon. Das prächtige rath haus der stadt Augspurg. 1733

Lundorp, Michael Caspar. Helden buch, oder beschreibung der vonembsten potentaten, keyser, königen, fürsten, graffen, kriegs-obersten, und helden, welche in nochwehrendem teutschen kriege ... sich gebrauchen lassen ... durch Nicolaum Bellum, [pseud] 1629

Murner, Thomas. Nebulo nebulonum, hoc est, jocoseria nequitiae censura. 1663

Scheible, Johann, ed. Die fliegenden blätter des XVI. und XVII. jahrhunderts. 1850.

18th century

Basedow, J. B. Elementarwerk mit den kupfertafeln Chodowieckis u. a. kritische bearbeitung. 1909

Boehn, Max von. Deutschland im 18. jahrhundert. 1922

Bonin, Lovis. Die neueste art zur galantin und theatralischen tantz-kunst: worinnen gründliche nachricht anzutreffen wie dieses ... exercitium. 1712

Brucker, J. J., and Haid, J. J. Bilder-sal heutiges tages lebender und durch gelahrheit berühmter schrift-steller. 1741-66

Callenbach, Franz. Almanach weltsittenstaat-marter-calender. 1714

Chodowiecki, D. N. Daniel Chodowiecki; 25 bisher unveröffentlichte handzeichnungen zu dem Moralischen elementarbuche von C. G. Salzmann. 1922

Chodowiecki, D. N. Daniel Chodowiecki; 62 bisher unveröffentlichte handzeichnungen zu dem Elementarwerk von Johann Bernhard Basedow. 1922

Chodowiecki, D. N. Von Berlin nach Danzig. 1895

Consentius, Ernst. Alt-Berlin, anno 1740. 1911

Gradmann, J. J. Habillemens berlinois. ca1780

Kleiner, Salomon. Representation au naturel des chateaux de Weissenstein au dessus de Pommersfeld et de celui de Gevbach appartenants a la maison des comtes de Schönborn ... Wahrhaffte vorstellung beÿder ... Schlösser Weissenstein ob Pommersfeld und Geibach. 1728

Kleiner, Salomon. Representation naturelle et exacte de la Favorite de son altesse electorale de Mayence ... Wahrhaffte und eigentliche abbildungen der ... chur fürstlich Mayntzischen Favorita. 1726

Kleiner, Salmon. Residences memorables ... ou Representation exacte des edifices et jardins de ... Monseigneur le Prince Eugene Francois, duc de Savoye ... Wunder würdiges kriegs- und siegslager. 1731-1740

Kleiner, Salomon. Vera et accurata delineatio omnium templorum et coenobiorum, quae tam in caesarea urbe ac sede Vienna Austriae, quam in circumjacentibus suburbijs ejus reperiuntur ... Wahrhaffte und genaue abbildung aller kirchen und clöster, welche sowohl in der keysserl. residenz-statt Wien, als auch in denen umliegenden vorstatten sich befinden. 1724-25

Leucorande, E. C. Die dem lieben frauen-zimmer sehr angenehmen auch commoden contusche und reiffen-röcke. 1717

Menzel, Adolph. Illustrations des oeuvres de Frédéric-le-grand. 1882

Misson, F. M. Herrn Maximilian Missons Reisen aus Holland durch Deutschland in Italien. 1701

Moser, J. P. Sammlung von bildnissen gelehrter männer und künstler. 1794

Neuestes gemälde von Berlin, auf das jahr 1798. 1798

Wörterbuch der mode, f. das schöne geschlecht u. seine freunde. 1782

Periodicals

Allgemeine modenzeitung; eine zeitschrift für die gebildete welt. 1799-1903

Allgemeines europäisches journal. 1794-98

Archiv weiblicher hauptkenntnisse für diejenigen jedes standes. 1787-90

Berlin; eine zeitschrift für freunde der schönen künste, des geschmacks und der moden. 1799-1800

Berlinischer damen-kalender. 1798-1810

Berlinisches archiv der zeit und ihres geschmacks. 1795-1800

Journal des dames et des modes. 1799-1848

Journal für fabriken, manufacturen, handlung, kunst, und mode. 1791-1808

Journal für literatur, kunst, luxus, und mode. 1786-1827

Magazin für frauenzimmer. 1782-86

Moden-gallerie. 1795

Germany—18th century—Periodicals—*Cont.*
Musarion, die freundin weiser geselligkeit und häuslicher freuden. 1799-1800
Neues magazin für frauenzimmer. 1787-89
Taschenbuch ... für damen. 1798-1831

Caricature and satire

Centi-folium stultorum in quarto. 1709
Conlin, A. J. Der christliche welt-weise beweinent die thorheit der neuentdeckten narrn-welt. 1706
Göz, J. F. von. Die heutige sichtbare körperwelt oder 100 charakter züge derer denen menschen ... äusserlich kennbar werdender, innerlich verborgener guter —oder böser leidenschafftlicher beschaffenheiten. 1783-85

19th century

Arndt, E. M. Ueber sitte, mode und kleidertracht. 1814
Bacher, Moritz. Trachtenpavillon der Berliner gewerbe-ausstellung 1896. 1896
Belin, A., and others. Costumes de Suède, Norvège, Danemark, Hollande et Allemagne. 186-?
Berlin vor hundert jahren. 1800. Secularheft von "Berliner leben". [1900]
Bettziech, Heinrich. Physiologie Berlins. 1846-47
Boehn, Max von. Biedermeier. 1911
Brückmann, H. W. Lehrkursus für damen-garderobe. 1878
Cocheris, Mme P. A. W. L'empire d'Allemagne. 1875
Dost, Wilhelm, and Stenger, Erich. Die daguerreotype in Berlin, 1839-1860. 1922
Endrulat, Bernhard. Das Schillerfest in Hamburg am 11., 12. u. 13. Novbr. 1859. 1860
Erich, O. A. Deutsche volkstrachten. 1934
Geissler, C. G. H. Leipziger meszscenen. 1804-1805
Grand-Carteret, John. La femme en Allemagne. 1887
Kerndörffer, H. A. Gallerie der stände. 1811
Kretschmer, Albert. Deutsche volkstrachten. 1887-90
Lewis, George. A series of groups illustrating the physiognomy, manners, and character of the people of France and Germany. 1823
Löffler, Ludwig. Berlin und die Berliner, in wort und bild. 1856
Oncken, Wilhelm. Das zeitalter des kaisers Wilhelm. 1890-92
Opiz, G. E. Leipzigermesse; 1. heft. ca1825
Ostwald, H. O. A. Berlin und die Berlinerin. 1911
Pniower, O. S. Alt-Berliner humor um 1830. 1919
Prospecte der vorzüglichsten gebäude in Berlin. ca1811
Weimar, Wilhelm. Die daguerreotype in Hamburg, 1839-1860. 1915
Wolf, G. J. Ein jahrhundert München, 1800-1900. 1935

See also Naval costume—Germany—19th century to 1914

Periodicals

Allgemeine modenzeitung; eine zeitschrift für die gebildete welt. 1799-1903
Allgemeine muster-zeitung; album für weibliche arbeiten und moden. 1844-65
Der Bazar. 1854+
Der Beobachter der herrenmoden. 1855+
Die Dame. 1873+
Damenkleider magazin vereinigt mit Musterzeitung und frauenzeitung. 1848-69
Die Damen-toilette. 1865-86?
Europa; chronik der gebildeten welt. 1835-85
Europäische modenzeitung. 1850+
Frauen reich; deutsche hausfrauen-zeitung. 1874-1910
Die Gartenlaube; illustriertes familienblatt. 1853+
Der Hausfreund. 1858-1901
Illustrirte frauen-zeitung; ausgabe der modenwelt mit unterhaltungsblatt. 1874-1908?
Illustrirte modenzeitung. 1873-79
Illustrirtes magazin. 1846-51
Iris; illustrirte blätter für mode, haushaltung und praktisches leben. 1849-65
Jahreszeiten, Hamburger neue mode-zeitung. 1842-74
Journal des dames et des modes. 1799-1848
Journal für literatur, kunst, luxus, und mode. 1786-1827
Journal für moderne stickerei, mode und weibliche handarbeiten. 1844-61
Ladies cabinet of fashion, music and romance. 1832-70
Moden-telegraph. 1861-1923
Die Modenwelt. 1865+
Das neue blatt; ein illustrirtes familienjournal. 1870-87
Neue illustrirte zeitung. 1873-87
Taschenbuch der liebe und freundschaft. 1800-40
Taschenbuch ... für damen. 1798-1831
Technische modenzeitung für damen, damenkleidermacher. 1844-51
Das Veilchen, ein taschenbuch. 1818-34
Victoria; illustrirte muster- und modenzeitung. 1851-79
Zeitung für die elegante welt. 1801-59
Zeitung für die elegante welt. 1872-85

See also subdivisions 1800-1824, 1825-1849, and 1875-1899, under Germany—19th century—Periodicals

Periodicals—1800-1824

Almanach der mode und des geschmacks für damen auf das jahr 1802. 1802
Almanach des luxus und der moden auf 1801 mit zehn illuminirten kupfern nach Hogarth. 1801?
Berlin; eine zeitschrift für freunde der schönen künste, des geschmacks und der moden. 1799-1800
Berlinischer damen-kalender. 1798-1810

Germany—Periodicals—1800-1824—*Cont.*

Journal für fabriken manufacturen handlung, kunst und mode. 1791-1808
Musarion, die freundin weiser geselligkeit und häuslicher freuden. 1799-1800
Neues journal für fabriken, manufakturen, handlungen, kunst und mode. 1808-11
Pariser und Hamburger damen, mode und kunst journal. 1803-05

Periodicals—1825-1849

Allgemeine weltchronik unserer zeit. 1832-34
Berliner modenspiegel in- und ausländischer originale. 1832-49
Eilpost für moden. 1837-43
Leipziger moden-journal. 1840-43
Museum der eleganten welt. 1836-38
Neue Pariser modeblätter. 1827-40
Neuestes Pariser moden-journal für herren und damen. 1843-48
Pariser moden journal. 1839-42
Schnellpost für moden. 1832-42
Vergiszmeinnicht; taschenbuch der liebe, der freundschaft und dem familienleben des deutschen volkes gewidmet. 1830-49

Periodicals—1850-1874

Bijou; original Pariser musterblätter weiblicher kunstarbeiten. 1851-52
Frauen-zeitung für hauswesen, weibliche arbeiten und moden. 1852-65
Freya; illustrirte blätter für die gebildete welt. 1861-67
Haus und welt. 1871-73
Die mode; journal für damentoilette mit Pariser original-modebildern, muster- und schnitt-beilagen. 1853-74
Pariser modelle für die selbst-anfertigung der gesammten damen-garderobe, leibwäsche und kinder-garderobe. 1858-70
Pariser moden-salon für damen-garderobe. 1853-69
Penelope; neue muster-zeitung für weibliche arbeiten und moden. 1853-61
Wiener modespiegel; wochenschrift für mode, schöne literatur, novellistik, kunst und theater. 1853-59

Periodicals—1875-1899

Berliner modenblatt. 1879-81
Butterick's modenblatt. 1896-1900
Deutsche modenzeitung. 1891+
Ebhardts' Moden-album. 1879-94
Die Elegante mode. 1890+
Grosse modenwelt. 1892-1920
Häuslicher ratgeber. 1886-1915
Kleine modenwelt. 1889-1910
Mode und haus. 1885-1920
Der Moderne kleidermacher. 1875-1923
Neue welt. 1876-87
Neueste moden für unsere damen. 1879-96
Sonntags-zeitung fürs deutsche haus. 1897-1919
Vom fels zum meer. 1881-1917
Wiener chic. 1891-1932

Caricature and satire

Borchardt, G. H, Die deutsche karikatur im 19. jahrhundert. 1901
Burger, Ludwig. Das emancipirte amazonenheer. ca1850
Detmold, J. H., and Schrödter, Adolph. Thaten und meinungen des herrn Piepmeyer. 1849
Dörbeck, F. B. Berliner redensarten. ca1830
Dörbeck, F. B. Berliner witze und anecdoten. ca1830
Eichler, Ludwig. Berlin und die Berliner. 1841-1842
Foltz, Philipp. IV blaetter aus dem Münchner volksleben. 1829
Friedrich, T. H. Deutsche volkstracht, oder Geschichte der kleiderreformation in der residenzstadt flottleben. Ein satyrisches gemälde. 1815
Glasbrenner, Adolf. Berlin wie es ist und trinkt. 1843-50
Glasbrenner, Adolf. März-almanach. 1849

20th century

Album moderner, nach kunstlerentwürfen ausgeführter damen-kleider. 1900
Bleyl, Fritz. Baulich und volkskundlich beachtenswertes aus dem kulturgebiete des silberbergbaues zu Freiberg, Schneeberg und Johanngeorgenstadt im sächs. erzgebirge. 1917
Bosselt, Rudolf. Krieg und deutsche mode. 1915
Brunner, Karl. Ostdeutsche volkskunde. 1925
Frucht, Lotte, and Schneehagen, Christian. Unsere kleidung. 1914
Geissler, C. G. H., and Menzel, A. Leipziger volksscenen. ca1830
Gratz, Josefine. So sollt ihr euch kleiden! 1910
Hielscher, Kurt. Picturesque Germany. 1924
Kiesewatter, Doris, and Steffahny, Hermine. Die deutsche frauenkleidung. 1904
Rapsilber, Maximilian. Berlin und die Hohenzollern. 1912
Reichel, Emil. Die frauenkleidung. 1912
Schramm, Fritz. Schlagworte der alamodezeit. 1914

See also Naval costume—Germany—19th century to 1914

Periodicals

Allgemeine modenzeitung; eine zeitschrift für die gebildete welt. 1799-1903
Der Bazar. 1854+
Die Dame. 1873+
Die deutsche Elite. 1924-30
Deutsche modenzeitung. 1891+
Die Elegante mode. 1890+
Europäische modenzeitung. 1850+
Frauen reich; deutsche hausfrauen-zeitung. 1874-1910
Die Gartenlaube; illustriertes familienblatt. 1853+
Grosse modenwelt. 1892-1920
Häuslicher ratgeber; illustrirte familien- und modenzeitung. 1886-1915
Illustrirte frauen-zeitung; ausgabe der modenwelt mit unterhaltungsblatt. 1874-1908?

Germany—20th century—Periodicals—*Cont.*
Kleine modenwelt. 1889-1910
Die Kunst in der mode. 1934+
Mode und haus. 1885-1920
Moden-telegraph. 1861-1923
Die Modenwelt. 1865+
Der Moderne kleidermacher. 1875-1923
Die Neue frauentracht. 1905-09
Der Silberspiegel. 1934+
Sport im bild. 1895-1934
Sonntags-zeitung fürs deutsche haus. 1897-1919
Styl; blätter für mode. 1922-24
Vom fels zum meer. 1881-1917
Wiener chic. 1891-1932

Caricature and satire

Gaudy, F. B. H. W., freiherr von. Karikaturenbuch. 1906

BY REGION OR PROVINCE

Deutsche bauerntrachten. 1924?
Deutsche volkskunst. 1923-33
Duller, Eduard. Das deutsche volk in seinen mundarten, sitten, gebräuchen, festen und trachten. 1847
Hansjakob, Heinrich. Unsere volkstrachten; ein wort zu ihrer erhaltung. 1892
Hürlimann, Martin. Deutschland; landschaft und baukunst. 1931
Julien, Rose. Die deutschen volkstrachten zu beginn des 20 jahrhunderts. 1912
Länder- und völker-schau; eine gallerie von bildern. 1847
Malerische landerschau in bildlichen darstellungen deutscher und schweizerischer stadte. ca1850
Opiz, G. E. Volks-trachten der Deutschen. ca1830
Pelser-Berensberg, Franz von. Mitteilungen über trachten, hausrat, wohn und lebensweise im Rheinland. 1909
Pessler, Wilhelm. Niedersächsisches trachtenbuch. 1922
Retzlaff, Hans. Deutsche bauerntrachten. 1935
Schreiber, A. W. Trachten, volksfeste und charakteristische beschäftigungen im grosherzogthum Baden. ca1825
XVII vorstellungen von deutschen nationaltrachten. 1800
Spiess, Karl. Die deutschen volkstrachten. 1911
Wegner, R. N. Volkslied, tracht und rasse; bilder und alte lieder deutscher bauern. 1934
Will, J. M., engr. Samlung europaeischer national trachten. ca1780

Alsace-Lorraine

See Alsace; Lorraine

Altenburg

See Germany—Thuringia

Baden

Badenia, oder das badische land und volk. 1859-62
Badenia, oder, Das badische land und volk; eine zeitschrift für vaterländische geschichte und landeskunde mit karten, lithographien und colorierten abbildungen und landestrachten. 1839-44
Badenia; zeitschrift des vereins für badische ortsbeschreibung. 1864
Bader, Joseph. Badische volkssitten und trachten. 1843-44
Badische volkstrachten. ca1870
Gageur, Karl. Das trachtenfest zu Haslach im Kinzigthal am 4. juni 1899. 1899
Gleichauf, R. Badische landestrachten im auftrage des Grossherzog. badischen handelsministeriums. 1862
Guinot, Eugène. L'été à Bade. 1847
Guinot, Eugène. A summer at Baden-Baden. 1853
Kley, Heinrich. Festzug; jubiläum der universität Heidelberg, 1386-1886. 1886?
Lallemand, Charles. Les paysans badois; esquisse de moeurs et de coutumes. 1860
Pingret, Edouard. Costumes du Grand Duché de Bade. 1828
Portrait- und costüme-gallerie aus der Badischpfälzischen revolution von 1849. 1849
Valerio, Théodore. Costumes du grand-duché de Bade et des bords du Rhin. 1840-42
Piton, Frédéric. Strasbourg illustré. 1855

See also Germany—Black Forest; Military costume—Germany—Baden

Caricature and satire

Darjou, H. A. Les plaisirs de Baden. ca1860

Bavaria

Adelmann, Leofrid. Bayerische trachten Mittelfranken. 1858
Adelman, Leofrid. Bayerischen trachten Unterfranken. 1856
Enhuber, Carl von. Deutsches volksleben in 13 bildern nach Melchior Meyr's erzählungen aus dem Ries. 1869
Heideloff, K. A. von, ed. Die kunst des mittelalters in Schwaben. 1855
Heksch, A. F. Die Donau von ihrem ursprung bis an die mündung. Eine schilderung von land und leuten des Donaugebietes. 1881
Heksch, A. F. Die Donau von ihrem ursprung bis an die mündung. Eine schilderung von land leuten des Donaugebietes. 1881
Jarwart, Sixtus, and Heinel, Eduard. Neun blatt slavische trachten im Bayreuther lande. 1860
Kellner, Joseph. Vorstellung der offentlichen sehbaren gebräuchen in Nürnberg. ca1780
Lipowski, F. J. Sammlung Bayerischer national-costume. ca1830
Lommel, Georg, and Bauer. Das Königreich Bayern in seinen acht kreisen bildlich ... bearbeitet. 1836

Germany—Bavaria—*Continued*

Quaglio, Lorenz. Studien nach der natur zur staffage von landschaften. 1812-20

Rheinwald, J. L. C. Baierische volkstrachten. 1805

Valério, Théodore. Souvenirs du Tyrol, du Vorarlberg et de la Haute Bavière ... Erinnerungen von Tyrol, Vorarlberg und Ober Baiern. 1842

Zell, Franz. Bauern-trachten aus dem bayerischen hochland. 1903

See also Germany—Palatinate; also subdivision Germany—Bavaria under Kings and rulers; Military costume

Ansbach

Fischer, J. B. Statistische und topographische beschreibung des burggraftums Nürnberg, unterhalb des gebürgs; oder des fürstentums Brandenburg-Anspach. 1787

Augsburg

Augspurgische kleider tracht. ca1720

Engelbrecht, Martin. La mode d'Augsbourg. Augsburgische kleider tracht. 1739

Grimm, Simon. Augusta Vindelicorum. 1678-81

Merz, J. G. Kleidungs arten in der stadt Augspurg. Modes de la ville d'Augsbourg. ca1710

Rohbausch, H. R. Samlung Augspurgischer kleider trachten ... Collection de divers habits, usités dans la ville d'Augsbourg par les deux sexes. ca1750

Roth, J. M. Wahrhaffte bildnüsse aller des heil. röm. reichs freyen stadt Augspurg, herren stadt-pfleger, welche ... seit ao. 1548 biss auf unsere zeitē regieret. 1731

Schmidt, Albrecht. Vorstellung der Augspurgischen kleiter tracht. ca1720

Munich

Regnet, C. A. München in guter alter zeit; nach authentischen quellen. 1879

Nuremberg

Alt-Nürnberg, schwänke, lieder und tänze d. Hans Sachs. 1918

Friderich, J. A. Costumes of Nuremberg. ca1720

Gabler, Ambrosius. 160 Nürnberger schimpfwörter. ca1795

Geschlecht buch dess heiligen reichs stat Nürnberg, darinen alle alte und neue adeliche geschlecht daraus der rath von 300 jahren hero erwölth wordn hierin zusam gebracht. 1610

Handwerks-umzüge und tänze, fischerstechen u. a. in Nürnberg. ca1770

Kleidungsarten und prospecten zu Nürnberg. La maniere de s'habiller à Nuremberg et les vues de cette ville. 1770

Luyken, Caspar. Deutliche vorstellung der Nürnbergischen trachten ... und anjetzo mit erklärungen versehen. 1766

Marx, L. W. Trachtenbuch zur Geschichte der reichsstadt Nürnberg. 1873

Mayer, M. M. Des alten Nürnbergs sitten und gebräuche in freud und leid. 1831-36

Menschenhold, C. G. Des gold- und silbergläntzenden himmels erlustigung und beschaffenheit ... benebenst der in des heil. reichs stadt Nürnberg üblichen und gewöhnlichen kleidungen mit schönen bildern und reimen vorgestellet. 1681

Nürnbergische kleider arten. 1669

Nürnbergische kleider-trachten der manns- und weibs-personen. 1689

Nürnbergische trachten. 1670?

Roth, J. F. Nürnbergisches taschenbuch. 1812-13

Schaeufelein, H. L. La danse des noces. 1865

Sostmann, Wilhelmine. Peter Vischer; romantischdramatisches gemälde aus der vorzeit Nürnbergs. 1832

Thaeter, Julius. Deutsche trachten aus dem sechzehnten jahrhundert. 1827

Wagenseil, J. C. Joh. Christophori Wagenseilii De Sacri rom. imperii libera Civitate noribergensi commentatio. 1697

Berlin

See Street venders—Germany—Berlin

Black Forest

Issel, Heinrich. Volkstrachten aus dem Schwarzwald. ca1890

Pettigrew, D. W. Peasant costume of the Black Forest. 1937

Retzlaff, Hans. Volksleben im Schwarzwald. 1935

See also Germany—By region or province—Baden

Brandenburg

Küster, G. G. Martin Friedrich Seidels Bilder-sammlung. 1751

See also Military costume—Germany—Brandenburg

Bremen

Kohl, J. G. Episoden aus der cultur- und kunstgeschichte Bremens. 1870

Brunswick

See Military costume—Germany—Brunswick

Danzig

See Danzig

Halle

See Germany—Prussia—Halle

Hamburg

Buek, F. G. Album hamburgische costüme. 1843-1847

Erinnerung an Hamburg. ca1840

Jessen, Heinrich. Trachten aus Alt-Hamburg. ca1850

Juhl, Ernst. Hamburg; land und leute der Nieder-Elbe. 1912

Lappenberg, J. M. Die miniaturen zu dem Hamburgischen stadtrechte vom jahre 1497. 1845

Suhr, Christoffer. Hamburgische trachten ... Costumes de Hambourg. 1808

Germany—Hamburg—*Continued*

Suhr, Christoffer. Hamburgische trachten. 1908. Reprint

Griese, Carl. Die Vierlande bei Hamburg. 1894

See also Military costume—Germany—Hamburg

Hanover

Bodemann, F. W. Denkwürdigkeiten der elinsel finkenwerder, sowie der benachbarten eilande und ortschaften. 1860

Lüpkes, Wiard. Ostfriesische volkskunde. 1925

Manninga, Unico. Ostfriesischen volks- und rittertrachten um 1500; in getreuer nachbildung. 1893

See also Military costume—Germany—Hanover

Helgoland

See Helgoland

Hesse

Hessler, Carl, ed. Hessische landes- und volkskunde. 1904-07

Justi, Ferdinand. Hessisches trachtenbuch. 1905

Retzlaff, Hans. Die Schwalm, kulturbild einer hessische landschaft. 1935

See also Military costume—Germany—Hesse

Wiesbaden

Hottenroth, Friedrich. Die nassauischen volkstrachten. 1905

Lübeck

Petersen, H. Bildnisse verdienter Lübecker, nebst deren biographien. 1843

Warncke, Johannes. Luebecker trachten. 1930

See Military costume—Germany—Lübeck

Lusatia

Bible. Wendic. Tv ie, vse svetv pismv, stariga inu Noviga Testamenta, slovenski tolmazhena, skusi Ivria Dalmatina; Bibel, das ist die gantze heilige schrifft windisch. 1584

Kuba, Ludvík. čtení o Lužici, cesty z roků 1886-1923. 1925

Müller, Ewald. Das Wendentum in der Niederlausitz. 1894

Mecklenburg

Lisch, G. C. F. Meklenburg in bildern. 1842-45

See also Military costume—Germany—Mecklenburg

Munich

See Germany—By region or province—Bavaria—Munich

Nassau

See Germany—Hesse

Nuremberg

See Germany—By region or province—Bavaria—Nuremberg

Oldenburg

Hamelmann, Hermann, comp. Oldenburgisch chronicon; das ist beschreibung der löblichen uhralten grafen zu Oldenburg und Delmenhorst &c. 1599

See also Germany—Lübeck

Palatinate

Becker, Albert. Pfälzer volkskunde. 1925

Prussia

See titles below; also Kings and rulers—Germany—Prussia. Also subdivisions Brandenburg; Hanover; Lusatia; Rhine Province; Westphalia, under Germany. And subdivisions Brandenburg, Hanover, Westphalia under Military costume—Germany

Frankfort on Main

Hottenroth, Friedrich. Altfrankfurter trachten von den ersten geschichtlichen spuren an bis ins 19. jahrhundert. 1912

Halle

Kirchhoff, Alfred. Die Halloren in ihrer alten tracht. 1890

Rhine Province

Diener, Walter. Hunsrücker volkskunde. 1925

Saxony

Abbildung derer VIII. ersten hertzogen zu Sachsen, Jülich, Cleve und Berg, Engern und Westphalen, des H. Römischen Reichs ertz-marschallen und chur-fürsten landgrafen in Thüringen. 1702

Batt. Teutsche denkmäler. 1820

Graenicher, Samuel, and Thiele, C. F. Costumes in Sachsen. 1807

Moré, G. Dresden types, 1895. 1895

Müller-Brauel, Hans. Das erste niedersächsische volkstrachtenfest zu Scheessel. 1904

Müller-Brauel, Hans. Niedersächsische volkstrachten. 1902

Schmidt; Seyffert, O., and Sponsel. Sächsische volkstrachten und bauernhäuser. 1897

See also Germany—Lusatia; also subdivision Germany—Saxony under Kings and rulers; Military costume

Leipzig

Richter, J. G. Costumes nationaux de Leipzig. 18—?

Richter, J. S. Unterweisung für anfänger beyderley geschlechts im zeichnen. 1790-91

Thuringia

Friese, Friedrich. Historische nachricht von den merkwürdigen ceremonien der altenburgischen bauern, 1703. 1887

Gerbing, Frau Luise. Die Thüringer trachten. 1925

Germany—Thuringia—*Continued*

Kronbiegel, C. F. Ueber die sitten, kleidertrachten und gebräuche der Altenburgischen bauern. 1806

Thümmel, Hans von. Historische, statistische, geographische und topographische beyträge zur kenntnisz. 1818

Vierland

See Germany—Hamburg

Westphalia

Jostes, Franz. Westfälisches trachtenbuch. 1904

See also Military costume—Germany—Westphalia

Württemberg

Eliat, F. Costumes du Wurtemberg. ca1830

Heideloff, K. A. von. Volkstrachten des königreichs Würtemburg. ca1810-15

Pflütz. Landliche gebräuche in Wurttemberg. ca1810

See also subdivision Germany—Wurttemberg under Kings and rulers; Military costume

Stuttgart

See Military costume—Germany—Wurttemberg—Stuttgart

Germany; architecture and landscape. See Hielscher, Kurt. Picturesque Germany

Germany's army and navy. See Sigel, G. A. Deutschlands heer und flotte

Germar, Ernst Friedrich

Reise nach Dalmatien und in das gebiet von Ragusa. Leipzig and Altenburg, F. A. Brockhaus 1817

xii,323p. 11pl.(9 col.) O.

Four of the colored plates show costume of Dalmatia

Colas 1232. Lipperheide 881

Gerson, Aldabert

Costume polonais, dessinés après nature par Gerson, lith. par E. Desmaisons. Varsovie, Daziaro ca1860

15? col.pl. Q.

Plates also exist in black and white

Colas 1233

Gerspach, Édouard

Les tapisseries coptes. Paris, Maison Quantin 1890

8p. 98pl.(8 col.) Q.

Lipperheide 3766. LC 10-30235

Gerstfeldt, Olga von

Hochzeitsfeste der renaissance in Italien. Esslingen, P. Neff 1906

51p. 5pl. O. (Führer zur kunst, bd.6)

Gerstmann, Maximilian

Das buch vom preussischen soldaten; kriegsbilder und friedensscenen ... In original-zeichnungen dargestellt von R. Meinhardt und A. Köhler. Berlin, Stuhr 1867

24p. 9 col.pl. Q.

Colas 2033

[Géruzez, Victor]

Paris à cheval, texte et dessins par Crafty [pseud.] Avec une préface par Gustave Droz. Paris, E. Plon 1883

xiii p. 404p. incl.illus. pl. Q.

Contents: Cavalerie parisienne; Au Bois de Boulogne; Aux courses; L'art de tomber de cheval

LC 22-15218

Die **gesammte** fachwissenschaft des schneiders. Müller, G. A.

Die **gesammte** kinder-garderobe. Klemm, Heinrich

Geschichte Babyloniens und Assyriens. Hommel, Fritz

Geschichte der babylonischen und assyrischen kleidung. Reimpell, Walter

Geschichte der bekleidung, bewaffnung und ausrüstung des königlich preussischen heeres. Prussia. Kriegsministerium

Geschichte der bekleidung und ausrüstung der königl. preussischen armee in den jahren 1808 bis 1878; zugleich eine ergänzungsschrift der uniformirungs-liste des deutschen reichs-heeres. Berlin, Mittler 1878

x,334p. O.

Geschichte der bildenden künste in der Schweiz. Rahn, J. R.

Geschichte der bulgarischen kunst unter der türkischen herrschaft und in der neueren zeit. Filov, Bogdan

Geschichte der deutschen frauen. See Scherr, Johannes. Kulturgeschichte der deutschen frau

Geschichte der deutschen kultur. Steinhausen, Georg

Geschichte der deutschen kunst. Berlin, G. Grote 1887-91

5v. illus. 237pl.(part col.) plans. Q.

Contents: v 1 Die baukunst, von Robert Dohme; v2 Die plastik, von Wilhelm Bode; v3 Die malerei, von Hubert Janitschek; v4 Der kupferstich und holzschnitt; von Carl von Lützow; v5 Das kunstgewerbe, von Jakob von Falke

Lipperheide 600

Geschichte der deutschen schauspielkunst. Devrient, Eduard

Geschichte der fremd-truppen im dienste Frankreichs. See note under Fieffé, Eugène. Histoire des troupes étrangères

Geschichte der handfeuerwaffen. Schön, Julius

Geschichte der Kaiser-garde. See Saint-Hilaire, É. M. H. Histoire anecdotique politique et militaire de la Garde impériale

Geschichte der kaiserl. königl. regimenter seit ihrer errichtung bis auf gegenwärtige zeiten worin die inhaber jedes regimentes ... angezeigt sind. Wien, Gräffer der jünger 1791-1792

2v. 377 col.pl. D.

Volume 2 has title *Genaue darstellung saemmtliche branchen der kaiserl. koenigl. armee* von C. Schütz, and Part one has half-title: *Costumes des uniformes de l'armée impériale et royale.* Ridder's *Catalogue* attributes the history to Auguste Gräffer, who in turn gives the author as Stéphanie le jeune

Colas 1235

Geschichte der Kirche St. Georg bei Räzüns und ihre wandgemälde. Jäklin, Dietrich

Geschichte der könige von Dänemark. Schlegel, J. H.

Geschichte der königlich deutschen legion. See Beamish, N. L. History of the King's German legion

Geschichte der kreuzzüge. Kugler, Bernhard

Geschichte der kriegsverfassung und des kriegswesens der Deutschen. Barthold, F. W.

Geschichte der liturgischen gewänder des mittelalters. Bock, Franz

Geschichte der neueren zeit. Philippson, Martin

Geschichte der Phönizier. Pietschmann, Richard

Geschichte der revolutionen. Conrady, Alexander

Geschichte der sächsischen armee in wort und bild. Hauthal, Ferdinand

Geschichte der sächsischen armee von ihrer reorganisation nach dem siebenjährigen kriege bis auf unsere zeit. See Hauthal, Ferdinand. Geschichte der sächsischen armee in wort und bild

Geschichte der Stuttgarten stadgarde zu pferd. Fischer, C. A.

Geschichte der tanzkunst. Czerwinski, Albert

Geschichte der waffen. Specht, F. A. K. von

Geschichte des ehemaligen weilers Affalterbach landgerichts Altdorf. Soden, Franz, freiherr von

Die **geschichte** des fächers. Frauberger, Heinrich

Geschichte des grotesk komischen. Flögel, K. F.

Geschichte des infanterie-regiments von Lützow. Stawitzky, E. H. L.

Geschichte des k.k. dragoner-regimentes Feldmarschall Alfred Fürst zu Windisch-Graetz nr. 14. Amon von Treuenfest, Gustav

Geschichte des k.k. 11. Huszaren-regimentes Herzog Alexander v. Wurttemberg, 1762 bis 1850. Amon Von Treuenfest, Gustav, ritter

Geschichte des k.k. Feldmarschall Graf Radetzky huszaren-regiments nr. 5. Amon von Treuenfest, Gustav, ritter

Geschichte des k.k. huszaren-regimentes Alexander Freiherr v. Koller, nr. 8. Amon von Treuenfest, Gustav, ritter

Geschichte des k.k. huszaren-regiments Freiherr von Edelsheim-Gyulai nr. 4. Amon von Treuenfest, Gustav, ritter

Geschichte des k.k. infanterie-regimentes hoch- und deutschmeister nr. 4. Amon von Treuenfest, Gustav, ritter

Geschichte des k.k. infanterie-regimentes nr. 50. Amon von Treuenfest, Gustav, ritter

Geschichte des k.k. infanterie-regimentes nr. 47. Amon von Treuenfest, Gustav, ritter

Geschichte des k.k. infanterie-regiments nr. 18. Amon von Treuenfest, Gustav, ritter

Geschichte des k.k. infanterie-regiments nr. 20. Amon von Treuenfest, Gustav, ritter

Geschichte des k.k. 12. Huszaren-regiments. Amon von Treuenfest, Gustav, ritter

Geschichte des k. und k. dragoner-regiments. Amon von Treuenfest, Gustav, ritter

Geschichte des k. und k. husaren-regimentes Kaiser nr. 1 (1756-1898) Amon von Treuenfest, Gustav ritter

Geschichte des k.u.k. husaren-regiments nr. 4, Arthur herzog von Connaught und Strathearn. Amon von Treuenfest, Gustav, ritter

Geschichte des k.u.k. huszaren-regimentes nr. 3. Amon von Treuenfest, Gustav, ritter

Geschichte des k.u.k. huszaren-regimentes nr. 15. Amon von Treuenfest, Gustav, ritter

Geschichte des k. und k. huszaren-regimentes nr. 10 Friedrich Wilhelm III. Amon von Treuenfest, Gustav, ritter

Geschichte des k.u.k. infanterie-regimentes nr. 46 feldzeugmeister Géza Frh. Fejervary de Komós-Keresztes. Amon von Treuenfest, Gustav, ritter

Geschichte des kaiserl. und königl. Kärnthnerischen infanterie-regimentes Feldmarschall Graf von Khevenhüller nr. 7. Amon von Treuenfest, Gustav, ritter

Geschichte des k. und k. uhlanen-regimentes Kaiser nr. 4 (1813-1900). Amon von Treuenfest, Gustav, ritter

Geschichte des königlich preuszischen dritten Dragoner-regiments. Schöning, K. W. von

Geschichte des königlich preuszischen kadattencorps. Crousaz, A. von

Geschichte des königlichen potsdamschen militärwaisenhauses, von seiner entstehung bis auf die jetzige zeit. Berlin & Posen, E. S. Mittler 1824
xvi,486,xviii p. front. 9pl.(4 col.) O.
Colas 1236. Lipperheide 2163

Geschichte des königlichen preuszischen regiments Garde du corps. Schöning, K. W. von

Geschichte des kostüms. Rosenberg, Adolf

Geschichte des kostüms. Weiss, Hermann

Geschichte des kunstgewerbes. See Blümner, Hugo. Das kunstgewerbe im altertum

Geschichte des männlichen barts unter allen völkern der erde bis auf die neueste zeit. . . nach dem französischen frey bearbeitet und mit einer theorie der haare nach ihren naturzwecken versehen [von Karl Gottlob Schelle] Leipzig, In der Weygandschen buchhandlung 1797
xxxii,305p. O.
Lipperheide 1684

Geschichte des magdeburgischen pionierbataillons nr 4, 1813 bis 1887. Volkmann, captain

Geschichte des mittelalterlichen, vorzugsweise des deutschen schachspieles. Massmann, H. F.

Geschichte des osmanischen reichs. See Cantemir, Dumitru. The history of the growth and decay of the Othman empire

Geschichte des ritterlichen ordens St. Johannis vom Spital zu Jerusalem. Winterfeld, A. W. E. von

Geschichte des sports aller völker und zeiten. Bogeng, G. A. E.

Geschichte des tanzes in Deutschland. Böhme, F. M.

Geschichte des volkes Israel. Stade, Bernhard

Geschichte des württembergischen kriegswesens. Stadlinger, L. J. von

Geschichte einiger geistlichen orden, besonders derer die in den kayserlichköniglichen erblanden bisher aufgehoben worden sind, nebst einem anhange von den Jesuiten- und Tempelherrn orden. Wien, 1783

254p. 13 col.pl. O.
Colas 1237. Lipperheide 1868

Geschichte und beschreibung des sächsischen bergbaues. Nebst .... abbildungen der sächsischen berg- und hüttenleute in ihren neuesten staats-trachten. Zwickau, Im literatur- und kunst-comptoir 1827

15p. 7 col.pl. Q.
Lipperheide 1995

Geschichte und bildliche vorstellung der königlich preussischen regimenter. Wien, Reilly 1796

28p. 159 col.pl. O.
Colas 1240

Geschichte und bildliche vorstellung der kurfürstlich saechsischen regimenter. Wien 1797

10p. 64 col.pl. O.
Thirty three plates show infantry, eighteen plates cavalry
Colas 1238. Lipperheide 2200

Geschichte und bildliche vorstellung der regimenter des erzhauses Oesterreich. Wien, Reilly 1796

27p. 170 col.pl. O.
Colas 1239. Lipperheide 2228

Geschichte u. statuten des rothen adlerordens und des königlichen kronenordens. Gravenhorst, C.

Geschichte und terminologie der alten spitzen. Ilg, Albert

Geschichte und verfassung aller geistlichen und weltlichen, erloschenen und blühenden ritterorden. Biedenfeld, F. L. C., freiherr von

Geschichtliche übersicht der schicksale und veränderung des grossherzogl. sächs. militairs. Müller, August

Die **geschichtlichen** uniformen des jetzigen Bad. Leib-Grenadier. Régiments. Freydorf, Rudulf von

Geschlecht buch dess heiligen reichs stat Nürnberg, darinen alle alte und neue adeliche geschlecht daraus der rath von 300 jahren hero erwölth wordn hierin zusam gebracht. No place, 1610

4 l. 81pl. F.
Each plate shows in full length a representative of an old Nuremberg family with coat of arms in color
This work appeared without date under title: *Patricij respublicae Nürenberg: Das ist 83. vhralte adeliche geschlächt daraus der rath von 300 jarn hero ervölt und noch das regiment füeren, zusamgebracht und an tag geben*
Lipperheide 773

Geschlecht register der durchleuchtigsten hertzogen in Bayern. See Kilian, Wolfgang. Genealogia serenissimor. Boiarlae ducum

Das **geschmeide**; schmuck- und edelsteinkunde. Barth, Hermann

Gesellschaft für bildende kunst und vaterländische altertümer, Emden. See Manninga, Unico. Ostfriesischen volks- und rittertrachten

Gesellschaft für die heereskunde. See Knötel, Herbert; Pietsch, Paul, and Jantke, Egon. Uniformkunde

Gesellschaft zur herausgabe der denkmäler des theaters, Vienna. See Denkmäler des theaters

Der **gesellschaftstanz** in der Renaissance. Bie, Oskar

Gespräch eines doctors in der theologie mit zweyen vornehmen frauen über die neue kleydertragten. München, M. M. Riedlin 1738

223p. O.
First edition: 1736
Lipperheide 3460

Gessler, Eduard A.

Die trutzwaffen der Karolingerzeit vom VIII. bis zum XI. jahrhundert. Basel, Basler buch- und antiquariatshandlung 1908

160p. O.
Quellenverzeichnis: p157-60

Gestickte kragen. Lescure, Alfred

Gestickte tücher aus der mitte des XIX[en] jahrhunderts. See Lescure, Alfred. Collection A. Lescure

Geszler, J.

Die moden des XIX jahrhunderts. Wien, E. Berté [1895-96]

2 l. 100 col.pl. Q.
Legends in German, French, and English
Colas 1241. Costume index. Lipp. 581

Getreue abbildung und beschreibung der 28 erzernen statuen, welche das grabmahl kaiser Maximilians I. umgeben, und in der hofkirche zu Innsbruck aufgestellt sind. Innsbruck, F. Unterberger [1841]

9 l. 28pl. O.
Title and text in German and French
Lipperheide 869

Die **geuerlicheiten** und eins teils der geschichten des lobliche̅ streitbaren und hochberümbten helds und ritters Tewrdannckhs. Theuerdank

Geuss, Joachim Michael

(tr.) Ólafsson, Eggert. Des vice-lavmands Eggert Olafsens und des landphysici Biarne Povelsens reise durch Island

Gevaerts, Jean Gaspard

Pompa introitus honori ... Ferdinandi Austriaci Hispaniarum infantis S.R.E. card ... a S.P.Q. Antverp. decreta et adornata; cum ... Antverpiam ... adventu suo bearet XV. kal. maii, ann. 1635. Antverpiae, apud I. Meursium 1642

189p. 47 illus. 42pl. F.
Lipperheide 2664

Die **gewandung** der alten Griechen und Römer. Amelung, Walther

Die **gewandung** der Christen in den ersten jahrhunderten. Wilpert, Josef

Gevartius, Casperius. See Gevaerts, J. G.

Gewirkte bildteppiche des xv. und xvi. jahrhunderts im Historischen museum zu Basel. Burckhardt, R. F.

Geyer, Andrea

Gründlicher abriss der jenigen zimmer in welchen bey noch fürwährendem reichs-tag der an. 1663. angefangen und biss dato continuiret die sessiones und deliberationes gehalten werden ... alles nach dem leben gezeichnet. Regensburg, J. B. Lang ca1722

1 l. 8pl. Q.
Lipperheide 682m

Gheltof, Giuseppe Marino Urbani de. See Urbani de Gheltof, G. M.

Gheyn, Jacob de

Die drillkunst; das ist kriegsübliche waffenhandlung der musqueten und piquẽ allen tapfern soldaten zu nutzlicher beliebüng. Nürnberg, P. Fürst 1664

49 l. 39 illus. Q.
This work is a new edition of *Künstlichen waffenhandlung der musqueten und piquen oder langer spiessen,* edited by Peter Isselburg in 1620. Gheyn's illustrations are in reduced size with the explanation and commands in French and German
Lipperheide 2061

The exercise of armes for calivres, muskettes, and pikes. The Hague 1608

117pl. F.

[Reiterübungen] no place, ca1600

22pl. F.
Plates show troopers practicing with swords, pistols, rifles, or lances
Lipperheide 2056

Trillinbuch; waffenhandlung von den röhren, muszquetten und spiessen. Franckfurt am Main, C. Corthoy [1610]

124 l. 117 illus. Q.
The illustrations are reduced copies from the author's *Wapenhandelinghe van roers musquetten ende spiessen* and are accompanied by an explanation and commands in German and French
Lipperheide 2060

Wapenhandelinghe van roers musquetten ende spiessen. SGrauen Hage 1607

3 l. 42, 43, 32 col.pl. F.
The text includes a brief explanation and the commands used at that period
French edition: *Maniement d'armes d'arquebuses, mousquetz, et piques* (Amsterdam, R. de Baudous, 1608. 28,43,32pl.). German edition: *Waffenhandlung von den rören, musquetten, undt spiessen* (Amsterdam, J. Janson 1640. 42,43,32pl.). English edition: *The exercise of armes for calivres, muskettes, and pikes*
Lipp. 2057-2059. LC 21-2713 (Fr. ed.)

See also Goltzius, Hendrick, jt. auth.

Gheyn, Jacques de. See Gheyn, Jacob de

Gheyn, Joseph van den

Cronicques et conquestes de Charlemaine: reproduction de 105 miniatures de Jean Le Tavernier. See entry under Le Tavernier, Jean

(ed.) Brussels. Bibliothèque royale de Belgique. Mss.(9967). L'ystoire de Helayne; reproduction des 26 miniatures du manuscrit

(ed.) Brussels. Bibliothèque royale de Belgique. Section des manuscrits. Deux livres d'heures (nos. 10767 et 11051 de la Bibliothèque royale de Belgique) attribués à l'enlumineur Jacques Coene

(ed.) Christine de Pisan. Épître d'Othéa

(ed.) Liédet, Loyset. Histoire de Charles Martel, reproduction des 102 miniatures by Loyset Liédet

Ghezzi, Pier Leone

Raccolta di xxiv caricature. Dresden, G. C. Walther 1750

24pl. F.
Two of the plates are dated 1722
Lipperheide 3723

Ghezzi, Pietro Leone. See Ghezzi, Pier Leone

Gholtz, Hubert. See Goltz, Hubert

Giacchieri, Pietro

Commentario degli ordini equestri esistenti negli stati di santa chiesa preceduto da un compendio storico dell' estinti istituzioni cavalleresche. Roma, Tipografia della S. C. de propaganda fide 1853

xxiv,231p. 24 col.pl. Q.
Colas 666. Lipperheide 1931

Giafferri, Paul Louis Victor de, marquis

L'histoire du costume féminin français de l'an 1037 à l'an 1870 ... Paris, Nilsson [1922-23]

80p. 120 col.pl. F.
Ten albums in portfolio, each containing 8 pages of text and 12 plates. Title on portfolio: *L'histoire du costume feminin de l'an 1037.* Covers illustrated in colors
Contents: Parures féminines au Moyen-Age; Influence latine sous la Renaissance; Modes de Henri III à Louis XIII; Etiquette somptuaire sous Louis XIV; La cour de la Regence et de Louis XV; Extravagance précieuse sous Louis XVI; Néo-grécisme sous la Révolution. Tanagras du Consulat et Premier Empire; Sobres atours de la Restauration; Grandes robes du Second Empire
Colas 1242. Costume index. LC 24-8646

L'histoire du costume feminin mondial de l'an 5318 avant J.-C. à nos jours. Paris, Nilsson 1925

160p. 200 col.pl. F.
Contents: Chinois, japonais, egyptien, assyrien, persan, indou, grecque, gréco-romains, orientaux, romain, gaulois, européen, France, Scandinavie, Britannique, Espagne, Italie, Allemagne, Russie, les trois Amériques, les races noires
For edition in English see below
Twenty parts in 2 portfolios, each part containing 8 pages of text and 10 plates in cover having illustrated title page
Colas 1243

Histoire du costume masculin français de l'an 420 à l'an 1870. Paris, Nilsson [1927]

80p. 100 col.pl. Q.
Colas 1244

The history of French masculine costume. New York city, Foreign publications [1927]

80p. illus. 100 col.pl. F.
Translated from the French
Ten parts (called volumes) in portfolio, each part, with cover-title illustrated in colors, containing 8 pages of text and 10 plates
Contents: Gallo-Roman togas and tunics; Monastic and Byzantine attire in the middle ages; Capes and collars, renaissance;

Giafferri, Paul L. V. de, marquis—*Continued*
Doublets and jerkins, Louis XIII and Louis XIV; Refined taste of the French garments, Louis XV; Masculine ideal, perukes and dress-coats, Louis XVI; Supreme good manners of the revolutionary "sans-culottes"; Napoleonic imperial official smartness; Romantic dandies and beaux of the restoration period; Appearance of the second empire fops
Costume index. LC 28-31152

The history of the feminine costume of the world, from the year 5318 B. C. to our century. New York, B. Westermann [1926-27]
160p. 200 col.pl. F. $50
Twenty parts in 2 portfolios, each part containing 8 pages of text and 10 plates and laid in cover having illustrated title page
Contents: v 1 China, Japan, Egypt, Assyria, Persia, India, Greece, Rome, Orient; v2 Rome, Gaul, Europe, France, Northern countries, Great Britain, Latin countries, Central Europe, The three Americas, The primitive races
English edition of *L'histoire du costume féminin mondial*
Costume index. LC 28-9067

Gibb, William
The royal house of Stuart; illustrated by a series of forty plates in colours drawn from relics of the Stuarts by William Gibb. London, Macmillan 1890
3 l. 40 col.pl. F.
The introductions to the plates are by Sir John Skelton
LC 3-30578

(illus.) Holmes, R. R. Naval & military trophies & personal relics of British heroes

Gibbon, Lardner. See Herndon, W. L., jt. auth.

La **Giberne**; publication mensuelle illustrée en couleurs. Fev. 1899-août 1914. Paris
Col.illus. col.pl. O.
Shows military uniforms
Colas 1245

Gibson, Charles Dana
People of Dickens; drawn by Charles D. Gibson. New York, R. H. Russell 1897
8 l. 6pl. F.

Gibson, Strickland. See Buxton, L. H. D., jt. auth.

Giem, A. C. S.
Blumen und kanten zum sticken als beitrag zum unterricht in zeichnen- und stickeschulen. Lüneburg, Herold and Wahlstab ca1810
32pl. Q.
Engraved by A. Bock
Lipperheide 3940

Giersberg
Die königlich preussische armée 1792. Berlin 1886
756 col.illus. Q.
Cataloged from Colas
Colas 1246

Giese, Fritz
Girlkultur, vergleiche zwischen amerikanischem und europäischem rhythmus und lebensgefühl. München, Delphin-verlag [c1925]
149p. pl. ports. Q.
LC 26-10662

Körperseele; gedanken über persönliche gestaltung. 2. aufl. München, Delphin verlag c1927
203p. 116 illus. O.

Gigault de La Bédollière, Émile. See La Bédollière, É. G. de

Gilbert, Oscar Paul
Men in women's guise; some historical instances of female impersonation. Translated from the French by Robert B. Douglas. London, John Lane [1926]
xv,284p. front. pl. ports. O.
Contents: Abbé de Choisy; Philip of Orleans and Abbé d'Entragues; The Chevalier d'Éon; Jenny de Savalette de Lange; Some men who still disguise themselves as women
LC 27-4407

Gilchrist, Helen Ives
A catalogue of the collection of arms and armor presented to the Cleveland museum of art by Mr. and Mrs. John Long Severance. See entry under Cleveland museum of art

Gilder, Rosamond, and Freedley, George
Theatre collections in libraries and museums, an international handbook. Published, under the auspices of the New York public library and the National theatre conference, with the cooperation of the American library association. New York, Theatre arts inc. [c1936]
182p. D.
Contains fourteen references to costume collections or to libraries which have special collections of books on costume. Contents: Introduction, by Rosamnd Gilder; The United States, Canada, Mexico, and South America, by Rosamond Gilder; Europe and Asia, by George Freedley; Fugitive material, its care and preservation, by George Freedley; Bibliography (p160-65)
LC 36-21492

Gildsmen
Ashley, Sir W. J. Introduction to English economic history and theory. 1893

Bem, Balcer. Die alten zunft- und verkehrs-ordnungen der stadt Krakau. 1889

Das goldene ehrenbuch der gewerbe und zunfte, enthaltend nachrichten uber ihr entstehen ... aus den zeiten Kaiser Maximilians I. 1834

Langenmantel, David. Histoire des regiments in des Heil. röm. reichs stadt Augspurg. 1725

Staley, J. E. The guilds of Florence. 1906

Trachten und wappen der zünfte und gilden von Bologna. ca1700

Vigne, Félix de. Moeurs et usages des corporations de métiers de la Belgique et du nord de la France, pour faire suite aux Recherches historiques sur les costumes civils et militaires des gilds et des corporations de métiers. 1857

Vigne, Félix de. Recherches historiques sur les costumes civils et militaires des gildes et des corporations de métiers, leurs drapeaux, leurs armes, leurs blasons. 1847

Giles, Edward Bowyer
The history of the art of cutting in England; preceded by a sketch of the history of English costumes. London, F. T. Prewett; New York, J. J. Mitchell 1887
192p. front. (part.) illus. 9 fold.pl. O.

Giles, Edward Bowyer, and others
The West-end system; 6th ed. London, F. T. Prewett [1887]
Q.

Giles, Godfrey Douglas
(illus.) Richards, Walter. Her Majesty's army ... various regiments now comprising the Queen's forces

Giles, J. W.
[Troupes carlistes] Printed by J. Graf ca1835
6 col.pl. ob.Q.
Legends in English
Cataloged from Colas
Colas 1247

Gille, Floriant
Musée de Tzarskoe-Selo, ou Collection d'armes de sa majesté l'empereur de toutes les Russies. Ouvrage ... lithographiées par Asselineau d'après les dessins ... de A. Rockstuhl ... avec une introduction historique par F. Gille. St. Pétersbourg & Carlsruhe, Velten 1835-53
36,35p. 184pl. F.
Lipperheide 2409

Gillig, Victor
Bayerische chevaux legers. München, G. Jaquet 1842
2 l. 6pl. ob.Q.
Colas 1248

Gillot, Claude
Nouveaux desseins d'habillements à l'usage des ballets, operas, et comédies. Paris, Dolibeau ca1726
1 l. 84pl. O.
Plates are engraved by Joullain after Gillot
Colas 1249

Gillum, Mrs Lulu Williams
Color and design, a practical art book. Kansas City, Mo. The Gillum publishing company 1931
207(i.e. 211)p. incl. col.pl. O.
"Treatise on color and design and their practical application to costume design, interior decoration, architecture, and landscape gardening." Preface
Bibliography: p195-200
LC 31-4154

Color secrets. Kirksville, Mo. The Journal printing company 1929
85p. col.pl. fold. tables. O.
"Treatise on color and its practical application to costume design, interior decoration, architecture and landscape gardening." Preface
Bibliography on color, costume design and house decoration: p83-85
LC 29-25752

Gimbel, Karl
Die reconstructionen der gimbel'schen waffensammlung. Berlin, E. S. Mittler 1902
45 l. 42pl. O.
Lipperheide 2460

Tafeln zur entwicklungsgeschichte der schutz -und trutz-waffen in Europa mit ausschluss der feuerwaffen vom VIII. bis XVII. jahrhundert. Baden-Baden, K. Gimbel 1894
15p. 2 illus. 7pl. (incl. 401 illus.) F.
Lipperheide 2447

Waffen und kunst-sammlung. Berlin 1904
70p. 36pl. Q.

Gimbrede, J. N.
(engr.) Grandville, J. I. I. G., called. The flowers personified

Ginguené, Pierre Louis. See Collection complète des tableaux historiques de la révolution française

Ginters, Valdis. See Dzērvītis, Arvēds, jt. auth.

Ginzrot, Johann Christian
Die wagen und fahrwerke der Griechen und Römer und anderer alten völker. München, J. Lentner 1817
2v. illus. 103pl. (part fold.) Q.
Lipperheide 117. LC 4-1480

Giorgi, Domenico
Degli abiti sacri del sommo pontefice paonazzi e neri in alc. sol. funzioni della chiesa. Roma 1724
4 l. 66p. Q.
Colas 1250

Giornale delle dame e delle mode di Francia. 1786-1794? [Italy]
Col.pl. O.
More than 600 colored plates, most of which show fashions and jewelry. Cataloged from Colas
Colas 1251

Giornale delle mode. v 1-? 1788-1795. Firenze, N. Pagni & G. Bardi
Col.pl. O.
Colas 1252. Lipperheide 4573

Giovio, Paulo, bp. of Nocera
Die moscouitische chronica, das ist ein grundtliche beschreibung oder historia desz mechtigen und gewaltigen grossfürsten in der Moscauw ... auch dess trefflichen landts zu Reussen von jrem herkommen, religion, sitten und gebreuchen ... ausz dem latein ins teutsch gebracht. Frankfurt am Mayn, J. Schmidt 1576
138 l. 15 illus. F.
Illustrations are by Jost Amman
This work first appeared in Basel in 1537 under title: *Pauli Jovii de legatione Basilii magni principis Moscoviae liber, in quo Moscovitarum religio, mores, etc. describuntur*
Lipperheide 1335

Musæi Ioviani imagines artifice manu ad vivum expressæ. Nec minore industria Theobaldi Mulleri Marpurgensis musis illustratæ. Basileæ, ex officina P. Pernæ 1577
130 port. on 66 l. O.
Each portrait accompanied by a verse in Latin
The same portraits are found in the author's *Elogia virorum bellica virtute illustrium*, of which this is the third edition
Lipperheide 485. LC 14-6949

Pauli Iovii Novocomensis episcopi nucerini Elogia virorum bellica virtute illustrium, septem libris iam olim ab authore comprehensa, et nunc ex eius-

Giovio, Paulo, bp. of Nocera—*Continued*
dem Musæo ad vivum expressis imaginibus exornata. [Basileæ] P. Pernæ opera ac studio 1575
391p. front. 129 ports. F.
The first edition appeared in Florence in 1551. The portraits, engraved by Tobias Stimmer, show 16th century costume
Lipperheide 484. LC 13-14335

Pauli Iovii Novocomensis episcopi nucerini Elogia virorum literis illustrium, quotquot vel nostra vel avorum memoria vixere. [Basileæ] P. Pernæ opera ac studio 1577
231p. 62 ports. F.
The portraits, engraved by Tobias Stimmer, are also included in Reusner's *Icones*
Lipperheide 486. LC 13-14336

Pauli Iovii Novocomensis episcopi nucerini Regionum et insularum atque locorum: descriptiones: videlicet Britanniae, Scotiae, Hyberniae. Basileae, ex officina P. Pernae 1578
156p. F.
Lipperheide 488

Pauli Iovii Novocomensis episcopi nucerini Vitae illustrium virorum. [Basileae] P. Pernae opera ac studio 1578
2v. 29 ports. F.
Most of the portraits were included in his *Elogia virorum bellica virtuta illustrium*
Lipperheide 487

Pauli Iovii Novocomensis Vitae duodecim vicecomitum Mediolani principum. Paris, R. Stephani 1549
199p. 10 ports. Q.
Portraits show dukes of Milan
This is the first edition with portraits from the original manuscript. There were numerous later editions including one printed at Venice in the same year. Lipperheide notes an Italian translation: *Le rite dei dodeci visconti che signoreggiarono Milano* (Milano, G. B. Bidelli 1645)
Lipperheide 1247 (Ital. ed.)

Gipsies
Gerard, Emily. The land beyond the forest: facts, figures and fancies from Transylvania. 1888

Hall, George. The gypsy's parson. 1915

Hoyland, John. A historical survey of the customs, habits, & present state of the Gipsies. 1816

Pennell, Mrs E. R. To gipsyland. 1893

Wlislocki, Heinrich von. Aus dem inneren leben der zigeuner; ethnologische mitteilungen. 1892

Girard, Pierre Jacques François
Traité des armes; [3. éd.] La Haye, P. de Hondt 1740
156p. 2 illus. 116pl. Q.
The first edition was published in Paris in 1736 and the second edition in 1737. A fourth edition was published at The Hague in 1755
Eighty-one plates show fencers of the period
Lipperheide 2971

Girard de Propiac, Catherine Joseph Ferdinand. See Propiac, C. J. F. G. de

Girardet, Karl. See Belin, A., and others. Costumes de Suède, Norvège, Danemark, Hollande et Allemagne

Giraud, Jean Baptiste
Documents pour servir à l'histoire de l'armement au moyen âge et à la renaissance. Lyon, L'auteur 1895-99
2v. Q.
Cover of v2 dated 1899-1904
"Table bibliographique": v 1 p241-258, v2 p285-303
Contents: v 1 La boutique et la mobilier d'un fourbisseur lyonnais en 1555. Nouv. éd. 1895. Les épées de Bordeaux, archéologie comparée des industries du fer dans la Biscaye française, le pays de Guyenne et le duché de Savoie; nouv. éd. 1896. Inventaire des épées et dagues du comte de Salm, conservées dans l'hôtel de Salm à Nancy, 1614. 1897. La boutique de Jean de Vouvray, armurier à Tours, en 1512. Les armuriers français et étrangers en Touraine. 1897. Documents sur l'importation des armes italiennes à Lyon à l'époque de la renaissance. 1897. Supplément aux Documents sur l'importation des armes italiennes à Lyon. Tables du premier volume. 1899; v2 Une armure de joute en 1514. Comptes de l'écurie de François d'Angoulême. 2. éd. 1899. Armerie des ducs de Lorraine, en 1629; nouv. éd. 1900. Notes pour servir à l'histoire de la sidérurgie en Lorraine: arsenal de Nancy, mines, forges, armes, etc. 1900. Les épées de Rives, étude archéologique sur les industries du fer en Dauphiné; nouv. éd. 1901. L'acier de Carme: notes sur le commerce de l'acier à l'époque de la renaissance, suivies des tables du second volume. 1904
LC 17-14905

Girdles. See Belts and belt buckles; Corset

Girke, Georg
Die tracht der Germanen in der vor- und frühgeschichtlichen zeit, mit einem anhange: Vom heutigen landläufigen germanenbildnisse. Leipzig, C. Kabitzsch 1922
2v. front. (port.) 71(i.e. 76)pl. on 38 l. Q. (Mannus-bibliothek, hrsg. von professor dr. Gustaf Kossinna. nr.23-24)
Contents: v 1 Von den ältesten zeiten bis zum ende der vorschriftlichen eisenzeit; v2 Vom 1. bis zum 8. jahrhundert nach Chr., und Anhang
Colas 1253. LC 32-30732

Girlkultur. Giese, Fritz

A **girl's** life eighty years ago. Bowne, Mrs. Eliza

Gironi, Robustiano
Le danze dei Greci descritte e pubblicate pel faustissimo imeneo di Sua Altezza imperiale e reale il serenissimo principe Ranieri, arciduca d'Austria ... con Sua Altezza serenissima la principessa Elisabetta di Savoja-Cariguano. Milano, Imperiale regia stamperia 1820
68p. 6 col.pl. (incl.front.) F.
Lipperheide 185. LC 15-8917

Saggio di Robustiano Gironi intorno alle costumanze civili dei Greci. Milano, G. Ferrario 1823
133p. 19 col.pl. Q.
The last pages of the text and the last five plates are concerned with the customs and dress of modern Greece
Plates are engraved by Gallina, Fumagalli, Raineri, and others
Colas 1254. Lipperheide 186

Giroux, Mme A.
Traité de la coupe et de l'assemblage des vêtements de femmes et d'enfants; 6. éd. Paris, Hachette 1907
251p. illus. D.
First edition: 1882

Girrane, Gustave
(illus.) Grand-Carteret, John. La femme en culotte

Giscard
Delineations of the most remarkable costumes of the different provinces of Spain, and also of the military uniforms, bull fights, national dances, &c. of the Spaniards. London, H. Stokes 1823
40 col.pl. (incl.front.) ob.Q.
Plates reproduced from sketches in water color. Most of the plates signed: Giscard
Colas 1255. Costume index. LC 10-17953

Giucci, Gaetano
Iconografia storica degli ordini religiosi e cavallereschi. Roma, 1836-47
9v. in 3. CDXXX(i.e. 431)pl. sq.F.
Colas 1256. Lipperheide 1850. LC 4-21305

Giustinian, Bernardo
Historie cronologiche dell' origine degl'ordini militari e di tutte le religioni cavalleresche. Venezia, Presso Cambi & Là Noù 1692
2v. illus. 35pl. F.
Colas 1257. Lipperheide 1895

Gladiators
Lipsius, Justus. Saturnalium sermonum libri duo, qui de gladiatoribus. 1598

Gladky, Serge, synthèse du costume théâtral. See entry under Salmon, André

Glasbrenner, Adolf
Berlin wie es ist und trinkt. Leipzig, I. Jackowitz 1843-50
32 parts. 32 col.fronts. O.
The contents, the edition, and the publication date of each part are noted in the Lipperheide *Katalog*
Lipperheide 3532

März-almanach; 2. aufl. Leipzig, J. G. Mittler 1849
1 l. 94p. 26 illus. O.
Illustrated by T. Hosemann, W. Scholz and others
Lipperheide 3539

Glaser, Rudolph
Denkbuch über die anwesenheit ihrer K. K. majestäten Franz des ersten und Caroline Auguste in Böhmen im jahre 1833. Prag, 1836
xxii,213p. 80pl. Q.
Lipperheide 2635

Glasgow. See Scotland—Glasgow

Glasgow ecclesiological society
Four Scottish coronations. See entry under Cooper, James

Glasgow men and women. Boyd, A. S.

[**Glasser**]
Catalogue d'une collection importante de costumes militaires français et étrangers, de costumes civils; recueils, suites, estampes détachées, aquarelles, livres; de livres illustrés des XVIIIe et XIXe siècles, de recueils de lithographies, estampes du XVIIIe siècle, œuvre de Félicien Rops. Paris, H. Leclerc 1910-11
2v. (255,80p.) incl.tables. col.pl. Q.
Colas 556-57. LC 12-15608 (under title)

Costumes militaires; catalogue des principales suites de costumes militaires français parures tant en France qu'à l'étranger depuis le règne de Louis XV jusqu'à nos jours, et des suites de costumes militaires étrangers parues en France; par un membre de la sabretache. Paris, H. Vivien, 1900
562p. 4 col.pl.(incl.front.) O.
A list of the sets of pictures of French military costume
Colas 1258. Lipperheide 2126. LC 4-8377 (under title)

Glasson, Ernest Désiré
Les origines du costume de la magistrature. Paris, L. Larose et Forcel 1884
29p. O.
From *La nouvelle revue historique de droit français et étranger*
Colas 1259

Gleanings from the past and memorials from the present. Davison, T. R.

Gleich
(engr.) Restif de La Bretonne. Tableaux de la vie, ou Les moeurs du dixhuitième siècle

[**Gleichauf, Rudolf**]
Badische landestrachten im auftrage des grossherzog. badischen handelsministeriums. Stuttgart, H. Müller [1862]
10 col.pl. F.
Colas 1260. Lipperheide 751

Gleichen-Russwurm, Alexander, freiherr von
Dandies and Don Juans; concerning fashion and love among the great ... translated from the German by Margaret M. Green. New York, London, A. A. Knopf 1928
xxiv,273p. front. pl. ports. O.
Translation of his *Könige des lebens*
LC 28-29777

Könige des lebens; von eleganz und liebe grosser herren. München, Drei masken verlag [1927]
495p. front. pl. ports. D.
Contents: Zur einführung: Vom stutzertum; Alkibiades; Demetrios; Publius Ovidius Naso; Petronius; Michael III. und Basilius; Wilhelm von Balaun; Ulrich von Liechtenstein; Petrarca; Ludwig graf von Valois; Conrad Celtis; Pietro Aretino; Walter Raleigh; Bassompierre; Anton van Dyck; Don Juan; Herzog von Lauzun; Graf von Brühl; Marschall von Richelieu; Graf Saint Germain; Jacob Casanova; Chevalier d'Eon; Das galante Leipzig; Graf Alfieri; Herault de Séchelles; Das klassische reich der dandies; Georg Brummel; Graf d'Orsay; Benjamin Disraeli; Barbey d'Aurévilly und Eugène Sue; Fürst von Metternich; Herzog von Morny; Ferdinand Lassalle; Oscar Wilde; Valentino; Vom stutzertum der lebenden
LC 29-21794

Glen, Jean Baptiste de
Des habits, moeurs, ceremonies, façons de faire anciennes & modernes du monde, traicté non moins utile, que delectable, plein de bonnes & sainctes instructions ... Partie première. Des principales nations, provinces, regions, & villes de l'Europe. Liege, I. de Glen 1601
168,13 l. 104 illus. O.
Part 2 not published. The illustrations are copies from previous works, especially Vecellio's *De gli habiti antichi et moderni.* Three new plates show the costume of Liège
Colas 1261. Lipperheide 27

Gliddon, George Robbins. See Nott, J. C., jt. auth.

Glimpses of Japan and Formosa. Franck, H. A.

Glimpses of life and manners in Persia. Sheil, M. L. W., lady

Globus; illustrierte zeitschrift für länder- und völkerkunde. [1.]-98. bd.; 1861/62-dez. 1910. Hildburghausen, Verlag des Bibliographischen instituts, 1862-66; Braunschweig, F. Vieweg und sohn, 1867-1910
98v. illus. pl. (part col.) maps. F.
Two vols. a year, containing 24 numbers each. Title varies slightly
Absorbed *Das Ausland* in 1894, *Aus allen weltteilen* in 1898. Merged into *Petermanns mitteilungen*
Lipperheide 4693. LC 19-1252

Les **gloires** de l'Opéra. Haguental and Fagonde

La **gloria** d'amore. Aureli, Aurelio

Glossaire archéologique du moyen âge et de la renaissance. Gay, Victor

Glossary of ecclesiastical ornament and costume. Pugin, A. W. N.

Glossary of terms used for articles of British dress and armour. Williams, John, ab Ithel

A **glossary** of the construction, decoration and use of arms and armor. Stone, G. C.

Glotz, Gustave
La civilisation égéenne. Paris, Renaissance du livre 1923
476p. illus. (incl. maps, plans) IV pl. D. (L'évolution de l'humanité, synthèse collective. [1. section. IX])
Contains a chapter on costume and some illustrations of Minoan dress
Bibliography: p[453]-57
LC 25-22885

Glover, Robert
The catalogue of honor, or Tresury of true nobility. See entry under Milles, Thomas
Nobilitas politica vel civilis. See entry under Milles, Thomas

Gloves
Beck, S. W. Gloves, their annals and associations. 1883
Franklin, A. L. A. La vie privée d'autrefois; arts et métiers, modes, moeurs, usages des Parisiens du XII. au XVIII. siècle. [v 16]
Guénot-Lecointe, Georges. Physiologie du gant. 1841
Der handschuh; ein vademecum für menschen von geschmack. 1914
Norton-Kyshe, J. W. The law and customs relating to gloves, being an exposition historically viewed of ancient laws, customs, and uses in respect of gloves, and of the symbolism of the hand and glove in judicial proceedings. 1901
Pacichelli, Giambattista. Schediasma juridico-philologicum tripartitum. 1693
Redfern, W. B. Royal and historic gloves and shoes. 1904
Smith, W. M. Gloves, past and present. 1917
Uzanne, L. O. L'ombrelle, le gant, le manchon. 1883
Uzanne, L. O. Les ornements de la femme ... L'éventail, l'ombrelle, le gant, le manchon. 1892

Gloves, Ecclesiastical
Barraud, P. C. Des gants portés par les évêques, par d'autres membres du clergé et même uar les laiques dans les cérémonies religieuses. 1867
Nicolai, Johann. Disquisitio de chirothecarum usu & abusu, in qua varii ritus, varia jura, & symbola illarum fuse exhibentur. 1701

Gloves, Papal
Barbier de Montault, Xavier. Les gants pontificaux. 1877

Gloves, past and present. Smith, W. M.

Gloves, their annals and associations. Beck, S. W.

Glück, E.
Fètes de Gutenberg; cortège industriel de Strasbourg 25. juin 1840. Strasbourg, E. Simon fils 1840?
50 col.pl. F.
Lipperheide 2829

[**Goater, Mrs Anne C.**]
A short treatise on head wear, ancient and modern, illustrated by Walter H. Goater. [New York, Lockwood press, c1885]
32p. illus. 17x14cm.
Issued as an advertising medium by R. Dunlap & co. hatters, New York
LC 9-7688
A short treatise on boots and shoes, ancient and modern. New York, J. & J. Slater [1884]
31p. illus. D.
LC 8-34479

Gobet, Nicolas
Recherches sur le sacre des rois de France. See note under Pichon, T. J., ed. Sacre et couronnement de Louis XVI roi de France. part 2

Goble, Warwick
(illus.) Van Millingen, Alexander. Constantinople

The **Gōda** collection of Japanese sword fittings. New York. Metropolitan museum of art

Godby, James
Italian scenery; representing the manners, customs, and amusements of the different states of Italy ... engravings by James Godby, from original drawings by P. van Lerberghi. The narrative by M. Buonaiuti. London, E. Orme 1806
74p. 32 col.pl. Q.
Text in English and French
Reprinted in 1823 (London, T. M'Lean)
Colas 2970. Lipperheide 1258

Goddard and Booth, London
(pub.) The military costume of Europe

Goddard, Eunice Rathbone
Women's costume in French texts of the eleventh and twelfth centuries. Baltimore, Md. Johns Hopkins press; Paris, Les Presses universitaires de France, 1927
263p. 7pl. O. (The Johns Hopkins studies in romance literatures and languages v7) pa $1.25
The introduction and plates alone were published as a thesis under the same title (Baltimore, Md., John Hopkins press; Paris, Les Presses universitaires 1927. 23p. 7pl. O. Colas 1262. LC 27-24192)
Bibliography p239-56
Costume index. LC 27-15102

Goddard, Pliny Earle
Indians of the Northwest coast. New York [American museum press] 1924
176p. front. illus. pl. fold.map. O. (American museum of natural history. Handbook series no10)
Second edition: 1934
Bibliography: p166-68
Costume index (2d ed.) LC 24-31104

Indians of the Southwest. New York, American museum of natural history, 1913
191p. front. illus. fold.map. D. (Handbook series, no2)
Second edition 1921, third ed. 1927
Dress of the Pueblo Indians p85-90, the nomadic peoples p140-43
Bibliography: p185-86
LC 14-2837; 22-26495; 29-9322

Godefroy, Adrien Pierre François
Armeés des souverains alliés, années 1814 et 1815. Paris, Martinet [1815?]
14 col.pl. F.
Colas 1263

Godey's lady's book. See Godey's magazine

Godey's magazine. v. 1-131; 1830-1898. Philadelphia & New York, L. A. Godey [etc.]
Illus. pl.(part col.) ports. O.
Published monthly
Title varies: 1830-39 *The Lady's book* [with which was united 1837, *The Ladies magazine*]; 1840-43 *Godey's lady's book and ladies American magazine*; 1844-June 1848 *Godey's magazine and lady's book;* July 1848-December 1853 *Godey's lady's book;* July 1854-December 1869 *Godey's lady's book and magazine;* October 1892-September 1898 *Godey's magazine.* Merged in *The Puritan,* October 1898
Editors: Sarah J. Hale, 1837-69; Lydia H. H. Sigourney, 1840-42; L. A. Godey, 1830-77; M. McMichael, 1842-46; J. H. Haulenbeek, 1883-85; Eleanor M. Hiestand, 1885-86; Jane C. Croly, 1887-88; H. W. Bates, 1894-95

Godfrey, Elizabeth, pseud. See Bedford, Jessie

Gods

Aztecs

Danzel, T. W. Mexiko. v1

Greece

Conze, A. C. L. Heroën- und göttergestalten der griechischen kunst. 1875

Goebels, W.
Der grosse cölnische maskenzug im jahre 1824. Cöln, H. Goffart [1824]
24 col.pl. F.
Lipperheide 2866

Göll, Hermann
Kulturbilder aus Hellas und Rom, 3. berichtigte und verm. aufl. Leipzig und Berlin, O. Spamer 1880
2v. O.
Volume 2, p151-206 has title: Die griechische und römische tracht

Göes, Damião de. See Boemus, Johann. Mores, leges, et ritus omnium gentium

Goethe, Johann Wolfgang
Das römische carneval. Berlin, J. F. Unger 1789
69p. 20 col.pl. Q.
Lipperheide 2859

Göttingen. See Street venders—Germany—Göttingen

Göttingische akademische annalen. Meiners, Christoph

Götz, Hermann
1826-1896. Der jubiläums festzug der haupt- und residenz-stadt Karlsruhe, zum siebenzigsten geburtstage seiner königlichen hoheit des grossherzogs Friedrich von Baden. Karlsruhe, A. Bielefeld [1896]
1 l. 23pl. F.
Lipperheide 2605

Goetz, Théodor
(illus.) Müller, August. Geschichtliche übersicht der schicksale und veränderungen des grossherzogl. sächs. militairs

Goetz, Walter Wilhelm
(ed.) Burckhardt, J. C. The civilization of the renaissance in Italy. 1929

Götze, Alfred
Die altthüringischen funde von Weimar (5.-7. jahrhundert nach Chr.) Berlin, E. Wasmuth 1912
72p. front illus. XVIII pl.(1 col.) map, plan. F. (Germanische funde aus der völkerwanderungszeit)
Issued in portfolio
Seven of the plates show jewelry of ancient times
LC 32-18744

Götzinger, Ernst
Reallexicon der deutschen altertümer; 2. vollständig umgearb. aufl. Leipzig, W. Urban 1885
viii,1151p. 157 illus. D.
First edition: 1881
Lipperheide 594 (1st ed.). LC 2-20460

Göz, Joseph Franz von
Die heutige sichtbare körperwelt oder 100 charakter züge derer denen menschen ... äusserlich kennbar werdender, innerlich verborgener guter-oder böser leidenschafftlicher beschaffenheiten. Augsburg, Handlung der kays. franziszischen reichsakademie Fr. K. und W. [1783-85]
7 l. 100 col.pl. Q.
The plates show in caricature fashions among society folk of Augsburg. They are engraved by R. Brichet, with the last 16 plates only engraved by J. F. von Göz
This suite is also found without the text, with the title: *Exércices d'imagination de différens caractères et formes humaines* which is the title of plate I
Colas 1277. Lipperheide 3521-22

Gohlke, Wilhelm
Die blanken waffen und die schutzwaffen, ihre entwicklung von der zeit der landsknechte bis zur gegenwart, mit besonderer berücksichtigung der waffen in Deutschland, Österreich-Ungarn und Frankreich. mit 115 abbildungen. Berlin und Leipzig, G. J. Göschen 1912
135p. 115 illus. D. (Sammlung Göschen. [631])
"Literatur und quellen": p[4]-6
LC 13-7375

Golbéry, Marie Philippe Aimé de
(tr.) Rugendas, J. M. Voyage pittoresque dans le Brésil

Gold, Charles
Oriental drawings: sketched between the years 1791 and 1798. London, G. and W. Nicoll 1806
[193]p. illus. col.pl. F.
LC 11-2554

Gold and silver jewelery and related objects. Williams, C. R.

A **gold** treasure of the late Roman period. Dennison, Walter

The **golden** age of classic Christian art. Richter, J. P., and Taylor, A. C.
The **golden** bough. Frazer, Sir J. G.

Golden fleece, Order of the
Kaschutnig, Anton. Vellis aureum burgundoaustriacum sive ... Ordinis torquatorum aurei velleris equitum ... relatio historica. 1728
Kervyn de Lettenhove, H. M. B. J. L., baron. La Toison d'or; notes sur l'institution et l'histoire de l'ordre (depuis l'année 1429 jusqu'à l'année 1559) 1907
Larchey, Lorédan. Ancien armorial équestre de la Toison d'or et de l'Europe au 15. siècle. 1890
Reprint of a 15th century mss.
Probszt, Günther. Der schatz des Ordens vom goldenen vliesse. 1926
Schlosser, Julius, ritter von. Der burgundische paramentenschatz des Ordens von goldenen vliesse. 1912
Vienna. K.K. Österreichisches museum fur künst und industrie. Die Burgundischen gewander der k.k. schatzkammer; messornat fur den Orden vom Goldenen vliess. 1864

Das **goldene** ehrenbuch der gewerbe und zünfte, enthaltend nachrichten über ihr entstehen ... aus den zeiten Kaiser Maximilians I. ... abbildungen nach zeichnungen Carl Heideloffs. Nürnberg, Riegel und Wiessner 1834
[210]p. 62 col.pl. Ti.

Das **goldene** gewand der Königin Margareta in der Domkirche, zu Uppsala. Branting, Agnes

Der **goldschatz** von Hiddensee. Paulsen, Peter

Goldschmidt, Ernst Philip
(ed.) Burchardus, abbot of Bellevaux. Apologia de barbis

Goldschmuck der renaissance. Luthmer, Ferdinand

Goldsmith, Oliver
(comp.) The world displayed

Goldstein, Harriet Irene, and Goldstein, Vetta
Art in every day life. New York, Macmillan 1925
xxvi,465p. illus. pl.(part col. part fold.) diagrs. O.
Pages 251-320 are on dress design
LC 25-19543

Goldstein, Vetta. See Goldstein, H. I., jt. auth.

Golebiowski, Lukasz
Ubiory w. Polsce od najdawniejszych czasów aż do chwil obecnych, sposobem dykcyonarza. Krakowie, Nakladem drukarni "Czasu" 1861
251p. 1 pl. O.
Describes costume in Poland from earliest times
Edited by K. J. Turowski
Colas 1264. Lipperheide 1394

Golf. Cotton, T. H.

Golf costume
Aldin, C. C. W. The omnibus book of sports for young and old. 1937 part 3
Darwin, B. R. M. A golfer's gallery by old masters. 1927?
Everard, H. S. C. A history of the Royal & ancient golf club, St. Andrews, from 1754-1900. 1907

A **golfer's** gallery by old masters. Darwin, B. R. M.

Golovackij, J. F. See Golovatskiĭ, ÎA. F.

Golovatskiĭ, ÎA. F.
O narodnoĭ odezhdîe ī ubranstvîe Rusīnov" īlī Russkīkh" v" Galīchīnîe i sîevero-vostochnoĭ Vengriī. S. Peterburg, tīp. V. Kīrshbauma 1877
85p. 5 illus. O.
On national dress and customs of the Ruthenians
Lipperheide 1371
Narodnyîa pîesnī Galītskoĭ ī Ugorskoĭ Rusī. Moskva, v" unīversītetskoĭ tīp. M. Katkov" 1878
3v. in 4. 20pl. O.
Plates show dress of the Ruthenians of Little Russia
Lipperheide 1372

Golovnin, Vasilii Mikhailovich. See Breton de la Martinière, J. B. J. Le Japon, ou moeurs, usages et costumes des habitans de cet empire

Goltz, Hubert
Les images presque de tous les empereurs, depuis C. Julius Caesar jusques à Charles v et Ferdinandus son frère, pourtraites au vif, prinses des médailles anciens ... par Hubert Gholtz. Anvers, G. Coppenius 1557
155pl. F.
Many editions are known

Goltzius, Hendrick, and Gheyn, Jacob de
[Officers and soldiers of a regiment of infantry of the Netherlands] No place 1587
12pl. F.
Each plate is signed H. Goltzius and J. de Gheyn
Colas 1266. Lipperheide 2052

Golubykh, Mikhail Dmitrievich
Kazach'îa derevnîa. Podred. M. Fenomenova. Moskva & Leningrad, Gosizdat 1930
323p. illus.
A monograph which describes the village of Timofeevsky, in the department of Cheliabinsk, Russia

Gomes, Edwin Herbert
Seventeen years among the Sea Dyaks of Borneo. Philadelphia, J. B. Lippincott 1911
343p. front. pl. port. fold.map. O.
LC 11-35364

Gómez Carrillo, Enrique
Psicologia de la moda femenina. Madrid, P. Villavicencio 1907
118p. S.
French translation has title *Psychologie de la mode* (Paris, Garnier 1910. 211p.)
Colas 1267-68

Gomez de Bedoya, Fernando
Historia del toreo, y de las principales ganaderias de España. Madrid, Imp. de A. Sta. Coloma y compañía 1850
380p. illus. pl. ports. Q.
LC 5-22736

Goncourt, Edmond Louis Antoine Huot de; Daudet, Alphonse, and Zola, Émile
Les types de Paris ... dessins de Jean-François Raffaëlli. Paris, E. Plon, Nourrit [1889]
162p. 138 illus.(46 col.) 17pl.(8 col.) F.
Lipperheide 1176m

Goncourt, Edmond Louis Antoine Huot de, and Goncourt, Jules Alfred Huot de
La femme au dix-huitième siècle; nouvelle éd., rev. augm. et illustrée ... par Dujardin. Paris, Firmin-Didot 1887
402p. 58pl.(10 col.) Q.
Lipperheide 1151

Histoire de la société francaise pendant la révolution. Paris, Quantin 1889
374p. 45pl.(9 col.) Q.
First edition: 1854
Lipperheide 1137m

Goncourt, Jules Alfred Huot de. See Goncourt, E. L. A. H. de, jt. auth.

Gonino, I.
(tr.) Charnay, Désiré. The ancient cities of the New World
(tr.) Perrot, Georges, and Chipiez, Charles. History of art in primitive Greece
(ed. and tr.) Perrot, Georges, and Chipiez, Charles. History of art in Sardinia, Judaea, Syria, and Asia Minor

González, Juana Natividad de Diego y. See Diego y González, Juana Natividad de

Good, Edward
Cameos and inspiration jewellery. London [The Press printers] 1914
2p.l. 11-46p. incl. illus. plates. col.front. col.pl. O.
LC 18-4971

Good form for all occasions. Hall, Mrs F. M. H.

Good taste in dress. McFarland, Mrs F. W.

Goodrich, Nathaniel Lewis
(ed.) American ski annual

Goodrich-Freer, Adela M.
Arabs in tent & town; an intimate account of the family life of the Arabs of Syria. London, Seeley, Service 1924
325p. front. pl. O.
LC 24-31304

Goodwin, Mrs Maud (Wilder)
Dolly Madison. New York, C. Scribner 1896
xiv,287p. front.(port.) D. (Half-title: Women of colonial and revolutionary times. [v2])
Styles in dress and hair dressing of the period are described in detail Mrs Madison lived from 1768 to 1849
LC 5-5428

Gopčević, Spiridion
Das fürstentum Albanien, seine vergangenheit, ethnographischen verhältnisse, politische lage und aussichten für die zukunft; 2. aufl. Berlin, H. Paetel 1914
364p. pl. ports. fold.map. O.
About half the plates show costume
LC 28-30133

Gordon, Anthony
A treatise on the science of defence, for the sword, bayonet, and pike, in close action. London, T. Egerton 1805
66p. 19pl.(1 fold.) sq.Q.
Second edition published in 1806
Lipperheide 2981 (2d ed.) LC 18-23674

Gordon, George Byron
In the Alaskan wilderness. Philadelphia, J. C. Winston 1917
247p. front.(port.) maps. 48pl.(1 fold.) O.

Gordon, William John
Bands of the British army; illus. by F. Stansell, with coloured plates of representative bandsmen and instruments and the drum-horses. London, F. Warne [1921]
25p. incl.col.front. pl. ob.Q.
Plates numbered 1-12

Gordon Highlanders. Milne, James

Gori, Antonio Francesco
Monumentum, sive columbarium libertorum et servorum Liviæ Augustae et cæsarum, Romæ detectum in Via Appia, anno 1726. Florentiae, typis Regiæ Celsitudinis 1727
2v. in 1. front. illus. pl. map, plans. O.
Lipperheide 227. LC 4-31273

Gorse, P.
Costumes de la région pyrénéenne française et espagnole. Paris, Imp. Becquet [18—]
1 p.l. 24 col. mounted pl. Q.
Four plates are missing from the Library of Congress copy. The title of the remaining plates follow: 1 Femme de pêcheur, Arcachon-La Teste; 2 Bergers des Landes; 3 Baigneur à Biarritz; 4 Cas carotte, Mde de poissons à St. Jean de Luz; 5 Paysan des environs de Pau; 8 Paysanne de Laruns, près les Eaux-Bonnes; 9 Musiciens à Laruns; 12 Bergers ossalois, près Le Pic du Midi; 13 Chasseur d'ours, vallée d'Ossau; 14 Paysan des environs de Cauterets; 15 Marchande de lait, a Cauterets; 16 Espagnol marchand de vin à Cauterets; 17 Homme & femmes de Bagnères, au marché; 18 Habitants de Luz, près Barèges; 19 Guide et chasseur d'izards à Luchon; 20 Espagnols revenant de Luchon; 21 Vénasquais descendant le port; 22 Pâtres Catalans, près La Maladetta; 23 Jeune femme de Bosost; 24 Aragonais
LC 30-33213

Souvenirs des Pyrénées. Pau, A. Bassy [1843]
16 col.pl. F.
Title appears at head of each plate. The following list of plates is taken from Colas's *Bibliographie:* 1 Grisette, Pau; 2 Le départ pour le marché, env. de Pau; 3 Scène du marché; 6 Marchands de lait et de beurre, Eaux-Bonnes; 7 Moissonneurs, Eaux-Bonnes; 8 Repos des faneurs, Eaux-Bonnes; 9 Jeune fille avouant son premier secret à sa mère, Eaux-Bonnes; 10 La demande, Eaux-Bonnes; 11 Porteuses d'eau Eaux-Bonnes; Famille de bergers, Eaux-Bonnes. 13 Chasseur à l'affut des isards au pied du Ger, Eaux-Bonnes; 14 Danse, Eaux-Bonnes; 15 Pendant la messe, Laruns; 16 La prière a la madonne du Hourat
Colas 2780

The **gospel** in the Old Testament. Copping, Harold

The **Gospel** story in art. La Farge, John

Gosse, Sir Edmund William. See Garnett, Richard, jt. auth.

Gosse, Philip Henry
Assyria; her manners and customs, arts and arms: restored from her monuments. London, Society for promoting Christian knowledge 1852
xviii,642p. illus. map. D. 8s
Pages 437-87 deal with costume. Some of the illustrations show costume
Costume index. LC 5-11566

Gosson, Stephen
Pleasant quippes for upstart newfangled gentlewomen. Imprinted at London by Richard Johnes. MDXCVI. To which is added, Pickings and pleasantries from The trumpet of warre. Totham, Printed at C. Clark's private press 1847
13 l. O.
Printed on one side of leaf only.
First published, London, 1595, with title *Quippes for upstart new-fangled gentlewomen.* The 2d edition, London, 1596, published with title *Pleasant quippes... The trumpet of warre* was first published, London, 1598, reprinted (London, C. Richards 1841)
LC 19-15361

Gostiaux, G.
(illus.) Du Fresnel, H. V. D. Un régiment à travers l'histoire

Gostling, Mrs Frances M. (Parkinson)
The Bretons at home ... with an introduction by Anatole Le Braz. New York, R. M. McBride; Methuen 1925
xxiii,264p. front 42pl.(12 col.) ports. D. $2.50; 10s 6d
Third edition. "Works consulted for this book": p [xvi]
LC 25-19001

Goths. See Europe—To 476

Gottesdientliche ceremonien, oder h. kirchengebräuche und religions-pflichten. See Picart, Bernard. Cérémonies et coutumes religieuses de tous les peuples du monde

Gottfrid, Joh. Ludov. See Gottfried, J. L.

Gottfried, Johann Ludwig
Joh. Ludov. Gottfridi Historische chronica; oder, Beschreibung der fürnehmsten geschichten so sich von anfang der welt biss auff das jahr Christi 1619 zugetragen. [Franckfurt am Mayn] Verlegt durch weiland M. Merianum seel., jetzo dessen erben 1674
1185,53p. 330 illus. XXXI pl. fold.map. fold.plan. F.
Engraved by Matthaeus Merian. The 31 plates each show 12 medallion portraits of Roman and German emperors up to Ferdinand III, also nobles and noted persons to the beginning of the 17th century
First edition: 1630
Lipperheide 313. LC 3-1468

Gottschalck, Friedrich
Almanach der ritter-orden. Leipzig, G. J. Goeschen 1817-19
3v. 29pl. O.
Lipperheide 1920

Goubarev. See Piratzky, A., jt. auth.

Goudeau, Émile
Tableaux de Paris. Émile Goudeau, Paris qui consomme; dessins de Pierre Vidal. Paris, impr. pour H. Béraldi par Chamerot et Renouard 1893
325p. col.illus. O.

Gouin, Édouard
L'Égypte au XIXe siècle. Histoire militaire et politique, anecdotique et pittoresque de Méhémet-Ali, Ibrahim-Pacha, Soliman-Pacha (Colonel Sèves). Illustrée de gravures peintes à l'aquarelle d'après les originaux de M. J. A. Beaucé. Paris, P. Boizard 1847
470p. front. 20 col.pl. Q.
Plates show costume
LC 1-22808

Goulart, Simon
(tr.) Bèze, Théodore de. Les vrais portraits des hommes illustres

Gould, Grace Margaret
The magic of dress. Illustrated by E. M. A. Steinmetz. Garden City, N. Y., Doubleday, Page 1911
166p. front. pl. D. $1
LC 11-27321

Goulet, Nicolas
Fêtes à l'occasion du mariage de S. M. Napoléon, empereur des Français ... avec Marie Louise, archiduchesse d'Autriche. Paris, L. C. Soyer 1810
48p. 54pl. O.
Lipperheide 2722

Goullin, Jean Antoine
La mode sous le point de vue hygiénique, médical, et historique; ou, conseils aux dames et à la jeunesse. Paris, chez l'auteur 1846
252p. D.

Goulven, Joseph Georges Arsène
Les mellahs de Rabat-Salé; préface de M. Georges Hardy ... dessins de Haïnaut. —Couverture de Jabin. Paris, P. Geuthner 1927
xii,163p. front. (plan) 1 illus XXXII pl. (part col.) sq.O.
LC 28-19377

Goupil Fesquet, Frédéric Auguste Antoine
Voyage d'Horace Vernet en Orient. Paris, Challamel [1843]
228p. 16 col.pl. (incl. front.) Q.
Plates lithographed by Challamel, C. Deshays, Bour and Loire after Goupil Fesquet present the costume of Egypt, Syria, Palestine, and Turkey. They show a variety of turbans
Colas 1275. Lipperheide 1597. LC 4-30810

Gourdaine, Jean Pierre Norblin de la. See Norblin de la Gourdaine, J. P.

Gourdon de Genouillac, Henri
Paris à travers les siècles. Histoire nationale de Paris et des Parisiens depuis la fondation de Lutèce jusqu'à nos jours. Paris, F. Roy 1879-82
5v. col.front. illus. 301pl.(part col.) ports. plans. Q.
Volume 1 covers the period from pre-Roman times to the death of Henry II; v2 from François II to Louis XIV; v3 from Louis XIV to Louis XVI; v4 from Louis XVI to Louis XVIII; v5 from Louis-Philippe to the death of Thiers
LC A12-827

Gourdon de Genouillac, Nicolas Jules Henri. See Gourdon de Genouillac, Henri

Le **goût** chinois en France au temps de Louis XIV. Belevitch-Stankevitch, H.

[Le **goût** du jour] Paris, Martinet ca1808
50 col.pl. ob.F.
Caricatures of Parisian costume of the first empire and the restoration. For a list of plates see Colas's *Bibliographie*
Colas 1276

Le **goût nouveau.** Devéria, Achille

Gower, Lord Ronald Charles Sutherland. See Clouet, Francois. Three hundred French portraits

Gowns and gossip. Almond, A. G.

Goya y Lucientes, Francisco José de
[Caprichos inventados y grabados al agua forte] Madrid, ca1799
80pl.(part col.) Q.
Lipperheide 3722

Goya y Lucientes, Francisco J. de—*Cont.*
Los desastres de la guerra von Goya; zweiundachtzig faksimile-wiedergaben in kupfertiefdruck nach den vorzugsdrucken des Kupferstichkabinetts in Berlin; herausgegeben von Hugo Kehrer. München, H. Schmidt 1921
13p. 82pl. sq.F.
LC 30-18226

Tauromachia; 43 faksimile-wiedergaben in kupfertiefdruck, herausgegeben von Hugo Kehrer. München, H. Schmidt [c1923]
15p. 43pl. F.
The original etchings were first published about 1815 with title: *Treinta y tres estampas que representan diferentes suertes y actitudes del arte de lidiar los toros*
Lipperheide names an undated French edition published in Paris with 40 plates: *La taureaumachie*
Lipp. 2862 (French ed.) LC 30-18233

About

Brunet, Gustav. Étude sur Francisco Goya. 1865

Die **grabdenkmale** während des mittelalters. Lind, Karl

Grad, Charles
L'Alsace; le pays et ses habitants. Paris, Hachette 1919
412p. front. illus. F.

Gradmann, Johann Jacob
Habillemens berlinois. Augsburg ca1780
6pl. F.

Graecorum ecclesiasticorum institutio et habitus. See Coronelli, M. V. Ordinum equestrium, ac militarium brevis narratio

Gräffer, Auguste
(pub.) Geschichte der kaiserl. konigl. regimenter

Graenicher, Samuel
Costumes suisses. Basle, C. de Mechel 1778-83
24 col.pl. Q.
Plates show folk costume of various Swiss cantons. For list of plates see Colas's *Bibliographie*
Colas 1278

(engr.) XVII vorstellungen von deutschen national-trachten

Graenicher, Samuel, and Thiele, C. F.
Costumes in Sachsen. Dresden, H. Rittner [1807]
26 col.pl. F.
For a list of the plates see Colas's *Bibliographie.* Lipperheide and Colas list another edition (ca1805) with 18 plates. This omits the plates engraved by Thiele
Colas 1279-1280. Lipperheide 823 (1805 ed.)

Gräter, Friedrich David
Bemerkungen über die monumente der ritter zu Vellberg; ein beytrag zur geschichte der sprache, kunst und sitten im 15ten und 16ten jahrhundert. Leipzig, H. Gräff 1797
50p. 3 illus. 4pl.(with 12 illus.) O.
Shows costume of the ladies of Vellberg, Germany, from 1496 to 1599
From *Bragur. Ein literarisches magazin der deutschen und nordischen vorzeit.* v5 pt2, 1797
Lipperheide 652

Graevius, Joannes Georgius
Thesaurus antiquitatum romanarum. See note under Raynaud, Théophile. Anselmus Solerivs Cemeliensis. De pileo

Graf, Henry
Vues des cérémonies les plus intéressantes du couronnement de Leurs Majestés Impériales l'empereur Nicolas Ier et l'impératrice Alexandra, à Moscou ... lithographiées à Paris par MM. L. Courtin et V. Adam. Paris, Firmin Didot 1828
14p. XIV pl. F.
Dedication signed: Henry Graf
Lipperheide 2786. LC 5-7032

Graf, Rainer
Die feste der republik Venedig. [Klagenfurt, J. Leon 1865]
64p. O.
From the 15th *Programm des K. K. Gymnasiums zu Klagenfurt*
Lipperheide 2492

Graf, Theodor
Antique portraits from the Hellenistic times. Vienna, T. Graf [1897]
2 l. [45]pl. F.
Useful for fashions in hair and head dress of the ancient Greeks

Graf, Urs
(illus.) Passio domini nostri Jhesu Christi

Grafström, Anders Abraham
Une année en Suède ou Tableaux des costumes, moeurs et usages des paysans de la Suède. Stockholm, L. J. Hjerta [1836]
116p. 47 col.pl. Q.
Translation of his *Ett år i Sverge.* Title and text in French and Swedish. Illustrated by J. G. Sandberg and engraved by C. D. Forssell
Colas 1281. Costume index (under Forssell) Lipperheide 1046n

Ett år i Sverge. Taflor af svenska almogens klädedrägt, lefnadssätt och hemseder, samt de för landets historia märkvärdigaste orter; tecknade af J. G. Sandberg, beskrifne af A. Grafström och utgifne af C. Forssell. Stockholm, J. Hörberg 1827
137p. 47 col.pl. Q.
Some of the plates are the same as in C. D. Forssell's *Album pittoresque du nord*
Reprinted: Stockholm, F. Svanström 1864 (104p. 48 col.pl. Q.)
Colas 1282. Lipp. 1046m, 1054. LC 5-11469

Graham, James A.
(tr.) Chu Chia-Chien. The Chinese theatre

Graham's American monthly magazine of literature, art, and fashion. v 1-53, 1826-1858. Philadelphia, G. R. Graham [etc.]
53v. illus. pl.(part col.) ports. O.-Q.
Title varies: Volume 1-7, 1826-30, *Casket;* 8-17, 1831-40 *Atkinson's Casket;* 18-21, 1841-42 *Graham's lady's and gentleman's magazine;* Ja-Je 1843 *Graham's magazine of literature and art;* July 1843-June 1844 *Graham's lady's and gentleman's magazine.*
Caption title: *Graham's magazine*
Continued as the *American monthly*

Graminaeus, Dietrich
Spiegel und abbildung der vergengligkeit. Darinnen was der toden recht und gebürnuss begriffen ... und wie ... Johan Wilhelm hertzog zu Gulich ... da ... hertzog Wilhelm am fünfften tag jannuarij, im jahr 1592 ... entschlaffen am zehenden tag martij in der collegiat kirchen zu Düsseldorff begraben und zur erden bestellen lassen. [Düsseldorff 1592]
58 l. 13 illus. F.
Lipperheide 2615

The **grammar** of ornament. Jones, Owen

Le **gran** cavalcata di Clemente VII. e Carlo V. della Sala Ridolfi. Riccio, Domenico

Gran simulacro dell' arte e dell' uso della scherma. Capoferro, R.

Grancsay, Stephen Vincent

Bashford Dean collection of arms and armor. See entry under New York. Metropolitan museum of art

Historical arms and armor. See entry under New York. Metropolitan museum of art

Le **Grand** calendrier, et compost des bergiers. Lyon, I. d'Ogerolles [1579]
83 l. 94 illus. Q.
The first edition of this calendar was printed in Paris by G. Marchand in 1493
Lipperheide 1104

Grand-Carteret, John

Les almanachs français: bibliographie—inconographie des almanachs—années—annuaires—calendriers—chansonniers—étrennes—états — heures—listes—livres d'adresses—tableaux—tablettes et autres publications annuelles éditées a Paris. (1600-1895) Paris, J. Alisie 1896
cx,846p. 306 illus. 5 col.pl. (incl.front.) Q.
Illustrations show 18th and 19th century costume
Limited to "almanachs imprimés ou édités à Paris". The proposed second volume, "consacré aux départements et à l'étranger", has not been published
Lipperheide 4873. LC 2-18916

XIXe siècle (en France); classes—mœurs—usages—costumes—inventions: ouvrage illustré ... d'après les principaux artistes du siècle. Paris, Firmin-Didot 1893
xii,774p. 487 illus. 16 col.pl. Q.
Colas 1284. Costume index. Lipperheide 1177. LC 13-13911

Les élégances de la toilette: robes—chapeaux—coiffures de style, Louis XVI—directoire—empire—restauration (1780-1825) 243 gravures de modes. Paris, A. Michel [1911]
xlviii p. 194 numb. l. [195]-198p. illus. 32 col.pl. O.
Notes bibliographiques: p xliii-xlviii
Costume index. LC 13-16769

La femme en Allemagne. Paris, L. Westhausser 1887
327p. 138 illus. 6pl.(2 col.) O.
Colas 1283. Lipperheide 601. LC 21-13206

La femme en culotte; 54 croquis originaux de Fernand Fau et Gustave Girrane. Paris, E. Flammarion [1899]
393p. illus. pl. ports. D.
Colas 1285

Les mœurs et la caricature en Allemagne —en Autriche—en Suisse; avec préface de Champfleury; 2.éd. Paris, L. Westhausser 1885
xx,491p. front. illus. 16pl.(3 col.) ports. Q.
Six plates, accompanied by guard sheets, with descriptive letterpress
"Bibliographie des journaux à caricatures": p[427]-49. "Liste des artistes caricaturistes": p[453]-82
Lipperheide 3511. LC 20-22662

Les moeurs et la caricature en France. Paris, La Librairie illustrée [1888]
xii,690p. 500 illus. 44pl.(8 col.) Q.
"Bibliographie et histoire des journaux à caricatures": p[557]-59. "Liste des journaux et almanachs à caricatures publiés à Paris (1830-1887)": p559-615. "Notices sur des journaux à caricatures des départements": p[616]-18. "Bibliographie des artistes caricaturistes": p[619]-75
LC 20-22661

Le **grand** cortége du couronnement de la reine Victoria. Londres, Fores [1838]
33 col.pl. O.
Lipperheide 2691

Grand magazin des plus nouveaux dessins françois de broderie. Silling, Karl

Le **grand** siècle; Louis XIV. Bourgeois, Émile

La **grande** danse macabre. Dance of death

La **grande** mascarade parisienne. Robida, Albert

La **grande** mode, journal des modes parisiennes. See Les modes parisiennes illustrées

La **grande** réforme. Sona, Ernest

La **grande** ville; nouveau tableau de Paris, comique, critique et philosophique, par Ch. Paul de Kock. Illustrations de Gavarni, Victor Adam, Daumier, d'Aubigny, H. Emy, etc. Paris, Bureau central des publications nouvelles 1842-43
2v. illus. pl. O.
Volume 2 has title: La grande ville . . . par H. de Balzac, Alex. Dumas, Frédéric Soulié, Eugène Briffault, Eugène de Mirecourt, Édouard Ourliac . . .
LC 4-26174

Les **grandes** dames d'aujourd'hui. Laincel-Vento, Alix, comtesse de

Les **grandes** manoeuvres. Hoff, Major, pseud.

Les **grandes** manoeuvres. Roy, Marius

Les **grandes** manoeuvres de cavalerie. Brunet, Romuald, and Chaperon, Eugène

Grandeur et suprématie de Peking. Hubrecht, Alph.

Grandmaison, Henri de

Fantassins et cavaliers sous Louis XV; croquis ... d'après des documents de la bibliothèque du ministère de la guerre; dessins de Parrocel, gouaches de Delaistre. [Paris, 1891]
82pl.(30 col.) Q.
Colas 1286

(illus.) Forbes-Leith, William. The Scots men-at-arms and life-guards in France

Grands voyages. Bry, Theodor de

Grandville, Jean Ignace Isidore Gérard, called

Un autre monde. Transformations, visions, incarnations ... et autres choses. Paris, H. Fournier [1844]
295p. 149 illus. 36 col.pl. Q.
Text by Taxile Delord
Lipperheide 3648

Grandville, Jean I. I. G., called—*Continued*

Cent proverbes par Grandville et par [vignette] Paris, H. Fournier 1845
400p. illus. 50pl.(incl.front.) O.
Vignette "représentant trois têtes dans un même bonnet." The authors of the text are P. É. D. Forgues (Old Nick), Taxile Delord, Arnould Frémy et Amédée Achard. cf. Quérard, Superch. littéraires, v3, col. 858
Lipperheide 3649. LC 15-2027

Le dimanche d'un bon bourgeois, ou Les tribulations de la petite propriété. Paris, Langlumé ca1827
12 col.pl. Q.
Lipperheide 3643

Les étoiles, dernière féerie; texte par Méry, astronomie des dames par le Cte. Foelix. Paris, G. de Gonet 1849
2v. 13 col.pl. Q.
Lipperheide 3180

Les fleurs animées; introductions par Alph. Karr, texte par Taxile Delord. Paris, G. de Gonet 1847
2v. 52 col.pl. O.
Thirty six of these plates are used in *Die pilgerfahrt der blumengeister* by Adolf Böttger
Lipperheide 3179

The flowers personified; being a translation of Grandville's "Les fleurs animées". By N. Cleaveland. New York, R. Martin 1847-49
2v. col.fronts. col.pl. Q.
Engraved on steel by J. N. Gimbrede, from designs by J. I. Grandville
LC 25-25472

Les métamorphoses du jour. Paris, Aubert [1830]
71 col.pl. Q.
First edition: 1829
Shows animals dressed in men's clothing
Lipperheide 3644

Petites misères de la vie humaine. Paris, H. Fournier 1843
390p. 165 illus. 49pl. Q.
Lipperheide 3647

Scènes de la vie privée et publique des animaux; études des moeurs contemporaines. Paris, J. Hetzel et Paulin 1842
2v. 120 illus. 200pl. O.
Lipperheide 3646

(illus.) Böttger, Adolf. Die pilgerfahrt der blumengeister

Granier de Cassagnac, Bernard Adolphe

Danaë, roman historique; suivi du costume des anciens, analyse raisonné de l'architecture, des meubles, de la vie intérieure, toilette, cuisine, poterie culinaire, du costume militaire, des armes offensives et défensives, et de la manière de combattre des Grecs homériques. Berlin, F. H. Morin 1840
205,77p. D.
Lipperheide 187

Granlund, Sten Alfred Agaton. See Holme, Charles, ed. Peasant art in Sweden, Lapland and Iceland

Grant, Sir Charles

The gazetteer of the Central Provinces of India; 2d ed. Na'gpu'r, Printed at the Educational society's press, Bombay 1870
clvii,582p. front.(fold.map) Q.
Contains some material on dress of the native tribes of India: Gadbás (p33), Máriás (p35), Márís (p36), and the inhabitants of Narsinghpúr (p360)
LC 9-34317

Grant, James

The tartans of the clans of Scotland; also an introductory account of Celtic Scotland; clanship, chiefs, their dress, arms, etc., and with historical notes of each clan. Edinburgh and London, W. & A. K. Johnston 1886
82 l. col.front.(port.) col.illus. 72 col.pl. map. F.
Each plate is accompanied by a leaf with descriptive letterpress and coat of arms in color
LC 2-12222

Grapheus, Cornille. See Schryver, Cornelis

Graphic illustrations of the dramatic works of Shakespeare. See Boydell, John. Boydell's Graphic illustrations

Grass. Cooper, M. C.

Grasset, Eugène

Costumes de guerre de l'âge du bronze et de l'ère gauloise. [Paris, Gillot 1886]
2v. 15 col.illus. O. (Cahiers d'enseignement illustrés, nr. 7, 8)
Edited by Gustave Dumoutier
Lipperheide 298

Grasset de Saint-Sauveur, André

Voyage dans les îles Baléares et Pithiuses; fait dans les années 1801, 1802, 1803, 1804 et 1805. Paris, L. Collin 1807
xvi,390p. fold.pl. O.
Colas 1288. LC 19-18068

Voyage historique, littéraire et pittoresque dans les isles et possessions ci-devant vénitiennes du Levant, savoir Corfou, Paxo, Bucintro, Parga, Prevesa, Vonizza, Sainte-Maure, Thiaqui, Céphalonie, Zante, Strophades, Cérigo et Cérigotte ... accompagné d'un atlas de ... planches ... des costumes et monuments anciens et des médailles et inscriptions grecques et romaines. Paris, Tavernier 1800
3v. O. and atlas 30pl. Q.
Colas 1287

Grasset de Saint-Sauveur, Jacques

L'antique Rome ou description historique ou pittoresque de tout ce qui concerne le peuple romain, dans ses costumes civiles, militaires et religieux ... depuis Romulus jusqu'à Augustule. Paris, Deroy 1796
222p. 48 col.pl. Q.
Plates, engraved by Labrousse, also exist in black and white
Italian edition: *L'antica Roma ovvero Descrizione storica e pittorica di tutto cio che riguarda il popolo romano né suoi costumi militari religiosi pubblici e privati da Romolo fino ad Augusto* (Bergamo, Mazzoleni 1825. 328p. 62 col.pl. F.)
Colas 1298-1299. Lipperheide 234 (Ital. ed.)

Collection des nouveaux costumes des autorités constituées civils et militaires. See entry under Garneray, J. F

Costumes civils actuels de tous les peuples connus, dessinés d'après nature, gravés et coloriés, accompagnés d'un

Grasset de Saint-Sauveur, Jacques—*Cont.*
abrégé historique de leurs coutumes, moeurs, religions, sciences, arts, commerce, monnoies. Paris, L'auteur 1784
575 l. 261 col.pl. Q.
Colas lists two other editions, (Paris, L'auteur 1784. 2v. 129,134 l. 120pl.) and (Paris, Knapen, 1784-87. 4v.)
Colas 1289-91. Lipperheide 40

Costumes civils actuels de tous les peuples connus, dessinés d'après nature, gravés et coloriés, accompagné d'une notice historique sur leurs coutumes, moeurs, religions ... Rédigés par Sylvain Maréchal. Paris, Pavard 1788
4v. 302 col.pl. Q.
After the rights of publication were sold to Pavard, the work was published without the name of the author
Contents: v 1-2 Europe; v3 Asie; v4 Afrique. Amerique
The second edition (Paris, Deterville ca1805. 298 col.pl. O.) is described by Colas as having the plates of inferior quality
The third edition *Costumes civils de tous les peuples* (3. éd. rev. & corr. Guincamp, B. Jollivet 1837-38. 5v. 294 col.pl. O.) has a shortened text and the plates revised and in a different order. Volume one has half-title: *Costumes civils des peuples connus.* Most of the plates are signed: A. Henry, lith. B. Jollivet, impr.
Colas 1979-1981. Lipperheide 42 (2d ed.)

Costumes des provinces françaises au 18eme siècle. Paris, H. Ernst [1932]
Cover-title, 36 col. mounted pl. sq.O.
Plates reproduced frov v 1 of the author's *Encyclopédie des voyages* (Paris, 1796)
Costume index. LC 33-33809

Costumes des représentans du peuple, membres des deux conseils, du directoire exécutif, des ministres, des tribunaux, messages d'état, huissiers, et autres fonctionnaires publics. Paris, Deroy 1795
20p. 15 col.pl. O.
Engraved by Labrousse
Translated into English under title: *Dresses of the representatives of the people* A German translation with title: *Amtskleidungen der stellvertreter des französischen volks und der übrigen staatsbeamten der republik Frankreich* (Paris, Deroy 1795) has text in German and French. Another German edition has title: *Trachten von den representanten des französischen volks* (Nürnberg, 1796) Translated into Italian under title: *Abito dei rappresentanti del popolo francese* (Nizza, Presso la Calcografia nazionale 1796) Colas notes an edition engraved by P. J. Maillart (Bruxelles, Maillart 1793. 19 col.pl.)
Colas 1294, 1296, 1297, 1947. Lipperheide 1781, 1782, 1783, 1784

Dresses of the representatives of the people, members of the two councils, and of the executive directory. London, E. and S. Harding 1796
12p. 16 col.pl. O.
A translation of the author's *Costumes des représentans du peuple*
Colas 1295

Encyclopédie des voyages, contenant l'abrégé historique des mœurs, usages, habitudes domestiques, religions, fêtes, supplices, funérailles, sciences, arts, et commerce de tous les peuples: et la collection complète de leurs habillemens civils, militaires, religieux et dignitaires, dessinés d'après nature. [Paris] Deroy 1796
5v. 432 col.pl. Q.
Part of the plates and part of the text are taken from his *Costumes civils actuels de tous les peuples connus*
A 3d edition was published under title: *Voyages pittoresques dans les quatre parties du monde* (Paris, Hocquart 1806. 2v. 154 col.pl.)
Colas 1292, 1302. Lipp. 41. LC 1-25030

Les fastes du peuple français, ou Tableaux raisonnés de toutes les actions héroïques et civiques du soldat et du citoyen français. Paris, Deroy 1796
139p. 139 col.pl. Q.
Illustrations by Labrousse show French military costume from 1789 to 1796
Colas 1300. Lipperheide 2303

Galerie dramatique, ou Acteurs et actrices célèbres qui se sont illustrés sur les trois grands théâtres de Paris. Paris, Hocquart 1809
2v. 60 col.pl. S.
Colas 1303

Mœurs, loix et costumes des Tatars-Usbeks. [Paris, 1795]
3p. 2 col.pl. O.
LC 25-22802

Recueil complet des costumes des autorités constituées, civiles, militaires, et de la marine. Paris, Deroy 1796
48p. 33 col.pl. Q.
Plates, engraved by Labrousse, are divided into two parts. Part I, with 17 plates, shows civil costume. Part II, with 16 plates shows military and naval costume
Colas 1293. Lipperheide 1780

Tableaux des principaux peuples de l'Europe, de l'Asie, de l'Afrique, de l'Amérique; et les découvertes des capitaines Cook, La Pérouse, etc. Paris, L'auteur 1798
5v. in 1. 10 fold.pl.(5 col.) Q.
The colored plates show groups of people of the four continents
Colas 1301

Grassi, Bartolomeo
Dei veri ritratti degl' habiti di tutte le parti del mondo; libro primo. Roma, 1585
52pl. F.
An edition is known with 49 plates and another with 57 plates. Each plate shows 3 full length figures
Colas 1304. Lipperheide 17

Grassi, Giacomo di
Ragione di adoprar sicuramente l'arme si da offesa, come da difesa. Venetia, G. Ziletti 1570
151p. 21 illus. 1 pl. Q.
Lipperheide 2949

Gratae et laboribus aequae posteritati. See Hogenberg, Nicolas. The procession of Pope Clement VII

Graterolle, Maurice
Du costume et de la toilette dans l'antiquité et de nos jours. Paris, Sauvaitre 1897
145p. 7pl. D.
Colas 1305

La **gratie** d'amore. See Negri, Cesare. Nuove inventioni di balli

Gratz, Josefine
Die Germanisierung der frauenkleidung; ein wort zur klärung der reformkleiderfrage. Leipzig, Verlag der frauenrundschau 1904
43p. 10 illus. O.
Colas 1306. Lipperheide 3320

Der gute geschmack in der frauenkleidung. München-Gladbach, Volksvereins verlag 1922
86p. O.

So sollt ihr euch kleiden! Ratgeber f. die frauendes mittelstandes einschiesslich der berufsfrauen. Dresden, Internat. Schnitt-Manufaktur 1910
93p. illus. O.

Die **graublauen** felduniformen der französischen armee und deren abzeichen, nach dem erlass des französischen kriegsministers vom. 9. dezember 1914. Leipzig, M. Ruhl [1915?]
14p. 4 col.pl. D.

Die **graue** felduniform der deutschen armee. Leipzig, M. Ruhl [1910]
2v. 20 col.pl. D.
Third edition 189? *Die grauen felduniformen ... nach originalzeichnungen von A. Schmidt.* Fifth edition: 1915

Die **grauen** felduniformen der italienischen armee und deren abzeichen. Leipzig, M. Ruhl [1915]
19p. 4 col.fold.pl. D.

Grauenhorst, C. See Gravenhorst, C.

Die **graugrünen** felduniformen der russischen armee und deren abzeichen. Leipzig, M. Ruhl [1912]
12p. 4 col.fold.pl. D.

Gravelot, Hubert François Bourguignon
[Four costume suites] London, ca1744
18pl.
A series of plates drawn from life and showing costume of the period: 1 Six plates of feminine costume, engraved by Truchy and Grignon; 2 Six plates of masculine costume, engraved by Truchy, 3 Three plates of masculine costume, engraved by Mayer; 4 Three plates of feminine costume
Colas 1307

Planches gravées d'après plusieurs positions dans lesquelles doivent se trouver les soldats, conformément à l'ordonnance du roi de l'exercice de l'infanterie, du 1er janvier, 1766. [Paris, 1766]
12pl. F.
Engraved by Guillaume de La Haye
Colas 1308. Lipperheide 2296

Gravenhorst, C.
Geschichte u. statuten des rothen adlerordens und des königlichen kronenordens. Festschrift zur feier des preussischen krönungs- und ordensfestes am 23. januar 1881. Berlin, Der verfasser 1881
32p. O.
Lipperheide 1938

Gravier, Jean
Recueil de toutes les uniformes qui se sont signalé durant le siège de Gènes. Gènes, Laziane 1752
3p. 21 col.pl. Q.
Colas 1309?

Gravot, Marius
(illus.) Gauthier, Joseph. La Bretagne

Les **gravures** de mode. Lyons. Bibliothèque municipale

Les **gravures** françaises du XVIIIe siècle. Bocher, Emmanuel

Gray, John Henry
China: a history of the laws, manners, and customs of the people; ed. by William Gow Gregor. London, Macmillan 1878
2v. fronts. pl. O.
Plates show people of various classes
LC 4-30845

Gray, Louis Herbert
(ed.) The mythology of all races

Gray, William
Social contrasts; portrayed in a series of twenty two coloured lithographic plates from pen and ink sketches, by William Gray. London, W. Oliver [1865]
2p.l. 22 col.pl. on 12 l. 27x36½cm.
LC 11-29565

Grazie e splendori dei costumi italiani. Massano, Gino

Great Britain. See England; Ireland; Scotland

Great Britain. Adjutant general's office
Historical records of the British army; comprising the history of every regiment in Her Majesty's service. See entry under Cannon, Richard

Great Britain. Admiralty
Uniform regulations for chief petty officers, men and boys of the fleet, and for boys in the training establishments. London, H. M. Stationery office 1907
83p. fold.plates, fold.diagrs. D.
LC 13-16218

Uniform regulations for officers of the fleet. London, H. M. Stationery office 1924
iv,28p. incl. tables. 18pl. F.
Officers' uniform regulations first issued in 1748 have since been published in the "London Gazette". They were first issued in book form, with plates, on the first of January 1825 and later editions have been published in 1879, 1891 and 1893. cf. Historical note, p iv
LC 25-5924

Uniform regulations for petty officers, men, & boys of the fleet, and for boys in the training ships. (Rev., embodying all corrections issued up to date) London, H. M. Stationery office 1904
71p. 11 fold.pl. S.
LC 13-16219

Great Britain. Board of trade. Committee on mercantile marine uniform
Report of the committee appointed by the Board of trade to advise as to the uniform to be adopted as the standard uniform for the mercantile marine. London, H. M. Stationery office 1918
9p. pl.(part col.) F. ([Parliament. Papers by command] Cd. 9030)
LC 18-14112

Great Britain. Civil service committee
Uniforms to be worn by Her Majesty's civil servants at home and in the colonies. London, Harrison [1859]
F.

Great Britain. Lord chamberlain
Dress and insignia worn at His Majesty's court. Ed. by Herbert A. P. Trendell. London, Harrison 1921
204p. col.front. illus. pl.(part col.) O.
LC 24-13809 (under ed.)

Great Britain—Lord chamberlain—*Cont.*

Dress and insignia worn at His Majesty's court, issued with the authority of the lord chamberlain ... Ed. by Austin Hertslet and George A. Titman. London, Harrison 1929
ix,[1]p. 2 l 246p. col.front.(port.) illus. pl.(part col.) O.
Costume index. LC 30-6814

Dress worn at His Majesty's court. Ed. by Herbert A. P. Trendell. London, Harrison 1912
165p. col.front. illus. pl.(part col.) O.
LC 13-1947 (under ed.)

Dress worn by gentlemen at His Majesty's court and on occasions of ceremony; collected from official sources with the sanction of the lord chamberlain. New ed. rev. and enl. edited by H. Graham Bennet. London, Harrison 1903
103p. col.front.(port.) 7pl.(part col.) O.
Cover-title: *Dress worn at court*

Uniforms to be worn by the queen's household. London, Harrison [1890?]
Col.pl. F.

Great Britain. War office

Dress regulations for the army. London, H. M. Stationery office 1911
134p. illus. 36pl. Q.
LC WAR12-50

Dress regulations for the army. 1934. London, H. M. Stationery office 1934
x,vii,192,xi-xxiv p. illus. Q.
LC 35-25711

Dress regulations for the army. (Provisional) 1928. London, H. M. Stationery office 1928
48p. illus. O.
LC 29-6300

Dress regulations for the officers of the army (including theh militia). London, H. M. Stationery office 1900
118p. 79pl. Q.

Dress regulations for the officers of the army (including the militia). London, H. M. Stationery office 1904
104p. 58pl. Q.

Inventory and survey of the armouries of the Tower of London. See entry under Ffoulkes, C. J.

The new German field service uniform. London, H. M. Stationery office 1916
9p. illus. D.
Plates show the new German field service uniform of the Prussian army

Great painters and their famous Bible pictures. Griffith, William, ed.

Great portraits, women. Hale, P. L.

Great races of mankind. Ridpath, J. C.

Greblinger, Georg

Wahre abbildungen der türckischen kayser und persischen fürsten so wol auch anderer helden und heldinnen von dem Osman biss auf den andern Mahomet ... auch ... eines jeden wandel kürtzlich mit versen beschrieben durch Georg Greblinger. Franckfurt, J. Ammon 1648
16p. 47pl. Q.
An abridged edition of Boissard's *Leben und contrafeiten der turckischen und persischen sultanen*
Lipperheide 1406

Greece

Dalon, Richard. Antiquities and views in Greece and Egypt. 1791

Davis, R. H. Rulers of the Mediterranean. 1894

Le Vacher de Charnois, J. C. Recherches sur le costumes et sur les théatres de toutes les nations, tant anciennes que modernes. 1790

Mahaffy, J. P. Greek pictures. 1890

See also Crete—Ancient; Ionian islands; also subdivision Greece under Arms and armor; Beads; Gods; Military costume

Mycenaean age

Perrot, Georges, and Chipiez, Charles. History of art in primitive Greece; Myçenian art. 1894

Schliemann, Heinrich. Mycenae; a narrative of researches and discoveries at Mycenae and Tiryns. 1878

Schliemann, Heinrich. Mykenae; bericht über meine forschungen und entdeckungen in Mykenae und Tiryns. 1878

Tsountas, Chrestos, and Manatt, J. I. The Mycenaean age. 1897

See also Rings—Greece—Mycenaean age; also Crete, Ancient

Homeric age

Helbig, Wolfgang. Das homerische epos aus den denkmälern erläutert. 1887

Quennell, Mrs M. C., and Quennell, C. H. B. Everyday life in Homeric Greece. 1930

Seymour, T. D. Life in the Homeric age. 1907

Ancient

General works

Abrahams, E. B. Greek dress, a study of the costumes worn in ancient Greece, from Pre-Hellenic times to the Hellenistic age. 1908

Amelung, Walther. Die gewandung der alten Griechen und Römer. 1903

Aragon, Henry. Le costume dans les temps anciens et au moyen âge. 1921

Barker, A. W. A classification of the chitons worn by Greek women as shown in works of art. 1923

Baxter, Thomas. Darstellung des aegyptischen, griechischen und römischen costums. 1815

Baxter, Thomas. An illustration of the Egyptian, Grecian, and Roman costume. 1810

Bieber, Margarete. Entwicklungsgeschichte der griechischen tracht von der vorgriechischen zeit bis zur römischen kaiserzeit. 1934

Bieber, Margarete. Griechische kleidung. 1928

Boehlau, Johannes. Quaestiones de re vestiaria Graecorum. 1884

Brummell, G. B. Male and female costume. 1932

Greece—Ancient—*Continued*
Carta, M. S. Tessuti fogge e decorazioni nell' abito muliebre in Grecia e a Roma. 1934
Evans, M. M. L., lady. Chapters on Greek dress. 1893
Gironi, Robustiano. Saggio di Robustiano Gironi intorno alle costumanze civili dei Greci. 1823
Heuzey, L. A. Histoire du costume antique d'après des études sur le modèle vivant. 1922
Horn, Rudolf. Stehende weibliche gewandstatuen in der hellenistischen plastik. 1931
Houston, M. G. Ancient Greek, Roman and Byzantine costume and decoration (including Cretan costume) 1931
Le Clerc, Sébastien. Divers habillemens des anciens Grecs et Romains. 1680
Mueller, Walther. Quaestiones vestiariae. 1890
Repond, Jules. Les secrets de la draperie antique de l'himation grec au pallium romain. 1931
Smith, J. M., comp. Ancient Greek female costume. 1882
Studniczka, Franz. Beiträge zur geschichte der altgriechischen tracht. 1886
Whibley, Leonard, ed. Companion to Greek studies. 1931
Willemin, N. X. Choix de costumes civils et militaires des peuples de l'antiquité. 1798-1802. v2

Supplementary material

Baumeister, August. Denkmäler des klassischen altertums. 1885-1888
Becker, W. A. Charicles; or, illustrations of the private life of the ancient Greeks. 1866
Becker, W. A. Charikles, bilder altgriechischer sitte. 1854
Beger, Lorenz. Cranae insula Laconica, Eadem & Helena dicta & Minyarum posteris habitata. 1696
Beger, Lorenz. Meleagrides et Aetolia, ex numismate Kyrieon apud Goltzium; interspersis marmoribus quibusdam, de Meleagri interitu, & apri Calydonii venatione. 1696
Blümner, Hugo. Home life of the ancient Greeks. 1893
Blümner, Hugo. Leben und sitten der Griechen. 1887
British museum. Department of Greek and Roman life. A guide to the exhibition illustrating Greek and Roman life. 1920
Brunn, Heinrich von. Greek vases: their system of form and decoration. 1879
Brunn, Heinrich. Griechische kunstgeschichte. 1893-97
Brunn, Heinrich von, and Krell, P. F. Die griechischen vasen ihr formen- und decorationssystem. 1877
Conze, A. C. L. Heroën- und göttergestalten der griechischen kunst. 1900
Daremberg, C. V., and Saglio, Edmond, eds. Dictionnaire des antiquités greques et romaines, d'après les textes et les monuments. 1877-1919
Effigies virorum ac foeminarum illustrium, quibus in Græcis aut Latinis monumentis aliqua ... pars datur. 1724?
Emmanuel, Maurice. La danse grecque antique d'après les monuments figures. 1896
Falke, Jakob von. Greece and Rome their life and art. 1882
Furtwängler, Adolf. Masterpieces of Greek sculpture. 1895
Furtwängler, Adolf. Meisterwerke der griechischen plastik. 1893
Furtwängler, Adolf, and Reichhold, Karl. Griechische vasenmalerei. 1904-1932
Gardner, E. A. The art of Greece. 1925
Gardner, Percy. Sculptured tombs of Hellas. 1896
Gerhard, Eduard. Auserlesene griechische vasenbilder. 1840-58
Graf, Theodor. Antique portraits from the Hellenistic times. 1897
Gronovius, Jacobus. Thesaurus Graecarum antiquitatum. 1732-37
Guhl, E. K., and Koner, W. D. Das leben der griechen und römer nach antiken bildwerken. 1862
Guhl, E. K., and Koner, W. D. The life of the Greeks and Romans described from antique monuments. 1889
Gulick, C. B. The life of the ancient Greeks, with special reference to Athens. 1902
Harrison, J. E., and MacColl, D. S. Greek vase paintings. 1894
Heuzey, L. A. Recherches sur les figures de femmes voilées dans l'art grec. 1873
Inghirami, Francesco. Pitture di vasi etruschi esibite dal cavaliere Francesco Inghirami, per servire di studio alla mitologia ed alla storia degli antichi popoli. 1852-56
Kekule von Stradonitz, Reinhard. Griechische thonfiguren aus Tanagra. 1878
Lermann, Wilhelm. Altgriechische plastik; eine einführung in die griechische kunst des archaischen und gebundenen stils. 1907
Lücken, Gottfried von. Greek vase paintings; peintures de vases grecques. 1923
Meiners, Christoph. Recherches historiques sur le luxe chez les Athéniens, depuis les temps les plus anciens, jusqu'à la mort de Philippe de Macédoine. 1823
Notor, G. La femme dans l'antiquité grecque. 1901
Opitz, Richard. Das häusliche leben der Griechen und Römer. 1894
Panofka, Theodor. Bilder antiken lebens. 1843
Panofka, Theodor. Manners and customs of the Greeks. 1849

Greece—Ancient—Supp. works—*Continued*

Petrograd. Ermitazh. Die alterthümer von Kertsch in der Kaiserlichen Eremitage ... direct nach den originalen photographirt und hrsg. von Carl Röttger ... mit erläuterndem text von Ludolf Stephani. I. lieferung: Das grab der Demeterpriesterin. 1873

Porträtköpfe auf antiken münzen hellenischer und hellenisierter völker. 1885

Quennell, Mrs M. C., and Quennell, C. H. B. Everyday things in archaic Greece 1931

Rehberg, Friedrich. Drawings faithfully copied from nature at Naples. 1794

Reinach, Salomon. Répertoire de la statuaire grecque et romaine. 1897-1910

Rich, Anthony. The illustrated companion to the Latin dictionary and Greek lexicon. 1849

Richter, G. M. A. Red-figured Athenian vases in the Metropolitan museum of art. 1936

Ridder, A. H. P. de. Catalogue des bronzes de la Société archéologique d'Athènes. 1894

Rochette, D. R. Peintures antiques inédites. 1836

Saburov, P. A. Die sammlung Sabouroff; kunstdenkmäler aus Griechenland. 1883-87

See also Funerals—Macedonia; Hairdressing—Greece, Ancient; Naval costume—Greece—Ancient times; Theatrical costume—Greece, Ancient

16th century

Nicolay, Nicolas de, sieur d'Arfeuille. The navigations, peregrinations and voyages, made into Turkie. 1585

Nicolay, Nicolas de, sieur d'Arfeuille. Les navigations, pérégrinations et voyages, faicts en la Turquie. 1576

Nicolay, Nicolas de, sieur d'Arfeuille. Les quatre premiers livres des Navigations et peregrinations orientales. 1568

18th century

Choiseul-Gouffier, M. G. A. F., comte de. Voyage pittoresque de la Grèce. 1782-1824

Moor, J. B. van. Wahreste und neueste abbildung des türckischen hofes. 1719-21

Tinney, John. A collection of eastern & other foreign dresses. ca1750

Tournefort, J. P. de. Relation d'un voyage du Levant. 1717

19th century

Bartholdy, J. L. S. Bruchstücke zur nähern kentniss des heutigen Griechenlands gesammelt auf einer reise. 1805

Cartwright, J. Selections of the costume of Albania and Greece. 1822

Dodwell, Edward. A classical and topographical tour through Greece, during the years 1801, 1805, and 1806. 1819

Dodwell, Edward. Views in Greece, from drawings by Edward Dodwell. 1821

Dupré, Louis. Voyage à Athènes et à Constantinople. 1825

Eton, William. W. Eton's Schilderung des türkischen reiches in politischer, moralischer, historischer, religiöser, wissentschaftl. statistischer, merkantiler, u.s.w. hinsicht. 1805

Friedel, Adam. The principal leaders in the Greek revolution. 1827

Krazeisen, Karl. Bildnisse ausgezeichneter Griechen und Philhellenen, nebst einigen ansichten und trachten. 1828-31

Latour, Antoine de. Voyage de S.A.R. Monseigneur le Duc de Montpensier à Tunis en Égypte, en Turquie et en Grèce. 1847

Le Blanc, T. P. Croquis d'après nature faits ... en Grèce et dans le Levant. 1833

Stackelberg, O. M., freiherr von. Trachten und gebräuche der Neugriechen. 1831

20th century

Ferriman, Z. D. Home life in Hellas. 1910

Holdt, Hanns. Greece; architecture, landscape, life of the people. 1928

Wace, A. J. B., and Thompson, M. S. The nomads of the Balkans, an account of life and customs among the Vlachs of northern Pindus. 1914

Greece and Rome their life and art. Falke, Jakob von

Greek dress. Abrahams, E. B.

Greek orthodox vestments and ecclesiastical fabrics. Riefstahl, R. M.

Greek pictures. Mahaffy, J. P.

Greek vase paintings. Harrison, J. E., and MacColl, D. S.

Greek vase paintings. Lücken, Gottfried von

Greek vases. Brunn, Heinrich von

Green, Mrs Alice Sophia Amelia (Stopford)
(ed.) Green, J. R. A short history of the English people

Green, Anna L. See Northrup, Belle, jt. auth.

Green, E. M.

La mode et la coquetterie. Paris, Devambez 1912
24p. 1 col.pl. D.
Colas 1310

Green, Henry

(ed. and tr.) Dance of death. Les simulachres & historiees faces de la mort

Green, John

(comp.) A new general collection of voyages and travels

Green, John Richard

A short history of the English people. Illustrated edition, edited by Mrs. J. R. Green and Miss Kate Norgate. New York, Harper 1893-95
4v. fronts. illus. (incl.facsims.) pl.(part col.) ports. maps, geneal. tables. Q.
Many of the illustrations show costume
Costume index. LC 30-30988

Green, Joyce M. Conyngham
Period costumes and settings for the small stage. London, G. G. Harrap [1936]
166p. pl. O.
A description of English costume, by reigns, from 1066 to 1830

Green, Margaret M.
(tr.) Gleichen-Russwurm, Alexander, freiherr von. Dandies and Don Juans

Greenleaf, Edward Hale
(tr.) Brunn, Heinrich von. Greek vases

Greeven, H.
Collection des costumes des provinces septentrionales du royaume des Pays-Bas. Amsterdam, F. Buffa; Paris, Engelmann 1828
23 l. 20 col.pl. Q.
Lithographed by H. Vallon de Villeneuve. Title and legends are in French and Dutch, text in French and English
Dutch title: *Verzameling der kleederdragten in de nordelyke provincien van het koningryk der Nederlanden*
Colas 1311. Lipperheide 960

Grego, Joseph
Rowlandson the caricaturist; a selection from his works, with anecdotal descriptions of his famous caricatures and a sketch of his life, times, and contemporaries. London, Chatto & Windus 1880
2v. front.(port.) illus. Q.
"Chronological summary of subjects, social and political caricatures, engraved by or after Thomas Rowlandson. With his contributions to book illustration in the order of publications": v2 p[387]-408. Lists of drawings by Rowlandson. v2 p412-31
Lipperheide 3508. LC 10-20031

(illus.) Gronow, R. H. The reminiscences and recollections of Captain Gronow

See also Vuillier, Gaston. A history of dancing

Grégoire, Gaspard
Explication des cérémonies de la Fête-Dieu d'Aix en Provence. Aix, Esprit David 1777
220p. 13pl. D.
Illustrated by Paul Grégoire
Lipperheide 2804

Grégoire, Paul
(illus.) Grégoire, Gaspard. Explication des cérémonies de la Fête-Dieu d'Aix en Provence

Gregor, Joseph
Wiener szenische kunst. [Wien] Wiener drucke 1924-25
2v. plans, pl.(part col.) ports.(part col.) F.

See also Denkmäler des theaters

Gregor, Joseph, and Fülöp-Miller, René
Das amerikanische theater und kino. Zürich, Amaltheaverlag [1931]
111p. illus. pl.(part col.) ports. plans, facsims. tables (1 fold.) sq.F.
Three plates show Indian masks, other plates theatrical costume
LC 31-19986

The Russian theatre: its character and history, with especial reference to the revolutionary period. Translated by Paul England. Philadelphia, J. B. Lippincott company [1929]
136p. pl.(part col.) ports. F.
Translation of the author's *Das russische theater*
LC 30-16694

Das russische theater. Zürich, Amalthea verlag 1928
137p. pl.(part col.) ports. F.

Gregor, William Gow
(ed.) Gray, J. H. China

Gregory, John Walter. See Hutchinson, H. N., jt. ed.

Greig, T. Watson
Ladies' dress shoes of the nineteenth century. Edinburgh, D. Douglas 1900
24 l. col.front. 21 col.pl. F.
Lipperheide 1746c

Ladies' old-fashioned shoes ... with ... illustrations from originals in his collection. Edinburgh, D. Douglas 1885
15 l. 9p. 11 col.pl. ob.Q.
A supplement was issued: *Supplement to Old-fashioned shoes* (Edinburgh, D. Douglas 1889. 9 l. 10p. pl.12-17. ob.Q.)
Colas 1312-13. Lipperheide 1744, 1744a. LC 14-16396

Grellmann, Heinrich Martin Gottlieb
Historische kleinigkeiten zum vergnügen und unterricht aus der zerstreuung gesammelt. Göttingen, Vandenhöck und Ruprecht 1794
246p. O.
Pages 175-88 are on costume of the 16th century
Lipperheide 651m

The **Grenadier** guards. Clayton, B.

Grenier, François
Album lithographié. Paris, C. Motte 1828
1 l. 12pl. Q.
Shows dress of the period as worn in the rural parts of France

XII sujets variés composés et dessinés sur pierre. Paris, C. Motte 1826
12pl. Q.
Lipperheide 1157e

Études et motifs d'après nature. Paris, F. Delarue ca1850
1 l. 36 col.pl. F.
Shows French folk costumes
Colas 1314

Le genre, études variées. Paris, Jeannin 1844
1 l. 24 col.pl. Q.
Shows French folk costumes
Colas 1315

Nouvelle collection variée de sujets de genre. Paris, F. Delarue ca1850
1 l. 36 col.pl. F.
Most of the plates show French folk costumes
Colas 1316

Greuze, Jean Baptiste
Divers habillements suivant le costume d'Italie, dessinées d'après nature. Paris, L'auteur 1768
24pl. F.
Legends in Italian and French. Engraved by P. E. Moitte
The plates show a youth of Savoy, three girls from Savoy, and women and girls from Piedmont, Genoa, Parma, Bologna, Florence, Pisa, Lucca, Naples, Calabria, and Frascati
Colas 1317; Lipperheide 1253

Grévedon, Pierre Louis Henri

Alphabet des dames, ou Recueil de vingt cinq portraits de fantaisie. Paris, Chaillou-Potrelle [1833]
25 col.pl. F.
Also known with plates in black and white
Half length portraits show feminine dress and coiffures in France in the 19th century
Colas 1320

Artisanne, grisette, jeune fille et dame. Paris, Aumont [183-?]
4 col.pl. F.
Also known with plates in black and white
Colas 1321

Les attraits; nouvelle collection de portraits. Paris, J. Bulla et F. Delarue [1839]
4 col.pl. F.
Also known with plates in black and white
Colas 1322. Lipperheide 1167m

Costumes des habitans de l'île de Java et des possessions hollandaises dans l'Inde. Paris, F. L. Cattier [1831]
10 col.pl. F.
Also known with plates in black and white. Legends are in English and French
Colas 1319

XII portraits d'enfants. Paris, Aumont [183-?]
12 col.pl. F.
Also known with plates in black and white
Colas 1326

Époques remarquables de la vie de la femme; suite de têtes. Paris, H. Jeannin [1831]
4 col.pl. F.
Also known with plates in black and white
Colas 1323

Les femmes cosmopolites, collection de têtes d'expressions dessinées d'après nature dans les costumes pittoresques de tous les pays. Paris, H. Jeannin ca1831
25 col.pl. F.
Cataloged from Colas's *Bibliographie*
Also known with plates in black and white
Colas 1319bis

Impératrices et reines. Paris, Aumont [184-?]
F.
Cataloged from Colas's *Bibliographie*
Colas 1324

Le miroir des dames, ou Nouvel alphabet français, collection gracieuse et variée de portraits. Paris, Aumont [1834]
25 col.pl. F.
Also known with plates in black and white
Colas 1325

Mosaïque de costumes, ou Alphabet étranger. Paris, Aumont ca1830
25 col.pl. F.
Also known with plates in black and white. A list of plates is in Colas's *Bibliographie*
Colas 1318

Les quatre éléments, portraits de femmes. Paris, Aumont [1833]
4 col.pl. F.
Also known with plates in black and white
Colas 1327

Les quatre parties du monde, portraits de femme. Paris, Aumont [1832]
4 col.pl. F.
Also known with plates in black and white
Colas 1328

Recueil de quelques portraits d'actrices des principaux théâtres de Paris. Paris, Chaillou-Potrelle; London, C. Tilt 1829
7pl. F.
Lipperheide 1159

Le vocabulaire des dames. Paris, Rittner et Goupil 1833
pl. F.
Cataloged from Colas's *Bibliographie*
Colas 1329

Grévin, Alfred

Costumes de fantaisie pour un bal travesti. Paris, Les Modes parisiennes 1870
24 col.pl. Q.
Colas 1330. Lipperheide 3186

Costumes de théâtre. Paris, Le Journal amusant ca1875
27 col.pl. Q.
Colas 1332. Lipperheide 3188

Les filles d'Ève; album de travestissements plus ou moins historiques. Paris Journal amusant [1867]
24 col.pl. Q.
Lipperheide 3650

Le monde amusant. Paris, E. Plon ca1873
27 col.pl. Q.
Lipperheide 3651

Les nouveaux travestissements parisiens. Paris, Les Modes parisiennes [1873]
1 l. 20 col.pl. Q.
Colas 1331. Lipperheide 3187

Grevin, Alfred, and Huart, Adrien

Les Parisiennes. Paris, M. Dreyfous [1879]
796p. 149 illus. (99 col.) Q.
Lipperheide 3652

Grey, A.

(tr.) Ivchenko, V. I. Anna Pavlova

Gridatori ed altri costumi popolari di Trieste. Bosa, Eugenio

Griechische kleidung. Bieber, Margarete

Griechische kunstgeschichte. Brunn, Heinrich

Griechische panzerung. Hagemann, Arnold

Griechische, römische und andere alterthümer für studirende. See Montfaucon Bernard de. L'antiquité expliquée

Griechische sitten und gebräuche auf cypern. Ohnefalsch-Richter, M. H.

Griechische thonfiguren aus Tanagra. Kekule von Stradonitz, Reinhard

Griechische und römische kriegsalterthümer. Rheinhard, Hermann

Griechische vasenmalerei. Furtwängler Adolf, and Reichhold, Karl

Die **griechischen** vasen ihr formen- und decorations- system. Brunn, Heinrich von, and Krell, P. F.

Grierson, Elizabeth Wilson
The children's book of Edinburgh; with 12 illustrations in colour, by Allan Stewart. London, A. and C. Black 1906
xi,379p. 12 col.pl.(incl.front.) O.
Contents: 1 Introductory; 2 Modern interests of Edinburgh; 3 The sights of Edinburgh; 4 Tales of long ago; 5 Mary, queen of Scots
LC 7-35148

Griese, Carl
Die Vierlande bei Hamburg; 50 lichtdrucke von Carl Griese, mit einer geschichtlichen einleitung u. erläuterndem text von dr. F. Voigt. Hamburg, C. Griese 1894
29p. illus. 47pl. 1 col.map. F.
Lipperheide 802

Grieve, James
(tr.) Krasheninnikov, S. P. The history of Kamtschatka

Griffin, Gerald
(tr.) Schebesta, Paul. Revisiting my pygmy hosts

Griffis, William Elliot
The Mikado's empire; 11. ed. with seven supplementary chapters including history to beginning of 1906. New York, Harper 1906
2v. illus. pl. O.
Earlier edition 1876

Griffith, William
(ed.) Great painters and their famous Bible pictures; the Bible story retold in one hundred masterpieces chronologically arranged, with sidelights on the life and work of the artists. New York, W. H. Wise 1925
223p. front. illus. Q.
LC 25-21185

Griggs, William
(illus.) Charles v, king of France. The coronation book of Charles v of France. 1899

Grille d'Angers, François. See Angers, F. G. d'

Les **grimaces.** Boilly, L. L.

Grimani, Breviaire. See Catholic Church Liturgy and ritual. Breviary. Breviaire Grimani de la Bibliothèque de S. Marco à Venise: reproduction photographique complète

Grimball, Elizabeth B., and Wells, Rhea
Costuming a play; inter-theatre arts hand-book. New York & London, D. Appleton-Century c1925
5p.l. 133p. illus. ob.O. $3
Costume index. LC 25-3105

Grimm, Simon
Augusta Vindelicorum ... Augstburg. Sambt dero vornembste kirchen, statthor, gebäüe und spring-brunnen, gezäichnet. [Augsburg] 1678-81
3v. 47pl. Q.
Landscapes with people in the background show costume of the various classes of Augsburg
Lipperheide 765

Grimm, Wilhelm
Ruolandes liet, mit einem facsimile und den bildern der Pfälzischen handschrift. Göttingen, Dieterich 1838
cxxviii,346p. 14pl. O.
Shows costume of the 12th century
Lipperheide 378

Grindlay, Robert Melville
Scenery, costumes and architecture, chiefly on the western side of India. London, R. Ackerman 1826-30
2v. 36 col.pl. sq.F. 168s
Volume 2 published by Smith, Elder & co
Plates are engraved by J. Baily, C. Bentley, T. Edge and others after drawings by W. Daniel, Fielding, Grindlay and others
Colas 1333-34. Lipp. 1487. LC 5-14060

Grinnell, George Bird
The Indians of to-day. Chicago and New York, H. S. Stone 1900
185p. front. ports. F. $5, o.p.
Costume index. LC 0-1811

Les **grisettes.** Monnier, Henri

Grisier, Augustin Edme François
Les armes et le duel ... Dessins par E. de Beaumont; 2. éd. Paris, Garnier frères 1847
583p. pl. 2 port.(incl.front.) Q.
LC 18-23672

Grisone, Federico
Ordini di cavalcare, et modi di conoscere le nature de' cavalli, emendare i vitii loro, & ammaestrargli per l'uso della guerra, & comodità de gli huomini ... ricoretta, & migliorata da gli errori delle prime impressioni. Pesaro, B. Cesano 1558
56,26 l. 50 illus. Q.
First Italian edition: Rome, 1550
Translated freely into German by Veit Tufft and Hans Frölich in 1566. A second German translation, by Johann Fayser, was published in 1570 under title: *Künstlicher bericht und allerzierlichste beschreybung ... wie die streitbarn pferdt ... zum ernst und ritterlicher kurtzweil geschickt und volkommen zumachen.* (Augspurg, M. Manger 1573. 235p. 21 l. 88 illus. F.) Also same publisher 1580. This also was a free translation from the Italian original. Revisions of Fayser's translation were published in 1580, 1599, 1623. Illustrations of the German editions, by an unknown artist and sometimes wrongly attributed to Jost Amman, differ from the original illustrations
Lipperheide 2892-93. LC 7-17172 (Ger. ed.)

Griswold, Lester Everett
Handbook of craftwork in leather, horsehair, bead, porcupine quill and feather, Indian (Navajo) silver and turquoise; 4th ed. [Colorado Springs, The Out West printing and stationery company] c1928
167p. illus. D. 50c
LC 29-8459

Griswold, Rufus Wilmot
The republican court; or, American society in the days of Washington; a new ed., with the author's last additions and corrections. New York Appleton 1868
481p. front.(ports.) Q. o.p.
First edition published 1855
Costume index. LC 8-3861

[Los **gritos** de Madrid] Madrid, ca1810
72pl. D.
The plates, 18 series of 4 plates each, are not signed. They show the street vendors of Madrid and have legends in Spanish. For a list of plates see Colas's *Bibliographie*
Colas 1335

Gritzner, Max
Handbuch der ritter- und verdienstorden aller kulturstaaten der welt innerhalb des XIX. jahrhunderts. Leipzig, J. J. Weber 1893
xiii,618p. 760 illus. D. (Webers illustrierte katechismen no146)
Nachweis der benutzten litteratur: on verso of p xiii
Lipperheide 1943. LC 18-22145

Landes- und wappenkunde der brandenburgisch-preussischen monarchie, geschichte ihrer einzelnen landestheile, deren herrscher und wappen. Berlin, C. Heymann 1894
xxii,310p. illus.(coats of arms) 1 pl. 15 fold.geneal.tab. O.
LC 3-16642

Gröber, Karl
Kinderspielzeug aus alter zeit, eine geschichte des spielzeugs. Berlin, Deutscher kunstverlag 1928
67p. col.front. illus. pl.(part col.) Q.
Illustrations show many German toys including many different kinds of dolls
LC 28-18390

Palestine and Syria. New York, Via-Lens publications c1926
xiv p. 192pl. on 96 l. map. F.
Sold also (New York, Westermann $4.50)
Costume index

Picturesque Palestine, Arabia and Syria; the country, the people and the landscape. New York, Brentano's; London, Jarrolds c1925
xvi p. 304pl. on 152 l. map. F. (Orbis terrarum) 25s
German edition: *Palästina, Arabien und Syrien* (Berlin, E. Wasmuth [1925])
LC 26-26403, 26-14313 (Engl. ed.)

Schwaben. See Deutsche volkskunst. v5

Grohmann, Adolf. See Arnold, Sir T. W., jt. auth.

Grohmann, Johann Gottfried
Gebräuche und kleidungen der Chinesen dargestellt in bunten gemälden von dem mahler Pu-Qúa in Canton als zusatz zu Macartneys und van Braams reisen. 60 kupfer mit erklärung in deutscher und französischer sprache. Leipzig, Industrie-comptoir [1800-10]
[128]p. 60 col.pl. ob.Q.
Added t.-p. in French: *Moeurs et coutumes des Chinois*
According to Quérard, Heinsius, and Grässe, done in collaboration with Frédéric Hempel: the work is based on G. H. Mason's *The costume of China*
An account of Earl Macartney's travels was published from his papers by Sir G. L. Staunton, and van Braam's journal was issued in French at Philadelphia (later at Paris) by Moreau de Saint-Méry with title: *Voyage de l'embassade*
Colas 1336. Lipperheide 1521 LC 1-23245

Grolier club, New York
The fan in all ages; a brief history of its evolution. To accompany an exhibition of fans, mostly French, of the XVIIIth century, illustrating the decorative art of that period as applied to fans. Exhibited at the Grolier club ... New York, from April 21 to May 5, 1891. [New York, De Vinne press 1891]
21p. illus. S.
LC A17-1179

Groll, Andr. See Sacken, Eduard, freiherr von. Die vorzüglichsten rüstungen und waffen der K.K. Ambraser-sammlung in original-photographien

Groneman, Isaäc
Der kris der Javaner. Leiden, 1910
19,39,33p. 10pl. Q.

Gronovius, Jacobus
Thesaurus Graecarum antiquitatum, [etc.]; 2. ed. Venetiis, typis Bartholomaei Javarina 1732-37
13v. illus. pl. F.
"Effigies virorum ac foeminarum illustrium quibus in Graecis aut Latinis monumentis aliqua memoriae par datur." Subtitle
Volumes 1-3 show ancient Greek dress and coiffures

Gronow, Rees Howell
The reminiscences and recollections of Captain Gronow; being anecdotes of the camp, court, clubs, and society, 1810-1860, with ... illustrations from contemporary sources, by Joseph Grego. London, J. C. Nimmo 1892
2v. fronts. 31 col.pl. O.
Plates show French and English costume of 1810-1860

Het **groote** tafereel der dwaasheid, vertoonende de opkomst, voortgang en ondergang der actie, bubbel en windnegotie, in Vrankryk, Engeland, en de Nederlanden, gepleegt in den jaare MDCCXX. Zynde een verzameling van alle de conditien en projecten van de opgeregte compagnien van assurantie, navigatie, commercie, &c. in Nederland, zo wel die in gebruik zyn gebragt, als die door de h. staten van eenige provintien zyn verworpen. [Amsterdam?] 1720
25,8,10,52,31p. 75pl.(part fold.) F.
Various pieces in prose and verse on the financial transactions of John Law and others, brought together under a general title-page. Plates show eighteenth century costume
Another edition, published the same year, with slightly different collation, is described by Lipperheide
Lipperheide 3550. LC 6-17039

Gropp, Ignatius. See Gropp, Ignaz

Gropp, Ignaz
Monumenta sepulchralia ecclesiae Ebracensis. Wirceburgi, P. W. Fuggart 1730
112p. 12pl. Q.
"Deinde Gertrudis Augustae, & eiusdem filii Friderici ducis Suevorum, Irenes item Augustae et aliorum quorundam nobilium figuris aeneis illustrata." Subtitle
Shows costume from the 12th to the 14th century. Engraved by G. F. Weigant
Lipperheide 367

Grosch, Henrik August. See Oslo. Kunstindustrimuseet. Gamle norske billedtaepper

Grose, Francis
Military antiquities respecting a history of the English army, from the conquest to the present time; new ed. London. T. Egerton & G. Kearsley 1801
2v. 77pl. Q.
Plates show English arms and armor and military dress before the introduction of uniforms
First edition: London, Printed for S. Hooper, 1786-88 (2v. 80pl. Q.) The new edition contains a supplement: *A treatise on ancient armour and weapons,* also issued separately in 1786
Colas 1338-39. Lipperheide 2263

A treatise on ancient armour and weapons, illustrated by plates taken from the original armour in the Tower of London, and other arsenals, museums, and cabinets. London, S. Hooper 1786
118,xviii p. 49pl. Q.
Engraved by J. Hamilton
Colas 1337. Lipperheide 2401

Groslier, George
Danseuses cambodgiennes anciennes et modernes ... Préface de Charles Gravelle. Paris, A. Challamel [1913]
178p. 15pl. Q.
Colas 1340

Recherches sur les Cambodgiens d'après les textes et les monuments depuis les premiers siècles de notre ère. Paris, A. Challamel 1921
x,432p. illus. XLVIII pl. (incl.front.) fold. map. F.
Chapters 5-9 are on costume and armor
LC 21-13243

Grosse, Ernst
Die anfänge der kunst. Freiburg, J. C. B. Mohr 1894
301p. 32 illus. 3pl. O.

The beginnings of art. New York, D. Appleton 1897
xiv,327p. 32 illus. III fold.pl. D. (The Anthropological series, [4])
Translated from the German title: *Die anfänge der kunst.* Chapters 5-6 show dress and ornamentation among primitive peoples
LC 4-8997

Das **grosse** carrosel und prächtige ringrännen. Klöcker von Ehrenstahl, David

Der **grosse** cölnische maskenzug im jahre 1824. Goebels, W.

Der **grosse** maskenball in Berlin zur feier des geburtstages ... der regierenden königin von Preussen ... 1804. Dahling, illus.

Grosse modenwelt. 1.-29. jahrg., 1892-1920. Berlin, Deutsche verlags-gesellschaft dr. Russak & co.
29? v. col.illus. F.
Published semi-monthly. No more published?
Colas 1341. Lipperheide 4809

Grossherzoglich badisches militair. Völlinger, Joseph

Grossherzoglich hessisches militair. Müller, F. H.

Grossherzoglich - Mecklenburg - Schwerin'sche und Mecklenburg strelitz'sche truppen. Berlin, L. Sachse 1831
16 col.pl. F.
Colas 1342. Lipperheide 2212

Gross-Hoffinger, Anton Johann
Wien wie es ist; illus. von Th. Hosemann. Leipzig, Jackowitz 1847
4v. 4 col.pl. O.

Grosvenor, Gilbert Hovey
(ed.) Scenes from every land. ser. 1-4. Washington, D. C., Nat. geographic soc. 1907-18
4v. pl.(part col.) Q. v 1-3, o.p.; v4 $1
Plates printed on both sides
Costume index

Groszbritannien und Irland. Stenzel, Alfred

Groszes magazin für stickerei. See Silling, Karl. Grand magazin des plus nouveaux dessins françois de broderie

Groteske gestalten. Hoffman, C. T. A.

Groupes de costumes de différens pays. Colin, Mme Anaïs

Groupes de costumes de la cour de France. Colin, Mme Anaïs

Grove, Henry M., jt. auth. See Dobson, George

Groves, John Percy
History of the 42nd Royal Highlanders —"The Black watch" now the first battalion "The Black watch" (Royal Highlanders) ... 1729-1893 ... Illustrated by Harry Payne. Edinburgh and London, W. & A. K. Johnston 1893
30p. 5 col.pl.(incl.front.) sq.F. (Illustrated histories of the Scottish regiments. book no 1)
Frontispiece and three of the plates accompanied by guard sheet with descriptive letterpress
LC 18-27434

Grubauer, Albert
Unter kopfjägern in Central-Celebes; ethnologische streifzüge in Südost- und Central-Celebes. Leipzig, R. Voigtländer 1913
xi,608p. illus. XVI pl.(incl.front., 2 fold. maps) O. M.14.50
Illustrations show costume
LC 14-428

Grubb, Wilfrid Barbrooke
An unknown people in an unknown land; an account of the life and customs of the Lengua Indians of the Paraguayan Chaco, with adventures and experiences met with during twenty years' pioneering and exploration amongst them ... ed. by H. T. Morrey Jones. Philadelphia, J. B. Lippincott company; London, Seeley 1911
329p. front. 11 illus. 31pl. fold.map. O.
LC A11-1326

Gruber, Johann Gottfried
Sitten, gebräuche, und kleidung der Russen, in St Petersburg. Leipzig, Industrie comptoir [1801-03]
95p. 40 col.pl. O.
Drawings by C. G. H. Geissler; text by J. G. Gruber
Added title page in French: *Costumes, moeurs et coutumes des Russes.* French and German text on alternate pages
Colas 1207

Gründ- und umständlicher bericht von denen römisch-kayserlichen wie auch ottomannischen grosz - bothschafften wodurch der friede ... zwischen dem

Gründ und umständlicher ... —*Continued*
... römischen kayser Leopoldo primo und dem sultan Mustafahan III. den 26. januarii, 1699. Zu Carlowiz in Sirmien auf 25. jahr geschlossen. Wien, J. B. Schönwetter 1702
132p. 12pl. F.
Plates show mainly Turkish costumes
Lipperheide 1411

Gründliche nachricht von denen ceremonien, welche jederzeit nach dem absterben eines pabstes ausser und in dem conclave bis zur wahl und crönung eines neuen pabstes vorgehen. Ingleichen von dem ursprung, hoheit und würde der cardinäle. Frankfurt und Leipzig, G. P. Monath 1769
166p. 12pl. O.
Lipperheide 2478

Gründlicher abriss der jenigen zimmer. Geyer, Andrea

Gründlicher selbstunterricht die damenbekleidungskunst. Büchner, Elise

Gründtliche beschreibung der freyen ritterlichen unnd adelichen kunst des fechtens. Meyer, Joachim

Grüner, Joseph Sebastian
Über die ältesten sitten und gebräuche der Egerländer, 1825 für J. W. von Goethe niedergeschrieben; hrsg. von Alois John. Prag, J. G. Calve 1901
137p. 8 col.pl. O. (Beiträge zur deutschböhmischen volkskunde ... IV. bd. 1. hft.)
Plates show costume of Bohemia
LC A28-2081

Grüner, V. R.
[Böhmische volkstrachten.] Prag, C. W. Enders ca1830
34 col.pl. Q.
Colas 1344. Lipperheide 874

Grünwald-Zerkovitz, Frau Sidonie
Die mode in der frauenkleidung. Wien, G. Szelinski 1889
43p. O.
Colas 1345. Lipperheide 3298

Grunauer, E. A.
(tr.) Ortiz Echagüe, José. Spanische kopfe

Grund, Johann Gottfried
Afbildning af Nordmands-Dalen, i den kongelige lyst-hauge ved Fredensborg ... Abbildung des Normannsthals, in dem königlichen lustgarten zu Friedensburg. Kiøbenhavn, N. Møller 1773
16p. 17pl.(incl. 33 illus.) F.
Illustrations show statues of Norwegian peasants. Engraved by A. Heckel
Lipperheide 1041

Die **grundlagen** und die neuesten fortschritte der zuschneidekunst. Mottl, Wendelin

Grundmann, Günther, and Hahm, Konrad
Schlesien. See Deutsche volkskunst. v8

Grundzüge einer philosophie der tracht. Schurtz, Heinrich

Gruner, Erich
Der historische festzug, anlässlich der jubelfeier des 500 jährigen bestehens der universität zu Leipzig ... mit kurzem begleitendem text v. Carl Chun. Leipzig, J. J. Weber 1909
2 l. 25pl. ob.O.

Grupen, Christian Ulrich
Teutsche alterthümer, zur erleuterung des sächsischen auch schwäbischen land- und lehn-rechts, wobey der gebrauch der dresdenschen, wolfenbüttelschen, und oldenburgschen ... durch einige abbildungen ... unter augen gestellet worden. Hannover und Lüneburg, J. W. Schmidt 1746
128p. 13 illus. 1 pl. Q.
Shows 14th century costume
Lipperheide 369

Gruppi di costumi napolitani. Dura, Gaetano

Gruppi pittoreschi modellati in terra-cotta. Pinelli, Bartolommeo

Gruyer, François Anatole
Chantilly. Notices des peintures; les quarante Fouquet. Paris, Plon-Nourrit 1900
190p. 40pl. Q.

Gualdo Priorato, Galeazzo, conte
Historia di Ferdinando Terzo imperatore. [Parte prima] Vienna, M. Cosmerovio 1672
616,12p. fold.pl. ports. fold.maps. F.
This volume is introductory, closing with the death of Ferdinand II in 1637. According to Clement (Bibl. curieuse, v9) the second volume was never published. Plates show costume of the seventeenth century
Lipperheide 539. LC 4-29129

Historia di Leopoldo Cesare, continente le cose piu memorabili successe in Europa, dal 1656 fino al 1670. Vienna, G. B. Hacque 1670
2v. 209pl. F.
Most of the plates are engraved by Conrad Meysens. Contains 142 portraits of nobles, military leaders, and ministers of state
Lipperheide 538

Vite, et azzioni di personaggi militari, e politici. Vienna, M. Thurnmayer 1673
669p. 61 illus. 66pl. F.
Most of the plates are portraits of noted people of the 17th century
Lipperheide 540

Gual-el-Jelû, Marqués de
(ed.) Clonard, S. M. de S. y A., conde de. Album de la infantiera española desde sus primitivos tiempos hasta el dia

Gualla, Giacopo
Papie sanctuarium. [Pavia, J. de Burgofrancho 1505]
92 l. 69 illus. port. Q.
Woodcuts of saints, bishops, and other dignitaries show costume of the early 16th century

Gualterotti, Raffaello
Descrizione del regale apparato per le nozze della serenissima Madama Cristiana di Loreno, moglie del serenissimo Don Ferdinando Medici III. granduca di Toscana. Firenze, A. Padouani 1589
35p. 46 l. 67 illus. O.
Lipperheide 2742. LC 18-8599

Feste nelle nozze del serenissimo Don Francesco Medici gran duca di Toscana; et della sereniss. sua consorte ... Bianco Capello. Firenze, Stamperia de' Giunti 1579
58,24p. 16pl. Q.
Lipperheide 2740

Guards, Papal. See Papal guards

Guarinos, Juan Sempere y. See Sempere y Guarinos, Juan

Guasco, Fráncesco Eugenio
Delle ornatrici, e de' loro uffizi, ed insieme della superstizione de' gentili medesima presso le antiche donne romane. Napoli, G. Gravier 1775
x,180p. 82 illus. Q.
Interesting for the history of feminine coiffures in ancient Rome
Colas 1346. Lipperheide 231

Guatemala
Domville-Fife, C. W. Guatemala and the states of Central America. 1913
Textile arts of the Guatemalan natives. 1935

Gülich, Ludwig von
Erb-huldigung so ... Josepho dem ersten von denen gesambten nider-oesterreichischen ständen ... an dem auff den 22. dess monats septembris anno 1705 angesetzten tag abgelegt und ... zusammen getragen worden. Wienn, J. J. Kürner [1705?]
46p. 11pl. F.
Plates from drawings by J. C. Hackhofer, engraved by J. A. Pfeffel and C. Engelbrecht. They also appear in J. B. von Mairn's *Beschreibung*
Lipperheide 2624

Guénot-Lecointe, Georges
Physiologie du gant ... vignettes de Lepaulle, C. J. Travies, Baron, R. Pelez, gravées par Porret. Paris, Desloges 1841
127p. S.
Colas 1347

Günther, Gustav Biedermann
Ueber den bau des menschlichen fusses und dessen zweckmässigste bekleidung. Leipzig, C. F. Winter 1863
34p. 65 illus. O.
Colas 1364. Lipperheide 1741

Guer, Jean-Antoine
Moeurs et usages des Turcs, leur religion, leur gouvernement civil, militaire et politique, avec un abregé de l'histoire ottomane. Paris, Coustelier 1746-47
2v. fronts. 28pl.(7 fold.) Q.
Plates are engraved by C. Duflos after F. Boucher and N. Hallé
Colas 1348-49. Lipp. 1418. LC 5-13706

Guérard, Eugène
Les annales de la danse et du théâtre. Paris, Goupil et Vibret [1840]
6pl. F.
Cover title
Colas 1352

Guérard, Nicolas
Diverses petitte figure des cris de Paris, désigné et gravé par N. Guérard, le fils. Paris, Guérard ca1730
18? pl. O.
Appeared in three parts with the title on the first plate of each part
Colas 1351

Livre à dessiner; les exercices de Mars, Dédiés et présentés à Monseigneur le duc de Bourgogne. Paris, N. Guérard [169-?]
1 l. 23pl. D.
Colas 1350

Guérinet, Armand
(ed.) Union centrale des arts décoratifs, Paris. Le costume

Guerra, Cristoforo
(illus.) Vecellio, Cesare. De gli habiti antichi

Guerra, Giovanni
Varie acconciature di teste usate da nobilissime dame in diverse cittadi d'Italia. Venise, ca1570
40pl. O.
Colas 1353. Lipperheide 1644

Guerre, Alice
Dress cutting: theoretical and practical. An exposition of the Guerre system of drafting, cutting-out, and making-up ladies' garments. Leeds, E. J. Arnold [1914]
xiii,128p. illus. O.

La **guerre** à toutes les époques. Quesnoy, Ferdinand

Le **guerre** festive nelle reali nozze de' ... re di Spagna Carolo secondo, e Maria Luisa di Borbone. Maggio, Pietro

Guhl, Ernest Karl, and Koner, Wilhelm David
Das leben der griechen und römer nach antiken bildwerken. Berlin. Weidmann 1862
407p. illus. O.

The life of the Greeks and Romans described from antique monuments; tr. from the 3d German ed. by F. Hueffer. New ed. London, Chatto & Windus 1889
1 p.l. ix,620p. illus. O. 7s 6d, o.p.
Translation of their *Das leben der griechen und römer*
Costume index. LC 4-14840

Guiaud
(lithgr.) Delbecchi, Amedée. Nice; vues et costumes

Guibaudet, François
(tr.) Clément, Nicolas, de Treille. Austrasiae reges et duces epigrammatis

Guichard, Édouard
Dessins de décoration des principaux maîtres; quarante planches réunies et reproduites sous la direction de Ed. Guichard ... avec une étude sur l'art décoratif et des notices par M. Ernest Chesneau. Paris, A. Quantin 1881
23,iv p. XL pl. F.
Each plate accompanied by leaf with descriptive letterpress not included in paging
Lipperheide 4369. LC 26-18680

Les petits alphabets du brodeur; compositions originales inspirées de nos grandes époques décoratives. Paris [187-?]
24pl. F.
Lipperheide 4192

Les tapisseries décoratives du Garde-meuble (Mobilier national); choix des plus beaux motifs, par Éd. Guichard ... texte par Alfred Darcel. Paris, J. Baudry [1881]
16p. 100 l. 100pl.(part col.) F.
Issued in 10 parts, 1878-81
Tapestries show European costume of the 16th and 17th centuries
Lipperheide 3763. LC 10-2708

Guide à l'usage des artistes et des costumiers. Malibran, H.

Guide des amateurs d'armes et armures anciennes. See Demmin, A. F. Encyclopédie d'armurerie avec monogrammes

Guide to antiquities of the early iron age. British museum. Department of British and mediaeval antiquities

Guide to the antiquities of the bronze age. British museum. Department of British and mediaeval antiquities

A **guide** to the Babylonian and Assyrian antiquities. British museum. Department of Egyptian and Assyrian antiquities

Guide to the collection of costumes. Victoria and Albert museum, South Kensington

Guide to the collection of lace. Victoria and Albert museum, South Kensington

Guide to the Egyptian collections in the British museum. British museum. Department of Egyptian and Assyrian antiquities

Guide to the English costumes presented by Messrs. Harrods ltd. See Victoria and Albert museum, South Kensington. Guide to the collection of costumes

Guide to the exhibition illustrating Greek and Roman life. British museum. Department of Greek and Roman life

Guide to the Japanese textiles. Victoria and Albert museum, South Kensington

Guide to the Maudslay collection of Maya sculptures. British museum. Department of ceramics and ethnography

Guide to the principal gold and silver coins of the ancients, from circ. B. C. 700 to A.D. 1. British museum. Department of coins and medals

Guignes, Joseph de

(ed.) Amiot, J. M., comp. and tr. Art militaire des Chinois

Guignols et marionnettes; leur histoire. Petite, J. M.

Guigue de Champvans, Frédéric

Histoire et législation des ordres de chevalerie, marques d'honneur et médailles du Saint-Siège, d'après les sources officielles, avec une introduction sur les ordres religieux et militaires, par le marquis Frédéric Guigue de Champvans de Farémont. Paris, Institut historique et héraldique de France 1932-33

2v. illus.(incl.ports. coats of arms, facsims.) F.

Included in the paging are specimen pages of the volume containing biographies of persons whose portraits are found in the *Livre d'or des chevaliers pontificaux* or in the *Livre d'or de la famille pontificale*

Previously published in 1913. Volume II has title: *Histoire et législation ... avec une introduction sur la cour laïque du pape et les camériers secrets et d'honneur de cape et d'épée*

LC 34-8804

The **Guild** of play book for little children. See Kimmins, Mrs G. T. H. The Guild of play book of festival and dance

The **Guild** of play book of festival and dance. Kimmins, Mrs G. T. H.

The **Guild** of play book of national dances. See Kimmins, Mrs G. T. H. The Guild of play book of festival and dance

The **guilds** of Florence. Staley, J. E.

Guildsmen. See Gildsmen

Guilhermy, Roch François Ferdinand Marie Nolasque, baron de, and Lasteyrie du Saillant, Robert Charles

Inscriptions de la France du v. siècle au XVIII. Paris, Impr. nat. 1873-83

5v. illus. pl. facsims. Q.

Illustrations include church windows of the 13th to 18th century and show religious costume

Guilino, Simon. See Guillain, Simon

Guillain, Símon

(engr.) Carracci, Annibale. Le arti di Bologna

(engr.) Carracci, Annibale. Diverse figure

Guillaume, Albert

Mon sursis; album militaire inédit en couleurs. Préface de Richard O'Monroy. Paris, S. Empis 1901

28p. 29 col.illus. Q.

Shows French army uniforms of this period

Guillaumet, Gustave Achille

Tableaux algériens; ouvrage illustré ... par Guillaumet, Courtry, Le Rat ... précédé d'une notice sur la vie et les oeuvres de Guillaumet par Eugène Mouton. Paris, Plon, Nourrit 1888

322p. illus. pl. port. O.

Guillaumot, Auguste Etienne

Costumes anglais du temps de la révolution et du premier empire 1795-1806. Paris, A. Levy 1879

2 l. 25 col.pl. Q.

Twenty plates showing feminine costume of 1795 to 1799 are from the *Gallery of fashion.* The last five plates show dandies of the period

Colas 1357. Lipperheide 1013

Costumes de la Comédie française XVIIe-XVIIIe siècles; avec une préface de G. Monval. Paris, J. Lemonnyer 1885

11p. 50 col.pl. F.

Colas 1359

Costumes de l'opéra, XVIIe-XVIIIe siècles, avec une préface de Ch. Nuitter. [Paris, A. Levy] 1883

11p. 50pl.(part col.) F.

Plates accompanied by guard-sheets with descriptive letterpress

Colas 1358. Lipperheide 3227

Costumes des ballets du roy; Archives de l'opéra XVIIIe siècle. Avec une notice de C. Nuitter. Paris, E. Monnier 1885

3 l. 20 col.pl. Q.

Plates accompanied by guard-sheets with descriptive letter-press

Colas 1360. Lipperheide 3228

Costumes du directoire, tirés des Merveilleuses, avec une lettre de m. Victorien Sardou. 20 eaux-fortes de A. Guillaumot fils avec un portrait de m. V. Sardou dessiné et gravé par m. Guillaumot père. Dessins de mm. Eugène Lacoste et Draner [pseud] d'après des estampes du temps. Tiré chez Chardon ainé. Paris, Rouquette, 1875

5 l. 12p. 30 col.pl. Q.

Costumes worn by the actors in producing Sardou's Les merveilleuses, first performed at the Variétés on December 16, 1873

Notice sur les costumes du directoire, by Albert de La Berge p 1-12

Earlier edition (Paris, J. Claye 1874) has 20 colored plates only

Colas 1699-1700. Costume index. Lipperheide 1143. LC 16-24888

Guillaumot, Auguste E.—*Continued*

Costumes du XVIIIe siècle, d'après les dessins de Watteau fils, Desrais, Leclere, Cochin, etc. Tirés de collections particulières. Paris, H. Cagnon [187-?]
60pl. F.
Costume index

Costumes du XVIIIe siècle tirés des près Saint-Gervais ... d'après les dessins de m. Draner [pseud.] Paris, P. Rouquette 1874
3 l. 7p. 20pl. Q.
Colas 895. Costume index. Lipp. 1141

Costumes du temps de la révolution, 1790-1791-1792-1793; tirés de la collection de m. V. Sardou. Préface de m. Jules Claretie. Paris, A. Levy 1876
2 l. 40 col.pl. F.
Plates are reproduced from *Cabinet des modes, Magasin des modes nouvelles, and Journal de la mode et du goût*
Colas 1356. Lipperheide 1147

Costumes of the time of the French revolution 1790-1793, together with English costumes during the years 1795-1806, drawn from the collection of Victorien Sardou, with an introduction by Clarence Cook. New-York, J. W. Bouton 1889
[7]p. 65 col.pl. F.
Forty plates of French costume are from his *Costumes du temps de la révolution, 1790-1793*. Twenty five plates of English costume are from his *Costumes anglais du temps de la révolution et du premier empire, 1795-1806*
Costume index. LC 4-6445

Guillonet, Octave Denis Victor
(illus.) Funck-Brentano, Frantz. Jeanne d'Arc

Guilmard, Désiré
Les maîtres ornemanistes, dessinateurs, peintres, architectes, sculpteurs et graveurs; écoles française,—italienne,—allemande,—et des Pays-Bas (flamande & hollandaise). Paris, E. Plon 1880-81
xvi,560p. illus. facsim. and atlas of 180pl. Q.
Lipperheide 4368. LC 3-3587

Guimaraes, A. L.
Plano a que se refere o decreto no. 1829 de 4 de outubro de 1856 para os uniformes dos officiaes do corpo da armada e das classes annexas. Rio de Janeiro, Brito et Braga 1857
2 l. 20 col.pl. ob.F.
Shows uniforms of the Brazilian navy
Colas 1361

Guiana. See Indians of South America—Guiana

Guiana, French. See French Guiana

Guinot, Eugène
L'été à Bade. Paris, Furne 1847
300p. illus. pl.(part col.) map. Q.
Illustrated by Johannot, Lamy, Français, and Jacquemot

A summer at Baden-Baden. Illustrated by Messrs. Tony Johannot, Eug. Lamy, Français, and Jacquemot. London, J. Mitchell [1853]
299p. front. pl. 1 port. Q.
Translation of his *L'été à Bade*
Costume index. LC 4-28789

La **Guirlande**; album mensuel d'art et de littérature sous la direction littéraire de monsieur Jean Hermanovits, sous la direction artistique de monsieur Brunelleschi. 1.-11. livraison, Oct. 1919-Nov. 1920. Paris, F. Bernouard
11 pts. illus.(part col.) pl.(part col.) O.
Contains fashion plates
Colas 1362

Guirlande des mois. 1.-5. année; 1917-1921. Paris, J. Meynial
5v. 29 col.pl. T.
Contains fashion plates by Georges Barbier
Colas 1363

Gulick, Charles Burton
... The life of the ancient Greeks, with special reference to Athens. New York, D. Appleton 1902
xii,373p. col.front. illus.(incl. plans) pl. map. D. $2.50 (Twentieth century textbooks. Classical section)
Clothing p153-70; The warrior p188-205
Bibliography: p310-20
Costume index. LC 3-734

Gummere, Mrs Amelia (Mott)
The Quaker; a study in costume. Philadelphia, Ferris & Leach 1901
232p. front. illus 12pl. 16 ports. O. $3, o.p.
Plates accompanied by guard sheet with descriptive letterpress
LC 1-27729

Gunsaulus, Helen Cowen
Japanese costume. Chicago, Field museum of natural history 1923
26p. pl. O. (Field museum of natural history. Anthropology leaflet, no12) pa 22c
LC 26-1553

Japanese sword-mounts in the collections of Field museum. See entry under Field museum of natural history, Chicago

Guppy, Henry Brougham
The Solomon islands. London, S. Sonnenschein, Lowrey 1887
vii,152p. front. II pl. maps. Q.
Pages 130-40 deal with dress, personal ornamentation, and tattooing
LC 1-3206

Guptill, Mrs Elizabeth Frances (Ephraim) and Wormwood, Edyth M.
Amateur's costume book. Franklin, O. Eldridge entertainment house [c1917]
iv p. 1 l. 106p. illus. O.
LC 17-29487

Gurdon, Philip Richard Thornhagh
The Khasis. With an introduction by Sir Charles Lyall. (Published under the orders of the government of Eastern Bengal and Assam) London, D. Nutt 1907
xxvii,227p. 11pl.(1 col.) 6 col.port. (incl. front.) O.
LC 7-40869

Gurk, Eduard
48 erinnerungs-blätter an die krönuung S.K.H. des erzherzogs kronprinzen Ferdinand zum könig von Ungarn in Presburg, den 28. september 1830. Wien, T. Mollo 1830
44 col.pl. F.
Lipperheide 2634

Gurlitt, Cornelius
Deutsche turniere, rüstungen und plattner des XVI. jahrhunderts. Dresden, Gilbers'sche königl. hof-verlagsbuchhandlung 1889
114p. 18 illus. O.
Lipperheide 2438

Das französische sittenbild des achtzehnten jahrhunderts im kupferstich. Berlin, J. Bard 1913
100 l. 59p. 100pl.(incl.ports.) F.
Plates show costume
LC 14-15836

Gussmann, Paul
Lehrbuch für den perückenmacher und tischarbeiter, mit ca. 480 abbildungen. Leitfaden für fachschulen, anfänger und vorgeschrittene. 3. verb. aufl. Leipzig, P. Gussmann 1909
444p. incl.front.(port.) illus. O.
LC 10-2580

Zeichenvorlagen für den fachschul-unterricht im perückenmachergewerbe. Serie I-III. Leipzig, P. Gussmann [c1910-]
3pt. pl.(part fold.) sq.F.
LC 10-11398

Die **gute** alte zeit. Lehmann, Hans

Die **gute** alte zeit geschildert in historischen beiträgen. Scheible, Johann

Der **gute** geschmack in der frauenkleidung. Gratz, Josefine

Gutenberg-feier Mainz 1900. Sutter, Conrad

Gutiérrez de Lara, Lazaro, and Pinchon, Edgcumb
The Mexican people: their struggle for freedom; illustrated from photographs. Garden City, New York, Doubleday, Page 1914
xi,360p. front. pl. ports. maps(1 fold.) O.
Plates printed on both sides. Also published in Spanish (Los Angeles, Calif. [19-?])
LC 14-8758

Guts-Muths, Johann Christoph Friedrich
Gymnastik für die jugend. Schnepfenthal, Buchhandlung der erziehungsanstalt 1793
xviii,663p. front. pl. O.
Plates engraved by C. Westermayer after H. Lips

Turnbuch für die söhne des vaterlandes. Frankfurt am Mayn, Gebrüder Wilmans 1817
17 l. xxxxii,300p. 4pl. O.
Lipperheide 3044

Gutter-snipes. May, Phil

Guttry, Alexander von
(tr.) Łoziński, Władysław. Polnisches leben in vergangenen zeiten

La **Guyane,** ou histoire, moeurs et costumes des habitants de cette partie de l'Amérique. Denis, Ferdinand

Guyot
(engr.) Watteau, L. J. Cris et costumes de Paris

Guyot, Antoine Patrice, and Debacq, Alexandre
Album des théâtres. Paris, Guyot 1837
246p. 80 col.pl. O.
Colas 1365

Gymnasium dress
Guts-Muths, J. C. F. Gymnastik für die jugend. 1793
Guts-Muths, J. C. F. Turnbuch für die söhne des vaterlandes. 1817
Mercuriale, Girolamo. De arte gymnastica libri sex: in quibus exercitationum omnium vetustarum genera, loca, modi facultates, & quidquid denique ad corporis humani exercitationes pertinet diligenter explicatur. 1672
Pascha, J. G. Kurtze jedoch gründliche beschreibung des voltiger. 1666
Schreber, D. G. M. Ärtzliche zimmer gymnastik, oder System der ohne gerä ... ausführbahren heilgymnastischen freiübungen. 1890
Walker, Donald. Exercises for ladies 1836

Gymnastik für die jugend. Guts-Muths, J. C. F.

Gynaeceum, sive Theatrum mulierum. Amman, Jost.

Gynäkatoptron, oder Blicke in die weibliche garderobe in bezug auf körperliche wohlseyn. Frankfurt am Main, P. W. Eichenberg 1805
viii,61p. O.
Colas 1366. Lipperheide 3247

Gypsies. See Gipsies

The **gypsy's** parson. Hall, George

H

H., D. M. J. See Les modes anciennes et modernes

H., J. S. See Stripes and types of the Royal Navy

Haagen, Carl Ernst Casimir
Dissertatio historica de Saxo-Vinariensi vigilantiae ordine, praemissa quorundam hujus seculi ordinum recensione, quam ... in Academia Salana praeside m. Carlo Ern. Casim. Haagen. [Jena litteris Horniansi 1734
24p. 1 illus. 1 pl. Q.
Lipperheide 1907

Die **haartracht** des mannes in archaischer griechischer zeit. Bremer, Walther

Haas, Johann Baptist
(engr.) Gerbert, Martin, freiherr von Hornau. De translatis Habsburgo austriacorum principum

Haberlandt, Michael
Textile volkskunst aus Österreich. Wien J. Löwy 1912
2 l. 45pl. F.

Völkerschmuck, mit besonderer berücksichtigung des metallischen schmuckes nebst einführungen und erläuterungen. Wien und Leipzig, Gerlach & Wiedling [1906]
22p. 109pl. sq.Q. (Die quelle, hrsg. von M. Gerlach. VII)
In portfolio
Costume index. LC 22-3835

Habermann, Franz, edler von
Kriegs-scenen. c in VI blättern. Wien & Leipzig, Trentsensky & Vieweg ca1840
6pl. F.
Lipperheide 2236

Habillemens à la mode de Paris en l'année 1761. Saint-Aubin, Augustin de

Habillemens berlinois. Gradmann, J. J.

Habillemens de plusieurs nations. Aa, Pieter van der

Habillemens des états de S. M. l'Empereur roi. See Kininger, V. G. Kleidertrachten der kaiserl. könig̈. staaten

Habillemens des païsans et païsannes de Hollande, de Frise de Braband et autres provinces. Allard, A.

Habillemens, moeurs et coutumes dans les provinces septentrionales des Pays-Bas. Maaskamp, Evert, ed.

Habillemens moscovites et crieurs à St. Petersbourg. See Dahlstein, Augustin. Russische trachten und ausrufer in St Petersburg

Habitants de l'Inde. Saltykov, A. D., kniaz'

Habiti antichi, et moderni di tutto il mondo. See Vecellio, Cesare. De gli habiti antichi

Habiti delle donne venetiane. Franco, Giacomo

Habiti delle donne venetiane intagliate in rame nouvamente. Franco, Giacomo

Habiti d'huomeni et donne venetiane. Franco, Giacomo

Habits and men. Doran, John

Habits de diverses nations. See Bruyn, Abraham de. Omnium pene

Habitudes et moeurs privées des Romains. Arnay, J. R. d'.

Habitus academicorum Oxoniensium a doctore ad servientem. London, I. Oliver ca1680
1 l. 10pl. Q.
According to Colas the engraver is probably John Oliver
Colas 1369. Lipperheide 2019

Habitus praecipuorum populorum. Weigel, Hans

Habitus variarum orbis gentium. Boissard, J. J.

Habitz ed nations estrãges. See Boissard, J. J. Habitus variarum orbis gentium

Hacault, P.
(tr.) Richter, J. G. Spiele und belustigungen der Russen

Hackhofer, Johann Cyriak
(illus.) Gülich, Ludwig von. Erb-huldigung so ... Josepho dem ersten

Hacklaender, Friedrich Wilhelm
Das caroussel welches am 27. Oktober 1846 aus veranlassung der hohen vermaelung ... des kronzprinzen Karl von Würtemberg mit ... der gross-fürstin Olga Nikolajéwna in Stuttgart abgehalten wurde. Stuttgart, C. F. Autenrieth'schen kunsthandlung [1846?]
1,26 l. 28 col.pl. F.
Lipperheide 2597

Erinnerungen an die feldzüge der k. k. oester. armee in Italien in den jahren 1848-49 ... lithogr. und hrsg. von den Brudern Adam. München 1851
24pl. F.

Hacouni
Patmouthiun hin haj tarazin patkerazard. [History of Armenian costume] Venedig, S. Lazzaro 1923
10,470p. front. 137 illus. 9pl.(1 col.) Q.
Text in Armenian. Bibliography: p445-52

Hacquet, Balthasar
Abbildung und beschreibung der südwest- und östlichen Wenden, Illyrer und Slaven ... deren sitten, gebräuche, handthierung, gewerbe, religion u.s.w. Erster theil. Leipzig, Industrie-comptoir [1802-1805]
12,246p. 34 col.pl. Q.
The first volume only appeared, in five parts. Plates are by C. G. H. Geissler and 28 of them show costume
Colas 1370. Lipperheide 878

Hacquet's neueste physikalisch-politische reisen in den jahren 1788 und 1789 durch die dacischen und sarmatischen oder nördlichen Karpathen. Nürnberg, Rasp 1790
4v. illus. pl. O.
Lipperheide 892

L'Illyrie et la Dalmatie, ou Moeurs usages et costumes des habitants et des ceux des contrées voisines; tr ... par M. Breton; augmentée d'un mémoire sur la Croatie militaire. Paris, Nepveu 1815
2v.(151,171p.) 32 col.pl. D.
Colas 1371. Lipperheide 879

Hadaczek, Karol
Der ohrschmuck der Griechen und Etrusker. Wien, A. Hölder 1903
84p. illus. O. (Archäologisch epigraphischen seminars der Universität Wien Abhandlung v14)

Haddon, Alfred Cort
Iban or sea Dayak fabrics and their patterns; a descriptive catalogue of the Iban fabrics in the Museum of archaeology and ethnology, Cambridge, by Alfred C. Haddon and Laura E. Start. Cambridge [Eng.] The University press 1936
xv,157p. front. illus. xxxv pl. on 18 l. diagrs. sq.Q.
Bibliography: p156-57
LC 37-1499

Haeberlin, Carl
Inselfriesische volkstrachten vom XVI. bis XVIII. jahrhundert. Kiel, Gesellschaft fur schleswig-holsteinische geschichte 1926
p171-251. pl.(part col.) O.
Reprint from *Zeitschrift der Gesellschaft für schleswig-holsteinische geschichte,* Bd 56
Bibliographical footnotes

Trauertrachten und trauergebräuche auf der insel Föhr. Berlin 1909
21p. illus. O.
From: *Mitteilungen des Vereins der k. sammlung für deutsche volkskunde zu Berlin,* v3, pt2 1909, p87-107

Volkstrachten d. nordfriesischen inseln v. anfang d. XVIII. d. anfang d. XIX. jahrhunderts. Wyck 1909?
Cover-title, 25 mount.col.pl. F.
Text in Danish and German

Haecht Goidtsenhoven, Laurens van
Chroniicke van de hertoghen van Brabant, waer in hun leuen, oorloghen, ende acten perfectelijk beschreuen zijn. Met oock de gheleghentheyt des lants, de manieren ende handel des volcks. Andtvverpen, I. B. Vrients 1606
116 l. 42 illus. (ports.) Q.
At end: Typis Hieronymi Verdussen. In double columns; gothic type; the illustrations are full-page engravings
Portraits of the Dukes of Brabant to about 1604
Lipperheide 928. LC 19-12462

Häckel-vorlagen für schule und haus. Rausche-Rauss, Frieda

Haegy
Collection de costumes suisses des XXII antons. See entry under Reinhart, J. C.

Häkel-, strick-, und stickmuster. Hennings, Emma

Häkel- und stickmuster der modenwelt. I. sammlung. Berlin, E. Lipperheide 1897
32p. 84 illus. Q.
Lipperheide 4179

Häkel-buch. Korn, Minna

Häkelmuster-album der "Wiener mode". Wien, Verlag der "Wiener mode" [1896]
29p. 32pl. Q.
Lipperheide 4177

Das **häkeln.** Georgens, J. D.

Das **häkeln.** Hochfelder, Frau B. L.

Häkelschule fur damen. Hennings, Emma

Haelwegh, Adrian
(engr.) Funeral ceremonies for George II. Landgrave of Hesse, June 1661

Haelwegh, Albert
Regum Daniae icones accuratê expressae. Hafnia, A. Haelwegh [1648]
103p. 105pl. F.
Head and shoulder portraits of the Danish kings and their queens, to Friedrich III. The text, in verse, is in Latin, Danish and German
Lipperheide 1036

Händel, Ernst
Schablonen in natürlicher grösse für decken, wände, säulenschäfte etc. aus dem ende des XV. und anfang des XVI. jahrhunderts; ausgeführt auf der K. Albrechtsburg zu Meissen. Weimar, B. F. Voigt 1888
1 l. 25 col.pl. F.
First edition 1883
Lipperheide 4371

Haenel, Erich
Alte waffen. 2. aufl. Berlin, R. C. Schmidt 1920
xii,176p. illus. O. (Bibliothek für kunst- und antiquitätensammler bd 4)
First edition 1913
"Literatur": p[162]-65
LC 26-24426

Kostbare waffen aus der Dresdner rüstkammer. See entry under Dresden. Historisches museum und gewehrgalerie

Der sächsischen kurfürsten turnierbücher. Frankfurt am Main, H. Keller 1910
51p. 52 col.pl. ob.F.

Haenen, F. De. See De Haenen, F.

Haenfler, Johann
Ists auch mode? Wenn wil mode modus werden? Frankfurt an der Oder, J. Schrey & H. J. Meyers seel. erbe 1693
7 l. 243p. 6 l. Q.
Lipperheide 3449

Haenle, S. See Stillfried und Rattonitz, R. M. B., graf von, jt. auth.

Hård
(illus.) Costumes nationaux des provinces de la Suède
(illus.) Svenska folkdrägter; med text lithocromierade plancher af Hård m. fl. Stockholm, Rs. och A. J. Salmson 185-
12p. 10 col.pl. Q. 7.50
(illus.) Swedish costumes; with text coloured plates by Hård a. o. Berlin Sacco 1858
10p. 10 col.pl. Q. 7.50
English edition of his *Svenska folkdräg ter.* Plates engraved by Salmson, in Stockholm

Haerlems ivweel, tot nut vande oude armen uyt liefde ten thoon ghestelt nae de voorghegevene caerte van 't speelcorentken. Zwol, Z. Heyns, drucker 1608
[63]p. 1 illus. fold.pl. O.
Lipperheide 2854. LC 15-16943

Häublin, N.
(engr.) Nürnbergische kleider arten

Das **häusliche** leben der europäischen kulturvölker. Schultz, Alwin

Das **häusliche** leben der Griechen und Römer. Opitz, Richard

Häuslicher ratgeber; illustrirte familien und modenzeitung. Begr. im jahr 1886 v. Rob. Schneeweisz. 1.-29. jahrg 1886-sept. 1915. Berlin, H. Hillger
29v. illus. Q.-F.
Published weekly
Subtitle varies: v 1-20 1886-1906, praktisches wochenblatt für hauswirtschaft und gesundheitspflege
Lipperheide 4789

Hagemann, A. See Franceschini, G., jt. auth.

Hagemann, Arnold
Griechische panzerung: eine entwicklungsgeschichtliche studie zur antiken bewaffnung. 1. theil, Der metallharnisch. Leipzig & Berlin, B. G. Teubner 1919
160p. illus. O.

Hagen, Friedrich Heinrich von der
Bilder aus dem ritterleben und aus der ritterdichtung nach elfenbeingebilden und gedichten des mittelalters. Berlin, J. A. Stargardt 1856
p487-500. 6pl. Q.
Costume of the age of chivalry, twelfth to fourteenth centuries, from carved ivories of the period
From the *Abhandlungen der philosophisch-historischen klasse* der K. Akademie der wissenschaften 1855
Lipperheide 385

Hagen, Friedrich H. von der—*Continued*
Bildersaal altdeutscher dichter; bildnisse, wappen und darstellungen aus dem leben und den liedern der deutschen dichter des XII. bis XIV. jahrhunderts. Berlin, J. A. Stargardt 1856-[1861]
xviii,279p. and atlas of 54pl. Q. (Minnesinger Deutsche liederdichter des XII. bis XIV. jahrhunderts. 5. Theil)
Reproductions of miniatures from the Manesse, Weingartner, Berlin and Nagler lieder manuscripts. The text includes discussion of clothing and armour
Lipperheide 386

Handschriftengemälde und andere bildliche denkmäler der deutschen dichter des 12.-14. jahrhunderts. Berlin, K. Akademie der wissenschaften 1853
27p. 7pl. Q.
From the *Königlichen Akademie der wissenschaften, Berlin. Abh. philol. hist. kl.* 1852 p813-39. The plates are reproductions of miniatures from the Manesse and Weingartner Minnesinger manuscripts with explanatory text
Lipperheide 384

Haghe, Louis
(lithgr.) Brockedon, William. Egypt & Nubia
(lithgr.) Croly, George. The Holy Land, Syria, Idumea, Arabia, Egypt & Nubia

Hague, Marian. See Morris, Frances, jt. auth.

Haguental, and Fagonde
Les gloires de l'Opéra; poses et portraits des principales danseuses de Paris et de Londres. Paris, Aubert n.d.
1 l. 12 col.pl. F.
Plates are signed Haguental or Haguental et Fagonde
Colas 1372

Hahm, Konrad. See Grundmann, Günther, jt. auth.

Haid, Johann Jacob
(engr.) Ehren-tempel der deutschen gelehrsamkeit

See also Brucker, J. J., jt. auth.

Haigh, Arthur Elam
The Attic theatre; a description of the stage and theatre of the Athenians, and of the dramatic performances at Athens. 3d ed. rev. and in part re-written. Oxford, Clarendon press 1898
xv,420p. illus.(incl.plans) 3pl.(incl.front.) O.
LC 3-25297

Hailsbronnischer antiquitäten-schatz. Hocker, J. L.

Hailstone, Edward, the Younger
(ed.) Walker, George. The costume of Yorkshire

Hailstone, S. H. Lilla
Designs for lace making. London, E. J. Francis 1870
7p. 40 col.pl. Q.
Lipperheide 4029

Hainaut
(illus.) Goulven, J. G. A. Les mellahs de Rabat-Salé

Haines, Herbert
A manual of monumental brasses: comprising an introduction to the study of these memorials and a list of those remaining in the British Isles. Oxford and London, J. H. and J. Parker 1861
2v. col.front. illus. O. 21s, o.p.
"The former part is based on the Introduction written by the author for the *Manual for the study of monumental brasses* issued about twelve years ago by the Oxford architectural society." Preface
English costume from the 14th to the 17th century
Costume index. LC 11-19799

Hair-dressing
Almanach de la toilette et de la coëffure des dames françoises, suivie d'une dissertation sur celle des dames romaines. 1777
Apologie des dames, les jolies françaises, leurs coëffures et habillemens. 1781
Le bijou des dames. 1779
Das buch der haare und bärte. 1844
Bysterveld, Henri de. Album de coiffures historiques. 1863-67
Child, T. Wimples and crisping pins. 1895
Cortambert, Richard. Essai sur la chevelure des différents peuples. 1861
Dulaure, J. A. Pogonologie, ou Histoire philosophique de la barbe. 1786
Eze, Mme M. G., and Marcel, A. Histoire de la coiffure des femmes en France. 1886
Franklin, A. L. A. La vie privée d'autrefois; arts et métiers, modes, moeurs, usages des Parisiens du XII. au XVIII. siècle. [v 1]
Grand-Carteret, John. Les élégances de la toilette: robes—chapeaux—coiffures de style, Louis XVI—directoire—empire—restauration (1780-1825). 1911
Handke, Hermann. Der bubikopf von Agamemnon bis Stresemann. c1926
Henning, Johann. Trichologia, id est De capillis veterum collectanea historico-philologica. 1678
Janik, Franz. Lehrbuch zur gründlichen erlernung des damenfrisirens. 1896
Lacroix, Paul, and others. Le livre d'or des métiers. 1850-58. v5
Mineur, A. E. A charitable remonstrance addressed to the wives and maidens of France, touching their dissolute adornments. 1887
Müller, Ernst, and Baumgärtner, F. G. Versuch einer ästhetik der toilette oder winke für damen sich nach den grundregeln der malerei geschmackwoll zu kleiden. 1805
Nissy, E. Album de coiffures historiques avec descriptions. 1927?
Pacichelli, Giambattista. Schediasma juridico-philologicum tripartitum. 1693
Paris. Exposition des arts de la femme. Histoire de la coiffure. 1892
Recueil des coëffures depuis 1589 jusqu'en 1778. 1779
Recueil général de coeffures de différents gouts. 1778

Hair-dressing—*Continued*

Rimmel, Eugene. The book of perfumes. 1867

Speight, Alexanna. A lock of hair: its history, ancient and modern, natural and artistic; with the art of working in the hair. 1871

Stéphane. L'art de la coiffure féminine, son histoire à travers les siècles. 1932

Stewart, James. Plocacosmos: or, The whole art of hair dressing. 1782

Vassetz, de. Traité contre le luxe des coeffures. 1694

Villermont, Marie, comtesse de. Histoire de la coiffure féminine. 1891

See also Beard; Wigs

Ancient times

Krause, J. H. Plotina, oder Die kostüme des haupthaares bei den völkern der alten welt mit berücksichtigung einiger kostüme neuerer völker in kosmetischer, ästhetischer und artistischer beziehung dargestellt. 1858

Raynaud, Théophile. Anselmus Solerivs Cemeliensis. De pileo, caeterisque capitis tegminibus tam sacris, quàm profanis. 1671

Stellartius, Prosper. De coronis et tonsuris paganorum, Judaeorum, Christianorum, libri tres. 1625

16th century

Guerra, Giovanni. Varie acconciature di teste usate da nobilissime dame in diverse cittadi d'Italia. ca1570

Hotman, Antoine. Jucundus & verè lectu dignus de barba et coma. 1628

17th century

Hollar, Wenceslaus. Reisbuchlein von allerlei gesichter und etlichen frembden trachten. 1636

Junius, Hadrianus. Hadriani Iunii Hornani Medici animadversorū libri sex, omnigenae lectionis thesaurus ... Ejusdem de coma commentarium. 1556

Rango, K. T. De capillamentis seu vulgo parucquen. 1663

Saumaise, Claude de. Ober het lang haair der mannen en de lokken der vrouwen. 1645

18th century

Boxhorn, M. Z. van. Spiegeltjen, vertoonende 't lanck ende cort hayr, by de Hollanders ende Zeelanders ghedragen. 1742

Copia eines unbedachtsamen schreibens über die heutige fontangen-tracht und entblössung des halses. 1704

Costumes françois et la parure des dames. 1776-?

Depain. Coeffures de dames. 17-?

Les différens goûts et nouvelles modes de coeffures. ca1775

Etrennes des jolies femmes, ou almanach de la beauté. 1783

Gallerie des modes et costumes françai dessinés d'après nature, gravés par le plus célèbres artistes en ce genre, e colorés avec le plus grand soin par Madame Le Beau. 1778-1788

Garsault, F. A. P. de. Art du perruquier 1767

Lathrop, Barnabas. Poem on the absurdity and sinfulness of wearing high rolls 1782?

Lefèvre, maître coiffeur. Traité des principes de l'art de la coëffure des femmes 1738

Legros, coiffeur. L'art de la coëffure de dames françoises, avec des estampes, o sont représentées les têtes coeffées 1768

Manuel des toilettes; dedié aux dames 1777-78

Marchand, J. H. L'enciclopédie car cassiere: ou Tableaux des coiffures la mode: gravés sur les desseins des pe tites-maîtresses de Paris. 1763

Marchand, J. H. L'enciclopédie perru quiere. 1757

Mark, Quirin. Coiffures de femmes ca1710?

Les modes parisiennes; ou Manuel d toilette. 1781

Nénot. La toilette des graces, ou Jo recueil des coëffures nouvellement. 178

Souvenir à l'Angloise et recueil de coif fures. 1780

Le trésor des grâces ou la parure d Vénus, mis au jour par le favori du bea sexe. 1784

Uzanne, L. O. Coiffures de style; l parure excentrique, epoque Louis xv 1895

Woestyn, Eugène. Le livre de la coiffur ca1850

19th century

Ackermann, Rudolph. Changeable ladies being an assemblage of moveable huma features. 1819

The art of dress; or Guide to the toilette with directions for adapting the vario parts of the female costume to the com plexion and figure. 1839

Coiffures de femmes. ca.1825

Creer, Edwin. Lessons in hairdressing 1887

Croisat, ed. Les cent-un coiffeurs de to les pays. 1836-41

Croisat. Méthode de coiffure. 1831

Croisat. Théorie de l'art du coiffeur, o méthode à suivre, pour approprier l coiffure aux traits, l'âge et la statur 1847

Debucourt, P. L. Recueil de têtes et coi fures modernes à l'usage des jeunes pe sonnes qui dessinent. 1801-04

Duchesne, coiffeur. De la necessité de coiffure pour les hommes distingués: s rapports avec la civilisation suivi de manière de mettre son chapeau. 1826

Ellett, Mrs E. F. L. The queens American society. 1867

Hair-dressing—19th century—*Continued*
Ellet, Mrs E. F. L. The court circles of the republic. 1869
Galland, V. A. Der vollkommene damenfriseur. 1830
Grévedon, P. L. H. Alphabet des dames ou Recueil de vingt cinq portraits de fantaisie. 1833
Grévedon, P. L. H. Artisanne, grisette, jeune fille et dame. 183-?
Die kunst in der liebe und freundschaft eine glückliche wahl zu treffen 1816
Lafoy, J. B. M. D. The complete coiffeur. 1817
Lanté, L. M. Costumes et coiffures de Paris haute et moyenne classes. ca1830
Lichtenfeld, Joseph. Principles of modern hairdressing. ca1882
Mallemont, A. Album de coiffures travesties, première série; modèles de la coiffure française illustrée, 1889-1898. 1907
Mallemont, A. Manuel de la coiffure de dames. 1898
Rothe de Nugent, D. Anti-Titus, ou La critique de la mode des cheveux coupés, pour les femmes. 1809
Rowland, Alexander. The human hair, popularly and physiologically considered, with special reference to its preservation, improvement and adornment and the various modes of its decoration in all countries. 1853
Villaret, P. L'art de se coiffer soi-même enseigné aux dames. 1828
Villaret, P. Le coiffeur de la cour et de la ville. 1829

Periodicals

Die Coiffure. 1868-1901
Illustrirte coiffure. 1878-92
Neue Wiener friseur-zeitung. 1887+
Palette, J. N. Journal de coëffure ou l'art du coëffeur. 1802-10

20th century

Alexandre, Paul. La beauté de la chevelure. 1924
Foan, G. A., ed. The art and craft of hairdressing. 1931
Gussmann, Paul. Lehrbuch für den perückenmacher und tischarbeiter ... Leitfaden für fachschulen, anfänger und vorgeschrittene. 1909
Korf, Frederick. Art and fundamentals of hairdressing. c1923
Ledoux, Hector. 50 leçons de coiffure: coupe, mise en plis, ondulation. 1931
Müller, F. R. Das moderne friseurgewerbe in wort und bild. 192-?
Woodbury, W. A. Hair dressing and tinting. c1915

Periodicals

Le Coiffure de Paris. 1910+
Women; the hairstyle and beauty review. 1933+

Arabs

Baker, Sir S. W. The Nile tributaries of Abyssinia. 1868

China

Blondel, Spire. L'art capillaire dans l'Inde, à la Chine et au Japon. 1889

France

Brittany

Bigot, Maurice. Les coiffes bretonnes, 100 modèles différents. 1928

Normandy

Canel, Alfred. Histoire de la barbe et des cheveux en Normandie. 1859

Poitou

Gelin, Henri. Les coiffes poitevines, les bijoux poitevins. 1898

Greece, Ancient

Bremer, Walther. Die haartracht des mannes in archaischgriechischer zeit. 1911
Gronovius, Jacobus. Thesaurus Graecarum antiquitatum. 1732-37
British museum. Department of coins and medals. Guide to the principal gold and silver coins of the ancients, from circ. B.C. 700 to A.D. 1. 1895

India

Blondel, Spire. L'art capillaire dans l'Inde, à la Chine et au Japon. 1889

Japan

Blondel, Spire. L'art capillaire dans l'Inde, à la Chine et au Japon. 1889
I͡Akoviev, Aleksandr, and Elis͡eev, S. G. Le théâtre japonais (kabuki). 1933

Rome, Ancient

Du Choul, Guillaume. Discours de la religion des anciens Romains, de la castrametation & discipline militaire d'iceux, des bains & antiques exercitations grecques & romaines. 1567
Guasco, F. E. Delle ornatrici, e de' loro uffizi, ed insieme della superstizione de' gentili nella chioma. 1775
Hulsius, Levinus. XII. primorum caesarum et LXIII. ipsorum uxorum et parentum ex antiquis numismatibus, in aere incisae, effigies. 1597
Steininger, Rudolph. Die weiblichen haartrachten im ersten jahrhundert der römischen kaiserzeit. 1909
British museum. Department of coins and medals. Guide to the principal gold and silver coins of the ancients, from circ. B.C. 700 to A.D. 1. 1895

Spain

Hispanic society of America. Spain costume details: women's coiffure. 1931?
Hispanic society of America. Women's coiffure: Candelario, Salamanca. 1931

Hair dressing and tinting. Woodbury, W. A.

Haire, Frances Hamilton
The American costume book, by Frances H. Haire ... illustrations by Gertrude Moser. New York, A. S. Barnes 1934
xi,164p. illus. col.pl. Q. $5
Costume index. LC 34-27110

Haire, Frances H.—*Continued*
The folk costume book; illustrated by Gertrude Moser. Rev. and enl. ed. New York, A. S. Barnes and company 1934
150p. 22 col.pl. Q.
First edition, 1926. New edition has two new plates (Austria and Portugal) and references to pattern numbers of Pictorial review, McCall's etc.
Bibliography: 2d leaf before p3
Costume index. LC 34-6430, 26-5370 (1926 ed.)

The **hairstyle** and beauty review for all women. See note under Women, the hairstyle and beauty review

Hairstyle review. See Women, the hairstyle and beauty review

Hake, Ormond. See Heathcote, J. M., and others. Skating

Hale, Philip Leslie
Great portraits, women. Boston, Mass. Bates & Guild 1909
83p. front. ports. Q. $1.50
LC 9-30058

Hale, Sara Josepha
(ed.) Godey's magazine

Halévy, Ludovic. See Meilhac, Henri, jt. auth.

Halkett, George Roland
(illus.) Hunt, Mrs M. R. Our grandmothers' gowns

Hall, Mrs Florence Marion (Howe)
Good form for all occasions; a manual of manners, dress and entertainment for both men and women. New York and London, Harper 1914
228p. D.
LC 14-10610

Hall, George
The gypsy's parson: his experiences and adventures. London, S. Low, Marston & co. 1915
xii,307p. front. pl. ports. O.
LC 16-6512

Hall, James. See McKenney, T. L., jt. auth.

Hall, Joseph Sparkes
The book of the feet; a history of boots and shoes. London, Simpkin, Marshall & co 1846
2 l. 148p. illus. pl. D.
"With illustrations of the fashions of the Egyptians, Hebrews, Persians, Greeks, and Romans; and the prevailing style throughout Europe, during the Middle-ages down to the present period." Subtitle
Published also "from the second London edition with a history of boots and shoes in the United States" (New York, W. H. Graham 1847)
Also in German translation: *Das illustrirte schusterbüchlein. Mit einem anhang: Die entstehung der hühneraugen* (Leipzig, O. Spamer 1852)
Colas 1373, 1374 (German tr.). Lipperheide 1739 (German tr.) LC 8-36578 (1847 ed.)

Hall, Mabel Lillian
Fashion drawing and dress design, a handbook dealing with proportion, construction, pose and draping of the adult and child figure. London, New York [etc.] I. Pitman & sons 1928
xvi,163p. front. illus. O.
LC 28-20325

Hall, Maud R.
English church needlework; a handbook for workers and designers. London G. Richards; New York, E. P. Dutton 1901
139p. illus. pl. front. Q.
LC 2-17261

Hall, Thomas
"Effects" and adventures of Raby Rattler gent. [with illus. by S. P. Fletcher London, Saunders & Otley 1845
645p. 28pl. O.
Plates show European dress of the nineteenth century as worn in Ireland

Halle. See Germany—Prussia—Halle

Hallé, N.
(illus.) Guer, J. A. Moeurs et usages des Turcs

Hallett, Holt Samuel. See Colquhoun, A. R. Amongst the Shans

Hallmar, Karel
(tr.) Lexová, Irena. Ancient Egyptian dances

[**Hallmark, Harrydele**]
The well-dressed woman, by Anne Rittenhouse [pseud.] New York and London Harper 1924
xii,216p. O.
LC 24-19911

Hallock, Gerard. See Sayles, Alexander jt. auth.

Die **Halloren** in ihrer alten tracht. Kirchhoff, Alfred

Hambly, Wilfrid Dyson
The history of tattooing and its significance, with some account of other forms of corporal marking. London, H. F & G. Witherby 1925
346p. front. 16 illus. 16pl. fold.map. O 25s
LC 26-2827

Hambridge, Ethel R.
Simple dressmaking explained and illustrated. New York, E. P. Dutton [1917]
vii,200p. illus. O.
LC A19-94

[**Hambro, Charles Joachim, baron**]
Edda; or, The tales of a grandmother History of Denmark, from the earliest ages to the accession of the Oldenburg dynasty, A. D. 1448. Ed. by Philojuvenis [pseud.] London, J. Nisbet 1875
3p.l. 398p. illus. O.
LC 4-35912

Hamburg. See Germany—Hamburg; Street venders—Germany—Hamburg

Hamburg. Stadtbibliothek. Mss.
Huon Capet. Der Huge Scheppel der gräfin Elisabeth von Nassau-Saarbrücken. 1905

Hamburger pflanzen-bilder. Koch, Rud.

Das **hamburgische** militär bis zum jahre 1811 und die hanseatische legion. Gaedechens, C. F.

Hamburgische trachten. Heckscher, Joseph

Hamburgische trachten. Suhr, Christoffer

Hamburgs bürgerbewaffnung. Gaedechens C. F.

Hamburgs bürger-bewaffnung. Rosmäsler F. H. W.

Hamckem, Martin
Frisia, seu De viris rebusque Frisiae illustribus libri duo. Amstelodami, apud J. Janssonium 1623
16,131 l. illus. 54 ports. Q.
Lipperheide 932

Hamconius, Martin. See Hamckem, Martin

Hamdī, O., bey, and Launay, Marie de
Les costumes populaires de la Turquie en 1873. Ouvrage publié sous le patronage de la Commission impériale ottomane pour l'Exposition universelle de Vienne ... Phototypie de Sébah. Constantinople, Impr. du "Levant times & shipping gazette" 1873
319,vii p. 74pl. 37x28½cm.
Colas 1375. Lipperheide 1441. LC 8-32179

Hamdī, O., bey, and Reinach, Théodore
Une nécropole royale à Sidon; fouilles de Hamdy bey. Paris, E. Leroux 1892
413p. illus. F. and portfolio of XLVI(i.e. 45) pl.(part col.; incl.plans) F.
"Note bibliographique": p[125]-26
"Observations anthropologiques sur les crânes de la nécropole royale de Sidon et sur le corps du roi Tabnit, par M. Ernest Chantre" p[401]-09
LC 10-4743

Hamdy, bey. See Hamdi, O., bey

Hamelmann, Hermann
(comp.) Oldenburgisch chronicon. Das ist beschreibung der löblichen uhralten grafen zu Oldenburg und Delmenhorst &c. Von welchen die jetztige könige zu Dennmarck u. hertzogen zu Holstein entsprossen. Oldenburg, W. Berendts erben 1599
42 l. 494p. 8 l. 123 illus. F.
Lipperheide 704

Hamilton, Angus
Afghanistan, by Angus Hamilton. London, W. Heinemann 1906
xxi,562p. incl.front.(port.) illus. pl. 2 plans. fold.map. O.
"Authorities consulted": p [xiii]-xiv
LC 6-41815

Korea. New York, Scribner 1904
xliii,313p. front. pl. fold.map. O.
LC 4-7337

Hamilton, Augusta, lady
Marriage rites, customs and ceremonies of all nations of the universe. London, Chapple 1822
400p. O.
Ceremonies and dress are described for countries in various parts of the world

Hamilton, Emma, lady
Lady Hamilton's attitudes. See Rehberg, Friedrich. Drawings faithfully copied from nature at Naples

Hamilton, J.
(engr.) Grose, Francis. A treatise on ancient armour and weapons

Hamilton, Louis
Canada. New York, Westermann 1926
xxxii p. 288pl. map. Q. $4.50 (Orbis terrarum)
Shows Canadian Indians and Eskimos
Costume index

(tr.) Boerschmann, Ernst. Picturesque China

(tr.) Tilke, Max. Oriental costumes

Hammarstedt, Edvard
Allmogens byggnadssätt, boningsinredning och dräkt, af N. E. Hammarstedt. [Stockholm, 1907?]
[28]p. illus. O.
From *Uppland. Skildring av land och folk* v2, p321-48
LC 21-14253

Hammer, Armand
The quest of the Romanoff treasure; foreword by Walter Duranty. New York, W. F. Payson [c1932]
x,241p. front. pl. ports. facsims. O.
LC 32-33389

Hammer, F. W.
(comp.) Das königlich preussische heer in seiner gegenwärtigen uniformirung. Berlin, E. H. Schroeder [1862-1865]
1 l. 30 col.pl. F.
Published in 15 parts. Plates are after A. von Werner and R. Meinhardt. Parts 1-9 published by Hammer
Colas 1376. Lipperheide 2183

Hammerstein, Hans von
Trachten der Alpenländer in zehnfarbigen wiedergaben von vierhundert vorbildlichen trachtenstücken aus privaten und öffentlichen sammlungen. Wien, H. Reichner 1937
60p. col.illus. O.
Shows costume worn in the Austrian Alps
LC 38-1835

Hammerton, Sir John Alexander
(ed.) Manners & customs of mankind. London, Amalgamated press; New York, W. H. Wise 1931-32
1356p. illus. col.pl. Q. $14.85, o.p.
Cover-title. Paged continuously. Issued in parts. Some plates printed on both sides. At head of title: "Entirely new pictorial work of great educational value, describing the most fascinating side of human life." Pictures costume of many parts of the world. Index
Costume index. LC 37-15872

(ed.) Peoples of all nations

(ed.) Wonders of the past; the romance of antiquity and its splendours; with more than 1000 illustrations including many full page plates in colour. New York and London, G. P. Putnam's sons, 1923-24
4v. col.front. pl.(part col.) Q. ea $5
Has a few good color plates showing costume of ancient Egypt
Costume index. LC 23-12917

Hammond, Edith Cary
Industrial drawing for girls; design principles applied to dress. New York, Redfield brothers 1912
103p. illus.(part col.) O.
LC 12-16968

Hammond, William
Masonic emblems and jewels, treasures at Freemasons' hall, London. London, G. Philip; [etc.] 1917
xi,91p. col.front. pl.(part col.) port. facsims. O.
LC 17-21927

Hampe, Theodor
Die fahrenden leute in der deutschen vergangenheit, mit 122 abbildungen und beilagen nach originalen, grösstenteils

Hampe, Theodor—*Continued*
aus dem fünfzehnten bis achtzehnten jahrhundert. Leipzig, E. Diederichs 1902
127p. 117 illus. pl. port. facsim. Q. (Monographien zur deutschen kulturgeschichte. bd. 10)
Lipperheide 605e. LC 3-9256

Der zinnsoldat; ein deutsches spielzeug; mit 186 abbildungen. Berlin, H. Stubenrauch 1924
116p. illus. 36pl. on 18 l. 20x16½cm. (Kleine volkskundliche bücherei. 1. bd.)
LC 25-11537

(ed.) Weiditz, Christoph. Das trachtenbuch

Hampel, József
Alterthümer der bronzezeit in Ungarn. Budapest, F. Kilian 1887
16p. 127pl.(incl. ca 1300 illus.) O.
A second edition was published 1890
Lipperheide 300

Han, Weygand, and Rab, Georg
Modelbůch neuw aller art nehens uñ stickens. Franckfurt am Mayn, [The authors] 1562
42,41 l. 81p. illus.(designs) Q.
Lipperheide 3890

Hanau, Ch.
Fourrures et pelleteries. Paris, Comité français des expositions à l'étranger [1913]
102p. illus. pl. O.
"Exposition internationale des industries et du travail de Turin, 1911. Groupe XX Classe 133A." Subtitle

Hanauer, Charles Auguste
Les paysans de l'Alsace au moyen-âge; études sur les Cours colongères de l'Alsace. Paris, Durand; Strasbourg, Salomon 1865
xv,351p. O. 6fr.

Hand-made laces from the South Kensington museum. Cole, A. S.

Handbook of American Indians north of Mexico. Hodge, F. W., ed.

Handbook of arms and armor, European and oriental. New York. Metropolitan museum of art

A **handbook** of Christian symbols. Waters, Mrs C. E. C.

Handbook of court and hunting swords, 1660-1820. Carrington-Peirce, P.

Handbook of craftwork. Griswold, L. E.

Handbook of embroidery. Higgin, L.

The **hand-book** of needlework. Lambert, Miss A.

Handbook of plain and fancy needlework; containing a description of all the stitches used in plain needlework. London, Ward, Lock & co. ca1886
178p. 234 illus. O.
Lipperheide 4153

Handbook to the ethnographical collections. British museum. Department of British and mediaeval antiquities

Handbuch der ballspiele. Schnell, H.

Handbuch der deutschen alterthumskunde. Lindenschmit, Ludwig

Handbuch der deutschen tracht. Hottenroth, Friedrich

Handbuch der germanischen alterthumskunde. Klemm, G. F.

Handbuch der kostümkunde. Quincke, Wolfgang

Handbuch der ritter- und verdienstorden. Gritzner, Max

Handbuch der uniformkunde. Knoetel, Richard

Handbuch der waffenkunde. Boeheim, Wendelin

Handbuch einer geschichte des kriegwesens. Jähns, Max

Handbuch fürs schöne geschlecht, zum nutzen und vergnügen. 1.-2. jahr. 1785-1786. Altona, J. D. U. Eckhardt 1785-1786
58p. 16 col.pl. D.
Beschreibung und abbildung der nonnen und münch- orden; ein beytrag zur kirchengeschichte volume 1, p153-84; v2 p177-202
Lipperheide 1869

Handbuch fur frauenarbeiten. See Journal des demoiselles. Manuel

Handiwork in modern homes, Woman's. Harrison, Mrs C. C.

Handke, Hermann
Der bubikopf von Agamemnon bis Stresemann; mit 60 zeichnungen von Friedrich Winckler-Tannenberg. Berlin, Verlag für kulturpolitik [c1926]
98p. O.
LC 27-15515

Handkerchiefs
Lescure, Alfred. Collection A. Lescure. Gestickte tücher aus der mitte des XIXe jahrhunderts. 1919?
Lescure, Alfred. Collection A. Lescure. Mouchoirs brodés, milieu du dixneuvième siècle. 190?

Handschriftengemälde und andere bildliche denkmäler der deutschen dichter des 12.-14. jahrhunderts. Hagen, F. H. von der

Der **handschuh**; ein vademecum für menschen von geschmack. Berlin, R. & P. Schaefer [c1914]
96p. illus. O.
LC 14-9383

Der **handwerker** in der deutschen vergangenheit. Mummenhoff, Ernst

Handwerks-umzüge und tänze, fischerstecher u. a. in Nürnberg. A. J. Trautner, ex cud. Noriberga ca1770
12pl. Q.
Lipperheide 782m

Handy, Mrs Willowdean Chatterson
Tattooing in the Marquesas. Honolulu, Hawaii, The museum 1922
32p. 38pl. on 19 l.(1 col.) Q. (Bernice P. Bishop museum. Bulletin 1)
Bibliography: p26
LC 23-15100

Handzeichnungen im königlichen museum zu Berlin. Dürer, Albrecht

Hangard-Maugé
(ed.) Louandre, C. L. Les arts somptuaires

Hannay, James Owen
Irishmen all, by George A. Birmingham [pseud.] ... with twelve illustrations in colour by Jack B. Yeats. London & Edinburgh, T. N. Foulis 1913
224p. 12 mounted col.pl.(incl.front.) O.
LC A14-587

Hannay, James Owen—*Continued*
The lighter side of Irish life, by George A. Birmingham [pseud.] ... Illus. by H. W. Kerr. New York, Frederick A. Stokes [1912]
270p. 16 col.pl.(incl.front.) D.
LC 12-29041

Hannema, Dirk, and Schendel, A. van
Noord- en zuid-nederlandsche schilderkunst der XVII. eeuw. Amsterdam, Bigot en Van Rossum [etc. 1936]
31p. 104pl. F.
Each plate accompanied by leaf with descriptive letterpress. Bibliography p22

Hanover. See Germany—Hanover; also Military costume—Germany—Hanover

Hans majestät konung Carl XV^s vapensamling. Stockholm, P. A. Norstedt 1861
7,34 l. 40pl. F.
Lipperheide 2415

Hans Sachs und seine zeit. Genée, Rudolf

Hansard, George Agar
The book of archery. London, Orme, Brown, Green and Longmans 1840
xxi,456p. 38pl. O.
Also published by H. G. Bohn (1841)
Plates show archers of various countries and periods both men and women, military and sport, and various kinds of bows. Some of the plates are portraits
Lipperheide 3005. LC 5-23441 (1841 ed.)

Hansen, Gotthard von
Die sammlungen inländischer alterthümer und anderer auf die baltischen provinzen bezüglichen gegenstände des Estländischen provinzial-museums, beschrieben. Reval, gedr. bei Lindfors' erben 1875
124p. illus. 11pl. O.
Lipperheide 5036

Hansjakob, Heinrich
Unsere volkstrachten; ein wort zu ihrer erhaltung. Freiburg im Breisgau, Herder 1892
24p. O.
Colas 1377. Lipperheide 3300

Hantich, Henri. See Tyršová, R. F., jt. auth.

Happel, Eberhard Werner
Historia moderna Europae, oder eine historische beschreibung dess heutigen Europae. Ulm, M. Wagner. 1691
968p. 38pl. F.
Plates are by J. B. Homann, W. P. and J. Kilian. They include 24 portraits and ten scenes of battles, celebrations, etc.
Lipperheide 545

(ed.) Thesaurus exoticorum; oder Eine mit ausslåndischen raritåten und geschichten wohlversehene schatz-kammer, fůrstellend die asiastische, africanische und americanische nationes ... Darauff folget eine umståndliche beschreibung von Tůrckey: der Türcken ankunfft; aller sultanen lebens-lauff und bildnůss; aller hohen staats-bedienten ... wie auch ihres propheten Mahomets lebensbeschreibung, und sein verfluchtes gesetz-buch oder Alkoran. Hamburg, T. von Wiering 1688
[879]p. illus.(incl.ports.) 25pl.(19 fold.) 3 fold.maps. F.
Shows costume figures from various parts of the world especially from Turkey
LC 5-7220

Haraeus, Franciscus
Francisci Haræi Annales ducum seu principum Brabantiæ totiusq. Belgii. Tomi tres: quorum primo solius Brabantiæ, secundo Belgii uniti principum res gestæ; tertio belgici tumultus, usque ad inducias anno M.DC.IX. pactas, enarrantur. Antverpiæ, ex officina Plantiniana apud B. Moretum et viduam I. Moreti et I. Meursium 1623
3v. in 2. ports. Q.
Lipperheide 933. LC 17-13852

Harbottle, Thomas Benfield
(tr.) Baye, Joseph, baron de. The industrial arts of the Anglo-Saxons

Harding, D.
(lithgr.) Johnson, John. The costumes of the French Pyrenees

Harding, George Perfect, and Moule, Thomas
Gallery of English historical personages, painted by Hans Holbein, Joseph Van Cleeve, Sir Antonio More ... [and others] from the original paintings by G. Harding, engraved .., by J. Brown, W. and G. Greatbach, accompanied by short biographical sketches by Thomas Moule. London, G. P. Harding 1844
29p. 15pl. F.
Lipperheide 1004

Harding, James Duffield
(illus.) Broke, Sir A. de C., 2d bart. Winter sketches in Lapland

Hardoin, Georges
Les cuirassiers (1672-1886) esquisses anecdotiques; texte et dessins par Dick de Lonlay [pseud.]. Paris, L. Baschet [1887]
39p. 46 illus.(part col.) O. (Cahiers d'enseignement illustré. No. 32, 33)
Lipperheide 2346

Nos gloires militaires; texte et dessins par Dick de Lonlay [pseud.]. Tours, 1888
? p. col.front. illus. O.

Hardouin, E.
(illus.) Ritter, W. L. Java tooneelen uit het leven, karakterschetsen en kleederdrachten van Java's bewoners

Hardy, Edouard Alexandre
Le musée de l'armée. Section des armes et armures. Collections renfermées dans les salles d'armures et dans la galerie des costumes de guerre. Paris, Berger-Levrault 1911
68p. illus. pl. O.

Hardy, Edward John
John Chinaman at home; sketches of men, manners and things in China. New York, Scribner [Woking and London printed] 1905
335p. front. pl. O. $1.50, o.p.
Costume index. LC 5-39529

Hardy, Norman H.
(illus.) Elkington, E. W. The savage South Seas

Hare, T. Leman
(ed.) Macfall, Haldane. Beautiful children immortalised by the masters

Harff, Arnold, ritter von
Die pilgerfahrt des ritters Arnold von Harff von Cöln durch Italien, Syrien, Aegypten, Arabien, Aethiopien, Nubien, Palästina, die Türkei, Frankreich und Spanien, wie er sie in den jahren 1496 bis 1499 vollendet, beschrieben und durch zeichnungen erläutert hat. Nach den ältesten handschriften und mit deren 47 bildern in holzschnitt ... hrsg. von dr. E. von Groote. Cöln, J. M. Heberle (H. Lempertz) 1860
li,280p. 47 illus. O.
The illustrations are taken from manuscripts and show costume of the countries thru which the author travelled
Lipperheide 456. LC 5-8228

The **harim** and the purdah. Cooper, Mrs E. G.

Harkness, Henry
A description of a singular aboriginal race inhabiting the summit of the Neilgherry Hills, or Blue Mountains of Coimbatoor in the southern peninsula of India. London, Smith, Elder, and co. 1832
175p. front. pl. Q.
LC 5-15823

Harlequin
Beaumont, C. W. The history of Harlequin. 1926
Driesen, Otto. Der ursprung des harlekin. 1904
Stockholm. National museum. Recueil de plusieurs fragments des premières comédies italiennes qui ont esté représentées en France sous le regne de Henri III ... présenté par Agne Beijer ... suivi de compositions de m. don Arlequin présentées par P. L. Duchartre. 1928
Stümcke, Heinrich. Die deutsche theaterausstellung, Berlin 1910. 1911

Harlequin crochet. Myra and son

Harman, Ellen Beard
Dress reform: its physiological and moral bearings. A lecture delivered at the hall of the Young men's Christian association, Washington city, February 10, 1862. New York, Davies & Kent 1862
33p. D.
LC CA16-724

Harmand, Adrien
Jeanne d'Arc, ses costumes, son armure. Paris, E. Leroux 1929
400p. illus. F.
Shows French dress of 1425-1450 and 15th century armor of several countries

Harmon, Dudley. See Carpenter, F. G., jt. auth.

Harmonie universelle: musique militaire. Perrot, Émile

Les **harmonies** du son et l'histoire des instruments de musique. Rambosson, J. P.

Harmsworth, Sir Alfred. See Northcliffe, A. C. W. H., 1st viscount

[**Harper, C. D., and Mussey, William P.**]
The pictorial base ball album. Chicago, Mussey & Harper c1888
[62]p. incl.illus. ports. D.
LC 5-24069

Harper's bazaar. v 1+ Nov. 1867+ New York, Harper
Illus. pl. ports. patterns. O.-F.
Published monthly. Weekly to April 1901. Current 1938. Title varies slightly

Harraden, Richard B.
Costume of the various orders in the University of Cambridge, drawn by R. Harraden. Cambridge, R. Harraden 1805
22p. 17 col.pl. F.
Colas 1379

Harrington, Mark Raymond
Certain Caddo sites in Arkansas. New York, Museum of the American Indian, Heye foundation 1920
349p. col.front. illus. 137pl.(part fold.) S. (Indian notes and monographs)
Bibliography: p298-305
LC 21-7827

Old Sauk and Fox beaded garters. New York, Museum of the American Indian, Heye foundation 1920
2p.l. p39-41. pl. D. (Indian notes and monographs, v10, no4)
LC 21-4568

Religion and ceremonies of the Lenape. New York, Museum of the American Indian, Heye foundation 1921
249p. col.front. illus. IX pl.(2 col.) S. (Indian notes and monographs. [Miscellaneous, no19])
Shows masks and dress of the Lenape
Bibliography: p201-05
LC 21-19423

Harriot, Thomas
Admiranda narratio fida tamen, de commodis et incolarum ritibus Virginiae, nuper admodum ad Anglis, qui à dn. Richardo Greinvile ... eò in coloniam anno. .M.D.LXXXV. deducti sunt inventae, sumtus faciente Waltero Raleigh ... Anglico scripta sermone à Thoma Hariot, eiusdem Walteri domestico, in eam coloniam misso ut regionis situm diligenter observaret nunc autem primum Latio donata à C. C. A. Francoforti ad Moenum, typis I. Wecheli, sumtibus vero T. de Bry 1590
34p. 28 col.pl. F. (In Bry, Theodor de. [Grands voyages] pt 1)
Most of the plates are signed T. B. (Theodor de Bry), four are signed with the name of the engraver Gisbert van Veen. Translated by C. de L'Écluse (Carolus Clusius Atrebatensis)
English edition: *A briefe and true report of the Newfoundland of Virginia, of the commodities and of the nature and manners of the naturall inhabitants.* 1590. (very rare). French edition: *Merveilleux et estrange rapport, toutesfois fidele, des commoditez qui se trouvent en Virginia, des façons des naturels habitans dicelle.* 1590. German edition: *Wunderbarliche, doch wahrhafftige erklärung, von der gelegenheit und sitten der wilden in Virginia.* 1590
Lipperheide 1609. LC 1-20221

[**Harris, John, bp. of Llandaff**]
A treatise upon the modes; or A farewell to French kicks. London, J. Roberts 1715
vii,64p. O.

Harris, Vida Agnes. See Gallemore, Margaret, jt. auth.

Harrison, Charles
Theatricals and tableaux vivants for amateurs. London, L. U. Gill 1882
126p. 92 illus. D.
"Giving full directions as to stage arrangements, 'making up', costumes, and acting." Subtitle

Harrison, Mrs Constance (Cary)
Woman's handiwork in modern homes; illus. and five colored plates from designs by Samuel Colman, Rosina Emmet, George Gibson, and others. [New York] Scribner 1881
xii,242p. pl.(part col., incl.front. port) O.
Lipperheide 4135. LC 12-3574

Harrison, Herbert Spencer. See note under Rawling, C. G. The land of the New Guinea pygmies

Harrison, Jane Ellen, and MacColl, Dugald Sutherland
Greek vase paintings; a selection of examples, with preface, introduction and descriptions, by J. E. Harrison & D. S. MacColl. London, T. F. Unwin 1894
32p. col.front. illus. XLIII(i.e. 44)pl.(2 double) sq.F.
Each plate, except the 2 double plates, accompanied by leaf, with descriptive letterpress
LC 1-1000

Harrison, William Henry
The tourist in Portugal ... Illus. from paintings by James Holland. London, R. Jennings; New York, D. Appleton 1839
x,290p. pl. O. (Added t.-p.: Jennings' landscape annual for 1839)
Lipperheide 1226. LC 16-10184

Harrisse, Henry
L.-L. Boilly ... 1761-1845 ... étude suivie d'une description de treize cent soixante tableaux, portraits, dessins et lithographies de cet artiste. Paris, Société de propagation des livres d'art 1898
228p. illus. port. 30pl. Q.
LC 8-11779

Harrwitz, Max
(ed.) Danckwerth, Caspar. Helgoland einst und jetzt

Hart, Albert Bushnell and Hazard, Blanche Evans
Colonial children; selected and annotated by Albert Bushnell Hart ... with the collaboration of Blanche E. Hazard ... New York, Macmillan; [etc.] 1901
xvii,233p. incl.illus. pl. ports. front. D. (Source-readers in American history no. 1)
Original imprint 1901 corrected in manuscript to 1902
LC 2-17870

Hart, Lockyer Willis
Character and costumes of Affghanistan. London, Graves 1843
26 col.pl. F. 84s
Colas 1380

Harting, James Edmund
Bibliotheca accipitraria; a catalogue of books ancient and modern relating to falconry. London, B. Quaritch 1891
xxviii,289p. illus. 26pl.(1 col.) O.
378 titles in 19 languages, arranged chronologically under each language; bibliographical, descriptive, and historical notes, followed by an index to authors, printers, engravers, etc.
Plates are portraits of falconers of various countries and periods and show how the birds were carried. Notes to the illustrations, p241-73
Lipperheide 3034. LC 3-14632

Hartknoch, Christoph
Alt- und neues- Preussen, oder preussische historien. Königsberg, M. Hallervorden 1684
18 l. 668p. 83 illus. 16pl. 2 maps. F.
"Zwey theile: In derer erstem von des landes vorjähriger gelegenheit und nahmen wie auch der völcker so darinnen vor dem Teutschen orden gewohnet ... in dem andern aber von dess Teutschen ordens ursprung desselben wie auch der nachfolgenden herrschaft vornehmsten thaten und kriegen, erbauung der städte ... religion, müntzordnung, rechten und policeywesen gehandelt wird." Subtitle
Views of Prussian cities with figures in the background, and thirty-five portraits of officers of the Teutonic Knights. The portraits of members of the Teutonic Order are reproductions of those in Caspar Henneberger's *Erklerung der preussischen grössern landtaffel oder wapen*
Lipperheide 811

Hartley, D. See Braun, A. A. Figures, faces, and folds, a practical reference book on woman's form and dress

Hartley, Dorothy
Mediæval costume and life; a review of their social aspects arranged under various classes and workers with instructions for making numerous types of dress ... with an introduction and notes by Francis M. Kelly. New York, Scribner; London, B. T. Batsford 1931
xiv,142p. col.front. illus. pl. O. $5; 12s
Colas 1382. Costume index. LC 32-26058

Hartley, Dorothy, and Elliot, Margaret, M. V.
Life and work of the people of England; a pictorial record from contemporary sources. New York, Putnam; London, B. T. Batsford ltd. [1926-31]
6v. fronts. illus.(incl.music) pl. O. (The "People's life & work" series)
Maps and illustrations on lining-papers
Contents: [I] The eleventh to thirteenth centuries, A. D. 1000-1300. [1931] [II] The fourteenth century. [1928] [III] The fifteenth century. [1926] [IV] The sixteenth century. [1926] [V] The seventeenth century. [1928] [VI] The eighteenth century. [1931]
Costume index. LC 26-11647

Hartman, Emil Alvin
Instructive costume design. 1st ed. Pelham, N. Y., E. C. Bridgman [1922]
170p. illus. Q.
LC 23-8523

Hartmann, Anton Theodor
Die Hebräerin am putztische und als braut. Amsterdam, im kunst- und Industrie-comptoir 1809-10
3v. 9pl. O.
"Vorbereitet durch eine übersicht der wichtigsten erfindungen in dem reiche der moden bei den Hebräerinnen von den rohesten anfängen bis zur üppigsten pracht." Subtitle
Lipperheide 135

Hartmann, Robert
Les peuples de l'Afrique; 2. ed. Paris, G. Baillière 1884
260p. 91 illus. O.
Many pictures of men and women of various tribes

Hartmann, Robert—*Continued*
Die völker Afrikas. Leipzig, F. A. Brockhaus 1879
341p. illus. O.

See also Barnim, A. J. B. von, freiherr, jt. auth.

[**Hartshorne, Charles Henry**]
English medieval embroidery. London, J. H. Parker 1848
132p. col.front. 39pl. O.
Lipperheide 3857

Harttung, Julius Albert Georg von Pflugk-. See Pflugk-Harttung, J. A. G. von

Harva, Uno
Die religion der Tscheremissen, von Uno Holmberg; übersetzt von Arno Bussenius. Helsinki, Suomalainen tiedeakatemia 1926
207p. illus. map. O. (Folklore fellows. FF communications no61)
LC 37-3908

Harvey, Fred
American Indians; first families of the Southwest; ed. by J. F. Huckel; 2d ed. Kansas City, Mo. F. Harvey 1920
68p. col.illus. F.
Pictures of Pueblo, Navaho, Hopi, Pima, and Supai Indians
LC 21-19660

Harvey, Richard Seldon
Wig and gown. [New York, 19-?]
p31-36. illus. 2 port. O.
Caption title. Excerpt from *American lawyer*

Harwood, Edith. See Ashbee, C. R.

Haskell, Arnold Lionel
Prelude to ballet; an analysis and a guide to appreciation. London, T. Nelson 1936
x,120p. illus. O. (Little theatre ser.)
LC 37-1507

Hasluck, Paul Nooncree
(ed.) Tailoring; how to make and mend trousers, vests, and coats. London, New York [etc.] Cassell 1901
160p. diagrs. sq.D. (Work handbooks)
LC 2-15109

Haslund-Christensen, Henning
Tents in Mongolia (Yabonah) adventures and experiences among the nomads of Central Asia; translated from the Swedish by Elizabeth Sprigge and Claude Napier. New York, E. P. Dutton [c1934]
xvi,366p. front. illus. (incl. music) pl. ports. maps(1 double) O. $5
Costume index. LC 34-31958

Hassler, Konrad Dieterich
Ulms kunstgeschichte im mittelalter. (In Heideloff, K. A. von, ed. Die kunst des mittelalters in Schwaben)

Hastings, James
Dictionary of the Bible. Edinburgh, Clark; N. Y., Scribner 1898-1902
5v. illus. maps. Q. 130s
Volume 5 is an "extra" volume with indexes, maps and supplementary articles
Contains material on costume of Biblical times under anklet, crescent, dress, earring, embroidery, jewel, and ornament

Hasui, Kawase. See Kawase Hasui

Hatcher, Orie Latham
A book for Shakespeare plays and pageants; a treasury of Elizabethan and Shakespearean detail for producers, stage managers, actors, artists and students. New York, E. P. Dutton 1916
339p. front. illus.(incl. music) pl. ports. O.
Part 1, chapter 12 describes Elizabethan dress. Bibliography: p315-20
LC 16-9570

Hatin, Louis Eugène
Histoire pittoresque des voyages autour du monde. Paris [etc.] Martial Ardant 1847
2v. (fronts.(v2 col.) pl.(part col.) Q.
"Recueil des récits curieux, des scènes variées, des découvertes scientifiques, des moeurs et coutumes qui offrent un intérêt universel. Extrait de Magellan, Byron, Wallis, Bougainville, Surville, Marion, Cook, La Pérouse, d'Entrecasteaux, Peter Dillon, Dumont-d'Urville, etc." Subtitle
A reissue of v4-5 of the author's *Histoire pittoresque des voyages dans les cinq parties du monde* (1843) Plates are by L. Massard and F. Wachsmut and show costume
Lipperheide 574. LC 1-22036

Hats. See Headdress

Hats and how to make them. Patty, V. C.

The **hats** of humanity. Sala, G. A. H.

Hats of the world. Stylepark hats, inc.

Hatt, Gudmund
Arktiske skinddragter i Eurasien og Amerika; en etnografisk studie. København, J. H. Schultz 1914
255p. illus. 16pl. on 4 l. O.
"Litteratur": p[243]-49
LC 32-31944

Moccasins and their relation to the Arctic footwear. Lancaster, Pa. Published for the American anthropological association, the New era printing company [1916]
p149-250. illus. O. (Memoirs of the American anthropological association. v3, no3. July-Sept. 1916)
LC 18-6197

Hauff, H.
Moden und trachten; fragmente zur geschichte des costüms. Stuttgart & Tübingen, J. G. Cotta 1840
328p. O.
Contents: v 1 Vor und nach der revolution; v2 Die männliche tracht; v3 Physiognomie der männlichen welt sonst und jetzt. Eleganz; v4 Zoologisches fragment; v5 Volkstracht und modetracht; v6 Weibliche eleganz; v7 Der deutsche Pariser; v8 Typen der trachten; v9 Antike tracht und weibliche historische bildung; v10 Verfeinerung; v11 Der hut; v12 Der männliche haarputz
Colas 1383. Lipperheide 58

Hauff, Ludwig
Die menschliche schönheit; ihre entwickelung, förderung, vervollkommung und erhaltung. Regensburg, J. G. Bössenecker 1866
399p. O.
Lipperheide 3271

Hauptmomente aus dem leben Sr. majestät Franz I. kaisers von Oesterreich, apostol. königs. Höchle, J. N.

Haus und welt; blatt für Deutschlands frauen. 1.-3. jahrg. 1871-1873. Berlin, F. Ebhardt
3v. illus. F.
Lipperheide 4733

Hauser, Friedrich. See Furtwängler, Adolf, and Reichhold, Karl. Griechische vasenmalerei

Hauser, Ph.
(lithgr.) Mannheimer maskenzug im jahr 1841

Hausfrauen-zeitung, Deutsche. See Frauen reich

Der **Hausfreund.** 1.-44. jahrg. 1858-1901. Berlin, Schlesische buchdruckerei
44v. illus. Q.
Published weekly
Title change: v 1, 1859; v8-14, 1865-71 *Der illustrirte hausfreund; ein familienbuch für alle stände.* Superseded by: *Neue illustrierte wochen-zeitung*
Lipperheide 4685

Hauslab, Franz von
Darstellung der k. k. osterreichischen armee mit allen chargen. Wien, J. Trentsensky [1823]
36 l. 205,20pl. O.
Published in 36 parts. The last twenty plates were published as a supplement
Colas 1384-1385

Über die charakteristischen keunzeichen der geschichtlichen entwickelungs-abschnitte der kriegertracht vom beginn des XVI. bis zu jenem des XIX. jahrhunderts. Wien, C. Gerold's sohn 1864
13p. 6pl.(incl. 25 illus.) O.
"Separatabdruck aus der österreichischen militarischen Zeitschrift, Jahrgang 1864"
Lipperheide 2039

Hausleutner, Philipp Wilhelm Gottlieb
Gallerie der nationen. Stuttgart, J. F. Ebner 1792-1800
54 col.pl. F.
Contents: 1 Asiaten; 2 Amerikaner; 3 Europœer; 4 Afrikaner; 5 Asiaten; 6 Amerikaner; 7 Europäer
Plates are engraved by H. Dunker, L. Ebner, G. Gerhardt and Haas
Colas 1387. Lipperheide 45

Gemählde aller nationen. Frankfurt & Leipzig 1796-1800
4v. fronts. 42pl. D.
Contents: 1 Asiaten; 2 Amerikaner; 3 Afrikaner; 4 Europäer; 5 Asiaten, 2te abt.
Plates are copies in reduced size, of those in the author's *Gallerie der nationen*
Colas 1388. Lipperheide 46

Hausner, Josef
Die k. k. österr. ungar. armee, nach den neuesten adjustirungsvorschriften bildlich dargestellt. Wien, M. Perles [1886]
1 l. 22 col.pl. ob.F.
Colas 1386

Haussoullier, Charles
(tr.) Cole, A. S. Les dentelles anciennes. 1878

Hauthal, Ferdinand
Geschichte der sächsischen armee in wort und bild; 2. aufl. Leipzig, J. G. Bach 1859
172p. 60 col.pl. F.
The first edition *Geschichte der sächsischen armee von ihrer reorganisation nach dem siebenjährigen kriege bis auf unsere zeit* (Leipzig, H. E. Schrader 1858) has 42 colored plates
Colas 1389-1390. Lipperheide 2204 (1st ed.)

Hauttmann, H.
(illus.) Petersen, H. Bildnisse verdienter Lübecker

Havard, Henry
Les quatre derniers siècles: étude artistique; illus. par J. B. Madou. Haarlem, J. M. Schalekamp [1873]
161p. 14pl. F.
The plates are mounted photographic reproductions of pictures by Madou, which were issued 1837 under title: *Physionomie de la société en Europe, depuis 1400 jusqu'à nos jours*

Havell, Robert, and son
(engrs.) Cartwright, J. Selections of the costume of Albania and Greece
(engrs.) Meyrick, Sir S. R., and Smith, C. H. Costume of the original inhabitants of the British islands

Havin
Tracé des objets d'habillemens et d'équipement à l'usage de l'armée norvégienne. No place, ca1880
21pl. F.
Cataloged from Colas
Colas 1391

Hawaii and its people. Twombly, A. S.

Hawaiian feather work. Brigham, W. T.

Hawaiian Islands
Browne, G. W. The new America and the Far East. 1907 v 1-2
Carpenter, F. G. Through the Philippines and Hawaii. 1925
Olivares, José de. Our islands and their people. 1899-1900
Twombly, A. S. Hawaii and its people; the land of rainbow and palm. 1899

See also Featherwork—Hawaiian islands

Haweis, Mrs Mary Eliza (Joy)
The art of dress, by Mrs. H. R. Haweis. London, Chatto & Windus, 1879.
127p. 33 illus. D.
Colas 1392. Lipperheide 3283 LC 11-22645

Hawes, Charles Henry
In the uttermost East; being an account of investigations among the natives and Russian convicts of the island of Sakhalin, with notes of travel in Korea, Siberia, and Manchuria. London, Harper 1903; New York, C. Scribner 1904
xxx,478p. illus. pl. ports. maps(1 fold.) O.
LC 4-15374

Hawke, Pierre
(illus.) René I, d'Anjou, king of Naples and Jerusalem. Oeuvres complètes du roi René

Hawkers & walkers in early America. Wright, R. L.

Hawkes, Ernest William
... The Labrador Eskimo. Ottawa, Government print. bureau 1916
x,235p. illus. XXXV pl. fold.map(in pocket) 25cm. (Canada. Geological survey. Memoir 91. Anthropological series no14)
At head of title: Canada. Dept. of mines
Bibliography: p164-65
LC GS17-194

Hawking. See Falconers

Hawkins, Edward L.
(ed.) Mackey, A. G. An encyclopaedia of freemasonry and of its kindred sciences

Hawks, Francis Lister
(comp.) See Perry, M. C. Narrative of the expedition of an American squadron to the China seas and Japan. v 1

Hawkshaw, John Clarke
Japanese sword-mounts; a descriptive catalogue of the collection of J. C. Hawkshaw ... comp. and illus. by Henri L. Joly. London 1910
xxvi,300p. L pl. (incl.front.) F.
Bibliography: p ix
LC 15-22281

Hay, Augustin Eugène
Recueil des chartes, créations et confirmations des colonels, capitaines, majors, officiers, arbalestriers, archers, arquebusiers, et fusiliers de la ville de Paris ... rev. et augm. de plusieurs pièces jusqu'en l'an 1770. Paris, G. Desprez 1770
276p. 43pl. O.
Colas 1393. Lipperheide 2297

Haycraft, Frank W.
The degrees and hoods of the world's universities & colleges; London and Cheshunt, Cheshunt press 1927
viii,101p. illus. pl. (part col.) Q. 4s 6d, o.p.
LC 27-20230

Haye, Guillaume De La. See La Haye, Guillaume de

Hayes, M. A.
Costume of the British army. ca1850
52 col.pl. F.
Plates lithographed by James Henry Lynch
Cataloged from Colas
Colas 1394

Hayward, Arthur Lawrence
The days of Dickens; a glance at some aspects of early Victorian life in London. New York, E. P. Dutton; London, G. Routledge 1926
xiv,280p. XXXII pl. (incl.front. ports. facsims.) O.
LC 26-11845

Hazard, Blanche Evans. See Hart, A. B., jt. auth.

Hazard, Willis Pope
(ed.) Watson, J. F. Annals of Philadelphia

Head, Barclay Vincent
Guide to the principal gold and silver coins of the ancients. See entry under British museum. Department of coins and medals

Head, Mrs R. E.
The lace & embroidery collector; a guide to collectors of old lace and embroidery. New York, Dodd, Mead 1922
252p. XLIX pl. on 25 l. (incl.front.) D. (The collectors series)
"Books useful to the collector of embroidery and lace": p245-46
LC 22-26237

Head gear, antique and modern. Wadleigh, R. H.

Headdress
Franklin, A. L. A. La vie privée d'autrefois; arts et métiers, modes, moeurs, usages des Parisiens du XII. au XVIII. siècle. [v 17] p 147-320
Genin, J. N. An illustrated history of the hat. 1848
Goater, Mrs A. C. A short treatise on head wear, ancient and modern. c1885
Der hut; ein kulturhistorischer essay, mit benutzung einer amerikanischen arbeit. 1869
Luton, England. Public museum. The romance of the straw hat. 1933
Manchester, Herbert. Romance of men's hats. c1920
Nott, J. C., and Gliddon, G. R. Types of mankind. 1854
Rosenthal, Doris, comp. Pertaining to costume. 1929
Sala, G. A. H. The hats of humanity, historically, humorously and aesthetically considered. 1880?
Timidior, O. Der hut und seine geschichte. 1914
Wadleigh, R. H. Head gear antique and modern. 1879

See also Crowns; Hair-dressing; Helmets; Miters

Bibliography

United States. Library of Congress. Division of bibliography. Brief list of references on the history of hats and head-dresses. 1922

Middle ages

Falke, Jacob von. Zur costumgeschichte des mittelalters. 1861

15th-16th centuries

Karabacek, Josef, ritter von. Abendländische künstler zu Konstantinopel im XV. und XVI. jahrhundert. 1918

18th century

Dighton, Robert. [English heads and coiffures. 1778]

19th century

The art of dress; or Guide to the toilette: with directions for adapting the various parts of the female costume to the complexion and figure. 1839
Bayle-Mouillard, Mme É. F. C. Manuel des dames. 1827
Melton, Henry. Hints on hats adapted to the heads of the people. 1865
Woolley, E. M. A century of hats and the hats of the century. c1923

Periodicals

Der Kopfputz; mode-zeitung für damen. 1878-79
Millinery trade review. 1876+
La Modiste élégante. 1872-75
Panorama der damen-moden; journal-ausg. für kopfputz und lingerie. 1859-65

20th century

Aiken, C. R. Millinery. 1922
Alensis, A. d'. L'enseignement professionel de la mode; méthode moderne et pratique permettant d'exécuter ses chapeaux soimême et les réparer. 1911
The art and craft of ribbonwork. 1921
Hill, Clare. Millinery, theoretical and practical. 1909

Headdress—20th century—*Continued*
Lyon, H. B. Modern millinery. 1922
Patty, V. C. Hats and how to make them. 1925
Reeve, A. J. Practical home millinery. 1912
Stylepark hats, inc. Hats of the world. c1935
Woolley, E. M. A century of hats and the hats of the century. c1923

Periodicals

Chapeaux du Très parisien. 1921-36
Chapeaux élégants. 1927+
Chapeaux modernes. 1904?+
Contemporary modes; the magazine of millinery and accessories. 1934+
Millinery trade review. 1876+

BY COUNTRY

Czechoslovakia

Úprka, Joža. Vazani šátků. 1924?

France

Almanach de la toilette et de la coëffure des dames françoises, suivie d'une dissertation sur celle des dames romaines. 1777

Beytrag zur unterhaltung beim nachttische für frauenzimmer vom stande. 1782

Le bijou des dames. 1779

Costumes françois et la parure des dames. 1776-?

Dergny, Dieudonné. Usages, coutumes et croyances ou livre des choses curieuses. 1885-88

Gagnier, G. Survivance du culte solaire dans les coiffures féminines en Bretagne, Auvergne, Savoie, Bourbonnais, etc. 1910

Grand-Carteret, John. Les élégances de la toilette: robes—chapeaux—coiffures de style, Louis XVI—directoire—empire—restauration (1780-1825). 1911

Langlade, Émile. La marchande de modes de Marie-Antoinette, Rose Bertin. 1911

Langlade, Émile. Rose Bertin, the creator of fashion at the court of Marie-Antoinette. 1913

La modiste universelle. 1876-97?

Recueil des coëffures depuis 1589 jusqu'en 1778. 1779

Recueil général de coeffures de différents gouts. 1778

Italy

Rica, Giuseppe. L'arte del cappello et della berretta a Monza e a Milano nei secoli XVI-XVIII. 1909

Mexico

Nuttall, Mrs Zelia. Ancient Mexican feather work at the Columbian historical exposition at Madrid. 1895

Nuttall, Mrs Zelia. Standard or headdress? An historical essay on a relic of ancient Mexico. 1888

Philippine islands

Miller, H. H. Philippine hats. 1910

Rome—Ancient

Hulsius, Levinus. XII. primorum caesarum et LXIII. ipsorum uxorum et parentum ex antiquis numismatibus, in aere incisae, effigies. 1597

Headdress, Military
Margerand, J. Les coiffures de l'armée française. 1909-24

Headland, Isaac Taylor
The Chinese boy and girl. New York, Chicago [etc.] Fleming H. Revell [1901]
176p. incl.front. illus. pl. O.
LC 1-26211

Heads of the people. Meadows, Kenny

Health. See Hygiene of dress

Health and beauty in dress. Ballin, A. S.

Health-culture. Jaeger, Gustav

Heard, Gerald
Narcissus, an anatomy of clothes, by Gerald Heard. New York, E. P. Dutton c1924
150p. illus. D. (To-day and to-morrow series)
LC 24-31296

The **heart** of Africa. Schweinfurth, G. A.

Heath, Charles
Beauty's Costume. See entry under Ritchie, Leitch

The Shakspeare gallery; containing the principal female characters in the plays of the great poet. Engraved ... from drawings by the first artists, under the direction and superintendence of Mr. Charles Heath. London, C. Tilt [1836-37]
48 l. front. 44pl. Q.
Plates dated 1836 and 1837. Each plate accompanied by leaf with quotation from the play represented
LC 12-13730

Heath, Miss F.
Pattern-making by paper folding; a simple method of cutting-out underclothing and children's dresses as used in the schools of the London school board. New ed. London, Longmans, Green & co 1895
64p. 18pl. O.

Heath, Henry
The caricaturist's scrap book. Drawn & etched by H. Heath. [London, C. Tilt 1840]
1 l. 59pl. sq.F.
Contents: Omnium gatherum; Demonology & witchcraft; Old ways and new ways; Nautical dictionary; The art of tormenting; Scenes in London; Sayings & doings
Lipperheide 3557. LC 11-29570

Heath, William
British military costume. London, T. McLean 1824
1 p.l. 6 col.pl. 26x37cm.
Colas 1395. LC 29-3848

A collection of interesting subjects of military occurences, costumes, etc. London, T. MacLean ca1823
84 col.pl. Q.
Colas 1396

Health, William—*Continued*

Foreign military costume. London, T. McLean 1823
1 p.l. 6 col.pl. F.
Uniforms of Austria, France, Russia, Prussia, Spain, Persia, Greece, China and Turkey
Colas 1397. LC 29-3847

The life of a soldier; a narrative and descriptive poem. London, Printed for W. Sams 1823
150p. 18 col.pl. Q.
Plates are duplicated in black and white. Shows English military costume of the 19th century
LC 16-278

Military costumes of the British cavalry. London, J. Watson 1820
18 col.pl. F.
Shows members of the Life guards, Horse guards, Seventh hussars, Ninth lancers, Tenth hussars, Twelfth lancers, Thirteenth Light dragoons and other regiments

Parish characters in ten plates, by Paul Pry, esq. [pseud.] [London] T. McLean, 1829
10 col.pl. 26½x37½cm.
Contents: Mr George King—the parish overseer; Mr Primate the churchwarden; Dusty Bob—the parish dustman; Master Fang the parish beadle; Attorney in general to the parish; Master Dogberry the parish watchman; One of the select vestry; Leo Sacks—one of the charity crabs; Caleb Quotem the parish factotum; One of the poor employed to mend the high ways
LC 25-19218

(illus.) Jenkins, James. Martial achievements of Great Britain and her allies. 1815

Heathcote, John Moyer, and others

Skating, by J. M. Heathcote and C. G. Tebbutt; figure-skating by T. Maxwell Witham; with contributions on curling (Rev. John Kerr). tobogganing (Ormond Hake), ice-sailing (Henry A. Buck), bandy (C. G. Tebbutt) Illus. by Charles Whymper and Captain R. M. Alexander and from photographs. London, Longmans, Green 1892
xiv,464p. front. illus. 11pl. D. (The Badminton library of sports and pastimes)
LC 5-23909

Heaton, Harriet A.

The brooches of many nations; ed. by J. Potter Briscoe. With 78 illustrations by the authoress. Nottingham, Murray's Nottingham book co. [etc., etc.] 1904
ix-xv,50p. front. 31pl. Q. o.p.
Costume index. LC 15-7101

Heawood, William

The manner and solemnite of the coronation of His Most Gracious Majestie King Charles the Second at Manchester ... 1661 ... Also the ... coronation of their Most Gracious Majesties King George III, and Queen Charlotte at Manchester ... 1761. With biographical notices of the principal persons taking part in each celebration. [Manchester, Imprinted by A. Ireland and co. 1861]
23p. Q.
LC 17-11517

Hebler, C.

(tr.) See note under Sommerlatt, C. V. von. Beschreibung der XXII Schweizerkantone

Die **Hebräerin** am putztische und als braut. Hartmann, A. T.

Hebräische archäologie. Benzinger, Immanuel

Hebrews. See Jews

Heckel, A.

(engr.) Grund, J. G. Afbildning af Nordmands-Dalen, i den kongelige lyst-hauge ved Fredensborg

Heckenauer, Leonhard

(engr.) Eigentliche abbildungen beeder römm. kayserl. wie. auch der röm. königl. majestäten und dann sämtlicher ... churfürsten dess H. Röm. Reichs wie selbige auf dem röm. königl. wahltag in ... Augspurg im jahr 1689 und 1690

Heckscher, Joseph

Chr. Suhrs Hamburgische trachten; eine kunst- und kulturgeschichtliche studie, nebst einem bibliographischen verzeichnis sonstiger hamburgischer trachtenwerke. Berlin, H. Barsdorf 1909
52p. incl.col. pl. F.
List of plates of the original work in German, French and English. "Bibliographisches verzeichnis": p47-52
Also contained in C. Suhr's *Hamburgische trachten,* 1908
LC 15-8906

Hecquet, F.

Tracé descriptif des divers objets d'habillement, d'équipement, de harnachement à l'usâge de l'armée française en 1828 executé d'après les ordres de ... le vicomte de Caux, ministre de la guerre. 1. partie: Armée de ligne. Paris, Langlume 1828
60pl.(5 col.) F.
No more published
Colas 1399

Hedin, Sven Anders

Transhimalaja. Entdeckungen und abenteuer in Tibet. Leipzig, F. A. Brockhaus 1909-12
3v. fronts. pl.(part fold. part col.) ports. maps(part fold.) O.
LC 9-32495

Heemskerk, Martin van

(illus.) Panvinio, Onofrio. Amplissimi ornatissimique triumphi

Das **heer.** Hoppenstedt, Julius

Das **heer** des blauen königs. Hoffmann, Anton

Das **heer,** Österreich-Ungarn. Kählig, Eduard von

Das k. k. **heer** und die österr. und ung. landwehren. Maly, A. von

De **heeren** stadhonderen van Vriesland. Bosch, Johannes van den

Hefner-Alteneck, Jakob Heinrich von

Original-zeichnungen deutscher meister des sechzehnten jahrhunderts zu ausgeführten kunstwerken für könige von

Hefner-Alteneck, Jakob H. von—*Continued*
Frankreich und Spanien und andere fürsten. Frankfurt a. M., H. Keller 1889
8p. 18pl. F.
In portfolio. Contains designs for helmets, shields and other armor. First edition 1865 had title: *Originalentwürfe deutscher meister für prachtrüstigen französicher könige*
Lipperheide 2417. LC 14-15857

Trachten des christlichen mittelalters. Nach gleichzeitigen kunstdenkmalen. Frankfurt am Main, H. Keller; Darmstadt, W. Beyerle 1840-54
3v. in 4. 320 col.pl. Q.
Contents: v 1 Von der ältesten zeit bis zum ende des dreizehnten jahrhunderts. 2v; v2 Vierzehntes und fünfzehntes jahrhunderts. 2v; v3 Sechzehntes jahrhundert. 2v
Published simultaneously with a French title: *Costumes du moyen-âge chrétien d'après les monumens contemporains* (Frankfurt am Main, H. Keller; Darmstadt, W. Beyerle 1840-54)
Colas 1401. Costume index (French ed.) Lipperheide 321

Trachten, kunstwerke und geräthschaften des siebzehnten und achtzehnten jahrhunderts. Frankfurt am Main, H. Keller 1889
28p. 72 col.pl. Q.
Part of the author's *Trachten, kunstwerke und geräthschaften vom frühen mittelalter bis ende des achtzehnten jahrhunderts* including plates 649-720
Colas 1404. Costume index

Trachten, kunstwerke und geräthschaften vom frühen mittelalter bis ende des achtzehnten jahrhunderts nach gleichzeitigen originalen; 2. verm und verb. aufl. Frankfurt am Main, H. Keller 1879-89
10v. 720 col.pl. F.
In portfolios. Combined edition of the author's *Trachten des christlichen mittelalters nach gleichzeitigen kunstdenkmalen* and of *Kunstwerke und geräthschaften des mittelalters und der renaissance* von C. Becker und J. H. von Hefner-Altneck
Also published in French with the title: *Costumes, oeuvres d'art et utensiles depuis le commencement du moyen âge jusqu'à la fin du 18e siècle.* Plate numbers correspond in both sets
Colas 1402-03. Costume index. Lipperheide 323. LC 10-13514

Waffen; ein beitrag zur historischen waffenkunde vom beginn des mittelalters bis gegen ende des siebzehnten jahrhunderts; hundert tafeln nach gleichzeitigen originalen. Frankfurt am Main, H. Keller 1903
58p. 100pl. F.
In portfolio
LC 4-17750

See also Becker, C. jt. auth.

Heger, Franz
(engr.) Debrois, Johann. Urkunde uber die ... kronung ... des königs von Böhmen Leopold des zweiten

Hegi, Franz
Das costume des mittelalters. Zürich, Selbst-verlag 1807
6pl. Q.
Each plate shows four types of Swiss costume of the twelfth to the sixteenth centuries
Colas 1405

Sammlung von schweitzertrachten. Collection des costumes suisses. Zürich, D. Mahler n.d.
29 col.pl. O.
Lipperheide 910

Heicke, Josef
Oesterreichische und russische truppen aus dem ungarischen feldzuge 1849. Wien, L. T. Neumann [1849]
8 col.pl. O.
Colas 1406

Seressaner und Croaten. Wien, L. T. Neumann [1849]
8 col.pl. O.
Colas 1407

Heidelberg university. See Academic costume—Heidelberg university

[**Heideloff, Karl Alexander von**]
Aux héros polonais. Nuremberg, F. Campe ca1830
12 col.pl. Q.
Each plate has title: *Militaires polonais.* They are engraved by Fleischmann after Heideloff's designs
Colas 1410

Costum des deutschen ritterthums. Heideloff, del. Campe ex. Fleischmann sc. Nürnberg, ca1830
12pl. F.
Plates show costume of knights and noblemen from the ninth to the thirteenth centuries
Colas 1409. Lipperheide 348

Gedenkblätter der Universitäten Heidelberg, Prag und Wien, darstellend die ursprünglichen trachten der landmannschaften mit den rektoren, siegeln und schutzpatronen nebst theilweiser stadtansicht im hintergrund. Nürnberg, J. L. Lotzbeck [1848]
3 l. 20 illus. 3pl. Q.
Plates, designed by Heideloff and engraved by Alex. Marx, show academic costume of these universities from their founding
Lipperheide 2032

Volkstrachten des königreichs Würtemburg; nach der natur gezeichnet. Stuttgart, G. Ebner ca1810-15
11 col.pl. Q.
Colas 1408. Lipperheide 796

(ed.) Die kunst des mittelalters in Schwaben. Denkmäler der baukunst, bildnerei und malerei. Hrsg. von C. Heideloff ... unter mitwirkung von architect C. Beisbarth. Mit erläuterndem text von prof. Fr. Müller. Stuttgart, Ebner & Seubert 1855
121p. illus. 30pl.(2 col.) incl.plans F.
"Die Cisterzienser-abtei Bebenhausen im Schönbuch, aufgenommen und beschrieben von dr. Heinrich Leibnitz": p[63]-80. Plates XXIII-XXVII and many of the illustrations show dress
Pages 81-121 have special title page: *Ulms kunstgeschichte im mittelalter,* beschrieben von professor dr. K. D. Hassler ... Zugleich text zu den drei ersten, Ulm betreffenden supplementheften der *Kunst des mittelalters in Schwaben.* Stuttgart, Ebner & Seubert 1864
LC 10-3952

(ed.) [Polnisches militair] Heideloff del. Fleischmann sc. Nürnberg, F. Campe [1832]
11 col.pl. Q.
Lipperheide 2385

Heideloff, Karl A. von—*Continued*
(illus.) Goldene ehrenbuch der gewerbe und zunfte ... aus den zeiten Kaiser Maximilians I

Heideloff, N.
(illus.) Eben, Frédéric, baron d'. The Swedish army; Modèles de l'uniforme militaire adopté dans l'armée royale de Suède

Heiden, Max
Motive. Sammlung von einzelformen aller techniken des kunstgewerbes als vorbilder und studienmaterial. Leipzig, A. Seemann [1892]
7 l. 300pl. F.
Lipperheide 4383

Heider, Gustav
Liturgische gewänder aus dem Stifte St. Blasien im Schwarzwalde, dermalen aufbewahrt im Stifte St. Paul in Kärnten. Wien, K. K. hof- und staatsdruckerei 1860
66p. 10 illus. 10 col.pl. Q.
Taken in part from *Jahrbuch der k. k. Central-Commission zur erforschung und erhaltung der baudenkmale* volume 4
Pictures of garments worn in the twelfth and thirteenth centuries
Lipperheide 1831

Das **heidnische** zeitalter in Schweden. Hildebrand, Hans

Heidrich, Karl
(illus.) Timidior, O. Der hut und seine geschichte

Heierli, Frau Julie
Die Klettgauer- oder Hallauertracht des kantons Schaffhausen; ihr ursprung und ihre entwicklung zur volkstracht, ihr niedergang und weiterbestehen als hallauische bzw. klettgauische festtracht. Basel, Schweizerische gesellschaft für volkskunde 1915
31p. xx pl.(part col.) O.

Schweizer-trachten, vom XVII-XIX jahrhundert. Zürich, Brunner & Hauser [1897-98]
13 l. 70 illus. 36 col.pl. F.
Colas 1412. Costume index. Lipperheide 915

Die volkstrachten der Schweiz. [Erlenbach-Zürich, E. Rentsch,] c1922-32
5v. about 900 illus. pl.(part col.) ports. (part col.) ob.Q.
Contents: v 1 Innerschweiz; v2 Thurgau, St Gallen, Glarus, Appenzel; v3 Bern, Freiburg, Wallis; v4 Zurich, Schaffhausen, Graubunden und Tessin; v5 Mittel- und Westschweiz: Luzern, Zug, Aargau, Solothurn, Basel, Waadt, Neuenburg und Genf
Each volume contains appendices of illustrations separately paged
Colas 1413-1414(v 1-2 only) LC 23-15112

Heikel, Axel Olai
... Mordvalaisten pupuja ja kuoseja. Trachten und muster der Mordvinen. Helsingissä, Suomalen keyallisunden seurankujakamni osakeyhtio [1879]-99
xxviii,43p. 208pl.(part col.) F.

Die volkstrachten in den Ostseeprovincen und in Setukesien. Helsingfors, Druckerei der Finnischen literaturgesellschaft 1909
2v. in 1. illus. 31pl. F. (Suomalais-ugrilainen seura, Helsingfors. Kansatieteellisiä julkaisuja. Travaux ethnographiques. IV Ethnographische forschungen auf dem gebiete der finnischen völkerschaften III)
Translated by E. W. Palander from Finnish and Swedish into German
Contents: v 1 Übersicht; v2 Verzeichniss der zu den trachten gehörenden gegenstände nebst trachtenbildern und tafeln
LC 10-24949

Heilige und selige der römischkatholischen kirche. See Doyé, F. von S. Die alten trachten der mannlichen und weiblichen orden sowie der geistlichen mitglieder der ritterlichen orden

Die **heiligen** monogramme. Versteyl, H. A.

Die **heilkunde** in geschichte u. kunst. Rosenthal, Oskar

[**Heimbucher von Bikessy, J.**]
A Magyar és Horváth országi leg nevezetesebb nemzeti oltözetek hazai gyüjteménie ... Vaterländische vollständige sammlung der merkwürdigsten national costume des königreichs Ungarn und Croatien nach der natur; gezeichnet von einem K.K. ingenieur-office. Herausgegeben von Carl Timlich. Wien, Cappischen kunsthandlung 1816
1 l. 66 col.pl. F.
Colas 1415. Lipperheide 892z

Pannoniens bewohner in ihren volksthümlichen trachten ... nebst ethnograph. erklärung von J. Heinbucher edler von Bikessy. Wien, 1820
Text, and atlas of 78 col.pl. Q.-F.
Second edition of the author's *A Magyar* with a text added and twelve new colored plates. Plates have legends in Hungarian and German. The last twelve are signed Heinbucher Edler Pikessy, pinxit, Carl Beyer, sculpsit. They show popular Hungarian costume and military uniforms, dress of ecclesiastics and nobles, also dress of Czechoslovakia, Yugoslavia and Rumania. Only 200 copies were printed
Colas 1416. Lipperheide 893

Heinbucher von Bikessy, J. See Heimbucher von Bikessy, J.

Heindorf, Auguste
Praktischer unterricht im massnehmen und zuschneiden aller arten weiblicher kleidungs-stücke, sowie auch der hauptsächlichsten männlichen. Quedlinburg & Leipzig, G. Basse 1832
xi,65p. 4pl. O.
"Nebst anweisungen zur verfertigung der vorzüglichsten und schönsten weiblichen handarbeiten und stickereien." Subtitle
Lipperheide 3788

Heine, Emmy
Lehrbücher der handarbeit; die gesammten handarbeitsarten für schule und haus. Leipzig, F. Wagner 1879-80
6v. illus. O.
Contents: Die schule des 1 Strickens; 2 Häkelns; 3 Filet-, knup- und frivolitätenarbeiten; 4 Tapisserie-arbeit [usw.] 5 Wäschenähens [usw.] 6 Tull-durchzugs, stopf- spitzen- [usw.]
Lipperheide 4126

Heine, Ferdinand
Abbildungen der neuen uniformen der königlich sächsischen armee, gezeichnet und lithographirt von Ferdinand Heine, gedruckt von L. Zöllner. Dresden, Morasch und Skerl [1834]
16 col.pl. Q.
Cover title
Colas 3119

Heine, Heinrich
Shakespeares mädchen und frauen, mit erläuterungen. Paris & Leipzig, Brockhaus & Avenarius 1839
228p. 45 ports. O.
Published with revision of text by E. Loewenthal (Berlin, Hoffmann & Campe 1921)

Shakespeare's maidens and women. New York, Printed for subscribers only by Croscup and Sterling [190-]
243-441p. 4 port.(incl.front.) O. (The works of Heinrich Heine, tr. by Charles Godfrey Leland. v2)
Plates accompanied by guard sheet with descriptive letterpress
Translation of his *Shakespeares mädchen und frauen*
LC 16-23784

Heinel, Eduard. See Jarwart, Sixtus, jt. auth.

Heinemann, Franz
Der richter und die rechtspflege in der deutschen vergangenheit; mit 159 abbildungen und beilagen nach den originalen aus dem fünfzehnten bis achtzehnten jahrhundert. [Leipzig, E. Diederichs 1900]
144p. illus. pl. facsims.(part fold.) Q. (Monographien zur deutschen kulturgeschichte, hrsg. von Georg Steinhausen. IV. bd.)
Pictures show judges, courts of justice, prisoners. Many of the illustrations show administration of punishment
Lipperheide 2013. LC G-1099

Heirlooms in miniatures. Wharton, A. H.

Heizo, Ise
Iseke Iwai No Sho. Costume and toilet accessories of a lady of the family of the Count Nobel Ise. 1764
100p. col.illus. Q.
Cataloged from card of the Ryerson library, Chicago

Heksch, Alexander Franz
Die Donau von ihrem ursprung bis an die mündung. Eine schilderung von land und leuten des Donaugebietes. Wien [etc.] A. Hartleben 1881
791p. 172 illus. 25pl. fold.maps. O.
"Verzeichniss der werke und manuscripte, welche bei abfassung dieses buches als quellen dienten": p[v]-vi
The illustrations show costume
Lipperheide 840. LC 19-8293

Helbig, Wolfgang
Das homerische epos aus den denkmälern erläutert. Archäologische untersuchungen von W. Helbig. 2. verb. und verm. aufl. Leipzig, B. G. Teubner 1887
x,470p. illus. 2pl.(1 fold.) O.
Contents: Die quellen. Das homerische zeitalter. 1 Tektonisches; 2 Die tracht; 3 Die schmucksachen; 4 Die bewaffnung; 5 Geräte und gefässe, Tracht; 6 Die kunst
Lipperheide 198. LC 5-3857

Helbing, K.
Spitzen-album. Wien, R. v. Waldheim [1877-80]
2v. 40pl. F.
Series 1, 1877; series 2, 1880
Lipperheide 4039

Helden buch. Lundorp, M. C.

Heldenthaten von soldaten der k.k. armee in den Feldzügen gegen die franzosen in den jahren 1792 bis 1799. Bartsch, Adam von, and Kininger, V. G.

Heldt, Sigmund
Abcontersaittung, allerlei ordenspersonen in iren klaidungen und dan viler alten klaidungen, so vor zeiten von fursten, furstin and herrn, auch burger and burgerin, alhie zu Nurmberg and vilen andern orten getragen sinnt worden, und an eins theils orten noch getragen werden. Dessgleichen allerlei turnier und gestech von hohen und nidern stenden. Letzlich die bauerschafft wass ihre klaidung, grosse arbeit, und widerum ergetzlichkeit gewesen ist. Nürnberg 1560-80
506 l. 867 col.illus. F.
Manuscript from the Lipperheide collection now in the possession of the Staatliche kunstbibliothek in the Staatliche museen, Berlin
Lipperheide 4

Helgoland
Danckwerth, Caspar. Helgoland einst und jetzt. 1891
Lindemann, Emil. Das deutsche Helgoland. 1913

Helgoland einst und jetzt. Danckwerth, Caspar

Heligoland. See Helgoland

Hellwag, Fritz
Die polizei in der karikatur. Berlin, Gersbach 1926
125p. illus. pl.(part col.) O. (Die polizei in einzeldarstellungen. Bd. 12)

Hellwald, Friedrich Anton Heller von
Centralasien. Landschaften und völker in Kaschgar, Turkestan, Kaschmir und Tibet. 2. verm. und verb. ausg. Leipzig, O. Spamer [1880]
viii,446p. front.illus. fold.maps. O. (Otto Spamer's Illustrirte bibliothek der länder- u. völkerkunde)
LC G-821

Helm, Rudolf
Deutsche bauerntrachten. See entry under Retzlaff, Hans

Deutsche volkstrachten, aus der sammlung des Germanischen museums in Nürnberg ... mit 115 trachtenbildern auf 48 schwarzen und 8 farbigen tafeln. München, J. F. Lehmann 1932
20p. 56pl.(8 col.) on 32 l. O.
Costume index. LC 34-22349

Helm, Seb., and Ströbel, Christian
Die feldgraue friedens- und kriegs- bekleidung d. k. bayer. armee. München, T. Riedel 1918
225 l. 74p. col.pl. Q.
Contents: I Offiziere und obere beamte; II Mannschaften; III Einheitsmantel

Helm und mitra. Seesselberg, W. F., ed.

Der **helm** von seinem ursprunge bis gegen die mitte des siebzehnten jahrhunderts. Suttner, Gustav, freiherr von

Helman, Isidore Stanislas
Abrégé historique des principaux traits de la vie de Confucius ... orné de 24 estampes ... gravees par Helman d'après des dessins originaux de la Chine. Envoyés à Paris par M. Amiot ... et tirés du Cabinet de Mr Bertin. Paris, L'auteur ca1790
24 l. 24pl. Q.
Also published in the series *Collection des moralistes anciens* with same collation
Lipperheide 1519

Helman, Isidore S.—*Continued*
Faits mémorables des empereurs de la Chine, tirés des annales chinoises ... estampes ... gravées par Helman d'après les dessins originaux de la Chine. Paris, L'auteur et M. Ponce 1788
24 l. 24pl. O.

Helmets
Dean, Bashford. Helmets and body armor in modern warfare. 1920
Suttner, Gustav, freiherr von. Der helm von seinem ursprunge bis gegen die mitte des siebzehnten jahrhunderts, namentlich dessen hauptformen in Deutschland, Frankreich und England. 1878

Ancient times

Benndorf, Otto. Antike gesichtshelme und sepulcralmasken. 1878

Gauls

Fourdrignier, Edouard. Notes archéologiques. Double sépulture gauloise de la Gorge-Meillet, territoire de Somme-Tourbe (Marne). Étude sur les chars gaulois et les casques dans la Marne. 1878

Middle ages

Seesselberg, W. F., ed. Helm und mitra; studien und entwürfe in mittelalterlicher kunst. 1905?

Helmets and body armor in modern warfare. Dean, Bashford

Helmin, Margaretha
Kunst- und fleiss- übende nadel-ergötzungen, oder neü-erfundenes neh- und stick-buch, worin dem solche schöne wissenschafft liebendem, frauenzimmer, allerhand, zu vielen tachen anständige, muster und risse, nach der neuesten façon. Nürnberg, J. C. Weigel ca1700
3v. 156pl. Q.
Lipperheide 3924

Heluicus, Nicolaus. See Helwig, Nicolaus

Die **Helvetische** legion, 1798-1804. Escher, A. von

Helvicus, Nicolaus. See Helwig, Nicolaus

Helwig, Nicolaus
Theatrum hystoriae universalis Catholico Protestantiv. Das ist wahrhafftige hÿstorische beschreibung aller gedenckwürdigen geschichten, welche sich von dem 1517 jahr und von anfang des religionstreits zwischen der Römischen Catholischen kirchen und D. Martino Luthero ... zugetragẽ v: unter weÿland den römischen käyss: wie dann auch andern ausländischen und inheÿmischen königen und potentaten biss auff das 1641 jahr verlauffen. [Frankfurt a. M., J. G. Schönwetter 1641]
22 l. 592,551p. 96 illus. 64pl. F.
The illustrations are portraits of noted men of the time and are by Sebastian Furck. The plates are picutres of sieges, battles and other historical events
Lipperheide 531

[Hélyot, Pierre]
Histoire des ordres monastiques, religieux et militaires, et des congregations seculieres de l'un & l'autre sexe, qui ont esté establies jusqu'à present ... avec des figures qui representent tous les differens habillemens de ces ordres & de ces congregations. A Paris, N. Gosselin 1714-19
8v. 810 col.pl. sq.D.
Usually found with plates in black and white only. Vols. 7-8 have imprint: Paris, Chez J. B. Coignard. Volumes 1-5 written by Pierre Hélyot; v6-8 generally attributed to Maximilien Bullot. Plates are engraved by Cl. Duflos, P. Giffart, de Poilly, et Thomassin
Reprinted (Paris, J. B. Coignard 1721) There are many other French editions with slightly different titles.
Italian edition: *Storia degli ordini monastici religiosi e militari* (Lucca 1737-39) Edition in German *Ausführliche geschichte aller geistlichen und weltlichen kloster und ritterorden* (Leipzig, Arkstee & Merkus 1753-56)
Contents: v 1 Préface. Catalogue des livres qui traitent des ordres monastiques, religieux, militaires, & des congregations seculieres, que l'auteur a consultés (p.xxxv-xcviii) Dissertation préliminaire sur l'origine et sur l'antiquité de la vie monastique. Les ordres de saint Antoine, de saint Basile, & des autres fondateurs de la vie monastique en Orient, avec les ordres militaires qui ont suivi leur regle; v2 Les congregations des chanoines reguliers & des chanoinesses regulieres, avec les ordres militaires qui y ont raport; v3-4 Toutes les differences congregations, & les ordres militaires qui ont été soumis à la legle de s. Augustin; v5-6 Toutes les differentes congregations, & les ordres militaires qui ont été soûmis à la regle de s. Benoît; v7 Les ordres de saint François, & autres qui ont des regles particulieres; v8 Toutes les congregations seculieres de l'un & de l'autre sexe, & les ordres militaires & de chevaleries qui ne sont soûmis à aucune des regles de religion
Colas 1417-21. Lipp. 1846-47. LC 17-22660

See also Perugini, G. Album ou collection complète et historique des costumes de la cour de Rome

Hemelryck, Johannes Lodewyk van
Costumes de l'armée belge. Bruxelles, Van den Burggraaff 1828-31
28(?) col.pl. Q.
May be a part of Madou and Hemelryck's *Costumes belgiques*
Colas 2969

See also Madou, J. B., jt. auth.

Hempel, Friedrich
Abbildung merkwürdiger menschen, mit rücksicht auff die trachten verschiedener zeitaltern nach den gemählden und zeichnungen eines Van Dyk, Holbein, Rubens, Hollart und andrer meister. Leipzig, C. F. Hempel 1810?
15 illus. Q.

Die strafen der Chinesen auf XXII ausgemalten kupfern dargestellt und nach dem englischen mit rückseit auf die ältern und neuern werke über China. Châtiments usetés chez les Chinois. Leipzig, Im industrie comptoir [1804]
22 l. 22 col.pl. Q.
Plates are copies of those in G. H. Mason's *The punishments of China*
Colas 1424

See also Geissler, C. G. H. Mahlerische darstellungen der sitten

Hempel, Friedrich, and Geissler, Christian Gottfried Heinrich
Abbildung und beschreibung der völkerstämme und völker unter des russischen kaisers Alexander I. regierung. Leipzig, im Industrie-Comptoir [1803]
136p. 66 col.pl. Q.
Published also in a French edition: *Description de tous les peuples qui se trouvent sous la domination bienfaisante d'Alexandre I;* tr. par M. de Lestiboudois (Paris, Fuchs [1803])
Colas 1422. Lipperheide 1342m

Hempstead, Laurene
Color and line in dress; [with] sketches by Mary Highsmith. New York, Prentice-Hall 1931
xiii,355p. col.front. illus. O.
LC 31-19240

Hendel, Johann Christian
Archiv für deutsche schützengesellschaften. Halle, J. C. Hendel 1802
3v. 90 illus. 12pl. O.
Lipperheide 3003

Henderson, George F.
(tr.) Garcia Cubas, Antonio. The republic of Mexico in 1876

Henderson, Harold Gould
(tr.) Minamoto, Hoshu. An illustrated history of Japanese art

[**Hendrickx**]
Uniformes de l'armée belge, publiés d'après les dessins originaux exécutés par ordre de S. A. R. mgr. le duc de Brabant et sur les documents fournis par le départment de la guerre. Bruxelles, Muquardt 1855
4 col.pl.
A broadsheet with four pictures of Belgian uniforms of 1855
Colas 1425

Henne am Rhyn, Otto
Kulturgeschichte des deutschen volkes. Berlin, G. Grote 1886
2v. 1049 illus. 134pl.(part fold. part col.) ports. facsims.(part fold. part col.) plans(1 fold.) Q.
2. neu bearb. und verm. aufl. 1892-93
Some of the plates are accompanied by guard sheets with descriptive letterpress
Pictures show German costume of various periods, dated. The earlier periods are represented by illustrations from manuscripts and woodcuts of Amman, Hefner-Alteneck and others
Costume index. Lipperheide 604 (2d ed.)
LC 29-15696; A12-1089 (2d ed.)

Henneberg, Alfred, freiherr von
The art & craft of old lace. London, B. T. Batsford [1931]
49p. illus. pl.(part col.; 2 double) F. (The art handicrafts encyclopaedia series)
Descriptive letterpress in German, English, French and Italian on versos facing plates
Bibliography: p49
LC 32-25130

Henneberg, Caspar
Erclerung der preüssischen grössern landtaffel oder wappen. Königsberg 1595
F.
Contains 35 portraits of Prussian noblemen, most of them in their dress as officers of the Teutonic Knights. Copies of the portraits are in Christoph Hartknock's *Alt- und neues Preussen*

Hennebert, Eugène
Nos soldats: infanterie, cavalerie, artillerie, marine, etc. Illus. de F. Hussenot. Paris, Librairie illustrée 1887-88
1016p. illus. O.
Published originally in 127 parts at 10 centimes each

Hennell, Sir Reginald
The history of the King's body guard of the yeomen of the guard (valecti garde domini regis), the oldest permanent body guard of the sovereigns of England, 1485 to 1904. Westminster, A. Constable 1904
xvi,343p. col.front. illus.(incl. plan) pl. (part col.) ports. map, facsims. Q.
LC 4-24736

Hennezel, Henri d'
La mode féminine au XVIIIe siècle. Lyon, Grange et Giraud 1924
xiv,98p. illus. pl. O.
"Ce petit livre . . . est composé de différentes études qui ont paru en 1922-23 et 24 dans la Soierie de Lyon." Introduction
Colas 1426. LC 25-14168

Hennin. See Headdress—15th-16th centuries

Henning, Johann
Trichologia, id est De capillis veterum collectanea historico-philologica. Magdeburgi, J. D. Müller 1678
160p. D.
Lipperheide 1657

Hennings, Emma
Anweisung zur kunst-strickerei zusammengestellt von Charlotte Leander, [pseud.] Erfurt, Hennings & Hopf 1843-47
16v. illus. pl. O.
Each volume a booklet of less than 100 pages with woodcut illustrations, and plates
The first edition of part 1 was published 1842. The seventeenth edition of the set consisted of 12 volumes (Leipzig, H. Wolfert 1874-78)
Lipperheide 4075-4076

Bunte stickmuster in weiss; gezeichnet von Charlotte Leander [pseud.] Erfurt, Hennings & Hopf 1846-47
5v. 30 col.pl. O.
Lipperheide 3953

Filet-schule, oder Gründliche anweisung alle vorkommenden netz-arbeiten anzufertigen; von Charlotte Leander [pseud.] Erfurt, Hennings & Hopf 1843
97p. 13 illus. 11pl. D.
Lipperheide 4080

Häkel-, strick-, und stickmuster gesammelt von Charlotte Leander [pseud.] Erfurt, Hennings & Hopf [1842-43]
8v. 126pl. O.
Lipperheide 4077

Häkelschule für damen; von Charlotte Leander [pseud.] Erfurt, Hennings & Hopf 1850
13v. illus. pl. O.
In thirteen hefte. First edition of hefte 1, 1843
Lipperheide 4081

Kleine häkel-schule, oder die kunst sämmtlich häkelarbeiten zu erlernen; von Charlotte Leander [pseud.] Erfurt, Hennings & Hopf 1849
75p. 26 illus. O.
Lipperheide 4089

Hennings, Emma—*Continued*

Die knöpfel-schule, oder Ausführliche beschreibung von seide, band, perlen und seinen bindfaden: taschen, börsen, kragen, jagdtaschen ... zu knöpfeln. Von Charlotte Leander [pseud.] Erfurt, Hennings & Hopf 1845
2v. 38 illus. 6pl. O.
Lipperheide 4084

Modenheft ... Weibliche handarbeiten, im stricken, sticken, häkeln, filetstricken und andern brauchen. Von Charlotte Leander [pseud.] Erfurt, Hennings & Hopf [1845]-48
6v. illus. pl. O.
First edition of Volume 1, published 1843
Lipperheide 4082

Die neuesten und elegantesten stickmuster in weiss; gezeichnet von Charlotte Leander [pseud.] Erfurt, Hennings & Hopf [1845-46]
13v. 130pl. O.
Lipperheide 3951

Vorlegeblätter zu model-tüchern; von Charlotte Leander [pseud.] Erfurt, Hennings & Hopf [1846]
2v. 16pl. Q.
Lipperheide 3952

Weisshäkel-muster. Als anhang zur häkelschule für damen; gezeichnet von Charlotte Leander [pseud.] 1. heft. Erfurt, Hennings & Hopf 1850
12pl. Q.
Lipperheide 4090

Henricpetri, Adam

General historien der aller namhafftigsten ... geschichten, thaten und handlungen, so sich bey ubergebung und ende des ... keyser Carols des Fünfften und anfange Ferdinanden seines bruders regierung. Basel, S. Henricpetri [1577]
12 l. 615p. illus.(incl.ports.) fold.pl. F.
A history of the period 1555-1561

Henricy, Casimir, and Lacroix, Frédéric

Les moeurs et costumes de tous les peuples d'après les documents les plus authentiques, les voyages les plus récents et les matériaux inédits. Rédigé par Henricy sous la direction de Lacroix. Paris, Librairie ethnographique 1847
2v. 75 col.pl. O.
Volume 1 Afrique; v2 Océanie
Colas 1427

Henriet, Israel

(pub.) Callot, Jacques. Les fantasies de Noble I. Callot

(pub.) Callot, Jacques. Les misères et les mal-heurs de la guerre

Henrion, Mathieu Richard Auguste, baron

Histoire des ordres religieuses. Bruxelles, Société nationale pour la propagation des bons livres 1838
415p. 8pl. D.
Colas 1428. Lipperheide 1880

Henry, Elisa

La charme, suite de compositions gracieuses; lith. par Regnier et Bettanier d'après Elisa Henry. London, Gambart, Junin & co. ca1840
1 l. 6 col.pl. F.
Plates show groups of women in the costume of the time
Colas 1429

Henry, Pierre François

(tr.) Voyages au Pérou, faits dans les années 1791 à 1794

Henry VIII and the English monasteries. Gasquet, F. A., cardinal

Henschel, F. A.

(engr.) Iffland, A. W. Ifflands mimische darstellungen für schauspieler und zeichner

See also Henschel, W., jt. auth.

Henschel, W.

(engr.) Iffland, A. W. Ifflands mimische darstellungen für schauspieler und zeichner

Henschel, W., and Henschel, F. A.

[Cries of Berlin. Berlin] ca1810
24 col.pl. Q.
Colas 1432. Lipperheide 817m

Les Gardes impériales et royales de l'armée française en 1810. [Berlin] ca1810
12 col.pl. Q.
Glasser gives a list of the plates. A modern reproduction was published (Paris, Schulz 1904. 75fr.)
Colas 1431

Kostüme der ganzen preussischen armee. Berlin, J. B. Schiavonetti 1806
24 col.pl. F.
Published in four parts, of six plates each, each part with separate cover. Plates engraved by F. A. Henschel after W. Henschel
Colas 1430. Lipperheide 2156

Hense, Otto

Die modifizierung der maske in der griechischen tragödie; 2. aufl. Freiburg im Breisgau, Herder 1905
38p. illus. Q.
First edition (Freiburg im Breisgau, G. Ragoczy 1902 p207-36) a separate from *Festschr. d. Univ. Freiburg z. 50 jähr. Reg.-Jub. d. Grossh. Friedrich von Baden*

Hensel, Wilhelm

Die lebenden bilder und pantomimischen darstellungen bei dem festspiel: Lalla Rukh, aufgeführt auf dem königlichen schlosse in Berlin den 27sten januar 1821 ... nach der natur gezeichnet von W. Hensel. Berlin, L. W. Wittich 1823
11 l. 12pl. F.
Lipperheide 2537c

Hepke, Felix Victor von

Frankreich. Das heer am ende des neunzehnten jahrhunderts, von Hepke ... Mit einer karte der truppenstandorte und einer armee-einteilung, von Exner. Berlin, A. Schall [1900]
xx p. 2 l. 604p. illus. pl.(part col.) ports. 2 fold.maps, fold.plan, fold.tab. O. (Die heere und flotten der gegenwart v.)
The colored plates show officers and men of various branches including gendarmerie and sapeur-pompiers and the badges and insignia of different ranks
Bibliography: p[599]-600
LC 19-5744

Her Majesty's army, Indian and colonial forces. Richards, Walter

Her Majesty's army ... various regiments now comprising the Queen's forces. Richards, Walter

Heræus, Carl Gustav
Bildnisse der regierenden fürsten und berühmter männer vom vierzehnten bis zum achtzehnten jahrhunderte in einer folgereihe von schaumünzen. Wien, J. G. Heubner 1828
xii,99p. 1 illus. 63pl.(part double) F.
Most of the portraits are of German princes and bishops
Ed. by Anton v. Steinbüchel. "Stellen über Heraeus und dessen nachgelassenes werk": p[vi]-x
Lipperheide 317. LC 16-21675

Heraldic costume
This term is used to indicate costume on which armorial bearings are shown
Ambrosoli, Solone. Numismatica. 1891
Bry, Theodor de. Emblemata nobilitatis. 1894
Bry, J. T. de. Emblemata secularia, mira et iucunda varietate seculi hujus mores. 1611
Burgkmair, Hans. Hans Burgkmair des jüngeren turnierbuch von 1529. 1910
Larchey, Lorédan. Ancien armorial équestre de la Toison d'or et de l'Europe au 15. siècle. 1890
Larchey, Lorédan. Costumes vrais. 1899.

England

Dallaway, James. Inquiries into the origin and progress of the science of heraldry in England. 1793

Germany

Gritzner, Max. Landes- und wappenkunde der brandenburgisch-preussischen monarchie, geschichte ihrer einzelnen landestheile, deren herrscher und wappen. 1894
Mair, P. H. Bericht und anzeigen aller Herren Geschlecht der loblichen Statt Augspurg. 1538?
Zangemeister, K. F. W. Die wappen, helmzierden und standarten der Grossen Heidelberger liederhandschrift (Manesse-codex). 1892

Italy

Freschot, Casimir. La nobilta' veneta, o' sia Tutte le famiglie patrizie con le figure de suoi scudi & arme. 1707-1722?

Heralds
Fox-Davies, A. C. The art of heraldry. 1904

Herbé, Charles Auguste
Costumes français civils, militaires et religieux ... depuis les Gaulois jusqu'en 1834. Paris, Herbé 1835-37
95p. 105 col.pl. Q.
"Avec les meubles, les armes, les armures, l'architecture domestique, les ordres de chevalerie, les étendards et les blasons les plus historiques ... dessinés d'après les historiens et les monumens." Subtitle
Published in 20 parts. According to Colas the plates are drawn in a fanciful manner in the taste of the period of publication
Colas 1433. Lipperheide 1082

Herberger, Theodor
Die ältesten glasgemälde im Dome zu Augsburg mit der geschichte des Dombaus in der romanischen kunstperiode. Augsburg, J. P. Himmer'schen buchdruckerei 1860
38p. 6pl.(5 col.) Q.
According to the author the paintings belong to the end of the 10th or the beginning of the 11th centuries. Costume is described on pages 33-34
Lipperheide 390

Herberstein, Sigmund, freiherr von
Picturae variae quae generosum ac magnificum domi. dominum Sigismundum liberum baronem in Herberstain Neyperg & Guttenhag etc. varias legationes obeuntem exprimunt. Viennae Austriae excudebat R. Hofhalter 1560
11 l. 21 col.illus.(6 full page) Q.
Herberstein was born in Wippach, Carniola, in 1486, and died in Vienna in 1566. The six large illustrations (woodcuts), three of which belong to the year 1559, show Herberstein in different costumes worn by him as an ambassador in foreign countries. Nine of the smaller illustrations show noblemen of the time
Lipperheide 632

Herbillon, A.
(tr.) Lange, Gustav. L'armée allemande sous l'empereur Guillaume II

Hercolani, Antonio
Storia e costumi delle contrade di Siena. Firenze, A. Hercolani 1845
83p. 40 col.pl. F.
Lipperheide 2873

Herder, Natalie von
Album für weisse und bunte häkel- und filetarbeiten; 3. aufl. Berlin, S. Mode [1870]
2 l. 24pl.(4 col.) F.
Lipperheide 4105

Herdtle, Eduard
Stilisirte blumen aus allen kunstepochen ... Vorbilder für das freihand- und musterzeichnen; 2. aufl. Stuttgart, F. Loewe [1881]
2 l. 21pl. F.
First edition 1877
Lipperheide 4366

Hergsell, Gustav
Die fechtkunst im XV. und XVI. jahrhunderte. Prag, C. Bellman 1896
631p. 48 illus. 48pl. O.
Lipperheide 2996b

Hering, George Edwards
Sketches on the Danube, in Hungary and Transylvania. London, 1838
1 l. 26 col.pl. F.

Hérisset
(engr.) Acteurs du theatre italien

The **heritage** of dress. Webb, W. M.

Herlaut, Auguste Philippe
Le costume militaire en France; par le lieutenant Herlaut. 1-5. series. Paris, G. Vitry 1912-13
5v. O.
At head of title: *Enseignement par les projections lumineuses*... 1re ser. Des origines à Henri IV; 2e ser. Le XVIIe et le XVIIIe siècles, jusqu'à la Révolution; 3e ser. La Révolution. L'Empire; 4e ser. La restauration. Louis-Philippe; 5e ser. Le second Empire
Colas 1434

Hermann, George, pseud. See Borchardt, Georg Hermann

Hermes, E.
Der dom zu Halberstadt; seine geschichte und seine schätze. Halberstadt, L. Koch 1896
150p. front. illus. O.
Bibliography: p3-4
The Cathedral dates from the thirteenth century and the treasure is rich in vestments, reliquaries, and other art objects of the Middle Ages
Lipperheide 1842. LC 14-8361

Hermits
Vos, Martin de. Oraculum anachoreticum. 1600

Herndon, William Lewis, and Gibbon, Lardner
Exploration of the valley of the Amazon, made under direction of the Navy department. Washington, R. Armstrong [etc.] public printer, 1853-54
2v. illus. 52pl.(incl.fronts.) and 2 atlases with 5 fold.maps. O. ([U.S.] 32d Cong., 2d sess. Senate. Ex. [doc.] 36)
Volume 1 by Herndon; v2 by Gibbon. Imprint of v2: Washington, A. O. P. Nicholson, public printer. Also issued (Washington, 1854) as House ex. doc. 33d Cong. 1st sess.
Ten of the plates show natives of the Amazon valley, most of them Indians of various tribes
Lipperheide 1632. LC 1-1101

Herodianus
Der fürtrefflich griechisch geschichtschreiber Herodianus ... Wellicher Herodianus von Marco Elio Antonino philosopho an untz auff Gordianum de jüngern römischen keysern unnd irer regierung die sich wunderbarlich zůtragen geschriben hatt. Augspurg, H. Steyner 1532
lxx l. 2 illus. F.
First edition 1531
One picture by Hans Burkmair, shows the emperors, Mark Antony and Gordain, as members of the Roman equites. The other is by the Illustrator of Petrarch
Lipperheide 620

Heroën- und götter-gestalten der griechischen kunst. Conze, A. C. L.

Heron-Allen, Edward
Codex chiromantiae. Appendix A. Dactylomancy; or, Finger-ring magic, ancient, mediæval, and modern. London, C. W. H. Wyman 1883
32p. O. (O. V. miscellanies. no2)
Edition limited to 20 copies
LC 17-17768

Hérouard
(illus.) Costumes européens du XVIIe au XIXe siècle

Der **herr** von heute. Becker, W. M. F.

Herrad von Landsberg, abbess of Hohenburg
Hortus deliciarum publié aux frais de la Société pour la conservation des monuments historiques d'Alsace. Texte explicatif commencé par le chanoine A. Straub, 1891, et achevé par le chanoine G. Keller. 1879-1899. Strasbourg, Imprimerie strasbourgeoise, en commission chez Trübner [1879-99]
xxv,59,6,7p. col.front. 111pl. F.
Issued in 11 parts
Reproduction of copies of the miniatures of a twelfth century manuscript which was destroyed in 1870
A notable source book for costume of that period. The pictures of the Divinity, Christ, angels, prophets and ancient Christian art, as in the old mosaics, but all the other figures are in costume of the author's period, the latter half of the twelfth century
LC 14-6328

Herrad von Landsperg. Engelhardt, C. M.

Herrliberger, David
Baslerische ausruff-bilder. Zürich, D. Herrliberger 1749
6 col.pl. F.
A later edition with nine pictures on each plate
Lipperheide 917a

Baslerische ausruff-bilder, vorstellende diejenige personen, welche in Basel allerhand so wol verkäuffliche als andere sachen. Zürich, D. Herrliberger 1749
18pl.(52 illus.) O.
Original edition with three pictures on each plate
Colas 1437. Lipperheide 917

Zürcherische ausruff-bilder, vorstellende diejenige personen, welche in Zürich allerhand so wol verkäuffliche, als andere sachen, mit der gewohnlichen land- und mund-art ausruffen. Zürich, D. Herrliberger 1748-51
54 col.pl.(156 illus.) ob.Q.
In three suites of 18 plates each
Colas 1435. Lipperheide 918

Zürcherische kleider-trachten oder eigentliche vorstellung der dieser zeit in der statt und landschaft Zürich. Les modes de Zurich. Zürich, D. Herrliberger 1749-51
6 col.pl.(52 illus.) F.
Also known with plates in black and white
Colas 1436. Lipperheide 919

Hermann, Max
Forschungen zur deutschen theatergeschichte des mittlalters und der renaissance ... Hrsg. mit unterstützung der general-intendantur der Königlichen schauspiele. Berlin, Weidmann 1914
xiv,541p. illus. Q.
LC 16-15295

Hertel, Louise
Neueste vollständige und gründliche anweisung zum häkeln der spitzen, manschetten, hauben, börsen, tücher, handschuhe; 4. aufl. Hildburghausen, Kesselring'sche hofbuchhandlung [1867]
2v.(54,54p.) 16 col.pl. O.
Lipperheide 4094

Hertslet, Austin
(ed.) Great Britain. Lord Chamberlain. Dress and insignia worn at his majesty's court

Der **hertzogen** und königen in Hungarn, leben, regierung und absterben, von dem ersten hertzogen Keve an biss auf den jetztregirenden könig Leopold den ersten. Nürnberg, J. Hofmann; Neustadt an der Aysch, J. C. Drechsler 1685
567,5p. 60 ports. D.
Lipperheide 858

Herwologia anglica. Holland, Henry

Herz, Alfred
Tätowirung, art und verbreitung. Leipzig, Schmidt & Baumann 1900
180p. O.
Inaugural dissertation

Herzegovina. See Yugoslavia—Bosnia and Herzegovina

Hesekiel, George

Das siebenkönigsbuch; die könige von Preussen geschildert von G. Hesekiel. Darmstadt, Literarisch- artistische anstalt; Berlin, P. Scheller 1874
308p. 10pl. Q.
Lipperheide 733

Hess

[Scenes of Neapolitan life;] Hess, f[ecit] No place, ca1815
24 col.pl. O.
The name of the artist is given on plate 18
Lipperheide 1293w

Hess, Carl Adolph Heinrich

Abbildung der chursächsischen truppen in ihren uniformen unter der regierung Fried.-Aug. III. Dresden, 1805-07
8 col.pl. F.
Colas 1439

Reitschule oder darstellung des natürlichen und künstlichen ganges des campagnepferdes. Leipzig, T. Seeger 1800-02
2v. col.pl. Q.
Published in two series
Lipperheide 2930

[Hess, David]

Hollandia regenerata. [London 1796]
20 l. 20pl. Q.
Caricatures from drawings by David Hess, engraved by Humphries. Text in French, Dutch and English
Another edition *La rigenerazione dell' Olanda* (Venezia, Appresso G. Zatta di Antonio Librajo 1799) has text in French and Italian. Also legends in Italian have been added on the plates
Lipperheide 3524-25

Der scharringgelhof, oder regeln der guten lebensart ... Zu nutz und frommen junger herren und bürger, die sich züchtiglich gebärden wollen ... von Daniel Hildebrand, [pseud.] [1801]
6pl. F.
Plates are signed D. H.
Lipperheide 3526

Hesse. See Germany—Hesse

Hesse-Wartegg, Ernst von

Siam, das reich des weissen elefanten. Leipzig, J. J. Weber 1899
252p. col.front. 120 illus. 18pl.(incl.ports. facsims.) double map. Q.
"Litteratur über Siam von 1627 bis 1899," 1 p preceding p 1
LC 5-9746

Tunis, land und leute. Wien, Pest; Leipzig, A. Hartleben 1882
234p. illus. pl. ports. maps. O.

Tunis: the land and the people. New York, Dodd, Mead [1882]
302p. front. illus. pl. O.
Translation of his: *Tunis, land und leute*
LC 3-13404

Hessen, Wilhelm

Uniformen der verschiedenen truppen der churfürstlich sächsischen armee. Erfurt, W. Hennings 1797
2 l. 31 col.pl. ob.Q.
Colas 1440

Hessische landes- und volkskunde. Hessler, Carl ed.

Hessisches trachtenbuch. Justi, Ferdinand

Hessler, Carl

(ed.) Hessische landes- und volkskunde; das ehemalige Kurhessen und das hinterland am ausgange des 19. jahrhunderts. In verbindung mit dem Verein für erdkunde zu Cassell und zahlreichen mitarbeitern hrsg. von Carl Hessler ... Marburg, N. G. Elwert, 1904-07 (v. 1: 1906-07)
2v. in 3. fronts.(2 col. and 1 fold.) illus. (incl.ports. plans) pl. maps(partly fold.) O.
"Notenanhang zur hessischen landes- und volkskunde ... Einige hessische volkslieder u. a. bearbeitet von kantor Becker": bd II p[655]-62
Contents: v 1 Hessische landeskunde. 1. hälfte: 1906. 2. hälfte: 1907; v2 Hessische volkskunde. 1904
Costume photographs in volume 2 which contains 100 illus. and 9 plates
Lipperheide 802i. LC 9-14138

Hetzel, Pierre Jules. See Gavarni, G. S. C. Œuvres choisies

Heuchler, Eduard

Die bergknappen in ihren berufs- und familienleben, bildlich dargestellt und von erläuternden worten begleitet. Dresden, R. Kuntze 1857
12p. 48pl. ob.Q.
Lipperheide 1996. LC GS15-756

Heuer

(illus.) Uniformes de l'armée danoise

[Heumann, Georg Daniel]

Dei in Göttingen herüm schriende lühe, od. der göttingische ausruf. Nürnberg, G. D. Heumann ca1740
28pl. F.
Lipperheide lists also another edition with only 26 plates and minor differences
Colas 1441. Lipperheide 804-05

Heures. Catholic church. Liturgy and ritual. Hours

Heussler, Sebastian

Künstliches abprobirtes und nutzliches fecht-buch von ein-fachen und doppelten degenfechten, damit ein jeder seinen leib defendirn kan. Nürnberg, P. Fürsten 1665
229p. 120 illus. 22pl. Q.
Illustrations are borrowed from early Italian books by Capoferro, Fabris and others
Lipperheide 2964

New künstlich fechtbuch ... Als dess: Sign. Salvator. Fabri de Padua und Sign. Rudol. Capo di Ferr, wie auch anderer italienischen und frantzösischen fechter beste kunststücklein im dolchen unnd rappier. Nürnberg, S. Halbmayern in verlegung B. Caymoxen 1630
61p. 39 illus. Q.
This is third edition. First edition 1615 or 1616. Pictures are etched by Gabriel Weyer
Lipperheide 2957

Die **heutige** sichtbare körperwelt. Göz, J. F. von

Das **heutige** Sina. Le Comte, L. D.; Le Gobien, Charles, and Bouvet, Joachim

Heuzey, Jacques. See Heuzey, L. A., jt. auth.

Heuzey, Léon Alexandre

Du principe de la draperie antique. Paris, Firmin-Didot 1893
40p. illus. pl. O.

Heuzey, Léon A.—*Continued*

Histoire du costume antique d'après des études sur le modèle vivant; avec une préface par Edmond Pottier. Paris, É. Champion 1922
xv,308p. illus. 8pl.(incl.front.; 5 col.) Q.
Colas 1442. Costume index. LC 23-7648

Recherches sur les figures de femmes voilées dans l'art grec. Paris, G. Chamerot 1873
44p. 3pl. F.
Illustrated with photographs of Greek sculpture

Heuzey, Léon Alexandre, and Heuzey, Jacques

Histoire du costume dans l'antiquité classique. L'Orient: Égypte—Mésopotamie—Syrie—Phénicie. [Paris] Société d'édition Les Belles lettres 1935
vii,156p. col.front. illus. 58(i.e. 59)pl.(part col.) Q. 150fr.
Based on articles by Leon Heuzey published posthumously in the *Gazette des beaux-arts* 1926, and in the *Revue d'assyriologie* v22 (1925)
"Bibliographie sommaire" p[133]-34
LC 36-13028

Hewitt, John

Ancient armour and weapons in Europe: from the iron period of the northern nations to the end of the seventeenth century: with illustrations from contemporary monuments. Oxford and London, J. Henry and J. Parker 1855-60
3v. fronts. (v 1-2) illus. pl. O.
Contents: [v 1] To the end of the thirteenth century; v2 The fourteenth century; [v3] Supplement. Comprising the 15th, 16th, and 17th centuries
LC 1-4205

Heyberger, G., and Füsslen, J.

Festzug zur vollendung des [Ulmer] Münsters 1377-1890. Ulm, J. Ebner [1890]
8p. 17pl. O.
Lipperheide 2815

Heyck, Eduard. See Rosenberg, Adolf. Geschichte des kostüms

Heyden, August von

Die tracht der kulturvölker Europas vom zeit-alter Homers bis zum beginne des XIX jahrhunderts. Mit ... teilweise vom verfasser gezeichneten abbildungen. Leipzig, E. A. Seemann 1889
xvi,262p. 222 illus. O. (Seemanns kunsthandbücher. IV)
Colas 1443. Lipperheide 95

Heyden, August von

(ed.) Blätter für kostümkunde

[Heyden, Jacob van der]

Pugillus facetiarum iconographicarũ ... 1618. Allerhand kurtzweilige stücklein, allen studenten furnemblich zu lieb aufs ihren eigenen stambüchern zusamen gelesen. Strasburg 1618
27pl. Q.
Plates are signed with the monogram of Jacob van der Heyden. They contain pictures of students, soldiers, knights, scholars and women of various ranks
Lipperheide 678

Heyden, Jan van der, 1637-1712, and Heyden, Jan van der, 1662-1726

Beschryving der nieuwlijks uitgewonden en geoctrojeerde slang-grand-spuiten, en haare wijze van brand-blussen ... nevens beschrijving der brand-ordres der stad Amsterdam. Amsterdam, J. Rieuwertsz 1690
50p. 20pl. F.
Most of the plates show firemen and fire-engines in Amsterdam
Lipperheide 1954

Heyden, Jan van der, 1662-1726. See Heyden, Jan van der 1637-1712, jt. auth.

Heye foundation, New York. See New York. Museum of the American Indian, Heye foundation

Heymann, Mme Alfred

Lunettes et lorgnettes de jadis. Préface de M. Georges Lafenestre. Paris, J. Leroy 1911
x,65,58p. front. illus. pl.(part col.) ports. facsim.(1 fold.) F.
"Productions littéraires ayant trait à l'optique": p[49]-50
Advis aux curieux de la conservation de leur veüe. Sur les lunettes dyoptiques, nouvellement mises en usage, pour l'utilité publique. Par Iacques Bourgeois (Paris, Et sé vendent chez le dit Bourgeois, 1645. 11p. D) Facsimile reprint inserted between p62 and 63
LC 12-25593

Heyne, Moritz

Fünf bücher deutscner hausaltertümer von den ältesten geschichtlichen zeiten bis zum 16. jahrhundert. Leipzig, S. Hirzel 1901-03
3v. illus. O.
Volume 3: *Körperpflege und kleidung bei den Deutschen* (373p. 96 illus.)
Colas 1444. Lipperheide 362e

Hicfelt, Eberhard

Aucupatorium Herodiorum; eine deutsche abhandlung über die beizjagd aus der ersten hälfte des 15. jahrhundertes. Nach der einzigen erhaltenen handschrift der K.K. Hofbibliothek zu Wien herausgegeben von Ernst, ritter von Dombrowski. Wien, Selbstververlag des herausgegebers, Druck von J. Roller 1886
lxxviii p. 3 illus. 1 col.pl. Q.
Lipperheide 3016

Hicks, Mrs R. (Mrs John Hicks)

Dress cutting and making on tailors principles, as taught in the London board schools. London, J. Williamson [1894]
47p. O.

Hielscher, Kurt

Dänemark, Schweden, Norwegen; landschaft, baukunst, volksleben; mit geleitworten von Karin Michaelis, Selma Lagerlöf und Sigrid Undset. Leipzig, F. A. Brockhaus 1932
xvi,v,vii p. 88,102,101p. of illus. F.
Contains several plates showing costume of Norway, Sweden, Denmark and Lapland
LC 33-11529

Picturesque Germany; architecture and landscape; prefatory note by Gerhart Hauptmann. New York, Brentano's [1924]
xii p. 304pl. on 152 l. map. F.
A new edition (New York, Westermann 1931. 280p. illus. $7.50) is available in the Orbis terrarum series
English edition: *Germany; architecture and landscape.* (London. Studio c1924)
LC 24-24171, 29-6477 (Eng. ed.)

Hielscher, Kurt—*Continued*
Picturesque Spain; architecture, landscape, life of the people. New York, Brentano [1922]
xxiii,304p. illus. F.
Published also in England (London, T. F. Unwin [1922]) republished with title: *Spain* (London, Studio c1928) Spanish edition: *La España incógnita* ([Madrid] Espasa-Calpe 193-?) German edition: *Das unbekannte Spanien; baukunst, landschaft, volksleben* (Berlin, Atlantis [1928-29]; New York. Westermann 1930)
Costume index (German ed.) LC 23-1267 (Engl. ed.) 29-6476 (1928 ed.) 33-4649 (Span. ed.)

Picturesque Yugo-Slavia; Slavonia, Croatia, Dalmatia, Montenegro, Herzegovinia, Bosnia and Serbia; landscape, architecture, life of the people. New York, Westermann [c1926]
xiv p. 192pl. on 96 l. map. F. (Orbis terrarum) $5.50
Published in England with title: *Yugo-Slavia; Slavonia, Croatia, Dalmatia* (London, The Studio)
Costume index. LC 27-7165, 29-6475 (Engl. ed.)

Rumania; landscape, buildings, national life, preface by Octavian Goga. Leipzig, F. A. Brockhaus 1933
xxxii p. illus. 304pl. on 152 l. F.
Published at the same time with German title-page: *Rumänien,* same publisher and collation; also (New York, Westermann $7.50) French edition: *Roumanie, son paysage* (Paris, Société du livre d'art ancien et moderne. c1933. 263pl. on 132 l. map)
LC 35-1807 (German ed.) LC AC34-4133 (French ed)

Higgin, L.
Art as applied to dress, and to harmonious colour. London, Virtue 1885
S. 2s 6d

Handbook of embroidery, by L. Higgin; ed. by Lady Marian Alford. Pub. by authority of the Royal school of art needlework. London, S. Low, Marston, Searle, and Rivington; New York, Scribner and Welford 1880
xii,106p. incl.illus. 16pl.(part col.) O.
Lipperheide 4000. LC 17-20945

High Albania. Durham, M. E.

The **high** priest of Israel. Rhind, W. G.

The **Highland** clans of Scotland. Eyre-Todd, George

Highland dress, arms and ornament. Campbell, Lord Archibald

The **Highlanders** at home. See Logan, James. Gaelic gatherings

Highlanders of Scotland. Macleay Kenneth

The **highlands** of central India. Forsyth, James

Highlands of Scotland. See Scotland, Highlands of

Highmore, Joseph
[Plates illustrating the "Pamela" of Samuel Richardson, engraved by L. Truchy and A. Benoist from the designs of Joseph Highmore. London 1745?]
12 double pl. F.

The **high-road** of empire. Murray, A. H. H.

Highways and homes of Japan. Lawson, Kate, lady

Hilaire, Émile Marc Hilaire. Saint-. See Saint-Hilaire, É. M. H., known as Marco de

Hildebrand, Daniel, pseud. See Hess, David

Hildebrand, Hans Olof Hildebrand
Das heidnische zeitalter in Schweden; eine archaeologisch-historische studie. Nach der 2[en] schwedischen originalausgabe uebersetzt von J. Mestorf. Hamburg, O. Meissner 1873
xii,228p. 44 illus. map. O.

Den kyrkliga konsten under Sveriges medeltid; 2. omarb. uppl. med 300 figurer. Stockholm, P. A. Norstedt [1907]
195p. illus. O.
Shows costume of the middle ages in Sweden
LC 22-2692

Hiler, Hilaire
From nudity to raiment; an introduction to the study of costume. New-York, F. Weyhe 1929
10p.l. viii,303p. front.(map) illus. 24pl. (12 col.) ob.Q. $7.50, o.p.
Contents: The origin of clothing; Prehistoric dress; The primitives; The Bronze Age and the Early Iron Age; and Costumes in Mexico, Central America and Peru
Bibliography: p277-80
Colas 1445. Costume index. LC 30-7263

Theater und balletentwürfe. See entry under Gehrig, Oscar. Hiler theater und balletentwürfe

Hiler theater- und balletentwürfe. Gehrig, Oscar

Hill, Clare
Millinery, theoretical and practical. 5th ed. London, Methuen [1909]
xvi,168p. illus. pl. diagrs. D.
LC 12-29388

Hill, Georgiana
A history of English dress from the Saxon period to the present day. New York, G. P. Putnam's sons 1893
2v. fronts. ports. O. $7.50, o.p.
Colas 1446. Costume index. Lipperheide 1018. LC 22-7165

Hill, J. C.
Die chinesische armee in ihrer neuorganisation und neu-uniformierung. Nach der amtlichen ausgabe: "Ta ch'ing kuo Lu Chün yi chih tu shuo" (die uniformen der chinesischen armee des "Lu Chün Pu") Leipzig, M. Ruhl [1910]
24p. 16 col.pl. D.
Colas 2596

Hill-Tout, Charles
British North America: I. The far West, the home of the Salish and Déné. London, A. Constable 1907
xiv,263p. front. 32pl. fold.map. O. 6s, o.p. (The native races of the British empire)
Bibliography. p254
Costume index. LC 7-28166

Hillardt, Gabriele
Stickmuster in altdeutschem stile für leinenstickerei (holbeintechnik) und löchleinstickerei in verbindung mit fullstichen und plattstich. Leipzig, Leipziger lehrmittel-anstalt 1883
2v. 24 illus. 20 col.pl. Q.
Lipperheide 4005

Hillert, Adolph
Der Schwanenorden; seine geschichte, statuten und bedeutung. Berlin, Im selbstverlage ... & in Commission der Voss'schen buchhandlung 1844
27p. 1 col.pl. O.
Plate shows the collar of the order
Lipperheide 1927

Hilleström, Pehr
Costumes des paysans de divers cantons en Suède ... gravés par J. F. Martin. Stockholm? ca1802
10 col.pl. ob.Q. 8 riksd
Published also with plates in black and white at 4 riksd
Legends on the plates are in Swedish and French. Contents: Scanie, Blekingie, Smalandie, Westrogothie, Wingaker en Sudermannie, Savolax, Karelie, Dalekarlie (2), Lapons en Herjedale
Colas 1447

Hilliard d'Auberteuil, Michel René
(ed.) Costumes et annales des grands théâtres de Paris. v 1

Hilterbrandt, Jodoco Andrea
Der unwürdige communicant. Stuttgart, J. N. Ernst [1705]
92p. D.
'Nebst einem anhang was von schminken, schön-flecken, haar-zöpffen nacketem halse, blossen brüsten &c des welt-gesinneten frauen-zimmers zu halten?" Subtitle
Lipperheide 3450e

Hiltl, Georg
Die waffensammlung Sr. königlichen Hoheit des prinzen Carl von Preussen ... Durch lichtdruck von A. Frisch in Berlin. Nürnberg, Verlag von S. Soldan [1879]
[18]p. 100pl. F.
After the owner's death the collection was transferred to the Zeughaus in Berlin
Lipperheide 2429. LC 6-39098

Waffen-sammlung Sr. koniglichen Hoheit des prinzen Carl von Preussen; mittelalterliche abtheilung. Berlin, W. Moeser, 1877.
199p. incl. about 250 illus. 2pl.
Lipperheide 2426

(comp.) Preussens heer

Hilton-Simpson, Melville William
Among the hill-folk of Algeria; journeys among the Shawía of the Aurès mountains. New York, Dodd, Mead 1921
248p. front. 1 illus. (map) pl. O.
LC 21-21410

Hincks, Marcelle Azra
The Japanese dance. London, W. Heinemann 1910
31p. 8pl. O.

Hind, Arthur Mayger
An introduction to a history of woodcut, with a detailed survey of work done in the fifteenth century. London, Constable 1935
2v. front. illus. Q.
Illustrations show 15th century costume. Bibliographical references at the end of each chapter and in the foot-notes
LC 36-5506

Hind, Henry Youle
Explorations in the interior of the Labrador peninsula, the country of the Montagnais and Nasquapee Indians. London, Longman, Green, Longman, Roberts, & Green 1863
2v. col.front. illus. pl.(part col.) maps. O.
LC 1-27524

Hindoostan. Shoberl, Frederic, ed.

Les **Hindoûs.** Solvyns, F. B.

L'**Hindoustan.** Pannelier, J. A.

Hindus. See India

Hinton, Henry L.
Selected historical costumes; compiled from the most reliable sources. New York, Wynkoop & Sherwood 1868
Unp. 30pl. O.
Most of the plates show costume of the middle ages

Hint's about men's dress, right principles economically applied. Barrett, W. H.

Hints on dress. Gale, E. C.

Hints on hats adapted to the heads of the people. Melton, Henry

Hints to the bearers of walking sticks and umbrellas. London, Murray 1808
O. 2s 6d

Hinz, A.
Die schatzkammer der Marienkirche zu Danzig mit ... abbildungen von G. F. Busse. Danzig, A. W. Kafemann 1870
2v. 103pl. O.
The church was begun in 1343, finished in 1509, and contains a rich collection of ecclesiastical vestments from the twelfth to the sixteenth centuries
Lipperheide 1838

Hirn, Yrjö
The origins of art; a psychological & sociological inquiry. London & New York, Macmillan 1900
xi,331p. O.
Contains material on the psychology of dress
Authorities quoted: p[307]-22
LC 3-1003

Hiroa, Te Rangi. See Buck, P. H.

Hirschgasse, Chronik de. See Chronik der Hirschgasse

Hirschhoff, Alexander
(ed.) Hollar, Wenceslaus. Strassburger ansichten und trachtenbilder

Hirt, Aloys Ludwig
Dädalus und seine statuen; eine pantomimischer tanz. Bei gelegenheit einer carnevals-feierlichkeit, welche am 23sten März 1802 im palais ... des Prinzen Ferdinand von Preussen statt hatte. Berlin, J. D. Sander 1802
24p. 12 col.pl. Q.
Plates show fancy dress
Lipperheide 2533

Hirt, Aloys Ludwig, and Brühl, Karl Friedrich Moritz Paul, graf von
Die weihe des Eros Uranios; ein festlicher aufzug mit tänzen gegeben den 8ten januar 1818 im weissen saale des königlichen schlosses, zur vermählungsfeuer ... des prinzen Friederich von Preussen ... und der prinzessin Wilhelmine Luise von Anhalt-Bernburg. Berlin, L. W. Wittich 1818
21p. 13pl.(12 col. 1 fold.) ob.O.
Drawings for the ancient costumes were provided by A. L. Hirt and for costumes of the middle ages and modern period by K. F. M. P. graf von Brühl
Lipperheide 2535. LC 25-24429 (under title)

Hirth, Georg
Album für frauen-arbeit enthalend klassische motive für weisstickerei, bunt-, gold-, und applikationstickerei, spitz-

Hirth, Georg—*Continued*
en-, verschnürungs- und knüpfarbeit, sowie weberei, passementrie und stoffbemalung. München & Leipzig, G. Hirth 1880
iv p. 1 illus. 40pl. Q.
Lipperheide 3864

(ed.) Bilder aus der Lutherzeit; eine sammlung von porträts aus der zeit der Reformation in getreuen facsimilenachbildung. München, G. Hirth [1883]
36p. 63 illus. F.
Lipperheide 667e

(ed.) Kulturgeschichtliches bilderbuch aus drei jahrhunderten. Leipzig & München, G. Hirth [1881-90]
6v. illus. ports. pl. (part fold.) F.
Facsimiles of woodcuts, copperplates, etchings [etc.] by German, French, Dutch and other artists, illustrative of the history and customs of the 16th to 18th century. No text. Introductions to v 1-4
Lipperheide 481. LC G-601

Hirth, Georg, and Muther, Richard
(eds.) Meister-holzschnitte aus vier jahrhunderten. München & Leipzig, G. Hirth 1893
xliv columns. 200(i.e. 177)pl. (part col. port double, incl. ports) on 176 l. F.
In portfolio
Lipperheide 345. LC 13-6608

His, Eduard
(engr.) Holbein, Hans, the elder. Hans Holbein's des aelteren feder- und silberstift-zeichnungen

Hishigawa Moronobu
(illus.) Kopon Bushido Ye - Zupushi. Pictures of ancient Japanese warriors

Hispanic society of America
Choricero costume; Candelario, Salamanca; from photographs in the collection of the Hispanic society of America. New York, The society 1931
1 fold sheet(12 illus.) D. pa 5c
Men's dress of Candelario, called Choricero because the men used to travel about selling sausages (chorizos) made by the women. "No one now wears habitually the old dress"
Costume index

Costume of Candelario, Salamanca, from colour plates in the collection of the Hispanic society of America. New York, Printed by order of the trustees 1932
[12]p. illus.(map) VI col.pl. Q. (Half-title: Hispanic notes & monographs)
Issued in portfolio
LC 32-23897

Extremadura costume: women's festival dress at Montehermoso, Caceres. New York, The society 1931?
10pl.(in envelope) D. pa 25c
Costume index

Jewelry: Brazaleras, La Alberca, Salamanca. New York, The society 1931
1 fold sheet(20 illus.) D. 5c
Costume index

Jewelry: necklaces, La Alberca, Salamanca. New York, The society 1931
1 folded sheet(23 illus.) D. pa 5c
Costume index

Men's capes and cloaks: La Alberca, Salamanca. New York, The society 1931
1 folded sheet(11 illus.) D. pa 5c
Costume index

Spain costume details: jewelry. New York, The society 1931?
10pl.(in envelope) D. pa 25c
Costume index

Spain costume details: women's coiffure. New York, The society 1931?
10pl.(in envelope) D. pa 25c
Costume index

Wedding costume: La Alberca, Salamanca. New York, The society 1931
1 folded sheet(11 illus.) D. pa 5c
Costume index

Women's coiffure: Candelario, Salamanca. New York, The society 1931
1 folded sheet(12 illus.) D. pa 5c
"The coiffure of the women of Candelario is peculiar to this village." Plates show how the coiffure is achieved
Costume index

Women's dress for church: Candelario, Salamanca. New York, The society 1931
1 folded sheet(12 illus.) D. pa 5c
Costume index

Women's jewelry: Candelario, Salamanca. New York, The society 1931
1 folded sheet(5 illus.) D. pa 5c
The illustrations reproduce the jewelry in the original size
Costume index

(pub.) Obermaier, Hugo. Fossil man in Spain

Histoire ancienne de peuples de l'Orient classique. Maspero, Sir G. C. C.

Histoire anecdotique des fêtes et jeux populaires au moyen-age. Amory de Langerack

Histoire anecdotique du costume en France de la conquête romaine à nos jours. Deblay, A.

Histoire anecdotique politique et militaire de la Garde impériale. Saint-Hilaire, É. M. H.

Histoire chronologique du vêtement (Homme). Eck, Ch.

Histoire contemporaine par l'image. Dayot, A. P. M.

Histoire, costumes, décorations de tous les ordres de chevalerie, et marques d'honneur. See Loumyer, J. F. N. Ordres de chevalerie et marques d'honneur

Histoire curieuse de tout ce qui c'est passé à l'entrée de la reyne mere du roy treschrestien dans les villes des Pays Bas. La Serre, J. P. de

Histoire de Charles Martel. Liédet, Loyset

Histoire de Charles Martel et de ses successeurs. See Liédet, Loyset. Histoire de Charles Martel, reproduction des 102 miniatures de Loyset Liédet

Histoire de France contemporaine depuis la révolution jusqu'à la paix de 1919. Lavisse, Ernest, ed.

Histoire de France depuis les origines jusqu'à la révolution. Lavisse, Ernest, ed.

Histoire de la barbe et des cheveux en Normandie. Canel, Alfred

Histoire de la charpenterie ... par P. Lacroix, E. Bégin, et F. Seré. See Lacroix, Paul, and others. Le livre d'or des métiers, v2

Histoire de la chaussure. Lacroix, Paul, and Duchesne, Alphonse

Histoire des révolutions de la barbe des Français. Motteley, J. C.
Histoire des rois de France depuis Pharamond jusqu'à ... Louis xv. Fer, Nicolas de
Histoire des théâtres de Bruxelles depuis leur origine jusqu'à ce jour. Renieu, Lionel
Histoire des troupes étrangères. Fieffé, Eugène
Histoire du clergé séculier et régulier. Buonanni, Filippo
Histoire du corps des gardiens de la Paix. Rey, Alfred, and Féron, Louis
Histoire du costume. Blum, André
Histoire du costume antique d'après des études sur le modèle vivant. Heuzey, L. A.
Histoire du costume au théâtre. Jullien, Adolphe
Histoire du costume civil (de 80 avant J.-C. à 1930 après J.-C.) en France. Carlier, Alfred
Histoire du costume dans l'antiquité classique. Heuzey, L. A., and Heuzey, Jacques
Histoire du costume de l'antiquité à 1914. Leloir, Maurice
Histoire du costume de l'antiquité au XIX. siècle. Ruppert, Jacques
Histoire du costume en France. Blum, André
Histoire du costume en France. Quicherat, J. É. J.
Histoire du costume féminin de l'an 1037 a l'an 1870. See Giafferri, P. L. V. de, marquis. L'histoire du costume féminin français de l'an 1037 à l'an 1870
L'histoire du costume féminin français de l'an 1037 à l'an 1870. Giafferri, P. L. V. de, marquis
L'histoire du costume feminine mondial de l'an 5318 avant J.-C. à nos jours. Giafferri, P. L. V. de, marquis
Histoire du costume, les modes au XVII. et au XVIII. siècle. Blum, André
Histoire du costume; les modes au XIX. siècle. Blum, André
Histoire du costume masculin français de l'an 420 à l'an 1870. Giafferri, P. L. V. de, marquis
Histoire du point d'Alençon. Despierres, Mme G. B.
Histoire du sacre et du couronnement des rois et reines de France. Lenoble, Alexandre
Histoire du theatre italien. Riccoboni, Luigi
Histoire et costumes des ordres religieux, civils et militaires. Tiron, abbé
Histoire et législation des ordres de chevalerie. Guigue de Champvans, Frédéric
Histoire et tableau de la Russie. See Czynski, Jean. Russie pittoresque
Histoire generale de la danse. Bonnet, Jacques
Histoire générale de la marine. Van Tenac, Charles
Histoire generale des Turcs. Chalcondylas, Laonicus
Histoire générale du costume civil, religieux et militaire. Jacquemin, Raphael
Histoire générale du costume civil, religieux et militaire du IV. au XII. siècle: Occident (315-1100). Jacquemin, Raphael
Histoire générale illustrée du théâtre. Dubech, Lucien
Histoire militaire du prince Eugène de Savoye. See Dumont, Jean, baron de Carlscroon. Batailles gagnées par le serenissime prince Fr. Eugene de Savoye
Histoire-musée de la République française. Challamel, Augustin
Histoire nationale des Gaulois sous Vercingetorix. Bosc, Ernest, and Bonnemère, Lionel
Histoire philosophique, anecdotique et critique de la cravate, et du col, précédé d'une notice sur la barbe, par Gr. de M. Paris, M. Lévy 1854
107p. D.
Colas 1453. Lipperheide 1705
Histoire philosophique, politique et religieuse de la barbe. Phillippe, Adrien
Histoire pittoresque de l'équitation, ancienne et moderne. Aubry, Charles
Histoire pittoresque des voyages autour du monde. Hatin, L. E.
Histoire pittoresque, dramatique et caricaturale de la Sainte Russie. Doré, Gustave
Histoire populaire de la garde nationale de Paris, juillet 1789-juin 1832. Raisson, H. N.
Histoire universelle des voyages. Montémont, A. É. de.
Histoire universelle du costume. Thirifocq
Historia Americae, sive novi orbis. See Bry, Theodor de. Grands voyages
Historia de ducibus ac regibus Bohemiae. Balbin, Bohuslav
Historia de las cosas de Nueva Espana. Sahagún, Bernardino de
Historia de las Indias de Nueva-España y islas de Tierra Firme. Durán, Diego
Historia de Nueva-España. Cortés, Hernando
Historia del lujo y de las leyes suntuarias de España. Sempere y Guarinos, Juan
Historia del reyno de Portugal. Faria e Sousa, Manuel de
Historia del toreo. Gomez de Bedoya, Fernando
Historia di Ferdinando Terzo imperatore. Gualdo Priorato, Galeazzo, conte
Historia di Leopoldo Cesare. Gualdo Priorato, Galeazzo, conte
Historia diplomatica de statu religionis evangelica in Hungaria in tres periodos distincta. 1710
150,250,56p. 22pl. F.
Contains portraits of the men of the Reformation and of the Holy Roman emperors to Joseph I
Lipperheide 315
Historia ducum Styriae. Graecii, Widmanstad 1728
185,123,84p. 22pl. F.
Most of the portraits are signed Christ. Dietell
Lipperheide 862

Historia moderna Europae. Happel, E. W.

Historia organica de las armas de infanteria y caballeria españolas. Clonard, S. M. de S. y A., conde de

Historia overo vita di Elisabetta. Leti, Gregorio

Historia S. Joannis Evangelistae ejusque visiones apocalypticae. ca1465
48 l. of col. woodcut illus. F.
Illustrations of the visions described in The Apocalypse and events in the life of St. John the Evangelist. Explanatory text is in Latin
Lipperheide 405

Historia von Rhodis. Caorsin, Wilhelm

Historiae Bysant. Epitome. See Ker, F. B. Imperatores orientes

Historiarum veteris instrumenti icones. Holbein, Hans, illus.

Historiarum veteris testamenti icones ad vivum expressae. See Holbein, Hans, the younger. Hans Holbeins Alte Testament in funfzig holzschnitten

Historic beauties and their footwear. Manchester, Herbert

Historic costume. Lester, K. M.

Historic costume, a chronicle of fashion in western Europe. Kelly, F. M. and Schwabe, Randolph

Historic costume for the stage. Barton, Lucy

Historic costume plates. See Northrup, Belle, and Green, A. L. A short description of historic fashion

Historic costumes. Ditchett, S. H.

Historic costumes through the ages. Louden, Mrs A. B., and Louden, N. P.

Historic costuming. Truman, Nevil

Historic dress in America. See McClellan, Elisabeth. History of American costume, 1607-1870

Historic dress of the clergy. Tyack, G. S.

Historic, military and naval anecdotes of personal valour in the last war. London, 1815
40 col.pl. Q.
Scenes and uniforms of the Napoleonic wars. Plates by Atkinson, J. H. Clark, Heath, and others

Historic tales of olden time. Watson, J. F.

Historica narratio profectionis et inaugurationis. Boch, Ioannes

An **historical** account of the rise and progress of the Bengal native infantry, from its first formation in 1757, to 1796. Williams

An **historical** and geographical description of Formosa. Psalmanazar, George

Historical and statistical information respecting the history, condition and prospects of the Indian tribes of the United States. See Schoolcraft, H. R. Information respecting ... the Indian tribes of the United States, v 1

Historical arms and armor. New York. Metropolitan museum of art

Historical cartoons. Doré, Gustave

Historical costumes. See Pauquet, H. L. E., and Pauquet, P. J. C. Book of historical costumes

An **historical** essay on the dress of the ancient and modern Irish. Walker, J. C.

Historical record of coronation of their Majestics Edward VII. and Queen Alexandra. Burke, H. F.

Historical record of the coronation of Their Majesties King George the Fifth and Queen Mary, 1911. Burke, H. F.

The **historical** record of the imperial visit to India, 1911; comp. from the official records under the orders of the viceroy and governor-general of India. London, Pub. for the government of India by J. Murray 1914
xii,457p. col.front. illus.(part col.) pl. (part col. 1 double) ports. 2 plans(1 fold.) 2 maps. Q.
Most of the plates printed on both sides
LC 15-3424

An **historical** record of the Light Horse volunteers. Collyer, J. N., and Pocock, J. I.

Historical records of the British army. Cannon, Richard

Historical Russian costumes. Perleberg, H. C., comp.

A **historical** survey of the customs, habits, & present state of the gipsies. Hoyland, John

The **historie** booke, done to keep in lasting remembrance the joyous meeting of the Honourable artillery company of London ... 1903. Smith, J. H., ed.

Historie cronologiche dell' origine degl' ordini militari e di tutte le religioni cavalleresche. Giustinian, Bernardo

Historie des regiments in des Heil. Röm. Reichs stadt Augspurg. Langenmantel, David

Historie ofte wiider verclaringhe vande Nederlandsche. See Die cronycke van Hollant, Zeelant ende Vrieslant

Historie van alle ridderlyke en krygs-orders. Schoonebeek, Adriaan

Historie von Pontus und Sidonia; eyn rhumreich zierlich unnd fast fruchtbar histori von dem edlen, ehrn-reichen unnd mañhafftigen ritter Ponto des kunigsûn ausz Galicia, auch von der schönen Sidonia künigin auss Britannia; durch ... Heleonora küngin auss Schottenland ... aus frantzösischer zungen ... bracht. Strassburg, S. Bun 1539
64 l. 32 illus. F.
German translation of the French story *Le nouble roy Ponthus.* Illustrations are from several earlier works. The first edition in German was published in Augsburg, 1485
Another German edition *Historie von Puntus und Sidonia; von adelichen mannlichen tugenten.* (\[Augsburg, H. Steiner\] 1548) has 44 woodcuts
Lipperheide 626-27

Historien vom Gallier uñ der Römer burgerische krieg. Caesar, C. J.

Historique du 2. régiment de dragons. Bruyère, H. E. P.

Historique du 5e régiment de hussards. Castillon de Saint-Victor, M. É. de

Historique de 7e régiment de dragons. Cossé-Brissac, R. M. T. de

Historique du 9e régiment de dragons. Martinet, F. X.
Historique du 11e régiment d'infanterie. Vassal, B. M. J.
Historique du 12e régiment de chasseurs de 1788 à 1891. Dupuy, J. R.
Historique du 13me régiment de chasseurs et des chasseurs à cheval de la garde. Descaves, Paul
Historique du 14e régiment de chasseurs. Longin, A. H. É.
Historiques des corps de troupe de l'armée française (1569-1900). France. Ministère de la guerre
Historiques du 84e régiment d'infanterie de ligne. Loÿ, L. C. É. A.
Historiques et uniformes de l'armée française. Titeux, Eugène
Historisch interessante bildnisse und trachten nach alten meistern der letzten drei jahrhunderte. München, M. Kellerer [1893]
2v. 213pl. F.
Shows European costume of the 17th and 18th centuries
Historische alterthümer der Schweiz. Rodt, Eduard von
Historische beschreibung der fürstlichen kindtauff fräulein Elisabethen zu Hessen. Dilich, Welhelm
Historische chronica. Gottfried, J. L.
Der **historische** festzug ... des 500 jährigen bestehens der universität zu Leipzig. Gruner, Erich
Historische kleinigkeiten zum vergnügen und unterricht aus der zerstreuung gesammelt. Grellmann, H. M. G.
Historische nachricht von den merkwürdigen ceremonien der altenburgischen bauern. Friese, Friedrich
Historische nachricht von der röm. kays. gross-botschaft nach Constantinopel. Driesch, G. C. von den
Historische nachrichten zur kenntniss des menschen in seinem wilden und rohen zustande. Bastholm, Christian
Die **historische** schwarze tracht der ... Braunschweigischen truppen. Elster, O.
Historische, statistische, geographische und topographische beyträge zur kenntnisz. Thümmel, Hans von
Historischer festzug in Winterthur den 22. juni 1864. Jenny, Heinrich
Historischer festzug veranstaltet bei der feier der vollendung des Kölner domes am 16. October 1880. Avenarius, Toni
The **history** and poetry of finger-rings. Edwards, Charles
History of academic costume in America. Erwin, John
History of American costume, 1607-1870. McClellan, Elisabeth
History of art by its monuments. Seroux d'Agincourt, J. B. L. G.
A **history** of art in Chaldaea & Assyria. Perrot, Georges, and Chipiez, Charles
A **history** of art in ancient Egypt. Perrot, Georges, and Chipiez, Charles
History of art in Persia. Perrot, Georges, and Chipiez, Charles
History of art in Phoenicia. Perrot, Georges, and Chipiez, Charles
History of art in Phrygia, Lydia, Caria, and Lycia. Perrot, Georges, and Chipiez, Charles
History of art in primitive Greece. Perrot, Georges, and Chipiez, Charles
History of art in Sardinia, Judaea, Syria, and Asia Minor. Perrot, Georges, and Chipiez, Charles
History of British costume. Planché, J. R.
History of China. See Davis, Sir J. F., bart. The Chinese: a general description of the empire of China and its inhabitants
History of Chinese spectacles. Rasmussen, O. D.
History of chivalry and ancient armour. Kottenkamp, F. J.
History of costume design. Sellner, Eudora
A **history** of dancing. Vuillier, Gaston
History of domestic manners and sentiments in England during the middle ages. See Wright, Thomas. Homes of other days
The **history** of England. Macaulay, T. B. M., 1st baron
A **history** of England from the earliest times to the present day. Innes, A. D.
A **history** of English dress from the Saxon period to the present day. Hill, Georgiana
A **history** of everyday things in England. Quennell, Mrs M. C., and Quennell, C. H. B.
History of fashion in France. Challamel, Augustin
History of feminine costume; tracing its evolution from earliest times to the present. London & Paris, Liberty [1896]
39 l. O.
The **history** of French masculine costume. Giafferri, P. L. V. de, marquis
A **history** of hand-made lace. Jackson, Emily
History of Harlequin. Beaumont, C. W.
The **history** of harlequinade. See note under Sand, Maurice. Masques et bouffons
The **history** of human marriage. Westermarck, E. A.
The **history** of Kamtschatka. Krasheninnikov, S. P.
History of lace. Palliser, Mrs F. M.
A **history** of Madeira. Combe, William
The **history** of mankind. Ratzel, Friedrich
A **history** of mourning. Davey, R. P. B.
The **history** of Our Lord as exemplified in works of art. Jameson, Mrs A. B. M., and Eastlake, E. R., lady
History of prostitution. Lacroix, Paul
History of religious orders. Currier, C. W.
The **history** of Sumatra. Marsden, William
The **history** of tattooing and its significance. Hambly, W. D.

The **history** of the art of cutting in England. Giles, E. B.

History of the city of New York. Lamb, Mrs M. J. R. N.

The **history** of the colleges of Winchester, Eton, and Westminster. Ackermann, Rudolph

The **history** of the coronation of ... James II ... and of his royal consort Queen Mary. Sandford, Francis

The **history** of the corps of Royal Sappers and Miners. Connolly, T. W. J.

History of the crusades. Michaud, J. F.

History of the Delhi coronation Durbar ... 1903. Wheeler, Stephen

A **history** of the dress of the British soldier. Luard, John

The **history** of the dress of the Royal regiment of artillery, 1625-1897. Macdonald, R. J., comp.

A **history** of the English turf. Cook, T. A.

History of the fan. Rhead, G. W.

The **history** of the feminine costume of the world, from the year 5318 B. C. to our century. Giafferri, P. L. V. de, marquis

History of the First troop Philadelphia city cavalry from its organization Nov. 17th 1774 to its centennial anniversary, November 17th, 1874. Philadelphia city cavalry. First troop

History of the 42nd Royal Highlanders. Groves, J. P.

The **history** of the growth and decay of the Othman empire. Cantemir, Dumitru

History of the Highlands and of the Highland clans. Browne, J.

History of the Indian tribes of North America. McKenney, T. L., and Hall, James

History of the Indian tribes of the United States. See Schoolcraft, H. R. Information respecting ... the Indian tribes of the United States, v6

The **history** of the King's body guard of the yeomen of the guard. Hennell, Sir Reginald

History of the King's German legion. Beamish, N. L.

History of the New world. Benzoni, Girolamo

A **history** of the nineteenth century. Emerson, Edwin

History of the orders of knighthood of the British Empire. Nicolas, Sir N. H.

The **history** of the present state of the Ottoman Empire. Rycaut, Sir Paul

The **history** of the rebellion and civil wars in England, begun in the year 1641. Clarendon, E. H., 1st earl of

A **history** of the Royal & ancient golf club, St. Andrews. Everard, H. S. C.

The **history** of the royal residences. Pyne, W. H.

History of the Royal Sappers and Miners, from ... March 1772 to ... October 1856. See Connolly, T. W. J. History of the corps of Royal Sappers and Miners

The **history** of the Second dragoons, Royal Scots greys. Almack, Edward

The **history** of the spur. Lacy, C. de L

A **history** of the United States and its people. Avery, E. M.

History of the University of Cambridge Combe, William

History of the University of Dublin. Taylor, W. B. S.

History of the University of Oxford Combe, William

A **history** of theatrical art. Mantzius, Karl

The **history** of women. Alexander, William

The **history**, principles and practice of symbolism in Christian art. Hulme, F. E

Hitchcock, Alfred Marshall

Over Japan way. New York, H. Holt 1917
xii,274p. front. pl. O.
LC 17-31433

Hitomi, I.

Daï-Nippon. Le Japon; essai sur les mœurs et les institutions. Paris, Société du Recueil général des lois et des arrêts, L. Larose, 1900
306p. 2 l. illus. 74pl.(incl. front. ports.) O.
LC 6-6255

Hitorff, Jacques Ignace, and Lecointe, Jean François Joseph

Description des cérémonies et des fêtes qui ont eu lieu pour le baptême de ... Henri-Charles-Ferdinand-Marie-Dieudonné d'Artois, duc de Bordeaux ... Recueil des décorations ... d'après ... J. Hittorf et J. Lecointe. Paris, P. Renouard 1827
19p. 12pl. F.
Lipperheide 2724

Un **hiver** à Paris. Janin, J. G.

Die **hoch** fürstl: leichbegengnis des durchleuchtigsten furstẽ ... herrn Friederich erben zu Norwegen, hertzogẽ zu Sleszwig Holstein. Olearius, Adam

Das **hochbeehrte** Augspurg wie solches nicht allein mit beeder kayserl. als auch der ungaris. königl. majest. ingleichem der ... churfürsten und churfürstl. gesandten ... Ankunfft sondern auch darauf gefolgter der ... römischen kayserin und römischen königs Eleonorae und Josephi, krönungs-festivität beglücket worden ... Mit einem anhang und ... kupffern ... durch M. J. F. W. Augspurg, J. Koppmayer, stadt-buchdruckern 1690
229,39,32p. 18pl. Q.
Pictures of the election and coronation of 1690
Lipperheide 2514

Hochegger, Rudolf

(ed.) Liber regum

Hochfelden, Frau Brigitta (Langerfeldt)

Ebhardt's handarbeiten; anleitung zum erlernen der verschiedenen handarbeitstechniken. Berlin, F. Ebhardt [1894-1895]
7v. illus. pl. O.
Contents: Hohlsäume und leinendurchbruch; Stricken und strickschrift; Die canevashäkelei; Das spitzenklöppeln; Die bändchenspitze; Stricken und strickschrift II; Tülldurchzug
Lipperheide 4175

Hochfelden, Frau Brigitta L.—*Continued*

Das filet und das filettopfen. Berlin, F. Ebhardt [1889]
16p. 115 illus. 1 pl. Q.
Lipperheide 4161

Die gabelhäkelei; anleitung zur anfertigung zahlreicher hübscher und leichter muster. Berlin, F. Ebhardt [1885]
24 l. 64 illus. Q.
Lipperheide 4146

Das häkeln; ausführliche anleitung zur erlernung der häkelarbeit und handbuch der gesammten häkelkunst. Berlin, F. Ebhardt [1892]
103p. 924 illus. 1 pl. Q.
Lipperheide 4169

Hochstetter, C. von

Militair- und civil-reiter-schule neuerer zeit zur gründlichen anleitung der einzig wahren reiter-praxis. Berlin, F. Bergemann 1839
xvi,229p. XIV pl. O.

Hochzeitgebräuche aller nazionen der welt; aus dem französischen übersetzet. Schwabach, J. G. Mizler 1783
135p. O.
Lipperheide 2857m

Hochzeitsbuch. Reinsberg-Düringsfeld, Ida, freifrau von, and Reinsberg-Düringsfeld, Otto, freiherr von

Hochzeitsfeste der renaissance in Italien. Gerstfeldt, Olga von

Hocker, Johann Ludwig

Hailsbronnischer antiquitäten-schatz, enthaltend derer uralten burggrafen von Nůrnberg, dann derer von denenselben abstammenden herren chur-fůrsten und marggrafen von Brandenburg, auch einiger gråflich- und adelichen familien in der vormahligen closter-kirche zu Hailsbronn befindliche grabståtte, wappen und gedåchtnusschrifften. Onolzbach, J. V. Lůders 1731
2pt. in 1 v. illus. pl.(part fold.) fold. plan. facsim. F.
Part 2 has title: *Bibliotheca heilsbronnensis.* A supplement with same title as part 1 was published (Nürnberg, P. C. Monath 1739. 208p. illus. 4pl. F.)
Many of the plates show costume and armor of the 16th century
Lipperheide 720. LC 4-28942

Hockey costume

Sayles, Alexander. Ice hockey. 1931

Hodge, Frederick Webb

Turquois work of Hawikuh, New Mexico. New York 1921
30p. illus. 2 col.pl.(incl.front.) F. (Leaflets of the Museum of the American Indian, Heye foundation. no2)
"Notes" (bibliographical): p29-30
LC 21-6643

(ed.) Curtis, E. S. The North American Indian

(ed.) Handbook of American Indians north of Mexico. Washington, Govt. print. off. 1907-10
2v. illus.(incl.ports.) fold.map. O. (Smithsonian institution. Bureau of American ethnology. Bull. 30)
Most of the portraits are half length
LC 7-35198

(ed.) New York. Museum of the American Indian, Heye foundation. Indian notes and monographs

Hodgetts, J. Frederick

The English in the middle ages; from the Norman usurpation to the days of the Stuarts. Their mode of life, dress, arms, occupations, and amusements. As illustrated by the mediæval remains in the British museum. London, Whiting 1885
xvi,210p. O.
"List of works referred to": p. xvi
Contents: The Normans; The English; The monk; Armour; Civil dress; Sports and pastimes
LC 2-21360

Hodgkin, Eliot

Fashion drawing. London, Chapman and Hall [1932]
xii,114p. front. pl. ob.Q.
LC 33-4411

Hodous, Lewis

Folkways in China. London, A. Probsthain 1929
viii,248p. pl. D. (Probsthain's oriental series, v18)
List of works consulted: p[237]-41
LC 29-12220

Höchle, Johann Nepomuk

(illus.) Hauptmomente aus dem leben Sr. majestät Franz I. kaisers von Oesterreich, apostol. königs. Höchle, del.; Wolf, lith. Wien, 1835-1836
2 l. 20pl. F.
Title from legend on the plates. The names Alexius Jordanszky and Xaver Seidemann are signed as authors of the brief text
Lipperheide 834n

See also Stubenrauch, Ph. von, jt. auth.

Hoeffler, Anton Reinhard Franz

Philosophia Herbipolensis, aeternae episcoporum ... memoriæ devota ... Publicae disputationi Antonius Reinhardus Franciscus Höffling defendet. Herbipoli, J. M. Kleyer 1712
4p. 71pl. F.
Plates are by Joh. Salver. Pictures of bishops of Wurzburg from Saint Kilian of the seventh century to Georg Carl, 1808
Lipperheide 1805

Höffling, Antonius Reinhardus Franciscus. See Hoeffler, A. R. F.

Das **höfische** leben zur zeit der minnesinger. Schultz, Alwin

Höflich, Nannette

Die wohlerfahrene elegante stickerin. Nürnberg, F. Korn [1855-1878]
6v. illus. 5pl. O.
The first edition of volume 1 was published 1843
Lipperheide 4083

Hoes, Mrs Rose (Gouverneur)

The dresses of the mistresses of the White House as shown in the United States National museum; 3d ed. Washington, D.C. Historical publishing company [1931]
[69]p. illus. D. $1
On cover: George Washington bicentennial edition
The dresses are shown in chronological order, each with a brief description. Previous editions: *Catalogue of American historical costumes* (Washington 1915) and *The costumes of the mistresses of the White House* (2d ed. Washington 1925) contain practically the same illustrations
Costume index. LC 32-16019

Hoevenaar, W. P.
(illus.) Lennep, Jakob van. Galerij van beroemde nederlanders

Hoey, Mrs Cashel. See Hoey, Mrs F. S. J.

Hoey, Mrs Frances Sarah (Johnston)
(tr.) Challamel, Augustin. History of fashion in France

(tr.) Humbert, Aimé. Japan and the Japanese

(tr.) Robida, Albert. Yester-year

Hofdijk, Willem Jacob
De klooster-orden in Nederland, historiesch onderzocht; en geschetst door W. J. Hofdijk, en afgebeeld door D. Van der Kellen. Haarlem, A. C. Kruseman 1865
10,289p. 32 col.pl. O.
Also known with plates in black and white
Colas 1457. Lipperheide 1884

Ons voorgeslacht; in zijn dagelyksch leven geschilderd; 2. druk. Leiden, P. Van Santen 1873-75
6v. pl. facsim. O.
From the earliest times to the eighteenth century

De oude schutterij in Nederland ... met gravures. Utrecht, Kemink en Zoon 1875
182p. 15 illus. 15pl. Q.
On the Dutch shooting-guilds of the seventeenth century. Pictures of costumes and weapons
Lipperheide 3009

Schets van de geschiedenis der Nederlanden. Amsterdam, Gebroeders Binger 1857
222p. 118 illus. 40pl. 3 maps. O.
Lipperheide 969n

Hoff, Major, pseud.
Les grandes manœuvres. Paris, Boussod, Valadon 1884
32p. illus. 6pl.(1 double) sq.F.
Illustrations par Édouard Detaille
LC 1-F-3328

Das **hoffest** zu Ferrara in den saelen des koeniglichen schlosses zu Berlin. Lange, Eduard

Hoffinger, Anton Johann Gross-. See Gross-Hoffinger, A. J.

Hoffman, C. T. A.
Groteske gestalten. Berlin, A. Juncker 1922
14p. 3 col.illus. Q.
First edition 1908

Hoffmann, Anton
Die eroberung von Mexiko durch Ferdinand Cortez 1519-1521; zum 400sten jahrestag nach geschichtlichen quellen in wort und bild geschildert. Diessen vor München, J. C. Huber 1922
279p. col.front. illus. pl.(part col.) O.
Second edition, revised. Many of the illustrations show costume and weapons of the Aztecs
Bibliography: p279

Das heer des blauen königs; die soldaten des kurfürsten Max II. Emanuel von Bayern, 1682-1726, geschildert in wort und bild, von Anton Hoffmann. München, Piloty & Loehle [1909]
66p. 58pl.(3 col.) F.

Hoffmann, Martin
Annales Bambergensis episcopatus, aborigine ad an MDC. Fide tabularii publica scripti et ex quatuor codicibus manuscriptis emendati continuation ad MDCC ... Bambergensium episcoporum novissimi seculi continuatio, ab anno 1600 ad annum 1718 cum adnotationibus. Francofurti & Lipsiae 1718
256, 101 (numbered 1008-1109) columns. 24pl. F.
Published as part of volume 1 of *Scriptores rerum episcopatus Bambergensis*, edited by Johann Peter Ludewig. Plates show coats of arms of all the Bamberg bishops and portraits of seventeen of them
Lipperheide 1807

Hoffmann, Nicolas
Costumes de la cavalerie française suivant les ordonnances de 1775 et 1779, et costumes de diverses époques. No place, n.d.
44pl.
Colas 1457

Costumes militaires de France. No place, 1800?
110pl.
Contents: Garde et cavalerie, 103 plates (most of them from the series "suivant l'ordonnance de 1786"); Grand dignitaires civils du 1er empire, ceux de état-major, 7 plates
Colas 1457 (part)

Costumes militaires suivant l'ordonnance de 1786
Contents: Maison du roi et des princes, 89 plates; Infanterie, 106 plates; Régiments royaux et gardes-cotes, 13 plates; Cavalerie, 117 plates
Colas 1458

[Régiments suisses au service de la France. [Paris] Le Fort 1780?
12 col.pl. F.
Colas 1459

Uniformes du consulat. No place, 1804?
7 col.pl.
Colas 1458 (noted)

(illus.) Margerand, J. Les Hussards sous la révolution

Hoffmann, Wilhelm
Neues modelbuch, 1604. Berlin, E. Wasmuth 1891
1 l. 19pl. F.
Facsimile edition of his: *Newes vollkommenes modelbuch von vierhundert schönen ausserwehlten künstlichen und aussgeschnittenen so wol italianischen, frantzösischen, niderlandischen, engelländischen als teutschen mödeln* (Franckfurt am Mayn, W. Hoffmann 1604)
Lipperheide 3912

Spitzen-musterbuch; .. herausgegeben vom K.K. Oesterreichischen museum für kunst und industrie. Wien, K. K. Oesterreich. museum 1876
1 l. 19pl. O.
Facsimile edition of his: *Gantz new modelbuch künstlicher und lustiger visirung und muster von allerhand schöner artiger zügen und blumwerck* (Franckfurt am Mayn, W. Hoffmann 1607)
Lipperheide 3914

Hoffmann, Wilhelm, and Kellerhoven, Franz
Recueil de dessins relatifs à l'art de la décoration chez tous les peuples et aux plus belles époques de leur civilisation. Paris, A. Lévy fils 1858
2v. in 1. 78pl.(41 col. 2 double) F.
"Puisés aux sources les moins connues, recueillis dans les musées et les bibliothèques les plus riches de l'Europe, reproduits avec le caractère de la forme et l'identité de couleur des originaux; destinés à servir de motifs et de matériaux aux peintres décorateurs, peintres sur verre et aux dessinateurs de fabriques." Subtitle
Lipperheide 4362. LC 10-34215

Hofman, Ješek
(ed.) Wrschowitz, Austria. Knopf-museum Heinrich Waldes. Berichte

Der **hofmarschall** auf der bühne, schauspielern und regisseuren. Ebart, P. J. von

Hofmeister, Adolf
(ed.) Eyn loszbuch ausz der karten gemacht

Hogarth, William
The works of William Hogarth, consisting of one hundred and forty-eight engravings ... engraved ... by Cooke and Davenport, with descriptions ... by the Rev. John Trusler. London [18—]
2v. in 1. fronts. pl. ports. Q.
Plates dated 1806-09
LC 26-20835

The works of William Hogarth, from the original plates restored by James Heath ... with the addition of many subjects not before collected: to which are prefixed, a biographical essay on the genius and productions of Hogarth, and explanations of the subjects of the plates, by John Nichols. London, Baldwin and Cradock [1822]
42p. 118pl.(158 illus.) F.
The first edition of Hogarth's works had title: *Hogarth moralized* (London 1768)
German edition *Die werke von William Hogarth ... photolithographirt von Carl Haack* (Brünn & Wien, F. Karasiat 1878)
Lipperheide 3551-3552

(illus.) Almanach des luxus und der moden auf 1801

(illus.) Bowen, Marjorie, pseud. William Hogarth, the cockney's mirror

Hogarth moralized. See note under Hogarth, William. The works of William Hogarth, from the original plates

Hogenberg, Abraham
(engr.) Hollar, Wenceslaus. Reisbüchlein von allerlei gesichter und etlichen frembden trachten. 1636

Hogenberg, Franz
(engr.) Braun, Georg. Civitates orbis terrarum. 1572-1618

Hogenberg, Hans
The procession of Pope Clement VII. and the Emperor Charles V. after the coronation at Bologna on the 24th February MD.XXX, designed and engraved by Nicolas Hogenberg, and now reproduced in facsimile, with an historical introduction by Sir William Stirling Maxwell. Edinburgh, Edmonston & Douglas; [etc.] 1875
28p. illus. 40pl. F.
Original edition is a series of 40 engravings each accompanied by 6 Latin verses. This edition, mounted on a roll, is known by the first line of the first inscription: *Gratae et laboribus aequae posteritati* (Antwerp? 1532?) French edition: *Représentation de la cavalcade et des réjouissances qui eurent lieu à Bologne (en février 1530) à l'occasion du couronnement de Charles V comme empereur des Romains* (Anvers, n.d. 40pl.) At the beginning of the seventeenth century H. Hondius, the Hague, published two editions with plates retouched and cut down. Also published in German
Lipperheide 2737. LC 13-12666

[**Hohberg, Wolfgang Helmhard, freiherr von**]
Georgica curiosa aucta, das ist: Umständlicher bericht und klarer unterricht von dem adelichen land- und feldleben. Auf alle in Teutschland übliche land- und hauswirthschafften gerichtet. Nürnberg, M. Endters. 1701-1715
3v. illus. pl. F.
First edition (Nürnberg 1682. 2v.) The third volume was first published in 1715
The pictures show peasants at work and also some other workmen and artisans at their trades
Lipperheide 1987. LC AGR22-324

Hohenheim, A., and Richards, E.
Chic! Ein ratgeber für damen in allen toilettenfragen mit besonderer berücksichtigung der farben. Stuttgart, Greiner & Pfeiffer 1890
162p. D.
Colas 1460

Hohenheim, Bombast von. See Paracelsus

Hohfelder, Carl
Das bayerische bürger-militär in allen waffengattungen und uniformen vom jahre 1790 bis zum jahre 1852. München, 1853
38 col.pl. Q.
Colas 1461

Hohmann, J.
(engr.) Die belgische armee in ihrer gegenwärtigen uniformierung
(engr.) Die niederländische armee nebst den kolonialtruppen und freiwilligen korps in ihrer gegenwärtigen uniformierung

Hokusai
Hokusai. London, The Studio; New York, W. E. Rudge 1930
6p. VIII col.pl. sq.Q. (Masters of the colour print. 8)
Six plates show costume of Japan. Each plate accompanied by guard sheet with descriptive letterpress. Text signed: Malcolm C. Salaman
Many of the works of Hokusai show Japanese costume of the early 19th century. A collection of his drawings is described by Lipperheide (no1557)
LC 30-29006

Holbach
(lithgr.) Malerische landerschau in bildlichen darstellungen deutscher und schweizerischer stadte

Holbach, Maude M.
Bosnia and Herzegovina, some wayside wanderings; with 48 illustrations from photographs, by O. Holbach. London, J. Lane; New York, J. Lane company 1910 [1909]
248p. 48pl.(incl.front.) fold.map. D.
LC 10-2613

Holbein, Hans, the elder, 1450-1525
Hans Holbein's des aelteren feder- und silberstift-zeichnungen in den kunstsammlung zu Basel, Bamberg, Dessau, Donaueschingen, Erlangen, Frankfurt, Kopenhagen, Leipzig, Sigmaringen, Weimar, Wien; mit einer einleitung von Dr. Eduard His. In lichtdruck ... von W. Biede. Nürnberg, S. Soldan [1885]
x p. 76pl. F.
Lipperheide 668

Holbein, Hans, the younger, 1497-1543
Hans Holbeins Alte Testament in funfzig holzschnitten getreu nach den originalen copirt; hrsg. von Hugo Bürkner, mit einer einleitung von D. F. Sotzmann 1850. Leipzig, G. Wigands verlag 1850
20p. 50pl. O.
The first edition of the Holbein illustrations had Latin text: *Historiarum veteris testamenti icones ad vivum expressae* (Lyon, 1537)
Lipperheide 657

Recueil de XII costumes suisses, civils et militaires, hommes et femmes, du seizième siècle. Gravés d'après les dessins originaux du célèbre Jean Holbein. Basle, C. de Mechel 1790
12 col.pl. F.
Plates exist also in bister
Colas 1462. Lipperheide 899o

(illus.) Bible. German. Die gantze Bibel der ursprüngliche ebraischen und griechischen waarheyt nach auffs aller treüwlichest verteutschet

(illus.) Chamberlaine, John. Imitations of original drawings by Hans Holbein, in the collection of His Majesty, for the portraits of illustrious persons of the court of Henry VIII

(illus.) Chamberlaine, John. Portraits of illustrious personages of the court of Henry VIII

(illus.) Dance of death. Holbein's todtentanz in den wandbildern zu Chur

(illus.) Dance of death. Les simulachres & historiees faces de la mort

(illus.) Harding, G. P., and Moule, Thomas. Gallery of English historical personages

(illus.) Historiarum veteris instrumenti icones ... Ymagines de las historias del viejo testamento. Antverpiae, J. Steelsium 1540
48 l. 92 illus. Q.
The first edition was printed at Lyons, 1538. Here issued with Latin and Spanish text and the Holbein cuts closely copied... A series of Old Testament woodcuts each with Latin title and references to the Old Testament above and Spanish description below

Holbein's todtentanz in den wandbildern zu Chur. Dance of death

Holden, Angus
Elegant modes in the nineteenth century, from high waist to bustle. London, G. Allen & Unwin [1935]
123p. 12pl.(part col.) O. 7s 6d
LC 36-14303

Holden, Edward Singleton
(comp.) United States. Military academy, West Point. The centennial of the United States Military academy at West Point, New York, 1802-1902

Holding, Thomas Hiram
Ladies' cutting made easy. London, T. H. Holding 1885
51p. pl. Q.

Uniforms of British army, navy and court. London, The author [1894]
81p. 75pl. 1 port. ob.Q.
Information on British uniforms and a guide to tailors, giving instructions, patterns and illustrations

Holdt, Hanns
Greece; architecture, landscape, life of the people. New York, Westermann; London, The Studio [c1928]
xxi p. illus.(plans) 304pl. on 152 l. map. F.
An English edition was published by T. F. Unwin, ltd. in 1923 under title: *Picturesque Greece.* The introduction was by Hugo von Hofmannsthal, the illustrations from photographs by Hanns Holdt, Professor Hamann and M. Zachos. This is an enlarged edition with additional illustrations by others
Costume index. LC 29-20208

Holidays in Sweden. Philip, J. B.

Holländer, Eugen
Die karikatur und satire in der medizin, medico-kunsthistorische studie; 2.aufl. Stuttgart, F. Enke 1921
404p. 251 illus. 11 col.pl. O.

Wunder, wundergeburt und wundergestalt in einblattdrucken des fünfzehnten bis achtzehnten jahrhunderts. Kulturhistorische studie. Stuttgart, F. Enke 1921
xvi,373p. 202 illus. ob.O.
"Literaturverzeichnis": p[372]-73
LC SG22-150

Die **Holländer.** Ehrmann, T. F.

Hollaenderski, Léon
Les Israélites de Pologne. Paris, Dagetau 1846
xvi,342p. 6pl. O.

Holländische patrizierhäuser. Muller, Samuel, and Vogelsang, Willem

Holland. See Netherlands

Holland. Jungman, Mrs Beatrix

Holland, Clive
Things seen in Japan ... with fifty illustrations. New York, E. P. Dutton 1907
251p. incl.illus. 47pl. front. S.
Contents: The glamour of Japan; On many subjects; Home life in Japan; Country life in Japan; Town life in Japan; The future of Japan
LC 7-29128

Holland, Clive—*Continued*
Tyrol and its people; with sixteen illustrations in colour by Adrian Stokes, thirty-one other illustrations and a map. London, Methuen; New York, J. Potts 1909
xiii,336p. 47pl.(16 col. incl.front.) O.
LC w9-303

Holland, Henry
Herwologia anglica: hoc est, clarissimorum et doctissimorum aliqout Anglorum qui floruerunt ab anno Cristi M.D. usq' ad presentem annum M.D.C.XX. Arnheim, Impensis Crispini Passaei et Jansonii 1620
7 l. 240p. 63 illus.(on 1 l.) 4pl. F.
Lipperheide 974

Holland of to-day. Edwards, G. W.

Holland sketches. Penfield, Edward

Hollandia regenerata. Hess, David

Hollandiae comitum historia et icones. Baerland, Adriaan van

Hollandiae et Zelandiae comitum. See Baerland, Adriaan van. Hollandiae comitum historia et icones

Hollar, Wenceslaus
Aula veneris, sive Varietas foeminini sexus diversarum Europae nationum differentiag habituum. Londini, 1644
1 l. 100pl. O.
Includes the plates of his *Theatrum mulierum* with additions. This title is sometimes found with plates of later dates
Colas lists also four collections of plates which may or may not duplicate the contents of the two series described above
Colas 1467-71

Ornatus muliebris Anglicanus or The severall habits of English women, from the nobilitie to the contry woman, as they are in these times. Londini, 1640
26pl. O.
Each plate shows a full length figure, many of which appear to be portraits
Colas 1464. Lipperheide 975. LC 14-19595

Reisbuchlein von allerlei gesichter und etlichen frembden trachten, für die anfangenden jugendt sich darinnen zu üben, gradiert zu Cöllen durch Wentzeslaum Hollar vö Prag. 1636
1 l. 24pl. D.
"Abraham Hogenberg excudit"
Plates show styles in hair-dressing and neckwear of the period
Colas 1463. Lipperheide 1647

Strassburger ansichten und trachtenbilder aus der zeit des dreissigjährigen krieges, herausgegeben im auftrag des Wissenschaftlichen institutes der Elsass-Lothringer im Reich an der Universität Frankfurt, von Alexander Hirschhoff. Frankfurt am Main, Prestel-verlag g. m. b. h., 1931
[11]p. mounted pl. F.
Issued in portfolio. "Literatur-nachweis": p[11]
LC 32-5998

Theatru mulierum, sive Varietas atque differentia habituum foeminei sexus diversorum Europæ nationum hodierno tempore vulgo in usu a Wenceslao Hollar, etc. Bohemo delineatæ et aqua forti æri sculptæ Londini A 1643. London, H. Overton.
48pl. on 24 l. O.
48 numbered plates without separate text. Two plates on each page, with Latin inscription below (and English above in some cases) All but three are signed by Hollar and most of them dated 1642-44. The first 13 show the dress of English women; 14-44, that of other nationalities; 45-48 (dated 1663) that of religious orders. No. 24 is signed: I. van Gaenhals delinr. W. Hollar fecit
Plates are full-length pictures of women of all countries in seventeenth century dress. The first edition, with same title, has 36 plates, all signed W. Hollar and with the legend in Latin only
Other printings had different imprints, e.g. (London, Printed by Peter Stent 1643) and (London, sold by R. Sayer)
See also his *Aula veneris*
Colas 1465-1466. Lipp. 30. LC 14-19596

Holliday, Robert Cortes
Unmentionables, from figleaves to scanties. New York, R. Long & R. R. Smith 1933
317p. front. illus. pl. O.
"Illustrations by Sven Elven." "The undie fancier's annotated bibliography": p299-309
LC 33-36353

Holmberg, Uno. See Harva, Uno

Holmboe, Christopher Andreas
Tillæg til en afhandling om amuletter og om stormænds begravelse blandt Skandinaver i hedenold og blandt Mellemasiens Buddhister. (Aftryk af Videnskabsselskabets forhandlinger for 1862.) Christiania, Trykt hos Brøgger & Christie 1863
14p. illus. O.
LC 5-136

Holme, Charles
(ed.) Modern design in jewellery and fans; ed. by Charles Holme. London, New York [etc.] The studio 1902
[44]p. pl.(part col.) Q. $3, o.p.
Various pagings. Special winter number of *The Studio*, London 1901-02
Contents: Modern French jewellery and fans, by Gabriel Mowrey; Modern British jewellery and fans, by Aymer Vallance; Modern Austrian jewellery, by W. Fred; Modern German jewellery, by Christian Ferdinand Morawe; Modern Belgian jewellery and fans, by F. Khnopff; Modern Danish jewellery by Georg Brochner
Costume index. LC 2-7834

(ed.) Peasant art in Austria and Hungary. London, New York [etc.] The studio 1911
x,54p. illus.(map) 106pl.(14 col.) Q. 7s 6d, o.p.
The black-and-white plates printed on both sides. Plates show costume of Czechoslovakia and Hungary
Costume index. LC 11-35972

(ed.) Peasant art in Italy; ed. by Charles Holme. London, New York [etc.] The studio 1913
viii,39p. 92pl.(12 col.) Q. 7s 6d, o.p.
Special autumn number of *The Studio* 1913
The black-and-white plates printed on both sides
Contents: Introduction, by S. J. A. Churchill; Peasant art in the Abruzzi, by V. Balzano; Women's crafts, by Elisa Ricci; Peasant jewellery, The "Presepe," by S. J. A. Churchill
Costume index. LC 14-2882

Holme, Charles—*Continued*

(ed.) Peasant art in Russia. London, New York [etc.] The studio 1912
x p. 2 l. 3-52p. 1 illus.(map) 86pl.(12 col.) Q. 7s 6d, o.p.
Special number of the *International studio*, autumn, 1912
Contents: The peasant art of Great Russia, by Princess Alexandre Sidamon-Eristoff and Mlle. N. de Chabelskoy; The peasant art of Little Russia (the Ukraine) by N. Bilachevsky, tr. by V. Stepankowsky; The peasant art of Russian Poland, by Maryan Wawrzeniecki, tr. by A. B. Boswell; The peasant art of Lithuania, by Michael Brentsztejn
Costume index. LC 13-88

(ed.) Peasant art in Sweden, Lapland and Iceland. London, & New York, The Studio, ltd. 1910
48p. 88pl.(12 col.) Q. 7s 6d, o.p.
Shows costume, jewelry and embroidery of Sweden; costume of Lapland, and jewelry of Iceland
Contents: Sweden, by Sten Granlund (tr. by E. Adams-Ray); Lapland, Iceland, by Jarno Jessen [pseud.]
Costume index. LC 11-404

(ed.) Salaman, M. C. Shakespeare in pictorial art

Holme, Geoffrey

(ed.) A book of old embroidery, with articles by A. F. Kendrick ... Louisa F. Pesel & E. W. Newberry, ed. by Geoffrey Holme. London, New York [etc.] The Studio 1921
40p. col.front. 87pl.(7 col.) on 47 l. Q.
Contents: Introduction, by A. F. Kendrick; A note on stitchery, by L. F. Pesel and E. W. Newberry; List of useful books on embroidery (p40)
LC 22-2095

(ed.) Kommīssarzhevskiĭ, F. F. and Simonson, Lee. Settings & costumes of the modern stage

(ed.) Nevill, R. H. Old English sporting prints and their history

Holmes, Richard Rivington

Naval & military trophies & personal relics of British heroes; a series of water colour drawings by William Gibb, the descriptive notes by Richard R. Holmes. London, J. C. Nimmo 1896
3p.l. [158]p. 36 col.pl. F.
Contents which relate to costume: Bible and silk scarf of Major-General Charles George Gordon; Sword, axe, and gold mask captured in the Ashantee expedition; Crown of the king of Delhi; Dirk, sword, and cocked hat of Lord Nelson; Cloak of Napoleon I; Crown and chalice from Abyssinia; Sword with scabbard, found with the dead body of Tippoo Sahib at the gate of Seringapatam; Chair and cloak of Field-Marshal, the Duke of Wellington, with bearskin and sword of the Grenadier guards; Pistol of Sir Ralph Abercrombie, and sash by which the body of Sir John Moore was lowered to his grave; Swords of Oliver Cromwell and John Hampden; Cap of the emperor of China; Creese of the rajah of Assam, and powder horn; Tiger's head from the throne of Tippoo Sultan; Sword of John, duke of Marlborough; Telescope of the Duke of Wellington, and the sword and hat worn by him at Waterloo; Swords of General Wolfe and Captain Cook; Burmese gun from Mandalay; Indian belt and cartouche boxes; The bullet which killed Lord Nelson at Trafalgar; "George" worn by the dukes of Marlborough and Wellington; Jewelled bird from the throne of Tippoo Sultan; Sword and relics of Admiral Viscount Duncan; Swords surrendered at Delhi by the kings and princes to Major Hodson; Helmet and standard of Tippoo Sultan; Sword of Joseph Bonaparte and baton of Marshal Jourdan captured at Vittoria; Tippoo Sultan's gun; Crown of the king of Kandy; Lord Raglan's telescope, and a Russian bugle from Sebastopol; Drake's walking-stick, and the punch-bowl of Captain Cook; Eagle captured by the Scots Greys at Waterloo
Colas 1473. LC 5-16116

Holmes, Samuel

Voyage en Chine et en Tartarie à la suite de l'ambassade de lord Macartney ... Tr. de l'anglais avec quelques notes par L. Langlès. Paris, Delance et Lesueur 1805
2v. 51pl. O.
"Auquel on a joint les vues, costumes, etc., de la Chine, par M. W. Alexandre, les planches de l'atlas original de cette ambassade omises dans la traduction française, et leur explication." Subtitle
Plates are engraved by Simon and are copies of those in Alexander's *Vues, costumes, moeurs et usages de la Chine*
Colas 1472

Holt, Ardern

Fancy dresses described, or What to wear at fancy balls; illus. in colours and black and white, by Miss Lilian Young; 6th ed. London, Debenham & Freebody [etc., 1896]
xiii,312p. illus. pl.(part col.) O.
Second edition 1880
Colas 1474. LC 4-4630

Gentlemen's fancy dress: how to choose it; 4th ed. London, E. Arnold [1898]
viii,73p. pl. D.
Colas 1475. LC 4-12402

Holtmont, Alfred

Die hosenrolle; variationen über das thema das weib als mann. München, Meyer & Jessen [1925]
247p. front. illus. pl. sq.O.

Holtzmann, Oskar. See Stade, Bernhard. Geschichte des volkes Israel

Holtzmann, Th.

Das spanische militär in Hamburg 1807-8. Hamburg, Jürgensen & Becker 1907
29p. 5 col.pl. Q.

Holy Ghost, Order of the

L'office des chevaliers de l'Ordre du St. Esprit. 1740

Viel-Castel, Horace, comte de. Statuts de l'ordre du Saint Esprit au droit desir ou du noeud institué à Naples en 1352 par Louis d'Anjou ... Manuscrit du XIVme siècle conservé au Louvre. 1853

Holy Land. See Palestine

The **Holy** Land. Kelman, John

The **Holy** Land and Syria. Carpenter, F. G.

The **Holy** Land, Syria, Idumea, Arabia, Egypt & Nubia. Croly, George

Holy Roman empire. See Coronations—Germany; Kings and rulers—Germany

Die **holzschnitte** des 14. und 15. jahrhunderts im Germanischen museum. Nuremberg. Germanisches nationalmuseum

Holzschnitt-werk in auswahl. Dürer, Albrecht

Holzschnitte zum Alten Testament. Beham, H. S.

El **hombre** fócil. See Obermaier, Hugo. Fossil man in Spain

Home decoration. Ruutz-Rees, Mrs J. E. M.

Home dressmaking and the art of good dressing. Barras, Easton de

Home life in colonial days. Earle, Mrs A. M.

Home life in Hellas. Ferriman, Z. D.

Home life in Italy. Duff-Gordon, C. L.

Home life of the ancient Greeks. Blümner, Hugo

Home life under the Stuarts, 1603-1649. Bedford, Jessie

Homeric age. See Greece—Homeric age

Das **homerische** epos aus den denkmälern erläutert. Helbig, Wolfgang

Homerische waffen. Reichel, Wolfgang

The **homes** of other days. Wright, Thomas

L'homme primitif. Figuier, Louis

Hommel, Fritz

Geschichte Babyloniens und Assyriens. Berlin, G. Grote 1885-[88]
vi,802p. 114 illus. 115pl.(part col. part double) double map. O. (Allgemeine geschichte in einzeldarstellungen ... hrsg. von W. Oncken. 1. hauptabth. 2. th.)
Issued in 5 parts, 1885-1888
Lipperheide 143. LC G-2480

Les **hommes** célèbres de l'Italie. Legouvé, G. J. B. E. W., and others

Les **hommes** d'épée. Vaux, Ludovic, baron de

Les **hommes** illustres qui ont paru en France pendant ce siecle. Perrault, Charles

Les **hommes** illustres qui ont vecu dans le XVII. siecle. Hulle, Anselm van

Honan, Michael Burke

(ed.) Andalusian annual for MDCCCXXXVII

Hondert steden en dragten. See Allard, Carel. Orbis habitabilis oppida et vestitus

Hondius, Hendrik

Pictorum aliquot celebrium praecipue Germaniae inferioris effigies. Hagae-Comitis, H. Hondius [1610]
54pl. F.
Lipperheide 927m

Hone, William

(ed.) Strutt, Joseph. The sports and pastimes of the people of England

Honor military, and civill. Segar, Sir William

Honor redivivus. Carter, Matthew

Honoré Daumier, l'homme et l'oeuvre. Alexandre, Arsène

Hoogewerff, Godfried Joannes. See Byvanck, A. W., jt. auth.

Hooghe, Romein de

Figures à la mode; inventez et gravez par R. de Hooghe. Amsterdam, N. Visscher ca1700
12pl. O.
Plates show fashions in Holland at the end of the seventeenth century
Colas 1477. Lipperheide 941

(engr.) Chertablon, de. La maniere de se bien preparer a la mort

(engr.) Geelen, G. V. Relation succincte et veritable de tout ce qui s'est passé pendant le siège de Vienne

(engr.) Petter, Nicolaes. Klare onderrichtinge der ... worstel-konst

Hoop skirts

Abiet, Édouard. Réflexions sur la crinoline. 1865

Le blason des basquines et vertu-galles. 1563

The crown skirts; nouveautés für 1864. 1864

La Fizelière, A. P. de. Histoire de la crinoline au temps passé ... suivie de La satyre sur les cerceaux [etc] L'indignité et l'extravagance des paniers. 1859

Lamorillière, R. L. de. Crinolines et volants. 1855

See also Crinoline

Hooper, Elizabeth

Dolls the world over. Baltimore, Md. 1936
67p. incl.illus. pl. front. D.
Contents: The league of doll-dom nations, an essay on the history and delights of dolls; Poems about dolls; Bibliography (p[49]-53)—Important doll collections; Where to buy dolls
LC 37-2049

Hooper, William Eden

(comp.) The Central criminal court of London; being a survey of the history of the court and of Newgate, the Fleet and other jails ... from a distant period to the present day, issued to commemorate the opening of the present court by His Majesty King Edward VII on February 27th, 1907. London, Eyre and Spottiswoode 1909
xv,191p. 21pl.(4 col. incl.front.) 25 port. Q.
Each plate accompanied by guard-sheet with descriptive letterpress. Plates show English judges
LC 10-9271

Hoover, Herbert Clark, and Hoover, Mrs Lou Henry)

(trs.) Agricola, Georg. De re metallica

Hope, Thomas

Costume of the ancients; new ed. enl. London, H. G. Bohn 1841
2v. 321pl. Q. 52s, o.p.
Many editions: W. Miller, 1809 (200pl.) W. Miller 1812 (300pl.) Chatto and Windus 1875 (321pl.)
A French translation of the first (1809) edition was published: *Costumes des anciens* publiés par D. Vincent, L. Boëns, et J. Vanden Burggraaff, lithographes (Bruxelles 1826. 200pl.)
Colas 1478-81. Costume index. Lipperheide 127, 126z

Hope, Sir William Henry St John

On the tomb of an archbishop recently opened in the Cathedral church of Canterbury. Westminster, Nichols 1893
12p. 5 col.pl.(1 double) F. (Society of antiquaries of London. Vetusta monumenta v7, pt 1)
Shows stole, mitre, sandals, amice-apparel found in an archbishop's tomb at Canterbury. These date from the early 13th century

Hope, Sir William H. St J.—*Continued*
(ed.) Pageants of Richard Beauchamp, earl of Warwick. Pageant of the birth, life and death of Richard Beauchamp

Hope, Sir William Henry St. John, and Atchley, Edward Godfrey Cuthbert Frederic
English liturgical colours. London, Society for promoting Christian knowledge; New York, Macmillan 1918
xiii,3-273p. col.front. Q.
A large amount of information, gathered from church records, on colors used in and ordered for English church vestments. Includes also material on the dress of the "lesser ministers: the patener, the cross-bearer . . . the ruler of the quire" and a note on Scottish liturgical colors. Bibliography p232-41
LC A19-377

An introduction to English liturgical colours. London, Society for promoting Christian knowledge; New York, Macmillan 1920
90p. D.
LC 20-22181

[Hopffer, Bartholom.]
Icones, sive Effigies omnium & singulorum ecclesiae Augustanae A. Cillibatâ verbi praedicatione, & purâ verorum sacramentorum administratione inservientium ministrorum .... Das ist: Contrafeth und abbildungen eines gesambten ministerij und praedig-ampts evangelischer gemein Augustb. conf. in Augspurg ... 1656. Augspurg, J. Wehen 1656
14pl. F.
Plates after drawings by Hopffer, engraved by Bartholom. Kilian
Lipperheide 1802

Hopi Indians. See Indians of North America—Hopi Indians

Hopkins, Mrs Marguerite (Stotts)
Dress design and selection. New York, Macmillan 1935
vii,196p. illus. pl. diagrs. O.
"French and American designers": p176-83
Supplementary readings at end of most of the chapters; bibliography on historic costume: p158-67; bibliography of Fashion magazines: p184-86
LC 35-34870

Hoppenstedt, Julius
Das heer. Dachau, Mundt & Blumtritt [1913]
45p. illus. 1 pl. Q. (Das volk in waffen, v 1)

Horda Angelcynnan. Strutt, Joseph

Hōrin, Seisai
(illus.) Ota, Shintaro. Tokugawa ryaku denki

Horn, Émile
(tr.) Mikszáth, Kálmán. Scènes hongroises

Horn, Rudolf
Stehende weibliche gewandstatuen in der hellenistischen plastik. München, F. Bruckmann 1931
109p. 1 l. 44pl. on 22 l. Q. (Mitteilungen des Deutschen archaeologischen instituts. Roemische abteilung. 2. ergänzungsheft)
"Literaturnachträge": p[98]
LC 33-18123

Hornau Gerbert, Martin, freiherr von. See Gerbert, Martin, freiherr von Hornau

Hornblower, Florence S. See Houston, M. G., jt. auth.

Hornfeck, Fr.
Das deutsche schützenfest in Frankfurt am Main. Leipzig, J. J. Weber [1862]
20p. 1 pl.(25 illus.) F.
Reprinted from the *Leipziger illustrirte zeitung* nos 997-1003
Lipperheide 3007

Horn-Monval, Mme Madeleine. See Dubech, Lucien. Histoire générale illustrée du théâtre

Horologium devotionis circa vitam Christi [Koln] ca1480-90?
65 l. 36 illus. O.
Title is from leaf 1a. The book is thought to have been published about 1480-90. The illustrations are woodcuts of a still earlier period
Lipperheide 415

Horschelt, Theodor
Études militaires faîtes au Caucase (1858 Edition du Grand Duc Georges Michaïlovich. Saint-Petersbourg 1895-96
60pl. F.
Sixty plates of military costume, published in six parts
Colas 1482

[Hort, Sir John Josiah, 3d bart.]
The days when we had tails on us .. Dedicated to the officers of the British infantry; 2d ed. London, Newman 1849
viii,24p. 13 col.pl. O.
LC 22-6764

Hortleder, Friederich
Der römischen keyser- und koniglichen maiestetē, auch dess Heiligen Römischen Reich geistlicher und weltlicher stände ... Von den ursachen dess teutschen kriegs kaïser Carls dess V wider die Schmalkaldische bundsoberste chur- und fürsten Sachsen und Hessen und ihrer chur- und F. G. G mitverwandte anno 1546 und 47. Gota, W. Endters 1645
2v. illus. 60pl. F.
Volume 1, years 1546-47; v2 to about 1558
First edition (Frankfurt a. M. 1617-18)
Forty-one of the plates show noblemen and military leaders. The others picture sieges, battle scenes and other events
Lipperheide 503

Hortus deliciarum. Herrad von Landsberg, abbess of Hohenburg

Horvath, Carl Christian
(pub.) Friedrichs II königs von Preussen. Armee montirungen sauber gemahlt wie selbige unter dessen regierung waren

(pub.) Preussische armee-uniformen unter der regierung Friedrich Wilhelm II, königs von Preussen; Uniforms de l'armée prussienne sous le regne de Frédéric Guillaume II. Potsdam, C. C. Horvath 1789
22p. col.front. 135 col.pl. O.
Published in 13 parts, 1787-89. Forty one plates from this collection were later retouched and gathered together in *Uniformes de l'armée de la république française*
Colas 1484. Lipperheide 2151

(pub.) Preussische civil-uniformen. 1787-88

Horvath, Carl C.—*Continued*

(pub.) Uniformes de l'armée prussienne sous le règne de Frédéric-Guillaume II, roi de Prusse. [Potsdam, Horvath?] 1788
2 l. 159 col.pl. O.
Colas 1483

(pub.) Uniformes de l'armée prussienne sous le règne de Frédéric-Guillaume III, roi de Prusse. Potsdam, C. C. Horvath 1799-1800
2 l. 165 col.pl. and supplément 14 col.pl. O.
Plates engraved by L. Schmidt. Most of the plates are from *Preussische armee-uniformen ... Friedrich Wilhelm II* published by Horvath in 1889
Colas 1486 and 1487

Hose, Charles, and McDougall, William

The pagan tribes of Borneo; a description of their physical, moral and intellectual condition, with some discussion of their ethnic relations ... with an appendix on the physical characters of the races of Borneo, by A. C. Haddon. London, Macmillan 1912
2v. col.fronts. illus. pl.(2 col.) 4 fold. maps, tables(part fold.) O.
Many of the plates show costume and headdress
LC 13-12065

Hose

May hosiery mills, inc., Burlington, N. C. The story of hosiery. c1931

Hosedjaevelen paa Dansk ved Peder Palladius, 1556. Musculus, Andreas

Hosemann, Theodor

(engr.) Dörbeck, B. Berliner witze und anecdoten

(lithogr.) Eichler, Ludwig. Berlin und die Berliner

(lithogr.) Gross-Hoffinger, A. J. Wien wie es ist

Die **hosenrolle.** Holtmont, Alfred

Hosentuch, Johann

Johann Hosentuch's lustiges schneiderbüchlein, oder witze, anekdoten und curiositäten aller art ... nebst liedern für die schneider-zunft und den zehn geboten für schneider. Creutzburg, F. Fischer 1846
62p. O.
Lipperheide 3489

Hōshun, Chōkōrō. See Chōkōrō Hōshun

Hosie, Dorothea (Soothill) lady

Two gentlement of China; an intimate description of the private life of two patrician Chinese families. Philadelphia, J. B. Lippincott 1924
316p. front. pl. ports. O. $3.50
Second edition: London, Seeley 1924
Costume index. LC 24-11218

Hospital garments

Peek, Emily. Practical instruction in cutting out and making up hospital garments for sick and wounded (adopted by the Red Cross Society). 1914

Host, George Hjersing

Nachrichten von Marokos und Fes, im lande selbst gesammlet, in den jahren 1760 bis 1768; aus dem dänischen übersetzt. Kopenhagen, C. G. Prost 1781
xvi,312p. front.(port.) pl. maps. Q.
Ten plates show costume of various tribes of Morocco

Hostein, Hippolyte

Piémont, Sardaigne, Simplon. See Audot, L. E. L'Italie. v5

Venise, Milan, Royaume-Lombardo-Venitien et états voisins. See Audot, L. E. L'Italie. v4

Hotman, Antoine

Jucundus & verè lectu dignus de barba et coma. Rostochi, ex. off. Ferberiana 1628
28p. Q.
First edition: Antwerp, 1586
Lipperheide 1643

Hottenroth, Friedrich

Altfrankfurter trachten von den ersten geschichtlichen spuren an bis ins 19. jahrhundert, von Friedrich Hottenroth. Frankfurt am Main, H. Keller 1912
405p. illus. 68pl.(part col.) O.
Costume index

Le costume chez les peuples anciens et modernes; nouvelle sér. Tr. par John Bernhoff. Paris, A. Guérinet 189-?
213p. col.front. illus. 29 col.pl. O.
Issued as a supplement to his *Le costume, les armes* but contains German costume only. French edition of his *Handbuch der deutschen tracht*
Colas 1490. Costume index. LC AC35-164

Le costume, les armes, ustensiles, outils des peuples anciens et modernes. Paris, A. Guérinet [1886-91?]
2v. illus. 240 col.pl. F.
French edition of his *Trachten, haus-, feld- und kriegsgeräthschaften,* with the same plates. Volume 2 has title: *Le costume, les armes, les bijoux, la céramique, les ustensiles, outils, objets mobiliers, etc. chez les peuples anciens et modernes*
Contents: v 1 Antiquity & Oriental people. Egypt, Assyria, Babylonia, etc. Medes, Persians, etc. Greeks, Romans, etc. Gallo-Romans, Celts, Gauls, Germans, Scythians, Byzantines, Goths, Merovingian and Carlovingian epochs in France. Persia, Arabia, India, China, Siberia. Part of the Mongol tribes. Turks, Slavs; v2 Middle Ages to 1840. Germanic people, up to 1200, Latin races up to 1200, Germanic & Latin peoples from 1200 to end of the Middle Age, Roman Catholic Church. European costume, from end of 16th century to 1840
Colas 1489. Costume index

Deutsche volkstrachten vom XVI bis zum XIX jahrhundert; 2 aufl. Frankfurt am Main, H. Keller 1923
3v. in 1. illus. col.pl. O.
Reprint of his: *Deutsche volkstrachten, städtische und ländliche* (Frankfurt, H. Keller 1898-1902. 3v.)
Contents. v 1 Süd und südwest Deutschland; v2 West und nordwest Deutschland; v3 Nord und nordost Deutschland. Deutsch-Böhmen
Colas 1492-94 (1898-1902 ed.) Costume index. Lipperheide 742e (1898-1902 ed.) LC 3-6190 (1898-1902 ed.)

Handbuch der deutschen tracht. Stuttgart, G. Weise [1893-1896?]
983p. 272 illus. 30 col.pl. O.
Published in 20 parts (ea M.2)
A historical treatment of German costume
Colas 1491. Lipperheide 605

Hottenroth, Friedrich—*Continued*

Die nassauischen volkstrachten. Wiesbaden, Verein für nass. altertumskunde und geschichtsforschung 1905

29 col.pl. 2 maps. O.
Colas 1495

Trachten, haus-, feld- und kriegsgeräthschaften der völker alter und neuer zeit. Stuttgart, G. Weise [1884?]-91

2v. 123 illus. 240 col.pl. F.
Published in 20 parts, 1882-91. "Quellen": v 1 p184-86; v2 p215-17
Volume one is on ancient times and the orient, volume two medieval times and modern Europe
See also note under his *Le costume, les armes*
Colas 1488. Lipperheide 91. LC 4-20508

Hottentots

Kolb, Peter. The present state of the Cape of Good-Hope. 1731

Houbigant, A. C.

Moeurs et costumes des Russes . . . 50 planches ... executées ... par A. G. Houbigant. Paris, Treuttel & Wurtz 1817

20p. 50 col.pl. F.
Four of the plates are signed Hte Bé (Bellangé). Most of them are copies of those in Atkinson and Walker's *A picturesque representation ... of the Russians.* Lipperheide lists the same publication with date 1821
The author's *Recueil de trente croquis representant des scènes et costumes russes* (Paris, Engelmann 1821. 30pl.) is a partial new edition
Colas 1496-7, 2512. Lipperheide 1352-1353

Hough, Walter

Primitive American armor. (*In* U.S. National museum. Annual report. 1893. Washington, 1895. O. p625-651. illus. 22 pl.)

LC 14-19796

Racial groups and figures in the natural history building of the United States National museum. (*In* Smithsonian institution. Annual report, 1920. Washington, 1922. O. p611-656. 87 pl. on 44 l. $1.50)

Shows American Indians
Costume index. LC 22-12600

Hourticq, Louis

Costumes et coiffes de Bretagne. See entry under Lalaisse, Hippolyte

The House of Kuppenheimer, Chicago

Tempered clothing—an investment in good appearance. [Chicago] The House of Kuppenheimer 1921

42p. illus. D.
This firm's books for the trade show men's suits and overcoats and include samples of materials. Another is *Spring book of B. Kuppenheimer & co.* (Chicago, The company 1900)
LC 22-1527

The **household** history of the United States. Eggleston, Edward

Houston, Mary Galway

Ancient Greek, Roman and Byzantine costume and decoration (including Cretan costume). London, A. & C. Black; New York, Macmillan 1931

xi,106p. 97 illus. 8 col.pl. O. $3.50 (A technical history of costume. [2])
Contains references
Costume index. LC 32-523

Houston, Mary Galway, and Hornblower, Florence S.

Ancient Egyptian, Assyrian, and Persian costumes and decorations. London, A. & C. Black; New York, Macmillan 1920

xii,89p. illus.(16 col.) diagrs. 24cm. (A technical history of costumes. [1]) $3.50
The 16 colored illustrations are mounted and numbered as plates
Contains bibliographies
Colas 1498. LC 21-9992

Houtman, J. P.

Nederlandsche uniformen, door Houtman. No place, 1815-31

122 col.pl. Q.
In portfolio
5 typewritten leaves laid in, with incomplete list of plates. 2 facsimile manuscript leaves: "Amschrijving der vaandels" laid in
Plates show uniforms of the Dutch army at this period. Some of the plates are duplicated

De schutter-en jagerkorps en 1830. No place, 1830

58 col.pl.
Cataloged from R. A. Peddie's *Subject index of books*

Houville, Gerard d', pseud. See Regnier, Mme. M. L. A. de H. de

How the world is clothed. Carpenter, F. G.

How to cut, fit, and finish a dress. Löfvall, Mme J. H.

How to distinguish the saints in art by their costumes, symbols, and attributes. Bles, Arthur de

How to dress. Klickmann, Flora, ed.

How to dress on £15 a year. Cook, M. W.

How to dress well. See Story, Mrs M. McE.-F. Individuality and clothes

How to make crepe paper costumes. Dennison manufacturing company

How to make paper costumes. See note under Dennison manufacturing company. How to make crepe paper costumes

How to "make up". Fitz-Gerald, S. J. A.

How we are clothed. Chamberlain, J. F.

Howard, Frank

(illus.) The art of dress

Howard, Oliver Otis

My life and experiences among our hostile Indians; a record of personal observations, adventures, and campaigns among the Indians of the great West... Illus. chiefly from photographs supplied by the Bureau of ethnology, Washington, and a series of colored plates showing Indian objects of interest and curiosity in facsimile. Hartford, Conn., A. D. Worthington [c1907]

570p. front.(port.) illus. 29pl.(10 col.) O. $3.50, o.p.
One plate shows Indian dolls. Other plates show costume
Costume index. LC 7-38634

Howe, Fisher
Oriental and sacred scenes, from notes of travel in Greece, Turkey, and Palestine. New York, M. W. Dodd 1856
408p. col.front. pl.(5 col.) fold.map. D.
Also published under title: *Turkey, Greece, and Palestine in 1853* (Edinburgh, 1854)
Plates show costume of Turkey, Albania, Palestine
LC 4-13428

[**Hoyer, Johann Gottfried von**]
Pragmatische geschichte der saechsischen truppen; ein taschenbuch für soldaten. Leipzig, J. A. Barth 1792
120p. 32 col.pl. D.
Plates show 314 types of Saxon uniforms of past times. According to Colas the text is by J. G. Hoyer. The collection has also been attributed to J. A. Barth. A modern reprint of the plates exists
Colas 2417. Lipperheide 2199

Hoyer, K., and Brennecke, F.
Die uniformen des reichsheeres und der reichsmarine nebst amtlichen uniformtafeln. Charlottenburg, Verlag offene worte 1925
62p. 2 fold.col.pl. O.

Hoyland, John
A historical survey of the customs, habits, & present state of the Gipsies. York, The author, sold by W. Alexander [etc.] 1816
viii,[9]-265,[1]p. O.
Colas 1500. LC 13-2247

Hoynck van Papendrecht, J.
(illus.) Raa, F. J. G. ten. De uniformen van de nederlandsche zee en landmacht

Hoyos Sáinz, Luis de
Etnografía española; cuestionario y bases para el estudio de los trajes regionales. Madrid, Madariaga 1922
56p. 12pl. map. Q. (Sociedad española de antropologia) 2 pesetas

Hrotsvit, of Gandersheim
Opera. Nürnberg, 1501
82 l. 8 illus. F.
First edition of the works of Hrotsvit. Edited by Konrad Celtes. The illustrations are woodcuts and show German costume of the sixteenth century. They have been ascribed to Dürer
Lipperheide 434

Huart, Adrien. See Grevin, Alfred, jt. auth.

Huart, Louis
Muséum parisien; histoire physiologique, pittoresque, philosophique et grotesque de toutes les bêtes curieuses de Paris et de la banlieue, pour faire suite à toutes les éditions des œuvres de m. de Buffon ... 350 vignettes, par mm. Grandville, Gavarni, Daumier, Traviès, Lécurieur et Henri Monnier. Paris, Beauger 1841
395p. illus. Q.
Lipperheide 3653. LC 4-21510

Physiologie du garde national ... vignettes de mm. Maurisset et Trimolet; 3. ed. Paris, Aubert 1841
133p. illus. S. 1 fr.
Lipperheide 3713

Physiologie du médecin; vignettes de Trimolet. Paris, Aubert [1841]
127p. illus. T.
Lipperheide 3716. LC 19-18076

Physiologie du tailleur, par Louis Huart. Vignettes par Gavarni. Paris, Aubert [1841]
121p. 62 illus. S.
Colas 1501. Lipperheide 3718. LC 14-8567

Hubbard, Margaret
(illus.) Young women's Christian associations. Bureau of pageantry and the drama. National costumes of the Slavic peoples

Huber, Emil
Schweizer militär, ein Album von 24 farbigen blättern, originale von militärmaler Emil Huber ... L'armée suisse. Bern, F. Wyss 1915
1 l. 23 col.pl. F.

Huber, Johan Rudolf
Recueil de XXIV differens costumes de la ville et du canton de Basle, choisis dans les divers états de la société sur la fin du XVIIe siècle, gravés d'après les dessins de J. R. Huber, par J. R. Schellenberg. Basle, C. de Mechel 1798
24pl. Q.
Published originally with only twenty plates and the title: *Recueil de XX costumes.* The four supplementary plates are after designs by Holbein
Colas 1502

Huber-Liebenau, Theodor von
Denkmäler des hauses Habsburg in der Schweiz. Das Kloster Königsfelden. Zürich, 1867
4v.(liefgn) 76pl. Q.
Also published in Stuttgart by Ebner & Seubert

Hubrecht, Alph.
Grandeur et suprématie de Péking. Péking, Imprimerie des Lazaristes 1928
xi,607p. front. illus. pl.(1 col.) ports. plans. F.

Hucher, Eugène Frédéric Ferdinand
L'art gaulois, ou, Les Gaulois d'après leurs médailles. Paris, A. Morel 1868
63p. illus. 101 mounted pl. sq.F.
LC 10-7702

Huchtenburgh, Jan van
(illus.) Dumont, Jean, baron de Carlscroon. Batailles gagnées par le serenissime prince Fr. Eugene de Savoye

Huckel, J. F.
(ed.) Harvey, Fred. American Indians

Hudnall, Mrs Gladys (Frank). See Lyster, A. M., jt. auth.

Hübbe, Karl Johann Heinrich. See Suhr, Christoffer. Der ausruf in Hamburg

Huebner, Joseph Alexander, graf von
Ein spaziergang um die welt. Leipzig, H. Schmidt & C. Günther 1882
459p. 231 illus. 89pl. F.
The illustrations show scenes and costumes of North America, Japan and China
Lipperheide 1536

Hueffer, Francis
(tr.) Guhl, E. K., and Koner, W. D. The life of the Greeks and Romans described from antique monuments

Hünten, Emil
Die waffengattungen des preussischen heeres. Düsseldorf, Arnz 1860?
8 col.pl. Q.
Colas 1507

Hürlimann, Martin

Burma, Ceylon, Indo-China, Siam, Cambodia, Annam, Tongking, Yunnan; landscape, architecture, inhabitants. New York, Westermann; London, The Studio [c1930]
xxxix p. 288pl. on 144 l. illus.(maps, plans) F. $4.50 (Orbis terrarum)
Costume index. LC 30-19093

Deutschland: landschaft und baukunst; einleitung von Ricarda Huch; herausgegeben von Martin Hürlimann; textliche bearbeitung: prof. dr. F. Lampe und dr. Walther Meier; photos: Walter Hege, J. von Heimburg ... und andere. Berlin, Atlantis 1931
320p. incl.pl. Q. ($4.50 (Orbis terrarum)
Reprinted 1904. Some of the photographs show men and women in the dress of various sections
Costume index. LC 35-21393

Der erdkreis; ein orbis terrarum in einem band, landschaft, baukunst, volksleben. Berlin und Zurich, Atlantis verlag 1935
xxix,479p. illus.(maps) pl. Q.
LC 37-2350

India; the landscape, the monuments and the people. New York, Westermann; London, The Studio [c1928]
xxxiii p. 304pl. on 152 l. map. F. $5 (Orbis terrarum)
German edition published under title: *Indien; landschaft, baukunst und volksleben* (Berlin, Wasmuth, 1928)
Costume index. LC 29-4491

Hüsing, Georg

Die deutschen hochgezeiten. Wien, Eichendorff-haus 1927
xvi,144p. front.illus. pl.(part fold.) D.
Contents: Werden und wesen der Weihnacht; Drei könige und Berchtentag; Die Fasenachtszeit; Die Walbert-zeit (Osterzeit); Schützenfest (Pfingstzeit); Der Feuersprung; Die hailige Kümmernis [Wilgefortis]—Der Totensonntag. Allerseelen
LC 27-19024

Huet, Daniel Theodore

Inhuldiging van ... Willem Karel Hendrik Friso, prins van Oranje en Nassau ... als erf-heer von Vlissingen, op den v. junij MDCCLI. Amsterdam, I. Tirion 1753
73p. 1 illus.(port.) 8pl. F.
Lipperheide 2672

Der **Huge** Scheppel der gräfin Elisabeth von Nassau-Saarbrücken, nach der handschrift der Hamburger Stadtbibliothek. Huon Capet

Hughan, William James. See Mackey, A. G. An encyclopaedia of freemasonry and its kindred sciences

Hughes, Talbot

Dress design; an account of costume for artists & dressmakers; illus. by the author from old examples. London, New York [etc.] Sir I. Pitman & sons [1920]
xxx,33-361p. front.illus. XXXIII(i.e. 34)pl. D. $3.75 (The artistic crafts series of technical handbooks)
"Patterns to scale": p283-352
First published 1913 by Macmillan; reprinted 1920. A history of English dress, shoes, wigs, etc. from Roman to Victorian times. Illustrated with half-tones, line drawings and many patterns
Costume index. LC 21-11941

Old English costumes, selected from the collection formed by Talbot Hughes a sequence of fashions through the 18th & 19th centuries. Presented to the Victoria and Albert Museum, South Kensington. [London, 1914]
79p. 54 illus. 5 col.pl. F.
Reprinted from *The Connoisseur*
Costume index. LC A15-899 (under title

See also Seligman, G. S., jt. auth.

Hugo, Abel

(ed.) France militaire. Histoire des armées françaises de terre et de mer de 1792 à 1837. Ouvrage rédigé par une société de militaires et de gens de lettres, d'après les bulletins des armées le Moniteur, les documents officiel. [etc.] Paris, Delloye 1838
5v. 803pl. ports. maps. Q.
Lipperheide 2314. LC 21-3244

Hugo, Hermann

De militia equestri antiqua et nova .. libri quinque. Antverpiae, B. Moret 1630
344p. 29 illus. 6pl. F.
Lipperheide 2075

Huish, Marcus Bourne

Catalogue of an exhibition of the arms and armour of old Japan. See entry under Japan society, London

Samplers & tapestry embroideries ... 2d ed. London, New York [etc.] Longmans, Green 1913
xiv,176p. illus. pl. XXIV col.pl.(incl.front.) Q.
Twenty-three of the colored plates accompanied by guard sheets with descriptive letterpress
LC 14-4917

(ed) Bing, Samuel. Artistic Japan

Huish, Robert

An authentic history of the coronation of His Majesty, King George the Fourth: with a full and authentic detail of that august solemnity ... to which is prefixed a concise history of the coronations of the kings of England from the Saxon heptarchy to the present time. London, J. Robins 1821
314p. 5pl.(incl.front.) port. O.
LC 3-28029

Hulbert, Homer Bezaleel

The passing of Korea ... illus. from photographs. New York, Doubleday, Page 1906
xii,473p. front. pl. ports. Q. $3.80, o.p.
Some of the matter in this book has already appeared in the Korea review and elsewhere. The historical survey is a condensation from the writer's "History of Korea". cf. Preface
Costume index. LC 6-32372

Huldberg, Adolf

(pub.) Svenska arméens uniformer. Fahlun, A. Huldberg 1842
30 col.pl. ob.Q.
Colas 2842

Huldigungen ihren majestaeten Anton und Theresia könig und königin von Sachsen am 16n. October 1827, dargebracht von der bergstadt Annaberg und Buchholz. Dresden, J. H. G. Rau 1827?
7 col.pl. F.
Lipperheide 2582

Huldigungs-festzug der stadt Wien zur feier der silberne hochzeit ihrer majestäten des kaisers Franz Joseph I. Berggruen, Oscar

Hull, Edward

Costume of the British Army in 1828; lithographed by M. Gauci, from original drawing by E. Hull. London, Engelmann, Graf, Coindet & co. 1828-30

Front. 84 col.pl. F.
Colas 1503

Costume of the British navy in 1828; lithographed by M. Gauci, from the original drawings by E. Hull. London, Engelmann 1828

12 col.pl. Q.
Colas 1504

Hulle, Anselm van

Les hommes illustres qui ont vecu dans le XVII. siécle: les principaux potentats, princes, ambassadeurs & plenipotentiaires qui ont assisté aux conferences de Munster et d'Osnabrug, avec leurs armes et devises; dessinez et peints au naturel. Amsterdam, Pierre de Coup 1717

131pl. F.
Contains the portraits in his *Pacis antesignani* and, in addition, 25 pictures of nobles of the participating states and 20 of ambassadors
Lipperheide 534

Pacis antesignani, sive Icones legatorum plena potestate intructorum, qui ... ad pacem universalem constituendam monasterium Westphalorum et Osnabrugam convenerunt, magno studio ad vivum expressae. Antverpia, apud D. Middelerium 1648-50

87pl. F.
Lipperheide 533

(illus.) Aubry, Petrus. Effigies omnium legatorum deputatorum, consiliariorum, qui pacem universalem monasterij anno salutis 1648

Hullmandel, Charles. See Pinelli, Bartolommeo, jt. auth.

Hulme, Frederick Edward

The history, principles and practice of symbolism in Christian art; 2d ed. London, S. Sonnenschein; New York, Macmillan 1892

234p. illus. D. [The antiquarian library. 2]
LC 1-1711

Hulsen, Esaias von

Aigentliche warhaffte delineatio unnd abbildung aller fürstlichen auffzüg und rütterspilen bey dess ... Johann Friderichen hertzogen zu Württemberg ... jungen printzen und sohns hertzog Ulrichen ... kindtauff: und bey ... dess ... Ludwigen Friderichen hertzogen zu Württemberg &c. Mit ... Magdalena Elizabetha landtgräffin auss Hessen &c. hochzeytlichem frewdenfest celebrirt in Stuetgartt ... Julii, 1617. [Stuttgart], E. von Hulsen [1618]

84pl.(54 col.) F.
Engraved by Friedrich Brentel and Matthaeus Merian
Lipperheide 2586

Repræsentatio der furstlichen aufzug und ritterspil. So ... Johan Friderich hertzog zu Württemberg ... beij ihr ... neüwgebornen sohn Friderich ... kindtauffen ... 1616, Inn ... Stuetgarten ... gehalten. [Stuttgart 1616]

79pl. F.
Plates engraved by Matthaeus Merian
Lipperheide 2584

Hulsius, Levinus

XII. primorum caesarum et LXIII. ipsorum uxorum et parentum ex antiquis numismatibus, in aere incisae, effigies. Francoforti ad Moenum, typis Iohannis Collitii 1597

198p. 19pl. Q.
"Atque eorundem earundemque vitae & res gestae ex varijs authoribus collectae." Subtitle
Later edition 1599. The engraving is the work of Hans Sibmacher
Lipperheide 216

Hulst, L. van

De mode. Amsterdam, L. van Hulst 1781

30p. O.
Lipperheide 3477

The **human** hair. Rowland, Alexander

The **human** race. Figuier, Louis

Humbert, Aimé

Japan and the Japanese, illustrated; tr. by Mrs. Cashel Hoey and edited by H. W. Bates. London, R. Bentley 1874

xviii,378p. illus. Q.
Translation of his *Le Japon illustré*
LC 4-29866

Le Japon illustré. Paris, L. Hachette 1870

2v. illus. pl. map, 5 plans. F. 50fr.

Humbert, René. See Lienhart, jt. auth.

Humboldt, Alexander, freiherr von

Vues des Cordillères, et monumens des peuples indigènes de l'Amérique. Paris, F. Schoell 1810

16,350p. 69pl.(30 col.) F.
Plate 14 shows costume of the time of Montezuma, 52 and 53 of Mexican Indians. They are from Von Humboldt's sketches
An abridged edition (Paris, Librairie grecque-latine-allemande 1816. 19pl. O.) has only four plates of costume value
Lipperheide 1630. LC 4-1354 (abr. ed.)

Hume, James Ord. See Zealley, A. E., jt. auth.

Humphreys, David

(tr.) Montfaucon, Bernard de. Antiquity explained, and represented in sculptures

Humphreys, Henry Noel

The illuminated books of the middle ages; an account of the development and progress of the art of illumination, as a distinct branch of pictorial ornamentation, from the IVth. to the XVIIth. centuries. Illus. by examples ... from the most beautiful mss. of the various periods, executed on stone and printed in colours by Owen Jones. London, Longman, Brown, Green, and Longmans 1859

15p. 34 l. 40pl.(39 col.and mounted) F.
Useful for costume of the middle ages
LC 15-7625

Humphries, G. C.

(illus.) United States. War dept. Regulations for the uniform and dress of the army of the United States, June, 1851

160 Nürnberger schimpfwörter. Gabler, Ambrosius

A **hundred** wonderful years. Peel, Mrs D. C. B.

Hungarian & highland broad sword. Rowlandson, Thomas

Hungarian peasant costumes. See Pekáry, István. Magyar népviseletek

Hungarian peasant customs. Viski, Károly

Hungary. Földmívelésügyi ministerium
Kiváló diszitmények az 1881. évi Országos magyar nöiparkiállitából ... Ornements remarquables de l'Exposition hongroise industrielle des ouvrages de femmes en 1881. Budapest 1882
2 l. 25pl. F.
Hungarian and French
Lipperheide 3966

Hungary
L'art populaire hongrois. 1928
Budapest. Magyar nemzeti múzeum. Néprajzi osztályának értesítöje. 1900+
Colquhoun, A. R., and Colquhoun, Mrs E. M. C. The whirlpool of Europe, Austria-Hungary and the Habsburgs. 1907
"Eighty" club, London. Hungary, its people, places, and politics, the visit of the Eighty club in 1906. 1907
Hacquet, Balthasar. Hacquet's neueste physikalisch-politische reisen in den jahren 1788 und 1789 durch die dacischen und sarmatischen oder nördlichen Karpathen. 1790
Das Kaiser-album, viribus unitis. 1858
A magyarság tárgyi néprajza. 1934
Malonyay, Dezsö. A magyar nép müvészete. 1913-22
Masner, Carl. Die costüm-ausstellung im K. K. Oesterreichischen museum 1891. 1892-93
Nemes, Mihály. A magyar jelmez és fejlödése dióhéjban. 1903
Nemes, Mihály. A magyar viseletek tört'enete. 1900
Szendrei, János. A magyar viselet történeti fejlödése. 1905
Trachten-album. ca1860
Undi, Mariska. Magyar himvarró müvészet; a nemes magyar fonalasmunkák története, a honfoglalás korától napjainkig. 1934

See also Military costume—Austria; Naval costume—Austria; also subdivision Hungary under Coronations and coronation robes; Crown jewels; Decoration and ornament; Embroidery; Kings and rulers; Nobles; Regalia

17th century

Oertel, Hieronymus. Ortelius redivivus et continuatus, oder Der ungarischen kriegs-empörungen historische beschreibung ... Deszgleichen auch mit einer continuation, von dem 1607. bis an das 1665. jahr vermehret durch Martin Meyern. 1665

19th-20th centuries

Ferenczy, Ferenc. Magyaros ifjúsági ruhák. 1935
Heimbucher von Bikessy, J. A Magyar és Horváth országi leg nevezetesebb nemzeti oltözetek hazai gyüjteménie ... Vaterländische vollständige sammlung der merkwürdigsten national costume des königreichs Ungarn und Croatien. 1816
Heimbucher von Bikessy, J. Pannoniens bewohner in ihren volksthümlichen trachten. 1820
Heksch, A. F. Die Donau von ihrem ursprung bis an die mündung. Eine schilderung von land und leuten des Donaugebietes. 1881
Hering, G. E. Sketches on the Danube, in Hungary and Transylvania. 1838
Holme, Charles, ed. Peasant art in Austria and Hungary. 1911
Kellner, Leon; Arnold, Mme Paula, and Delisle, A. L. Austria of the Austrians and Hungary of the Hungarians. 1914
Lederer, Mrs C. B. Made in Hungary. 1933
Mikszáth, Kálmán. Scènes hongroises. 1890
Die Österreichisch-ungarische monarchie in wort und bild. 1886-1902
Pekáry, István. Magyar népviseletek ... Costumes hongrois ... Ungarische volkstrachten ... Hungarian peasant costumes ... Costumi ungheresi. 1933
Prónay von Tot-Próna und zu Blathnicza, Gabriel, freiherr. Skizzen aus dem volksleben in Ungarn. 1855
Smith, F. B. Budapest, the city of the Magyars. 1903
Stokes, Adrian. Hungary. 1909
Valério, Théodore. Costumes de la Hongrie et des provinces danubiennes, Dalmatie, Monténégro, Croatie, Slavonie, frontières militaires. 1885
Viski, Károly. Hungarian peasant customs. 1932

Periodicals

Családi Kör. 1865-66
Divat-Tükör. Képes közlöny a divat-es kézimunka köreböl. 1889-90
Der Spiegel; zeitschrift für die elegante welt, mode, literatur, kunst, theater. 1828-47

Hungary, its people, places, and politics, the visit of the Eighty club in 1906. "Eighty" club, London

Hunglinger von Yngue, Andreas Magnus
Abbildungen und beschreib. herumziehender krämer von Constantinopel, nebst andern stadteinwohner und fremden aus Aegypten, d. Barbarei und d. Archipelagus, nach d. natur gezeichnet. Wien, Degen 1803
2 hefte. illus. F.

Hunloke, Sylvia (Heseltine) lady, and Aldin, Cecil Charles Windsor
Riding (*In* Aldin, C. C. W. The omnibus book of sports for young and old. Part 2)

Hunsley, W.
Costume of the Madras army. 1841
36 col.pl. F.
Colas 1505

Hunsrücker volkskunde. Diener, Walter

Hunt, George. See Boas, Franz. The social organization and the secret societies of the Kwakiutl Indians

Hunt, Mrs Margaret (Raine) (Mrs. A. W. Hunt)
Our grandmothers' gowns; illus. by George R. Halkett. London, Field & Tuer [etc. 1884]
54 numb. l. 24 col.pl. O. o.p.
Colas 1506. Costume index. LC 29-4608

Hunter, James
(illus.) Picturesque scenery in the kingdom of Mysore, from forty drawings taken on the spot. London, W. Bulmer 1805
41 col.pl. ob.F.
Contains views with figures, and a portrait of Tippoo Sahib, sultan of Mysore
Colas 1508. Lipperheide 1478

Hunter, John, robe-maker
A concise description of the insignia of the orders of British knighthood. London, J. Hunter [1844]
71p. 49 illus. on 1 l. 20 col.pl. Q.
"With illustrations of all the collars, stars, badges, medals, clasps, and crosses ... Shewing the manner of wearing them on all occasions, also the proper mode of using them in heraldry, exemplifying how they should be emblazoned." Subtitle
An extract from Biedenfeld's *Geschichte ... aller geistlichen und weltlichen ... ritterorden* with the same plates and illustrations
Lipperheide 1926

Hunting costume
Alessandro, Giuseppe d'. Opera. 1723 p781-84
Aubry, Charles. Chasses anciennes d'après les manuscrits des XIV. & XV. siècles. 1837
Döbel, H. W. Heinrich Wilhelm Döbel's Neueröffnete jäger-practica. 1754
Dryden, Alice, ed. The art of hunting. 1908
Frost, A. B. Sports and games in the open. 1899
Lacombe, Fr. Encyclopédie méthodique; dictionnaire de toutes les espèces de chasses. 1795-1811

See also Falconers

England

Clapham, Richard. Foxhunting on the Lakeland fells. 1920
Nevill, R. H. Old English sporting prints and their history. 1923
Sparrow, W. S. British sporting artists from Barlow to Herring. 1922
Sparrow, W. S. Henry Alken. 1927
Thomas, Sir W. B. Hunting England. 1936

France

Paris. Bibliothèque nationale. Mss.(Fr. 616) Livre de la chasse

Caricature and satire

Deyeux, Théophile. Physiologie du chasseur. 1841

Germany

Edelmann, August. Schützenwesen und schützenfeste der deutschen städte vom 13. bis zum 18. jahrhundert. 1890

15th century

Maximilian I, emperor of Germany. Das jagdbuch kaiser Maximilians I. 1901
Paris. Musée national du Louvre. Les tapisseries des chasses de Maximilien. 1920

16th century

Amman, Jost. Künstliche wolgerissne new figuren, von allerlei jag und weidtwerch. 1582
Neuw jag unnd weydwerck buch, das ist ein grundtliche beschreibung vom anfang der jagten, auch vom jäger. 1582
Sebizius, Melchior. XV bücher von dem feldbaw und recht volkommenen wolbestellung eines bekömmlichen landsitzes. 1598

18th century

Fleming, H. F. von. Der vollkommene teutsche jäger ... Dann auch die ... hunde, und der völlige jagd-zeug. 1719
Mellin, A. W., graf von. Unterricht eingefriedigte wildbahnen oder grosse thiergärten anzulegen und zu behandeln, um dadurch das wildpret nützlicher und unschädlich zu machen. 1800
Mellin, A. W., graf von. Versuch einer anweisung zur anlegung, verbesserung, und nutzung der wildbahnen so wohl im freyen als in thiergärten. 1779

Italy

Borsa, Mario. La caccia nel Milanese. 1924
Raimondi, Eugenio. Delle caccie. 1626

Hunting England. Thomas, Sir W. B.

Huon Capet
Der Huge Scheppel der gräfin Elisabeth von Nassau-Saarbrücken, nach der handschrift der Hamburger Stadtbibliothek; mit einer einleitung von Hermann Urtel. Hamburg, L. Grafe 1905
25,57p. facsims. illus. 4 col.pl. F. (Hamburg. Stadtbibliothek. Veröffentlichungen bd. 1)
Illustrations show 15th century costume. Text paged in duplicate

Hurd, William
Oude en tegenwoordige staat en geschiedenis van alle godsdiensten, van de schepping af tot op den tegenwoordigen tijd. Uit het Engelsch vertaald ... Versierd met een prachtig stel kunstplaaten. Amsterdam, M. de Bruyn 1781-91
7v. pl. O.
Translation of the author's *Universal history*. The plates show costume worn in religious ceremonies in all parts of the world and also Dutch costume of the latter part of the eighteenth century
Lipperheide 1813. LC 30-13611

Hurgronje, Christian Snouck
The Achehnese, by Dr. C. Snouck Hurgronje ... trans. by the late A. W. S. O'Sullivan ... with an index by R. J. Wilkinson. Leyden, E. J. Brill; London, Luzac 1906
2v. fronts. illus. ports. 2 fold.maps, fold. plan. Q.
Illustrations show costume of natives of Sumatra
LC 6-39436

Hurlimann, Johann
(engr.) Lörer, and Vogel. Costumes suisses

Hurll, Estelle May
Child-life in art; 2d ed. Boston, L. C. Page 1898
xii,176p. illus. ports. 7pl.(incl.front.) D.
Bibliography: p[175]-76
LC 9-25569

The Madonna in art. Boston, L. C. Page 1897
217p. incl. 30pl. front. D.
LC 10-116

Hurlock, Elizabeth Bergner
Motivation in fashion. New York 1929
71p. 24cm. (Archives of psychology ... no 111)
Bibliography: p71
LC 30-22158

The psychology of dress; an analysis of fashion and its motive. New York, The Ronald press [c1929]
viii,244p. front.illus. O.
Bibliography: p233-36
LC 29-27918

Husher, Th. v.
Samling af danske militaire uniformer med 6 tillaegsblade. Collection des uniformes militaires danois; avec 6 feuilles supplémentaires, suivies d'un texte explicatif et d'un règlement de l'habillement des officiers. Kiöbenhavn, J. Hoffensberg [1858]
6 l. 26 col.pl. Q.
The six supplementary plates show details of equipment, uniforms and decorations
Colas 1509. Lipperheide 2279

Les **hussards,** les vieux régiments, 1692-1792. Choppin, Henri

Les **hussards** sous la révolution. Margerand, J.

The **Hussay** festival in Jamaica. Beckwith, M. W.

Hussenot, F.
(illus.) Hennebert, Eugène. Nos soldats

Huszka, József
Magyarische ornamentik. Verfasst und gezeichnet von Josef Huszka. Autorisierte deutsche übersetzung von dr. Willibald Semayer. Leipzig, K. W. Hiersemann 1900
19p. illus. L pl.(12 col.) F.
LC 10-28074

Der **hut;** ein kulturhistorischer essay, mit benutzung einer amerikanischen arbeit. Hamburg & Leipzig, J. P. F. E. Richter 1869
62p. 75 illus. O.
Lipperheide 1709

Der **hut** und seine geschichte. Timidior, O.

Hutchinson, Mrs Frances (Kinsley)
Motoring in the Balkans along the highways of Dalmatia, Montenegro, the Herzegovina and Bosnia. Chicago, A. C. McClurg 1909
xiii,17-341p. front. O.
LC 9-27939

Hutchinson, Henry Neville
Marriage customs in many lands. London, Seeley 1897
xii,348p. front. pl. O.
LC 13-12985

Hutchinson, Henry Neville; Gregory, John Walter, and Lydekken, Richard
(eds.) The living races of mankind; a popular illustrated account of the customs, habits, pursuits, feasts & ceremonies of the races of mankind throughout the world. London, Hutchinson [1901]
584p. col.front. illus.(incl. maps) col.pl. O.
Published in 18 parts. Issued as volumes 4-5 of *The people's natural history* (New York, University society 1903)
LC 4-9000

Hutchinson, Walter
(ed.) Customs of the world; a popular account of the manners, rites and ceremonies of men and women in all countries ... with contributions by eminent authorities. London, Hutchinson [1913]
2v. col.fronts. illus. col.pl. maps. Q. ea 7s 6d, o.p.
Costume index. LC w15-79

Huth, Philip Jakob
Von den verdiensten des durchleuchtigsten hauses Wittelspach um die kirche. Landshut, M. Hagen 1777
268p. 2 illus. 2pl. O.
The plates contain 18 portraits of dukes and electors of Bavaria
Lipperheide 725

Huttich, Johann
Imperatorum romanorum libellus. Una cum imaginibus ad vivam effiigiem expressis. Argentina, W. Cephalaeus 1526
89 l. 184 ports. O.
The author's name appears in the dedication
The illustrations show heads of Roman, Byzantine and German emperors to the time of Charles V and the crown prince Ferdinand
First edition (Strassburg 1525) The third edition with title: *Romanorum principũ effigies: cũ historiarum annotatione, olim ab Io. Hutchichio confecta* (Argentorati, apud V. Cephalaeum 1552) has 277 portraits, some enlarged from the second edition, and a few new ones. Also 83 portraits of Roman consuls have been added
Lipperheide 208, 209

Hutton, Alfred
Old sword-play; the systems of fence in vogue during the XVIth, XVIIth, and XVIIIth centuries. London, H. Grevel; New York, B. Westermann 1892
10,36p. 57pl. Q.
Lipperheide 2995m

Hutton, Alfred—*Continued*
The sword and the centuries; or, Old sword days and old sword ways ... With introductory remarks by Captain Cyril G. R. Matthey. London, G. Richards 1901
xxii,367p. front.(port.) illus. 10pl. O.
"Being a description of the various swords used in civilized Europe during the last five centuries, and of single combats which have been fought with them." Subtitle
LC 3-23074

Hutton, Samuel King
Among the Eskimos of Labrador. London, Seeley, Service & co. 1912
xviii,343p. front. pl. ports. 2 maps(1 fold.) O.
LC 12-9697

Hyatt, Hallett
(engr.) Morgan, J. P. Catalogue of the collection of jewels and precious works of art

Hygiène de la parisienne. Darfeu

Hygiene der kleidung. Jaeger, Heinrich, and Jaeger, Frau Anna

L'**hygiène** et la mode. Drouineau, Gustave

Hygiene of dress
Cleveland, W. F. The prophylactic clothing of the body chiefly in relation to cold. 1896
Creve, C. C. Medizinischer versuch einer modernen kleidung die brüste betreffend ... nebst einigen bemerkungen über das schminken. 1794
Debay, Auguste. Hygiène vestimentaire. 1857
Darfeu. Hygiène de la parisienne. 1884
Drouineau, Gustave. L'hygiène et la mode. 1886
Ecob, H. G. The well-dressed woman 1893
Flinn, D. E. Our dress and our food in relation to health. 1886
Goullin, J. A. La mode sous le point de vue hygiénique, médical, et historique; ou, conseils aux dames et à la jeunesse. 1846
Gynäkatoptron, oder blicke in die weibliche garderobe in bezug auf körperliches wohlseyn. 1805
Jaeger, Gustav. Health-culture. 1908
Jaeger, Gustav. Die normalkleidung als gesundheitschutz. 1881
Jaeger, Gustav. Selections from essays on health culture and the sanitary woolen system. 1891
Jaeger, Heinrich, and Jaeger, Frau Anna. Hygiene der kleidung. 1906
Jessop, C. M. Dress and health, an appeal to antiquity and common sense. 1895
Job, A., doctor. Le vêtement au point de vue de l'hygiène. 1880?
Kellogg, J. H. The evils of fashionable dress, and how to dress healthfully. 1876
Kratschmer, Florian. Die bekleidung. 1894
Kuhnow, Anna. Die frauenkleidung vom standpunkte der hygiene. 1893
Leighton, John. Madre Natura versus the Moloch of fashion. 1874
Marie de Saint-Ursin, P. J. L'ami des femmes, ou Lettres d'un médecin, concernant l'influence de l'habillement des femmes sur leurs moeurs et leur santé. 1805
Michelitz, Anton. Über den nachtheil, den die heutige frauentracht der gesundheit bringt. 1803
Muthesius, Anna. Das eigenkleid der frau. 1903
Pearse, T. F. Modern dress and clothing in its relation to health and disease. 1882
Peters, Emil. Kleidung und gesundheit. 1911
Rougemont, Josephus Claudius. Etwas über kleidertracht, in wie ferne sie einen nachtheiligen einfluss auf die gesundheit hat. 1784
Treves, Sir Frederick. The influence of clothing on health. 1886
Vaughan, Walter. An essay, philosophical and medical, concerning modern clothing. 1792
Velde, T. H. van de. Die frauenkleidung. 1909
Watt, Jeannie. Das zukunftskleid der frau; die gesundung der frauenmode. 1902
Woolson, Mrs A. L. G. Dress-reform: a series of lectures delivered in Boston, on dress as its affects the health of women. 1874

See also Corset

Hygiène vestimentaire. Debay, Auguste

Hyllested, Hans Chr.
Collection complète des uniformes de la marine et de l'armée danoise. Altona 1829
4 l. 115 col.pl. F.
Two plates are signed with the initials K. S. and the work is sometimes attributed to Christoffer Suhr
Colas 1510

Hymans, Louis
xxve anniversaire de l'inauguration du roi. Les fêtes de juillet ... celebrées à Bruxelles les 21, 22 et 23 juillet 1856. Bruxelles, A. Jamar 1856
104p. 53 illus. Q.
Lipperheide 2683

Hypnerotomachia Poliphili. See note under Colonna, Francesco. Poliphili Hypnerotomachia

I

I., H.
(illus.) Erinnerung an Hamburg

Iacovleff, A. See I͡Akovlev, Aleksandr

I͡Akovlev, Aleksandr, and Elisi͡eev, Sergi͡eĭ Grigorevich
Le théâtre japonais (kabuki). Paris, J. Meynial [1933]
94p. illus. XXXII col.pl. F.
At head of title: A Iacovleff et S. Elisséef. Descriptive letterpress on verso of each plate
Plates show theatrical costume and modes of dressing the hair in Japan
LC AC34-925

Îakovlev, A., and Eliesîeev, S. G.—*Cont.*
(illus.) Chu Chia-Chien. The Chinese theatre
(illus.) Chu Chia-Chien. Le théâtre chinois

Iban or sea Dayak fabrics. Haddon, A. C., and Start, L. E.

Ibo tribe
Basden, G. T. Among the Ibos of Nigeria. 1921

Ibsen, Henrik
Peer Gynt, by Henrik Ibsen, decorated by Elizabeth MacKinstry. Garden City, N. Y., Doubleday, Doran 1929
286p. col.front. illus. pl.(part col.) Q.
Translated by R. F. Sharp
LC 29-19565

Ice hockey. Sayles, Alexander

Iceland
Bruun, Daniel. Den islandske kvinde og hendes dragt. 1903
Ólafsson, Eggert. Des vice-lavmands Eggert Olafsens und des landphysici Biarne Povelsens reise durch Island, veranstaltet von der Königlichen societät der wissenschaften in Kopenhagen und beschrieben von ... Olafsen. 1774-75

Icones aliquot clarorum virorum Germaniae, Angliae, Galliae, Ungariae. See Reusner, Nicolaus. Icones sive images vivae, literis cl. virorum

Icones & effigies virorum doctorum. Boissard, J. J.

Icones et elogia virorum. See note under Küster, G. G. Martin Friedrich Seidels Bilder-sammlung

Icones & vitae principum ac regum Poloniae. Neugebauer, Salomon

Icones, id est verae imagines virorum doctrina simul et pietate illustrium. Bèze, Théodore de

Icones Livianae: praecipuas romanorum historias magno artificio. Amman, Jost

Icones omnium ad officinas aerarias pertinentium officialium et operariorum. Weigel, Christoph

Icones omnium ad rem metallicam spectantium officialium et operariorum. Weigel, Christoph

Icones operum misericordiae. Cartarius, Marius

Icones principum. Dyck, Sir Anthonie van

Icones quibus habitus omnium fere mundi gentium exprimitur. See Trachten oder Stambuch; dariñen alle fürneñste nationen, völckern, manns und weibs personen in ihren kleydern artlich abgemahlt

Icones sive effigies omnium & singulorum ecclesiae Augustanae A. Cillibatâ verbi praedicatione. Hopffer, Bartholom.

Icones sive imagines impp. regum, principum, electorum et ducum Saxoniae. Reusner, Nicolaus

Icones sive imagines vivae, literis cl. virorum. Reusner, Nicolaus

Icones virorum gentis et stirpis Ottiorum in Helvetia. Ott, J. C.

Iconografía española. Carderera y Solano, Valentín

Iconografia storica degli ordini religiosi e cavallereschi. Giucci, Gaetano

Iconographie des contemporains, ou portraits des personnes dont les noms se rattachent plus particulièrement, soit par leurs actions, soit par leurs écrits, aux divers évènements qui ont eu lieu en France, depuis 1789 jusqu'en 1829; publié par F. S. Delpech. Paris, L'éditeur 1832
200pl. O.
Portraits of illustrious Frenchmen, by contemporary artists. According to Lipperheide, copied in reduced size from an earlier folio edition. Some of these plates were copied in reduced size in *Célébrités contemporaines*
Lipperheide 1162

Iconographie du costume militaire. Sauzey, J. C. A. F.

Iconographie française et étrangée. Maurin, Antoine

Iconographie françoise, ou Portraits des personnages les plus illustres qui ont paru en France depuis François premier, (et quelques années avant) jusqu'à la fin du règne de Louis XVI. Paris, Delpech 1828-40
200pl. O.
Includes the period 1515-1715
Lipperheide 1079

Iconographie générale et méthodique du costume du IV. au XIX. siècle (315-1815) Jacquemin, Raphael

Iconographie Molièresque. Lacroix, Paul

Iconologia ovvero immagini di tutte le cose principali a cui l'umano talento ha finto un corpo. Pistrucci, Filippo

Iconum virorum virtute. See Boissard, J. J. Icones & effigies virorum doctorum

Ein **ideal** der frauenwelt. Brosin, Fr.

Ideen zu einer mimik. Engel, J. J.

Les **Idées** nouvelles de la mode. v 1-11 no5, 1922-1932. Paris
11v. col.illus. col.pl. F. 252fr.
Published monthly
Merged into *Très Parisien*

Ides, Evert Ysbrandszoon
Driejaarige reize naar China, te lande gedaan door den moskovischen afgezant. Amsterdam, F. Halma 1704
14 l. 244p. 23 illus. Q.
Illustrations show Tatars and Siberians
Also published (Amsterdam, P. de Coup, 1710)
Lipperheide 1516. LC 2-536 (1710 ed.)

Iffland, August Wilhelm
[Ifflands mimische darstellungen für schauspieler und zeichner] gez. und gest. von den gebrüdern Henschel. Berlin, 1819
2 l. 120pl. O.
The sketches were made 1808-1813
Lipperheide 3208

Igiena ţĕranului, locuinţa. Manolescu, M. N.

Igny, Jean de Saint-. See Saint-Igny, Jean de

Igorots. See Philippine islands

Ilchester, Mary Eleanor Anne (Dawson) countess of, and Ilchester, Giles Stephen Holland Fox-Strangways, 6th earl of
(eds.) Napier, Lady S. L. B. The life and letters of Lady Sarah Lennox

Ilg, Albert
Geschichte und terminologie der alten spitzen. Wien, Lehmann & Wentzel 1876
64p. illus. 4pl. O.
Lipperheide 4036

Spitzen-album ... hrsg vom K.K Oesterr. museum für kunst und industrie. Wien, Verlag des K.K. Oesterr. museums 1876
1 l. 30pl. Q.
Lipperheide 4037

Ilios. Schliemann, Heinrich

The **illuminated** book of needlework. Owen, Mrs Henry

The **illuminated** books of the middle ages. Humphreys, H. N.

The **illuminated** ladies' book of useful and ornamental needlework. See Owen, Mrs Henry. The illuminated book of needlework

Illustrated album of the French army and navy. See Album militaire

Illustrated catalogue of the extensive collection ... from the ... Blakeslee galleries. Blakeslee, T. J.

The **illustrated** companion to the Latin dictionary and Greek lexicon. Rich, Anthony

An **illustrated** history of arms and armour from the earliest period to the present time. See Demmin, A. F. Weapons of war

An **illustrated** history of Japanese art. Minamoto, Hoshu

An **illustrated** history of the hat. Genin, J. N.

The **Illustrated** household journal and Englishwoman's domestic magazine. no 1-16; 1880-1881. London
Successor to the *Englishwoman's domestic magazine.* Merged with *The Milliner, dressmaker and draper*

Illustrated London magazine. See Ladies cabinet of fashion, music and romance

The **Illustrated London news**
The coronation of King George and Queen Mary: the abbey ceremonies; the processions; and the naval review. Illustrated London news coronation panorama number. London, 1911
Cover-title, 28p. illus. (part col.) ob.F.
Special number of the *Illustrated London news,* June 27, 1911, no3766A
LC 12-17864

The funeral procession of King Edward VII. London [Illustrated London news and sketch, ltd.] 1910
Cover-title, 24p. illus. double pl. ob.O.
Special number of May 24, 1910
LC 11-14446

The Illustrated London news coronation record number. King George V. and Queen Mary; ed. by Bruce S. Ingram. London, Illustrated London news and sketch, ltd. [1911]
20[i.e. 28]p. illus. (part col.) 16pl. (part col. part mounted) F.
Special number of the Illustrated London news, May 27, 1911
LC 12-15101

The Illustrated London news record of the coronation service and ceremony. King Edward VII. and Queen Alexandra (June 26, 1902); with twenty-five coloured and other plates and many illustrations by R. Caton Woodville, & others. London, Illustrated London news and sketch [1902]
26,19-52p. col.front. illus. pl. (part col.) port. (part col.) map, tab. F.
LC 2-28655

Silver jubilee record number, King George V. and Queen Mary, 1910-1935. London, Illustrated London news and sketch, 1935
84p. col.front. illus. col.pl. ports. (part col.) F.
Colored plates show King George V and Queen Mary, also the royal crowns and sceptres of England
LC 35-37321

L'Illustrateur des dames et des demoiselles, journal des soirées de famille. 1.-14. année, 1861-1874. Paris
Col.pl. Q.
Title change: v11-14, 1871-74, *La mode de Paris, L'Illustrateur des dames ... réunis*
Colas 1512. Lipperheide 4692

Illustration. See note under Jardin des modes

Illustration de l'armée française depuis 1789 jusqu'en 1832. Cogniet, Léon, and Raffet

Illustration des modes. See Jardin des modes

An **illustration** of the Egyptian, Grecian, and Roman costume. Baxter, Thomas

Illustrationen zu den werken Friedrichs des Grossen. See Menzel, Adolph. Illustrations des oeuvres de Frederic-le-grand

Illustrationen zur rang und quartier-liste, oder Abbildungen der neuen uniformen in der preuss. armee. Berlin, Mittler 1844-45
16 col.pl. O.
Published in five parts

Illustrations des oeuvres de Frédéric-legrand. Menzel, Adolph

Illustrations of Alaskan clothing. United States. Quartermaster corps

Illustrations of China and its people. Thomson, John

Illustrations of English and foreign costumes from the fifteenth century to the present day. Pauquet, H. L. É., and Pauquet, P. J. C.

Illustrations of incised slabs on the continent of Europe. Creeny, W. F.

Illustrations of mediaeval costume. Lonsdale, H. W., and Tarver, E. J.

Illustrations of medieval costume in England. Day, T. A., and Dines, J. H.

Illustrations of monumental brasses. Ecclesiological society, Cambridge

Illustrations of Shakspeare. Douce, Francis

Illustrations of the Dramatic works of Shakspeare. Boydell, John, and Boydell, Josiah

Illustrations of the historical ball given by ... the Earl and Countess of Aberdeen in the Senate Chamber, Ottawa, 17th Feb. 1896; with a short historical introduction by J. G. Bourinot. Ottawa, J. Durie & Son 1896
46p. 12pl. S.
Reproductions of photographs show groups of people dressed in the costume of the period they represent. 1 Voyages of the Norsemen, ca986-1015; 2 Discovery of North America by John Cabot, 1497; 3 Discovery of Canada by Jacques Cartier 1534-36; 4 Foundation of Port Royal and settlement of Acadia 1604-1677; 5 Foundation of Montreal 1641-1670; 6 Days of settlement and exploration 1665-1698; 7 Days of Montcalm and Wolf 1754-1760; 8 From the fall of Mount Royal to the second taking of Louisbourg 1710-1758; 9 Coming of the United Empire Loyalists 1775-1792; 10 The Indian group

Illustrations of the liturgy. Skilbeck, C. O., illus.

Illustrations of the manners and costumes of France, Switzerland, and Italy. See note under Bridgens, Richard. Sketches

Illustrations of the manners, customs and condition of the North American Indians. Catlin, George

Illustrations of the mission, the camp, and the zenána. Mackenzie, Mrs H. D.

Illustrations of the occasional offices of the church in the middle ages. Kingsford, H. S.

Illustrations to Maximilian Prince of Wied's Travels in the interior of North America. See Wied-Neuwied, M. A. P., prinz von. Travels in the interior of North America

Illustrierte sittengeschichte vom mittelalter bis zur gegenwart. Fuchs, Eduard

Illustrierte völkerkunde. See Buschan, G. H. T. Die sitten der völker

Illustrirte coiffure; zeitschrift für kopfputz u. lingerie. 1.-15 jahrg. Oct. 1878-1892. Berlin, Bazar-Actiengesellschaft
15v. col.illus. col.pl. F.
Years 4 and 5 were published as a supplement to *Bazar.* Merged with *Die Coiffure*

Illustrirte frauen-zeitung; ausgabe der modenwelt mit unterhaltungsblatt. 1.-35. jahrg.; 1874-1908? Berlin, F. Lipperheide
35v. col.pl. F.
Contains fashion plates
Colas 1513. Lipperheide 4703

Die vermählung seiner königlichen hoheit des prinzen Wilhelm von Preuszen mit ihrer hoheit der prinzessin Augusta Victoria zu Schleswig-Holstein. Berlin, F. Lipperheide 1881
36p. 26 illus. F.
Extra number of the *Illustrirte frauen-zeitung*
Lipperheide 2551

Illustrirte geschichte der k. k. armee. Anger, Gilbert

Illustrirte geschichte der Trappisten order. Pfannenschmidt, F.

Der **Illustrirte** hausfreund; ein familienbuch für alle stände. See Der Hausfreund

Illustrirte kriegs-chronik; gedenkbuch an den deutsch-französischen feldzug von 1870-1871, geschrieben vom verfasser der Illustrirten kriegs-chronik von 1866 ... Leipzig, J. J. Weber 1871
456p. front. illus. ports. maps. F.
Lipperheide 2122. LC 30-1832

Illustrirte modenzeitung. 1.-6. jahrg. 1873/74-1878/79. Berlin, Victoria-verlag 1873-79
6v. illus. F.
Published monthly
Colas 1514. Lipperheide 4740

Illustrirte stamm- rang- und quartier liste. Schneider, Louis

Das **illustrirte** schusterbüchlein. See Hall, J. S. The book of the feet

Illustrirte zeitung

Die Kölner dom-feier. Leipzig, J. J. Weber 1880
p.401-420. 6 illus. F.
Lipperheide 2813

Illustrirtes archäologisches wörterbuch der kunst. Müller, H. A., and Mothes, Oscar

Illustrirtes magazin begleitet von der Schnellpost für moden; eine zeitschrift zur unterhaltung und belehrung, unter bes. rücksicht auf die interessen der gegenwart. Jahrg. 1-6, 1846-1851. Leipzig, Baumgärtner
6v. col.illus. Q.
Published weekly. Edited by F. A. Weise
Supersedes *Das Heller-magazin*
Lipperheide 4655

Illustrirtes wörterbuch der römischen alterthümer. See Rich, Anthony. The illustrated companion to the Latin dictionary and Greek lexicon

Illustrissimi Wirtembergici. Neyffer, J. C.

Illustrium Hollandiae & Westfrisiae ordinum alma Academia Leidensis. Lugduni Batavorum, apud I. Marci 1614
27 l. 231 p. 55 illus. Q.
Fifty four portraits show professors of Leyden university
Lipperheide 2016

Illustrium quos Belgium habuit pictorum effigies, ad vivum accurate delineatae. Antverpiae, apud T. Gallaeum ca1600
22pl. Q.
First edition: 1572 (25pl.); second edition: 1572 (23pl.)
Many of the illustrations are by Hieronymus Wierx
Lipperheide 927

Illyria

Costume of Illyria and Dalmatia. 1824

Hacquet, Balthasar. L'Illyrie et la Dalmatie, ou Moeurs usages et costumes des habitants et des ceux des contrées voisines. 1815

Hacquet, Balthasar. Abbildung und beschreibung der südwest- und östlichen Wenden, Illyrer und Slaven. 1802-1805

Shoberl, Frederic, ed. Illyria and Dalmatia. 1821

Illyria and Dalmatia. Shoberl, Frederic, ed.

L'**Illyrie** et la Dalmatie. Hacquet, Balthasar

Ilschen, Wilhelm Meyer-. See Meyer-Ilschen, Wilhelm

Im frauwenzimmer. Amman, Jost

Im herzen von Afrika. Schweinfurth, G. A.

Im Kaukasus 1862. Albrecht, prince of Prussia

Im reiche Kaiser Menelik's tagebuch einer abessinischen reise. Kulmer, Friedrich von

Im toilettenzimmer. Sydow, Johanna von

L'**image** de la femme. Dayot, A. P. M.

L'**imagerie** populaire. Duchartre, P. L., and Saulnier, René

L'**imagerie** populaire italienne. Bertarelli, Achille

Images de saints et saintes issus de la famille de l'Empereur Maximilian I. Burgkmair, Hans

Les **images** d'Epinal. Perrout, René

Les **images** presque de tous les empereurs. Goltz, Hubert

Imaginary figures. See Allegorical and imaginary figures

Imagines et elogia virorum. Orsini, Fulvio

Imagines professorum Tubigensium. Cell, Erhard

Imagines XLI virorum celebriorum in politicis, historicis, &c. Leide, P. Vander Aa ca1720-30
1 l. 41pl. F.
Portraits belong mainly to the 17th century
Lipperheide 553

Le **imagini** con tutti i riversi trovati et le vite de gli imperatori. Vico, Enea

Imagini degl' abiti con cui va vestita la nobilta' della serenis'ma Republica di Venezia. Balduino, Giacomo

Le **imagini** delle Donne Auguste. Vico, Enea

Imago principum Bohemiae LXI. Althann

Imatgeria popular catalana. See Amades, Joan; Colominas, Josep, and Vila, Pau. Els soldats

Imhoof-Blumer, Friedrich
Porträtköpfe auf antiken münzen hellenischer und hellenisierter völker. Leipzig, B. G. Teubner 1885
95p. VIII pl. F.
Lipperheide 199. LC 10-7697

Imitations of original drawings by Hans Holbein, in the collection of His Majesty, for the portraits of illustrious persons of the court of Henry VIII. Chamberlaine, John

Imperatores orientes. Ker, F. B.

Imperatorum a Iulio Caesare ad Carolum VI P. F. Aug. in gemmis antiqua partim, partim recenti manu affabre incisorum series. [No place] 1722
7pl. (incl. 163 ports.) F.
Contains portraits of Roman and German emperors
Lipperheide 225

Imperatorum romanorum libellus. Huttich, Johann

Impératrices et reines. Grévedon, P. L. H.

Imperial Japan. Knox, G. W.

The **imperial** macramé lace-book. Douglas, Mrs Fanny

Imperialis, Joannes Baptista
Musaeum historicum et physicum. Venetiis, apud Iuntas 1640
212,219p. 56 ports. Q.
Engraved by Andrea Salmincio. Portraits are half length
Lipperheide 528

Imperii ac sacerdotii ornatus. Bruyn, Abraham de

Imperium Romano-Germanicum. Avancinus, Nicolas

The **improved** American "Paragon" scientific system of dress cutting and dress fitting. American Paragon scientific system

Improved art of designing. Schuman, Julius

The **improved** tailors' aera. Jackson, John

The **improvised** stage. Somerscales, M. I.

Im Thurn, Sir Everard Ferdinand
Among the Indians of Guiana; being sketches chiefly anthropologic from the interior of British Guiana. London, K. Paul, Trench 1883
xvi,445p. illus. x pl. (3 col incl. front.) fold. map. O.
Three plates show costume
LC 2-11792

In espettazione delle loro altezze reali Ferdinando III ... gran duca di Toscana e Luisa Maria di Borbone ... sua consorte; feste pubbliche ... Siena 1791. Siena, T. P. Carli 1791
xviii,xxxvi p. 26pl. (24 col.) Q.
Lipperheide 2769

In joyful Russia. Logan, J. A.

In kleuren en kleeren. Algemeen handelsblad

In search of our ancestors. Boyle, M. E.

In the Alaskan wilderness. Gordon, G. B.

In the Andamans and Nicobars. Kloss, C. B.

In the golden nineties. See Valentine's manual of old New York

In the khalifa's clutches. See Neufeld, Charles. A prisoner of the khaleefa

In the land of Tolstoi. Stadling, J. J., and Reason, Will

In the uttermost East. Hawes, C. H.

In Tuscany. Carmichael, Montgomery

In Vanity Fair. Brainerd, Mrs E. H.

In viking land. Monroe, W. S.

Incas
Brehm, R. B. Das Inka-reich. 1885
Markham, Sir C. R. The Incas of Peru. 1910
Montell, Gösta. Dress and ornaments in ancient Peru. 1929
Reiss, Wilhelm, and Stübel, Alfons. Das todtenfeld von Ancon in Peru. 1880-87
Schmidt, Max. Kunst und kultur von Peru. 1929

See also Indians of South America—Peru

The **Incas** of Peru. Markham, Sir C. R.

Incoronazione di ... Ferdinando I. a re del Regno Lombardo-Veneto. Sanquirico, Alessandro

Incroyables et merveilleuses. Vernet, Horace

L'Inde des rajahs. Rousselet, Louis

L'Inde française. Burnouf, Eugène

Independent order of Odd-fellows. See Odd-fellows, Independent order of

Inderwick, Frederick Andrew

The king's peace; a historical sketch of the English law courts. London, S. Sonnenschein; New York, Macmillan 1895

xxiv,254p. front. 15 pl. map. D. (Social England series)

Descriptive letterpress on verso of plates. Plates show legal costume in England at the time of Henry VI

LC 1-18675

India. Army department

Photographs of types of the native Indian arms; views in Afghanistan, taken during the war of 1879; north-west frontier of Hindustan; Burmah, during the British operations in that country; miscellaneous Indian photographs. No place, [1895?]

97p. of photographs. ob.F.

India. Dept. of revenue and agriculture. See The Journal of Indian art

India ancient and modern. Simpson, William, and Kaye, J. W.

India and its native princes. Rousselet, Louis

India and the Indians. Elwin, E. F.

India and the war, with an introduction by Lord Sydenham of Combe. London & New York, Hodder & Stoughton 1915

xi,77p. col.front. 15 col.pl. 16 port. fold. map. O. o.p.

Plates accompanied by guard sheets with descriptive letterpress

"The coloured illustrations . . . are taken . . . from The armies of India, painted by Major A. C. Lovett, text by Major G. F. MacMunn . . . The explanatory notes which accompany these pictures have also been compiled wholly or mainly from the same work." page v

Shows costume of the native troups serving as part of the British army in India

Costume index. LC WAR15-130

India

Barbosa, Duarte. A description of the coasts of East Africa and Malabar in the beginning of the sixteenth century. 1866

Bentley, John. Essays relative to the habits, character and moral improvement of the Hindoos. 1823

Boeck, Kurt. Durch Indien ins verschlossene land Nepal. 1903

Crooke, W. Things Indian. 1906

Dunlop, John. Mooltan, during and after the siege. 1849

Eden, Emily. Portraits of the princes & people of India. 1844

Hürlimann, Martin. India; the landscape, the monuments and the people. 1928

Kühnel, Ernst. Miniaturmalerei im islamischen Orient. 1922

Le Bon, Gustave. Les civilisations de l'Inde. 1887

Manucci, Niccolò. Storia do Mogor; or, Mogul India, 1653-1708. 1907-08

Simpson, William, and Kaye, J. W. India ancient and modern, a series of illustrations of the country and people of India and adjacent territories

See also Brahmans; Durbars—Delhi; English in India; Nepal; Nicobar islands; also subdivision India under Arms and armor; Children; Embroidery; Hair-dressing; Religious costume

18th century

Gold, Charles. Oriental drawings: sketched between the years 1791 and 1798. 1806

Solvyns, F. B. A catalogue of 250 coloured etchings. 1799

Solvyns, F. B. A collection of two hundred and fifty coloured etchings descriptive of the manners, customs, and dresses of the Hindoos. 1796-99

Solvyns, F. B. The costume of Indostan ... with descriptions in English and French, taken in the years 1798 and 1799. 1804

19th century

Atkinson, G. F. "Curry & rice," on forty plates; or, The ingredients of social life at "our station" in India. 1859

Atkinson, G. F. Indian spices for English tables. 1860

Belnos, Mrs S. C. Twenty four plates illustrative of Hindoo and European manners in Bengal. ca1832

Buchanan, F. H. A journey from Madras through the countries of Mysore, Canara, and Malabar. 1807

Grindlay, R. M. Scenery, costumes and architecture, chiefly on the western side of India. 1826-30

Hunter, James, illus. Picturesque scenery in the kingdom of Mysore, from forty drawings taken on the spot. 1805

Indian costumes and scenes, drawn by a native of Calcutta, for F. W. Simms. 1848

The Journal of Indian art. 1886-1916

Luard, John. Views in India, Saint Helena and Car Nicobar. 1833

Mackenzie, Mrs H. D. Illustrations of the mission, the camp, and the zenána. 185-?

Noé, Amédée, comte de. Mémoires relatifs à l'expédition anglaise partie du Bengale en 1800 pour aller combattré en Égypte l'armée d'Orient. 1826

Pannelier, J. A. L'Hindoustan, ou Religion, moeurs, usages, arts et métiers des Hindous. 1816

Rousselet, Louis. L'Inde des rajahs, voyage dans l'Inde centrale et dans les presidences de Bombay et du Bengale. 1874

Rousselet, Louis. India and its native princes; travels in Central India and in the presidencies of Bombay and Bengal. 1876

India—19th century—*Continued*
Saltykov, A. D., kniaz'. Habitants de l'Inde. 1853
Shoberl, Frederic, ed. Hindoostan. 1822
Shoberl, Frederic, ed. Tibet, and India beyond the Ganges. 1824
Schlagintweit, Emil. Indien in wort und bild; eine schilderung des indischen kaiserreiches. 1880-81
Smith, Captain. Asiatic costumes. 1828
Solvyns, F. B. Les Hindoûs. 1808-12
Tayler, W. Sketches illustrating the manners and customs of the Indians and Anglo-Indians. 1842
Waldemar, prince of Prussia. Zur erinnerung an die reise des prinzen Waldemar von Preussen nach Indien in den jahren 1844-1846. 1853
Watson, J. F. The textile manufactures and the costumes of the people of India. 1866
Young, Marianne. Cutch; or, Random sketches, taken during a residence in one of the northern provinces of western India. 1839
Yule, Henry. A narrative of the mission sent by the governor-general of India to the court of Ava in 1855, with notices of the country, government and people. 1858

20th century

Carpenter, F. G. From Bangkok to Bombay. 1924
Bradley-Birt, F. B. Chota Nagpore, a little-known province of the empire. 1903
Conway, M. D. My pilgrimage to the wise men of the East. 1906
Coomaraswamy, A. K. Indian drawings. 1910
Coomaraswamy, A. K. Indian drawings: 2d series, chiefly Rājput. 1912
Crooke, William. Natives of northern India. 1907
Elwin, E. F. India and the Indians. 1913
Finnemore, John. Delhi and the durbar. 1912
Fisher, Mrs W. H. Twins travelogues. 1924. v3
The Journal of Indian art. 1886-1916
Malcolm, Sir I. Z. Indian pictures and problems. 1907
Menpes, Mortimer. India. 1905
Menpes, Mortimer. The people of India. 1910
Murray, A. H. H. The high-road of empire. 1905
Penfield, F. C. East of Suez: Ceylon, India, China and Japan. 1907
Penny, Mrs F. E. F. Southern India. 1914
Rothfield, Otto. Women of India. 1920

BY REGION OR PROVINCE

Assam

Butler, John. Travels and adventures in Assam. 1855
Del Mar, Walter. The romantic East: Burma, Assam, & Kashmir. 1906

Baluchistan

Bouillane de Lacoste, É. A. H. de. Around Afghanistan. 1909

Bengal

Dalton, E. T. Descriptive ethnology of Bengal. 1872

Burma

Carpenter, F. G. From Bangkok to Bombay. 1924
Cuming, E. W. D. With the jungle folk. 1897
Curtis, W. E. Egypt, Burma and British Malaysia. 1905
Del Mar, Walter. The romantic East: Burma, Assam, & Kashmir. 1906
Enríquez, C. M. D. A Burmese arcady. 1923
Foran, W. R. Changing horizons. 1937
Gascoigne, G. T. Among pagoda and fair ladies; tour through Burma. 1896
Malcolm, Sir I. Z. Indian pictures and problems. 1907

Central provinces

Forsyth, James. The highlands of central India. 1919
Grant, Sir Charles. The gazetteer of the Central Provinces of India. 1870

Kashmir

Del Mar, Walter. The romantic East: Burma, Assam, & Kashmir. 1906
O'Connor, V. C. S. The charm of Kashmir. 1920

Maharashtra

Broughton, T. D. The costume, character, manners, domestic habits, and religious ceremonies of the Mahrattas. 1813
Broughton, T. D. Les Marattes. 1817

Nilgiri hills

See India—Native tribes—Todas

Orissa

Campbell, Sir John. A personal narrative of thirteen years' service amongst the wild tribes of Khondistan. 1864

Travancore

Mateer, Samuel. Native life in Travancore. 1883

India—Native tribes
Thurston, Edgar. Ethnographic notes in southern India. 1906

Khasi

Gurdon, P. R. T. The Khasis. 1907

Mikirs

Stack, Edward. The Mikirs. 1908

Todas

Harkness, Henry. A description of a singular aboriginal race inhabiting the summit of the Neilgherry Hills, or Blue Mountains of Coimbatoor in the southern peninsula of India. 1832

India, French
Burnouf, Eugène. L'Inde française. 1827-35

India occidentalis. See Bry, Theodor de. Grands voyages

Indian and oriental armour. See Egerton, W. E., earl. Description of Indian and Oriental armour

Indian army. See Military costume—England—Indian army

Indian blankets and their makers. James, G. W.

Indian costumes and scenes, drawn by a native of Calcutta, for F. W. Simms. Calcutta 1848
3v. 121 col.pl. Q.
Manuscript. Plates 115-121 are the same as those in Orlich's *Reise in Ost Indien*
Lipperheide 1496

Indian costumes in the United States. Wissler, Clark

Indian days in the Canadian Rockies. Barbeau, C. M.

Indian designs. See Decoration and ornament—Indians of North America

Indian drawings. Coomaraswamy, A. K.

Indian handicraft. Mangam, E. W.

The **Indian** how book. Parker, A. C.

Indian notes. New York. Museum of the American Indian, Heye foundation

Indian notes and monographs. New York. Museum of the American Indian, Heye foundation

Indian pictures and problems. Malcolm, Sir I. Z.

Indian races of North and South America. Brownell, C. De W.

Indian spices for English tables. Atkinson, G. F.

Indian stories from the Pueblos. Applegate, F. G.

The **Indian** tribes of Guiana. Brett, W. H.

The **Indian** tribes of the upper Mississippi valley and region of the Great lakes. Blair, E. H., ed.

Die **Indianer** Nord-Amerikas. Catlin, George. See note under his North American Indians

Indianer, die indianerstämme des Ostens und der prärien Nordamerikas. See Dengler, Hermann. American Indians

Indianer und weisse in Nordostbolivien. Nordenskiöld, Erland

Indians (American)
American museum of natural history, New York. Anthropological papers. 1907+

Hough, Walter. Racial groups and figures in the natural history building of the United States National museum. 1922

New York. Museum of the American Indian, Heye foundation. Indian notes and monographs; a series of publications relating to the American aborigines. 1919+

New York. Museum of the American Indian, Heye foundation. Indian notes. 1924+

See also Indians of Mexico; Indians of North America; Indians of South America. Also Beadwork; Masks

The **Indians'** book. Burlin, Mrs N. C.

Indians of Canada
Barbeau, C. M. Indian days in the Canadian Rockies. 1923
Boaz, Franz. Facial paintings of the Indians of northern British Columbia. 1898
Hamilton, Louis. Canada. 1926

See also names of individual tribes such as Kutchin, under the heading Indians of North America

Indians of Central America
Bancroft, H. H. Native races of the Pacific states of North America. 1874-76
Benzoni, Girolamo. History of the New world ... shewing his travels in America, from A. D. 1541 to 1556: with some particulars of the island of Canary. 1857
Brasseur de Bourbourg, C. É. Histoire des nations civilisées du Mexique et de l'Amérique-Centrale, durant les siècles antérieurs à Christophe Colomb. 1857-59

See also Guatemala

Indians of Mexico
Bancroft, H. H. Native races of the Pacific states of North America. 1874-76
Brasseur de Bourbourg, C. É. Histoire des nations civilisées du Mexique et de l'Amérique-Centrale, durant les siècles antérieurs à Christophe Colomb. 1857-59
Charnay, Désiré. Les anciennes villes du Nouveau monde. 1857-82
Charnay, Désiré. The ancient cities of the New World. 1887
Garcia Cubas, Antonio. The republic of Mexico in 1876. 1876
Sahagún, Bernardino de. Historia de las cosas de Nueva Espana. 1905-07
Starr, Frederick. Indians of southern Mexico. 1899
Tozzer, A. M. A comparative study of the Mayas and the Lacandones. 1907

See also Aztecs; Mayas

Indians of North America
Adam, Leonard. Nordwest-amerikanische Indianerkunst. 1923
Bancroft, H. H. Native races of the Pacific states of North America. 1874-76
Bastholm, Christian. Historische nachrichten zur kenntniss des menschen in seinem wilden und rohen zustande. 1818-21
Bastian, Adolf. Amerika's Nordwestküste. 1883-84

Indians of North America—*Continued*

Blair, E. H., ed. The Indian tribes of the upper Mississippi valley and region of the Great lakes. 1911

Brownell, C. De W. Indian races of North and South America. 1853

Burlin, Mrs N. C. The Indians' book. 1923

Carr, Lucien. Dress and ornaments of certain American Indians. 1897

Catlin, George. Catlin's North American Indian portfolio. 1844

Catlin, George. Illustrations of the manners, customs and condition of the North American Indians. 1845

Catlin, George. Letters and notes on the manners, customs and condition of the North American Indians. 1841

Catlin, George. North American Indians. 1926

Catlin, George. Souvenir of the N. American Indians as they were in the middle of the nineteenth century. 1850

Curtis, E. S. The North American Indian. 1907-30

Dellenbaugh, F. S. The North-Americans of yesterday. 1901

Dengler, Hermann. American Indians, tribes of the prairies and the East. 1923

Dixon, J. K. The vanishing race. 1913

Dodge, R. I. Our wild Indians. 1882

Donaldson, Thomas. The George Catlin Indian gallery in the U.S. National museum. 1886

Garland, Hamlin. The book of the American Indian. 1923

Goddard, P. E. Indians of the Northwest coast. 1924

Grinnell, G. B. The Indians of to-day. 1900

Haire, F. H. The American costume book. 1934

Haire, F. H. The folk costume book. 1934

Harvey, Fred. American Indians. 1920

Hodge, F. W., ed. Handbook of American Indians north of Mexico. 1907-10

Howard, O. O. My life and experiences among our hostile Indians. 1907

Krieger, H. W. American Indian costumes in the United States National museum. (*In* Smithsonian institution. Annual report, 1928. p623-661)

Lafitau, J. F. Moeurs des sauvages amériquains comparées aux moeurs des premiers temps. 1724

McKenney, T. L., and Hall, James. History of the Indian tribes of North America. 1836-44

Mangam, E. W. Indian handicraft. c1930

Palmer, R. A. The North American Indians: an account of the American Indians north of Mexico. 1929

Parker, A. C. The Indian how book. 1927

Salomon, J. H. The books of Indian crafts & Indian lore. 1928

Schoolcraft, H. R. Information respecting the history, condition and prospects of the Indian tribes of the United States. 1851-57

United States. Bureau of American ethnology. Annual report and accompanying papers. 1881+

Wied-Neuwied, M. A. P., prinz von. Reise in das innere Nord-America in den jahren 1832 bis 1834. 1839-41

Wied-Neuwied, M. A. P., prinz von. Travels in the interior of North America. 1843-44

Wissler, Clark. Costumes of the Plains Indians. 1915

Wissler, Clark. North American Indians of the Plains. 1927

Wissler, Clark. Structural basis to the decoration of costumes among the Plains Indians. 1916

Wissler, Clark. Indian costumes in the United States. 1928

See also Eskimos; Footwear, Moccasins; Indians of Canada; Indians of Mexico; also subdivision Indians of North America under Arms and armor; Dance costume; Decoration and ornament; Jewelry, Medieval and modern

BY REGION

Florida

Le Moyne de Morgues, Jacques. Brevis narratio eorum quae in Florida Americae provĩcia Gallis acciderunt, secunda in illam navigatione, duce Renato de Laudõniere classis praefecto: anno MDLXIIII. Quae est secunda pars Americae. 1591

Labrador

Hind, H. Y. Exploration in the interior of the Labrador peninsula, the country of the Montagnais and Nasquapee Indians. 1863

Southwest, New

Goddard, P. E. Indians of the Southwest. 1913

James, G. W. The Indians of the Painted desert region; Hopis, Navahoes, Wallapais, Havasupais. 1903

Virginia

Harriot, Thomas. Admiranda narratio fida tamen, de commodis et incolarum ritibus Virginiae, nuper admodum ad Anglis, qui à dn. Richardo Greinvile ... eò in coloniam anno. M.D.LXXXV. 1590

Sams, C. W. The conquest of Virginia. 1916

BY TRIBE

Algonquian Indians

Willoughby, C. C. Antiquities of the New England Indians. 1935

Blackfoot

See Indians of North America—Siksika Indians

Indians of North America—*Continued*

Caddo Indians

Harrington, M. R. Certain Caddo sites in Arkansas. 1920

Dakota Indians

Album of drawings, in pencil and water-colors, made during the Sioux troubles of 1851-52, and the Sioux rising of 1863 under Little Crow. 1863?

Delaware Indians

Harrington, M. R. Religion and ceremonies of the Lenape. 1921

Fox Indians

Harrington, M. R. Old Sauk and Fox beaded garters

Hopi Indians

Applegate, F. G. Indian stories from the Pueblos. 1929

Bourke, J. G. Snake-dance of the Moquis of Arizona. 1884

Dorsey, G. A., and Voth, H. R. The Mishongnovi ceremonies of the snake and antelope fraternities. 1902

Dorsey, G. A., and Voth, H. R. The Oraibi Soyal ceremony. 1901

James, G. W. Indian blankets and their makers. 1914

United States. Census office. 11th census, 1890. Moqui Pueblo Indians of Arizona and Pueblo Indians of New Mexico. 1893

Kiowa Indians

Jacobson, O. B. Kiowa Indian art. 1929

Kutchin Indians

Osgood, Cornelius. Contributions to the ethnography of the Kutchin. 1936

Kwakiutl Indians

Boas, Franz. The social organization and the secret societies of the Kwakiutl Indians. 1897

Navaho Indians

James, G. W. Indian blankets and their makers. 1914

Pueblo Indians

Applegate, F. G. Indian stories from the Pueblos. 1929

United States. Census office. 11th census, 1890. Moqui Pueblo Indians of Arizona and Pueblo Indians of New Mexico. 1893

Salishan Indians

Hill-Tout, Charles. British North America. 1907

Sauk Indians

Harrington, M. R. Old Sauk and Fox beaded garters. 1920

Siksika Indians

Linderman, F. B. Blackfeet Indians. 1935

Tinne Indians

Hill-Tout, Charles. British North America. 1907

Indians of South America

Brownell, C. De W. Indian races of North and South America. 1853

Church, G. E. Aborigines of South America. 1912

Cieza de Leon, Pedro de. The travels of Pedro de Cieza de Leon, A. D. 1532-50, contained in the first part of his Chronicle of Peru. 1864

Crevaux, J. N. Voyages dans l'Amérique du Sud. 1883

Danielli, Iacopo. Contributo allo studio del tatuaggio negli antichi Peruviani. 1894

Herndon, W. L., and Gibbon, Lardner. Exploration of the valley of the Amazon. 1853-54

Koebel, W. H. The romance of the river Plate. 1914

Krieger, H. W. American Indian costumes in the United States National museum. (Smithsonian institution. Annual report, 1928. p623-661)

Landor, A. H. S. Across unknown South America. 1913

Orbigny, A. D. d'. Voyage pittoresque dans les deux Amériques; résumé général de tous les voyages de Colomb, Las-Casas, Oviedo. 1836

Schumacher, Karl von. Sudamerika, Westindien, Zentralamerika; landschaft, volksleben, bankunst. 1931

Verrill, A. H. The American Indian, North, South, and Central America. 1927

Vidal, E. E. Picturesque illustrations of Buenos Ayres and Monte Video. 1820

See also Featherwork—South America; also subdivision Indians of South America under Decoration and ornament; Jewelry, Medieval and modern

BY COUNTRY

Brazil

Ehrenreich, P. M. A. Anthropologische studien über die urbewohner Brasiliens vornehmlich der staaten Matto Grosso, Goyaz und Amazonas (Purus-Gebiet). 1897

Staden, Hans and Lery, Jean de. Americae tertia pars memorabilẽ provinciae Brasiliae historiam continẽs ... Nunc autem latinitate donatam à Teucrio Annaeo Privato ... Addita est Narratio profectionis Ioannis Lerij in eamdem provinciam, quae ille initio gallicè conscripsit, postea verò latinam fecit. 1597?

Wied-Neuwied, M. A. P., prinz von. Reise nach Brasilien in den jahren 1815 bis 1817. 1820-21

Guiana

Brett, W. H. The Indian tribes of Guiana. 1868

Im Thurn, Sir E. F. Among the Indians of Guiana. 1883

Indians of South America—*Continued*

Patagonia

Lothrop, S. K. Polychrome guanaco cloaks of Patagonia. 1929

Vignati, M. A. Restos del traje ceremonial de un "médico" patagón. 1930

Peru

Bastian, Adolf. Die culturländer des alten America. 1878-89

Dorsey, G. A. A copper mask from Chimbote, Peru. 1897

Mead, C. W. Old civilizations of Inca land. 1924

Montell, Gösta. Dress and ornaments in ancient Peru. 1929

Voyages au Pérou, faits dans les années 1791 à 1794. 1809

See also Incas

BY TRIBE

Araucanian Indians

Schmidtmeyer, Peter. Travels into Chile, over the Andes, in the years 1820 and 1821. 1824

Calchaqui Indians

Quiroga, Adán. Calchaqui; con ilustraciones de F. Gonzales. 1897

Chacobo Indians

Nordenskiöld, Erland. Indianer und weisse in Nordostbolivien. 1922

Incas

See Incas

Lengua Indians

Grubb, W. B. An unknown people in an unknown land. 1911

Ona Indians

Gallardo, C. R. Tierra del Fuego. 1910

Indians of southern Mexico. Starr, Frederick

Indians of the Northwest coast. Goddard, P. E.

The **Indians** of the Painted desert region. James, G. W.

Indians of the Southwest. Goddard, P. E.

The **Indians** of to-day. Grinnell, G. B.

India's fighters. Singh, S. N.

L'Indicateur; contenant toutes les productions de l'esprit, les pièces de poésie fugitives, les bon-mots ... et surtout les modes. 1.-3. année, 1778-1780. Bruxelles

Illus. O.
Superseded *La feuille sans titre*
Colas 1515. Lipperheide 4566

Indien in wort und bild. Schlagintweit, Emil

Indien; landschaft, baukunst und volksleben. See note under Hürlimann, Martin. India

L'indignité et l'extravagance des paniers. See La Fizelière, A. P. de. Histoire de la crinoline au temps passé

Indische miniaturen der islamischen zeit. Kheiri, Sattar

Individuality and clothes. Story, Mrs M. McE.-F.

Indo-China

Carpenter, F. G. From Bangkok to Bombay. 1924

Dubois de Jancigny, A. P. Japon, Indo-Chine, Empire Birman (ou Ava), Siam, Annam (ou Cochinchine), Péninsule Malaise, etc., Ceylan. 1850

See also Cambodia; Laos; Shans; Siam

Indumentaria antigua. Peñafiel, Antonio

Indumentaria española. Aznar y García, Francisco

The **industrial** arts of Denmark. Worsaae, J. J. A.

The **industrial** arts of the Anglo-Saxons. Baye, Joseph, baron de

Industrial drawing for girls. Hammond, E. C.

Industrias artísticas. Miquel y Badía, Francisco

Les **industriels**, métiers et professions en France. La Bédollière, É. G. de

Industries françaises de la mode. See Les elégances parisiennes

Inedited works of Bakst. Réau, Louis, and others

Inexpensive costumes for plays, festivals and pageants. Lamkin, N. B.

Infamy, Signs of

Robert, U. L. L. Les signes d'infamie au moyen âge: Juifs, Sarrasins, hérétiques, lépreux, Cagots et filles publiques. 1891

L'infanterie. Riols de Fonclare, J. É. de

Infanterie allemande. See Genty, firm, Paris, pub. Costumes militaires

Die **infanterie** Friedrichs d. G. 1785. Boltze, Eberh.

Infanterie prussienne. See Genty, firm, Paris, pub. Costumes militaires

Infanterie russe. See Genty, firm, Paris, pub. Costumes militaires

Infants. See Children

Infants' and children's review. v 1, 1926+ New York, Haire

Illus. F.
Published monthly. Current 1938

Infants' and children's wear. Kneeland, Natalie

The **influence** of clothing on health. Treves, Sir Frederick

Information respecting the history, condition and prospects of the Indian tribes of the United States. Schoolcraft, H. R.

Inghirami, Francesco

Pitture di vasi etruschi esibite dal cavaliere Francesco Inghirami, per servire di studio alla mitologia ed alla storia degli antichi popoli; 2. ed. Firenze, A. Tozzetti 1852-56

4v. front. (port.) CCCC pl. (part col.) Q.
Lipperheide 239. LC 14-18974

Ingram, Bruce S.

(ed.) The illustrated London news. The Illustrated London news coronation record number: King George v. and Queen Mary

The **inhabitants** of the Philippines. Sawyer, F. H. R.

Inhuldiging van ... Willem Karel Hendrik Friso, prins van Oranje en Nassau ... als erf-heer van Vlissingen, op den v. junij MDCCLI. Huet, D. T.

Das **Inka-reich.** Brehm, R. B.

De **inlandsche** kunstnijverheid in Nederlandsch Indië. Jasper, J. E., and Pirngadie, Mas

Inleidinge tot het ceremonieel. Alkemade, Kornelis van

Innes, Arthur Donald

A history of England from the earliest times to the present day; illus. from sources mainly contemporary and with maps. New York, G. P. Putnam's sons; London, T. C. & E. C. Jack [1913]

xxxvi,984p. col.front. illus.(incl. maps, facsims. geneal. tables) pl. ports. O. $3.50, 3s 6d

Plates show costume

Costume index. LC 23-26544

Innhausen und Knyphausen, Edzard, graf zu. See Manninga, Unico. Ostfriesischen volks- und rittertrachten um 1500

The **inn-play.** Parkyns, Sir Thomas, bart.

Innsbruck. Ferdinandeum. See Zingerle, I. V., edler von Summersberg. Freskensyklus des schlosses Runkelstein bei Bozen

Inquiries into the origin and progress of the science of heraldry in England. Dallaway, James

Inscriptions de la France du v. siècle au XVIII. Guilhermy, R. F. F. M. N., baron de, and Lasteyrie du Saillant, R. C.

Inselfriesische volkstrachten. Haeberlin, Carl

Les **insignes** royaux de Hongrie. Czobor, Bela

Insignia. See note under Amman, Jost. Stam und wapenbuch

Insignia sacrae Caesareae maiestatis. Amman, Jost

Die **insignien** und juwelen der preussischen krone. Seidel, Paul

Institut de France. See entry under Botta, P. E.

Institute of women's professional relations. See Federated council on art education. Costume design as an occupation

The **institution,** laws & ceremonies of the most noble Order of the Garter. Ashmole, Elias

Instruction book with diagram and measure book. Peyry, J. B.

L'**instruction** du roy, en l'exercice de monter a cheval. Pluvinel, Antoine de

Instructive costume design. Hartman, E. A.

Instructive tanzmeister für herren und damen. Casorti, Louis

Intemperance and tight lacing. Fowler, O. S.

International chalcographical society

The Master of the Amsterdam cabinet, by Max Lehrs. See entry under Master of the Amsterdam cabinet, 15th century

See also Lippmann, Friedrich. The seven planets

International congress of popular arts, Prague, 1928

Art populaire, travaux artistiques et scientifiques du 1er Congrès international des arts populaires, Prague, MDCCCCXXVIII; introduction par Henri Focillon. Paris, Éditions Duchartre [1931]

2v. col.front. illus.(incl. maps, music) pl.(part col.) sq.Q.

Includes bibliographies

Volumes 1-2 contain material on masks. Volume 2, pages 9-96 contains material on costume of various European peoples, with illustrations and on the theatrical costume of Japan

LC 32-30049

International exhibition of theatre art. New York. Museum of modern art

International health exhibition, 1884. See London. International health exhibition, 1884

International puppen-ausstellung, 1911. See Frankfort-on-Main. International puppen-ausstellung, 1911

Das **internationale** Rote kreuz. V. von Strantz. (In Boguslawski, Albrecht von. Deutschland. Das heer ... Die flotte)

Interpretive costume design. See Kerr, R. N. Miniature costume folios

Intimate apparel; publication of the undergarment and negligee trades. 1934+ New York, Intimate apparel pub. co.

Illus. Q. $2 a year

Published monthly. Current 1938

Intogt van Frederik Hendrik in s'Hertogenbosch in 1629. Jonge, J. K. J. de, jonkheer

De **intogt** van hertog Jan van Beijeren binnen Leyden, op den 18[den] augustus 1420, in maskerade voorgesteld door H. H. studenten der Leydsche hoogeschool, op den 8[sten] februarij 1840. Leyden, H. Schreuder [1840?]

19pl. Q.

Lipperheide 2828

Introduction to a history of woodcut. Hind, A. M.

Introduction to English antiquities. Eccleston, James

Introduction to English economic history and theory. Ashley, Sir W. J.

Introduction to English liturgical colours. Hope, Sir W. H. St. J., and Atchley, E. G. C. F.

L'**invasion,** le siège, la commune 1870-1871. Dayot, A. P. M.

Inventaire des épées et dagues du comte de Salm, conservées dans l'hôtel de Salm à Nancy, 1614. 1897. See Giraud, J. B. Documents pour servir à l'histoire de l'armement au moyen âge et à la renaissance

Inventarios de mobiliario litúrgico. Villa-amil y Castro, José

Inventarium ... was in ... herrn Marx Fuggers ... rüst: und sattel cammer an harnischen, büchsen, wehrn, spiessen, sättlen, zeugen schlitten sampt irer zugehörung und andrn vorhanden ... im monat julio anno 1599 beschriben worden. München und Leipzig, G. Hirth 1890
26p. 10 illus. Q.
Edited by A. F. Butsch. Most of the illustrations by Jost Amman
Lipperheide 2398

Inventorium sepulchrale. Faussett, Bryan

Inventory and survey of the armouries of the Tower of London. Ffoulkes, C. J.

Ionian islands
MacBean, Forbes. Sketches of character & costume in Constantinople, Ionian Islands, &c. 1854

Iorga, Nicoláe
România in chipuri şi verderi. La Roumanie en images. Showing Roumania. [Bucureşti] Cultura naţională [1926]
27,223p. illus. pl.(part col.,mounted) ports. maps. col.diagrs. Q.
Text in Rumanian, French, and English. Many of the plates show costume

Iovius, Paulus. See Giovio, Paolo, bp. of Nocera

Iraq
Heuzey, L. A., and Heuzey, Jacques. Histoire du costume dans l'antiquité classique. 1935
Porter, Sir R. K. Travels in Georgia, Persia, Armenia, ancient Babylonia, &c. &c. during the years 1817, 1818, 1819, and 1820. 1821-22

Ireland, Samuel
A picturesque tour through Holland, Brabant, and part of France, made in the autumn of 1789; 2d ed. with additions. London, T. Egerton 1796
2v. 48 pl.(16 col.) Q.
One plate in volume 1 shows dress of the north Hollanders
Lipperheide 951

Ireland
Carleton, William. Traits and stories of the Irish peasantry. 1852
Smith, C. H. Selections of the ancient costume of Great Britain and Ireland from the seventh to the sixteenth century. 1814
Walker, J. C. An historical essay on the dress of the ancient and modern Irish; to which is subjoined a memoir on the armour and weapons of the Irish. 1818

See also Celts; Lace—Irish; Monastic and religious orders—Ireland

Early to 1200
Joyce, P. W. A social history of ancient Ireland. 1903
Meyrick, Sir S. R., and Smith, C. H. Costume of the original inhabitants of the British islands, from the earliest periods to the 6th century; to which is added that of the Gothic nations of the western coasts of the Baltic, the ancestors of the Anglo-Saxons and Anglo-Danes. 1821
O'Curry, Eugene. On the manners and customs of the ancient Irish. 1873

16th century
See Military costume—Ireland—16th century

19th century
Carleton, William. Traits and stories of the Irish peasantry. 1852
Hall, Thomas. "Effects" and adventures of Raby Rattler, gent. 1845
Shoberl, Frédéric, ed. England, Scotland and Ireland. 1827

20th century
Barlowe, Jane. Irish ways. 1909
Hannay, J. O. Irishmen all. 1913
Hannay, J. O. The lighter side of Irish life. 1912
Lynd, Robert. Rambles in Ireland. 1912
Mason, T. H. The islands of Ireland; their scenery, people, life and antiquities. 1936
Mathew, F. J. Ireland. 1905
Skeat, W. W. The past at our doors. 1911

Irene. Klai, Johann

Irenico-polemographia. See Theatrum europaeum

Iribe, Paul
Les robes de Paul Poiret. Paris, P. Poiret [1908]
3 l. 10 col.pl. Q.
Colas 1517

L'**Iris**, album de l'élégance; journal pratique des modes des dames. 1.-3. année; 1. sept. 1832-1 oct. 1834. Paris
O.
According to Colas, after the second year the subtitle became: the magazine of the beau monde
Colas 1518

Iris; illustrirte blätter für mode, haushaltung und praktisches leben. 1849-1865. Wien & Berlin, Haack
17v. col.illus. O.
Subtitle varies: v 1-4, 1849-52: original-Pariser-moden; v4-7 Pariser-damen-zeitung; v8-16 Pariser und Wiener damen-moden-zeitung
Published Gratz, Ludewig & Wohlfarth, and Leipzig, Hübner-Spaner 1849-63; Wien, 1864-65. *Bijou* was published as a supplement 1851-52
Colas 790. Lipperheide 4659

Iris; journal périodique. no 1+ hiver, 1932+ Paris, Société graphique
Illus.(part col.) F.
Published semi-annually. Current 1938

Irische spitzen. See Cole, A. S., comp. Dentelles d'Irlande

Irish lace. See Lace—Irish

Irish lace, a history of the industry. Lindsey, Ben, and Biddle, C. H.

The **Irish** lace instructor. Riego de la Branchardière, Mlle Éléonore

Irish ways. Barlow, Jane

Irishmen all. Hannay, J. O.

Irmer, Georg. See Baldwin, of Luxemburg, abp. and elector of Treves. Die romfahrt Kaiser Heinrich's VII

Iron crown of Lombardy, Order of the
Bombelli, Rocco. Storia della corona ferrea dei re d'Italia. 1870
Statuten für den oesterreichisch-kaiserlichen Orden der eisernen krone ... Statuti per l'Ordine imperiale austriaco della corona di ferro. 1860

Irwin, William Henry
Old Chinatown; a book of pictures by Arnold Genthe, with text by Will Irwin. New York, M. Kennerley 1913
208p. front. illus. 71 pl. O.
LC A13-1465

'T **is** al verwart-gaaren. Quast, P. J.

Isabey, John Baptiste
Caricatures. Paris, A. Giroux 1818
12 col.pl. ob.Q.
Cover title
Colas 1519

Isachi, Alfonso
Relatione di Alfonso Isachi intorno l'origine, solennita, traslatione, et miracoli della Madonna di Reggio. Reggio, F. Bartoli 1619
237p. 11 pl. O.
Plates engraved by G. L. Valesio
Lipperheide 2790

Iseke Iwai No Sho. Heizo, Ise

Iselberg, Peter
Künstliche waffenhandlung der musqueten uñ piquen oder langen spiessen ... Maniement des mousquets & piques. Nürnberg, S. Halbmayer [1620]
36 pl. ob.Q.

Isenberg, Walther
Wie die mechtige erbkünigreich unnd fürstentumb Hispania, Hunngern unnd Gelldern zu den loblichen heüsern Osterreich uñ Burgundi kommen sein. Augspurg, H. Schönsperger 1520
32 l. 24 illus. F.
Lipperheide 613

Iskusstvo Sredneĭ Azii. Denike, B. P., ed.

The **Islamic** book. Arnold, Sir Thomas Walker, and Grohmann, Adolf

Island of Formosa past and present. Davidson, J. W.

Islands of Ireland. Mason, T. H.

Islands of the Adriatic. See Adriatic, Islands of the

Den **islandske** kvinde og hendes dragt. Bruun, Daniel

Isnard, P. Fr. d'
État général des uniformes de toutes les troupes de France représentés par un homme de chaque régiment dans le costume du nouveau règlement arrêté par le roi, pour l'habillement de ses troupes, le 21 février 1779. Strasbourg, J. H. Heitz 1779
181 l. incl. 168 col.illus. Q.
Colas 1523. Lipperheide 2300
La gendarmerie de France; son origine, son rang, ses prérogatives et son service. Paris, Durand 1781
86p. front. O.
Colas 1524
Les nouveaux uniformes de tous les régimens de cavalerie de France avec des planches ... représentant un cavalier à cheval de chaque régiment, selon l'ordonnance du roy du 31 mai 1776. No place, 1776
1 l. 24 col.pl. Q.
Colas 1520
Les nouveaux uniformes de tous les régimens de dragons de France, avec des planches ... representant un chasseur à cheval de chaque régiment, selon l'ordonnance du roi du 31 mai 1776. Strasbourg? 1776
1 l. 24 col.pl. Q.
Colas 1521
Régiments de hussards au service de France. Strasbourg, Levrault n.d.
1 l. 6 col.pl. Q.
Colas 1522

Israélites de Pologne. Hollaenderski, Léon

Issel, Heinrich
Volkstrachten aus dem Schwarzwald; 25 originalaquarelle nach der natur gezeichnet ... mit einem vorwort von dr. Hans Jakob, hrsg. von Johannes Elchlepp. Freiburg, J. Elchlepp ca1890
4 l. 25 col.pl. ob.O.
Colas 1525

Isselburg, Peter. See note under Gheyn, Jacob de. Die drillkunst

Ist auch mode? Haenfler, Johann

Istoria della perruche. See Thiers, J. B. Histoire des perruques

Istoritcheskoïe oppissanïe odéjedy i vooroujéniia rossiskich voïsk. Viskovatov, A. V.

Istromenti armonici d'ogni generi. See Buonanni, Filippo. Descrizione degl'istromenti armonici d'ogni generi

Italia nei cento anni del secolo XIX. Comandini, Alfredo

Italian beggars, men and women. Callot, Jacques

[**Italian** costumes. No place ca1600]
12pl. O.
Plates have the following titles: Habiti della nobiltá di Fiorenzo; Milanesi; Paesani de Genoa; Il Corso; Sardegni; Ornamenti delli contadini di Sicilia; Contadina di Lombardia; Habiti delle gentildonne venetiane; Vestimento della juuentû romana; Donzella di Frascati; Nettunesa; Napolitani
Lipperheide 1244m

Italian scenery. Godby, James

L'**Italie,** la Sicile ... Audot, L. E.

Italien: Die flotte. Paschen, Karl

Italien und seine bewohner. No place, ca1840
30p. 14 col.pl. F.
Especially good for costume of southern Italy
Lipperheide 1283

Die **italienische** armee in ihrer gegenwärtigen uniformirung ... nebst erläuterungen zu denselben und mittheilungen über organisation, eintheilung und stärke der italienischen armee. Leipzig, M. Ruhl [1890]
20p. 17pl.(16 col.) on fold. sheet. D.
Colas 2601. Lipperheide. LC CA17-2454

Die **italienische** armee in ihrer gegenwärtigen uniformierung; 2. aufl. Leipzig, M. Ruhl [1910]
21p. col. fold pl. D.

Die **italienische** armee, mit zahlreichen textskizzen, adjustierungsbildern, kulturbildern und charakteristischen landschaftsbildern. 5. veränderte aufl. Wien, L. W. Seidel 1915
159p. front. illus. 2pl.(1 col. 1 fold.) fold. map. D.
"Änderungen der uniform der italienischen offiziere während des krieges": 4p. laid in
LC 28-8047

Italienische Renaissancegewänder umgestaltet für neue frauentracht. Jäger, Julie, and Wolzogen, Isolde von

Italy. Ministero della casa reale

Catalogo della armeria reale. Illustrato con incisioni in legno, compilato dal maggiore Angelo Angelucci. Torino, G. Candeletti 1890
xvi,614p. illus. O.
Lipperheide 2440

Italy. Ministero della guerra

Calendario del esercito, 1936. [Roma, Sansini 1936]
78pl. ob.S.
Plates have descriptive letter-press on verso

Photographs of uniforms worn by officers and soldiers of the Italian army, used for the military uniform display at the Tercentennial exposition at Jamestown. No place [1907]
38 illus. ob.O.

Raccolta delle disposizioni sulla divisa degli ufficiali. Roma, E. Voghera 1890
128p. illus. O.

Regolamento sull' uniforme. Roma, Istituto poligrafico dello stato, Libreria 1931
126p. XXXII pl.

Italy. Papal states

Regolamento per le vestimenta ed armamento della Guardia Civica nello Stato Pontificio analogamente alle disposizioni della legge 30 luglio 1847. Roma, 1847
23p. 5pl. F.

Italy

Bertarelli, Achille. L'imagerie populaire italienne. 1929

Förster, Ernst. Denkmale italienischer malerei vom verfall der antike bis zum sechzehnten jahrhundert. 1870-1874

Litta, Pompeo. Famiglie celebri d'Italia. 1819-83

Rodocanachi, E. P. La femme italienne avant, pendant et après la renaissance. 1922

Storia delle mode: Italia dagli Etruschi circa 800 anni avanti l'era Christiana fino al secolo XVIII. 1854

See also Lace—Venice; Naples (Kingdom); Sardinia; Sicily; Tyrol; also subdivision Italy under Agricultural laborers; Arms and armor; Beggars; Ceremonial and festival costume; Coronations and coronation robes; Decoration and ornament; Embroidery; Etruria; Funerals; Head-dress; Heraldic costume; Hunting costume; Kings and rulers; Military costume; Nobles; Street venders; Theatrical costume; Weddings and wedding dress; Workmen

To 1200

Montelius, Oskar. La civilisation primitive en Italie depuis l'introduction des métaux. 1895

Middle ages

Ancona, Paolo d'. Les primitifs italiens du XI. au XIII. siècle. 1935

Ferrario, Guilio. Storia ed analisi degli antichi romanzi di cavalleria e dei poemi romanzeschi d'Italia. 1828

Romussi, Carlo. Milano ne' suoi monumenti. 1912-13

Wilpert, Josef. Die romischen mosaiken und malereien der kirchlichen bauten vom IV. bis XIII. jahrhundert. 1916

14th century

Lasinio, Carlo. Pitture a fresco del Campo Santo di Pisa. 1828

Merkel, Carlo. Come vestivano gli uomini del "Decameron"; saggio di storia del costume. 1898

15th century

Montalto, Lina. La corte di Alphonso I di Aragona; vesti e gale. 1922

Müntz, Eugène. La renaissance en Italie et en France à l'époque de Charles VIII. 1885

Renaissance, 1492-1559

Burckhardt, J. C. The civilization of the renaissance in Italy. 1929

Burckhardt, J. C. Die cultur der renaissance in Italien. 1885

Floerke, Hanns. Die moden der italienischen renaissance. 1917

Seventeenth century

Buoninsegni, Francesco. Satyra Menippea, oder straff-schrifft weiblicher pracht. 1683

Callot, Jacques. Capricci di varie figure. ca1617

Italian costumes. ca1600

Lioni, Ottavio. Ritratti di alcuni celebri pittori del secolo XVII. 1731

Negri, Cesare. Nuove inventioni di balli. 1604

Orilia, Francesco. Il zodiaco over idea di perfettione di prencipi, formata dall'heroiche virtù dell' ... Antonio Alvarez di Toledo ... rapresentata come in un trionfo dal fidelissimo popolo napoletano. 1630

18th century

Alessandro, Giuseppe d'. Opera. 1723

Barbault, Jean. 12 costumes d'Italie d'après les peintures faîtes par Barbault à Rome en 1750. 1862

Manuale dei pittori, ovvero Manuale di pittura ... per l'anno 1792 [and 1794]. 1792-94

Italy—18th century—*Continued*

Tinney, John. A collection of eastern & other foreign dresses. ca1750

Volpini, Angelo. Figurini di moda. Année 1797-1798. 1797-98

Periodicals

Giornale delle dame e delle mode di Francia. 1786-94?

Giornale delle mode. 1788-95

Caricature and satire

Ghezzi, P. L. Raccolta di XXIV caricature. 1750

19th century

Allom, Thomas. Character and costume in Turkey and Italy. Designed and drawn from nature by Thomas Allom ... with descriptive letterpress by Emma Reeve. 1845?

Baschet, Armand, and Feuillet de Conches, F. S. Les femmes blondes selon les peintres de l'école de Venise. 1865

Bridgens, Richard. Sketches illustrative of the manners and costumes of France, Switzerland, and Italy. 1821

Cerrone, F. Scenes from Italian life. ca1830

Commandini, Alfredo. L'Italia nei cento anni del secolo XIX (1801-1900) giorno per giorno illustrata. 1900-29

Costumes italiens. ca1810

Debret. Costumes italiens dessinés à Rome en 1807. n.d.

Edel, Vittorio. Ricordo delle nozze d'argento delle loro maestà Umberto I e Margherita di Savoi, 22 Aprile 1893. 1893

Ferrari, Filippo. Costumi popolari Italiani. 1825

Frizzi, Arturo. Cinquanta maschere italiane illustrate nei loro costumi. 1888

Italien und seine bewohner. ca1840

Labruzzi, Carlo. Figure originali. ca1800

Lasinio, Carlo. Serie di 12 ritratti di persone facete che servono a divertire il pubblico Fiorentino. ca1800

Legouvé, G. J. B. E. W., and others. Les hommes célèbres de l'Italie. 1845

Pinelli, Bartolommeo. Costumi diversi. 1822

Pinelli, Bartolommeo. Gruppi pittoreschi modellati in terra-cotta. 1834

Pinelli, Bartolommeo. Nuovo raccolta di cinquanta costumi pittoreschi. 1816

Pinelli, Bartolommeo. Raccolta di cinquanta costumi pittoreschi. 1809

Pinelli, Bartolommeo. Raccolta di costumi italiani i più interessanti. 1828

Pinelli, Bartolommeo. Twenty-seven etchings illustrative of Italian manners and costume. 1844

Periodicals

Margherita, giornale della signore italiane. 1878-87

Il Mondo elegante; giornale illustrato delle mode francesi. 1864-75

20th century

Costumi, musica, danze e feste popolari italiane. 1935

Cyriax, Tony. Among Italian peasants. 1919

Donna Clara, pseud. L'eleganza femminile. 1907

Duff-Gordon, C. L. Home life in Italy: Letters from the Apennines. 1908

Holme, Charles, ed. Peasant art in Italy. 1913

Jäger, Julie, and Wolzogen, Isolde von. Italienische Renaissancegewänder umgestaltet für neue frauentracht. 1910

Periodicals

DEA; revista mensile della moda. 1933+

La Donna, la casa, il bambino; revista mensile di ricamo, moda, biancheria. 1930+

Moda. 1919-1936?

Moda maschile; rivista mensile illustrata di tecnica professionale e commerciale ad uso del sarto da uomo. 1907+

Mode revue; rivista tecnica di moda. 1929+

BY REGION OR PROVINCE

Audot, L. E. L'Italie, la Sicile, les Iles Éoliennes, l'Ile d'Elbe, la Sardaigne, Malte, l'Ile de Calypso, etc ... Sites, monumens, scènes et costumes. 1834-37

Boilly, J. L. Collection de costumes italiens. 1827?

Busuttil, Salvatore. Raccolta di costumi dello Stato Pontificio. 1826

Calderini, Emma. Il costume popolare in Italia. 1934

Ciuli, E. Folk-costume of Rome and the provinces of Italy. 1830

Colin, Mme Anais. Costumes de diverses provinces d'Italie. 1830

Costumes des différens états de l'Italie. 1826

Dura, Gaetano. Raccolta di costumi di provincie diverse. 18—?

Ferrari, Filippo. Costumi no. XXX di Roma e di altre paesi dello Stato Pontificio. 1825

Godby, James. Italian scenery; representing the manners, customs, and amusements of the different states of Italy. 1806

Greuze, J. B. Divers habillements suivant le costume d'Italie, dessinées d'après nature. 1768

Lemercier, Charles. Costumes coloriés des différents peuples d'Italie. 1830

Natura; rivista mensile illustrata. 1928

Opera nazionale dopolavoro. Popular Italian costumes, music, dances and festivals. 1931

Raccolta di costumi antichi e moderni. ca1880

Rémond, C. Costumes des différents peuples de l'Italie dessinés d'après nature. 1828

Scheffer, J. G. Choix de costumes italiens. 1832

Italy—*Continued*

Abruzzi e Molise

Canziani, Estella. Through the Apennines and the lands of the Abruzzi. 1928

Campania

Allers, C. W. La belle Napoli. 1890

Bourcard, Francesco de. Usi e costumi di Napoli e contorni descritte e dipinti. 1853-58

Busuttil, Salvatore. Nuova raccolta di costumi di Napoli disegnati dal vero. 1828-1830

Busuttil, Salvatore. Raccolta di sessanta piu belle vestiture che si costumono nelle provincie del regno di Napoli. 1793

Cuciniello, Michele, and Bianchi, Lorenzo. Voyage pittoresque dans le royaume des deux Siciles. 1830-33

Dura, Gaetano. Gruppi di costumi napolitani. ca1835

Dura, Gaetano. Naples—Characters. 183-?

Dura, Gaetano. Napoli e contorni. ca1835

Dura, Gaetano. Nuova raccolta di costumi e vestiture di Napoli. 1833-53

Dura, Gaetano. Scènes populaires, 1840. 1840?

Dura, Gaetano. Tarantella ballo napolitano, disegnato da Gaetano Duro, diretto da Pasquale Chiodi. 1854

Hess. Scenes of Neapolitan life. ca1815

Jorio, Andrea de. La mimica degli antichi investigata nel gestire napoletano. 1832

Lindström, K. J. Costumi, e vestiture napolitani. 1843

Lundström. Panorama delle scene populare di Napoli. 1832

Migliorato. Neapolitan scenes. ca1850

Mörner, Hjalmar. Scenes from Naples, Rome, and Paris. 1829

Mörner, Hjalmar. Scènes populaires de Naples. 1828

Muller. Neapolitan costumes. ca1840

Samaritani, G. L. da. Raccolta di costumi di Napoli. ca1825

Cisalpine republic

See Military costume—Cisalpine republic

Emilia

Carracci, Annibale. Diverse figure al numero di Ottanta. 1646

Lombardy

Campo, Antonio. Cremona fedelissima citta. 1585

Raccolta di 30 costumi con altretante vedute le piú interessanti della cittá di Milano. ca1820

See also Crown jewels—Italy—Lombardy

Naples

See Italy—Campania

Piedmont

Canziani, Estella, and Rohde, Eleanour. Piedmont. 1913

Rome

To 476 A.D.

See Rome

17th century

Falda, G. B. Der römischen fontanen wahre abbildung, wie solche so wohl auf offentlichen plätzen und palatien als auch zu Frescada Tivoli und denen lust-gärten mit ihren prospecten der zeit allda zu ersehen sind. 1685

18th century

Gori, A. F. Monumentum, sive columbarium libertorum et servorum Liviae Augustae et caesarum, Romae detectum in Via Appia, anno 1726. 1727

Pierre, J. B. M. Figures dessinées d'après nature du bas peuple à Rome. 1756

Vleughels, Nicolas. Costumes romains. 1734

19th century

Antonioli, Giovanni. Raccolta di costumi di Roma e vicinanze: incisi all' acquaforte da Gio. Antonioli. ca.1820

Bertini, A. Costumi di Roma e dei contorni. 1846

Busuttil, Salvatore. Raccolta di costumi dello Stato Romano. [1836-1838]

Cipriani, G. B. Costumi di Roma. 1822

Cipriani, G. B. Piccoli costumi di vario disegno. 1821

Costumi popolari dello Statto Romano e Regno di Napoli tratti dal vero. ca1815

Cottafavi, Gaetano. Raccolta di N. costumi di Roma e dei contorni. 1828

Ferrari, Filippo. Nuova raccolta di costumi di Roma e suoi contorni. 1838

Kleinpaul, R. A. R. Rom in wort und bild. 1882-83

Marroni, Salvatore. Costumi di Rome e suoi contorni; disegnati da varj artisti. 1820?

Marroni, Salvatore. Nuova raccolta di no. 40 costumi popolari di Roma e sue vicinanze. 1840

Nuova raccolta di 56 costumi di Roma e contorni tratti dalla fotographia. ca1860

Pigal, E. J. Coup d'oeil sur Rome, en 1828. 1829

Pinelli, Bartolommeo. Nuova raccolta di cinquanta costumi de' contorni di Roma compresi diversi fatti di briganti. 1823

Pinelli, Bartolommeo. Nuova raccolta di cinquanta motivi pittoreschi, e costumi di Roma. 1810

Pinelli, Bartolommeo. Nuova raccolta di costumi di Roma e sue vicinanze. 1838

Pinelli, Bartolommeo. Raccolta de' costumi di Roma e suoi contorni primi pensieri di Bartolomeo Pinelli da lui inventati ed incisi nell' anno 1815. 1819

Pinelli, Bartolommeo. Raccolta di cinquanta costumi di Roma e sue vicinanze. 1826

Italy—Rome—19th century—*Continued*

Pinelli, Bartolommeo. Raccolta di quattordici motivi di costumi pittoreschi di Roma. 1814

Pinelli, Bartolommeo, and Hullmandel, Charles. Roman costumes drawn from nature by Pinelli and C. Hullmandel. 1820

Raccolta di varie composizioni ed alcuni motivi di costumi pittoreschi di Roma e delle sue vicinanze. 1850?

Thomas, J. B. Un an à Rome et dans ses environs. 1823

Tuscany

Bicci, Antonio. I contadini della Toscana, espressi al naturale secondo le diverse loro vestiture. 1796

Carmichael, Montgomery. In Tuscany. 1901

Forno, F. Storia e costumi delle diciassette contrade di Siena. 1887

Piattoli, Giuseppi. Raccolta di quaranta proverbi toscani espressi in figure. 1786-88

Polidori Calamandrei, E. Le vesti delle donne fiorentine nel quattrocento. 1924

Staley, J. E. The guilds of Flòrence. 1906

Venice

Molmenti, P. G. La storia di Venezia nella vita privata dalle origini alla caduta della repubblica. 1905-08

Molmenti, P. G. Venice, its individual growth from the earliest beginnings to the fall of the republic. 1906-08

Mutinelli, Fabio. Del costume veneziano sino al secolo decimosettimo. 1831

Yriarte, C. E. Venise: histoire—art—industrie—la ville—la vie. 1877-78

See also Dogaressas; Doges

14th century

Cecchetti, Bartolomeo. La vita dei Veneziani nel 1300. 1886

17th century

Franco, Giacomo. Habiti delle donne venetiane intagliate in rame nuovamente. 1610

Franco, Giacomo. Habiti d'huomeni et donne venetiane. 1610

Franco, Giacomo. Habiti delle donne venetiane. 1877

18th century

Freschot, Casimir. La nobilta' veneta, o' sia Tutte le famiglie patrizie con le figure de suoi scudi & arme. 1707-1722?

19th century

Bosa, Eugènio. Crieurs et autres costumes populaires de Venise. 1835

Dusi, C. Costumes vénitiens. 1840

Paoletti, Ermolao. Il fiore di Venezia; ossia, i quadri, i monumenti, le vedute ed i costumi veneziani. 1839-42

Perl, Frau Henriette. Venezia. 1894

Venezia, Giulia e Zara

Bosa, Eugenio. Gridatori ed altri costumi popolari di Trieste. 1835

Caprin, Giuseppe. I nostri nonni. 1888

Caprin, Giuseppe. Tempi andanti; pagine della vita Triestina, 1830-1848. 1891

Itinerant trades of London. See Wheatley, Francis. Cries of London

Itinerario, voyage ofte schipvaert ... naer Oost ofte Portugaels Indien. Linschoten, J. H. van

Itinerarium, das ist Historische beschreibung. Ehingen, Georg von

Itinerarius beatissimae Virginis Mariae. [Basel] L. Ysenhut ca1488
108 l. 59 illus. O.
German edition (Basel, L. Ysenhut 1489)
Lipperheide 418

Īvchenko, A.
Al'bom" russkīkh ī malorossiĭskīkh" rīsunkov". S. Peterburg", līt. Brat'ev" Shumakher" 1875
25 col.pl. Q.
Lipperheide 3957

[Ivchenko, Valerian Īākovlevich]
Anna Pavlova translated from the Russian by A. Grey, woodcuts by D. Galanis. Paris, M. de Brunoff 1922
194p. illus. pl.(8 col.) ports. F. $30
Author's pseudonym, V. Svetloff, at head of title
French edition, translated by W. Pétroff (Paris, M. de Brunoff, 1922)

Ivchenko, Valerīan Īākovlevich, and Bakst, Léon
Le ballet contemporain, ouvrage éd. avec la collaboration de L. Bakst, traduction française de M.-D. Calvocoressi. [St. Pétersbourg, Société R. Golicke et A. Willborg] 1912
134p. illus. pl.(part col. part mounted) ports.(part col. part mounted. F.
Author's pseud., V. Svétlow, at head of title. Editions are shown in Russian, English, and German
Colas 2847. LC 14-7036

Ivori, Joan d'
Vestidos típicos de España. Barcelona, Editorial "Orbis" 1936
28p. 100 col.pl. F.

Izor, Estelle Peel
Costume design and home planning. illus. by K. P. Brown and R. T. Dixon. Boston, New York [etc.] Atkinson, Mentzer [c1916]
x,[2],210p. illus. (part col.) D.
LC 16-17166

J

Jack, Robert Logan
The black blocks of China; a narrative of experiences among the Chinese, Sifans, Lolos, Tibetans, Shans and Kachins, between Shanghai and the Irrawadi. London, E. Arnold 1904
xxii,269p. XVI pl.(incl.front.) II fold. maps. O.
A few plates show men and women from various parts of China
LC 4-13602

Jackson, Abraham Valentine Williams
Persia past and present; a book of travel and research. New York & London, Macmillan 1906
xxxi,471p. front. 128 pl. ports. map, plans, facsims. O.
A few photographs of Parsian types are useful for costume. Also page 375 has a paragraph on the dress of the Zoroastrians
List of works of reference: p xxvi-xxix
LC 6-33596

Jackson, Emily, "Mrs F. Nevill Jackson"
A history of hand-made lace. Dealing with the origin of lace, the growth of the great lace centres, the mode of manufacture, the methods of distinguishing and the care of various kinds of lace ... with supplementary information by E. Jesurum. London, L. U. Gill; New York, C. Scribner 1900
x,245p. front. illus. pl. ports. O
Bibliography: p98-105
LC 1-3607

Jackson, Herbert J.
European hand firearms of the sixteenth, seventeenth & eighteenth centuries; with A treatise on Scottish hand firearms, by Charles E. Whitelaw. London, M. Hopkinson 1923
xvi,108p. front. illus. pl. sq.F.
Originally published (London, P. L. Warner 1923)
LC 23-9298

Jackson, John
The improved tailors' area, containing an original system for measuring and cutting to fit the shape for forty-three garments, (including regimentals, ladies habits, and pelisses). London, W. Smith 1829
274,15p. 14pl. O.
Colas 1526. Lipperheide 3787

Jackson, Lawrence Nelson. See Jackson, Margaret. What they wore

Jackson, Margaret
What they wore; a history of children's dress, by Margaret Jackson; with drawings by O. H. Lister and verses by L. N. Jackson. [London] G. Allen & Unwin [1936]
160p. illus. D.
History of the shoe: p139-155. Bibliography: p156-157
LC 37-2351

Jacobs, Michel
The art of colour, by Michel Jacobs. Garden City, N.Y., Doubleday, Page; Batsford 1923
xiv,90p. col.front. col.pl. Q. $7.50; 30s
Chapter 14: Colour as applied to costume design
LC 23-11636

Jacobsen, Lis Rubin
(ed.) Musculus, Andreas. Hosedjaevelen paa Dansk ved Peder Palladius, 1556

Jacobson, Oscar Brousse
Kiowa Indian art: watercolor paintings in color by the Indians of Oklahoma; the introduction by Oscar Brousse Jacobson. Nice (France) C. Szwedzicki [c1929]
11p. 30 col.pl. F.
Introduction in English and French in parallel columns
Contains reproductions of paintings by five young Indians, Spencer Asah, Jack Hokeah, Steve Mopope, Monroe Tsa-to-ke and Miss Bou-ge-tah Smoky, chosen from the collection of Oscar Brousse Jacobson. cf. Introduction
Costume index. LC 30-31898

Jacoby, Mrs Catherine (Murray)
On special mission to Abyssinia. New York, Pub. priv. Printed by Argus graphic arts service [c1933]
141p. front. plates. ports. facsims. O.
LC 34-6190

Jacottet, Henri, and Leclerc, Max
Colonies françaises. Paris, L. Baschet [1888]
176p. 87 col.illus. O. (Cahiers d'enseignement no. 65-71, 80-83)
The plates show natives of Senegal, French Congo, Guiana, the Antilles, and Madagascar
Lipperheide 1608

Jacottet, Louis Julien
Souvenirs des eaux de Baden-Baden et des environs ... dessinés d'après nature et lithographiés par J. Jacottet. Paris [1860]
1 l. 40pl. F.
Plates show views, with people in the dress of the period
Colas 1527

Jacovleff, Alexandre. See Íakovlev, Aleksandr

Jacquemin, Raphael
Histoire générale du costume civil, religieux et militaire du IV. au XIX. siècle (315-1815) Tome premier. Paris, L'auteur [1876]
409p. Q.
No more published. Tho not so entitled this volume can be used as the text to accompany the author's *Iconographie*
Colas 1532

Histoire générale du costume civil, religieux et militaire du IV. au XII. siècle: Occident. (315-1100). Paris, Ch. Delagrave [1879]
407p. 48pl.(40 in color) Q.
Colas 1533. Lipperheide 357

Iconographie générale et méthodique du costume du IV. au XIX. siècle (315-1815) collection gravée à l'eau forte d'après des documents authentiques & inédits. Paris, L'auteur [1863-68]
2p. l. 200 col.pl. F.
Plates 1-6, Temps ancien; 7-57 Moyen âge; 58-183 Période moderne; 184-200 Orientaux
A supplement was issued (Paris, Nadaud ca1872. 80pl. numbered 201-280. F.)
Issued in 50 parts of 4 plates each. The text (Introduction, etc.) was apparently never published. The plates appeared also in the author's *Histoire générale du costume civil, religieux et militaire du* IV. *au* XIX. *siècle,* 315-1815 (Paris [1876])
The second edition (Paris, Nadaud ca1880) has 280 col.pl. The third edition (Paris, Gastinger ca1910 281 col.pl.)
Colas 1528-31. Costume index (3. ed.) Lipperheide 337. LC 28-645

Jacquenod, Marie Louise
Cours de coupe pour dames. Dijon, L'auteur 1912
132p. 61 illus. F. 4 fr.

Jacquet, Eugène Vincent Stanislas. See Burnouf, Eugène, jt. auth.

Jaeger, Frau Anna. See Jaeger, Heinrich, jt. auth.

Jaeger, Gustav
Health-culture. Tr. and edited by Lewis R. S. Tomalin. New, rev. ed. London, Adams bros. & Shardlow, ltd. printers 1908
201p. front. (port.) illus. D.
LC 34-24428

Die normalkleidung als gesundheitschutz ... 2. verm. aufl. Stuttgart, W. Kohlhammer 1881
261p. 3 illus. O.
First edition 1880. First appeared as articles in the *Neuen deutschen familienblatt* 1872-1880
Advocated the use of all-wool clothing. The books listed here on health culture are English translations
Lipperheide 3284

Selections from essays on health culture and the sanitary woolen system. [Tr. from the German] 2d ed. rev and enl. New York, Dr. Jaeger's sanitary woolen system co. 1891
viii,216p. S.
LC 7-33397

Jaeger, Heinrich, and Jaeger, Frau Anna
Hygiene der kleidung. Stuttgart, E. H. Moritz 1906
232p. 94 illus. 15 pl.(2 col.) O. (Bücherei der gesundheitspflege)

Jäger, Julie, and Wolzogen, Isolde von
Italienische Renaissancegewänder umgestaltet für neue frauentracht. Jena, E. Diederichs 1910
2v. 24pl. O.

Jähns, Max
Entwicklungsgeschichte der alten trutzwaffen mit einem anhange über die feuerwaffen. Berlin, E. S. Mittler 1899
13,401p. 40pl.(636 illus.) O.
Lipperheide 2459

Handbuch einer geschichte des kriegwesens von der urzeit bis zur Renaissance. Technischer theil: bewaffnung, kampfweise, befestigung, belagerung, seewesen. Nebst einem atlas. Leipzig, F. W. Grunow 1878-1880
xliv,1288p. O. and atlas 100pl. Q.
The atlas is a pictorial history of military costume, and arms and armor from ancient times to the sixteenth century. Primitive peoples also are shown in war dress and equipment
Lipperheide 2040

Jäklin, Dietrich
Geschichte der Kirche St. Georg bei Räzüns und ihre wandgemälde. Chur & Winterthur, Selbst-verlage des verfassers 1880
31p. 34pl.(64 illus.) O.
Pictures of about 1400
Lipperheide 463

Jaennicke, Friedrich
Die farbenharmonie mit besonderer rücksicht auf den gleichzeitigen contrast in ihrer anwendung in der malerei, in der decorativen kunst, bei ausschmückung der wohnräume, sowie in kostüm & toilette. Stuttgart, P. Neff 1878
275p 9 col.pl. O.
Published as the second completely revised edition of E. Chevreul's *Farbenharmonie*
Lipperheide 3281

Das **jagbuch** kaiser Maximilians I. Maximilian I, emperor of Germany

Jager, A.
Costumes des Pays-Bas; [photographs] Amsterdam 1878?
12 col.pl. D.

Jahn
(lithgr.) [Sächische bürgerwehr und schützen] Dresden-Neustadt, J. Weber, druck von W. Koppenhagen ca1860
8 col.pl. ob.Q.
Some of the plates are signed Jahn lith. Each shows six to ten types of uniforms
Colas 1534

Jahn, Martin
Die bewaffnung der Germanen in der älteren eisenzeit, etwa von 700 v. Chr. bis 200 n. Chr. Würzburg, C. Kabitzsch 1916
x,275,[1]p. illus. 3pl.(incl. 2 fold. maps) Q. (Mannus-bibliothek, nr. 16)
"Verzeichnis der abkürzungen": p[261]-267
LC 32-30726

Der reitersporn, seine entstehung und früheste entwicklung. Leipzig, C. Kabitzsch 1921
vi,127p. illus. fold.pl. Q. (Mannus-bibliothek, hrsg. von Gustaf Kossinna. nr. 21)
LC 32-30730

Ein **jahr** aus Ursula's leben. Schellenberg-Biedermann, E.

Jahrbuch der Kunsthistorischen sammlungen des Allerhöchsten kaiserhauses hrsg. unter leitung des oberstkämmerers Seiner Kaiserlichen und Königlichen apostolischen Majestät ... vom Oberstkämmerer-amte. v 1+ 1883+
Each volue of costume value has been entered separately. Contents: Supplement to v 1-2, Dürer, Albrecht. Triumph des Kaisers Maximilian I; Supplement to v3-4, Dürer, Albrecht. Ehrenpforte des Kaisers Maximilian I; v 12 Boeheim, Wendelin. Augsburger waffenschmiede; v 16 Boeheim, Wendelin. Nürnberger waffenschmiede
Lipperheide 90. LC 12-13290-93

Jahreszeiten, Hamburger neue mode-zeitung. 1.-33. jahrg. 1842-1874. Hamburg, C. F. Vogel
Col.pl. O.
Colas 1535. Lipperheide 4641

Ein **jahrhundert** München, 1800-1900. Wolf, G. J.

Jaime, Ernest
Musée de la caricature ou recueil des caricatures les plus remarquables publiées en France depuis le quatorzième siècle jusqu'à nos jours; avec un texte historique et descriptif. Paris, Delloye 1838
2v. 214 illus.(57 col.) Q.
Lipperheide 3503

See also Charlet, N. T., jt. auth.

Jamaica
Belisario, L. M. Sketches of character in illustration of the habits, occupation and the costume of the Negro population in the Island Jamaica. 1837

See also subdivision Jamaica under Ceremonial and festival costume; Mummers

James, Charles
The military costume of India. London, T. Goddard 1813
35p. 35 col.pl. F. £4 4d
"In an exemplification of the manual and platoon exercises for the use of the native troops and the British army in general." Subtitle
Plates are engraved by Sawyer and dated 1813. Some examples bear the date 1814, on the title page. The same prints are also published in folio size
Colas 1536. Lipperheide 2265

James, Constantin
Toilette d'une Romaine au temps d'Auguste, et cosmétiques d'une Parisienne au XIXe siècle. Paris, L. Hachette 1865
300p. D.
Lipperheide 241. LC 8-8795

James, George Wharton
Indian blankets and their makers. Chicago, A. C. McClurg 1914
xvi,213p. front. illus. pl.(part col.) Q. $5
Deals principally with the Navaho Indians
LC 14-15372

The Indians of the Painted desert region; Hopis, Navahoes, Wallapais, Havasupais ... with numerous illustrations from photographs. Boston, Little, Brown 1903
xxi,268p. front. 38pl. O.
Bibliography: p[265]-268
LC 3-19707

Jameson, Mrs Anna Brownell (Murphy)
Legends of the monastic orders as represented in the fine arts, forming the second series of Sacred and legendary art; 5th ed. London, Longmans, Green 1872
xlvii,461p. front. illus. pl. O.
Illustrations show saints
LC 17-17687

Sacred and legendary art; 6th ed. London, Longmans, Green 1870
2v. fronts. illus. pl. O.
Shows many figures of saints
LC 17-17686

Jameson, Mrs Anna Brownell (Murphy), and Eastlake, Elizabeth (Rigby), lady
The history of Our Lord as exemplified in works of art: with that of His types; St. John the Baptist; and other persons of the Old and New Testament. Commenced by the late Mrs. Jameson, contined and completed by Lady Eastlake. London, Longman 1864
2v. illus. pl. O.
LC 10-3957

Jamieson, Thomas Hill
(ed.) Brant, Sebastian. The Ship of fools

Jamnig, C., and Richter, A.
Die technik der geklöppelten spitze; original-entwürfe und ausführingen. Wien, Spielhagen & Schurich [1886]
2 l. 41pl. F.
Published in five parts, each with text and eight plates
Lipperheide 4049

Jane Austen and her times. Mitton, G. E.

Janet, Ange Louis, called Janet-Lange
Uniformes de l'armée française en [1846-] 1848. Dessinés ... par Janet-Lange. Paris, Aubert 1848
64 col.pl. F.
Also known with plates in black and white
Colas 1537

Janet, G.
Vie d'une Parisienne; 1. partie. Paris, Librairie Maresq ca1854
56 illus. O. (Petits albums pour rire, no7)
Lipperheide 3654

Janet-Lange. See Janet, A. L.

Janik, Franz
Lehrbuch zur gründlichen erlernung des damenfrisirens mit besonderer berücksichtigung der neuesten Wiener, Pariser und englischen modefrisuren, nebst costumehistorischen, theater und nationalfrisuren. Wien, Im selbstverlag des Verfassers [1896]
89p. 228 illus. O.
Colas 1538. Lipperheide 1717

Janin, Jules Gabriel
Un hiver à Paris; tableau des moeurs contemporaines. Paris, Vve L. Janet 1846
282p. illus. pl. O.
First edition (Paris, Curmer 1842). Illustrated by Eugene Lami

See also Gauthier, Théophile. Les beautés de l'opéra; Pictures of the French

Janitschek, Hubert. See Geschichte der deutschen kunst

Jankó, Janós
(ed.) Budapest. Magyar nemzeti múzeum. Néprajzi osztályának értesítöje

Jannettaz, Édouard, and others
Diamant et pierres précieuses; cristallographie, descriptions, emplois, évaluation, commerce. Bijoux, joyaux, orfévreries au point de vue de leur histoire et de leur travail. Par Ed. Jannettaz ... E. Fontenay ... Em. Vanderheym ... A. Coutance. Paris, J. Rothschild 1881
xii,580p. col.front. illus. O.
First edition 1880
Lipperheide 1752. LC GS33-215

Janssen, Luplau
(ed.)) Lund, F. C. Danske nationaldragter

Jantke, Egon. See Knötel, Herbert, jt. auth.

Jantscha, Lorenz. See Schwarz, Ignaz, ed. Wiener strassenbilder im zeitalter des rokoko.

Jany, C.
(ed.) Menzel, A. F. E. von. Die armee. Friedrichs des Grossen

Japan

General works

Baret, L. Le costume et la toilette au Japon. 1892
Breton de la Martinière, J. B. J. Le Japon, ou moeurs, usages et costumes des habitans de cet empire. 1818
Ema, Tsutomu. Kimono, one hundred masterpieces of Japanese costumes. [193-?]

Japan—General works—*Continued*
Fuku sen shiryo kenkyi kai, Tokio. Specimens of Japanese classical dresses. 1935
Gunsaulus, H. C. Japanese costume. 1923
Heizo, Ise. Iseke Iwai No Sho. Costume and toilet accessories of a lady of the family of the Count Noble Ise. 1764
Jidai Fukusoku Sen. Old Japanese dresses and ornaments. 1935
Joly, H. L. Legend in Japanese art. 1908
Kawakatsu, Kenichi. Kimono. 1936
Kongow, Iwao. The costume of Nō play in Japan. 193-
Kongow, Iwao. Nō-isho; Japanese Nō-play costume. 1934
Ogawa, K. Japanese costume before the Restoration. 1893
Tokyo. Imperial museum. Album of the life sized figures exhibited in the Tokyo Imperial museum, showing costumes of different ages. 190-?

Supplementary works

Anderson, William. The pictorial arts of Japan. 1886
Arnold, Sir Edwin. Japonica. 1891
Arnold, Sir Edwin. Seas and lands. 1891
Batchelor, John. The Ainu and their folk-lore. 1901
Beauvoir, Ludovic, marquis de. Pékin, Yeddo, San Francisco. 1902
Bell, Archie. A trip to Lotus land. 1917
Bing, Samuel, ed. Artistic Japan. 1888-91.
Bishop, Mrs I. L. B. Unbeaten tracks in Japan. 1880?
Brinkley, Frank. The art of Japan. c1901
Brinkley, Frank, ed. Japan; described and illustrated by the Japanese. 1897-98
Brinkley, Frank. Japan, its history, arts and literature. 1901-02
Brinckmann, Justus. Kunst und handwerk in Japan. 1889
Brown, G. W. The new America and the Far East. 1907 v5-6
Browne, G. W. Japan, the place and the people. 1904
Caiger, G. Japan, a pictorial interpretation. 1932
Carpenter, F. G. Japan and Korea. 1925
Challaye, Félicien. Le Japan illustré. 1915
Chamberlain, B. H. Things Japanese. 1905
Chōkōrō Hōshun. ... Jimbuts' gafu. n.d.
Dubois de Jancigny, A. P. Japon, Indo-Chine, Empire Birman (ou Ava), Siam, Annam (ou Cochinchine), Péninsule Malaise, etc., Ceylan. 1850
Einstein, Carl. Der frühere japanische holzschnitt. 1922
Fisher, Mrs W. H. Twins travelogues. v2. 1924
Francisci, Erasmus. Neu-polirter geschicht- kunst- und sitten-spiegel ausländischer völcker. 1670
Franck, H. A. Glimpses of Japan and Formosa. 1924
Griffis, W. E. The Mikado's empire. 1906
Hitchcock, A. M. Over Japan way. 1917
Hitomi, I. Daï-Nippon. Le Japon; essai sur les moeurs et les institutions. 1900
Hokusai. Hokusai [sketches with text by M. C. Salaman] 1930
Holland, Clive. Things seen in Japan. 1907
Humbert, Aimé. Japan and the Japanese, illustrated. 1874
Humbert, Aimé. Le Japon illustré. 1870
Japan; eine schilderung von dem umfange, der lage, staatsverwaltung, kriegsmacht dieses reichs und von den sitten, gebräuchen, religion, künsten, wissenschaften, handel, ackerbau seiner bewohner. 1831
Das Kaiserreich Japan nach den besten vorhandenen quellen geschildert von einem vereine gelehrter. 1860
Knox, G. W. Imperial Japan. 1905
Kurth, Julius. Suzuki Harunobu. 1923
Lawson, Kate, lady. Highways and homes of Japan. 1910
Meijlan, G. F. Japan. 1830
Menpes, Mortimer. Japan, a record in colour. 1901
Minamoto, Hoshu. An illustrated history of Japanese art. 1935
Mohl, Ottmar von. Am japanischen hofe. 1904
Montanus, Arnoldus. Gedenkwaerdige gesantschappen der Oost-Indische maatschappy in 't Vereenigde Nederland, aan de kaisaren van Japan. 1669
Netto, Curt. Papier-schmetterlinge aus Japan. 1888
Northrop, H. D. The flowery kingdom and the land of the mikado. 1894
Ota, Shintaro. Tokugawa ryaku denki. n.d.
Perry, M. C. Narrative of the expedition of an American squadron to the China seas and Japan, performed in the years 1852, 1853 and 1854. 1856
Pompe van Meerdervoort, J. L. C. Vijf jaren in Japan; (1857-1863) Bijdragen tot de kennis van het Japansche keizerrijk en zijne bevolking. 1867-68
Shoberl, Frederic, ed. Japan. 1823
Siebold, P. F. von. Nippon. 1897
Silver, J. M. W. Sketches of Japanese manners and customs. 1867
Strange, E. F. Japanese illustrations. 1897
Titsingh, Isaac. Cerémonies usitées au Japon, pour les mariages, les funérailles, et les principales fêtes de l'année. 1822
Trautz, F. M. Japan, Korea and Formosa. 1931?

Japan—Supp. works—*Continued*
Venables, E. K. Behind the smile in real Japan. 1936

See also Amos; also subdivision Japan under Arms and armor; Ceremonial and festival costume; Coronations and coronation robes; Children; Court dress; Decoration and ornament; Hairdressing; Masks; Military costume; Sword; Theatrical costume; Weddings and wedding dress

Japan. Brinkley, Frank

Japan, a pictorial interpretation. Caiger, G.

Japan, a record in colour. Menpes, Mortimer

The **Japan** advertiser
Enthronement of the one hundred twenty-fourth emperor of Japan. Tokyo, The Japan advertiser 1928
xvi,179p. illus.(1 col., mounted) F.
"Enthronement edition, the Japan advertiser. Being a complete account of the enthronement ceremonies from December 25, 1926, to December 13, 1928."
LC 29-17357

Japan and Korea. Carpenter, F. G.

Japan and the Japanese illustrated. Humbert, Aimé

Japan described and illustrated by the Japanese. Brinkley, Frank

Japan; eine schilderung von dem umfange, der lage, staatsverwaltung, kriegsmacht dieses reichs und von den sitten, gebräuchen, religion, künsten, wissenschaften, handel, ackerbau seiner bewohner. Berlin, J. G. Hasselberg [1831]
158p. 20 col.pl. O.
Contains some costume pictures, some of them from J. B. J. Breton de la Martinière's *Le Japon.* This book is sometimes attributed to Breton
Colas 441. Lipperheide 1559

Japan, Korea and Formosa. Trautz, F. M.

Japan society, London
Catalogue of an exhibition of the arms and armour of old Japan, held ... London, in June 1905. London, The Japan society [1905]
147p. 40pl. Q.
Contents: Introduction: The arms and armour of old Japan, by M. B. Huish; Japanese arms and armour in the royal collection, by G. F. Laking; The Japanese sword, by A. Dobrée; The sword-guard, by A. H. Church; Decoration of the parts of the sword-hilt and scabbard (other than the guard) by M. B. Huish; Bows, arrows, and quivers, by W. Harding-Smith; Pictures illustrating arms and armour, by E. F. Strange; The Japanese soldier's uniform in 1905; Catalogue of exhibits.
LC 13-5878

Japan, the place and the people. Browne, G. W.

The **Japanese** bride. Tamura, Naomi

Japanese costume. Gunsaulus, H. C.

Japanese costume. New York. Metropolitan museum of art

Japanese costume before the Restoration. Ogawa, K.

The **Japanese** dance. Hincks, M. A.

The **Japanese** dolls, Gosho-ningyo. Kawase Hasui

The **Japanese** floral calendar. Clement, E. W.

Japanese illustrations. Strange, E. F.

Japanese plays and playfellows. Edwards, Osman

Japanese sword fittings. Naunton, G. H.

Japanese sword guards. Okabe-Kakuya

Japanese sword-mounts. Field museum of natural history, Chicago

Japanese sword-mounts. Hawkshaw, J. C.

Die **japanische** armee in ihrer gegenwärtigen uniformirung ... abbildungen von offizieren und soldaten aller truppengattungen, farbendarstellungen, chargen-abzeichen etc. Nebst erläuterungen und mittheilungen über organisation, eintheilung und stärke. Leipzig, M. Ruhl [1895]
15p. 13pl.(12 col.) on fold. sheet. D.
Colas 2602. Lipperheide 2397. LC CA17-2458

Die **japanische** armee in ihrer gegenwärtigen uniformierung ... Nebst mittheilungen über organisation, eintheilung und stärke der japanischen armee; 3. auf. Leipzig, M. Ruhl [1905]
18p. 13 col.pl. D.

Japanische masken. Perzyński, Friedrich

Japanische vorbilder. Dolmetsch, Heinrich.

Japanischer formenschatz. See Bing, Samuel. Artistic Japan

Japhet
(illus.) Félix, E., ed. What she wore

Le **Japon** artistique. See Bing, Samuel. Artistic Japan

Le **Japon** illustré. Challaye, Félicien

Le **Japon** illustré. Humbert, Aimé

Japon, Indo-Chine ... Dubois de Jancigny, A.P.

Le **Japon,** ou moeurs, usages et costumes des habitans de cet empire. Breton de la Martinière, J. B. J.

Japonica. Arnold, Sir Edwin

Le **jardin** de la noblesse françoise. Saint-Igny, Jean de

Jardin de Monceau. Carmontelle, L. C. dit

Jardin des modes. v 1, Oct. 21 1920-Nov. 1935. Paris, Condé Nast
Illus.(part col.) Q. 50 fr. a year
Published monthly. Supplement to *Illustration* (Paris)
Title varies: Volume 1-3 no.36, Oct. 21 1920-July 15 1922, *Illustration des modes.* Merged with *Chic et pratiques* Nov. 1935
The following periodicals are supplements: *Enfants du Jardin des modes; Lingerie du Jardin des modes*

Jarno Jessen, pseud. See Michaelson, Anna

Jarwart, Sixtus, and Heinel, Eduard
Neun blatt slavische trachten im Bayreuther lande. Bayreuth, C. Giessel [1860]
8 col.pl. O.
Colas 1539. Lipperheide 771m

Jaschke, Franz
National-kleidertrachten und ansichten von Ungarn, Croatien, Slavonien, dem Banat, Siebenbürgen und der Bukowina. Wien, A. Strauss 1821
15,14p. 69 col.pl. F.
Colas 1540. Lipperheide 894

Jasper, J. E., and Pirngadie, Mas
De inlandsche kunstnijverheid in Nederlandsch Indië. 's-Gravenhage, Mouton 1912-16
3v. illus. pl.(part col.) F.
Contents: v 1 Het vlechtwerk; v2 De weefkunst; v3 De batikkunst
LC 17-19605

Jauslin, Carl
Feier zur eröffnung des Schweizerischen landesmuseums 25 Juni 1898 Zürich; kostümirter festzug darstellend die schweizerischen volkstrachten in bildern aus dem volksleben. Zürich, Gebr. Fretz [1898]
6p. 26pl. F.
Lipperheide 2845

Jauslin, Carl, and Roux, G.
400 jährige jubelfeier der schlacht bei Murten am 22 Juni 1876; album des historischen zuges. Bern, Buri & Jeker [1877]
12p. 40 col.pl. F.
Lipperheide 2839

Java
Campbell, D. M. Java: past & present. 1915
Carpenter, F. G. Java and the East Indies. 1923
Daniell, Thomas, and Daniell, William. A picturesque voyage to India, by the way of China. 1810
Grévedon, P. L. H. Costumes des habitans de l'île de Java et des possessions hollandaises dans l'Inde. 1831
Pfyffer, J. J. X. Skizzen von der insel Java und den verschiedenen bewohnern. 1829
Raffles, Sir T. S. Antiquarian, architectural, and landscape illustrations of the history of Java. 1844
Ritter, W. L. Java tooneelen uit het leven, karakterschetsen en kleederdrachten van Java's bewoners. 1872

See also subdivision Java under Dance costume; Decoration and ornament

Java and the East Indies. Carpenter, F. G.

Java: past & present. Campbell, D. M.

Java tooneelen uit het leven, karakterschetsen en kleederdrachten van Java's bewoners. Ritter, W. L.

De **javaansche** danskunst. Lelyveld, T. B. van

Jazet, A.
Mon village. Paris, Goupil & Vibert ca1840
24 col.pl. Q.
Plates show types of people in a French village. Title appears on the plates
Lipperheide 3655

Je fais mes masques. See Parain, Nathalie. Mes masques

Jeaffreson, John Cordy
A book about doctors. New York, Rudd & Carleton; London, Hurst & Blackett 1861
x,[11]-490p. front. D.
Physicians' canes p 1-5, wigs p9-12
LC 34-37547

A book about lawyers. New York, G. W. Carleton 1867
2v. in 1. O.
Reprinted from the English edition (London, Hurst & Blackett 1867)
Chapters 19-24 discuss dress of English lawyers

Brides and bridals. London, Hurst and Blackett 1872
2v. O.
Volume 2, pages 138-160 deal with costume: Chapter 10, The wedding-ring; 11, The ring finger; 12, The Gimmal ring; 13, Costume of brides
LC 15-11334

Jean, René
Le costume au moyen âge et à la renaissance. Melun, Imprimerie administrative 1905
18p. D.
At head of title: Ministère de l'instruction publique. Bibliothèque office et musée de l'enseignement public
Colas 1541

Jean-Meyan, Maurice, and Socquet, Jean
Le dessus du panier; illus. de Z. de Borelli Vranska, M. de Borelli Vranska, G. de Colomès. Paris, L. Michaud [1914]
91p. 22 col.pl. O.
Plates show masculine and feminine costumes, styles of dressing the hair, and shoes
Colas 1542

Jeanne d'Arc. Boutet de Monvel, L. M.

Jeanne d'Arc. Feyel, Paul

Jeanne d'Arc. Funck-Brentano, Frantz

Jeanne d'Arc. Wallon, H. A.

Jeanne d'Arc, ses costumes, son armure. Harmand, Adrien

Jeaurat, E.
(engr.) Vleughels, Nicolas. Costumes romains

Jedina, Rudolf, ritter von
Die flotte. See Kählig, Eduard von. Österreich-Ungarn

Jefferys, Thomas
(pub.) A collection of the dresses of different nations, antient and modern

Jéglot, Cécile
La jeune fille et la mode. Paris, Editions Spec [1928]
31p.
Colas 1543

Jégoudez, Mme
La mode. Paris, J. B. Baillière [1926]
262p. 327 illus. D. (Bibliothèque professionnelle publiée sous la direction de René Dhommée)
Colas 1544

Jelgerhuis, J.
Theoretische lessen over de gesticulatie en mimiek, gegeven aan de kweekelingen van het fonds ter opleiding en onderrigting van tooneel-kunstenaars an den stads schouwburg te Amsterdam. Amsterdam, P. M. Warnars [1827-29]
xiv,314p. 93pl. Q.
Costume for many periods is pictured. The text is in Dutch
Lipperheide 3215

Jellicoe, John
(illus.) Swinburne, H. L. The royal navy

Jena university. See Academic costume—Jena university

Jenkins, James
The martial achievements of Great Britain and her allies; from 1799 to 1815. London, Printed for J. Jenkins, by L. Harrison & J. C. Leigh [1815]
122p. 51 col.pl. sq.F.
Plates of battles, after W. Heath, engraved by T. Sutherland, from Seringapatam to Waterloo, including Egyptian campaign, Peninsular war, etc.
LC 4-25219 (under title)

Jenks, Tudor
Our army for our boys; a brief story of its organization, development and equipment from 1775 to the present day; pictures by H. A. Ogden. New York, Moffat, Yard [1906]
98p. col.front. illus. 7 col.pl. sq.Q. $2, o.p.
Each plate accompanied by guard sheet with descriptive letterpress
Colas 1545. Costume index. LC 6-36475

Jennings' landscape annual for 1839. See Harrison, W. H. The tourist in Portugal

Jenny, Heinrich
Historischer festzug in Winterthur den 22. Juni 1864, erinnerungsfeier des 22. Juni 1264. Winterthur, J. W. Randegger [1864]
8 pl. O.
Lipperheide 2835

Jenny, Wilhelm Albert, ritter von, and Volbach, Wolfgang Friedrich
Germanischer schmuck des frühen mittelalters. Berlin, Verlag für kunstwissenschaft 1933
53p. 64pl. F.
LC 34-19379

Jensen, Christian
Die nordfriesischen insel Sylt, Föhr, Amrum und die Halligen, vormals und jetzt. Hamburg, Actien-gesellschaft 1891
392p. 7 col.pl. col.map. O.
Plates show twenty-seven types of North-Frisian costume
Colas 1546. Lipperheide 800

Jeremias, Alfred
Der schleier von Sumer bis heute. Leipzig, J. C. Hinrichs 1931
70p. illus. 8pl. on 4 l. O. (Der alte Orient. bd. 31 hft. 1/2)
LC 31-32014

Jerrold, Blanchard
The life of George Cruikshank, in two epochs. London, Chatto and Windus 1882
2v. fronts. illus. pl. facsim. D.
Illustrations are by G. Cruikshank and are caricatures of English costume of the 19th century
Lipperheide 3509. LC 10-18641

London; a pilgrimage. By Gustave Doré and Blanchard Jerrold. London, Grant 1872
xii,191p. front. illus. 52pl. F.
Issued originally in 13 parts
Lipperheide 1028. LC 3-11554

Jerrold, Douglas
Heads of the people. See entry under Meadows, Kenny

Jesse, William
The life of Beau Brummell, by Captain Jesse. New ed., with an introduction and twenty coloured plates. London, The Navarre society 1927
2v. col.fronts. col.ports. O.
First published 1844. Several editions. The text is interesting for descriptions of English men's dress from about 1790 to 1840
LC 30-7653

Jessen, Heinrich
Trachten aus Alt-Hamburg. Hamburg, B. S. Berendsohn & W. Jowien ca1850
50 col.pl. O.
On most of the plates the publisher is given as B. S. Berendsohn, on the rest Wilh. Jowien, Hamburg. Thirty-three of these plates are after drawings by H. Jessen and were published earlier in Buek's *Album hambürgische costüme*
Colas 1547. Lipperheide 809

(illus.) Buek, F. G. Album hambürgische costüme. 1843-1847

Jessen, Jarno, pseud. See Michaelson, Anna

Jessen, Karl Ludwig
Friesische heimatkunst; text von Momme Nissen. Glückstadt, M. Hansen [1913]
24p. 24 col.pl. F.
Plates show costume

Jessen, Peter
Das ornament des rococo und seine vorstufen; 120 tafeln nach zeichnungen von Franz Paukert, Ad. Lackner, M. Bertram u. a., mit erläuterndem text. Leipzig, E. A. Seemann 1894
24p. illus. 120pl. F.
Lipperheide 4384. LC 20-7403

(ed.) Bretschneider, Andreas. Neues modelbuch 1619

Jessop, Charles Moore
Dress and health, an appeal to antiquity and common sense. London, E. Stock 1896
47p. O.

Jessup, Elon Huntington
Snow and ice sports. New York, E. P. Dutton [c1923]
x p. 293p. front. illus. pl. diagrs. O.
LC 23-6390

Jesus Christ
Adelphus, J. A. P. Warhafftig sag; oder red von dem rock Jesu Christi. 1512

Chertablon, de. La maniere de se bien preparer a la mort par des considerations sur la cene, la passion, & la mort de Jesus-Christ. 1700

Cranach, Lucas. Passional Christi und Antichristi. 1521

Dodd, I. S. The pictorial life of Christ. 1912

Dürer, Albrecht. Albrecht Dürer's Kleine passion. 1859

Dürer, Albrecht. Dürer album. 1856-61

Dürer, Albrecht. Dürer vier holzschnittfolgen phototypisch nachgebildet in der grösse der originale. 1887

Elder, A. P. T. The light of the world; or, Our Saviour in art. 1896

French, J. L. Christ in art. 1900

Jameson, Mrs A. B. M., and Eastlake, E. R., lady. The history of Our Lord as exemplified in works of art. 1864

Jesus Christ—*Continued*
La Farge, John. The Gospel story in art. 1913
Passio domini nostri Jhesu Christi ex evangelistarum textu q̃ue accuratissime deprompta additis sãctissimis exquisitissimisque figuris. 1513

Die **jetzige** frauenkleidung und vorschläge zu ihrer verbesserung. Spener

La **jeune** armée. Lalaisse, Hippolyte

La **jeune** armée. Maillot, T. J. R.

La **jeune** fille au dix-huitième siècle. See Claretie, Leo. Nos petites grand'mères

La **jeune** fille et la mode. Jéglot, Cécile

Les **jeunes** fiancées. Llanta, J. F. G.

Jeux de cartes tarots et de cartes numérales du quatorzième au dix-huitième siècle, représentés en cent planches d'après les originaux avec un précis historique et explicatif par Duchesne, ainé. Paris, Crapelet 1844
22p. 99pl.(part col.) Q.
Reproductions of the backs of twelve playing cards of the years 1390 to 1794. They are of interest for costume to the end of the fifteenth century
Lipperheide 326

Jeux et divertissements du peuple russe. See Richter, J. G. Spiele und belustigungen der Russen

Jewel don'ts. Russell, Edmund

The **jewel** house. Younghusband, Sir G. J.

Jewellery. Davenport, C. J. H.

Jewellery. Smith, H. C.

Jewelry
Abbott, Mary. Jewels of romance and renown. 1933
Barth, Hermann. Das geschmeide; schmuck- und edelsteinkunde. 1903-04
Bassermann-Jordan, Ernst. Der schmuck. 1909
Baudouin, M. E., and Lacouloumère, Georges. Le coeur vendéen; bijou populaire ancien. 1903
Bayard, Émile. L'art de reconnaître les bijoux anciens, pierres précieuses, métal précieux. 1924
Boodt, A. B. de. Le parfait ioaillier, ou Histoire des pierreries. 1644
Burgess, F. W. Antique jewellery and trinkets. 1919
Cambridge. University. Corpus Christi college. Lewis collection. The Lewis collection of gems and rings. 1892
Carpenter, F. G. How the world is clothed. 1908
Castellani, Alessandro. Antique jewelry and its revival. 1862
Davenport, C. J. H. Jewellery. 1913
Davidson, P. W. Applied design in the precious metals. 1929
Eppler, Alfred. Edelsteine und schmucksteine. 1934
Fontenay, E. Les bijoux anciens et modernes. 1887
Good. Edward. Cameos and inspiration jewellery. 1914
Haberlandt, Michael. Völkerschmuck. 1906
Jannettaz, Édouard, and others. Diamant et pierres précieuses; cristallographie, descriptions, emplois, évaluation, commerce. Bijoux, joyaux, orfévreries au point de vue de leur histoire et de leur travail. 1881
Kunz, G. F. The magic of jewels and charms. 1915
Londesborough, U. L. G. B. D., baroness. Catalogue of a collection of ancient and mediaeval rings and personal ornaments. 1853
Matthias, J. Der menschliche schmuck; form, farbe und anwendung. 1871
Miquel y Badia, Francisco. Industrias artísticas; alfarería, terra cotta, mayólica, loza, porcelana, vidrio, bronce, orfebrería, joyería, armas. 1892
Morgan, J. P. Catalogue of the collection of jewels and precious works of art the property of J. Pierpont Morgan. 1910
Müller, Peter, praeses. Dissertatio de jocalibus; Vom weiber-schmuck. 1706
Pattern book for jewellers, gold- and silversmiths. 1880?
Percival, MacIver. Chats on old jewellery and trinkets. 1912
Perleberg, H. C., comp. Voelkerschmuck (Jewels of all nations). 1915?
Rathbone, R. L. B. Unit jewellery; a handbook for craftsmen. 1921
Russell, Edmund. Jewel don'ts. 1895
Selenka, Emil. Der schmuck des menschen. 1900
Smith, H. C. Jewellery. 1908

See also Bracelets; Brooches; Crown jewels; Ear-rings; Nose-rings; Pins; Rings

Bibliography

Chambre syndicale de la bijouterie, de la joaillerie et de l'orfèvrerie de Paris. Bibliothèque. Catalogue. 1914

Jewelry, Ancient
Bibra, E. Ueber alte eisen- und silberfunde; archäologisch-chemische skizze. 1873
Blanchot, I. L. Les bijoux anciens. 1929
Blümner, Hugo. Das kunstgewerbe im altertum. 1885
British museum. Department of British and mediaeval antiquities. Guide to the antiquities of the bronze age. 1920
British museum. Department of British and mediaeval antiquities. Guide to antiquities of the early iron age. 1925
British museum. Department of Greek and Roman antiquities. Catalogue of the jewellery, Greek, Etruscan, and Roman. 1911
Chantre, Ernest. Études paléoethnologiques dans le bassin du Rhone: Age du bronze. 1875-76
Chantre, Ernest. Premier âge du fer: nécropoles et tumulus: Album. 1880
Cocheris, Mme P. A. W. Les parures primitives avec une introduction sur les temps préhistoriques. 1894

Jewelry, Ancient—*Continued*

Davenport, C. J. H. On the history of personal jewellery from prehistoric times. 1902

Evans, Sir John. The ancient bronze implements, weapons, and ornaments, of Great Britain and Ireland. 1881

Evans, Sir John. The ancient stone implements, weapons and ornaments of Great Britain. 1897

Faussett, Bryan. Inventorium sepulchrale [antiquities found in Anglo-Saxon cemeteries] 1856

Hampel, József. Alterthümer der bronzezeit in Ungarn. 1887

Keller, Ferdinand. The lake dwellings of Switzerland and other parts of Europe. 1878

King, C. W. Antique gems and rings. 1872

Mertins, Oskar. Wegweiser durch die urgeschichte Schlesiens und der nachbargebiete. 1906

Montelius, Oscar. Antiquités suédoises. 1873-75

Montelius, Oscar. Les temps préhistoriques en Suède et dans les autres pays scandinaves. 1895

Nelidov, A. I. kniaz. Klassische-antike goldschmiedearbeiten im besitze Sr. Excellenz A. J. von Nelidow. 1903

New York. Metropolitan museum of art. Jewelry, the art of the goldsmith in classical times as illustrated in the museum collection. 1928

Paris. Musée national du Louvre. Catalogue sommaire des bijoux antiques. 1924

Peigné-Delacourt, Achille. Recherches sur le lieu de la Bataille d'Attila en 451. 1860

Waring, J. B. Stone monuments, tumuli and ornament of remote ages. 1870

Worsaae, J. J. A. Nordiske oldsager i det kongelige museum i Kjöbenhavn. 1859

See also Bracteates (Ornaments)

Asia

Chantre, Ernest. Recherches anthropologiques dans le Caucase. 1885-87

Egypt

Brunton, Guy. Lahun. 1920-23

Carter, Howard, and Mace, A. C. The tomb of Tut.ankh.Amen, discovered by the late Earl of Carnarvon and Howard Carter. 1923-33

Lythgoe, A. M. The treasure of Lahun. 1919

Petrie, Sir W. M. F. The arts & crafts of ancient Egypt. 1910

Vernier, E. S. La bijouterie et la joaillerie egyptiennes. 1907

Williams, C. R. Gold and silver jewelery and related objects. 1924

Winlock, H. E. The treasure of El Lāhūn. 1934

Europe

Deane, J. B. Remarks on certain ornaments of gold found near Quentin in Britany in 1832. 1838

Dennison, Walter. A gold treasure of the late Roman period. 1918

Klemm, G. F. Handbuch der germanischen alterthumskunde. 1836

Paulsen, Peter. Der goldschatz von Hiddensee. 1906

Rome

Riccio, Gennaro. Descrizione, storia, ed illustrazione degli ornamenti di una donna romana vissuta circa il 383 dell' era cristiana. 1838

Jewelry, Medieval and modern

Allemagne, H. R. d'. Les accessoires du costume et du mobilier depuis le treizième jusqu'au milieu du dixneuvième siècle. 1928

British museum. Department of British and mediaeval antiquities. Catalogue of the engraved gems of the post-classical periods. 1915

Götze, Alfred. Die altthüringischen funde von Weimar (5.-7. jahrhundert nach Chr.) 1912

Africa

Eudel, Paul. Dictionnaire des bijoux de l'Afrique du Nord, Maroc, Algérie, Tunisie, Tripolitaine. 1906

Eudel, Paul. L'orfévrerie algérienne et tunisienne. 1902

Asia

Marchal, Sappho. Costumes et parures khmèrs. 1927

Roth, H. L. Oriental silverwork, Malay and Chinese. 1910

Europe

Boehn, Max von. Das beiwerk der mode. 1928

Boehn, Max von. Modes & manners: ornaments; lace, fans, gloves, walking-sticks, parasols, jewelry and trinkets. 1929

Brown, G. B. The arts and crafts of our Teutonic forefathers. 1910

Bruck-Auffenberg, Frau Natalie. Dalmatien und seine volkskunst. 1911

Cesnola, L. P. di. Cyprus: its ancient cities, tombs, and temples. 1878

Eudel, Paul. L'orfévrerie algérienne et tunisienne. 1902

Evans, Joan. English jewellery from the fifth century A. D. to 1800. 1921

Evans, Joan. Magical jewels of the middle ages and the renaissance, particularly in England. 1922

Falke, Otto von. Der Mainzer goldschmuck kaiserin Gisela.. 1913

Gelin, Henri. Les coiffes poitevines, les bijoux poitevins. 1898

Hispanic society of America. Jewelry: brazaleras, La Alberca, Salamanca. 1931

Jewelry, Medieval and modern—Europe—*Continued*

Hispanic society of America. Jewelry: necklaces, La Alberca, Salamanca. 1931

Hispanic society of America. Spain costume details: jewelry. 1931?

Hispanic society of America. Women's jewelry: Candelario, Salamanca. 1931

Holme, Charles, ed. Modern design in jewellery and fans. 1902

Holme, Charles, ed. Peasant art in Italy. 1913

Holme, Charles, ed. Peasant art in Sweden, Lapland and Iceland. 1910

Jenny, W. A., ritter von, and Volbach, W. F. Germanischer schmuck des frühen mittelalters. 1933

Londesborough, U. L. G. B. D., baroness. Catalogue of a collection of ancient and mediaeval rings and personal ornaments. 1853

Luthmer, Ferdinand. Goldschmuck der renaissance, nach originalen und von gemälden des XV.-XVII. jahrhunderts. 1881

Luthmer, Ferdinand. Ornamental jewellery of the renaissance in relation to costume. 1882

Oslo. Kunstindustrimuseet. Gamle smykker i Norge, 1550-1900. 1928

Rose, A. F., and Cirino, Antonio. Jewelry making and design; an illustrated text book for teachers, students of design, and craft workers in jewelry. 1917

Rothschild, M. K., freiherr von. Der schatz des freiherrn Karl von Rothschild; meisterwerke alter goldschmiedekunst aus dem 14.-18. jahrhundert. 1883-85

Vever, Henri. La bijouterie française au XIXe siècle (1800-1900). 1906-08

Viollet-Le-Duc, E. E. Dictionnaire raisonné du mobilier français de l'époque carlovingienne à la renaissance. 1858-75

Wistrand, P. G. V. Svenska folkdräkter. 1907

Worsaae, J. J. A. The industrial arts of Denmark from the earliest times to the Danish conquest of England. 1882

Indians of North America

Bedinger, Margery. Navajo Indian silverwork. 1936

Hodge, F. W. Turquois work of Hawikuh. 1921

Indians of South America

Montell, Gösta. Dress and ornaments in ancient Peru. 1929

Wright, B. M. Description of the collection of gold ornaments from the "huacas" or graves of some aboriginal races of the north western provinces of South America. 1885

Oceanica

Finsch, Otto. Südseearbeiten. 1914

Jewelry making and design. Rose, A. F., and Cirino, Antonio

Jewelry, the art of the goldsmith in classical times. New York. Metropolitan museum of art

Jewels of all nations. See Perleberg, H. C., comp. Voelker-schmuck

Jewels of romance and renown. Abbott, Mary

The **Jewish** child in home and synagogue. See Levinger, Mrs E. C. E. With the Jewish child in home and synagogue

The **Jewish** encyclopedia; a descriptive record of the history, religion, literature, and customs of the Jewish people from the earliest times to the present day; prepared ... under the direction of ... Cyrus Adler [and others] New York and London, Funk & Wagnalls 1901-06

12v. fronts. (part col.) illus. pl. (part col.) ports. maps, plans, facsims. (part col.) tables. Q.

The article on Costume in volume 4 contains material on Jewish dress

LC 1-9359

Jewish life in the middle ages. Abrahams, Israel

Jewish life through its festivals. See Adlerblum, Mrs N. H. A perspective of Jewish life through its festivals

Jewish priests

Cooper, C. W. The precious stones of the Bible; with an account of the breastplate of the High Priest, the ephod and urim and thummim. 192-?

Rhind, W. G. The high priest of Israel, in his robes of glory and beauty, blessing the people. 1859

See also Ecclesiastical costume—Jews

Jews

De Quincey, Thomas. Toilette of a Hebrew lady. 1926

Hartmann, A. T. Die Hebräerin am putztische und als braut. 1809-10

The Jewish encyclopedia. 1901-06

Kaufmann, Isidor. Isidore Kaufmann [Reproductions of paintings of Jewish life] 1926

Kirchner, P. C. Jüdisches ceremoniel, oder beschreibung derer jenigen gebräuche, welche die Jüden so wol innals ausser dem tempel, bey allen und jeden festtägen. 1726

Liebe, G. H. T. Das Judentum in der deutschen vergangenheit. 1903

Lund, Johann. Die alten jüdischen heiligthümer gottes-dienste und gewohnheiten ... in einer ausführlichen beschreibung des gantzen levitischen priesterthums. 1701

Neue Franckfurter jüdische kleider-ordnung, dess gleichen wie es bey ihren verlölnüssen, hochzeiten, beschneidungen, gevatterschafften und anderen vorfällen hinführo soll gehalten werden. 1716

See also Biblical characters; Ceremonial and festival costume—Jews; Ecclesiastical costume—Jews; Jesus Christ; Palestine

Jews—*Continued*

Caricature and satire

Fuchs, Eduard. Die Juden in der karikatur. 1921

Ancient times

Benzinger, Immanuel. Hebraeische archäologie. 1927

Benzinger, Immanuel. Hebräische archäologie. 1907

Brown, William. Antiquities of the Jews. 1820

Brüll, Adolph. Trachten der Juden im nachbiblischen alterthume. 1873

Kritische anmerckungen über die fehler der maler wider die geistliche geschichte und das kostum. 1772

Nowack, Wilhelm. Lehrbuch der hebräischen archäologie. 1894

Paris. Bibliothèque nationale. Département des manuscrits. Antiquités et guerre des Juifs de Josèphe. 1906

Perrot, Georges, and Chipiez, Charles. History of art in Sardinia, Judaea, Syria, and Asia Minor. 1890

Pierotti, Ermete. Customs and traditions of Palestine, illustrating the manners of the ancient Hebrews. 1864

Rosenzweig, Adolf. Kleidung und schmuck im biblischen und talmudischen schrifttum. 1905

Schemel, Siegfried. Die kleidung der Juden im zeitalter der Mischnah, nebst einem anhange: Die priester-kleidung. 1912

Stade, Bernhard. Geschichte des volkes Israel. 1887-88

Middle ages

Abrahams, Israel. Jewish life in the middle ages. 1896

Robert, U. L. L. Les signes d'infamie au moyen âge: Juifs, Sarrasins, hérétiques, lépreux, Cagots, et filles publiques. 1891

Singermann, Felix. Ueber Juden-abzeichen; ein beitrag zur sozialen geschichte des Judentums. 1915

17th-20th centuries

Addison, Lancelot. The present state of the Jews. 1676

Fishberg, Maurice. The Jews: a study of race and environment. 1911

Goulven, J. G. A. Les mellahs de Rabat-Salé. 1927

Hollaenderski, Léon. Les Israélites de Pologne. 1846

Kaufmann, Isidor. Isidor Kaufmann. 1925?

Picart, Bernard. Scènes de la vie juive. 1884

Jidai Fukusoku Sen

Old Japanese dresses and ornaments; part 1. London, Kegan Paul 1935
12p. illus. 6 col.pl. Q. 7s 6d

Joachim, abbot of Fiore

Profetic dell' abbate Gioachino et di Anselmo, vescovo di Marsico con l'imagini in dissegno, intorno a' pontefici passati, e c'hanno à venire, con due ruote, & uń oracolo turchesco, fugurato sopra simil materia. Venetia, C. Tomasini 1646
88p. 34 illus. Q.
Lipperheide 1801

Joaillerie de la renaissance. See Luthmer, Ferdinand. Goldschmuck der renaissance

Joan of Arc, Saint. See France—15th century

Joan of Arc. Boutet de Monvel, L. M.

Joannis Physiophilus's Specimen of the natural history of the various orders of monks. Born, Ignaz, Edler von

Job. See Onfroy de Bréville, J. M. G., called Job

Job, A., doctor

Le vêtement au point de vue de l'hygiène; conférence populaire ... le dimanche 18 janvier 1880. Lunéville, Imprimerie nouvelle 1880?
32p. O.
Colas 1548

Jobin, Bernhard

New künstlichs modelbuch von allerhand artlichen und gerechten mödeln auff der laden zu wircken ... auff ein news wider getruckt und mit vielen newer mödel gemehret. Strassburg, B. Jobin 1589
1 l. 43pl. Q.
The first collection by Jobin was published 1579
Lipperheide 3897

Jockeys

American racing colors. 1884

Brown, Paul. Aintree; Grand nationals —past and present. 1930

Cook, T. A. A history of the English turf. 1901-04

Nevill, R. H. Old English sporting prints and their history. 1923

Jocosi

Costumi nazionali Dalmati. Zara, Spiridione Artale [184-?]
20 col.pl. Q.
Plates are identical with those in Carrara's *La Dalmazia*
Lipperheide 883

(illus.) Carrara, Francesco. La Dalmazia

Jode, Gerard de

(engr.) Panvinio, Onofrio. Amplissimi ornatissimique triumphi

Joest, Wilhelm

Tätowiren, narbenzeichnen und körperbemalen: ein beitrag zur vergleichenden ethnologie; illus ... nach originalzeichnungen von O. Finsch, Cl. Joest, J. Kubary und P. Preissler ... Berlin, A. Asher 1887
128p. illus. 12pl.(11 col.) ob.F.
LC 1-G-1312

Johann von St Wendel]
Fidelis certa verissimaqz narratio de Monasterio beate Marie ad littus martirum: de Tunica quoqz beate Marie vginis ceterisqz sacris ibidē reliquijs. [Metz, C. Hochfelder ca1512]
4 l. illus. Q.
Lipperheide 1792

John, Alois
(ed.) Grüner, J. S. Über die ältesten sitten und gebräuche der Egerländer

John Chinaman at home. Hardy, E. J.

Johnes, Thomas
(tr.) Froissart, Jean. Sir John Froissart's chronicles of England, France, Spain
(tr.) Monstrelet, Enguerrand de. The chronicles of Enguerrand de Monstrelet

Johnson, Cecil Webb- See Webb-Johnson, Cecil

Johnson, John
The costumes of the French Pyrenees; drawn on stone by D. Harding, from sketches by J. Johnson. London, J. Carpenter 1832
60p. 30 col.pl. Q.
Colas 1551. Lipperheide 1198

Johnson, Merle de Vore
(comp.) Pyle, Howard, illus. Howard Pyle's book of the American spirit

Johnson, Rossiter
Campfire and battle-field; a history of the conflicts and campaigns of the great civil war in the United States ... Illus. with the original photographs of the ... Brady collection. New York, Knight & Brown [1896]
551p. front.(port.) illus.(incl.ports.) maps, plans, facsims. sq.F.
LC 2-9070

Johnson, Samuel
(comp.) The world displayed

Johnson's England. Turberville, A. S., ed.

Johnston, Harold Whetstone
The private life of the Romans; rev. by Mary Johnston. Chicago, Atlanta [etc.] Scott, Foresman [c1932]
430p. col.front. illus. 2 double maps. O. $2.24 (The Lake classical series)
Books on Rome and Roman life: p409-412
Costume index. LC 32-7692

Johnston, Sir Harry Hamilton
George Grenfell and the Congo; a history and description of the Congo independent state and adjoining districts of Congoland, together with some account of the native peoples. London, Hutchinson 1908
2v. fronts. illus. pl. ports. maps(part fold.) facsims. O.
Shows dress, ornaments, weapons of the Congo tribes
LC 8-34210

Liberia, by Sir Harry Johnston. New York, Dodd, Mead; London, Hutchinson 1906
2v. col.fronts. illus. col.pl. ports. (part col.) maps(part fold.) O. $12.50; 42s, o.p.
Bibliography: v 1 p xiii-xvii
Costume index. LC 13-4161

Johnston, M. F.
Coronation of a king; or, The ceremonies, pageants and chronicles of coronations of all ages ... with illustrations reproduced from old prints. London, Chapman & Hall 1902
279p. 20pl. 2 port 2 plans. O.
Contents: The crowning of a king; Early coronations; Coronations in the Confessor's abbey; Coronations from 1272-1558; Coronations from 1604-1838; Concerning regalia; The Knights of the bath; Some memorable coronations; The coronation of the popes of Rome; Coronations in the Far east.
LC 6-24002

Johnston, Margaret Taylor
(tr.) Lefébure, Ernest. Les points de France

Johnston, Reginald Fleming
The Chinese drama; ... with six illustrations reproduced from the original paintings, by C. F. Winzer. Shanghai [etc.] Kelly and Walsh 1921
36p. incl. 6 col.mounted pl. sq.Q.
LC 29-13202

Joiner, Betty
Costumes for the dance; illus. by the author. New York, A. S. Barnes 1937
82p. illus. col.front. col.pl. Q.
LC 37-5311

Les **jolies** femmes de Paris. Beaumont, C. E. de

Les **jolies** Françaises. See Le quart d'heure des jolies Françaises

Les **jolis** soldats français. Bellangé, J. L. H.

[**Joly, Adrien**]
Les petits acteurs du grand théâtre, ou recueil des divers cris de Paris. Paris, Martinet ca1815
3 l. 62 col.pl. O.
Plates 56 to 60 are signed by Joly. The others are probably not his work. Some plates bear title: *Arts, métiers et cris de Paris*. For full description see Colas
Colas 1552

Joly, Henri L.
Legend in Japanese art; a description of historical episodes, legendary characters, folk-lore, myths, religious symbolism, illustrated in the arts of old Japan. London, J. Lane; New York, J. Lane 1908
xliii p. 453p. col.front. pl.(15 col.) Q.
Bibliography: p[421]-37
LC 8-15873
(comp.) Hawkshaw, J. C. Japanese sword-mounts
(comp.) Naunton, G. H. Japanese sword fittings. 1912

Jomard, Edme François
(ed.) Cailliaud, Frederic. Recherches sur les arts et métiers ... des anciens peuples de l'Égypte, de la Nubie et de l'Éthiopie

Jomard, Edme François
(ed.) Description de l'Égypt

Jonas, Lucien
L'armée américaine, 1918. [Paris, Dorbon-aîné, c1919]
62pl.(incl. ports.) F.
Shows uniforms worn during the European war
LC 19-11496

Jonas, Lucien—*Continued*
Les armées britanniques. [Paris, Dorbon-aîné, 1918?]
103pl. (part col.; incl. ports.) F.
Shows uniforms worn during the European war
LC 19-12308

Jonchère, Ermance Dufaux de la. See Dufaux de la Jonchère, Ermance

Jones, Humphrey Tudor Morrey
(ed.) Grubb, W. B. An unknown people in an unknown land

Jones, Inigo
Designs by Inigo Jones, for masques & plays at court; a descriptive catalogue of drawings for scenery and costumes mainly in the collection of His Grace the Duke of Devonshire ... with introduction and notes by Percy Simpson and C. F. Bell. Oxford, University press 1924
xi,158p. col.mounted front. illus. 51pl. F. (Walpole society, London. [Publications]12)

Jones, Marie M.
Woman's dress, its moral and physical relations. New York, Miller, Wood & co 1865
29p. illus. O.
German translation: *Die weibliche kleidung und ihre sittlichen und leiblichen beziehungen* (Berlin, T. Grieben 1870)
Lipperheide 3273 (German ed.)

Jones, Mrs Mary Cadwalader (Rawle). See La Farge, John. The Gospel story in art; also Flory, M. A. A book about fans

Jones, George
(illus.) Booth, John, comp. Battle of Waterloo, with those of Ligny and Quatre Bras

Jones, Owen
Examples of Chinese ornament selected from objects in the South Kensington museum and other collections. London, S. & T. Gilbert 1867
15p. illus. c col.pl. F.
Lipperheide 4363. LC 10-19717

The grammar of ornament, by Owen Jones. Illustrated by examples from various styles of ornament. London, Day and son [1865]
157p. illus. 111 pl.(part col.) F.
With contributions by J. B. Waring, J. O. Westwood, and M. Digby Wyatt
LC 4-11692

(illus.) Humphreys, H. N. The illuminated books of the middle ages

Jones, W., and company, tailors
Wholesale army, navy and volunteer, helmet, cap, and accoutrement makers, gold lace manufacturers and embroiderers. London, W. Jones ca1855
74 l. illus.(28 col.) F.
Shows uniforms and equipment of the British army, including colonial forces, about 1855
Colas 3076

Jones, William, F. S. A.
Crowns & coronations; a history of regalia. London, Chatto & Windus 1883
xxx,551p. front. illus. pl. D. 7s 6d o.p.
Reprinted 1898, 1902
Costume index. LC 2-18216

Finger-ring lore; historical, legendary, & anecdotal; new ed. ... London, Chatto & Windus 1898
xvi,567p. illus. O. 7s 6d, o.p.
First edition 1877; 2. ed 1890
Costume index. Lipperheide 1751 (2d. ed)
LC 1-13048

Jong, Jo de
50 eeuwen costuum ... met medewerking van dr. F. H. Fischer, en een voorrede van Huib Luns. Amsterdam, De Spieghel 1927
116p. illus. pl. Q.

Jonge, Johann Karel Jakob de, jonkheer
Intogt van Frederik Hendrik in s'Hertogenbosch in 1629; gecostumeerde vorstelling door de H.H. studenten der Leydsche hooge school den XI Junij van het jaar 1850. Leyden, J. Hazenberg, C. Zoon & J. H. Gebhard [1850]
3 l. 13pl. F.
Lipperheide 2834

Jongh, Francis de. See Camena d'Almeida, P. J., jt. auth.

Jonghe, Caroline Henriette de
Bijdrage tot de kennis van de Noord-Nederlandsche costuum-geschiedenis in de eerste helft van de XVI[e] eeuw. Utrecht, A. Oosthoek 1916
v 1 (96p.) illus. D.
Deel 1 Het mannencostuum
All kinds of North Netherlands costume of the sixteenth century are discussed in detail and defined, a list of works of art which illustrate each kind of costume is given, with the name of the museum in which each work may be found

Jonghe, Clement de
Trachten der Holländerinnen. See entry under Buyteweck, Willem

Jonghe, J. de, vicomte
Catalogue d'une très belle collection de recueils de costumes, XVIIIe et début du XIXe siècles. Aquarelles originales appartenant à m. le vicomte J. de Jonghe. Paris, L. Giraud-Badin 1930
51p. 12pl. O.
Colas 558

Jordan, Mrs Louise Estella (Bulger)
Clothing: fundamental problems; a practical discussion in regard to the selection, construction and use of clothing. Boston, M. Barrows 1927
xvi,379p. illus. col.pl. diagrs. O.
LC 27-14267

Jordanszky, Alexius, and Seidemann, Xaver
Hauptmomente aus dem leben Sr. majestät Franz I. kaisers von Oesterreich, apostol. königs. See entry under Höchle, J. N., illus.

Jorgen Garnaas og Nordmandsdalen. Lexow, E. J.

Jorio, Andrea de
La mimica degli antichi investigata nel gestire napoletano. Fibreno 1832
xxxvi,380p. 21 pl.(16 col.) O.
Colored plates by Baron de Clugny de Nuis. Sixteen of the plates show scenes of Neapolitan life
Colas 1555. Lipperheide 1296. LC 7-6352

Joshua, Joan
(tr.) Boehn, Max von. Modes and manners

Jossic, Yvonne Françoise
(comp.) A revival of the past ages; costumes, accessories, architecture, social life and various activities. pts 1-8. Philadelphia, H. C. Perleberg [1932-35]
8v. plates(part col.) 35x28cm. ea $7.50
List of sources from which the plates have been reproduced, on mounted slip in each volume. Issued in portfolios. Plates numbered continuously
Costume index. LC 34-1636

Jossot, Henri
Mince de trognes!!! Preface de H. Bauër. Paris, C. Hazard 1896
3 l. 50pl. F. 6 fr.

Jostes, Franz
Westfälisches trachtenbuch. Bielefeld, Berlin & Leipzig, Velhagen & Klasing 1904
208p. 256 illus. 24 col.pl. Q.
Plates after drawings by Johs. Gehrts
Colas 1556. Lipperheide 802h

Jou, Louis
À la danseuse. Paris, Lapina, 1925
15 l. 15pl. F.
Text by A. T'Serstevens

Les **joueurs** d'épée à travers les siècles. Letainturier-Fradin, Gabriel

Jouhanneaud, Paul
Album des voyages anciens et modernes. Limoges, M. Ardant 1854
208p. pl. F.
"Édition illus. de portraits des différents peuples de la terre." Subtitle

Joullain, François
(engr.) Gillot, Claude. Nouveaux desseins d'habillements a l'usage des ballets, opéras, et comédies

Jourdain, Amable
La Perse, ou Tableau de l'histoire, du gouvernement, de la religion, de la littérature, etc., de cet empire. Paris, Ferra 1814
5v. pl. D.

Jourdain, Margaret
(ed.) Palliser, Mrs F. M. History of lace

Journal de coëffure ou l'art du coëffeur. Palette, J. N.

Journal de la mode et du goût; ou, Amusemens du sallon et de la toilette, par m. Le Brun. [1.-4. année] 25 fév. 1790-1 avr. 1793. Paris, Buisson
4v. 112 col.pl. O.
Colas 1557

Journal der moden. See Journal für literatur, kunst, luxus, und mode

Journal des dames. No. 1-52; 1849-1857 Paris, Janet
Col.pl. O.
Fifty-two colored fashion plates by Anaïs Toudouze
Colas 1560

Journal des dames et des modes, 1797-1839. See Gazette des salons

Journal des dames et des modes. 1799-1848. Francfort sur le Mein
Col.illus. O.-Q.
Published at the rate of fifteen parts (livraisons) a year, each with one colored fashion plate. This revue was inspired by the *Journal des dames* illustrated by La Mésangère
Colas 1565. Lipperheide 4584

Journal des dames et des modes. 1.-3. année (v. 1-5, no. 1-79); 1 juin 1912-20 juillet 1914. Paris, Aux bureaux du Journal des dames
5v. 184 col.pl. O.
Published three numbers a month
June-Dec. 1912 are called t. 1 on title page; Jan.-June 1913, t. 2; July-Dec. 1913, t. 3; Jan.-June 1914, t. 4; t. 5 was not completed—4 parts (fascicules) were published consisting of 32 pages and eight colored plates
Colas 1567. LC 13-11934

Journal des dames et des modes, gazette des salons
Costumes-portraits des actrices des principaux théâtres de Paris. Paris, Bureau du Journal des dames An II (1803)
4 col.pl. O.
Colas 1564

See also Annuaire des modes de Paris

Journal des demoiselles. 1.-60. année; 1833-1892. Paris [& Bruxelles] Au bureau du Journal
60v. illus. pl.(part col.) Q.
Published monthly. Volumes for 1833-51 have title *Journal des dames et des demoiselles.* Some volumes include separately paged supplements issued the 16th of each month, under title, to June 1873: *Journal des demoiselles,* edition bi-mensuelle; July 1873-? *Journal des demoiselles et Petit courrier des dames réunis*
Colas 1568-69. Lipperheide 4622, 4656. LC (CA11-2644)

Manuel du Journal des demoiselles, explication des termes ... et méthodes pour les principaux travaux des dames; 6. éd. Paris, Au bureau du Journal des demoiselles 1883?
313p. 422 illus. O.
German translation: *Handbuch für frauenarbeiten; eine anweisung in der anfertigung der verschiedenen arten der stickerei, strickerei, häkelei* (2. aufl. Leipzig, Hoffmann & Ohnstein 1883. 282p. 397 illus. O.) Translated by Mathilde Clasen-Schmid
Lipperheide 4113-4115

Journal des jeunes personnes; education, littérature, science et industrie, modes, etc. par mlle Julie Gouraud. 1832-63? Paris
Col.pl. O.
Colas 1559

Journal des luxus und der moden. See Journal für literatur, kunst, luxus, und mode

Journal für fabriken, manufakturen, handlung, kunst und mode. v 1-35, 1791-1808. Leipzig, J. F. Gleditsch
35v. col.illus. O.
Title varies: v 1-4 *Journal für fabrik, manufaktur und handlung*
Superseded by: *Neues journal für fabriken ...*
Colas 1572. Lipperheide 4574

Journal für literatur, kunst, luxus, und mode. v 1-42, 1786-1827. Weimar, F. J. Bertuch & J. M. Kraus
42v. col.pl. O.
Published monthly. The plates show fashions in dress and also in furniture, carriages, etc. Thirty-six plates were published each year
Title varies: v 1. 1786, *Journal der moden;* v2-27 1787-1812 *Journal des luxus und der moden;* v28 1813, *Journal für luxus, mode und gegenstände der kunst*
Colas 1570. Lipperheide 4570

Journal für luxus, mode und gegenstände der kunst. See Journal für literatur, kunst, luxus, und mode

Journal für moderne stickerei, mode und weibliche handarbeiten. 1.-18 jahrg. 1844-1861. Weimar
18v. col.illus. Q.
Lipperheide 4648

Journal historique du sacre et du couronnement de Louis XVI. See Pichon, T. J., ed. Sacre et couronnement de Louis XVI

Journal militaire officiel. v 1-54, 1790-1817; ser.2 v 1-26, 1818-1830; ser3 v 1-54, 1831-1857; ser.4 v 1-?, 1858-1886. Paris, 1790-1886
Fold.pl. tab.
Interesting for uniforms. An index is available for 1790-1872
Continues *Journal militaire et politique* (v 1-85, 1790-June 1842). Continued as *Bulletin officiel du Ministère de la guerre*
A reprint of v 1-14, 1818-72 was published (Paris, J. Dumaine 1872. LC 3-7470)

Journal of a cruise among the islands of the western Pacific. Erskine, J. E.

Journal of a residence in Ashantee. Dupuis, Joseph

Journal of a second voyage for the discovery of a northwest passage from the Atlantic to the Pacific. Parry, Sir W. E.

The **Journal** of Indian art. London, 1886-1916
17v. illus. pl.(part col.) F.
Issued by the Department of revenue and agriculture of India. Many illustrations show costume and jewelry
Lipperheide 1508e

Journal of the American Asiatic association. See Asia; journal

La **journée** d'une jolie femme. See, Le quart d'heure des jolies Françaises

Journees révolutionnaires: 1830, 1848. Dayot, A. P. M.

A **journey** from Madras. Buchanan, F. H.

A **journey** to Ashango-Land. Du Chaillu, P. B.

Journey to Lhasa and central Tibet. Sarach-chandra Dāsa

Jovius, Paulus. See Giovio, Paolo, bp. of Nocera

Joy, Lilian
The well dressed woman. London, Cassell 1907
151p. D. 1s

Joyce, Patrick Weston
A social history of ancient Ireland; treating of the government, military system, and law; religion, learning, and art; trades, industries, and commerce; manners, customs, and domestic life, of the ancient Irish people. London, New York, and Bombay, Longmans, Green 1903
2v. front. illus.(incl. ports. plans) col.pl. map, facsims. O.
Volume 2 treats of dress and personal adornment
LC 3-30494

Joyce, Thomas Athol
Guide to the Maudslay collection of Maya sculptures (casts and originals) from Central America. See entry under British museum. Department of ceramics and ethnography

Handbook to the ethnographical collections. See entry under British museum. Department of British and mediaeval antiquities

Maya & Mexican art. London, The Studio 1927
191p. col.front. illus. pl. O.
Bibliography: p187-91
LC 27-5612

Joyce, Thomas Athol, and Thomas, Northcote Whitridge
(eds.) Women of all nations; a record of their characteristics, habits, manners, customs, and influence. New York, Funk & Wagnalls; London, Cassell 1915
2v. col.fronts. illus. col.pl. Q. $7.50
Paged continuously. Pictures women of this period in all parts of the world
Costume index. LC 18-18818

La **joyeuse** & magnifique entrée de Monseigneur Françoys, fils de France, et frere unique du roy ... duc de Brabant, d'Anjou, Alençon, Berri &c. en ... Anvers. Anvers, C. Plantin 1582
46p. 21 pl. F.
Lipperheide 2655

Juan Belmonte, killer of bulls. Belmonte y Garcia, Juan

Jubilaeum theatri europaei. See Theatrum europaeum

Jubinal, Achille
Les anciennes tapisseries historiées, ou, Collection des monumens les plus remarquables, de ce genre, qui nous soient restés du moyen-âge, à partir du XIe siècle au XVIe inclusivement ... Gravures par les meilleurs artistes, d'après les dessins de Victor Sansonetti. Paris, L'éditeur de la Galerie d'armes de Madrid 1838
2v. in 1. illus.(incl.ports.) 123pl. F.
Shows costume of the middle ages in France and Switzerland
Lipperheide 319. LC 12-15436

La Armeria real; ou Collection des principales pièces de la galerie d'armes anciennes de Madrid. Dessins de Gaspard Sensi ... Texte de Achille Jubinal ... Frontispices, lettres ornées, culs de lampe, par Victor Sansonetti, gravures sur bois par Faxardo, sur pierre, sur cuivre, sur acier par les meilleurs artistes de Paris. Paris, au bureau des anciennes tapisseries 1837-1842
3v. 97 illus. 126pl. F.
Volume 2 published by Challamel; v3: Supplement, published by Didron
Colas 1574. Lipperheide 2410. LC 12-14908

La Armeria real, ou collection des principales pièces du Musée d'artillerie de Madrid; dessins de Gaspard Sensi, texte de Achille Jubinal. Paris [1861]
3v. in 1. 125 col.pl. F.

Jucundus & verè lectu dignus de barba et coma. Hotman, Antoine

Die **Juden** in der karikatur. Fuchs, Eduard

Das **Judentum** in der deutschen vergangenheit. Liebe, G. H. T.

Judex, M.
Uniformen distinctions und sonstige abzeichen der gesammten k. k. osterr. ungar. wehrmacht sowie orden und ehrenzeichen Oesterreich-Ungarns. Troppau, A. Strasilla 1884
61p. 25 col.pl. O.
Several times reprinted (4 éd. Leipzig, M. Ruhl 1904) and (5. éd. Leipzig, M. Ruhl 1908)
Colas 1575

Jüdisches ceremoniel. Kirchner, P. C.

Jügel, Friedrich
(engr.) Dähling, illus. Der grosse maskenball in Berlin zur feier des geburtstages ... der regierenden königin von Preussen am 12ten Marz 1804
(engr.) Lieder, Friedrich. Darstellung der königl. preussischen infanterie
(engr.) Lieder, Friedrich, and Krüger, F. Darstellung der königlich preussischen cavallerie
(engr.) Wolf, L. Uniformen der Berliner bürgergarde

Jünger, Alexander
Kleidung und umwelt in Afrika; eine anthropogeographische studie, zugleich ein beitrag zur frage nach den grundprinzipien der tracht. Leipzig, R. Voigtländer 1926
viii,165p. illus. 10pl. 9 charts on 8 l. Q. Staatliche forschungsinstitute in Leipzig. Institut für völkerkunde. [Veröffentlichungen] Erste reihe: Ethnographie und ethnologie. 8. bd.)
"Literaturverzeichnis": p[147]-165
Colas 1580. LC 29-4634

Juhl, Ernst
Hamburg; land und leute der Nieder-Elbe. Hamburg, Boysen & Maasch [1912]
4 l. 90pl. F.

Jukowsky, Rudolph
Scènes populaires russes. Paris, Lemercier; Moscou & St. Pétersburg, Daziaro 1843
50 col.pl. ob.Q.
Title is taken from the legends on the plates
Colas 1576. Lipperheide 1359

Julien, Rose
Die deutschen volkstrachten zu beginn des 20 jahrhunderts. München, F. Bruckmann 1912
192p. col.front. 16 col.pl. O.
Colas 1577. Costume index

Julius-Maximillan-universitet. See Würzburg, Bavaria. Julius-Maximilian-Universitet

Jullien, Adolphe
Histoire du costume au théâtre depuis les origines du théâtre en France jusqu'à nos jours. Ouvrage orné de vingtsept gravures et dessins originaux tirés des archives de l'opéra et reproduits en facsimilé. Paris, G. Charpentier 1880
xii,356p. 24pl.(2 col. part double) F. 40 fr., sur papier de chine, 50 fr.
Colas 1578. Lipperheide 3226. LC 9-32431

Jundt, J.
(pub.) Album des costumes nationaux de la Suisse

Jung, Julius
Leben und sitten der römer in der kaiserzeit. Leipzig, G. Freytag; Prag, F. Tempsky 1883-84
2v. 150 illus. 2pl. O.
Lipperheide 255

Jungbluth
(illus.) Roger-Milès, Léon. Les créateurs de la mode

Jungendres, Sebastian Jacob
(ed.) Kirchner, P. C. Jüdisches ceremoniel

Junghans, F.
Bleuler, L. Collection des costumes de la Suisse et de ses pays limitrophes d'après F. Junghans

Jungman, Mrs Beatrix
Holland, by Nico Jungman; text by Beatrix Jungman. London, A. and C. Black 1904
ix,212p. 75(i.e. 76) col.pl.(incl. front.) O. 20s, o.p.
Many colored plates show costume of men, women and children of different regions
Costume index. LC 5-3823

Norway; text by Beatrix Jungman; il. by Nico Jungman. London, A. & C. Black 1905
x,199p. 75 col.pl. O. 20s, o.p.
Many of the plates show costume of various districts
Costume index

Jungman, Nico
(illus.) Jungman, Mrs Beatrix. Holland
(illus.) Jungman, Mrs Beatrix. Norway
(illus.) Mitton, G. E. Normandy

Jungmann, Robert
Costumes, moeurs et usages des Algériens ... Trachten, sitten, und gebräuche der Algierer. Strasbourg, J. Bernard 1837
84,84p. 36 col.pl. ob.Q.
Colas 1581

Jungwirth, Fr. Xav.
(illus.) Edlweckh, Johannes. Triumphus virtutum in funere Caroli VII ... anno ... MDCCXLV
(engr.) Funebris memoria Mariae Amaliae

Junius, Hadrianus
Hadriani Iunii Hornani Medici animadversorū libri sex, omnigenae lectionis thesaurus ... Ejusdem de coma commentarium quo haud scio an quicquam extet in eo genere vel eruditius vel locupletius, sive historiarum cognitionem, sive lectionis multifariae divitias spectes. Basileae, [Isingrin] 1556
27 l. 432p. O.
Treatise on the hair p302-432
Lipperheide 1642

Junta de museus de Barcelona
Catàleg de la collecció d'indumentària de Manuel Rocamora. See entry under Rocamora, Manuel

Jurnitschek, Alfred
Die wehrmacht der Oesterreichisch-ungarischen monarchie im jahre 1873. Wien, K. K. Hof- und staatsdruckerei 1873
cxxxi,723p. 8 col.pl. O.
Plates are after designs by Katzler
Colas 1582

Jusserand, Jean Adrien Antoine Jules
English wayfaring life in the middle ages (XIVth century), translated from the French by Lucy Toulmin Smith; a new ed., rev. and enl. New York, G. P. Putnam [1931]
464p. front. illus. pl. O.
First edition 1889; third edition 1925
Illustrations show costume of the 14th century
The original French edition with title *Les Anglais au moyen âge; la vie nomade* ... (Paris, Hachette 1884) was published without illustrations and is not useful for costume
LC 35-13702

Justa funebria serenissimo principi Ioanni Friderico Brunsvicensium et Luneburgeduci a revermo. et sermo fratre Ernesto Augusto ... duci Brunsv: et Luneb. persoluta. [Rinteln, G. C. Wächter 1685]
74,174p. 79pl. F.
Plates by Johann Georg Lange. The text contains prayers, poems, etc. with French and Latin text by G. W. Leibniz
Lipperheide 2610

Justi, Ferdinand
Hessisches trachtenbuch. Marburg, N. G. Elwert 1905
94p. 32 col.pl. F. (Veröffentlichungen der historischen kommission für Hessen und Waldech) M.24
Colas 1583. Lipperheide 802c

La **justice** et les tribunaux. See L'ancienne France: La justice et les tribunaux

Justinus, Marcus Junianus
Des hochberümptesten geschicht schreybers Justini warhafftige hystorien die er aus Trogo Pompeio gezogẽ ... darinn er von vil künigreychen der welt wie die auff und abgang genom̃en beschriben. Augsburg, H. Steyner 1532
cxix l. 50 illus. F.
Translated by Heronimus Boner from the Latin. Some of the plates are from Cicero's *Officia* and Petrarch's *Trostspiegel*
Lipperheide 621

Juvenell, Friedrich
(illus.) Delsenbach, J. A. Wahre abbildung der sämtlichen reichskleinodien welche in ... Nürnberg aufbewahret werden

Juynboll, Hendrik Hermann
Borneo. Leyden, 1909
2v. illus. 24pl.(3 col.) (Leyden. Rijks ethnographisch museum. Katalog. v1-2)

See also Rouffaer, G. P., jt. auth.

K

K., Ch.
(tr.) Die kunst in der liebe und freundschaft eine glückliche wahl zu treffen

Die **k. k.** österr. ungar. armee. Hausner, Josef

Kabinet van mode en smaak. 1.-8. deel. 1791-1794. Haarlem, A. Loosjes
Col.pl. O.
Colas 1584. Lipperheide 4575

Kabuki. Kincaid, Zoë

Kabuki, Le theatre japonais. Îakovlev, Alexandr, and Elisieev, S. G.

Kábul. See Afghanistan

Kählig, Eduard von
Österreich-Ungarn: Das heer, von E. von Kählig ... Die flotte, von R. ritter von Jedina. Berlin, A. Schall [1899]
xviii,568p. front. illus. 46pl.(part col.) ports. 3 fold.maps, fold.plan, fold.tab. O. (Die heere und flotten der gegenwart. [IV])
"Benutzte werke und schriften": 1p. at end
LC 19-5743

Die **kämme** aller zeiten. Winter, Ferdinand

Käysserliche freyhaitten d schneyder und ab cunderfectur irer matteri auf allerley stuck zue endwerffen und zue sagen &c. [Enns 1590]
55 l. illus.(part col.) Q.
An illuminated manuscript. Contains the law of Emperor Maximilian I of 1574, concerning tailors, and the clothing law of the emperor Rudolf II, 1579. The greater part of the book consists of patterns for men's and women's costume, ecclesiatical costume, and flags, and some costume pictures of townsmen and women, soldiers and others
Lipperheide 3777

De **Kaffers** aan de zuidkust van Afrika. Alberti, Lodewyk

The **Kaffirs** illustrated. Angas, G. F.

The **Kafir** wars and the British settlers in South Africa. Bowler, T. W.

Kafirs. See Africa, South; African tribes

Kahn, Anton Friedrich
Anfangsgründe der fechtkunst nebst einer vorrede, in welcher eine kurze geschichte der fechtkunst vorgetragen ... wird; neue & verm. ausg. Helmstädt, C. F. Weygand 1761
52,164,36p. 25pl. O.
First edition published (Göttingen, 1739). The appendix contains an account of the art of fencing as practiced in German universities
Lipperheide 2972

Kahr, Andreas
New modelbuch darinnen zum nehen allerhandt schone newe modelen zu finndenn seinn. [no place] 1626
51pl. O.
Some of the designs are borrowed from Sibmacher
Lipperheide 3918

Kaiser, Eduard
38 Steirmark's national-trachten und festanzüge jetztiger und vergangener zeit. [No place] J. F. Kaiser ca1820
38 col.pl. S.
Colas 1585. Lipperheide 887

Kaiser, Friedrich
Erinnerungen an den feldzug in der Rheinpfalz und Baden ... 1849. Berlin, L. Sachse ca1849
12pl. F.
Lipperheide 2178
(lithgr.) Stawitzky, E. H. L. Geschichte des infanterie-regiments von Lützow

Kaiser, Friedrich, and others
Per aspera ad astra; blätter zur erinnerung an die siegesthaten der preussischen armee ... 1866. Gezeichnet von F. Kaiser, L. Burger, H. Lüders & L. Koch. Berlin, W. Loeillot [1867]
1 l. 24pl. F.
Lipperheide 2185

Kaiser Maximilians I triumph. Burgkmair, Hans

Das **Kaiser-Album.** Viribus unitis; herausgegeben von der mechitharisten-congregation. Wien, Mechitharisten-buchdruckerei 1858
244p. 19pl. F.
Plates after P. J. N. Geiger engraved by W. Brown, Eduard Kretzschmar and J. Pannemaker show folk dress of various parts of the Austrian empire
Lipperheide 837

Kaiserer, Jakob. See Spalart, Robert von. Versuch über das kostum der vorzüglichsten völker

Die **kaiserkrönungen** in Rom und die Römer von Karl dem Grossen bis Friedrich II. (800-1220). Bäseler, Gerda

Die **kaiserlich** königlich oesterreichische armee; nach der neuesten uniformirung. Wien, J. Bermann [1839]
48 col.pl. Q.
Colas 1616

Die **kaiserl.** koenigl. oesterreichische armee seit dem jahre 1849. Gerasch, Franz

[**Kaiserlich** koeniglich oesterreichischen militair. Wien, J. Trentsensky ca1830]
60 col.pl. ob.F.
Colas 1587

[**Kaiser.** königl. preuss. garde-cavalerie.] Berlin, L. Sachse [1852]
6 col.pl. F.
Colas 1586

Kaiserl. mexicanisches corps österreichischer freiwilligen. Richter, Wilhelm, and Gerasch, August

[**Kaiserlich** russische soldaten. Wien, J. Cappi] ca1815
18 col.pl. Q.
Legends in German. Cataloged from Colas
Colas 1588

Die **K. u. K.** oesterreichisch-ungarische armee; bildlich dargestellt nach den neuesten adjustierungs-vorschriften. Wien, L. W. Seidel [1901]
Cover-title, XXIV col.pl. on fold.sheet. O.
Colas 1676. LC 20-23418

Der **kaisermantel** Otto's IV. Bock, Franz

Das **Kaiserreich** Japan nach den besten vorhandenen quellen geschildert von einem vereine gelehrter. Karlsruhe, Kunstverlag 1860
355,40p. 24pl.(incl. 6 col.costume pl.) Q. (Die ausser-europäische welt. 2. bd.)
Lipperheide 1561

Kaladlit assilialiait; or, Woodcuts, drawn and engraved by Greenlanders. Godthaab, Printed in the Inspectors printing office, by L: Møller and R: Berthelsen 1860
2p. l., 39pl. on 26 l. 2 col. sq.Q.
Published also with title: *Kaladlit assilialiait. Gronlandske træsnit*
LC 12-5902,5-24123

Kalitkin, N.

Ornament shit'ia kostromskogo polushubka. S predisl. Vas Smirnova. Kostroma, 1926g
Embroidery patterns used at Kostroma, Russia, on short winter coats

Kalotaszegi varrottas-album. Pentsy, Josef, and Szentgyörgyi, Ludwig

Kamar al-Shimas, pseud. See Brand, N. F.

Kamchatka. See Siberia

Kammer für handel, gewerbe und industrie, Vienna. See Austria, Lower. Kammer für handel, gewerbe und industrie, Vienna

Kan dai ga nō; A display of great "no" illustrations. Tokyo, Toko-do Shoten [1936]
98 col.pl. F.
Transliterated cover-title. Each plate accompanied by guard sheet with descriptive letterpress in Japanese

Kandel, David

(illus.) Mair, P. H. Bericht und anzeigen allen Herren Geschlecht der loblichen Statt Augspurg.

Kane, John, of the Royal artillery

List of officers of the Royal regiment of artillery as they stood in the year 1763, with a continuation to the present time. Greenwich, E. Delahoy 1815
95p. nar.F.
Pages 93-95, Appendix; extracts from general and garrison orders and memoranda relative to the dress of the members, of the Royal regiment of artillery ... 1743 [to 1813]
R. J. Macdonald's *The history of the dress of the Royal regiment of artillery, 1625-1897,* is a supplement

Kantemir, Dmitrii Konstantinovich, knyaź. See Cantemir, Dumitru

Kannel, David. See Kandel, David

Kany, Charles Emil

Life and manners in Madrid, 1750-1800. Berkeley, Calif. Univ. of California press 1932
xiii,483p. (incl.illus. pl. facsim.) front. pl. port. O. $7.50
Bibliography: p[397]-406
Costume index. LC 33-2611

Kappeller, Josef Anton

[Tiroler trachten, nach den zeichnungen des malers Josef Anton Kappeller, gestochen und illuminirt von J. Warnberger. Wien, in dem industrie-comptoir ca1800]
24 col.pl. Q.
Published in four parts of six plates each. On some plates the legend is in French and German, on some German only. Some of the plates are signed: I. A. K. del.—S. W. sculpt.
The author's [*Tiroler trachten ... gestochen von J. Georg Laminit*] (Augsburg, V. Zanna ca1800) contains copies of the same plates with legends in German only
Colas 9589-90. Lipperheide 888-89

Karabacek, Josef, ritter von

Abendländische künstler zu Konstantinopel im XV. und XVI. jahrhundert. I. Wien, A. Hölder 1918
89p. 55 illus.(incl. facsims.) 9pl. F. (Kaiserliche akademie der wissenschaften in Wien. Philosophisch-historische klasse. Denkschriften, 62. bd., 1. abh.)
I. Italienische künstler am hofe Muhammeds II. des Eroberers, 1451-1481. Anhang I: Der he(n)nin, eine burgundisch-französische kopftracht der frauen: I p67-89
Bibliographical foot-notes
LC A25-584

Karachaĭ; istorico-ekonomichesk. Aliev, U. D.

Karacteristische abbildungen des neu organisirten bürger-militairs in sammtlichen königlich baierischen staaten. Augsburg, Herzberg [1807]
7 col.pl. O.
Cataloged from Colas
Colas 1591

Die **karikatur** der europäischen völker. Fuchs, Eduard

Die **karikatur** und satire in der medizin. Holländer, Eugen

Karikaturenbuch. Gaudy, F. B. H. W., freiherr von

Karlin, G. Json
Skånsk textil konstslöjd. Lund, Kulturhistoriska föreningen 1886
28p. 43 illus. 1 col.pl. Q.
Lipperheide 3972

Karlinger, Hans
Bayern (In Deutsche volkskunst. v4)

Kartenspielbuch; Charta lusoria. Amman, Jost

Kaschutnig, Anton
Vellis aureum burgundo-austriacum sive . . . Ordinis torquatorum aurei velleris equitum ... relatio historica. Viennae Austriae, W. Schwendimann [1728]
112p. 11pl. front. F.
Lipperheide 1904

Kashmir. See India—Kashmir

Kassel, August
Über elsässische trachten. Strassburg, Du Mont Schauberg 1907
47p. 3pl. O.
Plates show women of Kochersberg, 1834; Mietesheim, 1903; and Schwindratzheim, 1907
Colas 1593

Kat Angelino, P. de.
Mudras auf Bali; handhaltungen der priester; zeichnungen von Tyra de Kleen. Hagen i. W., Folkwang-Verlag, 1923
70,59p. incl.pl. Q. (Kulturen der erde, bd. 15.)
Plates printed on both sides
Bibliography p62

Katalog der Freiherrlich von Lipperheide'schen kostümbibliothek. Lipperheide, F. J., freiherr von

Katalog der im Germanischen museum befindlichen deutschen kupferstiche des xv. jahrhunderts. Lehrs, Max

Katalog der im Germanischen museum befindlichen gewebe und stickereinen, nadelarbeiten und spitzen und älterer zeit. Nuremberg. Germanisches nationalmuseum

Katalog der im Germanischen museum befindlichen glasgemälde aus älterer zeit. Nuremberg. Germanisches nationalmuseum

Katalog der im Germanischen museum befindlichen kartenspiele und spielkarten. Nuremberg. Germanisches nationalmuseum

Katalog der im Germanischen museum befindlichen originalskulpturen. Nuremberg. Germanisches nationalmuseum

Katalog der im Germanischen museum vorhandenen zum abdrucke bestimmten geschnittenen holzstöcke vom XV-XVIII jahrhunderte. Bösch, Hans

Katalog der ... kunst-sammlung der herren C. und P. N. Vincent in Konstantz am Bodensee. Rahn, J. R.

Katalog der kunst- und waffen-sammlung. Berthold, F. R. von

Katalog des museums. Cologne, Germany. Städtisches museum Wallraff-Richartz

Kate, Herman Frederick Carel ten
(illus.) Lennep, Jakob van. Galerij van beroemde Nederlanders uit het tijdvak van Frederik Hendrik

Katechismus der kostümkunde. See Quincke, Wolfgang. Handbuch der kostümkunde

Katkoff, Paul
Manuel de l'enseignement de l'escrime au sabre à l'usage de la cavalerie Russe. Paris, Lahure 1895
58p. illus.(col.) O.

Katzler, Vinzenz
(illus.) Jurnitschek, Alfred. Die wehrmacht der Oesterreichisch-ungarischen monarchie im jahre 1873
(lithgr.) Franceschini, G. Caroussel zur anwesenheit J. J. K. K. majestäten in Prag den 5. juni, 1854

Kauffmann, Paul Adolphe
L'Alsace traditionaliste. Édité sous le patronage du Touring-club de France; préface de m. Henry Defert. Strasbourg (Bas-Rhin) Librairie "Union" [c1931]
157p. 114pl.(30 col.) F.
Issued in portfolio
LC 32-9139

Les costumes de l'Alsace. Paris, Goupil 1918
2 l. 6 col.pl. ob.F.
Text in French and English

Kaufmann, Isidor
Isidor Kaufmann. [Reproductions of paintings of Jewish life. Vienna, 1926]
10p. 16 col.pl. port. F.
In portfolio, no title-page. Introduction by Herman Menkes, preface by H. P. Chajes
Plates show Jews of various European countries

Der **kaufmann** in der deutschen vergangenheit. Steinhausen, Georg

Der **Kaufruf** in Wien. See Brand, C. Zeichnungen nach dem gemeinen volke besonders der kaufruf in Wien

Der **Kaukasus** und seine völker. Erckert, Roderich von

Kaulbach, Wilhelm von
Shakspere gallerie. Berlin, Nicolaische buchhandlung 1855-58
3v. in 1. 8pl. F.
Published also: London, Ackermann; New York, E. Seitz
Contents: Macbeth; Der Sturm; König Johann
Engraved by E. Eichens, C. von Gonzenbach, A. Hoffmann, L. Jacoby, and E. E. Schaeffer. "The same designs in photographic reproduction may be found in the author's *Shakespeare-album.*" Boston public library

(ed.) Dürer, Albrecht. Dürer album

Kawakatsu, Kenichi
Kimono. [Tokio] Board of tourist industry, Japanese government railways [1936]
101p. illus. pl.(part col.) D. (Tourist library. 13)
Cover title: Kimono, Japanese dress

Kawase Hasui

The Japanese dolls, Gosho-ningyo. Tokyo, Meiji-Shobo [1935]
3p.l. 24 mounted col.pl. F.
Woodcut prints by Jungi Kato of "Gosho" dolls (dolls in court dress)

Kay, John

A series of original portraits and caricature etchings, by the late John Kay. Edinburgh, H. Paton, Carver and Gilder 1837-38
2v. in 4. pl. ports. Q.
LC 9-26836

Kaye, John William. See Simpson, William, jt. auth.

Kay's Edinburgh portraits. Paterson, James

Kazach'îa derevnîa. Golubykh, M. D.

Keenan, Angela Elizabeth, sister

(ed.) Thasci Caecili Cypriani De habitu virginum. See Cyprianus, Saint, bp. of Carthage

Keene, Charles Samuel

(illus.) Pennell, Joseph. The work of Charles Keene

Keepsake-Breton. Coste, Z.

Keerl, Johann Heinrich

Ueber die ruinen Herculanums und Pompejis. See note under Saint Non, J. C. R. de. Voyage pittoresque

Keezer, Ro.

Feminine toilettes and knick-knacks of the romantic age. New York, French and European pub. 1930
1 l. 20 col.pl. F. $10
Plates signed: Ro Keezer. Shows feminine costume from 1830 to 1850. French edition: *La toilette féminine et les bibelots de l'époque romantique* (Paris, Nilsson 1930)
Colas 1597 (French ed.) Costume index

Kehrer, Hugo Ludwig

(ed.) Goya y Lucientes, F. J. de. Los desastres de la guerra

(ed.) Goya y Lucientes, F. J. de. Tauromachia

Keim, Aline

Les costumes du pays de France; presentés par Aline Keim, texte par Line Coline. Paris, Nilsson 1929
4p. 60 col.pl. O.
Colas 1598. Costume index

The costumes of France. New York, French & European pub. inc. [1930?]
7p. 60 col.pl. ob.Q.
Issued in portfolio
Original edition in French: *Les costumes du pays de France*
LC 31-20137

Keiser, James R.

The what, where, and how of a man's cravat, being a comprehensive and practical treatise on the cravat. New York, J. R. Keiser [c1902]
38p. illus. D.
LC 2-21272

Kekule von Stradonitz, Reinhard

Griechische thonfiguren aus Tanagra. Stuttgart, W. Spemann 1878
31p. illus. XVII mounted pl. (part col.) F.
"Im auftrag des Kaiserlich deutschen archäologischen instituts zu Berlin, Rom und Athen, nach aufnahmen von Ludwig Otto." Subtitle
Issued in 3 parts. Bibliographical footnotes
Lipperheide 193. LC 13-19972

Kelchner, Ernst

(ed.) Der Enndkrist der Stadt-bibliothek zu Frankfurt am Main; facsimilewiedergabe

[Kellam, Samuel Bruce]

Color in personality and dress characterizes charming and distinctive women. [Seattle, The author, c1933]
47p. D.
LC CA33-432

Kellen, David van der

Nederlands-oudheden. Amsterdam, F. Buffa en zonen 1861
6p.l. 48p. XCVII pl. F.
"Verzameling van afbeeldingen der voor wetenschap, kunst en nijverheid meest belangrijke voorwerpen uit vroegere tijden, berustende op raadhuizen, in gestichten openbare en bijzondere kabinetten, enz. naar de natur geteekend, geëtzt en opgedragen aan Z. M. Willem III." Subtitle
French and Dutch in parallel columns; added title in French: *Antiquités des Pays-Bas*
Published in 20 parts, 1858-1862
Lipperheide 970. LC 4-28529

(illus.) Hofdijk, W. J. De kloosterorden in Nederland

Keller, Diethelm

Kunstliche und aigendliche bildtnussen der rhömischen keyseren ihrer weybern und kindern auch anderer vorrümpten personen. . . . auss dem Latin jetz neüwlich vertheütst durch Diethelmē Kellern. Zürych, A. Gessner 1558
703p. 8 l. (incl. 720 illus.) O.
German edition of *Promptuarium* but indebted also to Jacob Strada's *Epitome thesauri antiquitatum.* The order is slightly changed, a number of portraits of doubtful authenticity are omitted, a few portraits are from new drawings, the rest are copied
Lipperheide 311

Keller, Ferdinand

The lake dwellings of Switzerland and other parts of Europe; 2d ed. greatly enl. Tr. and arranged by John Edward Lee. London, Longmans, Green, 1878
2v. fronts. illus. CCVI pl. (incl. maps, plans) O.
The 1st edition was a translation of the author's Pfahlbauten, six reports published in the *Mittheilungen* of the Antiquarian association of Zürich v9-15, 1854-66. In the present edition . . . the whole of Dr. Keller's seventh report in v19 of the *Mittheilungen* has been incorporated
Contents: I. [Text]; II. Plates, with explanations. Some of the illustrations show weapons, bracelets, rings and toilet articles of prehistoric Switzerland
LC 6-1761

Keller, Jh. Jak.

Taschenbuch über die Schweiz. Stuttgart & Ulm, Ebner 1800
16 col.pl. D.
Plates are after drawings by A. Dunker. Fourteen show costume
Colas 1599

Kellerhoven, Franz

(illus.) Lacroix, Paul. Les arts au moyen âge et à l'époque de la renaissance

(illus.) Lacroix, Paul. Manners, customs, and dress during the middle ages

(illus.) Lacroix, Paul. Moeurs, usages et costumes au moyen âge

See also Hoffmann, Wilhelm, jt. auth.

Kellermann, Bernhard
Sassa yo yassa; japanische tänze. Lichtdrucke und aetzungen nach studien von Karl Walser. Berlin, Cassirer [1920]
134p. illus. pl. (part col.) O.

Kelley, James Douglas Jerrold. See Wagner, A. L., jt. auth.

Kellner, Heinrich
Chronica, das ist: Wahrhaffte eigentliche und kurtze beschreibung aller hertzogen zu Venedig leben ... von den ersten biss auff den jetzt regierenden. Franckfurt am Mayne, P. Reffeler in verl. S. Feyerabends 1574
140 l. 103 illus. F.
Contains 84 half-length portraits of Doges, with their coats of arms, and nineteen pictures of tombs, by Jost Amman
Lipperheide 1240

Kellner, Joseph
Vorstellung der offentlichen sehbaren gebräuchen in Nürnberg. Nürnberg, J. Kellner ca1780
4v. 29pl. (17 col.) Q.
Lipperheide 784m

Kellner, Leon; Arnold, Mme Paula, and Delisle, Arthur L.
Austria of the Austrians and Hungary of the Hungarians. New York, C. Scribner; London, I. Pitman 1914
304p. front. pl. ports. fold.map. D. $1.50, o.p.; 6s, o.p. (Countries & peoples series)
Costume index. LC 14-30361

Kellogg, John Harvey
The evils of fashionable dress, and how to dress healthfully. Battle Creek, Mich. Office of the Health reformer 1876
38p. D.
LC 8-8797

Kelly, Francis Michael
The bibliography of costume, a review. London, 1918
89-95p. 2pl. F.
From the *Burlington magazine,* v33 Sept. 1918
An interesting article on the qualifications that give a picture costume value

Kelly, Francis Michael, and Schwabe, Randolph
Historic costume, a chronicle of fashion in western Europe, 1490-1790; 2d ed. rev. & enl. New York, Scribner; London, B. T. Batsford 1929
xv,305p. col.front. illus. pl. (part col.) ports. Q. $7.50
First edition 1925. Enlarged by ten new plates, additional notes and additions to the bibliography
Bibliography: p299-302
Colas 1600 (1st ed.) Cost. ind. LC 30-26655

A short history of costume & armour, chiefly in England, 1066-1800. New York, Scribner; London, B. T. Batsford 1931
2v. in 1. col.fronts. illus. pl. (part col. part double) O. $7.50; 25s
Contents: 1. 1066-1485; 2. 1485-1800
Bibliography: v 1 p75-77; v2 p81-83; "Iconography": v 1 p78-79; v2 p83
Costume index. LC 32-26357

Kelly, Mary
On English costume; illus. by C. Ouless. Enl. ed. London, Yearbook press; Boston, Mass., Baker [1934]
x,54p. illus. D. 2s 6d
First published 1925. A history of English costume from Saxon dress to Victorian. Each period illustrated with line drawings
Costume index. LC 35-4073

Kelly, Robert Talbot
Egypt painted and described. London, A. & C. Black 1902
xiii,239p. 75 col.pl. (incl.front.) O.
"Republished in part from *Black and white* and the *Century magazine.*" Author's note
LC 3-7332

Kelman, John
The Holy Land, painted by John Fulleylove; described by John Kelman. London, A. & C. Black; New York, Macmillan 1902
xv,301p. 92pl. (part col. incl.front.) O.
Plates accompanied by guard sheets with descriptive letterpress
LC 3-837

Kemp, Emily Georgiana
The face of China; travels in east, north, central and western China. New York, Duffield; London, Chatto & Windus 1909
xv,275p. 63pl. (47 col.) O.
Several of the plates show costume
LC 10-2332 (English ed.)

Kempe, Alfred John. See note under Stothard, C. A. The monumental effigies of Great Britain

Kendrick, Albert Frank
A book of old embroidery. See entry under Holme, Geoffrey, ed.

English embroidery. London, G. Newnes; New York, Scribner [1905]
xii,125p. 1 l. 60(i.e. 61)pl. 4 col.pl. (incl. front.) O. (Newnes' library of the applied arts)
"Some useful books of reference": p107-08
LC 5-29072

Guide to the collection of costumes. See entry under Victoria and Albert museum, South Kensington

Kennelly, M.
(tr.) Doré, Henri. Researches into Chinese superstitions

Kensington. Loftie, W. J.

Keppel, George Thomas, 6th earl of Albemarle. See Albemarle, G. T. K., 6th earl of

Ker, Francisco Borgia
Imperatores orientes, compendio exhibiti, e compluribus Graecis praecipue scriptoribus, a Constantino Magno, ad Constantinum ultimum, et expugnatam per Turcos Constantinopolim. Tyrnaviae, Typis Academicis societatis Jesu 1744
596p. 66 illus. F.
An earlier edition was published 1743 with title *Historiae Bysant. Epitome*
The illustrations are portraits of the Byzantine emperors, from coins and medals
Lipperheide 229

Kerckhoff, Émile
Le costume à la cour et à la ville; étiquette, tenue officielle et de fantaisie. Paris, Debuisson 1865
272p. O.
Page 215 to end is on the official costume at the court of Napoleon III
Colas 1602. Lipperheide 3269

Keresan Indians. See Indians of North America—Keresan Indians

Kerndörffer, Heinrich August
Gallerie der stände; ein unterhaltendes und belehrendes lese- und bilderbuch für die jugend zur erweiterung ihrer kenntnisse. Pirna, C. A. Friese [1811]
190p. 18col.pl. sq.S.
Plates show representatives of many classes, occupations, and regions of Germany at this period

Kerr, John. See Heathcote, J. M., and others. Skating

Kerr, Rose Netzorg
Miniature costume folios. [Waldwick, N. J., Fairbairn publishers c1937]
5pt. pl. S.
Cover-title. Each part is a portfolio containing 12 plates. Issued in box
Parts 1-4 previously issued as separate publications, each with twelve plates in a folder, with title *Interpretive costume design*
Contents: 1 Egypt, Greece and Rome; 2 The orient; 3 The age of Chivalry; 4 American costume, 1620-1820; 5 Renaissance and Elizabethan costumes
Costume index. LC 38-6772

Kervyn de Lettenhove, Henri Marie Bruno Joseph Léon, baron
La Toison d'or; notes sur l'institution et l'histoire de l'ordre (depuis l'année 1429 jusqu'à l'année 1559) 2. éd. Bruxelles, G. van Oest 1907
113p. front. pl. ports. Q.
"Noms des chefs et souverains et des chevaliers de la Toison d'or depuis 1429, date de la fondation de l'ordre, jusqu'en 1559, date du vingt-troisième chapitre": p101-11
LC 8-29304

Kettner, Friedrich Ernst
Kirchen- und Reformations-historie des kayserl. freyen weltlichen stiffts Quedlinburg. Quedlinburg, T. J. Schwan 1710
300,105,7p. 7 tab. 13pl. Q.
Three of the plates have nine half-length portraits of abbesses of Quedlinburg
Lipperheide 648

Keyser, Jacob Rudolph
Om nordmae klaededragt i aeldre tider ... Afbildninger af norske nationaldragter. Christiana, P. F. Steensballe 1847
21p. 10pl. Q.

Keyssler, Johann Georg
Neueste reisen durch Deutschland, Böhmen, Ungarn, die Schweiz, Italien und Lothringen, worinnen der zustand und das merkwürdigste dieser länder beschrieben ... wird; neu. und verm. aufl. Vorrede [von] Gottfried Schütze. Hannover, N. Försters & sohns erben 1751
2v. 10pl. Q.
Contains short descriptions of costume of these countries but no illustrative pictures
Lipperheide 564

Khanykov", D. D.
Russkīā bylīny. Moskva, v" tīp. Lazareoskago īnstītuta vostochnykh" īāzykov 1860
178p. O.
Russian folk tales in which early Russian costume is described. Section 10 is on dress and ornaments

Khasi. See India—Native tribes—Khasi

The **Khasis.** Gurdon, P. R. T.

Kheiri, Sattar
Indische miniaturen der islamischen zeit. Berlin, E. Wasmuth [1921]
17p. 48pl. on 24 l. Q. (Orbis pictus; weltkunst-bücherei, bd. 6)
Translated from the English by H. T. Bossert
LC 23:15022

Khevenhiller, Frantz Cristoph
Annales Ferdinandei, oder Wahrhaffte beschreibung, käysers Ferdinandi des Andern ... geburth, aufferziehung und bisshero in krieg und friedens-zeiten vollbrachten thaten ... von anfang des 1578 biss auff dass 1637. Leipzig, M. G. Weidmann 1721-26
12 parts. illus. pl. F.
Plates illustrate life of the seventeenth century
Lipperheide 554

Counterfet kupffer-stich ... deren jenigen regierenden grossen herren, so von käysers Ferdinand dess Andern geburt, biss zu desselben seeligisten tödtlichen abschied successivè regiert, davon ertz hertzog Carl, vatter käysers Ferdinand dess Andern zum ersten gestellet worden. Leipzig, M. G. Weidmann 1721
2v. illus. 391pl. F.
Portraits are valuable for costume of the seventeenth century
Lipperheide 555

Khevenhüller, Ludwig Andrea, graf von
Observations-puncten ... bey dem Ihme von Dero kayserl. königl. maj ... anvertrauten dragoner-regiment vorgeschrieben; ... 3. aufl. Wienn, J. P. Krauss 1749
[3]v. 9 illus. 21pl. Q.
First edition 1729, second 1739. Volume 3, entitled *Exercitium zu pferd und zu fuss*, contains all the illustrations
Lipperheide 2222

Khmuryĭ, V. See Petrytz'kyi, Anatol'. Theater-trachten

Khrīstianskīā drevnostī ī arkheologīā. Prokhorov", V. A.

Kick, Wilhelm
Preisgekrönte stickerei-arbeiten der württembergerischen frauenarbeitschulen aus der ... landes-schulausstellung. Stuttgart, W. Nitzschke [1891]
1 l. 60pl. F.
Lipperheide 4015

Kidd, Dudley
The essential Kafir. With one hundred full-page illustrations from photographs. London, A. and C. Black 1904
xv,435p. 100pl.(incl.col.front.) map. O.
Each plate preceded by guard sheet with descriptive letterpress
Bibliography: p417-28
LC 4-26907

Kidd, Dudley—*Continued*
Savage childhood; a study of Kafir children. With thirty-two full-page illustrations from photographs. London, A. and C. Black 1906
xvi,314p. 32pl.(incl.front.) O.
LC 7-7554

Kieffer, Fritz
(ed.) Les garnisons d'Alsace au 19. siècle ... pub. sous la direction de Fritz Kieffer avec la collaboration de Henri Ganier-Tanconville, Frédéric Regamey, Léon Schnug. Strasbourg, Imp. alsacienne 1911
8p. 100 col.pl. F.
Plates are signed. Each shows three or four uniforms of regiments stationed in Alsace from the reign of Napoleon I to 1870
Colas 1603

[**Kiel, L.**]
[Uniforms of the Russian army. St. Petersburg 1815-1820]
73 col.pl. F.
Plates engraved by Le Vachez and Paul
Colas 1604

Kiel. Universität. See Academic costume —Kiel university

Kiel. Universität. Schleswig-Holsteinisches museum vaterländischer altertümer
Vorgeschichtliche alterthümer aus Schleswig-Holstein. See entry under Mestorf, Johanna, ed.

Kielland, Thor Bendz. See Bugge, A. R. jt. auth.

Kiesewatter, Doris, and Steffahny, Hermine
Die deutsche frauenkleidung. Berlin, P. Ouack [1904]
30 l. 61 illus. Q.
Colas 1605. Lipperheide 3320a

Kilian, Lucas
Der neapolitanischen könig leben und bildnuss. Augusta Vindel. L. Kilian 1624
42 l. 33 illus. F.
Illustrations include half-length portraits of the twenty-six kings of Naples from Roger (1154) to Philip IV (1605)
Lipperheide 1245

Newes soldaten buchlein. Augspurg, L. Kilian 1609
13pl. Q.
Plates show a fifer, a drummer, a captain, standard-bearer, etc.
Colas 1606. Lipperheide 2064

(engr.) Custos, Dominicus. Fuggerorum et Fuggerarum quae in familia natae, quaeve in familiam transierunt

(engr.) Custos, Dominicus. Pinacotheca Fuggerorum

Kilian, Philip
(engr.) Corona duodecim Caesarem ex Augustissimâ domo Austriaca

(engr.) Fugger, J. J. Spiegel der ehren des ... erzhauses Osterreich

(engr.) Kurtze und eygentliche beschreibung dess jenigen so bey der verlöbnus, heimführ- und vermählung ... Caroli, pfaltzgrafens bey Rhein ... mit ... Wilhelmina Ernestina ... erb-princessin zu Dennemarck ... vorgangen

Kilian, W. P.
(illus.) Apin, S. J. Vitae et effigies procancellariorum Academiae Altorfinae

Kilian, Wolfgang
Dess aller durchleutigsten haus ostereichs herzogen, ertz hertzogen, könig und käyser eigentliche contrafacturen, samt historischer beschreibung. Augspurg, W. Kilian [1629]
72 l. illus. 3pl. ports. F.
Contains 47 half-length portraits and 48 coats of arms
Translation of *Serenissimorum Austriae ducum* (Augustae Vindelicorum, 1623) Engravings by Wolfgang Kilian
Lipperheide 848

Genealogia serenissimor. Boiarlae ducum. Augusta Vindelicorum, S. Mangiam 1620
18 l. 10 illus. F.
Portraits of Bavarian princes from Charlemagne to Maximilian
The German edition *Geschlecht register der durchleuchtigsten hertzogen in Bayern* (Augspurg, J. U. Schönigk 1629) contains one more portrait, of Louis II, and the picture of Maximilian shows him at a later period. The first German edition appeared in 1623
Lipperheide 705, 706

Serenissimorum Saxoniae electorum, et quorundam ducum Agnatorum genuinae effigies. Augusta Vindelicorum, impensis W. Kilian, excudit Vidua Sara Mangin 1621
31 l. 26 illus. F.
Contains half-length portraits of twenty-six Saxon rulers of the fifteenth and sixteenth centuries
The German edition was entitled: *Der cur und fürsten von Sachsen* (Augspurg, J. U. Schönigk 1629) and contains the same portraits
Lipperheide 707-708

(engr.) Corona duodecim Caesarem ex Augustissimâ domo Austriaca

(engr.) Custos, Dominicus. Fuggerorum et Fuggerarum quae in familia natae, quaeve in familiam transierunt

(engr.) Custos, Dominicus. Pinacotheca Fuggerorum

The **kilt.** Douglas, L. M.

The **Kilt** Society. See Comunn an Fheilidh

Kimmins, Mrs Grace Thyrza (Hannam)
The Guild of play book of festival and dance. Curwen's edition, 5634. Written by G. T. Kimmins, dances arranged by M. H. Woolnoth. London, J. Curwen 1907-12
4v. front. pl. F.
Part 3 has title: *The Guild of play book of national dances.* Part 4 has title: *The Guild of play book for little children*
LC 10-5080

Kimono. Ema, Tsutomu

Kimono. Kawakatsu, Kenichi

Kincaid, Zoë
Kabuki, the popular stage of Japan. London, Macmillan 1925
xvi,385p. col.front. illus. pl. ports. Q.
LC 26-26299

Kinderbildnisse aus fünf jahrhunderten der europäischen malerei. Sauerlandt, Max

Kindergarderobe; monatsschrift zur selbst anfertigung der kinderkleidung und kinderwäsche. 1.-26 jahrg. 1894-märz 1919. Berlin, J. H. Schwerin
26v. illus.(part col.) Q.
Published monthly. Subtitle varies: v 1-6, 1894-99: illustrirte monatsschrift
Lipperheide 4812

Kinderleben in der deutschen vergangenheit. Boesch, Hans

Kinder-modenwelt. See Baby; eine zeitschrift für mütter

Kinderspielzeug aus alter zeit, eine geschichte des spielzeugs. Gröber, Karl

Kindleben, Christian Wilhelm
Galanterieen der Türken. Frankfurt & Leipzig [1782]
2v. (340,136p.) 40 col.pl. O.
The plates show costume
Colas 1607. Lipperheide 1419

Kindler, Alfred
Die schweizerische armee in bildern; Album militaire suisse. Zürich, Frey 1903
60pl. Q.

King, Charles G. See Western reserve historical society, Cleveland, O. King collection. The Charles G. King collection of books on costume

King, Charles William
Antique gems and rings. London, Bell and Daldy 1872
2v. illus. 75pl. Q.
Contents: v 1 Text; v2 Illustrations
"Works upon the glyptic art and cabinets of gems": v 1 p462-70
LC 10-34200

King, E. M.
Rational dress; or, the dress of women and savages. London, Kegan Paul 1882
29p. O.
Colas 1608. Lipperheide 3287

King, Gregory. See Sandford, Francis, jt. auth.

King, Mrs John Alexander
Weddings; modes, manners & customs of weddings. New York, Delineator 1927
94p. illus. O.
On cover: Delineator home institute. Department of service
LC 28-14537

King, John Glen
The rites and ceremonies of the Greek church in Russia. London, W. Owen 1772
477,[5]p. pl. Q.
Pages 35-41 Of the vestments of the clergy used in divine service, illustrated with plates 3-10. Page 361-81 Of the office of taking the monastic habits, one plate showing nuns' dress

King and his navy and army. See Navy and army illustrated

Kings and queens of ancient Egypt; portraits by Winifred Brunton, history by eminent Egyptologists, foreword by Professor J. H. Breasted. New York, C. Scribner's sons 1926'
163p. mounted pl.(part col.) Q.
Plates accompanied by guard sheets with descriptive letterpress
Contents; Khafra, by T. Gray; Pepy I., by Winifred Brunton; Amenemhat III., by G. Brunton; Queen Tetasheri, by H. E. Winlock; Queen Hatshepsut, by Margaret Murray; Thothmes III., by G. Brunton; Akhenaten, Queen Ty, Queen Nefertete, Queen Mutnezemt, by T. E. Peet; Sety I., Rameses II., Rameses III., by Margaret Murray; Physiognomy as historical material, by Winfred Brunton
LC 26-9310

Kings and rulers
Bonney, Thérèse, ed. Remember when—a pictorial chronicle of the turn of the century and of the days known as Edwardian. 1933

Clerck, Nicolaes de. Princelyck cabinet. 1625

Ehingen, Georg von. The diary of Jörg von Ehingen. 1929

Ehingen, Georg von. Itinerarium, das ist Historische beschreibung. 1600

Huttich, Johann. Imperatorum romanorum libellus. Una cum imaginibus ad vivam effigiem expressis. 1526

Keller, Diethelm. Kunstliche und aigendliche bildtnussen der rhömischen keyseren ihrer weybern und kindern auch anderer verrümpten personen. 1558

Pichler, Le P. Joseph. Augusta quinque Carolorum historia ... Carolo VI. 1735

Promptuarium. Prima pars promptuarii iconum insigniorum a seculo hominum, subiectis eorum vitis, per compendium ex probatissimis, autoribus desumptis. 1553

Schrenck von Nozing, Jacob. Augustissimorum imperatorum, serenissimorum regum, atque archiducum, illustrissimorum principum ... gestarum succinctae descriptiones. 1601

Austria

Domanig, Karl. Porträtmedaillen des erzhauses Oesterreich von Kaiser Friedrich III. bis Kaiser Franz II. 1896

Bohemia

Althann. Imago principum Bohemiae LXI. 1673

Balbin, Bohuslav. Historia de ducibus ac regibus Bohemiae. 1735

Byzantine empire

Ker, F. B. Imperatores orientes, compendio exhibiti, e compluribus Graecis praecipue scriptoribus, a Constantino Magno, ad Constantinum ultimum, et expugnatam per Turcos Constantinopolim. 1744

Denmark

Andersen, C. C. T. The chronological collection of the kings of Denmark. 1878

Beuther von Carlstatt, Michael. Kurtz begriffene anzeigung, vom leben und wesen der könige zu Danemarck, Sueden, Nordwagen etc. 1587

Brock, P. M. J. Chronological museum of the Danish kings, in Rosenborg castle. 1899

Haelwegh, Albert. Regum Daniae icones accuratê expressae. 1648

Schlegel, J. H. Geschichte der könige von Dänemark aus dem oldenburgischen stamme ... mit ihren bildnissen nach den originalen. 1769-77

Kings and rulers—*Continued*

Egypt

Kings and queens of ancient Egypt. 1926

England

Amman, Jost. Ehebrecherbrücke des Königs Artus. 1883

The Illustrated London news. Silver jubilee record number, King George v. and Queen Mary, 1910-1935. 1935

Leti, Gregorio. Historia overo vita di Elisabetta, regina d'Inghilterra detta per sopranome la Comediante Politica. 1693

Strutt, Joseph. Regal and ecclesiastical antiquities of England. 1842

France

Bernard, Charles. Généalogie de la maison royal de Bourbon, avec les éloges et les portraits des princes qui en sont sortis. 1644

Boissevin, Louis. Portraits des rois de France. ca1660

Colin, Mme Anais. Costumes des reines de France. 1845

Comines, Philippe de, sieur d'Argenton. Mémoires. 1881

Cronica breve de i fatti illvstri de' re di Francia. 1588

Daret, Pierre. Tableaux historiques ou sont gravez les illustres Francois et estrangers ... remarquables par leur naissance et leur fortune, doctrine, pieté, charges et emplois. 1654

Effigies regum Francorum omnium, a Pharamundo, ad Ludovicum xiii. 1622

Fer, Nicolas de. Histoire des rois de France depuis Pharamond jusqu'à ... Louis xv. 1722

Der könige in Franckreich leben, regierung und absterben: aus bewehrten frantzösischen geschicht-schreibern übersetzet und biss auf instehendes 1671. jahr continuirt. 1671

Larmessin, Nicolas. Les augustes representations de tous les rois de France depuis Pharamond, jusqu'à Louys xiiii. 1679-83

Lejeune, Eugène, and Lacauchie, A. Les rois et reines de France en estampes; réprésentant par l'ordre chronologique leurs portraits et costumes depuis Pharamond jusqu'à nos jours. ca1860

Montfaucon, Bernard de. Les monumens de la monarchie françoise qui comprennent l'histoire de France, avec les figures de chaque règne. 1729-33

Montfaucon, Bernard de. Thresor des antiquitez de la couronne de France. 1745

Müller, Elisabeth. La monarchie française en estampes. ca1856

Pantaleon, Heinrich. Omnium regum Francorum a Pharamundo usque ad Carolum nonum. 1574

Rois et reines de France depuis l'origine de la monarchie jusqu'à nos jours. ca1845

Solis, Virgil, and Amman, Jost. Effigies regum Francorum omnium, a Pharamundo, ad Henricum usque tertium. 1576

See also Kings and rulers—Germany—Early to 911

Napoleon, 1799-1814

Bailly, J. T. H. Napoleon, illustrated with prints from contemporary and other portraits. 1908

Kircheisen, F. M. Napoléon i. und das zeitalter der befreiungskriege in bildern. 1914

Lacour-Gayet, Georges. Napoléon. 1921

Onfroy de Bréville, J. M. G. Napoléon. 1921

Germany

Avancinus, Nicolas. Imperium Romano-Germanicum, sive Quinquaginta imperatorum ac Germaniae regum elogia, imperatori Leopoldo. 1663

Cavalleriis, J. B. de. Romanorum imperatorum effigies. 1638

Corona duodecim Caesarem ex Augustissimâ domo Austriaca. 1654

Goltz, Hubert. Les images presque de tous les empereurs, depuis C. Julius Caesar jusques à Charles v et Ferdinandus son frère, pourtraites au vif, prinses des médailles anciens. 1557

Heraeus, C. G. Bildnisse der regierenden fürsten und berühmter männer vom vierzehnten bis zum achtzehnten jahrhunderte in einer folgereihe von schaumünzen. 1828

Historia diplomatica de statu religionis evangelica in Hungaria in tres periodos distincta. 1710

Huber-Liebenau, Theodor von. Denkmäler des hauses Habsburg in der Schweiz. Das Kloster Königsfelden. 1867

Imperatorum a Iulio Caesare ad Carolum vi P. F. Aug in gemmis antiqua partim, partim recenti manu affabre incisorum series. 1722

Kilian, Wolfgang. Dess aller durchleutigsten haus ostereich herzogen, ertz hertzogen, könig und käyser eigentliche contrafacturen, samt historischer beschreibung. 1629

Kohlrausch, Friedrich. Bildnisse der deutschen könige und kaiser von Karl dem Grossen bis Maximilian i. 1846

Pregitzer, J. U. Teutscher regierungs- und ehren-spiegel vorbildend des Teutschen Reichs. 1703

Vianen, Ioannes van. Effigies Romanorum imperatorum ex antiquis numismatibus ... a Iulio Caesare, ad Leopoldum. 1695

Early to 911

Amman, Jost. Bildnuss oder contrafactur der zwölff ersten alten teutschen königen und fürsten. 1622

Kings and rulers—Germany—*Continued*

1273-1740

Aquila austriaca; das ist historische beschreibung und abbildung alles römischen kaiser und könige welche von Rudolpho I. biss auff Leopoldum I. auss dem Hause des Graven von Habspurg sind erwöhlet worden. ca.1660

Bock, Franz. Der kaisermantel Otto's IV. 1860

Gottfried, J. L. Joh. Ludov. Gottfridi Historische chronica; oder, Beschreibung der fürnehmsten geschichten so sich von anfang der welt biss auff das jahr Christi 1619 zugetragen. 1674

16th century

Boccaccio, Giovanni. Forneṁste historien und exempel ... grozsmächtiger kayser, künig, fürsten. 1545

Breunner-Enkevoërth, A. J., graf von. Römisch kaiserlicher majestät kriegsvölker im zeitalter der landsknecht ... mit erläuterndem text von Jacob von Falke. 1883

Leti, Gregorio. La vie de l'empereur Charles V. 1710

17th-18th centuries

Driesch, G. C. von den. Historische nachricht von der röm. kays. grossbotschaft nach Constantinopel welche Damian Hugo von Virmondt verrichtet. 1723

Lundorp, M. C. Helden buch, oder beschreibung der vonembsten potentaten, keyser, königen, fürsten, graffen, kriegs-obersten, und helden, welche in nochwehrendem teutschen kriege ... sich gebrauchen lassen. 1629

Bavaria

Amman, Jost. Genuinae icones ducum Bavariae. [1583]

Kilian, Wolfgang. Genealogia serenissimor. Boiarlae ducum. 1620

Prussia

Hesekiel, George. Das siebenkönigsbuch; die könige von Preussen geschildert von G. Hesekiel. 1874

Pregitzer, J. U. Teutscher regierungs- und ehren-spiegel vorbildend des Teutschen Reichs. 1703

Saxony

Bible. German. Biblia, das ist die gantze Heilige Schrift. 1708

Kilian, Wolfgang. Serenissimorum Saxoniae electorum, et quorundam ducum Agnatorum genuinae effigies. 1621

Reusner, Nicolaus. Icones sive imagines impp. regum, principum, electorum et ducum Saxoniae. 1597

Württemberg

Pfaff, Karl. Biographie der regenten von Württemberg von herzog Eberhard im Bart bis zum könig Friederich. 1821

Hungary

Der hertzogen und königen in Hungarn, leben, regierung und absterben, von dem ersten hertzogen Keve an biss auf den jetztregirenden könig Leopold den ersten. 1685

Nádasdy, Ferencz, graf. Mausoleum potentissimorum ac gloriosissimorum regni apostolici regum & primorum militantis Ungariae ducum. 1664

Schad, J. A. X. Effigies ducum et regum Hungariae. 1687

Turoczi, Ladislaus. Ungaria suis cum regibus compendia data. 1768

Italy

Bianchini, G. M. Dei gran duchi di Toscana della reale casa de' Medici, protettori delle lettere, e delle belle arti, ragionamenti istorici. 1741

See also Kings and rulers—Naples

Lorraine

Clément, Nicolas, de Treille. Austrasiae reges et duces epigrammatis. 1591

Naples (Kingdom)

Kilian, Lucas. Der neapolitanischen könig leben und bildnuss. 1624

Norway

Beuther von Carlstatt, Michael. Kurtz begriffene anzeigung, vom leben und wesen der könige zu Danemarck, Sueden, Nordwagen etc. 1587

Persia

Gálâl ad-Dîn Mîrzâ. The book of the Hosroes, history of the kings of Iran from the beginning of the Abbadides until the end of the Sassanid dynasty. 1880

Poland

Neugebauer, Salomon. Icones & vitae principum ac regum Poloniae. 1626

Portugal

Faria e Sousa, Manuel de. Historia del reyno de Portugal. 1730

Vasconcellos, Antonio de. Anacephalaeoses, id est summa capita actorum regum Lusitaniae. 1621

Rome

Madden, F. W. On the imperial consular dress. 1861

Vico, Enea. Le imagini con tutti i riversi trovati et le vite de gli imperatori tratte dalle medaglie et dalle historie de gli antichi. 1548

Russia

Russia. Komitet dli͡a izdanii͡a drevnosteĭ Rossiĭkago gosudarstva. Drevnosti rossiĭskago gosudarstva. 1849-53. v2

Russia. Ministerstvo Imperatorskago dvora. Les solennités du saint couronnement. 1899

Kings and rulers—*Continued*

Sweden

Beuther, von Carlstatt. Kurtz begriffene anzeigung, vom leben und wesen der könige zu Danemarck, Sueden, Nordwagen etc. 1587

Branting, Agnes. Das goldene gewand der Königin Margareta in der Domkirche, zu Uppsala. 1911

Lindberg, C. F. Objets choisis de la garde-robe royale de Suède. 1888

Turkey

Bertelli, Pietro. Vite de gl'imperatori de Turchi. 1599

Boissard, J. J. Leben und contrafeiten der türckischen un persischen sultanen. 1596

Cantemir, Dumitru. The history of the growth and decay of the Othman empire. 1734-35

Driesch, G. C. von den. Historische nachricht von der röm. kays. gross-botschaft nach Constantinopel welche Damian Hugo von Virmondt verrichtet. 1723

Greblinger, Georg. Wahre abbildungen der türckischen kayser und persischen fürsten so wol auch anderer helden und heldinnen von dem Osman biss auf den andern Mahomet. 1648

Spry, W. J. J. Life on the Bosphorus; doings in the city of the sultan. 1895

Young, John. A series of portraits of the emperors of Turkey, from the foundation of the monarchy to the year 1808. 1815

The **king's** peace. Inderwick, F. A.

[**Kingsborough, Edward King, viscount**]

Antiquities of Mexico: comprising facsimiles of ancient Mexican paintings and hieroglyphics, preserved ... libraries of Paris, Berlin [etc] Together with the Monuments of New Spain, by M. Dupaix. The whole illustrated by many valuable inedited manuscripts, by Augustine Aglio. London, A. Aglio 1830-48

9v. pl.(part col.) sq.F.

Volumes 1-4: plates, volumes 5-9: text. Volumes 6-7 published by R. Havell; volumes 8-9, by H. G. Bonn

Lipperheide 1620. LC 4-8396

Kingsford, Hugh Sadler

Illustrations of the occasional offices of the church in the middle ages from contemporary sources. London [etc.] A. R. Mowbray; Milwaukee, Morehouse 1921

89p. illus. Q. 25s (Alcuin club collections, XXIV)

"A selection of contemporary pictures illustrating the life of the mediaeval layman from his birth to his death... The scenes are briefly described, and wherever possible illustrative passages from the Sarum manual and other service books are added." Prefatory note

Baptism, confirmation, penance, communion, burial etc. are shown. An authoritative book on the dress worn by priests at these ceremonies, and on medieval dress

LC 21-17830

Kingsland, Florence

The book of weddings; a complete manual of good form in all matters connected with the marriage ceremony. New York, Doubleday, Page 1902

x,245p. front. pl. O.

LC 2-26327

Kininger, Vincenz George

Costumes des différentes nations composant les états héréditaires de S.M. et R. dessinés par Kininger et gravés par les meilleurs artistes. [Vienna] T. Mollo ca1821

100 col.pl. Q.

The fifty plates of the author's *Kleidertrachten* form the first half of this collection

Colas 1611. Lipperheide 834

Kleidertrachten der kaiserl. königl. staaten. Habillemens des états de S.M. l'Empereur roi. Vienne, T. Mollo ca1830

50 l. 50 col.pl. Q.

Plates have legends in French and German. Some were copied for Bertrande de Moleville's *Costume* and for Alexander's *Picturesque representation ... of the Austrians*

Colas 1610

See also Bartsch, Adam von, jt. auth.

[**Kininger, Vincenz George**], **and Mansfeld, Jos. Georg**

Abbildung der neuen adjustirung der k.k. armee; seiner königlichen hoheit dem erzherzog Ferdinand Karl. Wien, T. Mollo 1796-1798

44 col.pl. F.

Plates are engraved by Mansfeld after Kininger

Colas 1609

Kinne, Helen, and Cooley, Anna Maria

Shelter and clothing; a textbook of the household arts. New York, Macmillan 1913

xv,377p. front.(port.) illus. D. $1.10

A school textbook. Contains chapters on History of costume, Costume design, Hygiene of clothing, Economics of dress, Care and repair, and Millinery

Bibliography:p viii-ix

LC 13-15751

Kinnear, David Mitchell

Mynheer van Schlichtenhorth and the old Dutch burghers; a tale of old and new Albany ... illus. by Robert Sheridan. Albany, N.Y., The author 1906

16 l. illus. O.

Shows costume of the Dutch in Colonial New York

Kinsey, William Morgan

Portugal illustrated; in a series of letters. London, Treuttel, Würtz, and Richter 1828

xvii,500p. front. 22pl.(9 col.) map. Q.

Each of the colored plates shows four types of costume. Second edition 1829

Lipperheide 1218. Colas 1612-13. LC 5-1683

Kiowa Indian art. Jacobson, O. B.

Kiowa Indians. See Indians of North America—Kiowa Indians

Király, János

(ed.) Divat-Tükör

Kircheisen, Friedrich Max
Napoleon I.; ein lebensbild. Stuttgart und Berlin, J. G. Cotta, 1927-29
2v. front. pl. ports. O.
Shows French costume at the time of Napoleon
LC 28-10532

Napoléon I. und das zeitalter der befreiungskriege in bildern ... mit nahezu sechshundert porträten, schlachtendarstellungen, abbildungen von medaillen, autographen und karikaturen nach den berühmtesten malern, zeichnern und stechern. München und Leipzig, G. Müller 1914
xii,340p. pl. ports. facsims. F.
Plates printed on both sides
LC 14-10911

Kirchen geschmuck. See Müller, Jacob. Ornatus ecclesiasticus

Kirchen- und Reformations-historie des kayserl. freyen weltlichen stiffts Quedlinburg. Kettner, F. E.

Kirchenschmuck, ein archiv für weibliche handarbeit, herausgegeben unter der leitung des christlichen kunstvereins der diöcese Rottenburg. Redigirt von Florian Riess, Pfarrer Laib, und Pfarrer Dr. Schwarz. Stuttgart, J. B. Metzler 1857-1870
27v. pl.(part col.) F.
Volumes 1-12 were published in monthly parts, 13-27 in quarterly. From volume 3 on, the name of Florian Riess is omitted from the title-pages. From volume 5 on, the subtitle is: *Archiv für kirchliche kunstschöpfungen und christliche alterthumskunde.* Index: Register-band (Ellwagen, J. Hess 1874. 17 l.)
The plates contain patterns for vestments and church linens
Lipperheide 1827

Kirchenschmuck, neue folge. Sammlung von vorlagen für kirchliche stickereien, holz & metallarbeiten & glasmalereien. Amberg, G. Dengler 1873-1895
4v. pl.(2 col.) Q.
From volume 3 part 5 on, published Regensburg & Amberg, F. Hubbel. Text is in English and French
Lipperheide 1828

Kircher, Athanasius
China monumentis, quà sacris quà profanis, nec non variis naturæ & artis spectaculis, aliarumque rerum memorabilium argumentis illustrata. Amstelodami, apud J. Janssonium à Waesberge & E. Weyerstraet 1667
237p. illus. 23pl.(part fold.) port. 2 fold. maps. F.
Chapter 4, De vario habitu, moribus & consuetudinibus hominum illorum regnorum, Albertus Dorville & P. Gruberus observarunt, depinxeruntque p66-77. Many plates and illustrations thruout the book have costume interest. Costume of various occupations is shown, including military dress from various districts
Lipperheide lists an edition of the same date (Antwerpiae, apud Jacobum à Meurs)
Lipperheide 1511. LC 4-12928

Kirchhoff, Alfred
Die Halloren in ihrer alten tracht; nach originalen gemacht; neue ausg. Halle, [Reichardt] 1890
23p. 8 col.pl. O.
Earlier edition 1888

Kirchhoff, E. See Beely, F. jt. auth.

Kirchliche gewänder und stickereien aus dem schatz der Marienkirche. Danzig. Stadtmuseum

Kirchliche gewänder und stickereien aus der Marienkirche. See Mannowsky, Walter. Der Danziger paramentenschatz

Das **kirchliche** kunstgewerbe der neuzeit. Weingartner, Josef

Die **kirchliche** leinwandstickerei. Versteyl, H. A.

Kirchliche verfassung der heutigen Juden, sonderlich derer in Deutschland. Bodenschatz, J. C. G.

Kirchmaier, George Caspar
De majestate juribusque barbae ... praeses G. M. Kirchmajerus ... respondens C. D. Morhofius. Wittenbergae, C. Schrödteri [1698]
15 l. Q.
Lipperheide 1663

Kirchner, Paul Christian
Jüdisches ceremoniel, oder Beschreibung derer jenigen gebräuche, welche die Jüden so wol inn- als ausser dem tempel, bey allen und jeden fest-tägen ... in acht zu nehmen pflegen ... neuen aufl. verm ... von S. J. Jungendres. Nürnberg, P. C. Monath 1726
226p. 11 l. 28pl. Q.
An earlier edition was published 1716
Lipperheide 1806

Kirn, G. M.
Das k. württ. militär in seiner neuen uniformirung 1865. Stuttgart [1865]
13 col.pl. O.
Cataloged from Colas
Colas 1614

Kitchens, Matilda
When underwear counted, being the evolution of underclothes. [Talladega, Ala. Brannon print. co. 1931]
Cover-title, 55p. illus. D. $1
Costume index. LC 31-19891

Kittel, P.
(pub.) Unser vaterland in waffen; ein patriotischer hausschatz für das deutsche volk

Kiváló diszitmények az 1881. évi Országos magyar nöiparkiállitából. Hungary. Földmívelésügyi ministerium

Kjøbenhavns kloededragter eller, Det daglige liv i hovedstaden. Lahde, G. L.

Klaatsch, K. H. See Bagensky, C. H. L. von, jt. auth.

Klaededragt. See Troels-Lund, T. F. Dagligt liv i Norden i dèt 16 de aarhundrede klaededragt

[**Klaederdragter** i Kiöbenhavn. Kiöbenhavn, faaes hos Lahde ca1808]
16 col.pl. Q.
Civil and military costume of Copenhagen. Legends on the plates are in Danish and German
Colas 1617

Klai, Johann
Irene, das ist Vollständige aussbildung dess zu Nürnberg geschlossenen friedens 1650. Nürnberg, W. Endters 1650
[2]v. 7pl. Q.
Lipperheide 2819

Klara, Winfried
Schauspielkostüm und schauspieldarstellung; entwicklungsfragen des deutschen theaters im 18. jahrhundert. Berlin, Selbstverlag der Gesellschaft für theatergeschichte 1931
xvi,252p. pl. O. (Schriften der Gesellschaft für theatergeschichte bd. 43)
"Verzeichnis der abgekürzt zitierten literatur": p[ix]-xi
LC 32-16936

Klare onderrichtinge der ... worstel-konst. Petter, Nicolaes

Klassisch-antike goldschmiedearbeiten. Nelidov, A. I., kn͡iaz

Klatte, Cph.
Vorschule der soldaten-reiterei, oder Wahres reiter exercitium zu fuss. Berlin, Nauck 1825
60p. 17pl. O.
Lipperheide 2164

Klaua, Alvin
(ed.) Der Kopfputz

Kleederdragten, en typen der bewoners van Nederland. Amsterdam, P. G. Van Lom ca1850
16 col.pl. O.
Mostly women's costumes
Colas 1618. Lipperheide 969

De **kleeding** der vrouw. See Velde, T. H. van de. Die frauenkleidung

De **kleeding** van de vrouw. See Stratz, C. H. Die frauenkleidung

Das **kleid** der frau. Mohrbutter, Alfred

Kleidertracht in Hamburg. See Suhr, Christoffer. Hamburgische trachten

Kleidertrachten der kaiserl. könig. staaten. Kininger, V. G.

Die **kleidung** der Juden im zeitalter der Mischnah. Schemel, Siegfried

Kleidung und gesundheit. Peters, Emil

Kleidung und putz der frau. Winter, Max

Kleidung und schmuck der Römer zur zeit des Horaz. Strimmer, Hermann

Kleidung und schmuck im biblischen und talmudischen schrifttum. Rosenzweig, Adolf

Kleidung und umwelt in Afrika. Junger, Alexander

Kleidungs arten in der stadt Augspurg. Merz, J. G.

Kleidungsarten und prospecten zu Nürnberg. La manière de s'habiller à Nuremberg et les vues de cette ville. Nürnberg, P. C. Monath [1770]
52pl. O.
The plates show costume. Legends are in German and French
Colas 1619. Lipperheide 783

Kleine häkel-schule. Hennings, Emma

Das **kleine** kind. Ploss, H. H.

Kleine modenwelt. 1.-22. jahrg. 1889-1910. Berlin, J. H. Schwerin
22v. col.illus. Q.
Published monthly
Colas 1620. Lipperheide 4797

Kleine passion. Dürer, Albrecht

Die **kleine** puppenschneiderin. Lesser, Friederike

Kleiner, Salomon
Das prächtige rath haus der stadt Augspurg. Augspurg, J. Wolffen seel. erben 1733
16pl. F.
Plates are by Kleiner, engraved by Joh. Georg Pinz. Persons of all ranks are shown in the pictures. Legends on the plates are in German and French
Lipperheide 769

Representation au naturel des chateaux de Weissenstein au dessus de Pommersfeld et de celui de Gevbach appartenants a la maison des Comtes de Schönborn ... Wahrhaffte vorstellung beÿder ... Schlösser Weisenstein ob Pommersfeld und Geibach. Augspurg, J. Wolffens seel. erben 1728
27pl. F.
Lipperheide 685

Representation naturelle et exacte de la Favorite de son altesse electorale de Mayence ... Wahrhaffte und eigentliche abbildungen der ... chur fürstlich Mayntzischen Favorita. Augspurg, J. Wolffens seel. erben 1726
1,2 l. 14pl. F.
The pictures contain costume figures
Lipperheide 684

Residences memorables ... ou Representation exacte des edifices et jardins de ... Monseigneur le Prince Eugene François, duc de Savoye ... Wunder würdiges kriegs- und siegslager. Augspurg, J. Wolffs seel. erben 1731-1740
11v. 102pl. F.
Costume figures appear in the pictures
Lipperheide 686

Vera et accurata delineatio omnium templorum et cœnobiorum, quæ tam in cæsarea urbe ac sede Vienna periuntur ... Wahrhaffte und genaue abbildung aller kirchen und clöster, welche sowohl in der keysserl. residenz-statt Wien, als auch in denen umliegenden vorstätten sich befinden. Augspurg, J. A. Pfeffel 1724-25
v 1-2. pl.(part fold.) ob.F.
Plates are engraved by G. D. Heumann, J. A. Corvinus and H. Sperling. Figures in the pictures are interesting for eighteenth century costume
Lipperheide 683. LC 14-3539

Kleinere kunst und industrie im alterthum. Friederichs, Karl

Kleines magazin von mustern zu weiblichen kunstarbeiten. Leipzig, C. A. Friese ca1830
20pl.(part col.) D.
Lipperheide 4069

Die **kleinodien** des Heil. Römischen Reiches deutscher nation nebst den kroninsignien Böhmens, Ungarns und der Lombardei. Bock, Franz

Kleinpaul, Rudolf Alexander Reinhold
Das mittelalter. Bilder aus dem leben und treiben aller stände in Europa. Leipzig, H. Schmidt & C. Günther [1895]
2v. in 1. illus. pl.(part col.) Q.
LC 5-15621

Kleinpaul, Rudolf A. R.—*Continued*
Rom in wort und bild. Eine schilderung der ewigen stadt und der Campagna. Leipzig, H. Schmidt & C. Günther 1882-83
2v. fronts. 326 illus. 93pl. fold.plan. sq.F.
Lipperheide 1315. LC 11-13370

Kleinwächter, Friedrich
Zur philosophie der mode. Berlin, C. Habel 1880
44p. O. (Deutsche zeit- und streitfragen. heft 129)
Lipperheide 3285

Kleist, Heinrich von
Der zerbrochene krug; eingeleitet von Franz Dingelstedt. Mit 30 illustrationen und 4 photographien nach original-compositionen von Adolph Menzel. Berlin, A. Hofmann [1877]
xvi,71p. 32 illus. 4 mounted pl. sq.F.
A play, the action of which takes place in a Netherlands village. The plates show the characters dressed in the style of the end of the previous century
Lipperheide 972. LC 28-16357

Klemm, Gustav Friedrich
Handbuch der germanischen alterthumskunde. Dresden, Walthereche hofbuchhandlung 1836
xxxii,448p. 23pl. O.
Dress and jewelry, pages 54-73. The plates show implements and weapons
Lipperheide 277

Werkzeuge und waffen. Leipzig, J. A. Romberg 1854
393p. illus. O.
Volume 2 of the author's *Allgemeine culturwissenschaft*

Klemm, Heinrich
Buch der livreen; eine übersichtliche zusammenstellung der gebrauchlichsten herrschaftlichen livreen jeder gattung. 6. aufl. Dresden, H. Klemm [1895]
55p. 161 illus. tab. O.
First edition 1860
Lipperheide 3792

Die geistlichen gewänder katholischer und evangelischer konfession in mathematisch genauen schnitt-zeichnungen. 2. aufl. Dresden, H. Klemm 1890
29p. 88 illus. Q.
First edition 1881
Colas 1626. Lipperheide 3823

Die gesammte kinder-garderobe; eine vollständige belehrung über zuschnitt und anfertigung der geschmackvollsten knaben- und mädchen-anzüge. Dresden, H. Klemm [1876]
92p. 90 illus. 1 pl. Q.
Colas 1623. Lipperheide 3806

Lehrbuch für uniformschneider zur selbstbelehrung; 2. verb. aufl. bearbeitet von Albert Thiel, neue ... verb. durch R. Tiesler. Dresden, H. Klemm [1896]
2v. 379 illus. Q.
First edition 1885. Volume 1 is on German city, state and officials' uniforms, and uniforms of the mine and foundry personnel; Volume 2 on army and naval uniforms
Colas 1627. Lipperheide 3834

Neueste und vollständige schule der damenschneiderei. Dresden, H. Klemm [1871]
211p. 60 illus. 14pl. Q.
The 4th edition 1875, and 7th edition 1880 were considerably enlarged by additional illustrations
Lipperheide 3800-02

Unterricht im arrangement der damentoiletten von standpunkte der kleideraesthetik und der farben-harmonie. Dresden, H. Klemm [1876]
114p. 87 illus. 1 pl. Q.
Colas 1624. Lipperheide 3807

Versuch einer urgeschichte des kostüms mit beziehung auf das allgemeine culturleben der ältesten völker der erde; mitt abbildungen nach denkmälern der vorzeit. Dresden, H. Klemm [1860
136p. front. 6pl. D.
Colas 1622. Lipperheide 121

Vollständiges handbuch der höhern bekleidungskunst für civil, militär und livree; 26. aufl. Dresden, H. Klemm 1870
2v. 22pl. O.
First edition (Leipzig 1846) had title *Carl und Heinrich Klemm Vollständiges lehrbuch der praktischen zuschneidekunst*
Lipperheide 3789

Der vorschriftmässige talar der justizbeamten im Königreiche Preussen mit den abweichungen für richter, staatsanwälte, rechtsanwälte und gerichtsschreiber in bild und schnitt dargestellt. Dresden, H. Klemm [1885]
2 l. 7 illus. Q.
Colas 1625. Lipperheide 3833

Die **Klettgauer-** oder Hallauertracht des kantons Schaffhausen. Heierli, Frau Julie

[**Kley, Heinrich**]
Festzug; jubiläum der Universität Heidelberg, 1386-1886. Heidelberg, Bangel & Schmitt (O. Petters) [etc.] 1886?
Cover-title, fold.pl. sq.O.
On inside of back cover: Der von herrn Carl Hoff ... entworfene und unter seiner persönlichen leitung ausgearbeitete historische festzug bringt die fünf jahrhunderte seit gründung der Universität zur darstellung ... Das vorliegende festzugs-album selbst wurde von herrn maler H. Kley ... unter leitung des herrn professor Hoff entworfen und gezeichnet
Lipperheide 2840. LC 15-8904

Klickmann, Flora
(ed.) How to dress; a handbook for women of modest means. London, Ward, Lock & co. [1900]
128p. 1 pl. O.

Klikspaan, pseud. See Kneppelhout, Johannes

Klimsch, Ferdinand Karl. See Klimsch, Karl

Klimsch, Karl
(engr.) Gedenkbuch zu Friedrich v. Schiller's 100 jähriger geburtsfeier, begangen in Frankfurt a. M. den 10 november 1859
(lithgr.) Weismann, Heinrich. Das allgemeine deutsche schützenfest zu Frankfurt am Main, juli 1862

Kling, G.
(ed.) Prussia. Kriegsministerium. Geschichte der bekleidung, bewaffnung und ausrüstung des königlich preussischen heeres

Klinger, J. H.
(engr.) Delsenbach, J. A. Wahre abbildung der sämtlichen reichskleinodien welche in ... Nürnberg aufbewahret werden

Klingsohr, Chr. F.
Kurze geschichte des ehemaligen klosters Heilsbronn, und biographien derer sämtlich in der münsterkirche daselbst beigesetzten fürsten und kurfürsten aus dem burggraflichen fürsten hause, Nürnberg Hohenzollern. [Heilbronn?] Der verfasser 1806
99p. 20pl. Q.
Plates for the first part are borrowed from Hocker's *Hailbronnischem antiquitätenschatz,* the others are new engravings by P. W. Schwarz
Lipperheide 726

Klodt, Michael. See Clodt von Jürgensburg, M. P., baron

Kloeber, August von
(engr.) Kopisch, August. Die kunstheroen der vorzeit

Klöcker von Ehrenstrahl, David
Das grosse carrosel und prächtige ringrännen ... was ... zu sehen war alss ... Carl der Eylffte ... anno M.DC.LXXII. den XVIII. decembris ... zu Stockholm antratt. Stockholm, J. G. Eberdt [1672?]
13p. 62pl. F.
Lipperheide 2698

Klöppelbuch. Rasmussen, Sara

De **klooster-orden** in Nederland. Hofdijk, W. J.

Kloss, C. Boden
In the Andamans and Nicobars. London, J. Murray 1903
xvi,373p. front. illus. pl. maps. O.
Describes and pictures the dress of the Andaman and Nicobar islands
LC 3-15207

Die **kloster-orden** der heiligen katholischen kirche. Brockhoff, L. E. D.

Knanishu, Joseph
About Persia and its people; a description of their manners, customs, and home life, including engagements, marriages, modes of traveling, forms of punishments, superstitions, etc. Rock Island, Ill., Lutheran Augustana book concern, printers 1899
300p. front.(ports.) illus. D.
LC 0-643

Kneeland, Natalie
Aprons and house dresses, by Natalie Kneeland. Chicago & New York, A. W. Shaw company; [etc.] 1925
xxi,141p. illus. O. (Merchandise manuals for retail salespeople, W. W. Charters, editor)
Contains "References"
LC 25-9782

Infants' and children's wear. Chicago & New York, A. W. Shaw company; [etc.] 1925
xxi,187p. illus. O. (Merchandise manuals for retail salespeople, W. W. Charters, editor)
"References" at end of some of the chapters
LC 25-11195

Negligees. Chicago & New York, A. W. Shaw company; [etc.] 1925
xxii,156p. illus. O. (Merchandise manuals for retail salespeople, W. W. Charters, editor)
"References" at end of some of the chapters
LC 25-11193

Waists. Chicago & New York, A. W. Shaw company; [etc.] 1924
xxi,149p. illus. O. (Merchandise manuals for retail salespeople, W. W. Charters, editor)
Contains "References"
LC 24-32114

[**Kneppelhout, Johannes**]
Studenten-typen; [by Klikspaan, pseud.] Geillustrierd door Johan Braakensiek. 8. ed. Leiden, A. W. Sijthoff [1904]
287p. pl. O.
The ordinary dress of students in Dutch universities, 1839-41

Kniffin, Herbert Reynolds
Masks. Peoria, Ill. Manual arts press [c1931]
140p. front. illus. O. (Books on the arts; ed. by W. G. Whitford) $3
"A history and exposition of the technical process of mask-making, presented in practical form for the use of students, stage workers and anyone who wishes to learn the art of mask-making." B. M. Baker's Dramatic bibliography."
Bibliography: p137
LC 31-22773

Knight, Charles
(ed.) London. London, H. G. Bohn 1851
6v. in 3. illus. O.
First published, 1841-1844, in 150 numbers. Written in greater part by J. C. Platt, J. Saunders, W. Weir, G. L. Craik, and the editor
LC 3-7547

(ed.) Old England: a pictorial museum of regal, ecclesiastical, baronial, municipal, and popular antiquities. London, C. Knight 1845
2v. illus. col.pl. F.
Among the illustrations are hundreds showing English costume from the earliest times to the time of Hogarth
Costume index. LC 2-10764

See also Craik, G. L., and MacFarlane, Charles. Pictorial history of England

Knights
Hagen, F. H. von der. Bilder aus dem ritterleben und aus der ritterdichtung nach elfenbeingebilden und gedichten des mittelalters. 1856
Larchey, Lorédan. Costumes vrais. 1899
Mansberg, Richard, freiherr von. Wâfen unde wîcgewaete der deutschen ritter des mittelalters. 1890

See also Europe—Middle ages

A **knight's** life in the days of chivalry. Meller, W. C.

Knights of Malta. See Malta, Knights of

Knights of Pythias. See Pythias, Knights of

Knights of the Maccabees. See Maccabees, Knights of

Knights Templars. See Templars

Knitting
Album de modèles de tricot. 1881
Albums pour ouvrages au tricot. 1886
Allerhand mödel zum stricken und nähen. 1748
Andreä, Nanette. Sammlung von leicht ausführbaren vorschriften zu den schönsten und elegantesten strumpfrändern und andern seinen strickereien. 1843
Die arbeitstunden im stricken, nähen und sticken. 1810
Cottagers' comforts and other recipes in knitting & crochet. 1882
Dillmont, Thérèse de. Die strickarbeit. 1893?
Fischerin, Dorothea. Strick buch. Worinnen nicht nur viele neue zwickel, sondern nebst dem alphabet und zahlen auch viele zierrathen befindlich. 1803
Georgens, J. D. Das stricken. 1882-85
The lady's knitting-book. 1875-76
Lambert, Miss A. My knitting book. 1847
Leach, Mrs. Mrs Leach's knitting lessons, how to knit fancy and useful articles. ca1877
Myra and son. Myra's Knitting lessons. 1889
Netto, August. Neue original-desseins für die neuerfundene stickerei über stricknadeln. 1809
Netto, J. F., and Lehmann, F. L. L'art de tricoter ... ou Instruction complète et raisonnée sur toutes sortes de tricotages simples et compliqués. 1802
Neu gezeichnete muster zum stricken in garn, wolle, seide und zur perlstrickerei. 1811
Neue praktische strickschule; vollständige anleitung zum erlernen des strickens mit ... strick-mustern. 1879
Pauker, Juliane. Neuestes musterbuch von ... strick-muster-touren. 1835-38
Sylvia's book of new designs in knitting, netting, and crochet, containing a selection of useful articles in crochet, knitting, tatting, and netting, with minute details. 1881
Wilhelmi, Helene. Muster für strümpfe und muster für socken. 1869

Knitting lessons. Myra and son

Die **knöpfel-schule.** Hennings, Emma

Knötel, Herbert, and Sieg, Herbert
(eds.) Knötel, Richard. Handbuch der uniformkunde

Knötel, Herbert; Pietsch, Paul, and Jantke, Egon
Uniformkunde; das deutsche heer, friedens-uniformen bei ausbruch des weltkrieges. Im auftrag der Gesellschaft für heereskunde e.V. bearbeitet von Herbert Knötel ... text-band von Major a. D. Baron Collas. Hamburg, Diepenbroick-Grüter & Schulz 1935-37
v 1-2, 4. illus. col.pl. Q.
In portfolio. In progress
The following volumes have appeared: v 1 Generalstab und kriegsministerium. Infanterie. Jäger und schützen (64 col.pl.); v2 Kavallerie (58 col.pl.); v4 Text-band

Knoetel, Richard
Handbuch der uniformkunde; die militärische tracht in ihrer entwicklung bis zur gegenwart, begründet von prof. Richard Knötel, grundlegend überarbeitet, fortgeführt und erweitert von Herbert Knötel d. j. und Herbert Sieg. Mit 1600 uniform-darstellungen nach zeichnungen von Richard Knötel und Herbert Knötel d. j. Hamburg, Von Diepenbroick-Grüter & Schulz c1937
438p. illus. O.
First edition (Leipzig, J. J. Weber 1896) The present edition has been brought up to date
Colas 1632 (1896 ed.) Lipperheide 2125 (1896 ed.) LC 38-9707

Die türkische armee und marine in ihrer gegenwärtigen uniformirung. Rathenow, M. Babenzien [1897]
19p. 12 col.pl. O.
Colas 1633. Lipperheide 2389

Uniformenkunde: lose blätter zur geschichte der entwickelung der militärischen tracht. Rathenow, M. Babezien 1890-1914
18v. 1060 col.pl. O.
Volumes 1 and 2 show German uniforms, and contain one hundred colored plates; volumes 3-18 show uniforms of all nations including North and South America and have sixty plates in each volume
Colas 1631. Lipperheide 2123

(illus.) Vogt, Hermann. Das buch vom deutschen heere

(illus.) Vogt, Hermann. Die europäischen heere der gegenwart

Knoll, Carl, and Reuther, Fritz
Die kunst des schmückens; eine klärung des schmuck-problems durch wort und bild für schaffende und geniessende. Dresden, G. Kühtmann 1910
146p. 74pl.(part col.) O. M.12
LC 10-28019

Knoll, Eduard. See Arnold, Xaver, jt. auth.

Knorr, Georg Wolfgang
Auserlesenes blumen-zeichen-buch für frauenzimmer aus welchen das blumenzeichnen ... erlernt werden kan. Nürnberg, G. W. Knorr ca1750
2v. 23pl. F.
Lipperheide 4360

Knorre, Fr.
Costumes russes representés en groupes charactéristiques ... lith. par les premiers artistes de Paris. St Petersbourg, Velten ca1850
12 col.pl. ob.F.
Legends on the plates are in Russian and French
Colas 1630. Lipperheide 1364

Knox, George William
Imperial Japan; the country & its people. London, G. Newnes 1905
xi,294p. col.front. pl. O.
"I have used in this volume, chapters VII. IX. and X. portions of my translations from Japanese books which have been printed in the *Transactions* of the Asiatic society of Japan, and, chapter VIII. in the *Independent.*"
LC 5-36150

Die **knüpfarbeit.** Dillmont, Thérèse de

Kobbé, Gustav
Opera singers; a pictorial souvenir, with biographies of some of the most famous singers of the day. Boston, Oliver Ditson company; New York, C. H. Ditson [1913]
[95]p. illus. pl. F.
First published 1901
LC 4-37067

Koch, Joseph
(illus.) Valvasor, J. W. Die ehre desz hertzogthums Crain

Koch, L. See Kaiser, Friedrich, jt. auth.

Koch, Ludwig
Die reitkunst im bilde. Wien, Campagne reitergesellschaft 1923
249p. illus. 92 col.pl.

Koch, Rud.
Hamburger pflanzen-bilder; hrsg. von der Abtheilung fur kunstgewerbe des Hamburger gewerbe-vereins. Hamburg und Leipzig, L. Voss 1882
15pl. F.
Lipperheide 4370

Kock, Charles Paul de. See La grande ville; nouveau tableau de Paris

Koebel, William Henry
Portugal, its land and people ... illus. by Mrs. S. Roope Dockery. London, A. Constable 1909
xvii,405p. 21 col.pl.(incl.front.) O.
LC 9-31740

The romance of the river Plate. illus. by ... plates and numerous illustrations and maps dating from the sixteenth century. London, H. Ponsonby 1914
2v. fronts. illus. pl.(26 col.) ports. map. sq.F.
Useful for the costumes of Buenos Aires and for the dress of the Indians of Patagonia, Tierra del Fuego, Uruguay, Paraguay, and the Argentine
Bibliography: v 1, p19-22
LC 16-20528

Koehler, A.
(illus.) Gerstmann, Maximilian. Das buch vom preussischen soldaten

Köhler, Bruno
Allgemeine trachtenkunde. Leipzig, P. Reclam [1900-1902]
7v. 112pl. O.
Contents: v 1 Das altertum; v2-4 Das mittelalter; v5-7 Neuere zeit
Colas 1638. Lipperheide 98e

Trachtenbilder für die bühne. Berlin, M. Pasch 1890-92
2v. 120 col.pl. Q.
Colas 1637. Lipperheide 3231

Koehler, Heinrich Karl Ernst von
Masken, ihr ursprung und neue auslegung einiger der merkwürdigsten auf alten denkmälern die bis jetzt unerkannt und unerklärt geblieben waren. St. Petersburg, K. Academie der wissenschaften 1833
26p. pl. Q.

Koehler, Johann David
Dissertatio historico-critica de imperiali sacra lancea non inter reliquias imperii sed clinodia referenda cum problemate de novo S.R.I. Officio archi-lanciferatu. Altorfii, D. Meyer 1731
36p. 2pl. Q.
Contains one plate from contemporary miniatures, which shows Charles the Bald, Frankish emperor 823-877, surrounded by his court
Lipperheide 1757

Köhler, Karl
Die entwickelung der tracht in Deutschland während des mittelalters und der neuzeit. Nürnberg, F. Heerdegen 1877
226p. 100pl. O.
Contents: 1 Die fussbekleidung; 2 Kopfputz und kopfbedeckung; 3 Halsbekleidung und halsschmuck; 4 Das kleid; 5 Die jetzige tracht in bezug auf das unterscheidende der einzelnen stände
Colas 1636. Lipperheide 590

A history of costume; ed. and augmented by Emma von Sichart; tr. by A. K. Dallas. London G. G. Harrap [1928]
463p. illus. XVI col.pl.(incl.front.) O.
A translation of the German edition *Praktische kostumkunde.* The English edition has the same plates but the paging of the text differs from the German edition and the illustrations are rearranged
Bibliography p457-58
Costume index. LC 29-26370

Praktische kostümkunde in 600 bildern und schnitten. München, F. Bruckmann 1926
2v. 572 illus. 16 col.pl. O.
Edited and augmented by Emma von Sichart. A new edition of the author's *Die trachten der völker in bild und schnitt* (Dresden, Müller, Klemm & Schmidt 1871-73. 3v. illus.)
A history of costume from ancient times to 1870
Colas 1634-35, 2741. Lipperheide 79

Köller, Friedrich Ludwig von
Uniformzeichnung d. königl. dänischen armee. Schleswig, Röhss 1805
9p. 28 col.pl. O.

Uniformzeichnung der vorzüglichsten europäischen truppen. Kiel, C. F. Mohr 1802
4 l. 10 col.pl. Q.
Colas 1640. Lipperheide 2114

Die **Kölner** dom-feier. Illustrirte zeitung

König, Franz Niklaus
Collection de costumes suisses tirés du cabinet du m. Meyer d'Aarau. Unterseen, chez l'auteur; Berne, J. J. Bourgdorfer 1802-04
5,48 l. O. 24 col.pl. Q.
This collection is known as the "Grand König". It is a series of pictures drawn by Reinhardt, showing Swiss people in the costume of their cantons. For a list of plates see Colas's *Bibliographie*
This work, reproduced with plates in octavo is known as the "Moyen König", same title, publisher, and collation
Colas 1644-1645. Lipperheide 902

Neue sammlung von schweizertrachten ... Nouvelle collection de costumes suisses. Zürich, Orell, Füssli 1811
201p. 50 col.pl. D.
Text in German and French. Legends on the plates are in German. This work is known as the "Petit König"
The same illustrations, copied in reduced size, were published (Zürich, Füssli ca1812. 193p. 50 col.pl. S.)
Colas notes an earlier edition with the same title (Zürich, Füssli 1803. 147p. 40 col.pl. D.); and an edition, with French title only, containing the same plates as the 1803 edition (Paris, Lefuel ca1820. 40 col.pl. S.)
Colas 1646-47, 1650-51. Lipperheide 904

König, Franz Niklaus—*Continued*
Nouvelle collection de costumes suisses. Berne, J. J. Burgdorfer ca1810
25 l. 24 col.pl. O.
Colas notes an edition (Berne, J. J. Burgdorfer 1811. 24 col.pl.)
Colas 1648-49. Lipperheide 903m

Nouvelle collection de costumes suisses des XXII cantons d'après König, Lory et d'autres. Neue sammlung von schweizertrachten aus den XXII cantonen. Züric, Orell-Füssli ca1818
223p. 60 col.pl. S.
Text in French and German
Colas notes editions of 1803-1805 and ca1812, both with 60 colored plates, and also a new edition under title: *Collection complette de costumes et occupations suisses* (Berne, chez l'auteur ca1830. 42pl. Q.)
Colas 1652-1654, 1656

Kœnig, Marie
Poupées et légendes de France ... Préface de Maurice Bouchor. Illus. d'après les dessins de P. Mathey. Paris, Librairie centrale des beaux-arts [1900?]
viii,156p. col.pl. Q.
LC F-2513

König Otto I und die K. Bayerischen truppen in Griechland im jahre 1833. Kraus, G.

König Wilhelm und sein heer. Sellmer, Carl

Könige des lebens. Gleichen-Russwurm, Alexander, freiherr von

Der **könige** in Franckreich leben, regierung und absterben: aus bewehrten frantzösischen geschicht-schreibern übersetzet und biss auf instehendes 1671. jahr continuirt. Nürnberg, J. Hofmann 1671
16 l. 395p. 66pl. D.
"Und sambt ihren bildnüssen nach Boissevins Conterfäten ans liecht gegeben." Subtitle
Lipperheide 1067

Königl. bayerische armée. Diez, W.

Königl. bayerische kadetten-korps von der gründung bis zur gegenwart. Teicher, Friedrich

Königl. hannov. militair. Mentzel, C.

Königlich bayerisches linien und bürger militair. Kraus, G.

[Die **königlich** preussische armée. Berlin, Romolini 1845]
6 col.pl. F.
Colas 1657

Die **königl.** preussische armee in ihrer neuesten uniformirung. Burger, Ludwig

Die **königlich** preussische armée 1792. Giersberg

Die **königlich** preussische armee. Verdy, L., freiherr von

Das **königlich** preussische heer in seiner gegenwärtigen uniformirung. Hammer, F. W., comp.

Der **königlich-preussischen** crönung hoch feyerliche solemnitäten. See Besser, Johann von. Preussische krönungsgeschichte

Königlich sächsische armee. Schubauer, F.

Die **königlich** sächsische armee in ihrer neuesten uniformirung. Beck, August

Das **königliche** böhmische crönungs-ceremoniel. Rink, E. G.

Das **königliche** münzkabinet. Friedlaender Julius, and Sallet. A. F. C. von

Königliche württembergische armee. Braun Reinhold

Koenigliche württembergische garde du corps, infanterie, chevau-leger. Seele J. B.

Das **königreich** Bayern in seinen acht kreisen bildlich ... bearbeitet. Lommel, Georg, and Bauer

Könnecke, Gustav
Bilderatlas zur geschichte der deutschen nationallitteratur; 2. verb. und verm. aufl. Marburg, N. G. Elwert [1895]
xxvi,423p. front. illus. pl. port. facsim. (part col.) F.
Lipperheide 602. LC G-2445

Köppe, Joachim
Neuer discurs von der rittermessigen und weitberümbten kunst des fechtens sowol im rapier alleine als in dolcher und rapier pede firmo und per caminada ... beschrieben. Magdeburg, A Betzel 1619
73 l. 46 illus. 1 pl.
Lipperheide 2958

Köppen, Fedor von
Armies of Europe; tr. and rev. by Count Gleichen. London, W. Clowes 1890
81p. 20 col.pl. O. 12s, o.p.
Costume index

Körber, Philipp
Volksbelustigungen und mummenschanz der alten ehemaligen reichsstadt Nürnberg. Fürth, Löwensohn 1859
21p. 9 col.pl. F.
Illustrated by Oscar Schäffer

Körperpflege und kleidung bei den Deutschen. See Heyne, Moritz Fünf bücher deutscher hausaltertümer

Körperseele. Giese, Fritz

Kohfeldt, Gustav, and Ahrens, Wilhelm
(eds.) Ein rostocker studenten-stammbuch von 1736/37, mit 23 bildern aus dem studenten-leben in farbiger wiedergabe. Rostock, G. B. Leopold 1919
23 l. 65p. 23 col.pl. O.
Shows student life in Germany in the first half of the 18th century
Lipperheide notes a manuscript copy for the years 1736-38: *Stammbuch eines Rostocker studenten* (124 l. 30 col.illus.)
Lipperheide 2023

Kohl, Johann Georg
Episoden aus der cultur- und kunstgeschichte Bremens. Bremen, C. E. Müller 1870
x,161p. 18pl.(7 col.) Q.
This is part 2 of *Denkmale der geschichte und kunst der freien Hansestadt Bremen.* Chapter 5 is a history of costume in Bremen in the 16th and 17th centuries
Lipperheide 803

Die völker Europas ... Mit vignetten und farbendruck tafeln, nach acquarellen von A. Kretschmer u.a. Hamburg, B. S. Berendsohn 1872
408p. illus. 8 col.pl. Q.
Treats various countries of Europe and has a chapter on southern neighbors. Contents of the color plates: Araber, Mauren; Polen; Spanier; Schotten; Norweger; Deutsche (2)

Kohlrausch, Friedrich
Bildnisse der deutschen könige und kaiser von Karl dem Grossen bis Maximilian I. nach siegeln, münzen, grabmälern, denkmälern und originalbildnissen gezeichnet von Heinrich Schneider. Hamburg, und Gotha, F. und A. Perthes 1846
680p. 37 port. (incl.front.) Q.
Lipperheide notes a new edition (Gera, C. B. Griesbach 1877. 29pl.)
Lipperheide 731. LC 14-15296

Kok, W.
[Illumination in Amsterdam am 8. märz 1788] W. Kok del. De Wed: J: Dóll, excud. No place, 1788?
12pl. Q.
Inscriptions on plates in Dutch
Lipperheide 2677

Kolb, Ambrosius
Kriegs unnd friedens unserer zeiten kurtz begriffene history dessen was im Heil. Röm. Reich und durch gantz Europam denckwürdiges sich zugetragen bisz in das jahr 1653. Cölln, In verlegung I. A. Kinchii 1653
188,67,410,30p. 68pl. D.
Lipperheide 536

Kolb, Johann Christoph
(illus.) Conlin, J. R. Roma sancta sive Benedicti XIII

Kolb, Peter
The present state of the Cape of Good-Hope. Written originally in High German, by Peter Kolben; done into English, from the original, by Mr. Medley. London, W. Innys 1731
2v. fronts. pl.(2 fold.) fold.map, plan. D.
Volume 1 contains material on the dress of the Hottentots
LC 5-19297

Kolb, Valentin
Das Münchener bürger militär in allen waffengattungen und uniformen von den jahren 1790 bis gegenwärtige zeit. München, zu haben bei dem herausgeber 1834
1 l. 30 col.pl. Q.
Colas 1639. Lipperheide 2193

Kolbenheyer, Erich
Motive der hausindustriellen stickerei in der Bukowina ... Motifs de la broderie paysanne en Bukovine ... Designs of the home-industry embroideries in Bukovina. Wien, K. K. Hof- und staatsdruckerei 1912
121p. 76pl. map. F.
Shows many embroidery designs used in Bukovina, Rumania

Kolberg, Oskar
Pieśni ludu Polskiego zebrał i wydał. Warszawa, J. Jaworski 1857-80
13v. illus. 26pl. (20 col.) O.
Plates show national costume of Poland from photographs and drawings by W. Gerson, T. Konopki and B. Hoff
Lipperheide 1393

Kolinovics, Gabriel
Chronicon militaris ordinis, Equitum Templariorum e bullis papalibus, diplomatibus regiis ... collectum. Pestini, Litteris Trattnerianis [1789]
20,301,140p. 3pl. O.
Lipperheide 1910

Kollarz, and others. See Trachten-album

Kollmann, Ch.
Costumes russes, vues de Saint-Pétersbourg et de ses environs. St Pétersbourg, A. Pluchart 1822
2v. 20 col.pl. F.
Colas 1641. Lipperheide 1353e

(lithgr.) Collection de cris et costumes de paysans et paysannes de St. Pétersbourg

Komisarjevsky, Theodore. See Kommissarzhevskiĭ, F. F.

Kommissarzhevskiĭ, Fedor Fedorovich
The costume of the theatre, by Theodore Komisarjevsky. London, G. Bles [1931]
xii,178p. front. 31pl. Q. 25s
Colas 1642. LC 32-26508

Kommissarzhevskiĭ, Fedor Fedorovich, and Simonson, Lee
Settings & costumes of the modern stage. London, The Studio; New York, The Studio 1933
132p. illus. pl. (part col.) Q.
The Studio winter number, edited by C. G. Holme
LC 34-679

Komste van Zyne Majesteit Willem III. koning van Groot Britanje, enz. in Holland. Bidloo, Govard

Kondakov, Nikodim Pavlovich
Histoire de l'art byzantin considéré principalement dans les miniatures; éd. française originale, publiée par l'auteur, sur la traduction de M. Trawinski, et précédée d'une préface de M. A. Springer. Paris, Librairie de l'Art 1886-91
2v. in 1. illus. pl. ob.F. (Bibliothèque internationale de l'Art)
Lipperheide 261. LC 3-18545

Koner, Wilhelm David. See Guhl, E. K., jt. auth.

Kongl. lifrustkammaren och därmed förenade samlingar. Stockholm. Livrustkammaren

Kongl. Svenska arméens uniformer. No place, 1824-25
2 l. 23 col.pl. F.
Lithographed by Müller after Wettering, I. H. Sjokölm and Schützercrantz
Cataloged from Colas's *Bibliographie*
Colas 1643

Kongl. svenska arméens uniformer. Söderberg, Gustaf

De **kongl.** svenska riddare-ordnarne. Wrangel, F. U., grefve

Kongl. svenska riddare ordnarnes drägter 1833. Schützercrantz, Adolph

Kongow, Iwao
The costume of Nō play in Japan. Tokyo, Meiji-Shobo [193-]
2 l. 50 col.pl. sq.F.
Added title page in Japanese

Nō-isho; Japanese Nō-play costume. Tokyo, Meiji-Shobo [1934]
2v. 100 col.pl. F.
Preface and explanatory text in Japanese
Plates accompanied by guard sheets with descriptive letterpress

Konrad, Karl Gustav
Zur bilderkunde des deutschen studentwesens. Breslau, W. Finsterbusch 1921
64p. illus. O.
Cover title: Studenten-lebens

Das **konzert.** Meyer, Kathi

Der **Kopfputz;** mode-zeitung für damen; hrsg. im auftrage der akademie für damenkopfputz von Alvin Klaua. 1.-2. jahrg. 1878-1879. Berlin
2v. illus.(part col.) Q.
Published monthly. Volume 1 published by Hohorst in Comm.

Kopisch, August
Die kunstheroen der vorzeit, ein geisterzug, bei der 25. stiftungsfeier des Berliner Kunstlervereins am 18. october 1839 . . . scenisch vorgeführt von August Kopisch ... gezeichnet von August von Kloeber. Berlin, E. H. Schroeder 1840
2 l. 5pl. F.
Lipperheide 2827s

Kopon Bushido Ye-Zupushi
Pictures of ancient Japanese warriors, illustrated by Moronobu. Edo, Uropoya 1685
70 l. illus. Q.

Kopp, Ulrich Friedrich
Bilder und schriften der vorzeit. Mannheim, Auf kosten des verfassers 1819-21
2v. illus. col.pl.(part fold.) facsims.(part fold.) O.
Miniatures from the *Heidelberger Handschrift des Sachsenspiegels* which show 13th century costume
Lipperheide 374. LC 11-34877

Kopparberg. See Sweden-Kopparberg

Korea
Carpenter, F. G. Japan and Korea. 1925
Bishop, Mrs I. L. B. Korea and her neighbors. 1898
Fisher, Mrs W. H. Twins travelogues. 1924. v1
Hamilton, Angus. Korea. 1904
Hulbert, H. B. The passing of Korea. 1906
McLeod, John. Voyage of His Majesty's ship Alceste, along the coast of Corea, to the island of Lewchew, with an account of her subsequent shipwreck. 1818
Northrop, H. D. The flowery kingdom and the land of the mikado. 1894
Trautz, F. M. Japan, Korea and Formosa. 1931?

Korea and her neighbors. Bishop, Mrs I. L. B.

Korf, Frederick
Art and fundamentals of hairdressing; a text-book for professionals and a student's guide. New York, Wilfred academy of hair and beauty culture [c1923]
81p. illus. D. (Blue book series of hair and beauty culture v2)
LC 23-13561

Korio, Japanese artist
Ye zu gaku no. [Pictures of the No dance] Tokyo, Matsumoto Heipichi, Mey 35th yr.
200 col.pl. F.
Cataloged from card of the Ryerson library, Chicago

Korn, Minna
Minna Korn's Häkel-buch; neue bearbeitung. Leipzig, H. Hartung 1867
108p. 16 col.pl. O.
Lipperheide 4095

Korsov, G.
(tr.) Russia. Ministerstvo Imperatorskago dvora. Les solennités du saint couronnement

Korstogenes historie. Øverland, O. A.

Korte leevensschets en afbeeldingen der graaven van Holland. Smids, Ludolf

Kosacheva, Ol'ga P.
Ukrainskiĭ narodnyĭ ornament, obraztsy, vyshivok", tkaneĭ i pīsanok, izdanie vtoroe. Kiev", tip. S. V. Kul'zhenko 1879
19p. 15 col.pl. Q.
Lipperheide 3962

Die **Kosaken,** oder Historische darstellung ihrer sitten, gebräuche, kleidung, waffen und art krieg zu führen. Wien und Prag ca1812
31p. 1 col.pl. O.
Colas 1658. Lipperheide 1349

Kosmetische receptirkunst. Dachauer, Gustav

Kosmetisches taschenbuch für damen. Schreger, C. H. T.

Kostbare waffen aus der Dresdner rüstkammer. Dresden. Historisches museum und gewehrgalerie

Koster, Henry
Travels in Brazil. London, Longman, Hurst, Rees, Orme, and Brown 1816
ix,501p. col.pl. maps. Q.
LC 2-16499

Das **kostüm** der blütezeit Hollands, 1600-1660. Thienen, F. W. S. van

Das **kostum** der meisten völker des alterthums. Lens, A. C.

Das **kostüm** in vergangenheit und gegenwart. Buss, Georg

Kostümbilder für bühnenspiele des mittelalters. Schiller, Hermann

Kostüme aus der zeit Ludwigs XIV. Bonnart, J. B. and Bonnart, R.

Kostüme der ganzen preussischen armee. Henschel, W., and Henschel, F. A.

Kostüme der kaiserl. königl. National- und der anderen privil. theatern in Wien. Wien, J. Geistinger 1807-12?
138 col.pl. O.
This series appeared in parts with six plates each
Colas 1659. Lipperheide 3207

Kostueme, plakate und dekorationen. Schnackenberg, Walther

Kostümkunde. Weiss, Hermann

Kostümkunde für sammler. Mützel, H. H. H. E.

Die **kostümreform** unter der intendanz des grafen Brühl an den kgl. theatern zu Berlin. Schaffner, Hermann

Kottenkamp, Franz Justus
History of chivalry and ancient armour, with descriptions of the feudal system, the usages of knighthood, the tournament, and trials by single combat. Longon, Willis & Sotheran 1857
110p. 62 col.pl.(part fold.) ob.O.
Translated by A. Löwy from the author's *Der rittersaal*

Kottenkamp, Franz J.—*Continued*
Der rittersaal; eine geschichte des ritterthums, seines entstehens und fortgangs, seiner gebraüche und sitten. Artistisch erläutert von Friedrich Martin von Reibisch, historisch beleuchtet von dr. Franz Kottenkamp. Stuttgart, C. Hoffmann 1842
170p. 62 col.pl.(part fold.) Q.
Plates show mounted men in full armor
Colas 2525. Lipperheide 2096

Die verschiedenen trachten; aus dem englischen von dr. Franz Kottenkamp. [Stuttgart, Scheible, Rieger & Sattler 1847]
121p. 31 illus. O.
Issued as nos. 64-66 of *Wochenbände für das geistige und materielle wohl des deutschen volkes*
Colas 1660. Lipperheide 64

Koula, Jan
Výběr národního českého vyšívání z českého průmyslového musea Náprstkových ... Auswahl böhmischer nationalstickerei. Praha, Nákladem českého průmyslového musea Náprstkových 1893
20 l. 25pl.(2 col.) Q.
Title and text also in English, French, and Russian
Lipperheide 3980

Kozłowski, Karol
Wojsko polskie w roku 1831 ... [Das polnische heer im jahre 1831 ... nach zeichnungen von Wł. Motty ... hrsg. von K. Kozłowski] Poznan, Nakladem wydawcy 1889
32p. 10 col.pl. Q.
Colas lists the same plates, showing 90 figures in the uniforms of the Polish army, in *Album wojska polskiego z 1831* (Poznan 1887. 32p. 12 col.pl. ob.F.)
Colas 72, 2144. Lipperheide 2386

Kožmínová, Amalie
Podkarpatská Rus; práce a život lidu po stránce kulturní, hospodářské a národopisné. Karlín, Nákladem vlastním 1922
121p. illus.(incl. music) pl.(part col.) map. F.
Shows Czechoslovakian embroidery and costume

Kozuchy. See Úprka, Joža. Peasants furs in Czechoslovakia

Krahmer, Gustav. See Pflugk-Harttung, J. A. G. von, ed. Napoleon I.: Das erwachen der völker

Kramer & co.
(pub.) Neue häkelmappe
(pub.) Neue praktische strickschule

Kramer, Jules Henri
Afbildningar af nordiska drägter. See entry under Afbildningar

Kramer, Ludwig von
Blüthenzauber. Berlin, F. Lipperheide [1885-87]
3 l. 24 col.pl. Q.
First published as a supplement of *Illustrirte frauenzeitung*
Colas 1661. Lipperheide 3193

Kramer's Bazar für stickerei auf leder- und silber-canevas in vorlagen von angefangenen arbeiten. Leipzig, Kramer ca1874
3pts. 24pl. Q.
Lipperheide 3987

Kramer's Handbuch für weibliche handarbeiten; 3. aufl. Leipzig, Kramer [1877]
64p. 117 illus. 4 col.pl. Q.
Lipperheide 3989

Krapf, Anton
Durchdachte frauenkleidung; eine schönheitsfibel. Mit bildern von Ita Baumann. Berlin, H. Schnakenburg 1934
viii,117p illus. D.
LC 35-5255

Krasheninnikov, Stepan Petrovich
The history of Kamtschatka, and the Kurilski Islands, with the countries adjacent; illustrated with maps and cuts. Published at Petersbourg in the Russian language ... translated into English by James Grieve. Glocester, R. Raikes; London, T. Jefferys 1764
280p. front. pl.(part fold.) fold.map. S.
An abridged translation. The original was published in 1755. Three plates show costume
LC 3-4225

Kratschmer, Florian
Die bekleidung. Jena, G. Fischer 1894
p359-414. O. (Handbuch der hygiene. 1.bd. 1.abt. 4. lfg.)

Kraus, Franz Xaver
Die miniaturen der Manesseschen liederhandschrift ... nach dem original der Pariser Nationalbibliothek. Strassburg i. E., K. J. Trübner 1887
16p. 142pl.(2 col.) F.
Shows costume of the 14th century
Lipperheide 402

Die miniaturen des Codex Egberti in der Stadtbibliothek zu Trier. Freiburg im Breisgau, Herder 1884
27p. 60pl. Q.
Title also in Latin: *Picturae Codicus Egberti*
Shows costume of the 10th century
Lipperheide 365

(ed. and tr.) Rossi, G. B. de. Roma sotterranea

Kraus, Georg Melchior
Nationaltrachten verschied. völker. Weimar 1805
hft. 1-6. Q.

Kraus, Gustav
Festzug zur feyer der jubel-ehe I.I.M.M. des königs Ludwig und der königin Therese beym october-feste zu München am 4. october 1835. München, I. C. Hochwind 1836
24 col.pl. F.
Lipperheide 2569

[König Otto I und die K. Bayerischen truppen in Griechland im jahr 1833. No place 1833?]
6pl. F.
Colas 1663

Königlich bayerisches linien und bürger militair, nach der neuesten ordonnanz vom 1825. München, Hochwind 1832
9 col.pl. ob.O.
Colas 1662

Krause, Gregor, and With, Karl
Bali: volk, land, tänze, feste, tempel; 3. aufl. München, G. Müller 1926
x,50,272p. illus. Q.

Krause, Johann Heinrich
Angeiologie; die gefässe der alten völker insbesondere der Griechen und Römer aus den schrift- und bildwerken des alterthums in philologischer, archäologischer und technischer beziehung dargestellt. Halle, G. Schwetschke 1854
xvi,488p. 6pl.(with 164 illus.) O.
Lipperheide 120

Plotina, oder Die kostüme des haupthaares bei den völkern der alten welt mit berücksichtigung einiger kostüme neuerer völker in kosmetischer, ästhetischer und artistischer beziehung dargestellt. Leipzig, Verlag der Dyk'schen buchhandlung 1858
xvi,270p. 5pl.(with 210 illus.) O.
A discussion of styles of dressing the hair among the ancient Greeks, Romans, Egyptians, Assyrians, Israelites, Phoenicians and Etruscans
Colas 1664. Lipperheide 1706

Die **krawatte.** Edel, Edmund

Krazeisen, Karl
Bildnisse ausgezeichneter Griechen und Philhellenen, nebst einigen ansichten und trachten. München, Linauer 1828-31
14p. 28pl. F.
Text in German and French. French title: *Portraits des Grecs et des Philhellènes les plus célèbres.* Plates show portraits of leaders in the Greek war of independence
Lipperheide 1447

Kreil, Marie
Taschenbuch zum eintragen der masse für damen-kleider; mit einer auswahl von übungsmassen, nach den verschiedenen körper-verhältnissen zusammengestellt. München, T. Ackermann 1884
85p. 2 illus. O.
Lipperheide 3829

Kreling, August von
(ed.) Dürer, Albrecht. Dürer album

Kretschmer, Albert
Deutsche volkstrachten; 2. verm. aufl. Leipzig, J. G. Bach 1887-90
166p. 90 col.pl. Q.
Text in German and French. French title: *Costumes du peuple en Allemagne*
First edition (Leipzig, J. G. Bach 1870) contains 80 unnumbered plates and 8 numbered. The second edition adds 10 plates on the costumes of Alsace, Lorraine, Schleswig-Holstein and East Prussia, but does not include the eight supplementary plates found in the first edition. Plate numbers do not correspond for the two editions
An extract from the first edition has title: *Album deutscher volkstrachten* (Leipzig, J. G. Bach 1870. 19 l. 20 col.pl.)
Colas 1669-1671. Cost. ind. Lipp. 740-742

(illus.) Kohl, J. G. Die völker Europas

(illus.) Reinsberg-Düringsfeld, Ida, freifrau von, and Reinsberg-Düringsfeld, Otto, freiherr von. Hochzeitsbuch

(illus.) Rohrbach, Carl. The costumes of all nations from the earliest times to the nineteenth century

(illus.) Rohrbach, Carl. Die trachten der völker vom beginn der geschichte bis zum 19. jahrhundert

Kretschmer, R.
(lithgr.) Verdy, L., freiherr von. Die königlich preussische armee

Kretzschmar, Eduard
(engr.) Menzel, A. F. E. von. Aus könig Friedrich's zeit, kriegs- und friedenshelden

Kreussler, Heinrich Gottlieb
Beschreibung der feierlichkeiten am jubelfeste der Universität Leipzig, den 4. december 1809. Nebst kurzen lebensbeschreibungen der herren professoren. Leipzig, C. A. Solbrig 1810
80,77p. 38pl.(11 col.) sq.O.
Shows academic costume at the University of Leipzig
Lipperheide 2028. LC 11-3219

Kreuzstich-muster für leinenstickerei. Teschendorff, Toni

Krickel, G., and Lange, G.
Das deutsche reichsheer in seiner neuesten bekleidung und ausrüstung. Berlin, H. Toussaint 1888-92
168p. 532 illus. 45 col.pl. Q.
Colas 1672. Lipperheide 2138

Krieg und deutsche mode. Bosselt, Rudolf

Krieger, Herbert William
American Indian costumes in the United States National museum (In Smithsonian institution. Annual report, 1928. Washington, 1929)
p623-61. 36pl. on 18 l. O. $1.75
Costume index. LC 29-28857

The collection of primitive weapons and armor of the Philippine islands in the United States National museum. Washington, Govt. print. off. 1926
128p. front.(map) 21pl. on 11 l. O. (Smithsonian institution. United States National museum. Bul. 137)
Bibliography: p113-14
LC 26-27664

Krieges-schule worinnen nach ... der alten Römer und Griechen zu wasser und land geführten. Dilich, Wilhelm

Kriegl, Georg Christoph
Erb-huldigung, welche ... Mariae Theresiae, zu Hungarn, und Böheim königin, als ertzhertzogin zu Oesterreich, von denen gesammten nider-oesterreichischen ständen ... abgeleget den 22. novembris anno 1740. Wien, J. B. Schilge [1742]
92p. 11pl. F.
Six plates are from Ludwig von Gülich's *Erbhuldigung*
Lipperheide 2629

Kriegs-manual von übung der reüterej und infanterej montier-erken- und -abrichtung der pferden. Lavater, H. C.

Kriegs-scenen. Habermann, F. w.

Kriegs unnd friedens unserer zeiten. Kolb, Ambrosius

Das **kriegs-wesen** des Heiligen Römischen Reiches. Leitner, Quirin, ritter von

Kriegsflugblätter der Liller kriegszeitung. Arnold, Karl

Kriegsscenen aus den jahren 1813 bis 1815. Beyer, Leopold

Die **kriegswaffen.** See Demmin, A. F. Encyclopédie d'armurerie avec monogrammes

Das **kriegswesen** der alten. Fickelscherer, Martin

Kriegswesen und kriegskunst der schweizerischen eidgenossen im XIV-XVI jahrhundert. Elgger, Karl von

Kriegszbuch. Fronsperger, Leonhard

Krippenstapel, Friedrich
Die preussische armee von den ältesten zeiten bis zur gegenwart. Berlin, F. Krippenstapel 1883
xvi,197p. 1 pl. Q.
Lipperheide 2187

Der **kris** der Javaner. Groneman, Isaäc

Kritische anmerckungen über die fehler der maler wider die geistliche geschichte und das kostum; aus dem französischen. Leipzig, in der Dyckischen buchhandlung 1772
440p. O.
Pages 104-124 discuss ancient Jewish costume
Lipperheide 131m

Krivenko, Vasiliĭ Silovich
Les solennités du saint couronnement. See entry under Russia. Ministerstvo Imperatorskago dvora

Die **kroenung** ihrer majestaeten des koenigs Wilhelm und der koenigin Augusta von Preussen zu Koenigsberg am 18. october 1861. Stillfried und Rattonitz, R. M. B., graf von

Die **krönung** in Mailand im jahr 1838. Lewald, August

Krönung und huldigung Oscar I. königs von Schweden und Norwegen. Silfwerskjöld, T. von

Krönungs-album. Falk, Max, and Dux, Adolf

Krönungs-album ihrer majestäten des königs Wilhelm, der konigin Augusta. Leipzig, L. Denicke [1861]
2 l. 4 illus. 7pl. F.
Lipperheide 2548

Kronbiegel, Carl Friedrich
Ueber die sitten, kleidertrachten und gebräuche der Altenburgischen bauern; 2. verb. aufl. Altenburg, C. F. Petersen 1806
x,181p. 15 col.pl. O.
Illustrated by Kronbiegel and F. Ullrich and engraved by Hoppe
First edition: 1796. Third edition edited by C. F. Hempel, has title: *Sitten, gebräuche, trachten, mundart, häusliche und landwirthschaftliche einrichtungen der Altenburgischen bauern* (Altenburg, Schnuphase 1839. 127p. 10pl.)
Colas 1673-1674. Lipperheide 824z, 825

Kronyk der koningen van Engeland. See Baker, Sir Richard. A chronicle of the kings of England

Krows, Arthur Edwin
Play production in America. New York, H. Holt 1916
x,414p. front. illus. pl. facsim. O.
Pages 195-200 discuss the technique of theatrical costuming
LC 16-23425

Krüger, F. See Lieder, Friedrich, jt. auth.

Kruger, E. G.
(engr.) Hess, C. A. H. Reitschule oder darstellung ... des campagneferdes

Kruijt, Alb. C. See Adriani, Nicolaus, jt. auth.

Kruse, Friedrich Carl Hermann
Necrolivonica, oder Geschichte und alterthümer Liv-, Esth- und Curlands; neue verb. und verm. ausg. Leipzig, Dyk 1859
v.p. fold.col.front. col.pl. F.
Beilage C has title: Analyse der kleidung, des schmucks und der bewaffnung der alten Waräger-Russen. The frontispiece shows costume of the Varangian Russians

Kuba, Ludvík
Čtení o Lužici, cesty z roků 1886-1923. V Praze, Vydavatelstvo Družstevní práce 1925
223p. illus.(incl. music) 60 col.pl. fold. map. D.
Many of the plates show costume of Lusatia
LC 32-31215

Kuchler, Balthasar
Repraesentatio der fürstlichen auffzug und ritterspil ... des ... Johann Friederichen, hertzogen zu Wurttenberg ... und ... Barbara Sophien geborne Marggravin zu Brandēburg r̄ hochzeitlich ehrnfest den 6 novemb. 1609. In Stutgarten ... gehalten worden. [Stuttgart] B. Kuchler [1611]
244pl. F.
Lipperheide 2583

Kübler, Maria Susanne
Leitfaden für die verschiedenen weiblichen arbeiten. Stuttgart, J. B. Metzler 1868
208p. 211 illus. O.
Lipperheide 4098

Kühn, Heinrich
Album moderner stick-muster ... für ornamentale stickereien; grosse ausg. Berlin, A. Seydel [1880]
8pl.(7 col.) F.
Lipperheide 4001

Kühnel, Ernest
Miniaturmalerei im islamischen Orient. Berlin, B. Cassirer 1922
68p. 5 illus. 154pl.(part col.) Q.
Abb. 1-22, Arabischer buchmalerei in Mesopotamien ... 13.-14. jahr. 23-47, Der mongolische malstil in Westturkestan und Persien 14.-15. jahr. 48-92, Persische 15.-17. jahr. 93-101 Türkische miniaturmalerei 15.-17. jahr. 102-42, Indische 16.-18. jahr. 143-54. Hindu-miniaturen aus Radjuputana um 1700-1800
Many of the paintings show costume
Published also with French title: *La miniature en Orient* (Paris, Cres)
LC 24-9849

Nordafrika; Tripolis, Tunis, Algier, Marokko, baukunst, landschaft, volksleben. Aufnahmen von Lehnert & Landrock. Berlin, E. Wasmuth [1924]
xiii,240p. illus. map. Q. (Orbis terrarum, reihe 3, bd. 1)

North Africa; Tripoli, Tunis, Algeria, Morocco, architecture, landscape, life of the people. Photographs by Lehnert & Landrock, the introduction by Ernst Kühnel. New York, Brentano [1924]
xii,240p. illus. map. F.
Printed in Germany. Legends in English, French, German, Spanish, Italian
Translation of his *Nordafrika.* Cover title: *Picturesque North Africa*
Costume index. LC A31-91 (under title)

Künste und gewerbe. Vliet, J. J. van der

Künstler-gestalten aus der blüthezeit der kunst. Schwanthaler, Ludwig

Die **künstlerische** hebung der frauentracht. Velde, Henry van de

Der **künstlerische** tanz unserer zeit. Aubel, Hermann, and Aubel, Marianne

Der **künstliche** ringer. See Petter, Nicolaes. Klare onderrichtinge der ... worstelkonst

Künstliche waffenhandlung der musqueten uñ piquen oder langen spiesen. Iselberg, Peter

Künstliche wolgerissne new figuren, von allerlei jag und weidtwerck. Amman, Jost

Künstlicher bericht und allerzierlichste beschreybung ... wie die streitbarn pferdt ... zum ernst und ritterlicher kurtzweil geschickt und volkommen zumachen. See Grisone, Federico. Ordini di cavalcare

Künstliches abprobirtes und nutzliches fecht-buch von. Heussler, Sebastian

Küp, Karl
Some early costume books. (In New York. Public library. Bulletin 40:926-32 November 1936)
Illus.

Die **kürschner** und ihre zeichen. Larisch, Paul

Das **kürschner-handwerk.** Larisch, Paul, and Schmidt, Joseph

Küsel, Matthaeus
(engr.) Churfürstlich bayrisches frewdenfest

Küsel, Melchior
(engr.) Churfürstlich bayrisches frewdenfest

Küster, Georg Gottfried
Martin Friedrich Seidels Bilder-sammlung, in welcher hundert gröstentheils in der mark Brandenburg gebohrne, allerseits aber um dieselbe wohlverdiente männer vorgestellet werden, mit beygefügter erläuterung, in welcher derselben merkwürdigste lebens-umstände und schrifften erzehlet werden. Berlin, Buchladen bey der Real-schule 1751
204p. front.(facsim.) 100 port. F.
With reproduction of title-page of 2d (1671) edition of Seidel's work: *Icones et elogia virorum aliquot praestantium qui multum studiis suis consiliisq Marchiam olim nostram iuverunt ac illustrarunt ex collectione Martini Friderici Seidel.* First edition (1670) of Seidel's work contained only 75 portraits
Lipperheide 813. LC 10-23875

[**Küstner**]
[Würtembergisches militairs.] Stuttgart, Untenrieth [1870?]
20 col.pl. F.
Colas 1679

Kuffenerovo Husitské vojsko. Kutina, B. K.

Kugler, Bernhard
Geschichte der kreuzzüge. Berlin, G. Grote 1880
444p. illus. pl. maps, facsim. O. (Oncken, Wilhelm, ed. Allgemeine geschichte in einzeldarstellungen. 2. hauptabth., 5. th.)
LC G-2476

Kuhn, Charles Louis
A catalogue of German paintings of the middle ages and renaissance in American collections. Cambridge, Mass., Harvard university press 1936
xvii,108p. LXXX pl.(incl.ports.) F. (Germanic museum studies, I)
Includes bibliographies
LC 36-5499

Kuhnow, Anna
Die frauenkleidung vom standpunkte der hygiene. Leipzig, P. Hobbing 1893
18p. O.
Colas 1675. Lipperheide 3303

Kulle, Jakob
Jakob Kulles Svenska mönster för konstväfnader och broderier. Stockholm, J. Kulle 1892
v.p. 36 col.pl. O.
Lipperheide 3978

Nordische muster-sammlung. Berlin, P. Lindhorst [1895]
5pts. 40 col.pl. O.
Lipperheide 3979

Kulmer, Friedrich von
Im reiche Kaiser Menelik's tagebuch einer abessinischen reise, bearbeitet von Emanuela baronin Mattl-Loewenkreuz. Leipzig, Klinkhardt & Biermann [1910]
236p. 35pl. 2 ports. O.
Shows costume of Abyssinia

Die **kultur** des weiblichen körpers. Schultze-Naumburg, Paul

Kultur- und sittengeschichte Berlins. See Ostwald, H. O. A. Berlin und die Berlinerin

Kulturbilder aus Hellas und Rom. Göll, Hermann

Kulturgeschichte der deutschen frau. Scherr, Johannes

Kulturgeschichte des deutschen volkes. Henne am Rhyn, Otto

Kulturgeschichtliches bilderbuch aus drei jahrhunderten. Hirth, Georg, ed.

Kulturhistorischer bilderatlas. Leipsic, A. Seemann 1883-88
3v. 220pl. ob.Q.
Contents: v 1 Altertum, bearbeitet von dr. Theodor Schreiber (2. aufl.); v2 Mittelalter, bearbeitet von dr. A. Essenwein; v3 Textbuch ... von Karl Bernhardi (388p. D.)
Lipperheide 89

Kulturno īstorījsko etnografskī atlas kraīevīne Srbīje. Lay, Felix

Kumsch, Emil
(ed.) Dresden. K. Kunstgewerbemuseum. Posamente des XVI.-XIX. jahrhunderts
(ed.) Dresden. K. Kunstgewerbemuseum. Spitzen und weiss-stickereien

Kunc, M.
Die toilette; neue populäre unterrichtsmethode für den zuschnitt der damenbekleidung. Laibach, Selbstverlag 1891
44p. 6pl. O.
Lipperheide 3845

Kungliga lifgardet till häst. Strokirch, Einar von, illus.

Die **kunst** der goldstickerei. Saint-George, Amalie von

Die **kunst** der toilette. Flittner, C. G.

Die **kunst** der weiss-stickerei. Schinnerer, Luise

Die **kunst** des mittelalters in Schwaben. Heideloff, K. A. von, ed.

Die **kunst** des schmückens. Knoll, Carl, and Reuther, Fritz

Die **kunst** in der liebe und freundschaft eine glückliche wahl zu treffen ... Aus dem französischen übersetzt von Ch. K**. Pesth, K. A. Hartleben 1816
70p. 32 col.pl. D.
Shows styles of hair dressing of the period
Lipperheide 1693

Die **Kunst** in der mode. Jahrg. 1934+ Berlin, G. Lyon
Absorbed *Wiener chic* 1933. Current 1937

Die **kunst** sich zu schminken. Schneider, Louis

Kunst- und fleiss- übende nadel-ergötzungen. Helmin, Margaretha

Kunst und handwerk in Japan. Brinckmann, Justus

Kunst und kultur von Peru. Schmidt, Max

Kunst und leben der vorzeit. Eye, August von, and Falke, Jacob von

Kunst und leben im altertum. Mužik, Hugo, and Perschinka, Franz

Kunst und lehrbüchlein. See note under Amman, Jost. Kunstbüchlin

Kunst und religion der Mayavölker. Dieseldorff, E. P.

Kunstbüchlin. Amman, Jost

Kunstdenkmäler des christlichen mittelalters in den Rheinlanden. Weerth, Ernst aus'm, ed.

Kunstgeschichte des alten Peru. Lehmann, Walter, and Doering, Heinrich

Das **kunstgewerbe** im altertum. Blümner, Hugo

Kunstgewerbliches aus der vom Mähr. gewerbemuseum im jahre 1885 veranstalteten ausstellung von waffen, kriegs- und jagdgeräthen, hrsg. . . unter August Prokop ... erläutert von Wendelin Boeheim. Brünn, W. Burkart 1886
28p. 27pl. F.
Part 2: Das kunsthandwerk ... von Carl Schirek; part 3: Die künstgewerblichen objecte ... von Wendelin Boeheim
Lipperheide 2434

Kunstgewerbliches modell- u- muster-buch. Matthias, J. C.

Die **kunstheroen** der vorzeit. Kopisch, August

Kunstliche und aigendliche bildtnussen der rhömischen keyseren. Keller, Diethelm

Des **kunstreichen** und weitberühmten Melchior Lorichs. Lorich, Melchior

Kunstreiter und gaukler. Lang, Heinrich

Kunstwerke und geräthschaften des Mittelalters und der Renaissance. Becker, C. and Hefner-Alteneck, J. H. von

Kunz, George Frederick

The magic of jewels and charms. Philadelphia & London, J. B. Lippincott 1915
xv,422p. col.front. illus. pl.(part col.) facsims. O. $8.50
Shows jewelry of all periods
Costume index. LC 15-24206

Rings for the finger, from the earliest known times to the present, with full descriptions of the origin, early making, materials, the archæology, history, for affection, for love, for engagement, for wedding, commemorative, mourning. Philadelphia & London, J. B. Lippincott 1917
xviii,381p. col.front. pl.(part col.) ports. facsims. O. $8.50
Most of the plates printed on both sides
Costume index. LC 17-7933

Kupfer zur Beschreibung aller nationen des russischen reichs. See Georgi, J. G. Beschreibung aller nationen des russischen reichs

Kupferstiche und holzschnitte aller meister in nachbildungen. Lippmann, Friedrich

Kuppelmayr, Hans

Waffen-sammlung Kuppelmayr. München, [Knorr & Hirth 1895]
1 l.(with 180 illus.) 30pl. Q.
Lipperheide 2450

Kuppenheimer, The House of. See The House of Kuppenheimer

Kurck, Arvid. See Wallgren, O. Skänska folk drägter

Kurth, Julius

Suzuki Harunobu; 2. ed. rev. München, R. Piper 1923
121p. front. 54pl. Q.
Shows Japanese costume of the 18th century

Kurth, Willi

(ed.) Dürer, Albrecht. The complete woodcuts of Albrecht Dürer

Kurtz begriffene anzeigung, vom leben und wesen der könige zu Danemarck, Sueden, Nordwagen etc. Beuther von Carlstatt, Michael

Kurtze jedoch deutliche beschreibung handlend vom fechten auf den stosz und hieb ... auffgesetzet. Pascha, J. G.

Kurtze jedoch gründliche beschreibung des voltiger. Pascha, J. G.

Kurtze und eygentliche beschreibung dess jenigen so bey der verlöbnus, heimführ- und vermählung ... Caroli, pfaltzgrafens bey Rhein ... mit ... Wilhelmina Ernestina ... erb-princessin zu Dennemarck ... vorgangen. Heidelberg, A. Lüls 1672
v.p. 8pl. F.
Illustrated by J. G. Wagner and engraved by P. Kilian
Lipperheide 2559

Kurtze und gründliche histori ... der Gottgeweyhten orden aller claster-jungfrauen. Schoonebeek, Adriaan

Kurtze und gründliche histori vom ursprung der geistlichen orden. See note under Schoonebeek, Adriaan. Nette afbeeldingen

Kurze beschreibung des königlich hannoverschen Guelphen-ordens. Schaedtler, Heinrich

Kurze geschichte des ehemaligen klosters Heilsbronn. Klingsohr, C. F.

Kurze zusammenstellung über die französische armee; 2. aufl. Berlin, E. S. Mittler 1914
34,29p. illus.(part col.) fold.map. S.

Kurze zusammenstellung über die polnische armee. Urban, K., pseud.

Kurzgefassete geschichte aller königlichen preussischen regimenter. Seyfart, J. F., sohn

Kurzgefaste geschichte der königlich preussischen armée, nebst vorstellung der uniform eines jeden regiments. Berlin 1786
13 l. 116 col.pl. O.
Manuscript. Shows Prussian uniforms in seven divisions: infantry, grenadiers, garrisons, cuirassiers, dragoons, hussars, other special regiments. Uniforms of the grenadiers, not found in earlier works, have especial value
Lipperheide 2150

Kurzinger, J.
(illus.) Fries, and Nachtmann. Quadrilles parées et costumées exécutées à la cour de sa majesté le roi de Bavière le 3 février 1835

Kutchin Indians. See Indians of North America—Kutchin Indians

Kutina, Baltazar Kaspar
Kuffenerovo Husitské vojsko. [Prague, Husnik & Häusler 1900?]
8 col.pl. ob.O. (Umélecké snahy. Svazek 10)
Shows Hussites in armor

Kutrzeba, Tadeusz. See Poland. General staff. Mars. Siły zbrojne niemiec

Kuyper, Jacques
Afbeeldingen van de kleedingen, zeden, en gewoonten in Holland. See entry under Masskamp, Evert
(illus.) Costumes populaires et villageois de la Hollande
(illus.) Stuart, Martinus. De mensch, zoo als hij voorkomt op den bekenden aardbol

Kwakiutl Indians. See Indians of North America—Kwakiutl Indians

Kyd, pseud. See Clarke, J. Clayton

Den **kyrkliga** konsten under Sveriges medeltid. Hildebrand, H. O. H.

Kyshe, James William Norton-. See Norton-Kyshe, J. W.

L

L*.** See Paris et ses modes

L., Ch.
(illus.) Garde Royale

L., M. R. See Nouveau manuel complet des gardes nationaux de France

Laban, Rudolf von
Die welt des tänzers. Stuttgart, W. Seifert 1920
3,262p. col.front. pl. O.
Third edition (1926)
Bibliography: p260-62
LC 22-23346

Labarte, Jules
Histoire des arts industriels au moyen âge et à l'époque de la renaissance. Paris, A. Morel 1864-66
4v. illus. O. and Album (2v.) of CXLVIII pl.(part col.) F.
The two volumes of plates reproduce paintings and other works of art. Especially useful for costume are the plates of paintings (nos77-98) which reproduce miniatures from French, Byzantine, Greek, and German manuscripts showing European costume from ancient Greek times to the sixteenth century. Plates are accompanied by leaves with descriptive letterpress
Contents: v 1 Sculpture, Orfévrerie; v2 Orfévrerie; v3 Peinture, Émaillerie; v4 Émaillerie, Mosaïque, Peinture en matières textiles, Damasquinerie, Art céramique, Verrerie, Art de l'armurier, Horlogerie, Mobilier civil et religieux
Colas 1683-4. Lipp. 4224. LC 12-3218

La Bédollière, Émile Gigault de
Histoire de la mode en France ... éd. autorisée pour la Belgique et l'étranger, interdite pour la France. Paris, Michel-Lévy 1858
188p S. (Collection Hetzel)
Published also Leipzig, A. Dürr and Bruxelles, Méline Cars et cie, same date
Colas 1685
Les industriels, métiers et professions en France; avec cent dessins par Henry Monnier. Paris, Vve L. Janet 1842
231p. illus. 30pl. O.

La Berge, Albert Marchais de
Notice sur les costumes du directoire (In Guillaumot, A. E. Costumes du directoire, tirés des Merveilleuses. p 1-12)

See also Renard, Jules. Costumes du XVIIIe siècle

Laborde, Alexandre de, comte
Versailles ancien et moderne. Paris, A. Éverat 1839
516p. 560 illus. 15pl. O.
Lipperheide 1083

Labrador. See Indians of North America—Labrador

The **Labrador** Eskimo. Hawkes, E. W.

La Branchardière, Mlle Éléonore Riego de. See Riego de la Branchardière, Mlle Éléonore

Labrousse
(engr.) Grasset de Saint-Sauveur, Jacques. L'antique Rome
(engr.) Grasset de Saint Sauveur, Jacques. Costumes des représentans du peuple
(illus.) Grasset de Saint-Sauveur, Jasques. Les fastes du peuples français
(engr.) Grasset de Saint Sauveur, Jasques. Recueil complet

Labruzzi, Carlo
Figure originali; dedicate a ... Generale Heruey. No place, ca 1800
13pl. O.
The etchings show groups of Italians
Colas 1686. Lipperheide 1257

Lacassagne, Alexandre
La signification des tatouages chez les peuples primitifs et dans les civilisations mediterranéenes. Lyon, A. Rey 1912
28p. illus. O.
From the *Archives d'anthropologie criminelle, de médicine légale et de psychologie normale et pathologique,* nos.226-27, oct.-nov. 1912
Les tatouages; étude anthropologique et médico-légale. Paris, J. B. Baillière 1881
115p. 15pl. O.

Lacauchie, Alexandre

Costumes de femmes. Paris, Jacomme [1853-54]
117 col.pl. Q.
Plates were probably published for advertising. They have no descriptive legends but bear the names of various dealers e.g. Lewis & Allenby, London; George Hooper Carroz & Tabourier, Paris, etc.
Colas 1690

Costumes historiques. Paris, Martinet 1846?
8 col.pl. F.
Binder's title. Six plates signed, A. Lacauchie; two signed H. Lalaisse

Galerie de costumes. Paris, Martinet [1851]
7 col.pl. Q.
Title appears on each plate and each is signed A. L. Contents: Jeune femme russe; Vivandière Louis XVI; Bouquetière; Algérienne; Camargo; Costume Louis XV; Dame de la cour de Louis XV
Colas 1688

Galerie des artistes dramatiques de Paris. Portraits en pied dessinés par Lacauchie, et accompagnés d'autant de portraits littéraires. Paris, Marchant 1841-42
3v. pl. O.

Les nations; album de costumes de tous les pays. Paris, Hautecoeur frères, Lith. de Godard [1853]
1 l. 24 col.pl. F.
Each plate has an example of masculine and feminine costume
Colas 1689. Lipperheide 67

(illus.) Bals masqués de Paris

(illus.) Galerie dramatique, costumes de théâtre

See also Lejeune, Eugène, jt. auth.

Lace

Alte spitzen. 1886

Aubé, Mme Antonine. Traité complet du filet et du filet-guipure. 1876

Aubry, Félix. Rapport sur les dentelles, les blondes, les tulles et les broderies, fait à la commission française du jury international de l'exposition universelle de Londres. 1854

Bayard, Émile. L'art de reconnaître les dentelles, guipures, etc. 1914

Besselièvre, de. Collection Besselièvre, spitzen & stickereien. 192-?

Blum, C. M. Old world lace; or, A guide for the lace lover. 1920

Bock, Franz. Beschreibender katalog einer sammlung von spitzen und kanten, darstellend den geschichtlichen entwickelungsgang der gesammten spitzen-industrie vom XVI. bis zum XIX. jahrhundert, nebst kurzem abriss der geschichte der fabrikation der "passements, dentelles et guipures." 1874

Boehn, Max von. Das beiwerk der mode. 1928

Boehn, Max von. Modes & manners: ornaments; lace, fans, gloves, walking-sticks, parasols, jewelry and trinkets. 1929

Caplin, J. F. The lace book. 1932

Champeaux, Alfred de. Dessins et modèles; les arts du tissu: Étoffes-tapisseries—broderies—dentelles, reliures. 1892

Claesen, Joseph. Alte kunstvolle spitzen. 1884

Clifford, C. R. The lace dictionary. c1913

Cole, A. S. Ancient needlepoint and pillow lace. 1875

Cole, A. S. Les dentelles anciennes. 1878

Cole, A. S. Hand-made laces from the South Kensington museum. 1890

Collection de dentelles antiques. 1874

Douglas, Mrs Fanny. The imperial macramé lace-book. ca1875

Dresden. K. Kunstgewerbemuseum. Posamente des XVI.-XIX. jahrhunderts. 1892

Dresden. K. Kunstgewerbemuseum. Spitzen und weiss-stickereien des XVI.-XVIII. jahrhunderts. 1889

Filet- und haeckel-spitzen-muster für kirchliche zwecke. 1867

Finck, Emil. Barbara Uttmann, die begründoun der spitzenindustrie im Erzgebirge. 1886

Flemming, E. R. Textile künste, weberei, stickerei, spitze, geschichte, technik, stilentwickelung. 1923

Foillet, Jacques. Das musterbuch. 1891

Geneva. Musée d'art et d'histoire. Section des arts décoratifs. Collection de dentelles anciennes. 190-?

Hailstone, S. H. L. Designs for lace making. 1870

Head, Mrs R. E. The lace & embroidery collector. 1922

Helbing, K. Spitzen-album. 1877-80

Henneberg, Alfred, freiherr von. The art & craft of old lace. 1931

Ilg, Albert. Geschichte und terminologie der alten spitzen. 1876

Ilg, Albert. Spitzen-album. 1876

Jackson, Emily. A history of hand-made lace. 1900

Jamnig, C., and Richter, A. Die technik der geklöppelten spitze; original-entwürfe und ausführingen. 1886

Lefébure, Ernest. Broderie et dentelles. 1904?

Lefébure, Ernest. Embroidery and lace. 1888

Lowes, Mrs E. L. Chats on old lace and needlework. 1908

Lyons. Musée historique des tissus. La collection de dentelles au Musée des tissus de Lyon. 1910

Maidment, Margaret. A manual of hand-made bobbin lace work. 1931

Mincoff-Marriage, Mrs Elizabeth, and Marriage, Mrs M. S. Pillow lace. 1907

Moore, Mrs H. H. The lace book. 1904

Morris, Frances, and Hague, Marian. Antique laces of American collectors. 1920-26

Müntz, Eugène. Tapisseries, broderies et dentelles; recueil de modèles anciens et modernes. 1890

Overloop, Eugéne van. Dentelles anciennes de la collection Alfred Lescure; Bruxelles, Malines, Valenciennes, Binche. 1914

Lace—*Continued*

Overloop, Eugène van. Dentelles anciennes des Musées royaux des arts décoratifs et industriels à Bruxelles. 1912

Palliser, Mrs F. M. A descriptive catalogue of the lace in the South Kensington museum. 1881

Palliser, Mrs F. M. History of lace. 1902

Paris. Musée des arts décoratifs. Les dentelles anciennes. 1907?

Pollen, Mrs. M. M. La P. Seven centuries of lace. 1908

The queen lace book: a historical and descriptive account of the hand-made antique laces of all countries. Part I: Mediaeval lacework and point lace. 1874

Sharp, A. M. Point and pillow lace. 1899

Strassen, Melchior zur. Spitzen des 16. bis 19. jahrhunderts aus den sammlungen des Kunstgewerbe- museums zu Leipzig. 1894

Tebbs, L. A. The art of bobbin lace. 1907

Treadwin, Mrs. Antique point and Honiton lace, containing plain and explicit instructions for making, transferring, and cleaning laces of every description. ca1875

Victoria and Albert museum, South Kensington. Guide to the collection of lace. 1930

Vienna. Österreichisches museum für kunst und industrie. Die Wiener spitzenausstellung 1906. 1906

Bibliography

Edinburgh. Royal Scottish museum. Library. List of books, &c. in the library of the Museum; part 2 Lace & needlework. 1892

16th century

Cocheris, H. F. J. M. Patrons de broderie et de lingerie du XVIe siècle, reproduits. 1872

Livres à dentelles & dessins d'ornements. 1882-87

Parasole, E. C. Teatro delle nobili et virtuose donne. 1891

Parasole, I. C. Studio delle virtuose dame; Roma, Antonio Facchetti, 1597. 1884

Sera, Domenico da. Le livre de lingerie. 1883-87

Vecellio, Cesare. Corona delle nobili et virtuose donne. 1876

Vecellio, Cesare. Corona delle nobili, et virtuose donne, libro quinto. 1891

17th-18th centuries

Hoffmann, Wilhelm. Spitzen-musterbuch. 1876

Lescure, Alfred. Collection A. Lescure: Barbes du dix-huitième siècle. 1919?

19th century

Lescure, Alfred. Collection A. Lescure. Gestickte kragen; mitte des XIXe jahrhunderts. 1910

Lipperheide, Frieda. Das spitzenklöppeln. 1898

Modèles nouveaux de crochet et filet, broderies en soie, broderies anglaises, plumetis, soutache, laine, etc. ca1850?

Myra and son. Myra's Crochet edgings; first series, containing the illustrations and descriptions of ... original designs of laces and borders. 1889

Rasmussen, Sara. Klöppelbuch; eine anleitung zum selbstunterricht im spitzenklöppeln. 1884

Traité de la dentelle irlandaise et des jours à l'aiguille (point d'Alençon.) ca1870

Vorlagen für handarbeiten von häkelspitzen und mignardisen. ca1880

20th century

Prévot, Gabriel. Stores dentelles & broderies dans le style moderne. 1901

Prévot, Gabriel, and Devresse, G. Dentelles et broderies d'art, stores & brisebise. 1905

BY COUNTRY AND KIND

Alençon

See Lace—France

Arabia

See Lace—Macramé

Austria

Haberlandt, Michael. Textile volkskunst aus Österreich. 1912

Burano

See Lace—Venice

Dalmatia

Bruck-Auffenberg, Frau Natalie. Dalmatien und seine volkskunst. 1911

France

Chaleyé, Joannes. Dentelles du Puy. 1910?

Despierres, Mme G. B. Histoire du point d'Alençon, depuis son origine jusqu'à nos jours. 1886

Drouet, P. L. M. Causerie sur les dentelles de Normandie au debut du XXe siècle. 1913

Laprade, Mme Laurence de. Le poinct de France et les centres dentelliers au XVIIe et au XVIIIe siècles. 1905

Lefébure, Ernest. Les points de France. 1912

Malotet, A. La dentelle à Valenciennes. 1927

Overloop, Eugène van. Dentelles anciennes de la collection Alfred Lescure; Bruxelles, Malines, Valenciennes, Binche. 1914

Paris. Musée Galliera. Dentelles, guipures, broderies ajourées. 1904

Renouf, Maurice. Oeuvre dentellière française; le point d'Alençon. 1913

Germany

Gebser, Clara. Leitfaden zum selbstunterricht im spitzenklöppeln nebst praktischen winken für erfahrenere klöppelerinnen. 1892

Lace—*Continued*

Irish

Cole, A. S. Dentelles d'Irlande. 1915?
Lindsey, Ben, and Biddle, C. H. Irish lace, a history of the industry. 1883
Riego de la Branchardière, Mlle Éléonore. The Irish lace instructor: containing original designs for Spanish point crochet, lace tatting, and modern point lace. 1886

Italy

Ricci, Signora Elisa. Antiche trine italiane ... Trine a fuselli. 1911
Ricci, Signora Elisa. Old Italian lace. 1913

Macramé

Travail arabe, dit macramé. ca1880

Russia

La dentelle russe, histoire, technique, statistique. 1895
Stasov", V. V. Russkiĭ narodnyĭ ornament"; vypusk" nervyĭ, shīt'e, tkanī, kruzheva ... S" ob"îâsnītel'nym" tekstom". L'ornement national russe; première livraison: Broderies, tissus, dentelles. 1872

Spain

Williams, Leonard. The arts and crafts of older Spain. 1907

United States

Morris, Frances. Notes on laces of the American colonists. 1926
Vanderpoel, Mrs E. N. American lace & lace-makers. 1924

Valenciennes

See Lace—France

Venetian

See Lace—Venice

Venice

Camerino, J. G. Collection J. G. Camerino, Paris: Les points de Venise. 1907
Cérésole, Victor. Origines de la dentelle de Venise et l'école du point de Burano en 1878. 1878
Franco, Giacomo. Nuova inventione; de diverse mostre cosi di punto in aere come de retticelli hoggi di usate per tutte le parte del mondo. Con merletti, mostrette da colari, e da maneghetі et merli per cantoni de fazoletti. 1596
Lucretia, Romana, pseud. Ornamento nobile, per ogni gentil matrona, dove si contiene bavari, frisi, d'infinita bellezza. 1876
Pagani, Mattio. Lhonesto essempio del vertuoso desiderio che hanno le donne di nobil ingegno, circa lo imparare i punti tagliati a fogliami. 1878
Parasole, I. C. Pretiosa gemma delle virtuose donne. 1879
Sera, Domenico da. Opera nova ... dove si insegna a tutte le nobili & leggiadre giovanette di lavorare di ogni sorte di puti, cusire, recamare. 1879
Urbani de Gheltof, G. M. Trattato storico tecnico della fabbricazione dei merletti veneziani (Venezia-Burano). 1878
Vavassore, G. A. Opera nova universal intitulato corona di racammi. 1879
Venetianische musterblätter. 1879

The **lace** & embroidery collector. Head, Mrs R. E.

The **lace** book. Caplin, J. F.

The **lace** book. Moore, Mrs H. H.

Lace dictionary. Clifford, C. R.

Lachaise

Costumes de l'Empire Turc, avec des notes explicatives; vues de Constantinople, des Dardanelles et de Smyrne, prises en 1817, 1818, 1819, 1820. Paris, Pelicier 1821
61 l. 61pl.(57 col.) Q. 30 fr.
The colored plates show costumes. They are lithographs after C. Fauconnier, Lachaise and P. Lecomte
Colas 1694. Lipperheide 1433

La Chanonie, Louis Chappot de

Le costume à l'armée de Condé. Vannes, Lafolye 1892
15p. O.
From *La revue de Bretagne, de Vendée et d'Anjou*
Colas 1696

Le costume dans les armées royalistes. Compiègne, H. Lefebure 1891
11p. O.
From *La revue de Bretagne, de Vendée et d'Anjou*
Colas 1695

La Chapelle, George de

Recueil de divers portraits de principales dames de la Porte du grand Turc tirée au naturel sur les lieux. Paris, A. Estienne 1648
12 l. 12pl. F.
Engraving of the plates has been attributed to Nicolas Cochin de Troyes
Colas 1697

La Chavanne, C. de.

Royaume de Naples. See entry under Audot, L. E. L'Italie. v2

Lacombe, Fr.

Encyclopédie méthodique; dictionnaire de toutes les espèces de chasses. Paris, H. Agasse [1795-1811]
456p. 33pl. Q.
Lipperheide 3029

Lacombe, Paul

Arms and armour in antiquity and the middle ages: also a descriptive notice of modern weapons. Tr. from the French ... with a preface, notes, and one additional chapter on arms and armour in England by Charles Boutell. New York, D. Appleton 1870
xvi,296p. front. illus. plates. D. [Illustrated library of wonders]
Also published (New York, Scribner 1871)
LC 13-15429, 10-25788 (1871 ed.)

Les armes et les armures; 3. éd. illus. de 60 vignettes sur bois, par H. Catenacci Paris, Hachette 1877
302p. 1 l. incl. illus. plates. D. (Bibliothèque des merveilles)
LC 26-22856

Lacoste, Émile Antoine Henri de Bouillane de. See Bouillane de Lacoste, É. A. H. de

Lacoste, Eugène
Costumes du directoire, tirés des Merveilleuses. See entry under Guillaumot, A. E.

Lacouloumère, Georges, jt. auth. See Baudouin, Marcel Édouard

Lacour-Gayet, Georges
Napoléon; sa vie, son œuvre, son temps. [Paris] Hachette [c1921]
587p. incl.illus. (maps) pl. ports. col.pl. col.ports. Q.
LC 21-13007

Lacretelle, Charles
Voyage pittoresque de Constantinople et des rives du Bosphore. See entry under Melling, A. I., illus.

Lacroix, A. See Lorentz, Mme E., jt. auth.

Lacroix, Désiré. See Geoffroy, J. Les bataillons scolaires

Lacroix, Frédéric. See Henricy, Casimir, jt. auth.

Lacroix, Paul
Les arts au moyen âge et à l'époque de la renaissance; 6. éd. Paris, Firmin Didot 1877
576p. 437 illus. 20 col.pl. Q.
Illustrated by F. Kellerhoven. First edition: 1868. Based on part of *Le moyen âge* by Lacroix and Seré
Lipperheide 328. LC 26-18677 (5th ed.)

The arts in the middle ages and at the period of the renaissance; tr. by James Dafforne. New York, D. Appleton 1870
xix,520p. front. pl.(19 col.) Q. $12, o.p.
Also published (London, Chapman & Hall 1870 and 1875) and (London, Bickers 1870) with same pagination
Translation of his *Les arts au moyen âge et à l'époque de la renaissance*
Costume index. LC 11-33895 (Eng. ed.)

Costumes historiques de la France. Paris, Administration de librairie [1852]
10v. 646pl.(part col.) O.
"D'après les monuments les plus authentiques, statues, bas reliefs, tombeaux, sceaux, monnaies, peintures à fresque, tableaux, vitraux, miniatures, dessins, estampes, &., &. avec un texte descriptif par le Bibliophile Jacob (Paul Lacroix)." Subtitle
Originally published in four volumes with title: *Costumes français depuis Clovis jusqu'à nos jours.* The author's *Histoire de la vie privée des Français* was published as an introduction, and his *Recueil curieux de pièces originales rares ou inédits* as an appendix to the work
Colas 1702. Costume index. Lipperheide 1087. LC 11-11951

Directoire, consulat et empire. Mœurs et usages, lettres, sciences et arts. France. 1795-1815. Ouvrage illustré ... d'après Ingres, Gros, Prud'hon ... etc. Paris, Firmin-Didot 1884
564p. front. illus. pl.(part col.) port. facsim. Q.
Reprinted 1885
Costume index. LC 2-29442

XVIIIme siècle; institutions, usages et costumes, France 1700-1789; ouvrage illustré ... d'après Watteau, Vanloo ... etc.; 2. éd. Paris, Firmin-Didot 1875
520p. col.front. illus. 52pl.(20 col.) Q.
First edition: 1874
Colas 1705 (1. ed.) Lipperheide 1145. LC 26-21685

XVIIIme siècle; lettres, sciences et arts, France 1700-1789; ouvrage illustré ... d'après Watteau, Vanloo, Largrillière ... [etc] Paris, Firmin-Didot 1878
xiii,560p. illus. 36pl.(16 col.) Q.
Lipperheide 1146. LC 4-20539

XVIIme siècle; institutions, usages et costumes, France 1590-1700. Paris, Firmin-Didot 1880
xiii,580p. col.front. illus. 36pl.(16 col., 1 double) F.
Colas 1704. Costume index. Lipperheide 1118. LC 26-21683

XVIIme siècle; lettres, sciences et arts, France 1590-1700. Paris, Firmin-Didot 1882
581p. illus. 33pl.(17 col.) Q.
Lipperheide 1119

The XVIIIth century; its institutions, customs, and costumes. France, 1700-1789, illus. ... after Watteau, Vanloo, Rigaud [etc.] London, Chapman and Hall 1876
xvi,489p. col.front. illus. 51pl.(20 col.) Q. 42s, o.p.
Translation of his *XVIIIme siècle; institutions, usages et costumes, France, 1700-1789*
Costume index. LC 4-23408

Histoire de la vie privée des Français depuis les temps les plus reculés jusqu'à nos jours, comprenant l'histoire des mœurs, usages et coutumes de la nation française. Paris, Administration de librairie, rue de Vaugirard, 82 [Imp. Lacour et comp. 1852]
441p. 6pl. port. O.
"Pour servir d'introduction aux *Costumes historiques de la France,* par le Bibliophile Jacob (Paul Lacroix)." Subtitle
Listed by Colas as [volume 9] of the author's *Costume historiques*
Colas 1702. Lipperheide 1087. LC 11-11952

History of prostitution among all the peoples of the world, from the most remote antiquity to the present day; trans. from the original French by Samuel Putnam. Chicago, Pub. for subscribers only, by P. Covici 1926
3v. fronts. O.
Contents: v 1 Antiquity, Greece and Rome; v2 Antiquity, Rome and Christian era; v3 Christian era
Chapter 73 (v2 p 1197-1224) is almost wholly concerned with fashion and dress, especially the erotic influences, to about the end of the sixteenth century
LC 27-5430

Iconographie Molièresque. 2. éd. rev. cor. et considérablement augm. Paris, A. Fontaine 1876
xliii,392p. front.(port.) fold.facsim. O.
A list of lithographs which illustrate the life and works of Molière. The following sections have costume interest: Costumes de Molière dans les rôles qu'il a joués p81-91; Portraits des comédiens et des comédiennes de la troupe de Molière p146-75; Estampes relatives à divers ouvrages de Molière p176-86; Suites de figures pour les oeuvres de Molière p264-82; Costumes et portraits des artistes ... dans les rôles des comédies de Molière p305-15
LC 19-968

Lacroix, Paul—*Continued*

Manners, customs, and dress during the middle ages and during the renaissance period. London, Chapman and Hall 1874

xviii,554p. 22pl.(15 col.) Q.

Translation of his *Moeurs, usages et costumes au moyen âge et à l'époque de la renaissance*

Costume index. LC 11-33897

Military and religious life in the middle ages and at the period of the renaissance. London, Chapman and Hall 1874

xx,504p. illus. pl.(14 col. incl.front.) Q. 31s 6d, o.p.

Translation of his *Vie militaire*

Contents: Feudalism; Wars and armies; Naval matters; The crusades; Chivalry; Military orders; Liturgy and ceremonies; The popes; The secular clergy; The religious orders; Charitable institutions; Pilgrimages; Heresies; The inquisition; Burials and funeral ceremonies

Costume index. LC 11-33896

Moeurs, usages et costumes au moyen âge et à l'époque de la renaissance; 6. éd. Paris, Firmin Didot 1878

603p. 437 illus. 15 col.pl. Q.

Illustrated by F. Kellerhoven. First edition: 1871. Based on part of *Le moyen âge* by Lacroix and Seré

Colas 1703 (2d ed.) Lipperheide 329. LC 26-21684 (4th ed.)

Recueil curieux de pièces originales rares ou inédites, en prose et en vers, sur le costume et les révolutions de la mode en France. Paris, Administration de librairie, rue de Vaugirard, 82 [Imp. Lacour et comp. 1852]

2p.l. 517p. O.

"Pour servir d'appendice aux *Costumes historiques de la France*, par le Bibliophile Jacob (Paul Lacroix)." Subtitle

1. ptie.: Lois somptuaires. "Bibliographie des costumes historiques": p[499]-514

Colas 1702. Lipperheide 1087. LC 11-11953

Sciences & lettres au moyen âge et à l'époque de la renaissance ... ouvrage illustré ... par Compère, Daumont, Pralon et Werner. 2. ed. Paris, Firmin-Didot 1877

612p. 420 illus. 13pl.(12 col.) Q.

Plates are by Compère, Daumont, Pralon, and Werner. First edition: 1877. Based on part of *Le moyen âge* by Lacroix and Seré

Lipperheide 331. LC 15-3541

Vie militaire et religieuse au moyen âge et à l'époque de la renaissance, par Paul Lacroix (Bibliophile Jacob). 2. éd. Paris, Firmin Didot frères 1873

577p. incl.illus. pl.(14 col.) ports. Q.

"Ouvrage illustré de 14 chromolithographies exécutées par F. Kellerhoven, Regamey et L. Allard et de 410 figures sur bois gravées par Huyot père et fils." Subtitle

Based on part of *Le moyen âge* by Lacroix and Seré

Lipperheide 330. LC A12-1212

Lacroix, Paul, and Duchesne, Alphonse

Histoire de la chaussure depuis l'antiquité la plus reculée jusqu'à nos jours; suivie de l'histoire sérieuse et drolatique des cordonniers. Éd. enrichie de 250 gravures sur bois, et de deux atlas contenant l'armorial des cordonniers et des savetiers formant 48 planches contenant 432 [i. e. 232] blasons, par Ferdinand Seré. Paris, A. Delahays 1862

271p. col.front. illus. pl. ports. Q.

The two atlases, consisting of XXXIV and XIV plates, respectively, are bound with the text

LC F-3232

Lacroix, Paul, and Séré, Ferdinand

Le moyen âge et la renaissance, histoire et description des mœurs et usages, du commerce et de l'industrie, des sciences, des arts, des littératures et des beaux-arts en Europe. . . Dessins facsimilé par M. A. Rivaud. Paris, Administration 1848-51

5v. illus. pl.(part col.) O.

This work, with text completely revised and many illustrations added, has been republished under four separate titles: *Les arts au moyen âge, Moeurs, usages et costumes au moyen âge, Vie militaire et religieuse au moyen âge,* and *Sciences & lettres au moyen âge*

Colas 1701. Lipperheide 327. LC 11-33898

Lacroix, Paul, and others

Le livre d'or des métiers. Paris, Librairie de Seré 1850-58

5v. illus. 126pl.(18 col.) Q.

Contents: v 1 Histoire de l'orfevrerie-joaillerie, by P. Lacroix and F. Seré; v2 Histoire de la charpenterie, by P. Lacroix, E. Bégin, and F. Seré; v3 Histoire. . . des arts et professions qui se rattachent à la typographie, by P. Lacroix, E. Fournier and F. Seré; v4 Histoire des cordonniers, by P. Lacroix, A. Duchesne and F. Seré; v5 Histoire de la coiffure, de la barbe, et de cheveux postiches, by P. Lacroix, A. Duchesne, F. Seré and others

Lipperheide 1957

Lacroix-Danliard, pseud.

La plume des oiseaux. Paris, J. B. Baillière 1891

368p. 94 illus. S.

Has sections on: Emploi de la plume aux usages guerriers, Usage de la plume dans les jouets, dans la parure et dans l'habillement

Lipperheide 1755

La Cuisse, de, 18th cent.

Le répertoire des bals, ou Theorie-pratique des contredanses. Paris, Cailleau 1762-65

4v. front.(v.2) fold.pl. diagrs. D.

Volumes 2-3 have title: *Suite du Répertoire des bals.* Volume 2 has folded plate showing French costume of the 18th century

Lipperheide 3078m. LC 12-29698

Lacy, Charles de Lacy

The history of the spur. [London] The Connoisseur [1911]

81p. illus. 47 (i. e. 50) pl.(incl. front.) Q.

"A few of the illustrations and part of the text of this book appeared in ... *Country life* in 1904"

LC 12-29351

Lacy, Thomas Hailes

(ed.) Female costumes, historical, national and dramatic in 200 plates collected and edited by T. H. Lacy. London and New York, S. French 1865

4p. 203 col.pl. Q. 204s, o.p.

Published in 34 parts of 6 plates each

Colas 1707. Costume index

Lacy, Thomas H.—*Continued*
(ed.) Male costumes, historical, national and dramatic, in 200 plates collected and edited by T. H. Lacy. London and New York, S. French 1868
200 col.pl. Q.
Colas 1708

Ladies cabinet of fashion, music and romance; edited by Margaret and Beatrice de Courcy. v 1-14, 1832-38; new ser. v 1-10, 1839-43; [ser.3] v 1-17, 1844-52; [ser.4] v 1-37, 1852-70. London, G. Henderson 1832-70
[78]v. illus. pl.(part col.) O.
Volumes for 1852-70 are identical in content with three other magazines of the time: *New monthly Belle assemblée, Ladies' companion, and Illustrated London magazine*
Colas 1709. Lipperheide 4616

Ladies' companion. See Ladies cabinet of fashion, music and romance

Ladies' cutting made easy. Holding, T. H.

Ladies' dress shoes, of the nineteenth century. Greig, T. W.

Ladies' home companion. See Woman's home companion

Ladies home journal. v 1+ Dec. 1883+ Philadelphia, Curtis pub. co.
Col.illus. F.
Lipperheide 4776

Ladies' home magazine of New York. v. 1, no. 1-5; Nov. 1904-Apr. 1905. New York [Ladies' home magazine company]
[73]p. illus. F.
Published monthly. Unpaged. Continued as the *American family journal*
LC 10-21450

The **ladies** magazine. See Godey's magazine

The **Ladies** magazine and literary gazette. See The American ladies' magazine

Ladies monthly magazine. See Monde élégant

Ladies' monthly museum. See Ladies' museum

Ladies' museum. v 1-16, 1798-1806; new ser. v 1-16, 1806-14; improved ser. (ser.3) v 1-28, 1815-28; [ser.4] v 1-4, 1829-30; new ser.(ser.5) v 1-3, 1831-32. London, J. Robins 1798-1832
[67]v. col.illus. Q.
Title varies: 1798-1814, *Lady's monthly museum;* 1815-28 *Ladies' monthly museum.* Merged into *Lady's magazine,* later *Lady's magazine and museum of the belles-lettres*
Colas 1714-18. Lipperheide 4586

Ladies' national magazine. See Peterson's magazine

Ladies' old-fashioned shoes. Greig, T. W.

Ladies pocket magazine. 1824-1840. London, Robin
Col.illus. O.
Published annually. Contains fashion illustrations
Colas 1710. Lipperheide 4605

Ladies' tailor; a monthly journal devoted to the scientific cutting and making of ladies' fashionable garments. v 1-52; 1884-May 1936. London, Tailor and cutter, ltd.
52v. illus. pl.(part fold. part col.) F.
Published monthly. Price without semi-annual plates 19s, with plates 27s. Merged with *Women's wear* (London) May 1936

Ladurner, A. See Charlemagne, A., jt. auth.

Lady Godiva. Langdon-Davies, John

Lady Hamilton's attitudes. See Rehberg, Friedrich. Drawings faithfully copied from nature at Naples

The **lady** of Godey's. Finley, Mrs R. E.

The **Lady's** bazaar & fancy fair book. London, Ward, Lock ca1880
xi,384p. 354 illus. O.
"Containing suggestions upon the getting-up of bazaars and instructions for making articles in embroidery, cane-work, crochet, knitting, netting, tatting, rustic-work, and cone-work." Subtitle
Lipperheide 4127

The **Lady's** book. See Godey's magazine

The **lady's** crochet-book; by E. M. C. London, Hatchards 1884-86
4v. 26 illus. O.
Lipperheide 4143

The **lady's** handbook of fancy needlework. London, Ward, Lock ca1880
11,384p. 418 illus. O.
Lipperheide 4128

The **lady's** knitting-book; by E. M. C. London, Hatchards 1875-76
4v. 13 illus. O.
Lipperheide 4111

Lady's magazine and museum of the belles-lettres. v 1-50, 1770-1819; new ser. v 1-10, 1820-1829; ser.3 v 1-5, 1830-32; ser.4 v 1-11, 1832-1837. London, Page 1770-1837
Col.illus. Q.
Subtitle varies, 1770-1832. Merged into *Court magazine and monthly critic and lady's magazine and museum of the belles-lettres*
Volumes 1-50 published by Robinson, later volumes by Baldwin, Cradoch and Joy
Colas 1711-13. Lipperheide 4565

See also Ladies' museum

Lady's monthly museum. See Ladies' museum

Lady's newspaper. See The Queen, the Lady's newspaper

Lady's newspaper, the queen and court chronicle. See The Queen, the Lady's newspaper

Lady's pictorial, a newspaper for the home. v 1-51, 1881-1907. [London]
51v. illus. F.
Lipperheide 4769

Lady's world. See Peterson magazine

The **Lady's** world, a magazine of fashion and society. See note under Woman's world

Länder- und völker-schau; eine gallerie von bildern; 1. abtheilung, Deutschland, 1. lieferung. Kempten, T. Dannheimer 1847
1 l. 6 col.pl. ob.F.
"Welche die ansichten der bedeutendeste städte, die trachten der volkerstämme, scenen aus dem volkleben . . . kurz eine characteristik jedes landes darstellen." Subtitle
See also *Malerische landerschau* which may be a continuation
Colas 1753-54. Lipperheide 739

La Farge, John
The Gospel story in art. New York, Macmillan 1913
xiii,417p. front. pl. O. $5.
Preface signed: Mary Cadwalader Jones
Reissued in a cheaper edition (1926. $2.50)
A review following the narrative in the four Gospels and illustrated with eighty full page reproductions from the great masters. Helpful in costuming religious plays or pageants
LC 13-24770

La Fargue, Paul Constantin
Lyk-staetsie van ... Anna kroon princesse van Groot-Brittanien princesse douariere van Orange en Nassau ... 1759. Gravenhage, P. Gosse 1761
27p. 16pl. F.
Plates engraved by S. Fokke. French text also, with title: *Convoi funebre de son altesse royale, Anne*
Lipperheide 2676

Lafaye, Georges Louis. See Daremberg, C. V., and Saglio, Edmond, eds. Dictionnaire des antiquités grecques et romaines, d'après les textes et les monuments

Lafitau, Joseph François
Moeurs des sauvages amériquains comparées aux moeurs des premiers temps. Paris, Saugrain l'aîné 1724
2v. 42pl. Q.
An abridged edition *Moeurs, coutumes et religions des sauvages américains* was published (Lyon & Paris, Périsse frères 1839. D. 2v in 1 pl. D.)
LC 18-3920 (abr. ed.)

Lafitte, pseud. See Lamorillière, R. L. de

Lafitte, Louis
Entrée triomphale ... le duc l'Angoulême, généralissime de l'armée des Pyrénees ... gravés par Normand fils. Paris, Firmin Didot 1825
1 l. 23pl. F.
Lipperheide 2725

La Fizelière, Albert Patin de
Histoire de la crinoline au temps passé ... suivie de la satyre sur les cerceaux [et] L'indignité et l'extravagance des paniers. Paris, A. Aubry 1859
106p. O. 2 fr.
Page 33-88: de Nisard's *Satyre sur les cerceaux, paniers, criardes* ... originally published Paris, 1727; page 89-104 *L'indignité et l'extravagance des paniers pour les femmes sensées et chrétiennes* and *Petite bibliographie des stoles, basquines, vertugales et paniers,* originally published Paris 1735
Colas 1719. Lipperheide 1731

Lafond, Jean. See Ritter, Georges, jt. auth.

Lafoy, John B. M. D.
The complete coiffeur; or, An essay on the art of adorning natural, and of creating artificial, beauty. New-York, Stereotyped for the Proprietors 1817
2v. in 1. pl. D.
English and French
Part 1, English (108p.) Part 2 (98p.) is a free somewhat abridged French version with title *Essai sur l'art de parer la beauté naturelle et de créer la beauté factice*
LC 8-34024

Lafrensen, Nicolas
(illus.) Bocher, Emmanuel. Les gravures françaises du XVIIIe siècle, v 1. 1875-82

Lagarrigue
Nouvelle suite de costumes des Pyrénées par Ferogio, d'après Lagarrigue, lith. d'Auguste Bry. Paris, Gihaut frères [1841]
12 col.pl. F.
Published in two parts (livraisons) each with cover. The plates exist also in black and white. The plates have titles at head: *Hautes Pyrénées, Pyrénées espagnol, or Basses Pyrénées*
"Appears to be intended as a continuation of *Costumes des Pyrénées* by E. Pingret." British museum
Colas 1720. Lipperheide 1228

Lagerlöf, Peter
(ed.) Dahlberg, E. J. Suecia antiqua et hodierna

Lagrelius, A.
Kongl. lifrustkammaren och därmed förenade samlingar. See entry under Stockholm. Livrustkammaren

La Guérinière, François Robichon
École de cavalerie. Paris, Huart & Moreau [etc.] 1751
318,[10]p. illus. pl. F.
Editions of 1733 and 1802 are also described by Lipperheide
Lipperheide 2922-24

La Haye, Guillaume de
(engr.) Gravelot, H. F. B. Planches gravées d'après plusieurs positions dans lesquelles doivent se trouver les soldats

Lahde, Gerhard Ludvig
Kjøbenhavns kloededragter, eller Det daglige liv i hovedstaden i characteristiske figurer tegnede efter naturen. Kjöbenhavn, C. Steen ca1800
1 l. 35 col.pl. Q.
Legends in Danish and German. Includes Danish civil and military costume, street venders and others of the period
Also published with German title: *Das tagliche leben in Kopenhagen* (Kopenhagen, Gyldendal 1810)
Another Danish edition with title: *Det daglige liv i hovedstaden, i karakteristiske figurer efter naturen ... med poetiske forklaringer af professor Sander* (Kjobenhavn, G. L. Lahde 1818. 12 l. 12 col.pl. Q.)
Colas 1721, 1173. Lipperheide 1044

Lahmann, Heinrich
Die reform der kleidung; 4. verm. aufl. Stuttgart, A. Zimmern 1903
132p. 30 illus. 15pl. O.
First edition: 1887
Colas 1722. Lipperheide 3296

Lahun. Brunton, Guy

Laib, Franz
(ed.) Biblia pauperum. Biblia pauperum; nach dem original in der lyceums bibliothek zu Constanz
(ed.) Kirchenschmuck, ein archiv für weibliche handarbeit

Laincel, Alice de. See Laincel-Vento, Alix, comtesse de

[Laincel-Vento, Alix, comtesse de]
L'art de la toilette chez la femme; bréviaire de la vie élégante. Paris, E. Dentu 1885
O. 6 fr.
At head of title: Violette
Colas 3023. Lipperheide 3293

Laincel-Vento, Alix, comtesse de—*Continued*
Les grandes dames d'aujourd'hui, illustrations de Saint-Elme Gautier; nouv. ed. Paris, E. Dentu 1886
422p. 64 illus. 32pl. O.
At head of title: Claude Vento (Violette)
Lipperheide 1174

Laitem, Mrs Helen (Hollman). See Miller, F. S., jt. auth.

The **lake** dwellings of Switzerland and other parts of Europe. Keller, Ferdinand

Lake Ngami. Andersson, K. J.

Laking, Sir Guy Francis, bart.
The armoury of Windsor castle; European section. London, Bradbury, Agnew & company [1904]
xiv,283p. front. 39pl. F.
Half-title: The royal collection
LC 30-15434

A record of European armour and arms through seven centuries ... with an introduction by the Baron de Cosson. London, G. Bell 1920-22
5v. fronts.(v. 1-2) illus.(incl. ports. facsims.) ob.Q.
Volumes 2-5 edited by Francis Henry Cripps-Day
Bibliography: v5 p275-304
LC 20-13583

Lalaisse, Hippolyte
Album militar. See note under Villegas, José. Album militar

L'armée et la Garde impériale, 1860-1870. Paris, Hautecoeur [1870]
72 col.pl. Q.
Includes some plates from his: *Empire français.* The number of each plate appears at the foot and most of them are marked "lith. chez Godard"
Colas 1736

L'armée française et ses cantinières. Paris, G. Orengo ca1857
28 col.pl. F.
Plates are lithographed and colored by Sorrieu or Fortuné after Lalaisse. There are many variations in different sets. The author's *Types de l'armée française* seems to be a later printing with a new title-page
Colas 1731. Lipperheide 2324

La Bretagne, scènes de moeurs, sujets pittoresques et traits caractéristiques de cette contrée. Nantes, Charpentier ca1840
12 col.pl. F. 30fr.
Published in two parts of which Colas gives the contents
Colas 1727

Collection complète des uniformes de l'armée et de la marine françaises. Paris, Hautecoeur-Martinet [1840-48]
124 col.pl. Q.
Each plate has title: *Armée française.* The same plates with variations in color and engraving are published as his *Album des uniformes de l'armée et de la marine françaises*
Colas 1724

Costumes de tous les corps de l'armée et de la marine françaises (sous Louis-Philippe I.) Paris, Martinet 1845-52
36 col.pl. F.
Colas 1726

Costumes et coiffes de Bretagne; cent phototypies d'après les compositions de Hippolyte Lalaisse. Préface de Louis Hourticq. Paris, H. Laurens [1932?]
16p. 100pl. map. F.
In portfolio
Colas 1740. Costume index. LC AC33-528

Empire français; l'armée et la Garde impériale. Paris, Hautecoeur [1853-66]
120 col.pl. Q.
Some of the plates are from his *Uniformes de l'armée ... 1848-1852.* The first printing has no title at head of plates, the second printing has title: *Empire français.* Collections containing selections from these plates are known
Colas 1733-35

La jeune armée. Paris, Hautecoeur-Martinet [1845]
12 col.pl. F.
Colas 1725

Types de l'armée française et de ses cantinières; dessins de MM. Lalaisse, Victor Adam et Blondeau; lithographie de MM. Victor Adam [and others] préface ... par M. Henri Derville. Paris, G. Orengo 1860
32pl.(part col.) 1 l. F.
Plates include 3 half-titles and poem within ornamental border
Colas 1732. LC 18-22629

Types militaires du troupier français. Paris, E. Morier ca1870
59 col.pl. F.
Uniforms of the second empire 1857 to 1870
Colas 1737. Lipperheide 2325

Uniformes de l'armée et de la marine françaises (1848-1852). Paris, Martinet 1852?
41 col.pl. Q.
Plates have at head the title: *République française.* Published later, with title at head: *Empire français,* they form part of his work of that title listed above
Colas 1729

(illus.) Benoist, Félix. Nantes et la Loire Inférieure

(illus.) Ducamp, Jules. Histoire de l'armée d'Orient et de tous les régiments qui ont pris part aux campagnes de la Mer Noire et de la Mer Baltique

(illus.) La Normandie illustrée

See also Lacauchie, A. Costumes historiques

Lalaisse, Hippolyte, and Benoist, Félix
Gallerie armoricaine: costumes et vues pittoresques de la Bretagne. Nantes, Charpentier [1820?]
2v. 125pl.(100 col.) F.
Text signed: J. C. Le Meder
Contents: v 1 Loire-Inférieure; v2 Morbihan; v3 Ille-et-Vilaine; v4 Finistère; v5 Côtes du Nord
The colored plates are by Lalaisse, those in black and white by Benoist
Colas 1728. Lipperheide 1201. LC 15-21222

Lalaisse, Hippolyte and Ropartz, Sigismond
Scènes de la vie rurale en Bretagne; lith. par ... Lalaisse, texte par Sigismond Ropartz. Nantes & Paris, Charpentier [1840]
12pl. ob.F.
"Choix de costumes, scènes de moeurs, sujets pittoresques et traits caractéristiques ... dessinés d'après nature." Subtitle
Cataloged from Colas
Colas 1723

Lalla Roûkh. See Brühl, K. F. M. P., graf von. Lalla Rûkh

Lalla Rukh. See Theatrical costume—Special plays, ballets, etc.—Lalla Rukh

Lalla Rûkh. Brûhl, K. F. M. P., graf von

Lallemand, Charles

Lettres sur les fêtes du couronnement à Koenigsberg et Berlin, October 1861. Strasbourg, G. Silbermann 1861
28p. 1 illus. 6pl. F.
Lipperheide 2547

Les paysans badois, esquisse de mœurs et de coutumes; texte et dessins par Charles Lallemand. Strasbourg, Salomon; [etc.] 1860
4p. l. 32p. illus. 16 col.pl. map. F.
Colas 1743. Lipperheide 750. LC 15-8899

[**L'Allemand, Fritz**]

Die k. k. oesterreichische armee im laufe zweyer jahrhunderte. Wien, J. Bermann ca1846
2 l. 40 col.pl. F.
Plates designed and lithographed by L'Allemand
Colas 1742. Lipperheide 2237

La Marche, Albert Lecoy de. See Lecoy de la Marche, Albert

La Martinière, Jean Baptiste Joseph, Breton de. See Breton de la Martinière, Jean Baptiste Joseph

Lamas

Forman, Harrison. Through forbidden Tibet; an adventure into the unknown. 1935

Waddell, L. A. The Buddhism of Tibet. 1934

Lamb, Charles, supposed author. See The book of the ranks and dignities of British society

Lamb, Mrs Martha Joanna Reade (Nash)

History of the city of New York: its origin, rise, and progress. New York and Chicago, A. S. Barnes 1877-[96]
3v. illus. 43pl. 2 maps, 3 plans. Q.
Contents: v 1 The period prior to the revolution closing in 1774; v2 The century of national independence, closing in 1880; [v3] History of the city of New York; externals of modern New York. By Mrs. Burton Harrison ... chapter XXI. volume II. Volume 3 is paged continuously with v2 and has cover-title: *Externals of N. Y.* Mrs. Burton Harrison
LC 1-1942

Lambert, Miss A.

Church needlework with practical remarks on its arrangement and preparation. London, J. Murray 1844
xvi,158p. 53 illus. Q.
Lipperheide 3856

The hand-book of needlework, decorative and ornamental, including crochet, knitting and netting; 4. ed. London, J. Murray 1846
xv,494p. 128 illus. O.
First edition: 1842
Lipperheide 4074

My crochet sampler; 8th ed. London, J. Murray 1847-48
2v. 82 illus. O.
Lipperheide 4088

My knitting book. London, J. Murray 1847
2v. 2 illus. O.
Lipperheide 4087

Lambert, André

Aus dem alten Rom. Stuttgart, Hoffmann [1912]
xi p. 12 col.pl. F.
The plates show scenes of ancient Rome, with costume figures

Lambert, Pierre de La Mothe, bp. of Beirut. See La Mothe Lambert, Pierre de, bp. of Beirut

Lambranzi, Gregorio

New and curious school of theatrical dancing ... with all the original plates by J. G. Puschner; tr. from the German by Derra de Moroda, edited ... by Cyril W. Beaumont. London, Imperial society of teachers of dancing 1928
2v. in 1. front. 101pl. Q.
Translation of his *Nuova e curiosa scuola de' balli theatrali*

Nuova e curiosa scuola de' balli theatrali ... Neue und curieuse theatralische tanzschul. Nürnberg, I. I. Wolrab 1716
2v. in 1. 101pl. Q.
Preface and description of the dances in Italian, followed by same preface in German. Each plate has at head the tune for the dance represented and at foot the description in German. Illustrated by J. G. Puschner
LC 10-13626

Lamé, Émile

Le costume au theatre; la tragedie depuis 1636 avec un avant-propos par Gustave Larroumet. Paris, A. Dupret 1886
32p. O.
From *Le present,* October 15, 1857, and *Revue d'art dramatique,* October 1, 1886
Colas 1746

Lameau. See Mallet, jt. auth.

La Mésangère, Pierre de

Costumes des femmes de Hambourg, du Tyrol. See entry under Lanté, L. M.

Costumes des femmes françaises du XIIe au XVIIIe siècle. See entry under Lanté, L. M.

Costumes orientaux. See entry under Pécheux and Manzoni

Galerie française de femmes célèbres. See entry under Lanté, L. M.

(illus.) Gazette des salons; journal des dames et des modes

See also Almanach des modes (attributed)

[**Lami, Louis Eugène**]

Quadrille de Marie Stuart, 11 mars 1829. Paris, A. Fonrouge 1829
26 col.pl. F.
Colas 1747

Tribulations des gens à équipages. Paris, Delpech 1827
6 col.pl. Q.
Lipperheide 3656

Voitures. Paris, lith. de Delpech ca 1825
12pl. Q.
Most of the plates are from drawings by Lami. They show various types of vehicles, most of them with servants
Lipperheide 1157

(illus.) Janin, J. G. Un hiver à Paris

See also Vernet, Horace, jt. auth.

Lami, Louis Eugène, and Monnier, Henry
Voyage en Angleterre. London, Colnaghi; Paris, Firmin-Didot 1829
4 l. 24 col.pl. F.
Colas 1748. Lipperheide 995

Laminit, J. Georg
(engr.) Kappeller, J. A. Tiroler trachten

Lamkin, Nina B.
Inexpensive costumes for plays, festivals and pageants. National recreation association
25c

Lamorillière, Raoul L. de
Crinolines et volants [par Lafitte pseud.] Bordeaux, Les principaux libraires 1855
63p. S.

La Mothe Lambert, Pierre de, bp. of Beirut.
See Bourges, Jacques de. Wahrhaffte und eigendliche erzehlung von der reise des bischofs von Beryte

La Mottraye, Aubry de
Voyages ... en Europe, Asie & Afrique. La Haye, T. Johnson & J. Van Duren 1727
2v. 47pl. maps. F.
"Où l'on trouve une grande varieté de recherches geographiques, historiques & politiques, sur l'Italie, la Grèce, la Turquie, la Tartarie Crime'e, & Nogaye, la Circassie, la Suède, la Laponie &c." Subtitle
Nineteen of the plates show costume. They are by Hogarth, B. Picart, D. Lockley, S. Parker and R. Smith
Lipperheide 556

Lampert, Kurt
Die völker der erde; eine schilderung der lebensweise, der sitten, gebräuche, fest und zeremonien aller lebenden völker. Stuttgart, Deutsche Verlags-Anstalt [1902]
2v. illus. pl.(2 col.) Q.

Lamy, J. P.
Costumes des cantons. Basle & Berne, J. P. Lamy n.d.
15 col.pl. Q.
Colas 1751

Lanciani, Rodolfo Amedeo
(ed.) Ramsay, William. A manual of Roman antiquities

Lançon, A.
Album de l'armée française. Paris, Arnauld de Vresse [1861]
20 col.pl. F.
Plates are marked: *Armée française* at the head, and signed Lançon
Colas 1752. Lipperheide 2328

Lancret, Nicolas
(illus.) Boucher, Emmanuel. Les gravures françaises du XVIIIe sièle, v4

The **land** beyond the forest. Gerard, Emily

The **land** in the mountains. Baillie-Grohman, W. A.

The **land** of the Dons. Williams, Leonard

The **land** of the lamas. Rockhill, W. W.

The **land** of the New Guinea pygmies. Rawling, C. G.

The **land** of the pigmies. Burrows, Guy

The **land** of Uz. Bury, G. W.

Landaluze, Victor Patricio de
(illus.) Bachiller y Morales, Antonio. Coleccion de artículos

Landes- und wappenkunde der brandenburgisch-preussischen monarchie. Gritzner, Max

Das **landes-zeughaus** in Graz. Pichler, Fritz, and Meran, F. graf von

Landliche gebräuche in Wurttemberg. Pfluz

Landor, Arnold Henry Savage
Across unknown South America. Boston, Little, Brown 1913
2v. fronts. pl.(part col.) ports. 2 fold. maps. O.
Black and white plates printed on both sides. The greater part of the work is devoted to the author's explorations in Brazil. Many pictures of Indians of South America
LC 13-23372

Across widest Africa, an account of the country and people of Eastern, Central and Western Africa as seen during a twelve months' journey from Djibuti to Cape Verde. New York, C. Scribner 1907
2v. fronts. pl. ports. maps(1 fold.) O.
LC 7-37973

Tibet & Nepal, painted & described by A. Henry Savage Landor. London, A. & C. Black [1905]
233p. col.front. 74pl.(part col.) fold.map. O. 20s, o.p.
Each plate accompanied by guard sheet with descriptive letterpress
Costume index. LC 5-10437

Landreise in das innere von Afrika. Damberger, C. F., pseud.

Lands and peoples; the world in color; editor-in-chief: Holland Thompson ... with an introduction by Isaiah Bowman ... and a chapter on The friendly North by ... Vilhjalmur Stefansson. New York, Grolier society; London, Educational bk. co. [c1932]
7v. illus.(incl. maps; part col.) O. $39.50
Reprint of the 1930 edition
Excellent pictures showing costume of natives of various parts of the world
Costume index. LC 33-931

Lands of the Caribbean. Carpenter, F. G.

Landsknechte. See Military costume—Germany—16th century; Military costume—Switzerland—16th century

Die **landsknechte.** Wessely, J. E.

[**Landsknechte** mit den bannern von Schweizer cantonen] No place, ca1550
16pl. F.
Lipperheide 2047

Das **landwehr-zeughaus** in München. Braun, Kaspar

Lane, Edward William
Account of the manners and customs of the modern Egyptians, written in Egypt during the years 1833, 34, and 35. 5th ed. edited by E. S. Poole. London, John Murray 1871
2v. illus. 8pl. D. 21s, o.p.
Illustrations differ slightly from 1st edition, 1846. Many editions
German translation by J. T. Zenker: *Sitten und gebräuche der heutigen Egypter* (2. ausg. Leipzig, Dyk [1856] 64pl.)
Costume index. Lipperheide 1602 (German ed.)

Lane, Mrs Rose (Wilder)
Peaks of Shala; profusely illustrated by photographs taken on a special expedition to Albania. New York and London, Harper 1923
349p. front. pl. O.
LC 23-8539

Lane-Poole, Stanley
Cairo, sketches of its history, monuments, and social life. With numerous illustrations on wood by G. L. Seymour, Harry Fenn, J. D. Woodward and others. London, J. S. Virtue 1892
xiv,320p. incl.front. illus. plan. O.
LC 5-8276

Social life in Egypt, a description of the country and its people ... a supplement to "Picturesque Palestine." London, J. S. Virtue [1884]
vi,138p. front. illus. pl. F.
LC 11-28903

Lang, Heinrich
Kunstreiter und gaukler ... original-feder und bleistift-zeichnungen aus dem circusleben. München, A. Ackermann 1881
4p. 28pl. F. (Der circusbilder, neue folge)

Lang, J. L.
Recueil de costumes. Zürich, ca1819
20 col.pl. O.
Plates show costume of different cantons
Colas 1756?

Langdon-Davies, John
Lady Godiva: the future of nakedness. New York & London, Harper 1928
117p. mounted front. mounted pl. O.
LC 28-25946

Lange, Eduard
Costüme des Königlichen hof-theaters zu Berlin; unter der general-intendantur des herrn grafen von Redern. 1. band. Berlin, G. Crantz 1839
16p. 18 col.pl. Q.
Plates after Franz Teichel
Colas 1757. Lipperheide 3220

Das hoffest zu Ferrara in den saelen des koeniglichen schlosses zu Berlin dargestellt am 28. februar 1843; entworfen und lith. durch Wilhelm Frenzel. Berlin, C. G. Lüderitz 1846
24p. 42 col.pl. F.
Plates show fancy dress
Colas 1758. Lipperheide 2545

Die soldaten Friedrich's des Grossen ... Mit 31 original-zeichnungen von Adolph Menzel. Leipzig, H. Mendelssohn [1853]
xx,599p. 31 col.pl.(incl. front.) Q.
Originally issued in 30 parts, 1851-53
Colas 1759. Lipperheide 2179. LC 17-3976

[**Lange, Gustav**]
L'armée allemande sous l'empereur Guillaume II; ouvrage traduit et annoté par P. de Balaschoff et A. Herbillon. Paris, Haar & Steinert 1890
207p. 45 col.pl. ob.F. 90fr.
Colas 152

Uniforms-tabellen und quartier-liste der deutschen armee und der kaiserlich deutschen marine. Breslau, Der verfasser 1877
3 col.pl. F.
Lipperheide 2133

See also Krickel, G., jt. auth.

L'Ange, Jean Daniel
Deutliche und gründliche erklärung der ... fecht-kunst. Heidelberg, A. Weingarten 1664
72p. illus. Q.

Lange, Johann Georg
(illus.) Justa funebria serenissimo principi Ioanni Friderico Brunsvicensium et Luneburge

Das **lange** bestrittene königreich Candia. Merian, Mattheus

Langenmantel, David
Historie des regiments in des Heil. röm. reichs stadt Augspurg. Franckfurt & Leipzig, D. R. Mertz & J. J. Mayer 1725
286p. 23 l. 3 illus. 21pl. F.
The 1934 edition, *ausgefertiget und verm. von Jacob Brucker,* contains 23 plates
Plates contain coats of arms of Augsburg military leaders and pictures of different officials and members of various gilds
Lipperheide 767-767a

Langerack, Amory de. See Amory de Langerack

Langfors, Arthur
Deux témoignages inédits sur le costume des élégants au XIVe siècle. Paris, E. Rahir 1913
8p. O.
Colas 1761

Langlade, Émile
La marchande de modes de Marie-Antoinette, Rose Bertin. Paris, A. Michel [1911]
336p. front. 17pl. 14 port. O.
Colas 1762

Rose Bertin, the creator of fashion at the court of Marie-Antoinette; adapted from the French by Angelo S. Rappoport. London, J. Long 1913
x,11-320p. front. pl. ports. O.
Translation of his *La marchande*

Langlès, Louis Mathieu. See Castellan, A. L. Moeurs, usages, costumes des Othomanes

Langley, Ernest Felix
Romantic figures in pen and color; a French portrait album of a century ago. Cambridge, Mass. Harvard university press 1935
12p. 9 port. F.
Reproductions of the original portraits of eight French writers of the 19th century made by Charles Cassal, 1838 and 1839, which, with a crayon of Charles Dickens, were bound together by Pierre Morand of Philadelphia in an album entitled, *Littérateurs français.* The text, descriptive of the album and the portraits, has been written by E. F. Langley. The illustrations show French masculine costume of 1838 and 1839
LC 36-674

Langlois, Eustache Hyacinthe
Recueil de quelques vues de sites et monuments de France, spécialement de Normandie, et des divers costumes des habitans de cette province. 1re livraison. Rouen, F. Mari 1817
20p. illus. 8pl. Q.
Colas 1763

Langlois, Victor
Voyage dans la Cilicie et dans les montagnes du Taurus; exécuté pendant les années 1852-1853. Paris, B. Duprat 1861
10,478p. 17 illus. 7 col.pl. map. O.
Plates show costume
Lipperheide 1463

Languedoc. See France—By region or province—Languedoc

La Nieppe, Edgar de Prelle de. See Prelle de la Nieppe, Edgar de

Lanier, Henry Wysham
Photographing the civil war. See note under Miller, F. T., and Lanier, R. S. The photographic history of the civil war

Lanier, Robert Sampson. See Miller, F. T., jt. ed.

Lanté, Louis Marie
Costumes des femmes de Hambourg, du Tyrol, de la Hollande, de la Suisse, de la Franconie, de l'Espagne, du royaume de Naples, etc. Dessinés, la plupart, par M. Lanté, gravés par M. Gatine ... avec une explication pour chaque planche. Paris, chez l'éditeur 1827
41p. 100 col.pl. Q.
Text by P. de Lamésangère. Title at head of plates: *Cost. de div. pays.* For list of plates see Colas's *Bibliographie*
Colas 1774. Lipperheide 571

Costumes des femmes du pays de Caux, et de plusieurs autres parties de l'ancienne province de Normandie. Dessinés la plupart par M. Lanté, gravés par M. Gatine et coloriés avec une explication pour chaque planche. Paris, chez l'editeur 1827
46p. 105 col.pl. Q.
Nineteen plates drawn by Pécheux. Explanatory text by P. de Lamésangère. For list of plates see Colas's *Bibliographie*
Colas lists an edition including only the first 11 plates under title: *Costumes féminins ... du pays de Caux, dessinés ... en 1811 et 1812* (Paris, Journal des dames 1814) Other editions: Paris, Eudes 1885 (105 col.pl.); Paris, Le Goupy 1925-26 (44p. 105 col.pl.) Also republished under title found on the frontispiece of the original edition: *Cent cinq costumes des départemens de la Seine Inférieure, du Calvados, de la Manche et de l'Orne* (Paris, Durand ca1830. 105 col.pl.)
Colas 1770-1773. Lipperheide 1196 (1830 ed.)

Costumes des femmes françaises du XIIe au XVIIIe siècle; nouvelle éd. imprimée en taille-douce par Ch. Wittmann, coloriée à la main par Nervet. Paris, Tallandier 1900
70 l. 70 col.pl. Q.
Explanatory text by Pierre de La Mésangère
Plates reproduced from the original edition, 1827 with the title: *Galerie française de femmes célèbres par leurs talens, leur rang ou leur beauté.* Engraved by Gatine
Colas 1769. Costume index

Costumes et coiffures de Paris des haute et moyenne classes. Lanté del., Gatine sculp. Paris ca1830
14 col.pl. Q.
Nine plates show coiffures. For list of plates see Colas's *Bibliographie*
Colas 1775. Lipperheide 1160

Costumes parisiens; les ouvrières de Paris. Paris, ca1824
47 col.pl. Q.
Drawings by Lanté, engraved by Gatine. For list of plates see Colas's *Bibliographie*
Lipperheide lists an incomplete edition with 32 plates
Colas 1764. Lipperheide 1184

Galerie française de femmes célèbres par leurs talens, leur rang ou leur beauté. Portraits en pied, par M. Lanté ... gravés par M. Gatine ... avec des notices biographiques et des remarques sur les habillemens [par P. de Lamésangère]. Paris, chez l'éditeur 1827
70 l. 70 col.pl. Q.
Includes French feminine costume of the 12th to 18th century
Other editions published 1832 and 1840
The same plates are in his *Costumes des femmes françaises du* XIIe *au* XVIIIe *siècle.* These plates are also in *Les femmes célèbres de l'ancienne France* by A. J. V. Le Roux de Lincy
Colas 1765-1767. Lipperheide 1077

Travestissemens. See entry under Gatine, G. J.

(illus.) Le Roux de Lincy, A. J. V., and Leynadier, Camille. Les femmes célèbres de l'ancienne France

La lanterne magique. Paris, Aubert ca1840
72pl. Q.
Pictures after drawings by Cham, Quillenbois, Ch. Vernier, and others
Lipperheide 3704

Lanza Di Scalea, Pietro
Donne e gioielli in Sicilia nel medio evo e nel rinascimento. Palermo-Torino, C. Clausen 1892
xvi,350p. 5 col.pl. Q.
Colas 1776. Lipperheide 1318

Laos
Backus, Mary, ed. Siam and Laos. 1884
Mouhot, Henri. Travels in the central parts of Indo-China (Siam), Cambodia, and Laos, during the years 1858, 1859, and 1860. 1864

Lapaume, Jean
De la parure au temps jadis; mémoire lu en 1865 à la Sorbonne. Grenoble, Prudhomme Giroud & cie 1866
46p. O. 1 fr. 25c
Colas 1777

[**Lapidoth, Frits**]
Een schoeisel verzameling, door Lynceus [pseud.] [Amsterdam, 1902]
11p. 46 illus. Q.
From *Elseviers Geïlustreerd maandschrift,* deel XXIII, no.3, Maart 1902
Lipperheide 1746e

La Placa, Pietro
La reggia in trionfo per l'acclamazione e coronazione ... di Carlo infante di Spagna, re di Sicilia. Palermo, A. Epiro 1736
236p. 22pl. F.
Plates are after designs by Niccola Palma, engraved by Jos. Vasi and Ant. Bova. They show triumphal arches, decorations and processions
Lipperheide 2758

Lapland
Broke, Sir A. de C., 2d bart. Winter sketches in Lapland. 1827
Broke, Sir A. de C., 2d bart. A winter in Lapland and Sweden, with various observations relating to Finmark and its inhabitants. 1826

Lapland—*Continued*

Düben, G. V. J. von. Om Lappland och Lapparne, företrädesvis de svenske. 1873

Hielscher, Kurt. Dänemark, Schweden, Norwegen; landschaft, baukunst, volksleben. 1932

Holme, Charles, ed. Peasant art in Sweden, Lapland and Iceland. 1910

Leems, Knud. Beskrivelse over Finmarkens Lapper, deres Tungemaal ... De Lapponibus Finmarchiae ... commentatio. 1767

Pettersson, C. A. Lappland, dess natur och folk. 1860

Scheffer, Johannes. Joannis Schefferi Argentoratensis Lapponia; id est, Regionis Lapponum et gentis nova et verissima descriptio. 1673

Lappenberg, Johann Martin

Die miniaturen zu dem Hamburgischen stadtrechte vom jahre 1497. Hamburg, J. A. Meissner 1845
55p. 18pl. sq.Q.
Illustrations are after original drawings by Otto Spekter. The introduction contains material on costume in Hamburg, and especially dress of officials
Lipperheide 453. LC 12-3774

Lappland, das ist: Neue und wahrhafftige beschreibung. See Scheffer, Johannes. Joannis Schefferi Argentoratensis Lapponia

Lappland, dess natur och folk. Pettersson, C. A.

Laprade, Mme Laurence de

Le poinct de France et les centres dentelliers au XVIIe et au XVIIIe siècles ... lettre-préface de M. Henry Lapauze. Paris, L. Laveur 1905
xxxvi,395p. incl.front. illus. pl. ports. O.
LC 13-4574

Lara, Lazaro Gutiérrez de. See Gutiérrez de Lara, Lazaro

Larchey, Lorédan

Ancien armorial équestre de la Toison d'or et de l'Europe au 15e siècle; facsimilé contenant 942 écus, 74 figures équestres, en 114 planches chromotypographiées, reproduites et publiées pour la première fois d'après le manuscrit 4790 de la Bibliothèque de l'Arsenal. Paris, Berger-Levrault 1890
xxvi,292p. 116 col.pl. F.
"The original manuscript dates before 1467." Lipperheide
Lipperheide 4388. LC 18-580

Costumes vrais; fac-similé de 50 mannequins de cavaliers en grande tenue héraldique, d'après le manuscrit d'un officier d'armes de Philippe le Bon, duc de Bourgogne. 1429-1467. Paris, 1899
xii,102p. illus. O.
Introduction signed: Lorédan Larchey. At head of title: Monde féodal. Europe, XV. siècle
The facsimile reproductions of the "mannequins" from ms. 4790, Bibliothèque de l'Arsenal, are printed, with descriptive notes, on the rectos of p 1-99, the versos being blank
Colas 1778. LC 20-19824

L'Ardèche, Paul Mathieu Laurent de. See Laurent de l'Ardèche, Paul Mathieu

Larisch, Paul

Die kürschner und ihre zeichen; beiträge zur geschichte der kürschnerei. [Berlin] Selbstverlag [1928]
7-180p. illus. Q.
Revised edition of the first part of *Das kürschner-handwerk,* by P. Larisch and J. Schmid, published in Paris, 1902-1904
"Fachliteratur": p160-63
LC 30-33289

Larisch, Paul, and Schmidt, Joseph

Das kürschner-handwerk. Paris, Les auteurs 1902-04
3v. illus. F.
Issued in parts, jahrg. 1-2, no. 1-18
Contents: v1 Die geschichte des kürschnerhandwerkes; v2 Herkunft und handel der felle; v3 Die verarbeitung der felle
Another edition of the first part entitled *Die kuerschner und ihre zeichen* (Berlin, Im selbstverlag [1928] 180p. illus.(incl. port.) col.pl. facsim. tables Q.)

Larisch, Rudolf von

Der "schönheitsfehler" des weibes, eine anthropometrisch-ästhetische studie; 2. aufl. München, J. Albert 1896
36p. 7 illus. 3pl. O.
First edition 1896
Lipperheide 3305

Larmessin, Nicolas

Les augustes representations de tous les rois de France depuis Pharamond, jusqu'à Louys XIIII. Paris, La veuve P. Bertrand 1679-83
64pl. Q.
Half-length portraits
Lipperheide 1068

Larned, Josephus Nelson

The new Larned History for ready reference, reading and research; the actual words of the world's best historians, biographers and specialists ... completely rev. enl. and brought up to date under the supervision of the publishers, by Donald E. Smith [and others] Springfield, Mass. C. A. Nichols 1922-24
12v. col.front. illus. pl. ports. maps. Q.
Many of the articles are illustrated with pictures which show dress of the period
LC 22-6840

Larsson, Carl

Åt solsidan; 2. ed. Stockholm, A. Bonnier [1914]
32p. 31 col.pl. Q.
The plates reproduce paintings of interiors with figures in large size, showing costumes of men, women and children. Most of the paintings are dated 1908-09

Andras barn. Stockholm, Bonnier [1913]
23p. illus. 32 col.pl. F.
Shows Swedish children of the late 19th and early 20th century

Ett hem; 5. upplagan. Stockholm, A. Bonnier [c1913]
31p. illus. 24 col.pl. Q. kr.2.80
LC 14-3140

Spad-arfoet, mitt lilla landtbruk. [Stockholm, A. Bonnier 1906]
10 l. illus. 24 col.pl. ob.F.

La Rue, Philibert Benoit

Nouveau recueil des troupes légères de France levées depuis la présente guerre, avec ... leur uniforme et leurs armes. Paris, F. Chereau 1747
12pl.(3 col.) F.
Colas 1780. Lipperheide 2292s

La Rue, Philibert Auguste De. See Delarue, P. A.

La Ruelle, Claude de
Decem insignes tabulae, complexae icones justorum ac honorum supremorum, corpori ... Caroli III ... Dix grandes tables, contenantes les pourtraictz des ceremonies, honneurs, et pompe funebres, faitz au corps de Charles 3 ... duc le Lorraine. Nancy. apud B. Andream, typis I. Garnich [1611?]
2v. 58pl. F.
Forty-eight plates showing the funeral procession are by Fr. Brentel
Lipperheide 2706

Las Cases, Philippe, vicomte de
(ed.) L'art rustique en France. Tome 1-5. Paris, Ollendorf [1920-33]
5v. illus. col.pl. col.ports. Q.
Contents: v 1 La Lorraine, texte par Ch. Sadoul; v2 L'Alsace; v3 La Bretagne; v4 Dauphiné et Savoie; v5 L'Auvergne
Includes a chapter on the costume, embroidery and jewelry of each section, with illustrations

La Serre, Jean Puget de
Histoire curieuse de tout ce qui c'est passé à l'entrée de la reyne Mere du roy treschrestien dans les villes des Pays Bas. Anvers, B. Moretus 1632
74p. 2 illus. 2pl. F.
Illustrations engraved by A. Paulus
Lipperheide 2661

Lasinio, Carlo
Pitture a fresco del Campo Santo di Pisa. Firenze, A. Bernardini 1828
28p. 44pl. F.
Earlier edition, 1812. The murals belong to the second half of the fourteenth century
Lipperheide 377

Serie di 12 ritratti di persone facete che servono a divertire il pubblico Fiorentino. Firenze, G. Calamandrei ca1800
12 col.pl. F.
Colas 1781. Lipperheide 1321

Lassalle, Louis
(illus.) Galerie dramatique, costumes de théâtre
(lithogr.) Desessarts, Alfred. L'univers illustré

See also Costumes suisses des 22 cantons (attributed)

Last, H. W.
Verzameling van nederlandsche kleederdragten. Collection des costumes des Pays-Bas. Gravenhage, D. van Lier 1850
32 col.pl. Q.
Colas 1783

The **last** fifty years in New York. See Valentine's manual of old New York

The **last** of the Tasmanians. Bonwick, James

Lasteyrie du Saillant, Robert Charles. See Guilhermy, R. F. F. M. N., baron de, jt. auth.

Laszowska, Jane Emily (Gerard) de. See Gerard, Emily

Latham, Robert Gordon
The native races of the Russian empire. London, H. Bailliere [etc.] 1854
viii,340p. col.front. fold.map. O. (The ethnographical library v2)
The frontispiece shows costumes
Colas 1784. Lipperheide 1366. LC 5-24010

Latham, Simon
The whole work of Mr. Latham's books of faulconry ... whereto is added this year 1662 an excellent treatise called The gentlemans exercise. London, Printed by S. Griffin, for W. Lee 1662
16 l. 176p.; 11 l. 144,[6]p.;96,[12]p. front. illus. pl. T.
Each part has a separate paging and also special t.-p.: 1 Latham's faulconry, or, The faulcons lure and cure; 2 Latham's new and second book of faulconry; 3 The gentlemans exercise; or, A supplement to Mr. Lathams bookes of faulconry
LC 35-18754

[**Lathrop, Barnabas**]
Poem on the absurdity and sinfulness of wearing high rolls. No place, [1782?]
8p. D.
LC 22-22205

Lathrop, George Parsons
Spanish vistas; illus. by Charles S. Reinhart. New York, Harper 1883
xii,210p. incl.front. illus. pl. O.
LC 4-25755

Latimer, Mrs. Elizabeth (Wormeley)
Russia and Turkey in the nineteenth century. Chicago, A. C. McClurg 1893
413p. front. 22 pl.(ports.) O.
LC 5-15163

Latomus, Sigismund
Schön newes modelbuch von 500. schönen ausserwehlten künstlichen so wol italiänichen frantzösischen niderländischen engeländischen als teutschen mödeln allen nätherin seydenstickeren &c. Franckfurt am Mayn, S. Latomus 1606
98pl. O.
A collection of embroidery designs copied from Quentel, Vecellio, etc. It served as a model for many later books
Lipperheide 3913

[**La Torre, F. de**]
Costumes bordelais. Bordeaux, Casati 1828
8 col.pl. F.
Plates lithographed by Gaulon
Colas 1785

Latour, Antoine de
Voyage de S.A.R. Monseigneur le Duc de Montpensier à Tunis en Égypte, en Turquie et en Grèce. Paris, A. Bertrand [1847]
261p. O. and atlas of 31pl. F.
Album by de Sinety, lithographed by Mrs Bayot, Dauzats, and others. The plates are views with costume figures
Lipperheide 1595

Lattré, publisher
Exercice et révolutions de l'infanterie françoise dédiés à Monseigneur le Maréchal duc de Biron. Paris, Lattré 1766
4p. 66 col.pl. S.
Colas 1786

Lattre, A. de
Costumes de Nice; dessinés d'après nature. [Paris] Lemercier 1849-68
10 col.pl. Q.
Colas 1787. Lipperheide 1201m

Latvia
Barons, Krišjānis, ed. Latwju dainas. 1894-1915
Bielenstein, Martha. Die altlettischen färbmethoden. 1935

Latvia—*Continued*
Dzērvītis, Arvēds, and Ginters, Valdis, eds. Latviešu tautas tērpi. 1936
Rutter, Owen. The new Baltic states and their future. 1926
Schlichting, E. H. Trachten der Schweden an den küsten Ehstlands und auf Runö. 1854
Spekke, Arnolks. Vecākie latvju tautas apĝērba zīmējumi. 1934

See also subdivision Latvia under Embroidery; Weddings and wedding dress

Latviešu tautas tērpi. Dzērvītis, Arvēds, and Ģinters, Valdis, eds.

Latvijas saule. Jan. 1923-Marts 1931, nos 1-99. Riga, E. Paegle 1923-31
v 1-9 illus. pl. (part col.) O.
Published monthly. Editor 1923-29, E. Paegle. Shows many designs of peasant embroidery

Latwju dainas. Barons, Krišjānis, ed.

Latzke, Alpha, and Quinlan, Elizabeth
Clothing, an introductory college course; edited by Benjamin R. Andrews. Chicago, Philadelphia, J. B. Lippincott company [c1935]
xiii,418p. illus. col.pl. diagr. O.
LC 35-16154

Lau, Theodor
(ed.) Brunn, Heinrich von. Greek vases: their system of form and decoration
(ed.) Brunn, Heinrich von, and Krell, P. F. Die griechischen vasen ihr formen- und decorations system

[**Lauber, Joseph**]
Denkmahl der vaterlandsliebe und fürstentreue. Wien, Thad. E. v. Schmidbauer u. Komp. 1797
476,122p. 8 col.pl. O.
Seven plates show uniforms of the Austrian Volunteer Corps from the outbreak of the French revolution to the dissolution of the corps, 4 April 1797
Lipperheide 2229

Lauder, Sir Thomas Dick, bart.
(ed.) Geikie, Walter. Etchings illustrative of Scottish character and scenery

Laufer, Berthold
Chinese clay figures, part I: Prolegomena on the history of defensive armour. Chicago, Field museum of natural history 1914
313p. illus. 64pl. O. (Publication 177. Anthropological series v 13 no2)
Contents: I History of the rhinoceros; II Defensive armor of the archaic period; III Defensive armor of the Han period; IV History of chain mail and ring mail; V The problem of plate armor; VI Defensive armor of the T'ang period; VII Horse armor and clay figures of horses
LC (15-8603)

Oriental theatricals. Chicago, Field museum of natural history 1923
59p. fold.front. pl. (part fold.) D. (Field museum of natural history, Chicago. Dept. of anthropology. Guide, pt.1)
Plates show Mask of Kiang Tse-Ya, China; Shadow-play figures, China (3pl.); Tibetan mask, Burial clay figures of actors from Kucha (A.D. 618-906) Tibetan mystery-play (3pl.) Mask of Chao Kung-Ming, China

Laugel, Anselme
Trachten und sitten im Elsass ... Illus. von Ch. Spindler. Strassburg, G. Fischbach 1902
xii,300p. 90 illus. 61 col.pl. Q.
Published also in French with title: *Costumes et coutumes d'Alsace,* same publisher and date
A reprint of the German edition was published (Leipzig, K. Hiersemann 1908. M.100)
Colas 1788-89. Lipperheide 795e

Laugier, Léon
(illus.) Stein, Henri. Archers

Launay, Edmond
Costumes, insignes, cartes, médailles des députés 1789-1898. Paris, Motteroz [1899]
257p. 13 col.pl. illus. (part col.) Q.
Colas 1791

Launay, Marie de. See Hamdī, O., bey, jt. auth.

Laurencin, Marie
(illus.) Dyagilev, S. P. Les biches

Laurent, and Perrot, Georges
Les femmes de l'Asie, ou description de leur physiognomie, moeurs, usages, et costumes. Paris, Le Fuel [18-?]
xvi,144p. 15pl. Ti.
Faces and hands are colored but costumes are not
Colas 1792

Laurent, J. See Museos de España. Cordova scenes

Laurent de l'Ardèche, Paul Mathieu
Histoire de l'Empereur Napoléon; illus. par Horace Vernet. Paris, J. J. Dubochet 1840
832p. 463 illus. 46 col.pl. O.
Earlier edition 1839. The 1840 edition has two more chapters and seven new illustrations by J. Lange, and new plates on French uniforms after Hippolyte Bellangé. Forty-four of these plates appeared later in Bellangé's *Collection*
Lipperheide 1166-67

Lauron, Marcellus
The cries of London ... being 72 humorous prints with addition and improvements by L. P. Boitard. London, R. Sayer ca1760
72pl. F.
Colas 1795

The cryes of the city of London, drawne after the life. [London 1711]
74pl. F.
Published also (London, Overton [1733])
Title also in French: *Les cris de la ville de Londres;* and in Italian: *L'arti communi che vanno per Londra*
Colas 1793-94

Lauture, Stanislas, comte d'Escayrac de. See Escayrac de Lauture, Stanislas, comte de

Lavanha, João Baptista
Viagem da catholica real magestade del rey D. Filipe II ... ao reyno de Portugal e rellação do solene recebimento que nelle se lhe fez. Madrid, T. Iunti 1622
78 l. 12 illus. 3pl. F.
Published also in a Spanish edition. The illustrations are engraved by Juan Schorquens
Lipperheide 2729

Lavater, Hans Conrad
Kriegs-manual von übung der reüterij und infanterej montier-erken- und -abrichtung der pferden. Schaffhausen, J. K. Sutern 1664
3v. (103p.) 24 illus. 18pl. O.
Lipperheide 2084

Le **lavater** des dames. Ladies lavater. Philipon, Charles

Laver, James
English costume from the fourteenth through the nineteenth century. See entry under Brooke, Iris
English costume of the eighteenth century. See entry under Brooke, Iris
English costume of the nineteenth century. See entry under Brooke, Iris
(tr.) Aretz, Frau G. K. D. The elegant woman, from the rococo period to modern times

See also Messel, Oliver. Stage designs and costumes

La Villeneuve, Aurélien Marie C. de Courson de. See Courson de La Villeneuve, Aurélien Marie C. de

Lavisse, Ernest
(ed.) Histoire de France contemporaine depuis la révolution jusqu'à la paix de 1919; ouvrage illustré de nombreuses gravures hors texte. [Paris] Hachette [c1920-22]
10v. front. illus.(map, plans) pl. ports. O.
The index (v10) covers also the author's *Histoire de France depuis les origines jusqu'à la révolution*
Contents: t 1 La révolution (1789-1792) par P. Sagnac; t2 La révolution (1792-1799) par G. Pariset; t3 Le consulat et l'empire (1799-1815) par G. Pariset; t4 La restauration (1815-1830) par S. Charléty; t5 La monarchie de juillet (1830-1848) par S. Charléty; t6 La révolution de 1848-le second empire (1848-1859) par Ch. Seignobos; t7 Le déclin de l'empire et l'établissement de la 3e république (1859-1875) par Ch. Seignobos; t8 L'évolution de la 3e république (1875-1914) par Ch. Seignobos; t9 La grande guerre, par H. Bidou, A. Gauvain, Ch. Seignobos. Conclusion générale, par E. Lavisse; t10 Tables générales des origines à la paix de 1919
LC 21-3103

(ed.) Histoire de France depuis les origines jusqu'à la révolution; publiée avec la collaboration de mm. Bayet, Bloch [e. a.] Paris, Hachette 1900-[c11]
9v. illus. maps(1 fold.) sq.O.
Each tome originally issued in 8 fascicules
Contents: t 1: I. Tableau de la géographie de la France, par P. Vidal de la Blache; II. Les origines; la Gaule indépendante et la Gaule romaine, par G. Bloch. t2: I. Le christianisme, les barbares, Mérovingiens et Carolingiens, par C. Bayet, C. Pfister, A. Kleinclausz; II. Les premiers Capétiens (987-1137) par A. Luchaire. t3: I. Louis VII—Philippe-Auguste—Louis VIII (1137-1226) par A. Luchaire; II. Saint Louis, Philippe le Bel, Les derniers Capétiens directs (1226-1328) par C. V. Langlois. t4: I. Les premiers Valois et la guerre de cent ans (1328-1422) par A. Coville; II. Charles VII, Louis XI et les premières années de Charles VIII (1422-1492) par C. Petit-Dutaillis; t5: I. Les guerres d'Italie, la France sous Charles VIII, Louis XII et François Ier (1492-1547) par H. Lemonnier; II. La lutte contre la maison d'Autriche, la France sous Henri II (1519-1559) par H. Lemonnier. t6: I. La réforme et la ligue, L'édit de Nantes (1559-1598) par J. H. Mariéjol; II. Henri IV et Louis XIII (1598-1643) par J. H. Mariéjol. t7: I. Louis XIV, La fronde, Le roi, Colbert (1643-1685) par E. Lavisse; II. Louis XIV, La religion, Les lettres et les arts, La guerre (1643-1685) par E. Lavisse. t8: I. Louis XIV. La fin du règne (1685-1715) par A. de Saint-Léger, A. Rébelliau, P. Sagnac, E. Lavisse; II. La règne de Louis XV (1715-1774) par H. Carré. t9: I. Le règne de Louis XVI (1774-1789) par H. Carré, P. Sagnac, E. Lavisse; II. Tables alphabétiques
Indexed in volume 10 of the author's *Histoire de France contemporaine*
Each volume originally issued in eight fascicules
LC F-2488

(ed.) Parmentier, A. É. E. Album historique. 1897-1907

The **law** and customs relating to gloves. Norton-Kyshe, J. W.

Lawley, Annie Allen (Cunard), lady
(illus.) Penny, Mrs F. E. F. Southern India

Lawrence, H. W., and Dighton, Basil Lewis
French line engravings of the late XVIII century. London, Lawrence and Jellicoe 1910
xxv,110p. front. 81pl. F.
Contains, p89-102, reproductions of plates from Restif de la Bretonne's *Monument du costume*, a notable series of etchings by Sigmund Freudenberger and J. M. Moreau
LC 11-2058

Lawrence-Archer, James Henry
The orders of chivalry; from the original statutes of the various orders of knighthood, and other sources of information. London, W. H. Allen 1887
xxviii,355p. 57pl. 2 port.(incl.front.) F.
LC 9-32634

Laws and regulations
Lipperheide nos. 3321-3423 list books on regulations governing clothing and dress in various countries of Europe, with special emphasis on the 16th to 18th centuries and on the laws of Germany. These Lipperheide entries have not been included in this Bibliography
Boileau, Etienne. Réglemens sur les arts et métiers de Paris, rédigés au XIIIe siècle. 1837
Daubert, Pierre. Du port illégal de costume et de décoration. 1904
Struve, G. A. Georgii Adami Struvii ... Tractatio juridica de eo quod justum est circa vestitum civium, von der bürger kleider-ordnung; in acad. Jenensi 1675 habita. 1724

See also Sumptuary laws

The **laws** and usages of the church and the clergy. Pinnock, W. H.

Lawson, Kate, lady
Highways and homes of Japan ... illustrations from photographs taken by the author. London [etc.] T. F. Unwin 1910
352p. col.front. illus. pl. ports. O.
LC 11-1228

Lawyers. See Legal costume

Lay, Felix
Kulturno īstorījsko etnografskī atlas kraīevīne Srbīje ... Culturhistorisch etnografischer atlas des Königreiches Serbien. Vienne, Stockinger & Morsack [1886]
2v. 20 col.pl. Q.
Plates show Serbian weaving and embroidery
Lipperheide 3973

Ornamenti jugoslovenske domaće i umjetne obŕtnosti sabrao i izdao Srećko Lay ... Ornamente südslavischer nationaler haus und kunst-industrie ... Ornaments des arts et metiers des Slaves du sud. Wien, Der herausgeber [1875-84]
20pt. pl.(part col., part fold.) F.
Cover-title. In portfolios
Lipperheide 3958. LC 10-19009

Sudslävische ornamente gesammelt ... und nebst einer abhandlung über die verbreitung und cultur der Südslaven; der ornamentale theil von Friedrich Fischbach. Hanau a. M., F. Fischbach [1872]
27p. 1 illus. 20pl. Q.
Lipperheide 3955

Layard, Sir Austen Henry
Nineveh and its remains: with an account of a visit to the Chaldæan Christians of Kurdistan, and the Yezidis, or devil-worshippers; and an inquiry into the manners and arts of the ancient Assyrians. New York, G. P. Putnam 1849
2v. fronts. illus. pl.(part fold.) fold.map. fold.plans. O.
The author's *A popular account of the discoveries at Nineveh* (London, J. Murray 1851. xxiii,360. illus. pl. D.) is an abridged edition
LC 28-10444

A second series of the Monuments of Nineveh; including bas-reliefs from the palace of Sennacherib and bronzes from the ruins of Nimroud. From drawings made on the spot, during a second expedition to Assyria. London, J. Murray 1853
viii,7p. 71pl.(part col. part fold.; incl. front.) F.
The story of the second expedition is given in his *Discoveries in the ruins of Nineveh and Babylon; with travels in Armenia, Kurdestan and the desert* (London, J. Murray 1853. xxiii,686p. illus. pl. maps. O.)
LC 10-3925

Layenspiegel. See Tengler, Ulrich. Der neü Layenspiegel

Lazari Bayfii annotationes in l. II. de captivis, et postliminio reversis. Baïf, Lazare de

Lazarini, Ludwig von
(ed.) Maximilian I, emperor of Germany. Das fischereibuch kaiser Maximilians I

Lazius, Wolfgang
De gentium aliquot migrationibus, sedibus fixis, reliquijs, linguarúmque; initijs & immutationibus ac dialectis, libri XII. In quibvs praeter caeteros populos, Francorum, Alemanorum, Svevorum, Marcomanorum, Boiorum, Carnorum, Tauriscorum, Celtarumq̄ve, atque Gallograecorum tribus, primordia & posteritas singulorū, quæque ex his insigniores principum comitumque, ac nobilitatis totius penè Germaniæ, Latijque & Galliæ stirpes processerunt, diligenti examine historiæ, denique autorum annaliumque cùm lectione tum collatione traduntur atque explicantur. Basileae, per I. Oporinum [1557]
844,[26]p. illus. pl. geneal.tables. F.
Shows Gauls, Vandals, Longobardi, Heruli, and Pict, in dress of the Middle ages and earlier, many in armor. The costume is described by Lipperheide as somewhat fantastic
The text is a history of the migrations of the Germanic tribes. Another edition is described by Lipperheide (Basileae, ex officina Oporiniana, 1572)
Lipperheide 273. LC 3-14379

Leach, Mrs
Mrs Leach's complete guide to crochet work. London, R. S. Cartwright [1890]
10 l. 51 illus. Q.
Lipperheide 4165

Mrs Leach's knitting lessons, how to knit fancy and useful articles; re-issue, enl. London, R. S. Cartwright ca1877
10 l. 45 illus. Q.
Lipperheide 4118

Leander, Charlotte, pseud. See Hennings, Emma

Leather in clothing
Biggart, Helen. Leathercraft and beading, adapted for Camp fire girls. 1930
Griswold, L. E. Handbook of craftwork in leather, horsehair, bead, porcupine quill and feather, Indian (Navajo) silver and turquoise. 1928

Leathercraft and beading. Biggart, Helen

Le Beau, Mme. See Gallerie des modes et costumes français dessinés d'après nature

Das **leben** Christi. Ludolphus de Saxonia

Das **leben** der griechen und römer nach antiken bildwerken. Guhl, E. K., and Koner, W. D.

Leben und contrafeiten der türckischen un persischen sultanen. Boissard, J. J.

Leben und sitten der Griechen. Blümner, Hugo

Leben und sitten der Römer in der kaiserzeit. Jung, Julius

Leben und tapffere thaten der aller-berühmtesten see-helden admiralen und landerfinder unserer zeiten. Francisci, Erasmus

Die **lebenden** bilder und pantomimischen darstellungen bei dem festspiel: Lalla Rukh, aufgeführt auf dem königlichen schlosse in Berlin den 27sten januar 1821. Hensel, Wilhelm

Leber, Friedrich Otto, edler von
Wien's Kaiserliches zeughaus, zum ersten male aus historisch-kritischem gesichtspunkte betrachtet, für alterthumsfreunde und waffenkenner. Leipzig, K. F. Koehler 1846
2v. in 1. fronts. O. (Rückblicke in deutsche vorzeit, II, III)
Paged continuously. "Rüsstmeister-vocabularium": p[175]-205. "Tabellarische übersicht sämmtlicher zierde-geschütze des Kaiserlichen zeughauses": p[443]-58
LC 20-13002

Leber, Jean Michel Constant
Des cérémonies du sacre, ou Recherches historiques et critiques sur les mœurs, les coutumes, les institutions et le droit public des Français dans l'ancienne monarchie. Paris, Baudouin frères; [etc.] 1825
xv,525p. 48pl.(part fold.) O.
Lipperheide 2484. LC 3-23580

Leberthais, Casimir
(illus.) Paris, Louis. Toiles peintes et tapisseries de la ville de Reims

Le Blanc, H.
The art of tying the cravat ... preceded by a history of the cravat. From the 11th London ed. New-York, S. & D. A. Forbes 1829
68p. incl.fold.front. fold.pl. T.
LC 32-6142

Le Blanc, Th. Prosper
Croquis d'après nature faits ... en Grèce et dans le Levant. Paris, Gihaut [1833]
1 l. 30 col.pl. F. 12fr.
Published also in black and white at 6fr. Published in five parts of six plates each. The plates show costume
Colas 1796

Le Blond, Albert Waning Lenfranc, and Lucas, Arthur
Du tatouage chez les prostituées. Paris, Société d'éditions scientifiques 1899
96p. 2 l. facsims. D.
"Bibliographie": 1 leaf at end
LC 17-1258

Le Bon, Gustave
Les civilisations de l'Inde ... illustré ... d'après les photographies, aquarelles et documents de l'auteur. Paris, Firmin-Didot 1887
743p. col.front. illus.(incl. 2 maps) col.pl. Q.
Book 2, Les races, p69-242 contains many pictures of various Indian races and portraits of notable men of various periods. Costumes of different occupations are shown, both masculine and feminine
LC 1-18605

Le Bondidier, Louis
Les vieux costumes pyrénéens. Pau, Garet-Haristoy [1917]
16p. O.
Colas 1797

Leborgne, Paul
Les chiffres au XIXme siècle. Paris, A. Calavas [1884-91]
377pl. F.
Lipperheide 4187

Leborne, Louis. See Rugendas, J. M., jt. auth.

Le Brun, Corneille. See Bruyn, Cornelis de

Le Brun, Tossa
(ed.) Journal de la mode et du goût

[Le Camus, Antoine]
Abdeker; ou, L'art de conserver la beauté. Amsterdam, Chez les Libraires associés 1774
2v. in 1. D.
Many other editions
LC 8-3912

Le Carpentier, Jean
(tr.) Nieuhof, Johan. L'ambassade de la Compagnie orientale des Provinces Unies vers l'empereur de la Chine

Le Chevallier-Chevignard, Edmond
Costumes historiques de femmes du XIVe au XVIIIe siècle; dessinés par Le Chevallier-Chevignard, gravés par Didier, Flameng, Laguillermie, etc. Paris, A. Lévy 1889
64p. col.pl. Q.
"Plates largely selected from Camille Bonnard's *Costumes historiques des XIIe, XIIIe, XIVe et XVe siècles and Duplessis's Costumes historiques des XVIe, XVIIe et XVIIIe siècles.*" Monro & Cook's Costume index
Costume index

(illus.) Duplessis, Georges. Costumes historiques des XVIe, XVIIe et XVIIIe siècles

Lechner, Hedwig, and Beeg, Gunda
Die anfèrtigung der damen garderobe. Berlin, F. Lipperheide 1891
10,186p 421 illus. Q. (Lehrbücher der modenwelt, 1. bd.)
Translated into Portuguese under title *O preparo do vestuario para senhora* (Rio de Janeiro, H. Lombaerts 1894. 163p. 405 illus. Q.)
Lipperheide 3835-36

Die anfertigung der kinder-garderobe. Berlin, F. Lipperheide 1891
124p. 248 illus. Q.
Lipperheide 3837

Leclerc, Max. See Jacottet, Henri, jt. auth.

Le Clerc, Sébastien
Divers costumes français du règne de Louis XIV. [Paris, ca1695]
20pl. O.
Plates are the same as those in his: *Les figures,* but in a different order
Colas 1804. Lipperheide 1114

Divers habillemens des anciens Grecs et Romains. [Paris, N. Langlois 1680]
25pl. O.
A second edition, plates retouched, was published (Paris, Jeaurat [1706])
Colas 1801-02. Lipperheide 152

Les figures à la mode. Paris, Audran [1685]
1 l. 17pl. O.
The second edition (Paris, Jeaurat [1695]) had three additional plates. It has also been published, the plates rearranged, as *Divers costumes français,* listed above
Colas 1802

Les sept anciennes modes de Metz. No place, ca1665
7pl. O.
Cataloged from Colas, who did not see the book
Colas 1799

Leclercq, Louis
Les décors, les costumes, et la mise en scène au XVIIe siècle, 1615-1680, par Ludovic Celler [pseud.] Paris, Liepmannssohn & Dufour 1869
162p. D.
Colas 567. LC 10-1340

Leclère, Adhémard
Cambodge; la crémation et les rites funéraires. Hanoi, F.-H. Schneider 1906
154p. pl. plans. Q.
LC 30-7233

Leclert, Louis
Le costume de guerre en Basse Champagne au XIIIe et au XIVe siècle d'après les effigies gravées sur les pierres tombales. Troyes, P. Nouel 1909
23p. illus. pl. O.
From *L'Annuaire de l'Aube*, 1909

Lecointe, Georges Guénot-. See Guénot-Lecointe, Georges

Lecointe, Jean François Joseph. See Hitorff, J. I., jt. auth.

Lecomte, Hippolyte
Costumes civils et militaires de la monarchie française depuis 1200 jusqu'à 1820. Paris, Delpech 1820
4v. 380 col.pl. Q.
Colas 1807. Lipperheide 1074

Costumes de théâtre de 1600 à 1820; dédiés à Monsieur le baron de Laferté, intendant des thèâtres royaux. [Paris, Imp. lith. de Delpech, 1824?]
104 col.pl. incl. engr. t.-p. F.
Colas 1809. Lipperheide 3211. LC 10-25010

Costumes européens. Paris, F. Delpech 1817-19
89 col.pl. F.
Plates show folk costume of Switzerland, The Tyrol, Spain, Baden, Russia, Holland, Balkan countries, Turkey and France
Lipperheide 52, 52a

Costumes français, de 1200 à 1715. London, Printed by C. Hullmandel for Rodwell & Martin ca1830
100pl. O.
Plates are reduced and reversed copies of those in his *Costumes civils et militaires de la monarchie française*
Colas 1808. Lipperheide 1080

Le Comte, Louis Daniel
Nouveaux memoires sur l'etat present de la Chine. Paris, J. Anisson 1696
2v. 22pl.(part fold.) incl.ports. D.
LC 5-9309

Le Comte, Louis Daniel; Le Gobien, Charles, and Bouvet, Joachim
Das heutige Sina ... durch curieuse an verschiedene hohe geist- und weltliche standes-personen ... gefertigte sendschreiben den liebhabern ... vorgestellt, auss dem frantzösischen übersetzt. Franckfurt & Leipzig, C. Riegeln 1699-1700
4v. 22pl. D.
Volume 1 contains a section on Chinese dress. Eight of the plates show costume. Volume 3: *Bericht des edictes welches der ... Kayser in Sina der christischen religion zum besten ergehen lassen*, is by Le Gobien; v4, *Abbildung der ... qualitäten des sinesischen regnanten Cham-Hy*, by J. Bouvet
Lipperheide 1515

Leçons de chic: souvenirs et traditions militaires, par une sabretache. Paris, Berger-Levrault 1894
31p. illus. O.
Colas 1805

Leçons de couture, crochet, tricot, frivolité ... Raymond, Mme Emmeline

Le Coq, Albert von
Bilderatlas zur kunst und kulturgeschichte Mittel-Asiens. Berlin, D. Reimer 1925
107p. illus. F.
Shows costume worn in central Asia from the 6th to 11th centuries
LC 29-2418

Chotscho: facsimile-wiedergaben der wichtigeren funde der ersten Königlich preussischen expedition nach Turfan in Ost-Turkistan, im auftrage der generalverwaltung der Königlichen museen aus mitteln des Baessler-institutes. Berlin, D. Reimer (E. Vohsen) 1913
vii,18,[148]p. illus. 75pl.(30 col.) F.
In portfolio. At head of title: *Ergebnisse der Kgl. preussischen Turfan-expeditionen*
LC 16-13418

Volkskundliches aus Ost-Turkistan; mit einem beitrag von O. v. Falke (mit unterstützung der Orlopstiftung) Berlin, D. Reimer 1916
vii,72p. 110 illus. 25pl.(4 col.; incl.fold. facsim.) F.
At head of title: *Königlich preussische Turfan-expeditionen*
LC 20-23518

Lecor, Luiz Pedro
Collecção de dezenhos das figuras de detalhes que designão os differentes uniformes para todos os corpos do exercito. Rio de Janeiro, E. Rensburg 1859
[4] l. 14 col.pl. F.
Each plate is included twice with no change except in coloring. The uniforms are those ordered in April 1850. Lithographed by A. de Pinho
Colas 1810

Lecoy de la Marche, Albert
Saint Martin. Tours, A. Mame 1881
xv,735p. 114 illus. 34pl.(6 col.) O.
Pictures of the saint, and views of churches and squares. Also copies of miniatures and woodcuts which show costume of the middle ages
Lipperheide 1840

Le treizième siècle artistique. Lille, Desclée, De Brower & cie 1892
422p. illus. Q.

Lecuyer, Camille
Collection Camille Lecuyer; terres cuites antiques, trouvées en Grèce et en Asie-Mineure. Paris, Rollin 1882-85
2v. 117pl. F.
Volume 1 contains 13 plates showing ancient Greek masks

Lederer, Mrs Charlotte (Bacskay)
Made in Hungary. Budapest, G. Vajna [1933]
96p. illus.(part col.) pl.(part col.) D.
Bibliography: p92
Costume index. LC 34-2307

Ledoux, A.
(lithogr.) Cerrone, F. Scenes from Italian life

Ledoux, Hector
(comp.) 50 leçons de coiffure: coupe, mise en plis, ondulation ... ouvrage comprenant de nombreux modèles avec démonstrations pratiques des meilleurs professeurs de Paris ... 248 figures explicatives et de nombreuses coiffures-mode. Paris [Éditions La Coiffure de Paris] 1931
[11]-78p. illus. 27x20½cm.
At head of title: La bibliothèque du coiffeur moderne
LC 31-25010

Lee, Frederick George
(ed.) Purchas, John. The directorium Anglicanum

Lee, Sir Sidney. See note under Shakespeare's England

Leech, John

Pictures of life & character, from the collection of Mr. Punch. ⌊1st⌋-5th series. London, Bradbury and Evans 1854-69
5v. illus. sq.F.
LC 11-29542

(illus.) À Beckett, G. A. The comic history of England

Leeder, S. H.

The Desert gateway, Biskra and thereabouts. London, New York ⌊etc.⌋ Cassell 1910
x,272p. 16pl.(incl.fold.front.) O.
LC 11-35161

Modern sons of the Pharaohs; a study of the manners and customs of the Copts of Egypt ... illustrated with photographs. London, New York ⌊etc.⌋ Hodder and Stoughton ⌊1918⌋
xvi,355p. fold.front. pl. port. O.
Bibliography: p347-48
Contents: 1 The people and their customs; 2 The people and their Oriental church, Their great dignitaries, Their social and political position
LC 18-20021

Leeds, Edward Thurlow

Two types of brooches from the island of Gotland, Sweden. London and Aylesbury, Hunt, Barnard & co 1910
Cover-title, p⌊235⌋-58. illus. 3pl. O.
Reprinted from the *Archaeological journal* v67 no267; 2d ser. v17, no3
LC 28-5236

Leemans, Conradus

Monumens égyptiens du Musée d'antiquités des Pays-Bas à Leyde. Leide, E. J. Brill 1839-67
5v. in 4. pl.(part col.) sq.F.

Leems, Knud

Beskrivelse over Finmarkens Lapper, deres Tungemaal ... De Lapponibus Finmarchiae ... commentatio. Kjøbenhavn, G. G. Salikath 1767
16,5,544,82p. 101pl. Q.
Text in Danish and Latin. Chapter 4, on costume of the Lapps, is illustrated with twelve plates
Lipperheide 1382

Lefébure, Ernest

Broderie et dentelles ... Nouv. éd., rev. et augm. Paris, A. Picard & Kaan ⌊1904?⌋
328p. illus. O. (Bibliothèque de l'enseignement des beaux-arts)
First edition 1887
LC 32-23336

Embroidery and lace ... their manufacture and history from the remotest antiquity to the present day; a handbook for amateurs, collectors and general readers. Tr. and enl., with notes by A. S. Cole. London, H. Grevel 1888
x,326p. illus. O.
Translation of his *Broderie et dentelles*

Les points de France; tr. by Margaret Taylor Johnston. New York ⌊Cambridge, Mass., The Riverside press⌋ 1912
98p. incl.front. pl. 2 port. Q.
Half-title: International exhibition, 1900, Paris. Retrospective collection, class 84. Lace. Report of Monsieur Ernest Lefébure
LC 12-16175

Lefèvre, maître coiffeur

Traité des principes de l'art de la coëffure des femmes. Paris, L'auteur 1738
168p. O.
"Où il est démontré qu'avec un peu de réflexion on peut apprendre avec facilité à coëffer & soi-même, & toute autre personne." Subtitle
2. édition, rev. & corr. (1783. 175,59p. O.)
Colas 1811-12. Lipperheide 1678

Lefferts, Charles Mackubin

Uniforms of the American, British, French and German armies in the war of the American revolution, 1775-1783, painted and described; ed. by Alexander J. Wall. New York, The New-York historical society 1926
viii,289p. incl. 50 col.mounted pl. front. (port.) fold.tab. F. (The New-York historical society. The John Divine Jones fund series of histories and memoirs, VI) $25, o.p.
Costume index. LC 26-13064

Lefler, Heinrich

(illus.) Schröder, Severin. Die farbenharmonie in der damen-toilette

Legal costume

Damhouder, Joost. Praxis rerum civilium. 1569
Damhouder, Joost. Praxis rerum criminalium. 1562
Damhouder, Joost. Pupillorum patrocinium. 1564
Fehr, H. A. Das recht im bilde. 1913
Glasson, E. D. Les origines du costume de la magistrature. 1884
Marchand, Louis. Du costume de l'avocat à travers les âges. 1911

See also Doges; Prisoners

Caricature and satire

Physiologie de l'homme de loi. 1841?
Veth, Cornelis. Der advokat in der karikatur. 1927

China

Mason, G. H. The punishments of China. 1808

England

Book of the bench. 1909
The book of the ranks and dignities of British society. 1924
Darling, C. J. D., 1st baron. A pensioner's garden. 1926
Hooper, W. E., comp. The Central criminal court of London. 1909
Inderwick, F. A. The king's peace; a historical sketch of the English law courts. 1895
Jeaffreson, J. C. A book about lawyers. 1867

France

L'ancienne France: La justice et les tribunaux; Impôts, monnaies et finances. 1888
Le Magasin pittoresque. v 1 p266-67

Germany

Heinemann, Franz. Der richter und die rechtspflege in der deutschen vergangenheit. 1900

Legal costume—Germany—*Continued*
Klemm, Heinrich. Der vorschriftmässige talar der justiz-beamten im Königreiche Preussen mit den abweichungen für richter, staatsanwälte, rechtsanwälte und gerichtsschreiber in bild und schnitt dargestellt. 1885

16th century

Des allerdurchleuchtigsten groszmechtigsten unüberwindlichsten Keyser Karls des Fünfften und des Heyligen Römischen Reichs peinlichs gerichts-ordnung auff den reichsstägen zu Augspurg und Regenspurg in jaren dreissig und zwey und dreissig gehalten auffgericht und beschlossen. 1559
Bambergensis constitutio criminalis. Bambergische halszgerichts und rechtlich ordnung iñ peinlichen sachen. 1531

United States

Harvey, R. S. Wig and gown. 19—?

Legend in Japanese art. Joly, H. L.

Legend of Saint Meinrad. See Meinrad, Saint. Von sant Menrat

Legenda der heiligen Hedwig. Breslau, C. Baumgarten 1504
114 l. 68 illus.(66 col.) F.
First line: *Alby hebet sich an dy grosse lege*

Légendes et curiosités des métiers. Sébillot, Paul

Le Gendre, Léonce
Album du cortège historique, qui aura lieu à Bruges le 31 aout 1853, à l'occasion du mariage de ... monseigneur le duc de Brabant avec ... Marie-Henriette-Anne, archiduchesse d'Autriche. Bruges, Daveluy [1853]
44p. 12pl. Q.
Lipperheide 2681

Legends of the monastic orders. Jameson, Mrs A. B. M.

Léger
(illus.) Pannelier, J. A. L'Hindoustan, ou Religion, moeurs, usages, arts et métiers des Hindous

Léger, Abel
Abel Léger. L'élégance masculine, présenté par André de Fouquières. Paris, Nilsson [1912]
x,179p. S. 3fr.
Colas 1813

Legg, John Wickham
Church ornaments and their civil antecedents. Cambridge, [Eng.] The University press 1917
xvi,96p. 12pl.(part double) D. (The Cambridge handbooks of liturgical study)
Bibliography, by T. R. Gambier-Parry: p [xii]-xvi
LC 17-20985
(ed.) The coronation order of King James I. London, F. E. Robinson 1902
cii,118p. front.(port.) D. [Stuart series, v. II]
LC 3-4783

Legg, Leopold George Wickham
(ed.) English coronation records. Westminster, A. Constable & co. 1901
lxxxviii,413p. col.front. 16pl.(1 double) facsim. Q. 31s 6d, o.p.
Bibliographical foot-notes
Costume index. LC 2-9183

La **Légion** portugaise, 1807-1813. Boppe, P. L. H.

Le Gobien, Charles. See Le Comte, L. D., jt. auth.

Legouvé, Gabriel Jean Baptiste Ernest Wilfrid, and others
Les hommes célèbres de l'Italie, by MM. Legouvé, Schloelcher, Ch. Didier, Fortoul, Ferrier, Mazou; 28 portraits dessinés par Deveria. Paris, A. Ledoux 1845
240p. 30pl.(ports.) Q.
Lipperheide 1284

Legrand, Augustin
Candeur et bonté, ou Les quatre âges d'une femme. Paris, H. Janet ca1820
1 l. 29 col.pl. D.
Colas 1814

Legros, coiffeur
L'art de la coëffure des dames françoises, avec des estampes, ou sont représentées les têtes coeffées. Paris, A. Boudet 1768
5v. 16,100pl. Q.
The five volumes consist of *L'art de la coëffure* and 1.-4. *supplément* and form the third edition of this work. First edition *L'art de la coëffure des dames dans le nouveau goût d'a-présent* (Paris, [1765] 8p. 28pl.)
The second edition *Livre d'estampes de l'art de la coëffure des dames françoises* (Paris 1765) has the plates showing coiffures engraved more carefully, and six new plates showing technique
The fourth edition *L'art de la coëffure* (Paris, A. Boudet 1768) and *Supplément* (1768) is an abridgement of the third and contains in all 45 colored plates of hair styles
Colas 1815-1818

Le Hay
Recueil de cent estampes representant differentes nations du Levant. See entry under Moor, J. B. van
Wahreste und neueste abbildung des turckischen hofes. See entry under Moor, J. B. van

Le Herissé, A.
L'ancien royaume du Dahomey: moeurs, religion, histoire. Paris, E. Larose 1911
384p. illus. 23pl. 1 plan, 1 map. Q.

Lehmann, F. L. See Netto, J. F., jt. auth.

Lehmann, Gustav
Forschungen und urkunden zur geschichte der uniformirung der preussischen armee 1713-1807; 1. theil. Berlin, E. S. Mittler 1900
xx,252p. O.
Lipperheide 2190
Die trophäen des preuss. heeres in der königl. hof. und garnisonkirche zu Potsdam. Berlin, E. S. Mittler 1898
132p. 24pl. O.

Lehmann, Hans
Brünne und helm im angelsächsischen Beowulfliede; ein beitrag zur germanischen alterthumskunde. Leipzig, A. Lorentz 1885
30p. 2 fold.pl. O.
The author's inaugural dissertation (Göttingen) Another edition of the same date is from the press of G. Naumann
Lipperheide 2433. LC 2-28070

Die gute alte zeit; bilder aus dem leben unserer vorväter. Illus. von H. Bachmann, A. Hoffmann, C. Leuenberger, H. Meyer-Cassel, H. und E. van Muyden. Vorwort von bundesrat, M. Ruchet. Neuenburg, F. Zahn [1906]
700p. 121pl. Q.
Pictures are dated and show costume from Roman times thru the nineteenth century

Lehmann, Walter, and Doering, Heinrich
The art of old Peru. London, E. Benn 1924
67p. illus.(incl.map) 140pl.(part col.) fold.tab. F.
Translation of his *Kunstgeschichte des alten Peru*
"List of recent and important publications": p66-[68]
Contents: Lehmann, W. Historical survey; Doering, H. Land, people and monuments
LC 24-9697

Kunstgeschichte des alten Peru, erläutert durch ausgewählte werke aus ton und stein, gewebe und kleinode. Berlin, E. Wasmuth 1924
67p. illus.(incl.map) 140pl.(part col.) fold.tab. F.
Veröffentlichung des Forschungsinstituts des Museums für völkerkunde, Berlin.
"Neuere literatur in auswahl": p66-[68]
A rich source for designs of the Indians of Peru as used in pottery and textiles
LC 26-1343

Lehr- und lesebuch für männer- und frauenkleidermacher. Austria, Lower. Kammer für handel, gewerbe und industrie, Vienna

Lehrbuch der damenschneiderei. Schroeder, Minna

Lehrbuch der hebräischen archäologie. Nowack, Wilhelm

Lehrbuch für den perückenmacher und tischarbeiter. Gussmann, Paul

Lehrbuch für uniformschneider zur selbstbelehrung. Klemm, Heinrich

Lehrbuch zur gründlichen erlernung des damenfrisirens. Janik, Franz

Lehrbücher der handarbeit. Heine, Emmy

Lehrer und unterrichtswesen in der deutschen vergangenheit. Reicke, Emil

Lehrgänge für weiszstickerei und knüpfarbeit. Schinnerer, Luise

Lehrkursus für damen-garderobe. Bruckmann, H. W.

Lehrs, Max
Die aeltesten deutschen spielkarten des königlichen kupferstichkabinets zu Dresden. Dresden, W. Hoffmann [1886]
42p. 3 illus. 29pl. Q.
Reproductions of playing cards of the latter half of the fifteenth century, which show costume of that period
Lipperheide 467

Katalog der im germanischen museum befindlichen deutschen kupferstiche des xv. jahrhunderts. Nürnberg, Verlag des germanischen museums 1887
64p. 10pl. Q.
Lipperheide 468

See also Master of the Amsterdam cabinet, 15th century. The Master of the Amsterdam cabinet, by Max Lehrs

Leib-beschirmende und feinden trotzbietende fecht-kunst. Schmidt, J. A., fencing master

Der **leichenwagen** Alexanders des Grossen. Müller, K. F.

Leicht fassliche anweisungen zu verschiedenen weiblichen kunstarbeiten. Andreä, Nanette

Leiden, Hans Karl
Waffensammlung konsul a. d. Hans C. Leiden/Köln; vorwort von dr. Hans Stöcklein. [Köln, Bachemdruck, 1934]
71p. 1 l. 45pl. F.
At head of title: . . . Math. Lempertz'sche kunstversteigerung. [Katalog] 364
Catalog of a collection auctioned at Cologne, 1934
LC 34-19409

Leiden university. See Academic costume —Leiden university

Leidinger, George
(ed.) Munich. Bayerische staatsbibliothek. Meisterwerke der buchmalerei

Leigel, Gottfried
(illus.) Bible. German. Biblia

Leighton, John
London cries and public edifices; by Luke Limner, [pseud.] London, 1851
24p. 25pl.

Madre Natura versus the Moloch of fashion. A social essay ... by Luke Limner, esq. [pseud.] 4th ed. London, Chatto & Windus 1874
119p. incl.front. illus. D.
LC 9-22402

Leipold, Victor
Leutzsch' universal-monogramm-werk für gold-, bunt-, and weiss-stickerei, holz-, und glasmalerei. Gera, Germany, G. Leutzsch 1893
486pl. Q.
Lipperheide 4190

Leipzig. Kunstgewerbemuseum
Musterbuch für ornamente und stickmuster. See entry under Quentel, Peter

Spitzen des 16 bis 19. jahrhunderts. See entry under Strassen, Melchior zur

See also note under Dresden. K. Kunstgewerbemuseum. Posamente des xvi.-xix jahrhunderts

Leipzig. See Germany—Leipzig; also Street venders—Germany—Leipzig

Leipzig university. See Academic costume —Leipzig university

Leipziger meszscenen. Geissler, C. G. H.

Leipziger moden-journal, zeitschrift für die elegante welt; red. und hrsg. von N. Büchner. 1.-4. jahrg. 1840-1843. Leipzig, Expedition
4v. col.illus. Q.
Published weekly

Leipziger moden-zeitung. See Deutsche modenzeitung

Das **Leipziger** putzmacher- und nähtermädchen. Leipzig, A. F. Böhme 1798
176p. O.
Lipperheide 3786

Leipziger volksscenen. Geissler, C. G. H., and Menzel, A.

Leipzigermesse. Opiz, G. E.

Leitfaden für den gründlichen unterricht im maassnehmen und façonzeichnen der zuschneidkunst für damen. Suhr, H.

Leitfaden für die verschiedenen weiblichen arbeiten. Kübler, M. S.

Leitfaden zum selbstunterricht im spitzenklöppeln. Gebser, Clara

Leitfaden zum theoretischen und praktischen unterricht der damenschneiderei. Thormann-Bechlin, Louise

Leitner, Quirin, ritter von

Das kriegs-wesen des Heiligen Römischen Reiches deutscher nation unter Maximilian I und Carl V ... componirt u. gezeichn. von A. Reumann. Leipzig, J. L. Schrag (A. G. Hoffmann) [1860]
2 l. 7pl. F.
Lipperheide 2097

Die waffensammlung des osterreichischen kaiserhauses im K.K. Artillerie-arsenalmuseum in Wien; mit zeichnungen von J. G. Fahrnbauer, C. Mangold, C. Poschinger [etc.] Wien, H. Martin 1866-70
40p. 68pl.(10 col.) F.
Illustrations printed at the K.K. Hof- und staatsdruckerei, text printed by A. Holzhausen
Lipperheide 2419

(ed.) Maximilian I, emperor of Germany. Freydal

Leizelt, Balth. Freder.

(engr.) Collection des prospects

Lejeune, Eugène, and Lacauchie, A.

Les rois et reines de France en estampes; réprésentant par l'ordre chronologique leurs portraits et costumes depuis Pharamond jusqu'à nos jours. Paris, Martinet-Hautecoeur ca1860
34p. 24 col.pl. Q.
Plates are lithographed after designs by Lejeune and Lacauchie
Colas 1824. Lipperheide 1089

Leland, Charles Godfrey

(tr.) Heine, Heinrich. Shakespeare's maidens and women

Leleux, A., and others

(illus.) Pitre-Chevalier, P. M. F. C., called. La Bretagne ancienne et moderne

(illus.) Pitre-Chevalier, P. M. F. C., called. Bretagne et Vendée

Leloir, Mme Héloïse

Le Sélam, galerie fashionnable de costumes, de fleurs et de femmes, de tous les pays. Paris, V. Delarue; London, Anaglyphic co. ca1840
[2] l. 30 col.pl. F.
Colas 1825

Leloir, Maurice

Histoire du costume de l'antiquité à 1914. v8-10. Paris, E. Henri 1934-35
v8-10. illus. pl.(part col.) F. ea 200fr.
Descriptive notes on the plates are in French, English, Spanish, German and Italian. An excellent detailed and well illustrated treatment of European costume of the period, strongest in French. Material on parts of costume: cravats, shoes, etc. can be found thru the index. Each item is dated
Contents: v8 Epoque Louis XIII (1610-1643); v9 Epoque Louis XIV (1re partie, 1643-1678); v10 Epoque Louis XIV (2me partie) 1678-1715, Époque régence 1715-1725 Costume index

Lelyveld, Theodore Bernard van

La danse dans le théâtre javanais. Préface de Sylvain Lévi. Paris, Floury 1931
162p. 48pl. Q.
LC 32-13857

De javaansche danskunst. Amsterdam, Van Holkema & Warendorf 1931
258p. front. pl. Q.
Plates show dance costume of Java

Lemarchand, Albert

Album vendéen. See entry under Drake, T.

Le Meder, J. C.

Gallerie armoricaine: costumes et vues pittoresques de la Bretagne. See entry under Lalaisse, Hippolyte, and Benoist, Felix

Lemercier, Charles

Costumes coloriés des différents peuples d'Italie. Paris, Chabert [1830]
8 col.pl. Q.
Colas 1826

Lemonnier, Thomas Paul Henri

Ordonnance et règlement de Mgr. l'évêque de Bayeux et Lisieux [Lemonnier] sur le costume ecclésiastique, et notamment sur l'habit de choeur. (6 mai 1909). Bayeux, G. Colas 1909
14p. O. (Actes de Mgr. Lemonnier . . . no 18bis)

Le Moyne de Morgues, Jacques

Brevis narratio eorum quae in Florida Americae provĩcią Gallis acciderunt, secunda in illam navigatione, duce Renato de Laudõniere classis praefecto: anno MDLXIIII. Quae est secunda pars Americae ... Latio verò donata a C. C. A. ... Francoforti ad Moenum, tÿpis I. Wecheli, sumtibus vero T. de Brÿ 1591
30p. 13 l. illus. 42 col.pl. map. F. (In Bry, Theodor de. [Grands voyages] pt.2)
An account of the French expeditions to Florida under Ribault, Laudonnière and de Gourgues
Second Latin edition: 1609. German edition: *Der ander theyl, der neulich erfundenen landtschaft Americae, von dreyem schiffahrten, so die Frantzosen in Floridam (die gegen nidergang gelegen) gethan.* 1591
Lipperheide 1610. LC CA9-309

Lempertz, Math., firm, booksellers, Bonn-Cologne. See Leiden, H. K. Waffensammlung konsul a. d. Hans C. Leiden/Köln

Lenfant, Jacques
Histoire de la guerre des Hussites et du concile de Basle. Amsterdam, P. Humbert 1731
2v. 24 illus. 10pl. Q.
The plates are portraits of Hussite leaders, nobles and generals
Lipperheide 2091

Lengua Indians. See Indians of South America—Lengua Indians

Leningrad. See Russia—Leningrad; also Street venders—Russia—Leningrad

Lennep, Jakob van
Galerij van beroemde Nederlanders uit het tijdvak van Frederik Hendrik; afbeeldingen van Herman ten Kate & W. P. Hoevenaar. Utrecht, L. E. Bosch ca1850
166p. 27 col.pl. Q.
Cover title: *Neerlands Roem het tijvak van Frederik Hendrik*
Portraits of illustrious men of the Netherlands. Prince Frederick Henry of Orange lived from 1584 to 1647
Lipperheide 968

Lenniger, F. F.
Die anfertigung der damen-kleider; praktischer unterricht zur gründlichen erlernung derselben. 2. aufl. Leipzig, O. Schneider 1882
48p. 12pl. Q.
First edition (1880) had title: *Praktische anleitung zur erlernung der damen-schneiderei*
Colas 1827. Lipperheide 3822

Lennox, Lord William Pitt
Fashion then and now, illustrated by anecdotes, social, political, military, dramatic, and sporting. With remarks on dress, elections, duelling, [etc.] London, Chapman and Hall 1878
2v. O.
LC CA15-960

Lenoble, Alexandre
Histoire du sacre et du couronnement des rois et reines de France. Paris, Gaultier-Laguionie 1825
xii,656p. 1 pl. O.
"Précédé d'une introduction dans laquelle l'auteur ... fait un tableau général du mode d'inauguration du souverain, adopté chez les nations tant anciennes que modernes." Subtitle
Lipperheide 2485

Le Noble, Henri
Traité d'équitation à l'usage des dames. Paris, A. Dupont 1826
xxviii,199p. 10pl. D.
Lipperheide 2932

Lenoir, Alexandre
Monumens des arts libéraux, mécaniques et industriels de la France, depuis les Gaulois jusqu'au règne de François Ier. Paris, J. Techener 1840
48,48p. XLV(i.e. 46)pl. F.
"Présentant une suite non interrompue de monumens d'architecture, de sculpture et de peinture; de monnaies, médailles, meubles, armes et armures, costumes civils, religieux et militaires; machines, inventions utiles, etc., classés par siècles, et de manière à présenter un tableau des connaissances des Français aux différentes époques de leur histoire. Précédés d'un texte où précis de l'histoire des arts libéraux, mécaniques et industriels en France, depuis les Celtes et les Francs jusqu'au règne de François Ier, et d'une explication et analyse particulière et raisonnée de chaque figure ou monument." Subtitle
Lipperheide 1085. LC 14-15839

Musée royal des monumens français, ou Mémorial de l'histoire de France. See entry under Paris. Musée des monumens français

Lens, André Corneille
Le costume des peuples de l'antiquité prouvé par les monuments; nouv. éd. corr. rectifiée, et augm. par G. H. Martini. Dresden, Walther 1785
lvi,418p. 17 illus. 57pl. Q.
Plates engraved by J. Balzer
First edition *Le costume, ou Essai sur les habillements et les usages de plusieurs peuples de l'antiquité, prouvé par les monuments* (Liège, J. F. Bassompierre 1776. xxxii,411p. 51pl. Q.) Plates, engraved by Pitre Martenasie, show 161 numbered costume figures
Colas 1830, 1828. Lipperheide 105, 105a. LC 19-18414 (1776 ed.)

Das kostum der meisten völker des alterthums ... aus dem französischen übersetzt; berichtiget, mit zusätzen ... von G. H. Martini. Dresden, Walther 1784
lxxii,482p. 17 illus. 57pl. Q.
The author's *Le costume,* translated by C. S. Walther. Seven plates and some illustrations have been added
Colas 1828. Lipperheide 106

Lensi, Alfredo. See Stibbert, Federigo. Abiti e fogge civili e militari dal I al XVIII secolo. 1914

Lentz, Samuel
Becmannus; enucleatus, suppletus et continuatus; oder, Historisch-genealogische fürstellung des hochfürstlichen hauses Anhalt, und der davon abstammenden marggrafen zur Brandenburg, herzoge zur Sachsen und Sachsen-Lauenburg. Cöthen und Dessau, Cörnerischen buchhandlung 1757
11 l. 993p. 60pl. F.
Contains portraits of members of the House of Anhalt. Beckmann's *Historie des fürstenthums Anhalt* was published 1710 to 1716
Lipperheide 722

Lenz, E. von
Die waffensammlung des grafen S. D. Scheremetew in St Petersburg. Leipzig, K. W. Hiersemann 1897
228p. 26pl. F.

[Léo]
Travestissements enfantins. Paris, Hautecoeur-Martinet. 1880?
10 col.pl. Q.
Colas 1831

Travestissements parisiens. Paris, Hautecoeur-Martinet 1880?
18 col.pl. Q.
Colas 1832

Léon, Paul. See entry under Paris. Exposition internationale des arts décoratifs et industriels modernes, 1925. Rapport général

Leon, Pedro de Cieza de. See Cieza de Leon, Pedro de

León Salmerón, Africa, jt. auth. See Diego y Gonzalez, J. N. de

Leonard, Gardner Cotrell
The cap and gown in America ... to which is added an illustrated sketch of the intercollegiate system of academic costume. Albany, N. Y., Cotrell & Leonard 1896
20p. illus. O.
Reprinted from the *University magazine* for December 1893
LC E10-1813

Leonhardi, Friedrich Gottlob
Bildliche darstellung aller bekannten völker nach ihren kleidertrachten, sitten, gewohnheiten. Leipzig, Industrie-comptoir 1798
32pts. 122 col.pl. Q.
"Mit beschreibung aus den besten englischen, französischen und italienischen werken." Subtitle
Lipperheide lists also a second edition of the first part, dated 1801
Colas 1833. Lipperheide 48

Costumes de tous les peuples connu avec une notice succinte de leurs moeurs et de leurs religions. Leipzig, Comptoir-industrie ca1815
2v. 80pl. O.
Published in 20 parts, 4 plates to a part. Translation, by M. de Lestiboudois, of his *Bildliche darstellung*
Colas 1834

Leonhardt-Lysèr, Caroline, and Seifer, Cäcile
Encyclopädie der sämmtlichen frauenkünste; 2. verm. aufl. Leipzig, A. R. Friese 1837
xvi,224p. 26pl.(1 col.) O.
Lipperheide 4073

Leonnec, Paul
Nos marins. Paris, Bureau du Journal amusant 1887
32 col.pl. Q. 8fr.

Leonowens, Mrs Anna Harriette (Crawford)
The English governess at the Siamese court: being recollections of six years in the royal palace at Bangkok. With illustrations from photographs presented to the author by the king of Siam. Boston, Fields, Osgood 1870
x,321p. XVI pl.(incl.front. ports.) O.
Contains portraits of the King of Siam, and a prince and princess
Lipperheide 1505. LC 5-9743

The romance of the harem. Boston, J. R. Osgood 1873
viii,277p. XVII pl.(incl.front. ports.) O.
English edition (London, Trübner) has title: *The romance of Siamese harem life*
The plates show types from the household of the King of Siam
Lipperheide 1508. LC 5-9742

Leopold, Franz, and Mentzel, C.
Abbildung der königlich hannoverschen armee. Hannover, J. G. Schrader ca1820
18 col.pl. Q.
Colas 1835

Leopold, Order of
Fischer, Joseph, and Lýchdorff, Vincenz. Der ornat der ritter des erhabenen kaiserl. österreichischen Leopolds ordens. 1892

Leopoldi Guilielmi, Archiducis Austriae ... virtutes. Avancinus, Nicolas

Leóty, Ernest
Le corset à travers les âges; illus. de Saint-Elme Gautier. Paris, Ollendorff 1893
xii,110p. 50 illus. Q.
Colas 1836. Lipperheide 1735

Lepage, P. C. See La décoration primitive

Lepape, Georges
Les choses de Paul Poiret, vues par Georges Lepape. Paris, Maquet 1911
12 col.pl. Q.
Colas 1837

Costumes de théâtre, ballets & divertissements. Paris, L. Vogel 1920
4p. 20 col.pl.

Le Pautre, Jacques
(engr.) Bérain, J. L. Costumes de ballet
(engr.) Bérain, J. L. Maskenanzüge

Le Pautre, Jean
(engr.) Félibien, André, sieur des Avaux et de Javercy. Les divertissemens de Versailles

Le Perche
L'exercice des armes ou le maniement du fleuret. Paris, F. Chereau [1750]
25 l. 40pl. O.
Earlier edition 1676
Lipperheide 2965m

Le Prince, Jean Baptiste
Divers ajustements et usages de Russie ... dessinés d'après nature. 1764
10pl. Q.
Colas 1838

Divers habillements des prêtres de Russie, les mêmes qui étoient general't en usage avant la désunion des deux eglises ... dessinés en Russie d'après nature. [1764]
10pl. O.
Colas 1839

Œuvres de Jean-Baptiste Le Prince; Contenant plus de cent soixante planches gravées à l'eau-forte, & à l'imitation des dessins lavés au bistre; le tout d'après ses compositions, représentant divers costumes & habillemens de différens peuples du Nord. Paris, Basan & Poignant [etc.] 1782
1 p.l. 157pl. on 62 l. F.
Also published with title *Oeuvre de J. B. Le Prince, sur les moeurs, les coutumes et les habillemens de différents peuples*
Plates are drawn from life. Le Prince lived from 1734-81
A collected edition made up of the following works which were first published separately: *Divers ajustements et usages de Russie* [1764] 10pl.; *Divers habillements des prêtres de Russie, les mêmes qui étoient généralement en usage avant la desunion des deux eglises* [1764] 10pl.; *Les strelits; encienne et seule milice de Russie jusqu'au temps de Pierre Le Grand, qui les detruisit entierement à cause de leurs seditions. Ces habillements donnent en même temps une juste idée de l'ancien costume de cette nation et sont encore en usage dans une grande partie de l'empire* [1764] 8pl.; *Divers habillemens des femmes de Moscovie* [1764] 6pl.; *Vue des environs de St. Petersbourg* [1764] 2pl.; *Premiere suite de cris et divers marchands de Petersbourg et de Moscou* [1765] 6pl.; *2me-3me Suitte de divers cris de marchands de Russie* [1765] 12pl.; *IIe suitte d'habillement des femmes de Moscovie* [1768] 6pl.; *Diverses vues de Livonie* [1765] 6pl.; *Habillements de diverses nations* [1765] 6pl.;

Le Prince, Jean Baptiste—*Continued*
Suitte de divers habillements des peuples du nord [and IIe suite] [1765] 12pl.; *Ire suitte de coeffures dessinées d'après nature* [1768] 6pl.
Colas 1838-50. Lipp. 1339-40. LC 24-13879

Lepsius, Richard
Denkmaeler aus Aegypten und Aethiopien nach den zeichnungen der von Seiner Majestaet dem koenige von Preussen Friedrich Wilhelm IV nach diesen laendern gesendeten und in den jahren 1842-1845 ausgefuehrten wissenschaftlichen expedition; auf befehl Seiner Majestaet hrsg. und erlaeutert von C. R. Lepsius. Berlin, Nicolai [1849-56]
12v. 900pl.(part col.) F.
A preliminary pamphlet was published with same title (Berlin, Nicolai 1849. 36p.) and caption title: Vorläufige nachricht über die expedition, ihre ergebnisse und deren publikation
LC 5-9008

Lerberghi, P. van
(illus.) Godby, James. Italian scenery

Lermann, Wilhelm
Altgriechische plastik; eine einführung in die griechische kunst des archaischen und gebundenen stils; mit 80 textbildern und 20 farbigen tafeln, enthaltend nachbildungen von gewandmustern der mädchenstatuen auf der Akropolis zu Athen. München, Beck 1907
xiii,231p. illus. 20 col.pl. F.
LC 8-12589

Leroux, A. See Darjou, H. A. Costumes de la Bretagne

Leroux, Pierre Albert
(illus.) Brécard, C. T. La cavalerie
(illus.) Payard, Pol. Les chasseurs à pied
(illus.) Riols de Fonclare, J. É. de. L'infanterie
(illus.) Vidal, J. J. G. P. L'artillerie

Le Roux de Lincy, Antoine Jean Victor, and Leynadier, Camille
Les femmes célèbres de l'ancienne France par Le Roux de Lincy continué par C. Leynadier. Paris, A. de Vresse 1858
2v. 77 col.pl. Q.
Seventy plates are engraved by Gatine after Lanté and are from his *Galerie française de femmes célèbres*. The other seven plates are lithographs in the manner of Lanté
Contents: v 1 Depuis le ve jusqu'à la fin du xve siècle; v2 Depuis le xvie jusqu'à la fin du xviiie siècle
Colas 1768. Lipperheide 1088. LC 11-19831 (v 1 only)

Leroy, A.
(engr.) Niel, P. G. J. Portraits des personnages français les plus illustres du xvie siècle

Leroy, Alphonse
Recherches sur les habillemens des femmes et des enfans, ou Éxamen de la maniere dont il faut vêtir l'un & l'autre sèxe. Paris, Le Boucher 1772
350p. O.
Published later with imprint (Paris, Onfroy 1777)
Colas 1851. Lipperheide 3237

Leroy, Jules
(ed.) L'Aspic, moniteur générale des modes

Leroy, Louis
Les pensionnaires du Louvre; dessins de P. Renouard. Paris, J. Rouam 1880
97p. illus. F.
Shows French feminine costume of the period

Lery, Jean de. See Staden, Hans, jt. auth.

Lesage, Louis Ernest
Paris au xixe siècle et la fin du xviiie; costumes, scènes et élégances parisiennes. Paris, Alisié 1907
12 col.pl. F. 150fr.
"Revolution 1790. Directoire 1796. Premier empire 1804. Restauration 1815-1820-1830. Monarchie de juillet 1842. Second empire 1856-1867. Troisième république 1880-1889-1900." Subtitle

Lescure, Alfred
Barbes du dix-huitième siècle. Paris, Librairie des arts décoratifs 1919?
3p. 40pl. F. (Collection A. Lescure)

Cols en broderies et en dentelles, milieu du dix-neuvième siècle. Paris, Librairie des arts décoratifs 1919?
3p. 40pl. F. (Collection A. Lescure)

Dentelles anciennes de la collection Alfred Lescure. See entry under Overloop, Eugène van

Fonds de bonnets du xixe siècle. Paris, H. Ernst 1919?
3p. 54 mounted pl. Q. (Collection A. Lescure)
Introduction by C. Estrade

Gestickte kragen; mitte des xixe jahrhunderts. Plauen i Vogtland, C. F. Schulze [1910]
2p.l. 40pl. sq.F. (Collection A. Lescure)

Gestickte tücher aus der mitte des xixen jahrhunderts. Plauen i. V., C. F. Schulz 1919?
4p. 40pl. F. (Collection A. Lescure)

Mouchoirs brodés, milieu du dix-neuvième siècle. Paris, Librairie des arts décoratifs [190-?]
2 l. 40pl. F. (Collection A. Lescure)

Lesdain, Louis Bouly de. See Bouly de Lesdain, Louis

Leser, Jac., and Leser, Oskar
Die ritter- und verdienst-orden, ehren-, verdienst- und denkzeichen sowie dienstalters-auszeichnungen des Königr. Bayern. Nach authent. quellen bearb. Straubing, C. Attenkofer's verl. [1910]
253p. illus. 18 col.pl. F.

Leser, Oskar. See Leser, Jac., jt. auth.

Leslie, Frank
(pub.) Frank Leslie's ladies' gazette
(pub.) Frank Leslie's modenwelt

Lespès, Leo
Les contes du jour de l'an pour 1852. Paris, 1852
2 l. 322p. 16 col.pl. O.
Plates, by Sharles and Compte-Calix, show costume of French provinces
Colas 1852

Lesser, Friederike
Die kleine puppenschneiderin. Berlin, Winckelmann 1861
32p. 12pl. Q.

Lessing, C. F., and Lessing, Ida
Muster-blätter als vorlagen für stickereien in wolle und perlen. Cöln, D. Wüste ca1850
8 col.pl. Q.
Lipperheide 3954

Lessing, Ida. See Lessing, C. F., jt. auth.

Lessing, Julius
Album de broderies anciennes. Mulhouse, Dollfus-Mieg [1879]
12p. 63 illus. 24pl. Q.
Lipperheide 3861

Mönster för korsstyngsbroderier. Malmö, J. G. Hedberg 1880
3p. 25pl. Q.
Lipperheide 3862

Muster altdeutscher leinenstickerei. Berlin, F. Lipperheide 1878-[93]
4v. pl. O. (Musterbücher für weibliche handarbeit, hrsg. von der Redaction der modenwelt)
Volumes of embroidery patterns published in many editions during the dates given above
Lipperheide 3860

Lessons in hair dressing. Creer, Edwin

Lessore, A. E., and Wyld, W.
Voyage pittoresque dans la régence d'Alger pendant l'année 1833 ... publié par Ch. Motte. Paris, C. Motte [1835]
20p. 50pl. F.

Lester, Katherine Morris
Historic costume; a résumé of the characteristic types of costume from the most remote times to the present day; illus. by Ila McAfee; rev. ed. Peoria, Ill. Manual arts press [c1933]
244p. col.front. illus. O. $2.50
First edition 1925. Same collation
Bibliography: p237
Costume index. LC 33-25173

Lesueur, Charles Alexandre
See note under Péron, François. Voyage de découvertes aux terres Australes

Letainturier-Fradin, Gabriel
Le duel à travers les âges: Histoire et législation, duels célèbres, code du duel; avec une preface de A. Tavernier. Paris, Flammarion [1892]
14,303p. 8pl. 9 ports. O. 12fr.

Les joueurs d'épée à travers les siècles: maîtres d'armes, escrimisseurs, capitans, rodomonts, bravaches et ferailleurs. Paris, E. Flammarion [1905]
xiv,599p. illus. O.
Lipperheide 2996f

Le Tavernier, Jean
Cronicques et conquestes de Charlemaine; reproduction des 105 miniatures de Jean Le Tavernier, d'Audenarde (1460) par J. van den Gheyn. Bruxelles, Vromant 1909
24p. 105pl. O.
In portfolio
Reproductions of miniatures in David Aubert's *Les Cronicques et conquestes de Charlemaine* preserved as mss 9066, 9067, 9068, in the Section des manuscrits of the Bibliothèque royale de Belgique, Brussels
LC 9-26479

Lethbridge, Alan Bourchier
The new Russia, from the White Sea to the Siberian steppe. London, Mills and Boon c1915
xv,314p. front. pl. 3 fold.maps. O. 16s
LC 15-22734

Leti, Gregorio
Historia, overo Vita di Elisabetta, regina d'Inghilterra detta per sopranome la Comediante Politica. Amsterdam, A. Wolfgang 1693
2v. 18 illus. 29pl. D.
Lipperheide 505

La vie de l'empereur Charles v. Brussells, J. De Grieck 1710
4v. 46pl. D.
Original edition in Italian (Amsterdam, 1700)
Lipperheide 506

Letronne, Jean Antoine. See Choiseul-Gouffier, M. G. A. F., comte de

Lettenhove, H. M. B. J. Kervyn de, baron. See Kervyn de Lettenhove, H. M. B. J. L., baron

Letters and notes on the manners, customs, and condition of the North American Indians. Catlin, George

Letters from France, written by a modern tourist. See Manners & customs of the French

Lettres à Sophie sur la danse. Baron, A. A. F.

Lettres critiques et morales sur les modes du tems. Avignon, 1760
10,117p. T.
Colas 1853

Lettres et entretiens sur la danse. See Baron, A. A. F. Lettres à Sophie sur la danse

Lettres familières écrites d'Italie en 1739 et 1740. Brosses, Charles de

Lettres sur la Suisse. Rochette, D. R.

Lettres sur les fêtes du couronnement à Koenigsberg et Berlin, October 1861. Lallemand, Charles

Letts, Malcolm Henry Ikin
(tr.) Ehingen, Georg von. The diary of Jörg von Ehingen

Leucht, Christian Leonhard
Augusti corona augustissima Augustae coronata; das ist: Die crone ... des Leopoldi ... käyserliche gemahlin ... Frau Eleonora Magdalena Theresia ... als römische käyserin ... in ... Augspurg den 9. (19.) jenner des 1690sten jahrs gesalbet ... worden; vorgestellt durch C. L. Thucelium D. Augspurg, in verlegung L. Kronigers & G. Göbels sel. erben buchhändl. [1690]
28p. F.
Lipperheide 2510

Austria s. r. imperii conjux; das ist: des Heil. Röm. Reichs mit dem ... herzoglichen ertz-haus Oesterreich beständige ehe welche ... als ... Herr Josephus ... den 14. (24.) januarii zum römischen könig ... erwöhlet ... wurde. Augsburg, L. Kronigers & G. Göbels sel. erben buchhändl. 1690
82,40p. F.
Lipperheide 2511

Cronen zur zierd und schutz des Heiligen Römischen Reichs auf denen häuptern ... Eleonorä und Josephi &c. so auf das richtigste beschrieben nach allen umständen der wahl- und crönungs-solennitäten die vor- mit- und nachge-

Leucht, Christian L.—*Continued*
gangen ... nebenst der wahl-capitulation; vorgestellet durch Sigismund. Ferrarium, pseud. Nürnberg, L. Loschge 1690
198,110p. 29pl. Q.
The author's *Der eröffnete teutsche audientz-saal; entworffen durch Sigismund Schmidt* [pseud] (Franckfurt & Leipzig, F. Gegenbach 1697) is another edition with the same plates
Lipperheide 2512-3

Leuckfeld, Johann Georg
Johan. Georg. Leuckfeldi ... Antiqvitates gandersheimenses, oder Historische beschreibung des uhralten käyserl. freyen weltlichen. reichs-stiffts Gandersheim. Nebst einer besondern vorrede tit: herrn Johann: Andreæ Schmidts abtens zu Marienthal. Wolffenbüttel, G. Freytag 1709
7p.l. 478,[10]p. front. pl.(part fold.) O.
Plates contain pictures of abbesses taken from buildings and tombs, and portraits of later abbesses and canonesses, in the dress worn at the abbey of Gandersheim
Lipperheide 1865. LC 25-4659

Leucorande, Eleonora Charlotta
Die dem lieben frauenzimmer sehr angenehmen auch commoden contusche und reiffen-röcke. Linden-stadt (Leipzig) 1717
136p. 1 pl. O.

Leuthold, H. F.
Costumes suisses en mignature, dessinés d'après nature avec texte explicatif, par F. Meyer. Zurich, H. F. Leuthold [1837]
144p. 24 col.pl. S.
Title on cover: *La Suisse et ses inhabitants*
Costume of various cantons
Colas 2049

Leutzsch' universal-monogramm-werk. Leipold, Victor

[**Le Vacher de Charnois, Jean Charles**]
Recherches sur les costumes et sur les théatres de toutes les nations, tant anciennes que modernes; ouvrage utile ... aux artistes de tous les genres; non moins utile pour l'etude de l'histoire des temps reculés, des mœurs des peuples antiques ... Avec des estampes ... dessinées par M. Chéry, et gravées par P. M. Alix. Paris, Drouhin 1790
2v. (150,175p.) col.front. 54pl.(47 col.) map. Q.
Continuation of *Costumes et annales des grands théâtres de Paris.* The 2. éd., published 1802, is the same with a portrait of the author added
Colas 717-18. Lipp. 3203. LC 19-11286

See also Costumes et annales des grands théâtres de Paris

Le Vaillant, François
Second voyage dans l'intérieur de l'Afrique, par le cap de Bonne-espérance, dans les années 1783, 84 et 85. Paris, H. J. Jansen 1794
3v. XVIII(i.e. XXII)pl.(part fold.) O.
Contains pictures of natives
Lipperheide 1572. LC 18-19670

Levant. See East (Near East)

L'Évêque, Henry
Campaigns of the British army in Portugal, under the command of General, the Earl of Wellington. London, Colnaghi and E. Lloyd 1812
18p. 13pl. F.

Costume of Portugal. London, Colnaghi 1814
52p. 50 col.pl. Q.
Colas 1854

Le Verrier, Jean. See Bontier, Pierre, jt. auth.

Leverton, Mrs Waldemar
Dressmaking made easy; with chapters on millinery. London, G. Newnes [1909]
xii,158p. illus. D.

Levilly
(lithgr.) Costumes des différens états de l'Italie

Levinger, Mrs Elma C. (Ehrlich)
With the Jewish child in home and synagogue. New York, Bloch 1930
124p. illus. D.
"Something to read" at end of each chapter; Reference books for teachers: p123
Contains drawings of phylacteries, talith and other ceremonial accessories and an explanation of their use
LC 30-16813

Levinson, Andreĭ I͡Akovlevich
Bakst, the story of the artist's life. London, Bayard pr. 1923
240p. 1 l. incl. illus.(part mounted, part col.) LXVIII pl.(part mounted, part col.; incl. ports.) F.
Translation of his *Histoire de Léon Bakst.* Each plate is accompanied by guard sheet with descriptive letterpress
LC 24-13977

La danse d'aujourd'hui. [Paris, Duchartre et Van Buggenhoudt 1929]
xiii,517p. illus. pl. ports. Q.

Histoire de Léon Bakst. Paris, H. Reynaud 1924
63pl. Q.
Colas 1855

Meister des ballets. Potsdam, Müller 1923
231p. front. illus.(part col.) pl.(part col.) ports. Q.
Translated from the Russian by Reinhold von Walter. Some of the illustrations show ballet costume of the 18th and 19th centuries

Serge Lifar; destin d'un danseur. [Paris], B. Grasset [1934]
64p. front. 60pl.(incl. ports.) Q.

Les visages de la danse. Paris, B. Grasset [1933]
334p. illus.(incl. ports.) O.
LC 34-11968

Lewald, August
Die krönung in Mailand im jahre 1838. Carlsruhe, W. Creuzbauer [1838]
77p. 5pl. F.
Plates are after drawings by Foltz, engraved by E. Schuler and Hesslöhl
Lipperheide 2774

Lewis, Albert Buell
New Guinea masks. Chicago, Field museum of natural history 1922
Cover-title, 9p. 6pl. O. (Field museum of natural history. [Anthropology leaflet no4])
LC 26-1548

Lewis, Dio
Curious fashions. New York, Clarke brothers 1883
Cover-title, 32p. illus. S.
LC 17-12667

Lewis, Dominic Bevan Wyndham
(tr.) Barbey d'Aurevilly, J. A. The anatomy of dandyism

Lewis, George
A series of groups illustrating the physiognomy, manners, and character of the people of France and Germany. London, J. and A. Arch 1823
v.p. [52]pl. O.

Lewis, John Frederick
Lewis's sketches and drawings of the Alhambra, made during a residence in Granada, in the years 1833-4; drawn on stone by J. D. Harding, R. J. Lane, W. Gauci, and John F. Lewis. London, Hodgson, Bays & Graves [1835]
1 l. 25pl. F.
Views with figures in costumes of Granada
Lipperheide 1221

Lewis's sketches of Spain and Spanish character, made during his tour in that country, in the years 1833-4. London, F. G. Moon and J. F. Lewis 1836
[2] l. 25pl. F.
According to Colas the book also exists with plates colored
Colas 1858. Lipperheide 1222

Lewis, Lady Maria Theresa (Villiers) Lister
(ed.) Berry, Mary. Extracts of the journals and correspondence of Miss Berry, from the year 1783 to 1852

Lewis, Samuel Savage
The Lewis collection of gems and rings. See Cambridge. University. Corpus Christi college. Lewis collection

Lewis collection of gems and rings. Cambridge. University. Corpus Christi college

Lexa, František
(ed.) Lexová, Irena. Ancient Egyptian dances

Lexikon des kleidermachers enthalend in einzelnen aufsätzen eine ausführliche darstellung des gesammten fachwissens des kleidermachers in wort und bild; hrsg. und verlegt von der Expedition der europäischen modenzeitung. Dresden, Klemm und Weiss 1895-1904
9v. illus. 34pl.(part col.) O.
Colas 1859. Lipperheide 3849

Lexová, Irena
Ancient Egyptian dances; with drawings made from reproductions of ancient Egyptian originals by Milada Lexová; tr. by K. Haltmar. Praha, Czechoslovakia, Oriental institute 1935
84p. illus. 78(i.e. 75)pl.(part fold.) O.
Edited by Dr. František Lexa. Bibliography: p75-77
LC 37-2057

Lexová, Milada
(illus.) Lexová, Irena. Ancient Egyptian dances

Lexow, Einar Jakob
Joh. F. L. Dreiers norskefolkedragter. Kristiania, Cammermeyer 1913
35p. illus. 24 col.pl. F. (Norsk folkmuseum. Gammel norsk kultur i tekst og billeder)
Shows costume of various sections

Jorgen Garnaas og Nordmandsdalen. [Bergen, J. Grieg 1916]
77p. illus. pl. O. (Bergens Museums aarbok. 1915-16. Historisk-antikvarisk raekke, nr 1)

Leyden. Hoogeschool. See Jonge, J. K. J. de, jonkheer. Intogt van Frederik Hendrik in s'Hertogenbosch in 1629; also Maskérade, gehouden door de Leden van het Leidsche studentencorps

Leyden. Rijks ethnographisch museum
Tentoonstelling van kleederdrachten in Nederlandsch Indië. Voorgesteld door poppen ... 2. verm. en verb. opl. April, 1894. [Leiden, Boekdrukkerij van E. J. Brill 1894]
33p. ob.O.
Signed: Serrurier
LC 6-23663

See also Juynboll, H. H. Borneo

Leyden. Rijksmuseum van oudheden
Beschreibung der aegyptischen sammlung des Niederländischen reichsmuseums der altertümer in Leiden. Haag, M. Nijhoff; [etc.] 1905-32
v 1-14. illus. pl.(part col.) F.
In portfolios. Text of the 1st volume measures 32cm., the atlas 70cm.; v2-14 measure 41cm. On title-page of 1st volume: Herausgegeben in auftrage des Ministeriums des innern. Text of 1st volume has imprint: Leiden, Buchhandlung und druckerei vormals E. J. Brill, 1905
From volume 1, Die denkmäler des alten reiches, to v 14, Die denkmäler des neuen reiches und der saitischen zeit-grabtafeln und Osirisfiguren. Volume 1 is accompanied by an atlas of plates
LC 12-14324

Leynadier, Camille. See Le Roux de Lincy, A. J. V.

Lezioni di declamazione e d'arte teatrale. Morrocchesi, Antonio

Lezius, Martin
Das ehrenkleid des soldaten; eine kulturgeschichte der uniform von ihrer anfangen bis zur gegenwart. Berlin, Ullstein [1936]
415p. illus. 108 col.pl. facsims. Q.

L'Heureux, Mme Marie Anne
Pour bien s'habiller ... Collectien publiée sous le patronage du Lyceum. Paris, P. Lafitte c1911
xii,337p. 12pl. O.

Lhonesto essempio del vertuoso desiderio che hanno le donne di nobil ingegno, circa lo imparare i punti tagliati a fogliami. Pagani, Mattio

Lhote, Andre. See Delaunay, Sonia. Sonia Delauney; ses peintures, ses objets, ses tissus simultané, ses modes

Liagno, Theodoro Philippo
[Différens soldats; suite de douze estampes] Napoli, G. Orlandi [1585?]
12 col.pl.

[Liang, Shê-kan]
Mei Lan-fang, foremost actor of China.

Liang, Shê-kan—*Continued*
Shanghai, Printed at the Commercial press 1929
xii,132p. front. col.pl. ports.(1 col.; part fold.) Q.
LC 30-6083

Libellus novus politicus emblematicus civitatum pars. See Meisner, Daniel. Politica-politica

Liber ad honorem Augusti. Petrus, de Ebulo

Liber cronicarum. See Schedel, Hartmann. Das buch der chroniken

Liber geneseos. Działynski, A. T.

Liber regalis. Catholic church. Liturgy and ritual

Liber pontificalis. Catholic church. Liturgy and ritual. Pontifical

Liber regum. Nach dem in der K. K. Universitäts-bibliothek zu Innsbruck befindlichen exemplare zum ersten male herausgegeben, mit einer historisch-kritischen und bibliographischen einleitung und erläuterung von dr. Rudolf Hochegger. Leipzig, O. Harrassowitz 1892
iv,6p. 20 facsim. F.
Lipperheide 407. LC 5-24528

Liber singularis. Modius, François

Liber singularis de bysso antiquorum. Forster, J. R.

Liberia. Johnston, Sir H. H.

Liberty and co. See History of feminine costume

Libro de geometria. Alcega, Juan de

Libron, Fernand, and Clouzot, Henri
Le corset dans l'art et les moeurs du XIIIe au XXe siècle. Paris, F. Libron 1933
178p. front. illus. pl.(part col.) facsims. Q.
Bibliography p 169-70

Liceti, Fortunio
De anulis antiquis librum singularem. Utini, N. Schiratti 1645
250p. 1 pl.(with 40 illus.) Q.
Lipperheide 103. LC GS33-340

Lichtenfeld, Joseph
Principles of modern hairdressing. London, The author ca1882
33p. 10pl. O.
Colas 1861. Lipperheide 1712

Lichtwark, Alfred
Der ornamentstich der deutschen frührenaissance nach seinem sachlichen inhalt. Berlin, Weidmann 1888
xv,224p. 177 illus. O.
Lipperheide 4379

Lieb, Christophorus
Practica et arte di cavalleria, of Oeffeningh en konst des rydens. Utrecht, J. Ribbius 1671
2v. in 1. illus. 10pl. F.
The original edition published in German; *Übung und kunst des reitens* (Dresden, 1616)
Lipperheide 2906

Liebe, Georg Hermann Theodor
Das Judentum in der deutschen vergangenheit; mit 106 abbildungen und beilagen nach originalen, grösstenteils aus dem fünfzehnten bis achtzehnten jahrhundert. Leipzig, E. Diederichs 1903
127p. illus. 3pl. Q. (Monographien zur deutschen kulturgeschichte. 11. bd.)
Lipperheide 605g. LC 3-23571

Der soldat in der deutschen vergangenheit, mit einhundertdreiundachtzig abbildungen und beilagen nach den originalen aus dem 15.-18. jahrhundert. Leipzig, E. Diederichs 1899
157p. illus. pl.(part double) Q. (Monographien zur deutschen kulturgeschichte. [bd. 1])
Lipperheide 2042. LC G1205

Liebusch, Georg
Die deutschen reichsinsignien in ihrer symbolischen bedeutung. Quedlinburg & Leipzig, Ernst 1871
22p. O.
Lipperheide 1767

Lieder, Friedrich
Darstellung der königl. preussischen infanterie in 36 figuren ... gezeichnet von Friedrich Lieder und ... gestochen vom Professor Jügel. Berlin, L. W. Wittich 1820
1 l. 14 col.pl. F.
Colas notes an edition dated 1825 and one dated 1827, with the same plates; also an edition of 1827, with 16 colored plates
Colas 1863-65. Lipperheide 2161

Darstellung der königl. preussischen infanterie und cavallerie. Berlin, L. W. Wittich ca1818
24 col.pl. F.
Engraved by Wachsmann. Eleven plates show infantry, thirteen cavalry. These plates have been included in the author's *Darstellung der königl. preussischen infanterie* and *Darstellung der königl. preussischen cavallerie*
Colas 1862

Lieder, Friedrich, and Krüger, F.
Darstellung der königlich preussischen cavallerie in 41 figuren ... gezeichnet von ... Lieder und Krüger und ... gestochen vom professor Jügel. Berlin, L. W. Wittich 1821
1 l. 37 col.pl. F.
Colas notes another edition of 1821 with some variation in the engravings
Colas 1866-67. Lipperheide 2162

Liédet, Loyset
Histoire de Charles Martel, reproduction des 102 miniatures de Loyset Liédet (1470); par J. van den Gheyn. Bruxelles, Vromant 1910
23p. 102pl. O.
Reproduction of the miniatures in the prose romance *Histoire de Charles Martel et de ses successeurs,* compiled by David Aubert (mss. 6, 7, 8 and 9 of the Bibliothèque royale de Belgique)
"Relevé complet des travaux d'enluminure de Loyset Liédet": p 11-12
Bibliographical foot-notes
LC 10-27282

Liège and the Ardennes. See Omond, G. W. T. Belgium

Lienhart, and Humbert, René
Les uniformes de l'armée française depuis 1690 jusqu'à nos jours. Leipzig, M. Ruhl 1897-99
5v. 395 col.pl. Q.
Colas 1868

Lieven, Peter. See Liven, P. A., kni͡aź

Liez, Émile. See Nouvion, Pierre de, jt. auth.

The **life** and letters of Lady Sarah Lennox. Napier, Lady S. L. B.

Life and manners in Madrid. Kany, C. E.

Life and work of the people of England. Hartley, Dorothy, and Elliot, M. M. V.

Life in Abyssinia. Parkyns, Mansfield

Life in ancient Egypt. Erman, Adolf

Life in ancient Egypt and Assyria. Maspero, Sir G. C. C.

Life in London. Egan, Pierce

Life in mediaeval France. Evans, Joan

Life in Regency and early Victorian times. Chancellor, E. B.

Life in the army. Simkin, Richard

Life in the Homeric age. Seymour, T. D.

Life in the middle ages. Coulton, G. G.

The **life** of a soldier. Heath, William

The **life** of Beau Brummell. Jesse, William

The **life** of George Cruikshank. Jerrold, Blanchard

The **life** of the ancient Greeks, with special reference to Athens. Gulick, C. B.

The **life** of the Greeks and Romans described from antique monuments. Guhl, E. K., and Koner, W. D.

Life on a mediaeval barony. Davis, W. S.

Life on the Bosphorus. Spry, W. J. J.

Lifgardet till häst. See Strokirch, Einar von, illus. Kungliga lifgardet till häst

The **light** of the world. Elder, A. P. T.

The **lighter** side of Irish life. Hannay, J. O.

Lilienfeld, C. J.

Die antike kunst. Magdeburg, E. Baensch 1875

184p. 69 illus. O.
Lipperheide 126. LC 4-6577

Liller kriegszeitung. See Arnold, K. Kriegsflugblätter der Liller kriegszeitung

Lilley, M. C., & co., Columbus, O.

Illustrated catalogue and price list; Knights of Pythias lodge paraphernalia and costumes for all three ranks. Adapted to the revised ritual ... Manufactured by the M. C. Lilley & co. [Columbus, The Berlin printing co. c1899]

230p. illus. 51 col.pl. O.
LC 99-4259

Knights of the Maccabees paraphernalia and uniforms. [Columbus, 1893]

cover-title, 56p. illus. O.
LC 9-32519

Supplies for Royal arch chapters and councils of R. and S. masters, manufactured by the M. C. Lilley & co. Columbus, O. The M. C. Lilley & co. [1899]

146p. illus. (part col.) O.
LC 99-5432

Lillie, John

(jt. tr.) Challamel, Augustin. History of fashion in France

Lilly's Stickmuster-album ... entworfen und gezeichnet in der Gewerbeschule für mädchen in Hamburg. Harburg, G. Elkan [1879]

12 col.pl. O.
Lipperheide 3995

Lilly's Stickmusterbüchlein; eine sammlung in farben ausgeführter stylvoller stickmuster bearbeitet von den lehrerinnen der Hamburger gewerbeschule. Harburg, G. Elkan [1879]

5pts. 50 col.pl. D.
Lipperheide 3994

Lima: esquisses historiques. See note under Fuentes, M. A. Lima, or Sketches of the capital of Peru

Lima, or Sketches of the capital of Peru. Fuentes, M. A.

Limiers, Henri Philippe de

(ed.) Chevigny, de. La science des personnes de la cour, de l'épée et de la robe

Limner, Luke, pseud. See Leighton, John

Linas, Charles de

Anciens vêtements sacerdotaux et anciens tissus conservés en France. Paris, Didron 1860-63

3v. 48pl. (4 col.) O.
Describes ecclesiastical costume including the mitre, gloves, and shoes
Colas lists the author's *Rapport sur les anciens vêtements sacerdotaux et les anciens tissus* (1857) and his *Rapport sur les anciens vêtements sacerdotaux et les anciennes étoffes dan l'est et le midi de la France* (1858?) both published by Didron, Paris, each with 4 colored plates
Colas 1869-71. Lipperheide 1832

Linati, C.

Costumes civils, militaires et religieux du Mexique. Bruxelles, C. Sattanino [1828]

[48]p. front. 48 col.pl. (incl.ports.) Q.
An extract has title: *Costumes et moeurs de Mexique* (London, Engelmann 1830. 33 col.pl.)
Colas 1872-73. Costume index (1830 ed.)
Lipperheide 1622. LC 5-14175

Lincy, Antoine Jean Victor Le Roux de. See Le Roux de Lincy, A. J. V.

Lind, Karl

Ein antiphonarium mit bilderschmuck aus der zeit des XI. und XII. jahrhunderts im stifte St Peter zu Salzburg befindlich. Wien, A. Prandel 1870

46p. 5 illus. 45pl. Q.
Illustrated by Albert Camesina
Lipperheide 393

Die grabdenkmale während des mittelalters. Wien, K. Gronemeyr 1870

53p. 63 illus. 1 pl. Q.
From *Berichte und mittheilungen des Alterthums-vereins zu Wien,* bd. 11)
Lipperheide 355

Lindberg, C. F.

Objets choisis de la garde-robe royale de Suède ... photographies par C. F. Lindberg ... texte par C. A. Ossbahr. Stockholm, I. Haeggström 1888

2 l. 36pl. F.
Shows costume of Gustavus Adolphus of Sweden and his successors up to the 19th century
Colas 2256. Lipperheide 1057

(illus.) Montelius, Oskar. Antiquités suédoises

(illus.) Rygh, Oluf. Norse oldsager

Lindblom, Gerhard

Fighting-bracelets and kindred weapons in Africa. Stockholm [Gernandts boktryckeri a.-b.] 1927

32p. illus. O. (Riksmuseets etnografiska avdelning. Smärre meddelanden. [n:o4])
LC 35-14171

Lindemann, Emil
Das deutsche Helgoland. Berlin-Charlottenburg, Vita, deutsches verlagshaus [c1913]
xv,271p. front. illus. pl.(part col.) ports. maps.(part fold.) Q. M.7
A revision of *Die nordseeinsel Helgoland in topographischer, geschichtlicher, sanitärer beziehung* (1889)
Literatur: p259-65
LC 13-24858

Lindenschmit, Ludwig
Die alterthümer unserer heidnischen vorzeit ... hrsg. von dem Römisch- Germanischen centralmuseum in Mainz. Mainz, V. von Zabern 1868-1900
4v. illus. 314pl.(part col.) Q.
Contains material on the jewelry, weapons, armor of several ancient civilizations, especially Roman. Shows some Roman costume
Lipperheide 284

Handbuch der deutschen alterthumskunde ... In drei theilen. I. th. Die alterthümer der Merovingischen zeit. Braunschweig, F. Vieweg 1880-89
xii,514p. illus. XXXVII pl. O.
No more published. Bibliography: p64-67
Lipperheide 293. LC 3-25626

Das Römisch-germanische central-museum in bildlichen darstellungen aus seinen sammlungen. Mainz, V. von Zabern 1889
57 l. 51pl. Q.
Contents: 1 Die alterthümer der merovingischen zeit, von der mitte des 5. bis in das 8. jahrhundert (pl. 1-15); 2 Die alterthümer ... vom 5. jahrhundert nach Christus bis zurück zu der zeit um 50 vor Christus (pl. 16-29); 3 Die alterthümer der frühgeschichtlichen und vorgeschichtlichen zeit von den letzten jahrhundert vor Chr. aufwärts bis in die unbestimmbare zeit der ersten besiedelung unseres landes (pl. 30-50)
Lipperheide 304

Tracht und bewaffnung des römischen heeres während der kaiserzeit, mit besonderer berücksichtigung der rheinischen denkmale und fundstücke. Braunschweig, F. Vieweg 1882
30p. 12pl. Q.
Colas 1874. Lipperheide 253

Linderman, Frank Bird
Blackfeet Indians; pictures by Winold Reiss. [St. Paul, Brown & Bigelow 1935]
65p. 49 col.illus. col.pl. F. $3.50
"The Great northern railway asked Frank Bird Lindermann ... to write the story of the Blackfeet."—Foreword
Costume index. LC 35-17050

Lindner, Werner
Mark Brandenburg. See Deutsche volkskunst. v2

Lindsey, Ben, and Biddle, C. Harry
Irish lace, a history of the industry. London, Cunningham [1883]
11p. 10 pl. map. O.
At head of title: Mansion House exhibition, 1883
Lipperheide 4042

Lindström, Karl Johan
Costumi, e vestiture napolitani. Napoli, C. Batelli 1843
40 col.pl. Q.
Colas 1875. Lipperheide 1302

Lineff, Mme Eugènie
Russian folk-songs as sung by the people, and peasant wedding ceremonies customary in northern and central Russia. Chicago, C. F. Summy c1893
63p. front. illus. O.
LC 6-10761

Lingerie du Jardin des modes. 1928+ Paris, Condé Nast
Illus.(part col.) Q. 15fr. per no.
Published annually. Current 1938. A periodical on fashions in underwear. Supplement to *Jardin des modes*

Lingerie moderne. 1917?+ Paris, [etc] Société graphique
Col.illus. F.-Q.
Published semi-annually. Current 1937
A periodical on fashions in underwear

La **Lingerie** parisienne. no.1, 1907?+ Vienne, Le Granc chic; New York, Classique modes
Illus. pl.(part col.) F.
Published annually. Number 30, [March, 1937] latest number examined

Linges, insignes et vêtements liturgiques. Roulin, E. A.

Link, Joh. Carol. Elisabetha
Frauenschule; das A B C der schneiderskunst. Schweinfurt, Selbst-verlag der verfasserin 1881
2v. O.
Lipperheide 3824

Linschoten, Jan Huygen van
Itinerario, voyage ofte schipvaert ... naer Oost ofte Portugaels Indien. Amsterdam, C. Claesz 1595-96
4v. in 1. illus. 35pl. maps. F.
Translated into French with title: *Histoire de la navigation de Iean Hugues de Linschot Hollandois* (Amsterdam, E. Cloppenburgh 1638. 3. éd. augm. 36pl.)
Lipperheide 1454-55. LC F-3630 (Fr. ed.)

Linthicum, Marie Channing
Costume in the drama of Shakespeare and his contemporaries. Oxford, University press; New York, Oxford univ. press 1936
307p. xx pl.(incl.front. ports.) O. $5; 15s
On cover: Costume in Elizabethan drama
A work on the colors, textiles, clothing in use in England in the 16th and early 17th centuries
"Short title list of principal works cited": p[284]-97
LC 36-27363

Lintum, Christ te
Onze schutter-vendels en schutterijen, van vroeger en later tijd, 1550-1908, in beeld en schrift, met inleidend woord van prof. Dr. P. J. Blok ... aquarellen van J. Hoynck van Papendrecht en geschiedkundigen tekst van Dr. C. te Lintum. S'-Gravenhage, W. P. van Stockum [1910]
22p. 50 l. 50pl.(part col.) F.

The **Lion;** a journal of gentlemen's newest fashions, published in Paris and London. v 1-4; 1845-1848. London, J. H. Chappel and J. S. Womach
4v. Q.
Published monthly. English edition of *Le Lion*
Colas 1877

Le **Lion;** journal des nouveautés et des modes d'hommes. 1.-12. année; avr. 1842-1853. Paris
Q.
Published monthly

Lioni, Ottavio
Ritratti di alcuni celebri pittori del secolo XVII; disegnati, ed intagliati in rame dal ... Ottavio Lioni ... si e' aggiunta La vita di Carlo Maratti scritta da Gio. Pietro Bellori ... all' anno 1689. Roma, A. de Rossi 1731
272p. 12 illus. 12pl. Q.
Half length portraits, engraved by Lioni, show masculine costume of the seventeenth century
Lipperheide 1251

Lipowsky, Félix Joseph
Bürger-militär almanach für das königreich Baiern, 1809-1810. München, E. A. Fleischmann 1809-10
2v. 22pl. (4 col.) O.
No more published
Lipperheide 2192

Nazional garde almanach für das königreich Baiern, 1811-1812. Ingolstadt, A. Attenkover 1811-12
2v. 14pl. O.
Lipperheide 2192a

Sammlung Bayerischer national-costume. München, Hermann & Barth ca1830
52p. 49 col.pl. F.
Also known with plates in black and white, without text
Colas 1879. Lipperheide 755-756

Lipperheide, Franz Joseph, freiherr von
Katalog der Freiherrlich von Lipperheide'schen kostümbibliothek. Berlin, F. Lipperheide 1896-1905
2v. fronts. illus. ports. facsims. Q.
Catalog issued in 32 parts. Cover-title (pt. 1-12): Katalog der Freiherrlich von Lipperheide'schen sammlung für kostümwissenschaft. Mit abbildungen. 3. abtheilung: Büchersammlung
Lists in all 5064 titles, in classified order with an author index and with a subject index to the classification. Besides costume of various countries and periods includes books on hygiene, aesthetics, laws relating to clothing, criticism of various periods, and caricature
Collection presented to the Prussian government and now in the Staatliche kunstbibliothek, Berlin
LC 1-16626

Lipperheide, Frieda
Die decorative kunst-stickerei. Berlin, F. Lipperheide 1890-96
72,20,20p. 286 illus. 26pl. (13 col.) Q.
Lipperheide 3873

Muster altitalienischer leinenstickerei. Berlin, F. Lipperheide 1881-83
2v. 159 illus. 60pl. Q.
Second edition: 1883-92
Lipperheide 3865-3866

Musterblätter für künstlerische handarbeiten. Berlin, F. Lipperheide 1889-95
5v. 66 col.pl. Q.
Plates show embroidery designs
Lipperheide 4012

Das spitzenklöppeln. Berlin, F. Lipperheide 1898
xvi,63,43p. 267 illus. Q.
Lipperheide 4058c

Lipperheide, Frieda, and Dorn, Anna
Die webe-arbeit mit hand-apparat. Berlin, F. Lipperheide 1886
x,93p. 208 illus. Q. (Musterbücher für weibliche handarbeit. Neue folge. [1. bd.])
Lipperheide 4151

Lipperheide, Frieda, and Marggraff, Clara
Die Smyrna-arbeit. Berlin, F. Lipperheide 1886
53p. 121 illus. 12 col.pl. (Musterbücher für weibliche handarbeit. Neue folge. [2. bd.])
Lipperheide 4152

Lippmann, Friedrich
Kupferstiche und holzschnitte aller meister in nachbildungen. Berlin, G. Grote 1889-95
6pts. 50pl. F.
Selections from artists of the 15th to 18th century
Lipperheide 343

The seven planets; tr. by Florence Simmonds. London, Asher 1895
13p. 38pl. F.
At head of title: International chalcographical society, 1895
Translation of his *Die sieben planeten.* Five series of planet-pictures, dating to the 15th and 16th centuries, show costume of those centuries

Die sieben planeten. [Berlin, Gedruckt in der Reichsdruckerei 1895]
14p. 4 illus. 38pl. F.
At head of title: Internationale chalkographische gesellschaft, 1895
Lipperheide 474

Lips, Johann Heinrich
(illus.) Guts-Muths, J. C. F. Gymnastik für die jugend

Lipsius, Justus
Iusti Lipsi Saturnalium sermonum libri duo, qui de gladiatoribus; editio ultima. Antverpiae, ex officina Plantiniana 1598
136p. 4pl. 8 illus. Q.
Lipperheide 215

Lisbon. See Street venders—Portugal—Lisbon

Lisbon. Centro de estudos filologicos. See Menino, Pero. Livro de falcoaria

Lisch, Georg Christian Friedrich
Meklenburg in bildern redigirt und mit erläuterndem texte. Rostock, J. G. Tiedemann 1842-45
96pl. (16 col.) O.
The colored plates show Mecklenburg costume
Colas 1881. Lipperheide 797

List of books, &c. in the library of the Museum. Edinburgh. Royal Scottish museum. Library

List of books, &c. relating to armour and weapons in the library of the Museum. Edinburgh. Royal Scottish museum. Library

List of officers of the Royal regiment of artillery. Kane, John, of the Royal artillery

List of references on dress reform. United States. Library of Congress. Division of bibliography

A **list** of works on costume. See Victoria and Albert museum, South Kensington. Costume

Lister, O. H.
(illus.) Jackson, Margaret. What they wore

Literature, Costume in. See Costume in literature

Lithographic views of military operations in Canada. Beauclerk, Lord Charles

Lithuania
Danilowicz, Casimir de. La Lituanie artistique. 1919
Holme, Charles, ed. Peasant art in Russia. 1912
Rutter, Owen. The new Baltic states and their future. 1926

La **litografia** en Mexico en el siglo XIX. Mexico (city) Biblioteca nacional

Litta, Pompeo
Famiglie celebri d'Italia. Milano, P. E. Giusti 1819-83
12v. illus. 4-25pl.(157 col.) maps. F.
Contains many portraits of prominent Italians and is valuable for Italian costume of the 16th-18th centuries
Lipperheide 1274

Litterateurs français. See note under Langley, E. F. Romantic figures in pen and color

Little, Alicia Helen Neva (Bewicke)
Round about my Peking garden; by Mrs. Archibald Little. London, T. Fisher Unwin; Philadelphia, J. B. Lippincott 1905
284p. col.front. 85pl. O.
Many of the plates show Chinese costume
LC w6-21

Little, Mrs Archibald. See Little, A. H. N. B.

Little, Mrs Frances
Eighteenth-century costume in Europe. See entry under New York. Metropolitan museum of art

The **Little** messenger of fashions and the Confident united. Juillet 1852-1854
O.
English edition of *Le Petit messager des modes*
Colas 2332

Little Russia. See Russia—Ukraine

Littret, Claude Antoine de. See Montigny, C. A. L. de

La **Lituanie** artistique. Danilowicz, Casimir de

Liturgische gewänder aus dem Stifte St. Blasien im Schwarzwalde. Heider, Gustav

Die **liturgische** gewandung im Occident und Orient. Braun, Joseph

Die **liturgischen** gewänder und kirchlichen stickereien. Cologne. Schnütgen-museum

Die **liturgischen** gewänder und kirchlichen stickereien des Schnütgenmuseums Köln. Witte, Fritz

Liturgy of funeral offerings
The liturgy of funerary offerings, the Egyptian texts with English translations, by E. A. Wallis Budge. London, K. Paul, Trench, Trübner 1909
xviii,268p. illus. D. (Books on Egypt and Chaldaea, v.25)
LC 10-13900

Lītvīnov", Pelageīâ Îakovlevna
IUzhno-russkiĭ narodnyĭ ornament ... Ornement national de la Russie meridional. Kiev, tip. M. P. Fritsa 1878
13p. 20 col.pl. Q.
Lipperheide 3960

Līven, Petr Aleksandrovīch, knîaz'
The birth of ballets-russes; translated by L. Zarine. London, G. Allen & Unwin [1936]
377p. col.front. 35pl.(1 col.) O.
LC 37-388

Livery
Baker, W. H. A dictionary of men's wear. 1908
Lami, E. L. Voitures. ca1825
Padiglione, Carlo. Delle livree, del modo di comporle e descrizione di quelle di famiglie nobili italiane. 1888

See also Servants

Middle ages

Ashley, Sir W. J. An introduction to English economic history and theory. 1923-25

19th century

Klemm, Heinrich. Buch der livreen. 1895
Prewett, F. T. & company, London. The West-End hand-book of liveries. 189-?
Rogers, Peet & co. New York. Livery, 1898. 1898
Saint-Épain, de. L'art de composer les livrées au milieu du XIX. siècle d'après les principes de la science heraldique précédé d'une notice historique. 1853

Livery, 1898. Rogers, Peet & co. New York

Lives and legends of the English bishops and kings. Bell, Mrs N. R. E. M.

The **living** races of mankind. Hutchinson, H. N.; Gregory, J. W., and Lydekker, Richard

Livische figuren. See Amman, Jost. Icones Livianae

Livius, Titus
Römische historien. Mainz, J. Schöffer 1505
3v. 235 illus. F.
A new edition (Mainz, J. Schöffer 1530. 445p. 274 illus.) has few changes in text but many changes in the illustrations
Lipperheide 438, 615

Titi Livii Patavini Romanae historiae principis, libris omnes quotquot ad nostram aetatem pervenerunt. Francofurti ad Moenum 1568
24,988,20p. illus. F.
Woodcuts by Jost Amman. The woodcuts are also contained in Jost Amman's *Icones livianae,* which see

Livonia. See Estonia; Latvia

Livre à dessiner; les exercices de Mars. Guerard, N.

Le **livre** à la mode. Caraccioli, L. A. de

Livre de dentelles. See Vecellio, Cesare. Corona delle nobili et virtuose donne

Le **livre** de desseins charmans. See Tuer, A. W. The book of delightful and strange designs

Livre de la chasse. Paris. Bibliothèque nationale. Mss. (Fr. 616)

Le **livre** de la coiffure. Woestyn, Eugène

Le **livre** de lingerie. Sera, Domenico da

Le **livre** de quatre couleurs. Caraccioli, L. A. de

Livre des métiers d'Étienne Boileau. See Boileau, Étienne. Réglemens sur les arts et métiers de Paris

Le **livre** des parfums. See Rimmel, Eugene. The book of perfumes

Livre d'esquisses. Callot, Jacques

Livre d'estampes de l'art de la coëffure des dames françoises. Legros, coiffeur

Le **livre** d'heures de la reine Anne de Bretagne. Catholic church. Liturgy and ritual. Hours

Livre d'or de la Légion étrangère. France. Armée. Infanterie. Légion étrangère

Le **livre** d'or des metiers. Lacroix, Paul, and others

Livre du sacre de l'empereur Napoléon. Masson, Frederic

Le **livre** du très chevalereux comte d'Artois et de sa femme, fille au comte de Boulogne. Barrois, J.

Livre nouveau de diverses nations. Baur, J. W.

Livres à dentelles & dessins d'ornements, reproduits & publiés par Amand-Durand sous la direction de Emmanuel Bocher. Paris, A. Durand 1882-87
113pl. F.
A facsimile reprint of three separate titles: *Ain new formbüchlin bin ich gnandt allen künstlern noch unbekandt,* by Schartzemberger (Augsburg, 1534); *La vera perfettione del disegno,* by G. Ostaus (Venetia 1591); *Le livre de lingerie,* by D. da Sera (Paris, 1584)
Lipperheide 3883

Livro de falcoaria. Menino, Pero

Llanta, Jacques François Gaudérique
Les jeunes fiancées; suite de portraits et costumes variés de tous les pays. Paris, V. Delarue [1834]
6 col.pl. F.
Lipperheide 571m

(illus.) Cogniet, Léon, and Raffet, D. A. M. Illustration de l'armée française depuis 1789 jusqu'en 1832

Lloyd's magazine. v 1+ 1887+ London, Hansard union
Illus. O.
Published monthly. Current 1938
Title varies: 1889-1915 *Baby, an illustrated magazine for mothers;* 1915-17 *Mother's magazine and Baby;* 1917+ *Lloyd's mothers magazine*

Lloyd's mothers magazine. See Lloyd's magazine

Das **lob** der mode, eine rede, gehalten und gedruckt nach der mode. No place, 1772
54p. O.
Lipperheide 3471

Lobrede auf die perrüquen. See Deguerle, J. M. N. Éloge des perruques

Lobspruch des fürstlichen freischiessens zu Innsbruck im Oktober 1569. Flexel, Lienhard

Locataires et proprietaires. Daumier, T. V.

Loch, Sophy. See Longman, E. D., jt. auth.

Locher, Jakob
Panegyricus ad Maximilianum. Strassburg, J. Grüninger 1497
62 l. 20 illus. Q.
Shows costume of the 15th century
Lipperheide 430

Locher, N. See Dinkel, M., jt. auth.

Lochom, Michiel van
La mode des habits et vestementz des femmes de diverses nations. M. van Lochem excu. No place, ca1640
17pl. O.
This engraver also published a suite of seventeen plates with title *Moeurs et costumes de femmes chez diverses nations*
Colas 2971

Lochon, Michel van. See Lochom, Michiel van

A **lock** of hair. Speight, Alexanna

Lodge, Edmund
Portraits of illustrious personages of Great Britain, engraved from authenic pictures in the galleries of the nobility and the public collections of the country. London, Harding and Lepard 1835
12v. 240pl. O.
Portraits date from early 16th until middle 19th centuries
Also published in Bohn's illustrated library (London, G. H. Bohn 1849-50. 8v.); American edition (Boston, D. Estes 1902. 12v.)
Lipperheide 998. LC 13-20077 (Bohn ed.) A10-2337 (Amer. ed.)

Lodi, Giacinto
Amore prigioniero in Delo; torneo fatto da' signori Academici torbidi in Bologna li XX. di marzo MDCXXVIII. Bologna, V. Benacci [1628?]
123p. 15pl. F.
Engraved by G. B. Coriolano
Lipperheide 2817

Loeber, Christophorus Gulielmus
(praeses) Dissertationem academicam de mutatione formarum in vestibus, i.e., Von veränderung der kleider-moden. Ienae, Litteris Wertherianis 1722
28p. Q.
Colas 1888. Lipperheide 3235

Löffler, Ludwig
Berlin und die Berliner, in wort und bild. Leipzig, J. J. Weber 1856
138p. 60 illus. O. (Webers illustrirte reisebibliothek, nr.5)

Löfvall, Mme J. H.
How to cut, fit, and finish a dress. Boston, A. Mudge 1892
67p. diagrs. S.
LC 8-31419

Löhneyss, George Engelhard
Bericht vom bergwerck wie man dieselben bawen und in guten wolstande bringen sol, sampt allen dazu gehörigen arbeiten. Stockholm und Hamburg 1690
343p. 16pl. F.
Lipperheide 1991

Loeillot, Karl. See Aubry, Charles, jt. auth.

[**Lörer, and Vogel**]
[Costumes suisses.] Berne, Bourgdorfer ca1825
12 col.pl. Q.
Plates engraved by Johann Hurlimann
Colas 1904

Löschenkohl, H.
(pub.) Schema aller uniform der kaiserl. königl. kriegsvölkern. Wien, H. Löschenkohl ca1791
86pl.(79 col.) O.
According to Colas these plates have some resemblance to those in the *Schema* published by Artaria & compagnie
Colas 1909

Löwenheim-Röhn, E.
Aesthetik und cynismus; eine entgegnung auf die Vischer'sche schrift "Mode und cynismus". Berlin, E. Stande 1879
30p. O.
Lipperheide 3496

Loewenkreuz, Emanuela Mattl-. See Mattl-Loewenkreuz, Emanuela

Löwy, Albert
(tr.) Kottenkamp, F. J. History of chivalry and ancient armour

Löwy, J.
(photographer) Masner, Carl. Die costüm-ausstellung im K. K. Oesterreichischen museum 1891

Loftie, William John
The coronation book of Edward VII. king of the Britains and emperor of India. London, Paris, New York & Melbourne, Cassell [1902]
1p. l. iv,188p. illus.(part in gold and colors) 24 col.pl. (incl. front. port.) Q.
LC 3-2241

Kensington, picturesque and historical. London, Field & Tuer 1888
xix,287p. illus. 6 col. pl. Q.

Logan, Cornelius Ambrose
Memoir. See note under Logan, J. A. The volunteer soldier of America

Logan, James
The clans of the Scottish Highlands, illustrated by appropriate figures, displaying their dress, tartans, arms, armorial insignia, and social occupations, from original sketches, by R. R. McIan, esq. With accompanying description and historical memoranda of character, mode of life, &c. ... by James Logan. London, Ackermann 1845-47
2v. col.fronts. 72 col.pl. Q.
Also published: London, Willis and Sotheran 1857
Colas 1892 (1857 ed.). Lipperheide 1032 (1857 ed.). LC 12-36289

Gaelic gatherings; or, The Highlanders at home, on the heath, the river, and the loch ... plates by R. R. M'Ian. London, 1848
24 col.pl. F.
Published in reduced size under title: *McIan's Highlanders at home; or Gaelic gatherings* (Glasgow, D. Bryce 1900. 268p. 24 col.pl. O.)
Colas 1891

McIan's costumes of the clans of Scotland; seventy-four coloured illustrations, with descriptive letterpress by James Logan. Glasgow, D. Bryce; New York, F. A. Stokes 1899
343p. 74 col.pl.(incl.front.) D.
With reproduction of t.-p. of original edition: *The clans of the Scottish Highlands*
"The original work in two large quarto volumes is given here complete and unaltered further than being reduced in size, properly paged, and indexed for easy reference." Subtitle
LC A29-394

The Scottish Gaël; or, Celtic manners, as preserved among the Highlanders: being an historical and descriptive account of the inhabitants, antiquities, and national peculiarities of Scotland ... ed., with memoir and notes, by the Rev. Alex. Stewart. Inverness, H. Mackenzie [1876?]
2v. col.fronts. illus. pl.(part col.) coat of arms. O.
Table of clan tartans: v2, p[417]-24
First edition: London, Smith, Elder 1831
Colas 1889-1890. Lipperheide 1033. LC 15-23694

Logan, John Alexander
In joyful Russia. New York, D. Appleton 1897
x,275p. col.front. pl.(part col.) ports. (part col.) D.
Shows Russian costume of the 19th century
LC 4-4161

The volunteer soldier of America. With Memoir of the author and Military reminiscences from General Logan's private journal. Chicago and New York, R. S. Peale 1887
706p. col.front. pl. ports. O.
Memoir by C. A. Logan
LC 15-10003

Lohmann, Hermann
Aussprüche der heiligen schrift und der kirchenväter über kleiderpracht und moden zur warnung und belehrung gesammelt. Düsseldorf, P. Roschütz 1844
80p. O. (Kleine katholische hausbibliothek, 1. bd.)
Colas 1893. Lipperheide 3488

Loliée, Frédéric Auguste
Les femmes du second empire (papiers intimes) Paris, F. Juven [1906]
xi,369p. ports. O.
LC 30-3534

Lombardy. See Italy—By region or province—Lombardy; also Crown jewels—Italy—Lombardy

Lommel, Georg, and Bauer
Das königreich Bayern in seinen acht kreisen bildlich und statistisch-topographisch sowie in acht historisch-geographischen spezialkarten bearbeitet. Nürnberg, J. T. Schubert 1836
68 l. 8 col.pl. F.
Plates show costume of Bavaria
Colas 1894. Lipperheide 757

Loncin, Albert Joseph. See Conlin, A. J. Der christliche welt-weise

Londerseel, Assuerus van
(engr.) Nicolay, Nicolas de, sieur d'Arfeuille. Les navigations, pérégrinations, et voyages, faicts en la Turquie

Londesborough, Ursula Lucy Grace (Bridgeman) Denison, baroness
Catalogue of a collection of ancient and mediæval rings and personal ornaments, formed for Lady Londesborough. [London] Printed for private reference 1853
88p. illus. 2 fold. pl. O.
LC 12-9799

London. See Street venders—England—London

London. Fanmakers
Catalogue of competitive exhibitions of fans. London, 1897
O.

London. International health exhibition, 1884. See Wingfield, L. S. Notes on civil costume in England

London. Lyceum theatre
Souvenir of Macbeth produced at the Lyceum Theatre, by Henry Irving, 29th December, 1888; illustrated by C. Cattermole and J. B. Partridge. London, Cassell [1888]
17 l. illus. pl. ob.S.

Souvenir of Shakespeare's historical play King Henry the Eighth, presented at the Lyceum theatre, 5th January, 1892, by Henry Irving; illustrated by J. B. Partridge, W. Telbin, J. Harker, Hawes Craven. London, Black and White pub. co. 1892

London. Museum
Costume. [London and Beccles, W. Clowes] 1934
211p. illus. LVI pl. O.
Prepared by Thalassa Cruso
On English dress from 1558 to 1933 including official robes, uniforms and vestments. Plates show costumes and parts of costume each dated
Costume index. LC 35-274

London. University. University college
Amulets, illustrated by the Egyptian collection in University college, London. See entry under Petrie, Sir W. M. F.

Tools and weapons illustrated by the Egyptian collection in University college, London. See entry under Petrie, Sir W. M. F.

London, a pilgrimage. Jerrold, Blanchard

London art fashions for ladies. Spring/summer 1937+ London, Women's wear
Illus. F.
Published semi-annually. Current 1938

London. Knight, Charles, ed.

London as it is. See Boys, T. S. Original views of London as it is

London characters. Cruikshank, George, and Cruikshank, I. R.

The **London** cries. See The cries of London

London cries and public edifices. Leighton, John

London in the eighteenth century. Besant, Sir Walter

London in the nineteenth century. Besant, Sir Walter

London in the time of the Stuarts. Besant, Sir Walter

London in the time of the Tudors. Besant, Sir Walter

London interiors, with their costumes & ceremonies; from drawings made by permission of the public officers, proprietors & trustees of the metropolitan buildings. London, J. Mead 1841
96p. 24pl. Q.
Illustrated by T. H. Shepherd and engraved by H. Melville, J. Shury, W. Radclyffe, and J. H. Le Keux
Lipperheide 1027

The **London journal**
Advice to young ladies from the London journal of 1855 and 1862, with illustrations from the same and other sources, selected by R. D. London, Methuen [1933]
vii,55p. front. illus. sq.O.

London, Paris und Wien. v 1-6, 1811-1815. Rudolstadt, Hof-buch- und kunsthandlung
6v. col.pl. O.
Continues *London und Paris*
Title varies: v 1-2, 1811, *Paris, Wien und London;* v3-5, 1812-13 *Paris und Wien*
Colas 1896. Lipperheide 4585

London tailor and record of fashion. v 1-38, 1876-Jan. 1914. London
Volumes 1-8 published as *Monthly record of fashion.* Absorbed *Gentleman's magazine of fashion* Dec. 1894. Merged into *Sartorial gazette*

London types. Nicholson, William

London und Paris. v 1-24, 1798-1810. Rudolstadt, Hof-buch und kunst-handlung
ca250 pl.(part col.) O.
Continued as *Paris, Wien und London,* later *London, Paris und Wien*
Colas 1895. Lipperheide 4585

Londoner ausrufer. Amiconi, Jacob

Long, Mrs Gabrielle Margaret Vere (Campbell). See Bowen, Marjorie, pseud.

Longchamps et Paris élégant reunis. See Le Paris élégant, journal de modes

Longchamps, revue des modes. See Le Paris élégant, journal de modes

Longin, Anatole Henri Émile
Historique du 14e régiment de chasseurs. Paris, E. Person 1907
303p. illus. col.pl. ports. Q.

Longman, Charles James, and Walrond, Henry
Archery, by C. J. Longman and Col. H. Walrond; with contributions by Miss Legh, Viscount Dillon, Major C. Hawkins Fisher, Rev. Eyre W. Hussey, Rev. W. K. R. Bedford, J. Balfour Paul, L. W. Maxson. London, Longmans, Green 1894
xvi,534p. front.illus. pl. ports., 2 maps(1 fold.) D. (The Badminton library of sports and pastimes)
Bibliography: p472-503
LC 1-18569

Longman, Eleanor D., and Loch, Sophy
Pins and pincushions. London & New York, Longmans, Green 1911
xx,188p. front. 1 illus. pl. O.
LC 12-36236

Longmans' historical illustrations; England in the middle ages. Barfield, T. C.

Lonicer, Johann Adam
Pannoniae historia chronologica. Franckfort, 1596
229p. 10 illus. 4pl. map. Q.
Illustrated by J. J. Boissard and engraved by T. de Bry. Shows military costume of the 16th century
Lipperheide 2054

Ständ und orden der H. Römischen Catholischen Kirchen. See entry under Amman, Jost

(tr.) Staden, Hans, and Lery, Jean de. Americae tertia pars

Lonicer, Phillip
(comp.) Chronicorum turcicorum. Francoforti ad Moenum, S. Feyerabendt 1578
3v. 209 illus. F.
A second Latin edition was published in 1584
The illustrations are woodcuts by Jost Amman, some from Amman's *Icones Livianae,* and some from Fronsperger's *Kriegsbuch*
Contents: v 1 Turcorum origo; v2 Diversorum regnorum; v3 Vita, indoles et adversus Turcas res gestae Georgii Castrioti, by Martinus Barletius
Lipperheide 1400. LC 5-13699

See also Amman, Jost. Icones Livianae; and Amman, Jost. Insignia

Lonicerus, Johann Adam. See Lonicer, J. A.

Lonigo, Michel
Delle vesti purpuree e d'altri colori con quali adorna la dignità cardinalitia. Venetia, E. Deuchino 1623
60p. O.

Lonlay, Dick de, pseud. See Hardoin, Georges

Lonsdale, H. W., and Tarver, E. J.
Illustrations of mediaeval costume. London, H. W. Lonsdale and E. J. Tarver 1874
12p. 50pl.(with 370 illus.) Q.
Colas 1898. Lipperheide 356

Looking backward at woman's fashionable dress. Bible, G. W., and Bible, D. P.

Loose, Walter
(ed.) Behaim, Paulus. Briefe eines Leipziger studenten aus den jahren 1572 bis 1574. 1880

Lopes, Duarte
Beschrijvinge van 't koninckrijck Congo met 't aenpalende landt Angola. Amsterdam, J. Hartgers 1650
96p. 6 illus. Q.
Lipperheide 1570

Lopez, Eduart. See Lopes, Duarte

[**Lopez, J. A.**]
Cabrera y su ejército; album de las tropas carlistas de Aragon. Madrid, 1844
14pl. ob.Q.
Colas 1899

Lorange, Anders Lund
Den yngre jernalds svaerd. Et bidrag til Vikingetidens histoire og teknologi. Efter forfatterens Dod udgivet ved Ch. Delgobe. Bergen, Bergens museum 1889
80p. 8pl. Q.

Lorch, Melchior. See Lorich, Melchior

Lord, William Barry
The corset and the crinoline: a book of modes and costumes from remote periods to the present time. By W. B. L. London, Ward, Lock, and Tyler [1868]
xii,227p. incl.illus. 46pl. O. 7s 6d, o.p.
Issued later with title *The freaks of fashion* ([1870] Ward, Lock and Tyler LC 16-25749)
Colas 692. Costume index. Lipperheide 1734. LC 16-25750 (under title)

Lorentz, Mme E., and Lacroix, A.
Cours complet d'enseignement professionel de la coupe du corset. Paris, École moderne de coupe de Paris. 1911?
152p. 1 pl. ob.Q. (Cours complet d'enseignement professionel de la coupe, ptie. 1)

Lorenzano y Butron, Francisco Antonio
(ed.) Cortés, Hernando. Historia de Nueva-España

Lorenzini, Paolo
Storia del costume dei popoli attraverso i secoli. Con quadri a colori di Tancredi Scarpelli. Firenze, Casa editrice Nerbini 1934
847p. illus.(incl. maps, plans) col.pl. Q.
LC AC36-3591

Les **lorettes.** Talin, H. M., and Dąmourette

Lorey, Eustache de, and Sladen, Douglas Brooke
Queer things about Persia. Philadelphia, J. B. Lippincott 1907
xix,381p. front. pl.(1 col.) ports. O.
LC 8-1464

Lorgnettes. See Eyeglasses and lorgnettes

Lorich, Melchior
Des kunstreichen und weitberühmtem Melchior Lorichs wolgerissene unnd geschnittene türckische figuren in kupffer und holtz. Hamburg, T. Gunderman 1641
2 l. 128pl. F.
This is the third edition of this work. plates of first edition with title *Wolgerissene und geschnittene figuren in kupffer und holz,* published 1619, bear dates 1570 to 1583. Second edition: *Figure disegnate* (Hamburg, M. Hering 1626. 128pl.) Third edition republished with slight change in title (Hamburg, T. Gundermann 1646. 128pl.) The Lipperheide copy of third edition has only 106 plates
Colas 1900-1903. Lipperheide 1405

Lorin, Henri. See Archinard, L. Q. L'autre France (Tunisie, Algérie, Maroc). 1914

[**Loritz**]
Dieppe. Dieppe, C. Motte ca1830
4pl. F.
Contents: Cauchoise, costume de Cany; Cauchoise, costume de Bacqueville; Biville sur mer, fille d'Auberge; Dentellière
Colas 1905

Lorraine
Roy, Hippolyte. La vie, la mode et le costume au XVIIe siècle, époque Louis XIII. 1924
Edwards, G. W. Alsace-Lorraine. 1918

See also subdivision Lorraine under Kings and rulers; Nobles

Metz

Le Clerc, Sébastien. Les sept anciennes modes de Metz. ca1665

Lorsay, Eustache
Galerie illustrée des célébrités contemporaines; les théâtres de Paris ... lithographiés par Colette. Paris, S. Raçon ca1840?
2v. 100 col.pl. O.
Colas 1906

Lory, Gabriel, and Moritz, F. W.
(eds.) Costumes Suisses, dédié à son Altesse Royale le prince royal de Prusse, dessinés d'après nature. Neufchatel, C. H. Wolfrath 1824
55 l. col.front. 55 col.pl. Q.
Text is by Monvert. Some of the plates are reproduced in J. B. B. Eyriès's *La Suisse*
Colas 1908. Lipperheide 909

Lose blätter zur geschichte der königlich sächsischen armee. Beck, August

Lostalot-Bachoué, E.
(ed.) Saint Prosper, A. A. C. de, and others. Histoire de tous les peuples et des revolutions du monde

Lostelneau, de
Le mareschal de bataille, contenant le maniment des armes, les evolutions, plusieurs bataillons, tant contre l'infanterie que contre la cavalerie. Paris, E. Migon 1647
459p. 448 illus. F.
Illustrations show the use of muskets and pikes
Lipperheide 2080

Eyn **loszbuch** ausz der karten gemacht und alleyn durch kurtzweyl erdacht, wer aber zu glauben sich daran wolt keren das selbig liesz sich unrecht leren ... mit einer einleitung von dr. Adolf Hofmeister. Rostock, Volckmann & Jerosch 1890
Cover-title, viii p. facsim.(15p. illus. diagr.) O.
"Photolithographische reproduction des einzigen bekannten exemplars im besitze von Volckmann & Jerosch, antiquariat im Rostock." Subtitle
The original, without printing place or date, was published by M. Schürer, Strassburg, between 1506 and 1520. Illustrations show people of the 15th and 16th century, wearing pointed shoes
Lipperheide 442. LC 19-19192

Lothar, Rudolph
Das Wiener burgtheater. Leipzig, Berlin, und Wien, E. A. Seemann 1899
212p. illus. Q.

Lothrop, Samuel Kirkland
Polychrome guanaco cloaks of Patagonia. New York, Museum of the American Indian, Heye foundation 1929
30p. illus. col.pl. LXV-LXVI. Q. (Contributions from the Museum of the American Indian, Heye foundation. v7, no.6)
Bibliography: p27-30
LC 29-17249

Lotus land. Thompson, P. A.

Louandre, Charles Léopold
Les arts somptuaires; histoire du costume et de l'ameublement et des arts et industries qui s'y rattachent, sous la direction de Hangard-Maugé, dessins de Cl. Ciappori, introduction générale et texte explicatif par Ch. Louandre, impressions in couleurs par Hangard-Maugé. Paris, Hangard-Maugé 1857-58
2v. in 1. col.fronts. and atlas of pl.(part col.) 2v. Q.
Originally edited by Ferdinand Séré, and completed under the direction of M. Hangard-Maugé. cf. v.2, p248
Colas 1910, 2712. Costume index. Lipperheide 333. LC 32-14662

Louden, Mrs Adelaide Bolton, and Louden, Norman P.
Historic costumes through the ages; a portfolio of 20 plates in color, representative costumes, historic ornament, annotations. Philadelphia, Pa., H. C. Perleberg [c1936]
20 col.pl. sq.F.
Bibliography: p[4]
LC 36-18695

Louden, Norman P. See Louden, Mrs A. B., jt. auth.

Louis IX, Saint, king of France. See Paris. Bibliothèque nationale. Mss.(Lat.10525) Psautier de Saint Louis

Louis XI. Montorgueil, Georges

Louis XIV. Dayot, A. P. M.

[**Louis Salvator, archduke of Austria**]
Die Serben an der Adria; ihre typen und trachten. Leipzig, F. A. Brockhaus 1870-78
9pts. in 1v. 45 col.pl. F.

Louisens und Friederikens, kronprinzessin, und gemahlin des prinzen Ludwig von Preussen, geborner prinzessinnen von Mecklenburg-Strelitz, ankunft und vermählung in Berlin im december 1793. Berlin, W. Dieteric 1794
116p. 6pl. O.
Lipperheide 2532

Louisiana. See United States—Louisiana

Loumyer, Jean François Nicolas
Moeurs, usages et costumes de tous les peuples du monde ... par Auguste Wahlen [pseud.] Bruxelles, Librairie historique-artistique 1843-44
4v. 211 col.pl. Q.
With the collaboration of J. J. Van Beveren. Illustrated and engraved by Doms, Duverger, Lisbet, Markaert, Mercier, and others
Contents: v 1 Asia; v2 Océanie; v3 Afrique, Amérique; v4 Europe
An Italian edition translated by N. Dally has title: *Usi e costumi sociali, politici e religiosi di tutti i popoli del mondo* (Torino, Stab. tip. Fontana 1844-47. 4v. 245 col.pl.)
Colas 3041-3042. Costume index. Lipperheide 61-62. LC It-95 (Italian ed.)

Ordres de chevalerie et marques d'honneur; publié par Auguste Wahlen [pseud.] Bruxelles, Librairie historique-artistique 1844
341p. 108 col.pl. Q.
Half-title: *Histoire, costumes, décorations de tous les ordres de chevalerie, et marques d'honneur*
Eighty four of the plates are also in Cibrario's *Descrizione*
Lipperheide 1928

See also Van Beveren, J. J., and Du Pressoir, Charles. Costume du moyen âge d'après les manuscrits les peintures et les monuments contemporains (Attributed)

Loutherbourg, Philippe Jacques de
1er recueil de modes et habits galans de différents pays ... gravés par J. F. Foulquier. No place, 1771
6 col.pl. Q.
Shows 18th century costume
Colas 1913

Première suite de soldats. Paris, chez d'auteur ca1770
6 col.pl. D.
Colas 1911

Loutherberg, Philippe J. de—*Continued*
Seconde suite des figures. Paris, chez l'auteur ca1770
6 col.pl. D.
Shows 18th century costume
Colas 1912

Louvel
Dernières créations parisiennes. No place, [1884]
24pl. F.
Colas 1914

Lovett, Alfred Crowdy
(illus.) India and the war
(illus.) MacMunn, Sir G. F. The armies of India

Lovett, Richard
Norwegian pictures, drawn with pen and pencil; containing also a glance at Sweden and the Gotha canal. New ed. rev. and partly re-written. London, Religious tract society 1890
224p. incl.front. illus. pl. fold.map. Q.
LC 4-25550

Pictures from Holland, drawn with pen and pencil by Richard Lovett. London, Religious tract soc. 1887
223p. front. illus.(incl. ports.) map. Q.
LC 4-28121

Low, Frances H.
Queen Victoria's dolls ... illustrated by Alan Wright. London, G. Newnes 1894
42 l. 44 illus.(40 col.) Q.
Lipperheide 3149

Lowes, Mrs Emily Leigh
Chats on old lace and needlework. London, T. F. Unwin 1908
386p. front. pl. ports. O.
Bibliography: p[10]
LC w9-1

Lowinsky, Thomas Esmond
Modern nymphs; being a series of fourteen fashion plates; with an introductory essay on clothes by Raymond Mortimer. London, F. Etchells & H. Macdonald 1930
69p. 2 l. incl.col.pl. ob.D. (The Haslewood books)
LC 31-21507

Lowrie, Walter
Monuments of the early church. New York, Macmillan 1923
432p. illus. O. (Handbooks of archaeology and antiquities)
Pages 383-413 discuss civil dress of the Christians during the first six centuries, and ecclesiastical dress toward the end of this period
Published also under title: *Christian art and archaeology*
Bibliography: p415-26
LC 1-25602 (1901 ed.)

Loyal volunteers of London and environs. Rowlandson, Thomas

Loÿ, Léon Charles Émile Auguste
Historiques du 84e régiment d'infanterie de ligne "Un contre dix", du 9e régiment d'infanterie légère "L'incomparable", et du 4e régiment de Voltigeurs de la Garde. 1684-1904. Lille, L. Danel 1905
620p. pl.(1 col.) ports. Q.
LC 24-23587

Loyd, Lady Mary Sophia (Hely-Hutchinson)
(tr.) Uzanne, L. O. Fashion in Paris

Loziński, Władysław
Polnisches leben in vergangenen zeiten. München, G. Müller [1917?]
xi,334p. 67pl.(1 col.) O. (Polnische bibliothek. Abt 1, Bd 1.)
Translated by A. v. Guttry
Shows Polish costume of the 16th, 17th, 18th centuries

Prawem i lewem; obyczaje na Czerwonej Rusi w pierwszej połowie XVII. wieku. Lwów, H. Altenberg 1904-13
2v. illus. O.
Contents: t. 1 Czasy i ludzie; t. 2 Wojny prywatne
Some of the plates show Polish costume of the 17th century

Zycie polskie w dawnych wiekach. Lwów, H. Altenberg 1921
261p. front. illus.(part col.) pl.(part col.) ports. Q.
Illustrated by M. Treter. Shows costume of Poland in various periods

Luard, John
A history of the dress of the British soldier, from the earliest period to the present time. London, W. Clowes 1852
xxiv,171p. 50pl. Q. 30s, o.p.
Bibliography: p[iii]-iv
Colas 1915. Costume index. Lipperheide 2271. LC 15-9988

Views in India, Saint Helena and Car Nicobar. London, J. Graf, printer 1833
60 l. 60pl. Q.
Includes some costume plates
Lipperheide 1490

Lubbaeus, Richard
(illus.) Coornhert, Dierick. Emblemata moralia

Lucas, Arthur. See Le Blond, A. W. L., jt. auth.

Lucet, J. J.
(ed.) La Correspondance des dames, ou Journal des modes et spectacles de Paris

Luchs, Hermann
Schlesische fürstenbilder des mittelalters ... nach originalaufnahmen von T. Blätterbauer, K. Bräuer, A. Bräuer, B. Mannfeld und A. Wöffl. Breslau, E. Trewendt 1872
xii,356p. illus. 47pl.(9 col.) Q.
Lipperheide 732

Ueber die bilder der Hedwigslegende. Breslau, Grasz, Barth & Comp. [1861]
28p. 25 illus. Q.
["Im Schlackenwerther codex von 1353, dem Breslauer codex von 1451, auf der Hedwigstafel in der Breslauer Bernhardinkirche und in dem Breslauer drucke von 1504."] Subtitle
Lipperheide 457

Luchu islands. See Riu Kiu islands

Luciano, Baldassarre
Cenni sulla Sardegna ovvero usi e costumi amministrazione, industria e prodotti dell' isola; 2. ed. Torino, C. Schiepatti 1843
280p. 26 col.pl. Q.
Colas 1916. Lipperheide 1317

Lucientes, Francisco José de Goya y. See Goya y Lucientes, Francisco José de

Lucretia, Romana, pseud.
Ornamento nobile, per ogni gentil matrona, dove si contiene bavari, frisi, d'infinita bellezza ... con ponti in aria fiamenghi, et tagliati; opera fatta ... in Venetia, appresso L. de' Vecchi MDCXX. Venedig, F. Ongania 1876
3 l. 14pl. F.
A facsimile reprint of the 1620 edition
Lipperheide 3917

Ludewig, Johann Peter von. See Hoffmann, Martin. Annales Bambergensis episcopatus

Ludolphus de Saxonia
Das leben Christi. Antwerpen, C. Leeu 1488
402 l. 145 col.illus. F.
A translation of his *Vita Christi*
Lipperheide 419

Ludwig XIV, der Sonnenkönig. Bourgeois, Emile

Lübeck. See Germany—Lübeck

Luebecker trachten. Warncke, Johannes

Lübeck's bürger-militair. Stolle, C.

Lübker, Friedrich Heinrich Christian
Friedrich Lübker's Reallexikon des classischen alterthums, für gymnasien; 7. verb. aufl. hrsg. von dr. Max Exler. Leipzig, B. G. Teubner 1891
1332p. illus. fold.pl. O.
First edition: 1855
Illustrations show ancient Greek and Roman costume
Lipperheide 169. LC 17-7283 (1874 ed.)

Lücken, Gottfried von
Greek vase-paintings; peintures de vases grecques. The Hague, M. Nijhoff 1923
16p. 120pl. F.
Issued in 4 portfolios. Originally issued with title page dated 1921. Shows ancient Greek costume

Lüders, H. See Kaiser, Friedrich, jt. auth.

Lüpkes, Wiard
Ostfriesische volkskunde. Emden, W. Schwalbe [1925]
xv,399p. illus. O.
Bibliography: p382-85
Shows costume and jewelry of East Friesland
First edition: 1907

Lützow, Karl Friedrich Arnold von
(ed.) Dürer, Albrecht. Albrecht Dürer's Holzschnitt-werk in auswahl

See also Geschichte der deutschen kunst

Lullin de Châteauvieux, Jacob Frédéric. See Forestier, Alc. de, ed. Les Alpes pittoresques

Lumbermen
Michiels, Alfred. Les bûcherons et les schlitteurs des Vosges. 1857

Lund, Frederik Christian
Danske nationaldragter; 3. oplag bearb. af figurmaleren Luplau Janssen, med forklarende tekst af kunsthistorikeren Sigurd Müller. Kolding, P. Blicher [1916]
3 l. 30 mounted col.pl. F.
In portfolio. Legends in Danish, French and English
First edition (Kjöbenhavn, ca1850 12 col.pl.); second edition (Kjöbenhavn, Dansk forlags-konsortium 1890. 30p. 31 col.pl.)
Colas 1917-1918 (1st-2d ed.) Costume index. Lipperheide 1048m-1048n (1st-2d ed.)
LC 16-24895

Lund, Frederik Troels. See Troels-Lund, T. F.

Lund, Johann
Die alten jüdischen heiligthümer gottesdienste und gewohnheiten ... in einer ausführlichen beschreibung des gantzen levitischen priesterthums. Hamburg, G. Liebernickel 1701
1090p. 68 l. front. pl. port. F.
Contains a chapter and two plates dealing with dress of Jewish high priests, also two plates showing Pharisees

Lundborg, Herman Bernhard
Svenska folktyper. Stockholm, H. W. Tullberg [1919]
235p. illus. col.pl. ports. F.
Issued in seven parts

Lundin, Claës, and Strindberg, August
Gamla Stockholm anteckningar ur tryckta och otryckta källor framletade. Stockholm, J. Seligmann [1882]
xii,639p. 222 illus. 3pl. map. O.
On social life in Stockholm 1730-1850. Some of the illustrations show dress
Lipperheide 1055

Lundorp, Michael Caspar
Helden buch, oder beschreibung der vonembsten potentaten, keyser, königen, fürsten, graffen, kriegs-obersten, und helden, welche in nochwehrendem teutschen kriege ... sich gebrauchen lassen ... zusampt aller deren wahren abbildungen und contrafeyten ... durch Nicolaum Bellum [pseud.] Franckfurt am Meyn, E. Kempffer 1629
356p. 38pl. illus. Q.
Lipperheide 519

Lundström
Panorama delle scene populare di Napoli. [Napoli, Lundström 1832]
16 col.pl. ob.T.

Lunettes et lorgnettes de jadis. Heymann, Mme Alfred

Lurine, Louis
(ed.) Les rues de Paris. Paris ancien et moderne; origines, histoire, monuments, costumes, mœurs, chroniques et traditions. Paris, G. Kugelmann 1844
2v. illus. 40pl. port. Q.
Published in 73 parts
Lipperheide 1188. LC 4-26482

Lusatia. See Germany—Lusatia

Lussan-Borel
Traité de danse avec musique contenant toutes les danses de salon avec une théorie nouvelle de valse et boston, du cotillon et du cake-walk. Paris, E. Flammarion [1903]
244p. 150 illus. O.
Lipperheide 3140c

Lustiges schneiderbüchlein. Hosentuch, Johann

Luther, Martin
(tr.) Bible. German. Biblia

Luthmer, Ferdinand
Goldschmuck der renaissance, nach originalen und von gemälden des xv.-xvii. jahrhunderts Berlin, E. Wasmuth 1881
71p. illus. 30pl. (18 col.) F.
In portfolio
French edition *Joaillerie de la renaissance* (Paris, A. Quantin 1882)
Lipperheide 1753. LC 10-27299

Ornamental jewellery of the renaissance in relation to costume. London, H. Sotheran 1882
4p. 30pl. F. 84s, o.p.
Translation of his *Goldschmuck der renaissance*
Costume index

(ed.) Rothschild, M. K., freiherr von. Der schatz des freiherrn Karl von Rothschild

Luton, England. Public museum
The romance of the straw hat, being a history of the industry and a guide to the collections. Luton, Public museum 1933
48p. illus. 15pl. on 8 l. O.
Bibliography p45-48

Lutz, Henry Frederick
Textiles and costumes among the peoples of the ancient Near east. Leipzig, J. C. Hinrichs; New York city, G. E. Stechert 1923
x,207p. illus. O. $2
Bibliographical foot-notes
Shows costume of ancient Egypt, Assyria, and Babylonia
Costume index. LC 24-13025

Le **luxe** français. Bouchot, H. F. X. M.

Luxus und modesucht der jezigen zeit von ihrer lächerlichen seite, und nach ihren schreklichen würkungen auf völker- und familienglück ... geschildert von einem wittwer. Leipzig und Frankfurt, 1799
125p. O.
Lipperheide 3482

Luyken, Caspar
Deutliche vorstellung der Nürnbergischen trachten ... und anjetzo mit erklärungen versehen. Nürnberg, J. D. Tyroff 1766
24p. 20pl. Q.
These plates were published without title or text (Nürnberg, C. Weigel 1701)
Colas 1919. Lipperheide 781a, 781 (1701 ed.)

See also Luyken, Johann, jt. auth.

Luyken, Johann, and Luyken, Caspar
Menschelyke beezigheeden bestaande in regeering, konsten en ambachten. Harlem, A. Schevenhuysen 1695
100pl. Q.
Lipperheide 1972

Lýchdorff, Vincenz. See Fischer, Joseph, jt. auth.

Lydekker, Richard. See Hutchinson, H. N., jt. ed.

Lyk-staetsie van ... Anna kroon princesse van Groot-Brittanien princesse douariere van Orange en Nassau. La Fargue, P. C.

Lyk-staetsie van ... Willem Carel Hendrik Friso, prince van Orange en Nassau. Cuyck, Pieter van, the younger

Lynceus, pseud. See Lapidoth, Frits

Lynch, Albert
(illus.) Uzanne, L. O. La Française du siècle

Lynch, James Henry
(lithgr.) Hayes, M. A. Costume of the British army

Lynd, Robert
Rambles in Ireland. Boston, D. Estes [1912]
312p. 29pl. (incl. front.) O.
Illustrated by J. B. Yeats
LC A13-790

Lyne, Robert Nunez
Zanzibar in contemporary times, a short history of the southern East in the nineteenth century. London, Hurst and Blackett 1905
xii,328p. 19pl. (incl. front. ports.) 2 maps. O.
Bibliography: p313-20
Several plates show native costume
LC 7-42033

Lyon, George Francis
A narrative of travels in northern Africa, in the years 1818, 19, and 20 ... with ... a variety of coloured plates, illustrative of the costumes of the several natives of northern Africa. London, J. Murray 1821
xii,383p. front. (fold. map.) 17 col.pl. Q.
Translated into French under title: *L'Afrique, ou Histoire, moeurs, usages et coutumes des Africains* (Paris, Nepveu 1821. 2v. 18 col.pl.)
Colas 1920 (French ed.) Lipp. 1582 (French ed.) LC 5-8287

Lyon, Hester B.
Modern millinery; a workroom text book containing complete instruction in the work of preparing, making and copying millinery, as actually practiced in the most advanced trade workrooms. New York, Millinery trade pub. co. [c1922]
200p. illus. O.
LC 23-1180

Lyonnais. See France—By region or province—Lyonnais

Lyonnet, Henry. See Les plaisirs et les fêtes

Lyons. Bibliothèque municipale
Les gravures de mode à la Bibliothèque de la ville de Lyon. [Lyon, A. Rey] 1928
22p. illus. F.
From *La soierie de Lyon*
Shows French costume of the 16th to 19th centuries

Lyons. Chambre de commerce
L'art de décorer les tissus d'après les collections du Musée historique de la Chambre de commerce de Lyon. See entry under Cox, Raymond

Lyons. Musée historique des tissus
La collection de dentelles au Musée des tissus de Lyon. [Paris, E. Hessling] 1910
3 l. 114pl. F.
Sixty seven plates show Spanish laces, others show laces of Flanders, France and Italy

Le **Lys**, chronique de la cour; modes, théâtres, littérature. Paris, 1830
17 col.pl. O.
Seventeen numbers appeared. Plates designed by Ch. Philippon
Colas 1921

Lysèr, Caroline Leonhardt-. See Leonhardt-Lysèr, Caroline

Lyster, Alba Margaret, and Hudnall, Mrs Gladys (Franks)
Social problems of the high school boy; reviewed for educational value by Benjamin Floyd Pittenger. Austin, Tex. Steck company 1935
340p. incl.illus. pl. diagrs. col.pl. plans(1 col.) tables(1 fold.) O.
Includes a chapter on dress entitled: How can a boy improve his personal appearance. Also references
LC 36-9552

[**Lythgoe, Albert Morton**]
The treasure of Lahun. [New York, Metropolitan museum of art c1919]
26,[2]p. incl. illus. (incl. map.) pl. O.
Part 2 of the *Bulletin* of the Metropolitan museum of art, December, 1919. Signed: Albert M. Lythgoe
LC 28-15127

M

M., F. W. R. See Stripes and types of the Royal navy

M., Gr. de. See Histoire philosophique

M., X. See Costumes of Bordeaux

Maas, Dirk
[Die reitschule.] No place, ca1700
9pl. Q.
Lipperheide 2918

Maaskamp, Evert
Afbeeldingen van de kleedingen, zeden en gewoonten in Holland, met den aanvang der negentiende eeuw. Tableaux des habillements, des mœurs et des coutumes en Hollande, au commencement du dixneuvième siècle. [Amsterdam, E. Maaskamp; London, Colnaghi & co., 1811?]
56p. col.front. 24 col.pl. sq.Q. 400fr.
Plates signed: J. Kuyper, Direx, L. Portman, Sculp. The first edition entitled: *Afbeeldingen van de kleeding zeden en gewoonten in de Bataafsche Republiek. Tableaux de l'habillement ... dans la Republique Batave* (1803-05) had 16 plates only
Some of the plates have been copied for Shoberl's *Netherlands*
Colas 1680-82. Costume index. LC 23-17053

Representations of dresses, morals and customs, in the kingdom of Holland, at the beginning of the nineteenth century. Amsterdam, E. Maaskamp 1808
[48]p. 21 col.pl. sq.F.

Voyage dans l'intérieur de la Hollande, fait dans les années 1807-1812. Amsterdam, E. Maaskamp [1812?]
2v. 37 col.pl.(incl. 13 costume plates) O.
The costume plates are copies, reduced in size, of those in his *Afbeeldingen*
Lipperheide 954

(ed.) Habillemens, moeurs et coutumes dans les provinces septentrionales des Fays-Bas. Amsterdam, E. Maaskamp ca1820
3 l. 20 col.pl. Q.
Plates are copies, reduced in size, of the engravings in his *Afbeeldingen*
Colas 1368

Macaire. See Daumier, H. V. Les cent Robert Macaire

Macalister, Robert Alexander Stewart
Ecclesiastical vestments; their development and history. London, E. Stock 1896
xvi,270p. illus. 1 pl. O. (The Camden library) 6s, o.p.
Colas 1922. Costume index

Macartney, George Macartney 1st earl
Travels. See note under Grohmann, J. G. Gebräuche und kleidungen der Chinesen

Macaulay, Thomas Babington Macaulay, 1st baron
The history of England, from the accession of James the Second; ed. by C. H. Firth. London, Macmillan 1913-15
6v. fronts.(part col.) illus. ports.(part col.) maps, plans, facsims. Q. $8.40; 21s
Paged continuously
English costume, 1685-1702
Costume index. LC 14-14308

MacBean, Forbes
Sketches of character & costume in Constantinople, Ionian Islands, &c. From the original drawings made on the spot; lithographed by J. Sutcliffe. London, T. McLean 1854
5p. l. 25 col.pl. F. 84s, o.p.
Colas 1923. Costume index. Lipperheide 1437. LC 18-3328

Maccabees, Knights of
Lilley, M. C., & co., Columbus, O. Knights of the Maccabees paraphernalia and uniforms. 1893

McCall fashion bi-monthly. See note under McCall fashion book

McCall fashion book. 1913+ New York, McCall Co.
Illus.(part col.) F. $1.25 a year
A periodical on fashions and art needlework. Published five times a year. Current 1938
Many changes of title: In 1925-26 issued as *McCall quarterly*, a separately paged section of the *Buyers yardgoods review;* 1933-35 *McCall fashion bi-monthly*

McCall quarterly. See note under McCall fashion book

McCann, Justin
(tr.) Roulin, E. A. Vestments and vesture, a manual of liturgical art

MacCann, William
Two thousand miles' ride through the Argentine provinces: being an account of the natural products of the country, and habits of the people; with a hisorical retrospect. London, Smith, Elder & co. [etc.] 1853
2v. col.fronts. pl. fold.map. D.
Colas 1924. LC 4-9081

McCarthy, Justin
Portraits of the sixties, by Justin McCarthy. New York and London, Harper 1903
339p. front. ports. facsim. O.
LC 3-28556

McClees, Helen. See New York. Metropolitan museum of art. The daily life of the Greeks and Romans

McClellan, Elisabeth
History of American costume, 1607-1870; with an introductory chapter on dress in the Spanish and French settlements

McClellan, Elisabeth—*Continued*
in Florida and Louisiana; illustrations ... by Sophie B. Steel ... and Cecil W. Trout; together with reproductions from photographs of rare portraits, original garments, etc. New York, Tudor 1937
661p. col.front. illus. pl.(part col.) ports. Q. $3.48
Running title: Historic dress in America. Previous editions published under title: *Historic dress in America*
Descriptive text on pages preceding frontispiece, colored plates and some of the uncolored plates and illustrations. "Authorities consulted": p[655]-61
Colas 2025-26. Costume index. LC 37-11641 (orig. ed. 4-33115, 10-29401)

MacColl, Dugald Sutherland. See Harrison, J. E., jt. auth.

McCormick, Olive
Water pageants, games and stunts. New York, A. S. Barnes 1933
xii,138p. incl.front. illus.(incl. music) diagr. O.
Bibliography of music: p37-39; reference material for the writing of original water pageants: p59; Bibliography: p131-34
LC 33-7820

McCrackan, William Denison
The new Palestine; an authoritative account of Palestine since the great war. Boston, Page; London, Cape. 1922
xiv,392p. col.front. pl.(part col.) ports. fold.map. O.
Frontispiece and colored plates accompanied by guard sheets with descriptive letterpress
LC 22-22174

The spell of Tyrol; illus ... by Woldemar Ritter. Boston, Page 1914
xx,328p. col.front. 53pl.(5 col.) O. [The spell series]
"... A new and enlarged edition, with illustrations in colour, of Mr. McCrackan's ... *The fair land Tyrol.*" Publisher's note
LC A16-637

Macdonald, John
Czar Ferdinand and his people. London, Edinburgh, T. C. & E. C. Jack; New York, Stokes [1913]
viii,344p. front. pl. ports. O.
Shows some Bulgarian costume
Bibliography: p341
LC A13-2031

Macdonald, Reginald James
(comp.) The history of the dress of the Royal regiment of artillery, 1625-1897. London, H. Sotheran 1899
xx,131p. col.front. illus. 24 col.pl. F.
"Written as a supplement to Kane's *'List of officers of the Royal regiment of artillery.'*" Preface
"Summary of authorities": p[xv]-xviii
LC 1-2716

Macdonell, Anne
Touraine and its story; with coloured illustrations, by A. B. Atkinson. London, J. M. Dent; New York, E. P. Dutton [1906]
xiii,366p. 50 col.pl.(incl.front.) 30 illus. map. Q.
LC w7-36

McDougall, William. See Hose, Charles, jt. auth.

Mace, Arthur Cruttenden. See Carter, Howard, jt. auth.

Macedonia. See Funerals—Macedonia

Macfall, Haldane
Beautiful children immortalised by the masters, by C. Haldane McFall, with 50 reproductions in colour of famous paintings; ed. by T. Leman Hare. New York, Dodd, Mead [1909]
xii,318p. incl. 49 col.pl. col.front. Q. $5, o.p.
Costume index. LC 9-28434

McFarland, Mrs Frieda Wiegand
Good taste in dress. Peoria, Ill., Manual arts press [c1936]
108p. illus. O.
"Reference reading": p 101-4

MacFarlane, Charles. See Craik, G. L., jt. auth.

McGovern, William Montgomery
To Lhasa in disguise; an account of a secret expedition through mysterious Tibet. New York, D. Appleton; London, T. Butterworth [1924]
352p. front. illus.(maps.) pl. ports. O. $5
Costume index. LC 24-30631

Macgowan, Kenneth, and Rosse, Herman
Masks and demons. [New York] Harcourt, Brace [c1923]
xiii,177p. illus. O. $5
A history of the use of masks in religious ceremonies and the theater
List of works dealing with masks: p168-73
LC 23-18349

Mach, Richard von
Die wehrmacht der Türkei und Bulgariens, mit einem vorwort des generals der infanterie freiherrn Colmar v. d. Goltz [von] Richard v. Mach. Berlin, A. Schall 1905
99p. incl.maps, tables. ports. O. (Die heere und flotten der gegenwart ... hrsg. von C. von Zeppelin)
LC 11-28289

McIan, Robert Ronald
(illus.) Eyre-Todd, George. The Highland clans of Scotland
(illus.) Logan, James. The clans of the Scottish Highlands
(illus.) Logan, James. Gaelic gatherings
(illus.) Logan, James. McIan's costumes of the clans of Scotland

Mack, Mrs R. E.
(illus.) Ellet, Mrs E. F. L. The court circles of the republic

Mackay, Constance D'Arcy
Costumes and scenery for amateurs; rev. ed. A practical working handbook. New York, H. Holt [c1932]
viii,257p. incl.pl. D. $2
Costume index. LC 32-3119

Mackay, John Gunn
The romantic story of the Highland garb and the tartan; with an appendix by Norman Macleod ... dealing with the kilt in the great war. Stirling, E. Mackay 1924
208p. col.front. illus. pl.(part col.) ports. (part col.) coat of arms. Q.
LC 25-6527

McKenney, Thomas Loraine, and Hall, James
History of the Indian tribes of North America, with biographical sketches and anecdotes of the principal chiefs. Embellished with one hundred and

McKenney, T. L., and Hall, James—*Cont.*
twenty portraits, from the Indian gallery in the Department of war, at Washington. Philadelphia, E. C. Biddle [etc.] 1836-44
3v. col.fronts.(v1, 3) col.pl. col.ports. map, facsims. F.
Volume 2 published by F. W. Greenough, 1838; v3, by D. Rice and J. G. Clark, 1844. Volume 2 includes biographical sketches of Keokuk and Neomonni, without portraits
Colas 2067. Lipperheide 1616. LC 16-4777

Mackenzie, Frederick
(illus.) Combe, William. History of the University of Cambridge
(illus.) Combe, William. History of the University of Oxford

Mackenzie, Mrs Helen (Douglas)
Illustrations of the mission, the camp, and the zenána. London, Appel [185-?]
21 l. 20pl. F.
Plates show natives of various parts of India

Mackey, Albert Gallatin
An encyclopædia of freemasonry and its kindred sciences ... new and rev. ed. prepared under the direction, and with the assistance, of the late William J. Hughan ... by Edward L. Hawkins. New York and London, The Masonic history co. 1912
2v. col.fronts. illus. pl. ports. Q. $12
Paged continuously. A source of information about the dress and regalia of Freemasons
LC 12-19343

Mackey, Margaret Gilbert, and Sooy, Louise Pinkney
Early California costumes, 1769-1847, and historic flags of California. Stanford University, Calif. Stanford university press; London, H. Milford, Oxford university press 1932
xii,136p. incl.front. illus. col.pl. O. $3
Bibliography: p133-36
Costume index. LC 32-21304

Mackinstry, Elizabeth
(illus.) Ibsen, Henrik. Peer Gynt

Macklin, Herbert Walter
The brasses of England. New York, E. P. Dutton $2.50; London, Methuen 1907 12s 6d, o.p.
xx,336p. illus. 3pl. O. (The antiquary's books)
Bibliography included in preface. Reprinted as 3d edition, 1913
Shows English costume from the 14th to 17th century
Costume index. LC 7-38576

Monumental brasses together with a selected bibliography, and county lists of brasses remaining in the churches of the United Kingdom. London, G. Allen 1913
194p. illus. pl. D.
Several editions were published. Second ed. (London, Swan, Sonnenschein 1891)
Shows English costume from the 13th to the 16th century
Bibliography: p136-42
LC A15-464

Macleay, Kenneth
Highlanders of Scotland; portraits illustrative of the principal clans and followings, and the retainers of the Royal Household at Balmoral, in the reign of ... Queen Victoria ... in coloured lithographs by V. Brooks. London, 1870[1860]
2v. ports. F.

McLeod, John
Voyage of His Majesty's ship Alceste, along the coast of Corea, to the island of Lewchew, with an account of her subsequent shipwreck; 2d ed. London, J. Murray 1818
114p. front. 5 col.pl. O.
Three of the plates show groups of natives: Islanders of Sir James Hall's group; Corean chief and attendants; and Lewchewan chief and attendants
Lipperheide 1529. LC 4-29883

A voyage to Africa; with some account of the manners and customs of the Dahomian people. London, J. Murray 1820
iv,162p. pl. D.
French translation: *L'Afrique, ou histoire, moeurs, usages et coutumes des Africains: Dahomey (Guinée).* (Paris, Nepveu 1821. xiv,148p. 4 col.pl. S.)
Colas 2068 (French ed.). Lipperheide 1583 (French ed.) LC 5-16362

Macleod, Norman. See Mackay, J. G. The Romantic story of the Highland garb and the tartan

Maclure, Andrew
(lithogr.) Dunlop, John. Mooltan, during and after the siege

MacMunn, Sir George Fletcher
The armies of India, painted by Major A. C. Lovett ... described by Major G. F. MacMunn. London, A. and C. Black 1911
xiv,224p. col.front. illus. col.pl. O.
Shows uniforms of each regiment of native troups. Guard sheets with descriptive letterpress are included
LC A13-982

See also note under India and the war

McNabb, Robert Leroy
The women of the Middle kingdom. Cincinnati, Jennings and Pye; New York, Eaton and Mains [1903]
160p. front. 17pl. D.
LC 3-20482

McNutt, Kathleen. See Bolmar, Lydia, jt. auth.

Macphail
[Portuguese costumes. Lisbon?, Lith. de L. da Costa 1841-42?]
40 col.pl. Q.
Plates signed: Macphail, lith.

Macquoid, Percy
Four hundred years of children's costume from the great masters, 1400-1800, by Percy Macquoid. London, Boston [etc.] Medici [1923]
140p. col.mounted front. pl.(part col. and mounted) Q. (The Medici picture books) $4.50; 15s
"The main object of this little book is to explain and elucidate some of the various costumes worn by the young in past times, by giving examples from well-known authentic pictures ... [as] a guide ... in the construction of 'Fancy Dress' [for children]" Introduction. Contents: XV & early XVI centuries; XVI & XVII centuries; XVIII & early XIX centuries
Colas 1926. Costume index. LC 24-19457

Macramé. See Lace—Macramé

Madagascar
Drury, Robert. Madagascar. 1890
Ellis, William. Three visits to Madagascar during the years 1853-1854-1856. 1858
Jacottet, Henri, and Laclerc, Max. Colonies françaises. 1888
Pappenheim, M. A. F. K. L., graf zu. Madagascar; studien, schilderungen und erlebnisse. 1906

Madame. v. 1-9, 1895-1897. London, The St Paul's co.
9v. illus. Q.
Lipperheide 4814

Madden, Frederic William
On the imperial consular dress; communicated to the Numismatic society of London. London, 1861
12p. front. O.
From the *Numismatic chronicle,* new ser. v 1, p231-40

Made in Hungary. Lederer, Mrs C. B.

Madeira
Bowdich, T. E. Excursion in Madeira and Porto Santo, during the autumn of 1823 while on his third voyage to Africa. 1825
Combe, William. A history of Madeira. 1821

Madonna. See Mary, Virgin

The **Madonna** in art. Hurll, E. M.

Madou, Jean Baptiste
Collection des costumes de l'armée belge en 1832 et 1833. Bruxelles, Dero-Becker [1833]
[4]l. 22 col.pl. F.
Each plate has title *Armée belge* and is signed: Madou, del., lith. de Dero-Becker
Colas 1933

Physionomie de la société en Europe, depuis 1400 jusqu'à nos jours. Bruxelles, A. de Wasme-Pletinckx 1837
1 p.l. 3p. 15pl. F.
The same plates have been copied for Henry Havard's *Le quatre derniers siècles*
Colas 1934. Lipperheide 318. LC 12-23626

Sujets composés et dessinés sur pierre. Paris, C. Motte 1835
12pl. Q.
The plates show scenes from society life
Lipperheide 1164

Madou, Jean Baptiste, and Courtois, A.
Militaire costumen van het koninkryk der Nederlanden. Brussel, J. Delfosse ca1824
45 col.pl. Q.
The second edition (Brussel, J. Delfosse ca1825. 53 col.pl.) is enlarged by eight plates
Colas 1928-1929. Lipperheide 2257

Madou, Jean Baptiste, and Eeckhout, J. J.
Collection de costumes du peuple des provinces de la Belgique, 1835. Bruxelles, Van den Burggraaff 1835
28 col.pl. Q.
First published as part of their: *Costumes du peuple de toutes les provinces du royaume des Pays-Bas*
Colas 1931. Lipperheide 963

Costumes du peuple de toutes les provinces du royaume des Pays-Bas. Bruxelles, Van den Burggraaff 1825-28
52 col.pl. Q.
Published in 13 parts of four plates each. Forty-six plates are lithographed by Madou, six by Eeckhout
After 1830 this collection was separated into one suite of costumes of Holland and one of Belgium. See other titles by these lithographers
Colas 1930

Madou, Jean Baptiste, and Hemelryck, Johannes Lodewyk van
Costumes belgiques, anciens et modernes, militaires civils et religieux. Bruxelles, Lith. royale de Jobard 1830
103 l. 124 col.pl. Q.
Published in 25 parts
Colas 1932. Costume index. Lipperheide 962

La **madre** de familia. Ferry, Ramon

Madre Natura versus the Moloch of fashion. Leighton, John

Madrid. See Street venders—Spain— Madrid

Madrid
Descripcion de los ornatos públicos con que la corte de Madrid ha solemnizado la feliz exâltacion al trono de los reyes nuestros Señores Don Carlos IIII. y Doña Luisa de Borbon, y la jura del serenisimo Señor Don Fernando, principe de Asturias. Madrid, Imprenta real 1789
60p. 9pl.(partly fold.) F.
Lipperheide 2731. LC 4-30059

Madrid. R. Academia de la historia. See Academia de la historia, Madrid

Madrid. Armería real
Catálogo de la Real armería, mandado formar por S. M., siendo director general de reales caballerizas, armeria y yeguada el excmo. señor don José María Marchesi. Madrid, Por Aguado, impresor 1849
xx,198,119p. 10pl. O.
LC 34-35762

Catálogo histórico-descriptivo de la Real armería de Madrid, por el conde V. de Valencia de Don Juan. Madrid [Estab. tip. Sucesores de Rivadeneyra] Fototipias de Hauser y Menet 1898
xv,447p. 2 l. illus. XXVI pl. Q.
A. F. Calvert's *Spanish arms and armour* is based on this catalog
Lipperheide 2458. LC 8-14037

Jubinal, Achille. La Armería real; ou Collection des principales pièces de la galerie d'armes anciennes de Madrid. 1837-42

Jubinal, Achille. La Armería real; ou Collection des principales pièces du Musée d'artillerie de Madrid. 1861

Spanish arms and armour. See entry under Calvert, A. F.

Madrid. R. Academia de ciencias morales y politicas
Discursos leidos ante la Real academia de ciencias morales y politicas en la recepcion publica. See entry under Carramolino, J. M.

Madsen, Karl Johan Vilhelm. See Eckersberg, C. V. Ti Tegninger af Christoffer-Wilhelm Eckersberg

Das **mächtige** kayser-reich Sina. Wagner, J. C.

Mähr. gewerbemuseum, Brünn. See Brünn. Mähr. gewerbemuseum

Die **männliche** kleidung in der süddeutschen renaissance. Christensen, S. F.

März-almanach. Glasbrenner, Adolf

Maes, Joseph

Aniota-kifwebe; les masques des populations du Congo Belge et le matériel des rites de circoncision. Anvers, Éditions de Sikkel 1924

63p. 32pl. on 16 l. O.
LC 26-19940

Maffei, Paolo Alessandro. See Rossi, Domenico de. Gemme antiche figurate ... colle sposizioni di Paolo Alessandro Maffei

Magalhães, Fernão de, supposed author. See Barbosa, Duarte. A description of the coasts of East Africa and Malabar

Magallon, J. D.

(ed.) L'Album, journal des arts, des modes et des théâtres

Magasin des modes nouvelles, françaises et anglaise. t 1.-4; 15 nov. 1785-21 déc. 1789. Paris

4v. 108 col.pl. O.
Title varies: 1. année 1785, *Cabinet des modes*. Superseded by *Journal de la mode et du gout*
Colas 500. Lipperheide 4569

Magasin för konst, nyheter och moder. 1823-1825. Stockholm, C. Deleen

Col.pl. Q.
Colas 1936. Lipperheide 4604

Le **Magasin** pittoresque. 1. année, 1833+ Paris, Jouvet

Illus. pl. F.
Published weekly or monthly 1833-48; monthly 1849-78; semi-monthly 1879+. Current 1937
Editors: 1833-1888, Édouard Charton (with Euryale Cazeaux, 1833-36); 1889-1895, Eugène Best (with Charles Mayet, 1891-95); 1896, Charles Mayet; 1897-1902, Charles Formentin (with Émile Fouquet 1901-1902); 1902-June 1905, Émile Fouquet, Ernest Beauguitte; July 1905+ Émile Fouquet, Louis Fouquet
Contains hundreds of articles on costume of various countries and periods, the greater part on France at an early period. Some titles are: Dixième siècle: seigneurs, commercants, artisans, soldats; Dames de la cours; Troubadour et page; Costume civil sous Charles VII; Costumes des avocats en France, XIIIe siècle à nos jours; Colors and dyes in antiquity. Material is available thru the indexes
Indexes v 1-40, 1833-72; v41-50, 1873-82
LC (11-12602)

Les **magasins** de nouveautés. Franklin, A. L. A. (*In* his La vie privée d'autrefois; arts et métiers, modes, moeurs, usages des Parisiens du XII. au XVIII. siècle. v 15-18)

Magazin des demoiselles. 1.-49. année; 15 oct. 1844-1893. Paris

49v. ca800 col.pl. O.
Colas 1935. Lipperheide 4649

Magazin des neuesten geschmackes in kunst und mode. See Allgemeine modenzeitung

Magazin für frauenzimmer. v 1-20, 1782-1786. Strasburg, Levrault

20v. col.illus. O.
Superseded by *Neues magazin für frauenzimmer*
1783, pt.3 published by Kehl, in druck ... der gelehrten zeitungs-expedition
Colas 1941. Lipperheide 4567

Maggi

(pub.) Costumes of Bordeaux

Maggi, Giovanni Battista

Uniformi militari dell'armata di S. M. Sarda. Torino, G. B. Maggi 1844

1 l. 30 col.pl. F.
Each plate shows several types of uniform. Plates are signed: Gonin, Pedrone, or C. Sereno
Colas 1944, 2301?

Maggio, Pietro

Le guerre festive nelle reali nozze de' ... re di Spagna Carolo secondo, e Maria Luisa di Borbone, celebrate nella ... Palermo ... MDCLXXX. Palermo, G. la Barbera, e T. Rummulo & Orlando 1680?

80p. 12 l. 10 illus. 1 pl. F.
The ten full-page illustrations show costume and the plate shows the procession
Lipperheide 2750

The **magic** of colour harmony in dress. Moncrieffe, Mona, pseud.

The **magic** of dress. Gould, G. M.

The **magic** of jewels and charms. Kunz, G. F.

Magical jewels of the middle ages and the renaissance. Evans, Joan

Magistretti, Marco

Delle vesti ecclesiastiche in Milano. Milano, L. F. Cogliati 1897

83p. 4pl.(1 col.) Q. (Ambrosiana; scritti varii publicati nei XV centenario dalla morte di S. Ambrogio XI)
Colas 1945

Magne, Emile. See Les plaisirs et les fêtes

La **magnifique** et sumptueuse pompe funèbre fait aux obsèques ... du Charles V[e]. See Cock, Hieronymus. Amplissimo hoc apparatu

Magre, Maurice. See Les plaisirs et les fêtes

Magyar designs. See Decoration and ornament—Hungary

A **Magyar** és Horváth országi leg nevezetesebb nemzeti oltözetik hazai gyüjteménie. Heimbucher von Bikessy, J.

Magyar himvarró müvészet. Undi, Mariska

A **magyar** jelmez és fejlödése dióhéjban. Nemes, Mihály

Magyar népviseletek. Pekáry, István

Magyar tudományas akadémia, Budapest. See Szendrei, János. A magyar viselet történeti fejlödése

A **magyar** viselet történeti fejlödése. Szendrei, János

A **magyar** viseletek tört'enete. Nemes, Mihály

Magyarische ornamentik. Huszka, József

Magyaros ifjúsági ruhák. Ferenczy, Ferenc

A **magyarság** tárgyi néprajza ... Írta: Bátky Zsigmond, Györffy István, Viski Károly. Budapest, Királyi Magyar egyetemi nyomda [1934?]

2v. illus. pl.(part col.) O.
Edited by Elemér Czakó. Includes many illustrations of Hungarian costume

Mahaffy, John Pentland

Greek pictures, drawn with pen and pencil by J. P. Mahaffy. London, Religious tract. soc. 1890

223p. incl.front. illus. pl. map. Q.
LC 4-34820

Maharashtra. See India—Maharashtra

Mahérault, Marie Joseph François, and Bocher, Emmanuel
L'oeuvre de Gavarni; . catalogue raisonné. Par J. Armelhault, [pseud.] et E. Bocher. Paris, Librairie des bibliophiles 1873
627p. 3pl. O.
A list of Gavarni's sets and plates which show Costumes et modes, p507-90

Mahlerische darstellungen der sitten, gebräuche und lustbarkeiten bey den russischen, tartarischen, mongolischen und andern völkern im russischen reich. Geissler, C. G. H.

Mahrattas. See India—Maharashtra

Maidment, James
(ed.) Paterson, James. Kay's Edinburgh portraits. 1885

Maidment, Margaret
A manual of hand-made bobbin lace work. London, New York [etc.] I. Pitman 1931
x,183p. incl.front. illus. diagrs. sq.O.
Foreword signed: W. G. Paulson Townsend
LC 32-2013

Maigron, Louis
Le romantisme et la mode, d'après des documents inédits. Paris, H. Champion 1911
viii,250p. pl.(1 col.) ports. O.
Colas 1946. LC 20-4423

[**Maillart, Philippe Joseph**]
Collection de costumes de tous les ordres monastiques, supprimés à differentes époques, dans la ci-devant Belgique. Chaque figure est accompagnée d'une note historique indicative de l'époque de leur institution, de celle de leur suppression, et du nom de leurs fondateurs ... Bruxelles, P. J. Maillart et sœur [1811]
1 p. l. 137 col.pl. O.
Colas 1948. LC 4-85

See also note under Grasset de Saint Sauveur, Jacques. Costumes des représentans du peuple

Maillot, Thomas Jules Richard
À la caserne; texte par J. Richard [pseud.] [Paris 1885]
2v. 19 illus.(part col.) O. (Cahiers d'enseignement illustrés, no.5-6)
Illustrated by Marius Roy
Lipperheide 2338

En campagne ... tableaux et dessins de A. de Neuville. Paris, Boussod, Valadon et cie, L. Baschet [1885-86]
2v. 156 illus. F.
Some French uniforms, mostly of the 1870's and 80's, by Detaille, Meissonier, and others
Lipperheide 2339

La jeune armée; texte par Jules Richard, illus. de L. Du Paty. Paris, Librairie illustrée 1890
312p. 40 col.pl. Q.
Published in 40 series at ea 50 centimes

See also Detaille, Édouard, jt. auth.

Maindron, Ernest
Marionnettes et guignols, les poupées agissantes et parlantes à travers les âges. Paris, F. Juven [1900]
381p. incl.illus. pl. 8 col.pl. (incl.front.) Q.
LC 11-34182

Maindron, Maurice Georges René
Les armes. Paris, May & Motteroz [1890]
343p. illus. O. (Bibliothèque de l'enseignement des beaux-arts)
An illustrated history of weapons and armor
Lipperheide 2442. LC F-3471

Mainz. Römisch-Germanisches zentral museum
Die alterthümer unserer heidnischen vorzeit. See entry under Lindenschmit, Ludwig
Das Römisch-germanische central-museum in bildlichen darstellungen aus seinen sammlungen. See entry under Lindenschmit, Ludwig

Der **Mainzer** goldschmuck der kaiserin Gisela. Falke, Otto von

[**Mair, Paul Hector**]
Bericht und anzeigen aller Herren Geschlecht der loblichen Statt Augspurg so vor Fünffhundert und mehr Jaren auch lenger dann yemandt wissen und erfaren kan daselbst gewonet und bis auff Achte abgestorben. Auch deren so an der abgestorbenen stat ein und angenom̃en auch erhöhet worden seind sampt eines jeden Geschlechts Schilt und Helm in künstliche possen uff art der alten Harnisch Waffen vnd Wören artlich gestellet. Straszburg, C. Widitz und David Kannel [1538?]
2v. in 1. 98 illus. F.
Part [2] has title: *Volgen jetzo weitter die Acht überbelibne*
Woodcuts show representatives of Augsburg families, in armor and with coats of arms
A later edition (Augsburg, M. Kriegstein, 1550) with additions, has at end as author's name Paul Hector Mair. Other editions: Frankfurt, S. Feyrabend, 1580, 4 parts, with title-pages by Jost Amman; also Frankfurt, J. W. Amman, 1661
"Contains 98 full-page woodcuts. No. LI (pt. 1, p. liiii) and XXXIX (pt. 2, p. xlviii) have signature CW, probably Christoffel Widitz (or Weyditz) to whom, with David Kannel (or Kandel) the wood-cuts are probably to be credited. The identification of Kannel with David Kandel of Strassburg has not been fully established." Library of Congress
Lipperheide 4390. LC 32-17697

Mairn, Johann Baptist von
Beschreibung was auf ableiben weyland ihrer keyserl. majestät Josephi, bisz nach vorgegangener erb-huldigung welche dem ... römischen keyser Carolo dem sechsten ... als erz-herzogen zu Oesterreich die gesamte nideroesterreichische stände den 8. novembris A:1712. Wien, J. J. Kürner 1712?
76p. 11 pl. F.
Plates are taken from Gülich's *Erbhuldigung* with slight changes
Lipperheide 2625

Maison du Roi, 1814. See Martinet, pub. Troupes françaises

Maison du roi et garde royale (Louis XVIII). Aubry, Charles, and Loeillot, Karl

Maiss, Karl. See Schulze, Heinrich, jt. auth.

Le **maître** à danser. Colin, Mme Anaïs

Les **maîtres** de la caricature française au XIXe siècle. Dayot, A. P. M.

Les **maîtres** ornemanistes. Guilmard, Désiré

Major, Richard Henry
(ed.) Bontier, Pierre and Le Verrier, Jean. The Canarian. 1872

Majorn, Johann Daniel
(tr.) Buoninsegni, Francesco. Satyra Menippea, oder straff-schrifft weiblicher pracht

Makart, Hans
Festzug zur feier der silbernen hochzeit des kaiserpaares Franz Joseph und Elisabeth, nach Hans Makart's entwürfen gez. von Raphael von Ambros. Vienna, R. v. Waldheim [1879]
1 l. 28pl. O.
Lipperheide 2643-2644

Festzug zur fünfundzwanzigjährigen vermählungs-feier des allerhöchsten kaiserpaares veranstaltet von der haupt- und residenzstadt Wien, April 1879. Wien, V. Angerer [1879]
36pl. F.
Lipperheide 2642

Make-up
Bitterlin, A. L'art du maquillage. 1925

Make-up, Theatrical
Fitz-Gerald, S. J. A. How to "make up." 1901
Foan, G. A., ed. The art and craft of hairdressing. 1931
Harrison, Charles. Theatricals and tableaux vivants for amateurs. 1882
Schneider, Louis. Die kunst sich zu schminken. 1831

Making the most of your looks. Stote, Dorothy

Malay archipelago
Barbosa, Duarte. A description of the coasts of East Africa and Malabar in the beginning of the sixteenth century. 1866
Forbes, H. O. A naturalist's wanderings in the Eastern archipelago. 1885

See also Borneo; New Guinea; also Religious costume—Malay archipelago

Malay peninsula
Carpenter, F. G. Java and the East Indies. 1923
Curtis, W. T. Egypt, Burma and British Malaysia. 1905
Skeat, W. W., and Blagden, C. O. Pagan races of the Malay Peninsula. 1906

Malaya. See Malay peninsula

Malaysia. See Malay archipelago

Malcolm, Sir Ian Zachary
Indian pictures and problems. New York, E. P. Dutton 1907
xiv,294p. front. pl. O.
LC WAR7-133

Malcolm, James Peller
Anecdotes of the manners and customs of London, during the eighteenth century ... with a review of the state of society in 1807. London, Longman, Hurst, Rees, and Orme 1808
iv,490,8p. 50pl.(12 col.) O.
Supplementary to the author's *Anecdotes of ... London from the Roman invasion to ... 1700*
Plates show costume from 1690 to 1807. The second edition (1810) has the same costume plaes
Colas 1949-1951. Lipperheide 1021. LC 3-8409

Anecdotes of the manners and customs of London from the Roman invasion to the year 1700. London, Longman, Hurst, Rees, Orme, and Brown 1811
576p. 18pl.(part col.) Q.
At end of text: The end of part I. A companion volume to the author's *Anecdotes ... of London during the eighteenth century*
LC 3-8408

Mâle, Émile
L'art religieux de la fin du moyen âge en France; étude sur l'iconographie du moyen âge et sur ses sources d'inspiration. Paris, A. Colin 1908
xii,558p. illus. Q.
A source book for French costume of the Middle ages
LC 9-5105

L'art religieux du XIIIe siècle en France. 7. éd. Paris, Librairie A. Colin 1931
ix,428p. illus. Q.
"Index bibliographique": p[411]-414
LC A32-663

Religious art in France, XIII century; a study in mediaeval iconography and its sources of inspiration; tr. from the 3d ed. <rev. and enl.> by Dora Nussey; with 190 illustrations. London, J. M. Dent; New York, E. P. Dutton 1913
xxiv,414p. 190 illus. Q.
Translation of his *L'art religieux du XIIIe siècle*
Bibliography: p407-10
LC 14-11607

Male and female costume. Brummell, G. B.

Male costumes, historical, national and dramatic. Lacy, T. H., ed.

Male character costumes. London, S. Miller [1884]
96p. Q.
A guide to gentlemen's costume suitable for fancy dress balls and private theatricals, etc.

Malerische ansichten aus dem Orient. Mayr, Heinr. von

Malerische landerschau in bildlichen darstellungen deutscher und schweizerischer stadte. Kempten, T. Dannheimer ca1850
12 col.pl. F.
Plates lithographed by Hohbach. Colas lists this suite and suggests that it may be a continuation of *Länder- und völker schau*
Colas 1754

Malerische reise in Brasilien. See Rugendas, J. M. Voyage pittoresque dans le Brésil

Malerische studien; eine reise um die welt, in ... photographien nach naturaufnahmen. Leipzig, Koehler [1899]
2v. col.pl. Q.
An explanatory text for each picture is found at the end of the second volume

Malet, Albert
Nouvelle histoire de France; l'antiquité, le moyen âge, les temps modernes, la révolution, l'empire, la France contemporaine, la grande guerre. Paris [etc.] Hachette [c1922]
543p. col.front. illus. col.pl. F. 145frs.
Plates accompanied by guard sheets with descriptive letterpress
Costume index. LC 23-2662

Malet, Georges
L'art de se raser; préface de Georges-Armand Masson. Paris, C. A. Bourquin 1927
95p. S. (Petite bibliothèque d'hygiène moderne)

Maleuvre
(engr.) Costumes des différens departemens de l'Empire français
(engr.) Le petit cosmopolite, ou Recueil des costumes de différents peuples
(engr.) Petite galerie dramatique

Malevolti, Domenico Angelo. See Angelo, Domenico, later name

Les **malheurs** d'un amant heureux. Bouchot, Frédéric

Malibran, Alphonse Marie
L'armée du duché de Varsovie. See entry under Chelminski, Jan V.

Malibran, H.
Guide à l'usage des artistes et des costumiers, contenant la description des uniformes de l'armée française de 1780 à 1848. Paris, Combet 1904
946,11p. O. and atlas 10, 248p. incl. CCXI pl. O.
Atlas is entitled *Album du Guide à l'usage des artistes et des costumiers, publié en 1904* (Paris, Boivin 1907)
Colas 1952. Lipp. 2356c (text) LC 31-6042

Malkasten künstler verein, Düsseldorf. See Shakspeare-album

Mallemont, A.
Album de coiffures travesties, première série; modèles de la coiffure française illustrée, 1889-1898. Paris, Brunet 1907
12 col.pl. Q.
Manuel de la coiffure de dames. Paris, E. Robinet 1898
115p. 56 illus.(incl.ports.) D. 3fr.
Colas 1953

Mallet, and Lameau
Collection des uniformes de l'armée française, comprenant chaque régiment de toute arme ... ouvrage exécuté par ordre de S. E. le Ministre de la guerre. Les figures par M. Mallet, le paysage par M. Lameau. Paris, C. Picquet [1817-18]
12 col.pl. F.
Planned, and stated in the title, to comprise all the regiments, but only these twelve plates on the uniforms of the guards appeared. Described by Glasser under title: *Garde royale*
Colas 1954

Mallet, Alain Manesson-. See Manesson-Mallet, Alain

Mallet, Joseph
Cours élémentaire d'archéologie religieuse. Mobilier. Paris, Poussielgue frères 1883
viii,341p. illus. O. (Alliance des maisons d'éducation chrétienne)
Vêtements liturgiques des catacombs et des basiliques p72-87; de l'époque romane p175-89; de la période ogivale p295-306
LC 34-24533

Malliot, Joseph, and Martin, P.
Recherches sur les costumes, les moeurs, les usages religieux, civils, et militaires des anciens peuples d'après les auteurs célèbres, et les monuments antiques; publié par P. Martin. Paris, Firmin-Didot 1804
3v. 297pl. Q.
German translation: *Gallerie der sitten, geräthschaften, religiösen, bürgerlichen und kriegerischen gebräuche der vornehmsten völker des alterthums und der Franzosen bis in das 17te jahrhundert* (Strasburg, Treutel & Würtz 1812)
Colas 1955-1956. Costume index. Lipperheide 111, 111a

Malo, Charles
Les femmes et les fleurs. Paris, Janet 1831
6 l. 12pl. S. 12fr.
Plates show women of different European countries with flowers which typify their beauty

Malo, Servan
Ceux de Yorktown; uniformes et drapeaux, d'après des documents officiels de l'epoque. [Paris] G. Bertrand [1918]
[20]p. illus. 7 col.pl. Q.
Second title page: *The men of Yorktown:* uniforms and flags drawn after official documents by Servan Malo 1918. Text is in French and English
Uniforms of French regiments which fought on the American side at the battle of Yorktown, 1781. Uniforms are copied from an album attached to the regulations laid down by the king of France February 21, 1779

Malonyay, Dezsö
A magyar nép müvészete ... Számos szakértö és müvész közremüködésével irta Malonyay Dezsö. Budapest, Magyar Irod. Intezet es Könyvnyomda; Paris, E. Hessling [1913]-22
5v. illus. pl.(part col.) Q.
Plates show Hungarian dress and embroidery designs

Malotet, A.
La dentelle à Valenciennes, avec le concours pour l'illustration de M. Adolphe Lefrancq. Paris, J. Schemit 1927
xvi,95p. facsims. front. illus. pl. port. F.
Bibliography: p90-92

Malpière, D. Bazin de
La Chine: moeurs, usages, costumes. Paris, L'éditeur 1825-27
2v. 181 col.pl. Q.
"Arts et métiers, peines civiles et militaires, ceremonies religieuses, monuments et paysages, d'après les dessins ... des ... Castiglione ... Pu-Qua, W. Alexandre, Chambers, Dudley, etc." Subtitle
This work reproduces many of the plates in *Picturesque representations of the dress and manners of the Chinese* by W. Alexander
Malpière's *La Chine et les Chinois* (2. éd. mise en un meilleur ordre. Paris, J. Caboche, Demerville et cie. 1848) has the same number of colored plates
Colas 1957-1958. Costume index. Lipperheide 1531. LC 4-36106 (2. éd.)

Malta
Davis, R. H. Rulers of the Mediterranean. 1894

Malta, Knights of
Becmann, J. C. Beschreibung des ritterlichen Johanniter-Orden und dessen absonderlicher beschaffenheit im Herrn-Meistertum in der Marck Sachsen Pommern und Wendland ... mit nöthigen Anmerckungen. 1726

Caorsin, Wilhelm. Historia von Rhodis. 1513

Cenni, Quinto. Gl' ordini equestri religioso-militari; studi storici sui loro costumi ed armi. 1909

Des Maltheser-ritter-ordens teutschen grosspriorats wappen calender, 1770. 1770

Osterhausen, Christian von. Eigentlicher und grundlicher bericht dessen was zu einer volkommenen erkantnusz und wissenschaft desz ... ritterlichen ordens S. Johannis von Jerusalem zu Malta vonnöthen. 1650

Statuta ordinis Sti. Joannis Hierosolimitani per fratrem Ptolemaeum Veltronium eiusdem ordinis militem cum figuris, earundemque sententiis, ac magnorum magistrorum imaginibus, nuper adiectus. 1588

Vertot, R. A. de, abbé. Histoire des Chevaliers hospitaliers de S. Jean de Jerusalem, appellez depuis les Chevaliers de Rhodes, et aujourd'hui les Chevaliers de Malte. 1726

Winterfeld, A. W. E. von. Geschichte des ritterlichen ordens St. Johannis vom Spital zu Jerusalem. 1859

Malté, Fr.
(engr.) Abbildungen des württembergischen militärs von der früheren bis zur gegenwärtigen zeit

Malval, de
(illus.) Mérignac, Émile. Histoire de l'escrime

Mameluks. See Military costume—Egypt

Maly, August, ritter von
Das k. k. heer und die österr. und ung. landwehren. Wien, L. T. Neumann [1884]
26 col.pl. F.
Colas 1960

Man and his clothes. v 1+ Sept. 1926+ London, Fairchild pub.
Illus. F.
Published monthly. Current 1938
Volume 1, no 1-4 (Sept.-Dec. 1926) issued as a supplement to *Fairchild's international magazine.* Subtitle varies. Later years lack subtitle. Sept. 1934-Jan. 1935 title reads: *Man and his clothes, incorporating the Sunshine review*

Manatt, James Irving. See Tsountas, Chrestos, jt. auth.

Manceau, A.
(illus.) Sand, Maurice. Masques et bouffons

Mancel, Georges. See La Normandie illustrée

Manchester, Herbert
The evolution of dress fastening devices from the bone pin to the koh-i-noor ... written by H. H. Manchester, for Waldes & co. Long Island city, N.Y. [c1922]
22p. illus. O.
LC 22-16450

Historic beauties and their footwear; written ... for Waldes Kohinoor, inc. Long Island city, N.Y. [Waldes Koh-i-noor, inc. c1927]
24p. front. illus. O.

Romance of men's hats; written for E. V. Connett and company from data and records in their possession. New York, E. V. Connett & co [c1920]
Illus. ports. O.

Manchuria
Georgi, J. G. Beschreibung aller nationen des russischen reichs. 1776-80

Georgi, J. G. Description de toutes les nations de l'empire de Russie, ou l'on expose leurs moeurs, religious, usages, maisons, habillemens et autres curiosites; tr. de l'allemand. 1776-80

Georgi, J. G. La Russie ouverte ou collection complette des habillemens de toutes les nations qui se trouvent dans l'empire de Russie. 1774-75

Georgi, J. G. Russland: beschreibung aller nationen des russischen Reiche. 1783

Hawes, C. H. In the uttermost East. 1904

Mandelgren, Nils Månsson
Monuments scandinaves du moyen âge avec les peintures et autres ornements qui les décorent. Paris [Vve J. Renouard] 1862
[15]p. XL pl.(part col.) F.
Issued in 5 parts, 1855-62; the first part was published at Copenhagen
LC 31-22090

Mandet, Francisque
L'ancien Velay. See note under Michel, Adolphe. L'ancienne Auvergne et le Velay

Mandres, Charles Nicolas Léonce Rozat de. See Rozat de Mandres, C. N. L.

Maneige royal. See Pluvinel, Antoine de. L'instruction du roy, en l'exercice de monter a cheval

Manejo del sable. Vernet, Horace, and Lami, L. E.

The **maner** of the tryumphe of Caleys and Bulleyn, and The noble tryumphaunt coranacyon of Quene Anne, wyfe unto the most noble kynge Henry VIII. Printed by Wynkyn de Worde, 1532-33; ed. by Edmund Goldsmid. Edinburgh, Priv. print. 1884
vii,37p. illus. D. (Bibliotheca curiosa)
Reprint of a book originally published 1532-33
LC 4-19793

Manesse, Rüdiger
Minnesänger aus der zeit der Hohenstaufen, im vierzehnten jahrhundert; gesammelt von Rüdger Maness von Maneck. Facsimile der Pariser handschrift von Bernard Carl Mathieu. Paris, 1850
xv p. 24 col.pl. F.
Plates contain a list of the Minnesingers, the first ten miniatures, and twelve leaves of text
Lipperheide 383

Manesse codex. See Zangemeister, K. F. W. Die wappen, helmzierden und standarten der grossen Heidelberger liederhandschrift

Manesson-Mallet, Alain. See Manuel des toilettes; dedié aux dames (attributed)

Mangam, Elliott W.
Indian handicraft. New York city, Boy scouts of America c1930
48p. illus. O. (Boy scouts of America service library)
Bibliography: p48
LC 30-18640

Manicuring. See Finger nails

Maniement d'armes d'arquebuses, mousquetz, et piques. See Gheyn, Jacob de. Wapenhandelinghe van roers musquetten ende spiessen

Le **maniement** d'armes de Nassau, avecq rondelles, piques, espees & targes. Breen, Adam van

Maniement des mousquets & piques. See Iselberg, Peter. Künstliche waffenhandlung der musqueten uñ piquen oder langen spiessen

La **maniere** de se bien preparer a la mort. Chertablon, de

La **manière** de s'habiller à Nuremberg. See Kleidungsarten und prospecten zu Nürnberg

Le **manifique** carousel fait sur le fleuve de l'Arno, a Florence, pour le mariage du Grand Duc. Paris, B. Moncornet ca1690
18pl. D.
Plates by Nicolaus Boquet are copied from those in *Battaglia navale rappresentata in Arno . . . 1608*
Lipperheide 2743

Mankell, Julius
Anteckningar rörande svenska regementernas historia. Orebro, N. M. Lindh 1866
82p. 32 col.pl. O.
Colas 1961

Manley, Dean V. R.
(ed.) Ford, H. A. Archery: its theory and practice

Mann, James Sumarez. See Traill, H. D., jt. ed.

Mann, Kathleen
Peasant costume in Europe, by Kathleen Mann, with notes by J. A. Corbin. New York, Macmillan; London, A. & C. Black 1931-36
v 1-2. col.front. 7 col.pl. Q. v 1 $2.50, v2 $4
Contents: v 1 France, Spain, Italy, Switzerland, Central Europe, Sweden, Russia; v2 Denmark, The Baltic states: Finland, Estonia, Latvia, Lithuania, The British isles, Holland, Poland, Germany, The Balkans: Yugoslavia, Bulgaria, Albania
Costume index. LC 31-21074

Le **mannequin.** Riotor, Léon

Manner and solemnite of the coronation of His Most Gracious Majestie King Charles the Second. Heawood, William

Manners & customs of mankind. Hammerton, Sir J. A.

Manners and customs of the ancient Egyptians. Wilkinson, Sir J. G.

Manners & customs of the French; facsimile of the scarce 1815 edition. London, H. Sotheran; New York, C. Scribner 1893
43p. 10 col.pl. (incl.front.) O.
Preface by Henry Sotheran. With reproduction of original t.-p.: *Letters from France, written by a modern tourist in that country* by M. S. (London, T. Sotheran 1815)
"Who the author was is doubtful; but the writer has heard his father say that he was one Benjamin Rotch." Preface
LC 1-1718

Manners and customs of the Greeks. Panofka, Theodor

Manners and customs of ye Englyshe. Doyle, Richard

Manners and monuments of prehistoric peoples. Nadaillac, J. F. A. du P., marquis de

Manners and movements in costume plays. Chisman, Isabel and Raven-Hart, H. E.

Manners, customs, and dress during the middle ages. Lacroix, Paul

Manners, lawes and customes of all nations. Boemus, Johann

Mannheimer maskenzug im jahr 1841; lithg. v. W. Beier u. Ph. Hauser. Mannheim 1841?
84pl. Q.
Part 1 shows the wedding procession of the Emperor Frederick II; part shows carnival types
Lipperheide 2872

Manninen, Ilmari
Eesti rahvariiete ajalugu. Tartu, Eesti rahva muuseum 1927?
Illus. 4 col.pl. O.
A work on Estonian costume published as volume 3 of *Aastaraamat* issued by the Eesti rahva muuseum, at Tartu

[**Manning, Samuel**]
Swiss pictures drawn with pen and pencil . . . illus. by Mr. E. Whymper. London, Religious tract soc. [1866]
214p. incl.illus. 15pl. col.front. Q.
LC 4-8900

Manning, Sibylla, and Donaldson, Anna M.
Fundamentals of dress construction, by Sibylla Manning . . . and Anna M. Donaldson . . . illus. by Mary Jane Russell. New York, Macmillan 1926
xvi,223p. illus. diagrs. O. $1.60
LC 26-5328

Manninga, Unico
Ostfriesischen volks- und rittertrachten um 1500; in getreuer nachbildung der originale des häuptlings Unico Manninga in der gräflich knyphausenschen hauschronik zu Lützburg. Mit einleitendem text von grafen Edzard zu Innhausen und Knyphausen . . . hrsg.

Mannice, Unico—*Continued*
von der Gesellschaft für bildende kunst und vaterländische altertümer zu Emden. Emden, W. Schwalbe 1893
82p. 17pl.(16 col.) O.
Reprint from the *Jahrbuch* of the Gesellschaft, 1893
Colas 1962. Lipperheide 801

Mannlich, Johann Christian von
Versuch über gebräuche, kleidung und waffen der ältesten völker bis auf Constantin den Grossen; nebst einigen anmerkungen über die schaubühne. München, Fleischmann 1802
117p. 3 illus. 29pl. Q.
Colas 1963. Lipperheide 110

Mannowsky, Walter
Der Danziger paramentenschatz; kirchliche gewänder und stickereien aus der Marienkirche. Berlin, Brandussche verlags-buchhandlung [1931-33]
4v. col.fronts. pl. F.
Contents: Halbbd 1 Die chormäntel; 2 Die gewebten kaseln; 3 Kaseln mit stickerei und dalmatiken; 4 Einzelstücke priesterlicher kleidung, Altar-ausstattung, Weitere kirchliche stickereien

Manolescu, M. Nicolae
Igiena ţĕranului, locuinţa, iluminatul şi incălḑitul el imbrăcămintea, incălţămintea, alimentaţiunea tĕranului in deosebitele epoce ale anului şi in deosebitele regiuni ale ţĕrei. Bucuresci, C. Göbl 1895
363p. illus. fold.pl. 2 fold.tab. O.
LC CA11-3155

Manoni, Alessandro
Il costume e l'arte delle acconciature nell'antichità. Milano, U. Hoepli 1895
xiv,178p. front. O.
Dress and styles of dressing the hair in ancient times
Colas 1964

Man's book; a magazine. v 1-4, Oct. 1908-Nov. 1910. New York
4v. illus. F.
A periodical of men's fashions. Published monthly
Title changes: Nov. 1908-Apr. 1909, *Fairchild's magazine;* May-Dec. 1909, *Gentleman's journal*

Mansberg, Richard, freiherr von
Wâfen unde wicgewaete der deutschen ritter des mittelalters. Dresden, W. Hoffmann 1890
67p. 1 illus. 9pl. F.
Lipperheide 2443

Mansfeld, Alfred
Urwald-dokumente: vier jahre unter den Crossflussnegern Kameruns. Berlin, D. Reimer 1908
xvi,309p. 32pl. maps, tab. Q.

Westafrika; aus urwald und steppe zwischen Crossfluss und Benue; geologischer teil von Dr. H. Reck. München, G. Müller 1928
75,144p. incl.pl. Q.
Plates printed on both sides. Bibliography p[76]

Mansfeld, Heinrich, and Biller, B.
Wien's bewaffnete bürger im jahre 1806 in ihren uniformen dargestellt. La bourgeoisie de Vienne formée en regimens. Vienne, Artaria ca1806
1 l. 26 col.pl. F.
Plates engraved by Mansfeld and Biller
Colas 1965. Lipperheide 2231

Mansfeld, J.
(illus.) Constitutiones insignis ordinis equitum S. Stephanis regis apostolici

Mansfeld, Jos. Georg. See Kininger, V. G., jt. auth.

[**Mansfield, Milburg Francisco**]
Rambles in Brittany, by Francis Miltoun [pseud.] Boston, L. C. Page 1906
xiii,376p. front. illus. pl. fold.map. O.
Published later with title *The spell of Brittany* (Boston, L. C. Page 1927. $3.75)
LC 5-38090

Mansion, L. M.
Fancy ball dress. London, W. Spooner 1831?
30 col.pl. F.
27 of the plates are by L. M. Mansion, one by R. W. Buss, and 2 unsigned

[**Mansion, L. M., and Saint-Eschauzier**]
L'armée anglaise vers 1830. London, W. Spooner [1830?]
60 col.pl. F.
Plates are lithographed by C. H. Martin after Mansion and Saint-Eschauzier
Colas 1967

Costume of the Royal navy and marines. London, Andrevos ca1825
16 col.pl. F.
Printed by Lefèvre and co.
Colas 1966

Les **manteaux.** Caylus, A. C. P., comte de

Die **manteltracht** im mittelalter. Wirsching, Joseph

Manteuffel, Erna von
Album altdeutscher leinenstickerei. Harburg a. d. Elbe, G. Elkan [1883]
5v. 55pl. O.
Contents: v 1 Kreuzstich; v2 Holbeintechnik; v3 Wiener kreuzstich; v4 Italien. kreuzstich; v5 Flechtenstich
Lipperheide 4006

Filet-guipure-album; eine sammlung stilvoller praktisch ausgeführter originalmuster. Harburg a. d. Elbe, G. Elkan [1881]
4 l. 1 illus. 41pl. Q.
Lipperheide 4136

Monogramm-album sechshundert stilvoll verschlungene buchstaben für plattstichstickerei. Harburg a. d. Elbe, G. Elkan [1881]
40pl. Q.
Lipperheide 4185

Mantilla, Manuel Florencio
Premios militares de la República Argentina. Buenos Aires, Saurez 1892
246p. O. 4 pesos

Mantuano, Judith Ma'rffy. See Ma'rffy-Mantuano, Judith

Mantzius, Karl
A history of theatrical art in ancient and modern times; with an introduction by William Archer; authorised translation by Louise von Cossel. London, Duckworth 1903-21
6v. fronts. pl.(part fold.) ports. plans, facsims. O.
Contains bibliographies
Contents: 1 The earliest times. 1903; 2 The middle ages and the renaissance. 1903; 3 The Shakespearean period in England. 1904; 4 Molière and his times; the theatre in France in the 17th century. 1905; 5 The great actors of the eighteenth century. 1909; 6 Classicism and romanticism, tr. by C. Archer. 1921
LC 5-18107

Manual of costume as illustrated by monumental brasses. Druitt, Herbert

Manual of hand-made bobbin lace work. Maidment, Margaret

Manual of knitting, netting, and crochet. Mee, Cornelia

Manual of monumental brasses. Haines, Herbert

Manual of regulations and specifications for chapter workers' uniforms & insignia. Red cross. United States. American national Red cross

Manual of Roman antiquities. Ramsay, William

Manual of uniforms and insignia. United States. Shipping board

Manuale dei pittori, ovvero Manuale di pittura ... per l'anno 1792 [and 1794]. Firenze, G. Pagani 1792-94
3v. illus. S.
The number for 1794 has title: *Almanacco pittorico anno III.* Text and title are also in French
Lipperheide 4477

Manuale di pittura. See Manuale dei pittori

Manuale, oder Handgriffe der infanterie wie solches ao 1735, nach dem demahlig alt kayserl. würtenb. regiment zu fuss bey dem ... schwäbische Craysz regiment eingeführet worden. Entworffen von H: A v. A. Jerem. Wachsmuth fecit, Martin Engelbrecht, excudit. Augusta Vindelicorum 1735?
26pl. F.
Lipperheide 2223

Manucci, Niccolò
Storia do Mogor; or, Mogul India, 1653-1708; tr., with introduction and notes, by William Irvine. London, J. Murray 1907-08
4v. fronts. pl.(2 col.) ports. map(in pocket) col.plan, 2 fold.tab. O. (The Indian texts series)
"List of authorities quoted or referred to": v4 p463-82
LC 8-17330

Manuel complet de la danse. Blasis, Carlo

Manuel complet de la toilette. Saint-Hilaire, É. M. H.

Manuel d'archéologie française depuis les temps mérovingiens jusqu'à la renaissance. Enlart, Camille

Manuel d'archéologie préhistorique celtique et gallo-romaine. Dechelette, Joseph

Manuel de la coiffure de dames. Mallemont, A.

Manuel de l'amateur de la gravure sur bois et sur métal au xve siècle. Schreiber, W. L.

Manuel de l'enseignement de l'escrime au sabre à l'usage de la cavalerie Russe. Katkoff, Paul

Manuel des dames. Bayle-Mouillard, Mme. É. F.

Manuel des toilettes; dedié aux dames. Paris, Valade; Liège, J. J. Tutot 1777-78
4v. 52 col.pl. S.
Sometimes attributed to Alain Manesson-Mallet. Also published with plates in black and white. The illustrations show coiffures of men and women. Copies of the plates of volume one were published with Italian text under title: *Enciclopedia delle donne; Plocamopoli*
Colas 1968. Lipperheide 1677

Manuel d'escrime à la baïonette, simplifiée. Capiaumont, A.

Manuel du Journal des demoiselles. Journal des demoiselles

Manuel du tailleur. Dartmann, G. H.

The **manufacturing** clothier. See note under Clothing trade journal

Manuscrits à peintures de l'école de Rouen. Ritter, Georges, and Lafond, Jean

Manuzzi, Giuseppe
(ed.) Trattato della messa e della maniera di assistervi, e Del paramento del prete; testi di lingua ora per la prima volta pubblicati dal cavaliere abate Giuseppe Manuzzi. Forli, Dai tipi di L. Bordandini 1850
19p. O.
LC 32-12549

Manzoni. See Pécheux, jt. auth.

Maori and Polynesian. Brown, J. M.

Maori, past and present. Donne, T. E.

Maoris
Angas, G. F. The New Zealanders illustrated. 1847
Brown, J. M. Maori and Polynesian, their origin, history and culture. 1907
Buck, P. H. The evolution of Maori clothing. 1926
Donne, T. E. Maori, past and present. 1927
Taylor, Richard. Te Ika a Maui; or, New Zealand and its inhabitants. Illustrating the origin, manners, customs, mythology, religion ... of the Maori and Polynesian races in general. 1870

See also Tattooing—Maoris

Marais, Paul
Trois causeries sur l'histoire du costume, faites aux soirées paroissiales de Saint-Germain-L'Auxerrois. [Poitiers, Société française d'imprimerie] 1914
39p. O.
Colas 1969

Les **Marattes.** Broughton, T. D.

Marbot, Alfred Charles Adolfe, baron de
Costumes militaires français depuis 1789 jusqu'à 1814. Paris, Clément; London, E. Gamart 1860
58p. 150 col.pl. F.
Supplementary to Dunoyer de Noirmont's *Costumes militaires* which covers the period 1439 to 1789. According to Colas the two form the most important work on French military costume
Colas 1970. Lipperheide 2313

Tableaux synoptiques de l'infanterie et de la cavalerie française et des régiments étrangers au service de la France de 1720 à 1789; dressés par Alfred de Marbot d'après les documens authentiques. Paris, Clément 1854
12 col.pl. F.
Colas 1971. Lipperheide 2312

See also Dunoyer de Noirmont, J. A. E. E., jt. auth.

Marceau, Antoine François Sergent-. See Sergent-Marceau, A. F.

Marçais, Georges

Le costume musulman d'Alger. Paris, Plon 1930

134p. illus. double tab. XXXVIII pl. (5 col.) Q. (Collection du centenaire de l'Algérie. Archéologie et histoire) 160fr.

At head of title: 1830-1930. Plates accompanied by guard sheets with descriptive letterpress

"Bibliographie": p[127]-30

Colas 1972. Costume index. LC 31-5090

Marcel, A. See Eze, Mme M. G., jt. auth.

Marcel, Gabriel Alexandre

Un éventail historique du XVIIIe siècle. Paris, 1901

11p. double pl. O.

From the *Revue hispanique,* v8

LC 12-12088

Marcel, M.

L'Égypte et la Syrie. See entry under Breton de la Martinière, J. B. J.

Marcelli, Francesco Antonio

Regole della scherma insegnate de Lelio, e Titta Marcelli, scritte da Francesco Antonio Marcelli. Roma, D. A. Ercole 1686

2v. 34 illus. Q.

Lipperheide 2966

Marchal, Antoinette Caroline. See Marchal document

Marchal, Gustave

Les uniformes de l'armée française sous le consulat. Paris, E. Dubois 1901

38p. O.

"Renseignements tirés de "l'État militaire de la République française pour l'année VIII par plusieurs officiers", et des états militaires de la République française, années X et XI, par l'adjutant-commandant Champeaux." Subtitle

Colas 1973

Marchal, Sappho

Costumes et parures khmèrs, d'après les devatâ d'Angkor-Vat ... avec une préface de M. Victor Goloubew. Paris & Bruxelles, Librarie nationale d'art et d'histoire, G. Vanoest 1927

xi,114p. 41pl. O.

Colas 1974. Costume index

Marchal document; couture, mode, conseille, renseigne. Année 1, 1929+ Genève, C. Comisetti

Illus. (incl. ports.) pl. (part col.) F. 15fr. a year

Published monthly (slightly irregular)

Current 1938

[**Marchand, Jean Henri**]

L'enciclopédie carcassiere: ou Tableaux des coiffures à la mode: gravés sur les desseins des petites-maitresses de Paris. Paris, Chez Hochereau 1763

xl p. IV pl. (3 fold.) D.

German translation entitled: *Der Madame Beaumont, berühmten putzmacherin zu Paris lehrreiches kopfzeugermagazin zum nutzen des schönen geschlechts in Deutschland eingerichtet* was issued by the same publisher

Colas 1977. Lipp. 1669-1670. LC 25-18223

L'enciclopédie perruquiere ... Par M. Beaumont, coëffeur dans les Quinze-vingts [pseud.] Amsterdam; et Paris, chez l'auteur, et chez Hochereau 1757

37p. 45pl. D.

Another edition (1762) has 40 pages and 4 plates showing 44 styles of masculine coiffures

The German edition had title: *Des herrn Beaumont, berühmten haarfrisirers zu Paris, lehrreiches Perüquenmagazin zur bildung deutscher köpfe eingerichtet* (Paris & Berlin, Hochereau 1762)

Colas 1975-1976. Lipperheide 1666-1667. LC 20-14750, 25-18224 (Ger. ed.)

Marchand, Louis

Du costume de l'avocat à travers les âges. Poitiers, Blais et Roy 1911

32p. O.

"Discours prononcé à la séance solennelle de réouverture de la conférence des avocats stagiaires le 17 décembre 1910." Subtitle

Colas 1978

La **marchande** de modes de Marie-Antoinette, Rose Bertin. Langlade, Émile

Marchandon de La Faye, P. See Prisse d'Avennes, A. C. T. É. Histoire de l'art égyptien

Marchesi, José María. Catálogo de la Real armería. See Madrid. Armería real

The **Marcus-säule** auf piazza Colonna in Rom. Petersen, E. A. H.; Domaszewski, Alfred von, and Calderini, Guglielmo, eds.

Mare, Pieter de

(engr.) Chalon, Christina. Tweeëndertig stuks studien ordonnantien. 1779

(engr.) Chalon, Christina. Zinspelende gedigtjes

Maréchal, Pierre Sylvain

(ed.) Grasset de Saint-Sauveur, Jacques. Costumes civils actuels de tous les peuples connus

Mareschal

Artillerie, Garde royale; collection des dessins lithographiés représentant les principales positions de canonnier. Paris, lith. Engelmann, typ. Didot 1824

1,5 l. 20pl. F.

Colas lists also Mareschal's *Collection de dessins lithographiés représentant les principales positions du canonnier ...* (Paris, Engelmann 1824. 18p. 37pl.)

Colas 1982-83

Mareschal, Louis Auguste. See Perrin, O. S., jt. auth.

Le **mareschal** de bataille. Lostelneau, de

Ma'rffy-Mantuano, Judith

(tr.) Viski, Károly. Hungarian peasant customs

Margaretha, Anthonia. See Anthonia Margaretha, pseud.

Margerand, J.

Les coiffures de l'armée française; revue mensuelle illustrée. Paris, Leroy 1909-24

4pt. illus. (part col.) 126 col.pl. F.

Cover-title. Issued in 41 numbers, from Apr. 1909 to Aug. 1913, and a 42d number, July 1924

Published at 25 francs for 12 numbers on ordinary paper, 75 francs on vellum

Contents: 1 État-major général, de 1815 à 1900; 2 Maison du roi, 1814-1830. Garde royale, 1815-30; 3 Infanterie, 1791-1815; Infanterie, 1815-1900; 4 Cavalerie, 1791-1815. Cavalerie, 1815 à nos jours

Colas 1985. LC 24-1796

Les cuirasses des carabiniers (1810-1870) avec des dessins de P. Benigni. Paris, J. Leroy 1911

32p. illus. 16pl. O.

LC 24-1792

Margerand, J.—*Continued*
Les Hussards sous la révolution, reconstitution des gouaches de Hoffmann, brûlées à la Bibliothèque du Louvre en 1871, représentant les régiments de Hussards de 1791 à 1795. Paris, J. Leroy 1907
15p. col.pl. F.
Colas 1984. LC 26-22849

Notes sur les tenues des Hussards de 1815 à 1870; illus. de J. Rouffet. Extrait du Carnet de la Sabretache. Paris, Plon-Nourrit 1922
74p. 5pl. O.
Colas 1986

Marggraff, Clara. See Lipperheide, Frieda, jt. auth.

Margherita; giornale delle signore italiane. Anno 1-9; 1878-1887. Milano, Treves
9v. col.pl. F.
Contains colored fashion plates
Colas 1987. Lipperheide 4760

Maria Vergine coronata. Certani, Giacomo

Un **mariage** impérial chinois; cérémonial, traduit par G. Devéria. Paris, E. Leroux 1887
186p. 1 l. incl.front. fold.plan. D. (Bibliothèque orientale elzévirienne. 51)
"Fourni par deux documents bien distincts. Le premier, émané du Ministère des rites, concerne tout ce qui précède et suit le mariage proprement dit ... [Le] second est le plus intéressant et est rédigé par l'Intendance de la cour ... il concerne les cérémonies qui ont lieu." Introduction
Description of the marriage of T'ung Chih, emperor of China, 1856-1875
LC 33-7905

Mariaux, E. See note under Paris. Musée de l'armee. Armes & armures anciennes

Marie, Aristide
Henry Monnier, 1799-1877. Paris, Floury 1931
290p. front.(port.) illus. pl.(part col.) ports. O.
Bibliography: p201-36
Lists works by Monnier and contains many of his lithographs

Marie de Medicis, entrant dans Amsterdam. Baerle, Kaspar van

Marie de Saint-Ursin, P. J.
L'ami des femmes, ou Lettres d'un médecin, concernant l'influence de l'habillement des femmes sur leurs moeurs et leur santé; 2. éd. corr. et très-augm. Paris, Barba 1805
xlviii,454p. 6 illus. O.
"Et la nécessité de l'usage habituel des bains en conservant leur costume actuel; suivies d'un appendix contenant des recettes cosmétiques et une thérapeutique appropriée au goût." Subtitle
First edition was published (Paris, 1804)
Colas 2630. Lipperheide 3246

Mariette, Pauline
L'art de la toilette; méthode nouvelle pour tailler, éxécuter ou diriger avec économie et élégance tous les vêtements de dames et d'enfants. Paris, Librairie centrale 1866
160p. 38 illus. 40pl. O.
The illustrations show patterns; the plates show fashions of the day
Colas 1988. Lipperheide 3795

Costumes français. Paris, Mariette ca1730
24pl. O.
Colas 1989

Marin, L. See Colin, Mme Anais, jt. auth.

La **marine,** arsenaux, navires, équipages ... Pacini, E. F. L. D.

Marine corps

United States

1812-1860

United States. Marine corps. Regulations for the uniform & dress of the Marine corps ... October, 1859; from the original text and drawings in the Quarter Master's Department. 1859

United States. Navy department. Regulations for the uniform and dress of the navy and marine corps of the United States. March, 1852. 1852

1860-1898

United States. Marine corps. Regulations for the uniform and dress of the Marine corps ... May, 1875. 1875

1898-1917

United States. Marine corps. Uniform regulations, United States Marine corps, together with uniform regulations common to both U. S. Navy and Marine corps. 1912, rev. 1917

United States. Marine corps. Uniform regulations, United States Marine corps, together with uniform regulations common to both U. S. navy and Marine corps. 1913

United States. Navy dept. Uniform regulations, United States navy, together with uniform regulations common to both Navy and Marine corps. 1913

Volk, C. G. United States officers' uniforms, army, navy, marine corps. 1917

1917-date

United States. Marine corps. Uniform regulations, United States Marine corps, 1922. Superseding Uniform regulations, United States Marine corps, 1917. 1922

United States. Marine corps. Uniform regulations, United States Marine corps, 1929. 1930

United States. Navy department. Uniform regulations, United States navy, together with uniform regulations common to both Navy and Marine corps ... 1913, rev. to January 15, 1917. 1917

La **marine** et les colonies. See L'ancienne France: La marine et les colonies

Marine française. Paris, L. Baschet 1886
2v.(15,14p.) 21 illus.(part col.) O. (Cahiers d'enseignement illustrés nos 11, 12)
Lipperheide 2341

Marionettes. See Puppets

Marionnettes et guignols. Maindron, Ernest

Marionettes, masks and shadows. Mills, Mrs W. H., and Dunn, Mrs L. M.

Mark, Quirin
[Coiffures de femmes] No place, ca1710?
6pl. S.
Each plate shows four styles of hairdressing. Plates are signed Q. Mark
Colas 1990

Markham, Sir Clements Robert
The Incas of Peru. London, Smith, Elder 1910
xvi,443p. front. illus. pl. fold.map. O.
LC 10-34090

Marks, W.
(engr.) Dinaux, A. M. Description des fêtes populaires données à Valenciennes les 11, 12, 13 mai 1851

Marot, Daniel
Nouveaux lieure de housses en broderie et en gallons. No place, ca1700
6pl. Q.
Title is from the legend on plate one
Lipperheide 3925

Maroto, Victoriano Pérez
(comp.) Estadística taurina anual

Marozzo, Achille
Arte dell' armi ... ricorretto, et ornato di nuove figure. Venetia, A. Pinargenti 1568
126p. 26 illus. Q.
Fourth edition. The first edition was published at Modena about 1536
Lipperheide 2947

Marquardt, Carl
Die tätowirung beider geschlechter in Samoa; mit 19 tafeln in lichtdruck und photolithographie nach in Samoa aufgenommenen original-zeichnungen und photogrammen. Berlin, D. Reimer 1899
31p. 19pl. F.
LC 3-4054

Marquardt, Karl Joachim
Das privatleben der Römer; 2. aufl. besorgt von A. Mau. Leipzig, S. Hirzel 1886
2v. in 1. illus. 2 fold.plans. O. (Handbuch der römischen alterthümer von Joachim Marquardt und Theodor Mommsen, 7. bd.)
Lipperheide 260. LC A12-1502

Die **Marquesaner** und ihre kunst. Steinen, Karl von den

Marquesas Islands
Christian, F. W. Eastern Pacific lands. 1910

Handy, Mrs W. C. Tattooing in the Marquesas. 1922

See also Tattooing—Marquesas islands

Marquez, José Micheli y. See Micheli y Marquez, José

Marriage, Ernest
(illus.) Mincoff-Marriage, Mrs Elizabeth, and Marriage, Mrs M. S. Pillow lace

Marriage, Mrs Margaret S. See Mincoff-Marriage, Mrs Elizabeth, jt. auth.

Marriage costume. See Weddings and wedding dress

Marriage customs in many lands. Hutchinson, H. N.

Marriage rites, customs and ceremonies of all nations of the universe. Hamilton, Lady Augusta

Marriott, Wharton Booth
Vestiarium Christianum; the origin and gradual development of the dress of holy ministry in the church. London [etc.] Rivingtons 1868
14,lxxxiv,252p. mounted front. illus. LXIII pl.(part mounted, part col.) Q. 38s
"Authors and editions quoted or referred to." p[11]-14
Colas 1991. Costume index. Lipperheide 1837. LC 33-9891

Marroni, Salvatore
Costumi di Roma e suoi contorni; disegnati da varj artisti ed incisi da Salvatore Marroni. Roma, Cuccioni [1820?]
30 col.pl. F.
Title vignette, colored
Cataloged from information from the Grosvenor library, Buffalo, N.Y.

Nuova raccolta di no. 40 costumi popolari di Roma e sue vicinanze, disegnati dal vero ed incisi da Salvatore Marroni, anno 1840. Roma, A. Depoletti [1840]
1 l. 39pl. Q.
Colas 1992

Raccolta dei principali costumi religio e militari, della corte pontificia. Roma, ca1840
40 col.pl. F.

Mars. Siły zbrojne niemiec. Poland. General staff

Marsan, Eugène
Pour habiller Eliante, ou Le nouveau secret des dames. Liège, La lamp d'Aladin; Lyon, impr. Audin 1927
69p. O.
Colas 1993

Marsden, William
The history of Sumatra; 3d ed. with corrections, additions, and plates. London, J. McCreery, sold by Longman, Hurst, Rees, Orme, and Brown 1811
479p. front.(port.) 19(i.e. 20)pl.(part fold.) fold.map. sq.Q.
LC 5-13396

Marsh, Bower
Memorial rings, Charles the Second to William the Fourth. See entry under Crisp, F. A.

Marshall, Frances, and Marshall, Hugh
Old English embroidery: its technique and symbolism. London, H. Cox 1894
xii,138p. 31 illus. 17pl. Q.
Lipperheide 3875

Marshall, Francis
(ed.) Football, the Rugby union game; rev and enl ed. London, Paris & Melbourne, Cassell [1895]
xvi,564p. front. illus.(incl.ports.) O.
LC 1-2374

Marshall, Frederick Henry
Catalogue of finger rings, Greek, Etruscan, and Roman. See entry under British museum. Department of Greek and Roman antiquities

Catalogue of the jewellery, Greek, Etruscan, and Roman. See entry under British museum. Department of Greek and Roman antiquities

Marshall, Hugh. See Marshall, Frances, jt. auth.

Marstaller, G. J.
(lithgr.) Merkwaardige historische beschryving van alle vreemde en onlangs eerst bekent gewordene krygsvolkeren (attributed)

Marston, Annie Westland
The children of India. London, Religious tract society [1883]
190p. illus. O.

Marston, Morrell
Memoirs relating to the Sauk and Foxes (*In* Blair, E. H., ed. The Indian tribes of the upper Mississippi valley and region of the Great lakes)

Marta, Luigi
Costumi della festa data da S. Maesta' il di 20 feb. 1854 nella reggia di Napoli. Naples, Bertauts 1854
[3] l. 31 col.pl. ob.F.
Plates show masquerade costume
Colas 1994. Lipperheide 2781

Martenasie, Pitre
(engr.) Lens, A. C. Le costume des peuples de l'antiquité prouvé par les monuments

Martens, H.
(illus.) Ackermann, Rudolph. Costumes of the British Army

Martha, Jules
L'art étrusque, illustré ... d'après les originaux ou d'après les documents les plus authentiques. Paris, Firmin-Didot 1889
635p. incl.illus. map. IV col.pl.(incl.front.) Q.
Shows Etruscan costume and jewelry
"Indications bibliographiques": 4th prelim. leaf.
LC F-3664

The **martial** achievements of Great Britain and her allies (1799-1815) Jenkins, James

Martigny, Joseph Alexandre, l'abbé
Dictionnaire des antiquités chrétiennes. Paris, L. Hachette 1865
676p. illus. Q.
Contains material on dress of the early Christians and their priests

Martin, Arthur. See Cahier, Charles, jt. auth.

Martin, C. H.
(lithgr.) Mansion, L. M., and Saint-Eschauzier. L'armée anglaise vers 1830

Martin, Charles, and Martin, Leopold
Civil costume of England, from the conquest to the present time drawn from tapestries, monumental effigies, illuminated manuscripts, portraits, &c. by Charles Martin, etched by Leopold Martin. London, Bohn 1842
[3] l. 61 col.pl. Q. o.p.
Colas 1995. Costume index. Lipp. 1003

Martin, Cornelis
Les genealogies et anciennes descentes des forestiers et comtes de Flandre, avec brieves descriptions de leurs vies et gestes ... par Corneille Martī Zelandoÿs, et ornees de portraicts figures et habitz selō les facons et guises de leurs temps, ainsi qu'elles ont este trouvees es plus anciens tableaux, par Pierre Balthasar, et par luimesme mises en lumiere. Anvers, J. B. Vrints [1608]
121p. illus.(incl. 41 full-page port. map, coats of arms) F.
Lipperheide 929. LC 25-12960

[**Martin, Eugène**]
[Les Bretons, moeurs et coutumes; eaux-fortes d'Eug. Martin. Paris, Cadart & Luce] 1868
1 l. 10pl. Q.
Colas 1996

Martin, Jean Baptiste
Collection de figures theatrales inventées et gravées par Martin cy devant dessinateur des habillements de l'Opéra. Paris, veuve Chereau ca1760
1 l. 20 col.pl. F.
The same plates were re-published in *Gallerie des modes et costumes français.*
Colas gives a list of plates
Colas 1997

Martin, Johann Friedrich
Svenska galeriet, eller portraiter af märkvärdige svenske herrar och fruntimer. Stockholm, Trykt i kongl. tryckeriet [1782-84]
2v. 12pl. O.
Half-length portraits of Swedish men and women of the seventeenth and eighteenth centuries
Lipperheide 1043

(engr.) Hilleström, Pehr. Costumes des paysans de divers cantons en Suède

Martin, John Joseph
America dancing; the background and personalities of the modern dance; illustrated with photographs by Thomas Bouchard. New York, Dodge [c1936]
320p. pl. O.
LC 36-28530

Martin, Leopold. See Martin, Charles, jt. auth.

Martin, P. See Malliot, Joseph, jt. auth.

Martinet, firm, publisher
Catalogue des collections des costumes de theatres, fantaisies, historiques et nationaux. Paris, Martinet (J. Hautecoeur) 1883
20p. O.
A list of costume suites published by Martinet during the nineteenth century
Colas 2005

[Costumes des franc-tireurs et des volontaires de 1870. Paris, Martinet 1870?]
25 col.pl. Q.
Colas 2003

Galerie des enfants de Mars, offrande à sa Majesté l'impératice et reine. Paris, Martinet [1811]
3 l. front. 45 col.pl. Q.
Plates have title *Troupes françaises* and are a part of the 296 published in *Troupes françaises: Premier empire* by the same publisher
Colas 1157

Galerie militaire. Paris, Martinet ca1815?
55 col.pl. Q.
Plates show uniforms of armies outside France during the period of the first empire. Each plate has one of the following titles at head: *Troupes étrangères, Troupes turques, troupes autrichiennes, Troupes russes*
Colas 2004

Martinet, firm, publisher—*Continued*
Galerie militaire: troupes françaises. Paris, Martinet [1816-22]
18, 7 col.pl. O.
Plates show uniforms of the Garde royale
Colas 2002

Troupes françaises; Maison du Roi, 1814. Paris, Martinet [1814]
14 col.pl. Q.
The list of plates is given in Glasser's *Costumes militaires*. He lists also a set with same title and four colored plates
Colas 2000-2001

Troupes françaises (Premier empire) Paris, Martinet [1807-1814]
296 col.pl. O.
Each plate shows costume of one military type. The list is given in Glasser. Forty-five of these plates were published separately with title *Galerie des enfants de Mars*
Colas 1998

Troupes françaises (Restauration) Paris, Martinet [1814-16]
18 col.pl. O.
Colas 1999

(pub.) Costumes des différens départemens de l'Empire français

(pub.) Godefroy, A. P. F. Armées des souverains alliés, années 1814 et 1815

(pub.) Le goût du jour

(pub.) Recueil de costumes suisses

Martinet, François Xavier
Historique du 9e régiment de dragons ... illus. par Roger Parquet. Paris, H. T. Hamel 1888
172p. 15pl.(13 col.) Q.
Lipperheide 2350

Martinet, J. J.
Essai, ou principes élémentaires de l'art de la danse. Lausanne, Monnier et Jaquerod 1797
72p. 9pl. D.
Lipperheide 3087

Martínez Baca, Francisco
Los tatuages; estudio psicológico y médico-legal en delincuentes y militares. México, Tip. de la Oficina impresora del timbre 1899
vii,292p. pl. tables(part fold.) Q.
LC 24-25967

Martini, Angela
Moda, 1790-1900. Milano, Rizzoli 1933
117p. illus. 102,20pl.(20 col.) on 71 l. Q.
Examples of European costume, masculine and feminine for almost every year of the period, are shown. Some children's dress is included

Martini, George Heinrich
(ed.) Lens, A. C. Das kostum der meisten völker des alterthums

Martini, Johann Jacob. See Neu-eingerichtete und vermehrte bilder-geographie

Martiniennes. See Chroniques dites Martiniennes

Martinoff, André. See Martuinov, A. E.

Martuinov, Andrei Evthimievich
[Folk-costumes of Asiatic Russia,] dessiné et gravé par A. Martinoff. [No place] 1808
28 col.pl. F.
Colas 2006. Lipperheide 1387m

Martyne, Charles. See Gazette du bon genre. Trente neuf aquarelles

Marx, Alex.
(engr.) Heideloff, K. A. von. Gedenkblätter der Universitäten Heidelberg, Prag und Wien

Marx, Leonhard Wilhelm
Trachtenbuch zur Geschichte der reichsstadt Nürnberg. Nürnberg, F. Heerdegen (Barbeck) 1873
14pl.(10 col.) Q.
Cover serves as title-page
Lipperheide 788

Mary, Virgin
Carpenter, M. B. The child in art. 1906
Dürer, Albrecht. Dürer album. 1856-61
Dürer, Albrecht. Dürer vier holzschnittfolgen phototypisch nachgebildet in der grösse der originale. 1887
Hurll, E. M. The Madonna in art. 1897
Itinerarius beatissimae Virginis Mariae. ca1488
Johann von St Wendel. Fidelis certa verissimaqz narratio de Monasterio beate Marie ad littus martirum: de Tunica quoqz beate Marie vginis ceterisqz sacris ibidē reliquijs. ca1512
Maynard, M. U., abbé. La Sainte Vierge. 1877

Mas, E.
(illus.) Dally, Aristide. L'armée hollandaise

Mascara real, executada por los colegios y gremios de Barcelona para festejar el feliz desseado arribo de ... dn. Carlos tercero y da. Maria Amalia de Saxonia, con el real principe e infantes [October, 1759] Barcelona, T. Piferrer 1764
14 l. 11pl. F.
The plates show groups of people and carriages which took part in the ceremonies
Lipperheide 2730

Mascarade à la grecque. Petitot, E. A.

Mascarade improvisée. Philipon, Charles

Mascarades. Boissard, J. J.

Mascarades monastiques et religieuses. Bar, J. C.

Mascaras mexicanas. Montenegro, Roberto

Mascardi, Vitale
Festa, fatta in Roma, alli 25. febraio MDCXXXIV. Roma [1635]
135p. 11pl. Q.
Plates show processions, carriages, and ships
Lipperheide 2818

Maschere italiane, Cinquanta. Frizzi, Arturo

Le **maschere** sceniche e le figure comiche d'antichi romani descritte brevemente. Ficoroni, Francesco

Masken. Utzinger, Rudolf

Masken der neueren attischen komoedie. Robert, Karl

Masken, ihr ursprung. Koehler, H. K. E. von

Die **masken** in der völkerkunde. Andree, Richard

Die **masken** und geheimbünde Afrikas. Frobenius, Leo.

Maskenanzüge. Bérain, J. L.

Masken-anzüge zu polter-abenden und bällen. Dörbeck, B.

Masken-costüme; 70 costüm-entwürfe für damen- u. kinder-masken ... nebst erläuterungen und beschreibungen. Paris, Bazar-actien-gesellschaft [1883]
16, 4 col.pl. F.
Colas 2007. Lipperheide 3191

Maskerade, gehouden door de Leden van het Leidsche studenten-corps den 22n Juni 1880, ter viering van den 305den verjaardag der Leidsche hoogeschool, voorstellende den intoch van Phillips de Schoone binnen Amsterdam, den 27sten Juni 1497. Geteekend en op steen gebracht door G. J. Bos. Leiden, S. C. van Doesburgh 1880
Illus. ob.F. fl.12.50
In portfolio

Masks

Andree, Richard. Die masken in der völkerkunde. 1886

Benndorf, Otto. Antike gesichtshelme und sepulcralmasken. 1878

Berger, C. H., edler herr von. Commentatio de personis vulgo laruis seu mascheris von der carnavals-lust. 1723

La décoration primitive. 1922-24

Dorsey, G. A. A copper mask from Chimbote, Peru. 1897

Downs, Harold, ed. Theater and stage; a modern guide to the performance of all classes of amateur dramatic, operatic, and theatrical work. 1934

International congress of popular arts, Prague, 1928. Art populaire. 1931

Kniffin, H. R. Masks. 1931

Koehler, H. K. E. von. Masken, ihr ursprung und neue auslegung einiger der merkwürdigsten auf alten denkmälern die bis jetzt unerkannt und unerklärt geblieben waren. 1833

Laufer, Berthold. Oriental theatricals. 1923

Macgowan, Kenneth, and Rosse, Herman. Masks and demons. 1923

The mythology of all races. 1916-32

Nicoll, Allardyce. Masks, mimes and miracles; studies in the popular theatre. 1931

Parain, Nathalie. Masques de la jungle. c1933

Parain, Nathalie. Mes masques. c1931

Utzinger, Rudolf. Masken. 1922

See also Mummers

Africa

Frobenius, Leo. Die masken und geheimbünde Afrikas. 1898

Maes, Joseph. Aniota-kifwebe; les masques des populations du Congo Belge et le materiel des rites de circoncision. 1924

Ratton, Charles. Masques africains. 1931

Ancient times

Dieterich, Albrecht. Pulcinella; pompejanische wandbilder und römische satyrspiele. 1897

Ficoroni, Francesco. Le maschere sceniche e le figure comiche d'antichi romani descritte brevemente. 1736

Hense, Otto. Die modifizierung der maske in der griechischen tragödie. 1905

Lecuyer, Camille. Collection Camille Lecuyer; terres cuites antiques, trouvées en Grèce et en Asie-Mineure. 1882-85

Robert, Karl. Die masken der neueren attischen komoedie. 1911

Catalonia

Amades, Joan. Gegants, nans i altres entremesos. [1934]

Germany

Stümcke, Heinrich. Die deutsche theaterausstellung, Berlin 1910. 1911

Indians of America

Burlin, Mrs N. C. The Indians' book. 1923

Dorsey, G. A., and Voth, H. R. The Oraibi Soyal ceremony. 1901

Gregor, Joseph, and Fülöp-Miller, René. Das amerikanische theater und kino. 1931

Harrington, M. R. Religion and ceremonies of the Lenape. 1921

Verrill, A. H. The American Indian, North, South, and Central America. 1927

Aztecs

Danzel, T. W. Mexiko. v2

Japan

Bing, Samuel. Artistic Japan. 1888-91

Perzyński, Friedrich. Japanische masken, nō und kyōgen. 1925

Mexico

Montenegro, Roberto. Mascaras mexicanas. 1926

New Guinea

Lewis, A. B. New Guinea masks. 1922

Salzburg

Andree-Eysen, Marie. Die perchten im Salzburgischen. 1905

Masks and demons. Macgowan, Kenneth, and Rosse, Herman

Masks, mimes and miracles. Nicoll, Allardyce

Masner, Carl

Die costüm-ausstellung im k. k. Oesterreichischen museum 1891 ... in lichtdrucken hrsg von J. Löwy. Wien, J. Lowy 1892-93
15 l. 50pl. 6 diagrs. ob.Q.
Especially rich in 17th and 18th century costume of Austria Hungary and the Balkan countries. A few plates show costume of Egypt, India, Siberia, and Syria
Colas 2008. Lipperheide 97

Mason, Augustus Lynch

The romance and tragedy of pioneer life. A popular account of the heroes and adventurers who, by their valor and war-craft, beat back the savages from the borders of civilization and gave the American forests to the plow and the sickle. Cincinnati, Chicago [etc.] Jones brothers 1883

1032p. front. illus. pl. ports. maps. O.
LC 5-40616

Mason, George Henry

The costume of China, illustrated by sixty engravings: with explanations of English and French. London, Printed for W. Miller 1800

[134]p. 60 col.pl. F. 6gns. o.p.
Added title page in French: *Costumes de la Chine*
Reprinted 1806. Plates are engraved by Dadley after designs by the Cantonese artist Pu-Qúa. They have been copied in Corti's *Chinesisches bilderbuch*
J. G. Grohmann's *Gebrauche und kleidungen der Chinesen* is based on Mason's book. Also E. C. Corti's *Chinesisches bilderbuch* contains illustrations from Mason
Colas 2009. Costume index. Lipperheide 1520. LC 15-3329

The punishments of China, illustrated by twenty-two engravings: with explanations in English and French. London, Printed for W. Miller, by S. Gosnell 1808

[54]p. 22 col.pl. F.
Published anonymously
Added title page in French: *Les punitions des Chinois.* Copies of these plates appear in Friedrich Hempel's *Die strafen des Chinesen*
Colas 2010-2012. Lipp. 1522. LC 10-34452

Mason, Rupert

Robes of Thespis; costume designs by modern artists, edited for Rupert Mason by George Sheringham and R. Boyd Morrison. London, E. Benn limited 1928

xv,143p. 1 l. illus. 109(i.e. 110)pl.(part col.) Q. £8 8s
Each plate accompanied by guard sheet with descriptive letterpress
Bibliography: p31-32
LC 28-12776

Mason, Thomas H.

The islands of Ireland; their scenery, people, life and antiquities. London, B. T. Batsford [1936]

135p. col.front. illus. pl. O.

Masonic emblems and jewels. Hammond, William

Masons (Secret order). See Freemasons

Maspero, Sir Gaston Camille Charles

Art in Egypt. New York, C. Scribner's sons 1912

xi,314p. col.front. illus. 3 col.pl. D. (Ars una; species mille)
Each plate accompanied by guard sheet with descriptive letterpress. "This volume is published simultaneously in America . . . in England . . . also in French . . . in German . . . in Italian . . . in Spanish . . ."—Verso of title page
Costume, including headdress and jewelry, is shown incidentally in the art of different periods
Bibliography at end of each chapter
LC 13-35275

Histoire ancienne de peuples de l'Orient classique. Paris, Hachette 1895-1908

3v. illus. 7 col.pl.(incl.fronts.) maps. Q.
Contents: [t 1] Les origines: Égypte & Chaldée; [t2] Les premières mêlées des peuples; [t3] Les empires
LC 9-9794

Life in ancient Egypt and Assyria. From the French. [Authorized ed.] New York, D. Appleton 1892

xv,376p. illus. O.
Contains numerous outline drawings which show the dress of these countries
LC 4-14830

The **masque** of the Edwards of England. Ashbee, C. R. and Harwood, Edith

Masquelier, C. L.

(engr.) Mongez, Antoine. Tableaux, statues, bas reliefs et camées de la Galerie de Florence et du Palais Pitti

Masquerade and carnival. Wandle, Mrs J. T.

Masquerade costume. See Fancy dress

Masques africains. Ratton, Charles

Masques de la jungle. Parain, Nathalie

Masques et bouffons. Sand, Maurice

Les **masques** et les personnages de la comédie italienne. Regnier, Mme. M. L. A. de H. de, and Brunelleschi, Umberto

The **mass** and vestments of the Catholic church. Walsh, John

Massachusetts. See Military costume—United States—Massachusetts

Massano, Gino

Grazie e splendori dei costumi italiani. Roma, Morpurgo 1930

? p. 64pl. S.

Massard, Jean Marie Raphaël Léopold

(engr.) Challamel, Augustin, and Ténint, Wilhelm. Les Français sous la révolution

Massard, L.

(illus.) Costumes français, depuis Clovis jusqu'à nos jours

Massmann, Hans Ferdinand

Geschichte des mittelalterlichen, vorzugsweise des deutschen schachspieles. Nebst vollständiger und fortlaufender literatur des spieles sowie abbildungen und registern. Quedlinburg und Leipzig, G. Basse 1839

224p. 15pl. O.
The plates are pictures of chessmen of the middle ages to the seventeenth century, some of them showing the costume of the period of their origin
Lipperheide 320

(ed.) Dance of death. Die Baseler todtentänze in getreuen abbildungen

Masson, Frédéric

Livre du sacre de l'empereur Napoléon. Paris, Goupil; Manzi, Joyant 1908

188p. col.front. illus. 43pl.(4 col. 7 double) O.
Each plate accompanied by descriptive text, not included in paging
The author's *Napoléon* (Vienne, M. Munk n.d. 36p. 12 col.illus. by F. Myrbach Q.) also has pictures of the costume of the period
LC 13-12668

Master of the Amsterdam cabinet, 15th century
The Master of the Amsterdam cabinet, by Max Lehrs. Paris, A. Danlos; New York, H. Wunderlich [etc] 1893-94
8p. 89pl. mounted on 67 l. F.
At head of title: International chalcographical society 1893 and 1894
Also published in German edition: *Meister des Amsterdam kabinets*
Woodcuts show costume of the Netherlands in the fifteenth century
Lipperheide 473 (German ed.) LC 14-11848 (German ed.)

Master tailor and cutters' gazette. v 1-16; 1893-1908. London
Illus.
Merged into *Sartorial gazette*

Masterpieces of Greek sculpture. Furtwängler, Adolf

Il **mastro** di casa. Pandini, Cesare

Mastroianni, Dominico
(illus.) Dodd, I. S. The pictorial life of Christ

Mateer, Samuel
Native life in Travancore. London, W. H. Allen 1883
xvi,434p. front. illus. pl. fold.map. O.
Shows costume in Travancore, India, one of the Madras States
LC 1-3112

Matejko, Jan
Ubiory w dawnej Polsce. Warszawa, B. Wierzbicki i S-ka 1901
82p. illus. ob.O.
Half-title: *Ubiory w Polsce 1200-1795*. First edition 1860 (Krakow, M. Salba). Second edition 1875
Pages consist of fullpage illustrations with a descriptive note for each figure. They show Polish costume of all kinds including academic and ecclesiastical
Colas 2013. Lipperheide 1396

Matenesius, Joannes Fridericus
De luxu et abusu vestium nostri temporis. Coloniae, J. Crithium 1612
121p. D.
"Discursus quadraginta ex sacrarum scripturarum, gravissimorumque auctorum fontibus." Subtitle
Colas 2014

Materials. See Bark as clothing; Feathers used in costume; Fur in costume; Leather in clothing

Materialy po īstoriī russkīkh odezhd" ī obstanovkī zhīznī narodnoī, izdavaemye po Vysochaīshemu soīzvoleniīū. Prokhorov", V. A.

Mathew, Frank James
Ireland, painted by Francis S. Walker, described by Frank Mathew. London, A. & C. Black [1905]
xix,212p. 79 col.pl.(incl.front.) O.
LC 5-35680

Mathey, Paul
(illus.) Koenig, Marie. Poupées et légendes de France

Mathieu, Bernard Charles
(pub.) Manesse, Rüdiger. Minnesänger aus der zeit der Hohenstaufen

Matina, Leone
Ducalis regiae lararium, sive Ser'me Reipv. Venetae principũ omniũ icones usque ad ... Ioannem Pisaurum qui nunc rerũ feliciter potitur, elogia. Patavii, typis Hertz 1659
10 l. 344p. 103 ports. F.
Contains head and shoulder portraits of the doges of Venice, engraved by Giacomo Piccini
Lipperheide 1250

Matrimonial ladder. Egerton, M.

Matthäus und Veit Konrad Schwarz. Reichard, E. C.

Matthesius, Christophorus Laurentius
(respondent) Loeber, C. G., praeses. Dissertationem academicam de mutatione formarum in vestibus

Matthew, Christine D.
(tr.) Obermaier, Hugo. Fossil man in Spain

Matthews, Mary Lockwood
Clothing; selection and care. Boston, Little, Brown 1936
xiii,407p. illus. col.pl. O.
Includes bibliographies
LC 36-11453

Matthias, J.
Der menschliche schmuck; form, farbe und anwendung. Ein beitrag zur bildung des geschmacks in häuslichen und gewerblichen kreisen. Liegnitz, M. Cohn 1871
xvii,114p. 16pl. O.
Lipperheide 1750

Matthias, J. Chr.
Kunstgewerbliches modell- u- musterbuch; eine sammlung charakterist. beispiele der decorativen und ornamentalen kunst aller völker und zeiten. Zunachst im anschluss an das Museum Minutoli. Leipzig, Seemann 1866-67
38p. 24 col.pl. O.

Mattl-Loewenkreuz, Emanuela
(ed.) Kulmer, Friedrich von. Im reiche Kaiser Menelik's tagebuch einer abessinischen reise

Maudslay, Alfred Percival
Archaeology. London, R. H. Porter and Dulau & co. 1889-1902
4v. illus. and atlas of 392pl.(part col. part fold.) ob.F. (Biologia centrali-americana)
Some of the plates show Maya costume
LC 5-19358

Guide to the Maudslay collection of Maya sculptures. See entry under British museum. Department of ceramics and ethnography

Maugé, Hangard-. See Hangard-Maugé

Maurer, Hans Rudolf
Denkmale des geschmaks der sitten und gebräuche der alten Schweizer; erstes heft: Der warme Hirsbrey und die verbindungen Zürichs mit Strassburg Zürich, 1792
xii,106p. 10 illus.(2 col.) Q.
Lipperheide 901

Maurer, Willibald
(illus.) Eye, August von, and Falke, Jacob von. Kunst und leben der vorzeit vom beginn des mittelalters bis zu anfang des 19. jahrhunderts

Maurice, C.
Les cantinières de France. [Paris, F. Sinnett 184-?]
1 folder of 25 col.pl. S.
The canteen-women wore a uniform adapted from that of the regiment to which each belonged

Costumes pittoresques. Paris, E. Morier [1859]
12pl. Q.
Shows dress of peasants from Grandville, Caen, Lisieux, Bayeux and other parts of Normandy
Colas 2016

[French military costumes] Paris, F. Sinnett [184-?]
1 folder of 25 col.pl. S.

Un mois dans les Pyrénées. Paris, F. Sinnett ca1850
12 col.pl. ob.Q.
"Album de sites, moeurs et costumes des Hautes et Basses-Pyrénées, peint d'après nature." Subtitle
Colas 2015

Maurin, Antoine
Iconographie française et étrangée ... lithographiée par de Ligny-Frères. Paris, Rosselin 1835-37
1 l. 92pl. Q.
A collection of portraits, principally of French statesmen and generals of the beginning of the nineteenth century
Lipperheide 1165

Maurisset, Théodore
(illus.) Physiologie de l'homme de loi

Maury, Louis Ferdinand Alfred
(ed.) Clarac, C. O. F. J. B., comte de. Musée de sculpture antique et moderne

Mausoleum potentissimorum ac gloriosissimorum regni apostolici regum & primorum militantis Ungariae ducum. Nádasdy, Ferencz, graf

Maximilian I, emperor of Germany
Das fischereibuch kaiser Maximilians I ... Unter mitwirkung von Ludwig freih. v. Lazarini, hrsg. von dr. Michael Mayr. Innsbruck, Verlag der Wagner'schen universitätsbuchhandlung 1901
xxviii,52p. 9pl.(8 col.) F.
Lipperheide 3018

Freydal. Des kaisers Maximilian I. turniere und mummereien. Wien, A. Holzhausen 1880-82
civ p. facsim.: [25]p. illus. 255pl. F.
The facsimile lettered: A-Z. Bibliographical foot-notes
"Hrsg. mit allerhöchster genehmigung Seiner Majestät des kaisers Franz Joseph I. unter der leitung des k. k. oberstkämmers, feldzeugmeisters Franz grafen Folliot de Crenneville, von Quirin von Leitner; mit einer geschichtlichen einleitung, einem facsimilirten namensverzeichnisse und 255 heliogravuren." Subtitle
Shows arms and armor and costume of the fifteenth century
Lipperheide 2884. LC 15-12303

Das jagdbuch kaiser Maximilians I. In verbindung mit Wm A. Baillie-Grohman hrsg. von dr. Michael Mayr. Innsbruck, Wagner 1901
xxxii,191p. pl.(part col.) facsims. F.
Lipperheide 3017. LC 13-2285

See also Theuerdank. Die geuerlicheiten

Maximilian, prince of Wied. See Wied-Neuwied, Maximilian Alexander Philpp prinz von

Maximilian, prince of Wied's Travels in the interior of North America, 1832-1834. See Wied-Neuwied, M. A. P., prinz von. Travels in the interior of North America

Maximis, Franc. Xavier de
Musei Etrusci quod Gregorius XVI. pont. max. in aedibus Vaticanis constituit monimenta linearis picturae exemplis expressa et in utilitatem studiosorum antiquitatum et bonarum artium publici juris facta. [Roma] ex aedibus Vaticanis [1842]
2v. 238pl. F.
Text is in Italian
Lipperheide 236

Maxwell, Sir William Stirling, bart. See Stirling-Maxwell, Sir William, bart.

May, Phil
Phil May's gutter-snipes. London, Leadenhall press [c1896]
4 l. front. 50pl. Q.
Shows children of the poor at their games
LC 8-14760

May hosiery mills, inc., Burlington, N.C.
The story of hosiery. Burlington, N.C. [c1931]
101p. illus. O.
"By Wesley Taylor." Label mounted on p[2]
LC 31-22778

Maya & Mexican art. Joyce, T. A.

Mayas
Brasseur de Bourbourg, C. E. Monuments anciens du Mexique; Palenqué et autres ruines. 1866
British museum. Department of ceramics and ethnography. Guide to the Maudslay collection of Maya sculptures (casts and originals) from Central America. 1923
Charnay, Désiré. Les anciennes villes du Nouveau monde. 1857-1882
Charnay, Désiré. The ancient cities of the New World. 1887
Charnay, Désiré. Cités et ruines américaines, Mitla, Palenqué, Izamal, Chichen-Itza, Uxmal. 1863
Dieseldorff, E. P. Kunst und religion der Mayavölker im alten und heutigen mittel-Amerika. 1926
Gann, T. W. F. Ancient cities and modern tribes. 1926
Joyce, T. A. Maya & Mexican art. 1927
Maudslay, A. P. Archaeology. 1889-1902
Shattuck, G. C. The peninsula of Yucatan. 1933

See also Indians of Mexico

Mayer, Joseph. See Faussett, Bryan. Inventorium sepulchrale

Mayer, Ludwig
Views in Egypt, from the original drawings in the possession of Sir Robert Ainslie, taken during his embassy to Constantinople, by Luigi Mayer. London, R. Bowyer 1804
102p. 48 col.pl. F.
"Engraved by and under the direction of Thomas Milton: with historical observations, and incidental illustrations, of the manners and customs of the natives of that country." Subtitle

Mayer, Ludwig—*Continued*

Translated into French with title: *Vues en Egypte* (Londres, T. Bensley 1802). Legends on the plates are in English and French

Colas 2018-2019. Lipp. 1577 LC 12-19066

Views in Palestine, from the original drawings of Luigi Mayer, with an historical and descriptive account of the country, and its remarkable places. Vues en Palestine, d'après les dessins originaux de Luigi Mayer. London, R. Bowyer 1804

47p. 24 col.pl. F.
English and French
Colas 2020. Lipperheide 1461. LC 12-19065

Views in the Ottoman dominions, in Europe, in Asia, and some of the Mediterranean islands, from the original drawings taken for Sir Robert Ainslie by Luigi Mayer, with descriptions historical and illustrative. London, R. Bowyer 1810

16p. 35 l. 35 col.pl.(1 fold.) F.
The descriptions of the plates are in English and French
Colas 2022. LC 12-19073

Views in the Ottoman empire, chiefly in Caramania, a part of Asia Minor hitherto unexplored; with some curious selections from the islands of Rhodes and Cyprus, and the celebrated cities of Corinth, Carthage, and Tripoli: from the original drawings in the possession of Sir R. Ainslie, taken during his embassy to Constantinople, by Luigi Mayer. London, R. Bowyer 1803

40p. 24 col.pl. F.
English and French. Added title-page in French: *Vues dans l'empire Ottoman, principalement dans la Caramanie partie de l'Asie Mineur*
Colas 2021. Lipperheide 1425. LC 12-19064

Views in Turkey, in Europe and Asia comprising Romelia, Bulgaria, Walachia, Syria and Palestine; selected from the collection of Sir Robert Ainslie. Drawn by Luigi Mayer and engraved by William Watts. London, W. Watts 1801

56 l. 56 col.pl. F.
Colas 2017

(illus.) L'Égypte et la Syrie. See entry under Breton de la Martinière, J. B. J.

Mayer, Moritz Maximilian

Das alten Nürnbergs sitten und gebräuche in freud und leid. Nürnberg, J. J. Lechner 1831-36

3v. 32 col.pl. Q.
Published in three volumes (hefte): 1 *Nürnbergisches schembartbuch, aus alten handschriften herausgegeben,* erstes heft; 2 ⌊Vermischte abhandlungen⌋ erstes heft; 3 *Nürnbergisches trachtenbuch,* erstes heft
Only the first section of each volume was published. The third volume contains nine costume pictures after Hans Weigel's *Trachtenbuch* of 1577, colored as in a copy in the Nuremberg archives
Lipperheide 787

Maynard, Michel Ulysse, abbé

La Sainte Vierge; ouvrage illustrée ... par l'abbé M. Maynard. Paris, Firmin-Didot 1877

xx,528p. 41pl. Q.

Mayr, Heinrich von

Malerische ansichten aus dem Orient, gesammelt auf der reise ... des herrn herzogs Maximilian in Bayern, im jahre 1837, nach Nubien, Aegypten, Palästina, Syrien, und Malta im j. 1838. Vues pittoresques de l'Orient. Leipzig, R. Weigel 1839-40

10 l. 60pl. F.
Published in ten parts. The plates show costume of the period and also that of earlier times, taken from paintings
Lipperheide 1589

(illus.) Fischer, Sébastien. Tableaux de genre recueillis pendant le voyage de ... Monseigneur le duc Maximilien de Bavière

Mayr, Johannes Baptista

Zwey-einiger Hymenaeus, oder Oesterreich-lüneburgischer ... vermählungsgott denen ... Josepho I ... und Wilhelminae Amaliae ... durch ruhm- oder ehrenpforten ... hierbefor eröffnet. ⌊Salzburg, 1699⌋

13,8,7 l. 9pl. F.
Lipperheide 2623

Mayr, Michael

(ed.) Maximilian I, emperor of Germany. Das fischereibuch kaiser Maximilians I

(ed.) Maximilian I, emperor of Germany. Das jagdbuch kaiser Maximilians I

Mazeret, Constantin, and Perrot, Aristide Michel

Miroir des graces, dédié aux dames; ou Dictionnaire de parure et de toilette. Paris, V. Lefuel ca1821

175p. 15 col.pl. Ti.
"Contenant le nom et la définition de tous les objets qui servent à l'habillement, la parure et la toilette des dames; etoffes, fourrures, bijoux, pierres fines, cosmétiques, etc., indiquant les pays, manufactures et fabriques d'où sortent les meilleurs et les plus beaux produits, avec la manière de les reconnaître, et les adresses des marchands les mieux assortis de Paris." Subtitle
Colas 2023. Lipperheide 570m

Mazo, Bondí di

La spada maestra ... libro dove si trattano, i vantaggi ... della scherma si del caminare, girare, & ritirarsi, come del ferire sicuramente, e difendersi. Venice, D. Lovisa ⌊1696⌋

173p. 81 illus. Q.
Lipperheide 2968

Mazuy, A.

Types et caractères anciens d'après des documents peints ou écrits; dessins par Th. Fragonard et Dufêy. Paris, Delloye 1841

86p. 41 illus. 20 col.pl. Q.
Pictures show types of the fifteenth to the eighteenth century, e.g. La courtisane de Venise, Le bravo, Le fou, Le nain
Colas 2024. Lipperheide 324

Mead, Charles Williams

Old civilizations of Inca land. New York ⌊American museum press⌋ 1924

117p. front. illus. fold.map. O. (American museum of natural history. Handbook ser. no. 11)
Bibliography: p110-11
LC 26-6461

Mead, Charles W.—*Continued*

Technique of some South American feather-work. New York, The Trustees 1907

17p. illus. 4pl. O. (Anthropological papers of the American museum of natural history. v 1 pt. 1)
LC 11-28859

Meadows, Kenny

Etchings to the illustrated Shakspere. London, Orr 1845

pl. O. 10s 6d

Heads of the people, or Portraits of the English drawn by Kenny Meadows, with original essays by distinguished writers. Philadelphia, Carey & Hart 1841

370p. front. pl. O.
Later edition has title: *Heads of the people... With original essays by Douglas Jerrold ...* &c. Philadelphia, Carey & Hart 1844
French translation: *Les Anglais peints par eux-mêmes ... dessins de M. Kenny Meadows, tr. de M. Émile de Labedollière* (Paris, L. Curmer 1840)
Lipperheide 3558 (Fr. ed.)

(illus.) Planché, J. R. Costume of Shakespeare's ... King John, King Henry the Fourth, As you like it, Hamlet, Othello, Merchant of Venice

Meadows, Robert

(comp.) A private anthropological cabinet of 500 authentic racial-esoteric photographs and illustrations; privately issued for mature subscribers only. New York, Falstaff press [c1934]

[104]p. illus. O.
"After the originals from scientific explorations, field studies and museum archives, portraying intimate rites and customs, racial types of beauty, phenomena of childbirth, freaks, ethnic mutilations and many other curiosities of the erotic life of savage and civilized races of mankind." Subtitle
LC 37-17540

Meakin, Budgett

The Moors; a comprehensive description. London, S. Sonnenschein; New York, Macmillan 1902

xxii,503p. incl.illus. pl. O. 15s, o.p.
Costume index. LC 2-12000

Méaulle, Fortuné Louis

(engr.) Child, Théodore. Les peintures de la jeunesse

Le **mécanisme** de la vie moderne. Avenel, Georges d'

Mechel, Christian von

Costumes suisses, contenant 28 figures d'après nature, coloriées avec soin. Basle, C. de Mechel 1791?

28 col.pl. Q.
Colas 2028

Costumes suisses ,des différens cantons. No place, ca1820

27 col.pl. T.
Colas 2029

Suite de différens costumes de paysans et paysannes de la Suisse. Basle, 1785

30 col.pl. O.
Lipperheide 901m. Colas 2027

(engr.) École du soldat et de peloton

(engr.) Exerzier-reglement für die Eidgenössische linien u. leichte infanterie

Mecklenburg. See Germany—Mecklenburg

Mediaeval costume and life. Hartley, Dorothy

Mediaeval England. Barnard, F. P., ed.

Mediaeval London. Besant, Sir Walter

The **mediaeval** stage. Chambers, Sir E. K.

Medical officers. See Public health service

Medicea hospes. See Baerle, Kaspar van. Marie de Medicis

Medici animadversorū. Junius, Hadrianus

A **medieval** garner. See note under Coulton, G. G. Life in the middle ages

Medieval period. See middle ages

Medio-evo pittoresco; supplemento alla Galleria universale di tutti i popoli del mondo. Venezia, Antonelli 1844

588p. 144pl.(140 col.) Q.
Colas 2030. Lipperheide 351

Meditatae à gloriosiss. Torquatus à Franzipani, A. J.

Medizinischer versuch einer modernen kleidung die brüste betreffend. Creve, C. C.

Medley, Guido

(tr.) Kolb, Peter. The present state of the Cape of Good-Hope

Mee, Cornelia

A manual of knitting, netting, and crochet. London, D. Bogue 1844

xvi,312p. 32pl. D.
LC 8-34114

Meerboth, A.

[Saxon uniforms in the year 1806.] A. Meerboth, del. T. Jucksch sc. Leipzig, A. Reil [1806?]

8 col.pl. O.
Colas 2031. Lipperheide 2202

Megerle, Johann Ulrich. See Abraham a Santa Clara

Megiser, Hieronymus

Ein tractat von dem dreyfachen ritterstand und allen ritter orden der Christenheit so viel deren bisz auff den heutigen tag gestifftet und angerichtet worden. Franckfurt am Meyn, M. Lechler 1593

142p. 16 illus. Q.
Seven of the plates which show military religious orders are from Amman's *Eygentliche beschreibung*
Lipperheide 1890

Megret, Jacques. See Gazette du bon genre. Trente neuf aquarelles

Mei Lan-fang. Liang, Shê-kan

Meijlan, G. F.

Japan, voorgesteld in schetsen over de zeden en gebruiken van dat ryk byzonder over de ingezetenen der stad Nagasaky ... uitgegeven door J. H. Tobias. Amsterdam, M. Westerman 1830

190p. 2pl. O.
Colas 2032

Meilhac, Henri, and Halévy, Ludovic

La vie parisienne; pièce en cinq actes, musique de M. J. Offenbach. Éd. illus. de costumes coloriés, dessinés par Draner [pseud]. Paris, Librairie illustré 1875

226p. illus. col.pl. ports. Q. (Bibliothèque des succès dramatiques)

Meine Tibetreise. Tafel, Albert

Meiners, Christoph
Göttingische akademische annalen; 1. bd. Hannover, Helwingischen handlung 1804
378p. 1 pl. O.
No more published. Part 5 Kurze geschichte der trachten und kleider-gesetze auf hohen schulen; 7 Kurze geschichte des waffen- und degen-tragens auf hohen schulen
Lipperheide 2027

Recherches historiques sur le luxe chez les Athéniens, depuis les temps les plus anciens, jusqu'à la mort de Philippe de Macédoine; mémoire traduit ... par C. S[olve]t. Suivi du Traité du luxe des dames romaines, par l'abbé Nadal, revu et corrigé; et des Extraits d'un grand ouvrage intitulé: L'antiquité pittoresque, ou Essai sur l'étude de l'antiquité réduite en tableaux, par m. Bayeux. Paris, A. Egron, imprimeur 1823
viii,198p. O.
LC 35-15063

Meinert, E.
Modethorheiten; 2. aufl. Leipzig, Duncker & Humblot 1893
44p. 25 illus. O. (Volkswohlschriften, heft 6)
Lipperheide 3499

Meinhardt, R.
(illus.) Gerstmann, Maximilian. Das buch vom preussischen soldaten

Meinrad, Saint, d861
Von sant Menrat ein hüpsch lieplich lesen was ellend uñ armůt er litten hat. Getrükt zů Basel by Michel furter 1496. Berlin, J. A. Stargardt 1890
48p. illus. O. n.10
Facsimile reprint of the legend of Meinrad
Lipperheide 429

Meisner, Daniel
Politica-politica, dass ist Newes emblematisches büchleĩ, darinen in acht centurijs die vornembstẽ stätt vestung, schlösser &c. der gantzen welt ... abgebiltet werden. Nürnburg, R. J. Helmers 1700
8v. 400pl.(800 illus.) F.
Volumes 2-8 have title *Libellus novus politicus emblematicus civitatum pars, altra ... Oder Newen politischen Stätt: und emblematabuchs*
Interesting for seventeenth century costume in various parts of the world. Many editions have been published
Lipperheide 549

[**Meister, Léonard**]
Beschreibung der gemeineidgenossischen truppensendung nach Basel und der abreise der Zürchessen mannschaft am 31ten May, 1792. Zürich, D. Burkli ca1792
16p. 50 col.pl. O.
Plates engraved by Engelbrecht
Colas 2034. Lipperheide 2252

Meister der waffenschmiedekunst vom XIV. bis ins XVIII. jahrhundert. Boeheim, Wendelin.

Meister des Amsterdam kabinets. See Master of the Amsterdam cabinet, 15th century. The Master of the Amsterdam cabinet, by Max Lehrs

Meister des ballets. Levinson, A. I.

Meister des eisenschnittes. Stöcklein, Hans

Meister-holzschnitte aus vier jahrhunderten. Hirth, Georg, and Muther, Richard, eds.

Meisterwerke der buchmalerei. Munich. Bayerische staatsbibliothek

Meisterwerke der griechischen plastik. Furtwängler, Adolf

Meklenburg in bildern. Lisch, G. C. F.

Melanchthon, Philipp
Passional Christi und Antichristi. See entry under Cranach, Lucas

Melanesia
Codrington, R. H. The Melanesians. 1891
Erskine, J. E. Journal of a cruise among the islands of the western Pacific, including the Feejees and others inhabited by the Polynesian negro races. 1853

See also Fiji islands; New Caledonia

Mélanges d'archéologie, d'histoire et de littérature. Cahier, Charles, and Martin, Arthur

Meleagrides et Aetolia, ex numismate Kyrieon apud Goltzium. Beger, Lorenz

Melfort, Louis Hector, comte de Drummond de. See Drummond de Melfort, L. H. comte de

Les **mellahs** de Rabat-Salé. Goulven, J. G. A.

Meller, Walter Clifford
A knight's life in the days of chivalry. London, T. W. Laurie limited 1924
xv,300p. col.front. pl. ports. Q.
LC 24-25546

Mellin, August Wilhelm, graf von
Unterricht eingefriedigte wildbahnen oder grosse thiergärten anzulegen und zu behandeln, um dadurch das wildpret nützlicher und unschädlich zu machen. Berlin, F. Maurer 1800
xvi,264p. 12 illus. 18pl. Q.
Illustrations are by the Count and Countess Ulrike
Lipperheide 3030

Versuch einer anweisung zur anlegung, verbesserung, und nutzung der wildbahnen so wohl im freyen als in thiergärten. Berlin und Stettin, J. Pauli 1779
xxi,356p. 117 illus.(116 col.) Q.
Published anonymously
Lipperheide 3028

Melling, [Antoine Ignace]
(illus.) Voyage pittoresque de Constantinople et des rives du Bosphore d'après les dessins de M. Melling ... Pub. par MM. Treuttel et Würtz. Paris [etc.] Chez les éditeurs 1819
10p. 64 l. 1 pl. and atlas 51pl. F.
Volume [2] has engraved half-title: *Voyage pittoresque de Constantinople et du Bosphore*
Issued in parts: 12 parts of 4 plates each, with descriptive letter-press by C. de Lacretelle; an additional part of maps, with accompanying topographical description, by J. D. Barbié du Bocage
Contains views of Constantinople and environs with costume figures, and a portrait of Sultan Selim III
Lipperheide 1431. LC 5-3026

Melton, Henry
Hints on hats adapted to the heads of the people. London, J. C. Hotten 1865
102p. illus. S.

Melusine. [Strassburg, H. Knoblochtzer ca1483]
67 col.illus. F.
First edition 1478
Lipperheide 414

Melville, Harden S.
Sketches in Australia and the adjacent islands. London, Dickinson ca1850
25 l. 25pl. Q.
"Selected from a number taken during the surveying voyage of H. M. S. 'Fly' and 'Bramble', under the command of Capt. F. P. Blackwood ... during the years 1842-46." Subtitle
Lipperheide 1640

Melzo, Lodovico
Regole militari del cavalier Melzo sopra il governo e servitio della cavalleria. Anversa, G. Trognaesio 1611
221p. 15pl. F.
Illustrations show types of riding equipment, and dragoons, lancers, cuirassiers, and other bodies of troops as they appeared in camp and battle
Lipperheide 2066

Memling, Jean
(illus.) Delepierre, Octave, and Voisin, Auguste. La chasse de Sainte Ursule gravée au trait par Charles Onghena d'après Jean Memling

Memoire di un viaggio pittorico nel littorale Austriaco. Selb, August, and Tischbein, A.

Mémoire sur les costumes des Perses sous la dynastie des rois Achéménides et celle des successeurs d'Alexandre. Mongez, Antoine

Mémoires. Comines, Philippe de, sieur d' Argenton

Mémoires concernant l'histoire, les sciences, les arts, les mœurs, les usages, &c. des Chinois: par les missionnaires de Pékin. Paris, Nyon 1776-91
15v. fronts. (v. 1, 15: ports.) pl.(part fold) maps, tables. Q.
Edited by C. Batteux and L. G. O. F. de Bréquigny. Volume 7 is *Art militaire de Chinois* comp. and tr. by J. M. Amiot and also published separately. "Les auteurs sont MM. Amiot, Bourgeois, Cibot, Ko & Poirot." Volume 10 p316
A *second supplement* was issued (Paris, Nyon 1786. 352p. 8pl. 1 fold.map. O.)
LC 5-8790

Memoires ... contenans les vies des hommes illustres & grands capitaines françois de son temps. Brantôme, Pierre de Bourdeille, seigneur de

Memoires ... contenant les vies de dames galantes de son temps. Brantôme, Pierre de Bourdeille seigneur de

Mémoires de César Chabrac. Onfroy de Bréville, J. M. G.

Mémoires pour servir à l'histoire de la barbe de l'homme. Fangé, Augustin

Mémoires pour servir à l'histoire de l'armée prussienne. See Seyfart, J. F., sohn. Kurzgefassete geschichte aller königlichen preussischen regimenter

Mémoires pour servir à l'histoire des moeurs et usages des Français. Caillot, Antoine

Mémoires sur la Chine. Escayrac de Lauture, Stanislas, comte d'

Memoirs of an Arabian princess. Ruete, Frau Emilie

Memoirs of Philip de Commines. See Comines, Philippe de, sieur d'Argenton. Mémoires

Memoirs of St George, the English patron, and of the most noble Order of the Garter. Dawson, Thomas

A **memorial** of the marriage of H. R. H. Albert Edward, prince of Wales. Russell, Sir W. H.

Memorial rings, Charles the Second to William the Fourth. Crisp, F. A.

Memorias para la historia de las tropas de la casa real de Espana. Clonard, S. M. de S. y A., conde de

Memorie ed omaggi funebri per la morte dell' Arciduchessa Maria Beatrice Vittoria di Savoja ... duchessa di Modena. Modena, R. D. Camera 1841
198p. 4pl. O.
Lipperheide 2777

Memorie istoriche della miracolosa immagine di Maria Vergine dell' Impruneta. Casotti, G. B.

Men in women's guise. Gilbert, O. P.

Men, maidens and manners a hundred years ago. Ashton, John

Men of the army and navy. Christy, H. C.

Men of the old stone age. Osborn, H. F.

The **men** of Yorktown. See Malo, Servan. Ceux de Yorktown

Men, women & manners in colonial times. Fisher, S. G.

Ménard, René Joseph
La vie privée des anciens; texte par René Ménard; dessins d'après les monuments antiques, par Cl. Sauvageot. Paris, E. Flammarion 1880-83
4v. illus. O.
Contains description and illustrations of the jewelry and costume of Egypt, Ethiopia, Persia, Syria, Greece and Italy during ancient times
Contents: [v 1] Les peuples dans l'antiquité; [v2] La famille dans l'antiquité; [v3] Le travail dans l'antiquité; [v4] Les institutions de l'antiquité
Costume index. LC 4-678

Méndez, Ramón Torres. See Torres Méndez, Ramón

Mendoza, Gumesindo
(ed.) Durán, Diego. Historia de las Indias Nueva-España y islas de Tierra Firme

[**Menestrier, Claude François**]
Des ballets anciens et modernes selon les regles du theatre. Paris, R. Guignard 1682
28p.l. 232(i.e. 323)p.
Errors in paging. The privilege, dated 1679, is for Menestrier's *Philosophie des images,* of which this forms a part
Pages 144-223 and 250 to end, relate to costume
Lipperheide 3062. LC 10-18134

Menestrier, Claude F.—*Continued*

Description de la belle et grande colonne historiée, dressée à l'honneur de l'empereur Theodose, dessinée par Gentile Bellin ... Elle est représentée en seize planches ... expliquées par ... Menestrier ... & gravées par Jerôme Vallet. Paris, G. Vallet 1702
2 l. 16pl. plan of Constantinople. F.
Lipperheide 223. LC 10-23079

Les rejouissances de la paix, faites dans la ville de Lyon le 20.mars 1660. Lyon, G. Barbier & J. Justet 1660
49p. 18pl. F.
Published anonymously
Lipperheide 2821

Menin, Lodovico

Il costume di tutte le nazioni e di tutti i tempi, descritto ed illustrato dall' abate Lodovico Menin. Padova, Presso una società editrice coi tipi della Minerva 1834-37
3v. front.(port.) 47x33cm and atlas (291 col.pl) 3v. 41x58cm.
Published in 85 parts, 1833-44. Parts 69-72: Coi tipi Cartallier e Sicca; pts73-85: Coi tipi di A. Sicca
Contents: pt 1 Costume antico, 1837; pt2 Costume del medio evo, 1834; pt3 Costume moderno, 1834
Colas 2035. Lipperheide 56. LC 2-29630

Menin, Nicolas

The form, order and ceremonies of coronations, used at the investiture of all the sovereign princes of Europe; with the whole ceremony of the grand anointing and coronation of the present king of France. Also, an historical and chronological account of these solemnities from their origin to this present time. Tr. from the French. London, W. Mears 1727
xvi,333p. front. D.
LC 36-6005

Traite historique et chronologique du sacre et couronnement des rois et des reines de France: depuis Clovis I. jusqu'à present, et de tous les princes souverains de l'Europe, augmenté de la relation exacte de la cérémonie du sacre de Louis XV. Paris, J. B. C. Bauche 1723
11 l. 507p. D.
Lipperheide 2473

Menino, Pero

Livro de falcoaria; publicado, com introdução, notas e glossário, por Rodrigues Lapa. Coimbra, Imprensa da Universidade 1931
lxvii,91p. illus. 3 facsim. O. (Junta de educação nacional. Centro de estudos filológicos)
Edited from manuscript 518 (fl. 30-67) Secção pombalina, Biblioteca nacional, Lisbon, written in the 14th century
LC 35-18750

Mennechet, Édouard

(ed.) Le Plutarque français; vies des hommes et femmes illustres de la France. Paris, Crapelet 1835?-41?
8v. col.pl. Q.
Full length portraits of notable French men and women from the middle ages (Clovis) to the Empire period. The last entry is Beauharnais (1781-1824) Kings, bishops, nobles, etc. are included
Volume 2 published 1835, v7 published 1840. Also found with plates in black and white (Paris, Crapelet 1838-40 8v.) and (Paris, Langlois & Leclerq 1844-47 6v.)

Mennell, Jacob

Images de saints et saintes issus de la famille de l'Empereur Maximilian I. See entry under Burgkmair, Hans

Menpes, Dorothy. See entries under Menpes, Mortimer

Menpes, Mortimer

Brittany; text by Dorothy Menpes. London, A. & C. Black 1905
254p. 75 col.pl.(incl.front.) O. 20s, o.p.
Plates accompanied by guard sheets with descriptive letterpress
Costume index. LC 5-40373

China; text by Sir Henry Arthur Blake. London, A. & C. Black 1909
137p. 16 col.pl. illus. Q. (Menpes crown series)

The Durbar, by Mortimer Menpes; text by Dorothy Menpes. London, A. and C. Black [1903]
xii,210p. 100 col.pl.(incl.front.ports.) O.
LC 4-2556

India; by Mortimer Menpes, text by Flora Annie Steel. London, A. & C. Black [1905]
xii,216p. 75 col.pl.(incl.front.) O. $2.50
Each plate is accompanied by guard sheet with descriptive letterpress. Thirty-two plates show costume
Costume index. LC w6-212

Japan, a record in colour, by Mortimer Menpes; transcribed by Dorothy Menpes. London, A. & C. Black [1901]
xiv,206p. 100 col.pl.(incl.front.) O. 20s, o.p.
Costume index. LC 2-18028

The people of India, painted by Mortimer Menpes, with introduction by G. E. Mitton. London, A. & C. Black 1910
12p. col.mounted front. col.mounted pl. O. (Peoples of many lands) 5s
Each plate accompanied by leaf with descriptive letterpress and illustration on verso
Costume index. LC w11-63

World's children. Text by Dorothy Menpes. London, A. & C. Black [1903]
x,246p. 100 col.pl.(incl.front.) O.
LC 3-19420

Men's capes and cloaks. Hispanic society of America

Men's clothes, The story of. See Price, Sir H. P. When men wore muffs

The men's outfitter

(pub.) Clucas, Charles. The etiquette of men's dress

Men's wear; the retailer's newspaper. v. 1, 1896+ New York & Chicago
Illus. col.pl. F.
Periodical of men's fashions. Published semi-monthly. Current 1938
Title varies: v 1-69 no6, 1896, *Chicago apparel gazette*

Der **mensch** in seinen verschieden. lagen und ständen für die jugend geschildert. Augsburg, J. J. Haid 1779
172p. O. and atlas 50pl. Q.
Lipperheide 1956e

Der **mensch** und seine tracht. Rumpf, Fritz

De **mensch**, zoo als hij voorkomt op den bekenden aardbol. Stuart, Martinus

Menschelyke beezigheeden bestaande in regeering, konsten en ambachten. Luyken, Johann, and Luyken, Caspar

Menschenhold, Christian Gottlieb
Des gold- und silber-gläntzenden himmels erlustigung und beschaffenheit ... benebenst der in des heil. reichs stadt Nürnberg üblichen und gewöhnlichen kleidungen mit schönen bildern und reimen vorgestellet. Nürnberg, 1681
8 l. 25 illus. Q.
Twenty-four of the illustrations show Nuremberg costumes
Lipperheide 776

Der **menschliche** fuss. Beely, F., and Kirchhoff, E.

Der **menschliche** fuss und seine naturgemässe bekleidung. Pestel, Bernhard

Der **menschliche** schmuck. Matthias, J.

Die **menschliche** schönheit. Hauff, Ludwig

Mentzel, C.
Königl: hannov: militair ... gezeichnet und lithografirt von C. Mentzel. Hannover, 1836
8 col.pl. Q.
Colas 2036

See also Leopold, Franz, jt. auth.

[**Menut, Adolphe**]
Les danseuses de l'Opéra; costumes des principaux ballets, dessinés par Alophe [pseud.] Paris, Les modes parisiennes [1850?]
Cover-title, 14 col.pl. F.
Colas 103. LC 23-15134

Menzel, Adolph Friedrich Erdmann von
Die armee Friedrich's des Grossen in ihrer uniformirung gezeichnet und erläutert von Adolph Menzel. Berlin, L. Sachse 1851-57
3v. 432 col.pl. Q.
Contents: v 1 Die cavallerie; v2 Die infanterie; v3 Rest der infanterie, die besonderen corps und chargen, anhang und ergänzungen
Only thirty copies were printed. The number of plates varies in each
Colas 2037. Lipperheide 2178m

Die armee Friedrichs des Grossen in ihrer uniformierung gezeichnet und erläutert von Adolph Menzel; eine auswahl von 100 tafeln in mehrfarbiger faksimiliereproduktion hrsg. von professor F. Skarbina und hauptmann C. Jany. Berlin, M. Oldenbourg [1906-08]
8,6 l. 100 mounted col.pl. sq.F.
Issued in 10 parts. Each plate accompanied by leaf with descriptive letterpress
A selection of plates reproduced from the rare edition of 1851-57
LC 14-9732

Aus könig Friedrich's zeit, kriegs- und friedens-helden; gezeichnet von Adolph Menzel in holz geschnitten von Eduard Kretschmar, hrsg. von Alexander Duncker. Berlin, A. Duncker 1856
12 l. 12 ports. F.
Lipperheide 692

Illustrations des oeuvres de Frederic-le-grand; gravées sur bois par O. Vogel, A. Vogel, Fr. Unzelmann, et H. Müller ... avec texte de L. Pietsch. Berlin, R. Wagner 1882
4v. 199pl. F.
The same plates are in the German edition: *Illustrationen zu den werken Friedrichs des Grossen* (1886) issued by the same publisher
Lipperheide 694-695

(illus.) Kleist, Heinrich von. Der zerbrochene krug

(illus.) Lange, Eduard. Die soldaten Friedrich's des Grossen

See also Geissler, C. G. H., jt. auth.

Meran, F., graf von. See Pichler, Fritz, jt. auth.

Mercenary troops. See Military costume—Germany—16th century

Merchant marine. See Naval costume—England—20th century—Merchant marine

Merchants
Cutts, E. L. Scenes and characters of the middle ages. 1872. p519-25
Steinhausen, Georg. Der kaufmann in der deutschen vergangenheit, mit ... abbildungen ... aus dem 15. bis 18. jahrhundert. 1899

Mercier, Louis
Le deuil, son observation dans tous les temps et dans tous les pays comparée à son observation de nos jours. Londres, P. Douvet 1877
80p. D.
LC 16-24905

Mercier, Louis Sébastien. Tableau de Paris. See entry under Dunker, B. A. Tableau de Paris

Mercure des salons, revue française et étrangère; album des modes. v 1-5; jan. 1830-mars 1831. Paris
5v. col.illus. O.
Colas 2038. Lipperheide 4614

Mercuri, Paul
(illus.) Bonnard, Camille. Costumes des XIIIe, XIVe et XVe siècles
(illus.) Bonnard, Camille. Costumes historiques des XIIe, XIIIe, XIVe et XVe siècles
(engr.) Bonnard, Camille. Costumi ecclesiastice, civili e militari d' secolo XIII, XIV e XV

Mercuriale, Girolamo
De arte gymnastica libri sex: in quibus exercitationum omnium vetustarum genera, loca, modi, facultates, & quidquid denique ad corporis humani exercitationes pertinet diligenter explicatur. Ed. novissima, aucta, emendata, & figuris authenticis Christophori Coriolani exornata. Amstelodami, Sumptibus A. Frisii 1672
387,[41]p. illus. pl.(part fold.) O.
The second edition was published 1573
Lipperheide 3036. LC 5-24280

Mercurio peruano de historia. See Voyages au Pérou

Mergenthaler linotype company
A true description of all trades; published in Frankfort in the year 1568, with six of the illustrations by Jobst Amman. Brooklyn, N. Y., Mergenthaler linotype co. 1930
19p. 6 illus. O.
A brief account of the *Eygentliche beschreibung aller stände* (Frankfurt am Main, 1568) Illustrations show the printer, bookbinder, typefounder, papermaker, draughtsman, and wood engraver

Merian, Caspar
Beschreibung und abbildung aller königl. und churfürstl. ein-züge wahl und crönungs acta, so geschehen zu Franckfurt am Mayn im jahr 1658. Sampt andern darzu gehörigen und beygefûgten sachen. Franckfurt am Mayn, C. Merian 1658
40 l. 32pl.(incl. 8 ports.) F.
The same plates are in the author's *Solemnia electionis et inaugurationis Leopoldi, Romanor: imperatoris ... seu Descriptio et repraesentatio eorum omnium, quae anno 1658, ante, in & post electionem regio-imperatoriam apud Moeno-Francofurtanos . . . evenerunt* (Francofurti ad Moenum, 1660. 105p. 31pl. F.) with text in Latin and French
Lipperheide 2508-09

Merian, Johann Jacob
(engr.) Dance of death. Todten-tanz

Merian, Mattheus
Das lange bestrittene königreich Candia, das ist ... beschreibung von dem anfange fort- und auszgange desz fünff und zwantzig jährigen und zwischen der durchl. republik Venedig und dem Türcken geführten sehr blutigen krieges in dem königreiche Candia und archipelago. Franckfurt, O. Fievet 1670
87p. 12pl. F.
Contains portraits of the Sultana Zaffira, her son Osman and the Grand-Vizier Achmet
Lipperheide 1409

(engr.) Dance of death. Todten-tanz

(engr.) Gottfried, J. L. Joh. Ludov. Gottfridi Historische chronica

(engr.) Hulsen, Esaias von. Repræsentatio der furstlichen aufzug und ritterspil

Méricourt, P. J. Fargès-. See Fargès-Méricourt, P. J.

Mérignac, Émile
Histoire de l'escrime dans tous les temps et dans tous les pays. Eaux-fortes de M. de Malval. Paris, Impr. réunies, C. [etc.] 1883-86
2v. front.(port.) illus. pl.(part double) O.
Volume 1: dessins de m. Dupuy; v2: dessins de mm. Récipon, Dupuy, Girardin, mlle Daniel. Volume 2 has imprint: Paris, Rouquette 1886
Contents: v 1 Antiquité; v2 Moyen âge, Temps modernes
Lipperheide 2993. LC 4-20472

Merkel, Carlo
Come vestivano gli uomini del "Decameron"; saggio di storia del costume. Roma, 1898
115p. Q.
Bibliographical foot-notes
LC 13-19247

Merkwaardige historische beschryving van alle vreemde en onlangs eerst bekent gewordene krygsvolkeren. Amsteldam, A. van Huissteen en Z. Romberg 1745
97p. 12pl. O.
"Als van de Hussaaren, Panduuren, Croaaten, Heydukken, Tolpatsen, Insurgenten, Warasdynen, Slavoniers, Lycaniers, Morlakken, Raitzen, Wallachers, Uskoken, enz." Subtitle
Plates on pages 23 and 43 are signed G. J. M. and according to Lipperheide may be the work of G. J. Marstaller
Lipperheide 2225

Merkwürdigkeiten der feierlichen krönung eines königs von Böhmen; nebst dem krönungszeremoniel einer königinn von Böhmen. Prag, In der Königlichen hofbuchdruckerey 1791
210p. 2pl.(1 col.) O.
The colored plate shows the Emperor Leopold II in coronation robes as king of Bohemia
Lipperheide 2480

Merrifield, Mrs Mary Philadelphia
Dress as a fine art, with suggestions on children's dress. With an introduction on head dress, by Prof. Fairholt. Boston, J. P. Jewett; Cleveland, O. Jewett, Proctor, and Worthington 1854
x,143p. 12pl.(incl.front.) O.
On the philosophy of dress and the principles that should govern styles
LC 11-22643

Merritt, Mrs M. Angeline
Dress reform practically and physiologically considered. Buffalo, Printed by Jewett, Thomas and co. 1852
171p. front.(port.) S.
LC 9-22400

Merritt, Wesley. See The Armies of today; a description of the armies of the leading nations at the present time. 1893

Mertins, Oskar
Wegweiser durch die urgeschichte Schlesiens und der nachbargebiete, hrsg. vom Verein für das Museum schlesischer altertümer. Breslau, Preuss & Jünger 1906
150p. illus. O.
Pictures show jewelry and ornaments of the bronze age

Les **merveilles** de l'autre France. Ricard, Prosper

Merveilleux et estrange rapport, toutesfois fidele, des commoditez qui se trouvent en Virginia, des façons des naturels habitans dicelle. See Harriot, Thomas. Admiranda narratio fida tamen

Méry, Joseph Pierre Agnès
Constantinople et la Mer Noire; illus. de MM. Rouargue frères. Paris, Belin-Leprieur et Morizot 1855
xi,495p. illus. 21pl.(6 col.) O.
The colored plates show costume
Lipperheide 1439

Les parures: Fantaisie par Gavarni, texte par Méry, histoire de la mode par le Cte Foelix [pseud]. Paris, G. de Gonet; Leipzig, C. Twietmeyer ca1850
300p. 16 col.pl. O.
Plates are engraved by Geoffroy after Gavarni
Colas 2041. Lipperheide 573

See also Grandville, J. I. I. G. Les étoiles

[**Merz, Joh. Georg**]
Kleidungs arten in der stadt Augspurg. Modes de la ville d'Augsbourg. [Augsburg?] J. G. Mertz ca1710
36 col.pl. O.
Colas lists the same title published by J. G. Bock and Lipperheide lists an edition published by M. G. Crophius
A facsimile reprint was published with same title (Berlin, Jahresgabe des freundeskreises der Bibliothek des Kunstgewerbe museums 1924)
Colas 2042-2043. Lipperheide 765m-o

Mes gens, ou Les commissionnaires ultramontains. Saint-Aubin, Augustin de

Mes masques. Parain, Nathalie

Mes souvenirs d'Égypte. Minutoli, W. von der S. von W., freiherrn von

Les **mésaventures.** Demange

Mesdames nos aïeules. Robida, Albert

Mesopotamia. See Iraq

Mesplès, E.
(illus.) Rouveyre, Édouard. Gazette anecdotique du règne de Louis XVI

Le **Messager** des salons, journal des modes et des nouveautés parisiennes. 1.-7. année, 1832-1838. Paris
O.
Absorbed in 1840 by *Colifichet*
Colas 2046

La **messe.** Rohault de Fleury, Charles

Messel, Oliver
Stage designs and costumes; with an introduction by James Laver and a foreword by Charles B. Cochran. With eight illustrations in colour and sixty-four in black-and-white. London, John Lane [1933]
3p.l. 37p. col.front. 55pl.(part col.) Q.
LC 34-17049

Messieurs nos fils & mesdemoiselles nos filles. Randon, Gilbert

Mestorf, Johanna
Die vaterländischen alterthümer Schleswig-Holsteins; ansprache an unsere landsleute. Voröffentlicht im auftrage des Königlichen ministeriums für geistliche-, unterrichts- und medicinal-angelegenheiten. Hamburg, O. Meissner 1877
32p. XV pl. O.
Plates printed on both sides. Pictures show armor, utensils and personal ornaments
Lipperheide 289. LC 22-9931

(ed.) Vorgeschichtliche alterthümer aus Schleswig-Holstein. Zum gedächtniss des fünfzigjährigen bestehens des Museums vaterländischer alterthümer in Kiel. [illus.] nach handzeichnungen von Walter Prell. Hamburg, O. Meissner 1885
34p. LXII pl.(765 illus.) Q.
Lipperheide 295. LC 21-5970

(tr.) Hildebrand, Hans. Das heidnische zeitalter in Schweden

Les **métamorphoses** de Melpomène et de Thalie. Whirsker

Les **métamorphoses** du jour. Grandville, J. I. I. G., called

Metcalf, Frederick
(tr.) Becker, W. A. Charicles; or, Illustrations of the private life of the ancient Greeks

(tr.) Becker, W. A. Gallus, or, Roman scenes in the time of Augustus

Meteren, Emmanuel von
Niederländische historien, oder Geschichten aller deren händel so sich zugetragen von anfangs des niederländischen kriegs bisz auff das jahr 1611 in niederländischer spraach beschrieben; jetzo aber vom autore selbst obersehen, gemehret und gebessert und in hochteutsch ubergesetzt. No place, 1611
1126,420,96p. 23pl. F.
Lipperheide 930

Methode complete de coupe d'habillements. See Compaing, Charles. The complete manual of cutting

Méthode de coiffure. Croisat

Methodische anleitung für geometrische zuschnittlehre. Schmidt, Carl, and Schmidt, Rosalie

Methodius, Saint, bp of Olympus
Revelationes. Basel, M. Furter 1498
68 l. 61 illus. Q.
Plates picture incidents from the Bible, beginning with the time of Adam, and from Jewish, ancient and medieval history and mythology up to the time of the crusades
Lipperheide 431

Methodus geometrica. Pfintzing, Paul

Métiers féminins. Augrand, Parfait

Metropolitan museum of art, New York. See New York. Metropolitan museum of art

Metropolitan repository of fashions. See Cyclopaedia of the British costumes

Metz, Heinz
Die Schwalm, kulturbild einer hessischen landschaft. See entry under Retzlaff. Hans

Metz. See Lorraine—Metz

Metzger, Christoph
(engr.) Fürstliches Hessen-Holsteinisches ehren-gedächtnuss

Meubles et costumes (XVIe, XVIIe, et XVIIIe siècles). Teissier, Octave

Meubles et objets divers du moyen âge et de la Renaissance. Asselineau, L. A.

Meurs, Johannes van
De luxu Romanorum, liber singularis; sive Commentarius uberior in locum Senecae epist. CXIV. Item Mantisa. Hagae-Comitis, H. Jacobi 1605
88p. Q.
Lipperheide 218

Meuss, Johann Friedrich. See Batsch, C. F., jt. auth.

The **Mexican** people. Gutiérrez de Lara, Lazaro, and Pinchon, Edgcumb

The **Mexican** southland. Brand, N. F.

Mexico (city). Biblioteca nacional
La litografia en Mexico en el siglo XIX; sesenta facsimiles de la mejores obras con un texto de Manuel Toussaint. Mexico, Estudios neolitho, M. Quesada B. 1934
xxvii p. 60pl. F. (Ediciones facsimilares [v 1])

Mexico
Charnay, Désiré. Le Mexique. 1863
Garcia Cubas, Antonio. The republic of Mexico in 1876. 1876
Linati, C. Costumes civils, militaires et religieux du Mexique. 1828
Mexico (City) Biblioteca nacional. La litografia en Mexico en el siglo XIX. 1934
México y sus alrededores, colección de vistas monumentales, paisajes y trajes del país. 1869

Mexico—*Continued*

Nebel, Carl. Voyage pittoresque et archéologique dans la partie la plus intéressante du Mexique. 1836

Peñafiel, Antonio. Indumentaria antigua; vestidos guerreros y civiles de los Mexicanos. 1903

Reinach-Foussemagne, H. de, comtesse. Charlotte de Belgique, impératrice du Mexique. 1925

See also Indians of Mexico; Mayas; also subdivision Mexico under Arms and armor; Decoration and ornament; Funerals; Headdress; Masks

20th century

Brand, Norton F. The Mexican southland. 1922

Bruehl, Anton. Photographs of Mexico. c1933

Carpenter, F. G. Mexico. 1924

Carson, W. E. Mexico. 1914

Gutiérrez de Lara, Lazaro, and Pinchon, Edgcumb. The Mexican people: their struggle for freedom. 1914

Rivera, Diego. Portrait of Mexico. c1937

Mexico. Carpenter, F. G.

Mexico et ses environs. See México y sus alrededores

Mexico; the wonderland of the south. Carson, W. E.

México y sus alrededores, colección de vistas monumentales, paisajes y trajes del pais; dibujados al natural y litografiados por los artistas mexicanos C. Castro, G. Rodríguez é J. Campillo, bajo la dirección de V. Debray. Los artículos descriptivos son de los señores d. Marcos Arronis, d. José T. de Cuellar [y otros] ... Mexico et ses environs. Nueva ed. aum. México, V. Debray 1869

67p. 47pl.(part col.) 2 fold.maps. F.

Spanish and French in parallel columns. Cover dated 1878. First edition (Mexico, Decaen 1855-56) has thirty plates, five on costume, the rest views with costume figures

Colas 547. Lipperheide 1624. LC 31-33649

Mexiko. Danzel, T. W.

Le **Mexique.** Charnay, Désiré

Meyan, Maurice Jean. See Jean-Meyan, Maurice

Meyendorff, Kondratiĭ Egorovĭch, and Meyendorff, Natalīiā Grĭgor'evna

L'empire du soleil, Pérou et Bolivie; ouvrage illustré de cent onze gravures et de douze planches en couleurs d'après les originaux de S. A. S. la princesse Marie Wolkonsky et de mm. Himona et Bobrowsky. [Paris] Hachette 1909

lvi,318,xii p. col.front. illus. pl.(part col.) fold.map, plans. Q.

At head of title: Baron & baronne Conrad de Meyendorff

LC 9-18062

Meyendorff, Natalīiā Grĭgor'evna. See Meyendorff, K. E., jt. auth.

Meyer, Adolf Bernhard, and Uhle, Max

(eds.) Seltene waffen aus Afrika, Asien und Amerika. Herausgegeben mit unterstützung der Generaldirection der königlichen sammlungen für kunst und wissenschaft zu Dresden. Leipzig, A. Naumann & Schroeder 1885

6p. illus. 10pl. F. (Königliches ethnographisches museum zu Dresden. [Publicationen] v)

In portfolio

LC 25-18220

Meyer, Edmund. See Pflugk-Harttung, J. A. G., von, ed. Napoleon I: Das erwachen der völker

Meyer, Eduard

(ed.) Reimpell, Walter. Geschichte der babylonischen und assyrischen kleidung

Meyer, F.

(illus.) Leuthold, H. F. Costumes suisses en mignature

Meyer, Georg Hermann von

Die richtige gestalt der schuhe; eine abhandlung aus der angewandten anatomie für aerzte und laien. Zürich, Meyer & Zeller 1858

30p. 26 illus. O.

Colas 2050. Lipperheide 1740

Meyer, Joachim

Gründtliche beschreibung der freyen ritterlichen unnd adelichen kunst des fechtens in allerley gebreuchlichen wehren mit vil schönen und nützlichen figuren gezieret und fürgestellet. Strasburg, T. Berger 1570

64,107,47 l. 74 illus. Q.

New editions were published in Augsburg, 1600 and 1660. The woodcuts are attributed to Tobias Stimmer

Lipperheide 2949m

Meyer, Kathi

Das konzert; ein führer durch die geschichte des musizierens in bildern und melodien. Stuttgart, J. Engelhorns nachf. [c1925]

165p. illus.(incl.facsims.) O. (Musikalische volksbücher / Sonderreihe, hrsg. von Adolf Spemann und Hugo Holle)

Contains music. "Quellennachweis": p160-[63]

LC 26-12487

Meyer-Döhner, Kurt

Die neue deutsche kriegsmarine, aufbau, gliederung, dienst und anderes wissenswerte mit flaggen- und uniformtafeln. Hamburg, Broschek 1935

69p. 3pl.(2 col.) D.

Meyer-Ilschen, Wilhelm

(ed.) Gerhäuser, Emil. Stuttgarter bühnenkunst

Meyers, Charles Lee

(comp.) Bibliography of colonial costume; compiled for the Society of colonial wars in the state of New-Jersey. [New York, c1923]

36p. pl. O.

LC 23-10871

Meÿssens, Jean

Effigies des forestiers et comtes de Flandres, sur les desseins de Jean Meÿssens, peintre, gravées par Cornille Meÿssens. Anvers, M. vanden Enden [1663]

48pl. F.

Lipperheide 938

Meyrick, Sir Samuel Rush
A critical inquiry into antient armour, as it existed in Europe, but particularly in England, from the Norman conquest to the reign of King Charles II, with a glossary of military terms of the middle ages. London, Printed for R. Jennings 1824
3v. 80pl.(part col.) F.
From the 11th to the 17th century
Also published (2d ed. corr. and enl. London, H. G. Bohn 1842. 3v. 80pl. [70 col.] Q.
Lipperheide 2093 (2.ed.) LC 11-20051

Engraved illustrations of antient arms and armour, from the collection of Llewelyn Meyrick ... at Goodrich Court, Herefordshire; after the drawings and with the descriptions of Dr. Meyrick, by Joseph Skelton. London, Printed for J. Skelton, Oxford 1830
2v. fronts.(v 1, port.) 150pl. F.
Each plate accompanied by leaf with descriptive letterpress
Translated into German with title: *Abbildung und beschreibung von alten waffen und rüstungen* (Berlin, G. Fincke 1836. 42p. 151pl. Q.) with the same plates but a shorter text
Lipperheide 2407-2408. LC 11-20052

Observations on the body-armour anciently worn in England. Communicated to the Society of antiquaries, by Samuel Rush Meyrick. London, Bensley and son 1818
28p. ob.O.
From *Archaeologia,* v19
LC 18-23682

Observations on the military garments formerly worn in England. Communicated to the Society of antiquaries, by Samuel Rush Meyrick. London, Printed by T. Bensley 1821
32p. ob.O.
From *Archaeologia,* v19
LC 18-23681

Meyrick, Sir Samuel Rush, and Smith, Charles Hamilton
Costume of the original inhabitants of the British islands, from the earliest periods to the 6th century; to which is added that of the Gothic nations on the western coasts of the Baltic, the ancestors of the Anglo-Saxons and Anglo-Danes. London, T. M'Lean 1821
43 l. 25 col.pl. Q. 170s 6d, o.p.
Plates are imprinted: Published June, 1915, by R. Havell, London
Contents: Ante-Roman period; Roman period; Post-Roman period; Inhabitants of the Baltic. The authors give the sources for each plate
Colas 2051. Costume index. Lipp. 276

Meysens, Conrad
(engr.) Gualdo Priorato, Galeazzo, conte. Historia di Leopoldo Cesare

Mézeray, Françoise Eudes de. See Chalcondylas, Laonicus. Histoire generale des Turcs

Mich
Costumes inédits de Aine-Montaillé, 1, Place Vendôme, Paris; dessins fantaisistes de Mich, hiver 1906. Paris, C. Davis 1906?
10 col.pl. O.
Colas 2052

Michaelis, Christian Friedrich
(tr.) Baxter, Thomas. Darstellung

Michaelson, Anna. See Holme, Charles, ed. Peasant art in Sweden, Lapland and Iceland

Michaud, Joseph François
History of the crusades, by Michaud ... illustrated with one hundred grand compositions by Gustave Doré, engraved by Bellenger, Doms, Gusman, Jonnard, Pannemaker, Pisan, Quesnel. Philadelphia, G. Barrie [189-]
2v. fronts. pl. F.
Translated from the French by William Robson
LC 20-15135

Michel, Adolphe
L'ancienne Auvergne et le Velay: histoire, archéologie, moeurs, topographie par Ad. Michel et une société d'artistes. Moulin, P. A. Desrosiers 1843-51
3v. and atlas of 134pl.(5 col.) 9 ports. F.
Volume 3 part 1 has separate title page: *Voyage pittoresque dans la Basse-Auvergne* by H. Doniol; volume 3 part 2 has separate title page: *L'ancien Velay,* by F. Mandet
The atlas contains many scenes with figures in the foreground, showing costume, also portraits which show coiffures and headdress in these provinces

Micheli y Marquez, José
Tesoro militar de cavalleria antiguo y moderno modo de armar cavalleros, y professar, segun las ceremonias de qualquier orden militar .... insignias y abito de cada una. Madrid, D. Diaz de La Carrera 1642
118 l. 90 illus. F.
"Con un breve discurso del origen de los sumos sacerdotes, religiosos de la ley escrita y de gracia, assi de monges, como de frailes y monjes: sus fundatores, y abitos, y de que pontifices fueron aprovados." Subtitle
Illustrations show insignia of the orders
Lipperheide 1845

Michelitz, Anton
Über den nachtheil, den die heutige frauentracht der gesundheit bringt Prag, Haase und Widtmann 1803
45p. O.
Lipperheide 3244

Michelsen, Poul Ulrich
21. bataillons historie 1788-1918. København, Hasselbalch 1918
232p. illus. Q.

Michiels, Alfred
Les bûcherons et les schlitteurs des Vosges ... dessins par Théophile Schuler. Strasbourg, E. Simon 1857
34p. 43pl. Q.
Colas 2053

Microcosm. Pyne, W. H.

The **microcosm** of London. Ackermann, Rudolph

The **microcosm** of Oxford. See Whittock, Nathaniel. A topographical and historical description of the university and city of Oxford

Microscope of fashion and folly. See The Bon ton magazine

Middlemore, Samuel George Chetwynd
(tr.) Burckhardt, J. C. The civilization of the renaissance in Italy. 1929

Middleton, John Henry
Lewis collection of gems and rings. See Cambridge. University. Corpus Christi college. Lewis collection

Midy, Adolphe
(illus.) Cogniet, Léon, and Raffet. Illustration de l'armée française depuis 1789 jusqu'en 1832

Miélot, Jean
Vie de Ste Catherine d'Alexandrie ... texte revu et rapproché du français moderne par Marius Sepet. Paris, G. Hurtrel 1881
342p. col.front. illus. pl.(part col.)
The illustrations (illuminated plates, miniatures, and tinted borders enclosing the text) are essentially reproductions (by modern artists) of those of the 15th century made by order of Philippe, duke of Burgundy, for Miélot's work. They show French costume of the middle ages
LC 3-7838

See also Christine de Pisan. Épître d'Othéa

Mieth, Michael
Neue curieuse beschreibung der gantzen artillerie, worinnen ... gehandelt wird ... wie ... man aus stücken ... glüend- und andere kugeln ... werffen soll. Dreszden und Leipzig, G. C. Hilscher 1736
192p. 33pl. F.
First edition, 1683; second edition, 1705
Lipperheide 2399

Mifliez, frères, publishers, Paris
Costumes français depuis Clovis jusqu'à nos jours

Migliorato
[Neapolitan scenes.] No place, ca1850
9 col.pl. O.
Legends on plates in Italian
Colas 2055. Lipperheide 1303

The **Mikado's** empire. Griffis, W. E.

Mikirs. See India—Native tribes—Mikirs

Mikszáth, Kálmán
Scènes hongroises; traduit par E. Horn. Paris, Librairies—imprimeries réunies 1890
99p. 15 col.pl. F.
Shows Hungarian dress of late 19th century

[**Milano, Giacomo Maria**]
Costumi diversi di alcune popolazioni de' reale domini di qua del Faro. Napoli, dalla Stamperia reale 1832
1 l. 39pl. F.
Engraved by Raf. Aloja
Colas 2056

Milano ne' suoi monumenti. Romussi, Carlo

Milès, Léon Roger-. See Roger-Milès, Léon

Milices révolutionnaires. Foussereau

Les **milices** suisses aux XVIIIe et XIXe siècles. See Escher, A. von. Die Schweizer milizen im 18 und 19 jahrhundert

Militär-album aller länder; heft 1. See Die deutsche armee; 2-3 Die oesterreichungarische armee

Militär-album des königlich preussischen heeres. Schindler, C. F.

Militärische gesellschaft, Zürich. See Samlung der neu-jahr-kupferen

Militair- und civil-reiter-schule neuerer zeit. Hochstetter, C. von

Militaire costumen van het koninkryk der Nederlanden. Madou, J. B., and Courtois, A.

Militaires polonais. See Heideloff, K. A. von. Aux héros polonais

Militairisches pracht-bilderbuch. Franceschini, Friedrich

Die **militarische** fechtkunst vor dem feinde. Ballassa, Constantin

Die **militarische** fussbekleidung. Salquin, S. A.

Militarischer almanach auf das jahr 1779. Altona 1779
79p. 12 col.pl. 2 maps. O.
Plates show soldiers of Prussia, Saxony, and Austria
Lipperheide 2112

Military and naval recognition book. Bunkley, J. W.

Military and religious life in the middle ages. Lacroix, Paul

Military antiquities respecting a history of the English army. Grose, Francis

Military cadets

France

Armand-Dumaresq, C. E. Uniformes des écoles du gouvernement. 1886

Geoffroy, J. J. H. Les bataillons scolaires. 1887

Germany

Geschichte des königlichen potsdamschen militärwaisenhauses, von seiner enstehung bis auf die jetzige zeit. 1824

Teicher, Friedrich. Das königl. bayerische kadetten-korps von der gründung bis zur gegenwart. 1889

United States

United States. Military academy, West Point. The centennial of the United States Military academy at West Point, New York, 1802-1902. 1904

United States. Quartermaster corps. The army of the United States; illustrated by forty-four fac-simile plates from water color drawings by H. A. Ogden. Text by Henry Loomis Nelson. 1885?

United States. Quartermaster corps. Uniform of the army of the United States (illustrated) from 1774 to 1907. 1890-1909

Military costume

Armont, Paul. Soldats d'hier et d'aujourd'hui. 1929-31

Bonnard, Camille. Costumi ecclesiastici, civili e militari d' secolo XIII, XIV e XV. 1827-1828

Edel, Vittorio. Ricordo delle nozze d'argento delle loro maestà Umberto I e Margherita di Savoia, 22 Aprile 1893. 1893

Études de types militaires. n.d.

Hampe, Theodor. Der zinnsoldat; ein deutsches spielzeug. 1924

Military costume—*Continued*

Hauslab, Franz von. Über die charakteristischen kennzeichen der geschichtlichen entwickelungs-abschnitte der kriegertracht vom beginn des XVI. bis zu jenem des XIX. jahrhunderts. 1864

Heath, William. A collection of interesting subjects of military occurrences, costumes etc. ca1823

Hugo, Hermann. De militia equestri antiqua et nova. 1630

Jacquemin, Raphael. Histoire générale du costume civil, religieux et militaire du IV. au XII. siècle (315-1815). [1876]

Jacquemin, Raphael. Histoire générale du costume civil, religieux et militaire du IV. au XII. siècle: Occident (315-1100). 1879

Jacquemin, Raphael. Iconographie générale et méthodique du costume du IV. au XIX. siècle (315-1815) collection gravée à l'eau forte d'après des documents authentiques & inédits. 1863-68

Jähns, Max. Handbuch einer geschichte des kriegwesens von der urzeit bis zur Renaissance. Technischer theil: bewaffnung, kampfweise, befestigung, belagerung, seewesen. 1878-1880

Knoetel, Richard. Handbuch der uniformkunde. 1937

Knoetel, Richard. Uniformenkunde; lose blätter zur geschichte der entwickelung der militärischen tracht. 1890-1914

Lavater, H. C. Kriegs-manual von übung der reüterej und infanterej montiererken- und -abrichtung der pferden. 1664

Lezius, Martin. Das ehrenkleid des soldaten; eine kulturgeschichte der uniform von ihren anfangen bis zur gegenwart. 1936

Nouveau recueil des costumes militaires français et autres nations tant anciennes et modernes. 1795

Quesnoy, Ferdinand. La guerre à toutes les époques. 1892

Seyboth, Adolf, and Binder, C. Album de l'Exposition militaire de la Société des amis des arts de Strasbourg (fondée en 1832). 1904

Steyert, André. Aperçu sur les variations du costume militaire dans l'antiquité et au moyen age. 1857

See also Arms and armor; Buttons, Military; Crusaders; Fencers, fighters with bayonets, etc.; Helmets; Heraldic costume; Military cadets; Naval costume; also Archers (Military)

Bibliography

Balsan, Auguste. Catalogue de costumes militaires français et étrangers. 1909

Colas, René. Bibliographie générale du costume et de la mode. 1933

Periodicals

Carnet de la sabre-tache; revue militaire retrospective. 1893+

La Giberne. 1899-1914

Ancient times

Willemin, N. X. Choix de costumes civils et militaires des peuples de l'antiquité. 1798-1802

16th century

Amman, Jost. Kunstbüchlin darinnenn neben fürbildung vieler geistlicher unnd weltlicher hohes und niderstands personen, so dann auch der türckischen käyser unnd derselben obersten, allerhandt kunstreiche stück und figuren. 1599

Cigogna, G. M. Il primo libro dél trattato militare. 1583

Fronsperger, Leonhard. Fünff bücher. Voñ kriegss regiment und ordnung wie sich ein jeder kriegzman inn seinem ampt und beuelch halten soll und was zů anfang eines kriegs zůerwegen unnd zubetrachten sei. 1555

Fronsperger, Leonhard. Kriegszbuch. 1565-73

Hogenberg, Hans. The procession of Pope Clement VII. and the Emperor Charles V. after the coronation at Bologna on the 24th February 1530. 1875

Liagno, T. P. Différens soldats; suite de douze estampes. 1585?

Lonicer, J. A. Pannoniae historia chronologica. 1596

Ruscelli, Girolamo. Precetti della militia moderna, tanto per mare, quanto per terra. 1568

Savorgnano, Mario, conte di Belgrado. Arte militare terrestre, e maritima; secondo la ragione, e l'uso de piu valorosi capitani antichi, e moderni. 1599

Vegetius Renatus, Flavius. Fl. Vegetii Renati viri illustris De re militari. 1532

17th century

Callot, Jacques. Exercices militaires. 1635

Crasso, Lorenzo. Elogii di capitani illustri. 1683

Dambach, Christoff. Büchsenmeisterey; das ist ... erklärung deren dingen so einem büchsenmeister fürnemlich zu wissen von nöthen. 1609

Della Bella, Stefano. Diverses exercices de cavalerie. 1642

Dilich, Wilhelm. Krieges-schule worinnen nach ... der alten Römer und Griechen zu wasser und land geführten ... streit-methode ... gewiesen wird. 1689

Du Praissac. Les discours militaires. 1612

Melzo, Lodovico. Regole militari del cavalier Melzo sopra il governo e servitio della cavalleria. 1611

18th century

Decker, Paul. Repraesentatio belli, ob successionem in Regno Hispanico ... gesti ... Der spanische successionskrieg unter drey keyszern Leopoldo I, Josepho I. und Carolo VI. 1714?

Military costume—18th century—*Continued*

Drummond de Melfort, L. H., comte de. Traité sur la cavalerie. 1776

Rugendas, G. P. Die belagerung der stadt Augsburg durch die französischen und bayerischen truppen im jahre 1704. 1705?

Rugendas, G. P. Reiter und gefechte. ca1825

Bibliography

Glasser. Catalogue d'une collection importante de costumes militaires français et étrangers. 1910-11

19th century

The Armies of to-day; a description of the armies of the leading nations at the present time. 1893

Beyer, Leopold. Kriegsscenen aus den jahren 1813 bis 1815, zür erinnerung für ehemalige krieger und zum nachzeichnen und illuminiren für kleine leute in 12 herrlichen skizzen. ca1815

Cenni, Quinto. Eserciti d'oltremare; skizzi militari. 1880

Cenni, Quinto. Eserciti europei; skizzi militari. 1880

Cenni, Quinto. Atlante militare organizzazione, uniforme e distintivi degli eserciti et delle armate d'Europa. 1890

Charakteristiche darstellung der vorzuglichsten europaeischen militairs. 1800-1810

LII figures en habit de guere des hussarts. ca1850

Finart, N. and others. Armées étrangères. ca1840

Godefroy, A. P. F. Armées des souverains alliés, années 1814 et 1815. 1815?

Heath, William. Foreign military costume. 1823

Historic, military and naval anecdotes of personal valour in the last war. 1815

Illustrirte kriegs-chronik; gedenkbuch an den deutsch-französischen feldzug von 1870-1871. 1871

Martinet, firm, publisher. Galerie militaire. ca1815?

Renard, Jules. Types militaires. 1862-71

Renard, Jules. Types militaires étrangers. 1893

Simpson, William. The seat of war in the East. 1855-56

Vernier, Charles. Costumes militaires des différentes nations. ca1850

Bibliography

Glasser. Catalogue d'une collection importante de costumes militaires français et étrangers. 1910-11

20th century

Blakeslee, F. G. Army uniforms of the world. 1919

Blakeslee, F. G. Uniforms of the world. c1929

Bley, Wulf. Moderne heere, moderne waffen. c1935

Bunkley, J. W. Military and naval recognition book. 1918

Falls, De W. C. Army and navy information. 1917

Williams, Dion. Army and navy uniforms and insignia. c1918

Alsace

See Military costume—France

Argentine republic

Argentine republic. Laws, statutes, etc Reglamento de uniformes para el ejercito. 1904

Argentine republic. Ministerio de guerra y marina. Reglamento propuesto por la comandancia jeneral de armas prescribiendo el uniforme que debe usar el ejército de la República. 1872

Mantilla, M. F. Premios militares de la República Argentina. 1892

Saguí, Francisco. Los últimos cuatro años de la dominacion española en el antiguo vireinato del Rio de la Plata desde 26 de junio de 1806 hasta 25 de mayo 1810. 1874

Australia

Australia. Department of defence. Clothing factory. Report

Published annually. First published 1912-13

Austria

Including material on Austria-Hungary 1867-1919

Anger, Gilbert. Illustrirte geschichte der k. k. armee. 1886-87

Gerasch, Franz. Das oesterreichische heer von Ferdinand II. römisch deutscher kaiser, bis Franz Josef I. kaiser von Oesterreich. ca1854

Geschichte der kaiserl. königl. regimenter seit ihrer errichtung bis auf gegenwärtige zeiten worin die inhaber jedes regiments ... angezeigt sind. 1791-1792

L'Allemand, Fritz. Die k. k. oesterreichische armee im laufe zweyer jahrhunderte. ca1846

Teuber, Oscar. Die österreichische armee von 1700 bis 1867. 1895

Zimburg, Wilhelm von. Osterreichische cavallerie, von 1600-1883. 1883

Bibliography

Ridder, G. de. Catalogue et description bibliographique d'une collection de livres et gravures sur les costumes militaires: Autriche Hongrie. 1928

Individual regiments

Amon von Treuenfest, Gustav, ritter. Geschichte des k. und k. dragoner-regimentes, General der cavallerie freiherr Piret de Bihain nr. 9, von seiner errichtung 1682 bis 1892. 1892

Amon von Treuenfest, Gustav, ritter. Geschichte des k.k. dragoner-regimentes Feldmarschall Alfred Fürst zu Windisch-Graetz nr. 14. 1886

Amon von Treuenfest, Gustav, ritter Geschichte des k. und k. husaren-regimentes Kaiser nr. 1 (1756-1898) 1898

Military costume—Austria—Individual regiments—*Continued*

Amon von Treuenfest, Gustav, ritter. Geschichte des k. u. k. Hussaren-regimentes nr. 3, feldmarschall Andreas graf Hadik von Futak. 1893

Amon von Treuenfest, Gustav, ritter. Geschichte des k.u.k. husaren-regiments nr. 4, Arthur herzog von Connaught und Strathearn. 1903

Amon von Treuenfest, Gustav, ritter. Geschichte des k.k. huszaren-regimentes Freiherr von Edelsheim-Gyulai nr. 4. 1882

Amon von Treuenfest, Gustav, ritter. Geschichte des k.k. Feldmarschall Graf Radetzky huszaren-regimentes nr. 5. 1885

Amon von Treuenfest, Gustav, ritter. Geschichte des k.k. huszaren-regimentes Alexander Freiherr v. Koller nr. 8 von seiner errichtung 1696-1880. 1880

Amon von Treuenfest, Gustav, ritter. Geschichte der k. und k. huszaren-regimentes nr. 10 Friedrich Wilhelm III. 1878

Amon von Treuenfest, Gustav, ritter. Geschichte des k. k. 11. Huszaren-regimentes Herzog Alexander v. Wurttemberg, 1762 bis 1850. 1878

Amon von Treuenfest, Gustav, ritter. Geschichte des k. k. 12. huszaren-regiments. 1876

Amon von Treuenfest, Gustav, ritter. Geschichte des k. u. k. huszaren-regimentes nr. 15. Feldmarschall-lieutenant Moriz Graf Pálffy ab Erdöd. 1894

Amon von Treuenfest, Gustav, ritter. Geschichte des k. k. infanterie-regimentes hoch- und deutschmeister nr. 4. 1879

Amon von Treuenfest, Gustav, ritter. Geschichte des kaiserl. und königl. Kärnthnerischen infanterie-regimentes Feldmarschall Graf von Khevenhüller nr.7. 1891

Amon von Treuenfest, Gustav, ritter. Geschichte des k.u.k. infanterie-regimentes nr. 18. 1882

Amon von Treuenfest, Gustav, ritter. Geschichte des k.k. infanterie-regiments nr. 20. Friedrich Wilhelm, Kronprinz. 1878

Amon von Treuenfest, Gustav, ritter. Geschichte des k. u. k. infanterie-regimentes nr. 46 feldzeugmeister Géza Frh. Fejervary de Komós-Keresztes. 1890

Amon von Treuenfest, Gustav, ritter. Geschichte des k.k infanterie-regimentes nr.47

Amon von Treuenfest, Gustav, ritter. Geschichte des k. k. infanterie-regimentes nr. 50, Friedrich Wilhelm Ludwig, grossherzog von B[aden] 1762 bis 1850 zweites Siebenbürger Romanen-Grenz-infanterie-regimentes nr. 17. 1882

Amon von Treuenfest, Gustav, ritter. Geschichte des k. und k. uhlanen regimentes Kaiser nr.4 (1813-1900) 1901

17th century

Duces supremi qui elapso saeculo decimo septimo, Caesareis augustissimae domus Austriacae exercitibus summa potestate praefuere. 1735

Geelen, G. V. Relation succincte et veritable de tout ce qui s'est passé pendant le siège de Vienne ... assiegée par les Turcs depuis le 14. juillet jusqu'au 12. de septembre 1683. 1684

18th century

Abbildung der verschiedenen corps des oesterreichischen allgemeinen aufgebothes. Représentation des différens corps de l'Insurrection générale d'Autriche. 1797

Artaria & compagnie, Vienna. Schema aller uniform der kaiserl. königl. kriegsvölkern. 1781

Balzer, Anton, and Walenta, J. Sammlung der merkwürdigsten städte und festungen, welche in den jahren 1788. 1789 und 1790 von den k.k. österreichischen, und kais: russischen armée der pforte abgenommen worden, nach ihrer wahren lage. 1790

Balzer, Johann. Schema der kaisl. königl. armee. 1784

Bartsch, Adam von, and Kininger, V. G. Heldenthaten von soldaten der k.k. armee in den feldzügen gegen die franzosen in den jahren 1792 bis 1799. ca1800

Dumont, Jean, baron de Carlscroon. Batailles gagnées par le serenissime prince Fr. Eugene de Savoye ... en Hongrie, en Italie, en Allemagne & aux Pais-Bas. 1725

Dumont, Jean, baron de Carlscroon, and Rousset de Missy, Jean. The military history of Prince Eugene of Savoy. 1736

Geschichte und bildliche vorstellung der regimenter des erzhauses Oesterreich. 1796

Khevenhüller, L. A., graf von. Observations-puncten ... bey dem Ihme von Dero kayserl. königl. maj ... anvertrauten dragoner-regiment vorgeschrieben. 1749

Kininger, V. G., and Mansfeld, J. G. Abbildung der neuen adjustirung der k.k. armee; seiner königlichen hoheit dem erzherzog Ferdinand Karl. 1796-1798

Lauber, Joseph. Denkmahl der vaterlandsliebe und furstentreue. 1797

Löschenkohl, H., pub. Schema aller uniform der kaiserl. königl. kriegsvölkern. ca1791

Manuale, oder Handgriffe der infanterie wie solches ao 1735, nach dem damahlig alt kayserl. würtenb. regiment zu fuss bey dem ... schwäbische Craysz regiment eingeführet worden. 1735

Merkwaardige historische beschryving van alle vreemde en onlangs eerst bekent gewordene krygsvolkeren. 1745

Militarischer almanach auf das jahr 1779. 1779

Military costume—Austria—18th century —*Continued*

Recueil des estampes et tableaux representant la cause des maux qui affligent l'Italie dans le temps où nous sommes. 1797

Schmalen, J. C. H. von. Accurate vorstellung der saemtlichen kayserlich koeniglichen armeen, zur eigentlichen kentniss der uniform von jedem regimente. 1762

Schmutzer, Jakob. Abbildungen der k. k. oesterreichischen infanterie. ca1765

Schmutzer, Jakob. Abbildungen der k. k. cavallerie-regimenter von 1765. ca1766

19th century

Adjustirungs-vorschrift für die generale, stabs- und ober-officiere ... der kaiserlich-königlichen armée (sanctionirt ... vom 17 februar, 1854) 1855

Adjustirungs-vorschrift für die generale, stabs- und ober-officiere ... der K. K. Armée, vom jahre 1837. 1837

Adjustirungs- und ausrüstungs-vorschrift für das k.k. heer. 1878

Amon von Treuenfest, Gustav, ritter. Armeealbum zur erinnerung an das 40jähr. regierungs-jubiläum ... Franz Joseph I. 1889

Austria. Kriegsministerium. Uniformen distinctions- und sonstige abzeichen der gesammten k.k. osterr.-ungar. wehrmacht sowie orden und ehrenzeichen Oesterreich-Ungarns. 1887

Barteau, L. R. Die k. k. oesterreichisch-ungarische armee. 1893

Bossoli, Carlo. The war in Italy. 1859

Engelbrecht, Martin. Costumes des armées française, bavaroise et autrichienne en 1809. 1809?

Dally, Aristide. Uniformes de l'armée autrichienne. 1887

Emphinger, Franz. Darstellung aller waffengattungen der kais. königl. osterreichischen armee im jahr 1839. ca1840

Franceschini, Friedrich. Militairisches pracht-bilderbuch. 1875-76

Die Freiwilligen-corps Österreich's im jahre 1859. 1860

Gerasch, Franz. Die kaiserl. koenigl. oesterreichische armee seit dem jahre 1849. 1851

Habermann, Franz, edler von. Kriegsscenen. C in VI blättern. ca1840

Hacklaender, F. W., ritter von. Erinnerungen an die feldzüge der k. k. oester. armee in Italien in den jahren 1848-49. 1851

Hauslab, Franz von. Darstellung der k.k. osterreichischen armee mit allen chargen. 1823

Hausner, Josef. Die k. k. österr. ungar. armee, nach den neuesten adjustirungsvorschriften bildlich dargestellt. 1886

Heicke, Josef. Oesterreichische und russische truppen aus dem ungarischen feldzuge 1849. 1849

Heicke, Josef. Serassaner und Croaten. 1849

Judex, M. Uniformen distinctions und sonstige abzeichen der gesammten k. k. osterr. ungar. wehrmacht sowie orden und ehrenzeichen Oesterreich-Ungarns. 1884

Jurnitschek, Alfred. Die wehrmacht der Oesterreichisch-ungarischen monarchie im jahre 1873. 1873

K. K. Oesterreichische armee nach der neuen adjustirung. 1837-48

Kählig, Eduard von. Österreich-Ungarn: Das heer, von E. von Kählig ... Die flotte, von R. ritter von Jedina. 1899

Die kaiserlich königlich oesterreichische armee. 1839

Kaiserlich koeniglich oesterreichischen militair. ca1830

Maly, A. von. Das k. k. heer und die österr. und ung. landwehren. 1884

Mollo, Tranquillo. Abbildung der neuen k. k. oesterreichischen armee uniformen. 1808

Oesterreichische landwehr. 1810

Die oesterreich-ungarische armee. 1892

Papin, Heinrich. Bildliche darstellung der k. k. oesterreichischen armee. 1820

Pettenkoffer, August. Das k.k. oesterreich. militär. 1847

Pettenkoffer, August, and Strassgschwandtner, A. Die k. k. österreich'sche armee nach der neuesten adjustirung. 1854

Portraits des Hongrois, des Pandoures ou Croates, des Waradins ou Esclavoniens, et des Ulans, &c. qui sont au service de ... la reine de Hongrie & le roi de Prusse. 1842

Richter, Wilhelm, and Gerasch, August Kaiserl. mexicanisches corps osterreichischer freiwilligen. ca1864

Stephanie, J. Abbildung der k. k. oesterreichischen armee durch alle waffengattungen, enthält jedes regiment, corps und militair branche in freyen gruppirungen. ca1820

Stubenrauch, Philipp von.; Schindler, J. J., and Höchle, J. N. Darstellung der k. k. österr. armee nach der neuesten adjustirung; mit bewilligung des k. k. hofkriegsrath. ca1821

Vienna militia

Franceschini, G., and Hagemann, A. Neueste adjustirung der Wiener bürger militärs. 1842

Mansfeld, Heinrich, and Biller, B. Wien's bewaffnete bürger im jahre 1806 in ihren uniformen dargestellt. La bourgeoisie de Vienne formée en regimens. ca1806

Wiener bürgermilitär. ca1805

20th century

Adjustierungs- und ausrüstungsvorschrift für die k. und k. trabantenleibgarde. 1904

Die K. u. K. oesterreichisch-ungarische armee. 1901

Righetti, Camillo. Adjustierungsblätter des k.u.k. oesterr.-ungar. heeres. 1900

Military costume—Austria—20th century —*Continued*

Sussmann, Anton. Die österreich-ungarische armee, ihre organisation, uniformen, ausrüstung, bewaffnung, distinktionen und sonstigen abzeichen. 1911

Belgium

Rouen, Charles. L'armée belge; exposé historique de son organisation, de ses costumes et uniformes, de son armement et de sa tactique depuis les temps primitifs jusqu'à nos jours. 1896

See also Military costume—Netherlands

18th century

Volontaires brabançons en 1797. ca1798

19th century

Évènements de Bruxelles. 1830

Hemelryck, J. L. van. Costumes de l'armée belge. 1828-31

Hendrickx. Uniformes de l'armée belge. 1855

Madou, J. B. Collection des costumes de l'armée belge en 1832 et 1833. 1833

Monnier, D. Uniformes de l'armée belge. ca1860

Payen, Camille. Costumes de l'armée belge. ca1873

Romberg, Maurice. Types de l'armée belge 1897-1900

Uniformes de l'armée belge; uniformen des belgischen heeres; uniforms of the Belgian army. 1893

Viatour, Gustave. Étude sur l'armée belge, 1896. 1896

20th century

Die belgische armee in ihrer gegenwärtigen uniformierung. 1908

Belgium. Ministère de la guerre. Tenues des officiers et assimilés. 1914

Bohemia

14th-15th centuries

Kutina, B. K. Kuffenerovo Husitské vojsko. 1900?

Lenfant, Jacques. Histoire de la guerre des Hussites et du concile de Basle. 1731

See also Military costume—Czechoslovakia

Brazil

Figurinos do exercito de conformidade com o decreto N. 3620, 28 fevereiro de 1866. 1866

Lecor, L. P. Colleccâo de dezenhos das figuras de detalhes que designâo os differentes uniformes para todos os corpos do exercito. 1859

Vilhena, L. dos S. Recopilação de noticias soteropolitanas e brasilicas. 1921

Bulgaria

Mach, Richard von. Die wehrmacht der Türkei und Bulgariens. 1905

Sussmann, Anton. Die armeen Rumäniens und Bulgariens; ihre organisation, bewaffnung, ausrüstung und uniformierung. 1914

Canada

Beauclerk, Lord Charles. Lithographic views of military operations in Canada under his excellency Sir John Colborne during the late insurrection. 1840

See also Military costume—England

China

Amiot, J. M. (comp. and tr.) Art militaire des Chinois. 1772

Hill, J. C. Die chinesische armee in ihrer neu-organisation und neu-uniformierung. 1910

Cisalpine republic

Zanoli, Alessandro, baron. Sulla milizia cisalpino italiana. Cenni storico-statistici, dal 1796 al 1814. 1845

Confederate army

See Military costume—United States —1860-1865—Confederate army

Costa Rica

Costa Rica. Laws, statutes, etc. Reglamento de uniformes. 1903

Costa Rica. Secretaría de la guerra. Reglamento de uniformes para el ejército San José. 1907

Czechoslovakia

Czechoslovakia. Minister of national defense. Change of the uniform regulations of the Czechoslovak armed forces. 1920?

See also Military costume—Bohemia

Denmark

Blom, Carl. Bidrag til den danske krigmagts historie. 1868-70

Danske uniformer: I Militaire. n.d.

Michelsen, P. U. 21. bataillons historie 1788-1918. 1918

Møller, Vald. Den danske armès uniformer i deres hovedforandringer i løbet af ca. 3 aarhundreder. 1892

Vaupell, O. F. Den danske haers historie til nutiden og den norske haers historie, indtil 1814. 1872-76

19th century

Bergh, Th. Den danske armee og marine. 1859

Bergh, Th. Die uniformen d. königl. dänischen armee. ca1860

Brock, Gustav. Den Danske haer og flaade. L'armée et la marine danoises. 1885

Bruun, Chr. Danske uniformer. 1837-1842

Dally, Aristide. L'armée danoise. 1887

Danske uniformer. 1864

Husher, Th. v. Samling af danske militaire uniformer med 6 tillaegsblade. 1858

Hyllested, H. C. Collection complète des uniformes de la marine et de l'armée danoise. 1829

Military costume—Denmark—19th century —*Continued*

Köller, F. L. von. Uniformzeichnung d. königl. dänischen armee. 1805

Steen, Chr. Den danske armee. 1858

Uniformes de l'armée danoise. ca1808

20th century

Christiansen, Rasmus. Danske uniformer for haer og flaade. 1911

Egypt

Wagner, J. C. Delineatio provinciarum Pannoniae et imperii Turcici in oriente. 1684-85

England

Almack, Edward. Regimental badges worn in the British army one hundred years ago ... The regiments identified, and notes bearing on their history added. 1900

Atkinson, J. A. A picturesque representation of the naval military and miscellaneous costumes of Great Britain. 1807

Clark, Christopher. British soldiers 1550 to 1906. 1907

Grose, Francis. Military antiquities respecting a history of the English army, from the conquest to the present time. 1801

Holmes, R. R. Naval & military trophies & personal relics of British heroes. 1896

Hort, Sir J. J., 3d bart. The days when we had tails on us. 1849

Luard, John. A history of the dress of the British soldier, from the earliest period to the present time. 1852

Nevill, R. H. British military prints. 1909

Richards, Walter. Her Majesty's army; a descriptive account of the various regiments now comprising the Queen's forces, 1889-9-?

Scott, Sir J. S. D., bart. The British army: its origin, progress, and equipment. 1868

Talbot-Booth, E. C. The British army; its history, customs, traditions and uniforms. 1937

See also Military costume—Canada; Military costume—Ireland; Military costume—Scotland

Periodicals

Navy and army illustrated. 1895-1915

Individual regiments

Almack, Edward. The history of the Second dragoons, Royal Scots greys. 1908

Beamish, N. L. History of the King's German legion. 1832-37

Broughton, U. H. R. The dress of the First regiment of life guards, in three centuries. 1925

Castell, graf. Die soldaten d. Königl. deutschen legion. 1906

Clayton, B. The Grenadier guards. 1854

Collyer, J. N., and Pocock, J. I. An historical record of the Light Horse volunteers of London and Westminster. 1843

Connolly, T. W. J. The history of the corps of Royal Sappers and Miners. 1855

Groves, J. P. History of the 42nd Royal Highlanders—"The Black watch" now the first battalion "The Black watch" (Royal Highlanders) ... 1729-1893. 1893

Hennell, Sir Reginald. The history of the King's body guard of the yeomen of the guard

Kane, John, of the Royal artillery. List of officers of the Royal regiment of artillery as they stood in the year 1763, with a continuation to the present time. 1815

Macdonald, R. J., comp. The history of the dress of the Royal regiment of artillery, 1625-1897. 1899

Milne, James. Gordon Highlanders. 1898

Scotland forever; a gift-book of the Scottish regiments. 1915?

Smith, J. H., ed. The historie booke, done to keep in lasting remembrance the joyous meeting of the Honourable artillery company of London and the Ancient and honorable artillery company of the Massachusetts in the towne of Boston, A. D. 1903. c1903

Indian Army

Ackermann, Rudolph. Costumes of the Indian army. 1844-1849

Atkinson, G. F. The campaign in India, 1857-58. 1859

Hunsley, W. Costume of the Madras army. 1841

India and the war. 1915

James, Charles. The military costume of India. 1813

MacMunn, Sir G. F. Armies of India, painted by Major A. C. Lovett. 1911

Moore, Joseph. Eighteen historical and local views illustrative of the operations and positions of the forces in the Birman territories. 1825

Richards, Walter. Her Majesty's army, Indian and colonial forces; a descriptive account of the various regiments now composing the Queen's forces in India and the colonies. 1891

Simkin, Richard. Our armies. 1891

Singh, S. N. India's fighters: their mettle, history and services to Britain. 1914

Williams. An historical account of the rise and progress of the Bengal native infantry, from its first formation in 1757, to 1796. 1817

SPECIAL PERIODS

18th century

British volunteers, or, a general history of the formation and establishment of the Volunteer and associated corps. 1799

Calver, W. L. The British army button in the American revolution. 1923

Military costume—England—18th century —*Continued*

Pictures of the uniforms, arms, and equipments of the cavalry of Great Britain as it existed in 1742 and 1745. 1745?

A representation of the cloathing of His Majesty's household, and of all the forces upon the establishments of Great Britain and Ireland, 1742. 1893

Rowlandson, Thomas. Loyal volunteers of London and environs; infantry and cavalry in their respective uniforms. 1798-99

19th century

Ackermann, Rudolph. Costumes of the British army. 1840-1858

Archibald, J. F. J. Blue shirt and khaki. 1901

Atkinson, G. F. The campaign in India, 1857-58. 1859

Beauclerk, Lord Charles. Lithographic views of military operations in Canada under his excellency Sir John Colborne during the late insurrection. 1840

Booth, John, comp. The battle of Waterloo, with those of Ligny and Quatre Bras. 1852

British army, by a lieutenant-colonel in the British army. 1899

The British military library; or, Journal: comprehending a complete body of military knowledge. 1799-1801

Busby, T. L. Civil and military costume of the city of London. 1824-25

Cannon, Richard. Historical records of the British army; comprising the history of every regiment in Her Majesty's service. 1837-1853

Costume of the army of the British Empire, according to the last regulations, 1812. 1813

Dally, Aristide. Uniformes de l'armée anglaise. 1886

Dunlop, John. Moolton, during and after the siege. 1849

Duplessi-Bertaux, Jean. Campaigns of ... Arthur, Duke of Wellington ... from Seringapatam to ... Waterloo. 1817?

Duplessi-Bertaux, Jean. Recueil des principaux costumes militaires des armées alliées. 1816

Die englische armee in ihrer gegenwärtigen uniformirung. 1894

Finart, N. Uniformes des armées alliées. ca1815

Genty, firm, Paris, pub. Costumes militaires. Infanterie anglaise (1815). 1815?

Hayes, M. A. Costume of the British army. ca1850

Heath, William. British military costume. 1824

Heath, William. The life of a soldier; a narrative and descriptive poem. 1823

Heath, William. Military costumes of the British cavalry. 1820

Holding, T. H. Uniforms of British army, navy and court. 1894

Hull, Edward. Costume of the British Army in 1828. 1828-30

Jenkins, James. Martial achievements of Great Britain and her allies (1799-1815). 1815

Jones, W., and company, tailors. Wholesale army, navy and volunteer, helmet, cap, and accoutrement makers. ca1855

L'Évêque, Henry. Campaigns of the British army in Portugal, under the command of General, the Earl of Wellington. 1812

Mansion, L. M., and Saint-Eschauzier. L'armée anglaise vers 1830. 1830?

Newhouse, C. B. Military incidents. ca1840

Perry, O. L. Rank and badges, dates of formation, naval and military distinctions, precedence, salutes, colours, and small arms, in Her Majesty's army and navy and auxiliary forces, including a record of the naval and military forces in the different countries of Great Britain and Ireland. 1888

Simkin, Richard. British military types. 1888-92

Simkin, Richard. Life in the army, every day incidents in camp, field, and quarters. 1889

Simkin, Richard. Our armies. 1891

Smith, C. H. Costume of the army of the British Empire according to the regulations, 1814. 1815

Stenzel, Alfred. Groszbritannien und Irland: Das heer ... die flotte. 1897

Thomas. Sketches of British soldiers. 1861-69

Periodicals

Gentleman's magazine of fashions, fancy costumes, and the regimentals of the army. 1828-94

1900-1913

Army and navy gazette, London. Coloured military types which were issued as supplements to the "Army and navy gazette" between March 1888 and September 1902. [1910?]

Die englischen armee- und marine-uniformen im kriege, sowie die abzeichen an denselben. 1912

Great Britain. War office. Dress regulations for the army. War office, 1911. 1911

Great Britain. War office. Dress regulations for the officers of the army (including the militia). War office, 1900. 190-?

Great Britain. War office. Dress regulations for the officers of the army (including the militia) War office, 1904. 1904

1914-date

Gale & Polden, Ltd. Regimental ribbons & buttons of the British army. 1915

Great Britain. War office. Dress regulations for the army. (Provisional) 1928. 1928

Great Britain. War office. Dress regulations for the army. 1934. 1934

Jonas, Lucien. Les armées britanniques. 1918?

Military costume — England — 1914-date —*Continued*

Rank at a glance in the army & navy, the air services, R. N. R., R. N. V. R., R. D., royal marines, volunteer training corps, etc., etc., with descriptive notes. 1915

Regimental nicknames and traditions of the British army. 1915

Wie sehen die armeen der gegner des dreibundes im kriege aus. 1914

Musicians

Gordon, W. J. Bands of the British army. 1921

Zealley, A. E., and Hume, J. O. Famous bands of the British Empire; brief historical records of the recognised leading military bands and brass bands in the Empire. c1926

Estonia

Estonia. Kaitsevägede staap. Pionerieeskiri. 1932

Ethiopia, Modern

Sambon, L. L'esercito abissino; usi e costumi. 1896

Europe

See also names of European countries

18th century

Eigentliche vorstellung aller, sich dermahlen (von anno 1741, da sich das kriegs theatrum eröffnet hat) auf teutschen boden, befindlichen fremden nationen. ca1745

État militaire de l'Europe en 1762. 1762?

19th century

Dally, Aristide. Les armées étrangères en campagne. 1885

Europa in Waffen. 1874

Finart, N. Troupes étrangères. ca1835

Galerie militaire. Armées européennes. 1845

Galerie militaire; collection des costumes militaires de toutes les nations. 1840-1855

Köller, F. L. von. Uniformzeichnung der vorzüglichsten europäischen truppen. 1802

Köppen, Fedor von. Armies of Europe. 1890

The military costume of Europe. 1822

Moltzheim, A. de. Collection des uniformes actuels de l'artillerie européenne, dessinés par un officier de l'armée française. ca1830

Raffet, D. A. M. Costumes militaires français & étrangers, portraits et sujets divers. 1860

Saint-Fal. Costumes militaires. ca1815

Suhr, Christoffer. Abbildungen der uniformen aller in Hamburg seit den jahren 1806 bis 1815 einquartiert gewesener truppen. ca1899

Vallet, Louis. A travers l'Europe; croquis de cavalerie. 1893

Valley, A. Album colorié des uniformes des grandes armées de l'Europe. 1888

Venturini, K. H. G. Russlands und Deutschlands befreiungskriege von der Franzosenherrschaft unter Napoleon Buonaparte in den jahren 1812-1815. 1816-19

Vogt, Hermann. Die europäischen heere der gegenwart; illustrationen von R. Knötel. 1886-90

20th century

United States. Army war college. Notes on uniforms and insignia, French, British, Belgian, German. 1917

France

General works

Album historique de l'armée et de la marine. 1905-1906

L'ancienne France. L'armée, depuis le moyen age jusqu'à la revolution. 1886

Arnoux, Guy. Les soldats français dans les guerres. 1916

Bastin, Ferdinand. Costumes militaires des armées françaises de 1790 à 1856. ca1857

Bottet, Maurice. Le bouton de l'armée française. 1908

Costumes & uniformes. 1912-1914

Dally, Aristide. La France militaire illustrée. [1886?]

Daniel, Gabriel. Histoire de la milice françoise, et des changemens qui s'y sont faits depuis l'etablissement de la monarchie françoise dans les Gaules, jusqu'à la fin du règne de Louis le Grand. 1724

Depréaux, Albert. Les affiches de recrutement du XVIIe siècle à nos jours. 1911

Depréaux, Albert. Les armées françaises d'outre-mer; les uniformes des troupes de la marine et des troupes coloniales et nord-africaines. 1931

Dunoyer de Noirmont, J. A. É. É., baron, and Marbot, A. C. A., baron de. Costumes militaires français, depuis l'organisation des premières troupes régulières en 1439 jusqu'en 1789. 1845

Fallou, Louis. Le bouton uniforme français (de l'ancien-régime à fin juillet 1914). 1915

Fieffé, Eugène. Histoire des troupes étrangères au service de France depuis leurs origine jusqu'à nos jours. 1854

France. Ministère de la guerre. Historiques des corps de troupe de l'armée française (1569-1900). 1900

Hardoin, Georges. Les cuirassiers (1672-1886). 1887

Hardoin, Georges. Nos gloires militaires 1888

Hay, A. E. Recueil des chartes, créations et confirmations des colonels, capitaines, majors, officiers ... de la ville de Paris. 1770

Herbé, C. A. Costumes français civils militaires et religieux ... depuis les Gaulois jusqu'en 1834. 1835-37

Herlaut, A. P. Le costume militaire en France. 1912-13

Military costume—France—*Continued*

Leçons de chic; souvenirs et traditions militaires; par une sabretache. 1894

Lienhart, and Humbert, René. Les uniformes de l'armée française depuis 1690 jusqu'à nos jours. 1897-99

Loy, L. C. É. A. Historiques du 84ᵉ régiment d'infanterie de ligne "Un contre dix", du 9ᵉ régiment d'infanterie légère "L'incomparable", et du 4ᵉ régiment de Voltigeurs de la Garde. 1684-1904. 1905

Malibran, H. Guide à l'usage des artistes et des costumiers, contenant la description des uniformes de l'armée française de 1780 à 1848. 1904

Moltzheim, A. de. Esquisse historique de l'artillerie française depuis le moyen âge jusqu'à nos jours. 1868

Montigny, C. A. L. de. Uniformes militaires. 1772

Onfroy de Bréville, J. M. G. Aquarelles de Job: Tenue des troupes de France à toutes les époques armées de terre et de mer. 1900-04

Paris. Musée d'artillerie. Notice sur les costumes de guerre. 1876

Pascal, Adrien, and others. Galerie des victoires et conquêtes de l'armée française et de tous les régiments depuis les premiers temps de la monarchie jusqu'à nos jours. 1847-49

Quarré de Verneuil, A. H. R. Le costume militaire en France et les premiers uniformes. 1876

Revol, J. F. Histoire de l'armée française. 1929

Sicard, François. Histoire des institutions militaires des français suivie d'un aperçu sur la marine militaire. 1834

Thoumas, C. A. Les anciennes armées françaises. 1890

Titeux, Eugène. Historiques et uniformes de l'armée française. 1895?

Vernier, Charles. Costumes de l'armée française depuis Louis XIV jusqu'à ce jour. 1846-50

Supplementary material

Alexandre, Arsène. Histoire de la peinture militaire en France. 1889

L'ancienne France: La marine et les colonies; Commerce. 1888

Arnoux, Guy. Tambours et trompettes. 1919

Bouchot, H. F. X. M. L'épopée du costume militaire français; aquarelles et dessins originaux. 1898

Montfaucon, Bernard de. Les monumens de la monarchie françoise qui comprennent l'histoire de France, avec les figures de chaque règne. 1729-33

Montfaucon, Bernard de. Thresor des antiquitez de la couronne de France. 1745

See also Military cadets—France

France—Bibliography

Glasser. Costumes militaires; catalogue des principales suites de costumes militaires français. 1900

Sauzey, J. C. A. F. Iconographie du costume militaire. 1901-03

Periodicals

Journal militaire officiel. 1790-1886

Le Passepoil. 1921+

Société de l'histoire du costume. Bulletin de la Société. 1907-1911

Special branches

See also titles listed under period divisions

Artillery

Vidal, J. J. G. P. L'artillerie. 1929

Cavalry

Armand-Dumaresq, C. É. Album de la cavalerie française, 1635-1881. 1881

Béchu, M. E. Nos vieux houzards. 1933

Brécard, C. T. La cavalerie. 1931

Castillon de Saint-Victor, M. É. de. Historique du 5ᵉ régiment de hussards. 1889

Choppin, Henri. Les hussards, les vieux régiments, 1692-1792. 1899

Cossé-Brissac, R. M. T. de. Historique de 7ᵉ régiment de dragons 1673-1909. 1909

Dachery (illus.) Uniformes de tous les regiments de Hussards. 1889

Descaves, Paul. Historique du 13ᵐᵉ régiment de chasseurs et des chasseurs à cheval de la garde. 1891

Dupuy, J. R. Historique du 12ᵉ régiment de chasseurs de 1788 à 1891. 1891

Fallou, Louis. Nos hussards (1692-1902). 1902

Isnard, P. Fr. d'. Régiments de hussards au service de France. n.d.

Longin, A. H. É. Historique du 14ᵉ régiment de chasseurs. 1907

Martinet, F. X. Historique du 9ᵉ régiment de dragons. 1888

Picard, L. A. Origines de l'École de cavalerie et de ses traditions équestres. 1889

Colonial troops

Depréaux, Albert. Les uniformes des troupes coloniales de 1666 à 1875. 1931

Guards

Alboise de Poujol, J. E., and Élie, Charles. Fastes des gardes nationales de France. 1849

Cudet, François. Histoire des corps de troupe qui ont été spécialement chargés du service de la ville de Paris depuis son origine jusqu'à nos jours. 1887

Forbes-Leith, William. The Scots men-at-arms and life-guards in France. 1882

Raisson, H. N. Histoire populaire de la garde nationale de Paris, juillet 1789-juin 1832. 1832

Infantry

Boppe, P. L. H. La Légion portugaise, 1807-1813

Du Fresnel, H. V. D. Un régiment à travers l'histoire. Le 76ᵉ, ex-1ᵉʳ léger. 1893

Military costume—France—Infantry—*Cont.*

France. Armée. Infanterie. Légion étrangère. Livre d'or de la Légion étrangère, 1831-1931. 1931

Musée rétrospectif de l'infanterie française, régiments de France, Rocroy, Fontenoy, Austerlitz. 1866

Payard, Pol. Les chasseurs à pied. 1930

Riols de Fonclare, J. É. de. L'infanterie. 1930

Simond, Émile. Le 28e de ligne. 1889

Susane, L. A. V. V. Histoire de l'ancienne infanterie française. 1849-53

Touchemolin, Alfred. Le régiment d'Alsace dans l'armée française. 1897

Touchemolin, Alfred. Strasbourg militaire. 1894

Vassal, B. M. J. Historique du 11e régiment d'infanterie. 1900

Mercenary troops

Hoffmann, Nicolas. Régiments suisses au service de la France. 1780?

Sapeurs-pompiers

Since the Sapeurs-pompiers are part of the army their uniforms will be found in many general books on French uniforms. See also the subject Firemen—France

Middle ages

Le Clert, Louis. Le costume de guerre en Basse Champagne au XIIIe et au XIVe siècle d'après les effigies gravées sur les pierres tombales. 1909

15th century

Belleval, René, marquis de. Du costume militaire des Français en 1446. 1866

17th century

L'art militaire françois, pour l'infanterie. 1696

Bosse, Abraham. Figures au naturel tant des vestements que des postures des gardes françoises du roy très chretien. 1660?

Collombon, Jacques. Traité de l'exercice militaire. 1650

Fallou, Louis. Album de l'armée française (de 1700 à 1870) 1902

Ganier, Henry. Costumes des régiments et des milices recrutés dans les anciennes provinces d'Alsace et de la Sarre, les républiques de Strasbourg et de Mulhouse, la principauté de Montbéliard et le duché de Lorraine pendant les XVIIe et XVIIIe siècles. 1882

Guerard, N. Livre à dessiner; les exercices de Mars. 169-?

18th century

Caran d'Ache, E. P., known as. Nos soldats du siècle. 1889

Fallou, Louis. Album de l'armée française (de 1700 à 1870) 1902

Ganier, Henry. Costumes des régiments et des milices recrutés dans les anciennes provinces d'Alsace et de la Sarre, les républiques de Strasbourg et de Mulhouse, la principauté de Montbéliard et le duché de Lorraine pendant les XVIIe et XVIIIe siècles. 1882

Hugo, Abel. France militaire. Histoire des armées françaises de terre et de mer de 1792 à 1837. 1838

Marbot, A. C. A., baron de. Tableaux synoptiques de l'infanterie et de la cavalerie française et des régiments étrangers au service de la France de 1720 à 1789. 1854

Transformation des uniformes de l'Armée française de 1789 à nos jours. 1890

1715-1774

Baudouin, S. R., comte de. Exercice de l'infanterie françoise ordonnée par le roy le VI may MDCCLV; dessiné d'après nature dans toutes ses positions et gravé par S. R. Baudouin. 1757

Baudouin, S. R., comte de. Exercice de l'infanterie françoise ... copié d'après l'original. 1759

Dubois, Edmond, pub. État général des troupes de France sur pied en mai 1748 (uniformes, drapeaux, étendards) 1901

Eisen, C. D. J. Nouveau recueil des troupes qui forment la garde et maison du roy, avec la date de leur creation, le nombre d'hommes dont chaque corps est composé, leur uniforme et leurs armes. 1756

État général des troupes sur pied en 1760 et 1761

Grandmaison, Henri de. Fantassins et cavaliers sous Louis XV. 1891

Gravelot, H. F. B. Planches gravées d'après plusieurs positions dans lesquelles doivent se trouver les soldats, conformément a l'ordonnance du roi de l'exercice de l'infanterie du 1er janvier, 1766. 1766

Lattré, pub. Exercice et révolutions de l'infanterie françoise. 1766

LaRue, P. B. Nouveau recueil des troupes légères de France levées depuis la présente guerre, avec ... leur uniforme et leurs armes. 1747

Loutherbourg, P. J. de. Premiere suite de soldats. ca1770

Mouillard, Lucien. Armée française: les regiments sous Louis XV. 1882

Recueil de toutes les troupes qui forment les armées françoises. 1761

Uniformes de l'infanterie française suivant le règlement arrête par le roy le 25 avril 1767. 1767

Uniformes des armées françoises suivant les reglements du roi. 1775

1774-1789

Hoffmann, Nicolas. Costumes de la cavalerie française suivant les ordonnances de 1775 et 1779, et costumes de diverses époques

Hoffmann, Nicolas. Costumes militaires de France. 1800?

Hoffmann, Nicolas. Costumes militaires suivant l'ordonnance de 1786

Military costume—France—1774-1789—*Cont.*

Isnard, P. Fr. d'. Les nouveaux uniformes de tous les régimens de dragons de France, avec des planches ... représentant un chasseur à cheval de chaque régiment, selon l'ordonnance du roi du 31 mai 1776. 1776

Isnard, P. Fr. d'. Les nouveaux uniformes de tous les régimens de cavalerie de France avec des planches ... représentant un cavalier à cheval de chaque régiment selon l'ordonnance du roy du 31 mai 1776. 1776

Nouveau recueil des troupes qui forment la garde et maison militaire du roy. ca1780

Uniformes militaires des troupes françoises et étrangères ... sous le règne de Louis XVI, suivant les derniers règlement de 1778. 1779

Uniformes militaires des troupes françoises et étrangères ... sous le règne de Louis XVI, suivant les derniers règlements donnés sous le ministère de monseigneur le prince de Mont-Barey; Augmentés des troupes qui forment la garde et maison du roy. 1780

France. Laws, statutes, etc. Ordonnance du Roi, pour régler l'exercice de ses troupes d'infanterie; du 1. juin 1776. 1776

Isnard, P. Fr. d'. État général des uniformes de toutes les troupes de France représentés par un homme de chaque régiment dans le costume du nouveau règlement arrêté ... le 21 fevrier 1779. 1779

Malo, Servan. Ceux de Yorktown; uniformes et drapeaux, d'après des documents officiels de l'epoque. 1918

Watteau, L. J. Première [et deuxième] suite de divers sujets militaires. Paris, Lenfant ca1787

See also Military costume—U.S.—1775-1783—French troops

1789-1799

L'art du militaire, ou traité complet de l'exercice de l'infanterie, cavalerie, du canon, de la bombe, et des piques. 1793

Bellangé, J. L. H. Collection des types de tous les corps et des uniformes militaires de la republique et de l'empire. 1844

Charlet, N. T. Costumes de corps militaires faisant partie de l'armée française avant et pendant la revolution, et de la garde imperiale. ca1842

Charlet, N. T. Costumes militaires 1789-1815. 1886

Dayot, A. P. M. Histoire contemporaine par l'image d'après les documents du temps. 1905

Description de quelques corps composant les armées françoises. 1794

Detaille, Édouard and Maillot, T. J. R. Types et uniformes: L'armée française. 1885-89

État militaire des troupes de France en 1789. 1789?

Garneray, J. F. Collection des nouveaux costumes des autorités constituées civils et militaires. ca1796

La Chanonie, L. C. de. Le costume à l'armée de Condé. 1892

La Chanonie, L. C. de. Le costume dans les armées royalistes. 1891

Marbot, A. C. A., baron de. Costumes militaires français depuis 1789 jusqu'à 1814. 1860

Margerand, J. Les Hussards sous la révolution. 1907

Poisson, S. J. C., baron. L'armée et la Garde nationale. 1858-62

Recueil des estampes et tableaux representant la cause des maux qui affligent l'Italie dans le temps où nous sommes. 1797

1799-1815

Adam, Victor. Cavalerie de la Garde impériale du 1er empire. ca1840

Armées françaises et étrangères (de 1800 à 1804). ca1804

Barrès, Maurice. La vieille garde imperiale; illus. par Job [pseud.] 1901

Basset, pub. Troupes françaises; 1er empire. 1805-1814

Bellangé, J. L. H. Collection des types de tous les corps et des uniformes militaires de la république et de l'empire. 1844

Berka, J. L'armée française représentée en 18 feuilles. ca1810

Booth, John, comp. The battle of Waterloo, with those of Ligny and Quatre Bras. 1852

Bucquoy, Eugène Louis. Les gardes d'honneur du premier empire. 1908

Challiot. Modèles pour les uniformes et l'équipement des officiers et fonctionnaires de l'armée française. ca1800

Charlet, N. T. Costumes de corps militaires faisant partie de l'armée française avant et pendant la revolution, et de la garde impériale. ca1842

Charlet, N. T. Costumes de l'ex-garde impériale. 1819-1820

Charlet, N. T. Costumes militaires français. 1818

Charlet, N. T. Costumes militaires 1789-1815. 1886

Charlet, N. T. L'empereur et la garde impériale. ca1845

Charlet, N. T. L'empereur et la garde impériale, avec un précis historique. 1853

Charlet, N. T. La vieille armée française. 1820

Chataignier. Costumes militaires et civil. 1800-1815?

Cogniet, Léon, et Raffet. Illustration de l'armée française depuis 1789 jusqu'en 1832. ca1837

Depréaux, Albert. Les gardes d'honneur d'Alsace et de Lorraine à l'époque du premier empire. 1913

Military costume—France—1799-1815—*Cont.*
Duplessi-Bertaux, Jean. Recueil de cent sujets de divers genres. 1814. Part 2
Duplessi-Bertaux, Jean. Suite de militaires de différents armes. 1807
École du soldat et de peloton. 1799
Engelbrecht, Martin. Costumes des armées française, bavaroise et autrichienne en 1809. 1809?
Etrennes aux héros futurs ou présent d'un militaire à son fils. ca1810
Faber du Faur, C. W. von. Blätter aus meinem portefeuille, im laufe des feldzugs 1812 in Russland ... Feuilles extraites de mon portefeuille, esquissées sur les lieux dans le courant de la campagne de 1812 en Russie. 1831-34
Fallou, Louis. La Garde impériale (1804-1815). 1901
Fieffé, Eugène. Napoléon 1er et la Garde impériale. 1859
Fort, E. Recueil d'uniformes. Gardes d'honneur du voyage imperial de 1808. n.d.
France. Ministère de la guerre. Règlement concernant les uniformes des généraux et officiers des etats-majors des armées de la République française. 1798
France. Ministère de la guerre. Règlement sur l'uniforme des généraux, des officiers des états-majors des armées et des places, des officiers du corps du génie [etc.] 1803
Das französisch kaiserl. militair, 1805. 1805
Garde des Consuls. 1799-1804
Grasset de Saint-Sauveur, Jacques. Les fastes du peuple français ou Tableaux raisonnés de toutes les actions héroïques et civiques du soldat et du citoyen français. 1796
Grasset de Saint Sauveur, Jacques. Recueil complet des costumes des autorités constituées, civiles, militaires, et de la marine. 1796
Henschel, W., and Henschel, F. A. Les Gardes impériales et royales de l'armée française en 1810. ca1810
Hoffmann, Nicolas. Uniformes du consulat. 1804?
Laurent de l'Ardèche, P. M. Histoire de l'Empereur Napoléon. 1840
Marbot, A. C. A., baron de. Costumes militaires français depuis 1789 jusqu'à 1814. 1860
Marchal, Gustave. Les uniformes de l'armée française sous le consulat. 1901
Martinet, firm, publisher. Galerie des enfants de Mars. 1811
Martinet, firm, publisher. Troupes françaises (Premier empire). 1807-1814
Mundt, Albert. Die freiheitskriege in bildern; eine zeitgenössische bilderschau der kriegsjahre 1806 bis 1815. 1913
Norvins, J. M. de, baron de Montbreton. Histoire de Napoléon. 1839
Reglement das exercitium und die manövres der französischen infanterie betreffend, vom lsten August 1791. 1812
Rembowski, Alexandre. Sources documentaires concernant l'histoire du regiment des chevau-légers de la garde de Napoléon Ier d'après des manuscrits originaux et des documents inédits. 1899
Saint-Hilaire, É. M. H. Histoire anecdotique politique et militaire de la Garde impériale. 1847
Troupes auxiliaires ou troupes françaises. 1810
Vernet, Carle, and others. Campagnes des français sous le consulat & l'empire. 1860
Vernet, Horace, and Lami, L. E. Collection des uniformes des armées françaises, de 1791 à 1814. 1822

19th century

Album militaire. 18—
Algeria. Commissariat général du centenaire. L'armée d'Afrique, 1830-1930. 1930?
Bastin, Ferdinand. Uniformes français sous Napoléon ler, la restauration et Napoléon III. 1860?
Beauvoir, H. R. de. Album-annuaire de l'armée française. 1889-1909?
Bellangé, J. L. H. Uniformes de l'armée française depuis 1815 jusqu'à ce jour. 1831
Bruyère, H. E. P. Historique du 2. régiment de dragons. 1885
Caran d'Ache, E. P., known as. Nos soldats du siècle. 1889
Dayot, A. P. M. Histoire contemporaine par l'image, d'après les documents du temps, 1789-1872. 1905
Defontaine, Henri. Du costume civil officiel et de l'uniforme militaire des officiers à la cour ou auprès des chefs d'état français depuis 1804 jusqu'à nos jours. 1908
Galerie des militaires français qui, à differentes époques, se sont distingués par leur courage. ca1820
Ganier, Henry. Les Alsaciens dans la Garde impériale et dans les corps d'élite. 1914
Guillaume, Albert. Mon sursis; album militaire inédit en couleurs. 1901
Hugo, Abel. France militaire. Histoire des armées françaises de terre et de mer de 1792 à 1837. 1838
Kieffer, Fritz, ed. Les garnisons d'Alsace au 19. siècle. 1911
Margerand, J. Les coiffures de l'armée française. 1909-24
Margerand, J. Les cuirasses des carabiniers (1810-1870). 1911
Margerand, J. Notes sur les tenues des Hussards de 1815 à 1870. 1922

Military costume—France—19th century—*Continued*

Nouveau manuel complet des gardes nationaux de France contenant l'école du soldat et de peloton ... les lois et décrets sur la garde nationale, jusqu'en 1852. 1853?

Onfroy de Bréville, J. M. G. Mémoires de César Chabrac, trompette de Houzards. ca1900?

Perrout, René. Les images d'Epinal. 1914

Rozat de Mandres, C. N. L. La France en campagne; un siècle de guerres (1800-1900). 1906

Transformation des uniformes de l'Armée française de 1789 à nos jours. 1890

See also Military costume—France—18th century—1799-1815; Canteen women—French army

Restoration, 1814-1830

Aubry, Charles. Collection des uniformes de l'armée française. 1823

Aubry, Charles and Loeillot, Karl. Maison du roi et garde royale (Louis XVIII). 1816-17

Basset, pub. Troupes françaises; Restauration. n.d.

Basset, pub. Uniformes français: Restauration [1830]

Bellangé, J. L. H. Les jolis soldats français, chant guerrier par Ch. Plantade. 1824

Blanc. Garde nationale en 1830. 1830

Canu. Collection des uniformes français. 1816-1825

Charlet, N. T. Costumes militaires. 1817-18

Chéreau, Mme Vve. Garde royale. 1825?

Cogniet, Léon, et Raffet. Illustration de l'armée française depuis 1789 jusqu'en 1832. ca1837

Feltre, H. J. G., duc de. Notice sur l'uniforme des officiers d'état-major général, et des aides-de-camp, du 22 mai 1816. 1816

Finart, N. Les alliés à Paris en 1815, scènes de moeurs. 1815?

Finart, N. Garde royale et maison du Roi. ca1816

Foussereau, J. M. L'artillerie française en 1829; Garde royale et ligne. n.d.

Garde Royale dessiné par Ch. L. n.d.

Gautier, Rodolphe. Troupes françaises. 1814-1816

Genty, firm, Paris, pub. Troupes françaises. 1814-16

Hecquet, F. Tracé descriptif des divers objets d'habillement, d'équipement, de harnachement à l'usâge de l'armée française en 1828. 1828

Mallet, and Lameau. Collection des uniformes de l'armée française. 1817-18

Mareschal. Artillerie, Garde royale. 1824

Martinet, firm, publisher. Galerie militaire: Troupes françaises. 1816-22

Martinet, firm, publisher. Troupes françaises: Maison du Roi, 1814. 1814

Martinet, firm, publisher. Troupes françaises (Restauration). 1814-16

Raffet, D. A. M. Collection de costumes militaires. 1825-26

Raffet, D. A. M. Garde royale, 1828

Raffet, D. A. M. Uniformes des troupes de ligne, 1829-1830. 1830?

Tardieu, Ambroise. Galerie des uniformes des gardes nationales de France. 1817

Titeux, Eugène. Histoire de la maison militaire du roi de 1814 à 1830. 1890

Vernet, Carle. Collection de chevaux de tous pays montés ... cavaliers avec leurs costumes et leurs armes. ca1820

Vernet, Carle, and Vernet, Horace. Recueil de chevaux de tout genre. ca1826

Vernet, Horace; Vernet, Carle, and Lami, L. E. Collection raisonnée des uniformes français de 1814 à 1824. 1825

1830-1848

Adam, Victor. Cavalerie sous le règne de Louis-Philippe. ca1840

Adam, Victor. Collection des costumes militaires, armée française, 1832. ca1840

Adam, Victor. Costumes de la république, de l'empire, de l'armée française et de l'armée d'Afrique de 1830 à 1840. ca1840

Ambert, J. M. J. J. A. J., baron. Esquisses historiques des différents corps qui composent l'armée française. 1835

Armée française (1844-1846). [184-?]

Basset, publisher. Uniformes français sous le règne de Louis-Phillippe. n.d.

Bastin, Ferdinand. L'armée française en 1848. 1848?

Bellangé, J. L. H. Costumes de l'armée française depuis 1830 jusqu'à nos jours. 1831

Cavalerie française en 1846. 1846?

Daigremont, J. H. Description de l'uniforme des sous-lieutenants de l'école d'application de l'artillerie et du génie. 1848

Eckert, H. A., Monten, Dietrich, and Schelver, F. Saemmtliche truppen von Europa in characteristischen gruppen dargestellt. 1836-43

Foussereau, J. M. Milices révolutionnaires sous le gouvernement provisoire [du 24 Février au 4 Mai 1848] 1848

Foussereau, J. M. Uniformes de la garde nationale de l'armée et de la marine françaises de 1830-1832. 1832?

Huart, Louis. Physiologie du garde national. 1841

Janet, A. L. Uniformes de l'armée française en [1846-]1848. 1848

Lalaisse, Hippolyte. Collection complète des uniformes de l'armée et de la marine françaises. 1840-48

Lalaisse, Hippolyte. Costumes de tous les corps de l'armée et de la marine françaises (sous Louis-Philippe I.). 1845-52

Lalaisse, Hippolyte. La jeune armée. 1845

Maurice, C. French military costumes. 184-?

Military costume—France—1830-1848—*Cont.*
Noguès, S. Garde municipale et garde nationale. ca1830
Raaslöff, W. R. von. Rückblick auf die militairischen und politischen verhältnisse der Algérie in den jahren 1840 und 1841. 1845
Raffet, D. A. M. Collection des costumes militaires de l'armée, de la marine et de la garde nationale françaises depuis août 1830. 1833
Swebach, Edouard. Armée française, 1831. 1831?

1848-1852

Charpentier, Eugène. Costumes militaires sous la deuxième république. ca1850
Lalaisse, Hippolyte. Uniformes de l'armée et de la marine françaises (1848-1852) 1852?

1848-1852—Musicians

La musique militaire. 1850?

1852-1870

Adam, Victor. Costumes de l'armée française 1860-1861-1862. ca1863
Album de l'armée française et la Garde impériale. ca1860
Armand-Dumaresq, C. E. A. Uniformes de la Garde impériale en 1857. 1858
Armand-Dumaresq, C. E. A. Uniformes de l'armée française en 1861. 1861
Bastin, Ferdinand. L'armée française en 1854. 1854?
Bossoli, Carlo. The war in Italy. 1859
Ducamp, Jules. Histoire de l'armée d'Orient et de tous les régiments qui ont pris part aux campagnes de la Mer Noire et de la Mer Baltique. 1858
Gaildrau, Jules. L'armée française: recueil contenant toutes les tenues des différentes armes, les écoles militaires et les écoles de marine, les equipages et les trains de l'armée, l'administration militaire etc. 1855-56
Hoff, Major, pseud. Les grandes manoeuvres. 1884
Lalaisse, Hippolyte. L'armee et la Garde imperiale, 1860-1870. 1870
Lalaisse, Hippolyte. Empire française; l'armée et la Garde impériale. 1853-66
Lalaisse, Hippolyte. Types militaires du troupier français. ca1870
Lançon, A. Album de l'armée française. 1861
Moraine, L. P. R. de. Album militaire de l'armée française en action. ca1870
Moraine, L. P. R. de. Napoléon III et son armée vers 1859. ca1860
Pajol, C. P. V., comte. Armée française. ca1850
Perrot, Émile. Harmonie universelle: musique militaire. 1867
Renard, Jules. Souvenirs du siège de Paris: les défenseurs de la capitale. 1871
Renard, Jules. Souvenirs du siège de Paris: les soldats de la République, l'armée française en campagne. 1872
Types militaires de l'armée française; infanterie, mès. ca1868

1870-1900

Album de l'armée française. ca1875
Armand-Dumaresq, C. É. Uniformes de l'armée française en 1884. 1885
Armand-Dumaresq, C. É. Uniformes de l'armée française en 1887. 1887
Brunet, Romuald, and Chaperon, Eugène. Les grandes manoeuvres de cavalerie. 1887
Brunet, Romuald, and Chaperon, Eugène. La science des armes dans la cavalerie. 1887
Chapuis, F. Uniformes de l'armée française. 1892?
Detaille, Édouard and Maillot, T. J. R. Types et uniformes: L'armée française. 1885-89
France. Ministère de la guerre. Description des effets d'habillement, de coiffure, de grand et de petit équipement, de petite monture, de pansage et objets divers à l'usage des corps de troupe. 1879
Die französische armee in ihrer gegenwärtigen uniformirung dargestellt. 1891
Hennebert, Eugène. Nos soldats: infanterie, cavalerie, artillerie, marine, etc. 1887-88
Hepke, F. V. von. Frankreich. Das heer am ende des neunzehnten jahrhunderts. 1900
Maillot, T. J. R. À la caserne. 1885
Maillot, T. J. R. En campagne. 1885-86
Maillot, T. J. R. La jeune armée. 1890
Martinet, firm, publisher. Costumes des franc-tireurs et des volontaires de 1870. 1870?
Moltzheim, A. de. La nouvelle armée française. 1875
Roy, Marius. Les grandes manoeuvres. 1887

20th century

Beauvoir, H. R. de. Album-annuaire de l'armée française. 1889-1909?
Brun, Charles. Uniformes militaires anciens et actuels ... Nos soldats. 1916
Bucquoy, E. L. Les uniformes de l'armée française. 1935
Depréaux, Albert. Les armées françaises d'outre-mer. Les uniformes des troupes de la marine et des troupes coloniales et nord-africaines. 1931
Die französische armee in ihrer gegenwärtigen uniformierung. 1903
Die graublauen felduniformen der französischen armee und deren abzeichen. 1915?
Kurze zusammenstellung über die französische armee. 1914
Wie sehen die armeen der gegner des dreibundes im kriege aus. 1914

Military costume—*Continued*

Germany

Barthold, F. W. Geschichte der kriegsverfassung und des kriegswesens der Deutschen. 1864

Deiss, F. W. Das deutsche soldatenbuch. 1926

Krippenstapel, Friedrich. Die preussische armee von den ältesten zeiten bis zur gegenwart. 1883

Lehmann, Gustav. Die trophäen des preuss. heeres in der königl. hof. und garnisonkirche zu Potsdam. 1898

Liebe, G. H. T. Der soldat in der deutschen vergangenheit. 1899

Militarischer almanach auf das jahr 1779. 1779

Prussia. Kriegsministerium. Deutsche heeres-uniformen auf der weltausstellung in Paris, 1900. 1900

Schneider, Louis. Präsentirt das gewehr! 1844

See also Military cadets—Germany

15th century

Soden, Franz, freiherr von. Geschichte des ehemaligen weilers Affalterbach landgerichts Altdorf in Mittelfranken des königreichs Bayern. 1841

16th century

Barthold, F. W. George von Frundsberg oder das deutsch kriegshandwerk zur zeit der reformation. 1833

Blau, Friedrich. Die deutschen Landsknechte; ein culturbild. 1882

Breunner-Enkevoërth, A. J., graf von. Römisch kaiserlicher majestät kriegsvölker im zeitalter der landsknecht ... mit erläuterndem text von Jacob von Falke. 1883

Burgkmair, Hans. Kaiser Maximilians I triumph. Le triomphe de l'empereur Maximilien I. 1796

Burgkmair, Hans. The triumphs of the Emperor Maximilian I. 1873

Dürer, Albrecht. Ehrenpforte des Kaisers Maximilian I. 1885-86

Dürer, Albrecht. Triumph des Kaisers Maximilian I. 1883-84

Leitner, Quirin, ritter von. Das kriegswesen des Heiligen Römischen Reiches deutscher nation unter Maximilian I und Carl V. 1860

Parrocel, C. Reitres et lansquenets. 1750?

Wessely, J. E. Die landsknechte, eine culturhistorische studie. 1877

17th century

Callot, Jacques. Les miseres et les malheurs de la guerre. 1633

Faulhaber, Johann. Neue geometrische und perspectinische inventiones etlicher sonderbahrer instrument die zum perspectinischen grundreissen der pasteyen unnd vestungen ... deszgleichen zur buchsenmeisterey ... gebrauchsam seynd. 1610

Gheyn, Jacob de. Reiterübungen. ca1600

Kilian, Lucas. Newes soldaten buchlein. 1609

18th century

Assner, Leopold. Neueste abbildung aller kayserl. königl. regimenter. 1778

Boltze, Eberh. Die infanterie Friedrichs d. G. 1785. 1927

Fleming, H. F. von. Der vollkommene teutsche soldat, welcher die gantze kriegs-wissenschaft, insonderheit was bey der infanterie vorkommt ... und ... die einem soldaten nöthige vorbereitungswissenschafften, künste und exercitia, die chargen und verrichtungen aller kriegs-bedienten, von dem mousquetier an bis auf den general. 1726

Lange, Eduard. Die soldaten Friedrich's des Grossen. 1853

Schmalen, A. von. Nachricht von den fränkischen craistrouppen, nebst einem anhang von den schwäbischen creisregimentern. 1782

19th century

Arnould, Georg. Das deutsche heer und die marine. 1891-94

Bekleidungs vorschrift für die kaiserlichen schutztruppen in Afrika. 1896

Boguslawski, Albrecht von. Deutschland. Das heer, von Boguslawski ... Die flotte, von R. Aschenborn. 1900

Brueck, O. von. Erinnerungen an Schleswig. 1850

Dally, Aristide. Uniformes de l'armée allemande. 1886

Die deutsche armee. 1915?

Die deutsche marine und die deutsche schutztruppe für Ost-Afrika in ihrer neuesten uniformirung. 1893

Die deutsche militair-musik auf der internationalen ausstellung für musik- und theaterwesen Wien 1892. 1892

Das deutsche reichsheer, graphische dargestellt ... nebst erläuternden und historischen bemerkungen. 1879

Die deutschen schutztruppen in Afrika (Sudwestafrika, Ostafrika, Kamerun und Togo) in ihrer gegenwärtigen uniformirung. 1897

Eckert, H. A., Monten, Dietrich, and Schelver, F. Saemmtliche truppen von Europa in characteristischen gruppen dargestellt. 1836-43

Elzholz, L.; Rechlin, Karl, and Schulz, J. Das preussische heer. 1830

Genty, firm, Paris, pub. Costumes militaires. 1814-1815. v3

Hammer, F. W., comp. Das königlich preussische heer in seiner gegenwärtigen uniformirung. 1862-1865

Hünten, Emil. Die waffengattungen des preussischen heeres. 1860?

Illustrationen zur rang und quartier-liste, oder Abbildungen der neuen uniformen in der preuss. armee. 1844-45

Klatte, Cph. Vorschule der soldatenreiterei, oder Wahres reiter exercitium zu fuss. 1825

Klemm, Heinrich. Lehrbuch für uniformschneider zur selbstbelehrung. 1896

Military costume—Germany—19th cent. —*Continued*

Die königliche preussisch armée. 1845

Krickel, G., and Lange, G. Das deutsche reichsheer in seiner neuesten bekleidung und ausrüstung. 1888-92

Lange, G. Uniforms-tabellen und quartierliste der deutschen armee und der kaiserlich deutschen marine. 1877

Lange, Gustav. L'armée allemande sous l'empereur Guillaume II. 1890

Lieder, Friedrich. Darstellung der königl. preussischen infanterie in 36 figuren. 1820

Lieder, Friedrich. Darstellung der königl. preussischen infanterie und cavallerie. ca1818

Lieder, Friedrich, and Krüger, F. Darstellung der königlich preussischen cavallerie in 41 figuren. 1821

Mundt, Albert. Die freiheitskriege in bildern; eine zeitgenössische bilderschau der kriegsjahre 1806 bis 1815. 1913

Osten-Sacken und von Rhein, Ottomar, freiherr von der. Deutschlands armee in feldgrauer kriegs- und friedens-uniform. 1917

Poten, Bernhard von. Unser volk in waffen; das deutsche heer in wort und bild. 1885-87

Das preussische heer unter Friedrich Wilhelm IV. 1845

Réunion des officiers. Les uniformes de l'armée allemand. 1877

Röchling, Carl. Unser heer. 1894

Schindler, C. F. Die cavallerie Deutschland's. 1882

Sigel, G. A. Deutschlands heer und flotte, in wort und bild ... Germany's army and navy, by pen and picture. c1899

Die uniformen der deutschen armee. 1885

Die uniformen der deutschen armee. Zur benutzung in der instructions-stunde. 1870?

Unser vaterland in waffen; ein patriotischer hausschatz für das deutsche volk. 1893

Vogt, Hermann. Das buch vom deutschen heere. 1891

Periodical

Der Soldaten-freund. 1833-1914

20th century (to 1914)

Conring, F. F. Das deutsche militär in der karikatur. 1907

Die graue felduniform der deutschen armee. 1910

Hoppenstedt, Julius. Das heer. 1913

Schlawe, Karl. Die organe der deutschen freiwilligen krankenpflege im kriege, ihre uniformierung und ausrüstung. 1903

Periodical

Der Soldaten-freund. 1833-1914

1914-18

Arnold, Karl. Kriegsflugblätter der Liller kriegszeitung. 1915

Die Deutsche armee; abbildungen von offizieren und soldaten. 1915

Great Britain. War office. The new German field service uniform. 1916

Knötel, Herbert; Pietsch, Paul, and Jantke, Egon. Uniformkunde; das deutsche heer, friedensuniformen bei ausbruch des weltkrieges. 1935-37

Weisz, Otto. Feldgrau in krieg und frieden. 1916-17

1919-date

Die deutsche reichswehr. Organisation, einteilung, truppenteile, bekleidung und ausrüstung d. deutschen reichsheeres. 1924

Eelking, Hermann, freiherr von. Die uniformen der Braunhemden (S. A., S. S., Politische leiter, Hitler-jugend, Jung-volk und B. D. M.). 1934

Hoyer, K., and Brennecke, F. Die uniformen des reichsheeres und der reichsmarine nebst amtlichen uniformtafeln. 1925

Die neue deutsche reichswehr. 1919

Pietsch, Paul. Die deutsche reichswehr in ihrer uniformierung. 1919

Poland. General staff. Mars. Siły zbrojne niemiec. 1931

Rosenfeld, Helmut. Deutsches erntedankfest, 1933. 1933

OF SPECIAL STATES

Baden

Freydorf, Rudulf von. Die geschichtlichen uniformen des jetzigen Bad. Leib-Grenadier. Régiments. 1903

Kaiser, Friedrich. Erinnerungen an den feldzug in der Rheinpfalz und Baden ... 1849. ca1849

Rosenberg, Marc. Badische uniformen 1807 und 1809. 1896

Schreiber, Guido. Der badische wehrstand seit dem siebenzehnten jahrhundert bis zu ende der französischen revolutionskriege. 1849

Völlinger, Joseph. Grossherzoglich badisches militair. 1824

Bavaria

Abbildung des churpfalzbaïerischen militairs nach voriger und gegenwaertiger uniform. 1787

Allgemeiner militär-almanach; erster jahrgang mit acht colorirten militär gruppen, nach zeichnungen von Monten, und vier portraits berühmter generals. 1828

Armée bavaroise vers 1840. 1840?

Baader, Joseph. Die fehde des Hanns Thomas von Absberg wider den schwäbischen bund; ein beitrag zur culturgeschichte des sechszehnten jahrhunderts. 1880

Behringer, Ludwig. Die bayerischer armee unter König Maximilian II

Behringer, Ludwig. Uniformen des bayerischen heeres nach der neuen bekleidungsvorschrift. ca1864

Military costume — Germany — Bavaria — *Continued*

Beschreibung und vorstellung des solennen stuck-schiessens, welches auf ... befehl eines ... raths des Heil. Röm. Reichs freyer stadt Nürnberg ... 1733 den 8 Junii ... gehalten ... worden. 1734

Diez, Wilhelm von. Königl. bayerische armée. ca1864

Engelbrecht, Martin. Costumes des armées française, bavaroise et autrichienne en 1809. 1809?

Gillig, Victor. Bayerische chevaux legers. 1842

Helm, Seb., and Ströbel, Christian. Die feldgraue friedens- und kriegs- bekleidung d. k. bayer. armee. 1918

Hoffmann, Anton. Das heer des blauen königs; die soldaten des kurfürsten Max II. Emanuel von Bayern, 1682-1726. 1909

Hohfelder, Carl. Das bayerische bürgermilitär in allen waffengattungen und uniformen vom jahre 1790 bis zum jahre 1852. 1853

Kaiser, Friedrich. Erinnerungen an den feldzug in der Rheinpfalz und Baden ... 1849. ca1849

Karacteristische abbildungen des neu organisirten bürger-militairs in sammtlichen königlich baierischen staaten. 1807

Kolb, Valentin. Das Münchener bürger militär in allen waffengattungen und uniformen von den jahren 1790 bis gegenwärtige zeit. 1834

Kraus, Gustav. König Otto I und die K. Bayerischen truppen in Griechland im jahre 1833. 1833?

Kraus, Gustav. Königlich bayerisches linien und bürger militair, nach der neuesten ordonnanz vom 1825. 1832

Lipowsky, F. J. Bürger-militär almanach für das königreich Baiern, 1809-1810. 1809-10

Lipowsky, F. J. Nazional garde almanach für das königreich Baiern, 1811-1812. 1811-12

Monten, Dietrich. Die bayerische armee, nach der ordonnanz von jahre 1825. 1825

Monten, Dietrich. Die neue uniformirung, rüstung und bewaffnung der königlich baierischen armee. ca1825

Müller, Karl, and Braun, Louis. Die bekleidung, ausrüstung und bewaffnung der königlich bayerischen armee von 1806 bis zur neuzeit. 1899

Münich, Friedrich, and Behringer, Ludwig. Die uniformen der bayerischen armee von 1682 bis 1848. 1863-64

Pfeiffer, Baptist. Uniformen der königlich-bayerischen armee nach der neuesten ordonnanz vom jahre 1825. 1838

Schiesl, Ferdinand. Uniformirung und organisation des bürger-militärs in dem Königreiche Baiern. 1807

Voltz, J. M. Costumes de l'armée bavaroise 1813-1825. 1825

Augsburg

Almanach des augsburgischen bürgermilitärs. 1796-1798

Brandenburg

Eickstedt, C. von. Reglements und instructionen für die churfürstlich-brandenburgischen truppen zur zeit der regierung Friedrichs des dritten (ersten) als churfürst und als könig. 1837

Brunswick

Elster, O. Die historische schwarze tracht der ... Braunschweigischen truppen. 1896

Hamburg

Buek, F. G. Album hambürgische costüme. 1843-1847

Gaedechens, C. F. Hamburgs bürgerbewaffnung. 1872

Das hamburgische militär bis zum jahre 1811 und die hanseatische legion. 1889

Rosmäsler, F. H. W. Hamburgs bürgerbewaffnung. 1816

Hanover

Accurate vorstellung der saemtlichen Churfürstl. Hanoverischen armeen, zur eigentlichen kentniss der uniform von jedem regimente. 1763

Leopold, Franz, and Mentzel, C. Abbildung der königlich hannoverschen armee. ca1820

Mentzel, C. Königl: hannov: militair. 1836

Osterwald, G. Abbildungen des königlich-hannoverschen militairs. 1840

Ronnenberg, J. G. F. Abbildung der churhannöverischen armée-uniformen. 1791

Tackmann, E. Uniformen d. kgl. Hannoverschen armee. ca1830

Hesse

Müller, F. H. Grossherzoglich hessisches militair. ca1830

Tackmann, E. Gallerie des kurhessischen militärs. ca1825

Lübeck

Stolle, C. Lübeck's bürger-militair. 1837

Mecklenburg

Grossherzoglich - Mecklenburg - Schwerin'sche und Mecklenburg strelitz'sche truppen. 1831

Prussia

Abbildung der veränderten monturen 1799. No date

Brügner, C. Abzeichen der koeniglich preussischen armee im jahre 1863. 1863

Burger, Ludwig. Die königl. preussische armee in ihrer neuesten uniformirung. 1860

Burger, Ludwig, and Müller, H. Garde royale prussienne, 1861. 1861

Ciriacy, L. F. von. Chronologische übersicht der geschichte des preussischen heers ... seit den letzen kurfürsten von Brandenburg bis auf die jetzigen zeiten mit vielen erläuternden zusätzen. 1820

Military costume — Germany — Prussia —*Continued*

Crousaz, A. von. Geschichte des königlich preussischen Kadatten-corps, nach seiner entstehung, seinem entwickelungsgange und seinen resultaten. 1857

Duplessi-Bertaux, Jean. Recueil des principaux costumes militaires des armées alliées. 1816

Genty, firm, Paris, pub. Costumes militaires. 1814-1815. v2

Finart, N. Uniformes des armées alliées. ca1815

Franckfurther burger-lust im stückschiessen, oder Aussführliche beschreibung was bey dem ... ertz-hertzog von Oesterreich ... Leopoldo zu ... ehren den 10. aug. 1716. gehaltenen stück-schiessen. 1716?

Friedrichs II königs von Preussen. Armee montirungen sauber gemahlt wie selbige unter dessen regierung waren. 1789

Gerstmann, Maximilian. Das buch vom preussischen soldaten; kriegsbilder und friedensscenen. 1867

Geschichte der bekleidung und ausrüstung der königl. preussischen armee in den jahren 1808 bis 1878. 1878

Geschichte und bildliche vorstellung der königlich preussischen regimenter. 1796

Giersberg. Die königlich preussische armée 1792. 1886

Henschel, W., and Henschel, F. A. Kostüme der ganzen preussischen armee. 1806

Horvath, C. C., pub. Preussische armeeuniformen unter der regierung Friedrich Wilhelm II, königs von Preussen; Uniformes de l'armée prussienne sous le regne de Frédéric Guillaume II. 1789

Horvath, C. C., pub. Uniformes de l'armée prussienne sous le règne de Frédéric-Guillaume II, roi de Prusse. 1788

Kaiser, Friedrich, and others. Per aspera ad astra; blätter zur erinnerung an die siegesthaten der preussischen armee ... 1866. 1867

Kaiser. königl. preuss. garde-cavalerie. 1852

Kurzgefaste geschichte der königlich preussischen armée, nebst vorstellung der uniform eines jeden regiments. 1786

Lehmann, Gustav. Forschungen und urkunden zur geschichte der uniformirung der preussischen armee 1713-1807. 1900

Menzel, A. F. E. von. Die armee Friedrich's des Grossen in ihrer uniformirung. 1851-57

Menzel, Adolph. Illustrations des oeuvres de Frédéric-le-grand. 1882

Menzel, A. F. E. von. Die armee Friedrichs des Grossen in ihrer uniformierung. 1906-08

Müller, C. F. Abbildung der königl. preussischen armee uniformen. 1788

Pietsch, Paul. Die formations- und uniformirungs-geschichte des preussischen heeres 1808-[1912]. 1911-12

Portraits des Hongrois, des Pandoures ou Croates, des Waradins ou Esclavoniens, et des Ulans, &c. qui sont au service de ... la reine de Hongrie & le roi de Prusse. 1742

Preussens heer. Seine laufbahn in historischer skizze entrollt von George Hiltl ... seine heutige uniformirung und bewaffnung gezeichnet von C. F. Schindler. 1875-76

Prussia. Kriegsministerium. Geschichte der bekleidung, bewaffnung und ausrüstung des königlich preussischen heeres. 1902-06

Rabe, Edmund. Uniformen des preussischen heeres in ihren hauptveränderungen bis auf die gegenwart. 1850

Rabe, Edmund, and Burger, Ludwig. Die brandenburg-preussische armee in historischer darstellung; ihre uniformierung und bewaffnung vom grossen kurfürsten bis auf Kaiser Wilhelm. 1884-85

Ramm, A. L. Stammliste aller regimenter der königlich-preussischen armee; nebst nachträgen und berichtigungen bis zum I. junius 1802. 1802

Ramm, A. L. Tabellarische nachweisung von allen regimentern und korps der königlich preussischen armee unter der regierung sr. majestät Friedrich Wilhelm III, zur erläuterung der abbildungen von denen militair uniformen. 1800

Randel. Armée royale de Prusse. 1845

Sachse, L. & co., Berlin. Die preussischen garden. 1830?

Schindler, C. F. Militär-album des königlich preussischen heeres nach der neuesten organisation, uniformirung und bewaffnung aller truppentheile. 1862

Schindler, C. F. Die uniformirung der königl. preussischen armee im jahre 1874. 1875?

Schmalen, J. C. H. von. Accurate vorstellung der sämtlichen koeniglich preussischen armee. 1759

Schneider, Louis. Illustrirte stammrang- und quartier liste der königlich preussischen armee. 1854

Schöning, K. W. von. Geschichte des königlich preuszischen dritten Dragoner-regiments und derjenigen Dragoner-regimenter, aus welchen dasselbe, bei der reorganisation der armee im jahre 1807, hervorgegangen ist. 1835

Schöning, K. W. von. Geschichte des königlichen preussischen regiments Garde du corps zu seinem hundertjährigen jubelfeste (1740-1840). 1840

Sebbers. Uniformes de la cavalerie prussienne. ca1850

Sellmer, Carl. König Wilhelm und sein heer. 1885

Military costume — Germany — Prussia —*Continued*

Seyfart, J. F., sohn. Kurzgefassete geschichte aller königlichen preussischen regimenter, zur erklärung der illuminirten abbildungen derselben. 1770

Stamm-album der brandenburgisch-preussischen armee. ca1844

Stawitzky, E. H. L. Geschichte des infanterie-regiments von Lützow (1. Rheinisches) nr. 25 bis zum jahre 1857 und seines stammes, der infanterie des von Lützow'schen freikorps. 1889

Die uniformen der preussischen garden von ihrem entstehen bis auf die neueste zeit. 1827-40

Verdy, L., freiherr von. Die königlich preussische armee ... L'armée prussienne. 1846-49

Volkmann, captain. Geschichte des magdeburgischen pionier-bataillons nr. 4., 1813 bis 1887. 1888

Walter, W. Das preuszische heer in bildern. 1834

Winckelmann. Garde royale prussienne. ca1835

Wolf, L. Abbildung der neuen königl. preuss. armee uniformen. 1813-15

Wolf, L. Uniformen der Berliner bürgergarde. ca1810

Saxony

Abbildung der churfürstlich-saechsischen armée uniformen. 1799

Abbildung der kurfürstlich sächsischen armée. ca1800

Abbildungen der neu organisirten königlichsächsischen armée. 1810

Abbildung derer VIII. ersten hertzogen zu Sachsen, Jülich, Cleve und Berg, Engern und Westphalen, des H. Römischen Reichs ertz-marschallen und chur-fürsten landgrafen in Thüringen. 1702

Accurate vorstellung der sämtlichen Chur. Furstl. Sachss regimenter und corps, worinnen zur eigentl: kenntniss der uniform von jedem regimente. 1769

Bartsch, Adam. Die verschiedenen uniformen der sächsischen armee 1806 und 1823. ca1823

Beck, August. Die königlich sächsische armee in ihrer neuesten uniformirung. [1867]

Beck, August. Lose blätter zur geschichte der königlich sächsischen armee [from 1806-1868] 1873

Geissler, C. G. H. Abbildung der Communal-Garde zu Leipzig in ihren verschiedenen uniformen. 1831

Geschichte und bildliche vorstellung der kurfürstlich saechsischen regimenter. 1797

Hauthal, Ferdinand. Geschichte der sächsischen armee in wort und bild. 1859

Heine, Ferdinand. Abbildungen der neuen uniformen der königlich sächsischen armee. 1834

Hess, C. A. H. Abbildung der chursächsischen truppen in ihren uniformen unter der regierung Fried.—Aug. III. 1805-07

Hessen, Wilhelm. Uniformen der verschiedenen truppen der churfürstlich sächsischen armee. 1797

Hoyer, J. G. von. Pragmatische geschichte der saechsischen truppen; ein taschenbuch für soldaten. 1792

Jahn, lithgr. Sächsische bürgerwehr und schützen. ca1860

Meerboth, A. Saxon uniforms in the year 1806. 1806?

Müller, August. Geschichtliche übersicht der schicksale und veränderungen des grossherzogl. sächs. militairs während der ... regierung ... des grossherzogs Carl August. 1825

Neu uniformirte königlich sächsische armee, nach der natur gezeichnet und in gruppen dargestsellt. 1811

Sauerweid, Alexandre. L'armée saxonne représentée en 30 feuilles. 1810

Schmid, H., and Patzschke, Carl. L'armée saxonne depuis ses origines jusqu'en 1832. 1832

Schubauer, F. Königlich sächsische armee. 1842

Westphalia

Sauerweid, Alexandre. Uniformes de l'armée westphalienne du roi Jérome. ca1810

Uniformes de la garde de sa majesté le roi de Westphalie. 1810

Württemberg

Abbildungen der kostüme und uniformen des würtemburgischen militärs von der zeit des 30 jährigen kriegs bis 1854. 1860

Abbildungen des württembergischen militärs von der früheren bis zur gegenwärtigen zeit. 1857

Braun, Reinhold. Königliche württembergische armee. 1840

Donat, F. M. von. Bekleidungs-vorschrift für offiziere, sanitätsoffiziere und obere militärbeamte der reserve und landwehr und mit uniform verabschiedete offiziere des XIII (königl. württ.) armeekorps. 1897

Fromm, F. L. v. Würtembergischer militäralmanach. 1825

Kirn, G. M. Das k. Württ. militär in seiner neuen uniformirung 1865. 1865

Küstner. Würtembergisches militairs. 1870?

Seele, J. B. Koenigliche württembergische garde du corps, infanterie, chevauleger. 1809-13

Stadlinger, L. J. von. Geschichte des württembergischen kriegswesens von der frühesten bis zur neuesten zeit. 1856

Stuttgart

Fischer, C. A. Geschichte der Stuttgarten stadgarde zu pferd. 1887

Military costume—*Continued*

Great Britain

See Military costume—England

Greece

Ancient times

Fickelscherer, Martin. Das kriegswesen der alten. 1888

Rheinhard, Hermann. Griechische und römische kriegsalterthümer für den gebrauch in gelehrtenschulen zusammengestellt. 1859

20th century

Sussmann, Anton. Die armeen der Türkei und Griechenlands, ihre organisation, bewaffnung, ausrüstung und uniformierung. 1914

Hungary

For Austria-Hungary see Military costume—Austria

Danzer, Alfonz. A mi hadseregünk. 1889?

Nouveau recueil ... des differends habillements des trouppes qui composent l'armée de la reine de Hongrie. 1742

Recueil des différents habillements des trouppes qui composent l'armée de la reine de Hongrie. 17—?

India

For native troops which are part of the English army see Military costume—England—Indian army

Ireland

16th century

Campbell, Lord Archibald. Craignish tales and others. 1889

See also Military costume—England

Italy

Zanelli, Severino. Il reggimento Piemonte reale cavalleria dalle origini ai nostri tempi. 1892

See also Military costume—Cisalpine republic; Military costume—Sardinia

18th century

Alessandro, Giuseppe d'. Opera. 1723

Gravier, Jean. Recueil de toutes les uniformes qui se sont signalé durant le siège de Gènes. 1752

19th century

Bisi, A. F. Uniformi militari Italiani al 1° Ottobre 1863. 1863

Bossoli, Carlo. The war in Italy. 1859

Cenni, Quinto. Album delle uniformi militari del regno: esercito e marino. 1879

Cenni, Quinto. L'esercito Italiano; schizzi militari. 1880

Dally, Aristide. Uniformes de l'armée italienne. 1887

Gaglier. Armée Toscane. 1827

Die italienische armee in ihrer gegenwärtigen uniformirung. 1890

Italy. Ministero della guerra. Raccolta della disposizioni sulla divisa degli ufficiali. 1890

Uniformi de' corpi dell' armata italiana. 1809

Zanoli, Alessandro, baron. Sulla milizia cisalpino italiana. Cenni storico-statistici, dal 1796 al 1814. 1845

20th century

Cenni, Quinto. L'arma del Genio nel 4°. esercito italiano. 1903

Cenni, Italo. L'esercito italiano. 1914

Die grauen felduniformen der italienischen armee und deren abzeichen. 1915

Die italienische armee. 1915

Die italienische armee in ihrer gegenwärtigen uniformierung. 1910

Italy. Ministero della guerra. Calendario del esercito, 1936. 1936

Italy. Ministero della guerra. Photographs of uniforms worn by officers and soldiers of the Italian army, used for the military uniform display at the Tercentennial exposition at Jamestown. 1907

Italy. Ministero della guerra. Regolamento sull' uniforme. 1931

Papal states

Piano di riforma e di organizzazione della milizia provinciale ponteficia, decreta li 8 maggio 1823. 1823

Japan

Japan society, London. Catalogue of an exhibition of the arms and armour of old Japan, held ... London, in June 1905. 1905

Die japanische armee in ihrer gegenwärtigen uniformierung. 1905

Die japanische armee in ihrer gegenwärtigen uniformirung ... abbildungen von offizieren und soldaten aller truppengattungen, farbendarstellungen, chargen-abzeichen etc. 1895

Kopon Bushido Ye-Zupushi. Pictures of ancient Japanese warriors, illustrated by Moronobu. 1685

Ogawa, K. Military costume in old Japan. 1893

Montenegro

Rottmann, Hans. Die armeen Serbiens und Montenegros. 1909

Sussmann, Anton. Die armeen Serbiens und Montenegros, ihre organisation, bewaffnung, ausrüstung und uniformierung. 1914

Naples (Kingdom)

Collezione degli uniformi del reale esercito, della real marina napoletana. 1844

Gatti. Uniformes de l'armée des Deux-Siciles. ca1840

Zezon, Antonio. Tipi militari dei differenti corpi che compongono il reale esercito e l'armata di mare di S. M. il R. L. del regno delle due Sicilie. 1850-54

Military costume—*Continued*

Netherlands

Lintum, Crist te. Onze schutter-vendels en schutterijen, van vroeger en later tijd, 1550-1908, in beeld en schrift. 1910

Vinkeroy, E. van. Costumes militaires belges du XIe au XVIIIe siècle. 1885

See also Military costume—Belgium

Wars of independence, 1556-1648

Eitzing, Michael, Freiherr von. 1588. Novus ... de leone belgico, eiusque topographia atque historica descriptione liber quinque partibus Gubernatorum Philippi Regis Hispaniarum ordine, distinctus Jn super & elegantissimi illius artificis Francisci Hogenbergii. 1596

Gheyn, Jacob de. Die drillkunst. Das ist kriegsübliche waffenhandlung der musqueten und piquē allen tapfern soldaten zu nutzlicher beliebüng. 1664

Gheyn, Jacob de. The exercise of armes for calivres, muskettes, and pikes. 1608

Gheyn, Jacob de. Trillinbuch. Waffenhandlung von den röhren, musquetten und spiessen. 1610

Gheyn, Jacob de. Wapenhandelinghe van roers musquetten ende spiessen. 1607

Goltzius, Hendrick, and Gheyn, Jacob de. Officers and soldiers of a regiment of infantry of the Netherlands. 1587

17th century

Buren, Hendrik van. Drilkonst, of hedendaaghsche wapen-oeffening. 1672

Commelin, Izaak. Histoire de la vie & actes memorables de Frédéric Henry de Nassau, Prince d'Orange; enrichie de figures en taille douce & fidelement translatée du flamand en françois. 1656

18th century

Afbeeldingen der monteeringen van de gewapende schutterije en burgercorpsen in Nederland. 1789

19th century

Beschrijving der kleeding, equipement en wapening van de Nederlandsche land-, zeemagt en schutterijen, zoo binnen het koningrijk, als in deszelfs overzeesche bezittingen. 1845

Brunings, P. F. Onze krijgsmacht met bijschriften. 1887

Dally, Aristide. L'armée hollandaise. 1887

Gedenk boek der inhuldiging en feesttogten van Zijne Majesteit Wilhelm II. 1840-1842. 1842?

Houtman, J. P. Nederlandsche uniformen. 1815-31

Houtman, J. P. De schutter-en jagerkorps en 1830. 1830

Madou, J. B., and Courtois, A. Militaire costumen van het koninkryk der Nederlanden. ca1824

Die niederländische armee nebst den kolonialtruppen und freiwilligenkorps in ihrer gegenwärtigen uniformierung. 1891

Raa, F. J. G. ten. De uniformen van de nederlandsche zee en landmacht hier te lande en in de kolonien

Teupken, J. F. Beschrijving hoedanig de koninklijke Nederlandsche troepen en alle in militaire betrekking staande personen gekleed, geëquipeerd en gewapend zijn. 1823

Teupken, J. F. Vervolg van de beschrijving hoedanig. 1826

Uniformes des Gardes d'honneur des différens corps dans les sept départements de la Hollande. 1904

Norway

Dally, Aristide. L'armée norvégienne. 1887

Dardel, F. L. von. Den svenske og den norske armees samt marines uniformer. 1863

Havin. Tracé des objets d'habillemens et d'équipement à l'usage de l'armée norvégienne. ca1880

Norska arméens nuvarande uniformer. 1866

Philippine islands

See Military costume—Spain—19th century—Philippine islands army

Poland

Chelminski, J. V. L'armée du duché de Varsovie. 1913

Dietrich, F. Ubiory Wojska Polskiego z csasow kosiestwa warszawskiego. 1831

État actuel de l'armée de Sa Majesté le roi de Pologne ainsi qu'il a été stipulé à la Diète tenue en 1775. 1781

Gembarzewski, Bronislaw. Wojsko Polskie. Krôlestwo Polskie 1815-1830. 1903

Gembarzewski, Bronislaw. Wojsko Polskie. Ksiestvoo Warszawskie 1807-1814. 1905

Heideloff, K. A. von. Aux héros polonais. ca1830

Heideloff, K. A. von, ed. Polnisches militair. 1832

Kozłowski, Karol. Wojsko polskie w roku 1831. 1889

Straszewicz, Joseph. Armée polonaise; révolution du 29 novembre 1830. 1835

Ubiory woyska krôlewsko polskiego. 1829

Urban, K., pseud. Kurze zusammenstellung über die polnische armee. 1931

Portugal

Album de uniformes exercito e armada. 1890

Bradford, William. Sketches of the country, character, and costume, in Portugal and Spain ... made in 1808 and 1809. 1812-1813

Portugal militar; album de uniformes exercito e armada, con decoraçoès militares. 1890

Military costume—*Continued*

Rome, Ancient

Du Choul, Guillaume. Discorso ... sopra la castrametatione, & bagni antichi de i Greci, & Romani. Con l'aggiunta della figura del Campo Romano. Et una informatione della militia turchesca, & de gli habiti de soldati Turchi, scritta da M. Francesco Sansovino. 1582
Du Choul, Guillaume. Discours de la religion des anciens Romains, de la castrametation & discipline militaire d'iceux, des bains & antiques exercitations grecques & romaines. 1567. part 2
Fickelscherer, Martin. Das kriegswesen der alten. 1888
Forestier, Amédée. The Roman soldier; some illustrations representative of Roman military life with special reference to Britain. 1928
Froehner, Wilhelm. La Colonne Trajane, d'après le surmoulage exécuté à Rome en 1861-1862. 1872-74
Lindenschmit, Ludwig. Tracht und bewaffnung des römischen heeres während der kaiserzeit. 1882
Pistolesi, Erasmo. La Colonna Trajana illustrata da ... Pistolesi, disegnata da Salvatore Busuttil. 1846
Rheinhard, Hermann. Griechische und römische kriegsalterthümer für den gebrauch in gelehrtenschulen zusammengestellt. 1859
Weese, Arthur. Die Cäsar-teppiche im Historischen museum zu Bern. 1911

Rumania

Ajduklewicz, T. L'armée roumaine. 1903
Albumul armatei romane. 1873
Sococu, A. J. V. Die rumänische armee in ihrer gegenwärtigen uniformierung. 1893
Sussmann, Anton. Die armeen Rumäniens und Bulgariens; ihre organisation, bewaffnung, ausrüstung und uniformierung. 1914
Uniformes de l'armée roumaine, 1830-1930. 1930

Russia

Balachev. Dessins d'uniformes de l'histoire du regiment de cuirassiers de la garde de S.M. l'Empereur, 1702-1871. 1872
Damaze de Raymond. Tableau historique, géographique, militaire et moral de l'Empire de Russie. 1812
Russia. Voennoîe mînîsterstvo. Peremîeny v" obmundîrovanîî î vooruzhenîî voĭsk" Rossiĭskoĭ împeratorskoĭ armiî. 1857-81
Viskovatov, A. V. Istoritcheskoïe oppissanïe odéjedy i vooroujéniia rossiskich voïsk. 1841-53

18th century

Balzer, Anton, and Walenta, J. Sammlung der merkwürdigsten städte und festungen, welche in den jahren 1788, 1789 und 1790 von den k.k. österreichischen, und kais: russischen armée der pforte abgenommen worden, nach ihrer wahren lage. 1790
Entwurf einer vorstellung der russisch-kayserlichen armee. ca1760
Geisler, C. G. H. Représentation des uniformes de l'armée impériale de la Russie en 88 estampes enluminées. 1793
Le Prince, J. B. Oeuvres de Jean-Baptiste Le Prince. 1782
Orlowski, A. O. Uniformes, drapeaux et voitures militaires russes vers la fin du XVIIIe siècle et au commencement du XIXe. 1882
Vorstellung der russich-kayserlichen armee sowohl infanterie als cavallerie in XVI nach dem leben gemahlten blatten. 1773

19th century (to 1917)

Adam, Georg. Russisches militair im jahr 1814 in Nürnberg nach dem leben. 1814?
Adam, Victor. Armée russe, cavalerie. ca1860
Army of Russia containing the uniforms in portrait of the Russian soldiery. 1807
Backmanson, H. L'empereur Nicolas Alexandrovitch en tenue de 10 régiments dont sa majesté est chef. n.d.
Camena d'Almeida, P. J., and Jongh, Francis de. L'armée russe d'après photographies instantanées exécutés par Mm. de Jongh frères. 1896
Characteristic portraits of the various tribes of Cossacks attached to the allied armies in the campaign of 1815. 1820
Charlemagne, A., and Ladurner, A. Garde impériale Russe. 1848-52
The costume of the Russian army, from a collection of drawings made on the spot, and now in the possession of the Right Honourable The Earl of Kinnaird. 1807
Costumes des troupes russes répresentées en (quatorze) gravures et notice sur les différens peuples qui composent l'armée russe. 1812
Dally, Aristide. L'armée russe. 1887
Drygalski, Albert von, and Zepelin, Constantin von. Russland. 1898
Duplessi-Bertaux, Jean. Recueil des principaux costumes militaires des armées alliées. 1816
Eckert, H. A., Monten, Dietrich, and Schelver, F. Saemmtliche truppen von Europa in characteristischen gruppen dargestellt. 1836-43
Finart, N. Uniformes des armées alliées. ca1815
Gebens. Armée russe 1854-1862. 1862?
Genty, firm, Paris, pub. Costumes militaires. 1814-1815 v 1
Die graugrünen felduniformen der russischen armee und deren abzeichen. 1912
Heicke, Josef. Oesterreichische und russische truppen aus dem ungarischen feldzuge 1849. 1849

Military costume—Russia—19th century (to 1917)—*Continued*

Horschelt, Theodor. Études militaires faîtes au Caucase (1858). 1895-96

Kaiserlich russische soldaten. ca1815

Kiel, L. Uniforms of the Russian army. 1815-1820

Orlowski, A. O. Uniformes, drapeaux et voitures militaires russes vers la fin du XVIIIe siècle et au commencement du XIXe. 1882

Pajol, C. P. V., comte. Armée russe, 1856. 1856

Piratzky, A., and Goubarev. Armée russe de 1855 à 1867. 1867?

Die russische armee in ihrer gegenwärtigen uniformirung. 1891

Sauerweid, Alexandre. Armée russe vers 1815. 1815?

Schadow, J. G. Costumes militaires russes. ca1815

Shenk, V. K. Tablitzi form obmundirovania Russkoy armîi. 1910

Sobranie mundīrov" Rossīĭskoĭ Īmperatorskoĭ Armiī. Izdannoe Chertezhnoĭu Ego Īmperatoskago Vysochestva generad", Īnspektora po Inzhenernoĭ chastī. ca1830

Tettau, Eberhard, freiherr von. Die neue bekleidung und ausrüstung der russischen kavallerie. 1897

Vernet, Pierre. Galerie militaire ou collection complète des uniformes de la Garde impériale russe. 1840-42

Wie sehen die armeen der gegner des dreibundes im kriege aus. 1914

Zimmermann, C. F. Russische militair gruppen. ca1825

1917-date

Russia (1922- (U. S. S. R.) New uniform of the red army. 1922

Sardinia

Bossoli, Carlo. The war in Italy. 1859

Galateri, Pietro. Armata sarda; uniformi antichi et moderni. 1844

Maggi, G. B. Uniformi militari dell'armata di S. M. Sarda. 1844

Pedrone. Uniformi delle truppe di S. S. R. M. il re di Sardegna. 1831-36

Stagnon, A. M. Etat général des uniformes des troupes de S. M. le roi de Sardaigne. 1789

Stagnon, Giuseppe. Uniformi delle truppe di S. S. R. M. (le roi de Sardaigne) 1821

Uniformi e standardi delle truppe di s. s. real maesta Vittorio Amedeo III, re di Sardegna. 1790?

Scotland, Highlands of

Representation of the High-landers, who arrived at the camp of the confederated army, not far off the city of Mayence the 13th of August, 1743. 1744

See also Military costume—England

Serbia

Rottmann, Hans. Die armeen Serbiens und Montenegros. 1909

Sussmann, Anton. Die armeen Serbiens und Montenegros, ihre organisation, bewaffnung, ausrüstung und uniformierung. 1914

Spain

Amades, Joan; Colominas, Josep, and Vila, Pau. Els soldats. 1933-36

Barado y Font, Francisco. Museo militar: historia del ejercito español armas, uniformes, sistemas de combate, instituciones, organizacion del mismo desde los tempos más remotos hasta nuestros diâs. 1889

Clonard, S. M. de S. y A., conde de. Album de la infantiera española desde sus primitivos tiempos hasta el dia. 1861

Clonard, S. M. de S. y A., conde de. Historia organica de las armas de infanteria y caballeria españolas. 1851-59?

18th century

Uniformes de cada regimiento assi de infanteria como de cavalleria de España. 1789

19th century

Album de la artilleria española. 1862

Album de la cavalerie de l'armée espagnole. ca1850

Album descriptivo del ejército y la armada de España. 1884

Barado y Font, Francisco. La vida militar en España. 1888

Bradford, William. Sketches of the country, character, and costume, in Portugal and Spain ... made in 1808 and 1809. 1812-1813

Castro, Fernández de. Cuadernos militares. 1886

Clonard, S. M. de S. y A., conde de. Album de la caballeria española. 1861

Clonard, S. M. de S. y A., conde de. Memorias para la historia de las tropas de la casa real de Espana. 1828

Dally, Aristide. Uniformes de l'armée espagnole. 1887

Giles, J. W. Troupes carlistes. ca1835

Holtzmann, Th. Das spanische militär in Hamburg 1807-8. 1907

Lopez, J. A. Cabrera y su ejército; album de las tropas carlistas de Aragon. 1844

Soldiers of the Carlist army. ca1835

Die spanische armee in ihrer gegenwärtigen uniformirung. 1896

Suhr, Christoffer. Sammlung verschiedener spanischer national-trachten und uniformen der division des Marquis de la Romana, 1807 und 1808 in Hamburg in garnison. ca1808

Vernet, Horace, and Lami, L. E. Manejo del sable. 1819

Villegas, José. Album militar; coleccion de uniformes del ejercito español. 1846

Zambrano, marques, de. Coleccion de uniformes del egercito español. 1830

Zarza, and Vallejo. Ordenes militares. 1884

Military costume—Spain—*Continued*

Philippine islands army

Album de la infanteria y caballeria española del ejercito de Filipinas. 1856

20th century

La Confianza, Madrid. Plates illustrating uniforms and insignia in the Spanish army. ca1919

Spain. Ministerio de la guerra. New uniform regulations of the Spanish army. 1908?

Sweden

Engelhart, Gustaf. Svenska armens och flottans officers—och civilmilitära uniformer jemte gradbeteckingar samt armens och flottans indelning. 1886

Mankell, Julius. Anteckningar rörande svenska regementernas historia. 1866

Schützercrantz, Adolf. Svenska krigsmaktens fordna och närvarande munderingar. 1849-53

Strokirch, Einar von, illus. Kungliga lifgardet till häst. 1914

Strokirch, Einar von. Svenska arméns munderingar 1680-1905. 1911-12

18th century

Roos, Cajetan. Samling af Swenska armeens uniformer. Recueil des uniformes de l'armée suédoise. 1788

19th century

Bagge, Göran. Armée suédoise. 1887

Burman, J. J. Anteckningar, förda under tiden från år 1785 till år 1816 jemte relation om Savolaks-brigadens operationer under 1808 och 1809 års krig. 1865

Dardel, F. L. von. Den svenske og den norske armees samt marines uniformer. 1863

Eben, Frédéric, baron d'. The Swedish army; Modèles de l'uniforme militaire adopté dans l'armée royale de Suède. 1808

Eckert, H. A., Monten, Dietrich, and Schelver, F. Saemmtliche truppen von Europa in characteristischen gruppen dargestellt. 1836-43

Eklund, P. B. Svenska arméns och flottans nuvarande uniformer ... Die schwedische armee und marine in ihrer gegenwärtigen uniformirung. 1890

Fritze, C. E., pub. Svenska arméens och flottans nuvarande uniformer. ca1880

Huldberg, Adolf, pub. Svenska arméens uniformer. 1842

Kongl. Svenska arméens uniformer. 1824-25

Nordmann. Svenska armeens. 1864

Nyblaeus, G. A. Scener ur indelta soldatens lif. 1867

Söderberg, Gustaf. Kongl. svenska arméens uniformer. 1834

20th century

Die schwedische armee in ihrer gegenwärtigen uniformierung. 1906

Switzerland

Arnoux, Guy. A la gloire des soldats suisses. 1917

Dictionnaire historique et biographique de la Suisse. 1921-34

Elgger, Karl von. Kriegswesen und kriegskunst der schweizerischen eidgenossen im XIV-XVI jahrhundert. 1873

Escher, A. von. Die Schweizer regimenter in fremden diensten 1515-1860; Les régiments suisses au service étranger. 1903

Perron, Ch. Armée suisse. 1862

Pochon, A., and Zesiger, A. Schweizer militär vom jahr 1700 bis auf die neuzeit. 1906

See also Swiss guards

16th century

Landsknechte mit den bannern von Schweizer cantonen. ca1550

17th century

Collection of New Year's plates of the Company of constabulary and firemen in Zurich, 1689-1779. 1780?

18th century

Collection of New Year's plates of the Company of constabulary and firemen in Zurich, 1689-1779. 1780?

Engelbrecht, Martin. Pictures of Swiss uniforms. ca1792

Escher, A. von. Die Schweizer milizen im 18 und 19 jahrhundert. Les milices suisses aux XVIIIe et XIXe siècles. 1903

Escher, A. von. Die Schweizerische cavallerie im XVII, XVIII und XIX jahrhundert. La cavalerie suisse de 1694 à 1880. ca1903

Feyerabend, Franz. Costumes militaires des cantons de la Suisse. 1792

Meister, Léonard. Beschreibung der gemeineidgenossischen truppensendung nach Basel und der abreise der Zürchessen mannschaft am 31ten May, 1792. ca1792

Samlung der neu-jahr-kupferen ausgegeben von der Militarischen gesellschaft in Zürich. 1744-98

Volmar, Émile. Officiers et soldats des différents contingents des cantons suisses réunis à Bâle en 1792. 1792?

19th century

Beck, August. Schweizer militair album. ca1860

Eckert, H. A., Monten, Dietrich, and Schelver, F. Saemmtliche truppen von Europa in characteristischen gruppen dargestellt. 1836-43

Escher, A. von. Die Helvetische legion, 1798-1804. 1903

Escher, A. von. Die Schweizer milizen im 18 und 19 jahrhundert. Les milices suisses aux XVIIIe et XIXe siècles. 1903

Escher, A. von. Die Schweizerische cavallerie im XVII, XVIII und XIX jahrhundert. La cavalerie suisse de 1694 à 1880. ca1903

Military costume—Switzerland—19th century—*Continued*

Escher, A. von. Uniformierung und ausrüstung der schweizerischen armee von II januar 1898. ca1900

Estoppey, D. L'armée suisse. 1894

Exerzier-reglement für die Eidgenössische linien u. leichte infanterie. Abt I. Soldaten-schule. 1799-1804

Wolf, E. Schweizerische armee; armée suisse. ca1850

20th century

Audeoud, Alfred. Notre armée. 1915

Huber, Emil. Schweizer militär, ein Album von 24 farbigen blättern, originale vom militär-maler Emil Huber ... L'armée suisse. 1915

Kindler, Alfred. Die schweizerische armee in bildern; album militaire suisse. 1903

Peter Cailler Kohler Swiss chocolates co., inc. Colored illustrations of Swiss soldiers showing uniforms and equipment, mobilization 1914. 1914?

Sommerfeld, F. Die schweizer armee, ihre organisation, bewaffnung, ausrüstung, uniformen und abzeichen. 1915

Uniformen und abzeichen der schweizerischen armee; Uniformes et insignes de l'armée suisse. 1927?

Turkey

16th century

Du Choul, Guillaume. Discorso ... sopra la castrametatione, & bagni antichi de i Greci, & Romani; con l'aggiunta della figura del Campo Romano, et una informatione della militia turchesca, & de gli habiti de soldati Turchi, scritta da M. Francesco Sansovino. 1582

18th century

The military costume of Turkey, illustrated by a series of engravings from drawings made on the spot. 1818

Vorstellung der vorzüglichsten gattungen des türckischen militairs und ihrer officiere. ca1760

19th century

Heicke, Josef. Serassaner und Croaten. 1849

Knoetel, Richard. Die türkische armee und marine in ihrer gegenwärtigen uniformirung. 1897

Uniformes de l'armée turque en 1828. 1828

20th century

Mach, Richard von. Die wehrmacht der Türkei und Bulgariens. 1905

Sussmann, Anton. Die armeen der Türkei und Griechenlands, ihre organisation, bewaffnung, ausrüstung und uniformierung. 1914

United States

Gardiner, A. B. The uniforms of the American army. 1877

Jenks, Tudor. Our army for our boys. 1906

Logan, J. A. The volunteer soldier of America. 1887

United States. Quartermaster corps. The army of the United States; illustrated by forty-four fac-simile plates from water color drawings by H. A. Ogden. Text by Henry Loomis Nelson. 1885?

United States. Quartermaster corps. Uniform of the army of the United States (illustrated) from 1774 to 1907. 1890-1909

Wagner, A. L., and Kelley, J. D. J. Our country's defensive forces in war and peace. The United States army and navy; their histories, from the era of the revolution to the close of the Spanish-American war; with accounts of their organization, administration, and duties. 1899

Walton, William. Army and navy of the United States from the period of the revolution to the present day. 1900

See also subdivision United States under Coast guard; Marine corps; Military cadets

Massachusetts

Prang, Louis & company, publishers. Military types of the U. S. militia and National guard, past and present. (State of Massachusetts.) 1893

Texas

Texas (Republic) War department. General regulations for the government of the army of the Republic of Texas. 1839

Revolutionary period 1775-1783

Bolton, C. K. The private soldier under Washington. 1902

Fitzpatrick, J. C. The Continental army uniform. 1920

Lefferts, C. M. Uniforms of the American, British, French and German armies in the war of the American revolution, 1775-1783. 1926

United States. George Washington bicentennial commission. George Washington play and pageant costume book. c1931

French troops

Malo, Servan. Ceux de Yorktown; uniformes et drapeaux, d'après des documents officiels de l'epoque. 1918

Philadelphia

Philadelphia city cavalry. First troop. History of the First troop Philadelphia city cavalry from its organization Nov. 17th 1774 to its centennial anniversary, November 17th, 1874. 1875

1812-1860

Album of drawings, in pencil and watercolors, made during the Sioux troubles of 1851-52, and the Sioux rising of 1863 under Little Crow. 1863?

Military costume—United States—1812-1860 —*Continued*

United States. War department. Regulations for the uniform & dress of the army of the United States, June, 1851. 1851

See also Military costume—U.S.—Texas

1860-1865

Johnson, Rossiter. Campfire and battlefield; a history of the conflicts and campaigns of the great civil war in the United States. 1896

United States. War department. Regulations for the uniform and dress of the army of the United States, 1861. 1861

Confederate army

Confederate States of America. War department. Regulations for the army of the Confederate States, and for the Quartermaster's and Pay departments. 1861

Confederate States of America. War department. Uniform and dress of the army of the Confederate States. 1861

1865-1898

Bresler, A. L. Die armee der Vereinigten Staaten von Nord-Amerika. 1891

Rodenbough, T. F., comp. From everglade to cañon with the second dragoons (second United States cavalry) 1875

United States. Quartermaster corps. Regulations for the uniform of the army of the United States. 1888

United States. Quartermaster corps. Report of the Quartermaster to the Secretary of war, 1876

United States. Quartermaster corps. Uniform of the arvmy of the United States, 1882. 1882

United States. War department. Regulations for the uniform and dress of the army of the United States, July 1872. 1872

1898-1917

Archibald, J. F. J. Blue shirt and khaki. 1901

Christy, H. C. Men of the army and navy; characteristic types of our fighting men. 1899

Falls, De W. C. Die armee der Vereinigten Staaten von Amerika. [1914]

Falls, De W. C. Army and navy information. 1917

New York (State) Adjutant general's office. Regulations relating to the uniform of the National guard of the state of New York 1899. 1899

United States. Army. Regulations for the uniform of the U. S. army, 1914

United States. Quartermaster corps. Specifications for the uniform of the United States army, 1915

United States. Quartermaster corps. Uniform of the army of the United States, October 1, 1908. 1908

United States. Shipping board. Manual of uniforms and insignia. 191-?

United States. War department. Regulations and decisions pertaining to the uniform of the army of the United States ... 3d ed. 1899

United States. War department. Regulations for the uniform of the United States army ... 1907

Volk, C. G. United States officers' uniforms, army, navy, marine corps. 1917

Warnock uniform company. Uniforms and equipments for officers' national guard. 1900

Army transport service

United States. Quartermaster corps. Regulations prescribing flags, signals, funnel marks, etc., also uniforms of the United States army transport service. 1899

United States. Quartermaster corps. Regulations prescribing uniforms of the United States army transport service and harbor boat service, including mine planters and cable boats, also flags, signals, funnel marks, etc. 1912

1917-date

Jonas, Lucien. L'armée américaine, 1918. c1919

United States. War department. Regulations for the uniform of the United States army. 1917

Women's uniforms

National society of the colonial dames of America. Report of the Committee on relics; uniforms of women worn during the war. 1922

Yugoslavia

Yugoslavia. Laws, statutes, etc. Uredba o odeći suvozemne vojske. 1924

See also Military costume—Montenegro

Croatia and Slavonia

Boppe, P. L. H. La Croatie militaire (1809-1813): Les régiments croates à la grande armée. 1900

Military costume in old Japan. Ogawa, K.

The **military** costume of Europe; exhibited in a series of highly-finished military figures, in the uniform of their several corps, with a concise description, and historical anecdotes; forming memoirs of the various armies at the present time. London, J. Booth 1822

2v. 96 col.pl. F.

Plates are inscribed: Published by T. Goddard ... and I. Booth. In addition to the French, Italian, Dutch, Austrian, Saxon, Prussian, Russian, Swedish, Danish and Spanish armies, the following British regiments are illustrated: 1st and 2d life guards; horse guards blue; 5th dragoon guards; 7th, 10th, 12th, 13th, 15th, 17th, 18th light dragoons; horse and foot artillery; 1st, 2d, 9th, 25th, 73d, 79th, 87th, 95th and 97th regiments of foot; besides groups of troops of the line, light troops and foreign troops in the pay of Great Britain

Colas notes an earlier edition (London, T. Goddard and J. Booth 1812. 2v. 96 col.pl. Q.)

Colas 2058 (1812 ed.) Lipperheide 2115 (1812 ed.) LC A27-214

The **military** costume of India. James, Charles

The **military** costume of Turkey, illustrated by a series of engravings from drawings made on the spot. London, T. McClean 1818
30 l. col.front. 29 col.pl. F.
Shows costume of late 18th century
Colas 2059. Lipperheide 2388

Military costumes of the British cavalry. Heath, William

Military footwear. See Footwear, Military

Military garments formerly worn in England. See Meyrick, Sir S. R. Observations on the military garments formerly worn in England

The **military** history of Prince Eugene of Savoy. Dumont, Jean, baron de Carlscroon, and Rousset de Missy, Jean

Military incidents. Newhouse, C. B.

Military religious orders

Bar, J. C. Coleccion de los trages de todas las ordenes religiosas y militares de todo el mundo. ca1790

Bar, J. C. Costumes religieux et militaires des Mameluks, Arabes, Turcs, Orientaux, etc; Costumes religieux et militaires des peuples de l'Orient, des templiers, des chanoins et chevaliers de la Syrie, de la Palestine, d'Egypte, d'Ethiopie, d'Afrique et de l'Inde (*In* his Receuil de tous les costumes des ordres religieux et militaires, avec un abrégé historique et chronologique enrichi de notes et de planches coloriées, v 1-2. 1779-1789)

Biedenfeld, F. L. C. freiherr von. Geschichte und verfassung aller geistlichen und weltlichen, erloschenen und blühenden ritterorden. Nebst einer übersicht sämmtlicher militär- und civilehrenzeichen, medaillen &. &. und einem atlas ... Zugleich als fortsetzung von dessen geschichte der mönchsund klosterfrauenorden im Orient und Occident 1841

Buonanni, Filippo. Ordinum equestrium et militarium catalogus in imaginibus expositus & cum brevi narratione. 1711

Buonanni, Filippo. Verzeichniss der geist und weltlichen ritter-orden in netten abbildungen und einer kurtzen erzehlung in lateinisch und italienischer sprache. 1720

Burke, Sir J. B. The book of orders of knighthood and decorations of honour of all nations. 1858

Dithmar, J. C. Justus Christoph Dithmars Nachrichten von dem ... englischen kriegs- und ritterorden des Budes, worinn desselben ursprung ... erkläret, und der ... ritter namen, titel und wapenschilder ... dargestellet werden. 1744

Doyé, F. von S. Die alten trachten der männlichen und weiblichen orden sowie der geistlichen mitglieder der ritterlichen orden. 1930

Giacchieri, Pietro. Commentario degli ordini equestri esistenti negli stati di santa chiesa. 1853

Giucci, Gaetano. Iconografia storica degli ordini religiosi e cavallereschi. 1836-47

Giustinian, Bernardo. Historie cronologiche dell' origine degl' ordini militari e di tutte le religioni cavalleresche. 1692

Guigue de Champvans, Frédéric. Histoire et législation des ordres de chevalerie. 1932-33

Lawrence-Archer, J. H. The orders of chivalry. 1887

Megiser, Hieronymus. Ein tractat von dem dreyfachen ritterstand und allen ritter orden der Christenheit. 1593

Micheli y Marquez, José. Tesoro militar de cavalleria antiguo y moderno modo de armar cavalleros, y professar, segun las ceremonias de qualquier orden militar ... insignias y abito de cada una. 1642

Perrot, A .M. Collection historique des ordres de chevalerie civils et militaires, existant chez les différens peuples du monde. 1820

Schoonebeek, Adriaan. Historie van alle ridderlyke en krygs-orders. 1697

See also Teutonic Knights

The **military** shoe. Salquin, S. A.

Military types of the U. S. militia. Prang, Louis & company, publishers

Millais, John Guille

(illus.) Prichard, H. V. H. Through the heart of Patagonia

Mille

(illus.) Thirifocq. Histoire universelle du costume

Mille, E. See Compte-Calix, F. C., jt. auth.

Miller, Edward Darley

Modern polo, ed. by L. V. L. Simmonds; 3d ed. rev. and enl. London, Hurst and Blackett [1911]
576p. front. illus. pl.
Illustrations show dress worn by polo players

Miller, Frances Sue, and Laitem, Mrs Helen (Hollman)

Personal problems of the high school girl. Lakewood, O. The Lakewood high school print shop [c1935]
141p. illus. O.
Contents: The high school girl and her clothes; The high school girl in relation to the family income; The health of the high school girl; The social life of the high school girl; The mental life of the high school girl; Bibliography p135-38
LC 35-23590

Miller, Francis Trevelyan, and Lanier, Robert Sampson

(eds.) The photographic history of the civil war ... thousands of scenes photographed 1861-65, with text by many special authorities. New York, Review of reviews 1911
10v. fronts. illus.(incl. ports.) maps. Q.
Another issue, without the narrative text, and with illustrative material rearranged, appeared under title: *Photographing the civil war,* by Henry Wysham Lanier, same publisher and date
LC 11-11566

Miller, Hugo H.
Philippine hats. Manila, Bureau of printing 1910
61p. illus. XXI pl. O. ([Philippine islands] Bureau of education. Bulletin no33, 1910)
LC E11-374

Miller, Jack Humphrey. See Carruthers, A. D. M. Unknown Mongolia

Miller, Mabel Verdilla. See Boyd, A. M., jt. auth.

Miller, René Fülöp-. See Fülöp-Miller, René

Miller, Ruth Scott
(tr.) Worth, J. P. A century of fashion

Miller, William
(pub.) Alexander, William. The costume of Turkey
(pub.) The costume of the Russian Empire, illustrated by a series of seventy-three engravings

[**Milles, Thomas**]
The catalogue of honor; or, Tresury of true nobility, peculiar and proper to the Isle of Great Britaine: that is to say: a collection historicall of all the free monarches as well kinges of England as Scotland (nowe united togither) with the princes of Walles, dukes, marquisses and erles; their wives, children, alliances, families, descentes & achievements of honor ... Translated out of Latyne into English. London, Printed by W. Iaggard 1610
5p.l. 99,[8],240,[289]-1130p. 1 l. incl. illus. pl. F.
"Epistle dedicatory" signed: Thomas Milles. The work was begun by R. Glover and left with Milles to translate and reduce to method. He was assisted in its preparation by Lord William Howard, Sir Robert Cotton, William Camden, Nicholas Charles, and others
English edition of *Nobilitas politica* much enlarged to form a register of the English nobility
LC 15-25140

Nobilitas politica vel civilis. Personas scilicet distinguendi et ab origine inter gentes, ex principium gratia nobilitandi forma ... quò tandem & apud Anglos, qui sint nobilium gradus, & quæ ad nobilitatis fastigia euchendi ratio, ostenditur. Londini, G. Jaggard 1608
190p. 9pl. F.
Lipperheide 1788

Miller, Thomas K. & co.
(pub.) American racing colors

Millin, Aubin Louis
Antiquités nationales, ou Recueil de monumens pour servir à l'histoire générale et particulière de l'empire françois, tels que tombeaux, inscriptions, statues, vitraux, fresques, etc.; tirés des abbayes, monastères, châteaux et autres lieux devenus domaines nationaux. Paris, Drouhin 1790-[99]
5v. pl. plans. Q.
Many of the illustrations show French costume from the middle ages to the 17th century
LC 3-23584

The **Milliner** and dressmaker, and warehouseman's gazette, and illustrated journal of the new modes. no 1-136; 1870-1881. London
Q.
Merged into *Moniteur de la mode*

The **Milliner,** dressmaker and draper. no 1-10, May 1881-Jan. 1882. London
Absorbed the *Illustrated household journal.* Merged into *Moniteur de la mode*

Millinery. Aiken, C. R.

Millinery, theoretical and practical. Hill, Clare

Millinery trade review. v 1, 1876+ New York, Millinery trade pub. co.
Illus. Q. $4
Published monthly. Current 1938

Millot, Claude François Xavier. See Paciaudi, P. M. Descrizione delle feste celebrate in Parma l'anno MDCCLXIX per le auguste nozze di ... l'infante Don Ferdinando colla ... arciduchessa Maria Amalia

Mills, Mrs Winifred (Harrington) and Dunn, Mrs Louise M.
Marionettes, masks and shadows; illus. by Corydon Bell. Garden City, N. Y., Doubleday, Page 1927
270p. incl. illus. pl. col.front. pl. double map. O.
Bibliography: p241-62
LC 28-594

Miln, Mrs Louise (Jordan)
When we were strolling players in the east. New York, Charles Scribner's sons 1894
xiv,354p. front. pl. O.
Some of the plates show costume of Ceylon, Burma, and India
LC A34-3160

Wooings and weddings in many climes. Chicago & New York, H. S. Stone 1900
xx,395p. front. pl. O.
LC A13-2663

Milne, James
Gordon Highlanders. London, J. Macqueen 1898
110p. illus. O. 1s

Milne, Mrs Leslie
Shans at home; with two chapters on Shan history and literature by the Rev. Wilbur Willis Cochrane. London, J. Murray 1910
xxiv,289p. col.front. illus. pl. ports. map, facsims. O.
LC A11-2006

1588. Novus ... de leone belgico. Eitzing, Michael, Freiherr von

Miltitz, Carl Borromäus Alexander Stephan von. See note under Retzsch, F. A. M. Gallerie zu Shakspeare's dramatischen werken

Milton, Thomas
(engr.) Mayer, Ludwig. Views in Egypt

Miltoun, Francis, pseud. See Mansfield, M. F.

La **mimica** degli antichi investigata nel gestire napoletano. Jorio, Andrea de

Mimische darstellungen für schauspieler und zeichner. Iffland, A. W.

Minamoto, Hoshu
An illustrated history of Japanese art; trans. from the Japanese by Harold G. Henderson. Kyoto, K. Hoshino 1935
ix,264p. col.front. pl.(part col. 1 double) Q.
Shows Japanese costume from early times until the 19th century
LC 36-9490

Mince de trognes!!! Jossot

Mincoff-Marriage, Mrs Elizabeth, and Marriage, Mrs Margaret S.
Pillow lace; with illustrations by Ernest Marriage and fifty patterns. London, J. Murray 1907
xii,231p. front. illus. pl.(2 fold.) O.
Shows lace of various countries in the 16th to 20th centuries
LC 8-5855

Miners
Der belehrende bergmann. 1830
Geschichte und beschreibung des sächsischen bergbaues. Nebst ... abbildungen der sächsischen berg- und hüttenleute in ihren neuesten staatstrachten. 1827

16th century

Agricola, Georg. Berckwerck buch, darinn nicht allain alle empte instrument gezeug und alles so zu diesem handel gehörig mit figuren vorgebildet und klärlich beschriben. 1580
Agricola, Georg. Bergwerck buch. 1621
Agricola, Georg. De re metallica. 1556
Agricola, Georg. De re metallica; tr. by H. C. Hoover and L. H. Hoover. 1912
Agricola, Georg. Vom Bergkwerck XII bucher darin alle empter, instrument, bezeuge, unnd alles zu disem handel gehörig ... beschriben seindt. 1557

17th century

Lohneyss, G. E. Bericht vom bergwerck wie man dieselben bawen und in guten wolstande bringen sol, sampt allen dazu gehörigen arbeiten. 1690

18th century

Weigel, Christoph. Icones omnium ad officinas aerarias pertinentium officialium et operariorum. 1710?
Weigel, Christoph. Icones omnium ad rem metallicam spectantium officialium et operariorum. 1710?

19th century

Heuchler, Eduard. Die bergknappen in ihren berufs- und familienleben. 1857
Rambosson, J. P. Les pierres précieuses et les principaux ornements. 1870

Mineur, Antoine Estienne
A charitable remonstrance addressed to the wives and maidens of France, touching their dissolute adornments, together with two curious elegies; translated from the French ... by William Rooke. Edinburgh, E. & G. Goldsmid, printers 1887
56p. O. (Collectanea adamantæa, 21)
Notes on fashion in dress (p38-56) give a survey of costume in England from early times until the middle 19th century, also a discussion of hair styles from the time of the ancient Egyptians, and three pages on the fan

La **miniature** carolingienne. Boinet, Amédée

Die **miniaturen** der Manesseschen liederhandschrift. Kraus, F. X.

Die **miniaturen** des Codex Egberti in der Stadt-bibliothek zu Trier. Kraus, F. X.

Miniaturen und silhouetten. Boehn, Max von

Die **miniaturen** zu dem Hamburgischen stadtrechte vom jahre 1497. Lappenberg, J. M.

Miniatures and silhouettes. Boehn, Max von

Miniatures choisies de la Bibliothèque du Vatican. See Beissel, Stephan. Vaticanische miniaturen

Miniaturmalerei im islamischen Orient. Kühnel, Ernst

Minister's Gazette of fashion. v 1, 1846+ London, E. Minister
Illus. col.pl. Q.
Title varies: 1846-88, *Gazette of fashion and cutting room companion*
Absorbed the *West End gazette*, Jan. 1930
Colas 1203. Lipperheide 4654

Un **ministre** des modes sous Louis XVI. Nouvion, Pierre de, and Liez, Émile

Minnesänger aus der zeit der Hohenstaufen. Manesse, Rüdiger

Minnesingers
Hagen, F. H. von der. Handschriftengemölde und andere bildliche denkmäler der deutschen dichter des 12.-14. jahrhunderts. 1853
Manesse, Rüdiger. Minnesänger aus der zeit der Hohenstaufen, im vierzehnten jahrhundert. 1850
Weingartner liederhandschrift. 1843
Zangemeister, K. F. W. Die wappen, helmzierden und standarten der Grossen Heidelberger liederhandschrift (Manesse-codex) 1892

Minoan costume. See Crete—Ancient

Minutoli, Wolfradine (von der Schulenburg) von Watzdorf, freiherrn von
Mes souvenirs d'Égypte; revus et publiés par M. Raoul-Rochette. Paris, Nepveu 1826
2v. 9 col.pl. S.
Also known with plates in black and white. German edition: Leipzig 1829
Colas 2060. Lipperheide 1585

Miomandre, Francis de
La mode. [Paris] Hachette [1927]
60p. S. (Notes et maximes)
Colas 2061. LC 28-362

Miquel y Badía, Francisco
Industrias artísticas; alfarería, terra cotta, mayólica, loza, porcelana, vidrio, bronce, orfebrería, joyería, armas. Su historia y descripción. 2. ed., ilustrada con 75 grabados. Barcelona, A. J. Bastinos 1892
2p.l. 260p. illus. pl. O. (Biblioteca Minerva)
LC 34-12314

Miró y Argenter, José Ignacio
Estudio de las piedras preciosas, su historia y caractéres en bruto y labradas con la descripcion de las joyas mas notables de la corona de España y del monasterio del Escorial. Madrid, Imprenta á cargo de C. Moro 1870
4p.l. xi,[12]-288,[3]p. 12pl. O.
LC GS33-225

Le **miroir** des dames. Grévedon, P. L. H.

Miroir des dames. Philipon, Charles

Miroir des graces. Mazeret, Constantin, and Perrot, A. M.

Le **miroir** des graces. See The mirror of the graces

Miroir des modes parisiennes. Paris, Janet ca1824
180p. 8 col.pl. O.
Colas 2066

Le **miroir** des plus belles courtisannes de ce temps. Passe, Crispijn van de

Miroir du salut humain. See Speculum humanæ salvationis. Speculum humanæ salvationis cum speculo S. Mariae virginis, latine et germanice

The **mirror** of the graces; or, the English lady's costume, combining and harmonizing taste and judgment, elegance and grace, modesty, simplicity, and economy with fashion in dress ... by a lady of distinction. London, B. Crosly 1811
241p. 4pl. D.
French edition has title: *Le miroir des graces* (Paris, Galignani 1811. 200p. 4pl. D.) The American edition (Boston, F. S. Hill 1831. 192p. S.) has no illustrations
Colas 2065 (Fr. ed.) Lipp. 3252 (Fr. ed.)

A **miscellany** of arms and armor, presented ... bashford. Armor and arms club, New York

Les **miseres** et les mal-heurs de la guerre. Callot, Jacques

The **miser's** daughter. Ainsworth, W. H.

The **Mishongnovi** ceremonies of the snake and antelope fraternities. Dorsey, G. A., and Voth, H. R.

Misson, François Maximilian
Herrn Maximilian Missons Reisen aus Holland durch Deutschland in Italien. Leipzig, T. Fritsch 1701
1136p. 4 illus. 51pl. O.
Plates show feminine costume of Nuremberg, Strasbourg, and Augsburg, also the doges of Venice and Genoa
Lipperheide 550

Missy, Jean Rousset de. See Rousset de Missy, Jean

Mrs Fitzherbert and George IV. Wilkins, W. H.

Mrs Leach's complete guide to crochet work. Leach, Mrs

Mrs Leach's knitting lessons. Leach, Mrs

Mistresses of the White House. See Hoes, Mrs R. G. Dresses of the mistresses of the White House

Mitelli, Giuseppe Maria
Entrata solenne dell' ... Confaloniero di Giustizia, che si fà ogni bimestre nel palazzo publico di Bologna. [Bologna 1700?]
6pl. F.
Lipperheide 2754

(illus.) Carracci, Annibale. L'arti per via

(illus.) Carracci, Annibale. Di Bologna, l'arti per via. 1660

Miters
Geldart, Ernest. Ecclesiastical decoration. 1889
Seesselberg, W. F., ed. Helm und mitra; studien und entwürfe in mittelalterlicher kunst. 1905?

[**Mitford, John**]
My cousin in the army: or Johnny Newcome on the peace establishment; a poem, by a staff officer. London, printed for J. Johnston 1822
316p. col.front. 15 col.pl. O.
Colored plates by C. Williams

Mitres. See Miters

Mitreuter, Heinrich Ditlev, and others
Croquis russes, par H. Mitreuter, W. Timm Svertschkoff & O. Ludwig. Paris, Lemercier 1844-45
17 col.pl. F.
Lipperheide 1361

Mitteilungen aus dem Germanischen national-museum. Nuremberg. Germanisches national museum

Das **mittelalter.** Kleinpaul, R. A. R.

Mittelalterliches hausbuch; bilderhandschrift des 15. jahrhunderts mit vollständigem text und facsimilierten abbildungen ... vorworte von dr. A. Essenwein. Frankfurt a. M., H. Keller 1887
xii,58p. 28pl. Q.
A source book for costume of the 15th century
Lipperheide 469

Mittheilungen aus dem museum für deutsche volkstrachten. See Berlin. Museum für deutsche volkstrachten und erzeugnisse des hausgewerbes

Mittheilungen über alte trachten und hausrath, wohn- und lebensweise der Saar- und Moselbevölkerung. See Pelser-Berensberg, Franz von. Mittheilungen über trachten

Mittheilungen über trachten, hausrat, wohn und lebensweise im Rheinland. Pelser-Berensberg, Franz von

Die **mittlere** reitschule. Anderson, E. L.

Mitton, Geraldine Edith
Austria-Hungary. London, A. and C. Black 1914
214p. col.front. col.pl. fold.map. O.
LC 15-1383

Jane Austen and her times. London, Methuen [1905]
viii,334p. 21pl. (incl.front. ports.) O.
Contains material on fashions of the late 18th century in England
LC 6-2322

Normandy; by Nico Jungman, text by G. E. Mitton. London, A. and C. Black [1905]
xii,192p. 40 col.pl. (incl.front.) O. 10s, o.p.
Costume index. LC w6-83

People of India. See entry under Menpes, Mortimer

Mobiliario liturgico. See Villaamil y Castro, José. Inventarios de mobiliario litúrgico

Mobilier. Duret, D., abbé

Mobisson, Ferdinand
(ed.) Costumes of the modern stage. London, J. C. Nimmo 1889-91
5pts. col.pl. F.
Each part contains a review of a play given at a Paris theater with portraits of some of the actors in costume

Moccasins. See Footwear, Moccasins

Moccasins and their relation to the Arctic footwear. Hatt, Gudmund

Mochetti, V.
(engr.) Bertini, A. Costumi di Roma e dei contorni

Moda. 1919-1936? Roma, Federazione nazionale fascista industria abbiglimento
Illus. F. 50 l., foreign 75 l.
Published monthly, September to June. Current 1938?

La **moda.** Boehn, Max von

Moda, 1790-1900. Martini, Angela

La **Moda** elegante illustrada, periodico de las familias. I.-XLIV. año, 1842-1885. Madrid
44v. col.pl. F.
Colas 2069. Lipperheide 4642

Moda maschile; revista mensile illustrata di tecnica professionale e commerciale ad uso del sarto da uomo. Anno 1, 1907+ Milano
Col.illus. pl.(part fold.) F. L.35
Periodical of men's fashions. Published monthly. Current 1938. Various numbers include supplementary plates and patterns

Die **Mode;** journal für damentoilette mit Pariser original-modebildern, muster- und schnitt-beilagen. 1.-22. jahrg; 1853-1874. Hamburg, Kittler
22v. illus.(part col.) Q.
Published weekly

La **mode.** Bizet, René

De **mode.** Hulst, L. van

La **mode.** Jégoudez, Mme

La **mode.** Miomandre, Francis de

La **Mode** artistique; publiée par Gustave Janet; recueil de modes nouvelles coloriées et gouachées à l'aquarelle. 1.-? années, 1869-1899? Paris, Bureaux de La Mode artistique
Col.illus. F.
Title change: 1897-99? *Les Nouveautés parisiennes et La Mode artistique réunies*
Colas 2074. Lipperheide 4728

Das **mode-buch.** See Caraccioli, L. A. de. Le livre à la mode

La **Mode** chic. Année 1, 1928+ Paris, G. P. Joumard
Illus.(part col.) pl. Q. 32fr., foreign 44fr.
Includes fashions for women and children and needlework patterns. Published monthly. Current 1938
Absorbed *Très parisien* Oct. 1936

La **mode** d'Augsbourg. Engelbrecht, Martin

La **Mode** de Paris. v 1-?; 1859-1882? [Paris]
Col.pl. F.
Colas 2076. Lipperheide 4688

La **Mode** de Paris, L'Illustrateur des dames ... réunis. See L'Illustrateur des dames et des demoiselles

La **mode** de Strasbourg. See Dieterlin, Petrus. Strasburgisch trachtenbuchlein

La **Mode** des demoiselles. Juillet 1845-mai 1848. Paris
Col.pl. F.
Colas 2077

La **mode** des habits et vestementz des femmes de diverses nations. Lochom, Michiel van

Mode du jour. Paris, Basset ca1815
16 col.pl. Q.
Plates show fashions of the period. The first twelve are after designs by Desrais and are engraved by Blanchard, Florion, Fortier, and Demonchy. For list of plates see Colas's *Bibliographie*
Colas 2078

La **mode** et la coquetterie. Green, E. M.

La **mode** et la couture. Dörig, James

La **mode** féminine à travers les âges. Rouit, H.

La **mode** féminine au XVIIIe siècle. Hennezel, Henri d'

La **Mode** féminine de 1490 à 1920. Paris, Nilsson 1926
240 col.pl. Q.
Contents: v 1 1490-1795; v2 1795-1900; v3 1900-1920
Each volume contains four series of 20 plates each. Colas notes an English translation of volume 2: *A century of French fashion and costume* (London, Batsford)
Colas 576. Costume index

La **Mode** française. 1.-12. année, 1875-1886? Paris
Col.pl. Q.
Colas 2081. Lipperheide 4753

La **Mode** illustrée. 1. année, 1860+ Paris, Firmin Didot; London, Asher
Illus. pl.(part col.) F. 40fr., foreign 56fr.
Published weekly. Current 1937
Contains patterns and designs for needlework
Colas 2082. Lipperheide 4690

Die **mode** im alten Rom. Frölich, Franz

Die **mode** in der frauenkleidung. Grünwald-Zerkovitz, Frau Sidonie

Die **mode** in der karikatur. Wendel, Friedrich

The **mode** in dress and home. Donovan, D. G.

Die **mode** in fünf jahrhunderten. Bruhn, Wolfgang

Mode in Paris. Porada, Käthe von

Die **mode;** menschen und moden im achtzehnten jahrhundert. Boehn, Max von

Die **mode;** menschen und moden im mittelalter. Boehn, Max von

Die **mode;** menschen und moden im neunzehnten jahrhundert. Boehn, Max von

Die **mode;** menschen und moden im sechzehnten jahrhundert. Boehn, Max von

Die **mode;** menschen und mode im siebzehnten jahrhundert. Boehn, Max von

La **Mode** nationale. 1. année, 1885-1930. Paris, 1885-1930
Illus. Q.-F. 18fr., foreign 30fr.
Published monthly
Colas 2083. Lipperheide 4783

La **Mode** nouvelle; littérature, religion, histoire [etc.] Oct. 1829-nov. 1862. Paris
Col.illus. O.
Title varies: Oct. 1829-15 sept. 1854, *La mode, revue des modes;* 25 sept.-5 dec. 1854 *La revue universelle.* Subtitle varies
Colas 2070-72. Lipperheide 4613

Mode nuove, rivista di alta moda. See Mode revue

La **mode** par l'image du XIIe au XVIIe siècle. Paris, A. Michel 1903
66 illus. D. 3fr. 50
Colas 2087

La **Mode** pratique; journal de la femme et de la maison. v 1, 1891+ Paris, Hachette
Col.pl. F. 50fr. a year, foreign 85fr.
Published weekly. Current 1937
Colored plates published separately 20fr. a year, foreign 28fr.
An English edition *La mode pratique, fashions of today* was published (May, 1892-Mar. 1894. London. Illus. col.pl. F.)
Colas 2088. Lipperheide 4808

La **mode,** revue des modes
(pub.) Almanach de la mode de Paris

See also La mode nouvelle

Mode revue; rivista tecnica di moda. 1929+ Milan, Aracne
Illus. F. L.30
Published quarterly. Current 1938
Spanish edition: *Mode nuove; rivista di alta moda* (Milano, F. Hayez)

La **mode** sous le point de vue hygiénique, médical, et historique. Goullin, J. A.

Mode und cynismus. Vischer, F. T. von

Mode und haus; illustrierte familienzeitung. 1.-36. jahrg., okt. 1885-apr. 1920. Berlin, J. Schwerin
36v. col.illus. col.pl. O.-F.
Published semi-monthly
Subtitle varies: v 1-6, 1885-90: praktische illustrirte frauenzeitung; v7-10, 1891-94: illustr. universalblatt für die familie; v16-19, 1899-1903: mode und familien-journal; v20-35, 1903-1918: illustriertes moden und familien-journal
Colas 2103. Lipperheide 4779

Mode und kultur. Stern, Norbert

La **Mode** universelle, journal illustré des dames. 1.-12. année; 1874-1885. Paris
Illus. col.pl. Q.
Colas 2104. Lipperheide 4745

Die **mode;** wesen, entstehen und wirken. Neuburger, Otto

Mode; zeitung für die elegante welt. See Zeitung für die elegante welt

Model, Julius, and Springer, Jaro
Der französische farbenstich des XVIII. jahrhunderts. Stuttgart & Berlin, Deutsche verlags-anstalt [1912]
70p. 50 col.pl.(incl.ports.) F.
Each plate accompanied by leaf with descriptive letterpress. Plates show French costume of the 18th century
LC 14-17717

Modelbûch aller art nehewercks und stickens. Egenolff, Christian

Modelbûch neuw aller art nehens uñ stickens. Han, Weygand, and Rab, Georg

Modelbûch Welscher Ober uñ Niderländischer arbait. Egenolff, Christian

Modèles de broderies genre moyen-âge. Bruges & Lille, Société Saint Augustin 1889-92
4v. 65 col.pl. Q.
Lipperheide 4011

Modèles de l'uniforme militaire adopté dans l'armée royale de Suède. See Eben, Frédéric, baron d'

Modèles nouveaux de crochet et filet, broderies en soie, broderies anglaises, plumetis, soutache, laine, etc. Paris, Aubert ca1850?
10p. 28pl. F.
Lipperheide 4091

Modèles pour les uniformes et l'équipement des officiers et fonctionnaires de l'armée française. Challiot

Die **moden** der alten und neuern zeit seit dem verfall der Griechen und Römer. Paris, Bureau für technische literatur in Basel 1869-70
2v. 12 col.pl. F.
The plates, with six figures each, show French costume from the 8th to the 18th century
Colas 2084. Lipperheide 1092

Die **moden** der italienischen renaissance. Floerke, Hanns

Die **moden** des XIX jahrhunderts. Geszler, J.

Moden-gallerie; 1. abtheilung eroeffnet von Fr. Nitze. 1795. Berlin
63 col.pl. Q.
A fashion journal. No more published
Colas 2085. Lipperheide 4582

Moden-telegraph. 1.-63. jahrg. 1861-1923. Dresden, Expedition d. europ. modenzeitung
63v. illus. F.
Absorbed by *Beobachter der herrenmoden* with v63, 1923

Moden und trachten. Hauff, H.

Modenheft. Hennings, Emma

Die **Modenwelt.** 1. jahrg., okt. 1865+ Berlin, Bazar-aktien-gesellschaft
Col. illus. patterns. F.
Subtitle: vereinigt mit *Elegante mode* und *Praktische Berlinerin* hrsg. von dr. Margarete Hausenberg. Subtitle varies v 1-26, Oct. 1865-Sept. 1891: illustrirte zeitung für toilette und handarbeiten
Published fortnightly. Each number 45 pfennig. Current 1937
Absorbed *Praktischen Berlinerin* v61; Oct. 1925
The following foreign editions of *Die Modenwelt* were published at various periods. American edition: *The Season; lady's illustrated magazine* (Colas 2703. Lipp. 4705 Czech edition: *Modni Svět; illustrovany časopis pro dámy* (Colas 2107. Lipp. 4714) English edition: *The Season; lady's illustrated magazine* (Colas 2704. Lipp. 4704) French edition: *La Saison; journal illustré des dames* (Colas 2631. Lipp. 4708) Hungarian edition: *Budapesti bazar* (Colas 480. Lipp. 4715) Italian edition: *La Stagione; giornale delle mode* (Colas 2793. Lipp. 4709) Polish edition: *Tygodnik mód i powieści* (Lipp. 4713) Portuguese edition: *Estaçâo; jornal illustrado para a familia* (Colas 984. Lipp. 4711) Spanish edition: *La Estaciôn; periôdico para señoras* (Colas 985. Lipp. 4710) Swedish edition: *Freja illustrerad Skandinavisk modetidning* (Colas 1116. Lipp. 4707) A Russian edition also was published (Lipp. 4712)
Colas 2086. Lipperheide 4702

Zum funfundzwanzigjährigen bestehen der Modenwelt, 1865-1890. Berlin, [Druck von O. Dürr in Leipzig] 1890
165p. front. illus. 1 col.pl. Q.
Fashion in various European countries between 1865 and 1890. Pages 75-158 give a history of costume from 1775-1890, by Fritz Bürmann
Bibliographie der deutschen modenzeitungen von 1865 bis 1890, p159-65
Lipperheide 577

Modenzeitung. See Allgemeine modenzeitung

The **modern** art of fencing. Rolando, Guzman

Modern design in embroidery. Crompton, Rebecca

Modern design in jewellery and fans. Holme, Charles, ed.

Modern dress and clothing in its relation to health and disease. Pearse, T. F.

Modern figure skating. Richardson, T. D.

Modern millinery. Lyon, H. B.

Modern nymphs. Lowinsky, T. E.

Modern polo. Miller, E. D.

Modern sons of the Pharaohs. Leeder, S. H.

The **modern** voyager. Adams, William

Moderna och drägtreformen. Dietrichson, L. H. S.

Die **moderne** damenschneiderei. Zeischke, Josef

Das **moderne** friseurgewerbe in wort und bild. Müller, F. R.

Moderne heere, moderne waffen. Bley, Wulf

Der **Moderne** kleidermacher. 1.-49. jahrg., 1875-1923. Dresden, Klemm & Weiss
49v. illus. (part col.) O.-Q.
Published monthly. No more published?
Colas 2089. Lipperheide 4751

Der **moderne** tanz. Brandenburg, Hans

Moderner album. See Album moderner, nach kunstlerentwürfen

Les **modes**; almanach des dames pour 1832; 1. année. Paris, Goetschy [1832]
227p. col.front. illus. S.
Colas 2091

Les **Modes**; revue mensuelle illustrée des arts decoratifs appliqués à la femme. 1. année, 1901+ Paris, Goupil
Illus. col.pl. Q. 60fr. a year
Published monthly. Current 1937. Volume numbering begins with 14 which covers 1914-16
Colas 2092. Lipperheide 4818

Les **modes** anciennes et modernes; coup d'oeil sur l'origine et les progrès du vêtement, depuis l'antiquité jusqu'à nos jours, par D. M. J. H. Perpignan, J. Alzine ca1860
161p. D.
Colas 2093

Modes and manners. Boehn, Max von

Modes & manners of the nineteenth century. Boehn, Max von

Modes & manners: ornaments. Boehn, Max von

Les **modes** au XVII. et au XVIII. siècle. Blum, André. Histoire du costume, les modes au XVII. et au XVIII. siecle

Les **modes** au XIX. siècle. See Blum, André. Histoire du costume

Modes-caricatures. No place, 1794
16 col.pl. O.
Colas 2095

Modes d'hommes et de femmes de l'époque Louis XVI. Basset, Paris, pub.

Modes de la femme de France (pub.) Nice-carnaval

Les **Modes** de la saison. I.-XV. année, 1871-1885? Paris
Col.illus. F.
Colas 2096. Lipperheide 4734

Modes de la ville d'Augsbourg. See Merz, J. G. Kleidungs arten in der stadt Augspurg

Modes de Paris
Costumes d'enfans. Paris, ca1810
24 col.pl. Q.
For list of plates see Colas's *Bibliographie*
Colas 2097

Les **modes** de Paris. Uzanne, L. O.

Les **modes** de Zurich. See Herrliberger, David. Zürcherische kleider-trachten

Les **modes** depuis 1515 jusqu'à 1834. Dielmann

Les **modes** du Directoire et du Consulat. Daragon, Henri

Les **modes** du Directoire et du Consulat. Garcia, G.

Modes et costumes historiques. Pauquet, H. L. É., and Pauquet, P. J. C.

Modes et costumes historiques étrangers. Pauquet, H. L. É., and Pauquet, P. J. C.

Les **modes** et les belles; almanach nouveau, rédigé par le Caprice. Paris, Janet 1822
6 col.pl. D.
Colas 2098

Les **modes** et les parures chez les français depuis l'établissement de la monarchie. See Debay, Auguste. Hygiène vestimentaire

Modes et manières d'aujourd'hui. [Paris, J. Meynial] 1912-23
7v. 84 col.pl. O.
Illustrated by G. Lepape, Martin, G. Barbier, A. Marty, R. Bonfils, and Siméon
Colas 2099

Modes et manières du jour à Paris à la fin du 18e siècle et au commencement du 19e. Debucourt, P. L.

Modes & travaux féminins. Année 1, 1919+ Paris, Éditions E. Boucherit
Illus. (part col.) O.-Q.
Published semi-monthly. Numbering continuous. Current 1938
Editor 1936+ Renée Boucherit. Année 18+ each issue includes a fashion supplement

Modes et usages au temps de Marie-Antoinette. Éloffe, Mme

Les **modes** féminines du XIXe siècle. Boutet, Henri

Modes françaises: leur origine et leurs variations jusqu'à nos jours. Paris, Eymery 1822
251p. S.
Colas 2100

Modes françaises, ou Histoire pittoresque du costume en France depuis 1818. Paris, P. Blanchart 1818-23
4v. 301 col.pl. O.
Plates are from *L'Observateur des modes*
Colas 2101. Lipperheide 1155m

Les **Modes** parisiennes illustrées; journal de la bonne compagnie. no 1-? 5 mars 1843-1868. Paris
Col.pl. Q.
Contains engravings by Comte-Calix
Title changes: To 29 Oct. 1843 *Le musée des modes parisiennes;* Nov.-31 Dec. 1843, *La grande mode, journal des modes parisiennes*
Colas 2164-2166. Lipperheide 4650

Les **modes** parisiennes; ou Manuel de toilette, avec tablettes economiques. Paris, Desnos [1781]
Front. 12 col.pl. T.
The plates show styles in hair dressing. They are from the *Recueil général de coeffures*
Colas 2102. Lipperheide 4456

Les **modes** parisiennes sous le Directoire. Compte-Calix, F. C.

Modes vrais. See note under Musée des familles

Modespiegel. Boehn, Max von

Modestus. See Vegetius Renatus, Flavius. Fl. Vegetii Renati viri illustris De re militari

Modethorheiten. Meinert, E.

Die **modifizierung** der maske in der griechischen tragödie. Hense, Otto

La **Modiste** élégante. 1.-4. année; 1872-1875. Paris, Walter frères
Col.pl. F.
Colas 2105. Lipperheide 4738

La **Modiste** universelle; édition de chapeaux-modèles. 1.-21? année; 1876-1897? Paris, A. Goubaud
Col.pl. F.
No more published?
Colas 2106. Lipperheide 4755

Modius, François

Cleri totius romanae ecclesiae. See entry under Amman, Jost

Francisci Modii Liber singularis: in quo cuiusque ordinis ecclesiastici origo, progressus, & vestitus ratio breviter ex variis historicis quasi delineatur. Francoforti, S. Feyrabendij 1585
98 l. 102 illus. port. Q.
Woodcuts by Jost Amman

Gynaeceum, sive Theatrum mulierum. See entry under Amman, Jost

Pandectae triumphales, sive, Pomparum, et festorum ac solennium apparatuum, conviviorum, spectaculorum, simulacrorum bellicorum equestrium, et pedestrium. Francofurti ad Moenum, S. Feyrabendij 1586
2v. in 1. illus. double pl. F.
Volume 1 describes festivals of ancient Greece and Rome, the middle ages and to the end of the 16th century. Volume 2 describes tournaments. Some of the illustrations are by Jost Amman
Lipperheide 2468. LC 9-16894

Modni Svět. See note under Die Modenwelt

Möller, Anton

Omnium statuum foeminei sexus ornatus et usitati habitus Gedanenses ... Der Dantzger frawen und jungfrawen gebreuchliche zierheit und tracht jetziger zeit zu sehen. Dantzig, J. Rhödo 1601
1 l. 20 illus. O.
Shows feminine costume of Danzig
Facsimile edition published under title: *Danziger frauentrachtenbuch* (Danzig, R. Bertling 1886. 16p. 20 illus. O.)
Colas 2113-2114. Lipperheide 822

Møller, Jens Schou

Folkedragter i Nordvestsjælland, deres forhold til folkedragterne i det øvrige Sjælland og til de skiftende moder. København, Det Schønbergske forlag 1926
231p. illus. XII col.pl. diagrs. Q. (Danmarks folkeminder, nr.34)
Bibliographical foot-notes
Costume index. LC AC34-1728

Møller, Vald.

Den danske armès uniformer i deres hovedforandringer i løbet af ca. 3 aarhundreder. Kiøbenhavn, V. Möller 1892
21 col.pl. ob.F.
Shows uniforms of the Danish army from 1578 to 1890
Colas 2115. Lipperheide 2288

Das **monchskleid** im christlichen altertum. Oppenheim, Philippus

Mönster för korsstyngsbroderier. Lessing, Julius

Mönsterbok för slojdundervisningen i hem och skolor; efter gamla nordiska allmogearbeten. Stockholm, I. Haeggström 1880-81
2v. 34pl. O.
Lipperheide 3964

Mörner, Hjalmar

Il carnevale di Roma, 1820. Roma, presso F. Bourlié [1820]
20pl. F.
Includes more than 250 costume figures
Colas 530. Lipperheide 2864

[Scenes from Naples, Rome, and Paris.] Stockholm, 1829
16pl.(4 col.) Q.
Lithographed by Gjöthström and Magnusson. Legends are in Swedish
Colas 2142. Lipperheide 1279

Scènes populaires de Naples. Paris, Gihaut frères 1828
12 col.pl. ob.Q.
Also known with plates in black and white
Colas 2141. Lipperheide 1294-1295

Moeurs administratives. Monnier, Henri

Moeurs, coutumes et religions des sauvages américains. See Lafitau, J. F. Moeurs des sauvages amériquains

Moeurs des sauvages amériquains. Lafitau, J. F.

Moeurs du temps. Paris, Genty ca1830
10 col.pl. Q.
Lipperheide 3705

Moeurs et costumes de différens peuples de la terre. Paris, Delarue ca1840
98p. 31 col.pl. S.
Colas 2108

Moeurs et costumes de femmes chez diverses nations. See note under Lochom, Michiel van. La mode

Les **moeurs** et costumes de tous les peuples. Henricy, Casimir, and Lacroix, Frédéric

Moeurs et costumes des Russes. Houbigant, A. C.

Moeurs et coutumes des Chinois. See Grohmann, J. G. Gebräuche und kleidungen der Chinesen

Moeurs et coutumes des Corses. Feydel, Gabriel

Moeurs et coutumes des peuples, ou Collection de tableaux représentant les usages remarquables, les mariages, funérailles, supplices et fêtes des diverses nations du monde. Paris, Veuve Hocquart 1811-14
2v. 145 col.pl. Q.
Costumes of Europe (23pl.), Asia (58pl.), Africa (23pl.), America (31pl.), and Australia and Polynesia (10pl.)
Colas 2109

Les **moeurs** et la caricature en Allemagne —en Autriche—en Suisse. Grand-Carteret, John

Les **moeurs** et la caricature en France. Grand-Carteret, John

Moeurs et monuments des peuples préhistoriques. Nadaillac, J. F. A. du P, marquis de

Moeurs et usages des corporations de métiers de la Belgique et du nord de la France. Vigne, Félix de

Moeurs et usages des Turcs. Guer, J. A.

Moeurs, loix et costumes des Tatars-Usbeks. Grasset de Saint-Sauveur, Jacques

Moeurs parisiennes. Pigal, E. J.

Moeurs, usages, costumes des Othomanes. Castellan, A. L.

Moeurs, usages et costumes au moyen âge. Lacroix, Paul

Moeurs, usages et costumes de tous les peuples de monde. Loumyer, J. F. N.

Moffat, Elizabeth Whitney. See Gardilanne, Gratiane de, jt. auth.

Mogul India, 1653-1708. See Manucci, Niccolò. Storia do Mogor

Mohammedans
Acta Mechmeti I saracenorum principis. Aussführlicher bericht von ankunfft zunehmen gesatzen regirung und jam̃erlichen absterben Mechmeti I. 1597

Kheiri, Sattar. Indische miniaturen der islamischen zeit. 1921

See also names of Mohammedan countries, e.g. Turkey

Mohl, Ottmar von
Am japanischen hofe. Berlin, D. Reimer 1904
239p. front. pl.(4 col.) D.

Mohler, Samuel Loomis
The cestus. Philadelphia, 1926
79p. O.
Thesis (Ph.D.) University of Pennsylvania, 1926
Bibliography: p78-79
LC 27-12604

Mohrbutter, Alfred
Das kleid der frau. Darmstadt & Leipzig, A. Koch [1904]
99p. 56pl.(7 col.) Q.
Colas 2110. Lipperheide 3320b

Un **mois** dans les Pyrénées. Maurice, C.

Moitte, P. E.
(engr.) Greuze, J. B. Divers habillements suivant le costume d'Italie

Moke, Henry Guillaume Philippe. See La Belgique monumentale, historique et pittoresque

Moko. Robley, H. G.

Moland, Louis Émile Dieudonné
Molière et la comédie italienne, ouvrage illustré de vingt vignettes représentant les principaux types du théatre italien; 2. éd. Paris, Didier 1867
xi,378p. front. illus. 18pl. D.
Illustrations show theatrical costume of Italy in the 16th and 17th centuries

Moldavia. See Rumania—Moldavia

Molé, Guillaume François Roger
Essais historiques sur les modes et sur le costume en France. Nouvelle éd. pour servir de supplément aux "Essais historiques sur Paris", par M. Saint-Foix. London and Paris, Costard 1776
xxvi,360p. S.
Published anonymously, originally published under title: *Histoire des modes françaises.* Sometimes attributed to L. Charpentier
Also published (Merigot 1777)
Colas 1450

Histoire des modes françaises, ou Révolutions du costume en France, depuis l'établissement de la monarchie jusqu'à nos jours. Amsterdam & Paris, Costard 1773
xxiv,360p. S.
"Contenant tout ce qui concerne la tête des Français, avec des recherches sur l'usage des chevelures artificielles chez les anciens." Subtitle
Published anonymously
Colas 1449. Lipperheide 1674

Molé, Mad. Adnet-. See Adnet-Molé, Mad.

Moleville, Bertrand de. See Bertrand de Moleville, Antoine François, marquis de

Molière. Flutre, Fernand

Molière, Jean Baptiste Poquelin
Plays. See Theatrical costume—Special plays, ballets, etc.—Molière, Jean Baptiste Poquelin

Molière et la comédie italienne. Moland, L. É. D.

Molitor, Ulrich
De lamiis et phitonicis mulieribus. Köln, C. von Zyrichzee ca1489
28 l. 7 illus. Q.
The illustrations show witches garbed as townfolk of the period
Lipperheide 420

Molkenboer, Theodoor
De nederlandsche nationale kleederdrachten. Amsterdam, J. M. Meulenhoff 1917
247p. front. pl. S.

Mollo, Tranquillo
Abbildung der neuen k. k. oesterreichischen armee uniformen. Wien, T. Mollo [1808]
36 col.pl. F.
Colas 2116

Molloy, Joseph Fitzgerald
The Russian court in the eighteenth century. London, Hutchinson 1905
2v. 18 port.(incl.fronts.) O.
LC 6-9635

Molmenti, Pompeo Gherardo

La storia di Venezia nella vita privata dalle origini alla caduta della repubblica; 4. ed. interamente rifatta. Bergamo, Istituto italiano d'arti grafiche 1905-08

3v. fronts. illus. pl.(part col.) maps. Q.
Contents: 1 La grandezza; 2 Lo splendore; 3 Il decadimento
Contains much material on Venetian costume of all periods. French edition has title *La vie privée à Venise* (Venise, F. Ongania 1895-97. 3v. in 1)
LC 10-20918, 20-22136 (French ed.)

Venice, its individual growth from the earliest beginnings to the fall of the republic; tr. by Horatio F. Brown. London, J. Murray; Chicago, A. C. McClurg 1906-08

6v. col.fronts. illus. pl.(part fold.) ports. plans(part fold.) O. 63s; $10, o.p.
Translation of the author's *La storia di Venezia*
Costume index. LC 6-37649

Moltke, Eliza (Moltke-Huitfeldt) von, comtesse

Richtig angezogen in Deutschland und im Ausland. Kiel, W. Handorff 1912

44p. O.

Moltzheim, A. de

Collection des uniformes actuels de l'artillerie européenne, dessinés par un officier de l'armée française. [Metz, Dupuy ca1830]

29 col.pl. Q.
Colas 2117-2118

Esquisse historique de l'artillerie française depuis le moyen âge jusqu'à nos jours. Strasbourg, E. Simon 1868

61p. 64 col.pl. F.
Plate 1 bears title: *Costumes, uniformes, matériel de l'artillerie française depuis le moyen âge jusqu'à nos jours*
Later edition has title: *L'artillerie française, costumes, uniformes, matériel depuis le moyen-âge jusqu'à nos jours* (Paris, J. Rothschild 1870)
Colas 2119-2120. Lipp. 2329 (1870 ed.)

La nouvelle armée française. Paris, Dusacq [1875]

32 col.pl. F.
Colas 2121. Lipperheide 2331

Mon sursis. Guillaume, Albert

Mon village. Jazet, A.

La **monarchie** française en estampes. Müller, Elisabeth

Monastic and ecclesiastical costume. Duckett, Sir G. F.

Monastic and religious orders

Amman, Jost. Cleri totius romanae ecclesiae. 1585

Amman, Jost. Ständ und orden der H. Römischen Catholischen Kirchen. 1585

Bar, J. C. Coleccion de los trages de todas las ordenes religiosas y militares de todo el mundo. ca1790

Bar, J. C. Mascarades monastiques et religieuses de toutes les nations du globe. 1793

Bar, J. C. Les ordres monastiques féminins (In his Receuil de tous les costumes des ordres religieux et militaires, avec un abrégé historique et chronologique enrichi de notes et de planches coloriées, v6. 1778-1789)

Bar, J. C. Les ordres monastiques masculins (In his Recueil de tous les costumes des ordres religieux et militaires, avec un abrégé historique et chronologique enrichi de notes et de planches coloriées, v4-5. 1778-1789)

Biedenfeld, F. L. C., freiherr von. Ursprung, aufleben, grösse, herrschaft, verfall und jetzige zustände sammtlicher mönchs- und klosterfrauen- orden im Orient und Occident. Nebst den illuminirten abbildungen von 77 verschiedenen geistlichen orden. 1837-1839

Born, Ignaz, Edler von. Joannis Physiophilus's Specimen of the natural history of the various orders of monks, after the manner of the Linnaean system. 1783

Bruyn, Abraham de. Imperii ac sacerdotii ornatus; diversarum item gētium peculiaris vestitus. 1578

Bruyn, Abraham de. Omnium pene Europae, Asiae, Aphricae atque Americae gentium habitus. ca.1610

Bruyn, Abraham de. Omnium pene Europae, Asiae, Africae et Americae gentium habitus ... quibus accedunt Romani pontificis, cardinalum, episcoporum, una cum omnium ordinum monachorum et religiosorum habitu. 1581

Bruyn, Abraham de. Sacri Romani imperi ornatus, item Germanorum diversarumq. gentium peculiares vestitus; quibus accedunt ecclesiasticorum habitus varii. 1588

Buonanni, Filippo. Histoire du clergé séculier et régulier, des congrégations de chanoines et de clercs et des ordres religieux de l'un et de l'autre sexe qui ont été établis jusques à présent. 1716

Buonanni, Filippo. Ordinum religiosorum in ecclesia militanti catalogus, eorumque indumenta in iconibus expressa. 1706-10

Buonanni, Filippo. Verzeichnüss der geistlichen ordens-personen in der streitenden kirchen in nette abbildungen und einer kurtzen erzehlung verfasset. 1720-24

Capparoni, Giuseppe. Raccolta degli ordini religiosi che esistono nella città di Roma. 1826

Capparoni, Giuseppe. Raccolta degli ordini religiosi delle vergini a Dio dedicate. 1828

Cibrario, G. A. L., conte. Descrizione storica degli ordini religiosi. 1845

Costumes of religious orders; sixty-one original colored drawings, with ms. descriptions. 184-?

Costumi degli ordini religiosi. 1848

Costumi delle ven: archiconfraternite. 1870

Creccelius, Johannes. Collectanea ex historijs, De origine et fundatione Omnium ferè monasticorum ordinum in specie: Simulq: De fundatione et donatione cathedralium ac collegiatarum ecclesiarum cum suis canonicatibus. 1614

Monastic and religious orders—*Continued*

Crépon, Théophile. Costume civil, costume ecclesiastique, costume monastique. 1900

Currier, C. W. History of religious orders. 1895

Cutts, E. L. Scenes and characters of the middle ages. 1872

Doyé, F. von S. Die alten trachten der männlichen und weiblichen orden sowie der geistlichen mitglieder der ritterlichen orden. 1930

Duckett, Sir G. F. Monastic and ecclesiastical costume. 1892?

Fialetti, Odoardo. De gli habiti della religioni, con le armi, e breve descrittion. 1626

Fragmente aus der geschichte der klöster und stiftungen Schlesiens von ihrer entstehung bis zur zeit ihrer aufhebung im november 1810. 1811

Geschichte einiger geistlichen orden, besonders derer die in den kayserlich-königlichen erblanden bisher aufgehoben worden sind, nebst einem anhange von den Jesuiten- und Tempelherrn orden. 1783

Handbuch fürs schöne geschlecht, zum nutzen und vergnügen. 1785-1786

Hélyot, Pierre. Histoire des ordres monastiques, religieux et militaires, et des congregations seculieres de l'un & l'autre sexe, qui ont esté establies jusqu'à present. 1714-19

Henrion, M. R. A., baron. Histoire des ordres religieuses. 1838

Hollar, Wenceslaus. Aula veneris, sive Varietas foeminini sexus diversarum Europae nationum differentiag habituum. 1644

Hollar, Wenceslaus. Theatru mulierum, sive Varietas atque differentia habituum foeminei sexus diversorum Europae nationum hodierno tempore vulgo. 1643

Micheli y Marquez, José. Tesoro militar de cavalleria antiguo y moderno modo de armar cavalleros, y professar, segun las ceremonias de qualquier orden militar ... insignias y abito de cada una. 1642

Modius, François. Francisci Modii Liber singularis: in quo cuiusque ordinis ecclesiastici origo, progressus, & vestitus ratio breviter ex variis historicis quasi delineatur. 1585

Oppenheim, Philippus. Das mönchskleid im christlichen altertum. 1931

Piolin, Paul. Du costume monastique antérieurement au XIII. siècle. 1865

Rammelsberg, J. W. Beschreibung aller sowohl noch heutiges tages florirenden als bereits verloschenen geist- und weltlichen ritter-orden in Europa; nebst denen bildnissen derer ordenszeichen. 1744

Schoonebeek, Adriaan. Histoire des ordres religieux de l'un & de l'autre sexe. 1695

Schoonebeek, Adriaan. Nette afbeeldingen der eyge dragten van alle geestelyke orders. 1688

Schwan, C. F. Abbildungen der vorzüglichsten geistlichen-orden in ihren gewöhnlichsten ordenskleidungen. 1791

Tiron, abbé. Histoire et costume des ordres religieux, civils et militaires. 1845

See also Military religious orders; Monastic and religious orders for women; Trappists

Catholic church

Das Bapstum mit seinen gliedern gemalet und beschrieben. 1563

Brockhoff, L. E. D. Die kloster-orden der heiligen katholischen kirche. 1875

Coronelli, M. V. Ordinum religiosorum in ecclesia militanti catalogus. 1708

Costumi religiosi della corte pontificia. ca1850

Perugini, G. Album ou collection complète et historique des costumes de la cour de Rome, des ordres monastiques, religieux et militaires et des congrégations séculières des deux sexes. 1862

Pinelli, Bartolommeo. Raccolta di costumi degl' ordini religiosi. 1828

Wietz, J. K. Abbildungen sämmtlicher geistlichen orden männlich- und weiblichen geschlechts in der katholischen kirche. 1821

Belgium

Maillart, P. J. Collection de costumes de tous les ordres monastiques, supprimés à differentes époques, dans ci-devant Belgique. 1811

England

Fosbroke, T. D. British monachism, or, Manners and customs of the monks and nuns of England. 1817

Gasquet, F. A., cardinal. English monastic life. 1904

Gasquet, F. A., cardinal. Henry VIII and the English monasteries. 1893

Ireland

Archdall, Mervyn. Monasticon hibernicum: or, A history of the abbeys, priories, and other religious houses in Ireland. 1873-76

Netherlands

Hofdijk, W. J. De klooster-orden in Nederland. 1865

Monastic and religious orders for women

Biedenfeld, F. L. C., freiherr von. Ursprung, aufleben, grösse, herrschaft, verfall und jetzige zustände sammtlicher mönchs- und klosterfrauen-orden im Orient und Occident. Nebst den illuminirten abbildungen von 77 verschiedenen geistlichen orden. 1837-1839

Costumes des communautés religieuses de femmes en Canada. 1854

Monastic and religious orders for women —*Continued*

Leuckfeld, J. G. Johan. Georg. Leuckfeldi ... Antiquitates gandershcimenses, oder Historische beschreibung des uhralten käyserl. freyen weltlichen reichsstiffts Gandersheim. 1709

Schoonebeek, Adriaan. Kurtze und gründliche histori von dem anfang und ursprung der Gott-geweyhten orden aller closter-jungfrauen. 1693

Monasticism in the orthodox churches. Robinson, N. F.

Monasticon hibernicum. Archdall, Mervyn

Moncorps, de Savigny de. Savigny de Moncorps, de

Moncrieffe, Mona, pseud.

The magic of colour harmony in dress, Sydney, Bebarfald's ltd. c1927
140p. illus.(part col., mounted) O.
LC 28-4384

Mondain, Georges Hippolyte. See Monval, G. H. Mondain, called

Le **monde** amusant. Grévin, Alfred

Le **Monde** élégant; estafette des modes. 1.-27. année, 1856-1882. Paris
Col.illus. F.
No more published?
According to Colas this periodical was preceded by *Le Monde élégante, litterature, modes, théâtre* (Paris, 16 oct. 1850-?)
Colas 2123. Lipperheide 4680

Le **Monde** élégant, journal des modes, des salons, des gens du monde, des théâtres et de la littérature; tous les dix jours. 15. avr. 1838-nov. 1839. Paris
O.
Absorbed by *Colifichet*, January 1840
Colas 2122

Monde élégant, or The world of fashion. v 1-68, 1824-1891. London
Col.illus. O.
Title varies: v 1-28, 1824-25, *World of fashion and continental feuilletons*; 29-56, 1852-79 *Ladies monthly magazine*
Colas 3100. Lipperheide 4606

Le **Monde** élégant, litterature, modes, theatre. See note under Le Monde élégant; estafette des modes

Le **monde** en estampes. Müller, Élisabeth

Le **monde** en estampes. Roujoux, P. G., baron de

Monde féodal. See Larchey, Lorédan. Costumes vrais

Le **monde** plein de fols, ou Le theatre des nains. See Il Callotto resuscitato, oder Neu eingerichtes zwerchen cabinet

Il **Mondo** elegante; giornale illustrato delle mode francesi. 1.-XII. anno; 1864-1875. Torino, G. Cassone
Illus. F.
Volumes 7-12 published by G. Candeletti, successor to Cassone
Colas 2124. Lipperheide 4697

Mongez, Antoine

Mémoire sur les costumes des Perses sous la dynastie des rois Achéménides et celle des successeurs d'Alexandre. Paris, Baudouin 1803
202p. 6pl. Q.
Lipperheide 134

Tableaux, statues, bas reliefs et camées de la Galerie de Florence et du Palais Pitti, dessinés par Wicar, peintre, et gravés sous la direction de C. L. Masquelier ... avec les explications, par Mongez. Paris, Lacombe 1789-1807
4v. 192pl. F.
Shows costume of ancient times and of the 16th and 17th centuries
New editions published 1827 and 1852-1856
Lipperheide 155

(ed.) Recueil d'antiquités, contenant, I Têtes antiques, ou Iconographie; II Costumes des différens peuples de l'antiquité, jusqu'au moyen-âge; III Figures antiques, ou Iconologie; rédigé par Mongez ... dessiné par Madame Mongez, gravé sous la direction de M. Bouilliard. Paris, H. Agasse 1804
2v. 380pl. Q. (Encyclopédie methodique. v12-13)
Shows costume and coiffures of ancient peoples

Mongolia

Carruthers, A. D. M. Unknown Mongolia. 1914

Consten, Hermann. Weideplätze der Mongolen im reiche der Chalcha. 1919-20

Haslund-Christensen, Henning. Tents in Mongolia (Yabonah). 1934

Tafel, Albert. Meine Tibetreise. 1914

See also Sungaria

Le **Moniteur** de la coiffure; journal mensuel de l'art du coiffeur: coiffures, travestissements, littérature, beaux-arts et théâtres. 1. nov., 1858-1891. Paris,
Pl.(part col.) O.
Published monthly. Illustrations show coiffures, hats and fashions, most of them in color
Editors: To January 1861, Croisat; April 1861-1891, Loisel
Colas 2125

Le **Moniteur** de la mode: a fashionable journal appearing monthly, with which is incorporated The Milliner and dressmaker. v 1-8; 1882-1889. London
F.
No more published

Le **Moniteur** de la mode; journal du grande monde. 1.-70. année; Apr. 1, 1843-1910. Paris
70v. col.illus. O.
United with *Le bon ton* and continued under title *Le bon ton and le Moniteur de la mode united*
In English and French
Colas 2126. Lipperheide 4646

Moniteur de la mode united. See Le Bon ton and le Moniteur de la mode united

Le **Moniteur** des dames et des demoiselles. 1845-1877/78. Paris, A. Goubaud
Col.pl. Q.
According to Hatin's *Bibliographie* this fashion journal began publication in 1845
Colas 2127. Lipperheide 4676

Monks. See Monastic and religious orders

[**Monnier, D.**]

Uniformes de l'armée belge. Paris, ca1860
8pl. O.
Colas 2128

Monnier, Henri

Album Henri Monnier. Paris, L. Pannier 1843
20 col.pl. Q.
Lipperheide 3666

Monnier, Henri—*Continued*

Les grisettes, leurs moeurs, leurs habitudes. Paris, Giraldon-Bovinet 1827
24 col.pl. Q.
Two other collections by H. Monnier have title *Les grisettes* (Paris, E. Ardit 1827. 8 col.pl.) and (Paris, Delpech ca1828. 5 col.pl.)
Colas 2129-2131. Lipperheide 3659-3661

[Moeurs administratives, dessinées d'après nature. Paris, Delpech 1828]
12 col.pl. F.
Lipperheide 3662

Rencontres parisiennes; Macédoine pittoresque. Paris, Gihaut frères 1839-40
26pl.(9 col.) O.
"Croquis d'après nature au sein des plaisirs des modes, de l'activité, des occupations, du désoeuvrement, des travers, des vices, des misères, du luxe, des prodigalités des habitants de la capitale." Subtitle
Lipperheide 3665

(illus.) La Bédollière, É. G. de. Les industriels, métiers et professions en France

(illus.) Marie, Aristide. Henry Monnier, 1799-1877

See also Lami, E. L., jt. auth.

Monnoyeur, J. B.

Recueil de costumes ... gravé par P. Schenck. Amsterdam [1590?]
Text in French and Dutch

Monografía histórica é iconográfica del traje. Puiggarí, José

Monogramm-album. Manteuffel, Erna von

Monograms. See Embroidery—Monograms and numerals

Monro, Isabel Stevenson, and Cook, Dorothy Elizabeth

(eds.) Costume index; a subject index to plates and to illustrated text. New York, The H. W. Wilson company 1937
x,338p. Q.
"The Index was begun under the editorship of Minnie E. Sears... After Miss Sears' death the work was completed by the present editors." Preface
An analytical subject index to costume material in 615 books (942 volumes). Indexes well-known costume books and also the costume material in books of history, travel, etc., the aim being to include those most available. Few special books of military and ecclesiastical costume have been included but as this material was found in general books it was indexed
"List of books indexed": p[295]-338
LC 37-7142

Monroe, Paul

(ed.) A cyclopedia of education. New York, Macmillan 1911-13
5v. illus. pl.(part col.) ports. maps, diagrs. Q.
Contains material on academic dress (v 1 p14-18 illus. 2 col.pl.)
LC 11-1511

Monroe, Will Seymour

Bulgaria and her people, with an account of the Balkan wars, Macedonia, and the Macedonian Bulgars, by Will S. Monroe. Boston, Page 1914
xxi,410p. front. pl. ports. fold.map. O.
Illustrated lining-papers. Bibliography: p397-99
LC 14-16238

In viking land; Norway: its peoples, its fjords and its fjelds. Boston, L. C. Page 1908
xxiv,332p. front. pl. ports. fold.map. O.
Published also under title: *The spell of Norway* (Syracuse, N.Y. Bardeen 1907. $2)
Bibliography: p314-15
LC 8-30604

Turkey and the Turks; an account of the lands, the peoples, and the institutions of the Ottoman empire. New rev. ed. Boston, L. C. Page 1907
xxii,369p. front. pl. ports. fold.map. O.
Select annotated bibliography: p352-55
LC 19-10612

Monsieur. Boulenger, J. R.

Monstrelet, Enguerrand de

The chronicles of Enguerrand de Monstrelet ... beginning at the year MCCCC, where that of Sir John Froissart finishes, and ending at the year MCCCCLXVII, and continued ... to MDXVI; tr. by Thomas Johnes. London, Longman, Hurst, Rees, Orme and Brown 1810
12v. D. and atlas (51pl.) sq.O.
Shows French nobles of the 15th century, many of them in armor

Monta

Bals bourgeois. Paris, Marescq [1854]
56pl. O. (Petits album pour rire, no14)
Lipperheide 3667

Montagnards des Pyrénées. Gavarni, G. S. C.

Montaillé

Le costume féminin, depuis l'époque gauloise jusqu'à nos jours; tome 1. Allant jusqu'à la fin du règne de Louis XVI. Paris, G. D. Malherbe 1894
62 l. 58 illus. O.
No more published
Colas 2132. Costume index. Lipp. 1103

See also Mich. Costumes inédits de Aine-Montaillé

Montalto, Lina

La corte di Alphonso I di Aragona. vesti e gale. Napoli, R. Ricciardi 1922
129p. 2pl. D. (Biblioteca napoletana di storia, letteratura ed arte. v4)
Contains two chapters on Italian costume of the 15th century

Montañeses de la Frontera de Francia. See Gavarni, G. S. C. Montagnards des Pyrénées

Montani, Francesco, count Fabi. See Fabi-Montani, Francesco, count

Montanus, Arnoldus

Gedenkwaerdige gesantschappen der Oost-Indische maatschappy in 't Vereenigde Nederland, aan de kaisaren van Japan. Amsterdam, J. Meurs 1669
456,14p. illus. fold.pl. fold.map. F.
A German translation has title: *Denckwürdige gesandtschafften der Ost-Indischen gesellschaft in den Vereinigten Niederländern, an unterschiedliche keyser von Japan* (Amsterdam, J. Meurs 1670)
Lipperheide 1552 (Ger. ed.) LC 5-7806 (Ger. ed.), 7-5230

Montault, Xavier Barbier de. See Barbier de Montault, Xavier

Montavon, William A.

Wearing apparel in Bolivia. See entry under United States. Bureau of foreign and domestic commerce

Montavon, William Frederick
Wearing apparel in Peru. See entry under United States. Bureau of foreign and domestic commerce

Montbrial, Jacques de. See Dubech, Lucien. Histoire générale illustrée du théâtre

Il **monte**: opera nova di recami ... nella quale si ritrova varie, & diverse sorti di mostre, di punti in aiere, à fogliami. Venetia, ca1557
16,15 l. illus. Q.
Contains fifteen leaves of designs
Lipperheide 3888

Montelius, Oscar
Antiquités suédoises ... dessinées par C. F. Lindberg. Stockholm, P. A. Norstedt 1873-75
2v. 732 illus. O.
Lipperheide 285m

La civilisation primitive en Italie depuis l'introduction des métaux. Stockholm, Imprimerie royale 1895
v 1(548 l. 96 illus. Q.) and atlas of 21+113pl
Wood engravings by Meyer and Hansen after drawings by Sörling. Volume one, on northern Italy, is the only volume published
Lipperheide 269. LC (3-18538)

Les temps préhistoriques en Suède et dans les autres pays scandinaves ... traduit par Salomon Reinach. Paris, E. Leroux 1895
vi,352p. illus. 20pl. map. O.
Illustrations show jewelry of prehistoric times
"Bibliographie": p5-6
LC 3-9281

Montell, Gösta
Dress and ornaments in ancient Peru; archaeological and historical studies. Göteborg, Elanders boktryckeri aktiebolag; London, Oxford university press 1929
262p. illus.(incl.map) pl.(part col.) O. 15s
"The first half of the English translation of my typescript was carried out by Mr. M. Leijer, the latter half by Dr. G. E. Fuhrken." Preface
Bibliography: p[245]-62
Costume index. LC 30-20442

Montémont, Albert Étienne de
Histoire universelle des voyages effectués par mer et par terre dans les cinq parties du monde ... contenant la description des mœurs, coutumes, gouvernements, cultes, science et arts. Paris, Armand-Aubrée [1833-37]
46v. 90 col.pl. O.
Quoted in various bibliographies as *Bibliothèque universelle des voyages effectués par mer ou par terre*
LC 3-27705

Monten, Dietrich
Die bayerische armee, nach der ordonnanz von jahre 1825. München, J. M. Hermann [1825]
30pl.(24 col.) F.
Colas 2133

Die neue uniformirung, rüstung und bewaffnung der königlich baierischen armee. Darmstadt, Eberhardt ca1825
xxii p. 8 col.pl. S.
Colas 2134

See also Eckert, H. A. jt. auth.

Montenegro, Roberto
Mascaras mexicanas. [Mexico, Talleres graficos de la nacion 1926]
cxxxiv p. 51pl.(3 col.) F.
Plates show Mexican masks
LC 27-16426

Montenegro. See Yugoslavia—Montenegro; also Military costume—Montenegro

Montfaucon, Bernard de
L'antiquité expliquée et représentée en figures; 2. éd. rev. et cor. Paris, F. Delaulne [etc.] 1722
5v. in 10. front. pl. F.
French and Latin. First edition 1719-1724
Contents: v 1 Les dieux des Grecs & des Romains: pt 1 Les dieux du premier, du second & du troisième rang, selon l'ordre du tems. pt2 Les heros parvenus à la divinité; v2 pt 1 Le culte des Grecs et des Romains. pt2 La religion des Egyptiens, des Arabes, des Syriens, des Perses, des Scythes, des Germains, des Gaulois, des Espagnols, & des Carthaginois; v3 Les usages de la vie: pt 1 Les habits, les meubles, les vases, les monoyes, les poids, les mesures, des Grecs, des Romains, & des autres nations. pt2 Les bains, les mariages, les grands & les petits jeux, les pompes, la chasse, la pêche, les arts, &c. v4 La guerre, les voitures, les grands chemins, les ponts, les aqueducs, la navigation; pt 1 Les levées des gens de guerre, les habits, les magazins, les travaux, les signes & les combats militaires, les armes de toutes les nations, les marches d'armées, les machines de guerre, etc. pt2 Les chemins publics, les aqueducs, & la navigation; v5 Les funerailles, les lampes, les supplices, etc: pt 1 Les funerailles des Grecs & des Romains. pt2 Les funerailles des nations barbares
There is also a *Supplement au livre de L'antiquite expliquée* (Paris, La veuve Delaulne 1724. 5v. pl. F.) with contents which correspond with those of the main work
The author's *Antiquitates graecae et romanae* (Norimbergensis, G. Lichtensteger 1517. 2v. pl. Q.) is an abridged edition with Latin text. Published also in 1767. Volume 1 contains text, volume 2, plates. His: *Griechische, römische und andere alterthümer für studirende* (Nürnberg, Riegel u. W. 1807) is a German translation of the abridged edition. For edition in English see his: *Antiquity explained*
Lipperheide 104. LC 5-1446-7

Antiquity explained, and represented in sculptures. Tr. into English by David Humphreys. London, J. Tonson & J. Watts 1721-22
5v. pl. F.
Translation of his *L'antiquité expliquée.* Each plate contains more illustrations than those in the French edition
There is also a supplement: *Supplement to Antiquity explained* (1725. 5v. pl. F.)
LC 4-35159

Les monumens de la monarchie françoise qui comprennent l'histoire de France, avec les figures de chaque règne. Paris, J. M. Gandouin et P. F. Giffart 1729-33
5v. 306pl. F.
Covers the period from the early middle ages to Henry IV. The illustrations are battle scenes and portraits
The same plates appear in his *Thresor des antiquitez*
Lipperheide 1070 (noted) LC 11-167

Montfaucon, Bernard de—*Continued*
Thresor des antiquitez de la couronne de France represente'es en figures d'après leurs originaux, soit en pierre ... en or ... ou autre metal ... en peinture, gravure, sculpture, et autres arts. La Haye, P. de Hondt 1745
2v. (34,36p.) 306pl. F.
The same illustrations are in his *Les monumens*
Subtitle: Tout ce qui concerne particulierement les rois, les reines ... les ducs ... et autres grands-seigneurs ... les usages & coutumes du roiaume ... par exemple les habillemens, les coëffures, les chaussures, les modes de toute expece, les mariages, les repas, les festins, les fetes publiques, les spectacles
Lipperheide 1070

Montfort
Souvenir de l'orient. Paris, Gihaut frères 1827-29
6 col.pl. ob.F.
Plates show Arabs, Bedouins, Turks and Greeks
Colas 2136. Lipperheide 1586

Montgeron, Louis Basile Carré de
La verité des miracles operés par l'intercession de m. de Paris, demontrée contre m. l'archevêque de Sens; 3. ed. Cologne, Chez les libraires de la Compagnie 1739
lxiv,480,252p. illus. pl. (1 fold.) Q.
Shows costume of the 18th century
Lipperheide 1121. LC 30-33829

Montigny, Claude Antoine Littret de
Uniformes militaires, ou se trouvent gravés en taille-douce les uniformes de la maison du roy, de tous les régiments de France ... avec la datte de leur création et les différentes figures de l'exercice tant de la cavalerie que de l'infanterie. Paris, L'auteur 1772
2 l. 175 col.pl. O.
Colas 2137. Lipperheide 2298

Montillot, Just Marie Nicolas. See Lacroix-Danliard, pseud.

Montorgueil, Georges
Louis XI. Texte de Georges Montorgueil, aquarelles de Job. Paris, Combet 1905
79p. col.illus. Q. (Collections d'albums historiques) 15fr.

See also Onfroy de Bréville, J. M. G. Napoléon

Les **monumens** de la monarchie françoise. Montfaucon, Bernard de

Monumens des arts libéraux, mécaniques et industriels de la France. Lenoir, Alexandre

Monumens égyptiens du Musée d'antiquités des Pays-Bas à Leyde. Leemans, Conradus

Monument de Ninive. Botta, P. E.

Monument du costume physique & moral de la fin du XVIIIe siècle. Moreau, J. M.

Monument du costume physique & moral de la fin du XVIIIe siècle. Restif de La Bretonne, N. E.

Monument esthématique du XIXe siècle. See Uzanne, L. O. Les modes de Paris

Monumenta landgraviorum Thuringiae et marchionum Misniae. Reyher, Samuel

Monumenta scenica. See Denkmäler des theaters

Monumenta sepulchralia ecclesiae Ebracensis. Gropp, Ignaz

Monumental brasses. Macklin, H. W.

Monumental brasses, Illustrations of. Ecclesiological society, Cambridge

The **monumental** brasses of England. Boutell, Charles

The **monumental** brasses of Lancashire and Cheshire. Thornely, J. L.

The **monumental** effigies of Great Britain. Stothard, C. A.

I **monumenti** dell' Egitto e della Nubia. Rosellini, Ippolito

Monumentos del arte mexicano antiguo. Peñafiel, Antonio

Monuments anciens du Mexique. Brasseur de Bourbourg, C. E.

Monuments de l'Égypte et de la Nubie. Champollion, J. F.

Monuments du moyen-âge et de la renaissance, dans l'ancienne Pologne depuis les temps les plus reculés jusqu'à la fin du XVII. siècle. See Przezdziecki, Aleksander, and Rastawiecki, Edward, baron. Wzory sztuki średniowiecznej i z epoki odrodzenia po koniec wieku XVII. w dawnej Polsce

Monuments égyptiens. Prisse d'Avennes, A. C. T. E.

Monuments français. Willemin, N. X.

Monuments of the early church. Lowrie, Walter

Monuments scandinaves du moyen âge. Mandelgren, N. M.

Monumentum, sive columbarium libertorum et servorum Liviae Augustae et caesarum, Romae detectum in Via Appia, anno 1726. Gori, A. E.

Monval, Georges Hippolyte Mondain, called
Costumes de la Comédie française XVIIe-XVIIIe siècles. See entry under Guillaumot, A. E.

Monval, Mme Madeleine Horn. See Horn-Monval, Mme Madeleine

Monvert. See Lory, Gabriel, and Moritz, F. W., eds. Costumes Suisses

Mooltan, during and after the siege. Dunlop, John

[**Moor, Jean Baptiste van**]
Recueil de cent estampes representant differentes nations du Levant tirées sur les tableaux peints d'après nature en 1707. et 1708. par les ordres de m. de Ferriol, ambassadeur du roi a la Porte. Et gravées en 1712. et 1713. par les soins de m[r]. Le Hay. Paris, Le Hay [etc.] 1714
1 p.l. 100 col.pl. (1 double) F.
Plates are engraved by C. Du Bosc, B. Barron, C. N. Cochin, J. de Franssières, Haussard, P. Rochefort, P. Simonneau fils and J. B. Scotin
Two extra plates: Interrement Turc, and Les Dervichs Danse are inserted in some copies
An accompanying pamphlet *Explication des cent estampes qui representent differentes nations du Levant; avec de nouvelles estampes de ceremonies turques qui ont aussi leurs explications* (Paris, J. Collombat 1715. 26p. 3pl. F.) has been ascribed to Charles Ferriol as author
Colas 1820. Lipperheide 1414. LC F-3788

Moor, Jean Baptiste van—*Continued*
Wahreste und neueste abbildung des türckischen hofes. Nürnberg, C. Weigel 1719-21
2v. 121 col.pl. Q.
Translation of the author's *Recueil de cent estampes* with the plates copied in reduced size and some plates, relating to Greece, added
Colas 1821. Lipperheide 1415

Moore, Frederick
The Balkan trail. New York, Macmillan 1906
xi,296p. front. 48pl. map. O.
LC w6-326

Catalog of brilliant old robes from the late court of the Manchus. New York, Anderson galleries 1917
100p. 19 illus. Q.
Cover title: *Robes from the Manchu court*

Moore, George Foot
(ed.) Mythology of all races

Moore, Mrs Hannah (Hudson)
Children of other days; notable pictures of children of various countries and times, after paintings by great masters. New York, F. A. Stokes [c1905]
76p. front. illus. Q.
LC 5-36126

The lace book ... with seventy engravings showing specimens of lace, or its wear in famous portraits. New York, F. A. Stokes [1904]
206p. front. LVIII pl.(incl.ports.) Q.
LC 4-33228

Moore, Joseph
Eighteen historical and local views illustrative of the operations and positions of the forces in the Birman territories, etc.; engraved from the designs taken at Rangon. London, T. Clay 1825
18 col.pl. F. 2s

Moors. See Morocco

The **Moors.** Meakin, Budgett

Moqui Pueblo Indians of Arizona and Pueblo Indians of New Mexico. United States. Census office. 11th census, 1890

Moraine, Louis Pierre René de
Album militaire de l'armée française en action. Paris, J. Vermot ca1870?
112 col.pl. ob.Q.
Shows uniforms of French soldiers at the time of Napoleon III
Colas 2139

Napoléon III et son armée vers 1859. Paris, Ledot ca1860
20 col.pl. Q.
Colas 2138

Moral emblems. Cats, Jacob, and Farley, Robert

Morales, Antonio Bachiller y. See Bachiller y Morales, Antonio

Moralische kinderklapper für kinder und nichtkinder. Musäus, J. K. A.

Morals. See Criticism

Moran, Patrick Francis, cardinal
(ed.) Archdall, Mervyn. Monasticon hibernicum

Morant, Georges de, comte
Le sang glorieux de Jeanne d'Arc, illustré d'un grand nombre d'armoiries ... des portraits du souverain pontife et de Jeanne d'Arc. Paris, Rédaction et administration [du Nobiliaire du XXe siècle] 1912
24,[312]p. illus. pl. ports. fold.geneal.tab. F. (Nobiliaire du XXe siècle. IVe vol.)
LC 26-7745

Moravia. See Czechoslovakia—Moravia; also Embroidery—Czechoslovakia—Moravia

Moravské slovensko. Prague. Národopisné museum československé

Mordvalaisten pupuja ja kuoseja. Heikel, A. O.

Mordvinians
Heikel, A. O. Mordvalaisten pupuja ja kuoseja. Trachten und muster der Mordvinen. 1879-99

Moré, G.
Dresden types, 1895. [Dresden, C. Tittmann, 1895]
Cover-title. 12 col.pl. F.
In portfolio
Colas 2140. Lipperheide 825s. LC 4-6331

Moreau
Souvenirs du théâtre anglais. See entry under Devéria, Achille, and Boulenger

Moreau, [Jean Michel], dit le jeune
Monument du costume physique & moral de la fin du XVIIIe siècle; ou, Tableaux de la vie pour servir à l'histoire des modes et du costume en France, année 1776, ornés de vingt-six figures dessinées et gravées par Moreau le jeune et par d'autres célèbres artistes. Stuttgart, J. Scheible [1888]
3p.l. iv,iv p. 38pl. F.
Contains also *Graveurs des douze estampes de l'Histoire des moeurs et du costume, gravées d'après Sigismond Freudenberg*
Reproduction of the plates in Moreau's *Seconde suite* and *Troisième suite* and Freudenberger's *Suite d'estampes.* Also published in two volumes, Moreau's volume with title as above (26pl.) Freudenberger's with title *Histoire des moeurs & du costume des Français* (12pl. LC 3-6634)
The same plates are reproduced in N. E. Restif de la Bretonne's *Monument du costume,* which see
LC 2-26599

Seconde suite d'estampes, pour servir a l'histoire des modes et du costume en France, dans le dix-huitième siècle Année 1776. Paris, Prault, imprimeur du roy 1777
12 l. 12pl. F.
Leaves and plates numbered 13-24. Each plate accompanied by guard sheet with descriptive letterpresse. Plates engraved by P. A. Martini and others. This second series shows the life of a court gallant There is an edition with plates reduced in size (Paris, Moreau [1776])
Colas 1119, 1121. Lipperheide 1123

Moreau, Jean Michel, dit le jeune—*Cont.*
Troisième suite d'estampes pour servir a l'histoire des moeurs et du costumes des François, dans le dix-huitième siècle. Année 1784. Paris, Prault 1784
12 l. 12pl. F.
Plates numbered 25-36
Masculine costume, The cavalier à la mode or Petit maître. Engraved by L. Halbou and others after Moreau's designs. Contains two new plates *La surprise* and *Le matin* from Restif de la Bretonne's *Monument du costume*
Colas 1120. Lipperheide 1124

(illus.) Boucher, Emmanuel. Les gravures françaises du XVIIIe siècle, v6. 1875-82

(illus.) Restif de La Bretonne, N. E. Estampes de Moreau-le-jeune

(illus.) Restif de La Bretonne, N. E. Monument du costume physique et moral de la fin du dix-huitième siècle

(illus.) Restif de La Bretonne, N. E. Tableaux de la bonne compagnie

Moreau, Jean Michel, dit le jeune, and Freudenberger, Sigmund
Trois suites d'estampes pour servir à l'histoire des modes et du costume des Français dans le 18. siècle. Nach d. orig.-ausg. hrsg ... von Max von Boehn. Berlin, Askanischer verlag 1920
xxiv p. illus. 38pl. sq.F.
Contains the same plates that are in Moreau's *Monument du costume*

Moreau-Nélaton, Étienne
Les Clouet et leurs émules. Paris, H. Laurens 1924
3v. ports. Q.
Shows French costume of the 16th century. Volume 1 includes bibliographies
LC 24-24017

Moreau le jeune, 1741-1814. Schéfer, Gaston

Moreck, Curt
Die musik in der malerei. München, G. Hirth [1924]
112p. illus. 147pl. on 74 l. O.
LC 25-12215

(ed.) Der tanz in der kunst; die bedeutendsten tanzbilder von der antike bis zur gegenwart. Stuttgart-Heilbronn, W. Seifert [1924]
xxxv,187p. front. pl. O.

Morel, S.
(pub.) Costumes suisses des 22 cantons

Morel-Fatio, Antoine Léon
(illus.) Pacini, E. F. L. D. La marine, arsenaux, navires, équipages, navigation, atterrages, combats

Morel-Retz, L. P. G. B.
Ces messieurs; travestissements fantaisistes; par Stop [pseud.] Paris, Journal amusant et Petit journal pour rire ca1870
1 l. 24 col.pl. Q.
Lipperheide 3185

Costumes nationaux. Paris, Hautecoeur-Martinet ca1875
102 col.pl. Q.
Shows costume of European and Asiatic nations. For list of plates see Colas's *Bibliographie*
Colas 2809

Morelli, Jacopo
Descrizione delle feste celebrate in Venezia per la venuta di S.M.I.R. Napoleone, il massimo imperatore de' Francesi. Venezia, Picotti 1808
32p. 4 col.pl. Q.
Lipperheide 2770

Moreno Rodriguez, Manuel
Tipos españoles; acuarelas de Manuel Moreno Rodriquez. Madrid, Romo y Füssel n.d.
25 l. of music. 20 col.pl. ob.O.
Plates, in pocket of back cover, show Spanish dress

Mores, leges, et ritus omnium gentium. Boemus, Johann

Morgan, Jacques Jean Marie de
Prehistoric man; a general outline of prehistory. New York, A. A. Knopf 1925
xxiii,304p. illus.(incl.maps) O. (The history of civilization. [Pre-history and antiquity])
"Translated by J. H. Paxton and V. C. C. Collum
Contains material on prehistoric costume and jewelry
Bibliography: p297-98
LC 30-24008

Morgan, John Hill
Early American painters; illustrated by examples in the collection of the New-York historical society. New York, The New-York historical society 1921
136p. illus.(incl.ports.) O. (The New-York historical society. The John Divine Jones fund series of histories and memoirs, IV)
Most of the plates show costume of the 17th and 18th centuries in the United States, found in famous portraits of these periods
Bibliography: p121-26
LC 21-2910

Morgan, John Pierpont
Catalogue of the collection of jewels and precious works of art the property of J. Pierpont Morgan; compiled at his request by G. C. Williamson. London, Priv. print. at the Chiswick press 1910
xxvii,183p. illus. XCIV pl. 46 col.pl. F.
Plates engraved by Hallett Hyatt
LC 10-28649

Morgan, William C.
Shoes and shoemaking illustrated; a brief sketch of the history and manufacture of shoes from the earliest time. Beverly, Mass. Kehew & Odell 1897
120p. illus. ports. D.

Morgenscenen im putzzimmer der Romerin Sabina. See Böttiger, K. A. Sabina, oder morgenscenen im putzzimmer einer reichen römerin

Morghen, Luigi
Programma e figure della mascherata dé quattro principali poeti d'Italia, mostratasi alla festa data in Napoli dalla nobile Accademia delle dame e dé cavalieri, la sera del 19 febbraio 1827. Neapel ca1830
2 l. 20 col.pl. F.
Lipperheide 2773

Morhofius, Caspar Daniel. See Kirchmaier, G. C. De majestate juribusque barbae

Moritz, F. W. See Lory, Gabriel, jt. ed.

Morlon, A. See Compte-Calix, F. C., jt. auth.

Mornay
(illus.) A picture of St. Petersburgh, represented in a collection of twenty interesting views of the city, the sledges, and the people

Moro, Vala. See Vala Moro, pseud.

Morocco
Archinard, L. Q. L'autre France (Tunisie, Algérie, Maroc). 1914
Bensusan, S. L. Morocco. 1904
Christian, Pierre. L'Afrique française, l'empire de Maroc, et les deserts de Sahara. 1846
Davis, R. H. Rulers of the Mediterranean. 1894
Geoffroy de Villeneuve, R. C. L'Afrique, ou histoire, moeurs, usages et coutumes des Africains: Le Senegal. 1814
Host, G. H. Nachrichten von Marákos und Fes, im lande selbst gesammlet, in den jahren 1760 bis 1768. 1781
Meakin, Budgett. The Moors; a comprehensive description. 1902
Pidou de Saint Olon, François. Relation de l'empire de Maroc. 1695
Ricard, Prosper. Les merveilles de l'autre France; Algérie, Tunisie, Maroc; le pays—les monuments—les habitants. c1924
Shoberl, Frederic. Africa, containing a description of the manners and customs, with some historical particulars of the Moors of the Zahara, and of the negro nations between the rivers Senegal and Gambia. 1821

See also Moors; also subdivision Morocco under Decoration and ornament

Morocco. Bensusan, S. L.

Moroda, Derra de
(tr.) Lambranzi, Gregorio. New and curious school of theatrical dancing

Moronobu. See Hishigawa Moronobu

Morpurgo, Salomone
Catholic Church. Liturgy and ritual. Breviary. Breviaire Grimani de la Bibliothèque de S. Marco à Venise: reproduction photographique complète
(ed.) El costume de le donne, incomenzando da la pueritia per fin al maritar

Morris, Frances
Notes on laces of the American colonists, with plates explanatory of lace technique from Antique laces of the American collectors. New York, Pub. for the Needle and bobbin club by W. Helburn 1926
14p. front. pl. ports. F.
On American laces of the 17th and 18th centuries
LC 28-15122

Morris, Frances, and Hague, Marian
Antique laces of American collectors. New York, Pub. for the Needle and bobbin club by W. Helburn 1920-26
5v. illus. 104pl. F.
This shows laces of many countries and periods, including American laces of the 17th and 18th centuries

Morris, Maria. See Gallemore, Margaret, jt. auth.

Morrison, R. Boyd, jt. ed. See Mason, Rupert. Robes of Thespis

Morrocchesi, Antonio
Lezioni di declamazione e d'arte teatrale. Firenze, Tip. all' insegna di Dante 1832
366p. 40pl. O.
LC 11-17622

Morse, Mrs Harriet (Klamroth)
(ed.) Elizabethan pageantry, a pictorial survey of costume and its commentators from c. 1560-1620. London, The Studio, ltd.; New York, The Studio publications, inc. 1934
128p. mounted col.front. illus.(incl.ports.) O. $4.50
Costume index. LC 34-29131

Mortimer, Raymond. See Lowinsky, T. E. Modern nymphs

Morton, Cavendish
The art of theatrical make-up. London, A. and C. Black 1909
x,137p. front. 31pl. O.
LC w10-119

Morton, William
(illus.) Procter, R. W. The barber's shop

Mosaïque de costumes ou Alphabet étranger. Grévedon, P. L. H.

Der **mosaikboden** in St Gereon zu Cöln. Weerth, Ernst aus'm, ed.

Die **moscouitische** chronica. Giovio, Paolo, bp. of Nocera

Moscow. Sinodal'naiâ (byvshaiâ patrïarshaiâ) riznitsa
Sacristie patriarcale dite synodale, de Moscou; 2. éd., rev., cor., et augm. ... pub. par Sabas évêque de Mojaisk. Moscou, W. Gautier 1865
32p. xv pl. F.
LC 17-853

Moseman, Hermann Fabronius. See Fabronius, Hermann

Moser, Henri
Collection Henri Moser—Charlottenfels ... oriental arms and armour. Leipzig, K. W. Hiersemann 1912
xvii p. illus. XLIV pl.(part col.) ports. sq.F.
Title also in Persian. Descriptive letterpress in French, German and English
Issued in portfolio
LC 34-41755

Moser, J. B.
Das Wiener volksleben, in komischen scenen mit eingelegten liedern. Wien C. F. Mörschner 1842-44
6pts. 6 col.pl. O.
Lipperheide 3536

Moser, Johann Philipp
Sammlung von bildnissen gelehrter männer und künstler, nebst kurzen biographien derselben. Nürnberg, bey dem verleger 1794
287 l. 96pl. O.
Shows costume of the period
Lipperheide 689

Moses, Henry
Designs of modern costume, &c. [London] H. Setchel [1823?]
29pl. incl.front. O.
Also published with title: *A series of twenty-nine designs of modern costume* (London, E. and C. M'Lean 1823) The title on the first plate is *Le beau monde*
Shows English dress of the period
Colas 2143. Lipperheide 994. LC A34-2342

Moskovskiĭ telegraf" ... īzdavaemyĭ Nīkolaem" Polevym". 1.-18; 1825-1827 Moskva, v" Unīversītetskoĭ tīp.
Col.illus. O.
Fashion periodical
Lipperheide 4608

Moss, Frank
The American metropolis, from Knickerbocker days to the present time; New York city life in all its various phases. New York, P. F. Collier 1897
3v. fronts. illus. pl. ports. O.
LC 1-14308

Mothe Lambert, Pierre de La, bp. of Beirut.
See La Mothe Lambert, Pierre de, bp. of Beirut

Mother's magazine and Baby. See Lloyd's magazine

Mothersole, Jessie
Czechoslovakia, the land of an unconquerable ideal. London, John Lane; New York, Dodd, Mead [1926]
xxi,296p. col.front. illus. pl.(part col.) port. O. $5
Colored plates accompanied by guard sheets with descriptive letterpress
Bibliography: p[289]-90
Costume index. LC 26-21341

Mothes, Oscar. See Müller, H. A., jt. auth.

Motifs de la broderie paysanne en Bukovine. See Kolbenheyer, Erich. Motive der hausindustriellen stickerei in der Bukowina

Motivation in fashion. Hurlock, E. B.

Motive. Heiden, Max

Motive der hausindustriellen stickerei in der Bukowina. Kolbenheyer, Erich

Motoring costume

1900-1910

Northcliffe, A. C. W. H., 1st viscount. Motors and motor-driving. 1904

Motoring in the Balkans. Hutchinson, Mrs F. K.

Motors and motor driving. Northcliffe, A. C. W. H., 1st viscount

Motte, Charles
(ed.) Lessore, A. E., and Wyld, W. Voyage pittoresque dans la régence d'Alger pendant l'année 1833

[**Motteley, J. Charles**]
Histoire des révolutions de la barbe des Français, depuis l'origine de la monarchie. Paris, Ponthieu 1826
46p. T.
LC 15-8924

Mottl, Wendelin
Die grundlagen und die neuesten fortschritte der zuschneidekunst; 3. neu bearb. aufl. Prag, W. Mottl 1895
378p. 321 illus. 1 pl. O.
First edition: 1893
Lipperheide 3846

Motty, Wladimir
(illus.) Kozłowski, Karol. Wojsko polskie w roku 1831

Mōtus, A.
(illus.) Tartu. Eesti rahva muuseum. Eesti rahvariiete album. Album estnischer volkstrachten

Mouchoirs brodés. Lescure, Alfred

Mouhot, Charles
(ed.) Mouhot, Henri. Travels in the central parts of Indo-China (Siam), Cambodia, and Laos

Mouhot, Henri
Travels in the central parts of Indo-China (Siam), Cambodia, and Laos, during the years 1858, 1859, and 1860. London, J. Murray 1864
2v. illus. pl.(part fold.) O.
Edited by Charles Mouhot, with a memoir of Henri Mouhot by J. J. Belinfante
Shows costume of Cambodia, Siam, and Laos
LC 5-10966

Mouillard, Lucien
Armée française: les regiments sous Louis XV. Paris, J. Dumaine 1882
120p. 57 col.pl. F.
Shows French military costume from 1737 to 1774
Colas 2145

Moule, Thomas. See Harding, G. P., jt. auth.

Mountain life in Algeria. Barclay, Edgar

Mouradgea d'Ohsson, Ignatius
Tableau général de l'Empire othoman, divisé en deux parties, dont l'une comprend la législation mahométane; l'autre, l'histoire de l'Empire othoman. Paris, F. Didot 1787-90
2v. 66pl.(8 fold.) 4 fold.geneal.tab. F.
Translated into German with title: *Allgemeine schilderung des othomanischen reichs* (Leipzig, Weidmann 1788-93. 2v. 18pl.)
Lipperheide 1421 (Ger. ed.) LC 5-7776

Mourning costume
Cuyck, Peter van, the younger. Lykstaetsie ... van ... Willem Carel Hendrik Friso, prince van Orange en Nassau ... Gehouden den IV. Februari MDCCLII. 1755
Davey, R. P. B. A history of mourning. 1890
Franklin, A. L. A. La vie privée d'autrefois; arts et métiers, modes, moeurs, usages des Parisiens du XII. au XVIII. siècle. [v 17] p 1-146
Mercier, Louis. Le deuil, son observation dans tous les temps et dans tous les pays comparée à son observation de nos jours. 1877

Moussinac, Léon
Tendances nouvelles du théâtre; choix de décors, costumes, détails de mise en scène utilisés dans les représentations les plus originales de ces quinze dernières années. Paris, A. Lévy 1931
35p. illus.(part col.) 124pl.(part col.) F.
Colas 2145bis. LC 31-33362

See also Gazette du bon genre. Le bon genre

Moustache. See Beard

Mowrey, Gabriel
Modern French jewellery and fans. See Holme, Charles. Modern design in jewelry and fans

Le **moyen** âge et la renaissance. Lacroix, Paul, and Séré, Ferdinand

Mozin, Charles
Costumes de marins de la basse Normandie. Paris, Rittner 1829
12 col.pl. Q.
Colas 2147. Lipperheide 1194

[Scènes de Normandie.] Paris, Rittner et Arrowsmith [1828]
6 col.pl. Q.
Colas 2146

Mucci, Dominoco
(pub.) Raccolta di scene carnevalesche di Roma

Mudras auf Bali. Kat Angelino, P. de

Müller
(lithgr.) K. Svenska arméens uniformer

Müller, Albert
Die trachten der Römer und Römerinnen nach Ovid und Martial. Hannover, C. Meyer 1868
38p. 1 pl. O.
Colas 2149. Lipperheide 244

Müller, August
Geschichtliche übersicht der schicksale und veränderungen des grossherzogl. sächs. militairs während der ... regierung ... des grossherzogs Carl August. Weimar, T. Goetz 1825
17 l. 20 col.pl. ob.F.
Plates designed and lithographed by T. Goetz
Colas 2150. Lipperheide 2212m

Müller, C. See Dopler, J., jt. auth.

Müller, C. F.
Abbildung der königl. preussischen armee uniformen. Leipzig, 1788
4 l. 111 col.pl. D.
Colas 2151

Müller, Carl
(tr.) See note under Rich, Anthony. The illustrated companion to the Latin dictionary and Greek lexicon

Müller, Christian
New modelbûch von vilen artigen und kunstreichen mödeln zûgericht. Straszburg, 1572
38 l. 75 illus. Q.
A little known pattern book with many original patterns
Lipperheide 3895

Müller, Elisabeth
La monarchie française en estampes ... dessins de M. Fossey. Paris, A. Bedelet ca1856
37p. 16 col.pl. ob.Q.
"Tableaux de tous les rois et empereurs des plus célèbres reines, impératrices, régentes, princes, princesses et des autres principales illustrations de l'histoire de France." Subtitle
Plates lithographed by Duruy and Bocquin
Colas 2152

Le monde en estampes; types et costumes des principaux peuples de l'univers, lithographiés par J. Bocquin d'après les dessins de mm. Leloir et Fossey. Paris, A. Bedelet [1858]
52p. 18 illus. 23 col.pl. Q.
Colas 2153. Lipperheide 70

Müller, Ernst, and Baumgärtner, Friedrich Gotthelf
Versuch einer ästhetik der toilette oder winke für damen sich nach den grundregeln der malerei geschmachwoll zu kleiden. Leipzig, Industrie-comptoir [1805]
142p. 18pl.(8 col.) O.
Plates 1-10 show 50 types of feminine coiffures of various periods
Colas 2154. Lipperheide 3248

Müller, Ewald
Das Wendentum in der Niederlausitz. Kottbus, M. Liebe [1894]
xi,192p. 11 pl. 1 map. O.
Lipperheide 815

Müller, F. H.
Grossherzoglich hessisches militair ... auf stein gezeichnet von J. Völlinger. Carlsruhe, J. Velten ca1830
3 l. 30 col.pl. F.
Colas 2155. Lipperheide 2211

Müller, Ferdinand Richard
Das moderne friseurgewerbe in wort und bild; 2. aufl. Leipzig und Nordhauser, H. Killinger [192-?]
xvi,701p. col.front. illus.(incl. 1 port.) pl.(part col.) O.

Müller, Franz Hubert
Beiträge zur teutschen kunst- und geschichtskunde durch kunstdenkmale mit vorzüglicher berücksichtigung des mittelalters; 2. aufl. Leipzig & Darmstadt, C. W. Leske 1837
2v. 41pl.(16 col.) O.
Shows costume of the 13th to 15th century
Lipperheide 350

Müller, Friedrich. See Heideloff, K. A. von, ed. Die kunst des mittelalters in Schwaben

Müller, Gustav Adolf, and Gunkel, Anton
Die gesammte fachwissenschaft des schneiders; 3. verb. und verm. aufl. Dresden, G. A. Müller [1870]
2v. 101pl. O.
First edition: 1859
Lipperheide 3791

Müller, H. See Burger, Ludwig, jt. auth.

Müller, Hermann Alexander, and Mothes, Oscar
Illustrirtes archäologisches wörterbuch der kunst des germanischen alterthums, des mittelalters und der renaissance, sowie ... kostümkunde, waffenkunde. Leipsic und Berlin, O. Spamer 1877-78
2v. col.front. 1521 illus. Q.
Text in German, French, English, and Latin
Lipperheide 86

Müller, Jacob
Ornatus ecclesiasticus ... Kirchen geschmuck ... in lateinischer und teutscher sprach. München, A. Berg 1591
143,168p. 72 illus. Q.
Lipperheide 1798

Müller, Karl, and Braun, Louis
Die bekleidung, ausrüstung und bewaffnung der königlich bayerischen armee von 1806 bis zur neuzeit. München, A. Oehrlein 1899
947p. 59 l. Q. and atlas 70pl.(24 col.) ob.F.
Colas 2157. Lipperheide 2197

Müller, Karl Otfried
Denkmäler der alten kunst; 2. bearbeitung durch Friedrich Wieseler. Göttingen, Dieterich 1854-56
2v. 150pl. ob.O.
Illustrated by K. F. W. Oesterley. First edition: 1832-56. Shows costume of the ancient Greeks and Romans
LC G-2537 (1st ed.)

Müller, Kurt F.
Der leichenwagen Alexanders des Grossen. Leipzig, E. A. Seemann 1905
75p. illus. double pl. O. (Beiträge zur kunstgeschichte, neue folge XXXI)
LC 6-26539

Müller, Peter, praeses
Dissertatio de jocalibus; Vom weiberschmuck. Jenae, typis Ehrichianis 1706
72p. D.
Dissertation, Jena (C. Creutzing, respondent)
Lipperheide 1747. LC GS33-344

Müller, Salomon
Verhandeling over de natuurlijke geschiedenis der nederlandsche overzeesche bezittingen. Leiden, S. and J. Luchtman 1839-44
472p. 90pl.(21 col.) F.
Thirty one plates show costume and weapons of the natives of the Dutch East Indies. Edited by C. J. Temminck
Colas 2158. Lipperheide 1492

Müller, Sigurd. See Lund, F. C. Danske nationaldragter

Müller, Sophus Otto
Ordning af Danmarks oldsager; système préhistorique du Danemark, résumé en français. Kjøbenhavn, C. A. Reitzel [1888-95]
2v. pl. F.
Illustrated by Magnus Petersen. Part of the illustrations show ancient Danish costume, jewelry, and weapons

Müller, Susanna
Neuer systematischer zuschneide-unterricht ... erster theil. Zürich, C. Schmidt 1883
vi,81p. 83 illus. O.
Lipperheide 3827

Zuschneidekurs. St Gallen & Herisau, C. T. Meisel [1875]
100p. 56 illus. O.
"V. und VI. stufe des Elementarunterrichtes in den weiblichen handarbeiten; anhang: das weiszsticken." Subtitle
Lipperheide 3805

Mueller, Walther
Quaestiones vestiariae. Scripsit Gualtherus Mueller lubecensis. Gottingae, apud Dieterich (L. Hortsmann) 1890
53p. O.
On dress in ancient Greece

Müller, William James
Müller's Sketches of the age of Francis I. London, H. Graves 1841
2 l. 25pl. F.

Müller, Wolfgang. See Tidemand, Adolph. Norwegisches bauernleben

Müller-Brauel, Hans
Das erste niedersächsische volkstrachtenfest zu Scheessel. Hannover, Gebrüder Jänecke 1904
58p. 29 illus. O. (Beiträge zur neidersächsischen volkskunde 2)
Colas 2156. Lipperheide 802k

Niedersächsische volkstrachten. Bremen, C. Schünemann [1902]
20p. 10 illus. O.
Lipperheide 802e

Müllerheim, Robert
Die wochenstube in der kunst; eine kultur-historische studie. Stuttgart, F. Enke 1904
xvi,244p. 139 illus. O.
Shows children in art throughout the ages
Lipperheide 2007d

Münchausen, A. F. von
Teppiche des jungfrauenstifts Marienberg bei Helmstedt. Quedlinburg, H. C. Huch 1874
28p. 9pl. Q.
"Als beigabe zum siebenten jahrgange der zeitschrift des Harzvereins für geschichte und alterthumskunde." Subtitle
Lipperheide 395

München in guter alter zeit. Regnet, C. A.

Der **Münchener** Boccaccio. See Durrieu, Paul, comte. Le Boccace de Munich

Münchener bilderbogen. See Zur geschichte der costume, nach zeichnungen von W. Diez, C. Fröhlich, C. Häberlin, M. Heil, A. Muller, F. Rothbart, J. Watter; Also Costumes of all nations

Das **Münchener** bürger militär in allen waffengattungen und uniformen. Kolb, Valentin

Münich, Friedrich, and Behringer, Ludwig
Die uniformen der bayerischen armee von 1682 bis 1848. München, Mey & Widmayer 1863-64
71 col.pl. Q.
Colas 275. Lipperheide 2195

Münster, Sebastian
Cosmographia, das ist: beschreibung der gantzen welt ... vermehrt und mit neuen indianischen figuren geziehret. Basel, Bey den Henricpetrinischen 1628
1752p. illus. 26 maps. F.
Published in many editions. This is the 14th German edition and contains more than 1400 woodcuts. Lipperheide describes the 10th German edition with title: *Cosmography, oder beschreibung aller länder* (Basel, 1588. 1420p. ca1200 illus. 26 maps.) Illustrated by J. T. Coriolanus, D. Kandel, H. R. Manuel, H. Magdeburg, C. Hofreuter, J. Clauser, C. Stimmer, L. Prig and H. Holzmüller
Lipperheide 493-494

Müntz, Eugène
La renaissance en Italie et en France à l'époque de Charles VIII. Paris, Firmin-Didot 1885
xi,560p. 311 illus.(incl. ports.) 38pl. facsim. Q.
Lipperheide 465. LC 2-21158

Tapisseries, broderies et dentelles; recueil de modèles anciens et modernes. Paris, Librairie de l'Art 1890
43p. front.illus. XCVI pl.(partly fold.) F. (Bibliothèque internationale de l'art)
Lipperheide 3767. LC 10-19004

La tiara pontificale du VIIIe au XVIe siècle. Paris, Imprimerie nationale 1897
92p. illus. pl. Q.
From *Institut de France. Académie des inscriptions et belles-lettres. Mémoires.* v36 pt 1

Müntz, Louis Frédéric Eugène. See Müntz, Eugène

Mützel, Hans Heinrich Hermann Eduard
Kostümkunde für sammler; 2. umgearb. und verm. aufl. Berlin, R. C. Schmidt 1921
248p. illus. O. (Bibliothek für kunst- und antiquitätensammler, bd. 15) M. 10
A history of costume with special mention of 20th century dress in Europe and Asia
Colas 2174. Costume index. LC 23-12706

Vom lendenschurz zur modetracht, aus der geschichte des kostüms. Berlin, Widderverlag 1925
321p. illus. 8 col.pl. O. M. 18.50
A history of costume, with many illustrations
Colas 2175. Costume index

Muffs
Uzanne, L. O. L'ombrelle, le gant, le manchon. 1883
Uzanne, L. O. Les ornements de la femme ... L'éventail, l'ombrelle, le gant, le manchon. 1892

Muhammedans. See Mohammedans

Las **mujeres** españolas, portuguesas y americanas ... Descripcion y pintura del caracter, costumbres, trajes ... de la mujer de cada una de las provincias de España, Portugal y Américas españolas. Madrid, M. Guijarro 1872-76
3v. 81 col.pl. F.
Colas 2148. Lipperheide 1237

Muller
[Neapolitan costumes.] No place, ca1840
27pl. F.
Plates have legends in Italian and are signed Lit. Muller
Colas 2159. Lipperheide 1301

Muller, Alexandre
Théorie sur l'escrime à cheval, pour se défendre avec avantage contre toute espèce d'armes blanches. Paris, Cordier 1816
67p. 51pl. Q.
Lipperheide 2983

Muller, Pieter Lodewijk
Onze gouden eeuw. De Republiek der Vereenigde Nederlanden in haar bloeitijd; geillustreerd onder toezich van J. H. W. Unger. Leiden, A. W. Sijthoff 1896-98
3v. fronts. illus. 115pl.(part col.) ports. Q.
Shows costume of the Netherlands in the 17th century

Muller, Samuel, and Vogelsang, Willem
Holländische patrizierhäuser. Utrecht, A. Oosthoek 1909
47p. illus. 40pl. F.
Shows dolls' costume

Muller, Theobald. See Giovio, Paolo, bp. of Nocera. Musæi Ioviani imagines artifice manu ad vivum expressae

Mummenhoff, Ernst
Der handwerker in der deutschen vergangenheit. Mit 151 abbildungen und beilagen nach den originalen aus dem fünfzehnten bis achtzehnten jahrhundert. Leipzig, E. Diederichs 1901
141p. illus. pl. fold.facsims. Q. (Monographien zur deutschen kulturgeschichte, bd. VIII)
Lipperheide 1982. LC 1-22362

Mummers

Jamaica

Beckwith, M. W. Christmas mummings in Jamaica. 1823

Spain

Amades, Joan. Gegants, nans i altres entremesos. [1934]

The **mummy.** Budge, Sir E. A. T. W.

Munch, Andreas. See Tidemand, Adolph. Norwegisches bauernleben

Mundt, Albert
Die freiheitskriege in bildern; eine zeitgenössische bilderschau der kriegsjahre 1806 bis 1815. München, Einhorn 1913
121p. illus. 128pl. 5 port. Q.
Shows French and German soldiers between 1806 and 1815

Mundus muliebris. Evelyn, John

Mundy, Peter
The travels of Peter Mundy, in Europe and Asia, 1608-1667; ed. by ... Sir Richard Carnac Temple, bart. Cambridge, Printed for the Hakluyt society, 1907-24
4v. in 5. illus. pl.(part fold.) maps(part fold.) fold.geneal.tab. facsim. O. (Works issued by the Hakluyt society, 2d ser. no17, 35, 45-46, 55)
Volumes 3 and 4 describe costume and hair styles of the Chinese, of the natives of Madagascar and of Danzig, as well as Dutch, German, and Russian dress in the 17th century
Bibliography in each volume
LC 8-2221

Munich. See Germany—Bavaria—Munich

Munich. Bayerische staatsbibliothek
Meisterwerke der buchmalerei; aus handschriften der Bayerischen staatsbibliothek, München, ausgewählt und hrsg. von dr. Georg Leidinger. München, H. Schmidt [c1920]
32p. 50 col.pl. F.
Plates are selections from illuminated manuscripts of the ninth to the sixteenth century
LC 21-10807

Munich. K. Graphische sammlung
Ornamente. See entry under Aldegrever, Heinrich.

Munich. K. Hof- und staats-bibliothek
Sammlung von initialen. See entry under Arnold, Xaver, and Knoll, Eduard

Munich. K.Vasen-sammlung
Greek vases: their system of form and decoration. See entry under Brunn, Heinrich von

Die griechischen vasen ihr formen- und decorations system. See entry under Brunn, Heinrich von, and Krell, P. F.

Munson, Edward Lyman
The soldier's foot and the military shoe; a handbook for officers and noncommissioned officers of the line ... approved by the War department. Fort Leavenworth, Kan. [Menasha, Wis., Press of the George Banta pub. co.] 1912
147p. illus. O. $1.35
LC 13-2995

Munter, Frédéric
Recherches sur l'origine des ordres de chevallerie du royaume de Dannemarc. Copenhague, A. Seidelin 1822
124p. 3pl. O.
Lippherheide 1921e

Muraz, Gaston
Sous le grand soleil, chez les primitifs; images d'Afrique équatoriale. Coulommiers, P. Brodard 1923
xix,197p. illus. pl. O.

Murner, Thomas
Nebulo nebulonum, hoc est, jocoseria nequitiae censura ... latinitate donata à Joanne Flitnero. Francofurti, G. Fickwirt 1663
164p. 33 illus. O.
Shows townspeople, scholars, soldiers, and others in 17th century costume
This is the 4th Latin edition of the author's *Schelmenzunft* published in 1512. First three Latin editions were published 1620, 1634, 1644
Lipperheide 681

Murr, Christoph Gottlieb von
Beschreibung der sämtlichen reichskleinodien und heiligthümer welche in Nürnberg aufbewahret werden. Nürnberg, in Commission der bauer- und mannischen buchhandlung 1790
92p. illus. 4pl. O.
This description applies especially to the crown jewels and relics which are pictured in Delsenbach's *Wahre abbildung der sämtlichen reichskleinodien.* Translated into French under the title: *Description des ornemens impériaux et des reliques de Saint Empire Romain* (Nuremberg, A. G. Schneider 1790)
Lipperheide 1761, 1762 (French ed.)

Murray, Alexandre Henry Hallam
The high-road of empire ... sketches in India. London, J. Murray 1905
xxviii,453p. illus. 47 col.pl. (incl. front.) O.
LC w6-153

Murs, Marc Athanase Parfait Oeillet des. See Oeillet des Murs, M. A. P.

Musæi Ioviani imagines artifice manu ad vivum expressae. Giovio, Paolo, bp. of Nocera

Musaeum historicum et physicum. Imperialis, J. B.

Musäus, Johann Karl August
Moralische kinderklapper für kinder und nichtkinder ... neue aufl. Gotha, Ettinger 1823
110p. 17 illus. O.
Shows children and family groups. First edition: 1794
Lipperheide 691

See also Dance of death. Freund Heins erscheinungen in Holbeins manier

Musarion, die freundin weiser geselligkeit und häuslicher freuden; ein monatsschrift für damen. v. 1-3, 1799-1800. Altona, J. F. Hammerich
3v. illus. O.
Published monthly. Contains fashion illustrations
Colas 2160. Lipperheide 4589

Musculus, Andreas
Hosedjaevelen paa Dansk ved Peder Palladius, 1556; udgivet ... originalen af Lis Jacobsen. København, Gyldendalske boghandel 1920
76p. illus. O.
Shows German costume of the 16th century

Musée chronologique des rois de Danemark au château de Rosenborg. See Brock, P. M. J. The chronological museum of the Danish kings, in Rosenborg castle

Musée cosmopolite. See Aubert & cie. Musée de costumes

Musée d'art et d'histoire, Geneva. See Geneva. Musée d'art et d'histoire

Musée de costumes. Aubert & cie.

Musee de la caricature. Jaime, E.

Le **musée** de la Comédie-française, 1680-1905. Dacier, Émile

Le **musée** de l'armée. Hardy, E. A.

Musée de sculpture antique et moderne. Clarac, C. O. F. J. B., comte de

Musée de Tzarskoe-Selo. Gille, Floriant

Musée des anciens costumes turcs de Constantinople. See Brindesi, Jean. Elbicei Atika

Musée des armes rares, ancieñs et orientales de Sa Majesté l'Empereur de toutes les Russies. Carlsruhe, J. Velten [1835?]
26 l. 108pl. F.
Shows European arms and armor of the 15th and 16th centuries and some oriental armor

Le **musée** des dames. Compte-Calix, F. C.

Musee des familles. 1.-67. année; oct. 1833-1891. Paris
Illus. pl. Q.
Published monthly. From 1850-91 published with a monthly supplement with title: *Modes vrais* which contains colored fashion plates
Colas 2163. Lipperheide 4625. LC 11-12612

Le **musée** des modes parisiennes. See Les modes parisiennes illustrées

Le **Musée** des théâtres. Paris, Le Fuel 1823
11 col.pl. S.
Plates are portraits of actresses

Musée historique des tissus de Lyon. See Lyons. Musée historique des tissus

Musée rétrospectif de l'infanterie française, régiments de France, Rocroy, Fontenoy, Austerlitz. Paris, Lebigre-Duquesne [1866]
2 l. 150 col.pl. O.
Plates are designed by Philippoteaux. The same plates are in L. Susane's *Histoire de l'ancienne infanterie française*
Colas 2167

Musée rétrospectif des classes 85 et 86. Paris. Exposition universelle, 1900

Musée royal Bourbon. See Naples. Museo nazionale

Musée royal des monumens français. Paris. Musée des monumen français

Le **musée** secret de la caricature. Fleury, Jules

Musées royaux des arts décoratifs et industriels. See Brussels. Musées royaux des arts décoratifs et industriels

Musei Etrusci ... monimenta. Maximis, F. X. de

Museo militar: historia del ejercito español. Barado y Font, Francisco

Museos de España
[Cordova scenes]; fotografiado directamente del original por J. Laurent. Madrid [18—]
67 pl. F.

Museum der eleganten welt; hrsg. von J. V. Müller. 1.-3? jahrg., 1836-1838. München, F. S. Hübschmann
138 col.pl. O.
Title change: v2, 1837, *Museum für kunst, literatur, musik, theater und mode*
Colas 2169. Lipperheide 4630

Museum für deutsche volkstrachten und erzeugnisse des hausgewerbes, Berlin. See Berlin. Museum für deutche volkstrachten und erzeugnisse des hausgewerbes

Museum für kunst, literatur, musik, theater und mode. See Museum der eleganten welt

Museum in Basel; catalog für die antiquärische abtheilung. Bernoulli, J. J. B.

Museum of the American Indian, Heye foundation, New York. See New York. Museum of the American Indian, Heye foundation

Muséum parisien. Huart, Louis

The **musical** entertainer. Bickham, George

Musicians
Cutts, E. L. Scenes and characters of the middle ages. 1872. p267-310
Ewers, H. H. Musik im bild. ca1920
Friese, Friedrich. Ceremoniel und privilegia derer trompeter und paucker. ca1720
Meyer, Kathi. Das konzert; ein führer durch die geschichte des musizierens. 1925
Moreck, Curt. Die musik in der malerei. 1924
Rambosson, J. P. Les harmonies du son et l'histoire des instruments de musique. 1878

See also Military costume—England —1914-date—Musicians; Military costume—France—1848-1852 — Musicians; Minnesingers

Ancient times

Cheyne, T. K., and Black, J. S. Encyclopaedia biblica. 1899-1903. p3234-3239

18th century

Buonanni, Filippo. Descrizione degl' istromenti armonici d'ogni generi. 1776

20th century

Weissmann, Adolf. Der dirigent im 20. jahrhundert. 1925
Zealley, A. E., and Hume, J. O. Famous bands of the British Empire; brief historical records of the recognised leading military bands and brass bands in the Empire. c1926

Musik im bild. Ewers, H. H.

Die **musik** in der malerei. Moreck, Curt

La **musique** militaire. Paris, Sinnett 1850?
25 col.pl. S.
Shows uniforms of musicians of the French army

Musique militaire. See Perrot, Émile. Harmonie universelle

Mussey, William P. See Harper, C. D., jt. auth.

Mustache. See Beard

Muster altchristlicher kunst in Egypten. Koptische stickereien. See Dillmont, Thérèse de. L'art chrétien en Egypte. Motifs de broderie copte

Muster altdeutscher leinenstickerei. Lessing, Julius

Muster altdeutscher und moderner stickereien; hrsg. von ... M. Beeg-Aufsess ... C. v. Braunmühl ... M. Meyer [and others]. Leipzig, E. Heitmann [1884]
72 col.pl. Q.
Lipperheide 4008

Muster altitalienischer leinenstickerei. Lipperheide, Frieda

Muster altslowakischer leinenstickerei. See Sochán, P. B., pub. Vzory staroslovenských vipiviek

Muster für strümpfe und muster für socken. Wilhelmi, Helene

Muster stilvoller handarbeiten fur schüle und haus. Bach, Emilie

Muster von couleurt gestickten bordüren, zu kleidungsstücken. Philipson, A.

Muster zur weiszen stickerei im neuesten geschmack. Regensb., Reitmayr 1829
2pts. O.

Muster-album für haekel- arbeiten. Anker, Erna

Muster-album von kreuz-stichmonogrammen. Freimann, Jenny

Muster-blätter als vorlagen für stickereien in wolle und perlen. Lessing, C. F., and Lessing, Ida

Musterblätter für kreuzstichstickereien. Burchard, A.

Musterblätter für künstlerische handarbeiten. Lipperheide, Frieda

Das **musterbuch.** Foillet, Jacques

Musterbuch für frauenarbeiten. Clasen-Schmid, Mathilde

Musterbuch für ornamente und stickmuster. Quentel, Peter

Muster-sammlung alter leinen-stickerei. Schulze, Heinrich, and Maiss, Karl

Mustoxidi, Theodore Mavroïdi
Qu'est-ce que la mode? Paris, Picart [1920]
96p. D. 5fr.
Colas 2171

Muther, Richard. See Hirth, Georg, jt. ed.

Muthesius, Anna
Das eigenkleid der frau. Krefeld, Krammer und Baum 1903
84p. 14pl. O.
Colas 2172. Lipperheide 3318

Muths, Johann Christoph Friedrich Guts-. See Guts-Muths, J. C. F.

N

Nadaillac, Jean F. A. du P., marquis de—*Continued*
Mœurs et monuments des peuples préhistoriques. Paris, G. Masson 1888
312p. front. illus. O. (Bibliothèque de la nature)
LC 3-13157

Nadal, Augustin. Traité du luxe des dames romaines. (*In* Meiners, Christoph. Recherches historiques sur le luxe chez les Athéniens)

Nádasdy, Ferencz, graf
Mausoleum potentissimorum ac gloriosissimorum regni apostolici regum & primorum militantis Ungariae ducum ... erectum [1663]. Norimbergae, M. J. F. Endteros [1664]
407p. 59 illus. F.
Contains full length portraits of the kings of Hungary to the time of Ferdinand IV
Lipperheide 853

Nadel-ergötzungen, Kunst- und fleissübende. Helmin, Margaretha

Nagel, Gustav
(tr.) Beamish, N. L. Geschichte der königlich deutschen legion. See note under his History of the King's German legion

Nagy, Géza. See Nemes, Mihály. A magyar viseletek tört'enete

Nails, Finger. See Finger nails

Nainfa, John Abel Felix Prosper
Costume of prelates of the Catholic church, according to Roman etiquette; new and rev. ed. Baltimore, Md., J. Murphy 1926
xii,293p. 15pl.(1 col.) O. $2
First edition: 1909
Colas 2178. Costume index. LC 9-13272 (1st ed.)

Nakedness. See Nudity

Nanook of the North. Bilby, J. W.

Nansen, Fridtjof
Eskimo life; tr. by William Archer. London, Longmans, Green 1893
xvi,350p. front. illus. 15pl. O.
Contains a chapter on appearance and dress
LC 4-7811

Eskimoleben; aus dem norwegischen übersetzt von M. Langfeldt. Illustrierte ausgabe. Berlin, Globus verlag, g. m. b. h. [1910?]
304p. front.(port.) illus. 15pl. O.
LC 34-7751

Nantes et la Loire inférieure. Benoist, Félix

Nanteuil, Célestin
(illus.) Cuendias, M. G. de, and Suberwick, Mme de. L'Espagne, pittoresque, artistique et monumentale
(illus.) Recuerdos de un viage por Espana

Napier, Lady Sarah (Lennox) Bunbury
The life and letters of Lady Sarah Lennox, 1745-1826, daughter of Charles, 2nd duke of Richmond, and successively the wife of Sir Thomas Charles Bunbury, bart., and of the Hon: George Napier ... ed. by the Countess of Ilchester and Lord Stavordale. London, J. Murray 1901
2v. fronts. pl. ports. O.
Shows costume of English nobility during the 18th and 19th centuries
LC 2-1251

Naples—Characters. Dura, Gaetano

Naples. Museo nazionale
Collection of the most remarkable monuments of the National museum. Naples, 1870
4v. in 2. 240pl.(part fold.) F.
Translation of its *Raccolta de' monumenti più interessanti del Museo borbonico* (1825)
LC 1-3432

Real museo borbonico. Napoli, Stamperia reale 1824-57
16v. fronts. pl.(part col. part fold.) plans (part fold.) Q.
Preface signed: Cav. Antonio Niccolini. The descriptive letterpress by A. Niccolini, G. Bechi, and others. Each volume includes "Relazione degli scavi di Pompei" by G. Bechi and others
"Elenco degli autori moderni, che trattarono delle città di Pompei e di Ercolano": v 1 p[1]-11
LC 9-13895

Recueil des monumens les plus intéressans du Musée national, et de plusieurs autres collections particulières, publiés par Raffaele Gargiulo; 3. éd. Naples, 186[3?]
4v. in 1 240pl.(part fold.) sq.Q.
An edition was issued in 1825 with Italian title page: *Raccolta de' monumenti più interessanti del Museo borbonico e di varie collezioni private*
Lipperheide 157. LC 2-7092

Naples (Kingdom)
Costumes du Royaume de Naples. 1825
Costumi popolari dello Statto Romano e Regno di Napoli tratti dal vero. ca1815
Damame-Démartrais, M. F. Collection de costumes du royaume de Naples. 1818
Fabris, Pietro. Raccolta di varii vestimenti ed arti del regno di Napoli. 1773
Milano, G. M. Costumi diversi di alcune popolazioni de' reale domini di qua del Faro. 1832
Pinelli, Bartolommeo. Raccolta di 50 costumi li piú interessanti delle cittá' terre e paesi in provincie diverse del Regno di Napoli. 1814
Raccolta delle diverse vestiture delle provincie del regno di Napoli. n.d.

See also subdivision Naples (Kingdom) under Coronations and coronation robes; Kings and rulers; Military costume; Naval costume

Naples. Real museo borbonico. See Naples. Museo nazionale

Napoleon I, emperor of the French. See Kings and rulers—France

Napoleon I: Das erwachen der völker. Pflugk-Harttung, J. A. G. von, ed.

Napoleon I; ein lebensbild. Kircheisen, F. M.

Napoleon I: Revolution und kaiserreich. Pflugk-Harttung, J. A. G. von, ed.

Napoléon I. und das zeitalter der befreiungskriege in bildern. Kircheisen, F. M.

Napoleon, illustrated with prints from contemporary and other portraits. Baily, J. T. H.

Napoléon Ier et la Garde impériale. Fieffé, Eugène

Napoléon III et son armée vers 1859. Moraine, L. P. R. de

Napoli e contorni. Dura, Gaetano

Le **Narcisse.** See L'Observateur des modes et Le Narcisse réunis

Le **Narcisse,** et L'Observateur réunis. See L'Observateur des modes et Le Narcisse réunis

Narcissus, an anatomy of clothes. Heard, Gerald

Narni da Fusoritto. See Fusoritto, reale da Narni

Narodnyi͡a pi͡esnī Galītskoĭ ī Ugorskoĭ Golovatskiĭ, I͡A. F.

Narratio profectionis. See Staden, Hans, and Lery, Jean de. Americae tertia pars

Narrative of the expedition of an American squadron to the China seas and Japan. Perry, M. C.

A **narrative** of the mission sent by the governor-general of India to the court of Ava in 1855. Yule, Henry

A **narrative** of travels in northern Africa. Lyon, G. F.

Narrazione delle solenni reali feste fatte celebrare in Napoli da Sua Maestà il re delle Due Sicilie Carlo infante di Spagna ... per la nascita del suo primogenito, Filippo, real principe delle Due Sicilie. Napoli, 1749

20p. front. xv fold. pl. F.

The plates are engraved by various artists from the drawings by Vincenzo Rè of the festival held November 4th to 19th, 1747

Lipperheide 2765. LC 12-17884

Narrenschiff. Brant, Sebastian

Nartow, van, alleged author. See Antiquitates sacrae & civiles Romanorum explicatae

Nash, Frederick

(illus.) Combe, William. History of the University of Oxford

Nassau. See Germany—Hesse

Die **nassauischen** volkstrachten. Hottenroth, Friedrich

Natalibus, Petrus de, bp. of Equilio

Catalogus Sanctorum. Lyon, J. Sacon 1514

246 l. 246 illus. F.

First edition: 1493

Illustrations show saints in the dress of the 15th century

Lipperheide 441

Nathansen, W.

Zur geschichte der Hamburger Schützengilde. Hamburg, O. Meiszner 1890

43p. 26 illus. 1 pl. O.

Lipperheide 3015

National beauties and their costumes; with explanatory text. New York, Kirchner ͺ1907?ͺ

32p. ports. Q.

The **national** costumes of Holland. Gardilanne, Gratiane de, and Moffat, E. W.

National costumes of the Slavic peoples. Young women's Christian associations. Bureau of pageantry and the drama

National dressmakers' association (incorporated). See Style, a monthly magazine of fashions for women

The **National** geographic magazine. v. 1, 1888+ Washington, D. C., The National geographic society 1889+

Illus. pl. (part col.) ports. maps. O.

Quarterly, 1889-90; irregular, 1891-95; monthly, 1896+

Shows costume of its period in all parts of the world

Cumulative index, v 1-60, 1899 to 1931 inclusive (Washington, D. C., National geographic society)

Costume index (v16-68, 1905-35). LC (14-7038)

National guard, United States. See Military costume—United States

National leisure hours institution. See Opera nazionale dopolavoro. Popular Italian costumes, music, dances and festivals

National society of the colonial dames of America

Report of the Committee on relics; uniforms of women worn during the war. Washington, 1922

Cover-title, 28p. O.

Signed: Carolyn Gilbert Benjamin, chairman

LC 22-16086

The **national** sports of Great Britain. Alken, H. T.

Nationaldragter. Fett, H. P.

National-kleidertrachten und ansichten von Ungarn, Croatien, Slavonien, dem Banat, Siebenbürgen und der Bukowina. Jaschke, Franz

Nationaltrachten verschied. völker. Kraus, G. M.

National-trachten verschied. völkerschaften in Dänemark. Hamburg, Gundermann 1815

O.

Nationaltrachten von Tirol und Vorarlberg. Schedler, J. G.

Les **nations.** Lacauchie, A.

Native life in Travancore. Mateer, Samuel

Native races. See African tribes; Australia—Native races; Primitive dress

Native races of the Pacific states of North America. Bancroft, H. H.

The **native** races of the Russian empire. Latham, R. G.

Natives of northern India. Crooke, William

Native's return. Adamic, Louis

Nattier, Jean Baptiste

(illus.) Rubens, Sir P. P. La Gallerie du Palais du Luxembourg

Nattier, Jean Marc

(illus.) Rubens, Sir P. P. La Gallerie du Palais du Luxembourg

Natüralich abschilderung des academischen lebens. Dendrono

Natura; rivista mensile illustrata. Milano, Soc. an. Stab. arti grafiche Alfieri & Lacroix; New York, Westermann 1928
2v. col.pl. F.
This volume of a monthly periodical contains colored plates by Bruno Santi which show women in the costume of various regions of Italy

Natural history museum, New York. See American museum of natural history, New York

A **naturalist's** wanderings in the Eeastern archipelago. Forbes, H. O.

Der **naturgemässe** stiefel ... mit specieller berücksichtigung der bekleidung und pflege des fusses bei der armee. Starcke, Paul

Naudet, C.
(engr.) Aubry, Charles. Cris de Paris

[**Naudet, Thomas Charles**]
[Costumes du directoire et du consulat.] Paris, chez Jean ca1799
12 col.pl. F.
For list of plates see Colas's *Bibliographie*
Colas 2182

Naue, Julius
Die bronzezeit in Oberbayern. München, Piloty & Löhle 1894
xv,292p. 163 illus. 50pl. Q.
"Ergebnisse der ausgrabungen und untersuchungen von hügelgräbern der bronzezeit zwischen Ammer- und Staffelsee und in der nähe des Starnbergersees." Subtitle
Lipperheide 308
(ed.) Prähistorische blätter

Nauen, Paul
Blumenkinder. Berlin, F. Lipperheide [1884-87]
3 l. 24 col.pl. O.
Colas 2183. Lipperheide 3192

Naukeurige beschryving van Asie. Dapper, Olfert

Naukeurige beschryving van gansch Syrie. Dapper, Olfert

Naunton, George Herbert
Japanese sword fittings; a descriptive catalogue of the collection of G. H. Naunton, comp. and illustrated by Henri L. Joly. London, The Tokio printing co. 1912
xxix,317p. LXXXVIII pl.(incl. front.) F.
Each plate accompanied by guard sheet with descriptive letterpress
LC 16-9284

Navajo Indians. See Indians of North America—Navajo Indians

Navajo Indian silver-work. Bedinger, Margery

Naval & military trophies & personal relics of British heroes. Holmes, R. R.

Naval costume
Francisci, Erasmus. Leben und tapffere thaten der aller-berühmtesten seehelden admiralen und land-erfinder unserer zeiten angefangen mit Cristoforo Colombo ... und geendigt mit ... M. A. de Ruyter. 1681

20th century

Bunkley, J. W. Military and naval recognition book. 1918

Falls, De W. C. Army and navy information. 1917

OF SPECIAL COUNTRIES

Argentine republic

Argentine republic. Ministerio de marina. Uniformes navales de la marina de guerra Argentina. 1901

Argentine republic. Ministerio de marina. Uniformes para el personal subalterno de la marina de guerra de la Republica Argentina. 1896

Australia

Australia. Department of defence. Clothing factory. Report. 1912/13+

Austria

Austria. Kriegsministerium. Uniformen distinctions- und sonstige abzeichen der gesammten k.k. osterr.-ungar. wehrmacht sowie orden und ehrenzeichen Oesterreich-Ungarns. 1887

Kählig, Eduard von. Österreich-Ungarn: Das heer, von E. von Kählig ... Die flotte, von R. ritter von Jedina. 1899

K. K. Oesterreichische armee nach der neuen adjustirung. 1837-48

Righetti, Camillo. Adjustierungsblätter des k.u.k. oesterr.-ungar. heeres, der kriegsmarine und der beiden landwehren. 1901

Teuber, Oscar. Die österreichische armee von 1700 bis 1867. 1895

Brazil

Guimaraes, A. L. Plano a que se refere o decreto no. 1829 de 4 de outubro de 1856 para os uniformes dos officiaes do corpo da armada e das classes annexas. 1857

China

20th century

China. President. Specifications for the uniforms of the Chinese navy. 1913

Cisalpine republic

Zanoli, Alessandro, baron. Sulla milizia cisalpino italiana. Cenni storico-statistici, dal 1796 al 1814. 1845

Denmark

Bergh, Th. Den danske armee og marine. 1859

Brock, Gustav. Den Danske haer og flaade. L'armee et la marine danoises. 1885

Christiansen, Rasmus. Danske uniformer for haer og flaade. 1911

Hyllested, H. C. Collection complète des uniformes de la marine et de l'armée danoise. 1829

Egypt

Ancient times

Dueminchen, Johannes. Die flotte einer aegyptischen koenigin aus dem XVII. jahrhundert vor unserer zeitrechnung; und altaegyptisches militair im festlichen aufzuge auf einem monumente aus derselben zeit abgebildet. 1868

Naval costume—*Continued*

England

Atkinson, J. A. A picturesque representation of the naval military and miscellaneous costumes of Great Britain. 1807
Bowen, F. C. The sea. 1927
Great Britain. Admiralty. Uniform regulations for officers of the fleet. 1924
Swinburne, H. L. The royal navy. 1907

Periodical

Navy and army illustrated. 1895-1915

19th century

Holding, T. H. Uniforms of British army, navy and court. 1894
Hull, Edward. Costume of the British navy in 1828. 1828
Mansion, L. M., and Saint-Eschauzier. Costume of the Royal navy and marines. ca1825
Perry, O. L. Rank and badges, dates of formation, naval and military distinctions, precedence, salutes, colours, and small arms, in Her Majesty's army and navy and auxiliary forces, including a record of the naval and military forces in the different countries of Great Britain and Ireland. 1888
Stenzel, Alfred. The British navy. 1898
Stenzel, Alfred. Groszbritannien und Irland: Das heer ... die flotte. 1897

20th century

Die englischen armee- und marine-uniformen im kriege, sowie die abzeichen an denselben. 1912
Great Britain. Admiralty. Uniform regulations for chief petty officers, men, and boys of the fleet, and for boys in the training establishments. 1907
Great Britain. Admiralty. Uniform regulations for petty officers, men, & boys of the fleet, and for boys in the training ships. 1904
Stripes and types of the Royal navy. 1909

Merchant marine

Great Britain. Board of trade. Committee on mercantile marine uniform. Report of the committee appointed by the Board of trade to advise as to the uniform to be adopted as the standard uniform for the mercantile marine. 1918

France

L'ancienne France: La marine et les colonies; Commerce. 1888
Depréaux, Albert. Les armées françaises d'outre-mer. Les uniformes des troupes de la marine et des troupes coloniales et nord-africaines. 1931
Fallou, Louis. Le bouton uniforme français (de l'ancien-régime à fin juillet 1914). 1915
Onfroy de Bréville, J. M. G. Aquarelles de Job: Tenue des troupes de France à toutes les époques armées de terre et de mer. 1900-04

18th century

Grasset de Saint Sauveur, Jacques. Recueil complet des costumes des autorités constituées, civiles, militaires, et de la marine. 1796
Hugo, Abel. France militaire. Histoire des armées françaises de terre et de mer de 1792 à 1837. 1838

19th century

Album militaire. 18—
Batsch, C. F., and Meuss, J. F. Frankreich. 1900
Ducamp, Jules. Histoire de l'armée d'Orient et de tous les régiments qui ont pris part aux campagnes de la Mer Noire et de la Mer Baltique. 1858
Foussereau, J. M. Uniformes de la garde nationale de l'armée et de la marine françaises de 1830-1832. 1832?
France. Ministère de la marine. Décret relatif à l'uniforme des officiers et fonctionnaires des differents corps de la marine, corps de troupe exceptés. 3 juin 1891, suivi d'un arrête ministériel 6 juin 1891. 1891
Gaildrau, Jules. L'armée française: recueil contenant toutes les tenues des différentes armes, les écoles militaires et les écoles de marine, les equipages et les trains de l'armée, l'administration militaire etc. 1855-56
Hennebert, Eugène. Nos soldats: infanterie, cavalerie, artillerie, marine, etc. 1887-88
Hugo, Abel. France militaire; histoire des armées françaises de terre et de mer de 1792 à 1837. 1838
Lalaisse, Hippolyte. Collection complète des uniformes de l'armée et de la marine françaises. 1840-48
Lalaisse, Hippolyte. Costumes de tous les corps de l'armée et de la marine françaises (sous Louis-Philippe I.). 1845-52
Lalaisse, Hippolyte. Uniformes de l'armée et de la marine françaises (1848-1852) 1852?
Leonnec, Paul. Nos marins. 1887
Marine française. 1886
Pacini, E. F. L. D. La marine, arsenaux, navires, équipages, navigation, atterrages, combats. 1844
Van Tenac, Charles. Histoire générale de la marine. 1853

20th century

Album historique de l'armée et de la marine. 1905-1906
Bucquoy, E. L. Les uniformes de l'armée française. 1935

Germany

19th century (to 1919)

Arnould, Georg. Das deutsche heer und die marine. 1891-94
Boguslawski, Albrecht von. Deutschland. Das heer, von Boguslawski ... Die flotte, von R. Aschenborn. 1900

Naval costume—Germany—19th century (to 1919)—*Continued*

Die deutsche marine und die deutsche schutztruppe für Ost-Afrika in ihrer neuesten uniformirung. 1893

Klemm, Heinrich. Lehrbuch für uniformschneider zur selbstbelehrung. 1896

Schlawe, Karl. Die deutsche marine in ihrer gegenwärtigen uniformierung. 1913

Sigel, G. A. Deutschlands heer und flotte, in wort und bild ... Germany's army and navy, by pen and picture. c1899

1919-date

Hoyer, K., and Brennecke, F. Die uniformen des reichsheeres und der reichsmarine nebst amtlichen uniformtafeln. 1925

Meyer-Döhner, Kurt. Die neue deutsche kriegsmarine, aufbau, gliederung, dienst und anderes wissenswerte mit flaggen- und uniformtafeln. 1935

Greece

Ancient times

Fickelscherer, Martin. Das kriegswesen der alten. 1888

Hungary

See Naval costume—Austria-Hungary

Italy

19th century

Cenni, Quinto. Album delle uniformi militari del regno: esercito e marino. 1879

Zanoli, Alessandro, baron. Sulla milizia cisalpino italiana. Cenni storico-statistici, dal 1796 al 1814. 1845

See also Naval costume—Cisalpine republic

20th century

Paschen, Karl. Italien: Die flotte. 1902

See also Naval costume—Cisalpine republic

Naples (Kingdom)

Collezione degli uniformi del reale esercito, della real marina napoletana. 1844

Netherlands

19th century

Beschrijving der kleeding, equipement en wapening van de Nederlandsche land-, zeemagt en schutterijen, zoo binnen het koningrijk, als in deszelfs overzeesche bezittingen. 1845

Raa, F. J. G. ten. De uniformen van de nederlandsche zee- en landmacht hier te lande en in de kolonien. 1900

Peru

Peru. Ministerio de guerra y marina. Uniformes de la marina de guerra Peruana. 1905

Portugal

Portugal militar; album de uniformes exercito e armada, con decoraçoès militares. 1890

Rome, Ancient

Fickelscherer, Martin. Das kriegswesen der alten. 1888

Russia

1800-1917

Drygalski, Albert von, and Zepelin, Constantin von. Russland. 1898

Sweden

19th century

Eklund, P. B. Svenska armens och flottans nuvarande uniformer ... Die schwedische armee und marine in ihrer gegenwartigen uniformirung. 1890

Fritze, C. E., pub. Svenska arméens och flottans nuvarande uniformer. ca1880

Turkey

Knoetel, Richard. Die türkische armee und marine in ihrer gegenwärtigen uniformirung. 1897

Mach, Richard von. Die wehrmacht der Türkei und Bulgariens. 1905

United States

Bowen, F. C. The sea. 1927

Bennett, F. M. The steam navy of the United States. 1896

Wagner, A. L., and Kelley, J. D. J. Our country's defensive forces in war and peace. The United States army and navy; their histories, from the era of the revolution to the close of the Spanish-American war; with accounts of their organization, administration, and duties. 1899

Walton, William. Army and navy of the United States from the period of the revolution to the present day. 1900

See also Coast guard, United States; Marine corps—United States

1812-1860

United States. Navy department. Regulations for the uniform and dress of the navy and marine corps of the United States. March, 1852. 1852

United States. Navy department. Regulations for the uniform and dress of the navy of the United States. 1841

1860-1898

United States. Navy department. Regulations for the uniform of the United States navy, December 1, 1866. 1866

United States. Navy department. Uniform for the United States navy. 1869

United States. Navy department. Uniform regulations. 1877

U. S. Navy department. Regulations relating to the uniforms of the officers of the United States navy ... January 22, 1883. 1883

Naval costume—United States—1860-1898—*Continued*

United States. Navy department. Regulations governing the uniform. 1886

United States. Navy department. Regulations governing the uniform. 1897

1898-1917

Christy, H. C. Men of the army and navy; characteristic types of our fighting men. 1899

United States. Marine corps. Uniform regulations, United States Marine corps, together with uniform regulations common to both U. S. Navy and Marine corps. 1912, rev. 1917

United States. Marine corps. Uniform regulations, United States Marine corps, together with uniform regulations common to both U. S. navy and Marine corps. 1913

United States. Navy department. Regulations governing the uniform of commissioned officers, warrant officers and enlisted men of the navy of the United States, 1905. 1905

United States. Navy dept. Uniform regulations, United States navy, together with uniform regulations common to both Navy and Marine corps. 1913

United States. Shipping board. Manual of uniforms and insignia. 191-?

Volk, C. G. United States officers' uniforms, army, navy, marine corps. 1917

1917-date

Falls, De W. C. Army and navy information. 1917

United States. Marine corps. Uniform regulations, United States Marine corps, 1922. 1922

United States. Navy department. Uniform regulations, United States navy, together with uniform regulations common to both Navy and Marine corps ... 1913, rev. to January 15, 1917. 1917

Naven. Bateson, Gregory

Le **navigationi** et viaggi nell Turchia. See Nicolay, Nicolas de, sieur d'Arfeuille. Les navigations, pérégrinations et voyages, faicts en la Turquie

Navigations et peregrinations orientales. Nicolay, Nicolas de, sieur d'Arfeuille

The **navigations,** peregrinations and voyages, made into Turkie. Nicolay, Nicolas, sieur d'Arfeuille

Les **navigations,** pérégrinations et voyages, faicts en la Turquie. Nicolay, Nicolas de, sieur d'Arfeuille

Navy. See Naval costume

Navy and army illustrated; a magazine descriptive and illustrative of everyday life in the defensive services of the British empire. Edited by Commander Charles N. Robinson. v. 1-21; Dec. 20, 1895-Dec. 30, 1905; new ser. v. 1-4 no. 41, Aug. 22, 1914-May 29, 1915. London, Hudson & Kearns [etc.] 1895-1915

25v. illus. ports. (part col.)
Published biweekly (irregular)
Suspended Dec. 1905-Aug. 1914. Title varies: Apr. 1903-Dec 1905, *King and his navy and army*
LC (6-5658)

Nayler, Sir George

The coronation of His Most Sacred Majesty King George the Fourth solemnized in the collegiate church of Saint Peter, Westminster ... By the late Sir George Nayler. London, H. G. Bohn 1837

lvi,134p. illus. 45pl. (42 col.) F.
Completed under direction of the publisher with the assistance of Sir William Woods and Charles George Young. A portion of the work was published by G. Nayler in two parts, 1824-27
Lipperheide 2690. LC 15-12539

Nazional garde almanach. Lipowsky, F. J.

Neale, John Mason

(comp.) Ecclesiological society, Cambridge. Illustrations of monumental brasses

Neander, Johann

Tabacologia: hoc est Tabaci, seu nicotianæ descriptio medicocheirurgicopharmaceutica vel ejus præparatio et usus in omnibus fermè corporis humani incōmodis. Lugduni Batavorum, ex officina I. Elzeviri 1626

19 l. 257p. pl. O.
Some of the plates show pipes
LC 7-19092

Neapel und Sizilien. See note under Saint Non, J. C. R. de. Voyage pittoresque

Der **neapolitanischen** könig leben und bildnuss. Kilian, Lucas

Near East. See East (Near East)

Nebel, Carl

Voyage pittoresque et archéologique dans la partie la plus intéressante du Mexique. Paris, M. Moench 1836

[82]p. 49pl. (20 col.) plan. F.
Eleven plates show Mexican costume
Colas 2184. Lipperheide 1623. LC 18-8421

Nebulo nebulonum. Murner, Thomas

Necessary qualifications of a man of fashion. Egerton, D. T.

Neckclothitania; or Tietania: being an essay on starchers, by one of the cloth. London, J. J. Stockdale 1818

38p. front. D.

Neckwear

Code de la cravate. 1828

Cravatiana, ou traité général des cravates considérées dans leur origine, leur influence politique, physique et morale, leurs formes, leurs couleurs et leurs éspèces. 1823

Histoire philosophique, anecdotique et critique de la cravate, et du col, précédé d'une notice sur la barbe. 1854

Le Blanc, H. The art of tying the cravat ... history of the cravat. 1829

Lescure, Alfred. Collection A. Lescure. Gestickte kragen; mitte des XIXe jahrhunderts. 1910

Neckwear—*Continued*

17th century

Hollar, Wenceslaus. Reisbuchlein von allerlei gesichter und etlichen frembden trachten. 1636

19th century

The art of dress; or Guide to the toilette: with directions for adapting the various parts of the female costume to the complexion and figure. 1839

Lescure, Alfred. Collection A. Lescure: Cols en broderies et en dentelles, milieu du dix-neuvième siècle. 1919?

Neckclothitania; or, Tietania: being an essay on starchers. 1818

Saint-Hilaire, É. M. H. L'art de mettre sa cravate de toutes les manières connues et usitées. 1827

Saint-Hilaire, É. M. H. Manuel complet de la toilette, ou L'art de s'habiller avec élégance et méthode, contenant L'art de mettre sa cravate. 1828

20th century

Edel, Edmund. Die krawatte. 1912

Keiser, J. R. The what, where, when and how of a man's cravat. c1902

Necrolivonica. Kruse, F. C. H.

Une **nécropole** royale à Sidon. Hamdī, O., bey, and Reinach, Théodore

De **Nederlanden**; karakterschetsen, kleederdragten, houding en voorkomen van verschillende standen. 's Gravenhage, Nederlandsche maatschappij van schoone kunsten 1841
168p. 126 illus. 42pl. O.
Colas 458, 2185. Lipperheide 965

Nederlandsche uniformen. Houtman, J. P.

Nederlands-oudheden. Kellen, David van der

Nederlandsch oost-indische typen. Pers, A. van

Nederlandsche kleederdragten. Bing, Valentyn, and Ueberfeldt, Braet von

Needlework

Antrobus, Mrs M. S. and Preece, Louisa. Needlework through the ages. 1928

Bach, Emilie. Neue muster im altem stil. [1894]

Dillmont, Thérèse de. Encyclopédie des ouvrages de dames. 1887

Dillmont, Thérèse de. Encyclopedia of needlework. 19—

Fréchon, Henri. Traité théorique et pratique de travaux à l'aiguille. 1913

Lowes, Mrs E. L. Chats on old lace and needlework. 1908

Schinnerer, Luise. Antike handarbeiten. 1895

Seligman, G. S., and Hughes, Talbot. Domestic needlework, its origins and customs throughout the centuries. 1926

Wilton, M. M. E., countess of. The art of needlework. 1841

See also Crocheting; Embroidery; Knitting; Lace; Needlework, Church; Tatting

Bibliography

Edinburgh. Royal Scottish museum. Library. List of books, &c. in the library of the Museum; part 2 Lace & needlework. 1892

Periodicals

Cendrillon. 1850-72

Frank Leslie's ladies' gazette of fashion and fancy needle work. 1854-57

Harper's bazaar. 1867+

Journal für moderne stickerei, mode und weibliche handarbeiten. 1844-61

La Mode illustrée. 1860+

Toilet; tijdschrift voor vrouwelijke handwerken. 1849-54

Ancient times

Brugsch, Émile. La tente funeraire de la princesse Ishimkheb provenant de la trouvaille de Déir el-Baharî. 1889

16th century

Beatus, M. G. and Bischius, J. L. Book of designs. 1601

Ciotti, G. B. Prima parte de' fiori, e disegni di varie sorti di ricami moderni. 1591

Franceschi, Domenico de. Serena opera nova di recami, nella quale si ritrova varie & diverse sorte di punti in stuora, & punti a filo, & medesimamenta di punto scritto & a fogliami, & punto in stuora a scacchetti, & alcuni groppi incordonati, & rosete. 1879

Han, Weygand, and Rab, Georg. Modelbůch neuw aller art nehens uñ stickens. 1562

Jobin, Bernhard. New künstlichs modelbuch von allerhand artlichen und gerechten mödeln auff der laden zu wircken. 1589

Livres à dentelles & dessins d'ornements. 1882-87

Müller, Christian. New modelbůch von vilen artigen und kunstreichen mödeln zůgericht. 1572

Ostaus, Giovanni. La vera perfettione del disegno di varie sorti di recami et di cucire punti a fogliami, punti tagliati, punti a fili e rimessi, punti in cruciati, punti a stuora, et ogni altra arte che dia opera a disegno. 1878

Quentel, Peter. Musterbuch für ornamente und stickmuster ... (1527-1529). 1880

Vinciolo, Frederic de. Les singuliers et nouveaux pourtraicts, du seigneur Frederic de Vinciolo, Venitien, pour toutes sortes d'ouvrages de lingerie. 1594

17th century

Florimi, Matteo. Fiori di ricami nuovamente posti in luce. 1603

Fürst, Paulus. Neues modelbuch von unterschiedlicher art der blumen und anderer genehten mödel nach itziger manier allen liebhaberinnen dieser kunst zumbesten vorgestellt. 1666-89

Hoffmann, Wilhelm. Neues modelbuch, 1604. 1891

Needlework—17th century—*Continued*
Kahr, Andreas. New modelbuch darinnen zum nehen allerhandt schone newe modelen zu finndenn seinn. 1626

18th century

Allerhand mödel zum stricken und nähen. 1748
Bildende künste für frauenzimmer, im sticken, waschen, stricken usw. 1785
Helmin, Margaretha. Kunst- und fleissübende nadel-ergötzungen, oder neu-erfundenes neh- und stick-buch. ca1700
Marot, Daniel. Nouveaux lieure de housses en broderie et en gallons. ca1700
Marot, Daniel. Nouveaux lieure de housses en broderie et en gallons. ca1700
Neue desseins zu der beliebten modearbeit in linon, nesseltuch und claar. 1792
Rieglin, Frau S. D. S. Neu-erfundenes modelbuch zum nähen, stricken, würcken und weben. 1757-61

19th century

Adnet-Molé, Mad. Steno-tricographie; das ist neueste französische methode stenographischer musterzeichnungen für kunst-und spitzenstrickerei. 1850
Alq, Louise d', pseud. Les ouvrages de main en famille. Le tricot—le filet—le filet-guipure—le crochet—la frivolité—le travail au métier. 1877
Album de divers travaux exécutés sur la fourche à franges, Deuxième. 1885
Album pour ouvrages de travaux à la fourche. 1883
Alford, M. Needlework as art. 1886
Andreä, Nanette. Leicht fassliche anweisungen zu verschiedenen weiblichen kunstarbeiten. 1843
Die arbeitstunden im stricken, nähen und sticken. 1810
Bach, Emilie. Muster stilvoller handarbeiten fur schüle and haus. 1879-1881
Bayle-Mouillard, Mme E. F. C. Nouveau manuel complet des demoiselles, ou Arts et métiers qui leur conviennent ... tels que la couture, la broderie ... etc. par Mme Celnart [pseud.] nouvelle ed. 1837
Beeton, S. O. Book of needlework. 1886
The book of fancy needlework. 1879
Caulfeild, S. F. A., and Saward, B. C. The dictionary of needlework, an encyclopedia of artistic, plain, and fancy needlework. 1882
Clasen-Schmid, Mathilde. Musterbuch für frauenarbeiten. 1881
Daul, A. Die beschäftigung des weiblichen geschlechts in der hand-arbeit. 1867
Dessins pour ouvrages de dames. ca1870
Dillmont, Thérèse de. Die knüpfarbeit. 1891
Dillmont, Thérèse de. Recueil d'ouvrages divers à exécuter avec les fils et les cotons D. M. C. 1888
Dorinda, pseud. Needlework for ladies for pleasure and profit. 1886
Georgens, J. D., and Gayette-Georgens, Frau J. M. von. Die schulen der weiblichen handarbeit. 1878
Handbook of plain and fancy needlework; containing a description of all the stitches used in plain needlework. ca1886
Heine, Emmy. Lehrbücher der handarbeit. Die gesammten handarbeitsarten für schule und haus. 1879-80
Hennings, Emma. Anweisung zur kunststrickerei. 1843-47
Hennings, Emma. Filet-schule, oder gründliche anweisung aller vorkommenden netz-arbeiten anzufertigen. 1843
Hennings, Emma. Häkel-, strick-, und stickmuster. 1842-43
Hennings, Emma. Die knöpfel-schule, oder Ausführliche beschreibung von seide, band, perlen und seinen bindfaden: taschen, börsen, kragen, jagdtaschen ... zu knöpfeln. 1845
Hennings, Emma. Modenheft ... Weibliche handarbeiten, im stricken, sticken, häkeln, filetstricken und andern brauchen. 1845-48
Hirth, Georg. Album für frauen-arbeit enthalend klassische motive für weissstickerei, bunt-, gold-, und applikationstickerei, spitzen-, verschnürungs- und knüpfarbeit, sowie weberei, passementrie und stoffbemalung. 1880
Hochfelden, Frau B. L. Ebhardt's handarbeiten; anleitung zum erlernen der verschiedenen handarbeitstechniken. 1894-95
Höflich, Nannette. Die wohlerfahrene elegante stickerin. 1855-1878
Journal des demoiselles. Manuel du Journal des demoiselles. 1883?
Kleines magazin von mustern zu weiblichen kunstarbeiten. ca1830
Kramer's Handbuch für weibliche handarbeiten. 1877
Kübler, M. S. Leitfaden für die verschiedenen weiblichen arbeiten. 1868
The lady's bazaar & fancy fair book. ca1880
The lady's handbook of fancy needlework. ca1880
Lambert, Miss A. The hand-book of needlework, decorative and ornamental, including crochet, knitting and netting. 1846
Leonhardt-Lysèr, Caroline, and Seifer, Cäcile. Encyclopädie der sämmtlichen frauen-künste. 1837
Lipperheide, Frieda, and Dorn, Anna. Die webe-arbeit mit hand-apparat. 1886
Lipperheide, Frieda, and Marggraff, Clara. Die Smyrna-arbeit. 1886

Needlework—19th century—*Continued*
Matthias, J. C. Kunstgewerbliches modell-u-muster-buch; eine sammlung charakterist. beispiele der decorativen und ornamentalen kunst aller völker und zeiten. 1866-67
Mee, Cornelia. A manual of knitting, netting, and crochet. 1844
Mönsterbok för slojdundervisningen i hem och skolor; efter gamla nordiska allmogearbeten. 1880-81
Netto, J. F. Taschenbuch der strick-, stick-, näh-, und anderer weiblichen arbeiten, ein toilettengeschenk für das jahr 1809. 1808
Owen, Mrs Henry. The illuminated book of needlework: comprising knitting, netting, crochet, and embroidery. 1847
Raymond, Mme Emmeline. Leçons de couture, crochet, tricot, frivolité, guipure sur filet, passementerie et tapisserie. 1868
Ruutz-Rees, Mrs J. E. M. Home decoration: art needle-work and embroidery; painting on silk, satin, and velvet; panel-painting; and wood-carving. 1881
Uebungstunden im stricken, nähen und sticken. 1810
Verboom, Agnès. La clef de tous les ouvrages de dames. 1866
The young ladies journal; complete guide to the work-table. 1888

20th century

Pour bien travailler chez soi. 1912

Needlework, Church
Antrobus, Mrs M. S. and Preece, Louisa. Needlework in religion. 1924
Cologne. Schnütgen-museum. Die liturgischen gewänder und kirchlichen stickereien. 1926
Dolby, Mrs A. M. Church embroidery, ancient and modern. 1867
Hall, M. R. English church needlework. 1901
Hulme, F. E. The history, principles and practice of symbolism in Christian art. 1892
Kendrick, A. F. English embroidery. 1905
Lambert, Miss A. Church needlework with practical remarks on its arrangement and preparation. 1844

Needlework as art. Alford, M.

Needlework for ladies. Dorinda, pseud.

Needlework in religion. Antrobus, Mrs M. S. and Preece, Louisa

Needlework through the ages. Antrobus, Mrs M. S. and Preece, Louisa

Neeffs, Emmanuel. See Geets, Willem. Ommegang de Saint-Rombaut (1875)

Neerlands Roem; het tijdvak van Frederik Hendrik. See Lennep, Jakob van. Galerij van beroemde Nederlanders

La **nef** des folz du monde. See note under Brant, Sebastian. Narrenschiff

Neff, Elizabeth Clifford
An Anglican study in Christian symbolism. Cleveland, O., The Helman-Taylor co. 1898
238,14p. 2 charts. D.
Describes church vestments from the time of the early Christians and church embroidery of various periods
LC 99-403

Negligees
Kneeland, Natalie. Negligees. 1925

Negri, Cesare
Nuove inventioni di balli ... conueneuoli a tutti i cavalieri e dame per ogni sorta di balletto, e brando d'Italia, di Spagna e di Francia. Milano, G. Bordone 1604
296p. front.(port.) illus. Q.
Illustrations show costume of the period
First edition, 1602, appeared under title: *Le gratie d'amore*
Lipperheide 3060. LC 12-18603

Negrillos. See Pygmies

Negritos. See Pygmies

Negrone, Giulio. See Baudouin, Benoît, jt. auth.

Nélaton, Étienne Moreau-. See Moreau-Nélaton, Étienne

Nelidov, Aleksandr Ivanovich, kni͡az
Klassisch-antike goldschmiedearbeiten im besitze Sr. Excellenz A. J. von Nelidow ... beschrieben und erläutert von Ludwig Pollak. Leipzig, K. W. Hiersemann 1903
x,197p. illus. xx col.pl. F.
LC 11-29337

Nelson, Henry Loomis
The army of the United States. See entry under United States. Quartermaster corps
Uniform of the army of the United States (illustrated) from 1774 to 1907. See entry under United States. Quartermaster corps

Nemeitz, Joachim Christoph
La vie de Paris sous la régence. See Franklin, A. L. A. La vie privée d'autre-fois. ser. 2, v 1

Nemes, Mihály
A magyar jelmez és fejlödése dióhéjban. Pozsony, K. Stampfel [1903]
103p. illus. nar.S. (Stampfelféle tudományos zsebkönyvtár, 147-148)
Shows Hungarian costume from the 4th to the 19th century
A magyar viseletek tört'enete ... szövegét vita Nagy Géza. Budapest, Franklin-társulat 1900
2v. in 1. 100pl.(39 col.) F.
A history of Hungarian costume

Nénot
La toilette des graces, ou Joli recueil des coëffures nouvellement. Cythère, Nénot [1789]
Front. 12 illus. T.
Colas 2186

Nepal
Boeck, Kurt. Durch Indien ins verschlossene land Nepal. 1903
Landor, A. H. S. Tibet & Nepal. 1905

Népies irodalmi társaság, Budapest
Transylvanian Hungarians, peasant art. See entry under Viski, Károly

Néprajzi osztályának értesítöje. Budapest. Magyar nemzeti múzeum

Nesfield-Cookson, Mrs Mary (Jones-Parry)
The costume book. New York, R. M. McBride [c1935]
278p. illus. D. $2
Bibliography: p272-78
Costume index. LC 35-27125

Nési, Marcel. See Archinard, L. Q. L'autre France (Tunisie, Algérie, Maroc). 1914

Nesselrode, Charles Robert, comte de
Armes et armures de la collection du comte de Nesselrode au château de Tzarevtchina Saratov (Russie) ... vente à Amsterdam le 28 avril 1909. Amsterdam [1909]
17p. 44pl. Q.
Shows Persian arms and armor from the 15th to 19th century

Netherlands (Kingdom, 1815-). Departement van binnenlandsche zaken
Beschreibung der aegyptischen sammlung. See entry under Leyden Rijksmuseum van oudheden

Netherlands
This subject includes material on Belgium 1815 to 1830. For later material see Belgium

Algemeen handelsblad. In kleuren en kleeren Nederlandsche volksdrachten. 1930
Anthonia Margaretha, pseud. Onze kleeding. 1910
Byvanck, A. W., and Hoogewerff, G. J. Noord-Nederlandsche miniaturen in handschriften der 14e, 15e en 16e eeuwen. 1922-25
Costumes civils français et hollandais de diverses époques. 1790?
Darwin, B. R. M. A golfer's gallery by old masters. 1927?
Durand-Gréville, Émile. Hubert et Jean van Eyck. 1910
Galle, Philippe. Les vies et alliances des comtes de Hollande et Zélande, seigneurs de Frise. 1586
Hofdijk, W. J. Ons voorgeslacht. 1873-75
Kellen, David van der. Nederlands-oudheden. 1861
Die oude tijd. 1869-74
Smids, Ludolf. Korte leevensschets en afbeeldingen der graaven van Holland, van Dirk de eerste, tot Koning Filip de twede, zynde de laatste. 1744
Vlaanderen door de eeuwen heen. 1912-1913

See also subdivision Netherlands under Academic costume; Agricultural laborers; Ceremonial and festival costume; Children; Coronations and coronation robes; Firemen; Funerals; Military costume; Monastic and religious orders; Naval costume; Nobles; Shooting costume; Students; Weddings and wedding dress

15th century

Biblia pauperum. Biblia pauperum; reproduced in facsimile from one of the copies in the British Museum. 1859
Maskerade, gehouden door de Leden van het Leidsche studenten-corps den 22n Juni 1880, ter viering van den 305den verjaardag der Leidsche hoogeschool, voorstellende den intocht van Phillips de Schoone binnen Amsterdam, den 27sten Juni, 1497. 1880
Master of the Amsterdam cabinet, 15th century. The Master of the Amsterdam cabinet, by Max Lehrs. 1893-94

16th century

Bol, Hans. The twelve months. ca1590
Die cronycke van Hollant, Zeelant ende Vrieslant. 1591
Jonghe, C. H. de. Bijdrage tot de kennis van de Noord-Nederlandsche costuumgeschiedenis in de eerste helft van de XVIe eeuw. 1916
Schaepkens, A. Choix de costumes de l'époque de Charles V à sa joyeuse entrée à Maestricht en 1520. 1851
Weiditz, Christoph. Das trachtenbuch des Christoph Weiditz, von seinen reisen nach Spanien (1529) und den Niederlanden (1531/32). 1927

17th century

Berge, P. A. van den. Costumes hollandois. 16—?
Buyteweck, Willem. Trachten der Holländerinnen. 1645
Cats, Jacob. Alle de werken. 1726
Cats, Jacob, and Farley, Robert. Moral emblems. 1860
Dyck, Sir Anthonie van. Icones principum, virorum doctorum, pictorum, chalcographorum, statuariorum nec non amatorum pictoriae artis numero centum ab Antonio van Dyck, pictore, ad vivum expressae eiusq. sumptibus aeri incisae. 1646
Eeckhout, Guilielmus vanden. Le nouvelle figure à la mode de ce tempts de fine. 1650
Hamckem, Martin. Frisia, seu De viris rebusque Frisiae illustribus libri duo. 1623
Hannema, Dirk, and Schendel, A. van. Noorden zuid- nederlandsche schilderkunst der XVII. eeuw. 1936
Hondius, Hendrik. Pictorum aliquot celebrium praecipue Germaniae inferioris effigies. 1610
Jonge, J. K. J. de, jonkheer. Intogt van Frederik Hendrik in s'Hertogenbosch in 1629. 1850
Lennep, Jakob van. Galerij van beroemde Nederlanders uit het tijdvak van Frederik Hendrik. ca1850
Muller, P. L. Onze gouden eeuw. De Republiek der Vereenigde Nederlanden in haar bloeitijd. 1896-98
Orlers, Jan. Genealogia illustissimorum comitum Nassoviae, in qua origo incrementa, & res gestae ab ijs, ab anno 682 ad praesentem hunc 1616, cum effigiebus XVI praecipuorum inter eos heroum. 1616

Netherlands—17th century—*Continued*

Post, Pieter. Begraeffenisse van ... Frederick Henrick ... prince van Orange, grave van Nassau ... En ghesneden door Pieter Nolpe. 1651

Quast, P. J. 'T is al verwart-gaaren, of afbeeldingen van vermomde redelaaren, en andere gespuis. 1640

Thienen, F. W. S. van. Das kostüm der blützeit Hollands, 1600-1660. 1930

18th century

Bosch, Johannes van den. De heeren stadhonderen van Vriesland. 1770

Chalon, Christina. Tweeëndertig stuks studien ordonnantien. 1779

Chalon, Christina. Zinspelende gedigtjes. 1806

Cuyck, Pieter van, the younger. Willem Carel Hendrik Friso, prince van Orange en Nassau ... Gehouden den IV. Februari MDCCLII. 1755

Ehrmann, T. F. Die Holländer; eine karakteristische skizze aus der völkerkunde. 1791

Ehrmann, T. F. Print-Geschenkjen voor myn kinderen, bestaande in afbeeldingen van Hollandsche, Friesche, Brabandsche en Fransche dragten en costumes. 1804

Hooghe, Romein de. Figures à la mode. ca1700

Hulst, L. van. De mode. 1781

Hurd, William. Oude en tegenwoordige staat en geschiedenis van alle godsdiensten, van de schepping af tot op den tegenwoordigen tijd. 1781-91

Ireland, Samuel. A picturesque tour through Holland, Brabant, and part of France, made in the autumn of 1789. 1796

Kleist, Heinrich von. Der zerbrochene krug ... illus. von Adolph Menzel. 1877

Nieuwe almanach, bestaande in eene verzameling van kleedingen en kapsels ... voor den jaare 1785. 1785

Nieuwe atlas der stad Amsterdam. 1787

Perkois, Jacobus, and Prins, J. H. Verzameling van verschillende gekleede mans- en vrouwen-standen. 1836

Riemer, Jacob de. Beschryving van 's Graven-hage, behelzende deszelfs oorsprong, benaming, gelegentheid, uitbreidingen, onheilen en luister. 1730-39

Swart, P. de. Afbeelding van de zaal en 't praalbed waar op het lyk van ... Willem Karel Hendrik Friso, prinse van Orange en Nassau ... in de manden November en December des jaars MDCCLI, ten toon is gesteld geweest. 1752

Troost, Cornelis. Tafereelen uit het burgerlijke leven van de Hollanders in de achttiende eeuw ... Scènes tirées de la vie domestique des Hollandais au dixhuitième siècle. 1811

Het vermaaklyk buitenleeven, of de zingende en speelende boerenvreugd. 1716

Periodicals

Kabinet van mode en smaak. 1791-94

Caricature and satire

Hess, David. Hollandia regenerata. 1796

19th century

Album de costumes des Pays-Bas. 1849

Belin, A., and others. Costumes de Suède, Norvège, Danemark, Hollande et Allemagne. 186-?

Bing, Valentyn, and Ueberfeldt, Braet von. Nederlandsche kleederdragten ... Costumes des Pays-Bas. 1857

Boughton, G. H. Sketching rambles in Holland. 1885

Costumes populaire et villageois de La Hollande. 1811?

A cruise; or, Three months on the continent by a naval officer. 1818

Esménard, Jeanne d'. Costumes des pays du Nord: Hollande et Danemark. ca1830

Greeven, H. Collection des costumes des provinces septentrionales du royaume des Pays-Bas. 1828

Hofdijk, W. J. Schets van de geschiedenis der Nederlanden. 1857

Jager, A. Costumes des Pays-Bas. 1878?

Kleederdragten, en typen der bewoners van Nederland. ca1850

Last, H. W. Verzameling van nederlandsche kleederdragten. Collection des costumes des Pays-Bas. 1850

Lovett, Richard. Pictures from Holland. 1887

Maaskamp, Evert. Afbeeldingen van de kleedingen, zeden en gewoonten in Holland, met den aanvang der negentiende eeuw. 1811?

Maaskamp, Evert, ed. Habillemens, moeurs et coutumes dans les provinces septentrionales des Pays-Bas. ca1820

Maaskamp, Evert. Representations of dresses, morals and customs, in the kingdom of Holland, at the beginning of the nineteenth century. 1808

Maaskamp, Evert. Voyage dans l'intérieur de la Hollande, fait dans les années 1807-1812. 1812?

De Nederlanden; karakterschetsen, kleederdragten, houding en voorkomen van verschillende standen. 1841

Semple, Miss. The costume of the Netherlands. 1817

Shoberl, Frederic, ed. Nederlands; containing a description of the character, manners, habits, and costumes. 1823

Periodicals

De Bazar; geillustreerd tijdschrift voor modes en handwerken. 1857-1900

Elegantia. 1807-10

20th century

Edwards, G. W. Holland of to-day. 1909

Jungman, Mrs Beatrix. Holland. 1904

Penfield, Edward. Holland sketches. 1907

Netherlands—*Continued*

BY REGION OR PROVINCE

Allard, A. Habillemens des paisans et paisannes de Hollande, de Frise, de Braband et autres provinces; Dragten der Boeren en Boerinner, in Holland, Vriesland, Braband, en elders. 1713

Gardilanne, Gratiane de and Moffat, E. W. The national costumes of Holland. 1932

Madou, J. B., and Eeckhout, J. J. Costumes du peuple de toutes les provinces du royaume des Pays-Bas. 1825-28

Molkenboer, Theodoor. De nederlandsche nationale kleederdrachten. 1917

Vries, R. W. P. de. Dutch national costumes. 1930

Netsukes

Brockhaus, Albert. Netsuke; versuch einer geschichte. 1905

Brockhaus, Albert. Netsukes. 1924

Nette afbeeldingen der eyge dragten van alle geestelyke orders. Schoonebeek, Adriaan

Nette afbeeldingen der eygene dragten van alle geestelyke vrouwen en nonnen orders. See Schoonebeek, Adriaan. Kurtze und gründliche histori ... der Gott-geweyhten orden aller closter-jungfrauen

Netto, August

Neue original-desseins für die neuerfundene stickerei über stricknadeln. Dresden, Hilscher [1809]
1 l. 12 col.pl. Q.
Lipperheide 3938

Netto, Curt

Papier-schmetterlinge aus Japan ... illustrirt von Paul Bender. Leipzig, T. O. Weigel. 1888
xiii,266p. 142 illus. 21pl.(2 col.) Q
Shows costume of Japan
Lipperheide 1565

Netto, Johann Friedrich

Taschenbuch der strick-, stick-, näh-, und anderer weiblichen arbeiten, ein toilettengeschenk für das jahr 1809. Leipzig, J. C. Hinrichs [1808]
xiv,58p. 27pl.(9 col.) O.
A supplement for the year 1811 was published under title: *Neuestes toilettengeschenk der ... strick-, stick-, näh- und andern weiblichen arbeiten* (Leipzig, J. C. Hinrichs [1810] 60p. 29pl.(11 col.)
Lipperheide 4064-65

Zeichen- mahler- und stickerbuch zur selbstbelehrung für damen. Leipzig, Voss 1795
38p. 24pl. F.
Lipperheide 3931

Netto, Johann Friedrich, and Lehmann, F. L.

L'art de tricoter ... ou Instruction complète et raisonnée sur toutes sortes de tricotages simples et compliqués. Leipzig, Voss 1802
51p. 50pl.(25 col.) Q.
Lipperheide 4062

Neu alamodische ritterliche fecht- und schirm-kunst. Doyle, Alexander

Neu eröffnete welt-galleria. Abraham a Santa Clara

Neu feldt und ackerbau. Crescenzi. Pietro de

Neu gestellter schreib-kalender auf das jahr ... 1748. Welper, Eberhard

Neu gezeichnete muster zum stricken in garn, wolle, seide und zur perlstrickerei. Pirna, C. A. Friese 1811
3pts. pl. Q.
Lipperheide 4068

Neu künstliches fechtbuch. Sutor, Jakob

Neu uniformirte königlich sächsische armee, nach der natur gezeichnet und in gruppen dargestellt. Dresden, 1811
16p. 8 col.pl. Q.
Plate 7 signed: J. Beger
Colas 2194

Neuburger, Otto

Die mode; wesen, entstehen und wirken. Berlin, F. Siemenroth 1913
96p. O.

Neue alamodische sitten-schul. See Alamodische hobelbanck

Die **neue** bekleidung und ausrüstung der russischen kavallerie. Tettau, Eberhard, freiherr von

Das **Neue** blatt; ein illustrirtes familien-journal. 1.-18. jahrg. 1870-1887. Leipzig, A. H. Payne
18v. illus. Q.
Lipperheide 4730

Neue curieuse beschreibung der gantzen artillerie. Mieth, Michael

Neue desseins zu der beliebten mode-arbeit in linon, nesseltuch und claar. Braunschweig 1792
1 l. 8pl. Q.
Lipperheide 3929

Die **neue** deutsche kriegsmarine, aufbau, gliederung, dienst und anderes wissenswerte mit flaggen- und uniformtafeln. Meyer-Döhner, Kurt

Die **neue** deutsche reichswehr. Leipzig, M. Ruhl [1919]
2v. 9 fold.col.pl. D.

Neue Europa. See Europa

Neue Franckfurter jüdische kleider-ordnung, dess gleichen wie es bey ihren verlölnüssehn, hochzeiten, beschneidung en, gevatterschafften und anderen vorfällen hinführo soll gehalten werden. Aus dem hebräischen ... übersetzet ... von Johann Jacob Schudt. Franckfurt am Mayn, M. Andreä 1716
62p. O.
Lipperheide 3343

Neue frauentracht. Buschmann, Hedwig

Die **Neue** frauentracht; monatschrift. v 1-6, no 12; okt. 1903-dec. 1909. München, G. D. W. Callwey
6v. illus. pl. patterns. O.
Published monthly. Volumes 2-3, subtitle reads: Mitteilungen der freien vereinigung für verbesserung der frauenkleidung

Neue geometrische und perspectinische inventiones. Faulhaber, Johann

Neue häkelmappe; eine anzahl schöner häkelmuster nebst genauer beschreibung. Leipzig, Kramer & co. [1879]
12 l. 29 illus. Q.
Lipperheide 4122

Neue häkel-vorlagen. Reinle, Sophie

Neue illustrirte zeitung; illustrirtes familienblatt. 1.-15. jahrg. 1873-1887. Wien, L. C. Zamarski
15 v. illus. F.
Lipperheide 4741

Neue kostüme auf den beiden königlichen theatern in Berlin. Brühl, K. F. M. P., graf von

Der **neü** Layenspiegel. Tengler, Ulrich

Neue macramé-vorlagen. See Reinle, Sophie. Neue häkel-vorlagen

Neue muster in altem stil. Bach, Emilie

Neue muster-vorlagen für farbige kreuzsticharbeiten. Scheffers, A.

Neue original-desseins für die neuerfundene stickerei über stricknadeln. Netto, August

Neue Pariser modeblätter. 1.-14. jahrg. 1827-40. Hamburg & Leipzig, Taubert
14v. col.illus. O.-Q.
Various publishers
Lipperheide 4609

Neue Pariser moden- und modell-zeitung für damen- und kinder-garderobe. Hauptorgan für geschmackvolle anfertigung aller einschlagenden bekleidungs-gegenstände in familienkreisen, sowie für damenkleidermacher, &c. 1.-11 jahrg; 1860-1870. Leipzig, Fries
11v. illus. Q.-F.
Twenty four numbers a year. Volumes 1-8 published: Dresden, Klemm

Neue praktische strickschule; vollständige anleitung zum erlernen des strickens mit ... strick-mustern. Leipzig, Kramer & co. [1879]
28p. 27 illus. O.
Lipperheide 4123

Neue sammlung von schweizer trachten. König, F. N.

Neue stickmuster. Zeissig, M. C.

Neue und curieuse theatralische tanz-schul. See Lambranzi, Gregorio. Nuova e curiosa scuola de' balli theatrali

Die **neue** uniformirung, rüstung und bewaffnung der königlich baierischen armee. Monten, Dietrich

Neue welt; illustrirtes unterhaltungsblatt für das volk. v 1-12 no.20; 1876-1887. Breslau, Geiser
12v. illus. Q.
Published monthly. Weekly, 1876-82; fortnightly, 1883-86
Changes of publisher: 1876, Leipzig, Genossenschaftsbuchdr.; 1877-86, Stuttgart, Dietz

Neue Wiener friseur-zeitung. 1. jahrg., 1887+ Wien
Illus. F.
Title varies: 1887, *Österreichisch-ungarische friseur- und razeur-zeitung*
Colas 2193. Lipperheide 4787

Neue zeichnungen zur weissen stickerey. [Hamburg, Herold 1820]
1 l. 6pl. F.
Lipperheide 3945

Neue zeitung für die elegante welt. See note under Zeitung für die elegante welt

Neue zuschneidekunst für damenbekleidung. Borchers, Fr.

Neu-eingerichtete und vermehrte bilder-geographie von Europa, Asia, Africa und America worinnen alle nationen nach ihrem habit in saubern figuren ... vorgestellt werden. Erffurth, J. M. Funck 1738
592p. 28 l. front. illus. O.
Foreword signed: J. J. Martini
A new edition, with additional woodcuts, of *Neu-eröffnetes amphi-theatrum*, (Erffurth, J. M. Funck 1723-28)
Colas 2187-88. Lipperheide 35-36. LC 5-22118 (1723-28 ed.)

Neuer discurs von der rittermessigen und weitberümbten kunst des fechtens. Köppe, Joachim

Neuer systematischer zuschneide-unterricht. Müller, Susanna

Neuerburg, firm, Cologne
(pub.) Cudell, Robert. Das buch vom tabak

Neu-erfundenes modelbuch zum nähen, stricken, würcken und weben. Rieglin, Frau S. D. S.

Neueröffnete jägerpractica. Döbel, H. W.

Neu-eröffnete samlung der mit ihren eigenen arbeiten und werckzeugen eingekleideten künstlern, handwerckern und professionen. See Engelbrecht, Martin. Assemblage nouveau des manouvriers habilles

Neu-eröffnetes amphi-theatrum. See Neu-eingerichtete und vermehrte bilder-geographie

Neues journal für fabriken, manufakturen, handlungen, kunst und mode. v 1-6, no 2; 1808-1811. Leipzig, J. F. Gleditsch
6v. ca600pl. (part col.) O.
A fashion periodical. Continues *Journal für fabrik*. Some of the plates carry samples of materials
Colas 1573. Lipperheide 4574

Neues magazin für frauenzimmer. v 1-7, 1787-89. Strasburg, Levrault
7v. col.illus. O.
Continuation of *Magazin für frauenzimmer*. "Hrsg. von Seybold"
Colas 1942. Lipperheide 4567

Neues modelbuch, 1604. Hoffmann, Wilhelm

Neues modelbuch 1619. Bretschneider, Andreas

Neues modelbuch von unterschiedlicher art der blumen. Fürst, Paulus

Neues polnisches pferd und reuter büchlein. Sandrart, S. M.

Neues stick-muster-buch. Oppenheim, Guido

Neues stick und zeichnungs-buch verschiedene neue desseins enthaltend. Nürnberg, A. G. Schneider [1818]
12pl. Q.
Lipperheide 3943

Neues system des zuschneidens der damenkleider. Clasen-Schmid, Mathilde

Neües türckisches pferd und reüter büchlein. Sandrart, S. M.

Neues uniform-reglement für die beamten der verwaltung der indirecten steuern. See Rumpf, C. Der preussische steuerbeamte in bezug auf seine dienst- und rechtsverhältnisse

Neues Wiener tagblatt
Festzug der stadt Wien zur silbernen hochzeit des kaiserpaares. Wien, 1879
8 l. 28 illus. F.
At head of title: Extra-ausgabe
Lipperheide 2645

Neuest physikalisch-politische reisen in den jahren 1788 und 1789. Hacquet, Balthasar

Neueste abbildung aller kayserl. königl. regimenter. Assner, Leopold

Neueste adjustirung der Wiener bürger militärs. Franceschini, G., and Hagemann, A.

Die **neueste** art zur galanten und theatralischen tantz-kunst. Bonin, Louis

Neueste beschreibung derer griechischen christen in der Türckey. Elssner, Jacob

Neueste englische und französische muster zu aller art der stickerei. Berrin, Emilie and Savin, J. C.

Neueste hof- und staats- trachten in Frankreich. See Costumes de la cour impériale de France

Neueste moden für unsere damen. 1879-1896. Leipzig, A. H. Payen
Illus. Q.
Colas 2190. Lipperheide 4737

Neueste Pariser moden. Balzer, Johann

Neueste reisen durch Deutschland, Böhmen, Ungarn, die Schweiz, Italien und Lothringen, worinnen der zustand und das merkwürdigste dieser länder beschrieben ... wird. Keyssler, J. G.

Neueste und geschmackvollste maskenanzüge. Leipzig, Baumgärtner 1839-53
9pts. 72 col.pl. ob.Q.
Colas 2192. Lipperheide 3177

Neueste und vollständige schule der damenschneiderei. Klemm, Heinrich

Neueste vollständige und gründliche anweisung zum häkeln der spitzen, manschetten, hauben, börsen, tücher, handschuhe. Hertel, Louise

Die **neuesten** und elegantesten stickmuster in weiss. Hennings, Emma

Neuestes costume der staats-beamten der Republik Frankreich nach dem befehl des ersten consuls Buonaparte. No place, 1802
5 col.pl. O.
Costume der ersten consuls Buonapart, des general sekretairs beim staats-rath, der minister der französischen republik, der staats-rathe, des staats sekretairs
Colas 2191

Neuestes gemälde der erde und ihrer bewohner, oder Schilderung der vorzüglichsten merkwürdigkeiten, der sitten und gebräuche, der lebensart und den kostümen der verschiedenen völkerschaften aller welttheile ... Die Schweiz. Schweidnitz, C. F. Stuckart 1824
199p. 14 col.pl. Q.
Half title: *Die Schweiz oder Sitten, gebräuche, trachten und denkmäler der Schweitzer*
Lipperheide 908

Neuestes gemälde von Berlin, auf das jahr 1798, nach Mercier. Kölln, P. Hammer 1798
174p. O.
Pages 3-20 are on fashions of the period
Lipperheide 817

Neuestes musterbuch von ... strick-mustertouren. Pauker, Juliane

Neuestes Pariser moden-journal für herren und damen. 1.-6. band; 1843-1848. Ulm, E. Nübling
6v. col.pl. O.
Superseded *Pariser moden-journal*
Colas 2277. Lipperheide 4634

Neuestes toilettengeschenk der ... strick-, stick-, näh- und andern weiblichen arbeiten. See Netto, J. F. Taschenbuch der strick-, stick-, näh-, anderer weiblichen arbeiten

Neufeld, Charles
A prisoner of the khaleefa; twelve years' captivity at Omdurman; 4th ed. New York, G. P. Putnam 1900
xiv,365p. front. pl. ports. map, plans. O.
Appeared in the *Wide world magazine,* June 1899 to March 1900, under title *In the khalifa's clutches*
Shows costume of the Anglo-Egyptian Sudan
LC 8-31281

Neugebauer, Salomon
Icones & vitae principum ac regum Poloniae. Francofurti, I. de Zetter 1626
144p. 44 illus. Q.
Lipperheide 1389

Neun blatt slavische trachten im Bayreuther lande. Jarwart, Sixtus, and Heinel, Eduard

Die **neunte** deutsche Bibel. Bible. German

Neu-polirter geschicht- kunst- und sittenspiegel ausländischer völcker. Francisci, Erasmus

Neureuther, L.
(illus.) Rheinwald, J. L. C. Baierische volkstrachten

Neustätter, O.
Die reform der frauenkleidung auf gesundheitlicher grundlage. München, F. P. Datterer 1903
109p. illus. 1 pl. O.

Neuville, Marie Alphonse de
(illus.) Maillot, T. J. R. En campagne

Neuw jag unnd weydwerck buch, das ist ein grundtliche beschreibung vom anfang der jagten, auch vom jäger. Franckfurt, S. Feyerabendt 1582
2v. 171 illus. F.
Illustrations by Jost Amman
Lipperheide 3020

Neuwied, Maximilian Alexander Philipp prinz von Wied. See Wied-Neuwied, M. A. P. prinz von

Nevill, Ralph Henry
British military prints. London, The Connoisseur publishing company 1909
lii,72p. col.front. illus. 23 col.pl. Q.
Shows English uniforms of the 18th and 19th centuries
"List of military prints and books with plates of military interest—By W. G. Menzies": p65-72
Colas 2195. LC A10-564

Nevill, Ralph Henry—*Continued*

Old English sporting prints and their history [by] Ralph Nevill, edited by Geoffrey Holme. London, The Studio, ltd. 1923
xv,23p. CIII pl. on 96 l.(part col.) F.
Most of the plates show hunting and horse racing in England during the 18th and 19th centuries
LC 23-14933

The world of fashion, 1837-1922. London, Methuen [1923]
280p. col.front. pl. O.
Colas 2196. LC 24-4062

The **New** America and the Far East. Browne, G. W.

New and curious school of theatrical dancing. Lambranzi, Gregorio

The **new** and simplified system of dress-cutting and tailoring. Browne, Miss M. P.

The **new** Baltic states and their future. Rutter, Owen

The **New** bon ton magazine; or, Telescope of the times. v. 1-6; May 1818-21. London, J. Johnston
6v. col.pl. O.
Published monthly. No more published?
LC 10-13304

New Caledonia

Anderson, J. W. Notes of travel in Fiji and New Caledonia. 1880

A **new** general collection of voyages and travels ... comprehending everything remarkable in its kind, in Europe, Asia, Africa, and America. London, T. Astley 1745-47.
4v. fronts. pl.(part fold.) maps(part fold.) plans(part fold.) 26½cm.
Compiled by John Green, but known as the Astley collection
Contents: v 1 First voyages of the Portugueze to the East Indies. 1418-1546; First voyages of the English to Guinea, and the East Indies, 1552-1598; First voyages of the English to the East Indies, set forth by the company of merchants, 1600-1620. Voyages to Africa and the islands adjacent, 1455-1721; v2 Voyages and travels along the western coast of Africa, 1637-1735. Voyages and travels to Guinea and Benin, 1666-1726. Description of Guinea; v3 Voyages and travels to Guinea, Benin, Kongo and Angola. Description of Loango, Kongo, Angola, Benguela, and adjacent countries. Description of the countries along the eastern coast of Africa, from Cape of Good Hope to Cape Guarda Fuy. Voyages and travels in China, 1655-1722; v4. Description of China, of Korea, eastern Tartary and Tibet. Travels through Tartary, Tibet, and Bukhâria, to and from China, 1246-1698
The narrators comment on the dress of people which they encounter. Plates and illustrations almost never show costume
For French translation see Prévost, A. F. *Histoire générale des voyages*
LC 6-3061

The **new** German field service uniform. Great Britain. War office

New Guinea

Bateson, Gregory. Naven; a survey of the problems suggested by a composite picture of the culture of a New Guinea tribe. 1936

Finsch, Otto. Ueber bekleidung, schmuck, und tätowirung der Papuas der südostküste von Neu-Guinea. 1885

See also subdivision New Guinea under Masks; Tattooing

New Guinea, Dutch. See Pygmies—New Guinea, Dutch

New Guinea masks. Lewis, A. B.

The **new** gymnosophy. Parmelee, M. F.

New künstlich fechtbuch. Heussler, Sebastian

New künstlichs modelbuch. Jobin, Bernhard

The **new** Larned History for ready reference. Larned, J. N.

New modelbuch darinnen zum nehen allerhandt schone newe modelen zu finndenn seinn. Kahr, Andreas

New modelbüch darinnen allerley künstliche viesirüng und müster artiger züege und schöner blümmen zu zierlichen uberschlegen. See Bretschneider, Andreas. Neues Modelbuch 1619

New modelbůch von vilen artigen und kunstreichen mödeln zůgericht. Müller, Christian

New monthly Belle assemblée. v 1-73; 1834-1870. London
Col.illus. col.pl. Q.
Supersedes *La Belle assemblée.* July 1852+ the volumes are identical with those of *Ladies cabinet of fashion, music and romance* and *Ladies companion and monthly magazine*

New Orleans. See Street venders—United States—New Orleans

New Orleans characters. Frémaux, L. J.

The **new** Palestine. McCrackan, W. D.

New Peterson magazine. See Peterson magazine

The **new** Russia. Lethbridge, A. B.

A **new** system of sword exercise. See O'Rourke, M. J. Sword exercise illustrated

New uniform regulations of the Spanish army. Spain. Ministerio de la guerra

New York. American museum of natural history. See American museum of natural history, New York

New York. Metropolitan museum of art

The Bashford Dean collection of arms and armor in the Metropolitan museum of art; introduction and biographical outline by Carl Otto v. Kienbusch ... catalogue by Stephen V. Grancsay. Portland, Me., Pub. by the Southworth press for the Armor and arms club of New York city 1933
270p. front. LXIII pl. tables(1 fold.) F.
LC 34-1270

Catalogue of a loan exhibition of arms and armor, by Bashford Dean ... New York, February the sixth to April the sixteenth, MCMXI [New York, The Gilliss press, c1911]
xxv,85p. front. illus. pl.
LC 11-2014

Catalogue of a loan exhibition of Japanese sword fittings. See entry under Armor and arms club, New York

New York. Metropolitan museum—*Cont.*

Catalogue of a loan exhibition of Japanese sword guards. See entry under Armor and arms club, New York

Catalogue of European arms and armor, by Bashford Dean. New York, The Metropolitan museum of art 1905
215p. illus. pl. Q. (Handbook. no15)
Bibliography: p[211]-15
LC 6-16292

Catalogue of the loan collection of Japanese armor, prepared by Bashford Dean. New York, The Metropolitan museum of art 1903
71p. illus. pl. O. (Hand-book no14)
LC 5-1449

Chinese textiles; an introduction to the study of their history, sources, technique, symbolism, and use, by Alan Priest and Pauline Simmons; new and rev. ed. New York, The Museum 1934
x,96p. illus. pl. O. $1.50, pa. $1
Bibliography: p95-96
Costume index. LC 34-38348

The daily life of the Greeks and Romans, as illustrated in the classical collections, by Helen McClees, with additions by C. Alexander. New York, 1933
xviii,143p. illus. O.
Fifth edition, with corrections. First edition published 1924
LC 34-20054

Eighteenth-century costume in Europe; a picture book. New York, The author 1937
20pl. on 10 l. D. pa 25c (Picture books)
Text signed Frances Little
LC 38-8533

The Gōda collection of Japanese sword fittings; catalogue, by Robert Hamilton Rucker. New York, The Museum 1924
lxviii,93p. front.(port.) illus. O.
Bibliography: p71
LC 24-17952

Handbook of arms and armor, European and oriental, by Bashford Dean; 4th ed. New York, The Museum 1930
xviii,331p. illus.(incl.ports.) 2 plans(1 fold.) O.
First edition: 1915 (161p. 65pl.)
LC 30-31293

Historical arms and armor; twenty plates. New York [The Museum press] 1935
[8]p. 20pl. on 10 l. D. [Picture books]
Text signed: Stephen V. Grancsay
LC 35-10419

Japanese costume; an exhibition of nō robes and Buddhist vestments, by Alan Priest; New York, February 18 through April 14, 1935. [New York] The Museum 1935
42p. 45pl. O.
Shows theatrical costume of Japan
Bibliography: p40-42
Costume index. LC 35-4064

Jewelry, the art of the goldsmith in classical times as illustrated in the museum collection, by Christine Alexander. New York, The Museum 1928
50p. illus. IV col.pl.(incl.front.) O.
LC 28-16058

Red-figured Athenian vases. See entry under Richter, G. M. A.

The treasure of Lahun. See entry under Lithgoe, A. M.

New York. Museum of modern art

International exhibition of theatre art, January 16-February 26, 1934. New York, The Museum of modern art [c1934]
68p. pl. O.
This material also issued as Lee Simonson's *Theatre art*
Contents: The designer in the theatre, by Lee Simonson; The masque designs of Inigo Jones, by Allardyce Nicoll; The Drottningholm theatre, lost and found, by John Anderson; Modern German theatre art, by P. A. Merbach; Russia, the designer as collaborator, by O. M. Sayler; The American theatre and its designers, by J. M. Brown
LC 34-33553

New York. Museum of the American Indian, Heye foundation

Indian notes. v. 1+ Jan 1924+ New York, Museum of the American Indian, Heye foundation 1924+
Illus. pl.(part fold.) D.
"Published occasionally." Current 1938
LC (24-11173)

Indian notes and monographs; a series of publications relating to the American aborigines. v. 1, no. 1+ New York, Museum of the American Indian, Heye foundation, 1919+
Illus. pl. T.
Current 1938. Edited, 1920+ by F. W. Hodge
LC (20-2329)

New York. Public library. See Baldwin, Muriel. Costume 1400-1600

New York (State). See United States—New York (State)

New York (State) Adjutant general's office

Regulations relating to the uniform of the National guard of the state of New York 1899. Albany, N. Y., Brandow 1899
38p. pl. D.

New York historical society. See Williams, C. R. Gold and silver jewelry and related objects

New York in the elegant eighties. See Valentine's manual of old New York

New York life insurance company

Colonial children's costumes. New York, New York life insurance co. 1900
1 l. 6 col.pl.

New Zealand

Carpenter, F. G. Australia, New Zealand and some islands of the South Seas. 1924

Cook, James. A voyage towards the South pole, and round the world. 1777

Native races

See Maoris

The **New** Zealanders illustrated. Angas, G. F.

Newberry, Percy Edward
Scarabs; an introduction to the study of Egyptian seals and signet rings. London, A. Constable 1906
xvi,218p. illus. XLIV pl.(incl.col.front.) Q. (University of Liverpool. Institute of archaeology. Egyptian antiquities)
LC 6-10481

Newe summarische welt historia. Fabronius, Hermann

Newen politischen Stätt: und emblemata-buchs. See Meisner, Daniel. Politica-politica

Newes modelbuch. Sibmacher, Johann

Newes soldaten buchlein. Kilian, Lucas

Newes vollkommenes modelbuch. See note under Hoffmann, Wilhelm. Neues modelbuch, 1604

Newest styles for men. Autumn 1924/Winter 1925, Spring/Summer 1926+ New York, Tailoring arts pub. co. 1924+
Illus. F.
Published semi-annually. Current 1938

Newfoundland
Carpenter, F. G. Canada and Newfoundland. 1924

Newhouse, C. B.
Military incidents. No place, ca1840
6 col.pl. ob.F.
Plates, engraved by R. G. Reeve after C. B. Newhouse, show English military uniforms of the period
Colas 2197

Newmark, Harris
Sixty years in Southern California, 1853-1913, containing the reminiscences of Harris Newmark, ed. by Maurice H. Newmark [and] Marco R. Newmark; 3d ed. rev. and augmented. Boston and New York, Houghton Mifflin 1930
xxxv,744p. front. pl. ports. facsims. O. $5
LC 16-17932

Newmark, Marco Ross
(ed.) Newmark, Harris. Sixty years in Southern California

Newmark, Maurice Harris
(ed.) Newmark, Harris. Sixty years in Southern California, 1853-1913

Neyffer, Johann Christoff
Illustrissimi Wirtembergici ducalis novi collegii quod Tubingae quâ situm quâ studia quâ exercitia, accurata delineatio; Ludwig Ditzinger sculpsit, Io. Christoff Neyffer pinxit. No place, ca1580
1 l. 9pl. O.
Lipperheide 2014

Niccolini, Antonio
Real museo Borbonico. See entry under Naples. Museo nazionale

Nice. See France—By region or province—Nice

Nice; vues et costumes. Delbecchi, Amedée

Nice-carnaval. [Paris, Modes de la femme de France 192-?]
31p. col.pl. F.

Nichols, John
The progresses, processions, and magnificent festivities, of King James the First, his royal consort, family, and court; collected from original manuscripts, scarce pamphlets, corporation records, parochial registers. London, J. B. Nichols 1828
4v. fronts. 32pl. facsims. Q.
Shows court dress at the time of James I
LC 3-29463

Nicholson, William
London types. London, W. Heinemann 1898
9 l. 12 col.pl. F.
Shows a coster, beefeater, barmaid, soldier, lady, flower girl, paper boy, hawker, drum major, policeman, bluecoat boy, sandwich man

Nick, Old, pseud. See Forgues, P. E. D.

Nicobar islands
Kloss, C. B. In the Andamans and Nicobars. 1903

Nicolaï, Friedrich
Über den gebrauch der falschen haare und perrucken in alten und neuern zeiten. Berlin und Stettin, 1801
xi,179p. 17pl. O.
The plates show sixty six types of wigs
A French translation by Henri Jansen has title: *Recherches historiques sur l'usage des cheveux postiches et des perruques, dans les temps anciens et modernes* (Paris, L. Collin 1809. 221p. 2pl. with 65 illus.)
Colas 2198-2199. Lipperheide 1686-1687

Nicolai, Johann
Disquisitio de chirothecarum usu & abusu, in qua varii ritus, varia jura, & symbola illarum fuse exhibentur. Giessæ-Hassorum, H. Mülleri 1701
12 l. 144p. T.
Lipperheide 1719. LC 4-8466

Nicolas, Sir Nicholas Harris
History of the orders of knighthood of the British Empire; of the Order of the Guelphs of Hanover; and of the medals, clasps, and crosses, conferred for naval and military services. London, J. Hunter 1842
4v. col.fronts. illus. col.pl. F.
Lipperheide 1925. LC 25-12116

Nicolas, S. R. See Chamfort, S. R.

Nicolay, Nicolas de, sieur d'Arfeuille
The navigations, peregrinations and voyages, made into Turkie ... tr. out of the French by T. Washington the younger. London, T. Dawson 1585
161 l. illus. pl. D.
A translation of his *Les navigations.* Edited by John Stell
LC 5-7290

Les navigations, peregrinations et voyages, faicts en la Turquie. Anvers, G. Silvius, imprimeur du roy 1576
305,[25]p. 60pl. D.
These plates, engraved by Assuerus van Londerseel, are taken in reduced size from the author's *Les quatre premiers livres des Navigations et pérégrinations orientales.* Another French edition has title: *Discours et histoire véritable des navigations ... en la Turquie* (Anvers, A. Coninx 1586. 61pl. O. LC 5-7291)
Many editions. Italian edition: *Le navigationi et viaggi nell Turchia* (Anversa, G. Silvio 1577. O. LC 5-7288) and (Venetia, F. Ziletti 1580. 67 illus. F. LC 5-7289)

Nicolay, Nicolas de—*Continued*
Dutch edition: *De schipvaert ende reysen gedaen int landt van Turckyen* (T' Antwerpen, W. Silvius 1576. Q.)
German edition: *Von der schiffart und rayss in die Türckey* (Nürnberg, D. Gerlatz 1572. F.) and (Autorff, durch W. Silvium 1576. 61 illus. Q.)
Colas 2201-2207. Lipperheide 1397z, 1398-1399b. LC 24-24221

Les quatre premiers livres des Navigations et peregrinations orientales ... avec les figures au naturel tant d'hommes que de femmes selon la diversité des nations, & de leur port, maintien, & habitz. Lyon, G. Roville 1568
181p. 60 col.pl. F.
Plates show costume of Turkey, Arabia, and Greece in the 16th century. Engravings are attributed to Louis Danet
Colas 2200. LC 5-8226

See also Chalcondylas, Laonicus. Histoire general des Turcs

Nicoll, Allardyce
Masks, mimes and miracles; studies in the popular theatre. New York, Harcourt, Brace 1931
407p. front. illus. Q.
Shows theatrical costume and masks of various periods
LC 31-34446

Nicoll, John Ramsay Allardyce. See Nicoll, Allardyce

Nicoll, Josephine, pseud. See Calina, Josephine

Nideck, A. van, alleged author. See Antiquitates sacrae & civiles Romanorum explicatae

Die **niederländische** armee nebst den kolonialtruppen und freiwilligenkorps in ihrer gegenwärtigen uniformierung ... gezeichnet von J. Hohmann. Leipzig, M. Ruhl [1891]
32p. 16 fold.col.pl. D.
Colas 2603

Niederländische historien. Meteren, Emmanuel von

Niederle, Lubor
(ed.) Prague. Národopisné museum československé. Moravské slovensko

Niedersächsisches trachtenbuch. Pessler, Wilhelm

Niedersächsische volkstrachten. Müller-Brauel, Hans

Niel, P. G. J.
Portraits des personnages français les plus illustres du XVIe siècle, reproduits, en facsimile, sur les originaux dessinés aux crayons de couleur par divers artistes contemporains. Paris, M. A. Lenoir 1848[-56]
2v. 48 col.pl. F.
Engraved by A. Riffaut and A. Leroy
Lipperheide 1117

Nieppe, Edgar de Prelle de la. See Prelle de la Nieppe, Edgar de

Niessen, Johannes
Apokalypsis; zehn lithographisch vervielfältigte federzeichnungen ... aus der Felix'schen sammlung, in die des Germanischen museums zu Nürnberg übergegangenen originalen. Köln, T. Fuhrmann [1886]
2p. 10pl. Q.
Shows 14th century costume
Lipperheide 401

Nieuhof, Hendrik
(ed.) Nieuhof, Johan. Joan Nieuhofs Gedenkwaerdige zee en lantreize door de voornaemste landschappen van West en Oostindien

Nieuhof, Johan
L'ambassade de la Compagnie orientale des Provinces Unies vers l'empereur de la Chine, ou grand cam de Tartarie, faite par les Srs. Pierre de Goyer, & Jacob de Keyser ... mis en françois ... par Jean Le Carpentier. Leyde, J. de Meurs 1665
2pt. in 1 v. illus. 33pl. fold.map. F.
Lipperheide 1510w. LC 3-9254

Joan Nieuhofs Gedenkwaerdige zee en lantreize door de voornaemste landschappen van West en Oostindien. Amsterdam, By de weduwe van J. van Meurs 1682
2v. illus. pl. port. maps. F.
Edited by H. Nieuhof
Each volume has also a special title page as follows: v 1 *Gedenkweerdige Brasiliaense zee- en lant-reize;* v2 *Zee en lant-reize, door verscheide gewesten van Oostindien*
Lipperheide 1472, 1627. LC 1-6772

Nieuhoff, Jean. See Nieuhof, Johan

Nieuwe almanach, bestaande in eene verzameling van kleedingen en kapsels ... voor den jaare 1785. Amsterdam, H. Gartman & J. van Gulik 1785?
Illus. T.
Lipperheide 4462

Nieuwe atlas der stad Amsterdam. [Amsterdam, P. Conradi 1787]
62 l. 103pl. F.
Illustrated by C. Borgerts, de Coppier, S. Fokke and others. Part of the plates date between 1760 and 1769 and bear legends in French and Dutch; some plates, dated 1787, have Dutch legends only. Plates include views of Amsterdam with figures showing costume
Lipperheide 948

Nieuwe geinventeerde Sineesen. Schenk, Peter

Nieuwe livische figuren. See Amman, Jost. Icones Livianae

Nieuwenhuis, Anton Willem
Quer durch Borneo; ergebnisse seiner reisen in den jahren 1894, 1896-97 und 1898-1900 ... unter mitarbeit von dr. M. Nieuwenhuis-von Üxküll-Güldenbandt. Leiden, E. J. Brill 1904-07
2v. fronts. pl.(part col. part fold.) fold. maps. O.
Shows costume of the natives of Borneo
LC 5-13573

Nieuwenhuis-von Üxküll-Güldenbandt, M. See Nieuwenhuis, A. W.

Nigrinus, Georg
Papistische inquisition und guldē flüs der römischen kirchen. Frankfurt a. M. 1582
61 l. 728p. 30 illus. F.
"Das ist: Historia und ankunft der römischen kirchen und sonderlich vom antichristischen wesen ... darinn aller römischen bischoffen, ertzbischoffen, patriarchen, bäpst, unnd entlich der antichristen leben und händel kürtzlich angezogen." Subtitle
Twenty-seven portraits of the popes are from O. Panvinio's *Accuratae effigies pontificum maximorum*
Second edition: 1589
Lipperheide 1797

Nigronus, Julius. See Negrone, Giulio

Nikolaus, Paul
Tänzerinnen. München, Delphin-verlag [1919]
89p. col.front. pl.(part col.) D.
Illustrated by E. E. Stern

Nile tributaries of Abyssinia. Baker, Sir S. W.

Nillson, W.
(engr.) Voltz, J. M. Costumes de l'armée bavaroise 1813-1825

The **1915** mode as shown by Paris Panama-Pacific international exposition. San Francisco. Panama-Pacific international exposition

Nineteenth century
Abbildungen verschiedener völker der erde in ihren eigenthümlichen trachten. 1826
Adams, William. The modern voyager and traveller, through Europe, Asia, Africa, and America. 1835-38
Berghaus, H. K. W. Die völker des erdballs nach ihrer abstammung und verwandtschaft, und ihren eigenthumlichkeiten in regierungsform, religion, sitte und tracht. 1845-47
Colin, Mme Anaïs. Groupes de costumes de différens pays. 1834
Costumes des différens départemens de l'Empire français. ca1815
Dress and address. By the author of The Greeks, Pigeons, Fashion, [etc] 1829
Galerie royale de costumes peints d'après nature par divers artistes et lithographiés par Alophe, Janet-Lange et Dollet. ca1842-1843
Gallerie der menschen. Ein bilderbuch zur erweiterung der kenntnisse über länder und völker. 1813
A geographical present; being descriptions of the principal countries of the world; with representations of the various inhabitants in their respective costumes. 1817
La géographie en estampes. 1816?
Grévedon, P. L. H. Époques remarquables de la vie de la femme; suite de têtes. 1831
Grévedon, P. L. H. Les quatre parties du monde, portraits de femme. 1832
Huebner, J. A., graf von. Ein spaziergang um die welt. 1882
Hutchinson, Walter, ed. Customs of the world. 1913
Kottenkamp, F. J. Die verschiedenen trachten. 1847
Leloir, Mme Héloïse. Le Sélam, galerie fashionnable de costumes, de fleurs et de femmes, de tous les pays. ca1840
Oberländer, Richard. Fremde völker, ethnographische schilderungen aus der alten und neuen welt. 1883
Oriental and occidental northern and southern portrait types of the Midway plaisance. 1894
Routledge's every girl's annual, 1886. 1886
Stuart, Martinus. De mensch, zoo als hij voorkomt op den bekenden aardbol. 1802-07
Vanauld, Alfred; Richomme, C. E. H., and Castillon, A. Nouvelle geographie en estampes, revue pittoresque de l'univers; nouvelles, contes, légendes et aperçus historiques sur les moeurs, usages, costumes des différents peuples. 1852
Vernet, Horace. Incroyables et merveilleuses de 1814. ca1815
Vollständige völkergallerie in getreuen abbildungen aller nationen mit ausführlicher beschreibung derselben. 1830-39
Wilkie, Sir David. Sir David Wilkie's sketches, Spanish & oriental. 1846

See also Europe—19th century; also names of other countries with subhead 19th century, e.g. France—19th century

Bibliography

Martinet, firm, publisher. Catalogue des collections des costumes de theatres, fantaisies, historiques et nationaux. 1883

Nineveh and its palaces. Bonomi, Joseph

Nineveh and its remains. Layard, Sir A. H.

Nineveh and Persepolis. Vaux, W. S. W.

Ninive et l'Assyrie. Place, Victor

Niox, Gustave Léon. See note under Paris. Musée de l'armée. Armes & armures anciennes

Nippon. Siebold, P. F. von

Nisard
Satyre sur les cerceaux. See La Fizelière, A. P. de. Histoire de la crinoline au temps passé

Nissen, Momme. See Jessen, K. L. Friesische heimatkunst

Nissy, E.
Album de coiffures historiques avec descriptions. Paris, Brunet [1927?]
30 col.pl. O.
Cover title. Plates accompanied by guard sheets with descriptive letter press

Nitze, Fr.
(ed.) Moden-gallerie

Nobilitas politica vel civilis. Milles, Thomas

Nobiltà di dame. Caroso, M. F.

La **nobilta'** veneta. Freschot, Casimir

Nobles

See also Kings and rulers

17th century

Buytewech, Willem. Sieben edelleute verschiedener nationen. 1926
Clerck, Nicolaes de. Princelyck cabinet. 1625
Hulle, Anselm van. Les hommes illustres qui ont vecu dans le XVII. siecle: les principaux potentats, princes, ambassadeurs & plenipotentiaires qui ont assisté aux conferences de Munster et d'Osnabrug, avec leurs armes et devises. Dessinez et peints au naturel. 1717

Nobles—17th century—*Continued*

Hulle, Anselm van. Pacis antesignani, sive Icones legatorum plena potestate intructorum, qui ... ad pacem universalem constituendam monasterium Westphalorum et Osnabrugam convenerunt, magno studio ad vivum expressae. 1648-50

Austria

Avancinus, Nicolas. Leopoldi Guilielmi, Archiducis Austriae ... virtutes. 1665

Beer, J. C. Der ... erz-hertzogen zu Oesterreich leben, regierung und grossthaten: von dem ... urheber ... Rudolpho, grafen von Habsburg ... erstem römischen kayser an biss in die ... regierung ... Leopoldi und Josephi. 1695

Fugger, J. J. Spiegel der ehren des ... erzhauses Osterreich, oder ausführliche geschicht schrift von desselben ... mit Käys. Rudolphi I geburts jahr 1212 anfahend und mit Käys. Maximiliani I todes jahr 1519 sich endend. 1668

Gebwiler, Hieronymus. ... Epitome regii ac vetustissimi ortus sacrae caesareae ac Catholice maiestatis ... principis ... Ferdinandi ... Bohemiae regis, omniumque archiducum Austriae, ac Habsburgensium comitum. 1530

Getreue abbildung und beschreibung der 28 erzernen statuen, welche das grabmahl kaiser Maximilians I. umgeben, und in der hofkirche zu Innsbruck aufgestellt sind. 1841

Historia ducum Styriae. 1728

Primisser, Alois. Der stammbaum des allerdurchläuchtigsten hauses Habsburg-Oesterreich (16th century) 1822

Roo, Gerardus de. Annales, oder historische chronick der ... fürsten und herren, ertzhertzogen zu Oesterreich ... fürnemlich von Rudolpho dem ersten ... bisz auff Carolum den fünfften. 1622

Belgium

Martin, Cornelis. Les genealogies et anciennes descentes des forestiers et comtes de Flandres, avec brieves descriptions de leurs vies et gestes. 1608

Meÿssens, Jean. Effigies des forestiers et comtes de Flandres. 1663

Vred, Oliverius. Genealogia comitum Flandriae a Balduino Ferreo usque ad Phillipum IV. hisp. regem. 1642

See also Nobles—Brabant

Bohemia

Althann. Imago principum Bohemiae LXI. 1673

Balbin, Bohuslav. Historia de ducibus ac regibus Bohemiae. 1735

Brabant

Dit is die Afcoemste ende Genalogie der Hertoghen ende Hertoginnen van Brabant. 1565

Haecht Goidtsenhoven, Laurens van. Chroniicke van de hertoghen van Brabant. 1606

Haraeus, Franciscus. Francisci Haraei Annales ducum seu principum Brabantiae totivsq. Belgii. 1623

England

The book of the ranks and dignities of British society. 1924

Boutell, Charles. The monumental brasses of England. 1849

Carter, Matthew. Honor redivivus; or, The analysis of honor and armory. 1673

Dyck, Sir Anthonie van. Les contesses de van Dyck. ca1660?

Milles, Thomas. The catalogue of honor, or Tresury of true nobility. 1610

Milles, Thomas. Nobilitas politica vel civilis. Personas scilicet distinguendi et ab origine inter gentes, ex principium gratia nobilitandi forma ... quò tandem & apud Anglos, qui sint nobilium gradus, & quæ ad nobilitatis fastigia euchendi ratio, ostenditur. 1608

Napier, Lady S. L. B. The life and letters of Lady Sarah Lennox, 1745-1826. 1901

Flanders

See Nobles—Belgium

France

Montfaucon, Bernard de. Les monumens de la monarchie françoise qui comprennent l'histoire de France, avec les figures de chaque règne. 1729-33

Montfaucon, Bernard de. Thresor des antiquitez de la couronne de France. 1745

15th century

Comines, Philippe de, sieur d'Argenton. Mémoires. 1881

Monstrelet, Enguerrand de. The chronicles of Enguerrand de Monstrelet. 1810

17th century

Félibien, André, sieur des Avaux et de Javercy. Les divertissemens de Versailles donnez par le roy a toute sa cour au retour de la conqueste de la Franche-Comté en l'année MDCLXXIV. 1676

Prime, Temple. Notes relative to certain matters connected with French history. 1903

Saint-Igny, Jean de. Le jardin de la noblesse françoise, dans lequel ce peut ceuillir leur manierre de vettement. 1629

Saint-Igny, Jean de. La noblesse françoise à l'eglise. ca1625

18th century

Rouveyre, Édouard. Gazette anecdotique du règne de Louis XVI. 1881

Nobles—*Continued*

Germany

Abbildung derer VIII. ersten hertzogen zu Sachsen, Jülich, Cleve und Berg, Engern und Westphalen, des H. Römischen Reichs ertz-marschallen und chur-fürsten landgrafen in Thüringen. 1702

Abcontrafactur und bildnis aller gross hertzogen chur und fürsten welche vom jahre nach Christi geburt 842 biss auff das jetztige 1599 jahr das land sachsen löblich und christlich regiert haben. 1599

Agricola, Johann. Warhafftige abcontrafactur und bildnüs aller gros herzogen, chur und fürsten, welche vom jahr ... 842 bis auff das jetzige ... jahr das landt Sachssen ... regieret haben. 1586

Basilica Carolina. 1760

Baumeister, J. S. Familienbilder des Hauses Hohenzollern. 1817

Brunner, Andrea. Excubiae tutelares LX heroum, qui ab anno Ch. DVIII. Theodonem in principatu Boariae secuti cum elogiis suis et rerum gestarum compendio ad felicissimas cunas serenissimi principis Ferdinandi Marli Francisci Ignatii Wolfgangi utr. Boiariae ducis. [1637]

Cernitius, Johannes. Decem, è familia burggraviorum Nurnbergensium, electorum Brandenburgicorum eicones ad vivum expressae, eorumque res gestae, una cum genealogiis, fide optima collectae pubblicataeque. 1626

Eigentliche abbildungen beeder röm. kayserl. wie auch der röm. königl. majestäten en und dann sämtlicher ... churfürsten dess H. Röm. Reichs wie selbige auf dem röm. königl. wahl-tag in ... Augspurg im jahr 1689 und 1690.

Fortitudo leonina in utraque fortuna Maximiliani Emmanuelis, V. B. ac Sup. Palat. ducis, comitis Palatini Rheni. 1715

Franck, Sebastian. Teutscher nation chronic alt und neu vorbilde. Des gantzen teutschenn landes und völcker anfenglich herkomen, grentze und gelegenheit der reiche, fürstenthumb, bisthumb, stett und herschafften. 1539

Henneberg, Caspar. Erclerung der preüssischen grössern landtaffel oder wappen. 1595

Huber-Liebenau, Theodor von. Denkmäler des hauses Habsburg in der Schweiz. Das Kloster Konigsfelden. 1867

Huth, P. J. Von den verdiensten des durchleuchtigsten hauses Wittelspach um die kirche. 1777

Lentz, Samuel. Becmannus; enucleatus, suppletus et continuatus; oder, Historischgenealogische fürstellung des hochfürstlichen hauses Anhalt, und der davon abstammenden marggrafen zur Brandenburg, herzoge zur Sachsen und Sachsen-Lauenburg. 1757

Reyher, Samuel. Monumenta landgraviorum Thuringiae et marchionum Misniae, quae adhuc in Thuringia Misnia Saxonia superiore Franconia et Hassia extant. 1692

Roehl, E. Die tracht der schlesischen fürstinnen des 13. und 14. jahrhunderts auf grund ihrer siegel. 1895

Schnelboltz, Gabriel. Warhaffte bildnis etlicher hochlöblicher fürsten und herren. 1562

Warnecke, Friedrich, ed. Sammlung historischer bildnisse und trachten aus dem stammbuch der Katharina von Canstein. 1885

Zimmermann, J. A. Series imaginum Augustae domus Boicae ad genuina ectypa aliaque monum. fide digna delin. 1773-92

Middle ages

Luchs, Hermann. Schlesische fürstenbilder des mittelalters. 1872

16th century

Amman, Jost. Insignia sacrae Caesareae maiestatis. 1579

Amman, Jost. Stam und wapenbuch hochs und niders standts, darinnen der römischen keys. mt. dess heiligen röm. reyches, churfürsten, fürsten, grafen, freyen und herrn ... wapen mit iren schilt und helmen mit angehengten vilen ledigen schildten und helmen. 1579

Amman, Jost. Stamm- und wappenbuch; neu herausgegeben und geordnet von Friedrich Warnecke. 1877.

Amman, Jost. Wapen und stammbuch darinnen der keys. maiest. chur und fürsten, graffen, freyherrn, deren vom adel, etc. mit kunstreichen figuren. 1589

Amman, Jost. Wappen- & stammbuch. Franckfort a. M. S. Feyrabend 1589. 1881

Boccaccio, Giovanni. Fornem̃ste historien und exempel ... groszmächtiger kayser, künig, fürsten. 1545

Boeheim, Wendelin. Philippine Welser. 1894

Breunner-Enkevoërth, A. J., graf von. Römisch kaiserlicher majestät kriegsvölker im zeitalter der landsknecht ... mit erläuterndem text von Jacob von Falke. 1883

Herberstein, Sigmund, freiherr von. Picturae variae quae generosum ac magnificum domi. dominum Sigismundum liberum baronem in Heberstain Neyperg & Guttenhag etc. varias legationes obeuntem exprimunt. 1560

Hortleder, Friederich. Der römischen Keyserund koniglichen maiestetē, auch dess Heiligen Römischen Reich geistlicher und weltlicher stände ... Von den ursachen dess teutschen kriegs kaiser Carls dess V. wider die Schmalkaldische bunds-oberste chur-und F.G.G. mitverwandte anno 1546 und 47. 1645

Nobles—Germany—*Continued*

17th century

Birken, Sigmund von. Chur- und Fürstlicher sächsischer helden-saal. 1687

Lundorp, M. C. Helden buch, oder beschreibung der vonembsten potentaten, keyser, königen, fürsten, graffen, kriegs-obersten, und helden, welche in nochwehrendem teutschen kriege ... sich gebrauchen lassen. 1629

Hungary

Abbildungen aller angeblich: und wirklichen regenten ungarns mit beygefügten kurzen historischen anmerkungen. 1815

Trophaeum nobilissimae ac antiquissimae domus Estorasianae. 1700

Italy

Bianchini, G. M. Dei gran duchi di Toscana della reale casa de' Medici, protettori delle lettere, e delle belle arti, ragionamenti istorici. 1741

16th century

Balduino, Giacomo. Imagini degl' abiti con cui va vestita la nobilta' della serenis'ma Republica di Venezia. 1702

Barbuò Soncino, Scipione. Sommario della vite de' duchi di Milano. 1574

Caroso, M. F. Il ballarino. 1581

Caroso, M. F. Nobiltà di dame; libro, altra volta, chiamato Il ballarino. 1600

Giovio, Paolo, bp. of Nocera. Pauli Iovii Novocomensis Vitae duodecim vicecomitum Mediolani principum. 1549

Lorraine

Callot, Jacques. La noblesse de Lorraine. 1624

Netherlands

Baerland, Adriaan van. Hollandiae comitum historia et icones. 1584

Die cronycke van Hollant, Zeelant ende Vrieslant. 1591

Meteren, Emmanuel von. Niederländische historien, oder Geschichten aller deren händel so sich zugetragen von anfangs des niederländischen kriegs bisz auff das jahr 1611. 1611

Vosmer, Michael. Principes Hollandiae et Zelandiae. 1578

See also Nobles—Brabant

Russia

Russia. Komitet dli͡a izdanii͡a drevnosteĭ Rossiĭkago gosudarstva. Drevnosti Rossiĭskago gosudarstva. 1849-53

Tyrol

Custos, Dominicus. Tirolensium. Principum comitum. Ab. an. ... 1229 usq. ad ann. 1599. 1599

Custos, Dominicus. Tirolensium principum comitum. Der gefürsten grafen zu Tyrol, von anno 1229 biss anno 1623. 1623

La **noblesse** de France aux croisades. Roger, P. A.

La **noblesse** de Lorraine. Callot, Jacques

Noblesse de robe. Bibesco, M. L. L. princesse

La **noblesse** françoise à l'eglise. Saint-Igny, Jean de

Noé, Amédée, comte de

Mémoires relatifs à l'expédition anglaise partie du Bengale en 1800 pour aller combattre en Égypte l'armée d'Orient. [Paris,] l'Imprimerie royale 1826

288p. 19 col.pl. 2 col.maps. O.

Plates show costume of India, Egypt, and Turkey

Many other collections of plates by Noé, published under the pseudonym Cham, show 19th century costume in caricature. Some of these titles are listed in Lipperheide, nos 3579-3611

Colas 2208. Lipperheide 1584

Nöhring, Johann

Vierundzwanzig statuen des Vaticanischen und Capitolischen museums zu Rom und der Uffizien in Florenz, nach den originalen photographirt. Hamburg, H. Grüning 1869

24p. 24pl. F.

Lipperheide 166

Nørlund, Poul

Buried Norsemen at Herjolfsnes, an archaeological and historical study. København, 1924

267p. illus. double pl. Q. (Kommissionen for ledelsen af de geologiske og geografiske undersøgelser i Grønland. Meddelelser om Grønland. Bind 67, p 1-270)

Pages 86-192 are on the costume of the Norsemen in Greenland during the middle ages

Viking settlers in Greenland and their descendants during five hundred years. London, Cambridge university press, Copenhagen, G. E. C. Gad 1936

160p. illus. O.

Translated from the Danish by W. E. Calvert

Pages 105-26 deal with costume of the Norsemen in Greenland during the middle ages

Bibliography: p156-157

LC 37-14674

Noevel, Simon van den

(engr.) Braun, Georg. Civitates orbis terrarum. 1572-1618

Nogales, Manuel Chavez. See Chavez Nogales, Manuel

Noguès, S.

[Garde municipale et garde nationale] Paris, Lith. de Genty ca1830

6 col.pl. F.

Colas 2209

Noirmont, Dunoyer de. See Dunoyer de Noirmont, J. A. É. É., baron

Nō-isho. Kongow, Iwao

Nolpe, Pieter

(engr.) Post, Pieter. Begraeffenisse van ... Frederick Henrick ... prince van Orange

The **nomads** of the Balkans. Wace, A. J. B., and Thompson, M. S.

Noord- en zuid nederlandsche schilderkunst der XVII. eeuw. Hennema, Dirk, and Schendel, A. van

Noord-Nederlandsche miniaturen. Byvanck, A. W., and Hoogewerff, G. J.

Noort, Adam van, and Snellinck, Joan
Costumes de divers pays d'Europe. No place, ca1630
12pl. Q.
Colas 2972

Nopcsa, Ferencz, báró
Albanien; bauten, trachten und geräte Nordalbaniens. Berlin und Leipzig, W. de Gruyter 1925
viii,257p. illus. IV pl. Q.
Literatur zur materiellen kultur Nordalbaniens: p[240]-46
LC 25-16261

Noppen, John George
Royal Westminster and the coronation. London, Country life, ltd. [1937]
147p. illus. Q.
Chapter 12 deals with the coronation chair, regalia, and vestments. Plates show scenes from several English coronations, also the crown of St Edward, the Imperial state crown, the Imperial crown of India, and Queen Mary's crown, as well as the king's and queen's sceptres and several coronation robes

Norblin de la Gourdaine, Jean Pierre
Zbior wzorowy rozmaitych Polskick .. Collection de costumes polonais ... gravés par Debucourt. Paris, C. Bance [1817]
Col.front. 49 col.pl. F.
For a list of plates see Colas's *Bibliographie*
Colas 2210. Lipperheide 1390

Nordafrika. Kühnel, Ernst

Nordenberg, Bengt
(illus.) Berg, J. A. Bilder ur svenska folklifvet

Nordenskiöld, Erland
Indianer und weisse in Nordostbolivien. Stuttgart, Strecker und Schröder 1922
221p. front. 90 illus. 34pl. O.
Especially good for costume of the Chacobo Indians of South America

Die **nordfriesischen** insel. Jensen, Christian

Nordische muster-sammlung. Kulle, Jakob

De **nordiska** guldbrakteaterna. Salin, Bernhard

Nordiska museet. See Stockholm. Nordiska museet

Nordiske oldsager i det kongelige museum i Kjöbenhavn. Worsaae, J. J. A.

Nordmann
Svenska armeens. Stockholm, Norstedt et Sôner 1864
? p. 32 col.pl. F.
Colas 2211

Die **nordseeinsel** Helgoland. See Lindemann, Emil. Das deutsche Helgoland

Nordwest-amerikanische Indianerkunst. Adam, Leonard

Norgate, Kate
(ed.) Green, J. R. A short history of the English people

Norlind, Tobias
Gamla bröllopsseder hos svenska allmogen. Stockholm, A. B. M. Bergvall [1919]
152p. illus. O.
Shows Swedish costume of the 19th century

Svenska allmogens lif i folksed, folktro och folkdiktning. Stockholm, Bohlin [1912]
Col.front. illus. 5 col.pl. O.
Shows Swedish costume of various periods

Die **normalkleidung** als gesundheitschutz. Jaeger, Gustav

Norman, Sir Henry, bart.
All the Russias; travels and studies in contemporary European Russia, Finland, Siberia, the Caucasus, and Central Asia; with one hundred and twenty-nine illustrations chiefly from the author's photographs. New York, C. Scribner's sons 1902
xii,476p. illus. pl. maps. O.
Useful for costume of the Finns and of Caucasian types
LC 2-22431

The peoples and politics of the Far East; travels and studies in the British, French, Spanish and Portuguese colonies, Siberia, China, Japan, Korea, Siam and Malaya. London, T. F. Unwin 1900
xvi,608p. col.front. pl. 4 maps(part fold.) O.
LC 1-5583

Normand, Louis Marie
(engr.) Lafitte, Louis. Entrée triomphale ... le duc d'Angoulême

La **Normandie** ancestrale. Chauvet, Stéphen

La **Normandie** ancienne et moderne. See note under Philippe, P. La Normandie en 1834

La **Normandie** en 1834. Philippe, P.

La **Normandie** illustrée. Monuments, sites et costumes de la Seine-Inférieure, de l'Eure, du Calvados, de l'Orne, et de la Manche, dessinés d'après nature par F^x^ Benoist ... les costumes dessinés et lithographiés par H^te^ Lalaisse ... texte par m. Raymond Bordeaux et mlle Amélie Bosquet, sous la direction de m. André Pottier ... pour la Haute-Normande, et par mm. Charma, Le Héricher, de la Sicotière, Travers et de Beaurepaire, sous la direction de m. Georges Mancel ... pour la Basse-Normandie. Nantes, Charpentier 1854, '52
2v. 96pl.(incl. 24 col.pl. of costume) F.
Volume 1, Seine-Inférieure, Eure, Costumes normands; v2 Calvados, Orne, Manche
Published in "livraisons". Each part (except pt3) has special engraved title page. "Cherbourg" (v2, pt6, p65-71) by Charles Mourain de Sourdeval
Colas 294. LC 4-25973

Normandy. See France—By region or province—Normandy

Noronha, Eduardo de
O vestuario, historia do traje desde os tempos mais remotos até á idade-média; compilação das obras de maior autoridade sobre o assunto. Lisboa, L. da Silva 1911
317p. illus. D.
LC 33-37612

Norris, Herbert
Costume & fashion. London and Toronto, J. M. Dent; New York, E. P. Dutton 1924-33
v 1-2, 6. col.fronts. illus.(incl.maps) pl. (part col.) O.
Volume 6 by Herbert Norris and Oswald Curtis
Contents: v 1 Evolution of European dress through the earlier ages; v2 Senlac to Bosworth, 1066-1485; v6 Nineteenth century
Colas 2212. Costume index. LC 25-2565

Norse oldsager. Rygh, Oluf

Norsemen. See Northmen in Greenland

Norsk bondeliv. See Tidemand, Adolph. Norwegisches bauernleben

Norsk klaedebunad. Garborg, Fru H. B.

Norska arméens nuvarande uniformer. Örebro, N. M. Lindh 1866
8 col.pl. F.
Colas 2213. Lipperheide 2282

Norske folkelivsbilleder. Tønsberg, N. C., ed.

Norske nationaldragter. Tønsberg, N. C., ed.

Norske nationale klaededragter. Senn, J.

North, Charles Niven McIntyre
... The book of the Club of true Highlanders. London, R. Smythson [1892]
2v. fronts. 70pl. F.
"A record of the dress, arms, customs, arts and science of the Highlanders; compiled from printed and ms. records and traditions and illustrated with etchings of Highland relics and the Keltic vestiges of Great Britain and Ireland." Subtitle
Gaelic title at head of English title

North Africa. See Africa, North

North America. See names of individual countries; also Indians of North America

The **North** American Indian. Curtis, E. S.

North American Indian portfolio. See Catlin, George. Catlin's North American Indian portfolio

North American Indians. Catlin, George

The **North** American Indians. Palmer, R. A.

North American Indians of the Plains. Wissler, Clark

The **North-Americans** of yesterday. Dellenbaugh, F. S.

Northcliffe, Alfred Charles William Harmsworth, 1st viscount
Motors and motor-driving, by Sir Alfred C. Harmsworth; with contributions by the Marquis de Chasseloup-Laubat ... and others. With illustrations by H. M. Brock, H. Tringham, and from photographs; 3d ed. London and Bombay, Longmans, Green 1904
xx,521p. front. illus. pl. plans. diagrs. D. (The Badminton library of sports and pastimes)
LC 4-31416

Northcote, James
(illus.) Boydell, John, and Boydell, Josiah. The American edition of Boydell's Illustrations of the Dramatic works of Shakspeare

Northcote, James Spencer
(ed.) Rossi, G. B. de. Roma sotterranea

Northmen in Greenland
Nørlund, Poul. Buried Norsemen at Herjolfsnes. 1924
Nørlund, Poul. Viking settlers in Greenland and their descendants during five hundred years. 1936

Northrop, Henry Davenport
The flowery kingdom and the land of the mikado; or, China, Japan, and Corea; containing their complete history down to the present time. Philadelphia, National pub. co. [1894]
624p. front.(ports.) illus. pl. Q.
LC 0-4092

Northrup, Belle
(comp.) The story of costume told in pictures. New York, Art education press, inc. [c1935]
1 l. XXII pl. on 11 l. F. pa 60c
Bibliography on verso of 1st prelim. leaf.
Shows costume from early times until the 19th century
Costume index. LC 35-22603

Northrup, Belle, and Green, Anna L.
A short description of historic fashion, with index and suggestions for using the accompanying thirty historic costume plates. New York city, Teachers college, Columbia university 1925
7p. XXX pl. Q. $1.60
In portfolio which has title: *Historic costume plates*
Costume index. LC 25-21806

Norton-Kyshe, James William
The law and customs relating to gloves, being an exposition historically viewed of ancient laws, customs, and uses in respect of gloves, and of the symbolism of the hand and glove in judicial proceedings. London, Stevens and Haynes 1901
xi,125p. front. pl. D.
LC 3-25253

Norvins, Jacques Marquet de, baron de Montbreton
Histoire de Napoléon; vignettes par Raffet. Paris, Furne 1839
648p. front. illus. pl. ports. O.
Shows French military dress at the time of Napoleon
LC 18-10527

Norway
Dahl, Hans. Et varsko til det norske folk og den nordiske rase. 1932
Fett, H. P. Nationaldragter. 1903
Garborg, Fru H. B. Norsk klaedebunad. 1917
Grund, J. G. Afbildning af Nordmands-Dalen, i den kongelige lyst-hauge ved Fredensborg ... Abbildung des Normannsthals, in dem königlichen lustgarten zu Friedensburg. 1773
Jungman, Mrs Beatrix. Norway. 1905
Keyser, J. R. Om nordmae klaededragt i aeldre tider... Afbildninger af norske nationaldragter. 1847
Lexow, E. J. Joh. F. L. Dreiers norske-folkedragter. 1913
Lexow, E. J. Jorgen Garnaas og Nordmandsdalen. 1916
Lovett, Richard. Norwegian pictures. 1890
Monroe, W. S. In viking land; Norway: its peoples, its fjords and its fjelds. 1908

Norway—*Continued*
Oslo. Kunstindustrimuseet. Gamle norske billedtæpper ... Altnorwegische bildteppiche. 1901
Rygh, Oluf. Norse oldsager, ordnede og forklarede. 1885
Senn, J. Norske nationale klaededragter. 1812
Svenska och norska folkdrägter. ca1885
Tidemand, Adolph. Norwegisches bauernleben. 1851
Tønsberg, N. C., ed. Norske folkelivsbilleder. 1854
Tønsberg, N. C., ed. Norske nationaldragter. 1852
Troels-Lund, T. F. Dagligt liv i Norden i de det 16de aarhundrede. 1880-1901
Visted, Kristofer. Vor gamle boudekultur. 1923

See also Northmen in Greenland; also subdivision Norway under Agricultural laborers; Ecclesiastical costume; Kings and rulers; Military costume; Sword

19th century

Belin, A., and others. Costumes de Suède, Norvège, Danemark, Hollande et Allemagne. 186-?
Buch, Leopold, freiherr von. Travels through Norway and Lapland. 1813
Buch, Leopold, freiherr von. Reise durch Norwegen und Lappland. 1810

Norwegian pictures. Lovett, Richard

Norwegisches bauernleben. Tidemand, Adolph

Nos gloires militaires. Hardoin, Georges

Nos hussards (1692-1902). Fallou, Louis

Nos jolies parisiennes. Beaumont, C. E. de

Nos marins. Leonnec, Paul

Nos petites grand'mères: La jeune fille au XVIII. siècle. Claretie, Leo

Nos soldats. Hennebert, Eugène

Nos soldats du siècle. Caran d'Ache, E. P., known as

Nos vêtements. Rosary, Eugène, pseud.

Nos vieux houzards. Béchu, M. E.

Nose-rings
Bartholin, Caspar. De inauribus veterum syntagma. 1676. Part 2
Wright, B. M. Description of the collection of gold ornaments from the "huacas" or graves of some aboriginal races of the north western provinces of South America. 1885

I **nostri** nonni. Caprin, Giuseppe

Notes archéologiques. Fourdrignier, Edouard

Notes of travel in Fiji and New Caledonia. Anderson, J. W.

Notes on civil costume in England. Wingfield, L. S.

Notes on laces of the American colonists. Morris, Frances

Notes on the Bedouins and Wahábys. Burckhardt, J. L.

Notes on uniforms and insignia. United States. Army war college

Notes pour servir à l'histoire de la sidérurgie en Lorraine; arsenal de Nancy, mines, forges, armes, etc. 1900. See Giraud, J. B. Documents pour servir à l'histoire de l'armement au moyen âge et à la renaissance

Notes relative to certain matters connected with French history. Prime, Temple

Notes sur les costumes chevaleresques et les armes offensives des XIIe, XIIIe et XIVe siècles. Prelle de la Nieppe, Edgar de

Notes sur les tenues des Hussards de 1815 à 1870. Margerand, J.

Nothwendige erinnerung vom miszbrauch der kleyder da viele Christen in defectu, viele in excessu sündigen. Ouw, Wolfgang

Notice historique sur la tapisserie brodée par la reine Mathilde, épouse de Guillaume le Conquérant. Paris, L'imprimerie des sciences et arts 1804
20p. 7pl. Q.
Reproductions of the Bayeux tapestry show French and English costume of the period of the Norman conquest
Lipperheide 363

Notice sur les costumes de guerre. Paris. Musée d'artillerie

Notice sur l'uniforme des officiers d'état-major général, et des aides-de-camp, du 22 mai 1816. Feltre, H. J. G., duc de

Notitia universitatis Francofurtanae. Becmann, J. C.

Notizie, storiche, politiche, geografiche e statistiche sulla Vallachia e sulla Moldavia. Sestini, Domenico

Notor, G.
La femme dans l'antiquité grecque. Paris, H. Laurens 1901
288p. illus. 17pl. F. o.p.
Bibliography: p275-76
Costume index

Notre armée. Audeoud, Alfred

Nott, Josiah Clark, and Glidden, George Robins
Types of mankind. Philadelphia, Lippincott, Grambo 1854
lxxvi,[49]-738p. front.(port.) illus. fold. pl.(1 col.) fold.tab. 2 maps. Q.
"Ethnological researches, based upon the ancient monuments, paintings, sculptures, and crania of races, and upon their natural, geographical, philological and Biblical history: illustrated by selections from the inedited papers of Samuel George Morton ... and by additional contributions from Prof. L. Agassiz, W. Usher, and Prof. H. S. Patterson." Subtitle
Illustrations show headdress, especially of the Jews and Egyptians in ancient times
Lipperheide 138. LC 5-31173

Le **nouble** roy Ponthus. See Historie von Pontus und Sidonia

Nougaret, Pierre Jean Baptiste
Beautés de l'histoire d'Angleterre, ou Époques intéressantes et remarquables, origines, usages et moeurs, batailles célèbres, depuis les commencements de la monarchie, jusqu'à la fin du règne de Georges II. Paris, chez Le Prieur 1811
408p. 15pl. D.
Plates show English costume from earliest times until the middle of the 18th century
Lipperheide 986

Nouveau calendrier du diocèse de Strasbourg. See Striedbeck. Representation des modes et habillements de Strasbourg

Nouveau calendrier du diocèse de Strasbourg pour l'an 1760. Weis, J. M.

Nouveau journal des dames, ou Petit courrier des modes. See Petit courrier des dames

Nouveau manuel complet de la broderie. Bayle-Mouillard, Mme E. F. C.

Nouveau manuel complet de l'armurier, du fourbisseur et de l'arquebusier. Paulin-Désormeaux, A. O.

Nouveau manuel complet des demoiselles. Bayle-Mouillard, Mme E. F. C.

Nouveau manuel complet des gardes nationaux de France contenant l'école du soldat et de peloton ... les lois et décrets sur la garde nationale jusqu'en 1852 ... par M. R. L.; nouvelle ed., rev. Paris, Roret [1853?]
132p. front. fold.pl. diagrs. O.
Many editions. Lipperheide lists an edition of 1831 (160p. 3pl. 1 col.)
Lipperheide 2310 (1831 ed.)

Nouveau memoires sur l'etat present de la Chine. Le Comte, L. D.

Nouveau recueil des costumes militaires français et autres nations tant anciennes et modernes. Paris, Duflos jeune 1795
6 col.pl. O.
"Dans lequel on a fait entrer des tableaux d'evolutions, d'attaque, de défense et de retraite avec les cartes géographiques des pays et les plans topographiques des endroits devenus célèbres par les batailles ou les victoires—Ouvrage elementaire destiné à l'education publique." Subtitle
The work was not completed
Colas 909

Nouveau recueil . . . des differends habillements des trouppes qui composent l'armée de la reine de Hongrie, ramassées sur les frontières de ce royaume. Paris, chez Mde Le Rouge 1742
21 col.pl. Q.
Colas 2218

Nouveau recueil des troupes légères de France levées depuis la présente guerre. La Rue, P. B. de

Nouveau recueil des troupes qui forment la garde et maison du roy. Eisen, C. D. J.

Nouveau recueil des troupes qui forment la garde et maison militaire de roy ... avec ... leurs uniformes et leurs armes. Paris, chez Juliette ca1780
1 l. 14 col.pl. Q.
Colas 2217

Nouveau traité de l'art des armes. Demeuse, Nicolas

Les **Nouveautés** parisiennes et La Mode artistique réunies. See La Mode artistique

Nouveaux costumes étrennes les plus utiles aux dames. Paris, Desnos 1781
Col.pl. Ti.
Cataloged from Colas
Plates show costume and styles of hair dressing
Colas 2221

Nouveaux cris de Paris. Roehn, Adolphe

Nouveaux desseins d'habillements à l'usage des ballets, opéras, et comédies. Gillot, Claude

Nouveaux lieure de housses en broderie et en gallons. Marot, Daniel

Nouveaux modèles. See Zeissig, M. C. Neue stickmuster

Nouveaux pourtraicts de point coupé. See Foillet, Jacques. Das musterbuch

Les **nouveaux** travestissements parisiens. Grévin, Alfred

Nouveaux travestissements pour le théâtre et pour le bal. Gavarni, G. S. C., and Devéria, Achille

Les **nouveaux** uniformes de tous les régimens de cavalerie de France. Isnard, P. Fr. d'

Les **nouveaux** uniformes de tous les régimens de dragons de France. Isnard, P. Fr. d'

La **nouvelle** armée française. Moltzheim, A. de

Nouvelle collection de costumes suisses. König, F. N.

Nouvelle collection de costumes suisses. Volmar, G.

Nouvelle collection de costumes suisses des XXII cantons. König, F. N.

Nouvelle collection variée de sujets de genre. Grenier, François

Nouvelle encyclopédie des arts et métiers; Art de la chaussure considéré dans toutes ses parties. Nancy, Haener 1824
382p. col.front. 24 col.pl. O.
Colas 2222

Le **nouvelle** figure à la mode de ce tempts de fine. Eeckhout, Guilielmus vanden

[**Nouvelle** galerie dramatique.] Paris, Martinet [1872-80]
300 col.pl. Q.
Plates each show one or sometimes two actors in theatrical costume. Plates bear name of a theater, the title of a play, the role, and the name of the artist. Plates drawn by A. Morlon, Grévin, Draner and others. This collection is a continuation of *Galerie dramatique* (1844-70)
Colas 2223

Nouvelle geographie en estampes. Vanauld, Alfred; Richomme, C. E. H., and Castillon, A.

Nouvelle histoire de France. Malet, Albert

Nouvelle suite de costumes des Pyrénées. Lagarrigue

Les **nouvelles** collections de l'Union ... au Musée du Louvre. See Union centrale des arts décoratifs, Paris. Le costume

Nouvelles étrennes curieuses des incroyables, merveilleuses, inconcevables, et des raisonnables de Paris ... la notice de 30 différentes perruques à la mode ... dans des pays divers. Paris, Libraires des raisonnables [1796]
S.
Shows the fashions of the period in caricature
Colas 2225

Nouvion, Pierre de, and Liez, Émile
Un ministre des modes sous Louis XVI; Mademoiselle Bertin, marchande de modes de la reine (1747-1813). Paris, H. Leclerc 1911
223p. 12 col.pl. Q.
Plates, engraved by G. Ripart, are reproductions of eighteenth century fashion plates
Colas 2226

Novelli
Raccolta dei riti, e ceremonie religiose di tutti i popoli del mondo con la spiegazione storica italiana, e francese per cadauna ceremonia. Venezia, T. Viero 1789
40pl. F.
Shows religious ceremonies of the Jews, Roman Catholics, Mohammedans, Kaffirs, Persians, and the Japanese. Most of the plates are engraved by Baratti
Lipperheide 1815

La **Novempopulanie,** croquis et souvenirs des Pyrénées. Aires, Doléac 1834
20 col.pl. Q.
Colas 2227

Novus thesaurus antiquitatum Romanorum. See note under Bossi, Gerolamo. De toga Romana

Nowack, Wilhelm
Lehrbuch der hebräischen archäologie. Freiburg i. B. und Leipzig, J. C. Mohr 1894
2v. in 1. illus. O. (Sammlung theologischer lehrbücher)
Contains material on Jewish dress and jewelry, v 1, p120-32; on the dress of the priests, v2, p116-20
LC 14-19112

Le **nozze** degli dei favola. Coppola, G. C.

Nubia
Brockedon, William. Egypt & Nubia. 1846-49
Cailliaud, Frédéric. Recherches sur les arts et métiers, les usages de la vie civile et domestique des anciens peuples de l'Égypte, de la Nubie et de l'Éthiopie, suivies de détails sur les moeurs et coutumes des peuples modernes des mêmes contrées. 1831
Champollion, J. F. Monuments de l'Egypte et de la Nubie. 1835-45
Gau, F. C. Antiquités de la Nubie, ou, Monumens inédits des bords du Nil, situés entre la première et la seconde cataracte, dessinés et mesurés, en 1819. 1822-27

See also Sudan, Anglo-Egyptian

Nudity
Langdon-Davies, John. Lady Godiva: the future of nakedness. 1928
Parmelee, M. F. The new gymnosophy, the philosophy of nudity as applied in modern life. 1927

Nürnberg. See Nuremberg

Nürnberger ausrufer mit darstellung der vornehmsten stadttheile Nürnbergs. Gabler, Ambrosius

Nürnberger waffenschmiede. Boeheim, Wendelin

Nürnbergisch thurnier und schönbartbuch. See note under Nürnbergisches schönbart-buch und gesellen-stechen

Nürnbergische kleider arten. Nürnberg, J. Kramer 1669
6 l. 40pl. ob.Q.
Costume of the peasants and nobility of Nuremberg. Plates are engraved by H. J. Schollenberger and N. Häublin
An edition, published ca1675, under title: *Nürnbergisches verändert- und unverändertes trachten-buch* (41pl.) reproduces part of the plates and contains some new ones
Colas 2232-2233. Lipperheide 774-775, 775a

Nürnbergische kleider-trachten der manns- und weibs-personen. Nürnberg, A. Bäner 1689
14p. 30pl. ob.Q.
Another edition (Nürnberg, A. Bäner 1690. 43pl.) duplicates the first 17 plates of the 1689 edition and adds 25 views of the city of Nuremberg
Colas 2234. Lipperheide 777-778

Das **nürnbergische** schönbartbuch nach der Hamburger handschrift hrsg. von Karl Drescher, mit 97 abbildungen auf 78 handkolorierten tafeln. Weimar, Gesellschaft der bibliophilen 1908
xii,20p. front.(port.) 78 col.pl.(6 fold.) F.
LC 10-1162

Nürnbergische trachten. Nürnberg [1670?]
40pl. ob.S.

Nürnbergisches schembart-buch. See Nürnbergisches schönbart-buch und gesellenstechen; also Mayer, M. M. Des alten Nürnsbergs sitten und gebräuche in freud und leid

Nürnbergisches schönbart-buch und gesellenstechen; aus einem alten manuscript zum druck befördert und mit benöthigten kupfern versehen. [Nürnberg, 1765]
104p. 10pl. Q.
The source of text and illustrations is a hand colored manuscript: *Nürnbergisch thurnier und schönbartbuch.* The illustrations show masqueraders of the years 1449 to 1539. Sometimes known under title: *Nürnbergisches schembart-buch*
Lipperheide 2851, 2850

Nürnbergisches taschenbuch. Roth, J. F.

Nürnbergisches trachtenbuch. See Mayer, M. M. Des alten Nürnbergs sitten und gebräuche in freud und leid

Nürnbergisches verändert- und unveränderte trachten-buch. See Nürnbergische kleider arten

Nützliches, in lauter auserlesenen, wohl-approbirt- und meistentheils neu-inventirten mustern bestehendes, weber-bildbuch. Frickinger, J. M.

Nuevo art de esgrima. See Rolando, Guzman. The modern art of fencing

Nugent, D. Rothe de. See Rothe de Nugent, D.

Nuis, baron de Clugny de. See Clugny de Nuis, baron de

Numa, pseud. See Bassaget, Pierre Numa

Numerals. See Embroidery—Monograms and numerals

I **numi** a diporto su l'Adriatico. Sartorio, B. C.

Numismatica. Ambrosoli, Solone

Nuns. See Monastic and religious orders

Nuova e curiosa scuola de' balli theatrali. Lambanzi, Gregorio

Nuova, et utilissima prattica di tutto quello ch' al diligēte barbiero s'appartiene. Amato, Cintio d', and Riccio, T. A.

Nuova inventione. Franco, Giacomo

Nuova raccolta di cento tavole rappresentante i costumi religiosi civili e militari degli antichi Egiziani, Etruschi, Greci e Romani. Roccheggiani, Lorenzo

Nuova raccolta di cinquanta costumi de' contorni di Roma compresi diversi fatti di briganti. Pinelli, Bartolommeo

Nuova raccolta di cinquanta costumi pittoreschi. Pinelli, Bartolommeo

Nuova raccolta di cinquanta motivi pittoreschi, e costumi di Roma. Pinelli, Bartolommeo

Nuova raccolta di 56 costumi di Roma e contorni tratti dalla fotographia. Roma, Presso i principali negozianti ca1860
1 l. 27 col.pl. D.
Colas 2231. Lipperheide 1313

Nuova raccolta di costumi di Napoli disegnati dal vero. Busuttil, Salvatore

Nuova raccolta di costumi di Roma e sue vicinanze. Pinelli, Bartolommeo

Nuova raccolta di costumi di Roma e suoi contorni. Ferrari, Filippo

Nuova raccolta di costumi e vestiture di Napoli. Dura, Gaetano

Nuova raccolta di no. 40 costumi popolari di Roma e sue vicinanze. Marroni, Salvatore

Nuova raccolta rappresentante i costumi religiosi, civili, e militari degli antichi Egiziani, Etruschi, Greci, e Romani. Pronti, Domenico

Nuove inventioni di balli. Negri, Cesare

Nuremberg. Germanisches nationalmuseum

Anzeiger des Germanischen nationalmuseums, hrsg. vom direktorium ... jahrg. 1884/86-date. Nürnberg, 1886-date
illus. pl.(part col.) port. plans. Q.
v 1 1884/1886. Latest volume 1934/1935
Reproductions of works of German artists, many of them very interesting as costume pictures
Lipperheide 598. LC 11-28917

Die holzschnitte des 14. und 15. jahrhunderts im Germanischen museum. Nürnberg, Verlag der literarisch-artistischen anstalt des Germanischen museums 1874
16p. CLXIV pl. F.
Introduction signed A. Essenwein. Woodcuts show 14th and 15th century costume
Lipperheide 461

Katalog der im germanischen museum befindlichen gewebe und stickereien, nadelarbeiten und spitzen aus älterer zeit. Nürnberg, im verlag der Literarischartistischen anstalt des germanischen museums 1869
38p. 1 illus. 20pl. Q.
Contains pictures of weaving and tapestry of the sixth to the sixteenth centuries and pictures of life during the middle ages
Lipperheide 591

Katalog der im Germanischen museum befindlichen glasgemälde aus älterer zeit. Nürnzerg, Verlag des Germanischen museums 1884
54p. illus. XIV pl.(2 double) Q.
Issued as supplement to the Museum's *Anzeiger* 1.bd. 1. hft. jahrg. 1884
Paintings on glass show costume of the middle ages and of the 16th century. Foreword signed A. Essenwein
Lipperheide 596. LC 11-28934

Katalog der im Germanischen museum befindlichen kartenspiele und spielkarten. Nürnberg, Verlag des Germanischen museums 1886
35p. XXXX pl.(1 double) Q.
Preface signed: A. Essenwein
Reproductions of playing cards of the 15th to the 19th century present a history of costume
Lipperheide 597. LC 13-14575

Katalog der im Germanischen museum befindlichen originalskulpturen. Nürnberg, Germanisches museum 1890
92p. 20 illus. 16pl. Q.
Introduction signed: Hans Bösch. The pictures show costume of the fifteenth and first half of the sixteenth century
Lipperheide 673. LC 13-4911

Katalog der im germanischen museum vorhandenen zum abdrucke bestimmten geschnittenen holzstöcke vom XV-XVIII jahrhunderte. See entry under Bösch, Hans

Mitteilungen aus dem Germanischen nationalmuseum, hrsg. vom direktorium ... jahrg. 1884/86-1920/21. Nürnberg, 1886-1921
Illus. pl.(part col.) ports. facsims. Q.
The first two parts of the *Mitteilungen* were issued as supplements to the *Anzeiger,* v 1, pts 1-2 1884-85. From 1900-08 the *Mitteilungen* and the *Anzeiger* were issued quarterly in the same covers (cover-title, *Anzeiger*) with special title pages and separate paging, the latter being paged in roman; in 1909 the two became independent, the *Mitteilungen* issued annually, the *Anzeiger* quarterly
Lipperheide 599. LC 11-28916

Nuremberg. See Germany—Bavaria—Nuremberg; Street venders—Germany—Nuremberg

Nurses. See Red cross

Nusbiegel, Johann

24 blatt colorierte Schweizer mädchentrachten; je eine ganze figur im hintergrund, eine ansicht der hauptstadt des betreffenden cantons. Nürnberg, F. Campe ca1800
24 col.pl. Q.
Colas 2235

Nussbiegel, J. See Nusbiegel, Johann

Nussey, Dora

(tr.) Mâle, Émile. Religious art in France, XIII century

Nuttall, Mrs Zelia
Ancient Mexican feather work at the Columbian historical exposition at Madrid ... from the Report of the Madrid Commission, 1892. Washington, Govt. print. off. 1895
p[329]-37. pl. O.
LC 10-31376

Standard or head-dress? An historical essay on a relic of ancient Mexico. Cambridge, Mass., Peabody museum of American archæology and ethnology 1888
52p. 3 col.pl. O. (Archaeological and ethnological papers of the Peabody museum. Harvard university, vol. I, no 1)
The relic is a unique piece of featherwork dating from the time of the conquest of Mexico and now preserved in the imperial ethnological collection in Vienna
Colas 2236. LC 5-5557

Nyblaeus, Gustaf Adolf
Scener ur indelta soldatens lif; tecknade af V. L. E. Sparre. Stockholm, H. Pettersson 1867
32p. 12 col.pl. ob.F.

Nystrom, Paul Henry
Economics of fashion. New York, Ronald press [c1928]
xiii,521p. illus. pl. diagrs. O. $5
Bibliography: p483-94
Costume index. LC 28-22952

O

O narodnoĭ odezhdi͡e ī ubranstvi͡e Rusīnov" īlī Russkīkh" v" Galīchīni͡e ī si͡evero-vostochnoĭ Vengriī. Golovatskĭ, I͡A. F.

Oakey, Maria Richards. See Dewing, M. R. O.

Ober het lang haair der mannen en de lokken der vrouwen. Saumaise, Claude de

Oberländer, Richard
Fremde völker, ethnographische schilderungen aus der alten und neuen welt. Leipzig und Wien, J. Klinkhardt 1883
486p. 280 illus. F.
Published in 24 parts, 1881-82
LC 3-13171

Obermaier, Hugo
Fossil man in Spain. London, Milford; New Haven, Pub. for the Hispanic society of America by the Yale university press; [etc.] 1924
xxviii,495p. illus. XXIII pl.(part col. incl. front. map) diagrs. O. 23s; $5
"Translated into English from the original text of *El hombre fósil,* Madrid, 1916 . . . with extensive additions and alterations by the author, up to June, 1922, incorporated in the text by the translator, Christine D. Matthew. Revised and approved for the Hispanic society of America by Henry Fairfield Osborn"
Notes and bibliography: p[373]-454
LC 24-25757

See also Breuil, Henri, jt. auth.

Objets choisis de la garde-robe royale de Suède. Lindberg, C. F.

L'**Observateur** des modes. 1.-6. année; août 1818 - 30 nov. 1823. Paris
Col.pl. O.
A fashion periodical. Absorbed by *L'Observateur des modes et Le Narcisse réunis.* For a reprint of some of the plates see *Modes françaises ou histoire pittoresque du costume en France*
Colas 2237. Lipperheide 4601

L'**Observateur** des modes et Le Narcisse réunis. 1.-29 année; mars 1830-mars 1856. Paris, Fontaine
29v. O.-Q.
Title varies: v 1-21, 1830-mars 1848: *Le Narcisse;* Oct. 1832-March 1848: *Le Narcisse, et L'Observateur réunis.* Subtitle varies
Colas 2180-81

Observations on the body-armour anciently worn in England. Meyrick, Sir S. R.

Observations on the military garments formerly worn in England. Meyrick, Sir S. R.

Observations sur les modes et les usages de Paris. Gazette du bon genre

Observations-puncten. Khevenhüller, L. A., graf von

Occupations
Amman, Jost. De omnibus illiberalibus sive mechanicis artibus, humani ingenii sagacitate atque industria iam inde ab exordio nascentio mundi usque ad nostram aetatem adinuentis. 1574

Amman, Jost. Eygentliche beschreibung aller stände auff erden hoher und nidriger, geistlicher und weltlicher, aller künsten, handwercken unnd händeln, &c. vom grössten biss zum kleinesten. 1568

Amman, Jost. Stände und handwerker. 1884

Amman, Jost. Das ständebuch. 1934

Boileau, Étienne. Réglemens sur les arts et métiers de Paris, rédigés au XIIIe siècle. 1837

Brandt, Paul. Schaffende arbeit und bildende kunst. 1927-28

Luyken, Johann, and Luyken, Caspar. Menschelyke beezigheeden bestaande in regeering, konsten en ambachten. 1695

Weigel, Christoph. Abbildung der gemein- nützlichen haupt-stände von denen regenten und ihren so in friedens- als kriegs- zeiten zugeordneten bedienten an bisz auf alle künstler und handwercker nach jedes ambts- und beruffs-verrichtungen ... gezeichnet. 1698

See also Artists; Barbers; Circus performers; Clowns; Cooks; Designing, as an occupation; Firemen; Fish-mongers; Lumbermen; Merchants; Miners; Physicians; Poets; Printers; Sailors; Surveyors; Waiters; Workmen

Middle ages

Salzman, L. F. English life in the middle ages. 1929

Salzman, L. F. English trade in the middle ages. 1931

Occupations—*Continued*

15th century

Bossert, H. T. Ein altdeutscher Totentanz. 1919. From 15th century drawings

Brant, Sebastian. Sebastian Brands Narrenschiff; ein hausschatz zur ergetzung und erbauung erneuert von Karl Simrock; mit den holzschnitten der ersten ausgaben und dem bildniss Brands aus Reusners Icones. 1872

Brant, Sebastian. The Ship of fools; tr. by A. Barclay. 1874

Crescenzi, Pietro de. Commoda ruralium. ca1493

Crescenzi, Pietro de. Neu feldt und ackerbau. 1602

16th century

Amman, Jost. Insignia sacrae Caesareae maiestatis. 1579

Amman, Jost. Stam und wapenbuch hochs und niders standts, darinnen der römischen keys. mt. dess heiligen röm. reychss, churfürsten, fürsten, grafen, freyen und herrn ... wapen mit iren schilt und helmen mit angehengten vilen ledigen schildten und helmen. 1579

Amman, Jost. Stamm- und wappenbuch; neu herausgegeben und geordnet von Friedrich Warnecke. 1877

Amman, Jost. Wappen- & stammbuch. Franckfort a. M. S. Feyrabend 1589. 1881

Amman, Jost. Wapen und stammbuch darinnen der keys. maiest. chur und fürsten, graffen, freyherrn, deren vom adel, etc. mit kunstreichen figuren. 1589

Garzoni, Tommaso. Piazza universale: Das ist: Allgemeiner schauplatz, marckt und zusammenkunfft aller professionen, künsten, geschäfften, händeln und handwercken. 1641

17th century

Hohberg, W. H., freiherr von. Georgica curiosa aucta, das ist: Umståndlicher bericht und klarer unterricht von dem adelichen land- und feld-leben. 1701-1715

18th century

Les costumes français répresentans les differens etats du royaume, avec les habillemens propres à chaque etat. 1776

Curiöser spiegel. 1804?

Engelbrecht, Martin. Assemblage nouveau des manouvriers habilles. 1730

Die fehler der menschen nebst deren verbesserung in saubern kupfern und moralischen versen vorgestellet. 1751

Der mensch in seinen verschieden. lagen und ständen für die jugend geschildert. 1779

19th century

Augrand, Parfait. Métiers féminins. ca1810

Bourcard, Francesco de, ed. Usi e costumi di Napoli e contorni descritti e dipinti. 1853-58

Costumes, arts, métiers et usages de l'Angleterre. 1817

Gavarni, G. S. C. Physionomie de la population de Paris. 1832

Kerndörffer, H. A. Gallerie der stånde. 1811

La Bédollière, É. G. de. Les industriels, métiers et professions en France. 1842

Philipon, Charles. Genre parisien (métiers). ca1830

Philipon, Charles. Les ouvrières de Paris. ca1830

Pyne, W. H. Microcosm; or, A picturesque delineation of the arts, agriculture, manufactures &c. of Great Britain. 1808

Raccolta di 30 costumi con altretante vedute le piú interessanti della cittá di Milano. ca1820

Sébillot, Paul. Légendes et curiosités des métiers. ca1875

China

Colored wood engravings showing scenes of social life in China, and of Chinese trades-people working at their trades. 1880?

Oceania

Christian, F. W. Eastern Pacific lands. 1910

Cook, James. A voyage towards the South pole, and round the world. 1777

Edge-Partington, James. Album of the weapons, tools, ornaments, articles of dress, etc. of the natives of the Pacific islands. 1890-95

Elkington, E. W. The savage South Seas. 1907

Henricy, Casimir, and Lacroix, Frédéric. Les moeurs et costumes de tous les peuples. 1847

Océanie, ou cinquième partie du monde. Domeny de Rienzi, G. L.

Péron, François. Voyage de découvertes aux terres Australes, fait par ordre du gouvernement, sur les corvettes les Géographe, le Naturaliste, et la goëlette le Casuarina, pendant les années 1800, 1801, 1802, 1803 et 1804. 1824

Shoberl, Frederic, ed. South Sea islands. 1824

See also Polynesia; Solomon islands

Océanie. Domeny de Rienzi, G. L.

Ocherk" dīeîatel'nostī Mīnīsterstva Īmperatorskago dvora po prīgotovlenīîam ... v" 1896. Russia. Mīnīsterstvo Īmperatorskago dvora

O'Connell, Charles

(ed.) The Victor book of the opera

O'Connor, Vincent Clarence Scott

The charm of Kashmir. London, New York [etc.] Longmans, Green and co. 1920

xi,182p. 40pl.(16 mounted col. incl.front.) Q. $27.50
LC 20-18523

Octavien, François
Figures françoises nouvellement inventées. Paris, L. Surugue 1725
O.
Contains four costume pictures of men and women
Cataloged from Colas
Colas 2243

O'Curry, Eugene
On the manners and customs of the ancient Irish ... Edited with an introduction, appendixes, etc., by W. K. Sullivan. London [etc.] Williams and Norgate; New York, Scribner, Welford & co.; [etc.] 1873
3v. illus. O.
Contains a chapter on Irish dress
Colas 2244. LC 4-3055

Odd-fellows, Independent order of
Ames sword company, Chicago. Regalia, paraphernalia, and supplies for encampments I. O. O. F 1893

Odezhda stavropol'skikh turkmenok. Samoĭlovich, A. N.

Odieuvre, Michael
(engr.) Dreux du Radier, J. F. L'Europe illustre

Oduaga-Zolarde, G.
Les courses de taureaux expliquées, manuel tauromachique à l'usage des amateurs de courses. Paris, Dentu 1854
xi,140,148p. 4pl. O.
Lipperheide 2875c

Oeconomia ruralis et domestica. Coler, Johann

Oeconomus prudens et legalis. Florin, F. P.

Oeffeningh en konst des rydens. See Lieb, Christophorus. Practica et arte di cavalleria

Die **öffentliche** maskerade in Bamberg am fastnachts-montage 1833. See Vorläufer zum ersten Theresienvolksfeste in Bamberg

Oeillet des Murs, Marc Athanase Parfait.
See Chenu, J. C., jt. auth.

Oelssner, Gottlieb
Philosophisch-moralisch- und medicinische betrachtung, ueber mancherley zur hoffart und schönheit hervorgesuchte, schädliche zwang-mittel ... nebst den schädlichen miszbrauche der schnürbrüste und planchette oder sogenannten blanckscheite der frauenzimmer. Breszlau & Leipzig, D. Pietsch 1754
80p. O.
Lipperheide 3465

Oeri, Johann Jakob
Der onyx von Schaffhausen; jubiläumsschrift des historisch-antiquarischen vereins Schaffhausen. Zürich, J. J. Hofer [1882]
5p. 4 col.pl. F.
Plates are by Hofer and Burger. The onyx is cut to show a female figure representing Peace and her dress is described. The plate is attributed to the first century after Christ
Lipperheide 254

Oertel, Hieronymus
Ortelius redivivus et continuatus, oder Der ungarischen kriegs-empörungen historische beschreibung ... Deszgleichen auch mit einer continuation, von dem 1607. bis an das 1665. jahr vermehret durch Martin Meyern. Nürnberg, Verlegt durch P. Fürsten; Franckfurt am Mäyn, D. Fievert 1665
2v. 104pl. F.
"Darinnen enthalten alles was sich ... zwischen ... ungarischen königen ... und dem Türcken ... in Ober- und Nider-Ungarn wie auch Siebenbürgen von dem 1395. bisz in das 1607. jahr ... dem ... Türckischen friedensschlusz ... zugetragen." Subtitle
The first edition (Nürnberg, 1603-15) contained the same plates. Contains 153 portraits, a number of views and pictures of battles. The views have costume pictures and are signed with Lucas Schnitzer's monogram
Lipperheide 891

Oesterlèy, Karl Friedrich Wilhelm
(illus.) Müller, K. O. Denkmäler der alten kunst

Oesterreich, Matthias
(engr.) Ghezzi, P. L. Raccolta di XXIV carricature

Die **oesterreich-ungarische** armee; 204 abbildungen in farbendruck. Leipzig, M. Ruhl [1892]
1 p.l. 16 col.pl. on fold.sheet. O. (Militär-album aller länder, 2. u. 3. hft.)
"Die regiments-od. egalisirungs-farben der oesterreich.- ungar. armee," 1 page mounted on page 2 of cover
Colas 2604. Lipp. 2247. LC CA11-3233

Die k. k. **österr.** ungar. armee. Hausner, Josef

Die **österreich-ungarische** armee. Sussmann, Anton

Österreich-Ungarn: Das heer. Kählig, Eduard von

Die k. k. **öesterreichisch-ungarische** armee. Barteau, L. R.

Österreichisch-ungarische friseur-und razeur-zeitung. See Neue Wiener friseurzeitung

Die **österreichisch-ungarische** monarchie in wort und bild. Wien, K. K. Hof- und staatsdruckerei 1886-1902
24v. illus. col.pl.(incl.front.) ports. facsims. Q.
Contents: Wien und Niederösterreich. 1.abth. Wien. 1886; v2 Übersichtsband. 1.abth. Naturgeschichtlicher teil. 1887; v3 Übersichtsband. 2.abth. Geschichtlicher teil. 1887; v4 Wien und Niederösterreich. 2.abth. Niederösterreich. 1888; v5 Ungarn v 1. 1888; v6 Oberösterreich und Salzburg. 1889; v7 Steiermark. 1890; v8 Kärten und Krain. 1891; v9 Ungarn v2. 1891; v10 Das küstenland (Görz, Gradiska, Triest und Istrien) 1891; v11 Dalmatien. 1892; v12 Ungarn v3. 1893; v13 Tirol und Vorarlberg. 1893; v14 Böhmen, 1.abth. 1894; v15 Böhmen, 2.abth. 1896; v16 Ungarn v4. 1896; v17 Mähren und Schlesien. 1897; v18 Ungarn v5, 1.abth. 1898; v19 Galizien. 1898; v20 Bukowina. 1899; v21 Ungarn v5, 2.abth. 1900; v22 Bosnien und Hercegovina. 1901. v23 Ungarn v6, 1902; v24 Croatien und Slavonien. 1902
Each volume has plates or illustrations, many in color, which show costume of the region treated
Lipperheide 842. LC 1-16685

Österreichisch-ungarische national-trachten. Gaul, Franz

Die k. k. **oesterreichische** armee im laufe zweyer jahrhunderte. L'Allemand, Fritz

K. K. **Oesterreichische** armee nach der neuen adjustirung. Wien, M. Trentsensky [1837-48]
6 l. 88 col.pl. F.
Contents: 1 Generalität und garden; 2 Infanterie; 3 Cavalerie; 4 Artillerie und fuhrwesen; 5 Extra-corps und marine; 6 Militair-branchen
Colas 1615. Lipperheide 2235

Die **österreichische** armee von 1700 bis 1867. Teuber, Oscar

Osterreichische cavallerie, von 1600-1883. Zimburg, Wilhelm von

Das **oesterreichische** heer von Ferdinand II. römisch deutschen kaiser, bis Ferdinand I. kaiser von Oesterreich. See Gerasch, Franz. Das oesterreichische heer von Ferdinand II. römisch deutschen kaiser, bis Franz Josef I. kaiser von Oesterreich

Das **oesterreichische** heer von Ferdinand II. römisch deutschen kaiser, bis Franz Josef I., kaiser von Oesterreich. Gerasch, Franz

Oesterreichische landwehr. Wien, J. Eder [1810]
12 col.pl. ob.F.
Colas 2245

Das k. k. **oesterreich.** militär. Pettenkoffer, August

Oesterr. national-trachten. See entry under Trachten-album

Oesterreichische und russische truppen aus dem ungarischen feldzuge 1849. Heicke, Josef

Österreichisches museum für kunst und industrie. See Vienna. K. K. Österreichisches museum für kunst und industrie

Die k. k. **österreich'sche** armée nach der neuesten adjustirung. Pettenkoffer, August, and Strassgschwandtner, A.

Oettinger, Wolfgang von
(ed.) Chodowiecki, D. N. Von Berlin nach Danzig

L'**oeuvre** de Gavarni. Mahérault, M. J. F., and Bocher, Emmanuel

L'**oeuvre** de Léon Bakst pour La belle au bois dormant. See Bakst, Léon. The designs ... for The sleeping princess

Oeuvre dentellière française. Renouf, Maurice

Oeuvres complètes du roi René. René I, d'Anjou, king of Naples and Jerusalem

Of dandyism and of George Brummell. Barbey d'Aurevilly, J. A.

L'**office** des chevaliers de l'Ordre du St. Esprit. [Paris] L'imprimerie royale 1740
97p. 4 illus. D.
Contains a picture of the collar of the Order of the Holy Ghost
Lipperheide 1908

Officia Ciceronis, Teutsch. See Cicero, M. T. Officia M. T. C. Ein buch so Marcus Tullius Cicero der Römer zů seynem sune Marco

Official tour through Bosnia and Herzegovina. Asbóth, János de

Officials

England

The book of the ranks and dignities of British society. 1924

France

Chataignier. Costumes militaires et civil. 1800-1815?

Chataignier. Costumes officiels des fonctionnaires du Directoire. 1796

Costumes des representants du peuple. n.d.

Costumes des représentans du peuple français et fonctionnaire public. n.d.

Defontaine, Henri. Du costume civil officiel et de l'uniforme militaire des officiers à la cour ou auprès des chefs d'état français depuis 1804 jusqu'à nos jours. 1908

Garneray, J. F. Collection des nouveaux costumes des autorités constituées civils et militaires. ca1796

Grasset de Saint Sauveur, Jacques. Costumes des représentans du peuple, membres des deux conseils, du directoire exécutif, des ministres, des tribunaux, des messagers d'état, huissiers, et autres fonctionnaires publics. 1795

Grasset de Saint Sauveur, Jacques. Dresses of the representatives of the people, members of the two councils, and of the executive directory. 1796

Grasset de Saint Sauveur, Jacques. Recueil complet des costumes des autorités constituées, civiles, militaires, et de la marine. 1796

Launay, Edmond. Costumes, insignes, cartes, médailles des députés 1789-1898. 1899

Neuestes costume der staats-beamten der Republik Frankreich nach dem befehl des ersten consuls Buonaparte. 1802

Germany

Die deutschen reichs- und königl. preuss. staats- und hofbeamten-uniformen. 1897

Klemm, Heinrich. Lehrbuch für uniformschneider zur selbstbelehrung. 1896

Langenmantel, David. Histoire des regiments in des Heil. röm. reichs stadt Augspurg. 1725

Lappenberg, J. M. Die miniaturen zu dem Hamburgischen stadtrechte vom jahre 1497. 1845

Preussische civil-uniformen. 1787-88

Officiers et soldats des différents contingents des cantons suisses réunis à Bâle en 1792. Volmar, Émile

O'Followell, Ludovic
Le corset: histoire, médecine, hygiène ... étude historique, avec une préface de m. Paul Ginisty. Paris, A. Maloine 1905
xi,222p. 199 illus. 7pl. Q. 5fr.

Ogawa, K.
Japanese costume before the Restoration; photographed by K. Ogawa, under the direction of Ko-Yu-Kai. Tokyo, K. Ogawa 1893
1 l. 16pl. F.
Colas 2245 bis. Costume index

Military costume in old Japan; photographed by K. Ogawa, under direction of Chitora Kawasaki of Ko-yu-kai. Tokyo, K. Ogawa 1893
2p. 15pl. F.
Colas 2245 ter

Ogden, Henry Alexander
(illus.) United States. Quartermaster corps. The army of the United States
(illus.) United States. Quartermaster corps. Uniform of the army of the United States

Ogilby, John
The entertainment of His most excellent Majestie Charles II, in his passage through the city of London to his coronation. [London] Printed for R. Mariot [etc.] 1662
192p. front. 11 fold.pl. F.
"Containing an exact accompt of the whole solemnity; the triumphal arches, and cavalcade, delineated in sculpture; the speeches and impresses illustrated from antiquity. To these is added, a brief narrative of His Majestie's solemn coronation: with his magnificent proceedings, and royal feast in Westminster-hall." Subtitle
LC 5-14722

Der **ohne** ursach verworffene und dahero von rechts wegen auff den thron der ehren wiederum erhabene barth. Permoser, Balthasar

Ohnefalsch-Richter, Magda H.
Griechische sitten und gebräuche auf Cypern. Berlin, D. Reimer 1913
xiii,369p. illus. 40pl. 2 maps. Q.
Some plates are photographs of groups and some show articles of dress

Der **ohrschmuck** der Greichen und Etrusker. Hadaczek, K.

Ohsson, Ignatius Mouradgea d'. See Mouradgea d'Ohsson, Ignatius

Okabe-Kakuya
Japanese sword guards. Boston, 1908
148p. 18pl. O. (Museum of fine arts, Boston. Chinese and Japanese art dept.)
Published in cooperation with the department of Chinese and Japanese art of the Museum of fine arts, Boston
Also published with title: *Special exhibition of sword guards, April 1907.* (Boston 1907. [139p.] illus. pl.)

Ólafsson, Eggert
Des vice-lavmands Eggert Olafsens und des landphysici Biarne Povelsens reise durch Island, veranstaltet von der Königlichen societåt der wissenschaften in Kopenhagen und beschrieben von ... Olafsen; aus dem dånischen ůbersetzt. Kopenhagen und Leipzig, Heinecke und Faber 1774-75
2pts. in 1 v. L(i.e. 51)pl.(part fold.) Q.
Edited by G. Schøning; translated by Joachim Michael Geuss
Five plates show costume of Icelanders
Lipperheide 1042. LC 5-8236

Olberg, Félix von. See Arnould, Georg. Das deutsche heer und die marine

Old and rare Scottish tartans. Stewart, D. W.

The **old** art of tatting; by an Englishwoman. Bath, Hollway ca1860
2v. 10pl. O.
Lipperheide 4025

Old Bohemian customs throughout the year. Fišer, Frant

Old Chinatown. Irwin, W. H.

Old Chinese spectacles. Rasmussen, O. D.

Old civilizations of Inca land. Mead, C. W.

Old court customs and modern court rule. Armytage, Mrs F. F. H. (Berkeley)

The **old** cryes of London. Bridge, Sir Frederick

Old Edinburgh beaux & belles ... with the story of how they walked, dressed and behaved themselves. Edinburgh, W. Paterson 1886
112p. illus.(part col.) col.pl. port. D. 1s

Old Edinburgh pedlars, beggars and criminals with some other odd characters. Edinburgh, W. Paterson 1886
107p. illus. S.

Old England. Knight, Charles, ed.

Old English costumes. Hughes, Talbot

Old English costumes. Schild, Marie

Old English embroidery. Marshall, Frances, and Marshall, Hugh

Old English peasant costumes. See Schild, Marie. Old English costumes

Old English sporting prints and their history. Nevill, R. H.

Old fans from Mr. R. Walker's cabinet. Walker, Robert

Old Italian lace. Ricci, Signora Elisa

Old Japanese dresses and ornaments. Jidai Fukusoku Sen

Old London street cries and the cries of today. Tuer, A. W.

Old Nick, pseud. See Forgues, P. E. D.

Old Sauk and Fox beaded garters. Harrington, M. R.

Old sword-play. Hutton, Alfred

Old time punishments. Andrews, William

Old times. Ashton, John

Old world lace. Blum, C. M.

Oldenburg. See Germany—Oldenburg

Oldenburgisch chronicon. Hamelmann, Hermann, comp.

[**Olearius, Adam**]
Die hoch fürstl: leichbegengnis des durchleuchtigsten furstẽ ... herrn Friederich erben zu Norwegen, hertzogẽ zu Sleszwig Holstein ... so gestorben den 10 aug 1659 beigesetzt den 30 janua 1661. No place, [1661]
31 l. 143pl. F.
Lipperheide 2614

O'Leary, Florence. See Downs, Marie, jt. auth.

[**Olenschlager, Johann Daniel von**]
Vollständiges diarium von der ... erwehlung des ... herrn Franciscus ... zum römischen könig und kayser. Frankfurt am Mayn, J. D. Jung 1746
2v. 1 illus. 39pl. F.
Plates show the procession, the coronation, fireworks, and portraits of the nobles
Lipperheide 2518

Oliphant, Mrs Margaret Oliphant (Wilson)
Dress. By Mrs. Oliphant. London, Macmillan and co., 1878.
3p.l. 103p. front. illus. D. (Art at home series)
A plea for common sense rather than fashion
LC 11-22662

Olivares, José de
Our islands and their people as seen with camera and pencil ... edited and arranged by William S. Bryan ... photographs by W. B. Townsend. St. Louis, New York [etc.] N. D. Thompson [1899-1900]
776p. col.front. illus. col.pl. ports. maps. sq.F. (Educational art series v13)
Issued in 24 parts
Also published later (St. Louis, N. D. Thompson 1904. 3v.)
LC 99-5187

Oliver, John
(engr.) Habitus academicorum Oxoniensium a doctore ad servientem

Oliver, Samuel Pasfield
(ed.) Drury, Robert. Madagascar

Olivier, J.
Fencing familiarized: or, A new treatise on the art of small sword. Illustrated by elegant engravings ... painted from life, and executed in a most elegant and masterly manner. A new ed., rev., cor., and augm. by an original set of prints. London, J. Bell 1780
xlvii,205p. fold.front. illus.(coat-of-arms, duplicated) XIV pl.(13 fold.) O.
First edition: 1771-1772. English and French on opposite pages. Added title page in French: *L'art des armes simplifié.* Plates are after drawings by J. Roberts
Lipperheide 2976. LC 19-17

Ollier, Charles
Original views of London as it is. See entry under Boys, T. S.

Olon, François Pidou de Saint. See Pidou de Saint Olon, François

Olschki, Leonardo
Die romanischen literaturen des mittelalters. Wildpark-Potsdam, Akademische verlagsgesellschaft Athenaion, m. b. h. c1928
259p. illus. VII pl.(part col. and mounted; incl. port., facsims.) double map. Q. (Handbuch der literaturwissenschaft. lfg. 106, 110, 115, 117, 125, 132, 139, 144)
Issued in 8 parts ("hefte") 1928-30. Illustrations show costume worn during the Middle Ages. Includes bibliographies
LC 30-33932

Om Lappland och Lapparne. Düben, G. V. J. von

Om nordmae klaededragt i aeldre tider. Keyser, J. R.

Oman, Charles Chichele
Catalogue of rings. See entry under Victoria and Albert museum, South Kensington

Omboni, Tito
Viaggi nell' Africa occidentale. Milano, Stabilimento Civelli e comp 1845
416p. 11 col.pl. O.
Nine plates show costumes of natives. Some have been taken from Douville's *Voyage au Congo*
Colas 2246. Lipperheide 1593

L'**ombrelle,** le gant, le manchon. Uzanne, L. O.

Ommegang de Saint-Rombaut (1875). Geets, Willem

The **omnibus** book of sports for young and old. Aldin, C. C. W.

Omnium Caesarum verissimae imagines. See Vico, Enea. Le imagini con tutti i riversi trovati et le vite de gli imperatori

Omnium fere gentium nostrae aetatis habitus, nunquam ante hac aediti. Bertelli, Ferdinando

Omnium fere gentium, nostræq. Deserpz, François

Omnium fere monasticorum ordinum in specie. See Creccelius, Johannes. Collectanea ex historijs, de origine et fundatione

Omnium pene Europae, Asiae, Africae et Americae gentium habitus. Bruyn, Abraham de

Omnium pene Europae, Asiae, Aphricae atque Americae gentium habitus. Bruyn, Abraham de

Omnium poene gentium imagines, ubi oris totiusque corporis & vestium habitus, in ordinis cuiuscunque, ac loci hominibus diligentissime exprimuntur. Bruyn, Abraham de

Omnium regum Francorum a Pharamundo usque ad Carolum nonum. Pantaleon, Heinrich

Omnium statuum foeminei sexus ornatus et usitati habitus Gedanenses. Möller, Anton

Omond, George William Thomson
Belgium; painted by Amédée Forestier. London, A. & C. Black 1908
390p. 77 col.pl.(incl.front.) fold.map. O.
Also published in three separate parts: *Bruges and West Flanders, Brabant and East Flanders,* and *Liège and the Ardennes*
Plates protected by guard sheets with descriptive letterpress
LC w9-41

Omont, Henri Auguste
(ed.) Paris. Bibliothèque nationale. Mss. fr. nouv. acq. 1098. Vie et histoire de Saint Denys
(ed.) Paris. Bibliothèque nationale. Mss. (Lat. 7899). Comédies de Térence
(ed.) Paris. Bibliothèque nationale. Mss. (Lat. 8846) Psautier illustré (XIIIe siècle)
(ed.) Paris. Bibliothèque nationale. Mss. (Lat.10525). Psautier de Saint Louis
(ed.) Paris. Bibliothèque nationale. Département des manuscrits. Antiquités et Guerre des Juifs de Josèphe

On English costume. Kelly, Mary

On special mission Abyssinia. Jacoby, Mrs C. M.

On tattooing. Buckland, A. W.

On the art of the theatre. Craig, E. G.

On the history of personal jewellery. Davenport, C. J. H.

On the imperial consular dress. Madden, F. W.

On the manners and customs of the ancient Irish. O'Curry, Eugene

On the tomb of an archbishop. Hope, Sir W. H. St J.

On the trail of the Bushongo. Torday, Emil

Ona Indians. See Indians of South America—Ona Indians

Oncken, Wilhelm
Das zeitalter des kaisers Wilhelm. Berlin, G. Grote 1890-92
2v. illus. fold.pl. ports. maps(part double) facsims.(part fold.) O. (Allgemeine geschichte in einzeldarstellungen ... Hrsg. von W. Oncken. 4. hauptabth., 6. th.)
Contains portraits of celebrated men of the time
Lipperheide 578. LC G-2457

Onfroy de Bréville, Jacques Marie Gaston, called Job
Aquarelles de Job: Tenue des troupes de France à toutes les époques armées de terre et de mer. Paris, Aux bureaux de la publication [1900-04]
4v. illus. 192 col.pl. F.
Published in 48 parts of four plates each which form four annual volumes
Volume 2, seconde année, 1901-02, has title: *Tenues des troupes de France ... Texte par des membres de la "Sabretache"* (Paris, Furne, Combet) Volume 3, troisième année, 1902-03. Volume 4, quatrième année, 1904, has title: *Tenues des troupes de France illus. de Job, texte par G. Cottreau* (Paris, J. Leroy)
Colas 1549. LC 2-29181 (v 1)

Mémoires de César Chabrac, trompette de houzards. Paris, Geffroy ca1900?
44p. col.illus. Q.

Napoléon. Paris, Boivin 1921
78p. 42 col.illus. F.

(illus.) Barrès, Maurice. La vieille garde imperiale

(illus.) Bouchot, H. F. X. M. L'épopée du costume militaire français; aquarelles et dessins originaux. 1898

(illus.) Costumes européens du XVIIe au XIXe siècle

(illus.) Montorgueil, Georges. Louis XI

Ongania, Ferdinando
(ed.) Franco, Giacomo. Habiti delle donne venetiane
(pub.) Franco, Giacomo. Nuova inventione; de diverse mostre cosi di punto in aere come de retticelli hoggi di usate per tutte le parte del mondo. Con merletti, mostrette da colari, e da manegheti et merli per cantoni de fazoletti

Onghena
(illus.) Barrois, J. Le livre du très chevalereux comte d'Artois et de sa femme, fille au comte de Boulogne

Onghéna, Charles
(engr.) Delepierre, Octave, and Voisin, Auguste. La châsse de Sainte Ursule gravée au trait par Charles Onghena d'après Jean Memling

Onions, Charles Talbut
(ed.) Shakespeare's England; an account of the life & manners of his age

Ons voorgeslacht. Hofdijk, W. J.

Onwhyn, J. and Onwhyn, T.
Costumes of the time of George II designed for Her Majesty's state ball. [London] J. Lee [1845]
11 col.ports. O.
Colas 2249. Lipperheide 3178

Onwhyn, T. See Onwhyn, J., jt. auth.

Der **Onyx** von Schaffhausen. Oeri, J. J.

Onze gouden eeuw. Muller, P. L.

Onze kleeding. Anthonia Margaretha, pseud.

Onze krijgsmacht met bijschriften. Brunings, P. F.

Onze schutter-vendels en schutterijen. Lintum, Crist te

Oort, Adam van. See Noort, Adam van

Opel, Peter
Warhafte und aigentliche contrafactur des löblichen freund und nachbarliche stahelschiessens so anno 1586 den 31. julii zu Regenspurg gehalten. Regenspurg, P. Opel 1587
5pl. F.
Copies of the plates are in Edelmann's *Schützenwesen*
Lipperheide 2999

Die **oper.** Bie, Oskar

L'**opéra** au XIXme siècle. Beaumont, C. E. de

Opera di Georgio Agricola de l'arte de metalli. See Agricola, Georg. De re metallica

Opera nazionale dopolavoro
... Popular Italian costumes, music, dances and festivals. Rome, National leisure hours institution 1931
219p. illus.(incl. facsims. music) O.
At head of title: National leisure hours institution
Rather small photographs show the folk dress as worn in various regions at this period
LC A33-72

Opera nova. Sera, Domenico da

Opera nova universal intitulata corona di racammi. Vavassore, G. A.

Opera singers. Kobbé, Gustave

Operatic costume
Beaumont, C. E. de. L'opéra au XIXme siècle. ca1845
Fischer, Carlos. Les costumes de l'Opéra. 1931
Gautier, Théophile. Les beautés de l'opéra. 1845
Gerhäuser, Emil. Stuttgarter bühnenkunst. 1917
Guillaumot, A. E. Costumes de l'opera, XVIIe-XVIIIe siècles. 1883
Kobbé, Gustave. Opera singers. 1913
Meilhac, Henri, and Halévy, Ludovic. La vie parisienne; pièce en cinq actes, musique de M. J. Offenbach. 1875
Seitz, Rudolf. Parsifal; costum studien zu Richard Wagner's oper. 1882
The Victor book of the opera. c1936

Opisanie pami͡atnīkov' drevnostī tserkovnago ī grazhdanskago byta russkago muzei͡a P. Koroanova. Filimonov", Georg

Opīsanie starīnnykh" russkīkh". Savvaītov", P. Ī.

Opīsanie v" lītsakh" torzhestva, proīskhodīvshago v" 1626 godu febralai͡a 5, prī brakosochetaniī Gosudari͡a Tsari͡a ī velīkago Kni͡azi͡a Mīkhaīla Feodorovīcha, s" Gosudaryneiu Tsarītseiu Evdokieiu Luk' i͡anovnoiu īz" rodv Strīeshnevykh". Moskva, tīp. Platona Beketova 1810
137p. 65 col.illus. Q.
Lipperheide 2783

Opīsanïe vsi͡ekh" obītai͡ushchīkh" v" Rossīiskom" gosudarstvi͡e narodov". See note under Georgi, J. G. Beschreibung aller nationen des russischen reichs

Opitz, G. See Opiz, G.

Opitz, Richard
Das häusliche leben der Griechen und Römer. Leipzig, A. Seemann 1894
302p. illus. fold.pl. D. (Kulturbilder aus dem klassischen altertume. VI)
Lipperheide 176. LC 4-20050

Opiz, Georg Emanuel
Leipzigermesse. 1. heft; von G. Opitz. Dresden, L. von Kleist ca1825
6 col.pl. F.
Plates, signed Opiz, show scenes at the Leipzig fair and persons in dress of the period. They are entitled: Die buden, Die geschäfte, Der landadel, Die messfreiheit, Der rossplatz, Der zahltag
Colas 2250. Lipperheide 830

Die Schweizer nach ihrer volksthümlichkeit; in sechs charakteristischen gruppen. Dresden, L. von Kleist ca1830
6 col.pl. F.
Plates are signed Opitz, del. and Hilscher, sc. and entitled: Basel, Madonna del Sasso (Cant. Tessin), Freiburg, Zurich, Appenzell, Solothurn
Colas 2251

Volks-trachten der Deutschen; G. Opiz, f. Leipzig, Breitkopf & Hartel ca1830
6 col.pl. F.
Peasant costumes of Hamburg, Saxony, Altenburg, The Palatinate, Bohemia and the Tyrol
Colas 2252. Lipperheide 736

Oplomachia. Pistofilo, Bonaventura

L'oplomachia pisana. Borghi, C. R.

Oppenheim, Guido
Neues stick-muster-buch. Frankft. a. M., Gottlieb & Müller 1878
1 l. 12pl. Q.
Lipperheide 3991

Oppenheim, Philippus
Das mönchskleid im christlichen altertum. Freiburg im Breisgau, Herder 1931
xii,279p. xx pl. Q. (Römische quartalschrift für christliche altertumskunde und für kirchengeschichte. 28. supplementheft)
"Die vorliegende arbeit ist aus meiner Breslauer dissertation erwachsen." Vorwort
"Weiteres bildmaterial für frühchristliches mönchtum": p278-79
LC 34-34416

Oprescu, George
Arta ţărănească la Români; lucrare însoţită de cincizeci şi opt tabele de ilustraţii. ₍Bucureşti, Cultura naţională, 1922₎
74p. pl. D. (Tara noastra, cvlegere de scrieri pe înţelesvl tvtvrora despre pamântvl şi poporvl românesc)
Descriptive letterpress on verso of each plate
LC 34-35766

Peasant art in Roumania. London, The Studio
xvii,182p. incl.illus.(1 col.mounted) pl. (part col.) map. Q. $4.50, o.p.
Special autumn number of the *Studio.* Some of the plates and illustrations appear also in the author's *Arta taraneasca* and the general plan of both works is the same
Costume index. LC 29-28677

Opus chyrurgicum. Paracelsus

Oraculum anachoreticum. Vos, Martin de

Oraibi Soyal ceremony. Dorsey, G. A., and Voth, H. R.

Orazi, Andrea Antonio
(illus.) Buonanni, Filippo. Ordinum equestrium et militarium catalogus in imaginibus expositus & cum brevi narratione
(illus.) Buonanni, Filippo. Ordinum religiosorum in ecclesia militanti catalogus
(illus.) Buonanni, Filiopo. Verzeichnuss der geist und weltlichen ritter-orden in netten abbildungen und einer kurtzen erzehlung in lateinisch und italienischer sprache
(illus.) Buonanni, Filippo. Verzeichnuss der geistlichen ordens-personen

Orbigny, Alcide Dessalines d'
(ed.) Voyage pittoresque dans les deux Amériques; résumé général de tous les voyages de Colomb, Las-Casas, Oviedo ... Humboldt ... Franklin ... etc., par les rédacteurs du Voyage pittoresque autour du monde; publié sous la direction de M. Alcide d'Orbigny ... Accompagné de cartes et ... gravures ... d'après les dessins de ... Sainson ... et Jules Boilly. Paris, L. Tenré ₍etc.₎ 1836
xvi, 568p. front. pl. port. 2 maps. Q.
Some of the pictures show Indians of various regions
Spanish edition: *Viaggio pittoresco nelle due Americhe* (Venezia, G. Antonelli, 1852-54. 2v. pl. Q.)
Lipperheide 1614. LC 5-43023

Orbis habitabilis oppida et vestitus. Allard, Carel

Orchamps, baronin d', pseud?
Die geheimnisse der frau, von baronin d'Orchamps; einzige autorisierte bearbeitung und uebersetzung. 1. bis 5. aufl. Berlin, G. Rieckes buchhandlung nachfolger ₍1908₎
379p. D.
LC 9-4074

Orchard, William C.
Beads and beadwork of the American Indians, a study based on specimens in the Museum of the American Indian, Heye foundation. New York, Museum of the American Indian, Heye foundation 1929
140p. illus. XXXI (i.e. XXXII)pl.(part col.) Q. (Contributions from the Museum of the American Indian, Heye foundation. v11)
LC 29-17107

Orchésographie. Tabourot, Jehan

Orchesography. Tabourot, Jehan

Orchestra, sive De saltationibus veterum dissertatio. Bilbergh, Joanne

Die **orden,** wappen und flaggen aller regenten und staaten in originalgetreuen abbildungen; 2. aufl. verm. durch die specielle beschreibung der sämmtlichen orden. Leipzig, M. Ruhl 1883-87
2v. 72 col.pl. Q.
Volume 1, 1883-84; v2 *Supplement,* 1887: The first edition (1880) contained the material of volume 1 only (63p. 38 col.pl.)
Lipperheide 1939

Ordenes militares. Zarza, and Vallejo

Ordenliche beschreibung des ... beylags oder hochzeit ... Herrn Carolen ertzhertzog zu Osterreich. Wirrich, Heinrich

Order, Royal Guelphic. See Royal Guelphic order

The **order** and ceremonies used for the solemn interment of ... George late Duke of Albemarle ... in the year ... 1670. No place, [1670]
3 l. 21pl. F.
Lipperheide 2687

Order of St John of Jerusalem. See Malta, Knights of

Orders, Military religious. See Military religious orders

Orders, Religious. See Monastic and religious orders; Monastic and religious orders for women

The **orders** of chivalry. Lawrence-Archer, James Henry

Orders of collars. See Segar, Sir William. Original institutions of the princely orders of collars

Orders of knighthood and chivalry

Bar, J. C. Les ordres de chevalerie d'Europe. (In his Recueil de tous les costumes des ordres religieux et militaires, avec un abrégé historique et chronologique enrichi de notes et de planches coloriées, v3. 1778-1789)

Biedenfeld, F. L. C., freiherr von. Geschichte und verfassung aller geistlichen und weltlichen, erloschenen und blühenden ritterorden. Nebst einer übersicht sämmtlicher militär- und civilehrenzeichen, medaillen &. &. und einem atlas ... Zugleich als fortsetzung von dessen geschichte der mönchsund klosterfrauenorden im Orient und Occident. 1841

Das buch der ritterorden und ehrenzeichen. 1848

Buonanni, Filippo. Ordinum equestrium et militarium catalogus in imaginibus expositus & cum brevi narratione. 1711

Buonanni, Filippo. Verzeichniss der geist und weltlichen ritter-orden in netten abbildungen und einer kurtzen erzehlung in lateinisch und italienischer sprache. 1720

Burke, Sir J. B. The book of orders of knighthood and decorations of honour of all nations. 1858

Burke, Sir J. B., and Burke, A. P. A genealogical and heraldic history of the peerage and baronetage, the Privy council, and knightage. 1935

Cibrario, G. A. L., conte. Descrizione storica degli ordini cavallereschi. 1846

Coronelli, M. V. Ordinum equestrium, ac militarium brevis narratio. 1715

Dorregaray, J. G., ed. Historia de las órdenes de caballería y de las condecoraciones españolas. 1865

Eichler, Gottfried. Abbildung und beschreibung aller hohen ritter-orden in Europa. 1756

Falke, Jacob von. Die ritterliche gesellschaft im zeitalter des frauencultus. 1872

Gelbke, C. H. von. Ritterorden und ehrenzeichen erlaütert durch die vorhandenen urkunden. Als anhang des werkes: Abbildung und beschreibung der ritterorden und ehrenzeichen sämmtlicher souveraine und regierungen ... I. Preussen. 1834

Giucci, Gaetano. Iconografia storica degli ordini religiosi e cavallereschi. 1836-47

Gottschalck, Friedrich. Almanach der ritter-orden. 1817-19

Gritzner, Max. Handbuch der ritter- und vertienstorden aller kulturstaaten der welt innerhalb des XIX. jahrhunderts. 1893

Lawrence-Archer, J. H. The orders of chivalry. 1887

Loumyer, J. F. N. Ordres de chevalerie et marques d'honneur. 1844

Megiser, Hieronymus. Ein tractat von dem dreyfachen ritterstand und allen ritter orden der Christenheit. 1593

Micheli y Marquez, José. Tesoro militar de cavalleria antiguo y moderno modo de armar cavalleros, y professar, segun las ceremonias de qualquier orden militar ... insignias y abito de cada una. 1642

Milles, Thomas. Nobilitas politica vel civilis; personas scilicet distinguendi et ab origine inter gentes, ex principium gratia nobilitandi forma ... quò tandem & apud Anglos, qui sint nobilium gradus, & quæ ad nobilitatis fastigia euchendi ratio, ostenditur. 1608

Die orden, wappen und flaggen aller regenten und staaten in originalgetreuen abbildungen. 1883-87

Perrot, A. M. Collection historique des ordres de chevalerie civils et militaires, existant chez les différens peuples du monde. 1820

Rammelsberg, J. W. Beschreibung aller sowohl noch heutiges tages florirenden als bereits verloschenen geist- und weltlichen ritter-orden in Europa; nebst denen bildnissen derer ordens-zeichen. 1744

Salmson, A. J. Rikssalen på Gripholms slott historiskt porträtt-galleri af konung Gustaf I. 1847

Schoonebeek, Adriaan. Historie van alle ridderlyke en krygs-orders. 1697

Schulze, H. Chronik sämmtlicher bekannten ritter-orden und ehrenzeichen, welche von souverainen und regierungen verliehen werden ... Chronique de tous les ordres de chevalerie et marques d'honneur. 1855-78

Schwan, C. F. Abbildungen derjenigen ritter-orden, welche eine eigene ordenskleidung haben. 1791

Segar, Sir William. Honor military, and civill. 1602

Orders of knighthood and chivalry—*Cont.*

Trost, L. J. Die ritter- und verdienst-orden, ehrenzeichen und medaillen aller souveräne und staaten seit beginn des XIX. jahrhunderts. 1910

Wietz, J. K. Abbildungen sämmtlicher geistlichen orden männlich- und weiblichen geschlechts in der katholischen kirche. 1821

Denmark

Andersen, C. C. T. The chronological collection of the kings of Denmark. 1878

Munter, Frédéric. Recherches sur l'origine des ordres de chevallerie du royaume de Dannemarc. 1822

England

Carter, Matthew. Honor redivivus; or, The analysis of honor and armory. 1673

Hunter, John, robe-maker. A concise description of the insignia of the orders of British knighthood. 1844

Milles, Thomas. The catalogue of honor, or Tresury of true nobility. 1610

Nicolas, Sir N. H. History of the orders of knighthood of the British Empire. 1842

Segar, Sir William. Original institutions of the princely orders of collars. 1823

France

Herbé, C. A. Costumes français civils, militaires et religieux ... depuis les Gaulois jusqu'en 1834. 1835-37

Germany

Gravenhorst, C. Geschichte u. statuten des rothen adler-ordens und des königlichen kronen-ordens. Festschrift zur feier des preussischen krönungs- und ordensfestes am 23. januar 1881. 1881

Heideloff, K. A. von. Costum des deutschen ritterthums. ca1830

Tracht der ehren-ritter des deutschen ritterordens. 1874

Tracht der ritter des hohen deutschen ordens. 1869

Bavaria

Leser, Jac., and Leser, Oskar. Die ritter-und verdienst-orden, ehren-, verdienst-und denkzeichen sowie dienstaltersauszeichnungen des königr. Bayern. 1910

Prussia

Schneider, Louis. Die preussischen orden. 1867-72

Russia

Russisch kaiserlich-königliches ordensreglement. ca1870

Sweden

Schützercrantz, Adolph. Kongl. svenska riddare ordnarnes drägter 1833. 1833

Silfwerskjöld, T. von. Krönung und huldigung Oscar I. königs von Schweden und Norwegen, und der königin Josephin ... in Stockholm am 28sten september 1844 ... nebst einem anhang: Ursprung, geschichte und beschreibung der swedischen ritterorden. 1845

Wrangel, F. U. grefve. De kongl. svenska riddare-ordnarne. 1899

See also Military religious orders; also names of individual orders: Bath, Order of; Black eagle, Order of; Elephant, Order of; Garter, Order of; Golden fleece, Order of; Holy Ghost, Order of; Iron crown, Order of; Iron crown of Lombardy; Leopold, Order of; Malta, Knights of; Royal Guelphic order; St. Stephen, Order of; Templars; White Falcon, Order of the

Orders of knighthood and chivalry, Papal

Guigue de Champvans, Frédéric. Histoire et législation des ordres de chevalerie. 1932-33

Ordini di cavalcare. Grisone, Federico

Gl' **ordini** equestri religioso-militari. Cenni, Quinto

Ordinum equestrium, ac militarium brevis narratio. Coronelli, M. V.

Ordinum equestrium et militarium catalogus in imaginibus expositus & cum brevi narratione. Buonanni, Filippo

Ordinum religiosorum in ecclesia mlitanti catalogus. Buonanni, Filippo

Ordinum religiosorum in ecclesia militanti catalogus. Coronelli, M. V.

Ordning af Danmarks oldsager. Muller, S. O.

Ordnung Weyland desz ... herrn Joachim Ernsten marggrafen zu Brandenburg ... anno 1625. Gärtner, Georg

Ordonnance du Roi, pour régler l'exercice de ses troupes d'infanterie; du 1. juin 1776. France. Laws, statutes, etc.

Ordonnance et règlement de Mgr. l'évêque de Bayeux et Lisieux [Lemonnier]. Lemonnier, T. P. H.

Ordres de chevalerie et marques d'honneur. Loumyer, J. F. N.

Orengo, Gustav

(pub.) Lalaisse, Hippolyte. Types de l'armée française et de ses cantinières

L'**orfévrerie** algérienne et tunisienne. Eudel, Paul

Die **organe** der deutschen freiwilligen krankenpflege im kriege, ihre uniformierung und ausrüstung. Schlawe, Karl

Orient. See Asia

L'**Orient:** Égypte—Mésopotamie—Syrie—Phénicie. See Heuzey, L. A., and Heuzey, Jacques. Histoire du costume dans l'antiquité classique

Oriental album. St. John, J. A.

Oriental album. Van Lennep, H. J.

Oriental and occidental northern and southern portrait types of the Midway plaisance ... with an introduction by Prof. F. W. Putnam. St. Louis, N. D. Thompson pub. co. 1894
2p.l. 80 port. F. (Educational art series. v2 no 1-10)
With descriptive letterpress
"A collection of photographs of individual types of various nations from all parts of the world who represented, in the Department of ethnology, the manners, customs, dress, religions, music and other distinctive traits and peculiarities of their race." Subtitle
LC 5-28626

Oriental and sacred scenes. Howe, Fisher

Oriental arms and armor. See Arms and amor—Asia

Oriental costumes. Tilke, Max

Oriental drawings. Gold, Charles

Oriental silverwork. Roth, H. L.

Oriental theatricals. Laufer, Berthold

Orientalische kostüme. Tilke, Max

Orientalische reyss ... in der Türckey. Breüning, H. J.

Orientálni ústav, Prague
Ancient Egyptian dances. See entry under Lexová, Irena

L'**Oriflamme** des modes, journal du grande monde et du commerce. no. 1-103; 1840-1844. Paris
O.
Continuation of *La Fashion, guide journal des gens du monde; édition des dames* (Paris, Aug. 1839-1840)
Colas 1039-40

The **origin** of the whale bone-petticoat; a satyr. Boston, August 2d. 1714. [Boston, 1925]
Facsimile: 8 l. O. [Americana series; photostat reproductions by the Massachusetts historical society. no141]
Caption title. One of 10 photostat copies reproduced from the original in the British museum, July 1925
LC 26-235

The **origin** of tragedy. Ridgeway, Sir William

Original institutions of the princely orders of collars. Segar, Sir William

Original-stickmuster der Renaissance in getreuen copien. Vienna. K.K. Österreichisches museum für kunst und industrie

Original views of London as it is. Boys, T. S.

Original-zeichnungen deutscher meister des sechzehnten jahrhunderts. Hefner-Alteneck, J. H. von

Origines de la dentelle de Venise et l'École de point de Burano en 1878. Cérésole, Victor

Les **origines** de la parure aux temps paléolithiques. Wetter, George van

Origines de l'École de cavalerie et de ses traditions équestres. Picard, L. A.

Les **origines** du costume de la magistrature. Glasson, E. D.

Origins of art. Hirn, Yrjö

Orilia, Francesco
Il zodiaco over idea di perfettione di prencipi, formata dall' heroiche virtù dell' ... Antonio Alvarez di Toledo ... rapresentata come in un trionfo dal fidelissimo popolo napoletano. Per opera del ... Francesco Antonio Scacciauento ... nella festa ... 1629. Napoli, O. Beltrano 1630
501p. 229 illus. Q.
Pictures representatives of various sections of Italy, offices and occupations
Lipperheide 1246

Orissa. See India—Orissa

Orlers, Jan
Genealogia illustrissimorum comitum Nassoviae, in qua origo incrementa, & res gestae ab ijs, ab anno 682 ad praesentem hunc 1616, cum effigiebus XVI praecipuorum inter eos heroum ... collecta ex varijs monumentis. Lugduni Batavorum, J. Orlers 1616
98p. 16 illus. map. F.
Head and shoulder pictures of illustrious men of Nassau. The plates are by Adrian Schoonebeck
Lipperheide 931

Orley, Bernard van
(illus.) Paris. Musée national du Louvre. Les tapisseries des chasses de Maximilien

Orlich, Leopold von
Reise in Ostindien in briefen an Alexander von Humboldt und Carl Ritter. Leipzig, Mayer und Wigand 1845
xvi,298p. 40 illus. 22pl.(10 col.) Q.
Lipperheide 1495

Orlowski, Aleksandr Ossipovich
Album russe ou fantaisies dessinées lithographiquement. St Pétersburg, A. Pluchart 1826
14 col.pl. F.
Plates show dress of Russian peasants and workmen
Colas 2254. Lipperheide 1353m

The costume of Persia drawn from nature by A. Orlowski ... and engraved ... by Hulman, Dighton. Costumes de la Perse. London, 1820
25 col.pl. F.
In four parts
Cataloged from Colas
Colas 902

Uniformes, drapeaux et voitures militaires russes vers la fin du XVIIIe siècle et au commencement du XIXe. No place, [1882]
1 l. 28pl. F.
Colas 2255

(illus.) Drouville, Gaspard. Atlas ou collection de 43 costumes persanes, militaires et civil

Orlowski, G.
Russian cries; in correct portraiture, from drawings done on the spot by G. Orlowski and now in the possession of ... Lord Kinnaird. London, E. Orme 1809
1 l. 8 col.pl. F.
Plates engraved by J. Swaine and J. Godby
Colas 2253. Lipperheide 1347

Orme, Edward
(pub.) The costume of the Russian army

Das **ornament** des rococo und seine vorstufen. Jessen, Peter

Ornament in European silks. Cole, A. S.

O'Rourke, Matthew J.

Sword exercise illustrated: containing forty engravings from photographs, including the motions in "draw swords," "salute," and "return swords," with descriptive letter press. New York, M. J. O'Rourke 1865

iv p. 40 illus. on fold.pl. O.
Later edition published with title: *A new system of sword exercise* (New York, J. Gray 1872)
LC 19-9, 19-8 (1872 ed.)

Orsini, Fulvio

Imagines et elogia virorum illustrium et eruditor ex antiquis lapidibus et nomismatib. expressa cum annotationib. Romae, Ant. Lafrerij Formeis

109p. 75 illus.(58 full-page) F.
A new edition was published (Antwerp, 1606)
Lipperheide 147

Ortiz Echagüe, José

España, tipos y trajes; prólogo de J. Ortega y Gasset, texto de Guillermo de Achaval, 120 láminas por J. Ortiz Echagüe. Barcelona, Sociedad general de publicaciones [1933]

35p. incl. mounted pl. 120pl. on 60 l. Q.
Descriptive letterpress in German, English, Spanish and French
The author's: *Tipos y trajes de España* (Bilbao, Espasa-Calpe 1930) contains eighty of the same plates
LC 35-20722, 30-30152 (1930 ed.)

Spain; types and costumes. Barcelona, Sociedad general de publicaciones, S. A. Borrell 1934

34p. mounted front. 160pl. on 80 l. F.
Descriptive letterpress in German, English, Spanish, and French
English translation of the author's: *España, tipos y trajes*
Costume index

Ortiz Echagüe, José—*Continued*
Spanische kopfe; bilder aus Kastilien, Aragonien und Andalusien, eingeleitet von Felix Urabayen, J. Garcia Mercadal José Maria Salaverría, J. Muñoz San Román. Berlin, E. Wasmuth [1929]
80pl. on 40 l.
Translated from the Spanish by E. A. Grunauer

Osborn, Henry Fairfield
Men of the old stone age, their environment, life and art. New York, C. Scribner 1916
xxvi,545p. 8pl. illus. maps. O.
Frontispiece is a drawing of two Neanderthal men. Text contains references to clothing

(ed.) Obermaier, Hugo. Fossil man in Spain

Osgood, Cornelius
Contributions to the ethnography of the Kutchin. New Haven, Yale university press; London, H. Milford, Oxford university press 1936
189p. illus.(incl.map) 10pl.(incl.port.) on 5 l. O. (Yale university publications in anthropology. no14)
Seven of the plates show men's and women's dress, snowshoes, moccassins and mittens of the Kutchin Indians
Bibliography: p189
LC 37-10593

Oslo. Kunstindustrimuseet
Gamle norske billedtaepper . . . Altnorwegische bildteppische . . . hrsg. von der direction des Kunstindustriemuseums, durch H. Grosch. Berlin, E. Wasmuth 1901
9p. 12 col.pl. F.
Text in Danish and German. Figures show old Norwegian costume

Gamle smykker i Norge, 1550-1900; katalog over utstillingen ved Erla Thornam. Oslo, E. Moestue 1928
79p. pl. O.
LC 31-12411

Ossbahr, Carl Anton
Kongl. lifrustkammaren och därmed förenade samlingar. See entry under Stockholm. Livrustkammaren

See also Lindberg, C. F. Objets choisis de la garde-robe royale de Suède

Ost-indische reyse. Schultze, Walter

Ostade, Adriaan van
(engr.) Het vermaaklyk buitenleeven

Ostaus, Giovanni
La vera perfettione del disegno di varie sorti di recami et di cucire punti a fogliami, punti tagliati, punti a fili e rimessi, punti in cruciati, punti a stuora, et ogni altra arte che dia opera a disegni. In Venetia, appresso G. Ostaus 1567. Venetia, F. Ongania 1878
3 l. 35pl. Q. (Raccolta di opere antiche sui disegni dei merletti di Venezia. VII)
The first edition, published 1564, is rare. Lipperheide lists an edition dated 1564 which he describes as falsely dated since it contains some designs that first appeared in the 1567 and 1591 editions. The latter was reprinted in *Livres à dentelles*
Lipperheide 3894, 3893

Ostdeutsche volkskunde. Brunner, Karl

Osten-Sacken und von Rhein, Ottomar, freiherr von der
Deutschlands armee in feldgrauer kriegs- und friedens-uniform . . . tafeln und textabbildungen gezeichnet von militärmaler Paul Casberg. Mit den amtlichen bestimmungen und einem erläuternden text von freiherr v. d. Osten-Sacken u. v. Rhein. Berlin, P. M. Weber [1917]
36p. illus. 25, VIII col.pl. ob.O.
In portfolio

Osterhausen, Christian von
Eigentlicher und gründlicher bericht dessen was zu einer volkommenen erkantnusz und wissenschaft desz . . . ritterlichen ordens S. Johannis von Jerusalem zu Malta vonnöthen; 2. ed. verb. vermehr. und mit ... kupfferstichen geziehret. Augspurg, A. Aperger 1650
844p. 10 l. 19pl. O.
The first edition was published in Frankfort in 1644
Lipperheide 1891

[**Osterwald, G.**]
Abbildungen des königlich-hannoverschen militairs in characteristischen gruppen dargestellt. Hannover, [1840]
24 col.pl. F.
Colas 2257

Osteuropäische volkstrachten. Tilke, Max

Ostfriesischen volks- und rittertrachten um 1500. Manninga, Unico

Ostfriesische volkskunde. Lüpkes, Wiard

Ostrander, W. L.
(comp.) United States. Military academy, West Point. The centennial of the United States Military academy at West Point, New York, 1802-1902

Ostwald, Hans Otto August
Berlin und die Berlinerin; eine kultur- und sittengeschichte. Berlin, H. Bondy 1911
496p. front. illus. pl.(part col.) ports. Q.
Contents: Die damen, p13-238; Die dienstboten, p239-86; Höker und hausierer, p287-302; Kleinburgertum und proletariat, p303-98; Die halbwelt, p399-487
A later edition with published *Kultur und sittengeschichte Berlins* (Berlin, H. Klemm 1923.) The contents are rearranged and chapters on Die Berliner burgerin and Berliner kinder added. Other chapters have been enlarged and new illustrations added. The work is on a poorer grade of paper and the illustrations less clear and in many cases reduced in size

O'Sullivan, Arthur Warren Swete
(tr.) Hurgronje, C. S. The Achehnese

Oswald
(tr.) Psalmanazar, George. An historical and geographical description of Formosa

Ota, Shintaro
Tokugawa ryaku denki. Tokyo, Ohashido n.d.
2pts. illus. col.pl. O.
Title in Japanese. A short history of the Tokugawa Dynasty by Ota Shintaro, illustrated by Seisai Hōrin
Lipperheide 1568

Ott, Johann Caspar
Icones virorum gentis et stirpis Ottiorum in Helvetia praesertim Tiguri litteris armis et toga clarorum propriis sumptibus aeri. Thuric, [1777-88]
23pl. Q.
Lipperheide 900

Ottesen, Louise
Danske folkedragter. [København,] S. Hasselbalch 1923
91p. illus. col.pl. O. 6kr.
Costume index

Otto, H. J.
(engr.) Statuten des königlichen preuszischen ordens vom Schwartzen adler

Otto, Hermann Waldemar
Pauvres saltimbanques. Düsseldorf, E. Lintz 1891
212p. illus. O.

Otto, L.
(ed.) Thormann-Bechlin, Louise. Leitfaden zum theoretischen und praktischen unterricht der damenschneiderei

Ottoman empire. See Turkey

Oude en tegenwoordige staat en geschiedenis van alle godsdiensten. Hurd, William

De **oude** schutterij in Nederland. Hofdijk, W. J.

Die **oude** tijd. Haarlem, A. C. Krusemann 1869-74
6v. 241 illus. 99pl. O.
Editors: 1869-70 David van der Kellen, jr., (met medewerking van Noord- en Zuid-Nederlandsche geschied- en oudheidkundigen en kunstenaars). 1871-84, J. Ter Gouw (met medewerking van Vanderlandsche geschieden oudheidkundigen)
Lipperheide 971

Our armies. Simkin, Richard

Our army for our boys. Jenks, Tudor

Our artist in Cuba. Carleton, G. W.

Our artist in Peru. Carleton, G. W.

Our country's defensive forces in war and peace. Wagner, A. L., and Kelley, J. D. J.

Our dress and our food in relation to health. Flinn, D. E.

Our fathers. See note under Bott, A. J. This was England

Our grandmothers' gowns. Hunt, Mrs M. R.

Our islands and their people. Olivares, José de

Our mothers. Bott, A. J., ed.

Our Saviour in art. See Elder, A. P. T. The light of the world

Our times. Sullivan, Mark

Our wild Indians. Dodge, R. I.

Ourselves, 1900-1930. Clephane, Irene

Outcasts. See Infamy, Signs of

Outline history of costume. Walkup, Mrs F. P.

Outlines to Shakspeare. See Retzsch, F. A. M. Gallerie zu Shakspeare's dramatischen werken

Outlines to Shakespeare's dramatic works. See Retzsch, F. A. M. Gallerie zu Shakspeare's dramatischen werken

Outlines to Shakspeare's Tempest. Shakespeare, William

Ouvrages de dames. Sajou, firm, publishers

Les **ouvrages** de main en famille. Alq, Louise d', pseud.

Les **ouvrières** de Paris. Philipon, Charles

Les **ouvrières** de Paris, Costumes parisiens. Lanté, L. M.

Ouw, Wolfgang
Nothwendige erinnerung vom miszbrauch der kleyder da viele Christen in defectu, viele in excessu sündigen. Hamburg, J. Naumann 1663
22 l. 217p. D.
Lipperheide 3439

Over Japan way. Hitchcock, A. M.

Overbeck, Johannes
Gallerie heroischer bildwerke der alten kunst. Erster band: Die bildwerke zum thebischen und troischen heldenkreis. Braunschweig, C. A. Schwetschke 1853
819p O. and atlas of 33pl. F.
No more published

Øverland, Ole Andreas
Korstogenes historie, med 60 helsides illustrationer af Gustave Doré, samt 80 i texten trykte billeder. Kristiania, J. M. Stenersen 1900-[01]
487p. illus. F.

Overloop, Eugène van
Dentelles anciennes de la collection Alfred Lescure; Bruxelles, Malines, Valenciennes, Binche. Bruxelles [etc.] G. van Oest 1914
27p. L pl. F. (Matériaux pour servir à l'histoire de la dentelle en Belgique. 3. sér.)
In portfolio
LC 23-17049

Dentelles anciennes des Musées royaux des arts décoratifs et industriels à Bruxelles. Bruxelles, G. Van Oest 1912
100pl. F. 1.25fr. (Matériaux pour servir à l'histoire de la dentelle en Belgique. 2.sér.)

Ovid
La bible des poètes metamorphosée. Paris, A. Vérard 1493
208 l. 33 illus. F.
Lipperheide 425

Owen, Mrs Henry
The illuminated book of needlework: comprising knitting, netting, crochet, and embroidery ... Preceded by a history of needlework, including an account of the ancient historical tapestries. Edited by the Countess of Wilton. London, H. G. Bohn 1847
405,xii,114p. 30 illus. 13pl.(12 col.) O.
Second title-page: *The illuminated ladies' book of useful and ornamental needlework*
Lipperheide 4086

Oxford. University
Ffoulkes, C. J. European arms and armour in the University of Oxford

See also Academic costume—Oxford university

Oxford architectural and historical society, Oxford, England
A manual of monumental brasses. See entry under Haines, Herbert

Oxford university ceremonies. Buxton, L. H. D., and Gibson, Strickland

Oyley, Sir Charles D'. See D'Oyley, Sir Charles

P

P., J. See The directorium anglicanum

P., L. I. See entry under Cérémonial de l'empire français

Pacheco, José Ramon
Descripcion de la solemnidad fúnebre con que se honraron las cenizas del héroe de Iguala, don Agustin de Iturbide, en octubre de 1838. Mexico, J. Cumplido 1849
66p. 1 illus. 4pl. F.
Lipperheide 2734

Pachinger, Anton Max
Die mutterschaft in der malerei und graphik. München, G. Müller 1906
212p. 130 illus. O.

Paciaudi, Paolo Maria
Descrizione delle feste celebrate in Parma l'anno MDCCLXIX per le auguste nozze di ... l'infante Don Ferdinando colla ... arciduchessa Maria Amalia. Parma, Stampería reale [1769]
76p. 31 illus. 36pl. F.
Italian by P. M. Paciaudi, and French by C. F. X. Millot, in parallel columns
Drawings by E. A. Petitot
Lipperheide 2768. LC 12-17883

Pacichelli, Giambattista
Schediasma juridico-philologicum tripartitum ... De larvis, De capillamentis, De chirothecis vulgo mascheris, perruchis, guantis. Neapoli, C. Cavalli 1693
10 l. 392p. 2pl. D.
Lipperheide 1662

Pacific, Islands of the. See Oceania

Pacini, Eugène François Louis Désiré
La marine, arsenaux, navires, équipages, navigation, atterrages, combats, ... illustrations de M. Morel-Fatio. Paris, L. Curmer 1844
240p. 120 illus. 31pl.(9 col.) Q.
Colas 2258. Lipperheide 2317. LC 13-4217

Pacis antesignani. Hulle, Anselm van

Packe, Edmund
Royal regiment of horse guards, or Oxford Blues. See Cannon, Richard. Historical records of the British army. v3

Padiglione, Carlo
Delle livree, del modo di comporle e descrizione di quelle di famiglie nobili italiane; ricerche storico-araldiche. Pisa, Presso la direzione del Giornale araldico 1888
51p. Q.
LC 13-4292

Pægle, E.
(ed.) Latvijas saule

Pagan races of the Malay Peninsula. Skeat, W. W., and Blagden, C. O.

Pagan tribes of Borneo. Hose, Charles, and McDougall, William

Pagani, Giovacchino
(pub.) Manuale dei pittori

Pagani, Mattio
Lhonesto essempio del vertuoso desiderio che hanno le donne di nobil ingegno, circa lo imparare i punti tagliati a fogliami. In Venetia ... 1550. Venezia, F. Ongania 1878
28pl. Q. (Raccolta di opere antiche sui disegni dei merletti di Venezia, 4)
Facsimile reprint
Lipperheide 3887

La processione del doge nella domenica delle palme; incisa in Venezia per Mattio Pagan (1556-1569). Venezia, F. Ongania 1880
8pl. F.
Facsimile reprint
Lipperheide 2788

Paganino, Alessandro
Burato, noua maestria gratiose donne ... Libro primo [secondo, terzo, quarto] de rechami ... et il modo de recamare. Venedig 1527. Venezia, F. Ongania 1878-80
4pts. 86pl. O. (Raccolta di opere antiche ... v9,14a-14c)
Facsimile reprint

Pageant of America; a pictorial history of the United States, ed. by R. H. Gabriel and others; Independence ed. New Haven, Yale univ. press 1925-29
15v. illus. pl.(part col.) ports.(part col.) maps. O. $75 (each vol. $5.50 to schools and libraries)
Contents: v 1 Adventurers in the wilderness, by Clark Wissler and others; v2 Lure of the frontier, by R. H. Gabriel; v3 Toilers of land and sea, by R. H. Gabriel; v4 March of commerce, by Malcolm Keir; v5 Epic of industry, by Malcolm Keir; v6 Winning of freedom, by William Wood, and R. H. Gabriel; v7 In defense of liberty, by William Wood, and R. H. Gabriel; v8 Builders of the republic, by F. A. Ogg; v9 Makers of a new nation, by J. S. Bassett; v10 American idealism by L. A. Weigle; v11 American spirit in letters by S. T. Williams; v12 American spirit in art, by F. J. Mather and others; v13 American spirit in architecture by T. F. Hamlin; v14 The American stage, by O. S. Coad, and Edwin Mims; v15 Annals of American sport, by J. A. Krout
Costume index

The **pageant** of British history. Parrott, Sir J. E.

The **pageant** of English literature. Parrott, Sir J. E.

The **pageant** of London. Davey R. P. B.

Pageant of the birth, life and death of Richard Beauchamp, earl of Warwick, K. G., 1389-1439. Pageants of Richard Beauchamp, earl of Warwick

Pageants of Richard Beauchamp, earl of Warwick
Pageant of the birth, life and death of Richard Beauchamp, earl of Warwick, K. G., 1389-1439; ed. by Viscount Dillon ... and W. H. St. John Hope ... photo-engraved from the original manuscript in the British museum by Emery Walker. London, New York Longmans, Green 1914
x,109p. incl.LV facsim. on 28 l. 2pl. Q.
Facsimiles printed on both sides of leaves
The Warwick pageant is a Cottonian ms. (Julius E IV). Of the authorship of these drawings nothing is known. Their usual ascription to John Rous can not be proved,

Pageants of Richard Beauchamp, earl of Warwick—*Continued*
but the draughtsman was no doubt an Englishman. This manuscript, probably done between 1485 and 1490, shows costume of that period
Another edition: *The Pageants of Richard Beauchamp, earl of Warwick, reproduced in facsimile* (Oxford, Priv. print. for presentation to the members of the Roxburghe club 1908. xvi p. LV facsim. F.)
LC 21-11032

Pagenstecher, Johann Friedrich Wilhelm
De barba, liber singularis, quarta vice editus, multo auctior & emendatior. Lemgoviae, J. H. Meyer 1746
277p. O.
First edition: 1715
Lipperheide 1665

Pagès, François Xavier. See Collection complète des tableaux historiques de la révolution française

Pages de mode. 1924-1936. Paris, Éditions Darroux
Illus. F. 9fr. per no.
Published quarterly. No more published?

Painting, Body. See Body painting

The **Paisley** shawl. Blair, Matthew

Pajol, Charles Pierre Victor, comte
Armée française. Paris, Martinet frères ca1850
8 col.pl. ob.F.
Colas 2261

Armée russe, 1856. Paris, A. Bry [1856]
22 l. 56 col.pl. F.
Colas 2260

Pajou, Augustin Désiré. See Pigal, E. J., jt. auth.

Palästina, Arabien und Syrien. See Gröber, Karl. Picturesque Palestine, Arabia and Syria

Palander, Edvard Vilhelm
(tr.) Heikel, A. O. Die volkstrachten in den Ostseeprovincen und in Setukesien

Palatinate. See Germany—Palatinate

Palencia, Isabel de
The regional costumes of Spain; their importance as a primitive expression of the aesthetic ideals of the nation ... with a prologue by D. Luis Pérez Bueno. Madrid, Editorial Voluntad; London, B. T. Batsford [1926]
160p. col.front. illus. pl.(part col.) O.
Some of the plates are printed on both sides
Translation of the author's *El traje regional de España*
Colas 2263. Costume index. LC 27-13071

El traje regional de España: su importancia como expresión primitiva de los ideales estéticos del país. Prólogo de d. Luis Pérez Bueno ... illustraciones de Loygorri. Madrid, Editorial Voluntad 1926
155p. 10 l. col.front. illus. pl.(part col.) O.
"Relación de obras ... que los interesados en la historia del traje en España pueden consultar": p139-42
LC 33-5044

Palestine
See also Jews

17th century

Dapper, Olfert. Naukeurige beschryving van gansch Syrie. 1677

18th century

Spilsbury, F. B. Picturesque scenery in the Holy Land and Syria, delineated during the campaigns of 1799 and 1800. 1823

19th century

Ferrario, Giulio. Descrizione della Palestina, o storia del vangelo. 1831
Howe, Fisher. Oriental and sacred scenes. 1856
Mayer, Ludwig. Views in Palestine ... Vues en Palestine. 1804
Pierotti, Ermete. Costumes de la Palestine. 1871

20th century

Carpenter, F. G. The Holy Land and Syria. 1922
Gröber, Karl. Palestine and Syria. c1926
Gröber, Karl Picturesque Palestine, Arabia and Syria. c1925
Kelman, John. The Holy Land. 1902
McCrackan, W. D. The new Palestine. 1922

Palestine and Syria. Gröber, Karl

Palette, J. N.
Journal de coëffure ou l'art du coëffeur. Brumaire an XI (nov. 1820)-fév. 1810. Paris, 1802-10
38 col.pl. D.
Absorbed by *Journal des dames et des modes, gazette des salons*
Colas 2264

Palladius, Peder
(tr.) Musculus, Andreas. Hosedjaevelen paa Dansk ved Peder Palladius, 1556

Pallas, Peter Simon
Bemerkungen auf einer reise in die südlichen statthalterschaften des Russischen reichs in den jahren 1793 und 1794. Leipzig, G. Martini 1799-1801
2v. in 1. illus.(part col.) sq.Q. and atlas of 52pl.(part col.) ob.Q.

Reise durch verschiedene provinzen des Russischen reichs. St. Petersburg, K. Academie der wissenschaften 1771-76
3v. 110pl. Q.
Nine plates show costume
Lipperheide 1336. LC 18-22722

Travels through the southern provinces of the Russian empire, in the years 1793 and 1794. London, T. N. Longman & O. Rees 1802-03
2v. col.illus. 52pl.(part fold.) maps(part fold.) fold.plan. Q.
Shows costume of Russia, with many plates on Crimea. Translation of his *Bemerkungen auf einer reise in die südlichen statthalterschaften des Russischen reichs in den jahren 1793 und 1794*
LC 5-10954

Pallavicini, Giuseppe Morsicato
La scherma illustrata. Palermo, D. d'Anselmo 1670
76p. 31 illus. F.
Lipperheide 2965

Palliser, Mrs Bury. See Palliser, Mrs. F. M.

Palliser, Mrs Fanny (Marryat)
A descriptive catalogue of the lace in the South Kensington museum; 3d ed. London, G. E. Eyre and W. Spottiswoode 1881
144p. 8 illus. 21pl. O.
First edition, 1870; second edition, 1873
Lipperheide 4030-4031

History of lace, by Mrs. Bury Palliser; entirely revised, rewritten, and enlarged under the editorship of M. Jourdain and Alice Dryden; [4th ed.] New York, C. Scribner's sons 1902
xvi,536p. front. illus. XCIII pl. on 107 l. Q.
First edition: 1864; third edition: 1875
Lipperheide 4026 (3d ed.) LC 2-15796

Pallmann, Heinrich
(ed.) Burgkmair, Hans. Hans Burgkmair des jüngeren türnierbuch von 1529

Palma, J., pseud. See Lapaume, Jean

Palmer, Rose Amelia
The North American Indians: an account of the American Indians north of Mexico, compiled from the original sources. [New York, Smithsonian institution] 1929
309p. col.front. illus. 85pl. on 61 l.(part col.) O. (Smithsonian scientific series, v4)
Part of the plates accompanied by guard sheets with descriptive letterpress
Costume index (Sms) LC 29-14349

Pálsson, Bjarni. See Ólafsson, Eggert. Des vice-lavmands Eggert Olafsens und des landphysici Biarne Povelsens reise durch Island

Pandectae triumphales. Modius, François

Pandini, Cesare
Il mastro di casa; ragionamento fatto tra il cavalier reale Fusorito da Narni ... ed esso mastro di casa. Venetia, A. de Vecchi 1610
22p. illus. Q.
Pictures of cooks and waiters. Also published in Bartolomeo Scappi's *Opera* and in his *Dell' arte del cucinare*

Panegyricus ad Maximilianum. Locher, Jakob

Die **Pangwe.** Tessmann, Günter

Paniagua, André de
L'âge du renne. Paris, P. Catin 1926
290p. illus. maps. O.
Chapter 4: Les arts et la parure. The reindeer age or Magdalénien period, is a part of the Pleistocene age

Pannelier, Jean Amable
L'Hindoustan; ou Religion, moeurs, usages, arts et métiers des hindous. Ouvrage orné de cent quatre planches, gravées la plupart d'après les dessins originaux faits sur les lieux pour feu M. Léger. Paris, A. Nepveu 1816
6v. 104 col.pl. S.
Published anonymously
Known also with plates in black and white. Copies of the plates are contained in Frederic Shoberl's *Hindoostan* in the World in miniature series which also contains a free translation of the text
Colas 2266. Lipperheide 1482

Pannoniae historia chronologica. Lonicer, J. A.

Pannoniens bewohner in ihren volksthümlichen trachten. Heimbucher von Bikessy, J.

Panofka, Theodor
Bilder antiken lebens. Berlin, G. Reimer 1843
52p. 20pl. sq.F.
Plates show ancient Greek costume

Manners and customs of the Greeks; tr. from the German ... illustrations by George Scharf taken chiefly from Greek fictile vases. London, T. C. Newby 1849
40p. front. 21pl. Q. 21s, o.p.
Costume index. LC 4-35180

(ed.) Terracotten des Königlichen museums zu Berlin. Berlin, G. Reimer 1842
163p. 64pl.(part col.) Q.
Lipperheide 161

Panoplia omnium illiberalium mechanicarum aut sedentarium artium genera. Amman, Jost. See note under his Eygentliche beschreibung

Panoplie. Carré, J. B. L.

Panorama delle scene populare di Napoli. Lundström

Panorama der damen-moden; journal-ausg. für kopfputz und lingerie. [1.]-7. jahrg. 1859-1865. Basel, Bureau für tecknische literatur
7v. illus. Q.
Published monthly
Subtitle changes: 1860-64, journal für die elegante welt; mit besonderer berücksichtigung für beruftreibende

Panorama dramatique: Casanova. Barbier, George

Pantaleon, Heinrich
Omnium regum Francorum a Pharamundo usque ad Carolum nonum. Basileae, Brylinger 1574
67p. 61 ports. F.
Lipperheide 1060

Teutscher nation heldenbuch: Inn diesem werden aller hochuerrümpten teütschen personen, geistlicher und weltlicher, hohen unnd nideren staths ... von anfang der welt. Basel, N. Brylingers erben 1567-71
3v. 1569 ports. F.
Latin edition: 1565-66
Lipperheide 634

Panvinio, Onofrio
Accuratae effigies pontificum maximorum, numero XXVIII ... Eygenwissenliche unnd wolgedenckwürdige contrafeytungen oder antlitzgstaltungē der römischen bäpst. Strassburg, durch B. Jobin 1573
46 l. 28 illus. Q.
Twenty seven of the portraits have been reprinted in *Papistische inquisition und guldē flüs der römischen kirchen,* by G. Nigrinus
Original edition had title: *XXVII pontificum maximorum elogia et imagines* (Rome, 1568)
Lipperheide 1795

Amplissimi ornatissimiq. triumphi, uti. L. Paulus de rege Macedonum perse capto, P. Africanus Æmilianus de Carthagenensibus excisis. C. N. Pompeius Magnus ex Oriente, Julius Augustus, Vespasianus, Traianus, et alij imperatores romani, triumpharunt; ex antiquissimis lapidum, nummorum et

Panvinio, Onofrio—*Continued*
librorum monumentis accuratissima descriptio. Antwerpiæ primum, nunc autem Romæ apud Godefredum de Scaichi edita 1618
1 l. 11pl. ob.Q.
Engraved thruout by G. de Jode, after drawings of M. van Heemskerk. First edition: Antwerp, 1596
Lipperheide 219. LC 31-30200

Onuphrius Panvinius, Veronensis, De ludis circensibus; cum notis Johannis Argoli ... et additamento Nicolae Pinelli. [Lugduni Batavorum? 169-?]
576 columns, pl. F.
Shows costume of the charioteers of ancient Rome
Lipperheide 217 (1600 ed.)

Paoletti, Ermolao
Il fiore Venezia; ossia, i quadri, i monumenti, le vedute ed i costumi veneziani. Venezia, T. Fontana, 1839-42
4v. 190pl.(1 fold.) D.
Volume 4 deals with Venetian costume
Colas 2268. Lipperheide 1333. LC 15-4271

Papal decorations. See Decorations of honor, Papal

Papal guards
Brosses, Charles de. Lettres familières écrites d'Italie en 1739 et 1740. 1929

Collezione dei costumi militari pontifici. 1834

Corte pontificia. ca1860

Costumi religiosi e militari della corte pontificia. ca1840

Ferrari, Filippo. Costumi ecclesiastici civili e militari della corte di Roma disegnati all' acquaforte. 1823

Italy. Papal states. Regolamento per le vestimenta ed armamento della Guardia Civica nello Stato Pontificio analogamente alle disposizioni della legge 30 luglio 1847. 1847

Repond, Jules. Le costume de la garde suisse pontificale et la Renaissance italienne. 1917

See also Papal uniforms

Papal orders. See Orders of knighthood and chivalry, Papal

Papal states. See Military costume—Italy—Papal states

Papal tiara
Müntz, Eugène. La tiara pontificale du VIIIe au XVIe siècle. 1897

Papal uniforms
Barbault, Jean. 12 costumes d'Italie d'après les peintures faîtes par Barbault à Rome en 1750. 1862

Busuttil, Salvatore. Raccolta di costumi religiosi e civile della corte pontificia. 1833?

Corte pontificia. ca1860

Costumi della corte pontificia. 1846

Costumi religiosi e militari della corte pontificia. ca1840

Ferrari, Filippo. Costumi ecclesiastici civili e militari della corte di Roma disegnati all' acquaforte. 1823

Marroni, Salvatore. Raccolta dei principali costumi religio e militari, della corte pontificia. ca1840

Perugini, G. Album ou collection complète et historique des costumes de la cour de Rome, des ordres monastiques, religieux et militaires et deś congrégations séculières des deux sexes. 1862

Pistolesi, Erasmo. Costumi della corte pontificia. 1853

Papendrecht, J. Hoynck van. See Hoynck van Papendrecht, J.

Papie sanctuarium. Gualla, Giacopo

Papier-schmetterlinge aus Japan. Netto, Curt

Le **Papillon,** journal des modes. 1842-48
O.

Papin, Heinrich
Bildliche darstellung der k. k. oesterreichischen armee. Wien, J. Trentsensky [1820]
2 l. 51 col.pl. F.
Colas 2269. Lipperheide 2234

Papistische inquisition und guldē flüs der römischen kirchen. Nigrinus, Georg

Pappenheim, Maximilian Albrecht Friedrich Karl Ludwig, graf zu
Madagascar; studien, schilderungen und erlebnisse. Berlin, D. Reimer 1906
xi,355p. illus. pl. fold.maps. O.

Papua. See New Guinea

Paracelsus
Opus chyrurgicum, des weitberumbten ... wund und artzney buch. Franckfurt am Mayn, S. Feyrabend und S. Hüter 1565
706p. 36 illus. F.
Illustrated by Jost Amman
Lipperheide 2004

[**Parades,** 1791-1826] Paris, ca1826
12 col.pl. Q.
Plates are caricatures of dress of the period
Lipperheide 3706

Paraguay
Carpenter, F. G. Along the Paraná and the Amazon, Paraguay, Uruguay, Brazil. 1925

Parain, Nathalie
Masques de la jungle; compositions de Nathalie Parain. Paris, Flammarion, c1933
[36]p. col.illus. Q. (Les albums du père Castor)
How to cut and make masks for masquerades
LC 34-2250

Mes masques, compositions de Nathalie Parain. [Paris] Flammarion c1931
[35]p. col.illus. F. (Albums du père Castor)
Cover-title: *Je fais mes masques*
How to make masks of Japanese, Negroes and Indians for masquerades
LC 32-4010

Paramentik. Stummel, Helene

Parasole, Elisabetta Catanea
Teatro delle nobili et virtuose donne ... In Roma ... 1616. Venezia, F. Ongania 1891
54pl. Q. (Raccolta di opere antiche sui disegni dei merletti)
Facsimile reprint
Lipperheide 3915

Parasole, Isabella Catanea

Pretiosa gemma delle virtuose donne, dove si vedono bellissimi lavori di punto in aria, reticella, di maglia, e piombini ... stampata in Venetia, ad instantia di L. Gargano, 1600-1601. Venezia, F. Ongania 1879
2pts. 35pl. Q. (Raccolta di opere antiche sui disegni dei merletti di Venezia, 12)
Facsimile reprint
Lipperheide 3907

Studio delle virtuose dame; Roma, Antonio Facchetti, 1597. London, B. Quaritch 1884
10p. 33pl. ob.D. (Quaritch's reprints of rare books)

Parducci, Amos

Costumi ornati; studi sugli insegnamenti di cortigiania medievali. Bologna, N. Zanichelli [1927]
xi,308p. O.

Paret, Jahial Parmly

The woman's book of sports; a practical guide to physical development and outdoor recreation. New York, D. Appleton 1901
167p. front. pl. D.
Shows costume worn by women in the early 20th century for tennis, golf, and bicycling
LC 1-8201

Le **parfait** ioaillier. Boodt, A. B. de

Les **parfums** et les fards à travers les âges. Uzanne, L. O.

Parigi, Alfonso

(illus.) Coppola, G. C. Le nozze degli dei

Paris, Louis

Toiles peintes et tapisseries de la ville de Reims; ou, La mise en scène du théâtre des Confrères de la passion. Paris, Le Vte H. de Bruslart 1843
2v. Q. and atlas of 32pl. F.
The illustrations, by C. Leberthais, show 15th century costume
Lipperheide 451. LC 16-20192

Paris. See subdivision France—Paris under Police; Street venders

Paris. Bibliothèque de l'Arsenal. Mss. (4790)

Ancien armorial équestre de la Toison d'or et de l'Europe au 15. siècle. See entry under Larchey, Lorédan

Costumes vrais. See entry under Larchey, Lorédan

Paris. Bibliothèque Mazarine

Patrons de broderie et de lingerie du XVIe siècle. See entry under Cocheris, H. F. J. M.

Paris. Bibliothèque nationale

Le cabinet d'estampes de la bibliothèque nationale. See entry under Bouchot, H. F. X. M.

Catalogue des bronzes antiques de la Bibliothèque nationale; publié sous les auspices de l'Academie des inscriptions et belles lettres, par mm. Ernest Babelon et J. Adrien Blanchet. Paris, E. Leroux 1895
xlv,764p. 1149 illus. O.
Illustrated by Saint-Elme Gautier
Lipperheide 181

Paris. Bibliothèque nationale. Département des estampes

Un siècle d'histoire de France par l'estampes, 1700-1871. Collection de Vinck. Inventaire analytique par François Louis Bruel. v 1-4 Paris, Imprimerie nationale 1909-29
4v. pl. port. Q.
Illustrated descriptive catalog of the collection of prints made by Baron Eugène de Vinck de Deux-Orp. Planned to be complete in 10 volumes
v 1 Ancien régime; v2 La constituant; v3 Le legislative et la convention; v4 Napoléon et son temps (Directoire, consulat, empire)

Paris. Bibliothèque nationale. Département des manuscrits

Album de portraits d'après les collections du Département des manuscrits, par Camille Couderc. Paris, Impr. Berthaud frères [1910]
86p. CLXVII pl. Q.
Shows ecclesiastical, costume and costume worn by nobles and royalty in France from the ninth to the nineteenth century
LC 17-30296

Antiquités et Guerre des Juifs de Josèphe; reproduction des 25 miniatures des Manuscrits français 247 et nouv. acq. 21013 de la Bibliothèque nationale. Paris, Impr. Berthaud frères [1906]
9p. 25 facsim. O.
In portfolio. Edited by Henri Omont
LC 8-15879

Comédies de Térence; reproduction des 151 dessins du Manuscrit latin 7899 de la Bibliothèque nationale. Paris, Berthaud [1907]
16p. 151 facsim. D.
Edited by Henri Omont. Shows theatrical costume of ancient Rome
LC 8-16445

Livre de la chasse, par Gaston Phébus, comte de Foix; reproduction réduite des 87 miniatures du Manuscrit français 616 de la Bibliothèque nationale. Paris, Berthaud [1909]
35p. 90pl. D.
Edited by C. Couderc. Shows hunting scenes in France in the 14th century

Psautier de Saint Louis; reproduction réduite des 92 miniatures du Manuscrit latin 10525 de la Bibliothèque nationale. Paris, Berthaud [190-]
19p. 92pl. D.
Edited by Henri Omont. Shows Biblical characters in the 13th century manner

Psautier illustré (XIIIe siècle) reproduction des 107 miniatures du Manuscrit latin 8846 de la Bibliothèque nationale. Paris, Berthaud [1906]
19p. 107pl. O.
Edited by Henri Omont. Shows Biblical characters
LC 8-15876

Vie et histoire de Saint Denys; reproduction des 30 miniatures du Manuscrit français n. a. 1098 de la Bibliothèque nationale. Paris, Berthaud [1905]
18p. XXX pl. O.
Edited by Henry Omont. Shows costume of the 13th century
LC 8-15878

Paris. Exposition coloniale international
(pub.) Depréaux, Albert. Les uniformes des troupes coloniales de 1666 à 1875

Paris. Exposition de l'art populaire tchéco-Slovaque, 1920
Exposition de l'art populaire tchéco-slovaque. Paris, Comité de l'exposition 1920
50p. illus. col.pl. O.
Shows costume of Czechoslovakia

Paris. Exposition des arts de la femme
Histoire de la coiffure. Paris, Syndicat général des coiffeurs de dames 1892
2 l. 62pl. O.
Preface signed: Marius Vachon
Cataloged from Colas's *Bibliographie*
Colas 2262

Paris. Exposition internationale des arts décoratifs et industriels modernes, 1925
Broderies russes, tartares, armeniennes. Paris, H. Ernst [1925]
3 l. 40 col.pl. F.
In portfolio. At head of title: U.R.S.S.
First page of text has title: Broderies populaires russes
Ornements et perles des peuples finnois et siberiens. Paris, H. Ernst [1927?]
3 l. 28 col.pl. F.
Shows beadwork on costumes of the Russians, Finns, and Eskimos
Rapport général présenté au nom de M. Fernand David ... par M. Paul Léon. Paris, Larousse 1927
108p. 96pl.(7 col.) Q.
Sixty five plates show fashions and the accessories of dress
Colas 1009

Paris. Exposition universelle, 1900
Le costume en Égypte du III. au XIII. siècle. See entry under Gayet, A. J.
Musée rétrospectif des classes 85 et 86; le costume et ses accessoires à l'Exposition universelle internationale de 1900, à Paris. St Cloud, Belin frères [1900?]
8pl. O.
"Notices-rapports de MM. G. Cain, H. Cain, J. Claretie, L. Duchet, F. Flameng, H. Lavedan, M. Leloir, J. Robiquet." Subtitle
Colas 2168
Les points de France. See entry under Lefébure, Ernest
Les toilettes de la Collectivité de la couture. Paris, Société de publications d'art 1900
63p. illus. O.
At head of title: Exposition universelle de 1900
Foreword signed: Le président de la Chambre syndicale de la confection et de la couture pour dames et enfants, L. Perdoux
Colas 1010. Lipperheide 1177i. LC 35-25503

Paris. International exhibition, 1900. See Paris. Exposition universelle, 1900

Paris. Musée d'artillerie
Catalogue des collections composant le Musee d'artillerie en 1889, par L. Robert. Paris, Imprimerie nationale 1889-93
5v. in 2. 11pl. D.
Lipperheide 2439
Notice sur les costumes de guerre. Paris, Imprimerie nationale 1876
31p. O.
Brief descriptions of military dress in France from the 9th century until the time of Louis XIV, arranged by period of the reigning monarch
Colas lists a later edition (Paris, 1901 59p.)
Colas 2162

Paris. Musée de l'armée
Album historique de l'armée et de la marine. See entry under Album historique de l'armée et de la marine.
Armes et armures anciennes et souvenirs historiques les plus précieux. Paris, Durand 1917-27
2v. pl. F.
Chiefly European armor, with some oriental
Volume 1 issued under the direction of General Niox; v2 under the direction of General Mariaux
Contents: v 1 Armures et armes défensives du XIVe au XVIIe siècle; v2 Armes offensives du XVe au XVIIIe siècle
Décorations, medailles, monnaies et cachets du Musée de l'armée. See entry under Sculfort, V. C. L. É.
Le musée de l'armée. Section des armes et armures ... collections renfermées dans les salles d'armures et dans la galerie des costumes de guerre. See entry under Hardy, E. A.

Paris. Musée des arts décoratifs
Broderies, tissus, soieries, dessins de tissus. Paris, Librairie d'art décoratif, A. Guerinet n.d.
[4]p. 289pl. F. (Les nouvelles collections, v12)
Les dentelles anciennes. Plauen i. V., C. Stoll 1907?
28pl. F.
Examples of laces of the 15th to 18th centuries in various countries
Dessins de broderies, fin du XVIIIe siècle & 1er empire ... dessins originaux et inédits récemment entrés à la Bibliothèque de l'Union centrale des arts décoratifs. Paris, 1922
48pl. F.

Paris. Musée des monumens français
Musée royal des monumens français, ou Mémorial de l'histoire de France et de ses monumens; par Alexandre Lenoir. Paris, L'auteur 1815
216p. D. [Markoe pamphlets, v36 no4]
"Notice sur les costumes français et l'usage de la barbe": p[161]-213
LC 11-9801

Paris. Musée Galliéra
Dentelles, guipures, broderies ajourées. Plauen, C. Stoll [1904]
4p. 36pl. F.

Paris. Musée national du Louvre
Catalogue sommaire des bijoux antiques, par André de Ridder. Paris, Musées nationaux 1924
xxiii,219p. illus.(plan) XXXII pl. on 16 l. D.
LC 28-4010
Musée de sculpture antique et moderne. See entry under Clarac, C. O. F. J. B., comte de

Paris. Musée national du Louvre—*Cont.*
Les tapisseries des chasses de Maximilien ... préface par Gaston Migeon. Paris, A. Lévy 1920
18p. illus. XII pl.(2 col. 12 double) F.
In portfolio. The designs are by the Flemish artist, Bernard van Orley. Plates show hunting and general European costume of the 15th and 16th centuries
Bibliographical foot-notes
LC 22-25199

See also Reinach, Salomon. Répertoire de la statuaire grecque et romaine

Paris à cheval. Géruzez, Victor

Paris assiégé. Renard, Jules

Paris au XVIIIe siècle. Fouquier, Marcel

Paris au XIXe siècle et la fin du XVIIIe. Lesage, L. E.

Paris charmant artistique. 1.-8. année; 1877-1884. [Paris]
Col.pl. Q.
Colas 2271. Lipperheide 4759

Paris dans l'eau. Briffault, E. V.

Paris de 1800 à 1900. Cleemputte, P. A. van

Paris de 1800 à 1900 d'après les estampes et les mémoires du temps. See Cleemputte, P. A. van. La vie parisienne à travers le XIXe siècle

Paris élégant et Longchamps réunis. See Le Paris élégant, journal de modes

Le **Paris** élégant, journal de modes. [1.]-19. année; 10 juillet 1836-15 déc. 1854. Paris
Col.pl. Q.
Published fortnightly 1849-54. Earlier numbers three times a month
Title varies: 10 juil. 1836-sept. 1840, *Longchamps, revue des modes;* 10 oct. 1840-20 fév. 1841, *Longchamps et Paris élégant réunis;* 10 mars 1841-31 déc. 1843, *Paris élégant et Longchamps réunis;* 6 jan.-17 fév. 1844, *Paris élégant, revue du grand monde;* 24 jan. 1844-15 juin 1849, *Revue de Paris élégant*
Colas 1897. Lipperheide 4631

Paris élégant, revue du grand monde. See Le Paris élégant, journal de modes

Paris et ses modes; nouvel almanach rédigé par le Caprice. Paris, L. Janet [1821]
6 col.pl. S.
Each plate shows two costumes
Colas 2281

Paris et ses modes, ou les soirées parisiennes, par L***. Paris, Michelet 1803
214p. col.front. D.
Colas 2280

Paris fashion book. See Style, combined with Paris fashion magazine

Paris-illustré. 1.-8. année (no.1-117) 1883-March 29, 1890. Paris, L. Baschet
8v. illus.(part col.) pl.(part col.) F.
Published weekly
Lipperheide 4775

Paris marié. Balzac, Honoré de

Paris pittoresque, 1800-1900. Barron, Louis

Paris qui crie. Société des amis des livres.

Paris und Wien. See London, Paris und Wien

Paris-vivant: Les coulisses 'de la mode. Coffignon, A.

Paris, Wien und London. See London, Paris und Wien

Pariser modelle für die selbst-anfertigung der gesammten damen-garderobe, liebwäsche und kinder-garderobe. 1.-13. jahrg., 1858-1870. Berlin, Expedition der Pariser modelle; Leipzig, F. Wagner
13v. illus. Q.
Thirty-six numbers a year
Colas 2275. Lipperheide 4686

Pariser moden-journal; eine uebersetzung der neuesten Pariser moden-berichte, nebst angabe des schnitts. 1.-4. jahrg., 1839-1842. Ulm, Siler
4v. col.illus. O.
Superseded by *Neuestes Pariser moden-journal*
Colas 2276. Lipperheide 4634

Pariser moden-salon für damen-garderobe; technische zeitschrift für damen-kleidermacher, mode-handlungen, &c. 1.-17 jahrg. 1853-1869. Dresden, Klemm
Col.illus. col.pl. O.
Colas 2278. Lipperheide 4669

Die **Pariser** toiletten; supplement zu dem journal "Pariser moden". 1.-3. jahrg; 1865-67. Basel, Bureau für tecknische literatur
3v. illus.(part col.) Q.
Published monthly. Contains patterns

Pariser und Hamburger damen, mode und kunst journal. 1.-3. jahrg. 1803-1805. Hamburg & Altona, Herold
3v. col.pl. O.
Colas 2279. Lipperheide 4593

Parish characters in ten plates. Heath, William

Parisian costumes. See Townsend's quarterly selection of French costumes

Les **Parisiennes.** 1897-Sept. 1929. New York, American Fashion co.
Illus. F.
Published monthly except July-Aug. 1921-23; 1924-29 except Jan. July and Aug. Text in English
Absorbed by *American ladies' tailor*

Les **Parisiennes.** Grevin, Alfred, and Huart, Adrien

Parker, Arthur Caswell
The Indian how book. New York, G. H. Doran [c1927]
335p. front. illus. O.
Section III: Dress and ornament
LC 27-19296

Parker, Eleanor
(ed.) Male and female costume. See Brummell, G. B.

Parkes, Joan
Travel in England in the seventeenth century. New York, Oxford university press; Oxford, Clarendon press 1925
xvi,354p. front. pl. port. fold.map, facsims. O. $8.50, 25s
Costume index. LC 25-19450

Parkyns, Mansfield
Life in Abyssinia: being notes collected during three years' residence and travels in that country. London, J. Murray 1853
2v. fronts. illus. pl. fold.map. O.
Volume 2 contains a chapter on dress
Some of the plates show costume
LC 5-8153

Parkyns, Sir Thomas, bart.
... The inn-play: or, Cornish-hugg wrestler; 3d ed., corr. with large additions. London, Printed for T. Weeks 1727
xviii,64,12p. illus. pl. O.

Parmelee, Maurice Farr
The new gymnosophy, the philosophy of nudity as applied in modern life ... with an introduction by Havelock Ellis. New York, F. H. Hitchcock [c1927]
xiii,303p. front. pl. O.
Notes and references: p263-94
LC 28-4682

Parmentier, André Émile Emmanuel
Album historique, publié sous la direction de m. Ernest Lavisse. Paris, A. Colin 1897-1907
4v. illus.(incl.ports.) sq.Q.
Shows costume in Europe. Contents: v 1 Le moyen âge (du IVe au XIIIe siècle); v2 La fin du moyen âge (XIVe et XVe siècles); v3 Le XVIe et le XVIIe siècle; v4 Le XVIIIe et le XIXe siècle
Costume index. LC 6-24926

Parnes, Roger de, pseud. See Rouveyre, Édouard

Parquet, Roger
(illus.) Martinet, F. X. Historique du 9e régiment de dragons. 1888

Parrocel
(illus.) Grandmaison, Henri de. Fantassins et cavaliers sous Louis XV

Parrocel, C.
Reitres et lansquenets. Paris, L'auteur 1750?
12pl. O.
Plates engraved by J. G. Wille. Published also with title in German: *Reuter und lanzenknechte*
Cataloged from Colas's *Bibliographie*
Colas 2283

Parrott, Sir James Edward
The pageant of British history. London, Edinburgh [etc.] T. Nelson 1911
384p. col.front. illus. pl.(part col.) O.
"Depicted by the following great artists: J. M. W. Turner, G. F. Watts, Benjamin West, Lord Leighton, Sir John Gilbert, Daniel Maclise, C. W. Cope, John Opie, William Dyce, Sir L. Alma-Tadema, Sir John Millais, Paul Delaroche, W. Q. Orchardson, E. M. Ward, Stanhope Forbes, F. Goodall, Seymour Lucas, Ford Madox Brown, W. F. Yeames, Clarkson Stanfield." Subtitle
LC A15-2386

The pageant of English literature. New York, Sully and Kleinteich [1914]
480p. col.front. col.pl. ports. O.
"Depicted by J. M. W. Turner, Daniel Maclise, Sir John Millais, Briton Riviere, Sir Lawrence Alma-Tadema, Ford Madox Brown, E. M. Ward, J. W. Waterhouse, Sir James Linton, George H. Boughton, J. A. M'Neill Whistler, Sir E. J. Poynter, W. F. Yeames, Horace Vernet, Sir E. Burne-Jones, J. Doyle Penrose, Edgar Bundy, J. C. Dollman, Louis E. Fournier, etc., and described by Edward Parrott." Subtitle
A history of English literature with reproductions of notable paintings and drawings which illustrate it. Shows English costume from the time of Beowulf to the end of the nineteenth century
LC A15-2567

Parry, Albert
Tattoo; secrets of a strange art as practised among the natives of the United States. New York, Simon and Schuster 1933
xii,171p. col.front. pl.(part col.) ports. facsims. O.
Bibliography: p 152-64
LC 34-469

Parry, Sir William Edward
Journal of a second voyage for the discovery of a northwest passage from the Atlantic to the Pacific; performed in the years 1821-22-23, in His Majesty's ships Fury and Hecla. London, J. Murray 1824
xxx,571p. front. pl.(4 fold.) maps(5 fold.) Q.
Eighteen plates show costume of the Eskimos
Lipperheide 1615. LC 5-28902

Parsifal: costum studien. Seitz, Rudolf

Parsons, Frank Alvah
The art of dress. Garden City, N.Y., Doubleday, Doran 1928
xxiv,358p. front. pl.
Published in 1920 under title: *The psychology of dress.* Shows costume from the middle ages to the 20th century in Europe and America
Colas 2284 (1920 ed.) Costume index. LC 29-19491

Particularités du costume des évêques de Poitiers au XIIe siècle. Barbier de Montault, Xavier

Particulars relative to that portion of the regalia of England which was made for the coronation of King Charles the Second. Cole, Robert

Partington, James Edge-. See Edge-Partington, James

La **parure** des dames, ou 1. collection des plus belles coëffures. See Costumes françois et la parure des dames

Les **parures.** Méry, J. P. A.

Les **parures** primitives. Cocheris, Mme P. A. W.

Pasatiempos eruditos. Villaamil y Castro, José

Pascal, Adrien, and others
Galerie des victoires et conquêtes de l'armée française et de tous les régiments depuis les premiers temps de la monarchie jusqu'à nos jours, par ... A. Pascal, J. Du Camp ... Brahaut ... et ... Sicard. Paris, Siège de l'administration des Frères-réunis 1847-49
5v. in 10. front. 152pl.(116 col.) O.
Illustrated by mm. Philippoteaux, H. Bellangé, Charpentier, Morel-Fatio and others
Republished under title: *Histoire de l'armée et de tous les régiments depuis les premiers temps de la monarchie française jusqu'à nos jours* (Paris, Dutertre 1860-64) The plates have been published separately under title: *Collection de types coloriés représentant les uniformes français* (Paris, Barbier 1850-52. 146 col.pl.)
Colas 2285-2287

Pascha, Johann Georg
Kurtze jedoch deutliche beschreibung handlend vom fechten auf den stosz und hieb ... auffgesetzet. Hall in Sachsen, M. Oelschlegel [1664]
32p. illus. 43pl. F.
Lipperheide 2963

Kurtze jedoch gründliche beschreibung des voltiger, so wohl auf den pferde als über den tisch. Hall in Sachsen, M. Oelschlegel [1666]
22p. illus. 36pl. F.
Lipperheide 3040

Pascha, Johann Georg—*Continued*
Vollständiges ring-buch. Hall in Sachsen, M. Oelschlegel [1664?]
22p. illus. 33pl. F.
This title combined with the author's *Kurtze jedoch gründliche beschreibung des voltiger* and *Kurtzer jedoch deutliche beschreibung handlend vom fechten* was published under title: *Vollständiges fecht-, ring- und voltigier-buch* (Leipzig, 1667. 3pts.)
Lipperheide 3039

Paschen, Karl
Italien: Die flotte, von C. Paschen. Berlin, A. Schall [1902]
x,140p. front. illus. pl.(part col.) port. fold.plan. O. (Die heere und flotten der gegenwart ... hrsg. von C. von Zepelin. [VII])
LC 19-5746

Passe, Crispijn van de, b. 1593
Le miroir des plus belles courtisannes de ce temps; Spieghel der alderschoonste cortisanen deses tyts; Spieghel der allerschönsten courtisannen dieser zeyt. [Amsterdam?] Ghedruckt voor den autheur 1631
3, 20 l. incl. 40 ports. front. ob.Q.
Portraits show feminine costume of the period. An edition of 1630 has French title only with plates not signed by the artist. Also known with colored portraits
Colas 2288-2289. Lipperheide 523-524

Les vrais pourtraits de quelques unes des plus grandes dames de la chrestiente, desguisees en bergeres ... Ware afbeeldinghe van eenige der aldergrootste ende doorchluchtigste vrouwen van heel christenrijck, vertoont in gedaente als herderinnen. Amsterdam, Gedruckt by J. Broersz 1640
4pts. 72 ports. ob.Q.
Published anonymously. Each plate, except the last, has two portraits in ovals, with rhymed descriptions in French and Dutch on verso of preceding plate. Parts 1-3 show half length portraits of noble ladies and patricians disguised as shepherdesses; part 4 shows a choir of the Muses
Colas 2290. Lipperheide 525. LC 24-7168

Die zwölf monate. [Amsterdam? ca1640]
12pl. Q.
Plates show two figures each from Russia, Lapland, Belgium, France, Italy, Spain, Turkey, West Indies, England, Germany, Austria, Hungary
Lipperheide 526

Le **Passepoil;** bulletin illustré de la Société d'études des uniformes. 1921+ Strasbourg & Nancy, Imprimerie alsacienne
Col.pl. Q. 60fr. a year
Published quarterly. Current 1937
Colas 2291

Le **passe-temps** des jolies Françaises. See Le quart d'heure des jolies Françaises

The **passing** of Korea. Hulbert, H. B.

Passio domini nostri Jhesu Christi ex evangelistarum textu q̃ue accuratissime deprompta additis sãctissimis exquisitissimisque figuris. [Strassburg, M. Hupfuff, printer 1513]
60p. 26 illus. Q.
Compiled by Matthias Ringmann; the woodcuts, with one exception, are by Urs Graf. Previously published by Knobloch, 1507
Lipperheide 607 (1508 ed.). LC 30-33320

Das **Passional**
Passional. Nürnberg, A. Koberger 1488
385 l. 259 col.illus. F.
Lipperheide 417

The **past** at our doors. Skeat, W. W.

Patagonia
Bove, Giacomo. Patagonia, Terra del Fuoco, mari australi. 1883
Prichard, H. V. H. Through the heart of Patagonia. 1902

See also Indians of South America —Patagonia

Paterson, James
Kay's Edinburgh portraits; a series of anecdotal biographies chiefly of Scotchmen ... edited by James Maidment. London, Hamilton, Adams; Glasgow, T. D. Morison 1885
2v. fronts. pl. O.
Shows Scotsmen of the 18th century

Patino, Carlo
Le pompose feste di Vicenza, fatte nel mese di giugno, del 1680. Padova, G. B. Pasquati 1680
p.95-113 5 illus. 3pl. Q.
Lipperheide 2792

Patmouthiun hin haj tarazin patkerazard. Hacouni

Paton, James
(ed.) Scottish history & life. Glasgow, J. Maclehose 1902
xxi,343p. front. illus.(incl. facsims.) XXIV pl.(incl. ports.) F. 42s, o.p.
Contents: History of Scotland: Prehistoric remains, by J. Anderson; Sculptured stones of Scotland, by R. C. Graham; Early Scottish history, by P. H. Aitken; Medieval history, by D. J. Medley; Mary queen of Scots, by D. H. Fleming; James the Sixth, by D. H. Fleming; King, kirk, and covenant, by D. H. Fleming; Before the union, by H. G. Graham; The union, by H. G. Graham; The Jacobite risings, by H. G. Graham; After the rebellion, by H. G. Graham; Aspects of Scottish life: Scottish burghs, guilds, and corporations, by J. Paton; Scottish burghal charters, by R. Renwick; Deer stalking, fishing, and falconry, by Sir H. Maxwell; Archery, golf, and curling, by J. Kerr; Scottish weapons, by C. E. Whitelaw; Old Scottish plate, by A. J. S. Brook; Records of freemasonry, by J. D. G. Dalrymple; Early literary manuscripts, by G. Neilson; Some Scottish ecclesiastical relics, by W. G. Black; Aspects of social life in Scotland, by H. G. Graham; The Scottish universities, by D. Murray; Memorials of Glasgow: Glasgow, by W. Young.
Costume index. LC 3-2036

Paton, Sir Joseph Noël
(illus.) Compositions from Shakespeare's Tempest. London and Edinburgh. W. P. Nimmo 1877
16 l. 15pl. ob.F.
Added title page and dedication dated 1845
Each plate accompanied by leaf with extract from, or reference to the scene described
LC 20-13611

Patricij respublicae Nürenberg: Das ist 83. vhralte adeliche geschlächt. See Geschlecht buch dess heiligen reichs stat Nürnberg

Patriotischer hausschatz II. jahrg. See Unser vaterland in waffen

Patrons de broderie et de lingerie du XVIe siècle. Cocheris, H. F. J. M.

Patrons de broderies, dentelles & guipures du XVIe siècle. See Cocheris, H. F. J. M. Patrons de broderie et de lingerie du XVIe siècle

Patten, William
(ed.) The book of sport. New York, J. F. Taylor & company 1901
xii,411p. front. illus. plates. ports. F.
LC 1-24443

Pattern book for jewellers, gold- and silversmiths. London, A. Fischer [1880?]
2 l. 202pl. F.
Forty four plates show designs of old Roman as well as modern French and Italian jewelry

Pattern construction for garment makers, The science of. Poole, B. W.

Pattern-making by paper folding. Heath, Miss F.

Patty, Virginia C.
Hats and how to make them. Chicago, New York, Rand McNally [c1925]
xii,194p col.front. illus. col.pl. diagrs. O.
LC 25-12368

Patzschke, Carl. See Schmid, H., jt. auth.

Pauker, Juliane
Neuestes musterbuch von ... strickmuster-touren. Augsburg, K. Kollmann 1835-38
3v. 10pl. O.
Parts 1-2, 4th ed., 1838
Lipperheide 4070

Paul, Howard, and Gebbie, George
(eds.) The stage and its stars, past and present; a gallery of dramatic illustration ... from the time of Shakespeare till to-day. Philadelphia, Gebbie 1887
7v. fronts. illus. pl. F.
Running title: *Stars of the stage*

Pauli, Fedor Khristīanovich
Description ethnographique des peuples de la Russie, par T. de Pauly ... publiée à l'occasion du Jubilé millénaire de l'empire de Russie. Saint-Pétersbourg. F. Bellizard 1862
xiv,154,30,78,13,15p. 63 col.pl. double map, double tab. F.
Contents: Peuples indo-européens; Peuples du Caucase; Peuples ouralo-altaïques; Peuples de la Siberie orientale; Peuples de l'Amérique russe
Colas 2292. Lipperheide 1367. LC 29-4922

Paulin-Désormeaux, A. O.
Nouveau manuel complet de l'armurier, du fourbisseur et de l'arquebusier, ou Traité complet et simplifié de ces arts; nouv. éd. corr. augm. Paris, Roret 1852
2v. fold.pl. T. (Manuels-Roret)

Paulsen, Peter
Der goldschatz von Hiddensee. Leipzig, C. Kabitzsch 1906
94p. 104 illus. 16pl. O. (Führer zur urgeschichte, hrsg. von Hans. Reinerth. Bd. 13)
Most of the jewelry pictured is from Viking times

Pauly, Théodore de. See Pauli, F. K.

Pauquet, Hippolyte Louis Émile, and Pauquet, Polydore Jean Charles
The book of historical costumes, drawn from specimens and the most authentic documents of each period. London, Cassell 1868
96pl. Q. £2 10s
Published anonymously. Translation of their *Modes et costumes historiques.* Cover title: *Historical costumes*

Illustrations of English and foreign costumes from the fifteenth century to the present day. London, H. Sotheran 1875
4p. 96 col.pl. Q.
English edition of their *Modes et costumes historiques étrangers*

Modes et costumes historiques. Paris, Aux bureaux des modes et costumes historiques [1864?]
4p. 96 col.pl. Q.
These plates show French costume from the 5th to the middle of the 19th century
Colas 2293. Costume index. Lipperheide 1090

Modes et costumes historiques étrangers. Paris, Aux bureaux des modes et costumes historiques [1875?]
4p. 96 col.pl. Q.
Colas 2294. Costume index. Lipperheide 338

Pauquet, Polydore Jean Charles. See Pauquet, H. L. É., jt. auth.

Pauquier, Louis
(illus.) Maillot, T. J. R. La jeune armée

Pauthier, Jean Pierre Guillaume
Chine; ou, Description historique, géographique et littéraire de ce vaste empire, d'après des documents chinois. Paris, Firmin Didot 1837
493p. 72pl. fold. map. O. (L'univers. Histoire et description de tous les peuples, t. 5)
Plates show costume
LC 19-16343

Pauvres saltimbanques. Otto, H. W.

Paxton, J. H.
(tr.) Morgan, J. J. M. de. Prehistoric man

Payard, Pol
Les chasseurs à pied, par le colonel Pol Payard; préface de monsieur le maréchal Franchet d'Espérey, aquarelles de Pierre-Albert Leroux. Paris, Société des éditions militaires 1930
116p. 20 col.pl. F. (L'armée française à travers les âges, ses traditions—ses gloires—ses uniformes. [3])
Colas 157c. LC 32-23928

Payen, Camille
Costumes de l'armée belge. Bruxelles & Leipzig, Mayer et Flatau ca1873
1 l. 8 col.pl. ob.F.
Each plate shows several types of soldiers on foot and mounted
Colas 2295

Payer von Thurn, Rudolf, ritter
Chinesische miniaturen. Erste folge: Aus dem leben einer chinesischen dame. Leipzig-Wien, Thyrsos-verlag 1924
2 l. 12 mounted col.pl. sq.F. (Erste veröffentlichung aus den schätzen der Familien-fideikommiss-bibliothek des ehem. kaisers von Österreich)
No more published
LC 28-9417

Payne, Harry
(illus.) Groves, J. P. History of the 42nd Royal Highlanders

Payne-Gallwey, Sir Ralph William Frankland, bart.
The crossbow, mediæval and modern, military and sporting; its construction, history and management, with a treatise on the balista and catapult of the ancients. London, New York, Longmans, Green 1903
xxii,328p. front. illus. F.
Lipperheide 2460A. LC 3-15090

Le **pays** basque: sites, arts et coutumes. Boissel, W.

Le **pays** des Basques, types et coutumes. Bernoville, Gaëtan

Le **paysan** tchèque. Tyršová, R. F., and Hantich, Henri

Les **paysans** badois, esquisse de moeurs et de coutumes. Lallemand, Charles

Les **paysans** de l'Alsace au moyen-âge. Hanauer, C. A.

Peake, Richard Brinsley
The characteristic costume of France; from drawings made on the spot, with appropriate descriptions. London, W. Sams [1819-22]
20 l. 19 col.pl. Q.
Original edition (London, 1816) has title: *French characteristic costumes.* Another edition (London, W. Farman 1819-22) has text and title also in French: *Costume caractéristique de France*
Colas 2296-97. Lipperheide 1155

Peaks of Shala. Lane, Mrs R. W.

Pearse, Thomas Frederick
Modern dress; and clothing in its relation to health and disease. London, Wyman 1882
67p. illus. D. 8s

Peasant art in Austria and Hungary. Holme, Charles, ed.

Peasant art in Europe. Bossert, H. T.

Peasant art in Italy. Holme, Charles, ed.

Peasant art in Roumania. Oprescu, George

Peasant art in Russia. Holme, Charles, ed.

Peasant art in Sweden, Lapland and Iceland. Holme, Charles, ed.

Peasant art in Switzerland. Baud-Bovy, Daniel

Peasant costume in Europe. Mann, Kathleen

Peasant costume of the Black Forest. Pettigrew, D. W.

Peasants' furs in Czechoslovakia. Úprka, Joža

Pease, Sir Alfred Edward, bart.
Travel and sport in Africa. London, A. L. Humphreys 1857
3v. front. illus. pl.(part col.) ports. maps, diagrs. F.
Contains illustrations which show dress of the Somalis and the Sudanese

Les **péchés** actuels. Boussenot, and Boudier

Pécheux
(illus.) Lanté, L. M. Costumes des femmes du pays de Caux

[**Pécheux, and Manzoni**]
Costumes orientaux inédits, dessinés d'après nature en 1796, 1797, 1798, 1802 et 1809. Paris, 1813
8p. 25 col.pl. Q.
Engraved by Gatine after Pécheux and Manzoni. Explanatory text by P. de Lamésangère
Colas 2298

Pecht, Friedrich
Shakespeare-galerie; charaktere und scenen aus Shakespeare's dramen. Gezeichnet von M. Adamo, H. Hofmann ... u. a. Leipzig, Brockhaus 1876
334p. 36 illus. Q.
Illustrations are the same as in *Shakespeare scenes and characters* by Edward Dowden

Peck, Esther. See Young women's Christian associations. Bureau of pageantry and the drama. National costumes of the Slavic peoples

[**Peck, John Lord**]
Dress and care of the feet: showing their natural perfect shape and construction; their present deformed condition; and how flat-foot, distorted toes, and other defects are to be prevented or corrected. New York, S. R. Wells 1871
202p. illus. D.
As first prepared, the matter, under a different title, was printed in the *Shoe and leather reporter,* in 1868
LC 8-36577

Pedrone
Uniformi delle truppe di S. S. R. M. il re di Sardegna. Torino, 1831-36
4p. front. 44 col.pl. Q.
Colas 2300

Peek, Emily
Practical instruction in cutting out and making up hospital garments for sick and wounded (adopted by the Red Cross Society); knitted articles and women's apparel including dressmaking. London, J. Bale, sons, & Danielsson 1914
109p. illus. diagrs. D. and diagrams. XXIII p. Q.

Peel, Mrs Dorothy Constance (Bayliff)
Designs for fancy dresses ... for ladies, gentlemen, and children. London, Beeton [1904]
64p. front. illus. XXI pl. Q.

A hundred wonderful years: social and domestic life of a century, 1820-1920. London, J. Lane [1926]
xxii,258p. front. pl. facsim. O. 8s 6d
Bibliography: p244-47
Costume index. LC 27-6982

Peeps at English folk-dances. Alford, Violet

Peer Gynt. Ibsen, Henrik

Peigné-Delacourt, Achille
Recherches sur le lieu de la Bataille d'Attila en 451. Paris, J. Claye 1860
58p. 7 col.pl. sq.F.
Show ornaments and arms of Theodoric, king of the Visigoths (451) and Childeric, king of the Franks (481), also crowns of King Recceswinth, 7th century

Le **peigne** à travers les âges. See Winter, Ferdinand. Die kämme aller zeiten

Peinliche gerichtsordnung. See Austria. Laws, statutes, etc. Constitution criminalis Theresiana, oder Der ... Mariä Theresiä Peinliche gerichtsordnung

Peintures antiques inédites. Rochette, D. R.

Les **peintures** de la jeunesse. Child, Théodore

Peintures de vases grecques. See Lücken, Gottfried von. Greek vase paintings

Peintures et ornements des manuscrits. Bastard d'Estang, Auguste, comte de

Peirce, P. Carrington. See Carrington-Peirce, P.

Pekáry, István

Magyar népviseletek ... Costumes hongrois ... Ungarische volkstrachten ... Hungarian peasant costumes ... Costumi ungheresi. Budapest, Tamás galéria [1933]

1 l. 8 col.pl. sq.F.
Plates dated 1932-1933. Issued in portfolio
LC 33-37608

Pékin, Yeddo, San Francisco; voyage autour du monde. Beauvoir, Ludovic, marquis de

Pelcoq, Jules

Souvenir de l'Exposition universelle de Vienne ... gravés par Morse. Paris, Les modes parisiennes, etc. [1873]

20 col.pl. Q.
Plates show costumes of Austria Hungary
Colas 2303. Lipperheide 839

Les **pèlerinages** à Saint Antoine. See Úprka, Joža. Na pouti u Sv. Antoníčka

Pelisses rustiques dans le territoire de la republique Tchéco-Slovaque. See Úprka, Joža. Peasants' furs in Czechoslovakia

Pellé, Clement

L'empire chinois. See entry under Allom, Thomas

La **pelleterie** et le vêtement de fourrures dans l'antiquité. Fougerat, L.

Pellier, Jules

La selle et le costume de l'amazone, étude historique et pratique de l'équitation des dames ... vignettes par mm Gavarni, F. Régamey, Tavernier, etc. Paris, J. Rothschild 1897

184p. front. illus. O.
Colas 2304

Pelser-Berensberg, Franz von

Mittheilungen über trachten, hausrat, wohn und lebensweise im Rheinland; 3. verb. und verm. aufl. Düsseldorf, L. Schwann 1909

71p. 12 col.pl. Q.
First edition (March 1901), second edition (July 1901) under title: *Mittheilungen über alte trachten und hausrath, wohn- und lebensweise der Saar- und Moselbevölkerung* (Trier, F. Lintz. 42p. 5pl.)
Colas 2305-2306. Lipperheide 802d (2d ed.)

Pelzel, Franz Martin, and Voigt, Adauctus

Abbildungen Böhmischer und Mährischer gelehrten und künstler, nebst kurzen nachrichten von ihren leben und werken. Prag, W. Gerle 1773-82

4v. 118pl. O.
Includes 30 portraits engraved by A. Niederhofer, J. Ott, and J. Balzer
Lipperheide 873

Peñafiel, Antonio

Alfabetos adornados; aplicaciones decorativas del arte mexicano antiguo. 2. ed. aumentada. México, 1898

2 l. 72pl. F.
In portfolio. Twenty five plates show costume with ornamental borders. Other plates show decorative designs
LC 2-27151

Indumentaria antigua: vestidos guerreros y civiles de los Mexicanos. México, Officina tip. de la Secretaria defomento 1903

136p. 198 pl.(part col.) F.
Colas 2307

Monumentos del arte mexicano antiguo. Berlin, A. Asher 1890

3v. in 5. 318pl.(part col. part fold.) F.
Text in Spanish, French and English. Includes one volume of text and two volumes (in 4) of plates. Some of the plates show dress, masks, and jewelry of the Aztecs
LC 8-3853

Penelope; neue muster-zeitung für weibliche arbeiten und moden. 1.-9. jahrg. 1853-1861. Glogau, C. Flemming

9v. col.pl. O.
Colas 2308. Lipperheide 4671

Penfield, Edward

Holland sketches. New York, C. Scribner 1907

147p. col.front illus.(part col.) col.pl. O.
Costume index. LC 7-36404

Spanish sketches. New York, C. Scribner 1911

146p. col.front col.illus. col.pl. O. $2.50, o.p.
Costume index. LC 11-26182

(illus.) Woolley, E. M. A century of hats and the hats of the century

Penfield, Frederic Courtland

East of Suez: Ceylon, India, China and Japan. New York, The Century co. 1907

xvii,349p. front. pl. ports. map. O.
Costume index. LC 7-8551

The **peninsula** of Yucatan. Shattuck, G. C.

Pennell, Mrs Elizabeth (Robins)

To gipsyland ... illustrated by Joseph Pennell. New York, The Century co. 1893

240p. front. illus. pl. D.
LC 13-2257

Pennell, Joseph

The work of Charles Keene; with an introduction & comments on the drawings illustrating the artist's methods, by Joseph Pennell; to which is added a bibliography of the books Keene illustrated, and a catalogue of his etchings, by W. H. Chesson. New York, R. H. Russell; London, T. F. Unwin 1897

289p front. illus. pl. F.
Lipperheide 3516. LC 10-18165

(illus.) Pennell, Mrs E. R. To gipsyland

Pennsylvania. See United States—Pennsylvania

Penny, Mrs Fanny Emily (Farr)
Southern India, painted by Lady Lawley. London, A. & C. Black [1914]
xi,257p. 50 col.pl(incl.front.) fold.map. O. 20s, o.p.
Plates accompanied by guard sheets with descriptive letterpress
Costume index. LC A16-1378

Penseurs & propos. Damourette

A **pensioner's** garden. Darling, C. J. D., 1st baron

Les **pensionnaires** du Louvre. Leroy, Louis

Pentsy, Josef, and Szentgyörgyi, Ludwig
Kalotaszegi varrottas-album (régi magyar himzés-minták gyüjteménye) Budapest, M. Deutsch 1888
32p. 6 illus. 100 col.pl. O.
Lipperheide 3976

People of Dickens. Gibson, C. D.

People of Egypt. Thackeray, Lance

People of India. Menpes, Mortimer

The **people** of the Polar north. Rasmussen, K. J. V.

People of Tibet. Bell, Sir C. A.

The **peoples** and politics of the Far East. Norman, Sir Henry

People's natural history. See note under Hutchinson, H. N., Gregory, J. W., and Lydekker, Richard, eds. The living races of mankind

Peoples of all nations; their life to-day and the story of their past, by our foremost writers of travel, anthropology & history. Illus. with upwards of 5000 photographs, [and] numerous colour plates. Ed. by J. A. Hammerton. London, Fleetway house [1922-24]
7v. illus. col.pl. maps. O. o.p.
Issued in 49 fortnightly parts at 1s 6d each
Costume index. LC 24-6018

Pepys, Samuel
The diary of Samuel Pepys ... with a life and notes by Richard, lord Braybrooke ... additional notes by Rev. Mynors Bright. New York, Dodd, Mead 1885
10v. facsims. plan. tab. D.
The diary, begun in January 1660 and completed May 1669, contains comment on all kinds of dress worn in England at this period

Per aspera ad astra. Kaiser, Friedrich, and others

Perabò, Gabrio
Ammirabile promozione all' arcivescovato di Milano, ed alla sagra porpora dell' ... Cardinale Don Gioseppe Pozzobonelli, e suo solenne ingresso adì 21. giugno 1744. Milano, G. R. Malatesta [1744]
84p. 4pl. F.
Lipperheide 2800

Die **perchten** im Salzburgischen. Andree-Eysen, Marie

Percier, Charles
(illus.) Description des cérémonies et des fêtes qui ont eu lieu pour le couronnement de ... Napoléon ... et Joséphine

Percier, Charles, and Fontaine, Pierre François Léonard
Description des ceremonies et des fêtes qui ont eu lieu pour le couronnement de ... Napoléon ... et Joséphine. Paris, Leblanc 1807
24p. 2 illus. 12pl. F.
Lipperheide 2719

Description des cérémonies et des fêtes qui ont eu lieu pour le mariage de S. M. l'empereur Napoléon avec S. A. I. Madame l'archiduchesse Marie-Louise d'Autriche. Paris, P. Didot l'aîné 1810
45p. 13pl.(incl. 2 plans) sq.F.
Most of the plates are engravings of Napoleon and Marie Louise of Austria
Lipperheide 2723. LC 12-17873

Percival, MacIver
Chats on old jewellery and trinkets. New York, F. A. Stokes; London, E. Benn 1912
334p. front. illus. pl. O. 10s 6d
Costume index

The fan book. New York, F. A. Stokes; London, T. F. Unwin [1921]
344p. front. XXXI pl. O. $6; 21s, o.p.
Some fan painters, printers, and designers: p269-87. Some books of interest to fan collectors: p289-94
Costume index. LC 21-6155

Perea, Daniel
Á los toros; album ... con la esplicación ... en español, francés e inglés. Barcelona, H. Miralles [1894]
27 l. 27 col.pl. F.
Plates show a Spanish bull fight from beginning to end
Lipperheide 2880

Perelle, Adam
A collection of engravings containing views ... by A. Perelle ... portraits, costumes ... by A. Dieu, N. Arnoult, N. Bazin, H. Bonnart, J. Bonnart, R. Bonnart and others. Paris, [1685?]
F.

Peremi͡eny v" obmundīrovaniī. Russia. Voennoi͡e mīnīsterstvo

Perfection. Byrne, J. J.

Perfection; album pratique de la mode. 1920+? Paris, Éditions Bell
Illus.(part col.) F. 22fr.
Published semi-annually. Current 1938

Die **perfekte** schneiderin; leichtfaszliche lehre des zuschnitts und der bearbeitung der gesammten frauen-, mädchen- und knaben-garderobe. Dresden, Klemm & Weisz [1896-97]
96p. 130 illus. 12pl. Q.
Lipperheide 3851

La **perfezione** e i difetti del cavallo. Eisenberg, Baron d'

Perfumery
Cooley, A. J. The toilet and cosmetic arts in ancient and modern times. 1866

Franklin, A. L. A. La vie privée d'autrefois; arts et métiers, modes, moeurs, usages des Parisiens du XII. au XVIII. siècle. [v 16]

Rimmel, Eugene. The book of perfumes. 1867

Uzanne, L. O. Les parfums et les fards à travers les âges. c1927

Perger, Sigmund
Tyroler. Vienne, T. Mollo ca1810
8 col.pl. ob.O.
Plates, engraved by Zincke, show groups of 3 to 5 people in costume of the Tyrol, Legends are in German and French
Colas 2309

Peringskiöld, Johan
Ättartal för Swea och Götha konunga hus efter trowärdiga historier och documenter. Stockholm, J. L. Horrn 1725
140p. 37 l. illus. 17pl. F.
Illustrations are from coins, seals, medallions, and tombstones. They show Swedish kings, queens, and knights of the middle ages
Lipperheide 1038

Perini, Antonio
Armeria reale di Torino. See entry under Turin. Armeria reale; also Catholic Church. Liturgy and ritual. Breviary. Facsimile delle miniature contenute nel Breviario Grimani conservati nella biblioteca di S. Marco esequito in fotografia da A. Perini

Period costumes and settings for the small stage. Green, J. M. C.

Periodicals
A considerable amount of costume is indexed in the periodical indexes: *Poole's index to periodical literature,* 1802-1906 (Boston, Houghton, o.p.) *Readers' guide to periodical literature* 1900+ (New York, The H. W. Wilson co.) and *The Art index* 1929+ (New York, The H. W. Wilson co.)
Union list of serials is a guide to the periodical holdings of American libraries
The fashion periodicals listed under period subdivisions below are arranged by the date when each began publication. For fuller information about any periodical see the main entry which is under the title, (E.g. Lady's magazine under Lady's etc. in the L's) Duplicate entries are made under the name of the country in which each fashion periodical is published, (E.g. See France—19th century—Periodicals)

Bibliography

Periodicals directory. 1935
Savigny de Moncorps, de. Les almanachs de modes de 1814 à 1830. 1897

18th-19th centuries

Lady's magazine and museum of the belles-lettres. 1770-1837
Journal für literatur, kunst, luxus, und mode. 1786-1827
Journal für fabriken, manufacturen, handlung, kunst und mode. 1791-1808
Gallery of fashion. 1794-1803
Berlinisches archiv der zeit und ihres geschmacks. 1795-1800
Gazette des salons; journal des dames et des modes. 1797-1839
Berlinischer damen-kalender. 1798-1810
Fashions of London & Paris; v 1, 1798/-1800—v3 1804/06
Ladies' museum. 1798-1832
London und Paris. 1798-1810
Taschenbuch ... für damen. 1798-1831
Allgemeine modenzeitung. 1799-1903
Berlin; eine zeitschrift für freunde der schönen künste, des geschmacks und der moden. 1799-1800
La Correspondance des dames, ou Journal des modes et spectacles de Paris. 1799-1800
Journal des dames et des modes. 1799-1848
Musarion, die freundin weiser geselligkeit und häuslicher freuden. 1799-1800

18th century

Courrier de la mode, ou Journal du goût. 1768
L'Indicateur; contenant toutes les productions de l'esprit, les pièces de poésie fugitives, les bon-mots ... et surtout les modes. 1778-80
Nouveaux costumes, étrennes les plus utiles aux dames. 1781
Magazin für frauenzimmer. 1782-86
Magasin des modes nouvelles, françaises et anglaise. 1785-89
Giornale delle dame e delle mode di Francia. 1786-94?
Archiv weiblicher hauptkenntnisse für diejenigen jedes standes. 1787-90
Neues magazin für frauenzimmer. 1787-89
L'amour badin, ou les ruses de Cupidon; dédiés a la jeunesse. 1788
Giornale delle mode. 1788-95
Journal de la mode et du goût. 1790-93
The Bon ton magazine; or, Microscope of fashion and folly. 1791-96
Kabinet van mode en smaak. 1791-94
Manuale dei pittori, ovvero Manuale di pittura ... per l'anno 1792 [and 1794] 1792-94
Allgemeines europäisches journal. 1794-98
Moden-gallerie. 1795
Tableau général du goût, des modes et costumes de Paris. 1797-99
L'Arlequin; journal de pièces et de morceaux. 1799

19th-20th centuries

Le Moniteur de la mode. 1843-1910
Minister's Gazette of fashion 1846+
Europäische modenzeitung. 1850+
The Queen, the Lady's newspaper. 1847+
Le Bon ton and le Moniteur de la mode united. 1851-1926
Die Gartenlaube; illustriertes familienblatt. 1853+
Der Bazar. 1854+
Der Beobachter der herrenmoden. 1855+
De Bazar; geillustreerd tijdschrift voor modes en handwerken. 1857-1900
Der Hausfreund. 1858-1901
La Mode illustrée. 1860+
Moden-telegraph. 1861-1923
La Vie parisienne. 1863+
The Young ladies' journal. 1864-1920
Die Modenwelt. 1865+
Tailor and cutter. 1866+
Harper's bazaar. 1867+
Die Coiffure. 1868-1901
Die Dame. 1873+
The Delineator. 1873-1937
Woman's home companion. 1873+
Frauen reich; deutsche hausfrauen-zeitung. 1874-1910
Illustrirte frauen-zeitung; ausgabe der modenwelt mit unterhaltungsblatt. 1874-1908

Periodicals—19th-20th centuries—*Cont.*

Sartorial art journal and American tailor and cutter. 1874-1929
Der Moderne kleidermacher. 1875-1923
Wiener hausfrauen-zeitung. 1875-1907
London tailor and record of fashion. 1876-1914
Millinery trade review. 1876+
Le Petit écho de la mode. 1879+
The St. James's budget. 1880-1911
Art et la mode; revue de l'élégance. 1881+
Élite; an illustrated society journal addressed to people of culture and fashion. 1881-1907
Lady's pictorial, a newspaper for the home. 1881-1907
Vom fels zum meer. 1881-1917
Ladies home journal. 1883+
Ladies' tailor; a monthly journal devoted to the scientific cutting and making of ladies' fashionable garments. 1884-1936
La Mode nationale. 1885-1930
Häuslicher ratgeber. 1886-1915
Mode und haus. 1885-1920
Lloyd's magazine. 1887+
Neue Wiener friseur-zeitung. 1887+
Wiener mode. 1887+
Die Elegante mode. 1890+
Deutsche modenzeitung. 1891+
La Mode pratique; journal de la femme et de la maison. 1891+
Wiener chic. 1891-1932
Grosse modenwelt. 1892-1920
Vogue, incorporating Vanity fair. 1892+
Master tailor and cutters' gazette. 1893-1908
Kindergarderobe. 1894-1919
Royal. 1895-1925
Sport im bild. 1895-1934
Men's wear; the retailer's newspaper. 1896+
Pictorial review fashion book. 1896+?
Les Parisiennes. 1897-1929
The Puritan. 1897-1901
Sonntags-zeitung fürs deutsche haus. 1897-1919
Women's wear, incorporating the Ladies tailor. 1898?+
Pictorial review combined with Delineator. 1899+

19th century

Allgemeine modenzeitung; eine zeitschrift für die gebildete welt. 1799-1903
Taschenbuch der liebe und freundschaft. 1800-40
Zeitung für die elegante welt. 1801-59
Allgemeine theaterzeitung und originalblatt für kunst, literatur, musik, mode und geselliges leben. 1806-56
La Belle assemblée, or Bell's court and fashionable magazine. 1806-32
The Repository of arts, literature, commerce, manufactures, fashions, and politics. 1809-29
Wiener zeitschrift für kunst, litteratur, theater und mode. 1816-48
Das Veilchen, ein taschenbuch. 1818-34
L'Album, journal des arts, des modes et des théâtres. 1821-28
Petit courrier des dames. 1821-68
Ladies pocket magazine. 1824-40
Monde élégant, or The world of fashion. 1824-91
Moskovskiĭ telegraf" ... īzdavaemyĭ Nīkolaem" Polevym". 1825-27
Townsend's monthly selection of Parisian costumes. 1825-88
Graham's American monthly magazine of literature, art, and fashion. 1826-58
Gentleman's magazine of fashions, fancy costumes, and the regimentals of the army. 1828-94
Le Follet, courrier des salons; journal des modes. 1829-75
La mode nouvelle. 1829-62
Godey's magazine. 1830-98
L'Observateur des modes et Le Narcisse réunis. 1830-56
Journal des jeunes personnes. 1832-63?
Ladies cabinet of fashion, music and romance. 1832-70
Musée des familles. 1833-91
Journal des demoiselles. 1833-92
Le Bon ton, journal des modes. 1834-74
Psyché, journal des modes, littérature, théâtres et musique. 1834-54
New monthly Belle assemblée. 1834-70
Europa; chronik der gebildeten welt. 1835-85
Le Caprice; journal de la lingerie, revue des modes, des théâtres et des arts. 1836-54
L'Estafette des modes. 1836-53
Le Paris élégant, journal de modes. 1836-54
La Fashion, guide-journal des gens du monde. 1839-52
La Sylphide; littérature, beaux-arts, modes. 1839-54
La Corbeille; journal des modes. 1840-55
Peterson magazine. 1840-98
Die Elegante. 1842-71
Jahreszeiten, Hamburger neue modezeitung. 1842-74
Le Lion; journal des nouveautés et des modes d'hommes. 1842-53
La Moda elegante illustrada. 1842-85
Le Petit messager des modes et le Confident réunis. 1842-54
Die Wiener elegante. 1842-67
Les Modes parisiennes illustrées. 1843-68
Allgemeine muster-zeitung; album für weibliche arbeiten und moden. 1844-65
Journal für moderne stickerei, mode und weiblicher handarbeiten. 1844-61
Magazin des demoiselles. 1844-93
Technische modenzeitung für damen, damenkleidermacher. 1844-51
Le Favori des dames. 1845-53
Le Moniteur des dames et des demoiselles. 1845-78
Illustrirtes magazin. 1846-51
Le Conseiller des dames et des demoiselles; journal d'économie domestique et de travaux l'aiguille. 1847-63?
Damenkleider magazin vereinigt mit Musterzeitung und frauenzeitung. 1848-69
Iris; illustrirte blätter für mode, haushaltung und praktisches leben. 1849-65

Periodicals—19th century—*Continued*

Journal des dames. 1849-57
Le souvenir. 1849-66?
Cendrillon. 1850-72
Victoria; illustrirte muster- und modenzeitung. 1851-79
The Englishwoman's domestic magazine. 1852-79
Le Monde élégante; estafette des modes. 1856-82
Le Moniteur de la coiffure. 1858-91
Pariser modelle für die selbst-anfertigung der gesammten damen-garderobe, leibwäsche und kinder-garderobe. 1858-70
La Mode de Paris. 1859-82?
Die Damen-toilette. 1865-86?
The Young Englishwoman. 1865-77
L'Aquarelle-mode; compositions, nouveautés. 1866?-76
Vsemirnaia illiustratsiia. 1869-97
Das neue blatt; ein illustrirtes familienjournal. 1870-87
Les Modes de la saison. 1871-85?
Revue de la mode: gazette de la famille. 1872-98
Zeitung für die elegante welt. 1872-85
Illustrirte modenzeitung. 1873-79
Neue illustrirte zeitung. 1873-87
Conseiller des familles: littérature, travaux à l'aiguille, modes, etc. 1874-79
La Mode universelle, journal illustré des dames. 1874-85
La Mode française. 1875-86?

1800-1825

Almanach des luxus und der moden auf 1801 mit zehn illuminirten kupfern nach Hogarth. 1801?
Almanach der mode und des geschmacks für damen auf das jahr 1802. 1802
Palette, J. N. Journal de coëffure ou l'art du coëffeur. 1802-10
L'art du coëffeur. 1803-07
Pariser und Hamburger damen, mode und kunst journal. 1803-05
Almanach des modes et de la parure. 1805
Le Beau monde; or Literary and fashionable magazine. 1806-09
Elegantia, of tidschrift van mode. 1807-10
Record of fashion and court elegance. 1807-09
Neues journal für fabriken, manufakturen, handlungen, kunst und mode. 1808-11
London, Paris und Wien. 1811-15
Almanach des modes. 1814-22
Annuaire des modes de Paris. 1814
The New bon ton magazine. 1818-21
L'Observateur des modes. 1818-23
Townsend's quarterly selection of French costumes. 1822-24
Magasin für konst, nyheter och moder. 1823-25
Miroir des modes parisiennes. ca1824

1826-1850

Neue Pariser modeblätter. 1827-40
The American ladies' magazine. 1828-36
Der Spiegel; zeitschrift für die elegante welt, mode, literatur, kunst, theater. 1828-47
Mercure des salons, revue française et étrangère; album des modes. 1830-31
Vergiszmeinnicht; taschenbuch der liebe, der freundschaft und dem familienleben des deutschen volkes gewidmet. 1830-49
Allgemeine weltchronik unserer zeit. 1832-34
Berliner modenspiegel in- und ausländischer originale. 1832-49
The Court magazine and monthly critic and lady's magazine, and museum of the belles lettres. 1832-47
L'Iris, album de l'élégance. 1832-34
Le Messager des salons, journal des modes et des nouveautés parisiennes. 1832-38
Schnellpost für moden. 1832-42
Almanach de la mode de Paris; tablettes du monde fashionable. 1834
Gazette des salons, journal des modes et de la musique. 1835-37
Museum der eleganten welt. 1836-38
L'Aspic, moniteur générale des modes, littérature, beaux-arts, théâtres. 1837-38
Eilpost für moden. 1837-43
Aujourd'hui; journal des modes ridicules et d'annonces illustrées. 1838-41
Le Colifichet, indicateur des modes et nouveautés manufacturieres. 1838-43
Le monde élégant; journal des modes. 1838-39
Pariser moden-journal. 1839-42
Dziennik domowy wydawany przez N. Kamieńskiego. 1840-48
Leipziger moden-journal. 1840-43
L'Oriflamme des modes. 1840-44
La Renaissance, journal du monde élégante. 1840-42
L'Avenir, revue politique, litteraire et des modes. 1841-42
Le Papillon, journal des modes. 1842-48
Le Boudoir; modes, théâtres, littérature, beaux-arts. 1843
Neuestes Pariser moden-journal für herren und damen. 1843-48
The Lion; a journal of gentlemen's newest fashions. 1845-48
La Mode des demoiselles. 1845-48

1851-1875

Bijou; original Pariser musterblätter weiblicher kunstarbeiten. 1851-52
La Bonne compagnie, sporting and fashionable review. 1852-55
Frauen-zeitung für hauswesen, weibliche arbeiten und moden. 1852-65
The Little messenger of fashions and the Confident united. 1852-54
Die mode; journal für damentoilette mit Pariser original-modebildern, muster- und schnitt-beilagen. 1853-74
Panorama der damen-moden; journalausg. für kopfputz und lingerie. 1859-65

Periodicals—1851-1875—*Continued*

Neue Pariser moden- und modell-zeitung für damen- und kinder-garderobe. 1860-70

Pariser moden-salon für damen-garderobe. 1853-69

Penelope; neue muster-zeitung für weibliche arbeiten und moden. 1853-61

Wiener modespiegel; wochenschrift für mode, schöne literatur, novellistik, kunst und theater. 1853-59

Frank Leslie's ladies' gazette of fashion and fancy needle work. 1854-57

L'Abeille impériale, littérature, poésie, beaux-arts, théâtres; messager des modes et de l'industrie. 1856-62

La Toilette de Paris. 1859-73?

Freya; illustrirte blätter für die gebildete welt. 1861-67

L'Illustrateur des dames et des demoiselles. 1861-74

Il Mondo elegante; giornale illustrato delle mode francesi. 1864-75

Családi Kör. 1865-66

Die Pariser toiletten. 1865-67

Le Coquet; journal de modes, spécial pour couturières. 1867-75?

La Mode artistique. 1869-99?

Frank Leslie's modenwelt. 1870-71

The Milliner and dressmaker, and warehouseman's gazette, and illustrated journal of the new modes. 1870-81

Haus und welt. 1871-73

La Modiste élégante. 1872-75

1876-1900

La Modiste universelle. 1876-97?

Neue welt. 1876-87

Le Salon de la mode. 1876-1900?

Paris charmant artistique. 1877-84

Illustrirte coiffure. 1878-92

Margherita, giornale della signore italiane. 1878-87

Sylvia's home journal. 1878-94

Berliner modenblatt. 1879-81

Ebhardts' Moden-album. 1879-94

Neueste moden für unsere damen. 1879-96

The Illustrated household journal and Englishwoman's domestic magazine. 1880-81

The Milliner, dressmaker and draper. 1881-82

Le Moniteur de la mode: a fashionable journal appearing monthly. 1882-89

Paris-illustré. 1883-90

Le Costume au théâtre et à la ville. 1886-88

Woman's world. 1888-90

Divat-Tükör. Képes közlöny a divat-es kézimunka köreböl. 1889-90

Madame. 1895-97

Butterick's modenblatt. 1896-1900

20th century

American gentleman and sartorial art journal. 1901+

Femina. 1901+

Les modes; revue mensuelle illustrée des arts decoratifs appliqués à la femme. 1901+

American ladies' tailor and Les Parisiennes. 1903+

To-day's woman and home. 1905-1928

Femme élégante à Paris; album spécial de haute mode pour tailleurs et couturières, costumes, manteaux, robes. 1907+

La Lingerie parisienne. 1907?+

Moda maschile; rivista mensile illustrata di tecnica professionale e commerciale ad uso del sarto da uomo. 1907+

Butterick fashion magazine. 1908+

Élite. 1908+

Femme chic. 1911+

Clothing trade journal. 1912+

McCall fashion book. 1913+

Progressive tailor; a national magazine of authority on merchant tailoring. 1913+

Vanity fair. 1913-36

Style, combined with Paris fashion magazine. 1916+

Costumes et manteaux. 1919+

Moda. 1919-1936?

Modes & travaux feminins. 1919+

American fur designer. 1920+

Fashion service magazine. 1920+

Jardin des modes. 1920-35

Perfection; album pratique de la mode. 1920+?

Très parisien; la mode, le chic, l'élégance. 1920-36

Chapeaux du Très parisien. 1921-36

Créations parisiennes. 1921+

Excella fashion quarterly. 1922-36

Les Idées nouvelles de la mode. 1922-32

Women's wear magazine. Eastern edition. 1923-32

Art, goût, beauté; feuillets de l'élégance féminine. 1924-33

Die deutsche Elite. 1924-30

Newest styles for men. 1924+

Pages de mode. 1924-36

1900-1924

Allgemeine modenzeitung. 1799-1905

Élégance parisienne; a journal of fashion and instruction for the benefit of ladies' tailors. 1900-24

Élite; an illustrated society journal addressed to people of culture and fashion. 1881-1907

Style, a monthly magazine of fashions for women. 1901-09

Figaro-modes, à la ville, au théâtre, arts décoratifs. 1903-06

Ladies' home magazine of New York. 1904-05

Die Neue frauentracht. 1905-09

Man's book; a magazine. 1908-10

Le Coiffure de Paris. 1910+

Kleine modenwelt. 1910

Journal des dames et des modes. 1912-14

Gazette du bon genre. 1912-25

Le Style parisien. 1915-16

Les élégances parisiennes; publication officielle des Industries françaises de la mode. 1916-24

Periodicals—1900-1924—*Continued*
Guirlande des mois. 1917-21
Lingerie moderne. 1917?+
Children's vogue. 1919-25
La Guirlande; album mensuel d'art et de littérature sous la direction littéraire de monsieur Jean Hermanovits, sous la direction artistique de monsieur Brunelleschi. 1919-20
Styl; blätter für mode. 1922-24

1925+

Adam; revue de l'homme. 1925+
Vogue pattern book. 1925+
Infants' and children's review. 1926+
Man and his clothes. 1926+
Styles for men. 1926+
Chapeaux élégants. 1927+
Les Enfants du Jardin des modes. 1928+?
Lingerie du Jardin des modes. 1928+
La mode chic. 1928+
Style trend; devoted exclusively to the interests of the washable garment, fabric and related industries. 1928+
Fashions of the hour. 1929+
Marchal document; couture, mode, conseille, renseigne. 1929+
Mode revue; rivista tecnica di moda. 1929+
La Donna, la casa, il bambino; revista mensile di ricamo, moda, biancheria. 1930+
Creations de manteaux. 1931?+
Iris; journal périodique. 1932+
Chic et pratique. 1933-35
DEA; revista mensile della moda. 1933+
Designer and manufacturer; a magazine devoted to the designing and manufacture of men's, boys' and children's clothing. 1933+
L'Élégance féminine. 1933+
Gaceta gentleman. 1933+
Robes elegantes. 1933+
Style reporter. 1933+
Voici la mode. 1933-36
Women; the hairstyle and beauty review. 1933+
The Bride's magazine; So you're going to be married. 1934+
Contemporary modes; the magazine of millinery and accessories. 1934+
Fashion age. 1934+
Fashions art. 1934-36
Intimate apparel; publication of the under-garment and negligee trades. 1934+
Die Kunst in der mode. 1934+
Plaisirs de France; art, ameublement, jardins, mode, tourisme, mondanités. 1934+
Der Silberspiegel. 1934+
Primerose. 1935+
California stylist. 1937+
London art fashions for ladies. 1937+

Periodicals directory; a classified guide to a selected list of current periodicals, foreign and domestic. 2. ed. rev. and enl. Edited by Carolyn F. Ulrich. New York, R. R. Bowker 1935
371 p. O.
Includes a list of current fashion periodicals. New edition in preparation, 1938
LC (32-16320)

Perkins, Charles Callahan
(ed.) See Champlin, J. D., ed. Cyclopedia of painters and paintings

Perkins, Jocelyn Henry Temple
The coronation book; or, The hallowing of the sovereigns of England; illustrated by Zillah Temple, together with reproductions of numerous ancient prints. London, Isbister 1902
xv,399p. front. illus. port. O.
LC 3-2239

The crowning of the sovereign of Great Britain and the dominions overseas; a handbook to the coronation. London, Methuen [1937]
x,207p. front. pl. D.

Perkins, Justin
A residence of eight years in Persia, among the Nestorian Christians. Andover, Allen, Morrill & Wardwell; New York, M. W. Dodd 1843
xviii,512p. front. 27pl.(part col.) ports. O.
LC 5-12121

Perkins, Mrs Lucy (Fitch)
(comp.) Robin Hood; his deeds and adventures as recounted in the old English ballads; selected and illustrated by Lucy Fitch Perkins. New York, A. Stokes [1906]
115p. col.front. illus. 11 col.pl. sq.O. (The dandelion classics for children)
LC 6-32850

Perkois, Jacobus, and Prins, Johannes Huibert
Verzameling van verschillende gekleede mans- en vrouwen-standen, ter oefening van jonge schilders en liefhebbers. Amsterdam, Gebroeders Koster 1836
2 l. 33 col.pl. F.
Engraved by M. de Sallieth
Colas 2311-12. Lipperheide 964

Perl, Frau Henriette
Venezia, by Henry Perl [pseud.]; adapted from the German by Mrs. Arthur Bell; with an introduction by H. D. Traill. London, S. Low, Marston & company 1894
248p. illus. F.
"Text illustrations from original drawings by Ettore Tito, Tony Grubhofer, Luigi Cima, Mainardo Pagani, Guglielmo Berti, Emanuele Brugnoli, Millo Bortoluzzi, Cesare Laurenti, Egisto Lancerotto." Subtitle
LC 3-8214

Perl, Henry, pseud. See Perl, Frau Henriette

Die **perle** auf Lindahaide. Förster, Friedrich

Perleberg, Hans Carl
(comp.) Historical Russian costumes, XIV-XVIII century, worn by the Russian imperial family and their guests at

Perleberg, Hans Carl—*Continued*
the ball in the Winter palace, St Petersburg, on February 27, 1903. New York [H. C. Perleberg, 1923?]
2 l. 50 port. F. $15
In portfolio
Costume index. LC 23:15129

(comp.) Persian textiles ... with an introduction by John Cotton Dana. [Jersey City] H. C. Perleberg 1919-31
2v. 100pl. sq.F.
Volume 1 shows designs of Persian and Paisley shawls
LC 19-4695

(comp.) Voelker-schmuck (Jewels of all nations). Jersey City, N. J., H. C. Perleberg [1915?]
55pl. ob.D.
In portfolio

(tr.) Delaunay, Sonia. Sonia Delaunay, ses peintures, ses objets, ses tissus simultané, ses modes

Permoser, Balthasar
Der ohne ursach verworffene und dahero von rechts wegen auff den thron der ehren wiederum erhabene barth ... sambt anhang eines schönen lustig und ausführlichen real-discurs von den bärthen ... durch M. Barbatium Schönbart. Franckfurth und Leipzig, 1714
96p. 1 pl. O.
Lipperheide 1664

Péron, François
Voyage de découvertes aux terres Australes, fait par ordre du gouvernement, sur les corvettes les Géographe, le Naturaliste, et la goëlette le Casuarina, pendant les années 1800, 1801, 1802, 1803 et 1804, historique; 2. éd., rev., cor. et augm. par M. Louis de Freycinet. Paris, A. Bertrand 1824
4v. in 2. front.(port.) O. and atlas of 59 pl(part col.) 5 maps, 4 plans. F.
Atlas has title: *Voyage de découvertes aux terres Australes ... historique; atlas* par mm. Lesueur et Petit
First edition: 1807-16
LC 7-34289, 4-32253 (1st ed.)

Perrault, Charles
Courses de testes et de bague faittes par le roy, et par les princes et seigneurs de sa cour, en l'année 1662. Paris, De l'imprimerie royale 1670
67p. 40pl. F.
Published anonymously
Latin edition: *Festiva ad capita annulumque decursio, a rege Ludovico* XVI ... *anno 1662* (Paris, E Typographia regia 1670. 144p. 85 illus. 7pl.)
Lipperheide 2708 (Latin ed.)

Les hommes illustres qui ont paru en France pendant ce siecle: avec leurs portraits au naturel. Paris, A. Dezallier 1696-1700
2v. in 1. front. 103 port. F.
Lipperheide 1115. LC 20-2471

Perret, Jean Jacques
La pogonotomie, ou L'art d'apprendre à se raser soi-même. Yverdon, 1770
xiv,154p. 2pl. O.
Lipperheide 1672

Perret, Louis
Catacombes de Rome ... ourage publié par ordre et aux frais du gouvernement sous la direction d'une Commission composée de mm. Ampère, Ingres, Mérimée, Vitet, membres de l'Institut. Paris, Gide et J. Baudry 1851-55
6v. 322pl.(part col.) F.
Volumes 1-5: plates; volume 6: text. Pictures of saints and Biblical characters may be found in volumes 1-4
LC 10-4482

Perrin, Narcisse, and Gauttier du Lys d'Arc, Louis Édouard
La Perse ou histoire, moeurs et coutumes des habitans de ce royaume. Paris, Nepveu 1823
7v. illus. 61 col.pl. D.
Also known with plates in black and white
Colas 2313

Perrin, Olivier Stanislas
(illus.) Bouët, Alexandre. Breiz-Izel

Perrin, Olivier Stanislas, and Mareschal, Louis Auguste
Galerie des moeurs, usages et costumes des Bretons de l'Armorique. Paris, L. P. Dubray 1808
48p. 48pl. Q.
Also included in A. Bouët's *Breiz-Izel*
Colas 2314

Perrochel
Le jardin de la noblesse françoise. See entry under Saint-Igny, Jean de

Perron, Ch.
Armée suisse; types militaires. Genève, F. Charnaux [1862]
1 l. 15 col.pl. F.
Legends in German and French
Colas 2318

Perrot, Aristide Michel
Collection historique des ordres de chevalerie civils et militaires, existant chez les différens peuples du monde. Paris, A. André 1820
xxiv,294p. 40 col.pl.(part fold.) Q.
Supplément, by L. T. Fayolle (Paris, J. P. Aillaud 1846. 84p. 10 col.pl.)
Colas 2319-20. Lipperheide 1921. LC 9-26292

See also Mazeret, Constantin, jt. auth.

Perrot, Émile
Harmonie universelle: musique militaire. Paris, Lemercier [1867]
[4]l. 8 col.pl. Q.
Colas 2321

Perrot, Georges. See Laurent, jt. auth.

Perrot, Georges, and Chipiez, Charles
Histoire de l'art dans l'antiquité. Paris, Hachette 1882-1914
10v. front. illus. pl.(part col. part fold.) Q.
Shows costume and jewelry of ancient times
Contents: v 1 L'Égypte; v2 Chaldée et Assyrie; v3 Phénicie, Cypre; v4 Judée, Sardaigne, Syrie, Cappadoce; v5 Perse, Phrygie, Lydie et Carie, Lycie; v6 La Grèce primitive, l'art mycénien; v7 La Grèce de l'epopée, la Grèce archaïque (le temple) v8 La Grèce archaïque, la sculpture; v9 La Grèce archaïque, la glyptique, la numismatique, la peinture, la céramique; v 10 La Grèce archaïque, la céramique d'Athènes
An English translation of the individual volumes is available in a slightly abridged form. See other titles by Perrot and Chipiez listed here
Lipperheide 128. LC 4-18236

Perrot, Georges, and Chipiez, Charles —*Continued*

A history of art in ancient Egypt ... tr. and ed. by Walter Armstrong. London, Chapman and Hall 1883
2v. illus. 14pl. (part col.) Q.
Translation of their *Histoire*, v 1
LC 4-11652

A history of art in Chaldæa & Assyria ... tr. and ed. by Walter Armstrong. London, Chapman and Hall; New York, A. C. Armstrong 1884
2v. illus. 15pl. (part col. 1 fold.) Q.
Translation of their *Histoire*, v2
LC 9-24573

History of art in Persia. London, Chapman and Hall; New York, A. C. Armstrong 1892
xii,508p. illus. XII pl. (4 col. 3 fold.) Q.
Translation of their *Histoire*, v5, part 1
LC 9-23954

History of art in Phœnicia and its dependencies ... tr. and ed. by Walter Armstrong. London, Chapman and Hall 1885
2v. illus. 10pl. (part col.) Q.
On cover: *History of art in Phœnicia and Cyprus*
Translation of their *Histoire*, v3
LC 9-24576

History of art in Phrygia, Lydia, Caria, and Lycia. London, Chapman and Hall; New York, A. C. Armstrong 1892
xii,405p. illus. pl. Q.
Translation of their *Histoire*, v5, part 2
LC 9-23955

History of art in primitive Greece; Myçenian art. London, Chapman and Hall; New York, A. C. Armstrong 1894
2v. illus. pl. (20 col. part fold.) Q.
Translator's note signed I. Gonino. Translation of their *Histoire*, v6-10 in abridged form
LC 9-24575

History of art in Sardinia, Judæa, Syria, and Asia Minor ... tr. and ed. by I. Gonino. London, Chapman and Hall; New York, A. C. Armstrong 1890
2v. illus. 8pl. (2 fold.) Q.
Translation of their *Histoire*, v4
LC 9-24574

Perrot, Nicolas

Memoir on the manners, customs and religions of the savages of North America (*In* Blair, E. H., ed. The Indian tribes of the upper Mississippi valley and region of the Great lakes)

Perrout, René

Les images d'Epinal; new ed. Paris, P. Ollendorff 1914?
x,160p. 5pl. (part col. 3 fold.) illus. (part col.) F.
Les images militaires, p87-115, shows French uniforms of the nineteenth century

Perry, Matthew Calbraith

Narrative of the expedition of an American squadron to the China seas and Japan, performed in the years 1852, 1853 and 1854, under the command of Commodore M. C. Perry, United States navy, by order of the government of the United States. Washington, A. O. P. Nicholson, printer 1856
3v. illus. pl. (part col.) ports. maps (17 fold.) facsims. (2 fold.) Q. (U. S. 33d Congress. 2d session. House executive document, v 12, nos. 802-04)
Volume 1 contains material on costume of China and Japan. It was compiled from the original notes and journals of Commodore Perry by Francis L. Hawks
Costume index. LC 1-4228

Perry, Ottley Lane

Rank and badges, dates of formation, naval and military distinctions, precedence, salutes, colours, and small arms, in Her Majesty's army and navy and auxiliary forces; 2d ed. rev. and enl. London, W. Clowes 1888
xv,416p. incl. tables. S.

Pers, A. van

Nederlandsch oost-indische typen. Types indiens neerlandais. S'Gravenhage, C. W. Mieling. 1856
22 l. 44 col. pl. F.
Colas 2973. Lipperheide 1501

Perschinka, Franz. See Mužik, Hugo, jt. auth.

La **Perse.** Drohojowska, A. J. F. A. S de L., comtesse

La **Perse.** Jourdain, Amable

La **Perse,** ou Histoire, moeurs et coutumes des habitans de ce royaume. Perrin, Narcisse, and Gauttier, du Lys d'Arc, L. E.

Persia

Jackson, A. V. W. Persia past and present. 1906

Jourdain, Amable. La Perse, ou Tableau de l'histoire, du gouvernement, de la religion, de la littérature, etc., de cet empire. 1814

See also subdivisions Persia under Arms and armor; Decoration and ornament; Kings and rulers

Ancient to A.D. 640

Houston, M. G., and Hornblower, F. S. Ancient Egyptian, Assyrian, and Persian costumes and decorations. 1920

Mongez, Antoine. Mémoire sur les costumes des Perses sous la dynastie des rois Achéménides et celle des successeurs d'Alexandre. 1803

Perrot, Georges, and Chipiez, Charles. History of art in Persia. 1892

Vaux, W. S. W. Nineveh and Persepolis: an historical sketch of ancient Assyria and Persia. 1850

640-1405

Boissard, J. J. Leben und contrafeiten der türckischen un persischen sultanen. 1596

Greblinger, Georg. Wahre abbildungen der türckischen kayser und persischen fürsten so wol auch anderer helden und heldinnen von dem Osman biss auf den andern Mahomet. 1648

Persia—*Continued*

1405-1736

Barbosa, Duarte. A description of the coasts of East Africa and Malabar in the beginning of the sixteenth century. 1866

Kühnel, Ernst. Miniaturmalerei im islamischen Orient. 1922

1736-date

Allemagne, H. R. d'. Du Khorassan au pays des Backhtiaris, trois mois de voyage en Perse. 1911

Arnold, Sir T. W., and Grohmann, Adolf. The Islamic book. 1929

Bouillane de Lacoste, É. A. H. de. Around Afghanistan. 1909

Bruyn, Cornelis de. Cornelis de Bruins Reisen over Moskovie, door Persie en Indie. 1711

Bruyn, Cornelis de. Travels into Muscovy, Persia, and part of the East-Indies. 1737

Bruyn, Cornelis de. Voyage au Levant; c'est-à-dire dans les principaux endroit de l'Asia Mineure, dans les isles de Chio, Rhodes, Chypre, etc., de même que dans les plus considérables villes d'Egypte, Syrie, & Terre Sainte. 1725

Chopin. Costumes persans. ca1830

Cooper, M. C. Grass. 1925

Drohojowska, A. J. F. A. S. de L., comtesse. La Perse, géographie, histoire, moeurs, gouvernement. 1885

Drouville, Gaspard. Atlas ou collection de 43 costumes persanes, militaires et civil; dessinés par A. Orlowski. 1823

Drouville, Gaspard. Voyage en Perse, fait en 1812 et 1813. 1825

Knanishu, Joseph. About Persia and its people. 1899

Lorey, Eustache de, and Sladen, D. B. Queer things about Persia. 1907

Orlowski, A. O. The costume of Persia, drawn from nature by A. Orlowski ... and engraved ... by Hulman, Dighton. 1820

Perkins, Justin. A residence of eight years in Persia, among the Nestorian Christians. 1843

Perrin, Narcisse, and Gauttier du Lys d'Arc, L. E. La Perse ou histoire, moeurs et coutumes des habitans de ce royaume. 1823

Porter, Sir R. K. Travels in Georgia, Persia, Armenia. ancient Babylonia, &c. &c. during the years 1817, 1818, 1819, and 1820. 1821-22

Sheil, M. L. W., lady. Glimpses of life and manners in Persia. 1856

Shoberl, Frederic, ed. Persia. 1822

Wattier, Émile. Costumes persans modernes. ca1840

Yonan, I. M. Persian women: a sketch of woman's life from the cradle to the grave. 1898

Persia past and present. Jackson, A. V. W.

Persian textiles. Perleberg, H. C., comp.

Persian women. Yonan, I. M.

Personal beauty. See Beauty, Personal

A **personal** narrative of thirteen years' service amongst the wild tribes of Khondistan. Campbell, Sir John

Personal problems of the high school girl. Miller, F. S., and Laitem, Mrs H. H.

Personnages de comédie. Flament, Albert

A **perspective** of Jewish life through its festivals. Adlerblum, Mrs N. H.

Pertaining to costume. Rosenthal, Doris, comp.

Peru. Ministerio de guerra y marina

Uniformes de la marine de guerra Peruana; declarados reglamentarios por decreto supremo de 11 de julio de 1905. Barcelona, Establecimiento grafico 1905

24p. pl.(part col.) F.

Peru

Bonnaffé, A. A. Recuerdos de Lima. 1855

Carleton, G. W. Our artist in Peru. 1866

Fuentes, M. A. Lima, or Sketches of the capital of Peru. 1866

Meyendorff, K. E., and Meyendorff, N. G. L'empire du soleil, Pérou et Bolivie. 1909

Skinner, Joseph, comp. and tr. The present state of Peru. 1805

United States. Bureau of foreign and domestic commerce. Wearing apparel in Peru. 1918

See also subdivision Peru under Decoration and ornament; Incas; Indians of South America; Naval costume

Peru nach seinem gegenwärtigen zustande. See Voyages au Pérou ... 1791 à 1794

Perucci, Francesco

Pompe funebri di tutte le nationi del mondo. Verona, F. Rossi 1639

98 p. 32 illus. Q.
Lipperheide 102

Perugini, G.

Album, ou Collection complète et historique des costumes de la cour de Rome, des ordres monastiques, religieux et militaires et des congrégations séculières des deux sexes ... accompagnées d'un texte explicatif tiré du P. Hélyot; 2. éd. Paris, E. Camerlinck 1862

68 l. 80 col.pl. sq.Q.

A work entitled *Collection complète des costumes de la cour de Rome ...* dessinée ... par G. Perugini, avec un texte explicatif ... par M. l'abbé I. B. E. Pascal, Paris, 1852, is presumably the 1st edition

Colas 2322-23. Costume index. Lipperheide 1825. LC 1-10097

Perzyński, Friedrich

Japanische masken, nō und kyōgen. Berlin und Leipzig, W. de Gruyter 1925

2v. front. illus. pl.(part col.) fold. tab. Q.
LC 26-9928

Pesel, Louisa Frances
English embroidery. London, B. T. Batsford [1931]
2v. col.fronts. illus. pl. ob.O.
LC 32-29851

See also Townsend, W. G. P., jt. auth.

Pessler, Wilhelm
Niedersachsen. See Deutsche volkskunst. v 1
Niedersächsisches trachtenbuch. Hannover, 1922
100p. col.front. 11pl. O.

Pestel, Bernhard
Der menschliche fuss und seine naturgemässe bekleidung ... bearbeitet von Max Richter. Glauchau, E. Diener 1885
xii,79p. 90pl. O.
Colas 2324. Lipperheide 1743m

Peter Cailler Kohler Swiss chocolates co., inc.
[Colored illustrations of Swiss soldiers showing uniforms and equipment, mobilization 1914. Vevey] 1914?
9pl. Nar.F.

Peter Vischer; romantischdramatisches gemälde aus der vorzeit Nürnbergs. Sostmann, Wilhelmine

Peters, Emil
Entwicklungs-geschichte der tracht. I. teil: das altertum. Köln, Neuenhagen 1907
63p. 18 illus. O.
No more published

Kleidung und gesundheit; die gesetze d. hygiene in d. männl. und weibl. bekleidung. Nenenhagen, Volkskraftverlag [1911]
37p. 36 illus. O.

Peters, Hermann
Der arzt und die heilkunst in der deutschen vergangenheit; mit 153 abbildungen ... aus dem 15.-18. jahrhundert. Leipzig, E. Diederichs 1900
136p. 150 illus. 3pl. Q. (Monographien zur deutschen kulturgeschichte, [3. bd.])
Lipperheide 2007. LC G-1207

Aus pharmazeutischer vorzeit in bild und wort; 2. verm. aufl. Berlin, J. Springer 1889-91
2v. 211 illus. 1 pl. O.
First edition: 1886. The illustrations are reproductions of miniatures, woodcuts, and copper engravings of the 15th-17th centuries, and show apothecary shops
Lipperheide 2006

Petersen, Eugen Adolf Hermann; Domaszewski, Alfred von, and Calderini, Guglielmo
(eds.) Die Marcus-säule auf piazza Colonna in Rom. München, F. Bruckmann 1896
125p. illus.(incl. ports. map) and atlas of 128 mounted pl. F.
Lipperheide 272b. LC 25-16713

Petersen, H.
Bildnisse verdienter Lübecker, nebst deren biographien ... gezeichnet und lithographirt von H. Hauttmann. Lübeck, Druck von gebr. Borchers 1843
6 l. 6pl. F.
Lipperheide 810

Petersen, Magnus
(engr.) Worsaae, J. J. A. Nordiske oldsager i det kongelige museum i Kjöbenhavn
(illus.) Müller, S. O. Ordning af Danmarks oldsager

Peterson magazine. v 1-113; 1840-1898. New York & Philadelphia
113v. illus. Q.
Title varies: v 1-3, 1840-May 1843, *Lady's world;* June 1843 *Artist and lady's world;* v4-14, July 1843, *Ladies' national magazine;* v 15-ns v8 *Peterson's magazine;* Dec. 1892-94 *New Peterson magazine.* Merged into *Argosy,* later *Argosy all story weekly.* v 103-12 also published as new ser. v 1-8

Peterson's magazine. See Peterson magazine

Peteva, Yelena
Ceintures populaires bulgares. Sofia, Imprimerie de l'état 1931
4p. 31 col.pl. ob.O.
Title and imprint also in Bulgarian. Bulgarian and French in parallel columns

Petit, L. M.
(engr.) Debret. Costumes italiens dessinés à Rome en 1807

Petit, Nicolas Martin. See note under Péron, François. Voyage de découvertes aux terres Australes

Petit, Victor
Souvenirs des Pyrénées; vues prises aux environs des eaux thermales de bagnères de Bigorre, bagnères de Luchon, Cauteretz, Saint Sauveur, Barèges, les Eaux bonnes, les Eaux chaudes & Pau. Pau, A. Bassy [186-?]
31 pl.(13 col. 2 fold.) F.
Twelve colored plates show costume

Petit album des peuples de l'Asie avec une description de leurs moeurs et usages. Paris, J. Langlumé et Peltier n.d.
64p. 11pl.(incl. front.) ob.D.
Cataloged from Colas's *Bibliographie*
Colas 2325

Le **petit** cosmopolite, ou Recueil des costumes de différents peuples. Paris, Martinet ca1830
3 l. front. 100 col.pl. Q.
Most of the plates are engraved by Maleuvre. They show French, Italian, Swiss, Tyrolese, Hungarian, Transylvanian, Spanish, Russian, and Peruvian costume
Colas 2326. Lipperheide 44

Petit courrier des dames. v 1-89; 1821-1868. Paris
89v. col.illus. O.-Q.
Includes masculine as well as feminine costume. At the beginning published one number every five days
Title varies: v 1, 1821, *Nouveau journal des dames, ou Petit courrier des modes.* Subtitle varies. Absorbed by *Journal des demoiselles*
Colas 2215-16. Lipperheide 4602

Le **Petit** écho de la mode. no. 1, 1879+ Paris
Col.illus. F. 18fr. 50 a year, foreign 55fr.
Published weekly. Current 1937
Colas 2327. Lipperheide 4763

Petit guide pratique de l'art du théâtre. Saint-Ursanne, René

Le **petit** magasin de modes dédié aux dames. Paris, Lefuel ca1826
191p. 12 col.illus. S.
Colas 2329

Le **petit** messager des modes et le Confident réunis. v 1-14, 1842-1854. Paris
14v. illus. Q.
The words: et le Confident réunis, were added to the title with v6, no 11. For English edition see *The Little messenger of fashions*
Colas 2331

Petit tableau de Paris et des français aux principales époques de la monarchie. Propiac, C. J. F. G. de

Petite, J. M.
Guignols et marionnettes; leur histoire. Paris, Societé d'édition et de publications [1911]
x,224p. illus. Q.

Petite bibliographie des stoles, basquines, vertugales et paniers. See La Fizelière, A. P. de. Histoire de la crinoline au temps passé

Petite galerie dramatique ou Recueil des différents costumes d'acteurs des théâtres de la capitale. Paris, Martinet [1796-1843]
1637 col.pl. O.
A collection of interest in the history of theatrical costume at the beginning of the 19th century. Many of the plates are engraved by Maleuvre. This collection is continued by *Galerie dramatique* (1844-70)
Colas 2328. Lipperheide 3204

Petite suite des costumes suisses des XXII cantons. See note under Reinhardt, J. C. A collection of Swiss costumes in miniature

Les **petites** misères. Randon, Gilbert

Petites misères de la vie conjugale. Balzac, Honoré de

Petites misères de la vie humaine. Grandville, J. I. I. G., called

Petitot, Ennemond Alexandre
Mascarade à la grecque. Parme & Milano, G. Bettalli 1771
1 l. 10pl. Q.
Illustrated by Petitot and engraved by B. Bossi. Plates show grotesque costume composed of ornaments of architecture in neoclassic style
Colas 2334. Lipperheide 3560

(illus.) Paciaudi, P. M. Descrizione delle feste celebrate in Parma l'anno MDCCLXIX per le auguste nozze di ... l'infante Don Ferdinando colla ... arciduchessa Maria Amalia

Les **petits** acteurs de grand théâtre, ou recueil des divers cris de Paris. Joly, Adrien

Les **petits** alphabets du brodeur. Guichard, Édouard

Les **petits** métiers de Paris. Doucet, Jérôme

Petitville, Mme de
Le costume des femmes en Bretagne. Rennes, B. Rault 1909
D. 0fr.50
Colas 2335

Petrarca, Francesco
Trostspiegel in glück und unglück ... aus dem lateinischen ... verteutscht und mit schönen figuren geziert. Franckfurt, C. Egenolffs erben 1584
222 l. 260 illus. F.
Five of the illustrations are from M. T. Cicero's *Officia*. The illustrations, by an unknown artist, show costume of the 16th century
A translation by Stephanus Vigilius of Petrarca's *De remediis utriusque fortunae*. A German edition with the same woodcuts was published with title: *Von der artzney beyder glück, des guten und widerwertigen* (Augsburg, H. Steiner 1532). Many editions
Lipperheide 642-643

Petrie, Sir William Matthew Flinders
Amulets, illustrated by the Egyptian collection in University college, London. London, Constable 1914
x,58p. 54pl. sq.F.
LC A15-706

The arts & crafts of ancient Egypt; 2d ed. Edinburgh & London, T. N. Foulis 1910
165p. front. illus. 46pl. D.
Pages 83-97 are on jewelry
First edition: 1909
LC 10-9085

Tools and weapons illustrated by the Egyptian collection in University college, London, and 2,000 outlines from other sources. London, British school of archaeology in Egypt 1917
71p. LXXIX pl. F. (British school of archaeology in Egypt and Egyptian research account. Publication no. 30)
LC 19-796

Petrizky, Anatol. See Petrytz'kyĭ, Anatol'

Petrograd. See Russia—Leningrad

Petrograd. Ėrmitazh
Die alterthümer von Kertsch in der Kaiserlichen Eremitage ... direct nach den originalen photographirt und hrsg. von Carl Röttger ... mit erläuterndem text von Ludolf Stephani. I. lieferung: Das grab der Demeter-priesterin. St Petersburg, H. Schmitzdorff 1873
20p. illus. Q. and atlas of 8pl. F.
Plates show costume of the women of ancient Greece and the jewelry of a priestess of Demeter
Lipperheide 190. LC (28-15100)

Petrus de Crescentiis. See Crescenzi, Pietro de

Petrus, de Ebulo
De rebus siculis carmen, a cura di Ettore Rota. Città di Castello, S. Lapi 1904
256p. 54pl. F. (Rerum italicarum scriptores. Raccolta degli storica italiani, tomo XXXI, parte 1)
Plates show costume of the 12th century
Lipperheide notes an edition with title: *Carmen de motibus siculis* (Basileae, typis E. Thurnisii 1746. 159p. 8pl.)
Lipperheide 368

Liber ad honorem Augusti ... secondo il codice 120 della Biblioteca civica di Berna; a cura di G. B. Siragusa. Roma, Forzani e.c., tipo. del Senato 1905-06
166p. Q. and atlas VIII p. 54pl. F. (Instituto storica italiano. Fonti per la storia d'Italia, v39-40)
Plates show 12th century costume

Petrus de Natalibus. See Natalibus, Petrus de, bp. of Equilio

Petrytz'kyĭ, Anatol'
Theater-trachten; text von B. Chmury. [Charkiw] Staatsverlag der Ukraine 1929
23p. incl.col.front. illus. mounted pl.(part col.) F.
Added title page in Ukrainian. Text in Ukrainian with German translation

Pettenkoffer, August
Das k.k. oesterreich. militär. Wien, A. Leykum 1847
24 col.pl. F.
Cover title. Each plate shows several soldiers
Colas 2336

Pettenkoffer, August, and Strassgschwandtner, A.
Die k. k. österreich'sche armée nach der neuesten adjustirung. Wien, A. Leykum [1854]
36 col.pl. F.
Colas 2337. Lipperheide 2238

Petter, Nicolaes
Klare onderrichtinge der ... worstelkonst. Amsterdam, J. Jansson 1674
16p. 71pl. Q.
Engraved by R. de Hooghe
German edition: *Der künstliche ringer* (Amsterdam, J. Jansson 1674). An edition with title: *Ring-kunst vom jahre 1674* (Heidelberg, 1887. 39p.) has text in German and Dutch
Lipperheide 3041-42

Pettersson, Carl Anton
Lappland, dess natur och folk. Stockholm, C. E. Fritze 1860
?p. illus. 21pl. map. ob.Q.

Pettigrew, Dora W.
Peasant costume of the Black Forest. London, A. & C. Black; New York, Macmillan 1937
89p. front. illus.(part col.) O. 7s 6d
LC 37-28611

Les **peuples** de la Russie. Rechberg und Rothenlöwen, Karl, graf von

Les **peuples** de l'Afrique. Hartmann, Robert

Peyry, Jean B.
Prof. Jean B. Peyry's instruction book with diagram and measure book; giving full and complete instructions for using Prof. Jean B. Peyry's system metrique; [ed. 1896 for ladies' garments] New Orleans, La. J. B. Peyry [1896]
65p. illus. diagrs. F.
French edition: *Livre d'instructions* (New Orleans, J. B. Peyry, 1896)
LC CA10-2255, CA10-2254 (Fr. ed.)

Pfälzer volkskunde. Becker, Albert

Pfaff, Karl
Biographie der regenten von Württemberg von herzog Eberhard im Bart bis zum könig Friederich mit deren abbildungen. Stuttgart, G. Ebner [1821]
30 l. 15pl.(14 col.) F.
Shows rulers of Württemberg from 1459 to 1816
Lipperheide 728

Pfalz. See Germany—Rhine Province

Pfannenschmidt, F.
Illustrirte geschichte der Trappisten order ... seit ihrem ursprunge bis auf unsere zeit. Paderborn, F. Schöningh 1873
x,134p. 9pl. O.
Colas 2338. Lipperheide 1887

Pfeffel, Johann Andreas
Schweitzerisches trachten-cabinet oder allerhand kleidungen, wie man solche in dem löblichen Schweitzer-canton Zürch zutragen pflegt; Le cabinet de toutes les modes d'habits, lesquels on porte dans le louable canton de Suisse qui s'appelle Zurich. Augsbourg, J. A. Pfeiffel ca1750
1 l. 20pl. F.
Shows costume of Zurich in the 18th century
Colas 2339. Lipperheide 920

(engr.) Gülich, Ludwig von. Erbhuldigung so ... Josepho dem ersten ... an dem auff den 22. dess monats septembris anno 1705 angesetzten tag abgelegt ... worden

Pfeiffer, Baptist
Uniformen der königlich-bayerischen armee nach der neusten ordonnanz vom jahre 1825. Augsburg, F. Ebner 1838
12 col.pl. Q.
Colas 2340

Pfeiffer, Franz
(ed.) Weingartner liederhandschrift. Die Weingartner liederhandschrift

Das **pferd** und seine darstellung in der bildenden kunst. Schoenbeck, Richard

Der **pfingsmontag,** lustspiel in Strasburger mundart. Arnold, J. G. D.

Pfintzing, Melchior. See Theuerdank. Die geuerlicheiten

Pfintzing, Paul
Methodus Geometrica; das ist: kurtzer wolgegründter unnd auszführlicher tractat von der feldtrechnung messung wie solche zu fusz, rosz und wagen an allen orten und enden ... zugebrauchen. Nürnberg, V. Fuhrmann 1598
xlv p. 23 col.pl. F.
Most of the plates printed on both sides. They show surveyors at work
Lipperheide 647

Pflugk-Harttung, Julius Albert Georg von
(ed.) Napoleon I.: Das erwachen der völker; herausgegeben von dr. Julius v. Pflugk-Harttung ... unter mitwirkung von Karl v. Bardeleben ... Hans Dechend ... dr. August Fournier ... Gustav Krahmer ... dr. Edmund Meyer. Berlin, I. M. Spaeth [1901]
xiv,499p. front. 410 illus. 2 fold. pl. 3 fold. maps, facsim. Q.
Lipperheide 1177k (pt. 2) LC 3-13538

(ed.) Napoleon I.: Revolution und kaiserreich. Berlin, I. M. Spaeth [1900]
558p. front.(port.) 464 illus. 3pl. Q.
Lipperheide 1177k (pt. 1) LC 1-G-1318

Pfluz
Landliche gebräuche in Wurttemberg. Stuttgart, Ebner, ca1810
10 col.pl. Q.
Illustrated by Pfluz and engraved by Hörmann and others
Colas 2341

Pfyffer, J. J. X.
Skizzen von der insel Java und den verschiedenen bewohnern; von J. J. X. Pfyffer zu Neuck. Schauffhausen, F. Hurter 1829
93,11p. 15 col.pl. map. F.
Full size colored plates show a farmer, dance girl, members of the army, etc. They are engraved by J. Schiess
Colas 2342. Lipperheide 1488

Phantasie-costüme. Bechstein, L.

Pharmacists. See Apothecaries

Phenicia
Hamdī, O., bey, and Reinach, Théodore. Une nécropole royale à Sidon. 1892
Heuzey, L. A., and Heuzey, Jacques. Histoire du costume dans l'antiquité classique. 1935
Perrot, Georges, and Chipiez, Charles. History of art in Phoenicia and its dependencies. 1885
Pietschmann, Richard. Geschichte der Phönizier. 1889

Philadelphia city cavalry. First troop
History of the First troop Philadelphia city cavalry from its organization Nov. 17th 1774 to its centennial anniversary, November 17th, 1874. Philadelphia, Printed by Hallowell & co. 1875
194p. 4pl.(1 col.) 13 ports. Q.
Colas 1456

Philalethe, Thimothée, pseud.
De la modestie des femmes et des filles chrétiennes, dans leurs habits & dans tout leur exterieur. Lyon, L. Plaignard M.DC.LXXXVI
307p. S.
LC 31-25497

Philip, John Bentley
Holidays in Sweden. London, Skeffington [1930]
316p. front. pl. D.
A reprint of the 1914 edition
LC 33-11709

Sommardagar i Sverige. Stockholm, C. E. Fritze [1915]
258p. 16pl.(incl. front.) O.
Many plates show costume of various parts of Sweden

Philipon, Charles
Genre parisien (métiers). Paris, Basset ca1830
30 col.pl. Q.
Plates, also known in black and white, show women of various occupations. There exists a different suite with the same title at head of plates (Paris, Martinet ca1830. 7 col.pl. Q.) For a list of plates in both suites see Colas's *Bibliographie*
Colas 2345-46. Lipperheide 1160c

Le lavater des dames. Ladies lavater. Paris, F. Janet; London, C. Tilt ca1830
6 col.pl. Q.
Lipperheide 1160e

Mascarade improvisée. Paris, Hautecoeur-Martinet ca1835
6 col.pl. Q.
Also known with plates in black and white
Colas 2348

Miroir des dames. Paris, Hautecoeur-Martinet ca1834
6 col.pl. Q.
Plates show feminine costume of the period
Colas 2347

Les ouvières de Paris. Paris, E. Janet; London, C. Tilt ca1830
51 col.pl. Q.
Plates show half length figures of women of many occupations; e.g., laundress, presser, conservatory student, etc. For list see Colas's *Bibliographie*
Colas 2344. Lipperheide 1160i

(ed.) La caricature

(illus.) Le Lys, chronique de la cour

See also Daumier, H. V. Les cent Robert Macaire

Philippe, P.
La Normandie en 1834; moeurs, usages, antiquités, costumes et statistique des cinq départemens composant cette ancienne province. Paris, Imprimerie de Fain 1834
76p. 5 col.pl. Q.
No more published. The author's *La Normandie ancienne et moderne* (Paris, 1851. 40p.) is a new edition of the historical introduction. It is signed: Comte Alexis de Saint Priest
Colas 2349-50

Philippi, Friedrich
Atlas zur weltlichen altertumskunde des deutschen mittelalters. Bonn & Leipzig, K. Schroeder 1923-24
20p. 123pl. F.
Shows German costume of the middle ages

Philippine hats. Miller, H. H.

Philippine Islands. Bureau of constabulary
Uniforms of Philippine constabulary. No place, n.d.
1 col.fold.pl. Q.
Cataloged from information from the library of the United States War department

Philippine Islands. Bureau of public health
Regulations governing the uniforms of officers and employees of the Philippine health service, 1915. Manila, Bureau of printing 1915
21p. illus. O.
LC 16-25713

Philippine Islands
El archipiélago filipino ... por algunos padres de la Misión de la Compañía de Jesús en estas islas. 1900
Browne, G. W. The new America and the Far East. 1907 v4-5
Carpenter, F. G. Through the Philippines and Hawaii. 1925
Cole, F. C. The Tinguian. 1922
Cole, F. C. The wild tribes of Davao district, Mindanao. 1913
Olivares, José de. Our islands and their people. 1899-1900
Russel, Mrs F. K. A woman's journey through the Philippines on a cable ship that linked together the strange lands seen enroute. 1907
Sawyer, F. H. R. The inhabitants of the Philippines. 1900
Vanoverbergh, Morice. Dress and adornment in the mountain province of Luzon, Philippine Islands. 1929
Worcester, D. C. The Philippine Islands and their people. 1898

See also subhead Philippine Islands under Arms and armor; Headdress; Military costume—19th century—Spain; Police; Uniforms, Civil

The **Phillippine** Islands and their people. Worcester, D. C.

Philippine Welser. Boeheim, Wendelin

Philippoteaux, Félix Henri
(illus.) Musée retrospectif de l'infanterie française
(illus.) Susane, L. A. V. V. Histoire de l'ancienne infanterie française

Philippson, Martin
Geschichte der neueren zeit. Berlin, G. Grote 1886-89
3v. 457 illus. 143pl. O.
Shows costume of 16th, 17th and 18th century Europe
Lipperheide 482

Philips, J. C.
(engr.) Description des principales rejouissances, faites à La Haye, à l'occasion du couronnement de sa majesté ... François I

Philipson, A.
Muster von couleurt gestickten bordüren, zu kleidungsstücken nach d. neuesten engl. geschmack. Leipzig, Ind. comt. 1799
Col.illus. O.

Phillippe, Adrien
Histoire philosophique, politique et religieuse de la barbe, chez les principaux peuples de la terre, depuis les temps les plus reculés jusqu'à nos jours. Paris, Martinon 1845
152p. front. O.
Lipperheide 1703

Phillips, Margaret, and Tomkinson, William Shirley
English women in life and letters. [London, New York] Oxford university press 1926
xviii,408p. front. illus. D. $4
The illustrations, which include portraits and facsimiles, are taken from manuscripts and books of the periods described. They show feminine costume in England from 17th to 19th century
Costume index. LC 27-26453

Phillips, Richard. See The British military library

Phillips, Richard Jones
Spectacles and eyeglasses; their forms, mounting and proper adjustment; 5th ed. rev. Philadelphia, P. Blakiston [c1923]
xii,89p. illus. diagrs. O. $1.50
LC 23-5684

Philojuvenis, pseud. See Hambro, C. J., baron

Philosophia herbipolensis. Hoeffler, A. R. F.

Philosophie der toilette. Claudius, G. K.

Philosophisch-medicinischer versuch über die moderne kleidung. See Vaughan, Walter. An essay, philosophical and medical, concerning modern clothing

Philosophisch-moralisch- und medicinische betrachtung. Oelssner, Gottlieb

Philosophy of clothing. Williams, W. M.

Philosophy of dress
Balzac, Honoré de. Traité de la vie élégante. 1922
Carlyle, Thomas. Sartor Resartus: The life and opinions of Herr Teufelsdröckh. 1897
Châtillon, Jérôme de. Brief et utile discours sur l'immodestie et superfluité des habits. 1577
Claudius, G. K. Philosophie der toilette. 1800
Gallo, Emanuele. Il valore sociale dell' abbigliamento. 1914
Heard, Gerald. Narcissus, an anatomy of clothes. c1924
Leroy, Alphonse. Recherches sur les habillemens des femmes et des enfans, ou Examen de la maniere dont il faut vêtir l'un & l'autre sèxe. 1772
Merrifield, Mrs M. P. Dress as a fine art, with suggestions on children's dress. 1854
Radau, Rodolphe. Les vêtements et les habitations dans leurs rapports avec l'atmosphère. 1884
Williams, W. M. Philosophy of clothing. 1890

See also Fashion; Psychology of dress

The **philosophy** of dress. Bonwit, Teller & co., New York

Phoenicia. See Phenicia

The **photographic** history of the civil war. Miller, F. T., and Lanier, R. S., eds.

Photographing the civil war. Lanier, H. W. See note under Miller, F. T., and Lanier, R. S. The photographic history of the civil war

Photographs of Mexico. Bruehl, Anton

Photographs of types of the native Indian arms. India. Army department

Photographs of uniforms worn by officers and soldiers of the Italian army. Italy. Ministero della guerra

Physicians
Amato, Cintio d', and Riccio, T. A. Nuova, et utilissima prattica di tutto quello ch' al diligēte barbiero s'appartiene. 1671
Corsini, Andrea. Il costume del medico nelle pitture fiorentine del rinascimento. 1912
Dryander, Johann. Artzenei spiegel gemeyner inhalt derselbigen wes bede einem leib unnd wundtartzt in der theoric, practic unnd chirurgei zusteht. 1557
Franklin, A. L. A. La vie privée d'autrefois; arts et métiers, modes, moeurs, usages des Parisiens du XII. au XVIII. siècle. [v11-12]
Jeaffreson, J. C. A book about doctors. 1861
Paracelsus. Opus chyrurgicum. 1565
Peters, Hermann. Der arzt und die heilkunst in der deutschen vergangenheit. 1900
Rosenthal, Oskar. Die heilkunde in geschichte u. kunst. 1926

See also Red cross

Caricature and satire
Album comique de pathologie pittoresque, recueil de vingt caricatures médicales dessinées par Aubry, Chazal, Colin, Bellangé et Pigal. 1823
Holländer, Eugen. Die karikatur und satire in der medizin. 1921
Huart, Louis. Physiologie du médecin. 1841
Veth, Cornelis. Der arzt in der karikatur. 1927

Physiologia barbae humanae. Ulmus, M. A.

Physiologie Berlins. Bettziech, Heinrich

Physiologie de l'homme de loi, par un homme de plume; vignettes de mm. Trimolet et Maurisset. Paris, Aubert 1841?
112p. 56 illus. D.
Lipperheide 3714

Physiologie du chasseur. Deyeux, Théophile

Physiologie du gant. Guénot-Lecointe, Georges

Physiologie du garde national. Huart, Louis

Physiologie du médecin. Huart, Louis

Physiologie du poëte. Texier, E. A.

Physiologie du tailleur. Huart, Louis

Physionomie de la population de Paris. Gavarni, G. S. C.

Physionomie de la société en Europe. Madou, J. B.

Physiophilus, John, pseud. See Born, Ignaz, Edler von

Piano di riforma e di organizzazione della milizia provinciale ponteficia, decreta li 8 maggio 1823. Roma, Poggioli 1823
31p. 6 col.pl. Q.
Four of the plates show uniforms of the army of the Papal states
Colas 2351

Piattoli, Gaetano
(illus.) Bicci, Antonio. I contadini della Toscana, espressi al naturale secondo le diverse loro vestiture

Piattoli, Giuseppi
Raccolta di quaranta proverbi toscani espressi in figure. Firenze, N. Pagni & G. Bardi 1786-88
2v. 80 col.pl. F.
Colas 2352. Lipperheide 1319

Piazza universale. Garzoni, Tommaso

La **piazza** universale di tutte le professioni del mondo. See Garzoni, Tommaso. Piazza universale

Picard, Bernard. See Picart, Bernard

Picard, Louis Auguste
Origines de l'École de cavalerie et de ses traditions équestres. Saumur, S. Milon 1889
2v. pl. O.
"Équitation, dressage, hippeatrique, maréchalerie, haras, remonte, harnachement, uniformes, organisation militaire, règlements de cavalerie." Subtitle

Picart, Bernard
Ceremonies and religious customs of the various nations of the known world, together with historical annotations. London, C. Du Bosc 1733-39
7v. in 6 pl. F.
Translation of his *Cérémonies et coutumes religieusès de tous les peuples du monde*

Ceremonies et coutumes religieuses de tous les peuples du monde ... avec une explication historique. Amsterdam, J. F. Bernard 1723-1743
11v. illus. 266pl. F.
Another French edition had title *Histoire generale des ceremonies, moeurs, et coutumes religieuses de tous les peuples du monde représentées en 243 figures dessinées de la main de Bernard Picard* (Paris, Rollin fils 1741. 7v.)
German edition: *Gottesdienstliche ceremonien, oder h. kirchen-gebräuche und religions-pflichten* (Basel, D. Eckenstein, 1746-58. 7v.) Plates by David Herrliberger are copies from the French original
Contents: v 1 Juifs et chrétiens catholiques; v2 Les catholiques; v3-4 Les peuples idolâtres; v5 Grecs et protestants; v6 Les anglicans, les quaquers, les anabaptistes; v7 Les mahometans; v8 Plusiers dissertations de les abbés Banier & Le Mascrier; v9 Un parallèle historique des cérémonies religieuses de tous les peuples anciens & modernes; v 10-11 Superstitions anciennes et modernes
Lipperheide 1808-1809. LC 30-13599 (under title, 9v)

Diverses modes dessinées d'après nature. Paris, Vve de F. Chéreau ca1710
30pl. O.
Twenty of these plates were published, unnumbered, between 1702 and 1708, and are dated and printed with the name of the artist, Bernard Picart, and of the publisher, G. Duchange. They were later combined with a title-page and nine new plates
Another collection with this title was published (The author, Amsterdam 1728. 69pl. O.) It contains the 29 plates of the earlier edition and also forty plates not signed but imprinted (Paris, J. Mariette). The number of plates varies in different examples. The one described is in the Cabinet d'estampes, Paris
Colas 2353-54. Lipperheide 477, 477a

Scènes de la vie juive dessinées d'après nature. Paris, A. Durlacher 1884
1 l. 16pl. F.
In portfolio
Plates show Jewish costume of the 18th century
LC 28-24075

(engr.) Eisenberg, Baron d'. Description du manège moderne

(illus.) Ehrmann, T. F. Die Holländer

La **picca,** e la bandiera. Alfieri, F. F.

Piccoli costumi di vario disegno. Cipriani, G. B.

[**Pichler, Fritz, and Meran, F. graf von**]
Das landes-zeughaus in Graz; hrsg. von der vorstehung des münzen- und antiken-cabinetes am St. L. Joanneum. Leipzig, F. A. Brockhaus 1880
176, XLV, 149p. 44pl.(3 col.) Q.
Lipperheide 2431

Pichler, Le P. Joseph
Augusta quinque Carolorum historia ... Carolo VI. humillimè consecrata a ... Adamo Patachich. Viennae Austriae, typis Mariae Theresiae Voigtin viduae 1735
416p. 16pl. F.
Contains portraits of six emperors with the name Charles, from seals, coins, etc.
Lipperheide 864

Pichon, Jérome Frédéric
(ed.) Le blason des basquines et vertugalles

[**Pichon, Thomas Jean**]
(ed.) Sacre et couronnement de Louis XVI. roi de France et de Navarre, à Rheims, le 11. juin 1775; précédé de Recherches sur le sacre des rois de France, depuis Clovis jusqu'a Louis XV; et suivi d'un Journal historique de ce qui s'est passé a cette auguste cérémonie. Enrichi ... de figures ...

Pichon, Thomas J.—*Continued*
gravées par le sieur Patas, avec leurs explications. Paris, Vente [etc.] Imprimé par Maillet 1775
xi,147,[40],91p. front. 9 fold.pl. 39 port. fold.map. Q.
Recherches sur le sacre des rois de France ... is by N. Gobet. *Journal historique du sacre et du couronnement de Louis XVI,* by Pichon, has separate paging
Lipperheide 2718. LC 25-19797

Picken, Mrs Mary (Brooks)
The secrets of distinctive dress. Scranton, Pa. [International textbook press 1918]
221p. front. col.pl. ports. tables(1 double) O.
"Harmonious, becoming, and beautiful dress, its value and how to achieve it. Comp. and written for the Woman's institute of domestic arts and sciences, inc." Subtitle
LC 18-15489

Picquenard, Charles Armand
De l'évolution moderne du chupen et du jilet dans le costume masculin, aux environs de Kemper. Vannes, Lafolye 1904
23p. O.
From the *Revue de Bretagne.* At head of title: Union régionaliste bretonne Congrès de Lesneven
Colas 2355

Picquet, Paris
(pub.) Aubry, Charles. Collection des uniformes de l'armée française. 1823 [and 1828]

A **pictorial** and descriptive record of the origin and development of arms and armour. Brett, E. J.

The **pictorial** arts of Japan. Anderson, William

The **pictorial** base ball album. Harper, C. D., and Mussey, W. P.

Pictorial history of California. Coy, O. C.

Pictorial history of England. Craik, G. L., and MacFarlane, Charles

Pictorial life of Christ. Dodd, I. S.

Pictorial review combined with Delineator. v 1, 1899+ New York
Illus. F.
Published monthly. Current 1938
Title was *Pictorial review* until May 1937, when it absorbed *The Delineator* and assumed present title

Pictorial review fashion book. 1896+? New York, Pictorial review pattern co.
Col.illus. F. $1
Published quarterly. Current 1938

Pictorial Sweden. Billow, Anders

Pictorial times. See note under The Queen, the Lady's newspaper

Pictorum aliquot celebrium praecipue Germaniae inferioris effigies. Hondius, Hendrik

Picturae Codicus Egberti. See Kraus, F. X. Die miniaturen des Codex Egberti in der Stadtbibliothek zu Trier

Picturae variae. Herberstein, Sigmund, freiherr von

Picture book of ancient & modern dolls. White, Gwen

Picture book of English embroideries, Elizabethan & Stuart. Victoria and Albert museum, South Kensington

Picture of St. Petersburgh, represented in a collection of twenty interesting views of the city, the sledges, and the people. London, Printed for E. Orme, by J. F. Dove 1815
34p. 20 col.pl. F.
"Taken on the spot at thé twelve different months of the year: and accompanied with an historical and descriptive account." Subtitle
Plates marked: Drawn by Mornay. Explanations on the plates in French and English

Picture of the manners, customs, sports and pastimes of the inhabitants of England. Aspin, Jehoshaphat

Pictures from Holland. Lovett, Richard

Pictures of ancient Japanese warriors, illustrated by Moronobu. Kopon Bushido Ye-Zupushi

Pictures of English society ... from "Punch". Du Maurier, G. L. P. B.

Pictures of life & character. Leech, John

Pictures of society, grave and gay; from the pencils of celebrated artists and the pens of popular authors. New York, Hurd & Houghton; London, Sampson Low, son, & Marston 1866
viii,226p. 95pl. Q.
Plates show costume of the period

Pictures of Swiss uniforms. Engelbrecht, Martin

Pictures of the English liturgy. London, Society of S.S. Peter and Paul 1916-22
2v. pl. F.
Contents: v 1 High mass, 1922; v2 Low mass, 1916

Pictures of the French: a series of literary and graphic delineations of French character. By Jules Janin, Balzac, Cormenin, and other celebrated French authors. With ... engravings, drawn on the wood by Gavarni, H. Monnier, and Meissonier, and engraved by Lavieille, etc. London, W. S. Orr 1840
xx,361p. mounted front. illus. mounted pl. O.
A translation of portions of *Les Français peints par eux-mêmes, encyclopédie morale du dix-neuvième siècle*
LC 15-12533

Pictures of the uniforms, arms, and equipments of the cavalry of Great Britain as it existed in 1742 and 1745; drawn up under the direction of the Earl of Albemarle in 1744. No place, 1745?
32 pl. Q.
Colas 2356

Picturesque beauties of Shakespeare. Smirke, Robert

Picturesque China. Boerschmann, Ernst

Picturesque Germany; architecture and landscape. Hielscher, Kurt

Picturesque Greece. See Holdt, Hanns. Greece

Picturesque illustration of ... Ceylon. Daniell, Samuel

Picturesque illustrations of Buenos Ayres and Monte Video. Vidal, E. E.

Picturesque North Africa. See Kühnel, Ernst. North Africa

Picturesque Palestine, Arabia and Syria. Gröber, Karl

Picturesque people. Simpson, William

Picturesque representation of the manners, customs and amusements of the Russians. Atkinson, J. A. and Walker, James

Picturesque representation of the naval military and miscellaneous costumes of Great Britain. Atkinson, J. A.

Picturesque representations of the dress and manners of the Austrians. Alexander, William

Picturesque representations of the dress and manners of the Chinese. Alexander, William

Picturesque representations of the dress and manners of the English. Alexander, William

Picturesque representations of the dress and manners of the Russians. Alexander, William

Picturesque representations of the dress and manners of the Turks. Alexander, William

Picturesque scenery in the Holy Land and Syria. Spilsbury, F. B.

Picturesque scenery in the kingdom of Mysore. Hunter, James, illus.

Picturesque Spain. Hielscher, Kurt

Picturesque tour through Holland, Brabant, and part of France. Ireland, Samuel

Picturesque voyage to India. Daniell, Thomas, and Daniell, William

Picturesque Yugo-Slavia. Hielscher, Kurt

Pidou de Saint Olon, François

Relation de l'empire de Maroc. Paris, La veuve Mabre Cramoisy 1695
[7]l. 127p. 9pl. S.

Pièces choisies. Watteau, J. A.

Piedmont. See Italy—Piedmont

Pieraccini, Francesco

(illus.) Costumes des différens états de l'Italie

Piergiovanni, Bruno

Enciclopedia dell'abbigliamento femminile. Milano, "Unitas" 1924
2v. illus. pl.(part col.) O.
Volume 1 Tecnica dell'abito fantasia; v2 L'arte nel vestito femminile, La pellicceria, Brevi rilievi estetici

Pierotti, Ermete

Costumes de la Palestine. Paris, L'auteur 1871
6 l. 12pl. Q.
Colas 2360

Customs and traditions of Palestine, illustrating the manners of the ancient Hebrews. Tr. by T. G. Bonney. Cambridge, Deighton, Bell, and co. [etc.] 1864
280p. O.
Pages 130 to 150 are on dress
LC 1-27992

Pierre, Jean Baptiste Marie

Figures dessinées d'après nature du bas peuple à Rome. Paris, Chés Lempereur graveur 1756
9pl. O.
Colas 2361. Lipperheide 1307

Les **pierres** précieuses et les principaux ornements. Rambosson, J. P.

Pieśni ludu Polskiego zebrał i wydął. Kolberg, Oskar

Piesse, Louis

Costumes algériens. Paris, A. Godard ca1835
19(?) col.pl. Q.
Plates are after designs by L. Piesse, lithographed by F. Levi, Gaildrau, Calvi, and others
Colas 2362

Pietsch, Ludwig

Illustrations des oeuvres de Frédéric-le-grand. See entry under Menzel, Adolph

Pietsch, Paul

Die deutsche reichswehr in ihrer uniformierung. Frankfurt, F. Rascher 1919
10p. 5 col.pl. O.

Die formations- und uniformirungsgeschichte des preussischen heeres 1808-[1912]. Berlin, Verlag für nationale·literatur [1911-12]
2v. illus. XIV col.pl.(incl.fronts.) 2 fold.pl. Q.
Contents: v 1 Fusstruppen (infanterie, jäger, schützen, pioniere) und deren landwehr; v2 Kavallerie, artillerie, train, generalität usw.
Colas 2363. LC 13-2997

See also Knötel, Herbert, jt. auth.

Pietschmann, Richard

Geschichte der Phönizier. Berlin, G. Grote 1889
313p. 78 illus. 8pl.(1 double, 1 col.) O. (Allgemeine geschichte in einzeldarstellungen . . . hrsg. von W. Oncken. 1. hauptabth. 4 th. 2 hälfte)
Lipperheide 146. LC G-2489

Pigal, Edme Jean

Collection de costumes des diverses provinces de l'Espagne, lithographiés d'après des dessins originaux par Pigal. Paris, Clement frères ca1825
100 col.pl. F.
Plates marked: Pigal, Lith. de Langlumé. They are signed: M. A. W., or White. Legends on the plates are in French and Spanish
Colas 2368

Coup d'oeil sur Rome, en 1828; affaires du jour. Paris, Gihaut frères 1829
1 l. 12 col.pl. Q.
Colas 2369. Lipperheide 1311

Moeurs parisiennes. Paris, Gihaut & Martinet, lith. de Langlumé ca1823
100 col.pl. Q.
Plates are known also in black and white. They show scenes with costume figures
Colas 2367. Lipperheide 3676

Scènes de société. Paris, Gihaut & Martinet, lith. de Langlumé [1822]
50 col.pl. Q.
Plates are known also in black and white. The title as given above appears at top of each. They are humorous pictures, each with two or three persons in costume of the period
Colas 2366

Scènes populaires. Paris, Gihaut & Martinet, lith. de Langlumé [1822]
50 col.pl. Q.
Plates show humorous scenes, each with two or three figures in Parisian costume of the period
Colas 2365

Vie d'un gamin. Paris, Gihaut, lith. de Langlumé ca1825
12 col.pl. Q.
Lipperheide 3675

Pigal, Edme Jean; Pajou, Augustin Désiré, and Arago, Jacques
Proverbes et bons mots mis en action d'après les moeurs populaires, composés et lithographiés par mm. Pigal, Pajou et J. Arago, avec le texte explicatif, rédigé par J. Arago. Paris, Noël et Dauty 1822-24
67 col.pl. Q.
Lipperheide 3677

Pigmies. See Pygmies

Pigot, Richard
(tr.) Cats, Jacob, and Farley, Robert. Moral emblems

Die **pilgerfahrt** der blumengeister. Böttger, Adolf

Die **pilgerfahrt** des ritters Arnold von Harff von Cöln. Harff, Arnold, ritter von

The **pilgrimage** to St. Anthony's. See Úprka, Joža. Na pouti u Sv. Antoníčka

Pilinski, Adam
(ed.) Cris de Paris au XVIe siècle. Paris, Vve. A. Labitte 1885
8p. 18 col.pl. Q.
"Dix-huit planches gravées et coloriées du temps, reproduits en fac-similé d'après l'exemplaire unique de la bibliothèque de l'Arsenal, par Adam Pilinski, avec une notice historique sommaire par Jules Cousin." Subtitle
Colas 756. Lipperheide 1190

Pillon, M. F. See Thirifocq. Histoire universelle du costume

Pillow lace. Mincoff-Marriage, Mrs Elizabeth, and Marriage, Mrs M. S.

Pinacotheca Fuggerorum. Custos, Dominicus

Pinacotheca scriptorum nostra aetate litteris illustrium. See Brucker, J. J. and Haid, J. J. Bilder-sal heutiges tages lebender

Pinchon, Edgcumb. See Gutiérrez de Lara, Lazaro, jt. auth.

Pinder, Ulrich
Speculum passionis domine nostri Ihesu christi. Nurenberg, 1507
xc l. 77 illus.(39 full-page) F.
The second edition, published in 1519 had only 78 leaves
Some of the illustrations are by Hans Schäufelein
Lipperheide 606

Pine, John
The procession and ceremonies observed at the time of the installation of the Knights Companions of the ... Military order of the Bath: Upon Thursday, June 17th 1725. With the armes ... as they are fix'd up in Henry VIIth's chapel in Westminster Abbey. London, S. Palmer & J. Huggonson 1730
18p. 21 illus. 20pl. F.
French title: *La procession & les ceremonies qui s'observérent ... à l'installation des chevaliers de l'Illustre ordre militaire du bain*
Plates by J. Pine, some after drawings by J. Highmore
Lipperheide 1906

Pinelli, Bartolommeo
Il carnavale di Roma. [Roma, Bourlié 1820]
20 col.pl. F.
Some of the pictures are reproduced in his *Twenty-seven etchings*
Colas 2381

Costumi diversi. Roma, L. Fabri 1822
25pl. F.
Scenes from Rome, Naples and other parts of Italy showing the dress of the lower classes. This collection is described by Lipperheide as the richest in figures and the most carefully engraved. Each plate dated 1820 or 1821
Colas 2383. Lipperheide 1267

Costumi e fatti dei briganti che infestano le compagne degl' Appenini fra Roma e Napoli; disegnati ed incisi per ordine di conte Nicola di Gourief. Roma, 1822
24pl. sq.F.
Colas 2384. Lipperheide 1269

Gruppi pittoreschi modellati in terracotta, da Bartolomeo Pinelli; ed incisi all' acqua-forte da lui medesimo. Roma, R. Gentilucci 1834
Cover-title,front. 20pl. F.
Some of the plates are dated 1835
Colas 2391. LC 11-32354

Nuova raccolta di cinquanta costumi de' contorni di Roma compresi diversi fatti di briganti ... cominciati l'anno 1819 compiti nel 1822. Roma, G. Scudellari 1823
50pl. Q.
Colas 2386

Nuova raccolta di cinquanta costumi pittoreschi. Roma, N. de Antoni & I. Pavon 1816
50pl. sq.F.
The collection with the same title published (Roma, G. Scudellari 1817. 50pl.) according to Lipperheide has plates from the foregoing, in reduced size, and seven plates that are new
Colas 2378-79. Lipperheide 1263-64

Nuova raccolta di cinquanta motivi pittoreschi, e costumi di Roma. Roma, L. Lazzari 1810
50pl. Q.
Shows costume worn in Rome and a few examples from provinces outside Rome
Colas 2373. Lipperheide 1261

Nuova raccolta di costumi di Roma e sue vicinanze tratti dalle opere di Bartolomeo Pinelli, incisi da Gaetano Cottafavi. Roma, Presso il Deposito di stampe e oggetti di belle arti 1838
1 p.l. 51pl. sq.O.
LC 16-13420

Pinelli's five last days of the Carnival of Rome, in a series of five plates, drawn on the spot. London, J. R. Nicol 1830
6 l. v pl. sq.F.
Lipperheide 2868. LC 13-16203

Raccolta de' costumi di Roma e suoi contorni primi pensieri di Bartolomeo Pinelli da lui inventati ed incisi nell' anno 1815; e publicati ora per la prima volta ... da Angiolo Bonelli. Roma, G. Scudellari 1819
50pl. sq.F.
Colas 2380. Lipperheide 1265

Pinelli, Bartolommeo—*Continued*

Raccolta de' fatti li più interessanti eseguiti dal Capo Brigante Massaroni per la strada che da Roma, conduce a Napoli, dall' anno 1818, fino al 1822. [Roma] 1823
10 col.pl. F.
Included also as part 3 of Pinelli's *Twenty-seven etchings*
Colas 2385. Lipperheide 1270

Raccolta di cento costumi antichi ricavati dai monumenti, e dagli autori antichi ... Tomo I. Roma, L. Fabbri [1809]
1 l. 52pl. sq.F.
No more volumes published
The plates show 100 figures. On the last plate are some pictures of fifteenth and sixteenth century costumes, after Vecellio and Picart
The author's *Raccolta di costumi antichi, disegnati da ... Pinelli, incisi ... da A. M.; parte prima* (Bologna, G. Zecchi 1830. 75p. 100pl. D.) contains the same 100 figures, reduced in size, and explanatory text, which is new
Colas 2371-72. Lipperheide 114-15

Raccolta di cinquanta costumi di Roma e sue vicinanze. Roma, 1826
50pl. O.
Plates engraved by Cottafavi after Pinelli
Colas 2388

Raccolta di 50 costumi li piú interessanti delle cittá' terre e paesi in provincie diverse del Regno di Napoli. Roma, L. Lazzari 1814
50pl. F.
Other editions were published
Colas 2375-76. Lipperheide 1262

Raccolta di cinquanta costumi pittoreschi. Roma, L. Lazzari 1809
50 col.pl. F.
Also exists with plates in black and white
The author's *Costumes et moeurs des Italiens d'après Pinelli en cinquante feuilles* (Creuzbauer, Depot d'Estampes [1823]) has copies of the same plates, reduced, and a few plates from the *Nuova raccolta* (1816)
Colas 2370. Lipperheide 1259-60

Raccolta di costumi degl' ordini religiosi. Roma, 1828
60 col.pl. Q.
Colas 2390

Raccolta di costumi italiani i più interessanti; disegnati ... nell' anno 1828. Roma, L. Fabbri 1828
front. 50pl. sq.F.
Shows dress worn in Rome, Naples, Northern Italy, Sardinia and the Tyrol
Colas 2389. Lipperheide 1272

Raccolta di quattordici motivi di costumi pittoreschi di Roma. Paris, Vallardi [1814]
14pl. Q.
Colas 2377

Raccolta di quindici costumi li piu interessanti della Svizzera. Roma, L. Fabri 1813
15pl. Q.
Plates show dress of various cantons
Colas 2374. Lipperheide 905.

Twenty-seven etchings, illustrative of Italian manners and costume, by B. Pinelli. Comprising: Picturesque costumes of Rome ... The carnival ... Adventures of Massaroni, the brigand. Rome, 1844
2p.l. 27pl. F.
The first and third series both have special engraved t.-p., in Italian and English, not included in collation
LC 12-28912

(il.) Antonioli, Giovanni. Raccolta

Pinelli, Bartolommeo, and Hullmandel, Charles

Roman costumes drawn from nature by Pinelli and C. Hullmandel: on stone by C. Hullmandel. London, Rodwell & Martin [1820]
24 col.pl. Q.
Plates reproduced, in reverse, from those in Pinelli's *Raccolta* (1809)
Colas 2382

Pinelli's five last days of the Carnival of Rome. Pinelli, Bartolommeo

Pingret, Edouard

Costumes des Pyrennées, dessinés d'après nature et lithographiés par Ed. Pingret. Paris, Gihaut frères 1834
1 l. 40 col.pl. Q.
Covers of some of the parts are imprinted Paris, Dero-Becker. Colas notes another edition (Tarbes, Dufour 1860)
Lagarrigue' *Nouvelle suite* appears to be a continuation
Colas 2394. Lipperheide 1220

Costumes du Grand Duché de Bade, dessinés d'après nature. Paris, Déro-Becker [1828]
20 col.pl. F.
Colas 2393. Lipperheide 744

Recueil de costumes suisses dessinés d'après nature. Paris, G. Engelmann 1824-25
1 l. 40 col.pl. Q.
Colas 2392. Lipperheide 908m

Voyage de S. M. Louis-Philippe Ier, roi des Français, au Château de Windsor. Paris, Pingret; London, Ackermann 1846
72p. 5 illus. 25pl. F.
Cover title *Voyage du roi à Windsor.*
Nineteen of the plates are by Pingret
Lipperheide 2694

Pinkerton, Robert

Russia: or, Miscellaneous observations on the past and present state of that country and its inhabitants. London, Seeley 1833
486p. col.front. 8 col.pl. O.
Plates show popular scenes
Colas 2395. Lipperheide 1356. LC 4-6770

Pinnock, William Henry

The laws and usages of the church and the clergy. Cambridge [Eng.] 1855-63
6v. D.
Paged continuously
Contents: Volume a The unbeneficed clerk. 2d ed. 1857; vol. b The officiating minister, and the preliminary rubrics, &c. 2d ed. 1860; vol. c The ornaments and goods of the church. 1855; vol. d Ecclesiastical vestments. 1856; vol. e-f The conduct, order, and ritual of public worship. 1858-63
LC 31-9287

Pins

Longman, E. D., and Loch, Sophy. Pins and pincushions. 1911

See also Brooches

Piolin, Paul
Du costume monastique antérieurement au XIII. siècle; lettre à un peintre d'histoire. Arras & Paris, Putois-Crétté 1865
20p. Q.
From the *Revue de l'art chrétien*
Colas 2396

Pioneer systems of cutting ladies' fashionable garments. Davies, J. F.

Pioneers

United States

Mason, A. L. The romance and tragedy of pioneer life. 1883

Pionerieeskiri. Estonia. Kaitsevägede staap

The **pipe** book. Dunhill, Alfred

Piper, Maria
Die schaukunst der Japaner dramen, szenenbilder und schauspieler porträts des altjapanischen volkstheaters. Berlin, W. de Gruyter 1927
203p. front. pl. ports. O.
Ninety-five photographs show costume and sets of old Japanese plays

Pipes and smokers' utensils
Blondel, Spire. Le tabac. 1891
Cudell, Robert. Das buch vom tabak. 1927
Dunhill, Alfred. The pipe book. 1924
Neander, Johann. Tabacologia. 1626
Schranka, E. M., comp. Tabak-anekdoten. 1914

[**Pippi, Giulio**]
L'entrée de l'empereur Sigismond a Mantouë; gravé ... d'après une longue frise exécutée en stuc dans le palais du T. de la même ville, sur un dessin de Jules Romain [Giulio Pippi], par Antoinette Bouzonnet Stella. Paris, Galleries du Louvre; & chez Chereau et Joubert 1675
25pl. F.
Celebrating the visit of the emperor in 1432
Published also with Latin title: *Sigismundi Augusti Mantuam adevntis profectio ac triumphus* (Roma, J. J. de Rubeis [1680])
Lipperheide 2735, 2736

[**Piratzky, A., and Goubarev**
Armée russe de 1855 à 1867. No place, lith. de Lemercier] 1867?
70 col.pl. F.
Plates show 103 different uniforms
Colas 2397

Pirngadie, Mas. See Jasper, J. E., jt. auth.

Pisan, Christine de. See Christine de Pisan

Pistofilo, Bonaventura
Il torneo. Bologna, Ferrone 1627
555p. 117 illus. 1 pl. Q.
Illustrations are by J. B. Coriolano. Each shows a man in armor and with weapons
Lipperheide 2959

Oplomachia di Bonaventura Pistofilo ... Nella quale con dottrina morale, politica, e militare, e col mezzo delle figure si tratta per via di teorica, e di pratica del maneggio, e dell' vso delle armi. Distinta in tre discorsi di picca, d'alabarda, e di moschetto. Siena, H. Gori 1621
315(i.e. 320)p. 56 illus. O.
The plates include portrait of Sir Kenelm Digby (second prelim. leaf); portrait of the author (fourth prelim. leaf); "misvre pedali," p32; "ordine de' tagli," p141; figures of exercises with the pike, numbered 1-89, the halberd 90-95, and musket 1-30. "Les gravures semblent avoir été gravées par Bertelli."—Brunet, *Manuel, Supplément*, v2, p243
Lipperheide 2073. LC 18-22626

Pistolesi, Erasmo
La Colonna Trajana illustrata da ... Pistolesi, disegnata da Salvatore Busuttil, incisa da Nicola Moneta con alcune indicazioni del Fabretti, Cecconi, Bellori. Roma, tipografia Menicanti 1846
11 l. 80pl. F.
Lipperheide 238

Costumi della corte pontificia; disegnati ed incisi [da Pistolesi] Roma, Fratelli d'Atri 1853
1 l. 137pl. Q.

Pistrucci, Filippo
Iconologia ovvero immagini di tutte le cose principali a cui l'umano talento ha finto un corpo ... colla traduzione francese di Sergent Marçeau. Milano, P. A. Tosi 1819-21
2v. 240 col.pl. Q.
Lipperheide 3170

Pitman, C. B.
(tr.) Bonvalot, Gabriel. Across Thibet

Piton, Camille
Le costume civil en France, du XIIIe au XIXe siècle. Paris, E. Flammarion [1895]
380p. illus. 12 col.pl.(incl.ports.) Q. 85fr. pa 60fr.
Published in 12 parts
Colas 2398. Costume index

Piton, Frédéric
Strasbourg illustré, ou Panorama pittoresque historique et statistique de Strasbourg et de ses environs. Strasbourg, L'auteur; Paris, J. B. Dumoulin; [etc] 1855
2v. 81pl.(20 col.) Q.
The colored plates show costumes of Alsace and Baden
Colas 2399

Pitrè, Giuseppe
(ed.) Biblioteca delle tradizioni popolari siciliane. [Palermo, L. Pedone-Lauriel 1871-1913]
25v. illus. pl.(part fold.) music, diagrs. D.
Half-title. Imprint of special title pages varies
The following volumes show costume: v14-17 Usi e costumi, credenze e pregiudizi del popolo siciliano. 1889; v25 La famiglia, la casa, la vita del popoli siciliano. 1913
LC 1-19842

Pitre-Chevalier, Pierre Michel François Chevalier, called
La Bretagne ancienne et moderne, illus. par A. Leleux, O. Penguilly, T. Johannot. Paris, W. Coquebert [1844]
656p. front.(port.) illus. pl.(part col.) maps. Q.

Bretagne et Vendée; histoire de la revolution française dans l'ouest; illus. par A. Leleux, O. Penguilly, T. Johannot. Paris, W. Coquebert [184-?]
648p. front. illus. 32pl. ports. map. Q.
"Complément de *La Bretagne ancienne et moderne.*" Subtitle

Nantes et la Loire Inférieure. See entry under Benoist, Félix

Pittaluga, A.
Royaume de Sardaigne: costumes. Paris, P. Marino n.d.
1 l. 25 col.pl. F.

Pittoreska folkdrägter fran sveriges provinser. See Costumes nationaux des provinces de la Suède

Pitture a fresco del Campo Santo di Pisa. Lasinio, Carlo

Pitture di vasi etruschi esibite dal cavaliere Francesco Inghirami. Inghirami, Francesco

Pitz, Henry C. See Warwick, Edward, jt. auth.

Pizzi antichi. See Vecellio, Cesare. Corona delle nobili et virtuose donne

Place, Victor
Ninive et l'Assyrie; ... avec des essais de restauration par Félix Thomas; ouvrage pub. d'après les ordres de l'empereur. Paris, Imprimerie impériale 1867-70
3v. 82(i.e. 87)pl.(incl.map, plans; part col. and fold.) F.
Issued in parts. Volume 3, plates
At head of title: Ministère de la maison de l'empereur et des beaux-arts
LC 10-99

Les **plaisirs** de Baden. Darjou, H. A.

Plaisirs de France; art, ameublement, jardins, mode, tourisme, mondanités. Année 1+ Oct 1934+ Paris, Le Rayonnement français
Illus. pl.(part col.) F.
Published monthly. Numbering continuous. Current 1938

Les **plaisirs** et les fêtes. Paris, Martin-Dupuis [1929-30]
2v. fronts. illus. pl.(part col. part double) ports. F.
Contains plates after old documents and famous paintings. Contents: Volume 1, Les fêtes en Orient et dans l'antiquité, by Maurice Magre and Henry Lyonnet; v2, Les fêtes en Europe au XVIIe siècle
LC 30-21827

Planché, James Robinson
Costume of Shakespeare's ... King John [King Henry the Fourth, As you like it, Hamlet, Othello, Merchant of Venice] selected from the best authorities ... with biographical, critical and explanatory notices. The figures designed and executed on stone by J. K. Meadows [and G. Scharf] London, J. Miller 1823-25
5v. in 1. col.pl. S.
Published in five parts, each with separate title-page. Compiled for The Theatre royal, Covent garden

A cyclopaedia of costume or dictionary of dress, including notices of contemporaneous fashions on the continent; a general chronological history of the costumes of the principal countries of Europe, from the commencement of the Christian era to the accession of George the third. London, Chatto and Windus 1876-79
2v. col.front. illus. 66pl.(24 col.) Q. ea 73s 6d, o.p.
Contents: v 1 The Dictionary; v2 A general history of costume in Europe
Colas 2404. Costume index. Lipperheide 84. LC PO30-63

History of British costume, from the earliest period to the close of the 18th century; new ed. corr. and enl. London, C. Cox 1847
xxiv,416p. 148 illus. D. 3s, o.p.
Reprinted 1881 and 1907. The first edition (1834, 1836, 1837, 1839, and 1846) contains almost the same number of illustrations but only 376 pages. An 1834 edition was published (London, C. Knight)
Colas 2401-2402. Costume index. Lipperheide 996-997. LC 4-4631 (1900 ed.)

Regal records: or, A chronicle of the coronations of the queens regnant of England. London, Chapman and Hall 1838
xii,170p. incl.front. illus. D.
LC 4-24758

(ed.) Strutt, Joseph. Complete view of the dress and habits of the people of England

(ed.) Strutt, Joseph. The regal and ecclesiastical antiquities of England

See also Tomkins, C. F., jt. auth.

Planché, James Robinson, and Smyth, Coke
Souvenir of the bal costumé given by ... Queen Victoria at Buckingham palace, May 12, 1842; the drawings from the original dresses by Mr. Coke Smyth; the descriptive letter press by J. R. Planché. London, P. and D. Colnaghi 1843
Pictures historical costumes designed for fancy dress use
29 l. col.front. 52 col.pl. F.
Colas 2403

Planches gravées d'après plusieurs positions dans lesquelles doivent se trouver les soldats. Gravelot, H. F. B.

Plano a que se refere o decreto no. 1829 de 4 de outubro de 1856 para os uniformes dos officiaes do corpo da armada e das classes annexas. Guimaraes, A. L.

Plant forms. See Decoration and ornament—Plant forms

Planta, Joseph
Catalogue of the manuscripts in the Cottonian library. See entry under British museum. Department of manuscripts

Platina, i.e. Bartolomeo de' Sacchi di Piadena
Le vite de' pontefici ... dal Salvator nostro fino a Clemente XI. da Onofrio Panvinio ... e da altri. Venetia, A. Bortoli [1701-03]
2v. 252 illus. Q.
Contains portraits of the Roman popes
Lipperheide 1804

Plattner, S. See Dance of death. Holbein's todtentanz in den wandbildern zu Chur

Plautus
Comoediae. Venedig, L. Soardus 1511
ccxxviii,lxxxix l. 319 illus.(1 full-page) F.
Text begins: Ex emendationibus, adque comentariis Bernardi Saraceni
Each scene is pictured, with the actors. Especially valuable for the picture of the theatre from the stage, showing the audience
Lipperheide 440

Play production in America. Krows, A. E.

Playing cards
Allemagne, Henry René d'. Les cartes à jouer du XIV. au XX. siècle. 1906
Bleich, G. H. Abdrücke eines vollständigen kartenspieles auf silberplatten. 1881

Pleasant quippes for upstart newfangled gentlewomen. Gosson, Stephen

Plegtige inhuldiging van zyne doorlugtigste hoogheidt, Willem Karel Henrik Friso, prinse van Oranje en Nassau. Andriessen, Andreas

Pleydenwurff, Wilhelm
(illus.) Schedel, Hartmann. Das buch der chroniken

Plion, Raymond
Fêtes et cérémonies siamoises. Paris, Firmin-Didot [1935]
v 1. pl. sq.D. (The author's *Le Siam pittoresque et religieux,* I)
LC 35-17062

Plocacosmos. Stewart, James

Ploss, Hermann Heinrich
Das kleine kind von tragbett bis zum ersten schritt. Berlin, A. B. Auerbach 1881
xii,120p. 122 illus. O.
"Ueber das legen, tragen und wiegen, gehen, stehen und sitzen der kleinen kinder bei den verschiedenen volkern der erde." Subtitle

Plotina. Krause, J. H.

La **plume** des oiseaux. Lacroix-Danliard, pseud.

Le **Plutarque** français. Mennechet, Édouard, ed.

Pluvinel, Antoine de
L'instruction du roy, en l'exercice de monter a cheval ... Reitkunst. Paris, M. Rvette 1629
8p.l. 253p. 57 double pl. ports. F.
German and French in parallel columns
Plates first appeared in 1623, under title: *Maneige royal,* and with a brief text by J. D. Peyrol. The present full text with the same plates was first published in 1625. Lipperheide lists another edition (Paris, P. Rocolet 1627. 53pl.)
Lipperheide 2907. LC 13-8223

Pniower, Otto Siegfried
Alt-Berliner humor um 1830. Potsdam, G. Kiepenheuer [1919]
10p. 70 col.pl. Q.

Pochon, A., and Zesiger, A.
Schweizer militär vom jahr 1700 bis auf die neuzeit. Bern, Scheitlin, Spring & cie 1906
64p. illus. 34 col.pl. Q.
Shows Swiss uniforms up to 1875 including the uniforms of Swiss guards and regiments in the service of other countries

Pocock, John Innes. See Collyer, J. N., jt. auth.

Podkarpatská Rus. Kožmínová, Amalie

Poem on the absurdity and sinfulness of wearing high rolls. Lathrop, Barnabas

Poets
Caricature and satire
Texier, E. A. Physiologie du poëte. 1842

Pogonologie. Dulaure, J. A.

La **pogonotomie,** ou L'art d'apprendre à se raser soi même. Perret, J. J.

Pogozhev″, Vladimir Petrovich
Ocherk″ dīeīatel′ nostī Mīnīsterstva Īmperatorskago dvora po prīzotovlenīiam ī ustroīstvu torzhestv″ svīashchennago koronovanīia Īkh″ Īmperatorskīkh Velīchestv″ v″ 1896. See entry under Russia. Mīnīsterstvo Īmperatorskago dvora

Le **poinct** de France. Laprade, Mme Laurence de

Point and pillow lace. Sharp, A. M.

Les **points** de France. Lefébure, Ernest

Les **points** de Venise. Camerino, J. G.

Poiré, Emmanuel. See Caran d'Ache, Emmanuel Poiré, known as

Poisson, J. B. Marie
Cris de Paris; dessinés d'après nature par M. Poisson. Paris, L'auteur 1769-75
1 l. 72 col.pl. O.
Published in twelve parts. The plates exist also in black and white. They are engraved by Poisson, H. Godin, Ch. Beurlier, etc. Colas gives a list of the plates
Colas 2405. Lipperheide 1181

Poisson, Siméon Jean Charles, baron
L'armée et la Garde nationale. Paris, A. Durand 1858-62
4v. O.
Contents: v [1] 1789-1792; v2 1792-1793; v3 1793-1794; v4 1794-1795
Lipperheide 2322

Poitou. See France—Poitou

Poland. General staff
Mars. Siły zbrojne niemiec. Warszawa, Wojskowy institytut naukowo-wydawniczy 1931
xii,127p. fold.pl. fold.maps. O.
Preface signed: Tadeusz Kutrzeba. Shows uniforms of the German army

Poland
Akademija umiejętności, Cracow. Ubiory ludu polskiego. 1904-09
Chodzko, L. J. B., ed. La Pologne historique, littéraire, monumentale et pittoresque. 1835-42
Eljasz, W. R. Ubiory w Polsce i u sasiadow. 1879-1905
Golebiowski, Lukasz. Ubiory w. Polsce od najdawniejszych czasów aż do chwil obecnych, sposobem dykcyonarza. 1861
Holme, Charles, ed. Peasant art in Russia. 1912
Łoziński, Władysław. Polnisches leben in vergangenen zeiten. 1917?
Łoziński, Władysław. Zycie polskie w dawnych wiekach. 1921
Matejko, Jan. Ubiory w dawnej Polsce. 1901
Przezdziecki, Aleksander, and Rastawiecki, Edward, baron. Wzory sztuki średniowiecznej i z epoki odrodzenia po koniec wieku XVII. w dawnej Polsce. 1853-62
Russia. Glavnoe upravlenīe semleustroistra ī zemledīe liīa. L'art populaire russe à la seconde exposition koustare. 1914
Schiemann, Theodor. Russland, Polen und Livland bis ins 17. jahrhundert. 1886-87

Poland—*Continued*
Ubiory ludu dawnej Polski. 1862
Winter, N. Ó. Poland of to-day and yesterday. 1913

See also subdivision Poland under Arms and armor; Kings and rulers; Military costume

16th century

Działynski, A. T., hrabia. Liber geneseos, illustris familie Schidlovicie. 1849

17th century

Łozínski, Władysław. Prawem i lewem; obyczaje Rusi w pierwszej połowie XVII. wieku. 1904-13

19th century

Gerson, Aldabert. Costumes polonais. ca1860
Kolberg, Oskar. Pieśni ludu Polskiego zebrał i wydął. 1857-80
Norblin de la Gourdaine, J. P. Zbior wzorowy rozmaitych polskick ... Collection de costumes polonais. 1817
Zienkowicz, Léon. Les costumes du peuple polonais. 1841

Periodicals

Dziennik domowy wydawany przez N. Kamieńskiego. 1840-48
Tygodnik illustrowany. 1859+

20th century

Periodicals

Album "Ziemi". 191-?
Tygodnik illustrowany. 1859+

Galicia

Die Österreichisch-ungarische monarchie in wort und bild. 1886-1902. v 19

Poland of to-day and yesterday. Winter, N. O.

Polanzani, Felix
Collection des différents portraits d' hommes illustres dans les sciences, et dans les arts tires des ouvrages du Chr. Antoine Wandych et de Joseph Nogari; choisis, dessinés et gravés par Felix Polanzani. On y en a ajouté d'autres, la plûpart peints par le Chr. Octave Leoni et gravés par d'habiles maîtres. Rome, V. Monaldini 1786
19pl. Q.
Fourteen of the portraits are copies after Anthonie van Dyck
Lipperheide 568

Police
Blakeslee, F. G. Police uniforms of the world. 1934

Caricature and satire

Hellwag, Fritz. Die polizei in der karikatur. 1926

France

L'ancienne France: La justice et les tribunaux; Impôts, monnaies et finances. 1888
Isnard, P. Fr. d'. La gendarmerie de France; son origine, son rang, ses prérogatives et son service. 1781

Paris

Cudet, François. Histoire des corps de troupe qui ont été spécialement chargés du service de la ville de Paris depuis son origine jusqu'à nos jours. 1887
Rey, Alfred, and Féron, Louis. Histoire du corps des gardiens de la Paix. 1896

Germany

Boehn, Max von. Polizei und mode. 1926

Berlin

Ballhorn, Albert. Das polizei-präsidium zu Berlin. 1852

Prussia

Bekleidungsvorschrift für die staatliche schutzpolizei Preussens. 1923

Philippine Islands

Philippine Islands. Bureau of constabulary. Uniforms of Philippine constabulary. n.d.

Police uniforms of the world. Blakeslee, F. G.

Polidori Calamandrei, E.
Le vesti delle donne fiorentine nel quattrocento. Firenze, Soc. anon. editrice "La Voce" 1924
162p. 80pl. (4 in color) O.
Colas 504

Poliphili Hypnerotomachia. Colonna, Francesco

Politica-politica, dass ist Newes emblematisches büchleī. Meisner, Daniel

Die **polizei** in der karikatur. Hellwag, Fritz

Das **polizei-präsidium** zu Berlin. Ballhorn, Albert

Polizei und mode. Boehn, Max von

Pollak, Ludwig. See Nelidov, A. I., kníaz. Klassisch-antike goldschmiedearbeiten

Pollen, Mrs Maria Margaret (La Primaudaye)
Seven centuries of lace ... preface by Alan Cole. London, W. Heinemann; New York, Macmillan 1908
xvi,58p. cxx pl. on 60 l. sq.F.
Describes different kinds of handmade lace, and illustrates them with photographs of lace in the author's collection
Contents: Preface; Introduction; Glossary; Needlepoint lace; Bobbin-made lace; Index
LC 9-4090

Polnisches leben in vergangenen zeiten. Łoziński, Władysław

Polnisches militair. Heideloff, K. A. von, ed.

Polo costume
Miller, E. D. Modern polo. 1911

La **Pologne** historique, littéraire, monumentale et pittoresque. Chodzko, L. J. B., ed.

La **Pologne,** scènes historiques, monumens, etc. Chodzko, L. J. B. See entry under his La Pologne historique, Littéraire, monumentale et pittoresque

Polska akademja, Cracow. See Akademija umiejętności, Cracow

Polychrome guanaco cloaks of Patagonia. Lothrop, S. K.

Polynesia
Anderson, J. W. Notes of travel in Fiji and New Caledonia. 1880
Angas, G. F. Polynesia. 1866
Bastholm, Christian. Historische nachrichten zur kenntniss des menschen in seinem wilden und rohen zustande. 1818-21
Brown, J. M. Maori and Polynesian. 1907
Carpenter, F. G. Australia, New Zealand and some islands of the South Seas. 1924
Erskine, J. E. Journal of a cruise among the islands of the western Pacific, including the Feejees and others inhabited by the Polynesian negro races. 1853
Stuart, Martinus. De mensch, zoo als hij voorkomt op den bekenden aardbol. 1802-07

See also Fiji islands; Marquezas islands; Tahiti

Polynesia. Angas, G. F.

Pomay, Fr.
Ein sehr artig büchlein von dem weydwerck und der falcknerey. Traitté fort curieux de la vénerie et de la fauconnerie. Wortgetreuer abdruck der originalausgabe, Lyon 1671 ... Mit holzschnittvignetten von Jost Amman. Stuttgart, J. Scheible [1886]
65p. 4 illus. O.
Text in German and French. Illustrations are from the *Neuw- jag unnd weydwerck buch*
Lipperheide 3024

Pompa funebris ... Albertii Pii, archiducis Austriae. Francquart, Jacques

Pompa introitus honori ... Ferdinandi Austriaci Hispaniarum infantis. Gevaerts, J. G.

Le **pompe.** See note under Venetianische musterblätter

Pompe funebri di tutte le nationi del mondo. Perucci, Francesco

Pompe van Meerdervoort, J. L. C.
Vijf jaren in Japan. (1857-1863) Bijdragen tot de kennis van het Japansche keizerrijk en zijne bevolking. Leiden, Firma van den Heuvell & van Santen, 1867-68
2v. col.fronts. 12pl.(10 col.) O.
Ten plates show costume
Lipperheide 1563. LC 4-29858

Die **pompejanischen** wanddecorationen. Presuhn, Emil

Pompeji. Presuhn, Emil

Le **pompose** feste di Vicenza. Patino, Carlo

Ponce, Nicolas
Apperçu sur les modes françaises par le citoyen Ponce. No place, ca1795
16p. D.
Colas 2406

Die **pontificalen** gewänder des abendlandes. Braun, Joseph

Pontificum romanorum effigies. Cavalleriis, J. B. de

Poole, B. W.
The science of pattern construction for garment makers; 2d ed. rev. and enl. London, New York [etc.] I. Pitman 1936
xix,489p. front. illus. XI pl. diagrs. sq.Q.
First edition: 1927
LC 28-7379 (1st ed.)

Poole, Stanley Lane-. See Lane-Poole, Stanley

Poole's index to periodical literature, 1802-1906. See note at head of subject: Periodicals

Popes
Barbier de Montault, Xavier. Le costume et les insignes du pape ... Extrait du Dimanche, semaine religieuse du diocèse d'Amiens. 1874
Das Bapstum mit seinen gliedern gemalet und beschrieben. 1563
Bertelli, Pietro. Diversarũ nationum habitus. 1589-1596. 3v.
Capellan, Antonio. Chronologia summor. romrum pontificum, in quâ habentur verae eor. effigies ex antiqis numismatib. et picturis delineatae, ac nomna cognomna patriae, anni, menses, ac dies, creatnis pontificat obit. ac sedes vactes. ca1800
Cavalleriis, J. B. de. Pontificum romanorum effigies. 1585
Cérémonial de l'empire français. 1805
Conlin, J. R. Roma sancta sive Benedicti XIII. 1726-30
Corte pontificia. ca1860
Costumi della corte pontificia. 1846
Cranach, Lucas. Passional Christi und Antichristi. 1521
Fabri, Alexandro de. Diversarum nationum ornatus. 1593
Joachim, abbot of Fiore. Profetie dell' abbate Gioachino et di Anselmo, vescovo di Marsico con l'imagini in disegno, intorno a'pontefici passati, e c'hanno à venire, con due ruote, & un' oracolo turchesco, figurato sopra simil materia. 1646
Johnston, M. F. Coronation of a king; or The ceremonies, pageants and chronicles of coronations of all ages. 1902
Nigrinus, Georg. Papistische inquisition und guldẽ flüs der römischen kirchen. 1582
Panvinio, Onofrio. Accurate effigies pontificum maximorum, numero XXVIII ... Eygenwissenliche unnd wolgedenckwürdige contrafeytungen oder antlitzgstaltungẽ der römischen bäpst. 1573
Platina, i.e. Bartolomeo de' Sacchi di Piadena. Le vite de' pontifici ... dal Salvator nostro fino a Clemente XI. 1701-03

See also Decorations of honor, Papal; Gloves, Papal; Papal guards; Papal tiara

Popular account of the ancient Egyptians. Wilkinson, Sir J. G.

Popular account of the discoveries at Nineveh. See Layard, Sir A. H. Nineveh and its remains

Popular Italian costumes, music, dances and festivals. Opera nazionale dopolavoro

Popular weaving and embroidery in Spain. Byne, Mrs. M. S.

Porada. Käthe von
Mode in Paris, von Käthe v. Porada. Frankfurt am Main, Societäts-verlag 1932
151p. incl.front. pl. ports. sq.O.
LC 32-34121

Porcacchi, Tommaso
Funerali antichi di diversi popoli, et nationi; forma, ordine et pompa di sepolture, di essequie, di consecrationi antiche et d'altro, descritti in dialogo. Con le figure in rame di G. Porro. Venetia [S. Galignani] 1574
109p. illus. Q.
First edition appeared in 1591
Lipperheide 101. LC 1-19927

Poritzky, J. E. See Ewers, H. H. Musik im bild

Le **port** du costume religieux. Crouzil, Lucien

Le **portail** de l'église de Mimizan. Beaurain, Georges

Das **portefeuille** des wissbegierigen. Chimani, Leopold

Porter, Sir Robert Ker
The costume of the inhabitants of Russia. London, Edington 1810
26 col.pl. Q.
Plates are copies of those in the author's *Travelling sketches* and are engraved by Stadler after Ker
Colas 2408

Travelling sketches in Russia and Sweden, during the years 1805, 1806, 1807, 1808. London, R. Phillips 1809
2v. 41 col.pl. Q.
Twenty-seven plates show Russian costume, four show Swedish. Copies of twenty-six of the plates of Russian costume were published separately under title *Costume of the inhabitants of Russia*
Colas 2407. Lipperheide 1346

Travels in Georgia, Persia, Armenia, ancient Babylonia, &c. &c. during the years 1817, 1818, 1819, and 1820; with ... engravings of portraits, costumes, antiquities, &c. London, Longman, Hurst, Rees, Orme, and Brown 1821-22
2v. fronts. illus. 87pl.(part col. part fold.) maps(part fold.) Q.
Colas 2409. LC 4-14688

Portes et fenêtres. Compte-Calix, F. C.

Portier, Adolphe
(engr.) Compte-Calix. F. C. Album keepsake des costumes de la cour française depuis Charles VII jusqu'à Louis XVI

Portman, Ludwig
Afbeeldingen van de kleedingen, zeden, en gewoonten in Holland. See entry under Maaskamp, Evert

Porto Rico. See Puerto Rico

Porträtköpfe auf antiken münzen hellenischer und hellenisierter völker. Imhoof-Blumer, Friedrich

Portrait of Mexico. Rivera, Diego

Portrait- und costüm-gallerie aus der Badischpfälzischen revolution von 1849. Karlsruhe, F. Nöldeke 1849
6pl. Q.
Colored portraits of the following leaders in the revolution: Böning, Frau von Struve, Madame Blenker, Mieroslawski, Willich, Germain Metternich
Colas 2411. Lipperheide 749

Portraits aller herren burger-meistern. Walch, Sebastian

Portraits authentiques des tzars Jean III., Basile son fils et Jean IV. le Terrible, et cinq ambassades de leur époque. Rovinskiĭ, D. A.

Portraits d'acteurs et d'actrices dans différents rôles. Colin, Mme Anais, and Marin, L.

Portraits des Grecs et des Philhellènes les plus célèbres. See Krazeisen, Karl. Bildnisse ausgezeichneter Griechen und Philhellenen

Portraits des Hongrois, des Pandoures ou Croates, des Waradins ou Esclavoniens, et des Ulans, &c. qui sont au service de ... la reine de Hongrie & le roi de Prusse; dessinés d'après la vie. La Haye, A. de Groot 1742
3 l. 6 col.pl. F.
"On y a ajouté des descriptions exactes des päis, des moeurs, de l'habillement, & des armes de ces peuples." Subtitle
Text and legends in French and Dutch
An English edition was published: *Portraits of the Hungarians, Croats, Sclavonians and Uhlans ... in the services of the Queen of Hungary and the King of Prussia* (1742. 9pl.)
Colas 2410. Lipperheide 2224

Portraits des personnages célèbres de la révolution. Bonneville, François, and Quénard, P.

Portraits des personnages français les plus illustres du XVIe siècle. Niel, P. G. J.

Portraits des rois de France. Boissevin, Louis

Les **portraits** du commun peuple à Vienne. See Adam, Jacques. Bildungen des gemeinen volks zu Wien

Portraits in Norfolk houses. Duleep Singh, Frederick, prince

Portraits of illustrious personages of Great Britain. Lodge, Edmund

Portraits of illustrious personages of the court of Henry VIII. Chamberlaine, John

Portraits of the Hungarians, Croats, Sclavonians and Uhlans ... in the services of the Queen of Hungary and the King of Prussia. See Portraits des Hongrois

Portraits of the princes & people of India. Eden, Emily

Portraits of the sixties. McCarthy, Justin

Porträtmedaillen des erzhauses Oesterreich von Kaiser Friedrich III. bis Kaiser Franz II. Domanig, Karl

Portugal
Souza, Alberto. O trajo popular em Portugal nos seculos XVIII e XIX. 1924

See also Madeira; also subdivision Portugal under Kings and rulers; Military costume; Naval costume; Street venders

Portugal—*Continued*

19th century

Album de costumes portuguezes. 1888

Bégin, É. A. N. J. Voyage pittoresque en Espagne et en Portugal. 1852

Breton de la Martiniere, J. B. J. L'Espagne et le Portugal. 1815

Costumes portuguezes, ou Collecao dos trajos, uzos, costumes mais motaveis, e caracteristicos dos habitantes de Lisbo e Provincias de Portugal. 1832

Denis, Ferdinand. Portugal. 1846

Harrison, W. H. The tourist in Portugal. 1839

Kinsey, W. M. Portugal illustrated. 1828

L'Évêque, Henry. Costume of Portugal. 1814

Macphail. Portuguese costumes. 1841-42?

Las mujeres españolas, portuguesas y americanas ... Descripcion y pintura del caracter, costumbres, trajes ... de la mujer de cada una de las provincias de España, Portugal y Américas españolas. 1872-76

Shoberl, Frédéric, ed. Spain and Portugal. 1825

Sketches of Portuguese life, manners, costume, and character. 1826

20th century

Bell, A. F. G. Portugal of the Portuguese. 1915

Gallop, Rodney. Portugal; a book of folk-ways. 1936

Koebel, W. H. Portugal, its land and people. 1909

Portugal. Denis, Ferdinand

Portugal illustrated. Kinsey, W. M.

Portugal, its land and people. Koebel, W. H.

Portugal militar; album de uniformes exercito e armada, çon decoraçoès militares. [Lisboa] 1890
1 l. 53 col.pl. D.
Colas 2412

Portugal of the Portuguese. Bell, A. F. G.

Porzel, Elias
(engr.) Curiöser spiegel

Posamente des XVI.-XIX. jahrhunderts. Dresden. K. Kunstgewerbemuseum

Post, Paul
Die französich-niederländische männertracht, einschliesslich der ritterrustung im zeitalter der spatgotik 1350 bis 1475; ein rekonstruktionsversuch auf grund der zeitgenossischen darstellungen. Berlin, H. S. Hermann 1910
xvi,112p. O.
Doctoral dissertation Friedrichs Universität, Halle-Wittenberg
Besides description of the dress contains a list of illustrative material and tells in what collection they can be found
Colas 2413

Post, Pieter
Begraeffenisse van ... Frederick Henrick ... prince van Orange, grave van Nassau ... En ghesneden door Pieter Nolpe. Amsterdam, N. van Ravesteyn 1651
40p. 30pl. F.
Plates show the funeral procession
Lipperheide 2666

Postans, Mrs Thomas. See Young, Marianne

Posy-rings. Evans, Sir John

Poten, Bernhard von
Unser volk in waffen; das deutsche heer in wort und bild; illustriert von Chr. Speyer. Berlin & Stuttgart, W. Spemann [1885-87]
xi,384p. 232 illus. 51pl.(5 col.) F.
Colas 2415. Lipperheide 2135

Potier, Othmar, baron
Führer durch die rüstkammer der stadt Emden. Emden, C. Zorn 1903
xxiv,98p. 12 illus. 7pl. O.
Lipperheide 2460c

Potrelle, Jean Louis
(pub.) Garde des Consuls

Pottier, André Ariodant
Monuments français. See entry under Willemin, N. X.

See also La Normandie illustrée

Pottier, Edmond. See Daremberg, C. V., and Saglio, Edmond, eds. Dictionnaire des antiquités grecques et romaines, d'après les textes et les monuments

Pougin, Arthur
Dictionnaire historique et pittoresque du théâtre et des arts qui s'y rattachent. Paris, Firmin-Didot 1885
xv,775p. incl.illus. pl. 8pl.(7 col. incl. front.) col.port. Q. 40fr.
"Poétique, musique, danse, pantomime, décor, costume, machinerie, acrobatisme. Jeux antiques, spectacles forains, divertissements scéniques, fêtes publiques, rejouissances populaires, carrousels, courses, tournois." Subtitle
Bibliography: p xiij-xiv
Colas 2416. Lipperheide 3229. LC 2-1534

Poulsen, Frederik
Etruscan tomb paintings, their subjects and significance; translated by Ingeborg Andersen. Oxford, Clarendon press 1922
x,63p. front. 1 illus. pl. Q.
Based upon investigations made in the Etruscan tombs at Corneto and Chiusi. "Originally published in Danish in 1919." Preface
LC 22-15499

Les **poupées** anciennes. Sézan, Claude

Poupées et légendes de France. Koenig, Marie

Pour bien s'habiller. L'Heureux, Mme M. A.

Pour bien travailler chez soi; préface de mme la baronne Maurice Fauqueux. Collection publiée sous le patronage du Lyceum. Paris, P. Lafitte [c1912]
xv,400p. 480 illus. O. (Femina-bibliothèque) 5fr.
LC 12-19387

Pour habiller Eliante ou Le nouveau secret des dames. Marsan, Eugène

Pour la danse. Divoire, Fernand

Pourrat, Henri
Ceux d'Auvergne; types et coutumes; dessins originaux de Ed. Elzingre. Paris, Horizons de France 1928
135p. col.illus. col.pl. sq.Q.

Pracht, Emil
(engr.) Carrousel, geritten in Potsdam am 13 July 1829

Pracht-muster für die weisse stickerei; neue aufl. Frankfurt a. M., Wesché 1833
2v. 12pl. F.
Lipperheide 3949

Die **prachtharnische** des goldschmiedes Heinrich Cnoep aus Münster i. W. Geisberg, Max

Practica et arte di cavalleria. Lieb, Christophorus

Practical dresscutting up to date. Reeve, A. J.

Practical hints on stage costume. Bowen, Cyril

Practical home millinery. Reeve, A. J.

Practical instruction in cutting out and making up hospital garments for sick and wounded. Peek, Emily

A **practical** method of dress cutting, especially designed for technical classes. Carlisle, E. M. F.

Practical tailoring. Byrne, J. J.

Practical work of dressmaking & tailoring. Browne, M. P.

Practical work of tailoring. See Browne, M. P. The practical work of dressmaking & tailoring

Das **prächtige** rath haus der stadt Augspurg. Kleiner, Salomon

Prähistorische blätter. Unter mitwirkung von forschern und freunden der prähistorischen wissenschaft hrsg. von Dr. Julius Naue. 1.-19. jahrg.; 1889-1907. München, Prähistorischen blätter 1889-1907
19v. illus. pl. O.
Published bimonthly
Lipperheide 303. LC 5-38948

Praehistorische varia. See Antiqua

Prael-treyn, plegtigheden, vreugde-feesten en vercieringen van het vyftig-jaerig jubilé der martelie van den Heyligen Rumoldus, apostel en patroon der stad Mechelen MDCCCXXV. Mechelen, Velsen van der Elst [1825]
65p. 14pl. map. Q.
Lipperheide 2805

Prael-treyn verrykt door ry-benden, praelwagens, zinne-beélden en andere oppronkingen toegeschikt aen het duyzend-jaerig jubilé van ... den Heyligen Rumoldus. Mechelen, Joannes-Franciscus vander Elst [1775]
34p. 15pl. Q.
Plates are from drawings by W. J. Herreyns, engraved by the brothers Klauber
Lipperheide 2803

Präsentirt das gewehr! Schneider, Louis

Praga, Mrs Alfred
What to wear and when to wear it. London, G. Newnes 1908
x,138p. 8pl. D.

Pragmatische geschichte der saechsischen truppen. Hoyer, J. G. von

Prague. Knopf-museum Heinrich Waldes. See Wrschowitz, Austria. Knopfmuseum Heinrich Waldes

Prague. Národopisné museum československé
Moravské slovensko ... red. L. Niederle. Prag, 1918-22
2pts. illus. 53pl. O.
Many of the plates show costume of the Czecho-Slovakian peasants

Prague. Orientálni ústav. See Orientálni ústav, Prague

Praissac, du. See Du Praissac

Praktische anleitung zum masznehmen. Rocholl, Meta

Praktische anleitung zur erlernung der damen-schneiderei. See Lenniger, F. F. Die anfertigung der damen-kleider

Praktische kostümkunde. Köhler, Karl

Praktische schule der zuschneidekunst für damen. See Suhr, H. Leitfaden für den gründlichen unterricht

Praktischer unterricht im massnehmen und zuschneiden aller arten weiblicher kleidungs-stücke. Heindorf, Auguste

Prang, Louis & company, publishers
Military types of the U. S. militia and National guard, past and present. (State of Massachusetts). Ser. no 1. [Boston, 1893]
Col.pl.
No more published. Contents: Boston Light infantry; 1st Corps of cadets; 2d Corps of cadets; Roxbury horse guards; Naval brigade

Prawem i lewem. Łozínski, Władysław

Praxis rerum civilium. Damhouder, Joost

Praxis rerum criminalium. Damhouder, Joost

Precetti della militia moderna. Ruscelli, Girolamo

Precious stones of the Bible. Cooper, C. W.

Précis historique des ordres religieux et militaires de S. Lazare et S. Maurice. See note under Cibrario, G. A. L. Descrizione storica degli ordini cavallereschi

Preece, Louisa. See Antrobus, Mrs M. S., jt. auth.

Le **pregi** della nobilta' veneta. See Freschot, Casimir. La nobilta' veneta, o' sia Tutte le famiglie patrizie con le figure de suoi scudi & arme

Pregitzer, Johann Ulrich
Teutscher regierungs- und ehren-spiegel vorbildend des Teutschen Reichs und desselben stånde ersten anfang, fortleitung hoheit macht recht und freyheit. Auch der chur-fůrsten fůrsten grafen und herren und derselben hohen håuser besonders des hauses Hohenzollern / ursprung, wůrde / und herrlichkeiten. Berlin, J. M. Růdiger 1703
234p. illus. ports. fold.pl. F.
Lipperheide 718. LC 24-12999

La **préhistoire.** Capitan, Louis

Prehistoric
Benvenuti, Leo. La situla Benvenuti nel Museo di Este. 1886
Bertrand, A. L. J. Les Celtes dans les vallées du Pô et du Danube. 1894

Prehistoric—*Continued*
Boyle, M. E. In search of our ancestors. 1927
Breuil, Henri, and Obermaier, Hugo. The cave of Altamira. 1935
Capitan, Louis. La préhistoire. 1925
Forrer, Robert. Reallexikon der prähistorischen, klassischen und frühchristlichen altertümer. 1907
Grasset, Eugène. Costumes de guerre de l'âge du bronze et de l'ère gauloise. 1886
Figuier, Louis. L'homme primitif. 1870
Hiler, Hilaire. From nudity to raiment. 1929
Morgan, J. J. M. de. Prehistoric man; a general outline of prehistory. 1925
Nadaillac, J. F. A. du P., marquis de. Manners and monuments of prehistoric peoples. 1892
Nadaillac, J. F. A. du P., marquis de. Moeurs et monuments des peuples préhistoriques. 1888
Naue, Julius. Die bronzezeit in Oberbayern. 1894
Obermaier, Hugo. Fossil man in Spain. 1924
Osborn, H. F. Men of the old stone age, their environment, life and art. 1916
Paniagua, André de. L'âge du renne. 1926
Prähistorische blätter. v 1-19. 1889-1907
Quennell, Mrs M. C., and Quennell, C. H. B. Everyday life in the new stone, bronze & early iron ages. 1923
Wetter, George van. Les origines de la parure aux temps paléolithiques. 1920
Zannoni, Antonio. Gli scavi della Certosa di Bologna. 1876-84

See also Europe—to 476; also subdivision Prehistoric under Arms and armor; Denmark

Prehistoric man. Morgan, J. J. M. de

Preisgekrönte stickerei-arbeiten der württembergerischen frauenarbeitschulen. Kick, Wilhelm

Preisler, Johann Martin
(engr.) Schlegel, J. H. Geschichte der könige von Dänemark

Prelle de la Nieppe, Edgar de
Notes sur les costumes chevaleresques et les armes offensives des XIIe, XIIIe et XIVe siècles. Nivelles, C. Guignardé 1901
35p. illus. O.
Extract from the *Annales* of La société archéologique de Nivelles

Prelude to ballet. Haskell, A. L.

Premier âge du fer. Chantre, Ernest

Premier cahier des différens habillements distinctifs de la ville de Berne. Freudenberger, Sigmund

Premier suite d'estampes, pour servir à l'histoire des modes et du costhume en France, dans le XVIII siècle. Freudenberger, Sigmund

Première [et deuxième] suite de divers sujets militaires. Watteau, L. J.

Les **Premières** illustrées ... notes et croquis. [1.-7. année]; 1881-1888. Paris, E. Monnier [1882-88]
7v. illus.(part col.) pl.(part col.) ports. Q.
Vols. [1-6] have title: *Les Premières illustrées* ... notes et croquis; saison théâtrale 1881/82-1886/87. The text of the issues for 1881/82-1883/84 is by Raoul Toché, that of the other issues is by various authors. Illustrations show costumes and sets used in plays which opened during the period covered. No more published?
LC 22-9281

Premios militares de la República Argentina. Mantilla, M. F.

O **preparo** do vestuario para senhora. See Lechner, Hedwig, and Beeg, Gunda. Die anfertigung der damen garderobe

Prescott, Jean François Vernes- See Vernes-Prescott, J. F.

Present state of Peru. Skinner, Joseph, comp. and tr.

Present state of the Cape of Good-Hope. Kolb, Peter

Present state of the Jews. Addison, Lancelot

Preston, Harriet Waters, and Dodge, Louise
The private life of the Romans. New York, B. H. Sanborn [1893]
vi,167p. front. illus. pl. D. (The students' series of Latin classics) $1.50
Costume index. LC 5-2565

Presuhn, Emil
Die pompejanischen wanddecorationen. Neue wohlfeile ausg. in sechs lieferungen. Leipzig, T. O. Weigel 1882
40p. XXIV col.pl. plan. F.
"Für künstler und kunstgewerbtreibende sowie freunde des alterthums... Mit 24 tafeln nach original-copien von Discanno, in farbendruck ausgeführt von Steeger, nebst einem plan der malereien Pompeji's." Subtitle
In portfolio. "Literatur": 1 p. preceding p 1. Lettered on portfolio: *Die wanddekorationen in Pompeji*
Lipperheide lists an edition dated 1877
Lipperheide 248. LC 20-7412

Pompeji; die neuesten ausgrabungen von 1874 bis 1881; für kunst- und alterthumsfreunde illustrirt. 2. verb. und verm. aufl. Leipzig, T. O. Weigel 1878[-82]
2v. 85 col.pl. F.
Plates are after water colors by G. Discanno and A. Butts
Lipperheide 250

Pretiosa gemma delle virtuose donne. Parasole, I. C.

Preuschen, Erwin
Darstellungen aus dem Nibelungen-liede. Giessen, Ferber'sche universitaetsbuchhandlung (E. Roth) 1847
4 l. 30pl. Q.
Lipperheide 381

Preussens heer. Seine laufbahn in historischer skizze entrollt von George Hiltl ... illus. nach skizzen von L. Burger, Menzel, H. Lüders u.a.; seine heutige uniformirung und bewaffnung gezeichnet von C. F. Schindler. Berlin, H. J. Meidinger [1875-76]
32p. 39 illus. 50 col.pl. F.
Colas 1448, 2663. Lipperheide 2186

Preussens vorzeit in lebenden bildern dargestellt. See Bender, Ferdinand. Fünf lebende bilder

Die **preussische** armee von den ältesten zeiten bis zur gegenwart. Krippenstapel, Friedrich

Preussische armee-uniformen unter der regierung Friedrich Wilhelm II. Horvath, C. C., pub.

Preussische civil-uniformen. Potsdam & Küstrin, C. C. Horvath & F. Oehmigke 1787-88
2v. 12 col.pl. O.
Colas 2419. Lipperheide 1772

Das **preussische** heer. Elzholz, L.; Rechlin, Karl, and Schulz, J.

Das **preussische** heer, herausgegeben und Sr Majestät dem Könige Friedrich Wilhelm III allerunterthänigst gewidmet. Elzholz, L.; Rechlin, Karl and Schulz, J.

Das **preussische** heer unter Freidrich Wilhelm IV. Mit besonderer berücksichtigung der neuesten uniformirung und bewaffnung aller truppentheile unter specieller leitung eines allerhöchsten ort ernannten sachverständigen. Berlin, L. Sachse & co. 1845
36 col.pl.(incl. ca. 200 figures) F.
Plates are after those in *Das preussische heer* by Elzholz, Rechlin and Schulz, with changes to bring them up to date
Published in 6 parts at 90fr. A *Supplement* (9 col.pl.) was also published
Colas 2420. Lipperheide 2174

Das **preussische** infanterie-gewehr. Bagensky, C. H. L. von, and Klaatsch, K. H.

Preussische krönungs-geschichte. Besser, Johann von

Der **preussische** steuerbeamte in bezug auf seine dienst- und rechtsverhältnisse. Rumpf, C.

K. **Preussische Turfan-expeditionen**
Chotscho. See entry under Le Coq, Albert von
Volkskundliches aus Ost-Turkistan. See entry under Le Coq, Albert von

Die **preussischen** garden. Sachse, L. & co., Berlin

Die **preussischen** orden. Schneider, Louis

Das **preuszische** heer in bildern. Walter, W.

Prévot, Gabriel
Stores dentelles & broderies dans le style moderne. Paris, A. Calavas [1901]
1 l. 20pl. F.
In portfolio. The plates show 115 designs
Second series of the author's *Stores guipures & broderies d'art.* The author's *Motifs modernes; stores, guipures et broderies d'art dans le style moderne* (Plauen, C. Stoll 1900-02. 3v. 105fr.) seems to be volumes 1-3 of the series
LC 2-27788

Prévot, Gabriel, and Devresse, G.
Dentelles et broderies d'art, stores & brise-bise. Paris, A. Calavas; Plauen, C. Stoll [1905]
20pl. F. (Motifs modernes, ser. 4) 35fr.

Prewett, F. T. & company, London
The West-End hand-book of liveries. London, F. J. Prewett [189-?]
33p. 1 col.pl. Q.

Preziosi, A.
Le Caire, mœurs et costumes, par Preziosi. Paris, Canson 1883
4 l. 20 col.pl. F. (Encyclopédie des arts décoratifs de l'Orient [ser. 8])
Drawn and lithographed by Preziosi. Text by Victor Champier
The plates were published earlier in the author's *Souvenir du Caire* (Paris, Lemercier 1862)
Colas 2424-2425. LC 1-20622

Stamboul, mœurs et costumes. Paris, Canson 1883
4 l. 29pl.(28 col.) F. (Encyclopédie des arts décoratifs de l'Orient [sér. 7])
Second edition, edited by Victor Champier. First edition, 1861
Drawn and lithographed by Preziosi. A reimpression of the author's *Stamboul, souvenir de l'Orient* (Paris, Lemercier 1858)
Colas 2422-2423. Lipp. 1440 (1858 ed.) LC 1-20623; 17-4635 (1858 ed. reprint 1872)

Price, George
Ancient and modern beards ... from the 'Friends' Quarterly Examiner, etc. [1893]
8p. O.

Price, Sir Henry Philip
When men wore muffs; the story of men's clothes. London, J. M. Dent [1936]
viii,184p. front. pl. ports. O.
LC 37-15875

Price, Julius Mendes
Dame Fashion, Paris—London (1786-1912) London, S. Low, Marston & company; New York, C. Scribner 1912
vii,180p. col.front. 207pl.(154 col.) on 181 l. Q. $12
The black and white plates are printed on both sides
Colas 2426. Costume index. LC 13-16770

Price, Lake, and Ford, Richard
Tauromachia, or the bull-fights of Spain, illustrated by ... plates, representing the most remarkable incidents and scenes in the arenas of Madrid, Seville, and Cadiz ... lithographed from studies made expressly for the work, by Lake Price; with preliminary explanations by Richard Ford. London, J. Hogarth 1852
16p. 26pl. F.
Lipperheide 2874

Prichard, Hesketh Vernon Hesketh
Through the heart of Patagonia ... with illustrations ... by John Guille Millais ... and from photographs. New York, D. Appleton 1902
xvi,346p. col.front. illus.(incl.ports.) pl. (part col.) 3 fold.maps. Q.
Contains many pictures of natives
LC 3-6523

Priest, Alan
Chinese textiles. See entry under New York. Metropolitan museum of art
Japanese costume. See entry under New York. Metropolitan museum of art

Die **priesterlichen** gewänder des abendlandes. Braun, Joseph

Priests, Jewish. See Jewish priests

Prima parte de' fiori, e disegni di varie sorti di ricami moderni. Ciotti, G. B.

Prime, Temple
Notes relative to certain matters connected with French history: on the feudal nobility, the appanage and the peerage; on the surnames of collateral branches of the house of France. New York, [De Vinne press] 1903
2v. front. pl. ports. O.
LC 4-1333

Prime du journal Les modes parisiennes. See Compte-Calix, F. C.: Les travestissements élégants (1864), Costumes historiques français (1865), Costumes de l'époque de Louis XVI (1869), Les modes parisiennes sous le Directoire (1871)

Primerose. Année 1+ Oct. 1935+ Paris, Éditions Bell
Illus. (part col.) F.
A fashion journal. Published monthly. Numbering continuous. Each issue includes pattern supplement

Primisser, Alois
Der stammbaum des allerdurchläuchtigsten hauses Habsburg-Oesterreich ... fürsten und fürstinnen von Rudolf I. bis Philipp dem Schoenen nach dem in der k. k. Ambraser sammlung befindlichen. [Wien, 1822]
14 l. 56pl. (54 col.) F.
Published in 14 parts. Brunet lists an edition published in 22 parts with 66 plates. Reproduction of plates painted for Ferdinand Archduke of Ambras and finished in 1584. It is based on an earlier work of the first decade of the sixteenth century, the property of the emperor Maximilian
Lipperheide 867

Les **primitifs** italiens du XI. au XIII. siècle. Ancona, Paolo d'

Primitive American armor. Hough, Walter

Primitive dress
British museum. Department of British and mediaeval antiquities. Handbook to the ethnographical collections. 1910
Cocheris, Mme P. A. W. Les parures primitives avec une introduction sur les temps préhistoriques. 1894
Crawley, A. E. Dress, drinks, and drums, further studies of savages and sex. 1931
Deniker, Joseph. Les races et les peuples de la terre. 1926
Frobenius, Leo. The childhood of man. 1909
Grosse, Ernst. Die änfange der kunst. 1894
Grosse, Ernst. The beginnings of art. 1897
Hiler, Hilaire. From nudity to raiment. 1929
Meadows, Robert, comp. A private anthropological cabinet of 500 authentic racial-esoteric photographs and illustrations. 1934
Reitzenstein, F. E., freiherr von. Das weib bei den naturvölkern. 1923
Thomas, W. I., ed. Source book for social origins. 1909

See also African tribes; Arms and armor, Primitive; Australia—Native races; Body painting; Decoration and ornament—Primitive

Il **primo** libro del trattato militare. Cigogna, G. M.

Princelyck cabinet. Clerck, Nicolaes de

Principal leaders in the Greek revolution. Friedel, Adam

Principe de la draperie antique, Du. Heuzey, L. A.

Principes d'allemandes. Dubois

Principes Hollandiae et Zelandiae. Vosmer, Michael

Principles of clothing selection. Buttrick, H. G.

Principles of correct dress. Winterburn, Mrs F. H.

Principles of harmony and contrast of colours. Chevreul, M. E.

Principles of modern hairdressing. Lichtenfeld, Joseph

Prins, Johannes Huibert. See Perkois, Jacobus, jt. auth.

Print-Geschenkjen voor myn kinderen. Ehrmann, T. F.

Printers
Mergenthaler linotype company. A true description of all trades. 1930

Prinzhorn, Hans
Bildnerei der gefangenen; studie zur bildnerischen gestaltung ungeübter. Berlin, A. Juncker c1926
60p. illus. 83pl. Q.
Pictures 76-88 show modern tattooing as found on prisoners

Prior, Edward Schröder, and Gardiner, Arthur
An account of medieval figure-sculpture in England, with 855 photographs. Cambridge, University press 1912
xi,734p. illus. sq.Q.
"Bibliography of English medieval sculpture": p[105]-108
LC 13-1943

Priorato, Galeazzo, conte Gualdo. See Gualdo Priorato, Galeazzo, conte

Le **Prisme;** encyclopédie moral du XIX. siècle. See entry under Les Français peints par eux-mêmes

A **prisoner** of the khaleefa. Neufeld, Charles

Prisoners
Adam, Victor. Album de Ste. Pélagie (dette); douze scènes intérieures dessinées et lithographiées d'après nature. ca1835
Andrews, William. Bygone punishments. 1899
Austria. Laws, statutes, etc. Constitutio criminalis Theresiana, oder Der ... Mariä Theresiä ... Peinliche gerichtsordnung. 1769
Bambergensis constitutio criminalis. Bambergische halszgerichts und rechtlich ordnung iñ peinlichen sachen. 1531
Damhouder, Joost. Praxis rerum criminalium. 1562
Des allerdurchleuchtigsten groszmechtigsten unüberwindlichsten Keyser Karls des Fünfften und des Heyligen Römischen Reichs peinlichs gerichts-ordnung auff den reichsstägen zu Augspurg und

Prisoners—*Continued*
Regenspurg in jaren dreissig und zwey und dreissig gehalten auffgericht und beschlossen. 1559
Heinemann, Franz. Der richter und die rechtspflege in der deutschen vergangenheit. 1900
Hempel, Friedrich. Die strafen der Chinesen auf XXII ausgemalten kupfern dargestellt. Châtiments usetés chez les Chiois. 1804
Mason, G. H. The punishments of China. 1808

Prisse, Émile. See Prisse d'Avennes, A. C. T. É.

Prisse d'Avennes, Achille Constant Théodore Émile
Histoire de l'art égyptien d'après les monuments, depuis les temps les plus reculés jusqu'à la domination romaine, par Prisse d'Avennes; ouvrage publié sous les auspices du Ministère de l'instruction publique, des cultes et des beaux-arts. Texte par P. Marchandon de La Faye ... (d'après les notes de l'auteur) Paris, A. Bertrand 1878-79
444p. illus. pl. and atlas of 159pl. incl. plans(part col. 1 fold.) F.
Text dated 1879. Plates, originally published in 40 parts, forming 2 volumes, in portfolio. The second volume shows costume, especially the sections on "Sculpture" and "Peinture." Each picture is dated by dynasty
LC 10-1932

Monuments égyptiens. Paris, Firmin Didot 1847
9p. 50pl.(part col.) F.
"Bas-reliefs, peintures, inscriptions, etc., d'après les dessins executés sur les lieux, pour faire suite aux *Monuments de l'Egypte et de la Nubie* de Champollion-le-Jeune. Ouvrage publié sous les auspices de m. le compte de Salvandy, ministre de l'instruction publique." Subtitle

(illus.) St. John, J. A. Oriental album

A **private** anthropological cabinet. Meadows, Robert, comp.

The **private** life of King Edward VII (Prince of Wales, 1841-1901) by a member of the royal household. New York, D. Appleton 1901
xi,306p. front. pl. ports. O.
Show English dress of the period
LC 1-30624

Private life of the Romans. Arnay, J. R. d'.

Private life of the Romans. Johnston, H. W.

Private life of the Romans. Preston, H. W., and Dodge, Louise

Private soldier under Washington. Bolton, C. K.

Das **privatleben** der Römer. Marquardt, K. J.

Privatus, Teucrius Anneaus, pseud. See Lonicer, J. A.

Prizelius, Johann Gottfried
Vollständige pferdewissenschaft. Leipzig, Weidmanns erben und Reich 1777
xxxii,606p. 51pl. port. Q.
Lipperheide 2928

Probst, Balthasar
(engr.) Schübler, J. J. Amor vehementer quidem flagrans

Probszt, Günther
Der schatz des Ordens vom goldenen vliesse. Augsburg, B. Filser 1926
47p. 25pl. O.

The **procession** and ceremonies observed at the time of the installation of the Knights Companions of the ... Military order of the Bath: Upon Thursday, June 17th 1725. Pine, John

La **procession** & les ceremonies qui s'observérent ... à l'installation des chevaliers de l'illustre ordre militaire du bain. See note under Pine, John. The procession and ceremonies

Procession of Pope Clement VII. and the Emperor Charles V. after the coronation at Bologna on the 24th February 1530. Hogenberg, Hans

La **processione** del Doge nella domenica delle palme. Pagani, Mattio

Procter, Richard Wright
The barber's shop ... with illustrations by W. Morton; rev. & enl. with an introduction by W. E. A. Axon. Manchester, Heywood & son 1883
xxxii,244 illus.(incl.ports.) O.
First edition 1856

Prod'homme, Jacques Gabriel
La toilette féminine à travers les ages (1490-1720) Paris, Éditions Nilsson [1932-33]
2v. 40 col.pl. O.
[Volume 1] 1490-1645, [v2] 1645-1720
Each plate is dated. The author does not give sources. Plates show women's dress as worn in France
Costume index. LC AC33-2793

Pröckl, Vincenz
Eger und das Egerland. Prag & Eger, C. W. Medau 1845
2v. 22pl.(8 col.) O.
On Eger, a part of Bohemia, distinguished from the rest of the population by its dress and language. Colored plates show costume of the period and of earlier times including costume worn at a peasant wedding, and the uniforms of the militia from 1660 to 1843
Colas 2428. Lipperheide 876

Profetie dell'abbate Gioachino et di Anselmo, vescovo di Marsico. Joachim, abbot of Fiore

Programma e figure della mascherata dé quattro principali poeti d'Italia. Morghen, Luigi

Progresses, processions, and magnificent festivities, of King James the First, his royal consort, family, and court. Nichols, John

Progressive tailor; a national magazine of authority on merchant tailoring. v 1, 1913+ New York, Tailoring arts pub. co.
Illus. F. $3
Published semi-annually, 1917+ (monthly 1913-14; quarterly 1915-16) Current 1938
Suspended publication, autumn 1932-33

Prokhorov", V. A.
Khrīstīanskīi͡a drevnostī ī arkheologīi͡a. Ezhemi͡esi͡achnyĭ zhurnal". S.-Peterbūrg", tīp. Īmperatorskoĭ akademīī nauk" 1864-76
4v. 324pl.(part col.) Q.
Volume 1 published in 12 parts, v2 in 7 parts. Lipperheide gives contents which includes ecclesiastical and general Russian costume
Lipperheide 1368

Prokhorov", V. A.—*Continued*
Materialy po īstoriī russkīkh odezhd" ī obstanovkī zhīznī narodnoī, izdavaemye po Vysochaīshemu soīzvoleniīu. Sanktpeterburg, tip. Īmperatorskoī akademiī nauk 1881-85
4v. 173 col.pl. Q.
Materials for a history of Russian costume and national customs
Lipperheide 1373

Pusskiīa drevnostī īzdavaemyīa no vysochaīshemu soīzvoleniīu nod" redakts ieīu V. Prokhorova. Sanktpeterburg", tip. Īmperatorskoī akademiī nauk" 1871-76
2v. 112 col.pl. Q.
A history of Russian costume from prehistoric times to the seventeenth century
Lipperheide 1369

Prokop, August
(ed.) Kunstgewerbliches aus der vom Mähr. gewerbe-museum im jahre 1885

[**Promis, Vincenzo**]
Le auguste alleanze fra le case sovrane di Savoia e di Baviera nei secolo XV, XVII, XVIII; documenti e memorie. Torino, V. Bona 1883
356p. 17pl.(1 col.) Q.
Lipperheide 2496m

Promptuarium
Prima pars promptuarii iconum insigniorum a seculo hominum, subiectis eorum vitis, per compendium ex probatissimis autoribus desumptis. Lugduni, G. Rovillium 1553
2v. 831 illus. Q.
Volume 2 has title: Promptuarii iconum pars secunda incipit a Christo nato, perpetuam ducens seriem ad usque. Christianissimū Francorum regem Henricum hoc nomine secundum, hodie feliciter regnantem
Contains 729 portraits in medallions, not all of which are historically accurate. The editions of 1578 and 1581 are enlarged by more portraits
For German translation with additions see D. Keller's *Kunstliche und aigendliche bildtnussen der rhömischen keyseren*
Lipperheide 310

Prônay von Tot-Próna und zu Blathnicza, Gabriel, freiherr
Skizzen aus dem volksleben in Ungarn; mit ... darstellungen von Barabâs Sterio und Weber. Pesth, H. Geibel 1855
106p. 25 col.pl. F.
Colas 2430. Lipperheide 896

Pronti, Domenico
Nuova raccolta rappresentante i costumi religiosi, civili, e militari degli antichi Egiziani, Etruschi, Greci, e Romani, tratti dagli antichi monumenti; disegnata, ed incisa in rame da Domenico Pronti. Roma, presso il Sud° incisore ca1805
1 p.l. 49pl. ob.Q.
Plates are copied from those in Roccheggiani's *Nuova raccolta.* They are described by Colas as mediocre copies
Colas 2431. Lipperheide 113. LC 14-6982

Propert, Walter Archibald
The Russian ballet in western Europe, 1909-1920; with sixty-three illustrations from original drawings. London, J. Lane 1921
xv,131p. front. illus. 52 mounted pl.(part col.) ports. sq.Q.
Shows ballet costumes from designs by Bakst, A. Benois, A. Derain, I. Fedorovski, N. Gontcharova, M. Larionov, Picasso, J. M. Sert, Soudeikine, and others
Colas 2434. LC 22-20707

Prophylactic clothing of the body chiefly in relation to cold. Cleveland, W. F.

Propiac, Catherine Joseph Ferdinand Girard de
Beautés historiques chronologiques politiques et critiques de la ville de Paris, depuis le commencement de la monarchie jusqu'au 1er novembre ... orné ... de 14 vignettes représentant les costumes des Français aux diverses époques de la monarchie. Paris, A. Eymery 1822
2v. col.fronts.(v 1: fold.plan) 13 col.pl. D.
LC 14-15922

Petit tableau de Paris et des français aux principales époques de la monarchie ... avec une notice explicative des vêtemens, coiffures et armures des français depuis Pharamond jusqu'à ce jour; orné d'un joli plan de Paris et de costumes. Paris, A. Eymery 1820
144p. 14 col.pl. D.
Colas 2435

Prospecte der vorzüglichsten gebäude in Berlin. Berlin, G. Weiss ca1811
17pl. ob.F.
Plates show buildings with people in costume and are from drawings by Catel, L. Serrurier and others
Lipperheide 818

Prostitutes
Le Blond, A. W. L., and Lucas, Arthur. Du tatouage chez les prostituées. 1899

Le **prototype** des ames sensibles, ou Les épargnes de la pudeur; almanach nouveau. Paris, Jubert 1789
32p. front. 12pl. O.
Plates show costume of the period
Colas 2437

Provence. See France—By region or province—Provence

Proverbes en action. Compte-Calix, F. C.

Proverbes et bons mots mis en action d'après les moeurs populaires. Pigal, E. J.; Pajou, A. D., and Arago, Jacques

Provinces de France, types et coutumes v2 See Spindler, Charles. Ceux d'Alsace; v7 See Bernoville, Gaëtan. Les pays des Basques

Provinces françaises costumes décoratifs. Gallois, Émile

Provincial Russia. Stewart, Hugh

Prozeclawski, C. See Rembowski, Alexandre. Sources documentaire concernant l'histoire du régiment des chevau-légers de la garde de Napoléon Ier

Prüfer, Theodor
Der todtentanz in der Marien-kirche zu Berlin und geschichte und idee der todtentanze-bilder. Berlin, T. Prüfer 1883
36p. 4 col.pl. Q.
Lipperheide 1968

Prussia. See Germany—Prussia; also subdivision Germany—Prussia under Military costume; Police

Prussia. Kriegsministerium

Deutsche heeres-uniformen auf der weltausstellung in Paris 1900; herausgegeben von dem Königlich preussischen kriegsministerium. Berlin und Leipzig, Giesecke & Devrient [1900]

115p. 83 illus. 10pl. O.

Description and pictures of the uniforms of the German army from 1680 to 1863. French edition has title: *Uniformes de l'armée allemande à l'Exposition universelle de Paris en 1900.* (Berlin, Giesecke & Devrient)

Colas 850. Lipperheide 2143

Geschichte der bekleidung, bewaffnung und ausrüstung des königlich preussischen heeres. Weimar, Putze & Hölzer 1902-06

2v. (278,502p.) col.illus. col.pl. port. F.

Contents: v 1 Die infanterie regimenter im jahre 1806 (1902); v2 Die kürassier und dragoner-regimenter seit anfang des 18. jahrhunderts bis zur reorganisation der armee 1808 (1906)

Colas 1628

Pry, Paul, pseud. See Heath, William

Przezdziecki, Aleksander, and Rastawiecki, Edward, baron

Wzory sztuki średniowiecznej i z epoki odrodzenia po koniec wieku XVII. w dawnej Polsce. Ser. 1-3. W Warszawie i w Paryżu, Druk. J. Unger, 1853-[62]

3v. pl. (part col.) Q.

Polish and French; added title page in French: *Monuments du moyen-âge et de la renaissance, dans l'ancienne Pologne depuis les temps les plus reculés jusqu'à la fin du XVII. siècle* (Varsovie & Paris)

Plates show products of the goldsmiths' art for church and secular use, monuments, paintings and miniatures, church vestments and armor

LC 10-29534

Psalmanazar, George

An historical and geographical description of Formosa ... Giving an account of the religion, customs, manners, &c., of the inhabitants ... 2d ed. cor. London, Printed for M. Wotton [etc.] 1705

28p.l. 288p. front. (fold.map) 17pl. fold. tab. O.

A fabrication. The author's real name is unknown. "Psalmanazar ... wrote in Latin, and the main portion of his manuscript was translated by Mr. Oswald ... What was not due to his own imagination he borrowed from Varenius's 'Descriptio regni Japoniæ et Siam' (Amsterdam, 1649) or Candidius's 'Voyages'." Dictionary of national biography

Lipperheide 1553. LC 5-6687

Das **Psalterium** aureum von Sanct Gallen. Rahn, J. R.

Psautier de Saint Louis. Paris. Bibliothèque nationale. Mss. (Lat. 10525)

Psautier illustré (XIIIe siècle). Paris. Bibliothèque nationale. Mss. (Lat. 8846)

Psicologia de la moda femenina. Gómez Carrillo, Enrique

Psyché, journal des modes, littérature, théâtres et musique. 1.-19. année; 12 juin, 1834-1854. Paris

19v. col.pl. O.

Title change: 12 juin 1834-12 fev. 1835, *La toilette de psyche, journal de modes, sciences, littérature et beaux-arts.* Subtitle change v2, 1835 *littérature, théâtre et beaux-arts*

Colas 2887-88. Lipperheide 4626

Psychological analysis of fashion motivation. Barr, E. De Y.

Psychologie de la mode. See Gómez Carrillo, Enrique. Psicologia de la moda femenina

Psychologie der mode. Wechsler, Alfred

Psychology of clothes. Flügel, J. C.

Psychology of clothing. Dearborn, G. Van N.

Psychology of dress

Barr, E. De Y. A psychological analysis of fashion motivation. 1934

Bousfield, Paul. Sex and civilization. 1925

Burton, Robert. The anatomy of melancholy. 1864-65

Carlyle, Thomas. Sartor Resartus: The life and opinions of Herr Teufelsdröckh. 1897

Dearborn, G. Van N. The psychology of clothing. c1918

Flügel, J. C. The psychology of clothes. 1930

Frazer, Sir J. G. Adonis, Attis, Osiris. 1906

Frazer, Sir J. G. The golden bough. 1935

Gilbert, O. P. Men in women's guise. 1926

Gómez Carrillo, Enrique. Psicologia de la moda femenina. 1907

Hirn, Yrjö. The origins of art. 1900

Hurlock, E. B. The psychology of dress; an analysis of fashion and its motive. c1929

Lewis, Dio. Curious fashions. 1883

Schurtz, Heinrich. Grundzüge einer philosophie der tracht. 1891

Thomas, W. I. Sex and society. 1907

Veblen, Thorstein. The theory of the leisure class. 1912

Wechsler, Alfred. Psychologie der mode. 1904

Westermarck, E. A. The history of human marriage. 1921

See also Philosophy of dress

Psychology of dress. Hurlock, E. B.

Psychology of dress. See Parsons, F. A. The art of dress

Public health service

United States

United States. Public health service. Regulations governing the uniforms of officers and employees of the United States Public health service. 1914

Puche, Claudius Ciappori-. See Ciappori-Puche, Claudius

Puckle, Bertram S.

Funeral customs; their origin and development. London, T. W. Laurie 1926

283p. front. illus. pl. (incl.facsims.) O.

LC 27-6498

Pudor, Heinrich

Die frauenreform-kleidung; ein beitrag zur philosophie, hygiene und aesthetik des kleides. Leipzig, H. Seemann 1903

58p. 58 illus. O.

Lipperheide 3319

Pueblo Indians. See Indians of North America—Pueblo Indians

Puerto Rico

Browne, G. W. The new America and the Far East. 1907 v 11-12

Olivares, José de. Our islands and their people. 1899-1900

Pufendorf, Samuel, freiherr von

Samuelis liberi baronis de Pufendorf De rebus a Carolo Gustavo Sveciæ rege gestis ... Norimbergæ, sumptibus C. Riegelii 1696

626,53,11p. illus. pl. ports. maps. plans. F.

Plates show battles, festivals, portraits of nobles and military commanders during the reign of Charles x of Sweden. Contains also thirteen plates of the funeral ceremony of this king, engraved by E. J. Dahlbergh, separately issued under the title: *Exequiae ... Caroli Gustavi Suecorum Gothorum et Wandalorum regis ... Holmiae celebratae*

Translated into German and French in 1697. Re-issued in Latin in 1729

Lipperheide 558 (1729 ed.) LC 13-13902

Pugillus facetiarum iconographicarū. Heyden, Jacob van der

Pugin, Augustus Charles

(illus.) Combe, William. History of the University of Cambridge

(illus.) Combe, William. History of the University of Oxford

Pugin, Augustus Welby Northmore

Glossary of ecclesiastical ornament and costume; 3d ed. enl. and rev. by Bernard Smith. London, B. Quaritch 1868

xvi,245p. 73(i.e. 74) col.pl. F. 126s, o.p.

First edition (London, H. G. Bohn 1844) Second ed. enl. and rev. by B. Smith (H. G. Bohn 1846)

The origin, history and significance of the various emblems, devices and colors used in the Christian churches during the middle ages, and especially the decoration of the vestments and altar furniture used in the Church of England

Colas 2439-2441. Costume index. Lipperheide 1823. LC 12-14934 (2 ed.)

Puiggari, José

Estudios de indumentario española concreta y comparada ... cuadro histórico especial de los siglos XIII y XIV. Barcelona, J. Jepús y Rovinralta 1890

380p. 46pl. O.

"Estado político-social, estética y artes, costumbres, lujo, modas, técnica y análisis de trajes y armas en sus diferentes variedades." Subtitle

Plates show costumes of the middle ages, taken from tombs and paintings. Published under the auspices of L'association artistico-arqueologica, Barcelona

Colas 2443. Lipperheide 1238e

Monografía histórica é iconográfica del traje. Barcelona, J. y A. Bastinos 1886

288p. 618 illus. Q.

Consists of four sections ("épocas") each of which is preceded by a half-title not included in the paging

Colas 2442. LC 33-16908

Puis, Auguste

En marge de l'histoire, 1re série: essai sur les moeurs, les goûts et les modes au XVIIIe siècle. Paris & Toulouse, E. Champion 1914

178p. col.front. 4pl. O. 4fr.

"Les voyages, les villégiatures, la vie de château, la chasse, les turqueries, l'anglomanie, les chinoiseries et l'orientalisme, les modes américaines." Subtitle

Colas 2444

Pulcinella. Dieterich, Albrecht

Pulszky, Károly

Ornamente der hausindustrie Ungarns. Text von Carl v. Pulszky; gezeichnet von Friedrich Fischbach. Budapest, Gedruckt in der Kön. Ung. universitätsbuchdruckerei 1878

8p. 34 l. 40 col.pl. F.

Explanation of plates in Hungarian, German, French

Lipperheide 3959

Punishments in the olden time. Andrews, William

Punishments of China. Mason, G. H.

Les **punitions** des Chinois. See Mason, G. H. The punishments of China

Punt, Jan

(engr.) Swart, P. de. Afbeelding van de zaal en 't praalbed waar op het lyk van ... Willem Karel Hendrik Friso, prinse van Orange en Nassau

(engr.) Cuyck, Pieter van, the younger. Lykstaetsie van ... Willem Carel Hendrik Friso, prince van Orange en Nassau

Pupillorum patrocinium. Damhouder, Joost

Puppen und puppenspiele. Boehn, Max von

Das **puppenbuch.** Berlin, E. Reiss 1921

19 l. 33 mounted pl. sq.D.

Contents: Schickele, R. Puppen; Edschmid, K. Zu puppen der Erna Pinner; Daeubler, T. Die puppen der Lotte Pritzel; Mierendorff, C. Der mensch ent "puppt" sich

Puppets

Boehn, Max von. Dolls and puppets. 1932

Boehn, Max von. Puppen und puppenspiele. 1909

Fleury, Jules. Le musée secret de la caricature. 1888

Maindron, Ernest. Marionnettes et guignols, les poupées agissantes et parlantes à travers les âges. 1900

Mills, Mrs W. H., and Dunn, Mrs L. M. Marionettes, masks and shadows. 1927

Petite, J. M. Guignols et marionnettes; leur histoire. 1911

Das puppenbuch. 1921

Rehm, H. S. Das buch der marionetten 1905

Pu-Qúa

(illus.) Corti, E. C. Chinesisches bilderbuch

(illus.) Grohmann, J. G. Gebräuche und kleidungen der Chinesen

(illus.) Mason, G. H. The costume of China

[**Purchas, John**]

The directorium Anglicanum; being a manual of directions for the right celebration of the Holy Communion, for the saying of matins and evensong, and for the performance of other rites and

Purchas, John—*Continued*
ceremonies of the Church; according to ancient uses of the Church of England ... 4th ed. edited by F. G. Lee. London, J. Hogg 1879
lxiv,379p. front. pl. O.
Preface signed: J. P. Glossary: p358-69
Third edition (London, T. Bosworth 1866)
LC 31-9974 (3d. ed.)

Purdom, Charles Benjamin
(ed.) Shakespeare, William. The Swan Shakespeare, a player's edition. 1930

Purdy, D. W.
Tattooing; how to tattoo, what to use. London, D. W. Purdy [1896]
16p. S.

The **Puritan.** v. 1-9; Jan. 1897-March, 1901. New York, F. A. Munsey
9v. in 7. illus. O.-F.
Published monthly
Absorbed *Godey's magazine,* Oct. 1898. Merged into the *Junior Munsey,* April, 1901
LC 1-27154

Puschner, Johann Georg
(illus.) Lambranzi, Gregorio. New and curious school of theatrical dancing
(illus.) Lambranzi, Gregorio. Nuova e curiosa scuola de' balli theatrali

Pusskiia drevnosti izdavaemyia no vysochaishemu soizvoleniiu nod" redaktsieiu V. Prokhorova. Prokhorov", V. A.

Der **putz-tisch.** See Technische modenzeitung für damen, damenkleidermacher

Puyo, C.
Costumes d'atelier. [London, Maisenbach 191-?
16 l. front. illus. O.
Illustrations by Bergon, Demachy, Lebègue, Puyo
Colas 2446

Pygmies

Africa

Schebesta, Paul. Revisiting my pygmy hosts. 1936

Schebesta, Paul. Der Urwald ruft wieder. 1936

New Guinea, Dutch

Rawling, C. G. The land of the New Guinea pygmies. 1913

Pyle, Howard
(illus.) Howard Pyle's book of the American spirit; the romance of American history, pictured by Howard Pyle, comp. by Merle Johnson, with narrative descriptive text from original sources, edited by Francis J. Dowd. New York & London, Harper 1923
xiii,344p. col.front. illus. col.pl. F.
Contents: Coming of the English and the Dutch; The French come upon the scene; The nation
Contains scenes from American history which show costume, for the most part masculine, from the sixteenth century to the close of the civil war. The illustrations are from paintings by Pyle and were originally published in *Harper's magazine* or in books. The narrative makes it possible to know exactly the period depicted
LC 23-14398

Pyne, William Henry
The costume of Great Britain. Designed, engraved, and written by W. H. Pyne. London, William Miller 1808
[120]p. 60 col.pl. F. 180s, o.p.
First published 1804
"Sixty-five colored plates beautifully done in fac-simile of the original drawings, depicting the manners and customs, trades, industries, etc., including pottery, leather dressing, yeoman of the king's guard, half penny showman, milk woman, baker, roundabout bill sticker, lord mayor, water cart, knife grinder, dragoon, country fair, knight of the garter, etc., with descriptive text."
Colas 2447-48. Lipp. 985. LC A30-1332

Etchings of rustic figures, for the embellishment of landscape. London, R. Ackermann 1815
8p. 60pl. O.
Plates show men and women of the laboring and farmer classes of rural England
The copy at New York public library is (London, Nattali [1814-19])
Lipperheide 989. LC 1-13755

The history of the colleges of Winchester, Eton, and Westminster. See entry under Ackermann, Rudolph

The history of the royal residences of Windsor castle, St. James's palace, Carlton house, Kensington palace, Hampton Court, Buckingham house, and Frogmore. London, Printed for A. Dry 1819
3v. 100 col.pl. (incl.front.) F.
"Illustrated by one hundred highly finished and coloured engravings, fac-similes of original drawings by the most eminent artists." Subtitle
The drawings were supplied by Mackenzie, Nash, Pugin, Stephanoff, and others. Plates show servants of the royal households
Contents: v 1 Windsor castle. Frogmore; v2 Hampton Court. Buckingham house. Kensington; v3 St. James. Carlton house
Lipperheide 993. LC 3-6219

Microcosm; or, A picturesque delineation of the arts, agriculture, manufactures &c. of Great Britain ... Drawn from nature by W. H. Pyne, and aquatinted by J. Hill [with] explanations ... by C. Gray. London, W. Miller 1808
2v. in 1. 121pl. Q.
Plates show the tools and processes of various occupations and men engaged in the work

(ed.) World in miniature. See entries under Shoberl, Frederic, ed.

Pyrenees
Arco, Ricardo del. Costumbres y trajes en los Pirineos. 1930

Dartiguenave, Alfred. Costumes des Pyrénées. ca1860

Gavarni, G. S. C. Montagnards des Pyrénées, françaises et espagnoles; Montañeses de la Frontera de Francia

Gorse, P. Costumes de la région pyrénéenne française et espagnole. 18--

Gorse, P. Souvenirs des Pyrénées. 1843

Johnson, John. The costumes of the French Pyrenees. 1832

Lagarrigue. Nouvelle suite de costumes des Pyrénées. 1841

Le Bondidier, Louis. Les vieux costumes pyrénéens. 1917

Pyrenees—*Continued*
Maurice, C. Un mois dans les Pyrénées. ca1850
La Novempopulanie, croquis et souvenirs des Pyrénées. 1834
Petit, Victor. Souvenirs des Pyrénées; vues prises aux environs des eaux thermales de bagnères de Bigorre, bagnères de Luchon, Cauteretz, Saínt Sauveur, Barèges, les Eaux bonnes, les Eaux chaudes & Pau. 186-?
Pingret, Edouard. Costumes des Pyrenées. 1834

Pythias, Knights of
Lilley, M. C., & co., Columbus, O. Illustrated catalogue and price list. 1899

La **pythonisse** de Lutèce, ou Les secrets découverts; almanach orné de figures. Paris, Joubert 1789
1 l. front. 12 illus. T.
Colas 2450

Q

Quadrille de Marie Stuart. Lami, E. L.

Quadrilles du carnaval à Berlin 1836. Berlin, A. Asher [1836]
1 l. 20 col.pl. F.
Lipperheide 2542

Quadrilles parées et costumées exécutées à la cour de sa majesté le roi de Bavière le 3 février 1835. Fries, and Nachtmann

Quaestiones de re vestiaria Graecorum. Boehlau, Johannes

Quaestiones vestiariae. Mueller, Walther

Quaglio, Lorenz
Studien nach der natur zur staffage von landschaften. München, 1812-20
12pl. Q.
Plates show costume of Upper Bavaria and are signed by the artist. Lipperheide lists eleven other plates, unsigned, similar in format and subject
Colas 2451. Lipperheide 754

The **Quaker**; a study in costume. Gummere, Mrs A. M.

Quakers. See Friends, Society of

Quarré de Verneuil, Alexandre Henri Raoul
Le costume militaire en France et les premiers uniformes; étude historique. Paris, J. Dumaine 1876
36p. O. 75c
From the *Journal des sciences militaires,* December 1876
Colas 2452

Le **quart** d'heure des jolies Françaises; etrennes aux Dames. Paris, Desnos [1782]
136p. 12pl. T.
According to Colas this almanac was republished under various titles: *Les jolies Françaises, leurs coiffures et habillemens* (1782); *Le passe-temps des jolis Françaises* (1786); *La journée d'une jolie femme* (1787)
Colas 2453-56

Quast, Pieter Jansz
Costumes d'hommes et de femmes ... gravés par Savery. Amsterdam, C. de Jonghe ca1630
12pl. O.
Colas 2457

'T is al verwart-gaaren, of afbeeldingen van vermomde redelaaren, en andere gespuis. Amsterdam, C. J. Visscher 1640
1 l. 26pl. Q.
Colas 2458. Lipperheide 1952

Les **quatre** derniers siècles. Havard, Henry

Les **quatre** éléments, portraits de femmes. Grévedon, P. L. H.

Les **quatre** nieces [et des autres, danses] Paris, n.d.
19pts. O.
This is a collection of dances by various French dance masters
Lipperheide 3081

Les **quatre** parties du monde, portraits de femme. Grévedon, P. L. H.

Quatrebarbes, Théodore, comte de
(ed.) René I, d'Anjou, king of Naples and Jerusalem. Oeuvres complètes du roi René

Quebec tercentenary commemorative history. Carrel, Frank, and Feiczewicz, Louis

The **Queen.** See note under The Queen, the Lady's newspaper

The **queen** lace book: a historical and descriptive account of the hand-made antique laces of all countries. Part I: Mediaeval lacework and point lace. London, The Queen office 1874
38p. 14 illus. 13pl. Q.
Lipperheide 4034

Queen Mary's psalter. British Museum. Department of manuscripts

Queen Matilda's tapestry. See Bayeux tapisserie de la Reine Mathilde

The **Queen,** the Lady's newspaper. v 1+ Jan. 2, 1847+ London
Illus. F.
Published weekly. Current 1938. Various issues 1931+ contain children's supplements
Title varies: v 1-33 (no 1-861), 1847-June 1863, *Lady's newspaper;* v34 (no862-87), July-Dec. 1863 *Lady's newspaper, the queen and court chronicle*
Absorbed *Pictorial times* Jan 15, 1848; absorbed *The Queen* Jan. 1864
Lipperheide 4656

Queen Victoria's dolls. Low, F. H.

Queens. See Kings and rulers

Queens and empresses
Grévedon, P. L. H. Impératrices et reines. 184-?
Rubens, Sir P. P. La Gallerie du Palais du Luxembourg. 1710
Vico, Enea. Le imagini delle Donne Augustèe intagliate in istampa di rame ... libro primo. 1557

Egypt, Ancient

Kings and queens of ancient Egypt. 1926

Russia

Zabi͡elin, Ī. E. Domashniĭ byt' russkīkh" tsari͡ts" v" XVI ī XVII st. 1901

The **queens** of American society. Ellett, Mrs E. F. L.

Queer things about Persia. Lorey, Eustache de, and Sladen, D. B.

Quellen zur geschichte der feuerwaffen. Essenwein, A. O.

Quénard, P. See Bonneville, François, jt. auth.

Quennell, Charles Henry Bourne. See Quennell, Mrs M. C., jt. auth.

Quennell, Mrs Marjorie (Courtney), and Quennell, Charles Henry Bourne

Everyday life in Anglo-Saxon, viking, and Norman times. New York, G. P. Putnam; London, B. T. Batsford 1927
xvi,216p. col.front. pl.(1 col.) fold.tab. O. (The everyday life series) $2.50, 5s
Shows costume of Anglo-Saxon England
Short list of authorities: p vii
Costume index. LC 27-10938

Everyday life in Homeric Greece. New York, G. P. Putnam; London, B. T. Batsford 1930
xviii,194p. col.front. pl. maps, plans. O. (The everyday life series) $2.50
London edition has title: *Everyday things in Homeric Greece*
Recommended books: p xi-xii
Costume index. LC 30-10167

Everyday life in Roman Britain. New York, G. P. Putnam; London, B. T. Batsford 1925
xxii,225p. col.front. pl.(part col.) fold. map, fold.tab. O. (The everyday life series) $2.50, 5s
Short list of authorities: p xiii-xiv
Costume index. LC 26-6283

Everyday life in the new stone, bronze & early iron ages. New York, G. P. Putnam; London, B. T. Batsford 1923
xxiii,237p. incl.col.front. pl. fold.map, fold.tab. O. (The everyday life series) $2.50, 5s
Published subsequently as part 2 of the author's *Everyday life in prehistoric times*
Short list of authorities: p xv-xvi
Costume index. LC 23-6388

Everyday things in archaic Greece. London, B. T. Batsford; New York, G. P. Putnam [1931]
145p. col.front. illus. pl. O. 7s 6d, $2.50
Recommended books: p viii
Costume index. LC 31-20210

A history of everyday things in England, 1066-1935. New York, C. Scribner; London, B. T. Batsford [1922-35]
4v. in 3. col.fronts. illus. pl.(part col. part double) fold.tab. O. $10, ea. 8s 6d
Costume index. LC 26-7074

Quennell, Peter

Victorian panorama; a survey of life & fashion from contemporary photographs, with a commentary. New York, C. Scribner's 1937
120p. front. pl. ports. O.
The photographs show various kinds of English costume including some theatrical costume and uniforms from the 1840's to the end of the nineteenth century

Quentel, Peter

Musterbuch für ornamente und stickmuster ... (1527-1529); 265 vorlagen für kunsthandwerker und weibliche handarbeiten hrsg. vom Leipziger kunst-gewerbe-museum. Leipzig, E. Schloemp [1880]
1 l. 93pl. Q.
Facsimile reprint of the edition of 1529 and a part of the edition of 1527
Lipperheide 3877

Quentin, Henri. See Almeras, Henri d', jt. auth.

Quer durch Borneo. Nieuwenhuis, A. W

Quesnoy, Ferdinand

La guerre à toutes les époques. Paris, Laurens 1892
309p. 128 illus. O. 3fr. 50 (Bibliothèque d'histoire et d'art)

Quest of the Romanoff treasure. Hammer, Armand

Qu'est-ce que la mode? Mustoxidi, T. M.

Quicherat, Jules Étienne Joseph

Histoire du costume en France depuis les temps les plus reculés jusqu'à la fin du XVIIIe siècle. Paris, Hachette 1875
680p. 481 illus. Q.
Engraved by Chevignard, Pauquet and P. Sellier. Second edition: 1877
Colas 2459. Costume index (2d ed.) Lipperheide 1095. LC 3-12682

Quigley, Dorothy

What dress makes of us; illustrations by Annie Blakeslee. New York, E. P. Dutton 1897
xv,133p. illus. D.
Includes articles contributed to the New York Sun, and the New York Journal
LC 11-22640

Quillenbois, pseud. See Sarcus, Ch. M. de

Quincke, Wolfgang

Handbuch der kostümkunde; 3.verb. und verm. aufl. Leipzig, J. J. Weber 1908
x,255p. illus. O.
First edition: *Katechismus der kostümkunde* (Leipzig, J. J. Weber 1889. 270p.)
Shows costume of all periods
Bibliography: p vii-viii
Colas 2460 (1st ed.) Costume index. Lipperheide 94 (1st ed.)

Quinlan, Elizabeth. See Latzke, Alpha, jt. auth.

Quippes for upstart newfangled gentlewomen. See Gosson, Stephen. Pleasant quippes for upstart newfangled gentlewomen

Quiroga, Adán

Calchaqui; con ilustraciones de F. Gonzales. Tucuman, Imp. Española 1897
492,xxiv p. illus. O. 10 pesos

R

R., G. D. See Ridder, G. de

Raa, F. J. G. ten

De uniformen van de nederlandsche zee- en landmacht hier te lande en in de kolonien; naar aquarellen of teekeningen van J. Hoynck van Papendrecht, W. C. Staring, en J. P. de Veer. Met tekst van F. J. G. ten Raa. 's Gravenhage, Gebr. van Cleef 1900
2v. 80 col.pl. F.
Plates show uniforms of the Dutch army and navy, 1795 to 1900

Raaslöff, Waldemar Rudolph von

Rückblick auf die militairischen und politischen verhältnisse der Algérie in den jahren 1840 und 1841, nebst einer geschichtlichen einleitung. Altona, J. F. Hammerich 1845
xvi,452p. 7 col.pl. O.
Plates show uniforms of the French colonial army of native African troops and are after Raffet
Colas 2461. LC 5-3626

Rab, Georg. See Han, Weygand, jt. auth.

Raban, Louis François. See Méry, J. P. A. Les parures

Rabat und chorrock. Clauss, J. M. B.

Rabe, Edmund

Uniformen des preussischen heeres in ihren hauptveränderungen bis auf die gegenwart. Berlin, L. Sachse 1850
1 l. 18 col.pl. F.
Twelve of the plates were published first in 1847. Plates show 165 types of uniforms of the Prussian army from 1700 to 1850
Colas 2462. Lipperheide 2176

Rabe, Edmund, and Burger, Ludwig

Die brandenburg-preussische armee in historischer darstellung; ihre uniformierung und bewaffnung vom grossen kurfürsten bis auf Kaiser Wilhelm. Berlin, H. J. Meidinger [1884-85]
1 l. 20 col.pl. F.
New edition of Rabe's *Uniformen des preussischen heeres* with two new plates by Burger which show changes in the uniforms of the cavalry and infantry from 1850 to 1884
Colas 2463. Lipperheide 2177

Rabel, Daniel

Voici comment l'on s'accomode. Paris, LeBlond ca1630
1 p.l. 11pl. Q.
A collection of costumes of the time of Louis XIII, published without a title page. The preliminary leaf contains ten lines beginning with the title as used above and continuing: Tant à la ville qu'à la court, Les mignonnes du temps qui court, N'ont d'autre soin qu'être a la mode
Colas 2464

Rabelli, Giacomo Carlo, pseud. See Bar, Jacques Charles

Raccolta de' costumi di Roma e suoi contorni. Pinelli, Bartolommeo

Raccolta de' fatti li più interessanti eseguiti dal Capo Brigante Massaroni. Pinelli, Bartolommeo

Raccolta de' monumenti più interessanti del Museo borbonico. See Naples. Museo nazionale. Collection of the most remarkable monuments of the National museum

Raccolta de' monumenti più interessanti del Museo borbonico e di varie collezioni private. See Naples. Museo nazionale. Recueil des monumens les plus intéressans du Musée national

Raccolta degli ordini religiosi che esistono nella città di Roma. Capparoni, Giuseppe

Raccolta degli ordini religiosi delle vergini a Dio dedicate. Capparoni, Giuseppe

Raccolta dei principali costumi religio e militari, della Corte Pontificia. Marroni, Salvatore

Raccolta dei riti, e ceremonie religiose di tutti i popoli del mondo. Novelli

Raccolta della disposizioni sulla divisa degli ufficiali. Italy. Ministero della guerra

Raccolta della gerarchia ecclesiastica considerata nelle vesti sagre, e civili usate da quelli li quali la compongono. Capparoni, Giuseppe

Raccolta delle diverse vestiture delle provincie del regno di Napoli. Napoli, Cuciniello & Bianchi n.d.
ca 100 col.pl. O.
Colas 2466

Raccolta di cento costumi antichi ricavati dai monumenti, e dagli autori antichi. Pinelli, Bartolommeo

Raccolta di cento tavole rappresentanti i costumi religiosi civili, e militari degli antichi Egiziani, Etruschi, Greci, e Romani. Roccheggiani, Lorenzo

Raccolta di 126 stampe, che rappresentano figure. Viero, Teodoro

Raccolta di cinquanta costumi di Roma e sue vicinanze. Pinelli, Bartolommeo

Raccolta di 50 costumi li più interessanti delle cittá' terre e paesi in provincie diverse del Regno di Napoli. Pinelli, Bartolommeo

Raccolta di cinquanta costumi pittoreschi. Pinelli, Bartolommeo

Raccolta di costumi antichi, disegnati da ... Pinelli, incisi ... da A. M. See Pinelli, Bartolommeo. Raccolta di cento costumi antichi

Raccolta di costumi antichi e moderni. Firenze, P. Smorti ca1880
1 l. 20 col.pl. D.
Published in two parts (livraisons) only. They show Italian peasant costume in 19th century
Colas 2467. Lipperheide 1286

Raccolta di costumi degl' ordini religiosi. Pinelli, Bartolommeo

Raccolta di costumi dello Stato Pontificio. Busuttil, Salvatore

Raccolta di costumi dello Stato Romano. Busuttil, Salvatore

Raccolta di costumi di Napoli. Samaritani, G. L. da

Raccolta di costumi di provincie diverse. Dura, Gaetano

Raccolta di costumi di Roma e vicinanze. Antonioli, Giovanni

Raccolta di costumi italiani i più interessanti. Pinelli, Bartolommeo

Raccolta di costumi religiosi e civile della corte pontificia. Busuttil, Salvatore

Raccolta di N. costumi di Roma e dei contorni. Cottafavi, Gaetano

Raccolta di quaranta proverbi toscani espressi in figure. Piattoli, Giuseppi

Raccolta di quattordici motivi di costumi pittoreschi di Roma. Pinelli, Bartolommeo

Raccolta di quindici costumi li piu interessanti della Svizzera. Pinelli, Bartolommeo

Raccolta di scene carnevalesche di Roma. [Roma] D. Mucci [18—]
9pl. ob.D.

Raccolta di sessanta piu belle vestiture. Busuttil, Salvatore

Raccolta di sessante tavole. See note under Roccheggiani, Lorenzo. Nuova raccolta

Raccolta di stampe che rappresentano figure ed abiti di varie nazioni. See A collection of the dresses of different nations

Raccolta di 30 costumi con altretante vedute le più interessanti della cittá di Milano disegnati ed incisi da diversi; Biasioli terminó all' acqta. Milano, Presso li fratelli Bettalli [ca1820]
30 l. 30 col.pl. O.
Pictures show street venders of Milan, small tradesmen, artisans and workmen
Lipperheide 1293. LC CA11-1779

Raccolta di varie composizioni ed alcuni motivi di costumi pittoreschi di Roma e delle sue vicinanze. Roma, T. Cuccioni 1850?
1 p.l. 49pl. sq.Q.
LC 11-2544

Raccolta di varie vestiture ... del regno di Napoli. See Busuttil, Salvatore. Raccolta di sessanta piu belle vestiture

Raccolta di varii vestimenti ed arti del regno di Napoli. Fabris, Pietro

Raccolta di varij balli fatti in occorenze di nozze, e festini. See Caroso, M. F. Nobiltà di dame

Raccolta di XXIV caricature. Ghezzi, P. L.

Les **races** et les peuples de la terre. Deniker, Joseph

Les **races** humaines. Figuier, Louis

Racial groups and figures in the natural history building of the United States National museum. Hough, Walter

Racine, Jean Baptiste
Plays. See Theatrical costume—Special plays, ballets, etc.—Racine, J. B.

Racinet, Albert Charles Auguste
Le costume historique. Paris, Firmin-Didot 1888
6v. 500 col.pl. tables. sq.O.
"Types principaux du vêtement et de la parure, rapprochés de ceux de l'intérieur de l'habitation dans tous les temps et chez tous les peuples, avec de nombreux détails sur le mobilier, les armes, les objets usuels, les moyens de transport, etc... avec des notices explicatives, une introduction générale, des tables en un glossaire." Subtitle
Volume 1 is mainly explanatory text with an "Introduction générale" by the author dated "Juin 1887". V2-6, each with half-title only, are mainly plates accompanied by descriptive text and were published in 20 "livraisons", 1877-1886. Plates are arranged as follows: L'antiquité classique, pl 1-59; Le monde en dehors de l'Europe, pl 60-180; Les peuples chrétiens à partir des Byzantins, pl 181-410; L'Europe des temps modernes par nationalités distinctes, pl 411-500
The edition described above is known as the small or "petite" edition. The same text and plates were published at the same time in a larger edition, folio size, usually described as the "grande édition". The only difference is in the size of the page and the color of the paper. Plates are printed from the same lithograph plates, but in the "grande édition" they are on tinted paper
"Bibliographie du costume" by Ernest Vinet: v 1 p[141]-65
"Glossaire": v 1 p[169]-246
Colas 2471-2472. Costume index. Lipperheide 93 (grande éd.) LC 2-824

(ed.) L'ornement polychrome ... contenant environ 2,000 motifs de tous les styles, art ancien et asiatique, moyen âge, renaissance, XVIIe et XVIIIe siècle; recueil historique et pratique ... avec des notices explicatives et une introduction générale. Paris, Firmin Didot [1869-73]
60p 103 l. 100 col.pl. F.
Issued in 10 parts
LC 10-19455

Raczyński, Edward, hrabia
Dziennik podróży do Turcyi odbytey w roku MDCCCXIV. Przez Edwarda Raczyńiskiego. W Wrocławiu, Drukiem Grassa, Bartha i kompanii 1821
204p. illus. 82pl. on 65 l. F.
Plates no20 and 45 not published; no28 repeated
LC 5-7252

Radau, Rodolphe
Les vêtements et les habitations dans leurs rapports avec l'atmosphère. Paris, Gauthier-Villars 1884
92p. D. 1 fr. 75

Radier, Jean François Dreux du. See Dreux du Radier, J. F.

Radisics, E. de. See Czobor, Bela. Les insignes royaux de Hongrie

Rätische trachtenbilder. Calvenfeier, Zürich. Organisations-comité

Raffet, Denis Auguste Marie
Collection de costumes militaires. Paris, Frérot [1825-26]
15 col.pl. Q.
Plates marked: Lith. de Villain
Colas 2473

Collection des costumes militaires de l'armée, de la marine et de la garde nationale françaises depuis août 1830. Paris, Frérot [etc.] 1833
6p. 32 col.pl. Q.
Each plate has title: *Uniformes français* and is labelled with the name of the regiment depicted. Nineteen of the plates were published in previous collections by Raffet and have slight revisions here. A longer text was planned but never published
Colas 2476

Costumes militaires français & étrangers, portraits et sujets divers. Paris, Lecomte 1860
1 l. 26pl. F.
Colas 2477

Garde royale, 1828. Paris, Frérot-Rigny 1828?
19 col.pl. Q.
Colas 2475

Uniformes des troupes de ligne, 1829-1830. Paris, Frérot-Rigny 1830?
15 col.pl. F.
Colas 2474

(illus.) Fieffé, Eugène. Napoléon Ier et la Garde imperiale

(illus.) Norvins, J. M. de, baron de Montbreton. Histoire de Napoléon

See also Cogniet, Léon, jt. auth.

Raffles, Sir Thomas Stamford
Antiquarian, architectural, and landscape illustrations of the history of Java. London, Bohn 1844
92pl.(part col. part fold.) fold.map. F.
First published by Black, Parbury and Allen 1817
French translation *Description géographique, historique et commerciale de Java et des autres îles de l'Archipel indien,* by Raffles et John Crawfurd; tr. de l'anglais par Marchal. (Bruxelles, H. Tarlier [etc.] 1824. xix,364p. 48pl.[col.] fold.maps Q.)

Rage-Brocard, Madeleine
Rites de mariage; la deductio in domum mariti. Paris, Les éditions Domat-Montchrestien 1934
142p. pl. O.
"Bibliographie": p[129]-34
On marriage customs in ancient Rome
LC 34-34089

Ragguaglio delle nozze delle maestà di Filippo quinto, e di Elisabetta Farnese ... celebrate in Parma l'anno 1714. Parma, Stamperia di S. A. S. 1717
115p. 5pl. F.
Lipperheide 2755

Ragguaglio delle solenni esequie fatte celebrare in Roma nella Basilica di S. Clemente alla sacra real maestà di Federigo Augusto e di Polonia. Roma, G. M. Salvioni 1733
xxxv p. 14 illus. 14pl. F.
Lipperheide 2756

Ragione di adoprar sicuramente l'arme si da offesa, come da difesa. Grassi, Giacomo di

Rahn, Johann Rudolf
Geschichte der bildenden künste in der Schweiz von den ältesten zeiten bis zum schlusse des mittelalters. Zürich, H. Staub 1876
xxvii,821p. illus. 11 fold.pl.(incl.plan) O.
Illustrations show costume of the Middle ages and many Biblical characters
LC 12-33734

Katalog der ... kunst-sammlung der herren C. und P. N. Vincent Konstanz am Bodensee. Köln, M. DuMont-Schauberg 1891
xxiii,133p. 30pl.(2 col.) Q.
Contains reproductions of Swiss paintings on glass, of 14th to 17th century origin. They show dress of the middle ages
Lipperheide 344

Das Psalterium aureum von Sanct Gallen; ein beitrag zur geschichte der karolingischen miniaturmalerei. St. Gallen, Zollikofer 1878
67p. 31 illus. 18pl.(11 col.) F.
The Psalter was written during the second half of the ninth century and illustrations show costume of this period
Lipperheide 364

Raimondi, Eugenio
Delle caccie. Napoli, L. Scoriggo [1626]
27 l. 635p. 21 illus. Q.
Lipperheide 3022

Raisson, Horace Napoléon
Code de la toilette; 3. éd. rev. et augm. Paris, J. P. Roret 1828
275p. S.
"Manuel complet d'élégance et d'hygiène, contenant les lois, règles, applications et exemples, de l'art de soigner sa personne, et de s'habiller avec goût et méthode." Subtitle
Published anonymously
Colas 2478. Lipperheide 3259

Histoire populaire de la garde nationale de Paris, juillet 1789-juin 1832 ... ornée ... d'après M. Eugène Lami. Paris, Knecht & Roissy 1832
xi,239p. 14pl. O.
Colas 2479

Raleigh, Sir Walter Alexander. See note under Shakespeare's England

Ram, Johannis de
Costumes de divers nations du monde. No place, 1690?
48 unnumbered pl. ob.Q.
Most of the plates are signed J. de Ram. A list is given in Colas
Another printing without Ram's signature, has on each plate "Cum privilegio ordinum Hollandiae et West Frisiae." According to Colas the Cabinet des estampes, Paris, catalogs this collection under title *Costumes des quatres parties du monde gravés dans la manière de Luycken*
Colas 2480

Rambles in Brittany. Mansfield, M. F.

Rambles in Ireland. Lynd, Robert

Rambles in Spain. Fitz-Gerald, J. D.

Rambles of an archaeologist among old books in old places. Fairholt, F. W.

Rambosson, Jean Pierre
Les harmonies du son et l'histoire des instruments de musique. Paris, Firmin-Didot 1878
582p. 233 illus. 5 col.pl. O.
Plates show musical instruments and musicians
Lipperheide 2001

Les pierres précieuses et les principaux ornements. Ouvrage illustré de 43 planches dessinées par Yan' Dargent et d'une planche chromolithographique. Paris, F. Didot 1870
298p. illus. pl. col.front. O.
Illustrations show miners in diamond and opal mines, etc. and pearl-divers
LC 30-33865

Ramelli, Agostino
Le diverse et artificiose machine. Parigi, Autore 1588
15,338 l. 195 illus. F.
Text in Italian and French. Plates show machines and the workmen who tend them
A German edition was published: *Schatzkammer mechanischer künste* (1620)
Lipperheide 1969

Ramhoffsky, Johann Heinrich
Drey beschreibungen, erstens: des königlichen einzugs, welchen ... Maria Theresia, zu Hungarn und Böheim königin ... in dero königliche drey Prager-städte gehalten; andertens: der erb-huldigung, welche ... die gesammte ... stände des königreichs Böheim ... abgeleget; drittens ... ihro ... majestät königlich-böhmischen crönung. Prag, C. F. Rosenmüller [1743]
21,12,70p. 1 illus. 14pl. F.
Plates are from drawings by J. J. Dietzler. They show the procession, administration of the oath of allegiance, the coronation, etc.
Lipperheide 2630

Ramm, Auguste Léopold
Stammliste aller regimenter der königlich-preussischen armee; nebst nachträgen und berichtigungen bis zum I. junius 1802. Berlin, zum besten der militär-erziehungs anstalten [1802]
24,298p. front. 140 col.pl. O.
Plates are those in his *Tabellarische,* with slight changes
Colas 2483

Tabellarische nachweisung von allen regimentern und korps der königlich preussischen armee unter der regierung sr. majestät Friedrich Wilhelm III, zur

Ramm, Auguste L.—*Continued*
erläuterung der abbildungen von denen militair uniformen. Berlin, J. F. Unger [1800]
45p. col.front. 142 col.pl. O.
Published also with title: *Abbildungen von allen uniformen der konigl. preuss. armee unter der regierung sr. maj. Friedrich Wilhelm III*
Colas 2481-82. Lipperheide 2154

Rammelsberg, Johann Wilhelm
Beschreibung aller sowohl noch heutiges tages florirenden als bereits verloschenen geist- und weltlichen ritter-orden in Europa; nebst denen bildnissen derer ordens-zeichen. Berlin, 1744
20,114p. 33pl. Q.
Plates engraved by G. P. Busch
Colas 2484. Lipperheide 1909

Ramsay, William
A manual of Roman antiquities; revised or partly re-written by Rodolfo Lanciani. 17th ed. London, C. Griffin 1901
xv,573p. illus. 2pl.(incl.front.) 2 fold. plans. O.
Prefatory note signed: C. L. H. Wedderburn Ogilvy. Edited by Lanciani with the assistance of T. Edmonston Charles
Has a section on dress. References at end of chapters II-XIV and at beginning of chapter I
LC 6-20244

[Randel]
Armée royale de Prusse. Berlin, Meyer & Hofmann. [1845]
6 col.pl. F.
Legends and titles on the plates are in German and French
Colas 2485

Randon, Gilbert
Messieurs nos fils & mesdemoiselles nos filles. Paris, Martinet ca1860
20 col.pl. Q.
Lipperheide 3680

Les petites misères. Paris, Martinet [1860]
20 col.pl. Q.
Lipperheide 3681

Randzeichnungen aus dem Gebetbuche des kaisers Maximilian I. Dürer, Albrecht

Rango, Konrad Tiburtius
De capillamentis seu vulgo parucquen; liber singularis. Magdeburgi, sumptibus Tobiae Schröteri impr. J. Millens 1663
254p. front. D.
Colas 2486. Lipperheide 1652

Rank and badges ... in Her Majesty's army. Perry, O. L.

Rank at a glance in the army & navy, the air services, R. N. R., R. N. V. R., R. N. D., royal marines, volunteer training corps, etc., etc., with descriptive notes. London, G. Philip [1915]
48p. col.illus. D.
LC WAR15-181

Raoul-Rochette, Désiré. See Rochette, D. R.

Rapport sur les anciens vêtements sacerdotaux. See Linas, Charles de. Anciens vêtements sacerdotaux et anciens tissus conservés en France

Rapport sur les dentelles, les blondes, les tulles et les broderies. Aubry, Félix

Rapsilber, Maximilian
Berlin und die Hohenzollern; ein gedenkbuch zum Hohenzollern-jubiläum. [Berlin] H. Tietz 1912
160p. illus.(incl.port.) Q.

Rasch, Albert
Das Eibenstocker stickereigewerbe unter der einwirkung der mode. Tübingen, H. Laupp 1910
166p. O. (Zeitschrift für die gesamte staatswissenschaft ... Ergänzungsheft xxxv)
"Literatur": p165-66
LC 11-15695

Rasmussen, Knud Johan Victor
The people of the Polar north; a record ... compiled from the Danish originals and edited by G. Herring; illustrations by Count Harald Moltke. London, K. Paul, Trench, Trübner 1908
xix,358p. illus. pl.(12 col. incl.front.) ports. fold.map. O.
Colored plates accompanied by guard sheets with descriptive letterpress
"Compiled from the Danish originals recently published by the author in Copenhagen, under the titles of 'New people' and 'Under the last of the north wind'. It deals with the three distinct Eskimo branches which make up the population of Greenland."—Editor's pref.
LC 8-36704

Rasmussen, Otto Durham
History of Chinese spectacles. Pub. by Scientific section of the American optical association. [Bangor, Me., T. W. Burr] 1915
Cover-title, [16]p. illus. O.
LC 15-16241

Old Chinese spectacles. Tientsin, N. China, North China Press c1915
33p. pl. D.

Rasmussen, Sara
Klöppelbuch; eine anleitung zum selbstunterricht im spitzenklöppeln. Kopenhagen, A. F. Höst 1884
48p. 47 illus. 12pl. O.
Lipperheide 4045

Raspi, Raimondo Carta. See Carta Raspi, Raimondo

Rastawiecki, Edward, baron. See Przezdziecki, Aleksandér, jt. auth.

Rathbone, Richard Llewelyn Benson
Unit jewellery; a handbook for craftsmen. London, Constable; New York E. P. Dutton [1921]
6v. fronts. illus. O.
Paged continuously
LC 22-5305

Rathgen, Bernhard
Das aufkommen der pulverwaffe. München, Verlag Die schwere artillerie 1925
72p. illus. O. (Sonderhefte d. verlages Die schwere artillerie. Nr. 2)

Rathier, L. See Beaunier, F. jt. auth.

Rational dress. King, E. M.

Ratton, Charles
Masques africains. Paris, A. Calavas [1931]
12 l. 24pl. O.

Rattonitz, Rudolf Maria Bernhard, graf von Stillfried und. See Stillfried und Rattonitz, R. M. B., graf von

Rattray, James
The costumes of the various tribes, portraits of ladies of rank, celebrated princes and chiefs, views of the principal fortresses and cities, and interior of the cities and temples of Afghaunistaun; from original drawings by James Rattray. London, Hering & Remington 1848
30(i.e. 34)p. 30 col.pl.(incl.front.) on 26 l. F.
Lettered on cover: *Costumes and scenery of Afghaunistaun*
Colas 2489. Lipperheide 1497. LC 18-22719

Ratzel, Friedrich
The history of mankind, tr. from the 2d German ed. by A. J. Butler; with introduction by E. B. Tylor. London & New York, Macmillan 1896-98
3v. col.fronts. illus. pl.(part col.) maps (part fold.) Q. $4, o.p.
Translation of his *Völkerkunde*
Costume index. LC 4-9003

Völkerkunde; 2., gänzlich neubearb. aufl. Leipzig und Wien, Bibliographisches institut 1894
2v. illus. pl.(part col.) maps. Q.
LC 10-385

Rauch, Ernst
(engr.) Allgemeiner militär-almanach. 1828

Rausche-Rauss, Frieda
Häckel-vorlagen für schule und haus. Pforzheim, O. Riecker [1892]
10pl. Q.
Lipperheide 4171

Rauss, Frieda Rausche-. See Rausche-Rauss, Frieda

Raven-Hart, Hester Emilie. See Chisman, Isabel, jt. auth.

Ravenet, F.
(engr.) Boucher, François. Recueil de diverses figures étrangères

Raverat, Achille, baron
Savoie; promenades historiques, pittoresques et artistiques en Maurienne, Tarentaise, Savoie-Propre, et Chautagne. Lyons, L'auteur 1872
695p. O. 10fr.

Rawling, Cecil Godfrey
The land of the New Guinea pygmies; an account of the story of a pioneer journey of exploration into the heart of New Guinea. London, Seeley, Service 1913
xvi,17-365p. front. pl. fold.map. O.
Chapter XIX, on the pygmies, by H. S. Harrison
LC 13-9449

Rawlinson, George
The five great monarchies of the ancient eastern world; or, The history, geography, and antiquities of Chaldæa, Assyria, Babylon, Media, and Persia. Collected and illustrated from ancient and modern sources. New York, Dodd, Mead 1871
3v. illus. O. 16s
LC 15-8486 (1881 ed.)

Ray, Edward Adams-. See Adams-Ray, Edward

Raymond, Damaze de. See Damaze de Raymond

Raymond, Mme Emmeline
Leçons de couture, crochet, tricot, frivolité, guipure sur filet, passementerie et tapisserie. Paris, Firmin Didot 1868
360p. 348 illus. 3pl. D.
Lipperheide 4099

Raynaud, Théophile
Anselmus Solerius Cemeliensis. De pileo, caeterisque capitis tegminibus tam sacris, quàm profanis; editio novissima. Amstelodami, sumptibus A. Frisii 1671
379p. 19 l. 26 illus. 4pl. D.
The first edition (Lyon, 1655) The text is included in *Thesaurus antiquitatum romanarum* by Joannes Georgius Graevius (Traject. ad Rhen., apud F. Halmam 1732. v6 columns 1221-1310)
Lipperheide 1650-51

Rè, Vincenzo
(illus.) Narrazione delle solenni reali feste fatte celebrare in Napoli da Sua Maestà il re delle Due Sicilie Carlo infante di Spagna

Read, Sir Charles Hercules
Guide to the antiquities of the bronze age. See entry under British museum. Department of British and mediaeval antiquities

Readers' guide to periodical literature, 1900+ See note at head of subject: Periodicals

Reading and reference list on costume. Brooklyn. Public library

A **reading** list. Boyd, A. M., and Miller, M. V., comps.

Réal, Antony, pseud. See Fernand-Michel, F. F.

Réal, Daniel
The batiks of Java, forty-six plates in collotype and colour with an introduction by Daniel Real. London, E. Benn 1924
15p. XLVI pl.(part col.) F.
LC 25-6210

See also La décoration primitive

Real museo borbonico. See Naples. Museo nazionale

Reallexicon der deutschen altertümer. Götzinger, Ernst

Reallexikon der prähistorischen, klassischen und frühchristlichen altertümer. Forrer, Robert

Reallexikon des classischen alterthums. Lübker, F. H. C.

Reason, Will. See Stadling, J. J., jt. auth.

Réau, Louis, and others
Inedited works of Bakst: Essays on Bakst by Louis Réau, Denis Roche, V. Svietlov and A. Tessier. New York, Brentano 1927
127p. 17 illus.(7 col.) 30pl.(part col.) F.
Published in Paris by G. Lang
Most of the illustrations and plates contain designs for the scenery and costuming of the Russian ballet
Colas 2490

[**Rechberg und Rothenlöwen, Karl, graf von**]
Les peuples de la Russie; ou, Description des moeurs, usages et costumes des diverses nations de l'empire de Russie, accompagnée de figures coloriées. Paris, Impr. de D. Colas. 1812-13
2v. col.fronts. col.pl. sq.F.
Dedicatory epistle signed by the author. Revised by G. B. Depping
Colas lists also an edition with title changed to read: . . . Accompagnée de 94 figures. With the same collation but inferior plates
Colas 2491-2492. Lipp. 1348. LC 28-8257

Recherches anthropologiques dans le Caucase. Chantre, Ernest

Recherches historiques sur le luxe chez les Athéniens. Meiners, Christoph

Recherches historiques sur les costumes civils et militaires des gildes et des corporations de métiers. Vigne, Félix de

Recherches historiques sur l'usage des cheveux postiches et des perruques, dans les temps anciens et modernes. See Nicolaï, Friedrich. Über den gebrauch der falschen haare und perrucken in alten und neuern zeiten

Recherches sur le lieu de la Bataille d'Attila en 451. Peigné-Delacourt, Achille

Recherches sur les arts et métiers, les usages de la vie civile et domestique des anciens peuples de l'Égypte, de la Nubie et de l'Éthiopie. Cailliaud, Frédéric

Recherches sur les Cambodgiens. Groslier, George

Recherches sur les costumes et sur les théatres de toutes les nations, tant anciennes que modernes. Le Vacher de Charnois, J. C.

Recherches sur les costumes, les moeurs, les usages religieux, civils et militaires des anciens peuples. Malliot, Joseph, and Martin, P.

Recherches sur les figures de femmes voilées dans l'art grec. Heuzey, L. A.

Recherches sur les habillemens des femmes et des enfans. Leroy, Alphonse

Recherches sur les superstitions en Chine. Doré, Henri

Recherches sur l'origine des ordres de chevallerie du royaume de Dannemarc. Munter, Frédéric

Rechlin, Karl. See Elzholz, L., jt. auth.

Das **recht** im bilde. Fehr, H. A.

Rechtschaffener tantzmeister. Taubert, Gottfried

Die **reconstructionen** der gimbel'schen waffensammlung. Gimbel, Karl

Recopilação de noticias soteropolitanas e brasilicas. Vilhena, L. dos S.

A **record** of armour sales. Cripps-Day, F. H.

A **record** of European armour and arms through seven centuries. Laking, Sir G. F., bart.

Record of fashion and court elegance for 1807, 1808-1809 published under the direction of Mrs. Fiske. London, Orme, Harris and Walker 1807-09
47 col.pl. col.port. O.
According to Colas the book seems to be the successor of *Fashions of London and Paris*
Colas 2493

A **record** of the dress, arms, customs, arts and science of the Highlanders. See North, C. N. M. The book of the Club of true Highlanders

Récréations et passe-temps. Allemagne, H. R. d'

Recueil choisi des plus belles vues de palais. See Rigaud, Jean. Recueil de cent vingt-une des plus belles vues

Recueil complet des costumes des autorités constituées, civiles, militaires, et de la marine. Grasset de Saint Sauveur, Jacques

Recueil curieux de pièces originales rares ou inédites, en prose et en vers, sur le costume et les révolutions de la mode en France. Lacroix, Paul

Recueil d'antiquités. Mongez, Antoine, ed.

Recueil de cent estampes representant differentes nations du Levant. Moor, J. B. van

Recueil de cent sujets de divers genres. Duplessi-Bertaux, Jean

Recueil de cent vingt-une des plus belles vues de palais, chateaux et maisons royales de Paris et de ses environs. Rigaud, Jean

Recueil de chevaux de tout genre. Vernet, Carle, and Vernet, Horace

Recueil de cinquante scènes de grisettes. See note under Scheffer, J. G. Ce qu'on dit et ce qu'on pense

Recueil de costumes. Lang, J. L.

Recueil de costumes. Monnoyeur, J. B.

Recueil de costumes étrangers. Boissard, J. J.

Recueil de costumes suisses. Paris, Martinet ca1818
23 col.pl. O.
Colas 2494

Recueil de costumes suisses. Pingret, Edouard

Recueil de dessins lithographiques. Boilly, L. L.

Recueil de dessins relatifs à l'art de la décoration. Hoffmann, Wilhelm, and Kellerhoven, Franz

Recueil de divers portraits de principales dames de la Porte du grand Turc. La Chapelle, George de

Recueil de diverses figures étrangères. Boucher, François

Recueil de XII costumes suisses. Holbein, Hans, the younger

Recueil de la diversité des habits qui sont de present en usaige tant es pays d'Europe, Asie, Affrique et Illes sauvages. Deserpz, François

Recueil de modes et habits galans de différents pays. Loutherbourg, P. J. de

Recueil de planches de costumes historiques de Charles VII à Louis XVI. See Compte-Calix, F. C. Costumes historiques français

Recueil de plusieurs fragments des premières comédies italiennes. Stockholm. Nationalmuseum

Recueil de plusrs. habillements espagnols. See note under Cruz Cano y Olmedilla, Juan de la. Collection des costumes espagnols anciens et moderns

Recueil de portraits et costumes suisses les plus élégants. Dinkel, M., and Locher, N.

Recueil de quelques portraits d'actrices des principaux théâtres de Paris. Grévedon, P. L. H.

Recueil de quelques vues de sites et monuments de France. Langlois, E. H.

Recueil de sujets moraux. Boilly, L. L.

Recueil de têtes et coiffures modernes à l'usage des jeunes personnes qui dessinent. Dubucourt, P. L.

Recueil de tous les costumes des ordres religieux et militaires. Bar, J. C.

Recueil de toutes les troupes qui forment les armées françoises, dessiné et illuminé d'après nature. Nuremberg, G. N. Raspe 1761
220 col.pl. Q.
Plates of the Troops of the king's household are reduced after those in Eisen's *Nouveau recueil.* The others show an officer and a soldier of each regiment
Colas describes an edition with date 1762 and 194 colored plates. *Uniformes des armées françoises suivant les règlements du roi* is another edition
Colas 2509-11. Lipperheide 2295

Recueil de toutes les uniformes qui se sont signalé durant le siège de Gènes. Gravier, Jean

Recueil de trente croquis representant des scènes et costumes russes. See Houbigant, A. C. Moeurs et costumes des Russes

Recueil de XX costumes. See Huber, J. R. Recueil de XXIV differens costumes

Recueil de XXIV differens costumes de la ville et du canton de Basle, choisis dans les divers états de la société sur la fin du XVIIe siècle. Huber, J. R.

Recueil des chartes, créations et confirmations des colonels, capitaines, majors, officiers ... de la ville de Paris. Hay, A. E.

Recueil des coeffures depuis 1589 jusqu'en 1778. Paris, Desnos [1779]
2 l. 48 col.pl. 48 l. T.
"Avec des vers analogues à chaque costume. Collection fort desirée des dames et la plus complète qui ait encore paru en ce genre, suivie du secrétaire à la mode, à l'usage du beau-sexe." Subtitle
A German copy exists *Recueil général des coëffures de Paris* (Berlin, J. Pauli 1779)
A new edition of *Almanach de la toilette et de la coëffure* and its second part *Le bijou des dames.* The same plates are in *Recueil général de coëffures de différents gouts*
Colas 92-93. Lipperheide 1679 (Ger. ed.)

Recueil des costumes de la Bretagne et des autres contrées de la France. Charpentier, H. D.

Recueil des costumes de tous les ouvrages dramatiques représentés avec succès sur les grands théâtres de Paris. Vizentini, Augustin

Recueil des costumes français. Beaunier, F., and Rathier, L.

Recueil des devotions et divertissements de ... Marie Elisabeth archiduchesse d'Aûtriche ... dans sa residence à Bruxelles. Bruxelles, G. Fricx 1736
15pl. Q.
Lipperheide 2669

Recueil des différentes modes du temps. Paris, Hérisset 1729
12pl. Q.
Colas 2502

Recueil des différents costumes des principaux officiers et magistrats de la porte. Paris, Onfroy ca1775
16 l. 96 col.pl. Q.
Plates known also in black and white
Colas 2501

Recueil des différents habillements des trouppes qui composent l'armée de la reine de Hongrie, ramassées sur les frontières de ce Royaume. Paris, Charpentier 17—?
21 col.pl. Q.
Colas gives a list of the plates
Colas 2504

Recueil des divers costumes des habitans de Bordeaux et des environs. Galard, Gustave de, and Géraud, S. E.

Recueil des estampes et tableaux representant la cause des maux qui affligent l'Italie dans le temps où nous sommes. Bassano, 1797
4 l. 36pl. (22 col.) Q.
Colas 2505

Recueil des habillements anciens et modernes des differents nations d'après les dessins de Holbein [and others] Sammlung von trachten bey verschiedenen ältern und neuern völkern. Leipzig, Au comptoir d'industrie [1805]
15p. 32 col.pl. Q.
Described by Colas as a mediocre copy of plates from *A collection of the dresses of different nations, ancient and modern.* Legends in French and German
Colas 2506. Lipperheide 49

Recueil des habillements de différentes nations, anciens et modernes. See Collection of the dresses of different nations, ancient and modern

Recueil des monumens les plus intéressans du Musée national. Naples. Museo nazionale

Recueil des principaux costumes militaires des armées alliées. Duplessi-Bertaux, Jean

Recueil des uniformes de l'armée suédoise. See Roos, Cajetan. Samling af Swenska armeens uniformer

Recueil d'estampes de costume du XVIIe siècle. Bonnart, Henri

Recueil d'estampes, représentant les grades, les rangs et les dignités, suivant le costume de toutes les nations existantes; avec des explications historiques, & la vie abrégée des grands

Recueil d'estampes—*Continued*
hommes qui ont illustré les dignités dont ils étoient décorés. Paris, Duflos le jeune 1779[-84]
17 l. 264 col.pl. F.
Published in 44 parts of six plates each. Copies exist with the plates in black and white. Colas lists nine of the plates, all engraved by Pierre Duflos, Mme Duflos or Marillier after Jean Touzé
Colas 2508. Lipperheide 38

Recueil d'idées nouvelles pour habiller suivant les règles du meilleur goût ses domestiques, jockeys, courriers, postilons, cochers, chasseurs, houssars, etc. London & Leipzig, Baumgartner ca1790
8 col.pl. ob.Q.
Shows servants dress and livery in use in St Petersburg, Russia, at this period
Colas 2513

Recueil d'ornements et de sujets pour être appliqués à l'ornementation des armes. Claesen, Charles

Recueil d'ouvrages divers à exécuter avec les fils et les cotons D. M. C. Dillmont, Thérèse de

Recueil d'uniformes; Gardes d'honneur. Fort, E.

Recueil général de coeffures de différents gouts ... sous différens règnes, a commencer en 1589 jusqu'en 1778 ... Suivi d'une collection de modes françoises; contenant les différens habillemens & coëffures des hommes & des femmes. Paris, Desnos [1778]
Cover title, 48pl. on 24 l. Q.
Forty-eight engravings of coiffures and 48 accompanying stanzas of text (engraved)
Recueil général de costumes et modes, contenant les différens habillemens et les coëffures les plus élégantes des hommes et des femmes (Paris, Desnos 1779) contains the same material in smaller format
Contains the same plates as the *Recueil des coeffures depuis 1589 jusqu'en 1778.* Plates 1 to 24 were also published in the *Almanach de la toilette et de la coëffure des dames françoises;* and 24-48 in *Le Bijou des dames*
Colas 2514-15. Lipp. 4452. LC 28-660

Recueil général de costumes et modes, contenant les différens habillemens et les coëffures les plus élégantes des hommes et des femmes. See note under Recueil général de coëffures de différents gouts

Recueil général des coëffures de Paris. See note under Recueil des coëffures depuis 1589 jusqu'en 1778

Recueil général des modes d'habillements des femmes des etats de sa majesté le roi de Sardaigne. Stagnon, A. M.

Recuerdos de Lima. Bonnaffé, A. A.

Recuerdos de un viage por España. Madrid, Mellado 1849-51
3v. illus. pl.(part col.) O.
Most of the illustrations are from *L'Espagne* by Cuendias and Suberwick, illustrated by Célestin Nanteuil
Lipperheide 1232

Recurring cycles of fashion 1760-1937. Young, A. B.

Red cross
Boguslawski, Albrecht von. Deutschland. Das heer, von Boguslawski ... Die flotte, von R. Aschenborn ... Anhang: Das internationale Rote kreuz, von V. von Strantz. 1900

Red cross. United States. American national Red cross. Manual of regulations and specifications for chapter workers' uniforms & insignia. 191-?

See also Hospital garments

Red cross. United States. American national Red cross
Manual of regulations and specifications for chapter workers' uniforms & insignia. Baltimore and New York, Thomsen-Ellis co. 191-?
31p. illus.(part col.) O.

Redfern, W. B.
Royal and historic gloves and shoes, illustrated and described. London, Methuen [1904]
x,110p. col.front. 78pl.(part col.) F. 42s, o.p.
Most of the examples are English but a few are from other countries
Costume index. LC 5-6664

Red-figured Athenian vases in the Metropolitan museum of art. Richter, G. M. A.

Redslob, Edwin
Thüringen. See Deutsche volkskunst. v7
(ed.) Deutsche volkskunst

Redtenbacher, M.
Farbige stickerei-vorlagen. Karlsruhe, J. Veith 1891-95
2v. 66pl.(30 col.) Q.
Lipperheide 4017

Rees, Mrs Janet Emily (Meugens) Ruutz-. See Ruutz-Rees, Mrs J. E. M.

Reeve, Amy J.
The elements of dress pattern-making: Magyar dresscutting for technical classes, home workers & professionals, as taught in the London County council technical schools and in the colonies. London, New York [etc.] Longmans, Green 1912
30p. diagrs. O.
LC 13-368

French pattern modelling for professionals. London, New York [etc.] Longmans, Green 1912
23p. illus. O.
LC 13-8268

Practical dresscutting up to date. For technical classes, home workers & professionals, as taught in the London County council technical schools, and in the colonies. London, New York [etc.] Longmans, Green 1912
30p. diagrs. O.
LC 13-367

Practical home millinery ... new and rev ed. London, New York [etc.] Longmans, Green 1912
xii,96p. illus. diagrs. O.
LC 13-15592

Reeve, Emma. See Allom, Thomas. Character and costume in Turkey and Italy ... with descriptive letterpress by Emma Reeve

Reeve, R. G.
(engr.) Newhouse, C. B. Military incidents

Réflexions sur la crinoline. Abiet, Édouard

Die **reform** der frauenkleidung. Neustätter, O.

Régiments de hussards au service de France. Isnard, P. Fr. d'

Régiments suisses au service de la France. Hoffmann, Nicolas

Les **régiments** suisses au service étranger. See Escher, A. von. Die Schweizer regimenter in fremden diensten 1515-1860.

Regional costume

Fontenouille, G. de. Le faux-luxe et l'abandon des costumes locaux dans les campagnes. 1913

See also names of countries with subdivision By region or province

The **regional** costumes of Spain. Palencia, Isabel de

Regionum et insularum atque locorum. Giovio, Paolo, bp. of Nocera

Reglamento de uniformes. Costa Rica. Laws, statutes, etc.

Reglamento de uniformes para el ejercito. Argentine Republic. Laws, statutes, etc.

Reglamento de uniformes para el ejército San José. Costa Rica. Secretaría de la guerra

Reglamento propuesto por la comandancia jeneral de armas prescribiendo el uniforme que debe usar el ejército de la República. Argentine republic. Ministerio de guerra y marina

Réglemens sur les arts et métiers de Paris, rédigés au XIIIe siècle. Boileau, Étienne

Règlement concernant les uniformes des généraux et officiers des etats-majors des armées de la République française. France. Ministère de la guerre

Reglement das exercitium und die manövres der französischen infanterie betreffend, vom 1sten August 1791; aus dem französischen für die königlich-westfälischen regimenter ... 3. aufl. Braunschweig, F. Vieweg 1812

2v. 44pl. D.
Earlier edition (Braunschweig, Vieweg 1808. 44pl.)
Shows French uniforms of this date. Volume 1 Die soldaten- und ploton-schule; v2 Die bataillons-schule
Lipperheide 2301

Règlement sur l'uniforme des généraux, des officiers des état-majors des armées et des places, des officiers du corps du génie [etc.] France. Ministère de la guerre

Reglements und instructionen für die churfürstlich-brandenburgischen truppen zur zeit der regierung Friedrichs des dritten (ersten) als chürfurst und als könig. Eickstedt, C. von

Regnard, Jean François

Œuvres complètes de Regnard; nouv. éd. augm. de deux pièces inédites, précédée d'une introduction ... par M. Édouard Fournier, ornée de portraits ... dessinés par MM. Émile Bayard et Maurice Sand. Paris, Laplace, Sanchez 1875

lxxxiii,560p. col.front.(port.) col.pl. facsim. F.
LC 19-967

Regnet, Carl Albert

München in guter alter zeit; nach authentischen quellen ... mit original-kupferradirungen von F. Bollinger, F. Schieszl u. a. nebst erklärungen hierzu aus der Baumgartner'schen uebersicht von 1805. München, G. Franz 1879

124p. 54pl. Q.
Lipperheide 772

Regnier

(lithgr.) Henry, Elisa. Le charme

Regnier, Mme. Marie Louise Antoinette (de Heredia) de, and Brunelleschi, Umberto

Les masques et les personnages de la comédie italienne; expliqués par Gérard d'Houville [pseud.] et interprétés par Brunelleschi en douze estampes. Paris, Le journal des dames et des modes 1914

2 l. 12 col.pl. ob.F.
Plates are engraved by H. Reidel after designs of Brunelleschi and show Harlequin, Dr. Bellanzone, Brigghela, Coralline, Florindo, Gicometta, Mezzenin and Colombine, Paulaton, Rosaura, Scaramouche, Tartaglia, Trivellino
Colas 1499

Regolamento per le vestimenta ed armamento della Guardia Civica nello Stato Pontificio. Italy. Papal states

Regolamento sull' uniforme. Italy. Ministero della guerra

Regole della scherma. Marcelli, F. A.

Regole militari del cavalier Melzo sopra il governo e servitio della cavalleria. Melzo, Lodovico

La **regratterie** de Hambourg. See Suhr, Christoffer. Der ausruf in Hamburg

Regulations and decisions pertaining to the uniform of the army of the United States 3d ed. 1899. United States. War department

Regulations for the army of the Confederate States. Confederate States of America. War department

Regulations for the uniform & dress of the army of the United States. United States. War department

Regulations for the uniform & dress of the Marine corps. United States. Marine corps

Regulations for the uniform and dress of the navy and marine corps of the United States. March, 1852. United States. Navy department

Regulations for the uniform and dress of the navy of the United States. 1841. United States. Navy department

Regulations for the uniform of the army of the United States. United States. Quartermaster corps

Regulations for the uniform of the United States army. United States. War department

Regulations for the uniform of the United States navy, December 1, 1866. United States. Navy department

Regulations governing the uniform of commissioned officers, warrant officers, and enlisted men of the navy of the United States. United States. Navy department

Regulations governing the uniforms of the United States Coast Guard. United States. Coast guard

Regulations governing the uniforms of officers and employees of the Philippine health service, 1915. Philippine Islands. Bureau of public health

Regulations governing the uniforms of officers and employees of the United States Public health service, 1914. United States. Public health service

Regulations prescribing flags, signals, funnel marks, etc., also uniforms of the United States army transport service. United States. Quartermaster corps

Regulations prescribing uniforms of the United States army transport service and harbor boat service, including mine planters and cable boats, also flags, signals, funnel marks, etc. United States. Quartermaster corps

Regulations relating to the uniform of the National guard of the state of New York 1899. New York (State) Adjutant general's office

Regulations relating to the uniforms of the officers of the United States navy ... January 22, 1883. United States. Navy dept.

Regum Daniae icones accuratê expressae. Haelwegh, Albert

Rehberg, Friedrich

Drawings faithfully copied from nature at Naples. [London] 1794

2 l. 24pl. sq.F.

Added title-page: Outlines of figures and drapery collected ... from antient statues, monuments, basreleivos &c. representing the principle characters in the plays of Racine, in the proper costume, forming an useful study for amateurs in drawing, from the most correct & chaste models of Grecian & Roman sculpture

On cover: *Lady Hamilton's attitudes*

LC 11-25483

Rehm, Hermann Siegfried

Das buch der marionetten. Ein beitrag zur geschichte des theaters aller völker. Mit 130 ... textillustrationen nach zeichnungen des verfassers. Berlin, E. Frensdorff [1905]

307p. illus. Q.

LC 34-19569

Reibisch, Friedrich Martin von

Deutscher ritter-saal, artistisch-historisch bearbeitet von F. M. Reibisch. Dresden, 1836

60p. 72 col.pl. ob.F.

First edition which was not put on sale. Plates show tournaments and knights in armor

Colas 2524

Eine auswahl merkwürdiger gegenstände aus der königl. sächsischen rüstkammer. Dresden, Walther [1825-27]

9pts. 35 col.pl. Q.

Lipperheide 2406

Der rittersaal. See entry under Kottenkamp, F. J.

Reichard, Elias Caspar

Matthäus und Veit Konrad Schwarz nach ihren merkwürdigsten lebensumständen und vielfältig abwechselnden kleidertrachten aus zwey im Herzoglich-Braunschweigischen kunst- und naturalien-kabinette befindlichen originalien ... Ein beytrag zur geschichte der kleidermoden. Magdeburg, 1786

14 l. 194p. O.

Describes two costume books in the Brunswick museum

Lipperheide 651

Reichardt, Johann Friedrich

Johann Friedrich Reichardt's Vertraute briefe aus Paris geschrieben in den jahren 1802 und 1803. Hamburg, B. G. Hoffmann 1804

3v. D.

The eighth and seventeenth letters are on dress of the period

Lipperheide 1153. LC 9-5283

Reichel, Emil

Die frauenkleidung. Leipzig, Quelle & Meyer [1912]

76p. illus. 2 col.pl. O.

Reichel, Wolfgang

Homerische waffen; archäologische untersuchungen, von Wolfgang Reichel. 2. völlig umgearbeitete und erweiterte aufl. Wien, A. Hölder 1901

x,172p. illus. Q.

Introduction containing biographical sketch of the author, by R. Heberdey

The first edition: *Über homerische waffen* (Wien, A. Hölder 1894) was published as Hft XI of the *Abhandlungen des archäologischepigraphischen Seminares der Universität Wien; hrsg. von O. Benndorf und E. Bormann*

Lipperheide 205, 205a. LC 3-5104

Reichhold, Karl. See Furtwängler, Adolph, jt. auth.

Reicke, Emil

Der gelehrte in der deutschen vergangenheit. Mit 130 abbildungen und beilagen nach den originalen aus dem fünfzehnten bis achtzehnten jahrhundert. Leipzig, E. Diederichs 1900

143p. 127 illus.(incl.ports.) 2pl.(1 double) Q. (Monographien zur deutschen kulturgeschichte [VII. bd])

Contains pictures of German scholars, professors, etc., to the middle of the eighteenth century

Lipperheide 2035. LC G-1204

Lehrer und unterrichtswesen in der deutschen vergangenheit; mit 130 abbildungen und beilagen nach originalen aus dem 15.-18. jahrhundert. Leipzig, E. Diederichs 1901

135p. illus. pl. facsim. Q. (Monographien zur deutschen kulturgeschichte bd.9)

Contains pictures of German students to about 1801

Lipperheide 2036. LC 2-5882

Reidel, H.

(engr.) Regnier, Mme. M. L. A. de H. de, and Brunelleschi, Umberto. Les masques et les personnages de la comédie italienne

Reigentänze. Rietmann, A.

Reimpell, Walter

Geschichte der babylonischen und assyrischen kleidung ... hrsg. von Eduard Meyer. Berlin, K. Curtius [1921]

xii,82p. pl. Q.

Plates printed on both sides

Bibliography, p ix-xii

Rein, Wilhelm

(ed.) Becker, W. A. Gallus, oder Römische scenen aus der zeit Augusts. 1863

Reinach, Salomon
Répertoire de la statuaire grecque et romaine. Paris, E. Leroux 1897-1910
4v. in 5. illus. D.
Contents: v 1 Clarac de poche, contenant les bas-reliefs de l'ancien fonds du Louvre et les statues antiques du *Musée de sculpture* de Clarac; v2 Sept mille statues antiques, réunies pour la première fois; v4 Quatre mille statues antiques
LC 1-7184

See also Clarac's *Musée*

Reinach, Théodore. See Hamdī, O., bey, jt. auth.

Reinach-Foussemagne, H. de, comtesse
Charlotte de Belgique, impératrice du Mexique. Paris, Plon-Nourrit [1925]
xviii,408p. front. illus. ports. O.
Charlotte became Empress of Mexico in 1864
Bibliography: p385-91
LC 26-2552

Reinhardt, Johann Christian
Collection de costumes suisses des XXII cantons, peints par J. Reinhard de Lucerne et publiés par Birmann et Huber. Basle, Birmann & Huber 1819
46 l. 46 col.pl. Q.
Described by Colas as the definitive edition of Reinhardt's collection. Colas gives a list of the plates. A reprint exists with same title and collation, *réimprimés par Lang et Laube* (Zürich, Helvetia verlag 1924)
The first edition, according to Lonchamps, has title: *Costumes suisses d'après les desseins de J. Reinhard* (Bâle, Schöll 1803)
Another edition has cover title: *Costumes suisses peint spar Reinhard et publiés par P. Birman et J. F. Huber* (Basle, 1810. 44 col.pl. Q.) Each plate is marked "Peint par Reinhard, dessiné par Hégy"
Colas 2528-29, 2526-27. Lipperheide 903 (1810 ed.)

A collection of Swiss costumes in miniature, designed by Reinhardt to which is added a description in French and English ... Collection de costumes suisses d'après les dessins de Reinhardt. London, Printed by G. Schulze for W. T. Gilling 1822
27 l. 30 col.pl. Q.
The second English edition with same title (London, Printed for J. Goodwin by W. Lewis [1828]) is described by Colas as using heavier paper and finer coloring
Another edition entitled: *Petite suite des costumes suisses des XXII cantons* (Basle, Birmann & Huber, 1819) is listed by Lonchamp
Colas 2530-32. Costume index (1828 ed.) Lipperheide 907

(illus.) König, F. N. Collection de costumes suisses

Reinle, Sophie
Neue häkel-vorlagen. Konstanz, J. A. Pecht [1892]
112pl. O.
Series III has title: *Neue macramé-vorlagen*
Lipperheide 4172

Reinsberg-Düringsfeld, Ida, freifrau von, and Reinsberg-Düringsfeld, Otto, freiherr von
Hochzeitsbuch. Brauch und glaube der hochzeit bei den christlichen völkern Europa's ... Mit XXIV illustrationen von Albert Kretschmer und einem symbolischen titelbilde von Marie v. Reichenbach. Leipzig, J. G. Bach 1871
272p. col.front. 24 col.pl. sq.Q.
Lipperheide 2878. LC 10-25006

Reinsberg-Dueringsfeld, Otto, freiherr von
Das festliche jahr; in sitten gebraüchen, aberglauben und festen der germanischen völker. 2. aufl. Leipzig, H. Barsdorf, 1898
487p. 4pl. O.
First edition 1863

See also Reinsberg-Düringsfeld, Ida, freifrau von, jt. auth.

Reisbuchlein von allerlei gesichter und etlichen frembden trachten. Hollar, Wenceslaus

Reise a. h. ihrer k. k. apostolischen majestäten Franz Joseph und Elizabeth durch Kärnthen im september 1856. Wien, K. K. Hof- und Staatsdruckerei 1859
91p. 34pl.(20 col.) F.
Lipperheide 2638

Reise des evangelischen missionar Christian Ferdinand Ewald. Ewald, Paulus

Reise durch Norwegen und Lappland. Buch, Leopold, freiherr von

Reise durch verschiedene provinzen des Russischen reichs. Pallas, P. S.

Reise in Dalmatien. Forti, Alberto

Reise in Nord-Ost Afrika. Barnim, A. J. B. von, freiherr, and Hartmann, Robert

Reise in Ostindien. Orlich, Leopold von

Reise nach Brasilien in den jahren 1815 bis 1817. Wied-Neuwied, M. A. P., prinz von

Reise nach Dalmatien und in das gebiet von Ragusa. Germar, E. F.

Reisen aus Holland durch Deutschland in Italien. Misson, F. M.

Reisen in Celebes. Sarasin, Paul, and Sarasin, Fritz

Reisen in der europäischen Türckey, Kleinasien, Syrien und Aegypten in den jahren 1799, 1800, 1801 und 1802. See note under Wittman, William. Travels

Reisen und entdeckungen in Nord- und Central-Afrika. See Barth, Heinrich. Travels and discoveries

Reiset, Gustave Armand Henri. Modes et usages au temps de Marie-Antoinette. See entry under Éloffe, Mme

Reisner, George Andrew
Amulets. Le Caire, Impr. de l'Institut français d'archéologie orientale 1907
198p. illus. xxv pl. F. (Catalogue général des antiquités égyptiennes du Musée du Caire. nos5218-6000 et 12001-12527. [v35])
At head of title: Service des antiquités de l'Égypte
LC A28-2203

[Reiss, Heinrich]
(ed.) Sammlung der schönsten miniaturen des mittelalters aus dem 14. u. 15. jahrhundert der blüthezeit jener meisterminiatoren, deren werke in den berühmtesten geistlichen und weltlichen biblio-

Reiss, Heinrich—*Continued*
theken Deutschlands als unica aufbewahrt und bewundert werden. Wien, L. Lott 1867
80 col.pl. O.
The copy in the Library of Congress has cover title: *Chromotypographisches album ... enthaltend 80 miniaturen des mittelalters ... (Lott'sche sammlung)* and the date: 1870, has been supplied
Lipperheide 459. LC 2-49

Reiss, Wilhelm, and Stübel, Alfons
Das todtenfeld von Ancon in Peru; ein beitrag zur kenntnis der kultur und industrie des Inca-Reiches. Berlin, A. Asher 1880-87
3v. 141pl.(135 col.) F.
The articles described are in the Museum für völkerkunde, Berlin
Contents: v 1 Das todtenfeld und seine gräber; v2 Gewänder und gewebe; v3 Schmuck, geräthe, thongefässe, entwickelung des ornaments
Lipperheide 1637

Reiss, Winold
(illus.) Linderman, F. B. Blackfeet Indians

Reisser
Avis important au sexe, ou Essai sur les corps baleinés pour former & conserver la taille aux jeunes personnes ... Par N. Reisser l'ainé ... Tr. de l'allemand en françois. Lyon, V. Reguilliat 1770
xvi,148p. 1 pl. O.
Colas 2534

Reistrup, K. Hansen
(illus.) Dally, Aristide. L'armée danoise
(illus.) Dally, Aristide. L'armée norvégienne

Reiter und gefechte. Rugendas, G. P.

Reiterinnen und radlerinnen. Schönberger, Käthe

Reiter-karikaturen. See Bunbury, H. W. Academy for grown horsemen

Der **reitersporn.** Jahn, Martin

Reiterübungen. Gheyn, Jacob de

Reitkunst. See Pluvinel, Antoine de. L'instruction du roi en l'exercice de monter a cheval. 1627

Die **reitkunst** im bilde. Koch, Ludwig

Reitres et lansquenets. Parrocel, C.

Die **reitschule.** Maas, Dirk

Reitschule oder darstellung des natürlichen und künstlichen ganges des campagnepferdes. Hess, C. A. H.

Reitz, A., and Reitz, E.
Farbige flachtisch-muster. Hamburg, G. W. Seitz 1891
10 col.pl. O.
Lipperheide 4016

Reitz, E. See Reitz, A., jt. auth.

Reitzenstein, Ferdinand Emil, freiherr von
Das weib bei den naturvölkern. Berlin, Neufeld & Henius [pref. 1923]
xi,483p. front. illus. Q.
LC 24-18465

Reizen van Cornelis de Bruyn, door de vermaardste deelen van Klein Asia. Bruyn, Cornelis de.

Les **rejouissances** de la paix, faites dans la ville de Lyon le 20. mars 1660. Menestrier, C. F.

Relacion de la entrada de los reyes nuestros señores en la ciudad de Barcelona, la mañana del 4 de diciembre de 1827, y de los demas festejos públicos, que tributó á ss. mm. la junta de reales obsequios, en nombre y representacion de dicha ciudad. Barcelona, A. Roca 1828
25p. 8pl. Q.
Lipperheide 2732

Relation de la feste de Versailles. Félibien, André, sieur des Avaux et de Javercy

Relation de l'empire de Maroc. Pidou de Saint Olon, François

Relation de l'inauguration solemnelle de ... Charles VI. empereur des Romains ... et troisiéme du nom roy des Espagnes, comme comte de Flandres, celebrée à Gand ... le XVIII. Octobre 1717. Gand, A. Graet 1719
32p. 6pl. F.
Lipperheide 2668

Relation des fêtes données par la ville de Strasbourg à leurs majestés impériales et royales, les 22 et 23 janvier 1806 ... rédigé et imprimée par ordre du corps municipal. Strasbourg, Levrault 1806
18p. 5pl. F.
Lipperheide 2721

Relation du voyage de Monseigneur l'évêque de Beryte. See Bourges, Jacques de. Wahrhaffte und eigendliche erzehlung von der reise des bischofs von Beryte

Relation du voyage de sa majesté Charles X en Alsace. Fargès-Méricourt, P. J.

Relation d'un voyage d'exploration au nord-est de la colonie du Cap de Bonne-Espérance. Arbousset, Thomas

Relation d'un voyage du Levant. Tournefort, J. P. de

Relation officielle des fêtes organisées par la ville de Paris pour la visite des officiers et marins de l'escadre russe de la Méditerranée les 17, 19, 20 et 24 Octobre 1893. Cadoux, Gaston

Relation succincte et veritable de tout ce qui s'est passé pendant le siège de Vienne. Geelen, G. V.

Relatione di Alfonso Isachi intorno l'origine, solennita, traslatione, et miracoli della Madonna di Reggio. Isachi, Alfonso

Relazione del funerale celebrato in Parma nella chiesa conventuale della Beata Vergine della Steccata ... il giorno 28 di febbrajo dell' anno MDCCL. dalla ... real maestà di Elisabetta Farnese regina vedova di Spagna. Venezia, B. Recurti 1750
xv,xvii,viii p. 6 illus. 4pl. F.
Lipperheide 2766

Relazione del funerale celebrato nella Chiesa Metropolitana di Milano il giorno 8. febraro 1741. Barbiani, Francesco

Relazione delle solenni esequie celebrate nel duomo di Milano a sua maestà la reina di Sardigna, Polissena Giovanna Cristina. Milano, G. R. Malatesta 1735
31p. illus. 11pl. F.
Lipperheide 2757

Die **reliefs** der Traianssäule. Cichorius, Conrad

Religion and ceremonies of the Lenape. Harrington, M. R.

Die **religion** der Tscheremissen. Harva, Uno

Religious art in France, XIII century. Mâle, Émile

Religious costume

Hurd, William. Oude en tegenwoordige staat en geschiedenis van alle godsdiensten, van de schepping af tot op den tegenwoordigen tijd. 1781-91

Novelli. Raccolta dei riti, e ceremonie religiose di tutti i popoli del mondo con la spiegazione storica italiana, e francese per cadauna ceremonia. 1789

See also Ecclesiastical costume

Egypt, Ancient

Book of opening the mouth. The book of opening the mouth, the Egyptian texts with English translations. 1909

India

Broughton, T. D. Les Marattes. 1817

Broughton, T. D. The costume, character, manners, domestic habits, and religious ceremonies of the Mahrattas. 1813

Malay archipelago

Kat Angelino, P. de. Mudras auf Bali; handhaltungen der priester. 1923

Religious orders. See Monastic and religious orders; Monastic and religious orders for women

Religious sects. See Friends, Society of; Mordvinians

Remarks on certain ornaments of gold found near Quentin in Britany in 1832. Deane, J. B.

Rembowski, Alexandre

Sources documentaires concernant l'histoire du régiment des chevau-légers de la garde de Napoléon Ier d'après des manuscrits originaux et des documents inédits; publiées et précédées d'une préface par Alexandre Rembowski (préface en française par C. Prozeclawski et E. Titeux). Varsovie, X. Rubieszewski et Ch. Wrotnowski 1899
clxviii,830p. illus. col.pl. O.
Colas 2535

Remember when. Bonney, Thérèse, ed.

Remington, Frederic

(illus.) Garland, Hamlin. The book of the American Indian

Reminiscences and recollections of Captain Gronow. Gronow, R. H.

Rémond, C.

Costumes des différents peuples de l'Italie dessinés d'après nature. Paris, Delpech [1828]
1 l. 20 col.pl. F.
Colas 2536

Remonstrance charitable aux dames et damoyselles de France sur leurs ornemens dissolus. Estienne, Antoine

Renaissance. See Europe—Renaissance period, 1453-1517

La **renaissance** en Italie et en France à l'époque de Charles VIII. Müntz, Eugène

La **Renaissance,** journal du monde élégante. 1.?-3. année, 1840-1842. Paris
Illus. O.
Published three times a month. Subtitle: no 1-17: journal des modes et du commerce
Colas 2537

Renan, Ary

Le costume en France. Paris, Librairies-imprimeries réunies [1890]
274p. illus.(incl.ports.) O. (Bibliothèque de l'enseignement des beaux-arts)
Colas 2538. Costume index. Lipperheide 1100. LC F-3452

Renard, F.

(illus.) Vanier, Léon. Costumes de carnaval

[**Renard, Jules**]

Costumes du directoire, tirés des Merveilleuses. See entry under Guillaumot, A. E.

Costumes du XVIIIe siècle, tirés des prés Saint-Gervais, avec l'autorisation de V. Sardou, Ph. Gille & Ch. Lecocq ... d'après les dessins de m. Draner [pseud.] tirées chez Ch. Chardon ainé. Paris, P. Rouquette 1874
7p. 20 col.pl. F.
Also known with plates in black and white. The introduction, on the costume of the eighteenth century, is by Albert de la Berge
Colas 895. Lipperheide 1141-1142

Paris assiégé; scènes de la vie parisienne pendant le siège; par Draner [pseud.] Paris, Au bureau de L'éclipse ca1871
1 l. 31 col.pl. Q.
Colas 892. Lipperheide 3625

Souvenirs du siège de Paris: les défenseurs de la capitale; par Draner [pseud.] Paris, Au bureau de L'éclipse [1871]
1 l. 31 col.pl. Q.
Colas 894. Lipperheide 3626

Souvenirs du siège de Paris: les soldats de la République, l'armée française en campagne; par Draner [pseud.] Paris, L'éclipse [1872]
1 l. 31 col.pl. Q.
Colas 893. Lipperheide 2330

Travestissements comiques. Paris, Hautecoeur-Martinet 1870?
20 col.pl. Q.
Colas 896

Types militaires, par Draner [pseud.] [Paris, Dusacq 1862-71]
136 col.pl. F.
In portfolio. Title from cover of portfolio
Contains 35 plates of French uniforms of the period, 19 English, 10 American, 2 Russian, 4 Belgian, 13 Prussian, 5 Italian, 2 Bavarian, 8 Austrian and 1 each of Hanover, Holland, Spain, Sweden, Turkey, China and Haiti
Colas 891. Lipperheide 3624. LC 17-12931

Types militaires étrangers. Paris, H. Sicard [1893]
20 col.pl. Q.
Cataloged from Colas's *Bibliographie*
Colas 897

(illus.) Guillaumot, A. E. Costumes du XVIIIe siècle tirés des près Saint-Gervais

(illus.) Meilhac, Henri, and Halevy, Ludovic. La vie parisienne

Renatus, Flavius Vegetius. See Vegetius Renatus, Flavius

Renaudot

Alger; tableau du royaume, de la ville d'Alger et de ses environs ... 3. ed. rev. & corr. Paris, P. Mongie 1830
xl,182p. 7pl.(2 fold.) O.
Colas 2539

Rencontres parisiennes. Monnier, Henri

René I, d'Anjou, king of Naples and Jerusalem

Œuvres complètes du roi René, avec une biographie et des notices par M. le comte de Quatrebarbes, et un grand nombre de dessins et ornements, d'après les tableaux et manuscrits originaux par M. Hawke. Angers, Cosnier et Lachèse, 1843-46
4v. in 2. 94pl. F.
René lived from 1409-1480, and the manuscripts reproduced show the costume worn in Burgundy at this period
Contents: v 1 Biographie de René d'Anjou, Pièces justificatives, Lettres du roi René (a selection of 37 letters, the greater part tr. from the originals in Latin, Catalan and Italian) Institution de l'ordre du Croissant, Testament du roi René, Testament de Jeanne de Laval, Pièces justificatives. 1845; v2 Étude historique sur la chevalerie, Description des cinq manuscrits du Livre des tournois de la Bibliothèque du roi, par P. Paris, Traictié de la forme et devis d'ung tournoy (with 21 plates, miniatures reproduced from ms. 2692, ancien no8351, of the Bibliothèque nationale) Le Pas de la bergière, Regnault de Jehanneton. 1843; v3 Notice sur le Livre du cuer d'amours, Description des manuscrits du Livre du cuer d'amours, par le marquis de Villeneuve, Le Livre du cuer d'amours espris, René d'Anjou et Charles d'Orléans, Pièces justificatives. 1864; v4 Mortiffiement de vaine plaisance, L'Abuzé en court, Procession de la fête-dieu et Jeux de la Tarasque, par Alexis Chevalier, Pièces justificatives, Épilogues. 1846
Lipperheide 452. LC 3-12436

Renier, Rodolfo

Il tipo estetico della donna nel medioevo. Ancona, A. G. Morelli 1885
xiii,192p. 11 illus. D.
Lipperheide 360

Renieu, Lionel

Histoire des théâtres de Bruxelles depuis leur origine jusqu'à ce jour; préface de Auguste Rondel. Paris, Duchartre & Van Buggenhoudt 1928
2v. illus. pl. ports.(part col.) plans, facsims. O.
Paged continuously
LC 30-28659

Renouard, Paul

La danse; vingt dessins. Paris, C. Gillot 1892
20 col.pl. F.

(illus.) Leroy, Louis. Les pensionnaires du Louvre

Renouf, Maurice

Oeuvre dentellière française; le point d'Alençon. Bagnoles-de-l'Orne, M. Renouf [1913]
30p. pl. S.

Renovirte und mercklich vermehrte alamodische hobel-bank. See Alamodische hobelbanck

Répertoire de la statuaire grecque et romaine. Reinach, Salomon

Le **répertoire** des bals. La Cuisse, de, 18th cent.

Repond, Jules

Le costume de la garde suisse pontificale et la Renaissance italienne. [Rome, Polyglotte Vaticane] Paris, Spithoever 1917
93p. illus. 63pl. Q. 50fr.
Colas 2540

Les secrets de la draperie antique de l'himation grec au pallium romain. Rome, Pontificio istituto di archeologia cristiana; Paris, Société d'édition Les belles-lettres 1931
156p. illus. Q. (Studi di antichità cristiana, III)
LC 33-33629

Report of the committee appointed by the Board of trade to advise as to the uniform to be adopted as the standard uniform for the mercantile marine. Great Britain. Board of trade. Committee on mercantile marine uniform

Report of the Committee on relics. National society of the colonial dames of America

The **Repository** of arts, literature, commerce, manufactures, fashions and politics. v 1-14, 1809-1815; ser.2 v 1-14, 1816-1822; ser.3 v 1-12, 1823-1828; [ser.4] no.1-9, 1829. London, R. Ackermann 1809-29
41v. col.pl. Q.
Published in all about 900 colored plates of views of London, and 450 showing costume of the day. Title varies
Colas 2541. Lipperheide 4598

Repraesentatio belli, ob successionem in Regno Hispanico. Decker, Paul

Repraesentatio der fürstlichen auffzug und ritterspil ... 1609. Kuchler, Balthasar

Repræsentatio der furstlichen aufzug und ritterspil ... 1616. Hulsen, Esaias von

Repraesentatio & explicatio duorum arcuum triumphalium. Bry, J. T. de

Representation au naturel des chateaux de Weissenstein au dessus de Pommersfeld. Kleiner, Salomon

Représentation de la cavalcade et des réjouissances qui eurent lieu à Bologne (en février 1530) à l'occasion du couronnement de Charles V comme empereur des Romains. See Hogenberg, Nicolas. The procession of Pope Clement VII

Representation de l'ancien habillement de Strasbourg. See Eigentliche vorstellung der heutiger strassburgische mode und kleÿdertrachten

Représentation des différens corps de l'Insurrection générale d'Autriche. See Abbildung der verschiedenen corps des oesterreichischen allgemeinen aufgebothes

Représentation des fêtes données par la ville de Strasbourg pour la convalescence du roy. Weis, J. M.

Representation des modes et habillements de Strasbourg. Stridbeck, J. F.

Représentation des modes et habillemens qui sont en usage à Strasbourg. See Eigentliche vorstellung der heutiger strassburgische mode und kleÿdertrachten

Représentation des modes et particularitez de l'habillement en Alsace ... quinze portraicts faits après le naturel. Strasbourg, G. Boucher 1705
13pl. D.

Representation des montagnards d'Ecosse. See Representation of the High-landers

Représentation des uniformes de l'armée impériale de la Russie en 88 estampes enluminées. Geissler, C. G. H.

Représentation des uniformes de toutes les troupes qui ont été casernées à Hambourg de l'année 1806 à l'année 1815. See Suhr, Christoffer. Abbildungen der uniformen

Representation naturelle et exacte de la Favorite de son altesse electorale de Mayence. Kleiner, Salomon

A **representation** of the cloathing of His Majesty's household, and of all the forces upon the establishments of Great Britain and Ireland, 1742. [London, 1893]
16 l. 94 col.pl. Q.
"Of this work 25 copies have been produced for subscribers only, from the original preserved in the British museum, 1893. (no16)" Leaves printed on one side only
Colas 2542. LC 24-6818

Representation of the High-landers, who arrived at the camp of the confederated army, not far off the city of Mayence the 13th of August 1743. Norimberga, C. Weigely vidua [1744]
5pl. F.
German title: *Vorstellung deren in dem lager der alliirten armee onferne Maynz, den 13 ten August 1743 angekomenen Berg-Schotten*, and French title: *Representation des montagnards d'Ecosse*
Colas 2543. Lipperheide 2262

Représentation, ou l'on voit un grand nombre des isles, côtes, rivières et ports de mer, comme aussi les habillemens & moeurs des peuples, les cérémonies, les pompes et le magnificences ... dessinées sur les lieux & gravées exactement ... par les célèbres, Luyken, Mulder [etc.] Leide, P. Vander Aa ca1730
1 l. 83pl. ob.F.
Interesting for costume of the eighteenth century, especially of the Asiatic peoples
Colas 2544. Lipperheide 559

Representations of dresses, morals and customs, in the kingdom of Holland. Maaskamp, Evert

Republic of Mexico in 1876. Garcia Cubas, Antonio

Republican court; or, American society in the days of Washington. Griswold, R. W.

Researches into Chinese superstitions. Doré, Henri

Residences memorables. Kleiner, Salomon

A **resident** of eight years in Persia. Perkins, Justin

La **Restauration.** See Bouchot, H. F. X. M. Le luxe française: La Restauration

Restif de La Bretonne, Nicolas Edme

Estampes de Moreau-le-jeune pour le monument du costume gravées par Dubouchet. Paris, L. Conquet 1881
xxiv,104p. 24pl. O.
Has an introduction by P. Burty
There is also an edition without text and with the plates in triple proof (Paris, L. Conquet 1881. 86pl. F.)
Colas 1129

Histoire des moeurs et du costume des Français dans le dix-huitième siècle ... Texte par Restif de La Bretonne; rev. and corr. par Charles Brunet. Preface par Anatole de Montaiglon avec la vie de Freudenberg, tr. de l'allemand pour la première fois. Paris, L. Willem 1878
x p. 12 l. 12pl. F.
Modern reproduction of the first suite of the *Monument du costume* with plates by Freudenberger. Plates are engraved by E. Chavanne and others, in the size of the originals. Contains J. J. Horner's biography of Freudenberg
Colas 1126. Lipperheide 1126

Monument du costume physique et moral de la fin du dixhuitième siècle, ou Tableaux de la vie, ornés de figures dessinées & gravées par M. Moreau le jeune ... & par d'autres célèbres artistes. Neuwied sur le Rhin, Société typographique 1789
36p. 26pl. F.
Published anonymously. Contains two plates by Freudenberger, *La matinée,* and *La surprise,* and 24 by Moreau reprinted from the original plates of the *Monument du costume*
An edition with same title published (Londres 1792 2v. 26pl.) Contains the same illustrations, reduced in size and adapted to the English taste
Colas 1124-1125. Lipp. 1124a. LC 24-7175

Monument du costume physique & moral de la fin du XVIIIe siècle, ou Tableaux de la vie ornés de vingt-six figures dessinées et gravées par Moreaux le jeune et par d'autres célèbres artistes; texte par Restif de La Bretonne, rev. et cor. par m. Charles Brunet—préface par Anatole de Montaiglon. Paris, L. Willem 1876
vii,74p. 26pl. F.
Modern reproduction of the second and third suites of the *Monument du costume.* Plates are by Moreau
Colas 1127. LC 10-24962

Tableaux de la bonne compagnie; ou, Traits caractéristiques, anecdotes secrettes, politiques, morales & littéraires, recueillies dans les sociétés du bon ton, pendant les années 1786, et 1787. Paris, 1787-88
2v. 16pl. S.
Published anonymously. Includes text by Restif de La Bretonne and four plates after Freudenberger; plus the twelve of Moreau's *Seconde suite.* New legends have been added and are listed in Colas's *Bibliographie*
Colas 1122. LC 25-21942

Tableaux de la vie, ou Les moeurs de dix-huitième siècle. Neuwied sur le Rhin, Société typographique, & Strasbourg, Treuttel [1791]
2v. 17pl. S.
Also published with title: *Les petites et les grands costumes de la dernière cour de France* (Paris, Royez)

Restif de la Bretonne, Nicolas E.—*Cont.*
Plates are reduced from those by Freudenberg and Moreau in the *Monument du costume*
Colas 1123

Restos del traje ceremonial de un "médico" patagón. Vignati, M. A.

Restout, Jean
Galerie françoise, ou Portraits des hommes et des femmes célèbres ... gravés ... par les meilleurs artistes, sous la conduite de M. Restout ... avec un abrégé de leur vie. Paris, Herissant 1771-72
2v. 40pl. F.
Volume two compiled under the direction of m. Cochin
French kings, statesmen, scholars, and military officers of the seventeenth and eighteenth centuries
Lipperheide 1071

Retratos de personajes del siglo XVI. Calvo y Sánchez, Ignacio

Retz, L. P. G. B. Morel-. See Morel-Retz, L. P. G. B.

Retzlaff, Hans
Deutsche bauerntrachten, beschrieben von dr. Rudolf Helm. Berlin, Atlantis verlag [c1935]
223p. incl.illus. pl. Q.
LC 35-14362

Die Schwalm, kulturbild einer hessischen landschaft; 107 bilder von Hans Retzlaff, mit einführendem text von Heinz Metz. Berlin, Bong [1935]
112p. illus. pl. Q. (Bilderwerke zur deutschen volkskunde; hrsg. von der Deutschen volkskunst-kommission)

Volksleben im Schwarzwald; 137 bilder und 4 farbenphotographien, mit einführendem text von Wilhelm Fladt. Berlin-Leipzig, Bong [1935]
136p. incl.illus. map, diagr. col.front. col.pl. Q. (Bilderwerke zur deutschen volkskunde, hrsg. von der Deutschen volkskunst-kommission)
LC AC36-3386

Retzsch, Friedrich August Moritz
Gallerie zu Shakspeare's dramatischen werken. Leipzig & London, [E. Fleischer] 1828-46
8v. 101pl.(incl.front.) Q.
Contains title-page in English: *Retzsch's Outlines to Shakspeare*
Explanatory text of Macbeth and Hamlet, by C. A. Boettiger; of Romeo and Juliet and King Lear, by C. von Miltitz; of the Winter's Tale, Othello, the Merry Wives of Windsor, and King Henry IV, by Hermann Ulrici
Contents: Hamlet, 17pl. Macbeth, 12pl. Romeo und Julia, 12pl. König Lear, 12pl. Der sturm, 12pl. Othello, 12pl. Die lustigen weiber von Windsor, 12pl. König Heinrich IV., I. und II. theil, 12pl.
Also published with titles: *Gallery to Shakespeare's dramatic works in outlines* (New York, B. Westermann 1849. 101pl.) and *Outlines to Shakespeare's dramatic works* (Boston, Roberts 1878. 101pl.)
LC 18-3135

Reumann, Anton
(illus.) Leitner, Quirin, ritter von. Das kriegs-wesen des Heiligen Römischen Reiches

Réunion des officiers
Les uniformes de l'armée allemand ... Supplement au Bulletin. Paris, Laloux fils et Guillot 1877
15p. 15 col.pl. D. 1fr. 25
Colas 2438

Reusens, Edmond. See Claesen, Joseph. Alte kunstvolle spitzen

Reusner, Nicolaus
Emblemata ... cum symbolis & inscriptionibus illustrium & clarorum virorum. Francoforti ad Moenum, I. Feyerabendt [1581]
12 l. 372p. 165 illus. O.
Lipperheide 491

Icones sive imagines impp. regum, principum, electorum et ducum Saxoniae. Jena, Typis T. Steinmanni; impensis H. Grossi 1597
23 l. 42 illus.(incl. 39 ports.) F.
Portraits of Saxon rulers from Wittekind to Johann Ernst. The source of the book is Gabriel Schnellholz's *Sammlung* and the pictures are ascribed to Lucas Cranach, the younger
Lipperheide 702

Icones sive imagines vivae, literis cl. virorum, Italiae, Graeciae, Germaniae, Galliae, Angliae, Ungariae. Basileae, C. Valdkirch 1589
144 l. 83 ports. O.
Includes a supplement *Anhang: Icones aliquot clarorum virorum Germaniae, Angliae, Galliae, Ungariae; cum elogiis & parentalibus factis Theodore Zvingero* (1589. 32 l. 9 ports.)
Portraits are from drawings by Tobias Stimmer
Lipperheide 495

Reuter und lanzenknechte. See Parrocel, C. Reitres et lansquenets

Reuther, Fritz. See Knoll, Carl, jt. auth.

Reutter kunst. See Ritterliche reutter kunst

Réveil, Étienne Achille
(engr.) Bouët, Alexandre. Breiz-Izel

Revelationes. Methodius, Saint, bp of Olympus

Revisiting my pygmy hosts. Schebesta, Paul

Revista penitenciaria
El tatuage en su evolución histórica. See entry under Salillas, Rafael

Revista storica suizzera. See Zeitschrift für schweizerische geschichte

A **revival** of the past ages. Jossic, Y. F.

Revol, Joseph Fortuné
Histoire de l'armée française. Paris, Larousse [1929]
viii,308p. illus.(incl.ports.) pl.(part col.) map. Q.
Begins with armor and uniforms of the Gauls and Romans and continues with French to the time of the World war, 1918
LC 30-1590

La **révolution** française. Alba, André

La **révolution** française. Dayot, A. P. M.

Revue de la mode: gazette de la famille. 1.-28. année; 1872-1898. Paris
28v. col.illus. F.
Colas 2545. Lipperheide 4739

Revue de Paris élégant. See Le Paris élégant, journal de modes

Revue d'histoire suisse. See Zeitschrift für schweizerische geschichte

La **revue** universelle. See La mode nouvelle

Rey, Alfred, and Féron, Louis
Histoire du corps des gardiens de la Paix. Ouvrage publié sous les auspices de L. Lépine ... Préface de Waldeck-Rousseau. Paris, Firmin-Didot 1896
x,735p. 13pl. Q.
At head of title: Ville de Paris

Reyher, Samuel
Monumenta landgraviorum Thuringiae et marchionum Misniae, quae adhuc in Thuringia Misnia Saxonia superiore Franconia et Hassia extant: historico-genealogica descriptione illustrata a Samuele Reyhero. In aes incisa et typis exscripta Gothae 1692
70 l. 61pl. F.
Plates show the tombs of the landgraves of Thuringia and the dukes of Saxony, and their wives, from the twelfth to the end of the sixteenth century, many with effigies
Lipperheide 717

Reynitzsch, Wilhelm
Uiber truhten und truhtensteine, barden, und bardenlieder, feste, schmäuse und gerichte des Teutschen. Gotha, Ettinger 1802
368,87p. 5 illus. 1 pl. O.
Lipperheide 275

Reynolds, Sir Joshua, first president of the Royal academy. Armstrong, Sir Walter

Rhead, George Woolliscroft
Chats on costume. London, T. F. Unwin; New York, F. A. Stokes 1906
304p. col.front. 117 illus. O. $4
"Begins with a general survey of the subject and follows with brief accounts of the development and history of the tunic, mantle, doublet and hose, kirtle or petticoat, crinoline, collars and cuffs, hats, caps and bonnets, dressing of the hair, mustachios and beard, and boots, shoes and coverings of the feet."
Bibliography: p15-16
Costume index. LC w7-41

History of the fan. London, K. Paul, Trench, Trübner 1910
xix,311p. col.front. illus. pl.(26 col.) nar.F. 84s, o.p.
Costume index. LC A10-1351

Rheinfeld, Felician, freiherr von Myrbach-
See Myrbach-Rheinfeld, Felician, freiherr von

Rheinhard, Hermann
Griechische und römische kriegsalterthümer für den gebrauch in gelehrtenschulen zusammengestellt ... Mit einem vorwort von Carl Ludwig v. Roth. Stuttgart, A. Liesching [1859]
2 l. XIX pl. ob.Q.
Lipperheide 163. LC 14-19091

Rheinwald, Jh. Ldw. Chr.
Baierische volkstrachten. München, Scherer (Fleischmann) 1805
11 l. 12 col.pl. F.
Plates after designs by L. Neureuther
Colas 2548. Lipperheide 753

Rhind, William Graeme
The high priest of Israel, in his robes of glory and beauty, blessing the people; 5th ed. London, S. Bagster 1859
32p. 2 col.pl.(incl.front.) F.
"With notes and annotations, in chronological arrangement, shewing the high priesthood, etc., from Aaron to Eli ... and closing with the prophecy of Caiaphas." Subtitle
LC 33-21443

Rhine Province. See Germany—Rhine Province

Rhodes, Knights of. See Malta, Knights of

Rhoe, Mrs Mary Jane
The dress you wear and how to make it. New York and London, G. P. Putnam 1918
xiv,173p. illus. D. $1.50
LC 18-20789

Rhyn, Otto Henne am. See Henne am Rhyn, Otto

Ribbon work. See The art and craft of ribbon-work

Ribeyrolles, Charles
Brazil pittoresco ... acompanhado de um Album de vistas, panoramas, paisagens, costumes, etc. etc. Por Victor Frond. Rio de Janeiro, Typographia nacional 1859-61
2v. F. and atlas of 75pl. on 69 l. sq.F.
French and Portuguese in parallel columns. Atlas has special title-page: *Brazil pittoresco. Album de vistas, panoramas ... accompanhados de tres volumes ... por* Charles Ribeyrolles. Paris, Imp. Lemercier, 1861
The plates show Brazilian scenes with people in costume
Colas 2549. LC 1-F-2902

Riboni, Giuseppe
Broadsword and quarter-staff without a master. Broadsword fencing and stick or quarter-staff play, after the latest European practice adopted in the military schools of France and Italy, and the United States. Chicago, E. B. Myers 1862
81p. illus. pl. S.
LC 19-3

Ribot, Josep
(illus.) Costumes de Catalunya

Ricard, Prosper
Les merveilles de l'autre France; Algérie, Tunisie, Maroc; le pays—les monuments—les habitants [Paris] Hachette [c1924]
439p. col.mounted front.(port.) illus. (incl.maps) col.mounted pl. sq.Q.
LC 25-6429

Ricci, Signora Elisa
Antiche trine italiane ... Trine ad ago. Bergamo, Istituto italiano d'arti grafiche-editore 1908
2v. front. 170pl.(part col.) F.
Shows Italian laces and 15th to 16th century costumes which are rich in lace

Antiche trine italiane ... Trine a fuselli. Bergamo, Istituto italiano d'arti grafiche-editore 1911
v.p. pl.(part col.) F.
Shows Italian laces and 15th to 16th century costumes which are rich in lace

Old Italian lace. London, W. Heinemann; Philadelphia, J. B. Lippincott 1913
2v. fronts. mounted illus. pl.(part mounted, 1 fold.) ports.(part col. part mounted) F.
Some of the plates accompanied by guard sheets with descriptive letterpress
Volume 1 is a translation of her *Antiche trine italiane ... Trine ad ago;* volume 2 is a translation of her *Antiche trine italiane ... Trine a fuselli*
LC 14-11605

Ricci, Seymour de
Catalogue d'une collection de miniatures gothiques et persanes. See entry under Rosenberg, Léonce

Riccio, Domenico, known as Il Brusasorci
La gran cavalcata di Clemente VII. e Carlo V. della Sala Ridolfi dipinta dal Brusasorci incisa a contorno ... dal ... Agostino Comerio. Verona, Failoni ca1825?
1 l. 8pl. F.
Shows the procession of Clement VII and Charles V thru Bologna after the coronation, February 24, 1530

Riccio, Gennaro
Descrizione, storia, ed illustrazione degli ornamenti di una donna romana vissuta circa il 383 dell' era cristiana. Napoli, Stamperia e cartiere del Fibreno 1838
12p. 1 pl.(14 illus.) O.
"Pendente il regno dell' imperatore Arcadio rinvenuti tutti insiemo in tenimento di somma nel gennajo 1837." Subtitle
Lipperheide 1749

Riccio, Tomaso Antonio. See Amato, Cintio d', jt. auth.

Riccoboni, Luigi
Histoire du theatre italien, depuis la decadence de la comedie latine; avec un catalogue des tragedies & comedis italiennes imprimées depuis l'an 1500. jusqu'à l'an 1660. & une dissertation sur la tragedie moderne. Avec des figures qui représentent leurs differens habillemens. Paris, A. Cailleau 1730-31
2v. 19pl.(1 fold.) O.
At end of Dissertation sur la tragedie moderne (v 1, p[247]-319): A Paris, De l'Imprimerie de Pierre Delormel . . . 1728.
Appended to v 1: *Dell' arte rappresentativa, capitoli sei,* di Luigi Riccoboni. Londra, 1728 (60p. in verse)
Colas 2550. Lipp. 3200. LC 14-9710

Rich, Anthony
The illustrated companion to the Latin dictionary and Greek lexicon; forming a glossary of all the words representing visible objects connected with the arts, manufactures, and every-day life of the Greeks and Romans, with representations of nearly two thousand objects from the antique. By Anthony Rich, jun. London, Longmans 1849
xi,754p. illus. D.
Subsequently published under title: *Dictionary of Roman and Greek antiquities*
French translation: *Dictionnaire des antiquités romaines et grecques ... tr. de l'anglais sous le direction de m. Chéruel* (Paris, Firmin Didot 1859)
German translation: *Illustrirtes wörterbuch der römischen alterthümer mit steter berucksichtigung der griechischen; ubersetzt ... von Carl Müller* (Paris & Leipzig, Firmin Didot 1862. 716p. 2000 illus. O.)
Lipperheide 164 (German ed.) LC 4-35152, 4-35153 (Fr. ed.)

Richard, Jules, pseud. See Maillot, T. J. R.

Richard, T.
(photogr.) Costumes suisses

Richards, Raoul
Catalogue de la riche collection d'armes antiques, du moyen âge, de la renaissance et des temps modernes ... appartenant à ... Raoul Richards. Rome, Imprimerie editrice romana 1890
xvi,251p. 29pl. O.
"Dont la vente aux enchères publiques aura lieu à Rome ... le 3 mars 1890." Subtitle
Lipperheide 2444

Richards, Walter
Her Majesty's army; a descriptive account of the various regiments now comprising the Queen's forces, from their first establishment. London, J. S. Virtue 1889-9?
2v. 29 col.pl.(incl.fronts.) sq.Q. ea 21s, o.p.
Plates signed: G. D. Giles
Colas 2551. Costume index. LC 3-15085

Her Majesty's army, Indian and colonial forces; a descriptive account of the various regiments now composing the Queen's forces in India and the colonies. London, J. S. Virtue [1891]
376p. 15 col.pl. Q.
Plates signed H. Bunnett
Costume index (Ri v3) LC 3-15084

Richardson, Albert Edward
Georgian England; a survey of social life, trades, industries & art from 1700 to 1820. London, B. T. Batsford; New York, C. Scribner [1931]
viii,202p. col.front. illus.(incl.facsims. music) XCIII pl. on 48 l. O. $6
Costume index. LC 31-15216

Richardson, Samuel. Pamela. Illustrations
Highmore, Joseph. Plates illustrating the "Pamela" of Samuel Richardson. 1745?

Richardson, T. D.
Modern figure skating. London, Methuen [1930]
xvi,200p. front. pl. ports. diagrs. O.

Richental, Ulrich
Das concilium so zů Constantz gehalten ist worden ... MCCCCXIII. Augspurg, H. Steyner, 1536
215 l. 1204 illus. F.
Illustrations show processions and groups of people attending the conference
Manuscripts of this book have many illustrations in color
Lipperheide 444, 443z

Richomme, Charles Eugène Honoré. See Vanauld, Alfred, jt. auth.

Richormme
(engr.) Dugazon, Gustave. Danses nationales de chaque pays

Richter, A. See Jamnig, C., jt. auth.

Richter, Gisela Marie Augusta
Red-figured Athenian vases in the Metropolitan museum of art ... with eighty-three drawings by Lindsley F. Hall. New Haven, Yale university press; London, H. Milford, Oxford university press 1936
2v. illus. 181pl.(part fold.) on 115 l. F. $40; £10
At head of title: The Metropolitan museum of art
LC 37-1494

Richter, Jean Paul, and Taylor, Alicia Cameron
The golden age of classic Christian art. London, Duckworth 1904
xviii,427p. 52pl.(part mounted and col. incl.front.) F.
LC 17-3405

Richter, Johann Gustaf

Costumes nationaux de Leipzig. No place, 18—?
24 col.pl. Q.
Colas 2552

Sitten, gebräuche und kleidung der Russen aus den niedern ständen. Leipzig, Industrie comptoir [1805]
63p. 28 col.pl. O.
Drawings by C. D. H. Geissler; text by J. G. Richter

Spiele und belustigungen der Russen aus den niedern volks-klassen ... beschrieben von J. Richter. Jeux et divertissements du peuple russe. Leipzig, Industrie-comptoir [1805]
32p. 12 col.pl. Q.
Text in German and French, the latter translated by P. Hacault
Colas 2554. Lipperheide 1345

See also Geissler, C. G. H. Mahlerische darstellungen der sitten ... bey den russischen, tartarischen, mongolischen und andern völkern im russischen reich

Richter, Johann Gustaf, and Geissler, Christian Gottfried Heinrich

Châtiments usités en Russie, représentés dans une suite de 10 gravures, enluminées et accompagnées d'une explication. Leipsic, comptoir d'industrie ca1805
13 l. 10pl. Q.
Cataloged from Colas's *Bibliographie*
Colas 2553

Richter, Johann Salomon

Unterweisung für anfänger beyderley geschlechts im zeichnen. Leipzig, J. B. Klein 1790-91
5pts. 66pl. F.
Part 5 has added title: *Leipziger national-trachten, 1. bis 3. lieferung* and shows street venders
Lipperheide 826

Richter, Magda H. Ohnefalsch. See Ohnefalsch-Richter, Magda H.

Richter, Max

(ed.) Pestel, Bernhard. Der menschliche fuss und seine naturgemässe bekleidung

Richter, Wilhelm, and Gerasch, August

Kaiserl. mexicanisches corps österreichischer freiwilligen; gem. v. Wilh. Richter, lith. v. Aug. Gerasch. Wien, L. T. Neumann ca1864
4 col.pl. F.
Colas 2555

Der **richter** und die rechtspflege in der deutschen vergangenheit. Heinemann, Franz

Richtig angezogen in Deutschland und im Ausland. Moltke, E. M.-H. von, comtesse

Die **richtige** gestalt der schuhe. Meyer, G. H. von

Ricke, Herbert. See Borchardt, Ludwig, jt. auth.

Ricordo delle nozze d'argento delle loro maestà Umberto I e Margherita di Savoia, 22 Aprile 1893. Edel, Vittorio

Ridder, André Henri Pierre de

Catalogue des bronzes de la Société archéologique d'Athènes. Paris, Thorin 1894
x,214p. 13 illus. 5pl. O. (Bibliothèque des Écoles françaises d'Athènes et de Rome, fasc.69)

Catalogue sommaire des bijoux antiques. See entry under Paris. Musée national du Louvre

[Ridder, G. de]

Catalogue et description bibliographique d'une collection de livres et gravures sur les costumes militaires: Autriche Hongrie. Paris, H. Leclerc, L. Giraud-Badin 1928
xvi,338p. 57pl. Q.
Preface signed G. D. R.
Lists the collections of plates showing uniforms of Austria Hungary, gives the titles of the plates and describes variations
Colas 2556

Ridgeway, Sir William

The origin of tragedy with special reference to the Greek tragedians. Cambridge [Eng.] University press 1910
x,228p. illus. O.
LC 11-4139

Riding. Hunloke, S. H., lady, and Aldin, C. C. W.

Riding and driving for women. Beach, Belle

Riding costume

Aubry, Charles. Histoire pittoresque de l'équitation, ancienne et moderne. 1833-1834

Pellier, Jules. La selle et le costume de l'amazone, étude historique et pratique de l'équitation des dames. 1897

Schoenbeck, Richard. Das pferd und seine darstellung in der bildenden kunst. 1912

Schönberger, Käthe. Reiterinnen und radlerinnen. 1901

See also Spurs

16th century

Bruyn, Abraham de. Equitum descripcio, quomodo equestres copie, nostra hac aetate in sua armatura, per cunttas, videlicet Europae, Asiae et Affrice. 1576

Bussemecher, Johann. Folge von reitern verschiedener volker. ca1590

Fiaschi, Cesare. Trattato dell' imbrigliare, maneggiare et ferrare cavalli. 1556

Fugger, Marx. Von der gestüterey, das ist ein grundtliche beschreibung wie unnd wa man ein gestüt von guten edlen kriegsrossen auffrichten, underhalten, und wie man die jungen von einem jar zu dem andern erziehen soll ... gestellet und an tag geben. 1584

Grisone, Federico. Ordini di cavalcare, et modi di conoscere le nature de' cavalli. 1558

Ritterliche reutter kunst ... in Teutschland. 1584

17th century

Delcampe, and Fouquet, Samuel. L'art de monter a cheval. 1663-1664

Riding costume—17th century—*Continued*
Galiberto, G. B. di. Il cavallo da maneggio. 1659
Lieb, Christophorus. Practica et arte di cavalleria, of Oeffeningh en konst des rydens. 1671
Pluvinel, Antoine de. L'instruction du roy, en l'exercice de monter a cheval ... Reitkunst. 1629
Rugendas, G. P. Diversi pensieri. 1699
Sandrart, S. M. Neues polnisches pferd und reuter büchlein. ca1690?
Sandrart, S. M. Neües türckisches pferd und reüter büchlein. ca1690?
Winter, G. S. De re equaria tractatio nova complectens. 1672

18th century

Bernard, Francisco. Arte de andar a cavallo. 1757
Bunbury, H. W. Academy for grown horsemen. 1825
Eisenberg, Baron d'. Description du manège moderne. 1727
Eisenberg, Baron d'. La perfezione e i difetti del cavallo. 1753
La Guérinière, F. R. École de cavalerie. 1751
Maas, Dirk. Die reitschule. ca1700
Prizelius, J. G. Vollständige pferdewissenschaft. 1777

19th century

Anderson, E. L. Die mittlere reitschule. 1889
Aubert, P. A. Equitation des dames. 1842
Géruzes, Victor. Paris à cheval. 1883
Hess, C. A. H. Reitschule oder darstellung des natürlichen und künstlichen ganges des campagnepferdes. 1800-02
Hochstetter, C. von. Militair- und civilreiter-schule neuerer zeit zur gründlicher anleitung der einzig wahren reiter-praxis. 1839
Le Noble, Henri. Traité d'équitation à l'usage des dames. 1826
Vallet, L. Le chic à cheval; histoire pittoresque de l'équitation. 1891

20th century

Aldin, C. C. W. The omnibus book of sports for young and old. 1937 Part 2
Beach, Belle. Riding and driving for women. 1912
Koch, Ludwig. Die reitkunst im bilde. 1923

Ridpath, John Clark
Great races of mankind. Cincinnati, Jones brothers [1893]
4v. illus. XIV col.pl. Q.
"An account of the ethnic origin, primitive estate, early migrations, social evolution, and present conditions and promise of the principal families of men." Subtitle
Many illustrations show costume in all parts of the world from primitive to modern times

Riecke, Erhard
Das tatauierungswesen im heutigen Europa. Jena, G. Fischer 1925
40,16p. illus. XXIV pl. F.

Riefstahl, Rudolf Meyer
Greek orthodox vestments and ecclesiastical fabrics. Chicago, 1932
p359-73. 10 illus. on 4pl. F.
Reprinted from the *Art bulletin*, 1932, v14 no4

Rieglin, Frau Susanna Dorothea (Schulzin)
Neu-erfundenes modelbuch zum nähen, stricken, würcken und weben. Nürnberg, Die verfasserin 1757-61
5v. 40pl. F.
Lipperheide 4060

Riego de la Branchardière, Mlle Éléonore
The Irish lace instructor: containing original designs for Spanish point crochet, lace tatting, and modern point lace. London, Simpkin, Marshall 1886
26p. 9pl. ob.D.

Riehl, Berthold. See Dürer, Albrecht, and Wolgemut, Michael. Die gemälde von Dürer und Wolgemut

Riemer, Jacob de
Beschryving van 's Graven-hage, behelzende deszelfs oorsprong, benaming, gelegentheid, uitbreidingen, onheilen en luister; mitsgaders stigtinge van het hof, der kerken, kloosters, kapellen, godshuizen, en andere voornaame gebouwen ... Met veele nieuwe afbeeldingen verçiert. Delft, R. Boitet 1730-39
2v. in 3. illus. pl.(part fold.) F.
"Costumen van 's Graven-hage": 78 pages at end of volume 2
LC 10-22334

Rienzi, Grégoire Louis Domeny de. See Domeny de Rienzi, G. L.

Riess, Florian
(ed.) Kirchenschmuck, ein archiv für weibliche handarbeit

[Rieter, Jakob]
Danske nationale klaededragter; Dänische national kleidertrachten. Kiobenhavn, Rothes boghandling [1805]
91? col.pl. O.
Published in parts (livraisons) of six plates each. Legends on the plates are in Danish and German. Also known with plates in black and white
Colas 2557. Lipperheide 1045

Rietmann, A.
Reigentänze: 21 charakter- und waffentänze zusammengestellt von A. Rietman. Leipzig, E. Strauch [1892]
248p. 284 illus. O.
Lipperheide 3133

Rieusseyroux, Louise Alquié de. See Alq, Louise d'

Riffaut, A.
(engr.) Niel, P. G. J. Portraits des personnages français les plus illustres du XVIe siècle

Rigaud, Jean
Recueil de cent vingt-une des plus belles vues de palais, chateaux et maisons royales de Paris et de ses environs; dessinées d'après nature ... et gravées par J. Rigaud. Paris, Treuttel & Würtz 1780
6p. 121pl. F.
Costume figures appear in the foreground
An earlier edition was published with title: *Recueil choisi des plus belles vues de palais* [etc] (1752)
Lipperheide 1131

La **rigenerazione** dell' Olanda. See Hess, David. Hollandia regenerata

Righetti, Camillo
Adjustierungsblätter des k. u. k. oesterr.-ungar. heeres, der kriegsmarine und der beiden landwehren; nach der natur gezeichnet. Leipzig, M. Ruhl [1901]
29 col.pl. Q. M.6
Colas 2558. Lipperheide 2249

Rigmaroll, Olio, pseud. See Egerton, M.

Rikssalen på Gripsholms slott historiskt porträtt-galleri af konung Gustaf I. Salmson, A. J.

Rimmel, Eugene
The book of perfumes ... with ... illustrations by Bourdelin, Thomas, etc.; 5 ed. London, Chapman & Hall 1867
xx,266p. 244 illus. 13pl.(1 col.) O.
First edition 1865. The book is interesting for the history of costume and hairdressing as well as of perfumes
French translation: *Le livre des parfums* (Paris, E. Dentu 1870)
Lipperheide 3270

'The **ring** of Nestor'. Evans, Sir A. J.

Ringer kunst. Auerswald, Fabian von

Die **ringer-kunst;** erneuert von G. U. Schmidt. Auerswald, Fabian von

Ring-kunst vom jahre 1674. See Petter, Nicolaes. Klare onderrichtinge der ... worstel-konst

Ringle, Johann Jakob
Amictus senatus tam politi: quam academ. mulierum, virgin. populique Basileensis acuraté delineatus. Basel, ca1650
18pl. Q.
Lipperheide 916

Ringmann, Matthias
(comp.) Passio domini nostri Jhesu Christi

Rings
British museum. Department of British and mediaeval antiquities. Franks bequest; catalog of the finger rings. 1912
Cambridge. University. Corpus Christi college. Lewis collection. The Lewis collection of gems and rings. 1892
Edwards, Charles. The history and poetry of finger-rings. 1855
Evans, Sir John. Posy-rings. 1892
Fairholt, F. W. Rambles of an archaeologist among old books and in old places. 1871. p71-157
Heron-Allen, Edward. Codex chiromantiae. 1883
Jeaffreson, J. C. Brides and bridals. 1872
Jones, William. Finger-ring lore. 1898
King, C. W. Antique gems and rings. 1872
Kunz, G. F. Rings for the finger, from the earliest known times to the present
Tarnóczy, Mme Gustave de. Catalogue descriptif et illustré de la collection de bagues. 1889
Teixeira de Aragão, A. C. Anneis. 1887
Victoria and Albert museum, South Kensington. Catalogue of rings. 1930

Ancient times
British museum. Department of Greek and Roman antiquities. Catalogue of the finger rings, Greek, Etruscan, and Roman, in the departments of antiquities. 1907
Liceti, Fortunio. De anulis antiquis librum singularem. 1645

Middle ages
Deloche, Maximin. Étude historique et archéologique sur les anneaux sigillaires et autres des premiers siècles du moyen âge. 1900

Egypt
Newberry, P. E. Scarabs; an introduction to the study of Egyptian seals and signet rings. 1906

England
Crisp, F. A. Memorial rings, Charles the Second to William the Fourth. 1908

France
Deloche, Maximin. La bague en France à travers l'histoire. 1929

Greece—Mycenaean age
Evans, Sir A. J. 'The ring of Nestor.' 1925

Rings for the finger. Kunz, G. F.

[**Rink, Eucharius Gottlieb**]
Das königliche böhmische crönungs-ceremoniel. Franckfurt & Leipzig, C. Riegel 1723
10 l. 284p. 8 illus. 9pl. O.
"In welchem, nebst einer allgemeinen abhandlung von dieser crönung, alle besondere crönungs-actus derer könige und königinnen aus dem ertz-haus Oesterreich ... enthalten." Subtitle
The plates show coronation ceremonies
Lipperheide 2474

Riols de Fonclare, Jacques Élie de
L'infanterie, par le général de Fonclare; préface de monsieur le maréchal Pétain; aquarelles de Pierre-Albert Leroux. Paris, Société des éditions militaires 1930
146p. 20 col.pl. F. (L'armée française à travers les âges; ses traditions—ses gloires—ses uniformes. [2])
Colas 157b. LC 36-5857

Riotor, Léon
Le mannequin; illustrations de Frédéric Front et divers documents anonymes. Préface d'Octave Uzanne. Paris, Bibliothèque artistique et littéraire 1900
xvi,98p. 13 illus.(4 col.) Q.
Colas 2559

Ripart, G.
(engr.) Nouvion, Pierre de, and Liez, Émile. Un ministre des modes sous Louis XVI

Ritchie, Leitch
Beauty's costume: a series of female figures in the dresses of all times and nations. Containing twelve engravings by the first artists ... With original descriptions by Leitch Ritchie. London, Longmans, Orme, Brown, Green, and Longmans [1838]
12p. 12pl. Q.
Colas 1398. Lipperheide 66

Rites and ceremonies of the Greek church in Russia. King, J. G.

Rites de mariage. Rage-Brocard, Madeleine

I **riti** nuziali degli antichi Romani. Becatelli, Lorenzo, ed.

Ritratti di alcuni celebri pittori del secolo XVII. Lioni, Ottavio

Ritratti di cento capitani illustri. Capriolo, Aliprando

Ritratti et elogii di capitani illustri. Roscio, Giulio, and others

Ritratti et elogii di capitani illustri. Totti, Pompilio

Ritratto de quelle che vano vendendo et lavorando per Roma. Brambilla, Ambrosius

Rittenhouse, Anne, pseud. See Hallmark, Harrydele

Ritter, Georges, and Lafond, Jean

Manuscrits à peintures de l'école du Rouen; livres d'heures normands; recueil de facsimiles et texte par G. Ritter, avec la collaboration de J. Lafond. Paris, A. Picard 1913

60p. 81pl. F. (Soc. de l'histoire de Normandie)

Ritter, Wilhelm Leonard

Java tooneelen uit het leven, karakterschetsen en kleederdrachten van Java's bewoners in afbeeldingen naar de natuur geteekend door E. Hardouin, met tekst van W. L. Ritter, en een voorwoord van M. T. H. Perelaer. Leyden, A. W. Sijthoff 1872

12,165p. illus. 16 col.pl. Q.

The first edition (1855) has a preface by H. M. Lange

Colas 1378. Lipperheide 1507

Die **ritter-** und verdienst-orden. Trost, L. J.

Die **ritter-** und verdienst-orden ... des königr. Bayern. Leser, Jac., and Leser, Oskar

Die **ritterlich** vñ lobrwirdig rayss des gestrengen. Varthema, Ludovico de

Die **ritterliche** gesellschaft im zeitálter des frauencultus. Falke, Jacob von

Ritterliche reutter kunst dariñen ordentlich begriffen wie mã zuvorderst die ritterliche und adeliche ubung der reutterey bevorab in Teutschland ... gezieret durch L. V. C. Franckfurt am Mayn, M. Lechner, in verlegung S. Feyrabends 1584

41,ccliiii l. 289 illus. F.

"Mit musterhafftigen geschmuck ritterspiel, mumerey, kleidung und allem andern so dero beides im schimpff und ernst anhängig gebrauchen und underscheiden möge. Auch wie die röm. keys. maiest. geistliche und weltliche chur und fürsten grauen freyherrn und die vom adel in vorhabenden solemniteten und gewohnlicher herrlichkeit sich zu pferd erzeigen pflegen." Subtitle

Illustrations show riders in masks and fancy dress, tournaments, and the emperor and his household riding. Eight woodcuts showing tournaments are from F. Grisone's *Künstlicher bericht*

Lipperheide 2902

Ritterorden und ehrenzeichen erlaütert durch die vorhandenen urkunden. Gelbke, C. H. von

Der **rittersaal.** Kottenkamp, F. J.

Ritz, Joseph

Franken. See Deutsche volkskunst. v6

Riu Kiu islands

McLeod, John. Voyage of His Majesty's ship Alceste, along the coast of Corea, to the island of Lewchew, with an account of her subsequent shipwreck. 1818

Riva, Giuseppe

L'arte del cappello et della berretta a Monza e a Milano nei secoli XVI-XVIII. Monza, t. Sociale 1909

286p. Q.

Rivera, Diego

Portrait of Mexico; paintings by Diego Rivera and text by Bertram D. Wolfe. New York, Covici, Friede c1937

211p. 249pl. on 127 l. O.

LC 37-27170

Robert, Edouard

(illus.) Uniformes de l'armée turque en 1828

Robert, Karl

Die masken der neueren attischen komoedie. Halle a. S., M. Niemeyer 1911

112p. illus. 1 pl. sq.Q. (Hallisches Winckelmanns-programm, 25)

Robert, L.

Catalogue des collections composant le Musée d'artillerie en 1889. See entry under Paris. Musée d'artillerie

Robert, Ulysse Léonard Léon

Les signes d'infamie au moyen âge: Juifs, Sarrasins, hérétiques, lépreux, Cagots et filles publiques. Paris, H. Champion 1891

189p. illus. VI pl.(2 col. 4 double) D.

Bibliography: p4-5

LC 20-14171

Roberts, David

Sketches of Spanish scenes and architecture. No place, 1833?

26 col.pl.mounted. F.

Figures in the foreground of each plate show Spanish costume

(illus.) Brockedon, William. Egypt & Nubia

(illus.) Croly, George. The Holy Land, Syria, Idumea, Arabia, Egypt & Nubia

Roberts, J.

(illus.) Olivier, J. Fencing familiarized

Roberts, Peter

The Cambrian popular antiquities; or, An account of some traditions, customs, and superstitions, of Wales, with observations as to their origin. London, Printed for E. Williams 1815

353p. 9 col.pl. plan. O.

Lipperheide 990. LC 3-17053

Roberts, William

The cries of London, by W. Roberts. London, The Connoisseur 1924

13p. 14pl.(13 col.) F. (The Connoisseur series of books for collectors)

The plates were painted by F. Wheatley and engraved by A. Cardon, T. Gaugain, N. Schiavonetti, jr., and G. Vendramini. They are included also in Wheatley's *Cries of London*

Costume index. LC 25-6207

Les **robes** de Paul Poiret. Iribe, Paul

Robes élégantes. No. 1, July? 1933+ Wien, Société graphique S. A. Éditions de mode
Illus. col.pl. F.
Published monthly. Current 1938. Text in French and German

Robes from the Manchu court. See Moore, Frederick. Catalog of brilliant old robes from the late court of the Manchus

Robes of Thespis. Mason, Rupert

Robida, Albert

Le XIXe siècle. Paris, G. Decaux 1888
404p. col.front. illus. pl.(part col.) F.
LC 15-16752

La grande mascarade parisienne. Paris, M. Dreyfous 1881-82
5v. 569 illus.(100 col.) Q.
Lipperheide 3683

Mesdames nos aïeules; dix siècles d'élégances. Paris, La librairie illustrée [1891]
254p. 107 illus. 29 col.pl. D.
Colas 2560. Lipperheide 1102

Le vingtième siècle. Paris, G. Decaux 1883
404p. front. illus. pl.(part col.) Q.
A forecast of twentieth century fashions
LC 23-6319

Yester-year, ten centuries of toilette; from the French ... by Mrs Cashel Hoey. New York, C. Scribner; London, Sampson Low, Marston 1891
xii,264p. col.front. illus. col.pl. D. $2.50; 7s 6d, o.p.
Translation of his *Mesdames nos aïeules*
Costume index. LC 15-3343

Robin

Travestissements. Paris, Hautecoeur-Martinet ca1868
104 col.pl. F.
Colas 2561

Robin Hood. See England—Medieval period, 1066-1485

Robin Hood. Perkins, Mrs L. F., comp.

Robins, Joseph

Robins's panoramic representation of the queen's coronation procession in Westminster abbey, on the 28th June, 1838. London, J. Robins & C. Tilt 1838?
1 col.pl. O.
Lipperheide 2692

Robinson, Charles Napier

The British tar in fact and fiction ... illustrated with ... reproductions of old prints, engravings, and woodcuts depicting the character, costume, and customs of the sailor afloat and ashore, as described by the historians, the poets, the novelists and the playwrights. London and New York, Harper 1909
xxiii,520p. 81pl.(incl.col.front.) O.
LC 9-23761

See also Swinburne, H. L. The royal navy

Robinson, Nalbro' Frazier

Monasticism in the orthodox churches, being an introduction to the study of modern Hellenic and Slavonic monasticism; and the orthodox profession rites ... with a Greek dissertation on the monastic habit, done into English. London, Cope & Fenwick 1916
x,175p. illus. pl. D.

Robiquet, Jean. See Gazette du bon genre. Le bon genre

Robley, Horatio Gordon

Moko; or, Maori tattooing, by Major-General Robley. London, Chapman and Hall 1896
xxi,216p. front. illus.(incl. ports. facsim.) sq.Q.
Lipperheide 1641e. LC 9-1086

Robson, William

(tr.) Michaud, J. F. History of the crusades

Rocamora, Manuel

Catàleg de la col·lecció d'indumentaria de Manuel Rocamora, exposada per l'Associació d'amics dels museus de Catalunya ... Barcelona, 2 de juny a 2 de juliol, 1933 [Barcelona? Seix i Barral 1933]
148p. illus. pl. O.
At head of title: Junta de museus
LC 34-35770

Roccheggiani, Lorenzo

Nuova raccolta di cento tavole rappresentante i costumi religiosi civili e militari degli antichi Egiziani, Etruschi, Greci e Romani ... disegnate da Lorenzo Roccheggiani ed incise da Pietro Ruga. Roma, A. Franzetti [1805-09]
100pl. Q.
A partial second edition of his *Raccolta*. Copies of 49 of the plates are in D. Pronti's *Nuova raccolta*
An extract entitled: *Raccolta di sessante tavole* was published 1806
Colas 2563. Lipperheide 112a

Raccolta di cento tavole rappresentanti i costumi religiosi civili, e militari degli antichi Egiziani, Etruschi, Greci, e Romani, tratti dagli antichi monumenti ... Disegnate, ed incise in rame de Lorenzo Roccheggiani. Roma, G. Raffaelli [1804]
2v. 200pl. ob.F.
Volume 1 Tratti degli antichi monumenti; v2 Tratti da antichi bassirilievi
Colas 2562. Lipperheide 112

Rochette, Désiré Raoul

Lettres sur la Suisse écrites en 1819, 1820 et 1821. 3. éd ... ornée de gravures d'après König et autres paysagistes célèbres. Paris, Nepveu 1823
6v. 37 col.pl. S.
Previous editions were published in two volumes with 26 colored plates. The fourth edition, revised and corrected was published (Nepveu, 1828. 3v. 30pl. part col. O.)
Colas 2487. LC 4-8907 (2. éd.)

Peintures antiques inédities, précédées de recherches sur l'emploi de la peinture dans la décoration des édifices sacrés et publics, chez les Grecs et chez les Romains. Paris, Imprimerie royale 1836
xv,470p xv pl.(14 col., 1 fold.) F.
Plates show ancient Greek costume
Lipperheide 160. LC 11-21501

(ed.) Minutoli, W. von der S. von W., freiherrn von. Mes souvenirs d'Égypte.

Rocholl, Meta

Praktische anleitung zum masznehmen, schnittzeichnen, zuschneiden und anfertigen weiblicher garderobegenstände. Kassel, T. Kay 1884
78p. 35 illus. O.
Lipperheide 3830

Rockhill, William Woodville
The land of the lamas; notes of a journey through China, Mongolia and Tibet. New York, The Century co 1891
399p. front. illus. 2 maps. O.
Shows costume of Tibet
LC 4-16692

(ed.) Sarachchandra Dāsa. Journey to Lhasa and central Tibet

Rockstuhl, A.
(illus.) Gille, Floriant. Musée de Tzarskoe-Selo, ou Collection d'armes de sa majesté l'empereur de toutes les Russies

Rococo. See Decoration and ornament—Rococo

Rodenbough, Theophilus Francis
(comp.) From everglade to cañon with the second dragoons, (second United States cavalry); an authentic account of service in Florida, Mexico, Virginia, and the Indian country, including the personal recollections of prominent officers. New York, D. Van Nostrand 1875
561p. col. front. illus. pl.(part col.) 2 fold maps. O.
LC WAR10-91

Rodier, Paul
The romance of French weaving. New York, F. A. Stokes 1931
xvii,356p. col. front. pl.(1 col.) ports. O.
Shows French costume in various periods
Costume index. LC 31-32893

Rodocanachi, Emmanuel Pierre
La femme italienne avant, pendant et après la renaissance; sa vie privée et mondaine, son influence sociale. Paris, Hachette 1922
439p. 65pl.(incl.front. ports.) on 33 l. F. pa 60fr.
Formerly published under title: *La femme italiene à l'époque de la renaissance* (Paris, Hachette 1907)
Bibliography: p[399]-405
Costume index. LC A33-447

Rodrigues Lapa, Manuel
(ed.) Menino, Pero. Livro de falcoaria

Rodriguez, A.
Colleccion general de los trages que en la actualidad se usan en España; principiada en el año 1801. Madrid, Las librerias de Castillo [1804]
116 col.pl. O.
Plates show costume of the provinces of Spain and are engraved by I. Albuerne, F. Marti, Rodriquez, and J. Vasquez after drawings by A. Rodriguez
Colas 2566. Lipperheide 1212

Colleccion general de los trages; que usan actualmente todas las naciones des mundo descubierto. Madrid, 1799
300pl. O.
Plates are engraved by I. Albuerne, F. Marti, J. Vasquez and A. Rodriguez after drawings by the latter
Colas 2565. Lipperheide 479

Rodríguez, G.
(illus.) México y sus alrededores

Rodriguez, Manuel Moreno. See Moreno Rodriguez, Manuel

Rodt, Eduard von
Historische alterthümer der Schweiz ... serie I. Bern, Im selbstverlage des histor. museums 1889
13p. 25pl. F.
Lipperheide 470

Röchling, Carl
Unser heer. Breslau, C. T. Wiskott [1894]
1 l. 51pl. on 41 l. F.
Colas 2564

Rödlich, Hieronymus Franciscus
Skizzen des physisch-moralischen zustandes Dalmatiens und der buchten von Cattaro. Berlin, Realschulbuchhandlung 1811
91p. 9pl.(5 col.) O.
The colored plates show costume
Lipperheide 880

Roehl, E.
Die tracht der schlesischen fürstinnen des 13. und 14. jahrhunderts auf grund ihrer siegel. Breslau, R. Nischkowsky 1895
25p. 18 illus. O.
"Beilage zu dem Jahresberichte der Viktoriaschule in Breslau, Ostern, 1895." Subtitle
Colas 2567. Lipperheide 402e

Roehn, Adolphe
Nouveaux cris de Paris. Paris, Nepveu 1817
10 col.pl. Q.
Lithographed by G. Engelmann. For list of plates see Colas's *Bibliographie*
Colas 2568. Lipperheide 1183

Röhn, E. Löwenheim-. See Löwenheim-Röhn, E.

Römer-Büchner, B. J.
Die wahl und krönung der deutschen kaiser zu Frankfurt am Main. Frankfurt a. M., H. Keller 1858
x,118p. illus. 9pl(4 col.) O.
Lipperheide 1763

Römisch kaiserlicher majestät kriegs-völker im zeitalter der landsknechte. Breunner-Enkevoërth, A. J., graf von

Das **römische** carneval. Goethe, J. W.

Römische historien. Livius, Titus

Römische hochzeits- und ehedenkmäler. Rossbach, August

Römische und byzantinische seiden-textilien aus dem gräberfelde von Achmim-Panopolis. Forrer, Robert

Der **römischen** fontanen wahre abbildung. Falda, G. B.

Der **römischen** keyser- und koniglichen maiestetē. Hortleder, Friederich

Die **römischen** mosaiken und malereien der kirchlichen bauten vom IV. bis XIII. jahrhundert. Wilpert, Josef

Die **römischen** privataltertümer. Blümner, Hugo

Das **Römisch-germanische** central-museum in bildlichen darstellungen aus seinen sammlungen. Lindenschmit, Ludwig

Rötter, Henriette
Für frauen und töchter; das kleidermachen zum selbstunterrichte; 2. verb. aufl. Wien, R. v. Waldheim 1892
62p. 53 illus. 1 pl. F.
First edition: 1888
Lipperheide 3841-42

Röttger, Carl
(ed.) Petrograd. Ėrmitazh. Die alterthumer von Kertsch in der Kaiserlichen Eremitage

Rogacion en detestacion de los grandes abusos en los traxes y adornos nuevamente introducidos en España. Carranza, Alonso

Roger, Paul André
La noblesse de France aux croisades. Paris, Derache 1845
339p. front. illus. pl. Q.
Many of the plates show French armor
LC 13-14535

Roger-Milès, Léon
Comment discerner les styles du VIIIe au XIXe siècle: histoire—philosophie—document. Paris, E. Rouveyre ca1906
152 l. 104pl. Q.
Many editions
Costume index. Colas 2569

Les créateurs de la mode; dessins et documents de Jungbluth, texte de L. Roger-Milès. Paris, C. Eggimann [c1910]
156p. illus. pl.(part col.) F. fr.25
Colas 1579. LC 11-1705

Rogers, Agnes
(comp.) The American procession, American life since 1860 in photographs, assembled by Agnes Rogers; with running comment by Frederick Lewis Allen. New York and London, Harper 1933
[190]p. of illus.(incl. ports.) F. $3
Costume index. LC 33-30802

Rogers, James Edward
Academic caps, hoods and gowns. Waukesha, Wis. 1911]
5p. pl. S.
Reprinted from *The Waukesha Freeman*, August 24, 1911

Rogers, William
(engr.) Segar, Sir William. Honor military, and civill

Rogers, Peet & co. New York
Livery, 1898. New York, Rogers, Peet [1898]
52p. incl. front. illus. D.
LC 10-1022

Things clerical; being some account of ecclesiastical vestments, their origin and early form ... and such vestments as are sold by Rogers, Peet & co. [New York, Rogers, Peet 1902]
87p. illus. pl. T.
LC 2-9151

Rohault de Fleury, Charles
La messe; études archéologiques sur ses monuments, par Ch. Rohault de Fleury ... continuées par son fils [George Rohault de Fleury] Paris, A. Morel 1883-89
8v. illus. DCLXXX (i.e. 688) pl. F.
In portfolios. The last three volumes show ecclesiastical costume of the Christian church in early times and through the middle ages
Colas 2570. LC 13-26016

Rohault de Fleury, Georges. See Rohault de Fleury, Charles. La messe

Rohbausch, Helena Regina
Sam̃lung Augspurgischer kleider trachten ... Collection de divers habits, usités dans la ville d'Augsbourg par les deux sexes. Augsbourg, J. M. Motz ca1750
1 l. 29 col.pl. D.
Most of the plates show feminine costume at the beginning of the 18th century
Colas 2571. Lipperheide 771

Rohde, Eleanour. See Canziani, Estella, jt. auth.

Rohr, G.
Costumes de femmes suisse. No place, ca1825
21 col.pl. Q.
Colas 2572

Rohrbach, Carl
The costumes of all nations from the earliest times to the nineteenth century: exhibiting the dresses and habits of all classes, regal, ecclesiastical, noble, military, judicial, and civil. London H. Sotheran 1882
4p. 104 col.pl. F.
Has the same plates as the German edition: *Die trachten der völker,* but no text. Illustrated by Albert Kretschmer
Colas 1667. LC 12-27754

Die trachten der völker vom beginn der geschichte bis zum 19. jahrhundert; in 104 tafeln ... von Albert Kretschmer, mit text von Carl Rohrbach; 2 aufl. Leipzig, J. G. Bach 1882
366p. 104 col.pl. Q.
Plates 1-77 of the first edition (Leipzig, J. G. Bach 1860-64. 342p. 100 col.pl.) correspond with these same numbers in the second edition
According to Colas the third German edition (Leipzig, A. Schumann 1906. 352p. 104 col.pl.) is a reproduction of the German edition of 1882
Colas 1665-1666, 1668. Costume index. Lipperheide 75-76. LC 12-29705 (1st ed.)

Les **rois** et ducs d'Austrasie. See Clément, Nicolas, de Treille. Austrasiae reges et duces **epigrammatis**

Rois et reines de France depuis l'origine de la monarchie jusqu'à nos jours; lithographiés d'après les médailles, sculptures et peintures les plus authentiques. Paris, Mme. Vve Delpech ca1845
132 pl. O.
Lipperheide 1086

Les **rois** et reines de France en estampes. Lejeune, Eugène, and Lacauchie, A.

Rokoko. Boehn, Max von

Rolando, Guzman
The modern art of fencing agreeably to the practice of the most eminent masters of Europe ... revised ... by J. S. Forsyth. London, S. Leigh 1822
xxxi,240p. 23 col. pl. D.
Illustrated by W. Derby and engraved by S. Hall
Spanish edition: *Nuevo art de esgrima* (Londres, R. Ackermann 1826)
Lipperheide 2985

Rolfe, Clapton Crabb
The ancient use of liturgical colours. Oxford and London, Parker 1879
xii,227p. front(fold.tab.) O.
Contains material on ecclesiastical vestments from the 1st to the 17th century
LC 17-3016

Roller, Théophile
Les catacombes de Rome; histoire de l'art et des croyances religieuses pendant les premiers siècles du christianisme. Paris, Vve A. Morel [1881]
2v. illus. C pl.(incl.plan.) sq.F.
Shows ecclesiastical costume of the early Christian church
Lipperheide 252. LC 3-14174

Rom in wort und bild. Kleinpaul, R. A. R.

Rom und römisches leben im alterthum. Bender, Hermann

Roma sancta sive Benedicti XIII. Conlin, J. R.

Roma sotterranea. Rossi, G. B. de

Romain, Jules, pseud. See Pippi, Giulio

Roman festivals of the period of the Republic. Fowler, W. W.

The **Roman** soldier. Forestier, Amédée

The **Roman** toga. Wilson, L. M.

Romanae historiae principis. See Livius, Titus. Titi Livii Patavini, Romanae historiae principis

Romance and tragedy of pioneer life. Mason, A. L.

Romance of French weaving. Rodier, Paul

Romance of men's hats. Manchester, Herbert

Romance of Siamese harem life. See Leonowens, Mrs A. H. C. The romance of the harem

Romance of the harem. Leonowens, Mrs A. H. C.

Romance of the river Platte. Koebel, W. H.

Romance of the shoe. Wright, Thomas

Romance of the straw hat. Luton, England. Public museum

România in chipuri şi vederi. Iorga, Nicoláe

Die **romanischen** literaturen des mittelalters. Olschki, Leonardo

Romanorum imperatorium effigies. Cavaleriis, J. B. de

Romanorum principŭ effigies: cŭ historiarum annotatione, olim ab Io. Hutchichio confecta. See Huttich, Johann. Imperatorum romanorum libellus

Romantic East. Del Mar, Walter

Romantic figures in pen and color. Langley, E. F.

Romantic story of the Highland garb and the tartan. Mackay, J. G.

Le **romantisme** et la mode. Maigron, Louis

Romberg, Maurice
Types de l'armée belge. Bruxelles, 1897-1900
10 col.pl. F.
Colas 2573

Rome

See also Military costume—Rome, Ancient; also subdivision Rome under Arms and armor; Ceremonial and festival costume; Charioteers; Hair-dressing; Headdress; Jewelry, Ancient; Street venders—Italy

To 476

Amelung, Walther. Die gewandung der alten Griechen und Römer. 1903

Amman, Jost. Icones Livianae: praecipuas romanorum historias magno artificio. 1573

Antiquitates sacrae & civiles Romanorum explicatae. Sive commentarii historici, mythologici, philologici, in varia monumenta prisca, & maxime in plures statuas, aras, tumulos, inscriptiones &c. 1726

Aragon, Henry. Le costume dans les temps anciens et au moyen âge. 1921

Arnay, J. R. d'. De la vie privée des Romains. 1757

Arnay, J. R. d'. Habitudes et moeurs privées des Romains. 1795

Arnay, J. R. d'. Private life of the Romans. 1761

Bartholin, Bertelli. De paenula; accessit ... Henrici Ernstii ejusdem argumenti epistola. 1670

Baumeister, August. Denkmäler des klassischen altertums. 1885-1888

Baxter, Thomas. Darstellung des aegyptischen, griechischen und römischen costums. 1815

Baxter, Thomas. An illustration of the Egyptian, Grecian, and Roman costume. 1810

Becatelli, Lorenzo, ed. I riti nuziali degli antichi Romani. 1762

Bender, Hermann. Rom und römisches leben im alterthum. [1880]

Bertolini, Francesco. Storia di Roma dalle origini italiche sino alla caduta dell'impero d'occidente. 1886

Blümner, Hugo. Die römischen privataltertümer. 1911

Böttiger, K. A. Sabina, oder morgenscenen im putzzimmer einer reichen Römerin. 1803

Bossi, Gerolamo. De toga Romana commentarius. 1671

British museum. Department of Greek and Roman life. A guide to the exhibition illustrating Greek and Roman life. 1920

Brummell, G. B. Male and female costume. 1932

Carta, M. S. Tessuti fogge e decorazioni nell' abito muliebre in Grecia e a Roma. 1934

Danz, A. H. E. Aus Rom und Byzanz. 1867

Daremberg, C. V., and Saglio, Edmond, eds. Dictionnaire des antiquités grecques et romaines, d'après les textes et les monuments. 1877-1919

Davis, W. S. A day in old Rome. 1925

Effigies virorum ac foeminarum illustrium, quibus in Græcis aut Latinis monumentis aliqua ... pars datur. 1724?

Eiler, J. G., praeses. Dissertatio philologica de toga & sago. 1671

Falke, Jakob von. Greece and Rome their life and art. 1882

Rome—To 476—*Continued*

Frölich, Franz. Die mode im alten Rom. 1884

Grasset de Saint-Sauveur, Jacques. L'antique Rome ou Description historique ou pittoresque de tout ce qui concerne le peuple romain, dans ses costumes civiles, militaires et religieux ... depuis Romulus jusqu'à Augustule. 1796

Guhl, E. K., and Koner, W. D. Das leben der griechen und römer nach antiken bildwerken. 1862

Guhl, E. K., and Koner, W. D. The life of the Greeks and Romans described from antique monuments. 1889

Heuzey, L. A. Histoire du costume antique d'après des études sur le modèle vivant. 1922

Houston, M. G. Ancient Greek, Roman and Byzantine costume and decoration (including Cretan costume). 1931

James, Constantin. Toilette d'une Romaine au temps d'Auguste, et cosmétiques d'une Parisienne au XIXe siècle. 1865

Johnston, H. W. The private life of the Romans. 1932

Jung, Julius. Leben und sitten der Römer in der kaiserzeit. 1883-84

Lambert, André. Aus dem alten Rom. 1912

Lowrie, Walter. Monuments of the early church. 1923

Le Clerc, Sébastien. Divers habillemens des anciens Grecs et Romains. 1680

Marquardt, K. J. Das privatleben der Römer. 1886

Martigny, J. A., l'abbé. Dictionnaire des antiquités chrétiennes. 1865

Meiners, Christoph. Recherches historiques sur le luxe chez les Athéniens, depuis les temps les plus anciens, jusqu'à la mort de Philippe de Macédoine. 1823

Meurs, Johannes van. De luxu Romanorum. 1605

Müller, Albert. Die trachten der Römer und Römerinnen nach Ovid und Martial. 1868

Naples (City). Museo nazionale. Real museo Borbonico. 1824-57

Nöhring, Johann. Vierundzwanzig statuen des Vaticanischen und Capitolischen museums zu Rom und der Uffizien in Florenz. 1869

Opitz, Richard. Das häusliche leben der Griechen und Römer. 1894

Orsini, Fulvio. Imagines et elogia virorum illustrium et eruditor ex antiquis lapidibus et nomismatib. expressa cum annotationib. 1570

Panvinio, Onofrio. Amplissimi ornatissimique triumphi, uti. L. Paulus de rege Macedonum perse capto, P. Africanus Aemilianus de Cathagenensibus excisis. C. N. Pompeius magnus ex Oriente, Julius Augustus, Vespasianus, Traianus, et alij imperatores romani, triumpharunt. 1618

Petersen, E. A. H.; Domaszewski, Alfre von, and Calderini, Guglielmo, ed Die Marcus-säule auf piazza Colonn in Rom. 1896

Preston, H. W., and Dodge, Louis The private life of the Romans. 18

Presuhn, Emil. Die pompejanische wanddecorationen. 1882

Presuhn, Emil. Pompeji; die neueste ausgrabungen von 1874 bis 1881. 187 82

Ramsay, William. A manual of Roma antiquities. 1901

Rehberg, Friedrich. Drawings faithfull copied from nature at Naples. 1794

Reinach, Salomon. Répertoire de l statuaire grecque et romaine. 1897 1910

Repond, Jules. Les secrets de la draperi antique de l'himation grec au palliur romain. 1931

Rich, Anthony. The illustrated com panion to the Latin dictionary an Greek lexicon. 1849

Rossbach, August. Römische hochzeits und ehedenkmäler. 1871

Rossi, G. B. de. Roma sotterranea: di römischen katakomben. 1879

Saint Non, J. C. R. de. Voyage pitto resque; ou, Description des royaume de Naples et de Sicile. 1781-86

Sandys, Sir J. E., ed. A companion t Latin studies. 1921

Showerman, Grant. Rome and the Ro mans. 1931

Simons, Theodor. Aus altrömischer zei 1872-78

Strimmer, Hermann. Kleidung un schmuck der Römer zur zeit des Hora 1889

Tertullianus, Q. S. F. De fuga in per secutione, De pallio. 1932

Weese, Arthur. Die Cäsar-teppiche in Historischen museum zu Bern. 1911

Wilpert, Josef. Die gewandung de Christen in den ersten jahrhunderten vornehmlich nach den katakomben malereien dargestellt. 1898

Wilpert, Josef. Die römischen mosaike und malereien der kirchlichen baute vom IV. bis XIII. jahrhundert. 1916

Wilson, L. M. The Roman toga. 1924

Wilson, L. M. A study of the Roma toga. 1924

See also Kings and rulers—Rome also subdivision Rome, Ancient unde Naval costume; Theatrical costume Weddings and wedding dress

Collection

Cologne, Germany. Städtisches museum Wallraff-Richartz. Katalog des mu seums. 1869

Empire, B.C. 30-A.D. 476

Becker, W. A. Gallus, oder Römisch scenen aus der zeit Augusts. 1863

Becker, W. A. Gallus; or, Roman scene in the time of Augustus. 1849

Rome—Empire, B.C. 30-A.D. 476—*Continued*

Bellermann, C. F. Über die ältesten christlichen begrabnissstatten und besonders die katakomben zu Neapel mit ihren wandgemälden. 1839

Crochet L. C. La toilette chez les Romaines au temps des empereurs. 1888

Rome and the Romans. Showerman, Grant

Rome (City). See Italy—Rome

Rome (City) Esposizione dell' ornamento femminile 1500-1800, 1907

L'évolution de l'art dans l'éventail aux 16. 17. et 18. siècles. See entry under Bojardi, F. de

Die **romfahrt** Kaiser Heinrich's VII. Baldwin, of Luxemburg, abp. and elector of Treves

Romme

Les douze mois de l'année. Paris, Sauvage 1928?
12 col.pl. Q.
In portfolio. Plates show fancy dress

Romussi, Carlo

Milano ne' suoi monumenti ... 3. ed. rinnovata e completata. Milano, Società ed. Sonzogno [1912-13]
2v. illus. 105pl.(part col.) F.
Opera premiata dalla Società pedagogica italiana. Bibliographical foot-notes
Contents: v 1 Delle origini all'anno 1000; v2 Dall'anno 1000 al 1400
LC 14-13805

Ronnenberg, Johann Gottlieb Ferdinand

Abbildung der churhannöverischen armée-uniformen. Hannover & Leipzig, 1791
72p. 34 col.pl. O.
Colas 2

Roo, Gerardus de

Annales, oder historische chronick der ... fürsten und herren, ertzhertzogen zu Oesterreich ... fürnemlich von Rudolpho dem ersten ... bisz auff Carolum den fünfften. Augspurg, J. Schultes 1622
x,482p. 478 illus. F.
First edition was published in Latin in 1592, translated into German by Conrad Dietz
Lipperheide 849

Rooke, William

(tr.) Mineur, A. E. A charitable remonstrance addressed to the wives and maidens of France, touching their dissolute adornments

Roos, Cajetan

Samling af Swenska armeens uniformer. Recueil des uniformes de l'armée suédoise. [Dresde, Neumann] 1788
33 col.illus. O.
Colas 2574

Roos, Gaetano. See Roos, Cajetan

Rosses, Max

(ed.) Vlaanderen door de eeuwen neen

Ropartz, Sigismond. See Lalaisse, Hippolyte, jt. auth.

Rosa, Gaetano de. See Roos, Cajetan

Rosa, Michele

Della porpore e delle materie vestiarie presso gli antichi. Modena, Dalla stamperia Ducale MCCLXXXVI (i.e. 1786)
xx,388p. 1 pl. Q.
Colas 2575. Lipperheide 108

Rosary, Eugène, pseud.

Nos vêtements. Rouen, Mégard 1881
O. fr.80

Roscio, Giulio, and others

Ritratti et elogii di capitani illustri, che ne' secoli moderni hanno gloriosamente guerreggiato ... descritto da G. Roscio, A. Mascardi, F. Leonida, O. Tronsarelli, & altri. Roma, 1646
404p. 132 illus. Q.
May be the same book as a similar title by Totti. Books not available for comparison
Lipperheide 312

Rose, Augustus Foster, and Cirino, Antonio

Jewelry making and design; an illustrated text book for teachers, students of design, and craft workers in jewelry. Providence, R. I., Metal crafts publishing co. [c1917]
xiii,463p col. front. illus. col. pl. O. $10.40
Part of the illustrations numbered as plates
Costume index. LC 17-31894

Rose Bertin. Langlade, Émile

Rose, L.

(engr.) Du Fresnel, H. V. D. Un régiment à travers l'histoire

Rosellini, Ippolito

I monumenti dell' Egitto e della Nubia. Pisa, N. Capurro 1832-44
9v. illus. pl.(part fold.) O. and 3 atlases of 395 pl.(part col.) F.
Plates show costume, also decoration and ornament in ancient Egypt
LC 5-9012

Rosenberg, Adolf

The design and development of costume from prehistoric times up to the twentieth century. London, W. & G. Foyle 1925
5v. 400pl(part col.) F.
In portfolios. Edited by Dominic C. Tiranti. Plates by Max Tilke
English edition of the author's *Geschichte des kostüms*
Costume index. LC 26-5371

Geschichte des kostüms; text von prof. dr. Eduard Heyck. Berlin, E. Wasmuth [1905-23]
5v. in 8. 400pl.(part col.) F.
Five volumes or portfolios of 80 plates each; each plate accompanied by historical and explanatory text. Issued originally in 40 parts of 10 plates each, one-half in colors. Plates by Max Tilke
Contents: v 1 Orientalisches und ägyptisches alterthum, plates 1-21; v2 Griechisch-römisches alterthum, plates 22-59; v3 Mittelalter, plates 60-120; v4 16. jahrhundert, plates 121-170; v5 17. jahrhundert, plates 171-220; v6 18. und 19. jahrh. bis 1820, plates 221-300; v7 Europäische volkstrachten, plates 301-364; v8 Volkstrachten in Asien, Afrika, und Amerika, plates 365-400
Colas 2576. LC 25-21985

Rosenberg, J. C. W.

Les cris de Berlin; zwölf merkwürdige ausrufer von Berlin mit ihrem geschrey. Berlin, J. Morino ca1790
1 l. 12pl. F.
Colas 2578 Lipperheide 816

Rosenberg, Léonce
Catalogue d'une collection de miniatures gothiques et persanes, appartenant à Léonce Rosenberg, par Seymour de Ricci. Paris, [Montassier et Odend'hal] 1913
63p. 32pl. Q.
Shows costume of the 12th-16th centuries

Rosenberg, Marc
Alte und neue fächer, aus der wettbewerbung und ausstellung zu Karlsruhe 1891; hrsg. vom bad. kunstgewerbe verein. Wien, Gerlach & Schenk 1892
14,xip. illus. 69pl. F.
Published in twelve parts (lieferung)

Badische uniformen 1807 und 1809. Karlsruhe, A. Bielefeld 1896
43p. 14pl. Q.
According to Colas these plates are adapted from Weiland's pictures of French uniforms of the Empire period
Colas 2577. Lipperheide 2210c

Rosenfeld, Helmut
Deutsches ernte-dankfest, 1933; das bekenntnis der nation zum bauerntum; dokumente in wort und bild ... mit einem geleitwort des reichsbauernführers und reichsernährungsministers R. Walther Darré. Potsdam, Akademische verlagsgesellschaft Athenaion [1933]
64p. illus. pl. ports. Q.
Shows Nazi uniforms
LC 36-8117

Rosenthal, Doris
(comp.) Pertaining to costume. New York, Brown-Robertson [1929]
50pl. F. $4.50
Shows costume, headdress, and footwear from the time of the ancient Egyptians to the 20th century
Costume index

Rosenthal, Oskar
Die heilkunde in geschichte u. kunst; abreiszkalender f. ärzte. Doemitz, E. Mattig [1926]
122 illus. O.

Rosenzweig, Adolf
Kleidung und schmuck im biblischen und talmudischen schrifttum. Berlin, M. Poppelauer 1905
130p. D.

Roskoschny, Hermann
Das asiatische Russland. Leipzig, Gressner & Schramm [1884]
2v. illus. 9pl.(part double) maps(part fold.) F.
Lipperheide 1388. LC 5-35480

Russland, land und leute. Leipzig, Gressner & Schramm [1882-84]
2v. illus. 12pl.(part double) F.
Lipperheide 1375. LC 22-4967

Rosmäsler, F. H. W.
Hamburgs bürger-bewaffnung. Hamburg, G. Noveletto 1816
6 l. 22 col.pl. Q.
Colas 2579. Lipperheide 2213

Ross und reiter. See note under Sport im bild

Rossbach, August
Römische hochzeits- und ehedenkmäler. Leipzig, B. G. Teubner 1871
xii,180p. 2 fold.pl. O.
Plates show old Roman costume
Lipperheide 245

Rosse, Herman. See Macgowan, Kenneth, jt. auth.

Rossi, Domenico de
Gemme antiche figurate ... colle sposizioni di Paolo Alessandro Maffei. Roma, Nella Stamperia alla Pace 1707-09
4v. pl. Q.
Shows costume, hair, and headdress of the ancient Greeks and Romans, from carvings on agates, onyxes, cameos and other stones
Lipperheide 153. LC 19-7780

Rossi, Giovanni Battista de
Roma sotterranea: die römischen katakomben ... mit zugrundelegung des werkes, von I. Spencer Northcote ... und W. R. Brownlow ... bearb. von dr. Franz Xaver Kraus. 2. verm. aufl. Freiburg im Breisgau, St. Louis, Mo., Herder 1879
xxx,636p. front. illus. XII pl.(part col.) O.
Six of the plates show costume worn in Rome in the first century
LC 13-12649

Rostand, Maurice
Casanova. See Theatrical costume—Special plays, ballets, etc.—Rostand, Maurice. Casanova

Ein **Rostocker** studenten-stammbuch von 1736/37. Kohfeldt, Gustav, and Ahrens, Wilhelm, eds.

Rota, Ettore
(ed.) Petrus, de Ebulo. De rebus siculis carmen

Rotch, Benjamin. See Manners & customs of the French (attributed)

Roth, Henry Ling
Oriental silverwork, Malay and Chinese; a handbook for connoisseurs, collectors, students and silversmiths. London, Truslove & Hanson 1910
300p. front. illus. Q. 21s, o.p.
Shows Malay belt buckles, also jewelry, Malay and Chinese
Costume index. LC CA11-3367D

Roth, Johann Ferdinand
Nürnbergisches taschenbuch. Nürnberg, J. L. Schrag 1812-13
2v. 6pl.(5 col.) O.
Lipperheide 786

Roth, Johann Michael
Wahrhaffte bildnüsse aller des heil. röm. reichs freyen stadt Augspurg, herren stadt-pfleger, welche ... seit ao. 1548 biss auf unsere zeitē regieret. Augspurg, [1731]
30pl. Q.
Portraits are half length figures
Lipperheide 768

Rothe de Nugent, D.
Anti-Titus, ou La critique de la mode des cheveux coupés, pour les femmes. Paris, P. Mongie 1809
31p. O.
Lipperheide 1691

Rothenlöwen, Karl, graf von Rechberg und. See Rechberg und Rothenlöwen, Karl, graf von

Rothenstein, Albert Daniel. See Rutherston, A. D.

Rothfeld, Otto. See Rothfield, Otto

Rothfield, Otto
Women of India, by Otto Rothfeld ... illustrated by M. V. Dhurandhar. London, Simpkin, Marshall, Hamilton, Kent [1920]
222p. col.front. col.pl. O.
Each plate accompanied by guard sheet with descriptive letterpress
Costume index. LC 21-7941

Rothschild, Mayer Karl, freiherr von
Der schatz des freiherrn Karl von Rothschild. Meisterwerke alter goldschmiedekunst aus dem 14.-18. jahrhundert; hrsg. von Ferdinand Luthmer. Frankfurt am Main, H. Keller 1883-85
2v. 100 mounted pl.(part col.) F.
LC 14-16273

Rottmann, Hans
Die armeen Serbiens und Montenegros, von leutnant Hans Rottmann. Leipzig, M. Ruhl [1909]
22p. 4 col.pl. D.

Rouargue, Adolphe
(illus.) Souvestre, Émile. La Bretagne pittoresque

Rouen, Charles
L'armée belge; exposé historique de son organisation, de ses costumes et uniformes, de son armement et de sa tactique depuis les temps primitifs jusqu'à nos jours. Bruxelles, E. Lyon-Claesen 1896
784p. illus. 150pl,100 col.) Q. 60fr.
Colas 2582. Lipperheide 2261c

Rouffaer, Gerrit Pieter, and Juynboll, Hendrik Herman
De batik-kunst in Nederlandsch-Indië en haar geschiedenis. Utrecht, A. Oosthoek 1914
15,xxxiv,534,lxv p. illus. 100pl.(part col. part double) 2 fold.maps. F. (Publicaties van's Rijks ethnographisch museum. ser.II, no. 1)
Dutch and German in parallel columns; added title page in German: *Die batikkunst in Niederländisch-Indien und ihre geschichte*
"Voorwoord" signed: Dr. J. D. E. Schmeltz, who, until his death, revised the translation into German, of his son, J. C. E. Schmeltz
Shows costume of the Dutch East Indies, and also many batik designs
Bibliography: p XXIV-XXXIV at beginning
LC 15-12289

Rouffet, J.
(illus.) Margerand, J. Notes sur les tenues des Hussards de 1815 à 1870

Rougé, Emmanuel, vicomte de
Études sur le rituel funéraire des anciens Égyptiens. Paris, Didier 1860
83p. illus. 3pl.(2 col.) O.
LC 19-18761

Rougé, Oliver Charles Camille Emmanuel. See Rougé, Emmanuel, vicomte de

Rougemont, Josephus Claudius
Etwas über kleidertracht, in wie ferne sie einen nachtheiligen einfluss auf die gesundheit hat. Bonn, J. F. Abshoven [1784]
36p. Q.

Rouit, H.
La mode féminine à travers les âges. Paris, Édition d'art 1925
1 l. 54 col.pl. Q.
"Tout ce qui concerne la toilette féminine depuis la plus haute antiquité jusqu'à nos jours; robes et patrons, tissus, chapeaux, coiffures, bijoux, chaussures, peignes, etc." Subtitle
Costume index. Colas 2583

Roujoux, Prudence Guillaume, baron de
Le monde en estampes, ou Géographie des cinq parties du monde. Paris, A. Nepveu 1830
2v. 79 col.pl. 12 maps. ob.O.
Volume 1 text; v2 plates. Most of the plates show costume
Colas 2584. LC 11-34487

Roulin, Eugène Augustin
Linges, insignes et vêtements liturgiques. Paris, P. Lethielleux 1930
xii,316p. illus. 8pl. O.
Bibliography: p XI-XII
Shows ecclesiastical vestments of the Roman Catholic Church
Colas 2585

Vestments and vesture, a manual of liturgical art ... translated by Dom Justin McCann. London, Sands; St. Louis, Mo., B. Herder 1931
xv,308p. front. illus. pl. O. 15s, $6.50
Translation of his *Linges, insignes et vêtements liturgiques*
Bibliography: p299-300
Costume index. LC 31-20101

Roumania. See Rumania

La **Roumanie** en images, v 1; publié sous la direction de M. P. A. Paris, Imprimerie a.-g. L'Hoir 1919
268p. incl. illus.(part col.) pl.(part col.) Q.
Shows Rumanian costume and embroidery

See also Iorga, Nicoláe. România in chipuri şi vederi

Roumanie, son paysage. See Hielscher, Kurt. Rumania

Round about my Peking garden. Little, A. H. N. B.

Rourke, Constance Mayfield
Troupers of the Gold Coast; or, The rise of Lotta Crabtree. New York, Harcourt, Brace [c1928]
xiii,262p. front. illus.(facsims.) pl. ports. O.
Shows 19th century dress in the United States
LC 28-22487

Rous, John. See Pageants of Richard Beauchamp, earl of Warwick. Pageant of the birth, life and death (supposed author)

Rous, Samuel Holland. See note under The Victor book of the opera

Rousselet, Louis
L'Inde des rajahs, voyage dans l'Inde centrale et dans les présidences de Bombay et du Bengale. Paris, Hachette 1874
807p. 317 illus. 6 maps. Q.

India and its native princes; travels in Central India and in the presidencies of Bombay and Bengal; revised and edited by Lieut.-Col. Buckle. London, Chapman and Hall; New York, Scribner, Armstrong 1876
xviii,579p. front. illus. pl. maps. F.
Translation of the author's *L'Inde des rajahs*
LC 5-10076

Rousset de Missy, Jean. See Dumont, Jean, baron de Carlscroon, jt. auth

Roussillon. See France—By region or province—Poitou; France—By region or province—Pyrenees

Routier, Gaston
Le couronnement d'Alphonse XIII, roi d'Espagne. Paris, A. Savaète [1902]
223p. front. illus. plates, ports. Q.
LC 3-31099

Routledge, Mrs Katherine (Pease). See Routledge, W. S., jt. auth.

Routledge, William Scoresby, and Routledge, Mrs Katherine (Pease)
With a prehistoric people, the Akikúyu of British East Africa, being some account of the method of life and mode of thought found existent amongst a nation on its first contact with European civilisation. London, E. Arnold 1910
xxxii,392p. front illus. CXXXVI pl. fold. map. O.
Many plates printed on both sides, and some accompanied by descriptive text on verso or on separate leaf
Bibliography: p363-65
LC 10-21763

Routledge's every girl's annual, 1886. London, G. Routledge 1886
570p. illus. 12 col.pl. O.
Plates show 19th century dress in the principal countries of Europe and in Egypt

Rouveyre, Édouard
Le directoire: portefeuille d'un incroyable publié par Roger de Parnes; avec préface par Georges d'Heylli. Paris, E. Rouveyre 1880
xviii,228p. illus. 4pl. O.
Lipperheide 1149

Gazette anecdotique du règne de Louis XVI; portefeuille d'un talon-rouge publié par Roger de Parnes, avec préface par Georges d'Heylli. Paris, E. Rouveyre 1881
xxx,243p. illus. 4pl.(3 double) O.
Illustrated by E. Mesplès
Lipperheide 1148

Roux, Claudius, and Brunel, Noré
La vie galante à Lyon au bon vieux temps, histoire anecdotique et illustrée des mœurs intimes lyonnaises à toutes les époques ... ouvrage orné ... d'une série documentaire de XCV planches phototypiques hors-texte ouvrées par Maurice Lescuyer. Lyon, Les Éditions du Fleuve 1928
xv,390p. fold. front. illus. pl. ports. facsims. sq.Q.
LC 29-14045

Roux, F. A. W. L.
Anweisung zum hiebfechten mit graden und krummen klingen; 2. aufl. Jena, F. Mauke 1849
57,60p. 18pl. O.
First edition: 1840
Lipperheide 2988

Roux, G. See Jauslin, Carl, jt. auth.

Roux, Jules Charles
Bibliothèque régionaliste: Le costume en Provence. Paris, Bloud 1909
250p. 58pl. D.
Colas 601

Le costume en Provence; criticism. See Aurouze, J. Le costume en Provence. 1908

Souvenirs du passé: Le costume en Provence. Paris, A. Lemerre 1907
2v.(251,241p.) ca600 illus. 22pl. Q.
Contents: v 1 Période ancienne; v [2] Période moderne
Colas 600. Costume index. LC 20-1472[illegible]

Roving through southern China. Franck, H. A.

Rovinskiĭ, Dmitriĭ Aleksandrovich
Portraits authentiques des tzars Jean III, Basile son fils et Jean IV. le Terrible et cinq ambassades de leur époque, reproduits d'après des gravures contemporaines. Saint-Pétersbourg, Expédition pour la confection des papiers de l'éta[t] 1882
16p. 47pl.(2 col.) F.
Text is in Russian. Plates are reproduced from various works of the 16th an[d] 17th centuries
Lipperheide 1374

Rowbotham, John Frederick
The troubadours and courts of love. London, S. Sonnenschein; New York, Macmillan 1895
xxiii,324p. fold. front. illus. 2 maps([1] fold.) D. (Social England series)
LC 4-16407

Rowland, Alexander
The human hair, popularly and physiologically considered, with special reference to its preservation, improvemen[t] and adornment and the various mode[s] of its decoration in all countries. London, Piper 1853
214p. front. 6pl. O.
LC 7-12190

Rowlands, Walter
(comp.) Boston. Public library. Costume a selected list of books in the Public library of the city of Boston

Rowlandson, Thomas
Characteristic sketches of the lower orders. London, S. Leigh 1820
iv p. col.front. 52 col.pl. S.
Colas 2588

Hungarian & Highland broad sword [London] H. Angelo 1799
3 l. III p col.pl. Q.
Colas 2587

Loyal volunteers of London and environs; infantry and cavalry in thei[r] respective uniforms. [London, Ackermann] 1798-99
45 l. 86 col.pl. Q.
Colas 2586

(engr.) Bunbury, H. W. Academy fo[r] grown horsemen

(illus.) Busby, T. L. Costume of the lower orders in Paris (attributed)

(illus.) Tuer, A. W. Old London stree[t] cries and the cries of to-day. 1885

Rowlandson the caricaturist. Grego, Joseph

Roworth, C.
The art of defence on foot with the broad sword and sabre. London Printed for T. Egerton 1798
108p. 10pl. O.
Lipperheide 2979

Roxburgh club, London
Liber regalis. See entry under Catholic church. Liturgy and ritual

Roy, Hippolyte
La vie, la mode, et le costume au XVIIe siècle, époque Louis XIII; étude sur la cour de Lorraine établie d'après les mémoires des fournisseurs et artisans. Paris, É. Champion 1924
xvi,553p. 27pl.(part col. part double) O.
Each colored plate accompanied by guard sheet with descriptive letterpress
Colas 2589. Costume index. LC 25-9443

Roy, Marius
Les grandes manoeuvres. Paris, L. Baschet [1887]
2v. 16 illus.(part col.) O. (Cahiers d'enseignement illustrés, no.23-24)
Lipperheide 2349

(illus.) Dally, Aristide. Les sapeurs-pompiers
(illus.) Dally, Aristide. Uniformes de l'armée allemande
(illus.) Dally, Aristide. Uniformes de l'armée anglaise
(illus.) Dally, Aristide. Uniformes de l'armée italienne
(illus.) Maillot, T. J. R. À la caserne

Royal. v 1-29, no 8; 1895-May 1925. New York, Condé Nast
29v. illus.
Title change: 1895-Mr 1924, *Costume royal.* Merged into *Today's housewife*

Royal and historic gloves and shoes. Redfern, W. B.

Royal Guelphic order
Schaedtler, Heinrich. Kurze beschreibung des königlich hannoverschen Guelphen-ordens. 1816

The **royal** house of Stuart. Gibb, William

Royal households

England

A representation of the cloathing of His Majesty's household, and of all the forces upon the establishments of Great Britain and Ireland, 1742. 1893

The **royal** navy. Swinburne, H. L.

Royal Westminster and the coronation. Noppen, J. G.

Royaume de Sardaigne: costumes. Pittaluga, A.

Rozat de Mandres, Charles Nicolas Léonce
La France en campagne; un siècle de guerres (1800-1900) Cent uniformes militaires, dessinés uniquement d'après des documeents authentiques et les œuvres des artistes du temps ... avec de courtes notices historiques par le commandant Sauzey. [Paris, J. Leroy 1906]
100p. 100 col.illus. D.
Colas 2591. LC 24-1789

Ruas de Lisboa. See Coleçaõ de estampas intitulada Ruas de, Lisboa

Rubenius, Alberti. See Rubens, Albert

Rubens, Albert
Alberti Rubeni. De re vestiaria veterum. Antverpiæ, B. Moreti 1665
15 l. 328p. illus. 2 fold. pl. O.
Colas 2592. Lipperheide 150. LC GS34-804

Rubens, Sir Peter Paul
La Gallerie du Palais du Luxembourg, peinte par Rubens, dessinée par les Ss. Nattier, et gravée par les plus illustres graveurs du temps. Paris, Duchange 1710
25 pl.(part double) ports. F.
Paintings dating from 1620-1625 extol the life of Marie de' Medici, wife of Henry IV of France
Lipperheide 1106m. LC 11-33358

Rubens, Philip. See Bossi, Gerolamo. De toga Romana commentarius

Rucker, Robert Hamilton
The Gōda collection of Japanese sword fittings. See entry under New York. Metropolitan museum of art

Rucker, Robert Hamilton
(comp.) See Armor and arms club, New York. Catalogue of a loan exhibition of Japanese sword guards

Rudnitzki, Paul
Der turnierroman "Livre des faits du bon chevalier Messire Jacques de Lalaing" in der Anholter handschrift, nebst einem exkurs über den verfasser. Münster in Westf., Aschendorff 1915
39,26p. col.front. 19pl.(1 col. 1 fold.) facsim. O. (Forschungen und funde ... bd. IV. hft. 1)
Appeared in part as the author's inaugural dissertation, Münster, 1914 (26p.)
Shows costume, arms and armor of the tournaments in 15th century
LC 19-204

Rue, Lena
Greek and Egyptian costumes. [Palms, Calif., W. T. Foster c1931]
Cover-title, [24]p. illus. F.
LC A33-1218

Rückblick auf die militairischen und politischen verhältnisse der Algérie in den jahren 1840 und 1841. Raaslöff, W. R. von

Les **rues** de Paris. Lurine, Louis, ed.

Ruete, Frau Emilie
Memoirs of an Arabian princess; tr. by Lionel Strachey. New York, Doubleday, Page 1907
xvi,227p. front. pl. ports. O.
Shows costume of Arabia in the late nineteenth century
LC 7-29873

Rüxner, Georg
Thurnier buch; von anfang, ursachen, ursprung, und herkommen der thurnuier im Heyligen römischen reich teutscher nation wie viel offentlicher landthurnier von keyser Heinrich dem Ersten dieses namens an biss auff den jetztregierenden keyser Maximilian den Andern. Franckfurt am Mayn 1566
243 numb. l. illus. fold.pl. F.
Woodcuts by Jost Amman show tournament scenes. Lipperheide notes other editions published 1530, 1532, 1578
Lipperheide 2887 (1578 ed.). LC 10-2242

Ruffonus, J.
(engr.) Ferrari, Ottavio. Octavii Ferrari. De re vestiaria libri septem

Ruga, Pietro
(engr.) Roccheggiani, Lorenzo. Nuova raccolta di cento tavole rappresentante i costumi religiosi civili e militari degli antichi Egiziani, Etruschi, Greci e Romani

Rugendas, Georg Philipp
Die belagerung der stadt Augsburg durch die französischen und bayerischen truppen im jahre 1704. Aug. Vind., J. Wolff 1705?
6pl. F.
Lipperheide 2105

Diversi pensieri. Aug. Vind., J. Wolff 1699
8pl. O.
Plates show figures on horseback
Lipperheide 2917

Reiter und gefechte gezeichnet von G. P. Rugendas, gestochen von C. G. Bodenehr; neuere aufl. Augsburg, Herzberg ca1825
24pl. Q.
First published ca1700
Lipperheide 2106

Voyage pittoresque dans le Brésil; tr. de l'allemand par Mr de Golbéry. Paris, Engelmann 1835
48,34,51,32p. 100pl. F.
Published in 20 "livraisons". Divided in 4 "divisions", each accompanied respectively by 30, 20, 30, 20 mounted lithographs after designs of the author
Original German edition (Paris, Engelmann 1827-32) has title: *Malerische reise in Brasilien*
Colas 2594. Lipperheide 1631. LC 2-30043

Rugendas, Johann Moritz, and Leborne, Louis
Tyrol; costumes modernes. Paris, Engelmann ca1828
16 col.pl. Q.
Colas 2593

Ruggieri, E. F. D.
Catalogue des livres rares et précieux composant la bibliothèque de m. E. F. D. Ruggieri. Sacres des rois et des empereurs, entrées triomphales, mariages, tournois, joutes, carrousels, fêtes populaires et feux d'artifice. Paris, A. Labitte 1873
280p. O.
Lipperheide 2494

Ruhl, Moritz, firm, publisher, Leipzig
(pub.) Die armeen der Balkan-staaten
(pub.) Die belgische armee in ihre gegenwärtigen uniformierung
(pub.) Bresler, A. L. Die armee der vereinigten Staaten von Nord-Amerika
(pub.) Die deutsche armee
(pub.) Die deutsche marine und die deutsche schutztruppe für Ost-Afrika in ihrer neuesten uniformirung
(pub.) Die deutsche reichswehr
(pub.) Die deutschen schutztruppen in Afrika
(pub.) Die englische armee in ihrer gegenwärtigen uniformirung
(pub.) Die englischen armee- und marine-uniformen im kriege, sowie die abzeichen an denselben
(pub.) Die graugrünen felduniformen der russischen armee und deren abzeichen
(pub.) Die französische armee in ihrer gegenwärtigen uniformirung dargestellt
(pub.) Die graublauen felduniformen der französischen armee und deren abzeichen
(pub.) Die graue felduniform der deutschen armee
(pub.) Die grauen felduniformen der italienischen armee und deren abzeichen
(pub.) Hill, J. C. Die chinesische armee in ihrer neu-organisation und neu-uniformierung
(pub.) Die italienische armee in ihrer gegenwärtigen uniformirung
(pub.) Die japanische armee in ihrer gegenwärtigen uniformirung
(pub.) Judex, M. Uniformen distinctions und sonstige abzeichen der gesammten k. k. osterr. ungar. wehrmacht
(pub.) Lienhart, and Humbert, René. Les uniformes de l'armée française depuis 1690 jusqu'à nos jours
(pub.) Die neue deutsche reichswehr
(pub.) Die niederländische armee nebst den kolonialtruppen und freiwilligenkorps in ihrer gegenwärtigen uniformierung
(pub.) Die oesterreich-ungarische armee
(pub.) Die orden, wappen und flaggen aller regenten und staaten in originalgetreuen abbildungen
(pub.) Righetti, Camillo. Adjustierungsblätter des k.u.k. oesterr.-ungar. heeres
(pub.) Rottmann, Hans. Die armeen Serbiens und Montenegros
(pub.) Die russische armee in ihrer gegenwärtigen uniformirung
(pub.) Schlawe, Karl. Die organe der deutschen freiwilligen krankenpflege im kriege
(pub.) Scholl, Edouard. Bekleidung und ausrüstung der preuszischen feuerwehren
(pub.) Die schwedische armee in ihrer gegenwärtigen uniformierung
(pub.) Socecu, A. J. V. Die rumänische armee in ihrer gegenwärtigen uniformierung
(pub.) Sommerfeld, F. Die schweizer armee
(pub.) Die spanische armee in ihrer gegenwärtigen uniformirung
(pub.) Sussmann, Anton. Die armeen der Türkei und Griechenlands
(pub.) Sussmann, Anton. Die armeen Rumäniens und Bulgariens
(pub.) Sussmann, Anton. Die armeen Serbiens und Montenegros
(pub.) Sussmann, Anton. Die österreich-ungarische armee
(pub.) Wie sehen die armeen der gegner des drei-bundes im krieg aus

Das **ruhmwürdige** triumvirat der Johannischen verehrung. Prag, Fürst-erzbischöftichen buchdruckerei 1829
12p. illus. 1 pl. Q.
Plate shows dress of three archbishops of Prague who aided in the canonization of St. John of Nepomuk in 1729
Lipperheide 1820

Rulers. See Kings and rulers

Rulers of the Mediterranean. Davis, R. H.

Rullmann, Ludwig
Costumes suisses. Paris, Ostervald [1822]
22 col.pl. Q.
Illustrated by various artists and engraved by Rullmann. For list of plates see Colas's *Bibliographie*
Colas 739

Rumänien. See Hielscher, Kurt. Rumania

Die **rumänische** armee in ihrer gegenwärtigen uniformierung. Socecu, A. J. V.

Rumania
Curtis, W. E. Around the Black Sea. 1911
Heimbucher von Bikessy, J. Pannoniens bewohner in ihren volksthümlichen trachten. 1820
Hielscher, Kurt. Rumania; landscape, buildings, national life. 1933
Iorga, Nicoláe. România in chipuri şi vederi. La Roumanie en images. Showing Roumania. 1926
Jaschke, Franz. National-kleidertrachten und ansichten von Ungarn, Croatien, Slavonien, dem Banat, Siebenbürgen und der Bukowina. 1821
Manolescu, M. N. Igiena ţĕranului, locuinţa, iluminatul şi incăldĭtul el imbrăcămintea, incaltămintea, alimentaţiunea tĕranului in deosebitele epoce ale anului şi in deosebitele regiuni ale ţĕrei. 1895
Die Österreichisch-ungarische monarchie in wort und bild. 1886-1902 v20
Oprescu, George. Arta ţărănească la Români; lucrare însoţită de cincizeci şi opt tabele de ilustraţii. 1922
Oprescu, George. Peasant art in Roumania. 1929
La Roumanie en images, v.1 1919
Stratilesco, Tereza. From Carpathian to Pindus; pictures of Roumanian country life. 1906

See also subdivision Rumania under Embroidery; Military costume

Moldavia

Sestini, Domenico. Notizie, storiche, politiche, geografiche e statistiche sulla Vallachia e sulla Moldavia. 1821

Transylvania

Boner, Charles. Transylvania; its products and its people. 1865
Hering, G. E. Sketches on the Danube, in Hungary and Transylvania. 1838
Viski, Károly. Transylvanian Hungarians, peasant art. 191-?

Wallachia

Bouquet, Michel. Album valaque; vues et costumes pittoresques de la Valachie. 1843
Diehl, C. P. Collection de costumes nationaux. 1853
Sestini, Domenico. Notizie, storiche, politiche, geografiche e statistiche sulla Vallachia e sulla Moldavia. 1821

Rumania. Fondation de S. A. R. le Prince Carol. See L'art du peuple roumain

Rumpf, C.
Der preussische steuerbeamte in bezug auf seine dienst- und rechtsverhältnisse. Ein handbuch für alle beamte der steuer-verwaltung, supernumerarien, dienst-anwärter, militair-invaliden &c. 3. umgearb. und verm. aufl. Berlin, J. Krampe 1859
2v. in 1. 4 fold.pl. O.
Cirkular-verfügung, betreffend das reglement für die uniform der steuerbeamten: 14, [2] pages at end of volume 1. This section published separately under title: *Neues uniform-reglement für die beamten der verwaltung der indirecten steuern* (14,2p. 4 fold.pl.)
LC 8-7133, 8-7134

Rumpf, Fritz
Der mensch und seine tracht ihrem wesen nach geschildert. Berlin, A. Schall [1905]
x,330p. 29pl. O.
Colas 2609. LC 22-22393

Rumpf, Fritz, and Erich, Oswald Adolf
(illus.) Spielzug der völker, dargestellt von F. Rumpf & Oswald A. Erich, nebst vorwort von Peter Jessen. Berlin, W. Weise 1922
[7]p. 50 col.pl. ob.F.

Runö, island, Russia
Schlichting, E. H. Trachten der Schweden an den küsten Ehstlands und auf Runö. 1854

Ruolandes liet. Grimm, Wilhelm

Ruppert, Jacques
Le costume. Paris, R. Ducher [c1930-31]
5v. illus.(incl.ports.) O. (Les arts decoratifs)
Contents: v 1 L'antiquité et le moyen âge; v2 La renaissance, Le style Louis XIII; v3 Époques Louis XIV et Louis XV; v4 Époques Louis XVI et directoire; v5 Consulat, Premier empire, Louis-Philippe, Napoléon III
Colas 2610. LC 32-8893

Histoire du costume de l'antiquité au XIX. siècle. Paris, R. Ducher 1930
5v. in 1. illus. port. O. (Les arts décoratifs)

Ruscelli, Girolamo
Precetti della militia moderna, tanto per mare, quanto per terra. Venetia, Appresso gli heredi di M. Sessa 1568
59 l. 30 illus. Q.
Lipperheide 2050

Russel, Mrs Florence Kimball
A woman's journey through the Philippines on a cable ship that linked together the strange lands seen en route. Boston, L. C. Page 1907
xii,270p. incl.front. 39pl. fold.map. D.
Partly reprinted from various periodicals
LC 7-23256

Russell, Edmund
Jewel don'ts. New York, Bramerton [1895]
101p. illus. ob.S.
On the art of wearing jewelry
LC 19-4317

Russell, Sir William Howard
A memorial of the marriage of H. R. H. Albert Edward, prince of Wales, and H. R. H. Alexandra, princess of Denmark. The various events and the bridal gifts illustrated by Robert Dudley. London, Day and son [1864]
121,x,xvii p. illus. 40pl. 2 port. facsims. F.
Lipperheide 2696. LC 4-7194

Russia. Glavnoe upravlenīe zemleustroīstra ī zemledīe liīa

L'art populaire russe à la seconde exposition koustare. Petrograd, Prokudīn Gorskiī 1914

84,12p. front. illus. 88pl.(part col.) F.
Russian title: *Russkow narodnoe iskusstvo na vtoroī...*

Russia. Komītet dlīa īzdaniīa drevnosteī Rossiīkago gosudarstva

Drevnostī Rossīīskago gosudarstva. Moskva, A. Semena 1849-53

6v. in 1. And atlas of 509? col.pl. 6v. in 4. F.
Rīsovany ak. F. Solntsevym"
Cataloged by Colas under title: *Antiquités de l'Empire de Russie.* Legends on the plates are in Russian and French. Contents: v 1 Icones, croix et ornements d'église; v2 Costumes des tzars; v3 Armes, armures, voitures, sellerie; v4 Costumes et portraits de tzars, boyards, etc.; v5 Coupes, aiguières et objets d'orfèvrerie; v6 Monuments civils et religieux, meubles
Colas 138. LC 34-35262 (Russian characters)

Russia. Mīnīsterstvo īmperatorskago dvora

Ocherk" dīeīatel'nostī mīnīsterstva īmperatorskago dvora po prīgotovleniīam" ī ustroīstvu torzhestv" svīashchennago koronovaniīa Īkh" Īmperatorskīkh" Velīchestv" v" 1896 godu, po poruchenīiū mīnīstra Īmperatorskago dvora general" -ad"īutanta grafa Ī. Ī. Vorontsova Dashkova ī prī uchastiī chinov" Koronatsionnoī kantselīariī, sostavīl" zavīedyvaīushchiī Koronatsionnoī kantselīarieīu d. s.s. V. P. Pogozhev" ... S.-Peterburg", Īzd. Koronatsionnoī kantselīariī [189-]

6v. illus.(incl.plans, diagrs.) fold.tables. F.
LC CA15-182 (Russian characters)

Les solennités du saint couronnement; ouvrage publié avec l'autorisation de Sa Majesté l'empereur par le Ministère de la maison impériale sous la direction de M. V. S. Krivenko ... illustré par M. N. Samokiche [et d'autres] planches hors texte de mm. A. Benois, C. Lébédew [et d'autres]; traduction française de M. G. Korsow. Saint-Pétersbourg, Expédition pour la confection des papiers de l'état 1899

xxxi,396p. col.front. illus. pl.(part col.) ports. facsims. sq.F.
A supplement is bound in
Shows coronation scenes and coronation robes of Russia as well as portraits of Russian emperors
LC 9-14386

Russia. Voennoīe mīnīsterstvo

Peremīeny v" obmundīrovaniī ī vooruzheniī voīsk" rossiīskoī īmperatorskoī armiī. Sanktpeterburg", Voennaīa tīp. 1857-81

111 parts in 10v. 661 col.pl.
Changes in military dress and arms of the imperial Russian army

Russia (1922- (U. S. S. R.)

[New uniform of the red army. Moscow, 1922]

147p. pl.(part col. part fold.) O.

Russia

Al'bom rīsunkov" russkīkh ī slavīanskīkh" narīadov" Vypusk" I. narīady Velīkoruskiī (Rīazanskoī) gub. ī chernogorskiī. 1884

Chalif, L. H. Russian festivals and costumes for pageant and dance. 1921

Filimonov", Georg. Opīsanie pamīatnīkov' drevnosti tserkovnago ī grazhdanskago byta russkago museīa P. Koroanova. 1849

Heikel, A. O. Die volkstrachten in den Ostseeprovincen und in Setukesien. 1909

Pauli, F. K. Description ethnographique des peuples de la Russie. 1862

Perleberg, H. C., comp. Historical Russian costumes, XIV-XVIII century, worn by the Russian imperial family and their guests at the ball in the Winter palace, St Petersburg, on February 27, 1903. 1923?

Prokhorov", V. A. Khrīstianskiīa drevnostī ī arkheologiīa. Ezhemīesīachnyī zhurnal. 1864-76

Prokhorov", V. A. Materialy po īstoriī russkīkh odezhd" ī obstanovkī zhīznī narodnoī, īzdavaemye po Vysochaīshemu soīzvoleniīu. 1881-85

Prokhorov", V. A. Pusskiīa drevnostī īzdavaemyīa no vysochaīshemu soīzvoleniīu nod" redaktsieīu V. Prokhorova. 1871-76

Rovinskiī, D. A. Portraits authentiques des tzars Jean III., Basile son fils et Jean IV. le Terrible, et cinq ambassades de leur époque. 1882

Russia. Glavnoe upravlenīe zemleustroīstra ī zemledīe liīa. L'art populaire russe à la seconde exposition koustare. 1914

Russia. Komītet dlīa īzdaniīa drevnosteī Rossiīkago gosudarstva. Drevnostī Rossīīskago gosudarstva. 1849-53

Russia. Mīnīsterstvo Īmperatorskago dvora. Ocherk" dīeīatelńostī Mīnīsterstva Īmperatorskago dvora po prīgotovleniīam" i ustroīstvu torzhestv" svīashchennago koronovaniīa Ikh" Imperatorskīkh" Velīchestv" v" 1896. 189-

Savvaītov", P. Ī. Opīsanie starīnnykh" russkīkh" utvareī, odezhd", oruzhiīa, ratnykh" dospīekhov" ī konskago prībora, v" azbuchnom" porīadkīe raspolozhennoe. 1896

Vasili, Paul, comte, pseud. La sainte Russie; la cour, l'armée, le clergé, la bourgeoisie et le peuple. 1890

Weibel, Walther. Ruszland. 1916

Volkov", N. E. Dvor" russkīkh" īmperatorov" v" ego proshlom" ī nastoīaschchem. 1900

Zabīelin, Ī. E. Domashniī byt' russkīkh" tsarīts v" XVI ī XVII st. 1901

See also Bokhara; Cheremisses; Cossacks; Estonia; Mordvinians; Queens and empresses; Russia in Asia; Sakhalin; Turkomans; Varangians; also subhead Russia under Ceremonial and festival costume; Coronations and coronation robes; Crown jewels; Decoration and ornament; Diplomatic costume; Embroidery; Funerals; Kings and rulers; Lace; Military costume;

Russia—*Continued*
Naval costume; Nobles; Orders of knighthood and chivalry; Sakhalin; Servants; Street venders; Theatrical costume; Weddings and wedding dress

To 15th century

Khanykov", D. D. Russkiiâ bylīny. 1860

See also Theatrical costume—Special plays, ballets, etc—Dimitri Donskoy

16th century

Giovio, Paolo, bp. of Nocera. Die Moscouitische chronica, das ist ein grundtliche beschreibung oder historia desz mechtigen und gewaltigen grossfürsten in der Moscauw ... auch dess trefflichen landts zu Reussen von jrem herkommen, religion, sitten und gebreuchen. 1576

17th century

Album du bal costumé au Palais d'hiver, février 1903. 1904

Schiemann, Theodor. Russland, Polen und Livland bis ins 17. jahrhundert. 1886-87

18th century

Bruyn, Cornelis de. Cornelis de Bruins Reizen over Moskovie, door Persie en Indie. 1711

Bruyn, Cornelis de. Travels into Muscovy, Persia, and part of the East-Indies. 1737

Bruyn, Cornelis de. Voyage au Levant; c'est-à-dire dans les principaux endroits, de l'Asie Mineure, dans les isles de Chio, Rhodes, Chypre, etc., de même que dans les plus considérables villes d'Egypte, Syrie, & Terre Sainte. 1725

The costume of the Russian empire, illustrated by a series of seventy-three engravings. London, W. Miller 1803

Costume of the Russian empire illustrated by upwards of seventy richly coloured engravings. London, E. Harding 1803

Eyriès, J. B. B. La Russie, ou costumes, moeurs et usages des Russes. ca1823

Georgi, J. G. Beschreibung aller nationen des russischen reichs. 1776-80

Georgi, J. G. Description de toutes les nations de l'empire de Russie, ou l'on expose leurs moeurs, religions, usages, maisons, habillemens et autres curiosites; tr. de l'allemand. 1776-80

Georgi, J. G. La Russie ouverte ou collection complette des habillemens de toutes les nations qui se trouvent dans l'empire de Russie. 1774-75

Georgi, J. G. Russland: beschreibung aller nationen des russischen Reiche. 1783

Le Prince, J. B. Divers ajustements et usages de Russie. 1764

Le Prince, J. B. Oeuvres. 1782

Molloy, J. F. The Russian court in the eighteenth century. 1905

Pallas, P. S. Bemerkungen auf einer reise in die südlichen statthalterschaften des Russischen reichs in den jahren 1793 und 1794. 1799-1801

Pallas, P. S. Reise durch verschiedene provinzen des Russischen reichs. 1771-76

Pallas, P. S. Travels through the southern provinces of the Russian empire, in the years 1793 and 1794. 1802-03

Will, J. M., engr. Samlung der ruszischen national-trachten. ca1780

19th century

Alexander, William. Picturesque representations of the dress and manners of the Russians. 1814

Atkinson, J. A. and Walker, James. A picturesque representation of the manners, customs and amusements of the Russians. 1803-04

Breton de la Martinière, J. B. J. La Russie, ou moeurs, usages et costumes des habitans de toutes les provinces de cet empire. 1813

Breton de la Martinière, J. B. J. Russland oder sitten, gebräuche und trachten. 1816

Buddeus, Carl. Volksgemälde und charakterköpfe des russischen volks. 1820

Chopin. Costumes russes modernes. ca1828

Clodt von Jürgensburg, M. P., baron. Costumes russes. 1865?

Collection de cris et costumes de paysans et paysannes de St Pétersbourg. 1823

Costumes des troupes russes répresentées en (quatorze) gravures et notice sur les différens peuples qui composent l'armée russe. 1812

Czynski, Jean. Russie pittoresque; histoire et tableau de la Russie. 1837

Damame-Démartrais, M. F. Collection complète des divers jardins et points de vue des maisons de plaisance impériales de Russie. 1811

Damame-Démartrais, M. F. Vues de Russie et usages divers des habitants de ce genre. ca1817

Geissler, C. G. H. Mahlerische darstellungen der sitten ... bey den russischen, tartarischen, mongolischen und andern völkern im russischen reich. 1804

Gruber, J. G. Sitten, gebräuche und kleidung der Russen, in St Petersburg. 1801-03

Hempel, Friedrich, and Geissler, C. G. H. Abbildung und beschreibung der völkerstämme und völker unter des russischen kaisers Alexander I. regierung. 1803

Houbigant, A. C. Moeurs et costumes des Russes. 1817

Jukowsky, Rudolph. Scènes populaires russes. 1843

Knorre, Fr. Costumes russes representés en groupes charactéristiques. ca1850

Kollmann, Ch. Costumes russes, vues de Saint-Pétersbourg et de ses environs. 1822

Latham, R. G. The native races of the Russian empire. 1854

Latimer, Mrs E. W. Russia and Turkey in the nineteenth century. 1893

Lineff, Mme Eugènie. Russian folk-songs as sung by the people, and peasant wedding ceremonies customary in northern and central Russia. 1893

Russia—19th century—*Continued*

Logan, J. A. In joyful Russia. 1897

Mitreuter, H. D., and others. Croquis russes. 1844-45

Orlowski, A. O. Album russe ou fantaisies dessinées lithographiquement. 1826

A picture of St. Petersburgh, represented in a collection of twenty interesting views of the city, the sledges, and the people. 1815

Pinkerton, Robert. Russia: or, Miscellaneous observations on the past and present state of that country and its inhabitants. 1833

Porter, Sir R. K. The costume of the inhabitants of Russia. 1810

Porter, Sir R. K. Travelling sketches in Russia and Sweden, during the years 1805, 1806, 1807, 1808. 1809

Rechberg und Rothenlöwen, Karl, graf von. Les peuples de la Russie. 1812-13

Richter, J. G. Sitten, gebräuche und kleidung der Russen aus den niedern ständen. 1805

Richter, J. G. Spiele und belustigungen der Russen aus den niedern volksklassen. Jeux et divertissements du peuple russe. 1805

Richter, J. G., and Geissler, C. G. H. Châtiments usités en Russie. ca1805

Roskoschny, Hermann. Russland, land und leute. 1882-84

Saint-Julien, Charles de. Voyage pittoresque en russie; suivi d'un voyage en Siberie par M. R. Bourdier. 1853

Savinov, V. N. Stseny īz" russkago narodnago byta, rīsovany s" natury ... tekst" napīsan" V. N. Savinovym; [illus. by Ī. S. Shchedrovskī.] 1852

Schellenberg-Biedermann, E. Ein jahr aus Ursula's leben. 1845

Schlatter, Daniel. Bruchstücke aus einigen reisen nach dem südlichen Ruszland, in den jahren 1822 bis 1828. 1830

Shoberl, Frédéric, ed. Russia. 1822-23

Stadling, J. J., and Reason, Will. In the land of Tolstoi; experiences of famine and misrule in Russie. 1897

Timm, W. Costumes russes. 1843-44

Ujfalvy, Marie. De Paris à Samarkand, le Ferghanah, le Kouldja et la Sibérie occidentale. 1880

Periodical

Moskovskiĭ telegraf" ... īzdavaemyĭ Nīkolaem" Polevym". 1825-27

20th century

Dobson, George; Grove, H. M., and Stewart, Huch. Russia; painted by F. De Haenen. 1913

Golubykh, M. D. Kazach'i͡a derevni͡a. Podred. M. Fenomenova. 1930

Holme, Charles, ed. Peasant art in Russia. 1912

Kalitkin, N. Ornament shit'i͡a kostromskogo polushubka. S predisl. Vas. Smirnova. 1926g

Lethbridge, A. B. The new Russia, from the White Sea to the Siberian steppe. 1915

Stewart, Hugh. Provincial Russia. 1913

Tilke, Max. The costumes of eastern Europe. 1926

Tilke, Max. Osteuropäische volkstrachten in schnitt und farbe. 1925

Young women's Christian associations. Bureau of pageantry and the drama. National costumes of the Slavic peoples. 1920

Zelenīn, D. K. Russische (ostslavische) volkskunde. 1927

Caricature and satire

Doré, Gustave. Histoire pittoresque, dramatique et caricaturale de la Sainte Russie. 1854

BY REGION OR PROVINCE

Armenia

See Armenia

Azerbaijan

Berger, A. K. V gorakh Vostochnogo Zakavkaz'i͡a Azerbaĭdzhan. 1927g

Caucasus

Albrecht, prince of Prussia. Im Kaukasus 1862. 1865

Aliev, U. D. Karachaĭ; istorico-ekonomichesk. i kul'turno-ekonomicheskiĭ ocherk. 1927g

Chantre, Ernest. Recherches anthropologiques dans le Caucase. 1885-87

Curtis, W. E. Around the Black Sea. 1911

Erckert, Roderich von. Der Kaukasus und seine völker. 1887

Gagarīn, G. G., kni͡az. Costumes du Caucase. ca1840

Gagarīn, G. G., kni͡az, and Stackelberg, Ernest, count. Le Caucase pittoresque. 1847

Norman, Sir Henry, bart. All the Russias; travels and studies in contemporary European Russia, Finland, Siberia, the Caucasus, and Central Asia. 1902

See also Circassians

Georgia

Curtis, W. E. Around the Black Sea. 1911

Porter, Sir R. K. Travels in Georgia, Persia, Armenia, ancient Babylonia, &c. &c. during the years 1817, 1818, 1819, and 1820. 1821-22

Leningrad

Dahlstein, Augustin. Russische trachten und ausrufer in St. Petersburg. Habillemens moscovites et crieurs à St Petersbourg. 1750

Dobson, George. St Petersburg. 1910

Petrograd

See Russia—Leningrad

St Petersburg

See Russia—Leningrad

Russia—*Continued*

Ukraine

Clodt von Jürgensburg, M. P., baron. Costumes petit-russiens. ca1865

Russia. Glavnoe upravlenīe zemleustroīstra ī zemledīe liīa. L'art populaire russe à la seconde exposition koustare. 1914

See also Czechoslovakia—Ruthenia; also subdivision Russia—Ukraine under Decoration and ornament

Russia and Turkey in the nineteenth century. Latimer, Mrs E. W.

Russia in Asia

Denike, B. P., ed. Iskusstvo Sredneĭ Azii. Sbornik stateĭ. 1930g

Gamba, J. F. Voyage dans la Russie méridionale et particulièrement dans les provinces situées au-delà du Caucase, fait depuis 1820 jusqu'en 1824. 1826

Martuinov, A. E. Folk-costumes of Asiatic Russia. 1808

Paris. Exposition internationale des arts décoratifs et industriels modernes, 1925. Ornements et perles des peuples finnois et siberiens. 1927?

Roskoschny, Hermann. Das asiatische Russland. 1884

See also Siberia

Russia; painted by F. De Haenen. Dobson, George; Grove, H. M., and Stewart, Hugh

Russian ballet. See Theatrical costume—Special plays, ballets, etc.—Russian ballet

The **Russian** ballet in western Europe, 1909-1920. Propert, W. A.

The **Russian** court in the eighteenth century. Molloy, J. F.

Russian cries. Orlowski, G.

Russian festivals and costumes for pageant and dance. Chalif, L. H.

Russian folk-songs as sung by the people. Lineff, Mme Eugènie

The **Russian** theatre. Gregor, Joseph, and Fülöp-Miller, René

La **Russie.** Eyriès, J. B. B.

La **Russie,** ou moeurs, usages et costumes des habitans de toutes les provinces de cet empire. Breton de la Martinière, J. B. J.

La **Russie** ouverte ou collection complette des habillemens de toutes les nations qui se trouvent dans l'empire de Russie. Georgi, J. G.

Russie pittoresque. Czynski, Jean

Russisch kaiserlich-königliches ordens-reglement. ca1870

205p. and atlas of 33 col.pl. F.
A manuscript owned by the Lipperheide library. Plates show costume of the Orders of St Andrew, Alexander Nevsky, the White Eagle, St Catherine, St Anne, St Vladimir, St George, St Stanislaus and other Russian orders
Lipperheide 1937

Die **russische** armee in ihrer gegenwärtigen uniformirung ... Nebst ausführlichen erläuterungen und mittheilungen über organisation, eintheilung und stärke der russischen armee; 2. aufl. Leipzig, M. Ruhl [1891]

34,xii p. 20 col.pl. O.
Third edition: Leipzig, M. Ruhl 1901
Colas 2606. Lipperheide 2379-80

Russische, kleinrussische, und südslavonische stickmuster. See Verkhovskoĭ, O. Uzory russkie

Russische militair gruppen. Zimmermann, C. F.

Russische (ostslavische) volkskunde. Zelenīn, D. K.

Das **russische** theater. Gregor, Joseph, and Fülöp-Miller, René

Russische trachten und ausrufer in St. Petersburg. Dahlstein, Augustin

Russisches militair im jahr 1814 in Nürnberg nach dem leben. Adam, Georg

Russisches musterbuch. Chrapovitsky, L.

Russkiī narodnyĭ ornament". Stasov", V.

Russkiī ornament" v" starīnnykh" obraztsakh" khudozhestvenno-promyshlennago proīzvodstva. Sīmakov, N.

Russkiīa bylīny. Khanykov", D. D.

Russkiīa vyshīvki. Dalmatov", K.

Russkow narodnoe iskusstvo na vtoroĭ ... Russia. Glavnoe upravlenīe

Russland. Drygalski, Albert von, and Zepelin, Constantin von

Russland, land und leute. Roskoschny, Hermann

Russland oder sitten, gebräuche und trachten. Breton de la Martinière, J. B. J.

Russland, Polen und Livland bis ins 17. jahrhundert. Schiemann, Theodor

Russlands und Deutschlands befreiungskriege. Venturini, K. H. G.

Russwurm, Alexander, freiherr Von Gleichen-. See Gleichen-Russwurm, Alexander, freiherr von

Ruth, John A., and Snyder, C. S.

(comps.) Decorum, a practical treatise on etiquette and dress of the best American society. Chicago, J. A. Ruth 1877

352p.
Republished, with additions, under title: *Social culture* (Springfield, Mass., The King-Richardson co. 1902)
LC 9-30984

Ruthenians. See Czechoslovakia—Ruthenia

Rutherston, Albert Daniel

Sixteen designs for the theatre. London, Oxford university press 1928

16p. 16pl.(part col. part fold.) sq.F.
Most of the plates are accompanied by guard sheets with descriptive letterpress
Fourteen plates show costumes designed between 1912 and 1914 for characters in well-known plays
LC 29-11243

Rutter, Owen
The new Baltic states and their future; an account of Lithuania, Latvia and Estonia. Boston and New York, Houghton Mifflin 1926
xi,274p. front. pl. port. O.
Contains one costume plate each for Latvia, Lithuania, and Estonia
Bibliography: p265-70
Costume index. LC 26-26735

Ruutz-Rees, Mrs Janet Emily (Meugens)
Home decoration: art needle-work and embroidery; painting on silk, satin, and velvet; panel-painting; and wood-carving ... with ... designs, mainly by George Gibson. New York, D. Appleton 1881
120p. 65 illus. O.
Lipperheide 4137

Rycaut, Sir Paul
The history of the present state of the Ottoman Empire; 6th ed. corrected. London, Printed for C. Brome 1686
406p. front. illus. pl. D.
The plates show costume
French edition: *Histoire de l'état present de l'Empire Ottoman* (Amsterdam, A. Wolfgank 1670)
Lipperheide 1408 (Fr. ed.)

Rydh, Hanna Albertina
Dosformiga spännen från vikingetiden. Stockholm, I. Hæggströms boktryckeri 1919
162p. illus. O.
Akademisk avhandling—Upsala
LC 22-16852

Rygh, Oluf
Norse oldsager, ordnede og forklarede ... tegnede paa træ af C. F. Lindberg Christiania, A. Cammermeyer 1885
2v. 74pl. F.
Added title page in French: *Antiquités norvégiennes;* Norwegian and French in parallel columns
Contents: v 1 Afbildninger og oversigter; v2 Oplysninger om de afbildede oldsager
Lipperheide 296. LC 6-4082

S

S., I. C. H. von. See Schmalen, J. C. H. von

S., M. See Manners & customs of the French

Sabina, oder Morgenscenen im putzzimmer einer reichen römerin. Böttiger, K. A.

Sabretache. See Carnet de la Sabre-tache

Saburov, Petr Aleksandrovich, 1835-
Die sammlung Sabouroff; kunstdenkmäler aus Griechenland, hrsg. von Adolf Furtwängler. Berlin, A. Asher & co., 1883-87.
2v. CXLIX pl.(part col.) nar.F.
In portfolios. The plates are pictures of sculpture, vases, terracottas and bronzes, useful for costume worn in ancient Greece
Lipperheide 196. LC 6-20687

Sabine, ou Matinée d'une dame romaine. See Böttiger, K. A. Sabina, oder Morgenscenen im putzzimmer einer reichen römerin

Sachs, Hans
Eygentliche beschreibung aller stände auff erden. See entry under Amman, Jost
Stände und handwerker. See entry under Amman, Jost
Das ständebuch. See entry under Amman, Jost

See also Alt-Nürnberg, schwänke, lieder und tänze d. Hans Sachs. 1918

Sachse, L. & co., Berlin
Die preussische garden. Berlin, L. Sachse [1830?]
18 col.pl. F.
Das preussische heer. See entry under Elzholz, L.; Rechlin, Karl, and Schulz, J.
(pub.) Kaiser. königl. preuss. garde-cavalerie

Sacken, Eduard, freiherr von
Die vorzüglichsten rüstungen und waffen der K.K. Ambraser-sammlung in original-photographien ... die photographien von A. Groll. Wien, W. Braumüller 1859-62
2v. 128pl. F.
Contents: v 1 Deutsche fürsten und herren; v2 Italiener, Spanier und einzelne waffenstücke
Lipperheide 2413

Le **sacre** de Louis XV. Danchet, Antoine, ed.

Le **sacre** de s. m. l'empereur Napoléon, dans l'Église métropolitaine de Paris le XI frimaire an XIII. dimanche 2 décembre 1804. Paris, L'imprimerie impériale [1804]
56p. 38 l. 38pl. F.
Plates are after drawings by Isabey, Fontaine and Percier. Besides the ceremonies they show costume of the emperor, the empress, the pope, and dignitaries of the church and state
Lipperheide 2720

Sacre de sa majesté Charles X. dans la métropole de Reims, le 29 mai 1825. Paris, Sazerac et Duval 1825
22,6 l. illus. 10pl. F.
Plates are lithographs after drawings by V. Adam, Arnout, Chapuy, Deroy and Maurin
Lipperheide 2726

Sacred and legendary art. Jameson, Mrs A. B. M.

Sacristie patriarcale dite synodale. Moscow. Sinodal'naía (byvshaía patriarshaía) riznitsa

Sacre et couronnement de Louis XVI. roi de France. Pichon, T. J., ed.

Sacri Romani imperi ornatus. Bruyn, Abraham de

Sadeler, Raphael
Bavaria sancta Maximiliani sereniss. principis imperii, comitis Palatini Rheni utriusq. Bav. ducis auspiciis coepta, descripta eidemq. Monaci, 1615
55pl. Q.

Sadoul, Charles
La Lorraine. See Las Cases, Philippe, vicomte de, ed. L'art rustique en France

Sächsische bürgerwehr und schützen. Jahn, lithgr.

Sächsische kleiderordnungen aus der zeit von 1450-1750. Bartsch, L.

Sächsische volkstrachten und bauernhäuser. Schmidt; Seyffert, O., and Sponsel

Der **sächsischen** kurfürsten turnierbücher. Haenel, Erich

Saeculum octavum, oder Acht-tägisches hochfeyrliches jubel-fest ... mit ungemeinen kirchen-gepräng ... processionen triumphierlicher einholung der heiligen zweyen römischen martyrer Marii und Caelestini. Augspurg, gedruckt bey Mar. Magdalena Utzschneiderin 1702
10 l. 222,40p. 17pl. Q.
Two plates, engraved by Joh. Christoph Hafner, show the procession
Lipperheide 2796

Sage, Elizabeth
A study of costume, from the days of the Egyptians to modern times. New York, Chicago [etc.] C. Scribner [c1926]
xvii,235p. illus. diagrs. O. $2
Bibliography: p229-30
Colas 2611. Costume index. LC 26-13519

Saggio di Robustiano Gironi intorno alle costumanze civili dei Greci. Gironi, Robustiano

Saggio di storia sulle vicendo della barba, con un' appendice sopra i mostacchj. Bologna, Tipographia ai Celestine [1801]
35p. O.
Lipperheide 1688

Saglio, Edmond. See Daremberg, C. V., jt. ed.

Sagnac, Philippe. See Lavisse, Ernest, ed. Histoire de France contemporaine

Saguí, Francisco
Los últimos cuatro años de la dominacion española en el antiguo vireinato del Rio de la Plata desde 26 de junio de 1806 hasta 25 de mayo 1810. Buenos Aires, Imprenta americana 1874
xiii,324p. 8pl.(2 col.) ports. Q.
Edited with introduction by M. Esteves Saguí. "Apendice de documentos": p[191]-317
The two colored plates show uniformes of the Argentine defense corps organized at this time for the defense of Buenos Aires against the English
Lipperheide 2396. LC 4-9345

Saguí, Miguel Esteves. See Esteves Saguí, Miguel

Sahagún, Bernardino de
Historia de las cosas de Nueva España. Madrid, Fototipia de Hauser y Menet 1905-07
v6-9 col.pl. F.
A facsimile reproduction of the manuscript of Sahagún's history. Volume 6 contains colored illustrations showing the dress of Mexican Indians from their ancient writings

Sahara
Carpenter, F. G. From Tangier to Tripoli. 1923
Christian, Pierre. L'Afrique française, l'empire de Maroc, et les deserts de Sahara. 1846

Sahib, E. L. S., pseud. See Lesage, L. E.

Saillant, Robert Charles Lasteyrie du. See Lasteyrie du Saillant, R. C.

Sailors
Adam, Victor. Costumes de marins, dessinés dans les ports de Dunquerque au Havre. 1828
Mozin, Ch. Costumes de marins de la basse Normandie. 1829
Robinson, C. N. The British tar in fact and fiction. 1909

Saint Martin. Lecoy de la Marche, Albert

Saint-Aubin, Augustin de
L'art du brodeur. [Paris, L. F. Delatour 1770]
50p. 10pl. F. (Acad. Royale des sciences. Description des arts et métiers, v23)
Lipperheide 3972

C'est ici les différens jeux des petits polissons de Paris. Paris, L'auteur [1766-70]
6pl. Q.
Colas 2615

Habillemens à la mode de Paris en l'année 1761. Paris, Ve de F. Chereau 1761?
6pl. F.
Colas 2613

Mes gens, ou Les commissionnaires ultramontains au service de qui veut les payer. Paris, Basan [1766-1770]
1 l. 6pl. Q.
Pictures of Savoyards employed as Paris street-venders. Engraved by J. B. Tillard after plates by Saint-Aubin
Colas 2614. Lipperheide 1182

[Types du dix-huitième siècle. Paris] ca1760
12pl. O.
Includes two suites of six plates each. Colas gives a list of the plates
Colas 2612

(illus.) Boucher, Emmanuel. Les gravures françaises du XVIIIe siècle; volume 5. 1875-82

Saint-Épain, de
L'art de composer les livrées au milieu du XIX. siècle d'après les principes de la science héraldique précédé d'une notice historique. Paris, Tours, imprimerie Bouserez 1853
44p. 6pl. D
Colas 2616

Saint-Eschauzier. See Mansion, L. M., jt. auth.

Saint-Fal
Costumes militaires. Saint-Fal del., Alix sculp. Paris, Noël ca1815
14 col.pl. F.
Uniforms of various European countries. Glasser gives a list of them
Colas 2617

Saint-George, Amalie von
Die kunst der goldstickerei; nebst einer anleitung zur verwendung der goldstickerei in verbindung mit application. Wien, Verlag der "Wiener mode" [1896]
54p. 136 illus. 6pl. Q.
Lipperheide 4022

Saint-Germain, Prosper
Costumes bretons. Paris, Jeannin [1841]
6 col.pl. F.
Colas 1231bis

(illus.) Souvestre, Émile. La Bretagne pittoresque

Saint-Hilaire, Émile Marc Hilaire, known as Marco de

L'art de mettre sa cravate de toutes des manières connus et usitées ... précédé de l'histoire complète de la cravate, depuis son origine jusqu'à ce jour, de considérations sur l'usage des cols, de la cravate noire et l'emploi des foulards. Paris, Impr. de H. Balzac 1827

122p. 4pl.(incl. 32 illus.) port. D.
Italian edition: *L'arte di mettere la propria cravatta in tutte le foggie conosciute* (Napoli, Porcelli 1828. 99p. 4pl.)
Colas 2618-2619. Lipperheide 1697

Histoire anecdotique politique et militaire de la Garde impériale; illustrée par H. Bellangé, E. Lamy, De Moraine, Ch. Vernier. Nouv. éd. Paris, E. Penaud 1847

712p. 108 illus. 50pl.(39 col.) O. (Histoire de Napoléon, du consulat et de l'empire, t 1-2)
Published in 50 parts (livraisons) at O fr. 30 each
Published also in German translation with the same illustrations and plates: *Geschichte der Kaiser-garde* (Leipzig, J. J. Weber 1848)
Colas 2620-21. Lipperheide 2319 (German ed.) LC 4-12318

Manuel complet de la toilette, ou L'art de s'habiller avec élégance et méthode, contenant L'art de mettre sa cravate ... par M et Mme Stop. Paris, La librairie française et étrangère 1828

172p. fold.front. S.
The frontispiece shows 25 ways of tying a cravat
Colas 2810

Saint-Igny, Jean de

Diversitez d'habillemens à la mode; naifuement portraits, sur la differente condition de la noblesse, des magistrats, et du tiers estat. Paris, E. Dauvel ca1630

1 l. 12pl. Q.
Plates engraved by Briot after drawings by Saint-Igny. A second state of the plates exists with same collation (Paris, J. Honervogt ca1630)
Colas 2627-28. Lipperheide 1109

Le jardin de la noblesse françoise, dans lequel ce peut ceuillir leur manierre de vettement. Paris, M. Tavernier 1629

1 l. 17pl. Q.
Plates show masculine and feminine costume of the time of Louis XIII. Eight of the plates are signed St-Igny, in.—A. Bosse fecit. Brunet attributes the suite to Perrochel and lists a volume containing both this suite and his *Le théâtre de France* (Paris, Estienne 1629)
Colas 2624. Lipperheide 1107

La noblesse françoise à l'église ... inventée par le sieur de S. Igny. Paris, L'auteur ca1625

1 l. 12pl. Q.
Plates are engraved by Abraham Bosse, and show French noblemen and women of the time of Louis XIII. A second state of the plates has the same collation (Paris, François l'Anglois 1630)
Colas 2622-23

Le théâtre de France contenant la diversitez des habits selon les qualitez & conditions des personnes. Dédié à messire Charles Perrochel seigneur de Grandchamp. Paris, E. Dauvel 1629

1 l. XXI pl. Q.
Plates show French masculine and feminine costume of the time of Louis XIII. They are engraved by Isaac Briot after designs by Saint-Igny
A second state exists with some landscapes added to the figures on the plates (Paris, Honervogt ca1630)
Colas 2625-26. Lipperheide 1108 (2d ed.)

The **St. James's** budget. v 1-62 (no 1-1597), July 3 1880-Feb. 3 1911. London

62v. illus. F.
Lipperheide 4767

St. John, James Augustine

Oriental album: characters, costumes, and modes of life, in the valley of the Nile; illus. from designs taken on the spot by E. Prisse with descriptive letter-press by J. A. St. John. London, J. Madden 1848

60p. col.front. 30pl. F.
Colas 2427. Lipperheide 1599

St John of Jerusalem, Order of. See Malta, Knights of

Saint-Julien, Charles de

Voyage pittoresque en Russie; suivi d'un voyage en Siberie par M. R. Bourdier; illus. de mm. Rouargue, Outwaith et Kernot. Paris, Belin-Leprieur & Morizot [1853]

540p. pl.(8 col.) O.
The colored plates show costume

St Maixent. Exposition rétrospective du mobilier et du costume poitevins, 20 sept. 1901

Ville de St-Maixent. See entry under Farault, Alphonse

Saint-Martin, J. de

L'art de faire les armes ... On y a joint un traité de l'espadon. Vienne, J. Schrämble 1804

2v. 72pl. Q.
Lipperheide 2980

Saint-Maurice

(ed.) Almanach de la mode de Paris

[Saint Non, Jean Claude Richard de]

Voyage pittoresque; ou, Description des royaumes de Naples et de Sicile. Paris [Impr. de Clousier] 1781-86

5pt. in 4v. illus. pl.(part double) ports. maps(part fold.) plans(part fold.) F.
Volume 1 issued in 2 parts, pt 2 taking the place of v2; v4 issued in 2 parts
Volume 1, part 2 describes the antiquities of Herculaneum and Pompeii and shows Roman costume as pictured in the ruins
German translation under title *Neapel und Sizilien* (Gotha, Ettinger 1789-1800. 12v. illus. O.) contains as volume 3 J. H. Keerl's *Uber die ruinen Herculanums und Pompejis* (196p. 8pl. O.)
Lipperheide 232 (German ed. v3). LC 4-19764

Saint Olon, François Pidou de. See Pidou de Saint Olon, François

St Petersburg. See Russia—Leningrad; also Street venders—Russia—Leningrad

St Petersburg. Dobson, George

Saint Priest, Alexis de Guignard, comte de. See note under Philippe, P. La Normandie en 1834

Saint Prosper, André Augustin Cassé de, and others
Histoire de tous les peuples et des revolutions du monde depuis les temps les plus reculés jusqu'à nos jours; par Saint-Prosper, de Saurigny, Duponchel, le baron de Korff, Belloc et l'abbé Martin. Paris, E. Penaud 1841?
4v. 76pl.(64 col.) O.
Each of the colored plates shows three or four types of costume
Second edition: *Histoire de tous les peuples depuis les temps les plus reculés . . .* rev. et continuée par M. E. de Lostalot-Bachoué (Paris, Lebigre 1856. 10v. 50 fr.)
Colas 1451-52

Saint Sauveur, Jacques Grasset de. See Grasset de Saint Sauveur, Jacques

St Stephen, Order of
Constitutiones insignis ordinis equitum S. Stephanis regis apostolici. 1764

Saint-Ursanne, René
Petit guide pratique de l'art du théâtre. Paris, E. Flammarion [c1925]
x,224p. incl.pl. D. (Nouveau répertoire des "Soirées honnêtes")
LC 25-16239

Saint-Ursin, P. J. Marie de. See Marie de Saint-Ursin, P. J.

Saint-Victor, Marie Émilien de Castillon de. See Castillon de Saint-Victor, M. É. de

La **sainte** Russie. Vasili, Paul, comte, pseud.

La **Sainte** Vierge. Maynard, M. U., abbé

Saints
Bell, Mrs N. R. E. M. Lives and legends of the English bishops and kings, mediaeval monks, and other later saints. 1904
Bles, Arthur de. How to distinguish the saints in art by their costumes, symbols and attributes. 1925
Burgkmair, Hans. Images de saints et saintes issus de la famille de l'Empereur Maximilian I. 1799
Catholic church. Liturgy and ritual. Hours. Le livre d'heures de la reine Anne de Bretagne. 1841
Delepierre, Octave, and Voisin, Auguste. La châsse de Sainte Ursule gravée au trait par Charles Onghéna d'après Jean Memling. 1841
Derrick, Freda. Tales told in church stones. 1935. p57-80
Drake, Maurice, and Drake, Wilfred. Saints and their emblems. 1916
Dürer, Albrecht. Albrecht Dürer's Randzeichnungen aus dem Gebetbuche des kaisers Maximilian I. 1850
Jameson, Mrs A. B. M. Legends of the monastic orders as represented in the fine arts. 1872
Jameson, Mrs A. B. M. Sacred and legendary art. 1870
Lecoy de la Marche, Albert. Saint Martin. 1881
Natalibus, Petrus de, bp. of Equilio. Catalogus Sanctorum. 1514
Das Passional. Passional. 1488
Perret, Louis. Catacombes de Rome. 1851-55
Sadeler, Raphael. Bavaria sancta Maximiliani sereniss. principis imperii, comitis Palatini Rheni utriusq. Bav. ducis auspiciis coepta, descripta eidemq. 1615
Tabor, M. E. The saints in art, with their attributes and symbols alphabetically arranged. 1908
Waters, Mrs C. E. C. A handbook of Christian symbols and stories of the saints as illustrated in art. 1886
Waters, Mrs C. E. C. Saints in art. 1899
Westwood, J. O. Fac-similes of the miniatures and ornaments of Anglo-Saxon and Irish manuscripts. 1868

Saints and their emblems. Drake, Maurice, and Drake, Wilfred

Saints in art. Tabor, M. E.

Saints in art. Waters, Mrs. C. E. C.

Sáinz, Luis de Hoyos. See Hoyos Sáinz, Luis de

La **Saison**; journal illustré des dames. See note under Die Modenwelt

Sajou, firm, publishers
Ouvrages de dames, dessins de broderies. Paris, Maison Sajou ca1880
100pl. Q.
Lipperheide 4184

Sakhalin
Hawes, C. H. In the uttermost East. 1904

Sala, George Augustus Henry
The hats of humanity, historically, humorously and æsthetically considered. Manchester, J. Gee, hatter 1880?
60p. 3 col.pl.(incl.front.) T.
LC 10-17951

Salaman, Malcolm Charles
Shakespeare in pictorial art. Text by Malcolm C. Salaman. Ed. by Charles Holme. London, New York [etc.] The Studio 1916
183p. incl.pl.(part col.) ports. Q.
Part of plates printed on both sides. On cover: Special number of the International studio, spring, 1916. Imprint on cover: John Lane company: Offices of the International studio . . . New York
LC 16-20922
Hokusai. See entry under Hokusai

Salamanca. See Spain—Salamanca; also Capes and cloaks

Salillas, Rafael
El tatuage en su evolución histórica, en sus diferentes caracterizaciones antiguas y actuales y en los delincuentes franceses, italianos y españoles. Madrid, E. Arias 1908
201p. tab. O.
Publication of the *Revista penitenciaria*

Salin, Bernhard
De nordiska guldbrakteaterna. Några bidrag till kännedomen om brakteaternas utbredning och kulturhistoriska betydelse. En arkeologisk studie af Bernhard Salin. [Stockholm, I. Hæggströms boktryckeri, 1895]
111p. incl.illus. tab. O.
Caption title. From *Antiqvarisk tidskrift för Sverige* del 14, nr. 2.
LC 25-6771
Svenska folkdräkter. See entry under Wistrand, P. G. V.

Salisham Indians. See Indians of North America—Salisham Indians

Sallengre, Albert Henry de
Novus thesaurus antiquitatum Romanorum. See note under Bossi, Gerolamo. De toga Romana commentarius

Sallet, Alfred Friedrich Constantin von. See Friedlaender, Julius, jt. auth.

Sallieth, Matheus de
(engr.) Perkois and Prins. Verzameling van verschillende gekleede mans- en vrouwenstanden

Salmagundi club, New York. Library
Catalogue of the costume books in the library of the Salmagundi club, New York. ⌈New York⌉ 1906
35p. 2 facsim. O.
LC 6-16639

Salmasius, Claudius. See Saumaise, Claude de

Salmerón, Africa León. See León Salmerón, Africa

Salmincio, Andrea
(engr.) Imperialis, J. B. Musaeum historicum et physicum

Salmon, André
Serge Gladky, synthèse du costume théâtral; texte par André Salmon. Paris, Ducros & Colas ⌈1927⌉
8 l. 32 col.pl. Q.
Colas 2632

Salmson, Axel Jacob
Rikssalen på Gripsholms slott historiskt porträtt-galleri af konung Gustaf I. Stockholm, Hörbergska 1847
54p. 28 col.pl. Q.
Colas 2633

(lithgr.) Wallgren, O. Skänska folk drägter

Salomon, Julian Harris
The books of Indian crafts & Indian lore; with many illustrations by the author and others. New York and London, Harper 1928
xvii,418p. front. illus. pl. ports. O. $3.50
This book was written for boys and girls who want to learn how to do the things the Indians did and also for camp directors to enrich their programs in handicraft, pageantry and ceremonial. cf. Preface
Contents: The Indians of the United States; War bonnets and head-dresses; War shirts, leggins and woman's costume; Moccasins and tanning methods; Bead work, breastplates, and necklaces; Tipis and wigwams; Bows, arrows, and quivers; Weapons and war paint; Pipes and bags; Musical instruments; Fire-making and cooking; Games; Dance steps and music; Dances and ceremonies; Producing an Indian pageant, Indian names
Bibliography: p405-10
LC 28-22308

Le **Salon** de la mode. 1.-25. année, 1876-1900. Paris, H. Petit
Col.pl. F.
No more published?
Colas 2634. Lipperheide 4756

Salons colonial and republican. Wharton, A. H.

Salquin, S. A.
Die militärische fussbekleidung. Bern & Basel, Georg 1883
125p pl. O.

The military shoe ... first prize in the official military competition in 1874; tr. by H. L. B. Washington, Govt. print. off. 1883
58p. illus. O.
At head of title: Office of the Quartermaster general

Les **saltimbanques.** Escudier, Gaston

Saltykov, Alekseĭ Dmitrievich, kniaz'
Habitants de l'Inde ... lithographiés à deux teintes par J. Trayer. Paris, H. Gache ⌈1853⌉
42 l. front. 41 col.pl. F.
Colas 2762

Salwey, Mrs Charlotte Maria (Birch)
Fans of Japan; with introduction by William Anderson ... and with ten full-page coloured plates, and thirty-nine illustrations in black and white. London, Kegan Paul, Trench, Trübner & co., ltd. 1894
xix,148p. illus. x col.pl.(incl.front.) sq.F. 31s 6d, o.p.
Costume index. Lipperheide 1729. LC 12-8564

Salzburg. See Masks—Salzburg

Salzman, Louis Francis
England in Tudor times, an account of its social life and industries. London, B. T. Batsford ⌈1926⌉
143p. illus. LXIII pl.(1 col.double; incl. ports. maps, facsims.) on 33 l. O. $3
Costume index. LC 26-17866

English life in the middle ages. London, Oxford univ. pr. H. Milford ⌈1929⌉
287p. front. illus. O. $2.75
First edition, 1926
Pictures from old books and manuscripts show English people of various ranks and occupations
Bibliography: p⌈283⌉-84
Costume index. LC 31-14297

English trade in the middle ages. Oxford, Clarendon 1931
xii,464p. front. illus. O. $4.50
"May be regarded as a sequel to my English industries of the middle ages (Oxford, 1923)" Preface
Illustrations are from manuscripts and show dress of the middle ages, especially representations of merchants, money minters, and other people engaged in various tasks
Costume index. LC 31-27204

Salzmann, Christian Gotthilf. Moralisches elementarbuch—Illustrations
Chodowiecki, D. N. Daniel Chodowiecki; 25 bisher unveröffentlichte handzeichnungen zu dem Moralischen elementarbuche von Christian Gotthelf Salzmann

Samaritani, G. L. da
Raccolta di costumi di Napoli. ⌈Naples⌉ Lit. della Sirena ca1825
18 col.pl. Q.
Shows dress worn in various localities near Naples and dress of street-venders. Colas gives a list of the plates
Colas 2635

Sambon, L.
L'esercito abissino; usi e costumi. Roma, Voghera Enrico 1896
64p. illus. 5pl. O.

Samling af danske militaire uniformer. Husher, Th. v.

Samling af Swenska armeens uniformer. Roos, Cajetan

Samlung Augspurgischer kleider trachten. Rohbausch, H. R.

Samlung der neu-jahr-kupferen ausgegeben von der Militarischen gesellschaft in Zürich. Zürich, 1744-98
1 l. 55pl. F.
Colas 2636. Lipperheide 2251

Samlung der ruszischen national-trachten. Will, J. M., engr.

Samlung europaeischer national trachten. Will, J. M., engr.

Sammlung Bayerischer national-costume. Lipowski, F. J.

Sammlung der merkwürdigsten städte und festungen, welche in den jahren 1788. 1789 und 1790 von den k.k. österreichischen, und kais: russischen armée der pforte abgenommen worden, nach ihrer wahren lage. Balzer, Anton, and Walenta, J.

Sammlung der Neujahrs-kupfer der gesellschaft der constabler und feuerwerker in Zürich, 1689-1779. See Collection of New Year's plates of the Company of constabulary and firemen in Zurich, 1689-1779

Sammlung der schönsten miniaturen des mittelalters. Reiss, Heinrich, ed.

Sammlung gehäkelter spitzen und einsätze; hrsg. von der handarbeits-abtheilung der Wiener mode. Wien, Verlag der "Wiener mode" [1896]
37p. illus. 28pl. Q.
Lipperheide 4178

Sammlung historischer bildnisse. Warnecke, Friedrich, ed.

Sammlung neuer muster zum sticken in plattstich und tambourin; gezeichnet von einer Hamburgerin. 1812-1830. Hamburg, Perthes & Besser 1812-30
Pl. ob.O.
Published annually. Lipperheide lists also an edition published (Hamburg, A. Campe [1809] 34pl.)
Lipperheide 3939, 3944

Die **sammlung** Sabouroff; kunstdenkmäler aus Griechenland. Saburov, P. A.

Sammlung verschiedener spanischer nationaltrachten. Suhr, Christoffer

Sammlung von bildnissen gelehrter männer und künstler. Moser, J. P.

Sammlung von initialen. Arnold, Xaver and Knoll, Eduard

Sammlung von leicht ausführbaren vorschriften zu den schönsten und elegantesten strumpfrändern und andern seinen strickereien. Andreä, Nanette

Sammlung von national-trachten und andern zu charakter-masken passenden kostümen. Berlin, L. W. Wittich 1826
1 l. 24 col.pl. O.
Eight plates show costume used in the play, Dimitri Donskoy. The others show masculine and feminine dress from Persia, Russia, Altenburg, and Corsica, and figures from Italian comedies. Sixteen of the plates are after drawings by Stürmer
Colas 2637. Lipperheide 3213

Sammlung von schweitzertrachten. Hegi, Franz

Sammlung von trachten bey verschiedenen ältern und neuern völkern. See Recueil des habillements anciens et modernes de differents nations d'après les dessins de Holbein [and others]

Die **sammlungen** inländischer alterthümer. Hansen, Gotthard von

Samoa—Tattooing. See Tattooing—Samoa

Samoïlovich, Aleksandr Nikolaevich
Odezhda stavropol'skikh turkmenok. Petrograd, 1923g
On dress of Turkoman women of Stavropol, Russia

Samoyeds
Georgi, J. G. Beschreibung aller nationen des russischen reichs. 1776-80
Georgi, J. G. Description de toutes les nations de l'empire de Russie, ou l'on expose leurs moeurs, religions, usages, maisons, habillemens et autres curiosites; tr. de l'allemand. 1776-80
Georgi, J. G. La Russie ouverte ou collection complette des habillemens de toutes les nations qui se trouvent dans l'empire de Russie. 1774-75
Georgi, J. G. Russland: beschreibung aller nationen des russischen Reiche. 1783

Samplers and stitches. Christie, Mrs Grace

Samplers and tapestry embroideries. Huish, M. B.

Sams, Conway Whittle
The conquest of Virginia: the forest primeval; an account, based on original documents, of the Indians in that portion of the continent in which was established the first English colony in America. New York and London, G. P. Putnam 1916
xxiii,432p. front. 1 illus. pl. fold.maps. O. $3.50, o.p.
Contains many pictures of Indians of Virginia as they appeared in the early part of the 17th century
Bibliography: p xvii-xviii
LC 16-10741

Sams, William
(pub.) A tour through Paris

Sánchez, Ignacio Calvo y. See Calvo y Sánchez, Ignacio

Sanchez-M. Navarro, Francisco
En la sala de armas y en el terreno. Tratado de esgrima de espada; de sable, á pie y á cabello, en su aplicación al combate individual; instrucción para el tiro de pistola y revólver. Madrid, Imprenta del Patronato de Huérfanos de Administración Militar 1907
xxiv,836p. 18pl. Q.
Plates show customary athletic costume worn by fencers at this period

Sand, George, and others. See Le diable à Paris

Sand, Maurice
Masques et bouffons, comédie italienne; texte et dessins par Maurice Sand, gravures par A. Manceau. Paris, M. Lévy 1860
2v. 50 col.pl. O.
Also published with imprint (Paris, A. Lévy 1862) Also published with plates in black and white
Shows not only clowns and harlequins but a variety of characters from Italian plays. The dress is both described and pictured
The English translation *The history of harlequinade* (London, M. Secker [1915]) omits the preface and "avant-propos" and includes only 16 of the 50 colored plates
Colas 2638. Lipperheide 3223. LC 22-1978 (Engl. ed.)
(illus.) Regnard, J. F. Oeuvres complètes

Sandberg, Johan Gustaf
(illus.) Forssell, C. D. Album pittoresque du nord
(illus.) Grafström, A. A. Ett år i Sverge
(illus.) Grafström, A. A. Une année en Suède

Sandby, Paul
Twelve London cries done from the life. Part 1st. [London] F. Vivarez 1760
12pl. Q.
Colas 2639. Lipperheide 1020m

Sander, Christian Levin
Kjøbenhavens kloededragter. See entry under Lahde, G. L.

Sandford, Francis, and King, Gregory
The history of the coronation of ... James II ... and of his royal consort Queen Mary ... on Thursday the 23 of April ... 1685. With an exact account of the several preparations in order thereunto ... by Francis Sandford. [London] T. Newcomb 1687
135p. illus. 27pl. 3 plans. F.
"[Gregory King] was consulted about the coronation ... and was the principal author of the ... volume containing descriptions and splendid engravings of that ceremony ... though he allowed Francis Sandford to affix his name to the title-page." Dictionary of national biography
Lipperheide 2688. LC 4-3138

Sandrart, Jacobus
(engr.) Sandrart, S. M. Neües türckisches pferd und reüter büchlein

Sandrart, Joachim von
(ed.) Falda, G. B. Der römischen fontanen wahre abbildung

Sandrart, Susanna Maria
Neües türckisches pferd und reüter büchlein ... Jacobus Sandrart excudit. [Nürnberg] ca1690?
8pl. Q.
Title is from the legend on plate 1. Plates are copied from numbers 28, 34, 29, 35, 30, 37, 27 and 36 in David Klöcker von Ehrenstrahl's *Das grosse carrosel.* They show the carrousel and riders which celebrated the accession to the throne of Charles XI in 1672
Lipperheide 2915
Neues polnisches pferd und reuter büchlein ... Jacobus Sandrart excudit. [Nürnberg] ca1690?
8pl. Q.
Title is from the legend on plate 1. Plates are copied from numbers 49, 42, 46, 43, 48, 44, 47, 39 in David Klöcker von Ehrenstrahl's *Das grosse carrosel* and show riders in the festivities which celebrated the accession to the throne of Charles XI of Sweden in 1672
Lipperheide 2916
(illus.) Curiöser spiegel

Sandringham House, Norfolk, England
Arms and armour at Sandringham. The Indian collection presented to King Edward VII when Prince of Wales, 1875-1876. London, W. Griggs 1910
55p. 32pl. Q.

Sandwich islands. See Hawaiian islands

Sandys, Sir John Edwin
(ed.) A companion to Latin studies, edited by Sir John Edwin Sandys; 3d ed. Cambridge [Eng.] University press; New York, Macmillan 1921
xxxv,891p. illus.(incl. facsims.) 2 fold. maps. O. $7
The following sections are of costume interest: Private antiquities: Birth, marriage and death, The position of women, Dress, Daily life. Public antiquities: The Roman army, by E. H. Alton; The Roman navy, by W. W. Tarn; Roman public games, The Roman theater, by J. H. Gray. Art: Architecture, by C. Gutch; Sculpture by A. J. B. Wace; Terracottas, by A. S. Smith; Engraved gems, by W. Ridgeway; Painting and mosaic, by F. R. Earp. Index of Latin words and phrases
Includes bibliographies
Costume index. LC 30-31962

San Francisco. Panama-Pacific international exposition
The 1915 mode as shown by Paris Panama-Pacific international exposition. New York, C. Nast 1915?
67p. illus. pl.(part col.) O.
Colas 1202

Le **sang** glorieux de Jeanne d'Arc. Morant, Georges de, comte

Sangster, William
Umbrellas and their history; with illustrations by Bennett. London, New York [etc.] Cassell, Petter, and Galpin [1871]
80p. front. illus. D.
LC 14-16385

San Lazzaro, G. di. See Cogniat, Raymond. Décors de théâtre

San-Marte, pseud. See Schulz, Albert

Sann, Hans von der
Altsteirische trachten; eine studie. Graz, P. Cieslar 1891
39p. S.
Reprint from *Grazer wochenblatt*
Lipperheide 887e

Sanquirico, Alessandro
Incoronazione di ... Ferdinando I. a re del Regno Lombardo-Veneto ... celebrata nell' insigne metropna. di Milano il VI settre. MDCCCXXXVIII. [Milano, B. Schiepatti 1838]
xiii l. 41pl.(part col.) sq.F.
Plates show Ferdinand in the regalia of the King of Lombardy, and processions, ceremonies, guards, heralds, etc.
Lipperheide 2775

Sansonetti, Victor
La Armeria real; ou Collection des principales pièces de la galerie d'armes anciennes de Madrid. See entry under Jubinal, Achille

Sansonetti, Victor—*Continued*
(illus.) Jubinal, Achille. Les anciennes tapisseries historiées

Sansovino, Francesco. See Du Choul, Guillaume. Discorso ... sopra la castrametatione, & bagni antichi

Les **sapeurs-pompiers.** Dally, Aristide

Sarachchandra Dāsa
Journey to Lhasa and central Tibet. By Sarat Chandra Das. Edited by the Hon. W. W. Rockhill. London, J. Murray 1902
x p. 285p. front (port.) illus. pl. maps plans. O.
Published by the Royal geographical society
LC 3-10830

Sarasin, Fritz. See Sarasin, Paul, jt. auth.

Sarasin, Paul, and Sarasin, Fritz
Reisen in Celebes, ausgeführt in den jahren 1893-1896 und 1902-1903. Wiesbaden, C. W. Kreidel 1905
2v. illus. 12pl.(4 col.) maps(3 fold.) O.
"Verzeichnis wichtigerer schriften über Celebes": v2 p[366]-375
LC AGR15-1518

Sarcus, Ch. M. de
Le conservatoire de la danse moderne; charges parisiennes. Paris, A. de Vresse 1844-45
12 col.pl. F.
The artist, under the pseudonym Quillenbois, gives caricatures of the most popular Parisian dances of the period
Lipperheide 3105

Sardinia
Bresciani, Antonio. Dei costumi dell' isola di Sardegna comparati cogli antichissimi popoli orientali. 1850

Carta Raspi, Raimondo. Costumi sardi. 1932?

Dalsani. Galleria di costumi Sardi. 1878

Ferrario, Giulio. Del costume antico e moderno del dottore Giulio Ferrario: Indice generale ... preceduto da un saggio di supplimento alla detta opera e dall' indicazione delle piu importante scoperte e relazioni fatte dai recenti viaggiatori dal 1820 al 1829. 1829

Luciano, Baldassarre. Cenni sulla Sardegna, ovvero Usi e costumi amministrazione, industria e prodotti dell' isola. 1843

Perrot, Georges, and Chipiez, Charles. History of art in Sardinia, Judaea, Syria, and Asia Minor. 1890

Pittaluga, A. Royaume de Sardaigne: costumes. n.d.

Stagnon, A. M. Recueil général des modes d'habillements des femmes des etats de sa majesté le roi de Sardaigne. ca1780

See also Military costume—Sardinia

Sardou, Victorien
Les merveilleuses. See Guillaumot, A. E. Costumes de directoire

See also Gazette du bon genre. Trente neuf aquarelles

Sargeaunt, Bertram Edward
Weapons. A brief discourse on hand-weapons other than fire-arms. London, H. Rees 1908
54p. 10pl. O. 2s 6d
Contents: Weapons for stunning; Weapons for cutting; Weapons for thrusting or stabbing; Miscellaneous weapons

Sarraute, Mme Inèz Gâches. See Gâches-Sarraute, Mme Inèz

Sartor Resartus. Carlyle, Thomas

Sartorial art journal and American tailor and cutter. v 1-54 no9, 1874-June 1929. New York
Q.
Published monthly except July and August
Title varies: 1881-87, *American fashion review*; 1888, *American fashion review and Tailor's art journal*
Merged with *American gentleman* which took the title: *American gentleman and Sartorial art journal* and continued as v55+, the volume numbering of the *Sartorial art journal*

Sartorial gazette. v 1, 1909+ London
Illus. patterns. Q. 19s 6d a year
Pattern with each number. Published monthly. Current 1938
Absorbed *Master tailor and cutters' gazette*, 1908; *London tailor and record of fashion*, 1914

[**Sartorio, Bernardo Canonico**]
I numi a diporto su l'Adriatico. Descrizione della regatta solenne disposta in Venezia a godimento dell' altezza serenissima di Ferdinando terzo prencipe di Toscanna. Unita la narrativa d'altri trattenimenti ordinati à divertimento della medisima altezza nel carnovale del MDCLXXXVIII. Venezia, A. Poletti [1688]
43p. 14pl. F.
Lipperheide 2752

Sarychev, Gabrïil Andreevich
Account of a voyage of discovery to the north-east of Siberia, the frozen ocean, and the north-east sea. By Gawrila Sarytschew ... Tr. from the Russian. London, Printed for R. Phillips by J. G. Barnard 1806-07
2v. in 1. 5pl.(part col. part fold.) O.
LC 6-23603

Sarytschew, Gawrila. See Sarychev, G. A.

Sassa yo yassa. Kellermann, Bernhard

Satirical songs and poems on costume. Fairholt, F. W.

Saturnalium sermonum libri duo, qui de gladiatoribus. Lipsius, Justus

Satyra Menippea. Buoninsegni, Francesco

Satyre sur les cerceaux. See La Fizelière, A. P. de. Histoire de la crinoline au temps passé

Sauerlandt, Max
Kinderbildnisse aus fünf jahrhunderten der europäischen malerei von etwa 1450 bis etwa 1850. Königstein im Taunus & Leipzig, K. Robert Langewiesche verlag 1921
viii,168,v p. illus. 8pl. Q. (Artis monumenta)

Sauerweid, Alexandre

Armée russe vers 1815. Paris, Nepveu 1815?

12 col.pl. Q.
Also published with plates in black and white. Plates are engraved by Alix and Jazet
Colas 2643

L'armée saxonne représentée en 30 feuilles, dessinée par Sauerweid, gravée par Granicher, coloriée par Bötticher. Dresden, H. Ritner 1810

30 col.pl. F.
"Cette série a été reproduite de nos jours sans nom d'éditeur" Colas
Colas 2640. Lipperheide 2202e

Uniformes de l'armée westphalienne du roi Jérome. No place, ca1810

19 col.pl. F.
Colas notes also a modern reprint
Colas 2641-42. Lipperheide 2220

Sauk Indians. See Indians of North America—Sauk Indians

Saulnier, René. See Duchartre, P. L., jt. auth.

Saultereau, Anthoine

(comp.) Chronologie et sommaire des souverrains pontifes, anciens pères, empereurs, roys, princes, et hommes illustres, dés le commencement du monde, iusques à l'an de grace mil six cens vingtdeux. Paris, Jean le Clerc 1631

280 l. illus. 2190 ports. 12 maps. F.
First edition 1622, had note: "chronologie collée, mis en ordre par J. L. B."

Published in 22 parts: 1 Portraicts des patriarches, roys, juges, princes, & conducteurs du peuple Hebrieu, depuis Adam, jusques à Herodes Agrippa; 2 XII. sibylles; 3 Faux dieux et deesses de l'ancien paganisme, tirez sur des medailles antiques; 4 Tous les monarques de Perse: depuis Ciaxare, jusques à Schah Abas; 5 Empereurs romains, & imperatrices, depuis Jules Cesar, & Costutia; 6 Empereurs d'orient, autrement dicts de Grece, ou de Constantinople, depuis l'an de grace 732; 7 Papes depuis s. Pierre apostre; 8 Roys et roynes de France, depuis Pharamond & Argote sa femme, jusques à Louys XIII. dit le juste, & d'Anne d'Austriche sa fémme; 9 Roys et roynes d'Espagne, depuis Athanaric roy des Goths

10 Roys d'Angleterre, depuis Brutus; 11 Brief recueil des vies & moeurs des roys et roynes de Portugal, depuis l'an 1088; 12 Roys de Naples; 13 Roys de Pologne, depuis l'an 550; 14 Princes de Mauritanie, comtes & ducs de Savoye, depuis l'an mil; 15 Princes et ducs de Venise, depuis l'an 679; 16 Ducs de Brabant, forestiers, & comtes de Flandres; 17 Grand maistres de l'ordre de S. Jean de Hierusalem; 18 Plusieurs hommes illustres qui ont flory en France, depuis l'an 1500; 19 Chanceliers et garde des sceaux de France

20 Interpretes du droict romain, depuis l'an 1130; 21 Poetes latins, pris des medailles antiques . . . depuis Linius Andronicus, jusques à Sidonius Apolinaris, & Michel Marulle; 22 Sommaire des temps, augmenté de nouveau
Lipperheide 29

Saumaise, Claude de

Ober het lang haair der mannen en de lokken der vrouwen. Dordrecht, 1645
O.

Saunders, Catharine

Costume in Roman comedy, by Catharine Saunders ... New York, Columbia univ. pr. 1909

x,145p. D. (Columbia university studies in classical philology)
Bibliography: p143-45
LC 9-19854

Saunders, Dorothy Lynne

Costuming the amateur show; a handbook for amateur producers. New York, S. French 1937

216p. illus. diagrs. D. $2.50
Contains patterns

Saurwein, Marx Treitz-. See Treitz-Saurwein, Marx, von Ehrentreitz

Sauvageot, Claude

(illus.) Ménard, R. J. La vie privée des anciens

Sauzey, Jean Camille Abel Fleury

La France en campagne. See entry under Rozat de Mandres, C. N. L.

Iconographie du costume militaire ... avec une préface de m. Henri Bouchot. Paris, E. Dubois 1901-03

3v. 2 col.pl. D. ea 10fr.
Volumes 2-3 published by R. Chapelot & cie. Preface to volume 3 by J. Margerand

Contents: [v 1] De la révolution et de l'empire; v2 Restauration & Louis-Philippe; v3 Deuxième république (1848-1852) et Napoléon III

Containing historical notes on more than 200 bodies of troops and 8000 references to more than 5000 colored plates which show uniforms. Subtitle (translated)
Colas 2644-46. LC 1-26475

Savage, William

(tr.) Billow, Anders. Pictorial Sweden. 1932

Savage and civilized dress. Balch, E. S.

Savage childhood. Kidd, Dudley

Savage life in the black Sudan. Domville-Fife, C. W.

The **savage** South Seas. Elkington, E. W.

Save, Gaston

Le costume rustique vosgien. Saint-Dié, L. Humbert 1888

46p. O.
From the *Bulletin de la société philomatique vosgienne,* 1887-88, v13
Colas 2647

Savigny, P.

(illus.) Fougerat, L. La pelleterie et le vêtement de fourrures dans l'antiquité

Savigny de Moncorps, de

Les almanachs de modes de 1814 à 1830; bibliographie dédiée aux dames. Paris, Leclerc & Cornuau 1897

Col.illus. Q. 4fr.
From *Bulletin du bibliophile*
Lipperheide 4876

Savin, Jacques Christophe. See Berrin, Emilie, jt. auth.

Savinov, V. N.

Stseny iz" russkago narodnago byta, rīsovany s" natury ... tekst" napīsan" V. N. Savīnovym". Sanktpeterburg", tip. I. Fishona 1852

47 l. 21 col.pl. F.
Scenes from Russian life
Colas 2648. Lipperheide 1365

Savoie; promenades historiques. Raverat, Achille, baron

Savorgnano, Mario, conte di Belgrado
Arte militare terrestre, e maritima; secondo la ragione, e l'uso de piu valorosi capitani antichi, e moderni ... hora ridotta ... da Cesare Campana ... con un essatissimo trattato à parte dell' artiglierie. Venetia, appresso gli heredi di F. de Franceschi 1599
266p. 23pl. F.
Plates show battles
Lipperheide 2055

Savoy. See France—By region or province —Savoy

Savva, abp of Tver. See Moscow. Sinodal' naía (byvshaía patrïarshaía) riznitsa. Sacristie patriarcale dit synodale

Savvaītov, Pavel Īvanovīch
Opīsanie starīnnykh" russkīkh" utvareĭ, odezhd", oruzhiía, ratnykh" dospíekhov" ī konskago prībora, v" azbuchnom" poríadkíe raspolozhennoe. Sanktpeterburg", tīp. Ī. Akademiī nauk 1896
184p. 16pl.(1 fold.) Q.
Describes and pictures ancient Russian implements, costumes, arms and riding dress

Saward, Blanche C. See Caulfeild, S. F. A., jt. auth.

Sawyer, Frederic Henry Read
The inhabitants of the Philippines. London, S. Low, Marston and company 1900
xxviii,422p. front. pl. ports. maps. O.
"Alphabetical list of works": p xiii-xiv
LC 1-3020

Sayles, Alexander, and Hallock, Gerard
Ice hockey; how to play and understand the game. New York, A. S. Barnes 1931
x,132p. illus. diagrs. D.
LC 31-28586

Scacciavento, Antonio. See Orilia, Francesco. Il zodiaco ... per opera del ... Francesco Antonio Scacciavento

Scalea, Pietro Lanza Di. See Lanza Di Scalea, Pietro

Scamozzi, Ottavio Bertotti
Descrizione dell' arco trionfale e della illuminazione fatta nella pubblica piazza di Vicenza la notte 12 novembre 1758 per la gloriosissima esaltazione alla dignita' cardinalizia di ... signor Antonio Marino Priuli Vescovo della medesima citta. Vicenza, C. Bressan e F. Mazzolini 1758
10p. 4pl. Q.
Lipperheide 2801

Scandinavia
Broke, Sir A. De C., 2d bart. A winter in Lapland and Sweden, with various observations relating to Finmark and its inhabitants. 1826

Falk, H. S. Altwestnordische kleiderkunde, mit besonderer berücksichtigung der terminologie. 1919

Hielscher, Kurt. Dänemark, Schweden, Norwegen; landschaft, baukunst, volksleben. 1932

Mandelgren, N. M. Monuments scandinaves du moyen âge avec les peintures et autres ornements qui les décorent. 1862

Skandinavien: Dänemark, Schweden, Norwegen, Finnland; baukunst, landschaft, volksleben. 1930

See also Denmark; Norway; Sweden; Varangians; Vikings; also Embroidery —Scandinavia

Periodicals

American Scandinavian review. 1913-

Scandinavians in Greenland. See Northmen in Greenland

Scappi, Bartolomeo
Dell' arte del cucinare, con Il mastro di casa [di C. Pandini; ragionamento del cavalier R. Fusorito ... con C. Pandini] e Trinciante [di V. Cervio] Venetia, 1643
636p. 21pl. Q.
The illustrations show cooks and waiters. The same work, including the works of Pandini and Cervio, and Fusoritto's illustrations, is found in the author's *Opera* (Venetia, 1622. 3v. illus. Q.) Separate editions of the works by Pandini and Cervio are listed under their names

Scarabs. Newberry, P. E.

Scarification
Baker, Sir S. W. The Nile tributaries of Abyssinia. 1868

See also Mutilation

Scarpelli, Tancredi
(illus.) Lorenzini, Paolo. Storia del costume dei popoli attraverso i secoli

Scarselli, A. A.
(engr.) Descrizione delle feste fatte in Bologna il giorno XVII agosto dell' anno MDCCXXXVIII ... in occasione delle ... nozze de' monarchi delle due Sicilie

Gli **scavi** della Certosa di Bologna. Zannoni, Antonio

Ščedrovskij, I. S. See Shchedrovskī, I. S.

La **Scène**; revue des succès dramatiques, v.1, no.1-24, 1877-1881. Paris, 1877-81
46 l. 95p. 24 col.pl. Q.
Colas 2649

Scener ur indelta soldatens lif. Nyblaeus, G. A.

Scenery, costumes and architecture, chiefly on the western side of India. Grindlay, R. M.

Scenes and characters of the middle ages. Cutts, E. L.

Scènes de jeunes gens. See note under Scheffer, J. G. Ce qu'on dit et ce qu'on pense

Scènes de la vie juive. Picart, Bernard

Scènes de la vie privée et publique des animaux. Grandville, J. I. I. G., called

Scènes de la vie rurale en Bretagne. Lalaisse, Hippolyte, and Ropartz, Sigismond

Scènes de société. Pigal, E. J.

Scènes des mémorables journées des 27, 28, 29 juillet 1830. Charlet, N. T., and Jaime

Scènes et costumes divers. Vernet, Carle

Scenes from every land. Grosvenor, G. H., ed.

Scenes from Italian life. Cerrone, F.

Scènes hongroises. Mikszáth, Kálmán

Scenes of Neapolitan life. Hess

Scenes, paysages, moeurs et costumes du Caucase. See Gagarin, G. G. kniaz. Costumes du Caucase

Scènes populaires. Pigal, E. J.

Scènes populaires de Naples. Mörner, Hjalmar

Scènes populaires, 1840. Dura, Gaetano

Scènes populaires russes. Jukowsky, Rudolph

Schabelitz, J. C.

Collection de 54 costumes originaux de la Suisse. Bâle, J. C. Schabelitz ca1820
54 col.pl. O.
Colas 2650

Schablonen in natürlicher grösse für decken, wände, säulenschäfte. Händel, Ernst

Schachner, Ignaz. See Duces supremi, qui elapso saeculo decimo septimo, Caesareis augustissimae domus Austriacae exercitibus summa potestate praefuere. Attributed author

Schad, Johann Adam Xaver

Effigies ducum et regum Hungariae. No place [1687]
61pl. F.
Contains full length portraits
Lipperheide 859

Schadow, Johann Gottfried

Costumes militaires russes. Berlin, G. Weiss ca1815
6 col.pl. F.
Engraved by Buchhorn or Jügel after designs by Schadow. Plates bear legends in Russian
Colas 2651

Schaedtler, Heinrich

Kurze beschreibung des königlich hannoverschen Guelphen-ordens. Hannover, S. L. Lamminger und Rosenbusch 1816
40p. 15pl. F.
Lipperheide 1918

Schäfer, Wilhelm. See Dilich, Wilhelm

Schäffer, Oscar

(illus.) Körber, Philipp. Volksbelustigungen und mummenschanz der alten ehemaligen reichsstadt Nürnberg

Schaepkens, A.

Choix de costumes de l'époque de Charles v à sa joyeuse entrée à Maestricht en 1520. Bruxelles, 1851
11pl. F.
Colas 2652

Schaeufelein, Hans Leonhard

La danse des noces, par Hans Scheufelein, reproduite par Johannes Schratt et publiée par Edwin Tross. Paris, Tross 1865
ix p. 21pl.(1 double) F.
Each plate shows two or three figures wearing the rich dress of the upper classes in Nuremberg at the time the original work was published, about 1530
Lipperheide 660. LC 22-6704

(illus.) Theuerdank. Die geuerlicheiten

Schaffende arbeit und bildende kunst. Brandt, Paul

Schaffhausen. See Switzerland—By region or province—Schaffhausen

Schaffner, Hermann

Die kostümreform unter der intendanz des grafen Brühl an den kgl. theatern zu Berlin 1814-1828. Krefeld, Worms & Lüthgen [1926]
109p. O.
Inaugural-dissertation, Erlangen. Bibliography: p6-10
LC 34-16294

Schall,

(illus.) Batissier, Louis. Les douze dames de rhétorique

Das **schaltjahr.** Scheible, Johann, ed.

Scharf, Sir George

(illus.) Le Comte, Hippolyte. Costumes français, de 1200 à 1715

(illus.) Panofka, Theodor. Manners and customs of the Greeks

(illus.) Planché, J. R. Costume of Shakespeare's ... King John [etc.]

Der **scharringgelhof.** Hess, David

Schartzemberger

Ain new formbüchlin. See note under Livres à dentelles

Der **schatz** des freiherrn Karl von Rothschild. Rothschild, M. K., freiherr von

Der **schatz** des Ordens vom goldenen vliesse. Probszt, Günther

Der **Schatzbehalter.** Nürnberg, A. Koberger 1491
354 l. 95 illus. F.
Woodcuts, by Michael Wohlgemuth, show costume of the 15th century
Lipperheide 421

Die **schatzkammer** der Marienkirche zu Danzig. Hinz, A.

Schatzkammer mechanischer künste. See Ramelli, Agostino. Le diverse et artificiose machine

Schaub, Charles. See La Suisse historique et pittoresque

Die **schaukunst** der Japaner dramen. Piper, Maria

Schauspielkostüm und schauspieldarstellung. Klara, Winfried

Schebesta, Paul

Revisiting my pygmy hosts; tr. from the German by Gerald Griffin. London, Hutchinson [1936]
288p. front. map. pl. O.
Translation of his: *Der Urwald ruft wieder*

Der Urwald ruft wieder; meine zweite forschungsreise zu den Ituri-Zwergen. Salzburg, A. Pustet 1936
208p. pl. map. O.
Contains material on the pygmies of the Congo

Schedel, Hartmann

Das buch der chroniken. Nürnberg, A. Koberger 1493
10, 286 l. 2000 illus. F.
Latin edition of 1493 has title: *Liber cronicarum.* Translated into German by Georg Alt; illustrated by Wilhelm Pleydenwurff and Michael Wohlgemuth

Schediasma juridico-philologicum tripartitum. Pacichelli, Giambattista

Schedler, Johann Georg

Nationaltrachten von Tirol und Vorarlberg. Innsbruck, ca1824
17 col.pl. Q.
Lipperheide 890a

Schéfer, Gaston
Documents pour l'histoire du costume de Louis XV à Louis XVIII; texte par Gaston Schéfer. Paris, Manzi, Joyant 1911
5v. illus. pl. (part col.) F.
Issued in 10 parts
Essai bibliographique sur les recueils de modes au XVIIIe et au début du XIXe siècle, par Paul Cornu: 32p in v 1
Colas 2653. LC 27-13072

Moreau le jeune, 1741-1814. Paris, Goupil 1915
172p. 74pl. 6 port. Q.

Scheffer, Jean Gabriel
Ce qu'on dit et ce qu'on pense, petites scènes du monde Paris [Gihaut, 1829]
1 l. 60 col.pl. ob.O.
Shows French life of the period in caricature. Lipperheide notes two other titles containing caricatures by the same artist: *Scènes de jeunes gens* (Paris, Martinet ca1825. 34 col.pl.) and *Recueil de cinquante scènes de grisettes* (Paris, Delpech ca1826. 50 col.pl)
Lipperheide 3684-86. LC 34-23921

Choix de costumes italiens. Paris, Mme A. Nepveu 1832
16 col.pl. O.
Plates show feminine costume in various parts of Italy. For a list of plates see Colas's *Bibliographie*
Colas 2654

Scheffer, Johannes
Joannis Schefferi Argentoratensis Lapponia; id est, Regionis Lapponum et verissima descriptio. Francofurti, C. Wolff 1673
378p. 25 illus. map. Q.
Shows costume of the Laplanders
German edition: *Lappland, das ist: Neue und wahrhafftige beschreibung von Lappland und dessen einwohnern* (Franckfurt und Leipzig, J. Andreä 1675)
Lipperheide 1380-81. LC 4-5798 (Ger. ed.)

Scheffers, A.
Neue muster-vorlagen für farbige kreuzstich-arbeiten. Leipzig, J. M. Gebhardt 1887
15p. 40 col.pl. Q.
Lipperheide 4010

Scheible, Johann
Die gute alte zeit geschildert in historischen beiträgen zur nähern kenntnisz der sitten, gebräuche und denkart ... in den letzten fünf jahrhunderten. Erster band: Zur geschichte hauptsächlich des stadtlebens, der kleidertrachten ... der kinderspiele, tanzfreuden. Stuttgart, Verlag des herausgebers 1847
xvi,1106p. 33 illus. 71pl. O.
Lipperheide 587

(ed.) Die fliegenden blätter des XVI. und XVII. jahrhunderts ... zunächst aus dem gebiete der politischen und religiösen caricatur; aus den schätzen der Ulmer stadtbibliothek wort- und bildgetreu herausgegeben. Stuttgart, J. Scheible 1850
334p. 88pl. (part fold.) S.
Lipperheide 587m. LC G-1758

(ed.) Das schaltjahr; welches ist der teutsch kalender mit den figuren, und hat 366 tag. Stuttgart, Verlag des herausgebers 1846-47
5v. front. illus. 104pl. S.
Shows fashions of the period. No more published
Lipperheide 586. LC 20-6624

(ed.) Sutor, Jakob. Neu künstliches fechtbuch

Schelle, Karl Gottlob
(tr.) Geschichte des männlichen barts unter allen völkern der erde bis auf die neueste zeit

Schellenberg, Johann Rudolf
(engr.) Dance of death. Freund Heins erscheinungen in Holbeins manier
(engr.) Huber, J. R. Recueil de XXIV differens costumes de la ville et du canton de Basle ... sur la fin du XVIIe siècle

Schellenberg-Biedermann, E.
Ein jahr aus Ursula's leben. Winterthur, Heger 1845
208p. 18pl. (2 col.) O.
Thirteen plates show Russian dress
Lipperheide 1362

Schelmenzunft. See Murner, Thomas. Nebulo nebulonum

Schelver, F. See Eckert, H. A., jt. auth.

Schema aller uniform der kaiserl. königl. kriegsvölkern. Artaria & compagnie, Vienna

Schema aller uniform der kaiserl. königl. kriegsvölkern. Löschenkohl, H., pub.

Schema der kaisl. königl. armee. Balzer, Johann

Schemel, Siegfried
Die kleidung der Juden im zeitalter der Mischnah, nebst einem anhange: Die priester-kleidung. Berlin, H. Itzkowski 1912
95p. O.
Dissertation, Rostock

Schenck, P.
(engr.) Monnoyeur, J. B. Recueil de costumes

Schendel, A. van. See Hannema, Dirk, jt. auth.

Schenk, Peter
Nieuwe geinventeerde Sineesen, met groote moeyte geteekent en in 't ligt gegeven. Amsterdam, ca1740
56pl. F.
Drawings of various aspects of Chinese life, including hunting scenes. Some of the plates bear a legend in German
Lipperheide 1517

La **scherma.** Alfieri, F. F.

La **scherma** illustrata. Pallavicini, G. M.

Scherr, Johannes
Kulturgeschichte der deutschen frau; 1. illustrierte ausg., nach der 2. aufl. des originals durchgesehen und herausgegeben von Max Bauer. Dresden, P. Aretz [1928]
344p. col.front. pl. (part col.) ports. (1 col.) Q.
First edition published 1860 under title: *Geschichte der deutschen frauen.* Also issued under title: *Weib, dame, dirne; kultur- und sittengeschichte der deutschen frau* (1928)
LC 30-17754

Schets van de geschiedenis der Nederlanden. Hofdijk, W. J.

Scheurer, J. E.
Wiener-costüme vom mittelalter bis zur gegenwart. Wien, A. Schroll [1890]
12pl. F.
Cover-title

Schidrowitz, Leo
Sittengeschichte des intimen: bett, korsett, hemd, hose, bad, abtritt. Wien, Verlag für kulturforschung 1926
319p. col.illus. O.

Sittengeschichte des theaters; eine darstellung des theaters, seiner entwicklung und stellung in zwei jahrtausenden. Mit zirka 200 ein und mehr- farbigen illustrationen und kunstbeilagen. Wien, Verlag für kulturforschung 1925
Published anonymously
319p. col.illus. O.

Schiemann, Theodor
Russland, Polen und Livland bis ins 17. jahrhundert. Berlin 1886-87
2v. illus. pl. port. maps. facsims. O.
Shows some costume and armor of Russia and Poland during the middle ages and the 16th-17th centuries

Schiesl, Ferdinand
Uniformirung und organisation des bürger-militärs in dem Königreiche Baiern. München, Zängl 1807
32p. col.front. 13 col.pl. 44p. of music. Q.
Half-title on frontispiece: *Uniformen des bürger-militairs in Baiern*
Colas 2660, 2944

Schild, Marie
Children's fancy costumes. London, S. Miller 1886
120p. illus. Q.

Old English costumes; ladies & peasants; [new & enl. ed.] edited by Marie Schild. An epitome of costumes from the 1st to the 19th century. London, M. Miller [1912]
80p. illus. Q. o.p.
Caption title: *British costume from the first to the nineteenth century*
First edition entitled: *Old English peasant costumes from Boadicea to Queen Victoria, suitable for fancy fairs, costume balls and bazaars* (1898. 124p. pl. O. 1s 6d)
LC 18-6502

Schilderung des türkischen reiches. Eton, William

Schiller, Heinrich Adelbert Konrad Karl Alexander. See Gleichen-Russwurm, Alexander, freiherr von

Schiller, Hermann
Kostümbilder für bühnenspiele des mittelalters. Leipzig, A. Strauch [1927]
18pl. O. (Jugend- und volksbuehne, heft 534-35)

Das **Schillerfest** in Hamburg am 11., 12. u. 13. Novbr. 1859. Endrulat, Bernhard

Schilling, Ign.
(illus.) Funebris memoria Mariae Amaliae ... rom. imperatricis, utriusque Bavariae ... ducis ... viduae, die 11. decembris 1756

Schindler, C. F.
Die cavallerie Deutschland's ... abbildungen der verschiedenen deutschen cavallerie-regimenter, ihre uniform und ausrüstung. Berlin, Steglitz 1882
2 l. 24 col.pl. Q.
Colas 2665

Militär-album des königlich preussischen heeres nach der neuesten organisation, uniformirung und bewaffnung aller truppentheile, entworfen und lithographirt von C. F. Schindler. Berlin, C. Glück 1862
1 l. 50 col.pl. F.
Second edition: Berlin, F. Sala 1873
Colas 2661-62

Die uniformirung der königl. preussischen armee im jahre 1874, gezeichnet von F. Schindler. Berlin, R. Lesser 1875?
1 l. 50 col.pl. F.
Colas 2664

(illus.) Preussens heer

Schindler, J. See Stubenrauch, Ph. von, jt. auth.

Schinnerer, Luise
Antike handarbeiten ... mit einer historischen einleitung ... von Alois Riegl. Wien, R. v. Waldheim [1895]
25p. 32 illus. Q.
Lipperheide 4176

Die kunst der weiss-stickerei. Wien, Verlag der Wiener mode [1896]
67p. 430 illus. Q.
Lipperheide 4023

Lehrgänge für weiszstickerei und knüpfarbeit. Stuttgart, Deutsche verlagsanstalt. 1893
152p. 212 illus. O.
Lipperheide 4020

De **schipvaert** ende reysen gedaen int landt van Turckyen. See note under Nicolay, Nicolas de, sieur d'Arfeuille. Les navigations ... en la Turquie

Schirek, Carl. See Kunstgewerbliches aus der vom Mähr. gewerbe-museum im jahre 1885

Schlackenwerth, Austria. Piaristenkollegium. Bibliothek
Die bilder der Hedwigslegende. See entry under Wolfskron, Adolf, ritter von. Die bilder der Hedwigslegende

Schlagintweit, Emil
Buddhism in Tibet illustrated by literary documents and objects of religious worship, with an account of the Buddhist systems preceding it in India. Leipzig, F. A. Brockhaus; London, Trübner 1863
xxiv,403p. illus. pl.(part fold.) facsims. (part fold.) Q. and portfolio of 20pl. F.
Shows costume of the Buddhist monks
French translation published as volume 3 of the *Annales du Musée Guimet* with title: *Le Bouddhisme au Tibet* (Paris, E. Leroux 1881)
Literature: p[331]-69
LC 1-12439

Indien in wort und bild; eine schilderung des indischen kaiserreiches. Leipzig, H. Schmidt & C. Günther 1880-81
2v. fronts. illus. pl. fold.map. F.
LC 24-2679

Schlagworte der alamodezeit. Schramm, Fritz

Schlatter, Daniel
Bruchstücke aus enigen reisen nach dem südlichen Ruszland, in den jahren 1822 bis 1828; mit besonderer rücksicht auf die Nogayen-Tataren am Asowschen meere. St Gallen, Huber 1830
xx,496p. 15pl.(11 col.) map. O.
Colas 2666. Lipperheide 1354

Schlawe, Karl
Die deutsche marine in ihrer gegenwärtigen uniformierung; genaue beschreibung der bekleidungs- und ausrüstungsstücke und der rang- und sonstigen abzeichen; 8. aufl. Leipzig, M. Ruhl [1913]
141p. 405 col.illus. on 28pl. O.

Die organe der deutschen freiwilligen krankenpflege im kriege, ihre uniformierung und ausrüstung. Leipzig, M. Ruhl [1903]
28p. 2 col.pl. D.

Schlegel, Johann Heinrich
Geschichte der könige von Dänemark aus dem oldenburgischen stamme ... mit ihren bildnissen nach den originalen gestochen von Johann Martin Preisler. Kopenhagen, Möller 1769-77
2v. 8pl. F.
Includes portraits of the Danish kings from Christian I to Christian IV
Lipperheide 1040. LC 2-22796

Der **schleier** von Sumer bis heute. Jeremias, Alfred

Schlesische fürstenbilder des mittelalters. Luchs, Hermann

Schlichtegroll, Franz von
Gallerie altteutscher trachten. Leipzig, Industrie-comptoir 1802
2pts. 25 col.pl. Q.
Shows court dress of the 16th century
Colas 2667. Lipperheide 654

Schlichtegroll, Nathanael
Talhofer; ein beytrag zur literatur der gerichtlichen zweykaempfe im mittelalter. München, Im verlage der lithographischen kunstanstalt 1817
36p. 6pl. F.
Lipperheide 2984

Schlichten, Ian Philips van der
Tableaux de la sainte messe. Mannheim, Imprimerie electorale 1738
36 l. 36 illus. Q.
Lipperheide 1812

Schlichting, Ernst Hermann
Trachten der Schweden an den küsten Ehstlands und auf Runö. Leipzig, T. O. Weigel 1854
2p. 10 col.pl. Q.

Schliemann, Heinrich
Ilios; stadt und land der Trojaner; forschungen und entdeckungen in der Troas und besonders auf der baustelle von Troja. Leipzig, F. A. Brockhaus 1881
xxiv,880p. 1570 illus. 32pl. 1 map. 6 plans. O.
Lipperheide 195

Ilios: the city and country of the Trojans: the results of researches and discoveries on the site of Troy and throughout the Troad in the years 1871-72-73-78-79. London, J. Murray 1880
xvi,800p. front. illus. pl.(part fold.) fold. map. VI fold.plans. O.
Translation of his *Ilios; stadt und land der Trojaner*
LC 18-5921

Mycenæ; a narrative of researches and discoveries at Mycenæ and Tiryns; representing more than 700 types of the objects found in the royal sepulchres of Mycenæ and elsewhere in the excavations. London, J. Murray 1878
lxviii,384p. illus. 25pl.(4 col.) O.
Translation of his *Mykenae*
LC 4-32589

Mykenae; bericht über meine forschungen und entdeckungen in Mykenae und Tiryns. Leipzig, F. A. Brockhaus 1878
lxvi,447p. 468 illus. 25pl.(4 col.) O.
Lipperheide 194

Schlosser, Julius, ritter von
Der burgundische paramentenschatz des Ordens von goldenen vliesse. Wien, A. Schroll 1912
27p. 1 illus. 31pl.(2 col. 3 double) F.

Schluymer, M.
(illus.) Description des principales rejouissances, faites à La Haye, à l'occasion du couronnement de sa majesté ... François I

Schmalen, A. von
Nachricht von den fränkischen craistrouppen, nebst einem anhang von den schwäbischen creisregimentern. Nürnberg, G. N. Raspe 1782
102p. 12 col.pl. O.
Colas 2668. Lipperheide 2127m

Schmalen, Johann Christ. Hermann von
Accurate vorstellung der saemtlichen kayserlich koeniglichen armeen, zur eigentlichen kentniss der uniform von jedem regimente. Nebst beygefügter geschichte worinne von der stiftung denen chefs, der staercke, und den wichtigsten thaten jedes regiments nachricht gegeben wird. Nürnberg, Raspe 1762
2pts in 1 v. 76p. 124 col.pl. O. 450fr.
Second part, the supplement, is by J. F. S[eyfart] and entitled *Kurzgefasste geschichte aller kaiserlich-königlichen regimenter zu pferde und zu fuss ... welche bis auf das jahr 1762 fortgesetzet.* Frankfurth und Leipzig, 1762. Supplement is included in the 1762 edition only
Editions of 1772, 1777, and 1787 are revised to show new uniforms adopted
Colas 20-26. Lipperheide 2226

Accurate vorstellung der sämtlichen koeniglich preussischen armee ... von I. C. H. von S. Nürnberg, Raspe 1759
117 col.pl. O.
"Worinnen zur eigentlichen kenntniss der uniform von jedem regimente ein officier und gemeiner in völliger montirung und ganzer statur nach dem leben abgebildet sind nebst beygefügter nachricht. 1 Von der stiftung, 2 Denen chefs, 3 Der staerke und 4 Der in friedenzeiten habenden guarnisons jedes regiments." Subtitle
Also published (Neue verm. und verbess. aufl. Nürnberg, Raspischen buchh. 1770. 110 col.pl.) and a reprint 1787. Text to explain the plates is contained in J. F. Seyfart's *Kurzegefassete geschichte aller ... regimenter zur erklärung der illuminirten abbildungen*
Colas 2669-71. Lipperheide 2144-46

Schmeltz, J. C. E.
(tr.) Rouffaer, G. P., and Juynboll, H. H. De batik-kunst in Nederlandsch-Indië en haar geschiedenis

Schmeltz, Johannes Diedrich Eduard
(ed.) Adriani, Nicolaus, and Kruipt, A. C. Geklopte boomschors als kleedingstof op Midden-Celebes

Schmid, David Aloys
Farbige schweizer trachten-bilder. Zug, E. Kalt-Zehnder [1929]
22 col.pl. sq.O.
Cover title

Schmid, H., and Patzschke, Carl
L'armée saxonne depuis ses origines jusqu'en 1832. Leipzig, J. G. Fritzsche [1832]
24 col.pl. ob.F.
Colas 2672

Schmid, Matilde Clasen-. See Clasen-Schmid, Mathilde

Schmidt; Seyffert, O., and Sponsel
Sächsische volkstrachten und bauernhäuser. Dresden, W. Hoffmann 1897
4 l. 40pl. F.
Lipperheide 825e

Schmidt, Albrecht
Vorstellung der Augspurgischen kleiter tracht. Augspurg, A. Schmidt ca1720
13 col.pl. F.
Includes twenty six costume pictures, of which twenty four show feminine dress
Colas 3034. Lipperheide 766

Schmidt, Arthur
(illus.) Die graue felduniform der deutschen armee

Schmidt, Carl, and Schmidt, Rosalie
Methodische anleitung für geometrische zuschnittlehre, weiszarbeiten, maschinennähen und praktisches kleidermachen; 2. verm. und verb. aufl. München, G. Schöpping 1883
81p. illus. 22pl. O.
First edition: *Theoretisch-praktischer unterricht für maschinennähen und weiszarbeiten* (München, P. Höpfner 1877)
Lipperheide 3808-09

Schmidt, Ferdinand August
Anleitung zu wettkämpfen, spielen und turnerischen vorführungen bei volks- und jugendfesten; 2. umgearb. aufl. Leipzig, R. Voigtländer 1900
144p. 49 illus. O. (Kleine schriften des Zentralausschusses zur förderung der volks- und jugendspiele in Deutschland, bd.2)
First edition: 1896
Lipperheide 3051

Schmidt, Georg Friedrich
(engr.) Elssner, Jacob. Neueste beschreibung derer griechischen christen in der Türckey

Schmidt, Johann Andreas, fencing master
Leib-beschirmende und feinden trotzbietende fecht-kunst ... Nebst einem curieusen unterricht vom voltigiren und ringen. Nurnberg, 1713
376p. 84pl. ob.O.

Mit ... bewilligung der hoch-fürstl. würtemb. ober-vormundschafft und administration, solte de ... fecht-kunst ... nebst einem ... unterricht vom voltigiren und ringen ... an das licht stellen. Stuttgardt, Faber 1737
376p. 73 illus. 13pl. O.
First edition: Nürnberg, C. Weigel 1713
Lipperheide 2970

Schmidt, Joseph. See Larisch, Paul, jt. auth.

Schmidt, Max
Kunst und kultur von Peru. Berlin, Propyläen-verlag [c1929]
621p. incl.illus. pl. map. XVIII col.mounted pl. Q.
LC 30-1916

Schmidt, Mrs Minna (Moscherosch)
400 outstanding women of the world and costumology of their time. Chicago, M. M. Schmidt 1933
xviii,583p. illus. pl. ports. facsims. O.
A group of plates shows costume figures of the principal countries of the world. Contains material also on coiffures and wigs, make-up, fans, jewels, wedding dress, costume of the crusaders, and academic dress
LC 33-18770

Schmidt, Rosalie. See Schmidt, Carl, jt. auth.

Schmidt, Sigismund, pseud. See Leucht, C. L.

Schmidt, W.
Die frühesten und seltensten denkmale des holz- und metall-schnittes aus dem vierzehnten und fünfzehnten jahrhundert nach den originalen im k. Kupferstich-cabinet und in der k. Hof- und staats-bibliothek in München. Nürnberg, S. Soldan [1886]
12p. 110 pl. F.
Shows 15th century costume
Lipperheide 466

Schmidtmeyer, Peter
Travels into Chile, over the Andes, in the years 1820 and 1821, with some sketches of the productions and agriculture; mines and metallurgy; inhabitants, history, and other features, of America; particularly of Chile, and Arauco. London, Longman, Hurst, Rees, Orme, Brown, & Green 1824
378p. pl.(part col.) fold.map, fold.plan. sq.Q. 42s, o.p.
Shows costume of Chile and of the Araucanian Indians of South America
Costume index. LC 4-11482

Schmuck, Frédéric
(illus.) Berger-Levrault, Oscar. Les costumes strasbourgeois

Schmuck, Frédéric Guillaume
(illus.) Berger-Levrault, Oscar. Les costumes strasbourgeois

Schmuck, Guillaume
(illus.) Berger-Levrault, Oscar. Les costumes strasbourgeois

Der **schmuck.** Bassermann-Jordan, Ernst

Der **schmuck** des menschen. Selenka, Emil

Die **schmuck-** und edelsteine. See Eppler, Alfred. Edelsteine und schmucksteine

Schmutzer, Jakob
Abbildungen der k. k. cavallerie-regimenter von 1765. No place, ca1766
129 col.pl. F.
Colas 2674

Abbildungen der k. k. oesterreichischen infanterie. No place, ca1765
55 col.pl. F.
Colas 2673

Schnackenberg, Walther
Ballett und pantomine, mit e. enleit. v. Alxdr. v. Gleichen-Russwurm. München, G. Müller 1920
7p. 22 col.pl. sq.F.

Kostueme, plakate und dekorationen ... mit begleitendem text von Oskar Bie. München, Musarion-verlag 1920
8p. 82pl. on 21 l.(part col.) F.
Shows fancy dress

Schneehagen, Christian. See Frucht, Lotte, jt. auth.

Schneider, Friedrich
Ein bischofsgrab des zwölften jahrhunderts im Wormser dom. Bonn, C. Georgi 1888
10p. 3pl. O.
Describes the dress of Bishop Konrad II of Sternberg, in the year 1192
Lipperheide 1841

Schneider, Heinrich Justus
(illus.) Kohlrausch, Friedrich. Bildnisse der deutschen könige und kaiser von Karl dem Grossen bis Maximilian I.

Schneider, Louis
Gallerie der costüme auf historischen nationellen und characteristischen grundlagen für das theater. Berlin, Winckelmann 1844-47
96p. 144 col.pl. Q.
Colas 2675. Lipperheide 3221

Illustrirte stamm- rang- und quartier liste der königlich preussischen armee. Berlin, A. Duncker 1854
6 col.pl. F.
Colas 2676. Lipperheide 2180

Die kunst sich zu schminken (physiographie für das theater) oder leitfaden für junge schauspieler. Berlin, A. W. Hayn 1831
x,70p. 10 illus. 6pl. O.
Lipperheide 3216

Präsentirt das gewehr! Anleitung zu militairischen spielen, mit ... abbildungen der uniformen des preussischen militairs von der zeit des grossen churfürsten bis auf die jetzige. Berlin, Stuhr [1844]
128p. 5 col.pl. O.
Lipperheide 2137m

Die preussischen orden ... geschichtlich, bildlich, statistisch. Berlin, A. W. Hayn's erben 1867-72
13pts. 53 illus. 47pl.(45 col.) Q.
Lipperheide 1936

(ed.) Der Soldaten-freund

Schnelboltz, Gabriel
Warhaffte bildnis etlicher hochlöblicher fürsten und herren. Wittenberg, 1652
Illus. Q.
"Welch zu der zeit da die heilige Göttliche schrift, so durch menschen satzunge vertunckelt gewesen, durch Gottes gnaden wider an tag komen ist, regieret und gelebet haben. [With explanatory verses.]" Subtitle
Latin edition (1563) has same illustrations. Two books, listed elsewhere in full, are based on Schnelboltz: *Abcontrafactur und bildnis aller gross hertzogen;* and Reusner's *Icones*

Schnell, H.
Handbuch der ballspiele. Leipzig, R. Voigtländer 1899-1901
3v. 78 illus. O.
Lipperheide 3052

Schnellpost für moden . 1.-5. jahrg., juli 1832-1836; neue folge 1-6, 1837-1842. Leipzig, Baumgärtner's buchh. 1832-42
[11]v. col.illus. col.pl. O.-F.
Published weekly
Title changes: 1834-40 *Schnellpost für moden und literatur.* Subtitle varies
The second year, 1833, contains fifty-two illustrations from the *Petit courrier des dames*
Colas 2677. Lipperheide 4619

Schnittmusterbuch; anleitung zum wäsche-zu-schneiden für schüle und haus ... hrsg. vom Wiener-frauen-erwerb-verein. Wien, R. v. Waldheim 1877
4 l. 27pl. Q.
Sixth revised edition: 1889
Lipperheide 3810-3811

Schnitzer, Lucas
Beschreibung und abrisz der fürstlichen leich procession ... desz ... herrn Christiani marggraffens zu Brandenburg ... leichbestättigung, so dienstags den 11 septembris anno 1655, zu Bayreuth vorgangen. No place, 1655?
39pl. F.
Lipperheide 2523

(illus.) Oertel, Hieronymus. Ortelius redivivus et continuatus

Schober, Anna
Vollständiges lehr- und hilfsbuch zum selbstunterricht für damen in der herstellung einer guten toilette, nach der methode Anna Schober ... 9 ... verm. aufl. Wien und Leipzig, H. Winkler 1884
35p. 11pl. O.
Lipperheide 3831

Een **schoeisel** verzameling. Lapidoth, Frits

Schön, Julius
Geschichte der handfeuerwaffen; eine darstellung des entwickelungsganges der handfeuerwaffen von ihrem entstehen bis auf die neuzeit. Dresden, R. Kuntze 1858
xviii,182p. 32pl. Q.
Lipperheide 2412

Schön newes modelbuch. Latomus, Sigismund

Schön neues modelbuch von allerly lustigen mödeln naazunehen zuwürcken uñ zustickẽ: gemacht im ... 1599. Basel, L. König 1606
39pl. Q.
First edition: 1599. Patterns are copies from Sibmacher's *Newes modelbuch*
Lipperheide 3906

Schönbarth, Barbatius. See Permoser, Balthasar. Der ohne ursach verworffene und dahero von rechts wegen auff den thron der ehren wiederum erhabene barth

Schoenbeck, Richard
Das pferd und seine darstellung in der bildenden kunst; 2. aufl. Leipzig, F. Engelmann 1912
203p. illus. 45pl. F.
Horses and riders in bronzes and paintings

Schönberg, Alfons Diener-. See Diener-Schönberg, Alfons

Schönberger, Käthe
Reiterinnen und radlerinnen; humoristische scenen aus dem Berliner sportleben. Berlin, Harmonie [1901]
25pl. F.

Eyn **schöne** kurtzweilige histori von eym mächtigẽ riesen auss Hispaniẽ. Fierabras

Schönhaar, Wilhelm Friderich
Ausführliche beschreibung des- zu Bayreuth im september 1748 vorgegangenen ... beylagers, und derer- ... heimführungs festivitaeten, des ... herrn

Schönhaar, Wilhelm F.—*Continued*
Carls, regierenden herzogs zu Württemberg ... und der ... frauen Elisabethae Fridericae Sophiae. Stuttgardt, In der Jenischen buchdruckerey 1749
144p. illus. 5pl. F.
Lipperheide 2592

Der **"schönheitsfehler"** des weibes. Larisch, Rudolf von

Schøning, Gerhard
(ed.) Ólafsson, Eggert. Des vice-lavmands Eggert Olafsens und des landphysici Biarne Povelsene reise durch Island

Schöning, Kurd Wolffgang von
Geschichte des königlich preuszischen dritten Dragoner-regiments und derjenigen Dragoner-regimenter, aus welchen dasselbe, bei der reorganisation der armee im jahre 1807, hervorgegangen ist. Berlin, F. Dümmler, 1835
xiv,438p. 2 col.pl. O.
Lipperheide 2168

Geschichte des königlichen preuszischen regiments Garde du corps zu seinem hundertjährigen jubelfeste (1740-1840). Berlin, 1840
328p. 7 col.pl. Q.
Colas 2678. Lipperheide 2171

Scholl, Edouard
Bekleidung und ausrüstung der preuszischen feuerwehren; kommunale berufsfeuerwehren u. kommunale feuerwehraufsichtsbeamte. Polizeilich anerkannte freiwillige feuerwehren u. pflichtfeuerwehren, fortges. und erg. v. Paul Stapusch; 3. erw. u. verb. aufl. Leipzig, M. Ruhl [1926]
31p. 8 col.pl. O.

Schollenberger, Johann Jakob
(engr.) Nürnbergische kleider arten

School dress. See Students

Schoolcraft, Henry Rowe
Information respecting the history, condition and prospects of the Indian tribes of the United States: collected and prepared under the direction of the Bureau of Indian affairs, per act of Congress of March 3d, 1847 ... published by authority of Congress. Philadelphia, Lippincott, Grambo 1851-57
6v. front. illus. pl.(part col.) port. maps (part fold.) sq.F. $90, o.p.
Half-title: *Ethnological researches, respecting the red man of America.* Volume 1 has title: *Historical and statistical information respecting the history, condition and prospects of the Indian tribes of the United States.* Volume 6 has title: *History of the Indian tribes of the United States: their present condition and prospects* and half-title: *General history of the North American Indians.* Illustrated by Capt S. Eastman and others
Costume index. LC 2-14425

Schools and masters of fence. Castle, Egerton

Schoonebeek, Adriaan
Histoire des ordres religieux de l'un & de l'autre sexe ... et les figures de leurs habits; 2. éd. cor. et augm. Amsterdam, A. Schoonebeek 1695
2v. 144 illus. O.
From the first French translation of his: *Nette afbeeldingen* enlarged in the text and by the addition of 71 figures. Does not include women's religious orders
Colas 2682. Lipperheide 1860

Historie van alle ridderlyke en krygsorders; behelzende haar instellingen, plegtelykheden, gebruyken, voornaamste daden, en levens der meesters; nevens desselfs dragten, wapens en zinteekenen. Amsterdam, A. Schoonebeek 1697
2v. 142 illus. S.
Translated into French under title: *Histoire de tous les ordres militaires ou de chevalerie* (Amsterdam, H. Desbordes 1699)
Colas 2686-87. Lipp. 1898. LC 9-19111

Kurtze und gründliche histori von dem anfang und ursprung der Gott-geweyhten orden aller closter-jungfrauen aus dem frantzösischen in das teutsche übersetzet. Augspurg, D. Steudner 1693
123p. 90pl. S.
Translation of *Courte description des ordres des femmes et filles religieuses* (Amsterdam, 1691) a French version of Adriaan Schoonebeek's *Nette afbeeldingen der eygene dragten van alle geestelyke vrouwen en nonnen orders* (Amsterdam, 1691)
Colas 2683-85. Lipp. 1861-62. LC 31-19750

Nette afbeeldingen der eyge dragten van alle geestelyke orders. Amsterdam, By den auteur 1688
144p. 73pl. O.
A French translation has title: *Courte et solide histoire de la fondation des ordres religieux, avec les figures de leurs habits* (Amsterdam, 1688) A German translation from the French edition has title: *Kurtze und gründliche histori vom ursprung der geistlichen orden* (Augspurg, A. Nepperschmid 1692) and (Augspurg, J. C. Wagner 1695)
Colas 2679-81. Lipperheide 1857-59

(illus.) Orlers, Jan. Genealogia illustrissimorum comitum Nassoviae

Schopper, Hartmann
Panoplia. See note under Amman, Jost. Eygentliche

See also Amman, Jost. De omnibus illiberalibus

Schotel, Gilles Dionysius Jacobus
Bijdrage tot de geschiedenis der kerkelijke en wereldlijke kleeding. 'sGravenhage, P. H. Noordendorp 1856
152, 237p. O.
Lipperheide 1826

Schott, Charles M.
Catalogue of the choice and valuable collection of rare antique guns and pistols, edge weapons, accessories, etc., formed by Mr. Charles M. Schott ... also a collection of scarce and important books on old arms, armour, etc; to be sold ... November 19th, 20th and 21st, 1918 ... by Scott & O'Shaughnessy, inc. ... New York. [New York, S. L. Parsons, printers 1918]
Cover-title, 102p. 45pl. on 23 l. O.
LC CA19-209

Schramm, Fritz
Schlagworte der alamodezeit. Strassburg, K. J. Trübner 1914
120p. 3pl. O. (Zeitschrift für deutsche wortforschung)

Schranka, Eduard Maria
(comp.) Tabak-anekdoten; ein historisches braunbuch aus den verschiedensten quellen im laufe der jahre zusammengetragen und nach den persönlichkeiten alphabetisch geordnet ... Im selbstverlag hrsg. von J. Feinhals, Cöln. Cöln, P. Neubner 1914
302p. incl.illus. pl. O. M.5
LC 14-11095

Schratt, Johannes. See Schaeufelein, H. L. La danse des noces

Schreber, Daniel Gottlieb Moritz
Ärtzliche zimmergymnastik, oder System der ohne gerät ... ausführbahren heilgymnastischen freiübungen; 24. aufl. durchgesehen und ergänzt von ... Rudolf Graefe. Leipzig, F. Fleischer 1890
122p. 45 illus. pl. O.
First edition: 1855
Lipperheide 3048

Schreger, Christian Heinrich Theodor
Kosmetisches taschenbuch für damen, zur gesundheitsgemäszen schönheitspflege ihres körpers. Nürnberg, J. L. Schrag [1810]
xii,272p. O.
Lipperheide 3251

Schreiber, Aloys Wilhelm
Trachten, volksfeste und charakteristische beschäftigungen im grosherzogthum Baden in XII malerischen darstellungen und mit historischtopographischen notizen. Freiburg, Herder ca1825
12 l. 12 col.pl. ob.F.
Colas 2688. Lipperheide 743

Schreiber, Lady Charlotte Elizabeth (Bertie) Guest
Catalogue of the collection of fans and fan-leaves presented by the Lady Charlotte Schreiber. See entry under British museum. Department of prints and drawings

Fans and fan leaves ... collected and described by Lady Charlotte Schreiber. London, B. Quaritch 1888-90
2v. 314pl. F. 120s
In 1891 Lady Schreiber presented her collection to the British museum. A catalogue, compiled by Lionel Cust, assistant in the Department of prints and drawings, was printed in 1893. See entry under British museum. Department of prints and drawings
Contents: [v 1] English; [v2]Foreign
Costume index. LC 18-23212

Schreiber, Guido
Der badische wehrstand seit dem siebenzehnten jahrhundert bis zu ende der französischen revolutionskriege. Karlruhe, Herder 1849
x,310p. 8 col.pl. map. Q.
Drawings by F. Dietz, L. Reich, M. von Schvind
Colas 2689. Lipperheide 2210

Schreiber, Theodor. See note under Kultur-historischer bilderatlas

Schreiber, Wilhelm Ludwig
Manuel de l'amateur de la gravure sur bois et sur métal au XVe siècle. Berlin, A. Cohn 1891-1911
8v. in 9. illus. CXXI pl.(part col.) on 104 l. O.-F.
Volumes 4-5: Leipzig, O. Harrassowitz
Volumes 6-8 contain plates showing costume of the 15th century
Lipperheide 4958. LC F-2363

Schrenck von Nozing, Jacob
Augustissimorum imperatorum, serenissimorum regum, atque archiducum, illustrissimorum principum ... gestarum succinctae descriptiones. Oeniponti, excudebat I. Agricola 1601
260p. 125 port. F.
Text on verso of portraits. Portraits engraved after J. B. Fontana, by D. Custodis
German edition: *Der aller durchleuchtigisten und grossmächtigen kayser ... als kriegszeiten verrichten fürnembsten thaten und handlungen* (Ynsprugg, D. Baur 1603)
Portraits show standing figures in armor
Colas 2690-91. Lipperheide 499 (Ger. ed.)
LC 25-6355

Schroeder, Minna
Lehrbuch der damenschneiderei. Hamburg, G. Kramer 1878
107p. 7 illus. 12pl. O.
Second edition: 1881
Lipperheide 3814-15

Schröder, Severin
Die farbenharmonie in der damen-toilette ... mit ... tafeln ... originale von Heinrich Lefler. Wien, E. Berté und S. Czeiger 1897
x,47p. 7 col.pl. O.
Lipperheide 3306

Schrödter, Adolph. See Detmold, J. H., jt. auth.

Schryver, Cornelis
La tresadmirable, tresmagnificque, & triumphante entree, du ... Prince Philipes, Prince d'Espaignes, filz de Lempereur Charles V^e^., ensemble la vraye description des spectacles, theatres, archz triumphaulx lesquelz ont este faictz ... en ... ville d'Anvers, anno 1549. Premierement ... descripte en langue Latine, par Cornille Grapheus [Cornelis Schryver] Anvers, G. van Diest 1550
55 l. 29 illus. F.
Latin edition published the same year has title: *Spectaculorum in susceptione Philippi Hisp. prin. divi Caroli. V... Antverpiae aeditorum, mirificus apparatus*
Lipperheide 2652-2653

Schubauer, F.
Königlich sächsische armee. Leipzig, P. del Vecchio; Wien, J. Trentsensky 1842
1 l. 9 col.pl. F.
Colas 2693

Schudt, Johann Jacob
(tr.) Neue Franckfurter jüdische kleiderordnung

Schübler, Jean Jacob
Amor vehementer quidem flagrans: artificiose tamen celatus, de Pantalonis custodiaque triumphans intendado certamine prudentum stultorum, sive Arlechin viva pictura ridiculusque Cupido. Augustae Vindelicorum, J. Wolff 1729
1 l. 12pl. F.
Plates, engraved by B. Probst after Schübler, show costume of Italian comedy
Colas lists another edition with title in Latin and German: *Die zwar hefftige entflammte doch aber kunstlich verborgene über Pantalons aufsicht thriumphirende amor* (Augspurg, J. M. Probst)
Colas 2694-95

Schütz, Carl. See Geschichte der kaiserl. konigl. regimenter sei ihrer errichtung; Also Schwarz, Ignaz, ed. Wiener strassenbilder im zeitalter des rokoko

Schützenwesen und schützenfeste der deutschen städte. Edelmann, August

Schützercrantz, Adolph
Kongl. svenska riddare ordnarnes drägter 1833. Stockholm, Gjöthström & Magnusson 1833
8 col.pl. F.
Colas 2697. Lipperheide 1922

Svenska krigsmaktens fordna och närvarande munderingar. Stockholm, J. F. Meyer 1849-53
36 col.pl. ob.F.
Shows uniforms of Swedish soldiers from 1687 to the middle of the 19th century
Colas 2698. Lipperheide 2278

Das **schuhmacher**-handwerk im seiner entwickelung. Flotow, Gustav von

Die **schulen** der weiblichen handarbeit. Georgens, J. D., and Gayette-Georgens, Frau J. M. von

Schuler, Théophile
(illus.) Michiels, Alfred. Les bûcherons et les schlitteurs des Vosges

Schulin, Johann Philipp
Vollständiges diarium der römisch-königlichen wahl und kayserlichen krönung ... Leopold des zweiten. Frankfurt am Main, Jager 1791
22 l. 350,76,28,60p. 22pl.(2 col.) F.
Contains portraits of the emperor, electors and their retinue, pictures of the Archbishop of Cologne in the robes of the Grand Master of the Teutonic order and as an Elector, and of the procession
Lipperheide 2520

Schultz, Alwin
Deutsches leben im XIV. und XV. jahrhundert; grosse ausg. Wien, F. Tempsky 1892
xiii,660p. 678 illus. pl.(33 col.) Q.
Lipperheide 361. LC 1-22929

Das häusliche leben der europäischen kulturvölker vom mittelalter bis zur zweiten hälfte des XVIII. jahrhunderts. München und Berlin, R. Oldenbourg 1903
viii,432p. illus. O. (Handbuch der mittelalterlichen und neueren geschichte, hrsg. von G. v. Below und F. Meinecke, abt. IV)
Bibliographical foot-notes
Lipperheide 345e. LC 5-42558

Das höfische leben zur zeit der minnesinger; 2. verm. und verb. aufl. Leipzig, S. Hirzel 1889
2v. fronts. illus. pl. O.
First edition: 1879-80
Lipperheide 396-397. LC 1-22834

Schultze, Walter
Ost-indische reyse ... beschreibung der fürnehmsten ost-indischen landschaften ... ihre gesetze, sitten, religion, kleidung ... Aus dem niederländischen ins hochteutsche übergesetzet durch J. D. Amsterdam, J. von Meurs & J. von Sommern 1676
196p. 40 illus. 21pl. Q.
Some of the plates show landscapes and harbor scenes with figures
Lipperheide 1471

Schultze-Naumburg, Paul
Die kultur des weiblichen körpers als grundlage der frauenkleidung. Jena, E. Diederichs 1922
xii,143p. illus. O.
Lipperheide 3313. LC 25-85

Schulz, Albert
Zur waffenkunde des älteren deutschen mittelalters; mit dreizehn abbildungen aus handschriften zur Parcivaldichtung; hrsg. von San-Marte (A. Schulz) Quedlinburg und Leipzig, G. Basse 1867
xiv,354p. 13pl. O. (Bibliothek der gesammten deutschen national-literatur, 2.abth. 4.bd.)
Lipperheide 2420. LC 1-G-659

Schulz, C.
(lithgr.) Clodt von Jürgensburg, M. P., baron Costumes russes

Schulz, J. See Elzholz, L., jt. auth.

Schulze, H.
Chronik sämmtlicher bekannten ritterorden und ehrenzeichen, welche von souverainen, und regierungen verliehen werden ... Chronique de tous les ordres de chevalerie et marques d'honneur. Berlin, W. Moeser 1855-78
3v. 96 col.pl. and atlas of 45 col.pl. F.
Lipperheide 1932

Schulze, Heinrich, and Maiss, Karl
Muster-sammlung alter leinen-stickerei. Leipzig, T. O. Weigel [1887-88]
100pl. Q.
Lipperheide 3869

Schumacher, Karl von
Sudamerika, Westindien, Zentralamerika; landschaft, volksleben, baukunst ... Photos: Fr. Ahlfeld, Hugo Brehme. Berlin, Atlantis-Verlag; New York, Westermann 1931
xlviiip. 256pl. map. F. (Orbis terrarum) $4.50
Many of the pictures show Indians of various regions. The legends on the plates are in English, Spanish, German, French and Portuguese
Costume index

Schuman, Julius
Schuman's improved art of designing; complete self instruction in all branches of tailoring. [Tacoma, Pioneer printing co.] 1919
3 l. 14 diagr. F. $15
LC 20-1492

Schundenius, Karl Heinrich
Erinnerungen an die festlichen tage der dritten stiftungsfeyer der Akademie zu Wittenberg. Wittenberg, Der verfasser 1803
13,94p. 32pl.(7 col.) O.
Thirteen plates show costume, including a dean and university rector in academic dress
Lipperheide 2026

Schurtz, Cornelius Nicolaus
(engr.) Francisci, Erasmus. Neu-polirter geschicht- kunst- und sitten-spiegel ausländischer völcker
(engr.) Fugger, J. J. Spiegel der ehren des ... erzhauses Osterreich

Schurtz, Heinrich
Grundzüge einer philosophie der tracht. Stuttgart, J. G. Cotta 1891
146p. 10 illus. O.
"Mit besonderer berücksichtigung der negertrachten." Subtitle
Bibliographical footnotes
Colas 2696. Lipperheide 3299

De **schutter**- en jagerkorps en 1830. Houtman, J. P.

Schutz- und trutzrede für die crinoline oder den steif- und reifrock. Genthe, F. W.

Schvindt, Theodor

Finnische volkstrachten. Helsingfors, Weilin & Göös 1905
20p. 16 col.pl. O.

Suomalaisia koristeita. Finnische ornamente. Volumes 1-2, no.1-2. Helsinki, Suomal. Kirjall. Seura 1895-1903
2v. illus. col.pl. Q.
Lipperheide 3983

Schwabe, Randolph. See Kelly, F. M., jt. auth.

Die **Schwalm.** Retzlaff, Hans

Schwan, Christian Friedrich

Abbildungen der vorzüglichsten geistlichen-orden in ihren gewöhnlichsten ordens-kleidungen. Mannheim, C. F. Schwan und C. G. Götz 1791
361p. 127 col.pl. Q.
Colas 2699. Lipperheide 1871-72

Abbildungen derjenigen ritter-orden, welche eine eigene ordenskleidung haben. Mannheim, C. F. Schwan und C. G. Götz 1791
256p. 57 col.pl. Q.
A few of the plates are copies from the works of J. C. Bar
Colas 2700. Lipperheide 1914-15

Schwanenorden. See Order of the Swan

Schwanthaler, Ludwig

Künstler-gestalten aus der blüthezeit der kunst ... in kupfer gestochen von Felsing. Gera, C. B. Griesbach 1879
12pl. F.
Portrait statues by Dürer, Holbein, Rubens, Titian, Michel Angelo, Van Dyck, Da Vinci, Van Eyck, Poussin, Ghirlandajo, Memling, Masaccio
Lipperheide 509

Schwartz, Julia Augusta

Famous pictures of children. New York & Cincinnati, American book company [c1907]
144p. illus. D. (Eclectic readings)
LC 7-36957

Schwarz, Franz Joseph

(ed.) Biblia pauperum. Biblia pauperum; nach dem original in der lyceums bibliothek zu Constanz

(ed.) Kirchenschmuck, ein archiv für weibliche handarbeit

Schwarz, Ignaz

(ed.) Wiener strassenbilder im zeitalter des rokoko; die Wiener ansichten von Schutz, Ziegler, Janscha, 1779-1798. Wien, Gilhofer & Ranschburg 1914
xlvi,101,57p. illus. 57pl.(6 col.) F.

Schwarz, Matthaus und Veit Konrad. See Reichard, E. C. Matthaus und Veit Konrad Schwarz

Schwatka, Frederick

The children of the cold; new ed. New York, Chicago Educational publishing company [1899]
212p. illus. pl. S.
Shows the dress of Eskimo children
LC 99-1898

Die **Schweden** ihre trachten, beschäftigungen und volksthümliche gebräuche in bild und wort. See Vallander, J. V. Svenska folket

Die **schwedische** armee in ihrer gegenwärtigen uniformierung. Leipzig, M. Ruhl [1906]
16p. 12 col.pl. D.

Schwedische armee und marine in ihrer gegenwärtigen uniformirung. See Eklund, P. B. Svenska arméns och flottans nuvarande uniformer

Schweiger-Lerchenfeld, Amand, freiherr von

Die frauen des Orients in der geschichte, in der dichtung und im leben. Wien und Leipzig, A. Hartleben 1904
792p. illus. pl(part col.) facsims. Q.
Shows dress and jewelry of women of Asia, in ancient and modern times
LC 22-3406

Das frauenleben der erde, mit ... zeichnungen von A. Wanjura. Wien, A. Hartleben 1881
640p. illus. 20pl. O.
Many of the illustrations show costume

Schweinfurth, Georg August

The heart of Africa, three years' travels and adventures in the unexplored regions of Central Africa, from 1868 to 1871; tr. by Ellen E. Frewer. London, S. Low, Marston, Low, and Searle; New York, Harper 1874
2v. fronts. illus. pl. maps(part fold.) O.
Translation of his *Im herzen von Afrika*
LC 4-16732

Im herzen von Afrika; reisen und entdeckungen im zentralen äquatorial-Afrika während der jahre 1868-1871; 3., vom verfasser verb. aufl. Leipzig, F. A. Brockhaus 1918
xviii,578p. illus. ports. fold.map. Q.
First edition: 1874
LC 23-204

Schweitzerisches trachten-cabinet. Pfeffel, J. A.

Die **Schweiz,** oder Sitten, gebräuche, trachten und denkmäler der Schweitzer. See Neuestes gemälde der erde und ihrer bewohner ... Die Schweiz

Die **schweizer** armee. Sommerfeld, F.

Schweizer militär. Huber, Emil

Schweizer militär vom jahr 1700 bis auf die neuzeit. Pochon, A., and Zesiger, A.

Schweizer militair album. Beck, August

Die **Schweizer** milizen im 18 und 19 jahrhundert. Escher, A. von

Die **Schweizer** nach ihrer volksthümlichkeit. Opiz, G. E.

Die **Schweizer** regimenter in fremden diensten 1515-1860. Escher, A. von

Schweizer, Johann

(engr.) Funeral ceremonies for George II. Landgrave of Hesse, June 1661

Die **schweizerische** armee. See Estoppey, D. L'armée suisse

Die **schweizerische** armee in bildern. Kindler, Alfred

Die **Schweizerische** cavallerie im XVII, XVIII und XIX jahrhundert. Escher, A. von

Schweizer-trachten. Maenedorf, Verlag von Schweizer-trachten & ansichten, legenden & genre-bildern. [18—]
14pl. Ti.
Mounted photographs

Schweizer-trachten, vom XVII-XIX jahrhundert. Heierli, Frau J. W.

Die **schwerter** und schwertknäufe der Sammlung Carl von Schwerzenbach—Bregenz. Schwerzenbach, Carl von

Schwerter-sammlung. Dreger, Max

Schwerzenbach, Carl von

Die schwerter und schwertknäufe der Sammlung Carl von Schwerzenbach—Bregenz. Mit einer geschichte von schwert und dolch; hrsg. von dr R. Forrer. Leipzig, K. W. Hiersemann 1905

62p. illus. LX pl. F.
LC 10-30233

Schwietering, Julius

Zur geschichte von speer und schwert im 12. jahrhundert. Hamburg, L. Gräfe & Sillem 1912

60p. illus. Q. (Museum für hamburgische geschichte. Mitteilungen, nr.3)

Schwind, Moritz von

Die wandgemaelde des landgrafensaales auf der Wartburg ... in holzschnitt ausgeführt von August Gaber; text von B. von Arnswalt. Stuttgart, F. Bruckmann [1863]

8 l. 8pl. F.
Lipperheide 391

La **science** des armes dans la cavalerie. Brunet, Romuald, and Chaperon, Eugène

La **science** des personnes de la cour, de l'épeé et de la robe. Chevigny, de

Science of dress. See Ballin, A. S. Health and beauty in dress

Science of dress in theory and practice. Ballin, A. S.

Science of pattern construction for garment makers. Poole, B. W.

Sciences & lettres au moyen âge. Lacroix, Paul

La **scienza** della scherma. Florio, Blasco

Scotland

Drummond, James. Ancient Scottish weapons. 1881

Paton, James, ed. Scottish history & life. 1902

See also England; Celts; Scotland, Highlands of; also subdivision Scotland under Arms and armor; Coronations and coronation robes; Funerals; Regalia

18th century

Kay, John. A series of original portraits and caricature etchings. 1837-38

Paterson, James. Kay's Edinburgh portraits. 1885

19th century

Geikie, Walter. Etchings illustrative of Scottish character and scenery. 1885

Kay, John. A series of original portraits and caricature etchings. 1837-38

Shoberl, Frederic, ed. England, Scotland and Ireland 1827

Edinburgh

Grierson, E. W. The children's book of Edinburgh. 1906

Old Edinburgh beaux and belles. 1886

Old Edinburgh pedlars, beggars and criminals. 1886

See also Street venders—Scotland—Edinburgh

Glasgow

Boyd, A. S. Glasgow men and women. 1905

Scotland forever; a gift-book of the Scottish regiments, with a preface by the Earl of Rosebery. London, New York, Hodder and Stoughton 1915?

xii,180p. mounted front. mounted col.pl. Q.
LC A16-836

Scotland, Highlands of

Adam, Frank. The clans, septs & regiments of the Scottish Highlands; 3d ed 1934

Adam, Frank. What is my tartan? or, The clans of Scotland, with their septs and dependents. 1896

Authenticated tartans of the clans and families of Scotland. 1850

Browne, J. History of the Highlands and of the Highland clans. 1849-50

Campbell, Lord Archibald. The children of the mist; or, The Scottish clansmen in peace and war. 1890

Campbell, Lord Archibald. Highland dress, arms and ornament. 1899

Comunn an Fheilidh. Comunn an Fheilidh (The Kilt society). 1932

Douglas, L. M. The kilt; a manual of Scottish national dress. 1914

Eyre-Todd, George. The Highland clans of Scotland: their history and traditions. 1923

Grant, James. The tartans of the clans of Scotland; also an introductory account of Celtic Scotland; clanship, chiefs, their dress, arms, etc. 1886

Logan, James. The clans of the Scottish Highlands, illustrated by appropriate figures. 1845-47

Logan, James. Gaelic gatherings; or, The Highlanders at home, on the heath, the river, and the loch. 1848

Logan, James. McIan's costumes of the clans of Scotland. 1899

Logan, James. The Scottish Gaël; or, Celtic manners, as preserved among the Highlanders. 1876?

Mackay, J. G. The romantic story of the Highland garb and the tartan. 1924

Macleay, Kenneth. Highlanders of Scotland; portraits illustrative of the principal clans and followings, and the retainers of the Royal Household at Balmoral, in the reign of ... Queen Victoria. 1870

North, C. N. M. ... The book of the Club of true Highlanders. 1892

The Scottish clans & their tartans. 1931

The Scottish tartans, with historical sketches of the clans and families of Scotland, the badges, arms, slogans, etc. of the clans. 1928

Scotland, Highlands of—*Continued*
Shepherd, James, pub. Shepherd's select Scottish costumes. 18—
Skeat, W. W. The past at our doors. 1911
Smibert, Thomas. The clans of the Highlands of Scotland. 1850
Stewart, D. W. Old and rare Scottish tartans. 1893
Stuart, J. S. S., and Stuart, C. E. The costume of the clans with observations upon ... the Highlands and Western Isles during the middle ages. 1845
Vestiarium scoticum. Vestiarium scoticum: from the manuscript formerly in the library of the Scots college at Douay. 1842

See also Military costume—Scotland, Highlands of

The **Scots** men-at-arms and life-guards in France. Forbes-Leith, William

Scott
(illus.) Darfeu. Hygiène de la parisienne

Scott, Sir James George
The Burman, his life and notions, by Shway Yoe [pseud.] London, Macmillan 1910
xii,609p. O.
First edition, 1882; second edition, 1896; third edition, 1910
Contains material on tattooing
LC 10-12440

Scott, Sir James Sibbald David, bart.
The British army: its origin, progress, and equipment. London & New York, Cassel, Petter & Galpin 1868
2v. 103pl. O.
Shows military dress and armor of England in various epochs
Colas 2702. Lipperheide 2273

Scott, Sir Walter, bart.
Description of the regalia of Scotland. Edinburgh, Printed by R. Anderson 1854
34p. D.
Published also under title: *The regalia of Scotland*
LC 10-11086

The **Scottish** clans & their tartans; 22d ed. History of each clan and full list of septs. Edinburgh and London, W. & A. K. Johnston 1931
55p. illus.(map) 96 col.pl. Ti.
Descriptive letterpress on versos facing the plates
LC 33-22278

Scottish coronations. Bute, J. P. C. S., 3d marquis of

The **Scottish** Gaël. Logan, James

Scottish history & life. Paton, James, ed.

The **Scottish** regalia. Twining, E. F.

The **Scottish** tartans, with historical sketches of the clans and families of Scotland, the badges, arms, slogans, etc. of the clans. Edinburgh, Scotland, W. & A. K. Johnston [1928]
120p. col.illus.(incl.coats of arms) ob.Ti.
LC 31-4297

Sculfort, Valéry Charles Lucien Édouard
Décorations, médailles, monnaies et cachets du Musée de l'armée. Paris, J. Leroy 1912
348p. illus. v col.pl. D.
LC 24-6508

Sculptured tombs of Hellas. Gardner, Percy

The **sea.** Bowen, F. C.

Sea Dayak fabrics. See Haddon, A. C., and Start, L. E. Iban or sea Dayak fabrics

Sea-kings of Crete. Baikie, James

Sears, Minnie Earl
Costume index. See entry under Monro, I. S., and Cook, D. E., eds.

Seas and lands. Arnold, Sir Edwin

The **season;** lady's illustrated magazine. See note under Die Modenwelt

Seat of war in the East. Simpson, William

Sebbers
Uniformes de la cavalerie prussienne. Berlin et Breslau, J. Kühr ca1850
8 col.pl. F.
Colas 2705

Sébillot, Paul
Légendes et curiosités des métiers. Paris, E. Flammarion ca1875
v.p. 214 illus. Q.
Lipperheide 1980m

Sebizius, Melchior
xv bücher von dem feldbaw und recht volkommener wolbestellung eines bekömmlichen landsitzes. Strassburg, B. Jobins erben 1598
763p. 53 illus. F.
Earlier editions were published 1580, 1588, and 1592. Illustrations by Tobias Stimmer show hunting scenes
Lipperheide 1984

Séchan, Louis
La danse grecque antique. Paris, E. de Boccard 1930
369p. illus. xix pl. sq.O.
Bibliography at end of each chapter
LC 31-12912

Le **second** empire. Dayot, A. P. M.

Second voyage dans l'intérieur de l'Afrique. Le Vaillant, François

Seconde suite d'estampes. Moreau, J. M.

Secret societies. See Freemasons; Maccabees, Knights of; Odd-fellows, Independent order of; Pythias, Knights of

Les **secrets** de la draperie antique de l'himation grec au pallium romain. Repond, Jules

Les **secrets** du cabinet de toilette, conseils et recettes. Alq, Louise d'

The **secrets** of distinctive dress. Picken, Mrs M. B.

Secrets of the tango. Chester, S. B.

Sects. See Friends, Society of; Mordvinians

Sée, Raymonde
Le costume de la revolution à nos jours. Paris, Éditions de la Gazette des beaux-arts 1929
168p. col.front. 87pl.(part col.) Q. 375fr.
Colas 2707. Costume index

Seele, Johann Baptist
Koenigliche württembergische garde du corps, infanterie, chevau-leger. Stuttgart, Ebner [1809-13]
10 col.pl. ob.F.
Colas 2708

Seelos, Ignaz
(illus.) Zingerle, I. V., edler von Summersberg. Fresken-cyklus des schlosses Runkelstein bei Bozen

Seesselberg, Wilhelm Friedrich
(ed.) Helm und mitra; studien und entwürfe in mittelalterlicher kunst. Berlin, E. Wasmuth 1905?
6,13p. 65pl.(3 col.) F.

Segar, Sir William
Honor military, and civill. London, R. Barker 1602
256p. illus. 8pl. Q.
"Contained in foure bookes. Viz. 1. Justice, and jurisdiction military. 2. Knighthood in generall, and particular. 3. Combats for life, and triumph. 4. Precedencie of great estates, and others." Subtitle
Plates, engraved by W. Rogers, show one complete costume of each of the following knightly orders: Golden Fleece, Saint Michael, Annunciation, Saint Esprit, Templars, Knights of the Band
LC 24-6058

Original institutions of the princely orders of collars. Edinburgh, Printed for W. H. Lizars 1823
viii,15p. 7 col.pl. Q.
Half-title: *Orders of collars*
LC 18-3338

Segovia. See Spain—Segovia

Ein **sehr** artig büchlein von dem weydwerck und der falcknerey. Pomay, Fr.

Siedel, L. W., and sohn
(pub.) Barteau, L. R. Die K. K. Oesterreichisch-ungarische armee
(pub.) Die K. u. K. oesterreichisch-ungarische armee

Seidel, Martin Friedrich
Icones et elogia virorum. See note under Küster, G. G. Martin Friedrich Seidels Bilder-sammlung

Seidel, Paul
Die insignien und juwelen der preussischen krone; mit einer einleitung von Reinhold Koser. Leipzig, Giesecke & Devrient [1913]
56p. illus. 24pl. F.
"Zum regierungs-jubiläum seiner majestät, des kaisers und königs, 1888-15. juni-1913"

Seidemann, Xaver. See Jordanszky, Alexius, jt. auth.

Seifer, Cäcile. See Leonhardt-Lysèr, Caroline, jt. auth.

Seitz, Rudolf
Parsifal; costum studien zu Richard Wagner's oper. München, A. Ackermann 1882
1 l. 5 col.pl. F.

Le **Sélam.** Leloir, Mme Héloïse

Selb, August, and Tischbein, A.
Memoire di un viaggio pittorico nel littorale Austriaco. Trieste, B. Linassi 1842
1 l. 20pl. F.
Plates show folk costume
Lipperheide 835

Select historical costumes. Hinton, H. L.

Selections from essays on health culture and the sanitary woolen system. Jaeger, Gustav

Selections of the ancient costume of Great Britain and Ireland from the seventh to the sixteenth century. Smith, C. H.

Selections of the costume of Albania and Greece. Cartwright, J.

Selenka, Emil
Der schmuck des menschen. Berlin, Vita 1900
72p. 90 illus. O.
Lipperheide 1756

Seligman, Georges Saville, and Hughes, Talbot
La broderie somptuaire; à travers les moeurs et les costumes. Paris, Firmin-Didot; London, Country life 1927
99p. col.front. 100pl.(part col.) F.

Domestic needlework, its origins and customs throughout the centuries, London, Country life [1926]
95p. col.front. illus. 131pl.(part col.) sq.F. 26s, o.p.
Costume index. LC 28-17943

La **selle** et le costume de l'amazone. Pellier, Jules

Sellers, Eugénie. See Strong, Mrs Eugénie (Sellers)

Sellier, P.
(illus.) Cocheris, Mme P. A. W. Les parures primitives

Sellmer, Carl
König Wilhelm und sein heer; erinnerungs-blätter an das fünfundzwanzigjährige jubiläum der ruhmreichen preuszischen armee-reorganisation im jahre 1860. Cassel und Berlin, T. Fischer 1885
2 l. 20pl. F.
Lipperheide 2188

Sellner, Eudora
American costumes; 150 years of style in America, 1775-1925, forty eight costumes with color notation. Worcester, Mass., School arts magazine c1925
Cover-title, 12pl. Q. $1
In portfolio
Costume index. LC 25-17266

History of costume design; 11th ed. Worcester, Mass., School arts magazine c1928
Cover-title, 24pl. Q. $1
Colas 2709. Costume index. LC 28-22682

Selous, Henry Courteney
(illus.) Shakespeare, William. Outlines to Shakspeare's Tempest

See also Burford, Robert. Description of a view of the city of Moscow, with the gorgeous entry of His Imperial Majesty the Emperor Alexander II. into the Kremlin

Seltene waffen aus Afrika, Asien und Amerika. Meyer, A. B., and Uhle, Max

Seltman, Charles Theodore. See Cambridge ancient history

Semayer, Vilibáld
(ed.) Budapest. Magyar nemzeti múzeum. Néprajzi osztályának értesítöje
(tr.) Huszka, József. Magyarische ornamentik

Sempere y Guarinos, Juan
Historia del lujo y de las leyes suntuarias de España. Madrid, Imprenta real 1788
2v. O.

Semple, Miss
The costume of the Netherlands displayed in thirty coloured engravings after drawings from nature. London, Ackermann's repository of arts 1817
30p. 30 col.pl. F.
Seven of these plates reproduced in Shoberl's *The Netherlands*
Colas 2710. Lipperheide 958. LC 10-4408

Senegal
Boilat, P. D., abbé. Esquisses sénégalaises. 1853
Jacottet, Henri, and Leclerc, Max. Colonies françaises. 1888

Senn, J.
Norske nationale klaededragter. Kjobenhavn, 1812
80 col.pl. Q.
Colas 2711. Lipperheide 1045m
(illus.) Jubinal, Achille. La Armeria real, ou collection des principales pièces du Musée d'artillerie de Madrid

Sepet, Marius Cyrille Alphonse. See Miélot, Jean. Vie de Ste Catherine d'Alexandrie

Les **sept** anciennes modes de Metz. Le Clerc, Sébastien

Sera, Domenico da
Le livre de lingerie ... nouvellement augmenté & enrichi de plusieurs excelents & divers patrons ... de M. Jean Cousin. Paris, Marnef 1584. [Paris, A. Durand 1883-87]
2v. 51pl. F.
Cover title: *Livres à dentelles,* 4-5
Opera nova ... dove si insegna a tutte le nobili & leggiadre giovanette di lavorare di ogni sorte di puti, cusire, recamare ... stampato in Vinegia per Matio Pagan ... e G. da Fontaneto di Monferrato, 1546. Venezia, F. Ongania 1879
45pl. Q. (Raccolta di opere antiche sui disegni dei merletti di Venezia, 8)
Facsimile reprint
Lipperheide 3885

Die **Serben** an der Adria. Louis Salvator, archduke of Austria

Serbia. See Yugoslavia—Serbia; also Military costume—Serbia

Séré, Ferdinand
(ed.) Louandre, C. L. Les arts somptuaires

See also Lacroix, Paul, jt. auth.

Serena opera nova di recami. Franceschi, Domenico de

Serenissimi principis Ferdinandi Hispaniarum. Becanus, Guilielmo

Serenissimorum Austriae ducum. See Kilian, Wolfgang. Dess aller durchleutigsten haus ostereich herzogen

Serenissimorum Saxoniae electorum, et quorundam ducum Agnatorum genuinae effigies. Kilian, Wolfgang

Seressaner und Croaten. Heicke, Josef

Serge Gladky, synthèse du costume théâtral. Salmon, André

Serge Lifar. Levinson, A. I.

[**Sergent-Marceau, Antoine François**]
Costumi dei popoli antichi e moderni ... con discorsi analoghi sulla forma degli abiti e la maniera di vestirli. Brescia, N. Bettoni 1813-17
10, 320p. 44 col.pl. Q.
Colas 2713

Serie di 12 ritratti di persone facete che servono a divertire il pubblico Fiorentino. Lasinio, Carlo

Series imaginum Augustae domus Boicae ad genuina ectypa aliaque monum. fide digna delin. Zimmermann, J. A.

Series of groups illustrating the physiognomy, manners, and character of the people of France and Germany. Lewis, George

Series of monumental brasses, from the thirteenth to the sixteenth century. Waller, J. G., and Waller, L. A. B.

Series of original portraits and caricature etchings. Kay, John

Series of portraits of the emperors of Turkey. Young, John

Series of tables and diagrams illustrating economy in cutting. Falconer, John

Series of the costumes of the members of the University of Oxford. Shrimpton, A. T., pub.

Series of twenty-nine designs of modern costume. See Moses, Henry. Designs of modern costume

Seroux d'Agincourt, Jean Baptiste Louis Georges
Histoire de l'art par les monumens, depuis sa décadence au IVe siècle jusqu'à son renouvellement au XIVe. Paris, Treuttel et Würtz 1823
6v. in 3. illus. 325pl. F.
Issued in 24 parts, 1810-23. Edited by L. Dufourny, T. B. Eméric-David, and L. F. Feuillet
Translated into English, German, Italian. Illustrations from architecture, painting and sculpture are valuable for the history of costume
Lipperheide 347. LC 10-101
History of art by its monuments, from its decline in the fourth century to its restoration in the sixteenth. London, B. Quaritch 1847
3v. in 1. 328pl.(incl.plans) sq.F.
Translation of his *Histoire de l'art par les monumens.* Also published (London, Longman, Brown, Green and Longmans 1847)
LC 21-1003, 10-100

Serrano, Eduardo
(illus.) Castro, Fernández de. Cuadernos militares

Serres, Marcel de
L'Autriche, ou Moeurs, usages et costumes des habitans de cet empire; suivi d'un voyages en Bavière et au Tyrol; ouvrage orné de quarante-huit gravures représentant plus de cent vingt personnages differens. Paris, A. Nepveu 1821
6v. 48 col.pl.(incl.fronts.) T.
New ed. of the author's *Voyage en Autriche* (Paris, A Bertrand 1814. 4v.) which did not include the plates
Contents: v 1-2 Précis historique de la maison d'Autriche ... jusqu'en 1792; v3-5

Serres, Marcel de—*Continued*
Description de l'Autriche; v6 Fragmens d'un voyage dans la Bavière et le Tyrol, en 1811
Some of the plates are also used in J. B. B. Eyriès's *L'Autriche*
Colas 2714. Lipperheide 833. LC 3-31656

Serrurier, Lindor
Tentoonstelling van kleederdrachten in Nederlandsch Indië. See entry under Leyden. Rijks ethnographisch museum

Serstevens, Albert T'. See T'Serstevens, Albert

Servants
Correct social usage. 1906

See also Livery

England

Pyne, W. H. The history of the royal residences of Windsor castle, St. James's palace, Carlton house, Kensington palace, Hampton Court, Buckingham house, and Frogmore. 1819

Russia

Recueil d'idées nouvelles pour habiller suivant les règles du meilleur goût ses domestiques, jockeys, courriers, postilons, cochers, chasseurs, houssars, etc. ca1790

Service regulations of the Czechoslovak army. See Czechoslovakia. Minister of national defense. Change of the uniform regulations of the Czechoslovak armed forces

Sestini, Domenico
Notizie, storiche, politiche, geografiche e statistiche sulla Vallachia e sulla Moldavia. Milano, Batelli e Fanfani 1821
71p. 2 col.pl. 1 map. O.
Lipperheide 1445

Sett of one hundred original etchings. See Duplessi-Bertaux, Jean. Recueil de cent sujets de divers genres

Settings & costumes of the modern stage. Kommissarzhevskiĭ, F. F. and Simonson, Lee

Seven centuries of lace. Pollen, Mrs M. M. La P.

Seven planets. Lippmann, Friedrich

Seventeen years among the Sea Dyaks of Borneo. Gomes, E. H.

Seventeenth century
Aubry, Petrus. Effigies omnium legatorum, deputatorum, consiliariorum, qui pacem universalem monasterij anno salutis 1648. ca1655
Baur, J. W. Costumes of various peoples. 1640
Baur, J. W. Livre nouveau de diverses nations. ca1630
Breüning, H. J. Orientalische Reyss ... in der Türckey. [1612]
Bruyn, Abraham de. Omnium pene Europae, Asiae, Aphricae atque Americae gentium habitus. ca1610
Bulwer, John. A view of the people of the whole world. 1658
Carracci, Annibale. Divers ouvrages de belles figures. 1690?
Hirth, Georg, ed. Kulturgeschichtliches bilderbuch aus drei jahrhunderten. 1881-90
Hulle, Anselm van. Les hommes illustres qui ont vecu dans le XVII. siecle: les principaux potentats, princes, ambassadeurs & plenipotentiaires qui ont assisté aux conferences de Munster et d'Osnabrug, avec leurs armes et devises; dessinez et peints au naturel. 1717
Hulle, Anselm van. Pacis antesignani, sive Icones legatorum plena potestate intructorum, qui ... ad pacem universalem constituendam monasterium Westphalorum et Osnabrugam convenerunt, magno studio ad vivum expressae. 1648-50
Imagines XLI virorum celebriorum in politicis, historicis, &c. ca1720-30
Imperialis, J. B. Musaeum historicum et physicum. 1640
Lochom, Michiel van. La mode des habits et vestementz des femmes de diverses nations. ca1640
Meisner, Daniel. Politica-politica, dass ist Newes emblematisches büchleĩ, darinen in acht centurijs die vornembstẽ stätt vestung, schlösser &c. der gäntzen welt ... abgebiltet werden. 1700
Mundy, Peter. The travels of Peter Mundy, in Europe and Asia, 1608-1667. 1907-24
Passe, Crispijn van de. Le miroir des plus belles courtisannes de ce temps; Spieghel der alderschoonste cortisanen deses tyts; Spieghel der allerschönsten courtisannen dieser zeyt. 1631
Polanzani, Felix. Collection des différents portraits d'hommes illustres dans les sciences, et dans les arts tires des ouvrages du Chr. Antoine Wandych et de Joseph Nogari. 1786
Quast, P. J. Costumes d'hommes et de femmes. ca1630

See also Europe—17th century

Severall habits of English women. See Hollar, Wenceslaus. Ornatus muliebris Anglicanus

Severall wayes of hunting, hawking, and fishing, according to the English manner. Barlow, F.

Severance, John Long. See Cleveland museum of art. A catalogue of the collection of arms and armor presented to the Cleveland museum of art by Mr. and Mrs. John Long Severance

Severs, Jan. See Die cronycke van Hollant, Zeelant ende Vrieslant (supposed author)

Sewing. See Needlework

Sewrin, Edmond
Costumes de femmes à Bordeaux. Bordeaux, Legé [1837]
10pl. Q.
Colas 2715

Sex and civilization. Bousfield, Paul

Sex and society. Thomas, W. I.

Seyboth, Adolf

Costumes des femmes de Strasbourg ,(XVIIe et XVIIIe siècles) Strasbourg, R. Schultz 1880
4p. 46pl. sq.D.
Colas 2716. Lipperheide 793. LC 3-3038

Costumes strasbourgeois (hommes) (XVIe, (XVIIe et XVIIIe siècles) Strasbourg, Schultz 1881
12p. 54pl. sq.D.
Colas 2717. Lipperheide 794. LC 3-3037

Seyboth, Adolf, and Binder, C.

Album de l'Exposition militaire de la Société des amis des arts de Strasbourg (fondée en 1832). Strasbourg, G. Fischbach 1904
25p. XXXII pl. F.
Plates show armor and uniforms from the middle of the 14th until the 19th century
Colas 2718

Seyfart, Johann Friedrich, sohn

Kurzgefassete geschichte aller königlichen preussischen regimenter, zur erklärung der illuminirten abbildungen derselben. Bey dieser 4.aufl. bis aus ende des jahres 1769 fortgesezt und mit der jetzigen generalität vermehret. Nürnberg, Raspe 1770
162p. O.
Text to explain the illustrations in Schmalen's *Accurate vorstellung* (1759)
A new abridged edition was published by the same publishers (1783. 108p.)
Appeared first with French title: *Mémoires pour servir à l'histoire de l'armée prussienne* (Amsterdam, 1759) and with German title the same year. New editions were published in Nuremberg in 1760 and 1762
Lipperheide 2147-48

Seyffert, O. See Schmidt, jt. auth.

Seymour, Thomas Day

Life in the Homeric age. New York, London, Macmillan 1907
xvi,704p. front. illus. pl. fold.map. O.
Dress and decoration: p153-77; Homeric arms: p629-82
LC 7-36949

Sézan, Claude

Les poupées anciennes. Paris, Les Éditions pittoresques 1930
196p. col.front. XL pl. on 20 l. O. (Collection des collectionneurs. [1. sér.])
LC 30-18642

Sgroppo

(illus.) Costumes des différens états de l'Italie. v2

Shakespeare, William

Outlines to Shakspeare's Tempest: a series of twelve plates; [by H. C. Selous] with the text in English, German, French and Italian. London, A. Schloss [1836]
12 l. XII pl. F.
Slip inserted gives name of the artist. Title in English and German on first preliminary leaf, in French and Italian on second preliminary leaf; each plate faced by leaf of text from play, in four horizontal columns
LC 20-14440

The Swan Shakespeare, a player's edition, introduction and notes on production by C. B. Purdom ... drawings of costumes and scenes by Jean Campbell. London and Toronto, J. M. Dent; New York, E. P. Dutton [1930]
3v. front. pl.(part double) O.
Text is that of the Cambridge edition
Contents: [v 1] Comedies; [v2] Tragedies; [v3] Histories, Sonnets, Poems, Glossary
LC 31-6742

Characters

See England—Tudor period, 1485-1603; Theatrical costume—Special plays, ballets, etc.—Shakespeare, William

Shakespeare in pictorial art. Salaman, M. C.

Shakespeare scenes and characters. Dowden, Edward

Shakespeare-galerie. Pecht, Friedrich

Shakespeare's comedy of the Merry wives of Windsor. Crane, Walter

Shakespeare's England; an account of the life & manners of his age. New York, Oxford univ. press; Oxford, Clarendon press 1916
2v. fronts. illus. pl. ports. maps, facsims. O. $14, 42s
In 1905 Sir Walter Raleigh sketched the plan of the book and in 1909 Sir Sidney Lee undertook its production by arranging for the writing of most of the treatises and by making a first selection of illustrations. The Clarendon press employed C. T. Onions for the completion of the work
Chapter XIX is on costume. Many plates thruout show costume of Elizabethan England
Bibliography at end of each chapter
Costume index. LC 17-26075

Shakespeare's heroes on the stage. Wingate, C. E. L.

Shakespeare's heroines on the stage. Wingate, C. E. L.

Shakespeares mädchen und frauen. Heine, Heinrich

Shakespeare's maidens and women. Heine, Heinrich

Shakespearian costumes. Bööcke, R. L.

Shakhovskaîa, Princess S. N.

Uzory starīnnago shīt'îa v" Rossiī ... s" predisloviem" F. Buslaeva. Dessins d'anciennes broderies en Russie. Moskva, 1885
6,6p. 9 col.pl. sq.F.
Lipperheide 3971

Shakspeare gallery. Heath, Charles

Shakspeare-album. See Kaulbach, Wilhelm von. Shakspere gallerie

Shakspeare-album containing all the characters in costume, as represented at the Shakspeare-festival celebrated April 23d 1864 by the Malkasten society of artists at Düsseldorf. See Shakspeare-album; sämmtliche costümfiguren

Shakspeare-album; sämmtliche costümfiguren aus dem Shakspeare-fest, veranstaltet am 23. april 1864 von der künstler-gesellschaft Malkasten in

Shakspeare-album—*Continued*
Düsseldorf ... Shakspeare-album containing all the characters in costume, as represented at the Shakspeare-festival celebrated April 23d 1864 by the Malkasten society of artists at Düsseldorf. Düsseldorf, Overbeck [1864]
64 illus. O.

Shakspere gallerie. Kaulbach, Wilhelm von

Shakspere gallery of engravings. See Tallis's Shakspere gallery of engravings

Shans
Colquhoun, A. R. Amongst the Shans. 1885
Milne, Mrs Leslie. Shans at home. 1910

Shans at home. Milne, Mrs Leslie

Sharf, George. See Scharf, George

Sharles, H. See Belin, A., and others. Costumes de Suède, Norvège, Danemark, Hollande et Allemagne

Sharp, A. Mary
Point and pillow lace; a short account of various kinds, ancient and modern, and how to recognize them. London, J. Murray 1899
xv,202p. front. pl. ports. O.
Bibliography: p xiii

Sharp, Robert Farquharson
(tr.) Ibsen, Henrik. Peer Gynt

Shattuck, George Cheever
The peninsula of Yucatan; medical, biological, meteorological and sociological studies, by G. C. Shattuck ... in collaboration with ... J. C. Bequaert ... F. G. Benedict [and others]. Washington, Carnegie institution 1933
xvii,576p. front. illus. pl.(incl.ports.) 2 fold.maps, diagrs. F. (Carnegie institution of Washington. Publication no431)
Contains description and illustrations of the costume and textile patterns of the present day Maya
Eight of the costume illustrations are reprinted with title: Costumes of present-day Maya in the *News service bulletin* v4 no8, Nov. 29, 1936 of the Carnegie institution of Washington
Contains references
LC 33-18284

Shaving
Malet, Georges. L'art de se raser. 1927
Perret, J. J. La pogonotomie, ou L'art d'apprendre à se raser soi même. 1770

Shaw, Henry
Dresses and decorations of the middle ages. London, W. Pickering 1843
2v. illus.(part col.) 93 col.pl. O. 147s, o.p.
Reprinted by Bohn, 1858
Shows French and English costume and jewelry from the 7th to the 17th century, from miniatures, tombs, stained glass windows, tapestries, etc.
Colas 2720. Costume index. Lipp. 325

Shaw, Z. W.
(ed.) Byrne, J. J. Practical tailoring

Shawls
Blair, Mathew. The Paisley shawl and the men who produced it. 1904
Perleberg, H. C., comp. Persian textiles. 1919-31

Shchedrovskĭ, Ī. S.
(illus.) Savinov, V. N. Stseny īz" russkago narodnago byta, rīsovany s" natury

Sheil, Mary Leonora (Woulfe) lady
Glimpses of life and manners in Persia; with notes on Russia, Koords, Toorkomans, Nestorians, Khiva, and Persia. London, J. Murray 1856
xi,402p. front. 6pl.(incl.ports.) D.
Colas 2721. LC 5-10116

Shelter and clothing. Kinne, Helen, and Cooley, A. M.

Shenk, V. K.
Tablitzi form obmundirovania Russkoy armiī. St Petersburg, Magazinizdaniy Glavnago Shtaba 1910
4p. col.pl. diagr. ob.S.

Shepherd, James
(pub.) Shepherd's select Scottish costumes. Edinburgh, J. Shepherd [18—]
17 col.pl. T.
Cover title
Thirteen plates show costume of the clans of Scotland

Shepherd, Thomas Hosmer
(illus.) London interiors

Shepherd's select Scottish costumes. Shepherd, James, pub.

Shepherdesses. See Fancy dress—Shepherdesses

Sheringham, George
(ed.) Mason, Rupert. Robes of Thespis

Sheringham, George and others
Design in the theater; commentary by George Sheringham and James Laver, together with literary contributions by E. Gordon Craig, Charles B. Cochran and Nigel Playfair; ed. by Geoffrey Holme. [London] The Studio 1927
31p. pl.(part col.) Q.
Designs of stage costumes, English and continental, most of them from 20th century productions
LC 28-2278

Sherring, Charles Atmore
Western Tibet and the British borderland; the sacred country of Hindus and Buddhists, with an account of the government, religion and customs of its peoples. London, E. Arnold 1906
xv,376p. illus. ports. maps, diagrs. Q.
Shows costume of Tibet
LC 7-19489

Ship of fools, tr. by A. Barclay. Brant, Sebastian

Shoberl, Frederic
Africa, containing a description of the manners and customs, with some historical particulars of the Moors of the Zahara, and of the negro nations between the rivers Senegal and Gambia. London R. Ackermann [1821]
4v. 43 col.pl. D. o.p. (World in miniature)
A free translation of *L'Afrique* by R. C. Geoffroy de Villeneuve, with the same plates
The whole series "World in miniature" was first published in 43 volumes at 186s (LC 5-7094)
Colas 2723. Costume index. Lipp. 1580

The Asiatic Islands and New Holland. London, R. Ackermann [1824]
2v. 26 col.pl. D. o.p. (World in miniature)
Colas 2733. Costume index

Shoberl, Frederic—*Continued*

Austria; containing a description of the manners, customs, character and costumes. London, R. Ackermann 1823
x,108p. incl.col.front. 30 col.pl. D. o.p. (World in miniature)
Colas 2728. Costume index. LC 3-31659

China. London, R. Ackermann 1823
2v. 30 col.pl. D. o.p. (World in miniature)
Colas 2729. Costume index

England, Scotland and Ireland. ed. by W. H. Pyne. London, R. Ackermann [1827]
4v. 83 col.pl. D. o.p. (World in miniature)
Colas 2736. Costume index

Hindoostan. London, R. Ackermann [1822]
6v. 104 col.pl. D. o.p.
A free translation of J. A. Pannelier's *L'Hindoustan* with copies of the same plates
Colas 2725. Costume index

Illyria and Dalmatia. London, R. Ackermann 1821
2v. 32 col.pl. D.
Colas asserts that the plates are probably after Hacquet
Colas 2722. Costume index

Japan. London, R. Ackermann 1823
286p. 20 col.pl. D. o.p. (World in miniature)
Colas 2730. Costume index

The Netherlands; containing a description of the character, manners, habits, and costumes. London, R. Ackermann [1823]
238p. 18 col.pl. D. o.p. (World in miniature)
Plates are copied from Semple's *Costume* and from Maaskamp's *Afbeeldingen*
Colas 2731. Costume index. Lipp. 959

Persia. London, R. Ackermann 1822
3v. 30 col.pl. D. o.p. (World in miniature)
Colas 2726. Costume index

Russia. London, R. Ackermann 1822-23
4v. 72 col.pl. D. o.p. (World in miniature)
Colas 2727. Costume index

South Sea islands. London, R. Ackermann 1824
2v. 26 col.pl. D. o.p. (World in miniature)
Colas 2732. Costume index

Spain and Portugal. London, R. Ackermann [1825]
2v.(302,281p.) 27 col.pl. D. o.p. (World in miniature)
Colas 2735. Costume index. Lipp. 1217

Switzerland. London, R. Ackermann 1828
287p. 18pl. D. o.p. (World in miniature)
Colas 2737. Costume index

Tibet, and India beyond the Ganges. London, R. Ackermann [1824]
xii,352p. 12 col.pl. D. o.p. (World in miniature)
Colas 2734. Costume index. Lipp. 1485

Turkey. London, R. Ackermann 1821-1822
6v. 73 col.pl. D. o.p. (World in miniature)
Translation of A. L. Castellan's *Moeurs,* as published by Nepveu, with the same plates
Colas 2724. Costume index

See also Combe, William. History of the University of Oxford; and Combe, William, History of the University of Cambridge

The **shoe** in romance and history. Towle, H. C.

Shönberg, and Geissler, Christian Gottfried Heinrich

Description des planches relatives aux crieurs publics de St Pétersbourg et explication des figures. St Petersbourg, C. Lissner 1794
7 l. 18 col.pl. Q.
Legends are in Russian, German and French
Colas 2738

Shoes. See Footwear

Shoes and shoemaking illustrated. Morgan, W. C.

Shooting costume

Flexel, Lienhard. Lienhard Flexel's Lobspruch des fürstlichen freischiessens zu Innsbruck im oktober 1569. 1885

Austria

Beschreibung des Kaiserl. gnaden- und frey-schiessen, welche von Ihro ... Majestät Carolo Sexto der wienerischen burgerschaft durch vierzehen täg gegeben worden. [1739]

Germany

Deutsches bundesschiessen. 7.-10. 1881-90
Festzeiting für das 10. Deutsche turnfest zu Nürnberg, 1903. 1903
Hendel, J. C. Archiv für deutsche schützengesellschaften. 1802
Hornfeck, Fr. Das deutsche schützenfest in Frankfurt am Main. 1862
Nathansen, W. Zur geschichte der Hamburger Schützengilde. 1890
Opel, Peter. Warhafte und aigentliche contrafactur des löblichen freund und nachbarliche stahleschiessens so anno 1586 den 31. julii zu Regenspurg gehalten. 1587
Weismann, Heinrich. Das allgemeine deutsche schützenfest zu Frankfurt am Main, juli 1862. 1863

Netherlands

Hofdijk, W. J. De oude schutterij in Nederland. 1875

Short description of historic fashion. Northrup, Belle, and Green, A. L.

Short historical sketch of fans. Waern, Cecilia

Short history of costume & armour, chiefly in England, 1066-1800. Kelly, F. M. and Schwabe, Randolph

Short history of the English people. Green, J. R.

Short treatise on boots and shoes, ancient and modern. Goater, W. H.

Short treatise on head wear, ancient and modern. Goater, Mrs A. C.

Shover, Edna Mann
Art in costume design; practical suggestions for those interested in art, sewing, history and literature. Springfield, Mass., M. Bradley 1920
150p. front. illus. pl. Q.
Colas 2739. LC 20-9480

Showerman, Grant
Rome and the Romans; a survey and interpretation. New York, The Macmillan company 1931
xxi,643p. front. illus. maps(2 double) O. $5
Bibliography: p593-95
Costume index. LC 31-24179

Showing Roumania. See Iorga, Nicolâe. România in chipuri şi vederi

Shrimpton, A. T.
(pub.) Shrimpton's series of the costumes of the members of the University of Oxford. Oxford, A. T. Shrimpton; London, Simpkin, Marshall 1885?
Cover-title, 24 col.illus. on 1 fold.pl. S.

Siam
Backus, Mary, ed. Siam and Laos. 1884
Belevitch-Stankevitch, H. Le goût chinois en France au temps de Louis XIV. 1910
Carpenter, F. G. From Bangkok to Bombay. 1924
Hesse-Wartegg, Ernst von. Siam das reich des weissen elefanten. 1899
Leonowens, Mrs A. H. C. The English governess at the Siamese court. 1870
Leonowens, Mrs A. H. C. The romance of the harem. 1873
Mouhot, Henri. Travels in the central parts of Indo-China (Siam), Cambodia, and Laos, during the years 1858, 1859, and 1860. 1864
Plion, Raymond. Fêtes et cérémonies siamoises. 1935
Thompson, P. A. Lotus land, being an account of the country and the people of southern Siam. 1907?

Siam and Laos. Backus, Mary, ed.

Siam das reich des weissen elefanten. Hesse-Wartegg, Ernst von

Le **Siam** pittoresque et religieux. See Plion, Raymond. Fêtes et cérémonies siamoises

Siberia
Der allerneueste staat von Siberien, einer grossen und zuvor wenig bekannten moscowitischen provinz in Asien. 1725
Atkinson, T. W. Travels in the regions of the upper and lower Amoor, and the Russian acquisitions on the confines of India and China. 1860
Baĭsutov, N. I. V strane samykh bol'shikh morozov; kak zhivut i chem promyshli͡a͡iut i͡akuty; oblozhka V. Berga. 1928
Czaplicka, M. A. My Siberian year. 1916
Hawes, C. H. In the uttermost East. 1904
Ides, E. Y. Driejaarige reize naar China, te lande gedaan door den moskovischen afgezant. 1704
Krasheninnikov, S. P. The history of Kamtschatka, and the Kurilski Islands, with the countries adjacent. 1764
Sarychev, G. A. Account of a voyage of discovery to the north-east of Siberia, the frozen ocean, and the north-east sea. 1806-07

See also Samoyeds

Sibmacher, Johann
Newes modelbuch in kupffer gemacht darinen aller hand arth newes mödel von dün mittel und dick auszgeschnidener arbeit, auch andern künstlichen nehwerck zu gebrauchen. Nürnberg, 1604
10 l. 58pl.(part mounted) ob.S.
Lipperheide 3909. LC 22-16658

Sicard, François
Histoire des institutions militaires des français suivie d'un aperçu sur la marine militaire, avec un atlas de 200 planches représentant les uniformes anciens et modernes. Paris, J. Corréard 1834
4v. and atlas of 200pl. O.
Colas 2740

See also Pascal, Adrien, and others. Galerie des victoires et conquêtes de l'armée française

Sichart, Emma von
(ed.) Köhler, Karl. A history of costume
(ed.) Köhler, Karl. Praktische kostümkunde

Sicily
Cuciniello, Michele, and Bianchi, Lorenzo. Voyage pittoresque dans le royaume des deux Siciles. 1830-33
Lanza Di Scalea, Pietro. Donne e gioielli in Sicilia nel medio evo e nel rinascimento. 1892
Pitrè, Giuseppe, ed. Biblioteca delle tradizioni popolari siciliane. 1871-1913

See also Naples (Kingdom). also subhead Sicily under Ceremonial and festival costume

Sieben edelleute verschiedener nationen. Buytewech, Willem

Die **sieben** planeten. Lippmann, Friedrich

87 abbildungen böhmischer und mährischer gelehrten und künstler. Balzer, Johann

Das **siebenkönigsbuch.** Hesekiel, George

Siebold, Philipp Franz von
Nippon. Archiv zur beschreibung von Japan und dessen neben- und schutzländern Jezo mit den südlichen Kurilen, Sachalin, Korea und den Liukiu-inseln. Hrsg. von seinen söhnen. 2. aufl. Würzburg und Leipzig, L. Woerl 1897
2v. front. illus. port. map, tab. Q.
Lipperheide 1560. LC 1-12931

XVII vorstellungen von deutschen national-trachten. Augsburg, verlegt von C. F. Bürglen 1800
17pl. O.
Shows costumes of the women and children in southern Germany, Austria, and Switzerland. Most of the plates engraved by S. Graenicher
Colas 3037 (1796 ed.) Lipperheide 735

Un **siècle** de modes féminines, 1794-1894. Paris, G. Charpentier & E. Fasquelle 1894
20p. 194 col.pl. on 97 l. O. (Collection polychrome) 15fr.
Colas 2742. Costume index. Lipp. 580

Un **siècle** d'histoire de France par l'estampes. Paris. Bibliothèque nationale. Département des estampes

Sieg, Herbert. See Knötel, Herbert, jt. ed.

Sieg-streit dess lufft und wassers freudenfest zu pferd zu dem ... beyläger ... Leopoldi dess Ersten, Römischen Kaysers ... und Margarita ... Infantin auss Hispanien dargestellet in ... Wienn, Wien, M. Cosmerovio 1667
19 l. 29pl. F.
Same festivities described in *Allerhöchstfeyerlichste festivitäten*, which see
The plates, by Carlo Pasetti, show scenes from the procession, a tournament and an equestrian ballet
Lipperheide 2621

Siemienowicz, Kazimierz
Vollkommene geschütz- feuerwerck- und büchsenmeisterey-kunst ... anitzo in die hochteutsche spraach übersetzet, von Thoma Leonhard Beeren; mit schönen kupffern und einem gantzen neuen theil vermehret durch Daniel Elrich. Franckfurt am Mayn, J. D. Zunners 1676
2v. in 1. 47pl.(part fold.) F.
Published first in Latin (Amsterdam, 1650) and translated into French ca1651. Plates show makers of artillery and gunpowder
Lipperheide 2082. LC 8-15645

Sigel, Gustav A.
Deutschlands heer und flotte, in wort und bild ... Germany's army and navy, by pen and picture. Akron, O., Werner co. c1899
181p. 41 col.pl. F.

Les **signes** d'infamie au moyen âge. Robert, U. L. L.

La **signification** des tatouages. Lacassagne, Alexandre

Signs of infamy. See Infamy, Signs of

Siksika Indians. See Indians of North America—Siksika Indians

Der **Silberspiegel.** jahrg. 1, Sept. 18, 1934+ Berlin, A. Scherl
Illus. F.
Fashion periodical. Published bi-weekly. Current 1938
Superceded *Sport im bild.* Jahrg. 1 nr6-jahrg.2, nr11 (Nov 27, 1934-Feb 4, 1936) also called jahrg.40 nr24-jahrg.42, nr3, continuing the numbering of *Sport im bild*

Silfwerskjöld, T. von
Krönung und huldigung Oscar I. königs von Schweden und Norwegen, und der königin Josephine ... in Stockholm am 28sten september 1844 ... nebst einem anhang: Ursprung, geschichte und beschreibung der schwedischen ritterorden. Berlin, F. H. Morin 1845
102p. 15 col.pl. Q.
Colored plates show dress of the Swedish orders of knighthood
Engraved by A. U. von Schützercrantz. New edition (Berlin, F. H. Morin 1846)
Lipperheide 2700-01

Silling, Karl
Grand magazin des plus nouveaux dessins françois de broderie ... Groszes magazin für stickerei. Leipzig, Industrie-comptoir ca1800
54 col.pl. Q.
Lipperheide 3934

Silver, Jacob Mortimer Wier
Sketches of Japanese manners and customs; illus. by native drawings, reproduced in facsimile. London, Day 1867
51p. illus. 27 col.pl. Q.
Colas 2743. Lipperheide 1562. LC 5-6668

Silver jubilee record number, King George v. and Queen Mary, 1910-1935. Illustrated London news

Silvestre, Charles François
Differents habillements de Turcs. Paris, ca1700
30pl. on 15 l. ob.Q.
Colas 2744. Lipperheide 1412

Silvius. See Bosch, Ant.

Sīmakov", N.
Russkii ornament" v" starīnnykh" obraztsakh" khudozhestvenno-promyshlennago proīzvodstva ... L'ornement russe dans les anciens produits de l'art industriel national. Publication de la Société impériale d'encouragement aux beaux arts de St. Petersbourg. S.-Peterburg", tīp V. Kīrshbauma 1882
24 col.pl. F.
Lipperheide 3967

Simkin, Richard
British military types; supplement to the Army and nazy gazette. London, 1888-92
2v. 179 col.pl. F.
Colas 2746

Life in the army, every day incidents in camp, field, and quarters. London, Chapman [1889]
20 col.pl. ob.F.
Colas 2747

Our armies, illustrated and described. London, S. Low, Marston [1891]
46 l. 100 col.illus. Q.
Shows uniforms of the English army and the army of India
Colas 2745. Lipperheide 2275

Simmonds, Florence
(tr.) Lippmann, Friedrich. The seven planets

Simmonds, L. V. L.
(ed.) Miller, E. D. Modern polo

Simmons, Pauline
Chinese textiles. See entry under New York. Metropolitan museum of art

Simond, Charles, pseud. See Cleemputte, P. A. van

Simond, Émile
Le 28e de ligne; historique du régiment d'après les documents du Ministère de la guerre. Rouen, Mégard 1889
394p. 12 illus. 7pl. O.
Lipperheide 2352

Simons, Theodor
Aus altrömischer zeit ... mit illustrationen von Alexander Wagner. Berlin, Gebrüder Paetel 1872-78
4pts. 96 illus. Q.
Lipperheide 246

Simons, Theodor—*Continued*
Spanien ... illustrirt von ... Alexander Wagner. Berlin, Gebrüder Paetel [1880]
xvi,347p. 200 illus. 38pl. F.
Lipperheide 1238

Simonson, Lee
(ed.) Theatre art ... contributions by Allardyce Nicoll, John Anderson, Paul Alfred Merbach, Oliver M. Sayler [and] John Mason Brown. New York, The Museum of modern art, W. W. Norton [c1934]
66p. pl. Q.
The same material is published as: *International exhibition of theatre art, January 16-February 26, 1934,* of the New York Museum of modern art
LC 34-27067

See also Kommīssarzhevskiĭ, F. F., jt. auth.

Simple dressmaking explained and illustrated. Hambridge, E. R.

A **simple** explanation of low mass, by a secular priest. London, Burns, Oates & Washbourne; New York, P. J. Kenedy [1934]
xxx,87p. 43 illus. D.
LC 35-34787

Simple garments for infants. Synge, M. B.

Simpson, Melville William Hilton-. See Hilton-Simpson, M. W.

Simpson, William
Picturesque people: being groups from all quarters of the globe. London, W. M. Thompson 1876
viii p. 18 l. 19pl.(18 col.) F.
LC 5-30103

The seat of war in the East. London, P. & D. Colnaghi 1855-56
2v. 79 col.pl. F.
Scenes from the Crimean war 1853-1856
Lipperheide 2121

Simpson, William, and Kaye, John William
India ancient and modern, a series of illustrations of the country and people of India and adjacent territories. London, Day 1867
100p. col.pl. F.
Colas 2748. Lipperheide 1504

Simrock, Karl
(ed.) Brant, Sebastian. Sebastian Brands Narrenschiff; ein hausschatz zur ergetzung und erbauung erneuert von Karl Simrock; mit den holzschnitten der ersten ausgaben und dem bildniss Brands aus Reusners Icones

Les **simulachres** & historiees faces de la mort. Dance of death

Sinety, de
(illus.) Latour, Antoine de. Voyage de S.A.R. Monseigneur le Duc de Montpensier à Tunis en Égypte

Singer, Hans Wolfgang. See Deutsche bauerntrachten

Singermann, Felix
Ueber Juden-abzeichen; ein beitrag zur sozialen geschichte des Judentums. Berlin, L. Lamm 1915
51p. 4 illus. Q.
Contains material on Jewish dress of the middle ages

Singh, Saint Nihal
India's fighters: their mettle, history and services to Britain. London, Sampson Low, Marston 1914
xii,252p. front. pl. D.
Shows uniforms of the native troops in the English service
LC A15-2169

Singleton, Esther
Dolls. New York, Payson & Clarke [c1927]
xvi,167p. col.front. LXXX pl. on 40 l. Q. (The collector's library) $7.50, o.p.
Costume index. LC 27-23681

Social New York under the Georges, 1714-1776; houses, streets and country homes, with chapters on fashions, furniture, china, plate, and manners. New York, D. Appleton 1902
xix,407p. front. illus. O. $5, o.p.
Costume: pages 171-249
Costume index. LC 2-28275

Les **singuliers** et nouveaux pourtraicts ... pour toutes sortes d'ouvrages de lingerie. Vinciolo, Frederic de

Sinnett, F.
(pub.) La musique militaire

Sintes, Giovanni Battista
(engr.) Buonanni, Filippo. Ordinum equestrium et militarium catalogus in imaginibus expositus & cum brevi narratione

(engr.) Buonanni, Filippo. Verzeichniss der geist und weltlichen ritter-orden in netten abbildungen und einer kurtzen erzehlung in lateinisch und italienischer sprache

Sioux Indians. See Dakota Indians

Siragusa, Giovanni Battista
(ed.) Petrus, de Ebulo. Liber ad honorem Augusti

Sitten, gebräuche, trachten, mundart, häusliche und landwirthschaftliche einrichtungen der Altenburgischen bauern. See Kronbiegel, C. F. Ueber die sitten

Sitten, gebräuche und kleidung der Russen aus den niedern ständen. Richter, J. G.

Sitten, gebräuche, und kleidung der Russen, in St Petersburg. Gruber, J. G.

Sitten, gebräuche und trachten der Osmanen. Castellan, A. L.

Die **sitten** der völker. Buschan, G. H. T.

Sitten und gebräuche der heutigen Egypter. See note under Lane, E. W. Account of the manners and customs of the modern Egyptians

Sittengeschichte des deutschen studententums. Bauer, Max

Sittengeschichte des intimen. Schidrowitz, Leo

Sittengeschichte des theaters. Schidrowitz, Leo

Sittl, Karl
Archäologie der kunst. München, C. H. Beck 1895-97
xx,953p. O. and atlas of 66pl. ob.O. (Handbuch der klassischen altertums-wissenschaft. 6.bd.)
Shows costume of ancient times
Lipperheide 129f. LC 12-12193

La **situla** Benvenuti nel Museo di Este. Benvenuti, Leo

Six mois chez les Touareg du Ahaggar. Benhazera, Maurice

Six tableaux. Compte-Calix, F. C.

Sixteen designs for the theatre. Rutherston, A. D.

Sixteenth century

Bertelli, Ferdinando. Ferdinando Bertelli's trachtenbuch. 1913

Bertelli, Ferdinando. Omnium fere gentium nostrae aetatis habitus, nunquam ante hac aediti. 1563

Bertelli, Pietro. Diversarũ nationum habitus. 1589-1596

Bèze, Théodore de. Icones, id est verae imagines virorum doctrina simul et pietate illustrium. 1580

Bèze, Théodore de. Les vrais portraits des hommes illustres. 1581

Blakeslee, T. J. Illustrated catalogue of the extensive collection of highly valuable paintings by the great masters of the early English, French, Flemish, Dutch, Italian and Spanish schools, from the ... Blakeslee galleries. 1915

Boemus, Johann. The manners, lawes, and customes of all nations. 1611

Boemus, Johann. Mores, leges, et ritus omnium gentium. 1582

Boissard, J. J. Iani Iacobi Boissardi Vesuntini emblematum liber. 1593

Boissard, J. J. Habitus variarum orbis gentium. 1581

Boissard, J. J. Recueil de costumes étrangers; faisant le 3e volume de la collection recueillie par J. J. Boissard après 1581? ca1585?

Braun, Georg. Civitates orbis terrarum. 1572-1618

Bruyn, Abraham de. Costumes civils et militaires du XVIe siècle. 1875

Bruyn, Abraham de. Diversarum gentium armatura equestris. 1617

Bruyn, Abraham de. Imperii ac sacerdotii ornatus; diversarum item gẽtium peculiaris vestitus. 1578

Bruyn, Abraham de. Omnium pene Europae, Asiae, Africae et Americae gentium habitus ... quibus accidunt Romani pontificis, cardinalum, episcoporum, una cum omnium ordinum monachorum et religiosorum habitu. 1581

Bruyn, Abraham de. Omnium pene Europae, Asiae, Aphricae atque Americae gentium habitus. ca1610

Bruyn, Abraham de. Omnium poene gentium imagines, ubi oris totiusque corporis & vestium habitus, in ordinis cuiuscunque, ac loci hominibus diligentissime exprimuntur. 1577

Bruyn, Abraham de. Sacri Romani imperi ornatus, item Germanorum diversarumq. gentium peculiares vestitus; quibus accedunt ecclesiasticorum habitus varii. 1588

Bry, J. T. de. Emblemata nobilitatis. 1894

Bry, Theodor de. Emblemata secularia, mira et iucunda varietate seculi hujus mores. 1611

Casa, Giovanni della, abp. Trattato de costumi. 1573

Cicero, M. T. Officia M. T. C. Ein buch so Marcus Tullius Cicero der Römer zů seynem sune Marco. 1531

Deserpz, François. **Omnium fere gentium**, nostræq. 1572

Deserpz, François. Recueil de la diversité des habits qui sont de present en usaige tant es pays d'Europe, Asie, Affrique et Illes sauvages, le tout fait aprés le naturel. 1562

Fabri, Alexandro de. Diversarum nationum ornatus. 1593

Giovio, Paolo, bp. of Nocera. Musæi Ioviani imagines artifice manu ad viuum expressae. 1577

Giovio, Paolo, bp. of Nocera. Elogia virorum bellica virtute illustrium, septem libris iam olim ab authore comprehensa. 1575

Giovio, Paolo, bp. of Nocera. Elogia virorum literis illustrium, quotquot vel nostra vel avorum memoria vixere. 1577

Giovio, Paolo, bp. of Nocera. Regionum et insula um atque locorum: descriptiones: videlicet Britanniae, Scotiae, Hyberniae. 1578

Giovio, Paolo, bp. of Nocera. Vitae illustrium vivorum. 1578

Grassi, Bartolomeo. Dei veri ritratti degl' habiti di tutte le parti del mondo. 1585

Heldt, Sigmund. Abcontersaittung, allerlei ordenspersonen in iren klaidungen und dan viler alten klaidungen, so vor zeiten von fursten, furstin and herrn, auch burger and burgerin, alhie zu Nurmberg and vilen andern orten getragen sinnt worden, und an eins theils orten noch getragen werden. 1560-80

Hirth, Georg, ed. Kulturgeschichtliches bilderbuch aus drei jahrhunderten. 1881-90

Justinus, Marcus Junianus. Des hochberümptesten geschicht schreybers Justini warhafftige hystorien die er aus Trogo Pompeio gezogẽ ... darinn er von vil künigreychen der welt wie die auff und abgang genom̃en beschriben. 1532

Vergilius, Polydorus. Von den erfyndern der dyngen. 1537

Weigel, Hans. Habitus praecipuorum populorum. 1577

See also Hoop skirts; also subdivision Sixteenth century under Europe; Military costume

Sixty years in Southern California. Newmark, Harris

Sjaelland. See Zealand

Skåne. See Sweden—Skåne

Skånsk textil konstslöjl. Karlin, G. J.

Skänska folk drägter. Wallgren, O.

Skandinavien: Dänemark, Schweden, Norwegen, Finnland; baukunst, landschaft, volksleben. Mit einer einleitung von Valdemar Rørdam, Ernst Klein, Theodor Caspari, Johannes Öhquist. Berlin, E. Wasmuth; New York, Westermann 1930
280p. pl. map. (Orbis terrarum) $4.50
A few plates show costume of Norway and Sweden. Plates printed on both sides
Costume index

Skarbina, Franz
(ed.) Menzel, A. F. E. von. Die armee Friedrichs des Grossen

Skating. Heathcote, J. M., and others

Skating costume
Curry, Manfred. The beauty of skating. 1935
Garcin, J. Le vrai patineur ou principes sur l'art de patiner avec grâce. 1813
Heathcote, J. M., and others. Skating. 1892
Richardson, T. D. Modern figure skating. 1930
Zindel, C. S., ed. Der eislauf oder das schrittschuhfahren, ein taschenbuch für jung und alt. 1825

Skeat, Walter William
The past at our doors; or, The old in the new around us. London, Macmillan 1911
xi,198p. front. illus. D. (Readable books in natural knowledge)
The story of our dress (p50-122) discusses English costume, liveries and uniforms from the 17th to 19th century, and the origins of the national dress of Wales, Scotland, and Ireland
LC 12-39010

Skeat, Walter William, and Blagden, Charles Otto
Pagan races of the Malay Peninsula. London, Macmillan 1906
2v. fronts. pl. ports. maps(2 fold.) plan, fold.tab. O.
Bibliography: v 1, p xxv-xl
Includes dress, jewelry, body painting
LC 7-11553

Skelton, Joseph
(engr.) Engraved illustrations of antient arms and armour. See Meyrick, Sir S. R.

Sketch-book by an American in Venice. See Bosa, Eugenio. Sogetti pittoreschi e costumi di Venezia incisi all' acqua forte

Sketches and drawings of the Alhambra. Lewis, J. F.

Sketches from the Basque Provinces of Spain. Crocker, Sydney, and Barker, Bligh

Sketches illustrating the manners and customs of the Indians and Anglo-Indians. Tayler, W.

Sketches illustrative of the manners and costumes of France, Switzerland, and Italy. Bridgens, Richard

Sketches in Afghaunistan. Atkinson, James

Sketches in Australia and the adjacent islands. Melville, H. S.

Sketches in colors showing costumes of the period. Dighton, Richard

Sketches in Turkey, Syria and Egypt, 1840 & 1841. Wilkie, Sir David

Sketches of British soldiers. Thomas

Sketches of character & costume in Constantinople. MacBean, Forbes

Sketches of character in illustration of the habits, occupation and the costume of the Negro population in the Island Jamaica. Belisario, L. M.

Sketches of China and the Chinese. Borget, Auguste

Sketches of Japanese manners and customs. Silver, J. M. W.

Sketches of military costume in Spain and Portugal. See note under Bradford, William. Sketches of the country, character, and costume, in Portugal and Spain

Sketches of Portuguese life, manners, costume, and character, by A. P. D. G. London, G. B. Whittaker 1826
xxv,364p. illus. 21pl.(20 col.) O.
Colas 2750. LC 4-25168

Sketches of Spain and Spanish character. Lewis, J. F.

Sketches of Spanish scenes and architecture. Roberts, David

Sketches of the age of Francis I. Müller, W. J.

Sketches of the country, character, and costume, in Portugal and Spain. Bradford, William

Sketches on the Danube, in Hungary and Transylvania. Hering, G. E.

Sketches, Spanish & oriental. Wilkie, Sir David

Sketches taken during ten voyages to Africa between the years 1786 and 1800. Adams, Capt. John

Sketching rambles in Holland. Boughton, G. H.

Skiing costume
American ski annual. 1936

Skilbeck, Clement O.
(illus.) Illustrations of the liturgy, being thirteen drawings of the celebration of the Holy Communion in a parish church. London, Mowbray [1912]
84p. pl. Q. (Alcuin club collections, 19)

Skinner, Joseph
(comp. and tr.) The present state of Peru ... drawn from original and authentic documents, chiefly written and comp. in the Peruvian capital; and embellished by twenty engravings of costumes. London, R. Phillips 1805
xiv,487p. xx col.pl.(incl.front.) sq.Q. 18s, o.p.
Colas 2751. Costume index. Lipperheide 1629. LC 4-7839

See also Voyages au Pérou, faits dans les années 1791 à 1794

Skinner, Robert Peet
Abyssinia of to-day; an account of the first mission sent by the American government to the court of the King of Kings (1903-1904). London, E. Arnold; New York, Longmans, Green 1906
xvi,227p. front. pl. ports. O. $3, o.p.
Costume index. LC 7-7544

Skirts. See Crinoline; Hoop skirts

Skizzen aus dem volksleben in Ungarn. Prônay von Tot-Próna und zu Blathnicza, Gabriel, freiherr

Skizzen des physisch-moralischen zustandes Dalmatiens. Rodlich, H. F.

Skizzen für künstler und kunst-liebhaber über Paris. See Dunker, B. A. Tableau de Paris

Skizzen von der insel Java und den verschiedenen bewohnern. Pfyffer, J. J. X.

Sladen, Douglas Brooke Wheelton

Carthage and Tunis, the old and new gates of the Orient. With 6 maps and 68 illustrations, including 6 coloured plates by Benton Fletcher. London, Hutchinson 1906
2v. col.fronts. illus. pl.(6 col. 1 fold.) maps, 2 plans(1 fold.) O.
Paged continuously
LC 7-7541

See also Lorey, Eustache de, jt. auth.

Slavin. Dobrovsky, Josef

Slavs

Al'bom rīsunkov" russkīkh ī slavīanskīkh" narīadov". Vypusk" I. narīady Velīkorusskiĭ (Rīazanskoĭ) gub. i chernogorskiĭ. 1884

Hacquet, Balthasar. Abbildung und Beschreibung der südwest und östlichen Wenden, Illyrer und Slaven. 1802-05

Die **Slawen** in Deutschland. Tetzner, F. O.

The sleeping princess. See Theatrical costume—Special plays, ballots, etc.—The sleeping princess

Slovenské národnie ornamenty. Sochâň, P. B., pub.

Slowakische national-ornamente. See Sochâň, P. B., pub. Slovenské národnie ornamenty

Sluperius, Jacobus. See Deserpz, François. Omnium fere gentium, nostræq

Smart, Christopher

(comp.) The world displayed

The **smartly** dressed woman. Burbank, Emily.

Smibert, Thomas

The clans of the Highlands of Scotland: being an account of their annals, separately & collectively, with delineations of their tartans, and family arms. Edinburgh, J. Hogg 1850
340p. col.front. 60 col.pl. Q.
Colas 2752. Lipperheide 1031. LC 3-28702

Smids, Ludolf

Korte leevensschets en afbeeldingen der graaven van Holland, van Dirk de eerste, tot Koning Filip de twede, zynde de Laatste. Haarlem, J. Marshoorn 1744
15 l. 200p. 37pl. Q.
Lipperheide 945

(ed.) Allard, Carel. Orbis habitabilis oppida et vestitus

Smirke, Robert

Picturesque beauties of Shakespeare, being a selection of scenes engraved under the direction of Charles Taylor. London, C. Taylor 1783-84
24 l. 24pl. O.
Twenty-four plates illustrating As you like it, Macbeth, Hamlet, Merry wives of Windsor, Much ado about nothing, and Twelfth night (4 plates to each play) each with a leaf of quotation. Engraved by Charles and Isaac Taylor, jun. (one by Joseph Thornthwaite) from drawings by Robert Smirke and Thomas Stothard. A number of the plates dated 1783-84
LC 22-11738

(illus.) Boydell, John, and Boydell, Josiah. The American edition of Boydell's Illustrations of the Dramatic works of Shakspeare

Smirnov, Vas. See Kalitkin, N. Ornament shit'īa kostromskogo polushubka

Smith, Captain

Asiatic costumes. London, R. Ackermann 1828
88p. 44 col.pl. O. 18s, o.p.
Shows dress worn in India at this period
Also published with Spanish title: *Trajes asiaticos*
Colas 2753, 2907. Costume index

Smith, A. D. Howell

Brief guide to the Chinese woven fabrics. See entry under Victoria and Albert museum, South Kensington

Brief guide to the oriental painted, dyed and printed textiles. See entry under Victoria and Albert museum, South Kensington

Brief guide to the Peruvian textiles. See entry under Victoria and Albert museum, South Kensington

Brief guide to the western painted, dyed and printed textiles. See entry under Victoria and Albert museum, South Kensington

Guide to the Japanese textiles. See entry under Victoria and Albert museum, South Kensington

Smith, Albert Richard

(ed.) Gavarni, G. S. C. Gavarni in London

Smith, Bernard. See Pugin, A. W. N. Glossary of ecclesiastical ornament and costume

Smith, Charles Hamilton

Costume of the army of the British Empire according to the regulations, 1814. London, W. Bulmer 1915
2 l. col.front. 60 col.pl. Q.
Engraved by J. C. Stadler
Colas 2754, 733

Selections of the ancient costumes of Great Britain and Ireland from the seventh to the sixteenth century. London, W. Bulmer 1814
63 l. col.front. 60 col.pl. Q.
First published in 15 numbers at 210s, 1811-13. Edition of 1813 has title: *Ancient costume of Great Britain and Ireland, from the seventh to the sixteenth century.* Reprinted 1818 and 1848
Colas 2755. Costume index (1813 ed.)
Lipperheide 988

See also Meyrick, Sir S. R., jt. auth.

Smith, Charles Roach
(ed.) Faussett, Bryan. Inventorium sepulchrale

Smith, Frank Berkeley
Budapest, the city of the Magyars. New York, J. Pott 1903
xii,292p. col.front. illus. pl. ports. D. $1.50, o.p.
Costume index. LC 3-32577

Smith, George
(ed.) The coronation of the Queen. The coronation of Elizabeth Wydeville

Smith, Sir Grafton Elliot
Tutankhamen and the discovery of his tomb by the late Earl of Carnarvon and Mr Howard Carter. London, G. Routledge; New York, E. P. Dutton 1923
133p. col.front. illus. O.
LC 23-12932

Smith, Harold Clifford
Jewellery. London, Methuen [1908]
xlvii,409p. illus. LIV pl.(3 col.) Q. (The connoisseur's library)
Bibliography: p371-79
Costume index. LC 8-20539

Smith, Jessie Willcox
(illus.) Dickens's children. New York, C. Scribner's 1912
[27]p. col.pl. O.
LC 12-22525

Smith, John Moyr
(comp.) Ancient Greek female costume ... with explanatory letterpress, and descriptive passages from the works of Homer, Hesiod, Herodotus, Aeschylus, Euripides, Aristophanes, Theocritus, Xenophon, Lucian, and other Greek authors. London, S. Low, Marston, Searle, & Rivington 1882
87p. illus. 112pl.(incl.front.) D.
LC 15-11963

Smith, John Thomas
The cries of London: exhibiting several of the itinerant traders of antient and modern times. London, J. B. Nichols 1839
xv,99p. front. 30pl. Q.
Text revised by Francis Douce after the author's death
Colas 2757. Lipperheide 1024

Etchings of remarkable beggars, itinerant traders, and other persons of notoriety in London and its environs. London, J. T. Smith 1815-16
48pl. Q.
An edition with introduction by Francis Douce was published under title: *Vagabondiana*
Colas 2756. Lipperheide 1023

Smith, Justin Harvey
(ed.) The historie booke, done to keep in lasting remembrance the joyous meeting of the Honourable artillery company of London and the Ancient and honorable artillery company of the Massachusetts in the towne of Boston, A. D., 1903. [Norwood, Mass.] Priv. print. at the Norwood press for the Ancient and honorable artillery company of the Massachusetts [c1903]
lvi,176p. front. illus. col.pl. ports. facsims. sq.F.
Illustrated by E. H. Garrett
Colored plates show uniforms of the officers of the Honourable artillery company of London. Other illustrations show soldiers of the same company in the uniforms of various periods
LC 3-26331

Smith, Lucy Toulmin
(tr.) Jusserand, J. A. A. J. English wayfaring life in the middle ages (XIVth century)

Smith, Reginald Allender
Guide to antiquities of the early iron age. See entry under British museum. Department of British and mediaeval antiquities

Smith, Willard M.
Gloves, past and present. New York, Sherwood press 1917
119p. O. $1.50
LC 17-25761

Smith, Winifred
The commedia dell' arte; a study in Italian popular comedy. New York, Columbia university press 1912
xv,290p. front. pl. O. (Columbia university studies in English and comparative literature) $2
Appendix A: Scenarios; Appendix B: Relations between English and Italian drama in the 16th, 17th and 18th centuries. Published also as thesis (Ph.D.) Columbia university, 1912
Bibliography: p255-79
LC 12-23493

Smithsonian institution
North American Indians. See entry under Palmer, R. A.

Smokers' accessories. See Pipes and smokers' utensils

Smorti, P. & ci.
(pub.) Raccolta di costumi antichi e moderni

Die **Smyrna-arbeit.** Lipperheide, Frieda, and Marggraff, Clara

Smyth, Coke. See Planché, J. R., jt. auth.

Snake-dance of the Moquis of Arizona. Bourke, J. G.

Snellinck, Joan. See Noort, Adam van, jt. auth.

Snoeck
Collection générale de costumes suisses; les 32 cantons représentés en 64 figures. No place, 1828
64 illus. ob.Q.
Colas 2758

Snow, Bonnie E. and Froehlich, Hugo B.
The theory and practice of color. New York, Chicago, The Prang company [c1918]
53p. col.front. pl.(part col.) Q.
Chapter XI deals with color in dress
Third edition: 1930
LC 19-26166

Snow and ice sports. Jessup, E. H.

Snowshoes
Davidson, D. S. Snowshoes. 1937

Snyder, C. S. See Ruth, J. A., jt. comp.

So sollt ihr euch kleiden! Gratz, Josefine

So you're going to be married. See The Bride's magazine

Sobranie mundīrov" Rossīĭskoĭ Īmperatorskoĭ Armiī. Izdannoe Chertezhnoĭu Ego Īmperatoskago Vysochestva generad"-Īnspektora po Inzhenernoĭ chastī. No place, ca1830
65 col.pl. F.
Collection of uniforms of Russian Imperial army
Lipperheide 2377

Socecu, Alexandru J. V.
Die rumänische armee in ihrer gegenwärtigen uniformierung. Leipzig, M. Ruhl ⌊1893⌋
24p. 16 col.pl. O.
Second edition: *Die rumänische armee, ihre ... uniformierung* (Leipzig, M. Ruhl ⌊1895⌋ 54p. 15 col.pl.) Also found with title page in Rumanian: *Uniformele amatei romana*
Colas 2605. Lipperheide 2390

Socháň, Pavel B.
(pub.) Slovenské národnie ornamenty ... Ornements nationales slovaques. Slowakische national-ornamente. Sv. Martine, P. B. Socháň ⌊1896⌋
1 l. 40pl. Q.
Continues his *Muster altslowakischer leinenstickerei*
Lipperheide 3982

(pub.) Vzory staroslovenských vipiviek. Muster altslowakischer leinenstickerei. Sv. Martine, P. B. Socháň ⌊1894⌋
1 l. 40pl. Q.
Lipperheide 3981

Social contrasts. Gray, William

Social culture. See Ruth, J. A., and Snyder, C. S. Decorum

Social England. Traill, H. D., and Mann, J. S., eds.

Social England under the regency. Ashton, John

Social history of ancient Ireland. Joyce, P. W.

Social life in Egypt. Lane-Poole, Stanley

Social life in the early republic. Wharton, A. H.

Social life in the reign of Queen Anne. Ashton, John

Social life of the Chinese. Doolittle, Justus

Social life under the Stuarts. Bedford, Jessie

Social New York under the Georges, 1714-1776. Singleton, Esther

Social organization and the secret societies of the Kwakiutl Indians. Boas, Franz

Social problems of the high school boy. Lyster, A. M., and Hudnall, Mrs G. F.

Sociedad española de amigos del arte, Madrid
Exposicion de "el abanico en España", catalogo general ilustrado, por D. Joaquin Ezquerra del Bayo, Madrid, mayo-junio, 1920. Madrid, Imprenta Blass ⌊1920⌋
100p. illus. LXVII pl. (part col.) F.
LC 30-918

Société archéologique d'Athènes. See Ridder, A. H. P. de. Catalogue des **bronzes de la** Société archéologique d'Athènes

Société archéologique du Finistère
Catalogue du musée archéologique et du musée des anciens costumes bretons de la ville de Quimper. Quimper, Caen 1885
178p. 8pl. O.
Colas 2759

Société de l'histoire du costume
Bulletin de la Société. Paris, Leroy 1907/09-1910/11
2v. 25pl. (part col.) O.
Published irregularly. Volume 1 includes numbers for June 1907, Jan. Apr. July and Oct. 1908, Jan. Apr. July 1909; v2, Jan. Mar.-Apr. May-June, July-Aug. 1910. Continued by *Costumes & uniformes*
Colas 484

Costumes & uniformes. See Costumes & uniformes

Société des amis des livres
Paris qui crie; notices par divers membres de la Société; dessins de Pierre Vidal. Paris, Chamerot 1890
Pl. Q.

Société des bibliophiles français. See Jeux des cartes tarots et de cartes numérales du quatorzième au dix-huitième siècle

Société d'études des uniformes. See Le Passepoil

La **société** du second empire. Fleury, Maurice, comte, and Sonolet, Louis

Société française de reproductions de manuscrits à peintures, Paris
Les très belles Heures de Notre-Dame du duc Jean de Berry. See entry under Durrieu, Paul, comte

Société française de reproductions de manuments historiques d'Alsace, Strassburg. See Herrad von Landsberg, Abbess of Hohenburg. Hortus deliciarum

Society of colonial wars, New Jersey
Bibliography of colonial costume. See entry under Meyers, C. L., comp.

Socquet, Jean. See Jean-Meyan, Maurice, jt. auth.

Soden, Franz, freiherr von
Geschichte des ehemaligen weilers Affalterbach landgerichts Altdorf in Mittelfranken des königreichs Bayern; beitrag zur kriegs- und sittengeschichte des mittelalters. Nürnberg, A. Recknagel 1841
166p. 3 col.pl. O.
Shows seven soldiers of the late 15th century
Lipperheide 2095

Söderberg, Gustaf
Kongl. svenska arméens uniformer. Stockholm, Gjöthström & Magnusson 1834
36 l. 35 col.pl. O.

Sogetti pittoreschi e costumi di Venezia incisi all' acqua forte. Bosa, Eugenio

Soieries marocaines. Vogel, Lucien

Sojka, Berta. See Sojková, Berta

Sojková, Berta
Vzory vyšwání lidu slovanského na Moravě ... ⌊Stickerei-muster des slavischen volkes in Mähren, nach originalen im patriotischen museum in Olmütz⌋ Olomouci, Tiskem knížecí arcibiskupské knih- a kamenotiskárny 1887-95
3v. 32 col.pl. Q.
Lipperheide 3975

Soldan, Sigmund
(ed.) Dürer, Albrecht, and Wolgemut, Michael. Die gemälde von Dürer und Wolgemut

Der **soldat** in der deutschen vergangenheit. Liebe, G. H. T.

Die **soldaten** d. Königl. deutschen legion. Castell, graf

Die **soldaten** der französischen Republik und des Kaiserreichs. See note under Bellangé, J. L. H. Collection des types

Der **Soldaten-freund;** illus. zeitschrift für faszliche belehrung und unterhaltung des deutschen soldaten. 1.-81. jahrg.; 1833-1914. Berlin, Mittler
81v. col.illus. O.-Q.
Published monthly. No more published?
Lipperheide 4624

Die **soldaten** Friedrich's des Grossen. Lange, Eduard

Els **soldats.** Amades, Joan; Colominas, Josep, and Vila, Pau

Les **soldats** français dans les guerres. Arnoux, Guy

Soldats d'hier et d'aujourd'hui. Armont, Paul

Soldiers' feet and footgear. Webb-Johnson, Cecil

The **soldier's** foot and the military shoe. Munson, E. L.

[**Soldiers** of the Carlist army] Paris, Ligny ca1835
6 col.pl. F.
Plates bear legends in English, French, and Spanish
Colas 2761. Lipperheide 2360

Solemnia electionis et inaugurationis Leopoldi, romanor: imperatoris. See note under Merian, Caspar. Beschreibung

Solemniteter ... i ... Stockholm, aren 1771 och 1772 Floding, P. G.

Les **solennités** du saint couronnement. Russia. Ministerstvo Imperatorskago dvora

Solerius, Anselm, pseud. See Raynaud, Théophile

Solis, Virgil, and Amman, Jost
Effigies regum francorum omnium, a Pharamundo, ad Henricum usque tertium. Noribergae, K. T. Gerlach 1576
64 l. illus. 62 ports. Q.
Portraits, half length, are by Virgil Solis, with five only by Jost Amman. German edition: Köln, J. Bussemacher 1587
Lipperheide 1061

Solntsev, Fedor Grigor'evich
(illus.) Russia. Komitet dlia izdaniia drevnosteĭ Rossiĭkago gosudarstva. Drevnostē Rossiĭskago gosudarstva

Solomon islands
Guppy, H. B. The Solomon islands. 1887

Solvet, Charles
(tr.) Meiners, Christoph. Recherches historiques sur le luxe chez les Athéniens

Solvyns, Mme. See note under Solvyns, F. B. Les Hindoûs

Solvyns, Frans Baltasar
A catalogue of 250 coloured etchings; descriptive of the manners, customs, character, dress, and religious ceremonies of the Hindoos. [Calcutta] Mirror press 1799
28p. O.
To accompany the author's *A collection of 250 coloured etchings descriptive of the manners, customs and dresses of the Hindoos*
Colas 2764. LC 31-8750

A collection of two hundred and fifty coloured etchings descriptive of the manners, customs, and dresses of the Hindoos. Calcutta, 1796-99
13 l. 250 col.pl. F.
Colas 2763

The costume of Indostan ... with descriptions in English and French, taken in the years 1798 and 1799. London, E. Orme 1804
60 l. 60 col.pl. F. 31s, o.p.
French title: *Costumes de l'Indostan*
These plates are from his *Collection of two hundred and fifty coloured etchings*
Colas 2765-2766. Costume index. Lipperheide 1479

Les Hindoûs. Paris, L'auteur 1808-12
4v. 288 col.pl.(part fold.) sq.F.
Half-title: *Les Hindoûs, ou description de leurs moeurs, coutumes et cérémonies.* French and English, text, the latter by Mme Solvyns
Colas 2767-68. LC 5-10075

Some drawings of ancient embroidery. Barber, Mrs Mary

Some early costume books. Küp, Karl

Some Italian scenes and festivals. Ashby, Thomas

Some old Flemish towns. Edwards, G. W.

Somerscales, Marjorie I.
The improvised stage. London, Sir I. Pitman 1932
viii,136p. illus. O.
Contains patterns for costumes to be used in amateur theatricals
LC 33-3386

Sommardagar i Sverige. Philip, J. B.

Sommario delle vite de' duchi di Milano. Barbuò Soncino, Scipione

Sommerard, Alexandre Du. See Du Sommerard, Alexandre

Sommerfeld, F.
Die schweizer armee, ihre organisation, bewaffnung, ausrüstung, uniformen und abzeichen. Leipsig, M. Ruhl [1915]
39p. 16 col.pl. D.

Sommerlatt, Christian Vollrath von
Beschreibung der XXII. Schweizer-kantone, von C. V. v. S', zu dessen in dreizehn karten ... erschienenen kleinen atlas der Schweiz. Basel, 1838
vii,524p. O. and atlas of pl.
French edition: *Description des XXII cantons de la Suisse, accompagnant le petit atlas ... publié par le même auteur ... tr. ... par C. Hebler* (Berne, 1840. vii, 570p. O. and atlas of pl. F.

Son altesse la femme. Uzanne, L. O.

Sona, Ernest
La grande réforme. [Paris, Imp. E. Dessossés, 1917?]
cover-title, 230p. O.
"La grande reforme [est] la fixation de la mode ou la militarisation de l'habillement civil." p16
"La variabilité de la mode a été la cause première de la terrible conflagration actuelle car elle a excité la cupidité des richesses, le goût du luxe, du superflu, ce qui a donné naissance à l'abus de crédit et celui-ci à son tour a provoqué le débordement dans la consommation et dans la production." p227
LC 19-1261

Sonderland, Johann Baptist. See Tidemand, Adolph. Norwegisches bauernleben

Sonnenschein, Adolf
(tr.) Stenzel, Alfred. The British navy

Sonntags-zeitung für Deutschlands frauen. See Sonntags-zeitung fürs deutsche haus

Sonntags-zeitung fürs deutsche haus; illustrierte familien und frauenzeitung. 1.-? jahrg., okt. 1897-1919. Leipzig, W. Vobach
Illus. col.pl. Q.
Published weekly
Title varies: Oct. 1897-Sept. 1907: *Sonntags-zeitung für Deutschlands frauen.* Subtitle varies
Lipperheide 4817

Sonolet, Louis. See Fleury, Maurice, comte, jt. auth.

Il **sontuoso** apparato, fatto dalla magnifica citta di Brescia nel felice ritorno dell' ... il cardinale Morosini. Fontana, Publio

Sooy, Louise Pinkney. See Mackey, M. G., jt. auth.

Sorel, Charles
(ed.) Bernard, Charles. Généalogie de la maison royal de Bourbon, avec les éloges et les portraits des princes qui en sont sortis

Soria, E.
(illus.) Album descriptivo del ejército y la armada de España

Sorrieu, Frédéric
Galerie des modes et costumes français, dessinés ... par les plus célèbres artistes dans ce genre (règne de Louis XVI). Paris, F. Janet 1867
2 l. 24 col.pl. Q.
Plates for the most part show feminine costumes of the 18th century
Colas 2770. Lipperheide 1138

(lithgr). Lalaisse, Hippolyte. L'armée française et ses cantinières

Sostmann, Wilhelmine
Peter Vischer; romantischdramatisches gemälde aus der vorzeit Nürnbergs. Nürnberg, G. Winter 1832
108p. 10 pl.(9 col.) O.
Nine plates show costume
Lipperheide 3217

Sotheran, Henry
(ed.) Manners & customs of the French

Soto, Maria de. See Clonard, Serafín Maria de Soto y Abbach, conde de

Sotzmann, Johann Daniel Ferdinand. See Holbein, Hans, the younger. Hans Holbeins Alte Testament in funfzig holzschnitten getreu nach den originalen copirt

Source book for social origins. Thomas, W. I.

Sources documentaires concernant l'histoire du régiment des chevau-légers de la garde de Napoléon Ier. Rembowski, Alexandre

Sous le grand soleil. Muraz, Gaston

Sous Louis-Philippe; les dandys. Boulenger, J. R.

Sousa, Manuel de Faria e. See Faria e Sousa, Manuel de

South Africa. See Africa, South

South America
Carpenter, F. G. South America, social, industrial, and political. 1900
Las mujeres españolas, portuguesas y americanas ... Descripcion y pintura del caracter costumbres, trajes ... de la mujer de cada una de las provincias de España, Portugal y Américas españoles. 1872-76

See also Bolivia; Brazil; Chile; Columbia; Paraguay; Patagonia; Peru; Tierra del Fuego; Uruguay; Venezuela; also Indians of South America

South America, social, industrial, and political. Carpenter, F. G.

South Australia illustrated. Angas, G. F.

South Kensington museum. London. See Victoria and Albert museum, South Kensington

South Sea islands. See Oceania; also Polynesia, New Guinea, and names of other islands of the south Pacific ocean

South Sea islands. Shoberl, Frederic, ed.

A **southern** girl in '61. Wright, Mrs L. W.

Southern India. Penny, Mrs F. E. F.

Souvenir à l'Angloise et recueil de coiffures. Paris, Desnos 1780
12pl. T.
Plates are from the second part of *Almanach de la toilette*
Colas 2774

Souvenir de Bretagne: costumes de Cornouaille. Quimper, Villard n.d.
16pl. O.
Each plate shows two costumes or groups of costumes
Colas 2776

Souvenir de l'Exposition universelle de Vienne. Pelcoq, Jules

Souvenir de l'orient. Montfort

Souvenir du Caire. See Preziosi, A. Le Caire, moeurs et costumes

Le **Souvenir**; littérature, beaux-arts, critique, modes. Oct. 1849-1866? Paris
O.
According to Colas was published only to 1855. Hatin (1866) writes of it as current
Subtitle varies: Volumes 1-4: revue des modes et des salons; v4-? journal de la noblesse
Colas 2773

Souvenir of Macbeth produced at the Lyceum Theatre. London. Lyceum Theatre

Souvenir of Shakespeare's historical play King Henry the Eighth. London. Lyceum Theatre

Souvenir of the bal costumé given by ... Queen Victoria at Buckingham palace, May 12, 1842. Planché, J. R., and Smyth, Coke

Souvenir of the N. American Indians as they were in the middle of the nineteenth century. Catlin, George

Souvenirs de Bretagne. Deshays, Célestin

Souvenirs de Constantinople. Brindesi, Jean

Souvenirs de la Haute-Albanie. Degrand, J. A. T.

Souvenirs de la monarchie autrichienne. See Valério, Théodore. Costumes de la Hongrie et des provinces danubiennes, Dalmatie, Monténégro, Croatie, Slavonie, frontières militaires

Souvenirs de l'ouest de la France: costumes bretons. Valerio, Théodore

Souvenirs d'Égypte. Bida, Alexandre, and Barbot, E.

Souvenirs des eaux de Baden-Baden et des environs. Jacottet, L. J.

Souvenirs des Pyrénées. Gorse, P.

Souvenirs des Pyrénées. Petit, Victor

Souvenirs du passé: Le costume en Provence. Roux, J. C.

Souvenirs du siège de Paris. Renard, Jules

Souvenirs du théâtre anglais. Devéria, Achille, and Boulenger

Souvenirs du Tyrol, du Vorarlberg et de la Haute Bavière ... Erinnerungen von Tyrol, Vorarlberg und Ober Baiern. Valério, Théodore

Les **souvenirs** et les regrets du vieil amateur dramatique. Arnault, A. V.

Souvestre, Émile

La Bretagne pittoresque, ou Choix de monuments, de costumes et de scènes de moeurs de la Bretagne, dessinés et lithographiés par MM. Rouargue et Saint-Germain. Nantes, C. Mellinet et H. Baudoux [1841]

Cover-title, 11 l. 10pl. F.
Colas 2781. LC 4-26282

Souza, Alberto

O trajo popular em Portugal nos seculos XVIII e XIX. [Lisbon, Sociedade nacional de tipografia; New York, E. Weyhe 1924]

252p. illus. col.pl. F.

Soyons chic et pratiques. See Chic et pratique

Soyons pratiques. See Chic et pratique

La **spada** maestra. Mazo, Bondí di

Spad-arfoet. Larsson, Carl

Spätgothische wohnräume und wandmalereien aus Schloss Issogne. Forrer, Robert

Spätt, F. I.

(engr.) Fortitudo leonina in utraque fortuna Maximiliani Emmanuelis, V. B. ac Sup. Palat. ducis, comitis palatini Rheni

Spain. Ministerio de la guerra

New uniform regulations of the Spanish army. No place, 1908?

v.p. pl. O.

Spain

Aznar y García, Francisco. Indumentaria española, documentos para su estudio desde la época visigoda hasta nuestros dias. 1881

Boehn, Max von. Spanien: geschichte, kultur, kunst. 1924

Carderera y Solano, Valentín. Iconografía española ... desde el siglo XI hasta el XVII. 1855-64

Clonard, S. M. de S. y A., conde de. Discurso histórico sobre el trajo de los Españoles, desde los tiempos más remotos hasta el rienado de los reyes catolicos. 1879

Danvila y Collado, Francisco. Trajes y armas de los españoles desde los tiempos prehistóricos hasta los primeros años del siglo XIX. 1877

Diego y González, J. N. de, and León Salmerón, Africa. Compendio de indumentaria española, con un preliminar de la historia del traje v el mobiliario en los principales pueblos de la antigüedad. 1915

Discurso sobre el luxô de las señoras, y proyecto de un trage nacional. De orden superior. 1788

Folklore y costumbres de España. 1931-33

Moreno Rodriguez, Manuel. Tipos españoles. n.d.

Sempere y Guarinos, Juan. Historia del lujo y de las leyes suntuarias de España. 1788

See also subdivision Spain under Arms and armor; Bull-fighters; Ceremonial and festival costume; Coronations and coronation robes; Crown jewels; Embroidery; Funerals; Hairdressing; Lace; Military costume; Mummers; Regalia; Weddings and wedding dress

Middle ages

Puiggari, José. Estudios de indumentaria española concreta y comparada ... cuadro histórico especial de los siglos XIII y XIV. 1890

15th century

Benzoni, Girolamo. Americae pars quarta [-sexta] 1594-96

16th century

Calvo y Sánchez, Ignacio. Retratos de personajes del siglo XVI, relacionados con la historia militar de España. 1919

Weiditz, Christoph. Das trachtenbuch des Christoph Weiditz, von seinen reisen nach Spanien (1529) und den Niederlanden (1531/32). 1927

17th century

Carranza, Alonso. Rogacion en detestacion de los grandes abusos en los traxes y adornos nuevamente introducidos en España. 1636

Lavanha, J. B. Viagem da catholica real magestade del rey d. Filipe II ... ao reyno de Portugal e rellação do solene recebimento que nelle se lhe fez. 1622

18th century

Brunet, Gustav. Étude sur Francisco Goya. 1865

Cruz Cano y Olmedilla, Juan de la. Colleccion de trajes de España, tanto antiguos como modernos, que comprehende todos los de sus dominios. 1777-1788

Spain—18th century—*Continued*

Cruz Cano y Olmedilla, Juan de la. Collection des costumes espagnols anciens et moderns. 1786

Williams, Leonard. The arts and crafts of older Spain. 1907

Caricature and satire

Goya y Lucientes, F. J. de. Caprichos inventados y grabados al agua forte. ca1799

Goya y Lucientes, F. J. de. Los desastres de la guerra. 1921

19th century

Avanda, Jim. Costumes espagnols. 1876

Bégin, É. A. N. J. Voyage pittoresque en Espagne et en Portugal. 1852

Becquier, José. Spanish costumes. 1830

Breton de la Martinière, J. B. J. L'Espagne et le Portugal. 1815

Brunet, Gustav. Étude sur Francisco Goya. 1865

Clerjon de Champagny. Album d'un soldat pendant la campagne d'Espagne en 1823. 1829

Coleccion de trages de España. 1832-1836

Cuendias, M. G. de, and Suberwick, Mme de. L'Espagne, pittoresque, artistique et monumentale. 1848

Davillier, J. C., baron. L'Espagne. 1874

Davillier, J. C., baron. Spain. 1876

Escosura, Patricio de la. España artística y monumental. 1842-50

Eyriès, J. B. B. Costumes, moeurs et usages de tous les peuples ... Espagne. ca1815

Gail, Wilhelm. Erinnerungen aus Spanien. Nach der natur und auf stein gezeichnete skizzen aus dem leben in den provinzen Catalonien, Valencia, Andalusien, Granada und Castilien. 1837

Giscard. Delineations of the most remarkable costumes of the different provinces of Spain, and also of the military uniforms, bull fights, national dances, &c. of the Spaniards. 1823

Lathrop, G. P. Spanish vistas. 1883

Lewis, J. F. Lewis's sketches and drawings of the Alhambra, made during a residence in Granada, in the years 1833-4. 1835

Lewis, J. F. Lewis's sketches of Spain and Spanish character, made during his tour in that country, in the years 1833-4. 1836

Las mujeres españolas, portuguesas y americanas ... Descripcion y pintura del caracter, costumbres, trajes ... de la mujer de cada una de las provincias de España, Portugal y Américas españolas. 1872-76

Museos de España. Cordova scenes. 18—

Pigal, E. J. Collection de costumes des diverses provinces de l'Espagne. ca1825

Recuerdos de un viage por España. 1849-51

Roberts, David. Sketches of Spanish scenes and architecture. 1833?

Rodriguez, A. Coleccion general de los trages que en la actualidad se usan en España, principiada en el año 1801. 1804

Shoberl, Frédéric, ed. Spain and Portugal. 1825

Simons, Theodor. Spanien. 1880

Williams, Leonard. The arts and crafts of older Spain. 1907

Periodical

La Moda elegante illustrada. 1842-85

20th century

Estadística taurina anual ... año [1], 1931+

Fitz-Gerald, J. D. Rambles in Spain. 1910

Hielscher, Kurt. Picturesque Spain; architecture, landscape, life of the people. 1922

Penfield, Edward. Spanish sketches. 1911

BY REGION OR PROVINCE

Hoyos Sáinz, Luis de. Etnografía española; cuestionario y bases para el estudio de los trajes regionales. 1922

Ivori, Joan d'. Vestidos típicos de España. 1936

Ortiz Echagüe, José. España, tipos y trajes. 1933

Ortiz Echagüe, José. Spain; types and costumes. 1934

Ortiz Echagüe, José. Spanische kopfe; bilder aus Kastilien, Aragonien und Andalusien. 1929

Palencia, Isabel de. The regional costumes of Spain; their importance as a primitive expression of the aesthetic ideals of the nation. 1926

Palencia, Isabel de. El traje regional de España: su importancia como expresión primitiva de los ideales estéticos del país. 1926

Twenty illustrations of Spanish costumes. 1832

Los Valencianos pintados por si mismos. 1859

Williams, Leonard. The land of the Dons. 1902

Andalusia

Andalusian annual for MDCCCXXXVII; edited by M. B. Honan. 1836

Aragon

Arco, Ricardo del. El traje popular Altoaragones. 1924

Asturias

Vigil, Fausto. Artículos de Fausto Vigil sobre los trajes y costumbres asturianas. 1924

Basque provinces

See Basque provinces

Catalonia

Amades, Joan. Gegantes, nans i altres entremesos. [1934]

Costums de Catalunya. 1935

See also Masks—Catalonia

Spain—*Continued*

Estremadura

Hispanic society of America. Extremadura costume: women's festival dress at Montehermoso, Caceres. 1931?

Madrid

Kany, C. E. Life and manners in Madrid, 1750-1800. 1932

See also Street venders—Spain—Madrid

Pyrenees

See Pyrenees

Salamanca

Hispanic society of America. Choricero costume: Candelario, Salamanca. 1931

Hispanic society of America. Costume of Candelario, Salamanca. 1932

Hispanic society of America. Women's dress for church: Candelario, Salamanca. 1931

See also Capes and cloaks

Segovia

Calvert, A. F. Valladolid, Oviedo, Segovia, Zamora, Avila, & Zaragoza. 1908

Spain. Davillier, J. C., baron

Spain. See Hielscher, Kurt. Picturesque Spain

Spain and Portugal. Shoberl, Frédéric, ed.

Spain costume details: jewelry. Hispanic society of America

Spain costume details: women's coiffure. Hispanic society of America

Spain; types and costumes. Ortiz Echagüe, José

Spalart, Robert von

Versuch über das kostum der vorzüglichsten völker ... bearbeitet von Robert von Spalart und fortgesetzt von Jakob Kaiserer ... hrsg. von Ignatz Albrecht. Wien, In der Ederischen kunsthandlung 1796-1837

2pts. in 10 vol. 423pl. O. and atlases (242 col.pl.) ob.Q.

Contents: Abt.1, Alterthum: t 1 Kostum der Aegypter und Griechen (27 pl.); t2 Kostum der barbarischen nationen, der Hebräer und Indier (40 pl.); t3 Kostum der Römer, der Etruscer, Lateiner, Samniter, der Marsen und Sabiner (43 pl.); t4 Anmerkungen und ergänzungen ... von Leopold Ziegelhauser (15 pl.)

Abt.2, Mittelalter: t 1 Kostum der Gothen, Sueven und Vandalen, der Hunnen, der Angelsachsen und Dänen (35 pl.); t2 Kostum der Franken vom fünften jahrhunderte bis in das zwölfte, und der Normänner (35 pl.); t3 Geschichte des ritterwesens im mittelalter (60 pl.); t4 Kostum der geistlichen orden (47 pl.); t5 Trachten der Franzosen, Italiener, Neiderländer, Schweizer, Burgunder und Deutschen (73 pl.); t6 Anmerkungen und ergänzungen ... von Leopold Ziegelhauser (48 pl.)

French edition: *Tableau historique des costumes, des moeurs, et des usages des principaux peuples de l'antiquité et du moyen âge* (Metz, Collignon 1804-09. 7v. 287 col.pl. O. and atlases of 213 col.pl. ob.Q.)

Colas 2782-2784. Lipperheide 47

Spallart, Robert de. See Spalart, Robert von

Spanien. Boehn, Max von

Spanien. Simons, Theodor

Spanien und die Spanier. See Cuendias, M. G. de. L'Espagne pittoresque, artistique et monumentale

Die **spanische** armee in ihrer gegenwärtigen uniformirung ... nebst erläuterungen und mittheilungen über organisation, eintheilung und stärke der spanischen armee. Leipzig, M. Ruhl [1896]

22p. 16pl.(incl. 108 col.illus.) O.
Colas 2607

Spanische kopfe. Ortiz Echagüe, José

Das **spanische** militär in Hamburg 1807-8. Holtzmann, Th.

Der **spanische** successions-krieg. See Decker, Paul. Repraesentatio belli

Spanish arms and armour. Calvert, A. F.

Spanish sketches. Penfield, Edward

Spanish vistas. Lathrop, G. P.

Sparre, V. L. E.

(illus.) Nyblaeus, G. A. Scener ur indelta soldatens lif

Sparrow, Walter Shaw

British sporting artists from Barlow to Herring. London, J. Lane; New York, C. Scribner [1922]

xvii,249p. col.front. pl.(part col.) sq.Q.
Shows English hunting dress from the 17th-19th centuries
LC 23-6120

Henry Alken. London, Williams and Norgate; New York, C. Scribner 1927

xxiv,55p. front. pl.(part col.) Q. (The sport of our fathers, v. I)
Shows English hunting dress of the 19th century
LC 29-10570

Ein **spaziergang** um die welt. Huebner, J. A., graf von

Specht, F. A. K. von

Geschichte der waffen. Leipzig, Luckhardt 1869-77

3v. 59pl. O.
Lipperheide 2424

Special exhibition of sword guards, April 1907. See Okabe-Kakuya. Japanese sword guards

Specifications for the uniform of the United States army, 1915. United States. Quartermaster corps

Specifications for the uniforms of the Chinese navy. China. President

Specifications for uniforms to be worn by civilians. United States. War dept.

Specimen monachologiae. See Born, Ignaz, Edler von. John Physiophilus's Specimen of the natural history of the various orders of monks

Specimen of the natural history of the various orders of monks. Born, Ignaz, Edler von

Specimens of English ecclesiastical costume. Carter, John

Specimens of Japanese classical dresses. Fuku sen shiryo kenkyi kai, Tokio

Specimens of the ancient sculpture and painting. Carter, John

Speckter, Otto

(illus.) Endrulat, Bernhard. Das Schillerfest in Hamburg am 11., 12. u. 13. novbr. 1859

Spectacles. See Eyeglasses and lorgnettes

Spectacles and eyeglasses. Phillips, R. J.

Spectacula ossia caroselli, tornei, cavalcate e ingressi trionfali. Forcella, Vincenzo.

Spectaculorum in susceptione Philippi Hisp. prin. divi Caroli. v ... Antverpiae aeditorum, mirificus apparatus. See Schryver, Cornelis. La tresadmirable, tresmagnificque, & triumphante entree

Speculum humanæ salvationis

Speculum humanae salvationis cum speculo S. Mariae Virginis, latine et germanice. [Augsburg, G. Zainer, 1472?]
269 l. 192 illus. F.
Third edition published ca1475. A facsimile reproduction of the third edition was published (London, C. J. Stewart 1861. 72,33p. 116 illus.) A French translation has title: *Miroir du salut humain* (ca1465-75. 54 l. 192 illus.) The French translation is a manuscript on parchment
Shows costume of the 15th century
Lipperheide 411, 408, 403. LC 10-1042 (1861 ed.)

Speculum passionis domine nostri Ihesu Christi. Pinder, Ulrich

Speight, Alexanna

A lock of hair: its history, ancient and modern, natural and artistic; with the art of working in the hair. London, 1871
122p. 24pl. O.

Spekke, Arnolks

Vecākie latvju tautas apgērba zīmējumi. Rīgā, A. Gulbis 1934
41p. 5pl. D.
Plates show Lettish costume

Spekter, Otto

(illus.) Lappenberg, J. M. Die miniaturen zu dem Hamburgischen stadtrechte vom jahre 1497

Speleers, Louis

Le costume oriental ancien. Bruxelles, [1923]
78p. VIII pl. O.
Deals with ancient Assyrian, Egyptian, Babylonian, and Persian costume
Colas 2785

Spell of Belgium. Anderson, Mrs I. W. P.

Spell of Brittany. See Mansfield, M. F. Rambles in Brittany

Spell of Norway. See Monroe, W. S. In Viking land, Norway

Spell of Tyrol. McCrackan, W. D.

Spencer, Herbert

Descriptive sociology; or, Groups of sociological facts, classified and arranged by Herbert Spencer. Comp. and abstracted by David Duncan ... Richard Scheppig ... and James Collier [and others] London, Williams and Norgate 1873-1934
17v. F.
Volumes 1-8 were issued also with American imprint (New York, D. Appleton 1873-1881)
Gives definite, brief information on clothing and weapons and traces their development in each country from early times to the middle of the 19th century. Primitive tribes are included. The following volumes have costume value: v 1 English (p58-61); v2 Ancient Mexicans, Central Americans, Chibchas, and ancient Peruvians (p65-7); v3 Types of lowest races, Negritto races, and Malayo-Polynesian races (p130-33, 138-40); v4 African tribes (p350-55, 366-71); v5 Asiatic races (p52-55); v6 Races of North and South America (p49-53); v7 Hebrews and Phoenicians (p112-116); v8 France (p144-46, 148-49); v9 Chinese (p268-74, 284-88); v11 Ancient Egyptians (p72-77); v12 Hellenistic Greeks (p74-6); v13 Mesopotamia (p44-7); v15 The Romans (p300-11, 155-59)
LC 9-34189, 10-5814 (Amer. ed.)

Spener

Die jetzige frauenkleidung und vorschläge zu ihrer verbesserung. Berlin, H. Walther 1897
36p. 10 illus. O.
Colas 2786. Lipperheide 3307

Speyer, Christian

(illus.) Poten, Bernhard von. Unser volk in waffen

Spiegel der ehren des ... erzhauses Osterreich. Fugger, J. J.

Spiegel der menschlichen behaltniss. Augsburg, H. Schönsperger 1492
295, 288 l. 253 illus. F.
Pictures of Lucifer's fall, life of the first men, Noah's ark, etc., the figures in fifteenth century costume. An edition of the *Speculum*
Lipperheide 422

Spiegel für kunst, eleganz und mode. See Der Spiegel, zeitschrift

Spiegel und abbildung der vergengligkeit. Graminaeus, Dietrich

Der **Spiegel;** zeitschrift für die elegante welt, mode, literatur, kunst, theater. 1.-20. jahrg., 1828-1847. Ofen, Verlegt und hrsg. von F. Wiesen
20v. col.illus. O.-Q.
Title varies: v 1-19, 1828-47: *Spiegel für kunst, eleganz und mode*
Colas 2787. Lipperheide 4610

Spiegeltjen, vertoonende 't lanck ende cort hayr. Boxhorn, M. Z. van

Spieghel der alderschoonste courtisanen deses tyts. See Passe, Crispijn van de. Le miroir des plus belles courtisannes

Spieghel der allerschönsten courtisannen dieser zeyt. See Passe, Crispijn van de. Le miroir des plus belles courtisannes

Spiele und belustigungen der Russen aus den niedern volks-klassen. Richter, J. G.

Spielzug der völker. Rumpf, Fritz, and Erich, O. A., illus.

Spiess, Karl

Die deutschen volkstrachten. Leipzig, B. G. Teubner 1911
138p. illus. D. (Aus natur und geisteswelt; sammlung wissenschaftlich-gemeinverständlicher darstellungen, 342. bdchen.) M. 1.25
Bibliography: p124-31
LC 11-5933

Spilsbury, F. B.

Picturesque scenery in the Holy Land and Syria, delineated during the campaigns of 1799 and 1800. London, G. S. Tregear 1823
viii,70p. col.front. 19 col.pl. Q.
Eight of the plates show costume
Colas 2788. Lipperheide 1460. LC 5-3522

Spindler, Charles

Ceux d'Alsace, types et coutumes; dessins originaux de Ed. Elzingre. Paris, Horizons de France 1928
135p. col.illus. col.pl. Q. (Provinces de France v2)

Spindler, Charles—*Continued*
(illus.) Laugel, Anselme. Trachten und sitten im Elsass

Spitzen des 16. bis 19. jahrhunderts. Strassen, Melchior zur

Spitzen und weiss-stickereien. Dresden. K. Kunstgewerbemuseum

Spitzen-album. Helbing, K.

Spitzen-album. Ilg, Albert

Das **spitzenklöppeln.** Lipperheide, Frieda

Spitzen-musterbuch. Hoffmann, Wilhelm

Sponsel. See Schmidt, jt. auth.

Spooner, Shearjashub
(ed.) Boydell, John, and Boydell, Josiah. The American edition of Boydell's Illustrations of the Dramatic works of Shakspeare

Der **sporn** in seiner formen-entwicklung. Zschille, Richard, and Forrer, Robert

Sport costume
Alken, H. T. The national sports of Great Britain. 1821
Allemagne, H. R. d'. Récréations et passe-temps. 1905
Barlow, F. Severall wayes of hunting, hawking, and fishing, according to the English manner. 1671
Boehn, Max von. Modes & manners of the nineteenth century. v4 p199-[226]
Bogeng, G. A. E. Geschichte des sports aller völker und zeiten. 1926
Frost, A. B. Sports and games in the open. 1899

See also Archers (Sport); Baseball costume; Bicycle costume; Bloomer costume; Boating costume; Bull-fighters—Spain; Cricketers; Falconers; Fencers, fighters with bayonets, etc; Fishermen; Football costume; Golf costume; Gymnasium dress; Hockey costume; Hunting costume; Jockeys; Motoring costume; Polo costume; Riding costume; Shooting costume; Skating costume; Skiing; Tennis costume; Wrestlers

Ancient times

Berlin. Staatliche museen. Sport und spiel bei Griechen und Römern. 1934

19th century

Aspin, Jehoshaphat. A picture of the manners, customs, sports and pastimes, of the inhabitants of England. 1825
Schmidt, F. A. Anleitung zu wettkämpfen, spielen und turnerischen vorführungen bei volks- und jugendfesten. 1900
Strutt, Joseph. The sports and pastimes of the people of England. 1876

20th century

Aflalo, F. G., ed. The sports of the world. 1903
Bonney, Thérèse, ed. Remember when—a pictorial chronicle of the turn of the century and of the days known as Edwardian. 1933
Dier, J. C. A book of winter sports. 1912
Giese, Fritz. Körperseele; gedanken über persönliche gestaltung. c1927
Jessup, E. H. Snow and ice sports. 1923
Paret, J. P. The woman's book of sports; a practical guide to physical development and outdoor recreation. 1901
Patten, William. The book of sport. 1901

Sport im bild. Jahrg. 1-40, 1895-Sept. 1934. Berlin, 1895-1934
Illus. F.
Published bi-weekly; weekly 1895-1928
Each number has a section on fashions
Absorbed *Ross und reiter,* April, 1904. Superseded by *Der Silberspiegel*

Sport und spiel bei Grieschen und Römern. Berlin. Staatliche museen

Sports and games in the open. Frost, A. B.

Sports and pastimes of the people of England. Strutt, Joseph

Sports of the world. Aflalo, F. G., ed.

Sprengel, David
Från det moderna Danmark. Stockholm, A. Bonnier [1904]
469p. front. (port.) illus. pl. facsims. O.
Many of the illustrations show costume
LC 5-22001

Springer, Jaro. See Model, Julius, jt. auth.

Spry, William James Joseph
Life on the Bosphorus; doings in the city of the sultan. Turkey, past and present, including Chronicles of the caliphs from Mahomet to Abdul Hamid II. London, H. S. Nichols 1895
xix,244,330p. front. illus. pl. ports. fold. map. Q. 21s, o.p.
Includes many portraits of the caliphs
Costume index. LC 1-2105

Spurs
Jahn, Martin. Der reitersporn, seine entstehung und früheste entwicklung. 1921
Lacy, C. de L. The history of the spur. 1911
Zschille, Richard, and Forrer, Robert. Der sporn in seiner formen-entwicklung, ein versuch zur characterisirung und datirung der sporen unserer kulturvölker. 1891-99

Staatliche museen zu Berlin. See Berlin. Staatliche museen

Stack, Edward
The Mikirs; from the papers of the late Edward Stack; ed., arranged and supplemented by Sir Charles Lyall. Published under the orders of the government of eastern Bengal and Assam. London, D. Nutt 1908
xvii,183p. col.front. pl.(part col.) map. O.
Pages 5-6 and the colored plates deal with costume of the Mikirs, a Tibeto-Burman race inhabiting the province of Assam
LC A11-1025

Stacke, Ludwig Christoph
Deutsche geschichte; in verbindung mit anderen von L. Stacke; 2. unveränderte aufl. Bielefeld und Leipzig, Velhagen & Klasing 1880-81
2v. illus. pl.(part col.) ports. maps(part fold.) facsims.(part fold.) O.
Contents: v 1 Von der ältesten zeit bis zu Maximilian I; v2 Von Maximilian I. bis zur neuesten zeit
Lipperheide 593. LC 2-24129

Stackelberg, Otto Magnus, freiherr von
Trachten und gebräuche der Neugriechen. Berlin, G. Reimer 1831
28,4p. col.front. xxx,x col.pl. F.
Shows Greek dress of the period
French edition: *Costumes & usages des peuples de la Grèce moderne* (Paris, P. Marino ca1835 30 col.pl.)
Colas 2790-2791. Lipperheide 1448-1449

Stade, Bernhard
Geschichte des volkes Israel. Berlin, G. Grote 1887-88
2v. illus. 30pl. maps. facsims. O. (Allgemeine geschichte in einzeldarstellungen, 1. hauptabth., 6. th.)
Contents: v 1 Geschichte Israels unter der königsherrschaft, von B. Stade; v2 Geschichte des vorschristlichen Judenthums bis zur griechischen zeit, von B. Stade. Das ende des jüdischen staatswesens und die entstehung des Christenthums, von O. Holtzmann
Lipperheide 145. LC G-2483

Staden, Hans, and Lery, Jean de
Americae tertia pars memorabilẽ provinciae Brasiliae historiam continẽs ... Nunc autem latinitate donatam à Teucrio Annaeo Privato ... Addita est Narratio profectionis Ioannis Lerij in eamdem provinciam, quae ille initio gallicè conscripsit, postae verò latinam fecit. Francofurti ad Moenum, apud I. Wechelum, impensis T. de Bry MDXCII [i. e. 1597?]
296p. 7 l. 49 col.illus. map. F. (In Bry, Theodor de [Grands voyages] pt.3)
Second Latin edition: 1605; third Latin edition: 1630. First German edition of Staden's narrative: *Warhafftige historia unnd beschreibung einer landtschafft der wilden ... leuten in der neuen welt* (Frankfurt-am-Main 1556) A German edition of 1593 has title: *Dritte buch Americae*
Lipperheide 1611. LC CA9-6424

Stadler, Joseph Constantine
(engr.) Porter, Sir R. K. The costume of the inhabitants of Russia
(engr.) Smith, C. H. Costume of the army of the British Empire according to the regulations, 1814.

Stadling, Jonas Jonsson, and Reason, Will
In the land of Tolstoi; experiences of famine and misrule in Russia. New York, T. Whittaker 1897
xiv,286p. front. illus. 11pl. 2 port. O.
LC 4-16671

Stadlinger, L. J. von
Geschichte des württembergischen kriegswesens von der frühesten bis zur neuesten zeit. Stuttgart, Verlag der K. Hofbuchdruckerei zu Guttenberg 1856
xii,682p. O. and atlas of 36 col.pl. Q.
Plates show military uniforms from 1638 to 1856. The atlas was published separately in 1860 with title: *Abbildungen der kostüme und uniformen des würtembergischen militärs*
Colas 2792

Staehelin, W. R.
Basler portraits aller jahrhunderte. 1. bd. Basel, Frobenius 1919
54 l. illus. 54pl.(1 col.) F.

Ständ und orden der H. Römischen Catholischen Kirchen. Amman, Jost

Stände und handwerker. Amman, Jost

Das **ständebuch.** Amman, Jost

The **stage** and its stars. Paul, Howard, and Gebbie, George, eds.

Stage costume. See Theatrical costume

Stage costumes. Fletcher, Ursula

Stage costuming. Young, A. B.

Stage designs and costumes. Messel, Oliver

Stage-coach and tavern days. Earle, A. M.

La **Stagione;** giornale delle mode. See note under Die Modenwelt

Stagnon, Antonio Maria
Etat général des uniformes des troupes de S. M. le roi de Sardaigne. Turin, 1789
4 l. 84 col.pl. Q.
Colas 2794

Recueil général des modes d'habillements des femmes des etats de sa majesté le roi de Sardaigne. Turin, Reijcends ca1780
43 col.pl. F.
Plates show feminine fashions of all classes of society
Colas 2795. Lipperheide 1255

Stagnon, Giuseppe
Uniformi delle truppe di S. S. R. M. (le roi de Sardaigne) Torino, 1821
91 pl.(89 col.) O.
Colas 2796

Stahl, M. P. J., pseud. See Hetzel, P. J.

Staley, John Edgcumbe
The dogaressas of Venice (the wives of the doges). New York, C. Scribner [1910]
xxxii,333p. col.front. 24pl.(incl. ports.) O. 12s 6d, o.p.
Costume index. LC 10-20381

The guilds of Florence ... illustrated after miniatures in illuminated manuscripts and Florentine woodcuts. London, Methuen [1906]
xxiii,662p. illus. 75pl.(incl. front.) Q.
Shows costume of the gilds of Florence in the 14th and 15th centuries, also other Florentine dress of the period
Bibliography: p585-99
LC 6-37191

Stam und wapenbuch. Amman, Jost

Stamboul, moeurs et costumes. Preziosi, A.

Stamboul, souvenir d'Orient. See Preziosi, A. Stamboul, moeurs et costumes

Stamm-album der brandenburgisch-preussischen armee. Berlin, F. Silber ca1844
20p. 9pl.(5 col.) F.
Lipperheide 2173

Stamm- und wappenbuch. Amman, Jost

Stamm und wappenbuch. See Bry, Theodor de. Emblemata nobilitatis

Der **stammbaum** der allerdurchläuchtigsten hauses Habsburg-Oesterreich. Primisser, Alois

Stammbuch eines Rostocker studenten. See Kohfeldt, Gustav, and Ahrens, Wilhelm, eds. Ein Rostocker studentenstammbuch von 1736/37

Stammliste aller regimenter der königlich-preussischen armee; nebst nachträgen und berichtigungen bis zum 1. junius 1802. Ramm, A. L.

Stanard, Mrs Mary Mann Page (Newton)
Colonial Virginia, its people and customs. Philadelphia and London, J. B. Lippincott 1917
375p. front. pl. ports. facsims. O. $6, o.p.
Costume index. LC 17-30734

Standard or head-dress? Nuttall, Mrs Zelia

Stanley of Alderley, Henry Edward John Stanley, 3d baron
(tr.) Barbosa, Duarte. A description of the coasts of East Africa and Malabar

Stapley, Mildred. See Byne, Mrs M. S.

Stapusch, Paul
(ed.) Scholl, Edouard. Bekleidung und ausrüstung der preuszischen feuerwehren

Starcke, Paul
Der naturgemässe stiefel ... mit specieller berücksichtigung der bekleidung und pflege des fusses bei der armee; 2. aufl. Berlin, E. S. Mittler 1881
88p. 15 illus. 2pl. O.
First edition, 1880
Lipperheide 1742m

Starr, Frederick
Indians of southern Mexico; an ethnographic album. Chicago, 1899
32p. 141pl. ob.Q. $18, o.p.
Costume index. LC 99-5335

Starr, Laura B.
The doll book. New York, The Outing pub. co. 1908
xii,238p. col. front. illus. pl.(part col.) O.
LC 9-45

Stars of the stage. See Paul, Howard, and Gebbie, George, eds. The stage and its stars

Start, Laura Emily
Coptic cloths. Halifax, F. King 1914
35p. front. illus. Q. (Bankfield museum notes, ser.2, no.4)
Contains text and illustrations of ancient Egyptian dress

See also Haddon, A. C., jt. auth.

Stasov, Vladimir Vasil'yevich
L'ornement slave et oriental d'après les manuscrits anciens et modernes. St Petersbourg, Illine 1887
78p. 156pl. F.
Text in Russian and French. Shows Russian decorative designs
Lipperheide 4912

Russkiĭ narodnyĭ ornament"; vypusk" nervyĭ, shīt'e tkanī, kruzheva ... S" ob"i͡asnītel'nym" tekstom". L'ornement national russe, première livraison: Broderies, tissus, dentelles. S.-Peterburg, tīp. tovarīshchestva obshchestvennai͡a pol'za 1872
25p. 35 illus. 82 col.pl. F.
Lipperheide 3956

Stassoff, W. See Stasov", V. V.

States of the Church. See Military costume—Italy—Papal states

Statistische und topographische beschreibung des burggraftums Nürnberg. Fischer, J. B.

Statuta Hospitalis Hierusalem. See Statuta ordinis Sti. Joannis Hierosolimitani

Statuta ordinis Sti. Joannis Hierosolimitani per fratrem Ptolemaeum Veltronium eiusdem ordinis militem cum figuris, earundemque sententiis, ac magnorum magistrorum imaginibus, nuper adiectus. Roma, 1588
203p. 20 illus. 19pl. F.
Originally appeared in 1586 with half title only: *Statuta Hospitalis Hierusalem.* Twelve plates, engraved by Philipp Thomassin, contain 48 portraits of grand masters of the Knights of Malta
Lipperheide 1889

Statuten des königlichen preuszischen ordens vom Schwartzen adler. Cölln, V. Liebpert [1701]
29p. 9pl. F.
Shows the dress of knights of the Order of the Black Eagle. Plates engraved by H. J. Otto
Lipperheide 1899

Statuten für den oesterreichisch-kaiserlichen Orden der eisernen krone ... Statuti per l'Ordine imperiale austriaco della corona di ferro. [Wien, 1860]
16p. 7 l. 6pl. F.
Lipperheide 1933

Statuti per l'Ordine imperiale austriaco della corona di ferro. See Statuten für den oesterreichisch-kaiserlichen Orden der eisernen krone

Statuts de l'ordre du Saint-Esprit au droit desir ou du noeud institué à Naples en 1352 par Louis d'Anjou. Viel-Castel, Horace, comte de

Stavordale, Lord. See Ilchester, G. S. H. F.-S., 6th earl of

Stawitzky, E. H. Ludwig
Geschichte des infanterie-regiments von Lützow (1. Rheinisches) nr. 25 bis zum jahre 1857 und seines stammes, der infanterie des von Lützow'schen freikorps; 2. aufl. Berlin, E. S. Mittler 1889
412p. 5 col.pl. O.
Shows Prussian uniforms in 1813, 1815, 1830, 1849 and 1857. Lithographed by F. Kaiser
Lipperheide 2182

The **steam** navy of the United States. Bennett, F. M.

Stecher, J. See Vigne, Félix de. Recherches historiques sur les costumes civils et militaires des gildes et des corporations de métiers

Steel, Mrs Flora Annie (Webster)
India. See entry under Menpes, Mortimer

Steen, Chr.
Den danske armee. Kjöbenhavn, C. Steen 1858
40 col.pl. O.
Cover-title
Colas 2797

Stefánsson, Vilhjálmur
My life with the Eskimo. New York, Macmillan 1913
538p. front. pl. ports. 2 fold. maps. O.
LC 13-24327

Steffahny, Hermine. See Kiesewatter, Doris, jt. auth.

Stehende weibliche gewandstatuen in der hellenistischen plastik. Horn, Rudolf

Stein, Frédéric Alexandre Henri. See Stein, Henri

Stein, Henri

Archers d'autrefois; archers d'aujourd'hui ... illustrations par Léon Laugier. Paris, D. A. Longuet 1925
305p. illus. xx pl.(incl. facsims.) Q.
Shows military archers and archery as a sport
LC 26-6989

See also Gay, Victor. Glossaire archéologique

Steinbüchel, Anton von

(ed.) Heraeus, C. G. Bildnisse der regierenden fürsten und berühmter männer

Steinen, Karl von den

Die Marquesaner und ihre kunst; studien über die entwicklung primitiver südseeornamentik nach eigenen reise ergebnissen und dem material der museen ... Berlin, D. Reimer 1925-28
3v. illus.(incl.maps) F.
Volume 1 shows tattooing done in the Marquesas Islands
LC 25-13309

Steinhausen, Georg

Geschichte der deutschen kultur. Leipzig und Wien, Bibliographisches institut 1904
x,747p. 205 illus. 22pl.(10 col.) O.
Many of the illustrations show costume worn at various periods
Lipperheide 605i. LC 5-8055

Der kaufmann in der deutschen vergangenheit, mit ... abbildungen ... aus dem 15. bis 18. jahrhundert. Leipzig, E. Diederichs 1899
131p. 139 illus. 11pl. O. (Monographien zur deutschen kulturgeschichte, 2. bd.)
Lipperheide 1983

Steininger, Rudolph

Die weiblichen haartrachten im ersten jahrhundert der römischen kaiserzeit. München 1909
48p. O.
Inaugural dissertation, Munich
Colas 2798

Steinlen, Theophile Alexandre

(illus.) Bruant, Aristide. Dans la rue. 1889-95

Stell, John

(ed.) Nicolay, Nicolas, sieur d'Arfeuille. The navigations, peregrinations and voyages, made into Turkie

Stellartius, Prosper

De coronis et tonsuris paganorum, Judaeorum, Christianorum; libri tres. Duaci, B. Belleri 1625
262p. 5 illus. O.
Lipperheide 1646

Stenger, Erich. See Dost, Wilhelm, jt. auth.

Steno-tricographie. Adnet-Molé, Mad.

Stenzel, Alfred

The British navy. London, T. F. Unwin 1898
xi,327p. front. illus.(incl. ports.) pl.(part col.) fold. maps. O.
Translation by A. Sonnenschein of part 2 of the author's *Groszbritannien und Irland: Das heer ... die flotte*
LC 1-10083

Groszbritannien und Irland: Das heer ... die flotte. Berlin, Schaff & Grund 1897
537p. illus. pl.(part col.) fold. maps. O. (Die heere und flotten der gegenwart, 2. bd.)

Stéphane

L'art de la coiffure féminine, son histoire à travers les siècles, par Stéphane, coiffeur de s. m. la reine Élisabeth de Belgique; préface de René Rambaud. Paris, La Coiffure de Paris [1932]
xiii,200p. illus.(incl. ports.) sq.Q. 70fr.
Bibliography: p190
Colas 2800. Costume index. LC 32-19792

Stephani, Ludolf. See Petrograd. Ermitazh. Die alterthümer von Kertsch in der Kaiserlichen Eremitage

Stephanie, le jeune. See Geschichte der kaiserl. königl. regimenter, attributed author

[**Stephanie, J.**]

Abbildung der k. k. oesterreichischen armee durch alle waffengattungen, enthält jedes regiment, corps und militair branche in freyen gruppirungen. Wien, W. Waniek ca1820
36 col.pl. F. 170 fr.
Issued in six parts each with cover-title: *Bildliche darstellung der k.k. oesterreichischen armee aller waffengattungen;* lithografirt von Stephanie
Colas 2801. Lipperheide 2233

Das **sterbende** Afrika. Frobenius, Leo

Sterling, Ada

(ed.) Clay-Clopton, Mrs Virginia. A belle of the fifties. 1905

Stern, Ernst E.

(illus.) Nikolaus, Paul. Tänzerinnen. 1919

Stern, Henry Aaron

Wanderings among the Falashas in Abyssinia; together with a description of the country and its various inhabitants. London, Wertheim, Macintosh, and Hunt 1862
322p. front. illus. pl. ports. fold. map. O.
LC 5-8148

Stern, Norbert

Mode und kultur. Dresden, Expedition der europäischen modenzeitung c1915
2v. illus. pl.(part col.) O.
LC 16-15352

Steuart, Archibald Francis

(ed.) Bury, Lady Charlotte (Campbell) The diary of a lady-in-waiting

Stewart, Alexander

(ed.) Logan, James. The Scottish Gaël

Stewart, Allan

(illus.) Grierson, E. W. The children's book of Edinburgh. 1906

Stewart, Donald William

Old and rare Scottish tartans, with historical introduction and descriptive notices. Edinburgh, G. P. Johnson 1893
61p. 46 l. 1 illus. XLV col.pl. Q.
Plates are mounted samples. Notes on works treating of tartans: p[57]-61
LC 12-29772

Stewart, Hugh
Provincial Russia, painted by F. De Haenen, described by Hugh Stewart. London, A. and C. Black 1913
172p. 32pl.(16 col. incl. front.) fold. map. O.
Colored plates accompanied by guard sheets with descriptive letterpress
LC 15-7303

See also Dobson, George, jt. auth.

Stewart, James
Plocacosmos: or, The whole art of hair dressing. London, Printed for the author 1782
435p. front. 10pl. O.
Plates are engraved by Delegal
Colas 2802. Lipperheide 1681. LC 7-16184

Steyert, André
Aperçu sur les variations du costume militaire dan l'antiquité et au moyen age. Lyon, L. Perrin 1857
46p. 4 col.pl.(incl. 26 illus.) O.
Colas 2803. Lipperheide 2038

Stibbert, Federigo
Abiti e fogge civili e militari dal I al XVIII secolo; raccolta di disegni del cav. Fed. Stibbert ... con pref. e note illustrative di Alfredo Lensi. Bergamo, Instituto d'arti grafiche 1914
9p. 217pl. Q.

Stick-album des Berliner modenblatt. Berliner modenblatt

Die **stickerei** auf netz-canavas. Dillmont, Thérèse de

Stickerei-album des Bazar. Fischbach, Friedrich

Stickerei-muster des slavischen volkes in Mähren, nach original im patriotischen museum in Olmütz. See Sojková, Berta. Vzory vyšwání lidu slovanského na Moravě

Stickmuster für kirchl. linnenzeug im styl des XII.-XIII. jahrhunderts. Stiff, A.

Stickmuster für schule und haus. Stuhlmann, A.

Stickmuster in altdeutschem stile für leinen-stickerei. Hillardt, Gabriele

Sticks, walking sticks. See Canes

Stiff, A.
Stickmuster für kirchl. linnenzeug im styl des XII.-XIII. jahrhunderts. Marienwerth bei Maastricht, Holland, Im selbstverlag d. verf. [1884]
4p. 25 col.pl. F.
Lipperheide 4007

Stil im kinderkleid. Donner, Mizi, ed.

Der **stil** unserer kleidung. Bruns, M. S.

Stilisirte blumen aus allen kunstepochen. Herdtle, Eduard

Stilistiche muster für stickerei und hakelei. Fischbach, Friedrich

Stillfried und Rattonitz, Rudolf Maria Bernhard, graf von
Die attribute des neuen deutschen reiches. Berlin, A. Duncker 1872
29p. 16pl. Q.
Third edition: 1882
Lipperheide 1768-69

Die kroenung ihrer majestaeten des koenigs Wilhelm und der koenigin Augusta von Preussen zu Koenigsberg am 18. october 1861. Berlin, R. v. Decker 1868
174p. 10 l. 84p. 22 illus. 15pl. F.
Lipperheide lists an edition of 1873 with the same text and 12 plates
Lipperheide 2549-50

Stillfried und Rattonitz, Rudolph Maria Bernhard, graf von, and Haenle, S.
Das buch vom Schwanenorden. Berlin, W. Moeser 1881
238p. 40pl. Q.
Lipperheide 1940

Stillman, Ernest Goodrich
(ed.)Brockhaus, Albert. Netsukes

Stimmer, Tobias
(engr.) Giovio, Paolo, bp. of Nocera. Pauli Iovii Novocomensis episcopi nucerini Elogia virorum bellica virtute illustrium
(engr.) Giovio, Paolo, bp. of Nocera. Pauli Iovii Novocomensis episcopi nucerini Elogia virorum literis illustrium
(illus.) Crescenzi, Pietro de. Neu feldt und ackerbau
(illus.) Reusner, Nicolaus. Icones sive imagines vivae, literis cl. virorum
(illus.) Sebizius, Melchior. XV bücher von dem feldbaw

Stirling-Maxwell, Sir William, bart. See Hogenberg, Hans. The procession of Pope Clement VII. and the Emperor Charles V.

Stitches. See Needlework

Stockholm. Hallwylska palatset
Catalogue of the collection of arms and armour at Hallwyl house, Stockholm. Stockholm, Central tryckeriet 1928
117p. illus. XVI pl. D.
Translated by Edward Adams-Ray
Contents: Group XXXIV Arms and armour, European; Group XXXV Arms and armour, Oriental
LC 28-21027

Stockholm. Livrustkammaren
Kongl. lifrustkammaren och därmed förenade samlingar planscher ... utforda ... under ledning af A. Lagrelius, text af C. A. Ossbahr. Stockholm, Generalstabs. litogr anstalt 1897-1901
2v. illus. 95pl.(1 col.) F.
French title-page: *L'armurie royale et les collections y incorporées*

Stockholm. Nationalmuseum
Recueil de plusieurs fragments des premières comédies italiennes qui ont esté représentées en France sous le regne de Henri III ... conservé au Musée national de Stockholm ... présenté par Agne Beijer ... suivi de compositions de m. don Arlequin présentées par P. L. Duchartre. Paris, Duchartre et Van Buggenhoudt [1928]
33p. 62p. of illus.(part col.) F.
Chiefly full-page illustrations. Each shows several figures from the Italian comedies of the 16th century, including many harlequin costumes

Stockholm. Nordiska museet
Svenska allmogedräkter. See entry under Cederblom, Gerda, ed.
Svenska folkdräkter. See entry under Wistrand, P. G. V.
Svenska folklivsbilder. See entry under Cederblom, Gerda, ed.

Stockings. See Hose

Stöcklein, Hans
Meister des eisenschnittes; beiträge zur kunst- und waffengeschichte im 16. und 17. jahrhundert. Esslingen a. N., P. Neff 1922
156p. col.front. mounted illus. pl. Q.
The illustrations show swords

Störcklin, J. H.
(engr.) Deyerlsperg, G. J. von. Erb**huldigung**

Stokes, Adrian
Hungary; painted by Adrian & Marianne Stokes, described by Adrian Stokes. London, A. and C. Black 1909
xix,320p. 75 col. pl.(incl. front.) fold. map. O. 20s, o.p.
Each plate accompanied by guard sheet with descriptive letterpress
Costume index. LC w10-123

Stokes, Mrs Marianne (Preindlsberger)
(illus.) Stokes, Adrian. Hungary

Stolle, C.
Lübeck's bürger-militair. Lübeck, Borchers 1837
9 col.pl. F.
Colas 2805

Stone, Mrs Elizabeth
Chronicles of fashion, from the time of Elizabeth to the early part of the nineteenth century, in manners, amusements, banquets, costume, &c. London, R. Bentley 1845
2v. 15 ports.(incl. fronts.) O.
Colas 2806. Lipperheide 1005. LC 3-19731

Stone, George Cameron
A glossary of the construction, decoration and use of arms and armor in all countries and in all times, together with some closely related subjects. Portland, Me. The Southworth press 1934
694p. front. illus. F.
Bibliography: p687-94
LC 34-38895

Stone, Melicent
The Bankside costume book for children. London, W. Gardner, Darton & co. [1913]
xii,173p. front. illus. pl. diagrs. D. 5s
Also published (Akron, O., Saalfield 1915. $1)
Colas 2807. Costume index. LC 14-13977

Stone monuments, tumuli and ornament of remote ages. Waring, J. B.

Stop, pseud. See Morel-Retz, L. P. G. B.

Stop, M et Mme, pseud. See Saint-Hilaire, É. M. H.

Stores dentelles & broderies dans le style moderne. Prévot, Gabriel

Stores, guipures et broderies d'art dans le style moderne. See Prévot, Gabriel. Stores dentelles & broderies dans le style moderne

Storia degli ordini monastici religiosi e militari. See Hélyot, Pierre. Histoire des ordres monastiques, religieux et militaires

Storia del costume dei popoli attraverso i secoli. Lorenzini, Paolo

Storia della corona ferrea dei re d'Italia. Bombelli, Rocco

La **storia** della mode. Genoni, Rosa

Storia delle mode: Italia dagli Etruschi circa 800 anni avanti l'era Cristiana fino al secolo XVIII; Francia dal secolo XV al 1854. Milano, Corriere delle dame 1854
134p. 48 illus. 67pl. O.
Colas 2811. Lipperheide 1285

Storia di Roma dalle origini italiche sino alla caduta dell' impero d'occidente. Bertolini, Francesco

La **storia** di Venezia nella vita privata dalle origini alla caduta della repubblica. Molmenti, P. G.

Storia do Mogor. Manucci, Niccolò

Storia e costumi delle contrade di Siena. Hercolani, Antonio

Storia e costumi delle diciassette contrade di Siena. Forno, F.

Storia ed analisi degli antichi romanzi. Ferrario, Giulio

Story, Alfred Thomas
Swiss life in town and country. New York and London, G. P. Putnam's sons 1902
282p. front. 19pl. D. (Our European neighbours) $1.20, o.p.
Costume index. LC 2-3099

Story, Mrs Margaret (McElroy-Frost)
Individuality and clothes, the blue book of personal attire ... illustrated by Dale Adams. New York and London, Funk & Wagnalls 1930
xxvi,454p. front. illus. pl.(part double, part col.) O.
A revision of her *How to dress well* (New York and London, Funk & Wagnalls 1924) Many of the chapters have been rewritten and the rest are brought up to date
LC 30-12012, 24-22282 (1924 ed.)

Story of Arthur and Guinevere. E., G. R.

Story of costume told in pictures. Northrup, Belle, comp.

Story of hosiery. May hosiery mills, inc., Burlington, N. C.

Story of the stick in all ages and lands. Fernand-Michel, F. F.

Stote, Dorothy
Making the most of your looks ... with ... illustrations by Dorothy Cochran Boardman. New York, F. A. Stokes 1935
x,218p. front.(port.) illus. O.
Earlier edition, illustrated by Judy Bushnell (New York, Brentano's 1926)
LC 36-27031

Stothard, Charles Alfred
The monumental effigies of Great Britain; selected from our cathedrals and churches ... from the Norman conquest to the reign of Henry the Eighth. London, Printed by J. M'Creery 1817
23, 112p. col.front. illus. 144pl.(part col.) port. F.
Introductions and descriptions by A. J. Kempe, 1932. Illustrations show English kings, queens, princes, and heroes of the 12th to 15th century
Lipperheide 992. LC 17-8789

Stothard, Thomas. See Smirke, Robert. Picturesque beauties of Shakespeare

Strachey, Lionel
(tr.) Ruete, Frau Emilie. Memoirs of an Arabian princess

Die **strafen** der Chinesen. Hempel, Friedrich

Strange, Edward Fairbrother
Japanese illustrations; a history of the arts of wood-cutting and colour printing in Japan. London, G. Bell 1897
xx,155p. col.front. illus. pl.(part col.) O. (The Connoissuer series)
Shows Japanese dress from the 17th to the 19th century
LC 4-11710

Strantz, Victor von
Das internationale Rote kreuz (*In* Boguslawski, Albrecht von. Deutschland)

Strasbourg. See Alsace—Strasbourg

Strasbourg. Municipal council. See Relation des fêtes données par la ville de Strasbourg à leurs majestés impériales et royales, les 22 et 23 janvier 1806

Strasbourg illustré. Piton, Frédéric

Strasbourg militaire. Touchemolin, Alfred

Strasburger trachtenbuechlein darinnen von man und weibs personen aussgangen ihm jhar 1660. [Strassburg] P. Aubry 1660
57pl. O.
Many reprints at different dates, e.g. 1668, 1680. Some of the plates are reproduced in *L'Alsace françoise*
Colas 2812-14. Lipperheide 789w

Strasburgisch trachtenbuchlein. Dieterlin, Petrus

Strassburger ansichten und trachtenbilder aus der zeit des dreissigjährigen krieges. Hollar, Wenceslaus

Strassburger Sackkalender. See Berger-Levrault, Oscar. Les costumes strasbourgeois

Strassen, Melchior zur
Spitzen des 16. bis 19. jahrhunderts aus den sammlungen des Kunstgewerbemuseums zu Leipzig. Leipzig, K. W. Hiersemann 1894
2pts. 50pl. F. (Ornamentale und kunstgewerbliche sammelmappe, ser. 4-5)
Lipperheide 4057

Strassgschwandtner, A. See Pettenkoffer, August, jt. auth.

[**Straszewicz, Joseph**]
Armée polonaise; révolution du 29 novembre 1830. Paris, chez l'éditeur 1835
8p. 2 col.pl. Q.
Colas 2815

Stratilesco, Tereza
From Carpathian to Pindus; pictures of Roumanian country life. London, T. F. Unwin 1906
xii,379p. front. illus. pl. 2 maps. O.
LC 7-28495

Stratz, Carl Heinrich
Die frauenkleidung. Stuttgart, F. Enke 1900
x,186p. 102 illus. O.
Several editions. Also published with Dutch title: *De kleeding van de vrouw* (Amsterdam, Scheltema & Holkema 1901. 118 illus.)
Colas 2816-17. Lipperheide 3309-3311

Straub, A. See Herrad von Landsberg, abbess of Hohenburg. Hortus deliciarum

Street venders
Curiöser spiegel. 1804?

Austria

Vienna

Brand, C. Zeichnungen nach dem gemeinen volke besonders der kaufruf in Wien. 1775

Danzig

Deisch, Matthaeus. Danziger ausrufbilder. ca1780

East (Near East)

Hunglinger von Yngue, A. M. Abbildungen und beschreib. herumziehender krämer von Constantinopel, nebst andern stadteinwohner und fremden aus Aegypten, d. Barbarei und d. Archipelagus, nach d. natur gezeichnet. 1803

England

London

Amiconi, Jacob. Londoner ausrufer. 1739
Bridge, Sir Frederick. The old cryes of London. 1921
Busby, T. L. Costume of the lower orders of London. 1820
Busby, T. L. Costume of the lower orders of the metropolis. ca1820
The cries of London. 1839
Les cris de Londres au XVIIIe siècle. 1893
Description of the plates, representing the itinerant traders of London in their ordinary costume. 1804
Lauron, Marcellus. The cries of London ... being 72 humorous prints. ca1760
Lauron, Marcellus. The cryes of the city of London. 1711
Leighton, John. London cries and public edifices. 1851
Nicholson, William. London types. 1898
Roberts, William. The cries of London. 1924
Rowlandson, Thomas. Characteristic sketches of the lower orders. 1820
Sandby, Paul. Twelve London cries done from the life. 1760
Smith, J. T. The cries of London: exhibiting several of the itinerant traders of antient and modern times. 1839
Smith, J. T. Etchings of remarkable beggars, itinerant traders, and other persons of notoriety in London and its environs. 1815-16
Tuer, A. W. Old London street cries and the cries of to-day. 1885
Wheatley, Francis. Cries of London. 1925

France

Paris

Alphabet des cris de Paris. 1840
Aubry, Charles. Cris de Paris. 1818
Bonnart, J. B. [Cris de Paris] ca1700

Street venders—France—Paris—*Continued*

Bosse, Abraham. Les cris de Paris. ca1640

Bouchardon, Edme. Études prises dans le bas peuple, ou Les cris de Paris. 1737

Bouchardon, Edme. Les cris de Paris en 9 suites. 1768

Boucher, François. Les cris de Paris. ca1735

Brebiette, Pierre. Les cris de Paris. ca1640

Busby, T. L. Costume of the lower orders in Paris. ca1820

Cris de Paris. ca1825

Doucet, Jérôme. Les petits métiers de Paris. 1901

Duplessi-Bertaux, Jean. Recueil de cent sujets de divers genres. 1814. Part 4

Fournel, F. V. Les cris de Paris, types et physionomies d'autrefois. 1887

Franklin, A. L. A. La vie privée d'autrefois; arts et métiers, modes, moeurs, usages des Parisiens du XII. au XVIII. siècle. [v 2]

Guerard, N. Diverses petitte figure des cris de Paris. ca1730

Joly, Adrien. Les petits acteurs du grand théâtre ou recueil des divers cris de Paris. ca1815

Lurine, Louis, ed. Les rues de Paris. 1844

Poisson, J. B. M. Cris de Paris; dessinés d'après nature par M. Poisson. 1769-75

Roehn, Adolphe. Nouveaux cris de Paris. 1817

Saint-Aubin, Augustin de. Mes gens, ou les commissionnaires ultramontains au service de qui veut les payer. 1766-1770

Société des amis des livres. Paris qui crie. 1890

Vernet, Carle. Cris de Paris. ca1820

Watteau, L. J. Cris et costumes de Paris. 1786

Wattier, Édouard. Les cris de Paris. 1822

Germany

Berlin

Dörbeck, F. B. Berliner ausrufer, costume und locale gebräuche. ca1830

Henschel, W., and Henschel, F. A. Cries of Berlin. ca1810

Rosenberg, J. C. W. Les cris de Berlin. ca1790

Göttingen

Heumann, G. D. Die in Göttingen herüm schriende lühe, od. der göttingische ausruf. ca1740

Hamburg

Suhr, Christoffer. Der ausruf in Hamburg. 1808

Leipzig

Richter, J. S. Unterweisung für anfänger beyderley geschlechts im zeichnen. 1790-91

Nuremberg

Gabler, Ambrosius. Nürnberger ausrufer mit darstellung der vornehmsten stadttheile Nürnbergs. 1789

Italy

Bologna

Carracci, Annibale. Le arti di Bologna. 1646

Carracci, Annibale. L'arti per via. ca1740

Carracci, Annibale. Di Bologna, l'arti per via. 1660

Carracci, Annibale. Diverse figure al numero di ottanta. 1646

Rome

Brambilla, Ambrosius. Ritratto de quelle che vano vendendo et lavorando per Roma con la nova agionta de tutti quelli che nelle altre mancavano sin al presente. 1582

Villamena. Cris de Rome. ca1620

Trieste

Bosa, Eugenio. Gridatori ed altri costumi popolari di Trieste. 1835

Venice

Bosa, Eugenio . Crieurs et autres costumes populaires de Venise. 1835

Bosa, Eugenio. Sogetti pittoreschi e costumi di Venezia incisi all' acqua forte. ca1840

Zompini, Gaetano. Le arti che vanno per via nella città di Venezia. 1785

Portugal

Lisbon

Coleçaõ de estampas intitulada ruas de Lisboa. 1820

Russia

Orlowski, G. Russian cries. 1809

Leningrad

Collection de cris et costumes de paysans et paysannes de St. Pétersbourg. 1823

Le Prince, J. B. Oeuvres de Jean-Baptiste Le Prince. 1782

Shönberg, and Geissler, C. G. H. Description des planches relatives aux crieurs publics de St Pétersbourg. 1794

Scotland

Edinburgh

Old Edinburgh pedlars, beggars and criminals. 1886

Spain

Madrid

Los gritos de Madrid. ca1810

Kany, C. E. Life and manners in Madrid, 1750-1800. 1932

Switzerland

Zürich

Herrliberger, David. Züricherische ausruffbilder. 1748-51

Street venders—*Continued*

Turkey

Constantinople

Hunglinger von Yngue, A. M. Abbildungen und beschreib. herumziehender krämer von Constantinopel, nebst andern stadteinwohner und fremden aus Aegypten, der Barbarei und d. Archipelagus, nach d. natur gezeichnet. 1803

United States

New Orleans

Frémaux, L. J. New Orleans characters. 1876

Les **strelits**; encienne et seule milice de Russie. See Le Prince, J. B. Oeuvres

Strick buch. Fischerin, Dorothea

Die **strickarbeit.** Dillmont, Thérèse de

Das **stricken.** Georgens, J. D.

Stridbeck, Johann Friedrich

Representation des modes et habillements de Strasbourg. [Strasbourg] Le Roux 1756

1 l. 15pl. S.

Plates are signed: Striedbeck

The same plates are republished in *Nouveau calendrier du diocèse de Strasbourg ... pour l'année bissextile 1780* (Strasbourg, J. F. Leroux 1780)

Colas 2819-20

Striedbeck, Johann Friedrich. See Stridbeck, J. F.

Strimmer, Hermann

Kleidung und schmuck der Römer zur zeit des Horaz, nach dessen gedichten zusammengestellt. Meran, Im selbstverlage des gymnasiums 1889

31p. O.

From *Programm des K. K. Ober-gymnasiums in Meran* (1888-89)

Lipperheide 264

Strindberg, August. See Lundin, Claës jt. auth.

Stripes and types of the Royal navy ... showing the dress and duties of all ranks from Admiral to Boy Signaller; by F. W. R. M. and J. S. H. London, Gale and Polden 1909

62p. illus. D. 1s

Stroebe, Lilian Luise

Die altenglischen kleidernamen; eine kulturgeschichtlich-etymologische untersuchung. Borna-Leipzig, R. Noske 1904

84p. O.

Inaugural dissertation—Heidelberg

LC 5-31902

Ströbel, Christian. See Helm, Seb., jt. auth.

Stroganov, Sergîeĭ Grīgor'evich, graf. See Russia. Komītet dlîa îzdanîia drevnosteĭ Rossiĭkago gosudarstva. Drevnostī Rossīĭskago gosudarstva

Strokirch, Einar von

Kungliga lifgardet till häst; regementets historia i kort sammanfattning. Stockholm, Aftonbladets 1914

28 pl.(16 col.) O.

Svenska arméns munderingar 1680-1905. Stockholm, A. Bonnier 1911-12

5v. 152pl.(part col.) Q.

Strong, Mrs Eugénie (Sellers)

(ed.) Furtwängler, Adolf. Masterpieces of Greek sculpture

Structural basis to the decoration of costumes among the Plains Indians. Wissler, Clark

Strutt, Joseph

Complete view of the dress and habits of the people of England ... New and improved ed with critical and explanatory notes by J. R. Planché. London, H. G. Bohn [1842]

2v (v 1: x p, 2 l. cxvii,117p. v2: 6, 279p.) 151pl.(147 col.) Q. 84s, o.p.

First edition was published 1796 to 1799. A French edition was begun but never finished

Pictures are from manuscripts in the British museum and in the Bodleian library at Oxford, and are in excellent coloring. They show English costume from the earliest times to the beginning of the 17th century

Jehoshaphat Aspin's *Picture of the manners,* etc. is based on the work of Strutt and contains many of the same illustrations, much reduced in size

Colas 2824-25. Lipperheide 1001

Horda Angelcynnan: or A compleat view of manners, customs, arms, habits &c. of the inhabitants of England from the arrival of the Saxons to the present time. London, Printed for W. Shropshire 1775-76

3v. 158pl. Q.

A French translation of volumes 1-2 had title: *Angleterre ancienne* (Paris, Maradan 1789 68pl.)

Colas 2821-2822. LC 2-30219 (Fr. ed.)

The regal and ecclesiastical antiquities of England ... A new and improved ed. with critical and explanatory notes, by J. R. Planché. London, H. G. Bohn 1842

152p. 72 col. pl. Q. 42s o.p.

"Containing the representations of all the English monarchs from Edward the Confessor to Henry the Eighth; and of many persons that were eminent under their several reigns ... carefully edited from ancient illuminated manuscripts." Subtitle

Also known with plates in black and white only. First published 1773 with 60 plates; and a supplement, 1792, with 12 plates. New editions were issued 1777 and 1793

Colas 2823. Lipperheide 1002. LC 5-15803

The sports and pastimes of the people of England ... from the earliest period to the present time. London, Chatto & Windus 1876

12,530p. 137 illus. 39 col.pl. Q.

"Including the rural and domestic recreations, May games, mummeries, shows, processions, pageants, and pompous spectacles." Subtitle

The plates are from miniatures in old English manuscripts

First issued 1901. Many editions, including one edited by J. Charles Cox (new ed. enl. & corr. London, Methuen [1903] 41pl. F.)

Colas 2826. Lipperheide 1012, 1012a. LC 3-31738 (1903 ed.)

Struve, George Adam

Georgii Adami Struvii ... Tractatio juridica de eo quod justum est circa vestitum civium, von der bürger kleider-

Struve, George Adam—*Continued*
ordnung; in acad. Jenensi 1675 habita; editio novissima. Halae Magdeb. typis et impensis J. C. Hendelii [1724]
78p. Q.
Lipperheide 3321

Stseny îz" russkago narodnago byta, risovany s" natury. Savinov, V. N.

Stuart, Charles Edward. See Stuart, J. S. S., jt. auth.

Stuart, Henry Windsor Villiers. See Stuart, Villiers

Stuart, John Sobieski Stolberg
(ed.) Vestiarium scoticum

Stuart, John Sobieski Stolberg, and Stuart, Charles Edward
The costume of the clans with observations upon the ... Highlands and Western Isles during the middle ages. Edinburgh, J. Menzies 1845
lxiii,171p. 36pl. F.
According to *Halkett and Laing,* the above names are pseudonyms of John Hay Allan and Charles Stuart Hay Allan. Library of Congress form has been followed
Plates show costume of the clans from the 13th to the 18th century
Also published: Edinburgh, J. Grant 1892
Colas 2804. Lipperheide 1030. LC 11-19832

Stuart, Martinus
De mensch, zoo als hij voorkomt op den bekenden aardbol ... afgebeeld door J. Kuyper. Amsterdam, J. Allart, 1802-07
6v. col.front. 43pl.(41 col.) O.
Contents: v 1-2 Zuidzee eilanders; v3-4 Australia, America; v5-6 Africa
Lipperheide 1576. LC 2-160

Stuart, Villiers
The funeral tent of an Egyptian queen; printed in colours, in facsimile, from the author's drawings taken at Boulak. London, J. Murray 1882
xii,163p. fold.front. illus. pl.(part col. part fold.) Q.
"A remarkable piece of Egyptian needlework, the funeral tent of Isi em Kheb (21st dynasty) discovered at Deir el Bahri. It is a mosaic of leatherwork, pieces of gazelle hide of several colours, stitched together." Encyclopaedia Brittannica
The funeral tent shows decorative designs. Other colored illustrations show costume of the period
LC 2-13045

Stubenrauch, Philipp von; Schindler, Johann Josef, and Höchle, Johann Nepomuk
Darstellung der k. k. österr. armee nach der neuesten adjustirung; mit bewilligung des k. k. hofkriegsrath. Wien, Artaria ca1821
16 col.pl. F.
Contains eight plates from drawings by von Stubenrauch, four from Schindler and four from Höchle. Plates are engraved by H. Mansfield, Erhard and Beyer. According to Colas the twelve plates by Stubenrauch and Schindler were reprinted about 1902 without the name of the publisher
Colas 2827. Lipperheide 2232

Stuber, Nikolaus Gottfried
(illus.) Edlweckh, Johannes. Triumphus virtutum in funere Caroli VII ... anno ... MDCCXLV

Studenten-lebens. See Konrad, K. G. Zur bilderkunde des deutschen studentwesens

Studenten-typen. Kneppelhout, Johannes

Das **studentenleben** in 30. kupfern vorgestellet. Winterschmidt, A. W.

Students

See also Military cadets

England

Ackermann, Rudolph. The history of the colleges of Winchester, Eton, and Westminster; with the Charter-house, the schools of St. Paul's, Merchant Taylors, Harrow, and Rugby and the Free-school of Christ's hospital. 1816

Germany

Fabricius, Wilhelm. Die deutschen corps. 1898

Fick, Richard, ed. Auf Deutschlands hohen schulen. 1900

Reicke, Emil. Lehrer und unterrichtswesen in der deutschen vergangenheit. 1901

16th century

Behaim, Paulus. Briefe eines Leipziger studenten aus den jahren 1572 bis 1574. 1880

Neyffer, J. C. Illustrissimi Wirtembergici ducalis novi collegii quod Tubingae quâ situm quâ studia quâ exercitia, accurata delineatio. ca1580

18th century

Dendrono. Natüralich abschilderung des academischen lebens. ca1725

Kohfeldt, Gustav, and Ahrens, Wilhelm, eds. Ein Rostocker studenten-stammbuch von 1736/37. 1919

19th century

Geiling, F. W. Bilder aus dem deutschen studentenleben. 1865

20th century

Konrad, K. G. Zur bilderkunde des deutschen studentwesens. 1921

Netherlands

Kneppelhout, Johannes. Studenten-typen. 1904

Studien nach der natur zur staffage von landschaften. Quaglio, Lorenz

Studien zu der entwicklungsgeschichte des orientalischen kostüms. Tilke, Max

Studien zur kostümgeschichte der blütezeit Hollands. See Thienen, F. W. S. van. Das kostüm der blütezeit Hollands, 1600-1660

Studies in East Christian and Roman art. pt. II. See Dennison, Walter. A gold treasure of the late Roman period

Studies in the Chinese drama. Buss, Kate

The **Studio, periodical**
Beauty's awakening. See entry under Art workers guild, London
A book of old embroidery. See entry under Holme, Geoffrey, ed.
Chronicler of European chivalry. See entry under Coulton, G. G.
Modern design in jewellery and fans. See entry under Holme, Charles, ed.

Studio, periodical—*Continued*
Peasant art in Italy. See entry under Holme, Charles, ed.
Peasant art in Roumania. See entry under Oprescu, George
Peasant art in Russia. See entry under Holme, Charles, ed.
Settings & costumes of the modern stage. See entry under Kommīssarzhevskiĭ, F. F., and Simonson, Lee
Shakespeare in pictorial art. See entry under Salaman, M. C.

Studio delle virtuose dame. Parasole, I. C.

Studniczka, Franz
Beiträge zur geschichte der altgriechischen tracht. Wien, C. Gerold's sohn 1886
143p. 47 illus. O. (Abhandlungen des Archäologisch-epigraphischen seminares der Universität Wien, hft. VI, 1. t.)
Bibliographical foot-notes
Colas 2828. Lipperheide 200

A **study** of costume. Sage, Elizabeth

A **study** of the Roman toga. Wilson, L. M.

Stübel, Alfons. See Reiss, Wilhelm, jt. auth.

Stümcke, Heinrich
Die deutsche theaterausstellung, Berlin 1910. Berlin, Gesellschaft für theatergeschichte 1911
xii,58p. XLV pl. O. (Schriften der Gesellschaft für theatergeschichte, bd. XVII)
Shows masks of the 16th century, harlequin costume of the 17th century, and theatrical costume of the 19th century

Stürmer, Heinrich
(illus.) Sammlung von national-trachten und andern zu charakter-masken passenden kostümen

Stürmer, Karl
(illus.) Förster, Friedrich. Die perle auf Lindahaide

The **stuffs** of China. Ardenne de Tizac, J. H. d'

Stuhlfeld, Willy
(ed.) Devrient, Eduard. Geschichte der deutschen schauspielkunst. 1929

Stuhlmann, A.
Stickmuster für schule und haus. Stuttgart und Berlin, W. Spemann 1890-93
2v. illus. 149pl. Q.
Lipperheide 4014

Stummel, Helene
Paramentik. Kempten, J. Kösel & F. Pustet 1923
4v. pl. Q.
Issued in 15 parts, 1914-23. Explanatory text in English, French, and German. Volumes 1-2 show ecclesiastical vestments of various periods

Sturm, Florentine
(ed.) Georgens, J. D. Das häkeln
(ed.) Georgens, J. D. Das stricken

Sturm, Marie
(ed.) Georgens, J. D. Das häkeln
(ed.) Georgens, J. D. Das stricken

Stuttgart. See Military costume—Germany—Wurttemberg—Stuttgart

Stuttgarter bühnenkunst. Gerhäuser, Emil

Stuyvesant, Rutherfurd
The collection of arms and armor of Rutherfurd Stuyvesant, 1843-1909; by Bashford Dean. [New York] [The De Vinne press] 1914
xiv,174p. front.(port.) illus. LI mounted pl. F.
LC 15-26842

Styl; blätter für mode und die angenehmen dinge des lebens. Jahrg. 1-3, 1922-1924. Berlin, O. v. Holten
3v. col.illus. col.pl. Q.
Published bi-monthly

Style, a monthly magazine of fashions for women. v. 1-7, v. 8, no. 1-6; Oct. 1901-Aug. 1909. New York [Morse pub. co. etc]
8v. illus. pl.(part col.) F.
Title varies: Oct. 1901-Jan. 1905, *The American dressmaker.* Feb. 1905-July 1907, *Style and American dressmaker.* Jan. 1908-Aug. 1909, *Style* (Subtitle varies)
Editors: Oct. 1901-Jan. 1904, E. DeW. Morse; Feb. 1904-Apr. 1906, Mme. Baker and others; May 1906-July 1907, Mrs. Linda R. Wade; Jan. 1908-Aug. 1909
Official organ of the National dressmakers' association, 1905-06
No more published?
LC 11-24777

Style, combined with Paris fashion magazine. v 1, 1916+ New York, Style institute
Illus.(part col.) F. $2 a year
Published bi-monthly. Current 1938
Present title since 1933 when it absorbed *Paris fashion book,* with Oct./Nov. 1933 issue, and added the subtitle

Le **Style** parisien. no. 1-7; août 1915-fev. 1916. Paris, Librairie centrale des beaux-arts
1v. illus. pl.(part col.) F.
Published monthly. No more issued. Editor, L. Vogel. Superseded by *Les élégances parisiennes*

Style reporter. v 1, June 12 1933+ New York, W. Friedman, inc.
Illus. Q. $10
An underwear fashion journal. Published semi-monthly; monthly Aug.-Sept. 1933; weekly (irregular) June 12-July 1933. Current 1938
Planographed

Style trend; devoted exclusively to the interests of the washable garment, fabric and related industries. v 1+ March 1928+ New York, Modes and fabrics, inc.
Illus. Q. $12 a year
Published eight times a year. Current 1938

Stylepark hats, inc.
Hats of the world; interesting styles in hats worn in many lands, compliments of your Stylepark dealer. [Philadelphia, Pa., The Bingham co. c1935]
Cover-title, 19p. illus. D.
LC A35-1807

Styles for men. Spring/Summer 1926+ New York, American gentleman pub. corp.
Pl. F.
Published semi-annually. A folder of plates supplementary to *American gentleman and sartorial art journal.* Current 1938

Styria

Ancient

Sann, Hans von der. Altsteirische trachten. 1891

Styria—*Continued*

Modern

See Austria—Styria

Suberwick, Mme de. See Cuendias, M. G. de, jt. auth.

Succession de el rey D. Phelipe. Ubilla y Medina, Antonio, marqués de Rivas

Sudamerika, Westindien, Zentralamerika. Schumacher, Karl von

Sudan, Anglo-Egyptian

Neufeld, Charles. A prisoner of the khaleefa; twelve years' captivity at Omdurman. 1900

See also Nubia

Sudslävische ornamente. Lay, Felix

Suecia antiqua et hodierna. Dahlberg, E. J.

Les **Suédois,** moeurs et coutumes, tableaux et legendes. See Vallander, J. V. Svenska folket

Südseearbeiten. Finsch, Otto

Suffling, Ernest Richard

English church brasses from the 13th to the 17th century. London, L. U. Gill 1910

xii,456p. front. illus. pl. O.
Shows English costume and armor
LC A11-2069

Suhr, Christoffer

Abbildungen der uniformen aller in Hamburg seit den jahren 1806 bis 1815 einquartiert gewesener truppen. [Paris] ca1899

158 col.pl. Q.
Reissued with a French title: *Représentation des uniformes de toutes les troupes qui ont été casernées à Hambourg de l'année 1806 à l'année 1815* (Leipzig, K. W. Hiersemann 1902)
Shows military uniforms of Spain (30pl.), Italy (4pl.), France (58pl.), Holland (35pl.), Westphalia (7pl.), the allies of France (5pl.), the allies of Germany (5pl.), Denmark (3pl.), Sweden (1 pl.), Russia (7pl.)
Colas 8-9

Der ausruf in Hamburg; vorgestellt in ein hundert und zwanzig colorirten blättern, gezeichnet, radirt und geäzt von professor Suhr, mit erklärung begleitet. Hamburg, C. Miller 1808

8, 146p. 120 col.pl. O.
Published in 10 livraisons at 3 marks (Hamburg) each. Text is by K. J. H. Hübbe. Each plate has letterpress with words
Also published in reprint edition (Berlin, H. Barsdorf 1908. 22,146p. 120 col.pl. O.) with an introduction by Joseph Heckscher entitled *Der ausruf in Hamburg in literatur, kunst und geschichte*
Suhr's *La regratterie de Hambourg* (Hambourg, 1808. 3 l. 120 col.pl. O.) contains the same plates. Three preliminary leaves give a translation of the German letterpress
Colas 2829-2830. Lipperheide 807m. LC 14-7663 (1908 reprint)

Hamburgische trachten gezeichnet und gestochen von C. Suhr ... Costumes de Hambourg. [Hambourg] 1808

2 l. 36 col.pl. F.
Plates are stamped: Suhr. Colas gives a list of the plates

The same title published 1912 also contains 36 plates of which nos. 8 to 36 are the same as in the edition above. Plates 1-7 are new and entitled *Kleidertracht in Hamburg*
Colas 2831-32

Hamburgische trachten, gezeichnet und gestochen von C. Suhr ... Costumes de Hambourg ... Costumes of Hamburg ... Hamburg, 1838. [Berlin, H. Barsdorf 1908]

52p. L col.pl. F.
"Diese in 10 lieferungen erfolgte subscriptionsausgabe ... erschien in im verlage von Hermann Barsdorf in Berlin ... Derselben lagen die originalausgaben von 1806, 1808, 1815, 1822 und 1838 zugrunde. Sie ist gegen diese um 14 blatt, davon 4 handzeichnungen, vermehrt und enthält ausserdem eine einleitung von dr. J. Heckscher: *Suhrs Hamburgische trachten*"
"Bibliographisches verzeichnis": p47-52
LC 16-8661

—Heckscher, Joseph. Chr. Suhrs Hamburgische trachten; criticism. 1909

Sammlung verschiedener spanischer nationaltrachten und uniformen der division des Marquis de la Romana, 1807 und 1808 in Hamburg in garnison; gezeichnet von Christ. Suhr, radirt und geätzt von Corn. Suhr. [Hamburg], ca1808

1 l. 18 col.pl. F.
Colas 2833. Lipperheide 2357

See also note under Hyllested, H. C. Collection complète des uniformes de la marine et de l'armée danoise

Suhr, Cornelius

(engr.) Suhr, Christoffer. Sammlung verschiedener spanischer national-trachten

Suhr, H.

Leitfaden für den gründlichen unterricht im maassnehmen und façonzeichnen der zuschneidekunst für damen. Berlin, 1878

16p. 4pl. O.
Second edition has title: *Praktische schule der zuschneidekunst für damen; leitfaden zur erlernung des maassnehmens, façonzeichnens u. zuschneidens der damenkleider* (32p. 10pl.(2 col.)
Lipperheide 3816-17

La **Suisse.** Eyriès, J. B. B.

Suisse—Costumes anciens. Föhn, Michael

Suisse—Costumes modernes. Föhn, Michael

La **Suisse** et ses inhabitants. See Leuthold, H. F. Costumes suisses en mignature

La **Suisse** historique et pittoresque, comprenant l'histoire, la geographie et la statistique de ce pays, avec un precis des antiquités, du droit public, de la littérature, des arts et de l'industrie des vingt-deux cantons. Genève, C. Gruaz 1855-56

2v. illus. pl. Q.
Some of the plates show military uniforms and costume
Contents: v 1 La Suisse historique, par E. H. Gaullieur; v2 La Suisse pittoresque, par C. Schaub
LC 5-8538

Suisse—jeux et usages. Föhn, Michael

Les **Suisses.** Suter, Jakob

Suite de differens costumes de paysans et paysannes de la Suisse. Mechel, Christian von

Suite de mendiants. See Duplessi-Bertaux, Jean. Recueil de cent sujets de divers genres

Suite de militaires de différentes armes. See Duplessi-Bertaux, Jean. Recueil de cent sujets de divers genres

Suite de militaires de différentes armes. Duplessi-Bertaux, Jean

Suite de nouvelles modes françoises; avec les différentes grandeurs de boucles, chapeaux retapez à la Suisse, à la Corse; bourses longues, crapeaux, etc. Paris, P. Laurent 1776
6pl. Q.
Colas 2834

Suite de soldats, Première. Loutherbourg, P. J. de

Suite des cris des marchands ambulants de Paris, par J. D. Bertaux. See Duplessi-Bertaux, Jean. Recueil de cent sujets de divers genres

Suite des figures, Seconde. Loutherbourg, P. J. de

Suite d'estampes, pour servir à l'histoire des modes, et du costume en France, dans le XVIIIe siècle. Paris, Bligny 1778
10 col.pl. D.
Plates, without legend or signature of the artist, are sometimes attributed to Desrais. Each plate shows a man and woman in the costume of the period
Cataloged from Colas
Colas 2835

Suite d'ouvriers de différentes classes. See Duplessi-Bertaux, Jean. Recueil de cent sujets de divers genres

Suites des nouvelles modes françoises depuis 1778 jusqu'à ce jour. Desrais, C. L.

Suites d'estampes pour servir à l'histoire des moeurs et du costume des Français dans le dix-huitième siècle. Freudenberger, Sigmund

Sujets composés et dessinés sur pierre. Madou, J. B.

Sulla milizia cisalpino italiana. Cenni storico-statistici, dal 1796 al 1814. Zanoli, Alessandro, baron

Sullivan, Mark
Our times; the United States, 1900-1925 New York, C. Scribner 1926-35
6v. illus. (incl.ports, maps, facsims. music) O.
Other editions
Contents: v 1 The turn of the century, 1900-1904; v2 America finding herself; v3 Pre-war America; v4 The war begins, 1909-1914; v5 Over here, 1914-1918; v6 The twenties
LC 26-7896

Sullivan, William Kirby
(ed.) O'Curry, Eugene. On the manners and customs of the ancient Irish

Sulzbach, Franz Philipp, pfalzgraf von. See note under Florin, F. P. Oeconomus prudens et legalis

Sumatra
Hurgronje, C. S. The Achehnese. 1906
Marsden, William. The history of Sumatra. 1811

Summer at Baden-Baden. Guinot, Eugène

Sumptuary laws
Lipperheide (nos.3321-3423) gives a list of regulations governing clothing and dress in various countries of Europe, with special emphasis on the 16th to 18th centuries and on the laws of Germany. The Lipperheide entries have not been repeated here
Advis sur l'usage des passements d'or et d'argent. 1610
Bartsch, L. Sächsische kleiderordnungen aus der zeit von 1450-1750. 1882
Berlepsch, H. A. von. Chronik vom ehrbaren und uralten schneidergewerk. 1850
Evelyn, John. Tyrannus, or The mode, in a discourse of sumptuary laws. 1661
Vincent, J. M. Costume and conduct in the laws of Basel, Bern, and Zurich, 1370-1800. 1935

Sunder, Lucas. See Cranach, Lucas

The **Sundhya,** or the daily prayers of the Brahmins. Belnos, Mrs. S. C.

Sungaria
Carruthers, A. D. M. Unknown Mongolia. 1914

Suomalaisia koristeita. Schvindt, Theodor

Suomalaisia pukuja. Appelgren-Kivalo, Hjalmar

Supplies for Royal arch chapters and councils of R. and S. masters. Lilley, M. C., & co., Columbus, O.

Sur la meilleure forme des souliers. Camper, Petrus

Surveyors
Pfintzing, Paul. Methodus geometrica. 1598

Survivance du culte solaire dans les coiffures féminines en Bretagne, Auvergne, Savoie, Bourbonnais, etc. Gagnier, G.

Susane, Louis Auguste Victor Vincent
Histoire de l'ancienne infanterie française, par Louis Susane. Paris, J. Corréard 1849-53
8v. O. and atlas of 8p. 152 col.pl. Q.
Plates are from designs by Philippoteaux. They were later published separately with title: *Musée retrospectif de l'infanterie française*
Colas 2838. LC 25-5938

Sussmann, Anton
Die armeen der Türkei und Griechenlands, ihre organisation, bewaffnung, ausrüstung und uniformierung. Leipzig, M. Ruhl [1914]
20p. 7 col.pl. D. (Die armeen der Balkan-staaten, v2)
Die armeen Rumäniens und Bulgariens; ihre organisation, bewaffnung, ausrüstung und uniformierung. Leipzig, M. Ruhl [1914]
32p. illus. 3 col.pl. D. (Die armeen der Balkan-staaten, v3)
Plates show the Bulgarian army only
Die armeen Serbiens und Montenegros, ihre organisation, bewaffnung, ausrüstung und uniformierung. Leipzig, M. Ruhl [1914]
11p. 6 col.pl. D. (Die armeen der Balkan-staaten, v 1)

Sussmann, Anton—*Continued*
Die österreich-ungarische armee, ihre organisation, uniformen, ausrüstung, bewaffnung, distinktionen und sonstigen abzeichen. Leipzig, M. Ruhl [1911]
53p. incl. 186 illus. on 16 col.pl. O.

Suter, Jakob
Costumes suisses. Paris, London, New York. Goupil ca1840
24? col.pl. F.
Colas 2839

Les Suisses; ses types et costumes. Paris & New York, Goupil [1858]
12 col.pl. F.
Cataloged from cover. Plates show feminine figures, half-length, in medallions. Lithographed by Sirowy, Regnier, E. Desmaisons and Thielley after J. Suter
Colas 2840. LC 5-13849

Sutor, Jakob
Neu künstliches fechtbuch ... gedruckt zu Franckfurt am Mayn durch Johann Bringern, in verlegung Willhelm Hoffmans, 1612; neu hrsg ... durch J. Scheible. Stuttgart, J. Scheible 1849
104p. 93 illus. Q.
Lipperheide 2956

Sutter, Conrad
Gutenberg-feier Mainz 1900; offizielle darstellung des historischen festzuges nach den originalentwürfen. Mainz, L. Wilckens [1900]
1 l. 18 col.pl. sq.Q.
Lipperheide 2849

Suttner, Gustav, freiherr von
Der helm von seinem ursprunge bis gegen die mitte des siebzehnten jahrhunderts, namentlich dessen hauptformen in Deutschland, Frankreich und England. Wien, C. Gerold's sohn 1878
52p. illus. 48pl.(38 col.) Q.
Lipperheide 2427

Suzuki Harunobu. Kurth, Julius

Svedman, Karl Villhelm
Costume of Sweden. London, Rodwell and Martin 1823
22 col.pl. F.
Lithographed by D. Dighton
Colas 2841. Lipperheide 1046

Svenska allmogedräkter. Cederblom, Gerda, ed.

Svenska allmogens lif i folksed, folktro och folkdiktning. Norlind, Tobias

Svenska armeens. Nordmann

Svenska arméens och flottans nuvarande uniformer. Fritze, C. E., pub.

Svenska arméens uniformer. Huldberg, Adolf, pub.

Svenska arméns munderingar 1680-1905. Strokirch, Einar von

Svenska arméns och flottans nuvarande uniformer ... Die Schwedische armee und marine in ihrer gegenwärtigen uniformirung. Eklund, P. B.

Svenska armens och flottans officers. Engelhart, Gustaf

Svenska folkdrägter. Hård, illus.

Svenska folkdräkter. Wistrand, P. G. V.

Svenska folket. Vallander, J. V.

Svenska folkets seder. Dahlström, C. A.

Svenska folklivsbilder. Cederblom, Gerda, ed.

Svenska folktyper. Lundborg, H. B.

Svenska galeriet. Martin, J. F.

Svenska konungar och deras tidehvarf. Arvidsson, A. I.

Svenska krigsmaktens fordna och närvarande munderingar. Schützercrantz, Adolf

Svenska mönster för konst-väfnader och broderier. Kulle, Jakob

Svenska national drägter. Ekman, R. W.

[**Svenska** national-dräkter] No place, A. E. Strand 1894
20 col.pl. O.
Colas 2844

Svenska och norska arméerna samt flottorna i deras nuvarande uniformering. See Dardel, F. L. von. Den svenske og den norske armees

[**Svenska** och norska folkdrägter] Fot. af Eurenius & Quist. No place, ca 1885
18 col.pl. O.
Plates show 40 Swedish and Norwegian costumes
Colas 2846. Lipperheide 1056

Den **svenske** og den norske armees samt marines uniformer. Dardel, F. L. von

Svetloff, V. pseud. See Ivchenko, V. I.

Swan, Order of the
Hillert, Adolph. Der Schwanenorden; seine geschichte, statuten und bedeutung. 1844
Stillfried und Rattonitz, R. M. B., graf von, and Haenle, S. Das buch vom Schwanenorden. 1881

The **Swan** Shakespeare. Shakespeare, William

Swart, P. de
Afbeelding van de kaamer en 't paradebed waar op het lyk van ... Anna, kroon princesse van Groot-Brittanje, princesse douariere van Orange en Nassau ... 1759 Gravenhage, P. Grosse 1759
4p. 4pl. F.
Text and title also in French. French title: *Description de la chambre et lit de parade sur lequel le corps d'Anne, Princesse Royale de Grande-Bretagne ... a été exposé*
Lipperheide 2675

Afbeelding van de zaal en 't praalbed waar op het lyk van ... Willem Karel Hendrik Friso, prinse van Orange en Nassau ... in de manden November en December des jaars MDCCLI, ten toon is gesteld geweest. Amsterdam, F. Changuion 1752
3 l. 40p. 43pl.(part col.) F.
Lipperheide 2673

Swebach, Bernard Edouard. See Swebach, Edouard

Swebach, Edouard
Armée française, 1831. Paris, Engelmann 1831?
12 col.pl. ob.F.
Colas 2848

Sweden
Billow, Anders. Pictorial Sweden; nature and culture of the past and present. 1932
Brenner, Eli. Thesaurus nummorum Sueo-Gothicorum. 1731
Cederblom, Gerda, ed. Svenska allmogedräkter. 1921

Sweden—*Continued*

Cederblom, Gerda, ed. Svenska folklivsbilder. 1923

Costumes nationaux des provinces de la Suède. 1850

Dahlberg, E. J. Suecia antiqua et hodierna. 1691-1715

Hård, illus. Svenska folkdrägter med tio lithocromierade plancher af Hård m. fl. 1857

Hård, illus. Swedish costumes. 1858

Holme, Charles, ed. Peasant art in Sweden, Lapland and Iceland. 1910

Lundborg, H. B. Svenska folktyper. 1919

Norlind, Tobias. Svenska allmogens lif i folksed, folktro och folkdiktning. 1912

Pufendorf, Samuel, freiherr von. Samuelis liberi baronis de Pufendorf De rebus a Carolo Gustavo Sveciae rege gestis ... 1696

Wistrand, P. G. V. Svenska folkdräkter. 1907

See also subhead Sweden under Ceremonial and festival costume; Children; Funerals; Kings and rulers; Military costume; Naval costume; Orders of knighthood and chivalry

Primitive and early

Hildebrand, Hans. Das heidnische zeitalter in Schweden; eine archaeologisch-historische studie. 1873

Peringskiöld, Johan. Ättartal för Swea och Götha konunga hus. 1725

14th to 15th centuries

Hildebrand, H. O. H. Den kyrkliga konsten under Sveriges medeltid. 1907

16th-19th centuries

Afbildningar af nordiska drägter; utgifna af H. Thulstrup, met en kort svensk och fransk text af J. H. Kramer. 1888-89

Afbildningar af svenska national dräkter. 1907

Arnz & compagnie, Düsseldorf. Bilder aus dem schwedischen volksleben. 1855

Arvidsson, A. I. Svenska konungar och deras tidehvarf, en samling af porträtter öfver namkunniga personer med bifogade korta lefnadsteckningar. 1830-1843

Belin, A., and others. Costumes de Suède, Norvège, Danemark, Hollande et Allemagne. 186-?

Berg, J. A. Bilder ur svenska folklifvet. 1855

Camino, Charles, and Régamey, Frederic. Costumes suédois. 187-?

Dahlström, C. A. Svenska folkets seder, bruk och klädedrägter. 1863

Ekman, R. W. Svenska national drägter. 1847-49

Forssell, C. D. Album pittoresque du nord; tableaux des costumes, moeurs et usages des paysans de la Suède. 1843

Grafström, A. A. Ett år i Sverge. 1827

Grafström, A. A. Une année en Suède ou Tableaux des costumes, moeurs et usages des paysans de la Suède. 1836

Lovett, Richard. Norwegian pictures. 1890

Lundin, Claës, and Strindberg, August. Gamla Stockholm anteckningar ur tryckta och otryckta källor framletade. 1882

Martin, J. F. Svenska galeriet, eller porträiter af märkvärdige svenske herrar och fruntimer. 1782-84

Norlind, Tobias. Gamla bröllopsseder hos svenska allmogen. 1919

Porter, Sir R. K. Travelling sketches in Russia and Sweden, during the years 1805, 1806, 1807, 1808. 1809

Svedman, K. V. Costume of Sweden. 1823

Svenska national-dräkter. 1894

Svenska och norska folkdrägter. ca1885

Periodical

Magasin für konst, nyheter och moder. 1823-25

20th century

Larsson, Carl. Åt solsidan. 1914

Larsson, Carl. Ett hem. 1913

Larsson, Carl. Spad-arfoet, mitt lilla landtbruk. 1906

Philip, J. B. Holidays in Sweden. 1930

Philip, J. B. Sommardagar i Sverige. 1915

BY REGION OR PROVINCE

Hilleström, Pehr. Costumes des paysans de divers cantons en Suède. ca1802

Vallander, J. V. Svenska folket sådant det ännu lefver vid elfvom på berg och i dalom. 1864-65

Kopparberg (Dalecaria)

Bosaeus, Ernst. Tafvelgalleri fråm stugor i Dalom. 1905

Skåne

Wallgren, O. Skänska folk drägter. 1872

Uppland

Hammarstedt, Edvard. Allmogens byggnadssätt, boningsinredning och dräkt. 1907

Swedes in the United States

Clay, J. C. Annals of the Swedes on the Delaware. 1858

The **Swedish** army. Eben, Frédéric, baron d'

Swedish costumes. Hård, illus.

The **Swedish** people their customs and manners in pictures and legends. See Vallander, J. V. Svenska folket

Swinburne, Henry Lawrence
The royal navy, painted by Norman L. Wilkinson, described by H. Lawrence Swinburne; with some notes on the costume of the sailors of the past by Commander Charles N. Robinson, illus. by J. Jellicoe. London, A. and C. Black 1907
xx,378p. 61 col.pl.(incl.front.) O.
Plates accompanied by guard sheets with descriptive letterpress
LC 8-15739

Swiss guards
Escher, A. von. Die Schweizer regimenter in fremden diensten 1515-1860. Les régiments suisses au service étranger. 1903

See also Papal guards

Swiss life in town and country. Story, A. T.

Swiss pictures. Manning, Samuel

Switzerland
Baud-Bovy, Daniel. Peasant art in Switzerland. 1924
Collection des costumes suisses. n.d.
Costumes de la Suisse. n.d.
Costumes suisses; T. Richard, phot., Maenedorf. n.d.
Föhn, Michael. Suisse—costumes anciens. 18—?
Hegi, Franz. Sammlung von schweitzertrachten; Collection des costumes suisses. n.d.
Heierli, Frau J. W. Schweizer-trachten, vom XVII-XIX jahrhundert. 1897-98
Lehmann, Hans. Die gute alte zeit; bilder aus dem leben unserer vorväter. 1906
Maurer, H. R. Denkmale des geschmaks der sitten und gebräuche der alten Schweizer. 1792
Vincent, J. M. Costume and conduct in the laws of Basel, Bern, and Zurich, 1370-1800. 1935

See also subdivision Switzerland under Agricultural laborers; Arms and armor; Ceremonial and festival costume; Military costume; Tyrol

Periodical

Zeitschrift für schweizerische geschichte. 1921+

Caricature and satire

Grand-Carteret, John. Les moeurs et la caricature en Allemagne—en Autriche —en Suisse. 1885

Early period

Bernoulli, J. J. B. Museum in Basel; catalog für die antiquärische abtheilung. 1880
Hegi, Franz. Das costume des mittelalters. 1807
Rodt, Eduard von. Historische alterthümer der Schweiz. 1889

14th-16th centuries

Biblia pauperum. Biblia pauperum; nach dem original in der lyceums bibliothek zu Constanz. 1867
Recueil de XII costumes suisses. Holbein, Hans, the younger. 1790

18th century

Aberli, J. L. Costumes de Berne et paysans des environs. ca1782
Mechel, Christian von. Costumes suisses, contenant 28 figures d'après nature, coloriées avec soin. 1791?
Mechel, Christian von. Costumes suisses des différens cantons. ca1820
Mechel, Christian von. Suite de différens costumes de paysans et paysannes de la Suisse. 1785
Ott, J. C. Icones virorum gentis et stirpis Ottiorum in Helvetia praesertim Tiguri litteris armis et toga clarorum propriis sumptibus aeri. 1777-88

19th-20th centuries

Album des costumes nationaux de la Suisse. 1837
Barnard, George. Switzerland; scenes and incidents of travel in the Bernese Oberland. 184-?
Bégin, E. A. N. J. Voyage pittoresque en Suisse, en Savoie et sur les Alpes. 1852
Bleuler, L. Collection des costumes de la Suisse et de ses pays limitrophes. ca1810
Bridgens, Richard. Sketches illustrative of the manners and costumes of France, Switzerland, and Italy. 1821
Collection des costumes de la Suisse et de ses pays limitrophes. 1820?
Costumes suisses ... Costumes of Schwitzerland. ca1830
Eyriès, J. B. B. La Suisse, ou costumes, moeurs et usages des Suisses. 1825
Föhn, Michael. Suisse—Costumes modernes. 1826
Föhn, Michael. Suisse—jeux et usages. 1827
Forestier, Alc. de, ed. Les Alpes pittoresques; description de la Suisse. 1837-38
Fuchslin. Costumes suisses. ca1860
Füssli, R. H. Les costumes suisses les plus origineaux et les plus intéressants dessinés d'après nature. 1830
Jauslin, Carl. Feier zur eröffnung des Schweizerischen landesmuseums 25 juni 1898 Zürich; kostümirter festzug darstellend die schweizerischen volkstrachten in bildern aus dem volksleben. 1898
Keller, J. J. Taschenbuch über die Schweiz. 1800
Lörer, and Vogel. Costumes suisses. ca1825
Lory, Gabriel, and Moritz, F. W., eds. Costumes suisses dédié à son Altesse Royale le prince royal de Prusse. Dessinés d'après nature. 1824
Malerische landerschau in bildlichen darstellungen deutscher und schweizerischer stadte. ca1850
Manning, Samuel. Swiss pictures. 1866

Switzerland—19th-20th centuries—*Cont.*

Neuestes gemälde der erde und ihrer bewohner ... Die Schweiz. 1824
Opiz, G. E. Die Schweizer nach ihrer volksthümlichkeit. ca1830
Recueil de costumes suisses. ca18188
Rochette, D. R. Lettres sur la Suisse écrites en 1819, 1820 et 1821. 1823
Rohr, G. Costumes de femmes suisse. ca1825
Schabelitz, J. C. Collection de 54 costumes originaux de la Suisse. ca1820
Schmid, D. A. Farbige schweizer trachtenbilder. 1929
Shoberl, Frederic, ed. Switzerland. 1828
XVII vorstellungen von deutschen nationaltrachten. 1800
Suter, Jakob. Costumes suisses. ca1840
Suter, Jakob. Les Suisses; ses types et costumes. 1858
Wisard. Collection de costumes suisses dans leurs genres actuels. ca1818
Wisard. Types et costumes féminins de la Suisse. 1818

Periodicals

Marchal document; couture, mode, conseille, renseigne. 1929+
Die Pariser toiletten. 1865-67

BY REGION OR PROVINCE

Cahier de costumes suisses. 1833
Collection de costumes suisses. ca1820
Costumes des cantons de la Suisse. ca1830
Costumes suisses. ca1870
Costumes suisses des 22 cantons. ca1850
Dictionnaire historique et biographique de la Suisse. 1921-34
Dinkel, M., and Locher, N. Recueil de portraits et costumes suisses les plus élégants, usités dans les 22 cantons. ca1820
Graenicher, Samuel. Costumes suisses. 1778-83
Heierli, Frau Julie. Die volkstrachten der Schweiz. ca1922-32
König, F. N. Collection de costumes suisses, tirés du cabinet du M. Meyer d'Aarau. 1802-04
König, F. N. Neue sammlung von schweizertrachten ... Nouvelle collection de costumes suisses. 1811
König, F. N. Nouvelle collection de costumes suisses. ca1810
König, F. N. Nouvelle collection de costumes suisses des XXII cantons. ca1818
Lamy, J. P. .Costumes des cantons. n.d.
Lang, J. L. Recueil de costumes. ca1819
Leuthold, H. F. Costumes suisses en mignature, dessinés d'après nature avec texte explicatif, par F. Meyer. 1837
Nusbiegel, Johann. 24 blatt colorierte Schweizer mädchentrachten. ca1800
Pinelli, Bartolommeo. Raccolta di quindici costumi li piu interessanti della Svizzera. 1813
Pingret, Edouard. Recueil de costumes suisses. 1824-25
Reinhardt, J. C. Collection de costumes suisses des XXII cantons. 1819
Reinhardt, J. C. A collection of Swiss costumes in miniature, designed by Reinhardt ... Collection de costumes suisses d'après les dessins de Reinhardt. 1822
Rullmann, Ludwig. Costumes suisses. 1822
Schweizer-trachten. 18—
Snoeck. Collection générale de costumes suisses; les 32 cantons représentés en 64 figures. 1828
Sommerlatt, C. V. von. Beschreibung der XXII. Schweizer-kantone. 1838
Story, A. T. Swiss life in town and country. 1902
La Suisse historique et pittoresque. 1855-56
Vigneron, P. R. Costumes suisses. 1822
Volmar, G. Collection de costumes des cantons de la Suisse. 1819?
Volmar, G. Nouvelle collection de costumes suisses. 1819
Will, J. M., engr. Samlung europaeischer national trachten. ca1780
Yosy, A. Switzerland, as now divided into nineteen cantons ... with picturesque representations of the dress and manners of the Swiss. 1815
Yves. Costumes suisses des 22 cantons. ca1860

See also Switzerland—18th century; Switzerland—19th century

Basel

Basler kleidung aller hoh und nidriger standts, persone nach deren grad auff jetzige art fleissig corrigiert. 1634
Herrliberger, David. Baslerische ausruffbilder. 1749
Huber, J. R. Recueil de XXIV differens costumes de la ville et du canton de Basle, choisis dans le divers états de la société sur la fin du XVIIe siècle. 1798
Ringle, J. J. Amictus senatus tam politi: quam academ. mulierum, virgin. populique Basileensis acuraté delineatus. ca1650
Staehelin, W. R. Basler portraits aller jahrhunderte. 1919

Bern

Freudenberger, Sigmund. Premier cahier des différens habillements distinctifs de la ville de Berne. 1785

Schaffhausen

Heierli, Frau Julie. Die Klettgauer- oder Hallauertracht des kantons Schaffhausen. 1915

Zürich

Herrliberger, David. Zürcherische kleidertrachten ... Les modes de Zurich. 1749-51

Switzerland—Zürich—*Continued*
Pfeffel, J. A. Schweitzerisches trachten-cabinet, oder allerhand kleidungen, wie man solche in dem löblichen Schweitzer-canton Zürch zutragen pflegt. ca1750
Walch, Sebastian. Portraits aller herren burger-meistern, der vortrefflichen republique, stadt und vor-orths Zürich, von dem 1336ten bisz auf das 1742te jahr. 1756

See also Street venders—Switzerland—Zurich

Switzerland. Barnard, George

Switzerland, as now divided into nineteen cantons. Yosy, A.

Sword
Andersen, C. C. T. The chronological collection of the kings of Denmark. 1878
Berlin. Staatliche museen. Die bronze-schwerter des Königlichen museums zu Berlin. 1878
Bottet, Maurice. L'arme blanche de guerre française au XVIIIe siècle. 1910
Carrington-Peirce, P. A handbook of court and hunting swords, 1660-1820. 1937
Dreger, Max. Schwerter-sammlung ... Collection of swords. 1927
Emerson, Edwin. German swordplay. c1936
Hutton, Alfred. The sword and the centuries. 1901
Rowlandson, Thomas. Hungarian & Highland broad sword. 1799
Stöcklein, Hans. Meister des eisenschnittes; beitrage zur kunst- und waffengeschichte im 16. und 17. jahrhundert. 1922
Wilczek, J. N., graf von. Erinnerungen eines waffensammlers. 1908

Japan
Armor and arms club, New York. Catalogue of a loan exhibition of Japanese sword fittings. c1924
Armor and arms club, New York. Catalogue of a loan exhibition of Japanese sword guards. c1922
Field museum of natural history, Chicago. Japanese sword-mounts in the collections of the Field museum. 1923
Hawkshaw, J. C. Japanese sword-mounts. 1910
Naunton, G. H. Japanese sword fittings. 1912
New York. Metropolitan museum of art. The Gōda collection of Japanese sword fittings. 1924
Okabe-Kakuya. Japanese sword guards. 1908

Norway
Lorange, A. L. Den yngre jernalds svaerd. Et bidrag til Vikingetidens historie og teknologi. 1889

The **sword** and the centuries. Hutton, Alfred

Sword exercise. O'Rourke, M. J.

Syber, Nicolas
(tr.) Bible. German. Die neunte deutsche Bibel

Sydow, Johanna von
Im toilettenzimmer; plaudereien und enthüllungen aus dem gebiete der eleganz und aus dem salon ... 2. ausg. Leipzig, O. Spamer [1882]
254p. 40 illus. O.
Lipperheide 3288

La **Sylphide**; littérature, beaux-arts, modes. 1839-1854? Paris
Pl. (part col.) Q.
Absorbed 1855 by *La Revue parisienne*
Colas 2849

Sylvia's book of new designs in knitting, netting, and crochet, containing a selection of useful articles in crochet, knitting, tatting, and netting, with minute details. London, Ward, Lock [1881]
p97-192. 107 illus. O.
Lipperheide 4132

Sylvia's book of the toilet: a ladies' guide to dress and beauty, with a fund of information of importance to gentlemen. London, Ward, Lock ca1880
106p. 27 illus. O.
Lipperheide 3286

Sylvia's crochet book. London, Ward, Lock ca1879
96p. 48 illus. O.
Lipperheide 4121

Sylvia's home journal. 14 v., 1878-1891; 1 v. 1892; new ser. no 1-24 1893-1894. London, 1878-94
O.
Superseded *The Young Englishwoman*

Sylvia's illustrated embroidery book, containing ... ornamental designs in broderie anglaise, appliqué, cross stitch and the new Holbein work. London, Ward, Lock 1879
p193-288. 139 illus. O.
Lipperheide 3993

Sylvius. See Texier, E. A.

Symonds, Mary. See Antrobus, Mrs M. S.

Symptoms of being amused. Alken, H. T.

Synge, Margaret Bertha
Simple garments for infants ... with paper patterns comprising 52 pieces and ... other illustrations by Miss D. Payne. London, New York, Longmans, Green 1914
xii,49p. col.front. illus. paper patterns in pocket. O.
LC A15-183

Synopsis of ancient costume. Fosbroke, T. D.

Synthèse de l'oeuvre du maître. Bakst, Léon

Syria
Carpenter, F. G. The Holy Land and Syria. 1922
Heuzey, L. A., and Heuzey, Jacques. Histoire du costume dans l'antiquité classique. 1935
Wittman, William. Travels in Turkey, Asia-Minor, Syria, and across the desert into Egypt during the years 1799, 1800, and 1801, in company with the Turkish army, and the British military mission. 1803

Syria—*Continued*

Ancient times

Perrot, Georges, and Chipiez, Charles. History of art in Sardinia, Judaea, Syria, and Asia Minor. 1890

17th century

Dapper, Olfert. Naukeurige beschryving van gansch Syrie. 1677

18th century

Spilsbury, F. B. Picturesque scenery in the Holy Land and Syria, delineated during the campaigns of 1799 and 1800. 1823

19th century

Breton de la Martinière, I. B. J. L'Égypte et la Syrie, ou moeurs, usages, costumes et monumens des Égyptiens, des Arabes et des Syriens. 1814

Wilkie, Sir David. Sir David Wilkie's sketches in Turkey, Syria and Egypt, 1840 & 1841. 1843

20th century

Bell, G. L. The desert and the sown. 1907

Gröber, Karl. Palestine and Syria. c1926

Gröber, Karl. Picturesque Palestine, Arabia, and Syria. c1925

Système préhistorique du Danemark. See Müller, S. O. Ordning af Danmarks oldsager

Système théorique et pratique de la coupe des vêtements pour dames. Fulop, Jean

Szalatnay, Rafael D.
(ed.) Fišer, Frant. Old Bohemian customs throughout the year. 192-?

Szendrei, János
A magyar viselet történeti fejlődése. 174 szövegközti képpel és hat táblával. A Magyar tudományos akadémia Régészeti bizottsága megbizásából irta Dr Szendrei János. Budapest, Kiadja a Magyar tudományos akadémia 1905
223p. col.front. illus. 4 col.pl.(1 fold.) 1 fold.pl. F.
Plates show Hungarian dress including uniforms, from the eleventh to the eighteenth centuries
LC 6-7268

See also Tarnóczy, Mme Gustave de. Catalogue descriptif et illustré de la collection de bagues

Szentgyörgyi, Ludwig. See Pentsy, Josef, jt. auth.

T

Le **tabac.** Blondel, Spire

Tabacologia. Neander, Johann

Tabak-anekdoten. Schranka, E. M., comp.

Tabellarische nachweisung von allen regimentern und korps der königlich preussischen armee unter der regierung sr. majestät Friedrich Wilhelm III, zur erläuterung der abbildungen von denen militair uniformen. Ramm, A. L.

Tableau de Paris. Dunker, B. A.

Tableau des moeurs et des usages ... des Russes. See Buddeus, Carl. Volksgemälde und charakterköpfe des russischen volks

Tableau du royaume de Caboul. See Elphinstone, Mountstuart. An account of the kingdom of Caubul

Tableau général de l'Empire othoman. Mouradgea d'Ohsson, Ignatius

Tableau général du goût, des modes et costumes de Paris par une société d'artistes et gens de lettres. v 1-[3] An V-VII [1797-1799] Paris, L'imprimerie des amis réunis (Belin)
Pl.(part col.) O.
Continued by *La Correspondance des dames*
Volume 2-3 An VI-VII [1798-99] published by Gide
Colas 2850

Tableau historique des costumes, des moeurs, et des usages des principaux peuples de l'antiquité et du moyen âge. See Spalart, Robert von. Versuch über das kostum der vorzüglichsten völker

Tableau historique des monumens, costumes et usages des Français, depuis les Gaulois jusqu'à nos jours; ouvrage rédigé d'après Ducange, Montfaucon, Legendre, Sainte-Foix, et Legrand-d'Aussy. Paris, Thieriot et Belin 1822
xii,372p. 16pl. O.
"Orné de 16 planches dessinées d'après Gaignières, représentant la collection des portraits de nos rois depuis Clovis, et 80 sujets curieux." Subtitle
Especially interesting for French costume from the 5th to the 16th centuries
Colas 2851. Lipperheide 1075

Tableau historique, géographique, militaire et moral de l'Empire de Russie. Damaze de Raymond

Tableaux algériens. Guillaumet, G. A.

Tableaux de genre recueillis pendant le voyage de ... Monseigneur le duc Maximilien de Bavière. Fischer, Sébastien

Tableaux de la bonne compagnie. Restif de La Bretonne, N. E.

Tableaux de la sainte messe. Schlichten, I. P. van der

Tableaux de la vie. Restif de La Bretonne, N. E.

Tableaux de l'habillement ... dans la République batave. See Maaskamp, Evart. Afbeeldingen van de kleeding, zeden, en gewoonten in Holland

Tableaux de Paris. Delarue, Fortuné

Tableaux de Paris. Goudeau, Émile

Tableaux des habillemens, moeurs et coutumes dans les provinces septentrionales du royaume de Pays-Bas au commencement du dix-neuvième siècle. See Maaskamp, Evert. Afbeeldingen van de kleedingen, zeden en gewoonten in Holland

Tableaux des principaux peuples de l'Europe, de l'Asie, de l'Afrique, de l'Amérique. Grasset de Saint-Sauveur, Jacques

Tableaux historiques. Daret, Pierre

Tableaux of national character, beauty, and costume. Finden, William, and Finden, E. F.

Tableaux pittoresque des moeurs, des usages, et des divertissements des Russes, Tartares, Mongols et autres nations de l'empire russe. See Geissler, C. G. H. Mahlerische darstellungen

Tableaux synoptiques de l'infanterie et de la cavalerie française. Marbot, A. C. A., baron de

Tablitzi form obmundirovania Russkoy armiî. Shenk, V. K.

Tabor, Margaret Emma
The saints in art, with their attributes and symbols alphabetically arranged. London, Methuen [1908]
xxxi,208p. front. 19pl. D.
LC A11-1029

Tabourot, Jehan
Orchésographie. Réimpression précédée d'une notice sur les danses du XVIe siècle, par Laure Fonta. Paris, F. Vieweg 1888
xxxv,104p. illus. O.
Reprint of the first edition (Lengres, Jehan de preyz 1589)
Lipperheide 3057

Orchesography, a treatise in the form of a dialogue whereby all manner of persons may easily acquire and practice the honourable exercise of dancing, by Thoinot Arbeau [pseud.] Now first translated from the original edition published at Langres, 1588, by Cyril W. Beaumont. London, C. W. Beaumont 1925
xv,17-174p. illus.(incl.music) O.
LC 25-21997

Die tänze des XVI. jahrhunderts und die alte französiche tanzschule vor einführung der menuet; nach Jean Tabourot's Orchesographie herausgegeben von Albert Czerwinski. Danzig 1878
140p. 35 illus. O.
Translation of the *Orchesographie*
Lipperheide 3058

Tackmann, E.
Gallerie des kurhessischen militärs. No place, ca1825
1 l. 40 col.pl. F.
Colas 2853

Uniformen d. kgl. Hannoverschen armee. No place, ca1830
10 col.pl. F.

Tänzerinnen. Nikolaus, Paul

Taeschner, Franz
Alt-Stambuler hof- und volksleben, ein türkisches miniaturenalbum aus dem 17. Jahrhundert. Hannover, H. Lafaire 1925
v 1. pl.(mounted, part col.) F.

Tätowiren, narbenzeichnen und körperbemalen. Joest, Wilhelm

Tätowirung, art und verbreitung. Herz, Alfred

Die **tätowirung** beider geschlechter in Samoa. Marquardt, Carl

Tafel, Albert
Meine Tibetreise; eine studienfahrt durch das nordwestliche China und durch die innere Mongolei in das östliche Tibet. Stuttgart [etc.] Union deutsche verlagsgesellschaft 1914
2v. fronts.(1 col.) illus. pl.(part fold.) fold.map. Q. M.24
LC 15-14555

Tafeln zur entwicklungsgeschichte der schutz und trutz- waffen in Europa mit ausschluss der feuerwaffen vom VIII. bis XVII. jahrhundert. Gimbel, Karl

Tafereelen uit het burgerlijke leven van de Hollanders. Troost, Cornelis

Tafvelgalleri från stugor i Dalom. Bosaeus, Ernst

Das **tagliche** leben in Kopenhagen. See Lahde, G. L. Kjøbenhavns kloededragter

Tahiti
Christian, F. W. Eastern Pacific lands. 1910

Le **tailleur** sincère, contenant ce qu'il faut observer. Boullay, Benoît

Le **tailleur** sincere, contenant les moyens pour bien pratiquer. Boullay, Benoît

Tailor and cutter. v 1+ Oct 6, 1866+ London, J. Williamson
Illus. pl. Q.-F. 19s
Published monthly. Current 1938
Accompanying semi-annual plates of men's fashions are published. With these the price is 27s

Tailoring. Hasluck, P. N., ed.

Tailoring and cutting
Berlepsch, H. A. von. Chronik vom ehrbaren und uralten schneidergewerk. 1850
Giles, E. B. The history of the art of cutting in England. 1887

Periodicals

Clothing trade journal. 1912+
Élégance parisienne; a journal of fashion and instruction for the benefit of ladies' tailors. 1900-24
Ladies' tailor; a monthly journal devoted to the scientific cutting and making of ladies' fashionable garments. 1884-1936
Master tailor and cutters' gazette. 1893-1908
Progressive tailor; a national magazine of authority on merchant tailoring. 1913+
Sartorial gazette. 1909+
Tailor and cutter. 1866+

16th century

Alcega, Juan de. Libro de geometria practica y traça. 1580
Käysserliche freyhaitten d schneyder und ab cunderfectur irer matteri auf allerley stuck zue endwerffen und zue sagen &c. 1590

17th century

Boullay, Benoît. Le tailleur sincère, contenant ce qu'il faut observer. 1671
Boullay, Benoît. Le tailleur sincere, contenant les moyens pour bien pratiquer toutes sortes de pieces d'ouvrage pour les habits d'hommes, & la quantité des estoffes qu'il y doit entrer en chaque espece. 1671

Tailoring and cutting—*Continued*

18th century

Garsault, F. A. P. de. L'art de la lingère. 1771

Garsault, F. A. P. de. Art du tailleur, contenant le tailleur d'habits d'hommes; les culottes de peau; le tailleur des corps de femmes & enfants: la couturière; & la marchande des modes. 1769

Das Leipziger putzmacher- und nähtermädchen. 1798

19th century

Agdá. Tratado sobre o ensino do córte das vestes de ambos os sexos. 1897

American Paragon scientific system. The improved American "Paragon" scientific system of dress cutting and dress fitting. 1884

American scientific system of dress cutting. 1883-84

Aubé, Mme Antonine. Traité de couture. 1875

Austria, Lower. Kammer für handel, gewerbe und industrie, Vienna. Lehr- und lesebuch für männer- und frauen-kleidermacher. 1880

Barde, F. A. Traité encyclopédique de l'art du tailleur. 1834

Barras, Easton de. Home dressmaking and the art of good dressing. 1898

Bautz, Rudolf. Formenstudien; musterzeichnungen für schule, haus und gewerbe. 1891

Becker, Hermann. Das Dortmunder wandschneider-buch. 1871

Bonetti, Emilia. Disegno, taglio e confezione di biancheria. 1894

Borchers, Fr. Neue zuschneidekunst für damenbekleidung. 1889

Browne, Miss M. P. The new and simplified system of dress-cutting and tailoring. 1896

Büchner, Elise. Grundlicher selbstunterricht die damen-bekleidungskunst. ca. 1865

Byrne, J. J. Perfection; an illustrated manual for artist tailors. 1889

Byrne, J. J. Practical tailoring. 1895

Byron, E. Art of dressmaking. 1897

Carlisle, E. M. F. A practical method of dress cutting, especially designed for technical classes. 1893

Clasen-Schmid, Mathilde. Neues system des zuschneidens der damenkleider auf grundlage des dreiecks. 1880

Compaing, Charles, and Devère, Louis. The complete manual of cutting. 1883-84

Couts, Joseph. A practical guide for the tailor's cutting-room. 1848

Cova, Emilia. Confezione d'abiti par signora e l'arte del taglio. 1895

Dartmann, G. H. Manuel du tailleur. 1837

Davies, J. F. Pioneer & systems of cutting ladies' fashionable garments, of the latest London, Paris, and New York styles. 1881

Dessault, Marcel. Traité pratique de la coupe et de la confection des vêtements pour dames et enfants. 1896

Dobson, W. L. £20 prize essay on cutting by block patterns. 1884

Engelmann, Gustav. The American garment cutter for women's garments. 1913

Falconer, John. A series of tables and diagrams illustrating economy in cutting. 1889

Ferry, Ramon. La madre de familia o tratado de corte para confeccion de trajes de senora y ninos basado en la geometria. 1882

Fulop, Jean. Système théorique de la coupe des vêtements pour dames. 1896

Giles, E. B., and others. The West-end system. 1887

Giroux, Mme A. Traité de la coupe et de l'assemblage des vêtements de femmes et d'enfants. 1907

Heath, Miss F. Pattern-making by paper folding; a simple method of cutting-out under-clothing and children's dresses as used in the schools of the London school board. 1895

Heindorf, Auguste. Praktischer unterricht im massnehmen und zuschneiden aller arten weiblicher kleidungs-stücke, sowie auch der hauptsächlichsten männlichen. 1832

Hicks, Mrs R. Dress cutting and making on tailors principles, as taught in the London board schools. 1894

Holding, T. H. Ladies' cutting made easy. 1885

Jackson, John. The improved tailors' aera. 1829

Klemm, Heinrich. Neueste und vollständige schule der damenschneiderei. 1871

Klemm, Heinrich. Vollständiges handbuch der höhern bekleidungskunst für civil, militär und livree. 1870

Kreil, Marie. Taschenbuch zum eintragen der masse für damen-kleider. 1884

Kunc, M. Die toilette; neue populäre unterrichtsmethode für den zuschnitt der damenbekleidung. 1891

Lechner, Hedwig, and Beeg, Gunda. Die anfertigung der damen garderobe. 1891

Lechner, Hedwig, and Beeg, Gunda. Die anfertigung der kinder-garderobe. 1891

Lenniger, F. F. Die anfertigung der damenkleider. 1882

Link, J. C. E. Frauenschule; das A B C der schneiderskunst. 1881

Löfvall, Mme J. H. How to cut, fit, and finish a dress. 1892

Mariette, Pauline. L'art de la toilette; méthode nouvelle pour tailler, éxécuter ou diriger avec économie et élégance tous les vêtements de dames et d'enfants. 1866

Mottl, Wendelin. Die grundlagen und die neuesten fortschritte der zuschneidekunst. 1895

Müller, G. A. Die gesammte fachwissenschaft des schneiders. 1870

Müller, Susanna. Neuer systematischer zuschneide-unterricht. 1883

Tailoring and cutting—19th century—*Cont.*
Müller, Susanna. Zuschneidekurs. 1875
Die perfekte schneiderin; leichtfaszliche lehre des zuschnitts und der bearbeitung der gesammten frauen-, mädchen- und knaben-garderobe. 1896-97
Peyry, J. B. Prof. Jean B. Peyry's instruction book with diagram and measure book. 1896
Rocholl, Meta. Praktische anleitung zum masznehmen, schnittzeichnen, zuschneiden und anfertigen weiblicher garderobegegenstände. 1884
Rötter, Henriette. Für frauen und töchter; das kleidermachen zum selbstunterrichte. 1892
Schmidt, Carl, and Schmidt, Rosalie. Methodische anleitung für geometrische zuschnittlehre, weiszarbeiten, maschinennähen und praktisches kleidermachen. 1883
Schnittmusterbuch; anleitung zum wäschezuschneiden für schüle und haus. 1877
Schober, Anna. Vollständiges lehr- und hilfsbuch zum selbstunterricht für damen in der herstellung einer guten toilette, nach der methode Anna Schober. 1884
Schroeder, Minna. Lehrbuch der damenschneiderei. 1878
Suhr, H. Leitfaden für den gründlichen unterricht im maassnehmen und façonzeichnen der zuschneidkunst für damen. 1878
Thormann-Bechlin, Louise. Leitfaden zum theoretischen und praktischen unterricht der damenschneiderei. 1893
Walker, W. E. The tailor's philosophy; or, Science complete in the art of cutting. 1839
Zeischke, Josef. Die moderne damenschneiderei. 1888

Caricature and satire

Hosentuch, Johann. Johann Hosentuch's lustiges schneiderbüchlein, oder witze, anekdoten und curiositäten aller art ...; nebst liedern für die schneiderzunft und den zehn geboten für schneider. 1846

20th century

Bonetti, Emelia. L'arte del taglio e la confezione d'abiti per signora: manuale teorico-pratico. 1908
Browne, M. P. Dress-cutting, drafting, and French pattern modelling. 1902
Browne, M. P. Practical work of dressmaking & tailoring. 1908
Browne, Miss M. Prince. "Up-to-date" dress cutting and drafting. 1907-1908
Butterick publishing company, limited. The dressmaker. c1916
Collins, Harry. The A B C of dress. 1923
Dessault, Marcel. Études variés sur la coupe. 1903
Donovan, D. G. The mode in dress and home. 1935
Fales, Jane. Dressmaking, a manual for schools and colleges. 1917
Fleming, J. A. Garment making; the cutting-out and making-up of commonsense comfortable clothing for children. 1912
Field, Bradda. Clothes that count and how to make them. 1923
Guerre, Alice. Dress cutting: theoretical and practical. 1914
Hambridge, E. R. Simple dressmaking explained and illustrated. 1917
Hasluck, P. N., ed. Tailoring. 1901
Jacquenod, M. L. Cours de coupe pour dames. 1912
Latzke, Alpha, and Quinlan, Elizabeth. Clothing, an introductory college course. 1935
Leverton, Mrs Waldemar. Dressmaking made easy; with chapters on millinery. 1909
Manning, Sibylla, and Donaldson, A. M. Fundamentals of dress construction. 1926
Piergiovanni, Bruno. Enciclopedia dell' abbigliamento femminile. 1924
Poole, B. W. The science of pattern construction for garment makers. 1936
Reeve, A. J. The elements of dress pattern-making. 1912
Reeve, A. J. French pattern modelling for professionals. 1912
Reeve, A. J. Practical dresscutting up to date. 1912
Regal, Samuel. The American garment cutter. 1924
Rhoe, Mrs M. J. The dress you wear and how to make it. 1918
Schuman, Julius. Schuman's improved art of designing. 1919

Tailor's philosophy. Walker, W. E.

Taiwan. See Formosa

Talbot
(ed.) Auvergne, Puy-de-Dôme. Clermont-Ferrand, Lausedat ca1865
52 col.pl. F.
Plates show folk dress
Colas 2854. Lipperheide 1205

Talbot-Booth, Eric Charles
The British army; its history, customs, traditions and uniforms. All the black and white and colour drawings are by the author. London, S. Low, Marston [1937]
xvi,512p illus. pl.(part col.) S.
Most of the colored plates accompanied by leaves with descriptive letterpress not included in paging
LC 38-4371

Tales told in church stones. Derrick, Freda
Talhofer. Schlichtegroll, Nathanael
Talin, Henri Meilhac, and Damourette
Les lorettes; 1re partie. Paris, Maresq et Philipon fils [ca1855]
56 pl. O.
Lipperheide 3615

See also Damourette, jt. auth.

Talismans. See Amulets and talismans

Tallis, John
(pub.) Tallis's Shakspere gallery of engravings

Tallis's Shakspere gallery of engravings, parts 1-20. [London, J. Tallis 1852-53]
20 pts. pl. O.

Tallyrand-Périgord, Charles Maurice Camille, duc de Dino. See Cosson, C. A., baron de. Le cabinet d'armes de Maurice Tallyrand-Périgord

Tam gde rastet khlopok. Baïsutov, N. I.

Tambours et trompettes. Arnoux, Guy

Tamura, Naomi

The Japanese bride. New York, Harper 1893
92p. front. 3pl. T.
LC 13-12918

Der **tanz.** Becker, M. L.

Der **tanz.** Bie, Oskar

Der **tanz.** Boehn, Max von

Tanz. Vala Moro, pseud.

Der **tanz** der zukunft. Böhme, Fritz

Der **tanz** der zukunft. Duncan, Isadora

Der **tanz** in der kunst. Moreck, Curt, ed.

Die **tanze** des XVI. jahrhunderts und die alte französiche tanzschule vor einführung der menuett. Tabourot, Jehan

Die **tanzkunst** des Euripides. Buchholtz, Hermann

Tapisseries, broderies et dentelles. Müntz, Eugène

Les **tapisseries** coptes. Gerspach, Édouard

Les **tapisseries** décoratives du Garde-meuble (Mobilier national). Guichard, Édouard

Les **tapisseries** des chasses de Maximilien. Paris. Musée national du Louvre

Tarantella ballo napolitano. Dura, Gaetano

Taraval, Gustave

(engr.) Danet, Guillaume. L'art des armes

Taraval, Louis Gustave. See Taraval, Gustave

Tardieu, Ambroise

Galerie des uniformes des gardes nationales de France. Paris, A. Tardieu 1817
32p. col.front. 27 col.pl. O.
Colas 2856

Tarnóczy, Mme Gustave de

Catalogue descriptif et illustré de la collection de bagues de madame Gustave de Tarnóczy ... Par dr. Jean Szendrei. Paris, A. Lévy, 1889
lvi,384p. 300 illus. D.
LC GS34-274

Tartans. See Scotland, Highlands of

Tartans of the clans of Scotland. Grant, James

Tartars. See Tatars

Tartu. Eesti rahva muuseum

Aastaraamat. v3. See Manninen, Ilmari. Eesti rahvariiete ajalugu

Eesti rahvariiete album. Album estnischer volkstrachten. Tartu [Trükk. H. Laakmanni graafiline kunstiasutus] 1927
[6]p. x col.pl. Q.
At head of title: Eesti rahva muuseum. Illustrations by A. Mõtus
LC CA32-522

Tarver, E. J. See Lonsdale, H. W., jt. auth.

Taschenbuch der liebe und freundschaft. 1800-1840. Frankfurt am Mayn, F. Wilman
Illus. S.-D.
Lipperheide 4508

Taschenbuch der strick-, stick-, näh-, und anderer weiblichen arbeiten. Netto, J. F.

Taschenbuch ... für damen, von Huber, Lafontaine, Pfeffel, J. P. Fr. Richter u. anderen. 1799-1822, 1828-1831. Tübingen, J. G. Cotta 1798-1831
Illus. S.
No volumes were published for 1823-27
The volume for 1799 has title *Taschenkalender für damen* with added title-page *Taschenbuch für damen*
Lipperheide 4497

Taschenbuch über die Schweiz. Keller, J. J.

Taschenbuch zum eintragen der masse für damen-kleider. Kreil, Marie

Tasmanians. See Australia—Native races

Tatars

Ides, E. Y. Driejaarige reize naar China, te lande gedaan door den moskovischen afgezant. 1704

See also Embroidery—Tatary

Das **tatauierungswesen** im heutigen Europa. Riecke, Erhard

Le **tatouage** en Belgique. Vervaeck, L.

Les **tatouages.** Lacassagne, Alexandre

Tatting

Albums pour ouvrages en frivolité. 1886

The old art of tatting; by an Englishwoman. ca1860

Sylvia's book of new designs in knitting, netting, and crochet, containing a selection of useful articles in crochet, knitting, tatting, and netting, with minute details. 1881

Tattoo. Parry, Albert

Tattooing

Bailliot, Marcel. Du detatouage. 1894

Brown, J. M. Maori and Polynesian, their origin, history and culture. p 178-90

Buckland, A. W. On tattooing. 1888

Cerchiari, G. L. Chiromanzia e tatuaggio, note di varietà, ricerche storiche e scientifiche. 1903

Cocheris, Mme P. A. W. Les parures primitives avec une introduction sur les temps préhistoriques. 1894

Danielli, Iacopo. Contributo allo studio del tatuaggio negli antichi Peruviani. 1894

Fletcher, Robert. Tattooing among civilized people. 1883

Frobenius, Leo. The childhood of man. 1909 p31-55

Hambly, W. D. The history of tattooing and its significance. 1925

Herz, Alfred. Tätowirung, art und verbreitung. 1900

Joest, Wilhelm. Tätowiren, narbenzeichnen und körperbemalen. 1887

Lacassagne, Alexandre. La signification des tatouages chez les peuples primitifs et dans les civilisations mediterranéenes. 1912

Tattooing—*Continued*

Lacassagne, Alexandre. Les tatouages; étude anthropologique et médico-légale. 1881

Le Blond, A. W. L., and Lucas, Arthur. Du tatouage chez les prostituées. 1899

Martínez Baca, Francisco. Los tatuages; estudio psicológico y médico-legal en delincuentes y militares. 1899

Parry, Albert. Tattoo; secrets of a strange art as practised among the natives of the United States. 1933

Prinzhorn, Hans. Bildnerei der gefangenen; studie zur bildnerischen gestaltung ungeübter. c1926

Purdy, D. W. Tattooing; how to tattoo, what to use. 1896

Riecke, Erhard. Das tatauierungswesen im heutigen Europa. 1925

El tatuage en su evolución histórica, en sus diferentes caracterizaciones antiguas y actuales y en los delincuentes franceses, italianos y españoles. 1908

See also Body painting; Scarification

Africa

Frobenius, Leo. Das sterbende Afrika. 1923

Verrier, Eugène. Du tatouage en Afrique; ses variétés, sa signification, des survivances du tatouage en Europe. 1895

Belgium

Vervaeck, L. Le tatouage en Belgique. 1906

Burma

Scott, Sir J. G. The Burman. 1910

Maoris

Robley, H. G. Moko; or, Maori tattooing. 1896

Marquesas islands

Handy, Mrs W. C. Tattooing in the Marquesas. 1922

Steinen, Karl von den. Die Marquesaner und ihre kunst. 1825-28

New Guinea

Finsch, Otto. Ueber bekleidung, schmuck, und tätowirung der Papuas der südostküste von Neu-Guinea. 1885

Samoa

Marquardt, Carl. Die tätowirung beider geschlechter in Samoa. 1899

Tattooing among civilized people. Fletcher, Robert

Tattooing in the Marquesas. Handy, Mrs W. C.

El **tatuage** en su evolución histórica. Salillas, Rafael

Los **tatuages;** estudio psicologico y medicolegal en delincuentes y militares. Martinez Baca, Francisco

Taubert, Gottfried

Rechtschaffener tantzmeister, oder Gründliche erklärung der frantzösischen tantzkunst. Leipzig, F. Lanckischens erben 1717

1176,[55]p. front. pl. O.

The plates are included in the pagination, each numbered as one page

"Chorégraphie, das ist, Die kunst einen tantz durch characteres ... von Mons. Feüillet ... ins teutsche übersetzet ... von dem authore dieses buches" (p745-915) has reproduction of title-page of French edition of 1701

Lipperheide 3068m. LC 13-4473

Taunay, Hippolyte, and Denis, Ferdinand

Le Brésil ... Ouvrage orné de nombreuses gravures d'après les dessins faits dans le pays par M. H. Taunay. Paris, Nepveu 1822

6v. in 3. fronts.(part fold.) 52pl.(part fold.) T.

Plates exist in black and white or in color

Colas 2857. LC A26-778

La **taureaumachie.** See Goya y Lucientes, F. J. de. Tauromachia

Taurinius, Zacharias, pseud. See Damberger, C. F., pseud.

Tauromachia. Goya y Lucientes, F. J. de

Tauromachia. Price, Lake, and Ford, Richard

Tayler, W.

Sketches illustrating the manners and customs of the Indians and Anglo-Indians, drawn on stone from the original drawings from life. London, 1842

6 col.pl. F.

Cataloged from Colas's *Bibliographie*

Colas 2858

Taylor, Alicia Cameron. See Richter, J. P., jt. auth.

Taylor, Charles

(engr.) Smirke, Robert. Picturesque beauties of Shakespeare

Taylor, Mrs Emily (Drayton). See Wharton, A. H. Heirlooms in miniatures

Taylor, Richard

Te Ika a Maui; or, New Zealand and its inhabitants. Illustrating the origin, manners, customs, mythology, religion ... of the Maori and Polynesian races in general. 2d ed. London, W. Macintosh; [etc.] 1870

xv,713p. col.front. illus. 9pl(part col.) port. O.

LC 4-32535

Taylor, Wesley

The story of hosiery. See entry under May hosiery mills, inc., Burlington, N. C.

Taylor, William Benjamin Sarsfield

History of the University of Dublin ... Illustrated by views of its buildings, and the academic costumes, etc. London, Printed for T. Cadell; [etc.] 1845

xix,540p. col.front. pl.(partly col.) O.

Lipperheide 2031. LC 7-16551

Tcheremisses. See Cheremisses

Te Ika a Maui; or, New Zealand and its inhabitants. Taylor, Richard

I **teatri** di Roma nel secolo decimosettimo. Ademollo, Alessandro

Teatro critico universal. See Feyjoo, B.-J. Théâtre critique

Teatro delle nobili et virtuose donne. Parasole, E. C.

Tebbs, Louisa Augusta
The art of bobbin lace ... Illustrated with original designs in Italian, point de Flandre, Bruges guipure, duchesse, Honiton, "raised" Honiton, appliqué, and Bruxelles. London, Chapman & Hall 1907
xvi,111p. incl.pl. Q.
LC 8-5860

Tebbutt, C. G. See Heathcote, J. M., and others. Skating

Die **technik** der geklöppelten spitze. Jamnig, C., and Richter, A.

Technique of some South American featherwork. Mead, C. W.

Technische modenzeitung für damen, damenkleidermacher. 1.-8. jahrg., 1844-1851. Weimar, B. F. Voigt
8v. col.pl. O.-Q.
Title varies: 1844-1850, v 1-7 *Der putztisch;* zeitung für damenschneider, modehandlungen, stickerinnen
Colas 2445. Lipperheide 4652

Teichel, Franz
(illus.) Lange, Eduard. Costüme des Königlichen hof-theaters zu Berlin

Teicher, Friedrich
Das königl. bayerische kadetten-korps von der gründung bis zur gegenwart. München, T. Ackermann 1889
xii,136p. 28 illus. O.

Teissier, Octave
Meubles et costumes (XVIe, XVIIe, et XVIIIe siècles). Paris, H. Champion 1904
79p. O.
Colas 2859

Teixeira de Aragão, Augusto Carlos
Anneis. Lisboa, Typ. da Academia real das sciencias 1887
25p. II pl. O.
LC 35-34265

Tejidos y bordados populares españoles. Byne, Mrs M. S.

Telesio, Antonio. See Baïf, Lazare de. Lazari Bayfii annotationes

Temminck, C. J.
(ed.) Müller, Salomon. Verhandelingen over de natuurlijke geschiedenis der nederlandsche overzeesche bezittingen

Tempered clothing. The House of Kuppenheimer, Chicago

Tempiandanti. Caprin, Giuseppe

Templars
Kolinovics, Gabriel. Chronicon militaris ordinis Equitum Templariorum e bullis papalibus, diplomatibus regiis ... collectum. 1789

Temple, Sir Richard Carnac, bart
(ed.) Mundy, Peter. The travels of Peter Mundy, in Europe and Asia, 1608-1667

Temple, Zillah
(illus.) Perkins, J. H. T. The coronation book

Les **temps** préhistoriques en Suède. Montelius, Oscar

Tenac, Charles van. See Van Tenac, Charles

Tendances nouvelles du théâtre. Moussinac, Léon

[**Tengler, Ulrich**]
Der neü Layenspiegel von rechtmässigen ordnungen in burgerlichen und peinlichen regimenten; mitt additōn. Augspurg, H. Othmar 1511
18, cclviii l. illus. F.
Illustrations are woodcuts by H. F. (Hans von Freiburg?) and show the dress of judges, court attendants, clerks and others of this time
First published 1509 with title: *Layenspiegel.* Lipperheide lists another edition (Strassburg, 1536)
Lipperheide 610-611. LC 15-21885

Ténicheva, Mariya Klavdiyevna Pyatkovskaya, knyaginya
Broderies des paysannes de Smolensk, exécutées sous la direction de la princesse Marie Ténichev. Paris, Librairie centrale des beaux-arts [1907]
Preface by Denis Roche
11p. 60 col.pl. Q.

Ténint, Wilhelm. See Challamel, Augustin, jt. auth.

Tennis costume
Aldin, C. C. W. The omnibus book of sports for young and old. 1937 Part 1
Schnell, H. Handbuch der ballspiele. 1899-1901

La **tente** funeraire de la princesse Isimkheb. Brugsch, Émile

Tentoonstelling van kleederdrachten in Nederlandsch Indië. Leyden. Rijks ethnographisch museum

Tents in Mongolia (Yabonah). Haslund-Christensen, Henning

Tenue des troupes de France à toutes les époques armées de terre et de mer. See Onfroy de Bréville, J. M. G. Aquarelles de Job

Tenues des officiers et assimilés. Belgium. Ministère de la guerre.

Der **teppich** aus dem kloster Drübeck. Friederich, Adolf

Teppiche des jungfrauenstifts Marienberg bei Helmstedt. Münchausen, A. F. von

Terence
Comédies de Térence. See entry under Paris. Bibliothèque nationale. Mss. (Lat. 7899)
[Works.] Strassburg, J. Grüninger 1496
6,173 l. 166 illus.(8 full-page) F.
First line: Terenti' cū directorio vocabulorū
Illustrations show costume worn in Strasbourg at the end of the fifteenth century, and how the characters were dressed for these plays. Almost every scene is shown with the participating actors
Lipperheide 428

Terracotten des Königlichen museums zu Berlin. Panofka, Theodor, ed.

Terres cuites antiques. Lecuyer, Camille

Terrien de Lacouperie, Albert Étienne Jean Baptiste. See Colquhoun, A. R. Amongst the Shans

Terry, Daniel
British theatrical gallery; a collection of whole-length portraits. London, H. Berthoud 1825
38 l. 20 col.pl. F.
With biographical notes of famous English actors and actresses in the costumes of their best known dramatic rôles
Colas 2862

Tertullianus, Quintus Septimius Florens
De fuga in persecutione, De pallio; recensuit Josephus Marra. Aug. Taurinorum [etc.] in aedibus Io. Bapt. Paraviae et sociorum 1932
xix,103p. D. (Corpus scriptorum latinorum Paravianum. n. 59)
LC 33-31203

Teschendorff, Toni
Kreuzstich-muster für leinenstickerei. Berlin, E. Wasmuth 1879-84
2pts. 20 col.pl. F.
Lipperheide 3997

Tesoro militar de cavalleria antiguo y moderno. Micheli y Marquez, José

Tessmann, Günter
Die Pangwe; völkerkundliche monographie eines westafrikanischen negerstammes; ergebnisse der Lübecker Pangwe-expedition 1907-1909 und früherer forschungen 1904-1907. Berlin, E. Wasmuth 1913
2v. illus. XXVIII pl.(incl.front. part col.) 2 fold.maps. Q.
LC 27-6018

Tessuti fogge e decorazioni nell' abito muliebre in Grecia e a Roma. Carta, M. S.

Tettau, Eberhard, freiherr von
Die neue bekleidung und ausrüstung der russischen kavallerie. Leipzig, Zuckschwerdt 1897
28p. 14 illus. O.
Supplement to the author's *Die russische kavallerie in krieg und frieden*
Lipperheide 2381

Tetzner, Franz Oskar
Die Slawen in Deutschland; beiträge zur volkskunde der Preussen, Litauer und Letten, der Masuren und Philipponen, der Tschechen, Mährer und Sorben, Polaben und Slowinzen, Kaschuben und Polen. Braunschweig, F. Vieweg 1902
xx,520p. illus.(incl. music) pl. fold.maps, fold.plans. O.
Shows costume of various Slavic peoples in Germany from the 17th to 20th century
LC 3-3686

Teuber, Oscar
Die österreichische armee von 1700 bis 1867; illus. von Rudolf von Ottenfeld. Wien, E. Berté & S. Czeiger 1895
867p. 102 col.pl. Q.
Contains a chapter entitled Die kriegsmarine
Colas 2863. Lipperheide 2248

Teucrius Annaeus Privatus, pseud. See Lonicer, J. A.

Teupken, J. F.
Beschrijving hoedanig de koninklijke Nederlandsche troepen en alle in militaire betrekking staande personen gekleed, geëquipeerd en gewapend zijn. Gravenhage & Amsterdam, Gebroeders Van Cleef 1823
10,110,20p. front. 51pl.(48 col.) F.
Plates are engraved by K. Portman, D. Sluyter, A. L. Zeelander, A. Zürcher, John Bemme, after B. Van Hove, Bukhuyzen, N. Heideloff, and others
Colas 2864. Lipperheide 2255

Vervolg van de beschrijving hoedanig. Gravenhage, Gebroeders Van Cleef 1826
54p. 18 col.pl. Q.
Supplement to his *Beschrijving*. Plates are numbered 52-68, one is unnumbered. Most of the plates are by B. Van Hove
Colas 2865. Lipperheide 2256

Teutonic Knights
Bujack, Georg. Zur bewaffnung und kriegsführung der ritter des Deutschen Ordens in Preussen. 1888
Hartknoch, Christoph. Alt- und neues-Preussen, oder preussische historien. 1684
Henneberg, Caspar. Erclerung der preüssischen grössern landtaffel oder wappen. 1595
Schulin, J. P. Vollständiges diarium der römisch-königlichen wahl und kayserlichen krönung ... Leopold des zweiten. 1791

Teutonic Order. See Teutonic Knights

Teutsche alterthümer, zur erleuterung des sächsischen auch schwäbischen land- und lehn-rechts. Grupen, C. U.

Teutsche denkmäler. Batt.

Teutscher nation chronic alt und neu vorbilde. Franck, Sebastian

Teutscher nation heldenbuch. Pantaleon, Heinrich

Teutscher regierungs- und ehren-spiegel. Pregitzer, J. U.

Texas (Republic) War department
General regulations for the government of the army of the Republic of Texas; printed in accordance with a joint resolution of Congress, approved January 23rd 1839. Houston, S. Whiting, printer 1839
187,16p. T.
"Uniform of the army of the republic of Texas," 16 pages at end

Texas (Republic). See Military costume—United States—Texas

Texier, André Louis Victor
(engr.) Clarac, C. O. F. J. B., comte de. Musée de sculpture antique et moderne

Texier, Édmond Auguste
Physiologie du poëte, par Sylvius; illustrations de Daumier. Paris, J. Laisné 1842
124p. 56 illus. D.
Lipperheide 3717

Textile arts of the Guatemalan natives. Washington, Carnegie institution 1935
p[157]-68 illus.(2 col.) Q. (News service bull. v3 no 20 Feb. 3 1935)
Describes and pictures dress as well as textile patterns

Textile color card association of the United States
Colonial colors for the bicentennial year; approved by the United States George Washington bicentennial commission, Washington, D. C. 1732[-]1932. [New York? 1932?]
cover-title, [8]p. Q.
Contains colored mounted samples. "The colors portrayed in this card have been reproduced from original costumes worn by George and Martha Washington and other famous personages in early American history. They have been taken from the famous costume collection on exhibition in the United States National museum and are authentic and historically correct." Page [2] of cover
LC A33-569

Textile künste, weberei, stickerei, spitze. Flemming, E. R.

Textile manufactures and the costumes of the people of India. Watson, J. F.

Textile volkskunst aus Österreich. Haberlandt, Michael

Textiles and costumes among the peoples of the ancient Near east. Lutz, H. F.

Textiles and costume design. Ellsworth, E. P.

Thackeray, Lance

People of Egypt. London, A. & C. Black 1910

10p. fronts. pl.(part col.) O. (Peoples of many lands) 5s

Costume index

Thaeter, Julius

Deutsche trachten aus dem sechzehnten jahrhundert, 1. heft. No place, 1827

6pl. Q.

No more published. Plates show only the costume of Nuremberg and are from Jost Amman's *Trachtenbuch*

Colas 2866. Lipperheide 656

Thaten und meinungen des herrn Piepmeyer. Detmold, J. H., and Schrödter, Adolph

Thausing, Moritz

(ed.) Callot, Jacques. Livre d'esquisses. 1880

Das **theater.** Bie, Oskar

Das **theater** der gegenwart. Bab, Julius

Theater-trachten. Petrytz'kyĭ, Anatol'

Theater zeitung. See Allgemeine theaterzeitung und originalblatt

The **theatre.** Cheney, Sheldon

Théâtre. Corneille, Pierre

Le **théâtre** à Paris au XVIIIe siècle. Aghion, Max

Theatre and stage. Downs, Harold, ed.

Theatre art. Simonson, Lee, ed.

Le **théâtre** chinois. Chu Chia-Chien

Theatre collections in libraries and museums. Gilder, Rosamond, and Freedley, George

Théâtre critique. Feyjoo, B. J.

Le **théâtre** d'amateurs. Villard, Georges

Le **théâtre** de France. Saint-Igny, Jean de

Le **théâtre** en France au moyen âge. Cohen, Gustave

Théâtre français: recueil de costumes. Alaux, M. M. J., and Duponchel, L.

Le **théâtre** japonais (kabuki). IAkovlev, Aleksandr, and Elisieev, S. G.

Le **théâtre**: mystères, tragédie, comédie et la musique. See L'ancienne France. Le théâtre

The **theatre** of women. Amman, Jost.

Le **théâtre** profane. See Cohen, Gustave. Le théâtre en France au moyen âge

Le **théâtre** religieux. See Cohen, Gustave. Le théâtre en France au moyen âge

Les **théâtres** libertins au XVIII. siècle. Almeras, Henri d', and Quentin, Henri

Theatrical costume

L'ancienne France. Le théâtre: mystères, tragédie, comédie, et la musique: instruments, ballet, opera, jusqu'en 1789. 1887

Aria, Mrs E. D. Costume: fanciful, historical and theatrical. 1906

Arlington, L. C. The Chinese drama. 1930

Bie, Oskar. Die oper. 1913

Bie, Oskar. Das theater. 1912

Boehn, Max von. Das bühnenkostüm in altertum. 1921

Bouchot, H. F. X. M. Catalogue de dessins relatifs à l'histoire du théâtre conservés au département des estampes de la Bibliothèque nationale avec la description d'estampes rares sur le même sujet. 1896

Chalmers, Helena. Clothes, on and off the stage. 1928

Chambers, Sir E. K. The mediaeval stage. 1903

Cheney, Sheldon. The theatre; three thousand years of drama, acting and stagecraft. 1929

Cogniat, Raymond. Décors de théâtre. c1930

Denkmäler des theaters. 1926-30

Devéria, Achille. Costumes historiques de ville ou de théâtre et travestissemens. 1831

Devéria, Achille, and Boulenger. Souvenirs du théâtre anglais. ca1830

Engel, J. J. Ideen zu einer mimik. 1785-86

Harrison, Charles. Theatricals and tableaux vivants for amateurs. 1882

Holtmont, Alfred. Die hosenrolle; variationen über das thema das weib als mann. 1925

Jelgerhuis, J. Theoretische lessen over de gesticulatie en mimiek, gegeven aan de kweekelingen van het fonds ter opleiding en onderrigting van tooneelkunstenaars an den stads schouwburg te Amsterdam. 1827-29

Lamé, Émile. Le costume au theatre; la tragedie depuis 1636. 1886

Lecomte, Hippolyte. Costumes de théâtre de 1600 à 1820. 1824?

Le Vacher de Charnois, J. C. Recherches sur les costumes et sur les théatres de toutes les nations, tant anciennes que modernes. 1790

Mantzius, Karl. A history of theatrical art in ancient and modern times. 1903-21

Mills, Mrs W. H., and Dunn, Mrs. L. M. Marionettes, masks and shadows. 1927

Nicoll, Allardyce. Masks, mimes and miracles; studies in the popular theatre. 1931

Paul, Howard, and Gebbie, George, eds. The stage and its stars, past and present. 1887

Pougin, Arthur. Dictionnaire historique et pittoresque du théâtre et des arts qui s'y rattachent. 1885

Schidrowitz, Leo. Sittengeschichte des theaters; eine darstellung des theaters, seiner entwicklung und stellung in zwei jahrtausenden. 1925

Theatrical costume—*Continued*
Whirsker. Les métamorphoses de Melpomène et de Thalie. ca1770

See also Harlequin; Make-up, Theatrical; Masks; Operatic costume; Puppets

Middle ages

Schiller, Hermann. Kostümbilder für bühnenspiele des mittelalters. 1927

15th century

Plautus. Comoediae. 1511
Terence. Works. 1496

17th century

Bérain, J. L. Costumes de ballet. ca1690
Costa, Margherita. Li buffoni. 1641

18th century

Martin, J. B. Collection de figures theatrales. ca1760

19th century

Bab, Julius. Das theater der gegenwart; geschichte der dramatischen bühne seit 1870. 1928
Bloch, Eduard. Eduard Bloch's album der bühnen-costüme. 1859-1860
Bowen, Cyril. Practical hints on stage costume. 18-?
Costenoble, C. L. Dramatische spiele von C. Costenoble; ein taschenbuch für 1811. 1811
Mobisson, Ferdinand, ed. Costumes of the modern stage. 1889-91
Morrocchesi, Antonio. Lezioni di declamazione e d'arte teatrale. 1832
Sammlung von national-trachten und andern zu charakter-masken passenden kostümen. 1826
Schneider, Louis. Gallerie der costüme auf historischen nationellen und characteristischen grundlagen für das theater. 1844-47

20th century

Bab, Julius. Das theater der gegenwart; geschichte der dramatischen bühne seit 1870. 1928
Craig, E. G. On the art of the theatre. 1912
Dabney, Edith, and Wise, C. M. A book of dramatic costume. 1930
Downs, Harold, ed. Theater and stage; a modern guide to the performance of all classes of amateur dramatic, operatic, and theatrical work. 1934
George, Waldemar. Boris Aronson et l'art du théâtre. 1928
Grimball, E. B., and Wells, Rhea. Costuming a play: inter-theatre arts handbook. c1925
Guptill, Mrs E. F. E. and Wormwood, E. M. Amateur's costume book. c1917
Kommīssarzhevskiĭ, F. F. The costume of the theatre. 1931
Kommīssarzhevskiĭ, F. F., and Simonson, Lee. Settings & costumes of the modern stage. 1933
Levinson, A. I. Bakst, the story of the artist's life. 1923
Levinson, A. I. Histoire de Léon Bakst. 1924
Mason, Rupert. Robes of Thespis; costume designs by modern artists. 1928
Messel, Oliver. Stage designs and costumes. 1933
Morton, Cavendish. The art of theatrical make-up. 1909
Moussinac, Léon. Tendances nouvelles du théâtre. 1931
New York. Museum of modern art. International exhibition of theatre art, January 16-February 26, 1934. 1934
Rutherston, A. D. Sixteen designs for the theatre. 1928
Saint-Ursanne, René. Petit guide pratique de l'art du théâtre. c1925
Schnackenberg, Walther. Ballett und pantomime. 1920
Simonson, Lee, ed. Theatre art. c1934
Sheringham, George, and others. Design in the theater. 1927
Young, A. B. Stage costuming. 1927

BY REGION OR COUNTRY

Asia

Laufer, Berthold. Oriental theatricals. 1923

See also Theatrical costume—China; Theatrical costume—Japan

Austria

Bäuerle, Adolf, ed. Gallerie drolliger und interessanter scenen der Wiener-bühnen. 1827-28
Gregor, Joseph. Wiener szenische kunst. 1924-25
Kostüme der kaiserl. königl. National- und der anderen privil. theatern in Wien. 1807-12?
Lothar, Rudolph. Das Wiener burgtheater. 1899

Belgium

Renieu, Lionel. Histoire des théâtres de Bruxelles depuis leur origine jusqu'à ce jour. 1928

China

Buss, Kate. Studies in the Chinese drama. 1922
Chu Chia-Chien. The Chinese theatre. 1922
Chu Chia-Chien. Le théâtre chinois. 1922
Johnston, R. F. The Chinese drama. 1921
Liang, Shê-kan. Mei Lan-fang, foremost actor of China. 1929

England

Caractères dramatiques ou portraits divers du théâtre anglois. 1770
Jones, Inigo. Designs by Inigo Jones, for masques & plays at court. 1924
Terry, Daniel. British theatrical gallery: a collection of whole-length portraits. 1825

Theatrical costume—*Continued*

Europe

Dubech, Lucien. Histoire générale illustrée du théâtre. 1931-34

See also names of European countries under subject Theatrical costume

France

Alaux, M. M. J., and Duponchel, L. Théâtre français: recueil de costumes. n.d.
Arnault, A. V. Les souvenirs et les regrets du Vieil amateur dramatique [pseud.], ou lettres d'un oncle à son neveu sur l'ancien théâtre français. 1861
Bapst, Germain. Essai sur l'histoire du théatre; la mise en scène, le décor, le costume, l'architecture, l'éclairage, l'hygiène. 1893
Dacier, Émile. Le musée de la Comédie-français, 1680-1905. 1905
Galerie théâtrale, ou Collection des portraits en pied des principaux acteurs des premiers théâtres de la capitale. 1812-1834
Jullien, Adolphe. Histoire du costume au théâtre depuis les origines du théâtre en France jusqu'à nos jours. 1880

Middle ages

Cohen, Gustave. Le théâtre en France au moyen âge. 1928-31

17th century

Guillaumot, A. E. Costumes de la Comédie française XVIIe-XVIIIe siècles. 1885
Leclercq, Louis. Les décors, les costumes, et la mise en scène au XVIIe siècle, 1615-1680. 1869

18th century

Aghion, Max. Le théâtre à Paris au XVIII. siècle. 1926?
Almeras, Henri d' and Quentin, Henri. Les théâtres libertins au XVIII. siècle. 1905
Chefs-d'oeuvre dramatiques du XVIIIe siècle, ou choix des pièces les plus remarquables de Régnard, Lesage, Destouches, Beaumarchais, Marivaux. 1872
Costumes et annales des grands théâtres de Paris. 1786-1789
Gillot, Claude. Nouveaux desseins d'habillements à l'usage des ballets, opéras, et comédies. ca.1726
Guillaumot, A. E. Costumes de la Comédie française XVIIe-XVIIIe siècles. 1885

19th century

Cernuschi, and others. Le costume au théâtre. 1865
Colin, Mme Anais, and Marin, L. Portraits d'acteurs et d'actrices dans différents rôles. ca.1825
Costumes de theatre. ca1815
Damourette, and Talin, H. M. Les actrices. ca1855
Devéria, Achille. Actrices des principaux théâtres de Paris. 1832
Duplessi-Bertaux, Jean. Recueil de cent sujets de divers genres. 1814. Part 6
Galerie dramatique, costumes de théâtres. 1844-70
Grasset de Saint-Sauveur, Jacques. Galerie dramatique ou acteurs et actrices célèbres qui se sont illustrés sur les trois grands théâtres de Paris. 1809
Grévedon, P. L. H. Recueil de quelques portraits d'actrices des principaux théâtres de Paris. 1829
Grévin, Alfred. Costumes de théâtre. ca1875
Guérard, Eugène. Les annales de la danse et du théâtre. 1840
Guyot, and Debacq, A. Album des théâtres. 1837
Journal des dames et des modes. Costumes-portraits des actrices des principaux théâtres de Paris. 1803
Lacauchie, A. Galerie des artistes dramatiques de Paris. 1841-42
Lorsay, Eustache. Galerie illustrée des célébrités contemporaines; les théâtres de Paris. ca1840?
Le musée des théâtres. 1823
Nouvelle galerie dramatique. 1872-80
Petite galerie dramatique ou Recueil des différents costumes d'acteurs des théâtres de la capitale. 1796-1843
Les Premières illustrées. 1882-88
La Scène; revue des succès dramatiques, v.1, no.1-24, 1877-1881. 1877-81
Vizentini, Augustin. Recueil des costumes de tous les ouvrages dramatiques représentés avec succès sur les grands théâtres de Paris. 1819-25?

20th century

Barbier, George. Vingt-cinq costumes pour le théâtre. 1927
Flament, Albert. Personnages de comédie. 1922
Lepape, Georges. Costumes de théâtre, ballets & divertissements. 1920
Salmon, André. Serge Gladky, synthèse du costume théâtral. 1927

Germany

Devrient, Eduard. Geschichte der deutschen schauspielkunst. 1929
Herrmann, Max. Forschungen zur deutschen theater-geschichte des mittelalters und der renaissance. 1914
Hoffman, C. T. A. Groteske gestalten. 1922

16th-18th centuries

Bolte, Johannes. Das Danziger theater im 16. und 17. jahrhundert. 1895
Bonin, Louis. Die neueste art zur galanten und theatralischen tantz-kunst: worinnen gründliche nachricht anzutreffen wie dieses ... exercitium. 1712
Klara, Winfried. Schauspielkostüm und schauspieldarstellung; entwicklungsfragen des deutschen theaters im 18. jahrhundert. 1931

19th century

Brühl, K. F. M. P. graf von. Neue kostüme auf den beiden königlichen theatern in Berlin. 1819-1831

Theatrical costume—Germany—19th cent. —*Continued*

Gallerie dramatischer künstler der königlichen hofbühne zu Berlin. I. heft, Charlotte von Hagn. 1838

Iffland, A. W. Ifflands mimische darstellungen für schauspieler und zeichner. 1819

Köhler, Bruno. Trachtenbilder für die bühne. 1890-92

Lange, Eduard. Costüme des Königlichen hoftheaters zu Berlin. 1839

Stümcke, Heinrich. Die deutsche theaterausstellung, Berlin 1910. 1911

Greece, Ancient

Bieber, Margarete. Das Dresdner schauspielerrelief. Ein beitrag zur geschichte des tragischen kostüms und der griechischen kunst. 1907

Bieber, Margarete. Die denkmäler zum theaterwesen im altertum. 1920

Haigh, A. E. The Attic theatre. 1898

Ridgeway, Sir William. The origin of tragedy with special reference to the Greek tragedians. 1910

Robert, Karl. Die masken der neueren attischen komoedie. 1911

Italy

Allmanacco illustrato delle maschere italiane dalla loro origine sino ai nostri tempi. 1863

Duchartre, P. L. La comedie italienne. c1924

Riccoboni, Luigi. Histoire du theatre italien, depuis la decadence de la comedie latine. 1730-31

Sand, Maurice. Masques et bouffons, comédie italienne. 1860

Schübler, J. J. Amor vehementer quidem flagrans: artificiose tamen celatus, de Pantalonis custodiaque triumphans intentado certamine prudentum stultorum. 1729

Smith, Winifred. The commedia dell' arte; a study in Italian popular comedy. 1912

16th century

Moland, L. É. D. Molière et la comédie italienne. 1867

Stockholm. Nationalmuseum. Recueil de plusieurs fragments des premières comédies italiennes qui ont esté représentées en France sous le regne de Henri III ... présenté par Agne Beijer ... suivi de compositions de m. don Arlequin présentées par P. L. Duchartre. 1928

17th century

Ademollo, Alessandro. I teatri di Roma nel secolo decimosettimo. 1888

Callot, Jacques. Balli di Sfessania. 1621

Moland, L. É. D. Molière et la comédie italienne. 1867

18th-20th centuries

Acteurs du théâtre italien. ca1730

Regnier, Mme. M. L. A. de H. de, and Brunelleschi, Umberto. Les masques et les personnages de la comédie italienne. 1914

Japan

Edwards, Osman. Japanese plays and playfellows. 1901

I͡Akovlev, Aleksandr, and ElīsI͡eev, S. G. Le théâtre japonais (kabuki). 1933

International congress of popular arts, Prague, 1928. Art populaire. 1931

Kan dai ga nō. A display of great "no" illustrations. 1936

Kincaid, Zoë. Kabuki, the popular stage of Japan. 1925

Kongow, Iwao. The costume of Nō play in Japan. 193-

Kongow, Iwao. Nō-isho; Japanese Nō-play costume. 1934

Korio, Japanese artist. Ye zu gaku no. Mey 35th yr.

New York. Metropolitan museum of art. Japanese costume; an exhibition of nō robes and Buddhist vestments, by Alan Priest. 1935

Piper, Maria. Die schaukunst der Japaner dramen, szenenbilder und schauspielerporträts des altjapanischen volkstheaters. 1927

Rome, Ancient

Bieber, Margarete. Die denkmäler zum theaterwesen im altertum. 1920

Paris. Bibliothèque nationale. Mss. (Lat. 7899). Comédies de Térence. 1907

Saunders, Catharine. Costume in Roman comedy. 1909

Russia

Gregor, Joseph, and Fülöp-Miller, René. The Russian theatre: its character and history, with especial reference to the revolutionary period. 1929

Gregor, Joseph, and Fülöp-Miller, René. Das russische theater. 1928 1929

Petrytz'kyĭ, Anatol'. Theater-trachten. 1929

United States

Gregor, Joseph, and Fülöp-Miller, René. Das amerikanische theater und kino. 1931

Krows, A. E. Play production in America. 1916

SPECIAL PLAYS, BALLETS, ETC.

Bakst, Leon. Leon Bakst. 1927

Menut, Adolphe. Les danseuses de l'Opéra; costumes des principaux ballets. 1850?

See also Dance costume

Corneille

Corneille, Pierre. Théâtre. 1776

Dmitri Donskoy

Sammlung von national-trachten und andern zu charakter-masken passenden kostümen. 1826

Ibsen, Henrik

Ibsen, Henrik. Peer Gynt. 1929

Theatrical costume—Special plays—*Cont.*

Hiler. Kleine Klaus

Gehrig, Oscar. Hiler theater und balletenwürfe. 1922

Lalla Rukh

Brühl, K. F. M. P., graf von. Darstellung d. festspiels Lalla Rukh. 1822
Brühl, K. F. M. P., graf von. Lalla Rûkh. 1822
Hensel, Wilhelm. Die lebenden bilder und pantomimischen darstellungen bei dem festspiel: Lalla Rukh, aufgeführt auf dem königlichen schlosse in Berlin den 27sten januar 1821. 1823

Molière

Boucher, Françoise, illus. Les oeuvres de Molière. 1741?
Flutre, Fernand. Molière. 1925

Bibliography

Lacroix, Paul. Iconographie Molièresque. 1876

Racine, Jean Baptiste

Rehberg, Friedrich. Drawings faithfully copied from nature at Naples. 1794

Regnard, Jean François

Regnard, J. F. Oeuvres complètes de Regnard. 1875

Rostand, Maurice. Casanova

Barbier, George. Panorama dramatique: Casanova; décors et costumes. 1921

Russian ballet

Bakst, Léon. L'art décoratif de Léon Bakst. 1913
Bakst, Léon. Synthèse de l'oeuvre du maître. 1928
Brunoff, Maurice de, and Brunoff, Jacques de, eds. Collection des plus beaux numéros de Comoedia illustré et des programmes consacrés aux ballets & galas russes, depuis le début à Paris, 1909-1921. 1922?
Deakin, Irving. Ballet profile. 1936
Haskell, A. L. Prelude to ballet; an analysis and a guide to appreciation. 1936
Ivchenko, V. I. Anna Pavlova. 1922
Ivchenko, V. I., and Bakst, Léon. Le ballet contemporain. 1912
Liven, P. A., kníaz'. The birth of ballets-russes. 1936
Propert, W. A. The Russian ballet in western Europe, 1909-1920. 1921
Réau, Louis, and others. Inedited works of Bakst. 1927

Shakespeare, William

Bööcke, R. L. Shakespearian costumes. 1889-189-?
Boydell, John, and Boydell, Josiah. The American edition of Boydell's Illustrations of the Dramatic works of Shakspeare. 1852
Boydell, John, and Boydell, Josiah. Boydell's graphic illustrations of the dramatic works of Shakespeare. 1798
Darley, F. O. C. The Darley gallery of Shakespearean illustrations. 1884
Douce, Francis. Illustrations of Shakspeare, and of ancient manners. 1807
Dowden, Edward. Shakespeare scenes and characters. 1876
Hatcher, O. L. A book for Shakespeare plays and pageants. 1916
Heath, Charles. The Shakspeare gallery; containing the principal female characters in the plays of the great poet. 1836-37
Heine, Heinrich. Shakespeare's mädchen und frauen. 1839
Heine, Heinrich. Shakespeare's maidens and women. 190-
Kaulbach, Wilhelm von. Shakspere gallerie. 1855-58
Meadows, Kenny. Etchings to the illustrated Shakspere. 1845
Pecht, Friedrich. Shakespeare-galerie. 1876
Planché, J. R. Costume of Shakespeare's ... King John [King Henry the Fourth, As you like it, Hamlet, Othello, Merchant of Venice] selected from the best authorities. 1823-25
Retzsch, F. A. M. Gallerie zu Shakspeare's dramatischen werken. 1828-46
Salaman, M. C. Shakespeare in pictorial art. 1916
Shakespeare, William. The Swan Shakespeare, a player's edition. 1930
Shakspeare-album; sämmtliche costümfiguren aus dem Shakspeare-fest, veranstaltet am 23. april 1864 von der künstler-gesellschaft Malkasten in Düsseldorf ... Shakspeare-album containing all the characters in costume. 1864
Smirke, Robert. Picturesque beauties of Shakespeare. 1783-84
Tallis's Shakspere gallery of engravings. 1852-53
Wingate, C. E. L. Shakespeare's heroes on the stage. c1896
Wingate, C. E. L. Shakespeare's heroines on the stage. 1895

King Henry VIII

Costumes in Shakspeare's historical play of King Henry the Eighth. 18-?
London. Lyceum Theatre. Souvenir of Shakespeare's historical play King Henry the Eighth, presented at the Lyceum theatre, 5th January, 1892, by Henry Irving. 1892

Macbeth

London. Lyceum theatre. Souvenir of Macbeth produced at the Lyceum theatre, by Henry Irving, 29th December, 1888. 1888

Merry wives of Windsor

Crane, Walter. Shakespeare's comedy of the Merry wives of Windsor. 1894

Richard III

Tomkins, C. F., and Planché, J. R. Twelve designs for the costume of Shakespeare's Richard the Third. 1830

Theatrical costume—Shakespeare, William —*Continued*

Tempest

Crane, Walter. Eight illustrations to Shakespeare's Tempest. 1894

Paton, Sir J. N., illus. Compositions from Shakespeare's Tempest. 1877

Shakespeare, William. Outlines to Shakespeare's Tempest; a series of twelve plates by H. C. Selous. 1836

Two gentlemen of Verona

Crane, Walter. Eight illustrations to Shakespeare's Two gentlemen of Verona. 1894

Winter's tale

Costumes in Shakespeare's play of the Winter's Tale, as represented at the Princess's Theatre. 1861?

The sleeping princess

Bakst, Léon. Designs of Leon Bakst for The sleeping princess. 1923

Victor

Gérard. Costumes de principaux personnages des Scandinaves tragédie en 5 actes de M. Victor. 1824

Theatrical costume, Amateur

Bates, E. W. The art of producing pageants. 1925

Chubb, Percival. Festivals and plays in schools and elsewhere. 1912

Fletcher, Ursula. Stage costumes. n.d.

Lamkin, N. B. Inexpensive costumes for plays, festivals and pageants

Mackay, C. D'A. Costumes and scenery for amateurs. 1932

Nesfield-Cookson, Mrs M. J.-P. The costume book. 1935

Saunders, D. L. Costuming the amateur show. 1937

Somerscales, M. I. The improvised stage. 1932

Theatricals and tableaux vivants for amateurs. Harrison, Charles

Theatrũ Mulierum. Hollar, Wenceslaus

Theatrum europaeum, oder Aussführliche und warhafftige beschreibung aller und jeder denckwürdiger geschichten so sich hin und wieder in der welt fürnemblich aber in Europa, und Teutschlanden ... vom jahr Christi 1617 biss auff das jahr ⌊1718⌋ Franckfurt am Mayn, D. Fievet 1646-1738

32pt. in 21v. illus. 981pl.(part fold.) maps(part fold.) plans, tab. F.

A continuation of J. L. Gottfried's *Historische chronica.* Title varies: th. 7-10 have title: *Irenico-polemographia, sive Theatri europaei continuati septennium;* th. 21: *Jubilaeum theatri europaei*

Plates show portraits, battles, sieges, historical events, triumphs, festivals, tournaments, funerals, etc. in Europe during the 17th and 18th centuries

Contributors to the various parts and the period covered by each: 1. th. J. P. Abelin, 1617-29; 2. th. J. P. Abelin, 1629-32; 3. th. H. Oraeus, 1633-38; 4. th. I. P. A. ⌊Abelin?⌋ 1638-42; 5. th. J. P. Lotichius, 1643-47; 6. th. J. G. Schleder, 1647-50; 7. th. J. G. Schleder, 1651-57; 8. th. M. Meyer, 1657-60; 9. th. M. Meyer, 1660-65

10. th. W. J. Geiger, 1665-71; 11. th. 1672-79; 12. th. 1679-86; 13. th. 1687-90; 14. th. 1691-95; 15. th. 1696-1700; 16. th. ⌊D. Schneider⌋ 1701-03; 17. th. ⌊D. Schneider⌋ 1704-06; 18. th. ⌊D. Schneider⌋ 1707-09; 19. th. ⌊D. Schneider⌋ 1710-12

20. th. 1713-15; 21. th. 1716-18. cf. Meusel's Bibl. hist. and Zedler's Universal-lexicon

Lipperheide 527. LC 3-1466

Theatrum hystoriae universalis Catholico Protestantiv. Helwig, Nicolaus

Their Majesties' courts holden at Buckingham palace and at the palace of Holyroodhouse, 1934-35. With particulars of the courts and toilettes worn. Presentations to Their Majesties. London, Newbery publications 1934-35

v⌊1-2⌋ front. pl. ports. sq.Q.

Editor: 1934-35, F. B. Fawcett. Advertising matter interspersed. 1935 volume published by Belgravia publications

LC (35-16921)

Théodore, L.

Costumes du Finistère. Quimper, Lafage 1848?

8pl. O.

Colas 2868

Theoretisch-practische anleitung zur fechtkunst. Chappon, Louis

Theoretisch-praktischer unterricht für maschinennähen und weiszarbeiten. See Schmidt, Carl, and Schmidt, Rosalie. Methodische anleitung für geometrische zuschnittlehre

Theoretische lessen over de gesticulatie en mimiek. Jelgerhuis, J.

Théorie de l'art du coiffeur. Croisat

Théorie pratique du danseur de société. Brunet

Théorie sur l'escrime à cheval. Muller, Alexandre

Theory and practice of color. Snow, B. E., and Froehlich, H. B.

Theory of fencing. Corbesier, A. J.

Theory of the leisure class. Veblen, Thorstein. 1912

Thesaurus antiquitatum romanarum. See Raynaud, Théophile. Anselmus Solerivs Cemeliensis. De pileo

Thesaurus exoticorum. Happel, E. W., ed.

Thesaurus Graecarum antiquitatum. Gronovius, Jacobus

Thesaurus nummorum Sueo-Gothicorum. Brenner, Eli

Theuerdank

Die geuerlicheiten und eins teils der geschichten des loblichẽ streitbaren und hochberümbten helds und ritters Tewrdannckhs. Augspurg, Gedruckt durch den eltern Hansen Schönsperger 1519

580p. 118 illus. F.

The work of Maximilian I, of Germany, and his secretaries, Melchior Pfintzing and Marx Treitz-Sauerwein. The woodcuts are chiefly by Hans Schaeufelein. They show 16th century dress

First edition: 1517. This is the second printing of the second edition

Lipperheide 612. LC 15-12291

Thiele, C. F. See Graenicher, Samuel, jt. auth.

Thienen, Frithjof Willem Sophi van
Das kostüm der blütezeit Hollands, 1600-1660. Berlin, Deutscher kunstverlag. 1930
180p. illus. pl.(part fold.) O. (Kunstwissenschaftliche studien, bd. VI)
Folded maps in pocket
Issued also in part as the author's "proefschrift", Utrecht, under title: *Studien zur kostümgeschichte der blütezeit Hollands* (1929. 112p.)
Costume index. LC 36-6539, 35-36431 (1929 ed.)

Thiers, Jean Baptiste
De stola in archidiaconorum visitationibus gestanda à parœcis, disceptatio, in quâ multa ad archidiaconorum munus, jurisdictionem ac visitationes attinentia curiosè pertractantur. Parisiis, apud J. Du Puis 1674
391,[13]p. S.
Caption and running title: *Disceptatio de stola*
LC 31-30581

Histoire des perruques; où l'on fait voir, leur origine, leur usage, leur forme, l'abus & l'irregularité de celles des ecclesiastiques. Paris, Aux dépens de l'auteur 1690
12 l. 544p. S.
Another edition (Avignon, L. Chambeau 1777) Italian edition: *Istoria della perruche* (Benevento, 1702)
Colas 2869-70. Lipperheide 1660-1661. LC 25-3693

Thimm, Carl Albert
A complete bibliography of fencing and duelling, as practised by all European nations from the middle ages to the present day ... illustrated with numerous portraits of ancient and modern masters of the art, title-pages & frontispieces of some of the earliest works. London and New York, J. Lane 1896
xvi,537p. front. illus. pl. ports.(part col.) facsims. O.
Lipperheide 2996. LC 1-2640

Things as they are in America. Chambers, William

Things clerical. Rogers, Peet & co. New York

Things Indian. Crooke, W.

Things Japanese. Chamberlain, B. H.

Things seen in China. Chitty, J. R.

Things seen in Japan. Holland, Clive

Thirifocq
Histoire universelle du costume par Thirifocq d'après,les grands peintres de chaque époque et les documents authentiques, avec la collaboration artistique et littéraire de m. Mille dessinateur et de M. F. Pillon. Paris, 1863-64
20p. 15pl.(10 col.) Q.
Colas 2871

This was England. Bott, A. J.

[**Thomas**]
[Sketches of British soldiers. London, 1861-69]
6 col.pl. F.
Colas 2873

Thomas, Jean Baptiste
Un an à Rome et dans ses environs; recueil de dessins lithographiés, représentant les costumes, les usages et les cérémonies civiles et religieuses des états romains. Paris, F. Didot 1823
44p. 72 col.pl. F.
Also found with plates in black and white. Second edition: 1830
Colas 2872. Lipperheide 1309. LC 4-31443

Thomas, Northcote Whitridge. See Joyce, T. A., jt. ed.

Thomas, Sir William Beach
Hunting England; a survey of the sport and of its chief grounds. London, B. T. Batsford; New York, C. Scribner [1936]
120p. col.front. illus. pl.(part col.) O. 7s 6d, $3.50
"Illustrated from old prints and pictures, and from modern photographs." Subtitle
Illustrations show fox-hunting

Thomas, William Isaac
Sex and society; studies in the social psychology of sex. Chicago, Univ. of Chicago press 1907
325p. D.
Contains a chapter: The psychology of modesty and clothing p 201-220
LC 7-7162

(ed.) Source book for social origins; ethnological materials, psychological standpoint, classified and annotated bibliographies for the interpretation of savage society. Chicago, The University of Chicago press 1909
xvi,932p. illus. O.
Contains some material on dress and armor of primitive peoples
LC 9-27970

Thomassin, Henri Simon
(engr.) Watteau, J. A. Figures de modes

Thompson, Grace E. See Boehn, Max von. Modes & manners of the nineteenth century. v4

Thompson, Maurice Scott. See Wace, A. J. B., jt. auth.

Thompson, Peter Anthony
Lotus land, being an account of the country and the people of southern Siam. Philadelphia, J. B. Lippincott company; [etc. 1907?]
xii,312p. col.front. illus. pl. fold.map. O.
LC 7-37975

Thomson, Hugh
(illus.) Dobson, Austin. The ballad of Beau Brocade

Thomson, John
Illustrations of China and its people; a series of two hundred photographs, with letterpress descriptive of the places and people represented. London, S. Low, Marston, Low, and Searle 1873-74
4v. 96pl. sq.F. 126s, o.p.
Costume index. Lipperheide 1535. LC 5-3761

(tr.) Davillier, J. C., baron. Spain

Thomson, Richard
(ed.) A faithful account of the processions and ceremonies observed in the coronation of the kings and queens of England, exemplified in that of

Thomson, Richard—*Continued*
Their late most sacred Majesties King George the Third, and Queen Charlotte. London, Printed for J. Major 1820
99p. fold.front. 3pl. O.
Caption title: *An account of the ceremonial of Their late Majesties' coronation, and the other heraldic proceedings connected therewith*
Folding frontispiece shows form of the procession to the coronation of the sovereigns of England
LC 2-27349

Thormann-Bechlin, Louise
Leitfaden zum theoretischen und praktischen unterricht der damenschneiderei; 9. aufl. hrsg. von L. Otto. Straszburg, Im selbstverlage 1893
50 illus. 1 pl. O.
Lipperheide 3844

Thornam, Erla
Gamle smykker i Norge, 1550-1900. See entry under Oslo. Kunstindustrimuseet

Thornely, James L.
The monumental brasses of Lancashire and Cheshire, with some account of the persons represented. Hull, W. Andrews; London, Simpkin, Marshall, Hamilton, Kent 1893
322p. pl. O.
Shows English costume of the 15th, 16th, and 17th centuries
LC 7-6973

Thoumas, Charles Antoine
Les anciennes armées françaises; exposition rétrospective militaire du Ministère de la guerre en 1889. Paris, H. Launette 1890
2v. illus. 19pl. Q.
Shows French uniforms from the middle ages to 1870
Colas 2874

Three gringos in Venezuela and Central America. Davis, R. H.

Three hundred French portraits. Clouet, François

Three visits to Madagascar. Ellis, William

Thresor des antiquitez de la couronne de France. Montfaucon, Bernard de

Through Corsica with a camera. Este, Margaret d'

Through forbidden Tibet. Forman, Harrison

Through the Apennines and the lands of the Abruzzi. Canziani, Estella

Through the heart of Patagonia. Prichard, H. V. H.

Through the lands of the Serb. Durham, M. E.

Through the Philippines and Hawaii. Carpenter, F. G.

Thucelium, C. L. See Leucht, C. L.

Thümmel, Hans von
Historische, statistische, geographische und topographische beyträge zur kenntnisz. Altenburg, 1818
112p. 41pl.(38 col.) 2 maps. F.
Shows dress in Altenburg from the 15th to the 18th century
Lipperheide 824

Thüringer trachten. Gerbing, Frau Luise

Thulstrup, H.
Afbildningar af nordiska drägter. See entry under Afbildningar

Thuringia. See Germany—Thuringia

Thurn, Rudolf Payer von. See Payer von Thurn, Rudolf, ritter

Thurnier buch. Rüxner, Georg

Thurston, Edgar
Ethnographic notes in southern India. Madras, Printed by the superintendent, Government press 1906
580p. front. XXXVIII pl. O.
Contains material on the dress of the natives of southern India
LC 6-41736

Thylesius, Antonius. See Telesio, Antonio

Ti Tegninger af Christoffer Wilhelm Eckersberg. Eckersberg, C. V.

La **tiara** pontificale. Müntz, Eugène

Tibet
Ahmad Shāh. Four years in Tibet. 1906
Bell, Sir C. A. People of Tibet. 1928
Bonvalot, Gabriel. Across Thibet. c1891
Bouillane de Lacoste, É. A. H. de. Around Afghanistan. 1909
Candler, Edmund. The unveiling of Lhasa. 1905
Forman, Harrison. Through forbidden Tibet; an adventure into the unknown. 1935
Hedin, S. A. Transhimalaja. 1909-12
Landor, A. H. S. Tibet & Nepal. 1905
McGovern, W. M. To Lhasa in disguise; an account of a secret expedition through mysterious Tibet. 1924
Rockhill, W. W. The land of the lamas; notes of a journey through China, Mongolia and Tibet. 1891
Sarachchandra Dāsa. Journey to Lhasa and central Tibet. 1902
Sherring, C. A. Western Tibet and the British borderland. 1906
Shoberl, Frederic, ed. Tibet, and India beyond the Ganges. 1824
Tafel, Albert. Meine Tibetreise. 1914

See also Buddhist monks

Tibet & Nepal. Londor, A. H. S.

Tidemand, Adolph
Norwegisches bauernleben ... lithographirt von J. B. Sonderland, mit deutschem text von Wolfgang Müller und norwegischem text von A. Munch. Düsseldorf, E. Schulte 1851
11p. 10 illus. ob.F.
Norwegian title: *Norsk bondeliv*
Colas 2876. Lipperheide 1049

(illus.) Tønsberg, N. C., ed. Norske folkelivsbilleder

Tierra del Fuego
Bove, Giacomo. Patagonia, Terra del Fuoco, mari australi. 1883

Tierra del Fuego. Gallardo, C. R.

Ties (Neckties). See Neckwear

Tietz, Friedrich
(ed.) Bloch, Eduard. Eduard Bloch's album der bühnen-costüme

Tiffany, Ruth Moulton
(comp.) The Charles G. King collection of books on costume. See entry under Western reserve historical society, Cleveland, O. King collection

Tikkanen, Johan Jakob
Finnische textilornamentik. Leipzig, Duncker & Humblot 1901
2pts. 10pl.(2 col. 3 double) O.
From *Finnländische rundschau* I: 3-4
Lipperheide 3984

Tilke, Max
The costumes of eastern Europe. London, E. Benn; Berlin, E. Wasmuth 1926
32p. illus. 96 col.pl. F. 105s, o.p.
Obtainable from E. Weyhe, New York at $17.50. Translation of the author's *Osteuropäische volkstrachten*
Costume index. LC 26-13136

Oriental costumes, their designs and colors. London, K. Paul, Trench, Trubner [1923]
32p. 128 col.pl. Q. 52s 6d, o.p.
Translated by L. Hamilton, from the French edition of his *Orientalische kostüme*
Costume index. LC 24-5826

Orientalische kostüme in schnitt und farbe. Berlin, E. Wasmuth 1923
32p. 128 col.pl. F.
Shows costume of Syria, Arabia, Palestine, Turkey, Caucasus, Persia, Afghanistan, Kashmir, India, Indo-China, Tibet, Turkestan, China, Japan, Algeria, Egypt, Tunisia, and African tribes
Translated into French with title: *Le costume en orient* (Paris, G. Hue 1922)
Colas 2878 (Fr. ed.)

Osteuropäische volkstrachten in schnitt und farbe. Berlin, E. Wasmuth [1925]
35p. illus. 96 col.pl. Q.
Shows costume of northern and southern Russia as well as all the Balkan states
French edition: *Le costume de l'Europe orientale* (Berlin, E. Wasmuth 1926)
Colas 2879 (Fr. ed.)

Studien zu der entwicklungsgeschichte des orientalischen kostüms. Berlin, E. Wasmuth 1923
71p. Q.
Colas 2877

(illus.) Rosenberg, Adolf. The design and development of costume from prehistoric times up to the twentieth century

(illus.) Rosenberg, Adolf. Geschichte des kostüms

Tillæg til en afhandling om amuletter og om stormænds begravelse blandt Skandinaver i hedenold og blandt Mellemasiens Buddhister. Holmboe, C. A.

Timidior, O.
Der hut und seine geschichte; eine kulturgeschichtliche monographie. Wien, A. Hartleben [1914]
160p. 85 illus. O.
Illustrated by Karl Heidrich

Timlich, Carl
(ed.) Heimbucher von Bikessy, J. A Magyar és Horváth országi leg nevezetesebb nemzeti oltözetek hazai gyüjeteménie

Timm, W.
Costumes russes. Moscou et St Pétersbourg, Daziaro; Paris, Lemercier [1843-44]
28 col.pl. F.
Colas 2880. Lipperheide 1360

The **Tinguian.** Cole, F. C.

Tinne Indians. See Indians of North America—Tinne Indians

Tinney, John
A collection of eastern & other foreign dresses. London, J. Tinney ca1750
10pl. F.
Feminine costume of the 18th century in France, Italy, and Greece
Colas 2881. Lipperheide 562

Tipi militari. Zezon, Antonio

Il **tipo** estetico della donna nel medioevo. Renier, Rodolfo

Tipos españoles. Moreno Rodriguez, Manuel

Tipos y costumbres de la isla de Cuba. See Bachiller y Morales, Antonio. Coleccion de artículos

Tipos y trajes de España. See note under Ortiz Echagüe, José. España, tipos y trajes

Tiranti, Dominic C.
(ed.) Rosenberg, Adolf. The design and development of costume from prehistoric times up to the twentieth century

Tirard, Mrs Helen Mary (Beloe)
(tr.) Erman, Adolf. Life in ancient Egypt

Le **tiroir** du diable. See Le diable à Paris

Tirolensium. Custos, Dominicus

Tiroler trachten. Kappeller, J. A.

Tiron, Abbé
Histoire et costumes des ordres religieux, civils et militaires 2. ed. Bruxelles, Librairie historique-artistique 1845
2v. front. col.pl. Q.
Engraved by E. Duverger
For an Italian version see Cibrario's *Descrizione*
Colas 2882. Costume index. Lipperheide 1881

Tischbein, A. See Selb, August, jt. auth.

Titeux, Eugène
Histoire de la maison militaire du roi de 1814 à 1830, avec un résumé de son organisation et de ses campagnes sous l'ancienne monarchie. Paris, Baudry 1890
2v. 84 col.pl. Q.
Colas 2883. Lipperheide 2354

Historiques et uniformes de l'armée française. Paris, E. Levy 1895?
11 pts. col.illus. 20 col.pl. F.
Shows uniforms of several French regiments at various periods
Colas 2884

Titian. See Vecellio, Cesare. Coleccion; also note under his De gli habiti

Titsingh, Isaac
Cerémonies usitées au Japon, pour les mariages, les funérailles, et les principales fêtes de l'année; suivies d'anecdotes sur la dynastie régnante des souverains de cet empire; ouvrage traduit du japonais par feu M. Titsingh. Paris, Nepveu 1822
3v. 24 col.pl.(incl. fronts.) S.
Also known with plates in black and white. First edition (Paris, A. Nepveu 1809. 2v. 19pl.)
Colas 577-78. LC 4-35022

Tizac, Jean Henri d'Ardenne de. See Ardenne de Tizac, J. H. de'

Tiziano Vecelli. See Vecellio, Cesare. Coleccion de trages que usaron todas las naciones conocidas hasta el siglo xv; also note under Vecellio, Cesare. De gli habiti antichi

To gipsyland. Pennell, Mrs E. R.

To Lhasa in disguise. McGovern, W. M.

Tobacco pipes. See Pipes and smokers' utensils

Tobias, J. H.
(ed.) Meijlan, G. F. Japan

Toché, Raoul
(ed.) Les Premières illustrées

Todas. See India—Native tribes—Todas

Today's housewife. See To-day's woman and home

Today's magazine. See Today's woman and home

To-day's woman and home. v.1-24 no.6; Mar. 1905-Sept. 1928. New York, Canton magazine co.
24v. illus. Q.-F.
Published monthly
Title varies: Mar. 1905-Jan. 1917, *Today's magazine;* Feb. 1917-May 1927, *Today's housewife;* June-Dec. 1927 *Today's housewife and woman and home;* Jan.-Sept. 1928 *Today's woman and home*
Published at Yonkers, N. Y., 1905; Warren, Pa., 1906-10; Canton, O., 1910-14
Absorbed *Dressmaking at home,* Aug. 1911; *The Housewife,* Feb. 1917; *Royal* 1925. Publication suspended May-July 1922

Todd, George Eyre-. See Eyre-Todd, George

Das **todtenfeld** vom Ancon in Peru. Reiss, Wilhelm, and Stübel, Alfons

Der **todtentanz.** See Dance of death. Les simulachres & historiees faces de la mort

Todtentanz der stadt Basel. See Dance of death. Todten-tantz wie derselbe in der löblichen und weit berühmten statt Basel ... zu sehen ist

Der **todtentanz** in der Marien-kirche zu Berlin. Prüfer, Theodor

Todten-tantz wie derselbe in der löblichen und weitberühmten statt Basel ... zu sehen ist. Dance of death

Tønsberg, Nils Christian
(ed.) Norske folkelivsbilleder. Christiania, Winckelmann 1854
14 l. col.front. 12 col.pl. ob.F.
Text in Norwegian, German, English. Illustrations by A. Tidemand show Norwegian costume
Colas 2894

(ed.) Norske nationaldragter. Christiania, Winckelmann 1852
54p. 33 col.pl. Q.
Text in Norwegian, German and English. Illustrated by Joachim Frich and J. F. Eckersberg
New edition: *Udvalgte norske nationaldragter* (Christiania, Udgiverens forlag. 1861. 31p. 15 col.pl.)
Colas 2893. Costume index. Lipperheide 1050. LC 34-33438 (1861 ed.)

Toga. See Rome

Toga, The Roman. Wilson, L. M.

Toga, A study of the Roman. See Wilson, L. M. A study of the Roman toga

Toiles peintes et tapisseries de la ville de Reims. Paris, Louis

Toilet. See Beauty, Personal; Combs; Shaving

Toilet and cosmetic arts in ancient and modern times. Cooley, A. J.

Toilet in ancient and modern times. See Cooley, A. J. The toilet and cosmetic arts in ancient and modern times

Toilet; tijdschrift voor vrouwelijke handwerken. Jahrg. 1849-1854. Utrecht, N. de Zwaan
Pl. O.

Die **toilette.** Kunc, M.

La **toilette** à la cour de Napoléon, 1810-1815. Bouchot, H. F. X. M.

La **Toilette** de Paris. 1. annee, 1859-1873? Paris
Col.pl. Q.
Hatin gives the beginning date as 1858
Colas 2886. Lipperheide 4689

La **toilette** de Psyche. See Psyché, journal des modes, littérature, théâtres et musique

La **toilette** des femmes depuis l'époque gallo-romaine jusqu'à nos jours. See Challamel, Augustin. Histoire de la mode en France

La **toilette** des graces, ou Joli recueil des coëffures nouvellement. Nénot

La **toilette** chez les Romaines au temps des empereurs. Crochet, L. C.

Toilette d'une Romaine au temps d'Auguste. James, Constantin

La **toilette** féminine à travers les ages. Prod'homme, J. G.

La **toilette** féminine et les bibelots de l'époque romantique. See Keezer, Ro. Feminine toilettes and knick-knacks of the romantic age

Toilette of a Hebrew lady. De Quincey, Thomas

Les **toilettes** de la Collectivité de la couture. Paris. Exposition universelle, 1900

Toilettes de nos grand'mères d'après les meilleurs journaux du temps: Le journal des dames et Le petit courrier des dames. Paris, Au bureau du Journal les modes parisiennes [1860]
20 col.pl. Q.
Shows feminine costume from 1801 until 1830
Colas 2890. Lipperheide 1172

La **Toison** d'or. Kervyn de Lettenhove, H. M. B. J. L., baron

Tokugawa ryaku denki. Ota, Shintaro

Tokyo. Imperial museum
Album of the life sized figures exhibited in the Tokyo Imperial museum, showing costumes of different ages. 190-?
32p. 18pl. O.
Title taken from typewritten table of contents. Title page and text in Japanese

Tollius, Adrianus
(ed.) Boodt, A. B. de. Le parfait ioaillier

The **tomb** of Tut.ankh.Amen. Carter, Howard, and Mace, A. C.

Tomb of two sculptors at Thebes. Davies, N. de G.

Tomkins, C. F., and Planché, James Robinson
Twelve designs for the costume of Shakespeare's Richard the third by C. F. Tompkins; after the drawings and with the descriptions of J. R. Planché. London, Colnaghi 1830
20p. 12 col.pl. Q.
Colas 2892

Tomkinson, William Shirley. See Phillips, Margaret, jt. auth.

Tools and weapons illustrated by the Egyptian collection in University college, London. Petrie, Sir W. M. F.

Topf, Jakob. See An Almain armourer's album

Topographical and historical description of the university and city of Oxford. Whittock, Nathaniel

Torday, Emil
On the trail of the Bushongo; an account of a remarkable & hitherto unknown African people, their origin, art, high social & political organization & culture, derived from the author's personal experience amongst them. London, Seeley, Service 1925
286p. front. illus. pl. fold. map. O.
LC 25-10203

Il **torneo.** Pistofilo, Bonaventura

Il **torneo** di Caserta nel carnevale dell' anno 1846. Ventimiglia, Domenico

Torquatus à Frangipani, Alexander Julius
Meditatae à gloriosiss. Memoriae in Cembrica chersoneso academiae divo Friderico Cimbrorum duce ... & providentia ... Christiani Alberti ... Kiloniae fundatae. Ejusdem inaugurationis panegyrica descripto. No place [1666]
134p. 27pl. F.
Twenty-three plates show costume of professors and students at the University of Kiel
Lipperheide 2017

[**Torres Méndez, Ramón**]
Costumbres santafereñas. [Leipzig, E. V. Sperling 1910?]
[60]pl. ob.O.
Binder's title
LC 35-24108

Tott, François, baron de
Nachrichten con den Türken und Tataren, mit herrn von Peyssonnel's verbesserungen und zusätzen; aus dem französischen. Frankfurt und Leipzig, C. Weigel und A. G. Schneider 1788
2v. 26pl. O.
Many of the plates are copied from J. B. van Moor's *Recueil de cent estampes.* They show Turkish dress
Colas 2895. Lipperheide 1420

Totti, Pompilio
Ritratti et elogii di capitani illustri. Roma, P. Totti 1635
296p. 129 port. O.
"Dedicati all' A. S. di Francesco d'Este duca di Modena"
Head and shoulder portraits of distinguished European men. Some show armor. May be the same book as a similar title entered under Roscio. We have not been able to compare the two books

Touaregs. See Tuaregs

Touchemolin, Alfred
Le régiment d'Alsace dans l'armée française. Paris, A. Hennuyer 1897
100 illus.(6 col.) O.
Colas 2897

Strasbourg militaire. Paris, A. Hennuyer 1894
147p. 40 col.pl. Q.
Colas 2896

Toudouze, Anaïs
(illus.) Journal des dames

Touissant y Ritter, Manuel. See Mexico (City) Biblioteca nacional. La litografia en Mexico en el siglo XIX

Le **tour** du monde: album des costumes. Albert, A.

Tour du monde; nouveau journal des voyages, publié sous la direction de m. Edouard Charton et illustré par nos plus célèbres artistes. v 1-68, 1860-1894; new ser. v 1-20, 1895-1914. Paris, Hachette
Illus. F.
With new ser. v 1, sub-title changes to: journal des voyages et des voyageurs
Many parts of the world are described and pictured with illustrations ranging from those by Doré, Catlin, and others, to modern photographs. Many costumes are shown
A travers le monde v 1-20, 1895-1914, is a supplement; and also a continuation of *Nouvelles géographiques*

A **tour** through Paris. London, W. Sams [1822-24]
21 l. 21 col.pl. F.
Plates show various street scenes in Paris. Four of them are from Peake's *The characteristic costume of France*
Colas 2898. Lipperheide 1187

Touraine. See France—By region or province—Touraine

Touraine and its story. Macdonell, Anne

The **tourist** in Portugal. Harrison, W. H.

Le **touriste** ou souvenir de l'ouest de la France. Valerio, Théodore

The **tournament.** Clephan, R. C.

Tournament costume
Allerhöchst-feyerlichste festivitäten ... bei dem ... beylager ... Leopoldi I. Römischen Kaysers ... und Margaritae ... Infantin von Hispanien 1667

Borghi, C. R. L'oplomachia pisana, ovvero La battaglia del ponte di Pisa. 1713

Clephan, R. C. The tournament; its periods and phases. 1919

La description et ordre du camp & festiem̃t & ioustes des ... roys de France et Dangleterre la mil.ccccc. et vingt au moys de iuing. 1864

Hänel, Erich. Der sächsischen kurfürsten turnierbücher. 1910

Tournament costume—*Continued*

Lodi, Giacinto. Amore prigioniero in Delo; torneo fatto da' signori Academici torbidi in Bologna li xx. di marzo MDCXXVIII. 1628?

Modius, François. Pandectae triumphales, sive, Pomparum, et festorum ac solennium apparatuum, conviviorum, spectaculorum, simulacrorum bellicorum equestrium, et pedestrium. 1586

Perrault, Charles. Courses de testes et de bague faittes par le roy, et par les princes et seigneurs de sa cour, en l'année 1662. 1670

Pistofilo, Bonaventura. Il torneo. 1627

Ritterliche reutter kunst ... in Teutschland. 1584

Rudnitzki, Paul. Der turnierroman "Livre des faits du bon chevalier Messire Jacques de Lalaing" in der Anholter handschrift. 1915

Rüxner, Georg. Thurnier buch; von anfang, ursachen, ursprung, und herkommen der thurnuier im Heyligen römischen reich teutscher nation wie viel offentlicher landthurnier von keyser Heinrich dem Ersten dieses namens an biss auff den jetztregierenden keyser Maximilian den Andern. 1566

Sieg-streit dess lufft und wassers freuden-fest zu pferd. 1667

Tournefort, Joseph Pitton de

Relation d'un voyage du Levant. Paris, Imprimerie royale 1717

2v. illus. 88pl. O.
Twenty-five plates show costume of Greece and the Greek islands. Also published in Amsterdam, 1718
Lipperheide 1442. LC 12-16506

Tournier, Albert. See Arène, P. A., jt. auth.

Toussaint, Maurice

(illus.) Bucquoy, E. L. Les uniformes de l'armée française. 1935

Tout, Charles Hill. See Hill-Tout, Charles

Touzé, Jean

(illus.) Recueil d'estampes, représentant les grades, les rangs et les dignités, suivant le costume de toutes les nations existantes

The **tower** of London. Benham, William

Tower of London; guide to the armouries. Ffoulkes, C. J.

Towle, Herbert Chester

The shoe in romance and history. [San Francisco, A. Carlisle c1915]

24p. illus. O.
Illustrations are reproductions from paintings for the United shoe machinery company by Josef Urban
LC 15-25842

Townsend, W. G. Paulson, and Pesel, Louisa F.

Embroidery; or, The craft of the needle ... with preface by Walter Crane. New York, F. A. Stokes 1908

xx,308p. col.front. illus. pl. D.
First edition: London, 1899
LC 8-36170

Townsend's monthly selection of Parisian costumes. v. 1-336, 1825-52; new ser. v. 1-417, 1853-88. London, J. Townsend 1825-88

Col.pl. Q.
Supersedes *Townsend's quarterly selection*
Colas 2899. Lipperheide 4607

Townsend's quarterly selection of French costumes, nos 1-9, 1822-24. London, 1822-24

Col.illus. O.
Superseded by *Townsend's monthly selection of Parisian costumes.* Binders title: *Parisian costumes*

Tozzer, Alfred Marston

A comparative study of the Mayas and the Lacandones. New York & London, Macmillan 1907

xx,195p. illus. XXIX pl. O. (Archaeological institute of America. Report of the fellow in American archaeology, 1902-1905)
Bibliography: p191-95
Shows costume of the Indians of Mexico
LC 7-9604

Tracé des objets d'habillemens et d'équipement à l'usage de l'armée norvégienne. Havin

Tracé descriptif des divers objets d'habillement ... de l'armée française en 1828. Hecquet, F.

Tracht der ehren-ritter des deutschen ritterordens. Wien, Verlag der Deutschen ordens kanzlei 1874

4 l. 4pl. O.
Colas 2900. Lipperheide 1937m

Die **tracht** der Germanen in der vor- und frühgeschichtlichen zeit. Girke, Georg

Die **tracht** der kulturvölker Europas vom zeitalter Homers bis zum beginne des XIX jahrhunderts. Heyden, August von

Tracht der ritter des hohen deutschen ordens. Wien, Verlag der Deutschen ordens-kanzlei 1869

3 l. 4pl. O.
Lipperheide 1936m

Die **tracht** der schlesischen fürstinnen. Roehl, E.

Tracht und bewaffnung des römischen heeres während der kaiserzeit. Lindenschmit, Ludwig

Trachten-album, nach der natur gezeichnet und lithogr. von Ranftl. Kollarz, Gerasch, Kaliwoda, etc. Wien, F. Paterno ca1860

140 col.pl. F.
Running title: *Oesterr. national-trachten*
Plates show costume of various provinces of Austria-Hungary
Cataloged from Colas's *Bibliographie*
Colas 2901

Trachten aus Alt-Hamburg. Jessen, Heinrich

Trachten-bilder ... aus der Albertina. Dürer, Albrecht

Trachten der Alpenländer. Hammerstein, Hans von

Trachten der Holländerinnen. Buyteweck, Willem

Trachten der Juden im nachbiblischen alterthume. Brüll, Adolph

Die **trachten** der Römer und Römerinnen nach Ovid und Martial. Müller, Albert

Trachten der Schweden an den küsten Ehstlands und auf Runö. Schlichting, E. H.

Die **trachten** der völker. Rohrbach, Carl

Die **trachten** der völker in bild und schnitt. Köhler, Karl. See note under his Praktische kostumkunde

Die **trachten** der XII kirchspiele des Oeselschen kreises. Arensberg auf der insel Oesel ca1840[?]
20 col.pl. O.
Colas 2902. Lipperheide 1358

Trachten des christlichen mittelalters. Hefner-Alteneck, J. H. von

Die **trachten** des polnischen volkes. See Zienkowicz, Léon

Trachten, haus-, feld- und kriegsgeräthschaften der völker alter und neuer zeit. Hottenroth, Friedrich

Trachten, kunstwerke und geräthschaften des siebzehnten und achtzehnten jahrhunderts. Hefner-Alteneck, J. H. von

Trachten, kunstwerke und geräthschaften vom frühen mittelalter. Hefner-Alteneck, J. H. von

Trachten macherley völcker des erdskreyss. See Boissard, J. J. Habitus variarum orbis gentium

Trachten oder Stambuch: dariñen alle fürneṁste nationen, völckern, manns unnd weibs personen in ihren kleydern artlich abgemahlt nach jedes landes sitten und gebrauch. S. Gallen, G. Straub 1600
4 l. 90 illus. ob.O.
Illustrations each show two or three costume figures. Latin edition (ca1600) has title: *Icones quibus habitus omnium fere mundi gentium exprimitur*
Colas 2903. Lipperheide 26

Trachten, sitten, und gebräuche der Algierer. See Jungmann, Robert. Costumes, moeurs et usages des Algériens

Trachten und gebräuche der Neugriechen. Stackelberg, O. M., freiherr von

Trachten und muster der Mordvinen. See Heikel, A. O. Mordvalaisten pupuja ja kuoseja

Trachten und sitten im Elsass. Laugel, Anselme

[**Trachten** und wappen der zünfte und gilden von Bologna] Bologna, ca1700
18 col.pl. F.
Lipperheide 1974

Trachten, volksfeste ... im Baden. Schreiber, A. W.

Trachten von den representanten des französischen volks. See note under Grasset de Saint Sauveur, Jacques. Costumes des représentans du peuple

Trachtenbilder fur die bühne. Köhler, Bruno

Trachtenbuch. Bertelli, Ferdinando

Das **trachtenbuch.** Weiditz, Christoph

Trachtenbuch. See Weigel, Hans. Habitus praecipuorum populorum

Trachtenbuch der furnembsten nationen und volcker kleydungen. See Bruyn, Abraham de. Omnium pene Europae, Asiae, Aphricae atque Americae gentium habitus

Trachtenbuch des mittel-alters. Wagner, Heinrich

Trachtenbuch zur Geschichte der reichsstadt Nürnberg. Marx, L. W.

Die **trachtenbücher** des 16. jahrhunderts. Doege, Heinrich

Das **trachtenfest** zu Haslach im Kinzigthal am 4 juni 1899. Gageur, Karl

Trachtenpavillon der Berliner gewerbe-ausstellung 1896. Bacher, Moritz

Ein **tractat** von dem dreyfachen ritterstand und allen ritter orden der Christenheit. Megiser, Hieronymus

Tractatio juridica de eo quod justum est circa vestitum civium, von der bürger kleider-ordnung; in acad. Jenensi 1675 habita. Struve, G. A.

Trades. See Occupations

The **traditional** dance. Alford, Violet, and Gallop, Rodney

Trages y costumbres de la provincia de Buenos Aires. Buenos Aires, Bacle 1833-34
33 col.pl. Q.
Colas 2905

Traiectensium episcoporum catalogus et eorum res gestae. See Baerland, Adriaan van. Hollandiae comitum historia et icones

Traill, Henry Duff, and Mann, James Sumarez

(eds.) Social England. [New illustrated ed.] London, New York, Cassell 1901-04
6v. fronts. illus. col.pl. ports.(part col.) maps, plans, facsims. Q. 82s, o.p.
Reprinted by Cassell in 1909. Also reprinted with title *Building of Britain and the empire* (London, Waverly book co.)
Contents: v 1 From the earliest times to 1273; v2 1274-1509; v3 1509-1603; v4 1603-1714; v5 1714-1815; v6 From the battle of Waterloo to the general election of 1885
Costume index. LC 4-17441

Training in commercial art. Danvers, V. L.

Traité complet du filet et du filet-guipure. Aubé, Mme Antonine

Traité contre le luxe des coeffures. Vassetz, de

Traité contre l'amour des parures, et le luxe des habits. Gauthier, F. L.

Traité de couture. Aubé, Mme Antonine

Traité de danse. Lussan-Borel

Traité de la coupe et de l'assemblage des vêtements de femmes et d'enfants. Giroux, Mme A.

Traité de la dentelle irlandaise et des jours à l'aiguille (point d'Alençon). Paris, Aux bureaux du journal La Saison ca1870
6p. 117 illus. 1 pl. O.
Lipperheide lists a second edition (75p. 125 illus. n.d.)
Lipperheide 4027-28

Traité de la vie élégant. Balzac, Honoré de

Traité de l'exercice militaire. Collombon, Jacques

Traité d'équitation à l'usage des dames. Le Noble, Henri

Traité des armes. Girard, P. J. F.

Traité des edifices, meubles, habits, machines et ustensiles des Chinois. Chambers, Sir William

Traité des principes de l'art de la coëffure des femmes. Lefèvre, maître coiffeur

Traité des remèdes ... pour la guérison des chevaux. See Delcampe, and Fouquet, Samuel. L'art de monter a cheval

Traité élémentaire théorique et pratique de l'art de la danse. Blasis, Carlo

Traité encylopédique de l'art du tailleur. Barde, F. A.

Traite historique et chronologique du sacre et couronnement des rois et des reines de France. Menin, Nicholas

Traité pratique de la construction, de l'ameublement et de la décoration des églises. Barbier de Montault, Xavier

Traité pratique de la coupe et de la confection des vêtements pour dames et enfants. Dessault, Marcel

Traité sur la cavalerie. Drummond de Melfort, L. H., comte de

Traité théorique et pratique de travaux à l'aiguille. Fréchon, Henri

Traitté fort curieux de la vénerie et de la fauconnerie. See Pomay, Fr. Ein sehr artig büchlein

Traits and stories of the Irish peasantry. Carleton, William

El **traje** popular Altoaragones. Arco, Ricardo del

El **traje** regional de España. Palencia, Isabel de

Trajes asiaticos. See Smith, Captain. Asiatic costumes

Trajes y armas de los españoles. Danvila y Collado, Francisco

Trajes y costumbres asturianas. See Vigil, Fausto. Artículos de Fausto Vigil sobre los trajes y costumbres asturianas

O **trajo** popular em popular nos seculos XVIII e XIX. Souza, Alberto

Traktat von der reith-kunst. See Winter, G. S. De re equaria tractatio nova complectens

[**Transformation** des uniformes de l'Armée française de 1789 à nos jours. No place, 1890]

72 col.pl. sq.Ti.
LC CA17-3086

Transhimalaja. Hedin, S. A.

Transylvania. See Rumania—Transylvania

Transylvania; its products and its people. Boner, Charles

Transylvanian Hungarians, peasant art. Viski, Károly

Traphagen, Ethel

Costume design and illustration; 2d ed. New York, J. Wiley; London, Chapman & Hall 1932

248p. front. illus.(part col.) col.pl. Q. (The Wiley technical series for vocational and industrial schools) $5
First edition: 1918
Pages 165-223, *A reading and reference list on costume* first published by Brooklyn Public Library 1909, revised 1932; p225-29, *Decorative art of the Indians of the Southwest,* a list of publications comp. by K. M. Chapman (Santa Fé, N. M. 1931); p231-35, Artists whose work has bearing on period fabrics or costume. Contains also an outline of historic costume from the 4th dynasty in Egypt until the late 19th century, illustrated by the predominant modes of each period
Colas 2908. Costume index. LC 32-14766

Trappists

Pfannenschmidt, F. Illustrirte geschichte der Trappisten order ... seit ihrem ursprunge bis auf unsere zeit. 1873

Li **trastulli** guerrieri. Bresciani, Marin

Tratado sobre o ensino do córte das vestes de ambos os sexos. Agdá

Trattato de costumi. Casa, Giovanni della, abp.

Trattato dell' imbrigliare, maneggiare et ferrare cavalli. Fiaschi, Cesare

Trattato della messa e della maniera di assistervi, e Del paramento del prete. Manuzzi, Giuseppe, ed.

Trattato di scientia d'arme. Agrippa, Camillo

Trattato storico tecnico della fabbricazione dei merletti veneziani. Urbani de Gheltof, G. M.

Trattato su la commedia dell' arte. Valentini, Francesco

Trauertrachten und trauergebräuche auf der insel Föhr. Haeberlin, Carl

Trautner, A. J.

(engr.) Handwerks-umzüge und tänze, fischerstechen u. a. in Nürnberg

Trautz, Friedrich Max

Japan, Korea and Formosa. New York, Westermann; London, The Studio [1931?]

xxix p. 256pl.(incl. ports.) on 128 l. F. (Orbis terrarum)
Costume index. LC 31-14497

Travail arabe, dit macramé; ouvrages de dames, dessins, fournitures, modèles. Paris, Sajou ca1880

16p. 10pl. O.
Lipperheide 4129

Le **travail** manuel. Dufaux de la Jonchère, Ermance

Travancore. See India—Travancore

Travel and sport in Africa. Pease, Sir A. E., bart.

Travel in England in the seventeenth century. Parkes, Joan

Travelling sketches in Russia, and Sweden. Porter, Sir R. K.

Travels and adventures in the province of Assam. Butler, John

Travels and discoveries in North and Central Africa. Barth, Heinrich

Travels and researches in the interior of China. Baber, E. C.

Travels in Brazil. Koster, Henry

Travels in Brazil, in the years 1815, 1816, 1817. See Wied-Neuwied, M. A. P., prinz von. Reise nach Brasilien

Travels in Georgia, Persia, Armenia, ancient Babylonia, &c. Porter, Sir R. K.

Travels in the central parts of Indo-China (Siam), Cambodia and Laos. Mouhot, Henri

Travels in the interior of North America. Wied-Neuwied, M. A. P., prinz von

Travels in the interior of South Africa. Chapman, James

Travels in the interior of southern Africa. Burchell, W. J.

Travels in the regions of the upper and lower Amoor. Atkinson, T. W.

Travels in Turkey, Asia-Minor, Syria. Wittman, William

Travels into Chile. Schmidtmeyer, Peter

Travels into Muscovy, Persia, and part of the East-Indies. Bruyn, Cornelis de

Travels into the interior of southern Africa. Barrow, Sir John

The **travels** of Pedro de Cieza de Leon. Cieza de Leon, Pedro de

The **travels** of Peter Mundy. Mundy, Peter

Travels through Norway and Lapland. Buch, Leopold, freiherr von

Travels through the southern provinces of the Russian empire, in the years 1793 and 1794. Pallas, P. S.

Travestissemens. Gatine, G. J., engr.

Travestissemens. Gavarni, G. S. C.

Travestissements. Robin

Travestissements comiques. Renard, Jules

Les **travestissements** élégants. Compte-Calix, F. C.

Travestissements enfantins. Léo

Travestissements parisiens. Léo

Travestissements parisiens. Vernier, Charles

Trawinski, Florentin

(tr.) Kondakov, N. P. Histoire de l'art byzantin considéré principalement dans les miniatures

Treadwin, Mrs

Antique point and Honiton lace, containing plain and explicit instructions for making, transferring, and cleaning laces of every description. London, Ward, Lock, & Tyler ca1875

71p. 84 illus. 3pl. Q.
Lipperheide 4035

Treasure of El Lāhūn. Winlock, H. E.

Treasure of Lahun. Lythgoe, A. M.

Treatise on ancient armour and weapons. Grose, Francis

See also note under Grose, Francis. Military antiquities respecting a history of the English army, from the conquest to the present time

Treatise on the science of defence, for the sword, bayonet, and pike, in close action. Gordon, Anthony

Treatise upon the modes. Harris, John, bp. of Llandaff

Trébutien, Guillaume Stanislas

(ed.) Discours de l'entrée faicte par ... Henry IIII ... en ... Caen, au mois de septembre 1603

Treinta y tres estampas que representan differentes suertes y actitudes del arte de lidiar los toros. See note under Goya y Lucientes, F. J. de. Tauromachia

Treitz-Saurwein, Marx, von Ehrentreitz

Der weisz kunig, eine erzehlung von den thaten Kaiser Maximilian des ersten ... hrsg. aus dem manuscripte der kaiserl. königl. hofbibliothek. Wien, J. Kurzböcken 1775

308p. 237pl. F.
Shows 16th century costume. Illustrations by Hans Burgkmair, and others
A supplement of eight plates by Hans Burgkmair was published (Paris, Tross 1869) with title: *Der weisz kunig; tableau des principaux evénements de la vie et du règne de l'empereur Maximilien Ier*
Lipperheide 649-50

See also Theuerdank. Die geuerlicheiten

Le **treizième** siècle artistique. Lecoy de la Marche, Albert

Trendel, P. G.

Catalogue of English ecclesiastical embroideries of the XIII. to XVI. centuries. See entry under Victoria and Albert museum, South Kensington

Guide to the collection of lace. See entry under Victoria and Albert museum, South Kensington

Trendell, Herbert Arthur Previte

(ed.) Great Britain. Lord chamberlain. Dress and insignia worn at His Majesty's court

(ed.) Great Britain. Lord chamberlain. Dress worn at His Majesty's court

Trente neuf aquarelles. Gazette du bon genre

Trentsensky, Matthias

(pub.) Costumes in Shakespeare's play of the Winter's tale, as represented at the Princess's Theatre

(pub.) K. K. Oesterreichische armee nach der neuen adjustirung

Les **très** belles Heures de Notre-Dame du duc Jean de Berry. Durrieu, Paul, comte

Les **très** belles miniatures. Brussels. Bibliothèque royale de Belgique. Section des manuscrits

Très parisien; la mode, le chic, l'élégance. v 1, 1920-1936. Paris

Col. illus. col.pl. Q. 142 fr. a year
Published monthly (irregular) 1920-Sept, 1935; quarterly, Oct. 1935-Summer 1936. October 1935-Summer 1936 also called new series v 1-4. Absorbed by *La Mode chic*, Oct. 1936
Chapeaux du Très parisien is a supplement

Les **très** riches heures de Jean de France, duc de Berry. Durrieu, Paul, comte

La **tresadmirable** ... du ... Prince Phillipes, Prince d'Espaignes ... en ... ville d'Anvers, anno 1549. Schryver, Cornelis

Trésor de l'abbaye de Saint-Maurice d'Agaune. Aubert, Édouard

Le **trésor** des grâces, ou La parure de Vénus, mis au jour par le favori du beau sexe. Paris, Esnauts et Rapilly 1784

?p. front. 12 illus. T.
Cataloged from Colas's *Bibliographie*. Illustrations show coiffures
Colas 2910

Treter, Mieczysław
(illus.) Łoziński, Władysław. Zycie polskie w dawnych wiekach

Treter, Tomasz
Romanorum imperatorium effigies. See entry under Cavalleriis, J. B. de

Treuenfest, Gustav Amon von. See Amon von Treuenfest, Gustav, ritter

Treuttel & Würtz
(pub.) Melling, A. I., illus. Voyage pittoresque de Constantinople et des rives du Bosphore

Treves, Sir Frederick
The influence of clothing on health. London, New York, Cassell [1886]
112p. 15 illus. D.

Tribes, African. See African tribes

Tribulations des gens à équipages. Lami, E. L.

Trichet du Fresne, Raphael
De gli habiti della religioni. See entry under Fialetti, Odoardo

Trichologia. Henning, Johann

Trieste. See Street venders—Italy—Trieste

Trillinbuch. Gheyn, Jacob de

Trilling, Mabel Barbara, and Nicholas, Mrs Florence (Williams)
Art in home and clothing; edited by B. R. Andrews ... costume illustrations by Carol Howard Spindler; interior illustrations by James Graham. Chicago, Philadelphia, J. B. Lippincott [c1936]
xi,450p. illus.(incl. plans) col.pl. D.
LC 36-7535

Trimolet, Anthelme
(illus.) Physiologie de l'homme de loi

Il **trinciante.** Cervio, Vincenzo

Le **triomphe** de l'Empereur Maximilien I. See Burgkmair, Hans. Kaiser Maximilians I triumph

Trip to Lotus land. Bell, Archie

Tripolitania
Ewald, Paulus. Reise des evangelischen missionar Christian Ferdinand Ewald, von Tunis über Soliman, Nabal, Hammamet, Susa, Sfar, Gabis, Gerba nach Tripolis, und von da wieder zurück nach Tunis, im jahre 1835. 1837

Triumph des Kaisers Maximilian I. Dürer, Albrecht

Triumphs of the Emperor Maximilian I. Burgkmair, Hans

Triumphus virtutum in funere Caroli VII ... anno ... MDCCXLV. Edlweckh, Johannes

Troels-Lund, Troels Frederik
Dagligt liv i Norden i det 16de aarhundrede. Kjøbenhavn, C. A. Reitzel 1880-1901
13v. illus. O. (Danmarks og Norges historie i slutningen af det 16de aarhundrede. I. Indre historie. 2.-14. bog)
Volume 3: *Klaededragt* (1882. 307p. 65 illus.)
Lipperheide 1055e (v3) LC 5-9222

Trois causeries sur l'histoire du costume. Marais, Paul

Trois suites d'estampes pour servir à l'histoire des modes et du costume des Français dans le 18. siècle. Moreau, J. M., dit le jeune, and Freudenberger, Sigmund

Troisième suite d'estampes. Moreau, J. M., dit le jeune

Trollope, Mrs Frances (Milton)
Vienna and the Austrians; with some account of a journey through Swabia, Bavaria, the Tyrol, and the Salzbourg. London, R. Bentley 1838
2v. fronts. pl. O.
LC 3-31660

Troost, Cornelis
Tafereelen uit het burgerlijke leven van de Hollanders in de achttiende eeuw ... Scènes tirées de la vie domestique des Hollandais au dix-huitième siècle. Amsterdam, E. Maaskamp 1811
2 l. 32pl. of.F.
Plates show Dutch costumes of the early 18th century. They are engraved by Delfos, S. Fokke, J. Houbraken, R. Muys, Pelletier, A. Radigues, P. Tanjé
Colas 2912. Lipperheide 957

Die **trophäen** des preuss. heeres. Lehmann, Gustav

Trophaeum nobilissimae ac antiquissimae domus Estorasianae. Viennae, L. Voigt 1700
210 l. 96p. 92 l. 165pl. Q.
Plates show members of the House of Esterházy from the time of Attila to 1699
Lipperheide 891m

De **tropische** natuur in schetsen en kleuren. Blaauw, A. H.

Tross, Edwin
(pub.) Schaeufelein, H. L. La danse des noces

Trost, Andreas
(engr.) Valvasor, J. W. Die ehre desz hertzogthums Crain

Trost, L. J.
Die ritter- und verdienst-orden, ehrenzeichen und medaillen aller souveräne und staaten seit beginn des XIX. jahrhunderts. Wein, Braumüller 1910
xii,198p. pl.(part col.) ob.Q.

Trostspiegel in glück und unglück. Petrarca, Francesco

Troubadours
Rowbotham, J. F. The troubadours and courts of love. 1895

Troupers of the Gold Coast. Rourke, C. M.

Troupes autrichiennes. See Martinet, pub. Galerie militaire

Troupes auxiliaires, ou Troupes françaises. Paris, Noel 1810
5 col.pl. O.
Colas 2913

Troupes carlistes. Giles, J. W.

Troupes étrangères. Finart, N.

Troupes étrangères. See Martinet, pub. Galerie militaire

Troupes françaises. See entries under Basset, pub.; Gautier, pub.; Genty, firm, Paris, pub.; and Martinet, pub.

Troupes françaises (Premier empire). Martinet, pub.

Troupes françaises (Restauration). Martinet, pub.

Troupes russes. See Martinet, pub. Galerie militaire

Troupes turques. See Martinet, pub. Galerie militaire

Trouvain, Antoine

Les appartements du roi Louis XIV. Paris, A. Trouvain 1694-96
6pl. F.
Plates show masculine and feminine dress at the court of Louis XIV
Colas 2918

Troy

Schliemann, Heinrich. Ilios; stadt und land der Trojaner. 1881

Schliemann, Heinrich. Ilios: the city and country of the Trojans. 1880

Troyen, I.

(engr.) Eeckhout, Guillielmus vanden. Le nouvelle figure à la mode de ce tempts de fine

Troyes, Nicolas Cochin de. See Cochin de Troyes, Nicolas

Truchy, L.

(illus.) Highmore, Joseph. Plates illustrating the "Pamela" of Samuel Richardson

True description of all trades. Mergenthaler linotype company

Trützler, Hans von

(ed.) Vogt, Hermann. Die europäischen heere der gegenwart; illustrationen von R. Knötel

Truman, Nevil

Historic costuming; with a foreword by C. B. Cochran. London, Sir I. Pitman 1936
xii,152p. front.(port.) illus. col.pl. O.
LC 37-1508

Trusler, John. See Hogarth, William. The works of William Hogarth

Die **trutzwaffen** der Karolingerzeit. Gessler, E. A.

La **tryumphante** et solemnelle entree faicte sur le nouvel et joyeux advenement de ... Charles prince des Hespaignes. Dupuys, Remy

T'Serstevens, Albert. See Jou, Louis. À la danseuse

Tsountas, Chrestos, and Manatt, James Irving

The Mycenaean age; a study of the monuments and culture of pre-Homeric Greece. Boston and New York, Houghton, Mifflin 1897
xxxi,417p. front. illus. pl. map, plans. O.
Pages 159-216 deal with dress, personal adornment, and armor in pre-Homeric Greece
LC 4-14844

Tuaregs

Benhazera, Maurice. Six mois chez les Touareg du Ahaggar. 1908

Tudor costume. See England—Tudors, 1485-1603

Tübingen university. See Academic costume—Tübingen university

Tuer, Andrew White

The book of delightful and strange designs; being one hundred facsimile illustrations of the art of the Japanese stencil-cutter. London, Leadenhall press; New York, C. Scribner [1893]
24,27,26p. front. illus. 104 designs on double leaves. Q.
English, German and French, each part having special title-page and separate paging. German title: *Das buch reizender und merkwürdiger zeichnungen;* French title: *Le livre de desseins charmans*
Lipperheide 4385. LC CA14-259D

The follies and fashions of our grandfathers (1807); embellished with ... plates including ladies' and gentlemen's dress. London, Field & Tuer; New York, Scribner & Welford, 1886-87
366p. col.front. 30pl.(10 col.) 6 port. O.
Colas 2919. Lipperheide 1016. LC 11-19842

Old London street cries and the cries of to-day, with heaps of quaint cuts including hand-coloured frontispiece. London, Field & Tuer; New York, Scribner & Welford 1885
137p. col.front. illus. Ti.
Ten of the illustrations, by ... Thomas Rowlandson, are copied in facsimile from a scarce set ... published in 1820. cf. p117
LC 3-26679

Die **türkische** armee und marine in ihrer gegenwärtigen uniformirung. Knoetel, Richard

Tun, Li-ch'ên

Annual customs and festivals in Peking as recorded in the Yen-ching Sui-shih-chi by Tun Li-ch'en; tr. and annotated by Derk Bodde. Peiping, H. Vetch 1936
xxii,147p. illus. pl.(part col.) O.
Bibliography: p[128]-30
LC 37-3907

Tunis. Hesse-Wartegg, Ernst von

Tunis, land und leute. Hesse-Wartegg, Ernst von

Tunisia

Archinard, L. Q. L'autre France (Tunisie, Algérie, Maroc). 1914

Chassiron, Charles, baron de. Aperçu pittoresque de la régence de Tunis. 1849

Ewald, Paulus. Reise des evangelischen missionar Christian Ferdinand Ewald, von Tunis über Soliman, Nabal, Hammamet, Susa, Sfar, Gabis, Gerba nach Tripolis, und von da weider zurück nach Tunis, im jahre 1835. 1837

Hesse-Wartegg, Ernst von. Tunis, land und leute. 1882

Hesse-Wartegg, Ernst von. Tunis: the land and the people. 1882

Latour, Antoine de. Voyage de S.A.R. Monseigneur le Duc de Montpensier à Tunis en Égypte, en Turquie et en Grèce. 1847

Ricard, Prosper. Les merveilles de l'autre France; Algérie, Tunisie, Maroc; le pays—les monuments—les habitants. c1924

Sladen, D. B. W. Carthage and Tunis, the old and new gates of the Orient. 1906

Turberville, Arthur Stanley
English men and manners in the eighteenth century; an illustrated narrative; 2d ed. New York, Oxford univ. press; Oxford, Clarendon press 1929
xxiii,539 p. front. illus. ports. facsims. O. $4; 10s
First edition: 1926
Costume index. LC 26-20277 (1st ed.)

(ed.) Johnson's England; an account of the life & manners of his age. New York, Oxford univ. press; Oxford, Clarendon press 1933
2v. fronts. illus. pl. ports. maps, plans, facsims. O. $14, 42s
Costume index. LC 34-592

Turberville, George
The booke of falconrie or hawking ... collected out of the best authors, as well Italians as Frenchmen, and some English practises withall concerning falconrie; now newly reviued, corrected, and augmented. London, Printed by T. Purfoot 1611
370p. illus. D. LC 10-23082

Turin. Armeria reale
Armeria reale di Torino. [Photographs, with descriptive letterpress] Venezia 1865
55 illus. Q.
Compiled by Antonio Perini

Turin. Exposition internationale, 1911. See Hanau, Ch. Fourrures et pelleteries

Turkestan
Curtis, W. E. Turkestan: the heart of Asia. 1911
Le Coq, Albert von. Chotscho: facsimilewiedergaben der wichtigeren funde der ersten Königlich preussischen expedition nach Turfan in Ost-Turkistan. 1913
Le Coq, Albert von. Volkskundliches aus Ost-Turkistan. 1916

Turkey
Arif Pasha. Les anciens costumes de l'Empire ottoman, depuis l'origine de la monarchie jusqu'à la réforme du sultan Mahmoud. [1864]
Chalcondylas, Laonicus. Histoire generale des Turcs. 1662
Davis, R. H. Rulers of the Mediterranean. 1894
Franck, H. A. The fringe of the Moslem world. 1928
Lonicer, Phillip, comp. Chronicorum turcicorum
Wittman, William. Travels in Turkey, Asia-Minor, Syria, and across the desert into Egypt during the years 1799, 1800, and 1801, in company with the Turkish army, and the British military mission. 1803

See also Byzantine empire; also subdivision Turkey under Decoration and ornament; Kings and rulers; Military costume; Naval costume

1300-1596

Boissard, J. J. Leben und contrafeiten der türckischen un persischen sultanen. 1596
Greblinger, Georg. Wahre abbildungen der türckischen kayser und persischen fürsten so wol auch anderer helden und heldinnen von dem Osman biss auf den andern Mahomet. 1648

15th century

Barletius, Martinus. Des aller streytparsten vñ theüresten fürsten und herrn Georgen Castrioten genañt Scanderbeg ... ritterliche thaten. 1533
Karabacek, Josef, ritter von. Abendländische künstler zu Konstantinopel im XV. und XVI. jahrhundert. 1918

16th century

Acta Mechmeti I saracenorum principis. Aussführlicher bericht von ankunfft zunehmen gesatzen regirung und jam̃erlichen absterben Mechmeti I. 1597
Lorich, Melchior. Des kunstreichen und weitberühmten Melchior Lorichs wolgerissene unnd geschnittene türckische figuren in kupffer und holtz. 1641
Nicolay, Nicolas de, sieur d'Arfeuille. The navigations, peregrinations and voyages, made into Turkie. 1585
Nicolay, Nicolas de, sieur d'Arfeuille. Les navigations, pérégrinations et voyages, faicts en la Turquie. 1576
Nicolay, Nicolas de, sieur d'Arfeuille. Les quatre premiers livres des Navigations et peregrinations orientales. 1568

17th century

Gründ- und umständlicher bericht von denen römisch-kayserlichen wie auch ottomannischen grosz-bothschafften, wodurch der friede ... zwischen dem ... römischen kayser Leopoldo primo und dem sultan Mustafahan III. den 26 Januarii, 1699. Zu Carlowiz in Sirmien auf 25. jahr geschlossen. 1702
Happel, E. W., ed. Thesaurus exoticorum. 1688
La Chapelle, George de. Recueil de divers portraits de principales dames de la Porte du grand Turc. 1648
Merian, Mattheus. Das lange bestrittene königreich Candia. 1670
Rycaut, Sir Paul. The history of the present state of the Ottoman Empire. 1686
Taeschner, Franz. Alt-Stambuler hof- und volksleben, ein türkisches miniaturenalbum aus dem 17. jahrhundert. 1925
Wagner, J. C. Delineatio provinciarum Pannoniae et imperii Turcici in oriente. 1684-85

18th century

Guer, J. A. Moeurs et usages des Turcs, leur religion, leur gouvernement civil, militaire et politique, avec un abregé de l'histoire ottomane. 1746-47
Kindleben, C. W. Galanterieen der Türken. 1782

Turkey—18th century—*Continued*

Moor, J. B. van. Recueil de cent estampes representant differentes nations du Levant tirées sur les tableaux peints d'après nature en 1707. et 1708. 1714
—Explication. 1715

Moor, J. B. van. Wahreste und neueste abbildung des türckischen hofes. 1719-21

Mouradgea d'Ohsson, Ignatius. Tableau général de l'Empire othoman. 1787-90

Recueil des différents costumes des principaux officiers et magistrats de la porte. ca1775

Silvestre, C. F. Differents habillements de Turcs. ca1700

Tott, François, baron de. Nachrichten von den Türken und Tataren, mit herrn von Peyssonnel's verbesserungen und zusätzen. 1788

Vien, J. M. Caravanne du sultan à la Mecque; mascarade turque donnée á Rome par messieurs les pensionnaires de l'Académie de France et leurs amis, au carnavale de l'année 1748. 1749

19th century to date

Alexander, William. The costume of Turkey, illustrated by a series of engravings; with descriptions in English and French. 1802

Alexander, William. Picturesque representations of the dress and manners of the Turks. 1814?

Allom, Thomas. Character and costume in Turkey and Italy. Designed and drawn from nature by Thomas Allom ... with descriptive letterpress by Emma Reeve. 1845?

Allom, Thomas. Constantinople and the scenery of the seven churches of Asia Minor. 1838

Brindesi, Jean. Elbicei Atika; musée des anciens costumes turcs de Constantinople. [1855]

Brindesi, Jean. Souvenirs de Constantinople. 1860

Castellan, A. L. Moeurs, usages, costumes des Othomanes. 1812

Castellan, A. L. Sitten, gebräuche und trachten der Osmanen. 1815

Deval, Charles. Deux années à Constantinople et en Morée (1825-1826). 1828

Dupré, Louis. Voyage à Athènes et à Constantinople. 1825

Eyriès, J. B. B. La Turquie ou costumes, moeurs et usages des Turcs. ca1827

Hamdī, O., bey, and Launay, Marie de. Les costumes populaires de la Turquie en 1873. 1873

Howe, Fisher. Oriental and sacred scenes. 1856

Lachaise. Costumes de l'Empire Turc. 1821

Langlois, Victor. Voyage dans la Cilicie et dans les montagnes du Taurus. 1861

Latimer, Mrs E. W. Russia and Turkey in the nineteenth century. 1893

Latour, Antoine de. Voyage de S.A.R. Monseigneur le Duc de Montpensier à Tunis en Égypte, en Turquie et en Grèce. 1847

MacBean, Forbes. Sketches of character & costume in Constantinople, Ionian Islands, &c. 1854

Mayer, Ludwig. Views in the Ottoman empire, chiefly in Caramania, a part of Asia Minor hitherto unexplored. 1803

Mayer, Ludwig. Views in the Ottoman dominions, in Europe, in Asia, and some of the Mediterranean islands. 1810

Mayer, Ludwig. Views in Turkey, in Europe and Asia comprising Romelia, Bulgaria, Walachia, Syria and Palestine. 1801

Melling, A. I., illus. Voyage pittoresque de Constantinople et des rives du Bosphore. 1819

Méry, J. P. A. Constantinople et la Mer Noire. 1855

Monroe, W. S. Turkey and the Turks. 1907

Noé, Amédée, comte de. Mémoires relatifs à l'expédition anglaise partie du Bengale en 1800 pour aller combattre en Égypte l'armée d'Orient. 1826

Preziosi, A. Stamboul, moeurs et costumes. 1883

Raczyński, Edward, hrabia. Dziennik podrózy do Turcyi odbytey w roku MDCCCXIV. 1821

Shoberl, Frédéric, ed. Turkey. 1822

Van Lennep, H. J. Oriental album. 1862

Van Millingen, Alexander. Constantinople. 1906

Wilkie, Sir David. Sir David Wilkie's sketches in Turkey, Syria and Egypt, 1840 & 1841. 1843

Constantinople

See Street venders—Turkey—Constantinople

Turkey and the Turks. Monroe, W. S.

Turkey, Greece, and Palestine in 1853. See Howe, Fisher. Oriental and sacred scenes

Turkey. Commission impériale ottomane pour l'Exposition universelle de Vienne, 1873

Les costumes populaires de la Turquie en 1873. See Hamdi, O., bey, and Launay, Marie de

Turkomans

Baĭsutov, N. I. Tam gde rastet khlopok; kak zhivut i chem promyshlîaîut uzbeki. 1927

Baĭsutov, N. I. V peschanykh stepîakh. kak zhivut i chem promyshlîaîut turkmeny. 1927g

Samoĭlovich, A. N. Odezhda stavropol'skikh turkmenok. 1923g

Turnbuch fűr die söhne des vaterlandes. Guts Muths, J. C. F.

Turnierbuch. Burgkmair, Hans

Der **turnierroman** "Livre des faits du bon chevalier Messire Jacques de Lalaing". Rudnitzki, Paul

Turoczi, Ladislaus
Ungaria suis cum regibus compendio data ... novissima ... editione. Tyrnaviae, typis Collegii academici societatis Jesu 1768
631p. 39pl. Q.
Thirty-two plates are from J. A. X. Schad's *Effigies ducum et regum Hungariae*
Lipperheide 866

Turowski, Kazimierz Józef
(ed.) Golebiowski, Lukasz. Ubiory w. Polsce od najdawniejszych czasów aź do chwil obecnych, sposobem dykcyonarza

La **Turquie.** Eyriès, J. B. B.

Turquois work of Hawikuh, New Mexico. Hodge, F. W.

Tuscany. See Italy—Tuscany

Tutankhamen and the discovery of his tomb. Smith, Sir G. E.

Tv ie, vse svetv pismv. Bible. Wendic

Tv ie, vse svetv pismv, stariga inu Noviga Testamenta, Slovenski, tolmazhena, skusi ivria Dalmatina. Bible

Tweeëndertig stuks studien. Chalon, Christina

Twelve designs for the costume of Shakespeare's Richard the third. Tomkins, C. F., and Planché, J. R.

Twelve London cries. Sandby, Paul

The **twelve** months. Bol, Hans

Twentieth century
Avenel, Georges d'. Le mécanisme de la vie moderne. 1902
Carpenter, F. G. How the world is clothed. 1908
Chamberlain, J. F. How we are clothed. 1923
Le costume, la mode: Encyclopédie populaire illustrée du vingtième siècle. 1899
Grosvenor, G. H., ed. Scenes from every land. 1907-18
Joyce, T. A., and Thomas, N. W., eds. Women of all nations. 1915
Stratz, C. H. Die frauenkleidung. 1900

See also subdivision Twentieth century under Europe; Jewelry, Medieval and modern

Twenty four plates illustrative of Hindoo and European manners in Bengal. Belnos, Mrs S. C.

Twenty illustrations of Spanish costumes. London, R. Havell 1832
20 col.pl. ob.Q. 12s
Shows costume of various regions. For list of plates see Colas's *Bibliographie*
Colas 2920

Twenty-four subjects exhibiting the costume of Paris. Chalon, J. J.

£20 prize essay on cutting by block patterns. Dobson, W. L.

Twenty-seven etchings illustrative of Italian manners and costume. Pinelli, Bartolommeo

Twici, William. See Dryden, Alice, ed. The art of hunting

Twining, E. F.
The English coronation ceremony. London, Simpkin Marshall 1937
144p. front. pl.(part col.) Q.
Shows coronation robes and crowns

The English regalia and crown jewels in the Tower of London. London, Street & Massey 1935
72p. col.front. pl. D.
Illustrations show English regalia and coronation robes
LC 37-21488

The Scottish regalia. London, Street & Massey 1936
33p. col.front. D.
Frontispiece shows the Scottish crown

Twins travelogues. Fisher, Mrs W. H.

Two centuries of costume in America. Earle, Mrs A. M.

Two gentlemen of China. Hosie, D. S., lady

Two hundred sketches, humorous and grotesque. Doré, Gustave

Two thousand miles' ride through the Argentine provinces. MacCann, William

Two types of brooches from the island of Gotland, Sweden. Leeds, E. T.

Twombly, Alexander Stevenson
Hawaii and its people; the land of rainbow and palm. New York & Boston, Silver, Burdett 1899
384p. front.(map) illus.(incl. ports.) D. (The world and its people, book IX)
LC 99-5762

Tyack, George Smith
Historic dress of the clergy. London, W. Andrews [1897]
134p. front. illus. D. 3s 6d, o.p.
Colas 2921. Costume index. LC 2-14033

Tygodnik illustrowany. v 1, 1859+ Warsawa, Gebethner i Wolff [etc.]
Illus. pl(part col.) F.
Published monthly. Current 1938
1859-94 numbered as v1-15, 1859-67; ser2 v1-16, 1868-75; ser3 v1-14, 1876-82; ser4 v1-14, 1883-89; ser5 v1-10, 1890-94; 1895-1910 (yr. 36-51) unnumbered; 1911+ as v52+
Index: 1859-75

Tygodnik mód i powiésci. See note under Die Modenwelt

Tymms, William Robert
(illus.) Westwood, J. O. Fac-similes of the miniatures and ornaments of Anglo-Saxon & Irish manuscripts

Types de l'armée belge. Romberg, Maurice

Les **types** de Paris. Goncourt, E. L. A. H. de; Daudet, Alphonse, and Zola, Émile

Types du dix-huitième siècle. Saint-Aubin, Augustin de

Types et caractères anciens d'après des documents peints ou écrits. Mazuy, A.

Types et costumes féminins de la Suisse. Wisard

Types et uniformes; l'armée française. Detaille, Édouard and Maillot, T. J. R.

Types indiens neerlandais. See Pers, A. van. Nederlandsch oost-indische typen

Types militaires. Renard, Jules

Types militaires de l'armée française; infanterie, mès. Paris, Lemercier ca1868
15 col.pl. Q.
For list of plates see Colas's *Bibliographie*
Colas 2922

Types militaires du troupier français. Lalaisse, Hippolyte

Types militaires étrangers. Renard, Jules

Types of mankind. Nott, J. C., and Gliddon, G. R.

Tyrannus, or The mode. Evelyn, John

Tyrol
Calvenfeier, Zürich. Organisations-comité. Rätische trachtenbilder. 189-?
Costumes du Tyrol. ca1805
Erinnerung an süd Tirol. 186-?
Holland, Clive. Tyrol and its people. 1909
Kappeller, J. A. Tiroler trachten. ca1800
McCrackan, W. D. The spell of Tyrol. 1914
Die Österreichisch-ungarische monarchie in wort und bild. 1886-1902 v 13
Perger, Sigmund. Tyroler. ca1810
Rugendas, J. M., and Leborne, Louis. Tyrol; costumes modernes. ca1828
Schedler, J. G. Nationaltrachten von Tirol und Vorarlberg. ca1824
Tyrol. ca1805
Valério, Théodore. Souvenirs du Tyrol, du Vorarlberg et de la Haute Bavière ... Erinnerungen von Tyrol, Vorarlberg und Ober Baiern. 1842

See also Nobles—Tyrol

Tyrol. Vienne, Artaria ca1805
24 col.pl. Q.
Each plate bears the title as above, and a legend in German and French, and shows one person in costume
Colas 715

Tyrol and its people. Holland, Clive

Tyroler. Perger, Sigmund

Tyršová, Renata (Fügnerová)
Broderies et décoration populaires tchécoslovaques. See entry under Broderies

Tyršová, Renata (Fügnerová), and Hantich, Henri
Le paysan tchèque: Bohême, Moravie, Silésie, costumes et broderies. Préface par Camille Mauclair. Paris, Lamm 1911
42p. 6 col.pl. Q. 6fr.
Colas 2923

Tzigara-Samurcas, Alexandru. See L'art du peuple roumain

U

Ubilla y Medina, Antonio, marqués de Rivas
Succession de el rey D. Phelipe v. nuestro Señor en la corona de España. Madrid, J. G. Infanzon, impressor de Su Magestad 1704
672[38]p. fold.pl. port. tab. Q.
"Diario de sus viages desde Versalles a Madrid; el que executó para su feliz casamiento; jornada a Napoles, a Milan y a su exercito; successos de la campaña, y su buelta a Madrid." Subtitle
Plates show battle scenes, on land and sea with costume figures, and ceremonies
Lipperheide 551. LC 4-26810

Ubiory ludu dawnej Polski. Krakowie, 1862
12 col.pl. O.
Catalogued from Colas
Colas 2924

Ubiory ludu polskiego. Akademija umiejętności, Cracow

Ubiory w dawney Polsce. Matejko, Jan

Ubiory w Polsce 1200-1795. See Matejko, Jan. Ubiory w dawnej Polsce

Ubiory w Polsce i u sasiadow. Eljasz, W. R.

Ubiory w Polsce od najdawniejszych czasów aż do chwil obecnych, sposobem dykcyonarza. Golebiowski, Lukasz

Ubiory Wojska Polskiego z csasow kosiestwa Warszawskiego. Dietrich, F.

Ubiory woyska krôlewsko polskiego. Warszawie, A. Dal-Trozzo 1829
1 l. 132 col.pl. Q.
Cataloged from Colas's *Bibligoraphie*
Colas 2926

Ubrici, Hermann. See note under Retzsch, F. A. M. Gallerie zu Shakspeare's dramatischen werken

Udvalgte norske nationaldragter. See Tønsberg, N. C., ed. Norske nationaldragter

Uebe, Rudolf
Westfalen. See Deutsche volkskunst. v9

Ueber alte eisen- und silber-funde. Bibra, E., freiherr von

Ueber bekleidung, schmuck, und tätowirung der Papuas der südostküste von Neu-Guinea. Finsch, Otto

Ueber den bau des menschlichen fusses und dessen zweckmässigste bekleidung. Günther, G. B.

Über den gebrauch der falschen haare und perrucken in alten und neuern zeiten. Nicolaï, Friedrich

Über den nachtheil, den die heutige frauentracht der gesundheit bringt. Michelitz, Anton

Über die ältesten christlichen begrabnissstatten und besonders die katakomben zu Neapel mit ihren wandgemälden. Bellermann, C. F.

Über die ältesten sitten und gebräuche der Egerländer. Grüner, J. S.

Ueber die bilder der Hedwigslegende. Luchs, Hermann

Über die charakteristischen kennzeichen der geschichtlichen entwickelungs-abschnitte der kriegertracht. Hauslab, Franz von

Ueber die falsche, gewöhnliche schuhform und über die richtige form der fussbekleidung. Braatz, Egbert

Ueber die ruinen Herculanums und Pompejis. Keerl, J. H. See entry under Saint-Non, J. C. R. de. Voyage pittoresque

Ueber die sitten, kleidertrachten und gebräuche der Altenburgischen bauern. Kronbiegel, C. F.

Über elsässische trachten. Kassel, August

Über homerische waffen. See Reichel, Wolfgang. Homerische waffen

Ueber Juden-abzeichen. Singermann, Felix

Ueber sitte, mode und kleidertracht. Arndt, E. M.

Ueberfeldt, Braet von. See Bing, Valentyn, jt. auth

Übung und kunst des reitens. See Lieb, Christophorus. Practica et arte di cavalleria

Uebungstunden im stricken, nähen und sticken. Leipzig, G. Vosz 1810
28p. 18pl. Q.
Lipperheide 4067

Üxküll-Güldenbandt, M. Nieuwenhuis-von. See Nieuwenhuis, Anton Willem

Uganda to the Cape. Carpenter, F. G.

Uhle, Max. See Meyer, A. B., jt. ed.

Uiber truhten und truhtensteine. Reynitzsch, Wilhelm

Uizhno-russkiĭ narodnyĭ ornament. Lītvīnov", P. IA.

Ujfalvy, Marie
De Paris à Samarkand, le Ferghanah, le Kouldja et la Sibérie occidentale, impressions de voyage d'une Parisienne. Par mme. de Ujfalvy-Bourdon. Paris, Hachette 1880
487p. illus. maps. O.

Ukraine. See Russia—Ukraine; Decoration and ornament—Russia—Ukraine

Ukrainskiĭ narodnyĭ ornament. Kosacheva, O. P.

Ulmus, Marcus Antonius
Physiologia barbæ humanæ; in tres sectiones divisa. Hoc est de fine illius philosophico, & medico. Bononiæ, apud I. B. Bellagambam 1602
10p. l. 318 (i. e. 310)p. illus. Q.
Lipperheide 1645. LC 8-21212

Ulrich, Carolyn Farquhar
(ed.) Periodicals directory

Ulrike, count
(illus.) Mellin, A. W., graf von. Unterricht eingefriedigte wildbahnen

Los **últimos** cuatro años de la dominacion española en el antiguo vireinato del Rio de la Plata. Saguí, Francisco

Umbrellas and parasols
Cazal, R. M. Essai historique, anecdotique sur la parapluie, l'ombrelle et la canne et sur leur fabrication. 1844
Clyde and Black, firm, New York. Umbrellas and their history. 1864
Sangster, William. Umbrellas and their history. 1871
Uzanne, L. O. L'ombrelle, le gant, le manchon. 1883
Uzanne, L. O. Les ornements de la femme ... L'éventail, l'ombrelle, le gant, le manchon. 1892

Umbrellas and their history. Clyde and Black, firm, New York

Umbrellas and their history. Sangster, William

Umständliche beschreibung der ... salbung und crönung der ... frauen, Anna Joannowna kayserin und selbstherrscherin von gantz Ruszland ... 28. april 1730, in Moscau. St. Petersburg, Kayserl. academie der wissenschafften 1731
28p. 2 illus. 16pl. F
"Nach dem reiszischen original teutsch übersetzet und mit denen dazu gehörigen kupffern versehen." Subtitle
Plates show the coronation and regalia
Lipperheide 2784

Unbeaten tracks in Japan. Bishop, Mrs I. L. B.

Das **unbekannte** Spanien. See Hielscher, Kurt. Picturesque Spain

Underwear
Barker, A. W. A classification of the chitons worn by Greek women as shown in works of art. 1923
Fuchs, Eduard. Illustrierte sittengeschichte vom mittelalter bis zur gegenwart. 1909-12
Holliday, R. C. Unmentionables, from figleaves to scanties. 1933
Kitchens, Mathilda. When underwear counted. 1931
Schidrowitz, Leo. Sittengeschichte des intimen: bett, korsett, hemd, hose, bad, abtritt. 1926

Periodicals

L'Élégance féminine. 1933+
Intimate apparel; publication of the undergarment and negligee trades. 1934+
Lingerie du Jardin des modes. 1928+
Lingerie moderne. 1917?+
La Lingerie parisienne. 1907?+
Panorama der damen-moden; journal-ausg. für kopfputz und lingerie. 1859-65
Style reporter. 1933+

Undi, Mariska
Magyar himvarró müvészet; a nemes magyar fonalasmunkák töténete, a honfoglalás korától napjainkig; általános elméleti és gyakorlati vezérkönyv mindenfokú magyar kézimunkaoktatás számára. Budapest, Kiadja a szerzö [1934]
102p. illus. pl. (part col.) F.
Shows Hungarian costume and embroidery from early times. Some patterns are included

Ungaria suis cum regibus compendio data. Turoczi, Ladislaus

Ungarische volkstrachten. See Pekáry, István. Magyar népviseletek

Unger, Joh. Carl
(ed.) Das Veilchen, ein taschenbuch

Unger, Johan Hendrik Willem
(illus.) Muller, P. L. Onze gouden eeuw

Uniform and dress of the army of the Confederate States. Confederate States of America. War department

Uniform for the United States navy, 1869. United States. Navy dept.

Uniform of the army of the United States, 1882. United States. Quartermaster corps

Uniform of the army of the United States (illustrated) from 1774 to 1907. United States. Quartermaster corps

Uniform of the army of the United States, October 1, 1908. United States. Quartermaster corps

Uniform regulations. United States. Marine corps

Uniform regulations for chief petty officers, men, and boys of the fleet, and for boys in the training establishments. Great Britain. Admiralty

Uniform regulations for officers of the fleet. Great Britain. Admiralty

Uniform regulations for petty officers, men, & boys of the fleet, and for boys in the training ships. Great Britain. Admiralty

Uniform regulations for the United States navy, 1877. United States. Navy dept.

Uniform regulations, United States Marine corps, together with uniform regulations common to both U. S. Navy and Marine corps. 1912, rev. 1917. United States. Marine corps

Uniform regulations, United States navy, together with uniform regulations common to both Navy and Marine corps United States. Navy department

Uniformele amatei romana. See Socecu, A. J. V. Die rumänische armee in ihrer gegenwärtigen uniformierung

Uniformen d. kgl. Hannoverschen armee. Tackmann, E.

Die **uniformen** d. königl. dänischen armee. Bergh, Th.

Die **uniformen** der bayerischen armee von 1682 bis 1848. Münich, Friedrich, and Behringer, Ludwig

Uniformen der Berliner bürgergarde. Wolf, L.

Die **uniformen** der Braunhemden. Eelking, Hermann, freiherr von

Die **uniformen** der chinesischen armee des "Lu Chün Pu". See Hill, J. C. Die chinesische armee in ihrer neu-organisation und neu-uniformierung

Die **uniformen** der deutschen armee. Leipzig, M. Ruhl 1885
2v. 45 col.pl. O.
First edition: 1876. Many later editions. The edition of 1894-95 has title: *Die uniformen und fahnen der deutschen armee*
Contents: I Uebersichtliche farbendarstellungen der uniformen der deutschen armee; II Darstellungen der abzeichen der militairischen grade, sowie der sonstigen auszeichnungen
Lipperheide 2130

See also Die deutsche armee

Die **uniformen** der deutschen armee. Zur benutzung in der instructions-stunde. Neu-Ruppin, G. Kühn [1870-]
11pl. F.
Plates show almost 250 types of German uniforms
Cataloged from Colas
Colas 2927

Die **uniformen** der deutschen marine. See Die Deutsche marine und die deutsche schutztruppe für Ost-Afrika in ihrer neuesten uniformirung

Uniformen der königlich-bayerischen armee nach der neuesten ordonnanz vom jahre 1825. Pfeiffer, Baptist

Die **unformen** der preussischen garden von ihrem entstehen bis auf die neueste zeit, nebst einer kurzen geschichtlichen darstellung ihrer verschiedenen formationen, 1704-1836. Berlin, G. Gropius 1827-40
v. p. 106 col.pl. Q.
Colas 2928. Lipperheide 2170

Uniformen der verschiedenen truppen der churfürstlich sächsischen armee. Hessen, Wilhelm

Uniformen des bayerischen heeres nach der neuen bekleidungsvorschrift. Behringer, Ludwig

Uniformen des belgischen heeres. See Uniformes de l'armée belge

Uniformen des bürger-militairs in Baiern. See Schiesl, Ferdinand. Uniformirung und organisation des bürger-militärs in dem Königreiche Baiern

Uniformen des preussischen heeres. See Rabe, Edmund, and Burger, Ludwig. Die brandenburg-preussische armee

Uniformen des preussischen heeres in ihren hauptveränderungen bis auf die gegenwart. Rabe, Edmund

Die **uniformen** des reichsheeres und der reichsmarine nebst amtlichen uniformtafeln. Hoyer, K. and Brennecke, F.

Uniformen distinctions und sonstige abzeichen der gesammten k. k. osterr. ungar. wehrmacht. Judex, M.

Uniformen distinctions- und sonstige abzeicher. Austria. Kriegsministerium

Uniformen und abzeichen der schweizerischen armee; Uniformes et insignes de l'armée suisse. Bern, G. Kollbruner 1927?
12pl. O.

Die **uniformen** und fahnen der deutschen armee. See Die uniformen der deutschen armee

De **uniformen** van de nederlandsche zee en landmacht. Raa, F. J. G. ten

Uniformenkunde. Knoetel, Richard

Uniformes de cada regimiento assi de infanteria como de cavalleria de España. No place, 1789
49 col.pl. O.
Colas 2929

Uniformes de la cavalerie prussienne. Sebbers

Uniformes de la garde civique et de corps militaires nationaux aux Pays Bas en 1789. See Afbeeldingen der monteeringen van de gewapende schutterije en burgercorpsen in Nederland

Uniformes de la garde de sa majesté le roi de Westphalie. No place, 1810
1 l. 19 col.pl. Q.
Shows uniforms of different ranks and units. Sometimes ascribed to Gautier
Colas 2930

Uniformes de la Garde impériale en 1857. Armand-Dumaresq, C. E. A.

Uniformes de la garde nationale de l'armée et de la marine françaises de 1830-1832. Foussereau

Uniformes de la marine de guerra Peruana. Peru. Ministerio de guerra y marina

Uniformes de l'armée allemande. Dally, Aristide

Les **uniformes** de l'armée allemande. Réunion des officiers

Uniformes de l'armée allemande à l'Exposition universelle de Paris en 1900. See Prussia. Kriegsministerium. Deutsche heeres-uniformen auf der weltausstellung in Paris 1900

Uniformes de l'armée anglaise. Dally, Aristide

Uniformes de l'armée autrichienne. Dally, Aristide

Uniformes de l'armée belge. Hendrickx

Uniformes de l'armée belge. Monnier, D.

Uniformes de l'armée belge; uniformen des belgischen heeres; uniforms of the Belgian army. Bruxelles, Kiesseling 1893
38p. 12 col.pl. Q.
Plates are signed F. K. Each shows five uniforms
Colas 2931

Uniformes de l'armée danoise. Kiöbenhavn, L. Boglade ca1808
15 col.pl. Q.
One plate is signed: Heuer, sc.
Colas 2932

Uniformes de l'armée des Deux-Siciles. Gatti

Uniformes de l'armée espagnole. Dally, Aristide

Uniformes de l'armée et de la marine françaises (1848-1852) Lalaisse, Hippolyte

Les **uniformes** de l'armée française. Bucquoy, E. L.

Uniformes de l'armée française. Chapuis, F.

Uniformes de l'armée française depuis 1815 jusqu'à ce jour. Bellangé, J. L. H.

Les **uniformes** de l'armée française depuis 1690 jusqu'à nos jours. Lienhart, and Humbert, René

Uniformes de l'armée farnçaise en [1846-] 1848. Janet, A. L.

Uniformes de l'armée française en 1861. Armand-Dumaresq, C. E. A.

Uniformes de l'armée française en 1884. Armand-Dumaresq, C. É.

Uniformes de l'armée française en 1887. Armand-Dumaresq, C. É.

Les **uniformes** de l'armée française sous le consulat. Marchal, Gustave

Uniformes de l'armée italienne. Dally, Aristide

Uniformes de l'armée prussienne sous le regne de Frédéric-Guillaume II, roi de Prusse. Horvath, C. C., pub.

See also note under Horvath, C. C., pub. Preussische armee-uniformen unter der regierung Friedrich Wilhelm II

Uniformes de l'armée prussienne sous le règne de Frédéric-Guillaume III, roi de Prusse. Horvath, C. C., pub.

Uniformes de l'armée roumaine, 1830-1930. Bucarest, 1930
65 col.pl. F.
Explanations in French and Rumanian
Colas 2934

Uniformes de l'armée turque en 1828, d'après des dessins authentiques; publié par Ch. Motte. Paris, Gihaut frères [1828]
22 col.pl. O.
The first plate is signed: Edouard Robert. Glasser gives a list of the plates
Colas 2935

Uniformes de l'armée westphalienne du roi Jérome. Sauerweid, Alexandre

Uniformes de l'infanterie française suivant le règlement arrête par le roy le 25 avril 1767. Paris, Lattré [1767]
101 col.pl. O.
Glasser gives a list of 99 plates
Colas 2936

Uniformes de tous les regiments de Hussards. Dachery (illus.)

Uniformes des armées alliées. Finart, N.

Uniformes des armés françoisas suivant les reglements du roi. Nuremberg, Raspe 1775
11p. 159 col.pl. O.
Plates copied, in reduced size, from *Recueil de toutes les troupes qui forment les armées françoises*
Colas 2511

Uniformes des écoles du gouvernement. Armand-Dumaresq, C. E.

Uniformes des Gardes d'honneur des différens corps dans les sept départements de la Hollande formés pour la réception de sa majesté l'empereur et roi. [Reproduction of an edition published in 1811] Amsterdam, E. Maaskamp; Paris, La Giberne [1904]
12 l. 12 col.pl. Q.
Colas 2937

Les **uniformes** des troupes coloniales de 1666 à 1875. Depréaux, Albert

Uniformes des troupes de ligne, 1829-1830. Raffet, D. A. M.

Uniformes, drapeaux et voitures militaires russes vers la fin du XVIIIe siècle et au commencement du XIXe. Orlowski, A. O.

Uniformes du consulat. Hoffmann, Nicolas

Uniformes et costumes officiels de la 3e République Service militaire du chemins de fer. Aubry, A.

Uniformes et insignes de l'armée suisse. See Uniformen und abzeichen der schweizerischen armee

Uniformes français. Basset, pub.

Uniformes français. See Raffet, D. A. M. Collection des costumes militaires de l'armée, de la marine et de la garde nationale françaises

Uniformes français sous le règne de Louis-Phillippe. Basset, publisher

Uniformes français sous Napoléon 1er, la restauration et Napoléon III. Bastin, Ferdinand

Uniformes militaires. Montigny, C. A. L. de

Uniformes militaires anciens et actuels ... Nos soldats. Brun, Charles

Uniformes militaires des troupes françoises et étrangères ... sous le règne de Louis XVI, suivant les derniers règlement de 1778. [Paris] Juillette [1779]
5 l. 166 col.pl. map. Q.
Colas 2938

Uniformes militaires des troupes françoises et étrangères ... sous le règne de Louis XVI, suivant les derniers règlements donnés sous le ministère de monseigneur

Uniformes militaire des troupes françoises et étrangères—*Continued* le prince de Mont-Barey. Augmentés des troupes qui forment la garde et maison du roy. Paris, Onfroy 1780
5 l. 182 col.pl. map. Q.
Second edition of the preceding title. Gives uniforms as they were after the ordinance of 1779, adding especially the Chasseurs à cheval and Chevauléger
Colas 2939

Uniformes navales de la marina de guerra Argentina. Argentine Republic. Ministerio de marina

Uniformes para el personal subalterno de la marina de guerra de la Republica Argentina. Argentine Republic. Ministerio de marina

Uniformi de' corpi dell' armata italiana. Milano, 1809
1 l. 32 col.pl. Q.
Colas 2942

Uniformi delle truppe di S. S. R. M. il re di Sardegna. Pedrone

Uniformi delle truppe di S. S. R. M. (le roi de Sardaigne) Stagnon, Giuseppe

Uniformi e standardi delle truppe di s. s. real maesta Vittorio Amedeo III, re di Sardegna. No place, 1790?
30 col.pl. F.
Colas 2943

Uniformi militari dell'armata di S. M. Sarda. Maggi, G. B.

Uniformi militari Italiani al 1. Ottobre 1863. Bisi, A. F.

Uniformierung und ausrüstung der schweizerischen armee von II januar 1898. Escher, A. von

Die **uniformirung** der königl. preussischen armee im jahre 1874. Schindler, C. F.

Uniformirung und organisation des bürgermilitärs in dem Königreiche Baiern. Schiesl, Ferdinand

Uniformirungs-vorschrift für die k.k. finanzwache. Wien, K. K. Hof- und staatsdruckerei. 1870-80
1 l. 10pl. F.
Colas 2945

Uniformkunde. Knötel, Herbert; Pietsch, Paul, and Jantke, Egon

Uniforms. See Livery; Marine corps—United States; Military costume; Musicians; Naval costume; Papal uniforms; Police; Red cross

Uniforms, Civil

Blakeslee, F. G. Uniforms of the world. c1929

See also Public health service

Austria

Uniformirungs-vorschrift fur die k.k. finanzwache. 1870-80

England

Busby, T. L. Civil and military costume of the city of London. 1824-25

Great Britain. Civil service committee. Uniforms to be worn by Her Majesty's civil servants at home and in the colonies. 1859

Great Britain. Lord Chamberlain. Uniforms to be worn by the queen's household. 1890?

France

Aubry, A. Uniformes et costumes officiels de la 3e République Service militaire du chemins de fer. 1909

Hoffmann, Nicolas. Costumes militaires de France. 1800?

Germany

Bildliche darstellung der königlich preussischen civil-uniformen ... nebst ausführlicher erklärung. 1804

Rumpf, C. Der preussische steuerbeamte in bezug auf seine dienst- und rechtsverhältnisse. 1859

Philippine islands

Philippine Islands. Bureau of public health. Regulations governing the uniforms of officers and employees of Philippine health service, 1915. 1915

United States

United States. War department. Specifications for uniforms to be worn by civilians employed by the War department for duty in education and recreation work, and by certain of the national welfare societies. 1920

Uniforms and equipments for officers' national guard. Warnock uniform company

Uniforms de la garde civique et de corps militaires nationaux aux Pays Bas en 1789. See Afbeeldingen der monteeringen van de gewapende schutterije en burgercorpsen in Nederland

Uniforms of British army, navy and court. Holding, T. H.

Uniforms of Philippine constabulary. Philippine Islands. Bureau of constabulary

Uniforms of the American army. Gardiner, A. B.

Uniforms of the American, British, French and German armies in the war of the American revolution. Lefferts, C. M.

Uniforms of the Belgian army. See Uniformes de l'armée belge

Uniforms of the world. Blakeslee, F. G.

Uniforms of women worn during the war. See National society of the colonial dames of America. Report of the Committee on relics

Uniforms to be worn by Her Majesty's civil servants. Great Britain. Civil service committee

Uniforms to be worn by the queen's household. Great Britain. Lord Chamberlain

Uniforms-tabellen und quartier-liste der deutschen armee und der kaiserlich deutschen marine. Lange, G.

Uniformzeichnung d. königl. dänischen armee. Köller, F. L. von

Uniformzeichnung der vorzüglichsten europäischen truppen. Köller, F. L. von

Union centrale des arts décoratifs, Paris
Le costume. Paris, A. Guérinet [190-]
1 p.l. 48pl. F. (Les nouvelles collections de l'Union... au Musée du Louvre ... 17. série.)
Shows feminine costume of France during the eighteenth century
Colas 2224

See also Paris. Musée des arts décoratifs. Dessins de broderies, fin du XVIIIe siècle & 1er empire

Unit jewellery. Rathbone, R. L. B.

United Ladies' tailoring association of America. See entry under Élégance parisienne

United States. Army
Regulations for the uniform of the U. S. army; rev. ed. 1914. Washington, Govt print. off. 1914
68p. illus. S. (War department document no 468)

See also Military costume—United States

United States. Army war college
Notes on uniforms and insignia, French, British, Belgian, German; comp. and ed. at the Army war college, December 1917. [Washington, D. C. Govt. print. off. 1917]
30p. illus. D. (National army training pamphlets no 194. War dept. doc. no.726)

United States. Bureau of American ethnology
Annual report [and accompanying papers] 1st+ 1879/80+ Washington, Govt. print. off. 1881+
Illus. (part col.) Q.
Contains material on costumes, tattooing, masks, labrets, etc. of the North American Indians and Eskimos. Many plates and illustrations show details
The General index vols. 1-48 (1879-1931) compiled by Biren Bonnerjea [i.e. Vīrendra Vandyopādhyāya] (Washington, D.C. 1881-1933) is a detailed index in which material on the Indian is listed by tribe
An administrative *Annual report* is also issued

United States. Bureau of foreign and domestic commerce
Wearing apparel in Bolivia. Prepared by William A. Montavon. Washington, Govt. print. off. 1918
84p. incl.tables. O. (Miscellaneous series no 69)
LC 18-26689

Wearing apparel in Peru. Washington, Govt. print. off. 1918
64p. O. (Miscellaneous series no 74)
LC 19-26093

United States. Census office. 11th census, 1890
Moqui Pueblo Indians of New Mexico; by Thomas Donaldson. Washington, United States census printing office 1893
136p. col.front. pl. (part col.) maps (part fold.) Q. At head of title: Eleventh census of the United States. Extra census bulletin
Costume index. LC 7-18865

United States. Coast guard
Regulations covering the uniforms for commissioned and warrant officers and enlisted men of the United States Coast guard, 1930. Washington, Govt. print. off. 1930
v,75p. incl.illus. tables. O.
LC 31-26118

Regulations governing the uniforms for enlisted persons of the United States Coast guard, 1922. Washington, Govt. print. off. 1922
20p. incl. tables. 3pl. on 2 l. O.
LC 22-26410

Regulations governing the uniforms for warrant officers and enlisted persons of the United States Coast guard, 1916. Washington, Govt. print. off. 1916
27p. pl. O.
LC 16-26540

United States. Commission to the Madrid exposition, 1892
Ancient Mexican feather work. See entry under Nuttall, Mrs Zelia

U. S. George Washington bicentennial commission
George Washington play and pageant costume book ... Washington, D. C., United States George Washington bicentennial commission c1931
24p. illus. F. o.p.
"Authorities consulted": p24
Contents: pt I Costume in the time of George Washington; pt II Military uniforms and stage properties
Costume index. LC 32-26413

United States. Library of Congress. Division of bibliography
Brief list of references on the history of hats and head-dresses. August 5, 1922. [Washington, 1922]
4 l. Q. [Select list of references. no. 678]

List of references on dress reform. Washington 1920
5 l. Q. (Select list of references no. 435)
Typewritten

United States. Marine corps
Regulations for the uniform & dress of the Marine corps ... October, 1859; from the original text and drawings in the Quarter Master's Department. 1st ed. Philadelphia, Desilver [1859]
9p. pl. (part col.) F.
Colas 2522. Lipperheide 2393

Regulations for the uniform and dress of the Marine corps ... May, 1875. Washington, Govt. print. off. 1875
9p. 10pl. (part col.) F.
Report and drawings made by a board of officers, convened under the instructions of the Navy department, to revise the uniform of the Marine corps
Colas 2522. Lipperheide 2393. LC 8-16970

Uniform regulations, United States Marine corps, 1922. Superseding Uniform regulations, United States Marine corps, 1917. Washington, Govt. print. off. 1922
ix,112p. O.
LC 22-24140

United States—Marine corps—*Continued*

Uniform regulations, United States Marine corps. 1929 ... Washington, Govt. Print. off. 1930
vi,136p. O.
Superseding Uniform regulations United States Marine corps, 1922
LC 30-26546

Uniform regulations, United States Marine corps, together with uniform regulations common to both U.S. navy and Marine corps. Headquarters United States Marine corps, 1912. Washington, Govt. print. off. 1913
104p. 60pl. O.
LC 13-35418

Uniform regulations, United States Marine corps, together with uniform regulations common to both U. S. Navy and Marine corps. Headquarters United States Marine corps, 1912. Rev. 1917 ... Washington, Govt. print. off. 1917
111p. 60 (i. e. 64) pl. O.
LC 17-29007

United States. Military academy, West Point

The centennial of the United States Military academy at West Point, New York, 1802-1902. Washington, Govt. print. off. 1904
2v. fronts. illus. 42pl. ports. maps. Q. (58th Cong., 2d sess. House. Doc. no. 789)
Volume 1 Addresses and histories, v2 Statistics and bibliographies
Plates show uniforms worn at the academy from its founding to 1900
LC 5-17621

United States. National museum

Primitive American armor. See entry under Hough, Walter

United States. Navy department

Regulations for the uniform and dress of of the navy and marine corps of the United States. March, 1852 ... Washington, C. Alexander 1852
38p. D.
"From the original text and drawings in the Navy department"
LC 13-13292

Regulations for the uniform and dress of the navy of the United States. [Washington] J. & G. S. Gideon 1841
14p. fold.pl. D.
Extract from the General regulations for the government of the navy of the United States, approved February 19, 1841
LC CA17-785

Regulations for the uniform of the United States navy. December 1, 1866. Washington, Govt. print. off. 1866
16p. 29 col.pl. O.
LC CA17-790

Regulations governing the uniform of commissioned offiçers, warrant officers, and enlisted men of the navy of the United States ... Washington, Govt. print. off. 1897
37p. XXVII pl.(part col.) O.
LC 13-16223

Regulations governing the uniform of commissioned officers, warrant officers and enlisted men of the navy of the United States, 1905. With plates. Washington, Govt. print. off. 1905
54p. XXXV (i. e. 36) pl. O.
LC 32-633

Regulations governing the uniform of commissioned officers, warrant officers, and enlisted men of the navy of the United States. With plates. Washington, Govt. print. off. 1886
26p. 54 col.pl. O.
LC 9-15839

Regulations relating to the uniforms of the officers of the United States navy, Navy department, January 22, 1883. Washington, Govt. print. off. 1883
14p. V pl.(3 col.) O
LC CA17-787

Uniform for the United States navy, prepared under direction of the secretary of the navy. Washington, Govt. print. off. 1869
12p. 9pl.(8 col.) F.
The same title was published in O. size without the plates
Colas 2941. Lipperheide 2391. LC 32-617

Uniform regulations. [Washington, Govt. print. off. 1877]
cover-title, 20p. O.
LC CA17-788

Uniform regulations, United States navy, together with uniform regulations common to both Navy and Marine corps. Navy department, 1913. Washington, Govt. print. off. 1913
76p. 29 (i. e. 31) pl. O.
LC 13-12711

Uniform regulations, United States navy, together with uniform regulations common to both Navy and Marine corps. Navy department, 1913. (Rev. to January 15, 1917) Washington, Govt. print. off. 1917
76p. 30 (i. e. 33) pl. O.
LC 17-26370

United States. Public health service

Regulations governing the uniforms of officers and employees of the United States Public health service ... 1914. Washington, Govt. print. off. 1914
35p. 26pl. O.
LC 14-30839

United States. Quartermaster corps

The army of the United States [1774-1889] Illustrated by forty-four fac-simile plates from water color drawings by H. A. Ogden. Text by Henry Loomis Nelson. Prepared and executed by the Quartermaster general of the United States, under the authority of the secretary of war. New York, B. M. Whitlock 1885?
2v. 44 col.pl. F.
Volume 1 text; v2 plates. The same plates are published in volume 1 of *Uniform of the army of the United States,* also issued by the Quartermaster corps

Illustrations of Alaskan clothing. Washington, Govt. print. off. 1914
32. l. illus. O.
Shows fur coats and civilian clothing issued to American troops stationed in Alaska
LC WAR14-79

The military shoe. See entry under Salquin, S. A.

Regulations for the uniform of the army of the United States ... Compiled by direction of the Secretary of War under the

United States. Quartermaster corps—*Cont.*
supervision of the Quartermaster general and Inspector general. Philadelphia. I. Friedenwald, printer 1888
3 l. 25pl.(12 col.) F.
Colas 2523. Lipperheide 2394

Regulations prescribing flags, signals, funnel marks, etc., also uniforms of the United States army transport service. Washington, [Govt. print. off.] 1899
14 l. pl. O.

Regulations prescribing uniforms of the United States army transport service and harbor boat service, including mine planters and cable boats, also flags, signals, funnel marks, etc. Washington, Govt. print. off. 1912
49p. LXV pl. O. (Circular no 7)

Report of the Quartermaster to the Secretary of war, 1876
Contains colored plates of uniforms, caps, belt buckles, aguilettes, etc.
Also published in U. S. War department. *Annual report of the secretary, 1876*

Specifications for the uniform of the United States army, 1915. Washington, Govt. print. off. 1915
61p. D. (War dept. doc. no. 484)
LC WAR15-117

Uniform of the army of the United States, 1882. Philadelphia, T. Hunter [1882]
4p. 19pl.(part col.) ob.F.

Uniform of the army of the United States (illustrated) from 1774 to 1907. Authorized by the secretary of war, and prepared and published by the quartermaster general. [New York, Lith. by G. H. Buek, American lithograph co. c1885-1909]
2v. 68 col.pl. F.
Contents: v 1 From 1774 to 1889, 44 plates with index, and 71p. giving uniform orders from that period; v2 From 1898 to 1907, plates 45-47, and 1-23
Volume 1 with text by H. L. Nelson is also published by the Quartermaster corps with title: *Army of the United States*
Costume index. War 10-14

Uniform of the army of the United States, October 1, 1908. Washington, D. C., lith. by Eckert 1908
2 l. 143 col.pl. Q.

United States. Shipping board
Manual of uniforms and insignia. Boston, [191-?]
34p. pl. D.

United States. War department
Regulations and decisions pertaining to the uniform of the army of the United States ... 3d ed. Washington, Govt. print. off. 1899
48p. O. (War department. Document no. 38. Office of the quartermaster-general)
LC 9-27717

Regulations for the uniform & dress of the army of the United States, June, 1851. Philadelphia, W. H. Horstmann [1851]
13p. 25 col.pl. F.
Plates by G. C. Humphries, lithographed by Schuessele at P. G. Duval's
Colas 2520? LC 8-34917

Regulations for the uniform and dress of the army of the United States, 1861. Philadelphia, Horstmann; New York, Horstmann & Allien [1861]
23p. front. D.
"Copied from pamphlet issued by the War department"
LC 32-10687

Regulations for the uniform and dress of the army of the United States, July, 1872. Washington, Govt. print. off. 1872
10p. 8 col.pl. F.
LC 9-3297

Regulations for the uniform of the United States army, 1917. Washington, Govt. print. off. 1917
87p. incl.tab. D. (Special regulations. no. 41)

Regulations for the uniform of the United States army. General orders, no. 169, August 14, 1907. Washington, Govt. print. off. 1907
66p. D.
LC 7-35347

Specifications for uniforms to be worn by civilians employed by the War department for duty in education and recreation work, and by certain of the national welfare societies; revised 1920. Washington, Govt. print. off. 1920
13p. illus. O. (Special regulations. no. 105)

United States
Avery, E. M. A history of the United States and its people, from their earliest records to the present time. 1904-10

Earle, Mrs A. M. Two centuries of costume in America, MDCXX-MDCCCXX. 1903

Eggleston, Edward. The household history of the United States and its people, for young Americans. 1901

Haire, F. H. The American costume book. 1934

Haire, F. H. The folk costume book. 1934

Hoes, Mrs R. G. Dresses of the mistresses of the White House. 1931

Kerr, R. N. Miniature costume folios. c1937. v4

Lamb, Mrs. M. J. R. N. History of the city of New York. 1877-96

McClellan, Elisabeth. History of American costume, 1607-1870. 1937

Morgan, J. H. Early American painters. 1921

Pageant of America; a pictorial history of the United States. 1925-29

Pyle, Howard, illus. Howard Pyle's book of the American spirit; the romance of American history. 1923

Rogers, Agnes, comp. The American procession, American life since 1860 in photographs. 1933

Sellner, Eudora. American costumes; 150 years of style in America, 1775-1925. c1925

Sullivan, Mark. Our times; the United States, 1900-1925. 1926-1935

Wharton, A. H. Heirlooms in miniatures. 1898

United States—*Continued*

Wright, R. L. Hawkers & walkers in early America, strolling peddlers, preachers, lawyers, doctors, players, and others, from the beginning to the civil war. 1927

See also subdivision United States under Academic costume; Embroidery; Lace; Legal costume; Naval costume; Theatrical costume; Uniforms, Civil; Weddings and wedding dress; also Indians of North America

Foreign population

See Chinese in the United States

Public health service

See Public health service

Colonial period (to 1775)

Allard, Carel. Orbis habitabilis oppida et vestitus. 1705? pl.77-100

Bayley, F. W. Five colonial artists of New England. 1929

Bruce, P. A. Economic history of Virginia in the seventeenth century. 1935

Earle, Mrs A. M. Costume of colonial times. 1894

Earle, Mrs A. M. Home life in colonial days. 1913

Earle, Mrs A. M. Stage-coach and tavern days. 1905

Fisher, S. G. Men, women & manners in colonial times. 1898

Griswold, R. W. The republican court; or, American society in the days of Washington. 1868

Stanard, Mrs M. M. P. N. Colonial Virginia, its people ad customs. 1917

Textile color card association of the United States. Colonial colors for the bicentennial year. 1932?

United States. George Washington bicentennial commission. George Washington play and pageant costume book. c1931

Warwick, Edward, and Pitz, H. C. Early American costume. c1929

Wharton, A. H. Salons colonial and republican. 1900

Wharton, A. H. Colonial days & dames. 1895

See also Children—United States—Colonial period

Bibliography

Meyers, C. L., comp. Bibliography of colonial costume. 1923

Dutch in New York

Kinnear, D. M. Mynheer van Schlichtenhorth and the old Dutch burghers. 1906

Watson, J. F. Historic tales of olden time: concerning the early settlement and advancement of New York city and state. 1832

1775-1783

The costumes of America. 1852

Ellet, Mrs E. F. L. The women of the American revolution. 1900

Goodwin, Mrs M. W. Dolly Madison. 1896

Warwick, Edward, and Pitz, H. C. Early American costume. c1929

1783-1865

Bowne, Mrs Eliza. A girl's life eighty years ago. 1887

Chambers, William. Things as they are in America. 1854

Clay-Clopton, Mrs Virginia. A belle of the fifties. 1905

Goodwin, Mrs M. W. Dolly Madison. 1896

Wharton, A. H. Salons colonial and republican. 1900

Wharton, A. H. Social life in the early republic. 1902

See also Pioneers—United States

Periodicals

The American ladies' magazine. 1828-36

Graham's American monthly magazine of literature, art, and fashion. 1826-58

19th century

Clucas, Charles. The etiquette of men's dress. 1888

Finley, Mrs R. E. The lady of Godey's. 1931

Pictures of society, grave and gay. 1866

Rourke, C. M. Troupers of the Gold Coast; or, The rise of Lotta Crabtree. c1928

Walker, Isaac. Dress: as it has been, is, and will be. 1885

See also United States—1783-1865

Periodicals

Le Bon ton and le Moniteur de la mode united. 1851-1926+?

The Delineator. 1873-1937

Élite; an illustrated society journal addressed to people of culture and fashion. 1881-1907

Frank Leslie's ladies' gazette of fashion and fancy needle work. 1854-57

Frank Leslie's modenwelt. 1870-71

Godey's magazine, 1830-98

Harper's bazaar. 1867+

Ladies home journal. 1883+

Les Parisiennes. 1897-1929

Pictorial review combined with Delineator. 1899+

Pictorial review fashion book. 1896+

The Puritan. 1897-1901

Royal. 1895-1925

Sartorial art journal and American tailor and cutter. 1874-1929

Vogue, incorporating Vanity fair. 1892+

Woman's home companion. 1873+

Civil war period 1861-1865

Andrews, E. F. The war-time journal of a Georgia girl, 1864-1865. 1908

Clay-Clopton, Mrs Virginia. A belle of the fifties. 1905

Miller, F. T., and Lanier, R. S., eds. The photographic history of the civil war. 1911

Wright, Mrs L. W. A southern girl in '61. 1905

United States—*Continued*

20th century

Baldt, L. I. Clothing for women; selection and construction. c1935

Burbank, Emily. The smartly dressed woman; how she does it. 1925

Kneeland, Natalie. Aprons and house dresses. 1925

Lyster, A. M., and Hudnall, Mrs G. F. Social problems of the high school boy. 1935

National beauties and their costumes; with explantory text. 1907?

See also Children—United States—20th century; Motoring costume—1900-1910

Periodicals

American gentleman and sartorial art journal. 1901+

American ladies' tailor and Les Parisiennes. 1903+

Butterick fashion magazine. 1908+

California stylist. 1937+

The Delineator. 1873-1937

Designer and manufacturer; a magazine devoted to the designing and manufacture of men's, boys' and children's clothing. 1933+

Élite; an illustrated society journal addressed to people of culture and fashion. 1881-1907

Excella fashion quarterly. 1922-36

Fashion service magazine. 1920+

Fashions art. 1934-36

Fashions of the hour. 1929+

Harper's bazaar. 1867+

Ladies home journal. 1883+

Ladies' home magazine of New York. 1904-05

McCall fashion book. 1913+

Man's book; a magazine. 1908-10

Men's wear; the retailer's newspaper. 1896+

Newest styles for men. 1924+

Les Parisiennes. 1897-1929

Pictorial review combined with Delineator. 1899+

Pictorial review fashion book. 1896+?

Royal. 1895-1925

Sartorial art journal and American tailor and cutter. 1874-1929

Style, a monthly magazine for women. 1901-[09]

Style trend; devoted exclusively to the interests of the washable garment; fabric and related industries. 1928+

Styles for men. 1926+

To-day's woman and home. 1905-1928

Vanity fair. 1913-36

Vogue, incorporating Vanity fair. 1892+

Vogue pattern book. 1925+

Woman's home companion. 1873+

Women's wear magazine. Eastern edition. 1923-32

BY REGION OR STATE

California

Coy, O. C. Pictorial history of California. c1925

Mackey, M. G., and Sooy, L. P. Early California costumes, 1769-1847. 1932

Newmark, Harris. Sixty years in Southern California, 1853-1913. 1916

Louisiana

Frémaux, L. J. New Orleans characters. 1876

New England

Felt, J. B. The customs of New England. 1853

New Orleans

See Street venders—United States—New Orleans

New York (State)

Moss, Frank. The American metropolis, from Knickerbocker days to the present time. 1897

Singleton, Esther. Social New York under the Georges, 1714-1776; houses, streets and country homes, with chapters on fashions, furniture, china, plate, and manners. 1902

Valentine's manual of old New York. 1916-28

Pennsylvania

Watson, J. F. Annals of Philadelphia, and Pennsylvania, in the olden time. 1898

See also Military costume—United States—Revolutionary period—Philadelphia

Southern states

Avary, Mrs M. L. Dixie after the war. 1906

United States army and navy. See Wagner, A. L., and Kelley, J. D. J. Our country's defensive forces in war and peace

United States eastern amateur ski association. See American ski annual

United States eastern ski annual. See American ski annual

United States officers' uniforms. Volk, C. G.

L'**univers** illustré. Desessarts, Alfred

Gli **universali** de i belli recami antichi e moderni. Zoppino, N. d'A.

Universities and colleges. See Academic costume; Students

Unknown Mongolia. Carruthers, A. D. M.

An **unknown** people in an unknown land. Grubb, W. B.

Unmentionables. Holliday, R. C.

Unser heer. Röchling, Carl

Unser vaterland in waffen; ein patriotischer hausschatz für das deutsche volk. Berlin, P. Kittel [1893]

2v. 109pl. (part col.) O.

First published in 28 parts with title: *Patriotischer hausschatz II. jahrb.* Contains pictures of soldiers in uniform

Lipperheide 2141

Unser volk in waffen. Poten, Bernhard von

Unsere kleidung. Frucht, Lotte, and Schneehagen, Christian

Unsere volkstrachten. Hansjakob, Heinrich

Unter den fahnen. See Danzer, Alfonz. A mi hadseregünk

Unter kopfjägern in Central-Celebes. Grubauer, Albert

Untererdische hofhaltung. See Ercker, Lazarus. Aula subterranea domina dominantium subdita subditorum

Unterricht eingefriedigte wildbahnen. Mellin, A. W., graf von

Unterricht im arrangement der damentoiletten von standpunkte der kleideraesthetik und der farben-harmonie. Klemm, Heinrich

Unterweisung für anfänger beyderley geschlechts im zeichnen. Richter, J. S.

Unveiling of Lhasa. Candler, Edmund

Der **unwürdige** communicant. Hiltebrandt, J. A.

Uppland. See Sweden—Uppland

Úprka, Joža

Na pouti u Sv. Antoníčka ... Les pèlerinages à Saint Antoine ... The pilgrimage to St. Anthony's ... Die wallfahrt zum hl. Antonius. Kroměříž, 1924?
13p. 15 col.pl. O.
Shows dress of Czechoslovakia

Peasants' furs in Czechoslovakia ... Texte original par François Kretz. Kroměříž, The first Czech bookselling and pub. house [1920]
12p. 30 col.pl. ob.F.
Text and titles in English, French: *Pelisses rustiques dans le territoire de la république Tchéco-Slovaque;* German: *Bauernpelze in der tschechoslowakischev republik;* and Bohemian: *Kozuchy*

Vazani šátků; slovem doprovázi Frant. Kretz ... Tr. by O. Zahrade. Kroměříž, J. Pithart 1924?
[20]p. 25 col.pl. Q.
Second title page and letterpress description of plates in French, English and German: *Comment on noue les fichus de tête, The binding of kerchiefs in Moravia and Slovakia,* and *Das bunden von kopftüchern in Mähren und der Slowakei*

"Up-to-date" dress cutting and drafting. Browne, Miss M. P.

Urban, Josef

(illus.) Towle, H. C. The shoe in romance and history

Urban, K., pseud

Kurze zusammenstellung über die polnische armee. Berlin, R. Eisenschmidt 1931
79p. illus. pl.(1 fold.) diagrs. O.

Urbani de Gheltof, Giuseppe Marino

Trattato storico tecnico della fabbricazione dei merletti veneziani (Venezia-Burano). Venezia, F. Ongania 1878
69p. 31 illus. 7pl. Q.
Title-page, by error, has Venezia-Murano
Lipperheide 4041

Urbium totius Germaniae superioris illustriorum clariorumque tabulae antiquae & novae accuratissimè elaboratae. Braun, Georg

Urgeschichtliche nachrichten und forschungen. See Antiqua

Uredba o odeći suvozemne vojske. Yugoslavia. Laws, statutes, etc.

Uriarte, José R. de

(ed.) Los baskos en la Nacion Argentina. Buenos Aires [pref. 1919]
482p. illus.(part col.) col.pl. ports. F.
Includes a general account of the Basques, their history, customs, art, music, etc.
LC 30-12827

Urkunde über die ... krönung ... des königs von Böhmen Leopold des zweiten und ... der gemahlinn des königs Maria Louise. Debrois, Johann

Urlin, Ethel Lucy Hargreave

Dancing, ancient and modern. London, Herbert & Daniel [1911]
xvi,182p. 14pl.(2 col.) 8 port.(1 col.) D.
Many of the illustrations show dance costume as represented in famous paintings
LC A12-1480

Urquhart, Sir Richard. See note under Vestiarium scoticum

Ursinus, Fulvius. See Orsini, Fulvio

Ursprung, aufleben, grösse, herrschaft, verfall und jetzige zustände sammtlicher mönchs- und klosterfrauen- orden. Biedenfeld, F. L. C., freiherr von

Der **ursprung** des harlekin. Driesen, Otto

Ursprung, geschichte und beschreibung der schwedischen ritterorden. See Silfwerskjöld, T. von. Krönung und huldigung Oscar I. königs von Schweden und Norwegen

Uruguay

Carpenter, F. G. Along the Paraná and the Amazon, Paraguay, Uruguay, Brazil. 1925

MacCann, William. Two thousand miles' ride through the Argentine provinces. 1853

Vidal, E. E. Picturesque illustrations of Buenos Ayres and Monte Video. 1820

Urville, Jules Sebastien César Dumont d'. See Dumont d'Urville, J. S. C.

Der **Urwald** ruft wieder. Schebesta, Paul

Urwald-dokumente. Mansfeld, Alfred

Usages, coutumes et croyances ou livre des choses curieuses. Dergny, Dieudonné

Usi e costumi antichi e moderne, di tutti i popoli del mondo. Bellinzoni, Luigi

Usi e costumi di Napoli e contorni descritte e dipinti. Bourcard, Francesco de

Usi e costumi di tutti i popoli dell' universo, ovvero Storia del governo, delle leggi, della milizia, della religione di tutte le nazioni dai più remoti tempi fino ai nostri giorni; opera compilata da una società di letterati italiani. Milano, Borroni e Scotti 1856-62
7v. in 8. col.fronts. illus. pl.(part col.) Q.
Issued in 270 parts. Volumes 2-7 have imprint: Milano, F. Sanvito
Contents: v 1-4 Europa: 1 Grecia, 2 Italia, 3 Italia insulare e Svizzera, Spagna, Portogallo, Belgio, Olanda, Svezie, Norvegia, e Danimarca, 4 Francia, Inghilterra, Austria, Russia, Turchia, Prussia e Confederazione Germanica; v5 America ed Oceania; v6 Asia; v7 Africa
Lipperheide 69. LC 25-25346

Usi e costumi sociali, politici e religiosi di tutti i popoli del mondo. See Loumyer, J. F. N. Moeurs, usages et costumes de tous les peuples du monde

Utting, R. B.
(illus.) Boutell, Charles. The monumental brasses of England

Utzinger, Rudolf
Masken [von] Rudolf Utzinger. Berlin, E. Wasmuth a. g. [1922]
26p. 48pl. on 24 l. Q. (Orbis pictus; weltkunst-bücherei bd. 13)
"Literatur": p24
LC 24-1692

Uwins, Thomas
Costume of the University of Oxford. London, R. Ackermann 1815
18p. 18 col.pl. F.
Extract from William Combe's *History of the University of Oxford*
Colas 2947. Costume index

(illus.) Combe, William. History of the University of Cambridge

(illus.) Combe, William. History of the University of Oxford

(illus.) Costume of the ladies of England, 1810-1829

Uz, Land of. Bury, G. W.

Uzanne, Louis Octave
Coiffures de style; la parure excentrique, époque Louis XVI. Paris, E. Rouveyre 1895
38p. 100 col.pl. D.
Plates show feminine hair fashions
Colas 2951. Lipperheide 1716

L'éventail; illus. de Paul Avril. Paris, A. Quantin 1882
143p. illus.(part col.) Q.
Lipperheide 1725. LC 15-8932

The fan; [translated from the French] illus. by Paul Avril. London, Nimmo & Bain 1884
143p. illus. Q.
Translation of his *L'eventail*

Fashion in Paris; the various phases of feminine taste and aesthetics from 1797 to 1897; from the French by Lady Mary Lloyd. London, W. Heinemann 1898
xv,180p. 100 col.pl. 250 illus. O. 36s, o.p.
Translation of his *Modes de Paris* (1898) with same plates and illustrations
Issued also in 1901 by Heinemann with the same text but only 24 coloured plates. First published at 36s
Colas 2953 (1908 ed.) Costume index. LC 16-8656 (1901 ed.)

La Française du siècle. La femme et la mode, métamorphoses de la Parisienne de 1792-1892; tableau des mœurs et usages aux principales époques de notre ère républicaine. Édition illus ... par A. Lynch et É. Mas, frontispice en couleurs Félicien Rops. Paris, Librairies-imprimeries réunies 1892
viii,246p. front.illus. O.
Imprint date on cover: 1893
First edition published in 1886 under title: *La Française du siècle; modes, moeurs, usages*
Colas 2948-49. Lipperheide 1175-1176. LC 15-8934 (1886 ed.), 28-647

The Frenchwoman of the century; fashions—manners—usages, by Octave Uzanne. Illustrations in water colours by Albert Lynch, engraved in colours by Eugène Gaujean. London, J. C. Nimmo 1886
xxii,273p. col.front. col.pl. Q. o.p.
Translation of his *La Française du siècle*
Costume index. LC 34-9154

Les modes de Paris, variations du goût et de l'esthétique de la femme, 1797-1897; illus. originales de François Courboin ... d'après des documents inédits. Paris, Société française d'Éditions d'art, L. H. May 1898
242p. illus. 100 col.pl. O.
At head of title: *Monument esthématique du XIXe siècle*
Colas 2952. Lipperheide 1177e. LC 23-15121

L'ombrelle, le gant, le manchon; illus. de Paul Avril. Paris, A. Quantin 1883
138p. 79 illus.(part col.) Q.
Lipperheide 1726. LC 15-8933

Les ornements de la femme ... L'éventail, l'ombrelle, le gant, le manchon. Éd. complète et définitive. Paris, Quantin 1892
270p. illus. D. (Petites monographies d'art)
Colas 2950. LC 14-16376

Les parfums et les fards à travers les âges; illustrations de Léon Carré. Genève, C. Blanc [c1927]
74p. 4 col.pl. D.
LC 28-8624

Son altesse la femme; illustrations de Henri Gervex, J. A. Gonzalès, L. Kratkè, Albert Lynch, Adrien Moreau et Félicien Rops. Paris, A. Quantin 1885
xii,312p. illus.(part col.) 10 col.pl. Q.
Contents: Préface; Le vray mirouer de sorcellerie; La mie du poete; La précieuse; La caillette; La citoyenne française; Les galanteries du directoire; Sous la restauration; L'amour aux champs; La Parisienne moderne; Mulieriana
Describes and pictures French women of the 16th, 17th, and 18th centuries, time of the revolution, the directory, the empire and the restoration, women from the provinces and from Paris
Lipperheide 1099. LC 3-9464

Uzory russkie, malorossiĭskie, i i͡uzhnoslavi͡anskie. Verkhovskoĭ, O.

Uzory starīnnago shīt'i͡a v" Rossiī ... s" predisloviem" F. Buslaeva. Shakhovskai͡a, Princess S. N.

V

V strane samykh bol'shikh morozov. Baĭsutov, N. I.

V gorakh Vostochnogo Zakavkaz'i͡a Azerbaidzhan. Berger, A. K.

V" pami͡at' svi͡ashchennago koronovanii͡a Īkh" Īmperatorskīkh" Velīchestv" v" Moskvi͡e 1896g. V" Peterburgi͡e, H. Hoppe 1896?
100,210p. illus. ports.(2 fold.) fold.pl. F.
Published in two parts
On the coronation of Nicholas II
LC CA15-186 (Russian characters)

V peschanykh stepi͡akh. Baĭsutov, N. I.

Vachon, Marius
La femme dans l'art, les protectrices des arts, les femmes artistes. Paris, J. Rouam 1893
2v. illus. F.
Feminine costume shown in art

See also Paris. Exposition des arts de la femme. Histoire de la coiffure

Vade-mecum du peintre, ou Recueil de costumes du moyen-âge, pour servir à l'histoire de la Belgique et pays circonvoisins. Vigne, Félix de

Vagabond voyage through Brittany. Chase, Mrs Lewis

Vagabondiana. See Smith, J. T. Etchings of remarkable beggars

Vaillant
Costumes algériens. Paris, Dubos et Marest 1847-49
7pl. Q.
Colas 2954

Vala Moro, pseud.
Tanz; [einl. von Samuel Saint-Yves] Wien, M. Wolf [1924]
4p. 10 col.pl. F.

Valegio, Francisco
[Costumes d'hommes et de femmes du temps de Louis XIII] No place, ca1635
14pl. F.
Colas 2955

Valekoff, C.
Ornaments and vestments of the church of Russia and Constantinople. London, Talbot [189-?]
21p. illus. S.

Valencia de Don Juan, Viudo de
Catalogue histórico-descriptivo de la Real armería de Madrid. See entry under Madrid. Armería real

Los **Valencianos** pintados por si mismos; obra de interes y lujo escrita por varios distinguidos escritores. Valencia, I. Boix 1859
396p. 44pl. O.
Lipperheide 1235

Valentine's manual of old New York, 1916/17-1917/18, 1919-1928. New York, Valentine's manual, inc. 1916-28
Col.fronts. illus.(incl.facsims.) pl.(part col. part fold.) ports. D.
The following years, issued with special titles, have costume interest: 1926, *The last fifty years in New York;* 1927, *New York in the elegant eighties;* 1928, *In the golden nineties* by Henry Collins Brown. All show costume worn in New York City during the periods treated
Title varies: 1916/17-1917/18, *Valentine's manual of the city of New York*
LC 16-14583

Valentini, Francesco
Trattato su la commedia dell' arte, ossia improvvisa maschere italiane, ed alcune scene del carnevale di Roma. Berlino, L. G. Wittich 1826
x,32,36p. 20 col.pl. Q.
Text in Italian and German. German title: *Abhandlung über die comödie aus dem stegreif und die italienischen masken*
Colas 2956. Lipperheide 3171

Valério, Théodore
Costumes de la Hongrie et des provinces danubiennes: Dalmatie, Monténégro, Croatie, Slavonie, frontières militaires ... avec une notice par Henri Vuagneux. Paris, Librairie centrale des beaux-arts [1885]
4 l. 79pl. F.
First published in six series with title: *Souvenirs de la monarchie autrichienne* (Paris, Pieron et Delâtre 1853-64. 78pl.)
Colas 2962-63. Lipperheide 836 (1st ed.)

Costumes du grand-duché de Bade et des bords du Rhin Paris, Gehaut [1840-42]
Col.front. 36 col.pl. Q.-F.
For list of plates see Colas's *Bibliographie*
Colas 2957

Souvenirs de l'ouest de la France: Costumes bretons. Nantes, Mellinet [1843-44]
12 col.pl. Q.
Each plate shows two figures in costume of Brittany
Colas 2959

Souvenirs du Tyrol, du Vorarlberg et de la Haute Bavière ... Erinnerungen von Tyrol, Vorarlberg und Ober Baiern. Paris, Gihaut [1842]
Col.front. 12 col.pl. F.
Also found with plates in black and white
Colas 2958

Le touriste ou souvenir de l'ouest de la France. Nantes, P. Sebire [1843-44]
6 col.pl. Q.
Colas 2960

Valesio, Giovanni Luigi
(engr.) Isachi, Alfonso. Relatione di Alfonso Isachi intorno l'origine ... della Madonna di Reggio

Valladolid. Calvert, A. F.

Vallander, Josef Vilhelm
Svenska folket sådant det ännu lefver vid elfvom på berg och i dalom ... Les Suédois, moeurs et coutumes, tableaux et légendes ... Die Schweden ihre trachten, beschäftigungen und volksthümliche gebräuche in bild und wort ... The Swedish people their customs and manners in pictures and legends. Stockholm, A. Bonnier 1864-65
50 l. 17 col.pl. F.
Colas 3047

Vallejo. See Zarza, jt. auth.

Vallet, Jérôme
(engr.) Menestrier, C. F. Description de la belle et grande colonne historiée, dressée à l'honneur de l'empereur Theodose

Vallet, Louis
A travers l'Europe; croquis de cavalerie. Paris, Firmin-Didot 1893
xvi,300p. 300 illus. 50 col.pl. Q.
Lipperheide 2124

Le chic à cheval; histoire pittoresque de l'équitation. Paris, Firmin-Didot 1891
xi,274p. 254 illus. 50 col.pl. Q.
Lipperheide 2939

(illus.) Cossé-Brissac, R. M. T. de Historique du 7ᵉ régiment de dragons

Valley, A.
Album colorié des uniformes des grandes armées de l'Europe. Paris, A. Duquesne 1888
24p. 12 col.pl. O.
Colas 2964

Vallon de Villeneuve, H.
(lithgr.) Greeven, H. Collection des costumes des provinces septentrionales du royaume des Pays-Bas

Il **valore** sociale dell' abbigliamento. Gallo, Emanuele

Valvasor, Johann Weichard
Die ehre desz hertzogthums Crain. Nürnberg, W. M. Endter 1689
4v. 524 illus. 23pl. F.
Some of the plates show costume of Carniola and are engraved by Andreas Trost after drawings by Joseph Koch
Lipperheide 886

Van vrijen en trouwen op 't boerenland. Ven, D. J. van der

Vanauld, Alfred; Richomme, Charles Eugène Honoré, and Castillon, A.
Nouvelle geographie en estampes, revue pittoresque de l'univers; nouvelles, contes, légendes et aperçus historiques sur les moeurs, usages, costumes des différents peuples. Paris, Bédelet 1852
12 col.pl. O.

Van Beveren, Jacques Joseph
Moeurs, usages et costumes de tous les peuples du monde. See entry under Loumyer, J. F. N.

Van Beveren, Jacques Joseph, and Du Pressoir, Charles
Costume du moyen âge d'après les manuscrits les peintures et les monuments contemporains. Brussels, Libraire historique et artistique 1847
2v. (382,164p.) 150 col.pl. O.
Colas 2965. Costume ind. Lipperheide 352

Van den Berge, P. A. See Berge, P. A. van den

Van der Heide, Jan. See Heyden, Jan van der

Vanderheym, Émile. See Jannettaz, Édouard, jt. auth.

Van der Kellen, David. See Kellen, David van der

Vanderpoel, Mrs Emily (Noyes)
American lace & lace-makers ... ed. by Elizabeth C. Barney Buel. New Haven, Yale university press 1924
xx,14p. col.front. 110pl. F.
Description of each plate on verso of preceding plate
LC 24-28973

Van der Ven, Dirk Jan. See Ven, D. J. van der

Van de Velde, Henry. See Velde, Henry van de

Van Dyck, Sir Anthony. See Dyck, Sir Anthonie van

Van Hemelryck, Johannes Lodewyk. See Hemelryck, J. L. van

Vanier, Léon
Costumes de carnaval; album de 16 nouveaux costumes en couleurs, dessinés par F. Renard. Paris, [1885]
16 col.illus. O.

The **vanishing** race. Dixon, J. K.

Vanity fair. v. 1-45, no.6; Sept. 1913-Feb. 1936. [New York, The Vanity Fair pub. co]
Illus. F.
Published monthly. Volume numbering irregular
Formed by the union of *Dress* and *Vanity fair.* Title varies: Sept.-Dec. 1913, *Dress and Vanity fair;* Jan. 1914-Feb. 1936, *Vanity fair.* Absorbed by *Vogue,* March 1, 1936
Editor: March, 1914-Feb. 1936, Frank Crowninshield

Van Lennep, Henry John
Oriental album. New York, A. D. F. Randolph 1862
48p. 20pl. F. o.p.
Costume index

Van Lerberghi, P. See Lerberghi, P. van

Van Lochom, Michiel. See Lochom, Michiel van

Van Millingen, Alexander
Constantinople, painted by Warwick Goble, described by Alexander Van Millingen. London, A. & C. Black 1906
ix,282p. 63 col.pl.(incl.front.) fold.map. O.
Each plate is accompanied by a guard sheet with descriptive letterpress
LC 6-45156

Van Noort, Adam. See Noort, Adam van

Van Oort, Adam. See Noort, Adam van

Vanoverbergh, Morice
Dress and adornment in the Mountain province of Luzon, Philippine islands. Washington, D. C., Catholic anthropological conference 1929
Cover-title, p181-242. illus.(incl.map) O. (Publications of the Catholic anthropological conference, v. I no5)
LC 31-1061

Van Pers, A. See Pers, A. van

Van Tenac, Charles
Histoire générale de la marine; comprenant les naufrages célèbres, les voyages autour du monde ... jusqu'au bombardement de Tanger et la prise de Mogador par le prince de Joinville; ed. splendidement illustrée. Paris, E. et V. Penaud [1853]
4v. fronts. pl.(part col.) Q.
First edition appeared in parts 1847-1848
LC 1-22168

Van Vinkeroy, E. See Vinkeroy, E. van

Van Wetter, George. See Wetter, George van

Varangians
Kruse, F. C. H. Necrolivonica, oder Geschichte und alterthümer Liv-, Esth- and Curlands. 1859

Les **variantes** dans les armoiries. Bouly de Lesdain, Louis

Varie acconciature di teste usate da nobilissime dame in diverse cittadi d'Italia. Guerra, Giovanni

Varie figure. Callot, Jacques

Varthema, Ludovico de
Die ritterlich vñ lobwirdig rayss des gestrengen vñ über all ander weyt erfarnen ritters und lantfarers herzen Ludowico vartomans vo Bolonia Sagent vo den landen Egypto, Syria vo bayden Arabia Parsia India uñ Ethiopia vo den gestalte syte vñ dero menschen leben und gelauben; auch von manigerlay thyeren vöglen und vil andern in denselben landen seltza-

Varthema, Ludovico de—*Continued*
men wüderparlichen sachen; das alles er selbs erfaren vñ in aygner person gesehen hat. Augsburg, H. Miller 1515
76 l. 46 illus. Q.
Translated from the original Italian edition which appeared in 1510. A translation into Latin is also known
Lipperheide 1453

Vasconcellos, Antonio de
Anacephalaeoses, id est summa capita actorum regum Lusitaniae. Antverpiae, P. & I. Belleros 1621
597p. 25 illus. Q.
Contains head and shoulder portraits of the kings of Portugal until 1605, also two queens of Portugal
Lipperheide 1207

Vasili, Paul, comte, pseud.
La sainte Russie; la cour, l'armée, le clergé, la bourgeoisie et le peuple. Paris, Firmin-Didot 1890
550p. front. illus. pl.(part col.) ports. Q.
Illustrations show Russian costume of various periods, with the 19th century predominant

Vassal, Bonaventure Marie Joseph
Historique du 11e régiment d'infanterie ... pub. sous la direction de MM. les colonels Konne et Frère, 1635-1900. Montauban, É. Forestié 1900
301p. front. pl.(part col.) port. fold.maps. Q.
LC 21-14658

Vassetz, de
Traité contre le luxe des coeffures. Paris, E. Couterot 1694
16 l. 251p. S.
LC CA35-883

Vaterländische vollständige sammlung der merkwürdigsten national costume des königreichs Ungarn und Croatien nach der natur. See Heimbucher von Bikessy, J. A Magyar

Die **vaterländischen** alterthümer Schleswig-Holsteins. Mestorf, Johanna

Vatican. Biblioteca Vaticana
Vaticanische miniaturen. See entry under Beissel, Stephan

Vatican staff. See Papal uniforms

Vaticanische miniaturen. Beissel, Stephan

Vaughan, Walter
An essay, philosophical and medical, concerning modern clothing. Rochester, W. Gillman 1792
x l. 114p. O.
Translated into German under title: *Philosophisch-medicinischer versuch über die moderne kleidung* (Leipzig, C. G. Hilscher 1793. 118p.)
Lipperheide 3241 (Ger. ed.)

Vaupell, Otto Frederik
Den danske hærs historie til nutiden og den norske hærs historie, indtil 1814. Kjøbenhavn, Gyldendal (F. Hegel) 1872-76
2v. illus. col.pl. maps(part fold.) plans. O.
Illustrations by F. C. Lund show uniforms of the Danish army from the time of its origin
Colas 2975. Lipperheide 2283. LC 13-9002

Vaux, Ludovic, baron de
Les hommes d'épée; préface par Aurélien Scholl. Paris, É. Rouveyre 1882
xxxii,167p. front. illus. pl. ports. O.
Contents: Dédicace; Préface; Maîtres d'armes parisiens; Amateurs parisiens, (1. sér.) Amateurs parisiens, (2. sér.) 1. suppl. Le baron de San Malato; 2. suppl. Maîtres d'armes divers
LC F-1943

Vaux, William Sandys Wright
Nineveh and Persepolis: an historical sketch of ancient Assyria and Persia, with an account of the recent researches in those countries. London, A. Hall, Virtue 1850
436. front. illus. pl. fold.map. D.
Illustrations show dress of the Assyrians and ancient Persians
LC 5-12901

Vavassore, Giovanni Andrea
Opera nova universal intitulata corona di racammi ... stampato in Vinegia per M. Pagan e G. da Fontenato di Monferrato, 1546. Venezia, F. Ongania 1879
45pl. Q. (Raccolta di opere antiche sui disegni dei merletti di Venezia, 8)
Facsimile reprint
Lipperheide 3886

Vazani šátků. Úprka, Joža

Veblen, Thorstein
The theory of the leisure class; an economic study of institutions. [New ed.] New York, Macmillan 1912
404p. D.
First edition: 1899
Chapter VII: Dress as an expression of pecuniary culture
LC 12-5177

Vecākie latvju tautas apgērba zīmējumi. Spekke, Arnolks

Vecellio, Cesare
Coleccion de trages que usaron todas las naciones conocidas hasta el siglo XV, diseñados por el gran Ticiano Vecellio, y por Cesar su hermano. Madrid, Barco y Quirago 1794
2v. 275 col.pl. O.
Also known with plates in black and white. A reproduction of plates from earlier titles by C. Vecellio, with the addition of 25 plates of Spanish costume
The title of volume 2 is modified to carry the work up to the 16th century
Colas 2979. Lipperheide 24

Corona delle nobili, et virtuose donne, libro quinto ... In Venetia, 1596. Venezia, F. Ongania 1891
1 l. 11pl. F. (Raccolta di opere antiche sui disegni dei merletti di Venezia, 1 bis)
Facsimile reprint
Lipperheide 3900

Corona delle nobili et virtuose donne ... nelqual si dimostra in varij dissegni, tutte le sorti di mostre di punti tagliati, punti in aria, punti à reticello, et d'ogni altra sorte ... In Venetia, 1600. Venedig, F. Ongania 1876
110pl. Q.
Facsimile reprint. Includes the first four books of the *Corona*
Lipperheide lists an edition, books 2-4 (Venetia, 1592-1608. 82pl.) Reprints of books 1-4 from an edition of 1617 have titles: *Livre de dentelles* (Paris, Veuve Pairault 1882. 116pl.) and *Pizzi antichi* (Milano, U. Hoepli 1886. xiv p. 116p.)
Lipperheide 3899, 3901-03

Vecellio, Cesare—*Continued*
Costumes anciens et modernes; Habiti antichi et moderni di tutto il mondo, di Cesare Vecellio, précédés d'un essai sur la gravure sur bois, par M. Amb. Firmin Didot. Paris, Firmin Didot 1860
2v. 513 illus. O.
Fourth edition of the author's *De gli habiti antichi et moderni.* Includes reproductions of costumes found in the three previous editions, engraved by E. F. Huyot, after the designs of Catenacci, Felmann and Gérard Seguin. Didot's essay was printed separately: *Essai typographique et bibliographique sur l'histoire de la gravure sur bois* (Paris, 1863. LC 12-6438)
Colas 2980. Costume index. Lipperheide 25. LC PO30-66

De gli habiti antichi, et moderni di diverse parti del mondo. Venetia, Presso D. Zenaro 1590
24, 499 l. 420 illus. S.
Second edition: *Habiti antichi, et moderni di tutto il mondo* (Venetia, B. Sessa 1598. 506 illus.); third edition: *Habiti antichi* (Venetia, per Combi & La Noù 1664. 415pl.)
The first part, 361 illustrations, shows European costumes; the second part, 59 illustrations, shows dress in Asia and Africa. The woodcuts after designs by C. Vacellio are by Cristoforo Guerra. According to the Library of Congress he may be identical with Christoph Chrieger. In the 3d edition the designs are ascribed to Tiziano Vecelli (Gran Ticiano); however, the participation of Titian is doubtful
Colas 2976-78. Lipp. 21-23. LC 28-31181

Veen, Gisbert van
(engr.) Harriot, Thomas. Admiranda narratio fida tamen, de commodis et incolarum ritibus Virginiae, nuper admodum ad Anglis, qui à dn. Richardo Greinvile ... eò in coloniam anno M.D.LXXXV

Veer, Ellert de. See Die cronycke van Hollant, Zeelant ende Vrieslant

Vegetius Renatus, Flavius
Fl. Vegetii Renati viri illustris De re militari libri quatuor. Sexti Iulii Frontini De strategematis libri totidem. Aeliani De instruendis aciebus liber unus. Modesti De vocabulis rei militaris liber unus ... collata sunt omnia ad antiquos codices, maxime Budaei. Lutetiae, apud C. Wechelum 1532
279p. 124 illus. F.
First translated into German (Ulm, 1475. 63 illus.) Also published in German (Erfurt, 1511. 121 illus.) Lipperheide lists a reprint of the 1511 edition with title: *Vier bücher der ritterschafft* (Augspurg, H. Stainer 1529. 123 illus.) The Latin edition of 1532 and another Latin edition of 1553 have the same illustrations as the German edition of 1511
Lipperheide 2043-45

Das **Veilchen;** ein taschenbuch guten menschen geweiht von Joh. Carl Unger. 1.-17. jahrg., 1818-1834. Wien, H. Buchholz
17v. illus. D.
Lipperheide 4536

Veils
Jeremias, Alfred. Der schleier von Sumer bis heute. 1931

Velde, Henry van de
Die künstlerische hebung der frauentracht. Krefeld, Kramer & Baum 1900
33p. O.
Colas 2968. Lipperheide 3312

Velde, Frau Maria van de. See Album moderner, nach kunstlerentwürfen ausgeführter damen-kleider

Velde, Theodoor Hendrik van de
Die frauenkleidung ... dem holländischen übersetzt von F. P. Augustin. Haarlem, E. F. Bohn 1909
80p. illus. O.
First published with title: *De kleeding der vrouw* (Haarlem, Bohn 1908)

Vellis aureum burgundo-austriacum sive ... Ordinis torquatorum aurei velleris equitum. Kaschutnig, Anton

Velten, Johann
(pub.) Clodt von Jürgensburg, M. P., baron. Costumes petit-russiens
(pub.) Clodt von Jürgensburg, M. P., baron. Costumes russes
(pub.) Völlinger, Joseph. Grossherzoglich badisches militair

Ven, Dirk Jan van der
Van vrijen en trouwen op 't boerenland. Amsterdam-Mechelen, De Spieghel 1929
187p. pl. Q.
LC 32-6156

Venables, Ernest Kendrick
Behind the smile in real Japan. London, G. G. Harrap [1936]
319p. front. illus.(map) pl. O. 10s 6d
LC 37-4887

Vendée. See France—By region or province—Poitou

Venetianische musterblätter aus dem XVI. jahrhundert für passementerie-arbeiten und verwandte techniken, nach dem original-musterbuche im besitze ... des k. k. oesterr. museums. Wien, F. Paterno's nachfolger 1879
30pl. O.
Facsimile edition of *Le pompe,* second book (Venetia 1562)
Lipperheide 3891

Venezia. Perl, Frau Henriette

Venezia, Giulia e Zara. See Italy—Venezia, Giulia e Zara

Venezuela
Davis, R. H. Three gringos in Venezuela and Central America. 1896

Venice. See Italy—Venice; also Lace—Venice; Street venders—Italy—Venice

Venice, its individual growth. Molmenti, P. G.

Venise: histoire—art—industrie. Yriarte, C. E.

Venne, Adriaen van de
(illus.) Cats, Jacob. Alle de werken
(illus.) Cats, Jacob, and Farley, Robert. Moral emblems.

Le **Venti** giornate dell' agricoltura. Gallo, Agostino

Ventimiglia, Domenico
Il torneo di Caserta nel carnevale dell' anno 1846 descritto ed illustrato. Napoli, 1850
31p. 75pl.(1 col.) F.
Lipperheide 2780

Vento, Claude, pseud. Laincel-Vento, Alix, comtesse de

Venturini, Karl Heinrich Georg
Russlands und Deutschlands befreiungskriege von der Franzosen-herrschaft unter Napoleon Buonaparte in den jahren 1812-1815. Leipzig und Altenburg, F. A. Brockhaus 1816-19
4v. fronts. pl. (part col.) fold.maps. O.
Lipperheide 2118. LC 4-11405

Vera et accurata delineatio omnium templorum et coenobiorum. Kleiner, Salomon

La **vera** perfettione del disegno. Ostaus, Giovanni

Verboom, Agnès
La clef de tous les ouvrages de dames. Bruxelles, Bruylanf-Christophe; Paris, A. Goubaud [1866]
204p. 105 illus. O.
Lipperheide 4119

Verdun, Paul
Les costumes originaux des provinces de France. Paris, Bibliothèque des Soirées en famille 1897
31p. 14pl. O.
Colas 2981

Verdy, L., freiherr von
Die königlich preussische armee ... L'armée prussienne ... lithographies de R. Kretschmer. Berlin, C. G. Lüderitz 1846-49
12 col.pl. F.
Colas 2982. Lipperheide 2175

Verein der königlichen sammlung für deutsche volkskunde, Berlin. See Berlin. Museum fur deutsche volkstrachten und erzeugnisse des hausgewerbes. Mittheilungen

Verein für historische waffenkunde. See Zeitschrift für historische waffenkunde

Vergil. See Vergilius Maro, Publius

Vergilius, Polydorus
Von den erfyndern der dyngen ... jetzt- und newlich durch Marcum Tatium Alpinũ ... jñs Teutsch transferiert. Augspurg, H. Steyner 1537
17,ccx l. 147 illus. F.
First published in Latin (Venice, 1499). A second German edition was published in 1544
Lipperheide 625

Vergilius Maro, Publius
Opera. Strassburg, J. Grüninger 1502
ccccx,xxxiiii l. 214 illus. F.
Illustrations show costume of the latter part of the 15th century
Lipperheide 435

Vergiszmeinnicht; taschenbuch der liebe, der freundschaft und dem familienleben des deutschen volkes gewidmet; hrsg von C. Spindler. 1.-20.? jahrg.; 1830-1849. Stuttgart, Frankh
Illus. O.
Lipperheide 4556

Vergnaud, Paul
(tr.) Blasis, Carlo. Manuel complet de la danse

Verhandelingen over de natuurlijke geschiedenis der nederlandsche overzeesche bezittingen. Müller, Salomon

La **vérité** aux femmes sur l'excentricité des modes et de la toilette. Drohojowska, A. J. F. A. S. de L., comtesse

La **verité** des miracles operés par l'intercession de m. de Paris. Montgeron, L. B. C. de

Verkhovskoĭ, O.
Uzory russkie, malorossiĭskie, ī ı͡uzhnoslavi͡anskie. Ornements russes, petitrussiens et slaves méridionaux. Russische, kleinrussische, und südslavonische stickmuster. S. Peterburg", Kartogr. zav. A. Īl"īna 1882
20 col.pl. F.
Lipperheide 3968

Het **vermaaklyk** buitenleeven, of de zingende en speelende boerenvreugd. Haarlem, W. H. van Hulkenroy 1716
64p. 21 illus. 4pl. Q.
Most of the plates are copies in reverse of engravings by Adriaan van Ostade
Lipperheide 943

Die **vermählung** des prinzen Friedrich Wilhelm v. Preussen und der königl. prinzessin Victoria von England. Leipzig, J. J. Weber 1858
32p. 27 illus. 3pl. F.
"Separat-abdruck aus der Illustrirten zeitung." Subtitle
Lipperheide 2546

Die **vermählung** seiner königlichen hoheit des prinzen Wilhelm von Prueszen. illustrirte frauenzeitung

Verneau, René
Cinq années de séjour aux îles Canaries. Paris, A. Hennuyer 1891
xvi,412p. illus. pl. fold.map. O.
LC 1-25946

Vernes-Prescott, Jean François
L'Abbaye des Vignerons, son histoire et ses fêtes jusqu'à et y compris la fête de 1865, les toillettes de bal de 1783 à 1865 ... 3. éd. rev. et augm. Vevey, Loertscher 1865?
150p. 10pl. O.
Lipperheide 2877

Vernet, Carle
Collection de chevaux de tous pays montés ... cavaliers avec leurs costumes et leurs armes. Paris, C. de Lasteyrie ca1820
49pl. F.
Colas 2991

Collection de costumes ... gravés par Debucourt. Paris, C. Bance; London, Bossange-Masson 1814-24
15 l. 56 col.pl. F.
A collection of plates which show European dress, English, Scottish, and other, including many plates of military uniforms and street venders. Also known with plates in black and white. Explanatory text of plates 1-46 in French and English. For a list of plates see Colas's *Bibliographie*
Colas 2984

Cris de Paris. Paris, Delpech ca1820
100 col.pl. F.
For list of plates see Colas's *Bibliographie*
Colas 2986. Lipperheide 1186

Scènes et costumes divers de Carle Vernet, lithographiés par Victor Adam. Paris, Aumont; London, C. Tilt 1831
12pl. O.
Contains 36 figures from the author's *Collection de costumes*, copied in reduced size and lithographed on 12 plates by Victor Adam
Colas 2985

See also Vernet, Horace, jt. auth.

Vernet, Carle, and Vernet, Horace
Recueil de chevaux de tout genre ... gravés par Le Vachez. Paris, ca1826
60 col.pl. ob.F.
Plates show French army officers
Colas 2990

Vernet, Carle and others
Campagnes des français sous le consulat & l'empire. Paris, Librairie rue Visconti 22 1860
58pl. F.
"Album de cinquante-deux batailles et cent portraits des maréchaux, généraux et personnages les plus illustres de l'époque et le portrait de Napoléon Ier." Subtitle
Plates are after designs by Vernet, Swebach, Couché fils, Baugean, Le Compte and Roehn and are engraved by Duplessi-Bertaux, Couché fils, Bovinet, and Pigeot
Lipperheide 2326

Vernet, Horace
[Incroyables et merveilleuses de 1814] Paris, no. pub. ca1815
33 col.pl. F.
Plates are designed by Horace Vernet, except the last two which are by Lanté. Each plate has title *Paris, Incroyables* or *Merveilleuse* (for those on feminine costume) Colas gives a list of the plates
Colas 2992. Lipperheide 1154

(illus.) L'Empire de la mode

(illus.) Laurent de l'Ardèche, P. M. Histoire de l'Empereur Napoléon

See also Goupil Fesquet, F. A. A. Voyage d'Horace Vernet en Orient; also Vernet, Carle, jt. auth.

Vernet, Horace, and Lami, Louis Eugène
Collection des uniformes des armées françaises, de 1791 à 1814, dessinés par Horace Vernet et Eug. Lami. Paris, Gide 1822
xv,[169]p. incl.tables. 108 col.pl. Q.
Colas 2987. Lipperheide 2308. LC 34-19770

Manejo del sable; coleccion de 40 diseños lithograficos que representan las diversas posiciones de este exercicio a caballo. [Madrid] Engelmann 1819
40 col.pl. F.
Also known with plates in black and white. This suite was reprinted (Barcelona, J. E. Montfort ca1820)
Colas 2993

Vernet, Horace; Vernet, Carle, and Lami, Louis Eugène
Collection raisonnée des uniformes français de 1814 à 1824. Paris, Anselin et Pochard 1825
41 l. 50 col.illus. O.
Colas 2988. Lipperheide 2309

Vernet, Pierre
Galerie militaire, ou Collection complète des uniformes de la Garde impériale russe. Saint-Pétersbourg, U. Steinbach 1840-42
58 col.pl. F.
Colas 2994

Verneuil, Alexandre Henri Raoul Quarré de. See Quarré de Verneuil, A. H. R.

Vernier, Charles
Au quartier Latin. Paris, Destouches ca1860
29 col.pl. Q.
Lipperheide 3691

Costumes de l'armée française depuis Louis XIV jusqu'à ce jour. Paris, Aubert 1846-50
66 col.pl. ob.F.
Each plate shows six or seven uniforms. Plates cover the period 1680-1850
Colas 2995. Lipperheide 2318

Costumes militaires des différentes nations. Paris, Aubert ca1850
4pl. ob.F.
Plates show uniforms of French, English, Belgian, Austrian, Prussian, and Russian soldiers. For contents of plates see Colas's *Bibliographie*
Colas 2996

Travestissements parisiens. Paris, Aubert ca1850
50 col.pl. Q.
Lithographed by Charles Vernier, Victor Dollel, and Janet Lange
Colas 2997

Vernier, Émile Séraphin
La bijouterie et la joaillerie egyptiennes. Le Caire, Impr. de l'Institut français d'archéologie orientale 1907
156p. 25pl. Q. (Institut français d'archéologie orientale du Caire. Memoires, v2)

Verrier, Eugène
Du tatouage en Afrique; ses variétés, sa signification, des survivances du tatouage en Europe. Paris, J. André 1895
30p. illus. O. 1 fr. 50

Verrill, Alpheus Hyatt
The American Indian, North, South and Central America. New York, D. Appleton 1927
xxvii,485p. front.(port.) illus. pl. maps (1 double) O. $4
Shows costume of the Indians of South America; Indian masks p142; Moccasin types p259; Indian headdresses Central and South America p395
Costume index. LC 27-4104

Versailles ancien et moderne. Laborde, Alexandre de, comte

Verschiedene gewerbe. Wael, Cornelis de

Die **verschiedenen** trachten. Kottenkamp, F. J.

Die **verschiedenen** uniformen der sächsischen armee 1806 und 1823. Bartsch, Adam

Versteyl, Heinrich Anselm
Die heiligen monogramme. Düsseldorf, L. Schwann [1879]
4p. 15pl. Q.
Lipperheide 4183

Die kirchliche leinwandstickerei. Düsseldorf, L. Schwann 1879-83
3pts. 69pl.(2 col.) Q.
Lipperheide 3996

Versuch einer ästhetik der toilette. Müller, Ernst, and Baumgärtner, F. G.

Versuch einer anweisung zur anlegung, verbesserung, und nutzung der wildbahnen so wohl im freyen als in thiergärten. Mellin, A. W., graf von

Versuch einer urgeschichte des kostüms. Klemm, Heinrich

Versuch über das kostum der vorzüglichsten völker. Spalart, Robert von

Versuch über gebräuche, kleidung und waffen der ältesten völker bis auf Constantin den Grossen. Mannlich, J. C. von

Vertot, René Aubert de, abbé
Histoire des Chevaliers hospitaliers de S. Jean de Jerusalem, appellez depuis les Chevaliers de Rhodes, et aujourd'hui les Chevaliers de Malte. Paris, Rollin 1726
4v. 70pl. 6 maps. Q.
Lipperheide 1903

Vertraute briefe aus Paris. Reichardt, J. F.

Die **vertreibung** der Salzburger protestanten. Arnold, C. F.

Vervaeck, L.
Le tatouage en Belgique; communication faite à la Société de anthropologie de Bruxelles. Bruxelles, Hayes 1906
239p. 9pl. Q.
Reprinted from *Memoires de la Société d'anthropologie de Bruxelles,* v25

Verveer, Elchanon. See Belin, A., and others. Costumes de Suède, Norvège, Danemark, Hollande et Allemagne

Vervloet, J.
Cavalcade religieuse à l'occasion du jubilé de 850 ans célébré ... en l'honneur de Notre Dame d'Hanswyck à Malines pendant la dernière quinzaine du mois d'août 1838. Mechelen, P. J. Hanicq 1838
20pl. O.
Lipperheide 2806

Vervloet, Victor
Album du jubilé de 875 ans, en l'honneur de Notre Dame d'Hanswyk, ou description historique de la grande cavalcade et des fêtes publiques qui seront célébrées ... à Malines pendant la dernière quinzaine du mois d'aout 1863. Malines, H. Dierickx-Beke fils [1863]
40p. 20 col.pl. Q.
Lipperheide 2810

Vervolg van de beschrijving hoedanig. Teupken, J. F.

Verzameling der kleederdragten in de nordelyke provincien van het koningryk der Nederlanden. See Greeven, H. Collection des costumes des provinces septentrionales du royaume des Pays-Bas

Verzameling van nederlandsche kleederdragten. Last, H. W.

Verzameling van verschillende gekleede mans- en vrouwen-standen. Perkois, Jacobus, and Prins, J. H.

Verzeichniss der geist und weltlichen ritterorden. Buonanni, Filippo

Verzeichnüss der geistlichen ordens-personen. Buonanni, Filippo

Le **vesti** delle donne fiorentine nel quattrocento. Polidori Calamandrei, E.

Vestiarium Christianum. Marriott, W. B.

Vestiarium scoticum
Vestiarium scoticum: from the manuscript formerly in the library of the Scots college at Douay; with an introduction and notes, by John Sobieski Stuart. Edinburgh, W. Tait 1842
109p. 76 col.pl.(75 mounted) F.
Mounted plates accompanied by guard sheets with descriptive letterpress
Professes to be from a sixteenth-century manuscript book by Schyr Richard Urquharde, knycht
LC 23-14544

Vestidos típicos de España. Ivori, Joan d'

Vestitus sacerdotum hebraeorum. Braun, Johannes

Vestments, Church. See Ecclesiastical costume

Vestments and how to make them. Weston, Mrs L. B. N. F.

Vestments and vesture. Roulin, E. A.

O **vestuario,** historia de traje desde os tempos mais remotos até á idade-média. Noronha, Eduardo de

Vesuntini emblematum. Boissard, J. J.

Le **vêtement** au point de vue de l'hygiène. Job, A., doctor

Le **vêtement** de la Parisienne au XIX. siècle. See Cabris. Le costume de la Parisienne au XIX. siecle

Les **vêtements** du grand prêtre et des Levites, le sacrifice des colombes, d'après les peintures et les monuments. See Ancessi, Victor. L'Egypte et Moïse

Les **vêtements** et les habitations dans leurs rapports avec l'atmosphère. Radau, Rodolphe

Veth, Cornelis
Der advokat in der karikatur, hrsg. von Cornelis Veth, mit einer einleitung von Max Alsberg. Berlin, O. Stollberg 1927
119p. illus. Q.
LC 28-23854

Der arzt in der karikatur, hrsg. von Cornelis Veth, mit einer einleitung von Friedrich Krauss. Berlin, O. Stollberg 1927
153p. illus. Q.
LC 28-23853

Vever, Henri
La bijouterie française au XIXe siècle (1800-1900). Paris, H. Floury 1906-08
3v. illus. pl. ports. Q.
Contents: 1 Consulat. Empire. Restauration. Louis-Philippe; 2 Le second empire; 3 La troisième république
LC 10-27886

Viadrina university. See Academic costume —Viadrina university

Viagem da catholica real magestade del rey d. Filipe II. Lavanha, J. B.

Viaggi nell' Africa occidentale. Omboni, Tito

Viaggio pittoresco nelle due Americhe. See entry under Orbigny, A. D. d', ed. Voyage pittoresque

Viaje pintoresco al rededor del mundo á las dos Amérigas, Asia y África. See Dumont d'Urville, J. S. C., ed. Voyage pittoresque autour du monde

Vial, Eugène
Costumes lyonnais du XIVe au XXe siècle; illustrations de Jean Coulon, enluminées par François Garnier; préface de Édouard Herriot. Lyon, Les éditions "Provincia" 1935
[11]p. 1 l. 25 col.pl. sq.O. 75fr. (Collection "Choses et gens du Lyonnais")
Each plate accompanied by leaf with descriptive text, not included in paging
LC 36-24751

Vianen, Ioannes van

Effigies Romanorum imperatorum ex antiquis numismatibus ... a Iulio Caesare, ad Leopoldum. Excudit Trajecti Batavorum, F. Halma 1695
14pl. incl. 160 ports. F.
First edition show portraits of emperors up to 1705. A second edition (ca1795. 14pl. incl. 167 ports.) brings the list down to Francis II
Lipperheide 221-22

Viatour, Gustave

Étude sur l'armée belge, 1896. Gand, J. Vanderpoorten 1896
2v. 36pl. F.
Illustrated by Louis Geens
Colas 2998

Vice et virtu. David, Jules

Vico, Enea

Le imagini con tutti i riversi trovati et le vite de gli imperatori tratte dalle medaglie et dalle historie de gli antichi, libro primo. E. Vico, Parm. 1548
14 l. 41pl. Q.
No more published. The British Museum attributes the text to Antonio Zantani
Twelve plates show Roman emperors from Julius Caesar to Domitian (d. 96 A.D.) Thirty-three plates printed on both sides. Plates are engraved by Vico
Latin edition: *Omnium Caesarum verissimae imagines* (1554. 16 l. 46pl.)
Lipperheide 210-11

Le imagini delle Donne Auguste intagliate in istampa di rame ... libro primo. In V. Vinegia appresso e. Vico Parmigiano, et V. Valgrisio, all' insegna d'Erasmo 1557
212p. illus. pl. O.
No more published. Shows the Roman empresses
LC 28-16733

The **Victor** book of the opera; stories of the operas, with illustrations and descriptions of Victor opera records. [Camden, N. J., RCA manufacturing company c1936]
526p. illus. (incl. ports. music) O.
Ninth edition revised by Charles O'Connell
The 4th to the 8th edition, inclusive, were published under title: *The Victrola book of the opera.* The 4th edition, 1917, and at least one subsequent edition were published under the name of Samuel Holland Rous
LC 37-10322

Victoria and Albert museum, South Kensington

An Almain armourer's album. See Almain armourer's album

Brief guide to the Chinese embroideries. London, H. M. Stationery off. 1921
12p. VIII pl. D. (Publication no 144 T)
Bibliographical references: p8
LC 23-17012

Brief guide to the Chinese woven fabrics. London, Pub. under the authority of the Board of education 1925
34p. front. XVI pl. on 8 l. D. (Publication no175t)
"This brief guide ... is the work of Mr. A. D. Howell Smith."—Prefatory note.
Bibliography: p24-26
LC 26-1487

Brief guide to the oriental painted, dyed and printed textiles. London, Pub. under the authority of the Board of education 1924
32p. front. XVI pl. on 8 l. D. (Publication no170t)
Prepared by A. D. Howell Smith. Bibliography: p23-25
LC 25-6746

Brief guide to the Persian woven fabrics. London, Pub. under the authority of H. M. Stationery off. 1922
14p. XVI pl. on 8 l. D. (Publication no148t)
Works for fuller information on subject: p8-9
LC 24-13895

Brief guide to the Peruvian textiles. London, Pub. under the authority of the Board of education 1926
39p. front. XVI pl. on 8 l. D. (Publication no176t)
"The preparation of this brief guide ... has been undertaken by Mr. Howell Smith." Prefatory note (signed: Eric Maclagan)
Bibliography: p22-26
LC 26-13443

Brief guide to the Turkish woven fabrics. London, Pub. under the authority of H. M. Stationery off. 1923
22p. XVI pl. on 8 l. D. (Publication no148t)
Works for fuller information on subject: p15-16
LC 24-13894

Brief guide to the western painted, dyed and printed textiles. London, Pub. under the authority of the Board of education 1924
30p. front. XVI pl. on 8 l. D. Publication no165T)
Prepared by A. D. Howell Smith. Bibliography: p21-22
LC 27-13409

Catalogue of English ecclesiastical embroideries of the XIII. to XVI. centuries. London, Pub. under the authority of the Board of education, 1930
xvi,17-68p. front. XL pl. on 20 l. O. (Publication no117t)
First printed, 1907; 2. ed. 1911; 3. (illus.) ed. 1916; 4. (illus.) ed. 1930
Bibliography: p57-60
LC 33-168

Catalogue of rings, by C. C. Oman. London, Published under the authority of the Board of Education 1930
xvi,154p. front. 1 illus. XXXIX pl. on 20 l. O. (Publication no190m)
List of the principal works referred to: p xv-xvi
Costume index. LC 31-9109

Costume; an index to the more important material in the library. Rev. ed. London, 1936
236 l. F.
Mimeographed. A guide to the museum's collection of costume illustration, consisting of a classified catalog of books in the library, with notes about the illustrations, plates, etc., followed by appendices: 1 List of costume material available in the Department of textiles; 2 A chronological list of paintings in the museum showing costumes; 3 Costume material in the Department of engraving, illustration and design
An earlier edtion was entitled *A list of works on costume* compiled by R. H. Soden Smith (London, Eyre & Spottiswoode 1881. 70p.)
Colas 1882 (1881 ed.) LC 37-29139

Victoria and Albert museum—*Continued*

Descriptive catalogue of the collections of tapestry and embroidery. See entry under Cole, A. S.

Guide to the collection of costumes; rev. and enl. London, Pub. under the authority of the Board of education 1924

viii,42p. front. XXXVI pl. on 18 l. O. (Publication no90t)

First published 1913 under title *Guide to the English costumes presented by Messrs. Harrods ltd.* Revised and enlarged to include the other costumes in the museum collection. "In the preparation of the first guide Mr Francis Birrell gave much assistance. Mr A. D. Howell Smith of the Department of textiles has collaborated in its revision." Note, signed: A. F. Kendrick

Costume index. LC 24-21276

Guide to the collection of lace, by P. G. Trendell. London, Published under the authority of the Board of education 1930

viii,18p. front. XXXII pl. on 16 l. O. (Publication no189t)

"List of useful books on lace in the library of the museum": p15-16

LC 31-6415

Guide to the Japanese textiles. London, H. M. Stationery off. 1919-20

2v. in 1. fronts. illus. pl. D. (Publication no119t-120t)

"List of works useful for reference: pt I p[51]-53; pt II p[55]-56

Contents: pt I Textile fabrics, by A. D. Howell Smith; pt II Costume, by A. J. Koop

LC 21-10147

Hand-made laces. See entry under Cole, A. S.

Old English costumes. See entry under Hughes, Talbot

A picture book of English embroideries, Elizabethan & Stuart. London, Board of education 1926

[4]p. 20pl. (Publication no. PB5)

Victoria book of the opera. See The Victor book of the opera

Victoria; illustrirte muster- und modenzeitung. 1.-29. jahrg. 1851-1879. Berlin, F. Ebhart

29v. col.illus. F.

Colas 2999. Lipperheide 4664

Victorian costumes; A record of ladies' attire 1838 to 1897. London, S. Miller [1897]

70p. illus. O.

The book consists of illustrations of women's dress for various occasions, with descriptive notes on the materials

Victorian panorama. Quennell, Peter

La **vida** militar en España. Barado y Font, Francisco

Vidal, E. E.

Picturesque illustrations of Buenos Ayres and Monte Video. London, R. Ackermann 1820

xxviii,115p. 24 col.pl. sq.Q.

Church of San Domingo, and female costumes p45-50, Pampa Indians p53-60. Soldiers, country people, etc. are also shown

Also published in Buenos Aires. Universidad nacional. Instituto de investigaciones históricas. *Colección de viajeros y memorias geográficas.* (Buenos Aires. 1923. Q. v 1 p[77]-243 pl. [part double]) with Spanish and English text. Plates in black and white

Colas 3000. LC 4-9331

Vidal, J., publisher

Collection des costumes du Roussilon dédiée à la ville de Perpignan. J. Vidal [1833-34]

1 l. 11 col.pl. Q.

Plates are lithographed by A. Bayot

Colas 3001

Vidal, Jean Jacques Gomer Paul

L'artillerie, par le général Vidal; aquarelles de Pierre-Albert Leroux. Paris, Société des éditions militaires 1929

158p. 20 col.pl. F. (L'armée française à travers les âges: ses traditions, ses gloires, ses uniformes. [v 1])

Colas 157a. LC 32-31267

Vidal, Pierre

(ilus.) Société des amis des livres. Paris qui crie

Vidal de la Blache, Paul Marie Joseph. See Lavisse, Ernest. Histoire de France depuis les origines jusqu'à la révolution

Vie civile, politique et militaire du caporal Valentin. Charlet, N. T.

Vie de Confucius. See Helman, I. S. Abrégé historique des principaux traits de la vie de Confucius

La **vie** de l'empereur Charles V. Leti, Gregorio

Vie de Ste Catherine d'Alexandrie. Miélot, Jean

Vie des Bretons de l'Amorique. See Bouët, Alexandre. Breiz-Izel

Vie d'un gamin. Pigal, E. J.

Vie d'une Parisienne. Janet, G.

Vie élégante de la société parisienne. Compte-Calix, F. C.

Vie élégante, Traité de la. Balzac, Honoré de

Vie et histoire de Saint Denys. Paris. Bibliothèque nationale. Mss. fr. nouv. acq. 1098

La **vie** galante à Lyon au bon vieux temps. Roux, Claudius, and Brunel, Noré

La **vie** hors de chez soi (comédie de notre temps). Bertall, C. A. d'A.

La **vie,** la mode, et le costume au XVIIe siècle. Roy, Hippolyte

Vie militaire et religieuse au moyen âge. Lacroix, Paul

La **vie** parisienne. Meilhac, Henri, and Halévy, Ludovic

La **vie** parisienne à travers le XIXe siècle. Cleemputte, P. A. van

La **Vie** parisienne; moeurs élégantes, choses du jour, fantaisies, voyages, théâtres, musique, modes. 1. année, 1863+ Paris,

Illus.(part col.) pl. Q.

Published weekly. Current 1937. No numbers issued Sept. 17, 1870-July 1, 1871 inclusive

LC 9-30955

La **vie** parisienne pendant le siège et sous la commune. Alméras, Henri d'

La **vie** parisienne sous la republique de 1848. Almeras, Henri d'

La **vie** parisienne sous la restauration. Almeras, Henri d'

La **vie** parisienne sous la révolution et le directoire. Alméras, Henri d'

La **vie** parisienne sous le consulat et l'empire. Alméras, Henri d'

La **vie** parisienne sous le règne de Louis-Philippe. Almeras, Henri d'

La **vie** parisienne sous le second empire. Alméras, Henri d'

Vie politique et militaire de Napoléon. Arnault, A. V.

La **vie** privée à Venise. See Molmenti, P. G.

La **vie** privée d'autrefois. Franklin, A.L.A.

La **vie** privée des anciens. Ménard, R. J.

La **vieille** armée française. Charlet, N. T.

La **vieille** garde imperiale. Barrès, Maurice

Viel-Castel, Horace, comte de

Collection des costumes, armes et meubles pour servir à l'histoire de France depuis le commencement du v. siècle jusqu'à nos jours. Paris, Treuttel & Wurtz; Londres, Colnaghi 1827-1845

4v. 420 col.pl. Q.

Volume 4 has title: *Collection ... depuis le commencement du V. siècle jusqu'à 1814*. This volume also published with title: *Collection de costumes, armes et meubles pour servir à l'histoire de la revolution française et de l'empire* (Paris, Canson n.d.)

Published in 73 parts (livraisons). Also known with plates in black and white

Colas 3003-04. Lipperheide 1078. LC 23-15109 (v 1-3)

Statuts de l'ordre du Saint-Esprit au droit desir ou du noeud institué à Naples en 1352 par Louis d'Anjou ... Manuscrit du XIVme siècle conservé au Louvre ... avec une notice sur la peinture des miniatures et la description du manuscrit. Paris, Engelmann et Graf 1853

45p. 17 col.pl. F.

Contains 51 miniatures which show costume of the order and general costume of the period

Lipperheide 387

Vien, Joseph Marie

Caravanne du sultan à la Mecque; mascarade turque donné à Rome par messieurs les pensionnaires de l'Académie de France et leurs amis, au carnaval de l'anné 1748. Paris, [1749]

1 l. 31 col.pl. Q.

Reprinted (Paris, Fessard 1768) and according to Colas, at least twice more, with same collation

Colas 3005-06

Vîenchanie russīkh" gosudareĭ na Tsartsvo, nachīnaīa s" tsarīa Mīkhaīla Fedorovīcha do Īmperatora Aleksandra III ... Couronnement des souverains Russes à partir du tsar Michel Fédorovitch jusqu'à l'empereur Alexandre III. S.-Peterburg", Izdanie H. Hoppe 1883

283p. 217 illus. F.

Lipperheide 2498

Vienna. See Austria; Austria—19th century—Vienna; also Street venders—Austria—Vienna

Vienna. Albertina. See Callot, Jacques. Livre d'esquisses

Vienna. K. K. Hofbibliothek. MSS. (2831)

Freydal. Des kaisers Maximilian I. turniere und mummereien. See entry under Maximilian I, emperor of Germany

Vienna. K. K. Kunsthistorisches hof-museum

Wien's Kaiserliches zeughaus, zum ersten male aus historisch-kritischem gesichtspunkte betrachtet, für alterthumsfreunde und waffenkenner. Leber, F. O., edler von

Vienna. K. K. Österreichisches museum für kunst und industrie

Die burgundischen gewänder der k. k. schatzkammer; messornat für den Orden vom Goldenen vliess. Wien, K.K. Österreichisches museum 1864

2 l. 12 pl. F.

According to tradition these vestments, notable for their embroidery, were ordered by Philip the Good of Burgundy for the Order of the Golden fleece for church use at its festivals. They date from about 1450

Colas 489. Lipperheide 1835

Die costüm-ausstellung im K. K. Oesterreichischen museum 1891. See entry under Masner, Carl

Original-stickmuster der Renaissance in getreuen copien. Wien, Selbstverlag des museums. 1874

2 l. 50pl. Q.

Lipperheide 3859

Die Wiener spitzenausstellung 1906 ... Lichtdrucktafeln und einleitung von M. Dreger. Leipzic, K. W. Hiersemann 1906

28p. 68pl. F. (Ornamentale und kunstgewerbliche sammelmappe. Ser. 9-10)

Vienna. Nationalbibliothek. See Denkmäler des theaters

Vienna. Neues Wiener tagblatt. See Neues Wiener tagblatt

Vienna and the Austrians. Trollope, Mrs F. M.

Vienna militia. See Military costume—Austria—Vienna militia

IV blaetter aus dem Münchner volksleben Foltz, Philipp

400 jährige jubelfeier der schlacht bei Murten am 22 Juni 1876. Jauslin, Carl, and Roux, G.

Vierland. See Germany—Hamburg

Die **Vierlande** bei Hamburg. Griese, Carl

24 blatt colorierte Schweizer mädchentrachten. Nussbiegel, J.

Viero, Teodoro

Raccolta di 126 stampe, che rappresentano figure, ed abiti di varie nazioni, secondo gli originali, e le descrizioni dei piu celebri recenti viaggiatori, e degli scopritori di paesi nuovi. Venetiis, T. Viero 1783-1791

3v. 360 col.pl. F.

Volumes 1-2 Europe; v3 Asie, Afrique, Amérique

Colas 3007. Lipperheide 39

Vierundzwanzig statuen des Vaticanischen und Capitolischen museums zu Rom und der Uffizien in Florenz. Nöhring, Johann

Les **vies** et alliances des comtes de Hollande et Zélande. Galle, Philippe

Les **vieux** costumes pyrénéens. Le Bondidier, Louis

A **view** of the people of the whole world. Bulwer, John

Views and costumes of the city and neighbourhood of Rio de Janeiro, Brazil. Chamberlain

Views in ancient Egypt and Nubia. See Croly, George. The Holy Land, Syria, Idumea, Arabia, Egypt & Nubia

Views in Egypt. Mayer, Ludwig

Views in Greece, from drawings by Edward Dodwell. Dodwell, Edward

Views in India, Saint Helena and Car Nicobar. Luard, John

Views in Palestine. Mayer, Ludwig

Views in the Holy Land, Syria [etc] See Croly, George. The Holy Land, Syria, Idumea, Arabia, Egypt & Nubia

Views in the Ottoman dominions. Mayer, Ludwig

Views in the Ottoman empire, chiefly in Caramania. Mayer, Ludwig

Views in Turkey. Mayer, Ludwig

Views of the remains of ancient buildings in Rome and its vicinity. Dubourg, Matthew

Vigeant, Arsène

La bibliographie de l'escrime ancienne et moderne. Paris, Imprimé par Motteroz 1882
172p. 10 illus.(incl.port.) O.
Vignettes de Chégaray et A. Deville. Gravures sur bois de Pannemaker
Lipperheide 2992. LC 22-24018

Vigenère, Blaise de

(tr.) Chalcondylas, Laonicus. Histoire générale des Turcs

Vigil, Fausto

Artículos de Fausto Vigil sobre los trajes y costumbres asturianas. Oviedo, Imp. La Cruz 1924
33p. O.
"Publicados por el Boletín del Centro de estudios asturianos, julio y octubre 1924"
LC 35-24634

Vigilance, Order of. See White falcon, Order of the

Vigilius, Stephan

(tr.) Petrarca, Francesco. Trostspiegel in glück und unglück.

XXVII pontificum maximorum elogia et imagines. See Panvinio, Onofrio. Accuratae effigies pontificum maximorum, numero XXVIII

Vignati, Milcíades Alejo

Restos del traje ceremonial de un "médico" patagón. Buenos Aires, Imprenta de la Universidad 1930
52,[12]p. incl.illus. 2pl. 3 maps. VI pl. O. (Facultad de filosofía y letras de la Universidad de Buenos Aires. Notas del Museo etnográfico, número 4)
Bibliographical foot-notes
LC 31-24974

Vignay, Jean

(tr.) Cessolis, Jacobus de. The game of chesse

La **vigne.** Bertall, C. A. d'A.

Vigne, Félix de

Mœurs et usages des corporations de métiers de la Belgique et du nord de la France, pour faire suite aux Recherches historiques sur les costumes civils et militaires des gildes et des corporations de métiers. Gand, Busscher 1857
145p. 34pl.(part col.) Q.
Colas 3010. Lipperheide 1979. LC 3-5907

Recherches historiques sur les costumes civils et militaires des gildes et des corporations de métiers, leurs drapeaux, leurs armes, leurs blasons, etc ... avec une introduction historique par J. Stecher. Gand, F. et E. Gyselynck [1847]
82p. 35pl.(26 col.) Q.
The author's *Moeurs et usages* is a supplement
Colas 3009. Lipperheide 1978. LC 3-5929

Vade-mecum du peintre, ou Recueil de costumes du moyen-âge, pour servir à l'histoire de la Belgique et pays circonvoisins. 2.ed. Gand, Busscher 1844
2v. 206pl.(part col.) Q.
First edition 1835-40 has same collation
Colas 3008. Lipperheide 967

(illus.) Busscher, Edmond de. Album du cortège des comtes de Flandre

Vigneau, H.

(ed.) Brantôme, Pierre de Bourdeille, seigneur de. Oeuvres de Brantôme

Vigneron, Pierre Roch

[Costumes suisses] Paris, Delpech [1822]
56 col.pl. Q.
No title page. Some of the plates are signed Vigneron
Colas 3012

Vijf jaren in Japan (1857-1863). Pompe van Meerdervoort, J. L. C.

50 eeuwen costuum. Jong, Jo de

Viking age. Du Chaillu, P. B.

Viking settlers in Greenland and their descendants during five hundred years. Nørlund Poul

Vikings

Du Chaillu, P. B. Viking age. 1889

Vilà, Pau. See Amades, Joan, jt. auth.

Vilhena, Luiz dos Santos

Recopilação de noticias soteropolitanas e brasilicas contidas em XX cartas, que da cidade do Salvador Bahia de Todos os Santos escreve hum a outro amigo em Lisboa, debaixo de nomes alusivos, noticiando-o do estado daquella cidade, sua capitania, e algumas outras do Brasil: feita e ordenada para servir na parte que convier de elementos para a historia brasilica ... Divididas em trez tomos, que ao soberano e augustissimo princepe regente ... anno de 1802. [v 1] Bahia, Imprensa official do estado, 1921
v 1. pl.(part col. part fold.) fold.maps, plans(part fold.) fold.tables. O.
Cover-title: *Cartas de Vilhena, noticias soteropolitanas e brasilicas,* por Luiz dos Santos Vilhena; annotadas pelo Prof. Braz do Amaral ... e mandadas publicar pelo Exmo. Sr. Dr. J. J. Seabra ... governador do estado do Bahia no anno do 1.° centenario da independencia do Brasil, 1922. Bahia, Imprensa official do estado, 1922
From the manuscript in the Rodrigues collection of the Biblioteca nacional, Rio de Janeiro
Colored plates show military uniforms of Brazil
LC 28-29658

Villa-Amil, Genaro Perez de
(ed.) Escosura, Patricio de la. España artística y monumental

Villaamil y Castro, José
Inventarios de mobiliario litúrgico (Catedral de Mondoñedo, años 1579 y 1572. Colegiata de Ribadeo, año 1564. Catedral de Santiago, año 1509. Catedral de Sevilla, siglos XIV á XVII. Catedral de Oviedo, año 1385. Catedral de Toledo, último tercio del siglo XIII. Catedral de Salamanca, año 1275). Madrid, Nueva imp. de San Francisco de Sales 1906
105p. O.
Cover dated 1907. Also published as an appendix to the author's *Pasatiempos eruditos. Colección de artículos en su mayoría sobre el mobiliario litúrgico* (Madrid, 1907)
LC 34-12343

Pasatiempos eruditos. Colección de artículos en su mayoría sobre el mobiliario litúrgico de las iglesias gallegas, en la edad media, publicados por José Villaamil y Castro, en el espacio de treinta y tres años (desde 1872 á 1905) Madrid, Nueva impr. de San Francisco de Sales 1907
xxxvi,400,82p. incl.illus. port. pl. diagrs. O.
Appended, with special title-page and separate pagination, the author's *Inventarios de mobiliario litúrgico*. Madrid, 1906; also issued separately (Madrid, 1906)
LC 34-12342

Villain
(lithgr.) Charlet, N. T. Croquis à la manière noire dédiés à Bèranger

(lithgr.) Les Contretems

(lithgr.) Raffet, D. A. M. Collection de costumes militaires

Villalba, J.
Broderies populaires espagnoles. Paris, H. Ernst, 1929?
3 l. 30 col.pl. F. (Éditions art et couleurs)
Signed: J. Villalba

Villamena
[Cris de Rome] No place, ca1620
6pl. F.
Plates engraved by David after Villamena
Colas 3013

Villanueva, Antolín P.
Los ornamentos sagrados en España, su evolución histórica y artística. Barcelona [etc.] Editorial Labor, s. a. [1935]
332p. illus. XL pl. on 20 l. D. (Colección Labor. Sección IV: Artes plásticas. no356-57)
Illustrations show vestments worn in Spanish churches
LC 36-15439

Villard, Georges
Le théâtre d'amateurs; manuel d'art théâtral. Paris, A. Lesot [c1919]
252p. illus. pl.(part col.) D.
Pages 114-34 deal with costume and include eight colored plates, each showing fifteen to eighteen costume figures from the 4th century to 1835. Other black and white illustrations show footwear and headdress by period
LC 20-13327

Villaret, P.
L'art de se coiffer soi-même enseigné aux dames; suivi du manuel du coiffeur. Paris, Roret 1828
230p. 2pl.(1 fold.) D.
Colas 3014

Le coiffeur de la cour et de la ville; démontrant, par un grand nombre d'examples, l'art de composer la coiffure, de l'orner et de la mettre en harmonie avec les différents caractères de physionomie. Paris, Lepetit 1829
304p. 11pl. D.
Colas 3015. Lipperheide 1699

Ville de St-Maixent (Deux-Sèvres). Farault, Alphonse

Villegas, José
Album militar; coleccion de uniformes del ejercito español pintados por d. J. Villegas, y litografiados por V. Adam. Madrid, Godard 1846
36 col.pl. Q.
Colas lists also *Album militar; album del ejercito español* (Madrid, estamperias de los Suizos ca1846. 34 col.pl.) Plates lithographed and colored by V. Adam and H. Lalaisse
Colas 3016-17. Lipperheide 2361

(lithogr.) Clonard, S. M. de S. y A., conde de. Album de la caballeria española

(lithogr.) Clonard, S. M. de S. y A., conde de. Album de la infantiera española desde sus primitivos tiempos hasta el dia

Villeneuve, H. Vallon de. See Vallon de Villeneuve, H.

Villeneuve, René Claude Geoffroy de. See Geoffroy de Villeneuve, R. C.

Villepelet, Ferdinand
Du luxe des vêtements au XVIe siècle; étude historique. Périgueux, Dupont 1869
22p. O.
Reprint from *Annales de la Société d'agriculture des sciences et arts de la Dordogne* April and June 1869
Colas 3018. Lipperheide 508

Villermont, Marie, comtesse de
Histoire de la coiffure féminine. Bruxelles, A. Mertens 1891
xiii,830p. col.front. 570 illus. 10pl. O.
Also published (Paris, librairie Renouard, H. Laurens, éd. 1892)
Colas 3019-20. Costume ind. Lipp. 1715

[**Villiers, Henri de**]
Essais historiques sur les modes et la toilette française; par le Chevalier de *** [pseud] Paris, Lecointe et Durey 1824
2v. 4pl. S.
Colas 3021. Lipperheide 1076

Vincent, C.
Katalog der ... kunst-sammlung der herren C. und P. N. Vincent in Konstanz am Bodensee. See entry under Rahn, J. R.

Vincent, Charles
Histoire de la chaussure, de la cordonnerie et des cordonniers célèbres depuis l'antiquité jusqu'à nos jours. Antiquité. Edition ornée de ... gra-

Vincent, Charles—*Continued*
vures sur bois ... dessinés par A. Racinet, Dumont fils, gravés par A. Lavieille et L. Dumont. Paris, J. Lecuir & aux bureaux du Moniteur de la cordonneries. 1880
676p. 201 illus. O.
Colas 3022. Lipperheide 1743

Vincent, John Martin
Costume and conduct in the laws of Basel, Bern, and Zurich, 1370-1800. Baltimore, Johns Hopkins 1935
xii,170p. front. illus.(incl.facsims) diagrs. O. (The Johns Hopkins historical publications) $2.50
"Selected bibliography": p159-60. "Illustrations": p161
Costume index. LC 35-12466

Vinciolo, Frederic de
Les singuliers et nouveaux pourtraicts, du seigneur Frederic de Vinciolo, Venitien, pour toutes sortes d'ouvrages de lingerie ... pour la troisiesme fois augmentez. Paris, Jean le Clerc 1594
2v. 1 illus. 72pl. Q.
First edition 1587. The note: "de rechef et pour la 3.fois augmentée" appeared also on the editions from 1601 to 1612
Lipperheide 3896

Vinck de Deux-Orp, Eugène, baron de. See Paris. Bibliothèque nationale. Département des estampes. Un siècle d'histoire de France par l'estampes, 1700-1871

Vindel, Pedro
Estampas de toros; reproducción y descripción de las más importantes publicadas en los siglos XVIII y XIX relativas a la fiesta nacional; con una introducción de Gregorio Corrochano. Madrid, P. Vindel 1931
xii p. 40 l. col.front.(port.) ccc pl.(part col. part double, incl. ports. facsims.) F.
Plates show bull-fighters
LC 32-12131

Vindler, Hans
Flores virtutum, oder das buch der Tugent. Augsburg, J. Plaubirer 1486
213 l. 234 illus. F.
Illustrations show costume of the early fifteenth century
Lipperheide 416

Vinet, Ernest
Bibliographie du costume. (In Racinet, A. C. A. Le costume historique. v 1 p 141-65)

Bibliographie méthodique et raisonnée des beaux-arts: esthétique et histoire de l'art, archéologie, architecture, sculpture, peinture, gravure, arts industriels ... pub. sous les auspices du Ministère de l'instruction publique, des cultes et des beaux-arts. [1.-2. livr.] Paris, Firmin-Didot 1874-77
2pts. O.
Half-title, pt 1: *Complément du Manuel du libraire et de l'amateur de livres.* No more published
Pages 231-32, 265-88 contain a bibliography of costume
Lipperheide 4861. LC 10-32796

Vingt-cinq costumes pour le théâtre. Barbier, George

XXVe anniversaire de l'inauguration du roi. Les fêtes de juillet. Hymans, Louis

Le **28e** de ligne. Simond, Émile

27 avril 1879, cortège historique. See Berggruen, Oscar. Huldigungs-festzug der stadt Wien

Le **vingtième** siècle. Robida, Albert

Vinkeroy, E. van
Costumes militaires belges du XIe au XVIIIe siècle. Braine-le-Comte, Zech et Cornet [1885]
190p. illus. O. 2fr. 50

Vinkhuijzen, Hendrik Jacobus
Gl' ordini equestri religioso-militari. See entry under Cenni, Quinto

Violette, pseud. See Laincel-Vento, Alix, comtesse de

Viollet-le-Duc, Eugène Emmanuel
Antiquités américaines (In Charnay, Désiré. Cités et ruines américaines, p 1-104)

Dictionnaire raisonné du mobilier français de l'époque carlovingienne à la renaissance. Paris, Bance 1858-75
6v. 2007 illus. 118pl.(43 col.) maps, diagrs. O.
Reprinted (Paris, Gründ & Maguet 1914)
Issued in parts. Volumes 2-6 have imprint: Paris, Ve A. Morel
Partial contents: t3-4 Vêtements, bijoux de corps, objets de toilette; t5-6 Armes de guerre offensives et défensives
Colas 3024. Costume index. Lipperheide 1093. LC 32-17318

Virgilius, Publius. See Vergilius Maro, Publius

Virgin Mary. See Mary, Virgin

Visages de femmes. Beaunier, André

Les **visages** de la danse. Levinson, A. I.

Vischer, Friedrich Theodor von
Mode und cynismus; beiträge zur kenntniss unserer culturformen und sittenbegriffe. 2. abdruck. Stuttgart, K. Wittwer 1879
108p. O.
Lipperheide 3495. LC 23-15127

Visigoths
Barrière-Flavy, C. Le costume et l'armement du Wisigoth aux cinquième et seizième siècles. 1902

Viski, Károly
Hungarian peasant customs. Budapest, G. Vajna 1932
194p. incl.pl. O.
Translated from the Hungarian by Judith de Márffy-Mantuano
Costume index. LC 32-30616

Transylvanian Hungarians, peasant art. Budapest, Popular literary society [191-?]
19p. pl.(part col.) F.
Signed: Charles Viski. Many of the colored plates show costume
Also published with title: *Erdélyi magyarság. Transylvanian Hungarians. Nepművészet. Peasant art.* (Budapest, Népies irodalmi társaság, Popular literary society [192-])
LC 27-20982

Viskovatov, Alexsandr Vasil'evich
Istoritcheskoïe oppissanïe odéjedy i vooroujéniia rossiskich voïsk. Description historique des uniformes et des armes des troupes russes; par le general-major Viskovatoff. St Petersburg, Imp. militaire 1841-53
11v. pl. F.
According to information received from the Lipperheide library, there is a set by

Viskovatov, Alexsandr V.—*Continued*
Viskovatov (or Wiskovatoff) and others with title: *Description historique de l'habillement et de l'armement des troupes russes de 862-1855* (St Petersburg, 1841-62. 30v. 3953pl. F.) This set is not listed in the Lipperheide *Katalog*
Colas 840

Visted, Kristofer
Vor gamle boudekultur; ny forøket utgave. Kristiania, J. W. Cappelens [1923]
374p. illus. col.pl. Q.
Pages 75-105 are on Norwegian costume, and illustrations show costume by region
Bibliography p367-74

Vita Christi. See Ludolphus de Saxonia. Das leben Christi

La **vita** dei Veneziani nel 1300. Cecchetti, Bartolomeo

Vita, indoles et adversus Turcas res gestae Georgii Castrioti (In Lonicer, Phillip, comp. Chronicorum turcicorum, v3)

See also note under Barletius, Martinus. Des aller streytparsten

Vitae duodecim vicecomitum Mediolani principum. Giovio, Paolo, bp. of Nocera

Vitae et effigies procancellariorum Academiae Altorfinae. Apin, S. J.

Vitae et icones Sultanorum Turcicorum. See Boissard, J. J. Leben und contrafeiten der türckischen un persischen sultanen

Vitae illustrium virorum. Giovio, Paolo, bp. of Nocera

Vite de gl'imperatori de Turchi. Bertelli, Pietro

Le **vite** de' pontefici. Platina, i.e. Bartolomeo de' Sacchi di Piadena

Le **vite** dei dodeci visconti che signoreggiarono Milano. See Giovio, Paolo, bp. of Nocera. Pauli Iovii Novocomensis Vitae duodecim vicecomitum Mediolani principum

Vite, et azzioni di personaggi militari, e politici. Gualdo Priorato, Galeazzo, conte

Vizentini, Augustin
Recueil des costumes de tous les ouvrages dramatiques représentés avec succès sur les grands théâtres de Paris. Paris, Vizentini [etc.] 1819-25?
3v. 374 col.pl. Q.
Published periodically in parts ("livraisons"). Each part is on one play of the period and contains from five to twenty plates. Many plates are signed A. G. and are attributed to A. Garneray. Contents of the parts is given by Colas who also uses 1822 as the final date. The name of Vizentini is given in manuscript on the first twelve parts
Colas 2500. Lipperheide 3209

Vlaanderen door de eeuwen heen, door F. van Cauwelaert, A. de Cock [and others] Onder leiding van M. Rooses. Amsterdam Uitgevers-maatschappy Elsevier 1912-1913
2v. pl. port. Q.
Bibliography v 1, p417-18

Vlachs. See Greece—20th century

Vleughels, Nicolas
Costumes romains. No place, 1734
5pl. Q.
Plates signed: N. Vleughels, pinx. E. Jeaurat, sculp.
Colas 3025

Vliet, Jan Joris van der
Künste und gewerbe von J. G. van Vliet. Antwerp, C. Dankerts excud. 1635
18pl. F.
Lipperheide 1970

Le **vocabulaire** des dames. Grévedon, P. L. H.

Die **völker** Afrikas. Hartmann, Robert

Die **völker** der erde. Lampert, Kurt

Die **völker** des erdballs nach ihrer abstammung und verwandtschaft, und ihren eigenthumlichkeiten in regierungsform, religion, sitte und tracht. Berghaus, H. K. W.

Die **voelker** des oestlichen Asien. Bastian, Adolf

Die **völker** Europas. Kohl, J. G.

Völkerkunde. Ratzel, Friedrich

Völkerschmuck. Haberlandt, Michael

Voelker-schmuck. Perleberg, H. C., comp.

Völlinger, Joseph
Grossherzoglich badisches militair; nach der natur. Karlsruhe, J. Velten 1824
2 l. 30 col.pl. F.
Colas 3026. Lipperheide 2209

(illus.) Müller, F. H. Grossherzoglich hessisches militair

Voetsch, August
Fussleiden und rationelle fussbekleidung. Stuttgart, J. B. Metzler 1883
xiv,77p. 17pl. O.
Lipperheide 1743e

Vogel. See Lörer, jt. auth.

Vogel, Lucien
Soieries marocaines, les ceintures de Fès; cinquante planches en couleurs, introduction par Lucien Vogel. Paris, A. Lévy [1921]
4p. 50 mounted col.pl. F.
In portfolio
LC 21-17785

Vogelsang, Willem. See Muller, Samuel, jt. auth.

Vogt, Hermann
Das buch vom deutschen heere dem deutschen volkegewidmet ... 2. verm. und bis auf die neueste zeit fortgeführte aufl. bearbeitet durch Hanns von Zobeltitz. Mit ... illustrationen von R. Knötel. Bielefeld und Leipzig, Velhagen & Klasing 1891
475p. 176 illus. port. O.
First edition 1895
Lipperheide 2136

Die europäischen heere der gegenwart; illustrationen von R. Knötel. Rathenow, M. Babenzien 1886-90
444p. illus. O.
Published in 39 parts (hefte). Parts 31-39 edited by Hans von Trützler

Vogue, incorporating Vanity fair. v 1, Dec. 17, 1892+ New York, Paris & London, Condé Nast
Illus. F. $5 a year
Published weekly Dec. 17, 1892-Feb. 1910; semi-monthly March 1910+. Numbered continuously 1+. Current 1938
American, British and French editions
Absorbed *Vanity fair* March 1, 1936 and continued under present title

Vogue pattern book. v 1, Oct. 1925+ Greenwich, Conn., Condé Nast
Col.illus. F. $1.50
Published bi-monthly. Current 1938
Formed by the union of *Children's vogue* and *Vogue pattern book*. Oct. 1925-July 1927, title reads: *Vogue fashion bi-monthly*

Voici comment l'on s'accomode. Rabel, Daniel

Voici la mode. Mai 1933-sept. 1936. Paris, E. Boucherit
Illus. pl.(part col.) Q. 36fr.
Published monthly. Successor to *Art, goût, beauté; feuillets de l'élégance féminine*. The number for May 1933, is called 13e année, continuing the numbering of *Art, goût, beauté*. This numbering was dropped in later volumes

Voigt, Adauctus. See Pelzel, F. M. jt. auth.

Voigt, F. See Griese, Carl. Die Vierlande bei Hamburg

Voisin, Auguste, jt. auth. See Delepierre, Octave

Voitures. Lami, E. L.

Volbach, Wolfgang Friedrich. See Jenny, William Albert, jt. auth.

Volgen jetzo weitter die acht überbelibne. See Mair, P. H. Bericht und antzeigen aller Herren geschlecht der loblichen Statt Augspurg

Volk, Charles G.
United States officers' uniforms, army, navy, marine corps, drafted according to the latest regulations. New York, International tailor 1917
56p. 2pl. illus.(incl.diagr.) F. o.p.
Plates printed on both sides
Costume index

Volkmann, captain
Geschichte des magdeburgischen pionierbataillons nr. 4., 1813 bis 1887. Berlin, E. S. Mittler 1888
166p. 1 col.pl. 2 maps. O.
The two plates show soldiers in the uniforms of 1813 and 1887
Lipperheide 2189

Volkov", Nīkolaĭ Egorovīch
Dvor" russkīkh" īmperatorov" v" ego proshlom" ī nastoíāshchem". S. Peterburg", Pechatnīā R. Golīke 1900
x,246p. Q.
On the court of the Russian emperors past and present
LC CA 15-1123 (Russian characters)

Volksbelustigungen und mummenschanz der alten ehemaligen reichsstadt Nürnberg. Körber, Philipp

Volksgemälde und charakterköpfe des russischen volks. Buddeus, Carl

Volkskundliches aus Ost-Turkistan. Le Coq, Albert von

Volkskunst in Europa. Bossert, H. T.

Volksleben im Schwarzwald. Retzlaff, Hans

Volkslied, tracht und rasse. Wegner, R. N.

Volkstrachten aus dem Schwarzwald. Issel, Heinrich

Volkstrachten d. nordfriesischen inseln. Haeberlin, Carl

Volks-trachten der Deutschen. Opiz, G. E.

Die **volkstrachten** der Schweiz. Heierli, Frau Julie

Volkstrachten des konigreichs Würtemburg. Heideloff, K. A. von

Die **volkstrachten** in den Ostseeprovincen und in Setukesien. Heikel, A. O.

Der **vollkommene** damen-friseur. Galland, V. A.

Vollkommene geschütz-feuerwerck-und büchsenmeisterey-kunst. Siemienowicz, Kazimierz

Der **vollkommene** teutsche jäger. Fleming, H. F. von

Der **vollkommene** teutsche soldat. Fleming, H. F. von

Vollständige beschreibung aller feste und huldigungen ... zur vermählungsfeier des kronprinzen Friedrich Wilhelm von Preussen. 1824

Vollståndige beschreibung der ceremonien, welche sowohl bey den englischen crônungen ûberhaupt vorgehen, besonders aber bey dem ... crônungsfest ... Georgii des II. und Wilhelminae Carolinae, von Gross-Britannien, Frankreich und Irrland ... Am 11/22. octob. dieses 1727. jahres. Hanover, N. Fôrster und sohn, 1728
144p. illus. 5pl. sq.O.
Lipperheide 2689. LC 1-G-1553

Vollständige bildliche darstellung der gesammten löblichen uniformirten bürgerschaft der k. auch k. k. haupt- und residenz-stadt Wien nach dem neuesten costume 1806. Dopler, J. and Müller, C.

Vollständige pferdewissenschaft. Prizelius, J. G.

Vollständige völkergallerie in getreuen abbildungen aller nationen mit ausführlicher beschreibung derselben. Meissen, F. W. Goedsche [1830-39]
3v. 244 col.pl. Q.
Contents: v 1 pt 1 Asien, pt2 Afrika; v2 pt 1 Amerika, pt2 Australien; v3 Europa
Colas 3027. Lipperheide 55. LC 2-5428

Vollständiges diarium, alles dessen was vor, in und nach denen ... wahl- und crönungssolennitaeten ... Caroli des VI. erwehlten römischen kaysers. Frankfurt am Mayn, J. D. Zunners seel. erben und J. Adam 1712
2v. 19pl. F.
Contains ten portraits of the emperor, the electors and their followers, by Jos. v. Montalegre. The other plates show the coronation and ceremonies, some by Montalegre and the rest by P. Fehr
Lipperheide 2516

Vollständiges diarium der römisch-königlichen wahl und kayserlichen krönung ... Leopold des zweiten. Schulin, J. P.

Vollständiges diarium von den merckwürdigsten begebenheiten, die sich vor, in und nach der ... wahl und crönung ... Carls. des VII. erwehlten römischen kaysers ... Im gantzen Heil. Röm. Reich, und sonderlich in ... Franckfurt am Mayn zugetragen; nebst ... beschreibung der ein- und aufzüge, freuden-feste, und übrigen feyerlichen handlungen. Frankfurt am Mayn, J. D. Jung 1742-43
3v. 1 illus. 37pl. F.
Volume 3: Vor, in, und nach der ... crönung der frauen Maria Amalia, gecrönten römischen kayserin
Plates show procession, fireworks and portraits of those present
Lipperheide 2517

Vollständiges diarium von der ... erwehlung des ... herrn Franciscus ... zum römischen könig und kayser. Olenschlager, J. D. von

Vollständiges fecht-, ring- und voltigierbuch. See Pascha, J. G. Vollständiges ring-buch

Vollständiges handbuch der höhern bekleidungs-kunst für civil, militär und livree. Klemm, Heinrich

Vollständiges lehr- und hilfsbuch zum selbstunterricht für damen in der herstellung einer guten toilette. Schober, Anna

Vollständiges lehrbuch der praktischen zu schneidekunst. See Klemm, Heinrich. Vollständiges handbuch der höhern bekleidungskunst für civil, militär und livree

Vollständiges ring-buch. Pascha, J. G.

Volmar, Émile

Officierst et soldats des différents contingents des cantons suisses réunis à Bâle en 1792, dessinés et coloriés par Émile Volmar d'après les originaux de F. Feyerabend. No place 1792?
2 l. 26 col.pl. Q.
After Feyerabend's *Costumes militaires*
Colas 3028

Volmar, G.

Collection de costumes des cantons de la Suisse, dessinés par Volmar. Berne, Lamy 1819?
17 col.pl. Q.
Plates shows masculine and feminine folk dress
Colas 3029. Lipperheide 912

Nouvelle collection de costumes suisses. Berne, J. L. Lang 1819
18 l. 24 col.pl. F.
Colas 3030

Volontaires brabançons en 1797. No place, ca1798
10 col.pl. Q.
Colas 3031

Volpini, Angelo

Figurini di moda. Année 1797-1798. Firenze, La societa calcografica 1797-98
2v. 24 col.pl. Q.
One plate published each month. The first six are from the press of the Magazzino di Mobilia. Plates are engraved by Lasinio and Volpini after designs by Volpini. They show scenes from home and social life
Colas 3032. Lipperheide 1256

Voltz, Johann Michael

Costumes de l'armée bavaroise 1813-1825. Augsburg, Herzberg [1825]
14 col.pl. F.
Plates engraved by W. Nillson
Colas 3033

The **volunteer** soldier of America. Logan, J. A.

Vom bergkwerck. Agricola, Georg

Vom costume an denkmälern. Becker, W. G.

Vom fels zum meer; illustrirte zeitschrift für das deutsche haus. v 1-36; oct. 1881-1917. Stuttgart
36v. illus.
Welt der frau issued as a supplement beginning Sept. 1905. United with *Gartenlaube* Sept. 1905, the two being continued under their former titles with contents identical. A weekly edition was published with title: *Weite welt*

Vom kaiserreich zur republik. Boehn, Max von

Vom lendenschurz zur modetracht. Mützel, H. H. H. E.

Vom tabakblatt zur zigarette. See note under Cudell, Robert. Das buch vom tabak

Von Berlin nach Danzig. Chodowiecki, D. N.

Von den erfyndern der dyngen. Vergilius, Polydorus

Von den verdiensten des durchleuchtigsten hauses Wittelspach um die kirche. Huth, P. J.

Von der artzney beyder glück, des guten und widerwertigen. See Petrarca, Francesco. Trostspiegel in glück und unglück

Von der gestüterey. Fugger, Marx

Von der schiffart und rayss in die Türckey. See Nicolay, Nicolas de, sieur d'Arfeuille. Les navigations, pérégrinations et voyages, faicts en la Turquie

Von himmeln entzindete und durch allgemainen zuruff der erde sich himmelwerts erschwingende frolokhungs flammen zur begegnus des hochzeitlichen beylägers ... Leopoldi des Ersten, Römischen Kaisers ... und Margarita, geborner Infantin aus Hispanien, 1666. [Wien 1666]
4 l. 3pl. F.
The same festivities are described in *Allerhöchst-feyerlichste festivitäten*
An Italian translation entitled *Le fiamme accese del cielo* ([Wien] M. Cosmerovio [1666]) Same collation
Lipperheide 2619, 2620

Von sant Menrat ein hüpsch lieplich lesen was ellend uñ armůt er litten hat. Meinrad, Saint

Vor gamle boudekulture. Visited, Kristofer

Vorgeschichtliche alterthümer aus Schleswig-Holstein. Mestorf, Johanna, ed.

[**Vorläufer** zum ersten Theresienvolksfeste in Bamberg, oder] Die öffentliche maskerade in Bamberg am fastnachtsmontage 1833. In kolorirten abbildungen dargestellt von G. D. v. W. Bamberg, Drausnick 1833?
28 col.pl. Q.
Lipperheide 2869

Vorlagen für die plattstich-arbeit. Dillmont, Thérèse de

Vorlagen für handarbeiten von häkelspitzen und mignardisen. No place, ca1880
2pts. 30pl. O.
Lipperheide 4130

Vorlagen für nadelarbeiten. See Ciotti, G. B. Prima parte de' fiori, e disegni di varie sorti di ricami moderni

Vorlegeblätter zu model-tüchern. Hennings, Emma

Vornehmste reiche und staaten der welt. Engelbrecht, Martin

Der **vornehmsten** künstler und handwercker ceremonial-politica. Friese, Friedrich

Der **vorschriftmässige** talar der justizbeamten im Königreiche Preussen. Klemm, Heinrich

Vorschule der soldaten-reiterei. Klatte, Cph.

Vorstellung der alten strassburger kleidertracht. See note under Eigentliche vorstellung der heutiger strassburgische mode und kleÿdertrachten

Vorstellung der Augspurgischen kleiter tracht. Schmidt, Albrecht

Vorstellung der offentlichen sehbaren gebräuchen in Nürnberg. Kellner, Joseph

Vorstellung der russich-kayserlichen armee sowohl infanterie als cavallerie in XVI nach dem leben gemahlten blättern. Petersburg, 1773
2 l. 16 col.pl. Q.
Colas 3035

Vorstellung der vorzüglichsten gattungen des türckischen militairs und ihrer officiere. No place, ca1760
1 l. 28 col.pl. O.
Colas 3036. Lipperheide 2387

Vorstellung deren in dem lager der alliirten armee onferne Maynz, den 13 ten August 1743 angekomenen Berg-Schotten. See Representation of the High-landers

Vorstellung stuttgartischer jüngst-gehaltener hochfürstl. Würtemberg-Hessischer heimführungs-begängnis: samt zweyfachem kurtzem bericht von beyder hohen vermählten. Stuttgart, J. W. Röszlin 1675
118,80,66,32p. 6pl.(3 ports.) F.
Describes and pictures the wedding of Count Wilhelm Ludwig of Württemberg and Magdalena Sibylla of Hesse
Lipperheide 2588

Die **vorzüglichsten** rüstungen und waffen der K.K. Ambraser-sammlung in original-photographien. Sacken, Eduard, freiherr von

Vos, Martin de
Oraculum anachoreticum ... Martī de Vos figur. Joā Sadeler sculpsit. Venetijs, 1600
25pl. Q.
Lipperheide 1799

Vosges. See France—By region or province—Lorraine

Vosmer, Michael
Principes Hollandiae et Zelandiae, domini Frisiae ... a Theodorico Aquitaniae ad Iacobam Bavariae. Antwerp, C. Plantin 1578
87p. 36pl. illus.(ports.) Q.
The portraits are reproduced in Baerland's *Hollandiae comitum*
Lipperheide 923

Voss, Albert
(ed.) Die bronzeschwerter des Königlichen museums zu Berlin. See Berlin. Staatliche museen

Voth, Henry R. See Dorsey, G. A., jt. auth.

Voyage à Athènes et à Constantinople. Dupré, Louis

Voyage au Congo. Douville, J. B.

Voyage au Levant. Bruyn, Cornelis de

Voyage autour du monde. See Beauvoir, Ludovic, marquis de. Pékin, Yeddo, San Francisco

Voyage dans la Cilicie. Langlois, Victor

Voyage dans l'intérieur de l'Amérique du Nord. See entry under Wied-Neuwied, M. A. P., prinz von. Reise

Voyage dans la Russie méridionale. Gamba, J. F.

Voyage dans la Levant en 1817 et 1818. Forbin, L. N. P. A., comte de

Voyage dans les îles Baléares et Pithiuses; fait dans les années 1801, 1802, 1803, 1804 et 1805. Grasset de Saint-Sauveur, André

Voyage dans l'intérieur de la Hollande. Maaskamp, Evert

Voyage de découvertes aux terres Australes. Péron, François

Voyage de s. a. r. monseigneur le Duc de Montpensier à Tunis en Égypte, en Turquie et en Grèce. Latour, Antoine de

Voyage de s. m. Louis-Philippe Ier ... au Château de Windsor. Pingret, Édouard

Voyage d'Horace Vernet en Orient. Goupil Fesquet, F. A. A.

Voyage du roi à Windsor. See Pingret, Édouard. Voyage de S. M. Louis-Philippe Ier, roi des Français au Château de Windsor

Voyage en Angleterre. Lami, E. L., and Monnier, Henry

Voyage en Autriche. See Serres, Marcel de. L'Autriche

Voyage en Chine et en Tartarie. Holmes, Samuel

Voyage en Norvège et en Laponie. See Buch, Leopold, freiherr von. Reise durch Norwegen und Lappland

Voyage en Perse. Drouville, Gaspard

Voyage historique, littéraire et pittoresque dans les isles et possessions ci-devant vénitiennes du Levant. Grasset de Saint-Sauveur, André

Voyage of His Majesty's ship Alceste. McLeod, John

Voyage pittoresque. Saint Non, J. C. R. de

Voyage pittoresque autour du monde. Dumont d'Urville, J. S. C., ed.

Voyage pittoresque dans la régence d'Alger. Lessore, A. E., and Wyld, W.

Voyage pittoresque dans le Brésil. Rugendas, J. M.

Voyage pittoresque dans le royaume des Deux Siciles. Cuciniello, Michele, and Bianchi, Lorenzo

Voyage pittoresque dans les deux Amériques. Orbigny, A. D. d', ed.

Voyage pittoresque de Constantinople et des rives du Bosphore. Melling, A. I., illus.

Voyage pittoresque de la Grèce. Choiseul-Gouffier, M. G. A. F., comte de

Voyage pittoresque en Asie et en Afrique. Eyriès, J. B. B.

Voyage pittoresque en Espagne et en Portugal. Bégin, É. A. N. J.

Voyage pittoresque en russie. Saint-Julien, Charles de

Voyage pittoresque en Suisse, en Savoie et sur les Alpes. Bégin, E. A. N. J.

Voyage pittoresque et archéologique dans la partie la plus intéressante du Mexique. Nebel, Carl

Voyage to Africa. McLeod, John

Voyage towards the South Pole, and round the world. Cook, James

Voyages au Pérou, faits dans les années 1791 à 1794, par les pp. Manuel Sobreviela, et Narcisso y Barcelo; précédés d'un tableau de l'état actuel de ce pays ... publiés à Londres en 1805, par John Skinner, d'après l'original espagnol; traduits par P. F. Henry; ornés d'un atlas de 12 planches coloriées et d'une belle carte du Pérou, dressée d'après Lacruz et les documens les plus nouveaux, par P. Lapie. Paris, J. G. Dentu 1809

2v. O. and atlas (12 col.pl. fold.map) Q.

"A periodical known as *Mercurio peruano* was published at Lima, 1791-95 in 12 vols. Joseph Skinner, having obtained the first 4 volumes, translated selections from them, which he published under title *The present state of Peru,* in 1805. A German edition appeared at Hamburg, 1806. In 1807-08 there was published at Weimar a work entitled *Peru nach seinem gegenwärtigen zustande,* under the editorship of F. J. Bertruch. Volume 1 was a translation of Skinner, v2 a translation of selections from v5-10 of *Mercurio peruano.* The present work is a translation, v 1 from Skinner's English work and v2 from Bertuch's second volume." Library of Congress

Contents: Tableau de l'état actuel du Pérou; Voyages des pères Manuel Sobreviela et Narcisse Girbal-y-Barcelo; Description de différentes provinces du Pérou

LC F-3611

Voyages dans l'Amérique du Sud. Crevaux, J. N.

Voyages de Corneille Le Brun par la Moscovie, en Perse et aux Indes Orientales. See Bruyn, Cornelis de. Cornelis de. Cornelis de Bruins Reisen over Moskovie, door Persie en Indie

Voyages ... en Europe, Asie & Afrique. La Mottraye, Aubry de

Voyages par la Moscovie en Perse et aux Indes Orientales. See note under Bruyn, Cornelis de. Voyage au Levant

Voyages pittoresques dans les quatre parties du monde. See Grasset de Saint-Sauveur, Jacques. Encyclopédie des voyages

Le **vrai** patineur ou principes sur l'art de patiner avec grâce. Garcin, J.

Les **vrais** portraits des hommes illustres. Bèze, Théodore de

Les **vrais** pourtraits de quelques unes des plus grandes dames de la chrestiente, desguisees en bergeres. Passe, Crispijn van de

Vred, Oliverius

Genealogia comitum Flandriae a Balduino Ferreo usque ad Phillipum IV. hisp. regem; variis sigillorum figuris repraesentata. Brugis Flandrorum, J. Baptistam & L. Kerchovios 1642

1897 to date

170, 414p. 617 illus. F.

The illustrations, many of them from coins, show the counts and countesses. Many of them show armor

Lipperheide 934

Vrients, Joannes Baptista

(ed.) Martin, Cornelis. Les genealogies et anciennes descentes des forestiers et comtes de Flandre

Vries, R. W. P. de

Dutch national costumes. Amsterdam, J. M. Meulenhoff 1930

Unp. 48pl. O. fl.3

At head of title: *Beautiful Holland*

Twelve illustrations of costume masculine and feminine, and descriptive text

Costume index

Vries, Scato Gocko de

(ed.) Catholic Church. Liturgy and ritual. Breviary. Breviaire Grimani de la Bibliothèque de S. Marco à Venise: reproduction photographique complète

Vsemirnaia illiustratsiia. v 1-58? 1869-1897. St. Peterburg", H. A. Hoppe

Illus. F.

Lipperheide 4729

Vue des environs de St. Petersbourg. See Le Prince, J. B. Oeuvres

Vues, costumes, moeurs et usages de la Chine. Alexander, William

Vues dans l'empire Ottoman. See Mayer, Ludwig. Views in the Ottoman empire

Vues de la Chine et de la Tartarie. See Alexander, William. Costumes et vues de la Chine

Vues de Russie et usages divers des habitants de ce genre. Damame-Demartrais, M. F.

Vues des cérémonies les plus intéressantes du couronnement de Leurs Majestés Impériales l'empereur Nicolas 1er et l'impératrice Alexandra, à Moscou. Graf, Henry

Vues des Cordillères. Humboldt, Alexander, freiherr von

Vues en Egypte. See Mayer, Ludwig. Views in Egypt

Vues en Palestine. See Mayer, Ludwig. Views in Palestine

Vues et costumes pittoresques du départ. des Deux-Sèvres. Gellé, P., and Arnaud, Ch.

Vues pittoresques de l'Orient. See Mayr, Heinr. von. Malerische ansichten aus dem Orient

Vuillier, Gaston

La danse. [Paris] Hachette 1898

390p. illus. pl. ports. F.

Lipperheide 3135. LC 3-27304

Vuillier, Gaston—*Continued*

A history of dancing from the earliest ages to our own times; from the French. With a sketch of dancing in England, by Joseph Grego. Twenty full-page plates and 409 illustrations. [2d ed.] New York, D. Appleton 1898

xvi,446p. front. illus. pl. port. music. F.
Translation of the author's *La danse*. The sketch of dancing in England forms pages 381-440, and like the rest is well illustrated with reproductions of the works of famous artists
Lipperheide 3136. LC 3-450

Výběr národního českého vyšívání. Koula, Jan

Vzory staroslovenských vipiviek. Muster altslowakischer leinenstickerei. Socháň, P. B., pub.

Vzory vyšwání lidu slovanského na Moravě. Sojková, Berta

W

W. G. D. von. See Vorläufer zum ersten Theresienvolksfeste in Bamberg

Wace, Alan John Bayard

A Cretan statuette in the Fitzwilliam museum, a study in Minoan costume. Cambridge [Eng.] The University press 1927

49p. 1 illus. XIII pl.(incl.col.front.) diagr. sq.Q.
LC 28-10945

Wace, Alan John Bayard and Thompson, Maurice Scott

The nomads of the Balkans, an account of life and customs among the Vlachs of northern Pindus. London, Methuen [1914]

x,332p. XXIV pl. 2 maps(1 fold.) O.
Shows costume of the Aromunes of modern Greece
Notes and bibliography: p297-303
LC 15-15272

Wachsmann

(engr.) Lieder, Friedrich. Darstellung der königl. preussischen infanterie und cavallerie

Wachsmuth, Jerem.

(engr.) Manuale, oder Handgriffe der infanterie

Waddell, Laurence Austine

The Buddhism of Tibet; or, Lamaism, with its mystic cults, symbolism and mythology, and in its relation to Indian Buddhism ... 2d ed. Cambridge [Eng.] W. Heffer 1934

1, 598p. front. illus. fold.pl. O.
First edition (London, W. H. Allen 1895)
Bibliography: p578-83
LC 35-5423, 24-4665 (1st ed.)

Wadleigh, R. H.

Head gear antique and modern. Boston, Coleman & Maxwell 1879

41p. O.

Wael, Cornelis de

Verschiedene gewerbe, bilder aus dem italienischen volksleben. ca1650

15pl. sq.O.
Lipperheide 1953

Waern, Cecilia

A short historical sketch of fans. New York, The author 1895

29p. 8 illus. S.

Wâfen unde wîcgewaete der deutschen ritter des mittelalters. Mansberg, Richard, freiherr von

Die **waffen** der völker des alten Orients. Bonnet, Hans

Die **waffen** der Wartburg. Diener-Schönberg, Alfons

Waffen; ein beitrag zur historischen waffenkunde. Hefner-Alteneck, J. H. von

Waffen und kunst-sammlung. Gimbel, Karl

Die **waffengattungen** des preussischen heeres. Hünten, Emil

Waffenhandlung von den rören, musquetten, undt spiessen. See Gheyn, Jacob de. Wapenhandelinghe van roers musquetten ende spiessen

Waffensammlung. Leiden, H. K.

Die **waffensammlung** des grafen S. D. Scheremetew in St Petersburg. Lenz, E. von

Die **waffensammlung** des osterreichischen kaiserhauses. Leitner, Quirin, ritter von

Waffen-sammlung Kuppelmayr. Kuppelmayr, Hans

Waffen-sammlung sr. koniglichen hoheit des prinzen Carl von Preussen. Hiltl, Georg

Die **wagen** und fahrwerke der Griechen und Römer und anderer alten völker. Ginzrot, J. C.

Wagenseil, Johann Christoph

Joh. Christophori Wagenseilii De Sacri rom. imperii libera Civitate noribergensi commentatio. Altdorfi Noricorum, typis J. W. Kohlesii 1697

576p. front. pl.(part fold.) ports. sq.O.
Shows some costume of Nuremberg
Lipperheide 779. LC 6-44327

Wagner, Alexander

(illus.) Simons, Theodor. Spanien

Wagner, Arthur Lockwood, and Kelley, James Douglas Jerrold

Our country's defensive forces in war and peace. The United States army and navy; their histories, from the era of the revolution to the close of the Spanish-American war; with accounts of their organization, administration, and duties. The army, by Lieutenant-Colonel Arthur L. Wagner ... The navy, by Commander J. D. Jerrold Kelley. Akron, O., & New York, Werner 1899

241p. 42 col.pl. ob.F. $10, o.p.
On cover: *The U. S. army and navy 1776-1899*. Each plate accompanied by leaf with descriptive letterpress
Colas 3040. Costume index. LC 99-3702

Wagner, Heinrich

Trachtenbuch des mittel-alters, eine sammlung von trachten, waffen, geraethen. München, Lindauer 1830-33

6pts. 48pl. sq.F.
Colas 3039. Lipperheide 349

Wagner, J. G.
(illus.) Kurtze und eygentliche beschreibung dess jenigen so bey der verlöbnus, heimführ- und vermählung ... Caroli, pfaltzgrafens bey Rhein ... mit ... Wilhelmina Ernestina ... erb-princessin zu Dennemarck ... vorgangen

Wagner, Johann Christoph
Delineatio provinciarum Pannoniae et imperii Turcici in oriente; eine ... beschreibung ... wie auch allerhand seltenheiten welch sich an kleidertrachten ... befinden. Augspurg, J. Koppmayer 1684-85
2v. 21 illus. 83pl. F.
Contains five woodcuts showing costume of the Turks, a portrait of Mahommed IV of Turkey (1648-87) and one plate showing Mamelukes
Lipperheide 1410

Das mächtige kayser-reich Sina und die asiatische Tartarey vor augen gestellet. Augspurg, J. Koppmayer 1688
168,84p. illus. 34pl. F.
Nine plates showing Chinese costume are copied from A. Kircher's *China monumentis*
Lipperheide 1514

Wahabees. See Arabia

Die **wahl** und krönung der deutschen kaiser zu Frankfurt am Main. Römer-Büchner, B. J.

Wahlen, Auguste, pseud. See Loumyer, J. F. N.

Wahre abbildung der sämtlichen reichskleinodien welche in ... Nürnberg aufbewahret werden. Delsenbach, J. A.

Wahre abbildungen der türckischen kayser un persischen fürsten. Greblinger, Georg

Wahreste und neueste abbildung des türckischen hofes. Moor, J. B. van

Wahrhaffte bildnüsse aller der Heil. Röm. Reichs freyen stadt Augspurg. Roch, J. M.

Wahrhaffte eigentliche und kurtze beschreibung aller hertzogen zu Venedig leben. See Kellner, Heinrich. Chronica

Wahrhaffte und eigendliche erzehlung von der reise des bischofs von Beryte auss Franckreich ... nach China. Bourges, Jacques de

Wahrhaffte und eigentliche abbildungen der ... chur fürstlich Mayntzischen Favorita. See Kleiner, Salomon. Representation naturelle et exacte de la Favorite

Wahrhaffte und genaue abbildung aller kirchen und clöster. See Kleiner, Salomon. Vera et accurata delineatio

Wahrhaffte vorstellung beÿder ... Schlösser Weissenstein ob Pommersfeld und Geibach. See Kleiner, Salomon. Representation au naturel des chateaux de Weissenstein

Wahrhafftige hÿstorische beschreibung aller gedenckwürdigen geschichten, welche ... von dem 1517 jahr. See Helwig, Nicolaus. Theatrum hystoriae universalis Catholico Protestantiv

Wahrhafftige unnd eygentliche beschreibung der allerschrecklichsten verrätherey ... wieder die Königliche Majestät ... zu Londen. Bry, J. T. de, and Bry, J. I. de

Waists
Kneeland, Natalie. Waists. 1924

Waiters
Cervio, Vincenzo. Il trinciante. 1581
Pandini, Cesare. Il mastro di casa. 1610
Scappi, Bartolomeo. Dell' arte del cucinare, con Il mastro di casa di C. Pandini; ragionamento del cavalier R. Fusorito ... con C. Pandini; e Trinciante by V. Cervio. 1643

Walch, Sebastian
Portraits aller herren burger-meistern, der vortrefflichen republique, stadt und vor-orths Zürich, von dem 1336ten bisz auf das 1742te jahr. Kempten, 1756
24p. 3 illus. 61pl. F.
Lipperheide 921

Waldeck, Jean Frederic Maximilien, comte de
Monuments anciens du Mexique; Palenqué et autres ruines. See entry under Brasseur de Bourbourg, C. E.

Waldemar, prince of Prussia
Zur erinnerung an die reise des prinzen Waldemar von Preussen nach Indien in de jahren 1844-1846. Berlin, Decker 1853
2v. 104pl.(1 double) port. maps. F.
Volume 1 edited by Heinrich Mahlmann; v2 by Graf von Oriolla
Of the more than one hundred plates from sketches by the Prince, more than four-fifths are by Bellermann, and the remainder by Kretzchmer; they were lithographed by Bellermann, Tempeltei, Haun and Klaus
Lipperheide 1500. LC 29-20195

Walenta, J. See Balzer, Anton, jt. auth.

Wales
Roberts, Peter. The Cambrian popular antiquities; or, An account of some traditions, customs, and superstitions, of Wales. 1815
Skeat, W. W. The past at our doors. 1911
Welsh costumes. 1853

Walker, Mrs A.
Female beauty as preserved and improved by regimen, cleanliness and dress; and especially by the adaptation, colour and arrangement of dress ... Rev. and amended by an American editor. New York, Scofield and Voorhies [c1840]
400p. 12 col.pl.(incl.fronts.) D.
Published also (London, Hurst 1837)
Part III deals with the art of dress

Walker, Donald
Exercises for ladies; calculated to preserve and improve beauty, and to prevent and correct personal defects, inseparable from constrained or careless habits: founded on physiological principles. London, T. Hurst, 1836
xx,228p. front. XXXIII pl. D.
Shows gynasium dress
Lipperheide 3047. LC 15-22455

Walker, E. K.
(tr.) Boehn, Max von. Miniatures and silhouettes

Walker, Sir Edward
A circumstantial account of the preparations for the coronation of His Majesty King Charles the Second, and a minute detail of that splendid ceremony ... to which is prefixed, an account of the landing, reception, and journey of His Majesty from Dover to London. London, T. Baker 1820
131p. 10pl. O.
Lipperheide 2686. LC 3-26237

Walker, Francis S.
(illus.) Mathew, F. J. Ireland

Walker, G.
(pub.) Cyclopaedia of the British costumes, from the Metropolitan repository of fashions

Walker, George
The costume of Yorkshire ... being facsimiles of original drawings, with descriptions in English and French. Leeds, R. Jackson 1885
106p. col.front. 40 col.pl. F.
Added title-page: *Costumes du comté d'York*. Lettered: *The costumes of Yorkshire in 1814* ... edited by Edward Hailstone. First edition (London, T. Bensley 1814)
Colas 3044-45. Lipp. 1015. LC 2-29500

Walker, Isaac
Dress: as it has been, is, and will be. New York, I. Walker 1885
210p. front. illus. pl. D.
A short history of masculine dress from ancient times until the 19th century, with emphasis on the 19th century in the United States

Walker, James. See Atkinson, J. A., jt. auth.

Walker, Joseph Cooper
An historical essay on the dress of the ancient and modern Irish; to which is subjoined a memoir on the armour and weapons of the Irish ... 2d ed. Dublin, J. Christie 1818
2v. front. illus. pl. (1 col.) O. o.p.
Costume index

Walker, Robert
Old fans from Mr. R. Walker's cabinet. [London? 1882?]
52pl. ob.F.
Cover title. Plates printed on white silk and mounted. Shows English fans of the 18th century and French fans of the 17th-18th centuries

Walker, William Edward
The tailor's philosophy; or, Science complete in the art of cutting. London, Longman; Dublin, E. Madden 1839
100p. 3pl. O.
Colas 3046

Walking sticks. See Canes, walking-sticks, etc.

Walkup, Mrs Fairfax (Proudfit)
Outline history of costume, based on authentic and historic sources, illustrated by plates with patterns. Pasadena, Calif., Pasadena playhouse press 1933
45 l. pl. Q.
Mimeographed
Bibliography: numbered leaves 38-45
LC 35-12042

Wall, Alexander James
(ed.) Uniforms of the American, British, French and German armies in the war of the American revolution, 1775-1783. See Lefferts, C. M.

Wallachia. See Rumania—Wallachia

Wallander, J. W. See Vallander, Josef Vilhelm

Waller, John Green, and Waller, L. A. B.
A series of monumental brasses, from the thirteenth to the sixteenth century. London, J. B. Nichols 1864
xiii,65p. illus. 62pl. (part col.) F.
Issued in parts, 1840-1864
Shows English costume of the 13th to 16th century
LC 17-27813

Waller, L. A. B. See Waller, John Green, jt. auth.

Die **wallfahrt** zum hl. Antonius. See Úprka, Joža. Na pouti u Sv. Antoníčka

Wallgren, O.
Skänska folk drägter, tecknade af O. Wallgren utgifne med text af Arvid Kurck. Stockholm, I. Haeggström 1872
22col.pl. F.
Plates lithographed by A. J. Salmson
Colas 1678

Wallon, Henri Alexandre
Jeanne d'Arc ... éd. illustrée d'après les monuments de l'art depuis le quinzième siècle jusqu'à nos jours. Paris, Firmin-Didot 1876
552p. col.front. illus. (incl.music) pl. (part col.) ports. maps. F.
Lipperheide 1096. LC 17-1146

Walrond, Henry. See Longman, C. J., jt. auth.

Walser, Carl
(illus.) Bie, Oskar. Das theater. 1912
(illus.) Kellermann, Bernhard. Sassa yo yassa

Walsh, John
The mass and vestments of the Catholic church; liturgical, doctrinal, historical and archæological. Troy, N.Y., Troy times art press 1909
539p. front. illus. O.
LC 9-18052

Walsh, Robert. See Allom, Thomas. Constantinople and the scenery of the seven churches of Asia Minor

Walter, Reinhold von
(tr.) Levinson, A. I. Meister des ballets. 1923

Walter, W.
Das preuszische heer in bildern, nach zeichnungen von L. Elsholz gestochen von Fr. Bolt und Karl Funke; ein lesebuch für die jugend. Berlin, J. G. Hasselberg 1834
138p. 25 col.pl. O.
Colas 3050. Lipperheide 2167

Walterstorff, Emelie Wilhelmina von
(illus.) Cederblom, Gerda, ed. Svenska allmogedräkter
(illus.) Wistrand, P. G. V. Svenska folkdräkter

Walther, C. S.
(tr.) Lens, A. C. Das kostum der meisten völker des alterthums

Walton, William
Army and navy of the United States from the period of the revolution to the present day; rev. and enl. Boston, Philadelphia, New York, G. Barrie 1900
2v. illus. col.pl. F. o.p.
First published 1889-95 in parts. Revised edition has been enlarged in volume 2
Costume index. LC 2-23192 (1st ed.)

Die **wanddekorationen** in Pompeji. See Presuhn, Emil. Die pompejanischen wandecorationen

Wandering in northern China. Franck, H. A.

Wanderings among the Falashas in Abyssinia. Stern, H. A.

Die **wandgemaelde** des landgrafensaales auf der Wartburg. Schwind, Moritz von

Wandle, Mrs Jennie Taylor
Masquerade and carnival: their customs and costumes; rev. and enl. London and New York, Butterick pub. co. 1892
176p. illus. pl. Q.
LC 8-2275

Wangner, Jacob
(engr.) Schönhaar, W. F. Ausführliche beschreibung des- zu Bayreuth im september 1748 vorgegangenen ... beylagers

Wanjura, A.
(illus.) Schweiger-Lerchenfeld, Amand, freiherr von. Das frauenleben der erde

Wapen und stammbuch. Amman, Jost

Wapenhandelinghe van roers musquetten ende spiessen. Gheyn, Jacob de

Wappen- & stammbuch. Amman, Jost

Die **wappen,** helmzierden und standarten der Grossen Heidelberger liederhandschrift (Manesse-codex). Zangemeister, K. F. W.

War in Italy. Bossoli, Carlo

Warhaffte bildnis etlicher hochlöblicher fürsten und herren. Schnelboltz, Gabriel

Warhaffte relation und ... discours uber dess ... Herzen Johann Friderichen. Martij, Anno 1616. Assum, J. A.

Warhafftig sag; oder red von dem rock Jesu Christi. Adelphus, J. A. P.

Warhafftige abcontrafactur und bildnüs aller gros hertzogen, chur und fürsten, welche ... das landt Sachssen ... regieret haben. Agricola, Johann

Warhafftige historia unnd beschreibung einer landtschafft der wilden ... leuten in der neuen welt. See Staden, Hans, and Lery, Jean de. Americae tertia pars

Waring, John Burley
Stone monuments, tumuli and ornament of remote ages. London, J. B. Day 1870
x,96p. 108pl. F.
Contains material on prehistoric jewelry of the British isles
LC 15-3359

Der **warme** Hirsbrey und die verbindungen Zürichs mit Strassburg. See Maurer, H. R. Denkmale des geschmaks der sitten und gebräuche der alten Schweizer

Warnberger, J.
(engr.) Kappeller, J. A. Tiroler trachten

Warncke, Johannes
Luebecker trachten. Lübeck, Gebrüder Borchers 1930
72p. col.front. illus.(part col.) O.

Warnecke, Friedrich
(ed.) Sammlung historischer bildnisse und trachten aus dem stammbuch der Katharina von Canstein, unter mitwirkung des frhn. dr. E. R. v. Canstein. Berlin, H. S. Hermann 1885
20p. 115pl. F.
Includes portraits of the nobility from the end of the 16th to the beginning of the 18th century in Saxony, Hesse and Westphalia
Lipperheide 696

Warnock uniform company
Uniforms and equipment for officers' national guard. New York, The Warnock uniform co. 1900
Cover-title, 56p. illus. D.
LC 0-2170

Wartegg, Ernst Von Hesse. See Hesse-Wartegg, Ernst von

The **war-time** journal of a Georgia girl, 1864-1865. Andrews, E. F.

Warwick, Edward, and Pitz, Henry C.
Early American costume. New York, London, The Century co. [c1929]
xiv,319p. illus. LXIV pl. O. (Century library of American antiques) $4
Sources and authorities: p299-302; Bibliographical notes: p303-12
Costume index. LC 29-23781

Warwick, Richard, earl of. Pageants. See Pageants of Richard Beauchamp, earl of Warwick

Washington, Thomas
(tr.) Nicolay, Nicolas, sieur d'Arfeuille. The navigations, peregrinations and voyages, made into Turkie

Wassmansdorff, Carl. See Auerswald, Fabian von. Die ringerkunst; erneuert von G. U. Schmidt

Watchmen

France

Cudet, François. Histoire des corps de troupe qui ont été spécialement chargés du service de la ville de Paris depuis son origine jusqu'à nos jours. 1887

Water colours. See Cruikshank, George. Cruikshank's water colours

Water pageants, games and stunts. McCormick, Olive

Waters, Mrs Clara (Erskine) Clement
Angels in art. Boston, L. C. Page 1898
267p. front. 33pl. D.
LC 0-4936

A handbook of Christian symbols and stories of the saints as illustrated in art ... ed. by Katherine E. Conway. Boston, Ticknor 1886
xiv,349p. front. illus. 31pl. O.
Contains many pictures of saints
LC 9-28686

Saints in art. Boston, L. C. Page 1899
428p. front. 32pl. D. (Art lovers' series)
LC 99-3705

Wathy, Maria F.
(tr.) Brockhaus, Albert. Netsukes

Watson, John Fanning
Annals of Philadelphia, and Pennsylvania, in the olden time; being a collection of memoirs, anecdotes, and incidents of the city and its inhabitants, and of the earliest settlements of the inland part of Pennsylvania; enlarged, with many revisions and additions, by Willis P. Hazard. Philadelphia, E. S. Stuart 1898
3v. fronts. illus. pl. ports. plan. O.
Originally published in 1830 in one volume with title: *Annals of Philadelphia, being a collection of memoirs.* Many editions
Contains material on dress worn in Philadelphia
LC 1-10550, 1-10546(1830 ed.)

Historic tales of olden time: concerning the early settlement and advancement of New York city and state. New York, Collins and Hannay 1832
214p. front. pl. D.
Pages 143-58 discuss dress in New York state before the Revolution. The same material is included in the author's *Annals and occurrences of New York city and state* (Philadelphia, H. F. Anners 1846)
LC 1-14317, 2-8916 (1846 title)

Watson, John Forbes
The textile manufactures and the costumes of the people of India. London, G. E. Eyre and W. Spottiswoode 1866
xxi,173p. 12pl.(8 col., part mounted) F. 65s, o.p.
Colas 3051. Costume index. Lipperheide 1503. LC 32-21027

Watt, Jeannie
Das zukunftskleid der frau; die gesundung der frauenmode. Berlin-Leipzig, W. Vobach 1902
25p. 30 illus. O.
Lipperheide 3317

Watteau, Antoine. See Watteau, Jean Antoine

Watteau, Jean Antoine
Diverses figures chinoises et tartares. Paris, F. Chereau ca1740
3pts. 30pl. F.
First twelve plates engraved by Jeaurat, second twelve by Boucher, and last six plates by Aubert
Colas 3055-56

A drawing book of figures. London, J. Clark 1728
18pl. O. 6d
Plates are copied from his *Figures de modes* and *Figures françoises et comiques*
Colas 3054

Figures de modes. Paris, Duchange ca1720
7pl. O.
Part of the plates engraved by A. Watteau, others by H. S. Thomassin
Colas 3052. Lipperheide 1120

Figures françoises et comiques. Paris, Duchange ca1720
7pl. O.
Colas 3053

Gemälde und zeichnungen. Berlin, Mitschler und Röstell [1886-89]
168pl. F.
Lipperheide 1120b

Pièces choisies ... gravées par W. Marks. Paris, A. Delâtre 1850
43pl. Q.
Lipperheide 1137

Watteau, Louis Joseph
Cris et costumes de Paris; dessiné par Watteau, gravé en couleur par Guyot. Paris, Lecampion 1786
1 l. 6 col.pl. Q.
Colas 3057

Première [et deuxième] suite de divers sujets militaires. Paris, Lenfant ca1787
10pl. Q.
Colas 3058

Wattier, Édouard
Les cris de Paris. Paris, Engelmann 1822
12 col.pl. O.
Colas 3060

Wattier, Émile
Costumes persans modernes. [Paris, Engelmann] ca1840
30 col.pl. Q.
Colas 3059. Lipperheide 1467

Watty, M. F. See Wathy, Maria F.

Weapons
Edge-Partington, James. Album of the weapons, tools, ornaments, articles of dress, etc. of the natives of the Pacific islands. 1890-95

Essenwein, A. O. Quellen zur geschichte der feuerwaffen. 1877

Inventarium ... was in ... herrn Marx Fuggers ... rüst: und sattel cammer an harnischen, büchsen, wehrn, spiessen, sättlen, zeugen schlitten sampt irer zugehörung und andrn vorhanden. 1890

Jähns, Max. Entwicklungsgeschichte der alten trutzwaffen mit einem anhange über die feuerwaffen. 1899

Klemm, G. F. Werkzeuge und waffen. 1854

Payne-Gallwey, Sir R. W. F., bart. The crossbow, mediaeval and modern, military and sporting. 1903

Rathgen, Bernhard. Das aufkommen der pulverwaffe. 1925

Sargeaunt. Weapons; a brief discourse on hand-weapons other than fire-arms. 1908

Schweitering, Julius. Zur geschichte von speer und schwert im 12. jahrhundert. 1912

See also Arms and armor; Creese; Sword

Prehistoric

Chantre, Ernest. Études palèoethnologiques dans le bassin du Rhone: Age du bronze. 1875-76

Chantre, Ernest. Premier âge du fer: nécropoles et tumulus: Album. 1880

Evans, Sir John. The ancient bronze implements, weapons, and ornaments, of Great Britain and Ireland. 1881

Evans, Sir John. The ancient stone implements, weapons and ornaments of Great Britain. 1897

Keller, Ferdinand. The lake dwellings of Switzerland and other parts of Europe. 1878

Weapons of war. Demmin, A. F.

Wearing apparel in Bolivia. United States. Bureau of foreign and domestic commerce

Wearing apparel in Peru. United States. Bureau of foreign and domestic commerce

Webb, Wilfred Mark
The heritage of dress; being notes on the history and evolution of clothes ... new and rev. ed. London, The Times book club 1912
xxiv,299p. illus. XII pl.(incl.front.) O. o.p.
First edition (London, E. G. Richards 1907. 393p. 11pl.)
Bibliography: p271-73
Costume index. LC 12-29350, 8-12147 (1st ed.)

Webb-Johnson, Cecil
The soldiers' feet and footgear. Calcutta, Thacker, Spink; London, W. Thacker 1915
34p. illus. D.
Compiled from articles published in the *British medical journal* and from lectures delivered in England and elsewhere
LC 19-5750

Die **webe-arbeit** mit hand-apparat. Lipperheide, Frieda, and Dorn, Anna

Weber
(lithgr.) Föhn, Michael. Suisse—jeux et usages

Weber, J. See Dance of death. Holbein's todtentanz in den wandbildern zu Chur

Wechsler, Alfred
Psychologie der mode, von W. Fred [pseud.] [Berlin] Bard, Marquardt [1904]
79p. front. illus. pl.(1 fold.) ports.(2 fold.) sq.S. (Die kunst, 28.bd.)
Colas 1114. LC 34-23931

Wedding embassy, inc.
Wedding embassy year book. See entry under Brennig, M. C.

Weddings; modes, manners and customs. King, Mrs J. A.

Weddings and wedding dress
Aria, Mrs. E. D. Costume: fanciful, historical and theatrical. 1906. p211-24
Berlepsch, H. A. von. Chronik vom ehrbaren und uralten schneidergewerk. 1850
Brennig, M. C. Wedding embassy year book. c1935
The bride's own book. c1922
Hamilton, Lady Augusta. Marriage rites, customs and ceremonies of all nations of the universe. 1822
Hochzeitgebräuche aller nazionen der welt. 1783
Hutchinson, H. N. Marriage customs in many lands. 1897
Jeaffreson, J. C. Brides and bridals. 1872
Miln, Mrs L. J. Wooings and weddings in many climes. 1900
Reinsberg-Düringsfeld, Ida, freifrau von, and Reinsberg-Düringsfeld, Otto, freiherr von. Hochzeitsbuch; brauch und glaube der hochzeit bei den christlichen völkern Europa's. 1871

Austria

Allerhöchst-feyerlichste festivatäten ... bey dem ... beylager ... Leopoldi I. Römischen Kaysers ... und ... Margaritae ... Infantin von Hispanien. 1667

Sieg-streit dess lufft und wassers freudenfest zu pferd. 1667

Von himmeln entzindete und durch allgemainen zuruff der erde sich himmelwerts erschwingende frolockhungs flammen zur begengnus des hochzeitlichen beylägers ... Leopoldi des Ersten, Römischen Kaisers ... und Margarita, geborner Infantin aus Hispanien 1666. [1666]

Belgium

Cérémonies et fêtes du mariage de ... Duc de Brabant, et de ... Marie Henriette Anne Archiduchesse d'Autriche, célébre à Bruxelles le 22 aout, 1853. 1853

China

Un mariage impérial chinois; cérémonial, traduit par G. Devéria. 1887

England

Russell, Sir W. H. A memorial of the marriage of H. R. H. Albert Edward, prince of Wales, and H. R. H. Alexandra, princess of Denmark. 1864

Germany

Abbildung und repraesentation der fürstlichen inventionen, auffzüge, ritterspiel, auch ballet, so in des Herren Johann Georgen, Fürsten zu Anhalt, Hofflager zu Dessa, bey des Herrn Georg Rudolph, Hertzogen in Schlesien mit Fraw Sophia Elizabeth, Hertzogin in Schlesien ... hochzeitlichem frewdenfest ... beylager. 1614

Beschreibung der feierlichkeiten, welche bei der vermählung des Kronprinzen von Preussen K.H. mit der Prinzessin Elisabeth von Bairen K.H. so wie bei der ankunft der Prinzessin K.H. in Berlin und an andern orten statt gefunden haben. 1824

Beschreibung der festlichkeiten, welche bei der zu Dessau vollzogenen vermählung ... des Erbprinzen Ernst von Sachsen-Altenburg Herzogs zu Sachsen ... und der Prinzessin Agnes von Anhalt-Dessau ... so wie bei höchstderen einzuge in Altenburg stattgefunden haben. 1853

Beschreibung der illumination zu Dreszden bey der königlichen Sicilianischen in vollmacht vollzogenen vermählung, nebst andern dahin gehörigen vorstellungen. 1738

Beschreibung der reisz: Empfahuñg desz ritterlichen ordens; volbringung des heyraths. 1613

Frischlin, Jacob. Drey schöne und lustige bücher von der Hohen Zollerischen hochzeyt. 1599

Illustrirte frauen-zeitung. Die vermählung seiner königlichen hoheit des prinzen Wilhelm von Preuszen mit ihrer hoheit der prinzessin Augusta Victoria zu Schleswig-Holstein. 1881

Die vermählung des prinzen Friedrich Wilhelm v. Preussen und der königl. prinzessin Victoria von England. 1858

Weddings and wedding dress—Germany—*Continued*

Vorstellung stuttgartischer jüngst-gehaltener hochfürstl. Würtemberg-Hessischer heimführungs-begängnis: samt zweyfachem kurtzem bericht von beyder hohen vermählten. 1675

Italy

Agnelli, Jacopo. Descrizione delle ... solennita celebrate ... 12. febbrajo 1736 ... in Ferrara per le ... nozze di S.A.R. Francesco Steffano Duca di Lorena e della Serenissima Arciduchessa Maria Teresa d'Austria. 1736

Albo pittorico di alcune feste modenesi nella fausta occasione delle nozze auguste tra l'A. R. dell'arciduca Francesco Ferdinando, principe ereditario di Modena e S. A. R. la principessa Adelgonda di Baviera. 1842

Gerstfeldt, Olga von. Hochzeitsfeste der renaissance in Italien. 1906

Maggio, Pietro. Le guerre festive nelle reali nozze de' ... re di Spagna Carolo secondo, e Maria Luisa di Borbone, celebrate nella ... Palermo ... MDCLXXX. 1680?

Massano, Gino. Grazie e splendori dei costumi italiani. 1930

Japan

The ceremonies of a Japanese marriage. 19—?

Tamura, Naomi. The Japanese bride. 1893

Latvia

Barons, Krišjānis, ed. Latwju dainas. 1894-1915

Netherlands

Ven, D. J. van der. Van vrijen en trouwen op 't boerenland. 1929

Rome, Ancient

Rage-Brocard, Madeleine. Rites de mariage; la deductio in domum mariti. 1934

Russia

Opīsanie v" lītsakh" torzhestva, proīskhodivshago v" 1626 godu febralaꙗ 5, prī brakosochetaniī Gosudarꙗ TSarꙗ ī velīkago Knꙗzꙗ Mīkhaīla Feodorovīcha, s" Gosudaryneꙋ TSarītseꙋ Evdokieꙋ Luk'ꙗnovnoꙋ īz" rodv Strꙗshnevykh." 1810

Spain

Hispanic society of America. Wedding costume. 1931

United States

King, Mrs J. A. Weddings. 1927

Kingsland, Florence. The book weddings. 1902

Periodical

The Bride's magazine; So you're going to be married. 1934+

De **weelde** in Nederland. Bosch, Bernardus

Weerth, Ernst aus'm

(ed.) Kunstdenkmäler des christlichen mittelalters in den Rheinlanden. Leipzig, T. O. Weigel 1857-80
2pts. in 5v. 102pl.(13 col.) Q. & F.
Volume 3 published at Bonn by M. Cohen. The second part has especial value for costume of the middle ages
Lipperheide 389

(ed.) Der mosaikboden in St Gereon zu Cöln, restaurirt und gezeichnet von Toni Avenarius, nebst den damit verwandten mosaikböden Italiens. Bonn, Gedr. auf kosten des Vereins 1873
22p. illus. XII pl.(2 col.) F. (Verein von altertumsfreunden im Rheinlande, Bonn. Fest-programm zu Winckelmanns geburtstage, 1872-73)
Contains material on costume of the 11th century
Lipperheide 394. LC 17-20110

Weese, Arthur

Die Cäsar-teppiche im Historischen museum zu Bern; hrsg. vom Verein zur förderung des museums. Tafeln. Bern, A. Francke 1911
23p. 4 col.pl. F.
Legends in German and French. Plate 1, Caesar und Crassus verreisen in ihre provinzen; plate 2, Caesars sieg über Ariovist; plate 3, Caesars überschreitung des Rubikon; plate 4, Caesar zieht als triumphator in Rom ein

Wegner, Richard Nikolaus

Volkslied, tracht und rasse; bilder und alte lieder deutscher bauern. München, Knorr & Hirth [1934]
51p. front. illus. sq.F.
LC 36-25665

Wegweiser durch die urgeschichte Schlesiens. Mertins, Oskar

Die **wehrmacht** der Oesterreichisch-ungarischen monarchie im jahre 1873. Jurnitschek, Alfred

Die **wehrmacht** der Türkei und Bulgariens. Mach, Richard von

Das **weib** bei den naturvölkern. Reitzenstein, F. E., freiherr von

Weib, dame, dirne; kultur- und sittengeschichte der deutschen frau. See Scherr, Johannes. Kulturgeschichte der deutschen frau

Das **weib** im leben der völker. Friedenthal, Albert

Das **weib** in der antiken kunst. Ahrem, Maximilian

Weibel, Walther

Ruszland. München, Delphin-verlag 1916
xxix,96p. illus. Q. (Die ganze welt im bilde)
Some of the plates show Russian costume of various periods
Bibliography: p xxix

Die **weibliche** kleidung und ihre sittlichen und leiblichen beziehungen. See Jones, M. M. Woman's dress

Die **weiblichen** haartrachten im ersten jahrhundert der römischen kaiserzeit. Steininger, Rudolph

Weideplätze der Mongolen im reiche der Chalcha. Consten, Hermann

Weiditz, Christoph

Das trachtenbuch des Christoph Weiditz, von seinen reisen nach Spanien (1529) und den Niederlanden (1531/32), nach der in der Bibliothek des Germanischen nationalmuseums zu Nürnberg aufbewahrten handschrift, hrsg. von dr. Theodor Hampe. Berlin, W. de Gruyter 1927
164p. illus. 154pl.(part col.) F. (Historische waffen und kostüme, bd.2)

Weidmann, Franz Carl

Der costum-ball am schlusse des carnevals 1826 bey ... dem k. groszbrittannischen bothschafter Sir Henry Wellesley ... Description du bal paré en costume. Wien, A. Strausz 1826
12p. 13 col.pl. Q.
Lipperheide 2825

Weigall, Arthur Edward Pearse Brome

Ancient Egyptian works of art ... London, T. F. Unwin [1924]
xxii,353p. illus. Q.
LC 25-10127

Weigant, G. F.

(engr.) Gropp, Ignaz. Monumenta sepulchralia ecclesiae Ebracensis

Weigel, Christoph

Abbildung der gemein-nützlichen hauptstände von denen regenten und ihren so in friedens- als kriegs-zeiten zugeordneten bedienten an bisz auf alle künstler und handwercker nach jedes ambts- und beruffsverrichtungen ... gezeichnet. Regenspurg, 1698
676p. 211pl. Q.
Eighty-six of the plates are from J. and C. Luyken's *Menschelyke beezikheeden*
Lipperheide 1973

Icones omnium ad officinas aerarias pertinentium officialium et operariorum; Bildnisse aller hütten-beambten und bedienten. Nürnberg, C. Weigel 1710?
16p. 24 col.pl. D.
Many of the illustrations show German miners
German edition: *Abbildung und beschreibung derer sämtlichen schmelt-hutten-beamten und belienten* (Nürnberg, C. Weigel 1721)
Colas 14. Lipperheide 1993. LC CA29-702

Icones omnium ad rem metallicam spectantium officialium et operariorum; Bildnisse aller berg-beambten und bedienten. Nürnberg, C. Weigel 1710?
23p. 24 col.pl. D.
Many of the illustrations show German miners
German edition: *Abbildung und beschreibung derer sämtlichen berg-wercks-beamten und bedienten* (Nürnberg, C. Weigel 1721)
Colas 13. Lipperheide 1992. LC CA29-702

(engr.) Centi-folium stultorum in quarto

(pub.) Moor, J. B. van. Wahreste und neueste abbildung des türckischen hofes

Weigel, Hans

Habitus praecipuorum populorum, tam virorum quam foeminarum singulari arte depicti. Trachtenbuch: darin fast allerley und der fürnembsten nationen, die heutigs tags bekandt sein, kleidungen, beyde wie es bey manns und weibspersonen gebreuchlich, mit allem vleiss abgerissen sein, sehr lustig und kurtzweilig zusehen. Nürmberg, H. Weigel 1577
4 l. 220pl. F.
Woodcuts, after drawings by Jost Amman, show full-length figures of men and women
Reprinted (Ulm, J. Gölin 1639)
Colas 113-14. Lipperheide 7-8

Die **weihe** des Eros Uranios. Hirt, A. L., and Brühl, K. F. M. P., graf von

Weimar, Wilhelm

Die daguerreotypie in Hamburg, 1839-1860; ein beitrag zur geschichte der photographie. Hamburg, O. Meissner 1915
81p. illus. 49 numb.pl.(incl.ports.) sq.Q. (Veröffentlichungen des Hamburgischen museums für kunst und gewerbe)
Many plates show 19th century dress as worn in Hamburg
LC 29-549

Weinberg, Louis

Color in everyday life; a manual for lay students, artisans and artists; the principles of color combination and color arrangement, and their applications in dress, home, business, the theatre and community play. New York, Moffat, Yard 1918
xvi,343p. XVI pl.(incl.front.) O.
Thirty colored papers in pockets at end. Pages 70-102 are on color in dress
LC 18-22834

Weingartner, Josef

Das kirchliche kunstgewerbe der neuzeit. Innsbruck-Tyrolia a.-g. 1927
489p. illus. Q.
Many illustrations show ecclesiastical vestments worn in Europe from the 15th to the 18th centuries

Weingartner liederhandschrift

Die Weingartner liederhandschrift; hrsg. von Franz Pfeiffer und F. Fellner. Stuttgart, Literarischer verein 1843
xiv,338p. col.front. 25 col.illus. O. (Bibliothek des Literarischen vereins in Stuttgart, [bd.] v, [1])
Lipperheide 379. LC 2-9096

Weis, Johann Martin

Costumes d'hommes et de femmes de Strasbourg. No place, [1740]
24pl. O.
Colas 3066

Nouveau calendrier du diocèse de Strasbourg pour l'an 1760 avec une représentation des modes et habillements de Strasbourg. Strasbourg, 1745
S.
Colas 3067

Représentation des fêtes données par la ville de Strasbourg pour la convalescence du roy; à l'arrivée et pendant le séjour de sa majesté en cette ville. Paris, L. Aubert 1750?
20p. front. 11 double pl. F.
Lipperheide 2715

Weismann, Heinrich

Das allgemeine deutsche schützenfest zu Frankfurt am Main, juli 1862 ... unter mitwirkung verschiedener künstler auf stein gezeichnet von Ferd. Carl Klimsch. Frankfurt am Main, H. Keller 1863
170p. 23pl.(19 col.) Q.
Lipperheide 3008

Weiss, Hermann
Geschichte des kostüms ... 1. abt. Geschichte des kostüms der vornehmsten völker des alterthmus ... 1. theil: Afrika. Berlin, F. Dümmler 1853
xxii,406p. O.
No more published
Colas 3062. Lipperheide 137

Kostümkunde. Stuttgart, Ebner und Seubert 1860-72
3v. in 5. illus. O.
A second enlarged edition (Stuttgart, Ebner & Seubert 1881-83. 2v.) was never completed
Contents: v 1 Handbuch der geschichte der tracht ... der völker des alterthums; v2 Geschichte der tracht ... im mittelalter vom 4ten bis zum 14ten jahrhundert; v3 Geschichte der tracht ... vom 14ten jahrhundert bis auf die gegenwart
Colas 3063-65. Costume index. Lipp. 71-72

Weiss, Jean Martin. See Weis, Johann Martin

Weiss, Johann Martin. See Weis, Johann Martin

Weisshäkel-muster. Hennings, Emma

Weissmann, Adolf
Der dirigent im 20. jahrhundert. Berlin, Propyläen-verlag 1925
195p. illus. pl. ports. O.
LC 26-8790

Weisz, Otto
Feldgrau in krieg und frieden; uniformtafeln. Berlin, H. S. Hermann 1916-17
3pts. col.illus. ob.S.

Der **weisz** kunig. Treitz-Saurwein, Marx, von Ehrentreitz

Weite welt. See note under Vom fels zum meer

The **well-dressed** woman. Ecob, H. G.

The **well-dressed** woman. Hallmark, Harrydele

The **well** dressed woman. Joy, Lilian

Wellman, Katharine
Beauty begins at home; how to make and use cosmetics. New York, Covici-Friede [c1936]
xii,336p. O.
LC 36-21291

Wells, Jane Warren
Dress and look slender. Scranton, Pa., Personal arts company [c1924]
185p. illus. O.
LC 24-24467

Wells, Margery
Clothes economy for well dressed women. New York, Dodd, Mead 1927
95p. D.
LC 27-24961

Wells, Rhea. See Grimball, E. B., jt. auth.

Wells, Rosalie
Fans. Washington, D. C., 1928
42p. front. pl. D.
LC 29-6323

Wellstein
(illus.) Exerzier-reglement für die Eidgenössische linien u. leichte infanterie

Welper, Eberhard
Neu gestellter schreib-kalender auf das jahr ... 1748. Strassburg, M. Bauschinger 1749?
16pl. T.
Colas 3068

Welsh, Silvia M.
(tr.) Dürer, Albrecht. The complete woodcuts of Albrecht Dürer

Welsh costumes. London, Rock and co. 1853
16 col.pl. ob.Ti.
Cover title

Die **Welt** der frau. See Die Gartenlaube

Die **welt** des tänzers. Laban, Rudolf von

Weltliche lustige newe kunststück der jetzigen welt. See Bry, J. T. de. Emblemata secularia

Wendel, Friedrich
Die mode in der karikatur. Dresden, P. Aretz 1928
300p. col.front. illus. 16 col.pl. Q.
Colas 3069

Das **Wendentum** in der Niederlausitz. Müller, Ewald

Wends. See Germany—Lusatia

Wentzel, Johann Friedrich
(illus.) Besser, Johann von. Preussische krönungs-geschichte

Die **werke** von William Hogarth. See note under Hogarth, William. The works of William Hogarth, from the original plates

Werkzeuge und waffen. Klemm, G. F.

Werner, Edward Theodore Chalmers
Chinese weapons. Shanghai, The Royal Asiatic society North China branch 1932
41p. 59pl. on 30 l. Q.
LC 33-19341

Wessely, Joseph Eduard
Die landsknechte, eine culturhistorische studie. Görlitz, C. A. Starke 1877
11p. 30pl. F.
Colas 3070. Lipperheide 2100

Westafrika. Mansfeld, Alfred

Westall, William
(illus.) Combe, William. History of the University of Cambridge
(illus.) Combe, William. History of the University of Oxford

The **West-End** hand-book of liveries. Prewett, F. T. & company, London

The **West-end** system. Giles, E. B., and others

West Indies
Carpenter, F. G. Lands of the Caribbean. 1925

See also Puerto Rico

Westerberg, Ludwik
Europeiska nationerna, deras seder, bruk och klädedrägter. Stockholm, 1848
29 col.pl. Q.
Colas 3071

Westerhout, Arnold von
(engr.) Buonanni, Filippo. Ordinum religiosorum in ecclesia militanti catalogus

Westermarck, Edvard Alexander
The history of human marriage ... 5th ed., rewritten. London, Macmillan 1921
3v. O.
Bibliographical foot-notes
Contains material on the psychology of dress
LC 22-10725

Westermayer, C.
(engr.) Guts-Muths, J. C. F. Gymnastik für die jugend

Western reserve historical society, Cleveland, O. King collection
The Charles G. King collection of books on costume. Cleveland, O. [Columbus, O. The Champlin press] 1914
48p. 6pl.(incl.col.front.) O. (Tract no93, Western reserve historical society)
Annotated. Foreword signed: R. M. T. [i.e. Ruth M. Tiffany]
LC 14-17882

Western Tibet and the British borderland. Sherring, C. A.

Westfälisches trachtenbuch. Jostes, Franz

Westlake, Mrs Inez B.
American Indian designs. Philadelphia, H. C. Perleberg [c1925-30]
2v. pl.(part col.) F.
Contents: [1st ser.] Thirty-six plates of which sixteen are in color, containing 200 designs from prehistoric times to modern, with explanatory index; 2d ser. Containing more than 200 designs illustrating the gradual development into modern forms; thirty-six plates of which six are in color; explanatory text
LC 25-9212

Weston, Mrs Lilla Belle Norton (Folts)
Vestments and how to make them. Milwaukee, The Young churchman co. 1914
xi,89p. front.(port.) illus. diagrs. Q. $2
LC 14-12590

Westphalia. See Germany—Westphalia

Westwood, John Obadiah
Fac-similes of the miniatures and ornaments of Anglo-Saxon & Irish manuscripts; drawn on stone by W. R. Tymms, chromo-lithographed by Day and Son. London, Quaritch [1868]
xv,155p. 53 col.pl. F.
Added title page in French: *Les manuscrits Anglo-Saxons et Irlandais fac-similes de miniatures et ornements du VIIe au Xe siècle*
Shows saints and Biblical characters as depicted in manuscripts from the 7th to the 10th century

Wetter, George van
Les origines de la parure aux temps paléolithiques. Bruxelles, Lamertin 1920
170p. illus. pl. Q. (Académie royale de Belgique. Classe des beaux-arts)

Weyditz, Christoffel. See Widitz, Christoffel

Weyer, Gabriel
(illus.) Heussler, Sebastian. New künstlich fechtbuch

Wharton, Anne Hollingsworth
Colonial days & dames; with illustrations by E. S. Holloway. Philadelphia, J. B. Lippincott 1895
248p. front. illus. D.
LC 2-5482

Heirlooms in miniatures; with a chapter on miniature painting by Emily Drayton Taylor. Philadelphia & London, J. B. Lippincott 1898
xix,11-259p. col.front. 90 port. on 51 l. O.
Reproduces miniature portraits of Americans from Colonial days to the middle of the nineteenth century. Head and shoulder portraits which show styles of hair dressing and neckwear of various periods
"Authorities consulted": p ix
LC 10-12605

Salons colonial and republican, by Anne Hollingsworth Wharton, with numerous reproductions of portraits and miniatures of men and women prominent in colonial life and in the early days of the republic. Philadelphia & London, J. B. Lippincott 1900
xv,11-286p. col.front. ports. O.
LC 0-2172

Social life in the early republic, by Anne Hollingsworth Wharton ... with numerous reproductions of portraits, miniatures, and residences. Philadelphia & London, J. B. Lippincott 1902
xvi,13-346p. col.front. pl. ports. O.
LC 2-29033

What dress makes of us. Quigley, Dorothy

What is my tartan? Adam, Frank

What she wore. Felix, E.

What they wore. Jackson, Margaret

What to wear and when to wear it. Praga, Mrs Alfred

The **what,** where, when and how of a man's cravat. Keiser, J. R.

Wheatley, Francis
Cries of London; in aid of the "Daily news" wireless for hospitals fund ... Music arranged by Hubert Sullivan Ryan. [London, no publisher, 1925]
30 l. pl.(mostly colored) port. F.
Issued in 14 parts. Facsimile of a collection published about 1790. Another edition was issued in 1804 (London, B. Johnson o.p.) Published also under title: *Itinerant trades of London.* Many editions are known. The same plates are in William Roberts' *Cries of London*
Colas 3072

(illus.) Roberts, William. The cries of London

Wheeler, Stephen
History of the Delhi coronation Durbar held on the first of January 1903, to celebrate the coronation of His Majesty King Edward VII, emperor of India, comp. official papers by order of the viceroy and governor-general of India. London, J. Murray 1904
xiv,347p. ports. pl. plans, maps. sq.F.
LC A13-2101

When men wore muffs. Price, Sir H. P.

When underwear counted. Kitchens, Matilda

When we were strolling players in the east. Miln, Mrs L. J.

Whibley, Leonard
(ed.) A companion to Greek studies. 4th ed. rev. and enl. Cambridge, Univ. press 1931
xxxvi,787p. illus. maps(part fold.) O. $8
Bibliography at end of each article
The following chapters have costume interest: Engraved gems, by H. B. Walters p366-69: Minoan and Mycenean period, 7th and 6th centuries, 5th & 4th centuries, Hellenistic period; Arms and armor p548-52; Dress, by A. J. Wace and Lady Evans p618-32
Costume index. LC 17-3148

The **whirlpool** of Europe, Austria-Hungary and the Habsburgs. Colquhoun, A. R., and Colquhoun, Mrs E. M. C.

Whirsker
Les métamorphoses de Melpomène et de Thalie, ou caractères dramatiques des comédies françoise et italienne. Paris, L'auteur ca1770
2 l. 23 col.pl. O.
Published also in England, with same collation (Londres, R. Sayer 1772) The collection is reproduced in Arnault's *Souvenirs*
Plates also exist in black and white. They show "scènes théâtrales"
Colas 3073-74

White, Gwen
A picture book of ancient & modern dolls, written and illustrated by Gwen White. New York, Macmillan; London, A. & C. Black 1928
44p. front. illus.(part col.) col.pl. Q. $1.75; 5s, o.p.
Dolls of various countries and periods
Costume index. LC 29-7127

White falcon, Order of the
Haagen, C. E. C. Dissertatio historica de Saxo-Vinariensi vigilantiae ordine. 1734

Whitelaw, Charles Edward. See Jackson, H. J. European hand firearms of the sixteenth, seventeenth & eighteenth centuries

Whittock, Nathaniel
Costumes of the members of the University of Cambridge. London, N. Whittock 1840?
1 fold.pl.(23 col.illus.) Ti.
The costumes of the members of the University of Oxford. London, N. Whittock 1840?
17 col.pl. T.
Plates apparently are copied from Whittock's *Topographical and historical description*
A topographical and historical description of the university and city of Oxford ... to which is added, correct delineations of the costume of the members of the university. London, I. T. Hinton 1828
102p. front. pl.(1 fold. part col.) Q.
Added engraved title-page: *The microcosm of Oxford containing a series of views* (Oxford, N. Whittock, etc.)
Plates drawn and lithographed by the author

The **whole** art of dress, or The road to elegance and fashion ... being a treatise upon ... gentlemen's costume ... explaining ... the most becoming assortment of colours and style of dress and undress in all their varieties ... accompanied by hints for the toilette ... by a cavalry officer. London, E. Wilson royal exchange 1830
100p. col.front. 6pl. D.
Colas 3075. Lipperheide 3261

The **whole** work of Mr. Latham's books of faulconry. Latham, Simon

Wholesale army, navy and volunteer, helmet, cap, and accoutrement makers. Jones, W., and company, tailors

Whymper, E.
(illus.) Manning, Samuel. Swiss pictures

Wicar, Jean Baptiste Joseph
(illus.) Mongez, Antoine. Tableaux statues, bas reliefs et camées de la Galerie de Florence et du Palais Pitti

Wideman, Elias
Comitium gloriae centum qua sanguine qua virtute illustrium heroum iconibus instructum. Ed. corr. [Augsburg, 1649]
2v. 202pl. F.
Two hundred half-length portraits showing dress of 1642 to 1649
Lipperheide 680

Widitz, Christoffel
(illus.) Mair, P. H. Bericht vnd anzeigen aller Herren Geschlecht der loblichen Statt Augspurg.

Wie die mechtige erbkünigreich unnd fürstentumb ... kommen sein. Isenberg, Walther

Wie sehen die armeen der gegner des dreibundes im kriege aus. Leipzig, Ruhl [1914]
12p. fold.col.pl. D.

Wied-Neuwied, Maximilian Alexander Philipp, prinz von
Reise in das innere Nord-America in den jahren 1832 bis 1834. Coblenz, J. Hœlscher 1839-41
2v. illus. F. and atlas of 81 col.pl.
Also published in French: *Voyage dans l'intérieur de l'Amérique du Nord* (Paris, A. Bertrand 1840-43. 3v. illus. pl. fold. map, plan. O. and atlas of 81 col.pl.)
LC 2-5381, 2-5383 (French ed.)
Reise nach Brasilien in den jahren 1815 bis 1817; von Maximilian, prinz zu Wied-Neuwied. Frankfurt a. M., H. L. Brönner, 1820-21
2v. pl. F. and portfolio of 22pl.(5 col.) 3 maps. F.
Plates show some Indians of Brazil. Colored plates show weapons
The English translation is entitled: *Travels in Brazil, in the years 1815, 1816, 1817.* (London, H. Colburn 1820)
LC 12-20444
Travels in the interior of North America. Tr. from the German, by H. Evans Lloyd. To accompany the original series of eighty-one elaborately-coloured plates. London, Ackermann 1843-44
x,520p. illus. F. and atlas of 80 col.pl.
Translation of his *Reise in das innere Nord-America*
Atlas has title: *Illustrations to Maximilian Prince of Wied's Travels in the interior of North America* (1844) The plates are by Karl Bodmer. They also exist in black and white
Also reprinted in the series: Early western travels, edited by R. G. Goldthwaites, with title *Maximilian, prince of Wied's Travels in the interior of North America, 1832-34.* (Cleveland, O., A. H. Clark 1906. 3v. pl. facsim. O. and atlas of 81pl.)
LC 2-5382, 6-19696 (reprint)

Wien wie es ist. Gross-Hoffinger, A. J.

Wiener bürgermilitär. Wien, J. Eder ca1805
10 col.pl. D.
Plates are not numbered
Colas 3077

Das **Wiener** burgtheater. Lothar, Rudolph

Wiener chic. Jahrg 1, 1891-1932. Wien, G. Lyon
Illus. col.pl. F.
Published monthly. Irregular. Absorbed by *Die Kunst in der mode*
Colas 3078. Lipperheide 4805

Wiener-costüme vom mittelalter bis zur gegenwart. Scheurer, J. E.

Die **Wiener** elegante; zeitschrift für kunst, literatur und industrie. 1.-26. jahrg. 1842-1867. Wien, Prandel
26v. col.illus. Q.
Thirty-six numbers a year

Wiener frauen-erwerb-verein. See Schnittmusterbuch; anleitung zum wäschezuschneiden

Wiener hausfrauen-zeitung; organ für hauswirtschaftl. interessen. 1.-33. jahrg. 1875-1907. Wien, Perles
33v. col.illus. Q.-F.
Published weekly
Subtitle, 1875-1890: organ des Wiener hausfrauen-vereines
Lipeprheide 4750

Wiener mode. 1. jahrg, 1887+ Wien, Rob-verlag
Illus. Q.
Published semi-monthly. Current 1937
Colas 3079. Lipperheide 4788

Wiener moden-zeitung und zeitschrift für kunst, schöne litteratur und theater. See Wiener zeitschrift für kunst, litteratur, theater und mode

Wiener modespiegel; wochenschrift für mode, schöne literatur, novellistik, kunst und theater. 1.-7. jahrg., 1853-1859. Wien, J. F. Gresz
7v. illus. col.pl. Q.
Published weekly
Colas 3081. Lipperheide 4670

Wiener spitzenausstellung 1906. Vienna. Österreichisches museum für kunst und industrie

Wiener strassenbilder. Schwarz, Ignaz, ed.

Wiener szenische kunst. Gregor, Joseph

Wiener theater zeitung. See Allgemeine theaterzeitung und originalblatt

Das **Wiener** volksleben. Moser, J. B.

Wiener zeitschrift für kunst, litteratur, theater und mode. 1816-1848. Wien
Col.illus. O.
Title change: 1816-June 1817, *Wiener moden-zeitung und zeitschrift für kunst, schöne litteratur und theater*
Colas 3080. Lipperheide 4600

Wienerstadt, lebensbilder aus der gegenwart; geschildert von Wiener schriftstellern, gezeichnet von Myrbach, Mangold, Zasche, Engelhart und Hey. Wien, F. Tempsky; Leipzig, G. Freytag 1895
466p. 328 illus. 5pl.(3 col.) O.
Text by V. Chiavacci, and others
Lipperheide 899

Wien's bewaffnete bürger im jahre 1806. Mansfeld, Heinrich, and Biller, B.

Wien's Kaiserliches zeughaus. Leber, F. O., edler von

Wierx, Hieronymus
(illus.) Illustrium quos Belgium habuit pictorum effigies

Wierzbicki, Ludowik
Wzory przemysłu domowego ... włościani na rusi wydane przez muzeum Przemsyłowe miejskie ... Ornamente der hausindustrie ... ruthenischern bauern; hrsg. vom Stadtischen gewerbe-museum. Lwów. 1880-89
10v. 2 illus. 107 col.pl. Q.
Volumes 1, 2 and 8: Stickereimuster
Lipperheide 3965

Wiesbaden. See Germany—Hesse

Wieseler, Friedrich. See Müller, K. O. Denkmäler der alten kunst

Wietz, J. K.
Abbildungen sämmtlicher geistlichen orden männlich- und weiblichen geschlechts in der katholischen kirche; hrsg. von Peter Bohmanns erben ... Text von F. K. Wietz. Prag, Sommer 1821
3v. 233 col.pl. O.
Volume 3 has title: *Abbildungen sämmtlicher geistlichen und weltlichen ritter- und damenorden*
Colas 3082. Lipperheide 1849

See also Doyé F. von S. Die alten trachten der männlichen und weiblichen orden sowie der geistlichen mitglieder der ritterlichen orden mit erläuterungen zu Peter Bohmanns abbildungen von F. K. Wietz

Wig and gown. Harvey, R. S.

Wigs
Biographie einer perüque. 1806
Creer, Edwin. Board work; or the art of wig-making. 1887
Deguerle, J. M. N. Éloge des perruques, enrichi de notes plus amples que le texte; par le docteur Akerlio [pseud.] 1799
Garsault, F. A. P. de. Art du perruquier. 1767
Gussmann, Paul. Zeichenvorlagen für den fachschul-unterricht im perückenmachergewerbe. 1910
Nicolaï, Friedrich. Über den gebrauch der falschen haare und perrucken in alten und neuern zeiten. 1801
Nouvelles étrennes curieuses des incroyables, merveilleuses, inconcevables, et des raisonnables de Paris ... la notice de 30 différentes perruques à la mode ... dans des pays divers 1796
Pacichelli, Giambattista. Schediasma juridico-philologicum tripartitum. 1693
Rango, K. T. De capillamentis seu vulgo parucquen. 1663
Thiers, J. B. Histoire des perruques. 1690

See also Hair-dressing

Wilczek, Johann Nepomuk, graf von
Erinnerungen eines waffensammlers; 2. verb. aufl. Wien, R. Lechner 1908
24p. front.(port.) 69 illus. on 16pl. O.
A collection of swords of the 11th to the 19th centuries

Wild tribes of Davao district, Mindanao. Cole, F. C.

Wilde, Oscar
(ed.) Woman's world

Wilhelmi, Helene
Muster für strümpfe und muster für socken mit anleitung, dieselben zu stricken. Stuttgart, R. Roth 1869
1 l. 30 illus. Q.
Lipperheide 4102

Wilkie, Sir David
Sir David Wilkie's sketches in Turkey, Syria and Egypt, 1840 & 1841. London, Graves and Warmsley 1843
25pl. F.
Lipperheide 1436

Wilkie, Sir David—*Continued*
Sir David Wilkie's sketches, Spanish & oriental, drawn on stone by Joseph Nash. London, H. Graves 1846
3p.l. 26pl. F.
Lipperheide 1230. LC 11-29134

Wilkins, William Henry
Mrs. Fitzherbert and George IV. New York [etc.] Longmans, Green 1905
xx,476p. front. pl. ports. facsims. O.
List of authorities: p464-66
LC 5-37590

Wilkinson, Sir John Gardner
The Egyptians in the time of the Pharaohs. London, Bradbury & Evans 1857
xvi,282p. 2pl. illus. D.

The manners and customs of the ancient Egyptians. New ed. rev. and cor. by Samuel Birch. New York, Dodd, Mead [1879]
3v. fronts.(2 col. 1 fold.) illus. pl.(part col. part fold.) O. $8, o.p.
Costume index. LC 9-14353

A popular account of the ancient Egyptians. London, J. Murray; New York, M. Bradley 1854
2v. fronts. illus. D. o.p.
Originally published by Harper at $2
An abridgment of his *Manners and customs of the ancient Egyptians,* with some material added
Costume index. Lipp. 139. LC 3-22256

Wilkinson, Norman L.
(illus.) Swinburne, H. L. The royal navy

Will, Jean Martin
(engr.) Les différens goûts et nouvelles modes de coeffures

(engr.) Samlung der ruszischen nationaltrachten. Collection de manières de se vêtir de la nation russienne. Aug. vind. ca1780
22pl. sq.Q.
Each plate shows two costume figures. Explanations are in German and French
Colas 3083. Lipperheide 1338

(engr.) Samlung europaeischer national trachten. Collection de manières de se vêtir des nations de l'Europe. Aug. Vind. ca1780
3v. 96pl. O.
Shows town and folk dress of Germany, Austria and Switzerland of this period. Each plate has two costume figures, a man and a woman. Legends are in German and French
Colas 3084. Lipperheide 565

Wille, Johann Georg
(engr.) Parrocel, C. Reitres et lansquenets

Willemin, Nicolas Xavier
Choix de costumes civils et militaires des peuples de l'antiquité, leur instrumens de musique, leurs meubles, et les décorations intérieures de leurs maisons, d'après les monumens antiques, avec un texte tiré des anciens auteurs. Paris, auteur, an VI-X, 1798-1802
2v. 180pl.(incl. added engr. t.-p.) F.
Colas 3085. Costume index. Lipperheide 109. LC 11-19835

Monuments français inédits pour servir à l'histoire des arts depuis le VIe siècle jusqu'au commencement du XVIIe. Choix de costumes civils et militaires, d'armes, armures, instruments de musique, meubles de toute espèce, et de décorations intérieures et extérieures des maisons, dessinés, gravés et coloriés d'après les originaux, par N. X. Willemin ... Classés chronologiquement et accompagnés d'un texte historique et descriptif, par André Pottier. Paris, Mlle. Willemin 1839
2v. 300pl.(part col.) sq.F.
Colas 3086. Costume index. Lipperheide 1084. LC 2-5401

(engr.) Engelhardt, C. M. Herrad von Landsperg ... und ihr werk: Hortus deliciarum

William Hogarth, the cockney's mirror. Bowen, Marjorie, pseud.

Williams
An historical account of the rise and progress of the Bengal native infantry, from its first formation in 1757, to 1796. London, J. Murray 1817
387p. 4 col.pl. O.
Plates show uniforms
Lipperheide 2266

Williams, C.
(engr.) Dress and address

Williams, Caroline Ransom
Gold and silver jewelery and related objects. New York, N. Y. historical society 1924
xi,281p. 38pl. Q. (New York historical society. Catalogue of Egyptian antiquities, no 1-160) $10
Includes bibliographies
Costume index

Williams, Dion
Army and navy uniforms and insignia; how to know rank, corps and service in the military and naval forces of the United States and foreign countries. New York, F. A. Stokes [c1918]
302p. front. illus. pl.(part col.) ports. D. $1.75, o.p.
Part of the plates printed on both sides
Costume index. LC 18-2798

Williams, John, ab Ithel
Glossary of terms used for articles of British dress and armour. London, Pickering 1851
68p. O.

Williams, Leonard
The arts and crafts of older Spain. London [etc.] T. N. Foulis 1907
3v. fronts. illus. 170pl. D. (The world of art series)
Contents: v 1 Gold, silver, and jewel work, Iron-work, Bronzes, Arms; v2 Furniture, Ivories, Pottery, Glass; v3 Textile fabrics
Volume 3 contains material on costume of the eighteenth and nineteenth centuries, and on lace
Bibliography: v3 p[259]-68
LC 8-15871

The land of the Dons. London, Cassell 1902
xii,398p. pl. port. O. 15s, o.p.
Photographs show regional costume of Spain
Costume index. LC 3-3224

Williams, William Mattieu
Philosophy of clothing. London, T. Laurie 1890
155p. O. 4s

Williamson, George Charles
(comp.) Morgan, J. P. Catalogue of the collection of jewels and precious works of art

Williamson, Thomas
The costume and customs of modern India; from a collection of drawings by Charles Doyley, esq. engraved by J. H. Clark and C. Dubourg; with a preface and copious descriptions, by Captain Thomas Williamson. London, E. Orme [1823]
xxiii p. 38 l. 20 col.pl. F.
Plates bear the date of an earlier edition published under title *The European in India* (London 1813)
Colas 887-888. Lipp. 1486. LC 11-20568

Willoughby, Charles Clark
Antiquities of the New England Indians, with notes on the ancient cultures of the adjacent territory. Cambridge, Mass. Peabody museum of American archaeology and ethnology, Harvard university 1935
314p. illus.(incl.maps) diagrs. O.
LC 35-12177

Wilpert, Josef
Die gewandung der Christen in den ersten jahrhunderten; vornehmlich nach den katakomben-malereien dargestellt. Köln, J. P. Bachem 1898
58. 11pl. O.
Plates printed on both sides, numbered 1-22. Bibliographical foot-notes
Colas 3087. Lipperheide 272e

Die römischen mosaiken und malereien der kirchlichen bauten vom IV. bis XIII. jahrhundert. Freiburg im Breisgau, Herder 1916
4v. illus. 300 col.pl.(24 fold.) F.
The 2 vols. of text paged continuously
Bibliographical foot-notes
LC 22-20034

Wilson, Effingham
(pub.) The whole art of dress

Wilson, Lillian May
The Roman toga. Baltimore, Johns Hopkins press 1924
132p. 2 illus.(1 col.) pl. diagrs. O. (Johns Hopkins university studies in archaeology, no 1)
Bibliography: p129
Costume index. LC 25-2260

A study of the Roman toga. Baltimore, Johns Hopkins press 1924
38p. illus. pl. O.
Thesis, Johns Hopkins university 1924. An extract from the author's *The Roman toga*
LC 25-6863

Wilson, The H. W., company, firm, publishers
Costume index. See entry under Monro, I. S., and Cook, D. E., eds.

Wilton, Mary Margaret (Stanley) Egerton, countess of
The art of needle-work, from the earliest ages; 3d ed. London, H. Colburn 1841
ix,405p. O.
Also included in Owen, Mrs Henry. *The illuminated book of needlework.* 1847
Lipperheide 3855

The book of costume: or, Annals of fashion, from the earliest period to the present time. By a lady of rank. Illustrated with upwards of two hundred engravings on wood, by the most eminent artists. New ed. London, H. Colburn 1847
xii,482p. col.front. illus. O. 10s 6d, o.p.
Published anonymously. First edition 1846
Colas 386. Costume index. Lipperheide 63. LC 20-14742

Wimples and crisping pins. Child, T.

[**Winckelmann**]
[Garde royale prussienne] Winckelmann ca1835
12 col.pl. Q.
Colas 3088

Winckler, E.
(engr.) Dergny, Dieudonné. Usages, coutumes et croyances ou livre des choses curieuses

Winckler-Tannenberg, Friedrich
(illus.) Handke, Hermann. Der bubikopf von Agamemmon bis Stresemann

Wingate, Charles Edgar Lewis
Shakespeare's heroes on the stage ... with illustrations from photographs and rare prints. New York and Boston, T. Y. Crowell [c1896]
x,348p. incl.front. pl. D.
LC 12-40424

Shakespeare's heroines on the stage ... with illustrations from photographs and rare prints. New York and Boston, T. Y. Crowell [1895]
ix,355p. front. ports. D.
LC 12-40425

Wingfield, Lewis Strange
Notes on civil costume in England from the conquest to the regency, as exemplified in the International health exhibition, South Kensington. London, W. Clowes 1884
xxxiv,38p. col.front. col.pl. Q. 10s 6d, o.p.
Colas 3089. Costume index. Lipperheide 1014. LC 17-28754

Winkler, Friedrich
Die flämische buchmalerei des XV. und XVI. jahrhunderts; künstler und werke von den brüdern van Eyck bis zu Simon Bening. Leipzig, E. A. Seemann 1925
210p. illus. F.
"Die handschriftenverzeichnis nach orten": p[155]-209
Shows Flemish dress
LC A33-1090

Winlock, Herbert Eustis
The treasure of El Lāhūn. New York, 1934
xvi,80p. illus.(incl.plans) XVI pl. sq.F. (The Metropolitan museum of art. Department of Egyptian art. [Publications] v. IV)
Each plate accompanied by guard sheet with descriptive letterpress
"Key to references cited": p xiii-xvi
LC 34-20192

Winslow, Leon Loyal. See De Garmo, Charles, jt. auth.

Winter, Ferdinand
Die kämme aller aller zeiten von der steinzeit bis zur gegenwart ... The combs of all times from the stone age to the present day (the "rake's progress"); a collection of reproductions

Winter, Ferdinand—*Continued*
with notes ... Le peigne à travers les âges. Leipzig, H. A. L. Degener [1907]
12p. 84pl. F.
German, English and French text
Colas 3090. LC 21-17318

Winter, Georg Simon
De re equaria tractatio nova complectens. Norimbergae, J. Andrea & W. Endter 1672
34pl. F.
Also exists in a German translation: *Traktat von der reith-kunst* (Ulm, 1678)

Winter, Max
Kleidung und putz der frau nach den altfranzösischen chansons de geste. Marburg, N. G. Elwert 1886
65p. O. (Ausgaben und abhandlungen aus dem gebiete der romanischen philologie 45)
"Verzeichnis der abkürzungen des gelesenen texte": p[3]-7
Colas 3091. Lipperheide 401m. LC 22-18488

Winter, Nevin Otto
Poland of to-day and yesterday. Boston, L. C. Page 1913
xii,349p. front. pl. ports. fold.map. O. $3, o.p.
Bibliography: p342-43
Costume index. LC 13-21031

Winter in Lapland and Sweden. Broke, Sir A. De C., 2d bart.

Winter sketches in Lapland. Broke, Sir A. De C., 2d bart.

Winter- und sommer-gärtlein aller wolkönnenden jungfrauen; aus welchen unterschiedliche frücht und blumen abzubrocken auch zu einem däntzerl gegenwärtiges als musicalische noten allen embsigen frau-und jungfrauen. [Linz] 1691
14 l. 36pl. sq.D.
Lipperheide 3923

Winterburn, Mrs Florence (Hull)
Principles of correct dress; including chapters by Jean Worth and Paul Poiret. New York and London, Harper 1914
245p. D.
LC 14-6810

Winterfeld, Adolf Wilhelm Ernst von
Geschichte des ritterlichen ordens St. Johannis vom Spital zu Jerusalem. Berlin, M. Berendt 1859
xvi,896p. 16pl. 2 maps. Q.

Winterschmidt, Adam Wolffgang
Das studentenleben ... Nurnberg, ca1760
30pl. sq.O.
Lipperheide 2025

Winzer, C. F.
(illus.) Johnston, R. F. The Chinese drama

Wirrich, Heinrich
Ordenliche beschreibung des ... beylags oder hochzeit so da gehalten ist worden durch ... Herrn Carolen ertzhertzog zu Osterreich ... mit ... Maria zu Bayrn den XXVI. Augusti in ... Wienn. Wienn, durch B. Eberum 1571
Lipperheide 2618

Wirsching, Joseph
Die manteltracht im mittelalter. München, Hübschmann 1915
37p. 6pl. Q.
Würzburg dissertation, 1915

Wisard
Collection de costumes suisses dans leurs genres actuels. Berne, ca1818
24pl. Q.
Published also in reduced size
Colas 3092

Types et costumes féminins de la Suisse. [Berne] 1818
16pl. Q.
Colas 3093

Wise, Claude Merton, jt. auth. See Dabney, Edith

Wiskovatoff. See Viskovatov, A. V.

Wissendorffs, Henri. See Barons, Krišjānis, jt. ed.

Wissenschaftlichen institut des Elsass-Lothringer im Reich, Frankfurt am Main
Strassburger ansichten und trachtenbilder aus der zeit des dreissigjahrigen krieges. See Hollar, Wenceslaus

Wissler, Clark
Costumes of the Plains Indians. New York, American museum of natural history 1915
p39-91. illus. O. (Anthropological papers of the American museum of natural history. v17, pt2) pa 50c
Costume index. LC 17-28721

Distribution of moccasin decorations among the Plains tribes. New York, American museum of natural history 1927
23p. illus. O. (Anthropological papers of the American museum of natural history. v20, pt 1)
LC 27-17285

Indian costumes in the United States; a guide to the study of the collections in the museum; 2d ed. New York, American museum of natural history 1928?
32p. illus. O. ([American museum of natural history] Guide leaflet, no63) pa 15c
"Sources of information": p32
Costume index. LC 28-25732

North American Indians of the Plains; 3d ed. New York, American museum of natural history 1927
147p. illus. O. (American museum of natural history. Handbook ser. no 1) $1
Earlier editions, 1912 and 1920, differ slightly in pagination and illustrations
Bibliography: p143-44
Costume index. LC 22-26496 (2. ed.)

Structural basis to the decoration of costumes among the Plains Indians. New York, American museum of natural history 1916
p93-114. illus. O. (Anthropological papers of the American museum of natural history. v17, pt3)
Costume index. LC 17-28717

Wistrand, Per Gustaf Vilhelm
Svenska folkdräkter; kulturhistoriska studier. Med 30 färgtryck efter original af E. von Walterstorff, utgifna genom Nordiska museet. Stockholm, Aktiebolaget Hiertas bokförlag [1907]
160p. illus. 30 col.pl. Q.
Förord sigend: Bernard Salin
Swedish dress and jewelry of various regions
Costume index

With, Karl. See Krause, Gregor, jt. auth.

With a prehistoric people. Routledge, W. S., and Routledge, Mrs K. P.

With the Jewish child in home and synagogue. Levinger, Mrs E. C. E.

With the jungle folk. Cuming, E. W. D.

Witham, T. Maxwell. See Heathcote, J. M., and others. Skating

Witt, Henriette (Guizot) dame de

Les chroniqueurs de l'histoire de France depuis les origines jusqu'au XVIe siècle; texte abrégé, coordonné et traduit par Mme de Witt, née Guizot. Paris, Hachette 1883-95

4v. col.fronts. illus.(incl.facsims.) pl. (part col.) ports. Q.

"Liste chronologique des auteurs cités dans les Chroniqueurs de l'histoire de France": v4, p[641]-45

Contents: 1. sér. De Grégoire de Tours à Guillaume de Tyr. 1883; [2. sér.] Saint Louis et les croisades, Les premiers Valois. 1895; [3. sér.] Jeanne d'Arc et la guerre de cent ans. 1895; [4. sér.] Charles VII et Louis XI, La première guerre d'Italie. 1895

LC 4-27224

Witte, Fritz

(ed.) Die liturgischen gewänder und kirchlichen stickereien. See Cologne. Schnütgen-museum

Colas 3094

Wittman, William

Travels in Turkey, Asia-Minor, Syria, and across the desert into Egypt during the years 1799, 1800, and 1801, in company with the Turkish army, and the British military mission. London, R. Phillips 1803

xvi,595p. fold.front. 16 col.pl. fold. map, fold.facsim. Q.

The plates show costume

Published also in German translation *Reisen in der europäischen Türckey, Klein-asien, Syrien und Aegypten in den jahren 1799, 1800, 1801 und 1802 ... ubersetzt von J. A. Bergk* (Leipzig, W. Rein 1804-05. 2v. 18pl. [16 col.] O.)

Lipperheide 1426 (German ed.) LC 5-7121

Witze und anecdoten, Berliner. See Dörbeck, B. Berliner witze und anecdoten

Wlislocki, Heinrich von

Aus dem inneren leben der zigeuner; ethnologische mitteilungen. Berlin, E. Felber 1892

220p. 28 illus. O.

Lipperheide 897. LC 5-7446

Die **wochenstube** in der kunst. Müllerheim, Robert

Wocher, T.

(engr.) Forti, Alberto. Abbate Alberto Fortis Reise in Dalmatien

Woeiriot, Pierre

(illus.) Clément, Nicolas, de Treille. Austrasiae reges et duces epigrammatis

Wörterbuch der bekleidung. Eckardt, Theodor

Wörterbuch der mode, f. das schöne geschlecht u. seine freunde. Hamburg, Möller 1782

2v.

Woestyn, Eugène

Le livre de la coiffure. Paris, C. Ploche ca1850

46p. O.

A study of fashions in hair dressing in the second half of the 18th century

Colas 3095. Lipperheide 1704

Wohleingerichtete reitschule. See Eisenberg, Baron d'. Description du manége moderne

Die **wohlerfahrene** elegante stickerin. Höflich, Nannette

Wohlgemuth, Michael

(illus.) Der Schatzbehalter

(illus.) Schedel, Hartmann. Das buch der chroniken

Wojsko Polskie. Krôlestwo Polskie 1815-1830. Gembarzewski, Bronislaw

Wojsko Polskie. Ksietvoo Warszawskie 1807-1814. Gembarzewski, Bronislaw

Wolf, E.

Schweizerische armee; armée suisse. Basel, G. Wolf ca1850

13 col.pl. Q.

Colas 3096, 2701

Wolf, Georg Jacob

Ein jahrhundert München, 1800-1900; 3. aufl. Leipzig, H. Schmidt & C. Günther 1935

532p. illus. pl. ports. plan, facsims. O.

LC AC35-1362

Wolf, L.

Abbildung der neuen königl. preuss. armee uniformen. Berlin, N. Weiss 1813-15

71 col.pl. F.

Engraved by Jügel, Meyer, and Leopold

Colas 3098

Uniformen der Berliner bürgergarde; L. Wolf del: F. Jügel sc. Berlin, ca1810

10pl. Q.

Colas 3097. Lipperheide 2158

Wolf, Walther

Die bewaffnung des altägyptischen heeres. Leipzig, J. C. Hinrichs 1926

108p. illus. pl. O.

Bibliography: p106-08

Wolfe, Bertram D.

Portrait of Mexico. See entry under Rivera, Diego

Wolffgang, Andreas Matthaeus

Costumes algériens. Aug. Vind. ca1796

6pl. Q.

Colas 3099

(engr.) Fortitudo leonina in utraque fortuna Maximiliani Emmanuelis

Wolffgang, Johann Georg

(engr.) Besser, Johann von. Preussische krönungs-geschichte

Wolfskron, Adolf, ritter von

Die bilder der Hedwigslegende, nach einer handschrift vom jahre MCCCLIII in der bibliothek der p. p. Piaristen zu Schlackenwerth. Mit einem auszuge des originaltextes und historisch-archäologischen anmerkungen. Als versuch eines beitrages zur deutschen alterthumskunde hrsg. von Adolf ritter von Wolfskron. Wien, M. Kuppitsch 1846

lii,138 columns. 32 col.pl. 2 geneal.tab. (1 fold.) F.

"Historische beiträge zur genealogie der heiligen Hedwig": columns [1]-38

Lipperheide 380. LC 15-3505

Wolgemut, Michael. See Dürer, Albrecht, jt. auth.

Wolgerissene und geschnittene figuren in kupffer und holz. See Lorich, Melchior. Des kunstreichen ... türckische figuren

Wolkonsky, Marie

(illus.) Meyendorff, K. E., and Meyendorff, N. G. L'empire du soleil, Pérou et Bolivie

Wolzogen, Isolde von. See Jäger, Julie, jt. auth.

Woman as decoration. Burbank Emily

Womankind in western Europe. Wright, Thomas

Woman's book of sports. Paret, J. P.

Woman's dress. Jones, M. M.

Woman's handiwork in modern homes. Harrison, Mrs C. C.

Woman's home companion. v 1, 1873+ Springfield, O.

Illus.(part col.) F.
Published monthly. Current 1938
Title varies: 1873-95, *Ladies' home companion*

Woman's institute fashion service. See Fashion service magazine

Woman's institute of domestic arts and sciences, inc., Scranton, Pa. See Picken, Mrs M. B. The secrets of distinctive dress

A **woman's** journey through the Philippines. Russel, Mrs F. K.

Woman's world; edited by Oscar Wilde. v 1-3, Dec. 1887-1890. London [etc.]

3v. illus. Q.
Preceded by *The Lady's world, a magazine of fashion and society* (v 1, 1887. London, Cassell)
Lipperheide 4795, 4790

Women; [the hairstyle and beauty review] 1933+ New York, Capitaine pub. co.

Illus. Q. $1 a year
Published quarterly. Edited by Joseph Capitaine
Title change: published as *Hairstyle review* 1933-37
At head of title on cover: The hairstyle and beauty review for all women

Women, Canteen. See Canteen women

Women, fashionable gallery. See Deveria, Achille. Les femmes

Women of all nations. Joyce, T. A., and Thomas, N. W., eds

The **women** of Egypt. Cooper, Mrs E. G.

Women of India. Rothfield, Otto

The **women** of the American revolution. Ellet, Mrs E. F. L.

Women of the Middle kingdom. McNabb, R. L.

Women's coiffure. Hispanic society of America

Women's costume in French texts of the eleventh and twelfth centuries. Goddard, E. R.

Women's dress for church. Hispanic society of America

Women's jewelry. Hispanic society of America

Women's uniforms. See Military costume—United States—1917-date—Women's uniforms

Women's wear, incorporating the Ladies tailor. v 1, 1898?+ London, The tailor and cutter

Illus. O.-F.
Published weekly. Numbering continuous. Each issue includes "tailor-cut pattern" supplement Current 1938 (volume 40)
Title varies: Jan-April 1938, *Women's wear, fashions and patterns* (running title: *Women's wear fashions*)
Absorbed the *Ladies tailor,* May 1 1936

Women's wear magazine; Eastern edition. v 1-18; 1923-1932. New York, Women's wear magazines

18v. illus. O.
Published semi-monthly
Title varies: 1923-March 5, 1924 *Eastern women's wear magazine.* Absorbed by *Women's wear* Feb. 5, 1932

Wonders of the past. Hammerton, Sir J. A., ed.

Wood, Thomas William

The degrees, gowns, and hoods of the British, colonial, Indian, and American universities and colleges. London, T. Pratt [1883]

36p. O.
LC 1-14523

Woodbury, William A.

Hair dressing and tinting; a text-book of the fundamental principles showing the ready adaptability of the ever changing mode of wearing the hair, for professional and private use. New York, G. W. Dillingham [c1915]

85p. illus. pl. D. 50c
LC 15-12259

Woodcutters. See Lumbermen

Wooings and weddings in many climes. Miln, Mrs L. J.

Woolley, Edward Mott

A century of hats and the hats of the century ... illustrated by Edward Penfield. Danbury, Conn., The Mallory hat company, inc. [c1923]

46p. front. illus. pl. ports. O.
LC 23-10527

Woolson, Mrs Abba Louisa (Goold)

(ed.) Dress-reform: a series of lectures delivered in Boston, on dress as it affects the health of women. Boston, Roberts 1874

xviii,263p. front. illus. pl. D.
Five lectures by Mary J. Safford-Blake, Caroline E. Hastings, Mercy B. Jackson, Arvilla B. Haynes, Abba Goold Woolson
LC 9-22396

Worcester, Dean Conant

The Philippine Islands and their people; a record of personal observation and experience, with a short summary of the more important facts in the history of the archipelago. New York, London, Macmillan 1898

xix,529p. front. illus. 2 fold.maps. O.
LC 98-1283

The **work** of Charles Keene. Pennell, Joseph

Workmen

Ercker, Lazarus. Aula subterranea domina dominatium subdita subditorum. Das ist: Untererdische hofhaltung ... zusambt-angehängter auszlegung der terminorum und redarten der bergleute. 1672

Workmen—*Continued*
Friese, Friedrich. Der vornehmsten künstler und handwercker ceremonial-politica. 1708
Lacroix, Paul, and others. Le livre d'or des metiers. 1850-58
Ramelli, Agostino. Le diverse et artificiose machine. 1588
Siemienowicz, Kazimierz. Vollkommene geschütz-feuerwerck-und büchsenmeistereykunst. 1676
Vliet, J. J. van der. Künste und gewerbe. 1635

See also Occupations; Gildsmen

China

Arts, métiers et cultures de la Chine. 1814-1815

England

The young tradesman; or, Book of English trades. 1839

France

Adam, Victor. Les arts et métiers; avec vignettes par Victor Adam. ca.1830
Bertall, C. A. D'A. La vigne; voyage autour des vins de France; étude physiologique, anecdotique, historique, humoristique et même scientifique. 1878
Duplessi-Bertaux, Jean. Recueil de cent sujets de divers genres. 1814. Part 1, Part 3

Germany

Agricola, Georg. De re metallica. 1556
Agricola, Georg. De re metallica; tr. by H. C. Hoover and L. H. Hoover. 1912
Dresdner spielzeug aus den Dresdner werkstätten für handwerkskunst. 1904
Mummenhoff, Ernst. Der handwerker in der deutschen vergangenheit. 1901

Italy

Wael, Cornelis de. Verschiedene gewerbe, bilder aus dem italienischen volksleben. ca1650

Works of William Hogarth ... explanations by John Nichols. Hogarth, William

Works of William Hogarth ... with descriptions by the Rev. John Trusler. Hogarth, William

The **world** displayed; or, A curious collection of voyages and travels, selected and compiled from the writers of all nations; by Smart, Goldsmith, & Johnson. 1st American ed., cor. & enl. Philadelphia, Dobelbower, Key, and Simpson 1795-96
8v. fronts.(v 1,4,6,8) pl.(part fold.) fold. map. O.
This edition contains the same material, with a few additions, as the 20-vol. edition published by T. Carman and F. Newbery, London (L.C. set, partly 3d and partly 4th edition, 1762-90)
LC 36-24726

World in miniature. See entries under Shoberl, Frederic, ed.

World of fashion and continental feuilletons. See Monde élégant

The **world** of fashion, 1837-1922. Nevill, R. H.

World-noted women. Cowden-Clarke, Mary

World's children. Menpes, Mortimer

Wormwood, Edyth M. See Guptill, Mrs E. F. E., jt. auth.

Worsaae, Jens Jakob Asmussen
Forestillingerne paa guldbracteaterne. Kjøbenhavn, Thieles bogtrykkeri 1870
38p. illus. pl. 14-23. O.
LC 22-16672

The industrial arts of Denmark from the earliest times to the Danish conquest of England. London, Chapman & Hall 1882
2v. in 1. D. (South Kensington museum. Art handbook)
Contains some materials on prehistoric jewelry of Denmark

Nordiske oldsager i det kongelige museum i Kjöbenhavn ... tegnede og raderede af Magnus Petersen. Kjöbenhavn, Kittendorf & Aagaard 1859
200p. 621 illus. O.
Shows jewelry and ornaments of the stone, iron, and bronze ages
Lipperheide 285

Worth, Jean Philippe
A century of fashion ... tr. by Ruth Scott Miller. Boston, Little, Brown 1928
xviii,229p. col.front. pl.(part col.) ports. Q. $7.50, o.p.
The history of the House of Worth with reminiscences of its famous customers
Costume index. LC 28-23629

Wrangel, Fredrik Ulrik, grefve
De kongl. svenska riddare-ordnarne. [Stockholm] Generalstabens litografiska anstalts förlag [1899]
38p. 19 col.pl. Q.
Colas 3101. Lipperheide 1944c

Wrestlers
Auerswald, Fabian von. Ringer kunst. 1539
Auerswald, Fabian von. Die ringerkunst; erneuert von G. U. Schmidt. 1869
First published 1539
Parkyns, Sir Thomas, bart. The innplay: or, Cornish-hugg wrestler. 1727
Pascha, J. G. Vollständiges ring-buch. 1664?
Petter, Nicolaes. Klare onderrichtinge der ... worstel-konst. 1674

Wright, Agnes (Foster)
(ed.) The Bride's magazine

Wright, Alan
(illus.) Low, F. H. Queen Victoria's dolls

Wright, Bryce [M'Murdo]
Description of the collection of gold ornaments from the "huacas" or graves of some aboriginal races of the north western provinces of South America, belonging to Lady Brassey. London, C. Whittingham 1885
Cover-title, 49p. illus. pl. O.
LC 2-28586

Wright, Mrs D. G. See Wright, Mrs Louise (Wigfall)

Wright, George Newnham
(ed.) Allom, Thomas. China, in a series of views
(ed.) Allom, Thomas. The Chinese empire

Wright, Mrs Louise (Wigfall)
A southern girl in '61; the war-time memories of a Confederate senator's daughter, by Mrs. D. Giraud Wright. New York, Doubleday, Page 1905
xii,258p. front. ports. O.
LC 5-29989

Wright, Mrs Marie (Robinson)
Bolivia, the central highway of South America, land of rich resources and varied interest. Philadelphia, G. Barrie c1907
450p. front.(port.) illus. pl. sq.F.
LC 7-20755

Wright, Marion Logan
Biblical costume, with adaptations for use in plays. London, Society for promoting Christian knowledge 1936
4v. in 1. illus. O.
Includes bibliographies
Contents: Palestinian; Roman costume, the wise men, and angels; Hebrew, Egyptian, Assyrian and Persian; Beard making, stencilling, papier mâché properties, wings and armour
LC 36-34845

Wright, Richardson Little
Hawkers & walkers in early America, strolling peddlers, preachers, lawyers, doctors, players, and others, from the beginning to the civil war. Philadelphia, J. B. Lippincott 1927
317p. front. illus. pl. ports. facsims. O.
Bibliography: p275-89
LC 27-7004

Wright, Thomas
The homes of other days; a history of domestic manners and sentiments in England from the earliest known period to modern times. New York, D. Appleton; London, Trübner 1871
xv,511p. 333 illus. O. $7.50, o.p.
Earlier edition published under title: *History of domestic manners and sentiments in England during the middle ages* (London, Chapman & Hall 1862) has practically the same **illustrations**
Costume index. Lipperheide 1010. LC 15-10907, 2-16366 (1862 ed.)

The romance of the shoe, being the history of shoemaking in all ages, and especially in England and Scotland. London, C. J. Farncombe 1922
xvi,323p. front. pl. ports. facsims. O.
Plates printed on both sides
LC 23-10532

Womankind in western Europe from the earliest times to the seventeenth century. London, Groombridge 1869
xii,340p. col.front. illus. 10 col.pl. sq.O.
Lipperheide 77. LC 9-3468

See also Doré, Gustave. Historical cartoons

Wrschowitz, Austria. Knopf-museum Heinrich Waldes
Berichte. May 1916-1919. Prag, Vršovic, selbstverlag 1916-19
4v. illus. pl.(part col.) O.-Q.

Wüllner
(lithogr.) Diehl, C. P. Collection de costumes nationaux

Wüppermann, W. E. A.
Beschrijvend programma van den feestelijken optocht, gehouden te Haarlem, op Maandag 1 April 1872, ter viering van Nederland's 300 jarig vrij en onafhankelijk volksbestaan. Haarlem, Haeseker & Woest [1872]
11p. O. 12 double col.pl. F.
Lipperheide 2838

Würtembergischer militär-almanach. Fromm, F. L. v.

Würtembergisches militairs. Küstner

Das k. **Württ.** militär. Kirn, G. M.

Württemberg. See Germany—Württemberg; also Ceremonial and festival costume—Germany—Württemberg

Württemburgisches militär ... von 1800 bis 1857. See Abbildungen des württembergischen militärs von der früheren

Würzburg, Bavaria. Julius-Maximilian-Universitet
Alma Iulia; illustrirte chronik ihrer dritten säcularfeier. Wurzburg, Thein' schen druckerei 1882
184p. illus. F.
Lipperheide 2033

Wunder würdiges kriegs- und siegs-lager. See Kleiner, Salomon. Residences memorables

Wunder, wundergeburt und wundergestalt. Holländer, Eugen

Wunderbarliche, doch wahrhafftige erklärung, von der gelegenheit und sitten der wilden in Virginia. See Harriot, Thomas. Admiranda narratio

Wurzburg, Bavaria. University. See Academic costume—Wurzburg, Bavaria. University

Wyatt, Edward Gerald Penfold. See A directory of ceremonial

Wyld, W. See Lessore, A. E., jt. auth.

Wzory przemysłu domowego. Wierzbicki, Ludowik

Wzory sztuki średniowiecznej i z epoki odrodzenia po koniec wieku XVII. w dawnej Polsce. Przezdziecki, Aleksander, and Rastawiecki, Edward, baron

Y

Ye zu gaku no. Korio, Japanese artist

Yeats, Jack B.
(illus.) Lynd, Robert. Rambles in Ireland

Yester-year. Robida, Albert

Ymagines de las historias del viejo testamento. Holbein, Hans, illus.

Den **yngre** jernalds svaerd. Lorange, A. L.

Yoe, Schway, pseud. See Scott, Sir J. G.

Yonan, Isaac Malek
Persian women: a sketch of woman's life from the cradle to the grave, and missionary work among them. Nashville, Cumberland Presbyterian pub. house 1898
xii,224p. front. 14pl.(incl.ports.) D.
LC 5-12114

Yosy, A.
Switzerland, as now divided into nineteen cantons ... with picturesque representations of the dress and manners of the Swiss. London, Printed for J. Booth 1815
2v. 50 col.pl. Q.
Part of the plates are copied from F. N. Königs *Neue sammlung*
Colas 3102. Lipperheide 906. LC 11-20571

Young, Agnes Brooks
Recurring cycles of fashion 1760-1937. New York & London, Harper 1937
230p. illus. diagrs. O.
An analysis of trends in women's dress through an examination of typical styles during the last 175 years

Stage costuming. New York, Macmillan 1927
216p. front. illus. pl. diagrs. D. $1.90
A reference bibliography for period costume: p171-73
Reprinted 1933
Costume index. LC 27-12537

Young, George Malcolm
(ed.) Early Victorian England, 1830-1865. London, Oxford university press 1934
2v. fronts. 1 illus. pl. plan, facsims.(part double) O. $14
Contents: v 1 Work and wages, by J. H. Clapham; Homes and habits, by Mrs. C. S. Peel; Town life and London, by R. H. Mottram; Life in the new towns, by J. H. Clapham and M. H. Clapham; Country life and sport, by Bernard Darwin; The navy, by Admiral G. A. Ballard; The army, by Sir John Fortescue; The mercantile marine, by Basil Lubbock. v2 The press, by E. E. Kellett; Art, by A. P. Oppé; Architecture, by A. E. Richardson; Music, by E. J. Dent; Drama, by Allardyce Nicoll; Holidays and travel, by Mona Wilson; Charity, by E. Lascelles; Expansion and emigration, by D. Woodruff; Portrait of an age, by G. M. Young
Costume index. LC 35-27045

Young, John
A series of portraits of the emperors of Turkey, from the foundation of the monarchy to the year 1808; engraved from pictures painted at Constantinople by command of Sultan Selim the Third. London, R. Ackermann 1815
130p. 30 col.pl. F.
Lipperheide 1429

Young, Marianne
Cutch; or, Random sketches, taken during a residence in one of the northern provinces of western India ... by Mrs. Postans. London, Smith, Elder 1839
xvii,283p. 7 illus. 7pl. col.map. O.
Colas 2414. Lipperheide 1491

The **Young** Englishwoman; a volume of pure literature, new fashions, and pretty needlework designs. 4 v., 1865-1866; new ser. 3 v. 1867-1869; new ser. [ser. 3] 8 v. 1870-1877. London, Ward, Lock and Tyler 1865-77
Col.illus. O.
Superseded by *Sylvia's home journal*
Lipperheide 4731

The **Young** ladies' journal, an illustrated magazine of entertaining literature, original music, toilet & household receipts, Paris fashions and needlework ... full-size patterns for ladies' and children's dresses, etc. Colored plates of fashion and Berlin work, direct from Paris. v. 1, 1864-1920. London, E. Harrison
Illus. col.pl. F.
Published weekly, Apr. 13 1864-Mar. 14 1866; monthly, Apr. 1866-1920
Subtitle varies. Incorporated in 1920 with *Leach's Lady's companion*
Colas 3103. Lipperheide 4696. LC 11-34624

The **Young** ladies journal; complete guide to the work-table, containing instructions in Berlin work, crochet, drawn-thread work, embroidery, knitting, knotting or macramé, lace, netting, poonah painting, & tatting; 5th ed. London, E. Harrison 1888
136p. 505 illus. 4 col.pl. O.
Lipperheide 4158

The **young** tradesman; or, Book of English trades: being a library of the useful arts, for commercial education; new ed. London, Whittaker 1839
454,18p. 85pl. D.
Lipperheide 1977

Young women's Christian associations. Bureau of pageantry and the drama
National costumes of the Slavic peoples, drawings by Margaret Hubbard, descriptive notes and color plate by Esther Peck, comp. by the Bureau on pageantry and the drama, National board, Young womens Christian associations. New York, The Womans press 1920
17,7p. illus. col.pl. ob.O. 50c
Shows costume of Russia, Czechoslovakia, and Yugoslavia
Colas 2299. Costume index. LC 21-2827

Younghusband, Sir George John
The jewel house, an account of the many romances connected with the royal regalia, together with Sir Gilbert Talbot s account of Colonel Blood's plot here reproduced for the first time. New York, G. Doran 1920?
256p. col.front. pl.(part col.) ports. double plan, facsims. O.
LC 21-3674

Younghusband, Sir George John, and Davenport, Cyril James Humphries
The crown jewels of England. London, New York, Cassell 1919
viii,84p. front.(port.) illus. XVIII col.pl. F.
Each plate accompanied by guard sheet with descriptive letterpress
LC 20-17390

Yriarte, Charles Émile
Venise: histoire—art—industrie—la ville —la vie. Paris, J. Rothschild 1877-78
xii,328p. front. illus. 50pl. Q.
Issued in parts
Lipperheide 1334. LC 4-29955

L'**ystoire** de Helayne; reproduction des 26 miniatures du manuscrit. Brussels. Bibliothèque royale de Belgique. Mss. (9967)

Yugoslavia. Laws, statutes, etc.
Uredba o odeći suvozemne vojske ... Beograd Shtamparska radīonītsa Mīnīstarstva vojske ī mornarītse, 1924
62p. illus. D.
Regulations concerning uniforms for the Yugoslavian army
LC CA32-859 (title in Yugoslav)

Yugoslavia

Adamic, Louis. Native's return. 1934

Heimbucher von Bikessy, J. Pannoniens bewohner in ihren volksthümlichen trachten. 1820

Hielscher, Kurt. Picturesque Yugo-Slavia; Slavonia, Croatia, Dalmatia, Montenegro, Herzogovina, Bosnia and Serbia. 1926

Hutchinson, Mrs F. K. Motoring in the Balkans along the highways of Dalmatia, Montenegro, the Herzegovina and Bosnia. 1909

Jaschke, Franz. National-kleidertrachten und ansichten von Ungarn, Croatien, Slavonien, dem Banat, Siebenbürgen und der Bukowina. 1821

Die Österreichisch-ungarische monarchie in wort und bild. 1886-1902 v8, 10-11, 22, 24

Young women's Christian associations. Bureau of pageantry and the drama. National costumes of the Slavic peoples. 1920

See also Illyria; also subdivision Yugoslavia under Embroidery; Military costume

BY REGION OR PROVINCE

Bosnia and Herzegovina

Asbóth, János de. An official tour through Bosnia and Herzegovina, with an account of the history, antiquities, agrarian conditions, religion, ethnology, folk lore, and social life of the people. 1890

Capus, Guillaume. À travers la Bosnie et l'Herzégovine. 1896

Holbach, M. M. Bosnia and Herzegovina, some wayside wanderings. 1910

Carniola

Valvasor, J. W. Die ehre desz hertzogthums Crain. 1689

Dalmatia

Bruck-Auffenberg, Frau Natalie. Dalmatien und seine volkskunst. 1911

Carrara, Francesco. La Dalmazia. 1846

Costume of Illyria and Dalmatia. 1824

Dalmatien und das österreichische küstenland. 1911

Forti, Alberto. Abbate Alberto Fortis Reise in Dalmatien. 1776

Germar, E. F. Reise nach Dalmatien und in das gebiet von Ragusa. 1817

Hacquet, Balthasar. Abbildung und beschreibung der südwest- und östlichen Wenden, Illyrer und Slaven. 1802-1805

Hacquet, Balthasar. L'Illyrie et la Dalmatie, ou Moeurs usages et costumes des habitants et des ceux des contrées voisines. 1815

Jocosi. Costumi nazionali Dalmati. 184-?

Rödlich, H. F. Skizzen des physisch-moralischen zustandes Dalmatiens und der buchten von Cattaro. 1811

Shoberl, Frederic, ed. Illyria and Dalmatia. 1821

Valério, Théodore. Costumes de la Hongrie et des provinces danubiennes, Dalmatie, Monténégro, Croatie, Slavonie, frontières militaires. 1885

See also subdivision Yugoslavia—Dalmatia under Decoration and ornament; also Lace—Dalmatia

Montenegro

Durham, M. E. Through the lands of the Serb. 1904

Valério, Théodore. Costumes de la Hongrie et des provinces danubiennes, Dalmatie, Monténégro, Croatie, Slavonie, frontières militaires. 1885

Serbia

Durham, M. E. Through the lands of the Serb. 1904

Louis Salvator, archduke of Austria. Die Serben an der Adria. 1870-78

Yugo-Slavia, Slavonia, Croatia, Dalmatia. See Hielscher, Kurt. Picturesque Yugo-Slavia

Yule, Henry

A narrative of the mission sent by the governor-general of India to the court of Ava in 1855, with notices of the country, government, and people. London, Smith, Elder 1858
391p. 49 illus. 30pl. Q.
Lipperheide 1502

Yves

Costumes suisses des 22 cantons. Paris, Wild ca1860
Front. 12 col.pl. F.
Colas 3105

Études contemporaines; types parisiens. Paris, C. Bowin; London, E. Gambart 1850
7(?)pl. F.
Colas 3104

Z

Zabi͡elin, Īvan" Egorovīch"

Domashniĭ byt' russkīkh" tsarīts" v" XVI ī XVII st . . . 3. īzd. s" dopolnenīi͡amī. Moskva, T-vo tīp. A. Ī. Mamontova 1901
788p. 8pl.(2 fold.) Q.
On the home life of the Russian Tzarinas of the 16th and 17th centuries
LC CA15-1130 (Russian characters)

Žalud, August

Česká vesnice. Praze, B. Koči 1919
127p. illus. sq.Q.
Pages 71-85 deal with costume of Bohemia
Bibliography: p129-30

Zamacoïs, Miguel

Le costume . . . texte inédit. [Paris] Flammarion c1936
63p. 142 illus.(incl.ports.) Q. (Voir et savoir)
Contents: Les Égyptiens; Les Hébreux; Assyriens. Mèdes et Perses, Lydiens, Etrusques, Phrygiens; Les Grecs et les Romains; Byzance; Les Gaulois, les Germains; Les Francs; Les peuples asiatiques; Les

Zamacoïs, Miguel—*Continued*
Chinois; Les Russes, les Scandinaves et les Anglais; La France; Charles VII, Louis XI; La renaissance; Henri IV et Louis XIII; Louis XIV; Au XVIIIe siècle; La révolution et le directoire; Le consulat et l'empire; La restauration; Napoléon III; Et aujourd'hui
LC 37-9246

Dernière lettre persane mise en français par M. Zamacoïs et accompagnée de douze dessins exécutés dans le goût persan par Benito. Paris, Imprimée par Draeger Fres, ed. par la maison de fourrures Max ca1925
4 l. 12 col.pl. Q.
Contents: Schéhérazade, Princesse Lointaine, Florentin, Diane, Idole, Triomphe, Condottiere, Dogaresse, Geisha, Goyesca, Adieu New York, Boabdil
Colas 3106

Zambrano, marques de
Coleccion de uniformes del egercito español. Madrid, 1830
1 l. 21 col.pl. F.
Colas 3107

Zanelli, Severino
Il reggimento Piemonte reale cavalleria dalle origini ai nostri tempi. Città di Castello, S. Lapi 1892
235,47p. 6pl. F.
Colas 3108

Zanetti, Girolamo Francesco
Della berretta ducale volgarmente chiamata corno che portasi da' serenissimi dogi di Penezia. [Venezia] 1779
12p. 1 pl. O.
Lipperheide 1759

Zangemeister, Karl Friedrich Wilhelm
(ed.) Die wappen, helmzierden und standarten der Grossen Heidelberger liederhandschrift (Manesse-codex) Görlitz, C. A. Starke; [etc.] 1892
xii,28,[2]p. 62 col.pl. F.
LC 2-2518

Zangrius, Jean Baptiste
(engr.?) Album amicorum habitibus mulierum omniv nationv Europae

Zannoni, Antonio
Gli scavi della Certosa di Bologna descritti ed illustrati. Bologna, Regia tipografica 1876-84
479p. 2 illus. 150pl.(45 col.) on 56 l. F.
The illustrations show soldiers, a procession carrying animals to be sacrificed, workers in the field and the home, trappers and musicians
Lipperheide 247

Zanoli, Alessandro, baron
Sulla milizia cisalpino italiana. Cenni storico-statistici, dal 1796 al 1814. Milano, Borroni e Scotti 1845
2v. O. and atlas 5 col.pl. F.
Plates are after Robert Focosi and show reviews with uniforms of the army and navy of the Cisalpine republic and the Kingdom of Italy 1797 to 1812
Colas 3109. Lipperheide 2366

Zantani, Antonio. See note under Vico, Enea. Le imagini con tutti i riversi trovati et le vite de gli imperatori

Zanzibar
Lyne, R. N. Zanzibar in contemporary times, a short history of the southern East in the nineteenth century. 1905

Zanzibar in contemporary times. Lyne, R. N.

Zarīn, Leonīd Sergīeevich
(tr.) Liven, P. A., kníaź. The birth of ballets-russes

Zarys dziejów uzbrojenia w Polsce. Dziewanowski, Władysław

Zarza, and Vallejo
Ordenes militares. Paris, Lemercier 1884
Col.front. 14 col.pl.
Cataloged from Colas
Colas 3111

Der **zauber** des fleisses. Banze, Angela

Zawilinski, Roman
Ubiory ludu polskiego. See entry under Akademija umiejętności, Cracow

Zbior wzorowy rozmaitych polskick. Norblin de la Gourdaine, J. P.

Zealand
Møller, J. S. Folkedragter i Nordvestsjælland, deres forhold til folkedragterne i det øvrige Sjælland og til de skiftende moder. 1926

Zealley, Alfred Edward, and Hume, James Ord
Famous bands of the British Empire; brief historical records of the recognised leading military bands and brass bands in the Empire ... with historical sketch of the evolution of the military band by Colonel J. A. C. Somerville London, J. P. Hull c1926
62p. illus.(incl.ports.) sq.F.
LC 29-12556

Zee en lant-reize, door verscheide gewesten van Oostindien. See Nieuhof, Johan. Joan Nieuhofs Gedenkwaerdige zee en lantreize door de voornaemste landschappen van West en Oostindien

Zeichen- mahler- und stickerbuch zur selbstbelehrung für damen. Netto, J. F.

Zeichenvorlagen für den fachschul-unterricht im perückenmachergewerbe. Gussmann, Paul

Zeichnungen nach dem gemeinen volke besonders der kaufruf in Wien. Brand, C.

Zeischke, Josef
Die moderne damenschneiderei ... 2. verb. aufl. Dresden, Selbstverlag des verfassers [1888]
40p. 19pl. Q.
First edition: 1878
Lipperheide 3818

Zeissig, M. C.
Neue stickmuster zu allen gegenständen welche in weisz gestickt werden ... Nouveaux modèles. [Hamburg] ca1815
12pl. sq.F.
Lipperheide 3941

Das **zeitalter** des kaisers Wilhelm. Oncken, Wilhelm

Zeitschrift für bildende kunst ... 1.-24. jahrg.; [jan.] 1866-sept. 1889; [25.]-65. jahrg. (neue folge, 1.-[42.] jahrg.), okt. 1890-märz 1932. Leipzig [etc.] E. A. Seemann 1866-1931/32
65v. illus. pl.(part col.) ports. plans. Q.-F.
An art periodical published monthly. Illustrations show dress of various countries and periods
LC 8-18255

Zeitschrift für historische waffen- und kostümkunde; organ des Vereins für historische waffenkunde. bd 1, 1896+ Dresden
Illus. pl. (part col.) Q.
Volume 1-7 published as *Zeitschrift für historische waffenkunde.* Volume 9- also as new ser. v 1+
Lipperheide 2455

Zeitschrift für historische waffenkunde. See Zeitschrift für historische waffen- und kostumkunde

Zeitschrift für schweizerische geschichte. jahrg. 1, 1920+ Zurich, Gebr. Leemann 1920+
Published quarterly. Current 1938
Title and text also in French: *Revue d'histoire suisse* and in Italian: *Revista storica suizzera*
Published by Allgemeine geschichtforschende gesellschaft der Schweiz. Official organ of the Société suisse des professeurs d'histoire and the Association des archivistes suisses

Zeitung für die elegante welt. 1.-59. jahrg., 1801-1859. Berlin, Janke
59v. col.illus. col.pl. Q.
Forty-eight numbers a year
Title change: v47-48, *Mode; zeitung für die elegante welt*
Colas 3112. Lipperheide 4591

Zeitung für die elegante welt; illustrirtes hauptorgan d. deutschen, franz. u. engl. modegeschmacks in frauen- und kindergarderobe. Red. H. Klemm. 1.-14. jahrg. 1872-1885. Dresden, Exped. der Europ. modenzeitung
14v. illus. (part col.) Q.-F.
Published monthly; v 1-4, twenty-four numbers a year. Contains patterns
Title change: v 1-5: *Neue zeitung für die elegante welt*

Zeitung für theater, musik und poesie. See Allgemeine theaterzeitung und originalblatt

Zelenīn, Dimītriī Konstantīnovīch
Russische (ostslavische) volkskunde. Berlin und Leipzig, W. de Gruyter 1927
xxvi,424p. illus. v col.pl. fold.map. O. (Grundriss der slavischen philologie und kulturgeschichte, bd.3)
Shows Russian peasant costume
LC 35-1580

Zell, Franz
Bauern-trachten aus dem bayerischen hochland. München, Verlag der vereinigten kunstanstalten a.-g. 1903
4 l. 13 illus. 30 col.pl. F.
Colas 3113. Lipperheide 760e

Zepelin, Constantin von. See Drygalski, Albert von, jt. auth.

Der **zerbrochene** krug. Kleist, Heinrich von

Zerkovitz, Frau Sidonie Grünwald- See Grünwald-Zerkovitz, Frau Sidonie

Zesiger, A. See Pochon, A., jt. auth.

Die **zeugdrucke** der byzantinischen, romanischen, gothischen und spätern kunstepochen. Forrer, Robert

Zezon, Antonio
Tipi militari dei differenti corpi che compongono il reale esercito e l'armata di mare di S. M. il R. L. del regno delle Due Sicilie. Napoli, 1850-54
2v. col.front. 80 col.pl. F.
Colas 3114

Zíbrt, Čeněk
(ed.) Český lid

Zíbrt, Čeněk, and Winter, Zikmund
Dějiny kroje v zemích českých. Praze, 1892-93
2v. illus.
A history of Czech costume. Contents: v 1 Od dob nejstarších až po války husitské, sepsal Čeněk Zíbrt; v2 Od počátku století xv. až po dobu bělohorské bitvy, sepsal Zikmund Winter

Zichy
(illus.) Description du sacre et du couronnement de ... l'empereur Alexandre II et l'impératrice Marie Alexandrovna, MDCCLVI.

Ziegelhauser, Leopold. See Spalart, Robert von. Versuch über das kostum der vorzüglichsten völker

Ziegler, Johann. See Schwarz, Iznaz, ed. Wiener strassenbilder im zeitalter des rokoko

Zienkowicz, Léon
Les costumes du peuple polonais. Paris, Librarie polonaise; Leipzig, F. A. Brockhaus 1841
126p. 40 col.pl. sq.F.
German edition: Die trachten des polnischen volkes (Paris, 1841. 120p. 40 col.pl.)
Colas 3115-16. Costume index. Lipp. 1391

Zimburg, Wilhelm von
Osterreichische cavallerie, von 1600-1883. M. Weisskirchen, F. Kunza [1883]
18 col.pl. Q.
Colas 3117

Zimmermann, Carl Friedrich
Russische militair gruppen ... lithographirt von L. Förster. Berlin, C. G. Lüderitz ca1825
5pl. Q.
Colas 3118. Lipperheide 2376

Zimmermann, Joseph Anton
Series imaginum Augustae domus Boicae ad genuina ectypa aliaque monum. fide digna delin. Monachii, 1773-92
155pl. F.
Contains half length portraits of Bavarian nobles from 948 to 1792
Lipperheide 724

Zimmern, Alice
(tr.) Blümner, Hugo. Home life of the ancient Greeks

Zincke
(engr.) Perger, Sigmund. Tyroler

Zindel, Christian Siegmund
(ed.) Der eislauf oder das schrittschuhfahren, ein taschenbuch für jung und alt. Nürnberg, F. Campe 1825
180p. 6pl. O.
Lipperheide 3046

Zingerle, Ignaz Vincenz, edler von Summersberg
Fresken-cyklus des schlosses Runkelstein bei Bozen, gezeichnet und lithografirt von dr. Ignaz Seelos, erklaert von dr. Ignaz Vinzenz Zingerle; hrsg. von dem Ferdinandeum in Innsbruck. [Innsbruck, Wagner'sche buchdr. 1857]
10 l. 23pl. (6 col.) plan. ob.F.
The frescoes date from the early 15th century. Many of them show the nobility in games, at the dance, and hunting
Lipperheide 455. LC 12-1608

Zink, Theodor
Die Pfalz. See Deutsche volkskunst. v 12

Der **zinnsoldat.** Hampe, Theodor

Zinspelende gedigtjes. Chalon, Christina

Zobeltitz, Fedor von
(ed.) Gaudy, F. B. H. W., freiherr von. Karikaturenbuch

Zobeltitz, Hanns E. von
(ed.) Vogt, Hermann. Das buch vom deutschen heere

Il **zodiaco.** Orilia, Francesco

Zöllner, L. See Heine, Ferdinand. Abbildungen der neuen uniformen der königlich sächsischen armee

Zola, Émile. See Goncourt, E. L. A. H. de, jt. auth.

Zolarde, G. Oduaga- See Oduaga-Zolarde, G.

Zoll, K.
(illus.) Berg, J. A. Bilder ur svenska folklifvet

Zompini, Gaetano
Le arti che vanno per via nella città di Venezia. Venezia, 1785
3 l. 60pl. F.
At the foot of each plate is the street cry which it illustrates
First edition: 1753. Also published (London, Lackington, Allen 1803) with binder's title in English: *Cries of Venice*
Colas 3120-21. Lipperheide 1330. LC 11-19889, 1-15381 (Eng. ed.)

Zoppino, Nicolo d'Aristotile, called
Esemplario di lavori dove le tenere fanciulle & altre donne nobile potranno facilmente imparare il modo & ordine di lavorare ... [Stampato in Vinegia ... 1530] Venezia, F. Ongania 1878
50pl. Q. (Raccolta di opere antiche sui disegni dei merletti di Venezia, 11)
Lipperheide 3880

Gli universali de i belli recami antichi e moderni ... 1537. Venezia, F. Ongania 1876
1 l. 50pl. Q. (Raccolta di opere antiche sui disegni dei merletti di Venezia, 4)
Lipperheide 3884

Zschille, Richard, and Forrer, Robert
Der sporn in seiner formen-entwicklung, ein versuch zur characterisirung und datirung der sporen unserer kulturvölker. Berlin, P. Bette 1891-99
2v. 10 illus. 30pl. F.
Lipperheide 2940

Zürcherische ausruff-bilder. Herrliberger, David

Zürcherische kleider-tracten. Herrliberger, David

Das **zukunftskleid** der frau. Watt, Jeannie

Zungaria. See Sungaria

Zum fünfundzwanzigjährigen bestehen der Modenwelt. Die Modenwelt

Zur bewaffnung und kriegsführung der ritter des Deutschen Ordens in Preussen. Bujack, Georg

Zur bilderkunde des deutschen studentwesens. Konrad, K. G.

Zur costumgeschichte des mittelalters. Falke, Jacob von

Zur cultur und kunst. Falke, Jacob von

Zur erinnerung an die reise des prinzen Waldemar von Preussen. Waldemar, prince of Prussia

Zur geschichte der deutschen kleidertrachten. Gallenstein, Anton von

Zur geschichte der Hamburger Schützengilde. Nathansen, W.

Zur geschichte der costüme, nach zeichnungen von W. Diez, C. Fröhlich, C. Häberlin, M. Heil, A. Müller, F. Rothbart, J. Watter. München, Braun & Schneider [1895?]
125 col. double pl. F. (on plates: Münchener bilderbogen)
"Sachregister" ([8]p. O.) laid in
Plates show costume of Europe and Asia from the 4th to the 19th century. The same plates are included in *Costumes of all nations*
Colas 1234. Costume index. Lipperheide 83. LC 1-21852

Zur geschichte von speer und schwert im 12. jahrhundert. Schwietering, Julius

Zur philosophie der mode. Kleinwächter, Friedrich

Zur Strassen, Melchior. See Strassen, Melchior zur

Zur waffenkunde des älteren deutschen mittelalters. Schulz, Albert

Zurich. See Switzerland—By region or province—Zurich; also Street venders —Switzerland—Zurich

Zuschneidekurs. Müller, Susanna

20 hamburg. volkstrachten. See Erinnerung an Hamburg

Die **zwar** hefftig entflammte doch aber kunstlich verborgene über Pantalons aufsicht thriumphirende amor. See Schübler, J. J. Amor vehementer

Zwey-einiger Hymenaeus. Mayr, J. B.

Zwinger
(lithgr.) Föhn, Michael. Suisse—jeux et usages

Die **zwölf** monate. Passe, Crispijn van de

Zycie polskie w dawnych wiekach. Łoziński, Władysław